THE ENCYCLOPEDIA OF
The Musical Theatre
L-Z

KURT GÄNZL

SCHIRMER BOOKS
An Imprint of Macmillan Publishing Company
New York

Maxwell Macmillan Canada
Toronto

This American edition published in 1994 by Schirmer
Books, An Imprint of Macmillan Publishing Company.

Schirmer Books
An Imprint of Macmillan Publishing Company
866 Third Avenue
New York, NY 10022

First published in Great Britain by
Blackwell Publishers
108 Cowley Road
Oxford OX4 1JF
UK

Macmillan Publishing Company is part of the Maxwell
Communications Group of Companies.

Library of Congress Catalog Card Number: 93-48237

Printed in the United States of America

Printing number
    3   4   5   6   7   8   9   10

Library of Congress Cataloging-in-Publication Data

Gänzl, Kurt.
The encyclopedia of the musical theatre/Kurt Gänzl. –
American ed.
        p.   cm.
Includes bibliographical references.
ISBN 0-02-871445-8 : $150.00
1. Musicals – Encyclopedias.   I. Title.
ML102.M88G3   1994   93-48237
                                              CIP
                                              MN

This book is printed on acid-free paper

Contents

Organization of the encyclopedia

Alphabetization

Entries are arranged in a single alphabetical sequence, using a letter-by-letter system, as follows

MANNEQUINS
DER MANN MIT DEN DREI FRAUEN
MANNSCHAFT AN BORD
MANNSTÄDT, William
MAN OF LA MANCHA

For alphabetization purposes, the following conventions have been followed:
- ■ the definite and indefinite articles A, The, L', Le, La, Les, Das, Der, Die etc. are ignored where they appear at the beginning of show headwords.
- ■ the Scots or Irish prefixes 'Mac', 'Mc' and 'M' are all treated as if they were spelt out 'Mac'.
- ■ all accented letters are treated as English unaccented letters.

Cross references appear as follows:

MAYTIME   *see* WIE EINST IM MAI

with the large capital letter indicating the letter under which the entry may be found.

Introductory and supplementary sections to people entries

The articles are written and ordered under the name in which their subject was active in the theatre. When that name is simply an easily shortened version of the subject's real full name, the rest of that real name is given in square brackets: for example,

BROWN, Jon[athan Frederick]

When the bold headword is not simply a shortened form of the real full name or when the nom de théâtre/nom de plume is not that with which the subject was born, the real full name (where known) is given separately, again in square brackets. For example,

BROWN, John [BROWN, Jonathan Frederick]
BROWN, John [BRAUNSTEIN, Johann Friedrich]

The name is followed by the places and dates of birth and death, where known, in parentheses. For example,

(b London, 6 February 1933; d unknown)

On a number of occasions, a birth year is included but is marked with a query. This is generally where a death certificate or obituary has given the subject's age at death, but a birth certificate and/or date has not been found to confirm that information. For example,

(b Paris, ?1946; d Nice, 10 August 1980).

The bibliographies given at the end of entries include a representative selection of biographies, autobiographies or other significant literature devoted to the subject. I have not attempted to list every published work – not least because many of the people who have the most works written about them are those whose principal activity was not the musical theatre.

Introductory and supplementary sections to show entries

The introductory sections to show entries give the title (and subtitle where relevant) under which the show was normally played, followed by any considerably used alternative title, then the credits as given on the playbill, and the date and place of the first production. As in the worklists that appear at the end of people articles (see below), this information refers to the first metropolitan performance. In the case of modern works, the date of the official 'first night', rather than that of the first preview performance, is given. Out-of-town try-out dates are shown only when there is an appreciable gap between the initial out-of-town production and any later metropolitan production, or when the show failed to find its way to town at all. For example,

> **NO, NO, NANETTE** Musical comedy in 3 acts by Frank Mandel, Otto Harbach and Irving Caesar based on *My Lady Friends* by Mandel and Emil Nyitray (and *Oh, James!* by May Edgington). Music by Vincent Youmans. Garrick Theater, Detroit, 23 April 1923; Harris Theater, Chicago, 7 May 1923; Globe Theater, New York, 16 September 1925.

The supplementary sections at the end of the show entries consist of a record of the dates and places of the first productions of the show in what, for the purposes of this book, are treated as the 'main centres' (Berlin, Budapest, London, Melbourne, New York, Paris, Sydney, Vienna) other than that in which it was first performed. When the show was, on these occasions, given in France, Austria, Britain, America, Australia, Hungary or Germany under a title other than its original, the altered or translated title is given, along with the date and place of the production. For example,

> Austria: Theater in der Josefstadt 15 May 1952; France: Théâtre Marigny *Feu d'artifice* 1952; UK: Bristol Old Vic *Oh, My Papa!* 2 April, Garrick Theatre, London 17 July 1957
> Recordings: selection (Ariola-Eurodisc); selection in English (Parlophone EP)

Mention is also made of films and recordings of, and books on, individual shows. I have made no attempt to give details of recordings, as labels and serial numbers of recordings vary from country to country and a complete list of all the show recordings in question would fill a vast volume. I have merely tried to indicate which of the shows dealt with can be found on record, at least some of the labels that have been responsible for those recordings, and whether 'original cast' or foreign-language recordings are included amongst them. Similarly, I have mentioned books only in the rare instances where a book is wholly, or very largely, devoted to the show in question.

Authors' and composers' worklists

The worklists attached to the articles on librettists, lyricists and composers are intended to include all of each writer's credited works for the book musical theatre.

Works for which a writer was not credited on the playbills are not included, and neither are works written for such adjacent musical and theatrical areas as opera, ballet, pantomime and revue.

The original works in the list are given in chronological order of their first production.

When a show has been played under more than one title, the title in bold type is the title under which its main metropolitan run was given, with alternative titles in italic type in parentheses. Titles discarded in try-out are noted as 'ex-'. For example,

> 1988 **Ain't Broadway Grand** (ex- *Mike*)

Post-metropolitan changes of title are indicated by the prefix 'later-'. Where the title change was part of a significant rewrite, the rewrite will have a separate entry as 'revised version of [original title]'.

The year and title of the piece are followed by the names of the writer's credited collaborators on the show in question, in the order: composer(s)/lyricist(s)/librettist(s). Writers who collaborated with the writer in his or her area are shown by a 'w' indicating 'with'. Thus (Smith/w Brown/w Green) would mean that the person who is the subject of the article worked on the show's lyrics with Brown and its book with Green, and the music was by Smith. The names of the subject's collaborators are given in full on their first mention in a worklist, and thereafter by surname only except where a duplicated surname could lead to confusion, such as in the case of contemporaneous text-writers H B Smith, R B Smith and E Smith. Any variants occurring in a show's author/composer credits are included in square brackets. Major revisions of a show are credited separately in the worklist.

In the case of short works only, the names of the authors are followed by an indication such as '1 act' or '3 scenes'. Otherwise all works are 'full-length' pieces (in the loosest possible meaning of the term when some works from the 19th-century days of very long evenings are in question) in a minimum of two acts.

Each original work entry on the worklist ends with the place and date of the first metropolitan performance. In the case of modern works, the date of the official 'first night' rather than that of the first preview performance is used. Out-of-town try-out dates are shown only when there is an appreciable gap between the initial out-of-town production and any later metropolitan production, or when the show failed to find its way to town at all. In the case of shows initially staged in other cities and subsequently remounted in what, for the purposes of this book, are accounted the 'main centres' (Berlin, Budapest, London, Melbourne, New York, Paris, Sydney, Vienna), both dates are given. When the theatre in which the show's première is given is not based in the city that may be regarded as being/having been the writer's base, the name of the city is included alongside the theatre. So, for example, a Vienna-centred author will be credited with works at the Carltheater, the Theater an der Wien or the Raimundtheater without further elaboration, but for productions at the Theater am Gärtner-platz, Munich, the Népszinház, Budapest, or the Thalia-Theater, Berlin, the cities would be specified. For example,

> 1890 **Erminy** (*Erminie*) German version w Heinrich von Wald-
> berg (Carltheater)
> 1890 **Der bleiche Gast** (Josef Hellmesberger, Zamara/w von
> Waldberg) Carl-Schultze Theater, Hamburg 6 September

Shows which are not the original work of the writer in question, but simply adaptations of a musical originally written and produced by other writers in another language, are listed under the year of their production in the version by the subject of the worklist. The year is followed by the title given to the piece in the subject's adaptation, followed in parentheses by the title of the original piece in its original language, a description of the nature of the adaptation (where applicable) and the theatre where the adaptation was first staged. For example,

> 1889 **Capitän Wilson** (*The Yeomen of the Guard*) German version
> w Carl Lindau (Carltheater)

On the occasions where I have been unable to trace or to confirm that a show credited to a writer was in fact produced, rather than just being announced for production, I have listed the title at the end of the worklist under the heading 'Other titles attributed'. Conversely, shows which were definitely produced, but for which my details are incomplete, are included in the worklist, with their details as complete as I have been able to make them. Any dubious dates, places or credits are indicated with a question mark, thus, ?1849.

Occasionally circumstances arose which could not be adequately dealt with by the arrangements described above. In these cases, it has been my main care simply to make whatever the situation and credits might be as clear as possible without clinging too unbendingly to a 'standard' layout.

KURT GÄNZL

Abbreviations

(X) ad (Y)	the work of (X) adapted by (Y), adapter	ly	lyric(s)
add	additional	md	musical director
aka	also known as	mus	music
(X) arr (Y)	the work of (X) arranged by (Y), arranger	nd	no date known
b	born	np	no place known
ch	choreographed by, choreographer	posth	posthumous
d	died	rev	revival
Eng	English/England	scr	screenplay
fr	from	Sp	Spanish/Spain
Fr	French/France	sq/sqq	and that/those following
Frln	Fräulein	sr	senior
Ger	German/Germany	t/o	takeover (of a rôle)
Hun	Hungarian/Hungary	UK	United Kingdom
jr	junior	u/s	understudy
Lat	Latin	USA	United States of America
lib	libretto		

L

LÁBASS, Juci (b Zilah, 22 July 1896; d Budapest, 25 August 1932). Popular Hungarian soubrette whose career as a musical star was cut short by a premature death.

Juci Lábass left stage school to make her début at the Király Színház, at the age of 17, in Jean Gilbert's *Buksi* (*Puppchen* 1913, Lori), and subsequently became a favourite operett soubrette and leading lady in Budapest, appearing in local productions of such pieces as *Die geschiedene Frau* (Gonda van der Loo), *Die keusche Susanne* (1913, Susanne), *Rund um die Liebe* (1915, Stella), *Die Rose von Stambul* (1916, Midili), *Bacchusnacht* (1924, Chloris), *Gräfin Mariza* (1924, Mariza) *Der Orlow* (1925, Nadja), *Die Zirkusprinzessin* (1926, Fedora) and *Die Blume von Hawaii* (1932, Princess Lilia), and in such classic rôles as Eurydice, Serpolette, Lisbeth (*Rip*) and Boccaccio.

She also created the principal soubrette rôles in several notable Hungarian operetts including the lead rôle of *Nemtudomka*, the part of Sarah, paired with the Poire of Márton Rátkai, in *Szibill* (though in her later post-soubrette days she would play the title-rôle), Rolla in *Mágnás Miska* (1916) and Katinka in *Pillangó főhadnagy* (1918). She also appeared in the soubrette rôle of Szirmai's *Gróf Rinaldo*, as Hortense Schneider in the Hungarian biomusical *Offenbach* (1920), and starred in such other home-made pieces as *Chopin* (1926, Aurora), *A királynő rózsája* (1926, Suzy), *Aranyhattyú* (1927, Elinor), *Eltörött a hegedüm* (1928, Rozsika), *Cigánygrófné* (Panni), *Pesti család* (1929, Margit), *Alvinci huszárok* (1930), *Fehér orchideák* (1931, Elena), *Hajnali csók* (1931) and *Éjféli tangó* (1932) and made a Vienna appearance in *Die Herzogin von Chicago* (1929, t/o Mary) before her death at the age of 36.

LABICHE Eugène [Marie] (b Paris, 6 May 1815; d Paris, 22 January 1888).

Like George Bernard Shaw, the apparently tone-deaf French vaudevillist and co-author of *Un chapeau de paille d'Italie* (1851, w Marc-Michel) and *La Station Champbaudet* avowed a certain lofty distaste for the musical theatre. However, unlike the Irish author he was tempted from time to time, by the monetary gains possible, to dip into the despised area. He wrote his libretti largely for composers at the opéra-comique end of the musical theatre scale – Delibes, Massé, Poïse – and, most significantly, for François Bazin. Bazin's comical musical play *Le Voyage en Chine*, composed to a brightly humorous Labiche and Delacour text, became an enormous international success and served as the model for a number of pieces in the budding English-language musical-comedy tradition. An attempt to pair Labiche with Offenbach failed when the playwright (purposely?) wrote his libretto for the intended opérette, *Les Trente Millions de Gladiateur* (w Philippe Gille), at such length that there was no space for musical numbers, and the show in question was finally presented as a straight play.

Apart from *Le Voyage en Chine*, the nearest Labiche came to authoring a regular musical was with a vaudeville, *Le Roi dort* for the Théâtre des Variétés. It was presented with sufficient of the accessories of a féerie, and with a substantial enough musical score by the theatre's former musical director, Marius Boullard, for the latter to assert that it was a genuine opérette. Labiche also co-authored the féerie-vaudeville *Les Secrets du Diable* (w Clairville, Jules Cordier) for the Théâtre du Vaudeville (23 February 1850), had his 1868 *Le Roi d'Amatibou* (w E Cottinet) at the Palais-Royal illustrated musically by Hervé, and also wrote a handful of short vaudevillesque texts, subsequently produced as one-act opérettes.

Needless to say, in the manner of the time, many of Labiche's original vaudevilles were illustrated with a handful of pasticcio couplets, but in his later days he tried, where he could, to avoid any musical portions in his plays. Again like Shaw, but largely posthumously, his works later became the meat for musical-comedy authors, but unlike Shaw no *Der tapfere Soldat* or *My Fair Lady* came as a result. Labiche musicals have not precisely flourished.

Un chapeau de paille d'Italie was originally produced as a vaudeville with songs attached, the pasticcio score of more than 20 items including music from Auber's *Le Serment*, Hérold's *Zampa*, from other vaudevilles of the 1830s and 1840s, and even items from shows of the previous season. This score has not endured, but *Un chapeau de paille d'Italie* has been the most frequently adapted of Labiche's works, notably in a version by W S Gilbert who, with George Grossmith as composer, musicalized his own London version of the play, *The Wedding March* (itself played, like the original, with interpolated songs), as *Haste to the Wedding*. In Italy, Giovanni Maria Sala, Mario Borciani and Lores produced a *Capello di paglia di Firenze* at Verona's Teatro Ristori and Nino Rota later provided the music for a light operatic version under the same title, whilst in France Guy Lafarge and André Grassi turned out a musical *Un chapeau de paille d'Italie* at the Opéra de Strasbourg in 1966 (22 October). Hungary got a *Florentin kalap* in an adaptation by István Békeffy, music by Tibor Polgár, at Budapest's Fővárosi Operettszinház (19 April 1946) and a second in 1979 at the same theatre (lyrics: Iván Szenes, music: Szabolcs Fényes, 30 March), and the piece has also appeared in two American versions, a disastrous off-Broadway piece called *That Hat* (1964, Cy Young) which ran one performance, and a rather more successful one by Alfred Uhry and Robert Waldman with an even nippier title, *Chapeau* (John Houseman Theater, Saratoga 24 July 1977). *Un chapeau de paille d'Italie* would seem also to have been the source for Genée's comic opera *Rosina* and for the German pasticcio *Hochzeit mit Hindernissen* (Offenbach arr K Martens) produced in 1930 at the Leipzig Altes Theater (16 February).

The next most musically popular Labiche piece, *La Cagnotte*, became the Posse mit Gesang *Vergnügungszügfer* (Karl Stix/C F Stenzl, Carltheater) in Austria in 1870, *Die Sparbüchse* (Ludwig Kusche/Charles Regnier Saarbrücken Stadttheater 31 December) in Germany in 1953 and, in France, *La Cagnotte* (Jack Ledru/Guy Lafarge) produced at Lille in 1983. It was also apparently plundered, without credit, for a shabby British musical called *Instant Marriage*. *Le Voyage de M Perrichon* was made into an Italian musical *Il viaggio di Perrichon* with music by the Contessa Cento della Morea and into an American off-off-Broadway one, *Bon Voyage*, with a pasticcio Offenbach score (York Players ad V B Lawrence/Edward Mabley 18 November 1978), and Guy Lafarge adapted a third Labiche piece as a musical when he combined with Grassi on a version of *Les Noces de Bouchencoeur*, produced at the Théâtre de Besançon in 1966.

The 1874 Lecocq pasticcio put together by H B Farnie as *The Black Prince* for the London stage and said to be based on a combination of three separate French plays, credited Labiche and Delacour as its source and clearly owed part, at least, of its plot to *Le Voyage en Chine*, whilst another piece, the little *A Professional Beauty* played by Letty Lind in London, was apparently taken from his *Un mari qui lance sa femme* (Théâtre du Gymnase, 23 April 1864). Other Labiche derivatives were only nebulously credited. *Die Doppelhochzeit* (Hellmesberger/Léon, von Waldberg) produced at Vienna's Theater in der Josefstadt in 1895 (21 September) was given as based on Labiche, without being more specific, and the same went for *Auf der Rax* (w Martin) played at the Theater an der Wien in a version by Theodore Taube with music by the younger Adolf Müller, *Die Familie Pfifferling* (Ringtheater, 3 December 1881, music: A Grüber), for Hungary's *Az első és masodik* (Béla Szabados/Jenő Rakosi, Népszinház 8 April 1891), and the one-act vaudeville *Sein Bebe* (ad H Paul) to which Hugo Felix composed a score (15 January 1898). None, however, had a success of the kind that would indicate that Labiche's often very full evenings of comedy were, or are, ideal sources for musical plays.

1859 **L'Omelette à la Follembuche** (Léo Delibes/w Marc-Michel) 1 act Théâtre des Bouffes-Parisiens 8 June

1865 **Le Voyage en Chine** (François Bazin/w Alfred Delacour) Opéra-Comique 9 December

1867 **Le Fils du brigadier** (Victor Massé/w Delacour) Opéra-Comique 25 February

1868 **En manches de chemise** (A Villebichot/w Auguste Lefranc, Eugène Nyon) Alcazar 2 April

1868 **Le Roi d'Amatibou** (Hervé/w Edmond Cottinet) Palais-Royal 27 November

1868 **Le Corricolo** (Fernand Poïse/w Delacour) Opéra-Comique 27 November

1876 **Le Roi dort** (Marius Boullard/w Delacour) Théâtre des Variétés 31 March

1879 **Embrassons-nous Folleville** (Avelino Valenti/w Lefranc) Opéra-Comique 6 June

DER LACHENDE EHEMANN Operette in 3 acts by Julius Brammer and Alfred Grünwald. Music by Edmund Eysler. Wiener Bürgertheater, Vienna, 19 March 1913.

In a period when the Viennese musical theatre was casting its first glances towards the more sombrely romantic, less frivolous dramatic and musical styles which would become even more marked a trend after the First World War, Edmund Eysler and his collaborators remained cheerfully and successfully attached to the comic, light-hearted and brightly tuneful mode which had characterized the past decade of Viennese triumphs. After successes at the Bürgertheater with *Der unsterbliche Lump* and *Der Frauenfresser* they produced there, in *Der lachende Ehemann*, a piece with an air of traditional Parisian comedy in its libretto and everything that the name of Eysler meant in indubitably Viennese, dancing, melodious music as a score.

Novelist Heloïse Bruckner (Betty Myra) loves her husband Ottokar (Fritz Werner), but he seems to take her for granted and is interested only in his business – the manufacture of artificial butter. So to find someone with whom she can share her interest in modern music, art and literature, Heloïse strikes up a friendship with the amorous Graf Selztal (Ludwig Herold). Ottokar's maiden cousin, Lucinde (Viktoria Pohl-Meiser), warns him that for the good of his marriage he must get some culture, and the butter-maker announces that he will go to Italy for the very purpose. In fact, he simply slips away to his hunting lodge. It is there, however, that, in his putative absence, Heloïse decides to have an arty party. Events wind up to a pitch where Ottokar, urged on by his two-faced friend Pipelhüber (Leopold Strassmayer) who has himself designs on the faithful wife, is about to sue for a divorce, but when he becomes aware that the figure of fun in Heloïse's latest novel, 'Der lachende Ehemann', is not the husband but the lover, he realizes that Heloïse truly loves him. Pipelhüber, by way of retribution, is snared by the acidulous Lucinde.

The score of the piece ranges through the gamut of dance rhythms from a polka-duet in Act I, via mazurka, gavotte and a snatch of Ländler, to the most successful piece of the evening, Ottokar's temptingly lazy second-act waltz 'Fein, fein schmeckt uns der Wein', a march 'Wohl dem, der meine Lehr benützt' and a parody of Italian gondola-music in Lucinde and Ottokar's first-act duet 'Am Molo dort beim Canaletto'.

Der lachende Ehemann followed happily in the footsteps of the previous Eysler/Bürgertheater successes. It was played for 201 performances in its first run, then returned for a further series the following year, with Vincenz Bauer starring. It received a third run in 1915 at the Raimund-theater with Franz Glawatsch and Rosa Mittermardi in the leading rôles, and at the same time set off on an international career. Hungary was quickest off the mark, with a localized production (ad Adolf Mérei) at the Népopera which featured Imre Szirmai as Ottokár Bárdos and Nelly Hudacsek as Etelka (ex-Hella) alongside Ferenc Pázmán as gróf Szapolczay (ex-Selztal), Lili Berky as Charlotte (ex-Lucinde), Lajos Ujváry as Kakuk Istók (Pipelhüber) and Sándor Horti as Dr Rosenroth. The show, however, found its perhaps biggest success in Germany where, both before and following a three-month season at Berlin's Neues Operetten-Theater, it proved one of the most popular and widely played of all Eysler's long list of Operetten.

Its English-language productions proved less fortunate. Philip Michael Faraday's London mounting (ad Arthur Wimperis) starred Courtice Pounds (Ottokar), Daisie Irving (Hella) and Georges Carvey (Selztal) with James Blakeley in the stand-out comic rôle of the lawyer who effects the reconciliation not only of the leading pair but also of three other pairs in the final act. It started indifferently, and Faraday took it off after 78 performances, revised it, and restaged it at his own Lyric Theatre, where his production of Straus's *Love and Laughter* had foundered, under the more provocative title of *The Girl Who Didn't* (18 December). The second try lasted no longer than the first before being put on the road.

In America, where *The Laughing Husband* was produced under the management of Charles Frohman, a different script, adapted by Harry B Smith, was used and Eysler's score was botched with local additions, four of which came from the pen of Jerome Kern. One of these, 'You're Here and I'm Here', survived to be shifted into another show when Courtice Pounds (Ottokar), Betty Callish (Hella), Fred Walton (Andreas Pipelhuber), Gustave Werner (Selztal), William Norris (Mr Rosenrot) and the lovely Frances Demarest and Venita Fitzhugh left Broadway after 48 performances.

Hungary: Népopera *A nevető férj* 26 September 1913; UK: New Theatre *The Laughing Husband/The Girl Who Didn't* 2 October 1913; USA: Knickerbocker Theater *The Laughing Husband* 2 February 1914; Germany: Neues Operetten-Theater 17 February 1921; Film: 1926 Rudolf Walther-Fein

LACÔME, Paul [LACÔME D'ESTALEUX, Paul Jean-Jacques] (b Houga (Gers), 4 March 1838; d Houga, 12 December 1920). 19th-century Parisian composer who scored two attractive successes in the musical theatre.

The son of a wealthy Gascon family, Lacôme studied music at Aire-sur-l'Ardour in his native Gers and, at the age of 22, won a composing competition, promoted by a magazine, with his one-act opérette *Le Dernier des paladins*. This success encouraged him to move to Paris (dropping his patronym and, so some say, his circumflex accent en route) to pursue a career in music.

Over the next decade he composed songs and orchestral and chamber music as well as contributing articles and criticism to various journals, but it was not until 1870 that his first stage work, the one-act *Épicier par amour*, was staged at the Folies-Marigny. He collaborated on a pair of further short works, produced at the Café Tertulia, with librettist Georges Mancel, before the two men turned out their first full-length piece, the opéra-bouffe *La Dot mal placée* (1873). It was produced at the Théâtre de l'Athénée, where it proved sufficiently successful for Louis Cantin to give Lacôme the opportunity to compose a small part of the score for a Clairville/Delacour libretto for which he was having difficulty in finding suitable music. It had been effectively turned down by Offenbach, whose hesitance, apparently, was not unconnected with the fact that *Jeanne, Jeannette et Jeanneton*, as its title suggests, had not one, but three, prima donnas. Seven other attempts to find a composer for what had become a virtual Cantin audition piece had also failed.

Lacôme took the libretto, and swiftly wrote two whole acts. When he presented his music to Cantin, the director happily agreed that he should complete the score alone. *Jeanne, Jeannette et Jeanneton* (1876), presented at the Folies-Dramatiques with Mme Prelly, Berthe Stuart and the novice Marie Gélabert as its three heroines, was a great success, and was subsequently played in London, New York, Vienna and a long list of other centres as well as coming round again in a series of revivals.

Over the next two decades Lacôme produced a well-spaced series of elegantly tuneful and well-orchestrated scores for all types of musical plays which were shared amongst practically all of the major Parisian musical theatres. However, only with the spicy tale of *Madame Boniface* did he ever again approach the sizeable success of *Jeanne, Jeannette et Jeanneton*. His one-act *La Nuit de Saint-Jean* was played at the Opéra-Comique (1882, 1889), whilst *Ma mie Rosette* (1890), a Paris failure, found some friends, particularly in Australia, in a rewritten London version with much of the score replaced by Ivan Caryll and, like the attractive *Madame Boniface* (1883) – which was seen for two performances at the Theater an der Wien in 1891 as *Madame Bonbon* (ad Heinrich Thalboth, Richard Genée) following its Paris success – it won itself revivals in France.

Le Beau Nicolas was given two performances in Vienna as *Der schöne Nikolaus* but, when a version of *La Gardeuse d'oies* was produced in America, a hackwork score replaced the original music. *Les Quatre Filles d'Aymon*, Lacôme's final work at the age of 60, achieved a respectable run and a production at Budapest's Magyar Színház (*Négy meny-asszony* ad Ferenc Rajna 16 March 1901) but, although the composer continually found some partisans for his music amongst the cognoscenti, none of his later works survived long beyond their usually brief first runs.

Lacôme's other stage works included a ballet, *Le Rêve d'Élias* (1898), and incidental music to Pesquidoux's dramatic poem *Salomé* (1898), and his non-theatrical work a large number of songs and instrumental pieces and several books on musical subjects.

1870 **Épicier par amour** (Georges Mancel) 1 act Théâtre des Folies-Marigny 16 July
1872 **J'veux mon peignoir** (Mancel) 1 act Café Tertulia 11 May
1872 **En Espagne** (Mancel) 1 act Café Tertulia 10 May
1873 **La Dot mal placée** (Mancel) Théâtre de l'Athénée 9 March
1873 **Le Mouton enragé** (Jules Noriac, Adolphe Jaime) 1 act Théâtre des Bouffes-Parisiens 27 May
1875 **Amphytrion** (Charles Nuitter, Alexandre Beaumont) 1 act Théâtre Taitbout 5 April
1876 **Jeanne, Jeannette et Jeanneton** (Clairville, Alfred Delacour) Théâtre des Folies-Dramatiques 27 October
1877 **La Chaste Suzanne** (w Jules Bariller/Paul Ferrier) Palais-Royal 4 July
1879 **Pâques fleuries** (Clairville, Delacour) Théâtre des Folies-Dramatiques 21 October
1880 **Le Beau Nicolas** (Eugène Leterrier, Albert Vanloo) Théâtre des Folies-Dramatiques 8 October
1882 **La Nuit de Saint-Jean** (Erckmann-Chatrian ad Delacour, J de Lau-Lusignan) 1 act Opéra-Comique 13 November
1883 **Madame Boniface** (Ernest Depré, Charles Clairville) Théâtre des Bouffes-Parisiens 20 October
1885 **Myrtille** (Erckmann-Chatrian, 'Maurice Drack' [ie A Poitevin]) Théâtre de la Gaîté 27 March
1887 **Les Saturnales** (Albin Valabrègue) Théâtre des Nouveautés 26 September
1888 **La Gardeuse d'oies** (Leterrier, Vanloo) Théâtre de la Renaissance 26 October
1890 **Ma mie Rosette** (Jules Prével, Armand Liorat) Théâtre des Folies-Dramatiques 4 February
1890 **La Fille de l'air** (Cogniard brothers ad Liorat, Hippolyte Raymond) Théâtre des Folies-Dramatiques 20 June

1891 **Mademoiselle Asmodée** (w Victor Roger/Ferrier, C Clairville) Théâtre de la Renaissance 23 November

1893 **Le Cadeau de noces** (Liorat, Fernand Hue, Stop [ie Morel-Retz]) Théâtre des Bouffes-Parisiens 20 January

1895 **La Bain de Monsieur** (Octave Pradels, Mancel) 1 act Eldorado 12 September

1896 **La Fiancée en loterie** (w André Messager/Camille de Roddaz, Alfred Douane) Théâtre des Folies-Dramatiques 13 February

1898 **Le Maréchal Chaudron** (Henri Chivot, Georges Rolle, 'Jean Gascogne' [ie E Ratoin]) Théâtre de la Gaîté 27 April

1898 **Les Quatre Filles d'Aymon** (w Roger/Liorat, Albert Fonteny) Théâtre des Folies-Dramatiques 20 September

LA-DI-DA-DI-DA Farcical musical in 2 acts based partly on the musical *That's a Pretty Thing* by Stanley Lupino. Additional dialogue by Barry Lupino and Arty Ash. Music by Noel Gay. Victoria Palace, London, 30 March 1943.

To follow the successes of *Me and My Girl* and *Twenty to One* at the Victoria Palace, Lupino Lane produced a fresh vehicle for himself which, without ever reaching the level of the two earlier shows, carried on his run of good fortune. *La-di-da-di-da* was a new version of the 1933 musical *Paste*, a piece written by his cousin Stanley Lupino around a multiplicity of stolen or pawned jewels. Retitled *That's a Pretty Thing*, it had been played for 103 performances at Daly's Theatre (22 November 1933) with a comic cast headed by Bobbie Comber, Sara Allgood, George Gee and Jerry Verno.

Reorganized by another member of the family, Barry Lupino, and with 'additional dialogue by' jokes specialist Arty Ash, the show was again retitled, this time as *La-di-da-di-da*. The excuse for this was that it was the name of the original show's most successful number, a comical piece recommending deep breathing for what ails you. The new version re-routed the jewelled action into a nightclub (nightclubs being currently in fashion, and helpfully allowing the introduction of a cabaretful of speciality acts) and to Scotland for a picturesque finale to the accompaniment of some old and some new Noel Gay songs. It ran for 318 performances largely on the popularity of its star and his team, a team which included brother Wallace Lupino and wife Violet Blythe.

LADY, BE GOOD! Musical play in 2 acts by Guy Bolton and Fred Thompson. Lyrics by Ira Gershwin. Music by George Gershwin. Liberty Theater, New York, 1 December 1924.

One of the most successful of the American dance-and-comedy musicals of the 1920s, *Lady, Be Good!* gave its composer, George Gershwin, paired here for the first time on a Broadway score with brother Ira as lyricist, his first notable musical comedy success, and confirmed the newly established stardom of Fred Astaire and his sister Adele.

Guy Bolton and Fred Thompson's book cast the duo as brother and sister, Dick and Susie Trevor, an impecunious pair thrown out of their lodgings by the machinations of beastly, rich Josephine Vanderwater (Jayne Auburn), who thinks that this is the way to throw discomforted Dick into her money-padded embrace. But Dick is in love with gentle Shirley (Kathlene Martyn). As for Susie, she takes a fancy to a tattered passer-by called Jack Robinson (Alan Edwards). Most of the evening's action is precipitated by

the comical lawyer, Watty Watkins (Walter Catlett), who, for reasons connected with guilt and a very big Mexican with a knife, gets Susie to impersonate an imprisoned Mexican lady who is anxious to collect the fortune of her rich and 'accidentally' deceased husband. Of course, the husband in question is Jack, who escaped his 'accident' and who is only a temporarily disinherited millionaire, so by the final curtain everyone is as rich and happy as they have been since the invention of musical comedy final curtains.

The liveliest of the songs which punctuated the comedy included the jaunty title-song vamped out by Catlett, the stars' duet 'Hang on to Me', Fred Astaire's delightfully exasperated 'The Half of it Dearie, Blues', and, above all, the incidental 'Fascinating Rhythm' performed by stand-up performer Cliff Edwards (aka Ukelele Ike) who had no place or character in the action, but who appeared to sing two or three numbers during the course of the evening ('Little Jazz Bird', and at one stage his own 'Insufficient Sweetie') with considerable success. The loveliest piece, in a show where lovely songs were not really required, was Susie and Jack's winning 'So Am I', but another, cut on the road, eventually proved more memorable: 'The Man I Love'.

In a season that included *Rose Marie* and *The Student Prince*, the stars and the songs of *Lady, Be Good!* nevertheless outpointed such other light-footed musical comedies as the much-boosted *Louie the 14th*, *Mercenary Mary*, and the Duncan Sisters' virtually two-handed version of *Uncle Tom's Cabin* (*Topsy and Eva*). The show had a 41-week, 330-performance run on Broadway before producers Alex Aarons and Vinton Freedley arranged with Alfred Butt to take it to London, where the Astaires had been so well received in *Stop Flirting*. A few minor changes were made for the production at the Empire Theatre, with the stars garnering an extra duet, 'I'd Rather Charleston' (lyric: Desmond Carter). William Kent took on Catlett's rôle and Buddy Lee was the incidental Jeff, taking the place previously occupied by Ukelele Ike. The piece and its stars won London's approval as much as they had New York's, and the production ran for 326 performances. Whilst the Empire Theatre then shuttered its dressing-rooms and took in movies, *Lady, Be Good!* went out for a season's touring around Britain.

An Australian production, mounted by Hugh J Ward, featured the favourite team of soubrette Elsie Prince and comedian Jimmy Godden (Watty) and introduced a ukelele player called Jack Smith to take the moments originally belonging to Ike. However, the show did not take off as well as it had with its original stars. It managed only a fair-to-medium seven weeks in Melbourne, and later played Sydney under the auspices of Sir Benjamin and John Fuller (St James Theatre 30 July 1927). It was given a brief revival at Melbourne's Apollo Theatre in 1936.

Lady, Be Good! has remained in the regional repertoire of English-speaking countries over the years as a favourite example of a 1920s musical comedy, but it has been played almost invariably in heavily souped-up versions. Both of the major productions of recent years – an unfortunate London revival (Saville Theatre 25 July 1968) starring Lionel Blair and Aimi MacDonald, and a Goodspeed Opera House version (3 June 1974) – have filled up the piece's song list with additional Gershwin numbers culled from other shows, revues and films (five in the case of the first, four for the second). What passed for a film version, inevitably, did the same, using Kern's 'The Last Time I Saw Paris' and the Arthur Freed/Roger Edens 'You'll Never Know' alongside bits of Gershwin's score, as Eleanor Powell and Robert Young played out what was, in any case, a different story under the show's title.

Lady, Be Good! put in its most recent metropolitan appearance at London's Open Air Theatre in 1992 (28 July).

UK: Empire Theatre 14 April 1926; Australia: Princess Theatre, Melbourne 18 September 1926; Germany: Städtische Bühnen, Dortmund 19 September 1976; Film: MGM 1941

Recordings: London cast (WRC, part record), archive collection (Smithsonian/Columbia), studio cast (Elektra-Nonsuch)

LADY BEHAVE

LADY BEHAVE Musical comedy in 2 acts by Stanley Lupino. Additional dialogue by Arty Ash. Lyrics by Frank Eyton. Music by Edward Horan. His Majesty's Theatre, London, 24 July 1941.

Jack Hylton's wartime production *Lady Behave* chose the currently popular Ruritania of Hollywood for its setting, presenting the stories of a film-star (Bernard Clifton) in love with a humble stand-in (Sally Gray), and of a comic stunt man (Stanley Lupino) rivalled for the love of his soubrette (Pat Kirkwood) by a gangster (Arthur Gomez). The whole affair was topped with some further comedy gleaned from the antics of a scriptwriter (Hartley Power) who is forced into feminine clothes for a mock wedding in one of the oldest turns in the history of musical theatre.

Stanley Lupino's libretto was a hotch-potch of used themes, not in the same class as his Gaiety musical comedies of the 1930s, but *Lady Behave* was bright and escapist entertainment which gave the opportunity for some light if insignificant songs (of which Lupino's own 'I'm a Nil' proved the most popular) and rather less dancing than had been the habit in his Laddie Cliff series of shows. It wisely played a twice-daily schedule, at 2 pm and 5.15 pm, for an audience which had no wish to be out on the night-time streets of wartime London and, as the only new musical in town alongside reprises of *Me and My Girl* and *Chu Chin Chow*, it succeeded in holding up for nine months (401 performances). During the run Lupino fell ill and was temporarily replaced by Bobby Howes, who then headed a touring company into the provinces when the star/librettist returned, but Lupino was still ill and he died shortly after the show closed, as *Lady Behave* continued its second tour around the provinces.

A Lupino sequel to *Lady Behave*, *The Love Racket*, which used what were allegedly, at least, the same set of characters for a second Hollywood adventure, was posthumously produced at the Victoria Palace (21 October 1943). With Arthur Askey starring, it proved even more successful than the first piece, playing through good runs both in Britain and, under the management of David N Martin, in Australia (Tivoli, Melbourne 23 December 1949).

LADY IN THE DARK

LADY IN THE DARK Musical play in 2 acts by Moss Hart. Lyrics by Ira Gershwin. Music by Kurt Weill. Alvin Theater, New York, 23 January 1941.

The piece which became *Lady in the Dark* was originally conceived by author Moss Hart as a play for Katharine Cornell, but during its writing he became convinced that the fantastical dream sequences he envisaged as a part of the psychoanalysis of his heroine would be better played with music, and he approached Ira Gershwin and Kurt Weill to turn the play into a musical for Gertrude Lawrence.

Miss Lawrence played Liza Elliott, a smart and successful New York magazine editor who, in spite of her healthy material and business position and an apparently uncomplicated love-life with the rich if married Kendall Nesbitt (Bert Lytell), finds herself sufficiently ill at ease to consult a psychiatrist (Donald Randolph). It is finally resolved that Liza has a hang-up left over from a childhood in which her father overstressed the beauty of her mother, and this hang-up has led her to push herself to excel in life to make up for what she sees as an inability to compete as an attractive woman. Once she understands the whys of her uneasiness and dissatisfaction, she can finally give up the safe, unavailable Kendal, refuse the men who need her rather than want her, and start afresh on a less aggressive and defensive business- and love-life.

The musical portion of *Lady in the Dark* was, as Hart planned, virtually restricted to four dream sequences, three long and one brief, which made up the backbone of the show. The first ('O Fabulous One in Your Ivory Tower'/'The World's Inamorata'/'Only One Life to Live'/'Girl of the Moment'/'It Looks Like Liza') presented Liza as a matchless beauty, until blown apart by a portrait of the stern, besuited woman of business; the second ('Mapleton High Chorale'/'This is New'/'The Princess of Pure Delight'/'This Woman at the Altar') visited schooldays, saw her involved with film-star Randy Curtis (Victor Mature) and then threatened with a marriage which she knows she does not want; and the third ('The Greatest Show on Earth'/'He Gave Her the Best Years of his Life'/'Tschaikowsky'/'Jenny') mixed a circus, featuring office photographer Russel Paxton (Danny Kaye) as ringmaster, with a court scene in which her employee Charley Johnson (Macdonald Carey) pounded out accusations. It was this third (originally written as a minstrel show, with the principal number being a piece about the signs of the zodiac) that introduced two of the show's three set songs. Kaye caused a sensation with a madly pattering nonsense song of composers' names ('Tschaikowsky'), and Miss Lawrence followed with the saga of 'Jenny' the girl who would make up her mind, and, by a purposefully pianissimo performance, topped Kaye's number. The third and most popular number in the score came in the final dream. 'My Ship' was the melody which represented Liza's fears and which reappeared at her moments of crisis. It was also the one number of the score in which Weill's music was able to come to the fore over Gershwin's character- and plot-important words.

Hassard Short's production of *Lady in the Dark* was a fine Broadway success. If the work was seemingly somewhat daunting in its subject matter – although dream sequences were as old as the musical theatre and mental processes had been explored as recently as Herbert Fields's *Peggy-Ann* – it was produced with considerable glamour both in its dream portions and in the part of the play set in Liza's fashion magazine's offices, and it had three strong songs and as many outstanding players. Miss Lawrence, in spite of a psychoanalysable tendency to play the clown and upstage her fellow players, gave one of her finest performances as Liza, whilst Kaye's explosion of patter in 'Tschaikowsky' was his first step to stardom. Victor Mature who appeared as the soft piece of beefcake was on the same track. The show ran through 467 Broadway performances, with a two months-plus summer break during which the leading men were replaced.

The cost of the production and wartime conditions were surely at least partly responsible for the failure of *Lady in the Dark* to win a first-class production outside America, and any possibility of this being remedied in the postwar years was wiped out by the release of Paramount's 1944 film in which Ginger Rogers starred as Liza Elliott in a version 'based on' the Broadway show. The dream sequences were filleted and supplemented with Victor Schertzinger's 'Dream Lover' and the Johnny Burke/ Jimmy van Heusen 'Suddenly it's Spring'. These alterations were, however, made good for a 1954 television production in which Ann Sothern was featured.

A German version was produced in Kassel in 1951 under the give-away title of *Das verlorene Lied* (the lost song, ad Maria Teichs, R A Stemmle). As in Germany, when *Lady in the Dark* was finally played in Britain, 40 years after its initial production, it was in a provincial theatre, without a chorus, with an orchestra of nine, and with a cast of mostly expatriate Americans (Kenneth Nelson, Don Fellowes, Edward Wiley) supporting the specially imported Celeste Holm. Shorn of its production values, and with Hart's once ever-so-slightly daring psychoanalytic details seeming banal and almost jokey in an age where the stereotypical New Yorker is known to see a psychiatrist more often than he sees the sky, it proved singularly less workable than it had in the 1940s.

Germany: Staatstheater, Kassel *Das verlorene Lied* 24 May 1951; UK: Playhouse, Nottingham 9 December 1981; Film: Paramount 1944

Recordings: original cast (RCA, Columbia, AEI), TV cast (RCA), film soundtrack (Curtain Calls), selections (Columbia, Decca) etc

LADY LUCK Musical play in 2 acts by Firth Shephard, based on the libretto *His Little Widows* by William Cary Duncan and Rida Johnson Young. Additional scenes by Greatrex Newman. Lyrics by Desmond Carter. Music by H B Hedley and Jack Strachey. Carlton Theatre, London, 27 April 1927.

Producer Laddie Cliff followed up his semi-successful début show *Dear Little Billie* with another musical written by the same team. Firth Shephard, who had done the anglicization of Duncan and Young's *His Little Widows* for the London stage, borrowed the plot from the American musical and used it as the backbone for a vehicle for Cliff, a second dancing light comedian in Cyril Ritchard, and an out-and-out comic star in Leslie Henson as three American stockbrokers who invest in the 'Lady Luck' mine. After jagged fortunes, it renders pay-dirt at the final curtain. There was a theatrical sub-plotline which involved little Jane the milliner's assistant (Phyllis Monkman) becoming a sudden leading lady, and another – the *Little Widows* one – in which Henson inherits a fortune from a Mormon uncle on the condition that he weds all his wives.

Each element was a well-used one, but the appeal of *Lady Luck* was in the telling rather than the tale or, more accurately in the star comedy performances and in the

dancing which was one of the show's main attractions. Cliff did a gracefully eccentric turn to a number called 'Syncopated City', Ritchard performed a smooth routine to 'Happy' and paired with his long-legged Australian partner Madge Elliott in 'I've Learned a Lot', Phyllis Monkman sang and danced 'Blue Pipes of Pan' and the John Tiller Girls did their bit in unison. The suitably dance-rhythmed 'tinkling tunes' of Hedley and Strachey were supplemented, in the fashion of the time, by two American songs: 'Sing' and 'If I Were You' culled from Rodgers and Hart's Broadway flop *Betsy*.

Lady Luck opened the new and short-lived (as a live theatre) Carlton Theatre in London's Haymarket, and Cliff and Shephard proved to have gauged the public taste well. Alongside the town's other, and more romantic, musical hits, *The Desert Song* and *The Vagabond King*, their show ran for 324 performances and established Cliff and his team for a series of popular musicals in the same dance-and-laughter vein over the following years. Two *Lady Luck* companies went into the country whilst the London run continued, followed soon by a third, and the show held its place on the touring lists through into 1929 before being superseded by other British and American musicals in the same style.

LADY MADCAP Musical comedy in 2 acts by Paul Rubens and N Newnham Davis. Lyrics by Paul Rubens and Percy Greenbank. Music by Paul Rubens. Prince of Wales Theatre, London, 17 December 1904.

Following the success of the winsome *Three Little Maids*, George Edwardes commissioned another musical comedy from author-composer Paul Rubens. *Lady Madcap* had a tiresome little heroine (Adrienne Augarde) of the madcap variety beloved by Victorian and Edwardian playgoers, who fools her father into hurrying away from the country on fake business so that she can entertain a whole lot of soldiers and trick a French Count (Maurice Farkoa) and a couple of burglars pretending to be millionaires (Aubrey Fitzgerald, Fred Emney) into mistakenly flirting with her disguised maid, Gwenny (Delia Mason). She herself goes for one Trooper Smith (G P Huntley) who is, of course, a millionaire in disguise. The libretto was even weaker than that for *Three Little Maids* had been, and it was supported by a score which was occasionally pretty, often inane, and at its most popular when pinkly suggestive, as in Maurice Farkoa's serenade 'I Like You in Velvet' with its clear indication that he would prefer the lady without her velvet, or indeed anything else, on. Farkoa 'wore a pale mauve suit and a diamond ring and was voted fascinating' and, although now plumpish and 40, was as much of an attraction as the charmingly comical Huntley and the pretty girls of the cast.

In spite of its weaknesses (which were obviously not considered such), *Lady Madcap* found itself an audience as Edwardes poured into the cast some of his most attractive artists as periodic replacements (Madge Crichton, Zena Dare, Marie Studholme, Lily Elsie, Gabrielle Ray, Maud Hobson, Mabel Russell, Blanche Massey). Nine months in, he revamped the show thoroughly and advertised 'a new edition' which included several new numbers, amongst them Blanche Ring's pair of hits 'Sammy' and 'Bedelia' performed by Farkoa in French. *Lady Madcap* maintained its popularity for nearly a year (354 performances) before going on the road in two companies (soon reduced to one) for one season's touring, and beginning overseas productions. The Shuberts produced the show on Broadway in an americanized version (ad Edward Paulton, R H Burnside, Percy Greenbank) as *My Lady's Maid* with several of the London cast (Madge Crichton, Delia Mason, George Carroll) repeating their rôles and Joe Coyne as the disguised hero. It was scolded by the critics and lasted only 44 performances. Australia's version, the following year, featured Daisy Wallace and Myles Clifton and found little more popularity.

USA: Casino Theater *My Lady's Maid* 20 September 1906; Australia: Princess Theatre, Melbourne 3 August 1907

LADY MARY Musical play in 3 acts by Frederick Lonsdale and J Hastings Turner. Lyrics by Harry Graham. Music by Albert Szirmai. Additional numbers by Phil Charig, Richard Myers and Jerome Kern. Daly's Theatre, London, 23 February 1928.

Producers Lee Ephraim (*The Desert Song, Sunny*) and Jack Buchanan lined up an impressive writing team for *Lady Mary*, with Hungary's Albert Szirmai, who had recently been represented in London by *Princess Charming* (*Alexandra*) and by *The Bamboula*, his first made-for-Britain piece, as theoretically principal composer. If the libretto was rather conventional in its plotting (heir-to-earldom wins pretty lady from rotter) the show's action was peopled with enjoyable characters, notably the kindly self-made millionaire Hatpin Pinge (George Grossmith), who proposes to the heroine's sister (Dorothy Field) 68 times before being accepted, and his sidekick Waghorn (Herbert Mundin), who has to fight a fearsome butler (Thomas Weguelin) to win Lady Mary's maid (Vera Bryer). The incipient Earl was played by Paul Kavanagh and Lady Mary by star soprano Helen Gilliland. Some originality was obtained by setting the first act in Australia, but the effect was apparently rather spoiled by a male chorus of jackaroos 'who', the *Observer* critic noted, 'left me with the impression that if a little woolly lamb said "Baa" to them, they would fall into a deep swoon'.

The jigsaw score for the piece was very curiously credited. Some of the songs were labelled as the joint work of Szirmai and of Richard Myers, an American show-songwriter who must still just about hold the highest strike-out average of pre-Broadway closures, others of Szirmai and a second and slightly more successful trans-Atlantic composer, Phil Charig. Who did what and to whom must remain a mystery. The most winning song of the evening, Mary's pretty farewell to Australia, 'Calling Me Home', was credited to Szirmai and Myers. Unlike 'Calling Me Home', a number of the tunes – in spite of the Australian and British settings of the piece – strove towards being or, with the help of a half-dozen further American contributors, really were American and up-to-date, but no one semed to worry too much about such incongruities, and numbers such as Kalmar and Ruby's 'You Can't Have My Sugar for Tea' duly found a place in the entertainment. Szirmai and Charig supplied a jaunty duet, 'I've Got a Feeling for Somebody', for Mundin and Miss Bryer, and the soubrette had another catchy, bouncy number, 'What About Me?' (Szirmai unaided), both of which were more fun than the other songs given to Grossmith ('You Came Along', Charig's 'Why Should I Feel

Lonely') and to Miss Gilliland (Charig's 'I'll Go Where You Go', Jerome Kern's 'If You're a Friend of Mine' formerly played in *Stepping Stones* as 'In Love with Love').

The libretto of the show was very well reviewed and, although there were general reservations about the potpourri score *Lady Mary*, with Grossmith and Mundin as draws, began well, even breaking Daly's Theatre's house record in an early performance. However, something failed to click, and the show resolutely refused to become a hit. It was closed after 181 striving performances and sent on the road in two companies, but there too it simply failed to take and it ultimately closed in indifference.

THE LADY OF THE SLIPPER, or a Modern Cinderella Musical comedy in 3 acts by Anne Caldwell and Lawrence McCarthy. Lyrics by James O'Dea. Music by Victor Herbert. Globe Theater, New York, 28 October 1912.

Charles Dillingham's spectacular fairy-story show top-billed comedians Montgomery and Stone as a couple of jolly fellows from a cornfield called Punks and Spooks who more or less help their modern Cinderella (Elsie Janis) to get first to the ball and then into her prince's arms, much in the same way that the same two comedians had helped Dorothy and her dog get to the Emerald City nearly a decade previously. With three stars who had little in the way of singing ability, Herbert channelled his most attractive writing into the dance numbers (Witches' Ballet, Harlequinade) and descriptive music. Stone was left to take out his energies on a burlesque routine, the Punch Bowl Glide, whilst Miss Janis encompassed an A sharp below the stave to an E on its top edge in her 'Princess of Far Away', duetted with Mouser, her cat (David Abrahams), in 'Meow! Meow! Meow!' and droned away on Cs and Ds whilst her more vocally equipped Prince Maximilan (Douglas Stevenson) scampered up, in compensation, to a baritone G in 'A Little Girl at Home', in spite of this Cinderella having cornfield help, there was still a fairy godmother (Vivian Rushmore) in the story, not to mention a couple of creatures called, in a fashion which sounded more *Rocky Horror Show* than 1912, Dollbabia (Lillian Lee) and Freakette (Queenie Vassar), whose performances were rather for the delectation of the older children in the audience.

The Lady of the Slipper was Dillingham's third successive production with Montgomery and Stone, following *The Red Mill* and *The Old Town*, and their third success together. It ran for 232 performances on Broadway, apparently saved the producer from severe difficulties brought about by losses recently incurred on less popular shows, and served the comic partners and their promoter splendidly for good runs in Chicago and Boston and for two seasons of touring throughout America, until they traded it in for a newer model, based this time on Aladdin.

THE LADY SLAVEY Musical go-as-you-please in 2 acts by George Dance. Music by John Crook et al. Theatre Royal, Northampton, 4 September 1893; Avenue Theatre, London, 20 October 1894.

One of the earliest pieces in the new modern-dress 'musical comedy' style, and also one of the most phenomenally successful. H Cecil Beryl's production of

The Lady Slavey immediately post-dated George Edwardes's mounting of *In Town* and Frank Harris's hit *Morocco Bound* and it leaned in the same direction as these two pieces by unashamedly including a large variety content in its second act. However, in *The Lady Slavey* the Act-II 'concert' was dressed up in rather more of a genuine storyline than it had been in either of the earlier musicals.

The first act set up the show's plot in which youngest daughter Phyllis (Kitty Loftus) dons a maid's cap and apron to give 'tone' to her under-funded family home when the tinned-tomato millionaire Vincent Evelyn (J C Piddock) comes around in search of a wife. The kindly bailiff Roberts (Witty Watty Walton) agrees to pose as butler, in the hope of getting his money if the can-man is hooked. Of course, Evelyn chooses neither one of Phyllis's sisters (Amy Thornton, Florence Wilson) nor the determinedly pursuing music-hall star Flo Honeydew (producer's wife Edith Rosenthal), but Phyllis. He calculatedly lets it slip out that it is Roberts who is the real millionaire, in disguise, and as the ladies set their sights on the comical bailiff, things begin to go sufficiently unsmoothly to allow the show to run into a second act in which an 'entertainment', in which each of the performers has a number or a spot, is staged for the benefit of the house-guests before the happy ending is tied up.

George Dance's book was accurately aimed at the tastes and predilections of *The Lady Slavey*'s provincial audiences, and John Crook's score, a compound of lively pieces from which the concerted music and a comic number for Roberts called 'The Big Boss Dude' stood out, was perforated with a series of interpolated numbers including such popular songs as 'Daisy Bell', 'After the Ball', 'Wotcher' and 'The Seventh Royal Fusiliers', an original piece by Miss Rosenthal called 'Paddy Murphy Had a Pig', and a song Dance had written with Charles Graham two years earlier called 'In Friendship's Name'. The mixture proved a vast success in its first 14-week tour, in a simultaneous number-two tour run by William Greet, and also in a number-three company under Charles K Chute. All three tours were resumed after the Christmas pantomime season had passed and Greet's tour eventually ran virtually non-stop for 11 years, Chute's for four and Beryl's for no less than 15.

The *Lady Slavey* that totted up such amazing totals was, however, a rather different piece from the original, for in October 1894, after having long hesitated to bring such an unsophisticated show before Londoners, Beryl produced his musical at the Avenue Theatre with Americans May Yohé (Phyllis) and Jenny McNulty (Flo) starred alongside Charles Danby (Roberts) and Henry Beaumont (Evelyn). The libretto was little changed, although one new comedy character was introduced, but the score was largely remodelled and the popular songs replaced by some new material by Crook and by some modern interpolations. Miss Yohé sang 'What's a Poor Girl to Do?' (Joseph and Mary Watson), ''Tis Hard to Love and Say Farewell' (Frank Isitt), and a plantation song 'The Land of Dreams' (Albert Cammeyer/Herbert Walther), but she had her biggest success in duet with Danby in Crook's topical 'It's a Very Wise Child that Knows'. Danby, however, topped the lot with his 'Big Boss Dude'. The hero retained 'In Friendship's Name' and scored with 'Wanted a Wife for a Millionaire' in the first-act finale whilst Adelaide Astor, as one of the

sisters, danced and sang a little number called 'Dorothy Flop' written by her more famous sister Letty Lind.

Handicapped by Miss Yohé, who not only gave a disappointing performance but also hit the headlines in a less than happy manner when her husband Sir Francis Hope (owner of the infamous Hope diamond) was declared bankrupt and she thereafter declared herself off sick, the show ran for only 96 London performances. But *The Lady Slavey* left Miss Yohé and her diamond to their inexorable downward path and hurried back to its home on the road, there to continue its upward and onward perambulations in its new and improved version.

The Lady Slavey went round the English-speaking world, being played alongside the blossoming musicals of the Gaiety Theatre repertoire on the African, Pacific and Oriental circuits (where it was many years a feature of the repertoire of the children's company, Pollard's Lilliputians) and in 1896 George Lederer and Thomas Canary presented what passed for a version of the show (variously attributed) on Broadway. Little remained of Dance's dialogue and – according to the billing – nothing of Crook's score, which had been replaced by some Gustave Kerker pieces. However, London's 'Whoop-de-dooden-do' and 'The Harmless Little Girlie With the Downcast Eye' still appeared on the programmes. Virginia Earle (Phyllis), Dan Daly (Roberts) and Marie Dressler (Flo) were featured in a satisfactory run of 128 performances, which was followed by a second season two years later (72 performances). John F Sheridan introduced *The Lady Slavey* in Australia some years later, starring himself as Roberts and Celia Mavis as Phyllis in a version which had been 'increased in size', and he played it there through several seasons in repertoire. Nowhere, however, did the show harvest the same rewards as in Britain, where the London version of *The Lady Slavey* just went on and on. Even after the end of its two marathon tours, it continued to be played in Britain's provincial houses right through into the 1920s.

USA: Casino Theater 3 February 1896; Australia: Criterion Theatre, Sydney 2 August 1902

LÀ-HAUT Opérette-bouffe in 3 acts by Yves Mirande and Gustave Quinson. Lyrics by Albert Willemetz. Music by Maurice Yvain. Théâtre des Bouffes-Parisiens, Paris, 31 March 1923.

The musical comedy *Là-haut*, written and produced to be music-hall star Maurice Chevalier's follow-up to the highly successful *Dédé* as a legitimate stage vehicle, was a piece well and truly in the insouciant, sexy and dance-filled style that was the rage of the Parisian années folles. Yves Mirande (in a nominal collaboration with producer Quinson) supplied a suavely comical rôle for the star and Maurice Yvain, riding high after the triumph of *Ta bouche* at the Théâtre Daunou, and the ubiquitous Albert Willemetz provided a set of songs in a suitably insinuating music-hall mode.

The late Evariste Chanterelle (Chevalier) arrives in Heaven and learns that his widowed wife Emma (Mary Malbos) is already being amorously pursued by her horrid little cousin, Martel (Louis Blanche). He begs St Peter (Gabin père) to let him have 24 hours extra on earth to put the pest in his place. He is allowed to go, accompanied by a guardian angel called Frisoton (another major music-hall

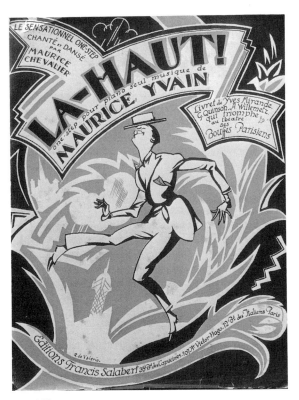

Plate 155.

star, Dranem), but when his time – mostly spent romancing his widow – is up, he brings the pregnant Emma back with him. Horrified at the thought of a celestial birth, St Peter throws the pair out of Heaven. Then Evariste wakes up.

Yvain's score was a bundle of catchy, comical songs made to the measure of his two stars, who shared the bulk of the musical content of the show between them. Chevalier was well served with a fox-trotting paean to Paris ('C'est Paris') which compared it favourably with Paradise, a very funny and catchy plea for sexual tolerance, 'Si vous n'aimez pas ça', which encouraged 'just because you don't like "ça", don't put other folk off', the lively title-song and the incidental 'Ose Anna', whilst Dranem sighed over the naughty things a guardian angel has to watch his client do without being able to partake himself, giggled over some ghastly puns in 'L'Hilarité céleste', took literally the phrase 'C'est la vie', ran through some literary burlesques in the clipping 'Aime-moi, Emma', and cheeked St Peter in 'J'm'en balance' as well as indulging in a pantomime scene of heavenly drunkenness. In the smaller feminine part of the show, Mlle Malbos lined up the advantages and disadvantages of widowhood and explained 'Parce que', whilst Simone Montalet, as an amorous angelette, swooned over Chevalier in the Duo de la tentation.

Là-haut was a splendid success, and Chevalier's triumph in *Dédé* seemed confirmed, but the star was not happy. Dranem, in what was theoretically the second rôle of the angel, had made a stunning major musical-theatre début and Chevalier, quickly noticing that his partner was gathering the largest applause of the night for his characterful and often liberty-taking performance, stamped his foot. Since there could be no question of reducing

Dranem's rôle or crushing his hugely popular extravagances, it did no good. So Chevalier walked out of the show and out of a career in the musical theatre, whilst Dranem went on to become one of the great comic stars of the French musical stage.

The show did not suffer noticeably from its star's departure, and Boucot and Harry Arbell both replaced him happily, first opposite Dranem and then alongside his replacement, the comedian Serjius, as the show played out the year at the Bouffes-Parisiens. The initial run was followed by a quick revival at the Folies-Dramatiques (14 April 1924), before *Là-haut* began a long and enduring career in the French provinces, where it still wins productions 70 years later.

Recording: complete (Decca)

LAHR, Bert [LAHRHEIM, Irving] (b New York, 13 August 1895; d New York, 4 December 1967).

The clownish, flappy-faced comic, who started his performing life in vaudeville and burlesque, made his first appearances in the musical theatre as a wobbly boxer in *Hold Everything!* (1928, Gink Schiner), as an incompetent air mechanic in *Flying High* (1930, Rusty Krause) and in *Hot-Cha!* (1932, Alky Schmidt) before extending his Broadway fame in revue. He had his best Broadway musical part as the little chappie who dreams he is Louis XV in Cole Porter's *Dubarry was a Lady* (1939), joining with Ethel Merman to celebrate 'Friendship', and his last, after a quarter of a century in mostly non-musical shows (*Waiting for Godot, Hotel Paradiso, The Winter's Tale* etc) and the occasional revue, was the title-rôle of *Foxy*, a musical-comedy version of Ben Jonson's *Volpone*, in 1964.

Lahr was seen on television in *Let's Face It* and *The Fantasticks*, but his most famous screen musical portrayal remains his Cowardly Lion in the cinematic version of *The Wizard of Oz* ('If I Were King of the Forest').

Biography: Lahr, J: *Notes on a Cowardly Lion* (Knopf, New York, 1969)

LAJTAI, Lajos (b Budapest, 13 April 1900; d Budapest, 12 January 1966).

Lajtai studied in Budapest and Vienna and, after a period in the army, made his first efforts as a theatre composer with music for the revues *Das nackte Ballet* and *Der Liebestrompeter*, produced at the Vienna Trocadero. The bulk of his work thereafter was mounted in Budapest, where his first book musicals, including an adaptation of Paul Gavault and Robert Charvay's 1904 Paris success *Mademoiselle Josette, ma femme* (*Az ártatlan özvegy*), were staged in the early 1920s. He wrote liberally for all kinds of stages throughout the decade, supplying songs for children's shows, and scores or part-scores for several spectacular operett-revues or revue-operetts or unqualified revues such as *A meztelen Pest* (Budapesti Színház 1925) and the Fővárosi Operettszínház's *Nézze meg az ember* (1926).

Lajtai's 1927 musical comedy *Mesék az írógépről* ran up more than 50 performances at the Városi Színház, but his first international success came with the 1928 *A régi nyár* (once upon a time in summer), a Budapest triumph with a first run of over 100 performances, and subsequently seen under the title *Sommer von Einst* (ad Hans Hellmut Zerlett,

Swariowsky) at Nuremberg (9 November 1929) and then at Stuttgart (12 May 1931). Thereafter, a fine series of successful musicals followed, several of which won subsequent productions beyond Hungary. *Sisters*, created by Rózsi Bársony and Ilona Titkos as two little girls from Pest who become a sister act at the Moulin-Rouge before going home to happiness, was played for two months in German (ad Bela Jenbach) at Vienna's Johann Strauss-Theater (22 October 1930) with Irén Biller and Grete Hornik starred; the musical comedy *Az okos mama*, whilst being revived several times in Budapest after its original successful run with Sári Fedák as the 'clever mama' of the title, appeared as *Die kluge Mama* (ad Jenbach) at the Vienna Volksoper in 1931 (6 April); and the costume piece *Őfelsége frakkja* (His Majesty's overcoat), a 300-performance hit with Emmi Kosáry, Márton Rátkai and István Gyergyai in Budapest, became *Katinka* (ad André Barde) on the Paris stage. At home, there were further successes with the revusical *Régi orfeum* (Old Time Music Hall) and a piece about the Rothschilds, starring Vilma Medgyasszay as a musical Mama Rothschild, watching her youngest son, Jacob, getting entangled with a Parisian singer (Hanna Honthy) before coming back to his hometown Betty.

Lajtai's output, and virtually his career in the theatre, came to an end at the age of 35. With the rise of Nazism, he left Hungary and, after a detour via Paris, where he capitalised on his success with *Katinka* by supplying some further music to the Théâtre des Nouveautés, settled in Sweden. Although he returned regularly to his homeland after the end of the War, his only 'new' stage show produced thereafter was *Három tavasz* (three springtimes), a piece which re-used favourite songs from his previous shows as its score.

1923 **Az asszonyok bolondja** (István Bródy) Budai Színkör 9 May

1924 **Az alvó feleség** (Mátyás Feld, Imre Harmath) Budapesti Színház 13 July

1925 **Az ártatlan özvegy** (Paul Gavault, Robert Charvay ad Harmath) Városi Színház 25 December

1927 **Mesék az írógépről** (István Békeffy, István Szomaházy) Városi Színház 8 October

1927 **Mackó urfi kalandjai** (Gyula Komor) Fővárosi Operettszinház 19 November

1928 **A Jégkirály kincse** (Arthur Lakner) Fővárosi Operettszinház 6 January

1928 **Postás bácsi szerencséje** (Károly Breitner) Fővárosi Operettszinház 4 March

1928 **A régi nyár** (I Békeffy) Budai Színkör 15 June

1928 **Dörmögő Dömötör** (Károly Beretvás) Fővárosi Operettszinház 17 November

1928 **Párizsi divat** (I Békeffy) Városi Színház 22 December

1929 **Sisters** (I Békeffy, László Vadnai) Belvárosi Szinház 2 March, Király Színház 10 January 1930

1930 **Lila test, sárga sapka** (I Békeffy, László Békeffy) Nyári Operettszinház 7 June

1930 **Az okos mama** (I Békeffy, Béla Szenes) Fővárosi Operettszinház 26 November

1931 **Őfelsége frakkja** (I Békeffy) Király Színház 19 September

1932 **A régi orfeum** (I Békeffy, Jenő Faragó) Fővárosi Operettszinház 12 March

1932 **A Rotschildok** (I Békeffy, Ferenc Martos/Martos) Fővárosi Operettszinház 25 November

1932 **Amikor a kislányból nagylány lesz** (I Békeffy) Budai Színkör 10 June

1932 **A fekete lány** Labriola Színház (Városi Színház) 16 October

1933 **Az a huncut postás bácsi** (Beretvás) Fővárosi Operettszínház 1 January

1933 **Katinka** (revised French *Őfelsége frakkja*, ad André Barde) Théâtre de l'Empire, Paris, 22 February

1933 **Tánc a boldogságért** (Andor Szénes/Adorján Bónyi) Budai Színkör 14 June

1933 **Sült galamb** (László Szilágyi) Király Színház 7 October

1934 **Nápolyi kaland** (I Békeffy, Vadnai) Fővárosi Operettszínház 10 November

1935 **Tonton** (Barde) Théâtre des Nouveautés, Paris, 19 March

1936 **La Poule** (w Henri Christiné/Henri Duvernois/ad Barde) Théâtre des Nouveautés, Paris, 9 January

1958 **Három tavasz** (Dezső Kellér) Fővárosi Operettszinház 19 December

LALOR, Frank (b Washington, DC, 20 August 1869; d New York, 15 October 1932).

Comedian Lalor made his first stage appearances as a child in variety and played as an adult at Tony Pastor's in New York (1892) before beginning a long and ultimately prominent career in musical comedy. He was first seen on Broadway in *The Show Girl* (1902, Dionysius Lye), as Bliffkins in *An English Daisy* (1904) and as Shamus O'Scoot in *Mr Wix of Wickham* (1904), played in vaudeville houses in *The Athletic Girl* (1905, Captain O'Shiver), in Chicago in *The Filibuster* (Bunny) and went on the road in Karl Hoschna's early *Prince Humbug*. In his forties, he played in such pieces as *Comin' Thru the Rye*, *The Candy Shop* and the *The Bachelor Belles* before making a big success as the comical-satyrical 'Donny' Dondidier, in Ivan Caryll's hit musical *The Pink Lady* ('I Like It!', 'Donny Didn't, Donny Did'), a part which he repeated on the London stage.

A series of good comic rôles followed this success, as Lalor appeared in the short-lived but admired *Iole* (1913, Clarence Guildford), as the philandering professor of Caryll's *Papa's Darling* (1914, Achille Petipas), in Irving Berlin's revusical *Stop! Look! Listen!* (1915, Gideon Gay) and as the chief comic of Marc Connelly's Broadway début show, *The Amber Express* (1916, Percival Hopkins). He featured alongside Fred Stone and Charlotte Greenwood in the Mormon musical *His Little Widows* (1917, Abijah Smith), and in the Chicago musical *Good Night Paul* (aka *Oh! So Happy* 1917, Frank Hudson), but he had to return to London to find himself another real winner. In 1918 he appeared as Prosper Woodhouse ('All Line Up in a Queue') in the long-running West End hit *The Lilac Domino*, and he remained in London to take part in the quick-flop import *Nobody's Boy* (1919, Colonel Bunting).

Lalor's last shows brought no such hits, whether in America – *The Cameo Girl* (1921, Jones), *Suzette*, the botched *Phi-Phi* (Phi-Phi), *Luckee Girl* (1928, Pontavès), a brief appearance in Busby Berkeley's *The Street Singer* or Friar Tuck in a 1932 revival of *Robin Hood* – or in London, where he played, subordinate to W H Berry, as Oliver J Oosenberry in Szirmai's *The Bamboula*, and when time came to tally up it was seen that the memorable shows of his career finally totalled few, even though the leading rôles had been many.

LAMBELET, Napoleon (b Corfu, 27 February 1864; d London, 25 September 1932). Corfiot composer and conductor in the London theatre.

Trained at the Naples Conservatoire, Lambelet took his first steps as a conductor and theatre composer in Greece, where he was chef d'orchestre at Athens's principal theatre and had an operetta, *M Pardarmenos*, produced in 1890. He later went to Alexandria where he became head of the local conservatoire, and then, in the mid-1890s, moved to Britain. He worked in London as musical director at the Coronet Theatre, Notting Hill Gate, and at the Alhambra Theatre under Charlot and Leveaux, and he also had several musicals staged, the most substantial of which were the basic replacement score for Seymour Hicks's much-touted 'Armenian opera' *The Yashmak*, the early revue *Pot Pourri* ('Mary Was a Housemaid') and the successful touring show *The Transit of Venus*.

Lambelet provided additional songs for a number of West End shows ('I Can't Refrain from Laughing' in *The Geisha* etc), incidental music and one-act operettas for several music halls, music for pantomime at the Coronet Theatre, and also turned out a patriotic Boer War piece called *The Gentleman in Khaki* which won several benefit showings. An attempt in 1918 to produce his own very old-fashioned comic opera *Valentine* ended in an expensive failure.

His brother, George Lambelet (1875–1945) was also a composer and musicologist.

1890 **M Pardarmenos** Athens
1897 **The Yashmak** (Seymour Hicks, Cecil Raleigh) Shaftesbury Theatre 31 March
1898 **The Transit of Venus** (Adrian Ross, James T Tanner) Dublin 9 April
1900 **A Gentleman in Khaki** (Preston Hope) 1 act Theatre Royal, Drury Lane 15 May, Coronet Theatre 17 May
1904 **The Last Load** (Arthur Sturgess) 1 act London Coliseum 24 December
1905 **Fenella** (Arthur Rackham Cleveland) 1 act London Coliseum 18 December
1915 **A Bit of Khaki** (Cleveland) 1 scene Empress, Brixton 17 May
1918 **Valentine** (Harry Davenport/Charles Wibrow) St James's Theatre 24 January

LAMY, Charles [CASTARDE, Charles] (b Lyon, 28 August 1857; d 1940).

The son of the director of Lyon's celebrated Théâtre des Célestins and the foremost of a family of light-tenor vocalists of charm (his brother Maurice and his son Adrien followed the same path), Charles Lamy had a 40-year career in the musical theatre, at first as a sweet-voiced tenor juvenile, and later as a full-blooded comedy player of some finesse. After beginning his career in the theatre as an orchestral violinist at the Théâtre de Saint-Étienne, he made his first stage appearances at the same house, but he began his lyric career in earnest, after some studies at his local conservatoire, playing opérette in Marseille (1876–7), touring in Italy (1877–8) and playing at the Galeries Saint-Hubert in Brussels (1879) before he was engaged at the Paris Théâtre des Bouffes-Parisiens in 1880.

His first rôle at the Bouffes was probably his most memorable of all for, in December 1880, he created the high tenorino-cum-comedy part of the Prince Fritellini in Audran's *La Mascotte* ('Le Je ne sais quoi poétique'), but there were other fine parts to follow. Prince Olivier in Audran's next work, *Gillette de Narbonne* (1882), and the goofy Egyptian Putiphar Bey in Victor Roger's comical *Joséphine vendue par ses soeurs* (1886) were his most memorable creations in the first part of a career which also

included such new works as *Coquelicot* (1882, Pérez), Lacôme's successful *Madame Boniface* (1883, Fridolin), *La Dormeuse éveillée* (1883, Saturnin), Serpette's *La Gamine de Paris* (1887), Lecocq's *Les Grenadiers de Mont-Cornette* (1888, Canut), Audran's *Miette* (1888), Pugno's *Le Valet de Coeur* (1888), Roger's *Le Fêtiche* (1890, Valentin des Hauts-Crénaux), Varney's *La Fille de Fanchon la vielleuse* (1891, Jules), *La Famille Vénus* (1891) and Paul Vidal's *Eros* (1892).

The vocal demands grew progressively less and the comic ones more prominent as he moved on through such pieces as Pessard's *Mam'zelle Carabin* (1893, Monsieur Chose), Messager's *Madame Chrysanthème* (1893, Kangourou), Varney's *Les Forains* (1894, Jules César), Banès's *Le Bonhomme de neige* (1894), Diet's *Fleur de vertu* (1894, Casimir), *L'Élève de Conservatoire* (1894, Gédau), *La Saint-Valentin* (1895), *La Belle Épicière* (1895, Pomponneau), the winning vaudeville *La Dot de Brigitte* (1895, Mulot), Audran's successful *L'Enlèvement de la Toledad* (1895, Gaston Lombard) and the part of the secret agent in *Monsieur Lohengrin* (1896, Boussard) to what was undoubtedly the best new rôle of this later period of his career as the joyously silly-âne Duc Jehan de Beaugency of *Les Fêtards* (1897).

In 1897 Lamy became a member of the company at the Palais-Royal, where *Les Fêtards* was included amongst the occasional musical productions, but he still made intermittent forays on to other musical stages, creating memorably the part of a low-comical Paris in Claude Terrasse's *Paris, ou le bon juge* (1906, revived 1922), and latterly onto the cinema stage. He played in Terrasse's *Le Coq d'Inde* (1908), appeared in revue and, in 1920, took the rôle of Ischabod in the production of *Rip!* which opened the new Théâtre Mogador and in which his son, Adrien, played the small part of Pickly. He died alongside that same son under German bullets in 1940 at the age of 83.

Adrien LAMY (d 1940), a clean-necked, boyish, light vocalist, dancer and actor had a lively career in the Paris musical theatre of the 1920s, playing in the French version of *The Pink Lady*, replacing Urban in the title-rôle of *Dédé*, and appearing in prominent juvenile parts in a full list of other popular jazz-age musicals including the Théâtre Marigny's *Je t'veux* (1923, Vignac, 'C'est fou la place que ça tient', 'Si c'était pour en arriver la' and the shimmy orientale 'Là-bas'), Szulc's *Le Petit Choc* (1923, Alfred de Marigny, 'L'Ouverture de la pêche', 'Il faut savoir prendre les femmes'), and Moretti's *En chemyse* (1924) and *Trois jeunes filles ... nues!* (1925). In 1926 he was the first French Tom in *No, No, Nanette*, introducing Paris to 'Thé pour deux' and 'J'ai confessé à la brise' in partnership with Loulou Hégoburu, with whom he teamed again in Paris's *Tip-Toes* (Steve Burton), performing 'La Femme que j'aimais' (a reverse-sex 'The Man I Love') and 'Un sentiment' ('That Certain Feeling'). He played the put-upon young hero Étienne Fanoche in *Zou!* (1930), appeared in Moretti's *Rosy* (1930) and was Orphée to the Eurydice of Marise Beaujon in the Mogador's starry 1931 revival of *Orphée aux enfers*. In the subsequent 1930s he appeared in the Parisian-Hungarian *Katinka* (1933 'En écoutant les petits oiseaux' with Lyne Clevers), as Frontignac in the Josephine Baker *La Créole* (1934) and in such productions as *Un p'tit bout de femme* (1936), *Les Soeurs Hortensia* (1937) and *Les Jolies Viennoises* (1938).

Maurice LAMY (b ?1863; d April 1930) created two major musical comedy rôles – the bedazzled shop-boy Aristide in Messager's *Les P'tites Michu* and the comical Loustot of the same composer's *Véronique* – in a career which ran closely alongside that of his brother Charles. He also appeared in the premières of such pieces as *Les Pommes d'or* (1883), Serpette's *Cousin-Cousine* (1893) and *Shakespeare!* (1899, Jack), Pessard's *La Dame de trèfle*, Lecocq's *La Belle au bois dormant* (1889, Le Taupier), the French version of *Donna Juanita* and *Cliquette* (1893, Nicolas), played des Toupettes in the 1897 revival of *Les Douze Femmes des Japhet*, and created parts in *Sa Majesté l'amour* (1897, Tricala) and *La Fille de la mère Michel* (1903). He later appeared in supporting rôles in several of Louis Ganne's works including *Hans, le joueur de flûte* (Petronius) and *Rhodope* at Monte-Carlo, where he was, from 1913 director of the Casino, in *Cocorico* (Margrave Jean-François) and in Banès's *Léda* (1909, Ménélas) and, in his sixties, took a four-line rôle as Le Directeur du Casino in Hahn's *Le Temps d'aimer* (1926).

DAS LAND DES LÄCHELNS Romantic Operette in 3 acts by Ludwig Herzer and Fritz Löhner-Beda based on the libretto *Die gelbe Jacke* by Victor Léon. Music by Franz Lehár. Metropoltheater, Berlin, 10 October 1929.

Die gelbe Jacke, written to a libretto by the partner of Lehár's earliest success, *Der Rastelbinder* (1902), and of his greatest triumph, *Die lustige Witwe* (1905), and produced by Karczag at the Theater an der Wien in 1923 (9 February), was another version of the East-has-difficulty-meeting-West theme so popular in such turn-of-the-century works as *The Geisha*. Hubert Marischka appeared as the Chinese Prince Sou-Chong Chwang whose marriage to the Viennese Lea von Limburger (Betty Fischer) threatens to founder when she cannot cope with oriental customs. Luise Kartousch as his sister, Mi, was paired with Josef König (Claudius von Wimpach) in a parallel soubret story.

Die gelbe Jacke won some appreciative comments for its attractive mixture of Chinese and Viennese tones (one critic apparently nicknamed it *Monsieur Butterfly*) and it proved a tidy, unspectacular success, running for three months and 98 performances at the Theater an der Wien. Just before its closure there, it was produced at Budapest's Király Színház (*A sárga kabát*, 5 May 1923) with Tivadar Uray, Erzsi Péchy, Árpád Latabár, Márton Rátkai and Hanna Honthy starred. It was not a success, however, to compare with the previous year's *Frasquita* or with the Theater an der Wien's other recent Operetten, *Der letzte Walzer*, *Die Frau im Hermelin* or Lehár's own *Die blaue Mazur* and *Wo die Lerche singt*, and it was positively overshadowed in the two following seasons by the huge successes of *Gräfin Mariza* and *Der Orlow*, all of which may help to explain why the myth has developed that *Die gelbe Jacke* was a thorough failure.

When Lehár moved into his tenor-dominated Tauber era of writing, *Die gelbe Jacke* was given a second chance. Tauber's greatest successes of the 1920s had been in Berlin, and the Rotter brothers of the Metropoltheater, who had hosted the tenor's success in *Paganini* and *Friederike*, asked the composer for another Tauber vehicle. Never loath to re-use the scores of his less enduring shows, Lehár had already produced a second version of *Wiener Frauen* and third versions of *Die Göttergatte* and *Der*

Plate 156. *East fails to meet West for longer than two acts. Günter Neubert as Sou-Chong and Gail Steiner as Lisa in the Nuremberg Städtische Bühnen production of* **Das Land des Lächelns***.*

Sterngucker, and now, to follow his successes with the lushly sentimental *Paganini*, *Der Zarewitsch* and *Friederike*, he decided on a romantic tenor remake of the tale of either *Endlich allein*'s mountaineering prince or of *Die gelbe Jacke*'s Chinese one. It was the Chinaman who won, but instead of returning the libretto to Léon to be Tauberized, Lehár instead handed the seven-year-old work to Ludwig Herzer and Fritz Löhner, the librettists of *Friederike*, for a rewrite. He himself revamped part of his score, principally to turn the rôle of the Prince into the kind of all-singing, all-throbbing Tauber-rolle which the previous Operetten had made a sine qua non.

The most obvious alteration to the *Die gelbe Jacke* book was the exchange of Léon's original reconciliatory ending for the now obligatory and fashionably unhappy one, in line with the bruised-to-brokenhearted final curtains featured in the three last Operetten. The most obvious change in the score was a large new number for the star, written in the ringing style of *Paganini*'s 'Gern hab' ich die Frau'n geküsst' or *Friederike*'s 'O Mädchen, mein Mädchen'. 'Dein ist mein ganzes Herz' was to turn out to be the most successful of all Lehár's songs for Tauber.

In *Das Land des Lächelns* (the title was already an improvement), the impassive Prince Sou Chong (Tauber) weds Viennese Lisa (Vera Schwarz) and takes her back to his homeland. There she discovers that the Prince is expected by custom to take Chinese brides as well. He is unable to defy the traditions of his country and she, in spite of her love for him, cannot bend to them. Aided by Sou Chong's sister, Mi (Hella Kürty), a trapped little soubrette who longs for a taste of the freedom that she sees Western women have, and by her Viennese friend Graf Gustl von Pottenstein (Willi Stettner), she plans an escape. When the Prince catches the fleeing foreigners he realizes that it is better to let Lisa go. Broken-hearted but impassive, he remains to rule his country.

Although the applause-tugger of Tauber's rôle was the new song, the part of Sou Chong contained some less obvious but more beautiful pieces, notably his two first-act songs, the philosophical 'Immer nur lächeln' and the gentle love song 'Von Apfelblüten einen Kranz', as well as some ringingly dramatic moments in the long and two-handed second-act finale which the tenor shares with the soprano. The prima donna, too, had many other fine moments, ranging from her light-hearted first-act entry song and the tiptoeing duet 'Bei einem Tee à deux' to the romantic duet 'Wer hat die Liebe', but it was the powerful light-operatic 'Ich möcht wieder einmal die Heimat seh'n', in which Lisa pours out her longing for her homeland in tones which have nothing to do with the usual Do-you-remember-Vienna type of song, which was her great moment and is, in spite of all the tenorizing propaganda to the contrary, arguably the musical highlight of the score. The soubrette rôle of Mi was equally well parted, the little princess's shy longing for Western freedom, expressed trippingly in the song 'Im Salon zur blau'n Pagoda', and her gently comical duos with Gustl ('Meine Liebe, deine Liebe', 'Zig, zig, zig') contrasting breath-catchingly with the powerful emotions and big singing of the other two principals.

The Berlin première of *Das Land des Lächelns* was an outstanding success, the hit song quickly became a favourite, and productions of the show flourished throughout Germany in the years that followed, with Tauber guesting as the star in several of the main centres. Hungary, as usual, was first off the mark with a foreign production, opening *A mosoly országa* at Budapest Opera-ház with Ferenc Székeleyhidy (Szu Csong), Margit Nagy (Liza), Júlia Orosz (Mi) and Lajos Laurisin (Feri Hat-faludy), just a few days before the Theater an der Wien premièred their Viennese production, with Tauber again starring opposite Vera Schwarz and Hella Kürty again as Mi. The two original stars did not stay long with this production, and Margit Suchy and Otto Maran soon succeeded to their rôles, whilst Luise Kartousch, the original Mi of *Die gelbe Jacke*, took up the new version of her old part during the 101 performances that Vienna's version played. The production was reprised for a fortnight the following year, but, in spite of this limited first Viennese run, *Das Land des Lächelns* established itself as a repertoire favourite in Austria just as it did in Hungary.

Paris was once again beaten to the nod by the Belgians who produced the first *Le Pays de sourire* (ad André Mauprey, Jean Marietti) at Ghent (Théâtre Royale, 1 April 1932) with Louis Izar and Germaine Roumans in the lead-ing rôles, but the French production, mounted six months

later, with Willy Theunis and Georgette Simon starred, was a prodigious success, securing *Le Pays de sourire* a prominent place in the permanent repertoire of the French musical theatre where it has remained, through regular revivals, ever since.

In spite of its success in Europe, however, the Operette did not catch on in Britain or in America. Tauber himself introduced his show to London's Theatre Royal, Drury Lane, with Renée Bullard as his Lisa and Hella Kürty again as Mi, but *The Land of Smiles* (ad Harry Graham) failed to appeal. It was not simply Tauber's well-publicized absences from the cast that deterred British audiences of the dawning 1930s from patronizing the show, it was simply that their pleasure was found in the then-popular dance-and-laughter musicals and their taste at the time did not run to a Very Big Romantic Operette. The show closed after 71 performances. Tauber repeated his Sou Chong in London in 1932 (Dominion Theatre 31 May) and again ten years later (Lyric Theatre 18 June 1942), each time paired with Josie Fearon and Miss Kürty, but the show never won a London run. In 1959 it was produced by the Sadlers Wells Opera Company (Charles Craig, Elizabeth Fretwell, June Bronhill, ad Christopher Hassall) but it did not remain in their repertoire.

In America, Graham's version was further adapted (ad Harry B Smith, Edgar Smith, Harry Clarke) and the resultant piece produced as *Prince Chu Chang* with Clifford Newdahl and Gladys Baxter starring in a bowdlerized tale in which the Prince and Lisa did not actually get married, and she ended up finding consolation in the arms of Gustl. It folded on the road. It was only after a St Louis Muny production and a second prematurely folding stab at a Broadway version (26 December 1932, w Charles Hackett, Nancy McCord) that the Shuberts finally got yet another adaptation (ad Ira Cobb, Karl Farkas, Felix Günther) of the show to Broadway in 1946 under the title *Yours is My Heart*. Sixteen years on, Tauber again starred, alongside Stella Andreva and Lillian Held (equipped with a Paul Durant interpolation explaining 'Paris Sings Again') but, yet again, an English-language version of *Das Land des Lächelns* failed.

Tauber put his *Das Land des Lächelns* on film soon after the show had been produced, and in 1952 another version (scr: Axel Eggebrecht, Hubert Marischka) with the music adapted by Alois Melichar, was produced with Jan Kiepura and Marta Eggerth starring. Prince Sou became a singer who falls in love with his Lissy over a duet and the pair produce a little Chrysanthemum on their way to their unhappy ending. Ludwig Schmitz featured as Chief Eunuch Kato.

Das Land des Lächelns remains a prominent fixture in the repertoire in Germany and in Austria, where it was played at the Staatsoper in 1938 (again with Tauber) and from 1985 at the Volksoper where Siegfried Jerusalem and Nicolai Gedda have both appeared at various times as Sou Chong. It also holds a continuing place both in France and in Hungary (ad Zsolt Harsányi) but in spite of regular exposure through recordings and through broadcasting, and the wide popularity of its tenor bon-bon, *The Land of Smiles* remains generally unplayed in English-language countries.

Hungary: Magyar Királyi Operaház *A mosoly országa* 20 September 1930; Austria: Theater an der Wien 26 September 1930;

UK: Theatre Royal, Drury Lane *The Land of Smiles* 8 May 1931; France; Théâtre de la Gaîté-Lyrique 15 November 1932; USA: Shubert Theater *Yours Is my Heart* 5 September 1946; Films: Max Reichmann 1931, Berolina/Union Films 1952

Recordings: complete (Columbia, EMI, Eurodisc), complete in French (EMI), selections (Philips, Polydor, EMI, Preiser, Telefunken etc), selection in Hungarian (Qualiton), selection in English (HMV), selections in French (Decca, Philips), selection in Italian (Fonit-Cetra) etc.

LANDESBERG, Alexander (b Grosswardein, 15 July 1848; d Vienna, 14 June 1916).

At first a journalist in Budapest and then in Vienna, Landesberg was also for some 20 years a librettist and lyricist mostly for the Viennese stage. He had his one great success with the text for Heinrich Reinhardt's Operette *Das süsse Mädel*, a long-running Carltheater hit in 1901 prior to productions around the world, but never approached the record established by *Das süsse Mädel* with his other works. Amongst these, several collaborations with Eugen von Taund brought forth two reasonably successful pieces in *Der Wunderknabe* (later seen in Britain as *The Little Genius*) and *Die Lachtaube*, which was exported to Berlin (Theater Unter den Linden 10 August 1895) after its 51-performance Viennese run, whilst a version of the French comedy *Nelly Rosier*, entitled *Fräulein Präsident* and composed by Alfred Müller-Norden, went on from its 25 nights in Vienna to be seen in Budapest as *Elnök kisasszony* (ad Károly Stoll, Fővárosi Nyari Színház 20 July 1900).

He had a number of works produced at the Theater an der Wien where his *Die Blumen-Mary* played 40 nights, *Der Lebemann* was seen 31 times, Reinhardt's *Der Generalkonsul* with Girardi in its starring rôle reached its 78th night before going on to Budapest as *A főkonsul, Das Garnisonsmädel* (*Huszárvér* in Hungary) played 53 performances consecutively, and *Der schöne Gardist* lasted just a month prior to its Hungarian production (*Szép gárdista*). *Clo-Clo*, with Fritzi Massary in the title-rôle, also played a month at Danzers Orpheum, whilst a further Reinhardt work, *Der liebe Schatz*, played 45 nights at the Carltheater, the best run of three latter-day Landesberg Operetten produced there.

1886 **Fioretta** (Max von Weinzierl, Alfred Strasser) Deutsches Theater, Prague 3 April
1889 **Das Familie Wasserkopf** (Julius Stern/w D Schild) Carltheater 24 March
1889 **Page Fritz** (von Weinzierl, Strasser/w Richard Genée) Deutsches Theater, Prague 24 November
1889 **Das Paradies** (Adolphe Ferron/w Leo Sendach) Brünn 21 May
1893 **Münchner Kindl** (Carl Weinberger/w Leo Stein) Theater Unter den Linden, Berlin 7 November
1895 **Die Lachtaube** (Eugen von Taund/w Stein as 'Otto Rehberg') Carltheater 14 April
1896 **Im Pavilion** (Karl Kappeller/Blum, Toché ad w Ludwig Fischl) Theater in der Josefstadt 6 March
1896 **Der Wunderknabe** (von Taund/w Stein) Theater an der Wien 28 March
1897 **Das rothe Parapluie** (*Le Voyage de Corbillon*) German version w Fischl w music by Kappeller Theater in der Josefstadt 27 February
1897 **Die Blumen-Mary** (Carl Weinberger/w Stein) Theater an der Wien 18 November
1897 **Der Prokurist** (von Weinzierl/w Leo Gerhard) Raimundtheater 25 September

1898 **Der Dreibund** (von Taund/w Stein) Theater an der Wien 28 April
1899 **Fräulein Präsident** (Alfred Müller-Norden/w Fischl) Theater an der Wien 6 May
1901 **Die Primadonna** (Müller-Norden/ad w Fischl) Carltheater 31 January
1901 **Das süsse Mädel** (Heinrich Reinhardt/w Stein) Carltheater 25 October
1902 **Der liebe Schatz** (Reinhardt/w Stein) Carltheater 30 October
1902 **Clo-Clo** (Ferdinand Pagin/w Stein) Danzers Orpheum 23 December
1903 **Der Lebemann** (Alfred Grünfeld/Josef Stolba ad w Fischl) Theater an der Wien 16 January
1904 **Der Generalkonsul** (Reinhardt/w Stein) Theater an der Wien 29 January
1904 **Das Garnisonsmädel** (Raoul Mader/w Stein) Theater an der Wien 29 October
1907 **Der selige Vincenz** (Mader/w Stein) Carltheater 31 January
1908 **Der schöne Gardist** (Heinrich Berté/w E Limé, A M Willner) Theater an der Wien 4 April
1908 **Der Glücksnarr** (Heinrich Berté/E Limé ad w Willner) Carltheater 7 November

THE LAND OF NOD Musical comedy in 2 acts by Frank R Adams and Will Hough. Music by Joe Howard. Additional material by George V Hobart and Victor Herbert. Opera House, Chicago, 17 June 1905; New York Theater, New York, 1 April 1907.

A children's extravaganza on the accepted model of the period, *The Land of Nod* was first produced by the Majestic Extravaganza Company in Chicago, where authors Hough, Adams and Howard had already combined to produce a long line of highly successful shows. It was named after a song from their earlier hit, *His Highness, the Bey*. Too big a piece for the little La Salle Theater, it was shifted instead to the Chicago Opera House where Mabel Barrison, the original babe heroine of *Babes in Toyland*, and wife to composer Howard, appeared as little Bonnie who goes to sleep and dreams herself into a series of lavishly staged adventures in the land of Nod – much in the same way that little Dorothy had got herself into her adventures in Oz a few seasons earlier, and Miss Barrison and her fellow babe had travelled through Toyland the following year. May de Sousa (Jack of Hearts) was the jeune premier of the evening, Juliet Wood was soubrette Rory Bory Alice and the main credit for the evening's visuals went to designer Ansel Cook.

Two years after its first Chicago production, *The Land of Nod* was taken up by the Will J Block Company and, suitably revamped by George Hobart, it was produced in New York. The baddie of the piece, the Sandman, out to steal the hearts from the pack of cards, was played by William Burress, the goodies were Miss Barrison as little Bonnie and Helen Bertram as her beloved Jack of Hearts, and the outcome, of course, was a picturesque and happy ending. Composer Howard appeared as the Moon, originally played in Chicago by Miss Barrison's *Babes in Toyland* partner, William Norris. To add a little more adult interest to the show, the producers squeezed a scene which Hobart and Victor Herbert had written for performance at the Lamb's Club into the loose fabric of the show. *The Song Birds* was a topical operatic burlesque which made fun of the current rivalry between operatic producers Oscar

Hammerstein of the Manhattan Opera House and Hans Conried of the Metropolitan.

Like most Chicago products, *The Land of Nod* did not find itself a run on Broadway, but this time it was not public indifference which did the show down. *The Land of Nod* was closed after 17 performances when a fire struck the New York Theater. The show, however, did not go wholly under. A decade on from its first staging, Australia's William Anderson put out a version in Melbourne. Although the American authors still got billing, and much of their work was still on view, the Australian *Land of Nod* was played at the pantomime season and additions and alterations accrued accordingly. Anna McNab was Bonnie, Tom Cannan the Sandman, Maudie Chetwynd made a hit as Rory Bory Alice, Tom Armstrong was the Man in the Moon, and such established hits of the period as 'You Made Me Love You', 'M.I.S.S.I.S.S.I.P.P.I' and 'Same Old Moon' were performed alongside 'Australia Calls' and 'Mine's Australia' through a fine 70 Christmas season performances, followed by a six-week season at Sydney's Palace Theatre (28 February 1914).

The title *The Land of Nod* was used in Britain for an 1897 musical written by and as a vehicle for popular singer Albert Chevalier. The score was provided by his accompanist Alfred H West. After touring for 29 weeks, it was brought to the West End's Royalty Theatre (24 September 1898) where it collapsed in six performances at a loss of £2,500.

Australia: King's Theatre, Melbourne 20 December 1913

DIE LANDSTREICHER
Operette in 2 acts and a Vorspiel by Leopold Krenn and Carl Lindau. Music by Carl Michael Ziehrer. Venedig in Wien, Vienna, 29 July 1899.

When the tramps August (Anton Matscheg) and Bertha (Frln Augustin) Fliederbusch are arrested on suspicion of theft, they escape from the police-station disguised in the overcoats of Count Adolar Gilka (Karl Tuschl) and the dancer, Mimi (Frln Dorn), who have come there to report a jewel robbery. In fact, Mimi's jewels have been found by August and Bertha and they would be more than happy, if they were permitted, to return them and win the 5,000-mark reward offered. But the problem is that the canny Count had intended that Mimi should have only paste copies and, before he can stop it, August has given the dancer the real jewels. In the midst of a masked ball, the clever pair effect the exchange only to find, in the end, that the second set of jewels is as phoney as the first!

Ziehrer's score to Krenn and Lindau's crook musical was one of his most successful. The first-act closer, the waltzing tenor solo 'Sei gepriesen du lauschige Nacht', sung by Roland (Sigmund Steiner), the official responsible for the escape of the two *Landstreicher* but also the piece's love interest, as a 'number' in the incidental celebration around a rustic golden wedding, proved the success of the evening and became a half-million seller. A march-duet for two extravagant soldiers (Anna Bachler, Ludmilla Gaston) 'Das Leutnant Rudi Muggenhain und Fähnrich Mucki Rodenstein ...', describing 'Der Zauber der Montur' – the magic of a uniform – in attracting girls, turned out to be the other take-away hit of the evening whilst a can-can duet for the Count and Mimi ('Wie war entzückt ich neulich'), another march ('Ich komme von Marokko')

Plate 157. **Die Landstreicher:** *August (Heinz Zimmer) and Bertha (Helga Schulze-Margraf) Fliederbusch make their hurried escape from the police (Mario Dehne) in the Dresden Staatsoperette's production.*

performed by the tramps and the count, all disguised in the same Arab outfit for their tricks at the ball, a Spanisches Lied for Mimi, Roland's love song ('Mein herzliche Bua') and a comical trio for Mimi and the two officers ('Der Soldat muss stets marschieren') all contributed tunefully to the success of the piece.

Die Landstreicher was first produced on the stage of the Englisher Garten 'Venedig in Wien', Gabor Steiner's outdoor summer theatre in the Prater which operated during the main theatres' closed season, and it was mounted by its producer with considerable spectacle, including a ballet of 200 which performed 'grosse militärische Evolutionen' staged by choreographer Louis Gundlach in the styles of ten countries (topped by Austria) in the second act. It was the most successful among a number of durable pieces which librettists Carl Lindau and Leopold Krenn, who were by way of being house writers to Steiner's enterprise, turned out during the manager's years of activities in Vienna. Following its summer season in 1899 it was repeated in the Prater in 1900 and was played the next year at Steiner's winter house, Danzers Orpheum (8 February 1901) before being given for nine performances at the Theater an der Wien (26 March 1902). It was later played at the Raimundtheater (w Franz Glawatsch, Gerda Walde) in 1909 and in 1920 at the Bürgertheater (12 October, w Josef Viktora, Rosa Koppler, Emmy Stein, Richard Waldemar).

In Germany *Die Landstreicher* became far and away the most popular of Ziehrer's works, and it has been produced regularly throughout the country through the 90 years since its creation, most recently in a rearranged version (ad Hans Fretzer, Herbert Mogg Staatsoperette, Dresden 8 March 1985), whilst in Hungary (ad Aurel Föld, Adolf Mérei), after beginning its career at the Városligeti Színkör, it moved on to the Magyar Színház and then to other theatres with equal popularity.

In America, the story of *Die Landstreicher* was retained as the libretto for the musical comedy *The Strollers* (ad H B Smith, Knickerbocker Theater, 24 June 1901), a George Lederer vehicle put together for comedian Francis Wilson, but in a fashion of the time which undoubtedly had something to do with finances, Ziehrer's score was replaced by a new one by Ludwig Englander. Wilson sang an English coon song ('Little Daffy Pipedreams') burlesquing Leslie Stuart's 'Little Dolly Daydream' and annexed a larger part of the now shorter score ('Song of the Strollers', 'When the Orchestra Plays'). Roland (Harry Fairleigh), who had descended to being a bass, had to be content with a waltz 'Song of Loretta' which did not compensate for his lost hit. Irene Bentley gave 'A Lesson in Flirtation' as Bertha, Marie George was the dancer and one Edwin Foy had a supporting rôle as a comedy jailor (developed from Franz Glawatsch's part of Kampel in the original script). A piece called 'The Kaiser's Bold Hussars' supplied a more Ziehrer-ish and Continental flavour, elsewhere submerged, which recalled the show's origins. *The Strollers* had a reasonable Broadway run of 70 nights without ever looking like equalling the success of *Die Landstreicher*.

Hungary: Városligeti Színkör *A svihákok* 19 July 1901; Germany: Luisen-Theater 2 May 1902

LANE, Burton [LEVY, Burton] (b New York, 2 February 1912). Film songwriter whose handful of ventures on to the stage produced a bundle of popular numbers.

Lane joined the Remick music publishing company as a staff pianist and writer at an early age, and he published his first songs at the age of 19. In the early 1930s he provided material for several revues (*Three's a Crowd, Earl Carroll's Vanities of 1931, The Third Little Show, Americana*), a couple of musicals – the flop *Singin' the Blues*, and the Shubert remake of the British show *Dear Love* as the revusical *Artists and Models* (w Sam Lerner) – and to films, scoring an early success with 'Everything I Have is Yours' (lyric: Harold Adamson) in *Dancing Lady* (1933). During the rest of the 1930s and 1940s he contributed songs to filmed musicals such as *Dubarry Was a Lady* ('Madam, I Love Your Crêpe Suzette' w Ralph Freed, Lew Brown; 'Salome') and for over more than 20 years wrote music for Hollywood screenplays including *Swing High, Swing Low* (title-song for Dorothy Lamour, w Ralph Freed), *Some Like it Hot* (1939, 'The Lady's in Love with You', w Frank Loesser), *Babes on Broadway* (1941, 'How About You?', w Freed), *Wedding Bells* (US: *Royal Wedding* 1951, 'Too Late Now', 'How Could You Believe Me When I Said I Loved You When You Know I've Been a Liar All My Life', w Alan Jay Lerner for Fred Astaire and Jane Powell), *College Swing*, and *Dancing on a Dime* ('I Hear Music', w Loesser).

Lane's first major stage venture, *Hold on to Your Hats*, a vehicle for the ageing Al Jolson who was returning to Broadway after a ten-year absence, saw the principal score ('There's a Great Day Coming', 'Don't Let it Get You Down', 'Walkin' Along Mindin' My Business') peppered with Jolson standards as desperation set in. The show ran for 158 fairly unsatisfactory performances. The composer had a slightly happier time with Olsen and Johnson's revue *Laffing Room Only* ('Feudin' and Fightin''), and then a considerable Broadway success with his next book musical, *Finian's Rainbow*. Although the show subsequently failed in productions outside America, it won a long initial run in New York and considerable popularity at home and its score produced a solid phalanx of Lane's most popular songs ('How Are Things in Glocca Morra?', 'Old Devil Moon', 'Look to the Rainbow', 'When I'm Not Near the Girl I Love', 'If This isn't Love').

It was nearly two decades before Broadway heard another Lane musical comedy score. *On a Clear Day You Can See Forever* had a respectable if unprofitable New York run and, like *Finian's Rainbow*, was made into a film, but it won out mainly by the enduring nature of its principal songs ('Come Back to Me', 'On a Clear Day You Can See Forever'). Lane returned only once more to Broadway, as the composer of *Carmelina* (1979), a musical version of the screenplay *Buona Sera Mrs Campbell*. It had a very short run, but it also threw up several attractive songs ('Someone in April', 'One More Walk Around the Garden') which, nevertheless, did not outlive their show or travel as the best numbers from his last two shows had done.

1940 **Hold on to Your Hats** (E Y Harburg/Guy Bolton, Matt Brooks, Eddie Davis) Shubert Theater 11 September
1947 **Finian's Rainbow** (Harburg/Fred Saidy) 46th Street Theater 10 January
1965 **On a Clear Day You Can See Forever** (Alan Jay Lerner) Mark Hellinger Theater 17 October
1979 **Carmelina** (Lerner/Joseph Stein) St James Theater 8 April

LANE, Lupino [LUPINO, Henry George] (b London, 16 June 1892; d London, 10 November 1959).

Born into a famous family of dancers and acrobats, Lane was trained in the family business from early childhood and appeared on the stage from the age of 11 in music hall and variety, performing at first under the name of 'Nipper'. He came to the theatre by way of revue at the beginning of the dancing-craze years, appearing in Irving Berlin's *Watch Your Step*, in *Follow the Crowd, We're All in It* and *Extra Special*, before tasting first the straight stage and then the musical. He was first seen in a book musical under the management of C B Cochran, when he played the rôle of Coucourli alongside Alice Delysia in the London version of *Afgar* (1919), and he journeyed to America with the French star to repeat his part briefly on Broadway the following year.

After several further years in revue on both sides of the Atlantic (*League of Notions, Brighter London, Ziegfeld Follies of 1924*), he returned to the musical stage as an acrobatic and unconventional Ko-Ko in a New York revival of *The Mikado* and in Willie Edouin's famously extravagant rôle of George Medway in a musical version of the farce *Turned Up* (1926). He took leading comic parts in London's version of *Der Orlow* (*Hearts and Diamonds*, Jefferson), in the Dominion Theatre's spectacular operetta *Silver Wings* (1930, Jerry Wimpole), in the London version of Broadway's *Smiles*, played under the title *The One Girl* (1932, Freddy Stone), and in the London Coliseum Schumann pasticcio *The Golden Toy* (1934, the Barber) before going into management himself to present a racing farce with songs called *Twenty to One*.

Lane starred in *Twenty to One* as a cheeky little bowler-hatted chappie called Bill Snibson and he scored a fine success, first on the road and then – with the show slimmed and recast – at London's Victoria Palace as a Christmas attraction which ran for six months. Lane then took his show on the road, and when it was done he started back towards the West End with a soi-disant 'sequel' (actually, the only continuing feature was the name of Lane's character) called *Me and My Girl*. A major wartime hit, in which its star introduced 'The Lambeth Walk' and the title-song, *Me and My Girl* provided Lane with a considerable fortune and with a vehicle to which he would return time and again in the remainder of his career. For the next ten years he and his company (including a good number of his family) occupied the Victoria Palace through a revival of *Twenty to One*, *La-di-da-di-da*, *Meet Me Victoria* and *Sweetheart Mine* in which, after being called 'Bill' in all the other shows Lane finally became 'Harry'.

The line of shows ended in 1947, and Lane's fortunes turned expensively sour when he bought the old, war-damaged Gaiety Theatre for the huge sum of £200,000, with a dream of restoring it to its Edwardesian splendour. The Gaiety drank his money greedily, but it never re-opened and was ultimately destroyed by the city council. Lane rarely appeared on the stage thereafter. He was seen in pantomime and the odd play and occasionally as Bill Snibson in revivals of *Me and My Girl* before he died, whilst still in his sixties.

Parallel to his stage career, Lane ran another in films. Having made early silents as a young man, he subsequently appeared in such British stage musicals-turned-movies as *The Lady of the Rose*, *The Yellow Mask* (Sam Slipper) and *The Lambeth Walk* (ie *Me and My Girl*, Bill Snibson), and he also visited Hollywood, where he was seen in a number of non-musical films and, with Maurice Chevalier and Jeanette MacDonald, in *The Love Parade*. In Britain he directed several early sound movie musicals, including *Love Lies* and *The Maid of the Mountains* and the non-musical version of the stage musical *The Love Race*.

Lane's wife, Violet Blythe, at first a buxom showgirl in Robert Courtneidge's shows (*The Pearl Girl*, *The Cinema Star*) and later a supporting principal at the Adelphi (*High Jinks*, *Who's Hooper?*), appeared with her husband in *Afgar* in America (Musauda) and in small, aristocratic rôles in the series of shows at the Victoria Palace. His son Lauri Lupino Lane (b London, 26 July ?1921; d London, 4 June 1986), also a performer, began as a child at the Victoria Palace and appeared in his father's rôle in later revivals of *Me and My Girl*.

1944 **Meet Me Victoria** (Noel Gay/Frank Eyton/w Lauri Wylie) Victoria Palace 8 April

1946 **Sweetheart Mine** (Gay/Eyton/Albert Chevalier, Arthur Shirley ad w Eyton) Victoria Palace 1 August

Biography: Dillon White, J: *Born to Star* (Heinemann, London, 1957)

LANG, Harold [Richard] (b Daly City, Calif, 21 December 1923; d Cairo, Egypt, 16 November 1975). Dancing actor who created one important rôle and re-created another to great effect.

Lang worked as a dancer with the Ballets Russes de Monte-Carlo and the American Ballet Theater before his first appearances in Broadway musicals in *Mr Strauss Goes to Boston* (1945) and *Look Ma, I'm Dancin'* (1946). In 1948 he had his one major new rôle when he created the part of the trouble-making dancer Bill Calhoun in *Kiss Me, Kate* and he then teamed with Helen Gallagher as the number-two pair (with dances) in the less successful *Make a Wish* (1951), before taking the title-rôle in the revival of *Pal Joey* (1952), which established this show as a fashionably unfrilly item in the standard repertoire. He appeared subsequently in *Shangri-La* (1956), as Gabey in a 1959 revival of *On the Town*, and as garment salesman Teddy Asch in *I Can Get it for You Wholesale* (1962).

LANNER, Josef (b Vienna, 12 April 1801; d Ober-döbling, 14 April 1843).

The great Viennese dance music composer of his time, Lanner wrote only occasionally for the theatre – a pantomime, a ballet and a fairytale piece for the Theater in der Josefstadt, a divertissement for the Kärntnertör Theater – but his melodies, arranged by Emil Stern, were used as the basis for the score for the successful Operette *Alt-Wien* (Carltheater, 23 December 1912) written to a libretto by Gustav von Kadelburg and Julius Wilhelm. He was also made the subject of a biomusical (labelled a Genrebild), *Josef Lanner*, produced at the Theater in der Josefstadt in 1880 (musical arrangements: Ludwig Gothov-Grüneke and Philipp Fahrbach; text: Franz von Radler, 30 September) which was later reprised at the Carltheater (1887, with Carl Adolf Friese as Lanner), the Theater in der Leopoldstadt (1888), at the Rudolsheim Colosseumtheater (1894) and at the Volksoper (1900). He was also portrayed on the Carltheater stage in 1894 by Siegmund Natzler in the Festspiel *Sein erster Walzer* celebrating Johann Strauss's 50 years in the theatre.

His daughter **Kathi** [later Katti] **LANNER** (b Vienna, ?1831; d London, 15 November 1908) was a highly successful dancer who appeared as a soloist in Austria, Germany (*Sitala das Gauklermädchen*, *Uriella, der Dämon der Nacht* etc), Hungary and other European countries as well as in New York, where she was star dancer at Niblo's Garden (*Leo and Lotos*, *Azraël* etc) and choreographed *A Midsummer Night's Dream* with G L Fox and a version of *The Black Crook*. She ultimately settled in London, where she had first performed as Giselle in 1870, and became celebrated as a choreographer (the original production of *Dorothy* and of Planquette's *Nell Gwynne*, *Toledo* etc) and teacher. She was in charge of the ballets at the Empire Theatre from its opening until 1905, and some of her choreography for that house was reproduced in parallel Paris establishments (*Brighton* Olympia, 1898 etc).

The American adapters of *Walzer aus Wien* introduced Kathi (sic) Lanner into their version of the show as a character.

LANSBURY, Angela [Brigid] (b London, 16 October 1925).

Miss Lansbury moved from Britain to America during the Second World War and there began an eminently successful career in films (*Gaslight*, *National Velvet* as Elizabeth Taylor's sister, *The Picture of Dorian Gray*, *The Harvey Girls*, *Till Clouds Roll By*, *The Court Jester*, *The Long Hot Summer*, *The Dark at the Top of the Stairs*, *The Manchurian Candidate* etc). In 1964 she made her first musical-stage appearance as the voracious Cora Hoover Hooper in the short-lived *Anyone Can Whistle*, but she found singular success and a Tony Award shortly afterwards when she introduced the title-rôle of the musicalization of *Auntie Mame* (*Mame*, 1966 'If He Walked into My Life', 'Bosom Buddies').

She subsequently starred as the Madwoman of Chaillot in Jerry Herman's musical version of Giradoux's play entitled *Dear World* (1969) and closed out of town in *Prettybelle* (1971) before scoring a fresh personal success in the rôle of Rose, created on Broadway by Ethel Merman, in a revival of *Gypsy*, first on the West End stage and then on Broadway where the performance earned her a second

Tony Award. In 1977 she took over the rôle of Anna, opposite Yul Brynner, in a revival of *The King and I* and in 1979 created the part of Mrs Lovett in Stephen Sondheim's musical melodrama *Sweeney Todd*, hawking 'The Worst Pies in London' which end up containing 'A Little Priest' before her blood-bespattered end in her own furnace.

In between her stage appearances, she continued a film career (*Bedknobs and Broomsticks* etc) and since 1984 she has appeared constantly on the world's television screens as small-town super-sleuth Jessica Fletcher, America's answer to Miss Marple, in the enormously successful *Murder She Wrote*.

LATABÁR

The founding father of five generations of Latabárs in the Hungarian theatre was **Endre LATABÁR** (b Kiskunhalas, 16 November 1811; d Miskolc, 10 July 1873), who, in a career which involved performing, directing and writing, was the translator of some of the earliest opérasbouffes and opérettes to be played in Hungary. His adaptation credits include *Nőnövelde* (*Das Pensionat*), *Szép Dunois lovag* (*Le Beau Dunois*), *Párizsi élet* (*La Vie parisienne*), *Szép Galathea* (*Die schöne Galathee*), *Tiz leány, egy férj* (*Zehn Mädchen und kein Mann*), *Szép Helena* (*La Belle Hélène*), *Orfeusz az alvilágban* (*Orphée aux enfers*), *Utazás Kínába* (*Le Voyage en Chine*) and *Genoveva* (*Geneviève de Brabant*).

Endre's son Kálmán Latabár (1855–1924) worked only in the non-musical theatre, but his son **Árpád LATABÁR** (b Miskolc, 19 September 1878; d Budapest, 22 August 1951) had a long career as a performer on the musical stage. He played in *Das verwunschene Schloss* at the age of 18, and joined the company at the Budapest Király Színház in his early thirties, making his first appearance there in the local version of *The Balkan Princess* and going on to appear in a long line of important character rôles in both Hungarian and foreign musicals. These ranged from the classic Viennese repertoire – *Die Rose von Stambul* (Müller), *Die Csárdásfürstin* (Feri), *Die Zirkusprinzessin* (Sergius Wladimir), *Eva*, *Der Zigeunerprimás*, *Die Bajadere* – to the American imports of the 1920s – *Rose-Marie* (Mountie Malone), *Mersz-e Mary?* (Harry) or the curious *Amerikai lányok* – up-to-date imports like Katscher's *Wunder-Bar* or Ábrahám's *Die Blume von Hawaii*, and a whole range of Hungarian pieces, including such pieces as *Leányvásár* (gróf Rottenberg), *Szibill* (The Governor), *Pillangó főhadnagy* (Morvay), *Alexandra* (gróf Szuvarov), *Éva grófnő* (Guido Bonyhády), *Aranyhattyú* (Dicky), *Mágnás Miska* (Korláth gróf), *Eltörött a hegedűm* (Lojzi), *Sisters* (Müller), *Alvinci huszárok*, *Lámpaláz*, *Hajnali csók*, *Sültgalamb*, *Kék Duna*, *Ördöglovas*, *Csak azért*, *Bécsi tavasz*, *Josephine császárnő*, *Gólyaszanatórium*, *Éva a paradicsomban*, *Ki gyereke vagyok én?* and *Becskereki menyecske*, a series which carried on through into his sixties.

The two long-faced sons of the tall moon-faced comedian, **Kálmán LATABÁR** (b Kecskemét, 24 November 1902; d Budapest 11 January 1970) and **Árpád LATABÁR** (b Sátoraljaújhely, 22 November 1903; d Budapest, 1 December 1961) both became popular musical theatre comedians. Árpád, after an early career which took him from Hungary (*Szeretlek*, *Lámpaláz* etc) to Africa, the Netherlands and Italy, returned to Budapest and,

through the 1930s and 1940s, took over some of his father's creations, such as Rottenberg and Feri bácsi, Zsupán in *Der Zigeunerbaron*, Château-Gibus in *Mam'zelle Nitouche* and the head waiter in *Ball im Savoy*, and played in and created a long list of new rôles in Hungarian works (*Száz piros rózsa*, *Kata*, *Kitty*, *Katinka*, *Bástyasétány 77* etc). From 1954 he was a member of the company at the Fővárosi Operettszinház.

Kálmán stayed closer to home, although he created the rôle of Graf Sacha Karlowitz in *Schön ist die Welt* at the Theater an der Wien (1931) and paired with his brother in Vienna's *Lady vom Lido* (1927, Dr Hitschi-Harschi/Buster Keaton), and he made a memorable career on stage and screen as a gangling, monocled and light-footed comic actor. His rôles, over the years, included Offenbach's Menelaus, General Boum, Fritz in *Leányvásár*, Zsupán in *Gräfin Mariza*, Basil in *Der Graf von Luxemburg* as well as a long line of both other imports (Christiné's *Szeretlek*, Jim in *Mr Cinders*, Yvain's *Cserebere* and several of the Russian musicals played in Budapest under communism), and more than 30 years of native pieces from the classically styled to the pseudo-American shows of the 1930s (*Weekend*, *Manolita*, *Amit a lányok akarnak*, *Bolondóra*, *Szegény ördög*, *n és kisöcém*, *Történnek még csodák*, *Szépségkirálynő*, *Budapest-Wien*, *A nagyhercegnő és a pincér*, *Eső után köpönyeg*, Benatzky's *Egy lány, aki mindenkié*, *Romantikus asszony*, *Antoinette*, *Kávé habbal*, *Egy bolond százat csinál*, *Pusztai szerenád*, *Pozsonyi lakodalom*, *Handa Banda*, *Sárgarigófeészek*, *Bécsi gyors*, *Fiatlalság-bolondság*, *Ilyenek a férfiak*, *Fityfiritty*, *Múzsák muzsikája*, *Maya*, *Mária főhadnagy*, *Csicsónénak három lánya*, *ŷayy?*, *VIII osztály*, *Ipafai lakodalom*, *Bécsi diákok*, *Szelistyei asszonyok*, *Kard és szerelem*), in some of which he appeared alongside his brother. In *Csak azért* (1934), *Zimberi, Zombori szépasszony* (1938) and *Fekete Liliom* (1946) the three Latabárs all appeared together in the same show.

Kálmán Latabár also directed a number of new musical shows, and continued to appear at the Operettszinház into the 1960s, appearing as Pietro in a *Boccaccio* rewritten to provide rôles for him and for Hanna Honthy as his wife (1961), as Don Moskitos in a version of Offenbach's *Les Brigands*, as Frosch, Negus (*Die lustige Witwe*) and – now alongside his son, the third Kálmán Latabár – as Saint-Hypothèse in *Lili* in the last years of a career in which he was, alongside Honthy, the most popular representative of the glorious bygone years of the musical theatre.

He also appeared in the comic rôles of 38 Hungarian films between 1937 and 1962.

Biography: *A Latabárok: egy szinészdinasztia a magyar Színháztörténetben* (NPI, Budapest, 1983)

LATOUCHE, John [Treville] (b Richmond, Va, 13 November 1917; d Calais, Vt, 7 August 1956). American lyricist whose best work won special praise for its literacy and ingenuity.

Early examples of Latouche's lyrics were heard in revue in 1939 when he contributed a song to *Pins and Needles* and several to *From Vienna* and *Sing for Your Supper* ('Ballad for Americans' w Earl Robinson) before he made a notable first appearance in the musical theatre with the lyrics to Vernon Duke's music for the negro fantasy *Cabin in the Sky* (1940). Even though the words for the most durable song of the score 'Taking a Chance on Love' came from the pen of Ted Fetter, Latouche was responsible for the lyrics to the show's title-song and 'Honey in the Honeycomb'. Further success, however, did not come quickly. Additional collaborations with Duke on a musical version of *Three Men on a Horse* (*Banjo Eyes*) for Eddie Cantor and on *The Lady Comes Across* were less productive, and a turn into pastiche operetta with pieces based on the music of Kreisler and Chopin did no better, whilst a rewrite of *The Beggar's Opera* in collaboration with Duke Ellington (*Beggar's Holiday*) found only a limited circle of admirers.

It is the 1954 musical *The Golden Apple* (music: Jerome Moross), a piece that has remained a strong favourite with musical theatre intellectuals since its first production, on which Latouche's continuing reputation almost wholly rests. A written-through piece using classical mythology, in time-honoured style, to poke fun at modern society and institutions, it had only a limited stage life, but it yielded up some particularly attractive pieces of writing and composing ('Windflowers', 'Lazy Afternoon', 'It's the Going Home Together', 'The Judgement of Paris' etc), many of which were pieces not safely extractable from the fabric of the show. Disappointingly, *The Golden Apple* was to be almost without tomorrow. A spectacular Hollywood burlesque, *The Vamp* (1955), encouraged camp rather than wit, and Vernon Duke's *The Littlest Revue* (1956) went the way of most of Duke's later works. By the time the first genuine success with which Latouche had been involved since *Cabin in the Sky* was produced, he was dead, having suffered a heart attack at the age of 38. His posthumous lyrical contribution to Leonard Bernstein's *Candide* was, in fact, his only work to ensure him a lasting place in the repertoire.

Latouche's other credits ranged from special material for New York night-club performer Spivy to the texts for Douglas Moore's opera *The Ballad of Baby Doe* (Colorado, 1956), and for three dance plays called *Ballet Ballads*, containing songs, composed by Moross (Music Box Theater, 1948).

1940 **Cabin in the Sky** (Vernon Duke/Lynn Root) Martin Beck Theater 25 October

1941 **Banjo Eyes** (Duke/w Harold Adamson/Joe Quillan, Izzy Ellinson) Hollywood Theater 25 December

1941 **The Lady Comes Across** (Duke/Fred Thompson, Dawn Powell) 44th Street Theater 9 January

1944 **Rhapsody** (Kreisler arr Robert Russell Bennett/w Bennett, Leonard Levinson, Arnold Sundgaard) Century Theater 22 November

1945 **Polonaise** (Chopin arr Bronislaw Kaper/Gottfried Reinhardt, Anthony Veiller) Alvin Theater 6 October

1946 **Beggar's Holiday** (Duke Ellington) Broadway Theater 26 December

1954 **The Golden Apple** (Jerome Moross) Alvin Theater 20 April

1955 **The Vamp** (James Mundy/w Sam Locke) Winter Garden Theater 10 November

1956 **Candide** (Leonard Bernstein/w Richard Wilbur, Dorothy Parker/Lillian Hellman) Martin Beck Theater 1 December

LATTÈS, Marcel (d 1943).

A much-liked young musician who moved around to good effect in Parisian society, Lattès wrote several short scores for both opérettes and opéras-comiques before making his full-length début with *La Jeunesse dorée*, a piece set in the 1830 Paris of the 'dandys' and starring Henri Defreyn and Brigitte Régent as an English lord and a dancer entangled in a rather curious, paedophilic plot. In the midst of the fashion – particularly at the Théâtre Apollo, where it was staged – for Viennese Operette, *La Jeunesse dorée* won some compliments for its distinctly French music. It won none for its book, however, and after 17 performances the Apollo hastened back to *La Veuve joyeuse* and *Le Comte de Luxembourg*.

Lattès's second piece was produced not in France, but in London, where C B Cochran mounted an English version of his musical comedy *Maggie* at the Oxford Theatre in succession to the wartime hit *The Better 'Ole*. Handicapped by an 'inventive' chief comic and the switch in the kind of fare at the Oxford, *Maggie* lasted only 108 performances, but it was exported with some success to Australia (Tivoli, Melbourne 30 October 1920) and was later given a kinder production at Paris's Théâtre de la Gaîté-Lyrique where, with Yane Exiane starring as *Nelly* (ad Jacques Bousquet, Henri Falk), it played for a reasonable run.

In a career which embraced both the stage and the cinema as well as the composition of occasional and salon music, Lattès later turned out several further musical plays which found some success. Mlle Régent was again the star of *Monsieur l'Amour* at the Gaîté, *Le Diable à Paris* featured Dranem as the 'diable' at the head of a starry cast including Edmée Favart, Raimu and Jeanne Cheirel, *Arsène Lupin, banquier* featured René Koval as the famous criminal aborting a fabulous plan for the sake of the pretty smile of his victim's niece, and *Xantho chez les courtisanes*, adapted from Jean Richepin's successful play, starred Gabrielle Ristori as an ancient Greek femme honnête learning about love from a team of courtesans headed by Arletty.

Each of Lattès's works was praised for its musicality and its melodic distinction, and he was considered a fine and ever-promising composer, but, in spite of some success, he did not manage to turn out a *Ciboulette* or a *Véronique* for the Parisian 1930s (which didn't really want one, anyhow), and his export rate was low to non-existent.

1908 **Fraisidis** (Jacques Redelsperger) 1 act Comédie-Royale 16 November

1912 **La Cour mauresque** (Fernand Nozière) privately, Maisons-Lafitte 21 June

1913 **Il était une bergère** (André Rivoire) 1 act Opéra-Comique 16 April

1913 **Pas davantage** (Nozière) 1 act Théâtre Michel 25 April

1913 **La Jeunesse dorée** (aka *Les Dandys*) (Henri Verne, Gabriel Faure) Théâtre Apollo 29 May

1919 **Maggie** (Adrian Ross/Fred Thompson, H F Maltby, Étienne Rey, Jacques Bousquet) Oxford Theatre, London 22 October

1921 **Nelly** (ad Bousquet, Henri Falk) revised French version of *Maggie* (Théâtre de la Gaîté-Lyrique)

1922 **Monsieur l'Amour** (Falk, René Peter) Théâtre Mogador 18 February

1927 **Le Diable à Paris** (Alfred Willemetz, Robert de Flers, Francis de Croisset) Théâtre Marigny 27 November

1930 **Arsène Lupin, banquier** (Yves Mirande) Théâtre des Bouffes-Parisiens 7 May

1932 **Xantho chez les courtisanes** (Jacques Richepin) Théâtre des Nouveautés 16 March

1935 **Pour ton bonheur** (Leopold Marchand, Albert Willemetz) Théâtre des Bouffes-Parisiens 20 September

LAURENT DE RILLÉ, [François Anatole] (b Orléans, 1828; d Paris, 26 August 1915).

Inspector of vocal music for the Parisian school area, de

Rillé was also the composer of a regular flow of songs, choral pieces and short opérettes, the majority of which last were written for and produced at Hervé's Folies-Nouvelles in the late 1850s. He had a more substantial success, however, on the few occasions that he stretched to full-length works, notably with the setting of Leterrier and Vanloo's *Le Petit Poucet* (subsequently played in Austria and Germany as *Der Däumling*), and with the little rustic tale of *Babiole* which, following its Parisian production, was played both in Britain and, with its original star, Paola Marié, in America. Of his shorter pieces, however, it was *Les Pattes-blanches*, a little two-handed tale of a couple of white folk adrift in a black country, introduced by Potel and Édouard Georges at the Bouffes-Parisiens in 1873, which proved his most popular.

An anecdote says that it was he who first set what ultimately became Offenbach's *Apothicaire et perruquier*. Offenbach the manager lost the score he had commissioned, so he put on his other hat and composed a new one himself.

1855 **Le Sire de Framboisy** 1 act Folies-Nouvelles 2 February
1857 **Aimé pour lui-même** (Machiat de la Chesneraye) 1 act Folies-Nouvelles 3 February
1857 **Bel-Boul, ou une métempsychase** (Chesneraye) 1 act Folies-Nouvelles 14 March
1857 **Achille à Skyros** (Ernest Alby, Delmare [ie Commerson]) 1 act Folies-Nouvelles September
1857 **La Demoiselle de la Hoche-Trombelon** (Jules Moinaux) 1 act Folies-Nouvelles 20 October
1858 **Trilby** (Chesneraye) 1 act Folies-Nouvelles 1 January
1858 **Le Moulin de Catherine** (Alby) 1 act Folies-Nouvelles 1 September
1858 **Frasquita** (Alfred Tranchant) 1 act Théâtre des Bouffes-Parisiens 3 March
1859 **Le Sultan de Mysapouf** 1 act Folies-Nouvelles 12 February
1859 **Le Jugement de Paris** (Alby, Commerson) 1 act Folies-Nouvelles 11 February
1859 **Elle a des bottes** (G Albert, Eugène Audray-Deshortier) 1 act Folies-Nouvelles 30 March
1859 **Au fond du verre** (Ernest Dubreuil) 1 act Baden-Baden, Théâtre Déjazet March 1861
1868 **Le Petit Poucet** (Eugène Leterrier, Albert Vanloo) Théâtre de l'Athénée 8 October
1873 **Les Pattes-blanches** (Marc Constantin, Léon Coron) 1 act Théâtre des Bouffes-Parisiens 21 May
1873 **La Liqueur d'or** (William Busnach, Armand Liorat) Théâtre des Menus-Plaisirs 11 December
1878 **Babiole** (Clairville, Octave Gastineau) Théâtre des Bouffes-Parisiens 16 January
1880 **La Princesse Marmotte** (Clairville, Busnach, Gastineau) Nouvelles Galeries St-Hubert, Brussels 24 January
1882 **Frasquita** (Lucien Solvay, Georges de Boesch) 1 act Galeries St-Hubert, Brussels October
1891 **La Leçon de chant** (Eugène Adénis) 1 act Théâtre de la Galerie Vivienne 21 June

LAURENTS, Arthur (b New York, 14 July 1918).

The author of several plays and screenplays in the 1940s and early 1950s, Laurents scored his most considerable early successes with the stage play *The Time of the Cuckoo* (1952, subsequently filmed as *Summer Madness*), the Alfred Hitchcock film *Rope* (1948) and the Twentieth Century-Fox movie version of *Anastasia* (1956) which netted an Academy Award for Ingrid Bergman.

His first venture into the musical theatre was as librettist

for *West Side Story* (1957), a venture which hoisted him immediately to the top of another section of his professions, and he confirmed this success when he collaborated with lyricist Stephen Sondheim a second time in the writing of *Gypsy*, a musical based on the tale of iconised stripper Gypsy Rose Lee and her stage mother. A third collaboration between the two, this time with Sondheim acting as composer as well as lyricist, resulted in a curious, grotesque parable called *Anyone Can Whistle* which was a quick failure (9 performances).

In 1965 Laurents adapted his *The Time of the Cuckoo* as a musical, with Richard Rodgers and Sondheim supplying the score but, in spite of top-class work from all the writers involved, *Do I Hear a Waltz?* hit concept problems on the road and ended up not being a success. Given the markedly superior quality of Laurents's earlier works, the libretto for *Hallelujah, Baby!* (1967) was a disappointment. A piece which mixed a conventional tale of making good in showbiz with some simplistic racial and civil rights elements and a dose of 1960s -isms, it followed all-purpose Georgina – an eternal 25 – through four decades of situations on her way to the present day. Its 293 Broadway performances, nevertheless, outdid the 220 of the more sophisticated *Do I Hear a Waltz?*.

In 1962, whilst still working on all three fronts as a dramatist, Laurents began a parallel career as a director for the musical theatre with the production of *I Can Get it for You Wholesale* and he subsequently directed *Anyone Can Whistle* (1964), the London (1973) and Broadway (1974) revivals of *Gypsy* and *La Cage aux Folles* (1983).

Laurents proved himself, with his eminently theatrical and intelligent libretti for *West Side Story*, *Gypsy* and *Do I Hear a Waltz?*, to be one of the most effective librettists of his era but, in the quarter of a century since *Hallelujah, Baby!*, his only further authorial contribution to the musical theatre has been *The Madwoman of Central Park*, a one-woman entertainment written with and for Phyllis Newman (22 Steps Theater, 13 June 1979) and the text for the disappointing and short-lived *Thin Man* musical *Nick and Nora* (1991, also director).

1957 **West Side Story** (Leonard Bernstein/Stephen Sondheim) Winter Garden Theater 26 September
1959 **Gypsy** (Jule Styne/Sondheim) Broadway Theater 21 May
1964 **Anyone Can Whistle** (Sondheim) Majestic Theater, 4 April
1965 **Do I Hear a Waltz?** (Richard Rodgers/Sondheim) 46th Street Theater 18 March
1967 **Hallelujah, Baby!** (Styne/Comden, Green) Martin Beck Theater 26 April
1991 **Nick and Nora** (Charles Strouse/Richard Maltby jr) Marquis Theater 8 December

LAURILLARD, Edward (b Rotterdam, 20 April 1870; d New York, 7 May 1936). Cinema owner turned musical producer who scored several London hits in partnership with George Grossmith and launched two West End theatres.

From his early twenties Dutchman Laurillard worked as a company manager with theatrical managements in Britain, under Fred Harris and C J Abud on their West End production of *King Kodak* and then on tour, at first for William Greet, and then for Hardie, von Leer and Gordyn. He moved into production on his own account in 1897 with the play *Oh! Susannah* and made his first venture into the musical theatre with George Grossmith's musical *The Lovebirds*, which he produced unsuccessfully at the Savoy Theatre in 1904.

Laurillard subsequently moved sideways, into the cinema world, and there he expanded his interests until he controlled some two dozen film theatres. Thus enriched, he turned back to the theatre and formed a partnership with Grossmith for producing plays and musical comedies. For some six years, from 1914 on, the two men mounted many successful pieces, beginning with the wartime comedy *Potash and Perlmutter* and continuing with the musicals *Tonight's the Night*, *Theodore & Co*, the London production of Victor Herbert's *The Only Girl*, *Mr Manhattan*, *Yes, Uncle!*, a version of Broadway's *Oh, Boy!* played in London under the title *Oh, Joy!*, and *Baby Bunting*. Their partnership culminated in the building of the Winter Garden Theatre and its opening with the successful importation of Ivan Caryll's Broadway musical *The Girl Behind the Gun*, remade for London under the title *Kissing Time*.

The partners produced Friml's *The Little Whopper* for a short run and Cuvillier's *The Naughty Princess* (*La Reine s'amuse*) for a longer one, and in 1920 mounted a second highly successful Winter Garden show, an original musical version of the famous farce *L'Hôtel du Libre-Échange* played as *A Night Out*. Around this time they were reported to have purchased the Gaiety and the Adelphi Theatres and to have made plans for the production at the latter for Lincke's *Gri-gri*, but, in fact, Grossmith and Laurillard made only one further venture together, a disastrous attempt to bring burlesque back to the post-Edwardes Gaiety Theatre with *Faust on Toast*, before the partnership was dissolved.

Whilst Grossmith continued to run the Winter Garden in tandem with Pat Malone, Laurillard took on the Apollo Theatre, and essayed a number of other producing ventures including a disastrous English version of Künneke's Berlin hit *Love's Awakening* (*Wenn Liebe erwacht*), a happier one of his *The Cousin from Nowhere* (*Der Vetter aus Dingsda*), and the revusical *The Smith Family* (w Alfred Butt), before attempting to export *A Night Out* to America. It closed expensively out of town. In 1928 he opened a second new London theatre, the Piccadilly, where he arranged with Lee Ephraim for the production of what would be his final musical show, the Jerome Kern costume operetta *Blue Eyes*. He maintained an active interest in the theatre up to his death, but in his later years, although he was to be seen 'shopping' around Broadway from time to time, he did not bring any further productions to the stage.

LAVALLIÈRE, Ève [FENOGLIO, Eugènie Pascaline] (b Toulon, 1 April 1866; d Thuillières, Vosges, 10 July 1929). A gentlemen's delight of the turn-of-the-century years on the Paris musical stage who quit the stage for a convent after a career of three decades.

Orphaned at the age of 18 by the murder of her mother and the suicide of her father, the pretty, diminutive Mlle Fenoglio was taken on as a member of a touring theatre troupe where she found experience, a fairly rich protector and her new name. She kept the name when she headed for Paris and won herself a job in revue at the Théâtre des Variétés. Soon after she replaced the fairly rich protector with a very influential one – Fernand Samuel, the new manager and director of the theatre. Samuel turned

Svengali, and the following year Mlle Lavallière scored her first stage success as Orèste in a revival of *La Belle Hélène*. She appeared regularly at the Variétés from then on, in revue, as the Baronne in *La Vie parisienne* and in a series of the travesty boy rôles for which her small stature and attractive figure fitted her: Adolphe de Valladolid (*Les Brigands*), Siebel (*Le Petit Faust*), Cupidon (*Orphée aux enfers*), Ernest (*L'Oeil crevé*), Orèste, and Prince Orlofsky in the first French production of *La Chauve-Souris*.

The birth of her daughter and a serious accident interrupted her career in the late 1890s, but she created rôles in the spicy Variétés spectaculars *Le Carnet du Diable* (1895, Jacqueline) and *Le Carillon* (1896, Prince Colibri), in *Madam Satan* (1893, Olympe), *Le Pompier de service* (1897, Mimile), *Les Petites Barnett* (1898, Lucie), *Mademoiselle George* (1900, Josette) and a number of other pieces. She had important parts in the original productions of the two most popular works of Claude Terrasse – *Le Sire de Vergy* (1903, where, in the rôle of Mitzy, she caused a sensation with her belly-dance and a dromedary-dance) and *Monsieur de la Palisse* (1904, Inésita) – appeared as Mimi in Henri Hirschmann's *La Petite Bohème* (1905), as La Collégienne in *L'Age d'or* (1905), and also took part in a series of plays, whilst at the same time playing a regular round of revivals (Hermia in *Barbe-bleue*, *Miss Helyett* etc).

In 1917 she starred in Emile Lassailly's *Carminetta* and then, still apparently in fine form at over 50, and after nearly 30 years a member of the Variétés company, suddenly (or opportunely, depending which version you believe) took religion. She retired from the stage and spent the remainder of her life first as a missionary in Tunisia and then in a closed Franciscan convent.

Biography: Engelbert, O: *La Vie et conversion d'Ève Lavallière* (Librairie Plon, Paris, 1936) etc

LAVERNE, Pattie (b London; d London, 24 April 1916).

A popular leading lady of the British opéra-bouffe and burlesque stage, Pattie Laverne was seen in prominent rôles in a decade of productions which ranged from the works of Offenbach and Hervé, through British extravaganza and burlesque and the earliest English light operas, to the first Viennese pieces to be staged in English-speaking houses.

She made her début as a singer in concert at the Hanover Rooms in 1871, appeared in oratorio and was then picked up by John Russell to star in his tour of *La Grande-Duchesse*. Thereafter, she appeared in London in *L'Oeil crevé* (1872, Dindonette), Lauber's little operetta *Lisette* (1873, Lisette), the Offenbach pasticcio *The Bohemians* (Guillerette), in the title-rôles of *Kissi-Kissi* (1873, *L'Île de Tulipatan*) and the burlesque *Tom Tug* (1873), as Clairette to the Lange of Blanche Tersi in Liston's *La Fille de Madame Angot* Company, as Margotte in *The Broken Branch* (1874), Ixion in the Opera Comique revival *Ixion (Rewheeled)* (1874) and Cunégonde in the Hervé piece *Dagobert* (1875). She also created the rôle of Nell Gwynne in Cellier's musical of that name at Manchester (1876) and that of Trainette in Mrs Liston's production of Bucalossi's *Pom* (1876). She subsequently played in the extravaganza *Wildfire* (1877) at the Alhambra, where she also took over the title-rôle of *Fatinitza*, and she appeared in the title-rôle of the British production of de

Rilléy's *Babiole* (1879), but she made her greatest success when she was recruited by Australia's George Musgrove as the leading lady of his first comic-opera company. She starred as Stella in Musgrove's landmark Australian production of *La Fille du tambour-major* (1880), and then, through 1881, in the title-rôles of his mountings of *Madame Favart* and *Olivette* and as Serpolette in *Les Cloches de Corneville* before quitting Australia and vanishing from the theatre-bills of the world to married life as Mrs James Hadley Laver.

LAW, [William] Arthur [aka West CROMER] (b Northrepps, 22 March 1844; d Parkstone, Dorset, 2 April 1913).

The son of a country clergyman, Law took up a commission in the Royal Scots Fusiliers at the age of 20 and he served with the regiment for eight years, in Britain and Burma, before resigning his commission in 1872 to become an actor. After touring for two years in stock with Joseph Eldred, he joined the German Reed company at London's St George's Hall and, during and after a period of more than two years acting with the company, he wrote the libretti of many of the short operettas which made up the Reeds' entertainments.

He later also wrote several successful plays for the regular theatre, including *The Mystery of a Hansom Cab* (1888) and *The New Boy* (1894), and four full-length musical plays, amongst which were Kate Santley's touring vehicle *Chirruper's Fortune* – rather an extended version of the polite and traditional little stories which made up his German Reed pieces – and *The Magic Opal*, a comic opera in the old brigands-and-witches style set to music by Albéniz. His play *The New Boy* gave him one additional and, probably, unwitting musical theatre credit. It apparently underwent some musical decoration on its voyage from London's Court Theatre to Australia (Palace Theatre, Sydney 22 December 1906) where Harry Macdona billed it as a farcical musical comedy.

Married to Fanny Holland, the soprano of the German Reed company, Law toured for a period with his wife in a drawing-room entertainment (*Wanted, a Ladies' Companion, Victoria Villa*).

1877 **A Night Surprise** (Thomas German Reed) 1 act St George's Hall 12 February
1877 **A Happy Bungalow** (King Hall) 1 act St George's Hall 11 June
1878 **An Artful Automaton** (Hall) 1 act St George's Hall 10 July
1879 **£100 Reward** (R Corney Grain) 1 act St George's Hall 17 March
1880 **Castle Botherem** (Hamilton Clarke) 1 act St George's Hall 16 February
1880 **A Flying Visit** (Grain) 1 act St George's Hall 31 May
1880 **A Merry Christmas** (Hall) 1 act St George's Hall 26 December
1881 **All at Sea** (Grain) 1 act St George's Hall 28 February
1881 **Uncle Samuel** (George Grossmith) 1 act Opera Comique 3 May
1881 **A Bright Idea** (Arthur Cecil) 1 act St George's Hall 30 May
1881 **Cherry Tree Farm** (Clarke) 1 act St George's Hall 30 May
1882 **The Head of the Poll** (Eaton Fanning) 1 act St George's Hall 28 February
1882 **Nobody's Fault** (Clarke) St George's Hall 5 June

1882 **Mr Guffin's Elopement** (Grossmith) 1 act Alexandra Theatre, Liverpool 29 September
1882 **A Strange Host** (Hall) 1 act St George's Hall 13 December
1883 **A Treasure Trove** (Alfred J Caldicott) 1 act St George's Hall 6 June
1883 **A Moss Rose Rent** (Caldicott) 1 act St George's Hall 17 December
1884 **A Double Event** (Grain/w Alfred Reed) 1 act St George's Hall 18 February
1884 **A Terrible Fright** (Grain) 1 act St George's Hall 18 June
1884 **A Peculiar Case** (Grossmith) 1 act St George's Hall 8 December
1885 **The Great Taykin** (Grossmith) 1 act Toole's Theatre 30 April
1885 **Chirruper's Fortune** (Florian Pascal, Georges Jacobi, Grossmith, Caldicott et al) Theatre Royal, Portsmouth 31 August
1889 **John Smith** (Caldicott) 1 act Prince of Wales Theatre 28 January
1890 **All Abroad** (Caldicott) 1 act Prince of Wales Theatre 21 February
1893 **The Magic Opal** (aka *The Magic Ring*) (Isaac Albéniz) Lyric Theatre 19 January
1898 **The Showman's Sweetheart** (George Byng/w Guy Eden) Queen's Theatre, Crouch End 29 August
1900 **Punch and Judy** (Byng, Arthur Meredyth) Theatre Royal, Croydon 25 June

LAWRENCE, Gertrude [KLASEN, Gertrud Alexandra Dagmar Lawrence] (b London, 4 July 1898; d New York, 6 September 1952). British revue performer and actress who introduced several major Broadway rôles in musical plays.

Gertrude Lawrence began her life on the stage as a child in pantomime and variety, and had her earliest musical theatre experience dancing in the Liverpool Repertory Company's fantasy *Fifinella*. She toured minor dates in the provincial musical comedies *Miss Lamb of Canterbury* and *Miss Plaster of Paris* and more worldly ones as Blanche-Marie in *Les P'tites Michu* and made her first London appearance at the age of 18 as understudy to the ill-fated Billie Carleton in the revue *Some*. For several years thereafter, she played in revue – *Cheep, Tabs, Buzz-Buzz, A to Z* – and in the newly fashionable cabaret *The Midnight Frolics*, establishing herself on the way as a singing comedienne of charm.

Miss Lawrence had her first major musical-comedy rôle as Denise in the London version of *Dédé* (1922) before returning to revue for a second series of engagements, now at the top of the bill: *Rats, London Calling* (creating 'Limehouse Blues'), *Charlot's Revue of 1924* on Broadway, *Charlot's Revue* (London) and *Charlot's Revue of 1926* (New York). Later in 1926, she created the comical (and suitably English) Lady Kay in Gershwin's *Oh, Kay!* introducing 'Someone to Watch Over Me' and 'Do, Do, Do' and scoring a singular success. She repeated that rôle and success the following year in London.

In 1928, after playing her first adult part in a non-musical show as Jane Crosby in *Icebound*, she returned to New York to star in Gershwin's less-successful *Treasure Girl* (1928, Ann Wainwright) and the *International Revue* (1930). From that time on, with her revue days now behind her, she appeared largely in plays (of which *Private Lives* with Noël Coward remains the best remembered), returning only episodically to the musical stage, first in 1933 to create the starring rôle of Cole Porter's short-lived *Nymph Errant* ('The Physician'), then to pair again with Noël Coward in the series of short and intermittently musical playlets of *Tonight at 8.30* (London, New York and revival) and in 1939 as Moss Hart's psychoanalysable heroine in *Lady in the Dark* ('My Ship', 'Jenny').

In 1951 Lawrence created her last and best remembered musical rôle as Anna Leonowens, the 'I' of Rodgers and Hammerstein's *The King and I*, performing the songs written especially to suit her sweet but slightly frayed and short-ranged voice – 'I Whistle a Happy Tune', 'Hello, Young Lovers', 'Getting to Know You' and 'Shall We Dance' (w Yul Brynner). She was forced out of the show by illness and died from cancer whilst the piece which she had dreamed up continued its run.

An approximative Hollywood film about her life was produced in 1968 as *Star!*, with Julie Andrews playing Miss Lawrence and Daniel Massey her Noël Coward.

Autobiography: *A Star Danced* (Doubleday, Doran, New York & W H Allen, London, 1945); Biography: Aldridge, R: *Gertrude Lawrence as Mrs A* (Greystone, New York, 1954), Morley, S: *Gertrude Lawrence* (Weidenfeld & Nicolson, London, 1981)

LAWRENCE, Jerome (b Cleveland, 14 July 1915).

In collaboration with **Robert E[dwin] LEE** (b Elyria, Ohio, 15 October 1918), Lawrence wrote two highly successful plays: the dramatization of the tale of the bible-belt Bertram Scopes 'Monkey Trials' as *Inherit the Wind*, and that of Patrick Dennis's comic novella about his extravagant *Auntie Mame*. This latter piece provided the pair with the basis for their most successful musical play, *Mame*.

Before their play successes, Lawrence and Lee had already ventured into the musical theatre when they provided the libretto to the songs of Hugh Martin for *Look Ma, I'm Dancin'!*, a vehicle for comedienne Nancy Walker as a rich lady who drags a ballet company into modern dance which had run through 188 performances on Broadway. They subsequently adapted James Hilton's famous *Lost Horizon* into a short-lived musical called *Shangri-La*, and Giraudoux's *The Madwoman of Chaillot* as a second vehicle for *Mame* star Angela Lansbury. Produced under the title *Dear World*, it ran for a disappointing 132 performances.

1948 **Look Ma, I'm Dancin'!** (Hugh Martin/w Lee) Adelphi Theater 29 January
1956 **Shangri-La** (Harry Warren/w Lee, James Hilton) Winter Garden Theater 13 June
1966 **Mame** (Jerry Herman/w Lee) Winter Garden Theater 24 May
1968 **Dear World** (Herman/w Lee) Mark Hellinger Theater 6 February

LAYE, Evelyn (b London, 10 July 1900). Beautiful British ingénue whose additional gift of a sweet and strong soprano voice made her the West End's outstanding musical leading lady between the wars.

Miss Laye made her first stage appearance at the age of 15, and played in her first book musical a year later when she went on tour with her father, Gilbert Laye, in Robert Courtneidge's production of *Oh, Caesar!* (1916). She appeared on the West End stage for the first time as a 17-year-old when she took over a supporting rôle in *The Beauty Spot* at the Gaiety Theatre (1918, Leonie Bramble), and she remained there to take her first leading ingénue

Plate 158. **Evelyn Laye:** *London's loveliest ingénue of the years between the wars.*

rôle in the London production of *Going Up* (1918, Madeline Manners). With only the occasional break for a play or revue, she then continued over the following years to sweep many of the best of the West End's ingénue rôles before her, beginning with Dollis Pym in *The Kiss Call*, Bessie Brent in *The Shop Girl* revival, Mary in Louis Hirsch's *Mary*, and Helen in C B Cochran's botched *Phi-Phi*. She moved to a different calibre of music when she went to Daly's Theatre in 1923 to star in Jimmy White's revivals of *The Merry Widow* and *The Dollar Princess* and she scored one of her greatest successes there in the made-for-Massary title-rôle of Fall's *Madame Pompadour* (1923–4). White's subsequent production of Straus's *Die Perlen der Kleopatra* (1925, Cleopatra), in which she appeared in another Massary title-rôle, was, however, not a success.

The star mixed musical weights merrily as she starred in the title-rôles of two light musical comedies, *Betty in Mayfair* (1925, Betty) and *Merely Molly* (1926, Molly), took over in Szirmai's *Princess Charming* (1927, *Alexandra*, Princess Elaine), appeared in the lead soprano part in *Lilac Time* for two London seasons and then starred in the opening attraction at the Piccadilly Theatre, Jerome Kern's *Blue Eyes* (1928, George Ann Bellamy) as the girl who saved Scotland, before moving to Drury Lane to take the leading lady's rôle in London's production of *The New Moon* (1929, Marianne Beaunoir).

Having refused the part of Sarah Millick in the original production of Noël Coward's *Bitter-Sweet* in London because of a quarrel with the author, whom she suspected

LAYTON

at the best of being on the other woman's side in the recent luring-away of her husband, she later agreed to play it on Broadway. Following an enormous personal success, she then returned to play the same part in the last part of the run in London. She was Helen of Troy in an all-star C B Cochran rehash of Max Reinhardt's rehash of Offenbach's *La Belle Hélène* (1932) and then, in contrast, appeared with Flanagan and Allen in the variety musical comedy *Give Me a Ring* (1933, Peggy). In 1937 she starred opposite Richard Tauber in the very vocal rôle of the Princess Anna Elisa in the London production of Lehár's *Paganini* and then moved to Broadway to appear in the very differently toned Dietz and Schwartz musical comedy *Between the Devil* (1937, Natalie).

Now in her forties, Miss Laye made her final London appearances as juvenile lady on the musical stage in Edna May's famous rôle of Violet Grey in a revival of *The Belle of New York*, in Sigmund Romberg's short-lived *Sunny River* (1943, Marie Sauvinet) and, as a bonne-bouche, in a performance fit to challenge Yvonne Printemps in the rôle the French star had made her own in an English adaptation of *Three Waltzes* (1945, Katherine). After this she appeared in plays, in pantomime where she was a much-prized principal boy, and in revue, but she finally returned, no longer an ingénue but a dashing leading lady, to star with Anton Walbrook in the successful musical *Wedding in Paris* (1954, Marcelle Thibault, 'In the Pink').

In her sixties, she played Annie Besant in the short-lived *Strike a Light* and, having temporarily replaced Anna Neagle in the rôle of Lady Hadwell in Harold Fielding's production of *Charlie Girl*, had a star rôle built for her in the next Fielding show, *Phil the Fluter* (1969, Mrs Fitzmaurice). The show ran but briefly, but Miss Laye's 'They Don't Make Them Like That Any More' nevertheless became an anthology piece. She later appeared in the British provinces as Madame Armfeldt in a tour of *A Little Night Music* in the final episode of one of the most remarkably long and successful careers in the British musical theatre.

Autobiography: *Boo, to My Friends* (Hurst & Blackett, London, 1958)

LAYTON, Joe [LICHTMAN, Joseph] (b New York, 3 May 1931). Choreographer-turned-director who won international success with his dances for *The Sound of Music* and his direction of the circus musical *Barnum*.

After an early career as a dancer in Broadway shows (*Oklahoma!*, *High Button Shoes*, *Gentlemen Prefer Blondes*, *Miss Liberty*, *Wonderful Town*), Layton joined the US Army where he was given his first opportunities to direct and choreograph musical productions. One of his earliest efforts in his post-forces period was the burlesque *The Princess and the Pea* (1958), but his New York choreography career began with the 1959 revival of *On the Town* and the off-Broadway development of *The Princess and the Pea* into *Once Upon a Mattress* (also London). He subsequently created the dances for the original production of *The Sound of Music* (Broadway and London), for *Greenwillow* (1960), *Tenderloin* (1960) and for Noël Coward's *Sail Away* (Broadway and London).

Layton's first Broadway directing assigment was on Richard Rodgers's *No Strings* (1962) and, although the show itself had a limited success, his contribution won him

half of the year's Tony Award for choreography. He subsequently directed another *On the Town* revival (London 1963), Coward's *The Girl Who Came to Supper*, *Drat! The Cat!*, *Sherry!* and the George Cohan biomusical *George M!*, which brought his total to four exclamation points in three shows and won him a second choreographer's Tony Award, as well as *Dear World* and another Richard Rodgers piece, *Two by Two*. He visited Japan in 1970 to stage the musical *Scarlett*, based on *Gone with the Wind*, and in 1973 he directed an English-language *Gone With the Wind* musical at London's Theatre Royal, Drury Lane.

Following a period devoted largely to revue, television, and nightclub work, Layton returned to Broadway to direct the musical *Platinum* (1978) before creating his greatest success with the all-circus staging of *Barnum* (1980), a staging subsequently repeated in various versions in the show's many productions around the world. In 1988 he directed and choreographed the London extravaganza *Ziegfeld*.

LEANDER, Zarah [HEDBERG, Zarah Stina] (b Lake Vaner, Karlskrona, Sweden, 15 March 1907; d Stockholm, 23 June 1981).

Daughter of a provincial Swedish pastor, Zarah Leander, equipped with a limited and extremely low singing voice of a highly individual character, seemed scarcely set to take her stage talents into the musical field. However, after beginnings in revue she made a success of Lehár's 'glada anken' (merry widow) in a Stockholm production which tactfully lowered the entire rôle into her range, and it was thereafter as a singing actress that she established herself in Sweden.

She made her Vienna début as the star of Benatzky's successful musical comedy *Axel an der Himmelstür* (1936) at the Theater an der Wien and, as a result of the film version that followed, began a prominent career in musical films, to the accompaniment of a series of successful songs. After the Second World War, she returned to the screen and later to the stage, starring in Vienna in Peter Kreuder's *Madame Scandaleuse* (1958) and as Mrs Erlynne in his musical version of *Lady Windermere's Fan*, *Lady aus Paris* (1964). Her final Vienna appearance was as Madame Armfeldt in *A Little Night Music*, produced at the Theater an der Wien in 1975, nearly 40 years after her first starring rôle there in *Axel an der Himmelstür*, and her final stage appearance was in the same rôle in a Swedish production.

In 1992 (3 July) the singer was the subject of a 'one-person musical' staged at Greifswald's Stadttheater as *Zarah 47-Das tote Lied*. The musical part of the evening was a selection of Leander's best screen songs.

Autobiography: *Es war so wunderbar* (Berlin, 1983)

LEÁNYVÁSÁR Operette in 3 acts by Miksa Bródy and Ferenc Martos. Music by Viktor Jacobi. Király Színház, Budapest, 14 November 1911.

Viktor Jacobi, although still only 28 years of age, was already well established as one of Budapest's most appreciable composers of operett, with half a dozen shows including the successful *Tüskerózsa* and *Van, de nincs* to his credit, by the time he wrote *Leányvásár*, the piece which would open up the international theatre scene to him. This expansion was not unpremeditated for, in the climate of that time, when central European Operette was the rage of

826

London and New York, many Viennese and Hungarian composers were writing their works more with a view to export than for the home market. Jacobi's librettists purposely set out their book to *Leányvásár* on 'English' principles and persuaded the composer to do the same with his score.

The story of the show was a sort of not-very-wild West version of the much-used tale which, up till now, had had its apotheosis in von Flotow's *Martha*. Lucy Harrison (Sári Petráss), the daughter of a millionaire San Francisco congressman (Endre Boross), is destined unenthusiastically to become the wife of Fritz (Márton Rátkai), the son of Count Rottenberg (Árpád Latabár sr). One day, she goes off for a bit of fun to the marriage market at 'a village near San Francisco' and there she gets herself paired off with a handsome vagabond called Tom Migles (Ernő Király). Migles turns out to be Tom Fleetwood, the son of a once wealthy San Franciscan gentleman who was ruined by playing the money market opposite Lucy's father. Lucy thinks that he has entrapped her into what is apparently a binding marriage as a form of revenge and she angrily and unhappily agrees to follow her father's wishes and wed Fritz. However, by the time the last scenes are reached it turns out that the little nobleman has already tied himself to Lucy's maid, Bessy (Sári Fedák), so the way is left clear for a pretty reconciliation and a happy if conventional ending.

Jacobi's score may have been lined up in an 'English' shape, with its two central singing lovers, its supporting pair of soubrets and its accent on comedy, but its flavour was unmitigatedly Hungarian with, advisedly, a rather more prominent ration of Viennese waltzes than was hitherto usual out east. It was also easily his best score to date, a mixture of light romantic and dancing comic melodies which produced a whole line of successful single numbers as well as some memorable ensembles. The best of the romantic music was in the prima donna's rôle, a swooping, rhythmic entrance waltz (Lucy belépője) and a lovely third-act solo 'Tele van a szívem' as well as a series of duets with the tenor Tom, of which the waltzes of the first-act finale ('De nagyot iramodtam') and the second act ('Mondjad igazán') stood out, but it was the light comic music of the show which supplied the real hits. Fedák and Rátkai scored in the first act with the tripping song-and-dance 'Kettecskén', again with the jaunty waltz duo 'No, de méltóságos úr', and topped the set with the bristling 'Dzsilolo', accompanied by a lively dance routine choreographed by the theatre's balletmaster Izsó Geiger which became famous in itself. Fedák hit the heights again with a marching sailor song (Tengerész-dal) in a rôle of proportions altogether out of line with her part in the plot, but altogether in line with her star status.

Leányvásár was one of the greatest successes that the Király Színház had known in its six years as Budapest's principal theatre for both imported and original Operette. It topped Jacobi's own previous works and such pieces as Rényi's *A kis gróf*, produced with great success earlier the same year, and outdid all but the very particular *János vitéz* of the works of earlier composers. It established itself firmly as a part of the basic Hungarian repertoire and promptly began the march around the world which had been hopefully planned for it. That march started disappointingly, for Victor Palfi's Berlin production at the Neues Operetten-Theater (ad Fritz Moss) was only a very relative success – being distinctly outpointed by Fall's *Der liebe Augustin* at the Theater des Westens – and *Das Mädchenmarkt* did not ever really establish itself in Germany. Perhaps as a result, although the Király Színház company introduced their show to Vienna in a season at the Carltheater in 1913, it was 1915 before Vienna saw the German version, and then it was produced not at one of the major houses but at Ronacher with Susanne Bachrich (Lucy), Mizzi Freihardt (Bessy), Karl Pfann (Tom), Carlo Böhm (Fritz) and Oskar Sachs (Rottenberg) featured.

If the German-language version failed to live up to the original success, however, the targeted British one did not. In London, George Edwardes mounted *The Marriage Market* at Daly's Theatre, following the line of Viennese successes there which descended from *The Merry Widow* through *The Dollar Princess* and *The Count of Luxemburg* to *Gipsy Love*. But, in spite of the authors' efforts to be English, the show which he staged had undergone some significant alterations. Gladys Unger's libretto beefed up the amount of comedy by making the first soubrette rôle a new 'heroine's best friend' called Kitty for top-billed Gertie Millar to whom 'Dzsilolo' was allotted as one of four solos, a total which later included a tacked-in piece called 'Silly Billy' written by Paul Rubens. Kitty went with Mariposa (as the heroine was now called) to the fair and won a Lord Hurlingham (comedian G P Huntley) as a prize. Bessy the maid did not quite disappear, although Emma (Avice Kelham) was now largely there to be paired off with the show's other star comic, Bill Berry, who appeared in a wholly new rôle as Huntley's valet, Blinker, and appropriated 'No, de méltóságos úr' made over as a song called 'A1'. He also had his part expanded by Rubens with a number called 'I Don't Believe in Fairies Now' and later with a Lionel Monckton piece called 'Joy Bells'.

With all this comedy and these comedy solos padding out the piece, Mariposa (Sári Petráss, repeating her original rôle) and Jack (Robert Michaelis) were limited to duets – although they did have four of them. Lucy belépője was no longer a belépője (entrance) but appeared in the second-act finale, whilst 'Kettecskén' became a quartet. Vocalist Harry Dearth as an incidental seaman rendered a baritone song which was also eventually replaced by one by Rubens during alterations intended to freshen the show six months into its run. The piece as made over proved strongly to London tastes – more so than either of the Viennese works which had preceded it at Daly's – and, in a 14-month run, Edwardes won 423 London performances from Jacobi's operett before sending it on the road.

In America, Charles Frohman had no such good fortune with an even further botched version which was based on the London one, but which wandered much further away from the original. If 'Kettecskén' ('Hand-in-Hand'), 'Ha lennék' ('The One I Love') and the Sailor Song were still there, the Rubens and Monckton interpolations had also been retained at the expense of much of the rest of Jacobi's score which was replaced by songs by Jerome Kern (three), Edwin Burch (two), Pedro de Zulueta (one) and leading man Donald Brian (one). Venita Fitzhugh was the heroine, and Moya Mannering and Percival Knight headed the comedy for a ten-week Broadway run.

J C Williamson Ltd returned to what was largely the London version when *The Marriage Market* was produced in Australia with Ethel Cadman (Mariposa), Thelma Raye (Kitty), Derek Hudson (Jack), Leslie Holland (Hurlingham) and Phil Smith (Blinker) featured for seasons in Melbourne and Sydney (Her Majesty's Theatre 3 July 1915), but it was Lionel Monckton's English 'Joy Bells' and Smith's Jerome and Schwartz ragtime song 'You Can't Get Away from It' which caught on best from the now internationally composite score, rather than the markedly rhythmic remaining Hungarian numbers.

Leányvásár took its time to reach France, where Jacobi never succeeded in gaining the foothold that he had in Britain, but it was ultimately produced by Charles Montcharmont at his Lyon theatre, in a version by Charles Quinel and Pierre d'Aumier, a dozen years after its Hungarian début. The French version, although crediting only the original librettists, was, however, based on the English text and Lilian Backson (Cécile Dessaud) and Jack Grims (Géo Bury) romanced, Ketty (Gabrielle Ristori) and Comte Montegrisky (Armand Franck) soubretted and comedian Morton played the valet Brichton opposite Denise Cam as the English maid Phoebe. The score, whilst ignoring the English incrustations, again underwent some alterations, but Ketty retained 'Psilolo' and Brichton and Phoebe got back most of their pilfered duets. *Le Beau Voyage* did not, however, make it to Paris where, by this time, the one-step and the foxtrot were reigning instead of the waltz and Hungarian novelties were not à la mode.

Germany: Neues Operetten-Theater *Das Mädchenmarkt* 7 April 1912; Austria: Carltheater (Hun) 7 May 1913, Ronacher *Das Mädchenmarkt* 1 March 1915; UK: Daly's Theatre *The Marriage Market* 17 May 1913; USA: Knickerbocker Theater *The Marriage Market* 22 September 1913; Australia: Her Majesty's Theatre, Melbourne 20 May 1915; France: Théâtre des Célestins, Lyon *Le Beau Voyage* 15 March 1923
Recording: Selection (Qualiton)

LEAVE IT TO JANE Musical comedy in 2 acts by Guy Bolton and P G Wodehouse based on George Ade's play *The College Widow*. Music by Jerome Kern. Longacre Theater, New York, 28 August 1917.

F Ray Comstock and Morris Gest planned to follow the successful production of *Oh, Boy!*, at the little Princess Theater, with another Bolton/Wodehouse/Kern collaboration and, to that end, they purchased the rights to musicalize George Ade's comedy *The College Widow*, an ingenuous piece of schooldays romance with footballing frills which had run up a fine 278-performance sequence at the Garden Theater in 1904–5 under the management of Henry Savage. The plot of the original play was retained as the central story of the more jovially titled musical *Leave it to Jane*, which told of how Jane Witherspoon (Edith Hallor), daughter of the President of Atwater College, uses her charms to make footballing star Billy Bingham (Robert Pitkin) abandon his own father's alma mater and secretly attend Atwater to be near his girl. Billy wins the big match for Atwater and then discovers the treachery, but the repentant Jane comes good for a happy ending. There were plenty of comic incidentals surrounding this tale, with Oscar Shaw as Stub Talmadge and Ann Orr as Bessie Tanner playing a football-mad pair of students, Georgia O'Ramey sweeping up the low comedy as a landlady's daughter determined to get romantic and/or financial

satisfaction from an ex-boarder, the weedy Harold Hicks (Olin Howland), who has grown too big for his boots and for her, and Will C Crimans as Billy's rampaging papa, dashed off by the students on a happily youthful spree so that he will not notice that his son is playing on the wrong side in the big match.

Kern supplied a suitably feather-light, youthful set of songs, some of which were left-overs from earlier works, to match the libretto. The title trio, performed by Misses Orr and Haller and Pitkin, was a rewritten version of *Ninety in the Shade*'s 'Whistling Dan', 'When the Orchestra is Playing Your Favorite Waltz'/'There it is Again' was an *Oh, Boy!* cut-out, whilst the delightful ensemble 'I'm Going to Find a Girl' re-used a melody Kern had written for a silent film score. The favourite numbers, however, were custom-made: the revusical 'Cleopatterer', performed by Miss Ramey, the incidental comedy trio 'Sir Galahad' (Shaw, Ramey, Howland), a pretty duo 'The Crickets Are Calling' for Pitkin and Miss Hallor and, most notably, the languid Siren's Song performed with intent by the girls of Atwater. These were supplemented by some jolly, lively pieces, principally for Shaw and Miss Orr ('Just You Watch My Step', 'The Sun Shines Brighter') which ensured that the collegiate spirits of the show never slackened.

Leave it to Jane started out of town happily, was given a smart wash-and-brush-up on the way to town (including the wiping of four numbers, only two of which were replaced), and, given that *Oh, Boy!* was still happily running at the Princess Theater, opened on Broadway at the much larger Longacre instead. It did well enough, holding its place there for 167 performances before moving on to the touring circuits in no less than three separate companies, but it did not establish itself in the same way that the rather less ingenuous *Oh, Boy!* had done, and its post-Broadway career was, with one exception, confined to America.

That exception was Australia. J C Williamson Ltd took up *Leave it to Jane* and presented Genevieve Davis/Margery Hicklin (Jane), Maude Fane (Bessie), Winnie Collins (Flora), Leyland Hodgson (Stub) and Athol Tier (Bub) for a fine 11 weeks in Sydney, six in Melbourne (Theatre Royal, 5 June 1926) and a subsequent trip to New Zealand.

In 1959 Joseph Beruh and Peter Katz produced a revival of *Leave it to Jane* at off-Broadway's Sheridan Square Theater (25 May 1959). A few alterations were made to the score, including the reinstating, for the benefit of top-billed Dorothy Greener as Flora, of 'Poor Prune', a number cut on the road, and the dropping of a couple of other songs, but by and large the revival reproduced the show much as it had been originally played on Broadway, if on a smaller scale. Kathleen Murray (Jane), Vince O'Brien (Billy), Angelo Mango (Stub) and George Segal (Ollie) were amongst the cast of the show which found an appreciative audience for a splendid 928 performances amongst those who appreciated a little nostalgic relaxation from the bigger and slicker products of contemporary Broadway. In 1985 a Goodspeed Opera House revival (2 October) with Rebecca Luker (Jane), Faith Prince (Flora), David Staller (Billy) and Michael O'Steen (Stub) was sent on tour with Broadway as a goal, but it petered out before reaching New York.

Australia: Her Majesty's Theatre, Sydney 24 October 1925
Recording: 1959 revival cast recording (Strand)

LEAVE IT TO ME! Musical comedy in 2 acts by Bella and Sam Spewack based on their play *Clear All Wires*. Music and lyrics by Cole Porter. Imperial Theater, New York, 9 November 1938.

Mrs Alonzo P Goodhue (Sophie Tucker) had ambitions for her husband (Victor Moore), so she dug into her deep bank accounts and backed Mr Roosevelt for President. As a result, with Roosevelt safely in the White House, Alonzo has been nominated as US Ambassador to Russia. But he doesn't want to be Ambassador to Russia, and once he gets there he tries everything in his power to get himself sacked. He has some help from a young newspaperman called Buckley Joyce Thomas (William Gaxton), an employee of tycoon J H Brody who had thought himself a shoo-in for the ambassadorial job, and who has sent his minion to Moscow under orders to try to get Goodhue disgraced. But no matter how badly Alonzo the ambassador behaves, things always seem perversely to turn out in his favour. It is only when he has ruefully settled in and is concocting a Goodhue plan for world peace that the State Department takes fright, and it is deemed advisable to get rid of him. Next thing Mrs Goodhue will have him standing for president. The feminine interest in this mostly masculine plot was provided by giving Mrs Goodhue a troupe of dancing girls to export 'culture' to Russia, Thomas a girl called Colette (Tamara), and introducing a nymphet of his (and Brody's) called Dolly Winslow (Mary Martin) with a song.

That song came out at the top of a not-really-top-notch score which nevertheless rendered up a couple of Porter durables. Miss Martin's singing of 'My Heart Belongs to Daddy', whilst delicately removing her furs, and all oblivious to the Siberian cold, established both the number and the artist as hits. Elsewhere, Tamara insisted 'Get Out of Town' and Miss Tucker disserted on the fact that 'Most Gentlemen Don't Like Love' with rather less relevance (probably because the number was a cut-out rescued from an earlier show) than her punning declaration in the first act that she was 'taking the Steps to Russia' and 'making Communism thwing', whilst Moore simply cried 'I Want to Go Home' and, in a typical Porter catalogue of fun, listed some reasons why. The finale of the first act hailed 'Comrade Alonzo' and had Joseph Stalin (Walter Armin) doing a little dance to a jazzed-up version of the Internationale.

Although the authors actually had the experience of having been journalists in Russia, *Leave it to Me!* was just another colourful Ruritanian song and dance show pretending to be 'biting satire', and just another on the recent heap of (mostly better) musical comedies which had decided that Presidents and politics – preferably ridiculed – were smart material for the musical stage. With the best of Porter's songs and its fine cast, headed by the inimitable *Of Thee I Sing* and *Anything Goes* pairing of Moore and Gaxton, as advantages, Vinton Freedley's production stayed 291 performances on Broadway before going on the road. By this stage, however, events had moved on in Europe and Stalin's rapprochement with the Nazis had not only rather messed up one bit of the plot, it had changed a few of even the most enthusiastically liberal Americans' thoughts on the Russian leader. It was judged wiser to expunge the dancing dictator from the show.

Britain and Australia did not take up *Leave it to Me!*, and the piece was laid to rest, leaving its favourite songs to carry on alone. However, it finally did find its way further afield in 1987 when, on the crest of the revived fashion for Porter's work, a German production, which swapped the show's original catchphrase title for the more apt and amusing *Wodka Cola* (ad Michael Kunze, Dietrich Hilsdorf, Michael Quast, Dieter Glawaschnig), was put together at Stuttgart. *Wodka Cola* used the plot and much of the score of *Leave it to Me!* but, in the musical jigsaw manner of modern Porter productions, interpolated numbers from *Seven Lively Arts*, *Out of this World* and *Anything Goes*. In a reverse of this process, four numbers from *Leave it to Me!* were inserted into a Porter pasticcio score for an unfortunate London musical based on the film *High Society*.

The title *Leave it to Me!* had been used previously for the 1925 out-of-town try-out of a musical comedy which ultimately came to Broadway in a revised version as *Sweetheart Time* (19 January 1926).

Germany: Staatstheater, Stuttgart *Wodka Cola* 9 December 1987
Recordings: original cast recordings (Decca, Smithsonian), *Wodka Cola* (Boyer)

LECOCQ, [Alexandre] Charles (b Paris, 3 June 1832; d Paris, 24 October 1918). The most potent musician in the development of the French opérette tradition in the 1870s, and for a decade the musical theatre's most successful composer.

A sickly child, Charles Lecocq has long been said to have suffered from an illness which left him with a permanent limp and the need to use crutches. It appears, however, that in truth his handicap was the result of his having been dropped, by his sister, whilst a baby. During his youngest years the physically limited boy developed the interest in music which led him to prefer a musical education to a general college one, and at the age of 16 he entered the Paris Conservatoire. The need to earn a living ultimately obliged him to give up his studies and devote himself to teaching and to work as an occasional pianist, but at the same time he made his first steps as a composer with a series of piano pieces. He was able to find a publisher for some of these, however, only when he pretended that they were the work of a fashionably German composer.

The struggling young man first came to general notice as a composer at the age of 24 when his setting of a Léon Battu/Ludovic Halévy text called *Le Docteur Miracle* tied for first place with that by his Conservatoire contemporary, Georges Bizet, in a contest organized by Offenbach for the Théâtre des Bouffes-Parisiens. The winning pieces were produced at the Bouffes, and Lecocq's stage career was launched. That launching was, however, to prove to be a very slow one. Although he continued to write regularly for the theatre and, during the next 15 years, succeeded in placing as many pieces – principally one-act opérettes but also several longer pieces – on the Paris stage, Lecocq did not manage to force his way through to a position in the first rank of opérette composers.

The most substantial and successful of these early pieces was the three-act oriental opéra-comique *Fleur de thé* (1868), a piece written to a swingeingly saucy libretto by Henri Chivot and Alfred Duru, librettists of a different class from those with whom Lecocq had previously been able to ally himself. *Fleur de thé* was produced at the

Théâtre de l'Athénée, under the management of the eccentric William Busnach, an earlier collaborator of the composer and a sometime producer. It was, in fact, Busnach who had given Lecocq – whom he had engaged on the music staff at his short-lived theatre – his first opportunity with a larger piece, a couple of seasons earlier. The two-act *L'Amour et son carquois* had been a semi-success which had been sufficient to win him an alliance with such authors as the rising Chivot and Duru, recently the librettists of Hervé's *Les Chevaliers de la table ronde*. *Fleur de thé* was given a good Parisian run in its unfashionable little house, and, at the height of the fashion for French opéra-bouffe, it went on to be played in most of the main theatrical centres of the world. Lecocq's name and reputation had begun to get around, but in a theatrical world where star composers were made within years of coming out of short pants and the Conservatoire, he was already heading for his 40th birthday.

Thereafter, however, his works began to win more attention. Three short pieces produced at the Théâtre des Bouffes-Parisiens – *Gandolfo*, *Le Rajah de Mysore* and *Le Testament de M Crac* – were given productions throughout Europe and sometimes beyond, and the two-act *Le Beau Dunois* went on from its Paris production to be played both in Vienna and in Budapest, where it was the first of Lecocq's works to be produced. However, Lecocq still had to struggle for commissions and productions, and the closest he got to a new production in Paris was the announcement that he was to write a new opéra-bouffe, entitled *Gesier XIV*, with Jules Moinaux for the Folies-Dramatiques. Apparently because of legal complications, *Gesier XIV* was never produced, and it was not until the Franco-Prussian War encouraged Lecocq temporarily to quit Paris that he found the opportunity that would set him on the road to real international success.

His fourth collaboration with Chivot and Duru, and this time with the famous vaudevilliste Clairville as well, was *Les Cent Vierges*, an extravagantly comical piece of musical farce writing which was accepted for production by the enthusiastic Eugène Humbert at Brussels's Théâtre des Fantaisies-Parisiennes. Splendidly mounted, *Les Cent Vierges* was a grand success in Belgium, and within two months of its first Brussels performance it appeared on the Paris stage before being exported world-wide (*To The Green Isles Direct*, *The Island of Bachelors*, *Hundert Jungfrauen*, *Szaz szüz* etc). A second piece for Humbert, *La Fille de Madame Angot* (1872), was even more successful. A combination of a splendidly shapely libretto and a score which offered one sveltely melodious song and ensemble after another, it went swiftly to Paris and then around the world several times. On the way, it proved itself the most consequent work of the period, and it firmly and finally established Lecocq and his light comic opera style of writing at the forefront of the French and international musical theatre scene, a position previously occupied by the outrageous frivolities of the opéras-bouffes of Offenbach and Hervé.

The success of *La Fille de Madame Angot* and *Les Cent Vierges* sent theatre directors off in the same kind of spin searching for more Lecocq works that they had earlier displayed in chasing Offenbach pieces. They dug back and, in London for example, where the new rage burned brightest, his *Le Carnaval d'un merle blanc* was produced in

a botched version as *Loo, or The Party Who Took Miss*, whilst such short pieces as *Les Ondines au champagne* (Folly, 1877) and *Le Rajah de Mysore* (Gaiety, 1878) were given belated first showings. Less scrupulous directors fabricated their own Lecocq opérettes from music from his old works (*The Black Prince*, 1874, *Una*, 1875, *Angela*, 1878).

The composer's next piece, *Giroflé-Girofla*, was also produced in Belgium. A delicious comic opera, much more in the old-fashioned, low-comic vein of *Les Cent Vierges* than in the dramatic and historic/political mode of *La Fille de Madame Angot* with its true-to-life characters, it proved a third consecutive international hit for Lecocq. With the Parisian theatres crying out for the services of the composer of *La Fille de Madame Angot* and *Giroflé-Girofla*, Lecocq – after an aborted start on a fourth show, *Le Grand Frédéric* (w Prével, Saint-Albin) for Humbert – now returned to France. There, his first new works had a mixed reception. A distinctly more polite comic opera, *Les Prés Saint-Gervais* (1874), written to a text by Sardou and Philippe Gille and produced at the Théâtre des Variétés, had neither the comic flavour nor the drama of his more popular pieces, but, after a disappointing Paris run, it nevertheless followed its predecessors on to the international circuit (*Prinz Conti*, *Conti herceg* etc). A bandit piece, *Le Pompon* (1875) was firmly rejected by the Paris public, but it too won some exposure away from home (*Tivolini*) and scored a long-lasting success in Hungary where, as *A kis doktor*, it was given a respectable first run at the Király Színház and remained more than 15 years in the general repertoire.

Following these two less-than-wholly-successful pieces, Lecocq teamed up again with his *La Fille de Madame Angot* collaborator, wheeler-dealer Victor Koning, who was now spending his royalties on being the director of the Théâtre de la Renaissance. Over the next six years Lecocq composed, Koning presented, and the reigning queen of Parisian opérette, Jeanne Granier, mostly starred in eight new opéras-comiques, beginning with *La Petite Mariée* (1875), peaking with *Le Petit Duc* (1878) and including such other internationally played pieces as *La Petite Mademoiselle*, *La Marjolaine*, *La Jolie Persane* and *La Camargo*. These Théâtre de la Renaissance shows, written to texts by a variety of librettists and lyricists, were a remarkably consistent body of works musically and they confirmed Lecocq's position at the head of his profession, but the dismal failure of *Janot* (1881), written after a period of illness and unhappiness, led to a split between the composer and his producer, and it was bruited about that Lecocq, accused now of turning out works which were all too much musically alike, might be on the downward slope.

A change of venue, of producer and of cast, however, proved to be a salutary one and Lecocq, who had already had some lively success at other houses with his music for the vaudevilles *Le Grand Casimir* and *La Roussotte* (w Hervé, Marius Boullard) at the Variétés, and his accompaniment to the grandiose spectacle of *L'Arbre de Noël* at the Porte-Saint-Martin, moved back into top gear with his next two pieces, *Le Jour et la nuit* (1881) and *Le Coeur et la main* (1882), both produced by Brasseur at the Théâtre des Nouveautés. Both, equipped with the kind of dashingly farcical libretti which suited him so well, were splendid successes which, like his earlier triumphs, were swiftly played throughout the world. Chivot and Duru's *La*

Princesse des Canaries (1883), which followed quickly on the heels of this pair of hits, had a more limited home success, but it, too, exported well, and the same authors' *L'Oiseau bleu* also found some takers at home and abroad without ever looking like challenging the composer's most popular works.

Thereafter Lecocq genuinely did become somewhat bogged down in his own style and, deprived by the depredations of time of the support of his favourite authorial teams of Leterrier/Vanloo, Chivot/Duru and Meilhac/Halévy, the shows and scores he produced became less and less successful. *Plutus*, his first work premièred at the Opéra-Comique, was a failure, *Les Grenadiers de Mont-Cornette* disappeared in 18 performances at the Bouffes-Parisiens, and *L'Égyptienne* (1890) did even worse. Only one work, *Ninette* (1896), his version of the Cyrano de Bergerac story, had any kind of a run, but even it did not begin to approach the composer's great works of the 1870s and 1880s.

A master of the charming and even the beautiful in light theatre music, as is best witnessed by the melodies written for the hero and heroine of *Le Petit Duc*, Lecocq could also turn his hand to lustier strains, such as those of the celebrated Quarrelling Duet and 'Marchande de marée' in *La Fille de Madame Angot*, and to swirling dance music as epitomized in the waltzing finale to the second act of the same piece. His work did not in any way lack comical strains, but his musical turn of phrase in comic situations was always more genteel than the cheerfully vulgar and belly-laugh burlesque effects of such musicians as Hervé. It is perhaps this lack of very obvious colouring that has led to his works being disproportionately neglected in modern times where only *La Fille de Madame Angot* and, to a lesser extent, *Le Petit Duc* remain in the repertoire in France.

1857 **Le Docteur Miracle** (Léon Battu, Ludovic Halévy) 1 act Théâtre des Bouffes-Parisiens 8 April

1859 **Huis-clos** (Adolphe Guénée, Adolphe Marquet) 1 act Folies-Nouvelles 28 January

1864 **Le Baiser à la porte** (Jules de la Guette) 1 act Folies-Nouvelles 26 March

1864 **Liline et Valentine** (de la Guette) 1 act Théâtre des Champs-Élysées 25 May

1865 **Les Ondines au champagne** (Hippolyte Lefèbvre, Jules Pélissié [ie Victorien Sardou], Merle) 1 act Folies-Marigny 5 September

1866 **Le Myosotis** ('Cham', William Busnach) 1 act Palais-Royal 2 May

1867 **Le Cabaret de Ramponneau** (Lesire) 1 act Folies-Marigny 11 October

1868 **L'Amour et son carquois** (Marquet, Delbès [ie Busnach]) Théâtre de l'Athénée 30 January

1868 **Fleur de thé** (Henri Chivot, Alfred Duru) Théâtre de l'Athénée 11 April

1868 **Les Jumeaux de Bergame** (Busnach) 1 act Théâtre de l'Athénée 20 November

1868 **Le Carnaval d'un merle blanc** (Chivot, Duru) Palais-Royal, 30 December

1869 **Gandolfo** (Chivot, Duru) 1 act Théâtre des Bouffes-Parisiens 16 January

1869 **Deux portières pour un cordon** (w Hervé/Isidore Legouix et al/'Lucian' [ie Lefèbvre, L Dubuis]) 1 act Palais-Royal 15 March

1869 **Le Rajah de Mysore** (Chivot, Duru) 1 act Théâtre des Bouffes-Parisiens 21 September

1870 **Le Beau Dunois** (Chivot, Duru) Théâtre des Variétés 13 April

1871 **Le Testament de M Crac** (Jules Moinaux) 1 act Théâtre des Bouffes-Parisiens 23 October

1871 **Le Barbier de Trouville** (Adolphe Jaime, [Jules Noriac]) 1 act Théâtre des Bouffes-Parisiens 19 November

1871 **Sauvons la caisse** (de la Guette) 1 act Tertulia 22 December

1872 **Les Cent Vierges** (Chivot, Duru, Clairville) Fantaisies-Parisiennes, Brussels 16 March

1872 **La Fille de Madame Angot** (Clairville, Victor Koning, Paul Siraudin) Fantaisies-Parisiennes, Brussels, 4 December

1874 **Giroflé-Girofla** (Eugène Leterrier, Alfred Vanloo) Fantaisies-Parisiennes, Brussels 21 March

1874 **Les Prés Saint-Gervais** (Victorien Sardou, Philippe Gille) Théâtre des Variétés 14 November

1875 **Le Pompon** (Chivot, Duru) Théâtre des Folies-Dramatiques 10 November

1875 **La Petite Mariée** (Leterrier, Vanloo) Théâtre de la Renaissance 21 December

1876 **Kosiki** (Busnach, Armand Liorat) Théâtre de la Renaissance 18 October

1877 **La Marjolaine** (Leterrier, Vanloo) Théâtre de la Renaissance 3 February

1878 **Le Petit Duc** (Henri Meilhac, Halévy) Théâtre de la Renaissance 25 January

1878 **La Camargo** (Leterrier, Vanloo) Théâtre de la Renaissance 20 November

1879 **Le Grand Casimir** (Jules Prével, Albert de St-Albin) Théâtre des Variétés 11 January

1879 **La Petite Mademoiselle** (Meilhac, Halévy) Théâtre de la Renaissance 12 April

1879 **La Jolie Persane** (Leterrier, Vanloo) Théâtre de la Renaissance 28 October

1880 **L'Arbre de Noël** (Leterrier, Vanloo, Arnold Mortier) Théâtre de la Porte-Saint-Martin 6 October

1881 **Janot** (Meilhac, Halévy) Théâtre de la Renaissance 22 January

1881 **La Roussotte** (w Marius Boullard, Hervé/Meilhac, Halévy, Albert Millaud) Théâtre des Variétés 25 January

1881 **Le Jour et la nuit** (Leterrier, Vanloo) Théâtre des Nouveautés 5 November

1882 **Le Coeur et la main** (Charles Nuitter, Alexandre Beaumont) Théâtre des Nouveautés 19 October

1883 **La Princesse des Canaries** (Chivot, Duru) Théâtre des Folies-Dramatiques 9 February

1884 **L'Oiseau bleu** (Chivot, Duru) Théâtre des Nouveautés 16 January

1885 **La Vie mondaine** (Paul Ferrier, Émile de Najac) Théâtre des Nouveautés 13 February

1886 **Plutus** (Millaud, Gaston Jolivet) Opéra-Comique 31 March

1887 **Les Grenadiers de Mont-Cornette** (Daunis, Delorme, Édouard Philippe) Théâtre des Bouffes-Parisiens 4 January

1887 **Ali-Baba** (Vanloo, Busnach) Théâtre de l'Alhambra, Brussels, 11 November (revised version Théâtre de l'Eden, Paris 28 November 1889)

1888 **La Volière** (Nuitter, Beaumont) Théâtre des Nouveautés 11 February

1890 **L'Égyptienne** (Chivot, Nuitter, Beaumont) Théâtre des Folies-Dramatiques 8 November

1894 **Nos bons chasseurs** (Paul Bilhaud, Michel Carré) 1 act Nouveau-Théâtre 10 April

1896 **Ninette** (Charles Clairville, Eugène Hubert, Christian de Trogoff) Théâtre des Bouffes-Parisiens 28 February

1898 **Ruse d'amour** (Stéphane Bordèse) 1 act Casino, Boulogne-sur-Mer 26 June

1900 **La Belle au bois dormant** (Vanloo, Georges Duval) Théâtre des Bouffes-Parisiens 19 February

1903 **Yetta** (Fernand Beissier) Galeries Saint-Hubert, Brussels, 7 March

1904 **Rose mousse** (André Alexandre, Peter Carin) 1 act Théâtre des Capucines 28 January

1905 **La Salutiste** (Beissier) 1 act Théâtre des Capucines 14 January

1905 **Les Poupées de M Dupont** (Paul Gavault) 1 act Théâtre des Variétés 26 May

1910 **La Trahison de Pan** (Bordèse) 1 act Théâtre du Cercle, Aix-les-Bains 13 September

Biography: Schneider, L: *Les Maîtres de l'opérette française: Hervé, Charles Lecocq* (Librairie Académique Perrin et Cie, Paris, 1924)

LEDERER, George W (b Wilkes-Barre, Pa, 1861; d Jackson Heights, NY, 8 October 1938). Turn-of-the-century Broadway producer, 'twice worth about a million', who had his best moments at the head of the Casino Theater, but also lot of bad ones.

Having dipped first into acting, playwriting and journalism, Lederer made his maiden venture as a theatrical producer at the age of 22, in partnership with the barely reliable Sydney Rosenfeld on a Philadelphia piece called *Florinel* (1883). He worked in variety and burlesque in the 1880s, allied in turn with M Ben Leavitt and Abe Leavitt, and with the Rentz–Santley company, and later toured May Yohé and Zelma Rawlston in 'George W Lederer's Players' with *U and I* (1891), but he became more thoroughly respectable when, in September 1893, he and Thomas Canary took over Broadway's Casino Theater after the squeezing out of its founder, Rudolf Aronson, from its directorial chair. At the Casino, Lederer and his partner produced a series of musical shows beginning with the local musicals *The Princess Nicotine*, *Prince Kam* and *The Little Trooper*, and including the early revue, *The Passing Show*, before he took over briefly, as sole manager. He soon allied himself with George B McLellan, brother of the librettist C M S McLellan, but by the end of 1899 that partnership too was dissolved. In spite of many precarious moments, Lederer managed to keep control of the theatre, both as a letting proposition and also as a producing management until 1904.

Amongst the long list of new musicals, revues and imports which Lederer produced (either alone or in partnership) and/or directed at the Casino during his decade in charge were the home-made *In Gay New York*, *The Whirl of the Town*, *An American Beauty*, *The Belle of Bohemia*, *The Casino Girl*, Alice Neilsen's production of Victor Herbert's *The Singing Girl*, and, ultimately the most successful of his own productions there, *The Belle of New York*, as well as American versions of the British hit *The Lady Slavey* (on which he grabbed an author's credit), the French *La Demoiselle du téléphone* (*The Telephone Girl*), *La Falote* and *Les Fêtards* (*The Rounders*), and the Austrian *Heisses Blut* (*A Dangerous Maid*).

Lederer also expanded outwards, and he mounted pieces at Broadway theatres other than the Casino – *The Strollers* (*Die Landstreicher*), *The Blonde in Black* and *The Wild Rose* at the Knickerbocker Theater, *The Man in the Moon* at the New York Theater, *The Jewel of Asia* (1903) at the Criterion, and *Sally in Our Alley* (1902) at the Broadway Theater – as well as taking an interest in the London productions of his pieces, notably the hugely successful version of *The Belle of New York* organized in London by George Musgrove, and even touring the Casino Theater company to the Continent.

He took the semi-black musical *The Southerners* on the road (also director) and, after getting his breath and presumably at least part of his purse back after the awkward end of his Casino adventure and this unprofitable exercise, he once again went back into producing. He toured such pieces as *The Smiling Island* and *The Girl Rangers* and then, partnered with the young H H Frazee, he produced and directed the highly successful *Madame Sherry* (1910 w A H Woods). The same kind of success did not, however, come again. In the 1910s he (co-)produced and/or directed W T Francis and Jeff de Angelis's unfortunate *The Ladies' Lion*, Richard Carle's *Jumping Jupiter* (co-producer only), *The Charity Girl*, *Madame Moselle* and *Angel Face*, but spent more time in employed positions, managing Chicago's Colonial Theater, working for Klaw and Erlanger on the west coast and/or travelling as an advance rep in vaudeville. He mounted his last Broadway production, Victor Herbert's *The Girl in the Spotlight*, in 1920. Several subsequent productions, such as *Peaches* (1923) and *The Pajama Lady* (1930), designed for New York, foundered on their way in.

In his last years Lederer became general manager for producer Sam Harris.

Lederer was at one stage married to Rene Davies, sister to the more famous Marion. His son, Charles Lederer, a screen and stage author, was co-adaptor of Edward Knoblock's play *Kismet* as the libretto for the successful musical of the same name which he presented on Broadway in 1953 and worked on the movie versions of *Red, Hot and Blue*, *Gentlemen Prefer Blondes* and *Can-Can*, whilst an elder son, George W Lederer jr (d New York, 17 December 1924) worked as a New York theatre agent until an early death, aged 33. Lederer's nephew, Norman J Norman (b Philadelphia 12 November 1870; d London 10 October 1941), who went to Britain as the company manager of the *Belle of New York* company, remained there and became European manager for the Shuberts and an occasional producer or general manager. He was also associated with the construction of the Apollo Theatre, and the opening of the Waldorf Theatre.

LEE, Alfred [Augustus] (b ?1839; d Walworth, 14 April 1906).

At first a piano tuner for Messrs Peachey, later a music-hall piano player, an arranger for the publishing house of Charles Sheard and a sometime musical director both for burlesque and touring musical comedy (*Larks*, *Pat* etc) and at London's Duke's and Astley's Theatres, Lee had some singular successes as a popular songwriter. In a long list of music-hall songs 'Champagne Charlie' and 'The Man on the Flying Trapeze' (w George Leybourne) proved the most enduring. As a theatre composer, he arranged the music for a number of burlesques and pantomimes, and also composed several original scores and part-scores, including a fresh set of songs for an expanded version of Burnand's record-breaking burlesque *Black-Eyed Susan*, mounted by William Holland at the Alhambra in 1884, and additional numbers for two decades of shows (*Rustic Roses* (1872), *Spectresheim* (1874), *Pat* (1886) etc). His music-hall hits also found their way into the scores of many a burlesque, pantomime and touring show.

1870 **Pom Pom** (A C Shelley) 1 act
1877 **The Lying Dutchman** (Frederick Hay, Arthur Clements) Strand Theatre 21 December
1884 **Black-Eyed Susan** (F C Burnand) Alhambra Theatre 2 August
1886 **Larks** (w John Crook, Oscar Barrett et al/J Wilton Jones) Winter Garden, Southport, 22 February

LEE, Bert [Albert George] (b Ravensthorpe, 11 June 1880; d Llandudno, 23 January 1946). Songwriter and musical-comedy man-of-all-parts in the British years between the wars.

Yorkshire-born Bert Lee played the organ from a young age, and cemented his connection with music when he took his first employment as a piano-tuner in Manchester at the age of 15. He subsequently joined a concert party as a pianist and, when he was 19, began to try his hand composing songs. In 1910 he had a major hit with 'Joshua' (lyric: George Arthurs), and he made an early appearance in the West End musical theatre when his song 'I Feel So Lonely' was interpolated into the musical *The Islander*. He supplied some additional songs for the inveterately touring *The Lady Slavey* (1913) and hit the bullseye again in the same year with the song 'Hello! Hello! Who's Your Lady Friend?' (w Worton David, Harry Fragson) before, in 1915, under the guidance of music publishers Francis, Day and Hunter, he came together with fellow songwriter R P Weston. The two then began a partnership which was to produce a 20-year run of hit songs, a considerable list of stage musicals and revues (both as joint-composers and text writers), as well as screenplays and musical scores for a number of films.

Weston and Lee began in the musical theatre supplying interpolations for *A Night Out* (1920) and the score for Herbert Clayton's touring revue *Sunshine and Laughter* (1923) before contributing the lyrics for Clayton's next venture, a touring musical version of the play *Tilly of Bloomsbury* produced in collaboration with Joe Waller. *Tilly* was played for one week at the Alhambra, giving the pair a first real West End credit. They supplied 'additional material' for C B Cochran's *Turned Up* and then, with their producer pals Clayton and Waller suddenly having become big news thanks to their canny purchase of *No, No, Nanette*, they were pitchforked into the West End as adaptors of the mélange of American musicals which their mentors staged under the title *The Girl Friend*. In the following decade, Lee – and Weston up till his death – worked steadily for Clayton and/or Waller. Lee's final full West End show, in 1938, was, like his first, under Waller's management.

In between, he had contributed libretti and lyrics to Waller's own shows, including the producer/composer's *Virginia* ('Roll Away Clouds'), his Bobby Howes comedy musicals *Tell her the Truth* ('Horrortorio', 'Sing, Brothers') and *He Wanted Adventure* ('Smile and Be Bright'), the Howes–Binnie Hale hit *Yes, Madam?* ('Sitting Beside o' You', 'Dreaming a Dream', 'Czechoslovakian Love'), *Please, Teacher* ('Song of the Cello') and its successors at the Hippodrome, as well as to the Flanagan and Allen show *Give Me a Ring* and many other successful inter-war comedy musicals. He also collaborated on the screenplays for the movie versions of the stage musicals *Hold My Hand* and *Yes, Madam?*.

The extensive list of Lee's song hits encompasses 'Any Complaints? No!', 'In a Land Fit For Heroes', 'Goodbyee', 'Paddy McGinty's Goat', 'What I Want is a Proper Cup of Coffee', 'My Word, You Do Look Queer', Stanley Holloway's comical 'With Her Head Tucked Underneath Her Arm' and 'Brahn Boots', 'Stop and Shop at the Co-Op' as performed by Gracie Fields, 'Shall I Have it Bobbed or Shingled?', the melodrama classic 'And the Great Big Saw Came Nearer', 'Sister Susie's Sewing Shirts', Violet Loraine's 'The Gipsy Warned Me' and 'Fancy You Fancying Me', and his contribution to the revue stage included doctoring, adding to or just plain writing for *Who's Who*, *Looking Around* with Jack Norworth, *Cheep* with Harry Grattan, *US* with Hastings Turner, *Back Again*, *Brighter London*, *Carte Blanche*, *Pot Luck* and, after Weston's death, George Black's *London Rhapsody*.

A compilation show written by Roy Hudd based on the life and songs of Weston and Lee was produced at the Haymarket Theatre, Leicester, under the title *Just Another Verse and Chorus*.

1924 **Tilly** (Haydn Wood, Jack Waller/w Weston/Herbert Clayton, Con West) Alhambra 3 November
1924 **Mr Tickle MP** (w Weston) Grand Theatre, Blackpool 29 September
1926 **King Rags** (Harry Weston/w Weston) Empire Theatre, Leeds 23 August
1927 **The Girl Friend** English adaptation of the libretto of *Kitty's Kisses* w Weston (Palace Theatre)
1928 **Billy Blue** (w Joseph A Tunbridge, Fred Elkin, Weston/Harold Dyne) Empire Theatre, Newcastle 6 August
1928 **Lucky Girl** (Phil Charig/w Douglas Furber, Weston) Shaftesbury Theatre 14 November
1928 **Virginia** (Waller, Tunbridge/w Furber, Weston/Clayton, Waller) Palace Theatre 24 October
1929 **Merry, Merry** English adaptation and new lyrics w Weston (Carlton Theatre)
1929 **Hold Everything!** English adaptation w Weston (Palace Theatre)
1929 **Here Comes the Bride** (Arthur Schwartz/Desmond Carter, Howard Dietz/w Weston) Opera House, Blackpool 7 October; Piccadilly Theatre, London 20 February 1930
1930 **Sons o' Guns** English lyrics w Weston (London Hippodrome)
1930 **Little Tommy Tucker** (Vivian Ellis/w Carter, Caswell Garth, Weston) Daly's Theatre 19 November
1932 **Tell Her the Truth** (Waller, Tunbridge/w Weston) Saville Theatre 14 June
1933 **He Wanted Adventure** (Waller, Tunbridge/w Clifford Grey, Weston/w Weston) Saville Theatre 28 May
1933 **Give Me a Ring** (Martin Broones/Graham John/w Guy Bolton, Weston) London Hippodrome 22 June
1934 **Yes, Madam?** (Waller, Tunbridge/w K Browne/w Weston) London Hippodrome 27 September
1935 **Please, Teacher** (Waller, Tunbridge/w Browne, Weston) London Hippodrome 2 October
1936 **Certainly, Sir!** (Waller, Tunbridge/w Weston) London Hippodrome 17 September
1937 **Big Business** (Waller, Tunbridge/w Carter/w Carter, Browne) London Hippodrome 18 February
1937 **Oh! You Letty** (Paul Sharon/Grey/w Geoffrey Kerr) Palace Theatre 8 December
1938 **The Fleet's Lit Up** (Vivian Ellis/w Thompson, Bolton) London Hippodrome 17 August
1938 **Bobby Get Your Gun** (Waller, Tunbridge/w Grey, Carter, Bolton, Thompson) Adelphi Theatre 7 October
1940 **Present Arms** (Noel Gay/Thompson) 'additional dialogue' Prince of Wales Theatre 13 May

LEE, Gypsy Rose [HOVICK, Rose Louise] (b Seattle, 9 January 1914; d Los Angeles, 26 April 1970).

Labelled and classified in showbusiness history as the archetypal stripper, Miss Lee was once a player in vaudeville, and was subsequently seen in a handful of 1930s Broadway shows (*Hot-Cha!*, *Melody*, *Ziegfeld Follies*). In the early 1940s she suceeded Ethel Merman in the star rôle of *Dubarry Was a Lady*, and appeared alongside Bobby Clark as the principal attraction of the burlesque revue *Star and Garter* (1942).

Her memoirs, *Gypsy*, became the basis of the Styne/Sondheim/Laurents musical of the same title which, ultimately, was more about the ambitions and staunchly stentorian heartaches of the star's mother, and in which 'Louise' was played by Sandra Church.

Miss Lee's sister, **June HAVOC** (b 8 November 1916), the 'Baby June' of the musical *Gypsy*, had a longer but equally intermittent career in the musical side of the theatre. She played in musicals at the St Louis Muny at the age of 19, appeared on Broadway in *Forbidden Melody* (1936, Rozsa), *Pal Joey* (1940, Gladys), *Mexican Hayride* (1944, Montana) and *Sadie Thompson* (1944, Sadie) and as late as 1982 starred in *Sweeney Todd* on tour. She also authored a musical, *Oh Glorious Tintinnabulation* (Actors Studio 23 May 1974).

Miss Lee was married to film director Otto Preminger.

Autobiography: *Gypsy* (Harper, New York, 1957); Literature: Preminger, E L; *Gypsy and Me* (Little, Brown, Boston, 1984)

LEE, Robert E[dwin] *see* LAWRENCE, JEROME

LEE, Sammy [LEVY, Samuel] (b New York, 1890; d Woodland Hills, Calif, 30 March 1968).

After appearing in his twenties as a dancer in *The Firefly* and *The Belle of Bond Street*, Lee made a career as a choreographer, providing the dances for more than two dozen musical comedies and revues during a decade of Broadway work. Amongst the most important shows on which he worked were the Astaires' *Lady, Be Good!* (1924), the subsequent Gershwin shows *Tell Me More!*, *Tip-Toes* (with its ex-ballet-dancer heroine, Queenie Smith) and *Oh, Kay!*, *No, No, Nanette*, the Marx Brothers vehicle *The Cocoanuts*, the spectacular *Rio Rita* with its call for everyone to do 'The Kinkajou', the original production of *Show Boat* and the 1927 edition of the *Ziegfeld Follies*. Lee subsequently went to Hollywood, where his work from the early 1930s was in films.

LEE, Vanessa [MOULE, Winifred Ruby] (b London, 18 June 1920; d London, 15 March 1992).

Miss Lee made her first appearance on stage at the age of 12, and on the London musical stage when she was 15 as a schoolgirl in Anne Croft's twice-a-day *Tulip Time* (as Ruby Moule). She toured in the leading soprano parts of *Chu Chin Chow* and *The Belle of New York* and then returned to London to take over a small part in Richard Tauber's *Old Chelsea*. In 1947 she understudied Jessica James as Maria Ziegler in *The Dancing Years* and was subsequently given the principal soprano rôle in the post-London *Perchance to Dream*, playing opposite Novello in his tour of South Africa and Britain. When Novello's last show, *King's Rhapsody*, was produced, she again played opposite the author, creating the rôle of the Princess Cristiane and the song 'Some Day My Heart Will Awake'. She appeared as Lady Windermere in *After the Ball*, Noël Coward's musical version of *Lady Windermere's Fan*, toured as *The Merry Widow* and played Maria in *The Sound of Music* in Australia, but thereafter limited her stage appearances to the straight stage for a number of years before retiring.

Miss Lee was the wife of actor **Peter GRAVES** [Lord] (b London, 21 October 1911) who appeared in several of Novello's musicals, sometimes understudying and playing for the star and, in *Arc de Triomphe* (1943), creating the lead rôle of Pierre Bachelet built on Novello lines. He played in the original productions of Novello's *Glamorous Night* (Nico), *Careless Rapture* (Jimmy Torrence), *The Crest of the Wave* (Lord William Gantry) and *The Dancing Years* (Franzel). Graves was Lord Windermere to his wife's Lady in *After the Ball*, appeared as Orlofsky in *Gay Rosalinda*, starred as Valentine Brown in the musical of *Quality Street*, *Dear Miss Phoebe*, and played Danilo to the Widow of Margaret Mitchell (1952). He later appeared in the stage-musical version of *The Water Gipsies* and a re-run of *Old Chelsea*. In a long parallel career in British films he was seen in the screen versions of *Waltz Time* (1945) and *Derby Day* (1952).

LEFTWICH, Alexander (b Baltimore, 24 December 1884; d Hollywood, 13 January 1947).

A former actor and production assistant, Sandy Leftwich worked behind the scenes first in variety and then in the theatre, for Daniel Frohman and later for the Shuberts. In a bright Broadway career as a director, the heart of which lasted only the half-dozen years before filmland started claiming the talents of the musical theatre, Leftwich staged a heavy schedule of revues and musicals from which his first book show, Al Jolson's *Big Boy* (1925), and the later *Hit the Deck* (1927) and *A Connecticut Yankee* (1927), both for Lew Fields, *Strike Up the Band* (1930) and Aarons and Freedley's *Girl Crazy* (1930) emerged as the most interesting and/or successful.

LEGOUIX, Isidore [Edouard] (b Paris, 18 April 1834; d Boulogne, 15 September 1916).

A Conservatoire-trained musician and composer, Isidore Legouix was an early purveyor of one-act entertainments to the Paris theatre. He had a wider success with the little piece *La Tartane*, played in Britain, Australia and in America (Brooklyn Opera House 31 March 1873) in H B Farnie's version as *The Crimson Scarf* and Farnie was also responsible for *Deux portières pour un cordon*, another one-act piece to which Legouix contributed, getting a wider showing under the title *Retained on Both Sides*.

1863 **Un Othello** (Charles Nuitter, Alexandre Beaumont) 1 act Théâtre des Champs-Elysées 20 June
1864 **Le Lion de Saint-Marc** (Nuitter, Beaumont) 1 act Théâtre Saint-Germain 24 November
1866 **Ma fille** (Alexis Bouvier) 1 act Délassements-Comiques 20 March
1867 **Marlborough s'en va-t-en guerre** (w Georges Bizet, Léo Delibes, Émile Jonas/William Busnach, Paul Siraudin) Théâtre de l'Athénée 15 December
1868 **Le Vengeur** (Nuitter, Beaumont) 1 act Théâtre de l'Athénée 20 November
1869 **Deux portières pour un cordon** (w Charles Lecocq,

Hervé et al/'Lucian' [ie Hippolyte Lefèbvre, L Dubuis])
1 act Palais-Royal 15 March

1869 **L'Ours et l'amateur de jardins** (Busnach, Adolphe
Marquet) 1 act Théâtre des Bouffes-Parisiens 1 September

1871 **La Tartane** done as *The Crimson Scarf* (ad H B Farnie)
1 act Alhambra, London 24 April

1874 **Les Dernières Grisettes** (Nuitter, Beaumont) Fantaisies-
Parisiennes, Brussels 12 December

1876 **Le Mariage d'une étoile** (Eugène Grangé, Victor
Bernard) 1 act Théâtre des Bouffes-Parisiens 1 April

1877 **Madame Clara, sonnambule** (Albert Vanloo, Eugène
Leterrier) 1 act Palais-Royal 15 March

Other title attributed: *Le Clef d'argent*

LEHÁR, Franz [LEHÁR, Ferencz] (b Komárom,
Hungary, 30 April 1870; d Bad Ischl, Austria, 24 October
1948). The celebrated composer of *Die lustige Witwe*, who
switched with almost equivalent success to writing romantic Operette in the years between the wars, and whose
works remain an important part of the backbone of the
20th-century Viennese repertoire.

The son of an orchestral horn-player and bandmaster,
Franz Lehár studied music, and principally the violin, at
Sternberg and, from the age of 12, at the Prague Conservatorium. He worked first as a teenaged violinist in the
theatre orchestra of Barmen-Elberfeld then, when he was
19, joined a regimental band, subsequently becoming a
military bandmaster in Losoncz. During this period he first
tried his hand at composing opera (*Der Kurassier*, *Kukuka*)
without success, although the latter work, written to a text
by Felix Falzari, was produced at Leipzig and Königsberg
in 1896 and at Budapest's Magyar Kiralyi Operaház in
1899, and was subsequently revised (ad M Kalbeck) and
re-presented under the title *Tatjana*.

Lehár held several army posts before finally quitting the
military to take up a position as a theatre conductor at
Trieste and there, putting aside his ambitions as an
operatic composer, he made his first attempts at writing for
the lighter musical theatre. After several false starts
(*Arabella die Kubanerin*, *Fräulein Leutnant*, *Das Club Baby*)
one of his works was accepted by his fellow Hungarian,
Wilhelm Karczag, the recent lessee of Vienna's Theater an
der Wien, and it was under Karczag's management that
Wiener Frauen was produced at the Theater an der Wien in
1902, with the composer waving the baton.

Fashionably admitting to be 'partly based on French
material', *Wiener Frauen* featured Alexander Girardi,
Oscar Sachs, soubrette Lina Arbarbanell, tenor Karl
Meister, and grande dame Sarolta von Rettich-Birk, with
Julius Brammer, who would later serve Lehár as a librettist
listed amongst the 'wedding guests' in a frothy evening's
entertainment. It was given a reasonable reception, played
out precisely 50 performances (a favourite contractual
number) and was then removed, returning the following
year for another ten performances into which were interpolated an act by Mlle Celia Galley 'of the Nouveautés,
Paris' doing her imitations of Sarah Bernhardt, Réjane,
Yvette Guilbert, la Belle Otéro and other such 'Wiener
Frauen'. It played its 75th and last performance at the
Theater an der Wien on 14 September 1905. The piece
was also mounted at Budapest's Budai Színkör in a version
which made the Frauen into local ones – *Pesti nők* and later
Pesti asszonyok.

In the meanwhile, however, Lehár's reputation had been

well and truly made. Just a month after the production of
Wiener Frauen, Andreas Aman produced the composer's
second Operette, the folksy tale of *Der Rastelbinder*, at the
opposition Carltheater, with the young comic actor and
singer Louis Treumann starring as the onion-seller Wolf
Bär Pfefferkorn. The piece was an immediate and major
hit. Whilst other Operetten came and went from the Carltheater stage and repertoire, *Der Rastelbinder* continued to
be heavily featured in the theatre's Spielplan. By the end of
the following year it had been played 189 times, it passed
its 300th performance in late 1908 and continued for
decades as a popular part of the Viennese repertoire whilst
also winning a very long list of productions throughout
Europe. Franz Lehár had his first major hit in the musical
theatre.

He followed up with further shows for both Vienna's
principal stages. *Der Göttergatte*, a comical retelling of the
mythological Amphytrion tale, gave him a semi-success,
being played for a decade (latterly in a revised version) in
the repertoire of the Carltheater, but *Die Juxheirat* was a
39-performance failure at the Theater an der Wien in spite
of the presence of Girardi at the head of its bill. It was no
better liked back home in Hungary (*Mókaházasság*, Magyar
Színház 7 September 1906) even though it managed to
knock up its half-century at Berlin's Centraltheater (28
January 1905). This serious flop temporarily damped the
composer's élan. Karczag, however (apparently with some
persuasion), stuck by the musician whose only real hit to
date had been at the opposition theatre, and when a composer was needed for Léon and Stein's libretto to *Die
lustige Witwe* it was to Lehár that the assignment was
eventually given.

Lehár's *Die lustige Witwe* was not just the musical-
theatre sensation of its time, both in Vienna and beyond
(*The Merry Widow*, *La Veuve joyeuse*, *A víg özvegy* etc). It was
also the show which gave the all-important outward-
moving impetus to the Viennese and Hungarian school of
Operette which, as a consequence, was to dominate the
world's stages for the following decade and hold a fine
place on them for even longer. And as the composer of *Die
lustige Witwe*, Lehár would remain the standard-bearer of
that school through the days of its greatest popularity.

Further hits did not follow immediately. There was a
remake of *Wiener Frauen*, the first of many occasions on
which Lehár would work on revisions of his moderately
successful or unsuccessful shows; there was a children's
piece, *Peter und Paul reisen ins Schlaraffenland*, played for a
dozen matinées at the Theater an der Wien in 1906 and
again for the two following Christmases, and the first and
most successful of a handful of one-acters written for the
same theatre's studio theatre, Hölle, called *Mitislaw der
moderne*, an opérette-bouffe which had fun with the grisettes of *Die lustige Witwe* and a Danilo clone called Mitislaw.

It was two years after the production of *Die lustige Witwe*
before Lehár presented his next major work, *Der Mann mit
den drei Frauen*, again written with *Juxheirat* librettist Julius
Bauer, and again mounted at the Theater an der Wien.
Rudolf Christians starred as the man of the title and Mizzi
Günther as the wife whom he finally keeps, but this piece
of modern-day musical beds had few of the attractions of
its famous predecessor and was played out in a two-part
Vienna run of 90 performances. Nevertheless, as the next
work by the internationally worshipped composer of *Die*

lustige Witwe, Der Mann mit den drei Frauen won its ration of foriegn productions.

Success returned more surely when Lehár returned to the land of princes and princesses and counts and countesses to turn out the scores for *Das Fürstenkind*, which featured *Die lustige Witwe* stars Treumann and Mizzi Günther through a first run of 200 performances at the Johann Strauss-Theater and *Der Graf von Luxemburg*, a recomposed version of a libretto first set by Johann Strauss, which clocked up 179 Vienna performances with Lehár's melodies attached to it before going on to a fine national and international career.

Some rather more sombre and dramatic colouring crept into much of Lehár's score for the often turbulent love story of *Zigeunerliebe* which, when it was produced in early 1910 at the Carltheater, for a period gave the composer the monopoly of Vienna's three major musical theatres: the Carltheater, the Johann Strauss-Theater (*Das Fürstenkind*) and the Theater an der Wien (*Der Graf von Luxemburg*). *Zigeunerliebe*'s score was a foretaste of the more sentimental and romantic style of show that Lehár would give to the postwar musical theatre, but the tones the composer gave to the music of this early 'romantische Operette' were the freshest and most exciting of all that he would accomplish in a field in which he would later linger a little more self-indulgently. Mizzi Zwerenz top-billed, and *Zigeunerliebe* did even better than the composer's other two Operetten in 1910 Vienna, ending its first run after 232 performances before going on to productions around the world.

The Theater an der Wien followed up with Treumann and Günther in *Eva*, a less colourful piece which nevertheless confirmed the previous run of success with a fine 226 performances, and, after a short interlude in which Lehár composed music for two little pieces for the Hölle studio theatre and an incidental minuet for Árpád Pásztor's Budapest play *A lányom*, the composer followed up with *Die ideale Gattin* (a rewrite of *Die Göttergatte*), which had only an indifferent run (111 performances), and the decidedly individual 'mountain musical' *Endlich allein* in which Mizzi Günther and Hubert Marischka spent time up a Swiss alp working out their love story for the same number of first-run performances. If Vienna did not decide between the two, the rest of the world did, and *Endlich allein* had the generally better career of the pair until it was put down by becoming Lehár's latest candidate for a remake. The Theater in der Josefstadt's production of *Der Sterngucker* (1916) proved it Lehár's least welcomed piece since the days of *Die Juxheirat* (79 performances), and even when it was rewritten and restaged later the same year at the Theater an der Wien, it had no more success. The music duly went into the drawer of 'scores to be recycled' and, like the preceding two pieces, it would be, frequently.

Following this period of less than triumphant shows on the Viennese stage, Lehár's next première took place in his native Hungary. *A pacsirta* (the lark), a piece composed to a libretto by Ferenc Martos, was produced at Budapest's Király Színház and the slim Hungarian tale ran for a season there, with Emmi Kosáry, Ilona Dömötör and Ernő Király starring, before being produced in Vienna the following month. At the Theater an der Wien the retitled *Wo die Lerche singt* took off solidly and it ran with all the vigour typical of a well-liked and escapist wartime show, to such effect that it piled up the longest initial season of any Lehár musical since *Die lustige Witwe* (379 performances). When the fighting died, however, the piece did not prove to be as attractive as many of his others and it did not have a significant international career.

After the First World War, however, the kind of success Lehár had achieved with *Wo die Lerche singt* continued. The up-to-date musical comedy *Die blaue Mazur* (1920) kept the Theater an der Wien occupied for 11 months, Carlo Lombardo's revusical-spectacular remake of *Der Sterngucker* as *La danza delle libellule* did well enough in Italy finally to put Lehár's score, with its hit number 'Gigolette', into international orbit at the third time of asking, and the Spanish story of *Frasquita* allowed Betty Fischer to vamp her way through the composer's not very serious attempt at Iberian-flavoured music opposite Hubert Marischka and take-over Richard Tauber for some six months at a Theater an der Wien where the repertoire (*Eva, Die lustige Witwe, Zigeunerliebe, Die blaue Mazur, Der Graf von Luxemburg, Wo die Lerche singt, Der Rastelbinder*) in late 1922 seemed to be entirely made up of Lehár works, old, very old and new.

A Chinese Operette, *Die gelbe Jacke*, played 104 performances at the Theater an der Wien, and another musical comedy piece, apparently aimed at the international market and featuring Theater an der Wien star Luise Kartousch as the eponymous Parisian revue star of *Cloclo* (1924), was played at the Bürgertheater for two and a half months before reaching its hundredth performance at the Johann Strauss-Theater later in the year and duly going out for export.

It was now, however, that the receipt of an unsolicited manuscript sent Lehár out on a track leading far from the French farcicalities of *Cloclo* and into an area of which intimations had been heard more than a decade earlier, in *Zigeunerliebe*. Paul Knepler's libretto for *Paganini* was a piece written squarely in the romantic mode, and Lehár set it with a lushly romantic score in which the leading tenor rôle, created by actor-turned-opera-star Carl Clewing, was paramount. The show had a five-month run in Vienna, but it did better in Berlin where Richard Tauber appeared as *Paganini* and made 'Gern hab' ich die Frau'n geküsst' his own. That song ('Girls Were Made to Love and Kiss'), went around the world and ultimately became more widely popular than the Operette, the success of which remained limited to Germany and France.

Paganini's Berlin season, however, had made a notable effect and, from this time on, Lehár's new works were mounted in Germany. They also stuck textually close to the kind of romantic Operette outline which *Paganini* had used and which was very quickly to become a sine qua non and, eventually, a cliché. Boy (tenor and Tauber, for preference) loves girl, wins girl and ultimately has to renounce girl for reasons of state, career or some other shade of incompatibility at the final curtain. The unhappy ending was obligatory, and only once in the following years, in a remake of the old *Endlich allein*, did Lehár and his librettists allow an 'old-fashioned' happy ending as a climax to one of their works. The result of all this textual unhappiness was to set the composer loose on a lot of often sad and dramatic sentiments, and it was romantic music often deeply dyed with misery which made up much of the scores of Lehár's later Operetten. Much of it, also, was tenor music, for Lehár's on- and off-stage friendship with Tauber meant that the starring rôles in these Operetten were custom-made for the popular singer. Much of it, again, was splendid music and Lehár's talent shone as brightly in his postwar scores as in his pre-war ones, even if the colour of the shine was a different one.

The first, and deepest dyed, of the series that followed *Paganini* was a version of Gabryela Zapolska's romantic novella about a Russian princeling *Der Zarewitsch* who, having been slow to find his sexuality and romance, has to give it up in *Alt-Heidelberg* fashion, when the time comes to take up his crown (1927). The second, which put the poet Goethe into the same kind of sorry love affair already inflicted on poor Paganini and the semi-historical Russian, allowed his sweet *Friederike* (1928) to do the renouncing whilst he secured the vocal bon-bon of the show 'O Mädchen, mein Mädchen'. Once again, the bon-bon travelled better than the show, but both Operetten were thoroughly appreciated in their original productions and have remained popular in central Europe for more than half a century.

The most successful of the Lehár romantic musicals, however, was none of these new pieces but another remake. *Das Land des Lächelns* (1929), was a Tauberized version of *Die gelbe Jacke* with the happy ending of the original changed to an unhappy one to fit the formula, and a new tenor number, 'Dein ist mein ganzes Herz', prominent in the star rôle. A major hit in several languages in Europe and one of the bastions of the European Operette repertoire to this day, it did not, however, make itself a career beyond. 'Dein ist mein ganzes Herz', under the titles 'You Are My Heart's Delight' (UK) and 'Yours is My Heart Alone' (USA), like Lehár's previous tenor solos, did very much better with English-speaking audiences than the show that hosted it. The successor to *Das Land des Lächelns* was another remake, this time of *Endlich allein*. Once again, however, although *Schön ist die Welt* proved to be a long-running hit at home, it turned out to be of little interest outside Europe.

This line of deeply sentimental and musically lush costume pieces, each with its modish downbeat ending and far, even in their lighter moments, from displaying the sparkling frivolity of Lehár's earlier works, culminated in the composer's biggest-sing Operette of all, the tempestuous 'musikalische Komödie' *Giuditta*, produced at the Vienna Staatsoper with Tauber starring opposite cruiser-weight soprano Jarmila Novotna. *Giuditta* had a limited life in its unlikely home (42 performances), although, like its predecessors, it left a legacy of several beautiful songs – soprano ones, this time – to the light-opera repertoire.

Giuditta was Lehár's last original work. The striving towards an operatic Operette already evidenced in his re-arrangement of *Frasquita* for Paris's Opéra-Comique, and in his angling of the score of *Giuditta* towards operatic voices, was continued in a rewrite of *Zigeunerliebe* as an opera for the Budapest Operaház, but otherwise he limited himself, in the years running up to the Second World War, to a handful of film scores (*Grossfürstin Alexandra, Die ganze Welt dreht sich um Liebe, Eine Nacht in Wien, Die Gefährten des Odysseus*) and to efforts to re-assemble the publishing of his work under the banner of his own firm, Glocken Verlag.

Lehár's non-operettic stage music included a share in the score for the wartime Volksstück (w Eysler) *Komm, deutscher Bruder*, accompanying waltz-music for the 1916 György Ruttkay play *Keringő* (*Walzer*, Magyár Színház 23 September 1916) and 'musikalische Illustrationen' to Heinrich Ilgenstein's Schwank *Der Walzer von heute Nacht* (Kleines Theater, Berlin 17 January 1930).

Lehár's body of work, one of the most important in the 20th-century European Operette at the period of its greatness, falls clearly into two halves. The earlier contains his most attractive work, the later, deliberately more pretentious, his most impressive. But, although the individual songs from his romantic Operetten still have international success and the best of the shows which housed them still win regular performances in Europe, it is the gaily glittering *Die lustige Witwe* which, with Strauss's *Die Fledermaus*, remains the world-wide epitome of Viennese Operette and Lehár's enduring monument.

1902 **Wiener Frauen** (Ottokar Tann-Bergler, Emil Norini) Theater an der Wien 21 November

1902 **Der Rastelbinder** (Victor Léon) Carltheater 20 December

1904 **Der Göttergatte** (Léon, Leo Stein) Carltheater 20 January

1904 **Die Juxheirat** (Julius Bauer) Theater an der Wien 22 December

1905 **Die lustige Witwe** (Léon, Stein) Theater an der Wien 30 December

1906 **Der Schlüssel zum Paradies** (revised *Wiener Frauen*) Stadttheater, Leipzig October

1906 **Peter und Paul reisen ins Schlaraffenland** (Fritz Grünbaum, Robert Bodanzky) Theater an der Wien 1 December

1907 **Mitislaw der moderne** (Grünbaum, Bodanzky) 1 act Hölle 5 January

1908 **Der Mann mit den drei Frauen** (Bauer) Theater an der Wien 21 January

1909 **Das Fürstenkind** (Léon) Johann Strauss-Theater 7 October

1909 **Der Graf von Luxemburg** (aka *Der Graf von Luxenburg*) (A M Willner, Bodanzky) Theater an der Wien 12 November

1910 **Zigeunerliebe** (Willner, Bodanzky) Carltheater 8 January

1911 **Die Spieluhr** (T Zasche) 1 act Hölle 7 January

1911 **Eva (das Fabriksmädel)** (Willner, Bodanzky) Theater an der Wien 24 November

1912 **Rosenstock und Edelweiss** (Bauer) 1 act Hölle 1 December

1913 **Die ideale Gattin** (revised *Der Göttergatte*) Theater an der Wien 11 October

1914 **Endlich allein** (Willner, Bodanzky) Theater an der Wien 30 January

1914 **Komm, deutscher Bruder** (w Edmund Eysler/Carl Lindau, August Neidhart) Raimundtheater 4 October

1916 **Der Sterngucker** (Fritz Löhner-Beda, Willner) Theater in der Josefstadt 14 January (revised version Theater an der Wien 26 September)

1918 **A Pacsirta** (*Wo die Lerche singt*) (Ferenc Martos) Király Színház, Budapest 1 January

1920 **Die blaue Mazur** (Stein, Bela Jenbach) Theater an der Wien 28 May

1921 **Die Tangokönigin** (revised *Der Göttergatte*) Apollotheater 9 September

1922 **Frühling** (Rudolf Eger) 1 act Hölle 20 January

1922 **Libellentanz** (aka *Die drei Grazien*) (revised *Der Sterngucker*, as *La danza delle libellule*) (ad Carlo Lombardo) Teatro Lirico, Milan 3 May

1922 **Frasquita** (Willner, Heinz Reichert) Theater an der Wien 12 May

1923 **Die gelbe Jacke** (Léon) Theater an der Wien 9 February

1924 **Cloclo** (Jenbach) Bürgertheater 8 March

1925 **Paganini** (Paul Knepler, Jenbach) Johann Strauss-Theater 30 October

1926 **Gigolette** (revised *La danza delle libellule*) (ad Lombardo, Gioacchino Forzano) Teatro Lirico, Milan 30 October

1927 **Der Zarewitsch** (Jenbach, Reichert) Deutsches Künstlertheater, Berlin 21 February

1928 **Friederike** (Ludwig Herzer, Löhner-Beda) Metropoltheater, Berlin 4 October

1929 **Das Land des Lächelns** (revised *Die gelbe Jacke*) (Herzer, Löhner-Beda) Metropoltheater, Berlin 10 October

1930 **Das Frühlingsmädel** (pasticcio/Rudolf Eger) Theater am Zoo, Berlin 29 May

1930 **Schön ist die Welt** (revised *Endlich allein*) Metropoltheater, Berlin 3 December

1932 **Der Fürst der Berge** (revised *Das Fürstenkind*) Theater am Nollendorfplatz, Berlin 23 September

1934 **Giuditta** (Knepler, Löhner-Beda) Staatsoper, Vienna 20 January

Biographies: Czech, S: *Franz Lehár: sein Weg und sein Werk* (Franz Perneder, Berlin, 1942) and as *Schön ist die Welt: Franz Lehars Leben und Werk* (Berlin, 1957), Grün, B: *Gold and Silver: the Life and Times of Franz Lehár* (David McKay, New York, 1970), Decsey, E: *Franz Lehár* (Drei Masken Verlag, Berlin, 1924) etc

LEHMANN, Liza [LEHMANN, Elizabeth Nina Mary Frederika] (b London, 11 July 1862; d Pinner, Middlesex, 19 September 1918).

The daughter of the painter Rudolf Lehmann, Liza Lehmann was brought up in a home where the famous and fashionable of London were often to be found. Thoroughly educated in all the arts, she was at first a concert singer, and then a composer, becoming well known for her compositions of parlour music and, in particular, the song cycles 'In a Persian Garden' (1896) and 'The Daisy Chain' and an 'In Memoriam' based on Tennyson's poem. In 1904 she was commissioned by Frank Curzon, who had just had record-breaking success with the musical comedy *A Chinese Honeymoon*, to provide the score for another piece in a similar vein. Teamed with top librettist Owen Hall and lyricist James Hickory Wood, Miss Lehmann turned out a fine set of popular-styled songs for the musical comedy *Sergeant Brue* without writing anything that was likely to wear out the barrel organs of the town.

Sergeant Brue had a good London run and a Broadway production (1905) but, irritated at the way Curzon had interpolated other composers' music into her score despite her announced willingness to supply any extra music, Miss Lehmann wrote no more for the musical comedy stage. She did, however, provide an elegant score to a text by Laurence Housman for a comic opera version of *The Vicar of Wakefield* (1906). This time it was the librettist who flounced angrily out when his over-long book was cut to make room for the vast amount of music his composer had supplied. *The Vicar of Wakefield* was produced in the West End by vocalist David Bispham with some success, but once again the composer ventured no further. She moved on instead to compose the score for an opera, *Everyman*, which was played by the Beecham Opera Company in 1916.

1904 **Sergeant Brue** (Owen Hall, James Hickory Wood) Strand Theatre 14 June

1906 **The Vicar of Wakefield** (Laurence Housman) Prince of Wales Theatre 12 December

Biography: *The Life of Liza Lehmann By Herself* (T Fisher Unwin, London, 1919)

LEHMANN, Maurice (b Paris, 14 May 1895; d Paris, 17 May 1974). Paris's champion of the opérette à grand spectacle through several decades, particularly at the helm of the vast Théâtre du Châtelet.

Originally an accountant in an automobile emporium, then an actor (at first as 'Dormel') at the Comédie Française and then at the Théâtre de la Porte-Saint-Martin, Lehmann became the director of the Nouvel-Ambigu and of the Porte-Saint-Martin in the early 1920s. In 1928 he was taken on as the partner of Alexandre Fontanes at the head of the Théâtre du Châtelet and, soon after, was left at the sole head of the management of that great auditorium. He was to run it for most of the next 40 years and, during his tenancy, bring to Paris a long series of musical productions with a heavy accent on spectacular staging.

The series began in 1929 with the production of the French version of *Show Boat* (*Mississippi*) and continued through its first decade with *Robert le Pirate* (*The New Moon*), Joseph Szulc's North African extravaganza *Sidonie Panache*, a long run of *Nina Rosa* and an original work commissioned from that show's composer, Sigmund Romberg, for the Châtelet stage and entitled *Rose de France*. These were followed by the picturesque *Au temps des merveilleuses*, Yvain's *Au soleil du Mexique*, *Yana*, Romberg's *Le Chant du tzigane* (*Forbidden Melody*) and the comical and (of course) scenery-filled chase after the contents of *Le Coffre-fort vivant*, mixed with occasional productions of such Châtelet traditionals as the everything-that-moves mounting of the stage version of Verne's *Le Tour du monde en 80 jours*.

The war years were filled, as war years so often are, with revivals as well as two new shows, *Valses de France* and *Le Beau Voyage d'un enfant à Paris*, the years following the War brought the film-land *Les Chasseurs d'images*, *La Maréchale Sans-Gêne* and *Annie du Far-West* (*Annie Get Your Gun*) as well as revivals of, in particular, the frequently recalled *L'Auberge du Cheval Blanc* and *Valses de Vienne*, before in 1950 Lehmann called in composer Francis Lopez, the newly popular writer of *La Belle de Cadix*, to supply him with his next piece. Lopez became, for a period, chief supplier of music to the Châtelet, following the romantic Hispanneries of *Pour Don Carlos* with the 905-performance run of Luis Mariano's newest star-vehicle *Le Chanteur de Mexico*, musical adventure in oil-rich Turkestan in *La Toison d'or* and a saga of smuggling skulduggery in song amid the islands of the *Méditerranée* with Corsican star Tino Rossi at its head. In the late 1950s, Lehmann mounted *Maria Flora*, the Lehár pasticcio *Rose de Noël* and Lopez's *Le Secret de Marco Polo*, and in the 1960s a French version of *Some Like It Hot* (*La Polka des Lampions*), *Eugène le Mystérieux* and Charles Aznavour's *Monsieur Carnaval* amongst continuing reprises of the most popular older pieces. *Monsieur Carnaval* was Lehmann's last production at the Châtelet from which he retired in 1966.

From 1933 Lehmann turned the Porte-Saint-Martin over to musical shows as well, staging opera, opéra-comique and opérette and including amongst his productions both grandiose revivals of the classic repertoire, modern imports (*La Dubarry*, *Valses de Vienne*, *Violette de Mont-martre*), such new pieces as Pierné's *Fragonard* and, with more success than any of these, the musical comedy *Ignace* with Fernandel starred, until he handed over the management in 1938. At this stage he took over the Théâtre Mogador where, alongside his Châtelet shows, he produced further large-scale musical shows – the British *Balalaïka*, the ex-Austrian *Billy et son équipe* and a revival of the eternal *Rose Marie* – before the wartime closures intervened.

After the War he was engaged in the reopening of the Paris Opéra and the Opéra-Comique, and he later returned to this arena between 1952 and 1955, but his principal fame in the Paris theatre was won in his long tenancy of the Châtelet and his championing there of the opérette à grand spectacle.

1948 **La Maréchale Sans-Gêne** (Pierre Petit/Albert Willemetz/Victorien Sardou, Emil Moreau ad) Théâtre du Châtelet 18 February

Autobiography: *Trompe l'oeil* (Editions de la pensée moderne, Paris, 1971)

LEICHTE KAVALLERIE Comic Operette in 2 acts by Karl Costa. Music by Franz von Suppé. Carltheater, Vienna, 21 March 1866.

Following the success of his short pieces *Das Pensionat*, *Zehn Mädchen und kein Mann*, *Flotte Bursche* and *Die schöne Galathee*, Suppé ventured for the first time into a two-act Operette format, in collaboration with the prolific and successful playwright Karl Costa, on *Leichte Kavallerie*.

The orphan Vilma (Frln Mayer) has grown up so pretty that the wives of the Burgermeister Bums (Grois) and city official Pankraz (Josef Matras) cannot bear to have her around, even though the girl has eyes only for her own Hermann (Telek). When the lascivious Burgermeister refuses to allow her to wed Hermann, the boy enlists the help of two Hungarian cavalry officers, János (Carl Treumann) and Carol (Frln Voll), to stage a series of rendezvous which will allow the jealous wives (Fr Walter, Fr Bachmann) to catch their husbands misbehaving. János plays his part in the charade, but, as he does, he cannot help thinking of his old, lost love and the song they sang together. Then he hears that song. It is Vilma singing – the orphan is an orphan no longer, she has found her father and he is only too happy for her to wed Hermann. Then the trumpets sound and, their duty done, the Light Cavalry leave town.

Of Suppé's score to this, one of the most successful of his earliest Operetten, only the celebrated overture is heard today, but the rest of the score, put together with the aid of some popular Hungarian military melodies, produced a number of attractive and/or humorous pieces of which a number mocking jumped-up local officials ('Wie gescheit, wie gescheit, wir von der G'meind') proved a favourite.

After its first season at the Carltheater, *Leichte Kavallerie* was regularly reproduced in Vienna, appearing at the Hietzing 'Zur neuen Welt' (20 July 1870), returning to the Carltheater in 1872 (11 performances), 1873 (11 performances), 1874 (1 performance), 1875 (4 performances) and in 1876 (5 performances) with Blasel (Bums) and Karoline Finaly (Vilma). Later it played at the Theater an der Wien,

first from 17 January 1888, then in 1898 in a double-bill with *La Chanson de Fortunio* with Joseffy as János and Streitmann as Hermann, and as late as 1914 (paired with *Flotte Bursche*), as well as appearing on a bill at Ronacher (9 August 1896), and again at the Carltheater in 1905 with Blasel still playing Bums.

The show was first seen in Hungary in 1867, being performed at the Budai Színkör one night in the original German and the next, as *Magyar huszárok*, in Hungarian, by István Benyei's company. It was subsequently played there also under the title *Könnyü lovasság*, and duly appeared in Germany and in the German theatres in America, but, apart from that eternal overture, it did not evoke sufficient interest anywhere else outside central Europe to win productions in an era of musical theatre which was very largely devoted to the many and very available works of Offenbach. A French-language version was made by Gustave Lagye but, although it may have been performed in Belgium, there is no record of a first-class professional staging of *Cavalerie légère* in France.

Germany: ?1866; Hungary: Budai Színkör (Ger) 10 May 1867, *Magyar huszárok* 11 May 1867; USA: Stadttheater 1 October 1869

LEIGH, Carolyn [Paula] (b New York, 21 August 1926; d New York, 19 November 1981).

At first a writer of radio link material and advertising copy, Carolyn Leigh won her first contract to compose song lyrics in 1951 and subsequently produced a number of successful songs including 'Young at Heart' (w Johnny Richards) sung in the 1954 Frank Sinatra film of the same title, 'The Day the Circus Left Town' (w E D Thomas), 'Witchcraft' (w Cy Coleman) and 'You Fascinate Me So' (w Coleman). She made her first input to the musical theatre when, on the initiative of Mary Martin, she was invited to supply the lyrics to Moose Charlap's songs for the 1954 Broadway version of *Peter Pan* ('I'm Flying', 'I Won't Grow Up').

She contributed to the revues *Shoestring '57* (w Phillip Springer), *Take Five* (1957, w Springer), *The Ziegfeld Follies of 1957* (w Springer) and *Demi-Dozen* (1958 w Coleman) and later to the unhappy attempt to write a new *Hellzapoppin* (1976 w Coleman, Jule Styne), but her principal successes on the musical stage came with two collaborations with Coleman, the Lucille Ball vehicle *Wildcat*, in which the star introduced 'Hey, Look Me Over', and the Neil Simon burlesque *Little Me* from which 'Real, Live Girl', 'I've Got Your Number' and 'The Other Side of the Tracks' added to her palette of song hits. Her fourth and final Broadway musical was *How Now, Dow Jones*, written with composer Elmer Bernstein, who had supplied additional music to *Peter Pan*.

1954 **Peter Pan** (Moose Charlap, Jule Styne/w Adolph Green, Betty Comden) Winter Garden Theater 20 October
1960 **Wildcat** (Cy Coleman/N Richard Nash) Alvin Theater 16 December
1962 **Little Me** (Coleman/Neil Simon) Lunt-Fontanne Theater 17 November
1967 **How Now, Dow Jones** (Elmer Bernstein/Max Shulman) Lunt-Fontanne Theater 7 December

LEIGH, Gracie [ELLIS, Grace] (b ?1875; d Box, Glos, 24 June 1950). Musical comedienne who had nearly 30 years of stage stardom in Britain.

Gracie Leigh first came to notice in her first London rôle in the musical *Little Miss Nobody* in which she succeeded to the principal soubrette part during a cast reshuffle in rehearsals and went on to make a personal success as the music hall's common little Trixie Triplet. When Ada Reeve walked out of *San Toy*, again in rehearsals, Leigh was again called in as an emergency, and again scored a personal hit in the show's chief feminine comic rôle of Dudley. She was kept on the payroll by George Edwardes for whom she then created the important female comedy rôles in *A Country Girl* (1902, Madame Sophie) and *The Cingalee* (1904, Peggy Sabine) at Daly's, as she quickly became one of the town's most popular musical comediennes. In between time she also played in Edwardes's unfortunate *The Merry-Go-Round*, several comedies and short musical pieces, and took over from Marie Dainton for a period as Mrs Pineapple in the long-running *A Chinese Honeymoon*.

She appeared in the short-lived London production of *The Gay Lord Vergy* (1905, *Le Sire de Vergy*) in the rôle of the belly-dancing Mitzy created in Paris by Ève Lavallière, dropped out of the small-scale *The White Chrysanthemum*, and was seen in a typical low-comedy rôle in the popular *The Dairymaids* (1906, Eliza) before she was contracted by Frank Curzon for the Prince of Wales Theatre. There she scored her biggest success of all in the comedy-soubrette role of Mina in *Miss Hook of Holland* (1907, 'A Pink Petty from Peter', 'The Flying Dutchman'). Similar clowning, song-and-dance rôles followed in Broadway's *The Parisian Model*, alongside Anna Held (1907), and at the Prince of Wales in *My Mimosa Maid* (1908, Popotte), *King of Cadonia* (1908, Militza) and *Dear Little Denmark* (1909, Ophelia), before she returned to the Edwardes stable to create the lead comedy parts of *The Quaker Girl* (1912, Phoebe), Kálmán's *Autumn Manoeuvres* (1912, Lady Larkin), *The Dancing Mistress* (1912, Jeannie McTavish), and *The Girl from Utah* (1913, Clancy). In 1913 she visited America again to star alongside Hazel Dawn in Ivan Caryll's *The Little Café* (Katziolinka).

During the First World War Miss Leigh appeared in a revival of *Miss Hook of Holland* and the revue *Airs and Graces*, but thereafter abandoned the stage for several years. She returned in 1921 to take the comedy rôle of Wei Wa Shei in *Cairo*, Oscar Asche's successor to *Chu Chin Chow*, and appeared in the quick flop *Almond Eye* (1923) and in several plays before scoring the best and last success of the second part of her career as the maid, Pauline, in the London production of *No, No, Nanette* (1925).

Her husband, the successful musical-comedy actor Lionel Mackinder, was killed in action in the War.

LEIGH, H[enry] S[ambrook] (b London, 29 March 1837 ; d London, 16 June 1883).

Sometime journalist, adaptor, stagewriter and lyricist, the bohemian bachelor Leigh was known as a man of culture and wit in the purlieus of London's Savage Club. His speciality was the writing and performing of satirical verses and of songs, set to simple melodies, which he played and sang himself and, with the coming of opéra-bouffe, he turned that talent to the theatre, being responsible for the English-language stage versions of a number of popular large-scale opéras-bouffes and Operetten of the 1870s and 1880s. Leigh also published several collections of lyrics (*Gillot and Goosequill*, *Carols of Cockayne* – including the famous 'Uncle John', *A Town Garland*, *Strains from the Strand*) and authored an operatic version of *Cinderella* (music: John Farmer, Harrow, 1883) before his death at the age of 46.

1871 **Falsacappa** (*Les Brigands*) English version (Globe Theatre)
1872 **Le Roi Carotte** English version (Alhambra Theatre)
1872 **Le Pont des soupirs** English version (St James's Theatre)
1876 **Le Voyage dans la lune** English version (Alhambra Theatre)
1878 **Fatinitza** English version (Alhambra Theatre)
1879 **La Petite Mademoiselle** English version w Robert Reece (Alhambra Theatre)
1879 **Le Grand Casimir** English version (Gaiety Theatre)
1883 **Lurette** (*Belle Lurette*) English lyrics (Avenue Theatre)
1883 **Prince Methusalem** (*Prinz Methusalem*) English version (Folies Dramatiques)

LEIGH, Mitch [MITCHNIK, Irwin] (b Brooklyn, NY, 30 January 1928). The composer of one major Broadway hit who never came near repeating that success.

Leigh studied music at Yale and began a career in 1954 as a composer of television and radio commercial music. He subsequently founded the commercial production house Music Makers. He wrote incidental music for several plays in the early 1960s (*Too True to Be Good*, *Never Live Over a Pretzel Factory*) and set music to Sean O'Casey's *Purple Dust*, before breaking through as a Broadway composer with his score for *Man of La Mancha* (1965, 'The Impossible Dream', 'Man of La Mancha', Tony Award). Whilst *Man of La Mancha* continued to travel around the world's stages, Leigh's subsequent efforts at stage musicals foundered, with two shows closing on the road and two others closing after one and eight performances respectively on Broadway.

A 1979 musical *Sarava*, based on *Dona Flor and Her Two Husbands*, which never officially opened on Broadway nevertheless lasted several months there, whilst a Mike Todd biomusical produced in Philadelphia in 1988 and seen subsequently on Broadway as *Ain't Broadway Grand* also got into double figures.

In recent times, whilst *Man of La Mancha* continues to make repeated appearances worldwide, Leigh has operated more successfully as a producer. His Mitch Leigh Company was behind the highly successful Yul Brynner revival of *The King and I* of the 1980s, but it failed in an effort to bring his *Chu Chem* from a revival at the Jewish Repertory Theater to Broadway (w William D Rollnick, 44 performances).

1965 **Purple Dust** (Sean O'Casey) Goodspeed Opera House, East Haddam August
1965 **Man of La Mancha** (Joe Darion) Goodspeed Opera House, East Haddam 28 June; ANTA Washington Square Theater, New York 22 November
1966 **Chu Chem** (Jim Haines, Jack Wohl/Ted Allan) New Locust Street Theater, Philadelphia 15 November; Ritz Theater, New York, 17 March 1989
1970 **Cry for Us All** (William Alfred, Phyllis Robinson/Alfred, Albert Marre) Broadhurst Theater 8 April
1972 **Halloween** (Sidney Michaels) Bucks County Playhouse 20 September
1976 **Home Sweet Homer** (aka *Odyssey*) (Forman Brown, Charles Burr/Roland Kibbee, Marre) Palace Theater 4 January

1979 **Sarava** (N Richard Nash) Mark Hellinger Theater 13 February

1980 **An April Song** (Sammy Cahn/Marre) John Drew Theater 25 August

1988 **Ain't Broadway Grand** (ex- *Mike*) (Lee Adams/Thomas Meehan) Walnut Street Theater, Philadelphia 26 March; Lunt-Fontanne Theater, New York 18 April 1993

LENO, Dan [GALVIN, George Wild] (b London, 20 December 1860; d London, 31 October 1904).

The famous music-hall clog-dancer, acrobat and comic singer began by parodying the musical theatre (his perversion of Cellier's 'Queen of My Heart' as 'Queen of the Tarts' was withdrawn after a complaint from the composer) and ended up playing in it. His first venture as a musical-comedy actor was at a matinée performance where he appeared as Pitcher to the Tosser of Rutland Barrington, vying for the affections of Kate Everleigh's *Penelope* (1889) in Edward Solomon's musical version of the popular farce *The Area Belle*. His regular start came when provincial producer Milton Bode signed him for a musical comedy at a vast salary of £125 a week and commissioned Basil Hood and Walter Slaughter to write *Orlando Dando* (1898), featuring the little comic in a suitably protean rôle.

Although he played *Orlando Dando* for only a short season, owing to more lucrative commitments, he returned the following year for a longer tour of another piece commissioned by Bode, *In Gay Piccadilly* (Clarence Corri/George Sims), and a third time in 1902 with a piece by Herbert Darnley, who had previously written music-hall songs for him, as the benighted little hero of *Mr Wix of Wickham*. None of the three pieces ventured near the West End, and Leno (perhaps warned by the less-than-successful venture of fellow music-hall star Little Tich in a London musical) never appeared in a regular London production other than his highly successful pantomimes at the Theatre Royal, Drury Lane.

Biography: Wood, J Hickory; *Dan Leno* (Methuen, London, 1905), Brandreth, G: *The Funniest Man on Earth* (Hamilton, London, 1977)

LENYA, Lotte [BLAMAUER, Karoline Wilhelmina] (b Vienna, 18 October 1898; d New York, 27 November 1981).

During her early career as an actress in Berlin, Lenya appeared there in the several pieces composed by her husband, Kurt Weill: the *Mahagonny* Singspiel, *Die Dreigroschenoper*, first as Jenny ('Seeräuber-Jenny', 'Barbara-Lied') and subsequently as Lucy, and the full-scale *Aufstieg und Fall der Stadt Mahagonny* (1931, Jenny).

She left Germany together with her husband in 1932, and made her way to Paris (Anna I in *Die sieben Todesünden*, 1933), London, and finally New York, where the couple settled in 1937. There she appeared in several plays and in Weill's *The Firebrand of Florence* (1945, Duchess) and found an enthusiastic following with her performance as Jenny in the 1954 revival of *The Threepenny Opera* which brought the piece tardily to the notice of the English-language world. In a subsequent career which was angled very largely towards the works of Weill and of his sometime collaborator, Bertolt Brecht, she created a single Broadway musical rôle as the Berlin landlady, Fräulein Schneider, in *Cabaret* (1966).

Lenya appeared in the 1930 film version of *Die Dreigroschenoper*, but made her most memorable screen appearance in a non-singing rôle as the arch-villainess Elsa Krebs (equipped with a dagger in her toes) in the James Bond film *From Russia with Love* (1964).

Biography: Spoto, D: *Lenya: a Life* (Little, Brown, Boston, 1989)

LEON, Francis [GLASSEY, Patrick Francis] (b New York, 21 November 1844 (?1840); d unknown). Minstrel performer who was the finest travesty player of his era, and who introduced a number of important burlesque musicals to America and to Australia.

Leon made his first stage appearance as a boy soprano at Buckley's Music Hall, and joined up with Christy and Wood's Minstrels at the age of 14. He worked the minstrel circuits, billed as 'the Ethiopian Cubas' and 'the wonderful danseuse and soprano singer', for a number of years before going into partnership with Edwin Kelly in 1864 to form the company known as Kelly and Leon's Minstrels. The company did well and Leon quickly made himself a reputation as the outstanding minstrel 'prima donna' of his day, starring in the lavishly produced burlesques (advertised as 'Africanised opéra-bouffe') which formed the heart of Kelly and Leon's minstrel programmes. He appeared in the lead female rôles of their burlesques *My-deah Restore Her*, *Lucrezia Borgia*, *The Great Black Crook Burlesque*, *Kill Trovatore*, *La Belle LN*, *The Grand Dutch-S*, *Frow-Frow*, *Barber-blu* and *Gin-nevieve de Graw* (mimicking Rose Bell, the current star of the real *Geneviève de Brabant*), as Marguerite in Hervé's *Le Petit Faust* and also in the feminine leads of such Offenbach pieces as *Lischen et Fritzchen*, *Ba-ta-clan* and *La Rose de Saint-Flour* and as the vocally perilous Ernestine of *Monsieur Choufleuri, or Prima Donna for a Night*. He played Limonia in Suppé's *Zehn Mädchen und kein Mann* and Galatea in his *Die schöne Galathee*, top-featured in Legouix's *The Crimson Scarf*, burlesqued Jenny Lind in the celebrated parody of the operatic star called *Leatherlungs*, and appeared as a man-hunting widow in Kelly's musical comedy *His Grace the Duke* and as three different girls and one boy in the made-to-measure tale of *The Pretty Detective*.

After more than a decade as favourites in New York and throughout America, Kelly and Leon were taken to New Zealand and Australia in 1878 by Hiscocks and Hayman. There they found less competition and further success, particularly when they produced an early and unofficial version of *HMS Pinafore* with Leon featured as Little Buttercup. When J C Williamson, the official rights-holder of the work, stopped these performances, they announced a sequel, *Sir Joseph at Sea*, and produced a burlesque *Pin-a-4* (the difference in attitude was marked by the fact that Leon now played Josephine). They also presented such pieces as *The Sorcerer* (Aline), *Trial by Jury* (Plaintiff), *Rose Michon, or the Little Bride* (ie *La Jolie Parfumeuse*, Rose Michon), the Vokes's famous *Belles of the Kitchen* and a burlesque *Norma on a Half Shell* (Norma) and the 'prima donna' drew the comment 'Mr Leon's female impersonations are certainly exceedingly clever, and although he has no great vocal power, except in the upper range of a falsetto voice, he has extraordinary execution and in his imitation of di Murska took some florid runs in a remarkable manner. He is an excellent light comedian, and plays the female parts without the slightest vulgarity, which has been the bane of most female impersonators'. In other words, instead of burlesquing womanhood in the manner of the music-halls, Leon was quite simply playing a woman.

In 1880 Kelly and Leon split up. The 'divine and only' Leon continued briefly to lead a minstrel company under the Kelly and Leon banner but soon returned to America where he joined Haverley's minstrels at a reputed salary of $200 a week. However, after having 'made a round of the earth', he returned to Australia in 1886 in a combination with a new leading man, Frank Cushman. Their features included the burlesques *Ill-fed Dora* and *A Tough Gal-atea*, the musical extravaganza *Vassar Girls* and a production of *Uncle Tom's Cabin* mounted to allow Leon to play the popular rôle of Topsy to the Tom of Cushman. A local journal noted 'his make-up was perfect and his voice as good as ever' but the difference in the style of the company was seen in their repertoire: instead of playing Suppé's Galatea, Leon now appeared alongside Cushman's Hogmalion in a broad, traditional burlesque.

After touring through New Zealand, Leon returned at the end of the year to America. There he had a continuing career in minstrelsy (as 'The Only Leon') at first with Cushman, then with Billy Sweatnam's San Francisco Minstrels and other groups, in vaudeville and occasionally – though still in feminine garb – in the musical theatre, as in his performance as Pomona Potter Pommery in Edward Kidder's musical farce *On the Stage* (1888). An 1890 attempt to revive Kelly and Leon's Minstrels (without Kelly) in Chicago was not a success, and whilst his old partner worked out the end of his career as a busy character actor in Australia, Leon donned his skirts one last time to play in *A High Roller* (1891) with Barney Fagan, and then retired from the theatre.

LÉON, Victor [HIRSCHFELD, Viktor] (b Vienna, 4 January 1858; d Vienna, 3 February 1940).

Vienna-born journalist Victor Léon adopted a French name for his career in the theatre, whilst his brother, Leo, opted for a definitely German one as Leo Feld. Léon's choice turned out to be a significant one, for, during a career as an operettic librettist which took him to the top level of his profession at the time when Austrian Operette was the most popular kind of musical theatre throughout the world, his first and his greatest successes were based on works borrowed from the French comic theatre.

Léon's earliest stage works, written while he was in his twenties, were in the usual beginner's mould: one-act pieces for Vienna houses and full-sized texts for regional theatres, in his case the important Carl-Schultze Theater in Hamburg, which produced Rudolf Raimann's setting of Léon's first substantial work – already based on a French original, Dumas's *Les Trois Mousquetaires* – and the Deutsches Theater in Pest which hosted Emil Rosé's *Tizianello*.

The first major work from Léon's pen to be presented in Vienna was Alfred Zamara's *Der Doppelgänger*, which was brought from its Munich production to the Theater an der Wien in 1887 prior to a mass of further showings throughout Germany, and later the same year his musical-comedy adaptation of Grimmelhausen's *Simplicius Simplicissimus*, set by Johann Strauss as *Simplicius*, was produced at the same theatre. Both were, however, Vienna failures,

Der Doppelgänger playing for just two weeks and the collaboration with Strauss, which had seemed like an engraved-not-printed passport to success, a disastrous 31 performances.

Another such opportunity did not come quickly. During the 1890s Léon tried his hand at opera – supplying texts to Josef Beer (*Friedl mit der leeren Tasche, Der Strike der Schmiede*), Ignaz Brüll (*Gringoire, Schach dem König, Der Husar*) and Julius Stern (*Narciss Rameau*) – adapted several foreign musical texts for the Carltheater, wrote Possen and Volksstücke, and spent a period as dramaturg at the Theater in der Josefstadt where his operettic contribution was limited to adapting French musicals for the Vienna stage and the composition of an early biomusical on the father of his erstwhile collaborator, *Johann Strauss*.

He was represented on the Vienna stage of the later 1890s, however, by several original Operetten of which two found some small measure of success: Dellinger's *Die Chansonette*, imported from Dresden, lasted only a fair 37 performances at the Theater an der Wien before going on to be seen in Munich and Berlin, whilst Suppé's *Das Modell* was played intermittently in the Carltheater repertoire for some three years. Another collaboration with Suppé and Ludwig Held, *Die Pariserin* fell flat in 11 performances.

Léon's next contribution to the Carltheater was not an original text, but an adaptation: a version of Bayard and Scribe's *La Frontière de Savoie*. As *Der Cognac-König*, it fell flatter than ever in just ten performances in Vienna and in a production at Berlin's Theater Unter den Linden, but Léon continued to delve into the French theatrical libraries as Zell and Genée had so successfully done before him, and at his next essay he came up trumps. After 20 not very impressive years in the business, he finally got his hit. The breakthrough came with an adaptation of the famous farce *Les Dominos roses*, written with his co-author of a decade, the Baron von Waldberg, and set to music by the unproven Richard Heuberger, with whom Léon had worked a couple of years previously on a ballet-pantomime *Struwwelpeter* (6 January 1897) for Dresden. Produced at the Theater an der Wien, *Der Opernball* was a singular success, and Léon dipped further into the French opus to turn out texts based on Scribe's *La Bataille des femmes* (set by the youngest Johann Strauss as *Katze und Maus*), on Alfred Hennequin and Albert Millaud's *Niniche* (*Ihre Excellenz*), and on Meilhac's *Décoré* (*Der Sechsuhrzug*). None found anything like the same success as *Der Opernball*. He also dipped, with rather more success, back into the Strauss family's works and produced a French-style Viennese text to a Johann jr pasticcio score under the title *Wiener Blut* for the Carltheater and another to be illustrated by a pasticcio of the same Strauss's *Simplicius* and *Blindekuh* music, played at Venedig in Wien as *Gräfin Pepi* for a fair season.

However, there were other successes for him in those turn of the century years, and the first and most important of these was a first collaboration with the young Franz Lehár on the composer's earliest success, *Der Rastelbinder*. He combined again with Lehár on a wilfully Offenbachian classical burlesque, *Der Göttergatte*, and with another young composer on the way up, Leo Ascher, on the Theater an der Wien's *Vergeltsgott* (42 performances), but he returned to French sources for his next success. Whilst

Heuberger, whom Léon had apparently wanted to set his adaptation of Meilhac's *L'Attaché d'ambassade* for the Theater an der Wien, instead composed his Volksoper *Barfüssele* for Dresden, it was Lehár who turned Léon and Leo Stein's version of Meilhac's piece into *Die lustige Witwe*, a success which eclipsed not only *Der Opernball* but every other Operette of the past decades.

The years which followed *Die lustige Witwe* housed Léon's other greatest and most enduring successes – the original *Der fidele Bauer* and the French-borrowed *Die geschiedene Frau* with Leo Fall and *Das Fürstenkind* with Lehár – but thereafter major success avoided him. In the 1910s and up to his last venture in 1925, his output continued at the same staunch level as before, but not one outstanding hit emerged from amongst the two dozen titles, large and small, to which his name was affixed. Two works written with Péter Stojanovits had good runs at the Carltheater (*Liebchen am Dach* 183 performances, *Der Herzog von Reichstadt* 111 performances), but collaborations with Straus brought nothing more durable than *Liebeszauber* (77 performances), those with Fall produced at best 55 nights of *Der Nachtschnellzug*, with Granichstädten 60 of *Glück bei Frauen* and with Nedbal 52 of *Donna Gloria*. The only other one of his pieces to clear the 100 performance mark was his sole further work with Lehár, *Die gelbe Jacke* (104 performances). It was five years after Léon's last contribution to the Viennese stage when Fritz Löhner-Beda and Ludwig Herzer remade his libretto into the rather more successful *Das Land des Lächelns*. If Léon had really not, as the tale goes, wanted Lehár as his partner on *Der Rastelbinder* and/or *Der lustige Witwe*, the composer was now, in some small way, revenged. He returned to Léon, however, two years later for a revision of the librettist's text to *Das Fürstenkind*, staged in Berlin as *Der Fürst der Berge*. It was no *Land des Lächelns* and it was Léon's last stage credit.

From 1908, in parallel to his work as a librettist, Léon acted as director for many of his Operetten. He mounted the original Vienna production of *Der fidele Bauer* (1908), *Gold gab' ich für Eisen* (1915) and of *Die gelbe Jacke* (1923) at the Theater an der Wien, the premières of *Das Fürstenkind* (1909), *Das erste Weib* (1910) and *Der Nachtschnellzug* (1913) at the Johann Strauss-Theater, *Der gute Kamerad* (1911) and *Liebeszauber* (1916) at the Bürgertheater, *Die geschiedene Frau* (1908), *Liebchen am Dach* (1917), *Der Herzog von Reichstadt* (1921), *Glück bei Frauen* (1923) and *Donna Gloria* (1925) at the Carltheater. He also directed his *Der Millionendieb* with Mizzi Günther and Louis Treumann at Ronacher.

Léon was also the author of a number of non-musical plays including *Gebildete Menschen*, *Die Rheintochter* (w Waldberg), *Der grosse Name* (w Leo Feld, music by Robert Stolz), *Ein dunkler Ehrenmann*, *Man sagt* (w Waldberg) and *Toeff-Toeff* (w Alexander Engel), as well as further operas, among them a version of Erckmann-Chatrian's famous play as *Der Polnische Jude* (1902, music by Karl Weis w Richard Batka) and *Die Schönen von Fogaras* (1907, Alfred Grünfeld). *Toeff-Toeff* was later musicalized by Zsolt Harsányi and composer Adorjan Ötvös under the title *Özvegy kisasszony* (Budai Színkör 1 September 1916).

In spite of the fact that very many of his pieces had short lives, Léon left a solid handful of often first-rate pieces which remain in the European repertoire nearly a century

after their first productions: *Der Opernball*, *Wiener Blut*, *Der Rastelbinder*, *Der fidele Bauer*, *Die geschiedene Frau*, and *Das Land des Lächelns*, for which he must be allowed at least a slice of the credit. However, it is as the librettist of *Die lustige Witwe* that he principally remains amongst the star names of the Viennese Operette tradition.

His brother, Leo Hirschfeld (b Augsburg, 14 February 1869; d Florence, 9 September 1924), who wrote for the theatre under the name of **Leo Feld**, was Léon's partner on the successful *Der grosse Name* and also supplied libretti for the comic operas *Kleider machen Leute* (Zemlinsky/w Keller, Volksoper 2 December 1910) and *Die Stunde* (Lafite, Volksoper 25 October 1932).

1880 **Beim Schützenfest in Wien** (Max von Weinzierl) 1 act Ronacher 17 July

1881 **D'Artagnan** (*Die drei Musketiere*) (Rudolf Raimann) Carl-Schultze Theater, Hamburg 18 September

1883 **Tizianello** (Emil Rosé) Deutsches Theater, Pest 29 March

1883 **O diese Götter!** (Karl Stix) 1 act Ronacher 8 August

1884 **Die Königin von Arragon** (Alfred Zamara) 1 act Ronacher 1 May

1886 **Der Doppelgänger** (Zamara) Theater am Gärtnerplatz, Munich 18 September; Theater an der Wien 1 October 1887

1887 **Simplicius** (Johann Strauss) Theater an der Wien 17 December

1888 **Der Savoyarde** (Ottokar Feith/w Josef Brackl) Theater am Gärtnerplatz, Munich 19 June

1889 **Der Herr Abbé** (Zamara/w Brackl) Theater am Gärtnerplatz, Munich 10 August

1889 **Capitän Wilson** (*The Yeomen of the Guard*) German version w Carl Lindau (Carltheater)

1890 **Erminy** (*Erminie*) German version w Heinrich von Waldberg (Carltheater)

1890 **Der bleiche Gast** (Josef Hellmesberger, Zamara/w von Waldberg) Carl-Schultze Theater, Hamburg 6 September

1892 **Der Bajazzo** (Alfons Czibulka/w von Waldberg) Theater an der Wien 7 December

1894 **Tata-Toto** (*Toto*) German version w F Zell (Theater in der Josefstadt)

1894 **Johann Strauss** (Strauss arr Klimsch) 1 act Theater in der Josefstadt 12 October

1894 **Die Chansonette** (Rudolf Dellinger/w von Waldberg) Residenztheater, Dresden 16 September

1895 **Die eiserne Jungfrau** (*Le Brillant Achille*) German version w add mus by Karl Kappeller (Theater in der Josefstadt)

1895 **Die Doppelhochzeit** (Hellmesberger/w von Waldberg) Theater in der Josefstadt 21 September

1895 **Das Modell** (Franz von Suppé/w Ludwig Held) Carltheater 4 October

1896 **Toledad** (*L'Enlèvement de la Toledad*) German version w Waldberg (Theater in der Josefstadt)

1897 **Der Cognac-König** (Franz Wagner/w Held) Carltheater 30 February

1898 **Der Opernball** (Richard Heuberger/w von Waldberg) Theater an der Wien 5 January

1898 **Die Pariserin** (von Suppé/w Held) Theater an der Wien 28 March

1898 **Katze und Maus** (Johann Strauss III/w Ferdinand Gross) Theater an der Wien 23 December

1899 **Ihre Excellenz** (*Die kleine Excellenz*) (Heuberger/w von Waldberg) Centraltheater, Berlin 17 January

1899 **Wiener Blut** (Strauss arr Müller/w Leo Stein) Carltheater 26 October

1899 **Die Strohwitwe** (Albert Kauders/w von Waldberg) Theater an der Wien 4 November

1899 **Tohu-Bohu** (*L'Auberge du Tohu-bohu*) German version

(Theater in der Josefstadt)

1900 **Frau Leutnant** (*La Dot de Brigitte*) German version w von Waldberg (Theater in der Josefstadt)

1900 **Der Sechsuhrzug** (Heuberger) Theater an der Wien 20 January

1901 **Die verwünschene Prinzessin** (Eduard Gärtner) Carltheater 4 January

1901 **Das Medaillon** (Walter Mortier) 1 act Friedrich-Wilhelm-städtisches Theater, Berlin 31 March

1902 **Tarok** (Rudolf Raimann) Raimundtheater 8 February

1902 **Das gewisse Etwas** (Weinberger/w Stein) Carltheater 15 March

1902 **Gräfin Pepi** (Strauss arr Ernst Reiterer) Venedig in Wien 5 July

1902 **Der Rastelbinder** (Franz Lehár) Carltheater 20 December

1903 **Der Herr Professor** (Béla von Ujj) Theater an der Wien 4 December

1904 **Der Göttergatte** (Lehár/w Leo Stein) Carltheater 20 January

1905 **Kaisermanöver** (von Ujj) Carltheater 4 March

1905 **Vergeltsgott** (aka *Der Bettlerklub*) (Leo Ascher) Theater an der Wien 14 October

1905 **Barfüssele** (Heuberger) Königliches Operntheater, Dresden 11 March

1905 **Die lustige Witwe** (Lehár/w Stein) Theater an der Wien 30 December

1907 **Der fidele Bauer** (Leo Fall) Hoftheater, Mannheim 27 July

1907 **Der Frauenmörder** (Oscar Straus) 1 act Danzers Orpheum 8 November

1908 **Die geschiedene Frau** (Fall) Carltheater 23 December

1909 **Das Fürstenkind** (Lehár) Johann Strauss-Theater 7 October

1909 **Little Mary** (Straus/ad Auguste Germain, Robert Trébor) 1 act Comédie-Royale, Paris, 8 January

1909 **Didi** (Straus) Carltheater 23 October

1910 **Das erste Weib** (Bruno Hartl) Johann Strauss-Theater 22 October

1910 **Die Post im Walde** (Oehl) 1 act Colosseum October

1911 **Der andere Herr war nicht so** (Straus) 1 act Hölle 1 February

1911 **Der gute Kamerad** (*Az Obsitos*) German version (Wiener Bürgertheater)

1911 **Die eiserne Jungfrau** (Robert Stolz) Raimundtheater 11 November

1913 **Die Studentengräfin** (Fall) Theater am Nollendorfplatz, Berlin 18 January

1913 **Der Nachtschellzug** (Fall/w Stein) Johann Strauss-Theater 20 December

1914 **Gold gab ich für Eisen** revised German version of *Az Obsitos* (Theater an der Wien)

1915 **Das Lumperl** (Stolz) Operntheater, Graz 4 April

1915 **Man steigt nach!** (Straus/w Heinz Reichert) Carltheater 2 May

1915 **Otto oder Otto** (Hans Tegern) 1 act Apollotheater 7 September

1916 **Im Apollo** (Tegern) Apollotheater 1 act 2 January

1916 **Liebeszauber** (Straus) Wiener Bürgertheater 28 January

1916 **Die Wachsfigur** (Oskar Stalla) 1 act Apollotheater 1 April

1917 **Wiener Kinder** (Johann Schrammel arr Stalla/w Reichert) Johann Strauss-Theater 16 May

1917 **Liebchen am Dach** (Péter Stojanovits) Carltheater 19 May

1917 **Der weisse Adler** (Chopin arr Raoul Mader/w Hugo H Regel) Volksoper 22 December

1918 **Der Millionendieb** (Friedrich Mayer) 3 scenes Ronacher 30 September

1920 **Die Pawlatsch'n** (Robert Mahler) Raimundtheater 19 May

1920 **Wiener Volkssänger** (Mahler) Raimundtheater 21 May

1920 **Hol' mich der Teufel** (Leopold Reichwein/w Reichert) Wiener Bürgertheater 29 October

1921 **Der Herzog von Reichstadt** (Stojanovits/w Reichert) Carltheater 11 February

1923 **Die gelbe Jacke** (Lehár) Theater an der Wien 9 February

1923 **Glück bei Frauen** (Bruno Granichstädten/w Reichert) Carltheater 4 December

1925 **Donna Gloria** (Oskar Nedbal/w Reichert) Carltheater 30 December

1930 **Das Land des Lächelns** revised *Die gelbe Jacke* by Fritz Löhner-Beda, Ludwig Herzer, Theater an der Wien 26 September

1932 **Der Fürst der Berge** revised *Das Fürstenkind* Theater am Nollendorfplatz, Berlin 23 September

LEONCAVALLO, Ruggiero (b Naples, 8 March 1858; d Montecatini, 9 August 1919).

The composer of *I Pagliacci* dipped on a number of occasions into the light musical theatre, reasoning if that Lehár, whom he judged his musical inferior, could make such a killing there, there was a place for him too. It turned out that there wasn't, although Leoncavallo made regular attempts, ranging from an early *Songe d'une nuit d'été* which was not played publicly, through a charming *Reginetta delle rose* (played in Paris as *La Petite Reine des roses*, Théâtre Réjane 10 May 1913, ad Claude Berton, Charles Maral), a disastrous attempt to break into London with a telephone-girl musical comedy mis-staged by revue specialist Albert de Courville, who also mounted the composer's short opera *I Zingari* on a variety bill, to a series of pieces in his later years, following the failure of his operatic ventures to produce another *I Pagliacci*.

1910 **Malbruck** (Angelo Nessi) Teatro Nazionale 19 January

1912 **La reginetta delle rose** (Gioacchino Forzano) Teatro Costanzi 24 June

1913 **Are You There?** (Edgar Wallace/Albert de Courville) Prince of Wales Theatre, London 1 November

1915 **La candidata** (Forzano) Teatro Nazionale 6 February

1916 **Prestami tua moglie** (Edmondo Corradi) Casino, Montecatini 2 September

1919 **A chi la giarrettiera?** (Corradi) Teatro Adriano 16 October

1923 **Il primo bacio** (Luigi Bonelli) 1 act Kursaal, Montecatini

1925 **Emile Collet** (Polieri, Bonelli) Politeama, Naples July

1925 **La maschera nuda** (ad Salvatore Allegra)

LÉONCE [GENIOT, Léon] (d Arras, ?April 1922). Slim, bespectacled (off-stage) low comedian with a musical education whose particularity apparently was that in spite of playing and singing in what one critic called his 'voix de flûte', with much ad-libbing and physical foolery, he managed always to keep in tune.

Engaged at the Bouffes-Parisiens in the 1850s, Léonce created a number of rôles in opéras-bouffes both large and small including Offenbach's *Tromb-al-ca-zar* (1856, Vert-Panné), *Dragonette* (1857), *Croquefer* (1857, Boutefeu), *Les Deux Pêcheurs* (1857, Madame Schabrauqe), *Vent du soir* (1858, Le Lapin Courageux), *Mesdames de la Halle* (1858, Madame Poiretapée) and *Orphée aux enfers* in which he introduced the part of Pluton/Aristée (1858), as originally played for its comedy rather than tenorial values. He introduced two more of his gallery of grotesque ladies as the Baronne de Follembuche in Delibes's *L'Omelette à la Follembuche* and Madame Potichon in his *Deux vieilles gardes*, and yet another as the gushing guest, Madame Balandard, in *Monsieur Choufleuri* (1861), took further Offenbach rôles as Patrocle, the younger Dunanan, in *Le Voyage de MM Dunanan père et fils* (1862), Boboli in *Les Géorgiennes* (1864) and the Marquis de Fonrose in *Les Bergers* (1865), and appeared in Hervé's first full-length opéra-bouffe *Les Chevaliers de la table ronde* (1866) before leaving the Bouffes-Parisiens and moving to William Busnach's Théâtre de l'Athénée. If much of the work he found there was of a lesser quality than at the Bouffes (Archiduc in *Marlbrouk s'en va-t-en guerre*, 1867, *Les Horreurs de la guerre*, 1868, Legouix's *Le Vengeur*, 1868) the engagement did allow him to appear in two of the earliest full-scale works by the young Lecocq, *L'Amour et son carquois*, and as the mandarin Ka-o-lin in *Fleur de thé* (1868).

He played the same rôle in a revival of *Fleur de thé* at the Théâtre des Variétés the following year, as well as appearing there as Volteface in Delibes's *La Cour du Roi Pétaud* and, in perhaps his greatest creation in a full-sized musical play, as Antonio, the harmless-seeming caissier with a womanful past in *Les Brigands* (1869). Thereafter, he made his artistic home at the Variétés and over the next two decades created a long list of rôles in, at first, opéra-bouffe, then opéra-comique, and in latter days in the vaudeville-opérettes which became the rage of the early 1880s. Amongst his parts were included Caprican in *Le Beau Dunois* (1870), Buckingham in *Le Trône d'Écosse* (1871), Briddidick in the Paris première of *Les Cent Vierges* (1872), Zizibar in *La Veuve du Malabar* (1873), Bibès in *Les Braconniers* (1873), Don Pedro in the expanded *La Périchole* (1874), Délicat in *La Boulangère a des écus* (1875), Ygène in *Le Docteur Ox* (1877), Tardivel in *Les Charbonniers* (1877), Sotherman, the lascivious clown in *Le Grand Casimir* (1880), Savarin in *La Roussotte* (1881), Bonpain in *Lili* (1882), the soldier Loriot with his virtual stand-up comedy routine in *Mam'zelle Nitouche* (1883) and Le consul d'Illyrie in *La Cosaque* (1884), as well as repeats of his Pluton and Caissier, Ménélas in *La Belle Hélène*, Alfred in *La Vie parisienne*, and a vast number of comedy rôles in the plays which made up an important part of the Variétés repertoire.

Léonce died in 1922 from injuries received in the First World War.

LERNER, Alan Jay (b New York, 31 August 1918; d New York, 14 June 1986). Librettist/lyricist to some of the happiest musicals of Broadway's postwar heyday.

Born into a well-off garment chain-store family and educated in Britain and at Harvard, Lerner first worked on college shows and, after graduation, as a radio writer. In 1942 he came together for the first time with composer Frederick Loewe when the two worked together on remaking a show called *Patricia*, a musicalized version of the successful play *The Patsy* done by George Grandee, J Keirn Brennan and Barry Connors, in which Dorothy Stone had played the previous season in San Francisco. Lerner was hired on this occasion to redo the libretto, with Earle Crooker (Loewe's partner on an earlier show) working on the lyrics of what was now called *The Life of the Party*. *The Life of the Party* got no nearer to Broadway than *Patricia* had done.

The following year Lerner and Loewe repeated their collaboration on *What's Up?*, a curious piece redolent of turn-of-the-century comic opera which did make it to Broadway but closed after eight weeks. A third effort together, *The Day Before Spring*, marked further progress: it had a life of 164 performances at Broadway's National Theater, and produced some fine (and some recyclable) songs in the midst of an uninteresting libretto which was weighted down with a barrage of ballets that were more *Oklahoma!* than *Oklahoma!*.

The curve of fortune continued to ascend and, when Lerner abandoned the little love lives of everyday people and reached into the world of romantic fantasy for his libretto for *Brigadoon*, a piece consciously constructed and written in the revived Broadway operetta style made fashionable by the success of *Oklahoma!*, the partners found a major success. The simple, charming tale of *Brigadoon* was illustrated with some particularly winning and suitable songs, both sentimental and comical ('Come to Me, Bend to Me', 'Almost Like Being in Love', 'The Heather on the Hill', 'There But for You Go I', 'The Love of My Life' etc), and these quickly found their way to as much popularity out of the show as in it.

In his next piece, *Love Life*, Lerner returned to more prosaic folk and their more prosaic relationships, but approached them in a less-than-straightforward way. His text followed its couple through 150 years of a slowly developing married life to a score by Kurt Weill which did not turn out any individual pieces to equal the popularity of those from *Brigadoon*. The show had a fair, if insufficient, run of 252 performances. A return to Loewe for the vigorously romantic go-west-young-woman *Paint Your Wagon* provided more songs that lingered ('They Call the Wind Maria', 'Wanderin' Star', 'I Still See Elisa', 'I Talk to the Trees') and a slightly longer, if still insufficient, run, at a time when the competition included such shows as *Guys and Dolls* and *The King and I*, but their 1956 work *My Fair Lady* both outshone and outran all and any competition. Lerner's adaptation of George Bernard Shaw's *Pygmalion*, and the score which he and Loewe devised to illustrate it, came together to produce a show which was as much the key show of its time as *Die lustige Witwe* had been half a century earlier in Vienna or *Orphée aux enfers* a century earlier in Paris. It was not that it was influential, or at the beginning of anything, it was simply a show which would spread itself, on stage and disc, to corners of the earth where few other Broadway musicals of the era had been, there to become accepted as the flag-bearer of this most successful age of the American musical stage.

To follow such a work was difficult, not to say impossible, but Lerner found fruitful material for adaptation in T H White's whimsical Arthurian tale *The Once and Future King*, and the result was another highly successful show. The stage musical which the authors called *Camelot* was ultimately more sentimental than whimsical, but it was full, once again, of tasty songs, both romantic and brightly and unforcedly comic ('I Loved You Once in Silence', 'How to Handle a Woman', 'If Ever I Would Leave You', 'The Simple Joys of Maidenhood'. 'Take Me to the Fair') and it proved a resounding and enduring international triumph.

With Loewe's subsequent retreat into real or imagined delicate health, Lerner was now forced to look for other collaborators, but in spite of his tying up with several writers of reputation the kind of success he had enjoyed with his first partner did not repeat itself. The first of his 'outside' collaborations, a musical about ESP, *On a Clear Day You Can See Forever*, written with composer Burton

Lane, did the best. It lasted for 280 performances on Broadway, provided the basis for a film, won subsequent regional productions, and launched both its title song and 'Come Back to Me' as singles. It did not, however, become an international property any more than did a biomusical on couturière Coco Chanel (*Coco*) mounted with Katharine Hepburn as an unlikely Chanel through 332 Broadway performances.

An attempt to make a musical out of Nabokov's much-discussed teeny-porn novella *Lolita* curled up out of town, and another nymphet musical – a stage version of Lerner and Loewe's enormously successful musical film of Colette's *Gigi* – failed to get off the ground in spite of several tries. *1600 Pennsylvania Avenue*, the umpteenth (but, alas, not the last) presidential musical, with an extended timespan and a score by Leonard Bernstein lasted a week before going nowhere except into the scrapbooks of those who adore one-week flops by superior writers, a pretty but impotent musical version of the screenplay *Buona Sera Mrs Campbell*, produced as *Carmelina*, lasted little longer and a final essay, an awkwardly updated version of the hit play *Idiot's Delight* as *Dance a Little Closer*, was a one-performance flop.

Always a very much better lyricist than a librettist, Lerner nevertheless wrote the texts for all his musicals. Given the success of his spot-on musical comedy slimming of Shaw's *Pygmalion*, there was no reason why he should not have. But many of his texts were inclined to wander and none, not even those for *Camelot* (subsequently severely altered in revival) or *Brigadoon*, reached the same level. His show songs, however, included a bookful of the most memorable of the 1950s and 1960s produce of Broadway's musical stage.

Five of Lerner's musicals reached the screen – *Brigadoon*, *My Fair Lady*, *Camelot*, *On a Clear Day You Can See Forever* and *Paint Your Wagon* – and he had further success on film, most notably with *Gigi* (subsequently turned into a stage piece) and with *An American in Paris* (1951, Academy Award). He also wrote an autobiography and a book of musical theatre history, both of which unfortunately showed evidence of a faulty memory and/or careless copy-editing. His collected lyrics (ed Benny Green) were published in 1987 under the title *A Hymn to Him: the Lyrics of Alan Jay Lerner*.

1942 **The Life of the Party** (Frederick Loewe et al/Earle Crooker et al) Detroit 8 October
1943 **What's Up?** (Loewe/w Arthur Pierson) National Theater 11 November
1945 **The Day Before Spring** (Loewe) National Theater 22 November
1947 **Brigadoon** (Loewe) Ziegfeld Theater 13 March
1948 **Love Life** (Kurt Weill) 46th Street Theater 7 October
1951 **Paint your Wagon** (Loewe) Shubert Theater 12 November
1956 **My Fair Lady** (Loewe) Mark Hellinger Theater 15 March
1960 **Camelot** (Loewe) Majestic Theater 3 December
1965 **On a Clear Day You Can See Forever** (Burton Lane) Mark Hellinger Theater 17 October
1969 **Coco** (André Previn) Mark Hellinger Theater 18 December
1971 **Lolita, My Love** (John Barry) Shubert Theater, Philadelphia 16 February
1973 **Gigi** (Loewe) Uris Theater 13 November
1976 **1600 Pennsylvania Avenue** (Leonard Bernstein) Mark Hellinger Theater 4 May
1979 **Carmelina** (Lane/w Joseph Stein) St James Theater 8 April
1983 **Dance a Little Closer** (Charles Strouse) Minskoff Theater 11 May

Autobiography: *On the Street Where I Live* (Hodder and Stoughton, London, 1978); Biographies: Lees, G: *Inventing Champagne* (St Martins Press, New York, 1990), Shapiro, D: *We Danced All Night* (Morrow, New York, 1990).

LESLIE, Fred [HOBSON, Frederick] (b Woolwich, London, 1 April 1855; d London, 7 December 1892).

The most popular British musical comedian of his era, Leslie – in tandem with 'boy' specialist Nellie Farren – fronted a series of musical burlesques at George Edwardes's Gaiety Theatre between 1885 and 1892 which were the centrepiece of the popular musical theatre of their time.

Leslie began acting as an amateur before being hired by Kate Santley (at the age of 22) to play old Colonel Hardy in the play *Paul Pry*. Miss Santley's main diet, however, was musicals, and a month later Leslie made his first London appearance as a musical-comedian as Agamemnon in *La Belle Hélène*, following this début with parts in *La Jolie Parfumeuse* (Poirot), the burlesque *Over-Proof* (Duc d'Aubeterre), *La Marjolaine* (Burgomaster) and *Tita in Thibet* (Po-Hi) with Santley, and *Les Dragons de Villars* (Thibaut), *La Périchole* (Panatellas) and the burlesque *Another Drink* (Folly Slantier) with Selina Dolaro. He joined the company at the Alhambra Theatre to play a leading rôle in *La Petite Mademoiselle* (Manicamp), toured as Hector in *Madame Favart* (with the young Beerbohm Tree as Pontsablé), and then returned to the Alhambra to appear in a group of widely differing rôles in French musicals – as the heroine's father in *La Fille du tambour-major* (aged all of 24), Faust in *Mefistofele II* (ie *Le Petit Faust*), the comic little Briolet in *Jeanne, Jeannette et Jeanneton* and Prince Toko in Auber's opéra-comique *The Bronze Horse*.

In 1881 Leslie was engaged to appear in America and visited Broadway for the first time to play for Comley and Barton in *Madame Favart* (now as Favart), *Manola* (Brasiero) and *Olivette* (Duc des Ifs). He returned to London to leading comic rôles in *Madame Favart* (a third different rôle, the aged comedy of Pontsablé this time) and Bucalossi's highly successful *Manteaux Noirs*. By this time he had become admired as a quite exceptional comic actor, and H B Farnie and Planquette, the composer of the record-breaking *Les Cloches de Corneville*, together wrote a vehicle for him in which he could star as a musical *Rip van Winkle*. Leslie's performance in this rôle placed him firmly at the head of his profession, but contractual quarrels led him eventually to quit the part and to return to America. There he starred in John McCaull's comic opera company in such pieces as *The Queen's Lace Handkerchief*, *The Beggar Student* (Ollendorf), *The Merry War* (Balthazar) and *Madame Favart* (Favart), returning home to repeat his Ollendorf at the London Alhambra, appear again as Rip and to play at the Comedy Theatre in *The Grand Mogul* (Ayala) and *Barbe-bleue* (Popolani).

Leslie was appearing in a feeble, fantastical piece called *Fay o' Fire* for a novice management when he was approached with a proposition to star opposite Gaiety Theatre favourite Nellie Farren in a burlesque on the Jack

Plate 159. **Fred Leslie** *as Rip van Winkle.*

Sheppard tale. Fortunately for his future, *Fay o' Fire* folded quickly and Leslie went to the Gaiety where his performance as Jonathan Wild in *Little Jack Sheppard* gave him the last fillip to megastardom. Thereafter, under the newly instituted management of George Edwardes, he starred with Nellie Farren in the Gaiety's series of 'new burlesques': as Noirtier to the Dantès of Miss Farren in *Monte Cristo Jr*, as the Monster to Nellie's Frankenstein in *Frankenstein* (the least successful of the series), as Don Caesar de Bazan to his partner's Ruy in *Ruy Blas and the Blasé Roué* and, finally, as 'the servant' who turns out to be the comedy value in *Cinder-Ellen Up-too-Late*, but this time not opposite Nellie, who was now incapacitated with rheumatism. The pair toured their successes through Britain and took them to America and to Australia, where they also appeared in *Miss Esmeralda*, one of the similar pieces with which Edwardes filled the Gaiety stage during his stars' hugely popular and lucrative touring absences. The partnership with Nellie Farren, hopefully only suspended for *Cinder-Ellen* was, however, never to be resumed. Whilst Leslie was planning his next piece – a burlesque of *Don Juan* – he was taken ill and, at the age of 37, died of typhus.

In the era of the creative comic actor, Leslie supplied much of the material with which his parts in the first Gaiety burlesques were made. As a result, he decided to turn author officially, and, under the fairly transparent pseudonym of 'A C Torr' co-wrote the libretti for his last three shows, as well as one on commission from fellow comedian Arthur Roberts (*Guy Fawkes Esq*, 1890).

Leslie's elder son, **Fred Leslie** [William Herbert Leslie HOBSON], had a good career in musical comedy as a light comedy supporting gentleman. He began in a small rôle in George Grossmith's *The Lovebirds* (1904), toured America in *The School Girl* and took over in *Lady Madcap* in the West End before spending some time on tour with George Edwardes's and Seymour Hicks's companies. He played in a revival of *The Dairymaids*, covered Joe Coyne as Danilo in *The Merry Widow*, and had his first good West End rôle as Nicola in Robert Courtneidge's *Princess Caprice* (*Der liebe Augustin*), a part he repeated in New York. After *Dancing Around* (USA) and *The Miller's Daughters* (London) he joined the company of *Theodore & Co* at the Gaiety Theatre, thus beginning an association with producers Grossmith and Laurillard which gave him good number-two light-comedy rôles in the hit musicals *Yes Uncle!*, *Kissing Time* and *A Night Out*. In 1922 he appeared with Jack Buchanan in *Battling Butler* and in 1924 visited Broadway one last time with Charlot's revue company.

Another Fred Leslie, an Australian dancer, actor and choreographer, worked on the revue and musical comedy stage in both Australia and Britain.

1887 **Miss Esmeralda** (Meyer Lutz/w Horace Mills) Gaiety Theatre 8 October
1889 **Ruy Blas** (Lutz/w Herbert F Clark) Gaiety Theatre 21 September
1890 **Guy Fawkes Esq** (George W Byng/'Doss Chidderdoss'/w Clark) Nottingham 7 April
1891 **Cinder-Ellen Up-too-Late** (Lutz et al/w W T Vincent) Princess's Theatre, Melbourne 22 August

Memoirs: Vincent, W T: *The Recollections of Fred Leslie* (2 vols) (Kegan, Paul, Trench, Trübner & Co, London, 1894)

LESLIE, Henry J (b London, ?1849; d London, 14 June 1900). Briefly but dramatically successful London producer and the builder of the West End's Lyric Theatre.

Originally an accountant with a musical and theatrical bent, Leslie worked in accounts at the Gaiety Theatre whilst occasionally inserting an original song into such of the theatre's shows as *Little Jack Sheppard* and *Monte Cristo Jr*, until the time that George Edwardes produced Alfred Cellier's comic opera *Dorothy*. After *Dorothy* had run an adequate season at the Gaiety, Edwardes transferred it to the Prince of Wales Theatre when his main company returned for the newest burlesque production. Soon he lost interest in the show and would have closed it had not Leslie offered to buy the production from him. For £500 the accountant became a producer and by recasting the old-style comic opera with some more vivacious performers, most notably the young Marie Tempest in the title-rôle, he turned it into the longest running London show of the century and made himself a fortune.

Leslie built Shaftesbury Avenue's Lyric Theatre on the proceeds of *Dorothy*, and there he produced Cellier's next piece *Doris* with sufficient if not equivalent returns whilst sending out long and large tours of both pieces. After the success of *Dorothy*, Leslie had put a lien on Cellier's future works and he took Lydia Thompson to court when she produced the 1874 *Sultan of Mocha*. He lost when *The Sultan of Mocha*, although heavily revised, was adjudged an 'old' work. He then abandoned Cellier, and turned for his next production to Edward Solomon, whose *The Red Hussar* he staged in 1889. Miss Tempest, with whom he had been carrying on a rather indiscreet affair which brought him again to court – this time as a co-respondent with

£5,000 in damages to pay to the wounded husband – again starred, and with an undoubted success. However the ex-accountant's finances became more and more parlous as he became more and more ambitious.

A hugely spectacular pantomime, *Cinderella*, which he set up at Christmas 1889 at Her Majesty's Theatre in a hopeless attempt to outdo the traditional Drury Lane one, lost him his fortune and his theatre, and, in spite of Miss Tempest's success in *The Red Hussar* on Broadway, he went further under when a surfeit of top notes forced her to cancel the tour. She returned to Britain, whilst he, having gone suddenly blind, remained in America. He later regained his sight, but his career in the theatre was over.

1887 **Jubilation** (w Ivan Caryll/'Richard Henry') 1 act Prince of Wales Theatre 14 May

1888 **Warranted Burglar Proof** (w Caryll/B C Stephenson) 1 act Prince of Wales Theatre 31 March

LESTER, Alfred [LESLIE, Alfred Edwin] (b Nottingham, 25 October 1872; d Madrid, Spain, 6 May 1925). Little British musical comedian who followed in the tradition set by Teddy Payne at the Gaiety.

Born into a theatrical family, Lester worked on the stage from his earliest years, and spent the first part of his career touring the provinces in comedy and drama. In 1904 he appeared in London in the musical comedy *The Officer's Mess* (of which he was also the director) and scored a success with a comic scene-shifting act which he had invented and interpolated in the show. When *The Officer's Mess* closed he was hired to repeat this 'act' at the Palace music-hall.

Lester successfully followed this variety stage performance with several others before he was drawn back into musical comedy by George Edwardes, who hired him to appear in the Gaiety show *The New Aladdin* (1906). Although this musical turned out to be one of the Gaiety's least popular, Lester scored a personal hit as a bewildered London bobby magicked into an ideal London. He returned to the Gaiety to take the principal comic rôle in *Havana* (1908, Nix) and then found a huge success when he created the part of the lugubrious jockey, Doody, in *The Arcadians* (1909) introducing the ludicrous song 'My Motter'. Kerker's *The Grass Widow* (1912) was a failure, but *The Pearl Girl* (1913), which cast him as a lovelorn shopboy, served him better and he had the second outstanding rôle of his career when he appeared as one of the Bing Boys, teamed with George Robey, in the triumphant Franco-English revue *The Bing Boys Are Here* at the Alhambra.

Lester subsequently played in the unsuccessful *Shanghai* and *The Eclipse*, and he made his last appearance in a musical comedy in Teddy Payne's rôle of Miggles, another little shop boy, in the year-long revival of *The Shop Girl*, before spending his final years playing in revue. He withdrew, ill, from the cast of *The Punch Bowl* and went to Spain in search of health, dying there at the age of 52.

LESTER, Edwin (b Providence, RI, 1895; d Beverly Hills, 13 December 1990). American producer responsible for much of the best action on that country's western seaboard through several decades.

A child singer and pianist, a sometime conductor and mounter of the prologues at Grauman's Chinese Theater, sales manager with a Los Angeles music company, then a talent agent, Lester began producing for the benefit of his clients. He founded the San Francisco Light Opera Association (w Homer Curran) in 1937 and the Los Angeles Light Opera Association the following year. Amongst the productions of their first years, which from the beginning attained a high level of staging and casting, were included *Blossom Time* with John Charles Thomas, a heavily reorganized *Gipsy Baron*, *A Waltz Dream*, Allan Jones in *The Desert Song*, *HMS Pinafore*, Jana Novotna as *The Merry Widow*, *The Red Mill*, Thomas and Irra Petina in *The Chocolate Soldier*, *Bitter-Sweet* with Muriel Angelus, *Music in the Air*, an 'adapted' version of *Die Fledermaus* as *The Rose Masque* and a Strauss pasticcio called *The Waltz King*.

Lester had a major success and a Broadway transfer with another original pasticcio, *Song of Norway*, and thereafter he hosted and commissioned a number of other pasticcio and arranged pieces including, most successfully, Wright and Forrest's *Kismet* (1953) and, after several attempts, a new version of *Walzer aus Wien* produced as *The Great Waltz*. Other productions included a Tchaikovsky pasticcio *Song Without Words* (aka *Music in My Heart*) with Margit Bokor starred, another made-over *Fledermaus* based on the Reinhardt-and-Korngoldized version and called *Rosalinda*, Wright and Forrest's Victor Herbert *Gypsy Lady* (1946) and Saint-Saëns *Dumas and Son*. He also mounted some new musicals, ranging from stage versions of *Gigi* (1973) and Robert Stolz's musical film *Two Hearts in Waltz Time* to a musical *Peter Pan* (1954), Wright and Forrest's *Magdalena* (1948) and *At the Grand*, and Vernon Duke's *Zenda*.

Separately, and later in tandem, the two companies flourished, although over the years the production schedule was forced down by rising costs and the season was ultimately obliged to include brought-in productions. Lester retired in 1976.

LET 'EM EAT CAKE Musical comedy in 2 acts by George S Kaufman and Morrie Ryskind. Lyrics by Ira Gershwin. Music by George Gershwin. Imperial Theater, New York, 21 October 1933.

Conceived as a sequel to the successful *Of Thee I Sing*, *Let 'em Eat Cake* followed the fortunes of President John P Wintergreen (William Gaxton), his winsome wife Mary (Lois Moran) and his ever-forgotten vice-president, Throttlebottom (Victor Moore) – partially recognizable in their new antics as the joyous folk of the former show – following their ejection from office after one term. In a plot redolent of 19th-century comic opera, they open a clothing store, espouse revolution in order to sell their blue shirts as the uniform of rebellion, end up back in power after toppling the legitimate president, and get court-martialled out of power and in the direction of the gibbet following a baseball match between the League of Nations and the Supreme Court (prize: double or nothing on the war debts). Mary's manipulation of feminine America saves their necks, and the ex-presidential pair end up going back into the garment trade whilst Throttlebottom becomes president.

Lightning did not strike twice. The happy, witty burlesque tone which had made the first piece a success was missing second time round: the Gilbertian sparkle replaced by a grey zaniness. From the score, only the extractable 'Mine' (which was indeed extracted and used in a later version of *Of Thee I Sing*) won notice. *Let 'em Eat Cake* ran for 90 performances, and its closing marked the end of George Gershwin's contribution to the light musical theatre.

Recording: 1987 concert (CBS)

LETERRIER, Eugène (b 1842; d Maisons-Lafitte, 22 December 1884). One of the most successful librettists for the Parisian opéra-comique in the years of its greatest prominence.

The young Leterrier, a clerk at the Paris Hôtel de Ville, began his theatrical career as he would finish it, in partnership with the even younger Albert Vanloo, who was at that time a not entirely enthusiastic law student. Their first work together, a version of the 'Tom Thumb' story set to music by Laurent de Rillé, was given a production by William Busnach – the manager who had recently given his first major opportunity to the young composer Charles Lecocq – at his short-lived Théâtre de l'Athénée. However, it was five years of occasional one-acters, burlesques and flops before the pair found their first really productive opportunity in the musical theatre – one which came courtesy of the same Lecocq, now the celebrated composer of *La Fille de Madame Angot*. Leterrier and Vanloo, his friends from the days when he had been accompanist at the Athénée, were given the opportunity to supply the text for the new Lecocq work which producer Humbert anxiously awaited to follow his explosive hit, and they did not let him down. Their hilariously foolish text for *Giroflé-Girofla*, with its double-headed prima-donna rôle, added greatly to the success of the show which confirmed the tonitruant arrival of Lecocq. It also marked the arrival of his new librettists.

Over the next decade, Leterrier and Vanloo – always working together – provided Lecocq with five further opéra-comique texts in the best and most intricately saucy farcical style of the time. Virtually all were successful, all were internationally played, with *Le Jour et la nuit*, *La Marjolaine* and *La Petite Mariée* each, in different areas, the most popular, and *La Jolie Persane* and *La Camargo* only a little in retreat. A sixth joint piece, in a different vein, was *L'Arbre de Noël* (w Arnold Mortier), a spectacular Christmas féerie in no fewer than 30 scenes, which was produced with considerable success at the Porte-Saint-Martin in 1880 and thereafter throughout Europe.

At the same time that they were turning out their Lecocq hits, the team also supplied texts to several of the other greats of the Paris musical stage, beginning, in the year following the production of *Giroflé-Girofla*, with Offenbach himself. Their *Le Voyage dans la lune* (w Mortier) proved a splendidly spectacular and durable piece of writing, but they worked on only one other occasion with Offenbach, and that was on a one-act piece which took many years to find its way to the stage. They also supplied the young Chabrier with the libretto for his *L'Étoile* – a libretto which subsequently went a good deal further than its score, being adapted to the uses of the American (*The Merry Monarch*), Hungarian (*Uff király*) and British (*The Lucky Star*) stages, without the benefit of Chabrier's music.

Later the same American writer, Cheever Goodwin, who had helped himself to *L'Étoile*, would also borrow the libretto of their *La Gardeuse d'oies* for his William Furst musical *A Normandy Wedding* (aka *Papa Gougou*).

Lacôme's *Le Beau Nicolas*, Lajarte's *Le Roi de carreau* and Messager's *La Béarnaise* all had respectable runs and travelled to productions overseas, but it was Leterrier and Vanloo's collaboration with Francis Chassaigne, *Le Droit d'aînesse*, which provided their biggest success of all outside France. Adapted by Henry Farnie as *Falka*, *Le Droit d'aînesse* was carried triumphantly across English-speaking stages from one side of the globe to the other, outdoing even *Giroflé-Girofla* in popularity and becoming easily the most often played of the partners' works in those areas.

Leterrier died at the age of 42 but, in an effective career of little more than ten years, he had made a significant contribution to the musical theatre of his time with a dozen notably well-made and internationally played works, a number of which still receive intermittent productions a century later.

1868 **Le Petit Poucet** (Laurent de Rillé/w Albert Vanloo) Théâtre de l'Athénée 8 October

1869 **Madeleine** (Henri Potier/w Vanloo) 1 act Théâtre des Bouffes-Parisiens 10 January

1869 **La Nuit du 15 Octobre** (Georges Jacobi/w Vanloo) 1 act Théâtre des Bouffes-Parisiens 25 October

1871 **Nabucho** (A Villebichot/w Vanloo) Folies-Nouvelles 13 September

1874 **Giroflé-Girofla** (Charles Lecocq/w Vanloo) Fantaisies-Parisiennes, Brussels 21 March; Théâtre de la Renaissance 12 November

1875 **Le Voyage dans la lune** (Jacques Offenbach/w Vanloo, Arnold Mortier) Théâtre de la Gaîté 26 October

1875 **La Petite Mariée** (Lecocq/w Vanloo) Théâtre de la Renaissance 21 December

1877 **La Marjolaine** (Lecocq/w Vanloo) Théâtre de la Renaissance 3 February

1877 **Madame Clara, sonnambule** (Isidore Legouix/w Vanloo) 1 act Palais-Royal 15 March

1877 **L'Étoile** (Emmanuel Chabrier/w Vanloo) Théâtre des Bouffes-Parisiens 28 November

1878 **La Camargo** (Lecocq/w Vanloo) Théâtre de la Renaissance 20 November

1879 **La Jolie Persane** (Lecocq/w Vanloo) Théâtre de la Renaissance 28 October

1880 **L'Arbre de Noël** (Lecocq/w Vanloo, Mortier) Théâtre de la Porte-Saint-Martin 6 October

1880 **Le Beau Nicolas** (Paul Lacôme/w Vanloo) Théâtre des Folies-Dramatiques 8 October

1881 **Der Weihnachtsbaum** German version of *L'Arbre de Noël* w music by Louis Roth (Theater an der Wien, Vienna)

1881 **Mademoiselle Moucheron** (Offenbach/w Vanloo) 1 act Théâtre de la Renaissance 10 May

1881 **Le Jour et la nuit** (Lecocq/w Vanloo) Théâtre des Nouveautés 5 November

1883 **Juanita** (*Donna Juanita*) French version w Vanloo (Galeries Saint-Hubert, Brussels)

1883 **Le Droit d'aînesse** (Francis Chassaigne/w Vanloo) Théâtre des Nouveautés 27 January

1883 **Le Roi de carreau** (Théodore Lajarte/w Vanloo) Théâtre des Nouveautés 26 October

1885 **Le Petit Poucet** (André Messager et al/w Vanloo, Mortier) Théâtre de la Gaîté 28 October

1885 **La Béarnaise** (André Messager/w Vanloo) Théâtre des Bouffes-Parisiens 12 December

1887 **La Gamine de Paris** (Gaston Serpette/w Vanloo) Théâtre des Bouffes-Parisiens 30 March

1888 **La Gardeuse d'oies** (Lacôme/w Vanloo) Théâtre de la Renaissance 26 October

LET'S FACE IT Musical comedy in 2 acts by Herbert and Dorothy Fields based on the play *Cradle Snatchers* by Russell Medcraft and Norma Mitchell. Music and lyrics by Cole Porter. Imperial Theater, New York, 29 October 1941.

The Fields, brother and sister, working here together for the first time, adapted the play *Cradle Snatchers* to wartime musical comedy conditions by a little switching of characters. In the original play, the three ladies of the piece go and get themselves a gigolo apiece when they think their husbands are cheating on them. In the musical version, the ladies (Vivian Vance, Eve Arden, Edith Meiser) pick themselves up three soldiers (Danny Kaye, Benny Baker, Jack Williams) who are already equipped with sweethearts (Mary Jane Walsh, Sunny O'Dea, Nanette Fabray), who are, in fact, being romanced by the husbands. All the combinations came to a peak in some farcical scenes which finally restored the status quo.

Cole Porter's score was built on a veritable parade of for-the-moment lyrics: Mary Jane Walsh hymned 'Jerry, My Soldier Boy' and the title-song had the army facing it 'for Uncle Sam' but, war or no war, the composer returned to his favourite style in 'Let's Not Talk About Love', a duo for Kaye and Miss Arden decorated with a bevy of topical and social names, a second name-dropper describing how celebrities go 'Farming', a catalogue song on 'You're the Top' lines called 'You Irritate Me So' which was shared by Williams and Miss Fabray, and a trio for the three girls advising each other always to have an 'Ace in the Hole'. The lyric of this last had to be altered when one of its plugged personalities, Carole Lombard, was killed during the show's Broadway run. However, the most winning lyric was one of the few that barely mentioned a star or brand-name: a weary trio for the three wives explaining why 'A Lady Needs a Rest'.

Danny Kaye came to the cast of *Let's Face It* direct from his big success in *Lady in the Dark*, and he was allowed to develop his rôle into a festival of personal comedy amongst the more general comedy of the rest of the show. He also interpolated a pair of songs written with his wife, Sylvia Fine: a travestied Fairytale, and a gobbledegook scena to music called 'Melody in 4F' in which he followed through the stages of the induction of an army recruit, and which proved to be amongst the comic highlights of the evening.

The piece was greeted as 'brisk and bright and continuously enjoyable ... swift and dry-humoured comedy, a good thing in the vein of high pressure fooling'. With appreciable help from Kaye and his comicalities during the first part of its run (he was later succeeded by José Ferrer) and, no doubt, also from the usual wartime long-run phenomenon, Vinton Freedley's lively production racked up a splendid 547 performances on Broadway. London gave the show an equally warm welcome, and Jack Waller and Tom Arnold's production, with Bobby Howes appearing in Kaye's rôle alongside Joyce Barbour, Noele Gordon and Babette O'Deal (wives), Pat Kirkwood, Pat Leonard and Zoe Gail (girls) and Jack Stanford and Leigh Stafford (soldiers), ran for 348 performances in the West End.

The score underwent alterations on Broadway when Kaye left the cast, and a number from *Dubarry Was a Lady*

was inserted to replace his double-talk material for the benefit of Ferrer. It was this un-Kayed version which was subsequently played both in Britain and in Australia where Yvonne Banvard/Marjorie Gordon, Marie La Varre and Lily Moore featured as the three ladies and Don Nicol (who kept the Fairytale), Ron Beck and Fred Murray the three fellows as the show played a two and a half months' season at Sydney's Theatre Royal and another the following year at Melbourne's Her Majesty's (20 November 1943) during a wartime period which saw few other new productions relieving the flow of revivals in the area.

A 1954 television version with a cast including Bert Lahr, Gene Nelson and Vivian Blaine snaffled two additional Porter songs ('It's De-Lovely' and 'I've Got You under My Skin'), whilst a film adaptation which starred Bob Hope alongside Betty Hutton and Miss Arden went the opposite way and shrunk the song content, retaining only the title-song and 'Let's Not Talk About Love' alongside some studio-baked songs.

Australia: Theatre Royal, Sydney 12 September 1942; UK: London Hippodrome 19 November 1942; Film: 1943
Recording: Archival reconstruction (CBS/Smithsonian Institution)

DIE LETZTEN MOHIKANER Komische Operette in 3 acts by F Zell. Music by Richard Genée. Theater am Gärtnerplatz, Munich, 29 September 1878; Friedrich-Wilhelmstädtisches Theater, Berlin, 8 May 1879.

Zell and Genée's Operette had nothing to do with J Fenimore Cooper's tale of American frontier life, but was set in Germany, with much of its action located around a rowing club and had for its chief characters a rowing photographer, a plumber, and his girfriend. Liberally played in Central Europe after its première in Munich (Leipzig, Vienna, Brünn, Berlin, Nuremberg, Prague etc) it lasted only 12 performances when it was mounted at Vienna's Theater an der Wien in spite of the presence of Albin Swoboda, Alexander Girardi and Hermine Meyerhoff in its principal rôles. It continued to win productions in Germany, however, and was mounted as a burlesque spectacular at Hamburg's Centraltheater in the 1885–6 season.

Austria: Theater an der Wien 7 January 1879

DER LETZTE WALZER Operette in 3 acts by Julius Brammer and Alfred Grünwald. Music by Oscar Straus. Berliner Theater, Berlin, 12 February 1920.

By 1920 more than a decade had passed since Oscar Straus's two big international hits with *Ein Walzertraum* and *Der tapfere Soldat* and, although he had subsequently composed Operetten and musical plays for the Austrian, German, British, French and Hungarian stages, including such not-inconsiderable pieces as the long-running *Rund um die Liebe*, *Die schöne Unbekannte*, *Die kleine Freundin*, *Eine Ballnacht*, *Liebeszauber* and *Dorfmusikanten*, none of these had achieved the same wide-ranging popularity that his two early hits had.

After the First World War Straus settled in Berlin, and his first work for the Berlin theatre was *Der letzte Walzer*, written to a libretto by Julius Brammer and Alfred Grünwald. Their plot centred on Vera Lisaweta (Fritzi Massary), eldest daughter of the widowed Countess Opalinski, who once rejected the pressing advances of the powerful Prince Paul and ultimately had to be rescued from his importunities by an unknown young man. Paul, however, has had his revenge. He has had the interfering Count Dmitri Sarrasow (Otto Storm) condemned to death and commanded the elderly General Krasinski to wed the so-very-particular Vera Lisaweta. Dmitri, under arrest in Krasinski's castle, is allowed a reasonable freedom on his honour and, on the night before his transfer to the death cell, he encounters the woman who is now the General's fiancée at a ball. Together they dance what will be his last waltz. Vera arranges an escape for him, but Dmitri refuses to break his word. Paul, however, does not mean to kill the Count, he means merely to humiliate both him and Vera, and the vehicles taking the prisoner to Warsaw and the bride to her wedding are rerouted to the Prince's palace. There, Vera gains the upper hand. She points out to the Prince that Dimitri is emerging in the eyes of the world as the hero of the affair and he as a petulant loser, a situation which can be turned around if he now orders Vera and Dmitri to be wed. The light comedy of the piece was ensured through the first two acts by Vera's sisters, notably the youngest, Babuschka, and by their suitor Baron Ippolith, a group who were then tactfully faded out of the picture to allow the final triangle to be worked out without interrruption.

Straus's score for *Der letzte Walzer* was one of his most sweepingly romantic and melodious and, if it did not bring forth such obvious bon-bons as *Ein Walzertraum*'s famous duet or *Der tapfere Soldat*'s 'My Hero' waltz, it was nevertheless filled with music in the very best and most beautiful contemporary Viennese vein. The best rôle and the bulk of the romantic music fell to the prima donna: her mirror song 'Tanze, Vera Lisaweta' as she persuades herself that she can convince Dmitri to flee, the waltzing 'Rosen die wir nicht erreichten', the csárdás of the second-act finale, the contrastingly taunting 'O du pikantes, süsses o-la-la' of her third-act encounter with the Prince, and her rousing waltz duets with the tenor ('Das ist der letzte Walzer', 'Hörst du die liebliche zwingende singende werbende Walzermusik'). The tenor rôle had its best moments in duet, and in Dmitri's carefree farewell to life, 'Bei Lied und Wein', but the other highlights of the show's score came in the light numbers, Ippolith's appreciation of Babuschka's dimples ('Du hast zwei Grübchen') and his polka-ed dilemma, before the appearance of the youngest, over which delicious sister to choose (Der Polkakavalier: 'O kommt, o kommt und tanz mit mir').

Der letzte Walzer scored a major success through 280 performances in Berlin, sealing a collaboration between Straus and Fritzi Massary which would last, to their great mutual advantage, through five further shows, and it soon found its way to the stages of the world in a way that only his two most popular pieces had previously done. Hungary, as almost always, was first off the mark with *Búcsúkeringő* (ad Zsolt Harsányi), followed by America and the Shuberts whose Broadway production of *The Last Waltz* (ad Edward Delaney Dunn, Harold Atteridge) starred Eleanor Painter and Walter Woolf, two of the most considerable musical-theatre vocalists of the time. In a fashion which had not yet, sadly, seen its day, they also botched Straus's score with interpolations by house-writer Al Goodman and by Ralph Benatzky. *The Last Waltz* was, nevertheless, a distinct success and played for 199 performances at the huge Century Theater.

Having taken its time to reach Vienna, *Der letzte Walzer* was no less of a hit when it finally appeared there, in the wake of Gilbert's not dissimilar *Die Frau im Hermelin*, with Betty Fischer (Vera), Hubert Marischka (Dimitry), Lilly Welly (Babuschka), Kurt Ehrle (Paul) and Walter Huber (Ippolith) starring at the Theater an der Wien for a first run of 221 performances and a 34-performance reprise. In Britain, the piece was picked up by Robert Evett as the first independent vehicle for *Sybil* star José Collins following her departure from Daly's Theatre. Played at the Gaiety in a version by Evett and Reginald Arkell, with Kingsley Lark as Dmitri and Miss Collins's Daly's Theatre co-star Bertram Wallis as Prince Paul, *The Last Waltz* set the new management off to a fine start with a 280-performance run which, if less than that achieved by *Sybil*, was to be the best that any of their ventures would achieve.

Oddly, it took six years for the show to reach France, the French version (ad Jean Marietti, Léon Uhl) being given first at Geneva, where Odette Sardo created the French Vera Lisaveta opposite Pagnoulle and Monval. When it did arrive in Paris, it was at Louis Masson's well-meaning repertoire theatre, the Trianon-Lyrique, where Germaine Revel, René Rudeau and Monval headed the cast. However *La Dernière Valse* received a more substantial showing a decade later when it was played at the Gaîté-Lyrique (21 May 1936), with Suzanne Laplace, Raymond Chanel and André Balbon at the head of its cast.

In spite of its obvious attractions and its strong initial runs *Der letzte Walzer* subsequently rather slipped from the standard repertoire, but it was filmed on two occasions, the first in 1934 with Camille Horn and Ivan Petrovitch starred, and the second in 1953. This version (ad Curt Braun, music arr Bruno Uher) kept a little (but not much) closer to the original story than the bulk of European Operette films, as Eva Bartok pleaded with O E Hasse for the life of Curd Jürgens. Robert Gilbert and Fritz Rotter wrote fresh text for new numbers interpolated into what remained of the score and maturing Operette star Christl Mardayn appeared as the heroine's mother.

Hungary: Városi Színház *Búcsúkeringő* 29 December 1920; USA: Century Theater *The Last Waltz* 10 May 1921; Austria: Theater an der Wien 27 October 1921; UK: Gaiety Theatre *The Last Waltz* 7 December 1922; France: Trianon-Lyrique *La Dernière Valse* 5 May 1926; Films: Georg Jacoby 1934, International Films 1953
Recording: selection (Period)

LEVEY, Ethel [FOWLER, Ethelia] (b San Francisco, 22 November 1880; d New York, 27 February 1955).

Ethel Levey made her first professional stage appearance at the age of 17, singing a coon song in a west coast production of the musical farce-comedy *A Milk White Flag*. She soon moved east, and she appeared in music-hall and burlesque at Koster and Bial's and Weber and Fields's music halls in New York before joining Hyde and Behman's company. This last shift was made in order to stay at the side of the man who shortly after became her husband, George M Cohan. She appeared with Cohan, between 1901 and 1907, in the musical comedies which he wrote, composed and starred in: *The Governor's Son* (1901, Emerald Green), *Running for Office* (1903, Gertie Gayland), *Little Johnny Jones* (as the persecuted heroine, Goldie Gates) and *George Washington Jr* (1906, Dolly

Johnson). During this period she also took over the title-rôle of Sidney Jones's much more musically substantial comedy opera, *My Lady Molly*, on the road.

After divorcing Cohan, Miss Levey appeared on Broadway in the musical *Nearly a Hero* (1908) and appeared with Laddie Cliff in the revusical *Gaby* (1911), but she worked largely in music hall and revue, both in America and in Europe, performing Blanche Ring's successful 'Rings on My Fingers' and 'Prairie Mary' at Vienna's Apollotheater and scoring a big success in London in 1912 when she starred in the early revue *Hullo, Ragtime!*, dancing Jack Mason's choreography to the 'Bacchanale Rag' with Checkers von Hampton. She subsequently spent a number of years in Britain where she devoted most of her time to revue but also appeared in the title-rôle of Ernest C Rolls's musical comedy production *Oh! Julie* (1920), and won a personal success in the show's medium run. In 1922 she was seen in New York as the Mabel of *Go Easy, Mabel* and three years later, back in London, as Totoche in *The Blue Kitten*, but her musical stage performances thereafter were few and, as far as Broadway was concerned, limited to character rôles in Romberg's *Sunny River* and Kálmán's *Marinka* when she was in her sixties.

LEVI, Maurice

Broadway conductor and songwriter of the turn-of-the-century variety and comedy musical stage.

After working under Klaw and Erlanger as musical director and utilitarian composer for the Rogers Brothers series of shows between 1899 and 1902, Levi moved across to the rival Weber (now without Fields) establishment to work in a similar capacity on *Higgledy-Piggledy*, a piece originally co-produced by Florenz Ziegfeld, who withdrew from the show along with his wife Anna Held when it was discovered that her rôle was no more prominent than those of the other stars of the show. Levi did not suffer, however, as he was subsequently retained by Ziegfeld to write the basic score for *The Soul Kiss*, a vehicle for ballerina Adeline Genée (Miss Genée brought her own large sections of dance music with her), and for three editions of the *Ziegfeld Follies* (1908, 1909, 1911). He won an isolated West End credit when Marie Dressler visited London, briefly playing *Philpoena* (an extended sketch from *Higgledy-Piggledy*) under circumstances which led to her discredit and a quick, permanent departure from the London stage for both star and musician.

1897 **At Gay Coney Island** (w J Sherrie Matthews, Harry Bulger/Levin C Tees) Columbus Theater 1 February
1899 **A Reign of Error** (J J McNally) Victoria Theater 2 March
1899 **Mlle Ka-za-za** (McNally) Victoria Theater 8 May
1899 **The Rogers Brothers in Wall Street** (McNally) Victoria Theater 18 September
1900 **The Rogers Brothers in Central Park** (McNally) Victoria Theater 17 September
1901 **The Rogers Brothers in Washington** (McNally) Knickerbocker Theater 2 September
1902 **The Rogers Brothers at Harvard** (J Cheever Goodwin/McNally) Knickerbocker Theater 1 September
1904 **Higgledy-Piggledy** (including *Philpoena*) (Edgar Smith) Weber's Music Hall 20 October
1905 **The College Widower** (E Smith) 1 act Weber's Music Hall 5 January
1906 **Twiddle Twaddle** (E Smith) Weber's Music Hall 1 January

1906 **The Squawman's Girl of the Golden West** (E Smith) 1 scene Weber's Music Hall 26 February
1908 **The Soul Kiss** (H B Smith) New York Theater 18 January

LEVIN, Herman (b Philadelphia, 1 December 1907; d New York, 27 December 1990).

A lawyer in New York, Levin entered theatrical production as co-producer of the revue *Call Me Mister* in 1946. His first musical play venture was a combination with Paul Feigay and Oliver Smith on *Bonanza Bound!* (1947) which closed on the road, his first Broadway musical was *Gentlemen Prefer Blondes* (1949) and he more than confirmed this promising start with his second, the triumphant *My Fair Lady* (1956), which he sponsored both in America and Britain.

Thereafter, however, the winning touch deserted him. Noël Coward's *The Girl Who Came to Supper* (1963), although patently geared to the *My Fair Lady* formula, failed to repeat that show's results, *Lovely Ladies, Kind Gentlemen*, a musical version of *The Teahouse of the August Moon*, was a quick flop in 1970, and *Tricks*, a musical-comedy adaptation of Molière, an even quicker one three years later.

LEWENSTEIN, Oscar (b London, 18 January 1917).

The manager of several British theatres (Unity Glasgow, Embassy, Royal Court), Lewenstein produced or co-produced a number of plays in the 1950s and the 1960s, often with a bias towards the experimental and/or the left-wing. His first musical theatre venture was a revival of *The Threepenny Opera* (1956), but, having commissioned a first original musical, the adventurous *Valmouth*, from Sandy Wilson as a vehicle for American star Bertice Reading, he did not ultimately produce it. Two years later, however, he did mount an original musical in the equally impressive *Expresso Bongo* (David Heneker, Julian More, Monty Norman/Wolf Mankiewicz) and, following its success, sponsored the same authors' next piece, *Make Me an Offer* (1959), a musical play which was, like its predecessor, one of the best British musicals of its time. *The Lily White Boys* at the Royal Court and the British production of Broadway's *Fiorello!* were unsuccessful and thereafter Lewenstein stuck principally to producing straight plays, making one last but unmemorable musical venture with the short-lived London version of the off-Broadway import *Your Own Thing* (1969).

LEWIS, Ada (b New York, ?1875; d Hollis, NY, 24 September 1925). One of the most effective character actresses of the Broadway musical theatre in the 1910s and 1920s.

Ada Lewis made her stage début walking on at $3 a week in *Siberia* at the Alcazar, San Francisco, before progressing to speaking rôles. She passed much of her juvenile days in the stock company at the same theatre, before catching the eye of Ned Harrigan during the star's guest appearance at the Alcazar. Harrigan wrote her into his *Reilley and the Four Hundred* and she scored a fine personal success in the rôle of the 'tough girl' Kittie Lynch. She appeared in another similar rôle in Harrigan's *The Last of the Hogans* (Mary Ann Brennan), and thereafter made herself a reputation and a pigeonhole as a strong lady in a string of farce comedies and variety musicals (Margie McIntyre in *A Country Sport*, Felicity Jones in *The Widow*

Jones, Mme Nocodi in *Courted into Court*, Mamie Muggins in *Cook's Tour*, Kate in *The Supper Club*, Clementine Clapper in *A Reign of Error*, Letitia Campbell in *Champagne Charlie*, Lotta Hintz in *The Rogers Brothers on Wall Street*, Fritz in *Tammany Hall*). She then moved 'up' to the Casino Theater where she took further rôles in the same line in *The Social Whirl* (Kitty La Verne), *Fascinating Flora* (Winnie Wiggins) and *Nearly a Hero* (Gwendolyn Doolittle).

In the following years, as she matured from 'tough girl' into a comical character actress, she played in such pieces as *Old Dutch* (Alma Villianyi), *The Summer Widowers* (Mrs McGuirk), the double-bill of *Gaby* and *Hell* and the burlesque *Bunty Bulls and Strings* (Susie Slimson), supported Al Jolson in *The Honeymoon Express* (Mme de Bressie), appeared briefly in the substandard *The Dancing Duchess* (Tilly), took over in Chicago's *One Girl in a Million* and then, at the age of 40, landed her best rôle to date as Madame Matroppo, the extravagantly forgetful singing teacher of *Very Good Eddie*.

Her next musical appearance was in the long-running *Listen, Lester* (1920, Tillie Mumm), after which she appeared in two further Jerome Kern musicals: as the gorgonic mother-in-law of *The Night Boat* (1920, Mrs Maxim), and the comical couturière of *Good Morning, Dearie*. In 1924 she starred alongside John E Hazzard as Madame Doremi, the American version of Jeanne Cheirel's celebrated rôle of the 'Comtesse' in *Ta bouche* (*One Kiss*) and she was signed to appear in a further Kern piece, *Sunny*, when, at a time and age when she might have been expected to have continued into a career as a major star older comedy/character lady, she collapsed with a nervous breakdown and died.

LEWIS, Bertha (b London, 12 May 1887; d Cambridge, 8 May 1931).

At first a supporting member and then, for many years, the principal contralto of the D'Oyly Carte Opera Company, the imposing, squarely built Bertha Lewis became identified with the heavy ladies of the Gilbert and Sullivan repertoire to a generation of British theatre-goers and early record buyers. She was killed in a car crash, aged 43, while touring with the company.

LEWIS, Catherine [neé **JEFFREYS-LEWIS**] (b London, ?1853; d Hove, 15 February 1942). Leading lady of the international musical stage who later transformed herself into a classic character actress.

Soprano Catherine Lewis made her first notable appearance on the London stage at the age of 19, when she took over from Selina Dolaro in the rôle of Clairette in *La Fille de Madame Angot* at the Philharmonic Theatre. The following year she took the feminine lead in the London production of Lecocq's *Les Prés Saint-Gervais*, playing Friquette to the Prince Conti of Pauline Rita, and appeared at Manchester as Dolly in the first revival of *The Sultan of Mocha*, and in 1875–6 she toured Britain in the double title-rôle of Mrs Liston's production of *Giroflé-Girofla*. In 1877 she visited Australia, starring in *Giroflé-Girofla*, *La Fille de Madame Angot* and *Madame l'Archiduc*, but she could not equal the popularity of the more incisively vivacious Emilie Melville and she soon moved on

to America. There, in 1878–9, she starred at Baldwin's Theater and Emerson's Opera House, San Francisco in a wide variety of musical pieces including *Fra Diavolo*, *Les Cloches de Corneville* (Serpolette), *Giroflé-Girofla* and *Zampa*, in opera and in burlesque, and then on tour for Alexander Henderson as Josephine in *HMS Pinafore*. She subsequently moved on to New York and performed with Augustin Daly's company in, amongst others, the lead rôle of a version of *Niniche* (*Newport*, Hon Mrs Peter Porter) and as Fanchette Michel in *The Royal Middy* (1880) at a reported salary of $150 a week. She earned her huge salary, however, as that version of Genée's *Der Seekadett* was a major hit and she its most appreciated star.

She scored another major Broadway hit when she starred as Audran's *Olivette* with the Comley-Barton troupe, then appeared in the title-rôles of *Madame Favart* (1881) and *Manola* (*Le Jour et la nuit*) and as Regina in *The Princess of Trébizonde* and featured as the first American-language *Prince Methusalem* (1883) before disappearing from the musical stage. However she returned to prominence 15 years later, playing both in classic plays – she was Daly's Maria in *Twelfth Night* – and also in character rôles in such musical productions as *A Runaway Girl* (1898, Lady Coodle), *The Cadet Girl* (1900, Madame Majeste) and Aimé Lachaume's *The Prima Donna* (Mrs Chumpley).

Her sister, Mary, had a fine career as an actress on the Broadway stage under the name Jeffreys Lewis.

LIBELLENTANZ Revue-Operette in 3 acts by Carlo Lombardo, a revised version of *Der Sterngucker* by Fritz Löhner-Beda and A M Willner. Music by Franz Lehár. Produced as *La danza delle libellule*, Teatro Lirico, Milan, 27 September 1922.

Franz Lehár's *Der Sterngucker*, produced at Vienna's Theater in der Josefstadt in 1916 (14 January), had a libretto in which an unworldly young astronomer gets involved simultaneously with three of his sister's girlfriends and has to be brought severely down to earth. Seventy-nine performances at the Theater in der Josefstadt were followed by a second attempt, with a 'Neubearbeitung', which played for a further 60 nights from September of the same year, with all the forces of the Theater an der Wien behind it (Hubert Marischka, Betty Fischer, Luise Kartousch, Ernst Tautenhayn) but, although the piece was substantially played in Germany (Montis Operettentheater) and won productions in Budapest (*A csillagok bolondja*, Népopera 10 October 1916) and in America (*The Star Gazer*, Plymouth Theater 26 November 1917, 8 performances), it was not anywhere considered a genuine success.

When the composer was subsequently approached for a score by Carlo Lombardo, Lehár, who was never chary of re-using 'wasted' music, exhumed *Der Sterngucker* and handed it over to the enterprising Italian manager and writer. Lombardo put together a wholly new libretto in which the disguised Charles, Duke of Nancy, finds himself a young widow for a Duchess during the course of some amateur theatricals, and he produced the resulting piece, under the description of a 'revue-operetta' and the title *La danza delle libellule*, in Milan. *La danza delle libellule* proved noticeably more successful than *Der Sterngucker*, and following its Italian production it was duly re-exported to

Vienna where it was mounted by Herbert Trau at the Neues Wiener Stadttheater, as *Libellentanz*, with Otto Storm starring as the Herzog von Nancy, Lia Lüdersdorff as his Hélène Cliquot, and Josef König, Lisa Rado and manager's wife Olga Bartos in the other principal rôles.

The show, as it now stood, consisted of a very light and slight story, which depended as much on the flirtations of the ex-chorus-girl wives of local gentlemen who join in the theatricals as on its main threadlet, decorated with many dances of which a Snowball Ballet was the feature, a parade of ladies' underwear, a classical burlesque, harp and violin solos, an extensive wardrobe and a very full score of no fewer than 25 musical numbers. From that score, which Lombardo (who was a composer and musical director as well as a librettist, adaptor, producer and performer) had remodelled to appeal to the international dance-music tastes of the time, there emerged one genuine international hit, the foxtrot 'Gigolette', sung by the two principals, as well as several other appreciated numbers amongst which the song-and-dance duo 'Bambolina' (Storm and Frau Trau), a waltz song for Frln Rado, a quartet in the form of a java-gavotte, and a Butterfly Duet in which König threatened to net Frau Trau.

If Germany and America, who had both previously hosted *Der Sterngucker*, refrained from taking up *Libellentanz*, Hungary had no such qualms, being both the first and the most successful to stage its version, but balking at Lombardo's title. The show, staged as *A harom grácia* (the three graces, ad Zsolt Harsányi), scored a major triumph at the Fővárosi Operettszinház with Irén Biller starring, and it was played more than 200 times there during 1923–4. Elsewhere, those countries which had passed on the original show moved in to try the revised one. In Paris, Mme Rasimi produced Roger Ferréol and Max Eddy's French version of the show at the Ba-ta-clan (the productrice being herself responsible for what she billed as 300 costumes), with Maria Kousnezoff and Jacques Vitry in the lead rôles and Marthe Ferrare, Marie Dubas and Félix Oudart in rich support, and it again won a comfortable success. If the French retained Lombardo's title – in spite of the fact that the word 'libellule' (dragon-fly) had suffered something of the same denaturization as the English 'gay' – England followed the Hungarians, calling its version of the piece *The Three Graces*. Produced by Joe Sacks in a version by the young playwright Ben Travers, with the well-known vocalists Thorpe Bates and Winifred Barnes starring, it suffered the fate of most of Lehár's middle and later works in Britain and managed only a mediocre run of two and a half months (121 performances) in a season in which Gilbert's *Lady of the Rose*, Kern's *Sally* and a variegated selection of revues dominated the London scene. It was sufficient time, however, for 'Gigolette' to become a London dance band hit.

The name value of this hit was sufficient, and sufficiently international, for the piece to be re-produced (in a further revised version) in Milan under the title *Gigolette* (Teatro Lirico, 30 December 1926), but the new version did not succeed in superseding the previous one.

Austria; Neues Wiener Stadttheater *Libellentanz* 1 April 1923; Hungary: Fővárosi Operettszinház *A harom grácia* 6 June 1923; France: Théâtre Ba-ta-clan *La Danse des libellules* 14 March 1924; UK: Empire Theatre *The Three Graces* 26 January 1924

LIDO LADY Musical comedy in 3 acts by Ronald Jeans based on a libretto by Guy Bolton, Bert Kalmar and Harry Ruby. Lyrics by Lorenz Hart. Music by Richard Rodgers. Gaiety Theatre, London, 1 December 1926.

In the post-*Nanette* period, when anything American that sang and danced was the rage in the London theatre, *Lido Lady* was commissioned by London producers Jack Hulbert and Paul Murray from the American songwriting team of Rodgers and Hart, hard on the heels of the duo's first Broadway successes with *The Garrick Gaieties*, *Dearest Enemy* and *The Girl Friend*, and before any of their shows had as yet been presented to the London public. The pair had their first experience of being presented with a ready-made book to illustrate (their earlier musicals had been evolved in collaboration with Herbert Fields) and a star team already in place (Hulbert, his wife Cicely Courtneidge and Phyllis Dare). The jolly, nonsensical book, which opened on the Lido at Venice, featured Miss Dare as Fay Blake, daughter of sporting-goods magnate, and revolved around a stolen formula for a tennis ball. It spent most of its time looking at various set-up efforts staged by the boys of the piece who are attempting to impress their chosen girls with their particular sporting prowesses, and took time off to enjoy the attempts of a budding starlet called Peggy Bassett (Miss Courtneidge) to find herself publicity.

Rodgers was less than happy with the situation (and also with the lack of fuss made over him by his employers), and this disenchantment came out in his work. The best number in *Lido Lady* was not composed for the show, it was none other than 'Here in My Arms', lifted from *Dearest Enemy* and here performed by Hulbert and Miss Dare. Miss Courtneidge duetted with Harold French (as Spencer Weldon) about 'A Tiny Flat Near Soho Square' and with Hulbert (playing her brother, Harry) in 'Try Again Tomorrow', whilst Miss Dare got the best of the new numbers, the 'Atlantic Blues', as well as a De Sylva, Brown and Henderson interpolation 'It All Depends on You', taken from Broadway's *Big Boy*. It shared the evening's honours with the other second-hand song as the best liked numbers in the show.

Lido Lady was carefully produced out of town (Alhambra, Bradford 4 October) and run in thoroughly in the provinces before moving into town where its brisk fun and star team won it a seven-and-a-half-month (261 performances) stay. It subsequently went on the road in 1928 with George Clarke and Ella Retford featured, was trotted out again in 1929, and was mounted by the Fuller organization in Australia with Elsie Prince (Peggy), Billy Leonard (Harry), Jimmy Godden (Bill), Yvette Armina as Fay, singing the 'Atlantic Blues', and director Charlton Morton as Spenser. A good Sydney run was followed by six weeks at Melbourne's Princess Theatre (10 May) where the show had the misfortune to follow in behind one of the biggest Australian hits of the era, *Rio Rita*.

Lido Lady also appeared briefly on the Paris stage (ad Charles Tutelier, Georges Gilbert, with additional songs by musical director Max Alexis) under the management of Edgard H Rietjens and advertised as a 'comédie musicale à grand spectacle'. Violet Warland (succeeded by Mireille) sang 'Atlantic Blues' and 'Tout ça dépend sur vous' with Lucien Mussière, who shared 'Reviens un autre jour' with Yvonne Louis. 'Here in My Arms' became 'Rien n'est plus doux' in the show but was given under its American title as the theme of the intermission music, arranged by M Alexis to feature trumpet and piano solos. The 16 Dolly Dorne's Girls and the 8 Apollo's Boys supported, and the second act featured 'La Parade de la Reine de Saba' as an entertainment at the Fête du Sporting Club. *Lido Lady* was not, however, transported back to America, where its best pieces had already been used, and the unused parts were, on the evidence, not reckoned by their writers to be recyclable on home ground.

Vienna did not take up London's *Lido Lady*, but soon after its closure in the West End the Johann Strauss-Theater came up with a Revue-Operette in seven scenes by Otto Florian and Robert Katscher, directed by Leo Strassberg and starring Luise Kartousch as Mister Quick the Detective in the tale of *Die Lady vom Lido* (12 August 1927). It didn't actually get to the Lido until scene seven, having spent its time in such revusical places as the High-school for Charlestonning, A Revuetheater in Rehearsal and Amongst Cannibals.

Australia: St James Theatre, Sydney 23 February 1929; France: Théâtre Apollo

DER LIEBE AUGUSTIN Operette in 3 acts by Rudolf Bernauer and Ernst Welisch, a revised version of their *Der Rebell*. Music by Leo Fall. Neues Theater, Berlin, 3 February 1912.

Leo Fall's first venture as a composer of Operette was *Der Rebell*, a piece written to a libretto by Bernauer and Welisch and produced in no less a venue than the Theater an der Wien (29 November 1905) with a cast headed by Louis Treumann, Karl Streitmann, Dora Keplinger, Gerda Walde and Franz Glawatsch. It was an utter failure, playing for just five performances before being withdrawn, leaving manager Karczag hurriedly to rehearse and replace it with a piece by another promising and slightly more experienced composer, Franz Lehár. The failure of *Der Rebell* was forgotten in the success of *Die lustige Witwe*.

Half a dozen years later, Fall, now the internationally idolized composer of *Der fidele Bauer*, *Die Dollarprinzessin* and *Die geschiedene Frau*, and pressed from all sides and all parts of the world for new shows and new compositions, exhumed his score for *Der Rebell* and reworked it, with the original librettists, under the title *Der liebe Augustin*, with its catchy reminiscence of the popular song. The beloved Augustin, in this story, was the piano teacher of Princess Helene (Fritzi Massary), daughter of the desperately impecunious Bogumil of Thessaly who is intent that his child wed the rich Prince Nicola of Mikolics to save the family furniture from the hands of the bailiffs. Helene attempts to dissuade her bridegroom with a display of temper tantrums, but he is set on the Thessalian throne, even if he is obliged to wed a shrewish wife to get it, and he already has his eye on Helene's maid Anna as a candidate for the post of an eligibly consoling royal mistress. Fortunately, it turns out that batty Bogumil and Anna's father Jasomirgott got their babies mixed up whilst fleeing from an old revolution, so Nicola gets both the crown and Princess Anna, whilst Helene goes off happily to picturesque poverty with her piano teacher.

Fall's score was made up from such a series of winning melodies that it was almost impossible to believe that they

had escaped popularity six years earlier. The big hit of the show was the duet for Helene and Augustin, blissfully dreaming of a paradise for two in the waltz 'Und der Himmel hängt voller Geigen', but there were many more. The same pair shared a jaunty duo in a soundless piano lesson after the bailiffs have taken the piano ('Es war einmal ein Musikus') and took the first steps to special friendship in the lilting 'Sei mein Kamarad', whilst Anna joined Jasomirgott and Augustin in the leaping 'Anna, was ist denn mit dir?' and there were splendid solos for Augustin ('Lass' dir Zeit'/'Was es Schönes gibt') and Helene ('Wenn die Sonnen schlafen geht') as well as bouncy, tuneful comic material for the comedy men ('Heut' Nacht, nach acht', 'Wo steht denn das Geschrieben').

Der liebe Augustin was a singular hit for the Neues Theater and, as its total of performances rose at a rate which would, within a decade, put it in the all-time top 20 of musical shows in Germany (Otto Keller's calculations, made to the early 1920s, placed it 16th with 3,660 performances), the foreign-language productions began.

The first of these was in Budapest, where Adolf Mérei's version was mounted at the Népopera, prior to the city seeing the piece in German during a guest appearance by the Carltheater company at the Király Színház the following year. The second was in London, where Robert Courtneidge produced a version entitled *Princess Caprice* (ad Alexander M Thompson, A Scott Craven, Harry Beswick, Percy Greenbank) with Harry Welchman and Clara Evelyn starring in the romantic rôles alongside top comedians Courtice Pounds (Jasomirgott) and George Graves (Bogumil) and Marie Blanche (Anna). Producer's daughter Cicely appeared in an added rôle as Nicola's sister, Clementine, which involved some reallocating of the score. The show was a fine London success through 265 performances before taking to the road for a provincial career which was somewhat handicapped by the First World War and the subsequent campaign mounted against shows by German and Austrian composers. In the meantime *Der liebe Augustin* had reached Vienna where, with Mizzi Zwerenz and Hubert Marischka starred alongside Richard Waldemar (Bogumil), Josef König (Nicola), Karl Schöpfer (Jasomirgott) and Magda Szécsy (Anna), Sigmund Eisenschütz's production won a fine reception and 66 first-run performances.

What was allegedly another English version (ad Edgar Smith, but including the character of Clementine and, inevitably, musically botched) was produced in America by the Shuberts. George Macfarlane and May de Sousa played the lovers and De Wolf Hopper headed the comedy whilst Fred Leslie repeated his London rôle as Nicola. Yet again, a botched Continental hit failed on Broadway, and *Lieber Augustin* was sent on the road after just five weeks, retitled *Miss Caprice*. It did, however, last longer than an Australian production of the British *Princess Caprice* version which was mounted in Melbourne with Elsie Spain (Helen), Derek Hudson (Augustin), John Ralston (Jasomir), Dorothy Brunton (Clementine), Jack Cannot (Digomir), Phil Smith (Nicola) and Olive Goodwin (Anna) featured. It played only six nights as a try-out, and J C Williamson Ltd decided not to persevere with it.

Der liebe Augustin became part of the standard repertoire for many years in central Europe, losing its place only when Fall, in his time perhaps the most saleable of all composers, faded as a money-making name.

Other Operetten with the same title were produced in Vienna at the Theater an der Wien (15 January 1887, Brandl/Klein) and at the Volksoper (11 June 1917, Julius Bittner), and in Germany at Brandenburg in 1906 (H Chemin-Petit/Hans Gaus, Sommertheater 2 September) and Berlin's Theater des Volkes in 1942 (Josef Rixner/ Rudolf Köller, Bruno Hardt-Warden 18 December).

Hungary: Népopera *Kedves Augusztin* 9 March 1912; UK: Shaftesbury Theatre *Princess Caprice* 11 May 1912; Austria: Carltheater 12 October 1912; USA: Casino Theater *Lieber Augustin* (aka *Miss Caprice*) 3 September 1913; Australia: Her Majesty's Theatre, Melbourne 17 October 1914

Recordings: Selection (EMI-Electrola)

LIEBE IM SCHNEE   Singspiel in 2 acts and a Nachspiel by Ralph Benatzky and Willy Prager. Music by Ralph Benatzky. Ronacher, Vienna, 2 December 1916.

When the time comes for Princess Gertrud (Mizzi Günther) to choose a husband, she is still going through the crush-phase of being passionately in love with the opera singer Hendryk van Rhyn (Karl Pfann). A taste for the theatre evidently runs in the royal family, for her father, the Landesfürst Dagobert of Landskron (Arthur Guttmann), is currently linked with the dancer Ellen Kramer (Margit Suchy). Both couples have spent some idyllic times in the snowy market-town of Saffen, in the inn run by another of the Landesfürst's old flames (Alma Sorel). However, the Herzog Kilian Dietrich von Parthey (Adolf Klein) is determined to win the Princess and when, during the court theatricals which precede the naming of her official fiancé, she goes so far as defiantly to kiss her leading man – Hendryk – on the lips, it is he who steps cleverly in to save the situation. After their marriage, he tactfully arranges for Hendryk to be offered a job he can't refuse in another city and, when he accompanies the Princess to the singer's farewell performance, she is able uncomplicatedly to say goodbye to her old love, secure in the presence of the new.

Waltz songs predominated: the title song, the lilting 'Was jede Köchin summt!', the Princess's declaration 'Ich will frei sein!' and 'Du, mein Geliebter' all moved the romance along in 3/4 time, contrasted with square-time songs of which the most popular were 'Im Januar, im Februar' and the march rhythms of the presentation of the Princess's suitors ('Wir vier Thronprätendenten').

Liebe im Schnee secured a very good reception in both Austria, where it was produced at Ronacher under Oscar Straus's management (director: Miksa Préger, md: Oskar Jascha), and in Germany, as well as in an Hungarian version (ad Zsolt Harsányi) which was played in Budapest with Erzsi Péchy, Ferenc Galetta and Aladár Sarkadi starred. In each centre it was recognized as being musically one of Benatzky's best works.

An American version (ad Rowland Leigh) produced by the Shuberts many years later, after the Broadway success of Benatsky's *Im weissen Rössl*, folded on the road.

Germany: ?1917; Hungary: Városi Színház *Hóvirág* 9 March 1918; USA: Bushnell Memorial Theater, Hartford *Love in the Snow* 15 March 1946

LIEBESWALZER   Operette in 3 acts by Robert Bodanzky and Fritz Grünbaum. Music by Carl Michael Ziehrer. Raimundtheater, Vienna, 24 October 1908.

A jealous Austrian Count, Graf Artur Wildenburg (Ludwig von der Bruch), his jealous wife, Jenny (Gisela Noris) and her glittering mantrap of a cousin, the Baroness Yella von Bernau (Flora Siding), a wealthy tradesman called Leopold Führinger (Franz Glawatsch) and his wife Kathi (Louise Lichten) and daughter Antschi (Rose Karin-Krachler), a seductive Italian violin virtuoso, Guido Spini (Franz Gross), and a non-existent ballerina called Lisa Lizza (to rhyme conveniently with the city of Nizza), all caught up in the lightly amorous complications provoked by the Italian's apparent duplicity during a stay on the French Riviera, made up the action of *Liebeswalzer*. Ziehrer's score featured the popular Viennese strains for which he was best known in a Fiaker-duett for father and daughter on 'Das Wien der alten Zeit', the tradesman's solo 'Wie ich einmal noch jünger war', his family trio 'Wenn man Geld hat' and a spanking entrance number for Yella, 'Mädel, guck, Mädel, schau', alongside a polka trio and a piece in praise of the usefulness of the newfangled motor car, a vehicle which played a vitally deus-exmachinal part in the complexities of the plot.

Produced by Wilhelm Karczag and Karl Wallner in repertoire at the Raimundtheater, *Liebeswalzer* reached its 50th performance there by the end of the year, its 100th on 28 October 1909, and ultimately its 150th almost five years after its first performance (29 September 1913). It was played in Paris as part of a 1911 repertoire season by the Viennese company, was well received in Germany where, following its initial production with Conrad Dreher in the rôle created by Glawatsch, it proved the most popular of Ziehrer's works behind the untouchable *Die Landstreicher*, whilst an American production (ad Edgar Smith, Matthew Woodward) was staged under the management of the Shuberts at the Casino Theater. Dissatisfied with the reaction to the piece in its May try-out at New Haven, the Shuberts ordered a face-lift, and by the time the show arrived in town four months later it had a score botched with five Jerome Kern and two Louis Hirsch numbers, alongside what remained of Ziehrer's music. With Flora Zabelle (Nella, ex-Yella), Adele Rowland, Robert Warwick and William Pruette starred, it ran for 88 performances before leaving town with the shapely Valeska Suratt starred to score a fine success on the tour circuits.

Germany: 4 February 1910; USA: Casino Theater *The Kiss Waltz* 18 September 1911; France: Théâtre du Vaudeville (Ger) 1911

LI'L ABNER   Musical comedy in 2 acts by Norman Panama and Melvin Frank based on the cartoon characters of Al Capp. Lyrics by Johnny Mercer. Music by Gene de Paul. St James Theater, New York, 15 November 1956.

Li'l Abner was a musical comedy built around the well-known cartoon characters who had peopled the extravagantly crazy cornseed town of Dogpatch, USA, in the *New York Daily Mirror*'s strip of the same name for more than 30 years: the bulgingly healthy and strappingly naïve Abner, the burstingly promising Daisy Mae, only just held in by her tiny, tattered dress, pipe-sucking, fly-attracting Mammy Yokum, and all those that get in their way. After several other better-known names, including Alan Jay Lerner, had dithered with the project, it was film men Norman Panama and Melvin Frank who ultimately put together a libretto which tri-centred on a love story, a patriotic-political story and a sex-and-secret-formula story. On the one hand there were the endless efforts of Daisy Mae (Edith Adams) to get herself L'il Abner (Peter Palmer) as a mate aided by that awesomely terrifying institution known as Sadie Hawkins Day, on which Dogpatch ladies go out and physically catch themselves a husband. On the second hand, there was the threat to the very existence of Dogpatch, nominated because of its utter uselessness as an atom-bomb test site, and, on the third hand, there were the attempts of the horrid General Bullmoose (Howard St John) to steal the recipe for Mammy's (Charlotte Rae) Yokumberry tonic, the elixir which turns the feeblest of men into specimens like Abner. After a disastrous Sadie Hawkins race in which Abner is cornered by Bullmoose's protegée, Appassionata von Climax (Tina Louise), and Daisy Mae is set to wed the aptly named Earthquake McGoon (Bern Hoffman), and after the bomb-carrying planes have circled Dogpatch with their cargo of doom, everything comes right, *Pirates of Penzance*-fashion, thanks to the magic of the name of Abraham Lincoln.

The film-land writing team was completed by director/choreographer Michael Kidd, who joined the authors both on the development of the project and as its producer, and his *Seven Brides for Seven Brothers* colleagues, songwriters Johnny Mercer and Gene de Paul, who were brought in to compose the songs. *Li'l Abner*'s score turned out a genuine hit in the lively tale of the town's founding father 'Jubilation T Cornpone' as sung by Stubby Kaye in the rôle of Dogpatch's Marryin' Sam and, if it proved a little difficult to endow the comic-strip folk with ballady sentiments ('Namely You'), they were more than happy with a series of wordful, topical songs ('The Country's in the Very Best of Hands', 'Progress is the Root of All Evil') and another number for Kaye celebrating the happy ending of the show with the 'Matrimonial Stomp'. A non-musical highlight of the evening was the hero's entrance, accompanied by a flock of real, live geese.

Li'l Abner had a fine Broadway success and a 693-performance run, but, perhaps because of its extremely broad outback American-ness, it failed to attract export propositions. It did, however, make its way back to Hollywood where, under the direction of the authors, ex-college footballer Palmer repeated his impersonation of the beefcake Abner alongside Kaye and Leslie Parrish (Daisy Mae) on film.

Film: Paramount 1959
Recording: original cast (Columbia), film soundtrack (Columbia)

LILAC TIME *see* DAS DREIMÄDERLHAUS

DER LILA DOMINO Operette in 3 acts by Emmerich von Gatti and Béla Jenbach. Music by Charles Cuvillier. Stadttheater, Leipzig, 3 February 1912.

An Operette by a French composer, produced in Germany, which made him for several years the most sought-after musician in Britain, *Der lila Domino* (or, more correctly, *The Lilac Domino*) was a curious theatrical phenomenon – a musical which wandered the world without notable success until it was six years old, and then became a major hit.

Before this explosion of interest in his music, Cuvillier had had an agreeably successful Parisian career, mostly in smaller theatres, with such pieces as the winningly witty

Son p'tit frère. Like many other French composers, he had also found some popularity in neighbouring Belgium, but history does not relate how he came suddenly to be involved in writing a score to a German-language libretto for Leipzig. It was an unexceptional, conventional libretto, more than a little redolent of the successful American comedy *Captain Jinks of the Horse Marines*, whose heroine Georgine gets into a lilac domino at a ball, gets kissed by a disguised Count Anatol de Saint-Vallé, and then has the stars in her eyes doused when she finds he has taken a wager to find a rich wife. By the final curtain she, naturally, also gets her man, who had, of course, regretted the bet from the moment of the kiss.

The Leipzig production was well enough received for *Der lila Domino* to be produced later the same year in Budapest, but it created little interest in Europe and neither Berlin nor Vienna nor Paris took it up. Its next major première was in America where it appeared, two years after its début, in a version adapted by Harry and Robert Smith, under the management of Andreas Dippel and his Opéra-Comique Company. Eleanor Painter (Georgine) was the girl in purple, John E Hazzard (Prosper) played the comedy, Wilfred Douthitt (André), Rene Dettling (Léonie), Jeanne Maubourg (Baroness de Villiers) and Robert O'Connor (Casimir) supported, the evening was enlivened by some coloured motion pictures depicting the carnival at Nice, and the show ran for a fair-to-all-right 110 performances on Broadway.

In spite of the show's only reasonable, rather than exceptional, record to date, the British rights to *Der lila Domino* were taken up by a maverick little Russian-South African producer called Joe Sacks, who had recently ventured onto the London stage with a nearly successful revue called *Three Cheers* (1916). He had the American lyrics given a facelift by journalist S J Adair Fitzgerald, popped in a few additional songs by musical director Howard Carr and lyricist Donovan Parsons, and produced his show at the Empire Theatre with what was, for wartime, some splendour. A fine soprano in Clara Butterworth was cast as Georgine, but the cast did not in any way glitter with known names. Out of the blue, *The Lilac Domino* became not just a success but a vast success, almost on the scale of the town's two monster war-aided hits *The Maid of the Mountains* and *Chu Chin Chow*. The show's title song, as performed by Miss Butterworth, Vincent Sullivan and R Stuart Pigott, became one of the hits of the day, and Cuvillier's 'What's Done You Never Can Undo' (Miss Butterworth, Jamieson Dodds) and Carr's 'For Your Love I Am Waiting' (Josephine Earle) and 'All Line Up in a Queue' (American comedian Frank Lalor as Prosper) all became popular. When Miss Earle's lyrical 'True Love Will Find a Way' was replaced by the saucier 'We Girls Don't Like Them Shy', another song success was added to the total.

Before the end of the year Sacks had two companies touring his hit show in the provinces and Cuvillier had put in an appearance in London to take part in concerts for André Charlot and to talk to managements about new shows. And while all this was going on, the London *The Lilac Domino* ran on until it reached a total of 19 months and 747 performances. Four weeks after its West End closure it was already back in town again for further performances, this time at the Palace Theatre (23 October). It was also exported, on the crest of its London success, to Australia, where West End hero Jamieson Dodds was paired with a young local soprano, Rene Maxwell, at the head of a cast featuring Marie La Varre, Ivy Shilling, A B Majilton, George Gee, Hugh Steyne, John Delacey and William Valentine. Once again the show was a major hit, running for 155 performances in three different theatres in Sydney, prior to playing in Melbourne (Theatre Royal 16 July 1921) and in New Zealand, where Miss Maxwell was paired with the robust ex-Savoyard Claude Flemming. It was revived on the Australasian stage on several occasions thereafter.

The Lilac Domino remained on the British touring circuits for many years, established itself as an operatic society favourite, and returned during the Second World War for a West End revival (ad Herbert Sargent, His Majesty's Theatre 5 April 1944) under the management of Jack Hylton. With his lady friend, Pat Taylor, starring as Georgine it once again proved popular and played for 224 performances in a run bisected by bombing. In between its two profitable wartimes, however, the piece's popularity had been thoroughly retained, even to the extent, in 1937, of its being made into a film. June Knight starred in the cinematic version alongside dashing Richard Dolman, Michael Bartlett and comedians Athene Seyler and Fred Emney.

Whether *The Lilac Domino* would have become the success it did without the aid of wartime circumstances to establish it as a favourite cannot be guessed. It is certainly not Cuvillier's best score, and it is attached to a much less imaginative libretto and lyrics than some of his Parisian works, but it nevertheless won the composer the international popularity which his other works were denied and became a durable English repertoire staple for many years.

Hungary: Népopera *A lila dominó* 5 November 1912; USA: 44th Street Theater *The Lilac Domino* 28 October 1914; UK: Empire Theatre 21 February 1918; Australia: Tivoli, Sydney 18 December 1920; Film: Grafton-Capitol-Cecil (Eng) 1937
Recording: selection in English (HMV 45EP)

LILI Comédie-opérette in 3 acts by Albert Millaud, Alfred Hennequin [and Ernest Blum]. Music by Hervé. Théâtre des Variétés, Paris, 10 January 1882.

One of the hugely successful series of Parisian vaudeville-opérettes produced in the late 1870s and early 1880s under the management of Eugène Bertrand, with Anna Judic, at the peak of her popularity, in the starring rôle, *Lili* followed *Niniche*, *La Femme à papa* and *La Roussotte* on to the stage of the Théâtre des Variétés and proved as successful as the best of them. Madame Judic appeared as the Lili of the title, in a rôle which permitted her to run the now-expected gamut: as a young woman in 1842, a middle-ageing married lady in 1850 and an aged grandmother of the 1880s.

Amélie Bouzincourt, known as Lili, a strictly-brought-up young lady of the provincial noblesse, is tactless enough to fall in love with Antonin Plinchard (José Dupuis), a poor soldier who had come to her home to court the kitchen-maid. They have their moment of passion, but then go their separate ways. Eight years on, when they meet again, Lili is the Baronne de Lagrange-Batelier and Plinchard has risen to the rank of lieutenant. Their moment of passion is still visible, in the person of Lili's daughter, Antonie

(also Judic), but it is now too late to upset the lives into which they have settled. Years later, General Plinchard and the Baronne meet once more, when it is now safe to reminisce over what happened, and what might have happened but did not. The stalwarts of the Variétés company – Baron (Vicomte St Hypothèse), Léonce (Professor Bompain) and Lassouche – had fine supporting comic rôles whilst Rosine Maurel appeared in the next-best feminine rôle as Madame Bouzincourt.

The score, largely devoted to its female star, more than filled its purposes. Hervé came up once again with the kind of hit song which Judic had made a feature of these shows, and his Chanson provençale ('Du Pont du Garde à la Durance') was the musical moment of the evening. The Duo de la reconnaisance between Lili and Plinchard also proved enormously popular, and the star also turned out a rondeau ('Celui que j'aime est un piou-piou') and a saucy song about 'Le plus beau jour de ma vie' (it begins as her wedding day, and in the last verse it's the day her husband decides on separate bedrooms), and there were some wistfully touching musical moments in the final act as the two lovers relived their early escapade.

Lili's success ran to 233 performances at the Variétés before it gave way to its successor, Hervé's latter-day masterpiece and another triumph for Judic, *Mam'zelle Nitouche*. The star, however, kept her splendid vehicle warm, and, in the years that followed, she reappeared in *Lili* on several occasions on the Paris stage. The first was a brief 1884 reprise following the indifferent run of *La Cosaque*, the second in 1885 when the actress, now engaged at the Palais-Royal, returned to the Variétés for a few performances of each of her fondly remembered rôles, the last in 1894 when, fatter and fortyish, she made one last appearance as Amélie-Lili. In the meanwhile, however, Judic had taken *Lili* and the rest of her repertoire around the world, appearing in London, Vienna and Budapest in 1883 and in America in 1885 with *Lili* always a part of her baggage.

Whether it was Judic's performance that dissuaded many folk from trying to produce *Lili* with another star or whether the piece simply had limited appeal for foreign producers, the show was little taken up outside France – with one very notable exception, in Hungary. A version by Lajos Evva and Béla J Fái was produced at the Budapest Népszinház ten months after the Paris première with that theatre's star vocalist Aranka Hegyi taking the Judic rôle opposite Miklós Tihanyi (Plinchard). Hegyi and *Lili* scored a triumph every bit as grand as Judic and *Lili* had done in Paris. The piece was revived in 1883 (13 December) and in 1894 (5 October) with Hegyi's successor Klara Küry at the Népszinház (100th performance 9 December 1898, 150th 2 February 1907), at the Népopera in 1915 and at the normally non-musical Nemzeti Színház with Gizi Bajor in 1926, and it became an oft-revived part of the Hungarian standard repertoire, reappearing as recently as 1967 at the Fővárosi Operettszinház (new ad Ernő Andai) with Zsuzsa Lehoczky starred, many years after its last sighting in France.

Vienna, which had first seen the piece in German (ad F Zell) with Frln Jona starred alongside Felix Schweighofer (Hypothèse), Alexander Girardi (Plinchard) and Carl Adolf Friese (Bompan), in advance of Judic's visit, also welcomed several reprises. The undaunted Marie

Geistinger played the rôle before Viennese audiences just months after Judic had departed and the city was also given Klara Küry's Hungarian version during her 1902 Vienna season with *Der kleine Günstling*. There was a Vienna revival of the German adaptation at the Theater in der Josefstadt as late as 1909.

Austria: Theater an der Wien 21 October 1882, Theater an der Wien 18 November 1883 (Fr); Hungary: Népszinház 17 November 1882; Germany: Teplitz 13 July 1884; UK: Gaiety Theatre (Fr) 4 June 1883; USA: Wallack's Theater 1885 (Fr)

LILI BÁRÓNÖ
Operett in 3 acts by Ferenc Martos. Music by Jenő Huszka. Városi Színház, Budapest, 7 March 1919.

One of the classics of the Hungarian musical comedy repertoire, *Lili bárónő* has remained a favourite on the stages of the country of its origin ever since its production just after the end of the First World War, even though it has rarely been staged outside Hungary. Although it had been some years since Huszka's biggest successes with *Bob herceg* (1902), *Aranyvirág* (1903) and *Gül Baba* (1905), the postwar musical tale of the Baroness Lili found him back on the top, with a fourth enduring piece to add to his already impressive list.

Ferenc Martos's libretto was made up of elements familiar to Victorian followers of musical theatre. The penniless Count Illésházy (Ferenc Galetta) dons the clothes of his valet and, in this disguise, woos young Lili (Erzsi Péchy), daughter of the Baron Malomszegi (Rezső Sik). But the jealous actress Clarisse (Manci Vigh) exposes the Count's identity and persuades Lili that he was making light with her. The little baroness returns chastened to her official fiancé, Frédi (Aladár Sarkadi). But one day on the racecourse her horse Tündér is left without a jockey and the Count appears to ride his way to victory and into Lili's arms. Clarisse, of course, gets Frédi.

The favourite pieces of the score included a Cigarette-Waltz duo for the hero and the soubrette and the heroine's 'Egy férfi képe', as well as Clarisse's saucy 'Gyere, csókolj meg', the lovers' duos 'Tündérkirálynő légy a párom' and 'Szellő szárnyán', the lighthearted 'Drágám engem sohase féltsen' for Clarisse and Frédi, and a choral Jockeys March in the final act.

Repeatedly played since its initial production, and several times recorded, *Lili bárónő* was most recently heard in Budapest in 1989 (14 September) played in a cut version as part of a Huszka double-bill, with *Gül Baba*, at the Fővárosi Operettszinház.

Recording: Selection (Qualiton)

LILLIE, Beatrice [Gladys]
(b Toronto, 29 May 1894; d Henley-on-Thames, 20 January 1989).

An outstanding revue comedienne with a special vogue, 'Bea' Lillie appeared rarely in the musical theatre. On the first (and best) occasion, which was also one of only two on the London stage, she took the leading comedy part of Jackie in the UK version of the Bolton–Wodehouse–Kern musical *Oh, Boy!* (played as *Oh, Joy!*, 1919). In 1921, again in London, she played a multiple comedy rôle in the short-lived revusical *Now and Then*. Five years later, following her Broadway success in the Charlot revues, she was seen there as the comical 'other woman' in Vincent Youmans's musical version of the Paris hit *La Présidente, Oh, Please!*,

and then as a masquerading maid (in one of the most over-used plots in the business) in the Rodgers and Hart *She's My Baby*. Neither was successful. She made one last musical-comedy appearance, 35 years later, in the rôle of the batty medium Madame Arcati in a musical version of Noël Coward's *Blithe Spirit* (*High Spirits*), giving more to the show than it gave to her.

Autobiography: *Every Other Inch a Lady* (Doubleday, New York, 1972); Biography: Laffey, B: *Beatrice Lillie: The Funniest Woman in the World* (Wynwood Press, New York, 1989)

THE LILY OF KILLARNEY
Opera in 3 acts by John Oxenford and Dion Boucicault based on Boucicault's play *The Colleen Bawn*. Music by Julius Benedict. Theatre Royal, Covent Garden, 8 February 1862.

Benedict's *The Lily of Killarney* was the third of the three basic romantic 'operas' which, with the marginally more popular *The Bohemian Girl* and *Maritana*, made up the basis of the repertoire of many English-language opera companies of the mid-19th century. Although called an opera – for its dramatic tale, even though it had a happy ending, forbade it at that stage any other kind of description – *The Lily of Killarney* was, musically at least, already a large step towards the romantic comic operas of later years and its most outstanding songs, the male duo 'The Moon Has Raised His Lamp Above', the beautiful tenor serenade to 'Eily Mavourneen' and the heroine's 'I'm Alone', for decades parlour favourites, were the fore-runners of many a sentimental song in 19th-century musical theatre writing in Britain and America.

Widely and frequently played on English-language stages of both hemispheres for several decades, the piece was also given in a German adaptation (ad F von Dingelstedt) throughout Germany. In the 20th century performances have become progressively less frequent as the fashion has militated against Victorian English works.

A film issued as *The Lily of Killarney* by A, P & B in 1934, with John Garrick, Gina Malo, Sara Allgood and Stanley Holloway amongst its cast, used some of Boucicault's plot and characters, but turned to old Irish melodies for its musical part rather than to Benedict's score.

Australia: Apollo Music Hall, Melbourne 2 August 1862; Germany: Brunswick *Die Rose von Erin* 28 January 1863, Berlin 9 February 1864; USA: Academy of Music 1 January 1868
Recording: selection (part-record) (HMV)

LINCKE, [Carl Emil] Paul
(b Berlin, 7 November 1866; d Clausthal-Zellerfeld, Germany, 3 September 1946). German revue and Operette composer who, in spite of the fact that he did not produce an international success, nor even one major full-length Operette, has become tagged as the landmark writer of the German musical theatre.

Musically trained in Wittenberg, Lincke worked his way through some menial musical jobs to the position, at the age of 18, of bassoonist in the orchestra of Berlin's Centraltheater. From there, he moved on to a similar post at the newly renamed Ostend-Theater (ex-National-theater), before he was given his first opportunities to conduct. Lincke the conductor moved from pleasure garden to second-class theatre, to touring company until, as a 26-year-old, he was engaged at the Apollotheater (Apollo-Variété-Theatre), a Berlin house formerly specializing in large musical and dance spectaculars and now become a more reasonable variety theatre. There he conducted the orchestra and supplied such music as was necessary to the running of its programmes, sometimes less, sometimes, as for Senefeld's Posse *Die Spreeamazone*, which made up part of one Apollo programme, a little more. At the same time, he also purveyed music to other Berlin houses, and an Eduard Jacobson 'ballet-phantasie', *Unter den Linden*, with music by Lincke, was mounted at the theatre of that name (14 November 1896).

It was, however, back at his old haunt, the Ostend-Theater, that he first found the feeling of genuine success as a composer. Carl Weiss produced the Posse *Der deutsche Michel*, a little tale of adventures in foreign parts which dropped the Berlin Bombach family and their army-officer son, Michel (Weiss), into darkest Africa. The show, equipped with a scoreful of songs and incidental music by Lincke, had a splendid run, topping the 100 performance mark which in those days signalled a genuine hit. However, this success was as nothing beside that which he made when he tried his hand at genuine (if small) Operette. The director of the Apollotheater decided to insert one-act Operette spectaculars into his variety programmes, and Lincke was given the job of writing the scores. One of these, the picturesque, topical *Venus auf Erden* (1897), with its splendid, saucy staging and bright music, turned out a major Berlin hit.

Lincke abandoned the Apollotheater for the siren calls of France and the French equivalent of the Apollo, the Folies-Bergère, but two seasons in Paris brought him little joy and in 1899 he returned home and to the Apollotheater where another and even more successful little Grosse Ausstattungs-Operette from his pen, *Frau Luna*, was produced soon after. The fantastical *Frau Luna* was followed by another fine success in *Im Reiche des Indra* ('Nimm mich mit in dein Kämmerlein'), by the rather less-liked *Fräulein Loreley*, and then by another eventual winner in *Lysistrata* (Glühwürmchen-Idyll), and the Siamese-flavoured *Nakiris Hochzeit*, all composed to libretti by his *Venus auf Erden* collaborator, Heinrich Bolten-Bäckers. This run of little pieces carried on through four Apollotheater seasons and Lincke, after a tour of Germany, Austria and the Netherlands with his repertoire, saw the most popular of them win further productions outside Germany, in a fashion that few German composers to that date had succeeded in achieving.

Increasingly rich, randy and lazy, Lincke devoted himself but episodically to his music from this time on, and these miniature successes were not followed by the full-length work that might have been expected. He returned to the Apollotheater in 1904 as conductor for the Operetten which now made up an increasingly important part of its programme, and he scored a fresh success with his scoreful of popular songs for the revusical *Berliner Luft* (1904, 'Das ist die Berliner Luft'). In the years that followed, he provided some long-running revue and Posse scores for Kren and Schönfeld at the Thalia-Theater and for the Metropoltheater (*Donnerwetter, tadellos!*, *Hallo! die grosse Revue*), where he subsequently became musical director, and some shorter pieces for the Apollotheater and for Vienna's Danzers Orpheum. He set music to comic scenes for variety and wrote individual songs with and for various star performers, but he still produced no genuine Operette.

Lincke's full-sized musical stage plays did finally come,

but not until he had composed his last theatre pieces fc Berlin. He was 44 years old when his musicalization of a Parisian farce was brought out at Cologne under the title *Gri-gri*. It was successful enough to win further productions, both in Germany and beyond, a little more successful than his second piece, *Casanova*, staged two years later at Chemnitz, and altogether more so than the third and a handful of further wartime pieces. Then Lincke, apparently at odds with the new, foreign dance rhythms invading the Continental stages, stopped writing.

He worked still occasionally as a conductor and at his publishing house, Apollo Verlag, and, as one of the very few successful German or Austrian composers with no apparent Jewish connection, found himself and his little turn-of-the-century Operetten prized and popular under the Nazi régime. But though he received honours from that régime and saw his old shows boosted into fresh productions, he lost everything in the final stages of the war and died soon after.

The high-spot of Lincke's curiously unambitious career as a composer of musical theatre lies in the three seasons he spent at the Apollotheater after his return from Paris. The most successful of his little pieces there, *Frau Luna*, altered, expanded and decorated to make it up into a full evening's entertainment, has survived into the modern German repertoire, and *Lysistrata*, on the back of its internationally popular glowworm number, has followed on a lesser scale. Of *Gri-gri* and its fellows little is heard. But, in spite of the paucity of his product, Lincke remains pinned into position as the rather infertile follower of the almost as infertile Dellinger at the beginning of what would be – with the arrival of such writers as Gilbert and Kollo – Germany's busiest years as a producer of original and internationally appreciated musical theatre.

1896 **Die Spreeamazone** (A Senefeld) Apollotheater, Berlin 16 May
1896 **Der deutsche Michel** (Rudolf Kneisel) Ostendtheater 4 September
1897 **Eine lustige Spreewaldsfahrt** (Alfred Schmasov) 1 act Apollotheater
1897 **Ein Abenteur in Harem** 1 act Apollotheater
1897 **Venus auf Erden** (Heinrich Bolten-Bäckers) 1 act Apollotheater 6 June
1899 **Frau Luna** (Bolten-Bäckers) 1 act Apollotheater 1 May
1899 **Im Reiche des Indra** (Bolten-Bäckers, Leopold Ely) Apollotheater 18 December
1900 **Fräulein Loreley** (Bolten-Bäckers) 1 act Apollotheater 15 October
1902 **Lysistrata** (Bolten-Bäckers) Apollotheater 1 April
1902 **Nakiris Hochzeit** (Bolten-Bäckers) Apollotheater 6 November
1903 **Am Hochzeitsabend** (Bolten-Bäckers) 1 act Danzers Orpheum, Vienna 31 March
1904 **Berliner Luft** (Benno Jacobson) Apollotheater 28 September
1905 **Ausser Rand und Band** (Carl Lindau, F Antony) 1 act Danzers Orpheum, Vienna 4 November
1905 **Prinzess Rosine** (Bolten-Bäckers) Apollotheater 18 November
1905 **Bis früh um Fünfe** (Jean Kren, Arthur Lippschitz) Thalia-Theater 26 August
1906 **Hochparterre-Links** (Alfred Schönfeld/Kren, Arthur Lippschitz) Thalia-Theater 7 April
1906 **Das blaue Bild** (Bolten-Bäckers) Apollotheater 18 May
1906 **Wenn die Bombe platzt** (Schönfeld/Kren, Lippschitz) Thalia-Theater 25 August

1906 **Eine lustige Doppel-Ehe** (Schönfeld/Kurt Kraatz) Thalia-Theater 27 November

1907 **Ihr sechs-Uhr-Onkel** (Schönfeld/Kren) Thalia-Theater 15 August

1908 **Immer oben auf** (Schönfeld/Kren, Bernhard Buchbinder) Thalia-Theater 22 January

1910 **Nu hat's geschnappt** (Oskar Sachs) 1 act Sans Souci 2 September

1911 **Gri-gri** (Bolten-Bäckers) Metropoltheater, Cologne, 25 March

1913 **Casanova** (Jacques Glück, Willi Steinberg) Altes Theater, Chemnitz, 5 November

1915 **Fräulein Kadett** (Julius Winckelmann) Olimpia-Theater, Dortmund, 25 December

1917 **Pst-Pst** (Steinberg/Leonhard Haskel) Neues Theater, Hamburg 12 January

1917 **Stahl und Gold** (Leo Leipziger) 1 act Stadttheater, Memel 29 September

1940 **Ein Liebestraum** (Alexander Erler, Max Neumann) Theater an der Reeperbahn, Hamburg 15 October

Biographies: Nick, E: *Paul Lincke* (Musikverlag Hans Sikorski, Hamburg, 1953), Schneidereit, O: *Paul Lincke und die Entstehung der Berliner Operette* (Henschelverlag, Berlin, 1974)

LIND, Letty [RUDGE, Letitia Elizabeth] (b Birmingham, 21 December 1861; d Slough, 27 August 1923).

The most successful of the five stageworthy Rudge sisters, Letty Lind was London's favourite musical-comedy soubrette at the peak of the George Edwardes era at Daly's Theatre. After apparently having her first contact with the theatre as a dresser for and, later, a performer with Howard Paul's entertainment, she spent a number of youthful years playing in the provinces, during which she was seen at one stage in Minnie Palmer's famous rôle of Tina in *My Sweetheart*, and then in several plays. She first played in London musical comedy in the chorus rôle of Phebe in the 1883 revival of Offenbach's *Le Voyage dans la lune*, then appeared in the secondary rôle of Clorinda in a revival of *Manteaux Noirs* (1885), but her main career began when she was noticed by author and journalist Henry Pottinger Stephens who plugged her extravagantly in his newspaper column and urged George Edwardes to take her on at the Gaiety.

She duly made her Gaiety début succeeding Lottie Collins in the rôle of Mariette in the burlesque *Monte Cristo Jr* (1886), and she had her first own rôle, with a featured dance, as the gypsy Fleur-de-Lis in *Miss Esmeralda* (1887). She played Lizzina in *Frankenstein* (1887), visited America and Australia with the first-named two shows and returned, now an accepted part of the Gaiety number-one team, to contribute a polka and a valse chantante to the next Gaiety burlesque, *Ruy Blas and the Blasé Roué*, and a hornpipe and a spot with farmyard imitations to *Carmen Up-to-Data* (Mercedes). Her first leading part came when, following the illness of Nellie Farren, she ultimately took over in the title-rôle of *Cinder-Ellen Up-too-Late*.

When burlesque gave way to musical comedy, Letty Lind appeared in one of the earliest such shows, *Morocco Bound*, performing the famous skirt dance which her erstwhile understudy, Loie Fuller, was later to glossy-up and win history's credit for, and then had her first full-blown top-of-the-bill rôle as the ballerina heroine of the next work by the *Morocco Bound* team, *Go-Bang* ('Di, Di, Di', 'The Chinee Dolly'). After she had successfully taken over the central rôle of *A Gaiety Girl* (following Maud Hobson

Plate 160. **Letty Lind** *with the skirt she made famous.*

and Marie Studholme) for the last part of the show's run, George Edwardes slated her as the juvenile leading lady of his Daly's Theatre production *A Naughty Girl*. However, the late hiring of Marie Tempest meant she had to share the top spot, and give up the title. *An Artist's Model* ('The Gay Tomtit', 'Daisy With the Dimple'), however, proved a triumph for both women and established the Daly's star team, Tempest/Lind/Hayden Coffin, who, with comic Huntley Wright, were to be the backbone of the theatre's famous series of musicals during the late 1890s.

After scoring huge successes in the soubrette rôle of Molly Seamore in *The Geisha* ('The Interfering Parrot', 'The Toy Monkey'), and Iris in *A Greek Slave* ('A Frog He Lived in a Pond') Miss Lind broke up the team by leaving Daly's. After an ill-starred appearance in the unfortunate *The Gay Pretenders* she came back to Edwardes's management for an incidental rôle in *The Girl from Kays*, after which, aged more than 40, she slipped from the forefront of the theatrical scene.

Miss Lind's eldest sister **Millie HYLTON** [Sarah Frances Louise RUDGE] (b Birmingham, 8 February 1870; d Steyning, 1 September 1920) also had a fine career, most notably as a star of the music halls. She also played principal rôles in pantomime and later in musical theatre where she created the title-rôle in the Gaiety burlesque *Don Juan* (1893), took over as Lord Clanside in *In Town*, toured as Mme Drivelli in *The Circus Girl* (1897) and was later seen in music-hall musicals including Walter

Slaughter's *S'Nero* (1906) in which she featured as Poppaea to the Nero of M R Morand.

Adelaide ASTOR [Elizabeth Gertrude RUDGE] (b Birmingham, 15 December 1873; d London, 24 May 1951) appeared as a dancer and in lighter soubrette rôles in such pieces as *Carmen Up-to-Data*, *Cinder-Ellen Up-too-Late*, *In Town*, *The Lady Slavey* (Maud), *Go-Bang* (Sarah Ann), *The Shop Girl* (UK and USA) and *Morocco Bound*. She became the wife of the celebrated performer/manager George Grossmith jr.

Lydia FLOPP [Lydia Agnes RUDGE] (b 11 February ?1875; d unknown) appeared alongside her sister in *Go-Bang* and *An Artist's Model*, created the rôle of the little midshipman Tommy Stanley in *The Geisha* and also appeared in *Mr Popple of Ippleton* in the West End, and as Sophia in *The Catch of the Season* in Australia in a full career of musical-comedy credits.

Fanny DANGO [Fanny RUDGE] (b ?1878; d 15 July 1972), the youngest sister, had the lengthiest career and the longest life. For a long time an understudy, take-over and touring player in such British shows as *A Runaway Girl*, *Little Miss Nobody*, *Florodora*, *The Silver Slipper*, *The Gay Cadets*, *Three Little Maids*, *The Girl from Kays*, *The Medal and the Maid*, *The Lovebirds* and *The Spring Chicken*, she came into her own in leading rôles when she visited Australia and New Zealand. She appeared there, during a three-year stay, as Angela in *The Catch of the Season*, Peggy in *The Dairymaids*, Anita in *Havana*, Illyrine in *Les Merveilleuses*, Mitzi in *The Girls of Gottenberg*, Tina in *The Red Mill*, in *The Prince of Pilsen*, as Franzi in *A Waltz Dream* and in the title-rôle of the *Merry Widow*. She survived into her nineties, dying almost half a century after her most famous sister.

The Rudge family's involvement in the musical theatre continued for one more generation when Millie's daughter **Millie SIM** appeared in *Riquette* (1925, Liane) and *Bitter-Sweet* (1929, Lotte) as part of her career as an actress.

LINDAU, Carl [GEMPERLE, Karl] (b Vienna, 26 November 1853; d Vienna, 15 January 1934). Prolific comic actor turned equally prolific librettist of the Viennese musical theatre.

Lindau went on the stage at the age of 17, playing the classic repertoire at Graz, and subsequently worked in Budapest, Frankfurt, Dresden, at Graz again and then at Olmütz before making his first Viennese appearances at the Theater an der Wien in supporting comic rôles such as Degomez in *Tag und Nacht* and Josse in *Doctor Ox*. He joined Josefine Gallmeyer's American tour company in 1882 in a comedy team with Tewele and Knaack, playing a range of shows from *Hamlet* (gravedigger) through Possen (*Die Näherin*, *Der Goldonkel*) to such opérettes and Operetten as *La Mascotte*, *Giroflé-Girofla*, *Les Cloches de Corneville*, *Der lustige Krieg*, *Gräfin Dubarry* and *La Princesse de Trébizonde*, and on his return he became a solid member of the Theater an der Wien company.

Over the next 15 years, with only one short break, he there created and played good supporting comic rôles in a long list of plays and Operetten including *Rip-Rip* (1883, Nick Vedder), *Eine Nacht in Venedig* (1883, Barbaruccio), *Der Marquis von Rivoli* (1884, Baptiste), *Der Feldprediger* (1884, D'Alencourt), *Pfingsten in Florenz* (1884, Lorenzi),

La Princesse de Trébizonde (1885, Trémolini), *Zwillinge* (1885, Avrillon), *Gillette de Narbonne* (1885, Barigoul), *Der Viceadmiral* (1886, Deodato), *Der Hofnarr* (1886, Der Kanzler), *Der liebe Augustin* (1887, Längler), *Bellman* (1887, Claasen Steen), *Die sieben Schwaben* (1887, Allgäuer), *The Mikado* (1888, Mikado), *Pagenstreiche* (1888, Pomposo), *Der Schlosserkönig* (1889, Herzog von Uak), *Capitän Fracassa* (1889, Ali), *Das Orakel* (1889, Glaukos), *Der arme Jonathan* (1890, Graf Nowalsky), *Mam'zelle Nitouche* (1890, Loriot), *Der Vogelhändler* (1891, Süffle, one of the two crazy professors), *Madame Bonbon* (1891, Fridolin), *Die Kosakin* (1891, Fürst Cyrill Macshinstoff), *Miss Helyett* (1891, Bacarel), *Das Sonntagskind* (1892, Sheriff Plunkett), *Fanchons Leyer* (1892, August), *Der Millionenonkel* (1892, Jovan Zingaliri) and *Der Bajazzo* (1892, Monstroso). He played Melchior in his own new version of *Simplicius* and Lord Plato in Strauss's new *Fürstin Ninetta* (1893), created the rôle of mine manager Zwack in *Der Obersteiger* (1894) and continued on in *Husarenblut* (1894, Pinter), *Jabuka* (1894, Sava), *Kneisel & Co* (1894, Eustachius Altgrübel), Millöcker's *Der Probekuss* (1894, Graf Pizzi), *Die Chansonette* (1895, Tromboni), *Der goldene Kamerad* (1895, Juba Bill), *Waldmeister* (1895, Sebastian), *General Gogo* (1896, Armand Charmant), *Mister Menelaus* (1896, Flips), *Der Wunderknabe* (1896, Graf Calmore), *Der Löwenjäger* (1896, Tonpin), *Der Schmetterling* (1896, Theodor de Saint Marco), *Die Schwalben* (1897, Satrapschil), *Der Blondin von Namur* (1898, General Fano), *Ihre Excellenz* (1899, Desablettes) and as Baron Bonifaz Nickel in *Ein durchgeganges Mädel* (*A Runaway Girl*), Calineau in *Fräulein Präsident* and Lord Fiddlepuds in *Der Grossmogul* (1900) as well as repeating such classic parts as Agamemnon, Frank, Scalza, Bliemchen, Sindulfo and Stanglmeier, or later Nachtfalter, in *Drei Paar Schuhe*.

Lindau began a concurrent career as a playwright, librettist and lyricist in 1885, writing short plays, then translating French pieces, and writing first songwords and then text and lyrics for Possen, including several with good rôles for his colleague Girardi. It was in this area that he found his first big successes as an author with *Ein armes Mädel* and, in particular, *Heisses Blut*, a genuine star vehicle with a rôle à tiroirs par excellence for its leading lady, which was later played throughout central Europe and in an American adaptation as *A Dangerous Maid*. *Der Nazi*, *In siebenten Himmel* (1896) for Girardi and *Die fesche Pepi* (1897) were amongst the other successful musical comedy pieces which he turned out in the 1890s.

Lindau's first operettic libretto, written at a time when one of his most successful rôles was that of Gilbert's *Mikado*, was for a version of *Der Schelm von Bergen* (1888). A libretto by Ignaz Schnitzer, also based on Heine's poem, had been originally accepted and partly set by Strauss, but it was ultimately rejected by him on the excuse that it was too like *The Mikado*. Lindau's version – originally announced for setting by the ageing Brandl – was ultimately set by the less famous Oelschlegl without success (17 performances). However, Lindau later worked with Strauss when he co-authored a revision of the libretto of his *Simplicius* (1894).

Writing mostly in collaboration with either Krenn or 'F Antony', Lindau translated and adapted many of the most popular British and American musical-comedy imports of the turn of the century – in particular for Gabor Steiner's theatres, the open-air stage of Venedig in Wien and the 'winter' house Danzers Orpheum – as well as the occasional Hungarian operett, or a Berlin show that needed to be 'localized' with Viennese references for presentation in the Austrian theatre.

Of the original Operetten on which he collaborated, amongst this busy writing schedule, the most successful were two pieces composed by Carl Michael Ziehrer, *Die Landstreicher* (1899) and *Der Fremdenführer* (1902), and three with music by Edmund Eysler, Girardi's vehicles *Die Schützenliesel* (1905) and *Künstlerblut* (1906) and *Der Frauenfresser* (1911). A pastiche of Josef Strauss music attached to a version of Jaime and Duval's French farce *Coquin de Printemps* won considerable success for Steiner as *Frühlingsluft* (1903), prompting several other such pasticcii including the adding of a fresh libretto to Johann Strauss's *Indigo* score under the title *Tausend un eine Nacht* (1906). Berény's much-travelled *Lord Piccolo* (1910) was another fine success, and a set of collaborations with Josef Hellmesberger brought forth that composer's longest-running work *Das Veilchenmädel* (1904), which Lindau not only wrote but directed in its first Vienna presentation. He also directed *Die drei Wünsche* (1901) and *Der Schnurrbart* (1905) at the Carltheater and the Hungarian hit *Der Sultan* (1909) at the Johann Strauss-Theater.

Lindau also worked on libretti for several foreign composers – Ivan Caryll, Paul Lincke, Viktor Holländer, Ludwig Englander – all of whom had original pieces produced in Vienna, and, in later days, with his performing well behind him, he also contributed texts to the Berlin stage.

1885 **Die beiden Wenzel** (Paul Mestrozzi/w Wilhelm Mannstädt) Theater in der Josefstadt 26 September

1885 **Eine gute Partie** (Franz Wagner) Theater in der Josefstadt 12 December

1886 **Der Aprilnarr** (Karl Kleiber/w F Antony) Theater in der Josefstadt 13 April

1886 **Humbug der Geist des Schwindels** (Kleiber/w Mannstädt) Theater in der Josefstadt 11 September

1886 **Der Stabstrompeter** Viennese version w Antony w music by Hanns Krenn (Theater in der Josefstadt)

1887 **Wien bleibt Wien** Viennese version w Antony w music by H Krenn Theater in der Josefstadt 1 October

1887 **Peter Zapfel** Viennese version w Antony w music by Kleiber Theater in der Josefstadt 17 December

1888 **Der Grasteufel** (Kleiber/w Mannstädt) Theater in der Josefstadt 3 April

1888 **Der Schelm von Bergen** (Alfred Oelschlegl/w Karl Löwe) Theater an der Wien 29 September

1888 **Ein Hundert Jahre** (Kleiber/w Franz von Radler) Theater in der Josefstadt 24 October

1889 **Capitän Wilson** (*The Yeomen of the Guard*) German version w Victor Léon (Carltheater)

1889 **Wiener Luft** (Carl Michael Ziehrer/ad w Heinrich Thalboth) Theater an der Wien 10 May

1889 **Der Wildfang** (*Mademoiselle Moucheron*) German version (Carltheater)

1890 **Das Paradies** (H Krenn/w Leon Treptow) Carltheater 11 January

1892 **Heisses Blut** (Heinrich Schenk/w Leopold Krenn) Theater an der Wien 17 April

1892 **Unser Volk unter Waffen** (Kleiber/w Antony, Thalboth) Theater in der Josefstadt 17 September

1893 **Ein armes Mädel** (Leopold Kuhn/w Krenn) Theater an der Wien 6 May

1894 **Simplicius** revised version Theater an der Wien 19 September

1895 **Wiener Touristen** (Karl Kappeller/w Antony) Theater in der Josefstadt 2 March

1895 **Der Nazi** (Kuhn/w Krenn) Theater an der Wien 3 October

1896 **In siebenten Himmel** (Ferdinand Pagin/w Krenn) Theater an der Wien 29 April

1897 **Die Ladenmamsell** (*The Shop Girl*) German version (Theater in der Josefstadt)

1897 **Die fesche Pepi** (Wilhelm Argauer/w Krenn) Theater an der Wien 23 January

1897 **Der Herr Pomeisl** (Max von Weinzierl/w Krenn) Raimundtheater 23 October

1898 **Moderne Weiber** (Kuhn, Johann Brandl/w Krenn) Carltheater 10 April

1898 **Der schöne Rigo** (Ziehrer/w Krenn) Venedig in Wien 24 May

1899 **Ein durchgegangenes Mädel** (*A Runaway Girl*) German version w Krenn (Theater an der Wien)

1899 **Die Landstreicher** (Ziehrer/w Krenn) Venedig in Wien 29 July

1899 **Der kleine Corporal** (*The Little Trooper*) German version w Golz brothers (Carltheater)

1900 **Die Schöne von New-York** (*The Belle of New York*) German version w Krenn (Venedig in Wien)

1901 **Die verkehrte Welt** (*Le Royaume des femmes*) (Kappeller/ad w Krenn) Danzers Orpheum 22 February

1901 **Die drei Wünsche** (Ziehrer/w Krenn) Carltheater 9 March

1901 **Die Reise nach Cuba** (Ivan Caryll/w Krenn) Venedig in Wien 3 August

1901 **Das Brautpaar vor Gericht** (*Trial By Jury*) German version (Danzers Orpheum)

1901 **Das Frauenduell** (Edmund Eysler/w Louis Gundlach) 1 act Danzers Orpheum 23 November

1901 **Das Gastmahl des Lucullus** (Eysler/w A Paulus) 1 act Danzers Orpheum 23 November

1902 **Eine feine Nummer** Austrian version w Krenn (Venedig in Wien)

1902 **Der kleine Günstling** (*Katalin*) German version (Carltheater)

1902 **Der Laufbursche** (*The Messenger Boy*) German version w Krenn (Danzers Orpheum)

1902 **Der Fremdenführer** (Ziehrer/w Krenn) Theater an der Wien 11 October

1902 **Das Cirkusmädel** (*The Circus Girl*) German version w Krenn (Danzers Orpheum)

1903 **Frühlingsluft** (Josef Strauss arr Ernst Reiterer/w Julius Wilhelm) Venedig in Wien 9 May

1904 **Das Veilchenmädel** (Josef Hellmesberger/w Krenn) Carltheater 27 February

1904 **Die Eisjungfrau** (*The Girl from Up There*) German version w Wilhelm, M Band and add mus by Hellmesberger (Venedig in Wien)

1904 **Jung Heidelberg** (Millöcker arr Reiterer/w Krenn) Venedig in Wien 9 July

1904 **Ein nasses Abenteuer** (Roth/w Krenn) Deutsches Volkstheater 27 August

1904 **'s Zuckergoscherl** (J Wolffsgruber/w Alfred Schönfeld, August Neidhart) Carltheater 15 October

1904 **Wien bei Nacht** (Hellmesberger/w Wilhelm) 1 act Danzers Orpheum 28 October

1905 **Der Schnurrbart** (*A bajusz*) German version w Leo Stein (Carltheater)

1905 **Die Ringstrassenprinzessin** (*Messalinette*) German lyrics (Danzers Orpheum)

1905 **Fesche Geister** (Ziehrer/w Krenn) Venedig in Wien 7 July

1905 **Frauenherz** (Josef Strauss ad Reiterer) Danzers Orpheum 29 September

1905 **Die Schützenliesel** (Eysler/w Stein) Carltheater 7 October

1905 **Ausser Rand und Band** (Paul Lincke/w Antony) 1 act Danzers Orpheum 4 November

1905 **Auf's in Orpheum** Viennese version (Danzers Orpheum)

1906 **Die drei Engel** (Hellmesberger/w Antony) Venedig in Wien 4 May

1906 **Kunstlerblüt** (Eysler/w Leo Stein) Carltheater 20 October

1906 **Tausend und Eine Nacht** (Johann Strauss arr Reiterer/w Stein) Venedig in Wien June

1906 **Das Scheckbuch des Teufels** (*Le Carnet du Diable*) German version w Antony and add mus Max R Steiner (Danzers Orpheum)

1906 **Über'm grossen Teich** (*Across the Big Pond*) Viennese version w Antony w music by Franz Ziegler (Theater an der Wien)

1907 **Der lustige Witwer** Austrian version w Antony (Danzers Orpheum)

1907 **Monte Carlo** (Ludwig Roman Ehmel/w Antony) Neues Operetten-Theater, Leipzig 7 April

1907 **Die kleine Prinzessin** (Bela von Ujj/w Antony) Venedig in Wien 5 May

1907 **Eine Sensation** (von Ujj/w Antony) 3 scenes Danzers Orpheum 20 December

1907 **Miss Hook von Holland** (*Miss Hook of Holland*) German version (Venedig in Wien)

1907 **Weiberlaunen** (*Leányka*) German version w Leo Stein (Frankfurt-am-Main)

1908 **Das Glücksschweinchen** (Eysler/w Stein) Venedig in Wien 26 June

1908 **Johann der zweite** (Eysler/w Stein) Carltheater 3 October

1909 **Der Ehemannerzug** (Kappeller/w Alexander Engel) Nuremburg

1909 **Der Sultan** (*A Szultan*) German version (Johann Strauss-Theater)

1909 **Tanzhusaren** (*A Táncos huszárok*) German version (Venedig in Wien)

1909 **Drei Stunden Leben** (von Ujj/w Antony) 1 act Apollotheater 1 November

1909 **Miss Gibbs** (*Our Miss Gibbs*) German version w Krenn, Max Baer (Ronacher) 12 November

1910 **Hupf mein Mädel** (Viktor Holländer/w Krenn) Ronacher 13 August

1910 **Lord Piccolo** (Henrik Berény/w Rudolf Schanzer) Johann Strauss-Theater 1 September

1910 **Die verhexte Wien(erstadt)** (*The New Aladdin*) German version w Antony (Ronacher)

1910 **Der Dumme hat's Glück** (von Ujj/w Krenn) Raimundtheater 10 September

1910 **Chantecler** (von Ujj/w Krenn) Ronacher 25 October

1911 **In fünfzig Jahren** (arr Ziehrer/w Krenn) Wiener Stadttheater 7 January

1911 **Die romantische Frau** (Carl Weinberger/w Béla Jenbach) Johann Strauss-Theater 17 March

1911 **Vielliebchen** (Ludwig Engländer/w Rudolf Österreicher) Venedig in Wien 5 May

1911 **Das geborgte Schloss** (Hermann Dostal/w György Verő) Stadttheater, Leipzig 15 May

1911 **Der Frauenfresser** (Eysler/w Stein) Wiener Bürgertheater 23 December

1912 **Autoliebchen** Viennese adaptation (Apollotheater)

1912 **Freddy und Teddy** (Digby-Latouche/H L Melbourne ad w Neidhart) Theater am Nollendorfplatz, Berlin 23 December

1913 **Mein Mäderl** (Berény/w Eugen Burg, Schanzer) Raimundtheater 21 January

1913 **Die verbotene Stadt** (Bruno Granichstädten/w Granichstädten) Montis Operetten-Theater, Berlin 23 December

1914 **Teresita** (Emile Waldteufel arr von Ujj) Venedig in Wien 27 June

1914 **Komm, deutscher Bruder** (Eysler, Franz Lehár/w Neidhart) Raimundtheater 4 October

1914 **Frühling am Rhein** (Eysler/w Fritz Löhner-Beda, Oskar Fronz) Wiener Bürgertheater 10 October

1915 **Das Weltenbummler** (Richard Fall/w Löhner-Beda) Montis Operetten-Theater, Berlin 18 November

1915 **Die ledige Frau** (Karl Eibenschütz/w Neidhart) Landestheater, Linz 3 December

1917 **Liebessport** (Eibenschütz/w Neidhart) Theater am Gärtnerplatz, Munich 26 May

1921 **Der keusche Heinrich** (Hans Duval-Diamant/w Löhner-Beda) Lustspieltheater 29 March

1926 **Donauweibchen** (Egon Neumann/w Krenn ad Karl Farkas) Wiener Bürgertheater 22 May

LINDSAY, Howard [NELKE, Herman] (b Waterford, NY, 29 March 1888; d New York, 11 February 1968). Broadway director and producer and the author, at 25 years' distance, of two of the most enduring musical plays of their times.

At first an actor and stage manager, Lindsay directed several productions for Margaret Anglin's company and made his Broadway début as a director (he also played a part) at the helm of George S Kaufman and Marc Connelly's highly successful *Dulcy* in 1921. The following year he directed the revue *The 49ers*, in which he made what would be his only Broadway appearance as a performer in a musical piece. Other directing assignments followed, including the 1932 Fred Astaire musical *Gay Divorce*.

Lindsay's initial stage play, *Tommy* (w Bertrand Robinson), was produced in 1927, and his first significant success as an author came six years later with Dwight Deere Wiman and Tom Weatherly's production of his play *She Loves Me Not* (1933), a piece which took in two Arthur Schwartz/Edward Heyman songs. He directed each piece, but did not perform.

Hired to direct the Cole Porter musical *Anything Goes* the following year, Lindsay became emergency librettist when events prompted a major rewrite. He was paired on this job with Russel Crouse and, following the enormous success of *Anything Goes*, the two worked together as a play- and musical-writing partnership for a 25-year stretch which was highlighted by some exceptionally big successes. Amongst their plays the Pulitzer Prize-winning *State of the Union* (1945) and the extremely long-running *Life with Father* (1939) were the most memorable, whilst the Irving Berlin musical which had Ethel Merman demanding that one *Call Me Madam* and Rodgers and Hammerstein's Mary Martin vehicle *The Sound of Music* gave them two major musical theatre hits.

Lindsay also authored film scripts (*The Great Victor Herbert* etc), continued occasionally to direct – staging both *Red, Hot and Blue* and *Hooray for What?* of his own musical shows – and later produced several Broadway plays (w Crouse), notably the long-running *Arsenic and Old Lace*.

Lindsay and Crouse's 1942 play *Strip for Action* was turned into a musical of the same name (Jimmy McHugh/Harold Adamson/Paul Streger, Eli Blaser) which folded out of town in 1956.

1934 **Anything Goes** (Cole Porter/w Russel Crouse, Guy Bolton, P G Wodehouse) Alvin Theater 21 November

1936 **Red, Hot and Blue** (Porter/w Crouse) Alvin Theater 29 October

1937 **Hooray for What?** (Harold Arlen/E Y Harburg/w Crouse) Winter Garden Theater 1 December

1950 **Call Me Madam** (Irving Berlin/w Crouse) Imperial Theater 12 October

1956 **Happy Hunting** (Matt Dubey, Harold Karr/w Crouse) Majestic Theater 6 December

1959 **The Sound of Music** (Richard Rodgers/Oscar Hammerstein/w Crouse) Lunt-Fontanne Theater 16 November

1962 **Mr President** (Berlin/w Crouse) St James Theater 20 October

Biography: Skinner, C Otis: *Life with Lindsay and Crouse* (Houghton Miflin, Boston, 1976)

LINGARD, W[illiam] H[orace] [NEEDHAM, William Horace Thomas] (b London, 20 June 1837; d London, 12 January 1927). Buccaneering musical comedian who purveyed musical theatre to all corners of the English-speaking world for more than half a century.

Horace Lingard made his first successes in Britain as a music-hall performer, singing about what happens 'On the Beach at Brighton on a Summer's Day' in an act built around a series of impersonations and comic songs. In 1866 he visited America and there caused a sensation with his songs, notably the number 'Captain Jinks of the Horse Marines', and with what was claimed to be the first quick-change act ever seen in the country. He became hailed, in Odell's words, as 'the best comic singer ever introduced to New York audiences'. He played at New York's Theatre Comique in farce and burlesque and, supported by his wife, former music-hall dancer Alice Dunning (d 25 June 1897) and her sister, Mrs Harriet Dalziel, who worked under the name of Dickie Lingard, he took over the management of the house (27 June 1868) for a short period until it was burned down. He then took over its homonym in Boston. The Lingards toured for a number of years in and out of New York with programmes which included plays, burlesques and later short operettas featured alongside Horace's own stand-up performance. A tale is told of family rivalry in which Alice and Horace, each considering themselves the main attraction, came to hard words. To prove his point, Horace withdrew from the bill, leaving Alice to head it alone. When the receipts went down and his wager was apparently won, he came back.

Lingard worked both with Thomas and Blanche Whiffen (née Galton) and their family group, the earliest purveyors of Offenbach in English to American audiences, and with the Howard Pauls, and travelled his company as far afield as the south Pacific, appearing in Australia in 1875 billed as 'the world-renowned comedian' in *Our Boys*, *David Garrick*, *Married in Haste*, the melodrama *Dead to the World* and a comic opera called *I Ladroni*, allegedly of his own making. However, *I Ladroni* (Theatre Royal, Sydney 19 February 1876), which he had mounted in St Louis several years earlier, and which was allegedly musically compiled by Giuseppe Operti of *Black Crook* fame, bore a remarkably close resemblance both textually and musically to Burnand and Sullivan's early piece *The Contrabandista*.

In February 1879, hot on the heels of the first startling Broadway performances of *HMS Pinafore*, Lingard starred as John Wellington Wells in New York's first *The Sorcerer* and later the same year the Lingards sailed off again to New Zealand and Australia, playing *HMS Pinafore* (he as Joseph Porter, she as Josephine) and *The Sorcerer*. He was pursued legally, in a stranger-than-fiction saga of court appearances, featuring flights and probably faked bankruptcy, by J C Williamson (who had played at the Theatre Comique under Lingard's management) who had bought the Australasian rights to Gilbert and Sullivan's show. Balked by the courts, Lingard eventually had to give up, but he continued to play in his repertoire his own 'sequel' *The Wreck of the Pinafore*, which ultimately found its way briefly to the London stage. He also performed a number of French works (Frimousse to Alice's *Le Petit Duc* etc), British pieces (*Our Boys*, *Old Bachelors*, Gilbert's *The Happy Land*, H B Farnie's *Pluto*) and the inevitable *I Ladroni*.

After touring the rest of the Pacific circuit – Japan, China, Hong Kong – the Lingards finally returned to Britain where Horace mounted a special Gaiety Theatre matinée to promote his wife as a star, but metropolitan success did not come their way and it was ultimately the provinces where Lingard found himself a very comfortable niche. In collaboration with cellist, actor and producer Auguste van Biene, he produced and subsequently toured endlessly with English versions of such reputable French pieces as *Le Droit d'aînesse* (*Falka*, Pelican), *Les Voltigeurs de la 32ème* (*The Old Guard*, Polydore Poupart) and *Pepita* (*La Princesse des Canaries*, Inigo). In a rare venture into the West End he tried *Pepita* at Toole's Theatre in 1888 and was gratified with a run of 102 performances before going back on the road. He also played one London week of Messager's *La Fauvette du Temple* (1891) and produced a revival of Offenbach's *Les Brigands*. For this revival he used a youthful translation by W S Gilbert, published by Boosey and Hawkes, and once again found himself in court, on the receiving end of a writ from the author who had no wish to see his juvenilia thus displayed (nor, perhaps, for its influence on *The Pirates of Penzance* and *The Mountebanks* in particular to be noticed). For once, this time, Lingard was on the right end of the law.

Lingard also co-wrote and produced a burlesque of his touring success *Falka* under the title *Brother Pelican* (1894) and mounted a new and short-lived show called *The Chorus Girl* as part of his repertoire in 1897 (Caractacus Tire). In 1899, now a widower, he was still to be found on the road, starring in the chief comic part of a musical called *An American Heiress*. He trouped his shows endlessly and, in his eighties, allowed himself to drop from star comic rôles to smaller parts, whilst also taking time off to direct amateur productions of the works which he had performed in his younger days. He died in his ninetieth year.

The two daughters of Horace and Alice Lingard both married music. Lulu became Lulu Wicks, and Nelly became the wife of Arthur Godfrey, composer of the successful *Little Miss Nobody* (1898) and nephew to the more famous bandsman and arranger Dan Godfrey.

1872 **I Ladroni** (Giuseppe Operti) 1 act De Bar's Opera House, St Louis 30 December

1880 **The Wreck of the Pinafore** (Luscombe Searelle) Princess's Theatre, Dunedin, New Zealand 29 November

1894 **Brother Pelican** (Operti, Ernest Allen, William C Levey/w Alfred Rae) Theatre Royal, Belfast 8 February

LINK, Antonie (b Budapest, 5 February 1853; d Vienna, June 1931). Star of some of the earliest Viennese Operetten who crammed a vast amount into a career which ended in her mid-twenties.

Having at first played children's rôles at the Bürgertheater and then sung in the chorus at the Vienna Hofoper, the statuesque and poised teenage mezzo-soprano became a member of the company at the Carltheater where, at the age of 23 (or 19, if some reports of her birth-date are to be believed), she created the title-rôle in *Fatinitza* (1876) and, subsequently, those of Johann Strauss's *Prinz Methusalem* (1877) and, her greatest rôle, Suppé's *Boccaccio* (1879).

Link also originated and/or played rôles in such early Viennese Operetten as Suppé's short-lived *Die Frau Meisterin* (Pierre), Conradin's *Flodoardo Wuprahall* (Donna Fiamina) and Zaytz's favourite *Mannschaft an Bord* (Grobecker's rôle of Max), appeared again in travesty as Frinke in *Flotte Bursche*, Pygmalion in *Die schöne Galathee*, as the midshipman Henrik in *Les Cent Vierges* (1873, with a song specially added for her in what was officially her début), Pedro in *Giroflé-Girofla* and the heroine's bridegroom Bavolet in *Schönroschen* (*La Jolie Parfumeuse*), and in skirts as Manon in *Die schöne Bourbonnaise*, as the slavegirl Nakahira in the spectacular *Reise um die Erde in 80 Tagen*, and opposite manager Franz Jauner as Constanze Mozart in a Singspiel called *Wolfgang und Constance*.

She was also Vienna's first and blessedly young Madame Lange in *La Fille de Madame Angot* (1873), the first German-language *Petit Duc* in Lecocq's opérette, the first Boulangère of Offenbach's *Margot die reiche Bäckerin* (1877) and the Rose Friquet of the Viennese *Les Dragons de Villars*. She visited the Theater an der Wien to star in Offenbach's *Der Jahrmarkt von St Laurent* (1877, Bamboche) and Pest to play at the German-language theatre in *Die Prinzessin von Trapezunt* (1875), and she also appeared in such lighter operatic rôles as Cherubino and Ännchen in *Der Freischütz*. At the age of 26 (surely not 22?), after playing just four long-remembered weeks in her final rôle as *Boccaccio*, she married and retired from the stage.

Antonie Link was introduced as a character in Willy Forst's film *Operette* where she was impersonated by Trude Marlen.

Her sister **Sophie LINK** (b Budapest, 1860; d New York, 1 October 1900) played some operettic rôles in Hamburg and Vienna in the 1880s, appearing as Princess Blanche de Coligny in *Capitän Fracassa* at the Theater an der Wien, and Josephine in *Josephine vendue par ses soeurs* at the Carltheater before moving on to an operatic career. Her brother, comedian **Adolf LINK** (b Pest, 15 September 1851; d New York, 24 September 1933), was a former child actor who played in Olmütz, Budapest and Hamburg and was for a while a small-part player at the Theater an der Wien (Nux in *Königin Indigo*, Tabellion in *Les Cloches de Corneville*, Curtius in *Der Jahrmarkt von St Laurent*, Lamotte in *Das verwunschene Schloss*, Baldrian in *Der letzte Mohikaner*, Biscontin in *Madame Favart*) and Ronachers Operetten-Theater (Simplicius in *Der Graf von Gleichen*, Stutzerl in *Kapitän Ahlstrom*, Zwickel in *Die weiblichen Jäger* etc). He later introduced and performed larger rôles in German-language Operette in America (Sebastiani in *Der lustige Krieg*, Sir Andrew in *Donna Juanita*, Fritellini in *La Mascotte*, Wenzel in *Der Chevalier von San Marco*, Prutschesko in *Apajune*, Anatol in *Hundert Jungfrauen*, Capitän Nicol w Geistinger, Taboreau in *Trompette*, *Der Vagabund* etc) before later moving into the English-speaking theatre. As late as 1923 he appeared in *Peaches* (Baron von Blowitz) in Philadelphia.

LINNIT & DUNFEE LTD

Originally a London talent agency headed by Jack Dunfee and S E Linnit, a former general manager to Edgar

Wallace, the firm began producing plays in 1936 with regular success. They made their first venture into the musical field with the small-scale *Cage Me a Peacock* (1948) but, in spite of mounting a couple of revue productions, did not again produce a musical until they picked up Julian Slade's *Salad Days* from the Bristol Repertory Company and brought it to the Vaudeville Theatre for what was to be the longest run of any musical piece up to that date.

Thereafter they produced Slade's further works (*Free as Air, Follow That Girl, Hooray for Daisy, Vanity Fair*) as well as the *Little Women* musical, *A Girl Called Jo*, written by the authors of their successful revue *Intimacy at 8.30*. Two Broadway imports, *Candide* and *High Spirits* (1964) were failures, and after the flop of another repertory theatre show, *The Matchgirls* (1966), the firm returned exclusively to producing plays.

LIONEL AND CLARISSA Comic opera by Issac Bickerstaff. Music by Charles Dibdin. Theatre Royal, Covent Garden, 28 February 1768.

One of the most enduring comic operas of its time, *Lionel and Clarissa* brought together a regular set of comic-opera characters in a lively, if regular comic opera-plot. Clarissa (Miss Macklin) is the daughter of Sir John Flowerdale (Mr Gibson), Lionel (George Mattocks) is the orphaned son of a friend brought up in Sir John's care. Before they can be happily paired off, Clarissa has to escape from a more advantageous match with the unwanted Lord Jessamy (Mr Dyer). The son of the boisterously old-English, wench-snatching Colonel Oldboy (Ned Shuter) and his affected, underwed Lady Mary, Jessamy has been raised by her brother as a powdered and painted exquisite of whom his own father is in horror. British salt-of-the-earth outdoes Frenchified pansy at every turn, and gets the girl. A subplot dealt with Oldboy's encouragement of the jaunty Frank Harman (Mr Mahoon) to elope with his girl, unaware that the girl in question is his own daughter, Diana (Mrs Baker).

Bickerstaff's merrily bristling script, which gave more than three-quarters of its scenes to the comical folk and only occasional moments to the amorous mopings of the title-characters, was illustrated with 24 musical numbers, mostly solos, and mostly original music from the pen of Dibdin.

An indifferent success on its ill-prepared first production, when it was played but 11 times in its first run, the show was seen at the Theatre Royal, Drury Lane, two seasons later, under the new title of *The School for Fathers* (8 February 1770). But if its initial London career was scarcely brilliant, the piece – in each of its versions – went the rounds of the world's English-speaking stages with great success and it was revived at Drury Lane in 1807 (12 December) and at several other houses in the early 1800s. A version of *Lionel and Clarissa* (mus arr Alfred Reynolds) was given a modern revival at the Lyric Theatre, Hammersmith (28 October 1925, 171 performances), during the management of Nigel Playfair, as one of his ballad-opera attempts to follow up the theatre's major success with a reorganized version of *The Beggar's Opera*.

USA: Southwark Theater, Philadelphia *A School for Fathers* 14 December 1772; New York 21 February 1794

LIORAT, Armand [DÉGAS, Georges] (b Sceaux, 10 January 1837; d Paris, 1898).

For more than 30 years both a civic accountant and a librettist and lyricist for the Parisian opérette stage, Liorat had a fair share of success, notably in his collaborations with the composer Varney, with whom he worked on *L'Amour mouillé*, *La Falote*, *Les Petites Brébis* and *La Fille de Fanchon la vielleuse*, all of which were also played through Europe and, occasionally, further afield after their Parisian successes. Others of his works which travelled beyond their original productions included Lecocq's *Kosiki*, Grisart's *Les Poupées de l'Infante* and *Le Petit Bois* (played in Hungary as *A kisasszony babui* and *A farkas meg a bárány* respectively), Lacôme's *Ma mie Rosette*, which was seen on the London stage and became a long-term favourite in Australia, and, most successfully of all, Francis Chassaigne's Hungarian tale of *Les Noces improvisées* which, reworked as *Nadgy*, found particular success in America.

Outside the operettic field, Liorat collaborated with Pierre Decourcelle on the libretto for d'Erlanger's 1897 opera *Inès Mendo* and contributed to the drama *La Belle aux cheveux d'or* (1882) on the one hand, and joined Clairville in writing revue for the Théâtre de l'Athénée (*De bric et de broc*, *Boum! Voilà!*, 1876) on the other.

1869 **Un mariage au gros sel** (Frédéric Barbier) 1 act Eldorado 10 July
1870 **Un souper chez Mlle Contat** (Barbier) 1 act Eldorado 5 February
1871 **Une entrevue** (Charles Lecorbeiller) 1 act Eldorado 1 October
1871 **Un drame à Nogent** (Paul Wachs) 1 act Alcazar 9 October
1872 **Les Brioches du Doge** (F Demarquette/w William Busnach) 1 act Folies-Bergère 16 March
1872 **Le Valet de chambre de Madame** (Olivier Métra) 1 act Folies-Bergère November
1872 **La Belle Kalitcha** (Wachs) 1 act Folies-Bergère December
1873 **La Belle Indiénne** (Wachs) 1 act Alcazar
1873 **La Rosière d'ici** (Léon Roques) Théâtre des Bouffes-Parisiens 27 March
1873 **Mariée depuis midi** (Georges Jacobi/w Busnach) 1 act Marseille 20 August, Théâtre des Bouffes-Parisiens 6 March 1874
1873 **La Leçon d'amour** (Wachs) 1 act Théâtre des Bouffes-Parisiens 14 September
1873 **La Liqueur d'or** (Laurent de Rillé/w Busnach) Théâtre des Menus-Plaisirs 11 December
1874 **Une pleine eau à Chatou** (Wachs) 1 act Folies-Bergère 21 November
1876 **Kosiki** (Lecocq/w Busnach) Théâtre de la Renaissance 18 October
1878 **Le Pont d'Avignon** (Charles Grisart) Théâtre des Bouffes-Parisiens 3 September
1879 **Le Petit Abbé** (Grisart/w Henri Bocage) 1 act Théâtre du Vaudeville 9 October
1881 **Les Poupées de l'Infante** (Grisart/w Bocage) Théâtre des Folies-Dramatiques 9 April
1883 **Le Pot au lait** (Wachs/w Busnach) 1 act Palais-Royal 1 May
1886 **Les Noces improvisées** (Francis Chassaigne/w Albert Fonteny) Théâtre des Bouffes-Parisiens 13 February
1887 **L'Amour mouillé** (Louis Varney/w Jules Prével) Théâtre des Nouveautés 25 January
1888 **Le Bossu** (Grisart/w Bocage) Théâtre de la Gaîté 19 March
1889 **La Vénus d'Arles** (Varney/w Paul Ferrier) Théâtre des Nouveautés 30 January

1890 **Ma mie Rosette** (Paul Lacôme/w Prével) Théâtre des Folies-Dramatiques 4 February
1890 **La Fille de l'air** (Lacôme/Cogniard brothers ad w Hippolyte Raymond) Théâtre des Folies-Dramatiques 20 June
1891 **La Fille de Fanchon la vielleuse** (Varney/Busnach, Fonteny) Théâtre des Folies-Dramatiques 3 November
1893 **Le Cadeau de noces** (Lacôme/w Fernand Hue, Stop [ie L Morel-Retz]) Théâtre des Bouffes-Parisiens 20 January
1893 **Le Petit Bois** (Grisart) 1 act Théâtre des Bouffes-Parisiens 7 March
1894 **La Fille de Paillasse** (Varney/w Louis Leloir) Théâtre des Folies-Dramatiques 20 April
1895 **Les Petites Brébis** (Varney) Théâtre Cluny 5 June
1896 **La Falote** (Varney/w Maurice Ordonneau) Théâtre des Folies-Dramatiques 17 April
1896 **Le Lézard** (Frédéric Toulmouche) 1 act Scala 29 August
1898 **Les Quatre Filles d'Aymon** (Lacôme, Victor Roger/w Fonteny) Théâtre des Folies-Dramatiques 20 September

THE LISBON STORY Play with music in 2 acts by Harold Purcell. Music by Harry Parr Davies. London Hippodrome, 17 June 1943.

George Black's wartime production of *The Lisbon Story* was a curious concoction of drama, sentiment and patriotism on the one hand and song and dance on the other – rather like a hybrid of an Ivor Novello romantic musical and a purposeful film melodrama. Harold Purcell's book was filmic in style, following episodically the career of Parisian prima donna Gabrielle Girard (Patricia Burke) who agrees to the insistent offers of Nazi cultural boss von Schriner (Albert Lieven) to return to the Paris stage only so that she can help a French scientist to escape with a vital wartime secret. On opening night, Gabrielle takes the place of the man's daughter in the show's ballet, a depiction of the rape of Innocence by Evil, whilst the pair escape, but when she steps forward to underline the ballet's message in words von Schriner shoots her. As she dies, the Allied bombs pound onto Paris and the cast joins in the Marseillaise.

Harry Parr Davies (in spite of being currently in the Life Guards) supplied a score in which, in good Novello style, the numbers were given to the prima donna and to some incidental vocalists, but not to the hero or the villain. Miss Burke had a successful waltz, 'Someday We Shall Meet Again', with an infallible wartime lyric, a fruit-seller sang the tenor 'We Must Never Say Goodbye' and a café singer rendered 'Music at Midnight'. However, *The Lisbon Story*'s most successful song was a late addition. Purcell's film-style writing made for some awkward scene-changes and it was decided that one was serious enough to require the front cloth to be dropped and the wait to be covered by a song. The Vincent Tildesley Mastersingers, who acted as backing vocalists, were given a whistling song called 'Pedro the Fisherman' which they harmonized effectively to cover the bumps and bashes of the scene change. 'Pedro' became one of the most popular songs of the war years. The show was also heavily equipped with dance, and the Polish dance stars Alicia Halama and Czeslaw Konarski were featured both in the ballet-within-the-opérette and in a long set-piece Portuguese festival routine in which Wendy Toye deftly mixed balletic and music-theatre dance to produce one of the highlights of the show.

Lisbon Story evoked some startled responses ('The Heroine Is Shot At the End ... at the Hippodrome of all

Plate 161. *The Vincent Tildesley Mastersingers sing the front-cloth hit of* **The Lisbon Story** *– 'Pedro, the Fisherman'.*

places!'). It was clearly not what a musical show should be. It was serious. There was hardly any comedy. And The Heroine Got Shot at the End. But the public didn't mind. *The Lisbon Story* ran through 492 performances before it was chased from town by some indignant German bombs. Three months later it returned, with Viennese soprano Maria Elsner and Karel Stepanek replacing the stars and Raymond Newell singing 'Pedro' as a baritone solo, but it failed to take off a second time and ended its run after 54 further performances. It went promptly on the road with Jessica James starring and in 1946 it was filmed.

British National determined to make *The Lisbon Story* an all-star affair and, if they failed after much trying to persuade the busy Sadler's Wells Ballet to take part, they ended up with a fair plateau including vocalists Richard Tauber, Harry Welchman and Lorely Dyer and violinist Stéphane Grappelly featured alongside Miss Burke, the Polish dance stars and Walter Rilla as the villain.

Film: British National 1946

LISCHEN ET FRITZCHEN Saynète (conversation alsacienne) in 1 act by Paul Boisselot (and Charles Nuitter?). Music by Jacques Offenbach. Théâtre du Kursaal, Bad Ems, 21 July 1863.

Lischen and Fritzchen was a two-handed 'conversation' for a pair of young folk who have the same Alsatian accent. Fritzchen (Jean-Paul) has been sacked because his 'improper' French has led him to mistake the word 'pierre' for 'bière' and commit an embarrassing error in front of his master's sweetheart. Lischen (Zulma Bouffar) is having a problem making ends meet selling brooms (probably because she pronounces 'balais' as 'palais'), and is thinking of giving up and going home. They meet on the road, and are rather taken with each other, only to discover that they have the same surname ... they are brother and sister! But the disappointed Fritzchen can read (which Lischen cannot), and he reads a letter which the girl has kept. It is from her mother, admitting that her so-called daughter is really the child of her unfortunate sister. And so Lischen and Fritzchen can head off towards Alsace and a happy un-brotherly-and-sisterly ending, arm in arm.

The musical part of the little piece consists of five portions, entry songs for Fritzchen ('Me chasser') and Lischen ('P'tits balais'), the girl's tale of the Rat de Ville and the Rat de Campagne, a duo finale, and, most effectively, the delightful duo in which the two discover their similar origins ('Je suis alsacien, je suis alsacienne').

First produced at Ems, where Offenbach spent many a holiday and where, from 1862, a number of his short pieces were given their first performance, the little saynète was a great success and it was taken into the repertoire of Offenbach's Théâtre des Bouffes-Parisiennes the following season with Désiré and Mlle Bouffar playing the two heavily accented sweethearts. Within months it was seen in Vienna (ad Poly Henrion) and in Berlin, and later in Budapest, but it was several years more before, with the slowly growing vogue for Offenbach's works in England and America, the piece was given its first performances there.

America was given *Lischen et Fritzchen* in French by Lucille Tostée and Dardignac in H L Bateman's repertoire (Academy of Music), and by Mlle Irma with James Fisk's company, whilst Kelly and Leon's minstrels performed their English adaptation (with Leon as Lischen) and the little English company of the Galton sisters and Thomas Whiffen purveyed a more normally cast vernacular version. Kelly and Leon later played their unisex *Lischen and Fritzchen* in Australia, half a dozen years after it had been seen there for the first time, played at Sydney's Royal Victoria Theatre for a handful of nights by Miranda Hirst and David Miranda who was billed as being 'from the Theatre Royal, Covent Garden'.

In London, which – like New York – had first been given the piece in French by a visiting company, one English version, *A Happy Result*, was given at the Gallery of Illustration in 1865, 1868 and again in 1869, a second, also in 1869 (ad W Guernsey, 9 August), at the newly opened Gaiety Theatre, and a third at Covent Garden, performed by Julia Mathews and Wilford Morgan as a forepiece to the Christmas pantomime, prior to intermittent performances around Britain over the following years.

Lischen et Fritzchen and its various national variants proved long popular as a part of multiple bills or as a benefit item, and the little piece still wins occasional performances today.

France: Théâtre des Bouffes-Parisiens 5 January 1864; Austria: Carltheater *Französiche Schwaben* 16 April 1864; Germany: Friedrich-Wilhelmstädtisches Theater 23 June 1864; UK: St James's Theatre (Fr) 2 June 1868, Gallery of Illustration *A Happy Result* 3 November 1865; Hungary: Budai Színkör *Liesl und Fritzl, oder Die Französichen Schwaben* 21 June 1866; USA: Academy of Music (Fr) 25 June 1868, Williamsburgh 8 October 1868 (Eng); Australia: Royal Victoria Theatre, Sydney, 9 March 1872

Recording: complete (Bourg)

LISTEN LESTER Musical comedy in 2 acts by Harry L Cort and George E Stoddard. Music by Harold Orlob. Knickerbocker Theater, New York, 23 December 1918.

Plate 162.

The comedian of the title (Hansford Wilson) and his pal (Fred Heider) gallivant lightheartedly around 'the Ritz Hotel, Palm Beach' attempting to get back some incriminating letters from Miss Arbutus Quilty (Gertrude Vanderbilt), warningly described on the theatre programme as 'a live one'. The juvenile songs and dances in Orlob's ultra-light score ('Waiting', 'For You – Just You' and the foxtrot 'Two is Company') featured the young Clifton Webb and Ada Mae Weeks, The Four Entertainers provided the harmony and Eddie Garr and Heider got the jolliest song of the evening in 'Who Was the Last Girl You Called By Her First Name?'

John Cort's cast played 272 performances of the featherweight comedy and frequent dance routines of *Listen Lester* at the Knickerbocker Theater in the 1918–19 season, the show toured in three companies in the following one, and encouraged the Corts to continue with a series of similar musical comedies (one, *Jim Jam Jems*, was temporarily called *Hello, Lester!* to emphasize a non-existent connection), none of which found anything like an equivalent success.

Listen Lester's announced C B Cochran production in London did not come off, but the show was given a mounting in Australia, under the J C Williamson Ltd banner, with a cast headed by Charles Norman, Renie Riano, Sydney Burchall and Jack and Sylvia Kellaway. The Sydney press sniffed that although it was 'not entirely dreary' and had 'some pleasant dancing' it also had 'hardly any plot ... and is a traditional mélange of "wisecracks", brightly dressed chorus girls, miscellaneous dancing and a pair of lovers'. Williamsons did not bother to take it on to Melbourne.

Australia: Criterion Theatre, Sydney 10 February 1934

LISTEN TO THE WIND   Musical play in 2 acts taken from the book by Angela Ainley Jeans. Music by Vivian Ellis. Oxford Playhouse, 15 December 1954; Arts Theatre, London, 16 December 1955.

A superior children's musical, in the best British tradition, *Listen to the Wind* was based on a pretty nursery tale which had a nasty butler conniving with gipsies to whisk three children away from their home. The children get help from the winds and they escape the baddies through a series of adventures with moonbeam, sunshine, thundercloud and a sea witch called Miranda before returning home in time for tea. Ellis decorated the tale with a suitable score which included 'The Bread and Butter Song', 'Listen to the Wind', 'Whistle Down the Chimney' and the traditional Suffolk 'Timothy's Under the Table'.

The Oxford production included several to-be-well-known names in its credits: director Peter Hall, designer Disley Jones, musical director Raymond Leppard, and amongst the cast Ronald (later to be Ronnie) Barker, Julia Smith (godmother to TV's *EastEnders*), Derek Francis, Vivienne Martin and Sylvia Coleridge. The following year Hall, appointed director of the Arts Theatre, brought *Listen to the Wind* to London for a season. This time the cast included Clive Revill as the butler, Roderick Cook (Gale Bird), Miriam Karlin (Miranda) and Barker. The changing taste in children's entertainment meant that *Listen to the Wind*'s life was not as long as it might have been and the show is perhaps best known today by record collectors – its 45 EP recording being (only just) the rarest commercially issued British show disc in existence.

Recording: studio cast selection (EP) (World Records)

LITOLFF, Henry Charles (b London, 6 February 1818; d Bois-Colombes, 6 August 1891).

Best known as a pianist and conductor, Litolff also composed overtures for the dramatic theatre and wrote several pieces for the opera and opérette stage. If his first attempt at a Parisian opérette, *La Boîte à Pandore*, was a failure, his second, a musical-comedy version of the medieval tale of *Heloïse et Abélard*, found a much happier outcome (both for Abélard and the composer), playing a good first run, being subsequently revived and also performed outside France. Litolff subsequently composed the music for the féerie *La Belle au bois dormant* at the Châtelet, which had previously mounted his 'symphonie dramatique' *Les Guelfes* (18 February 1872), and attempted several other lighter musical stage pieces, one of which, *L'Escadron volant de la reine*, was played at the Opéra-Comique.

He later composed the score for the opera *Les Templiers*, produced in Brussels in 1886, and music for other lyric-dramatic pieces.

1866 **Le Chevalier Nahal** (Édouard Plouvier) 1 act Baden-Baden 10 August
1871 **La Boîte à Pandore** (Théodore Barrière) Théâtre de Folies-Dramatiques 17 October
1872 **Heloïse et Abélard** (Clairville, William Busnach) Théâtre des Folies-Dramatiques 19 October
1874 **La Belle au bois dormant** (Busnach, Clairville) Théâtre du Châtelet 4 April
1874 **La Fiancée du roi de Garbe** (Adolphe d'Ennery, Henri Chabrillat) Théâtre des Folies-Dramatiques 29 October
1876 **La Mandragore** (Jules Brésil) Fantaisies-Parisiennes, Brussels 29 January

Plate 163. **The Little Café:** *Even when the book-based musical hit Broadway, there still had to be a line of leggy lassies to troop across the stage between the bits of plot.*

1888 L'Escadron volant de la reine (d'Ennery, Brésil) Opéra-Comique 14 December

THE LITTLE CAFÉ Musical comedy in 3 acts by C M S McLellan based on Tristan Bernard's play *Le Petit Café*. Music by Ivan Caryll. New Amsterdam Theater, New York, 10 November 1913.

Tristan Bernard's play, one of the popular playwright's best, had a memorable Parisian success when it was produced at the Palais-Royal (12 October 1911) with the comedian Le Gallo in its starring rôle and, in the era where French-language comedies were considered the most effective starting point for English-language libretti, it was a natural choice for musicalization. Composer Ivan Caryll, who had long shared his time between England and France before settling in America, had become something of a specialist in this area. He had had notable successes with adaptations of *Madame Sans-Gêne* (*The Duchess of Dantzic*), *Coquin de Printemps* (*The Spring Chicken*), *Le Prince Consort* (*S.A.R.*), *Le Satyre* (*The Pink Lady*) and *La Grimpette* (*Oh! Oh! Delphine*), and he was quick to snap up this latest piece for the same purposes. *The Little Café*, produced, like the last two named musicals, by Broadway's Klaw and Erlanger, gave him yet another hit.

The story centred on the little waiter Albert Loriflan (John E Young) who inherits a whole heap of money but who is unable to hand in his notice because of a very strict contract with his employer (Harold Vizard). And so, whilst he serves in the petit café by day, Albert leads a lively and extravagant life at night, getting into the clutches of not one but two colourful women and also of the crooked Bigredon (Tom Graves) before ending up safely in the arms of the boss's daughter, Yvonne (Alma Francis). The 'other women' were played by Hazel Dawn, repeating her famous demi-mondaine portrayal of *The Pink Lady*, as Gaby Gaufrette, Queen of the Night Restaurants, and English low comedienne Gracie Leigh as Katziolinka, an Hungarian singer.

Young had the jolly songs ('You Little Café, Good Day', 'They Found Me' and the well-plugged 'Serve the Caviar'

which returned as the piece's finale), Miss Francis the pretty ones ('I Wonder Whom I'll Marry', 'This Gay Paree'), and Miss Leigh the extravagantly comical as she chased after the little hero declaring 'I'm a Hunting Jaguar' or recommended Hungarian dancing instead of the clinch-and-crawl variety in 'You Call That Dancing?' The show's big number, however, was saved for Miss Dawn. She had scored a major hit with *The Pink Lady*'s famous waltz song, and here Caryll provided her with another, as near as was possible in style to the last one. Lightning did not strike again, and although 'Just Because it's You' was a charming piece it did not make the effect of the earlier number, perhaps by virtue of that very noticeable similarity.

The Little Café ran for 148 performances on Broadway before taking to the road but, unlike *The Pink Lady* and *Oh! Oh! Delphine*, it was not produced in London or in Continental Europe. The play, however, subsequently served as a libretto for further musical comedies both in Austria and in France. Ralph Benatzky's *Das kleine Café* was introduced under the management of Rolf Jahn at Vienna's Deutsches Volkstheater in 1934 with Max Hansen playing the waiter Franz, whilst librettist Jean Valmy, who had also readapted *Coquin de Printemps* as a musical, turned out a French piece produced as *Le Petit Café* at the Grand Theatre, Mulhouse (music: Guy Lafarge, Jack Ledru, 14 December 1980).

Le Petit Café also served as the basis for the musical film *The Playboy of Paris* (1930) in which Maurice Chevalier took the starring rôle.

THE LITTLE CHERUB Musical play in 3 acts by Owen Hall. Lyrics by Adrian Ross. Additional lyrics by George Grossmith jr and W H Risque. Music by Ivan Caryll. Additional music by Frank E Tours and Paul Rubens. Prince of Wales Theatre, London, 13 January 1906.

The Little Cherub was one of the very few pieces which issued from the pen of librettist Hall that was less than wholly successful, and also the only one which reckoned itself to be based on someone else's work. The supposed source was Henri Meilhac's play *Décoré* (earlier the basis of the 1900 Viennese musical *Der Sechs-Uhr-Zug*) but, in fact, only one insignificant subplot resembled the French play in a story which had a straight-laced earl (Fred Kaye) blackmailed by his daughters (Zena Dare, Gabrielle Ray, Lily Elsie, Grace Pindar) into letting them be coached in their amateur dramatics by a real actress (Evie Greene) who ultimately hooks their Papa. Maurice Farkoa featured as a lecherous Rajah, Lennox Pawle was the asinine Algy who, in the *Décoré* piece of plot, saves a drowning man who isn't, and the comedian W H Berry made his first stage appearance as a valet.

Ivan Caryll's attractive music was often weighed down by some tiresome and repetitively suggestive lyrics as Miss Greene scored the evening's hit singing coyly of having had 'Experience', Farkoa praised the 'Supper Girl', as opposed to the less easy girls who only accept invitations at lunchtime, and Gabs Ray aimed for yet another rich husband on 'Cupid's Rifle Range'. Berry got some topical comedy in 'I Wasn't Engaged for That' and the servant characters amusingly described 'Couples' on a dance floor.

The Little Cherub started dubiously. It opened on election night when the cast was salutorily booed for trying to bring politics into their ad libs, and thereafter it refused to become the usual kind of George Edwardes success. The producer tried some cosmetics, then acted more strongly by putting star comic Willie Edouin into the rôle of the Earl and replacing the less-than-manly matinée idol Farkoa with staunch Louis Bradfield. Still it didn't go. So, after 114 performances Edwardes took the show off, commissioned a major rewrite and ordered a half-dozen new songs from specialist interpolators Frank Tours and Jerome Kern. A week after closing, the show re-opened with the title *The Girl on the Stage*. Four weeks later it closed definitively.

In spite of this indifferent showing, Charles Frohman took *The Little Cherub* to Broadway. He put Hattie Williams and British comic Jimmy Blakeley in the leads, went mostly back to the original book, flung in a handful more new songs by Kern and Jean Schwartz, and produced the piece for a limited Broadway run prior to touring. But *The Little Cherub* refused to be limited. It remained at the Criterion Theater for a profitable five months and 169 performances before taking to the road on a tour which was eventually directed back to Broadway for a three-week return engagement, then carried on to a fine life on the American touring circuits, a life which had long since ended in Britain. Thus, *The Little Cherub* became one of the very few British musicals to have done better on and beyond Broadway than in its country of origin.

USA: Criterion Theater 6 August 1906

LITTLE CHRISTOPHER COLUMBUS

Burlesque opera in 2 acts by George R Sims and Cecil Raleigh. Music by Ivan Caryll. Lyric Theatre, London, 10 October 1893.

One of the latter-day London burlesques, *Little Christopher Columbus* had, in fact, very little to do with its alleged subject or hero, even though its Little Christopher did go from Europe to America – albeit a thoroughly discovered America, and disguised as a girl. Sims and Raleigh's Christopher (May Yohé) was a naughty cabin boy in love with Genevieve (Maud Holland), the daughter of Chicago meat king Silas Block (J Furneaux Cook). Pursued, for a complexity of reasons, by a Spanish policeman (George Tate) and an Irish detective called O'Hoolegan (E J Lonnen), he escapes across the water to the World's Fair (cue for the interpolation of such variety acts as were required) by swapping clothes with the dancer Pepita (Eva Moore). The convolutions of the book existed merely to house the songs and dances and a goodly dose of comical scenes, and the show depended for its success on these elements. Ivan Caryll, writing his first full score for the London theatre after doing some hefty but successful botching on *La Cigale* and *Ma mie Rosette*, provided two lively comedy songs for Gaiety burlesque star Lonnen ('The Indiarubber Shoe', 'Rumpty Tumpty') and a plantation song 'Oh, Honey, My Honey' and siesta song ('Lazily, Drowsily') for his co-star, Miss Yohé. The last three numbers all became major song successes, in spite of the fact that the lady's solos had all to be written within the ten tones that comprised her vocal range.

Little Christopher Columbus started indifferently, in spite of the quick popularity of its best numbers, and the blame was firmly to be laid before the libretto. Lonnen's role was a patchwork of his earlier successes and both story and dialogue were banal. George Edwardes set his team to work to straighten things out, but when the show was taken off after 74 performances 'for renovations' the wording seemingly covered a tactful closure. However *Little Christopher Columbus* re-opened shortly after ar d from then never looked back. It had, admittedly, been much improved since opening, and the biggest single improvement was the addition of American dame-comedian John Sheridan (the creator of Widow O'Brien in *Fun on the Bristol*) as the Second Mrs Block. This rôle, originally intended as a parody of the current play hit *The Second Mrs Tanqueray*, but ultimately a two-line part played by Adelaide Nelson, was worked up into a low-comic tour de force by and for Sheridan who became the show's star in all but pecking order (May Yohé had 'bought' her rôle and status with a large investment in the production). Sheridan helped *Little Christopher Columbus* to a run of 421 performances in 14 months before it took to the road.

Edward Rice produced the show in America with Helen Bertram (succeeded by Bessie Bonehill) in the title-rôle, London's George Walton in Lonnen's rôle, Harry McDonough as Mrs Block and eight songs by Gustave Kerker added to the score. The entertainment also included a 'sensational fantastic danseuse', a Royal Marionette Dance, an eccentric step dance, duet items by the Twin Sisters Abbott, a representation as 'The Puritan Maiden' by Miss Clara Lane, a tramp act, a topical song act, tableaux vivants by the Kilyani Troupe and a slide show between the acts showing 'novel and beautiful illustrations ... of the World's Columbian exposition'. This now vastly over-stuffed variety musical proved a jolly evening's entertainment and ran for 264 performances at the Garden and later Palmer's Theater. The show was subsequently and regularly played in Australia as part of Sheridan's repertoire during his later career in that country. It was, however, played in a version which he advertised as 'funnier than a pantomime', which warned on its bills that the score was 'arranged by George Gardener' and which seemed as if it might have come quite a long way (in more ways than one) since its days at the Lyric Theatre.

Little Christopher Columbus, not unsurprisingly, did not find his way to the Paris stage, but his two hit songs did. 'Lazily, Drowsily' turned up in a revue at the Variétés, whilst 'O Honey, My Honey' was re-used as part of Caryll's contribution to *La Marraine de Charley* – the French version of *Charley's Aunt* which was decorated with several songs of his making.

Christopher Columbus had already been present on the stage for several decades, as the hero of a run of Italian operas, and more recently of a Spanish one (*Cristóbal Colón* by Francisco Vidal y Careta, 1892), and he had also served as the star of a handful of musical-theatre pieces in both Britain and America. In London, after being first seen at Covent Garden in Morton's 1792 *Christopher Columbus* and then, grotesquely, in Tom Taylor's 1853 pantomime at the Olympic, he had been the star of an earlier burlesque *Columbus, or the Original Pitch in a Merry Key* (Alfred Thompson, Gaiety Theatre 17 May 1869) where he was played by Nellie Farren in breeches. In New York he had previously appeared in John Brougham's burlesque *Columbus Reconstructed*, in the person of the very American (and distinctly swishy) Sgr (otherwise John) Perugini and then British baritone John Peachey, in an R A Barnet/Pfluger piece called *1492* mounted by E E Rice's Surprise Party, and, as played by Edmund Shaftesbury – to the Isabella of Pauline Markham – in the 1890 extravaganza *Christopher Columbus or the Discovery of America* (Windsor Theater, 18 August).

Vienna saw the discoverer of America in the spectacular *Die Entdeckung Amerikas* (Emil Korolanyi/Karl Alexander Raida) at the Jantschtheater in 1904 (23 December), Cassel took pity on *Armer Columbus* in a 1928 opéra-bouffe (Artur Zeininger/Erwin Dressel) whilst Darius Milhaud put out a serious *Christophe Colombe* in the same year and Werner Egk devoted a three-part opera (1933 radio, 1942 stage) to *Columbus*. More recently, a winning *Christopher Columbus*, a pastiche Offenbach opéra-bouffe (ad Don White) was staged in Britain, and the Columbus demi-millennium provoked a gaggle of theatrical pieces using the mariner as a subject (or an excuse), ranging from the Metropolitan Opera's *The Voyage* (Philip Glass/David Henry Hwang 12 October) to a *Christopher Columbus, or Business as Usual*, 'a musical about multiculturalism and American history as seen through the eyes of a fourth grader' performed in a Brooklyn park. It would have been fun to see George Sims find a rhyme for 'multiculturalism'.

USA: Garden Theater aka *Little Christopher* 15 October 1894; Australia: Lyceum Theatre, Sydney 4 November 1899

LITTLE JACK SHEPPARD Burlesque operatic melo-drama in 3 acts by Henry Pottinger Stephens and William Yardley. Music by Meyer Lutz. Additional music by Florian Pascal, Arthur Cecil, Hamilton Clarke, Henry J Leslie, Alfred Cellier and R Corney Grain. Gaiety Theatre, London, 26 December 1885.

Little Jack Sheppard was the first full-length burlesque produced at the Gaiety Theatre, the first of the famous series of so-called Gaiety 'new burlesques', which went round the world in what was the last long-term period of success for the burlesque genre in the English-language

theatre. Earlier in 1885 John Hollingshead, ill, overworked and near the end of his career, accepted and staged a burlesque by his friends Bill Yardley and 'Pot' Stephens called *The Vicar of Wide-awake-field* which used an original score by music-publisher-cum-composer 'Florian Pascal' rather than the usual paste-up of popular melodies. Thanks largely to Arthur Roberts's and Laura Linden's imitations of Irving and Ellen Terry in the central rôles, it did fairly well, and Hollingshead planned a second piece – full-length this time – to follow it. By the time *Little Jack Sheppard* went on, however, his successor George Edwardes, who would lead the 'new burlesque' to its triumphs, had in effect taken over the running of the theatre.

Little Jack Sheppard burlesqued Harrison Ainsworth's novel and the old tale of the thief Sheppard, who was here made into a lovable scamp as a rôle for the Gaiety's favourite 'boy', Nellie Farren. The well-known comic actor David James played Blueskin, and the thief-taker, Jonathan Wild, was made into a large comedy rôle for the popular singing comedian Fred Leslie, a newcomer to the Gaiety. In later years, Hollingshead and Edwardes both claimed to have brought Leslie to the Gaiety where he created with Miss Farren the most famous musico-theatrical partnership of the century. The fact that the artist was rehearsing and playing in another (flop) show till three weeks before *Jack Sheppard*'s opening seems to give credence to Edwardes, but it is perfectly possible that Hollingshead had approached him earlier and found him unavailable.

The libretto of the new show was rhyming, metred and often punning, in line with the old burlesque tradition. However, sometimes it moved into a style more akin to legitimate comedy and its lyrics made no concession to burlesque style but remained staunchly popular songs. These lyrics also had original music for, in spite of the reservations of the press over the original songs in *The Vicar of Wide-awake-field*, Edwardes stuck to the principle and musical director Meyer Lutz composed (mostly) and collected from several colleagues a score of almost entirely new music. If the most successful number of the night turned out to be an arrangement of 'Botany Bay' made by Lutz for David James (one of only two non-original numbers out of 24) there were nevertheless bright moments for Leslie declaring 'I'm Jonathan Oscar Wild' and for Nellie Farren insisting irresistibly 'Jack Keeps 'em All Alive-o'.

The Fred-and-Nellie team, a splendid physical production of which the highlight was the escape of Jack and Blueskin from Newbury jail and the chase across the rooftops that followed, and a whole evening's feast of songs and dances secured the success of *Little Jack Sheppard*, the future of the 'new burlesque', Edwardes and the Gaiety Theatre. The piece ran for 155 performances and, when it was removed to allow the pre-booked summer season of French plays to come in, Edwardes sent it on the road with Fred and Nellie starring, giving the provinces a rare glimpse of such London stars.

Whilst Fred and Nellie toured, Messrs Miles and Barton opened a Broadway version of *Little Jack Sheppard* with Nat Goodwin (Wild) and Loie Fuller (Jack) in the starring rôles, a production which also passed its 100th performance, and the newly fledged Brough and Boucicault company produced the piece in Australia with

Brough himself starring opposite Fanny Robina and E W Royce, from the Gaiety, as Blueskin. Once again the result was a major success, leading Brough to repeat the piece the following year and again in 1888 before subletting it to other managers. In 1892 an Australian revival featured Billie Barlow and George Walton, with Royce repeating his Blueskin and another famous veteran, Edwin Kelly, as Trenchard.

Even when the later and rather better-made new burlesques came on the scene, *Little Jack Sheppard* continued to be fondly played throughout the English-speaking world and in 1894, when the new burlesque had become very old hat, Edwardes, needing a stop-gap in his programme at the Gaiety, surprisingly revived the old piece in the West End (18 August). Seymour Hicks was Wild and the music-hall artiste Jessie Preston played Jack, but memories of the adored Fred and Nellie partnership were still too fresh and 42 performances were all that the revival achieved.

A singing Jack Sheppard returned briefly to London, many years later, portrayed by Nicky Henson in the musical *Stand and Deliver* (Monty Norman/Wolf Mankowitz, Roundhouse 24 October 1972, 14 performances).

USA: Bijou Theater 13 September 1886; Australia: Opera House, Melbourne 19 October 1886

LITTLE JESSIE JAMES Musical comedy in 2 acts by Harlan Thompson. Music by Harry Archer. Longacre Theater, New York, 15 August 1923.

A bedroom-and-livingroom farce of the most cheerful and blissfully busy kind, *Little Jessie James* took place in a New York apartment (one set throughout) which housed rendezvous of both licit and apparently illicit kinds, as well as a series of business dealings, all of which got mixed up with each other amidst a welter of comic scenes, songs and dances from the small principal cast and eight-girl chorus. The highlight of the comic action was a scene with a retractable bed in which members of the cast disappeared in a frantic and farcical scene of semi-sexual shenanigans. The Jessie of the title was not a sharpshooting misprint, but the noisiest lady of the piece, one Miss Jessie Jamieson (Nan Halperin) who always gets her man. Jay Velie, Ann Sands, Allen Kearns and Miriam Hopkins were amongst the cast and the accompaniment to Harry Archer's score was provided by Paul Whiteman's band. That score produced Broadway's surprise hit song of the season, 'I Love You', sung by Velie and Miss Sands, a hit which helped to ensure the economy-sized *Little Jessie James* a magnificent run of 393 performances without, however, encouraging other producers to forsake large casts and spectacular productions in the search for similar results.

The show subsequently had a very much wider showing than was usual for American musical comedies of the period. The year after its production, it turned up in Germany, where the adapters took the show's original title at face value and rechristened their version variously *Das Wildwestgirl* or *Wildwestmädel*, and it also got a showing in Hungary where Jenő Faragó similarly dropped the title, whose joke clearly didn't work too well outside America, and simply christened his version *I Love You*. Australia followed up with its production, and was alone in keeping the original title when the Fuller–Ward management mounted the show with local star Dot Brunton as Jessie,

supported by Mary Gannon, Elsie Parkes, Leslie Pearce, Harry Angers, the Boys Symphonic jazz orchestra and with a couple of non-Archer songs edged into the score. It played a good ten weeks in Melbourne and seven in Sydney (Grand Opera House 27 July 1925).

A decade later, the show turned up in Britain. In 1929 Clayton and Waller had had some success with their version of another Archer/Thompson show *Merry, Merry* and now Leslie Henson and Firth Shephard followed where they had led and picked up *Little Jessie James* as a vehicle for Henson. The libretto was anglicized by Douglas Furber under the title *Lucky Break*, although its original outlines and the retractable bed remained, and the song schedule was reorganized by Archer with some of the *Jessie James* songs (more or less relyricked by Furber), complemented with other Archer songs written with Walter O'Keefe ('A Kick in the Pants'), Will B Johnstone ('You Can't Take It') and Wolsely Charles ('Hush, Hush'). Strangely, 'I Love You', which had already become popular ten years earlier when recorded by Whiteman and by Jackie Gleason and which had since been heard in the film *The Sun Also Rises*, was amongst those numbers dropped. Henson, Heather Thatcher, Adele Dixon, Richard Hearne, David Hutcheson, Sydney Fairbrother and nine athletic chorus girls who danced out of a bookcase as 'Bookworms' kept the fun and the show alive for 198 London performances.

In 1942 an attempt was made to revive *Little Jessie James* in America. It was rewritten by Thompson and Gladys Shelley into a wartime setting, equipped with what seem to have been new Archer songs ('I Just Want to Make Friends', 'Teach Me to Dance', 'Who's to Blame', 'Rainy Afternoon', 'Gotta Have a Man Around the House') and, apparently, little more than the famous scene with the bed remained. As *Heels Together* it was produced at Scarsdale, New York (15 September) and folded before making it to the metropolis. In 1953 Archer himself masterminded another attempt, with the old book, the new songs and the old title, but it too folded after three weeks on the road.

Hungary: Lujza Blaha Színház *I Love You* 31 August 1924; Germany: Stadttheater, Düsseldorf *Das Wildwestgirl* 16 December 1928; Australia: New Princess Theatre, Melbourne 11 April 1925; UK: Strand Theatre *Lucky Break* 2 October 1934

LITTLE JOHNNY JONES Musical play in 3 acts by George M Cohan. Liberty Theater, New York, 7 November 1904.

It was only three years since the young and multi-talented George M Cohan had first turned his hand to creating and playing full-length musical comedies rather than the comic song-and-dance sketches contained in the Cohan family's vaudeville act, and *Little Johnny Jones* was already his third such piece. Now more widely ambitious, however, he moved into an alliance with producer Sam H Harris, and stepped his sights up a notch to write, direct and perform *Little Johnny Jones* at Broadway's Liberty Theater, rather than at one of the less up-market houses which had housed his first two pieces.

The new show and Cohan's character in it were suggested by the exploits of the American jockey Tod Sloane who had ridden in the English Derby the previous year. Cohan appeared as jockey Johnny Jones, over in England to ride the colt 'Yankee-Doodle' in the blue riband of the turf. He doesn't have an easy time. He loses the race and beastly Anthony Anstey (played by Cohan's father, Jerry) revengefully gets the boy warned off for allegedly pulling his horse, whilst rich, crusading Mrs Kenworthy (mother Helen Cohan) arranges for her niece Goldie Gates (wife Ethel Levey), whom Johnny loves, to wed a titled Englishman. It takes two further acts of action and music, including some kidnapping high jinks in San Francisco's Chinatown, for Johnny to clear his name, defeat Anstey and rescue and win Goldie in a series of events which didn't seem too far away from the melodramatic moments of *Fritz, Our Cousin German* and other such old-time favourites.

Little Johnny Jones, however, had a different, rather insouciant flavour to it which contrasted wholly with *Fritz* and his ilk, just as Cohan himself contrasted with Emmet. It was also easily Cohan's best show and rôle to date and, through the many that followed, it remained one of his finest. The part of the bright and bouncy little 100-percent American jockey, idolized by the girls yet true to his Goldie, ill-done-by but determined, and ultimately true red-white-and-blue heroic, gave him every opportunity he needed, and the songs with which he furnished the character proved to be amongst his most popular. 'The Yankee Doodle Boy', 'Life's a Funny Proposition After All' and 'Give My Regards to Broadway' gave the author-star three hits in one production. Miss Levey had a fine rôle as Goldie, disguised variously as her own British fiancé and as a French girl and all but tied to the railway tracks in the last act, and several songs ('Goodbye Flo', 'Mademoiselle Fanchette'); the rising juvenile man Donald Brian complemented Cohan's plug for Broadway by singing in praise of 'Good Old California'; and Truly Shattuck played a busybody newspaper lady and sang apropos of nothing about 'Nesting in a New York Tree', whilst the plot was helped along by Tom Lewis as a detective disguised, variously, as a fop, a lady and a San Francisco 'Chink'. The show's lively selection of songs was complemented by several choruses and by a double sextet on *Florodora* lines for six London cabdrivers and six little American girls (''Op in Me 'Ansom').

Cohan's expertise also extended to the staging of the piece, and his second-act closing became famous. Johnny, left in Britain to clear his name, stands on the pier whilst the ship on which he should have sailed heads for America across the back of the stage. Then, from the ship, a rocket goes up – a message from his detective ally that he has found the evidence they need of Anstey's villainy – and Cohan leapt joyfully into action with a vigorous one-man reprise of 'Give My Regards to Broadway' in a finale which brought down the house. But although there was plenty of song and dance for the audience's entertainment, the admittedly melodramatic and episodic story was never out of sight for long, and all of the play's characters had a part and a purpose in that story. *Little Johnny Jones* did not tail away into a virtual variety show of acts and interpolated numbers like so many so-called musical comedies of the time. It also had, amongst the conventionalities of its disguises and horrid foreigners, some little originalities: rare was the musical-comedy hero who rode in the Derby and lost!

Little Johnny Jones was not destined for a long Broadway run. After just 52 performances Cohan uprooted his show

from the Liberty Theater and took it on the road, where the principal and most lucrative of his activities had always been, but he returned the show to New York the following May (New York Theater, 8 May), again in November (New York Theater, 13 November) and yet again in 1906, so that ultimately Broadway saw nearly 200 performances of *Little Johnny Jones*.

Very few of Cohan's works were ever produced abroad, and the career of *Little Johnny Jones*, with its starry-and-stripey chauvinism, was limited to America. It was given a major revival in 1980 (ad Alfred Uhry, 25 June) when it was produced at the Goodspeed Opera House with Tom Hulce in the rôle Cohan had written for himself. It was subsequently toured and brought to Broadway almost two years later (Alvin Theater 21 March 1982) with the popular vocalist Donny Osmond starring, where it played for one performance.

A 1923 film entitled *Little Johnny Jones* based itself on the character Cohan had invented rather than on the show. Johnny Hines played the jockey alongside Wyndham Standing as the Earl of Bloomsbury.

A one-act British piece called *Little Johnnie Jones* written by Harry Vernon with songs by Frank E Tours and Preston Wayne was played on the music-hall bill at the Tottenham Palace, London 9 May 1910.

LITTLE MARY SUNSHINE New musical about an old operetta in 2 acts by Rick Besoyan. Orpheum Theater, New York, 18 November 1959.

A little burlesque of bits plucked here and there from the Broadway musical theatre of the first 30 or 40 years of the century, *Little Mary Sunshine* was set amongst the same Rocky Mountains that had hosted *Rose Marie* where Forest Rangers who have wandered in from *Naughty Marietta* serenade the owner of the local pub (Eileen Brennan) before breakfast. Mary is a foundling, like *Sally*, and she sings similar songs with such titles as 'Look for a Sky of Blue'. Captain 'Big Jim' Warington (William Graham) is the head of the Rangers and a baritone who expresses himself in terms such as 'You're the Fairest Flower' to little Mary. He has a subordinate called Billy Jester (John McMartin) and she has a maid called Nancy Twinkle (Elmarie Wendel) to supply the soubret work, and the Viennese influence arrives with a vocalist called Mme Ernestine Liebich (Elizabeth Parrish), who describes 'Izzenschnooken on the Lovely Essenzook See' as if she had recently been to see *Music in the Air* and demands of a passing General (Mario Siletti) 'Do You Ever Dream of Vienna?' in predictable style. Some of the score's more direct parodies included a 'Colorado Love Call' echoing *Rose Marie*, a 'Naughty, Naughty Nancy' which recalled *Naughty Marietta* and, popping back to the 19th century, a *Florodora* double sextet called 'Tell a Handsome Stranger'. As for the plot, the piece's nasty Indian is reformed, its nice Indian is given a great chunk of Colorado, and all ends happily.

The show first saw the light of stage in a much shorter form during the mid 1950s, and it was subsequently extended to its full two-act form and produced by Howard Barker, Cynthia Baer and Robert Chambers at off-Broadway's Orpheum Theater. Staged by its author, a former light opera vocalist, in an imitation of the precious style of some of the worse and more stilted operatic and operettic productions of not only earlier years but of the present day, it proved highly popular, remaining at the Orpheum for three years and 1,143 performances. It was subsequently produced in Britain with Patricia Routledge (Mary), Terence Cooper (Jim), Bernard Cribbins (Billy), Joyce Blair (Nancy) and Gita Denise (Ernestine), but its parodies appeared more amateurish than endearing to the English and it became another on the long list of successful off-Broadway musicals to founder in the West End (44 performances). An Australian production under the management of the Elizabethan Theatre Trust and Garnet Carroll, featuring Geraldene Morrow and Myron Natwick, also flopped in just a month's run in Sydney.

UK: Comedy Theatre 17 May 1962; Australia: Palace Theatre, Sydney 10 February 1962

Recordings: Original cast (Capitol), London cast (Pye/DRG)

LITTLE ME   Musical comedy in 2 acts by Neil Simon based on the novel of the same name by Patrick Dennis. Lyrics by Carolyn Leigh. Music by Cy Coleman. Lunt-Fontanne Theater, New York, 17 November 1962.

Patrick Dennis's brilliantly funny and best-selling burlesque of the star autobiography genre, *Little Me*, was translated to the stage by Neil Simon, who had not long since had his first Broadway triumph with the comedy *Come Blow Your Horn*. Cy Coleman and Carolyn Leigh, whose first Broadway musical *Wildcat*, two years earlier, had produced some success and a hit song, provided the score. It proved to be an outstanding combination, with Coleman matching the extravagantly witty burlesque humour of the text with music that was equally as humorous, and displaying for the first time his unequalled ability amongst modern composers as a writer of genuine and sophisticated burlesque, as opposed to the soupy imitations of earlier styles involved in such pieces as the recent off-Broadway success, *Little Mary Sunshine*.

Little Me is Belle Poitrine (Nancy Andrews), née Schlumpfert on the very wrongest side of the tracks. The ageing Belle is dictating her autobiography, the story of her young self (Virginia Martin) and her attempt to acquire the wealth, culture and social position which the devastatingly rich, cultured and social mother (Nancy Cushman) of Noble Eggleston (Sid Caesar) had told her were indispensable for anyone with ambitions to be her son's wife. Armed with nothing more than the best and biggest pair of bazooms in Illinois, Belle went via slum landlord Mr Pinchley (money) and a spell in vaudeville (culture), to marriage first with a gormless GI called Fred Poitrine, thus acquiring her predestined name, and then with French singing star Val du Val whose demise in the sinking of the *Gigantic* brought her more money. Thus equipped, she entered films (more culture), won a Golden Turkey for her *Moses Takes a Wife* (even more culture), and had oil discovered on her back lot (even more money), before going off to Europe to find social position. In Monte Carlo she chummed up with a penniless Prince, helped him with his national debt and in return was given a Rosenzweigan title (definitely social position). All three aims accomplished after so many years, she returned to America and Noble. At last they could be wed! But the celebratory champagne turned teetotal Noble into a raving alcoholic and in no time the man whose life had been a double dose of success from

his cradle was a bum. Belle gave up and married George Musgrove (Swen Swenson) who'd been pursuing her since the beginning of Act I and settled down to her autobiography. All, however, is not yet over. It may have taken time, but there is a walk-in sunset waiting for our heroine at the final curtain.

The score included three take-away songs: Belle's determined carol to escaping from 'The Other Side of the Tracks', George Musgrove's song-and-dance seduction 'I've Got Your Number' which, on the stage, featured a memorably slick Bob Fosse solo routine for the handsome, gangstery Swenson, and Fred Poitrine's myopic meeting with 'A Real Live Girl' ('pardon me, Miss, but I've never been kissed by ...'), later reprised longingly by the entire American army. Amongst the rest, the most plot-worthy was the tune 'I Love You', which rang out every time Belle and Noble touched each other. Initially introduced at their first meeting in Drifter's Row with Noble covered in slops slung from Belle's rubbish-pail, it returns throughout, rising to operettic proportions as the pair duet magnificently on the rapidly subsiding deck of the *Gigantic*. Belle's insistence that old Pinchley is a real nice person 'Deep Down Inside', her vaudeville turn 'Dimples' and her film-starry 'Poor Little Hollywood Star', Val du Val's cabaret song 'Boom-Boom' and a title-song shared by the old and young Belles also contributed to the fun, whilst a crisply mannered dance to 'The Rich Kids Rag' turned up another memorable dance moment.

If the rôle of Belle cornered most of the score and much of the comedy, the largest share of the latter went to Sid Caesar who, in Simon's text, appeared as each and every one of the men in Belle's life with the exception of the ultimately unlucky George Musgrove. Caesar's top billing was justified by a virtuoso rôle which allowed him to impersonate the aged Pinchley, the Frenchman, the gormless Fred and the Rosenzweigian Prince in a gala of comic acting.

Even with the very popular Caesar at its masthead, *Little Me* did not have the success it might have done on Broadway. A fair rather than a fine run of 257 performances prefaced a London production sponsored by Bernard Delfont, Arthur Lewis and Tom Arnold in which Bruce Forsyth and Eileen Gourlay starred. This did better, with a run of ten months (334 performances), but it was clear that upmarket burlesque of this kind, whilst it had very strong partisans amongst its partisans ('the most witty and richly entertaining comedy musical to come to us from America since *Pal Joey*') did not have battalions of them.

In 1982 a clutch of seven individuals and corporations produced a Broadway revival of a lightly revised *Little Me* (Eugene O'Neill Theater 21 January 1982). Several numbers were removed ('Dimples', the vaudeville duet 'Be a Performer' and 'Poor Little Hollywood Star') whilst a new opening song for Belle ('Don't Ask a Lady') replaced the original one. More surprisingly, the Sid Caesar rôle was cut in two for Victor Garber and James Coco. The revival folded after 36 performances, but Bernard Delfont's office remounted the show at London's Prince of Wales Theatre (30 May 1984) with television comedy star Russ Abbott playing the reconstituted multiple rôle and Sheila White as a Belle who had got her 'Dimples' back. Once again, London welcomed the show more warmly through a run of 423 performances.

UK: Cambridge Theatre 18 November 1964
Recordings: Original cast (RCA), London cast (Pye)

THE LITTLE MILLIONAIRE   Musical comedy in 3
acts by George M Cohan. George M Cohan Theater, New
York, 25 September 1911.

Although not one of Cohan's most memorable shows,
The Little Millionaire, with its author at its head 'a human
dynamo of nervous energy', found itself a willing Broadway
public for 192 performances and a nationwide one for even
longer. The entertainment served up much the same mixture that Cohan had been serving up for the past decade to
a fond public which knew precisely what to expect. There
was a simplistic story of a father (Jerry Cohan) and son
(George Cohan) out to get themselves wed in order to
inherit, the author's usual lively and straightforward type of
songs and some colourful production numbers. George
ended up getting Goldie Grey (Lila Rhodes) and his
father, Mrs Prescott (Nellie Cohan), although neither got
any Cohan song hits from amongst 'The Musical Moon',
'Oh! You Wonderful Girl', 'Any Place the Old Flag Flies',
'Barnum Had the Right Idea', 'New Yorkers', 'We Do the
Dirty Work', The Little Millionaire' and 'Come with Me
to the Bungalow' (Cohan's Bungalow Song) to line up
alongside those from the best of the previous shows. The
busy Cohan and his partner, Sam H Harris, got a tidy
profit out of *The Little Millionaire* during a season in which
they had a mass of productions – mostly non-musical – on
the road, confirming, if it needed confirming, the continuing popularity of both the star and his style of show.

LITTLE MISS NOBODY   Musical comedy in 2 acts by
H Graham. Music by Arthur E Godfrey. Additional music
by Landon Ronald. Added songs by Paul and Walter
Rubens. Lyric Theatre, London, 14 September 1898.

In a London musical theatre dominated by George
Edwardes and a handful of other producers, unexpected
musical comedy hits from untried producers were few and
far between. *Little Miss Nobody* was one. Written by the
playwright H Graham, author of the comedy *The County
Councillor*, with music by ballad composer Arthur Godfrey,
the piece was played for one try-out performance at
Cheltenham's Opera House under the management of
actor and would-be producer Yorke Stephens. There it
was seen and taken up by Tom B Davis, a former solicitor
and theatre-manager, who had the show titivated with
some songs from Paul Rubens and his brother Walter, sold
the American rights to Charles Frohman, and then produced it himself at London's Lyric Theatre.

Kate Cutler starred as Elsie Crockett, the little
governess of the title, who wins noble Guy Cheviot (Yorke
Stephens), Fred Eastman was the money-lender Potter
and Gracie Leigh, Lydia West and Dora Dent three music-
hall artists, all of whom end up in a Scots castle mistaken
for aristocrats. The grand old comedian Lionel Brough
played the heroine's father and the Gaiety's dragon Maria
Davis was Guy's lofty aunt. The score was an unexceptional one, with some jolly, ephemeral numbers being
topped by one deprecating the ghastly 'Gay Excursionist'
as described by Miss Leigh. A later addition, however,
proved the most popular: 'Trixie of Upper Tooting', an
early Paul Rubens hit describing an unpleasant little lady to
a jaunty tune. Sung in the show by Lionel Mackinder and

Plate 164. **Little Miss Nobody:** *The poster-maker was a bit
premature. Top-billed Florence Perry dropped out of the cast, Kate
Cutler was upped to the title-rôle and Gracie Leigh brought in to play
Trixie and thus start a memorable career.*

later George Grossmith, it became a music-hall success in
the hands of Ada Reeve who later claimed to have written
the tasteless lyric which the sheet music attributed to
Rubens.

Frohman's production actually opened first, in Philadelphia, with ex-D'Oyly Carte chorister Ethel Jackson in
the title-rôle. It proved a disaster, and its one week at the
Broad Street Theater finished its American life. On
Shaftesbury Avenue, however, *Little Miss Nobody* became a
quick and comfortable success, running for more than six
months and 200 performances during which Davis's cast
went decidedly upmarket with the addition of such performers as comedian John Le Hay and operatic singer
John Coates, for whom the rôle of Guy was made into a
considerable singing one. Equally, the neophyte producer
did not shrink from enlivening his 'bill' with such plot-
irrelevant items as Loie Fuller doing what one paper described as 'posing in coloured lights'.

Before the show closed in London, Edward Compton's
Company took it on the road with Hettie Dene, Sidney
Barraclough and young Adrienne Augarde in the tiny rôle
of Maggie, and this was soon followed by a second com-
pany which played two seasons on the road. In 1903
George Walton produced the show in South Africa and in

1904 a revised version again played the British provinces. The authors of *Little Miss Nobody* never confirmed their success, but other *Little Miss Nobody* beginners did: Davis went on to produce *Florodora* the next year, whilst Gracie Leigh, who had won her London début only by the late drop-out of soprano Florence Perry from the cast, went on to become a musical comedy star, and Ethel Jackson became Broadway's 'merry widow'.

USA: Broad Street Theater, Philadephia 5 September 1898; Film: Carlton Productions/Wilfred Noy 1923 (silent)

LITTLE NELLIE KELLY   Song and dance show in 2 acts by George M Cohan. Liberty Theater, New York, 13 November 1922.

The only one of George M Cohan's long list of mostly successful American musical comedies to be internationally played, *Little Nellie Kelly* was a sentimental bog-American-Irish tale with considerable family resemblances to the *Irene/Sally* school of Cinderella musicals, and with perhaps rather less to the vigorous pieces Cohan had written for himself 15 and 20 years earlier. Little Nellie Kelly (Elizabeth Hines) is an American-Irish shopgirl who is courted by the wealthy Jack Lloyd (Barrett Greenwood) but who prefers to give her hand and heart to the rough and ready, but Irish, Jerry Conroy (Charles King), in spite of the fact that he sings dubious things like 'You Remind Me of My Mother' to her. The subplot involved Jerry in accusations of stealing some jewels from Jack's aunt, Mrs Langford (Georgia Caine). If it was all conventional-sounding stuff, it had to be noted that *Sally, Irene* and even *Mary*, the musical-comedy megaheroines of the era, all found their love with wealthy heroes, and giving up a life of musical-comedy luxury for a lad, even if he was Irish, was probably either old-fashioned or plain dumb. For the moment it was also, at least, different. The show's songs included such titles as 'Dancing My Worries Away', 'The Name of Kelly', 'The Hinky Dee', 'Until My Luck Comes Rolling Along' and 'All My Boys', but far and away the most successful piece of the evening was Jerry's love song 'Nellie Kelly, I Love You' which turned out to be Cohan's biggest song success in years.

Little Nellie Kelly ran for 274 performances at Broadway's Liberty Theater before heading not only out onto the American road, as was normal and expected with a Cohan show, but overseas, which was not. C B Cochran took up the London rights and produced the show at the Oxford Theatre, where he had recently had a considerable hit with *The Better 'Ole*. Ralph Whitehead outdid Roy Royston for the hand of June in a cast that also included Anita Elson, Maidie Hope and Sonnie Hale. It had taken 20 years for a Cohan show to play London, but, now, the one that did proved to be thoroughly to London's taste. With a score of 265 West End performances *Little Nellie Kelly* did nearly as well in Britain as on Broadway. In 1923 Hugh J Ward produced the show in Australia as a successor to his highly successful mountings of Broadway's *The O'Brien Girl* and *Tangerine* and, if it did not quite equal the splendid record put up by the former of those shows, Mamie Watson and Leyland Hodgson nevertheless starred in Australia's version of *Little Nellie Kelly* for a fine four months in Melbourne and two and a half in Sydney (Grand Opera House 9 August 1924).

In 1940 a film was made by MGM under the title *Little*

Nellie Kelly with Judy Garland starred as Nellie. Jack McGowan's screenplay kept virtually nothing of Cohan's story, and Roger Edens's songs made space only for 'Nellie Kelly I Love You' after the originally scheduled 'You Remind Me of My Mother' ended up on the cutting-room floor. The score did, however, include one song that would be considerably bigger than Cohan's not inconsiderable hit – 'Singin' in the Rain'.

UK: Oxford Theatre 2 July 1923; Australia: New Princess Theatre, Melbourne, 22 December 1923

LITTLE NEMO   Musical play in 3 acts by Harry B Smith. Music by Victor Herbert. New Amsterdam Theater, New York, 20 October 1906.

Little Nemo was one of the spectacular, variety-filled children's musical shows that prospered as family entertainment on Broadway in the early part of the 20th century much as pantomime prospered in Britain, and of which such pieces as *The Wizard of Oz* and *Babes in Toyland* were enduring examples. Harry Smith developed this one for Klaw and Erlanger from Winsor McKay's *New York Herald* comic strip of the same name.

In Smith's story, Little Nemo (Master Gabriel, not actually a child actor but a midget) goes off to Slumberland to find the elixir of youth. On his travels he encounters the nice King of the land, Morpheus (W W Black), but also the villainous Dr Pill (Joseph Cawthorn), and a great deal of scenery (Young brothers and Boss, Ernest Albert and John Young) and dancing. The scenic plot led Little Nemo through Slumberland, the Land of Saint Valentine, a Weather Factory in Cloudland, the shipwreck of the Ship of Dreams, the Island of the Table d'hôte, a Dream of the Fourth of July and a battleship where the entire company paraded in naval whites. One writer voted that it was rather 'like *Peter Pan* ... with the accompaniment of stirring and tuneful music, capital songs, glittering pageants, graceful ballets and clever fooling by those inimitable comedians Joseph Cawthorn, Billie B Van and Harry Kelly'. Victor Herbert's score did not produce any lasting pieces to equal his *Babes in Toyland* bon-bons, but such numbers as 'Won't You Be My Sweetheart?' for Nemo and the Little Princess (Aimée Erlich), 'If I Could Teach My Teddy Bear to Dance' as sung by the Candy Kid (Florence Tempest) and 'The Happy Land of Once Upon a Time' served their purpose in the show alongside orchestral music accompanying a Valentine sequence, a Will o' the Wisp routine, a Cannibal scene, a review of athletes, a barbecue, and a comical zouave march featuring Van and Kelly.

Richard Rodgers and Vincent Youmans apparently both remembered seeing *Little Nemo* as one of the earliest theatrical parts of their childhood, but it does not seem to have left any influence on their writing. However, an ad lib by Joseph Cawthorn in a catalogue of imaginary animals apparently introduced the 'whiffenpoof' into the American language, and the Yale University society which took up the creature as their name, and the title of their famous club song, lasted rather longer than anything else from *Little Nemo*'s 111 Broadway performances. These performances were followed by two seasons of touring, limited in scope by the amount of scenery that Herbert Gresham's production required to be carried.

In 1992 *Little Nemo (Adventures in Slumberland)* made his

way to the cinema screen, but producers Hemdale did not avail themselves of Herbert's music as an accompaniment.

A LITTLE NIGHT MUSIC   Musical comedy in 2 acts by Hugh Wheeler suggested by the screenplay *Smiles of a Summer Night* by Ingmar Bergman. Music and lyrics by Stephen Sondheim. Shubert Theater, New York, 25 February 1973.

Following on behind his two revusical American pieces of the early 1970s, *Company* and *Follies*, Stephen Sondheim expanded his talents as both lyricist and composer into a rather different sphere with the score to Hugh Wheeler's stage adaptation of the screenplay of the atmospheric 1955 Swedish film *Smiles of a Summer Night*.

Fredrik Egerman (Len Cariou) is a middle-aged lawyer whose second wife is the young and decidedly immature Anne (Victoria Mallory). It is an immaturity which means that Anne, in spite of months of marriage, is still a virgin, and she is showing no signs of becoming anything else. Whilst Fredrik holds back with decreasing patience from leaping amorously upon his wife, the theatre company in which Desirée Armfeldt (Glynis Johns) is playing comes to town. Desirée, who troupes the cities of Sweden whilst her young, illegitimate daughter, Fredrika (Judy Kahan), remains in the care of her grandmother, Madame Armfeldt (Hermione Gingold), is now in the throes of an affair with a bristling hussar, Carl Magnus Malcolm (Lawrence Guittard), a sexual despot with a total belief in the rights of man (as opposed to those of woman). The Count's predecessor, however, as witnessed in the name of Desirée's child, was the between-wives Fredrik. When Desirée hears of her ex-lover's predicament she offers, first, practical consolation, and then a different kind of invitation. And, thus, it happens that all the protagonists of this amorous sextangle turn up one weekend at the palatial home of Madame Armfeldt: Fredrik, Anne, Carl Magnus, his miserably maltreated wife Charlotte (Patricia Elliott), Desirée, and Fredrik's burstingly teenaged son, Henrik. As the young (Fredrika), the old (Mme Armfeldt) and the amused, uncomplicated servants (Petra, Frid) look on, the waltz of changing partners begins. Hearts and other parts are bared, realizations blossom, practicalities emerge in a series of events and encounters often more farcical than romantic, before Anne runs off with Henrik, Charlotte drags Carl Magnus at least temporarily back, and Fredrik and Desirée relax, with a little bit of Petra's practicality, into a comfortable, middle-aged partnership which is so much more suitable than their respective chases after exhaustingly active youth.

The wry, sophisticated comicalities of the show's script were dazzlingly echoed in a waltzing score which was musically far in advance of its predecessors. It skated excitingly through the full range of male and female voices, blending into some of the most fascinating ensembles heard on Broadway in decades, yet always in allegiance with its witty and elegant words, and at the same time both melodic and interesting. There were solos which touched on the style of Sondheim's earlier works – Petra (D Jamin Bartlett) explaining that she will naturally marry 'The Miller's Son' one day, but sees that as no bar to a healthy sex-life in the meanwhile, and Madame Armfeld mooning over the debased status of 'Liaisons' since the days when she was the plaything of royalty – but others took on a less set-

piece tone. Fredrik debates patteringly whether to make his move on his wife 'Now', whilst she promises in soaring soprano tones that 'Soon' she won't shy away, and pubescent Henrik, curdled with impatience at always being always told to wait till 'Later', supplies what becomes a frantic tenor and cello obbligato when the three solos interlace in a trio of musical frustrations. The rest of the ensemble music was highlighted by everyone's feelings over the prospect of 'A Weekend in the Country' – the reasons for not going are manifold, but no one would dream of missing out – and by two illustrative pieces for the quintet of vocalists which served the essentially intimate piece as a chorus ('Night Waltz', 'The Sun Won't Set'), whilst Fredrik enthused unenthusiastically to Desirée that 'You Must Meet My Wife', turned over comical maybes in his mind in parallel to Carl Magnus's different ones in 'It Would Have Been Wonderful', and Anne and Charlotte ran down marriage in 'Every Day a Little Death' in some of the evening's musical duologues.

The piece of the show's score which became a success, however, was none of these. It was a rueful, gentle, rather obscurely lyricked piece delivered by Desirée, in the midst of all the hurly-burly of the house party, as she sits and wonders if she hasn't rather made a mess of things. Before *A Little Night Music* had finished making use of it, 'Send in the Clowns' made its way into the repertoire of Frank Sinatra, on to the radios and gramophones of the world, and via cabaret and concert to the list of Broadway standards, where it stands alongside 'Don't Cry for Me, Argentina' as one of the unlikeliest out-of-context show hits of the era.

A Little Night Music took the season's Tony Awards for best musical, book and score (Sondheim's third consecutive win in this category), and for Miss Johns's performance, and went on to play for 601 performances on Broadway. It was only nine months into its run when an Australian production appeared, under the management of J C Williamson Ltd, with Tania Elg (Desirée), Bruce Barry (Fredrik), Tim Page (Henrik) and comedienne Anna Russell (Mme Armfeldt) starred in what proved to be one of the country's most outstanding musical productions in years. However, like its American counterpart (still in the red at the end of its run), it found that cash returns and artistic merits did not necessarily go together. It played but four months in Sydney and as many weeks in Melbourne (Her Majesty's Theatre 10 July 1974). These considerations prompted London to pull the plug on its already cast and prepared production, but the show did ultimately make it to London, in 1975, with Jean Simmons, who had been touring America in the rôle of Desirée, starring alongside Miss Gingold, repeating her original rôle, Joss Ackland (Fredrik), Terry Mitchell (Henrik) and Veronica Page (Anne) in a reproduction of the Broadway version. Once again the production created great enthusiasms, and once again it struggled to make ends meet through 406 performances.

An Austrian version, which again reproduced the ingenious and much-praised Broadway scenery and production, went back to the film title, *Das Lächeln einer Sommernacht*. Susanne Almassy starred as Desirée, performing 'Wo sind die Clowns', Gideon Singer played Fredrik, Zarah Leander supplied the marquee value in the rôle of Madame Armfeldt, and the young Dagmar Koller appeared as Petra through 65 performances. A film version, which featured several of the original cast, Elizabeth Taylor as Desirée and a lot of dubbing, went through all kinds of problems and finally sneaked out late, lavishly cut and low-profile.

Following its initial major productions, *A Little Night Music* went through a long and widespread series of stagings in regional theatres all around the world, becoming in the process a standard item in the international repertoire. In 1989 it was given a return season in London under the management of H M Tennent Ltd, in a production transferred from the Chichester Festival (Piccadilly Theatre, 10 October, 152 performances) with Dorothy Tutin (Desirée), Eric Flynn (Fredrik) and Lila Kedrova (Mme Armfeldt) and in 1991 the New York City Opera mounted a production, with Sally Ann Howes featured as Desirée.

Australia: Her Majesty's Theatre, Sydney 30 November 1973; Austria: Theater an der Wien *Das Lächeln einer Sommernacht* 14 February 1975; UK: Adelphi Theatre 15 April 1975; Film: New World/Sascha-Wien Films 1978

Recordings: Original cast (Columbia), London cast (RCA), Film soundtrack (Columbia), selection in German (Preiser, Austria) studio cast (TER)

LITTLER, Emile (Sir) (b Ramsgate, 9 September 1903; d Ditchling, 23 January 1985). British producer of London and provincial shows through more than three decades.

The son of a suburban theatre manager, Littler took his first theatrical job as assistant manager at the Ambassador's Theatre in Southend-on-Sea. He fulfilled a series of company management and stage management positions on both sides of the Atlantic before he took over the running of the Birmingham Repertory Theatre in 1931. In the mid-1930s he began a commercial producing career, touring both plays and musical comedies. The musicals were mostly revivals of proven favourites but occasionally, as with the South Seas musical *Aloma and Nutane* (1938) starring Carl Brisson and Gabrielle Brune, they were billed fatally as 'prior to London presentation' and didn't make it.

It was in the early 1940s that Littler made his first London ventures with wartime revivals of *The Maid of the Mountains* with Sylvia Cecil, *The Belle of New York* with Evelyn Laye and a successful, rewritten version of *The Quaker Girl* featuring Celia Lipton. He had less luck with his first London production of an original musical, when a version of the famous farce *When Knights Were Bold*, in which he himself had had a hand in the adaptation and the direction, was a ten-performance flop. Sigmund Romberg's *Sunny River* with which he followed it at the Piccadilly Theatre lasted only two months, but he had better fortune when he had a little interest in Lee Ephraim and Tom Arnold's presentation of the Cicely Courtneidge/Jack Hulbert musical *Something in the Air* (1943) and then joined them in the London version of Cole Porter's *Panama Hattie*.

His breakthrough in the London theatre came with the considerable success of two further imports, *Song of Norway* (1945) and *Annie Get Your Gun* (1947), although others, such as the revived *The Red Mill* (1947), failed to make the grade. Littler made several other attempts with original musicals, scoring successes with a pretty musi-

calization of *Quality Street* (*Dear Miss Phoebe* 1950), a comical one of the famous farce *Hurra! eine Junge!* (*Blue for a Boy* 1950) with Fred Emney, the George Formby *Brewster's Millions* show *Zip Goes a Million* (1951), and the *Daddy Long-Legs* with music entitled *Love from Judy* (1952). Others, such as the Robert Stolz spectacular *Rainbow Square* (1951), *Happy Holiday* (based on *The Ghost Train*) and *Romance by Candlelight* (from *Bei Kerzenlicht*) were unmitigated flops.

Littler took a ten-year tuck in his musical presentation schedule, returning to the West End in 1967 with three months of a Broadway import, *110 in the Shade*. A revival of *The Student Prince* with popular touring tenor John Hanson had a good run, but an attempt to bring back Littler's own idea of a sure-fire success with a version of *The Maid of the Mountains*, revamped in the same way that he had treated *The Quaker Girl* and *Miss Hook of Holland* 30 years earlier, was a costly disaster.

A major presence on the touring circuits throughout the 1940s and 1950s, Littler was also extensively and lucratively involved for many years with the presentation of Christmas pantomimes throughout Britain and owned both the Palace and Cambridge Theatres in London's West End. He was knighted in 1974.

His brother **Prince LITTLER** (b Ramsgate, 25 July 1901; d Henfield, 17 September 1973), originally a producer of mainly touring shows and pantomimes, was for many years the most influential theatre owner in Britain, whilst his sister **Blanche LITTLER** (b Ramsgate, 26 December 1899; d Brighton 7 June 1981) partnered Prince in early productions and subsequently became even more theatrically prominent as Lady Robey, the wife of comedian George Robey.

1943 **The Knight Was Bold** (ex- *Kiss the Girls*) (Harry Parr Davies/Barbara Gordon, Basil Thomas/w Thomas Browne) Piccadilly Theatre 1 July

LITTLE SHOP OF HORRORS Musical in 2 acts by Howard Ashman based on the film by Charles Griffith. Music by Alan Menken. WPA Theater, New York, 6 May 1982; Orpheum Theater, 27 July 1982.

The most internationally successful wholly off-Broadway musical since *The Fantasticks*, *Little Shop of Horrors* began its career at the little WPA Theater, where author Ashman was co-director, before moving up to off-Broadway's première house, the Orpheum, with the massed might of Cameron Mackintosh, the Geffen Organisation and the Shubert Organisation behind it, for the bulk of what was eventually a 2,209-performance run in more than five years.

The musical was a burlesque of the period horror-movie genre in general, and of the 1960 film *Little Shop of Horrors*, made by Roger (*Not of This Earth, Teenage Caveman, A Bucket of Blood*) Corman, in particular. It was written in a tightly controlled and tautly funny combination of dialogue and lyrics which lovingly, knowledgeably parodied its original whilst still making the show funny to those who had never seen a horror movie. The doom-laden newsreadery tones of the voice-over narrator, a period trio of girl singers just too girl-group to be true, and a set of impossibly wide-eyed characters featuring shopboy hero Seymour (Rick Moranis) and his beloved workmate, the vacuous blonded Audrey (Ellen Greene), her sadistic leather-clad dentist boyfriend, Orin (Franc Luz), and a man-eating plant (Ron Taylor/Martin P Robinson) which grew and grew and grew, all went to make up the flavour of the most winning small musical in ages.

Seymour and Audrey work for florist Mr Mushnik (Hy Anzell) on Skid Row, where Seymour nurses this strange and interesting plant which he has called Audrey II after his adored one. The plant proves a major attraction and clients start to pour in to the once neglected shop, but there is one problem: the plant doesn't drink water, it drinks blood. And when Seymour's fingers are whitened with pinpricks, it even talks! It says 'Feed Me!' The beastly Orin snuffs it whilst getting his kicks on laughing gas, and Seymour feeds him to the hungry plant, then Mr Mushnik gets on the trail, and he becomes the next victim. Seymour is becoming famous, but he's also losing control. Audrey is the next to fall, and finally Seymour realizes what is happening: this is not horticulture, it is a plan for Global Domination by Creatures From Outer Space. He attacks his plant, and is gobbled up in his turn, as Audrey II prepares to take over the world.

The musical part of the show was launched with the three girls boopsing out their harmonized history of 'Little Shop of Horrors', and went on to a row of endearingly funny pieces. Seymour encouraged the baby plant to 'Grow For Me', Audrey mooned over the fate of those who live 'Downtown', longed for sweet suburbia in 'Somewhere That's Green' and rose rhapsodically with Seymour to the heights of 'Suddenly Seymour', whilst the dentist laughed himself to death in song ('Now'/'It's Just the Gas'), but the musical highlight of the night came when Audrey II burst forth with a big, black, husky voice demanding 'Feed Me!' and gloating over making Audrey its 'Suppertime'.

Mackintosh took *Little Shop of Horrors* to London and was faced with the eternal dilemma of what to do with an off-Broadway show in a city with no equivalent area. He opted for the West End's little Comedy Theatre, made it littler by closing the dress-circle, but still could not quite reproduce the special atmosphere engendered by off-Broadway. Miss Greene repeated her original rôle alongside Barry James (Seymour), Harry Towb (Mushnik) and Anthony B Asbury/Michael Leslie (Audrey II) and although the show struggled, it nevertheless managed to put up a better performance than previous off-Broadway shows had done in London, playing 813 West End performances before recouping some extra cash when the complex Audrey II puppet proved a rental prospect in view of the rush of regional houses anxious to mount the nine-handed musical.

An Australian production, mounted at Sydney's unsuitably handsome, modern Theatre Royal and at Melbourne's Comedy Theatre (26 February 1985), performed disappointingly, before the show moved into its foreign-language showings. Hungary was, as so often, at the head of the field with a version adapted by Mária Révész and produced at the Városmajori Parkszínpad, and the following season France's Claude Martinez and Paul Ledermann gave *La Petite Boutique des horreurs* (ad Alain Marcel) a fine production with Vincent Vittoz (Seymour), Fabienne Guyon (Audrey) and Jacques Martial/Charles Philippe Klanit (Audrey II) in the starring rôles for a four-month Paris season. In Germany *Der kleine Horrorladen* (ad Michael Kunze) was played in Gelsenkirchen and in

Austria the Amstetten Festival Theater, which had done so finely by *La Cage aux Folles* the previous season, also mounted a German-language version. Japan, Scandinavia, South Africa, Israel, Iceland and other countries all saw productions, as the show moved into provincial and small-city houses around the world, and there often found an atmosphere more favourable to its success than in oversized or over-sophisticated metropolitan theatres.

In 1986 a film version was put out by the Geffen Company. Rick Moranis (Seymour) and Miss Greene featured in a glossy A-minus movie version of the parody of the musical based on a Z-movie, which topped up the main portions of the original score with several fresh musical pieces including a rip-roaring 'Mean Green Mother from Outer Space' for the plant.

UK: Comedy Theatre 12 October 1983; Australia: Theatre Royal, Sydney 8 November 1984; Hungary: Városmajori Parkszínpad *Rémségek kicsiny boltja* 15 August 1985; France: Théâtre Déjazet *La Petite Boutique des horreurs* 19 June 1986; Austria: Amstetten *Der kleine Horrorladen* 1990; Germany: Musiktheater im Revier, Gelsenkirchen 31 March 1989, Berliner Kammerspiele 4 April 1989; Film: Geffen Co 1986

Recordings: original cast (Geffen), French cast (Martinez Lederman), Icelandic cast (Steinar), Spanish cast (*La botica dels horrors*) (Musica per a Anna), German cast (Polydor), film soundtrack (Geffen)

LLEÓ, Vicente (b Valencia, 19 November 1870; d Madrid, 28 February 1922).

Composer, conductor and producer of zarzuelas, Vicente Lleó turned out a long list of scores for the Spanish stage over a period of more than 20 years, beginning with *Las de farandul* (lib: Lopez Marin, Teatro Maravillas 19 August 1898) and following up with a veritable rush of pieces over the next months, composed both in collaboration and alone: *Los cenceros* (Ramirez, Teatro Romea 11 February 1899), *Variétés* (w Zavala/Montesinos, Luis Pascual Frutos, Nuevo Teatro April 1899), *Extraje de boda* (w A Rubio/Miguel Palacios, Guillermo Perrin, 7 April 1899) *Los gladiatores* (w Chalons/Pazos, Gijon, Teatro Zarzuela 5 June 1899), *El estado di sitio* (w Calleja/Soriano, Falcado, Teatro Maravillas 20 June 1899), *Cambios naturales* (w Rubio/Ventura de la Vega, Teatro Maravillas 19 August 1899), *Venus Salón* (w Calleja/Limendoux, Lopez Marin, Teatro Romea 14 December 1899) and *La tiple mimada* (Enrique Prieto, Teatro Martin 17 October 1899).

He subsequently worked on a long list of pieces with Rafael Gomez Calleja, amongst which were included *La maestra* (1901, w Barrera), *Jilguero chico* (1901), *El dios Apolo* (1901), *Gubasta nacional* (1902), *Arlequin rey* (1903), *El mozo crúo* (1903), *Copito de nieve* (1903), *Gloria pura* (1904), *Quo vadis, montero* (1905), *La Golfa del Manzanares* (1908), *El rey del valor* (1914), *El premio de honor*, *El famoso Colirón*, *Los hijos del mar*, *Los presupuestos de Villapierde* and *Venus Kursaal*, but his most important success came well into his career with a piece composed alone, the 1909 zarzuela *La corte de faraón* (lib: Miguel Palacios, Guillermo Perrin).

Lleó's long list of further credits includes the following titles: *La pierras preciosas* (1905), *La taza de thé* (1906), *La guedeja rubia* (1905), *La loba* (1907), *Tupinamba* (1907), *Episodios nacionales* (1908 w Amadeo Vives), *Mayo florido* (1908), *La vuelta del presidio* (1908), *La república del amor*

(1908), *La balsa de aceite* (1908), *Si las mujeres mantasa* (1908, w Luis Foglietti), *Las molineras* (1908), *Ninfas y satiros* (1909), *La moral en peligro* (1909), *La partina della porra* (1911), *Livio* (1911), *El barrio latino* (1912), *La Tirrena* (1913), *La Pandereta* (1915, w Jiménéz), *Siera Morena* (1915), *To esta pagas* (1920), *La alegre trompetaria*, *La carne flaca*, *Apaga y vamonos*, *Ave Cesar*, *El metodo Gorriz*, *El crimen pasional*, *El ilustre Recóchez*, *El maestro Campanone* and *El principe sin miedo*.

LLOYD WEBBER, Andrew (Sir) (b London, 22 March 1948).

The son of William Lloyd Webber, musician, composer and principal of the London College of Music, Andrew Lloyd Webber began writing songs in his teens, soon in collaboration with an ephemeral law student, Tim Rice. In the wake of the success of the children-heavy musical *Oliver!*, the two attempted a stage musical based on the life of children's-homes founder Doctor Barnardo (a subject which would come to the London stage years later in other hands and disastrously), but their first produced piece was one of more modest proportions, brought out under modest circumstances. *Joseph and the Amazing Technicolor Dreamcoat* was a 15-minute staged cantata, written for and first played by a boys' school choir. It did, however, lay the bases for the style which its writers would follow thereafter with outstanding success: lively, colloquial lyrics illustrated by music which blended popular modern tones with more classic elements, and which found much of its humour in burlesque.

Joseph was subsequently expanded, little by little, into a full-length show, but it was a second biblically-based piece, produced before an evening-long *Joseph* had been developed, that made its composer's reputation. *Jesus Christ Superstar*, the story of the last days of the life of Christ as seen through the eyes of Judas Iscariot, was conceived as a stage musical, first heard as a two-record, pre-original-cast recording, and ultimately premièred at Broadway's Mark Hellinger Theater in 1971. Advisedly described as a 'rock opera', it took the modern-toned, written-through cantata style used in *Joseph* a step further, produced its composer's first hit songs ('Jesus Christ Superstar', 'I Don't Know How to Love Him'), scored an important success, became London's longest-running musical of all time and was played thereafter throughout the world, in productions varying from the extravagantly trendy to the wholly devotional.

After a sidewind into a conventional musical comedy with the period-piece set of songs for the short-lived *Jeeves*, Lloyd Webber returned to Rice and to the particular style they were developing with a musical show set this time not in the religious, but in the political arena. Maintaining the sung-through idiom, which was fast becoming accepted by other young writers as the modern style, and which they here further developed to fit a more substantial and modern dramatic subject, they told, to a musical score richer than before, the tale of Argentinian politician's wife Eva Peron, otherwise known as *Evita* ('Don't Cry for Me, Argentina', 'O What a Circus', 'Another Suitcase in Another Hall'). The world-wide triumph of *Jesus Christ Superstar* was more than confirmed as *Evita* triumphed over politically dying-to-be-correct howls about its subject

Plate 165. **Andrew Lloyd Webber.**

matter and joined its predecessor at the head of the list of the most internationally successful musicals of the 1970s.

Leaving, for the moment, historical and dramatic subjects and his collaboration with Rice, Lloyd Webber took a turn into a lighter vein with his musical setting of the Old Possum poems of T S Eliot, brought to the theatre in 1981 as the song-and-dance spectacular *Cats* ('Memory'). *Cats* was a piece far from the 20th-century traditions of the book musical in its layout and its staging, but it would become the theatrical sensation of its era, outrunning even its record-breaking predecessors on the London and New York stages and breeding productions throughout the world.

The composer essayed further into the area of the theatre spectacular and further away from the musical-dramatic style of *Jesus Christ Superstar* and *Evita* with the pop-orientated wheelie extravaganza *Starlight Express* (1984) and had another success with the equally unusual staged pairing of his solo song-cycle 'Tell Me on a Sunday' and a choreographed version of his cello variations on a theme by Paganini under the title *Song and Dance* (1982), before taking a turn into yet another field with the romantic musical melodrama *The Phantom of the Opéra* (1986). More musically substantial than his most recent works, Lloyd Webber's score for *The Phantom of the Opéra* paired opera pastiche and lush love songs with some highly developed ensembles, and produced no fewer than three hit-parade songs ('Music of the Night', 'All I Ask of You', 'The

881

Phantom of the Opéra') before following its composer's earlier works to outsized international success.

In spite of the popularity of this romantic costume piece, Lloyd Webber followed the lavishly staged *The Phantom of the Opéra* with a musical play which was of a wholly different genre, the comparatively intimate and sophisticated *Aspects of Love*, a piece based on a successful 1940s British novel dealing largely with the fairly unspectacular affairs of the heart of one family over some 20 years. Once again, Lloyd Webber's written-through score rendered up hit parade songs ('Love Changes Everything', 'Anything But Lonely') as the musical settled in for a run which gave its composer the unusual distinction of having five shows running concurrently in the London of the early 1990s (*Cats, Starlight Express, The Phantom of the Opéra, Aspects of Love, Joseph and the Amazing Technicolor Dreamcoat* revival), and three simultaneously on Broadway (*Cats, The Phantom of the Opéra, Aspects of Love*), a record not even Ivan Caryll and the other most outstanding (and much more prolific) musical theatre composers of the past had achieved.

In between the successes of *Cats* and *Starlight Express*, and at the termination of the management contract under which he had worked from his earliest days, Lloyd Webber founded the Really Useful Company as a production and exploitation company for his works. The company (which subsequently became for a period the Really Useful Group and a public company) has co-produced or produced each of his subsequent musicals, and has also produced both plays (*Daisy Pulls it Off, Lend Me a Tenor*) and, less successfully, musicals (*The Hired Man, Café Puccini*) by other writers. Embryonic versions of Lloyd Webber's own pieces have been tried out at his private Sydmonton Festival, and there too the works of other writers have been tested, including two (*Masquerade, Café Puccini*) that were subsequently played in London. Another stage piece, a collaboration with Rice on an occasional one-act operetta called *Cricket*, was also staged privately, and in 1985 he composed a requiem mass, performed first at New York's St Thomas's Church, later in London, and ultimately staged as a ballet. His other work includes two film scores (*Gumshoe, The Odessa File*).

The most important and innovative – not to say phenomenally successful – theatre composer of his era, Lloyd Webber has, in his nine full-length theatre shows to this date, displayed a considerable musical range within his preferred idiom, whilst always remaining not only accessible, but popular to the extent of placing regular numbers from his musicals in the pop charts, an area in which the musical-theatre music of the past 30 years has appeared less and less frequently.

1971 **Jesus Christ Superstar** (Tim Rice) Mark Hellinger Theater, New York 12 October

1972 **Joseph and the Amazing Technicolor Dreamcoat** (Rice) Edinburgh 21 August, Roundhouse, London 8 November

1973 **Jacob's Journey** (Rice) 1 act Albery Theatre 17 February

1975 **Jeeves** (Alan Ayckbourn) Her Majesty's Theatre 22 April

1978 **Evita** (Rice) Prince Edward Theatre 21 June

1981 **Cats** (T S Eliot ad) New London Theatre 11 May

1982 **Song and Dance** (Don Black) Palace Theatre 26 March

1984 **Starlight Express** (Richard Stilgoe) Apollo Victoria Theatre 19 March

1986 **The Phantom of the Opéra** (Charles Hart/w Stilgoe) Her Majesty's Theatre 9 October

1989 **Aspects of Love** (Hart, Black) Prince of Wales Theatre 17 April

1993 **Sunset Boulevard** (Black/Christopher Hampton) Adelphi Theatre 12 July

Biographies: Mantle, J: *Fanfare – The Unauthorised Biography of Andrew Lloyd Webber* (Michael Joseph, London, 1989): Walsh M: *Andrew Lloyd Webber* (Viking, London, 1989)

LOCK UP YOUR DAUGHTERS Musical play in 2 acts by Bernard Miles adapted from *Rape upon Rape* by Henry Fielding. Lyrics by Lionel Bart. Music by Laurie Johnson. Mermaid Theatre, London, 28 May 1959.

Bernard Miles, the brainfather and manager of the Mermaid Theatre in London's Puddle Dock, opened his newly built house in 1959 with a musical for which he himself had written the libretto. *Lock Up Your Daughters* was a lusty adaptation of Henry Fielding's 1730 tale *Rape upon Rape*, to which, after several writers had turned down the opportunity, the musical part was supplied by film composer Laurie Johnson and the 28-year-old Lionel Bart, the lyricist of *Fings Ain't Wot They Used t' Be*.

The rape of the story's title did not actually happen. 18th-century Hilaret (Stephanie Voss) has snuck out to meet her lover, Captain Constant (Terence Cooper), but become embroiled in the dangers of the city. One of these is Ramble (Frederick Jaeger), but when Hilaret deters his advances by squealing 'Rape!' both of them are dragged before Justice Squeezum (Richard Wordsworth). Squeezum is himself an even greater danger than the lowest streets of London, and while he is dribbling all over Hilaret, his wife (Hy Hazell) makes merry with Ramble. However Hilaret is not all winsomeness, and she arranges a booby-trapped rendezvous with the lascivious judge who, by the final curtain, ends up in his own jail. The songs ranged from a lusty title number, through two comical pieces for Mrs Squeezum (one demanding 'When Does the Ravishing Begin?' and the other vengefully threatening her prison-bound husband 'I'll Be There'), the gentle wonderings of the wine-sodden Sotmore (Keith Marsh) over Hilaret's smartness ('If I'd Known You'), and the heroine's ingenuously comical seduction of the boggling Judge, describing her deflowering on 'A Sunny Sunday Morning' as she removes her clothes.

Staged by the Mermaid's 29-year-old artistic director, Peter Coe, on a multiple-purpose setting constructed on scaffolding by the architect Sean Kenny, *Lock Up Your Daughters* was a singular success. Intended only for a six-week season at what was planned to be a house with a regular turnover of productions, it ran and ran, paying off the entire building cost of the theatre and setting the venture off on a very firm foot. But the house's trustees required productions, not success and profit, and they urged that the show be closed. Finally, after six months and 330 performances, it was taken off. The round of international productions began soon after in South Africa, but an American version, Broadway-bound under the management of Douglas Crawford, and with Harry Locke, Nancy Dussault and John Michael King teamed with Miss Hazell, folded on the road amidst little cries of horror at the show's indecent content. Australia proved less tender-eared and welcomed *Lock Up Your Daughters* the following year with Wordsworth in his original rôle and Miss Hazell in the part she had made all her own for an eight-week limited season in Melbourne and then in Sydney (Palace Theatre 8 June 1961).

In 1962, the Mermaid revived its most successful piece with Bernard Miles and Sally Smith featured, and after 111 more performances there it was shifted into the West End's Her Majesty's Theatre. Wordsworth and Miss Voss took up their original rôles again, and the piece played 15 further months and 553 performances. *Lock Up Your Daughters* was regularly mounted in English theatres thereafter. It played a tenth anniversary season at the Mermaid (31 March 1969) and it was to have been included in the first season of the newly rebuilt Mermaid in 1981. This production was cancelled when the ill-conceived, -cast and -staged new piece which this time opened the theatre proved such a failure that the rest had to be abandoned and Miles ultimately lost his theatre. Sydney's Q Theatre mounted a revival in 1977, and in 1982 Goodspeed Opera House made another attempt to interest America in the show (30 March), but the production, with Carleton Carpenter and Dena Olstad in its leading rôles, played its two-and-a-half-month regional season and ended.

Coe, whose directing assignment on *Lock Up Your Daughters* was his first musical in what was to be a distinguished career, later made a film under the same title which, in fact, used Johnson's score only as incidental music.

The success of *Lock Up Your Daughters* provoked a rash of attempts at Restoration musicals, none of which approached the success of the first. It also tempted the Mermaid into a number of other musicals, most of which – and particularly the last – were not on the same professional level, so that the musical theatre, which had been the original source of the Mermaid's financial and popular strength, ultimately proved its downfall.

USA: Shubert Theater, New Haven 27 April 1960; Australia: Princess Theatre, Melbourne 12 April 1961
Recording: original cast (Decca)

LOESSER, Frank [Henry] (b New York, 29 June 1910; d New York, 26 July 1969). Songwriter turned show-writer who, in spite of a very short theatrical output, turned out three of the most outstanding musical comedies of the postwar era.

The son of a piano teacher, Loesser evinced an early interest in popular music and songwriting, but he found little success in his early attempts to write songwords. When he finally broke into the world of popular music as a house lyricist for the publishing firm of Leo Feist, it was only to find himself dismissed after one year as inadequate, but it was, nevertheless, Feist who published his first printed song, 'In Love with the Memory of You' (music: William Howard Schuman) in 1931. In spite of working with such established names as Hoagy Carmichael and Joseph Meyer, Loesser found that success still slouched at coming, and the only one of his numbers to catch the ear, as he worked as a nightclub pianist to make ends meet in the years immediately following, was 'I Wish That I Were Twins' (w Joseph Meyer, Eddie de Lange).

In 1935 Loesser contributed lyrics to the quasi-amateur *The Illustrators' Revue* and as a result won the interest of Hollywood. He moved there in 1936 and, at first for Universal and then subsequently for Paramount, RKO and MGM, he provided seven years of lyrics for cinema songs.

Plate 166. **Frank Loesser.**

Here he at last built, albeit slowly, a genuine success and the series of popular songs on which he collaborated included several which were to become standards: 'Moon of Manakoora' (1937, Alfred Newman, *The Hurricane*), 'Says My Heart' (1938, Burton Lane, *The Cocoanut Grove*), 'Two Sleepy People' (1938, Hoagy Carmichael, *Thanks for the Memory*), 'The Lady's in Love with You' (1939, Lane, *Some Like it Hot*), 'The Boys in the Back Room' (1939, Frederick Hollander, *Destry Rides Again*), 'Say It' (1940, Jimmy McHugh, *Buck Benny Rides Again*), 'Dolores' (1941, Louis Alter, *The Gay City*), 'I'll Never Let a Day Pass By' and 'Kiss the Boys Goodbye' (1941, Victor Schertzinger, *Kiss the Boys Goodbye*), 'Katy Did, Katy Didn't' (1941, Carmichael, *Hoppity Goes to Town*), 'I Don't Want to Walk Without You' (1942, Jule Styne, *Sweater Girl*), 'Jingle, Jangle, Jingle' (1942, Joseph Lilley, *The Forest Rangers*), 'Touch of Texas', 'Can't Get Out of this Mood' and 'I Get the Neck of the Chicken' (1942, McHugh, *Seven Days Leave*), 'Let's Get Lost' and 'Murder, He Says' (1943, McHugh, *Happy Go Lucky*), 'They're Either Too Young or Too Old', 'How Sweet You Are', 'The Dreamer' and 'I'm Riding for a Fall' (1943, Arthur Schwartz, *Thank Your Lucky Stars*), 'Hello, Mom' (Arthur Jones, Eddie Dunstedter).

It was in 1942 that Loesser first made his mark as a composer. He was in the habit of composing his lyrics to dummy tunes, and when 'Praise the Lord and Pass the Ammunition' was not only accepted for publication with its 'dummy' melody unreplaced, but also became a major hit, he continued to write songs alone. Amongst those which he turned out and which were used by Hollywood over the following years were 'Spring Will Be a Little Late this Year' (1944, *Christmas Holiday*), 'I Wish I Didn't Love You

So', 'Poppa Don't Preach to Me', 'The Sewing Machine' (1947, *The Perils of Pauline*), 'Tallahassee' (1947, *Variety Girl*), 'Bloop Bleep', 'On a Slow Boat to China', 'Baby, it's Cold Outside' (1949, *Neptune's Daughter*) (Academy Award) and 'Now That I Need You' (1949, Betty Hutton in *Red, Hot and Blue*).

In 1948 Loesser came to the Broadway stage with a musicalized version of the famous farce *Charley's Aunt*. The lyrics and music for *Where's Charley?*, written to fit the elderly and extremely English play, included one which was popular at the time ('My Darling, My Darling') and another which lasted a little better ('Once in Love with Amy') but Loesser's score was only a supporting item to the joyous antics of Ray Bolger who led *Where's Charley?* to a long-running Broadway success. However, a second essay at the musical stage, one with a thoroughly American and New York subject, produced something very different. The bookful of colourful and characterful songs which Loesser provided for the adaptation of Damon Runyon's stories as the musical *Guys and Dolls* (1950) remains to this day one of the most outstanding of American musical theatre scores (Adelaide's Lament, 'Sue Me', 'Marry the Man Today', 'Take Back Your Mink', 'My Time of Night', 'I've Never Been in Love Before', 'A Bushel and a Peck', 'Sit Down, You're Rockin' the Boat', 'If I Were a Bell'). The show ran for 1,200 Broadway performances prior to an international career on English-language stages and a place amongst the classics of the musical theatre.

After a highly successful Hollywood venture with the score for the Danny Kaye film of *Hans Christian Andersen* ('The King's New Clothes', 'Thumbelina', 'Wonderful Copenhagen'), Loesser returned to Broadway with another outstanding musical play. *The Most Happy Fella* (1956), for which he provided both text and score, was once again a show that breathed 'America' from every pore. But it took a different turn from its toughly endearing predecessor, seamlessly mixing operatic vocalizing with broad Broadway show songs in a show score of considerable scope and substance, as an accompaniment to a gentle, intimate love story. 'Standing on the Corner', 'Big D', 'Ooh, My Feet' and 'Joey, Joey, Joey' were amongst the popular singles that emerged as *The Most Happy Fella* became a Broadway hit and a perennial favourite.

In the 1960 *Greenwillow* Loesser attempted to step too far away from the genre which had proven itself as his forte and, in the area of near fantasy, met failure for the first time, but his final Broadway musical, the brisk, modern *How to Succeed in Business Without Really Trying*, brought him back to the forthright American folk who suited him best, whilst allowing him to expose more fully the satirical facet of his style in its story of one ingenuous-seeming young man's drive to the very top of the business tree ('Brotherhood of Man', 'A Secretary is Not a Toy', 'Happy to Keep his Dinner Warm', 'Been a Long Day', 'I Believe in You'). *How To Succeed in Business Without Really Trying* gave Loesser his longest Broadway run (1,417 performances), his widest international coverage (it made it to a French production, for example, which few Broadway shows ever managed) and a Pulitzer Prize.

A final musical, *Pleasures and Palaces*, which went – in company with its sources, Sam and Bella Spewack's *Once There Was a Russian* – back to the days of Catherine the Great, closed out of town, but Loesser's total of musical-theatre successes was increased posthumously when his score for the 1952 film *Hans Christian Andersen* became the basis for a London stage musical, *Hans Andersen* in 1974. His works were also the bases for a compilation show *Perfectly Frank* played at Broadway's Helen Hayes Theater in 1980 (ad Kenny Solms, 30 November, 16 performances), and 1985 saw the mounting of *Señor Discretion Himself*, a piece to a text by Budd Schulberg, in a showcase at New York's Musical Theater Works.

The most versatile and inventive musical-comedy writer of his time, Loesser displayed a warmth and wit in creating the songs of the almost inevitably likeable, and always comprehensible American characters who people, in particular, his three great musical shows, each of which remains a classic and a solid part of the basic musical-theatre repertoire.

Loesser's first wife, Lynn, was co-producer of *The Most Happy Fella* (w Kermit Bloomgarden) and of several other shows (*The Carefree Heart*, *The Love Doctor*, *High Fidelity* etc) but is remembered principally for having inspired the irritated soubriquet 'the evil of two Loessers'. His second wife was soubrette Jo Sullivan, the creator of the rôle of Rosabella in *The Most Happy Fella*.

1948 **Where's Charley?** (George Abbott) St James Theater 11 October
1950 **Guys and Dolls** (Abe Burrows, Jo Swerling) 46th Street Theater 24 November
1956 **The Most Happy Fella** Imperial Theater 3 May
1960 **Greenwillow** (w Lesser Samuels) Alvin Theater 8 March
1961 **How to Succeed in Business Without Really Trying** (Burrows, Jack Weinstock, Willie Gilbert) 46th Street Theater 14 October
1965 **Pleasures and Palaces** (w Sam Spewack) Fisher Theater, Detroit 11 March
1974 **Hans Andersen** (Beverley Cross, Tommy Steele) London Palladium 17 November
1985 **Señor Discretion Himself** (Budd Schulberg) Musical Theatre Works 20 November.

Biography: Loesser, S: *A Most Remarkable Fella: Frank Loesser and the Guys and Dolls in his Life* (Donald I Fine, New York, 1993)

LOEWE, Frederick (b Berlin, 10 June ?1904 d; Palm Springs, Calif, 14 February 1988). Composer who combined with Alan Jay Lerner on the scores for several enduring hits, topped by *My Fair Lady*, during the peak years on postwar Broadway.

Frederick Loewe was born in Berlin, the son of Edmund Loewe, a popular Operette light comedian who appeared on the musical stage in Berlin and Vienna (Theater an der Wien as Célestin to Lina Arbarbanell's Nitouche, Alphonse in *Die Dame aus Trouville* etc), and in New York (1903, Florian in *Das süsse Mädel*, *Die Puppe* and *Die Geisha* with Ferenczy's Centraltheater Company, 1906 in *Mam'zelle Nitouche* with Abarbanell etc).

'Fritz' studied music, and, in particular, piano as a youth, but when he moved with his father to America at the age of 20, he found himself unable to make the kind of performing career he had hoped for. He also tried his hand at composing, but it was a decade more before he found any signs of hope in a career in the musical theatre. He managed to place occasional individual numbers, but his first produced shows, written in collaboration with Earle Crooker, did not set him off to a flourishing start. Richard Berger's production of *Salute to Spring*, with Guy Robertson starring, did not make it out of St Louis, whilst a piece called *Great Lady* – again with name value on the marquee in the persons of Irene Bordoni, Helen Ford and Norma Terris, and with an exhaustingly time-warping libretto – lasted just 20 performances on Broadway. He worked with Crooker again on a revised version of a musical entitled *Patricia* (itself a musicalized version of the successful play *The Patsy*) in which Dorothy Stone had played a reasonably successful season on the west coast in 1941. The doctor on the textual side was a young man named Alan Jay Lerner. *The Life of the Party*, again with Dorothy Stone starred, played a second season but kept away from Broadway.

After their work together on this project, Loewe and Lerner collaborated on two further pieces, *What's Up?* (63 performances) and, improving their hit-rate all the time, *The Day Before Spring* (165 performances), before they finally won success, in the wake of *Oklahoma!*, with a delightfully unpretentious piece of romantic Scottish fantasy. *Brigadoon* enchanted both Broadway and London as it set the partners on the road to even bigger triumphs. Loewe successfully submerged any signs of Vienna in such winning numbers as 'Come to Me, Bend to Me', 'It's Almost Like Being in Love' and 'I'll Go Home with Bonnie Jean', just as he turned thoroughly and believably Western for the dashing songs of the pair's next musical *Paint Your Wagon* ('Wand'rin' Star', 'They Call the Wind Maria', 'I Talk to the Trees', 'I Still See Elisa'). *Paint Your Wagon* did a little less well than *Brigadoon*, but the partnership's most memorable triumph came with their next and fifth Broadway show together, the musical adaptation of G B Shaw's *Pygmalion* as *My Fair Lady*.

My Fair Lady's record-breaking Broadway run, its world-wide productions, penetrating even countries where the American musical was otherwise little known, made it the most popular and played show of its era. Once again, Loewe successfully adapted his musical style to a foreign setting and, after being Scots and Wildish-Western, came up with some colourable if smooth-edged English music-hall numbers ('A Little Bit o' Luck', 'Get Me to the Church on Time') as well as a Spanish-flavoured trio, a serenade ('On the Street Where You Live'), which was related to European serenades only in being sung under a window, and sent his heroine off into pre-ball raptures to the memorable strains of 'I Could Have Danced All Night' not in a normally inevitable waltz time, but in 4/4.

Success came for a fourth consecutive time with the human and humorous retelling of the tale of Arthur, Lancelot and Guenevere in *Camelot* (1960, 'If Ever I Would Leave You', 'I Loved You Once in Silence', 'How to Handle a Woman'), before Loewe, convinced that he was unwell, retired from the theatrical scene. He emerged briefly in 1973 to supply additional material for an unfortunate first stage version of the partnership's 1958 film hit, *Gigi*, and combined again with Lerner on the film score *The Little Prince* (1975), but otherwise remained quiet. As is so often the case, he survived another 15 years, seeing his incessantly active partner pass away first before himself died at the fine age of 84.

Loewe's basically romantic music, staunchly rooted in the values (if not necessarily the styles) of the pre-war European operetta, had, like that of the latter-day Richard Rodgers, a substance which had often been absent in a musical theatre where the large proportion of show scores had, for many years, been the works of songwriters and modern-dance composers. Fresh, characterful and singable, and tidily in keeping with its subject, it helped give the Lerner/Loewe collaborations a fine cohesiveness, whilst still producing a large percentage of show standards.

1937 **Salute to Spring** (Earle Crooker) St Louis 12 July
1938 **Great Lady** (Crooker/Crooker, L Brentano) Majestic Theater 1 December
1942 **The Life of the Party** revised *Patricia* (w George Grandee/Earle Crooker, J Keirn Brennan/Barry Connors, Alan Jay Lerner) Detroit 8 October
1943 **What's Up?** (Lerner, Arthur Pierson) National Theater 11 November
1945 **The Day Before Spring** (Lerner) National Theater 22 November
1947 **Brigadoon** (Lerner) Ziegfeld Theater 13 March
1951 **Paint Your Wagon** (Lerner) Shubert Theater 12 November
1956 **My Fair Lady** (Lerner) Mark Hellinger Theater 15 March
1960 **Camelot** (Lerner) Majestic Theater 3 December
1973 **Gigi** (Lerner) Uris Theater 13 November

Biography: Lees, G: *Inventing Champagne: the Worlds of Lerner and Loewe* (St Martin's Press, New York, 1990)

LOFTUS, Kitty (b Carlisle, 16 June 1867; d London, 17 March 1927). Star soubrette of the British stage of the 1890s and 1900s.

The daughter of a touring actor, Kitty Loftus began a stage career as a child actor and in pantomime, before touring in new burlesque rôles (*Little Jack Sheppard*, *Faust Up-to-Date*, *Cinder-Ellen Up-too-Late*) and creating the title-rôle in the most successful of the early variety musical comedies, *The Lady Slavey* (1893). She made her first major London appearance starring as Emma, the housemaid, opposite the *Gentleman Joe* of Arthur Roberts (1895) and paired with the unreliable comic again in *Biarritz* (1896, Janet) and *The White Silk Dress* (1896, Mrs Bailey). She also starred in the allegedly Armenian musical *The Yashmak* (1897, Dora Selwyn), succeeded Kate Cutler to the title-rôle of *The French Maid* (1898) and appeared in New York in *In Gay Paree* (1899).

She went into court to challenge her old partner Roberts when he dropped her as co-star for his West End season of *HMS Irresponsible* after the pre-London tour. In the incomprehensible way of theatrical lawsuits, she somehow managed to lose, and, instead went off to play Shakespeare with Benson and the musical comedy *Bebe* on the road. In 1902 she brought her own touring musical, *Naughty Nancy*, written by Lord Tiverton, to the then-hallowed walls of the Savoy and scored a surprisingly good run with what was essentially a variety musical in the home of comic opera. In 1904 she appeared at Terry's Theatre in the burlesque *The Duchess of Silliecrankie* before going on to see out the last part of her career in variety and in the provinces.

LOGAN, Joshua [Lockwood] (b Texarkana, Tex, 5 October 1908; d New York, 12 July 1988). Broadway director of several major hits of the postwar era.

First an actor, then a director of plays and films, Logan made his bow as a director of Broadway musicals in 1938 with the Rodgers and Hart *I Married an Angel* and the Maxwell Anderson/Kurt Weill *Knickerbocker Holiday*. *Stars in Your Eyes* (1939), with Ethel Merman and Jimmy Durante, and Rodgers and Hart's *Higher and Higher*

(1940), in which Logan also took a hand in the libretto, did less well than his first essay, but success reared its head again when he staged the Rodgers and Hart classical burlesque *By Jupiter* (1942).

Logan subsequently directed Irving Berlin's wartime revue *This is the Army* and, in consequence, was employed for the same task on Berlin's book musical *Annie Get Your Gun*. Following the huge and worldwide success of that musical, he joined Rodgers and Hammerstein as co-producer, co-librettist and director of *South Pacific* with equally memorable results. He filled the same multiple role on two further Broadway successes: the easy-going summer-camp piece *Wish You Were Here* (1952) and the three-into-one musicalization of Pagnol's Marseille tales as *Fanny* (1954), but thereafter he returned for a long time solely to directing. However, the college musical *All American* (1962) and Berlin's *Mr President* (1962) measured their runs in months, *Hot September* (1965) didn't measure its at all, and a final engagement, *Look to the Lilies* (1970), counted its life in days. A last attempt at producing/writing/directing with a musical version of *The Corn is Green*, produced under the title *Miss Moffat*, folded out of town.

Logan had considerable success with several non-musical ventures both as an author (*Mr Roberts*) and a director (*The World of Suzie Wong*). He also directed the screen versions of *South Pacific* with its technicolor Pacific skies, *Camelot* and *Paint Your Wagon*, as well as the filmed *Fanny* without its music.

1940 **Higher and Higher** (Richard Rodgers/Lorenz Hart/w Gladys Hurlbut) Shubert Theater 4 April

1949 **South Pacific** (Rodgers/Oscar Hammerstein/w Hammerstein) Majestic Theater 7 April

1952 **Wish You Were Here** (Harold Rome) Imperial Theater, 25 June

1954 **Fanny** (Rome/w S N Behrman) Majestic Theater 4 November

1974 **Miss Moffat** (Albert Hague/Emlyn Williams/w Williams) Shubert Theater, Philadelphia 7 October

Autobiographies: *Josh* (Delacorte, New York, 1976); *Movie Stars, Real People and Me* (Delacorte, New York, 1978)

LÖHNER, Fritz [aka BEDA or LÖHNER-BEDA, Fritz] (b Wildenschwert, 24 June 1883; d Auschwitz, 4 December 1942).

Dr Löhner (he was a doctor of law) made a career as a musical theatre librettist, a writer of revue, and, under the pseudonym of 'Beda', the lyricist of a large number of popular songs of the 1910s and 1920s, both original German pieces – many in the American style – with titles ranging from 'Tutenkhamen Shimmy' to the 'Komm, meine kleine Colombine' foxtrot, and German versions of foreign numbers (amongst which a German translation of 'Yes, We Have No Bananas' as 'Ausgerechnet Bananen').

His first major stage work, produced (as by 'Fritz Beda') during the Great War, was Edmund Eysler's *Frühling am Rhein*, staged at the Bürgertheater with Louis Treumann starring through 62 performances, but it was well into the 1920s before Löhner found real theatrical success with his libretto for the Operette written around Fred Raymond's hit song *Ich hab' mein Herz in Heidelberg verloren* and the fictionalized romance of Goethe set by Lehár as *Friederike*. Thereafter, he was allotted the task of revising earlier Lehár works, Tauberizing *Die gelbe Jacke* into *Das Land des Lächelns* and *Endlich allein* into *Schön ist die Welt*, and he

also collaborated with Paul Knepler on the heavily dramatic libretto for Lehár's last work, *Giuditta*.

Löhner found a second fruitful collaboration with the Hungarian composer Pal Ábrahám, whose two most successful works he adapted from their original Hungarian into German (*Viktoria und ihr Husar*, *Die Blume von Hawaii*) before writing the text for the composer's third and last major hit, *Ball im Savoy*, and he later worked successfully with other Hungarian composers, Eisemann and Brodzsky, and with the Czechoslovakian Jára Beneš. Imprisoned in Auschwitz in late 1939, he died there three years later.

1910 **Die keusche Susanne** (Leo Ascher) 1 act Kabarett Fledermaus 1 February

1910 **Die fromme Silvanus** (Ascher) 1 act Kabarett Fledermaus 3 November

1911 **Rampsenit** (Ascher) 1 act Kabarett Fledermaus 1 January

1911 **Eine fidele Nacht** (Ascher) 1 act Colosseum 11 September

1913 **Die goldene Hanna** (Ascher) 1 act Apollotheater 4 January

1913 **Das Gartnerhäuschen** (Béla Lazsky) 1 act Künstlerspiele 1 December

1914 **Frühling am Rhein** (Edmund Eysler/w Carl Lindau, Oscar Fronz) Wiener Bürgertheater 10 October

1915 **Der Weltenbummler** (Richard Fall/w Lindau) Montis Operettentheater, Berlin 18 November

1916 **Der Sterngucker** (Franz Lehár) Theater in der Josefstadt 14 January

1917 **Die Dame von Welt** (R Fall/w Hans Kottow) Apollotheater 31 January

1917 **Die Anne-Marie** (Franz Schubert arr Max Egger) 1 act Ronacher 1 November

1918 **Muschi** (Robert Stolz) 1 act Gartenbau 1 January

1918 **Das Zuckergoscherl** (R Wagner, Arthur Guttmann) 1 act Hölle 31 August

1920 **Kikeriki** (Stolz/w Otto Hein) Rolandbühne 31 December

1921 **Der Herr der Welt** (Károly Hájos/w Carl Bretschneider, Franz Wolf) Komische Oper 4 October

1922 **Der schwarze Pierrot** (Hájos) Theater am Nollendorfplatz, Berlin 19 May

1923 **Die Brasilierin** (Oskar Jascha/w Max Neal) Carltheater 12 January

1923 **Der keusche Heinrich** (Hans Duval-Diamant/w Lindau) Jantschtheater 29 March

1924 **Revanche** (Jascha/Fritz Lunzer) Wiener Bürgertheater 8 November

1925 **Die Bojarenbraut** (Willy Engel-Berger/w Kottow) Carltheater 22 September

1927 **Ich hab' mein Herz in Heidelberg verloren** (Fred Raymond/Ernst Neubach/w Bruno Hardt-Warden) Volksoper 26 April

1928 **Friederike** (Lehár/w Ludwig Herzer) Metropoltheater, Berlin 4 October

1930 **Frühling in Wienerwald** (Ascher/w Lunzer) Neues Wiener Stadttheater 17 April

1930 **Viktoria und ihr Husar** (*Viktória*) German version w Alfred Grünwald (Stadttheater, Leipzig)

1930 **Das Land des Lächelns** (Lehár/Léon ad w Herzer) Theater in der Wien 26 September

1931 **Bei der Wirtin Rosenrot** (Ascher/w Paul Knepler) Theater des Westens, Berlin 14 March

1931 **Schön ist die Welt** (Lehár/ad w Herzer) Theater an der Wien 21 December

1931 **Die Blume von Hawaii** German version w Grünwald (Neues Theater, Leipzig)

1932 **Ball im Savoy** (Pál Ábrahám/w Grünwald) Grosses Schauspielhaus, Berlin 23 December

1933 **Rosen im Schnee** (Karl Loewe arr Jascha/w Hardt-Warden) Volksoper 20 January

1933 **Katz im Sack** (*Zsákbamacska*) German lyrics (Die Komödie)

1934 **Giuditta** (Lehár/w Paul Knepler) Hofoper 20 January

1934 **Märchen im Grand-Hotel** (Ábrahám/w Grünwald) Theater an der Wien 29 March

1934 **Der Sterne der Manege** (*Vadvirág*) German version w Hugo Wiener

1934 **Der Prinz von Schiras** (Josef Beer/w Herzer) Theater an der Wien 20 November

1934 **Die verliebte Königin** (*A szerelmes királynő*) German version w Grünwald (Scala Theater)

1935 **Dschainah, das Mädchen aus dem Tanzhaus** (Ábrahám/w Grünwald) Theater an der Wien 20 December

1935 **Der gütige Antonius** (Jára Beneš/w Wiener) Volksoper 23 December

1936 **Auf der grünen Wiese** (*Na t louce zelen*) (Beneš/V Tolarsky ad w Wiener) Volksoper 9 October

1937 **Polnische Hochzeit** (J Beer/w Grünwald) Stadttheater, Zurich 3 April

1938 **Grüss und Kuss aus der Wachau** (Beneš/w Wiener, Fritz Eckhardt/Wiener, Karl Breuer) Volksoper 17 February

LOLA MONTEZ Musical in 2 acts by Alan Burke. Lyrics by Peter Benjamin. Music by Peter Stannard. Union Theatre, Melbourne, 19 February 1958. Revised version Her Majesty's Theatre, Brisbane, 1 October 1958.

One of the periodic attempts in Australia to produce a musical with international possibilities, *Lola Montez* was sponsored by the financially pressed Elizabethan Theatre Trust, a straight theatre organization, which hoped to cash in with a run on the lines of those achieved by the profitable imported musicals of the time. It was written by one of their former producers, with songs by two young men whose principal experience had been in university revue. An early, small-scale version of the show was tried out, under the Trust's aegis, at the Union Repertory Company in Melbourne, with operatic vocalist Justine Rettick as Lola, and seven months later an enlarged and revised version, with one number cut and two fresh ones inserted, was produced at Brisbane, with English dancer Mary Preston as the heroine, before being brought to the Trust's Sydney Theatre. The much-publicized show (using the byline 'a gay, virile Australian musical') proved to be agreeable but undistinguished by anything except being 'local' and it folded with severe losses.

Ms Montes (sic) got an earlier showing as the heroine of an Amadeo Vives Zarzuela produced at Madrid's Teatro de la Zarzuela in 1903.

Recording: original cast (Columbia)

LOMBARDO, Carlo [aka BARD, Leon etc] (b Naples, 28 November 1869; d Milan, 19 December 1959). Italian musical man-of-all-parts who contributed to much of the best of his country's musical theatre for many years.

Lombardo began in the musical world as a writer of songs, and apparently made his first attempts at stage musical pieces in his early twenties. He became musical director of a touring operetta company, a job which he subsequently traded in for that of chief comedian in the same group before founding his own company, with himself as leading player and his brother Costantino taking over the post of musical director. For that company, he turned out Italian versions of a number of foreign musical

shows. The fidelity of those versions can only be guessed at, but given Lombardo's later depredations on other folk's works, it is unlikely that the originals survived in a very recognizable state. His company toured in Italy and in Northern Africa, where he trouped in 1907 with a repertoire consisting of versions of such pieces as *The Geisha*, *The Toreador* and *The Orchid*.

Lombardo had a singular success when (under the pseudonym of 'Leon Bard') he reorganized Bruno Granich-städten's *Majestät Mimi* into a piece which he called *La Duchessa del Bal Tabarin*, and another when he mixed some of the score of Josef Szulc's hit musical comedy *Flup..!* with pieces borrowed from Cuvillier's *Der lila Domino*, from Offenbach, Lehár and Vicente Lleó with a libretto set in a Paris nightclub, under the title *Madama di Tebe*. Other composers who came under his pasticcio-making hand included Vienna's Leo Ascher (*La Regina della fonografo*) and Budapest's Béla Zerkovitz (*La bambola della prateria*), but his cheeky request to Lehár for a new operetta won him instead the opportunity to rework an old one. The revue-operetta which he fabricated around the composer's *Der Sterngucker* score under the title *La danza delle libellule* proved sufficiently popular for the show to be retranslated into German and played in Vienna and elsewhere mostly with more success than *Der Sterngucker* had had.

Lombardo worked both as a musician and a text-writer, or sometimes as both, but his most successful operettas were those in which he had a proven composer as a partner. A collaboration with composer Mario Costa produced two of the most effective of Italian native operettas, *Scugnizza* and the pasticcio *Il re di Chez Maxim*, and another with Virgilio Ranzato produced two further Italian standards, *Il paese dei campanelli* and *Cin-ci-là*. The best of his later works, *La casa inamorata*, a collaboration with Renato Simoni, was another piece that became part of the Italian repertoire.

In the fashion of the time (or slightly earlier) Lombardo turned out a number of libretti based on French comedy texts. Amongst the famous plays which he borrowed were Feydeau's *La Dame de chez Maxim* (*La dama di Montmartra*), Moreau and Sardou's *Madame Sans-Gêne* (*Cri-cri*), de Flers and de Caillavet's *Primerose* (*Primarosa*) and, in the making of yet another pasticcio, this time of the music of Robert Stolz, a version of Hennequin and Veber's *La Présidente* (*La Presidentessa*).

His brother, Costantino Lombardo, also composed several operettas, including a musical version of Mélesville's *Sullivan* (1914), and works on such popular subjects as *Vita d'artista* (1916), *La Pompadour* (1918), *La Sirena delle Folies-Bergère* (1920) and *Diana al bagno* (1924).

1891 **Un viaggio di piacere** (E Favi) Teatro Gerbino, Turin, 30 January

1892 **I coscritti** (L Manna) Teatro Alfieri, Turin, 10 May

1892 **Il borgomastro** (w Achille Grafigna/G Maresca) Teatro Quirino, Rome 26 October

1896 **La milizia territoriale** (Maresca) Teatro Balbo, Turin, ?April

1910 **Amor de principi** (*Pufferl*) Italian version (Teatro Fossati, Milan)

1914 **La signorina del cinematografo** (*Der Schmetterling*) Italian version

1916 **La signora mia moglie** (Felice Checcacci) Teatro Miramar, Naples 2 September

1916 **Il marito decorativo** (Adolfo Bossi/ad)

1917 **La regina della fonografo** (Leo Ascher ad/w 'Gil Blas') Teatro Fossati, Milan 3 February

1917 **La Duchessa del Bal Tabarin** (*Majestät Mimi*) revised Italian version

1917 **Linotte** (Ernest Coop) Teatro Quirino, Rome, 3 July

1918 **Cloclo** (Emilio Gragnani) Politeama Nazionale, Faenza 7 November

1918 **Madama di Tebe** pasticcio based on the score of *Flup..!* et al (Teatro Fossati, Milan)

1918 **Il figlio in accomandita** (Carlo Nicolò) Teatro del Casino, Montecatini, September

1919 **Il re di chez Maxim** (Mario Costa arr/Arturo Franci) Teatro Fossati, Milan, 10 May

1919 **Si** (*La Dame des Folies-Bergère*) (Pietro Mascagni/Franci) Teatro Quirino, Rome, 13 December

1920 **Changez la dame** (Coop/Georges Berr ad) Politeama Chiarella 14 February

1922 **La danza delle libellule** revised Italian version of *Der Sterngucker* (Teatro Lirico, Milan)

1922 **Il paese dei campanelli** (Virgilio Ranzato) Teatro Lirico, Milan, 23 November

1922 **Scugnizza** (Costa) Teatro Alfieri, Turin, 16 December

1923 **La bambola della prateria** (Béla Zerkovitz ad) Teatro Fossati, Milan 12 May

1923 **La Presidentessa** (Robert Stolz arr)

1924 **Luna Park** (Ranzato) Teatro Lirico, Milan 26 November

1925 **La dama di Montmartre** (Ermete Liberati/Feydeau ad)

1925 **La Fornarina** (pasticcio ad/Giuseppe Adami)

1925 **Cin-ci-là** (Ranzato) Teatro dal Verme, Milan 18 December

1926 **Primarosa** (Guiseppe Pietri/w Renato Simoni)

1926 **Gigolette** revised *La Danza delle libellule* w Gioacchino Forzano Teatro lirico, Milan 30 December

1927 **La città rosa** (w Ranzato/Carlo Ravasio) Teatro Lirico, Milan 13 April

1927 **Miss Italia** (Alfredo Cuscina/w A Zorzi ad)

1928 **Cri-cri** (Ranzato) Teatro dal Verme, Milan 28 March

1928 **Il trillo del diavolo** (Cuscina/w A Lanocita) Teatro Lirico, Milan, 2 May

1928 **I Merletti di Burano** (w Ranzato/w Ravasio) Teatro Lirico, Milan 22 December

1929 **La casa inamorata** (Renato Simoni) Teatro Lirico, Milan 15 November

1929 **Zig-Zag** (Ivan Darclée) Teatro dal Verme, Milan, 2 February

1929 **L'isola verde** (Pietri/w Luigi Bonelli) Teatro Lirico, Milan, 16 October

1930 **Mille e un bacio** (Vittorio Mascheroni/w Lanocita) Teatro dal Verme, Milan, 1 February

1930 **La Duchessa di Hollywood** (Ranzato) Teatro dal Verme, Milan 31 October

1931 **Le tre lune** (Lombardo) Teatro Verdi, Florence 5 February

1932 **Parigi che dorme** (Lombardo) Teatro Argentina, Rome, 16 December

1932 **L'appuntamento nel sogno** (Simoni) Odeon, Milan 22 October

1932 **Prigioni di lusso** (Ranzato/w Ravasio) Odeon, Milan 26 March

1937 **I mulini di Pit-Lil** (w Colombini) Teatro Lirico, Milan 2 February

Other titles attributed: *Crema di chic, Il Viaggio di Perrichon, Tre studenti e una cocotte, Diavolo e jazz*, Italian versions of *Coqueli-cot, Fanfan la Tulipe, Der Fremdenführer* (*Cavaliere della luna*).

LONNEN, E[dwin] J[esse] (b Hull, 1861; d Ipsden, Warwickshire, 31 October 1901). Star comedian of the Gaiety new burlesques.

Born into a touring theatrical family, Lonnen played in stock companies in his teens, then took bit parts with the barnstorming Barry Sullivan in Shakespeare and on the road with Edward Terry. He had an early musical theatre experience in the comic opera *The Bachelors* (Sam Sleepy) at Manchester, but his first successful venture in London was in burlesque at the Avenue Theatre, where he appeared under the management of Alexander Henderson in the supporting rôle of Tony Foster in *Kenilworth* (1885) in a cast including Arthur Roberts, J J Dallas, Violet Cameron and the Broughton sisters. He played Skragge-stein in the same company's *Lurline* (1886) and appeared in Henderson's production of *Falka* (1886), then moved to the new Prince of Wales Theatre for Messager's *La Béarnaise* (1886, Girafo) after which he was promptly picked up by George Edwardes as a supporting comedian to Fred Leslie for the Gaiety's new burlesque productions.

Lonnen's first appearance at the Gaiety was as the policeman, de Villefort, in *Monte Cristo Jr* (1886). He made a great success singing Robert Martin's Irish song 'Bally-hooley' and, when Leslie and Nellie Farren took *Monte Cristo Jr* on tour, he remained behind to head the Gaiety's alternative company as Claude Frollo 'a monk and a villain of deepest dye' in *Miss Esmeralda* (1897). The French monk also had an Irish song, and 'Killaloe' proved even more popular than its predecessor as Lonnen quickly became one of the hottest comedy stars in town. He appeared as Visconti in *Frankenstein* (1887) and then as Mephistopheles in *Faust Up-to-Date* (1888 'Enniscorthy', 'McCarthy's Widow', 'Donegal', 'I Shall 'ave 'em') and, after Fred and Nellie had had their turn with *Ruy Blas and the Blasé Roué*, he returned from the road to create Don José to Florence St John's Carmen in *Carmen Up-to-Data* (1890). This time he sang of 'The Jolly Boys' Club' and, instead of the usual Irish song, tried a nigger minstrel number, 'borrowed' from the repertoire of the Christy Minstrels. 'Hush, the Bogie' turned out to be the greatest of his many great hit songs.

Lonnen took over John Shine's rôle of Charles VII in *Joan of Arc* when that show transferred to the Gaiety and caused a sensation with the rather-too-topical 'Jack the Dandy, Oh', but finally in *Cinder-Ellen Up-too-Late* (1891) the two Gaiety burlesque teams joined up again and Lonnen took second place in the comic cast as Prince Belgravia to Fred Leslie's Servant (ie Buttons), introducing Lionel Monckton's first Gaiety song, 'What Will You Have to Drink?' and the Irish 'Teaching McFaddyen to Dance'. At the end of *Cinder-Ellen* he headed the latest and last of the great Gaiety tours to Australia (1892) playing Frollo, Arthur de Richemont (*Joan of Arc*), Don José and Mephistopheles with a company including Marion Hood, Robert Courtneidge and Addie Conyers.

When he returned, it was to find that the new burlesque, of which he had been one of the brightest stars, was almost a thing of the past, but he had one last grand burlesque rôle – at the Lyric, and not at the Gaiety where he had passed his seven years of stardom – as the detective O'Hoolegan in *Little Christopher Columbus*, equipped with a mass of disguises and Ivan Caryll's 'The Indiarubber Shoe', 'I Pay No Attention to That' and the popular 'Rumpty Tumty'.

Lonnen never took to musical comedy as he had to burlesque. He went to South Africa with Alice Lethbridge under the management of Luscombe Searelle and ended up getting imprisoned by the Boers in Pretoria, he succeeded Shine as William White in London's *The New Barmaid* (1896), played large rôles in the adaptation of Eugen von Taund's *Der Wunderknabe* as *The Little Genius* (1896, Chevalier Tween) and the flop musicals *Man About Town* (1897, Frank Ennesleigh) and *The Maid of Athens* (1897, The O'Grady), he played Cabestan in Willie Edouin's production of *Toto and Tata* (1897) at Leeds and guested as a Huntsman in *Dorothy* for Furneaux Cook's benefit before renouncing musical comedy for the music-halls and an essay at a play. He returned, at the last, to the Gaiety when Edwardes cast him in a supporting rôle in *The Messenger Boy*, but at the end of the show's run he was taken ill and he died a few months later at the age of 40.

Lonnen's three brothers also partook of theatrical careers. Walter Lonnen was a supporting comedian in musicals, Lonnen Meadows was a musician, and Victor Champion (d 20 July 1910) was a conductor, mostly on the touring circuits and in suburban theatres but also, occasionally, at the Gaiety and other London houses. Edwin's daughter Jessie Lonnen also went on the stage and appeared in a number of musical comedies, both in Britain and in Australia.

LONSDALE, Frederick [LEONARD, Lionel Frederick] (b St Helier, Jersey, 5 February 1881; d London, 4 April 1954).

Variously a private soldier, an employee of the London and South Western Railway and a winning layabout, the young Lonsdale struggled for a number of years to make a career as a playwright until his wife, who had taken a job as a chorus girl for William Greet to make ends meet, got his work read by her employer. Greet sent it to fellow producer Frank Curzon, who not only put the young man on a retainer but eventually produced his first work: the musical play *King of Cadonia*, which he had set to music by none other than the composer of *The Geisha*, Sidney Jones, and the doyen of lyricists, Adrian Ross. It was, however, Lonsdale's very much more substantial than usual dialogue for the show's Ruritanian comic opera plot which both won *King of Cadonia* fine notices and helped the musical to a long career. After a couple of indifferent runs with straight plays, he turned out a second successful musical for Curzon. *The Balkan Princess* was basically little more than *King of Cadonia* with the sexes reversed, but it, too, had a good London run and a remarkably long and wide provincial and export life.

After a hiatus of some five years, during which Curzon turned down his author's newest text, Lonsdale reappeared on the London musical stage under the patronage of George Edwardes with the libretto for a third successful musical, *Betty*, at Daly's Theatre and following Edwardes's death he submitted the text Curzon had rejected to Daly's Theatre manager Bobby Evett. Evett staged it as *The Maid of the Mountains* and the show became one of the phenomena of the wartime London theatre, compiling one of the longest runs in the history of the musical theatre and establishing itself as a classic of the British musical stage.

As Lonsdale moved on towards a career which would establish him as one of London's favourite writers of classy comedy, he did not abandon the musical stage. He adapted Booth Tarkington's *Monsieur Beaucaire* as a highly success-

ful light opera for André Messager, he made the English versions for the enormously popular British productions of Jean Gilbert's *Die Frau im Hermelin* (*The Lady of the Rose*) and *Katja, die Tänzerin* and for Leo Fall's *Madame Pompadour*, but he wrote only two more original libretti. His Parisian tale of *The Street Singer*, commissioned by and devised for Phyllis Dare and with lyrics by his Jersey compatriot Ivy St Helier, told another conventional operetta tale in a manner that ensured it a more than conventional success, but his final piece, *Lady Mary*, 20 years after his splendid beginning with *King of Cadonia*, turned out to be the one musical venture which was rather less than a hit. From this time on Lonsdale wrote only plays but, after two decades of success, it seemed evident by the early 1930s that his era was past.

Remembered today principally for the four or five comedy hits of his career (*On Approval*, *The Last of Mrs Cheney* etc), Lonsdale, nevertheless, had considerably more, and more lucrative, successes in the musical theatre. He wrote the text for one of the greatest hits of the London musical stage in *The Maid of the Mountains*, and, if his other musicals are no longer played in Britain, *Monsieur Beaucaire* has remained in the repertoire in France for the 70 years since its original production.

Lonsdale's daughter Frances Donaldson became an author of, amongst other books, her father's biography, whilst his illegitimate daughter Angela became the mother of Britain's theatrical Fox family: actors Edward and James and producer Robert.

1908 **King of Cadonia** (Sidney Jones/Adrian Ross) Prince of Wales Theatre 3 September
1910 **The Balkan Princess** (Paul Rubens/Arthur Wimperis/w Frank Curzon) Prince of Wales Theatre 19 February
1915 **Betty** (Rubens/w Gladys Unger) Daly's Theatre 24 April
1916 **High Jinks** English adaptation (Adelphi Theatre)
1917 **The Maid of the Mountains** (Harold Fraser-Simson/Harry Graham) Daly's Theatre 10 February
1919 **Monsieur Beaucaire** (André Messager/Ross) Prince's Theatre 19 April
1922 **The Lady of the Rose** (*Die Frau im Hermelin*) English version (Daly's Theatre)
1923 **Madame Pompadour** English version (Daly's Theatre)
1924 **The Street Singer** (Fraser-Simson/Ivy St Helier) Lyric Theatre 27 June
1925 **Katja the Dancer** (*Katja, die Tänzerin*) English version w Harry Graham (Gaiety Theatre)
1928 **Lady Mary** (Albert Szirmai, Phil Charig/w John Hastings-Turner) Daly's Theatre 23 February

Biography: Donaldson, F: *Freddy Lonsdale* (Heinemann, London, 1957)

LOPEZ, Francis [LOPEZ, Francisco] (b Montbéliard, 15 June 1916). The brightest musical star of the postwar years in France, whose output frittered away into embarrassing imitations of himself after he had produced some of the happiest Parisian scores of the 1950s.

Trained as a dentist, Lopez had his first musical successes as a part-time songwriter before turning to the theatre for the first time in 1945. His initial opérette, *La Belle de Cadix*, a colourful, vivacious piece hastily written to play six weeks at the small Casino-Montparnasse, ran for two years and provided the French musical theatre with the same kind of new acceleration that *Oklahoma!* had recently provided in America. Lopez and his librettist/lyricist

Raymond Vincy followed up with a series of like pieces for larger Parisian stages over the next decade, pieces which, like *Oklahoma!*, returned to the classic romantic operettic proportions in a deft textual and musical mixture of the sentimental and the comic set in the most colourful of venues (*Andalousie, Pour Don Carlos, Le Chanteur de Mexico, À la Jamaïque, La Toison d'or, Méditerranée*). Unlike their American counterparts, however, the pair also worked on a number of more intimate comedy musicals such as *Quatre Jours à Paris* and *La Route fleurie* which were mounted at smaller venues with success equal to that won by their bigger shows, thus dominating the postwar musical theatre large and small.

After Vincy's death, Lopez continued writing ostensibly the same kind of pieces, to mostly much less able texts, supplying a series of often long-running if very obvious opérettes à grand spectacle to the large stage of Paris's Théâtre du Châtelet and only occasionally, as in *Viva Napoli* (1970), finding again the hearty freshness of his earlier work. Familiar strains set to what became thin and painfully predictable libretti and orchestrations became the order of the day in the 1980s as Lopez became his own producer at, successively, the Théâtre de la Renaissance, the Elysée Montmartre and the Eldorado, producing scrappily written and staged shows in which his wife, Anya, and son, Rodrigo, often took a hand. Madame Lopez and her son were credited with the score for *La Perle des Antilles* (1979) (nevertheless billed as 'opérette de Francis Lopez'), and the younger Lopez also composed the music for his father's production of *Aventure à Tahiti* (1988).

Whilst Lopez's more recent shows, and intermittent revivals of his earlier ones, play to their particular audience at his Parisian base, contributing no little to the falling reputation and image of 'opérette' amongst the French younger generation, the provincial theatres of France continue to welcome productions of his earlier works, and no season passes in the French theatre without numerous revivals of his best (and, occasionally, his less good) musicals being seen in all corners of the hexagon.

Several of Lopez's early opérettes were made into films (*La Belle de Cadix, Andalousie, Quatre Jours à Paris, Le Chanteur de Mexico, À la Jamaïque*), and the composer also supplied songs and scores for a good number of musical films of the 1940s and 1950s, including *Je n'aime que toi*, *L'Aventurier de Séville, Sérénade au Texas* and the musical film remake of *Violettes impériales*, composed for the theatre by Vincent Scotto.

Unsophisticated though it may often be, the rhythmic, sentimental and immensely singable music of his earliest opérettes is in the happiest tradition of popular light musical theatre, and his best scores as admirable as the last are inane. When these are attached to the best of Vincy's texts (*Quatre Jours à Paris, Andalousie*) they make up into delightful theatre pieces.

A 1987 autobiography concentrates on the composer's career as a ladykiller rather than on his work.

1945 **La Belle de Cadix** (Maurice Vaucaire/Raymond Vincy) Casino Montparnasse 24 December

1947 **Andalousie** (Vincy, Albert Willemetz) Théâtre de la Gaîté-Lyrique 25 October

1948 **Quatre Jours à Paris** (Vincy) Théâtre Bobino 28 February

1949 **Monsieur Bourgogne** (Vincy, Jean-Jacques Vital) Théâtre Bobino 12 March

1950 **Pour Don Carlos** (Vincy, André Mouëzy-Éon) Théâtre du Châtelet 17 December

1951 **Le Chanteur de Mexico** (Henri Wernert/Vincy, Félix Gandera) Théâtre du Châtelet 15 December

1952 **La Route fleurie** (Vincy) Théâtre de l'ABC 19 December

1953 **Soleil de Paris** (Vincy) Théâtre Bobino 7 March

1954 **À la Jamaïque** (Vincy) Théâtre de la Porte Saint-Martin 24 January

1954 **La Toison d'or** (Vincy) Théâtre du Châtelet 18 December

1955 **Méditerranée** (Vincy) Théâtre du Châtelet 17 December

1956 **El Aguila de Fuego** (Arturo Rigel, Francisco Ramos de Castro) Teatro Maravillas, Madrid 19 January

1957 **Tête de linotte** (Vincy) Théâtre de l'ABC December

1957 **Maria-Flora** (w Henri Betti/Vincy) Théâtre du Châtelet 18 December

1958 **S E la Embajadora** (Rigel, Jesus M de Arozamena) Teatro Alcázar, Madrid 21 November

1958 **La Cancion del amor mio** (M Brocey, A Quintero, Arozamena) Madrid

1959 **Le Secret de Marco Polo** (Vincy) Théâtre du Châtelet 12 December

1961 **Visa pour l'amour** (Vincy) Théâtre du Gaîté-Lyrique December

1963 **Cristobal le Magnifique** (Vincy) Théâtre de l'Européean December

1963 **Le Temps des guitares** (Vincy, Marc-Cab) Théâtre de l'ABC October

1967 **Le Prince de Madrid** (Jacques Plante/Vincy) Théâtre du Châtelet 4 March

1969 **La Caravelle d'or** (Plante/Jean Valmy) Théâtre du Châtelet 19 December

1970 **Viva Napoli** (Daniel Ringold/René Jolivet) Théâtre Mogador 4 September

1972 **Gipsy** (Ringold/Claude Dufresne) Théâtre du Châtelet 18 December

1974 **Les Trois Mousquetaires** (w Anja Lopez/Ringold/Jolivet) Théâtre du Châtelet 23 February

1975 **Fiesta** (Dufresne) Théâtre Mogador 23 February

1976 **Volga** (Plante, Ringold/Dufresne) Théâtre du Châtelet 26 November

1980 **Viva Mexico** revised *Fiesta* (Plante, Ringold/Dufresne) Théâtre de la Renaissance 22 February

1981 **Aventure à Monte-Carlo** (Ringold/Dufresne) Théâtre de la Renaissance

1981 **Soleil d'Espagne** (Ringold/Dufresne) Théâtre de la Renaissance 3 October

1981 **La Fête en Camargue** (Ringold/Dufresne) Théâtre de Saint-Étienne 3 December

1982 **Le Vagabond tzigane** (Ringold/Dufresne, Fernand Cayol) Théâtre de la Renaissance 2 October

1982 **Vacances au soleil** (Ringold/Dufresne, Cayol) Théâtre de Besançon 4 December

1983 **L'Amour à Tahiti** (Ringold/Dufresne) Théâtre de l'Élysée-Montmartre 1 October

1984 **Les Mille et une nuits** (Ringold/Dufresne) Théâtre de l'Élysée-Montmartre 6 October

1985 **Carnaval aux Caraïbes** (w Rodrigo Lopez/Ringold/Dufresne) Théâtre de l'Élysée-Montmartre 27 September

1986 **Le Roi du Pacifique** (Ringold/Dufresne) Théâtre de l'Élysée-Montmartre 24 September

1987 **Fandango** (Ringold/Dufresne) Théâtre de l'Élysée-Montmartre 16 January

1988 **Rêve de Vienne** (Ringold/Dufresne) Théâtre de l'Eldorado 30 September

1989 **La Marseillaise** (Ringold/Dufresne) Théâtre de l'Eldorado 7 July

1989 **La Belle Otéro** (Ringold/Dufresne) Théâtre de l'Eldorado 30 September

1990 **Portorico** (Ringold/Dufresne) Théâtre de l'Eldorado 30 September

1991 **Sissi** (Ringold/Dufresne, Nadine de Rotschild) Théâtre de l'Eldorado 8 September

1992 **Mariane mes amours** revised *La Marseillaise* Théâtre de l'Eldorado 26 September

Autobiography: *Flamenco: la gloire et les larmes* (Presses de la Cité, Paris, 1987)

LORD PICCOLO Operette in 3 acts by Carl Lindau and Rudolf Schanzer. Music by Henri Berény. Johann Strauss-Theater, Vienna, 1 September 1910.

Berény's most successful Operette, produced by Leopold Müller at the Johann Strauss-Theater, starred Lisa Weise as Daisy, the barmaid from the Parisian Tabarin dance-hall who pretends to be the little lost heir to the Scottish earldom of Goberdeen long enough to allow her foster-brother, Jim (Carlo Böhm), to be given his rightful place. Louis Treumann shared the top billing as the comical detective, Arsène Dupont, set on the trail of the missing heir by Lord Goberdeen (Oscar Sachs) and Eduard Rose was Gaston, Marquis de Champ d'Azur, who is Daisy's ultimate reward.

Berény's score, composed in classic proportions with numbers for Daisy (mostly), Gaston, Dupont and Lord Goberdeen featured alongside a ration of duets, a trio, a quartet and a full-scale first-act finale, was topped by a waltz duo for Gaston and Daisy in the first act.

Lord Piccolo played to its 50th performance on its first run, was brought back for some matinée showings the following year, and was later produced, without arousing too much enthusiasm, both in Germany and in Hungary. In America, however, it had a genuine success. Adapted in two acts by Edward Paulton and A E Thomas, with lyrics by Grant Stuart and a number of other folk, some additional numbers with a Scots flavour written and composed by Paulton and another two, one of which was a medley of popular Scots tunes, by musical director Arthur Weld, the piece was presented by Henry Savage under the title *Little Boy Blue*. A little-known actress, Gertrude Bryan, starred as Daisy and won herself praise as 'the musical comedy find of the season', as the production ran with singular vigour through a very appreciable 174 performances on Broadway before going on to a further fine life on the road.

Germany: ?1911; Hungary: Temesvár 18 April 1911, Budai Színkör 28 September 1911; USA: Lyric Theater *Little Boy Blue* 27 November 1911

LOSEBY, Constance (b London, 1850; d London, 13 October 1906). Star soprano of the British opéra-bouffe stage who introduced many important rôles to the 19th-century London stage.

Originally a music-hall performer in a double act ('Constance and Losebini') with her mother, Connie Loseby made early appearances in Sara Lane's variety bills at the Britannia, Hoxton, before progressing to such houses as the Alhambra where she came under the management of John Hollingshead.

When Hollingshead opened the Gaiety Theatre, he engaged the 18-year-old Miss Loseby as one of his original company and she appeared there on the opening night opposite Charles Lyall as Columbine in Jonas's *The Two Harlequins* and as Raimbault in Gilbert's *Robert the Devil* burlesque. She remained with the Gaiety for some seven years, appearing in burlesque (Don Diego in *Columbus*,

Ellen Tyler in *Wat Tyler MP*, Morgiana in *The Forty Thieves*, *Martha*, Tresham in *Guy Fawkes*, the remake of *MM Dunanan* as *The Great Metropolis*, Donna Anna in *Don Giovanni in Venice*), in comedy (*London Assurance*, *The Hypocrite*), drama (*Snae Fell*), ballad opera (Polly Peachum in *The Beggar's Opera*), English opera (*Letty the Basketmaker*) and in opéra-bouffe of all kinds. She appeared as Prince Raphaël in *The Princess of Trébizonde*, Princess Hermia in *Barbe-bleue*, Caesarine in *Malala* (ad fr *Fleur de thé*), Gabrielle in *The Island of Bachelors* (*Les Cent Vierges*), Clairette in *La Fille de Madame Angot*, Paris in *La Belle Hélène*, Gigolette in *Tromb-al-ca-zar*, as Galatea in the Gaiety's version of *Die schöne Galathee*, and in several of the earliest British musicals: as Princess Veloutine to the Aladdin of Nellie Farren in *Aladdin II*, as the 'ugly' sister Bellezza in *Cinderella the Younger*, and as Nicemis in Gilbert and Sullivan's *Thespis*.

In 1876 she went to Manchester to play the heroine of Cellier's *The Sultan of Mocha*, and in 1878 she joined the company playing London's most spectacular productions of opéra-bouffe at the Alhambra. With a few forays out, she remained at the Alhambra for five years starring as Geneviève in *Geneviève de Brabant*, Florine in *La Poule aux oeufs d'or*, Angelo in *Venice* (*Le Pont des soupirs*), Prince Raphaël, Countess Cameroni in *La Petite Mademoiselle*, Rothomago in *Rothomago*, Stella in *La Fille du tambour-major*, Marguerite in *Mefistofele II* (*Le Petit Faust*), Jeanneton in *Jeanne, Jeannette et Jeanneton*, Black Crook in the Alhambra's version of the *Biche au Bois/Black Crook* tale, Mistigris in *Babil and Bijou*, and Violetta in Strauss's *The Merry War*, returning after the fire which destroyed the theatre to star again as Sirene in *The Golden Ring*. Her outside engagements during this period included the leading rôles in two British pieces, the comic opera *The Lancashire Witches* (1882, Alizon) and the title-rôle of Luscombe Searelle's *Estrella* (1883). She toured in 1884 as *Nell Gwynne* and then, after a remarkable career of some 15 years as one of the West End's leading musical artists, retired from the stage.

LOST IN THE STARS Musical tragedy in 2 acts by Maxwell Anderson and Alan Paton based on Paton's novel *Cry, the Beloved Country*. Music by Kurt Weill. Music Box Theater, New York, 30 October 1949.

An 'operaticized' version of the highly successful South African novel *Cry, the Beloved Country*, *Lost in the Stars* told the tale of Absalom (Julian Mayfield), the son of a black minister (Todd Duncan), who murders the son of one of his father's white neighbours during an attempted robbery, and is sentenced to hang. In this racially orientated tale, however, the accent is not on the 'murder' and the 'robbery', but on the 'black' and the 'white', as the father of the killer and the suddenly liberalized father (Leslie Banks) of the victim come together, at the end of the evening, in some kind of an unsteadily improved understanding.

The bulk of Kurt Weill's musical score fell to the rôle of the churchman ('Lost in the Stars', 'Thousands of Miles' etc), whilst the feminine part of the musical entertainment rested largely with Absalom's mistress, Irina (Inez Matthews), and a prominent place was reserved for a chorus which narrated and commented on the action. In spite of the respected names attached to it, the Playwrights' Company production of this 'musical tragedy' had only a

891

respectable but ultimately insufficient run of 273 performances on Broadway.

A 1972 revival (Imperial Theater, 18 April) ran 39 performances, and a filmed version was made in 1974 with that production's lead man, Brock Peters, repeating his rôle. *Lost in the Stars* is played regularly in America, mostly in situations where its theme of the former South African apartheid politic and/or racial disharmony in general are fashionable, and occasionally under professional circumstances.

Film: AFT 1974

LOST, STOLEN OR STRAYED (aka *Lost, Strayed or Stolen*) Musical farce in 3 acts by J Cheever Goodwin based on the play *Le Baptême du petit Oscar* by Eugène Grangé and Victor Bernard. Music by Woolson Morse. Fifth Avenue Theater, New York, 21 September 1896.

On the day of his christening, the baby of Monsieur Bidart goes astray. The nursemaid gave him to a soldier in the Luxemburg Gardens to hold, and that soldier cannot be found. Bidart (Louis Harrison) and the three godfathers, the exuberant Chachignon (M A Kennedy), string-bean, misanthropic Courte Botte de Roquencourt (Joseph Herbert) and the bright little notary Godard, set out to find baby Oscar. They gallop through the barracks and through the boudoir of Mlle Rose d'Été (Georgia Caine), having to assume ridiculous disguises when found where they shouldn't be and braving the lady's irate Cuban guardian, the possessor of a poisonous handshake, on the way, before baby is found.

Morse and Goodwin illustrated the French antics with a score of lively songs, from which 'When Two Hearts Love' proved the favourite, and the show, with a cast completed by Irene Verona (Françoise), Rose Beaudet (Catherine), Cyril Scott (Gaston de Champignol, Rose's gentleman friend), Emma Janvier (Louise) and Fannie Bulkeley (Honorine Girardin, the baby's godmother), had a respectable stay of 77 nights through more than two months at the Fifth Avenue Theater before moving on both to the country and, a rare thing for an American musical at the time, to Britain.

Exported to a London at the peak of the British musical-theatre boom, *Lost, Strayed or Stolen* was mounted with South African comedian Frank Wheeler as Bidart, Decima Moore (Rose), Ethel Sydney (Honorine) and J H Barnes, Arthur Appleby and Herman de Lange as the three godfathers. It was well noticed as a jolly entertainment, and Johnnie D'Auban's eccentric dance routines won rave notices, but it failed to attract. The producers took no half-measures. They hired Louie Freear, the comic star of *The Gay Parisienne*, and wrote in a rôle for her, they changed other cast members and the show's title (*A Day in Paris*), souped up the second act, and what little remained of the original score ('When Two Hearts Love', 'Two Heads Are Better Than One', 'Jean and Jacques' etc) was complemented by a barrage of local numbers: Arthur Godfrey's 'Why Did the Little Fly Fly?' and 'Summer Tide', Leslie Stuart's 'The Goblin and the Fay', Herbert Darnley's 'Blowed if Father Ain't Commenced to Work' for Louie Freear, 'She Just Walks On' (Mills/Scott), 'An Extra Little Bit Thrown In' (Sidney Jones/Bowyer), 'It's Painfully True' (Roby/Cross). It was to little avail, and the show was shunted out to Islington after ten weeks.

UK: Duke of York's Theatre (aka *A Day in Paris*) 27 April 1897

LOUDON, Dorothy (b Boston, 17 September 1933). Versatile actress who came into her own in the musical theatre in character rôles.

After early work in stock and revue, Miss Loudon made her first Broadway appearance in the short-lived Izzy and Moe musical *Nowhere to Go But Up* (1962). In a career mixing straight and musical-theatre appearances, she toured as the *Unsinkable Molly Brown* and Reno Sweeney, in *The Apple Tree* and *High Spirits*, appeared on Broadway in *The Fig Leaves Are Falling* (1968, Lillian Stone) and stopped short in *Lolita My Love* (1971, Charlotte Haze), before memorably creating the rôle of the kiddie-loathing Miss Hannigan in a very different kind of nymphet musical, *Annie* ('Little Girls', 'Easy Street') in its metropolitan production.

She subsequently succeeded to the rôle of Mrs Lovett in Broadway's *Sweeney Todd*, starred opposite Vincent Gardenia as Bea Asher in *Ballroom* (1978) and repeated her *Annie* rôle in the 'Miss Hannigan Fights Back' version of the musequel *Annie 2*.

LOUISIANA PURCHASE Musical comedy in 2 acts by Morrie Ryskind based on a story by B G De Sylva. Music and lyrics by Irving Berlin. Imperial Theater, New York, 28 May 1940.

One of the later examples of the group of mostly 1930s musical comedies which liked to think they were politically satirical, *Louisiana Purchase* followed hopelessly clean Senator Oliver P Loganberry (Victor Moore) down to New Orleans where he has been ordered to carry out an investigation into the indubitably dubious activities of the Louisiana Purchase Company. The company's lawyer Jim Taylor (William Gaxton) sets out to divert and compromise Loganberry, bringing in such big guns as the sexy Marina van Linden (Vera Zorina) and Madame Bordelaise (Irene Bordoni) to knock him off his high moral standards. After some musical comedy ups and downs, and a lot of winning comedy from Moore – cast yet again as a buffonish politician, following his double helping of Throttlebottoms in *Of Thee I Sing* and *Let 'em Eat Cake* and the unable-to-do-wrong ambassador of *Leave it to Me!* – the lovable senator ends up wedding la Bordelaise, whilst Taylor gets Marina, in good, tidy Gilbert and Sullivan style.

Irving Berlin's score of a dozen numbers accompanied the story brightly, with Miss Bordoni's assertion that 'It's a Lovely Day Tomorrow' (always a winner of a title for wartime, even other people's wartime) coming out as the most popular single number, alongside her suggestive 'Latins Know How', a happy title-song, an opening called 'Sex Marches On' and some less louche lyrics such as 'You're Lonely and I'm Lonely', 'Outside of That, I Love You', 'What Chance Have I (with love)?' and 'Dance With Me (tonight at the Mardi Gras)'.

A winning combination of grand comedy, songs, production values and a fine cast, Buddy De Sylva's production of *Louisiana Purchase* settled down as the principal hit of 1940 (which nevertheless included *Panama Hattie*, *Pal Joey* and *Cabin in the Sky*), running through 444 performances on Broadway, and bundling directly into the movie studios where Mlles Bordoni and Zorina again vamped Moore who was pitted this time against Bob Hope in the rôle of Taylor. Only three of the show's songs ('It's a Lovely Day Tomorrow', 'You're Lonely' and the title-song) survived into a film which, since only one other number was added, was rather shorter on music than the original piece.

Moore, Gaxton and Miss Bordoni took up their rôles again for a tightened-up TV version in 1951, but *Louisiana Purchase* did not travel beyond America and ultimately none of its songs made its way into the Irving Berlin book of standards.

Film: Paramount 1941
Recording: compilation (JJA)

LOUIS XIV Opérette in 3 acts by Serge Veber. Music by Georges van Parys and Philippe Parès. Théâtre de la Scala, Paris, ?October 1929.

Serge Veber's musical comedy vehicle for the celebrated singing comedian Dranem cast him as a grocer in prey to a celluloid passion for film-star Diamond Black (Lily Zevaco). When a film-director spots in him the sosie of King Louis and stars him opposite his dreamgirl in a Louis XIV film, the grocer takes all his friends to filmland with him and Versailles becomes an on-screen havoc. In his royal garb, little Louis briefly succeeds in winning Miss Black before going back to grocering, and, since his battle-axe wife (Martine Lestac/Pauline Carton) has gone off with a svelte screen-star (Jacques Vitry/Pierre Dorly), he takes the faithful little shopgirl Odette (Suzette O'Nil) with him. Urban and Morton added to the comedy as two of Odette's soupirants.

Veber's script earned him accusations of plagiarism from André Vivolette, the French adaptor of *Merton of the Movies*, but the local piece got to the stage first and suffered not a whit from these aspersions. Henri Darcet's production at the Scala boasted 'la fleur des comiques' in its advertising and indeed the comedy of Veber's libretto and the cast of top comedy players did much towards the success of *Louis XIV*. It had a fine first run and was reprised at the Théâtre de l'Étoile in 1945, under the title *On cherche un roi*, with Champi in Dranem's rôle and Urban repeating the part he had created 16 years earlier.

A Florenz Ziegfeld Broadway show (Sigmund Romberg/Arthur Wimperis, Ziegfeld-Cosmopolitan Theater 2 March 1925) went in for phonetics, calling itself *Louie the 14th*. Like the French piece, it wasn't about the King of France at all, but was a version of the German play, *Ludwig XIV* (Theater des Westens 15 March 1918), by Julius Wilhelm and Paul Frank about an army chow-puncher who gets invited to a posh dinner to prevent there being an unlucky 13 guests at the table. Comedian Leon Errol performed his regular routines, whilst getting to imitate the cook, a mountain guide and a nobleman, alongside leading lady Doris Patston, without the show – which Ziegfeld had boomed as 'the greatest musical comedy ever' – really taking off. It played 79 performances on Broadway, and closed its subsequent tour in Chicago after the star had had time off with an injured leg.

LOVE FROM JUDY Musical comedy in 2 acts by Eric Maschwitz adapted from the play *Daddy Long-Legs* by Jean Webster. Lyrics by Hugh Martin and Timothy Gray. Music by Hugh Martin. Saville Theatre, London, 25 September 1952.

Love from Judy was an attempt to create an American musical in Britain in which producer Emile Littler teamed local librettist Eric Maschwitz with American stage and film composer Hugh Martin (*Meet Me in St Louis*, *Best Foot Forward* etc) and the 1914 Broadway play *Daddy Long-Legs*, a 264-performance success at New York's Gaiety Theater (28 September) and a triumph at London's Duke of York's Theatre two years later (514 performancs).

The sentimental story of an orphanage girl, Judy Abbott (Jeannie Carson), and her mysterious benefactor, Jervis Pendelton, whom she calls Daddy Long-Legs (Bill O'Connor), was a natural for adaptation into an equally sentimental musical. Maschwitz kept the well-known plot, in which Pendleton – who is not, as the girl supposes, an old man – eventually wins Judy's love as well as her gratitude, placed the action in more picturesque surroundings to supply some spectacle, and added 17 mostly incidental numbers including an old-fashioned concert scene and an obligatory dream-ballet on Agnes de Mille lines.

There was an orphans' chorus, a Mardi Gras number, a deep-south blackface 'Get Out Your Old Banjo', a black maid (Adelaide Hall) to sing of 'A Touch of Voodoo', a smooth title-song for the hero, a perky blonde soubrette (June Whitfield) to squawk out the most enjoyable piece of the evening with the denial that she was 'Dum-dum-dum' and a series of other pieces which all sounded like a purée of Broadway and Hollywood as illustration to a piece which, if unoriginal, proved, at least, likeable. The orphans, the sentiment, the liveliness and a winning performance from Miss Carson helped the made-to-formula *Love from Judy* to a 594-performance run in London, followed by four years of touring.

Recording: Original cast recordings on *Three by Hugh Martin* (JJA Records/Encore)

LOVE IN A VILLAGE Comic opera in 3 acts by Isaac Bickerstaff based on *The Village Opera* by C Johnson. Music composed, selected and arranged by Thomas Arne and Edward Toms. Theatre Royal, Covent Garden, London, 8 December 1762.

One of Bickerstaff's most popular comic operas, *Love in a Village* was based, like so many contemporary pieces, on a plot designed to get young aristocrats paired off as their hearts rather than their parents desire. Rossetta (Charlotte Brent) runs away and disguises herself as chambermaid to her friend, Lucinda Woodcock (Miss Hallam), rather than marry unseen the son of Sir William Meadows (Mr Collins), who himself runs away rather than obey his father's orders to wed Rossetta. Young Meadows (George Mattocks) ends up disguised as a gardener at the Woodcock's house, and predictably falls for the disguised Rossetta. In the meanwhile Lucinda is planning to elope with her beloved Jack Eustace (Mr Dyer), who is posing as a music master in the house, under the noses of Justice Woodcock and his tight-lipped maiden sister Deborah (Mrs Walker). Deborah catches them out, but Jack's credentials and Deborah's opposition combine to make the Justice permit the match. The supporting characters included a jolly country squire, Hawthorn (John Beard), and a pair of comical servants, Hodge (Mr Dunstall) and Madge (Miss Davies).

The accompanying musical part included some 30 to 43 numbers (added to, latterly, by a whole series of ad lib interpolations), including 'The Miller of Dee' as performed by Hawthorn as his entrance piece, and seven original pieces composed specifically for the piece by Arne (five) and Samuel Howard (two). This original contribution, and the more substantial nature of the score, it has been argued, disqualifies the piece from being considered a ballad opera and makes it 'the first English comic opera'.

Love in a Village was played 37 times in its first season in the repertoire at Covent Garden, was a major success, and was repeated on English language stages for many decades thereafter.

During the brief fashion for 18th-century musical shows in London during the 1920s, *Love in the Village* was given a revival at the Everyman Theatre (21 December 1923, mus arr Julian Herbage), and another at the Lyric Hammersmith (19 April 1928, 124 performances) in a version with a score rearranged by Alfred Reynolds. Rose Hignell (Rossetta), Sybil Crawley (Lucinda), Frederick Ranalow (Hawthorn), Una O'Connor (Deborah) and Nigel Playfair (Meadows) featured, with veteran Savoyard H Scott Russell in a small rôle.

USA: Southwark Theater, Philadelphia January 1767, New York 11 January 1768; Australia: Theatre Royal, Sydney 22 February 1836

LOVE LIES Musical play in 2 acts by Stanley Lupino and Arthur Rigby. Lyrics by Desmond Carter. Music by 'Hal Brody'. Gaiety Theatre, London, 20 March 1929.

Following his success with *Lady Luck* and a larger one with *So This is Love*, producer-performer Laddie Cliff continued with a third piece in the same dance-and-laughter mode, written by and played by the same team that had been involved in the previous show. Lupino and Rigby's silhouette-slight book involved the usual wealthy uncles and scallywag nephews who have got entangled with girls without asking the permission of those relations from whom they have expectations. The functions of each artist were maintained, Lupino going in for the low comedy and a whole lot of disguises, Cliff taking the tricky dancing and little-fellow comedy, and Cyril Ritchard and Madge Elliott being the romance and the graceful dancing. The songs, mostly by the team of British songwriters who were still pretending to be a fashionably American 'Hal Brody', were a bundle of the lightly dancing kind from which 'You've Made a Difference to Me' as delivered by Ritchard and Miss Elliott emerged as the best. As so often, however, it was the interpolations which proved the most popular: Billy Mayerl's 'A House on a Hill Top', Leslie Sarony's nonsensical 'I Lift Up My Finger (and say tweet-tweet)' as performed by Lupino, and De Sylva, Brown and Henderson's 'I'm on the Crest of a Wave' borrowed from one of *George White's Scandals*.

Cliff took *Love Lies* to the famous Gaiety Theatre, which had fallen onto sadly hard times, and the show gave that house its biggest success since *Going Up* a decade earlier. It won delighted notices, which compared it and its performers favourably with the recent *Funny Face*, a production which had featured no less artists than the Astaires and Leslie Henson, and it settled in for a run of 347 performances. Before the London run was done, there were two companies on the road taking *Love Lies* to the provinces, a total which rose to three when the London company took to touring at the end of its run, and the show was still to be seen on the provincial lists in 1931, by which time Cliff and his team had compounded their success with more of the same type of shows.

An Australian production under the management of Richard White and Eric Edgley featured Dan Agar, Bobby Gordon, Rita McLean, Clem Dawe and Compton Coutts, for four-week seasons in Melbourne and Sydney (Theatre Royal, 24 May 1930).

A 1931 BIP film version scripted by and starring Lupino, and directed by Lupino Lane, omitted the music.

Australia: King's Theatre, Melbourne 5 April 1930

LOVE LIFE Vaudeville in 2 acts by Alan Jay Lerner. Music by Kurt Weill. 46th Street Theater, New York, 7 October 1948.

Like Rodgers and Hammerstein's *Allegro* of the previous season, Alan Jay Lerner and Kurt Weill's *Love Life* sported a libretto which looked at its two principal characters, from a standpoint apart, more as the victims of their environment than as real people of action. The story of the love-life of Sam (Ray Middleton) and Susan (Nanette Fabray) Cooper was told in a revusical fashion, in a series of scenes which (after a prologue set in the present) took them through various periods of time from 1791 through 1821, 1857, 1890 and the 1920s, back to the present. Like the couple of *Allegro* they progress from a promising start to infidelity, and it is all the fault of the American way of life and its economic pressures which Lerner apparently considered – for the purposes of this piece, at least – to have been less in 1791 than in 1948.

The songs of *Love Life* included some which were set in the action, notably the winning first-scene duo for the two principals, 'Here I'll Stay', and others which were presented between the scenes, repeating in song what was played in the action in the style of traditional Jewish theatre ('Economics', 'Progress'). The second act, wholly set in present time, and including a dance sequence featuring Punch and Judy in the throes of divorce and a long scena played as a stylized minstrel show, ultimately gave forth some hope for the future of marriage in this hard, modern world. As long as you go into it with your eyes and wallet open. The other principal dance sequence of the entertainment was the first-act 'Green-Up Time', and the score also included a number entitled 'I Remember it Well' whose lyric was later made over for Maurice Chevalier and Hermione Gingold for re-use in the film *Gigi*.

In spite of being equipped with two fine star performances in its not very coherent leading rôles, with Michael Kidd's lively choreography and with much in the way of colourful spectacle to assist its unconventionally shaped tale and score, *Love Life* failed to become a success. It ran 252 Broadway performances without either breaking even or establishing itself in the exportable or revivable repertoire. It was given a 1990 staging at the American Music Theater Festival of Philadelphia (10 June) with Richard Muenz and Debbie Shapiro featured in a tinkered-with version.

Recording: selection on *Lyrics by Lerner* (Walden/DRG)

LOVE OFF THE SHELF

LOVE OFF THE SHELF Musical in 2 acts by Roger Hall. Lyrics by A K Grant. Music by Philip Norman. Fortune Theatre, Dunedin, New Zealand, 29 August 1986.

A revusical eight-hander written by New Zealand playwright Roger Hall, who had had a London stage success with his play *Middle-Age Spread* shortly before, *Love off the Shelf* took the romantic novel as its subject and source of fun. John is a serious but unpublished writer who has spent ages working on a book about a minor poet. Mary is his serious research assistant. On the side, each begins to write romantic fiction, and the action of the show sees the characters of their pink novellas come off the page to tangle with their authors and with each other in a series of comic scenes and songs which culminates in a suitably romantic ending. The score was in an ultra-light, revusical vein, producing comical moments as two wide-eyed and be-skied characters met on 'The Virgin Slopes of Love', as that novelist's sine qua non the 'Deux ex Machina' put in an appearance, or as a bemused stock character bewailed 'You'd Think it Was Fine to Be Virile'.

A successful New Zealand production was followed by a six-month tour and then by a production in Southampton, England. Marilyn Cutts and Barry James led the company in a more revue-like version of the show which cut some of the structure from the libretto whilst maintaining most of the score unchanged. Well received, it was mooted for a London showing which failed to get off the drawing-board in a period when West End audiences and producers were still concentrating on the large-scale musical spectaculars and pastiche shows that had been their diet for some years. *Love off the Shelf* nevertheless remains the first New Zealand-produced musical to have been played in Great Britain since *The Wreck of the Pinafore* over a century earlier.

UK: Nuffield Theatre, Southampton 17 December 1987
Recording: original cast (Kiwi Pacific Records)

LOVE O' MIKE

LOVE O' MIKE Musical comedy in 2 acts by 'Thomas Sydney' (Sydney Smith and Augustus Thomas). Lyrics by Harry B Smith. Music by Jerome Kern. Shubert Theater, New York, 15 January 1917.

The show which eventually became *Love o' Mike* was first produced at the Lyric Theater, Philadelphia (20 November 1916), under the title *Girls Will Be Girls*, as a joint production by the Shuberts and Elisabeth Marbury but, after an unsuccessful start, it was taken off after two weeks of performances and given a thorough overhaul. In just two further weeks major revisions were made to the text and the score (four songs were jettisoned and replaced by five others, in spite of the fact that Kern was working concurrently on another show), several of the lead rôles were recast and the show re-opened at New Haven (25 December 1916) under the new title of *Love o' Mike*. Three weeks later it was on Broadway.

English actor Lawrence Grossmith (brother to the more famous George) was the Mike of the title, an English soldier and Lord whose dashing presence cuts out all the other fellows at the house party run by Mrs Marvin (Alison McBain). Whilst the girls cluster, the boys try to discredit Mike, but the comical butler (George Hassell) spoils their plans and Mike comes out as heroic as ever at the end of the evening, with his choice of the girls (Vivian Wessell) to

boot. The pick of the songs turned out to be one of the additions, 'It Wasn't My Fault' (lyrics: M E Rourke) which Kern had lifted from the score of his 1915 flop *Ninety in the Shade* to be performed here by Grossmith and Miss Wessell. Grossmith's limited voice was not taxed much further, and the bulk of the songs went to the boys and girls of the house party amongst whom were to be found the young Peggy Wood singing of 'A Lonesome Little Tune', Clifton Webb duetting 'It's in the Book', and Luella Gear. Miss Wessel retained two of the best of the original songs, 'I Wonder Why' and 'The Baby Vampire'.

The two weeks of hard work proved to have been worth their while, and the bright and extremely lightweight piece of entertainment ran for 192 Broadway performances. On the road, however, it was less successful and did not confirm its happy New York run.

THE LOVE RACE

THE LOVE RACE Musical play in 2 acts by Stanley Lupino. Lyrics by Desmond Carter. Music by Jack Clarke. Additional numbers by H B Hedley and Harry Acres. Gaiety Theatre, London, 25 June 1930.

After the success of *Love Lies*, Laddie Cliff attempted to repeat the formula which George Edwardes had successfully used at the Gaiety Theatre in the 1880s by sending his star team on the road, with the original show to play and a new one to prepare, whilst holding the theatre open with a second team and another musical show. The second team and *Darling, I Love You* did not come up to hopes and expectations, and *The Love Race* promptly brought the A-team back to town.

Disapproving elders and youthful love were again the theme of the piece, with Cyril Ritchard as a film star and Madge Elliott playing the daughter of a socialist MP who disapproves of film stars, whilst Stanley Lupino was the son of a car magnate in love with Fay Martin as the daughter of a rival manufacturer. Laddie Cliff was her brother, Fred Conyngham and Esmé Tosh were a supporting song-and-dance pair, Drusilla Wills provided low comedy, Connie Emerald (Mrs Stanley Lupino) the soubrette comedy, and Violet Farebrother, Arthur Wotton and Arthur Rigby jr played the heavy parents.

The team was equipped with plenty of comedy, light and low, and nine mostly dance-orientated numbers of which the three star men singing and dancing 'You Can't Keep a Good Man Down' and Laddie Cliff's 'Spring is in the Air' proved the best. Lupino's 'I Stamp My Foot' did not come up to *Love Lies*'s 'I Lift Up My Finger'. The stars scored a repeat success, to which had to be added a success for costumier Irene Segalla who had, in the age of naked kneecaps, put her ladies back into long dresses, a decision perhaps not unconnected with the improving billing of the elegant and longline Miss Elliott. *The Love Race* ran 237 performances, rather short of the producers' most hopeful expectations, but it lasted for two provincial seasons and confirmed Cliff and Lupino in their successful ways.

J C Williamson Ltd mounted a production in Australia with Gus Bluett, Leo Frankyln, Alfred Frith, Elsie Prince and Josie Melville featured in a starry cast, but the piece proved to have no future beyond its Sydney season.

A 1931 film starring Lupino followed the pattern set with *Love Lies* and omitted the music.

Australia: Her Majesty's Theatre, Sydney 16 May 1931

THE LOVE RACKET Musical play in 2 acts by Stanley Lupino. Additional dialogue by Arty Ash. Lyrics by Frank Eyton, Barbara Gordon and Basil Thomas, and Leslie Gibbs. Music by Noel Gay. Additional numbers by Hubert Gregg and Freddie Bretherton. Victoria Palace, London, 21 October 1943.

Allegedly a successor to *Lady Behave*, in the same dubious style that *Me and My Girl* had been billed a sequel to *20 to 1*, *The Love Racket* repeated the names of some of the earlier piece's characters but without even the connection of having them played by the same artist. Author and *Lady Behave* star Stanley Lupino was, in fact, dead by the time Jack Hylton and Lupino Lane staged his last stage work, and his rôle was taken by Arthur Askey who starred alongside Roy Royston, Harry Milton, Valerie Tandy, Carole Raye and Peggy Carlisle as the six filmland folk of the earlier show, this time mixed up in problems over the making of a film which is apparently a cert to be the blockbuster of its era. The accompanying songs included 'Happy Days' (Harry Milton, Carol Raye) and 'Reaching for the Moon' (Carol Raye) amongst a pleasant dance-and-laughter set.

The Love Racket proved a viable vehicle, and Askey confirmed himself as the legitimate successor to Lupino Lane at the theatre where Lane had triumphed in *Me and My Girl*, but the show's run was interrupted by Lane's decision to return to 'his' theatre himself in *Meet Me Victoria*, which necessitated the removal of the still-profitable *Love Racket* to the Prince's Theatre. It was interrupted again by enemy bombing which, after eight and a half months and 324 performances, forced the show out of town. It was taken on an ENSA round of service entertainment, and then on a regular provincial tour, returning to London five months later for a Christmas season at the Adelphi Theatre (23 December 1944, 36 performances). Askey then took the show back on the ENSA trail, around the provinces again, before, after more than two years in his rôle, handing it over to Ernie Lotinga. However in 1949 he took up the part one more time for an Australian production which confirmed both his own popularity and that of his show.

Australia: Tivoli, Melbourne 23 December 1949

LOVE'S LOTTERY Comic opera in 2 acts by Stanislaus Stange. Music by Julian Edwards. Broadway Theater, New York, 3 October 1904.

History does not relate how producer F C Whitney persuaded 43-year-old Metropolitan Opera star Mme Ernestine Schumann-Heink away from her operatic and concert pursuits to appear on the musical stage. One can only suppose that the lure was either money, or the unusual opportunity for the contralto to play the heroine. The vehicle which Whitney provided was a comic opera which cast Mme Schumann-Heink as a German laundress called Lina (which took care of the hefty accent if not the lady's ingenuous acting style) and paired her with English baritone Wallace Brownlow, the original Luis of *The Gondoliers*, in a story of true love in the England of the Napoleonic wars.

Julian Edwards's score was by no means overwhelmingly written for his star, nor, curiously, did it seek to capitalize on her gifts. She had four songs, two in each act, but if 'She is the Right Girl for Your Money' gave her a little cadenza, and the closing 'Sweet Thoughts of Home' allowed a few cello-like low A-flats, 'Kind Fortune Smiles Today' and 'A Spanish Grandee' were pretty standard stuff with vocal lines which never ventured above the stave and rarely more than a tone or two below. Brownlow had a solo in each half and a duo and a trio with the star, Louise Gunning and George L Tallman were the number-two couple and John Slavin as Barney O'Toole provided the comedy ('The Blarney of Killarney'), but *Love's Lottery* was not sufficiently distinguished to win more than 50 performances on Broadway.

DES LÖWEN ERWACHEN Operette (comic opera) in 1 act by Julius Rosen. Music by Johann Brandl. Carltheater, Vienna, 26 April 1872.

A four-handed, one-act Operette on the Offenbach model, Rosen and Brandl's 18th-century piece centred on the young Gaston (Hermine Meyerhoff), the second son of the local lord, who has been brought up, without expectations, by the local teacher Placide (Karl Blasel). To keep his ward, Paquerette (Frl Guilleaume), safe from the pubescent boy, Placide locks her up in the mill, but when news comes that the Herzog's eldest son has died and that Gaston is now his heir, Placide decides that a boy with his expectations needs a different kind of education. Part of that education involves letting Paquerette out of the mill. By the time Placide discovers that the news was incorrect and bundles the girl back into the mill it is too late – the lion of the title has awakened. Fortunately the Herzog has given Gaston a commission, so he marches away leaving the girl safe with her rural lover (Herr Küstner).

The most enduring of the many pieces (few of which, however, were legitimate Operetten) written by Carltheater musical director Brandl, and one of the best of the early attempts at short 'French' Operetten by Viennese composers, *Des Löwen Erwachen* was played 18 times during 1872, and became a firm favourite in Vienna. It was reprised regularly at the Carltheater, and played at the Strampfertheater (25 December 1872), the Theater an der Wien (31 March 1886), the Hofoper (22 October 1893) and at Venedig in Wien (31 August 1900), as well as throughout Germany.

Germany; ?1873

LOWENFELD, Henry (b ?Poland; d Paris, 20 November 1931).

A wealthy businessman, owner of the Kops Ale brewery, of a stockbroking firm and, if word told true, of a fair chunk of the Isle of Wight, Lowenfeld moved into the musical theatre in 1893 when he picked up Albéniz's failing comic opera, *The Magic Opal*, had it rewritten, leased the Prince of Wales Theatre and reproduced it there. Its re-failure apparently daunted him not, and he continued to run musicals at the Prince of Wales, scoring notable successes with Arthur Roberts in *Gentleman Joe* (1895) and, above all, with the French musical *La Poupée* (1897), a long-running hit which he had picked up from Paris after most of London's managers had rejected it. He met with failure, however, when he put his trust in French composer Justin Clérice, first with the previously unproduced *The Royal Star* and then an English version of the composer's Portuguese success *O Moliero d'Alcala*, presented as *The Coquette* (1899). Infuriated by a section of the first-night gallery audience which drowned a perfectly adequate musical with their whistling and shouting, he went on stage and harangued the self-appointed arbiters of his show. Soon after, although *The Coquette* showed every signs of running, he removed it, sold his lease, and got himself and his money out of a business which did not behave like a business, but where profit and loss could be decided by a handful of irresponsible (or paid) whistlers.

LUDERS, Gustave [Carl] (b Bremen, 13 December 1865; d New York, 24 January 1913). One of the best and most successful composers for the comic opera stage at the turn of the American century.

Having spent his youth and study years in Germany, where he worked latterly as a band musician, Luders moved to America in 1888 and settled in Milwaukee. There he was engaged first as a theatre and pleasure-garden musician and later as a conductor and as a staff arranger for the music-publishing company of Witmark. Under Witmark's banner he found his first success when his transcription of Barney Fagan's song 'My Gal is a Highborn Lady' became a hit. The music publisher and songwriter Charles Harris encouraged him to move to the more musically active Chicago, where there was currently a shortage of trained musicians in the publishing trade, and it was there that Luders began his career as a theatre composer by placing the odd number in such pieces as *By the Sad Sea Waves* ('In Dear Old London') and by writing a stop-gap score for Harry B Smith's *Little Robinson Crusoe* (1895) for a Chicago theatre.

Having taken a taste for this new activity, he teamed with Frank Pixley, a Chicago journalist, to write a second piece. They were unable to find a producer for the completed *King Dodo*, but a second effort, *The Burgomaster*, was taken up by the Dearborn Theater and turned out to be a major Chicago success. It had but a brief Broadway run (33 performances) with Raymond Hitchcock and Zelma Rawlston featured, but proved highly popular through several years of touring for manager William Cullen. The previously unwanted *King Dodo* was now snapped up by Henry Savage, and it duly followed a similar path from Chicago to New York (64 performances) and to a long life on the lucrative road.

The third Luders/Pixley work, *The Prince of Pilsen*, turned out to be their best and their most successful. This time even Broadway took notice of the happily American-Continental comic opera with its fine 'Stein Song' and its pretty 'The Message of the Violet' and the piece, certainly one of the best of all early American comic operas, not only lived out many years on the road but returned for repeated revivals and even travelled to London and to Paris with some success after its initial 143 nights in New York.

This run of success finally prompted a call eastwards for Luders, and a commission to provide the score for Florenz Ziegfeld's production of *Mam'selle Napoléon*, a Jean Richepin piece he was having adapted as a vehicle for Anna Held. In 1905 Luders had a second Broadway job writing part of the score for the Hippodrome spectacular *A Society Circus* but, in between, he turned out two further pieces in his own Chicago vein. George Ade's *The Sho-Gun*, after splendid seasons in Chicago and New York (125 performances) and a long tour, proved to be another export when, by some chain of events, it was staged with notable success at the Király Színház in Budapest, and the

pretty fantasy *Woodland* (83 Broadway performances), written again with Pixley, also had a good life on the home circuits.

The last three of the Pixley/Luders team's shows were disappointing. Klaw and Erlanger's production of the old-fashioned *The Grand Mogul* (40 performances), *Marcelle* (68 performances) and *The Gypsy* (12 performances), all built on the same format of easy comedy and well-written, tuneful songs were simply a little less fresh than their first attempts, and they duly did increasingly less well. Luders' simultaneous collaborations with Ade on the college musical *The Fair Co-Ed* (136 performances), a follow-up to the librettist's *The College Widow* starring Elsie Janis, and on a Montgomery and Stone vehicle for Charles Dillingham, *The Old Town* (171 performances), each helped not a little by the popularity of its respective stars, had much longer Broadway lives.

With Pixley having gone into retirement after the flop of *The Gypsy*, Luders paired for his next Broadway show with the young Avery Hopwood, but Henry Savage's production of their *Somewhere Else* proved to be the composer's quickest-ever failure. Four days after the première Luders died, reportedly of a broken heart.

A composer of well-written, unpretentiously attractive music with a delightfully catchy lilt, ranging from bubble-light waltzes with a tinge of the old world right through the range of song styles to coon songs and politely ragtimey numbers which were wholly of the new world, as well as of thoroughly musical ensembles in the best comic-opera tradition, Luders was one of the most effective composers in the American musical theatre of his time. His best shows rank musically alongside those of Herbert and Caryll as the choice produce of the Broadway stage in the first decade and a bit of the century.

1895 **Little Robinson Crusoe** (Harry B Smith) Schiller Theater, Chicago, 21 June
1900 **The Burgomaster** (Frank Pixley) Dearborn Theater, Chicago 17 June; Manhattan Theater 31 December
1901 **King Dodo** (Pixley) Chicago; Daly's Theater 12 May 1902
1902 **The Prince of Pilsen** (Pixley) Tremont Theater, Boston, May; Broadway Theater 17 March 1903
1903 **Mam'selle Napoleon** (Joseph W Herbert) Knickerbocker Theater 8 December
1904 **Woodland** (Pixley) Tremont Theater, Boston 25 April; New York Theater 21 November
1905 **A Society Circus** (w Manuel Klein/Sydney Rosenfeld) Hippodrome 13 December
1904 **The Sho-Gun** (George Ade) Studebaker Theater, Chicago 4 April; Wallack's Theater 10 October
1906 **The Grand Mogul** (Pixley) Colonial Theater, Chicago 7 December; New Amsterdam Theater 25 March 1907
1908 **Marcelle** (Pixley) Casino Theater 1 October
1908 **The Fair Co-Ed** (Ade) Boston; Knickerbocker Theater 1 February 1909
1910 **The Old Town** (Ade) Globe Theater 10 January
1911 **Ladies' Day** (Vernon Cassard) Ladbroke Hall, London 4 October (copyright performance); Lyric Theater, Philadelphia 13 January, 1913
1912 **The Gypsy** (Pixley) Park Theater 14 November
1913 **Somewhere Else** (Avery Hopwood) Broadway Theater 20 January

LUIGINI, Pauline

The daughter of composer François Luigini (*Les Odalisques de la rue de Lancry, Faublas*) Pauline Luigini was a leading member of the company at the Brussels Fantaisies-Parisiennes under the management of Eugène Humbert in the early 1870s. As such, she became the creator of the rôle of Clairette Angot in *La Fille de Madame Angot* (1872), the title-rôle of *Giroflé-Girofla*, Marion in Vogel's *La Filleule du roi* (1875) and the leading rôle of French version of the Jonas's *Chignon d'or*. Having seen the first two rôles recast for Paris whilst she stayed with the Brussels company, she was finally given the third on its production in France, only to have the show prove very much less liked than its two brilliant predecessors.

Mlle Luigini subsequently appeared in the Parisian première of Offenbach's *La Boîte au Lait* (1876, Paméla), starred opposite Louise Théo as Bavolet in a revival of *La Jolie Parfumeuse* (1877) and in the opéras-comiques *Capitaine Fracasse* at the Théâtre Lyrique and *Scheinn Baba* (1879) at Nice, but she had her best metropolitan chances when her husband, Taillefer, took over the management of the Théâtre Cluny in 1881–2 and featured her as Bibletto in *Les Braconniers*, Stella in *La Fille du tambour-major*, and in the title-rôle of Michiels's new but unsuccessful opérette *Mimi Pinson* (1882).

In fact, Luigini's greatest moments had come in Brussels and in London, where, whilst Paola Marié and Jeanne Granier gleaned the real fame from the parts of Clairette and Giroflé-Girofla in Paris, she had travelled to play her famous rôles with the Brussels company.

LUISA FERNANDA

LUISA FERNANDA Zarzuela in 3 acts by Federico Romero and Guillermo Fernández Shaw. Music by Federico Moreno Torroba. Teatro Calderón, Madrid, 26 March 1932.

Although belonging to a later period than most of the best and longest-lived Spanish works, *Luisa Fernanda*, written in the early 1930s and towards the end of its composer's career, remains one of the most popular full-length pieces in the zarzuela repertoire.

Like that other staple of the zarzuela repertoire, *El barberillo de Lavapiés*, *Luisa Fernanda* mixed pictures of everyday Spanish life, particularly in Madrid, with a tale of royalty-versus-republican politics and plotting. Luisa Fernanda is a Madrid lass, whose soldier lover, Javier Moreno, has risen above her, to the rank of Colonel. Whilst he mixes in royal circles, she is assiduously courted by the wealthy Vidal Hernando, but she longs still for Javier. When a group of republicans stage an armed uprising, the apolitical Vidal fights with them solely to have the chance to challenge Javier in the field and he bests and imprisons his rival. The royal troops are finally victorious, but when Luisa sees Javier depart with the Queen's lady-in-waiting, the Duquesa Carolina, she at last agrees to marry the brave Vidal. Even wed, however, she cannot forget Javier, and when, following the Queen's deposition and Carolina's flight into exile, he seeks out his old love in Extremadura, Vidal realizes that he must lose the wife he loves to the subtle soldier.

The shape of the piece was interesting in that, like others of the zarzuela grande genre and unlike most traditional Operette libretti, it had no space for low comedy, and, although there were fine featured rôles for regular soubrettes (innkeeper Mariana, dressmaker Rosita) its male rôles were less predictable. Of its two leading men it was the less worthy Javier, rather than the brave and gentlemanly Vidal (who in a French or Viennese script would have been an ageing buffoon), who was capable of inspiring the love of the heroine.

The score included numbers in the popular dance rhythms – a habanera for an organ-grinder ('Marchaba á ser soldado'), a mazurka chorus ('A San Antonio') – alongside the main body of romantic and lyric numbers, the best and most of which fell to the men of the cast. Javier sang of his rise to high position in a romanza ('De este apacible rincón de Madrid'), responded to Carolina's come-hither ('Caballero del alto plumo') and forced a quarrel on Vidal and Luisa ('¡Cuanto tiempo sin verte, Luisa Fernanda!') before getting to his final love duet ('Cállate corazón'), whilst Vidal poured out his love to Luisa ('En mi terra estrameña'), spurned the flirtations of Carolina ('Para comprar á un hombre'), went into battle for his love ('Por el amor da una mujer') and rejoiced in heart-felt fashion over his marriage ('En una dehesa de la Extramadura') before being left, at the finish, to nothing but despair ('Si por el rido').

Recordings: complete (Columbia, Alhambra, Montilla, Hispavox, EMI etc)

LULU Opérette in 3 acts by Serge Veber. Music by George van Parys and Philippe Parès. Théâtre Daunou, Paris, 14 September 1927.

The first Parisian show of the young van Parys/Parès team of songwriters, mounted just a few months after their *La Petite Dame du train bleu* had seen stage-light in Brussels, *Lulu* was written to an up-to-date comedy script by another young writer, Serge Veber, who had already tasted Parisian success in collaboration with his father, the celebrated author of comedies Pierre Veber, on *Quand on est trois*.

Bernard (Pizella) and Yette (Davia) have been wed, he swearing to her all along that he has led a blameless youth, so when the little actress Lulu (Christiane Dor) bounces out of his past and into their home, Yette goes home to daddy (Paul Asselin). Then Bernard's rich Aunt Chloë (Marcelle Yvren) turns up with her son Jeff (Fernand Graavey) and a dowry and, presuming that Lulu is Bernard's new wife, destines Yette for Jeff. In the third act, everyone goes off to Venice where things get worse before they finally get better and the inevitable tidy pairing-off (equipped with happy financial arrangements) brings down the curtain.

The young composers' score included a foxtrot title-song for Pizella, who also pleaded liltingly 'Fais ça pour moi', whilst Mlle Davia went on pinkly about 'Un petit quelquechose', and Mlle Dor explained ('J'ai une nature') that whilst other performers had talent and could play Iphigenia or Mademoiselle Beulemans she got by very nicely on 'une nature, une bonne figure'.

Lulu was produced by Jane Renouardt on the stage of the little Théâtre Daunou and it scored an instant success. It held its place on the Paris stage for the best part of a year, being joined after just a few weeks by a quick transfer of *La Petite Dame du train bleu* and, when it was time for a change, it was replaced by the young team's next work, *L'Eau à la bouche*. The show went merrily into the provinces, and even travelled as far as Budapest where it was brought into the adventurous and eclectic Fővárosi Operettszinház (ad Adorján Stella, Zsolt Harsányi), following in behind no less adventurous a production: *Abris Rózsája* – otherwise *Abie's Irish Rose*.

Another musical of the same name written by Alain Monjardin and composed by Victor Alix was produced at Caen in 1922 (29 December), an Hungarian *Lulu* with a Szabolcs Fényes score was produced at Budapest's József Attila Színház in 1967 (20 May) and an American one, based on the plays of Wedekind, was played in New York in 1977. The title had also been previously used for what later became *The Girl in the Private Room* (Gitz Rice/Edward Clark, New Haven, 20 September 1920) and ultimately the Broadway success *The Blushing Bride*.

Hungary: Fővárosi Operettszinház 14 September 1928

LUNA [y Carné], Pablo (b Alhama de Aragón, 21 May 1880; d Madrid, 28 January 1942).

Pablo Luna worked as a violinist at the Teatro Apolo, and later as a conductor at the Teatro de la Zarzuela, whilst leading a career as a composer for the theatre which would make him, with Vicente Lleó and Federico Moreno Torroba, one of the main and most successful practitioners of the genero grande – the full-length zarzuela rather than the shorter and more widely popular genero chico.

He began his career, just before his 30th year, with several shorter pieces – *La reina de los mercados* (1909), *El club de las solteras* (1909, w Luis Foglietti), *Huelga de criados* (1910, w Foglietti) – one of which, the 1910 *Molinos del viento* (lib: Luis Pascual Frutos), produced at first in Seville and then the following year in Madrid, gave him his first popular success.

Amongst his longer works, the 1918 *El niño judío* (lib: Enrique Garcia Alvarez, Antonio Paso y Cano, Teatro Apolo, Madrid 5 February) proved to be his most successful single piece, but it was his 1916 *El asombro de Damasco* which became the only full-length zarzuela to be adapted for a commercial run on the British stage. It was produced by William J Wilson at the Oxford Theatre under the title *The First Kiss* (ad Boyle Lawrence) with a cast including Désirée Ellinger and Courtice Pounds (10 November 1924) for a run of 43 performances.

His other major works included *Los cadetes de la reina* (1913), *Benamor* (1923), *La pícara molinera* (1928), *La chula de Pontevedra* (1928, w Enrique Brú) and, in later years, *Un copla hecha mujer* (1939) and *Las calatravas* (1941) from a long list of works amongst which are numbered *Sangre y arena* (1911), *Canto de primavera* (1912), *La alegria de amor* (1913), *El rey del mundo* (1914), *El potro salvaje* (1914, w Joaquín Quirito Valverde), *La corte de Risalia* (1914), *Amores de aldea* (1915), *Ni rey, ni roque* (1915), *El boton de nácar* (1916), *Trina la clavellina* (1918), *Los Calabreses* (1918), *Munecos de trapo* (1919), *La mecanografa* (1919), *Pancho Virondo* (1919), *Llévame al' metro mama* (1919), *El suspiro de moro* (1919), *La Venus de las pieles* (1920), *Su Alteza se casa* (1921), *El sinverguenza en palacio* (1921, w Amadeo Vives), *Musetta, El rey flojo, La conquista de la gloria* and *El sapo enamorado*.

Luna also wrote for the musical screen.

Biography: Saguardia, A: *Pablo Luna* (Espasa-Calte, Madrid, 1978)

LUNZER, Fritz (b Prague, 19 October 1877; d Vienna, 16 March 1940).

The author of more than 30 years of libretti – many of which were short pieces – for the Viennese stage, Lunzer had a single international success with his libretto to the *Die Siegerin*, a tale of Catherine the Great set with a pasticcio score of Tchaikovsky music. Of his other pieces, another pasticcio, a Johann Strauss show called *Faschingshochzeit*, ran over 100 nights at the Carltheater in 1921, a remake of his early Ziehrer Operette *Manöverkind* as *Husarenblut* was played 51 nights at the Raimundtheater, Robert Stolz's *Prinzessin Ti-Ti-Pa* played 53 Viennese performances and *Revanche* lasted two and a half months at the Bürgertheater.

1901 **Die Luftzauberin** (Julius Eibenschütz/Richard Manz ad w Eduard Lunzer) Jantschtheater 27 November

1904 **Der jüngste Tag** (Georg Klammer/w E Lunzer) Jantschtheater 14 October

1908 **Ein Wiener Märchen** (Julius Heller) Wiener Colosseum 7 October

1911 **Die schöne Estrella** (Tomás Lopez Torregrosa/w Friedmann) 1 act Ronacher

1911 **Im Schilderhaus** (Donell/w Friedmann) 1 act Ronacher 22 February

1911 **Die Arkadier** (*The Arcadians*) German version w Oskar Friedmann (Ronacher)

1912 **Manöverkind** (Carl Michael Ziehrer/w Friedmann) Venedig in Wien 22 June

1912 **Adam und Eva** (A M Schweiger) 1 act Ronacher 1 March

1912 **Die Frau im Negligee** (*Die Frau im Hemd*) (Karl W Zeller/w Alfred Spitzer) Ronacher 1 March

1912 **Fräulein Bijou** (Richard Grünfeld/w Ludwig Rottmann) 1 act Wiener Colosseum 1 October

1912 **Kittys Ehemänner** (Ludwig Engländer/w Emil Kolberg) 1 act Hölle 1 November

1913 **Der dreifache Gatte** (Oskar Porges/w Friedmann) 1 act Intimes Theater 5 April

1913 **Die Ballkönigin** (*The Catch of the Season*) German version w Karl Tuschl (Theater an der Wien)

1913 **Das Liebesnest** (Nicolas Hédas) Strasbourg

1913 **Das grosse Abenteuer** (Hans May/w C Clermont)

1913 **Wie Frauen lieben** (Karl List/w Ludwig Johannes) Venedig in Wien 1 May

1913 **Husarengeneral** (revised *Manöverkind*) (Ziehrer/w Friedmann) Raimundtheater 3 October

1914 **Eine verschenkte Nacht** (Béla Laszky/w Gustav Beer) 1 act Deutsches Künstlertheater 1 February

1917 **Die Bauernprinzessin** (Robert Stolz/w Anton Aldermann) Volkstheater, Munich 2 March

1918 **Leute von heute** (Edmund Eysler, Stolz, Arthur M Werau/w Arthur Rebner) Bundestheater 22 June

1919 **Daniel in der Löwenhöhle** (Hans May) 1 act Kleinkunstbühne, Munich 1 December

1920 **Liebe auf den ersten Blick** (Robert Rakowianu/w Friedmann) Bundestheater 19 May

1920 **Ein alter Steiger** (Oskar Dub) 1 act Rolandbühne 1 June

1920 **Heimkegekehrt** (Károly Újvári) 1 October

1921 **Faschingshochzeit** (Johann Strauss arr Josef Klein/w Friedmann) Carltheater 25 May

1921 **Der Theatergraf** (Walter Bransen) Landestheater, Gotha 24 April

1922 **Die Siegerin** (Tchaikovsky arr Klein/w Jenbach, Friedmann) Neues Wiener Stadttheater 7 November

1923 **Der Hampelmann** (Stolz/w Beer) Komödienhaus 9 November

1924 **Die Afrikareise** new libretto (Bürgertheater)

1924 **Revanche** (Oskar Jascha/w Löhner-Beda) Bürgertheater 8 November

1928 **Prinzessin Ti-Ti-Pa** (Stolz/w Beer) Carltheater 15 May

1928 **Die singende Venus** (Eduard Künneke/w Beer) Schauspielhaus, Breslau 9 June

1930 **Das Amulet der Pompadour** (Eysler/w Emil von Meissner) Stadttheater, Augsburg 16 March
1930 **Frühling im Wienerwald** (Ascher/w Löhner-Beda) Stadttheater 17 April
1930 **Durchlaucht Mizzi** (Eysler/w Beer) Neues Wiener Schauspielhaus 23 December
1935 **Valentino, der Liebling vom Broadway** (Ludo Philipp/ Kurt Breuer) Volksoper 10 February

LUPINO, Stanley   (b London, 15 May 1894; d London, 10 June 1942). Startled-looking little star comedian and author of two decades of British musicals.

A member of a famous family of dancers and acrobats, Lupino worked as a child in an acrobatic act and in pantomime, and as a young man in revue, variety (his first musical comedy appearance being in the one-act *Go to Jericho* in a variety house) and at the Theatre Royal, Drury Lane, in animal rôles in pantomime. He had his first good musical-comedy rôle in 1917 at the age of 24 supplying the supporting comedy in the Gaby Deslys vehicle *Suzette* (Tibbs) and he made a notable success later the same year in the principal comic part of *Arlette* (Rono) in which he made the hit of the evening with his performance of Ivor Novello's 'On the Staff'.

Established as a leading comic, he mixed musicals and revues over the years that followed, appearing at the Gaiety in *The Kiss Call* (1919, Dr Pym), in *Oh! Julie* (1920, t/o Mumps), *His Girl* (1922, James Hicks) and Cochran's remade *Phi-Phi* (1923, Mercury), before making his American début alongside Vivienne Segal (pre-Broadway) and later Mitzi in the local version of Oscar Straus's *(Naughty) Riquette* (1925/6, Théophile Michu). He remained in America to play in the Jenny Lind biomusical *The Nightingale* (1927, Mr Carp). During this period he won his first West End credit as a writer when he supplied some material to C B Cochran's many-handed musical version of the famous comedy *Turned Up*.

Back in Britain, he was seen in the farcical *Up with the Lark* on the road before he teamed up with rising producer Laddie Cliff as co-librettist and co-star of the new style dance-and-laughter musical *So This is Love* (1928, Potiphar Griggs). The piece was a substantial success, and many of the team it created continued together over the following years, playing in a number of the further shows in the same vein, written and directed by Lupino, produced by Cliff and starring the pair as chief comedians (Jerry Walker in *Love Lies*, Reggie Powley in *The Love Race*, Percy Brace in *Sporting Love*, Tommy Teacher in *Over She Goes*, Bertie Barnes in *Crazy Days*) with decided success.

Lupino rewrote the rewritten libretto of the American musical *So Long, Letty!* for Cliff, in an unsuccessful attempt to get it into shape for town; wrote, directed and starred in *Hold My Hand* (1931, Eddy Marston); wrote and then rewrote *Paste/That's a Pretty Thing*, which was played at Daly's Theatre without him in the cast and without equivalent success, and was credited with the 'book' to the wartime revue *Funny Side Up* (1940) produced at His Majesty's Theatre with a score made up of a mass of songs mostly culled from American publishers.

After his winning partnership with Cliff and their series of shows together was ended by the little producer-dancer's premature death, Lupino went on to star at the Hippodrome in *The Fleet's Lit Up* (1938, Horatio Roper) and took the leading comic rôle in his own Hollywood saga, *Lady Behave* (1941, Tony Meyrick, also director). He himself was taken ill during the run of this last show, and died at the age of 48. He was represented posthumously as an author in two further shows, a remake of *That's a Pretty Thing* called *La-di-da-di-da* and *The Love Racket*, both successfully produced by his cousin, Lupino Lane, in 1943.

Lupino worked widely in early British musical films, both as an author and an actor, writing the screenplay with Arthur Rigby and Frank Miller for the cinema version of *Love Lies* and starring in that piece as well as in the screen versions of *The Love Race*, *Hold My Hand* and *Over She Goes*.

Lupino's wife Connie Emerald appeared in supporting rôles in several musicals in the provinces (*The Belle of New York*, *Our Miss Gibbs*, *The King's Bride*, *The Algerian Girl*), in Australia (*The Swiss Express*), in London (*The Prince of Pilsen*, *Nobody's Boy*, and alongside her husband in the majority of his 1920s and 1930s shows) and in New York (*Naughty Riquette*). His brother **Barry LUPINO** (b London, 7 January 1884; d Brighton, 26 September 1962) worked as a musical comedian in Australia (Eddie Kettle in *Very Good Eddie*), America (*The Love Call*, *The Red Robe*, *Babes in Toyland*) and in Britain where he also toured in good rôles in the family musicals (both Stanley's and Lupino Lane's) and played regularly in pantomime. He co-authored the libretti for the touring musical *Happy Birthday* and the London show *Runaway Love*.

1926 **Turned Up** (Joseph Tunbridge/w others/Arthur Rigby) New Oxford Theatre 11 January
1928 **So This is Love** ('Hal Brody'/Desmond Carter/w Arthur Rigby) Winter Garden Theatre 25 April
1928 **Oh, Letty!** (ex- *So Long, Letty!*, later *Change Over*) (Billy Mayerl/Frank Eyton/w Austin Melford) revised English version (Sheffield)
1929 **Love Lies** ('Hal Brody'/Carter/w Rigby) Gaiety Theatre 20 March
1930 **The Love Race** (Jack Clarke/Carter) Gaiety Theatre 25 June
1931 **Hold My Hand** (Noel Gay/Carter) Gaiety Theatre 23 December
1933 **That's a Pretty Thing** (ex- *Paste*) (Gay/Carter) Daly's Theatre 22 November
1934 **Sporting Love** (Mayerl/Carter, Eyton/w Rigby, Arthur Ash) Gaiety Theatre 31 March
1936 **Over She Goes** (Mayerl/Carter, Eyton) Saville Theatre 23 September
1937 **Crazy Days** (Mayerl/Carter, Eyton) Shaftesbury Theatre 14 September
1941 **Lady Behave** (Edward Horan/Eyton) His Majesty's Theatre 24 July
1943 **La-di-da-di-da** revised *That's a Pretty Thing* Victoria Palace 30 March
1943 **The Love Racket** (Gay/Eyton et al) Victoria Palace 21 October

Autobiography: *From the Stocks to the Stars* (Hutchinson, London, 1934)

DER LUSTIGE KRIEG   Operette in 3 acts by F Zell and Richard Genée based on the libretto to *Les Dames capitaines* by Mélesville. Music by Johann Strauss. Theater an der Wien, Vienna, 25 November 1881.

The eighth of Strauss's Operetten, *Der lustige Krieg* followed behind the disastrous *Blindekuh* and the much more successful *Das Spitzentuch der Königin*, and it reunited him with the Theater an der Wien's most successful librettists,

Zell and Genée (the veritable author of his *Die Fledermaus* book), with whom he had previously combined on the indifferent *Cagliostro in Wien*.

There is war between Massa-Carrara and Genoa, over the fact that these countries' rulers are each claiming a binding contract with a certain ballet star, but it is a war where no one has yet come to blows, even though battle-lines are drawn. Violetta (Karoline Finaly), niece of the Princess Artemisia (Therese Schäfer) who heads the all-female army of Massa-Carrara, is to be married to the Duke of Limburg, in exchange for reinforcements, but her voyage to the wedding ceremony is betrayed to the Genoese by the chattery Marchese Sebastiani (Alexander Girardi). The Genoese commander Umberto Spinola (Ferdinand Schütz) intercepts both Violetta and the proxy husband sent by Limburg, and, having fallen in love with the lady at first sight, he himself takes the deputy bridegroom's place in a hasty wedding. Spinola forces a little Dutchman, Balthasar Groot (Felix Schweighofer), who has unknowingly wandered into the war-lines, to pretend to be the Duke and he follows Violetta and her 'husband' to Massa-Carrara. There, Sebastiani recognizes him and uncovers Groot's impersonation, at which it becomes apparent that Violetta has married ... a Genoese! Since she is by now thoroughly in love with him, she has no objection, and since there seems no longer to be a need for battle-lines, the merry war is declared over.

The splendidly silly book – easily the best of those with which Strauss was supplied after *Die Fledermaus* – was based on that used for Reber's 1857 French opéra-comique *Les Dames capitaines*, and it spurred the composer to one of his most attractive and versatile scores. The musical numbers ranged from the glittering coloratura of Violetta's polka 'Für diese Kriegezugs Wohl und Wehe' to the bristling march strains of her 'Es war ein lustig' Abenteuer' to the warmly beautiful song for the Dutchman's little wife (Rosa Streitmann) who has lost her husband and his cargo of precious tulip-bulbs somewhere amongst the war ('Durch Wald und Feld'), their third-act duet, woefully and sweetly wondering when they will ever get out of this mess and back to their little Dutch family ('Zwei Monat sind es schon') and the first-act waltz quintet, 'Kommen und gehen'.

However, *Der lustige Krieg* had not only a delicious score, it had a hit number, one which (like so many of its fellows before and after) was not originally in the show. Alexander Girardi, one of the Theater an der Wien's principal comedians here cast as Sebastiani, threatened to strike unless he was given an additional number. Strauss wearily complied, Franz Wagner supplied the words which Genée was too busy to produce, and Girardi squeezed 'Nur für Natur' into the show's second act. The waltz turned out to be not only the hit of the show, but the biggest theatre song-hit in years. It played a significant part in initially helping *Der lustige Krieg* to success, and his light, comic tenor performance of it made Girardi – who had been around for a few years in worthwhile rôles – into a major star overnight.

Der lustige Krieg held the stage at the Theater an der Wien through the Christmas and New Year period before being removed to allow some guest performances to be played, but it returned later in the year to notch up its 100th performance at the beginning of September. By this time, however, it had run half way round the world. An

Plate 167. **Der lustige Krieg** *made its way to Belgium, but steered clear of Paris – possibly because Messrs Mélesville and Reber hadn't been consulted over the 'borrowing' of their text.*

extremely fine success in Germany – no fewer than 200 performances in 9 months at the Friedrich-Wilhelmstädtisches Theater – was quickly followed by an excellent reception in Budapest (ad Lajos Evva, Béla J Fái) where a topline Népszinház cast was headed by Aranka Hegyi, Mariska Komaromi, Zsöfi Csatay, Janós Kápolnai and Elek Solymossy and featured Vidor Kassai as the now all-important Sebastiani.

Six weeks later New York saw the piece in the original German as played by Jenny Stubel (Violetta), Marie Seebold (Else), Adolf Link (Sebastiani) Gustav Adolfi (Groot) and Alexander Klein (Umberto), and three months after that it was seen on Broadway in English (ad L C Elson) in the repertoire of J W Norcross's Opera Company. This production ended up transferring to the Metropolitan Alcazar and the company happily jettisoned the rest of its repertory for the season and simply played one and the same show for a remarkable seven consecutive weeks. W T Carleton, Dora Wiley, Belle Cole, Louise Paullin, Richard Golden and Adolfi (this time in English) headed this cast which brought the piece back for two further weeks later in the same season. New York was, however, far from finished with its favourite Strauss Operette, for in September 1882 *Der lustige Krieg* was remounted at the Thalia Theater, in October it was burlesqued by Irene Worrell and Lina Aberle (Aberle's Theater), and at the beginning of 1884 the Casino Theater staged a revival with Lilly Post starred as Violetta, which added two further months to *The Merry War*'s Broadway tally. Between 1885 and 1889 it was again played each season in repertoire in the German theatres, and William Carleton toured the English version throughout the country for several seasons.

Prague, Naples, Strasbourg and Stockholm had all hosted the show before London put out its version (ad Robert Reece) on the vast stage of the Alhambra, which had hosted *Die Fledermaus* and *King Indigo* without exceptional results. Constance Loseby (Violetta), Henry Walsham (Spinola), Vienna's Lori Stubel (Else) and Albert Lefevre headed the cast. Unfortunately Miss Stubel miscalculated London's tastes and, when she pulled up her partner's stocking-tops in what London first-nighters found a rather vulgar fashion, she drew the wrath of the audience on her. She promptly thumbed her nose back at them. Things Viennese did not impress some of the more hidebound London music critics either: 'dance music such as he writes is very attractive in the ballroom, but it is apt to weary the hearer when polka and waltz melodies are given throughout the entire opera'. However *The Merry War* (with Frln Stubel quickly replaced by Kate Sullivan) had settled in nicely when, five weeks into the run, the Alhambra was burnt down. It was 56 years before the piece got another London showing (New St Pancras Theatre 2 January 1939), and the show never recovered from the heated start which prevented it becoming popular in England.

La Guerre joyeuse (ad Alfred and Maurice Hennequin) was produced in Brussels (Alcazar Royale, Brussels 21 November 1885) with Claire Cordier as Violetta and Monsieur Minne singing 'Pour la nature' in a score which had been 'adapté par Maurice Kufferath', but it did not make its way to Paris. This may very well have been because Strauss was not keen, after the fuss that had been made over his librettist's unauthorized borrowing of *Le Réveillon* as the source for *Die Fledermaus*, similarly to tangle with the representatives of the original French author of the 'borrowed' *Les Dames capitaines*.

In Vienna, *Der lustige Krieg* was played in repertoire through 1882 and 1883, and in 1885 the Theater an der Wien mounted a new production with Girardi teamed with Marie-Theresia Massa and Josef Joseffy. It was revived at the Carltheater in 1898 with Ottilie Collin and Natzler and at the Johann Strauss-Theater in 1911–12 with Grete Holm, and it had a continuing success through the 19th and early 20th centuries holding an indubitable third place behind *Die Fledermaus* and *Der Zigeunerbaron* as the most popular of Strauss's works in central Europe. Only with the coming of increasingly sentimental and romantic tastes (as opposed to the continuous comedy this work displays) in the later 20th century did it give way to the revamped, scenery-worthy *Eine Nacht in Venedig* and to the pasticcio *Wiener Blut*, which are now played and recorded in preference to it.

A hacked-about version of the show rewritten by Wilhelm Sterk, with the music rearranged by Felix Günther, in which Balthasar (Richard Waldemar) became a strolling player, Else disappeared and Violetta (Anni Ahlers) acquired a sister called Nina (Marianne Küpfer) alongside Hans Heinz Bollmann's Umberto and Ernst Tautenhayn's Cipriani, was produced at the Johann

Strauss-Theater on 23 December 1929 by Erich Müller, and another partially rewritten version was produced at Augsburg in 1957 (Städtische Bühne 23 August ad Eugen Mühl) under the title *Fürstin Violetta*.

Germany: Friedrich-Wilhelmstädtisches Theater 19 January 1882; Hungary: Népszinház *A furcsa háboru* 31 January 1882; USA: Thalia Theater 15 March 1882, Germania Theater *The Merry War* 27 June 1882; UK: Alhambra Theatre *The Merry War* 16 October 1882

Recordings: selections (Philips etc)

DIE LUSTIGEN NIBELUNGEN Burlesque Operette in 3 acts by Rideamus. Music by Oscar Straus. Carltheater, Vienna, 12 November 1904.

Oscar Straus's first produced Operette, written in collaboration with the cabaret satirist 'Rideamus' (Fritz Oliven) with whom he had previously written a series of pieces described polyglottishly as 'lustige Chansons', was a burlesque of the legend which had been the basis for Richard Wagner's Ring Cycle or, more properly, of the material used for one plot strand of the last two operas – the marriage of Gunther and Brünnhilde and the fate of Siegfried.

In Rideamus's version, flabby Gunther (Friedrich Becker) is obliged to go into single combat with Brünnhilde (Hermine Herma) to win her as his bride. He is all for catching the first train out of town, but Herr Siegfried von Niederland (Willi Bauer) comes to his aid and, invisible under his magic nightcap, complies with the rules set down by referee Hagen (Karl Blasel) and floors Brünnhilde, both shoulders to the ground, all for the sake of Gunther's pretty sister Kriemhild (Helene Merviola). At the beginning of Act II the two couples are supposed to be getting wed, but there are plenty more troubles in store. Hagen tries to get Kriemhild to woo from Siegfried the secret of his dragon's blood baths and Gunther gets into a squabble with Brünnhilde over domestic matters and calls again for Siegfried's help as his invisible arm. But this time Hagen spots the marks left on the ground by the invisible man's gown and he fells his opponent with a nifty blow. Battered Siegfried goes off to have a restorative dragon's blood bath and while he is away Gunther confesses, Brünnhilde takes umbrage, Kriemhild gets a better offer, and they all decide to get rid of Siegfried. However, a friendly canary brings the Hero all this latest news and, fore-warned and -armed, he is finally able to win everyone around and Brünnhilde to bride.

Straus replaced Wagner's tonitruant score with one in very different rhythms, one from which a 'Rheingold' waltz-song, a Lindenblatt-duet ('Das ist die Stelle mit dem Lindenblatt'), and a round ('Nun lasst uns denn Siegfried ermordern') stood next to some more splendid music, which was paired with ridiculous words in the best traditions of burlesque. Siegfried emerged the best with two such numbers 'Ich bracht's auf dem Gymnasium' and 'Ich hab ein Bad genommen', alongside a catching march, which opened the second act declaring 'Das ist der Furor teutonicus'.

Die lustigen Nibelungen had only a fair reception at the Carltheater for, in spite of its gleefully foolish fun and its attractive, well-made music, it contained none of the well-rhythmed, take-away songs that the public expected from the composer of so many Überbrettl songs and Volkslieder.

And burlesque was scarcely in its heyday. Andreas Aman's production was withdrawn after a first run of 26 performances, although it was given occasional repertoire performances over the next three years. It was better received in Berlin, and was subsequently produced in Hungary (ad Adolf Merei), and kept a small place in the repertoire for a number of years, establishing Straus on the springboard from which he would shortly leap to fame with *Ein Walzertraum*. In 1987 it was seen again in Vienna in a production at the Wiener Kammeroper.

Germany: ?1905; Hungary: Király Színház *Vig Nibelungok* 30 August 1907

DIE LUSTIGE WITWE
Operette in 3 acts by Victor Léon and Leo Stein, based on *L'Attaché d'ambassade* by Henri Meilhac. Music by Franz Lehár. Theater an der Wien, Vienna, 30 December 1905.

Henri Meilhac's play *L'Attaché d'ambassade*, produced at Paris's Théâtre du Vaudeville in 1861, was not a success. It was played for just 15 performances in the French capital. Yet, in the way of the time, this failure did not affect its export prospects and the piece found its way to the Vienna stage the following year. There, played at the Carltheater in an adaptation by 'Alexander Bergen' as *Der Gesandschafts-Attaché*, it became not only a success but a piece which was popular enough to win regular revivals over a number of years.

The first years of the 20th century in the Viennese musical theatre were not rich in successes. The staple composers of earlier years – Suppé, Strauss, Millöcker – were gone, and the last real new successes which the Theater an der Wien had hosted had been Richard Heuberger's *Der Opernball*, a musical version of the French comedy *Les Dominos roses*, and the young Edmund Eysler's *Bruder Straubinger*. It was logical, then, that librettist Victor Léon, the co-author of *Der Opernball*, should present Theater an der Wien director Karczag with another French-flavoured libretto for Heuberger to set – a musical version of *Der Gesandschafts-Attaché*. One version of the story goes that Heuberger actually set Léon and Leo Stein's piece, but that Karczag did not like the score he provided and took back the libretto. On the encouragement of theatre secretary Emil Steininger, he then proposed to offer it to Lehár, whose début piece, *Wiener Frauen*, had been played at the Theater an der Wien three years earlier. Léon, however, objected. Although he had had a major success with Lehár on *Der Rastelbinder* at the rival Carltheater, he and Stein had subsequently worked with the composer on the barely successful *Der Göttergatte* in which the composer had clearly failed to catch the Offenbachian opéra-bouffe flavour the librettists intended their piece to have. But, in the end, he agreed that Lehár should be given the opportunity to set a portion of the piece, as a kind of an audition. When the composer played Léon the melody which he had set to the Hanna/Danilo duet 'Dummer, dummer Reitersmann', the librettist allowed himself to be convinced.

Karczag, however, showed little enthusiasm for the show. During 1905 little had gone right for him. Star comic Girardi had gone off after the production of *Pufferl* taking the most promising composer of the time, Edmund Eysler, with him, and if some performances of the second-hand Strauss pastiche *Wiener Blut* had filled a gap, neither

Plate 168. **Die lustige Witwe:** *The Pontevedrian ambassador and his staff of noble gentlemen have money problems ... and, some of them, woman problems too (Vienna Volksoper, 1987).*

a German version of Huszka's *Bob herceg* (10 performances) nor Léon's collaboration with another young composer, Leo Ascher, on *Vergeltsgott* (69 performances) had proved a hit. Another essay with an untried composer, Leo Fall's *Der Rebell*, had been a total disaster, folding after just five performances. There was little incentive for Karczag to invest heavily in another new piece in which he had little confidence, and so, when *Die lustige Witwe* was hurriedly produced to fill the gap left by the flop of *Der Rebell* (in preference, according to Harry B Smith's memoirs, to De Koven's *Robin Hood*, which was also on Karczag's waiting list), it was done so on the proverbial shoestring with recycled scenery and costumes. Four weeks after the closure of Fall's Operette, *Die lustige Witwe* opened.

Léon and Stein's piece, which was shyly announced only as being 'teilweise nach einer fremden Grundidee' (partly based on a foreign idea), was set in contemporary Paris at the Embassy of the Balkan state of Pontevedro rather than in the Germanic Birkenfeld of the original play or in Léon's originally posited, but too real, Montenegro. Baron Mirko Zeta (Siegmund Natzler) is desperate to find a Pontevedran husband for the 'merry widow', the young and hugely wealthy Hanna Glawari (Mizzi Günther) who is currently being chased by half of male Paris. He and the fatherland cannot afford to let Hanna's millions go into a foreign exchequer. He selects for this delicate patriotic task the womanizing, boozing but indubitably charming attaché Count Danilo Danilowitsch (Louis Treumann). Unfortunately Danilo and Hanna are rather more than old friends from the days before Hanna's wealthy marriage and Danilo has sworn that he will never again say 'I love you' to the woman he regards as venal. It soon becomes clear, however, what his feelings are, for when Hanna steps in to save the Ambassador's wife, Valencienne (Annie Wünsch), from an embarrassing if innocent exposure in a tête-à-tête with the sexy young Camille de Rosillon (Karl Meister), the furious Danilo sweeps off to Maxim's and consolation with the girls of that friendly establishment. Hanna sets up part of her mansion as an imitation of Maxim's and, there, the amazed Danilo comes to discover that the merry widow loses her money should she remarry. His pride assuaged, he now proposes, only to find that the money goes to the new husband.

Lehár's score gave his four principals plenty of opportunities, both the leading pair who, in good Gaiety Theatre tradition, were light-comedy actor/singers, and their straighter-singing secondary counterparts. Hanna made her first entrance to a cascading number ('Bitte meine Herr'n') which immediately established her as lustige, performed the mythological tale of the 'Vilja' as a party-piece, and shared the 'Dummer Reitersmann' duo and the evening's big waltz tune, 'Lippen schweigen', with Danilo, whilst he, apart from the duets, saluted the high-life in 'Da geh' ich zu Maxim' and the 'Ballsirenen' waltz. Valencienne and Camille shared three soprano/tenor set piece duets ('Zauber der Hauslichkeit', 'Ich bin eine anständige Frau' and the Pavilion duo with Camille's fine-spun solo 'Wie eine Rosenknospe'). The lower-comedy area, headed by Zeta and his colleagues Cascada (Carlo Böhm) and Saint-Brioche (Leo von Keller), came to the fore in a swinging march octet ('Ja, das Studium der Weiber ist schwer'), whilst Valencienne led the grisettes of Maxim's in a lively song-and-dance routine ('Ja, wir sind es die Grisetten'), choreographed by Professor van Hamme, alongside some particularly fine finales. Almost every portion of the *Die lustige Witwe* score became familar and popular in the years which followed, but it was, perhaps, the big waltz duet and the march octet which stood out at first.

The success of *Die lustige Witwe* was never in doubt. The show ran through the spring at the Theater an der Wien, totalling 119 performances by the time, at the end of April, that the traditional summer closure began. *Die lustige Witwe* did not, however, close but transferred first to the Raimundtheater and then to the Volksoper to continue its run with some 69 guest performances. The two stars held their places, but amongst the minor characters now appeared both Julius Brammer (Cascada, after having originally been Pritschitsch) and Robert Bodanzky (Pritschitsch), before long to be much better known as librettists. When the Theater an der Wien reopened in September, *Die lustige Witwe* resumed and on 11 January 1907 it passed its 300th, and on 24 April 1907 its 400th performance. Lehár composed a new overture ('Eine Vision') for the latter occasion, and conducted an expanded orchestra of a hundred players himself in celebration.

In the meanwhile, the foreign productions had begun. Max Monti opened *Die lustige Witwe* at Hamburg's Neues Operetten-Theater, with Marie Ottmann and Gustave Matzner starred and Poldi Deutsch as the Ambassador for 'Pontenegro', little more than two months after seeing it at the Vienna première and, soon after, the Hamburg company, which had played 250 performances on its home ground within seven months, introduced the show to Berlin. Their success was, again, indubitable, and the show was promptly taken up for a local production. The 400th performance was passed at the Theater des Westens on 10 December 1907.

Budapest followed with, as usual, the first foreign-language version, an Adolf Mérei adaptation produced at the Magyar Színház with Olga Turchányi (later Ilona Szoyer) and Ákos Ráthonyi starred. It passed its 200th performance at the end of May before the show was taken up by the Király Színház, where Ráthonyi was paired with Sári Fedák, and then at the Budai Színkör. *Die lustige Witwe* was translated into Czech, Norwegian, Russian, Swedish, Croatian and Italian (Milan, 27 June 1907) before it received its first English performance, at London's Daly's Theatre, in a version credited variously to Edward Morton (best known as the author of *San Toy*) or to Basil Hood, and lyricist Adrian Ross.

The book underwent some alterations for the London presentation. Some tended to the clichéd – Danilo became a Prince, for example – others removed things which would have seemed odd to English ears. In the British version the final scene takes place in the real Maxim's rather than a reproduction at the widow's home (yet years later the libretto for *Primrose* pinched precisely Léon and Stein's plotline). Lehár himself was on hand to help with the adaptation and, at Edwardes's request, he provided two additional songs, one to feature Mabel Russell as a third-act grisette ('Butterflies') and the second to give Bill Berry, cast in the small rôle of Nisch, a number declaring that although 'I was born, by cruel fate, in a little Balkan state' he had now become 'Quite Parisian'. There were other alterations, too. The 'Zauber der Hauslichkeit' duet was turned into a solo for Robert Evett as Camille, and the rôle of Valencienne (here called Natalie) was reduced further by giving the Grisetten-Lied of the last act to Gertrude Lister as another grisette.

Edwardes followed the light-comedy lead casting of the Viennese production by choosing American Joe Coyne, who had played light-comedy rôles for Edwardes in America before making his British début earlier in the year as the comic hero of *Nelly Neil*, to be his Danilo. Lily Elsie, who had been moving up through smaller rôles in Edwardes productions, was cast as a younger, prettier, and slimmer widow (now called Sonia) than previously and accredited comic George Graves was given leave to play up the rôle of Zeta (now called Popoff) which he did largely by sticking in a self-written chat about a fowl called Hetty and her propensity for producing bent eggs. The fine singing was left to Evett and another American, soprano Elizabeth Firth (Natalie). The English *Widow* proved as popular as her Continental counterpart, running solidly for two years and two months, a total of 778 performances, before beginning the round of tours, and it launched in Britain, as it would elsewhere, the rage for Viennese shows which would last until the war. Its songs and a bit of millinery merchandising called the 'Merry Widow Hat' became the hits of the day.

Henry Savage's New York production continued the series of *Merry Widow* triumphs. Savage used the London adaptation, now uncredited and with 'Quite Parisian' omitted, and cast the bright and friendly looking actor/dancer/singer Donald Brian as Danilo with Ethel Jackson, a former D'Oyly Carte chorine whose Broadway credits over half-a-dozen years were good if scarcely starry, as Sonia. The waltz, the hat, the stars and the strains of Vienna all came together in an enormous hit which produced 419 Broadway performances and, as in London, set up the fashion for all that's Viennese.

Theatrical mythology has every country unwillingly taking on *Die lustige Witwe* without any expectation of success. Given its untarnished record of triumph, this seems unlikely. Yet Paris did not welcome *La Veuve joyeuse* until more than four years after the Vienna production – by which time it had been seen in Cairo, in Shanghai, in Melbourne and in Johannesburg – and it was not one of the major Parisian musical producers but Alphonse Franck at the Théâtre Apollo who finally ventured. Franck gave the text to the most popular upmarket comedy writers of the day, Gaston de Caillavet and Robert de Flers, for adaptation and they, like the British, made their amendments to the original. The widow, now called Missia, became an American brought up in Marsovie (ex-Pontevedro, Pontenegro, Montenegro). Whether this was because Franck cast British soprano Constance Drever (a London take-over) in the rôle, or whether Miss Drever was cast because of the change of nationality (American, after all, at this period always meant rich), is not known, but to this day the French script of *La Veuve joyeuse* bears the instruction that Missia is to be played with an English (sic) accent, touched with a little Slav. The French Danilo is a Prince gone broke through gambling. In line with London, the Ambassador remained Popoff and the last act went to Maxim's, although the extra numbers disappeared along with Graves's excrescences and Hetty the Hen. The truly dashing light baritone Henry Defreyn was cast opposite Miss Drever, Charles Casella (Camille de Coutançon) and Thérèse Cernay (Nadia) had the duets, and Félix Galipaux was Popoff. Franck's production was an enormous success, played 186 times consecutively for its first run, and was regularly reprised at the Apollo in the years that followed with Defreyn repeating his rôle endlessly opposite Alice O'Brien and other Anglophone (and later not so very Anglophone) ladies.

Australia followed the personality-plus-singing style in casting its *Merry Widow* when local soubrette Carrie Moore, who had had considerable success on the London stage, introduced the rôle of the widow to audiences in Melbourne and later the rest of the country. The piece had a fine success, and it was regularly played thereafter, with the change in values from personality performance to singing ability being particularly noticeable as Australians such as Gladys Moncrieff and Joan Sutherland succeeded to the rôle of Hanna/Sonia.

The success of *Die lustige Witwe* prompted many burlesques throughout the world. In Germany, Julius Freund authored a pasticcio, *Der lustiger Witwer*, with music by Max R Steiner and others attached, which later played Danzers Orpheum in Vienna (ad Lindau, Anthony 9 February 1907), the Folies-Caprice presented a one-act *Die lästige Witwe* (20 August 1908) and a 'sequel' depicting *Die lustige Witwe in zweite Ehe* (the merry widow's second marriage), written by Max Hanisch and composed by Karl von Wegern, was played both in Vienna (Apollotheater 1907), where Annie Danninger and Eugen Borg challenged Günther and Treumann's creations, and in America (Deutsches Theater, Philadelphia 10 May 1909 and as *The Merry Widow Remarried*, Colonial Theater Chicago 4 August 1912). In Vienna, Lehár himself had fun with a little bit of his show, turning out a one-acter for the Theater an der Wien's studio theatre, Hölle, called *Mitislaw der moderne*, which allowed Louis Treumann to burlesque his own performance as Danilo.

Hungary saw *A vigadó özvegy* (Albert Heidelberg/Károly Ujváry, Emil Tábori, Budai Színkör 25 July 1907), France a dozen or so pieces including *La Veuve soyeuse* (Eugène Joullot, Henry de Farcy, 5 March 1909) at the Parisiana, *Moins veuve que joyeuse* and *Ni veuve, ni joyeuse*, whilst in New York Joe Weber produced a highly successful *Merry Widow Burlesque* which allowed Lulu Glaser and Blanche Ring an unlikely crack at the widow's rôle, and the show

His Honor the Mayor threatened in song 'I Wish I Could Find the Man Who Wrote the *Merry Widow* Waltz' and went on to say what he would do to him. In London, George Edwardes sued Pelissier's *Follies* not for burlesqueing the *Merry Widow* but for playing its music whilst he was still running the show. That problem, of course, raised its head elsewhere and a curious lawsuit arose in New York when Savage attacked one variety house for playing *The Merry Widow* without permission. The producers claimed that their production was not *The Merry Widow*, it was an adaptation of *L'Attaché d'ambassade* with music taken from Planquette's *Le Paradis de Mahomet* and other sources which just happened to sound like Lehár's score.

Inevitably, *Die lustige Witwe* made its way on to film. The first versions, including a Hollywood one with Mae Murray and John Gilbert, were silent, later versions proved not terribly faithful, whether emanating from America (MGM's 1934 version with Chevalier and Jeanette MacDonald and a 1952 repeat with Lana Turner and Fernando Lamas) or from Austria (1962 with Karin Hübner and Peter Alexander). A projected 1980s British film which, like this last, used the Operette as part of another story, vanished off the schedules without being made.

Major revivals have appeared regularly in all the main musical-theatre centres in the 85 years since the widow's first stage appearances as *Die lustige Witwe* established itself as the outstanding representatative of Vienna's Silver Age on the international stage. London saw Carl Brisson three times as Danilo, paired with Evelyn Laye, Nancie Lovat and Helen Gilliland, but if the last of these signalled a switch to a more legit singing widow, a reprise starring Madge Elliott and Cyril Ritchard put the ball squarely back in the light-comedy area. The last commercial London production of the piece was in 1969 with Lisbeth Webb. In New York, where revivals had passed in 1921, 1929 and 1931, musical film-stars Marta Eggerth and Jan Kiepura played the piece in 1943 before going on to repeat their performances around the world. In both countries the piece then passed into the opera houses, with June Bronhill initiating the Sadler's Wells Opera production with Christopher Hassall's new translation, and the New York City Opera and Beverley Sills putting the new very vocal slant on the piece in America. Since then the rôle of the widow has become meat for such operatic divas as Roberta Peters, Joan Sutherland, Lisa della Casa and Anna Moffo – a long way from the pretty-voiced personality performances of such as Mizzi Günther and Lily Elsie.

In Vienna the piece remains regularly in the repertoire of the Volksoper, which admits it finds it difficult to cast a Hanna with the personality the rôle has traditionally maintained in Austria but also with the now more solid vocal equipment modern tastes require, but the show stood up for a commercial run as recently as 1967 when the Theater an der Wien hosted a season of 309 performances with the ageing but ineffably dapper Johannes Heesters, repeating the Danilo on which Lehár had earlier posed 'best ever' laurels, playing opposite Ilona Szamos. In Germany, on the other hand, the piece, which has elsewhere suffered surprisingly little from the depredations of directors out to make themselves noticed by setting it in Greenland or the 14th century, has had some rather extreme treatments. An extravagantly reorganized and reorchestrated version (ad Rudolph Schanzer, Ernst Welisch), with Fritzi Massary and Max Hansen, was staged by Erik Charell at the Grosses Schauspielhaus in 1929, and in 1979 the Deutsches Oper hosted a version in which Wagnerian soprano Gwyneth Jones (who is not, in fact, the only Brünnhilde to have also played the widow in Germany) appeared as Hanna.

In Paris, with no operatic venue in which to retreat, *La Veuve joyeuse* has remained resolutely opérette through regular revivals, the most recent of which was at the Châtelet in 1982. After Mary Lewis (1925) and Corinne Harris (1934) the French productions stopped importing their Missias and Jeanne Aubert starred with Opéra-Comique baritone Jacques Jansen in 1942, followed by singing actress Marina Hotine (1951), Jenny Marlaine (1957) and the Opéra-Comique's Géori Boué (1962) before a multi-cast effort in 1982.

The score of *Die lustige Witwe* has been used as the basis for two ballets, one by Maurice Béjart (1963) and the second, with the score arranged by John Lanchbery, produced by the Australian Ballet. This latter arrangement, which included choral pit vocals, was played in New York and at the London Palladium with Marilyn Jones/Margot Fonteyn dancing the rôle of the widow.

Germany: Neues Operetten-Theater, Hamburg 3 March 1906, Berliner Theater, Berlin 1 May 1906; Hungary: Magyar Színház *Viz özvegy* 27 November 1906; UK: Daly's Theatre *The Merry Widow* 8 June 1907; USA: New Amsterdam Theater *The Merry Widow* 21 October 1907; Australia: Her Majesty's Theatre, Melbourne 16 May 1908; France: Théâtre Apollo *La Veuve joyeuse* 28 April 1909; Films: MGM 1925 (silent), MGM (Eng) 1934, MGM (Eng) 1952, Sacha Films/Herbert Grüber 1962 (Ger)

Recordings: 2-record 'complete' w Elisabeth Schwarzkopf, Erich Kunz (EMI) and many others; selection in English w June Bronhill (CSD) and many others; selection in French w Janette Vivalda (EMI-Pathé) and many others; 2-record 'complete' in Italian w Lia Origoni; 2-record 'complete' in Russian (Melodiya); selection in Swedish w Sonja Sternquist (London), selection in Spanish w Lily Berchmann (Montilla) etc

LUTE SONG Musical play (love story with music) in 2 acts by Sidney Howard and Will Irwin based on the play *Pi-Pa-Ki*. Lyrics by Bernard Hanighen. Music by Raymond Scott. Plymouth Theater, New York, 6 February 1946.

The musical *Lute Song* was based on a classic 14th-century Chinese play, adapted into English by Sidney Howard, the author of such outstanding successes as *They Knew What They Wanted* (subsequently musicalized as *The Most Happy Fella*), *The Silver Cord*, *The Late Christopher Bean* and *Alien Corn*, in collaboration with Will Irwin. The piece failed to find a production as a play, but producer Michael Meyerberg had it set as a 'love story with music' and it was finally produced, seven years after Howard's death, with Mary Martin as the Chinese wife Tschao-Ou-Niang whose husband Tsai-Yong (Yul Brynner) becomes too successful at court and who finds himself commanded to wed a royal Princess, Nieou-chi. Ultimately, the Princess realizes that her husband loves his first wife and relinquishes him.

The score included as much in the way of incidental and dance music as of vocal numbers, the most successful of

the latter being Miss Martin's opening song 'Mountain High, Valley Low'. In spite of a production which was praised for its beauty, *Lute Song* proved too far from the Broadway mainstream to attract the audiences needed, and it folded after 142 performances. It was, however, taken up by the once-proud London manager Albert de Courville, of *Hullo Ragtime!* and variety fame, and staged by him at the Winter Garden, a rather larger venue than Broadway's Plymouth Theater, with Brynner starred alongside Dolly Haas and Iris Russell. It failed in 24 performances.

Lute Song was seen once more when it was revived at New York's City Center in 1959.

UK: Winter Garden Theatre 11 October 1948
Recording: Selection (Decca, Ace of Hearts)

LUTZ, W[ilhelm] Meyer (b Mannerstädt, Kissingen, (?1822) 1829; d London, 31 January 1903). London conductor and composer of a half-century of all kinds of musical theatre.

Meyer Lutz was born in Germany, the younger brother of the Baron von Lutz, Prime Minister of Bavaria, whose principal claim to be remembered is that he was the 'villain' who committed the 'mad' King Ludwig of Bavaria. The younger Lutz studied music with his organist father, then at Würzburg under Eisenhöfer, and visited Britain for the first time in 1846 to conduct a series of concerts in Birmingham. He returned for a second visit in 1848 and this time he remained. He became, first, organist at St Chad's Church in Birmingham and then, successively, at St Ann's, Leeds, and St George's Catholic Cathedral in London, pairing this latter engagement with a post as conductor at Surrey Theatre (1850–55). There he conducted the Romer family's productions of operas (*Ernani, Robert le Diable, La Juive, Lucia di Lammermoor* etc) and composed, arranged and conducted the music for the house's dramatic productions. There, too, his own first composed works, including a light-operatic version of *Faust and Marguerite*, were played.

Over the following decade he toured as conductor of the London Grand Opera Company (1862, Sims Reeves, Elliot Galer, Rebecca Isaacs, Oliver Summers etc), of Henri Corri's English Opera Company (1864, *Faust, Maritana, No Song, No Supper, The Bohemian Girl, The Waterman, Lurline, The Rose of Castile* etc), and Galer and Fanny Reeves's Royal English Opera Company (1866, *La sonnambula, Il trovatore, Satanella, Faust, The Bohemian Girl*, Burnand's *Dido* etc) and with various concert combinations which included such artists as Mario and Mme Sainton Dolby. He appeared in London on a number of occasions, including seasons with Galer and his wife in burlesque and operetta at the Royalty Theatre in the mid-1860s.

At the same time, he turned out a steady stream of music ranging from a mass for Southwark Cathedral to a number of short operettas, notably for Galer and Miss Reeves who had mounted and starred in his *Zaida* as early as 1859 ('Herr Lutz has been known for some years as a graceful composer in the school of Auber'), and an 1864 Christmas cantata *King Christmas* was performed at the Oxford Music Hall under Charles Morton, with a cast including the young Emily Soldene, alternating with a potted version of *Orphée aux enfers*. When the craze for Minstrelsy struck, he was for a time the principal purveyor of songs, scenas and burlesque music to the Christy Minstrels and their Moore and Burgess successors.

His peripatetic life was stilled in February 1869 when John Hollingshead engaged him to replace Kettenus as musical director of the two-month-old Gaiety Theatre. There, in his first year, he composed and arranged the pasticcio scores for such burlesques as *Columbus* (1869, and including three original numbers by Lutz), *Linda di Chamouni* (1869) and *Wat Tyler MP* (1869) and the operetta *The Happy Village* (1869) and composed incidental music for several plays including the popular *Uncle Dick's Darling*. In the years following, he continued to turn out a liberal supply of mostly pasticcio burlesque scores, whilst also conducting the opéras-bouffes – including the Gaiety's original works *Aladdin II, Cinderella the Younger* and *Thespis* – on the programme of the theatre which was rapidly becoming recognized as London's top musical house. During the Gaiety's summer closure, he would conduct at seaside resorts, in later years on a regular basis at Scarborough, one of most charming and upmarket of such English holiday venues.

A conductor, répétiteur and musical amanuensis by day and evening, Lutz continued as a composer by night, working not only on the house pasticcio scores (*Little Don Caesar de Bazan, Ariel, The Bohemian G'yurl, Camaralzaman, Gulliver, The Forty Thieves, Little Doctor Faust, Robbing Roy, Little Robin Hood, Mazeppa* etc, etc), to which he supplied original melodies if and when necessary, but on some original, if distinctly old-fashioned little operettas and light operas, several of which were played on a matinée or benefit programmes at the Gaiety. His most successful compositions, at this stage, were two little pieces – *On Condition* and *Posterity* – played by Lila Clay's all-women concert party, and a song, 'Eyes of English Blue', performed by Alice Atherton in the touring scena *The Japs* (1885) and interpolated into most of her other shows.

After 35 years in the business and 15 at the Gaiety, it seemed unlikely that the ageing musician would suddenly become a hot property, but when pasticcio scores began to give way to original music at the Gaiety, under the management of George Edwardes, Lutz provided at first a portion (*Little Jack Sheppard*, 13 of 24 numbers) of the scores required and, very soon, virtually all the music for the hugely popular run of shows starring Nellie Farren and Fred Leslie and their contemporaries. He had a major hit with the barn-dance music for the pas de quatre in *Faust Up-to-Date*, but he also supplied the basic scores (into which interpolations were regularly made) for the whole series of new burlesques from *Monte Cristo Jr* and *Miss Esmeralda* through to the last, *Don Juan*.

At the same time, Lutz continued his conducting duties (notably as the original conductor of *Dorothy*) and also turned out a regular mass of contributions to mostly touring shows, including Willie Edouin's *Blackberries* and Harry Monkhouse's *Larks*, an activity which he pursued further when the burlesque fashion faded and newer composers stepped in to provide scores for the 'musical comedy' productions at the Gaiety. *Cupid & Co, Giddy Miss Carmen* (1894), *Baron Golosh, One of the Girls* (1896), *The Merry-Go-Round* (1899), *Hidenseek* (1901) and *The Girl from Kays* (1902) were amongst the shows to which he supplied more or fewer individual numbers.

Lutz conducted the early musical comedy *In Town* at the Gaiety before finally quitting his post there, although he continued to conduct some ill-advised ventures such as *Baron Golosh* (*L'Oncle Célestin*), Nellie Farren's attempt at management with his *A Model Trilby* and, at the age of 72, the desperate *Hidenseek*, as well as spending a period working under Edward Terry at the Strand Theatre.

A well-trained and versatile musician, and a prolific composer, who held an important place in the light musical theatre through the whole of the opéra-bouffe and burlesque eras and into that of Edwardesian musical comedy, Lutz leaned naturally to a somewhat polite and academic style in his writing, but he won his greatest successes with comic songs and lively dances of which the famous *Faust Up-to-Date* dance was the most enduring.

1852 **The Charmed Harp** (John Courtney) 1 act Surrey Theatre 30 August

1855 **Mephistopheles, or Faust and Marguerite** Surrey Theatre 16 May

1859 **Zaida, or The Pearl of Granada** (Oliver Summers) Liverpool Amphitheatre 14 February

1862 **Blonde or Brunette** (J P Wooler) 1 act Royalty Theatre 19 May

1865 **Felix, or The Festival of the Roses** (John Oxenford) 1 act Royalty Theatre 23 October

1872 **The Miller of Millberg** 1 act Gaiety Theatre 13 April

1874 **Cousin Kate** (Eliot Galer) 1 act Leicester 21 February

1881 **All in the Downs** (Douglas Jerrold ad) Gaiety Theatre 5 November

1882 **On Condition** (Robert Reece) 1 act Opera Comique 19 October

1882 **The Knight of the Garter** (J Sheddon Wilson) 1 act Gaiety Theatre 7 December

1884 **Posterity** (Augustus Moore) 1 act Newcastle 10 March

1885 **Won by a Trick** (Wilson) 1 act Gaiety Theatre 15 April

1885 **The Laundry Belle** (Wilson) 1 act Gaiety Theatre 2 May

1885 **Little Jack Sheppard** (w Florian Pascal et al/William Yardley, H Pottinger Stephens) Gaiety Theatre 26 December

1886 **Carl** (Wilson) 1 act Gaiety Theatre 3 May

1886 **Monte Cristo Jr** (w Ivan Caryll et al/'Richard Henry') Gaiety Theatre 23 December

1887 **Miss Esmeralda** (w Robert Martin et al/'A C Torr' [ie Fred Leslie], Horace Mills) Gaiety Theatre 8 October

1887 **Frankenstein** (w Martin et al/'Richard Henry') Gaiety Theatre 24 December

1888 **Faust Up-to-Date** (G R Sims, Henry Pettitt) Gaiety Theatre 30 October

1889 **Ruy Blas and the Blasé Roué** ('A C Torr', Herbert F Clark) Gaiety Theatre 3 September

1890 **Carmen Up-to-Data** (Sims, Pettitt) Gaiety Theatre 22 September

1891 **Cinder-Ellen Up-too-Late** Princess Theatre, Melbourne 22 August; Gaiety Theatre, London 24 December

1893 **Frasquita** (W Godfrey) 1 act Gaiety Theatre 29 May

1893 **Don Juan** (Adrian Ross/James T Tanner) Gaiety Theatre 28 October

1895 **A Model Trilby, or A Day or Two After Du Maurier** (C H E Brookfield, Yardley) 1 act Opera Comique 16 November

1896 **One of the Girls** (w John Crook, Sidney Jones/Herbert Darnley, J J Dallas) Birmingham 9 March

1899 **The Merry-Go-Round** (w others/Aubrey Hopwood/Seymour Hicks) Coronet Theatre 24 April

UN LYCÉE DE JEUNES FILLES Vaudeville-opérette in 3 acts by Alexandre Bisson. Music by Louis Gregh. Théâtre Cluny, Paris, 28 December 1881.

A lively piece from the pen of top comedy-writer Bisson which dealt with a young ladies' establishment, set up for the daughters of ... ladies of the night. The comedy, with established funny men Guy (Simplice) and Mesmaecker (headmaster Cavénécadas) in its lead rôles, with Blanche Ghinassi (Suzette) and Marguerite Luther (Tambourine) supplying the feminine moments, and accompanied by some self-effacing numbers from Louis Gregh, proved to be good for a run of more than 50 nights under Taillefer's management at the Théâtre Cluny on its first showing. It was also good for a series of repeats thereafter. Paris saw the piece again when Fernand Samuel mounted it at the Théâtre de la Renaissance in 1890, with Guy repeating his original lead comic rôle (3 May) and the 140 performances racked up by this reprise were sufficient encouragement for the director to repeat *Un Lycée de jeunes filles* when he took over at the Théâtre des Variétés (24 May 1892). Baron featured in this third production, alongside the young Ève Lavallière. This time it was a flop, but when the Folies-Dramatiques took the show up in 1895 (63 performances), followed by the Théâtre Déjazet in 1897 and, finally, the Gaîté-Lyrique in 1904, it was evident that the Variétés season had been the odd man out.

France was not the only country to welcome Bisson's tale of mildly immodest mix-ups in a girls' school. The Renaissance revival inspired an Hungarian mounting for a good 24 nights at the Népszinház (ad Lajos Evva, Viktor Rákosi as 'theatre school') within months, followed by performances at the Budai Színkör (1 June 1892) and elsewhere, and Berlin saw a version adapted by Richard Genée who also supplied some fresh music to supplement Gregh's score.

Hungary: Népszinház *Színitanoda* 7 November 1890; Germany: Thomas Theater *Mädchenschule* 25 September 1891

LYNNE, Gillian [PYRKE, Gillian Barbara] (b Bromley, 20 February 1927). Performer turned choreographer whose dances for *Cats* and other musicals of recent years have made her Britain's most internationally successful dance arranger since the days of E W Royce.

Miss Lynne made her earliest theatre appearances in ballet, dancing for seven years with the Sadler's Wells company (Lilac Fairy, Queen of the Wilis, Black Queen in *Checkmate*, *Adam Zero* etc) before moving into variety at the London Palladium and into jazz dance with her own group, Collages. She made her first major musical appearance in the West End in 1953 when she played the part of Claudine in the London production of *Can-Can*, and was subsequently seen as Wanda in a revival of *Rose Marie* and in several revues.

She began her career as a choreographer in 1962 with the Western Theatre Ballet, and choreographed several revues and films before taking on her first musical shows, *The Roar of the Greasepaint - the Smell of the Crowd* (England 1964, USA 1965) and *Pickwick* (USA 1965, TV 1970). She directed and choreographed the musical *The Matchgirls* at the Leatherhead Repertory Theatre (1965) and on its West End transfer and subsequently fulfilled the same double function in a 1969 production of Offenbach's *Bluebeard* at Sadler's Wells, the unlucky musical version of *Love on the Dole* (Nottingham, 1970) and a Westernized *She Stoops to Conquer* written by Caryl Brahms and Ned Sherrin (*Liberty Ranch*, 1972). She also choreographed

Broadway's *How Now Dow Jones* (1968) and London's *Phil the Fluter* (1969), *Ambassador* (1971), *The Card* (1973), *Hans Andersen* (1974), *My Fair Lady* revival (1979) and *Songbook* (1979).

In the late 1970s Miss Lynne had a personal success with her musical staging of two Royal Shakespeare Company productions, *A Comedy of Errors* and *Once in a Lifetime*, and she teamed again with RSC director Trevor Nunn to create the original production of the dance-based Andrew Lloyd Webber musical *Cats*. She subsequently directed and choreographed productions of *Cats* in many parts of the world, teamed with Hal Prince on *The Phantom of the Opéra* and with Nunn again on *Aspects of Love*, and directed and choreographed the compilation show *Tomfoolery* (1980), a London revival of *Cabaret* (1986) and the musicalized Shaw piece *Valentine's Day* (1992).

Miss Lynne choreographed the film versions of *Half a Sixpence* (1966) and *Man of La Mancha* (1972) and the screen's *Yentl* (1982). In 1985 she created a ballet, *Café Soir*, to the music of *A Little Night Music*, for the Houston Ballet and in 1990 the BBC-TV's *The Look of Love* (directed and choreographed) based on the songs of Burt Bacharach and Hal David.

Miss Lynne is married to actor and singer **Peter Land** [Peter Oliver WHITE b Taihape, New Zealand 9 July 1953] who has appeared on the London stage in *My Fair Lady* (1979, Freddy), *Galileo* (1980, Balladsinger), *Six for Gold* (1985), *Cabaret* (1986, Cliff) and *The Phantom of the Opéra* (t/o André).

LYSISTRATA Spectacular Operette with ballet in 2 acts by Heinrich Bolten-Bäckers. Music by Paul Lincke. Apollotheater, Berlin, 1 April 1902.

One of the successors to Lincke and Bolten-Bäckers' enormously successful spectacle-fantasy *Frau Luna* as part of the variety programme at Berlin's Apollotheater was a comic-burlesque treatment of Aristophanes' celebrated war-or-sex tale. Bolten's Lysistrata inflicted her 'Bettstreik' on her husband, Athenian generalissimo Themistokles, and encouraged her nieces Cypris and Bachis and the Apollotheater's glamour chorus to do the same to their husbands, to the accompaniment of a lively set of songs, dances, marches and ensembles. *Lysistrata* proved to have less attraction for the Apollotheater's audiences than *Frau Luna* or *Im Reiche des Indra*, but from amongst several agreeable pieces its score brought forth the number which was to become the most internationally successful single item in Lincke's opus. The Glühwürmchen-Idyll, a delicious, twinkling ensemble used as an intermezzo in the show, became a worldwide hit, travelling to all kinds of countries where *Lysistrata* itself did not go. On Broadway it was inserted into the production of *The Girl Behind the Counter*, sung as a solo by May Naudain.

Adolf Klein's Apollotheater production, with Lucie Medlon in the title-rôle, was taken to Vienna's Danzers Orpheum by Gabor Steiner in 1903. It shared the bill with a Lincke/Bolten-Bäckers one-acter *Am Hochzeitsabend* and a variety programme, and was played in repertoire with the Apollo's other pieces, *Frau Luna* and *Im Reiche des Indra*, for a season. The 'electric' ballet *Leuchtende Brillanten* 'by H Harndin from the Folies Bergères [sic] in Paris and the Alhambra-Theater in London' was interpolated into each of the three Operetten.

P-L Flers's French version was played at the Moulin-Rouge, in the wake of the Parisian success of Steiner's earlier success, *The Belle of New York*, with the beautiful, aggressively corseted soprano Germaine Gallois starred in the title-rôle and Angèle Gril and Sulbac featured. Flers added additional scenes and tableaux-vivants to the libretto and interpolated extraneous songs, turning the piece into a full evening's entertainment which showed off the scenic and feminine specialities of the Moulin-Rouge at their lushest. With typical theatrical mensongerie, the show was advertised as having been played nearly ten thousand times in America and Britain: it had actually been seen in neither. It had, however, reached Hungary (ad Ferenc Molnár, Jenő Farago), where it was played at the Király Színház in 1903.

In spite of an indifferent start, *Lysistrata* survived. It was revived at Budapest's Scala Színház as *Lysistratá* with Hanna Honthy in the title-rôle (14 August 1920), and it remains on the fringe of the German-language repertoire in one of those reorganized versions which, like Flers's effort, brings it up to the length of a full evening's entertainment. However, the 'Glow-Worm' is still heard more than the Operette.

Lysistrata has been seen on the musical stage on a number of other occasions since she was given Schubert music in 1861 in the little *Der Verschworenen, oder Der häusliche Krieg* (lib: I F Castelli, Frankfurt 29 August), and Aristophanes' sexy tale was a natural prey for musical-makers of the naughty-words-are-thrilling era. After a Frank Vinciguerra/Danny Liebstein rock musical *Lysistrata* had been played at Hunter College Theater Workshop in 1968, another American musical of the same title was played in New York in 1972 (Brooks Atkinson Theatre 13 November Peter Link/Michael Cacoyannis). A 1963 Romanian operetta by Nicouzor Constantinescu and George Voinescu, music by Gherase Dendrino and a 1971 Czechoslovakian piece (*Der schönste Krieg*) by Hana Čináková, Vladimir Renčin and composer Jiři Bedná also went to the same source, whilst a British piece mixed the tale with a cowboy setting and called itself *Wild, Wild Women* as it made its way from Richmond to Windsor to London's Astoria (ex-movie) Theatre. A piece called *Lysistrata 2001* appeared in Munich in 1986 (Musiktheater 21 December). So far none has come up to Bolten-Bäckers and Lincke's effort in durability nor produced anything to rival his Glühwürmchen-Idyll.

Austria: Danzers Orpheum 31 March 1903; Hungary: Király Szinház *Makrancos Hölgyek* 16 December 1903; France: Théâtre du Moulin-Rouge 15 April 1904

LYTTON, Henry A (Sir) [aka Henry HENRI] [JONES, Henry Arthur] (b London, 3 January 1865; d London, 15 August 1936). Light-comedy baritone who became long-time chief comedian of the D'Oyly Carte company.

Lytton made his earliest stage appearances (as H A Henri, pretending to be his wife's brother) as a chorister for Violet Melnotte in *Erminie* and Ivan Caryll's first musical *The Lily of Léoville*. He subsequently toured with one of D'Oyly Carte's companies, played briefly for George Grossmith in *Ruddigore* and George Temple in Broadway's *Gondoliers* and, after some eight years playing Gilbert and Sullivan in the provinces, came in to the town company to replace the failing Grossmith in the lead rôle of Carte's production of *His Majesty* (1897). Thereafter he remained at the Savoy Theatre to appear in D'Oyly Carte's main company in the Gilbert and Sullivan repertoire (Shadbolt, Dr Daly, Strephon, Mikado etc), as Prince Paul in the Savoy's revival of *The Grand Duchess*, and to create important rôles in *The Lucky Star* (1899, Baron Tabasco), *The Rose of Persia* (1899, Sultan Mahmoud), *The Emerald Isle* (1901, Pat Murphy), *Merrie England* (1902, Earl of Essex, 'The Yeomen of England') and *A Princess of Kensington* (1903, Jelf).

When William Greet took the Savoy company into musical comedy, Lytton starred as juvenile lead in *The Earl and the Girl* (Dick Wargrave, 'My Cosy Corner Girl') and continued in similar rôles in *The Talk of the Town* (Reggie Drummond), *The White Chrysanthemum* (Reginald Armitage), as a take-over for the younger George Grossmith in the Gaiety's *The Spring Chicken* (Boniface) and in *The Little Michus*. He was cast as a Seymour Hicks clone in *My Darling* (1907) in his last musical-comedy performances before rejoining the D'Oyly Carte company in 1908 (Mikado, Dick Deadeye, Strephon, Pirate King etc). He remained with the company for the rest of his long career, graduating from the Richard Temple rôles to the George Grossmith rôles, and making himself an enduring name as the comic star of the Gilbert and Sullivan repertoire over a quarter of a century. He retired in 1934.

Lytton's wife, Louie Henri, who had begun a career as a chorus singer before her husband (*The Merry Duchess* etc), played alongside him thereafter both with Miss Melnotte and then with Carte, firstly as a chorister and later as a soubrette during their eight years of touring. She appeared as Tessa in the 1891 revival of *The Gondoliers* before retiring to family life.

Their son Henry Lytton jr played in musical comedy and revue and was at one stage the husband of revue star Jessie Matthews.

Autobiographies: *Secrets of a Savoyard* (Jarrolds, London, 1922), *A Wandering Minstrel* (Jarrolds, London, 1933)

M

McCARTHY, Joseph (b Somerville, Mass, 27 September 1885; d New York, 18 December 1943). Lyricist of the 1910s and 1920s who scored sizeable hits both in and out of the theatre.

Described as having been variously a vocalist, a music publisher in Boston, and a scion of Tin Pan Alley, McCarthy poked his head out noticeably in the musical theatre for the first time in 1913 when Al Jolson used his 'You Made Me Love You' (w James Monaco) as part of his act in *Honeymoon Express*. He had further song successes with 'Ireland Must Be Heaven (for my mother came from there)' (w Fred Fisher, Howard Johnson), 'What Do You Want to Make Those Eyes at Me For?' (w Monaco, Johnson), which was interpolated both in Broadway's *Follow Me* and the London wartime musical *The Better 'Ole*, and 'They Go Wild, Simply Wild Over Me' (w Fisher) before, in 1918, he collaborated with Harry Carroll on the score of a first Broadway musical, *Oh, Look!* Although short-lived in New York, this piece proved much more of a success on the road with the Dolly Sisters featured at the top of its bill, and it produced another McCarthy piece that was to become a standard, 'I'm Always Chasing Rainbows' (music: Chopin ad).

The following year he provided the whole of the lyrics for a second show produced at the little Vanderbilt Theater. This time his musical collaborator was Harry Tierney, another *Follow Me* contributor with whom he had written two numbers for the Cohanized comic opera *The Royal Vagabond* earlier in the year, and the huge success of their *Irene* ('Alice Blue Gown'), cemented a partnership which was to last through five and a bit more musicals in the following decade. The comical *Kid Boots* and the spectacular, romantic *Rio Rita* (Rangers Song, 'Rio Rita') were both played internationally but, in spite of some considerable success, they did not approach *Irene* in either charm or in longevity. The 'bit' of the five and a bit was the Broadway production of the French opérete *Afgar* for which Tierney and McCarthy supplied a goodly number of interpolations.

McCarthy and Tierney also wrote for revue, contributing songs to the *Ziegfeld Follies* from 1919 on ('My Baby's Arms', 'They're So Hard to Keep When They're Beautiful', 'Take Oh Take Those Lips Away') and being billed as principal writers for the 1924 edition ('Adoring You', 'All Pepped Up', 'The Old Town Band'). They also composed the songs for *The Broadway Whirl* (1921).

The 1973 revival of *Irene*, which gave the show a second and even more prosperous Broadway, London and Australian life, used a selection of McCarthy's early song hits written with composers other than Tierney as part of a score which featured only a part of *Irene*'s original music.

1918 **Oh, Look!** (Harry Carroll/James Montgomery ad) Vanderbilt Theater 7 March

1919 **Irene** (Harry Tierney/Montgomery) Vanderbilt Theater 18 November

1922 **Up She Goes** (Tierney/Frank Craven) Playhouse 6 November

1922 **Glory** (Tierney/Montgomery) Vanderbilt Theater 25 December

1923 **Kid Boots** (Tierney/William A McGuire, Otto Harbach) Earl Carroll Theater 31 December

1927 **Rio Rita** (Tierney/Guy Bolton, Fred Thompson) Ziegfeld Theater 2 February

1928 **Cross My Heart** (Tierney/Daniel Kusell) Knickerbocker Theater 17 September

McCAULL, John A (b Scotland, 1846; d Greensboro, NC, 12 November 1894). Broadway's most energetic producer of comic opera in the 1880s.

Colonel McCaull (apparently a genuine Colonel, from the Confederate ranks) was a Baltimore lawyer and sometime member of the Virginian state legislature whose first link with the theatre was in handling a number of stage lawsuits. In 1879, in partnership with Charles E Ford and James Barton Key, he became a theatrical manager, setting up first at the Fifth Avenue Theater where the partners hosted D'Oyly Carte's production of *The Pirates of Penzance* and, from March 1880, at the newly remodelled Bijou Theater which was opened with a spectacle coupé of English operettas (*Charity Begins at Home*, *Ages Ago*, *The Spectre Knight*). After six months, Ford dropped out and McCaull continued alone, presenting Audran's *Olivette*, *La Mascotte* and *Le Grand Mogul* (*The Snake Charmer*), Gilbert and Sullivan's *The Sorcerer* and *Patience*, Solomon's *Billee Taylor* (as D'Oyly Carte's accredited American associate) and Lecocq's *Le Coeur et la main* (*Heart and Hand*), and scoring several notable successes. He hosted Willie Edouin's Sparks for a season with *Dreams* and also ventured briefly into comedy, but his career from this time on was virtually wholly in the musical theatre.

McCaull sponsored the Blanche Roosevelt Opera Company which folded after underprepared productions of Cellier's *The Sultan of Mocha* and *The Mask of Pandora* (1881), and he then set up the McCaull Opera Comique Company which became a much more significant and wide-ranging institution. For a while he joined forces with Rudolf Aronson, investing money in the Casino Theater under an agreement to supply the house with operettic product. That agreement foundered when the two came to disagreement over Aronson's attempts to influence the staging of the shows, and McCaull moved his company on to Wallack's (1884) and to other theatres. He numbered amongst his productions such imported pieces as *The Queen's Lace Handkerchief* (*Das Spitzentuch der Königin*), *The Sorcerer*, *La Princesse de Trébizonde*, *Der Bettelstudent*, *The Black Hussar* (*Der Feldprediger*), *Die Fledermaus*, *Falka*, *Jacquette* (*La Béarnaise*), *Bellman*, *Le Petit Duc*, Planquette's

Nell Gwynne, Indiana, Dellinger's *Don Cesar, Lorraine* and *Capitán Fracasse, Joséphine vendue par ses soeurs, The Crowing Hen (Serment d'amour), Die sieben Schwaben, Prince Methusalem, Boccaccio,* the Viennese musical comedy *Die Näherin* played as *Chatter* and Suppé's *Die Jagd nach dem Glück* produced under the title *Clover,* and also produced two early American comic operas, *The Lady or the Tiger* and *The Begum,* and the English-bred but American-produced *Virginia and Paul* (1883).

McCaull became disabled after an accident on the ice in Chicago and, by 1892, his circumstances had become so reduced that a benefit was given for him by the profession, raising $8,000 to help him through the last years of his life.

MacCUNN, Hamish (b Greenock, Scotland, 22 March 1868; d London, 2 August 1916).

A composer of orchestral music and of two operas (*Jeanie Deans, Diarmid*), MacCunn began his composing and conducting careers (Carl Rosa Opera, Moody-Manners Opera) in classical music before, in 1902, moving to the Savoy Theatre where, as principal conductor, he musically directed the original productions of *Merrie England* and *A Princess of Kensington*. When manager William Greet moved on from the Savoy and comic opera to the Lyric Theatre and musical comedy, MacCunn went with him as the conductor for *The Earl and the Girl* and *Little Hans Andersen*. He subsequently conducted *The Blue Moon* (1905), *The Talk of the Town* (1905), Liza Lehmann's light opera *The Vicar of Wakefield* (1906), *Tom Jones* (1907) and German's last musical *Fallen Fairies* (1909). He then joined the Beecham Opera Company with whom he was the musical director for Beecham's 1910 revival of C V Stanford's *Shamus O'Brien*.

MacCunn supplied occasional songs for interpolation into a number of West End shows and in 1905 he wrote the score for the musical comedy *The Golden Girl*, toured by H Cecil Beryl.

MacCunn's brother, Andrew MacCunn, at first a deputy conductor with the Moody-Manners Opera Company, later also worked as a musical director in the musical theatre. He toured for George Edwardes in South Africa, but made the large part of his career in Australia where he became established as the senior theatre conductor of his time.

1905 **The Golden Girl** (Basil Hood) Prince of Wales Theatre, Birmingham 5 August
1912 **The Sailor and the Nursemaid** (Charles Childerstone) 1 act Aldwych Theatre 27 June

MacDERMOT, Galt (b Montreal, 18 December 1928). The composer of the songs for *Hair*.

MacDermot's achievement at the age of almost 40 was sufficiently limited for him to list himself in the programme of his first musical, amongst the lists of credits of his companions, solely and briefly as 'piano player, organist, choir director, African and love-rock musicologist'. In fact, he had made some inroads into the popular-music world, and had had some success with a 1961 song, 'African Waltz', but that was small beans compared to the success which that first musical would bring him. *Hair* turned out to be an enduring international hit, and its favourite song 'Aquarius', became and has remained ever since the anthem of the 1960s people of every decade.

In spite of its huge success, *Hair* won no awards (the 1968 Best Musical Tony went to *Hallelujah, Baby!*), and it almost seemed like a slightly shamefaced acknowledgement of that fact that, in 1972, MacDermot's modern musical-comedy version of Shakespeare's *Two Gentlemen of Verona,* brought to Broadway, like *Hair,* from the New York Shakespeare Festival's Public Theatre, did take the principal award. *Two Gentlemen of Verona* proved quite successful – although not anywhere as successful as *Hair* – finding a good run on Broadway and a number of productions overseas.

Thereafter, however, MacDermot failed to find again the success that the 1960s and its trends, attitudes and tastes had brought him. *Dude,* mounted by *Hair* director O'Horgan (another whose triumphs lasted only those few years of the late 1960s and early 1970s), was a quick failure, an Andrew Lloyd Webber-style sung-through *Via Galactica* which was mounted by Peter Hall at the new Uris Theater was gone in a week and a version of Tirso de Molina's *El Burlador de Sevilla,* originally commissioned by Britain's Royal Shakespeare Company, was eventually seen only in Trinidad.

MacDermot returned to the musical theatre in the 1980s with another score for Joseph Papp and the Public Theatre, but *The Human Comedy* followed its 79 performances at the Shakespeare Festival with just 13 at Broadway's Royale.

MacDermot has also written ballet and church music and composed an operatic *Troilus and Cressida* (1969), as well as incidental music for the Public Theatre's productions of *Hamlet* and *Twelfth Night*.

1967 **Hair** (Gerome Ragni, James Rado) Anspacher Theater 17 October, Biltmore Theater 29 April 1968
1970 **Isabel's a Jezebel** (William Dumaresq) Duchess Theatre, London 15 December
1971 **Two Gentlemen of Verona** (John Guare, Mel Shapiro) St James Theater 1 December
1972 **Dude** (*The Highway Life*) (Ragni) Broadway Theater 9 October
1972 **Via Galactica** (Christopher Gore, Judith Ross) Uris Theater 28 November
1973 **The Karl Marx Play** (Rochelle Owens) American Place Theater 16 March
1973 **Aunt Harriet** (MacDermot) Theater for the New City 21 November
1974 **The Charlatan** (Derek Walcott) Mark Taper Forum, Los Angeles 23 May
1974 **The Joker of Seville** (Walcott) Little Carib Theater, Trinidad November
1983 **The Human Comedy** (Dumaresq) Public Theater 28 December, Royale Theater 5 April 1984
1985 **The Special** Jewish Repertory Theater 19 October

MACDONALD, Christie (b Pictou, Nova Scotia, 28 February 1875; d Westport, Conn, 25 July 1962). Pretty, sweet-voiced leading lady on the turn-of-the-century Broadway stage.

Born in Nova Scotia and educated in Boston, the palely pretty young Christie MacDonald made her first stage appearance as a chorus singer in *Erminie* and appeared with Francis Wilson's company in such comic operas as *The Lion Tamer* (*Le Grand Casimir*), *The Merry Monarch* (*L'Étoile*) and *Erminie* again (Marie) before being promoted to a slightly larger rôle in *The Devil's Deputy* (Babolin, 1894, Bob). She appeared in the Boston musicals *The Sphinx*

(1895, Shafra) and *The Walking Delegate* (1897, Woo Me), and featured alongside Wilson again both as Dolly Grigg in the Broadway version of Sullivan's *The Chieftain* and in *Half a King* (*Le Roi de carreau*, Lucinde), and had her best new rôle to date as the Princess Minutezza in Klaw and Erlanger's production of Sousa's *The Bride Elect* (1898).

Thereafter a string of leading ingénue rôles followed, both in American musical comedies – *The Man in the Moon* (1899, Diana), *In Gay Paree* (1899, Louisette), *The Princess Chic* (1900, Chic, which served her two whole seasons on the road), *The Sho-Gun* (1904, Princess Hunni-Bun), *Mexicana* (1906, Tita), *The Prince of Bohemia* (1910, Angela Tritton) – and in imports such as the Gaiety Theatre musical *The Toreador* (Nancy Staunton), *An English Daisy* (Daisy), *The Cadet Girl* (*Les Demoiselles de Saint-Cyriens*, Antoinette) and *The Belle of Mayfair* (playing the Juliet rôle created in London by Edna May). She found particular success in the title-rôle of *Miss Hook of Holland* and as the star of the long-running American production of Reinhardt's *The Spring Maid* (*Die Sprudelfee*). In 1913 she created the ingénue lead in Victor Herbert's *Sweethearts* before, no longer an ingénue at almost 40, disappearing from the musical stage.

She returned in 1920 to play the star character rôle of Lady Holyrood, created by Ada Reeve, in a revival of *Florodora*, before putting an end to her career.

MacDONALD, Jeanette [Anna] (b Philadelphia, 18 June 1901; d Houston, Tex, 14 January 1965). Hollywood's most successful soprano star of celluloid operetta.

After beginning her singing career as a teenager in the chorus of a New York revue, Miss MacDonald appeared in Jerome Kern's *The Night Boat* (1920), acted as understudy to the title-rôle of *Irene* in Chicago and played a chorus part at the Casino Theater in *Tangerine* (1921). She won improving rôles alongside Mitzi in *The Magic Ring* (1923, Irish Bellamy), and (sporting two 'n's in her Jeannette in the playbill) as Sylvia Metcalf, the second female part to Queenie Smith, in *Tip-Toes* (1925), accompanying another fine voice, Robert Halliday, in the strains of 'Nice Baby'. She had a leading rôle, alongside touring stars Cecil Lean and Cleo Mayfield, in a musical version of *Brewster's Millions* called *Bubbling Over* (1926) which stumbled out of town, and she moved on instead to the title-rôle (which was not quite as good as it sounded) of another fine farce, *Nothing But the Truth*, set to music as *Yes, Yes, Yvette* (1927). This one made Broadway, but she stopped short of New York once again in *The Studio Girl*, a flop version of the *Trilby* tale musicalized by the perennially flopping Will Ortmann, in which she had been cast as the mutable heroine.

Miss MacDonald continued in ingénue rôles in a further trio of undistinguished shows in 12 months – *Sunny Days* (1928, Ginette Bertin), *Angela* (aka *The Right Girl*, 1928, Princess Angela) and *Boom Boom* (1929, Jean), before moving on to a film career which made her one of the most famous leading ladies of the heyday of the musical screen. She starred in (not always recognizable) film versions of *The Vagabond King* (1930), *The Cat and the Fiddle* (1932), *The Merry Widow* (1934), *Naughty Marietta* (1935), *Rose Marie* (1936), *The Firefly* (1937), *Maytime* (1937), *Sweethearts* (1939), *Bitter-Sweet* (1940) and *I Married an Angel* (1942), as well as in such made-for-the-screen musi-

cal movies as *The Love Parade*, *One Hour With You*, *Love Me Tonight* and *San Francisco*. She later appeared on the stage in concert but never returned to the musical theatre where, *Tip-Toes* apart, she had drawn a fairly feeble lot of shows in her ingénue days.

MacDONOUGH, Glen (b Brooklyn, NY, 12 November 1870; d Stamford, Conn, 30 March 1924). Eclectic musical-theatre writer whose works ranged from touring comedy to fantasy to Viennese adaptations.

MacDonough began his theatre career as an actor, and subsequently wrote several farces before making his first essay into the musical theatre in a collaboration with Victor Herbert on a piece called *The Gold Bug* (1896). In spite of the last-minute interpolation of two lively and appreciated young performers called Bert Williams and George Walker into its cast, *The Gold Bug* expired after one week. MacDonough supplied farcical vehicles for Sam Bernard (*The Marquis of Michigan*) and May Irwin (the play with songs *Kate Kip, Buyer*, the musical comedy *The Belle of Bridgeport*), concocted a low-comical American-in-Paris text to star Dan Daly as one of *The New Yorkers* and adapted the Strauss pasticcio *Wiener Blut* for Rudolf Aronson, but he found his first major success only when he came back together with Herbert, seven years after their disastrous first collaboration, to write the spectacular children-of-all-ages extravaganza *Babes in Toyland*.

The association was pursued in a successful piece of Ruritanian musical comedy, *It Happened in Nordland*, in a pretty fantasy called *Woodland* (based on the Brothers Grimm tale *The Dancing Princesses*), which did not, in spite of a respectable career (73 performances), win the same audience that had clustered around *Babes in Toyland*, and an oriental comic opera called *Algeria*. Herbert's delightful score for this last piece was too good to jettison, so when the piece failed to come up to expectations MacDonough partly rewrote the libretto and it was given a second chance the following season as *The Rose of Algeria*. But it still failed to take off.

The end of MacDonough's collaboration with Herbert overlapped with the beginning of his contribution to a mostly successful series of 'summer musicals'. These were frivolous, light pieces of only fairly coherent comedy, illustrated by pluggable songs in the mode of the moment (at first by Raymond Hubbell, later by Baldwin Sloane), pretty girls, specialities and scenic effects, and intended for the businessman who was not only tired but hot, and also for his family. After the success of the first, *The Midnight Sons*, producer Lew Fields played the series summer and winter at the Broadway Theater until the vein ran out some three years later.

MacDonough subsequently adapted several of the freshly fashionable Viennese musical shows into American-style shows for Klaw and Erlanger with some success, remade Leo Birinski's *Narrentanz* as the libretto for a piece called *The Merry Martyr* without any, and had his last brush with something like a winner when he contributed the text to Raymond Hubbell's *The Kiss Burglar* in 1918. His last work for the musical theatre was in four songs (w Hubbell) for the 1919 *Come to Bohemia*, on the revues *As You Were* (American adaptation), *Hitchy Koo of 1920* (book and lyrics to the music of Jerome Kern) and *Snapshots of 1921*, and five projects that all stopped short of Broadway: De

Koven's last comic opera, May Irwin's last star vehicle, a musical version of the comedy *It Pays to Advertise*, a botch job on the Paris hit *Phi-Phi* and an unsuccessful musical-comedy vehicle for female impersonator Julian Eltinge, produced by Jacques Pierre as *The Elusive Lady*.

1896 **The Gold Bug** (Victor Herbert) Casino Theater 21 September

1898 **The Marquis of Michigan** (Edward W Townsend) Bijou Theater 21 September

1898 **Kate Kip, Buyer** (various) Bijou Theater 31 October

1899 **Sister Mary** (various) Bijou Theater 27 October

1900 **Chris and the Wonderful Lamp** (John Philip Sousa) Victoria Theater 1 January

1900 **The Belle of Bridgeport** (various) Bijou Theater 19 October

1901 **Vienna Life** (*Wiener Blut*) American version (Broadway Theater)

1901 **The New Yorkers** (Ludwig Englander/George V Hobart) Herald Square Theater 7 October

1903 **Babes in Toyland** (Herbert) Majestic Theater 13 October

1904 **It Happened in Nordland** (Herbert) Lew Fields Theater 5 December

1905 **Wonderland** (Herbert) Majestic Theater 24 October

1908 **Algeria** (Herbert) Broadway Theater 31 August

1909 **The Midnight Sons** (Raymond Hubbell) Broadway Theater 22 May

1909 **The Rose of Algeria** revised *Algeria* Herald Square Theater 20 September

1909 **The Girl from the States** (later *The Golden Widow*) (Hubbell, A Baldwin Sloane) Adelphi Theater, Philadelphia 11 October

1910 **The Jolly Bachelors** (Hubbell) Broadway Theater 6 January

1910 **The Summer Widowers** (Sloane) Broadway Theater 4 June

1911 **The Hen Pecks** (Sloane/E Ray Goetz) Broadway Theater 4 February

1911 **The Never Homes** (Sloane/Goetz) Broadway Theater 5 October

1912 **The Count of Luxemburg** (*Der Graf von Luxembourg*) American version (New Amsterdam Theater)

1912 **Eva** American version (New Amsterdam Theater)

1913 **The Merry Martyr** (Hugo Riesenfeld) Colonial Theater, Boston 8 September

1914 **The Queen of the Movies** (*Die Kino-Königin*) American version w Edward A Paulton (Globe Theater)

1918 **The Kiss Burglar** (Hubbell) George M Cohan Theater 9 May

1919 **Yesterday** (Reginald De Koven) Playhouse, Wilmington 10 March

1919 **Raising the Aunty** (aka *The Water's Fine*) (Ted Snyder/Joe Sam Lewis, Joe Young/w Aaron Hoffman) Poughkeepsie 19 March

1919 **Among the Girls** (Hubbell/w Henry Blossom/Blossom, Roi Cooper Megrue) Park Square Theater, Boston 19 May

1921 **Phi-Phi** American version w Harry Wagstaffe Gribble, Goetz (Globe Theater, Atlantic City)

1922 **The Elusive Lady** (Hubbell) Ford's Theater, Baltimore 2 October

MACÉ-MONTROUGE, Marguerite [née MACÉ].

Marguerite Macé began her career as an actress at the Gymnase and during the 1850s worked at the Délassements-Comique and at the Bouffes-Parisiens (from 1855) where she made up part of Offenbach's original little company. At one stage she was the only female member. She remained with the composer to create rôles in a number of his early works including *Une nuit blanche* (Fanchette), *La Chatte metamorphosée en femme* (Marianne) and, most notably, the part of L'Opinion Publique in *Orphée aux enfers*, and also created rôles in such little opérettes as Jonas's *Le Duel de Benjamin* (1855), the prize opérette *Le Docteur Miracle* (Véronique), *Les Ondines au Champagne* (1865, Coquilette), *Le Cabaret de Ramponneau* (1867, Bellhumeur) and *Sauvons la caisse* (1871).

She had a long career, successfully transferring to character parts in later years and creating two important senior musical-comedy rôles, the conniving Madame Jacob in *Joséphine vendue par ses soeurs* (1886) and La Señora, the vigorous duenna of *Miss Helyett* (1890). She also appeared as La Baronne in *Le Droit du seigneur* (1878), in *Mamselle Crénom* (1888), Pugno's *Le Valet de coeur* (1888) and a number of other musical shows amongst a busy programme of plays.

Her husband, **MONTROUGE** [Louis HESNARD], a comic actor in the musical theatre, had begun his working life as an architect. After being involved in the restoration of the Théâtre des Batignolles in 1855 he became its associate director and moved on from there to manage, at various times, the Théâtre Marigny, the Bouffes-Parisiens, the Châtelet and the Théâtre de l'Athénée-Comique. He simultaneously had a long career as a performer, making a particular mark as a compère in revue ('le roi des compères et des féticheurs') and creating many musical rôles, from early days in *Le Testament de M Crac* (1871, Capoulade) and alongside his wife in *Le Cabaret de Ramponneau* (Ramponneau) and *Les Ondines au Champagne* (Vent-Contraire), to good character rôles in *Le Droit du seigneur* (1878, the Baron), *François les bas-bleus* (1883, Marquis de Pontcornet), *Surcouf* (1887, Kerbiniou), *Le Valet de coeur* (1888), *Le Mari de la reine* (1889, Patouillard), *Miss Helyett* (1890, Smithson) etc.

McGOWAN, John P (b Muskegon, Mich, 1892; d New York, 28 May 1977). Juvenile lead man turned librettist for musical comedy.

McGowan had a first and distinctly prominent contact with the musical theatre as a performer, appearing on Broadway in a series of musical comedies from his teens. He had lead juvenile rôles in *Take It From Me* (1919, Tom Eggett), *Little Blue Devil* (1919, Philip Scarsdale) and *Mary* (1920, Jack Keene), took the principal comic rôle of Howard Rodney Smith in *The Rose of Stamboul* (1922), and appeared in *George White's Scandals*, in George M Cohan's *The Rise of Rosie O'Reilly* (1923) and, as takeover from Roy Royston, as Austin Bevans in *June Days* (1925).

He had a notable first success as a dramatist with the play *Mama Loves Papa* (1926) and later that year he turned his play, with altogether less success, into a musical, under the title *Sweet Lady*. After a couple more plays (*Tenth Avenue*, *Excess Baggage*), he returned to the musical scene, this time more happily, as the co-librettist on De Sylva, Brown and Henderson's boxing musical, *Hold Everything!* A collaboration with Rodgers and Hart on a thorough rewrite of the musical which ended up being called *Heads Up!* was less satisfactory, but *Girl Crazy* (1930) with the Gershwins and a second venture with De Sylva, Brown and Henderson on another quickly written piece, *Flying High*, helped turn the 1929–30 season into a spectacularly lucrative one for their librettist.

The run did not continue, however. A rather curious 'melodrama with music' called *Singin' the Blues* (1931), laced with black speciality acts, was a quick failure for producers Aarons and Freedley, as was *Pardon My English*, which McGowan directed for the same management, and a final Broadway venture, *Say When*, this time as co-producer as well as writer (w Ray Henderson), joined the revue *Strike Me Pink* on which the two men had worked together the previous season in the debit column of his career.

McGowan then abandoned Broadway for Hollywood, where he worked as a screenwriter (*Sitting Pretty*, *Little Nellie Kelly*, *Babes in Arms*, *Lady, Be Good!*, *Panama Hattie*, *Broadway Melody of 1936*, *Broadway Melody of 1938*, *Born to Dance*), as a director and a performer.

1926 **Sweet Lady** (Delos Owen/Bud Green) Weiting Theater, Syracuse 2 December
1928 **Hold Everything!** (Ray Henderson/B G De Sylva, Lew Brown/w De Sylva) Broadhurst Theater 10 October
1929 **Heads Up!** (Richard Rodgers/Lorenz Hart/w Paul Gerard Smith) Alvin Theater 11 November
1930 **Girl Crazy** (George Gershwin/Ira Gershwin/w Guy Bolton) Alvin Theater 14 October
1930 **Flying High** (Henderson/De Sylva, Brown) Apollo Theater 3 March
1931 **Singin' the Blues** (Jimmy McHugh/Dorothy Fields) Liberty Theater 16 September
1934 **Say When** (Henderson/Ted Koehler) Imperial Theater 8 November

MacGREGOR, Edgar J (b Rochester, NY, 1879; d New York, 3 April 1957).

For 30 years one of the busiest stage directors in the American musical theatre, McGregor began his career working in the straight theatre before directing his earliest Broadway musicals. *The Kiss Burglar* (1918) gave him a promising start, and Abe Erlanger's productions of Ivan Caryll's *The Girl Behind the Gun* and Victor Herbert's *The Velvet Lady*, May Irwin's *Raising the Aunty* and the 1919 edition of *George White's Scandals* helped to establish his reputation.

In 1920 MacGregor joined William Moore Patch to produce Hugo Felix's *The Sweetheart Shop* (director: Herbert Gresham), a fine success in Chicago and a respectable one in New York, before he returned to directing with John Cort's *Jim Jam Jems* and Sigmund Romberg's essay as a producer with *The Love Birds*. In 1922 he directed a piece called *Love and Kisses*, the first production by the young Laurence Schwab. After the show had been turned into *The Gingham Girl* and, at the same time, into a success, McGregor directed eight further shows for Schwab and his sometime partner Frank Mandel, in a collaboration that produced his most memorable triumphs – *The Desert Song*, (1926), *Good News* (1927) and *The New Moon* (1928) – as well as *Captain Jinks* (1925), *Queen High* (1926), *Follow Thru* (1929) and Gershwin's *Sweet Little Devil* (1924). Amongst a contrasting selection of less successful pieces, ranging from the Sissle and Blake show *Elsie* (1923), Gershwin's grim *Our Nell* (1922), *Adrienne* (1923, the show which didn't turn up at the theatre for its out-of-town first night) and the Tchaikovsky pasticcio *Natja* (1925) to the splashy vanity production *Fioretta* (1929), he also staged several hits for other producers: Eddie Dowling's ingenuous *Honeymoon Lane* (1926) and Aarons and

Freedley's production of *Funny Face* (1927) with Fred and Adele Astaire in its star rôles.

In the early 1930s MacGregor directed several Earl Carroll revues and Ziegfeld's *Hot-Cha!*, but after one last show, *Take a Chance*, for Schwab, he abandoned Broadway. He returned in 1939 to direct Cole Porter's *Dubarry Was a Lady*, and followed it up with three further fine successes in two seasons: Berlin's *Louisiana Purchase*, and Porter's next two pieces, *Panama Hattie* and *Let's Face It*, before fizzling away into a few failures (*My Dear Public*, *Nellie Bly*, *Louisiana Lady*) in his last Broadway assignments.

MacGregor has sometimes been listed as co-librettist of some of his shows, but these credits did not appear at the time of the productions, and it appears that his only effective input was directorial. He was also credited with a co-writer's share (w Otto Harbach) in the unproduced (screen)play which was transformed into the British musical *Here Comes the Bride*.

McGUIRE, William Anthony (b Chicago, 9 July 1885; d Beverly Hills, Calif, 16 September 1940). Broadway librettist and director who flourished in the 1920s, and floundered thereafter.

McGuire worked at first as a journalist on the *South Bend News* in Indiana, but he began to make his first efforts as a playwright in his teens and he had a dozen plays under his belt, without notable success, before he tackled the musical theatre. In the early 1920s he wrote sketches for such revues as *Frivolities of 1920*, *Ziegfeld Follies* (1924) and *No Foolin'* (1926), and worked on his first libretto, with Otto Harbach, for the successful Eddie Cantor vehicle *Kid Boots* (1923), whilst in the same period turning out the most successful of his straight plays, *Six-Cylinder Love* (1921) and *Twelve Miles Out* (1925).

McGuire directed the Broadway production of the Rodgers and Hart musical *Betsy* for Florenz Ziegfeld and, during 1928, doubled the functions of librettist and director on three shows, of which Friml's *The Three Musketeers* and Walter Donaldson's *Whoopee* both turned out to be sizeable hits. He had less success with a textual and directorial doctoring of Vincent Youmans's Broadway-bound *Great Day* (1929), the starry and lavish Ziegfeld *Show Girl*, and a *Rip van Winkle* vehicle for the fading Fred Stone and his daughter, *Ripples* (1930). Nor did he fare any better with his final effort, *Smiles*, for which Ziegfeld had again supplied all of what ought to have been the best in the way of music (Youmans), stars (Fred and Adele Astaire, Marilyn Miller) and physical production.

Suffering by this stage from what had finally become a severe drink problem, McGuire was all but sacked from *Smiles*. After nine productions for Ziegfeld, he never worked for him again nor, indeed, for anyone else in the musical theatre.

1923 **Kid Boots** (Harry Tierney/Joseph McCarthy/w Otto Harbach) Earl Carroll Theater 31 December
1928 **Rosalie** (George Gershwin, Sigmund Romberg/Ira Gershwin, P G Wodehouse/w Guy Bolton) New Amsterdam Theater 10 January
1928 **The Three Musketeers** (Rudolf Friml/Wodehouse, Clifford Grey) Lyric Theater 13 March
1928 **Whoopee** (Walter Donaldson) New Amsterdam Theater 4 December

1929 **Show Girl** (G Gershwin/I Gershwin, Gus Kahn) Ziegfeld Theater 2 July
1930 **Ripples** (Oscar Levant, Albert Szirmai/Irving Caesar, John Graham) New Amsterdam Theater 11 February
1930 **Smiles** (UK: *The One Girl*) (Vincent Youmans/Grey, Harold Adamson/w others) Ziegfeld Theater 18 November

MACK AND MABEL Musical romance (musical love story) in 2 acts by Michael Stewart. Music and lyrics by Jerry Herman. Majestic Theater, New York, 6 October 1974.

A primary-coloured almost-burlesque of the early days of the movies in America, through which runs the story of silent film-maker Mack Sennett (Robert Preston) and Mabel Normand (Bernadette Peters) the girl he takes from the deli, makes into a film heroine, seduces, then loses (after she's invented custard-pie-throwing) to a more-reel film-maker. This gap in his schedule makes Sennett invent his Bathing Beauties in time for a first-act closer. Boy and girl get together again five years later, but when he invents the Keystone Kops she leaves and goes off with her film-maker. Her ambition to be more than a speechless comic, and his determination that the kind of slapstick films he makes are the only kind he can and will make, mean that no happy ending is available.

The songs of *Mack and Mabel* – very largely devoted to the two stars – fell into three categories, the movie numbers, bright and usually comical, the production numbers, and the romantic ballads. Mack set the evening going, singing (before moving into the flashback that was the main part of the piece) of how 'Movies Were Movies' when he ran the show, insisted that, in face of the fashion for spectaculars, weepies and dramas his only credo was 'I Wanna Make the World Laugh', brought on the Bathers to 'Hundreds of Girls' and declared 'My Heart Leaps Up' every time a Keystone Kop falls down. Lisa Kirk, in the supporting rôle of Lottie Ames, also contributed to the showbizzy section with her description of the 'Big Time' and a parodic encouragement to 'Tap Your Troubles Away'. On the romantic side, Mack proposed sex with no attachments in 'I Won't Send Roses', whilst Mabel, who had set her evening off marvelling at herself on film in 'Look What Happened to Mabel', spat out her preference for being 'Wherever He Ain't' and torched her way through the disbelief that 'Time Heals Everything'. She also benefited from a 'Hello, Dolly!' style of entrance number as she was welcomed back to Mack's studio by the massed cast, hailing the effect that is made 'When Mabel Comes in the Room'.

Directed and choreographed, like *Hello, Dolly!*, by Gower Champion, the piece, with its uneasy mix of the two-dimensional and real feelings, proved not to have the same appeal for Broadway audiences as its block-busting predecessor, and it closed after 65 performances. However, several years later, a magistral piece of plugging gave *Mack and Mabel* a strange sort of second life. The original-cast recording of the show was outrageously pushed by one British disc jockey on one British radio station and, little by little, the songs gained currency, and the score a cult status amongst a particular group of English musical-theatre devotees. A British provincial production was staged, West End producers went to look, shook their heads, and librettist Stewart set to re-rewriting

the text which was being blamed for insufficiently supporting the now-familiar songs. Several times an announcement of a London production was whispered or even pronounced, but the nearest *Mack and Mabel* got to the London stage was a concert performance of the score. At Stewart's death, he had got no closer to making an attractive libretto out of the tale of the basically distasteful man and the rather silly girl who make up the title and most of the text of the show, and so *Mack and Mabel* lives on as a set of much-loved songs rather than as a musical show.

UK: Nottingham Playhouse 16 September 1981
Recordings: original cast (ABC/MCA), London concert (First Night)

MACKEBEN, Theo (b Stargard, 5 January 1897; d Berlin, 10 January 1953).

A composer, pianist and conductor in Berlin, Mackeben wrote a long series of scores for German films (*Bel-Ami, Es war eine rauschende Ballnacht, Das Herz der Königin, Eine Frau wird erst schön durch die Liebe, Bal-Paré, Tanz auf dem Vulkan, Heimat*) and also for a number of stage musicals, including a version of Jerome K Jerome's *Lady Fanny and the Servant Problem*. First produced in Germany, this piece was later mounted in London (1939) by the expatriate Lucie Mannheim and closed after one week. Mackeben is, however, best remembered as the original conductor of Weill's *Die Dreigroschenoper* and as the adapter of Millöcker's *Gräfin Dubarry* score and other music into the shape in which it became known to 20th-century audiences as *Die Dubarry*.

1931 **Die Dubarry** (Carl Millöcker ad/Paul Knepler, Ignaz M Welleminsky) Admiralspalast 14 August
1932 **Die Journalisten** (Felix Joachimson) Deutsches Theater May
1934 **Lady Fanny** (Erich Ernst, Peter Höll) Deutsches-Künstlertheater 16 February
1934 **Liebe auf Reisen** (R Frenzel) Plazatheater
1938 **Anita und der Teufel** (Géza von Cziffra, H F Beckmann) Komödienhaus
1943 **Der goldene Käfig** (Heinz Heutschke, Günther Schwenn) Admiralspalast 23 September
1950 **Versuchung der Antonia** (Schwenn, M Freytag) Städtische Bühnen, Bonn 16 September

McKENZIE, Julia [Kathleen Nancy] (b Enfield, 17 February 1941). Actress and vocalist who won a triple-headed success, unparalleled in modern British showbusiness, as an award-winning star of straight and musical theatre and television.

Originally trained as an operatic vocalist, Julia McKenzie made her earliest stage appearances on the road (*Rose Marie* tour, 1963) and in British regional theatres as well as appearing in the chorus and deputizing for Rachel Roberts in the lead rôle of *Maggie May* (1964) in London. She was subsequently seen in London in *Joey Joey* (1966), *Queenie* (1967), the showcase of the Worcester repertory theatre's musical production *A Present from the Corporation* (1967, Maggie Slater), *The Man with a Load of Mischief* and as a memorably simpering Gloria in *Mame* (1969). She took over the rôle of Marge in *Promises, Promises* (1970), appeared at the Old Vic in the York repertory theatre's production of *The Last Sweet Days of Isaac* (1971) and played the Ladybird in a Shaw Theatre production of *The Plotters of Cabbage Patch Garden* (1971) before, in 1972, she

Plate 169. **Julia McKenzie** *as Lily Garland to the Oscar Jaffee of Keith Michell in London's memorable reproduction of* On the Twentieth Century.

had her first contact with the works of Stephen Sondheim, a writer with whose works she was to have a special connection, when she took over the rôle of April in the London production of *Company* (1972).

Miss McKenzie subsequently appeared at Leatherhead in *I Do! I Do!* and at London's Mermaid Theatre in the musical compilation shows *Cowardy Custard* (1972) and *Cole* (1974), and she was one of the group which was instrumental in compiling and performing a similar show made up from the works of Sondheim, produced in London as *Side By Side By Sondheim* (1976). The notable success of this piece, which was largely reponsible for promoting a wider awareness of the author's work in Britain, was continued overseas, and the London team repeated their performances for an Equity-allowed period on Broadway. Miss McKenzie appeared there, by the will of that organization, as Julie N McKenzie.

After a period spent shunning the musical theatre in a purposeful attempt to establish herself as an actress in a country where, unlike others, ability as a vocalist is considered by the powers-who-cast to be a bar to acting ambitions (*Norman Conquests, Ten Times Table, Outside Edge* etc) Miss McKenzie returned to the musical stage in London's production of *On the Twentieth Century*, giving the performance of an era in the demanding mixture of comedy and vocal versatility which make up the rôle of Lily Garland. Over the following years she was largely claimed by television (*Blott on the Landscape, Fresh Fields, French Fields* etc), film (*Shirley Valentine* etc) and the non-musical stage (*Woman in Mind* etc) returning to the musical theatre only to play Adelaide in *Guys and Dolls* at the National Theatre (1982) and then two Sondheim works in the West End – as Sally in *Follies* (1987) and as the Witch in *Into the Woods* (1990) – and a third, *Sweeney Todd* (1993, Mrs Lovett), back at the National Theatre.

In recent years Miss McKenzie has varied her performing career with directing assignments, mounting the original production of the play *Stepping Out*, Britain's *Steel Magnolias* and musical pieces including *Just So* and a further Sondheim compilation *Putting it Together* (1992).

MACKINTOSH, Cameron [Anthony] (b London, 17 October 1946). The dominant producer of the international musical theatre of the 1980s and 1990s.

Cameron Mackintosh began his life in the theatre working as a teenaged stage-hand on *Camelot* at the Theatre Royal, Drury Lane, and as an ASM on the touring production of *Oliver!*. He moved into production with a season of plays (w Robin Alexander, Hubert Woodward) at Henley's Kenton Theatre, and touched London for the first time with a version of *Little Women* mounted by 'Bloomsbury Plays' at the Jeannetta Cochrane Theatre at Christmas 1967. Although the same year saw the 20-year-old neo-producer paragraphed in the press as preparing an Ireland Cutter/Tommie Connor musicalization of *A Portrait of Dorian Grey*, it was to be almost two years, spent whetting his teeth on the produce of such writers as Agatha Christie in the provinces, before Mackintosh got his first real West End production of a musical to the stage. It was a revival of a version of *Anything Goes*, mounted in collaboration with Laurier Lister at the Yvonne Arnaud Theatre, Guildford, and its stay at London's Saville Theatre was a brief one.

New and original musicals, however, were soon to follow. In partnership with Veronica Flint-Shipman, he brought a musical version of Pinero's *Trelawny of the Wells* (*Trelawny*) from the Theatre Royal, Bristol, to London for 177 performances in 1972, with Jimmy Wax he mounted a version of Arnold Bennett's *The Card* (1973) at Bristol and in London (130 performances), and with Mrs Flint-Shipman again, in the wake of *Jesus Christ Superstar*, he launched one of the biblical musicals which were briefly the rage, a *Rock Nativity* (1974, revised 1975 as *A New Tomorrow*) written by *Card* songwriters Tony Hatch and Jackie Trent. He also staged London seasons of two children's entertainments – Julian Slade's *Winnie the Pooh* and David Wood's *The Owl and the Pussycat Went to See* – whilst keeping up a busy schedule of touring activities.

After this burst of productivity, however, Mackintosh retrenched for a number of years into less adventurous, but slightly more profitable areas, and for the remainder of the 1970s he mounted no new musical play. He invested the touring circuits with a seemingly ceaseless touring version of *Godspell*, which returned on several occasions to London, and joined Michael White on a touring *The Rocky Horror Show*. He presented several seasonal editions of the popular children's musical *The Gingerbread Man*, brought the successful compilation show *Side By Side By Sondheim* (1976) to the Mermaid Theatre and then to the West End, and also produced fine revivals of several major classics: an *Oliver!*, that remained 1,139 performances at the Albery Theatre, and Arts-Council-backed versions of *My Fair Lady* and *Oklahoma!*, which both found their way to London for good seasons from the touring circuits for which they had been originally designed.

In 1980 Mackintosh put together and mounted another compilation show, this one made up from the works of humourist Tom Lehrer (*Tomfoolery*), but it was the following year that he made his major breakthrough to success when, following the disappearance from the London theatre scene of Robert Stigwood, the producer of *Jesus Christ Superstar* and *Evita*, he began an alliance with composer Andrew Lloyd Webber. The partnership was initiated by the production of *Cats*. The vast success of this piece, which spread long and large throughout the world

Plate 170. **Cameron Mackintosh.**

with results unparalleled in musical-theatre history, was compounded not only by two further pieces produced in collaboration with Lloyd Webber's Really Useful Company – the two-headed entertainment *Song and Dance*, and a second international blockbuster in the romantic operetta *The Phantom of the Opéra* (1986) – but by an involvement in the off-Broadway hit *Little Shop of Horrors* and, even more significantly, the production of the third of the three grandiose 'Cameron Mackintosh presents' musical plays which were to dominate the late 1980s and early 1990s on the world's stages: the English adaptation of the French musical *Les Misérables* (1985).

Whilst Mackintosh rose to the top of the international producing heap, bestriding not only the Atlantic but a few other of the world's oceans as carefully managed reproductions of his three big, spectacular musicals went from one corner of the globe to another, there were occasional less-profitable productions going on in their shadow. The 1983 *Blondel* was a failure, repeats of *Oliver!* in London and New York did not have the same success as his previous revival of the show, an awkwardly choreographed-up revival of *The Boy Friend* convinced no more, and a late West End version of the Broadway musical *Follies* had a respectable London life without ringing any bells.

In 1989 he produced a fourth mega-musical, a modernized *Madam Butterfly* written by the authors of *Les Misérables* and christened *Miss Saigon*. This piece took the stereophonic-sound-and-scenery kind of sub-operatic spectacular that the musical theatre seemed to be becoming, to (or perhaps beyond) bursting point but, as it set off – rather less sure-footedly than its three famous forebears – to the areas beyond the West End which those forebears

had established as almost an international circuit, Mackintosh had already begun what was evidently a change in policy. Like George Edwardes, the most outstanding musical-theatre producer of the last years of the 19th century, whose scale of international achievement and success Mackintosh was now emulating in the last days of the 20th century, he had his eye turned in advance on to the eternal public demand for novelty in its entertainments. Edwardes had managed, almost always and with few misjudgements, to keep ahead of the fashion. Mackintosh now similarly felt the moment right to make a switch. A switch away from the monolithic everything-that-moves musical towards smaller, more content-based pieces of entertainment.

During the past decade he had ventured several times into the field – the internationally popular *Little Shop of Horrors*, a highly successful children's show made up from the music of the then popular singing group Abba (*Abbacadabra*, 1983), a flop Puccini pasticcio *Café Puccini* – but in the 1990s, as the London productions of the three big hits and *Miss Saigon* all ran on in their original West End productions and in various other venues abroad, his new shows came in less voluminous packages: compilation shows (*Five Guys Named Mo*, *Putting it Together*) and original material (*Just So*, *Moby Dick, or a Whale of a Tale*) as well as a revival of the 1973 *The Card*. At the time of writing, he has yet to hit the bull's-eye in the same manner that he achieved with his big shows in the 1980s, but by the time this comes to print that will in all likelihood have changed.

Mackintosh has been active in other theatrical areas in the 1980s and 1990s. He founded the Chair of Contemporary Theatre at Oxford University, and his Mackintosh Foundation has sponsored musical-theatre productions both large – revivals of fashionable but uncommercial American musicals at Britain's National Theatre – and small, with provincial try-outs of new material at Oxford's Old Fire Station Theatre and Newbury's Watermill Theatre.

McLELLAN, C[harles] M[orton] S[tewart] [aka MORTON, Hugh] (b Bath, Maine, 1865; d Esher, Surrey, 22 September 1916). Adept Broadway librettist who began at the turn of the century writing variety musicals and revues, and ended up adapting French comedies as the libretti for a landmark set of musical comedies in the 1910s.

At first a journalist, and at one stage the editor of the New York journal *Town Topics*, McLellan made his first attempt at writing for the stage with the libretto to *Puritania*, an olde-American comic-opera vehicle for Pauline Hall as an English Earl out to save a 17th-century Salem girl accused of witchcraft. The piece did well enough, but McLellan chose to make his next ventures into musical theatre under the pseudonym Hugh Morton. After supplying some fresh lyrics for George Lederer's brutal remake of the British hit *The Lady Slavey*, he worked on a number of libretti and lyrics for Lederer and the Casino Theater. *In Gay New York*, *The Whirl of the Town* and *Yankee Doodle Dandy* professed to be revues, *An American Beauty* and *The Belle of New York* were billed as musical comedies, but no matter what they called themselves, they were all basically lively rag-bags of multi-coloured entertainment, whose plots took more preposterous turnings than a politician and whose dialogue was eased aside to allow the introduction of songs, specialities and dance numbers on the one hand, and what were little more than stand-up turns from the chief comedians on the other.

The Belle of New York, however, turned out to be a phenomenon. Introduced into Britain, it proved a novelty attraction of huge drawing power, and became established throughout the world in the earliest years of the 20th century as the representative of 'American musical comedy'. McLellan failed to repeat this out-of-the-blue success with two further vehicles for *Belle of New York* star Edna May, *The Girl from Up There* (which had the heroine emerging from a block of ice at the North Pole) and a truly silly London piece called *Nelly Neil*, or with a musicalized version of his own farce *Glittering Gloria* (1904) which had been discreetly produced at London's Wyndham's Theatre the year before. His one success in the decade following *The Belle of New York* was, in fact, not in the musical field, but in one of a handful of attempts at non-musical playwriting, with the drama *Leah Kleschna* (1904), which won productions throughout the world after its New York introduction by Minnie Maddern Fiske.

Musical comedy success returned when McLellan allied himself with Ivan Caryll, his partner on *Nelly Neil*, following the composer's removal to America. Caryll had a ready supply of first-rate French comedies optioned for musicalization, and it was McLellan whom he chose to do the English-language adaptations. *Marriage à la Carte*, at McLellan's old haunt, the Casino, was the first, but it was the next pair, *The Pink Lady* (*Le Satyre*) and *Oh! Oh! Delphine* (*La Grimpette*), two dazzling musical comedies which played an important part in establishing the more sophisticated book-based musical comedy on Broadway, which were both their librettist's biggest Broadway successes and the best of his writings. However, after one more successful collaboration with Caryll on a version of Tristan Bernard's *Le Petit Café*, McLellan reversed his partner's trail, and left America to go to live in Britain.

There, in the few years up till his death, he made little further contribution to the theatre, his final musical piece being a reversion to the now-fashionable revue form with *Round the Map* (music: Herman Finck, lyrics: Hartley Carrick, Clifford Grey) produced at the Alhambra in 1915.

McLellan was married to the actress and musician Yvonne Arnaud.

His brother, **George B[ilton] McLELLAN** (b Bath, Maine; d London, 1 February 1932) was for many years a theatrical manager. He teamed with George Lederer to produce several Casino Theater shows (*The Telephone Girl, Yankee Doodle Dandy* etc), was for a period manager of that house, and later moved to London where he was associated with the Shuberts in several productions and acted as their London and Continental representative. He also became the general manager for Sir Harold Wernher's London group of theatres, including the Adelphi, Shaftesbury, Gaiety, Apollo and His Majesty's Theatres. He was married successively to two particularly lovely Broadway musical stars in Pauline Hall and Madge Lessing.

1892 **Puritania** (Edgar Stillman Kelly) Fifth Avenue Theater 19 September
1896 **The Lady Slavey** American lyrics (Casino Theater)
1896 **In Gay New York** (Gustave Kerker) Casino Theater 25 May

1896 **An American Beauty** (Kerker) Casino Theater 28 December
1897 **The Whirl of the Town** (Kerker) Casino Theater 25 May
1897 **The Belle of New York** (Kerker) Casino Theater 28 September
1898 **The Telephone Girl** (*La Demoiselle du téléphone*) American libretto (Casino Theater)
1898 **Yankee Doodle Dandy** (Kerker) Casino Theater 25 July
1901 **The Girl from Up There** (Kerker) Herald Square Theater 7 January
1904 **Glittering Gloria** (Bernard Rolt) Daly's Theater 15 February
1907 **Nelly Neil** (Ivan Caryll) Aldwych Theatre, London 10 January
1911 **Marriage à la Carte** (Caryll) Casino Theater 2 January
1911 **The Pink Lady** (Caryll) New Amsterdam Theater 13 March
1912 **Oh! Oh! Delphine** (Caryll) Knickerbocker Theater 30 September
1913 **The Little Café** (Caryll) New Amsterdam Theater 10 November

McNALLY, John J (b Charleston, Mass, ?1854; d Brooklyn, NY, 25 March 1931). Librettist for farce comedy and variety musicals of the 19th and early 20th centuries.

Originally if briefly a lawyer, and subsequently a drama critic in his native Charleston and then in Boston (*Times, Herald*), McNally began his career as a dramatist in Boston when he supplied the young E E Rice and his 'Surprise Party' company with the loose-legged libretto for the early musical farce comedy *Revels* (1880). The piece, decorated with a set of songs gathered from hither and yon, served for many years of touring, and McNally followed it up with a run of like pieces – cheerful low comedies of the most unsophisticated kind, often in the German-accented style, and effectively adaptable to a changing musical and variety-turn content.

McNally wrote several such vehicles for May Irwin (who had appeared in his 1891 *Boys and Girls*), including *The Widow Jones* which brought her to stardom, and provided annual vehicles for the Rogers Brothers as part of Klaw and Erlanger's attempt to out-Weber-and-Fields Weber and Fields, beginning with the 1899 *A Reign of Error* and continuing to the last of the series in 1907. He also fabricated *Lola from Berlin* to feature Lulu Glaser in a Dutch comedy rôle, brought the *New York Herald*'s cartoon *Fluffy Ruffles* to the stage, and in 1909 put together *In Hayti* for the comedy team of McIntyre and Heath. McNally then took his distance from the theatre after 30 years of supplying almost inevitably reviled libretti which had, simply, the merit of allowing their performers to show off whatever it was that they did best to an audience who had really only come to see them do that.

1880 **Revels** (various/w Dexter Smith) 14th Street Theater 25 October
1880 **Evangeline** revised version
1891 **A Straight Tip** (various) Bijou Theater 26 January
1891 **Boys and Girls** (various) Park Theater 21 September
1892 **A Mad Bargain** (various/w Julian Mitchell) Bijou Theater 27 February
1893 **A Country Sport** (various) Bijou Theater 25 December
1895 **The Widow Jones** (various) Bijou Theater 16 September
1895 **The Night Clerk** (various) Bijou Theater 11 November
1896 **A Good Thing** (various) Casino Theater 12 October

1896 **Courted into Court** (various) Bijou Theater 29 December

1897 **The Good Mr Best** (Henry J Sayers, Tom Le Mack, Frederick Dene et al) Garrick Theater 30 August

1899 **A Reign of Error** (Maurice Levi) Victoria Theater 2 March

1899 **Mademoiselle Ka-za-za** (Levi) 1 act Victoria Theater 8 May

1899 **The Rogers Brothers in Wall Street** (Levi) Victoria Theater 18 September

1900 **The Rogers Brothers in Central Park** (Levi/J Cheever Goodwin) Victoria Theater 17 September

1900 **Star and Garter** (various) Victoria Theater 26 November

1901 **The Rogers Brothers in Washington** (Levi) Knickerbocker Theater 2 September

1901 **The Sleeping Beauty and the Beast** American version w Cheever Goodwin and Fred Solomon (Broadway Theater)

1902 **The Rogers Brothers at Harvard** (Levi/Goodwin, Edward Gardiner) Knickerbocker Theater 1 September

1903 **Mother Goose** American version w George V Hobart (New Amsterdam Theater)

1903 **The Rogers Brothers in London** (Max Hoffman, Melville Ellis/Hobart, Gardiner) Knickerbocker Theater 7 September

1904 **The Rogers Brothers in Paris** (Hoffman/Hobart) New Amsterdam Theater 5 September

1904 **Humpty Dumpty** American version (New Amsterdam Theater)

1904 **(Life) In Newport** (Bob Cole/James Weldon Johnson, J Rosamond Johnson) Liberty Theater 26 December

1905 **Lifting the Lid** (Jean Schwartz/William Jerome) New Amsterdam Theater 5 June

1905 **The Whole Damm Family** (various) 1 act Aeriel Gardens 26 June

1905 **The Rogers Brothers in Ireland** (Hoffman/Hobart) Liberty Theater 4 September

1905 **Fritz in Tammany Hall** (Schwartz/Jerome) Herald Square Theater 16 October

1907 **Lola from Berlin** (Schwartz/Jerome) Liberty Theater 16 September

1907 **The Rogers Brothers in Panama** (Max Hoffman) Broadway Theater 2 September

1908 **Fluffy Ruffles** (W T Francis/Wallace Irwin) Criterion Theater 7 September

1909 **In Hayti** (Schwartz/Jerome) Circle Theater 30 August

MACRAE, Arthur [SCHRÖPFER, Arthur] (b London, 17 March 1908; d Brighton, 25 February 1962).

An actor from an early age, Macrae appeared largely in plays but also in the musical *Song of the Drum* at the Theatre Royal, Drury Lane (1931, 'Babe'). His first play was produced when he was 24, and he subsequently contributed to a number of revues (*Charlot's Char-a-Bang!*, *Shall We Reverse*, *The Town Talks*) before collaborating on the texts for the long-running series of Cicely Courtneidge musical comedy vehicles which spanned the Second World War in Britain. He also supplied 'additional dialogue' for James Hadley Chase's nightclub mystery musical *Get a Load of This* (1941).

1938 **Under Your Hat** (Vivian Ellis/w Jack Hulbert, Archie Menzies) Palace Theatre 24 November

1942 **Full Swing** (George Posford, Harry Parr-Davies/w Hulbert, Menzies) Palace Theater 16 April

1943 **Something in the Air** (Manning Sherwin/Harold Purcell, Max Kester/w Hulbert, Menzies) Palace Theatre 23 September

1945 **Under the Counter** (Sherwin/Purcell) Phoenix Theatre 22 November

MADAME Comédie-opérette in 3 acts by Albert Willemetz. Music by Henri Christiné. Théâtre Daunou, Paris, 14 December 1923.

When Gustave Quinson chose to stage Maurice Yvain's *Là-haut* at the Bouffes-Parisiens, the way was left free for Jane Renouardt of the Théâtre Daunou to mount the latest work by Henri Christiné, the darling of the modern musical theatre and formerly monopolized by her very good friend Quinson. She produced *Madame* with considerable success, and it followed a good Parisian run – including a quick revival at Quinson's Théâtre des Bouffes-Parisiens (28 April 1924) – with an equally good provincial life.

Madame is – by the end of the play, at least – little Mlle Delicia (Andrée Alvar) who, with the encouragement of her friend Chicorée (Davia), tests her hold over her fiancé, Paul Fêtard (André Luguet), too far and loses him. Chicorée, trying to atone for her unfortunate interference, gets them together in the same hotel, along with Delicia's father Romulus (Gabin père) and his petite amie Blanche Farine (Christiane Dor), Paul's best friend Clichy de Lapinière (Louis Boucot) and Aunt Hortense (Jeanne Cheirel) and, after much in the way of farcical doings, everyone is safely and suitably paired off for the final curtain.

Christiné's score, abetted by some tasty Willemetz lyrics, had its most successful moment in Chicorée's rhythmic recipe for a plain girl's self-improvement, 'Ell' n'est pas si mal que ça', but there were plenty of other numbers of charm and wit, including Paul's description of how his eye first lit on Delicia because her father was such good fun ('Quand une fille possède un papa'), Delicia's waltz celebrating marriage 'Être Madame', Hortense's peremptory 'On l' dit ... sapristi!' and the ensemble 'L'annexe' in which Romulus at first protests against his off-hand, out-of-the-way accommodation, until he realizes that, in the annexe, he can entertain Mlle Farine without being overseen.

MADAME BONIFACE Opéra-comique in 3 acts by Ernest Depré and Charles Clairville. Music by Paul Lacôme. Théâtre des Bouffes-Parisiens, Paris, 20 October 1883.

Madame Boniface (Louise Théo), the wife of a little confectioner (Édouard Maugé), is altogether too pretty for her husband's peace of mind but, when he tries to send her off to the safety of Orléans, the rakish Comte Annibal de Tournedor (Piccaluga) takes the place of the coachman and whisks her off instead to his debauched home. Boniface goes after him and, unsuccessful in recapturing his wife, he then hurries to court to complain. The clever little Madame Boniface succeeds in keeping her virtue, but Tournedor's escapade costs him dear: whilst he has been trying to seduce the pretty confiseuse his own fiancée has gone off with his best friend, Fridolin (Charles Lamy). Désiré (Jacquot) and Mlle Levasseur (Isabelle) headed the support cast.

Apart from his star, who was well equipped with a Chanson Auvergnat in the final act and with a catchy 'Il faut s' taire', Lacôme's score most favoured the baritone rôle of the Count (the romance 'Comme la fleur', 'Moi, si j'étais époux'), with best-friend Fridolin supplying the tenor notes.

Tailor-made, very closely on the lines of her early success, *La Jolie Parfumeuse*, for the piquant, vocally limited

Théo, who was freshly back from one of her American tours, *Madame Boniface* was produced by Louis Cantin – much in need of a successor to *La Mascotte* at the Bouffes-Parisiens – and it won an agreeable success through 76 performances, followed by a further 23 in the next season (29 April 1884). When the star went back to America she took her show with her and it was played by Maurice Grau's troupe with Mezières (Boniface) and Gaillard (Tournedor) appearing alongside Mlle Théo at Wallack's Theater in 1884 and at the Star in 1885. In Paris, *Madame Boniface* was revived in 1916 (Théâtre Apollo, 29 March) with Jenny Syril starred, and it was played again in 1919 and in 1924 at the Trianon-Lyrique.

An 1891 production by Alexandrine von Schönerer at Vienna's Theater an der Wien (ad Heinrich Thalboth, Richard Genée) starred Therese Biedermann as the cutely renamed Friquette Bonbon, alongside Siegmund Natzler (Bonbon), Josef Joseffy (Tournedor) and Carl Lindau (Fridolin), but the piece proved not at all to Viennese tastes and was played only three times. It was, nevertheless, given an Hungarian showing (ad Károly Murai) under the title of *A kis cukrászné* (the little confectioner) in 1897.

USA: Wallack's Theater 8 April 1884; Austria: Theater an der Wien *Madame Bonbon* 15 May 1891; Hungary: Kisfaludy Színház *A kis cukrászné* 31 August 1897

MADAME CARTOUCHE Opérette in 3 acts by Pierre Decourcelle and William Busnach. Music by Léon Vasseur. Théâtre des Folies-Dramatiques, Paris, 19 October 1886.

The actress Sylvine (Mme Grisier Montbazon) is carried off by Labretèche (Vauthier), the lieutenant of the brigand Cartouche, to a fate not quite as bad as death, but when she is compulsorily installed as a brigandesse she gets her revenge by tricking her captor out of both the booty he has stolen from the wealthy Grippardin (Riga), and the pretty Olympe (Jeanne Becker), wife of the barkeeper Grégoire (Gobin), whom he was sure of winning into his bed. The heart of the opérette's action had the heroine masquerading as the Mexican Carmen de las Pampas, the betrothed bride of Grippardin, complete with entourage and a boléro sextet, in order to effect her anti-robbery. Vasseur's score paired the heroine musically with her baritone captor, and with Guy in the rôle of the violinist whom she loves, whilst the comic numbers fell principally to the almost-cuckolded Grégoire.

A disappointment at the Folies-Dramatiques, where it held the stage for just a month, *Madame Cartouche* was nevertheless staged in Britain when light opera soprano Giulia Warwick, the original Constance of *The Sorcerer* something more than a decade earlier, took it on the road in 1891 for eight weeks.

UK: Leicester 21 September 1891

MADAME CHRYSANTHÈME Comédie-lyrique in 4 acts, a prologue and an epilogue, by Georges Hartmann and André Alexandre, based on a work by Pierre Loti. Music by André Messager. Théâtre de la Renaissance (Théâtre-Lyrique), Paris, 30 January 1893.

Written during a period when Messager, with the successes of *La Fauvette du Temple* and the opéra-comique *La Basoche* a couple of years behind him, turned out half-a-dozen scores in as many years in quest of a financial suc-

cess, *Madame Chrysanthème* was a quick Paris failure (ten performances) when produced by Léonce Détroyat at his Théâtre Lyrique. However, in its short life it won many partisans for its elegant and extended opéra-comique score and its pretty story which prefigured in many ways that of John Luther Long and David Belasco's *Madam Butterfly* and Luigi Ilica's *Madama Butterfly*. During his service in the east, the Breton naval officer Pierre (Delaquerrière) 'weds' the oriental singing girl Chrysanthème (Jane Guy) through the offices of the marriage-broker Kangourou (Charles Lamy) and then finds himself falling in love with her. His jealousy is aroused and the idyll spoiled when she takes a sick colleague's place and sings in public once more, and again when he fancies an attachment between the girl and his best friend and fellow officer, Yves (Jacquin). But it is Chrysanthème whose love is the more real, and whose heart is almost broken when he finally sails away with his ship leaving his loving 'wife' behind him. Mlle Caisso (Madame Prune) and Declercq (Monsieur Sucre) helped the comedy along as Chrysanthème's temporary 'parents' and Nettie Lynds had the soubrette rôle as Oyouli, Prune's young daughter.

The success of *Madama Butterfly* (1904) precluded a revival of the earlier work mooted at the same time for the Opéra-Comique, but the piece has continued to be prized by musicians and is still occasionally played, most recently at Rochefort in 1990.

MADAME FAVART Opéra-comique in 3 acts by Henri Chivot and Alfred Duru. Music by Jacques Offenbach. Théâtre des Folies-Dramatiques, Paris, 28 December 1878.

Madame Favart was produced in 1878, at a time when Offenbach's nearest real success, *Le Voyage dans la lune*, was three years in the past, and his recent shows had been failures (*La Boîte au lait*, *Maître Péronilla*) or, at best, half-successes (*Le Docteur Ox* 42 performances, *La Foire Saint-Laurent* 48 performances). The new show set the composer's reckoning right with a vengeance.

He was much aided in this return to form by the libretto served to him by Chivot and Duru with whom, in spite of their eminence on the opérette stage, he had worked only once previously, almost a decade back on *L'Île de Tulipatan*. Their book to *Madame Favart* tacked the name of the famous actress, Justine Favart, who had already been the subject of a comédie-vaudeville at the Palais-Royal half a century earlier (Masson, Boniface 24 December 1836) on to a thoroughly comic-opera adventure, in much the same way English writers were inclined to do with Nell Gwynne or Peg Woffington. The action was intricately filled with disguises and situations in the best French mode, and at the same time it developed the character of Justine into a first-rate rôle à tiroirs for the show's leading lady, who was given the opportunity of appearing in turn as a serving wench, an elderly lady and an elegant actress during the course of the night.

Justine Favart (Juliette Simon-Girard) has adeptly avoided the carnal desires of the powerful Maréchal de Saxe and, as a result, both she and her celebrated actor husband, Charles Favart (Lepers), are on the run from his vengeance. At first they hide in an inn, he in the basement, she disguised as a maidservant, and then – after Justine has posed as the wife of young Hector de Boispréau (Simon-Max) effectively enough to win him a police appointment from the lecherous Marquis de Pontsablé (Édouard Maugé) – they masquerade as Hector's servants. When Pontsablé visits Hector, Justine is obliged to become 'wife' again – whilst the real wife, Suzanne (Marie Gélabert) temporarily becomes the maid – and then to impersonate a dowager who has threatened to expose her. Suzanne and Favart are triumphantly dragged off by Pontsablé to Fontenoy to appear before the mighty Saxe, followed by Justine and Hector, who are now disguised as Tyrolean peddlers, and things wind up to a pretty height before the vengeance of Saxe and Pontsablé is defused by none other than the king himself.

Offenbach's score – opéra-comique music to its last semiquaver, and without a touch of joshing opéra-bouffe from end to end – accompanied this ever-active tale delightfully, with Madame Favart scoring the hit of the evening with her fake-rustic sauce in 'Ma mère aux vignes m'envoyit', playing the little wandering minstrelette in 'Je suis la petite vielleuse', the elderly grande dame in 'Je passe sur mon enfance', and the Tyrolean peasant in 'Mon grand frèr' vend des mouchoirs', and finally relating the whole of her complex tale to the king in 'J'entrai sous la royale tente'. The baritone rôle of Favart was also well equipped with amusing songs, notably his 'Quand du four on le retire' recalling his father's life as a pastrycook, whilst Hector (tenor) and Suzanne (soprano) provided the ingénu duets and solos, and the buffo part of the musical entertainment was assured by Pontsablé and by Suzanne's father, Cotignac (Luco).

Juliette Simon-Girard, the heroine of *Les Cloches de Corneville*, had her second rôle of a lifetime as Madame Favart, and the show was a splendid success, running for more than 200 performances (interleaved with performances of the theatre's other main pieces) in its first year at the Bouffes-Parisiens and keeping away the following year solely because of the subsequent hit of Offenbach's next piece, *La Fille du tambour-major*. It was soon back, and in 1883 Marie Grisier-Montbazon succeeded to the rôle created by Mme Simon-Girard (34 performances) alongside the Favart of Piccaluga. Meanwhile, the show had set out swiftly on its international travels. Vienna's version (ad Julius Hopp), produced under Maximilian Steiner's direction, was on the stage six weeks after the Paris première. Marie Geistinger was his Madame Favart, with Girardi as her husband, Steiner and Hermine Meyerhoff as the young couple and Felix Schweighofer as Pontsablé. But even a cast of such voltage left Vienna unmoved: *Madame Favart* played only 23 times.

On the other hand, when Alexander Henderson produced the first English version (ad H B Farnie) at the Strand Theatre with the virtually unknown Florence St John starring alongside Claude Marius (Favart), Walter Fisher (Hector), Henry Ashley (Pontsablé) and Violet Cameron (Suzanne), he and his star both scored a sensational success. *Madame Favart* proved itself the genuine successor to the record-breaking *Les Cloches de Corneville*, running alongside that piece and *HMS Pinafore* until it reached 502 performances, a total excelled in London's theatre history to that time only by its two direct competitors. Camille Dubois relieved the now starry Miss St John late in the run, but the new London 'queen of comic

opera' returned to the West End with her show again in 1882, in 1887 and one last time in 1893.

In America, Marie Aimée and Paola Marié both played *Madame Favart* in the original French and Marie Geistinger gave her German version before the Comley-Barton Company brought the English *Madame Favart* to Broadway. The English pair Catherine Lewis and Fred Leslie starred as the Favarts with Australia's John Howson as Pontsablé, local star Marie Jansen as Suzanne and Alfred Cellier conducting, but New York sided with Vienna rather than with Paris and London, and the company was obliged to revert to Audran's *Olivette*, which Broadway had already certified as a hit, after only a short season. Only the French-speaking part of the American population continued to welcome *Madame Favart* as it was repeated by Aimée and Paola Marié on their regular returns to town. The English-language version was also later played in Australia, where Pattie Laverne starred alongside Fred Mervin, Alfred Brennir and Nellie Stewart in George Musgrove's production in Sydney and Melbourne (Opera House, 29 October 1881), similarly sharing a repertoire with *Olivette* and with the hit Australian production of *La Fille du tambour-major*. Stockholm, Leipzig, Berlin, Brussels and Naples all presented *Madame Favart* whilst it still held the stage in Paris, and in Hungary (ad Lajos Evva, Béla J Fái) it was given a fine 34 performances at the Népszinház with Lujza Blaha starred.

In spite of its great success, however, and the outstanding opportunities it offers to its star, *Madame Favart* has not become a genuine fixture in the 20th-century Offenbach repertoire. It has been given revivals in Paris (1911, 1913, 1934) and in Germany, where a revised version was produced in 1955 (Operetten-Theater, Leipzig 15 October), but it still exists a little in the shadow of *La Fille du tambour-major* amongst the composer's late works.

Austria: Theater an der Wien 7 February 1879; UK: Strand Theatre 12 April 1879; USA: Park Theater (Fr) 12 May 1879, Fifth Avenue Theater (Eng) 19 September 1881; Germany: Leipzig 1 June 1879, Friedrich-Wilhelmstädtisches Theater, Berlin 15 August 1879; Hungary: Népszinház *Favartné* 14 November 1879; Australia: Theatre Royal, Sydney, 17 September 1881

Recordings: 2-record sets (Discoreale, Rare Recorded Editions)

MADAME L'ARCHIDUC Opéra-comique in 3 acts by Albert Millaud (and Ludovic Halévy?). Music by Jacques Offenbach. Théâtre des Bouffes-Parisiens, Paris, 31 October 1874.

An agreeable Millaud/Offenbach piece, but one which had little in the way of outstanding features in book or score, *Madame l'Archiduc* had a very much better international career than a number of the composer's other equally good or better works, possibly due to the appeal the large central prima donna rôle had for lady stars.

Hotel workers Marietta (Anna Judic) and Giletti (Habay) have just been wed when the exiled Comte (Lucien Fugère) and Comtesse (B Perret) arrive at the inn. The aristocratic pair are plotting the downfall of the local Archiduc Ernest (Daubray), but their steward Riccardo (Desmonts) discovers that Ernest has got wind of their conspiracy and so the disguised Marietta and Giletti are bribed to go to the castle in the aristocrats' place. The effects of this swap are alarming. Ernest goes loopy over

Marietta, and before she knows what is happening she is under siege from the amorous overlord who even goes so far as to abdicate and promote her to Archiduc in a frantic attempt to win her favours whilst simultaneously bundling Giletti out of the way with a posting as Ambassador to Naples. However, when his ardour is continually doused by the newly married Marietta, Ernest gets sulky and, like the Grande-Duchesse de Gérolstein, he ends up joining the conspiracy against the one he has, with sexual self-interest, promoted. However, the moment Ernest gets to the conspiracy table and sees the real Comtesse, he transfers his affections so that, once Marietta is deposed and he is restored, it is the Comte who is bundled off to Naples whilst Marietta and Giletti, who have bought the inn where they worked with the money gained in the exercise, close it for three months and go to bed for a honeymoon. Laurence Grivot played the important, but not plotworthy, rôle of Fortunato, the young captain of the guard who is the hereditary favourite of the Archiduc's favourite.

Most of the solo highlights of Offenbach's score were for the benefit of his leading lady. Judic scored with the catchy 'Pas ça!' and her ridiculing of Fortunato's over-slicked appearance, 'P'tit bonhomme', described her husband's honeymoon arrangements (Couplets de la voyage de noces), spied on the Comte and Comtesse's heavy petting ('Pardonnez-nous, monsieur, madame') and joined Giletti in a Duo des rires, laughing at themselves in their fancy court clothes. Fortunato had a jolly entrance song (Chanson du petit capitaine), Ernest described himself as 'Original! Original', and the Comte and Comtesse, pretending to be English tourists, had a burlesque Duo anglais and joined in some foolish, comical plotting pieces with their fellow conspirators.

The first run of the show, in spite of its song hits and, in particular, of the presence of the enormously popular Mme Judic in the cast, was a just a little disappointing. After three and a half months Charles Comte's production ran out of audience. However, in spite of this, *Madame l'Archiduc* proved to have a remarkable amount of staying power and it was seen again on the same stage in 1876 and, much to the annoyance of the authors, who had arranged for a new production at the Variétés with Judic, Comte kept his hands legally on the piece by playing it again – lawsuit or none – in 1877 (18 May, 45 performances) with Louise Théo and later Mary Albert taking the part created by Judic and with the tiny Paola Marié (succeeded by the very tall Blanche Miroir) as Fortunato. Judic took up her rôle again in 1889 at the little Théâtre des Menus-Plaisirs, whilst a 1901 revival at the Bouffes-Parisiens starred Juliette Simon-Girard (20 December) and another, in 1920 at the Théâtre Mogador, featured Edmée Favart. A further revival was mounted at the Théâtre des Variétés in 1924 (10 October).

Madame l'Archiduc was seen far and wide after its Paris début. It was first performed in America in English (ad H B Farnie) by Emily Soldene's visiting company, with the diva taking the title-rôle alongside Lizzie Robson (Fortunato), Edward Marshall (Archduke) and E D Beverley (Giletti) for a week at the end of her season of *Chilpéric*, then later played in its original language by most of the opéra-bouffe repertoire companies, notably by Coralie Geoffroy with the Grau and Chizzola Company, and

by Louise Théo. Soldene eventually took the show back to base, in Britain, where she played an 1876 London season for Charles Morton with Kate Santley (Fortunato) and W J Hill in support. This was, ultimately, a distinctly slimmed-down version of Offenbach's original as the audience revolted loudly on the first night when the afterpiece *Trial By Jury* was cancelled at midnight. Thereafter London audiences got all of *Trial By Jury* and rather less of *Madame l'Archiduc* for the two months of the run.

Soldene also travelled her production to New Zealand and to Australia, where the piece had been introduced by Catherine Lewis (Marietta), Henry Bracy (Giletti) and Miss E A Lambert (Fortunato) just a few months earlier. She scored a solid success there (Theatre Royal, Sydney 15 September 1877) alongside Rose Stella (Fortunato), Marshall and Charles J Campbell (Giletti), and the piece was long retained in the Soldene repertoire, the buxom prima donna being responsible for taking *Madame l'Archiduc* to the largest part of the English-speaking world. The show was later repeated in Australia in a short season by Australian prima donna Lotty Montal and Annette Ivanova (Fortunato) in 1885.

In Vienna a version by Julius Hopp was mounted as *Madame 'Herzog'* at the Theater an der Wien with the theatre's co-manager Marie Geistinger starring alongside Karoline Tellheim (Fortunato), Carl Adolf Friese (Archduke) and Jani Szika (Giletti) and with the young Girardi playing a supporting conspirator, Scaevola. It played a splendid 51 performances and Geistinger then went on to repeat her performance in Berlin. A new and worked-over German version was later produced at the Stendal Landestheater (15 June 1929). Prague, Naples, Stockholm and St Petersburg were amongst the other cities to host *Madame l'Archiduc* before Hungary's version (ad Lajos Evva, Béla J Fái) was seen at the Budai Színkör in 1877 and the show was brought into the repertoire of the Népszinház in 1883 (23 April).

USA: Lyceum Theater 29 December 1874; Lyceum Theater (Fr) 6 September 1875; Austria: Theater an der Wien *Madame 'Herzog' (Die Verschwörung zu Montefiasco)* 19 January 1875; Germany: Friedrich-Wilhelmstädtisches Theater *Madame 'Herzog'* 3 July 1875; UK: Opera Comique 13 January 1876; Australia: Opera House, Melbourne 26 May 1877; Hungary: Budai Színkör *A hercegasszony (A Montefiasconei összeesküves)* 12 June 1877

Recording: complete (Gaîté-Lyrique)

MADAME POMPADOUR Operette in 3 acts by Rudolf Schanzer and Ernst Welisch. Music by Leo Fall. Berliner Theater, Berlin, 9 September 1922.

The most successful of the postwar works of Leo Fall, and one of his most delightful, *Madame Pompadour* was written for the Berlin theatre and as a vehicle for its reigning queen of the musical stage, Fritzi Massary. Like those of many Operetten before and since, the amorous adventures of the plot had little to do with the historical Madame Pompadour, but were simply tacked on to the recognizable and title-worthy figures of France's Louis XV and his mistress.

René, Comte d'Éstrades, who has come up to Paris for a dirty weekend over carnival time, picks up a pretty girl in an inn. She turns out to be the Marquise de Pompadour (Massary), out on the town in disguise, and he consequently finds himself arrested and condemned to ... her personal bodyguard. His drinking companion, Josef Calicot (Ralph Arthur Roberts), a would-be poet who had been singing rude songs about the royal mistress over his beer, is, in his turn, sentenced to write the amused Marquise a play. The jealous King Louis and his police chief get into a fiendish muddle trying to catch the Pompadour out with her unknown lover, but, after a series of bedroom-farcical incidents, the lady neatly extracts herself from trouble. The comical Calicot, who had ludicrously been under suspicion, is paired off with her maid Belotte and René, who turns out to be none other than the husband of the royal mistress's half-sister, is packed off back to his wife, leaving the Marquise with the King, not to mention the remainder of her personal bodyguard.

The score followed one sparkling song with another. The tripping duet between Massary and Roberts 'Josef, ach Josef' was a comical highlight, alongside Calicot's bouncing denunciation of 'Die Pom-, Pom-, Pompadour', whilst the leading lady made her entrance to the strains of 'Heut' könnt einer sein Glück bei mir machen', dazzled through her showy 'Madame Pompadour' and encouraged René's invitation to 'Ein intimes Souper' in her principal musical moments.

Bernauer and Meinhard's Berlin production of *Madame Pompadour* was a splendid success at the Berliner Theater and then at their Komödienhaus before Massary took the piece to Vienna's Carltheater. She starred there, alongside Ernst Tautenhayn (Calicot), Erik Wirl (René), Mimi Vesely (Belotte) and Ernst Rollé (King), for some 60 performances before Mimi Kott took over the star rôle and romanced first Willi Strehl and then Eric Deutsch-Haupt, with Ernst Arnold as Calicot, through to the end of the seven-month run. In Budapest Sári Fedák played the Pompadour, whilst in New York, after producer Dillingham had sacked leading lady Hope Hampton on the road as 'incompetent and insubordinate', Wilda Bennett headed what was ultimately a disappointing production (ad Clare Kummer) which lasted only 80 performances.

A much more successful English version of *Madame Pompadour*, adapted for the British stage by Frederick Lonsdale and Harry Graham, turned out to be the longest-running *Madame Pompadour* of all. Mounted at Daly's Theatre under Jimmy White's régime, with Evelyn Laye as the merry Marquise, Derek Oldham as René, the old Daly's favourite, Huntley Wright, as Calicot and Bertram Wallis (King Louis) and Elsie Randolph (Belotte) in support, it was an enormous hit, running for 13 months and 469 performances. Australia, too, welcomed this version of the show, with the Dutch soprano Beppie de Vries as its Pompadour teamed with Frank Webster (René) and Arthur Stigant (Calicot).

It took some years before Paris saw *Madame Pompadour*, but the Operette won itself a French showing in the wake of an extravagantly produced 'Revue-Operette' revival at Berlin's Grosses Schauspielhaus in 1926 into which, in line with that house's reputation for botching, Massary had introduced the Arthur Guttmann/Julius Freund 'Im Liebesfalle', first heard in *Die Herren von Maxim*, adapted by Schanzer and Welisch as an additional solo. The French version (ad Albert Willemetz, Max Eddy, Jean Marietti, with the lady punctiliously rechristened *Madame de Pompadour*) was lavishly and successfully presented at

the Théâtre Marigny by Léon Volterra. Raymonde Vécart, Robert Burnier and René Hérent starred, supported (in deference to the fashion for things American, even in period France) by 'les Merry Girls' and 'les Smart Boys', as well as an orchestra of 40.

In more recent times, *Madame Pompadour* has been seen at the Vienna Volksoper which brought back a version of the show in 1976 and again in 1986, and it holds a place on the fringe of the revivable and revived repertoire where it is looked at by musicians with particular favour.

The Pompadour has been utilized a number of times as a character on the musical stage even if she has proved a touch more discreet than such other members of her profession as Madame Dubarry. An operatic *Die Pompadour* by Emmanuel Mór was produced at Cologne in 1902, and an Italian operetta *La Pompadour* by Costantino Lombardo to a text by Antonio Lega was produced at the Teatro Alfieri, Turin (25 September 1918).

Austria: Carltheater 2 March 1923; Hungary: Fővárosi Operettszinház 28 November 1923; UK: Daly's Theatre 20 December 1923; USA: Martin Beck Theater 11 November 1924; Australia: His Majesty's Theatre, Brisbane 21 May 1927; Her Majesty's Theatre, Sydney 4 June 1927; France: Théâtre Marigny 16 May 1930
Recording: Selection (EMI Electrola)

MADAME SHERRY Operette in 3 acts by Benno Jacobson adapted from a libretto by Maurice Ordonneau [and Paul Burani]. Music by Hugo Felix. Centraltheater, Berlin, 1 November 1902.

Bachelor music teacher Anatole Mac Sherry has been supported for many years by his Canadian uncle, Epaminondas Mac Sherry, whom he has led to believe that he is an underfunded married man with two children. When the uncle inevitably and unexpectedly turns up, along with his pretty convent-bred niece Jane, Anatole has to produce an instant family. Housekeeper Catherine becomes the wife, the dancer Mistigrette with whom Anatole has been carrying on a flirtation is the daughter, and Leonard y Gomez, son of the president of Bolivia and Anatole's pupil, is the son. The pretence, complicated by the fact that Leonard's old flame, the tempestuous Pepita, is led to believe that Mistigrette is Madame Sherry junior – ie Leonard's wife – is given a hard time during a hair-raising evening out at the 'Golden Key' restaurant, but Uncle, who has finally to be told the truth, is mollified by the fact that Anatole and Jane have fallen in love and there will, at last, be a real Madame Sherry.

Felix's score was a pretty one, skipping merrily and effectively through the whole range of his performers' voices from top tenor and soprano to some basso rumblings from the men of the company. It was highlighted by the jaunty duet 'Youp-la! Catarina' for Catherine and her (real) husband Aurillac and a comical dagger number for the stalking Pepita, but most particularly by its ensembles, including a charming vocal nocturne and a second-act finale in which a befuddled policeman, called in to sort out the brouhaha in the restaurant, is 'youp-la-ed' off his feet by Catherine and waltzed through a laughing chorus by Jane.

A genuine hit in Berlin, the show was soon on its way around the world, and on the way it met a curious fate.

Andreas Aman produced *Madame Sherry* at the Carltheater with Karl Blasel as the elder Mac Sherry, Louis Treumann as the younger, Karl Streitmann as the Bolivian and Therese Biedermann (Catherine), the American divette Marie Halton (Jane), Else Stefans (Mistigrette) and Marie Gribl (Pepita) in the feminine rôles, but in spite of its fine cast the show managed only a dozen performances. Its Berlin success was, however, sufficient for it to reach London (ad Charles E Hands, Adrian Ross) where it arrived with vast pre-production ballyhoo. Florence St John (Catherine), Louis Bradfield (Andrew), Nigel Playfair (MacSherry) and Ruth Lincoln (Barbara, ex-Jane) headed George Edwardes's cast, the score was infiltrated by a couple of Paul Rubens ditties, and the agencies bought up thousands of pounds worth of tickets for the first six months of the run, only to find their fingers nastily burned when the show didn't run that long.

Success was reserved for America, but the *Madame Sherry* which was given to the Broadway public by A H Woods, George Lederer and H H Frazee was a decidedly different one from that which had been played in Europe (New Amsterdam Theater 30 August 1910). Otto Harbach's libretto (billed as 'a three-act French vaudeville') kept closely to Ordonneau's original plot but, with scenic and terpischorean considerations ever in view, it resituated the first act in a school of aesthetic dancing, and the remaining two ... on board a yacht. Felix's score was quite simply replaced by a wholly new one largely written by Karl Hoschna. It was one with a different level of ambition. Felix's finales were replaced by act-endings that were little more than tags, what ensembles there were were largely sung in unison, and the accent was on 'numbers' and, very specifically, on dances.

Frances Demarest (as Lulu, ex-Mistigrette) and Carl Martens (Leonard) performed a burlesque aesthetic dance to 'Every Little Movement (has a meaning all its own)', a melody which had been previously introduced in the opening chorus, and which was replugged both as a finale to the first act and in an intermezzo. It was this tune that became the most popular of the evening, in spite of a catchy waltz 'The Birth of Passion', which was given a similar treatment in the second act by the show's star, Lina Arbarbanell (Yvonne, ex-Jane), and Jack Gardner (Edward, ex-Anatole). Comic Ralph Herz played Uncle Sherry and English *Chinese Honeymoon* star Marie Dainton was Pepita. Amongst the interpolated numbers were the Albert von Tilzer/Junie McCree 'Put your Arms Around Me, Honey' and Harold Atteridge and Phil Schwarz's 'The Dublin Rag'. Whatever purists might have thought, the producers had judged their audiences aright in their remake of the show and Abarbanell, in particular, and *Madame Sherry* in general, were fine successes both on Broadway (231 performances) and on the road. As for 'Every Little Movement', it completed the full circle. Stripped of Harbach's lyric, Hoschna's melody turned up back in France – where Ordonneau had begun the whole thing – set to words by Lucien Boyer and purveyed to Parisians by Henri Leoni as 'Je n' sais comment!', and in Germany where it was billed as the 'Liebestanz aus *Madame Sherry*'.

In 1989 a revised version of the American version of show (ad John Peters, Joe Goss, Shawn McEnaney), which introduced several of Felix's numbers as well as Hoschna's 'Cuddle up a Little Closer' from *Three Twins* in preference to half-a-dozen pieces from the original score, was played at the Goodspeed Opera House (28 June).

Austria: Carltheater 10 October 1903; UK: Apollo Theatre 23 December 1903; Hungary: Magyar Színház *Sherry* 9 January 1904

MADAME SUZETTE Opérette in 3 acts by Maurice Ordonneau and André Sylvane. Music by Edmond Audran. Théâtre des Bouffes-Parisiens, Paris, 29 March 1893.

Suzette Gabillot (Biana Duhamel), the daughter of a provincial hotelier (Édouard Maugé), needs to win time in her battle not to wed her father's candidate for her hand, for her beloved, extremely moustachioed but unrich soldier (Dekernel) has to woo sufficient money from an old aunt to clear his hotel bill before they can announce his pretensions. When papa discovers that another, new pretender for Suzette's affections, William Robiquet (Piccaluga), is violently rich, he practically forces the young man into his daughter's bed, but William is a nice young man and he helps Suzette keep father quiet by pretending a liaison until her soldier returns, not from seeing any aunt but in reality from breaking off another affaire in Paris. Suzette then realizes that William is the better bargain of the two. A lightly pretty Audran score in his *Miss Helyett* vein, moulded to suit *Miss Helyett*'s star, Mlle Duhamel, illustrated the story deftly, and the piece was played 79 times at the Bouffes before going on to be seen in a German version in Berlin (ad Eduard Jacobson, Jean Kren) with Frln Schlüter and Thielscher starred, and in an Hungarian one in Budapest (ad Ferenc Rajna).

Germany: Adolf Ernst Theater 23 March 1895; Hungary: Magyar Színház *Menyecske kisasszony* 8 January 1898

DAS MÄDEL VON MONTMARTRE Operette in 3 acts by Rudolf Schanzer adapted from *La Dame de chez Maxim* by Georges Feydeau. Music by Henrik Bérény. Neues Theater, Berlin, 26 October 1911.

Feydeau's highly successful 1899 play *La Dame de chez Maxim*, with its showy comic rôles for both leading man and lady – the latter memorably created by Armande Cassive in the play's première at Paris's Théâtre des Nouveautés (17 January 1899) – was natural fodder for the musical-farce stage. When model husband Dr Petypon is reluctantly dragged out for a night on the tiles by a friend he ultimately rather overdoes things and wakes up squeamishly in the morning underneath the upturned sofa. There is an empty dress over the chair, and his bed is occupied by 'the girl from Montmartre'. Enter Madame Petypon, and the farcical complications and the crises of mistaken identity begin, galloping from Paris to a house party in the Touraine and ending only when, with his wife blissfully undeceived over the escapade which never really was one, Petypon succeeds in offloading the embarrassing 'la môme crevette'.

Das Mädel von Montmartre had only an average run in Berlin and it did not travel to Vienna or to Budapest but, in the wake of the splendid Broadway success of Bérény's previous Operette, *Lord Piccolo* (*Little Boy Blue*), not to mention the hit made by the production of the original, slightly musicalized play a decade earlier (*The Girl from Maxim's* Criterion Theater 29 August 1899, starring Josephine Hall) it was snapped up for New York by that production's sponsor, Charles Frohman. Adapted by Harry B and Robert B Smith, peppered with a good half-dozen Jerome Kern songs, a duet from *The Arcadians* and a Franz Wagner number relyricked as 'Something Like This' (thus leaving Berény represented by about 50 per cent of the score), with Richard Carle and Hattie Williams in the two juicy star rôles, and given an up-to-date touch by the use of a kinemacolor film section in the last act depicting the heroine's pursuit of the show's various characters, it had a modest 64 performances in town but served well enough on the road.

La Dama di Montmartre (1925), an Italian musical by Carlo Lombardo and Ermete Liberati and the Polish *Dama od Maxima* (1967) by Antoni Marianowicz and Ryszard Sielicki, were also later based on the same Feydeau play.

USA: Criterion Theater *The Girl from Montmartre* 5 August 1912

MADER, Raoul [MADER, Rezső] (b Pressburg, Hungary 25 June 1856; d Budapest 16 October 1940). Composer, conductor and administrator in the Austrian and Hungarian theatre.

The son of a schoolteacher, Mader showed an early preference for music and, after his first studies in his home town, he was sent to Vienna to attend the Conservatorium there. He won prizes in piano and composition, but was slow to make a career thereafter. His first musical theatre composition to be produced in Vienna was a Spieloper, *Die Flüchtlinge*, written with Bernard Buchbinder and staged at the Hofoper (19 February 1891), where Mader had for nearly a decade been a répétiteur, when the composer was already well into his thirties. This was followed by a burlesque of *Cavalleria rusticana* ('mit verschiedene skandalösen Auftritten') on the bill of which the musician was described, tongue-in-cheek, as the 'komponist der Mascagnischen Musik', and two ballets, also for the Hofoper (*Die Sirenen-Insel* 1892, *Hochzeit in Frisirsalon* 4 October 1894), before his first Operette, *Engelsherz*, was presented at the Carltheater in 1895 with Julie Kopácsi-Karczag and Karl Blasel starred. It was played just ten times.

In the same year Mader was engaged as a conductor at the Magyar Királyi Operaház in Budapest and he returned home to Hungary where his first new offerings to the theatre were further ballets (the highly successful *A piros cipő* 1897, *She* 1898). He had some success with an operett, *Kadétkisasszony*, written with Árpád Pásztor and produced at the Népszínház (31 performances), and rather less with a second, written with the same partner, and played later the same year at the Magyar Színház (*Primadonnák*), before taking over as Director of the Operaház in November 1901. During his six-year tenure there, he had two more Operetten produced, both to libretti by Landesberg and Stein, and both in Vienna. The first of these, *Das Garnisonsmädel*, gave him his most considerable run to date with 55 performances at the Theater an der Wien and productions at Berlin's Theater des Westens (8 July 1905) and Budapest's Magyar Színház under the title *Huszárvér* (ad Adolf Mérei, György Ruttkay 2 December 1904). *Der selige Vinzenz*, produced at the Carltheater with Girardi and Mizzi Zwerenz as stars, played for one month.

Mader subsequently became director of the shortlived

Népszínház-Vigopera (1907), and while there composed the musical score for his most enduring piece, Pásztor's musical version of Gergely Csiky's play *Nagymama*, in which the ageing Lujza Blaha scored one final triumph as the grandmother of the title. *Nagymama* went on to become Hungary's most popular vehicle for a senior female star. As Mader's career as a manager progressed from Budapest to Vienna's Volksoper (1916) and again to the Magyar Királyi Operaház (1922–5), his composing decreased, and his later works – another ballet, a puppet-play score for the Budapest opera house (*A bűvös bábú* 19 December 1924), and a Chopin pastiche for the Theater an der Wien – were few and far between.

1891 **Krawalleria musicana** (*Sizilianische Ehrenbauern*) (Alexander Weigl) 1 act Theater an der Wien 3 October
1895 **Engelsherz** (*Coeur d'ange*) (Hugo H Regel, Richard Genée) Carltheater 12 January
1900 **Kadétkisasszony** (Árpád Pásztor) Népszínház, Budapest 10 January
1900 **Primadonnák** (Pásztor) Magyar Színház, Budapest 29 December
1904 **Das Garnisonsmädel** (Alexander Landesberg, Leo Stein) Theater an der Wien 29 October
1907 **Der selige Vincenz** (Landesberg, Stein) Carltheater 31 January
1908 **A Nagymama** (Pásztor) Népszínház-Vigopera, Budapest 1 February
1917 **Die weisse Adler** (Chopin arr/Victor Léon, Regel) Theater an der Wien 3 October

MÄDI Operette in 3 acts by Alfred Grünwald and Leo Stein. Music by Robert Stolz. Berliner Theater, Berlin, 1 April 1923.

The titular heroine of *Mädi*, the Countess Mädi von Birkenhof (Claire Waldoff), gets her straying Count Anatol Welsberg (Fritz Werner) to marry her by a ruse that is a slight twist on a much-used plot. She enlists the help of his best friend, Baron Aristid ('Stidi') Stelzer (Hans Albers), who pretends that he wants to marry Mädi himself but, in order to inherit a fortune, he must only marry a divorcée. Will his good friend Anatol help him out by marrying his own ex-girlfriend for four weeks? It takes a honeymoon in a Wintersportshotel in the Swiss Alps (Act II) and a ride south on the Riviera-Express (Act III) before Mädi convinces the helpful but up-till-now chaste Anatol that the marriage should be left permanent. Stidi gets his reward for his helpfulness in the person of the soubrette, Clo Bernas (Hilde Wörner).

The 15 pieces of the show's score were shared out largely amongst the four principals, with Mädi and Anatol having the catch-number of the evening in their second-act 'what would you say if we were really husband and wife?' duo, 'Mädi, mein süsses Mädi'. Amongst the other numbers, Mädi sang of 'Was die kleinen Mädchen träumen' and joined in the night's other top number, the two-step 'Halt dich fest, dass du die Balance nicht verlierst' with Stidi and Clo and in a Bummeln-trio ('Wir fahren eine Strecke') with the two men, whilst Anatol hymned 'Die süssen Mäderln' and joined his wife with the Shimmy-invitation 'Nun komm doch, du kleine, du reizende Schampusfee'. But it was pretty, incidental Clo – who delivered an introductory number ('Das ist ja Clo'), another in the last act ('Wenn du nur Einen kennst'), led a march to get the second act going ('Auf ja und nein') and joined with Stidi in a pair of duets: the waltz 'Du brauchst nur treu zu sein' and 'Du darfst alles, was du willst, mein Schatz' – who had what seemed the lioness's share in the evening's music.

Mädi had a fine run in Berlin, passing its 100th night (9 July) at the Berliner Theater and in October it was seen in Vienna, produced under the management of Siegfried Geyer and Oscar Fronz at the Bürgertheater. Louis Treumann and Luise Kartousch played the lovers, Hans Albers was again their comic helpmate, Magda Garden was the ubiquitous Clo, and *Mädi* ran a little short of three months. It was produced at Budapest's Király Színház (ad Györy Verő), not unreasonably retitled *Huncut a lány* (the crafty girl) with Hanna Honthy starred, but London preferred to stress the picturesque accoutrements of the staging rather than the plot and called its version (ad Reginald Arkell, Dion Titheradge) *The Blue Train*. Jack Hulbert and Paul Murray's production boasted a toboggan slide on the stage in the alpine act, additional numbers by Ivy St Helier (3), Howard Carr (2), and Jay Gorney and Dion Titheradge (a title song), and the return to the stage of the much loved heroine of *The Merry Widow*, Lily Elsie, as the the crafty Mädi, here rechristened Eileen. Arthur Margetson was the man she married and comedian Bobby Howes helped her do it. However, a London mad for such novelties as *The Desert Song*, *The Vagabond King*, *Sunny* and the antics of Leslie Henson and Laddie Cliff in *Lady Luck* showed little interest in *The Blue Train* and, surprisingly, in Miss Elsie, and *The Blue Train* lasted only 116 performances.

A new version of *Mädi* with some additional numbers and revised lyrics by Robert Gilbert was produced in 1953. (Stadttheater, Zurich 9 April).

Austria: Wiener Bürgertheater 5 October 1923; Hungary: Király Színház *Huncut a lány* 19 April 1924; UK: Prince of Wales Theatre *The Blue Train* 10 May 1927

MAGGIE MAY Musical in 2 acts by Alun Owen. Music and lyrics by Lionel Bart. Adelphi Theatre, London, 22 September 1964.

Bart's successor to *Oliver!* and *Blitz!* had no exclamation mark and didn't need one. Having decided to construct a show around the old ballad character of Maggie May, Bart had a libretto written by the successful Liverpool playwright Alun Owen in which the docklands prostitute (Rachel Roberts) was really not central to the story. Her childhood sweetheart, docker Casey (Kenneth Haigh), dogged by having a famous union man for a father, is his own man. In spite of the jeers of his co-workers, to whom management is a born-not-bred enemy, he refuses to commit himself to unreasoning union action, but he ends up, in spite of himself, leading a wildcat strike and dying as he tries to ditch a cargo of guns intended for anti-riot police in South America.

In a strong if simplistic story (in which both bosses and union men were shown with plenty of warts), Owen created a set of colourful characters for whom Bart supplied an unusual collection of folky-sounding pieces and modern shanties which were far from making up a conventional musical-play score. The heroine's toughly pragmatic 'love' song 'It's Yourself I Want', her duo with a fellow whore, 'I Told You So', and their mockery of the men's self-important preoccupation with union affairs in 'There's

Only One Union' stood alongside such ballady pieces as 'Dey Don't Do Dat T'day' and 'Leave Her, Johnny, Leave Her' and, it being Beatles time, a number for a Liverpudlian pop group, in a score which accompanied the play very effectively, rather than the other way around.

Bernard Delfont and Tom Arnold's production of *Maggie May* ran through 501 London performances, during which time the unreliable Miss Roberts was first deputized for by 21-year-old chorister Julia McKenzie, and then succeeded by Georgia Brown. However, in spite of being announced for Broadway by Delfont and David Merrick, it did not move on to further productions.

Recordings: Original cast (Decca), original cast with additional songs (TER), selection (EP) (Capitol)

THE MAGIC OPAL Comic opera in 2 acts by Arthur Law. Music by Isaac Albéniz. Lyric Theatre, London, 19 January 1893. Revised version as *The Magic Ring*, Prince of Wales Theatre, 11 April 1893.

The music for *The Magic Opal* was composed by Albéniz whilst he was resident in Britain on a retainer from the wealthy banker and amateur author Francis Burdett Money-Coutts to set to music such libretti as the latter might write. In between Coutts's assignments, the composer wrote some additional music for interpolation into London's versions of *Le Coeur et la main* and *Der arme Jonathan* and also completed the full score for this comic opera, produced by Horace Sedger. Arthur Law's libretto followed a magic ring which makes the wearer irresistible as it affected a brigand chief (Wallace Brownlow) and his sister (May Yohé), an old hag (Susie Vaughan), the two juvenile leads (Aida Jenoure, John Child) and the heroine's father (Harry Monkhouse) to the accompaniment of a fairly straightforward comic-opera score. *The Magic Opal* was well enough received and reviewed, but it aroused little interest and closed after 44 performances, leaving its touring company, which had gone out counting on London success, adrift.

However, brewery tycoon Henry Lowenfeld liked the show, leased the Prince of Wales Theatre, got rid of Miss Yohé (in spite of her already distinct personal following) and half the original cast and reproduced the show as *The Magic Ring* with Monkhouse, Miss Vaughan, Norman Salmond and the American soubrette Marie Halton featured. The critics liked it again, but again it lasted for just 37 performances. Later in the year it surfaced a third time, but this time in Madrid where, in Eusebio Sierra's translation, it was played as *La Sortija*.

The title *The Magic Ring* was once more the second choice for a 1923 American musical comedy (Harold Levey/Zelda Sears, Liberty Theater 1 October) which had been originally produced by Henry Savage as *Minnie and Me* (Stamford, 2 April 1923), but it was first choice for a comic opera by Immanuel Liebich, tentatively produced in London in 1886 to a firm thumbs-down.

THE MAGIC SHOW Musical in 2 acts by Bob Randall. Music and lyrics by Stephen Schwartz. Cort Theater, New York, 28 May 1974.

A vehicle for the illusions of Doug Henning, *The Magic Show* cast the young magician as a young magician called Doug in a storyline which had him saving a failing nightclub from extinction by his performances. One of the evening's highlights came when Doug sawed his girlfriend (Anita Morris) in half, and his jealous wife promptly ran off with one half – the bottom half, at that. The magic was spaced out by 11 bright songs for a supporting cast of nine (Henning did not sing) and band of seven. Partly thanks to these manageable proportions, Henning (temporarily spelled by Joe Abbaldo) and his show ran through 1,859 performances on Broadway. The star returned to Broadway in 1983 with another but less successful show, in which he appeared as *Merlin*.

An Australian production, mounted under the auspices of the Elizabethan Theatre Trust and Garnet Carroll, did not have Henning, was a two-month failure in Melbourne and did not brave Sydney.

Australia: Princess Theatre, Melbourne 2 August 1975
Recording: Original cast (Bell)

MÁGNÁS MISKA Operett in 3 acts by Károly Bakonyi. Lyrics by Andor Gábor. Music by Albert Szirmai. Király Színház, Budapest, 12 February 1916.

Produced in Budapest during the most fecund period in Hungarian operett, Szirmai's wartime piece *Mágnás Miska* (Miska the magnate) stands alongside such pieces as Jacobi's *Leányvásár* and *Szibill* as one of the most successful products of its time and place.

During a sporty country-house weekend at the house of Count Kasimir Korláth (Kálmán Latabár), his daughter, Rolla (Juci Lábass), falls for the untitled Iván Baracs (Ernő Király) whose athletic prowesses have won him every event. Rolla's brother Gida (Ernő Szabolcs) and the other losers get it whispered about that she is simply leading the bourgeois fellow on, and in revenge Baracs introduces his groom, Miska (Márton Rátkai), to the dazzled aristocrats as the lofty Graf Amadée, just returned from darkest Africa. But Rolla, who is wise to his trick, in turn disguises her kitchen-maid, Marcsa (Sári Fedák), as Amadée's cousin, the Countess Lizzi. The antics of the two disguised 'aristocrats' and the clearing of a path towards both their union and that of Rolla and Baracs comprise the action of the second and third acts.

Szirmai's score was a vigorously tuneful one, ranging from the fiendishly bouncing and folksy 'Hoppsza Sári' and a rollicking march-time entry song for the heroine to some duets for the tenor and soprano which verged on the 'grand operette' style, yet which maintained a swinging sound which stopped them ever becoming too pretentious for their jolly little story. However, the heart of *Mágnás Miska* was its comedy, and the rôles of Miska himself, a part in joyous line of descent from the *Erminie* style of masquerading rogue of 19th-century comic opera, and of soubrette Marcsa.

A great success in Budapest, *Mágnás Miska* passed its 150th performance at the Király Szinház just eight months after its première, and it has continued to be regularly revived in Hungary, most recently at the Fővárosi Operettszinház in 1972 (27 October). The show was also briskly picked up for a German presentation (ad Robert Bodanzky) which ran through almost three months of performances at Berlin's Komische Oper, and this version was later played at Vienna's Apollotheater with Fedák repeating her original rôle (now called Rosi) alongside Josef König, Olga Bartos-Trau and Oskar Neruda. It apparently, however, went no further west.

Germany: Komische Oper *Der Pusztakavalier* 16 November 1916; Austria: Apollotheater *Der Pusztakavalier* November 1920; Film: 1948

THE MAID OF THE MOUNTAINS Comic opera in 3 acts by Frederick Lonsdale. Lyrics by Harry Graham. Additional lyrics by 'Valentine' and F Clifford Harris. Music by Harold Fraser-Simson. Additional music by James Tate and Merlin Morgan. Daly's Theatre, London, 10 February 1917.

One of the sensations of the London theatre during the First World War, *The Maid of the Mountains* arrived at Daly's Theatre just in time to save George Edwardes's once-great theatre from financial disaster. Bobbie Evett, representing the Edwardes estate as manager of Daly's, accepted the show (originally rejected some nine years previously by Frank Curzon) from author Frederick Lonsdale and had it set by composer Harold Fraser-Simson. He then mounted the tale of swashbuckling banditry and low comedy with the darkly attractive prima donna José Collins playing the part of Teresa, 'the maid of the mountains', whose love for her brigand chief, Baldasarre, is great enough for her to free him from his island prison to fly straight to the arms of her rival, the governor's daughter. *The Maid of the Mountains* followed the system which Lonsdale had set out in his first musical, *King of Cadonia*, by taking an old-fashioned comic-opera plot and characters and equipping them with rather better-made scenes and lines than was the custom, as well, in this case, as an unusual (at that stage) 'unhappy' ending – which he was ultimately not permitted to keep. Miss Collins objected damply to the unconventional (for her) unhappy (for her) ending to the piece as originally written and forced her producer and her writer to invert it so that she and her leading man (Arthur Wontner) could sail off into the sunset together at the final curtain.

Fraser-Simson's score, topped by two lovely waltzes, 'Farewell' and 'Love is My Life', for the prima donna, and some sprightly comic pieces ('I Understood', 'Husbands and Wives') for the supporting comedy couple (Lauri de Frece, Mabel Sealby), illustrated Lonsdale's work splendidly. During the show's Manchester try-out, however, Evett decided the score needed further strengthening and he added three numbers by Miss Collins's stepfather, songwriter James Tate, and one by musical director Merlin Morgan. Tate's songs included another hit for the star, 'Love Will Find a Way', a solo for principal baritone Thorpe Bates (the rôle of Baldasarre was a non-singing one) declaring 'A Bachelor Gay Am I', and a duet for the two of them, 'A Paradise for Two'. All three numbers subsequently became enormous favourites and ubiquitous concert items in English and colonial houses for half a century. Morgan's song didn't last out the run.

Oscar Asche, already the director (and author and star) of the West End's other great hit, *Chu Chin Chow*, staged the show, which, arriving in town after its Manchester Christmas season, caused nothing short of a sensation at Daly's Theatre. It played for 1,352 performances – a massive run for the time – and closed only when Miss Collins, who in spite of regular breaks was finding an endless run of Teresas nerve-racking, cried enough. She was so closely identified with the rôle that, although she had been ably deputized for by Dorothy Shale during

927

various absences, there was no thought of replacing her, and Evett took the only way out – he produced a new show, as like as possible to the old one, with Miss Collins starring, whilst *The Maid of the Mountains* went on the road. It proved as big a hit in the provinces – without its star – as it had in London with her and, at one stage, no fewer than 12 different companies were on the road touring *The Maid of the Mountains* around Britain. José Collins reappeared as 'the maid' in 1921–2 as a farewell to Daly's, and the show returned to London in 1930 with Annie Croft and again, and most successfully, in 1942 with Sylvia Cecil starred, but a 1972 Emile Littler version, embarrassingly rewritten and with the score plumped up with some operetta pops ('Song of the Vagabonds', 'Pedro the Fisherman') was a failure.

The Maid of the Mountains, similarly disfigured by unsuitable interpolations, also failed quickly (37 performances) when it was trekked down to America from a Canadian mounting, with Sidonie Espero in its title-rôle, but in Australia where it was played as written it proved, if anything, even more of a hit than in Britain. Soprano Gladys Moncrieff scored a huge personal success as Teresa and became as thoroughly identified with the rôle in Australia and New Zealand as Miss Collins had in Britain. Again and again she appeared on the Australian stage as 'the maid', always a reliable money-maker in a piece which producers J C Williamson Ltd re-mounted whenever another iffy venture had landed them in sharky waters ('Gladys, the ship is sinking ...'). She made her final appearance in the rôle of the gipsyish brigand-girl at the age of 59.

USA: Casino Theater 11 September 1918; Australia: Theatre Royal, Melbourne 21 January 1921

Recordings: original cast transfers (World Records), selection (World Records, Australia), revival cast 1972 (Columbia) etc

MAILLART, Aimé [MAILLART, Louis] (b Montpelier, 24 March 1817; d Moulins-sur-Allier, 26 May 1871).

Conservatoire-trained Aimé Maillart was the composer of a number of lyric theatre works including *Gastibelza, ou Le Fou de Tolède* (1847), *Le Moulin des Tilleuls* (1849), *La Croix de Marie* (1852), *Les Pêcheurs de Catane* (1860) and *Lara* (1864) produced variously at the Opéra-Comique and at Adolphe Adam's Théâtre Lyrique. His most notable success came with the opéra-comique *Les Dragons de Villars*, composed to a book by Lockroy and Cormon which mixed a light-hearted soldiers-and-peasant-girls tale of (attempted) naughty doings in the ruins of a hermitage with a more serious story of a *Sound of Music*-style attempt by some persecuted folk (without children) to escape through the mountains to political safety. The piece was illustrated by a score which leaned tunefully towards the light musical theatre rather than the grand operatic. Produced by Léon Carvalho at the Théâtre Lyrique in 1856, *Les Dragons de Villars* was subsequently taken into the repertoire of the Opéra-Comique (1868) and became one of the handful of opéras-comiques of the early and middle part of the 19th century to survive into the repertoires of the touring French opéra-bouffe companies when the works of Offenbach, Lecocq and their fellow composers of the latter part of the century dominated the musical stages

of the world to the exclusion of virtually all the musical works of the earlier sub-operatic stage.

MAJESTÄT MIMI Operette in 3 acts by Felix Dörmann and Roda Roda. Music by Bruno Granichstädten. Carltheater, Vienna, 17 February 1911.

Granichstädten's Operette presented Mizzi Zwerenz as a Parisian cabaret performer called Mimi who dances the can-can, insists that she is 'modern', has 'Temp'rament' and sings in praise of 'Walzer und Wein', and Willi Strehl as the cabaret-singer Prince of a mythical country called Bythinia who is unhappily whisked away from his happy bohemian life in Paris to Brussa (capital of Bythinia) to take up his royal duties in the same manner that Ivor Novello's Niki of Murania would be a few decades later. In spite of Granichstädten's penchant for music with a modern and even trans-Atlantic tinge, the two lovers spend most of the evening singing in 3/4 time and by the third-act finale they are encouraging each other to 'Küss mich in dreivierteltakt' as they waltz into their happy ending. Josef König was the patter-singing representative of Bythinia, the Fürst von Lepanto, Otti Dietze (Princess Xenia) and Rudolf Kumpa (Ferry) supplied the soubret moments, again largely in waltz time ('Komm mit mir auf meine kleine Segelyacht ...', 'O, jui jui jui') and veteran Karl Blasel had a virtual non-singing rôle.

Sigmund Eibenschütz's production of *Majestät Mimi* lasted but 27 performances at the Carltheater, and the piece was played without stirring too much interest in Hamburg. It did not, apparently, make it to Hungary where even the least of its composer's works was played. Broadway whispered that Lillian Russell would do it, if she didn't do *Der Opernball*, but in the end she did neither. However, the show did find its way to Italy where, in the hands of Carlo Lombardo, a specialist in concocting semi-original shows out of other people's works, it was turned into a piece called *La Duchessa del Bal Tabarin* – its heroine was now no longer Mimi but Frou-Frou of the Bal Tabarin – with a considerable success. Granichstädten's name was nowhere to be seen on the bill which described the piece as 'an operetta by Leon Bard' (Lombardo's occasional nom de plume). After cleaning up in Italy, where it was re-produced many times in years to come, it moved on to repeat its Italian success in Spain (ad Enrique Gomez Carillo, Jose Juan Cadenas).

Germany: Deutsches Operetten-Theater, Hamburg 1 April 1911

Recordings: Italian recording *La Duchessa del Bal Tabarin* (Fonit-Cetra), Spanish recording *La Duquesa del Bal Tabarin* (Montilla)

MAKE ME AN OFFER Musical in 2 acts by Wolf Mankowitz taken from his novel of the same name. Lyrics and music by David Heneker and Monty Norman. Theatre Royal, Stratford East, 17 October 1959; New Theatre, London, 16 December 1959.

Developed from a novel (and subsequent film) that author Mankowitz had written around his own collector-mania for Wedgwood china, *Make Me an Offer* was the tale of market stallholder Charlie (Daniel Massey), who loves and knows the stuff he sells, but who is not much of a chat-happy businessman. When he takes part in an auction ring at a big sale, he gets enough cash to buy a beautiful vase – it's something he's dreamed all his life of owning, but he finds he has grown up enough to be able to sell it. He is a professional dealer, and he needs the cash both to support his wife (Diana Coupland) and babes and to develop his business. Temptation was represented not only by the vase, but its pushy redheaded seller (Dilys Laye), whilst comedy was provided by the snappily professional, sell-you-anything Jewish market-vendors (Meier Tzelniker, Wally Patch) quarrelling day in, day out until they unite in the face of a common prey as represented by a pair of American buyers (Victor Spinetti, Chuck Julian).

The show's songs and ensembles, often flowing over into and out of the text, were from two-thirds of the team responsible for *Expresso Bongo* and the English version of *Irma la Douce*. They were highlighted by Massey's musical epitomizing of life's problems in 'Damn the Pram' and his longing for 'A Lock-Up in the Portobello Road', a first-act finale with Charlie on the phone to his wife and the red-head hovering dangerously near ('Make Me an Offer'), and a rhythmical set-piece auction scene. Like the writers' earlier work it was a show 'for grown ups of all ages' which almost never tumbled into the stage Sohoisms of such recent pieces as *Fings Ain't Wot They Used t' Be* and *The Crooked Mile*, and its quality showed through as it won a transfer from the suburban Theatre Royal, Stratford East, to the West End's New Theatre where it remained for 267 performances before going on to be reprised in provincial theatres.

A German adaptation (ad Kurt Barthel) mounted in Rostock under the unlikely title 'a breath of romance' elevated the previously un-named 'redhead' to being 'Lady Rotkopf' in what otherwise seemed a faithful version.

Germany: Rostock *Ein Hauch von Romantik* 27 March 1966
Recording: original cast (HMV/AEI).

MALONE, J A E (b Mhow, India; d London, 3 February 1929). George Edwardes's stage director through his greatest era of activity.

Pat Malone began his theatrical life as a performer before shifting to the stage management and directing side of the business, first at the Prince of Wales' Theatre in Liverpool (where he directed his first musical, W Duck's presentation of the comic opera *Herne's Oak*, in 1887), and later at the Opera Comique in London. From 1893, he worked under the wide-reaching management of the country's most important musical producer, George Edwardes, at a time when the Gaiety Theatre and Daly's Theatre were launching his double-headed series of musical plays towards the stages of the world.

Malone directed the initial production of *A Gaiety Girl* and in 1894 restaged *In Town*, *The Shop Girl* and *Gentleman Joe* for the Gaiety's world tour, with which he travelled as general manager. Returning to Britain, over the following two decades he directed the majority of Edwardes's productions at the Gaiety Theatre (*The Circus Girl*, *A Runaway Girl*, *The Messenger Boy*, *The Toreador*, *The Girls of Gottenberg*, *The Sunshine Girl*), at Daly's (*The Geisha*, *A Greek Slave*, *San Toy*, *A Country Girl*, *The Cingalee*, *The Merry Widow*), in various other venues in London (*Kitty Grey*, *Three Little Maids*, *The Merry-Go-Round*, *The School Girl*, *Lady Madcap*, *The Little Cherub*, *A Waltz Dream*, *The Quaker Girl*, *The Dancing Mistress*, *The Girl from Utah*) and on Broadway (*The Geisha*, *In Town*, *The Circus Girl*, *The Girls of Gottenberg*, *The Dollar Princess*, *The Quaker Girl*, *The Sunshine Girl*, *The Girl from Utah*).

After Edwardes's death, Malone continued as a director of Musical Plays Ltd, running the Adelphi Theatre where he directed the successful *High Jinks* (1916), *Who's Hooper?* (1919) and *The Naughty Princess* (*La Reine s'amuse*) for Alfred Butt. He also directed *The Beauty Spot* for Butt, with whom he was allied on the board of the Victoria Palace Theatre, at the Gaiety, Messager's *Monsieur Beaucaire* in London and New York and *The Maid of the Mountains* for Broadway, billed as 'Captain J A E Malone' on a self-conscious programme which also credited 'additional music by Lieutenant Gitz Rice'.

Alongside his directing activities, Malone was involved in various producing exercises from the time of joining Robert Courtneidge and Arthur Hart in 1904 on the management side of the first provincial production of *The Blue Moon*, and he deputized efficiently for the absent and ill Edwardes on *After the Girl* and *Adele* (1914) in the last days of the producer's Gaiety reign. However, he made his firmest effort in that area when, in 1920, he joined George Grossmith and Edward Laurillard in their production company and, on Laurillard's retirement from the partnership, teamed with Grossmith in the management of the Winter Garden, the Shaftesbury and His Majesty's Theatres and as the co-producer of the successful series of musicals staged at the Winter Garden (*Sally*, *The Cabaret Girl*, *The Beauty Prize*, *Tell Me More*, *Primrose*, *Kid Boots*) as well as such other London and provincial pieces as Jack Buchanan's *Toni* (1923).

Malone was for a period London representative of Australia's J C Williamson Ltd, for whom he was directing their London transfer of the musical *Mr Cinders* when he died in 1929.

MALTBY, H[enry] F[rancis] (b Ceres, Cape Colony, 25 November 1880; d London, 25 October 1963).

For many years an actor and, in late life, a favourite screen character performer, big, bullet-headed Maltby wrote a number of successful postwar plays, beginning with the splendid *A Temporary Gentleman*, and innumerable film screenplays, as well as several West End musicals. The first of these, C B Cochran's production of *Maggie* with music by the French composer Marcel Lattès, proved only a semi-success (108 performances) in London before going on to productions in Australia and (as *Nelly*) in Paris, but the second, the musical comedy *For the Love of Mike* – originally written as a straight comedy, but rejected by Tom Walls for whom it had been intended – proved a hit for star Bobby Howes and producer Jack Waller (239 performances) and initiated a happy series of 'plays with tunes' at the Saville Theatre in the early 1930s. *Jack o' Diamonds*, a comedy piece featuring Richard Dolman as a phony South African millionaire, won good notices for its text, but only a fair run (126 performances), and *Meet Me Victoria*, a Lupino Lane vehicle constructed on a Maltby storyline continued the star's successful series at the Victoria Palace.

1906 **Fannikin** (w Kathleen Barry) 1 act Pier Pavilion, Hastings May
1919 **Maggie** (Marcel Lattès/w Fred Thompson) Oxford Theatre 22 October
1931 **For the Love of Mike** (Jack Waller, Joseph Tunbridge/

Clifford Grey, Sonny Miller/w Grey) Saville Theatre 8 October

1935 **Jack o' Diamonds** (Noel Gay/w Grey) Gaiety Theatre 25 February

1942 **Susie** revised *Jack o' Diamonds* New Theatre, Oxford 13 June

1944 **Meet Me Victoria** (Gay/Frank Eyton/w Lupino Lane, Lauri Wylie) Victoria Palace 6 March

1948 **The Lilac Domino** (*Der lila Domino*) revised English libretto and lyrics

Autobiography: *Ring Up the Curtain* (Hutchinson & Co, London, 1950)

MAME Musical in 2 acts by Jerome Lawrence and Robert E Lee based on the novel *Auntie Mame* by Patrick Dennis and the play by Lawrence and Lee. Lyrics and music by Jerry Herman. Winter Garden Theater, New York, 24 May 1966.

The adventures of Patrick Dennis's extraordinary Auntie Mame, as she has ridden (doubtless bareback) from the printed page to the stage and the screen, have become as much part of American and international folklore as those of Rip van Winkle and the inhabitants of *Uncle Tom's Cabin*. Auntie Mame's first appearance on the stage – in the person of comedienne Rosalind Russell – was in a play version of her story, written by Lawrence and Lee and produced at the Broadhurst Theater (*Auntie Mame* 31 October 1956) for a triumphant run of 639 performances, and Miss Russell transferred her amiable antics to the screen in 1958 before, in 1966, Mame was given music by the newly celebrated composer of *Hello, Dolly!*, Jerry Herman.

Mame Dennis (Angela Lansbury) is a gourmand for all the latest fads and fancies, no matter how unsuitable they might seem for a nice middle-class American lady of middle years. If she thought at all, she could possibly be called a free-thinker. When she is suddenly given charge of her young, orphaned nephew she fights off a hidebound trustee who wants him to have a strictly conventional upbringing, and drags the boy with her via martinis, kook religion and the sloughs of showbusiness to young manhood. When he shows signs of marrying a horsey nincompoop, in spite of (or because of?) his off-the-elbow upbringing, Mame scuttles the liaison and Patrick (Jerry Lanning) ends up with a nice no-nonsense wife and, before the evening is over, a young son who, it seems, is going to give the ageing Mame the chance to be a madcap surrogate mother all over again.

Herman's score obligatorily sported an equivalent to the title song of *Hello, Dolly!*, and, if the cakewalky serenade of the entire southlands of America, all dressed in hunting red, to the 'Mame' who has just brought the fox back alive, didn't quite equal its predecessor in popularity, it very nearly disproved the old saw about lightning never striking twice. But if 'Mame' was the most obviously big number in the lively score, there were other pieces in a different vein: Mame ruminating on whether she has done the best for her boy ('If He Walked into My Life'), Patrick's plain nanny, Agnes Gooch (Jane Connell), hilariously relating her finally achieved skydive from virginity (Gooch's Song), Patrick's comforting hymn to his aunt, 'You're My Best Girl', or Mame and best-friend Vera Charles (Beatrice Arthur) declaring themselves 'Bosom Buddies' with only the odd gallon of bitchery.

Mame won a fine Broadway success, staying at the Winter Garden Theater for 1,508 performances, and returned for a second showing in 1983 with Misses Lansbury and Connell repeating their original rôles alongside Byron Nease (Patrick) and Anne Francine (Vera) (24 July, 41 performances). If it did not follow *Hello, Dolly!* on to the world's stages, it nevertheless had a highly satisfying run at London's Theatre Royal, Drury Lane, where Harold Fielding's production, with Ginger Rogers starred and Ann Beach (Gooch), Margaret Courtenay (Vera) and Tony Adams (Patrick) in support, played through 443 performances, closing only when Miss Rogers left the show. *Mame* was subsequently seen in South Africa with Joan Brickhill and in Australia with Gaylea Byrne starred as Mame alongside Geoff Hiscock (Patrick) and Sheila Bradley (Vera) for four months in Melbourne and, later, a rather shorter season in Sydney (Her Majesty's Theatre, 8 February 1969). A Spanish-language version (ad Berta Maldonaldo, Jose Luis Ibañez), with Silvia Pinal featured as *Mame* was a very long-running success in Mexico, where the show survives to this day with a great vigour.

In 1974 the musical version of *Mame* was filmed, with Lucille Ball starred as Mame alongside Misses Arthur and Connell. Robert Preston played the wealthy bluegrass husband who falls off an alp on their honeymoon, leaving Mame a well-equipped widow, and was given an additional song for the occasion.

UK: Theatre Royal, Drury Lane 20 February 1969; Australia: Her Majesty's Theatre, Melbourne 25 May 1968; Film: Warner Brothers 1974

Recordings: Original cast (Columbia), Mexican cast (Orfeon), film soundtrack (Warner Brothers)

MA MIE ROSETTE Opérette in 3 acts by Jules Prével and Armand Liorat. Music by Paul Lacôme. Théâtre des Folies-Dramatiques, Paris, 4 February 1890.

Lacôme's *Ma mie Rosette* was a pretty, if apparently run-of-the-mill, opérette based on a little adventure of 'lou nouste Henrique', France's fictionally philandering monarch. It had only a limited run in France, yet it won itself an afterlife overseas and, ultimately, became a long-lived repertoire piece with the J C Williamson company in Australia.

Rosette (Juliette Nesville) the daughter of the rustic Moustajon (Bellucci) is all set to be happily wed to her Vincent (Gobin) when King Henri, with whom she had played as a child, passes by and sees what has become of his little playmate. To the annoyance of the official royal mistress, Corisandre (Mlle Vernon), the tasty little Rosette is lured up to the King's castle to deliver the milk and, before she knows where she is, she's decked out in jewels and silks and attending a court ball. Vincent is conveniently sent off to the wars. However, the determined Corisandre makes sure that Vincent is brought back on the scene and, although swords are drawn momentarily, the final act brings its happy, everyone-in-his-place, ending. The comedy was supplied by the royal valet, who, disguised as a Duc, cocks an eye dangerously at Rosette's aunt, a dame in active search of a fourth husband.

The *Ma mie Rosette* which appeared in Britain was a little different from that seen in Paris. The piece had been done over into a two-act English version by George Dance, which turned the whole kingly episode into nothing but

Rosette's dream. It had also had its score adapted by Ivan Caryll, who added eight or nine new musical numbers of his own – including two finales – to the 13 or 17 remaining pieces of Lacôme's score (the totals varied through the run). In a cast full of Savoy Theatre favourites, very young French soubrette Juliette Nesville came to Britain to repeat her Rosette alongside Eugene Oudin (Henry IV), Courtice Pounds (Vincent), Jessie Bond (Martha), Lawrance D'Orsay, Frank Wyatt, Cairns James, Scott Fishe and American soubrette Jennie McNulty (Corisandre). William Boosey and John Lart's production was well received ('a pretty, sentimental story slashed with streaks of genuine comedy') and the show looked set for a fine run, but after an optimistic shift of theatre it suddenly faded and came off after just three months. During those months, however, it started a controversy in London's papers over the botching of French opérettes for the English stage. Teddy Solomon came out against, but Lacôme and Serpette – apparently more interested in royalties than integrity – announced themselves in (English) print as pro!

The London version was the one which was played in Australia. Nellie Stewart was the first Australian Rosette, with Wallace Brownlow as Henri alongside Howard Vernon (Cognac), George Lauri (Bouillon), Florence Young (Corisandre) and Clara Thompson (Marthe), and the opérette established itself as a sufficient favourite to be revived periodically by the Williamson organization as late as 1925, when Gladys Moncrieff appeared as Rosette.

UK: Globe Theatre 17 November 1892; Australia: Princess Theatre, Melbourne, 16 June 1894

MAMOULIAN, Rouben (b Tiflis, Russia, 8 October 1897; d Los Angeles, 4 December 1987). Director of several highly successful Broadway musicals of the 1940s.

Having spent the early part of his career working in the straight theatre, in opera and comic opera, Mamoulian became in the mid-1920s stage director with the Theatre Guild, in which capacity he directed the original production of the play *Porgy* (1928). He moved on to a striking career as a director of films (*Applause, City Streets, Dr Jekyll and Mr Hyde*, the Jeanette MacDonald musical film *Love Me Tonight, The Gay Desperado*, Garbo's *Queen Christina* etc) before he returned to Broadway where he directed, amongst other pieces, the original production of George Gershwin's musical version of *Porgy, Porgy and Bess* (1935).

In 1943 Mamoulian was responsible for the staging of the Theatre Guild's venture into the musical theatre, Rodgers and Hammerstein's *Oklahoma!*, and following the enormous worldwide triumph of that piece, he directed, and occasionally co-wrote, a series of musicals, several of which were more than usually interesting if not always successful: a version of Somerset Maugham's *Rain* as *Sadie Thompson* (1944), another adaptation of a tragi-comic classic, Ferenc Molnár's *Liliom*, as the highly successful *Carousel* (1945), Harold Arlen's dazzlingly musicked *St Louis Woman* (1946), the musical version of *Cry, the Beloved Country* written by Maxwell Anderson and composed by Kurt Weill as *Lost in the Stars* (1949) and the Theatre Guild's musical made out of their own play *The Pursuit of Happiness, Arms and the Girl* (1950). After the original productions of *Oklahoma!* and *Carousel*, he directed a number of further productions of each piece, notably in Britain and Germany.

His later film credits included the screen version of *Silk Stockings* (1957).

1944 **Sadie Thompson** (Vernon Duke/w Howard Dietz) Alvin Theater 16 November
1950 **Arms and the Girl** (Morton Gould/Dorothy Fields/w Herbert Fields, D Fields) 46th Street Theater 2 February
Biography: Milne, T: *Mamoulian* (Thames & Hudson, London, 1969)

MAM'SELLE QUAT' SOUS Opérette in 4 acts by Antony Mars and Maurice Desvallières. Music by Robert Planquette. Théâtre de la Gaîté, Paris, 5 November 1897.

A period piece, set in the markets of Paris at the turn of the 19th century (1804), *Mam'selle Quat' sous* told of the fortunes and misfortunes of a little fishmonger, Michel Borniche (Paul Fugère), in a tale which had considerable resemblances with Duru's *Les Deux Noces de M Boisjoli*. Borniche is engaged to the market-girl Marion (Mlle Cocyte), but they have sworn not to wed until they have a 10,000 franc nest egg. Marion zealously puts aside every sou that they can earn – thus earning herself the nickname of 'Quat' sous' – but while she is doing so the local Don Juan, baker Anatole (Lucien Noël), is getting Borniche into trouble. Anatole chaffs Borniche over his faithful virginity, and the fishmonger gets his revenge by taking the baker's place at one of his spare blindish dates and making love to pretty coal-merchant's niece Thérèsette Rascalou (Mariette Sully). Alas, he gets caught by the girl's uncle and condemned to marriage. The marriage is scheduled for the same day as his wedding with Marion (for she has saved up her sous at last) and, indeed, at adjoining restaurants. The double engagement inevitably comes to light, and the doubly dumped and downcast Borniche goes off to join the army. In the last act he comes back covered in glory, accompanied by the entire old guard, to reclaim his Marion. Thérèsette pairs off with Anatole, whilst pastrycook Isidore (Émile Soums) and little Denise (Mlle Deberio) make up the third pair.

Planquette's winning music included a jolly 'Cris de Paris' for Fugère and a number in praise of 'Les Fillettes de chez nous', whilst the military element of the tale once more gave the composer the opportunity to dip his pen into the martial strains which had found him fame with 'La Sambre et Meuse' and which he had utilized repeatedly on the operettic stage in such military pieces as *Les Voltigeurs de la 32ème, La Cantinière* and *Captain Thérèse*. The military scenes also supplied the opportunity for a display of marching, a parade of veterans and other such spectacular accoutrements, well suited to the large stage of the Théâtre de la Gaîté.

Mam'selle Quat' sous had a fine run at the Gaîté, and, although it proved not to be of the stuff revivals are made of, it nevertheless got itself seen throughout central Europe.

Budapest's Magyar Színház mounted its version (ad Emil Makai, Ferenc Rajna) the next year, and Munich got the first German version in 1901 before the show moved on to be seen in Austria. It was mounted at the Theater an der Wien (ad A M Willner, Robert Pohl) with Girardi starred in Fugère's rôle of Borniche and Betti Seidl (Thérèsette), Dora Keplinger (Marion) and Oskar Sachs (Rascalou) supporting, but the production had been hurried unwillingly on to meet contractual dates when the theatre held a big new hit with *Bruder Straubinger* in its repertoire and Planquette's piece was simply shoved in to play from 25 May till 5 June, leaving time for one last *Straubinger* before the season ended. It was played a handful more times in the autumn, but *Bruder Straubinger* dominated the bills, and after 17 performances *Die beiden Don Juans* was dropped.

Hungary: Magyar Színház *A garasos kisasszony* 12 November 1898; Germany: Theater am Gärtnerplatz, Munich *Die Sparmamsell* 10 October 1901; Austria: Theater an der Wien *Die beiden Don Juans* 23 May 1903

MAM'ZELLE CARABIN Opérette in 3 acts by Fabrice Carré. Music by Émile Pessard. Théâtre des Bouffes-Parisiens, Paris, 3 November 1893.

A vaudevillesque piece of character and comic scene, *Mam'zelle Carabin* featured Juliette Simon-Girard as Olga, a would-be medical student who prides herself on having all the advantages of the two sexes, but who faints at the sight of a pricked finger. She nevertheless proves a fine psychologist as she helps her handsome fellow student and neighbour Ferdinand (Piccaluga) to study his books, renounce the tarty Nini (Mlle Bokaï) and, finally, to take her hand instead. In parallel to this plotlet ran the comic story of cousin Adolphe (Félix Huguenet), the eternal failed student, who exchanged lovers' tokens with his already mature mistress, Olga's aunt Caroline Quillette (Rosine Maurel), 16 years ago, and now wants to break it off. He can't, because the tokens were 100-franc pieces and he doesn't have that much money to give back. Charles Lamy played the idiotic Monsieur Chose, equipped with a dandy's lingo and a rare coin which Adolphe manages to swallow at the right moment to tie up the plot.

The comedy – which was substantial enough to have played without songs – was nevertheless illustrated by a well-regarded score of songs and ensembles, which did not hesitate to make comic references to such pieces of the operatic repertoire as *Manon* or *Samson et Dalila*, and which was devoted largely to the five principals. 'Carabin' arrived in a whirl ('Je touche au terme du voyage'), was christened with her nickname ('Va pour Carabin'), explained to Adolphe the failings of man ('L'Être idéal, parfait en somme') and, loosened up by an unaccustomed glass of wine, gave out in praise of love ('Pourquoi donc que toutes les femmes'), but she had her most amusing moment in a rondeau ('La belle amoureuse') in which she described to the unbelieving Ferdinand the way in which Nini would pick herself up a man. As she sang, the cocotte, seen on the split stage meeting up with Monsieur Chose, was going through exactly the routine that was being described. In other musical moments, Mme Quillette drew her coin from her ample bosom ('Pendant seize ans') only to find Adolphe unable to respond with his, and Nini tempted Ferdinand ('Faut pas m'la faire') whilst Carabin pushed him to work ('Rien ne vaut le devoir austère'). A quartet for three students and a little Bichette in the first act ('Grand Salomon') was also picked out for mention by the critics, who found Pessard's educated and well-orchestrated music decidedly to their taste.

Mam'zelle Carabin scored a fine success in Paris, running for more than 150 nights at the Bouffes-Parisiens in its first series, returning for a second visit in October 1895 and again, to the Théâtre de la Renaissance, in September

Plate 171. **Mam'zelle Nitouche:** *By the end of the evening's entertainment, music master Célestin (Jean-Marie Proslier) is aware that little Miss Innocence (Fabienne Guyon) is nothing of the kind.*

1900 with Rosalia Lambrecht in its title-rôle for another 50 Parisian nights. It was also seen in Germany (ad Richard Genée, Richard Pohl), played in Munich under the title of *Mamselle Cerevis*.

Germany: Theater am Gärtnerplatz, Munich *Mamselle Cerevis* 6 October 1894

MAM'ZELLE NITOUCHE Comédie-vaudeville in 3 acts by Henri Meilhac and Albert Millaud [and Ernest Blum]. Music by Hervé. Théâtre des Variétés, Paris, 26 January 1883.

Of the series of enormously successful vaudevilles produced by Eugène Bertrand at the Théâtre des Variétés between *Niniche* and *La Cosaque*, with Anna Judic for their overwhelming female star, *Mam'zelle Nitouche* was, in the long run, the most enduringly successful of all.

Convent music master Célestin (Baron) leads a double life. Outside teaching hours he composes opérettes, and one of his frothy little works is about to be presented at the local theatre. Unfortunately for him, his secret is discovered by his most innocent-looking but diabolically frisky pupil, Denise de Flavigny (Anna Judic). Without too much use of blackmail she manages to get first backstage, and finally on stage, at the theatre, falls for a handsome soldier (Cooper), gets arrested climbing out of a window and is carried off to the barracks. She ends up, disguised as a soldier, on top of a table singing a jolly song before she is discovered, and she finally sneaks poor Célestin back into the convent in the early hours, blinking not an eyelash as she delivers a plausible story for the benefit of the Mother Superior. She now announces she is going to become a nun rather than wed the unknown man her father has lined up for her, until she discovers that that man is none other than her handsome soldier. But Mam'zelle Nitouche, little Miss Innocence, is perfectly able to do a volte face without anyone thinking anything but the very sweetest thoughts about her. Only her husband and her music master know the truth.

Hervé's light comic score provided Judic with her obligatory encorable chanson, this time the Légende de la grosse caisse, a thumpingly comical piece of tuneful foolery performed in her military disguise, and with a comical singing-lesson scene in which she and her music master sneak off into a duo from his opérette only to be recalled quickly to a 'Gloria' when the Superior heaves to. When the fire-breathing Major (Christian) with whom Nitouche has tangled both at the theatre and at the barracks turns up at the convent and accuses her of being one of his soldiers, she sweetly sings to him 'Que je n'ai rien de masculin'. Her soldier had a musical moment romancing over 'Un mariage de raison', and there was a stand-up comedy scene and number for a gormless soldier called Loriot (Léonce) at the opening of the third act ('Je suis de Saint-Étienne, Loire') but, if there was comedy for everyone, the music was mainly for Judic in a piece which was a genuine musical comedy in the straightforward meaning of the two words.

Mam'zelle Nitouche was an instant hit. It played through the whole spring and returned immediately after the summer recess, running on to its 212th performance before Judic set off on her international travels, and the theatre hastened to mount a non-Judic piece that Bertrand didn't want to lose from his repertoire. When her next year's piece, *La Cosaque*, proved shorter-lived than hoped, *Mam'zelle Nitouche* was promptly brought back, but after 19 performances Judic's husband died, and the run had to be ended. In the years that followed, Judic played *Mam'zelle Nitouche* all around the world, but Paris was given the most opportunities to see her portrayal of the archetypical Miss Innocence, for she reprised the rôle there in 1885, in 1888 and again as late as 1894. Mathilde Auguez (1892), Jeanne Pierny (1898), Juliette Simon-Girard (1901), Angèle Gril (1913–14), Mary Malbos (1921, 1923), Andrée Alvar (1924), Germaine Roger (1945, 1960) and Madeleine Vernon (1954) have been amongst those who have followed, and if some of these ladies were, like Judic, just a decade or two too old to play a perky schoolgirl, such an accusation cannot be made about Paris's 1984 Nitouche, Fabienne Guyon, who starred opposite Jean-Marie Proslier at the Bouffes-Parisiens in the most recent Paris production.

Both in America and in Britain, the piece was first seen in English. The American actress Lotta, a specialist in little-girl rôles though by then 37, latched on to *Nitouche* as a vehicle for herself and she starred as Denise with Frank Wyatt and Frederic Darrell supporting her in London, and C H Bradshaw and Darrell in New York. London gave her seven weeks, but Broadway sent her on her way in three. Both cities later had a chance to see the genuine article when Judic played her repertoire at the Gaiety Theatre, London (a matter of weeks after Lotta had closed) and at Wallack's Theater in New York. London saw a second season of the show in English when another American actress, May Yohé, gave her Nitouche at the Trafalgar Square Theatre in 1893 (6 May) for some of the run of 104 performances, and at the Court Theatre in 1896 (1 June) in a new and 'improved' version boasting two extra numbers by Carl Kiefert and one by Ivan Caryll. Polyglot New York had a second, post-touring season of Lotta, as well as a piece called *Papa's Wife* in which Anna Held used bits of both *Nitouche* and *La Femme à papa* to make up one show and, in 1906, a German version at the Irving Place Theater with Lina Abarbanell and Edmund Loewe starred.

That German-language version had been very slow to

get going. Although Vienna, Berlin, Hamburg and other centres had welcomed Judic's French seasons, it was apparently not until 1890 when the Hungarian star Ilka Pálmay came to the Theater an der Wien that Richard Genée's German adaptation of the show was first mounted. Pálmay was paired with Girardi as a perfect Célestin, Josef Joseffy was Fernand, Carl Lindau played Loriot and Sebastian Stelzer the roaring major. Over the next 12 years the piece resurfaced every year for further performances in the repertoire. Therese Biedermann and Annie Dirkens took turns at the star rôle, Juliette Méaly visited from France with her version, and Lina Abarbanell and Edmund Loewe gave theirs before the piece was finally taken from the repertoire after 122 performances. In the meanwhile it had also been played at the Theater in der Josefstadt – in Czech (1893). In 1910 Girardi took up his rôle again and paired with Gerda Walde and then Julie Kopácsi-Karczag, at the Raimundtheater, whilst in 1914 Mimi Marlow and Fritz Werner played the piece at the Johann Strauss-Theater where it was repeated by Ernst Tautenhayn and Luise Kartousch in 1926 (18 February).

In Germany, too, the Genée version was popular, and, following its introduction *Mam'zelle Nitouche* won regular revivals up until 1931 before the piece underwent several of the modern reorganizations dear to that country. One of these was played in 1954 at Berlin's Theater im Kurfürstendamm (ad Alexander Steinbrecher, Hans Weigel 25 February).

Pálmay, who introduced Nitouche to Vienna also introduced her to Budapest, at the Népszinház (ad Lajos Evva, Viktor Rákosi) with Béla Pusztai (Célestin) and Imre Szirmai (Fernand) in the other lead rôles. As elsewhere, the show was regularly seen thereafter, reaching its 100th performance in 1901, being revived at the Népopera in 1915 (28 February) and at the Városi Színház in 1927 (6 January) with Irén Biller, at the Fővárosi Operettszinház in 1928 and again in a new adaptation in 1959, at the Magyar Színház in 1930 and at the Vigszinház in 1946, as it confirmed itself as a permanent part of the opérette repertoire.

Australia was particularly slow to pick up on *Mam'zelle Nitouche*, but the piece duly arrived there in 1894, mounted at the Sydney Lyceum with Nellie Stewart as Nitouche, George Lauri as Célestin and Wallace Brownlow as Champlâtreux. The rôle which had been good enough for Judic was apparently not, however, good enough for Miss Stewart: it seems that she ousted La Légende de la grosse caisse, wrote herself a Drum Song, had it set by musical director, Leon Caron, and a local journal staunchly reported that it was 'the biggest hit' of the show. Miss Stewart gave her *Nitouche* in Sydney and in Melbourne (Princess Theatre, 10 November 1894) without it becoming a lasting feature of the Australian repertoire.

Mam'zelle Nitouche remains a feature of the European repertoire to the present day although, like virtually all other such comedy-based pieces, it has faded from the spectacle-orientated English-language stage.

The show has also been twice filmed in France, initially in 1931 with Janie Marèse as Nitouche and Raimu in the rôle of Célestin, and on the second occasion with Pier Angeli in the title-rôle and Fernandel starred as the music master.

UK: Opera Comique 12 May 1884, Gaiety Theatre (Fr) 13 June 1884; USA: Daly's Theater (Eng) 15 September 1884,

Wallack's Theater (Fr) 1885; Hungary: Népszinház *Nebantsvirág* 14 October 1887; Austria: Theater an der Wien 19 April 1890; Australia: Lyceum, Sydney 11 August 1894; Films: Paramount 1931; 1953

Recordings: complete (Decca), selections (EMI, Decca)

MANDEL, Frank (b San Francisco, 31 May 1884; d Hollywood, 20 April 1958). Broadway producer and writer who was behind some of the most successful musicals of the 1920s American stage.

Mandel attended the University of California and Hastings Law School before going east and finding his first employment as a journalist whilst he endeavoured to establish himself as a playwright. He made his first mark in the theatre when he collaborated with Helen Craft on an adaptation of Ludwig Fulda's play *Jugendfreude* under the title *Our Wives* (1912), and he made his début in the musical theatre as the librettist for John Cort's Chicago and New York production of *Miss Princess* (1912), a piece set to songs by the indefatigable and rarely successful Alexander and Will Johnstone.

Mandel followed up with several more plays, but, although Victor Herbert and Henry Blossom turned his *Our Wives* into *The Only Girl* (39th Street Theater, 1914) with some success, he did not venture back into the musical world for another seven years. When he did, he then simply deluged the musical stage with texts. After a good beginning with a slightly musical play called *My Lady Friends*, which put up a fine 228 performances at the Globe Theater with Clifton Crawford (with his own song) in its star rôle, Broadway saw no fewer than four musicals to which Mandel had contributed within nine months. The first, *Look Who's Here*, written with Edward Paulton and composer Silvio Hein for Spiegels Productions, visited the metropolis only briefly prior to going on the road where its stars, Cecil Lean and Cleo Mayfield, had a faithful public, but the second and third, both produced by Arthur Hammerstein, teamed Mandel with a pair of writing partners in Otto Harbach and Oscar Hammerstein II who were of a different class to the hacking Paulton. *Tickle Me* (it was not an invitation, but the name of a ship) was a piece of film-land foolery evolved as a vehicle for vaudeville favourite Frank Tinney, which its star's antics helped hold up for 207 performances, whilst *Jimmie*, which leaned on the old plot of putting a ringer in for a lost heiress, did rather less well (71 performances).

In between, however, Harbach and Mandel had found a genuine hit, one which would outdo even *My Lady Friends*, in a venture with producer George M Cohan. Their piece, which had started out on the road as *The House That Jack Built* even before *Tickle Me* had begun, cleaned up on the road, and by the time it came to town as *Mary*, their pretty if barely original little tale of a poor girl who weds a rich boy after two acts of minor difficulties was, no small thanks to the fact that the writers had allied themselves with a first-class composer in Louis Hirsch, already a sure-fire hit.

A second innocently Cinderellary show with the same team, *The O'Brien Girl*, also did well at home (164 performances) and in export; a vehicle for Nora Bayes as *Queen of Hearts* rather less (39 performances); but a piece called *Paradise Alley* which had Mandel's name on the credits in Rhode Island, Boston and Philadelphia in 1922,

no longer did so by the time the show reached Broadway in 1924. By that time, however, Mandel was pretty much in Paradise Alley himself, for he had well and truly hit pay dirt in the form of one of those outsized hits that come along in only a few folk's lifetimes. Harry Frazee, who had co-produced his play *My Lady Friends*, brought Mandel in to work on the musical version of that piece, and the resulting *No, No, Nanette* promptly became the hit of the era.

Before *No, No, Nanette* reached Broadway, Mandel had teamed up with a new writing partner. Lawrence Schwab, looking for a collaborator to work with on his new show, asked publishers Harms for a suggestion. They put forward Mandel and the two collaborated for the first time on the smart-talking modern text for the George Gershwin musical *Sweet Little Devil*. After that show's 120-performance Broadway run, the pair formed a producing partnership which they launched in 1925 with a play, *The Firebrand*, and with their own musical version of Clyde Fitch's play *Captain Jinks of the Horse Marines*. *Captain Jinks* was a big hit in Philadelphia, but Lewis Gensler and Stephen Jones's score didn't throw up any popular songs and the 167 performances the show eventually played on Broadway did not quite come up to the hopes that had been aroused on the road.

Mandel and Schwab were on the right tracks, however, and they hit the bull's-eye with their next production. *Lady Fair* didn't cause the stir pre-Broadway that *Captain Jinks* had done, but when it reached town, now retitled *The Desert Song*, it proved another *Nanette*-sized hit for Mandel, this time as both author and producer. The team followed their biggest hit with the production of another memorable musical in which Mandel had again some kind of hand in the writing (though quite what and how much is not sure) in *The New Moon*, but the producers also mounted several shows in which neither Mandel nor Schwab were involved authorially.

The first two were from the De Sylva, Brown and Henderson team, and both were hits: the favourite college musical of the day, *Good News* and the golfing piece *Follow Thru*. The next was Rodgers and Hart's filmland piece *America's Sweetheart*, which did well enough, but the up-to-now apparently charmed partners hit their first dud when they mounted a small-scale Richard Whiting musical, written to a text by Schwab and Hammerstein and entitled *Free for All*. After the opening on Broadway Mandel and Schwab offered to sell out the show to the cast for the weekly break-even figure of $5,100, but the cast declined and *Free for All* closed at the end of the week. Returning to the area of romantic operetta, Mandel co-wrote and co-produced *Always Young* ('it looks like Schwab and Mandel have a worthy successor to *The New Moon* ...') which became *East Wind* and flopped in 23 performances in New York.

Following this pair of failures Schwab and Mandel dissolved their association, and Mandel ventured only once more on to the Broadway musical stage, in 1935, when he adapted *The Happy Alienist*, a ludicrously old-fashioned romantic novel tricked out with a fashionable tinge of psychoanalysis, to Romberg's music as *May Wine*. The piece ran for a respectable 213 performances, but it was not in any way comparable with *The Desert Song* and *The New Moon*.

Mandel subsequently spent some time in 1937–8 as a film director with Warner Brothers, but he finally withdrew from the arena of show business in 1942 and went into retirement.

1912 **Miss Princess** (Alexander Johnstone/Will B Johnstone) Park Theater 23 December
1920 **Look Who's Here** (Silvio Hein/Edward Paulton) 44th Street Theater 2 March
1920 **Tickle Me** (Herbert Stothart/w Otto Harbach, Oscar Hammerstein II) Selwyn Theater 17 August
1920 **Mary** (Louis Hirsch/w Harbach) Knickerbocker Theater 18 October
1920 **Jimmie** (Stothart/w Harbach, Hammerstein) Apollo Theater 17 November
1921 **The O'Brien Girl** (Hirsch/w Harbach) Liberty Theater 3 October
1922 **Paradise Alley** (Harry Archer/Howard Johnson/Carle Carlton, Hale Francisco) Providence, RI, 18 September
1922 **Queen of Hearts** (Lewis E Gensler/w Oscar Hammerstein II) Cohan Theater 10 October
1923 **No, No, Nanette** (Vincent Youmans/Harbach, Irving Caesar/w Harbach) Garrick Theater, Detroit 23 April; Globe Theatre, New York, 16 September 1925
1924 **Sweet Little Devil** (George Gershwin/w Lawrence Schwab) Astor Theater 21 January
1925 **Captain Jinks** (Gensler, Stephen Jones/B G De Sylva/w Schwab) Martin Beck Theater 8 September
1926 **The Desert Song** (Sigmund Romberg/w Hammerstein, Harbach) Casino Theater 30 November
1928 **The New Moon** (Romberg/Hammerstein/w Hammerstein, Schwab) Imperial Theater 18 November
1931 **East Wind** (Romberg/w Hammerstein) Manhattan Theater 27 October
1935 **May Wine** (Romberg/Hammerstein) St James Theater 5 December

MANHATTAN MARY Musical comedy in 2 acts by William K Wells and George White. Music and lyrics by B G De Sylva, Lew Brown and Ray Henderson. Apollo Theater, New York, 26 September 1927.

When the mum (Dorothy Walters) of Manhattan Mary loses all her money, the show's comic helps the girl to get a job in the *George White Scandals* and set things aright. If this was a little different from the fate of most contemporary musical comedy heroines, who almost invariable ended up a the star of the *Ziegfeld Follies*, this was because *Manhattan Mary* was produced by George White, on the very stage which housed the *Scandals*. Manhattan Mary was Ona Munson, the comic in question was Ed Wynn and George White's contribution to the production included appearing in the show as himself. This was not as unlikely as it might have been in the case of some producers, as White had been a top-class international tap-dancing act before becoming a producer, and in the final act he showed that his talents were still intact. The McCarthy Sisters, who simply appeared as the McCarthy Sisters, also got into the musical action.

De Sylva, Brown and Henderson, whose *Good News* had opened with great success just three weeks earlier, supplied 'My Bluebird's Home Again', 'Just a Cozy Hideaway', 'Broadway', 'Manhattan Mary', 'I'd Like You to Love Me' and 'It Won't Be Long Now' without turning out anything to challenge the other show's 'Varsity Drag' or 'The Best Things in Life Are Free', but it didn't really matter. The priorities of *Manhattan Mary* were evident in the billing it proposed to the public: George White (70%)

presents Ed Wynn (200%) in *Manhattan Mary* (100%). There were also 100 George White Beauties, the George White Ballet, 24 Hudson Dusters, 17 scenes and curtains and costumes by Max Weldy from designs by Erté. Wynn lisped his way endearingly through his rôle without too much apparent regard for what was going on around him, and did it for 264 revusical performances.

MANINA Operette in 3 acts by Alexander Lix. Lyrics by Hans Adler. Music by Nico Dostal. Admiralspalast, Berlin, 28 November 1942.

Produced by Heinz Hentschke in wartime Berlin, *Manina* profited from a good-old-days libretto treating of turn-of-the-century Ruritanian royal romance and from a lavish physical production to run for a full season at Berlin's Admiralspalast. Lix's book centred on the lives of King Jalomir of Catatea (who is never seen) and Hella von Lichtenau (Carla Spletter), who are condemned to be royally wed. He carries on with a cabaret singer (Elvira Erdmann) and she ends up in bed with the poet Mario Zantis (Julius Katona), who the next day writes a satirical poem about the king and gets himself arrested and banished. Hella eventually becomes Queen when Jalomir abdicates, but she has to abdicate herself before she can, at last, officially have her Mario. The Manina of the title was another who never appeared: she was the ideal heroine of Mario's epic work.

Dostal's rather oddly coloured score aspired towards the big-sing Operette in the music for its principal lovers, notably in their ever-rising duet 'Niemand weiss, warum auf einmal süss und heiss', although, in contrast, Mario explained 'Ich such' in jeder Frau Manina' (I look for Manina in every woman) to a tango rhythm, and the sounds of film-land crept in frequently. A pair of soubrets, Hella's cousin Carla (Herta Mayen) and good friend Ronni (Karl Heigl) and a duo of comical elders (former prima donna Cordy Millowitsch and Kurt Seifert) provided the lighter moments in a 1940s version of traditional style.

Manina was staged in Vienna after the War, with Steffi Schafel and Rudolf Reimer in the romantic rôles and Fritz Imhoff as the comical Obersthofmarschall, through a run of five months, and it was subsequently seen in Norway, Switzerland and, in a French translation, in Belgium.

Austria: Raimundtheater 8 September 1947
Recording: selection (part-set) (Eurodisc)

MANKOWITZ, Wolf (b London, 7 November 1924). Librettist to the best of the British theatre's attempts at a 'Soho' musical in the 1950s.

The author of such East End of London novels as *Make Me an Offer* and *A Kid for Two Farthings*, Mankowitz had a first stage and film success with the play *The Bespoke Overcoat* (1953) and entered the musical theatre five years later when he expanded his newspaper novella, a piece transparently based on the career of popular cockney singer Tommy Steele, into a musical play under the title *Expresso Bongo*. *Expresso Bongo* and its successor, *Make Me an Offer* (based on Mankowitz's earlier book), both produced by Oscar Lewenstein, led the field in the trend towards the Soho, low-life musicals of the London 1950s, but they had about them a quality and a gritty taste of unpretentious realism which those that tried to follow them – including a piece on which Mankowitz later joined Lewenstein as co-producer, *The Lily White Boys* (1960) – almost inevitably failed to repeat.

Belle, an attempt to adapt the tale of the murderer Crippen into a musical told in music-hall terms, did not catch on, and Mankowitz then abandoned the toughly realistic style of his earliest pieces to mould a jolly musical entertainment out of Dickens's *The Pickwick Papers* as a vehicle for tenor comedian Harry Secombe. *Pickwick* had a fine London career and something of an afterlife. Mankowitz moved further away from the adult world of his earliest works in the 1960s with his last contributions to the musical theatre, two pieces produced to diminishing success: an adaptation of the successful teeny-fumbling novel *Passion Flower Hotel*, followed by an advertisedly 'bawdy' retelling of the Jack Sheppard tale, *Stand and Deliver*.

1958 **Expresso Bongo** (David Heneker, Monty Norman/Heneker, Norman, Julian More/w More) Saville Theatre 23 April
1959 **Make Me an Offer** (Heneker, Norman) New Theatre 16 December
1961 **Belle, or The Ballad of Doctor Crippen** (Norman/Beverley Cross ad) Strand Theatre 4 May
1963 **Pickwick** (Cyril Ornadel/Leslie Bricusse) Saville Theatre 4 July
1965 **Passion Flower Hotel** (John Barry/Trevor Peacock) Prince of Wales Theatre 24 August
1972 **Stand and Deliver** (Norman) Royal Lyceum, Edinburgh, 20 September; Roundhouse, 24 October

MANNEQUINS Féerie-opérette in 3 acts by Jacques Bousquet and Henri Falk. Music by Joseph Szulc. Théâtre des Capucines, Paris, 30 October 1925.

A happily sort-of-satirical small-scale piece, with a cast of 15, no chorus and accompanied just by composer Joseph Szulc at the piano, *Mannequins* was a shoestring hit at the little Théâtre des Capucines in 1925.

Shopboy Alfred (Louvigny) is more at home mooning over the pretty dummies in the shop's windows than in chatting up the real, live flowergirl Micheline (Edmée Favart). Then one night the mannequins all come to life. Alfred finds his attempts to win the glamorous Fleur de Pêcher (also Edmée Favart) impeded by the elegant Vicomte (Hiéronimus) and Marquis (Jean Périer) who are, each in turn, placed next to the lady mannequin as the chief window-dresser rearranges his display, and his hopes are finally ended by the arrival of a new dummy: the American millionaire. When Alfred wakes up, he realizes that Micheline is better value than a doll.

Christiane Dor as Rose, the Marquis's maid turned *poule de luxe*, scored the song success of the evening with the saucy 'Si ça n'est qu' ça' in a score which, although it was of the lightest kind, was, nevertheless, not undemanding. A second-act finale with the whole cast running up the stave in parallel semi-quavers (admittedly to an ah-ah lyric) was a more substantial piece of writing, for all its piano-only (and no conductor!) accompaniment, than much contemporary musical-comedy music.

The show was toured in France, produced at Budapest's Magyar Szinház (ad Zsolt Harsányi, István Zágon), announced for London by C B Cochran, in an adaptation by Eddie Knoblock, and purchased by E Ray Goetz for America. It was apparently, however, not produced in either English-language case. In 1948 a German-language piece (ad H Adler) taken from a work by Bousquet, Falk and Szulc turned up at Vienna's Theater in der Josefstadt under the title *Es schlägt 12, Herr Doktor* where it ran for 56 consecutive nights. Since the trio wrote nothing else together, this would seem to have been a version of *Mannequins*.

Hungary: Magyar Színház *Párizsi kirakat* 9 April 1926; Austria: Theater in der Josefstadt *Es schlägt 12, Herr Doktor* 15 November 1948

DER MANN MIT DEN DREI FRAUEN Operette in 3 acts by Julius Bauer. Music by Franz Lehár. Theater an der Wien, Vienna, 21 January 1908.

Lehár's first new full-scale Operette following the triumph of *Die lustige Witwe* moved far away from both the subject matter and the style of his big hit. Set, like the earlier piece, in the present time, it remained far from the ambassadorial circles of Paris in its tale of a Viennese rep for an international travel company. Hans Zipler (Rudolf Christians), in spite of having a happy home life with his wife (Mizzi Günther), acquires additional ladies in the branch-office cities of London (Mizzi Gribl) and Paris (Luise Kartousch). Generally reckoned a disappointment, the show lasted only 82 performances at the Theater an der Wien, and rendered up no re-usable parts to a composer who very often recycled his 'lost' music. It was still, however, picked up by overseas managements anxious for the latest Lehár show. In Budapest (ad Adolf Mérei) it was played a respectable 35 times. On Broadway (ad Paul Potter, Harold Atteridge, Agnes Bangs Morgan), where its score was dotted with interpolations including a ditty called 'Rosie' composed by *Chu Chin Chow*'s composer Frederic Norton, the Shuberts' production starred Cecil Lean (Hans) with Alice Yorke (Lori), Cleo Mayfield (Alice), Charlotte Greenwood (Sidonie) and Dolly Castles (Olivia) and lasted 52 performances.

Germany: Neues Operettenhaus 18 March 1908; Hungary: Népszinház-Vigopera *Három feleség* 31 March 1908; USA: Weber and Fields Theater *The Man with Three Wives* 23 January 1913

MANNSCHAFT AN BORD Komische Oper in 1 act by J L Harisch. Music by Giovanni von Zaytz ('mit freier Benützung der Englisch bootman songs'). Carltheater, Vienna, 15 December 1863.

Zaytz was, along with C F Conradin, Johann Baptist Klerr and Franz von Suppé, amongst the first composers of the German-language stage to follow the Offenbach-inspired fashion for short Operetten, and his little *Mannschaft an Bord* (crew on board) followed and joined Suppé's *Das Pensionat*, *Zehn Mädchen und kein Mann* and *Flotte Bursche* and Conradin's *Flodoardo Wuprahall* as one of the early Viennese successes in the genre. The little semi-nautical tale was set in a French harbour where an English frigate takes refuge. During the ship's stay, the old local cargo-man Piffard (Karl Treumann) helps one of the sailors, Max (Anna Grobecker), to win his steersman's ticket and, thus, the consent of the schoolmater, Profond (Grois), for the boy to wed his daughter, Emma (Frln Fischer). Wilhelm Knaack featured as the dentist Svermazet and Fr Raab was Frau Bibiana Piffard alongside a half-dozen shapely-legged chorus 'sailors'. The text was accompanied by a brightly catchy score, an effective part of which was made up of arrangements of English sea-shanties (endearingly billed as 'bootman-songs').

After its original, successful production *Mannschaft an Bord* remained some years in the Carltheater repertoire (50th performance, 16 February 1867), was picked up by the 'Zur neue Welt' at Hietzing and other minor theatres, and returned to the Carltheater in 1873 (10 June) with Treumann (Piffard), Karl Blasel (Jean), Therese Schäfer (Bibiana) and Adolf Link (Max) in the cast to play 25 times over the next four seasons. It was played at Ronacher in 1883, at the Jantschtheater in 1902, at Budapest's Royal Orfeum in 1903 (*Legényseg a födelzeten*) and at the Johann Strauss-Theater in 1915, surviving, thus, more strongly than any but Suppé's most popular pieces as a representative of its period.

USA: Germania Theater 30 November 1873; Hungary: Budai Színkör (Ger) 27 April 1867 and *Matrózok a fedélzeten* (*Matrózok a kikotoban*) 17 May 1867

MANNSTÄDT, Wilhelm (b Bielefeld, 29 May 1837; d Steglitz, 13 September 1904).

A polytalented artist – painter, composer, poet, actor and theatrical conductor, notably at Berlin's Woltersdorff Theater – Mannstädt's most significant contribution was as an author to the musical-comedy stage. He actually made his début in the musical theatre as a composer, supplying the songs for other folk's and then for his own pieces, but he soon found his niche as a librettist and over nearly 30 years' activity in the German theatre he wrote or co-wrote the texts of some 60 theatrical works of all kinds, the most and the best being Possen for the Berlin and Vienna stages. Amongst these, the Centraltheater Posse *Eine tolle Nacht* – the inspiration for George Edwardes's Gaiety musical *The Circus Girl* – was the most generally successful, whilst of the handful of Operetten to which he subscribed Czibulka's *Der Glücksritter*, played in Austria, Germany and in America (*The May Queen*), was the most widely seen.

1868 **Ein moderner Hexenmeister** (Fritz Mai) 1 act Theater in der Josefstadt, Vienna 6 September

1870 **Chor de mille fleurs** (Rudolf Hahn) 1 act Woltersdorff Theater

1875 **Luftschlösser** (Adolf Mohr/w A Weller) Woltersdorff Theater; Theater an der Wien, Vienna 11 July 1876 w music by Richard Genée

1875 **Eine resolute Frau** (Mohr/w Weller) Woltersdorff Theater

1876 **In harter Lehre** (Schramm, Michaelis/w Weller)

1877 **Die Tochter des Hollenfürsten** (w Henrik Delin/w Weller) Theater in der Josefstadt, Vienna 24 November

1878 **Schusserl, der Heiratsvermittler** (aka *Das Kind der Natur*) (w Delin/w Eduard Dorn) Theater in der Josefstadt, Vienna 2 March

1879 **Wildröschen** (Johann Brandl/w Weller) Carltheater, Vienna 4 July

1880 **Im Strudel** (Gustave Steffens/w Heinrich Sealsieb)

1881 **Unser Otto** (Steffens) Thalia-Theater

1882 **Eine neue Welt** (Steffens) Friedrich-Wilhelmstädtisches Theater

1882 **Der tolle Wenzel** (Steffens) Friedrich-Wilhelmstädtisches Theater

1883 **Die schöne Ungarin** (Steffens) Friedrich-Wilhelmstädtisches Theater

1883 **Ein Naturkind** (Karl Kleiber/w C B) Fürsttheater, Vienna 15 September

1884 **Die Millionenbraut von Sarajewo** (Kleiber/w Weller ad Bruno Zappert) Fürsttheater, Vienna 21 May

1885 **Die beiden Wenzel** (Paul Mestrozzi/w Carl Lindau) Theater in der Josefstadt, Vienna 26 September

1885 **Der Walzerkönig** (Brandl/w Karl Costa, Bruno Zappert) Carltheater, Vienna 9 October

1886 **Humbug, der Geist des Schwindels** (Kleiber/w Lindau) Theater in der Josefstadt, Vienna 11 September

1886 **Der Stabstrompeter** (Steffens/w Weller) Centraltheater; Theater in der Josefstadt, Vienna 2 October

1887 **Rikiki** (Josef Hellmesberger/w Genée) Carltheater, Vienna 28 September

1887 **Das Glücksritter** (Alfons Czibulka/w Genée, Zappert) Carltheater, Vienna 22 December

1887 **Der Spottvögel** (Steffens) Centraltheater

1887 **Der Waldteufel** (Steffens) Centraltheater

1887 **Höhere Töchter** (Steffens) Centraltheater 3 September

1887 **Die wilde Katze** (Steffens/w Weller) Centraltheater

1887 **Peter Zapfel** (Kleiber/ad Lindau, Antony) Theater in der Josefstadt, Vienna 17 December

1888 **Der Grasteufel** (Kleiber/w Lindau) Theater in der Josefstadt, Vienna 3 April

1891 **Der Tanzteufel** (Steffens/w Eduard Jacobson) Adolf-Ernst Theater 25 December

1892 **Berliner Pflaster** (Ludwig Gothov-Grüneke) Alexanderplatz Theater January

1892 **Modernes Babylon** (Steffens/w E Jacobson) Adolf-Ernst Theater 25 December

1893 **Monsieur Hannibal** (Alfons Czibulka/w Karl Dreher) Theater im Gärtnerplatz, Munich 5 September

1893 **Goldlotte** (Steffens/w E Jacobson) Adolf-Ernst Theater 4 April

1895 **Unsere Rentiers** (Einödshofer/w Julius Freund) Centraltheater 16 February

1895 **Frau Lohengrin** (Steffens/G Görss/w E Jacobson) Adolf-Ernst Theater 21 December

1895 **Eine tolle Nacht** (Einödshofer/w Freund) Centraltheater 4 September

1896 **König Chilperich** (*Chilpéric*) German version w E Jacobson (Carltheater)

1896 **Eine wilde Sache** (Einödshofer/w Julius Freund) Centraltheater 20 September

1897 **Ein fideler Abend** (Einödshofer/w Freund) Centraltheater 7 February

1897 **Berliner Fahrten** (Einödshofer/w Freund) Centraltheater 4 September

1897 **Metella** (*Le Capitole*) German version (Alexanderplatz Theater)

1898 **Die Tugendfalle** (Einödshofer/w Freund) Centraltheater 20 January

1898 **Sterzl in Berlin** (Einödshofer/w Freund) Theater an der Wien, Vienna 2 April

1902 **Der silberne Pantoffel** (*The Silver Slipper*) German version (Neues Königliches Opernhaus)

MAN OF LA MANCHA Musical play by Dale Wasserman based on his television play *I, Don Quixote* and on Miguel de Cervantes y Saavedra's *Don Quixote*. Lyrics by Joe Darion. Music by Mitch Leigh. Goodspeed Opera House, Connecticut, 28 June 1965; ANTA Washington Square Theater, New York, 22 November 1965.

A version of the *Don Quixote* tale, developed from a television play by author Wasserman, *Man of La Mancha* was laid out in a manner often used by a director of a piece of dubious value to take the curse off his material. It was framed, or made into a play-within-a-play, thus putting the main story of the evening and its characters at one step's remove from any need to run too close to a convincing reality. The technique was one that could prove powerful when used on fine material, as Peter Brook's previous year's production of the *Marat/Sade* had proven, and in the case of *Man of La Mancha*, where the material was anything but of dubious value, it worked most effectively once again. Wasserman's dramatically effective reduction of the Quixote story made up into a strongly projected play-within-a-play, equipped with a score which produced one hit song from amongst a set of vigorously written numbers and ensembles.

Cervantes (Richard Kiley) and his servant (Irving Jacobson) act out the story of the Knight of the woeful countenance as a sort of command performance before their fellow prisoners whilst waiting their turn to be called before the Inquisition. Cervantes impersonates the Don and the servant plays his servant Sancho Panza in their depiction of the adventures of the dream-a-day old Knight, living out his fine notions of the age of chivalry whilst struggling to keep clear of the clutches of the members of his greedily expectant family who are anxious to have him declared insane. Quixote and Sancho pass together by the famous encounter with the giant-cum-windmill, and arrive at an inn where Quixote pays homage to the vulgar wench Aldonza (Joan Diener) as his fair lady Dulcinea. His other-worldly idealism earns him only buffetings and robbings, and when Aldonza tries to follows his tenets of charity, chivalry and life led in keeping with a code of generosity, she too is made to suffer. But Quixote is undeterred, until he faces up to the great Enchanter. The Enchanter's weapon against Quixote is a mirror: the old man is forced to look at reality, at himself as he really is, and the great dream is chased away. The Enchanter is, of course, no Enchanter, but his son-in-law come to take him home. But the hope of a better world is never utterly extinguished. As Quixote lies dying, Sancho and Aldonza, the willing and the unwilling believers, come to him. With them at his side, the old man can go back into his dream for the last minutes of his life. Amongst the supporting cast, Ray Middleton (the original Frank Butler of *Annie Get Your Gun*) appeared as the Innkeeper and Robert Rounseville, the creator of Bernstein's Candide, was the family's hypocritical Padre.

Quixote's creed, The Quest, otherwise known as 'The Impossible Dream', a crazily philosophizing piece with a strong flavour of 1960s idealism about it, was the song success of the show, but amongst the rest of the score a lusty title song for the Knight, some gently humorous pieces for Sancho ('I Like Him', 'A Little Gossip'), Quixote's gentle dream of 'Dulcinea' and a particularly accurate, nagging trio for the family, 'I'm Only Thinking of Him', all contributed to the success of the show.

Albert Selden and Hal James's production of *Man of La Mancha* was a major hit. In a season which included *Sweet Charity* and *Mame* amongst its products, it virtually swept the board at the year's Tony Awards, taking prizes for best musical, score, libretto, Albert Marre's direction and for Kiley's thrilling, rich-voiced performance in its title-rôle, as it settled in at the ANTA Washington Square Theater for what would be one of the longest runs in Broadway history. By the time it closed, after 2,328 performances, *Man of La Mancha* had passed all but *Fiddler on the Roof, Hello, Dolly!* and *My Fair Lady* in Broadway longevity, and

like those three exceptional pieces it had spread itself triumphantly to all corners of the globe.

The first American touring company, with Broadway take-over José Ferrer starring as Quixote, went out ten months into the Broadway run, and the first foreign mounting appeared a year later, when an Australian production with Charles West and Sadler's Wells and Covent Garden soprano Suzanne Steele was mounted in Melbourne. Four months there were followed by four more in Sydney (Her Majesty's Theatre, February 1968), a tour through New Zealand, two repeat seasons at Melbourne's Comedy Theatre and one at Sydney's Theatre Royal (1 April 1971) as the piece established itself as a great favourite. In London, on the other hand, Donald Albery's reproduction of the Broadway staging failed wholly to catch on. Keith Michell (Quixote), Bernard Spear (Sancho) and Miss Diener headed a cast which included operetta favourites Oliver Gilbert and Alan Crofoot in its supporting ranks, but which could only keep the producer's theatre alight for 253 performances. Albery closed the show, but brought it back for a second attempt in June 1969 with Kiley crossing the Atlantic to repeat his original rôle. Again, it failed to take, and was shuttered in 118 performances. Michell, like Australia's West, however, went on to succeed to the rôle of Quixote in the continuing Broadway production.

France, which had not made a major hit of a Broadway musical since *Rose-Marie* and *No, No, Nanette*, gave *L'Homme de La Mancha* one of its more attentive hearings. Part of the reason for this, however, was its casting. The enormously popular Belgian vocalist Jacques Brel both adapted and starred in the Parisian production, with Jean-Claude Calon as Sancho and Miss Diener repeating in French the rôle she had already played in English in both America and Britain. *L'Homme de La Mancha* had sufficient success to be taken up in the French provinces and, in 1988, Paris saw a revival, brought in from Nantes, with Jean Piat as Quixote and Richard Taxy as Sancho (Théâtre Marigny 15 January).

If the show proved popular in French, it was even more so in its German-language version (ad Robert Gilbert). First produced by Vienna's Theater an der Wien (w Lawrence White, Paul Kijzer), with Josef Meinrad (Quixote), Fritz Muliar/Manfred Lichtenfeld (Sancho) and Blanche Aubry (Aldonza) in the leading rôles, it played a fine 143 nights between its original season and a return visit in 1970, before going on to be seen in Hamburg, with Gideon Singer, also the star of the Israeli version and later a Broadway replacement, as Quixote, Peter W Staub (Sancho) and Dagmar Koller (Aldonza), and then at Berlin's Theater am Kurfürstendamm. Thereafter it was seen throughout German-speaking areas where it is regularly played to the present day. An Hungarian version (ad Tamás Blum) was taken into the repertoire of Budapest's Fővárosi Operettszinház in 1971, but it did not find the same popularity there as the oft-repeated *Hegedüs a háztetön* (*Fiddler on the Roof*) or *My Fair Lady*.

A film version was produced by United Artists in 1972 with Peter O'Toole (singing dubbed by Simon Gilbert) cast as Don Quixote and James Coco as Sancho. Sophia Loren was a lushly beautiful Aldonza. The film version retained all but a couple of the show's songs but cut much of its other music.

On the stage somewhere at most times since it first appeared in the Connecticut countryside in 1964, with artists such as Howard Keel, Allan Jones and, for two New York reprises (1972, 1977), Kiley himself playing Quixote, *Man of La Mancha* ultimately returned to Broadway in a '25th anniversary' production (Marquis Theater 24 April 1992, 108 performances) which had originally been mounted on the American west coast. Raul Julia and British pop vocalist Sheena Easton featured in the lead rôles.

Australia: Comedy Theatre, Melbourne 30 September 1967; UK: Piccadilly Theatre 24 April 1968; France: Théâtre des Champs-Élysées *L'Homme de La Mancha* 1968; Austria: Theater an der Wien *Der Mann von La Mancha* 4 January 1968; Germany: Operettenhaus, Hamburg 1969, Theater am Kurfürstendamm 1969; Hungary: Fővárosi Operettszinház *La Mancha lovagja* 7 May 1971; Film: United Artists 1972

Recordings: original cast (Kapp/MCA), London cast (MCA), French casts (Barclay, Maison de la Culture de Loire Atlantique), Mexican cast (Decca), Austrian cast (Polydor), Hamburg cast (Polydor), Israeli cast (CBS), film soundtrack (United Artists), selection (Columbia) etc

MANSELL, Richard [MAITLAND, Richard Lauderdale] (b Ireland; d London, 28 February 1907).

A lively and popular Irishman whose theatrical ventures often ran short of money but rarely of skimpily clad girls, Mansell caused a sensation when he and his brother, William, produced Hervé's *Chilpéric* at London's Lyceum in 1868. Staged under Mansell's own direction, in a version by himself, Frederick Marshall and Robert Reece and with the author/composer performing in the title-rôle, this production largely helped set in motion the fashion for opéra-bouffe, and for original music scores for burlesque and musical comedy in general, in Britain.

Mansell subsequently produced Hervé's *Le Petit Faust*, with less success, and leased the St James's Theatre in the 1872–3 season to produce the first British version of Offenbach's *Le Pont des soupirs*. His management there ended after four months when the money ran out, but he was responsible, with Henry Herman, for running up in two days a libretto for a scandalous version of what claimed to be Offenbach's *Vert-Vert*, played at the same theatre the following year. He was briefly connected with the management of the Alexandra Theatre, Liverpool, and the Queen's, Manchester, toured in Russia with various companies, and put in a brief managerial appearance at the Theatre Royal in Kilburn before later taking employment as house manager at various suburban theatres, notably the Coronet Theatre, Notting Hill Gate, where he was responsible for the mounting of a 1903 revival of *Chilpéric* and reprises of those other classics of his heyday *La Fille de Madame Angot* and *La Fille du tambour-major*. He died at the age of 70 plus, as impecunious as ever.

1870 **Chilpéric** English version w Robert Reece, Frederick Marshall (Lyceum Theatre)
1874 **Vert-Vert** English version w Henry Herman (St James's Theatre)
1881 **La Belle Normande** (*La Famille Trouillat*) English version w Alfred Maltby (Globe Theatre)

MANSFIELD, Richard (b Heligoland, 24 May 1857; d New London, Conn, 30 August 1907). British musical comedian who turned himself into a classical actor on the other side of the water.

Mansfield made his first theatrical appearance at the age of 17, deputizing for Corney Grain as the Beadle in a revival of the operetta *Charity Begins at Home* in the German Reed entertainment at London's St George's Hall. He then joined the D'Oyly Carte touring companies and, as principal comedian of the A-company (Sir Joseph Porter, John Wellington Wells) played the role of Major General Stanley in the mocked-up, pre-production copyright performance of *The Pirates of Penzance* at Paignton. He appeared in London in supporting rôles in *La Boulangère* (1881, Coquebert), a revival of *Geneviève de Brabant* with Soldene (1881, Vanderprout), and in a Strand Theatre revival of *La Mascotte* (1882, Rocco) before going to America with Carte to play Harry Paulton's principal comedy part in *Manteaux Noirs* and Nick Vedder in *Rip van Winkle* on Broadway. He remained there, appearing in New York's first English-language *La Vie parisienne* (von Wienerschnitzel, ie Gondremarck) and *Gasparone* (Nasoni), but, increasingly, in non-musical pieces.

He only occasionally used his limited singing voice thereafter, in such plays as *Prince Karl* and *The First Violin*, as he spread himself through all areas of the straight theatre until he eventually became regarded as one of America's foremost classical leading men.

During his early days in Britain Mansfield was the author of a one-act musical play, *Ten Minutes for Refreshment*, and he later wrote another short opéra-bouffe under the title *Bouffes and Breezes*.

1882 **Ten Minutes for Refreshment** (James M Glover) 1 act Olympic Theatre 14 January

Biography: Winter, W: *The Life and Art of Richard Mansfield* (Moffat, Yard & Co, New York, 1910) etc

[LES] MANTEAUX NOIRS Comic opera in 3 acts by Walter Parke and Harry Paulton adapted from the libretto *Giralda, ou La Nouvelle Psyche* by Eugène Scribe. Music by Procida Bucalossi. Avenue Theatre, London, 3 June 1882.

Girola (Florence St John) has been needfully betrothed to the loutish miller Dromez (Charles Groves), but she sighs after the mysterious Luis (Henry Bracy), a gallant who one day rescued her from the hands of some ruffians. At the wedding, the equally unenthusiastic Dromez secretly sells his bridegroom's place to a stranger, but on the wedding night, spent in the blackness of the mill, the lecherous King Philip (Claude Marius) comes sneaking around the pretty country girl. In the dark, the king, his chancellor (Fred Leslie) and Luis all get involved in the series of comical encounters which make up the comic heart of the play's action, before everything is straightened out in time for the final curtain.

Bucalossi's straightforward, old-fashioned comic opera score was highlighted by a comedy serenade for the philandering king and his chancellor, but the bulk of the music fell to the heroine, in ballad ('The Heart Sighs Ever to Be Free'), fandango ('Anita is Sad'), rondo ('Six Months Ago') or air ('I Never Could, Like Some Girls, Smile'). If not top-class stuff, it was sufficient to effectively complement Paulton and Parke's highly comical book, which, in the hands of such accomplished players as Marius, Leslie and the enormously popular young Miss St John, who had recently come to fame as London's *Madame Favart*, played hilariously enough to win the show 190 London performances, an 1885 revival, and many years of touring in the British provinces and colonies.

D'Oyly Carte snapped up the American rights to this challenger to his domination of the musical West End, and presented the piece in New York with a largely British cast headed by Selina Dolaro, W T Carleton, Richard Mansfield, J H Ryley and Arthur Wilkinson. It didn't take, even when the two last-named actors decided to swap rôles, and ended its Broadway run after 37 performances. A Vienna production (ad M Röttinger, Franz Wagner) which starred Jenny Stubel, Karl Drucker, Thaller, Rösike and Kühle played just eight times.

Giralda, originally set as an opéra-comique by Adolphe Adam (Opéra-Comique, Paris 20 July 1850), and popularized later as a straight play in Dion Boucicault's English adaptation (*Giralda/A Dark Night's Work*), was also used as the basis for the Hungarian operett *A kis molnarné* (Jenő Sztojanovits/Antal Radó, Népsinház 29 January 1892).

USA: Standard Theater 26 September 1882; Austria: Carltheater *Drei Schwarzmäntel* 14 October 1882; Australia: Opera House, Sydney 11 July 1883

MARBURY, Elisabeth (b New York, 19 June 1856; d New York, 23 January 1933).

An important New York theatrical agent, 'Bessie' Marbury is said to have been the first to negotiate a percentage of the box-office returns for her playwright clients – a claim that Dion Boucicault, who, admittedly, is said to have done so on his own behalf, would doubtless have challenged.

Miss Marbury was involved in the turning of the intimate Princess Theater into a home for small musicals, and was associated with F Ray Comstock on the production of the first of the pieces staged there: *Nobody Home* (1915) and *Very Good Eddie* (1915). She was also the first producer to introduce Cole Porter to the professional musical stage when she mounted *See America First*, described as a comic opera, written by the young songwriter and his college chum, T Lawraston Riggs, and she later mounted several other musicals including Bartholomae's *Girl o' Mine* (Bijou, 28 January 1918, 48 performances) and the small-scale *Say When* (1928 w Carl Reed), a musical version of the Amélie Rives/Gilbert Emery play *Love in a Mist* put together by many hands, in a career in which she was first and foremost an artists' representative.

Autobiography: *My Crystal Ball* (Boni and Liveright, New York, 1923)

MARC-CAB [CABRIDENS, Marcel] (b Nice, 1900; d Bandol, 1978).

French author, librettist and lyricist, Marc-Cab wrote at first largely for the revue stage, turning out pieces both in the Casino de Paris style and in the Marseillais genre. He made his first appearance as a musical-comedy librettist on the Paris stage with the texts for two opérettes by the conductor of the Marseillais pieces, Georges Sellers. After collaborating with Raymond Vincy on the libretto for the landmark musical *La Belle de Cadix*, he was connected with many further Parisian productions, ranging from such large, romantic opérettes à grand spectacle as *Les Amants de Venise* and the Tino Rossi vehicle *Naples au baiser de feu*, mounted by Henri Varna at the Théâtre Mogador, to the

smaller-scale comedy musicals where he was particularly successful with such shows as the extremely long-running *Mon p'tit pote*, *Coquin de printemps* and the Frères Jacques' musical *La Belle Arabelle*.

1933 **Loulou et ses boys** (Michel Emer, Georges Sellers/w Paul Farges, Pierre Baylès) Théâtre Daunou 7 December

1940 **Ma belle marseillaise** (Sellers/w Audiffred, Charles Tutelier) Théâtre des Variétés 8 March (revised version 10 February 1978, Opéra de Toulon)

1945 **La Belle de Cadix** (Francis Lopez/Maurice Vandair/w Raymond Vincy) Casino Montparnasse 24 December

1949 **Symphonie Portugaise** (aka *Romance au Portugal*) (José Padilla/w Vincy) Théâtre de la Gaîté-Lyrique 9 October

1950 **Il faut marier maman!** (Guy Lafarge/w Lafarge/w Serge Veber) Théâtre de Paris 15 September

1952 **Schnock, ou L'École du bonheur** (Lafarge/w Jean Rigaux) Théâtre l'Européen

1953 **La Belle de mon coeur** (*The Belle of New York*) revised French version (Théâtre Mogador)

1953 **Les Amants de Venise** (Vincent Scotto/w Henri Varna, René Richard) Théâtre Mogador 5 December

1954 **Mon p'tit pote** (Jack Ledru/w Jean Valmy) Théâtre l'Européen 29 September

1954 **Les Chansons de Bilitis** (Joseph Kosma/w Valmy) Théâtre des Capucines 30 January

1955 **Les Amours de Don Juan** (Juan Morata/w Varna, Richard) Théâtre Mogador 23 December

1956 **La Belle Arabelle** (Lafarge, Pierre Philippe/w Francis Blanche) Théâtre de la Porte-Saint-Martin 4 October

1957 **Naples au baiser de feu** (Renato Rascel/w Varna, Richard) Théâtre Mogador 7 December

1958 **Coquin de printemps** (Guy Magenta/Fernand Bonifay/w Valmy) Théâtre l'Européen 30 January

1958 **Le Moulin sans souci** (Georges van Parys, Philippe Parès/S Veber) Opéra, Strasbourg 24 December

1959 **Sissi, futur Impératrice** [*Sissi*] French lyrics (w Richard) (Théâtre Mogador)

1961 **À toi de jouer** (Ledru/w Valmy) Théâtre l'Européen 24 November

1963 **Le Temps des guitares** (Francis Lopez/w Vincy) Théâtre de l'ABC October

1964 **Michel Strogoff** (Ledru/w Richard) Théâtre Mogador 5 December

1967 **SO6** (Jo Moutet/w Jacques Dambrois) Pacra/Théâtre du Marais

1967 **Vienne chante et danse** (Ledru, Strauss arr Ledru/w Varna, Richard) Théâtre Mogador 25 November

1971 **Hello, Dolly!** French version w Jacques Collard, André Hornez (Liège)

1972 **Le Pêcheur d'étoiles** (Alain Vanzo/w Francis Didelot, Marc Berthomieux) Théâtre Sebastapol, Lille September, Opéra-Comique, Paris 1973

1973 **Quand fleurissent les violettes** (*Wenn die kleine Veilchen blühen*) French version w Hornez (Liège)

1976 **Parade de printemps** (*Frühlingsparade*) French version w Hornez (Grand Théâtre, Bordeaux)

1977 **L'Oeuf à voiles** (Lafarge/Cami) Théâtre Graslin, Nantes 23 December

MARCH OF THE FALSETTOS Music and lyrics by William Finn. Playwrights Horizons, New York, 1 April 1981, Chelsea Westside Arts Theatre, 13 October 1981.

March of the Falsettos was the second of what ultimately became a trio of short musicals dealing with a self-centred, neurotic Jewish New Yorker called Marvin (Michael Rupert) who has left the wife, Trina (Alison Fraser), whom he had acquired in Part One (*In Trousers*, Playwrights Horizons, February 1979) to make his home and love-life with young Whizzer Brown (Stephen Bogardus). His psychiatrist, Mendel (Chip Zien, who played Marvin in *In Trousers*), moves in with Trina. The fifth character of the show is Marvin and Trina's young son, Jason (James Kushner).

At first staged – like *In Trousers*, under the auspices of Playwrights Horizons – as *Four Jews in a Room Bitching* (the title of the opening song from the finished show), the piece was developed by Finn and director James Lapine through a workshop production before being staged off-Broadway as *March of the Falsettos*. It was received with mixed feelings, but from those who liked its unconventional story-in-sort-of-songs style and were interested in and/or identified with its drivingly egotistic small group of characters and their dissected sentiments, it won high and enthusiastic praise. Played off-Broadway for 268 performances, it was subsequently produced in Britain, at first at Manchester, but failed when brought to London with Barry James, Simon Green, Martin Smith and Paddy Navin in its cast.

The success of *March of the Falsettos* won a second chance for *In Trousers*, which had not progressed beyond its two dozen try-out performances in New York in 1979, but which was now brought back to off-Broadway's Promenade Theater. It did not confirm its sequel's success, closing after 16 performamces.

Falsettoland (Lucille Lortel Theater, 14 September 1990), the third Marvin musical, moving with the preoccupations of the times, dealt with what develops when Whizzer turns out to have AIDS. Following its off-Broadway run the piece was mounted in a number of regional houses, before a combination of pieces number two and three was put together and produced on Broadway as *Falsettos* (John Golden Theater, 29 April 1992). Rupert, Bogardus and Zien all repeated the rôles which they had played a decade earlier, with Barbara Walsh as Trina, and director Lapine now had a co-librettist's credit. Barry and Fran Weissler's production picked up Tony Awards for music and lyrics (the 'best musical' citation went to the even older paste-up *Crazy for You*) as *Falsettos* established itself as one of the rare glimmers of musical-theatre light on a Broadway starved of well-written new works.

UK: Manchester Library Theatre 29 January 1987, Albery Theatre 24 March 1987
Recording: original cast (DRG)

LE MARIAGE AU TAMBOUR

Opéra-comique in 3 acts by Paul Burani adapted from the play by Alexandre Dumas père, Adolphe de Leuven and Brunswick. Music by Léon Vasseur. Théâtre du Châtelet, Paris, 4 April 1885.

In order to help her brother, Vicomte Charles d'Obernay (Marcelin), escape from the republican lines to carry battle orders to the army of the princes, the dashing, lovely Louise (Mlle Perrouze) disguises herself as a peasant-girl and, to keep up her masquerade, even goes through an in-the-field marriage with the attractive Sergeant Lambert (Vauthier). When order and the aristocracy are restored, and Charles is urging his sister to marry one of his comrades in arms, Lambert returns and proves to be the Marquis d'Argy.

Vasseur's musical score illustrated the military-spectacular part of the piece richly (the entire fourth tableau

of the second act was devoted to the army setting out to war in a regimental parade headed by officers on horseback and ending with the ragtag of 'volontaires, voltigeurs, tambours, clairons, cantinières'), whilst also supplying a varied selection of solos for Louise – in her various appearances as cavalier, peasant, vivandière and lady – and for her Lambert, and some perky pieces for the vivandière Gervaise (Mlle Dharville) and her comical suitors Fleurdes-Pois (Plet) and Spartacus (Romani).

Produced with plenty of spectacle at the Châtelet, the show proved to sit ill there. It was taken off after 11 performances, and shortly after was restaged at the Folies-Dramatiques (2 June 1885), with Félix Huguenet replacing Plet and Mlle Carlin as Gervaise. This time the result was altogether different and *Le Mariage au tambour* played happily for a good Paris run. It was subsequently translated into Hungarian (ad Béla J Fái, György Verő) for three performances at the Népszinház, and into German for a production at Berlin's Walhalla Theater.

Hungary: Népszinház *Esketés dobszóval* 1 May 1886; Germany: Walhalla Theater *Die Marketenderin* 26 February 1887

LE MARIAGE AUX LANTERNES

Opérette in 1 act by Michel Carré and Léon Battu, a revised version of *Le Trésor à Mathurin* by Battu. Music by Jacques Offenbach. Théâtre des Bouffes-Parisiens, Paris, 10 October 1857.

One of the most successful and influential of Offenbach's long series of short operéttes, *Le Mariage aux lanternes* was developed by Michel Carré from a 'tableau villageois' called *Le Trésor à Mathurin*, which Offenbach had composed to a text by Léon Battu at the very beginning of his career and which had been played at the little Salle Herz four years earlier (7 May 1853).

Pépito, *Les Deux Aveugles*, *Le Violoneux*, *Ba-ta-clan*, *Tromb-al-ca-zar*, *La Rose de Saint-Flour*, *Le 66*, *La Bonne d'enfant[s]* and *Croquefer* followed, all but the first staged under Offenbach's management at his Bouffes-Parisiens, before he introduced the made-over version of his little rustic opérette in which the farmer Guillot (Paul Geoffroy) and his cousin Denise (Mlle Mareschal) are brought together by a letter-writing uncle who sends them both to look for a treasure in the same place. The principal cast of the piece was completed by two gossiping-widow neighbours (Lise Tautin, Marie Dalmont) with an eye for the handsome and potentially wealthy farmer.

The score to *Le Mariage aux lanternes* had nothing of the burlesque extravagance of a *Ba-ta-clan*, but instead relied on the same kind of unpretentious melodic charm tasted with such widespread success in such pieces as *Le Violoneux* and *La Rose de Saint-Flour*, shot through with the comedy provided in the widows' pieces ('Mon cher mari quelquefois s'emportait', 'Ah! la fine, fine mouche'), and peaking in an Angelus Quartet in which Guillot digs on one side of the 'treasure' tree, Denise dreams on the other, and the prospecting widows watch eagerly and vocally from behind the hedge.

A fine success on its first production in France, where it remains one of the best-loved of Offenbach's non-burlesque pieces, *Le Mariage aux lanternes* was the first of Offenbach's opérettes to be played in Vienna in the German language and its great success there headed the invasion of the Viennese stage by French opéra-bouffe and opérette. Adapted by actor Karl Treumann, with the music 'eingerichtet und instrumentiert' by Carl Binder, it was presented under Johann Nestroy's management at the Carltheater with Treumann and Elise Zöllner as the treasures and Therese Braunecker-Schäfer and Anna Grobecker as the widows. It played for a splendid 14 straight nights and then another dozen between Possen and a Déjazet play season. Treumann later re-produced it at his Theater am Franz-Josefs-Kai (6 November 1860) with Anna Mareck playing Denise alongside himself and his original widows, and it was staged at several other houses in spectacles coupés including Ronacher (12 June 1880), the Fürsttheater (26 April 1884) and the Theater an der Wien (18 February 1889). It was brought back to the Carltheater in 1914 as part of an Offenbach season (1 June).

In Germany *Die Verlobung bei Laternenschein* proved easily the most popular of the large repertoire of Offenbach one-acters, whilst Hungary's version (ad Miklós Feléky), first seen in Kolozsvár, and then at Budapest's Nemzeti Színház with Kálmán Szerdahelyi, Vilma Bognár, Ida Huber and Ilka Markovics in its four rôles, was again instrumental in setting off a local fashion for Offenbach in particular and French musical shows in general. *Eljegyzés lámpafényél* was widely and long played thereafter, notably in the repertoire at the Budapest Operaház (12 December 1890).

England had its first sight of the piece when the Bouffes-Parisiens company visited London in 1860 with Geoffroy playing his original rôle, and several English versions were subsequently produced, including one at the Royalty Theatre (ad Benjamin Barnett) in 1862, a second, played by Frank Crellin, Bessie Lovell, Susan Pyne and Harriet Everard at the St James's in 1869, and another at the Gaiety Theatre (11 October 1871) in which Frank Wood, Constance Loseby and Annie Tremaine were featured. A British version was introduced to America by the Galton family's little company in 1868, but by that time New York had already been able to see the piece both in German and in French. It was played first at the Stadttheater with Hübner and the ladies Siedenburg, Meaubert and Auguste Steglich-Fuchs, and on several later occasions in the next decade in the other German-language houses, as well as being played in French by Paul Juignet's Théâtre Français company at Niblo's Saloon. Another English version entitled *Plighted by Moonlight* was produced by J Fred Zimmerman's company at the Metropolitan Alcazar (17 June 1882) with Fanny Wentworth, Adelaide Randolph, Rosa Cooke and Sgr Montegriffo.

Austria: Carltheater 16 October 1858; Germany: Krolls Theater *Hochzeit bei Laternenschein* 17 June 1858; Hungary: Kolozsvár 28 December 1859, Nemetzi Szinház *Eljegyzés lámpafényél* 21 November 1860, Budai Színkör (Ger) 1 May 1862; UK: Lyceum Theatre (Fr) 9 July 1860, Royalty Theatre *Marriage by Candlelight* 18 January 1862, St James's Theatre *Treasure Trove* 16 October 1869; USA: Stadttheater (Ger) 18 March 1860, Théâtre Français/Niblo's Saloon (Fr) 6 February 1864, Wood's Museum *Married By Lanterns* 31 August 1868; Australia: Theatre Royal, Melbourne *Love by Lantern Light* 8 December 1877

UN MARI À LA PORTE

UN MARI À LA PORTE Opéra-comique in 1 act by Alfred Delacour and Léon Morand. Music by Jacques Offenbach. Théâtre des Bouffes-Parisiens, Paris, 22 June 1859.

Un mari à la porte is a farcical little piece in which a husband called Henri Martel (Guyot) finds his newly wed wife, Suzanne (Coralie Geoffroy), has locked him out of their room. And there is a man in there with her. But Florestan (Paul Geoffroy), who has arrived over the roof and down the chimney, is only a silly fellow fleeing from a jealous husband and a bailiff, and his little flirtation is ultimately not with the wife, but with her pretty bridesmaid, Rosita (Lise Tautin). The show was a virtual three-hander, as the husband is heard but not seen until the final moments, when the door is at last opened. The features of the little score were a valse tyrolienne for Rosita ('J'entends, ma belle, la ritournelle'), some comical lamentations for Florestan who, it seems, is going to have to jump three floors to the ground to save the situation, a dilemma trio when the trellis he attempts to descend by breaks ('Juste ciel! Que vois-je?') and, the big set piece of the show, a quartet with the husband outside joining in to provide the bottom line.

This comical opérette did well in France, where it was introduced at Offenbach's Bouffes-Parisiens, but it also won a particularly strong and widespread popularity in Austria and in Hungary. Karl Treumann followed up his successes with his versions of *Le Mariage aux lanternes*, *Pépito*, *Le Savetier et le Financier*, *Le Violoneux* and *Le 66* by adapting *Un mari à la porte* for the Carltheater. With its adaptor playing the foolish Florian alongside Therese Braunecker-Schäfer and Helene Weinberger in a version which made great play of a lot of business with a painter's cradle and which seems to have been rather more joyously farcical than the French original, it gave him his biggest success since the first two – and still most popular – of his Offenbach rewrites. Treumann played *Der Ehemann vor der Thüre* both at the Carltheater and subsequently at his Theater am Franz-Josefs-Kai, and it was later taken up at the Variététheater and at other houses specializing in spectacles coupés, appearing at Ronacher in 1880 and at the Theater an der Wien in 1884 (13 January) and again in 1894 with Karl Wallner, Ferdinand Pagin and Frlns Devall and Häckl featured for a series of ten performances.

In Hungary, *Férj az ajto elött* (ad Kálmán Szerdahelyi) followed *Le Mariage aux lanternes* into the Nemzeti Színház. Thus, the second Hungarian-language Offenbach work in Budapest thoroughly confirmed the success of the first, and the piece was repeated regularly thereafter. Offenbach's company played *Un mari à la porte* there in French the same year, whilst István Benyey's team were seen in the Hungarian adaptation at the Budai Színkör (1867), where the show had been put on as early as 1860 in its German version, as the little piece made itself a firm place in the repertoire.

Although Europe enjoyed the piece (it was seen in Paris as recently as 1983, Théâtre Essaïon), it does not seem to have travelled significantly beyond there. America saw it in its German version, at the Stadttheater, several times with Minna von Berkel and Eugenie Schmitz featured, and later at the Germania (1873–4), but neither in America nor in Britain does it seem to have been staged in English in the century of its first appearance. That distinction seems to have fallen only to Australia where *The Wrong Side of the Door* was produced to considerable publicity as the first Offenbach opérette to play in the colony. The publicity was occasioned, however, more by the fact that local burlesque author William M Akhurst was announced as the 'author', and the show was spoken of as 'Mr Akhurst's long-promised operetta'. H Humphreys (Pythias Callicado), E Reeve (Tapper), Kate Ryder (Mrs Tapper) and Milly Parker (Rosella Parrott) introduced the show for a brief season at Melbourne's Duke of Edinburgh's Theatre.

London finally saw *A Husband on the Mat* in 1950 when Geoffrey Dunn's anglicization of the piece was played at the Fortune Theatre.

Austria: Carltheater *Der Ehemann vor der T(h)üre* 28 December 1859; Hungary: Budai Színkör *Der Ehemann vor der Tür* 16 June 1860, Nemzeti Színház *Férj az ajto elött* 12 March 1861; USA: Stadttheater *Der Ehemann vor der Tür* 1866; Australia: Duke of Edinburgh's Theatre, Melbourne *The Wrong Side of the Door* 7 November 1868; UK: Fortune Theatre *A Husband on the Mat* 21 February 1950

MARIANO, Luis [GONZALES, Luis] (b Irun, Spain, 12 August 1914; d Paris, 14 July 1970). Svelte little singing idol of the French opérette à grand spectacle of the post-war stage and screen.

The son of a Spanish garagiste and taxi-driver, brought up largely in Bordeaux, the young Mariano studied at the local Conservatoire whilst singing with a cabaret band. Jeanne Lagiscarde, a forceful lady who looked after the classical department at the local record shop, took him under her wing and finally sold up in order to take her 'discovery' to Paris and make him a star. Three years of meagre pickings in the popular music world and several performances of *Don Pasquale* intervened before that stardom came when Mariano was cast in the leading rôle of the film star Carlos Médina in *La Belle de Cadix* (1945), the first opérette by the composer Francis Lopez. As a sometime art student, Mariano also designed the sets for the *Belle de Cadix*'s purse-pinched mounting on the little stage of the Casino-Montparnasse, but it was his singing rather than his painting which won the enthusiasm of all when the show opened. He created the famous, lilting title-song 'La Belle de Cadix', the serenade to 'Maria Luisa' and the longing 'Une nuit à Grenade' and he made them and the show as famous as they, in turn, made him.

Thereafter, the slim, dark little tenor swiftly became one of the most loved stars of the French entertainment world, leading a high-profile career in alternate stage and film productions, always in large made-to-measure rôles full of ringing tenor songs in the popular vein, usually from the pen of the now-equally-famous Lopez. His films of the 1940s included *Histoire de chanter* (1946), *Cargaison clandestine* (1947), *Fandango* (1948), *Je n'aime que toi* (1949) and *Pas de weekend pour notre amour* (1949), whilst his stage successor to *La Belle de Cadix* was *Andalousie* (1947), a piece in similar vein to the former, and with an even brighter bag of tenor songs: 'Andalucia mia', 'Le Marchand d'alcarazas', 'Je veux t'aimer', 'La Fête a Seville', 'Olé torero' and the ringing prayer 'Santa Maria'.

Le Chanteur de Mexico (1951, 'Mexico', 'Acapulco', Il est un coin de France', 'Maïtechu', 'Quand on voit Paris d'en haut', 'Rossignol de mes amours') gave Mariano a third successive stage hit and, helped by the film versions of his stage opérettes and of *Violettes impériales*, perhaps his best film, it brought him to the peak of his career.

This record of unalloyed success had its first hiccough when Mariano essayed less suitable material: a weak musical, *Chevalier du ciel* (1954), which put him in uniform and

gave him virtually the entire score to sing, and a botched film version of Lehár's *Der Zarewitsch* which found its star happier with the character than the music. He filmed several further Lopez stage pieces: *Le Chanteur de Mexico*, and two others in which he had not appeared on the stage, *Quatre jours à Paris* and *À la Jamaïque*, appeared in the film musical *Sérénade au Texas*, and played five more of Lopez's works in the theatre: *La cancion del amor mio* in Madrid (1958), the indifferent *Le Secret de Marco Polo* (1959), the lively *Visa pour l'amour* (1961) in which he paired with Annie Cordy to sing and dance the twist, and two further spectaculars, *Le Prince de Madrid* (1967) which cast him as Goya and, finally, *La Caravelle d'or* (1969). Although each had a good run and a long tour, none was of the same class as the early pieces and, latterly, Mariano too lost some of his éclat. He died during the run of *La Caravelle d'or* at the age of 56.

Biography: Montserrat, J: *Luis Mariano* (Pac, Paris, 1984), Chardans, J-L; *J'ai connu un prince* (Table Ronde, Paris, 1976), *Luis Mariano* (Ramsay, Paris, 1980)

MARIÉ, Paola   Opéra-bouffe star of the French and American stages.

The tiny, dark and very lovely mezzo-soprano Paola Marié made her first appearance before the Paris public as a teenaged take-over in the rôle of Méphisto in *Le Petit Faust* (1869) before she became a member of the company at the Brussels Fantaisies-Parisiennes, with whom she visited London in 1871 (*La Chanson de Fortunio*, *Les Bavards*, *Les Chevaliers de la table ronde* etc). The following year she was seen again in Britain when she played Dindonette in *L'Oeil crevé* with the Folies-Dramatiques company.

She scored a considerable success when she appeared as the original Paris Clairette in *La Fille de Madame Angot* in 1873, and she remained in the French capital to appear as Fiorella in the 1874 remake of *Les Brigands*, and to create leading roles in Lecocq's *Les Prés Saint-Gervais* (1874, Friquette), Offenbach's *La Boulangère a des écus* (Toinon), as a very-last-minute replacement for the bereaved Mlle Luce in *Le Moulin du Vert-Galant* (1876, Jeanne), *La Boîte au lait* (1876, Mistigris), and such little pieces as Legouix's *Le Mariage d'une étoile*. She guested at the profitable theatre at St Petersburg in 1876, and on her return to Paris starred in Vasseur's *La Sorrentine* (1877, Theresina), opposite Louise Théo as the captain of the guard, Fortunato, in *Madame l'Archiduc*, created another major travesty rôle as Lazuli in *L'Étoile* (1877), and also starred in Laurent de Rillé's opérette villageoise *Babiole* (1878, Babiole) and in *La Marocaine*.

In 1879 Paola Marié went to America, making her first appearance there under the management of Maurice Grau as Clairette (15 September), and over the next four years she toured the country playing a vast repertoire of opéras-bouffes, including *Giroflé-Girofla*, *Barbe-bleue*, *Les Brigands*, *La Périchole*, *La Vie parisienne*, *Le Petit Faust*, *La Grande-Duchesse*, *Le Petit Duc*, *Madame Favart*, *Les Cloches de Corneville* and *Olivette*. She introduced several new pieces to America, among them *La Petite Muette* (Mercedès), *La Camargo* (Camargo), *La Fille du tambour-major* (Stella), *Les Mousquetaires au couvent* (Louise, later Simonne), *Babiole* and *Le Jour et la nuit* (Manola) and also

Plate 172. **Paola Marié**: *Star of Parisian and American opéra-bouffe.*

starred in Sardou's play *Divorçons* and in the title-rôle of Bizet's *Carmen*, created in Paris by her sister.

Mlle Marié returned to the Paris stage in 1884, now tiny, dark and distinctly tubby, and with her 33-year-old voice beginning to curl up a little at the edges, and she made her reappearance at the Bouffes as Régine in the short-lived *Le Chevalier Mignon*. She appeared in Paris in a revival of *La Grande-Duchesse*, but soon put an end to a career which had taken her through a large number of countries in its span of nearly 20 years.

The two sisters of Paola Marié were also singing stars. **Mlle Irma** (originally Irma-Marié), chosen by Offenbach to create his *L'Amour chanteur* (1864) and *Les Bergers* (1865, Daphne/Annette/La Rouge), was subsequently the prima donna at the short-lived Théâtre de l'Athénée where she created the rôle of Césarine in Lecocq's *Fleur de thé* and his *L'Amour et son carquois*. She made the most successful portion of her career in America where she was the first interpreter of Offenbach's Boulotte (*Barbe-bleue*) and *La Périchole* and played in a repertoire of touring opéra-bouffe, before returning home to take her place amongst the supporting casts at the Opéra-Comique.

Galli-Marié, whose career was in a different and more purely vocal area, was the creator of Ambroise Thomas's *Mignon* and Bizet's *Carmen*, the first Friday in Offenbach's *Robinson Crusoe*, Fantasio in his *Fantasio* and for a long time a prima donna at the Opéra-Comique. She appeared alongside sister Irma, in 1869, in the little opérette *Madeleine* at the Bouffes-Parisiens.

MARIETTE, ou Comment on écrit l'histoire Comédie musicale in 5 scenes by Sacha Guitry. Music by Oscar Straus. Théâtre Edouard VII, Paris, 1 October 1928.

Originally written by Sacha Guitry as a vehicle for Sarah Bernhardt, but ultimately rewritten for his then wife, Yvonne Printemps, and for himself, *Mariette* presented its star as a 100-year-old actress recalling her past to a journalist. Since her past is not quite what she would have liked it to have been, she improves on fact, and invents for herself a romance with Prince Louis Napoleon (Guitry). Her tale of that non-existent romance makes up the remainder of the show.

Mariette is seen as a girl of 20 in the 1848 of the first act, performing a boy's rôle in a provincial opérette (the audience saw the scene from behind the actors). The first contact with the Prince is made in a scene of pantomime, with the young woman initially refusing his advances, but ultimately accepting his invitation to 'supper'. The piece then followed their subsequent affair before, in the overture to the fourth scene, it advanced musically through the years from the can-can and the waltz to the boston, the foxtrot, one-step, charleston and blues of the present day.

The short score included musical pieces for several other artists (Jane Montange, Renée Sénac, Aquistapace) although not for the non-singing Guitry as the Prince, but it was the star who reaped the bulk of the music, ranging from a lovely Valse d'adieu ('Depuis trois ans passés') to a coon song in the final act.

Mariette was a full-scale hit in Paris, with the duo who had previously triumphed in *Mozart* triumphing all over again in a piece wholly different in style, and they subsequently played their piece in London, for a four-week season at His Majesty's Theatre, in the same way that they had done with the earlier show.

When *Mariette* was produced in Berlin, the Rotter brothers (who ran Berlin's musical theatre with a rubber glove) decided that Guitry's sweet spider's-web of a book was not sufficiently throat-tugging and they commissioned Alfred Grünwald to rewrite it, adding a melodramatic scene of self-sacrifice for the heroine. The scene sat like a pustule on the face of the play, as Käthe Dorsch and ex-opera baritone Michael Bohnen, supported by Ida Perry and Hermann Böttcher, played out a version of the show which had also introduced altogether more vocal music for the leading man, turning the show from a play with music into a full-blown, conventional Operette, without making anything like the same effect as the original had done. A Vienna production of the Grünwald version starred Rita Georg and Hubert Marischka along with Anny Coty and Fritz Imhoff through a total of 127 performances at the Theater an der Wien in 1929–30.

In America, an English-language version by Arthur Guiterman, with Helen Ford and Richard Hale featured, was produced under weekly stock conditions which were sufficiently uninspiring to damp its management's hopes that it might make its way to Broadway.

UK: His Majesty's Theatre (Fr) 3 June 1929; Germany: Metropoltheater *Marietta* 5 September 1929; Austria: Theater an der Wien *Marietta* 25 October 1929; USA: Stockbridge, Mass, 28 June 1937
Recording: items (HMV)

MARIETTI, Jean (d 1977).

The managing director of the music-publishing firm of M Eschig, long one of the foremost in French musical theatre publications, Marietti made a speciality of the translation of Austrian and German musical shows for the French market. It has been suggested, however, that his pen-wielding contribution to the actual writing of the list of Eschig publications on which his name appears may have been limited. The most successful of his list were *Le Pays du sourire* and *Valses de Vienne*.

1925 **La Dernière Valse** (*Der letzte Walzer*) French version w Léon Uhl (Geneva)

1927 **La Teresina** French version w Uhl (Théâtre Graslin, Nantes)

1928 **La Rose de Stamboul** (*Die Rose von Stambul*) French version w Uhl, Jean de Letraz

1930 **Madame Pompadour** French version w Albert Willemetz, Max Eddy (Théâtre Marigny)

1930 **Comtesse Maritza** (*Gräfin Mariza*) French version w Eddy (Mulhouse)

1931 **Frasquita** French version w Eddy (Théâtre du Havre)

1932 **Le Pays du Sourire** (*Das Land des Lächelns*) French version w André Mauprey (Ghent, Théâtre de la Gaîté Lyrique)

1933 **Valses de Vienne** (*Walzer aus Wien*) French version w André Mouëzy-Éon, Eddy (Théâtre de la Porte-Saint-Martin)

1934 **La Princesse du cirque** (*Die Zirkusprinzessin*) French version w Eddy (Théâtre du Havre)

1935 **Violette de Montmartre** (*Das Veilchen vom Montmartre*) French version (Théâtre de la Porte-Saint-Martin)

1959 **Sissi, futur impératrice** (*Sissy*) French version w Henri Varna, Marc-Cab, René Richard (Théâtre Mogador)

MARION, George F (b San Francisco, 16 July 1860; d Carmel, Calif, 30 November 1945). Actor turned musical-theatre director through three decades of Broadway productions.

At first a performer, Marion appeared on Broadway with Dockstader's minstrels and in several musical shows (Dr Dago Daggeri in *The Reign of Error*, Major Bombardos in *Papa's Wife*, *The Little Duchess*) before becoming a director in the 1890s (*A Brass Monkey*, *The Fencing Master*, *Papa's Wife*, *The Little Duchess*), notably for Ziegfeld and Anna Held. He was later for several years house director for Henry Savage and, in that capacity, directed such successful early American pieces as *The Prince of Pilsen* (USA and UK), *The Yankee Consul*, *Woodland* and *The Yankee Tourist*, as well as Eysler's *The Love Cure* (*Künstlerblut*) and, mostly notably, Broadway's version of *The Merry Widow*. He returned to the stage as an actor intermittently in such pieces as Victor Herbert's *Algeria* (C Walsingham Wadhunter, 1908).

In 1910 he directed the highly successful *The Spring Maid* for Werba and Luescher, then starred for the same management in their Broadway version of *Der fidele Bauer* (Matthaeus) the following year, and thereafter mounted a series of musicals for A H Woods, John Cort, Savage and other managements including local pieces *The Fascinating Widow*, *Tantalizing Tommy*, *The American Maid*, *The Debutante*, *Molly O*, *The Amber Express*, *The Love Mill* and *Head Over Heels* and American adaptations of the Continental *Gypsy Love*, *Modest Suzanne*, *The Rose Maid*, *The Woman Haters*, *The Purple Road*, *Sari*, *The Maids of Athens* and *Suzi*.

Although he was seen again as a performer in *The Grass Widow* (1917, Anton Pivert), his acting appearances from this time on were confined largely to plays (Christopherson in *Anna Christie*, 1921) and in films. As a director, however, he continued to be active in the musical theatre through the 1920s, staging musicals for the Shuberts and others up to his retirement (*The Right Girl*, *Tangerine*, *First Love*, *White Lilacs*, *Angela*, *Boom Boom*).

His son, **George Marion jr** (b Boston, 30 August 1899; d New York, 25 February 1968) wrote silent-movie scenarios, subtitles for the early film of *Irene*, screenplays for such films as *The Gay Divorcee* and *Love Me Tonight* and later libretti, including the books for an unfortunate version of *Der Zigeunerbaron* for San Francisco (1938 w Ann Ronell), *Too Many Girls* (1939), *Beat the Band* (w George Abbott), *Early to Bed* (1943), Kálmán's Mayerling musical, *Marinka* (1945), *Toplitzky of Notre Dame* (1946) and Guy Lombardo's *Arabian Nights* (Jones Beach 1954).

MARISCHKA, Ernst (b Vienna 2 January 1893; d Chur, Switzerland, 12 May 1963).

The brother of the Theater an der Wien's Hubert Marischka, Ernst also spent his life in the world of Operette. He began as a librettist, scoring his most important successes at the family theatres with *Der Orlow* and the pasticcio *Walzer aus Wien* and in his collaboration with Hubert on *Sissy*. He subsequently became a busy and important figure in the film world, writing and/or directing many musical films (screenplays for *Das Abenteuer geht weiter*, *Die Fledermaus*, *Mein Herz ruft nach dir*, *Ich liebe alle Frauen*, *Frühjahrsparade*, *Zauber der Bohème*, *Konfetti*, *Rosen in Tirol* [ie *Der Vogelhändler*], *Saison in Salzburg*, *Hochzeitsnacht im Paradies*, producer/director and screenplay for *Der Opernball*, *Dreimäderlhaus* with Rudolf Schock etc). His screenplay for *Frühjahrparade* (*Spring Parade*) was subsequently adapted as a stage musical.

1911 **Der Minenkönig** (Robert Stolz/w Gustav Beer) 1 act Apollotheater 1 November

1914 **Das Narrenhaus** (Tivadar Pallós, Hans Albert Cesek/w Beer) 1 act Hölle 1 February

1916 **Das Kammerkatzerl** (w Max Blau) 1 act Rideamus Kabarett 1 April

1920 **Der König heiratet** (Edmund Eysler/w Beer) 1 act Künstlertheater April

1923 **Die Bacchusnacht** (Bruno Granichstädten) Theater an der Wien 18 May

1923 **Eine Nacht in Venedig** revised text (Theater an der Wien)

1924 **Puszipajtások** (Pallós/w Beer ad Zsolt Harsányi) 1 act Lujza Blaha Színház, Budapest 9 October

1925 **Der Orlow** (Granichstädten) Theater an der Wien 3 April

1926 **Das Schwalbennest** (Granichstädten) Raimundtheater 2 September

1926 **Die Königin** (Oscar Straus) Künstlertheater, Berlin 5 November

1927 **Alles auf Liebe** (Ralph Benatzky/w Karl Farkas) Stadttheater 30 September

1930 **Reklame** (Granichstädten) Theater an der Wien 28 February

1930 **Walzer aus Wien** (Johann Strauss arr E W Korngold/w A M Willner, Heinz Reichert) Wiener Stadttheater 30 October

1932 **Sissy** (Fritz Kreisler/w Hubert Marischka) Theater an der Wien 23 December

1933 **Glück muss man haben** (Anton Profés/w Herman Feiner) Neues Wiener Stadttheater 10 March

1934 **Der singende Traum** (Richard Tauber/w Feiner) Theater an der Wien 31 August
1940 **Franzi** (Peter Kreuder) Leipzig 12 September
1949 **Frühling im Prater** (Stolz) Wiener Stadttheater 22 December
1964 **Frühjarsparade** (Stolz/w Hugo Wiener) Volksoper 25 March

MARISCHKA, Hubert (b Brünn, 27 August 1882; d Vienna, 4 December 1959). Long-time leading man and leading producer of the Viennese Operette theatre between the wars.

Marischka began his career as an actor and vocalist at St Pölten at the age of 21 and played at first in provincial theatres. During a successful engagement at Brünn, he was seen by librettist Victor Léon and in 1908 he both married Léon's daughter and made his first appearances in Vienna, playing in a revival of Léon's Strauss pasticcio *Wiener Blut* and featuring alongside Karl Streitmann in *Die lustige Witwe* at the Raimundtheater. From there he moved to the Carltheater and leading-manhood, and created the rôles of the temporarily divorced husband Karel van Lysseweghe in *Die geschiedene Frau*, the cabaret-director Olivier in Oscar Straus's *Didi*, the comical Kajetán in Lehár's *Zigeunerliebe*, and Tiborius in Fall's *Das Puppenmädel* (1910) as well as appearing as Hector to the Nanon of Mizzi Zwerenz in a revival of *Nanon* (1910). In 1912 he appeared in the title-rôle of the Viennese première of *Der liebe Augustin* and as Stephan to the *Susi* of Zwerenz before switching his allegiance to the Theater an der Wien for what was to be a long and eventful stay.

Marischka began his life at the Theater an der Wien starring in *Die ideale Gattin* (1913, Pablo de Cavaletti), *Endlich allein* (1914, Baron Frank Hansen), and opposite Betty Fischer in Léon's newest, patriotic version of Kálmán's *Az obsitos*, *Gold gab ich für Eisen* (1914). He appeared as Dumesnil in the revival of *Der Opernball* and as Konrad in Granichstädten's *Auf Befehl der Herzogin*, guested at the Apollotheater in Zerkowitz's *Das Finanzgenie* and a little scene called *Otto oder Otto*, and then returned to base to appear in *Der Sterngucker* (Paul von Rainer). He also took at turn at playing Schubert in the Raimundtheater production of *Das Dreimäderlhaus*, but scored his greatest success to date when he introduced the archetypal romantic tenor rôle of Achmed Bey in the Theater an der Wien's long-running wartime hit *Die Rose von Stambul* (1916, 'O Rose von Stambul', 'Ihr stillen süssen Frauen').

Marischka went on to play the rôle of Sándor Zapolja in the Vienna version of *Wo die Lerche singt* (1918), created the title-rôle of Friedl Pausinger in Straus's *Dorfmusikanten* (1919) and again visited the same management's Raimundtheater to star as Heinrich Heine in a biomusical made up of Mendelssohn music and called *Dichterliebe* (1920). He returned to the Theater an der Wien to create Count Julian Olinski in *Die blaue Mazur* (1920), the heroic Dimitri Sarrasow in *Der letzte Walzer* (1921), Armand Mirbeau (later to be taken by Richard Tauber) in *Frasquita* (1922) and Nero in Granichstädten's *Die Bacchusnacht*, and was also seen as Caramello in a revival of *Eine Nacht in Venedig* and starred as the prototype Prince Sou Chong (another rôle with which Tauber would later identify himself) in the first performances of *Die gelbe Jacke* (1923).

During the period that had seen him rising to the top of the list of romantic leading men in the Viennese operettic firmament, the widowed Marischka had married Lilian Karczag, the daughter of the director of the Theater an der Wien, and he had become progressively more and more involved in the running of the theatre. When Wilhelm Karczag died in 1923, his son-in-law (now billed as Marischka-Karczag) took over the management of the Theater an der Wien. He also soon took up the co-running of the Raimundtheater (1926), formerly under Karczag's control, where Rudolf Beer had again got himself into trouble producing admirable but unprofitable plays, and leavened that house's diet with some more popular Operette productions including the premières of *Das Schwalbennest* and *Die Liebe geht um*.

Marischka began his managership of the Theater an der Wien by staging Oscar Straus's *Die Perlen der Kleopatra* (1923, with playbills still giving Karczag as producer), and found major success producing and starring opposite Betty Fischer as Count Tassilo ('Grüss mir die süssen, die reizenden Frauen', 'Komm' Zigan!'), the impoverished nobleman in love with his employer, in Kálmán's *Gräfin Mariza* (1924). A first-rate hit which ran for a full year, *Gräfin Mariza* was followed up by the short-lived *Das Milliardensouper* (director) and a run of further splendid successes in *Der Orlow* (1925 Alex Dorotschinsky, director), *Die Zirkusprinzessin* (1926 Mister X, introducing 'Zwei Märchenaugen'), *Die Königin* (Nikola Tontscheff, director) and *Die gold'ne Meisterin* (1927, Christian, director, 'Du liebe gold'ne Meisterin').

In 1928 Marischka staged and starred in Kálmán's *Die Herzogin von Chicago* (1928, Sándor Boris), in 1929 did the same for Fall's posthumous *Rosen aus Florida* (Goliath Armstrong) and Straus's *Marietta* (Louis Napoleon), with Rita Georg as his partner, and in 1930 directed Granichstädten's *Reklame*. He was given the large-billed credit of 'künstlerische Oberleitung' (which he'd used on a few previous occasions) to the 'Regie' of house director Otto Langer on the the original Vienna production of *Das Land des Lächelns* (1930) in which Richard Tauber repeated his Berlin performance of Marischka's old rôle of Sou Chong.

He appeared in revivals of *Wiener Blut* and *Die lustige Witwe* with leading lady Betty Fischer, as Leopold in *Im weissen Rössl* and in Girardi's rôle in *Bruder Straubinger* and directed and starred in the Theater an der Wien's productions of the disappointing *Der Bauerngeneral* (1931, Fedor Gregorowitsch Irtitsch), his own *Sissy* (1932, Herzog Max to the Sissy of Paula Wessely), *Der Teufelsreiter* (1932, Rittmeister Graf Sándor) and *Zwei lachende Augen* (1933, Grossfürst Felician). In between these appearances, he left the star rôles in such of his theatre's productions as Miksa Preger's staging of *Viktoria und ihr Husar* ('künstlerische Gesamtleitung'), his own production of *Schön ist die Welt* (1931), Preger's mounting of *Die Blume von Hawaii*, *Das Veilchen vom Montmartre*, the Hungarian *Ein Liebestraum* (director), *Die Dame mit dem Regenbogen* (director) and Otto Preminger's visiting staging of *Märchen im Grand-Hotel* at his theatre to such artists as Louis Treumann, Otto Maran, Hans Heinz Bollmann and Wilhelm Klitsch whilst he occasionally guested elsewhere. In 1930 he directed and created the rôle of the younger Johann Strauss in *Walzer aus Wien* at the Stadttheater, and in 1934 he played Erzherzog Salvator in the Hungarian children's musical *Kadettenliebe*.

In 1935 Marischka gave up the active management of the Theater an der Wien, which had fallen into severe difficulties in the depression, retaining only his lease on the property, and he thereafter devoted much of his time to writing screenplays and libretti, directing films and appearing in screen rôles ranging from the heroic, such as his original part in *Gräfin Mariza* (1932), to the ageing, such as Féri in Georg Jacoby's version of *Die Csárdásfürstin*. However, he continued to work and to appear in the theatre in such pieces as Jessel's *Der goldene Mühle* (1936 Scala Theater), as author-director of *Die Straussbuben* (later staged in Hungary as *Tavaszi hangok*), as Ferdinand Lobmeyer to the Marie Geistinger of Elfie Meyerhofer in his own *Die Walzerkönigin*, in Schmidseder's *Abscheidswalzer* (Georg Ferdinand Waldmüller) and as director of Stolz's *Frühling im Prater*. In 1958, a little stouter, but not a lot balder (a lot would not have been possible), he appeared at the Raimundtheater in his own Operette *Deutschmeisterkapelle*.

Marischka was the outstanding figure of his age in the Viennese theatre, both from a managerial point of view and as the archetypal leading man of the Austrian Operette for over 20 years. In spite of his place as the creator of the star rôles and songs of some of the best Operetten of the Austrian stage canon, his reputation has been somewhat overshadowed outside Austria by the purely vocal talents of the better-publicized, -travelled and -recorded Richard Tauber, but it was Marischka who, whilst lacking the finer and more forceful vocal skills of a Tauber, a Bollmann or a Clewing, outshone and outlasted all his contemporaries as a complete performer: the darkly dashing romantic leading man (a tendency to baldness and squareness notwithstanding) with the winning tenor voice.

1932 **Sissy** (Fritz Kreisler/w Ernst Marischka) Theater an der Wien 23 December
1946 **Die Straussbuben** (Johann Strauss, Josef Strauss arr Oskar Stalla/w Rudolf Weys) Raimundtheater
1948 **Die Walzerkönigin** (Ludwig Schmidseder/w Aldo Pinelli) Wiener Bürgertheater 11 October
1949 **Abschiedswalzer** (Schmidseder/w Rudolf Österreicher) Bürgertheater 8 September
1954 **Der Feldernhügel** (Heinz Sandauer/Karl Farkas) Raimundtheater 24 March
1955 **Liebesbriefe** (Nico Dostal/w Österreicher) Raimundtheater 23 November
1958 **Deutschmeisterkapelle** (Carl Michael Ziehrer arr Max Schönherr/w Österreicher) Raimundtheater 31 May

MARITANA Opera in 3 acts by Edward Fitzball based on the play *Don César de Bazan* by Adolphe d'Ennery and Philippe Dumanoir. Music by Vincent Wallace. Theatre Royal, Drury Lane, London, 15 November 1845.

Wallace's vastly popular romantic opera was one of the three great standards of the English-language opera companies' repertoire in the middle years of the 19th century when such troupes provided an important part of popular theatrical entertainment. Based on a classic French play, which would later inspire a number of other musical theatre writers including W S Gilbert on his *The Yeomen of the Guard*, *Maritana*'s Spanish tale of a blindfold wedding was illustrated by a score that included such hit numbers as 'Ah! Let Me Like a Soldier Fall' and 'Scenes That Are Brightest', melodies which would be used over and over again as fodder for burlesque and other pasticcio scores.

Written in a spoken dialogue format with musical numbers, and boasting a happy ending, *Maritana* was, like its equally popular contemporary *The Bohemian Girl*, a legitimate ancestor of the English romantic operettas of later years.

The *Don Caesar de Bazan* story in general, and *Maritana* in particular, came in for a considerable amount of burlesque treatment during the 19th-century reign of the burlesque over the popular musical stage, notably in F C Burnand's *Mary Turner, or the Wicious Willin and Wictorious Wirtue* (Holborn Theatre, 1867, mus arr: George Richardson) in which Fanny Josephs appeared as Mary ('Our Bol'eroine') to the Don Caesar of Jenny Willmore, the Don Carlos of H J Montague, the Don Jose of Charlotte Saunders and the Queen Isabella of Mr Wilmott. An 1876 *Little Don Caesar de Bazan, or Maritana and the Merry Monarch* by H J Byron (Gaiety Theatre, 26 August 1876) presented Kate Vaughan as Maritana, with Nellie Farren (Don Caesar), E W Royce (Don Jose) and Edward Terry as the King of Spain.

The principal plotline of the show, the case of the convenience marriage with a condemned man who then doesn't die after all, was reprised as late as 1927 in Broadway's *Half a Widow*. In this case, the husband was going into battle.

Austria: Theater an der Wien 8 January 1848; USA: Bowery Theater 4 May 1848; Germany: Hamburg 16 February 1849; Australia: Royal Victoria Theatre, Sydney 19 April 1849; Hungary: Budai Színkör (Ger) 20 June 1850

MARIUS, Monsieur [DUPLANY, Claude Marius] (b Paris, 18 February 1850; d at sea, 25 January 1896). Dashing French actor and singer who made a fine career on the burlesque and opéra-comique stage in Britain.

'Mons' Marius began his theatrical career at the age of 15 as an extra, then a chorister at Paris's Théâtre des Folies-Dramatiques where he rose, through his teens, to small rôles, such as Anglo-Saxon in *Le Petit Faust*, and understudies. He was still only 19 when he was taken to Britain to play his first major rôle, as Landry to the Chilpéric of Hervé in *Chilpéric* (1870), and following the enormous success of Hervé's opéra-bouffe (in which the young, prettily accented Frenchman won more than his share of applause) he remained to play Siebel in London's *Le Petit Faust* before being hurried back to France to join the army.

Having done his bit against the Prussians, he returned to England and there appeared as Charles Martel (and later in the normally travesty star rôle of Drogan) in *Geneviève de Brabant* (1872). In 1873 he was contracted to the Strand Theatre and there he won major star status in the long run of burlesques presented by the Swanborough family: *Nemesis* (1873, Roland de Roncevaux Ramponneau), *El Dorado* (1874, Patatras), *The Field of the Cloth of Gold* (1874 revival), *Loo* (1874, Rimbombo), *Intimidad* (1875, Intimidad), *Flamingo* (1875, Hannibal Gobbler), *Antarctica* (1876, Amadis de Batignolles), *Dan'l Traduced* (1876), *Champagne* (1877, Chevalier de la Mayonnaise), *L'Africaine* revival (Nelustan), *Dora and Diplunacy* (Orloff) and *The Baby* (1879, Rajar Real Jam). He also appeared in the Strand's occasional productions of original musicals, playing Prince Doro in Gilbert and Clay's *Princess Toto* and François Frenchipani in *The Lying Dutchman*.

When Alexander Henderson brought French comic opera to replace burlesque at the Strand, Marius was a natural for the leading rôles. He paired with Florence St John as Charles Favart in *Madame Favart* (1879), and with Violet Cameron as Merimac in *Olivette* (1880) before moving with Henderson and Miss St John (who was by now Mme Marius à la ville) to play again in *Madame Favart* (1882), Don Philip of Aragon in *Manteaux Noirs* (1882), Malicorne in Offenbach's *Belle Lurette* (1883), and in revivals of *Olivette* and *Barbe-bleue* (Popolani) at the Avenue Theatre.

The Avenue engagement and the liaison with Miss St John both came to an end, and Marius went on to appear as Prince Grégoire in *La Cosaque* with Kate Santley (1884), in the operetta *The Casting Vote* (1885), *The Palace of Pearl* (1886) and *Mynheer Jan* (General Bombalo, 1887). Around this time, the journalist Jimmy Davis took his pen to the actor in the pages of *The Bat*, sneering at him as an ex-waiter and suggesting he return to his old trade. Marius sued, proved he had never been a waiter, and was awarded £110 damages. Nevertheless, thereafter he increasingly devoted his attention to directing. His production of *Nadgy*, with Arthur Roberts and Marie Vanoni featured, was not wholly successful, but he won a fine run with the very delicately balanced sauciness of *Miss Decima* (1891).

In the 1890s Marius ventured further afield. He appeared with Mrs Bernard Beere in America and Australia (1892), succeeded to the rôle of Galeazzo Visconti in Broadway's *The Fencing Master* (1892) and directed the production of E E Rice's successful Boston extravaganza *Venus* (1893). His last engagement, in spite of several years of intermittent illness, was with George Edwardes's South African company. He died of consumption on board ship on the way back to Britain.

LA MARJOLAINE   Opérette in 3 acts by Alfred Vanloo and Eugène Leterrier. Music by Charles Lecocq. Théâtre de la Renaissance, Paris, 3 February 1877.

Modest Marjolaine (Jeanne Granier) has won the Brussels May Queen title for eight years running, and even though she is now married she wins it a for a ninth, for her husband, old Baron Palamède (Berthelier), has to admit that his bride is still a virgin. Annibal (Vauthier), gayest of a band of gay young blades, bets the resigned husband that he will change that and, though he fails in his naughty designs, he manages to give the appearance that he has succeeded. The baron pays up ruinously and Marjolaine is thrown out of the castle. By the time the truth comes out, she is past accepting apologies, and goes off with a little clockmaker, Frickel (Félix Puget), who is a tenor.

Granier was this time equipped with a rôle which had not the farcical possibilities of a *Giroflé-Girofla* or a *La Petite Mariée*, but which nevertheless gave her plenty of opportunities to score points in dialogue as well as in song. Lecocq provided her with a pretty, coy first-act Rondo des Blés, a Duo des adieux and the Couplets des 'coucous' with her little tenor, and another duo of 'no's with the determined baritone, with whom she later shared a thought of what might have been, and finally a little tongue-in-cheek 'Complainte'. Vauthier had his chance in his Couplets de Printemps and Berthelier had a few comic

moments, but the best of the rest fell to Mlle Théo, as Aveline, the original girl who can't say no, who complained of a 'coeur trop sensible' explaining 'c'est ma nature qui veut ça!', and joined in a bell song with Puget which came dangerously near in lyrics at least to that of the soon-to-be-concurrent *Les Cloches de Corneville* ('sonne, sonne, donc maudit carillon').

If *La Marjolaine* was not adjudged quite up to its predecessors by the critics, it nevertheless pleased Victor Koning's Théâtre de la Renaissance public. It ran straight through the spring to packed houses (116 performances) and would have resumed after the summer recess had Granier not been taken ill. By the time she returned other shows were under way, and it was not until 1880 that she reprised *La Marjolaine* at the Renaissance. But, in spite of this accident, the show was already on its way. Brussels staged the piece which was set in its own town square just a few weeks after the Paris opening with Mlle Luce starred as Marjolaine, Bordeaux welcomed the Renaissance company headed by Mme Matz-Ferrare in the summer, and in the autumn the show began to appear further afield.

In September *Kisasszony feleségem* (ad Jenő Rákosi) opened at the Budapest Népszinház with no less a star than Lujza Blaha in the rôle of Marjolaine alongside János Kápolnai (Friquet), Elek Solymossy (Hannibal) and István Együd (Palamède) to great success and a series of 56 performances, the best for any opérette since the theatre's opening three years earlier, and outpointing both *La Fille de Madame Angot* and *Der Seekadet*. A firm hit, it was brought back in new productions in 1884 and in 1901. A few days later, London saw its version of *La Marjolaine* (ad Sutherland Edwards) starring Kate Santley alongside Fred Mervin, Lionel Brough and Walter H Fisher. London's critics, however, were not ready for a musical about virginity. They howled ('one of the most daring books in the long, dirty line of opéra-bouffe') at the doubles entendres which had looked safe to the Lord Chamberlain on paper but which la belle Kate imbued with very different meanings – ignoring the fact that the audience were howling too, but with delight. Newspaper correspondence flowed, and when *The Era* announced that the piece had been changed ('nearly all the naughty speeches and wicked suggestions have disappeared'), the director, Mrs Liston, hastened into print to deny 'the process of emasculation' suggested. *La Marjolaine* ran for a fine four months, and returned the following autumn for a second season.

In America, Marie Aimée was quick to add *La Marjolaine* to her repertoire, and she kept it there as a popular item for a number of years. Louise Théo followed her example from 1882, but apparently no one was game to try to produce it on Broadway in English. In German, the famous doubles entendres either didn't entendre or else were not liked. A mounting at Vienna's Carltheater (ad not credited) with Frln Horty cast as Marjolaine alongside Karl Blasel (Palamède), Franz Eppich (Hannibal), Antonie Schlager (Frickel) and Rosa Streitmann (Aveline) played just 13 times. A Spanish version was mounted under the title *Amapola*.

Another musical entitled simply *Marjolaine* (Hugo Felix/ Brian Hooker/Catherine Chisholm Cushing) produced in America (Broadway Theater 24 January 1922, 136 performances) and later played briefly in Britain, was a musical version of the Louis N Parker play *Pomander Walk* in which young love is thwarted by the fact that the lovers' parents had been involved in a jilt.

USA: Park Theater 3 May 1877; Hungary: Népszinház *Kisasszony feleségem* 14 September 1877; UK: Royalty Theatre 29 September 1877; Austria: Carltheater 18 October 1879

MARJORIE English comic opera in 3 acts by 'Lewis Clifton' (Clifton Lyne) and Joseph J Dilley. Revised by Robert Buchanan. Music by Walter Slaughter. Prince of Wales Theatre, London, 18 January 1890.

Marjorie was the first and only English musical produced by the Carl Rosa Light Opera Company, a British company set up by the famous operatic manager to attempt to pluck some of the pickings from the lighter musical theatre which had eaten into his audiences. Written by an authorial partnership with little track record and a composer whose only notable achievement to date had been a children's musical version of *Alice in Wonderland*, it was a period light opera, in the style of *Dorothy*, with a feudal background, telling the tale of an amorous earl's attempts to win and wed the titular Marjorie by sending her lover, his serf, off to the wars. Tried out at a matinée during the very successful run of *Paul Jones*, the company's initial presentation, it was subsequently revised for production by the poet Robert Buchanan and made into a vehicle for contralto Agnes Huntington, who had won fame in *Paul Jones*, as the serf, Wilfred.

Miss Huntington walked out shortly after the opening, in newspaperworthy circumstances, but *Marjorie*, with its pretty old-English score, some vigorous low comedy from resident funny man Harry Monkhouse, ringing singing from the handsome baritone Hayden Coffin as the villain ('For Love of Thee'), and the hero's rôle restored to its original tenor, had a six-and-a-half-month run in London, toured successfully with Miss Herbert, 'the lady baritone', as hero, and was played in the repertoire of J C Williamson's Royal Comic Opera Company in Australia and in South Africa.

Another musical under the same title credited to Fred Thompson, Clifford Grey and Harold Atteridge ('additional dialogue'), with music by Romberg, Herbert Stothart, Philip Culkin and Stephen Jones, was produced at Broadway's Shubert Theater (11 August 1924). Elizabeth Hines in the title-rôle vamped Roy Royston to charleston strains until he put her brother's play on the stage and married her 144 times.

Australia: Princess Theatre, Melbourne 20 December 1893

MARRE, Albert [MOSHINSKI, Albert] (b New York, 20 September 1925). Director whose several hits were big enough to make up for a welter of quick failures.

After posts in Cambridge, Massachusetts, and at the New York City Center as a director of drama, Marre made a successful start in the musical theatre when his first assignment, as director of the west coast production of *Kismet*, gave him a major national and international success. He had less joy with the *Lost Horizon* musical, *Shangri La*, a camped-up Offenbach *Belle Hélène* retitled *La Belle*, and with two further shows by the *Kismet* team of Wright and Forrest, *At the Grand* and *The Love Doctor*, but he moored up against success once again with Jerry Herman's maiden musical, *Milk and Honey* (1961) and, most notably, with the original production of the Don Quixote

musical *Man of La Mancha* (1965). His subsequent ventures with new musicals have been wholly unfortunate. Four later shows by *La Mancha* composer Mitch Leigh (*Chu Chem*, *Cry for Us All*, *Halloween*, *Home Sweet Homer*) and a British extravaganza called *Winnie*, based on the life of Winston Churchill, folded on the road or soon after.

Marre is married to performer Joan Diener who appeared as Lalume in *Kismet*, as Aldonza in *Man of La Mancha* (USA, UK, France), as Helen in *La Belle*, in *At the Grand* (1958), *Cry for Us All* (1970), *Home Sweet Homer* (1976) etc.

1970 **Cry for Us All** (Mitch Leigh/William Alfred, Phyllis Robinson/w Alfred) Broadhurst Theater 8 April
1976 **Home Sweet Homer** (aka *Odyssey*) (Leigh/Forman Brown, Charles Burr/Roland Kibbee) Palace Theater 4 January

MARS, Antony (b Vence, 22 October 1861; d Paris, 17 February 1915). Expert author of vaudevilles and comedies whose works won substantial and far-flung success around Europe in the 1890s and 1900s, and on several occasions around the world.

Before making a success as a dramatist, Mars worked first in a solicitor's office and then for the railways. His first significant hit in the theatre came with the play *Les Surprises du divorce* (1888, w Alexandre Bisson) and, as the play successes continued through the 1890s, he also began to write freely, both in collaborations and occasionally alone, for the musical theatre. He achieved a remarkable percentage of hits to productions, and his most enduring successes in the musical sphere came with two pieces with scores composed by Victor Roger: the vaudeville-opérette *Les Vingt-huit Jours de Clairette* with its tale of mistaken identities and a disguised lady loose in an army camp, and the superb *Les Fêtards*, with its comic/sentimental lesson on how to hold an errant husband. The libretto of *Les Fêtards* was later used as the basis for two further musicals, the highly successful *Kitty Grey* in England and *The Rounders* in America, as well as being played widely and long in Europe with Roger's original musical score attached, and on the West End stage as a straight play.

Three other Mars pieces originally set with scores by Roger for their French productions also travelled around Europe, sometimes with and sometimes without that music attached. *Le Voyage de Corbillon*, written by Mars alone, was adapted into German as *Das rothe Parapluie* (ad Alexander Landesberg, Ludwig Fischl) and played at Vienna's Theater in der Josefstadt with a score by Karl Kappeller (26 February 1897), and also appeared in Hungary as *Az orleansi szüzek* (ad Sándor Peterdi, Városligeti Nyári Szinkör 23 August 1906) with Roger's score intact. The vaudeville *Les Douze Femmes de Japhet*, written with Maurice Desvallières and played with some considerable success in France, Austria and Hungary, was also adapted into a German vaudeville, *Die zwölf Frauen des Japhet*, by Julius Freund and composer Viktor Holländer for the Berlin Metropoltheater. The later *La Poule blanche* (w Maurice Hennequin) turned up in Germany as *Das weisse Henne* (ad Bolten-Bäckers, Viktoria Theater 11 September 1898) and in Hungary as *Fehér csirke* (ad Emil Makai, Gyula Zempléni Népszinház 28 April 1899). Hungary also proved partial to one piece which France had cared less for: *Clary-Clara* had a fine run in Budapest as *Klári* (ad

Ferenc Rajna, Viktor Rákosi Népszinház 14 April 1894, 31 performances) before its libretto was borrowed by László Szilágyi to be made over into the text for Béla Zerkovitz's extremely successful *Csokos asszony* (Városi Színház 27 February 1926). Hungary also welcomed Mars and Raymond's *Nicol-Nick*, under the title *Vegye el á lányomat* (ad Gyula Komor).

Another vaudeville, *La Demoiselle du téléphone*, this one originally set with a score by Gaston Serpette, provided Mars with a further worldwide success in a variety of musicalized forms, whilst the Serpette/Roger *La Dot de Brigitte* was played in Vienna as *Frau Lieutenant* (ad Léon, Waldberg, Theater in der Josefstadt 13 January 1900, 14 performances), in Germany under the same title (ad Hermann Hirschel, Thalia-Theater 12 January 1898) and in Hungary as *Brigitta* (ad Emil Makai, Népszinház 19 October 1895, 22 performances).

The Robert Planquette vaudeville-opérette à grand spectacle *Mam'zelle Quat' sous* and the Louis Varney opérette *Les Forains* also won both German- and Hungarian-language productions as *Die beiden Don Juans/ A garasos kisasszony* and *Olympia, die Muskelvenus/Der Gaukler/Komediások* respectively. However, in spite of this outstanding strike rate in Europe, and in spite of the enormous popularity of versions of such of his plays as *Les Surprises du divorce*, *Le Truc de Séraphin* and *Fils à papa* in English-speaking countries, Mars's musical works works – *Les Fêtards* and *La Demoiselle du téléphone* apart – were largely bypassed in Britain and America. *Les Surprises du divorce*, however, eventually turned up on the Broadway stage in musical form, played under the title *Honeydew* (Efrem Zimbalist/Joseph W Herbert Casino Theater 6 September 1920).

In later years, Mars devoted his attention largely to the non-musical theatre, but he collaborated with his earliest partner, Maurice Desvallières, on the French versions of two highly successful Operetten, *Die Dollarprinzessin* and *Die keusche Susanne*, the latter a musical version of his own play *Fils à papa* and, in the long run, his most international credit in the musical theatre.

His *Veuve Durosel* (w Bisson, Théâtre du Vaudeville 7 March 1888) was made into a musical in Czechoslovakia as *Mama vom Ballet* (Bernard Grün/Rudolf Stadler, Ernst Stadler Deutsches Theater studio 20 February 1926) whilst another, unidentified work was quoted as the source of the American entertainment *Exceeding the Speed Limit* (Cohan's Grand Opera House, Chicago 23 December 1912).

A pretty little square, which once held Vence's one good second-hand bookshop, commemorates Mars in his hometown. Even if it spells his name wrongly on its bus-stop.

1888 **Quand on conspire!** (P Devos) 1 act Salle Lancry 22 January
1890 **Les Douze Femmes de Japhet** (Victor Roger/w Maurice Desvallières) Théâtre de la Renaissance 16 December
1891 **La Demoiselle du téléphone** (Gaston Serpette/w Desvallières) Théâtre des Nouveautés 2 May
1891 **Le Mitron** (André Martinet/w Maxime Boucheron) Théâtre des Folies-Dramatiques 24 September
1892 **Les Vingt-huit Jours de Clairette** (Roger/w Hippolyte Raymond) Théâtre des Folies-Dramatiques 3 May
1892 **La Bonne de chez Duval** (Serpette/w Raymond) Théâtre des Nouveautés 6 October

1893 **Catherinette** (Roger/w Raymond) 1 act Lunéville 17 July
1893 **Pierre et Paul** (Roger/w Raymond) 1 act Lunéville 17 July
1894 **Les Forains** (Louis Varney/w Boucheron) Théâtre des Bouffes-Parisiens 9 February
1894 **Le Troisième Hussards** (Justin Clérice/w Maurice Hennequin) Théâtre de la Gaîté 14 March
1894 **Clary-Clara** (Roger/w Raymond) Théâtre des Folies-Dramatiques 20 March
1895 **Nicol-Nick** (Roger/w Raymond, Henri Duru) Théâtre des Folies-Dramatiques 23 January
1895 **La Dot de Brigitte** (Serpette, Roger/w Paul Ferrier) Théâtre des Bouffes-Parisiens 6 May
1896 **Le Voyage de Corbillon** (Roger) Théâtre Cluny 30 January
1896 **Sa Majesté l'amour** (Roger/w M Hennequin) Eldorado 24 December
1897 **Les Fêtards** (Roger/w M Hennequin) Théâtre du Palais-Royal 28 October
1897 **Mam'zelle Quat' Sous** (Robert Planquette/w Desvallières) Théâtre de la Gaîté 5 November
1898 **La Geisha** (*The Geisha*) French version w Charles Clairville, Jules Lemaire (Théâtre de l'Athénée)
1899 **La Poule blanche** (Roger/w M Hennequin) Théâtre Cluny 13 January
1910 **La Vie joyeuse** (Henri Hirschmann) Valence 17 November
1911 **La Princesse Dollar** (*Die Dollarprinzessin*) French version w Desvallières
1913 **La Chaste Suzanne** (*Die keusche Susanne*) French version w Desvallières (Théâtre des Célestins, Lyon)

MARSH, Howard [Warren]   (b Bluffton, Ind; d Long Branch, NJ, 7 August 1969).

A good-looking leading man with a fine tenor voice, Marsh (who managed modestly to keep his birthdate a secret through 20 years of being anthologized) had his first good part on Broadway in 1917 as the leading man of Louis Hirsch's short-lived *The Grass Widow* (Comte Jacques de Cluny). He took over a supporting rôle in *Maytime*, toured the piece alongside Grace van Studdiford, and appeared in the *Greenwich Village Follies* (1920) before his next important appearance on Broadway. This time he was in a hit, cast as Franz Schober, the tenor who gets the girl and Schubert's 'Serenade' to sing in the American version of *Das Dreimäderlhaus* (*Blossom Time*, 1921). He followed this memorable performance with a second consecutive triumph when he created the star rôle of Sigmund Romberg's romantic operetta *The Student Prince* (Karl-Franz), a rôle equipped with another, almost as celebrated Serenade, and introducing the duets 'Deep in My Heart, Dear' and 'Golden Days'. Romberg's *Cherry Blossoms* (1927, Ned Hamilton) was a failure, but its closure at least made Marsh available to create the romantic lead of a third block-buster, as Gaylord Ravenal in *Show Boat*, joining Norma Terris in singing 'Make Believe', 'You Are Love' and 'Why Do I Love You?' for the first time on any stage. After this top-class trio of rôles, however, there were no more successes and Marsh's final Broadway appearance came when he was paired again with Miss Terris in a swift flop called *The Well of Romance* in 1930, little more than a decade after his first lead rôle.

MARTIN, Ernest [MARKOWITZ, Ernest H] (b Pittsburgh 28 August 1918).

Producer who, in collaboration with Cy Feuer, presented such Broadway musicals as *Where's Charley?*, *Guys and Dolls*, *Can-Can*, *The Boy Friend*, *How to Succeed in Business*

Without Really Trying, Little Me, Skyscraper and *Walking Happy* and the film version of *A Chorus Line*.

MARTIN, Hugh (b Birmingham, Ala, 11 August 1914).

At first a chorister and member of the singing group The Martins in musical comedy (*Hooray for What!, The Streets of Paris, Louisiana Purchase, The Lady Comes Across,* pre-Broadway in *My Dear Public* and *Three after Three*), Martin joined with fellow singer Ralph Blane to compose the songs for the successful musical comedy *Best Foot Forward* ('Buckle Down, Winsocki') and for a number of films, of which the most notable was *Meet Me in St Louis* ('Meet Me in St Louis', 'Trolley Song'). After the War, Martin returned to writing for the stage and supplied songs for *Look Ma, I'm Dancin'* (188 performances), *Make a Wish* (102 performances), Eric Maschwitz's neatly calculated attempt to write a British Broadway musical to the text of the play *Daddy Long-Legs* (*Love from Judy,* 594 performances), and a musicalization of Noël Coward's *Blithe Spirit* (375 performances, London 93 performances).

In 1989 an attempt to mount a Broadway stage-spectacular version of *Meet Me in St Louis* – first played as a stage piece at the St Louis Municipal Opera in 1960 – ran through an apparently forced 236 performances.

1941 **Best Foot Forward** (w Ralph Blane/John Cecil Holm) Ethel Barrymore Theater 1 October
1948 **Look Ma, I'm Dancin'** (Jerome Lawrence, Robert E Lee) Adelphi Theater 29 January
1951 **Make a Wish** (Preston Sturges) Winter Garden Theater 18 April
1952 **Love from Judy** (Timothy Gray/Eric Maschwitz) Saville Theatre, London 25 September
1964 **High Spirits** (w Gray) Alvin Theater 17 April
1989 **Meet Me in St Louis** (w Blane/ad Hugh Wheeler) Gershwin Theater 2 November

MARTIN, Mary [Virginia] (b Weatherford, Tex, 1 December 1913; d Rancho Mirage, Cal, 4 November 1990).

Broadway soubrette who became one of the American musical theatre's favourite leading ladies and who introduced two of Rodgers and Hammerstein's most memorable heroines.

Miss Martin first came to the fore at the age of 25 as the soubrette of *Leave it to Me!* in which, in the character of the popsie Dolly Winslow, she introduced Cole Porter's 'My Heart Belongs to Daddy'. It was, however some four years before she returned to Broadway, having closed out of town in the musicals *Nice Goin'* (1939, Billie Jackson) and *Dancing in the Streets* (1943, Mary Hastings) and spent some time in Hollywood where her film assignments had included *The Great Victor Herbert* (1939) and *The Birth of the Blues* (1941). The character in which she returned was that of the brought-to-life statue of the goddess of love in *One Touch of Venus,* introducing Kurt Weill's 'Speak Low' and 'I'm a Stranger Here Myself' for a long and successful run. She subsequently appeared as the Chinese heroine of *Lute Song* (1946, 'Mountain High, Valley Low') on Broadway and, miscast, as the prima donna heroine of Noël Coward's London musical *Pacific 1860* before going out to the rest of America as the star of the first touring company of *Annie Get Your Gun* (1947).

Miss Martin had her second great success when she created the rôle of Ensign Nellie Forbush, the button-bright little heroine of Rodgers and Hammerstein's *South Pacific* (1949, Tony Award), singing '(I'm in love with) A Wonderful Guy', 'I'm Gonna Wash that Man Right outa my Hair' and 'Honey Bun' to New York and London audiences. In 1954, now past the age of 40, she starred in a Broadway-style musical version of J M Barrie's *Peter Pan* which brought her a second Tony award and, thanks to a television recording, loving identification with this celebrated boyish rôle throughout America. However, her most memorable achievement came when she encouraged Rodgers and Hammerstein to write for her their musical version of the tale of Maria von Trapp and her singing family. As Maria in *The Sound of Music* ('My Favourite Things', 'Do-re-mi', 'The Sound of Music') Miss Martin scored another major triumph, took her third Tony Award, and launched a show which was to become – this time with a little help from someone else's film – one of the best-loved of all time.

If the star was less successful in the title-rôle of the short-lived *Jennie* (1963), it was perhaps partly because she herself had ordered a disinfecting rewrite of the libretto and character, and her version of the title-rôle of *Hello, Dolly!,* though well received on the touring circuits at home proved not to be to the taste of Londoners, but she turned up one final Broadway musical success in 1966 when she starred opposite Robert Preston in the two-handed tale of marriage, *I Do! I Do!* ('My Cup Runneth Over', 'Flaming Agnes').

I Do! I Do! turned out to be not only Miss Martin's last Broadway success, but her last Broadway musical. Although she appeared further on the stage over another 20 years, she did not move into senior rôles in musicals, leaving her image, in line with her oft-reseen television film appearance as Peter Pan, as a youngish and spiritedly soubretty one.

Miss Martin was married to Richard Halliday, producer of *Jennie,* and was the mother of actor Larry Hagman, best known as the 'JR' of television's *Dallas*.

Autobiography: *My Heart Belongs* (Morrow, New York, 1976); Literature: Newman, S: *Mary Martin On Stage* (Westminster Press, Philadelphia, 1969)

MARTIN, Millicent (b Romford, Essex, 8 June 1934).

Top British soubrette of the 1950s who later returned to play character rôles.

Originally a child performer (*Lute Song* etc), Millicent Martin made her first adult London appearance at the age of 21 when she took over as Fay/Lolita in *The Boy Friend,* and her first on Broadway as Nancy in the same show. She made her mark soon after as the little cockney stripper, Maisie, in *Expresso Bongo* (1958) but another, rather similar, rôle in the less successful *The Crooked Mile* (1959, Cora) was followed only by the flops of *The Dancing Heiress* (1960), *State of Emergency* (1962) and a curiously adapted musical version of *The Admirable Crichton* (*Our Man Crichton*) reorganized to make her character of Tweenie extravagantly prominent. Thereafter she was seen principally on television, but she appeared at the Chichester Festival as Polly Peachum (*Beggar's Opera*) and had her best new musical-theatre part since *Expresso Bongo* as Ruth Earp opposite the Denry Machin of Jim Dale in *The Card* (1975) before finding a fine success with *Side By Side By Sondheim,* a compilation show of material from Stephen Sondheim's

Plate 173. **Millicent Martin** *and the ladies' chorus in* The Crooked Mile.

shows of which she was one of the original group of instigators.

After some years away from the musical theatre, Miss Martin succeeded, in the 1980s, to the rôles of Dorothy Brock in Broadway's *42nd Street* and that of Phyllis in the London production of *Follies*.

On film, she paired with Tony Tanner in a cinematic version of *Stop the World – I Want to Get Off*.

MARTIN, Robert

Irish songwriter Bob Martin never had a musical-comedy score played in the professional theatre, and probably would not have been capable of writing one, but in the late 1880s his songs were amongst the greatest highlights of George Edwardes's Gaiety Theater new burlesques. Nellie Farren introduced 'I'm a Jolly Little Chap all Round' and Edwin Lonnen made major hits of his 'Bally-hooley' in *Monte Cristo Jr* (1886) and of his 'Killaloe' in *Miss Esmeralda* (1887). 'The Dispensary Doctor' written for the same artist in *Frankenstein* (1887) was, like the show, a little less successful, but 'Enniscorthy' sung by Lonnen as Mephistopheles, and the topical duet 'I Raise No Objection to That' in *Faust-Up-to-Date* (1888) were both serious hits.

Martin wrote lyrics for Teddy Solomon for two songs in *Ruy Blas and the Blasé Roué* (1889) and combined with Ernest Ford to produce an entire short musical called *Joan or the Brigands of Bluegoria* ('a story of the stock exchange') which was privately performed by himself and a group of 'name' friends including Sir George Power, David Bis-

pham, Cosmo Gordon Lennox and Gabrielle Enthoven at the Opera Comique, but thereafter, although he continued to write ('Mullingar', 'Mulrooney's Dog', 'Thru Darkest Ireland', 'On the Blatherumskite' etc) his name disappeared from London's playbills, emerging just once more, a decade later, on the programme of Edwardes's revusical *The Merry-Go-Round*.

MARTINOT, Sadie [MARTINOT, Sarah] (b Jamaica, NY, 19 December 1861; d Ogdensburg, NY, 7 May 1923). Singing beauty who played in musical theatre on both sides of the Atlantic.

At the age of 15 the glamorous Miss Martinot appeared as Cupid in a production of the burlesque *Ixion* at the Eagle Theater, and three years later, now a member of the company at the Boston Museum, she was the first American Hebe in *HMS Pinafore*. She then crossed to Britain where she played small rôles in the Alhambra productions of *Mephistopheles II* (*Le Petit Faust*, 1880, Spirit of the Brocken) and *Jeanne, Jeannette et Jeanneton* (1881, Céline) and created her one important musical part, the ingénue Katrina in Planquette's *Rip van Winkle*.

Returning to America, she concentrated largely on dramatic parts, but she appeared at the Casino Theater for Aronson and scored a major success in the title-rôle of Genée's *Nanon* (1885). Cast in the lead of the theatre's later production of *Nadgy*, she walked out of the show during rehearsals and appeared instead at the Amberg Theater playing Bettina in *La Mascotte* in German. Then she disappearing from the theatre for several years. She reappeared on the musical stage playing Suzette in *Le Voyage de Suzette* in 1893 and caused a sensation (more by her figure and revealing frock than anything else) as Lady Angela in a revival of *Patience* (1896). She later appeared in character rôles in such pieces as *Piff! Paff! Pouf!* (1905) on the road before going into a second retirement which ended, in the last five years of her life, in an insane asylum.

MARTOS, Ferenc (b Arad, 10 January 1875; d Budapest 24 November 1938). The most outstanding and successful librettist of the Hungarian musical theatre.

In a career of over 30 years which covered the most internationally flourishing years of the Hungarian musical theatre, Martos worked with virtually all the best local composers of his time, and he was responsible for the texts of a vast percentage of Hungary's most successful and enduring operetts.

Martos graduated as a Doctor of Law from Budapest university and took a post in the public service in the department of religious and public education. He began writing for the theatre in 1900 and his first produced piece, a verse comedy, *Balassa Bálint*, was staged in 1902 at the Nemzeti Szinház. Later the same year he moved into the musical theatre for the first time when he provided the text for Jenő Huszka's highly successful operett *Bob herceg*. It was a libretto which involved British royalty in the same kind of preposterous doings that British librettists persisted in inflicting on central European kings and princesses, and the Prince Bob of the title was no less than the son of Queen Victoria. *Bob herceg* turned out to be the biggest native operett success up to its time and thereafter, although Martos turned out a handful of successful plays and adaptations (including the Hungarian version of *His Official Wife*), the bulk of his career was spent as a librettist and lyricist for the musical theatre.

After further hits with Huszka (*Aranyvirág, Gül Baba*), he joined forces with the rising Viktor Jacobi. The pair had several home successes before they teamed on Jacobi's two most important shows, *Leányvásár* (*The Marriage Market*) with its Ruramerican-cowboy version of the *Martha* story, and the finely constructed combination of the romantic and comic that was *Szibill*. Both operetts would go round the world. Before they got there, however, *A kis gróf*, on which Martos had collaborated with the young Aladár Rényi, had already made it to Vienna and to Broadway under the title *Suzi*.

Martos wrote the texts for Kálmán's *A kis király* (*Der kleine könig*) and *Zsuzsi kisasszony* (*Miss Springtime*), and for Lehár's *A Pacsirta*, originally produced in Budapest but later more generally known under its German title of *Wo die Lerche singt*, and he paired with another young composer, Károly Komjáthy, on what would be, as it had been with Rényi, the most important hit of his career. The military operett *Pillangó főhadnagy* became another oft-revived staple in the Hungarian repertoire.

Martos then paired up with Albert Szirmai, for whom he provided the text for *Alexandra* (1925), one of his most internationally successful works, as well as *Éva grófnő* ('a combination of *Enoch Arden* and *Madame Butterfly* with a happy ending') and the successful *A Ballerina*. By the time of his final works, some of which were staged in translation in Vienna (the christmas show *Hanserl* – ex-*Jánoska* – and Komjáthy's Singspiel *Ein Liebestraum*), the height of the European operett period had passed, and his remarkable total of hits was no further increased.

Martos's name appeared attached to a 1923 American musical called *Peaches* (Max R Steiner/Robert B Smith/ad Harry B Smith Garrick Theater, Philadelphia 22 January) but producer George Lederer was not specific about the source of his borrowing and the Swiss maid/heiress identity-swap of the tale didn't belong to any of Martos's major plays.

1902 **Bob herceg** (Jenő Huszka/w Károly Bakonyi) Népszinház 20 December
1903 **Aranyvirág** (Huszka) Király Színház 6 November
1905 **A granadai vőlegény** (József Bahnert) Népszinház 11 February
1905 **Gül Baba** (Huszka) Király Színház 9 December
1905 **A legvitézebb huszár** (Viktor Jacobi) Magyar Színház 30 December
1907 **Tüskerózsa** (Jacobi) Király Színház 23 March
1907 **Tündérszerelem** (Huszka) Népszinház-Vigopera 20 December
1908 **Van, de nincs** (Jacobi) Király Színház 30 October
1909 **Jánoska** (Jacobi) Király Színház 7 May
1911 **A kis gróf** (Aladár Rényi) Király Színház 9 September
1911 **Leányvásár** (Jacobi/w Miksa Bródy) Király Színház 14 November
1913 **Szökik a nagysága** (w M Bródy) Budapesti Színház 22 March
1914 **A kis király** (Emmerich Kálmán/w Bakonyi) Népopera 17 January
1914 **Szibill** (Viktor Jacobi/w M Bródy) Király Színház 27 February
1915 **Zsuzsi kisasszony** (Kálmán/w M Bródy) Vigszinház 22 February
1917 **A pacsirta** (Franz Lehár) Király Színház 1 February
1918 **Pillangó fődhadnagy** (Károly Komjáthy/w Imre Harmath) Király Színház 7 June
1919 **Lili bárónő** (Huszka) Városi Színház 7 March
1920 **Cigánygrófné** (Zsigmond Vincze/Ernő Kulinyi) Király Színház 13 March
1925 **Anna-bál** (Robert Volkmann arr Vincze/Kulinyi) Király Színház 20 September
1925 **Alexandra** (Albert Szirmai) Kiräly Színház 25 November
1926 **Kitty és Kató** (Rényi) Király Színház 30 April
1926 **Hajtóvadászat** (Huszka) Városi Színház 22 October
1928 **Éva grófnő** (Szirmai) Király Színház 3 February
1929 **Katica** (Alfred Márkus) Városi Színház 7 December
1931 **A Ballerina** (Szirmai) Király Színház 7 March
1933 **Ein Liebestraum** (Komjáthy/w Szilágyi ad Heinz Reichert) Theater an der Wien 27 October
1935 **Szépségkirálynő** (József Paksy/w Andor Szenes) Király Színház 21 June

MARX BROTHERS

Chico MARX [Leonard MARX] (b New York, 22 March 1891; d Hollywood, 11 October 1961); Groucho MARX [Julius Henry MARX] (b New York, 2 October 1895; d Los Angeles, 19 August 1977); Harpo MARX [Adolph MARX] (b New York, 23 November 1893; d Hollywood, 28 September 1964); Zeppo MARX [Herbert MARX] (b New York, 25 February 1901; d Palm Springs, 29 November 1979).

The famous American comedy squad began their careers in vaudeville, before appearing (reduced to four, by this stage, with the early loss of fifth brother, Gummo, né Milton), on the almost legitimate stage in three musical comedies. The first of these, *I'll Say She Is* ('a musical comedy revue') written by Will B Johnstone in the form of

Plate 174. **The Marx Brothers** *surrounded by their chorines in* The Cocoanuts.

an extended variety sketch (songs: Tom Johnstone), allowed the team to gallivant through the kind of extravagant comedy for which they became famous, and included an hypnosis section which permitted Groucho to appear as Napoleon, a courtroom 'drama' and some spare moments for other specialities. It ran through 304 performances at the Casino Theater, encouraging the follow-up the next year with a vehicle written by an altogether classier team: George S Kaufman and Irving Berlin.

The equally zany and marginally more constructed *The Cocoanuts* was an even greater success than its predecessor (377 performances), and a third piece, *Animal Crackers*, again by Kaufman and Morrie Ryskind (songs: Bert Kalmar and Harry Ruby), presenting Groucho as the preposterous Captain Spalding, out to hunt down a stolen painting, also had a fine run (191 performances). The brothers then left Broadway to pursue the career which would give them international fame, in Hollywood. Amongst their screen ventures were included filmed versions of both *The Cocoanuts* and *Animal Crackers*.

Targets for often unimaginative impersonators for many years, the brothers finally won a clever and sympathetic treatment in the London revusical show *A Day in Hollywood, a Night in the Ukraine*, where Sheila Steafel stole the evening as an appealingly mute Harpo in a one-act Marx-

style perversion of *The Bear*. Perhaps just because it was successful, and success of course means money, this umpteenth imitation provoked a threat of legal action for plagiarism of the brothers' act. The team were also portrayed in the Broadway musical *Minnie's Boys* (Imperial Theater 26 March 1970), a *Gypsy*-ish tale of their ambitious stage mother, which avoided any such action by having a younger Marx on its writing team and paying Groucho Marx (Harpo and Chico were already departed) to be a 'production consultant'. It folded after 80 performances.

Autobiographies: Marx, G: *Groucho and Me* (Bernard Geis, New York, 1959), Marx, H w Barber, R: *Harpo Speaks* (Gollancz, London, 1961), *The Groucho Letters* (Simon & Schuster, New York, 1967); w Anobile, R: *The Marx Brothers Scrapbook* (Norton, New York, 1973); Biographies: Crichton, K: *The Marx Brothers* (Doubleday, New York, 1950), Marx, A: *Son of Groucho* (David McKay, New York, 1972), etc.

MARY Musical comedy in 2 acts by Otto Harbach and Frank Mandel. Music by Louis Hirsch. Knickerbocker Theater, New York, 18 October 1920.

The most successful of composer Louis Hirsch's successors to *Going Up*, *Mary* was one of the best in the prettily naïve 'Cinderella' line of Broadway shows which had been given such an impetus by *Irene* the previous season and which would be compounded a couple of weeks after *Mary*'s opening by *Sally*.

Mary's tiny story centred on Jack Keene (Jack McGowan) who is more interested in trying to make a fortune out of building 'portable houses' than in paying attention to his mother's little secretary, Mary (Janet Velie). Wealthy Madeleine (Florrie Millership) pursues Jack, and dashing Tommy (Alfred Gerrard) and womanizing Gaston (Charles Judels) pursue Madeleine, until the latter switches his attentions to Mary, but Jack finally gets around to recognizing true love round about the same time that his housing plot spouts oil, so whilst Gaston is gratefully grabbed by Mrs Keene (Georgia Caine), the happily-rich-and-wed ending expected since Act I, minute one, duly arrives.

George M Cohan's production, originally entitled *The House That Jack Built* (even though he apparently didn't) but rechristened doubtless with its producer's famous old song ('it's a grand old name') – which was then eased into the show – in mind, opened at Philadelphia in April. After four weeks the show headed for Boston for the summer, then it repeated Philadelphia, then it returned to Boston, and all the time its favourite songs – the delightful hymn to 'The Love Nest', the lively 'We'll Have a Wonderful Party' (strong shades of *Irene* here) and the jaunty 'Anything You Want to Do, Dear' – were becoming ingrained into the popular piano stool. By the time *Mary* eventually opened in New York, its score was well and truly whistled-in. Two tours were on the road and Joe Sacks had signed the piece for England within weeks of the Broadway opening, and the show looked set to be another *Irene*. But in the end *Mary* had a slightly disappointing metropolitan career.

Cohan's production played for a thoroughly respectable if not earth-shattering 219 performances at the Knickerbocker Theater, but Sacks's version with Evelyn Laye, Mabel Sealby (Madeleine), Ralph Lynn (Gaston), Alec Regan (Jack) and Bernard Granville (Tommy) lasted only 90 nights at London's not-so-big Queen's Theatre and soon after its closure the producer was declared bankrupt. Australia's production did not have such disastrous effects, and did rather better, all told. Maud Fane starred as Mary to the Jack of J Roland Hogue, with W S Percy (Gaston), Madge Elliott (Madeleine) and Ethel Morrison (Mrs Keene) through a try-out in Adelaide (30 September), a good ten-week run in two theatres in Melbourne, and seven weeks in Sydney (Her Majesty's Theatre 7 July 1923) the following year with Phyllis Beadon as Mary.

If all this was a little less than might have been hoped, *Mary*, nevertheless, had a long and happy life which was lived out largely in the areas where she had first found popularity, wearing a much-loved trail around the American touring circuits for many seasons.

UK: Queen's Theatre 27 April 1921; Australia: Theatre Royal, Melbourne 7 October 1922

MASCHWITZ, Eric [aka Holt MARVELL] (b Birmingham, 10 June 1901; d London, 27 October 1969). Librettist for several long-running London shows.

Cambridge-educated Maschwitz became first the editor of Britain's *Radio Times*, and subsequently director of variety programmes at the BBC in the years prior to the war. His position gave him reasonably unhampered access to the airwaves, which he used (and not for the last time) pseudonymously to give an airing to his own unproduced romantic musical play *Goodnight Vienna* (music: George Posford). *Goodnight Vienna* went on from its radio production to become a musical film with Jack Buchanan and Anna Neagle starred, whilst the pair turned out a second piece, *The Gay Hussar*, constructed on very similar plotlines, for the British touring circuits. Three years later, in the wake of Ivor Novello's great success with *Glamorous Night*, Maschwitz exhumed *The Gay Hussar*, rewrote it in a similar style, hired as many of Novello's team as he could to stage it, and scored a singular success with what was now called *Balalaika* ('At the Balalaika').

An attempt to follow up this winner with another large romantic musical, failed twice (*Paprika*, *Magyar Melody*), as did a musical version of *Nymph Errant* (*Evangeline*), for which he supplied lyrics only, and a Chopin pasticcio biomusical ripped off from a recent Hungarian show. The indifferent performance of the Chopin piece deterred producer Jack Buchanan from continuing with his announced plans to mount Maschwitz's pasticcii of Tchaikovsky, Offenbach and Mendelssohn, but the author found much more success with a year's run of another romantic piece, *Carissima* (1948), adapted from a Viennese musical by Armin Robinson and the expatriate composer Hans May and, above all, with two further adaptations: a musical version of *Brewster's Millions* with popular singer George Formby starred (*Zip Goes a Million*), and a built-for-Britain Broadway musical called *Love from Judy*, with a book taken from the play *Daddy Long-Legs*. Both held the London stage for over 500 performances. The vein, however, did not stay solid. Adaptations of Arnold Ridley's *The Ghost Train* (*Happy Holiday*) and of the musical version of Siegfried Geyer's widely successful play *Bei Kerzenlicht* (*Romance in Candlelight*) were both failures.

Over the years since *Goodnight Vienna* had been taken from the screen to be played by amateur groups (and ultimately, outside London, by professionals), Maschwitz had, simultaneously, turned out a steady list of adaptations and pasticcio pieces intended for the lucrative amateur market. One of these, a biomusical on (of all people) Dvořák, called *Summer Song*, was professionally produced in 1956. An extremely adept follower, adaptor, imitator of and borrower from whatever musical theatre styles and shows were in fashion, equipped with the position and the connections to plug his works, Maschwitz made himself a good career in the musical theatre, from which he emerged with several enduring song credits ('These Foolish Things', 'A Nightingale Sang in Berkeley Square') and a firm which purveys his product to operatic societies to this day.

1933 **The Gay Hussar** (George Posford) Manchester 2 October
1936 **Balalaika** (revised *The Gay Hussar*) Adelphi Theatre 22 December
1938 **Paprika** (Posford, Bernard Grün) His Majesty's Theater 15 September
1939 **Magyar Melody** (revised *Paprika*) His Majesty's Theatre 20 January
1942 **Waltz Without End** (Frederic Chopin arr Grün) Cambridge Theatre 29 September
1946 **Evangeline** (Posford, Harry Jacobson/Romney Brent) Cambridge Theatre 14 March
1946 **Goodnight Vienna** (Posford/w Harold Purcell) Pavilion, Bournemouth 22 July

1948 **Carissima** (Hans May/Armin Robinson ad) Palace Theatre 10 March

1949 **Belinda Fair** (Jack Strachey/w Gilbert Lennox) Saville Theatre 25 March

1951 **Zip Goes a Million** (Posford) Palace Theatre 20 October

1952 **Love from Judy** (Hugh Martin, Timothy Gray) Saville Theatre 25 September

1954 **Happy Holiday** (Posford) Palace Theatre 22 December

1955 **Romance in Candlelight** (*Bei Kerzenlicht*) English version with new songs by Sam Coslow Piccadilly Theatre 15 September

1956 **Summer Song** (Antonín Dvořák arr Grün) Prince's Theatre 16 February

MASCOTTCHEN Operette in 3 acts by Georg Okonkowski. Lyrics by Will Steinberg. Music by Walter Bromme. Thalia Theater, Berlin, 15 January 1921.

Georg Okonkowski supplied a fine farcical libretto to be the backbone of what would be the most successful of Walter Bromme's series of musical comedies for the Berlin stage. Its key rested in the fact that both the ladies of the piece – the young Countess von Castell-Steensdorf and the dancing-girl Fräulein de Lorm – have the same name, Marion. They also have the same man, for the young Count Eric von Friisenborg who is betrothed to the countess has previously been knocking about with the dancer. Worse, the fine house that Countess Marion's mama has purchased for the pair's honeymoon is none other than the former home of Marion the unaristocratic. The situation is obviously ripe for a bundle of mix-ups and misunderstandings, and when Marion the dancer's periodic sugar-daddy, sea-captain Krag von Westergaard, pulls into port with his nephew, Harald, a lad anxious to cast an eye (and probably something else) over uncle's bit of fluff, the trouble starts. Harald, of course, gets the wrong Marion. After a lot of shipboard and waterside comings and goings Eric goes back to the premarital Marion, Harald gets the upmarket one, and Krag (like all operettic over-30s) has to be content with his pipe and his grog.

Mascottchen ran past its 200th Berlin performance at the Thalia on 30 July before being taken off, and it was later seen in Vienna where Mimi Vesely and Klara Karry starred as the two Marions alongside Viktor Norbert (Eric), Paul Harden (Harald) and Oskar Sachs as the re-named Götz von Berlichingen through a season of 37 performances. The show was later revived at Berlin's Rosetheater.

Austria: Carltheater 26 September 1924

LA MASCOTTE Opéra-comique in 3 acts by Henri Chivot and Alfred Duru. Music by Edmond Audran. Théâtre des Bouffes-Parisiens, Paris, 28 December 1880.

Produced at Louis Cantin's Théâtre des Bouffes-Parisiens following the enormous success of Varney's *Les Mousquetaires au couvent*, Audran's successor to his splendid début with *Les Noces d'Olivette* was thus given two very difficult acts to follow. It triumphed unequivocally, giving the Bouffes-Parisiens another vast hit and going on to become and to remain one of the most popular French opérettes of all time.

The turkey-girl Bettina (Mlle Montbazon) is a 'mascot' – that is to say, she brings good luck to her household – and when she joins the working staff of the miserable farmer Rocco (Raucourt) his luck changes immediately. Bettina's boyfriend, Rocco's shepherd Pippo (Louis

Morlet), isn't allowed too close, however, for a mascot ceases to be a mascot if she ceases to be a virgin. Alas, when her virtues are discovered by the interminably unlucky King Laurent (Paul Hittemans), poor Bettina is dragged off to court, much to the displeasure of the Princess Fiametta (Mlle Dinelli) who, unaware of the rules of being a mascot, assumes the girl is her father's mistress. A whole barrage of complexities leads up to preparations for a double royal wedding, from which Pippo and Bettina escape just as Fiametta's rejected suitor, Fritellini (Charles Lamy), attacks the now-instantly-unlucky Laurent with his army. But luck has changed sides only for as long as it takes for Pippo and Bettina finally to get wedded and bedded. When all efforts to stop this disaster fail, both camps have to sit down and wait for nine months and hope for twins. It appears that mascotry is hereditary.

Chivot and Duru's joyously lubricious libretto built up to wilder and wilder comic scenes which, in the last act, bordered on the burlesques of earlier days, and the comedy was illustrated by a delicious Audran score. The hit number of the show was an ingenuous love duo for the shepherd and the turkey-girl with its 'glou-glou' and 'bé-bé' refrain, whilst Fritellini's melodic analysis of his own qualities ('Le je ne sais quoi poétique') and his bamboozling of the naïve Pippo ('Ah, mon cher, que vous êtes naïf') and Fiametta's appreciation of Pippo's muscles ('Ah! qu'il est beau!') boasted the piece's loveliest melodies. The comic side was topped by Laurent's declaration of his main advantage as a husband for Bettina – his impotence ('J'en suis tout à fait incapable').

La Mascotte was an overwhelming success at the Bouffes-Parisiens, playing for the entire season, and then for most of the next one. Cantin removed it in order to stage Louis Varney's *Coquelicot*, but when that piece failed to take, he promptly brought back *La Mascotte* which proved far from having exhausted its public. It was nearly two years from its opening night when the show was finally taken off and replaced with the next Audran work, *Gillette de Narbonne*. *Gillette de Narbonne* was another fine success, but *La Mascotte* was naturally brought back in 1883 (11 April) with Piccaluga, Mme Morlet and Edouard Maugé for another 92 performances, and it resurfaced again in 1889. Paris revivals were regular thereafter, including runs at the Menus-Plaisirs (1890), the Gaîté (1897, 1901 w Germaine Gallois, 1915 w Angèle Gril), the Apollo (1913, 1914), the Mogador (1921, 1944) and the Porte-Saint-Martin (1933 w Edmée Favart, 1935, 1968) as *La Mascotte* confirmed itself as one of the surest pillars of the opérette repertoire.

The piece also travelled with considerable success. Although Vienna hosted an uncredited (and apparently insufficient) adaptation of *Der Glücksengel* with Josefine Gallmeyer given top billing in the rôle of Fiametta alongside Girardi (Pippo), Karoline Finaly (Bettina) and Carl Adolf Friese (Lorenzo) for only 23 performances, and Germany extended it only a slightly warmer reception, in Hungary, where Lujza Blaha took on the rôle of the turkey-girl with Pál Vidor as her Pippo, János Kápolnai (Fritellini) and Vidor Kassai as Laurent, *Az udvöske* (ad Jenő Rákosi) was an undoubted winner and it followed its original production with many returns. Britain reacted similarly when, after an out-of-town try-out at Brighton (a most unusual thing at the time) Alexander Henderson brought *La Mascotte* (ad Robert Reece, H B Farnie) to the Comedy Theatre with Violet Cameron and the Frenchman Gaillard starred, Lionel Brough heading the comedy, and Lizzie St Quinten and Henry Bracy in the chief singing rôles. After a first run of 199 performances it came back after just a month for a further season with Clara Merivale and Gaillard starred, whilst Kate Santley took her production and her Bettina to the provinces. In 1884 Florence St John paired with Gaillard in a re-run, in 1885 Violet Cameron repeated her original rôle, in 1888 the French prima donna Mary Albert gave a performance in French and, finally, in 1893 the Gaiety Theatre staged a *La Mascotte* season with Miss St John (9 September), the sixth sighting of the show in London in a dozen years. Australia, in the meantime, had responded with equal delight to a J C Williamson production which featured his wife, Maggie Moore, as a truly lusty Bettina, alongside George Verdi (Pippo), W H Woodfield (Fritellini), Nellie Stewart (Fiametta), H M Harwood (Laurent) and Edwin Kelly (Rocco) in the first of what would be a long series of *La Mascotte* seasons.

The competition to get the first *La Mascotte* on to the American stage was all the hotter because of the vast success of the American version of *Les Noces d'Olivette*, but in the end it was the management of the Bijou Theater, which had staged the earlier piece, who won the race. They brought in their production, with Emma Howson (the original London Josephine of *HMS Pinafore*) and John Brand heading the cast, from Boston four days before a rival company appeared at the Park Theater with Helen Carter in the title rôle. Once again the Bijou had an over-sized hit on its hands, for *La Mascotte* ran there for 108 performances in an uninterrupted period of over three months, the Gobble Duet became, as it had in Britain, one of the hits of the season, and the floodgates were opened for productions of the show around the country.

Over the next 12 months Selina Dolaro appeared as Bettina in a quick revival at the Bijou, Geraldine Ulmar and H C Barnabee as Laurent headed the Bostonians' production at Booth's, Paola Marié introduced the original French version, which was also played in repertoire by Louise Théo, Jenny Stubel and Alexander Klein gave *Der Glücksengel* at the Thalia-Theater in German, whilst the young Fay Templeton appeared in the title-rôle of a production at the Windsor Theater. The flood slowed thereafter, but it did not stop for many years: Judic played Bettina during her 1885 tour, the Bijou revived the piece in 1887, a 1892 production at Palmer's Theater presented William Pruette as Pippo, Henry Dixey as Laurent and Camille D'Arville in the title rôle, and Raymond Hitchcock and his wife Flora Zabelle starred in a 1909 production at the New Amsterdam Theater. The last sight of *La Mascotte* on Broadway was in 1926 (1 December) when Jenny Syril and Servatius starred in a revival at the Jolson Theater, by which time the show had proven itself one of the standards of the American-French repertoire. Largely because Audran's name has not remained a fashionable one, it has not, however, followed Offenbach and Strauss's works into the modern opera houses.

A French film version was made in 1935 by Léon Mathot, with Germaine Roger as Bettina alongside Dranem, Lucien Baroux and Lestelly, but *La Mascotte* had undoubtedly its most curious film exposure in 1913 when it was presented as a three-reeler film starring Minnie Jarbeau 'in three six-minute acts' with accompanying sound 'by means of Edison's wonderful kinetophone'. The experiment was apparently successful enough for the manufacturers to subsequently serve up the customers a version of *Les Noces d'Olivette* recorded in the same style.

Austria: Theater an der Wien *Der Glücksengel* 12 February 1881; Hungary: Népszinház *Az üdvöske* 10 April 1881; USA: Bijou Theater 5 May 1881; UK: Comedy Theatre 15 October 1881; Germany: Friedrich-Wilhelmstädtisches Theater *Der Glücksengel* 25 October 1881; Australia: Theatre Royal, Sydney 25 October 1882

Recordings: complete (Clio, Decca), selection (EMI-Pathé) etc

MASKE IN BLAU Revue-Operette in 8 (later 6) scenes by Heinz Hentschke. Lyrics by Günther Schwenn. Music by Fred Raymond. Metropoltheater, Berlin, 27 September 1937.

A splendid success at Hentschke's Berlin Metropoltheater in 1937–8, the colourfully staged if textually feeble *Maske in Blau* followed the young artist Armando Cellini (Niko Stefanini) from San Remo to Argentina in pursuit of Evelyne (Carla Carlsen), the beautiful and rich plantation owner who is the subject of his painting. He takes along two pals and a noisy soubrette called Juliska (Clara Tabody) and together they foil the beastly Pedro who has caused the bust-up between the lovers in Scene Two. Then almost everyone (five into pairs doesn't go) pairs up for a multi-happy ending. Fred Raymond's score was mostly in a B-film vein, but it threw up two songs – both performed by the very prominent soubrette – which became highly popular: her insistence that she has 'temperament' ('Ja, das Temp'rament') and that she is 'Die Juliska aus Budapest'. Most of the rest of the music fell to the two lovers, she singing of 'Frühling in San Remo', he of 'Maske in Blau' and both of them of being 'Am Rio Negro', which didn't stop them being more than a little edged out by Juliska. The fourth scene also introduced the Maxixe for South American flavouring.

The piece remained popular in Germany and, in spite of its and Hentschke's Nazi connections, was introduced to Vienna after the Second World War, playing first at the Sophiensaal (1946), then at the Titania Theater (1947 with Stefanini, Desa Valoni and Mimi Urban) and in 1964–5 at the Raimundtheater with patented star Marika Rökk making Juliska even more prominent than before. It wins regional productions in Austria, and above all in Germany, up to the present day.

A 1953 film had nothing to do with the show's plot, except that its leading lady (Frln Rökk) was called Juliska. She was a 'revuestar' and never went near the Argentine. However, she was still 'Die Juliska, die Juliska aus Buda-Budapest', still had 'Temp'rament' and also sang with her painter (Paul Hubschmid) the principal soprano/tenor duet ('In dir hab ich mein Glück gefunden'). He retained his two main solos ('Maske in Blau', 'Schau einer schönen Frau') in a score which had rather more of *Maske in Blau* about it than the story.

Austria: Sophiensaal 15 June 1946; Film: Georg Jacoby 1953
Recordings: selections (Eurodisc, EMI, Telefunken, Philips) etc

MASSARY, Fritzi [MASSARIK, Friederike] (b Vienna, 21 March 1882; d Beverly Hills, Calif, 30 January 1969).

For 20 years the adored queen of the Berlin Operette

stage, Massary at the peak of her powers won appreciative comments from the press of the world ('in a class by herself ... the most finished operetta diva on the Continent') even though she did not venture beyond central Europe until she was past her best years.

She made her first appearances on stage as a child, then played in revue, toured to Russia in the chorus of an Operette company, worked in Linz, and in the 1900–1 season was a member of the company at the Carl-Schultze Theater, Hamburg, where she played her first good rôles as the classic soubrettes Christl (*Der Vogelhändler*) and Bronislawa (*Der Bettelstudent*). She appeared at the Carltheater as Molly in *The Geisha* and in 1901 she joined Gabor Steiner's company, performing both at his summer theatre, Venedig in Wien, and at his winter Danzers Orpheum, as Kitty, the heroine's maid, in Ivan Caryll's *Die Reise nach Cuba* (billed as Frln Massari), as Cora Angélique in *Die Schöne von New York* (1901), La Favorita in the English musical *Das Cirkusmädel* (1902), Ninetta in *Eine feine Nummer* (1902), in the title-rôle of Clotilde in Ferdinand Pagin's *Clo-Clo* (1902) and as 'Sie' in Paul Lincke's little *Am Hochzeitsabend* (1903).

Massary went on from here to play in Cologne and in Prague, and in 1904 she stopped in Berlin. It was there that she was to make the bulk of the rest of her career. She joined the company at Richard Schultz's Metropoltheater, made her début there in Viktor Holländer's *Die Herren von Maxims* ('Im Liebesfalle'), and performed thereafter in the revues which Lincke, Walter Kollo and Holländer supplied for the house. She revisited Vienna in 1908 to star in Eysler's *Das Glücksschweinchen* at her old haunt, Venedig in Wien, appeared as Helene in Leo Fall's *Der liebe Augustin* in its Berlin première, played in Vienna in Benatzky's vaudeville *Prinzchens Frühlingserwachen*, and at the Theater Gross-Berlin am Zoo in Gilbert's *So bummeln wir!* and *Die Studentengräfin*, but she returned each time to the Metropoltheater.

The war years brought the déclic which lifted Massary from stardom to megastardom. Her performance in the title-rôle of Leo Fall's *Die Kaiserin* (1915) won her stunning reviews and popularity, and thereafter the Metropoltheater mounted a series of Operetten specifically for her. Some were pieces already played in Vienna, but as the years went on she created, or in some cases had created for her, some of the greatest of the period's works, becoming to Straus and Fall what Hortense Schneider had been to Offenbach or the Savoy company to Gilbert and Sullivan. She starred successively in Betty Fischer's rôles in *Die Csárdásfürstin* and *Die Rose von Stambul*, as Offenbach's *Grande-Duchesse*, in Kálmán's *Die Faschingsfee* and in the character created by Sári Fedák in *Szibill* (1919) before creating the star rôle of the richly vocal Vera Lisaweta in Straus's *Der letzte Walzer* (1920), Dolores Belamor in Leo Fall's *Die spanische Nachtigall* and the title-rôle of his *Madame Pompadour* (1922).

Die Perlen der Cleopatra (1923) cast her as the queen of the Nile in Berlin and Vienna, and if *Geliebte seiner Hoheit* (1924), *Der Tanz um die Liebe* (1924), *Teresina* (1925) and *Die Königin* (1926) offered her fewer opportunities than a Vera Lisaweta or a Pompadour, she was able to return to the latter rôle in a splashy Erik Charell production at the Grosses Schauspielhaus in 1926. It was another Charell staging which, a few years later, resulted in her temporarily

leaving the musical theatre. A badly disfigured, over-staged version of *Die lustige Witwe* drew the public's and critics' scorn, and the star suffered. She withdrew to the straight theatre, and remained there for two years, playing lead rôles in Germany and in Austria. She came back to the musical stage to star in the outstanding mother rôle of Oscar Straus's *Eine Frau, die weiss, was sie will* (1932), creating the song which would remain, more than any other, her trademark, 'Jede Frau hat irgendeine Sehnsucht'. In 1933 she was obliged to quit Germany, and almost more than the flight of any or all the other Jewish makers of Operette, her departure signalled the end of an era in the German theatre.

The now-widowed Massary moved to London, where in 1938 she made her one appearance in the British musical theatre as the prima donna of Noël Coward's unfortunate *Operette*, and then to America. She ultimately retired to Beverly Hills to the home of her son-in-law where she died in 1969.

Massary was married to actor **Max Pallenberg** (b Vienna, 18 December 1877; d Prague, 20 June 1934), another Austrian who made much of his career in Berlin. He was regarded by many as Germany's foremost comedian, but he also took a number of comic rôles in Operette, with very limited vocal means but with considerable success.

MASSÉ, Victor [Félix Marie] (b Lorient, 7 March 1822; d Paris, 5 July 1884).

A winner of the celebrated Prix de Rome (1844), awarded to the outstanding composition student of the Paris Conservatoire, Massé did not ever fulfil the hopes this prize automatically placed in him for a career in serious music. He composed some attractive vocal pieces, one opera which was presented at the Paris Opéra, and nine works – full-length and short – which were produced at the Opéra-Comique. Two of the earliest of these, however, ensured that his musical survival was distinctly more marked than many more 'successful' winners of the Prix de Rome. The two-act comic opera *Galathée* (1852), dealing with the awakening of Pygmalion's statue, won considerable popularity (its libretto by Jules Barbier and Michel Carré later formed the basis for Poly Henrion's text for Suppé's *Die schöne Galathee*), whilst the little rustic opérette *Les Noces de Jeannette* (1853), written by the same authors, provoked a delightful score from the composer which has resulted in the piece being played throughout the world ever since, perched on the very cusp of the light opera and opérette repertoires.

MASTEROFF, Joe (b Philadelphia, 11 December 1919).

Masteroff worked as an actor (he appeared in one Broadway play) and as an assistant director to Howard Lindsay whilst making his first attempts as a playwright, and he reached Broadway as an author in 1959 with play *The Warm Peninsula* (86 performances). He moved into the musical theatre for the first time with his adaptation of the Hungarian play *Illatsertár* as the text for *She Loves Me*, but found his greatest success with a second adaptation, that of Christopher Isherwood's Berlin stories as the libretto for the internationally triumphant *Cabaret*. A third adaptation, of the classic British farce *Breath of Spring* as the confusingly titled *70, Girls, 70*, with songs by the composers of *Cabaret*, did not have the same success.

1963 **She Loves Me** (Jerry Bock/Sheldon Harnick) O'Neill Theater 23 April

1966 **Cabaret** (John Kander/Fred Ebb) Broadhurst Theater 20 November

1971 **70, Girls, 70** (Kander/Ebb) Broadhurst Theatre 15 April

1989 **Desire Under the Elms** (Edward Thomas) New York City Center 11 January

1992 **Six Wives** (E Thomas) York Theater 4 October

MATHEWS, Julia (b London, 14 December 1842; d St Louis, Mo, 18 May 1876). Top international prima donna of the English-language opéra-bouffe stage whose fame was extinguished by an early death.

Taken to Australia as a child, Julia Mathews made her first appearances on the stage (or whatever did duty for a stage) in Sydney and in the goldfields, appearing in comedy, drama, comic opera and burlesque whilst still in her earliest teens, and she subsequently made herself a considerable name as an actress and vocalist at the Princess Theatre in Melbourne ('the Queen of burlesque and song'). Amongst the musical shows in which she appeared were numbered *The Beggar's Opera* (Polly), *The Latest Edition of the Lady of Lyons*, *Midas*, *The Fair One with the Golden Locks* (Graceful), *Esmeralda* (Phoebus), *Bluebeard* (Alidor), *Prince Prettypet* (Prince), *Cinderella the Second* (Cinderella), *The Little Savage*, *Endymion* (Endymion), *Aladdin* (Aladdin), *The Daughter of the Regiment* (Marie), *The Queen of Beauty* (Queen) (all 1861), *The Miller and his Men* (Karl) and *Theseus and Ariadne* (Theseus) and, even in the theatre's production of dramas, a spot was usually found to break the action and allow Julia to sing a song or two.

She appeared at the Princess alongside a number of visiting stars, notably Joseph Jefferson, and she gained some additional notoriety when her name was linked with that of the ill-fated explorer R O'H Burke who apparently proposed marriage to her when she was 15 years old. After further performances in New Zealand (where she toured for W H Mumford and ended by becoming his wife) and in Australia, Julia left, in 1867, for Britain. There, she quickly became one of the most celebrated stars of the opéra-bouffe stage when she introduced the title-rôle in Offenbach's *La Grande-Duchesse de Gérolstein* to English audiences both in London (Theatre Royal, Covent Garden, 17 November 1867) and in a substantial tour around the provinces. She returned to Covent Garden in 1869 in a double bill of *Lischen and Fritzchen* and the pantomime *The Yellow Dwarf*.

The new singing star joined the Gaiety Theatre company to take the title-rôle in Émile Jonas's *Cinderella the Younger* (1871) and later appeared with them as *La Belle Hélène*, as Boulotte in *Barbe-bleue*, as Gigolette in *Tromb-al-ca-zar* and in the title-rôles of Balfe's *Letty the Basket-maker* and Offenbach's *Madame l'Archiduc*. She was the prima donna of the London version of Hervé's *L'Oeil crevé* in 1872, and in 1873 appeared as Mlle Lange to the Clair-ette of Selina Dolaro in the first English-language *La Fille de Madame Angot* at the Philharmonic, Islington. After this second sensational success, she followed up there in the title-rôle of the English version of *Giroflé-Girofla* (1874) and, at Christmas of the same year, she created the part of Alice Fitzwarren in Offenbach's *Whittington* at the London

Plate 175. **Julia Mathews** *came from the Australian goldfields to stun* London *as* La Grande-Duchesse de Gérolstein.

Alhambra. In 1875 she toured for Mrs Liston in the dual title-rôle of *Giroflé-Girofla*, visited Europe, and appeared in New York as Giroflé-Girofla, in *Perfection* and *Jenny Lind at Last*, before setting out on a tour of America with a repertoire including *Giroflé-Girofla*, *La Fille de Madame Angot*, *La Grande-Duchesse*, *Lurline* and *Aladdin*. In St Louis, what had already been a truly remarkable career was cut short by a premature death from rheumatic fever at the age of 33.

MATRAS, Josef (b Vienna, 1 March 1832; d Vienna, 30 September 1887). Star comic of the 19th-century Viennese stage.

Viennese-born Matras toured as a vocalist and chorister, playing in the Austrian provinces and at Pest before coming back to play in his home town, first of all at Fürsts Singspielhalle in the Prater, and then, in 1862, at the Carltheater. There he became a popular and highly paid leading comedian, appearing in some of the foremost comedies of the Austrian classic and modern repertoire, in Possen and Volksstücke and, with the coming of the French opéra-bouffe, in this new brand of entertainment.

Amongst his operettic assignments in the 1860s and 1870s were included the Viennese versions of the French *Les Deux Aveugles* (Terzabeck, paired with Franz Eppich), *Les Géorgiennes* (Paterno), *L'Île de Tulipatan* (Cactus), *Le Château à Toto* (Massepain), *Les Cent Vierges* (Rumpelmeier), *La Princesse de Trébizonde* (Casimir), *La Boulangère a des écus* (Flammèche to the Delicat of Blasel), *Le Soldat magicien* (Robin), *Monsieur Choufleuri* (the travesty Madame Balandard, invented by Léonce), *Vert-Vert* (Binet), *Boule de Neige* (The Corporal), *Cannebas* (Augustin), *La Cour du Roi Pétaud* (Confusius IX), *La Permission de dix heures* (Lanternik), *La Belle Bourbonnaise* (Anselme), *Le Grand Casimir* (Little Wheel, the clown), *Les Prés Saint-Gervais* (Harpin), *La Marjolaine* (Peterschop) and *Le Petit Duc* (Frimousse). He also appeared in a number of the earliest native Viennese works, playing Fleck in *Flotte Bursche*, Midas in *Die schöne Galathee*, Bitterich in Julius Hopp's *In der Sackgasse*, Hans der Gerechte in *Die Jungfrau von Dragant*, the title-rôle of *Flodorado Wuprahall* and Dr Tondolo in *Banditenstreiche*.

With the blossoming of the Austrian tradition, Matras found his finest musical rôles, creating the parts of Izzet Pascha in *Fatinitza* (1876), Satanas in *Der Teufel auf Erden* (1877) and Fürst von Trocadero in *Prinz Methusalem* (1877) as well as playing in *Die Mormonen*, but his career came prematurely to an end in 1880 when his memory failed him and he died a depressive in 1887, after spending the last five years of his life in a lunatic asylum.

Matras's daughter, actress Pepi Glöckner, was Vienna's first Mrs Peachum in *Die Dreigroschenoper*.

In the 1921 Wiener Bürgertheater Singspiel on *Josefine Gallmeyer*, Fritz Schrödter impersonated Matras in an operetticized retelling of the actor's love affair with his fellow star.

MATTHEWS, Jessie (b London, 11 March 1907; d London, 19 August 1981).

A petitely pretty and maniacally bright dancing soubrette, Jessie Matthews had a successful career as a star of London and occasionally New York revue in the 1920s and of British film musicals in the 1930s (*Evergreen*, *It's Love Again*, *The Good Companions*, *Waltzes from Vienna*, *Gangway* etc). She also made isolated appearances in stage musicals, performing as a child in *Bluebell in Fairyland*, teamed with Harry Milton and Sonnie Hale as the ingénue of Stanley Lupino's musical comedy *Hold My Hand* (1931), and starring in the Marilyn Miller rôle of Sally in a revised version of Kern's musical of the same name re-christened *Wild Rose* (1942). In her mid-sixties she appeared one final time on the London stage as Mrs Doasyouwouldbedoneby in a version of *The Water Babies* (1973). In 1939 she starred with Sonnie Hale (then her husband), and his father as Sue Merrick in their own production of a piece called *I*

Can Take It which died on the road, and in 1941 she disappeared from the cast of the Vernon Duke musical *The Lady Comes Across* between New Haven and New York, thus avoiding a three-night Broadway flop.

Autobiography: *Over My Shoulder* (W H Allen, London, 1974)

MAUPREY, André [J de] (d Paris, 1939).

Mauprey began his theatrical career at the turn of the century as the composer and author of a number of revues and other short pieces for such venues as the Bodinière, the Mathurins and the Divan Japonais. He subsequently doubled a career as a playwright (*Les Criminels*, the Mussolini piece *Les Cent Jours*, *Le Pont vivant*, *Abracadabra*, *Plus jamais ça*, *Le Masque*) with a busier one as a composer of opérettes, supplying the smaller Parisian, resort and provincial theatres with a regular flow of shows amongst which the military musicals *Le Lieutenant Cupidon* and *Le Cavalier Lafleur* both ran up good totals out of town. His combination of writing and composing talents later led naturally to a third career – the most successful – as the translator and adaptor of a wide variety of musical shows in the late 1920s and 1930s.

Mauprey's French versions included those of *Die Dreigroschenoper* and of American musical comedies on the one hand, and a number of romantic Viennese Operetten, of which *Princesse Csardas* and *Le Pays du sourire* were both major and enduring French-language successes, on the other. He also adapted *Der Zigeunerbaron* into French for the cinema screen.

Mauprey got a brief New York showing when his little three-handed *La Musique adoucit les coeurs* was played by Robert Casadesus's company at the Théâtre Parisien (15 December 1919) for 16 performances, followed later in the season by eight performances of the pair's *Miss Flirt* (8 February 1920).

1903 **L'Enfant du miracle** (Fernand Rouvray) Théâtre Déjazet 24 September
1905 **Y a de l'amour** (Claude Roland) 1 act Théâtre Bobino 27 October
1906 **L'Amour bohème** (Jules Oudot) 1 act Théâtre Bobino 27 February
1906 **Le Prince Diamant** (Roland) Troyes 24 March
1906 **Ah! Mon Colin** (Roland) Théâtre Bobino 1 act 3 August
1906 **Coeur de neige** (Seigle, Georges Montignac) Vichy 23 August
1907 **À qui le baiser?** (Roland) Théâtre Bobino 22 February
1907 **Ulysse** 1 act Little Palace 11 March
1907 **Joe** (Montignac) 1 act Théâtre Royal 22 September
1907 **La Fiancée du 59ème chasseurs** (Jean Kolb, Marcel Yver) Théâtre de la Gaîté-Rochechouart 31 August
1908 **Tout à la femme** (Mme Verdellet) 1 act Lyon 1 January
1908 **La Visite de nuit** 1 act Théâtre Bobino 21 January
1908 **Messaouda** (w H Jacquet/Davin de Champclos) 1 act Théâtre Moncey 9 March
1909 **Le Lieutenant Cupidon** (F Celval, Charles, Joubert) Marseille 19 November, Comédie Royale, Paris 14 January
1912 **Alcide** (Rouvray, Bail, Thuillier) Univers 1 November
1912 **L'arrière-petite fille de Madame Angot** Théâtre des Folies-Dramatiques 29 November
1913 **Toto la purée** (w Pougaud) 1 act La Fauvette 14 November
1914 **Rien que par les femmes** (w Pougaud)
1915 **L'amour à Seville** (w René Nazelles) 1 act
1915 **Miss Flirt** (Robert Casadesus) 1 act Chansonia 19 February

1915 **Soufflons nos dames** (Chagrin/w Pougaud) 1 act Chansonia 25 June

1915 **Les Petits Sansonnet** (R Vers) 1 act

1916 **La Reine de l'or** (Casadesus/w Nazelles) Trianon-Lyrique 5 March

1916 **La Petite Tonkinoise** (William Burtey) 1 act

1916 **Le Rosier de Banglie** (Nazelles)

1916 **La Belle au bois dormant** (Nazelles)

1917 **Monsieur Mouton** (Nazelles, Blondeau)

1917 **La Petite Detective** (w Burtey) Théâtre Cluny 22 February

1917 **La Reine de l'or** (Casadesus/w Nazelles) Trianon-Lyrique 5 March

1920 **Papa, maman et moi** (Pougaud)

1920 **Le Cavalier Lafleur** (L Raine) Casino Kursaal, Lyon 11 May

1921 **Son Altesse Papillon** (w H Jacquet/w Celval) Marseille January

1922 **L'amour en Chine** (Pougaud) Royan 22 August

1923 **Miria, ou l'amoureuse incomplète** (Nazelles) Théâtre le Perchoir 15 June

1929 **Mon prince chéri** (M Boisyvon) Nouveau-Théâtre 12 October

1929 **Tip-Toes** French version w Serge Veber, Robert de Mackiels (Folies-Wagram)

1930 **L'Opéra de quatre sous** (*Die Dreigroschenoper*) French version (Théâtre Montparnasse)

1930 **Princesse Csardas** (*Die Csárdásfürstin*) French version w René Peter (Trianon-Lyrique)

1932 **Le Pays du sourire** (*Das Land des Lächelns*) French version w Jean Marietti (Théâtre de la Gaîté Lyrique)

1934 **Les Jolies Viennoises** (*Wiener Blut*) French version (Trianon-Lyrique)

1935 **Giuditta** French version (Théâtre de la Monnaie, Brussels)

1935 **La Chanson du bonheur** (*Schön ist die Welt*) French version (Théâtre de la Gaîté-Lyrique)

1937 **Le Roi du cirque** (Max Alexys) Théâtre de la Gaîté-Lyrique 14 October

1945 **D'Artagnan** ('Bétove'/w André Mouëzy-Éon, de Mackiels, Maquet) Théâtre de la Gaîté-Lyrique 18 November

Other title: *La Musique adoucit les coeurs*

MAY, Alice (b England, 1847; d St Louis, Mo, 16 August 1887). The first prima donna of the Gilbert–Sullivan–Carte combine.

Australian-raised Alice May made her earliest appearances in her adopted homeland, appearing first in concert (18 June 1870) and then, under the banner of W S Lyster and Smith, in light opera (*The Daughter of the Regiment* 29 April 1871) and in prima donna rôles in opéra-bouffe and comic opera with Lyster and Cagli's company (Zerlina in *Fra Diavolo*, the Grande-Duchesse, Boulotte, Agathe in *Freischütz*, Elvira in *The Rose of Castille*, Maritana, Arline etc). She played a season with her own 'Gallery of Illustration', a group set up at Sydney's Masonic Hall on the lines of London's German Reed establishment, playing *Cox and Box*, *The Rose of Auvergne* and *The Belle of Wooloomooloo*, before going on to star as Drogan in a seasonal version of *Geneviève de Brabant*, as Eurydice in Australia's first *Orphée aux enfers*, and as Balfe's *Satanella*. She had established herself as Australia's foremost light opera star before she made her professional way back to Britain as leading lady of the Richard South's travelling opéra-bouffe troupe, which headed north playing its wares to the cities of the Orient.

She soon left that company to make an attempt at opera, performing Marguerite in *Faust* and the title-rôle in *Satanella* at Leicester, but she subsequently returned to lighter fare and established herself as one of the best opéra-bouffe sopranos of her time on the London stage, making herself a place in history by creating the rôle of Aline in Gilbert and Sullivan's *The Sorcerer*. Miss May left the *Sorcerer* company to appear again as Drogan in a revival of *Geneviève de Brabant* (1878) and, whilst fellow Australian Emma Howson introduced the rôle that would have been hers in *HMS Pinafore*, appeared in London's versions of Lecocq's *Le Petit Duc* (Duke), the revived *La Princesse de Trébizonde* (1879, Zenetta), *La Petite Mademoiselle* (1879, Madelon), *Les Mousquetaires au couvent* (1880, Simonne) and *Jeanne, Jeannette et Jeanneton* (1881, Jeanne), before going out in tandem with Emily Soldene to play her husband's comic opera *The Wicklow Rose* (1882) in the provinces. She appeared on the British road as Zanetta (*La Princesse de Trébizonde*) and Dolly (*The Sultan of Mocha*), before visiting New York where she appeared in *Satanella* with Barton's English Opera Company and played at the Casino Theater as Sophistica in *Prinz Methusalem*. Now, although only in her mid-thirties, she was already unwillingly abandoning heroines for character ladies. She toured with John Ford's comic-opera company (*Barbe-bleue*, *The Mikado*, *La Princesse de Trébizonde* etc) and, in her final appearances, exhibiting a thickened waistline and a voice that had clearly sunk somewhat, she was seen as Katisha in *The Mikado* and Lady Jane in *Patience*.

Miss May's first husband, the Australian conductor and composer **George B Allen** – one of those with a passion for putting letters after their names on playbills (it was MLC until he was able to make it Mus Bac (Oxon)) – was the original conductor of London's *The Sorcerer*. He had previously spent much time as a conductor in Australia, musically directing everything from the Sons of Temperance's concerts in Sydney in the late 1860s to Lyster and Cagli's productions of opéra-bouffe and opéra-comique in the early 1870s (*Barbe-bleue*, *Geneviève de Brabant*, *La Grande-Duchesse*, *Der Freischütz* etc) and working often with his wife. He also wrote several pieces for the musical stage, including the extravaganza *The Belle of Woolloomooloo* (1872) and two pieces played on the British stage, the one-act operetta *Castle Grim* (1865) and the full-length *The Wicklow Rose* mounted at Manchester with Emily Soldene starred alongside his wife.

MAY, Edna [PETTIE, Edna May] (b Syracuse, NY, 2 September 1878; d Lausanne, Switzerland, 2 January 1948). Palely pretty ingénue who made her name as The Belle of New York.

Having played in juvenile Gilbert and Sullivan companies and in plays in her home town, Edna May Pettie (still thus billed) made her first New York appearance at the age of 17 in the elder Oscar Hammerstein's comic opera *Santa Maria* (Clairette). After only a year on the professional stage she was hired by George Lederer to create the rôle of the Salvation Army lass Violet Gray in *The Belle of New York* ('They All Follow Me', 'The Purity Brigade'). She travelled to London with the show after its New York closure and there made an enormous personal hit, establishing herself in this one performance as one of the most popular and sought-after stars of the London musical theatre.

Plate 176. **Edna May:** *Broadway's Belle of New York.*

Miss May appeared in London in another American musical comedy, *An American Beauty*, and in both America and Britain in the title-rôle of *The Girl from Up There*, being largely responsible by her popular presence for the few months each piece held the stage. The following years were also spent in London where she starred opposite Evie Greene as the artless Baroness de Trègue in *Kitty Grey* (*Les Fêtards*), teamed with Hilda Moody and Madge Crichton as Paul Rubens's *Three Little Maids*, and created the title-rôle of Leslie Stuart's *The School Girl* (1903).

After playing on Broadway with the American production of *The School Girl*, Miss May remained there to play Alésia in a return season of *La Poupée* and the Cinderella rôle of Angela, written for Ellaline Terriss, in the imported *The Catch of the Season*. She went to London once more to star in the latest Leslie Stuart show, *The Belle of Mayfair*, but walked out of the production when her star billing was threatened by the novelty attraction represented by 'the Gibson Girl' Camille Clifford. As a replacement vehicle, Charles Frohman mounted *Nelly Neil*, a silly piece with a silly part calculatedly modelled for her on her *Belle of New York* rôle, but the piece failed and Miss May left the theatre in favour of an advantageous marriage at the age of 29.

MAY, Hans [MAYER, Johannes] (b Vienna, 11 May 1891; d Beaulieu, France, 1 January 1959). Viennese composer who had more success after emigrating to Britain.

May studied in Vienna and composed much accompanying music for silent films both in Germany and France as well as a list of small-scale Operetten in the 1910s and a handful of larger ones in the 1920s. He moved to Britain in 1930, an early part of the Jewish exodus which bled central

Europe of most of its operettic talent, and continued there to make the largest part of his career in the cinema, composing film scores (*The Stars Look Down, Thunder Rock, The Wicked Lady, Brighton Rock, The Gypsy and the Gentleman*) and later conducting film music, whilst still supplying some music to the German stage (*Kolonne Immergrün*, Theater am Schiffbauerdamm 1932 etc).

His 1935 Operette *Die tanzende Stadt*, played in Vienna at the Theater an der Wien (26 performances), was produced at the Coliseum by André Charlot with Lea Seidl starred as Maria Theresia without success, but two later pieces, an English adaptation of a piece written with Armin Robinson and called *Carissima* and, particularly, the attractive *Wedding in Paris* ('Light Another Match', 'I Have Nothing to Declare', 'Wedding in Paris') had fine runs, whilst a theatre version of his film *Waltz Time* had a reasonable touring career.

During his English years, May had song successes with 'My Song Goes Round the World', Vera Lynn's 'Love of My Life', 'The Windsor Waltz' and 'Throw Open Wide Your Window'.

1911 **Das süsse Gespenst** sketch Ronacher
1912 **Der Teufelswalzer** (Ernst Ress/Leopold Krenn) Ronacher ?February
1912 **Der Dreibund** (Alfred Spitzer) 1 act Hölle 1 March
1913 **Das grosse Abenteuer** (Fritz Lunzer, C Clermont)
1918 **Die schöne Blonde** (Hans Pflanzer) 1 act Hölle 1 October
1919 **Daniel in der Löwenhöhle** (Lunzer) 1 act Kleinkunstbühne, Munich 1 December
1922 **Miss Blaubart** (Alexander Pordes-Milo, Ernst Neubach) Jantschtheater 22 December
1926 **Drei Mädel von Heute** (Dengraf, Max Steiner-Kaiser) Komödienhaus, Berlin 20 July
1932 **Traum einer Nacht** (Willy Wolff/Behr) Theater am Nollendorfplatz, Berlin 4 March
1935 **Die tanzende Stadt** (Karl Rössler, Arthur Rebner) Theater an der Wien 4 October
1935 **The Dancing City** revised *Die tanzende Stadt* by Harold Plumptre, David Yates Mason (London Coliseum)
1948 **Carissima** (Armin Robinson ad Eric Maschwitz) Palace Theatre, London 10 March
1949 **Waltz Time** (Conrad Carter, Harry C James/Alan Stranks) Winter Gardens, Morecambe 2 May
1954 **Wedding in Paris** (Sonny Miller/Vera Caspary) London Hippodrome 9 March

MAYA Operett in 3 acts by Imre Harmath. Music by Szabolcs Fényes. Fővárosi Operettszinház, Budapest, 10 December 1931.

The most successful of Fényes's operetts, *Maya* was first mounted in Budapest in 1931 with Hanna Honthy, the favourite soubrette of the Hungarian stage, playing the rôle of the Arabian dancer of the show's title.

The show's tale was begun in Paris. The meddling mama of Charley (Gábor Kertész) is determined to put an end to his love affair with unsuitable Madelaine (Olly Szokolay). She persuades friend Dixie (István Békássy) to help her in her plans, and Dixie consequently confides in Charley that he's been having an affair with the girl. Charley pulls a gun, shoots Dixie, and runs off to join the Foreign Legion. He doesn't much like the Foreign Legion, and he is helped to escape from Tangiers and back to Paris by Maya, the little dancer he once defended from a nasty soldier. Maya follows the man with whom she has fallen in love by forming an acrobatic trio with a couple of friends and getting a job in a Paris music-hall. When Charley gets home, he quickly finds out that Dixie didn't fall down dead, just dead drunk, but whilst Charley's been gone he has really moved in with Madelaine. It takes Charley a whole further act, however, to realize that the little acrobat, who has meanwhile become a music-hall megastar in the metropolis, is the girl for him.

Maya went round Hungary, and proved a regular item in the repertoire at the Fővárosi Operettszinház where it was given new productions in 1945 (25 May), in 1957 (now billed as a 'revueoperett', 31 July) in a version from the Margitszigeti Szinpad, and in 1967 in a production from the Parkszinpad (ad József Romhányi). It also went further afield – something fewer Hungarian operetts were doing by the 1930s – and was seen in a German-language version at Vienna's Theater an der Wien (ad Schanzer, Welisch) with Mary Lossef featured as Maya (30 performances).

Austria: Theater an der Wien 16 November 1935.

MAYERL, Billy [MAYERL, Joseph William] (b London, 31 May 1902; d London, 27 March 1959).

A longtime popular light-entertainment pianist and composer of piano music ('Marigold'), Mayerl at one time made up part of the famous concert party team, the Co-Optimists, for whom he provided a considerable amount of performance material. He contributed music to a number of revues (*The Punch Bowl, The London Revue* etc) and appeared as a performer in others (*You'd Be Surprised, Shake Your Feet, White Birds*), and also had a career as a composer of the ultra-light kind of songs and dances popular in the interwars musical theatre.

Mayerl composed his first full show score, in collaboration with loyal lyricist Frank Eyton, for Laddie Cliff, recently risen to the top of London's producing tree, as replacement music for a new version of the American musical comedy *So Long, Letty!* In spite of several rewrites the show floundered out of town, but Cliff stuck with his composer, and after Mayerl had injected additional numbers into several London and touring shows during 1929–31 (*Love Lies, Darling, I Love You, Silver Wings, Meet My Sister*), Cliff hired him to compose the songs and/or act as musical director for several more of his musicals. *Sporting Love* and *Over She Goes* did splendidly, *The Millionaire Kid, Leave it to Love* and *Crazy Days* rather less well. Mayerl had his most substantial success, however, when he supplied the score for the long-running Lupino Lane comedy with songs, *Twenty to One*.

In 1939 he turned producer-composer-musical director with the production of a not terribly successful piece called *Runaway Love*. He fulfilled this triple rôle again on *Happy Birthday* (w Barry O'Brien), but this one failed to make it to town and its failure effectively ended his musical theatre career. His last musical contributions were to a touring musical comedy, *Kiki*, and a short-lived *Six Pairs of Shoes* at a minor London house.

Long eclipsed through the change in musical fashions, Mayerl's sometimes deceptively simple-sounding music has begun to again find aficionados amongst piano players in the 1990s.

1928 **So Long, Letty!** (later *Oh, Letty!*) (Frank Eyton/Austin Melford) Theatre Royal, Birmingham 22 October
1929 **Change Over** revised *Oh, Letty!* Hippodrome, Portsmouth 8 April
1930 **Nippy** (Arthur Wimperis, Eyton/Melford) Prince Edward Theatre 30 October
1931 **The Millionaire Kid** (Eyton/Norman Scott) Gaiety Theatre 20 May
1934 **Sporting Love** (Desmond Carter, Eyton/Arthur Rigby, Arty Ash, Stanley Lupino) Gaiety Theatre 31 March
1935 **Twenty to One** (Eyton/L Arthur Rose) London Coliseum 12 November
1936 **Over She Goes** (Eyton, Carter/S Lupino) Saville Theatre 23 September
1937 **Crazy Days** (Eyton, Carter/S Lupino) Shaftesbury Theatre 14 September
1939 **Runaway Love** (Eyton/Barry Lupino) Saville Theatre 3 November
1940 **Happy Birthday** (Eyton/Eyton, B Lupino, Rigby) Opera House, Manchester 9 September
1942 **Kiki** (Eyton/Martin Henry) Grand Theatre, Leeds 30 March
1944 **Six Pairs of Shoes** (w Harry Roy et al/Eyton et al/Monica Disney Ullman) Playhouse 10 April

THE MAYOR OF TOKIO Farcical Japanese opera in 2 acts by Richard Carle. Music by William Frederick Peters. Studebaker Theater, Chicago, 12 June 1905; New York Theater, New York, 4 December 1905.

Richard Carle's actor-manager vehicle was a latter-day *Chinese Honeymoon* which starred him as Marcus Orlando Kidder, the actor-manager of Kidder's Komiques, let loose in a barrage of misunderstandings and romantic complications in Tokio. Kow-Tow (Edmund Garvie) introduced himself as 'The Mayor of Tokio', and his daughter Oloto (Hortense Mazurette) insisted that one 'Pity My Pitiful Plight' before falling in love with the tenor of the Komique company (Edmund Stanley), who sang 'A Toast to the Moon'. Her father ended up in cahoots with the wardrobe mistress (Emma Janvier). Soubrette Birdie Talcum (Minerva Courtney) and Rusty (William Mock) provided the light moments alongside Betsy Lincoln, an American heiress (May Boley), and Ivan Orfulitch, a Russian spy (Charles Meyers), all of whom still left room for Carle to sing of 'Foolishness' and 'I Like You' and earn his billing.

The Mayor of Tokio played only 50 Broadway performances, but it proved a rich touring vehicle for Carle, and in 1914 it even made it to Australia. There, however, produced by George Willoughby with George H Bogues, Gilbert H Emery, Carrick Major (Kidder) and Amy Murphy (Oloto) in the lead rôles it was voted 'not as good as *The Tenderfoot*', another Carle piece which had preceded it, and did not stay around long.

Australia: Adelphi Theatre, Sydney 2 May 1914

MAYTIME *see* WIE EINST IM MAI

MÉALY, Juliette [JOSSERAND, Juliette] (b Toulouse).

Juliette Méaly 'with her abbreviated skirts, a wealth of rustling frills and a huge hat' not to mention a very fine soprano voice, led a full career in the European musical theatre, starring in many a Parisian rôle where a certain glamorous audacity was needed, yet proving herself in a wide range of parts, from the classics to the music-hall, through a long career.

She made her earliest appearances at a very young age at the Eldorado in 1884, but she first came into evidence as a young and appealing jeune première at the Théâtre des

Plate 177. **Juliette Méaly** – *with her clothes on.*

Menus-Plaisirs in 1891 when she took over from Yvonne Stella in the central rôle of Audran's *L'Oncle Célestin.* She followed up at the same house alongside Félix Huguenet in Roger's *Le Coq* and in Audran's *Article de Paris* (1892, Jeanne) before starring the following year on the rather larger Gaîté stage as Michelette in *Le Talisman.* She followed this distinct personal success by taking her new-found stardom to the rest of Europe, and later the same year she visited Vienna where she appeared as *Miss Helyett* and *Le Petit Duc,* and then London where she was featured in a pasted-in 'green-room scene' in *A Trip to Chinatown* at the Gaiety Theatre (August), alongside American whistler Tom Browne and impersonator Cissie Loftus.

Back in Paris, she starred as Christiane in *Le Troisième Hussards* (1894) at the Gaîté, and as the voluptuous Mimosa, nude scene and all, in the spectacular *Le Carnet du Diable* (1895, 1897, 1899) and another near-the-knuckle demoiselle, Paquerette in *Le Carillon* (1896), both at the Variétés where, under the direction of Fernand Samuel, she would make her 'home' for most of the next two decades. In between her appearances in osée opérette à grand spectacle, she played in the Variétés revivals of the classics (Dindonette in *L'Oeil crevé*, Gabrielle in *La Vie parisienne*, Marguerite in *Le Petit Faust* etc). In 1897 she created the rôle of Fanny in *Le Pompier de service*, but the years which followed brought no new rôles of value as Mlle Méaly appeared as Fragoletto to the Fiorella of Tariol-Baugé in *Les Brigands* and as Eurydice at the Variétés, and took another turn around central Europe, playing *Madame Méphisto*, Blondeau and Monréal's Parisian 'opérette-folie'

spectacle, which had her as a female demon taking vengeance on her underworld husband, *Mam'zelle Nitouche* and *L'Auberge du Tohu-bohu* (Flora) at Budapest's Magyar Színház (16–20 April 1901), Berlin's Friedrich-Wilhelmstädtisches Theater and Vienna's Theater an der Wien and Carltheater.

She had her best fresh rôle for a decade when she starred as the Princess Bengaline in Planquette's posthumous *Le Paradis de Mahomet* (1906), and then stepped aside from the Variétés to appear at the Moulin-Rouge alongside Mistinguett in *La Revue de la femme* (1907) and the following year as the star of the opérette *Son Altesse l'amour*, this time in competiton with Gaby Deslys. She was seen regularly on the Paris stage for another decade, repeating her best rôles (notably *La Vie parisienne*'s Gabrielle, but no longer those requiring a nude scene) and creating the occasional new rôle, as in *Les Merveilleuses* (1914) or, as late as 1921, in a return to the stage, in *La Galante Épreuve* at La Cigale.

ME AND JULIET Musical in 2 acts by Oscar Hammerstein II. Music by Richard Rodgers. Majestic Theater, New York, 28 May 1953.

A regulation backstage musical which busied itself with the love affairs of a regulation operetta pair of pairs: one romantic – between chorine (Isabel Bigley) and an ASM (Bill Hayes), which comes to a happy conclusion in spite of a lighting man (Mark Dawson) with the air of *Oklahoma!*'s Judd Fry – and one, between dancer Betty (Joan McCracken) and stage manager Mac (Ray Walston), which is comic. The authors of *Me and Juliet* (which was the title of the show within the show) considered that they had avoided the clichés of the backstage musical, using their theatre setting only as a colourful background to a pair of love affairs, but in throwing out the clichés (and it was not often evident that they had) they had also thrown out the colour, and the tale and the action of *Me and Juliet* looked a little pale in the wake of such bristlingly bright theatrical shows as *Kiss Me, Kate.*

The score turned out one number, the lilting 'No Other Love', adapted from Rodgers's theme music for the film *Victory at Sea* and performed by the leading lovers, which became a Rodgers and Hammerstein standard (it was later shifted over into their *Cinderella* in London, when *Me and Juliet* failed to travel), as well as a pleasing ballad with the rather ungrammatical title 'Marriage Type Love' for the leading man of the internal *Me and Juliet*. The characters and situations of the show did not allow its writers to stretch their ideas too far beyond the everyday in their numbers. But if the show was a touch unimaginative, it was also, as might have been expected, highly professional, and Rodgers and Hammerstein's names on the bill (they were producers as well as authors) gave it an extra impetus through 358 performances on Broadway.

Recording: original cast (RCA Victor)

ME AND MY GIRL Musical comedy in 2 acts by L Arthur Rose and Douglas Furber. Music by Noel Gay. Victoria Palace, London, 16 December 1937.

Following his success as the perky little hero of the musical comedy *Twenty to One*, Lupino Lane commissioned a second piece for himself which would allow him

Plate 178. **Me and My Girl:** *Robert Lindsay (Bill Snibson) and Emma Thompson (Sally) introduced the revival that set Arthur Rose's comedy musical off for a worldwide series of productions – 50 years after its first showing.*

to repeat the characterization of cheeky cockney Bill Snibson. Arthur Rose, the author of the first piece, teamed with librettist-lyricist Douglas Furber to write what was advertised as a sequel but which, in fact, apart from its general tone, had only Lane's character and his name in common with its predecessor. This time Lane was presented as the unwilling heir to an earldom, whisked from Lambeth and his girl, Sally (co-producer's wife Teddie St Denis), to suffer with due comicality being made into a 'fit and proper person' for his new position by the dragonistic Duchess of Hareford (Doris Rogers). Betty Frankiss played the Lady Jacqueline, seductively angling for the new Earl, whilst veteran comedian George Graves made a sympathetic aristocratic ally for the little fellow in the rôle of Sir John Tremaine.

Noel Gay's handful of songs – whittled down to just seven on a run into town which, in a fashion most untypical in Britain, also saw the disappearance of the original duchess, Mignon O'Doherty, and director Gene Gerrard – illustrated the comedy with vigour. Brother Wallace Lupino sang and danced about the duties of 'The Family Solicitor', Miss Frankiss looked to 'Me' and duetted comically with Lane that 'I Would if I Could', Sally kept a stiff upper lip and decided to 'Take it on the Chin' and the servants of the house had 'A Domestic Discussion'. However, it was Bill and Sally's title song and the jaunty dance number 'The Lambeth Walk' which proved the show's happiest numbers, and both became perennial favourites.

Me and My Girl played a twice-nightly schedule at the Victoria Palace and, boosted by a clever introduction of 'The Lambeth Walk' into the dance halls of the country, by broadcast and television versions and, ultimately, by wartime conditions which at first caused the show to take a

short break, it settled in for a fine run. In the early stages of the war, as 'The Lambeth Walk' went to the battlefields of Europe with the British troops, the production switched from evening performances to playing 1.45 and 4 pm matinées. Then, when 'We're Going to Hang Out the Washing on the Siegfried Line' joined 'The Lambeth Walk' at the top of the Tommies' marching songs, Lane interpolated that song into his show as well. By the time he had finished, the piece had racked up 1,646 performances on its 12-a-week schedule.

Me and My Girl became a perennial vehicle for Lane, who returned to London for a second season in 1941 (London Coliseum 25 June) a third, back at the Victoria Palace, in 1945 (6 August) and a fourth at the Winter Garden in 1949 (12 December), before his son Lauri took over to continue to troupe the piece around Britain and overseas.

In 1984, under the management of Richard Armitage, son of and publisher to the late Noel Gay, *Me and My Girl* was given a major revival in a revised version (ad Stephen Fry). The show's score was expanded to more conventional 1980s musical comedy proportions by the addition of a number of songs which the original writers had composed after the event to make their show more appealing to amateur musical companies, as well as several other Gay hits. Robert Lindsay in Lane's rôle (complete with some of the originator's well-known acrobatic comedy) was given 'Leaning on a Lampost', whilst his Sally (Emma Thompson) inherited the lovely ballad 'Once You Lose Your Heart' from the amateur score. The new version of *Me and My Girl* proved, nearly half a century on, to be even more popular than the first. It settled down at London's Adelphi Theatre (4 February 1985) where, whilst running through a veritable parade of mostly television-comedy names at the top of its bill (Karl Howson, Gary Wilmot, Les Dennis) it remained for nearly eight years, taking the show's London total past 4,000 performances.

Exported to Broadway, the new *Me and My Girl* once again conquered by its charm and high spirits, won Lindsay acclaim for his performance, and remained for 1,420 performances before being crowded out of its theatre in a booking jam. In the meanwhile, the show progressed to all kinds of places that Lane would never have dreamed of. It was seen in an under-cast production in Australia (which hadn't, curiously, bothered about it first time round), in Mexico (as *Yo y mi chica*), in Hungary (ad Iván Bradányi) with Sándor Szakácsi, Judit Kocsis and Görgy Bánffy featured at Budapest's József Attila Színház, and in a Japanese production mounted by the famed all-woman Takarazuka troupe, giving *Me and My Girl* its widest and most fruitful career more than half a century after that tempestuous run in from Glasgow to London.

With the Second World War and 'We're Going to Hang Out the Washing on the Siegfried Line' now expunged from the text, *Me and My Girl* (it retained its English title in Mary Miliane and Helmut Forche's adaptation) even ultimately appeared in Germany, having its first performance in Coburg with a cast headed by Roland Wagenführer (Bill), Carol Lentner (Sally) and Wilhem Eyberg-Wertenegg (Sir John).

A wartime film version was made under the title *The Lambeth Walk* in which Lane was teamed with Seymour Hicks (Sir John) and soubrette Sally Gray, whilst in 1956 a television version featured Lauri Lupino Lane alongside the Duchess of Marie Löhr.

USA: Marquis Theater 10 August 1986; Australia: State Theatre, Melbourne 3 January 1986; Hungary: József Attila Színház *Én és a kedvesem* 1988; Germany: Landestheater, Coburg 29 February 1992; Film: CAPAD-Pinebrook *The Lambeth Walk* 1939

Recordings: London revival cast (EMI), Broadway cast (MCA), Mexican cast (private), Hungarian cast (Qualiton), Japanese cast (TMP)

MECCA *see* CAIRO

MÉDITERRANÉE Opérette à grand spectacle in 2 acts by Raymond Vincy. Music by Francis Lopez. Théâtre du Châtelet, Paris, 17 December 1955.

Corsican singing star Tino Rossi came late in his career from the screen to the stage to play Corsican singing star Mario Franchi, who becomes mixed up in some dangerous Mediterranean smuggling when he joins a holiday cruise around his home islands. The criminal turns out to be the yacht's captain, the lovely Paola (Dominique Rika) returns to her island and to the arms of the singer's rash but reformed brother (Henri-Jacques Huet), and all the comical folk who have enlivened the evening of Corsican revelry – from the jolly campers Juliette (Aglaë) and Mimile (Pierjac) to the priest Père Padovani (Fernand Sardou), the local gendarme Cardolacci (Ardisson) and the determinedly widowed innkeeper (Andrée Delavel) he pursues – can get on with their lives as Mario heads back to the big world of showbusiness.

Vincy's colourful, comedy-filled book was illustrated by Lopez with a mixture of throbbing tenor solos for the star and sprightly comedy songs. Rossi serenaded 'Les Filles d'Ajaccio' and the 'Méditerranée', greeted the 'Campanella' of his home town, and invited Paola to a party with 'Demain c'est Dimanche' before bidding her farewell with the secret of their night out intact ('N'en dit rien à personne'), but he saved his biggest guns for one of the religious moments which had succeeded so well in Lopez's earlier *Andalousie*, as he prayed passionately for his brother's safety to the 'Vierge Marie'. Mimile jollied about 'Un p'tit verre du p'tit vin du pays', Juliette swaggered about disguised as a moll with 'C'est mon mataf' and the priest wondered over 'Les Paroissiens de mon village' in some of the evening's lighter moments.

Méditerranée and Rossi won a fine success, and the piece played through 572 performances at the huge Théâtre du Châtelet before finding itself a secure place in the repertoire of French provincial theatres. A 1964 revival at the same house (11 July) starred Rossi's legitimate successor, Rudy Hirigoyen, through a further 181 performances.

Recordings: Selection w Rossi (Pathé) Selection w Hirigoyen (CBS/Odéon) etc

MEET ME VICTORIA Musical play in 2 acts by Lupino Lane and Lauri Wylie based on a story by H F Maltby. Additional dialogue by Ted Kavanagh. Lyrics by Frank Eyton. Music by Noel Gay. Victoria Palace, London, 8 April 1944.

Meet Me Victoria brought Lupino Lane back to the Vic-

Plate 179.

toria Palace where he had triumphed in *Me and My Girl* and *Twenty to One*, and done fairly well in *La-di-da-di-da*, with a fourth musical in which he exploited his chirpy cockney 'Bill' character. Railwayman Bill Fish (Lane) needs cash and promotion to be able to wed his Dot (Phyllis Robins). He is befuddled into wedding a foreign strongwoman (Dorothy Ward) by a gang of traffickers in British Citizenship, but he wins his stationmaster's cap and a happy ending when he brings them to justice. Gay's bundle of songs didn't include a 'Lambeth Walk', but Lane did well with the comical 'You're a Nice Little Baggage' and a rôle which permitted all his favourite antics tucked inside a plot that was a mite more of a plot than those of his preceding shows. However, *Meet Me Victoria* was squeezed out of London by enemy action after 117 performances, and when it returned it managed only another 134 nights, suggesting that the line of shows Lane had produced in Victoria had seen its most popular days.

MEILHAC, Henri (b Paris, 21 February 1831; d Paris, 6 July 1897). Half of the most famous libretto-writing partnership of the heyday of opéra-bouffe.

Henri Meilhac began his working life behind the counter of a bookshop, and his writing career with humorous articles for magazines and newspapers. In 1855 he took his first steps into the theatre as an author of vaudevilles, and made his first appearance on the bill of an opérette in 1861 when he wrote the text for a one-act piece composed by Louis Deffès and produced at the spa town of Bad Ems. *Le Café du roi* was a fine little success and moved swiftly to Paris, where it was played at first at the Théâtre Lyrique and a few years later at the Opéra-Comique itself. In 1863 Meilhac met up with Ludovic Halévy, a schooldays contemporary at the Lycée Louis le Grand, and the two combined on a little one-act vaudeville *Le Brésilien*, produced at the Palais-Royal (9 May) with a cast featuring the young Hortense Schneider. For this vaudeville Jacques Offenbach wrote the brief musical part, including an original song with Meilhac/Halévy words 'Voulez-vous acceptez mon bras?' which, as sung by the rising star, became extremely popular.

This three-sided writing team continued their collaboration (Offenbach and Halévy had already worked episodically together for some eight years prior to this), and they had an immense success with their first full-length work, the classical burlesque *La Belle Hélène* (1864). *La Belle Hélène* was followed by a whole series of opérasbouffes and semi-bouffes of which *Barbe-bleue*, *La Vie parisienne*, *La Grande-Duchesse de Gérolstein*, *La Périchole* and *Les Brigands* all proved vastly popular, hoisting their writers to a pre-eminent theatrical position not only in France, but, as these pieces led the invasion of the world's stages by French musical plays during the 1860s and 1870s, throughout the entire world.

Meilhac and Halévy now worked almost exclusively together, both for the musical stage and for the comic theatre where they were represented during the decade and a half of their collaboration by a long list of plays including *Frou-Frou* (Gymnase, 1869), *Tricoche et Cacolet* (Palais-Royal, 1871), *Le Réveillon* (Palais-Royal, 1872), *Le Roi Candaule* (Toto chez Tata) (1 act, Palais-Royal, 1873), *La Petite Marquise* (Variétés, 1874), *L'Ingénu* (1 act, Variétés, 1874), *La Mi-Carême* (Palais-Royal, 1874), *La Boule* (Palais-Royal, 1874), *La Cigale* (Variétés, 1877), *Le Mari de la débutante* (Palais-Royal, 1879) and *La Petite Mère* (Variétés, 1880). However, each did occasionally work with other partners and, after the rise of Charles Lecocq, also together but with a composer other than Offenbach.

For Lecocq they prepared the text for the most successful of his Théâtre de la Renaissance works, *Le Petit Duc*, as well as for the internationally played *La Petite Mademoiselle* and the disastrous *Janot*. They also worked with Albert Millaud, to whom Halévy had allegedly supplied an uncredited part of the text for Offenbach's *Madame l'Archiduc*, on the book for the Théâtre des Variétés vaudeville *La Roussotte* (for which Lecocq supplied some of the music) and they made a memorable, rare venture into the opéra-comique when they adapted Prosper Mérimée's tale of *Carmen* as the libretto for Georges Bizet's celebrated work. Meilhac, alone, teamed again with Millaud on the text for Offenbach's *La Créole*, as he had with Nuitter on the text for the Opéra-Comique's *Vert-Vert* in his only two major musical 'infidelities' to his partner.

La Roussotte, in 1881, marked the end of the partnership between 'Meil and Hal' (as Offenbach apparently called them). Meilhac continued, with Millaud, to write two further vaudevilles for the Variétés and its star Anna Judic. One of these, *Mam'zelle Nitouche*, added to his alreadylong list of outstanding successes whilst the other, *La Cosaque*, which found the series fading, was, in itself, as fine and funny (if not perhaps as protean) as its predecessors and won several productions beyond France. With Arnold Mortier he fabricated the tale of *Madame le Diable* which was set to music by Gaston Serpette for Paris and, a number of years later, by Adolf Müller for Vienna (*Des Teufels Weib*, Theater an der Wien, 1890), and with Philippe Gille he worked on the version of Robert Planquette's British musical *Rip van Winkle* which has survived through a century in the French repertoire, as well as on the libretti for Massenet's opera *Manon* and Delibes's drame lyrique *Kassya*. After a decade away from the musical theatre, he was represented one final time, shortly before his death, by a collaboration with Albert Saint-Albin on the book for Robert Planquette's successful *Panurge*.

For a man reputedly lazy, late-rising, and of a gadabout nature, Meilhac accomplished a vast amount of theatrical work of all kinds in the 20 years which comprised the main part of his career. Much of his best work came in that partnership with Halévy of which it was said that 'Meilhac avait plus de cartouches mais Halévy avait un meilleur tir' (Meilhac had more bullets, but Halévy was the better shot), but he proved, when he moved on to work with other authors, that the esprit and ideas which he brought to his collaborations were no less effective when shaped by and with other partners. His range, too, was outstanding: from the extravagant bouffonneries of *La Belle Hélène* and *Barbebleue* to the crisp social comedy of *La Vie parisienne*, the wildly comic vaudeville tones of a *Mam'zelle Nitouche* to the often delicate sentiment found in a piece such as *Le Petit Duc* or moments of *La Roussotte*, the pathos of *Manon*, and the drama of *Carmen* and some parts of works such as *Rip!*, he covered the whole gamut of the musical theatre. And it was notable that, in an age when the turnover of shows was fast and furious and authors were not scared to fail, very few of the pieces to which he contributed were short-lived.

As well as providing a crop of landmark shows to the Parisian stage, Meilhac also had a share in what have nowadays become accepted as being the most representative shows of both the 19th- and the 20th-century Viennese stage. His play *Le Réveillon* (w Halévy) was the basis for Richard Genée's libretto for Johann Strauss's *Die Fledermaus* (1874), whilst the earlier *L'Attaché d'Ambassade*, written solo in 1862 before his association with Halévy began, became, in the hands of Victor Léon and Leo Stein, the book for Franz Lehár's *Die lustige Witwe*. Many other of his works, particularly in the wake of these two successes, were also adapted as libretti for the Austrian stage, although not always with acknowledgement. *La Boule* (w Halévy) became the Posse *Von Tisch und Bett* written and composed by Julius Hopp (Theater an der Wien 7 September 1875); *Tricoche et Cacolet* was given songs by Karl Treumann and Franz von Suppé (Carltheater 1876) and more liberally musicalized as *Spitzbub et Cie* by Wilhelm Ascher and Robert Pohl, with music by Josef Bayer, at the Lustspiel Theater (5 July 1907); *La Cigale* (w Halévy) was turned by H Osten and Julius Stern into *BumBum* (Carltheater 24 October 1896); his 1888 play *Décoré* was set to music as *Der Sechs-Uhr-Zug* (1900) by Léon, Stein and Richard Heuberger (as well as being professedly borrowed from for a portion of the British musical *The Little Cherub*), and *La Petite Marquise* (w Halévy) became Felix Albini's *Madame Troubadour* (1907). The delightfully comical *Le Mari de la débutante* was turned into two different Operetten at the Carltheater within eight months: Annie Dirkens played seven performances at both the home house and the Theater an der Wien in *Die Prima Donna* (Alfred Müller-Norden/Alexander Landesberg, Ludwig Fischl 31 January 1901) and Mizzi Günther played ten nights as Nina in *Die Debutantin* (Alfred Zamara/A M Willner, Waldberg 4 October 1901). *La Roussotte*, in one of its hurly-burly series of international remakings, was adapted by Franz von Schönthan and given a new score by Karl Millöcker under the title of *Ein süsses Kind* (Theater an der Wien 1 April 1882) and the Offenbach opérette *La Diva* was rewritten by Zell and Genée into a piece called *Die Theaterprinzessin* (Theater an der Wien 30 December 1872).

1861 **Le Café du roi** (Louis Deffès) 1 act Ems 17 August; Théâtre Lyrique, Paris 16 November

1862 **Les Bourgignonnes** (Deffès) 1 act Baden-Baden; Opéra-Comique, Paris 16 July 1863

1864 **La Belle Hélène** (Offenbach/w Halévy) Théâtre des Variétés 17 December

1866 **Barbe-bleue** (Offenbach/w Halévy) Théâtre des Variétés 5 February

1866 **La Vie parisienne** (Offenbach/w Halévy) Palais-Royal 31 October

1867 **La Grande-Duchesse de Gérolstein** (Offenbach/w Halévy) Théâtre des Variétés 12 April

1868 **L'Elixir du docteur Cornélius** (Émile Durand/w Arthur Delavigne) 1 act Fantaisies-Parisiennes 3 February

1868 **Le Château à Toto** (Offenbach/w Halévy) Palais-Royal 6 May

1868 **La Pénitente** (Mme de Grandval/w William Busnach) 1 act Opéra-Comique 13 May

1868 **La Périchole** (Offenbach/w Halévy) Théâtre des Variétés 6 October

1869 **Vert-Vert** (Offenbach/w Charles Nuitter) Opéra-Comique 10 March

1869 **La Diva** (Offenbach/w Halévy) Théâtre des Bouffes-Parisiens 22 March

1869 **Les Brigands** (Offenbach/w Halévy) Théâtre des Variétés 10 December

1875 **La Boulangère a des écus** (Offenbach/w Halévy) Théâtre des Variétés 19 October

1875 **La Créole** (Offenbach/w Millaud) Théâtre de Bouffes-Parisiens 3 November

1876 **Berengère et Anatole** (Jules Massenet/w Paul Poirson) 1 act Cercle de l'union artistique January

1878 **Le Petit Duc** (Lecocq/w Halévy) Théâtre de la Renaissance 25 January

1879 **La Petite Mademoiselle** (Lecocq/w Halévy) Théâtre de la Renaissance 12 April

1881 **Janot** (Lecocq/w Halévy) Théâtre de la Renaissance 21 January

1881 **La Roussotte** (Hervé, Lecocq, Marius Boullard/w Halévy, Millaud) Théâtre des Variétés 28 January

1882 **Madame le Diable** (Gaston Serpette/w Arnold Mortier [and Millaud?]) Théâtre de la Renaissance 5 April

1883 **Mam'zelle Nitouche** (Hervé/w Millaud) Théâtre des Variétés 26 January

1884 **La Cosaque** (Hervé/w Millaud) Théâtre des Variétés 1 February

1884 **Rip!** French version w Philippe Gille (Théâtre des Folies-Dramatiques)

1895 **Panurge** (Planquette/w Albert Saint-Albin) Théâtre de la Gaîté 22 November

MEINE SCHWESTER UND ICH Musical comedy in 2 acts, a Vorspiel and Nachspiel by Ralph Benatzky and Robert Blum based on the play *Ma soeur et moi* by Louis Verneuil and Georges Berr. Music and lyrics by Ralph Benatzky. Komödienhaus, Berlin, 29 March 1930.

A small-scale musical comedy with six principals and seven small-part players but with a full helping of songs, Benatzky's *Meine Schwester und ich* was adapted by its author-composer from a German version of Verneuil and Berr's 1928 comedy made by Robert Blum. A fine success on its first Berlin production, it travelled extensively thereafter.

Parisian Princess Dolly Saint-Labiche (Liane Haid) has fallen in love with the young professor Roger Fleuriot (Oskar Karlweis) who has been hired to catalogue her library. When he moves on to Nancy, she disguises herself as her sister, and placing herself as a shopgirl in Filosel's (Felix Bressart) provincial shoeshop, she woos, wins and weds her man. However, when he discovers the truth he demands a divorce. The prologue and epilogue of the piece took place in court, framing the tale of the couple's courtship in a scene reminiscent of *Trial By Jury* or *Die geschiedene Frau*, and ended, of course, in reconciliation.

The score of the show featured the fashionable dance rhythms of the time, Dolly moving seductively into tango time ('Mein Freund!'), and joining Roger in a foxtrot ('Wie kommt der Mann zu den Frau') and a shimmy ('Ich lade sie ein, Fräulein'), whilst he also took a turn through the slow fox ('Ich bin verliebt') and waltz ('Ich bin diskret') rhythms and scored his best as this last number moved into his catchy declaration that 'Mein Mädel ist nur ein Verkäuferin'. Irma, the shopgirl whom Dolly pays off to go absent, uses the opportunity to go off to Paris to become – like every good shopgirl in German films, in particular – a revue star and, thus, she was given the chance at the second-act opening to demonstrate her revusical talents in a 'Tanz-Revue-Parodie' and one-step.

Following its Berlin success, *Meine Schwester und ich* was produced by Rolf Jahn at Vienna's Die Komödie with Marita Streelen (Dolly), Karl Stepanek (Roger) and Josef Egger (Filosel) at the head of the cast of just ten, and it was later revived in a version revised by Benatzky as *Die Prinzessin auf der Leiter* (the princess on the ladder) at the Theater in der Josefstadt under Max Reinhardt (3 August 1934), the Scala Theater (4 September 1934) and at the Theater an der Wien (5 February 1935) with Gerda Maurus, Oskar Karlweis and Felix Bressart featured, for over a hundred performances. It returned to Berlin in 1939 (Renaissance Theater) with Johannes Heesters and Carola Höhn starring, and continued to be played throughout Germany and Austria in the decades that followed, returning to the Theater an der Wien once more in 1964 (20 November).

The Shuberts hired Walter Slezak from Berlin for their quickly arranged American production of *Meet My Sister* (ad Harry Wagstaffe Gribble), apparently in a case of mistaken identity, but he scored a personal success on Broadway, opposite the Dolly of Bettina Hall and George Grossmith as a comical Marquis, in a version which was recommended as a charming evening 'for folks weary of precision dancing and synthetic energy'. It ran for 167 performances, and Grossmith swiftly persuaded his old ally Edward Laurillard to export the piece to England. Gribble's text was readapted as *My Sister and I* by a team of writers (Lauri Wylie, Brandon Fleming, Desmond Carter, Frank Eyton) and the piece mounted with Francis Lederer and Alexa Engström featured alongside Grossmith and ageing star Joe Coyne as Filosel. A flop in town, it was put on the road after eight performances as *Meet My Sister* with Anne Croft and Roy Royston taking over alongside Coyne and Grossmith, and three additional songs by Billy Mayerl.

A 1954 film version had Bentazky's score 'adapted' by Friedrich Schröder.

Austria: Theater 'Die Komödie' 22 December 1930, Theater in der Josefstadt *Die Prinzessin auf dem Leiter* 3 August 1934; USA: Shubert Theater *Meet My Sister* 30 December 1930; UK: Shaftesbury Theatre *My Sister and I* (later *Meet My Sister*) 23 February 1931; Hungary: Andrássy-uti Színház *Exhercegnó* 28 January 1932; Film: 1954

MELFORD, Austin [Alfred] (b Alverstoke, 24 August 1884; d London, 19 August 1971). Actor, writer and director for the musical stage between the wars in Britain.

An actor from childhood, Melford appeared for many years in provincial and West End plays and the occasional touring musical (*The Talk of the Town, Faust Up-to-Date*) before making his first metropolitan musical appearances in revue and in the musical comedy *Mr Manhattan* (1916, Bobby Washington). In a long and fine subsequent career, which was shared equally between musical and non-musical comedies, he appeared in leading light-comedy rôles at the Gaiety in *Theodore & Co* (1916, taking over from George Grossmith as Theodore), *Going Up* (1918, 'Hoppy' Brown) and *The Kiss Call* (1919, Christopher Deare), and then as Maxime Paillard in Grossmith's production of *A Night Out* (1920) at the Winter Garden. After a first period as a member of the famous Co-Optimists concert party, operating as both a performer and a writer, he succeeded Grossmith as Otis in London's production of *Sally*.

Melford played further comic rôles in *Whirled into Happiness* (*Der Tanz ins Glück*, Horace Wiggs), as Algernon Hozier in the Jack Buchanan boxing musical *Battling Butler* (for which he also collaborated on the text), in *Up with the Lark* (1927, Jack Murray) and *Lucky Girl* (replacing star Gene Gerrard as Hudson Greener), returning to the Co-Optimists in between times. In 1948 he appeared alongside Leslie Henson in his own musical *Bob's Your Uncle* (Mandeville). He later played Sir John in a revival of *Me and My Girl* and appeared, in his sixties, as Dudley Leake in *Blue for a Boy* (the rôle he had created years previously in the play *It's a Boy* from which the musical was made), *Happy as a King* (Count Domboli) and *Happy Holiday* (1955, Admiral Dallas-Buckingham).

In parallel to his career as a comic actor, Melford also worked both as a writer and a director. He fulfilled both functions in the successful *Yes, Uncle!, Bob's Your Uncle* and *Blue for a Boy*, directed *Lucky Girl* (1928), *Oh, Letty!* (1928) and *Here's How* (1934), and wrote or contributed to the texts of several other London plays and musicals. His other writing credits included the Prince's Theatre extravaganza *Magic Carpet* and the Fred Karno company's touring musical farce *French Beans*.

Melford's brother **Jack MELFORD** (b London, 5 September 1899; d October 1972) also had a long and successful stage and film career, which included a regular dose of musical rôles. In 1926 he appeared with the Astaires in *Stop Flirting* (Perry Reynolds) and in the juvenile rôle of the musical version of his uncle's hit play *Turned Up* (Frank Steadley). He paired with Basil Howes as Binnie Hale's exquisite 'ugly' brothers in *Mr Cinders* (1929), played Hugh Posset in *Here's How!* (1934) and the titled hero of the ingenuous wartime *The Silver Patrol*, and toured in *Sunny, Tonight's the Night* and in the second

tryout of *Happy Birthday* (1945). In 1950 he was seen at the Theatre Royal, Drury Lane, as the Heavenly Friend in *Carousel*.

Both performers were the sons of actor Austin Melford [Alfred SMITH] (b Fareham, 11 April ?1855; d Twickenham, 23 January 1908), and the nephews of actor and playwright Mark Melford (d 4 January 1914) whose works included, apart from the enormously successful *Turned Up*, Alice Atherton's little musical entertainment *Blackberries* (1886), the romantic comic opera *Jackeydora* (1890) and the touring 'musical farcical comedy' *Black and White* (1898).

1917 **Yes, Uncle!** (Nat D Ayer/Clifford Grey/w George Arthurs) Prince of Wales Theatre 29 December

1921 **Yes, Papa** (Phil Braham/w Eric Blore) Coliseum, Cheltenham 21 February

1921 **French Beans** (Leslie Alleyne/w Blore, Fenton Mackay) Jubilee Hall, Weymouth 25 April

1922 **Battling Butler** (Braham/Douglas Furber/w Stanley Brightman) New Oxford Theatre 8 December

1924 **Patricia** (Geoffrey Gwyther/Dion Titheradge/w Denis Mackail, Arthur Stanley) His Majesty's Theatre 31 October

1928 **So Long, Letty!** (aka *Oh, Letty!*) English version w Frank Eyton, Billy Mayerl (Theatre Royal, Birmingham)

1930 **Nippy** (Mayerl/Eyton/w Arthur Wimperis) Prince Edward Theatre 30 October

1934 **Here's How!** (w Robert Nesbit, Eddie Pola, Robert Walker) Saville Theatre 22 February

1944 **Ring Time** revised *Battling Butler* w Noel Gay, Frank Eyton (Glasgow)

1945 **Gay Rosalinda** (*Die Fledermaus*) English version w Rudolf Bernauer, Sam Heppner (Palace Theatre)

1947 **The Birdseller** (*Der Vogelhändler*) English version w Bernauer, Harry S Pepper (Palace Theatre)

1948 **Bob's Your Uncle** (Gay/Eyton) Saville Theatre 5 May

1949 **Roundabout** (aka *Hat in the Air*) (Edward Horan, Ken Attiwill, Eyton/w Attiwill) Saville Theatre 4 August

1950 **Blue for a Boy** (Harry Parr Davies/Harold Purcell) His Majesty's Theatre 30 November

1953 **Happy as a King** (Ross Parker/w Fred Emney) Princes Theatre 23 May

MELNOTTE, Violet (b Birmingham, ?1853; d London, 17 December 1935). Producer and theatre manageress who launched one vast hit and one of her era's most important composers.

Originally an actress, Miss Melnotte began producing in the mid-1880s. She took the Avenue Theatre for a season in 1885, mounting amongst other items a revival of the comic opera *Manteaux Noirs* and the one-act operettas *A Professional Beauty* and *The Golden Wedding*, but she won a singular success with her production of the new comic opera *Erminie* (1885) at the Comedy Theatre. In her dual rôle of producer and second leading lady (Cerise Marcel) she saw *Erminie* through a good season in London before it moved on to more enormous triumphs in America and on the touring circuits. The following year she produced and played in Ivan Caryll's first full-length musical *The Lily of Léoville* and in 1887 she fulfilled the same double rôle with a new piece by the now-celebrated authors of *Erminie*, *Mynheer Jan*. A monetary disagreement with her authors during the run of the show resulted in *Mynheer Jan* being prematurely closed and the association ended.

In 1892 Miss Melnotte and her husband, Frank Wyatt (the original Duke of Plaza Toro in Gilbert and Sullivan's

The Gondoliers and co-star of *Erminie*), built the Trafalgar Square Theatre, which Miss Melnotte ran, or leased to other producers, for most of the next 40 years, under the names Trafalgar and, later, Duke of York's Theatre. She produced and/or housed and at various times appeared in a long and sometimes eccentric list of plays and musicals at her theatre, a list which included, in the early days, revivals of *Dorothy* and *Mam'zelle Nitouche*, Toulmouche's *The Wedding Eve* (*La Veillée de noces*), Audran's *Baron Golosh* (*L'Oncle Célestin*), the successful *The Gay Parisienne*, the American musicals *Lost, Strayed or Stolen* and *The Girl from Up There*, and later, after a long succession of plays, J M Barrie's unfortunate musical attempt *Rosy Rapture, Toto, The Girl for the Boy, Nicolette*, such successful revues as *London Calling* and *The Punch Bowl* and many of Barrie's other works, notably the first production of *Peter Pan*.

Right up until her death, at the age of about 80, the forceful Miss Melnotte, known – politely – as one of the 'characters' of London showbusiness, remained (with one gap of five years) at the helm of the theatre which sported her initials artistically linked in the pattern of its auditorium decor. When she died, after several rocky decades of management, it was more than half a century since she had been reponsible for producing, in *Erminie*, the most popular musical of the 19th-century American theatre, and for giving a start to an out-of-luck young Belgian musician and composer who called himself Ivan Caryll.

MELVILLE, Alan [CAVERHILL, William Melville] (b Berwick-upon-Tweed, 9 April 1910; d Brighton, 27 December 1983).

Best known as a witty sketch-writer and lyricist in revue (*Scoop, Sky High, Between Ourselves, À la Carte, At the Lyric, Going to Town, All Square* etc) and most notably for the famous *Sweet and Low/Sweeter and Lower/Sweetest and Lowest* series, Melville also made several forays into the musical theatre. He supplied the lyrics to Ivor Novello for the author/composer's last show, *Gay's the Word*, a vehicle for Cicely Courtneidge ('Vitality', 'It's Bound to be Right on the Night', 'Bees are Buzzin''), wrote book and lyrics for *Bet Your Life* to feature Arthur Askey ('I Love Being in Love', 'I Want a Great Big Hunk of a Man', 'All on Account of a Guy') and, less successfully, paired with his *Sweet and Low* colleague Charles Zwar on a musicalization of the romantic play *Marigold*.

1951 **Gay's the Word** (Ivor Novello) Saville Theatre 16 February
1952 **Bet Your Life** (Kenneth Leslie-Smith, Charles Zwar) London Hippodrome 18 February
1959 **Marigold** (Zwar) Savoy Theatre 27 May

Autobiographies: *Myself When Young* (Max Parrish, London, 1955), *Merely Melville* (Hodder & Stoughton, London, 1970)

MELVILLE, Emilie [SNYDER, Emily] (b Philadelphia, 1850; d San Francisco, 19 May 1932). Round-the-world star of 19th-century opéra-bouffe.

Emilie Melville was trained as an actress from toddling age by her mother, the former Julia Miles, who had had a fine career in comedy, extravaganza and opera on the New York stage (Kitty in *New York as it Is*, Jenny in *Olympic at a Glance*, Jenny Bogert in *Mysteries and Miseries of New York*, Rosa in *Linda di Chamonix*, Fatemma in *Oberon*, Fetuah in

Plate 180. **Emilie Melville:** *the globe-trotting American soprano dressed to play von Suppé's Boccaccio.*

Ganem etc). Emilie went on the stage young and she had already well and truly made herself a name – not only on America's western circuits, but also in New York, where she appeared as Brougham's *Pocohantas* at the age of 16 – before she moved to San Francisco in 1868 as soubrette at the old California Theater. She played rôles ranging from Shakespeare's Ophelia to Burnand's leggy Ixion before retiring to marriage as Mrs Thomas Derby. She was quickly back, however, to pick up a performing career which would ultimately stretch over three-quarters of a century.

Her youthful successes were in burlesque, opéra-bouffe and light opera, with which she toured indefatigably through America in the 1870s and early 1880s. She went out at first with companies like that run by C D Hess (Arline, Serpolette, Zerlina in *Fra Diavolo* and creating the rôle of Queen Elizabeth I to the Shakespeare of William Castle in the 'romantic opera' *A Summer Night's Dream*), then later with the 'Emilie Melville Comic Opera Company', and the 'Hess-Melville Opera Company', playing regularly in New York in opéra-bouffe, in Gilbert and Sullivan (*HMS Pinafore, The Pirates of Penzance*) and in Operette (Fanchette Michel in *The Royal Middy*, Natalitza in *Apajune der Wassermann* etc). At one stage she took over the management of San Francisco's Baldwin Theater.

Mme Melville did not restrict her touring to America. She also toured both westward and southward, and made an enormous success in Australia when she appeared with

W S Lyster in opéra-bouffe in 1875 ('the most successful vocalist that ever graced the Melbourne stage'). She returned there regularly thereafter, in spite of a contretemps with producer J C Williamson when she walked out of her position as prima donna in his 1882 season (*Giroflé-Girofla*, *Les Cloches de Corneville*) and launched the Emilie Melville Opera Company (*Fatinitza*, *The Royal Middy*, *La Périchole*, *Giroflé-Girofla*) in competition. In 1884–5 she took an extended tour of the orient with a vast baggage of musical shows (*Patience*, *La Mascotte*, *The Royal Middy*, *Fatinitza*, *La Périchole*, *La Belle Hélène*, *HMS Pinafore*, *The Pirates of Penzance*, *Maritana*, *Giroflé-Girofla*, *La Fille de Madame Angot*, *Les Noces d'Olivette*, *Madame Favart*, *Nell Gwynne* etc) playing in such venues as Calcutta, Bombay and Rangoon, but she soon found that the few thousand Europeans in these cities were not enough to fill her houses. She handed over the management to her baritone, Edward Farley, and Calcutta manager Frost, but stuck to it as prima donna, even though, when the season ended in April, Frost decamped and the company split up in disarray.

She returned to Australia and appeared there in *Falka*, *La Périchole*, *La Fille de Madame Angot* (Clairette), *The Royal Middy* and as Planquette's *Nell Gwynne*, and in 1887, her voice now showing signs of a hole in the middle, began to ease herself into non-singing rôles by playing *Masks and Faces*. The following year, however, she was back as *The Grand Duchess*, and in 1889 she set off for South Africa where, billed as the 'Australian nightingale', she delivered *La Périchole* and others of her repertoire through two seasons, sometimes under the management of local managers and sometimes under her own banner.

Ultimately news filtered back that she had thrown up the stage, married her baritone, George Verdi (né Green), and settled down to run an hotel in Capetown. Before long, however, the news was different: it reported that she was playing Rosalind in *As You Like It* in Johannesburg. She soon left South Africa and the hotel trade (and Mr Green?) and continued her career, now on the straight stage, appearing in Australia (she played there with Nat Goodwin's company in 1896), on Broadway (notably as the original Mrs Chichester in *Peg o' My Heart* and in 1904 in a small part in *Leah Kleschna*) but, latterly, mostly back in San Francisco, where she became an important and highly respected member of the city's Alcazar stock company with which she played major character rôles through into her seventies. At the age of nearly 80 she appeared in the film *Illusion* (1929), which must surely make her the only (or one of very few) contemporaries of Brougham to have been recorded for posterity.

THE ME NOBODY KNOWS Musical based on the book of the same name edited by Stephen M Joseph. Lyrics by Will Holt. Music by Gary William Friedman. Orpheum Theater, New York, 18 May 1970; Helen Hayes Theater, 18 December 1970.

Based on a book compiled by a New York ghetto schoolteacher which consisted of the writings of his pupils, *The Me Nobody Knows* had no linear shape, but was a collection of scenes, songs and impressions developed from the children's stories and played by a group of 12 young people. It ran for six months at off-Broadway's Orpheum Theater, and subsequently re-opened at the Helen Hayes Theater

where it remained until it had reached a total of 587 performances. It was later seen on American television, in Hamburg and Munich in a German adaptation and was produced at London's subsidized Shaw Theatre, where it was played 20 times. In the 1980s a sequel was mooted, but did not appear.

Germany: Hamburg *Ich bin ich* May 1971; UK: Shaw Theatre 31 May 1973

Recording: original cast (Atlantic), German cast (Global) etc

MERCENARY MARY Musical comedy in 3 acts by Isabel Leighton and William B Friedlander based on *What's Your Wife Doing?* by Herbert Hall Winslow and Emil Nyitray. Lyrics by Irving Caesar. Music by Con Conrad and William B Friedlander. Longacre Theater, New York, 13 April 1925.

A brightly typical 1920s musical comedy, *Mercenary Mary* was based on a 1923 play (in which authoress Leighton had appeared) full of the kind of marital and financial ins and outs that were overwhelmingly popular as subject matter for such shows. On the one hand, we have penniless Jerry (Allen Kearns) who can only marry millionaire's niece June Somers (Margaret Irving) if he earns a million and stays faithful. On the other we have Chris Skinner (Louis Simon) and his extravagant wife Mary (Winnie Baldwin), who was formerly engaged to Jerry, who stand to be disinherited by Chris's very rich grandfather (Sam Hearn) who disapproves of her. To earn his million, Jerry agrees to play the 'other man' in the temporary Chris-Mary divorce which needs to be staged to get the money rolling but, when grandpa is slow to show up for the prepared scene of infidelity, Mary gets a little tipsy and takes Jerry's acting for revived romance. It is another act before all ends happily with tills and marriage bells ringing.

The jazzy, dance-based score did not bring forth any enduring numbers from amongst pieces such as 'I'm a Little Bit Fonder of You', 'Honey, I'm in Love with You', 'Charleston Mad' and 'Beautiful Baby', and L Lawrence Weber's production of *Mercenary Mary* lasted only 17 weeks and 136 performances on Broadway before being shunted out of its producer's theatre and onto the road in duplicate. Before long one of the touring companies had folded in disappointment.

However, *Mercenary Mary*'s life did not by any means end with this semi-failure. Jack Waller and Herbert Clayton, who had scored an immense London hit with their production of *No, No, Nanette*, naturally wanted something in the same vein with which to follow up, and they selected *Mercenary Mary*. Produced at the London Hippodrome in an anglicized version by Fred Jackson with June (June), Sonnie Hale (Jerry), Peggy O'Neil (Mary), A W Baskcomb (Chris) and Lew Hearn (Grandpa) featured, and with Vivian Ellis's 'Over My Shoulder' and Vincent Youmans's 'Tie a String Around Your Finger' (first heard in *Lollipop*) boosting June's rôle and the score, it was a great success with a public avid for more of the latest transatlantic song-and-dance comedies. It was played for 446 performances and, if this was markedly less than the score notched up by *Nanette*, it was nevertheless the longest British run achieved by any other Broadway musical comedy of the time. It also prefaced first a good touring life (the show was still to be seen on the road during the second war) and then a production of the show, in its

English version, in Australia under the management of Hugh J Ward. Mai Bacon starred as Mary, alongside Jack Morrison (Chris), Florence Hunter (Joan), Sydney Smith (Harry) and Eddie Joyce (Grandpa) for two months in Melbourne before the company switched, with less success, to another Broadway import, *Betty Lee*. A Sydney season was sponsored by the Fullers in 1928 with Elsie Prince and Jimmy Godden starred (St James Theatre 11 February 1928).

Rather less expectedly, the show turned up next in another city anxious for more *No, No, Nanette*: Paris. Robert de Simone's production at the Théâtre des Bouffes-Parisiens (ad Yves Mirande, de Simone, Jean Bastia) starred Denise Grey as Mary alongside Bouffes regulars Sim-Viva (Jenny/June), René Koval (Charley/Jerry) and Edmond Roze (Christophe) and a large dancing chorus, all jazzily accompanied by Berson and Vauchant's Europa Ramblers. However, more remarkable was yet to come. From Paris, *Mercenary Mary* continued on to Budapest.

Now, somehow, somewhere, somewhy, *No, No, Nanette* had apparently become ambushed on its way to Hungary and, when *Mersz-e, Mary?* (ad Adorján Stella, Imre Harmath) arrived at Budapest's Király Színház towards the end of 1927, it was the first modern American musical comedy so to do. J C Piddock, the English ballet master of the Paris production was imported to stage the dances with 48 chorus girls equipped with 258 costumes, there were 48 orchestral players (one per chorus girl?), and a cast headed by acredited comics Márton Rátkai (Kristof) and Árpád Latabár sr (Harry), György Solthy (Charley), Erszi Péchy (Mary), Ilona Vaály (Souzy) and Vilma Orosz. *Mersz-e, Mary?* proved the same kind of sensation in Hungary that *Nanette* had been elsewhere. Budapest's *Mary* had, however, clearly undergone some changes since Broadway. Firstly, it had been expanded and spectacularized. Secondly, it was textually an adaptation of the French adaptation of the British adaptation. But, most notably, the one Vincent Youmans song included in London, which had given way to a co-composing credit in Paris (obviously in an attempt to capitalise on the famous names of *Nanette*'s writers), had now become a sole credit: 'music by Vincent Youmans and Irving Caesar'. Had Friedlander and Conrad's songs really disappeared? And, if so, where had the Youmans/Caesar songs come from? Had Mr Piddock brought bits of *Nanette* from Paris with him? Did he, in fact, give Budapest a mélange of *Mary* and *Nanette*? This would explain why, in spite of the vast success of *Mersz-e, Mary?*, *Nanette* was never played in Hungarian.

UK: London Hippodrome 7 October 1925; Australia: Princess Theatre, Melbourne 3 April 1926; France: Théâtre des Bouffes-Parisiens 5 April 1927; Hungary Király Színház *Mersz-e, Mary?* 5 November 1927

MERCER, Johnny [MERCER, John H] (b Savannah, Ga, 18 November 1909; d Los Angeles, 25 June 1976). Lyricist of many a popular song and filmland hit whose work for the stage musical was the less shining part of his career.

Having moved to New York in 1928, when the failure of the real-estate firm run by his lawyer father had brought down the shutters on the family's comfortable existence, Mercer at first made a living as a performer. He spent a period as a group vocalist with the Paul Whiteman band, but at the same time he was already writing song lyrics. He interpolated a number, 'Out of Breath' (music: Everett Miller), in *The Garrick Gaieties* (1930) and contributed to the score of George Lederer's out-of-town flop *The Pajama Lady* the same year, but his first successes came with non-theatre songs – 'Lazybones' (Hoagy Carmichael, 1933), 'I'm an Old Cowhand' (Mercer, 1936), 'Goody Goody' (Matty Malneck, 1936), 'Jeeper Creepers' (Harry Warren, 1938), 'You Must Have Been a Beautiful Baby' (Warren, 1938), 'Day in Day Out' (Rube Bloom, 1939), 'Fools Rush In' (Bloom, 1939) etc.

Mercer wrote a number of lyrics for revue songs, including the whole score (music: Bloom) for London's *Blackbirds of 1936*, and he supplied some words for Fred Astaire's tune to 'I'm Building Up to an Awful Let-Down', performed in the Drury Lane flop *Rise and Shine* (1936), before collaborating with Hoagy Carmichael, composer of his first hit 'Lazybones', on the score for the Shubert production *Walk with Music*. Six years and many hits later – 'Tangerine', 'Skylark', 'Dearly Beloved', 'You Were Never Lovelier', 'I'm Old Fashioned', 'That Old Black Magic', 'Dream' and the Academy Award-winning 'On the Atchison, Topeka and the Santa Fe' (1946, Harry Warren, *The Harvey Girls*) – he ventured a further theatre score in collaboration with Harold Arlen, his co-writer on 'That Old Black Magic'. Although the resulting show, *St Louis Woman*, did not have a long run on Broadway it added some superb songs and one major hit, 'Come Rain or Come Shine', to Mercer's long list of successes.

The 1949 musical *Texas L'il Darlin'* and Mercer's one attempt to write and compose a full show score on his own, *Top Banana* (1951), had much longer runs than *St Louis Woman* but brought forth no such single song successes. Ultimately, his biggest all-round theatre win came with the comic-strip musical *Li'l Abner* (1956) from which the song 'Jubilation T Cornpone' emerged as the comical hit.

Although there were plenty of further song hits in the next part of his career ('Autumn Leaves', 'Satin Doll', 'Sobbin' Women', 'Goin' Courtin'', 'Blues in the Night', 'Charade', 'Somethin's Gotta Give', 'Laura', 'Hooray for Hollywood' etc) as well as three further Academy Awards for 'In the Cool, Cool, Cool of the Evening' (1951, music: Carmichael), 'Moon River' (1961, music: Henry Mancini) and 'The Days of Wine and Roses' (1962, music: Mancini), the handful of stage shows with which Mercer was subsequently involved did not equal the successes of his ventures in the 1940s and 1950s.

Since his death his film score (music: Gene de Paul) for *Seven Brides for Seven Brothers* has been unsuccessfully adapted to the stage (1982), and his songs have been regularly used in such theatre compilations as *A Day in Hollywood*, *A Night in the Ukraine* and *Dancin'*.

1930 **The Pajama Lady** (Phil Charig, Richard Myers/w Robert B Smith/H B Smith, George Lederer) National Theater, Washington 6 October
1940 **Walk with Music** (ex-*Three After Three*) (Hoagy Carmichael/Parke Levy, Alan Lipscott) Barrymore Theater 4 June
1946 **St Louis Woman** (Harold Arlen/Arna Bontemps, Countee Cullen) Martin Beck Theater 30 March
1949 **Texas, L'il Darlin'** (Robert Emmett Dolan/John Whedon, Sam Moore) Mark Hellinger Theater 25 November
1951 **Top Banana** (Mercer) Winter Garden Theater 1 November

1956 **Li'l Abner** (Gene de Paul/Norman Panama, Melvin Frank) St James Theater 15 November

1959 **Saratoga** (Arlen/Morton da Costa) Winter Garden Theater 7 December

1964 **Foxy** (Dolan/Ian McLellan Hunter, Ring Lardner jr) Ziegfeld Theater 16 February

1974 **The Good Companions** (André Previn/Ronald Harwood) Her Majesty's Theatre, London 11 July

1982 **Seven Brides for Seven Brothers** (de Paul/Lawrence Kasha, David Landay) Alvin Theater 8 July

MERCIER, René [Yves Auguste] (d 1973).

Conductor and composer of dance and theatre music, Mercier contributed the scores to several Parisian musical comedies of the 1920s and 1930s, of which *Les Fifilles de Loth*, *Je t'veux* and *Déshabillez-vous* all had fine metropolitan careers and the second-named even got produced in Hungary. *Bégonia*, another piece which he illustrated, but in which the accent was firmly on comedy, also had a good run.

1920 **Le Béguin de la garnison** (Paul Murio) Théâtre des Capucines November

1922 **Les Fifilles de Loth** (Murio) Théâtre du Moulin-Bleu 4 or 11 February

1923 **Je t'veux** (w Fred Pearly, Gaston Gabaroche, Albert Valsien/Bataille-Henri/Wilned, Marcel Grandjean) Théâtre Marigny 12 February

1923 **Benjamin** (André Barde, Murio, Benjamin Rabier) Ba-ta-clan 11 April

1928 **Déshabillez-vous** (Barde) Théâtre des Bouffes-Parisiens 22 December

1930 **Bégonia** (René Pujol) Théâtre Scala 15 February

1934 **Elles font toutes l'amour** (Murio) Théâtre du Moulin-Bleu 7 May

1936 **Un p'tit bout de femme** (Daniel Normand, Charles Pothier, Belotti) Théâtre de la Gaîté-Lyrique

LA MÈRE DES COMPAGNONS Opérette in 3 acts by Henri Chivot and Alfred Duru. Music by Hervé. Théâtre des Folies-Dramatiques, Paris, 15 December 1880.

Juliette Simon-Girard appeared in *La Mère des compagnons* as Francine Thibault, the mascot of the local carpenter lads, who disguises herself as her aristocratic fiancé, Gaston (Simon-Max), while he escapes the agents of the republic. When he proves foolish and faithless, Francine returns to wed the solid carpenter lad, Marcel (Lepers), who has been sighing over her ever since the opening chorus. The comedy fell to Francine's outspoken mother (Mme Dharville), bumbling into the attempts of Gaston's family to make a lady of Francine, and to Édouard Maugé, as Marcel's impossible brother, venturing into extravagant disguise in his attempts to expose Gaston's shortcomings and ease his brother's aching heart. Hervé's lively score illustrated a thoroughly comical piece, which had more of the character of an old-fashioned ballad opera than of modern opéra-comique to it, most effectively and the piece ran for 58 nights before going on to be seen at Budapest's Népszinház (ad Béla J Fái, Lajos Evva).

Hungary: Népszinház *Az ácslegények gazdasszonykája* 26 March 1881

MÉREI, Adolf [MERKL, Adolf] (b Hatvan, 7 February 1876; d Budapest, 12 March 1918).

Dramaturg and chief stage director at the Magyar Színház from 1899, Mérei wrote or, more often, translated and adapted libretti and lyrics for the brisk flow of French, Austrian and British musicals and comedies staged at that house, amongst which were included such major hits as the Hungarian versions of *Der Rastelbinder* and *Die lustige Witwe*. In 1907 he moved on to fulfil a similar position at the Népszinház-Vigopera, then to the Király Színház and, ultimately, to the Népopera.

Although the bulk of his writing work was in adapting opérettes and Operetten, and such plays as Bilhaud and Hennequin's *Nelly Rosier*, Rudyard Stone's *Lotty ezredesei* and Grenet-Dancourt and Vaucaire's *Le Fils surnaturel* for local versions equipped with added songs – and Conan Doyle's *The Hound of the Baskervilles* without – he also wrote a number of original pieces, combining on several operetts with popular song- and show-writer Béla Zerkovitz and writing the text for Huszka's little *Tilos a bemenet* and Szirmai's *A sárga dominó*.

1899 **Tilos a bemenet** (Jenő Huszka) Magyar Színház 2 September

1901 **Lotty ezredesei** Hungarian version w songs w Jenő Faragó (Magyar Színház)

1901 **A postásfiu** (*The Messenger Boy*) Hungarian version w Ernő Salgó (Magyar Színház)

1901 **A szerencsecsillag** (*The Lucky Star*) Hungarian version w Emil Makai (Magyar Színház)

1901 **A vesztaszüzek** (*Les Petites Vestales*) Hungarian version (Magyar Színház)

1901 **Svihákok** (*Die Landstreicher*) Hungarian version w Aurél Föld (Magyar Színház)

1901 **Florodóra** Hungarian version w Dezső Bálint (Magyar Színház)

1902 **Herkules munkái** (*Les Travaux d'Hercule*) Hungarian version w Ernő Keszthelyi (Magyar Színház)

1903 **A szobalány** (*Nelly Rosier*) Hungarian version w songs (Magyar Színház)

1903 **A Drótostót** (*Der Rastelbinder*) Hungarian version w György Ruttkay (Magyar Színház)

1903 **Tavasz** (*Frühlingsluft*) Hungarian version (Magyar Színház)

1903 **Pesti nők** [later *Pesti asszonyok*] (*Wiener Frauen*) Hungarian version (Budai Színkör)

1904 **Sherry** (*Madame Sherry*) Hungarian version (Magyar Színház)

1904 **Hüvelyk Kató** (*La Petite Poucette*) Hungarian version (Magyar Színház)

1904 **A rikkancs** (*Das Marktkind*) Hungarian version w Ruttkay (Magyar Színház)

1904 **Pfefferkorn utazása** (*Pfefferkorns Reise*) Hungarian version (Magyar Színház)

1904 **Csak tréfa** (György Verő) Magyar Színház 10 September

1904 **A tórvénytelen apa** (*Le Fils surnaturel*) Hungarian version w songs (Király Színház)

1904 **A próféta álma** (Jenő Markus) Népszinház 25 November

1904 **Bebe hercegnő** (*Princesse Bébé*) Hungarian version (Magyar Színház)

1904 **Az ibolyáslány** (*Das Veilchenmädel*) Hungarian version (Magyar Színház)

1904 **Fecskefészek** (*Das Schwalbennest*) Hungarian version (Magyar Színház)

1904 **Huszárvér** (*Das Garnisonsmädel*) Hungarian version w Ruttkay (Magyar Színház)

1905 **A portugál** (Jenő Sztojanovits) Magyar Színház 3 January

1905 **A danzigi hercegnő** (*The Duchess of Dantzic*) Hungarian version (Király Színház)

1905 **Putifárné** (*Madame Potiphar*) Hungarian version (Magyar Színház)

1906 **A koldusgróf** (*Vergeltsgott*) Hungarian version (Magyar Színház)

1906 **Gyöngyélet** (*Tire-au-flanc!*) Hungarian version w Ferenc Molnár and music by Ferenc Békési Magyar Színház 21 April

1906 **Cserelányok** (*Les Filles Jackson*) Hungarian version (Király Színház)

1906 **A milliárdoskisasszony** (*Frauenherz*) Hungarian version (Magyar Színház)

1906 **A víg özvegy** (*Die lustige Witwe*) Hungarian version (Magyar Színház)

1907 **A századik asszony** (Izsó Barna) Budai Színkör 7 June

1907 **A sárga dominó** (Albert Szirmai) Népszinház-Vigopera 4 October

1907 **Három feleség** (*Der Mann mit den drei Frauen*) Hungarian version (Népszinház-Vigopera)

1907 **Paris almája** (*Paris, ou le bon juge*) Hungarian version (Népszinház-Vigopera)

1907 **Víg nibelungok** (*Die lustigen Nibelungen*) Hungarian version (Király Színház)

1907 **A varázskeringő** (*Ein Walzertraum*) Hungarian version (Király Színház)

1907 **Fuzsitus kisasszony** (*Ein tolles Mädel*) Hungarian version (Fővárosi Nyári Színház)

1909 **A szerencsemalac** (*Das Glücksschweinchen*) Hungarian version (Fővárosi Nyári Színház)

1909 **Az erdészlány** (*Die Försterchristl*) Hungarian version (Fővárosi Nyári Színház)

1909 **Színészvér** (*Künstlerblut*) Hungarian version (Fővárosi Nyári Színház)

1909 **Aranyhalacska** (*Der Goldfisch*) Hungarian version (Nagyvárad)

1911 **A muzsikus leány** (*Das Musikantenmädel*) Hungarian version (Fővárosi Nyári Színház)

1911 **A kék róka** (Béla Zerkovitz) Royal-Orfeum 29 September

1912 **Az asszonyfaló** (*Der Frauenfresser*) Hungarian version (Budapesti Színház)

1912 **Az ártatlan Zsuzsi** (*Die keusche Susanne*) Hungarian version (Budai Színkör)

1912 **Tengerész Kató** (*Die Marinengustl*) Hungarian version (Népopera)

1912 **A régi Pest** (*Alt-Wien*) Hungarian version (Budapesti Színház)

1912 **A kedves Augusztin** (*Der liebe Augustin*) Hungarian version (Népopera)

1912 **Ostromállapot** (*Ein Belagerungzustand*) Hungarian version (Royal Orfeum)

1913 **Aranyeső** (Zerkovitz/w Iszor Béldi) Népopera 21 February

1913 **Budagyöngye** (*Hoheit tanzt Walzer*) Hungarian version (Népopera)

1913 **A nevető férj** (*Der lachende Ehemann*) Hungarian version (Népopera)

1913 **Katonadolog** (Zerkovitz/w Béldi) Népopera 25 October

1913 **Finom família** (Zerkowitz) Royal Orfeum 31 January

1914 **Éjfélkor** (*Zwischen zwölf und eins*) Hungarian version (Népopera)

1914 **A mozitündér** (*Die Kino-Königin*) Hungarian version (Népopera)

1915 **Vándorfecskék** (Zerkovitz) Télikert 1 March; Royal Orfeum, Budapest 2 October

1915 **Kotnyeles naccsága** (*Botschafterin Leni*) Hungarian version (Népopera)

1916 **Marci** (Alfred Márkus/Engel, Horst ad) Fővárosi Nyári Színház 16 June

1917 **Az első feleség** (*Seine erste Frau*) Hungarian version (Budapesti Színház)

MERKÈS, Marcel (b Bordeaux, 7 July 1920).
MERVAL, Paulette [RIFFAUD, Paulette] (b La Roche Chalais, 3 November 1920).

Married during their student days at Bordeaux, baritone Merkès and soprano Merval subsequently led a large part of their careers in the musical theatre as a duo, appearing on Paris's larger stages as the stars of *Rêve de valse*, as Scotto's *Les Amants de Venise*, in *Les Amours de Don Juan* (1956), *Vienne chante et danse* (1967), *Rose-Marie*, *Michel Strogoff* and *Douchka* (1973). Merkès also created the hero of Scotto's *Violettes impériales* and appeared as Frank Butler in France's *Annie du Far-West* and as Danilo in *La Veuve joyeuse*.

Freely recorded and re-recorded and regularly re-released, constantly touring and/or televised in their later years in increasingly modest but spangled productions and, latterly, staged concerts, the couple known as the 'M et Mme Opérette' of France are the delight of their fans and the principal purveyors of the wrinkles, wobbles and glitter image of the opérette that became prevalent in France in the 1970s and 1980s.

MERMAN, Ethel [ZIMMERMAN, Ethel Agnes] (b Astoria, NY, 16 January 1909; d New York, 15 February 1984). Swingeing vocalist and queen-sized personality who moved smoothly from playing youthful wisecrackers to out-front mothers, taking her stardom with her all the way.

The young Miss Zimmerman worked first as a typist and a secretary and made her way into showbusiness in her late teens singing in cabaret and in vaudeville and appearing in some short films. She came to the notice of the general public with a bang when she made her first Broadway musical theatre appearance as the lusty, out-west Kate Fothergill in Aarons and Freedley's production of *Girl Crazy* (1930), introducing 'I Got Rhythm', 'Boy! What Love Has Done to Me' and 'Sam and Delilah' with all the oomph and vocal carrying-power that were to become her trademark. She appeared the following year in *George White's Scandals* ('Life is Just a Bowl of Cherries'), and in 1932 in a De Sylva, Brown and Whiting piece called *Humpty Dumpty* which ultimately came to town as *Take a Chance* (Wanda Brill). Although the show was far from its writers' best, Miss Merman confirmed the effect of her first Broadway musical appearance with the help of the songs 'Eadie was a Lady' and 'Rise 'n' Shine' and helped *Take a Chance* to a good run. The rôle of chanteuse-cum-evangelist Reno Sweeney in Cole Porter's *Anything Goes* (1934) gave her her best opportunities to date. As she wisecracked and walloped her way through a nightclubby prayer meeting to the strains of 'Blow, Gabriel, Blow', and got appreciatively personal over William Gaxton in 'You're the Top' and 'I Get a Kick Out of You', Miss Merman hoisted herself to a firm position amongst Broadway's favourite musical stars.

The built-to-bust-size rôles of Nails Duquesne in Porter's *Red, Hot and Blue* (1936, 'It's De-Lovely') and Jeanette Adair in *Stars in Your Eyes* (1939) did less for the star than she did for the shows in question, but she found another fine, comic part as another nightclub singer, May Daly, who is dreamed into the character of Madame Dubarry, in *Dubarry was a Lady* (1939, 'Friendship'). She had solo star-billing in two further Cole Porter shows, winning long-running success as nightclub owner Hattie Maloney in *Panama Hattie* (1940, 'Let's Be Buddies'), and rather less of a run as the chorus-girl-turned-munitions-worker heroine of *Something for the Boys* (1943, Blossom Hart).

Miss Merman moved out of her regular loud, jokey and lovable night-club-singer/chorus-girl mould of rôles when she was cast a little against type as the toughly innocent sharpshooter, Annie Oakley, in Rodgers and Hammerstein's production of *Annie Get Your Gun* (1946). If, as a result, Annie on the stage came out a bit different to Annie on the printed page, Miss Merman nevertheless triumphed in the part and in the songs with which Irving Berlin had supplied her: 'You Can't Get a Man with a Gun', 'Doin' What Comes Natur'lly', 'I Got the Sun in the Morning', 'They Say It's Wonderful', 'Moonshine Lullaby'. The star rôle of Berlin's next musical, *Call Me Madam*, was tailored perhaps better than any had yet been for its occupant. Miss Merman played the brash and bright, maddening and adorable Sally Adams, socialite turned ambassador, splashing cash and cheer around Ruritania ('You're Just in Love', 'The Hostess with the Mostes' on the Ball', 'The Best Thing for You') and scored another major success.

Call Me Madam also marked the advance of Miss Merman – now in her forties – from playing girls to playing women and, if *Happy Hunting* (1956, Liz Livingstone), which actually cast her as a mother – even though she got the man in the final reel – proved one of her few unsatisfactory shows, her second older-woman rôle brought her another triumph. Cast as the rampaging stage-mother of Gypsy Rose Lee in a musical which, for all that it was called *Gypsy*, centred firmly on her parent, Miss Merman performed 'Everything's Coming Up Roses', 'Some People' and an 11-o'clock act, Rose's Turn, which won itself a virtually legendary status, imitators (more male than female) and a consecration as the highlight of what has become, more in hindsight than at the time, regarded as the most popular and praised example of that peculiarly Broadway institution, the large lead rôle for a starry older woman with a scalding voice.

In fact, by this time Merman's voice was a little less scalding (its main quality had, apparently, never been actual volume, as the legend now has it, but a singular ability to project both notes and words with the utmost clarity to the last row of the gallery) and the artist a little less hungry. The star who had – unlike so many others – almost always stayed with her shows right throughout their often lengthy runs, began walking through performances of *Gypsy*. After 30 years at the very top of the tree, and as popular as ever, she had, nevertheless, created her last Broadway rôle. Her final musical stage appearances were again as Annie, in her mid-fifties (with an extra song for the occasion), and as Dolly Gallagher Levi in Broadway's *Hello, Dolly!*, a rôle which she had originally turned down but which she finally took up for a period in the show's seventh Broadway year and her 62nd (with two extra songs).

One of the most popular musical stage stars of her time, if not indeed the most popular, and certainly the one who aroused the most passionate following amongst her fans (and also amongst many who never ever saw her), Merman did not, however, manage to put herself across on the screen with the same success. She filmed versions of both *Anything Goes* (1936) and *Call Me Madam* (1953), but her other major rôles – Annie and Rose, in particular – were filmed by other artists. As film guru Leslie Halliwell summarized 'Her style was too outsize for Hollywood.'

Autobiographies: w Martin, P: *Who Could Ask for Anything More?* (Doubleday, Garden City, 1955), w Eells, G: *Merman – an Autobiography* (Simon & Schuster, New York, 1978) Biography: Thomas, B: *I Got Rhythm: the Ethel Merman Story* (Putnam, New York, 1985)

MERRICK, David [MARGULOIS, David] (b St Louis, Mo, 27 November 1911). Broadway's most up-front showman of the 1950s, 1960s, 1970s and 1980s and producer of a shower of hit shows.

At first a lawyer and subsequently on the staff of producer Herman Shumlin, Merrick moved into production in 1949 as associate producer on a comedy called *Clutterbuck* and entered the musical theater when he managed to get the rights to make Marcel Pagnol's celebrated trilogy of Marseillais novels/plays into a musical. The resultant piece, entitled *Fanny*, had an excellent Broadway run (888 performances) and was the starting point for a long series of Merrick productions of both plays and musicals. The latter included the Lena Horne vehicle *Jamaica* (1957), a second film adaptation with a score by *Fanny* composer Harold Rome, *Destry Rides Again* (1959), the highly successful *Gypsy* (1959) with Ethel Merman as the title-lady's mum, *Take Me Along* (1959), the English version of the French musical *Irma la Douce* (1960), the comedy musical *Do Re Mi* (1960), Michael Stewart and Bob Merrill's adaptation of the film *Lili* as *Carnival* (1961), the uncharacteristically unattractive *Subways Are for Sleeping* (1961), *I Can Get it for You Wholesale* (1962), the British musical successes *Stop the World – I Want to Get Off* (1962) and *Oliver!* (1962), and *110 in the Shade* (1963). This colourful and very largely successful selection came to its peak in 1964 with the record-breaking production of *Hello, Dolly!*, a musical version of the play *The Matchmaker* which Merrick had presented on Broadway a decade earlier.

The frenetic success rate sagged slightly in the mid-1960s, but amongst the Broadway failures of *Foxy* (1964) and *Pickwick* (1965), the pre-Broadway demises of *Hot September* (1965), *Breakfast at Tiffany's* (1966) and *Mata Hari* (1967) and the only average runs of *The Roar of the Greasepaint – the Smell of the Crowd* (1965), *How Now, Dow Jones* (1967) and *The Happy Time* (1968), Merrick still pulled out two further major hits with the two-handed *I Do! I Do!* (1966) and *Promises, Promises* (1968).

A reduced schedule in the reduced Broadway temperatures of the 1970s brought out an unprepossessing musical version of the screenplay *Some Like It Hot* (*Sugar*) which passed 500 performances on Broadway without establishing itself as a hit, the Hollywood tale of *Mack and Mabel* (1974) which lasted very much less long on stage but very much better off it, and a transfer of the Goodspeed Opera House production of *Very Good Eddie* (1975), whilst his production of another musicalized piece of Pagnol, *The Baker's Wife*, closed on the road. Merrick remarried success, however, in 1981, when he mounted a stage version of the famous film *42nd Street* which won him extended runs in both America and Britain.

The most loved, hated, feared, admired, but above all paragraphed producer on Broadway for many years, Merrick, in an era when musical theatre production was steadily becoming an affair for syndicates and bankers, remained staunchly and loudly a one-man producing band with his own ideas on his shows (even down to the picking of a replacement chorus girl) and his own colourful ways of publicizing both them and himself. At a time when the 'show' was falling rapidly out of 'showbiz' on Broadway he stuck with some success to the (to the 'enlightened') often corny and often transparent but eminently theatrical ways of the previous century.

A stroke, which left him with a severe speech impediment, depleted Merrick's energies only temporarily. In a saga worthy of a TV teatime mini-series, he fought off efforts to seize control of his affairs by having him declared incompetent to run them himself, kept his current productions running and before too long was back with a new one. If the transfer of a recoloured revival of Gershwin's *Oh, Kay!* (1990) proved an uncharacteristically gimmicky and unprofitable choice, it nevertheless allowed him to take on and severely stain the credibility of an over-powerful theatre critic, proving that he was still a presence to be counted on in the Broadway theatre.

MERRIE ENGLAND Comic opera in 2 acts by Basil Hood. Music by Edward German. Savoy Theatre, London, 2 April 1902.

When William Greet took over the Savoy Theatre from the D'Oyly Carte family, he determined to continue to run it on the same diet of high-class comic opera on which it had always thrived. He commissioned his first show from the men who had proven themselves, in the Savoy's previous show, to be the natural successors to Gilbert and Sullivan – Basil Hood and Edward German – and with *Merrie England* they produced a piece noticeably better than their initial *The Emerald Isle*.

Queen Elizabeth (Rosina Brandram) has her romantic eye on young Sir Walter Raleigh (Robert Evett), but Raleigh is in love with her lady-in-waiting, Bessie Throckmorton (Agnes Fraser). The jealous queen plans to poison Bessie, but she is shamed from her design by an apparition of Herne the Hunter, engineered by the the Earl of Essex (Henry Lytton), himself ambitious for the queen's attention, the witch Jill-all-Alone (Louie Pounds) and her forester lover. The tale was set in the forests of Windsor, peopled with the folk of the town, and with a troupe of players which provided the principal if incidental comic rôles of Walter Wilkins (Walter Passmore) and his sidekick Simkins (Mark Kinghorne).

Hood told his tale skilfully in a language amusingly redolent of ancient burlesque, full of puns and wordplay, of conceits and similes and three-quarter serious thee-ing and thou-ing, whilst German turned out a score full of beautiful ensembles and pluckable solos. Raleigh's tenor song 'The English Rose', Essex's baritone paean to 'The Yeomen of England', Bessie's soprano waltz song 'Oh Who Shall Say That Love is Cruel?', her lost-letter song 'She Had a Letter from Her Love', and the Queen's contralto summoning of 'O Peaceful England' all became concert and recording favourites over the half-century following.

However, *Merrie England*, in spite of comparing favourably with Sullivan's olde Englishe light opera *The Yeomen of the Guard*, did not find anything like the same degree of popularity as that piece at the Savoy. After 120 performances Greet took it on tour, and though it returned for a further 57 performances at the end of the year, its record remained a disappointment. Yet *Merrie England* remained

staunchly in the repertoire. Its principal songs remained omnipresent, and provincial, amateur and concert performances were numerous through the years. Then, in 1934, a professional revival was mounted at the Prince's Theatre (6 September) with star tenor Joseph Hislop (Raleigh) and Enid Cruickshank (Elizabeth) featured: it ran for 187 performances. Another decade later, a second revival (Winter Garden Theatre, 19 October 1944) was staged, and in 1945 a third, albeit of a rather badly adapted version (ad Edward Knoblock, Prince's Theatre 6 September). However, this last revival was produced by Jack Waller and cast to the hilt with Heddle Nash (Raleigh) and Dennis Noble (Essex) in the leading male rôles. This time *Merrie England* lasted for 365 West End performances, bringing its all-time West End score up to 782 nights, a figure rather more in keeping with its offstage popularity. Thereafter the show returned to London again briefly in 1951 (National Light Opera Co) and in 1960 when the Sadler's Wells Opera Company mounted another, less drastically revised, version (ad Dennis Arundell).

If *Merrie England* was reluctant to take off in Britain, it was equally so in the colonies. Australia did not see a professional *Merrie England* until 1921 when, finally persuaded by the relentless popularity of its music, J C Williamson Ltd mounted a production with ex-Savoyard C H Workman as Wilkins, Strella Wilson (Bessie), Ethel Morrison/Pearl Ladd (Elizabeth), Ralph Errolle (Raleigh) and Howett Worster (Essex) as part of their Gilbert and Sullivan Company's season. It played brief seasons in Melbourne and Sydney (Theatre Royal 13 January 1922) but was not brought back.

Australia: Her Majesty's Theatre, Melbourne 18 November 1921
Recording: Sadler's Wells company (HMV/EMI)

MERRILL, Bob [LAVAN, Henry] (b Atlantic City, 17 May 1921). Songwriter of many a novelty hit of the 1950s who transferred his talents to the theatre with mixed results.

Merrill was introduced to the theatre through various jobs at the Bucks County Playhouse in his teens, but his first attempts at writing for the stage were made during a spell in the army. He subsequently spent periods working at NBC (1943–4) and at Columbia Pictures as an author of short and secondary movies, as a caster and ultimately as a director, before turning his attention to the popular-music world.

He had his first song hit in 1950 with the words for '(If I Knew You Were Comin') I'd've Baked a Cake' (w Al Hoffman, Clem Watts) and this was followed by a veritable rush of 1950s song successes, including many winning novelties, for which he mostly provided both music and words: 'Candy and Cake' (1950), 'Me and My Imagination' (1950 w Hoffman), 'Christopher Columbus' (w Terry Gilkyson), 'Sparrow in the Treetop', 'A Beggar in Love' 'My Truly, Truly Fair', 'There's Always Room at Our House', 'Belle, Belle My Liberty Belle' (all 1951), 'We Won't Live in a Castle', 'There's a Pawnshop on the Corner', 'Walkin' to Missouri', 'Feet Up', 'That's Why' (all 1952), 'How Much is That Doggie in the Window', 'All the Time and Everywhere', 'She Wears Red Feathers', 'Look at That Girl', 'If I Had a Golden Umbrella', 'Chick a Boom' (all 1953), 'Mambo Italiano' (1954), 'Where Will the Dimple Be', 'Make Yourself Comfortable' (both 1955), 'Sweet Old Fashioned Girl', 'The Miracle of Love' (both 1956) and 'In the Middle of a Dark, Dark Night' (1957).

Merrill made his first appearance as a Broadway writer with the music and lyrics for the 1957 musical *New Girl in Town*, a version of Eugene O'Neill's *Anna Christie*, which had a year's run on Broadway, and he followed up with a second piece of musical O'Neill, *Take Me Along* (based on *Ah, Wilderness*), which ran up an equivalent life. The 1961 show *Carnival*, a charming and catchy musical version of Paul Gallico's *Lili*, had not only a fine New York run but a wider appeal which brought it a good number of overseas productions. It also had a hit song in 'Love Makes the World Go Round' which, with the help of Perry Como, became the highlight of a score which also included the wistful 'Mira', a swirling 'Grand Impérial Cirque de Paris' and 'Sword, Rose and Cape', the pretty 'Yes, My Heart' and 'A Very Nice Man' for the show's little heroine and the misanthropic 'I've got to Find a Reason' for its anti-hero.

Merrill supplied the lyrics to Jule Styne's music for the highly successful Fanny Brice biomusical *Funny Girl* ('People', 'I'm the Greatest Star', 'You Are Woman', 'When a Girl isn't Pretty', 'Don't Rain on My Parade'), which also earned him another pair of notches on his hit-parade tally, but subsequent ventures with music and lyrics (the unopened *Breakfast at Tiffany's*, 80 performances of *Henry, Sweet Henry*), book and lyrics (pre-Broadway closer *Prettybelle*) or all three (*The Prince of Grand Street*) were not successful. An adaptation of the screenplay *Some Like it Hot* under the title of *Sugar*, for which Merrill supplied the lyrics to another Styne score, did better than any of these with more than a year on Broadway and several foreign productions, but produced nothing in the way of memorable songs.

A television musical *The Dangerous Christmas of Little Red Riding Hood* was brought latterly to the off-Broadway stage and a compilation show of Merrill songs was produced at the Vineyard Theater in 1984 under the title *We're Home* (11 October).

1957 **New Girl in Town** (George Abbott) 46th Street Theater 14 May
1959 **Take Me Along** (Joseph Stein, Robert Russell) Shubert Theater 22 October
1961 **Carnival** (Michael Stewart) Imperial Theater 13 April
1964 **Funny Girl** (Jule Styne/Isabel Lennart) Winter Garden Theater 26 March
1966 **Breakfast at Tiffany's** (*Holly Golightly*) (Nunnally Johnson, Abe Burrows, Edward Albee) Forrest Theater, Philadelphia, 10 April; Majestic Theater previews only
1967 **Henry, Sweet Henry** (Johnson) Palace Theater 23 October
1971 **Prettybelle** (Styne) Shubert Theater, Boston, 1 February
1972 **Sugar** (Styne/Peter Stone) Majestic Theater 9 April
1978 **The Prince of Grand Street** Forrest Theater, Philadelphia 7 March
1990 **Hannah ... 1939** Vineyard Theater 31 May

MERRILY WE ROLL ALONG Musical in 2 acts by George Furth based on the play by George S Kaufman and Moss Hart. Music and lyrics by Stephen Sondheim. Alvin Theater, New York, 16 November 1982.

A musical version of Kaufman and Hart's fairly successful play (Music Box Theater 29 September 1934, 155 performances), a piece which presented the particularity of telling its tale in reverse. The successful, shiny New York folk who are seen gathered together at the party that opens the evening are tracked back, through the events which have led them to their present point in life, to their college days where, full of ideas, ideals and promise, they are about to set out into the world. The point of the exercise is to emphasize that, to gain success both worldly and personal, it is usually necessary to compromise on shiny ideals: the only question seems to be, how much?

The musical version was updated to the present day and the central figure, Franklin Shepard (Jim Walton), became a songwriter and Hollywood producer. In reverse to the play, where adult actors played 'down' in the final scenes, the show was also cast with college-age performers who played 'up' for the show's earlier scenes, thus allowing the young idealists to be still seen in the slick, disillusioned middle-aged characters they had become. Lonny Price played Charley Kringas, college friend and collaborator of Shepard until he falls by the hard wayside, Ann Morrison was Mary Flynn, best pal of always. The songs included a musical television interview ('Franklin Shepard Inc.') which was also a keystone in the tale, a hymn to 'Old Friends' and a pretty ballad, 'Not a Day Goes By'.

Produced by Lord Grade, Martin Starger, Robert Fryer and director Hal Prince, the musical *Merrily We Roll Along* flopped in 16 Broadway performances. However, the reputation and name value of Stephen Sondheim ensured that it did not rest there. It has since received repeated performances (particularly in places where its young casting is an attraction), some revisions as seen in a revival at California's La Jolla Playhouse, and even an announcement of a major revival, without yet being re-staged on Broadway.

In Britain, the show caused a small stir when it was played by students at London's Guildhall School for Music and Drama, leading to its being played regionally in Britain. It did not, however, in spite of much talk, progress further.

UK: Manchester Library Theatre 28 September 1984
Recordings: original cast (RCA), English cast (Leicester Haymarket Theatre) (TER)

THE MERRY DUCHESS Comic opera in 2 acts by George R Sims. Music by Frederick Clay. Royalty Theatre, London, 23 April 1883.

Kate Santley's continually brave production schedule included in 1883 a comic opera written by the respected journalist and playwright George Sims and Frederic Clay, whose music she had introduced in *Cattarina* and *Princess Toto* some years previously. *The Merry Duchess* was a racing drama-comedy, transparently based on the love affair between the famous jockey Fred Archer and the Duchess of Montrose. This Duchess (Kate Munroe) has to surmount such problems as the villainous Brabazon Sikes (Henry Ashley) and his wife and fellow horse-doper, Rowena (Miss Santley), an accusation of doping her own horse (already, in 1883!) and a horrid bet which pledges her hand to the ghastly masher Lord Johnnie (R Martin) should her horse lose the St Leger, before she can get to the arms of the victorious Freddy Bowman (W E Gregory).

Robust and lively in its text, the show's score was agreeable in its ballads ('The Captive Bird', 'Love's Messenger'), brightly amusing in its comical numbers ('An English

Jockey') and particularly successful in its wealth of ensembles and concerted music, but it brought forth no songs that made it to the barrel organs. The combination, however, seemed to please and *The Merry Duchess*, in a move unusual for the time, sent out a second, touring company whilst the London production moved on towards its fine 177-performance total. America, too, opened its production, starring Selina Dolaro as the Duchess and Henry Dixey and Louise Lester as the villains, whilst London's ran on, and it played a respectable 46 performances in New York before heading for the regions.

Australia followed suit the next year with Gracie Plaisted (Rowena) and Phil Day (Brabazon) starred and Nellie Stewart (Duchess), Hans Phillips (Freddie) and Edwin Kelly (Sir Lothbury Jones) heading the rest of the Royal Comic Opera Company's cast for seasons in Sydney and Melbourne (Princess Theatre 1 November 1884), helping to give *The Merry Duchess* a wider coverage than most of the best English comic operas of its era, the works of Messrs Gilbert and Sullivan, of course, apart.

USA: Standard Theater 8 September 1883; Australia: Theatre Royal, Sydney 23 August 1884

MERRY, MERRY Musical comedy in 2 acts by Harlan Thompson. Music by Harry Archer. Vanderbilt Theater, New York, 24 September 1925.

After the successes of *Little Jessie James* and *My Girl*, producer Lyle Andrews and writers Thompson and Archer followed up with a third piece in the same musical comedy mould: limited settings (originally one, but it grew to take in an impressive opening scene in a subway), much farcical action, and lively songs in an up-to-date dancing mood. *Merry, Merry* proved as good, if not better, than the previous season's effort and it was whisked in from its tryout in Providence, Rhode Island, with a lot of fuss being made over its ingénue, 21-year-old Marie Saxon, who was advertised as having invented a new dance step – a 'diagonal high kick' in which the right leg flirted with the left shoulder.

Miss Saxon featured as little Eve Walters who comes to New York to be a chorus girl in a Broadway show. She ends up sharing digs with one Sadie la Salle (Sacha Beaumont) who sets out to make enough money to wed her poor but favoured boyfriend by tempting a wealthy admirer into a close embrace and then suing him largely for cracking one of her ribs. Eve ends up renouncing showbiz and folks like Sadie for a boy called Adam. Archer's 13 songs, which he conducted from the pit with his band, were in the same joyously modern vein as those from his earlier shows, and *Merry, Merry* lived up to its title through 176 Broadway performances and a happy touring life.

Four years later, it turned up in London. The story was still recognizable but the score was not. Only three of Archer's songs survived ('You're in Love', 'Little Boy, Little Girl', 'I Was Blue'), supplemented by seven numbers by producer Jack Waller and his team of Joe Tunbridge, Bert Lee and Bob Weston plus Weston's brother Harris, and one, 'Blue Shadows' (a cue for a ballet in crinolines), by Louis Alter. There were now seven sets, a dance specialty and a chorus of 20 drilled by martial choreographer Ralph Reader. Gladys Cruickshank and Richard Dolman were

Adam and Eve, A W Baskcomb cracked Peggy O'Neil's ribs, and W H Berry was chief comic. The show was given 131 performances with a transfer to the Lyceum in the middle.

UK: Carlton Theatre 28 February 1929

THE MERRY WIDOW *see* DIE LUSTIGE WITWE

LES MERVEILLEUSES (aka *The Lady Dandies*) Comic opera in 3 acts by Basil Hood based on the play by Victorien Sardou. Lyrics by Adrian Ross. Music by Hugo Felix. Daly's Theatre, London, 27 October 1906.

The popularity of his English version of *Les P'tites Michu* at Daly's Theatre had led George Edwardes to the belief that a new round of success for the theatre which had so long housed his English comic operas lay in the import of French pieces. However, on the principle that it was more sensible to build one's own French piece than to buy one, he took a libretto made up by Victorien Sardou from his play *Les Merveilleuses*, had it adapted by Basil Hood, and commissioned Hugo Felix, the Austrian composer whose *Madame Sherry* had caused him some embarrassment by its unexpected failure, to provide the music.

Set in the *La Fille de Madame Angot* time of the Directoire (like the Lecocq hit, it introduced Citizen Barras into the plot), it dealt with the trials of the lovely Illyrine (Denise Orme), forced by the vicious régime to divorce her émigré husband (Robert Evett) and wed a vulgar Bulgar (W H Berry). Into this tale were introduced the merveilleuse Lodoiska (Evie Greene) and the ex-hairdresser Lagorille (Louis Bradfield) on the light comic/romantic hand, and two policemen (Fred Kaye, Fred Emney) on the low comic one. Felix's score, a well-crafted one with fine ensemble writing if without the catchier strains of Jones and Monckton's music for the older Daly's shows, or the pure charm and class of Messager's work, included several pieces which were well noticed, including Illyrine's 'The Cuckoo' and Lodoiska's 'Ring a Ring a Roses'.

Les Merveilleuses did not take off as it might have done. Edwardes changed the title to an English one (*The Lady Dandies*), and later brought old favourite Huntley Wright back, equipped with three Lionel Monckton songs, to attempt to add some of the appeal of earlier days, but the show had a run of only 196 performances. If this was more than fair in itself, it was disappointing when considered alongside the runs accumulated by the former Daly's musicals. However, Edwardes perservered with the Continental idea, and following the closure of *Les Merveilleuses* he tried another musical – already made, this time – by an Austrian composer. With *The Merry Widow* he did rather better.

Les Merveilleuses nevertheless did find an afterlife. It was played in Australia as *The Lady Dandies* with Florence Young (Lodoiska), Fanny Dango and, for a period, the young Rosina Buckman (Illyrine), Reginald Roberts (Dorlis), Edmund Sherras (Lagorille) and W S Percy in the featured rôles, it was toured through the Orient by Maurice Bandmann (1908), and was even later given a showing in Paris (ad Paul Ferrier) with Marthe Régnier and Juliette Méaly starred alongside a fine brochette of comics including Albert Brasseur and Guy.

Australia: Her Majesty's Theatre, Sydney *The Lady Dandies* 21 March 1908; France: Théâtre des Variétés 24 January 1914

MESDAMES DE LA HALLE Opérette bouffe in 1 act by Armand Lapointe. Music by Jacques Offenbach. Théâtre des Bouffes-Parisiens, Paris, 3 March 1858.

Mesdames de la Halle followed in the 'bouffe' tradition of *Ba-ta-clan*, *Tromb-al-ca-zar* and *Croquefer* but without taking advantage of their extravagant settings. It was a delicious piece of Parisian bouffonnerie, in which the burlesque was underlined by, and much of the comedy came from, the fact that the three ageing market-ladies of the title were played by male comedians. Madame Poiretapée (Léonce), Madame Madou (Désiré) and Madame Beurrefondu (Mesmacre) all lust after the little kitchen-lad, Croûte-au-pot (played in travesty by Lise Tautin), who himself loves pretty Ciboulette (Mlle Chabert) who sings coloratura behind her fruit stall. The sixth principal character of the piece is the drum-major Raflafla (Duvernoy) who, in a parody of operatic coincidences to match that of *HMS Pinafore*, discovers (after a few false starts) that he is the long-lost husband of one of the Mesdames and the father of Ciboulette, all in time for the flourishingly happy ending. Offenbach's score accompanied the tale in typically glittering comic fashion through an arietta for Ciboulette ('Je suis la petite fruitière'), two lively numbers for Raflafla, a duo for the principal boy and girl and a burlesque septet in which the ladies battle in extravagantly motherly style for the privilege of owning the lost girl.

Produced at the Bouffes-Parisiens, *Mesdames de la Halle* proved a delightful addition to the rapidly growing Offenbach catalogue of short opéras-bouffes, and it was revived regularly until, in 1940 (4 May), it was given the consecration of being played at the Opéra-Comique. It made its way briskly to Vienna, being played at Karl Treumann's Theater am Franz-Josefs-Kai first by the Bouffes company on tour, with Lucille Tostée as Croûte-au-pot and Léonce, Désiré and Desmonts as the ladies, and then in German (ad Alois Berla) with Johann Nestroy himself donning skirts to play Jungfer Barbara alongside Wilhelm Knaack and Grois and Treumann as Raflafla. Knaack later played the long-lost mother in a different adaptation (*Die Damen der Halle*) at the Carltheater, with Karl Blasel and Röhring as his commères and Anna Grobecker as the boy. Budapest, too, saw the Bouffes company tour before the piece was adapted into Hungarian (ad Mihály Havi), and there, as well, other productions followed. In spite of the English travesty and burlesque traditions, however, there does not ever seem to have been either a contemporary or a later production in the English language.

Germany: Krolls Theater (Fr) 7 July 1859, (Ger) 6 August 1867; Austria: Theater am Franz-Josefs-Kai (Fr) 11 June 1861, *Die Damen von Strand* 22 February 1862; Hungary: Nemzeti Színház (Fr) 12 July 1861; Budai Népszinház *A kofák* 3 October 1863
Recording: complete (revised) (EMI)

MESSAGER, André [Charles Prosper] (b Montluçon, France, 30 December 1853; d Paris, 24 February 1929). Composer and administrator whose favourite works largely held up the waning French opérette tradition in the early years of the 20th century.

The son of a civil servant, Messager entered the École Niedermeyer at an early age and completed his whole musical education there, both in Paris and during the school's exile in Switzerland in the time of the Franco-Prussian War, under Eugène Gigout (counterpoint), Adam Laussel (piano) and Clément Loret (organ). On leaving, aged 21, he became organist at Saint-Sulpice, a position he maintained until 1880 before moving on to the more expansive instruments at St-Paul-St-Louis (1881) and Sainte-Marie-des-Batignolles (1882–4). Whilst fulfilling these ecclesiastical duties, he began his wide-ranging career as a composer. A symphony was honoured by the Society of Composers and performed at the Concerts Colonne (20 January 1878), a dramatic scena, *Prométhée enchaîné*, was awarded runner-up laurels in the Concours Musical de la Ville de Paris, a cantata, *Don Juan et Haydée*, was performed in 1877 by the Société Académique de Saint-Quentin and, at the same time that these works were being produced, Messager was also providing ballet music for and conducting at the Folies-Bergère (*Les Vins de France*, *Fleur d'oranger*, *Mignons et vilains*). Then, in 1880, he left Paris for a year to take an engagement as conductor at the Eden-Théâtre at Brussels.

Messager made his entry into the musical theatre through the aegis of his publishers, Messrs Enoch. When the young composer Firmin Bernicat died before completing the score for his opérette *François les bas-bleus* (1883), the publishers nominated Messager to provide the music needed to get the show into a state for production. *François les bas-bleus* was a great success, and the management of the Théâtre des Folies-Dramatiques offered Messager, whose work had more than stood up alongside Bernicat's, the opportunity to write the entire score for their next production. *La Fauvette du Temple* (1885) and, a month later, *La Béarnaise* confirmed the happy impression of the first work, without quite winning an equivalent international success.

In 1886 Messager composed what would be his most successful ballet, *Les Deux Pigeons*, for the Paris Opéra, but an 1887 opéra-comique *Le Bourgeois de Calais* failed, and the composer was hard put to find a librettist willing to confide a new text to him. When he did, that author was none less than Catulle Mendès and the result was the poetic fairytale *Isoline*, a piece which, through a combination of circumstances, had but a short initial run but which has since found many champions amongst the lovers of light operatic music and which, in 1959, won itself a revival at the Opéra-Comique.

After an indifferent return to more standard opérette with *Le Mari de la reine* at the Bouffes-Parisiens, it was at the Opéra-Comique that Messager's next piece, *La Basoche*, was staged. It won a considerable success, making the nearest approach that the composer had yet achieved to equalling the wide public popularity of *François les bas-bleus*, but it did not bring forth another similar opportunity. In the years that followed, suffering from a need to make himself a living, Messager was present on all fronts with a ballet, *Scaramouche* (1890 w Georges Street) for the opening of the Nouveau-Théâtre, the incidental music to Paul Delair's *Hélène* (1891), the Parisian opérette *Miss Dollar* which, although far from unsuccessful, could not be ranged amongst his best works, and *Mirette*, a piece written to order for D'Oyly Carte at London's Savoy Theatre. This comic opera, for which he insisted that his new wife, the English songwriter Hope Temple, had contributed a small (and uncredited) portion of the music, did not fulfil Carte's hopes as *The Nautch Girl* (an earlier and more successful alternative to Gilbert and Sullivan) had done, and in spite of the best Savoy casting, a withdrawal, a rewrite and re-presentation, it failed to catch on. The most appreciable Messager work to emerge from this period was the Japanese-Parisian *Madame Chrysanthème* (1893), based on the novel by Pierre Loti and commissioned as the opening work for Détroyat's Théâtre-Lyrique de la Renaissance. It was another piece which, like *Isoline*, found more, and more expansive, admirers for its delicacy and musical intelligence in the years after rather than during its Paris run, and it has survived on the fringes of the played repertoire.

Messager returned to the Opéra-Comique in 1896 with *Le Chevalier d'Harmental*, a piece of which he was particularly proud, and he was devastated when it proved a total failure in Paris and did nothing to establish itself when mounted in the 1896-7 season at the Vienna Hofoper. A lighter piece, *La Fiancée en loterie*, produced at the Folies-Dramatiques (71 performances) and later at Munich's Theater am Gärtnerplatz (*Die Brautlotterie*, 12 April 1902), did better, but the composer was truly disheartened. He envisaged returning to Britain and abandoning composition, but the receipt of a delightful opérette libretto from Albert Vanloo and Georges Duval (a libretto which he was unaware had been refused by other composers) helped him to decide otherwise. His setting of that libretto with some of his most charming yet lively and melodious music ensured that *Les P'tites Michu* (1897) finally gave him the sizeable popular and international success that had so far eluded him in the musical theatre.

The same librettists provided Messager with another libretto which mixed refinement and gaiety in just the right proportions to appeal both to the general public and to the habitués of the Opéra-Comique: *Véronique*, with its Swing Song and Donkey Song ('Trot here, trot there' to two generations of English-language vocalists), scored an even more remarkable success, helping materially to extend the borders of the great period of classic French opéra-bouffe and opéra-comique which, after half a century, was touching its end.

Véronique, however, had no comparable successor. Once again the Opéra-Comique intervened. Albert Carré, librettist of *La Basoche* and newly named as director of the Salle Favart, invited Messager to become his musical director and, as a result, the composer's output over the next 20 years was limited first by his activities at the Opéra-Comique, and subsequently by periods as director of both London's Royal Opera House (1901-7) and the Paris Opéra (1908-14), and throughout as a theatre and concert conductor. A German remake of *Le Mari de la reine* as *Der Prinz gemahl* (ad Théo de Gillert, Neues Königlichen Operntheater 24 July 1904), and the productions of *Les Dragons de l'Impératrice* (1905) and the opéra-comique *Fortunio*, more in the vein of *La Basoche* than of his two great and happy hits, were his only contributions to his musical theatre oeuvre during this period, although he composed a ballet *Une aventure de la Guimard* (1900) for the Opéra-Comique to add to *Le Chevalier aux fleurs* (1897 w Raoul Pugno), written earlier for the Théâtre Marigny, incidental music for the Théâtre de la Porte Saint-Martin's féerie *La Montagne enchantée* (1897 w Xavier Leroux), an

opera, *Béatrice*, written to a text by de Flers and de Caillavet and produced both in Monaco and later at the Opéra-Comique, and a one-act opérette for the Concert Mayol.

After the war, however, Messager returned to the light musical theatre and, whilst the new-born rage for jazz-age musical comedy whirled around him, he turned out the pieces that, after his two famous works of the previous decade, have proved the most enduring of his stage pieces. In the last decade of his life, he collaborated with the distinguished playwright Frederick Lonsdale on the English light opera *Monsieur Beaucaire* (1919 'Philomel', 'Red Rose'), with Sacha Guitry on the exquisite musical play *L'Amour masqué* ('J'ai deux amants') and the comedy *Deburau* (incidental music) and, finally, with Albert Willemetz, the librettist à la mode, on two modern opérettes, *Passionnément* (1926) and *Coups de roulis* (1928).

In descriptions of the works of Messager the words 'elegant' and 'poetic' recur the most frequently. His natural habitat was, perhaps, the area of light opera formerly cared for by the Opéra-Comique, an area which has steadily faded away in more recent years in favour of the extremes of operatic and popular musical theatre. However, he proved in such pieces as *Les P'tites Michu* that he was capable of the most delightfully sparkling gaiety and even comical effects in his music, and if he never quite let himself rip in the style of some of the more frankly popular composers of the different eras of the 45 years through which he was active, he succeeded in giving those eras and their musical theatre some of their most beautiful melodies and ensembles.

1883 **François les bas-bleus** (Firmin Bernicat, completed) Théâtre des Folies-Dramatiques 8 November
1885 **Le Petit Poucet** (Eugène Leterriet, Albert Vanloo, Albert Mortier) Théâtre de la Gaîté 28 October
1885 **La Fauvette du Temple** (Paul Burani, Eugène Humbert) Théâtre des Folies-Dramatiques 17 November
1885 **La Béarnaise** (Leterrier, Vanloo) Théâtre des Bouffes-Parisiens 12 December
1887 **Le Bourgeois de Calais** (Paul Burani, Ernest Dubreuil) Théâtre des Folies-Dramatiques 6 April
1888 **Isoline** (Catulle Mendès) Théâtre de la Renaissance 25 December
1889 **Le Mari de la reine** (Ernest Grenet-Dancourt, Octave Pradels) Théâtre des Bouffes-Parisiens 18 December
1890 **La Basoche** (Albert Carré) Opera-Comique 30 May
1893 **Madame Chrysanthème** (Georges Hartmann, André Alexandre) Théâtre-Lyrique de la Renaissance 30 January
1893 **Miss Dollar** (Charles Clairville, Albert Vallin) Nouveau-Théâtre 22 December
1894 **Mirette** (Frederick E Weatherly/Michel Carré ad Harry Greenbank, revised by Adrian Ross) Savoy Theatre 3 July
1896 **La Fiancée en loterie** (w Paul Lacôme/Camille de Roddaz, Alfred Douane) Théâtre des Folies-Dramatiques 13 February
1896 **Le Chevalier d'Harmental** (Paul Ferrier) Opéra-Comique 5 March
1897 **Les P'tites Michu** (Vanloo, Georges Duval) Théâtre des Bouffes-Parisiens 16 November
1898 **Véronique** (Vanloo, Duval) Théâtre des Bouffes-Parisiens 10 December
1905 **Les Dragons de l'Imperatrice** (Vanloo, Duval) Théâtre des Variétés 13 February
1907 **Fortunio** (Robert de Flers, Gaston de Caillavet) Opéra-Comique 5 June
1914 **Béatrice** (de Flers, de Caillavet) Monte Carlo 21 March
1916 **Cyprien, ôte ta main d'la** (Maurice Hennequin) 1 act Concert Mayol

1919 **Monsieur Beaucaire** (Ross/Frederick Lonsdale) Prince's Theatre, London 19 April

1921 **La Petite Fonctionnaire** (Antoine Capus, Xavier Roux) Théâtre Mogador 14 May

1923 **L'Amour masqué** (Sacha Guitry) Théâtre Edouard VII 13 February

1926 **Passionnément** (Albert Willemetz, M Hennequin) Théâtre de la Michodière 19 January

1928 **Coups de roulis** (Willemetz) Théâtre Marigny 28 September

1930 **Sacha** (completed by Marc Berthomieu/André Rivoire) Monte Carlo

Biographies: Augé-Laribé, M: *André Messager: musicien de théâtre* (Vieux Colombier, Paris, 1951), Fevrier, H: *André Messager: mon maître, mon ami* (Amiot-Dumont, Paris, 1948), Wagstaff, J: *André Messager: a Bio-bibliography* (Greenwood Press, New York, 1991)

THE MESSENGER BOY Musical comedy in 2 acts by James T Tanner and Alfred Murray. Lyrics by Adrian Ross and Percy Greenbank. Music by Ivan Caryll and Lionel Monckton. Gaiety Theatre, London, 3 February 1900.

The first of George Edwardes's Gaiety Theatre 'girl' musicals to be a 'boy', *The Messenger Boy* top-billed comedian Teddy Payne as Tommy Bang, entrusted by the villainous Tudor Pyke (John Tresahar) with a promissory note in disfavour of his rival in love, Clive Radnor (Lionel Mackinder), to be delivered to the father of their beloved Nora (Violet Lloyd) in Egypt. Pyke thus intends to discredit his rival, but Tommy must get to Lord Punchestown with his letter before Clive does. Only after the boy has set out does Pyke discover that he has actually given him another of his 'useful' bits of paper: a compromising letter written by Lady Punchestown! So Nora, Lady Punchestown's maid, Rosa (Katie Seymour), and Pyke all set out to try to stop the messenger boy from delivering. Reorganization in the Gaiety's personnel meant that the star-billed old favourites were mostly not in the plot rôles. Miss Seymour, Payne's partner since *The Shop Girl* more than five years earlier, and Connie Ediss, as Tommy's Mum who discovers her long-lost husband passing himself off as Hooker Pasha (Harry Nicholls), were the female stars, and there were character parts for such as dance captain Willie Warde, Fred Wright and former Gaiety burlesque star E J Lonnen.

The show's songs gave Payne a jolly title number and the expected duos with Miss Seymour, including one in which they imitated 'Mummies', Miss Lloyd waxed patriotic in 'When the Boys Come Home Once More' (it was Boer War time) and Miss Ediss scored with a comical 'In the Wash', but it was a simple little piece called 'Maisie', breathlessly sung in a non-existent rôle by the exquisite ex-chorus girl Rosie Boote, which proved the show's hit. It was scarcely an outstanding number, but it caught on rageously, and little Miss Boote's reward was a coronet. She left the show to become the Marchioness of Headfort.

The Messenger Boy was a tremendous Gaiety success (429 performances) and, as was now the norm with Gaiety shows, immediately began a long and wide career beyond Britain. Budapest's Magyar Színház mounted *A postás fiu* (ad Ernő Salgó, Adolf Mérei) whilst London's version

Plate 181.

still ran, Frank Wheeler produced *The Messenger Boy* in South Africa shortly after, and, as three touring companies worked their ways around Britain, Nixon and Zimmerman starred James T Powers, Georgia Caine (Nora) and May Robson (Mrs Bang) in a highly successful Broadway run (129 performances) of a localized version which featured such additional songs as Pat Rooney's 'Pansy'.

Australia and New Zealand saw J C Williamson's production in 1902 with Fred Graham playing Tommy alongside Lillian Digges (Nora) and Rose Musgrove (Rosa), and Vienna's Gabor Steiner, who had had considerable success with *The Circus Girl*, mounted the show for three weeks at his Danzers Orpheum (ad Carl Lindau, Leopold Krenn), with his Oberregisseur Karl Tuschl starring as Tommy, Franz Glawatsch as Cosmos Bey and Frlns Felsen and Huemer as Nora and Mrs Bang. The second act featured a tarantella and an interpolated song, by Karl Kappeller, for Helene Merviola, in the rôle of Anita, an Italian street-singer, and a 'Frauen aus der ganzen Welt' display in which a waltz, 'Die Wienerin', the work of Broadway's Ludwig Engländer, was displayed by 'die gesammte Damenpersonal'.

Having played its run, long or short, in each area, *The Messenger Boy* then moved aside to make way for the newest Gaiety offering.

Hungary: *A postás fiu* Magyar Színház 24 January 1901; USA: Daly's Theater 16 September 1901; Australia: Palace Theatre, Sydney 8 October 1902; Austria: Danzers Orpheum *Der Laufbursche* 31 October 1902

MESTÉPÈS, Eugène (b 1818; d Paris, 15 May 1878).

For two decades a supplier of mostly little libretti to the budding French musical theatre of the mid-19th century, Eugène Mestépès doubled in a 'real job' as a theatrical administrator. He was in charge of the Théâtre des Bouffes-Parisiens from the little house's inception in 1855, and later ran the Théâtre de l'Ambigu. On the more substantial side of the musical theatre, he teamed with Victor Wilder to provide the libretto to Weber's *Sylvana* (1872).

1855 **Le Violoneux** (Jacques Offenbach/w Émile Chevalet) 1 act Théâtre des Bouffes-Parisiens 31 August

1855 **Le Duel de Benjamin** (Émile Jonas) 1 act Théâtre des Bouffes-Parisiens October

1856 **En revenant de la Pontoise** (Alfred Dufresne) Théâtre des Bouffes-Parisiens 20 February

1856 **En revenant de la revue** (Dufresne) Théâtre des Bouffes-Parisiens 20 March

1857 **Les Trois Baisers du Diable** (Offenbach) 1 act Théâtre des Bouffes-Parisiens 15 January

1857 **Le Roi boit** (Jonas/w Adolphe Jaime) 1 act Théâtre des Bouffes-Parisiens 9 April

1857 **Dragonette** (Offenbach/w Jaime) 1 act Théâtre des Bouffes-Parisiens 30 April

1857 **Maître Griffard** (Léo Delibes) 1 act Théâtre Lyrique 3 October

1857 **La Demoiselle d'honneur** (Théophile Semet/w A S Kaufmann) 1 act Théâtre Lyrique 30 December

1863 **Ondine** (Semet/w Lockroy) Théâtre Lyrique 7 January

1863 **Job et son chien** (Jonas) 1 act Théâtre des Bouffes-Parisiens 6 February

1864 **Le Manoir des Larenadière** (Jonas) 1 act Théâtre des Bouffes-Parisiens 29 September

1864 **La Fille du maître de chapelle** (Vauzanges/w Ventéjoul) Théâtre Déjazet 9 July

1865 **Avant la noce** (Jonas/w Paul Boisselot) 1 act Théâtre des Bouffes-Parisiens 24 March

1865 **Les Deux Arlequins** (Jonas) 1 act Fantaisies-Parisiennes 29 December

MEXICAN HAYRIDE Musical comedy in 2 acts by Herbert and Dorothy Fields. Music and lyrics by Cole Porter. Winter Garden Theater, New York, 28 January 1944.

The third successive collaboration and third successive long run (481 performances) for songwriter Cole Porter and librettists Herbert and Dorothy Fields, *Mexican Hayride* was a vehicle for popular comedian Bobby Clark, cast by the authors as a minor crook in a Mexican setting, and pursued by the authorities through a series of disguises to challenge the most ebullient musical comedies of half a century earlier. June Havoc (Montana) portrayed a lady bullfighter, Wilbur Evans (David Winthrop) was her baritonic diplomat boyfriend, George Givot (Lombos Campos) the comic's comical partner in crime, and Corinna Mura was an extraneous lady called Lolita who sang Mexicanish songs.

The score brought forth no new Porter bon-bons, although within the show 'Count your Blessings' as comicked by the two crooks and the matadoress scored a popular success, and Evans sang an 'I Love You' (allegedly as a result of a bet taken by Porter that he couldn't, or wouldn't dare, put out a piece with such a timeworn title) which became popular and pulled out a Porter catalogue of names and rhymes for 'There Must be Someone For Me'. Much of the musical material written for the show was, in fact, dropped on the way into town (notably Porter's latest dip into the celebrity telephone directory in 'It's Just Like the Good Old Days') and Porter wasn't happy with what was finally heard on Broadway, but, extravagantly produced by Mike Todd, with a large cast, crew, orchestra and publicity budget, *Mexican Hayride* proved popular wartime entertainment. The musical was not seen outside America, but its libretto (without the songs) was later made into an Abbott and Costello movie.

Recording: original cast (Decca/CBS)

MEYER, Joseph (b Modesto, Calif, 12 March 1894; d New York, 22 June 1987).

Songwriter Meyer flourished in the second half of the 1920s, supplying several major hit numbers to Broadway and London shows of which the most famous were 'California Here I Come' (lyric: B G De Sylva, Al Jolson) sung by Jolson in *Bombo* and again in *Big Boy*; 'A Cup of Coffee, a Sandwich, and You' (w Billy Rose, Al Dubin) introduced by Gertrude Lawrence in *Charlot's Revue of 1926*; 'If You Knew Susie' which was part of the score for *Big Boy*, on which Meyer collaborated, but was cut and handed over by Jolson to Eddie Cantor; 'Clap Hands, Here Comes Charlie' and 'Tonight's My Night with Baby'.

Meyer supplied music to Gallagher and Shean's musical comedy *In Dutch*, which only played out of town, but had major credits on four Broadway scores and placed songs in a number of other shows both in America (*Battling Butler, Ziegfeld Follies, Shuffle Along* etc) and in Britain (*Happy Go Lucky, Lucky Girl*) where his work was used to make up part-scores for *Merely Molly* and for the Jack Buchanan vehicle *That's a Good Girl* ('Fancy Our Meeting'). One Meyer song, 'Crazy Rhythm' (w Wolfe-Kahn, Caesar), originally played in Broadway's *Here's Howe*, actually appeared in both *That's a Good Girl* and *Lucky Girl* in London.

Although he continued to have occasional song successes ('Idle Gossip', 'I Wonder') through into the 1950s, Meyer's connection with the musical theatre did not go beyond 1930.

1924 **In Dutch** (w others/William Cary Duncan, Irving Caesar) Newark, NJ, 22 September

1925 **Big Boy** (w James F Hanley/B G De Sylva/Harold Atteridge) Winter Garden Theater 7 January

1926 **Merely Molly** (w Herman Finck/Harry Graham/J Hastings-Turner) Adelphi Theatre, London 22 September

1927 **Just Fancy** (w Phil Charig/Leo Robin/Joseph Santley, Gertrude Purcell) Casino Theater 11 October

1928 **Here's Howe** (ex- *And Howe!*) (w Roger Wolfe-Kahn/Irving Caesar/Fred Thompson, Paul Gerard Smith) Broadhurst Theater 1 May

1928 **That's a Good Girl** (w Charig/Douglas Furber, Desmond Carter et al/Furber) London Hippodrome 5 June

1929 **Lady Fingers** (Edward Eliscu/Eddie Buzzell) Vanderbilt Theater 31 January

1930 **Jonica** (Moss Hart, Dorothy Heyward) Craig Theater 7 April

MEYERHOFF, Hermine (b Braunschweig, Germany, 26 March 1848; d Waltendorf, 24 February 1926). Leading lady of the 19th-century Vienna stage.

Hermine Meyerhoff began her career as a dancer at the ducal theatre in her native Braunschweig, before turning actress and then, after a very short course of vocal studies, singer. She made her début as Ännchen in *Der Freischütz* at the age of 20, and went on to appear in opera at the Danzig Stadttheater and at Hamburg's Floratheater (Zerlina, Marie in *Der Waffenschmied*, Page in *Les Huguenots*, *Fra Diavolo*, *Zar und Zimmermann*) before winning herself a provincial success when she took Pepi Gallmeyer's original rôle in *Wiener Geschichten* opposite the guesting Albin Swoboda.

In 1869 Meyerhoff moved to Vienna's Carltheater, making her début there as Jeanne in Offenbach's *Toto* (*Le Château à Toto*). Over the following years she was seen in a series of further rôles in shows by Offenbach – who expressed a particular liking for her work – and by other opéra-bouffe composers. She starred as Zanetta to the Regina of Gallmeyer in *Die Prinzessin von Trapezunt*, as Gabrielle in *Hundert Jungfrauen*, as the first Viennese Clairette in *Angot die Tochter des Halle*, as Rose Michon in *Schönröschen* and in the title rôles of *Giroflé-Girofla* and *Prinz Conti* whilst also playing such rôles as Oleander in *Tulipatan*, Laurette in *Fortunio*, Chloë in *Daphnis and Chloë*, Mimi in *Kakadu*, Ernestine in *Salon Pitzelberger*, Schamyl in *Schneeball*, Corraline in *Der Regimentzauberer*, Cannebas in *Cannebas*, Princess Girandole in *Confusius IX*, Mme Jobin in *Urlaub nach Zapfenstreich* and Billette in *Die schöne Bourbonnaise* and guesting at the Theater an der Wien as Rubin in *König Carotte*.

During this period, Meyerhoff also appeared in such early Viennese Operette rôles as Lieschen in *Flotte Bursche*, Marianne in *Wein, Weib, Gesang*, Lisi in *In der Sackgasse*, Fanny in *Fitzliputzli*, Limonia in *Zehn Mädchen und kein Mann* and Calumba in *Die Frau Meisterin*. Then, as the Austrian tradition took off, she created the more significant rôle of Lydia in *Fatinitza*, and played Pulcinella in *Prinz Methusalem* and Amanda in *Der Teufel auf Erden* whilst still performing in such French pieces as *Jeanne, Jeannette et Jeanneton* (Jeanne) and *Der Kohlenhandler von Paris* (Thérèse).

In 1878, now established as one of Vienna's top operettic performers, if without the star status of a Gallmeyer or a Geistinger, she moved – though long billed as a guest artist – to the Theater an der Wien. There she succeeded Gallmeyer as Gabrielle in *La Vie parisienne*, was the first Viennese Haiderose (ie Serpolette) in *Die Glocken von Corneville* and starred as Marie in *Der letzte Mohikaner*, as Susanne to the Madame Favart of Geistinger in *Madame Favart*, and in the title-rôle of Millöcker's *Gräfin Dubarry*, and appeared as Namuna in *Die hübsche Perserin*, Donna Irene in *Das Spitzentuch der Königin*, Palmyra in *Ein Schotte* (*L'Écossais de Chatou*) and Betsy in Strauss's short-lived *Blindekuh*.

Meyerhoff then abandoned the Viennese theatre to star throughout Europe (Berlin, Hamburg, Dresden, Florence, Naples, Palermo, Moscow, St Petersburg, Odessa, Bucarest etc) in a long series of operettic productions. In 1886 she appeared as Strauss's Sáffi in Riga and then put a full stop to her career, retiring to married life as the Countess Tatischeff, the wife of a Russian aristocrat and diplomat.

MIAMI

Apparently a title which is considered more evocative outside America than in, *Miami* has been used as the name of musicals in Britain, France and Hungary, but not in the United States of America. In Britain it was used as the title

for a melodramatic opera by John Hollingshead based on the favourite drama *The Green Bushes* by J B Buckstone, with lyrics by E Warham St Leger and music by J Haydn Parry. Produced at the Princess's Theatre, London on 16 October 1893 in an unfortunate production which used the name of the ageing Hollingshead, the famous founder of the Gaiety Theatre (billed as manager, author and director), as a front, it folded in 11 performances. Violet Cameron played Buckstone's self-sacrificing Indian heroine (she was called 'Miami') alongside several D'Oyly Carte stars (Courtice Pounds, Jessie Bond, Richard Temple).

In Hungary the title was attached to an Operette in 3 acts by István Bródy and Lászlo Vajda, with music by Viktor Jacobi posthumously arranged by Zsigmond Vincze (Fővárosi Operettszinház, 27 November 1925) and featuring Jacobi's successful waltz 'On Miami Shore' (aka 'Golden Sands of Miami', ly: William Le Baron), a number which had already managed to get itself interpolated into not one but two Australian musical comedy productions – sung by Gladys Moncrieff in *Theodore & Co* and Cecil Bradley in *Yes, Uncle!*. The French *Miami* was a comédie musicale by René Pujol with lyrics by Saint-Granier and a score credited to De Sylva, Brown and Henderson with additional numbers by Maurice Yvain (Théâtre des Ambassadeurs, Paris 20 December 1930), which starred Milton and Janie Marèse and which just may have been a version of *Follow Thru*'s 'musical slice of country club life', but may equally well not have been.

MICHAELIS, Robert (b ?St Petersburg, 22 December 1884; d Bristol, 29 August 1965). The handsome, apparently French-bred (some sources give his birthplace as Paris) baritone had a fine career as a musical theatre leading man in his twenties and thirties in a career split by the First World War and more or less terminated with the coming of the all-dancing and very-little-singing shows of the mid-1920s.

Michaelis played in the British provinces in Serpette's *Amorelle (1798)* (1903, François), *The Gay Parisienne*, *The Belle of New York* and *Three Little Maids* before making his West End début, succeeding Louis Bradfield as the hero of *The Girl from Kays*. In his earliest twenties, he visited New York to appear in *The White Hen* (1907) and there replaced William Percival as the hero of *Mlle Modiste* opposite Fritzi Scheff, before returning to London where he succeeded Joe Coyne as Danilo to the Widow of Lily Elsie in London's *Merry Widow*. He played opposite Miss Elsie again as the hero of London's *The Dollar Princess*, beginning a series of romantic lead rôles in George Edwardes's productions, both in London and on the road: *A Waltz Dream* (Niki), *The Count of Luxembourg* (René), *Gipsy Love* (Joszi), *The Marriage Market* (Jack Fleetwood), *A Country Girl* revival (Geoffrey Challoner).

After serving in the War, Michaelis returned to the London stage as James in *Who's Hooper?* and as J P Bowden in the British production of *Irene* (1920), appeared in *The Golden Moth*, Ivor Novello's rewrite of *Erminie* (1921, Pierre Caravan) and took a second turn on Broadway in *Orange Blossoms* (1922, Baron Roger Belmont). He then joined prima donna José Collins to provide her love interest in *Catherine* (1923), *Our Nell* (1924) and *Frasquita* (1925), before moving on to his final West End appearances in the modern dance-and-comedy shows in *Dear Little Billie* (1925, Harry Somerset) and *Up with the Lark* (1927, Baron Frétigny).

Michaelis was married to soprano Phyllys LeGrand who played leading rôles for George Edwardes in town and on the road and appeared alongside him in Broadway's *Orange Blossoms* (Helène).

MICHELL, Keith [Joseph] (b Adelaide, 1 December 1927). Australian actor and singer who created and/or played several important rôles in London musical productions.

Formerly an art teacher, Michell trained as an actor in Britain and made his earliest London appearance as King Charles to the Samuel Pepys of Leslie Henson in the musicalized *And So to Bed* (1951). He played for a number of seasons with the Shakespeare Company at Stratford-on-Avon, returning to the musical stage in 1958 in the rôle of Nestor in the long-running English-language version of *Irma la Douce* in both London and in New York. The next of his liberally spaced musical rôles, as Robert Browning to the Elizabeth Barrett of June Bronhill in London's *Robert and Elizabeth* (1964), gave him another major success, but in the following years only *Man of La Mancha* (1968) in which he took the rôle created by Richard Kiley in London and as a replacement on Broadway, brought him again to the musical stage during a period in which he became not only one of Britain's best-known and most-admired stage and television actors, but also the director of the Chichester Festival Theatre.

He returned once more, after over a decade away from the musical stage, to star with Julia McKenzie in the London production of *On the Twentieth Century* (1980, Oscar Jaffee) but, in another decade since, his only fresh appearances in the musical theatre, apart from a dressed concert staging of his own 'Captain Beaky' poems, have been as Georges in *La Cage aux Folles* in America and Australia, and as George in *Aspects of Love* in Canada and America.

MICHEL STROGOFF Opérette à grand spectacle in 2 acts by Marc-Cab and René Richard based on the novel by Jules Verne. Music by Jack Ledru. Théâtre Mogador, Paris, 28 November 1964.

A popular and often-reprised Châtelet spectacular over the years, the 1880 stage adaptation by Jules Verne and Adophe d'Ennery of Verne's novel was turned into an opérette à grand spectacle equipped with 25 sets for Henri Varna's Théâtre Mogador in 1964. Marcel Merkès played Strogoff, riding across the wastes of Siberia, through the invading Tartar hordes, with his Nadia (Paulette Merval) ever near, suffering torture and imprisonment before finally delivering the vital letter to the Tsar of all the Russias. Accompanied by a romantico-scenic score very largely devoted to its hero and its heroine, *Michel Strogoff* ran for the best part of a year at the Mogador and has continued to win occasional provincial productions since.

Recording: original cast (CBS)

MIDAS Burletta (comic opera) in 2 acts by Kane O'Hara. Crow Street Theatre, Dublin, 22 January 1762; Theatre Royal, Covent Garden, London, 22 February 1764.

Variously described as a burletta or a comic opera, the extremely successful *Midas* was, in fact, a classical burlesque written in rhymed couplets and with its lyrical pieces set, in the style of the period, to borrowed music.

A marital squabble on Olympus results in Apollo (Mr Mattocks) being sent down to earth as punishment. There, disguised as a farm-hand, he gets mixed up in the randy efforts of squire and justice Midas (Mr Shuter) and his pimp Damaetas (Mr Fawcett) to lay hands and things on the local maidens, Daphne (Miss Miller) and Nysa (Miss Hallam), both of whom complicate matters by falling for the pretty newcomer. When Midas crookedly backs his pal Pan (Mr Dunstall) in a singing competition with the God of music, he brings down Apollo's wrath and finds himself changed into an ass. The 20 to 30 musical items introduced into the action included a booming number for the jealous Juno ('Your favourite jades I'll plunge to the shades or into cows metamorphose them ...'), a drinking song for Pan, a maypole number, a jealousy duet for the two sisters, several ensembles and the two competition songs, of which Apollo's was listed in the script as being 'introduced', and thus presumably of the artist's choice.

Produced at London's Theatre Royal, Covent Garden two seasons after its Dublin première, *Midas* was regularly revived thereafter. It was included in the touring baggage of dozens and dozens of road and repertoire companies, given revivals in London for well over a century and in the provinces for longer, at a time when very few burlesque pieces of former days (*The Beggar's Opera*, *Bombastes Furioso*, *Tom Thumb*) still found the stage. *Midas* was the most successful classical burlesque of its time, and stands historically as a fore-runner to Planché, to *Orphée aux enfers*, to *Thespis* and to the other classic-based musical comedies which have so often been important landmarks in the musical theatre.

What may have been the first American performance was seen at New York's John Street Theater in 1773 with Mr Goodman (Midas), Mr Woolls (Apollo), Miss Stover (Nysa) and Mrs Morris (Daphne) on the bill.

Author O'Hara wrote several other pieces thereafter – *The Golden Pippin*, *The Two Misers*, *April Day*, and a version of *Tom Thumb* amongst them – without finding again the same kind of success.

USA: John Street Theater 4 May 1773; Australia: Royal Victoria Theatre, Sydney 13 May 1839

MIDDLETON, Ray (b Chicago, 8 February 1907; d Panorama City, Calif, 10 April 1984). Broadway baritone who drew one outstanding rôle in 30 years of service.

Originally trained as an opera singer, Middleton made his first Broadway appearance as the giant in a version of *Jack and the Beanstalk* (1931) before taking a rather more conventional rôle as the all-American in Paris, John Kent, the juvenile leading man (surprisingly, without a song) of Jerome Kern's *Roberta* (1933). After a period which included some essays in opera, he returned to Broadway in 1938 as Washington Irving in *Knickerbocker Holiday*, then went through revue (*George White's Scandals*, *American Jubilee* at the World's Fair), film (*Lady for a Night*, *The Girl from Alaska*) and a period in the air-force, before returning to create his most important musical comedy rôle as Frank Butler in *Annie Get Your Gun* (1946, 'My Defences Are

Down', 'The Girl That I Marry', 'Anything You Can Do', 'They Say It's Wonderful').

Middleton subsequently starred on the musical stage as Samuel Cooper, the eternally married man of *Love Life* (1948), took over as Émile LeBecque in *South Pacific* from Ezio Pinza, and in his later years appeared in a character rôle in *Man of La Mancha* (1965, the Governor) and in *Purple Dust* at the Goodpeed Opera House. He was also seen in the film version of *1776* (McKean) and in the television version of *Damn Yankees* (Joe Boyd).

THE MIKADO, or The Town of Titipu Comic opera in 2 acts by W S Gilbert. Music by Arthur Sullivan. Savoy Theatre, London, 14 March 1885.

Of all the Gilbert and Sullivan musicals produced at the Savoy Theatre, *The Mikado* succeeded in building the longest West End run (672 performances), the most extensive European reputation, and the widest and most enduring afterlife. After more than a century of repeated productions it remains as popular as ever, undoubtedly the most generally loved of the Gilbert and Sullivan canon and, many would argue, the best.

Gilbert chose an oriental setting for the show with which he and Sullivan followed their remake of his old burlesque *The Princess* as *Princess Ida*. The extravagant and quaint orient had always been a popular and colourful choice of venue in comic opera, and since in the mid-1880s there was a new craze in Britain for 'all that's Japanese', Gilbert's decision to head east was a logical one. For his title he chose one announced and discarded nine years previously by Busnach and Liorat (they eventually gave the title of *Kosiki* to their *Le Mikado*) and for his plot he abandoned direct burlesque: the nautical and operatic burlesque of *HMS Pinafore*, the melodrama burlesque of *The Pirates of Penzance*, the aesthetic burlesque of *Patience*, the burlesque of faërie in *Iolanthe* or of Tennyson in *Princess Ida*. The story of *The Mikado* was in direct line of descent from previous British and French 'Japanese' comic operas and opéras-bouffes and built not around any specific parody but, with the help of many familiar elements from the comic opera tradition, around the company at the Savoy Theatre.

Leonora Braham was Yum-Yum, a Japanese schoolgirl (Gilbert said he made her a schoolgirl because she and her fellows Jessie Bond and Sybil Grey were all tiny) who is unwillingly engaged to Ko-Ko, the underworked Lord High Executioner of Titipu (George Grossmith). When Nanki-Poo (Durward Lely), the son of the Mikado (Richard Temple), comes to Titipu fleeing a forced marriage with the dragonistic Katisha (Rosina Brandram) and disguised as an itinerant trombonist, the little bride-to-be and the inept musician fall in love. Ko-Ko, finding himself forced to hold an execution to save his post from abolition, joins a plot to fake the death of Nanki-Poo only to find out, too late, that he is a royal, and that having 'executed' him he is in a worse spot than before. Ko-Ko is obliged to wed Katisha himself before the young man agrees to come safely back to life for a happy ending. Rutland Barrington was cast as Pooh-Bah, a venal nobleman and 'Lord High-Everything-Else', and Jessie Bond was the conspiring Pitti-Sing.

If the various elements of the tale were far from original, Gilbert brought them all together in his inimitable style

Plate 182. *Katisha (Heather Begg) shows her affection for Nanki-Poo (Peter Cousens) in the Australian Opera's production of* **The Mikado.**

and language and combined them into their most celebrated incarnation in *The Mikado*. Sullivan, back to his lightest and most winning style after the more weighty moments of *Princess Ida*, supplied a score in his best vein. Yum-Yum pondered her own beauty in 'The Moon and I' and joined her sisters declaring themselves 'Three Little Maids' in fluttering harmonies, Nanki-Poo tenorized fluently 'A Wandering Minstrel, I', and Katisha plumbed emotion with a slightly incongruous sincerity in the drawing-room ballad 'Hearts Do Not Break'. On the more regularly humorous side, Grossmith detailed a topical series of public nuisances in 'I've Got a Little List' and wrung hearts with his phoney tale of dying for love, 'Tit Willow', and Temple described how, as supreme magistrate, he would 'make the punishment fit the crime' (Mikado's Song). A jolly hymn to 'The Flowers that Bloom in the Spring' and an unaccompanied madrigal 'Brightly Dawns our Wedding Day' were amongst the most winning ensembles.

The Mikado was a superb success at the Savoy, setting up a new long-run record for a British musical play in London and a worldwide record for a Gilbert and Sullivan production which would last almost a century until a Broadway revival of *The Pirates of Penzance* topped it in 1981. In spite of the care D'Oyly Carte had taken to protect, in particular, the copy- and stage-rights of *The Pirates of Penzance* and *Iolanthe* in America, arrangements for *The Mikado* went rather curiously astray. The score and libretto were published, making them public domain, and several American impresarii promptly leaped into production with *Mikado*s. The irrepressible Sydney Rosenfeld opened his in Chicago, but found himself arrested when he tried to bring it to New York's Union Square Theater. When rumours of a first-class production hit Carte, he acted swiftly, secretly transporting a company headed by American prima donna Geraldine Ulmar, tenor Courtice Pounds and comic George Thorne from London to New York and opening at the Fifth Avenue Theater (19 August 1885) before the opposition J C Duff version was ready. Duff opened hurriedly the next night and Broadway was given the sight of two rival *Mikado*s playing side by side for three months. Then Duff took his company on tour, whilst Carte's ran on to its 250th performance.

At the same time, whilst Carte's touring companies continued to carry the show to the British public, *The Mikado* was staged by J C Williamson's Royal Comic Opera Company at Sydney's Theatre Royal with Nellie Stewart (Yum-Yum), Howard Vernon (Ko-Ko) and the Savoy company's Alice Barnett (Katisha). Australia later welcomed further Savoy members when Alfred Cellier conducted the Melbourne season, which ran for a remarkable 101 consecutive nights, and when Leonora Braham (dubbed by a down-under critic 'the yummiest Yum-Yum of them all') repeated her original rôle, alongside the Broadway Mikado, Federici. In South Africa, Frank Wheeler starred himself as Ko-Ko.

Success for *The Mikado* in Britain, America and the other English-speaking areas was fairly forseeable. What was not forseeable was the success it would have on the Continent. It was by no means the first Gilbert and Sullivan work to be played in German or in Hungarian, but it was the first to become a success on the same scale in those languages that it had been on home territory. Dresden and Berlin first saw the piece in English, when D'Oyly Carte's company, headed by several of his American cast (Pounds, Federici, Elsie Cameron) and David Fisher (who went mad, allegedly from playing Ko-Ko for too long, thus prompting a debate on 'are long runs injurious to the brain') visited the Wallner-Theater. The German version was produced, two years later, at the Friedrich-Wilhelm-städtisches Theater, following its splendid success in Vienna. It was again a notable hit, and established the piece as the second most popular English musical on 19th- and early 20th-century German stages (*The Geisha*, another oriental musical, was the number one). In 1900, Sullivan himself conducted *The Mikado* in Berlin before an audience including the German emperor.

Viennese theatre-goers also saw the Carte tour in 1886, in advance of Camillo Walzel's production of his own adaptation (w Richard Genée) at the Theater an der Wien in 1888 in which Sebastian Stelzer (Ko-Ko), Karl Streitmann (Nanki-Poo), Ottilie Collin (Yum-Yum), Therese Biedermann (Pitti-Sing) and Carl Lindau (Mikado) headed the cast. The show was played regularly in the theatre's repertoire over the next six years, passing its 100th performance on 27 May 1894, and it was brought back again in a 1901 production which included 'Harry Delaney's genuine Japanese Geisha Girls from Tokio, Japan' with four dance routines amongst its attractions. It was also played at the Theater in der Josefstadt in 1899 and produced at the Raimundtheater in 1909 with Franz Glawatch (Ko-Ko) and Marthe Dorda-Winternitz as a rather bulky Yum-Yum.

The Hungarian stage received the show late – Carte's company, which had toured freely through Holland, Scandinavia, Germany and Austria, cancelled its visit to Pest because of a cholera epidemic – but with the same vigour. First produced at the Népszinház (ad Jenő Heltai) with Aranka Hegyi playing Nanki Poo in travesty to the Yum-Yum of Ilka Pálmay and Célia Márgo (Katisha), József Németh (Ko-Ko), Vidor Kassai (Pooh-Bah) and Nina Fehér as a Peep-Bo renamed Pep-Si at the head of its cast, it was revived there in 1899 and again in 1905. Played in all the principal musical theatres of Hungary, it appeared notably at the Városi Színház (25 September 1924) in a new translation by Ferenc Molnár.

Moscow, Brussels (a first French version by Charles Kufferath at the Alhambra, 23 December 1889), Prague, Bucharest, Riga, Buenos Aires, Stockholm, Zagreb, Copenhagen and Florence all hosted various translations of *The Mikado*, and it ingrained itself into the principal international repertoire in a way no British comic opera had previously done.

Inevitably, given the magnitude of its success, attempts were made to burlesque *The Mikado* (*Der Mizekado, ein Tag in Pititu* 1 act, Otto Ewald/F Beier, Kassel 26 December 1886 etc), but the show, its characters and score were, from very early on, not so much burlesqued as squeezed into all kinds of improbable shapes, concepts and rhythms. Reports came back from America during the original London run of 'heartrending liberties' being taken with the show in Boston, where Richard Mansfield played Ko-Ko as an English fop, eyeglass and all. In Sweden, a hybrid was made from *The Mikado* and Lecocq's *Kosiki*, the show which had originally been called *Le Mikado*. In America it suffered from being blackened, with Chauncey Olcott as a burnt-cork Nanki-Poo, swung (*The Swing Mikado*, Chicago, 1938) and hotted (*The Hot Mikado*, 23 March 1939), in South Africa it was rearranged into a sort of jigaboo opéra-bouffe as another *The Black Mikado* for a successful London run (Cambridge Theatre 24 April 1975, 472 performances) and a season in Paris, whilst in Berlin the accredited librettists Bernauer and Österreicher remade the piece as something like a revue for the Grosses Schauspielhaus. Max Pallenberg starred as Ko-Ko in a witless version in which Nanki Poo became the son of an American sugar millionaire and filched Katisha's 'Hearts Do Not Break', relyricked as a love ballad. The lacerated score was re-orchestrated for a 'modern' band, and Erik Charell filled the stage with acrobats and charlestoning chorines to distract from the content. In Austria, Franz Reinl decided to give Nanki-Poo a boost in his 1954 version for Salzburg's Landestheater, and the resultant piece was called *Der Sohn des Mikado*. A successful English National Opera production of 1986 copied Richard Mansfield's example of a century earlier by throwing out the Japanese element and re-situating the action in Victorian England, whilst, most recently, New Jersey's Paper Mill Playhouse produced a *Mikado Inc* (16 May 1990) which equated Japan with commerce rather than cherry-blossoms.

In between the oddities and the remakes, however, many a talented director has been found capable of making Gilbert's enduring fun and unstringent satire ring through without eccentric aids, and *The Mikado* continues into its second century with its head as firmly on its shoulders as Ko-Ko's victims. London, which in one season in the 1980s welcomed no less than three different *Mikado*s, has most recently seen a production by the new D'Oyly Carte company, whilst Broadway saw its latest *Mikado* in a production brought from Stratford, Ontario, and played at the Virginia Theater (2 April 1987) for 46 performances, and the 1990s even saw *The Mikado* break through for its first showings in France.

Amongst the numerous film and television *Mikado*s have been a 1960 NBC-TV Bell Telephone Hour encapsulation with a cast including Groucho Marx (Ko-Ko), Helen Traubel (Katisha), Stanley Holloway (Pooh-Bah) and Dennis King (Mikado), a 1939 film with Martyn Green (Ko-Ko) and Kenny Baker (Nanki-Poo), a 1967 British film with Valerie Masterson (Yum-Yum) and a 1963 *Cool Mikado* made by Michael Winner, starring Frankie Howerd and with limited relevance to the original.

USA: Museum, Chicago 6 July 1885, Union Square Theater, New York 20 July 1885: Australia: Theatre Royal, Sydney 14 November 1885; Germany: Residenztheater, Dresden (Eng) 1886, Wallner Theater (Eng) 2 June 1886; Austria: Carltheater *Der Mikado, ein Tag in Titipu* 1 September 1886; Hungary: Népszinház *Mikádo* 10 December 1886; France: Opéra, Toulouse (Eng) 1991, Tours (Fr) 7 November 1992.

Recordings: complete (Decca, HMV), selection (TER) etc

MILHER [HERMIL, Ange Édouard] (b Marseilles, 25 September 1833; d Aix-les-Bains, 13 August 1898).

A popular comic actor-singer of the French stage, from the earliest days of opéra-bouffe until his death just before the turn of the century, Milher had fine rôles in many of Hervé's earliest works, creating parts in *Les Chevaliers de la table ronde* (1866, Le Duc Rodomont), *L'Oeil crevé* (1867, Géromé), *Chilpéric* (1868, Doctor Ricin), *Le Petit Faust* (1869, Valentin) and *Les Turcs* (1869, Ababoum), as well as in the later *La Belle Poule* (1875, Baron de la Champignole) and *Alice de Nevers* (1875, Sire de Courbaril). He also created the rôle of duped van Ostebal in Jonas's triumphant *Le Canard à trois becs*, the villainous Fulbert in Litolff's *Héloïse et Abélard*, the Prince de Soubise in *Jeanne, Jeannette et Jeanneton* (1876), Prince Ramollini in *La Foire St-Laurent*, and, above all, the unusually patheticodramatic role of the miser, Gaspard, in *Les Cloches de Corneville* (1877) at the Théâtre des Folies-Dramatiques.

Milher also played in such less successful pieces as *Fleur de Baiser*, *La Fiancée du roi de Garbe* (Zaïr) and *Le Pompon* (Don Melchior) before switching from the Folies-Dramatiques to the Palais-Royal and, if that house provided little in the way of musical shows, he guested outside on occasions, repeating his most famous rôles and appearing in such pieces as the spectacular *L'Arbre de Nöel* (Porte-Saint-Martin, 1880, Oscar de Pulna). Milher continued to play on the musical stage up till his last days, being seen at the Variétés as Tournesol XXIV in *Le Carillon* and in *L'Oeil crevé* in 1896 and as Le Commandant in *Le Pompier de Service* in 1897.

Alongside his career as an actor, Milher was also a prolific writer for the stage, under his real name of 'Hermil'. He provided a long run of mostly one-act entertainments – comedies, opérettes, revues, vaudevilles – for the Folies-Saint-Antoine, the Théâtre Cluny, La Cigale and for a considerable number of other small Parisian and provincial houses, many latterly written with his Palais-Royal confrère (and later Variétés director) Armand Numès.

1863 **Un mari qui fait des farces** (Eugène Moniot) Théâtre des Champs-Élysées 14 December

1864 **Un Troupier en bonne fortune** (Moniot) Théâtre des jeunes artistes 5 October

1866 **Encore un sapeur** (Camille Michel) 1 act Folies Saint-Antoine 1 September

1866 **Les Rendezvous interrompus** (Moniot) 1 act Théâtre du 19ème siècle 6 May

1873 **La Fille de Dagobert** (Moniot) 1 act Folies-Bergère 19 October

1873 **Dans le bain** (w Gardel) 1 act Eldorado 7 April

1874 **La Noce à Briochet** (Hervé/w Gardel) Délassements-Comique 26 April

1874 **Flon-flons et flic-flacs** (Moniot) Théâtre de la Tour d'Auvergne 20 February

1875 **Le Voyage du Prince Soleil** (Moniot/w Frantz Beauvallet, Henri Buguet) Théâtre du Parc 2 October

1879 **Un Concièrgicide** (Francis Chassaigne/w Armand Numès) 1 act Eldorado 23 August

1880 **Le Carnaval de Blizimard** (Charles Thony/w Numès) Alcazar 12 March

1880 **Atchi** (Frédéric Barbier/w Numès) 1 act Eldorado

1882 **Boum! Servi chaud!** (A de Villebichot/w Numès) 1 act Eldorado 20 June

1882 **Ma vieille branche** (Édouard Deransart/w Numès) 1 act Alcazar

1882 **Mon p'tit oncle** (Thony/Numès) 1 act Eldorado 9 September

1883 **Soupirs de coeur** (Jean Mitchell/w Paul Meyan, Numès) 1 act Eldorado 21 April

1883 **Politique en menage** (Thony/w Numès) 1 act Dijon 21 July

1883 **La Cuisinière** (Thony/w Numès) 1 act Dijon 21 July

1883 **Le Nègre de la Porte-Saint-Denis** (Louis Desormes/w Numès) 1 act Eldorado 25 August

1884 **Malbrough** (Deransart/w Numès) Casino de Bougival 24 June

1885 **L'École de Tatété-les-Nefles** (Thony/w Numès) 1 act Eden Concert 17 March

1885 **Suzette, Suzanne et Suzon** (Tac-Coën/w Numès) 1 act Eden Concert

1885 **Fièvre phyllaxérique** (Frantz Liouville/w Numès, Meyan) 1 act

1886 **Le Roi Mabouc** ('L Herpin' [ie L Perey]/w Numès) Scala 2 November

1889 **L'Étudiant pauvre** (*Der Bettelstudent*) French version w Numès (Théâtre des Menus-Plaisirs)

Other title attributed: *Tog* (Francis Chassaigne/w Numès),

MILK AND HONEY Musical play in 2 acts by Don Appell. Music and lyrics by Jerry Herman. Martin Beck Theater, New York, 10 October 1961.

The first book musical and first Broadway assignment of composer-lyricist Jerry Herman after three off-Broadway revues, *Milk and Honey* had its starting point in its writers' decision to make a musical set in Israel. As a result, they spent several weeks in Israel but they came up with a script which, in fact, used the country only as a background to a main story of middle-aged romance which was wholly American and, of course, Jewish. The principals were widowed Ruth (Mimi Benzell) and separated Phil (Robert Weede) who fall in love in the Middle East whilst he is visiting his daughter and she is touring with a ladies' group. Ultimately, they separate, but with the hope that a divorce will soon leave Phil free. Alongside them, Phil's daughter Barbara (Lanna Saunders) and her husband (Tommy Rall) face the wild-west challenge of making their home in a new land, whilst the comical widow Clara (Molly Picon) leads her consoeurs' search for a man.

The score was compiled of a combination of locally coloured numbers – of which Phil's directions on the meaning of 'Shalom' and the title song both proved highly successful, love songs for the two operatically experienced stars ('That Was Yesterday', 'As Simple as That') and for the rich-voiced young Rall ('I Will Follow You'), and what were virtual stand-up comic spots for Jewish theatre star Molly Picon ('Chin Up Ladies' and the pre-*Hello, Dolly!* monologue to her dead husband 'Hymn to Hymie').

Gerald Oestreicher's production ran for 543 performances on Broadway and toured thereafter, but *Milk and Honey* did not reach out to productions in the other main musical theatre centres.

Recording: original cast (RCA)

MILLAR, Gertie (b Bradford, 21 February 1879; d Chiddingford, 25 April 1952). Dainty, pretty musical-comedy star who became the Gaiety Theatre's headliner in the early part of the 20th century.

Gertie Millar made her first stage appearances as a child, playing the girl babe in the pantomime *Babes in the Wood* at St James's Theatre, Manchester, in 1892. As a teenager she began touring in musical comedy, appearing as Dora in *The New Barmaid* for Alexander Loftus (1898), in Frank Carlyon's musical comedy company playing ingénue in *The Silver Lining* (1898), as Sadie Pinkhose in *Bilberry of Tilbury* (1899) and then with the touring company of *The Messenger Boy* in which she was spotted by composer Lionel Monckton. As a result, she was taken to London to play the tiny part of Cora ('Captivating Cora') in *The Toreador* (1901), the rôle which would have gone to Rosie Boote had she not gone off to become a marchioness.

Twenty-two-year-old Gertie stole the show, much as Miss Boote had done last time round, but she was not in such a hurry for her coronet. For the meanwhile, she just saw her rôle enlarged as she set off on a road which would make her both a star and Mrs Lionel Monckton in double quick time. She appeared in increasingly important soubrette parts in *The Orchid* (1903, Violet Anstruther), *The Spring Chicken* (1905, Rosalie), *The New Aladdin* (1906, t/o Lally) and *The Girls of Gottenberg* (1907, Mitzi), then left the Gaiety to play Franzi in Edwardes's production of *A Waltz Dream*, visited America to repeat her *Girls of Gottenberg* part, and returned to star in the title-rôles of two of her most memorable shows: Edwardes's productions of *Our Miss Gibbs* (1909, Mary Gibbs 'Moonstruck') and *The Quaker Girl* (1910, Prudence 'The Quaker Girl', 'The Little Grey Bonnet'). She had a new rôle, Lady Babby, written for her in Edwardes's production of the otherwise too vocally hefty *Gipsy Love* (1912), then starred in *The Dancing Mistress* (1912, Nancy Joyce), *The Marriage Market* (1913, Kitty Kent) and in a revival of *A Country Girl* (1914, Nan).

With the change of temperature that came over the musical theatre around wartime, Miss Millar tried her hand at revue in Monckton's *Bric à Brac* and *Airs and Graces* and ventured two musicals by revue producers, Cochran's *Houp-la!* and Charlot's *Flora*. Both the musicals were solid flops, the first real disasters (*A Waltz Dream* being only a half-disaster) that she had known in her career as

Plate 183. *Gaiety star* **Gertie Millar** *in* The Girls of Gottenberg.

London's favourite musical-comedy soubrette of more than a decade's standing. She and Monckton both renounced the new-style musical theatre, retired, and, after her husband's death, Gertie finally followed Rosie Boote into the peerage, for a seven-year run as the Countess of Dudley.

MILLAR, Ronald [Graeme] (Sir) (b Reading, 12 November 1919).

Originally an actor and then a playwright, Millar had his first connection with the musical theatre when he was cast in the almost non-singing juvenile lead rôle of *Jenny Jones* (1944), a piece which he was later called upon to doctor (under the pseudonym John Jowett) on the road. He subsequently had considerable success as an author in the straight theatre (*Frieda*, *Waiting for Gillian*, *The Bride and the Bachelor*, *They Don't Grow on Trees*, *The Masters* etc) and as a screenwriter (his Hollywood credits included the rewritten *Rose Marie*), and found significant success on the musical stage in 1964 with his first attempt, an adaptation of *The Barretts of Wimpole Street*, the tale of the poets Browning and Barrett, as *Robert and Elizabeth* (libretto and lyrics). A second piece, *On the Level*, written in a very different idiom, was less successful, and when several proposed projects, including a musical version of Christopher Isherwood's Berlin stories, fell through he returned to the straight theatre, venturing back onto the musical stage only with a revusical biomusical, *Once More with Music* (Yvonne Arnaud Theatre, Guildford) for the aged Cicely Courtneidge and Jack Hulbert, and, in the same way that he had begun, as an uncredited play doctor (*Peg*).

He was knighted for services to politics after spending a number of years as speechwriter to Mrs Margaret Thatcher, PM, during which time he was responsible for coming up with many of the sometimes theatre-linked 'catchphrases' and images which have entered everyday speech and everyday journalese as a result.

1964 **Robert and Elizabeth** (Ron Grainer) Lyric Theatre 20 October
1966 **On the Level** (Grainer) Shaftesbury Theatre 19 April

Autobiography: *A View From the Wings* (Weidenfeld & Nicolson, London, 1993)

MILLAUD, [Arthur David Paul] Albert [Samuel] (b Paris, 13 January 1844; d Paris, 22 October 1892).

Alongside the famous 'duos' of the French musical stage – Meilhac and Halévy, Chivot and Duru, Leterrier and Vanloo, and even those celebrated writers such as Nuitter, Tréfeu or Clairville who popped in and out of less wholly faithful collaborations as they collected their hits – the name of Albert Millaud remains one which has much less éclat. Yet Millaud, too, wrote internationally successful shows with Offenbach, Hervé and Lecocq, and for a solid half-dozen years had his name attached to the biggest musical hits in town, as well as to the biggest star of the musical theatre.

In the mid-1870s, with only one opéra-comique to his credit, journalist (*Figaro*) and versifier (*Le Péché Veniel*, *Plutus*) Millaud became one of Offenbach's preferred collaborators. With, apparently, some uncredited help from Halévy he wrote the libretto and lyrics to *Madame l'Archiduc*, and in collaboration with Halévy's usual partner, Meilhac, he provided the composer with the text for *La Créole*, another Offenbach piece starring Anna Judic. He worked with Eugène Grangé on the text for the revue *Les Hannetons* (Bouffes-Parisiens 22 April 1875), wrote the one-act *Tarte à la crème* (in which Offenbach supplied a little music), and contributed without credit to *Le Voyage dans la lune* after Offenbach had dragged him in, as being the nearest handy writer, when he suddenly needed some words.

The couple of busy years of teaming with Offenbach past, Millaud found his future in the star they had shared. Between 1878 and 1884, in varying collaborations of which he was the continuing element, he provided the Théâtre des Variétés and its star, Anna Judic, with the series of vaudevilles which were the highlight of her career and also of that period of the French musical theatre. *Niniche, La Femme à papa, La Roussotte, Lili, Mam'zelle Nitouche* and *La Cosaque*, from the most flamingly successful (*Mam'zelle Nitouche*) to even the least long-lasting (*La Cosaque*), went around the world, played in a variety of languages whilst also becoming the bases for a number of other musicals and plays in Austria, Germany, Hungary, America and Britain. And Millaud compounded it all by becoming the new husband of Madame Judic.

When the famous run of vaudevilles was done, Millaud continued in the musical theatre, writing the Aristophanean libretto for Lecocq's *Plutus*, and two further – and this time not as successful – vaudevilles, *La Noce à*

Nini and *La Japonaise* (15 performances) for the Variétés. The genre had done its dash, but much of the dashing had been done by author Millaud.

1873 **La Quenouille de verre** (Charles Grisart/w Henri Heugel ['Henri Moreno']), Théâtre des Bouffes-Parisiens 7 November
1874 **Madame l'Archiduc** (Jacques Offenbach/[w Ludovic Halévy]), Théâtre des Bouffes-Parisiens 31 October
1875 **La Créole** (Offenbach/w Henri Meilhac) Théâtre des Bouffes-Parisiens 3 November
1875 **Tarte à la crème** (Offenbach) 1 act Théâtre des Bouffes-Parisiens 14 December
1878 **Niniche** (Marius Boullard/w Alfred Hennequin) Théâtre des Variétés 14 February
1879 **La Femme à papa** (Hervé/w Hennequin) Théâtre des Variétés 3 December
1881 **La Roussotte** (Hervé, Lecocq, Marius Boullard/w Henri Meilhac, Ludovic Halévy) Théâtre des Variétés 28 January
1882 **Lili** (Hervé/w Hennequin, Ernest Blum) Théâtre des Variétés 10 January
1883 **Mam'zelle Nitouche** (Hervé/w Meilhac) Théâtre des Variétés 26 January
1883 **Joséphine** (Louis Varney) 1 act Casino de Paramé (Trouville) 10 August, Théâtre des Variétés 16 March 1884
1884 **La Cosaque** (Hervé/w Meilhac) Théâtre des Variétés 1 February
1886 **Plutus** (Charles Lecocq/w Gaston Jollivet) Opéra-Comique 31 March
1887 **La Noce à Nini** (Hervé/w Émile de Najac) Théâtre des Variétés 19 March
1888 **La Japonaise** (Varney/w de Najac) Théâtre des Variétés 23 November

MILLER, Marilyn[n] [REYNOLDS, Mary Ellen or Marilynn] (b Evansville, Ind, 1 September 1898; d New York, 7 April 1936). Diminutive, blonde dancing star of the Broadway 1920s.

Marilyn(n) Miller spent the earliest part of her career in vaudeville as part of a family act, the Five Columbians, and made her first Broadway appearances in the *Passing Show* series of revues. Her first musical comedy rôle, at the age of 20, was in the Shuberts' unremarkable *Fancy Free* (1918, Betty Pestlethwaite) alongside Clifton Crawford, but it was under the management of Florenz Ziegfeld (she dropped the extra 'n', which she had originally sported, at his suggestion) that she made her mark, first in two editions of his *Follies* and then in the title-rôle of Jerome Kern's *Sally* (1920) where she introduced 'Look for the Silver Lining' and 'Wild Rose' in between her featured dance spots.

Miss Miller appeared on Broadway as J M Barrie's *Peter Pan* (1924), but had more success in the written-to-order title-rôle of Kern's *Sunny* (1925, 'Who?'), a patent and pretty attempt to photocopy *Sally*, before going on to star in two more shows for Ziegfeld, Sigmund Romberg and George Gershwin's *Rosalie* (1928, Rosalie) and, alongside the Astaires, in the Vincent Youmans musical comedy *Smiles* (1930), with rather less success. She then quit Broadway for Hollywood, where she starred in the screen versions of *Sally* and *Sunny* and in *Her Majesty Love* (1932), returning to Broadway for one final stage appearance in the revue *As Thousands Cheer* ('Easter Parade') before her early death.

The leading character of the Jerome Kern musical comedy *The Cabaret Girl* (London 1922), revealingly named Marilynn Morgan, and played by Dorothy Dickson, was lightly based on Miss Miller, and in 1988 she was portrayed on the musical stage in the London extravaganza *Ziegfeld* by six-foot red-headed Australian dancer/actress Amanda Rickard who was physically as far away from the original as had been Judy Garland (*Till the Clouds Roll By* 1946) and June Haver (*Look for the Silver Lining* 1949) who had been the Marilyn(n) Millers on the screen.

Biography: Harris, W G: *The Other Marilyn* (Arbor House, New York, 1985)

MILLÖCKER, Carl (b Vienna, 29 April 1842; d Baden bei Wien, 31 December 1899). One of the trio of Viennese composers who were responsible for the bulk of the outstanding Operetten of the 19th-century Austrian stage.

The son of a goldsmith, Millöcker worked, not very wholeheartedly, for his father whilst taking his first steps towards a career in music by studying the flute with a musician from the orchestra at the Theater an der Wien. He learned piano from books, and was given lessons in composition by an elderly official with musical connections who tutored young musicians in his free time. He later took flute lessons at the Vienna Gesellschaft der Musikfreunde, and finally began a theatre-music career at the age of 16, playing in the woodwind section of the orchestra at the Theater in der Josefstadt.

During his time as an orchestral player Millöcker wrote his first compositions, winning encouragement from no less an authority than Franz von Suppé, and over half a dozen years he turned out a regular stream of songs, orchestral music and theatre pieces. In 1864 Suppé was instrumental in getting him appointed as a conductor at the Thalia-Theater in Graz, and it was there that the young man's first stage works, the one-act burlesques *Der tote Gast* and *Die lustigen Binder*, were staged the following year. Towards the end of 1866 he left Graz, taking with him the theatre's leading lady, Fräulein Kling, who had become his wife, to go back to Vienna and employment at the Theater an der Wien, under the management of Friedrich Strampfer. This engagement, however, proved unproductive of the sort of opportunities for which he was looking as a composer and even as a conductor, and he moved on to a conducting job at the less up-market but more amenable Harmonietheater, a short-lived but enthusiastic establishment set up by the Countess von Pasqualati.

There Millöcker succeeded in getting a production for his first regular Operette, *Diana*, a medium-sized piece written to a mythological-satirical text by Josef Braun, the librettist of Suppé's *Flotte Bursche*. *Diana* was produced in January 1867, after its rather too daring libretto had at first led to its being postponed whilst it was sent back to the author for softening up. It was played for 13 successive nights, but then put away until a revised version was produced nearly a century later at Nuremberg (Städtische Bühnen, 21 March 1959). Millöcker also supplied the music for several Possen and Singspiele – the local versions of musical comedies in the true sense of the words – for the Harmonietheater, and he worked with the later-famous playwright Ludwig Anzengruber, at that stage an actor and house writer at the theatre, on several pieces. In 1868 he moved again, this time to Budapest, to take up a post as conductor at the Deutsches Theater, and it was there that he heard his first full-length score, a resetting of the Cogniard brothers' famous spectacular *Le Royaume des*

femmes as *Die Fraueninsel*, performed. He returned to Vienna again the following year to take up a position as number- two conductor at the Theater an der Wien and to place another full-length piece, *Der Regiments-Tambour*, at his youthful stamping-ground, the Theater in der Josefstadt.

During the 14 years which he spent at the Theater an der Wien, where he was ultimately promoted to first conductor, Millöcker turned out original music and songs for a wide variety of pieces – revues, plays, many Singspiele and Possen, and pieces described as 'ländliche Gemälde' (local pictures) or 'Lebensbilder' (life pictures), but all variants of the comedy with songs and music genre, and mainly from the highly successful pens of Alois Berla, O F Berg and Karl Costa. Amongst the musical plays, the 1871 musical comedy *Drei Paar Schuhe* was a major success, being subsequently revived many, many times and giving Millöcker a pair of genuine hits with 'I und meine Bua' and 'Bei Tag bin ich hektisch'. Further successes, in Vienna and beyond, came with Berla's *Abenteuer in Wien* (1873), the revusical *Erinnerung an bessere Zeiten* (1874), which introduced Alexander Girardi to the the Theater an der Wien, Berg's Possen *Der barmherzige Bruder* (1874) and *Der närrische Schuster* (1877) and Costa's *Ein Blitzmädel* (1875) and *Ihr Korporal* (1878).

In 1878, encouraged by the success of Strauss's *Die Fledermaus*, Millöcker ventured his nearest approach to date to a legitimate, full-sized Operette with the score for Berla's comical piece *Das verwunschene Schloss*. With Girardi and Gallmeyer in its starring rôles, *Das verwunschene Schloss* and its songs ('S is a Bisserl Liab' und a Bisserl Treu', 'Dalkata Bua!', 'O, du himmelblauer See!') were first-rate and international successes and, although he produced further winners in the following years in the Posse genre, notably the 1880 *Die Näherin*, Millöcker devoted himself, from here on, principally to writing musically substantial Operetten. *Gräfin Dubarry* (1879) was only a moderate success (27 performances), but *Apajune, der Wassermann* (1880), seen 45 times at the Theater an der Wien, gave him another internationally played success, and *Die Jungfrau von Belleville* (1881) confirmed that success before in 1882, after nearly 20 years of composing for the theatre, Millöcker had his greatest triumph of all with the production of *Der Bettelstudent*. *Der Bettelstudent* not only proved the Theater an der Wien's most important hit since and apart from *Die Fledermaus*, but it also launched one of Viennese Operette's all-time greatest song hits, the loping baritone waltz 'Ach, ich hab' sie ja nur auf die Schulter geküsst'.

From *Der Bettelstudent* on, Millöcker's works almost all won productions around the world: the swashbuckling *Gasparone*, which has remained in the repertoire in Austria and Germany for the century since its production, *Der Feldprediger*, for a while highly popular in America, *Der Vice-Admiral* which suffered a little in the shadow of the production of Strauss's *Der Zigeunerbaron* and was played only 30 times first up, *Die sieben Schwaben* and, his most successful piece after *Der Bettelstudent*, the comical *Der arme Jonathan*. *Der arme Jonathan* provided a particularly happy rôle for the theatre's adored star, Alexander Girardi, but in spite of worldwide success in the 1890s it has not survived in the repertoire with the strength of the more physically picturesque and endlessly revamped *Gasparone*.

Das Sonntagskind (1892) was another success and *Der Probekuss* (1894) played 55 times in its first run, but, in the year of its production, Millöcker suffered a stroke. Although he produced one more Operette thereafter, the indifferently received *Nordlicht* (1896), a part of which was reused to make up the score of the subsequent *Der Damenschneider*, the long and brilliant career which had placed him alongside Suppé and Johann Strauss as one of the three pillars of the 19th-century Viennese school of Operette was at an end.

Two of a number of pasticcio Operetten made from his music, *Jung Heidelberg* (arr Ernst Reiterer/Leopold Krenn, Carl Lindau, Raimundtheater 9 July 1904) and *Cousin Bobby* (arr L Sänger/Benno Jacobson, Franz Wagner, Theater des Westens, Berlin 29 December 1906) both found some success and productions in several countries.

Millöcker appeared as a character in the film *Operette* where, although subsidiary to theatre manager Franz Jauner in the text, he was played by Curd Jürgens.

1865 **Der tote Gast** (J L Harisch) 1 act Thalia-Theater, Graz 21 December

1865 **Die lustigen Binder** (Gustav Stolze) 1 act Thalia-Theater, Graz 21 December

1866 **Kleine Kinder** (Poly Henrion) 1 act Harmonietheater 20 October

1866 **Sachsen in Österreich** (Henrion) 1 act Harmonietheater 24 October

1866 **Wenn man Leben ins Haus bringt** 1 act Harmonietheater 3 November

1866 **Die Lehrbuben** (Josef Doppler) 1 act Harmonietheater 3 December

1866 **Stübenmädel-Geschichten, or Der junge Herr auf Nadeln** (Carl F Stix) 1 act Harmonietheater 8 December

1867 **(Die keusche) Diana** (Josef Braun) Harmonietheater 2 January

1867 **Die Neujahrstag** (Karl Elmar) 1 act Harmonietheater 5 January

1867 **Die Diamantengrotte** (Karl Riedl) Harmonietheater 7 January

1867 **Der Millionen-Bräutigam** (Doppler) Harmonietheater 19 January

1867 **Der Reformatürk** (Ludwig Anzengruber) Harmonietheater 26 January

1867 **Brave Stadtleute** (Henrion) Harmonietheater 6 February

1867 **Das Mädel aus Blitzblau** (Henrion) Harmonietheater 6 February

1867 **Die Eselshaut** (Eugen Sporck) Harmonietheater 10 February

1867 **Der Telegraphist in der Nacht** (Anzengruber) Harmonietheater

1867 **Der Sackpfeifer** (Anzengruber) 1 act Harmonietheater

1868 **Die Fraueninsel** (*Asszonyok szigete*) (Theodore Cogniard, Hippolyte Cogniard ad) Deutsches Theater, Budapest

1869 **Der Regiments-Tambour** Theater in der Josefstadt 23 October

1869 **Schottenfeld und Ringstrasse** (Alois Berla) Theater an der Wien 3 December

1870 **Bartelmanns Leiden** (Hugo Müller) Theater an der Wien 25 April

1870 **Wallach Menelaus** (Berla) Theater an der Wien 7 June

1870 **Die Kinder von Ungefahr** (Berla) Theater an der Wien 7 September

1870 **Grand Hotel** (Leopold Feldmann) Theater an der Wien 7 December

1871 **Drei Paar Schuhe** (Karl Görlitz ad Berla) Theater an der Wien 5 January

1871 **Die beiden Elfen** (Julius Feld) Theater an der Wien 19 March

1871 **In Paris** (Berla) Theater an der Wien 6 June

1871 **Gewonnen Herzen** (Müller ad Josef Böhm) Theater an der Wien 14 August

1871 **Der letzte Nationalgardist** (O F Berg) Theater an der Wien 23 September

1871 **Wähler und Quäler** (Berla) Theater an der Wien 21 October

1871 **Die Veilchendame** (Eduard Dorn) Theater an der Wien 26 December

1872 **Kläffer** (C Gärtner) Theater an der Wien 25 March

1872 **Ein nagender Wurm** (aka *Wechselbrief und Briefwechsel*) (Jules Moinaux ad Josef Weyl) Theater an der Wien 15 July

1872 **Das Haus Wiener und Sohn** (aka *Der Millionenschwindel*) (Dorn) Theater an der Wien 20 August

1873 **Abenteuer in Wien** (aka *Herr Bendels Abenteuer*) (Berla) Theater an der Wien 20 January

1873 **Theatralische Weltausstellungsträume** (Berla) Theater an der Wien 9 August

1873 **Die Tochter des Wucherers** (Anzengruber) Theater an der Wien 17 October

1873 **Gift** (J E Mand) Theater an der Wien 7 November

1874 **Die Prinzipien des Herrn Bezirksberger** (Julius Johann Krassnigg) Theater an der Wien 1 February

1874 **Durchgegangene Weiber** (Berla) Theater an der Wien 14 February

1874 **Erinnerung an bessere Zeiten** (Berg) Theater an der Wien 12 June

1874 **Die aufgeweckten Götter** (Berg) 1 act Theater an der Wien 12 July

1874 **Die Carlisten in Spanien** (Berla) Theater an der Wien 14 August

1874 **Der barmherzige Bruder** (Berg) Theater an der Wien 20 October

1874 **Die Frau von Brestl** (Berg) Theater an der Wien 25 December

1875 **Der Musik von Teufels** (Berla) Theater an der Wien 17 April

1875 **Dr Haslinger** (Berg) Theater an der Wien 1 November

1876 **Die schlimmen(de) Töchter** (Berg) Theater an der Wien 12 February

1876 **Der Confusionsrath** (Julius Rosen) Theater an der Wien 8 March

1876 **Der elegante Toni** (aka *Hass und Liebe*) (Alois Blank) 1 act Theater an der Wien 1 April

1876 **Die Reise durch Wien in 80 Stunden** (Hermann Salingré) Theater an der Wien 26 May

1877 **Ein Blitzmädel** (Karl Costa) Theater an der Wien 4 February

1877 **Der Löwe des Tages** (Heinrich Wilken) Theater an der Wien 1 April

1877 **Die Reise nach Sibirien** (Karl Bruno) Theater an der Wien 21 April

1877 **Hasemanns Tochter** (Adolphe L'Arronge) Carltheater 6 October

1877 **Ein Kassastück** (Costa) Theater an der Wien 21 October

1877 **Der närrische Schuster** (Berg) Theater an der Wien 31 October

1878 **Die Landpomeranze** (Alois Just) Theater an der Wien 12 January

1878 **Ihr Korporal** (Costa) Theater an der Wien 19 January

1878 **Das verwunschene Schloss** (Berla) Theater an der Wien 30 March

1878 **Die bezähmte Bisgurn** (Anton Langer) Theater an der Wien 10 April

1878 **Der Untaugliche** (Berg) Theater an der Wien 30 October

1878 **Die Trutzige** (Anzengruber) Theater an der Wien 8 November

1878 **Plausch net Pepi** (Berla) Theater an der Wien 23 November

1879 **Himmelschlüssel** (Costa) Theater an der Wien 15 March

1879 **Der Theaterteufel** (Berla) Theater an der Wien 29 March

1879 **Die umkehrte Freit** (Anzengruber) 1 act Theater an der Wien 4 April

1879 **Gräfin Dubarry** (F Zell, Richard Genée) Theater an der Wien 31 October

1879 **Aus'm g'wohnten Gleis** (Anzengruber) Theater an der Wien 25 December

1880 **Die Näherin** (Ludwig Held) Theater an der Wien 13 March

1880 **Vaterfreuden** (Theodore Taube) Theater an der Wien 12 November

1880 **Apajune, der Wassermann** (Zell, Genée) Theatre an der Wien 18 December

1881 **Herz-Ass** (Karl A Görner) Theater an der Wien 29 January

1881 **Ihre Familie** (Berla) Theater an der Wien 12 February

1881 **Die Jungfrau von Belleville** (Zell, Genée) Theater an der Wien 29 October

1882 **Der Mann im Monde** (Costa, Eduard Jacobson) Theater an der Wien 16 February

1882 **Ein süsses Kind** (Franz von Schönthan) Theater an der Wien 1 April

1882 **Der Bettelstudent** (Zell, Genée) Theater an der Wien 6 December

1884 **Gasparone** (Zell, Genée) Theater an der Wien 26 January

1884 **Der Feldprediger** (Hugo Wittmann, Alois Wohlmuth) Theater an der Wien 31 October

1886 **Der Dieb** (Berla) 1 act Vaudeville Theater April

1886 **Der Vice-Admiral** (Zell, Genée) Theater an der Wien 9 October

1887 **Die sieben Schwaben** (Wittmann, Julius Bauer) Theater an der Wien 29 October

1890 **Der arme Jonathan** (Wittmann, Bauer) Theater an der Wien 4 January

1892 **Das Sonntagskind** (Wittmann, Bauer) Theater an der Wien 16 January

1894 **Der Probekuss** (Wittmann, Bauer) Theater an der Wien 22 December

1896 **Nordlicht** (aka *Der rote Graf*) (Wittmann) Theater an der Wien 22 December

1898 **Der Maler Veri** (Bruno Hartl-Mitius) Theater an der Wien 5 February

1901 **Der Damenschneider** (Wittmann, Louis Hermann) Carl-theater 14 September

MILY-MEYER Impishly boyish, yet obviously feminine soubrette who became a major Parisian star.

The tiny, dark musical comedienne made her Parisian début in a barely comic rôle, as the petite Duchesse in Lecocq's hugely successful *Le Petit Duc* (1878, 'Je t'aime', 'Ah! Qu'on est bien') and went on from there to build an oustanding career of some 30 years in the musical theatre. In, at first, often theoretically secondary soubrette rôles she succeeded on a number of occasions in stealing a show before being confirmed herself as a top-billable name. Mily-Meyer followed up her success in *Le Petit Duc* by creating other supporting rôles at the Théâtre de la Renaissance as the piquant little Colombe, with a tiny number in the second act of *La Camargo* (1878), as Jacqueline, the innkeeper's wife, in *La Petite Mademoiselle*, and in breeches as the little sergeant Flambart in Planquette's *Les Voltigeurs de la 32ème* (1880). She played Aveline in the revived *La Marjolaine* (1880), introduced the comic washerwoman Marceline in Offenbach's posthumous *Belle Lurette* (1880), played soubrette rôles in *Ninette*

and *Janot* (1881, Suzon), created Offenbach's *Mademoiselle Moucheron* (1881), the rôle of Catherine in the play *La Cigale* and that of Carmen in Jonas's opérette *La Bonne Aventure* (1882).

She then moved in turn from the Renaissance to the Théâtre des Nouveautés where she appeared as Lucinde in *Le Roi de carreau* (1883), and to the Folies-Dramatiques to play Kate in the French première of *Rip!*, stole the show as the unplotworthy Bagatella in *Babolin* (1884) and appeared in breeches again in *La Vie mondaine* (1885, Tom). She played at the Bouffes-Parisiens as the deceived Bianca in *La Béarnaise* (1885), as Mimosa in *Les Noces improvisées* (1886) and then, in the most successful rôle of her entire career, created the part of the youngest sister, Benjamine, in Ferrier and Carré's richly comical *Joséphine vendue par ses soeurs* (1886).

Now confirmed as a top-rank star, she was seen in the years that followed in virtually all the principal musical theatres of Paris: at the Bouffes-Parisiens in *La Gamine de Paris* (1887), at the Variétés in a revival of *La Princesse de Trébizonde* (1888), at the Folies-Dramatiques in the French version of Millöcker's *La Demoiselle de Belleville* (Virginie Troupeau), at the Bouffes again in Messager's *Le Mari de la reine* (1889, Justine), at the Nouveautés in *Samsonette* (1890), star-billed as *Cendrillonnette* and *La Petite Poucette*, in *Le Petit Bois* (1893), *Fleur de vertu* (1894, Lucrèce), Serpette's *La Bonne de chez Duval* (1894) and the made-to-measure *L'Élève de conservatoire* (1894, Friquette), at the Eldorado in the spectacular *Le Royaume des femmes* (1896, Xéressa), at the Athénée-Comique in *Madame Putiphar* (1897, Lota), at the Châtelet as Catiche in *La Poudre de Perlinpinpin* (1898), and in the title-rôle of the reprised *Les 28 Jours de Clairette* (1900), all the time repeating her most successful creations, notably her Benjamine, which she played on the Paris stage as late as 1906, and all the time an adored favourite of public and critics.

MINNELLI, Liza [May] (b Los Angeles, 12 March 1946).

The daughter of film director Vincente Minnelli and film actress and vocalist Judy Garland, Miss Minnelli made appearances on the musical stage as a teenager in *The Fantasticks* and *Carnival* on the road, and off-Broadway in the 1963 Stage 73 revival of *Best Foot Forward*. She made her Broadway début at the age of 19 in the title-rôle of the short-lived Kander and Ebb musical *Flora, the Red Menace*, but thereafter her career blossomed in other directions, taking her away from the theatre to the variety and night-club stages and to the recording and film studios. In 1972 she took the starring rôle of Sally Bowles in the film version of Kander and Ebb's *Cabaret* (Academy Award), transforming the girl of the book and of the stage musical into an altogether different character in one of the stage-to-screen's most memorable musical play performances.

When she finally returned to the stage, it was in highly theatrical circumstances, deputizing for several weeks for the indisposed Gwen Verdon in Kander and Ebb's *Chicago*. She made a more regular return to the musical stage with two further pieces by the same team (*The Act*, *The Rink*), but neither provided the wheels that would carry her to the Broadway success on which the star has to date somehow missed out.

Biographies: Parish, J R; *Liza!* (Simon & Schuster, New York,

1975), Petrucelli, A W: *Liza! Liza!* (Karlz-Cohl, New York, 1983), Leigh, W: *Born a Star* (Dutton, New York, 1993)

MINNIE MOUSTACHE Comédie musicale in 2 acts by Jean Broussolle and André Hornez. Lyrics by Broussolle. Music by Georges van Parys. Théâtre de la Gaîté-Lyrique, Paris, 13 December 1956.

This spoofish Western about a donkey called Pittypat, which is to gold what a truffle hound is to truffles, featured Ginette Baudin in its title-rôle as the keeper of a Nevada City saloon. However, the chief attraction of *Minnie Moustache* was the appearance in the cast of the favourite singing group Les Compagnons de la Chanson, who played nine Frenchmen wandering through the action in a variety of disguises, trying to rescue both the donkey and its little owner Calico (Thérèse Laporte) from the clutches of the outlaw Maguire. In the process, they sang 'La Berceuse de l'inconnu', 'Avant de nous embarquer', 'L'Amour c'est de l'or', 'Mariage Indien' and 'San Francisco'. One of them (Fred Mella) ended up with Calico, Minnie paired off with a singing coachman called Wells Fargo (Yves Thomas), and Germaine Roger-Montjoye's production ran for seven months.

Recording: original cast (Columbia)

MIRANDE, Yves [LE QUERREC, Anatole Charles] (b Lannion, Côtes-de-Nord, 8 March 1875; d Paris, 20 March 1957).

Parisian boulevardier, spinner of bons mots and the author of a long list of successful comedies, for 20 years in a nominal collaboration with theatre magnate Gustave Quinson (*Le Chasseur de chez Maxim* being 'their' greatest hit), Mirande was also one of the most successful authors of libretti for the musical comedies of 'les années folles', many of which Quinson mounted at his Théâtre des Bouffes-Parisiens.

Mirande's first dip into the musical theatre, in the earliest days of his career, was with a little thriller-sketch called *Ma gosse* (w Henri Cain), a tongue-in-cheek piece invented basically as a vehicle for the fashionable apache dance routine and introduced in Paris by Polaire. It sported, at various times, music by one van Oosternyck, a score composed and arranged by the Moulin-Rouge's Maurice Jacobi, and when played by Polly Goss at Vienna's Apollotheater (*Der schwarze Mali* 1909), interpolations by Bela von Ujj. *Ma gosse* was also seen at London's Palace Music-Hall (18 October 1909 ad J N Raphael), performed by Edmé Mollon and Gaston Silvestre, and for 48 nights at New York's American Music Hall (10 January 1910) and later at the Plaza Music Hall with the same partnership featured.

It was not, however, until more than a decade later, following his alliance with Quinson, and the production by his ally of the blockbusting *Phi-Phi*, that Mirande entered seriously into the manufacture of libretti and lyrics. When he did, his very first effort was a major hit. *Ta bouche*, with its tiny cast and no chorus, was built on the same proportions as *Phi-Phi*, but it was wholly French and wholly contemporary in its display of its subject matter – a perfect whirligig of sexual-cum-financial relationships – and its crisp, merrily sexphisticated dialogue helped set the tone

for the musical theatre of the next decade. Mirande himself played a major part in that decade, for he followed *Ta bouche* with another hit, the Maurice Chevalier/Dranem show *Là-haut* and several other delightful musical comedies, of which *Trois jeunes filles ... nues!* was probably the most successful, while continuing his heavy output as a writer of comedy for the Quinson theatres. His last contributions to the musical stage were an adaptation of his 1921 play *Simone est comme ça* for the Bouffes-Parisiens and the libretto for Nikola Bobrykine's opera *Inès*.

Mirande's *Le Chasseur de chez Maxim* was metamorphosed into the Broadway musical *The Blue Kitten* (1922, Rudolf Friml/Otto Harbach, William Cary Duncan), whilst his name also appeared as source on the credits for Budapest's *Parizsi espress* (Markus Park Színház, 1942, Béla Csanak/Andor Pünkösti) and recent musicalized versions of two of his 1920s plays: *Uraim, cask egymás után* (Szabolcs Fényes/Adorján Stella, Városmajori Színpad 28 June 1984) and *Az utolsó bölény* (Gyula Bodrogi, József Vinkó, Vidám Színpad 1 June 1990).

Alongside his stage credits, Mirande also worked for film in both France and in Hollywood where he was responsible for the screenplays for some of the early Maurice Chevalier films.

1909 **Ma gosse** (various/w Henri Cain) 1 act Théâtre du Moulin-Rouge 20 August
1922 **Ta bouche** (Maurice Yvain/w Gustave Quinson) Théâtre Daunou 1 April
1923 **Là-haut!** (Yvain/Albert Willemetz/w Quinson) Théâtre des Bouffes-Parisiens 31 March
1923 **La Dame en décolleté** (Yvain/w Lucien Boyer) Théâtre des Bouffes-Parisiens 22 December
1924 **Troublez-moi** (Raoul Moretti) Théâtre des Bouffes-Parisiens 17 September
1925 **Riri** (Charles Borel-Clerc/w Willemetz, Quinson) Théâtre Daunou 4 November
1925 **Trois jeunes filles ... nues!** (Moretti/Willemetz) Théâtre de Bouffes-Parisiens 3 December
1927 **Mercenary Mary** French version w Robert de Simone, Jean Bastia (Théâtre des Bouffes-Parisiens)
1930 **Arsène Lupin banquier** (Marcel Lattès) Théâtre des Bouffes-Parisiens 7 May
1936 **Simone est comme ça** (Moretti/Willemetz/w Alex Madis) Théâtre des Bouffes-Parisiens 5 March

Autobiography: *Souvenirs d'Yves Mirande* (Fayard, Paris, 1932)

LES MISÉRABLES Musical tragedy by Alain Boublil and Jean-Marc Natel based on the novel by Victor Hugo. Music by Claude-Michel Schönberg. Palais des Sports, Paris, 17 September 1980.

After the production of their first musical spectacular, *La Révolution française* (w Raymond Jeannot, Jean-Max Rivière), mounted at the Palais des Sports in 1973, composer Claude-Michel Schönberg and librettist Alain Boublil, this time in collaboration with poet Jean-Marc Natel, attacked another over-sized French subject for their second work: Victor Hugo's dramatic novel *Les Misérables*. Following the procedure successfully used with *Jesus Christ Superstar*, *Evita* and *La Révolution française*, *Les Misérables* was at first performed as a recording (April 1980), and it was subsequently brought to the Paris stage, at the same Palais des Sports, in a staging by Robert Hossein, France's specialist in vast, popular theatrical productions. Many of the cast from the recording repeated their rôles for the stage production in a version which followed fairly closely the layout which was presented on the record.

This musical reduction of *Les Misérables*, which took on the challenge of slimming Victor Hugo's novel, with its huge cast of characters, its wide time-span and its momentous happenings and personal stories, into a few-hour spectacle, did not take the same line as that chosen for *La Révolution française*. Whereas the earlier piece had skipped through its even wider span sketching most of its characters as extravagant near-caricatures in a comic-strip retelling of history, *Les Misérables* was played straight. Its characters and the events in which they were caught up were given their full dramatic import, and the music that illustrated the show was largely dramatic and romantic in tone.

Jean Valjean (Maurice Barrier) is released from prison, where he was long condemned for petty theft, on a ticket of leave, and over the years he struggles his way back to respectability and ultimately to the position of mayor in a provincial town. However, he has broken the terms of his ticket of leave, and the policeman Javert (Jean Vallée) has made it his mission to track the law-breaker down and return him to prison. When one of Valjean's employees, Fantine (Rose Laurens), is sacked, sinks into prostitution, and finally dies, the mayor takes on the responsibility of her child, Cosette (Fabienne Guyon). He rescues the girl from her crooked foster parents, the Thénardiers (Yves Dautin, Marie-France Roussel), and, keeping one pace ahead of the pursuing Javert, takes her to Paris.

Cosette is already in her teens by the time the stirrings of armed revolt begin in the capital. A band of students, amongst them the young Marius (Gilles Buhlmann), join the anti-government fighting. But Marius has met and fallen in love with Cosette, and she with him, and Valjean is determined that the boy shall come to no harm. When the barriers go up in the streets of Paris, Valjean joins the street-fighters and, as the scrappy revolt fails bloodily, he is able to carry the wounded Marius away to safety. But during the fighting he has also come up against the dogged Javert, still intent on capturing the escaped criminal. Circumstances put Javert in Valjean's power, and when the latter not only does not kill his 'enemy' but sets him free, the uncomprehending policeman falls to pieces. Justice is on its head, the notions of right or wrong seem to have vainished in a world which Javert cannot any longer understand – there is nothing left but for him to leave it to its anomalies. Javert jumps from a bridge and drowns himself in the Seine.

Fantine is dead, Javert is dead, Marius's foolishly idealistic friends are all dead, and little Eponine (Marianne Mille), the Thénardiers' child, who was shot delivering a love-letter for the Marius she herself loved, is dead. Even the urchin Gavroche is dead, killed scavenging for bullets for the empty guns of the street-fighters. But Cosette and Marius come at last to their joyful ending, and Valjean can himself die secure in the knowledge that he has made his child happy.

The sung-through score of the piece mixed a number of solo songs with musical scenes, as it moved from its beginnings in 1821, at the factory where Fantine is employed (chorus: 'La journée est finie') through the various stages of its epic tale. Fantine sang her Air de misère ('J'avais des si joli defauts') and tore her heart out thinking of what

might have been ('J'avais revé d'une autre vie'), the little Cosette piped out her pauper's day-dream 'Mon prince est en chemin', Thénardier roughly pounded out his 'devise du cabaratier' and, backed by his wife, waltzed insinuatingly through his bartering with Valjean for Cosette (La Valse de la fourberie). In the Paris scenes, Marius delivered a stinging paean to the 'Rouge et noir' and his companion Enjolras hymned 'la volonté du peuple', before Marius and Cosette joined together in romance ('Dans ma vie'). There were also songs for Eponine ('L'un vers l'autre') and for the boy Gavroche ('Bonjour Paris, c'est moi Gavroche', 'La Faute à Voltaire') before the drama rose to its pre-fight height in the ensemble 'Demain'. The final scenes featured Javert's final dilemma, powerfully expressed in the monologue 'Noir ou blanc'.

Hossein's production played for a predestined season of 105 performances in Paris, and closed. As in the case of *La Révolution française*, things might have ended there, had not the piece come to the attention of Cameron Mackintosh, riding high as the London producer of *Cats*. Mackintosh took the piece up and, in collaboration with *Cats* director Trevor Nunn, at that time chief of Britain's Royal Shakespeare Company, and his colleague John Caird, teamed initially with *Times* theatre critic James Fenton and later with Herbert Kretzmer as lyricist, began the process of turning the rather unwieldy piece of French-language spectacular entertainment into something more resembling an at least relatively conventional English stage musical in the tradition of *Evita*. The alterations were to be many, and the time long.

The Royal Shakespeare Company joined Mackintosh as co-producer of the new *Les Misérables*, with Nunn and Caird (who had teamed on the internationally successful *Nicholas Nickelby*) as joint directors, and the production had its first performances on the Shakespeare Company's stage at London's Barbican complex. Those performances ran nearer to four hours than to three in comparison with the $2\frac{1}{4}$ hour version played in Paris. Between the Palais des Sports and The Barbican well over an hour of new material had been dug from Hugo's text and eased into the telling of his story. The new *Les Misérables* concentrated rather less on skating almost filmically through the familiar (to the French) high spots of the famous tale and focused itself very much more firmly and deeply on the novel's central characters, almost all of whom had been given additional numbers in which to express themselves. Several scenes and characters originally omitted also now reappeared. The rôle of Jean Valjean (Colm Wilkinson) had been given some dramatic new music ('What Have I Done?' 'Who Am I?', the pianissimo 'Bring Him Home'); Javert (Roger Allam) had a second solo, early in the piece ('Stars'), as did Thénardier (Alun Armstrong), halting the action as he scavenged through the sewers of Paris to deliver a 'Dog Eats Dog', and Marius (Michael Ball), achingly looking at the 'Empty Chairs and Empty Tables' where his friends had joyously planned their little war. Eponine (Frances Ruffelle) had a replacement number ('On My Own', originally Fantine's Air de misère) for her original. Fantine (Patti Lu Pone) had versions of two numbers from the original score, and Cosette – the rôle split between a child and soprano Rebecca Caine as the grown-up girl – had English adaptations of her childish song ('My

Castle in the Clouds') and her love duo ('In My Life').

The production, too, took the same attitude, focusing on the individual stories and characters within the piece and, as a result, the whole piece became eminently more theatrical, rather than merely spectacular. It was, of course, too long. But where to cut? A 12-minute section detailing Javert's pursuit of Valjean and Cosette from Monfermeil to Paris had already been excised in preview – what else would go? One character who went for nothing to English audiences was the obvious target – but to make the French authors understand that Gavroche, almost the most loved and famous character of the novel, had little place in the proceedings and looked and sounded as if he'd wandered in from a production of *Oliver!*, was tough. Eventually almost all of Gavroche's original part went under the knife, leaving the gamin moments to the more attractive Eponine, and the comedy to Thénardier and his wife (Susan Jane Tanner) whose rôles had been coloured-up (though coloured-down since Paris) into low-comedy relief, as the show was reduced by only a handful of minutes.

Les Misérables was not an instant success. More of the London critics had hard words for it than had encouragement following its opening, and the planned move to the West End's Palace Theatre was for a while in doubt. The cast recording was postponed, and those involved waited to hear whether they were to close at the end of the Barbican season. Ultimately, Mackintosh decided to go for it. The show transferred, with only a little in the way of alterations, and opened at the Palace Theatre on 4 December 1985. At the time of writing (1992) it is still there and promising to be so a while more.

The success that was won so slowly in London was won without the same suspense elsewhere as reproductions of Caird and Nunn's staging of the show appeared round the world in the years that followed. Broadway's production (Tony Awards Best Musical, book, score, directors, set, lighting), with Wilkinson and Miss Ruffelle (Tony Award) repeating their London performances, also featured Terrence V Mann (Javert), David Bryant (Marius), Judy Kuhn (Cosette), Michael Maguire (Enjolras, Tony Award), Randy Graff (Fantine) and Leo Burmester and Jennifer Butt as the Thénardiers in the first cast of a production which has changed a number of times in the six years that the show has held its place at the Broadway and then (16 October 1990) at the Imperial Theater. A Los Angeles company (Shubert Theater 1 June 1988) ran simultaneously with the Broadway production, followed by a bus-and-truck touring company which took the show around America, again whilst the Broadway production continued.

Australia's production, which opened later the same year in Sydney, featured former pop singer Normie Rowe as Valjean and Philip Quast as Javert. Two years later, after a Sydney run which was one of the longest in that city's musical theatre history, it progressed to Melbourne (Princess Theatre 9 December 1989) with Rob Guest and John Diedrich in the central rôles. Vienna's Raimundtheater launched a German version (ad Heinz Rudolf Kunze) in 1988 with Reinhard Brussmann (Valjean), Norbert Lamla (Javert) and Felix Martin (Marius) in its principal rôles, and in the same year Budapest's Rock Színház produced an Hungarian version (ad Miklós Tibor) with Gyula Vikidál (Valjean), Pál Makrai (Javert), Sándor

Sasvári (Marius), Anikò Nagy (Eponine) and Zsuzsa Csarnóy (Cosette) featured.

In 1991, more than a decade after those first 105 performances at the Palais des Sports, *Les Misérables* finally arrived back where it had started when it was staged in Paris, at the Théâtre Mogador. It was, of course, the 'new' *Les Misérables*, honed by thousands of performances around the world into something very different in tone and style to the version played initially, and some of the original pieces of the text that remained were not adapted back into the original French, but rewritten by the French authors. Michel Pascal (Valjean) and Patrick Rocca (Javert) starred alongside Jérome Pradon (Marius), Marie Zamora (Cosette) and Stéphanie Martin (Eponine) with Marie-France Roussel of the original cast repeating her Madame Thénardier, in a fine production which held up for but seven months in a Paris which, yet again, displayed its disinterest in modern musical theatre, even when essentially home-made.

Elsewhere round the world the Franco-English show found a much warmer welcome. As the original London and Broadway productions totted up their runs into the thousands of performances, versions of *Les Misérables* were seen in Japan (Imperial Theatre, Tokyo 17 July 1987), Israel (Cameri Theatre, Tel Aviv 9 August 1987), Iceland (National Theatre, Reykjavik 26 December 1987), Norway (Det Norske Teatre, Oslo 17 March 1988), Canada (Royal Alexandra Theatre, Toronto 15 March 1989), Poland (Teatr Muzyczny, Gdynia 30 June 1989), Sweden (Cirkus Theater 12 September 1990), Netherlands (Carré Theater, Amsterdam 28 February 1991), Denmark (Odense Theater 20 April 1991), New Zealand (Aotea Theatre, Auckland 29 May 1991), Czechoslovakia (Vnohrady Theatre, Prague 25 June 1992) and Spain (Nuevo Apolo, Madrid 16 September 1992), as others lined up to follow them.

UK: Barbican Theatre 30 September (8 October) 1985; USA: Broadway Theater 12 March 1987; Australia: Theatre Royal, Sydney, 27 November 1987; Austria: Raimundtheater 15 September 1988; Hungary: Rock Színház, Szeged *A Nyomorulták* 14 August 1987, Rock Színház, Budapest 14 September 1987; France: Théâtre Mogador 12 October 1991; Recordings: pre-production (Tréma etc), London cast (First Night), Broadway cast (Geffen), Japanese cast (Pony Canyon), Austrian cast (Polydor), Hungarian cast (Radioton), Israeli cast (Hed-Arzi), Swedish recording (CBS), 'Complete Symphonic Recording' (First Night), Dutch cast (Mercury), French cast (Tréma) etc

MISS DUDELSACK Operette in 3 acts by Fritz Grünbaum and Heinz Reichert. Music by Rudolf Nelson. Neues Schauspielhaus, Berlin, 3 August 1909.

The most successful of Rudolf Nelson's stage works, *Miss Dudelsack* was based on a familiar operettic story, given a special colour by a Scots setting. Sir Francis MacHumber's will leaves much of his estate to his nephew Lieutenant John Jack MacHumber on condition that he weds his cousin, Kitty Sommerset. John Jack prefers poor and pretty Mary (otherwise 'Miss Bagpipes'!) to riches, and his decision turns out to be right all round when Sir Francis turns up alive and turns out to be Mary's father.

Nelson's score gave most opportunities to Mary and her man, with John Jack's waltz song 'Eine dunkel Rose' proving the favourite of the evening alongside his entrance number 'Reite, roter Leutnant', Mary's introduction 'Ich bin das Fräulein Dudelsack', their 'English' duo 'Oh du my darling, du, du, du' and their tale of the castle ghost (Das Schlossgespenst), but it also included two amusing sextets for the MacHumber relations and two substantial finales – a kind of writing which might have been less than expected from the pen of a man known mostly as a cabaret writer and performer.

Following its Berlin run, the piece went on to be played in Hungary (ad Jenő Faragó), in Vienna's summer theatre in the Prater with Annie Münchow as Mary, Grete Mayer as Kitty and Josef Victora as John Jack, and later the same year in America, where Louis F Werba and Mark A Luescher's production (ad Grant Stewart) featured Lulu Glaser as its heroine and Joseph Herbert at the head of the comedy as her unwanted suitor, Peter (ex-Patrick). Miss Glaser and her bagpipes failed to make it to Broadway.

Hungary: Városligeti Színkör *Dudakisasszony* 8 May 1910; Austria: Venedig in Wien 17 August 1911; USA: Boston Theater, Boston 16 October 1911

MISS ESMERALDA, or The Monkey and the Monk melodramatic burlesque in 3 acts by 'A C Torr' (Fred Leslie) and Horace Mills. Music by W Meyer Lutz. Additional songs by Robert Martin and Frederick Bowyer. Gaiety Theatre, London, 8 October 1887.

The third of the Gaiety 'new burlesques', following behind *Little Jack Sheppard* and *Monte Cristo Jr*, this loose-limbed parody of Victor Hugo's *Notre Dame de Paris* and its derivatives was written by the Gaiety's star comedian, Fred Leslie, who dragged in a city-gent chum from his local amateur theatre group to help. Leslie, in fact, didn't initially play in *Miss Esmeralda*, for he and his team-mate, Nellie Farren, went on the road with their previous success and it was Edwin Lonnen who appeared at the Gaiety in the rôle of the mad monk, Claude Frollo, and Fannie Leslie who took the breeches part of Captain Phoebus. Marion Hood, the Mabel of Gilbert and Sullivan's *Pirates of Penzance*, was Esmeralda, and another Savoyard, Frank Thornton, played the lovelorn hunchback. Lutz composed a lively score which won approving notices, but the hit of the night was Bob Martin's interpolated Irish song 'Kilalloe' as delivered by Lonnen, who played the star rôle Leslie had constructed for himself with an eccentric ghoulishness which confirmed his rise to the top of the Gaiety's B-team.

The show had a curiously cut-about run, as it was taken off as soon as Fred and Nellie were ready to return with their Christmas show, but was then restaged as an afternoon piece when the new show proved less popular. Lonnen led a company on the British road, whilst Leslie got to grips with the part of Frollo and Miss Farren with that of Phoebus in a Gaiety company tour through Australia and the United States in 1888–9. The piece continued to tour in Britain for some years thereafter (Little Tich appeared as Quasimodo in one tour) and it was given a second Australian tour (with Lonnen starred). As a postscript, city-gent turned librettist Horace Mills ended up handing in his three-piece suit and becoming a comedian at the Gaiety!

Australia: Princess Theatre, Melbourne 1 August 1888; USA: Standard Theater 17 December 1888

MISS HELYETT Opérette in 3 acts by Maxime Boucheron. Music by Edmond Audran. Théâtre des Bouffes-Parisiens, Paris, 12 November 1890.

Miss Helyett gave composer Audran the greatest Parisian success of the second part of his career, a decade after his initial triumphs with *Les Noces d'Olivette* and *La Mascotte*. But although his score was written in his most charming vein, much of the credit for the show's success had to be given to the piece's librettist, Maxime Boucheron, for his delicately humorous if basically 'schocking' book.

Miss Helyett (Biana Duhamel) is a pubescent little American Salvation Army lass, whose pastor father (Montrouge) has inculcated her with a very firm morality. So when she goes walking in the mountains, slips over a cliff, is left hanging upside down from a branch with her skirts over her head, then tactfully left in a deep faint on the edge of the ravine by her rescuer, she simply has to find and wed the unknown saviour who has seen a portion of her anatomy that only a husband should see. She mistakenly lights on a cowardly bullfighter (Tauffenberger) who is already engaged to a dramatic Spanish lady (Mlle St-Laurent) with a fearsome mother (Mme Macé-Montrouge), then on her own dreary fiancé (Jannin), before discovering that the right man is the artist Paul (Piccaluga) for whom she had sighed all along. Musically, the rôle of the teenaged heroine was undemanding, though not short, and the principal singing moments fell to her baritone artist – notably in his duo d'album with his friend Bacarel (Désiré), sighing over the sketch he made of the young lady's predicament before rescuing her ('Ah! ah! le superbe point de vue!') – and particularly to the volatile trio of Spaniards.

Miss Helyett was a triumph at the Bouffes-Parisiens, making a star of the 21-year-old Mlle Duhamel, and playing there for virtually all of 1891 and 1892. It returned in 1893, in 1895 with Alice Favier in her début as a very young Miss Helyett (900th performance, 11 January 1896), again later in 1896 with Mlle Favier, and yet again in 1901, whilst in the meanwhile having been played at the Théâtre des Menus-Plaisirs with Mariette Sully and by Duhamel, Mlle Deliane and Evelyne Jeanney (1900) at the Renaissance. In 1904 Eve Lavallière played the rôle of Helyett at the Variétés, whilst Juliette Méaly took her version round the Continent in 1893 and rare was the rising ingénue of the French turn-of-the-century stage who didn't have a *Miss Helyett* credit on her curriculum vitae before she turned 20.

In next to no time the piece went round the world, virtually all the main centres hastening the hit of the Parisian period on to the stage whilst its career in the French capital still continued. If neither Germany (ad Richard Genée) nor Hungary (ad Lajos Evva, Viktor Rákosi) showed the same delight in the adventures of Miss Helyett, and the Theater an der Wien, in spite of an acclaimed performance by Lilli Lejo in the star rôle and the featuring of Girardi as the bullfighter, played the piece only 16 times, a British *Miss Decima*, as directed by the Gallic Mons Marius, had a fine 191-performance run at London's little Criterion and then the larger Prince of Wales Theatres. It was, however, as might have been expected, an Anglo-Saxonic deodorized version, F C Burnand having turned 'a scandalously suggestive French piece into a harmless but exceedingly amusing operatic

comedy' to feature the young French artist Juliette Nesville alongside David James as the pastor, Charles Conyers as Paul, Mary Ann Victor as the dragonistic Señora and American tenor Chauncey Olcott in a part called the Chevallier Patrick Julius O'Flanagan, fabricated on the bones of the bullfighter. When the show transferred, Decima Moore and Hayden Coffin took over the lead rôles, and some additional Edward Solomon music, including a duo for James and Miss Victor, was added to the score.

David Belasco and Charles Frohman's American production took advantage of the fact that the vocal demands of the star rôle were limited, and cast the well-publicized, red-haired neophyte actress Mrs Leslie Carter (aged 30) as Miss Helyett alongside Mark Smith (Paul), Joseph Herbert (Jacques ie James) and Laura Clement as the fiery Manuela. After passing its 50th performance at the Star Theater (17 December), it moved to the Standard (11 January) to complete a good if not spectacular run of 116 performances.

Australia chose the British adaptation for its production, and local soubrette Juliet Wray was teamed with a virtually all-British star cast: Jack Leumane (Chevallier), Henry Bracy (Marmaduke), Wallace Brownlow (Paul), Clara Thompson-Bracy (Señora) and George Lauri (pastor) for seasons in Sydney and Melbourne (Princess Theatre 16 May 1896).

Although the English-language productions fared well, nowhere else in the world did *Miss Helyett* have the vast success it achieved in France. There it remained a favourite item in the repertoire for many years, until the arrival of the Viennese Operette, and of the jazz age when the naughtiness of the 1890s and a few blushes over a bare bottom seemed altogether pale alongside the modern parade of theatrical comico-permissiveness. Even then, however, *Miss Helyett* continued to be revived, appearing in 1926 at the Gaîté and maintaining a presence in the provinces long after that.

Germany: Wallner-Theater 7 February 1891; Hungary: Népszinház *Miss Heliett* 25 April 1891; UK: Criterion Theatre *Miss Decima* 23 July 1891, USA: Star Theater 3 November 1891; Austria: Theater an der Wien 25 December 1891; Australia: Lyceum Theatre, Sydney *Miss Decima* 7 March 1896

Recording: complete (Gaîté-Lyrique)

MISS HOOK OF HOLLAND

MISS HOOK OF HOLLAND Dutch musical incident in 2 acts by Paul Rubens and Austen Hurgon. Music and lyrics by Paul Rubens. Prince of Wales Theatre, London, 31 January 1907.

One of the most likeable and certainly the most successful of Paul Rubens's musical comedies, *Miss Hook of Holland* was completed by writer-director Austen Hurgon when Rubens's ill-health meant that the show was not ready on time. The collaboration proved a fine one, for the resultant libretto avoided all the 'coy sallies of innuendo and dollops of bad taste' which had infected most of Rubens's early shows, in a strong and entertaining 'Dutch musical incident' set with a series of catchy set of what the songwriter called 'jingles and tunes'.

When the adorably vague distiller Hook (G P Huntley) loses his precious recipe for 'Cream of the Sky' whilst taking it out for a walk, it is found by the professionally unemployed Slinks (George Barrett), who sells it to Cap-

Plate 184. *G P Huntley as Mr Hook, the daffy Dutch papa of* **Miss Hook of Holland.**

tain Papp (Herbert Clayton), the unfavoured suitor of Sally Hook (Isabel Jay). However, after an actful of high jinks in the liquor factory at Amsterdam, Sally discomforts Papp, wins her beloved bandmaster Van Vuyt (Walter Hyde) and retrieves the missing formula. If comedy was high in *Miss Hook*, largely through the acclaimed creation of the elderly Hook by the not-elderly Huntley and the routines of the comic maid Mina (Gracie Leigh), Rubens supported it with some charming songs. Miss Leigh wondered why all the fellows give her underwear as a gift in 'A Pretty Pink Petty from Peter' and explained why 'The Flying Dutchman' (whose home life wasn't so hot) flew, Miss Jay sang 'Fly Away, Kite' (apropos of very little) and joined operatic tenor Hyde in 'The Sleepy Canal', one of a series of lyrically Dutch songs ('Little Miss Wooden Shoes', 'Soldiers of the Netherlands') whilst Harry Grattan, in a supporting comedy rôle, had a good old-fashioned topical song, 'From Harwich to Hook'.

Frank Curzon's production of *Miss Hook of Holland* stayed at the Prince of Wales Theatre for 462 performances, and if it lost Huntley and Miss Jay during its run it gained matinée idol Maurice Farkoa for whom the rôle of the bandmaster was expanded by several extra songs. Curzon produced a concurrent Christmas season, played by a cast of children at matinées (Ida Valli was Mr Hook) and the piece set out on the first of countless tours, under the management of George Dance, as the overseas productions began. Gabor Steiner played the show (ad Carl Lindau) at his Vienna summer theatre in both 1907 and 1908, for a total of over 100 performances. His production boasted two outstanding stars, but in succession, for both Ilka Pálmay and Annie Dirkens preferred the fun of Gracie Leigh's rôle to the title part. The second act featured an 'Hollandisches Fest' in which three songs and a routine called 'In Amsterdam' danced by '8 Original-Engländerinnen' were featured. Having performed *Miss Hook* at 8 pm, most of the cast then proceeded to perform Lincke's *Frau Luna* at 11 for the later-night pleasure-seekers in the Prater. When Vienna had done, it was Hungary's turn, and Miksa Bródy's version of *A Hollandi lány* (the joke about the Hook of Holland was clearly untranslatable) worryingly described as a 'nagy oper' or grand opera, had a good season at Budapest's Király Színház, where the latest novelties had been *Ein Walzertraum* and *Die Dollarprinzessin*.

Charles Frohman's Broadway production suffered an attempt to pre-empt its little bit of novelty, when Reginald De Koven's on-the-way-in *The Snowman* switched its title to *The Girls of Holland* under its nose, and also a sticky start when both the lead comedians were sacked on the road. However, with a cast which featured Christie MacDonald (Sally), Georgia Caine (Mina), Bertram Wallis (Papp) and Tom Wise as Hook it ultimately ran up 119 Broadway performances before going on to a fine road life. Australia welcomed Clarke, Meynell and Gunn's production, with husband and wife team Edwin Brett (Hook) and Emmeline Orford (Mina) and soprano Ruth Lincoln (Sally) from England starred, for an enormously successful run, in spite of the competition of *The Merry Widow*. It went on to a quick revival, and a tour of New Zealand. *Miss Hook* was also revived in London in 1914 for a wartime run, again in 1932 as part of a season of past glories, and in 1945 it was given a major tour in a revised version by producer Emile Littler which nevertheless did not follow his revamped *A Quaker Girl* into London. It also remained a great favourite with provincial houses and operatic societies for many more years.

Austria: Venedig in Wien *Miss Hook von Holland* 22 June 1907; USA: Criterion Theater 31 December 1907; Australia: Theatre Royal, Melbourne 18 April 1908; Hungary: Király Színház *A Hollandi lány* 19 September 1908

MISS LIBERTY Musical comedy in 2 acts by Robert Sherwood. Music and lyrics by Irving Berlin. Imperial Theater, New York, 15 July 1949.

Irving Berlin's follow-up to *Annie Get Your Gun* did not prove to be the same kind of success, in spite of being based on an amusing premise which was turned into a libretto by top-flight playwright Robert Sherwood (*Idiot's Delight*, *Reunion in Vienna*).

In the atmosphere of a newspaper circulation war, little photographer Horace Miller (Eddie Albert) goes off to France to find the original lady who modelled for the statue of Liberty. His publicity coup looks assured when he brings back pretty Monique Dupont (Allyn McLerie) but it turns out he has the wrong girl. Since he thus makes one newspaper magnate look foolish, Horace is assured of a job with the other. Mary McCarty played Horace's reporter helpmate, Maisie, and aged Ethel Griffies was the elderly and comical mother of the lassie who isn't 'Miss Liberty'.

Berlin's score did not bring forth any numbers to add to his list of standards, although Monique's final singing of the statue's motto 'Give Me Your Tired, Your Poor' and the old lady's cynical and lively description of opportunism in 'Only for Americans' both went down well in the show. It was an outcut, 'Mr Monotony' (previously cut also from a film score), which was given the most enduring life when it was included in the retrospective compilation show staged as *Jerome Robbins' Broadway* (1989).

Moss Hart, Berlin and Sherwood's production, directed by Hart, choreographed by Robbins, and designed by Oliver Smith and Motley, was eagerly awaited and opened with a very large advance sale, but the show proved to have few of the attractions of *Annie Get Your Gun* for the theatre-going public. Although it ran on for 308 performances, *Miss Liberty* was generally voted a disappointment.

Recording: original cast (Columbia), selections (RCA Victor, Decca)

MISS SAIGON Musical in 2 acts by Alain Boublil. Lyrics by Boublil and Richard Maltby jr. Music by Claude-Michel Schönberg. Theatre Royal, Drury Lane, London, 20 September 1989.

Miss Saigon is a modern version of the tale made famous as *Madame Butterfly* in the story by John Luther Long (1898), the play by David Belasco (5 March 1900) and the subsequent opera by Giacomo Puccini (1904), all in their turn borrowed at least in part from a Pierre Loti tale previously utilized in the lighter musical theatre in André Messager's *Madame Chrysanthème* (1893). This newest incarnation of the story followed the fashion of the 1980s for anything that allowed a little safely distanced breast-beating over the Vietnam War by resetting the once-Japanese tale in the Saigon of the 1970s. Alain Boublil's text, however, made some significant changes to the best-known version of the romantic and tragic history of Loti's and Long's oriental bride, changes which were ultimately less in storyline than in character and in motivation.

Kim (Lea Salonga) is an unenthusiastic tyro tart in a Saigon brothel run by a pimp known as the Engineer (Jonathan Pryce) when she is bought for a first night by GI Chris (Simon Bowman). During that night the two fall lickety-split in love, but the American army is being evacuated from Vietnam and Chris, although he had really intended to stay behind, is taken with it. He returns to America and weds Ellen (Claire Moore). Kim's cousin and promised husband, Thuy (Keith Burns), now powerful in the new régime, seeks her out and discovers that she has borne a son. When he tells her that this evidence of her past must be got rid of, she shoots him. From now on the girl's sole mission in life is simply to get United States citizenship for her son and, when Chris and Ellen go to 'Ho Chi Minh City' to find her, she deliberately kills herself to oblige the father to take his son home with him.

The authorial team of Schönberg and Boublil had, in their previous collaboration, taken the original French version of their *Les Misérables*, sharpened it and made it both more characterful and more theatrical for the English-language stage whilst always maintaining the strong forward-going storyline of the original. This process was missing in the case of *Miss Saigon*, which, commissioned for the English-language stage, had not been staged in the French in which Boublil had at first written it and the result was a piece much less coherent and effective than the earlier one. A curious piece of structuring had the scene of Chris's departure from Saigon, confusingly missing from its first-act place in the chronology, turning up – apparently for spectacular reasons, as it sported a particularly impressive practical helicopter – as a flashback in the middle of the second act, Kim's murder of Thuy had no apparent consequence, and the climax of the first part came on a piece of disconnected spectacle rather than on a moment of drama. In the inevitable comparison with *Madama Butterfly*, the imaginative transformation of the marriage-broker Goro into the Faginesque Engineer and the priestly Bonze into the vehement Thuy worked well, but the pushing-forward of the American wife (barely seen in the opera) served only to diffuse the principal story, and the metamorphosis of the heroine's motive for suicide from love and, above all, trust, to motherly and material ambition gave a tartly sour taste to the new piece, in contrast to the tragic romance of the earlier one. That taste was confirmed in the style of the English lyrics which were often coarse and 'realistic', particularly in the mouths of the American servicemen-characters and the Engineer, and almost never in the vein of vaguely unreal lyricism which had served so well in *Les Misérables*.

Schönberg's score to the piece which, like the pair's two previous works, was virtually sung-through, took a similar turn and, as a result, the lyrical moments, headed by the repeated 'I Still Believe' (Kim and Chris), proved to be less memorable than those of *Les Misérables*, and the main accent was placed on the incidental music and on such pieces as the Engineer's thumpingly cruel paean to 'The American Dream', played and staged in a harsh parody of Broadway, and his 'If You Want to Die in Bed' – a kind of bitter oriental version of Fagin's dilemma from *Oliver!*

Produced at London's Theatre Royal, Drury Lane (the first production of a new musical to be housed there in some 15 years), under the management of *Les Misérables* producer Cameron Mackintosh, *Miss Saigon* was received with some very fine notices, with Pryce, a former National Theatre leading actor, gaining particularly appreciative criticisms for his depiction of the pimp. It was a characterization which came over rather like a burlesque of 1960s musical-comedy star Anthony Newley then currently appearing just down the road in a revival of *Stop the World – I Want to Get Off*, but Newley was soon gone, whilst *Miss Saigon* ran on. The harshness, all and any references to politics and the almost contemporary setting also pleased the papers, and, even without its songs making any particular impression on a chart world that was now used to show-music intrusions, *Miss Saigon* was quickly established as a success.

The London production was followed by a Broadway one in which the show itself almost went unnoticed under the swathes of newspaperworthy side issues which it provoked. The one that gained the most column inches was over casting. Mackintosh proposed to bring both Pryce and Miss Salonga from the original cast to repeat their rôles in America, as he had done previously with the stars of *The Phantom of the Opéra*. However, egged on by a racist group within their ranks, Actors' Equity put a ban on the artists, claiming – in spite of the fact that their own president had been starring in a revival of *The Good Woman of Szechuan* – that it was immoral/illegal for a white actor to play a

Eurasian. Mackintosh promptly responded that he would not cast his shows on racial considerations, cancelled the production, and Equity, faced with putting their musical Asian members out of the best jobs they'd had since the last tour of *The King and I*, was forced into a shamed backdown. There were less column inches given to a more disturbing tale: allegations that the *New York Times* critic, who had been plugging the show vehemently since well before he was due to review it, had been in touch with the producers with some input to offer on the piece's construction. These allegations didn't appear until well after *Miss Saigon* had been thoroughly launched (with an excellent notice from the *Times*) and Broadway had confirmed London's opinions of the performance which had largely caused all the kerfuffle by awarding Pryce the year's Tony Award for the best Actor in a musical. The next *Saigon* story – and there never seemed to be long without one – came when the producers were accused of buying up unsold tickets in an effort to keep up what was allegedly an illusion of a sell-out success, but all the time that the incidental stories flowed wearisomely on London's and New York's *Miss Saigon* ran comfortably on, and – with Japan first off the mark – further productions began to appear in other areas eager for the latest product from the *Cats/Les Misérables/Phantom of the Opéra* production house.

A slightly earlier musical theatre version of the *Madame Butterfly* tale was produced at the Belvoir Street Theatre, Sydney (23 April 1987) under the title *Cho-Cho-San* (Dalmazio Babare, Boris Conley/Daniel Keene). A small-cast piece featuring mime and puppets, it was praised as 'visually splendid, musically exciting and ... innovative' but apparently went no furher.

USA: Broadway Theater 11 April 1991
Recording: original cast (Geffen)
Literature: Behr, E, Steyn, M: *The Story of Miss Saigon* (Jonathan Cape, London, 1991)

MITCHELL, Julian (b 1854; d Long Branch, NJ, 24 June 1926). Ubiquitous director and choreographer of all types of musical plays through more than three Broadway decades.

A nephew of star actress Maggie Mitchell, Julian Mitchell got some of his earliest opportunities thanks to his aunt's fame. Originally a dancer and actor, he made his first steps as a director and choreographer in his early twenties and, from 1884, he doubled as an actor and stage director/choreographer for Charles Hoyt. As such, he directed the productions of such of Hoyt's musical shows as *The Maid and the Moonshiner* (1886), the long-running *A Trip to Chinatown* (1891) and *A Black Sheep* (1896). He subsequently became stage director at Weber and Fields' Music Hall where, between 1897 and 1902, he staged such revusical spectacles as *Poussé Café*, *Hurly-Burly*, *Helter Skelter*, *Whirl-I-Gig*, *Fiddle-dee-dee*, *Hoity-Toity* and *Twirly-Whirly* and their burlesque inserts. In between times, he also directed legitimate comic opera for Alice Nielsen (*The Fortune Teller*, *The Singing Girl*), less legitimate comic opera (*The Idol's Eye* with Frank Daniels, *The Princess Chic*) and Casino Theater musical comedy (*The Girl from Up There*, Ziegfeld's *Papa's Wife*).

Mitchell put an end to his career on the boards after a tour of Australia with Hoyt's *A Milk White Flag* and *A Trip to Chinatown* (1900) and thereafter he devoted himself wholly to directing, choreographing and, briefly, producing for another 25 years. He scored an enormous success with his direction of the Fred Hamlin extravaganza *The Wizard of Oz* (1903) and it was on the heels of this success that he joined Hamlin to produce that show's follow-up, *Babes in Toyland* (1903). He then paired with Lew Fields to sponsor Victor Herbert's subsequent *It Happened in Nordland*, before going it alone as producer of the less successful *Wonderland*. Its comparative failure convinced him to stick to directing.

Mitchell staged the revusical *About Town* and the imported musical comedy *The Girl Behind the Counter* for Fields, choreographed *The Red Mill* with *Wizard of Oz* stars Montgomery and Stone, and then rejoined Florenz Ziegfeld to direct Anna Held in *A Parisian Model*. Thereafter he directed Ziegfeld's *Follies* between 1907 and 1914 (making a brief return to the stage in the 1910 version), as well as such of his musicals as *Miss Innocence* (1908), the unsuccessful *A Winsome Widow* and the Adeline Genée vehicle *The Soul Kiss* (w Herbert Gresham) for which the ballerina, however, supplied her own choreographer. In a kaleidoscope of shows which ranged from one end of the musical theatre scale to the other, he acted as director for the Ivan Caryll musicals *The Pink Lady* and *Papa's Darling* and choreographed (and/or co-directed) the same composer's *The Girl Behind the Gun* and *Little Miss Raffles*, choreographed the American versions of the Continental Operetten *Die Kino-Königin*, *Eva*, *Der Graf von Luxemburg* and *Zsuzsi kisasszony* (although he did not direct a Viennese import until *The Yankee Princess* in 1922) and directed Hirsch's *The Rainbow Girl*, Herbert's *The Velvet Lady* and George M Cohan's productions of the comic-opera burlesque *The Royal Vagabond* (1919), *Mary* (1920, w Sam Forrest), *The O'Brien Girl* (1921, w John Meehan), *Little Nellie Kelly* (1922) and *The Rise of Rosie O'Reilly* (1923).

Other directing and/or choreographing credits (the two were sometimes credited jointly with a collaborator without being more specific) included *Forward March* (1914), *Some Night* (1918), *The Kiss Burglar* (1918), Ed Wynn's *The Perfect Fool* (1921), the black shows *In Bamville* (1923) and *The Chocolate Dandies* (1924), *Daffy Dill* and *Molly Darling* as well as the out-of-town flop *Lola in Love* (1922). Mitchell had his final Broadway assignment at the age of 71 when, as an 'old reliable', he was brought in to replace Julian Alfred as the choreographer on *Sunny*, providing the dances for star hoofer Marilyn Miller.

One of the most important dance stagers of his day, Mitchell, along with such contemporaries as Edward Royce (jr), set the tone for the musical theatre dance of the early years of the 20th century. It was not complex or highly technical choreography, nor did it rely on the drilling or the novelty dancing which would later become popular, but it did require some talent and teaching, and there was no place in Mitchell's shows for the old-time 'walker' who filled the rows of the chorus simply to show off her figure. Whether for chorus or for principals, his dances were almost always energetic on the one hand or graceful on the other, with plenty of room kept for the comical, as so often used in his earliest work with Hoyt and as featured in his days with a Cohan who was quite capable of staging his own dances if he wished.

As a director, he naturally leaned towards the choreographer-director's eternal penchant for favouring the visual over the textual but, once again, early experiences in the Hoyt pieces, where comedy was nearly all, meant that he was able to stage such finely constructed comic pieces as *The Pink Lady* when occasionally called upon to do so. By and large, however, his directing assignments were on less tightly book-orientated pieces, and his principal groups of works were all in the loose-limbed area: the Hoyt shows, the Weber and Fields burlesques, the Ziegfeld revues and revusical musical comedies and his latter-day works for Cohan.

Mitchell was married to leggy dancer Bessie Clayton who played in *A Trip to Chinatown*, *A Black Sheep* and other Hoyt shows, then at Weber and Fields' (*Helter Skelter*, *Fiddle-dee-dee*, *Hoity-Toity* right up to the final *Roly Poly*), and in such musical comedies as *The Belle of Mayfair* (1906, Pincott) and the *Merry Widow Burlesque* (1908).

MITISLAW DER MODERNE Operette in 1 act by Robert Bodanzky and Fritz Grünbaum. Music by Franz Lehár. Hölle, Vienna, 5 January 1907.

One of the few short Operetten composed by Franz Lehár, *Mitislaw der moderne*, produced whilst Vienna was still in the throes of *Die lustige Witwe*, was a little bit of an in-joke. The character of Mitislaw, the prince whose mama always told him to be 'modern', was a burlesque on the Danilo of the more famous show, and he arrived on the scene – in the person of no less than the original Danilo, Louis Treumann – accompanied by no less an escort than Lolo, Dodo, Joujou, Cloclo, Margot and Froufrou, the ladies from Maxims. In a little plot which hinged on virtue and the undoing of it, Mitislaw shared the limelight and the nine numbers which made up the show's musical part, with two leading ladies, Tina and Amaranthe, the professedly feeble Graf Jerzabinka, and the girls. Treumann delivered an entrance number ('Man sagte mir') with his girls, and a Marschlied ('Ich schaff mir einen Musterstaat') about being modern, and Amaranthe a mazurka and a minuet-cum-waltz.

First staged at the Theater an der Wien's little Hölle studio theatre, the piece proved to the liking not only of Vienna, but to the rest of the world. It was given in a proper theatre in Hungary, six months after the opening of *Die lustige Witwe*, but elsewhere it found itself a home in variety theatres – Berlin's Apollotheater, London's Hippodrome with Maurice Farkoa in the rôle of Mitislaw etc.

Hungary: Király Színház *Micislav* 3 April 1907; Germany: Apollotheater 1 February 1908; UK: Hippodrome *Mitislaw, or the Love Match* November 1909

MLLE MODISTE Comic opera in 2 acts by Henry Blossom. Music by Victor Herbert. Knickerbocker Theater, New York, 25 December 1905.

Operatic vocalist Fritzi Scheff had been taken from the Metropolitan Opera and introduced to the musical stage whilst only in her earliest twenties, first of all starring in Victor Herbert's comic opera *Babette*. Neither that nor the *She Stoops to Conquer* musical *The Two Roses* brought her the kind of success that the other operatic refugee of the time, Emma Trentini, found with *Naughty Marietta* and *The Firefly*, but Herbert's second piece for the little prima donna ran these hits close, and *Mlle Modiste* turned out to be easily the best of the six new Broadway (and some pre-Broadway) musicals in which the star featured during her career.

Henry Blossom's libretto introduced Miss Scheff as Fifi, an industrious little milliner who is beloved by aristocratic Étienne (Walter Percival) – to the fury of his father (William Pruette) – and coveted by her employer Madame Cécile (Josephine Bartlett) as a useful wife for her fairly useless son Gaston (Leo Mars). A gift from a kindly American gentleman (Claude Gillingwater) who likes giving pretty girls gifts allows Fifi to quit millinery, and she goes off and becomes a singing star instead. When she returns to sing at a bazaar on the old Count's property she is so clever and so charming that he is wholly happy to hand over the son he had once forbidden her company.

Herbert's score gave Miss Scheff some splendid opportunities, from the *Fledermaus*-ish audition scene 'If I Were on the Stage' with its extension waltz (taken from Herbert's bottom drawer) 'Kiss Me Again', to the show-piece 'The Nightingale and the Star' and the jaunty 'The Mascot of the Troop', whilst both Percival, with the delightful solo 'The Time, the Place and the Girl' and, above all, Pruette with his basso march-song 'I Want What I Want When I Want It', had hit material in their rôles as well.

Charles Dillingham's production of *Mlle Modiste* had a very fine run of 202 performances on Broadway before going to the country for three years of touring. Miss Scheff returned to New York in her best vehicle on a number of occasions, both during that time – in 1906 (Knickerbocker Theater, 1 September) and 1907 (Academy of Music 20 May, Knickerbocker Theater, 9 September) – after (Globe Theater 26 May 1913), and one final time, almost a quarter of a century after the first (Jolson Theater 7 October 1929). However, in spite of the piece's popularity throughout America, no Broadway productions were played without the original star, and *Mlle Modiste* did not, apparently, travel into first-class productions outside the United States.

A film based on *Mlle Modiste* and using the title of its favourite song, 'Kiss Me Again', was produced in 1931. Bernice Claire appeared as Fifi alongside Walter Pidgeon as Paul St Cyr, Edward Everett Horton as René and original cast member Claude Gillingwater. The action was set in part in glamorous Algiers.

Film: *Kiss Me Again* (1931)
Recording: selections (part-record Reader's Digest, RCA)

THE MOCKING BIRD Musical play in 3 acts by Sydney Rosenfeld. Music by A Baldwin Sloane. Bijou Theater, New York, 10 November 1902.

The Mocking Bird's record of 64 New York performances and a brief return season at the same house in the following year (May 1903) was scarcely that of a hit, but the piece, written by two men often dismissed as hacks, contained some work that was very much better than a lot of the imported material which Broadway audiences were gobbling up eagerly in the turn-of-the-century years.

Rosenfeld's book prefigured *Naughty Marietta* and *A New Moon* with its tale of 18th-century romance and swashbuckling in New Orleans. Mabelle Gilman was Yvette Millet, the ward of the wealthy and importunate Maxime Grandpré (Robert Rogers), Frank Doane was Jean Villiers, otherwise 'a gentlemanly pirate' called Jean Le Farge, and the plot was carried through some wholesome colonial rebellion (pro-France and anti-Spain) to a happy ending in which the heroine frees the heroic pirate

Plate 185.

and wins herself the Governor's tenor secretary (Sydney Deane) for a final duet.

Sloane wove into his score the old minstrel song 'Listen to the Mocking Bird', used by the pirate band as their rallying call and by the composer as a delightful concerted finale to the second act, and came together with Rosenfeld on a kind of New Orleans coon song, 'What's the Matter With the Moon Tonight' which, both in its irresistible melody and charmingly picturesque words, flew well above its authors' reputations. The rest of the score, ranging from a marching salute to 'France, Glorious France', to the waltzing love duet 'Just a Kiss', the saucy tale of 'Musette, Coquette' and the tenor parlour ballad 'In Silence' was a touch more conventional than the two top numbers, but as good as anything else of its kind and period. Yet Broadway rejected *The Mocking Bird* and, in the same season, Julian Edwardes's costume Civil War musical *When Johnny Comes Marching Home*, whilst showing favour to the British fantasy *The Silver Slipper*, the vigorous fun of *The Sultan of Sulu*, the combination of both with large amounts of spectacle in *The Wizard of Oz*, and the tuneful mixture of Ruritania and Dutch comedy in *The Prince of Pilsen*. The costume comic opera with a recognizable American setting had not yet found its day.

DAS MODELL Operette in 3 acts by Victor Léon and Ludwig Held. Music by Franz von Suppé. Carltheater, Vienna, 4 October 1895.

The little washergirl Coletta (Julie Kopácsi-Karczag) will not act as a model for the painter Tantini (Willi Bauer) any more, for she is being true to her promised Niccolo

(Julius Spielmann), the peddler. But Niccolo finds a letter which has been dropped by Riccardo (Grinzenberger) the prospective husband of the lovely Stella (Betty Stojan), and he decides to return it to Stella's mother, Silvia (Adolphine Ziemaier), for whom he has a deep – and, for Coletta's taste, too deeply expressed – admiration. He turns up with the paper at a party where the piqued Coletta has agreed to pose in Tantini's living pictures, is mistaken for Riccardo and then, when the truth is discovered, ridiculed by all. Niccolo plots revenge on Tantini and on Silvia's husband Stirio (Karl Blasel), but he is finally soothed by a job in the latter's salami factory and the hand of the repentant Coletta.

Suppé's last major Operette, completed by Julius Stern and Alfred Zamara, *Das Modell* was produced by Blasel at the Carltheater, where it was played for seven straight weeks and thereafter remained in the repertoire for six years under the management of Blasel and then under Jauner, with Betty Stojan playing her original rôle. It was also one of the earliest pieces brought into the repertoire at the new Johann Strauss-Theater (1908) where it was given occasional performances up to 1912. It won a certain popularity in Germany, and, similarly, played a respectable 29 times at Budapest's Népszinház (ad György Ruttkay, Emil Makai).

Another Operette of the same title with text by Kallenberg and music by Moritz (father of Leo) Fall was produced at Berlin's Theater Unter den Linden just shortly before Suppé's work appeared in Vienna (December 1892).

Germany: Carl-Schultze Theater, Hamburg 21 March 1896; Hungary: Népszinház *A Modell* 1 February 1901

DIE MODERNE EVA Operette in 3 acts by Georg Okonkowski and Alfred Schönfeld, based on *Place aux femmes!* by Maurice Hennequin and Albin Valabrègue. Music by Jean Gilbert. Neues Operetten-Theater, Berlin, 18 October 1911.

The modern ladies of the title of Okonkowski and Schönfeld's text are Niniche Cascadier, Doctor of Law (Poldi Augustin), and her daughters Renée, a painter (Mizzi Wirth), and Camille, a doctor (Lisa Weise). When Renée weds the rich young Pontgirard (Karl Pfann) her husband finds that her professional interests leave her insufficient time for him and he soon begins to play around, taking the pseudonym of Count Castel-Bajour for the purpose. His long-subdued father-in-law takes to the idea too, and he adopts the same pseudonym for his adventures until, inevitably, there is a double-whammy backlash. Niniche's law firm takes both an action against the mysterious Castel-Bajour and then Renée's divorce case to court, and it takes a few twists and turns before a happy marital ending is arrived at. Camille's partner is the young lawyer Cibolet (Karl Bachmann).

Gilbert's score was topped by Renée's duo with her husband claiming 'Ich bin eine moderne Frau' and the dance duo 'Liebchen, lass uns tanzen'.

Coming after it's composer's *Polnische Wirtschaft* and *Die keusche Susanne* and before his *Autoliebchen* and *Puppchen* – all premièred in the space of three years and all very big hits – the slightly less appealing *Die moderne Eva* slipped a little from view after its original and well-received Berlin showing. Gilbert's own company took it on tour and it won

several foreign productions, but comparatively little total exposure. Even Britain and George Edwardes, who leaped for Gilbert works until the First World War came, for some reason didn't take this one on. In Vienna it was produced by Karczag in a Viennesed version by E Rudy at the Raimundtheater, with Therese Tautenhayn as the renamed Sybilla, Rosa Mittermardi and Paula Zulka as the daughters, Franz Glawatsch as father and Robert Nästlberger as the philandering son-in-law. Gilbert billed himself under his Germanic wartime name as 'Hans Winterfeld' (but with Jean Gilbert still in brackets, just to be sure) and the show lasted one week.

America's Midwest however, showed a distinct taste for Okonkowski's up-to-date ladies. Mort Singer introduced an American version of the show (ad Will M Hough) in Chicago in 1912 with great success, winning a run of over 200 performances at the Princess Theater, but without encouraging anyone to take the piece east. It was three years before John Cort picked up the rights and took a version of that version, now with most of Gilbert's score replaced by tunes by Viktor Holländer and also a couple by Jerome Kern, to New York. Produced at the Casino Theater with Leila Hughes (Renée), Georgie Drew Mendum (Niniche) and William Norris (Cascadier) in the lead rôles, it played 56 performances.

Britain had its *A Modern Eve*, in fact, but it was a different musical. Ada Reeve reproduced her *Winnie Brooke, Widow* in 1916 and put it out under Okonkowski's title.

Austria: Raimundtheater 14 November 1914; USA: Garrick Theater, Chicago 21 April 1912, Casino Theater *A Modern Eve* 3 May 1915

MOINAUX, Jules [MOINEAUX, Joseph Désiré] (b Tours, 29 October 1815; d Saint-Mandé, 4 December 1895).

A stenographer at the Paris law courts, Moinaux wrote comic pieces for Parisian magazines before venturing into the theatre. He was the partner of Offenbach on a number of his earliest short pieces, including the landmark *Les Deux Aveugles*, and later moved on to write several important full-scale musicals – the early musical comedy *Le Voyage de MM Dunanan père et fils* and the opéra-bouffe *Les Géorgiennes* with Offenbach, and the enjoyably ridiculous and long-popular *Le Canard à trois becs* with Émile Jonas.

Moinaux's *Le Ver rongeur* (Théâtre des Variétés 30 March 1870, w Henri Bocage, P Bocage) was used as the basis for the Singspiel *Ein nagender Wurm* (*Wechselbrief und Briefwechsel*) by Josef Weyl and Carl Millöcker, produced at the Theater an der Wien, 15 July 1872.

His son, under the nom de plume Georges Courteline, became one of the French theatre's most famous comic playwrights.

1853 **Pépito** (Jacques Offenbach/w Léon Battu) 1 act Salle Herz 27 February; Théâtre des Variétés 28 October

1855 **Oyayaie, ou la reine des îles** (Offenbach) 1 act Théâtre des Folies-Nouvelles 26 June

1855 **Les Deux Aveugles** (Offenbach) 1 act Théâtre des Bouffes-Parisiens 5 July

1855 **Deux sous de charbon** (Léo Delibes) 1 act Théâtre des Folies-Nouvelles 9 February

1857 **La Demoiselle de la Hoche-Trombelon** (Laurent de Rillé) 1 act Théâtre des Folies-Nouvelles 20 October

1858 **Les Désespérés** (François Bazin/w Adolphe deLeuven) 1 act Opéra-Comique 26 January

1862 **Le Voyage de MM Dunanan père et fils** (Offenbach/w Paul Siraudin) Théâtre des Bouffes-Parisiens 23 March

1864 **Les Géorgiennes** (Offenbach) Théâtre des Bouffes-Parisiens 16 March

1864 **Le Joueur de flûte** (Hervé) 1 act Théâtre des Variétés 16 April

1869 **Le Canard à trois becs** (Émile Jonas) Théâtre des Folies-Dramatiques 6 February

1869 **L'Astronome du Pont-Neuf** (Émile Durand) 1 act Théâtre des Variétés 18 February

1871 **Le Testament de M Crac** (Charles Lecocq) 1 act Théâtre des Bouffes-Parisiens 23 October

1872 **L'Alibi** (Adolphe Nibelle) Théâtre de l'Athénée 10 October

1874 **Les Parisiennes** (Léon Vasseur/w Victor Koning) Théâtre des Bouffes-Parisiens 31 March

1875 **La Cruche cassée** (Vasseur/w Jules Noriac) Théâtre Taitbout 27 October

1877 **La Sorrentine** (Vasseur/w Noriac) Théâtre des Bouffes-Parisiens 24 March

MOINEAU Opérette in 3 acts by Henri Duvernois and Pierre Wolff based on their play *La Noce*. Lyrics by Guillot de Saix. Music by Louis Beydts. Théâtre Marigny, Paris, 13 March 1931.

The most successful work of the composer Beydts, a pupil and disciple of Messager, *Moineau* was a Parisian period piece which strove to be in the manner of Messager's *Véronique* to the extent of setting its second act in the same Restaurant du Tourne-bride at Romainville which was featured in the middle act of the earlier piece, and even to plugging the older composer's name in its lyrics.

A Montmartre layabout, Gaston Gilbert (Robert Burnier), makes it a rule to change his mistress each three months and in Act I he swaps Léontine (Nilda Duplessy) for little Moineau (Marcelle Denya), who makes wedding crowns for a living. His friends Chadec (Serjius) and Mme Froumentel (Nina Myral), thus cued, suggest an imitation wedding for the new lovers, and off they go to Romainville to celebrate. Moineau is a little sad that it is not for real, but when the three months are up Gaston finally finds that he cannot let her go, so there is a happy ending after all.

Beydts's score was in the Messager mode, with reminiscences of the more famous composer arising frequently, and with some attractive songs for Gaston ('Chaque souvenir d'amour'), Moineau ('De tous les voyages de noces') and the lively Madame Froumentel ('Ce petit coquin de printemps') set alongside some well-built concerted music and finales.

Produced by Léon Volterra at the Théâtre Marigny, the piece ran for a set season, but in spite of the appeal that it had for those who liked their opérette made in the soigné if not precisely popular mode, it was not brought back.

MOLLISON, Clifford (b London, 1897; d Cyprus, 5 June 1986). Light-comedy leading man of the West End interwar stage.

After 15 years working in the straight theatre, Mollison made his first West End musical appearance as Adolar in Lehár's *The Blue Mazurka* (1927). Thereafter he played light comedy leads in many British stage and screen musicals including *The Girl Friend* (1928, Richard Dennison), *Lucky Girl* (1929, King Stephan), *Here Comes the Bride* (1930, Frederick Tile) and *Nippy* (1931, Bob Deering) opposite Binnie Hale. He played the rôle of Leopold in the British *White Horse Inn* (1931) in which he introduced Harry Graham's English version of Robert Stolz's added song 'Goodbye', and during the 1930s featured in *Out of the Bottle* (1932, Peter Partridge), *The Gay Deceivers* (*Toi c'est moi*, 1935, Pat Russell), *Twenty to One* (1935, Timothy), *No, No, Nanette* (1936 rev, Billy Early) and *Balalaika* (1936, Nicki). On the screen he appeared in, amongst others, Bobby Howes's rôle of Jim in *Mr Cinders*.

After five years in the wartime army Mollison returned to the theatre and appeared in the Offenbach pasticcio *Can-Can* (1946, Paul Latour) but thereafter he appeared largely in non-musical pieces. He returned to musical comedy in his sixties to play in *A Funny Thing Happened on the Way to the Forum* in Australia and Britain.

MOLLISON, William (b London, 24 December 1893; d London, 19 October 1955). British director of a quarter of a century of interwars musicals.

After an early career as an actor and service during the First World War, Mollison spent a period in South Africa and Australia doubling as a jobbing actor and director. Jack Waller and Herbert Clayton hired him to direct the London production of *No, No, Nanette* (1925, also Paris 1926), and thus set in motion his long career as a director of London musical plays. The list of his credits in the later 1920s included *Mercenary Mary* (1925), *Princess Charming* (1926), *The Girl Friend, Hit the Deck* (1927), *Good News, Virginia* (1928), *Merry, Merry, Hold Everything!, Dear Love* (1929), *Silver Wings, Sons o' Guns* and *Little Tommy Tucker* (1930). He staged *Meet My Sister* for the Shuberts and Al Jolson's *Wonder Bar* on Broadway at the turn of the decade before returning to London for *The Cat and the Fiddle, Tell Her the Truth* (1932), *Jolly Roger, He Wanted Adventure, Give Me a Ring, Command Performance* (1933), *Lucky Break, Jill Darling* (1934), *Gay Deceivers, Seeing Stars* (1935), *Going Places* (1936), *The Laughing Cavalier* (1937), *Bobby Get Your Gun* (1938) and *Magyar Melody* (1939). He mounted wartime touring revivals of *No, No, Nanette, The Duchess of Dantzic* and *The Merry Widow* (1943), *Panama Hattie* (1943), reprises of *Irene* and *Merrie England* (1945), the pasticcio *Can-Can* (1946), *The Kid from Stratford* (1948) and in 1950 his last new musical, the touring *Caprice* for the same Jack Waller who had launched his London career 25 years earlier.

One of the most important and efficient musical theatre directors in Britain between the wars, both with American musical comedies and with the new British pieces built around such comedy stars as Bobby Howes, George Robey, Flanagan and Allen and Leslie Henson, Mollison was increasingly bedevilled in his later days by persistent drunkenness and such postwar work as he found was largely for the faithful Waller.

MOLNÁR, Ferenc (b Budapest, 12 January 1878; d New York, 1 April 1952). Internationally successful Hungarian playwright whose career touched on the musical stage at each of its ends.

Playwright (from 1902), dramatic translator and adapter, novelist, short-story writer and a war correspondent in the First World War, Molnár pursued an eclectic and all-embracing career through the years of his greatest early successes with the plays *Az Ördög* (the devil, 1907), *Liliom, egy csirkefogó élete és halála* (Liliom, the life and death of a

1003

lout, 1909) and *Az testőr* (the guardsman, 1910). In his earliest years as a writer, he produced a flood of translations and adaptations of the plays of such authors as Maurice Hennequin, Georges Duval, de Flers and de Caillavet, Paul Gavault, Georges Berr and Jerome K Jerome for the Király Színház and the Magyar Színház, a list which included Hungarian versions of both French and German musical works as well as such musicalized French comedies as *Kati bácsi* (*Le Sursis*) and *Gyöngyélet* (*Tire-au-flanc!*).

His *The Phantom Lover* (*A farkas*, 1912) was used as the source for fellow Hungarian Victor Jacobi's 1921 Broadway musical *Love Letters*, but it was many years later, after Molnár had gone to live in America, before he had his next contact with the musical stage when others of his plays became the bases for musical shows. If Billy Rose's commission to Rodgers and Hart to make a musical from his *The Play's the Thing* (*Színház*) was aborted when the work was only half complete, Rodgers more than compensated with his collaboration with Hammerstein on *Carousel* (1945), based on Molnár's *Liliom*. *Make a Wish* (Hugh Martin/Preston Sturges, Winter Garden Theater, New York 18 April 1951) was based on his 1930 play *A jo tündér* (the good fairy), his 1929 one-act play *Egy, kettő, három* became the basis for a German musical *Eins, zwei, drei* (Theater des Westens, 12 November 1989 Birger Heyman/Volker Kühn/Helmaut Baumann) which dealt with the 1960s, and the outline of *Az testőr* was used as the book for the film version of *The Chocolate Soldier* after G B Shaw had effectively prevented the use of *Arms and the Man*.

Between 1922 and 1925 Molnár was the husband of the Hungarian musical-theatre star Sári Fedák from whom he was divorced with much noise and filling of newspaper front pages and a considerable and uncontested out-of-court settlement, made when Fedák threatened to 'tell the whole truth', whatever that might have been, before the Budapest divorce judge.

1900 **Veronka** (*Véronique*) Hungarian version (Magyar Színház)
1900 **Felfordult világ** (*Le Royaume des femmes*) Hungarian version w Emil Makai (Fővárosi Nyari Színház)
1901 **Az ikrek** (*Les Soeurs Gaudichard*) Hungarian version (Magyar Színház)
1901 **Korhelykirály** (*Le Roi frelon*) Hungarian version w Makai (Fővárosi Nyari Színház)
1903 **Lysistrata** Hungarian version (Király Színház)
1905 **Kati bácsi** (*Le Sursis*) Hungarian version w songs Király Színház 20 January
1906 **Gyöngyélet** (*Tire-au-flanc!*) Hungarian version w songs by Adolf Mérei, Ferenc Békési Magyar Színház 21 April
1911 **A ferencvárosi angyal** (Alfred Szirmai/w Jenő Heltai) Royal Orfeum 31 December
1912 **Ábraham a menyországban** (*Casimirs Himmelfahrt*) Hungarian version w Heltai (Fővárosi Nyari Színház)
1924 **Mikádó** (*The Mikado*) new Hungarian version (Varósi Színház)

Autobiography: *Companion in Exile: Notes for an Autobiography* (Gaer, New York, 1950)

MONCKTON, [John] Lionel [Alexander] (b London, 18 December 1861; d London, 15 September 1924). Composer for the heyday of the Gaiety and Daly's Theatres musicals.

The son of London's town clerk, Sir John Monckton, and of Lady Monckton, an enthusiastic amateur actress, Lionel Monckton was educated at Charterhouse and at Oxford University where he took part in theatricals and composed music for the dramatic society's productions. He began his working life in the legal profession, but worked on the side as a theatre and music critic on the *Pall Mall Gazette* and, subsequently, the *Daily Telegraph*, and all the time continued to write songs. He was 30 years old before he placed his first number in a professional musical show when George Edwardes put his 'What Will You Have to Drink?', with a lyric by no less a collaborator than Basil Hood, into the burlesque *Cinder-Ellen Up-too-Late* (1891) where it was sung by Edwin Lonnen. Monckton subsequently supplied interpolations for Edwardes's *Don Juan* (1893, 'Some Do It This Way' w Horace Lennard), contributed to the hotch-potch collection of songs which illustrated *King Kodak* (1894, 'We've Faith in the Old Flag Still' etc) and wrote half of the music for Arthur Roberts's burlesque *Claude Du-Val* (1894) before supplementing Ivan Caryll's score for the Gaiety Theatre's *The Shop Girl* (1894) with such successful pieces as George Grossmith's 'Beautiful Bountiful Bertie' and 'Brown of Colorado' (w Adrian Ross).

The association with Edwardes and Caryll (later as co-composers rather than Monckton being 'additional music by') begun on *The Shop Girl* was to continue for 15 years – 15 years in which the Gaiety Theatre was the world's centre of musical comedy and Caryll and Monckton's songs for *The Circus Girl* ('A Simple Little String', 'The Way to Treat a Lady'), *A Runaway Girl* ('Soldiers in the Park', 'Society', 'The Sly Cigarette', 'The Boy Guessed Right' also lyric, 'Not the Sort of Girl I Care About'), *The Messenger Boy* ('Maisie', 'In the Wash', 'When the Boys Come Home Once More' also lyrics as 'Leslie Mayne'), *The Toreador* ('Captivating Cora', 'I'm Romantic', 'When I Marry Amelia', 'Keep Off the Grass', 'Archie'), *The Orchid* ('Liza Ann', 'Little Mary', 'Pushful', 'Fancy Dress'), *The Spring Chicken* ('I Don't Know, But I Guess', 'Alice Sat By the Fire', 'Under and Over Forty'), *A New Aladdin*, *The Girls of Gottenberg* ('Two Little Sausages' also lyric, 'Rheingold', 'Berlin on the Spree') and *Our Miss Gibbs* ('Moonstruck', 'Mary', 'In Yorkshire', 'Our Farm') were amongst the most widely played and sung numbers of the contemporary light musical theatre.

Although, during this period, Monckton occasionally supplied single or multiple numbers for several other producers and shows (*L'Auberge du Tohu-bohu*, *The Scarlet Feather*, *A Modern Don Quixote*, *Biarritz* etc), his principal activity outside the Gaiety Theatre was in a similar capacity at Edwardes's other important musical house, Daly's Theatre, where the producer offered a more substantial, romantic-comic-opera kind of musical play than was presented at the Gaiety. At Daly's, rather than supplementing the work of Caryll, he operated in support of the other outstanding theatre composer of the contemporary London scene, Sidney Jones. They came together first on the score for Jones's greatest hit *The Geisha* (1896) for which Monckton provided the jaunty 'Jack's the Boy' and Letty Lind's 'pop' hit 'The Toy Monkey' alongside Jones's beautiful romantic numbers, more traditional comedy songs, finales and ensembles. The mixture was repeated in *The Geisha*'s successor, *A Greek Slave* (1898, 'I Want to Be Popular', 'I Should Rather Like to Try', 'What Will Be the End of It?')

and, with an equivalent international success, in *San Toy* ('Rhoda and Her Pagoda', 'Sons of the Motherland').

Edwardes put Monckton to work on one musical without Caryll or Jones, but still as an adept of the additional number, in the delightful *Kitty Grey* (1900/1, 'Little Zo-Zo', 'Kitty Grey') but it was not until 1902 that the composer was given his first opportunity to write a full score himself. A little surprisingly, perhaps, this was not at the Gaiety, for which his lively and exceptionally catchy melodies seemed the best suited, and where he had for so long supplied his wife, the Gaiety's brightest star Gertie Millar, with her material, but for Daly's Theatre. With lyricist Harry Greenbank dead and composer Jones deployed elsewhere, Monckton teamed with librettist James Tanner, more connected to date with the Gaiety, and with ubiquitous lyricist Adrian Ross to produce *A Country Girl*.

The piece proved an enormous success, launched several hit songs ('Molly the Marchioness', 'Try Again, Johnny', 'Under the Deodar') both by Monckton and by Paul Rubens who now filled the 'additional songs by' line on the credits, and led to another Daly's musical from the same team, *The Cingalee*. However, *The Cingalee*, although successful, persuaded Edwardes to change his style at Daly's and, as Messager's *Les P'tites Michu*, Hugo Felix's *Les Merveilleuses* and ultimately *The Merry Widow* took over that stage, Monckton found, for the moment, no further outlet for his newly discovered vocation as principal composer. He had to content himself with working on more additional material – *The Girl from Kays* ('Papa'), *Les Merveilleuses* ('Publicity', 'A Lady With a Dowry', 'It's Only a Matter of Time') – and part-scores, including more special material for his wife at the Gaiety. Then Edwardes decided to make a change at the Gaiety as well. He signed up Leslie Stuart, composer of *Florodora* and the 1908 Gaiety show *Havana*, as lead composer for the Gaiety musical to follow Caryll and Monckton's *Our Miss Gibbs*, and redirected Monckton down to the Adelphi Theatre, recently added to his chain of musical houses.

In the meanwhile, Monckton had found other collaborators. Before his first Adelphi show was seen, Robert Courtneidge had produced the first Lionel Monckton musical for many years not to have been mounted under the Edwardes banner. *The Arcadians* (1909), co-composed with his *Kitty Grey* colleague, Howard Talbot, was also the best musical of the whole Edwardian age – arguably the best musical of the whole Edwardian age – and it scored an enormous worldwide success. Monckton's 'The Pipes of Pan', 'The Girl with the Brogue' and 'All Down Piccadilly' became, in the age where the fashion was for 'anything one sees that's Viennese' as big hits as any of his previous show songs. When Edwardes produced Monckton's first Adelphi musical, *The Quaker Girl* ('The Quaker Girl', 'Come to the Ball', 'Tony from America') with Miss Millar, who had followed her husband away from the Gaiety, starring in its title-rôle, the composer – approaching 50, and with nearly two decades of almost unbroken success in the musical theatre behind him – found himself basking in his most outstandingly successful period of all.

However, it was a peak period which was not enduring. Monckton next combined with Talbot again on some enchanting music for another musical, *The Mousmé*

('I Know Nothing of Life', 'The Little Japanese Mamma', 'The Temple Bell', 'The Corner of My Eye'), for Courtneidge, and repeated for the Adelphi, Edwardes and Miss Millar with *The Dancing Mistress*. Both pieces had respectable rather than outstanding runs, before the composer took part in one last huge success – the musical-comedy version of Pinero's *The Magistrate*, *The Boy* ('I Want to Go to Bye-Bye', 'The Game That Ends with a Kiss', 'Powder on Your Nose') produced at the Adelphi by Alfred Butt during the war and after Edwardes's death. And then, having tried his hand, not unsuccessfully, at the newfangled revue in partnership with Herman Finck and others (*Bric à Brac*, *We're All in It*, *Airs and Graces*) he withdrew from the world of the musical theatre. Unable and unwilling to adapt his style of writing to the newly popular dance rhythms and 'noisy numbers' which were invading the theatre, he simply stopped writing.

Monckton showed, through a quarter of a century of shows and songs, that, perhaps more than any other British songwriter of the great period of Gaiety and Daly's musical comedy, he had the ability to produce individual musical-comedy songs which stood out as hit singles in scores by the most appreciable composers of the time. But he also subsequently showed, in *A Country Girl* and *The Quaker Girl*, that he was capable of composing a complete, or quasi-complete score for a show with equal felicity and equal popular success, and even of venturing occasionally into writing the concerted and ensemble music which had previously been largely the domain of his colleagues (though Monckton's arrangements and orchestrations were inevitably left to the useful Carl Kiefert). His contribution to the English-speaking musical theatre was vast, and his individual songs, from 'Soldiers in the Park', 'Jack's the Boy' and 'Try Again, Johnny' to 'Moonstruck', 'Come to the Ball' and 'The Girl with the Brogue', lasted as favourites for many decades

1894 **Claude Du-Val** (Blend 1664–1894) (w John Crook/ Frederick Bowyer, 'Payne Nunn' (Arthur Roberts)) Prince of Wales Theatre 25 September

1896 **The Circus Girl** (w Ivan Caryll/Adrian Ross, Harry Greenbank/James T Tanner, Walter Pallant) Gaiety Theatre 5 December

1898 **A Runaway Girl** (w Caryll/Aubrey Hopwood, H Greenbank/Seymour Hicks, Harry Nicholls) Gaiety Theatre 21 May

1900 **The Messenger Boy** (w Caryll/Ross, Percy Greenbank/ Tanner, Alfred Murray) Gaiety Theatre 3 February

1901 **The Toreador** (w Caryll, Paul Rubens/Ross, P Greenbank/Tanner, Nicholls) Gaiety Theatre 17 June

1901 **Kitty Grey** (w Howard Talbot, Augustus Barratt, Rubens/Ross, Rubens/J Smyth Piggott) Apollo Theatre 7 September

1902 **A Country Girl** (Ross, P Greenbank/Tanner) Daly's Theatre 18 January

1903 **The Orchid** (w Caryll/Ross, P Greenbank/Tanner) Gaiety Theatre 26 October

1904 **The Cingalee** (Ross, P Greenbank/Tanner) Daly's Theatre 14 May

1905 **The Spring Chicken** (w Caryll/Ross, P Greenbank/ George Grossmith jr) Gaiety Theatre 30 May

1906 **A New Aladdin** (w Caryll, Frank E Tours/Ross, P Greenbank, Grossmith, W H Risque/Tanner, Risque) Gaiety Theatre 24 November

1907 **The Girls of Gottenberg** (w Caryll/Ross, Basil Hood/ Grossmith, L E Berman) Gaiety Theatre 15 May

1909 **Our Miss Gibbs** (w Caryll/Ross, P Greenbank/'Cryptos', Tanner) Gaiety Theatre 23 January
1909 **The Arcadians** (w Talbot/Arthur Wimperis/Mark Ambient, Alexander M Thompson) Shaftesbury Theatre 28 April
1910 **The Quaker Girl** (Ross, P Greenbank/Tanner) Adelphi Theatre 5 November
1911 **The Mousmé** (w Talbot/Wimperis, P Greenbank/Thompson, Robert Courtneidge) Shaftesbury Theatre 9 September
1912 **The Dancing Mistress** (Ross, P Greenbank/Tanner) Adelphi Theatre 19 October
1914 **The Belle of Bond Street** revised *The Girl from Kays* ad Harold Atteridge (Shubert Theater, New York)
1917 **The Boy** (w Talbot/Ross, P Greenbank/Fred Thompson) Adelphi Theatre 14 September

MONCRIEFF, Gladys (b Bundaberg, Queensland, Australia, 13 April 1892; d Benowa, Queensland, 8 February 1976). Australia's favourite musical-comedy star between the wars.

A rangy, true-voiced soprano, Gladys Moncrieff worked at first in vaudeville before being signed at the age of 20 to a long-term contract by J C Williamson Ltd, Australia's most important producers of musical theatre. She began with 'the firm' in the chorus, and worked as a small part player and understudy before progressing to larger rôles (O Mimosa San in *The Geisha*, Yum-Yum, Sombra, *The Merry Widow* etc) in Australia and on Williamsons' tours of New Zealand and South Africa. She made her first big personal success in the title-rôle of *Katinka* (1918) and was featured as Delphine in *Oh! Oh! Delphine*, Ottilie in *Maytime*, Pansy in *Theodore & Co*, Diana in *The Boy* and Georgette in *Kissing Time* before, in 1921, she was starred in José Collins' famous rôle of Teresa in *The Maid of the Mountains*. *The Maid of the Mountains* was Gladys's greatest success and she repeated her Teresa regularly for the rest of her career, becoming identified with the part even more strongly than Collins had in Britain. Whenever 'the firm' was in trouble, they would call up Gladys ('Gladys, the ship is sinking ...') and remount the infallible *Maid of the Mountains*. She is said to have played Teresa 2,289 times and used up 18 different leading men.

Miss Moncrieff followed up in José Collins's other starring rôles in *Sybil* and *A Southern Maid*, as well as appearing in *The Naughty Princess*, *The Merry Widow*, a revival of *Ma mie, Rosette* (Rosette), *The Lady of the Rose* (Mariana) and *The Street Singer* (Yvette). Then, her contract with Williamsons having expired, she decided to try her luck in London. She was given lead rôles there in Künneke's disastrous *Riki-Tiki* and Lehár's indifferent *The Blue Mazurka* and returned to Australia disappointed. However, another gipsyish lady quickly put her right back on top. Her first new home engagement, for the Fuller Brothers, was to play the title-rôle in *Rio Rita*, and as Rita she made a success second only to her *Maid of the Mountains* triumph.

In the years that followed, several attempts were made to create a native Australian musical around the country's biggest singing star, but *Collits' Inn* (1933), Dudley Glass's *The Beloved Vagabond* (1934, but 1927 in Britain) and *The Cedar Tree* (1934) did not prove any more successful than the half-New Zealand show *Jolly Roger* (1936). Otherwise, oddly starved by the all-powerful Williamsons of new rôles, she appeared largely in revivals of her most successful rôles

– Teresa, Rio Rita, the Merry Widow or as Viktoria in Ábrahám's operette of the same name – before putting an end to a career unequalled in the 20th-century Australian musical theatre where 'our Glad', as she was adoringly known, was a star like no other.

Autobiography: *My Life in Song* (aka *Our Glad*) (Rigby Ltd, Melbourne, 1971)

MONKHOUSE, Harry [McKIE, Harry] (b Newcastle-upon-Tyne, May 1854; d London, 18 February 1901). British comedy star of Victorian musical theatre.

Monkhouse made his first appearance on the stage as a child at Blyth, and as an adult at London's suburban Elephant and Castle Theatre under Marie Henderson's management. He played at other secondary theatres, including the Victoria, the Marylebone and the Grecian, before making his West End début at the Alhambra as King Octopus in the 1882 revival of *Babil and Bijou*. It was not a performance which won him any further London work, and he returned to the provinces where he made a successful venture as a producer in 1886 with a farcical piece called *Larks* which he ran on the number-two circuits for several seasons.

Monkhouse's career took a London turn when he was hired as principal comedian by the newly formed Carl Rosa Light Opera Company, and was featured as the old smuggler, Bouillabaisse, in their highly successful *Paul Jones* (1889) at the Prince of Wales Theatre. He remained at the Prince of Wales under Horace Sedger's management for lead comedy rôles in *Marjorie* (1890, Gosric), *Captain Thérèse* (1890, Duvet), *The Rose and the Ring* (1890, Valoroso), and the British version of De Koven's *Robin Hood* (Maid Marian, Sheriff of Nottingham). By now established amongst the town's top musical comedians, he then proceeded to rack up a series of further London credits in *La Cigale* (1891, Matthew Vanderkoopen t/o), *The Mountebanks* (1892, Bartolo), *Incognita* (1892, Don Pedro), *The Magic Opal* (1893, Telemachus Ulysses Carambollas) and *Poor Jonathan* (1893, Jonathan). During this period he took time off to launch another provincial musical comedy of his own, a jolly piece of Irish musical comedy called *Pat* (1892). *Pat* served several seasons on the British road and won a production in Sydney, Australia (Theatre Royal, 21 December 1895), by which time the names of Sir Arthur Sullivan and Adrian Ross had become attached to the list of songwriting contributors.

Monkhouse moved on to take the senior comic rôle in George Edwardes's musical comedy *A Gaiety Girl* (1893, Rev Montague Brierly), and thereafter he played for Edwardes in the Gaiety tour of Australia and America, and in a series of important rôles in important London shows: *The Shop Girl* (1895, t/o Hooley), *An Artist's Model* (1895, t/o Smoggins), *The Geisha* (1896, Marquis Imari), *A Circus Girl* (1896, Sir Titus Wemyss), *A Runaway Girl* (1898, Brother Tamarind), *The Messenger Boy* (1900, t/o Hooker Pasha) and *Kitty Grey* (1900, King of Illyria). He then succeeded Willie Edouin's as Tweedlepunch in Tom Davis's *Florodora*, but died during his tenancy of the rôle. His estate revealed that he was bankrupt, a fact which probably had something to do with his unfortunate attempt to produce his own comic opera *La Rosière* a few years earlier (1893 w Marie Halton).

1892 **Pat** (Edward Jakobowski, John Crook et al/Mark Ambient,

Frederic Wood/w George Roberts) Aquarium, Yarmouth 1
August
1893 **La Rosière** (Jakobowski) Shaftesbury Theatre 14 January

MONKMAN, Phyllis [HARRISON, Phyllis] (b London,
8 January 1892; d London, 2 December 1976). Dancer
and light-comedy actress who played several London leading rôles in the 1920s and 1930s.

A teenaged dancer (a little girl in *Lady Madcap*, a Mon-
tezuma dancer, with her sister Dorothy, in *The Belle of
Mayfair*, a soloist in *Butterflies*) and then a small-part player
(*Dear Little Denmark*, *The Girl in the Train*, *The Quaker Girl*,
The Dancing Viennese) in musical comedy, Miss Monkman
made her mark in revue and with the Co-Optimists concert party. She appeared in occasional musicals (*The Wild
Geese*, as the naughty maidservant of *A Night Out*), before
being given her first leading rôles in the productions of
Dear Little Billie (1925, Billie), *Lady Luck* (1926, Jane Juste)
and *So Long, Letty!* (1928, Letty Robbins) each produced
by her husband, Laddie Cliff. In a later career which
mixed musical appearances with some dramatic ones, she
played Lucille in a revival of *No, No, Nanette* (1936), took
over in *The Two Bouquets*, appeared in Noël Coward's
Operette (1938, Maisie Welbey), played the leading female
rôle in the wartime musical *Present Arms* (1942, Babette)
and was seen in a West End musical for the last time as
Lady Jane in a revival of *Rose Marie*.

MONNOT, Marguerite [Angèle] (b Decize, France,
28 May 1909; d Paris, 12 October 1961).

A student of Nadia Boulanger and a youthful concert
pianist, Monnot won early laurels as a songwriter with
'L'Étranger' and 'Mon Légionnaire' (1935) and thereafter
composed numerous successful songs, notably for Edith
Piaf, several of which became international hits – 'The
Poor People of Paris', 'Milord', 'The Left Bank' ['C'est à
Hambourg'], 'If You Love Me' ['Si tu m'aimes'], 'Un coin
tout bleu', 'Hymne à l'amour' etc.

Monnot made her entry into the musical theatre with the
score for a vehicle for Piaf and Eddy Constantine called *La
P'tite Lili*, but she scored her greatest theatrical triumph
with the songs for a musical which had more than a little of
Piaf about its leading character. *Irma la Douce* ('Ah! dis-
donc', 'Avec les anges', 'Y a que Paris pour ça') proved the
most internationally successful French musical play for
decades. It was still playing in Paris, five years after its
première, when its composer died.

1951 **La P'tite Lili** (Marcel Achard) Théâtre de l'ABC 10
March
1956 **Irma la Douce** (Alexandre Breffort) Théâtre Gramont 12
November

MONSIEUR BEAUCAIRE Romantic opera in 3 acts
by Frederick Lonsdale founded on the story by Newton
Booth Tarkington and the play by Tarkington and Evelyn
Greenleaf Sutherland. Lyrics by Adrian Ross. Music by
André Messager. Prince's Theatre, London, 19 April
1919.

The play *Monsieur Beaucaire* (1901), originally produced
in America with Richard Mansfield in the starring rôle and
since then a vehicle for many a matinée idol and romantic
leading man, most particularly Britain's Lewis Waller, was
a natural for transubstantiation as a romantic light opera.
The men who took on the task, equally, seemed the natural

choices: Freddie Lonsdale, the most literate of Britain's
librettists and the author of the megahit *The Maid of the
Mountains*, and the 65-year-old leader of the French light
opera tradition, André Messager, supported by lyricist
Ross, director Pat Malone and designer Percy Anderson –
each the doyen of his profession. The result came up to all
but the most extravagant expectations.

Beaucaire (Marion Green), a French barber living in
Bath, has been expelled from the Pump Rooms for
presumptiousness. But he is determined to meet the
beautiful Lady Mary Carlisle (Maggie Teyte), and when he
catches the louche Duke of Winterset (Robert Parker)
cheating at cards, the barber blackmails the aristocrat into
taking him to a society ball, disguised as the Duc de
Châteaurien. When Beaucaire and Lady Mary find a fast
affinity, the furious Winterset first forces him into a duel,
then exposes him. But Lady Mary holds to her love, and
Winterset is confounded when Beaucaire turns out to be
the exiled and incognito heir to the French throne.

The solos of Messager's score were written very largely
for the two romantic leads, and that total was increased
further when he added one more number for operatic diva
Teyte, Debussy's admired Mélisande, between the
Birmingham tryout and the London opening. The waltz-
song 'Philomel', learned by the prima donna in 24 hours,
turned out to be the bon-bon of a score in which she had
several other fine romantic and dramatic pieces and duets
with her baritone. Green, slightly over-parted as a singing
Lewis Waller, had several attractive ballads – 'Under the
Moon', 'Red Rose', 'English Maids' – whilst a soubrette
couple, woven neatly into the main story (John Clarke,
Alice Moffat), had two duos in Messager's lightest and
brightest style.

Produced during the postwar rage for revue and ragtime, *Monsieur Beaucaire* put up a remarkable London run
of 221 performances (no such light opera in memory had
done so well) before Gilbert Miller handed over his entire
production to Broadway's Abe Erlanger. Mme Teyte and a
young supporting performer called Dennis King, who had
been replaced during the run, did not go to Broadway, and
Green starred opposite Blanche Tomlin for a respectable
143 performances at the New Amsterdam Theater before
the show was taken around America.

Six years after its London première, Messager's piece
(ad André Rivoire, Pierre Veber), only slightly retouched,
was produced in Paris with André Baugé and Marcelle
Denya starred. Paris gave *Monsieur Beaucaire* its strongest
welcome of all. The piece was played for more than 200
performances in its initial season, revived for three and a
half months at the Gaîté-Lyrique in 1929 with René Ger-
bert and Louise Dhamarys (1 October), again in 1935 (31
August), and was ultimately mounted at the Opéra Comique, with Jacques Jansen and Denise Duval, in 1954.
Britain hosted revivals in the West End in 1931 (Daly's
Theatre 16 November) with Raymond Newell and Barbara
Pett-Fraser, and on the road, under Tom Arnold's banner,
in 1945 with Derek Oldham and Lisa Perli.

Like most other English light operas, *Monsieur Beaucaire*
has slipped from the repertoire in its original language, but
it still finds occasional playing in its French translation, the
most recent of which was seen at the Grand Théâtre,
Nancy with François Le Roux and Véronique Dietschy
featured in 1980 (5 April).

USA: New Amsterdam Theater 11 December 1919; France: Théâtre Marigny 20 November 1925

Recordings: original cast (Opal/Pearl), French selection (EMI-Pathé)

MONSIEUR CHOUFLEURI RESTERA CHEZ LUI LE (24 JANVIER 1833) Opérette-bouffe in 1 act by Mr *** (Duc de Morny et al). Music by Mr de St Rémy (Morny) and Jacques Offenbach. Privately, 31 May 1861; Théâtre des Bouffes-Parisiens, 14 September 1861.

A little piece, barely more than a sketch, originally evolved by Offenbach's friend-in-high-places, the Duc de Morny, as a vehicle for some extravagant parody of the Italian opera, *Monsieur Choufleuri* was re-organized and, it would seem, largely composed by Offenbach and his friends (allegedly MM Meilhac, Halévy and Lépine) and, after a private production, ultimately put into Offenbach's company's repertoire and on the stage at the Bouffes-Parisiens. It proved to be a thoroughly delightful piece of burlesque nonsense, and it has survived the 130 years since its first appearance with, at first, a rush of and, latterly, regular performances, the most recent in Paris being as part of a three-part Offenbach evening inaugurated at the Salle Favart in December 1979 (w *Pomme d'api* and *Mesdames de la Halle*).

The bourgeois Monsieur Choufleuri (Désiré) has pretensions. He keeps a butler, even if he is only a Belgian (Marchand), and he won't let his daughter Ernestine (Lise Tautin/Mlle Auclair) wed anyone so unimpressive as her composer boyfriend Chrysodule Babylas (Potel). Monsieur Choufleuri decides to launch himself socially by giving a soirée to which he will invite the operatic stars Sonntag, Rubini and Tamburini. They will, of course, be expected to sing. The guests arrive, but the singers don't, and Ernestine, Babylas and Choufleuri are obliged to imitate them to save face. The guests, headed by Balandard (Bache) and his wife (Léonce in travesty) are as foolish as their host and go away thinking they have seen the real thing, whilst Babylas gets his reward for saving Choufleuri's face in the hand of Ernestine. The musical part consisted of an overture and seven numbers of which the central burlesque Italian trio ('Italia la bella'), Choufleuri's lesson on how to fake Italian in the trio 'Babylas, Babylas', and a rollicking boléro for the two lovers ('Pedro possède une guitare') were the highlights.

Monsieur Choufleuri proved as popular in other parts of Europe as it did at home. Offenbach's company introduced it to Vienna prior to its Bouffes opening (and with the same cast) as the highlight of an evening with *La Rose de Saint-Flour* and *Vent du soir*, and soon after Karl Treumann staged a German-language version as *Narren-Abend im Salon Pitzelberger* in which he himself played Baptist (ie Babylas) to the Pitzelberger (Choufleuri) of Grois. Knaack was the Belgian butler, Anna Marek played Ernestine, and there were no fewer than 84 guests, a mazurka, a waltz, a quadrille, a 'magellone' and a finale galoppade performed by the cast to music that was 'arranged by C F Stenzl' included in this 'crazy evening at the Pitzelberger at-home'.

Berlin rechristened Choufleuri (whose jolly name seemed not to work in the German language) as the harsh-sounding Herr Jaschke, but Hungary's Pál Tarnay allowed him to keep his name in the Hungarian version, and for his brief appearance at London's Gaiety Theatre the English christened him Mr Nightingale. America saw *Choufleuri* regularly, but mostly in French. Tostée appeared as Ernestine in H L Bateman's production, Irma in James Fisk's, and Jacob Grau included *Choufleuri* in his company's repertoire, but Alice Oates could be relied upon to give the piece in English (as *Primadonna for a Night*), and the little piece was also a favourite item on the bills of the Kelly and Leon Minstrels in both America and on the Australian/New Zealand circuit. Female impersonator Leon tackled the stratospheric 'Sonntag' soprano line allotted to Ernestine, Kelly was Choufleuri and his son, Edwin Lester, played Babylas.

Austria: Theater am Franz-Josef-Kai (Fr) 6 July 1861, *(Narren-Abend im) Salon Pitzelberger* 17 October 1861; Germany: *Salon Jaschke* 1862; Hungary: Budai Népszinház *Choufleuri úr otthon lesz* 18 April 1863; Budai Színkör *Salon Pitzelberger* 8 July 1868; USA: Théâtre Français (Fr) 5 March 1869; Olympic Theater *Primadonna for a Night* 20 October 1873; UK: St James's Theatre (Fr) 14 November 1871, Gaiety Theatre *Nightingale's Party* 27 March 1880; Australia: Queen's Theatre, Sydney *Primadonna for a Night* 16 February 1878

MONSIEUR DE LA PALISSE Opérette in 3 acts by Robert de Flers and Gaston de Caillavet. Music by Claude Terrasse. Théâtre des Variétés, Paris, 2 November 1904.

Baron Placide de la Palisse (Albert Brasseur) has banned love amongst his tenants, since women in general and wives in particular only complicate your life and cause you problems and misery. Finally, however, he gives in and decides to marry his cousin, Heloïse de la Verdure, who is safely ageing and plain. But his plans go awry when his cousin Bertrand (Alberthal), who is scheduled to take part in a Congress at Seville, twists his ankle and calls upon Placide to take his place. The poor Baron, hastening away from the extravagantly amorous and anxious-to-be-wed Heloïse, heads for Spain and there he encounters an explosive little creature called Inésita (Ève Lavallière), the daughter of the Governor, Don Diego (Claudius). If the honour of the family is made safe by Placide's mission accompli, the wife he brings home is a guarantee that his peace of mind is gone for ever. The other principal female rôle was that of Dorette (Mlle Lanthelmy), the danseuse girlfriend of Bertrand.

Terrasse accompanied the piece with an opéra-bouffe score in the *Sire de Vergy* mould, from which the doubletalk duo 'Mon coeur est rempli d'un tendre tambour' between Inésita and Palisse, with the pair saying 'tambour' when they mean 'amour' and 'fauteuil' instead of 'baiser' in order to get around Palisse's hang-ups, Dorette's waltz 'Ce sont des châteaux en Espagne' and Inésita's saucy couplets 'Comm' ça' with their 'tra-la-la-la pfuut' consummation were the favourites, alongside the antihero's version of the old song of Monsieur de la Palisse ('La Palisse eut peu de bien pour soutenir sa naissance') which had given the piece its title and its hero.

Produced by Fernand Samuel at the Théâtre des Variétés, *Monsieur de la Palisse* lasted only some 30 performances, in spite of the praises lavished on Terrasse's work and that of his highly admired and successful librettists. However, it was revived in 1913 and 1914 at the Apollo, on the first occasion with Henri Defreyn and Polaire (39 performances), on the second with Henri Fabert and Mlle Docin, and it was brought back again, in 1930, at the Gaîté-Lyrique with Robert Allard and Janie Marèse top-billed, and with Duvaleix in the rôle of Don Diego.

A German production was staged in Munich, and Budapest saw 11 performances of Jenő Faragó's Hungarian version with a cast headed by Sári Petráss, but a version published under the title of *The Ambassador* (ad John Haliwell Hobbes) in America does not seem to have been produced on the professional stage.

Germany: Theater am Gärtnerplatz, Munich *Der Kongress von Sevilla* 21 April 1906; Hungary: Népszinház *Az erényes nagykövet* 12 January 1907

MONSIEUR ET MADAME DENIS Opérette in 1 act by Laurencin [Paul Aimé Chapelle] and Michel Delaporte. Music by Jacques Offenbach. Théâtre des Bouffes-Parisiens, Paris, 11 January 1862.

M et Mme Denis don't actually appear in this little piece. Their ward Gaston d'Amboise (Juliette Darcier) has taken advantage of their absence to whisk away their niece Lucile de Tondray (Mlle Pfotzer) from her pension, and the law, in the person of Sergeant Bellerose (Potel), has followed them to the Denis house. The maid, Nanette (Mlle Simon), dresses them up as M and Mme Denis, but the clumsy Gaston ruins the trick and it is left to Nanette to get the sergeant drunk to enable the runaways to run away further.

The short score which illustrated this tiny tale actually produced a hit number. Lucile's 'Dansons la chacone', a showpiece waltz which tingled up to a top C before the rest of the cast joined in, turned out to be a show-stopper, did much to ensure the show's afterlife and was culled from its original place to make up the part of many pasticcio entertainments in the years that followed.

Successful enough in Offenbach's repertoire, *M et Mme Denis* proved even more popular in the German language. Karl Treumann produced it at his Kai-Theater (ad Alois Berla) with Anna Grobecker (Nanette), Helene Weinberger (Gaston), Anna Marek (Lucile) and himself as the Sergeant before Offenbach's own troupe visited with the French original, and the German version was later played at the Kärntnertor Theater (1870), the Hofoper (1881), the Raimundtheater (1881), at Ronacher (1883) and, in 1904, at a benefit at the Theater an der Wien with Elise Elizza as Lucile. Hamburg, Berlin and Prague all followed, whilst Budapest's Nemzeti Színház chose the piece (ad Kálmán Szerdahelyi) as one of the short list of opérettes which they introduced in Hungarian in the early 1860s. It was later played in Budapest in German, and this Berla version continued to be performed throughout Central Europe for many years. It was also, apparently, the only version to be seen in America, where Louise Lichtenay featured as Nanette in a production at the German-language Terrace-Garten in 1873.

Austria: Theater am Franz-Josefs-Kai *Monsieur und Madame Denis* 31 March 1862; Germany: Hamburg 22 May 1862, Friedrich-Wilhelmstädtisches Theater, Berlin 22 June 1862; Hungary: Nemzeti Színház *Denis úr neje* 31 July 1862, February 1963 (Ger); USA: Terrace-Garten *Herr und Madame Denis* 16 July 1873

MONTALAND, Céline [Marie Henriette] (b Ghent, 1843; d Paris, 8 January 1891). Handsome actress-who-sang, who appeared in opéra-bouffe in Europe and America.

The daughter of provincial actors, Céline Montaland began in the theatre as a child performer. She played at the Comédie Française at the age of six and made herself a name at seven in Labiche's *La Fille bien gardée* at the Palais-Royal. At 17 she was seen at the Porte-Saint-Martin, at 20 at the Gymnase, before she rejoined the Palais-Royal where, in 1866, with the tag of 'one of the most beautiful women in Paris' attached to her, she created the rôle of the Baronne Gondremarck in *La Vie parisienne*. In 1870 she visited America with an opéra-bouffe company, starring as Marguerite in *Le Petit Faust* and Fiorella in America's first *The Brigands*. She provoked enough interest to be burlesqued and paragraphed, but did not challenge the opéra-bouffe image established by Aimée and Tostée and soon returned home.

She appeared in opérette at the Théâtre Taitbout (Javotte in *La Cruche cassée*) and the Nouveautés (*Fleur d'oranger*, *Les Deux Nababs*), in féerie at the Châtelet, and caused a small sensation when she visited St Petersburg, but she angled herself thereafter increasingly towards the non-musical theatre and in 1884, to surprise in some quarters, became a member of the Comédie-Française. She remained there until her death, from measles, six years later.

[GRISIER-]MONTBAZON, Marie (d Paris, 18 October 1922). 'The perfect all-rounder' of the Parisian opérette of the 1880s.

The daughter of a popular provincial actor who went insane after failing to make good in Paris, Mlle Montbazon similarly began her career in regional theatres. However, unlike her father, she not only made good in Paris, but scored a sensation in her very first metropolitan appearance. She had the good fortune, it must be said, to make her début at the Théâtre des Bouffes-Parisiens in one of the best rôles and opérettes of recent years – as the farmgirl Bettina in *La Mascotte* – but she soon confirmed the triumph of her first rôle, winning great praise for her pretty mezzo-soprano voice and delightful acting style as she guested at the Folies-Dramatiques as Suppé's *Boccaccio*, then returned to the Bouffes to star as Audran's *Gillette de Narbonne* (1882). She took up the rôle of Simonne in the Bouffes' other current hit, *Les Mousquetaires au couvent*, and, now billed as Mme Grisier-Montbazon, following her marriage to Georges Grisier (later to be manager of the Bouffes-Parisiens) revived *Madame Favart* and took the lead rôles in such new pieces as *La Dormeuse éveillée* (1883, Suzette) and *Le Chevalier Mignon* (1884, Mignon).

In 1886 she created the rôle à tirors which was the central part of *Madame Cartouche* (1886, Sylvine), but although she repeated her early great rôles and appeared in the classic repertoire (Serpolette etc), pieces such as *Le Valet de coeur* (1888), *Les Délégués* (1888), *Mam'zelle Crénom* (1889) and *Le Mitron* (1891) did not bring her any new triumphs. In 1893 she visited Vienna as the star of a company playing *Orphée aux enfers*, *La Belle Hélène*, *La Fille de Madame Angot*, *La Mascotte* and *La Périchole*.

MONCHARMONT, Charles

Originally an actor, Montcharmont became the co-director (1906) and then the sole director (1912) of the Théâtre des Célestins at Lyon which, during 30 years at its head, he brought to a position as one of the most important provincial theatres in France. Simultaneously, he ran a play agency in Paris through which he obtained the rights to many of the foreign, and most particularly Viennese, Operetten of the 1910s and 1920s. Thus, pieces such as *Le Soldat de chocolat* (1911, *Der tapfere soldat*), *La Chaste Suzanne* (1913, *Die keusche Susanne*), *La Bayadère* (1925) and *Le Tsarewitsch* (1929) were presented at Lyon prior to being sold or transferred for Paris productions, and others, such as *Manoeuvres d'automne* (*Tatárjárás*) and Cuvillier's German Operette *Flora Bella* (1921), which were never played at Paris, were nevertheless seen in Lyon.

In an ever-adventurous programme, Montcharmont mounted the revised Cuvillier/Barde *La reine s'amuse* (1912) which he had originally produced at Marseille, and sent it Paris-ward and, from there, to overseas productions. He produced the first French-language version of Lionel Monckton's *The Quaker Girl* (1913), the first French *Flup..!* (following its Belgian première), a number of major revivals of often neglected classic works, the initial seasons of several of the Marseillais opérettes (*Les Gangsters du Château d'If*, *Le Roi des galéjeurs*) and even an opérette by a local Lyonnais composer.

MONTE CARLO Musical comedy in 2 acts by 'Sydney Carlton' (Harry Greenbank). Lyrics by Harry Greenbank. Music by Howard Talbot. Avenue Theatre, London, 27 August 1896.

A rare venture into libretto-writing by Daly's Theatre lyricist Harry Greenbank and a step up the ladder for the novice composer Howard Talbot, *Monte Carlo* arrived in London in the busiest year of the Victorian musical theatre (*The Geisha*, *The Circus Girl*, *My Girl*, *The Grand Duke*, *Shamus O'Brien* plus eight more new musicals in the West End), won fine reviews and folded after 76 performances.

Mrs Carthew (Lottie Venne) found her old husband (E W Garden), daughter Dorothy (Kate Cutler) paired off with her dashing Fred (Richard Green) and French soubrette Suzanne (Emmie Owen) with the whole male chorus at the end of an evening of complex romancing on the Riviera, livened by some common music-hall folk (Robb Harwood, the Belfrey sisters, Lalor Shiel), in what was little more than a superior variety musical. The entertainment included a representative array of songs from the ballad to the bouncing, and the hits of the evening were made by the diminutive Miss Shiel's music-hally 'I'm Jemima' and the Belfrey sisters' imitation of 'The Sisters Gelatine'. After the early closure, the show went on the road, but it was also picked up by E E Rice for Broadway. There, duly americanized by the addition of some variety acts, an animated music sheet, an imitation of a striptease trapeze artist and some biograph pictures of a patriotic nature, and with a cast including Marguerite Sylva (Dorothy) and Marie Cahill as half of the Gelatine sisters, it lasted 48 performances.

Another musical by the same title was produced at the Neues Operetten-Theater, Leipzig (Ludwig Roman Ehmel/Carl Lindau, F Antony) on 7 April 1907.

USA: Herald Square Theater 21 March 1898

MONTE CRISTO JR Burlesque melodrama in 3 acts by 'Richard Henry'. Music by Meyer Lutz, Ivan Caryll, Hamilton Clarke, G W Hunt, Henry J Leslie and Robert Martin. Gaiety Theatre, London, 23 December 1886.

Following the success of *Little Jack Sheppard* at the Gaiety Theatre, George Edwardes launched a series of what came to be called 'new burlesques', of which *Monte Cristo Jr* was the next in line. It was 'new' in that it eased away a little from the old burlesque restrictions of rhyme and punning in its text (although both elements were still used here, they would soon largely vanish) and in that, like *Jack Sheppard*, it used custom-written songs for its score. The libretto, written by journalists Richard Butler and Henry Chance Newton as 'Richard Henry', burlesqued Dumas's *Le Comte de Monte Cristo*. Nellie Farren played Edmond Dantès, the imprisoned count, and Fred Leslie was Noirtier, the arch plotter with whom Dantès escapes from the Château d'If. In a plethora of disguises, the two set out to wreak vengeance on the bent policeman de Villefort (E J Lonnen), the nasty Danglars (George Honey) and the unpleasant Fernand (Fay Templeton) who has been sniffing around after Dantès's girl, Mercedes (Agnes de la Porte).

The plot took sufficient breaths for everyone to do his or her number: the unplotworthy Sylvia Grey danced gracefully, Lottie Collins danced vigorously, Mlle de la Porte sang a waltz and Miss Templeton gave a décolleté parlando number, whilst Nellie and Fred took the bulk of the evening's material, topical, comic and variety. Leslie's best 'spot' came as he delivered a song called 'Imitations', an ever-changing series of impersonations which apparently ran, on a good night, to 22 verses. The hit songs of the show, however, proved to be two added during the run of this ever-mobile show. Robert Martin contributed a number for Lonnen about a phoney temperance group called the Ballyhooley Blue Ribbon army ('Ballyhooley') and a lively piece, 'I'm a Jolly Little Chap All Round' for Nellie Farren, and these two became the take-away tunes of the night.

Monte Cristo Jr ran through till the end of the season, then went on the road – without Miss Templeton, who had been sacked for incessantly trying to expose more of herself than was permitted – whilst the Gaiety hosted its annual summer season of French plays.

On the road, the company began to prepare its next piece, but *Monte Cristo* was not forgotten. The following year the company, headed by Nellie, Fred, Charles Danby, Marion Hood and Letty Lind, took it to Australia and to America (including two visits to Broadway), following which several 'versions' sprouted in America, including one toured by Jennie Kimball for two seasons, whilst the Gaiety team moved on to further pieces in the same vein.

Another piece under the same title was mounted on Broadway in 1919. Charles Purcell starred as Monte Cristo jr in a Harold Atteridge dream-sequence piece which whisked him, comedian Ralph Herz, and a bundle of variety acts back to Dumas's days, to the accompaniment of songs by Jean Schwartz and Sigmund Romberg, through 254 performances at the Winter Garden Theater (12 February).

USA: Standard Theater 17 November 1888; Australia: New Princess Theatre, Melbourne 20 June 1888

MONTGOMERY, David [Craig] (b St Joseph, Mo, 21 April 1870; d Chicago, 20 April 1917). Star comedian of the Broadway musico-spectacular stage.

Paired with his partner of always, Fred Stone, Montgomery had a fine career in variety before the twosome turned to the musical theatre where their first engagement was in the Casino Theater musical comedy *The Girl from Up There*. Montgomery appeared as Solomon Scarlet to the Christopher Grunt of Stone, a pair of grotesquely made-up, knockabout clowns in the style of an earlier era, in the show's productions in both New York and in London. If *The Girl from Up There* did little for anyone but top-billed Edna May in its title-rôle, the pair quickly found a vehicle that did. In 1903 Montgomery appeared as the Tin Man to Stone's Scarecrow in Fred Hamlin's spectacular production *The Wizard of Oz*, and the team were immediately promoted to a major stardom which they confirmed in no small fashion when, in 1906, Montgomery created the rôle of Kid Connor – Stone was Con Kidder – in *The Red Mill* ('The Sidewalks of New York').

Montgomery starred alongside Stone again in *The Old Town* (1909, Archibald Hawkins), in the modernized Cinderella-tale *The Lady of the Slipper* (1912, Punks) and the updated Aladdin, *Chin-Chin* (1914, Chin Hop Lo), a series which combined to confirm them as Broadway's most popular musical comedy funmakers, but in 1917, during the preparations for their next show, *Jack o' Lantern*, Montgomery died, leaving Stone to continue through five further Broadway musicals alone.

MONTGOMERY, James H (b 27 April 1882; d New York, 17 June 1966).

Actor-turned-playwright James Montgomery wrote 12 Broadway plays of which he himself, alone or in collaboration, remade four as musicals, almost always with inverse results to those won on the straight stage. The first of his musicals, *Going Up*, based on his 1910 play *The Aviator*, scored an immense success both in America and overseas, but the second, *Oh, Look!*, taken from his hit play *Ready Money* (1912), had none of the same success, even if it had the consolation of including Harry Carroll and Joseph McCarthy's 'I'm Always Chasing Rainbows' in its score. Montgomery outpointed even his *Going Up* success in 1919 with the most winning of (Irish) Cinderella stories in *Irene*, which he extracted from his short-lived play *Irene O'Dare* (1916), but an attempt to repeat the same formula with an original libretto for the same songwriting team of Tierney and McCarthy in *Glory* proved a flop. In 1925 he adapted *The Fortune Hunter*, a play which he had not written, but in which he had appeared during his acting days, under the title *The City Chap*, but neither this nor *Yes, Yes, Yvette*, a musical based on Montgomery's most enduring play, *Nothing But the Truth*, added to his total of two major musical hits.

Nothing But the Truth was also made over by others hands, becoming *Tell Her the Truth* in a British adaptation (Jack Waller, Joseph Tunbridge/R P Weston, Bert Lee) produced at London's Saville Theatre (14 June 1932) and briefly on Broadway. It was also adapted by Michael Stewart, Mark Bramble and Cy Coleman in 1988 (unproduced).

Montgomery latterly worked as a writer for MGM, retiring as a playwright and as a producer in 1939.

1917 **Going Up** (Louis Hirsch/w Otto Harbach) Liberty Theater 25 December
1918 **Oh, Look!** (Harry Carroll/Joseph McCarthy) Vanderbilt Theater 7 March
1919 **Irene** (Harry Tierney/McCarthy) Vanderbilt Theater 18 November
1922 **Glory** (Tierney, McCarthy) Vanderbilt Theater 25 December
1925 **The City Chap** (Jerome Kern/Anne Caldwell/w William Cary Duncan) Liberty Theater 26 October
1927 **Yes, Yes, Yvette** (Phil Charig, Ben Jerome, Irving Caesar/w Duncan) Harris Theater 3 October

MONTI, Max (b Sopron, Hungary, 11 April 1859; d Vienna, 14 January 1929). Berlin producer of the early 20th century.

An actor and light baritone vocalist, Monti appeared as a performer at the Theater an der Wien (1884, Ein Hausirer in *Der Feldprediger*), the Deutsches Theater in Budapest (1886–8), briefly at the Carltheater and at Berlin's Friedrich-Wilhelmstädtisches Theater as well as at a number of provincial houses. He played at Hamburg's Carl-Schultze Theater (1893), toured America with the Ferenczy Operette company (1893–4, Stanislaus in *Der Vogelhändler*, *Lachende Erben*) and then, in 1897, became manager of Dresden's Tivoli Theater. He subsequently moved back to Hamburg to take over the management of the Carl-Schultze Theater, followed in 1904 by that of the Centralhallen-Theater, and in 1906 he made his happiest move of all when he secured the German rights to *Die lustige Witwe* which he produced at his Hamburg Neues Operetten-Theater and subsequently took to Berlin for a guest season at the Theater des Westens with huge success.

He followed up *Die lustige Witwe* with other Operetten including premières of such as Fall's *Der liebe Augustin*, Winterberg's *Die Dame in Rot*, Jessel's *Die beiden Husaren* and Chantrier's *Gräfin Fifi*, establishing himself at the Theater des Westens and at the head of Berlin's musical theatre. In the process, he squeezed out his main competitor, Victor Palfi, and moved in to what had been the Neues Theater, renaming it Montis Operetten-Theater (1912). Amongst his productions there were Granichstädten's *Die verbotene Stadt*, Fall's *Jung England* and Goetze's *Die liebe Pepi*. When the Theater des Westens was destroyed by fire in 1912, Monti moved his operations to the Theater am Nollendorfplatz, and later leased the rebuilt Westens to Carl Beese and Carl Bieber.

In 1916, he took the course that so few very impresarii have been able to take: successful and extremely wealthy, he sold up and got out of the business taking his profits with him. He was not rewarded for his acumen, alas, for he then lost his fortune in the shuddering inflation which ravaged postwar Germany.

MOODY, Ron [MOODNICK, Ronald] (b London, 8 January 1924).

After an early career in revue, Moody appeared on the musical stage in the brief London production of *Candide* (1959, Governor of Buenos Aires) before being cast in the rôle for which he is remembered, as the original Fagin in Lionel Bart's *Oliver!* (theatre 1960, film 1968).

He subsequently wrote and played the title-rôle of a musicalized life of the famous historical clown in *The Great Grimaldi* (aka *Joey* and *Joey, Joey*), appeared as Aristophanes in a provincial musical based on *Lysistrata* which called her *Liz* (1968), and fell victim to the *Hair* syndrome with an effortlessly trendy piece called *Saturnalia*.

He took the lead in *The Showman* at the Theatre Royal, Stratford East, returned on several occasions to a broadening performance of his most famous part, and in 1989 created his first London musical part in 20 years in the title-rôle in a short-lived London musical version of *Sherlock Holmes*.

1962 **Joey** Theatre Royal, Bristol 26 December
1966 **Joey, Joey** (aka *The Great Grimaldi*) revised *Joey* Saville Theatre 11 October
1971 **Saturnalia** Belgrade Theatre, Coventry 4 August

MOORE, [Lilian] Decima (b Brighton, 11 December 1871; d London, 18 February 1964).

A scholarship student at the Blackheath Conservatory, Decima Moore was discovered by D'Oyly Carte and given the rôle of Casilda in the original production of *The Gondoliers* at the age of 16. She did not remain at the Savoy, however, but moved on to succeed Juliette Nesville in the title-rôle of *Miss Decima* (*Miss Helyett*) and Edith Chester as Violet Eaton-Belgrave in *A Pantomime Rehearsal*, before starring in the title-rôle of a revival of *Dorothy* (1892). She top-billed as Yvonette in the short-lived *The Wedding Eve* (1892), returned to the Savoy to play the schoolgirl, Bab, in *Jane Annie* (1893) and played Clairette to the Lange of Amy Augarde in a revival of *La Fille de Madame Angot* before she came under George Edwardes's crook, and moved into the world of musical comedy to create the ingénue rôle of Rose Brierly in *A Gaiety Girl*.

In 1894 she went to Australia as the star of Edwardes's musical comedy company to play Rose, Bessie Brent in *The Shop Girl*, Kitty Hetherton in *In Town* and Emma in *Gentleman Joe*. Back in Britain, however, she did not stay in the Edwardes stable, but starred opposite Arthur Roberts in *The White Silk Dress* (1896), as Rose d'Été in the American musical comedy *Lost, Strayed or Stolen* (1897) and as Renée in George Musgrove's production of *The Scarlet Feather* (*La Petite Mademoiselle*). Covering the whole gamut of musical theatre styles, she played Lucia in the burlesque *Great Caesar* (1899), succeeded to the rôles of Scent-of-Lilies in Sullivan's *The Rose of Persia* and Angela in *Florodora*, played in the Christmas musical *The Swineherd and the Princess* (1901), toured in *The Gay Cadets* (1902) and created the ingénue to Sybil Arundale's *My Lady Molly* on the road, a rôle she repeated when the show came successfully to London in 1904. Then, after 15 years as a favourite singing ingénue, she effectively put her musical career to rest, turning to non-musical theatre for the remainder of her career.

Her sister **Eva MOORE** (b Brighton, 9 February 1870; d nr Maidenhead, 27 April 1955) began a career as an actress at the age of 17, spending a considerable time touring with Johnnie Toole, but during her twenties appeared in several musicals. She created the rôle of Minestra in Gilbert's *The Mountebanks*, succeeded to that of Violet Eaton-Belgrave (previously played by Decima) in *A Pantomime Rehearsal* at the Court, introduced the part of the dancer, Pepita, in *Little Christopher Columbus* and took over the title-rôle of *The Shop Girl* at the Gaiety before going on to a substantial career as an actress. She also appeared in both British and American films, notably in the 1922 silent movie of *Chu Chin Chow*. She was the mother of actress Jill Esmond.

Another sister, Jessie Moore, was the wife of the Savoy performer and teacher Cairns James.

Autobiography: *Exits and Entrances* (Chapman & Hall, London, 1923)

MOORE, Grace (b Del Rio, Tenn, 5 December 1901; d nr Copenhagen, Denmark, 25 January 1947). Operatic vocalist who appeared in lighter fare on film and occasionally on the stage.

Grace Moore made her first Broadway appearance in the revue *Hitchy Koo of 1920* and performed in two editions of the *Music Box Revue* and as Jean Jones, the disguised film-star heroine of Joseph Gaites's musical comedy production *Up in the Clouds/Above the Clouds* (1922), before moving into the operatic world. She re-emerged in 1932 to take the title-rôle in Broadway's version of *The Dubarry*, but her non-operatic appearances were largely on film where she starred in the screen version of *The New Moon* (1930), as Jenny Lind in *A Lady's Morals* (1930), in *One Night of Love* (1934), *Love Me Forever* (1935), *The King Steps Out* (1936), *When You're in Love* (1937), *I'll Take Romance* (1937), and *Louise* (1940). She was killed in an air crash in 1947.

A biographical film, *The Grace Moore Story* (*So This is Love*) was made in 1953 with Kathryn Grayson impersonating Miss Moore.

Autobiography: *You're Only Human Once* (Doubleday, Doran, Garden City, 1944)

MOORE, Victor [Frederick] (b Hammonton, NJ, 24 February 1876; d East Islip, NY, 23 July 1962). One of the great comic actors of the Broadway musical stage, blessed with a long list of fine rôles in which to display his talents.

Ex-office boy Moore started out in the theatre as a teenaged super, and made his way through minor rôles in plays and musicals (*The Girl from Paris*) to a four-year stint in vaudeville, playing an act called 'Change Your Act, or Back to the Woods'. He moved straight from vaudeville to his first substantial Broadway rôle as the smart-talking Kid Burns, introducing the title-song in George M Cohan's *Forty-Five Minutes from Broadway* (1905) to New York and, for two years thereafter, to the rest of the country. He followed up in the same character in the sequel *The Talk of New York* (1907), in a poor imitation of the same style of piece mounted by Frazee and Lederer and called *The Happiest Night of His Life* (1910–11), and in *Shorty McCabe* (1911–12) before returning to his act and the vaudeville stage for several years.

Moore appeared in Chicago in the ex-French musical *See You Later* in 1919 but his virtual second career in the musical theatre began when he was 50 years old, when he created the principal comedy rôle of Shorty McGee in *Oh, Kay!*. After appearing in the 1927 revue *Allez Oop!*, he continued with a series of further Broadway rôles, mostly in musical comedies, creating comic parts in several memorable shows and being himself memorable in several less durable ones. He appeared as the bungling burglar Herbert in *Funny Face* (1927), as Nosey Bartlett in the De Sylva, Brown and Henderson boxing musical *Hold Everything!* (1928), as the rum-running Skippy Dugan in Rodgers and Hart's *Heads Up!* (1929), as Irving Huff in the

Plate 186. **Victor Moore** *apparently dressed to go hunting in* Anything Goes.

American version of Albert Szirmai's *Alexandra, Princess Charming* (1930), and as the wonderfully befuddled vice-president, Throttlebottom, in *Of Thee I Sing* (1931).

This last piece paired him to enormous effect with William Gaxton, whose forthright, edgy comedy contrasted effectively with Moore's deceptively gentler, muddly style. The partnership was repeated in a sequel, *Let 'em Eat Cake* and again in the production of *Anything Goes* in which Moore created the rôle of Moon-face Mooney, the foolish and harmless public enemy number 13 (but with ambitions to rise in the rankings) and introduced 'Be Like the Blue-bird'. He next created the part of the lost-lamblike Ambassador Alonzo P Goodhue (with Sophie Tucker as his wife and Gaxton as his rival) in Cole Porter's *Leave it to Me!* (1938), appeared as the investigative Senator Oliver P Loganberry, again pitted against Gaxton, in Irving Berlin's *Louisiana Purchase* (1940) and as Joseph W Porter to Gaxton's Dick Live-Eye in George S Kaufman's short-lived burlesque of *HMS Pinafore, Hollywood Pinafore* (1945).

His last Broadway appearance was in 1946, at the age of 70, when he was seen in the unsuccessful *Nellie Bly* as Phineas T Fogerty, racing the show's heroine around the world under the orders of Gaxton, although he was later seen as the Starkeeper in a City Center revival of *Carousel*.

Moore appeared in silent films and later in such musical movies as *Romance in the Rain* (1934), as a memorable Pop Cardetti in *Swing Time* (1936), in *Gold Diggers of 1937*, in his original rôles in the screen versions of *Heads Up!* and of *Louisiana Purchase* (1941) and, at nearly 80, in *The Seven Year Itch* (1955).

A MOORISH MAID, or The Queen of the Riffs Comic opera in 2 acts by J Youlin Birch. Music by Alfred Hill. His Majesty's Theatre, Auckland, New Zealand, 26 June 1905.

Written by Auckland journalist Birch and composed by Hill, the most successful and considerable New Zealand composer of his generation, *A Moorish Maid* was produced for a week in Auckland, where, billed as a 'romantic opera', and with Lillian Tree, Marion Mitchell and Frederick Graham heading the cast it won a fine success. It was repeated in Wellington, with the young Rosina Buckman in the title-rôle and a company was then set up by George Stephenson to take the piece to Australia. The show was considerably rewritten for the occasion (the tenor part was cut out because there was no suitable singer available!) and Australia's version was labelled 'a comic opera'. Efforts to get *A Moorish Maid* staged in London failed, in spite of an audition in which the soon-to-be-famous Miss Buckman sang her rôle of La Zara, but it was repeated in both Australia (1910, ad David Souter) and New Zealand, and proved one of the few successful pieces to emerge from the pre-war antipodean musical theatre.

Hill wrote a number of other theatre pieces including *Tapu, or the Tale of a Maori Pah* and *The Rajah of Shivapore* which won local productions but which did not bring him the same kind of success that his orchestral and vocal writings did.

Australia: Palace Theatre, Sydney 28 April 1906
Biography: (Alfred Hill) Thompson, J M: *A Distant Music* (OUP, Auckland, 1980)

MORE, Julian (b Llanelli, 15 June 1928). Author or co-author of several of the most successful musicals of the London 1950s.

Cambridge-educated More wrote material for the University Footlights shows before his first professional pieces, the adult pantomimes *Puss-in-Red-Riding-Breeches* (1952) and *Arabian Nightmare* (1953, music: Geoffrey Beaumont) were produced at London's little Watergate Theatre. He collaborated on the revue *The World's the Limit* (1955) at the Theatre Royal, Windsor, and it was at that house that his first musical comedy, *Grab Me a Gondola*, was produced the following year, subsequently transferring to London for a good run. He had further successes, in collaboration with David Heneker and Monty Norman, on the English-language version of *Irma la Douce* and on the impressive *Expresso Bongo*, but a second teaming with *Grab Me a Gondola* composer James Gilbert was a swift flop.

His five subsequent musical shows did not play London, although *Quick, Quick, Slow*, an amusing tale of the competition ballroom dancing world, teetered for many years on the brink of a West End showing and *R Loves J* was seen at Munich's Theater am Gärtnerplatz following its Chichester festival début (ad Peter Goldbaum, Uwe Mund 4 May 1974). In 1979 More had a fresh success with *Songbook*, a burlesque of the flood of composer compilation shows at that time infesting the British theatre, but *Roza*, an adaptation of the Romain Gary screenplay *La Vie devant soi*, with a score by French songwriter Gilbert Bécaud, originally announced for London but subsequently produced on Broadway, did not take off.

1956 **Grab Me a Gondola** (James Gilbert) Lyric Theatre 26 December

1958 **Irma la Douce** English version w David Heneker, Monty Norman (Lyric Theatre)

1958 **Expresso Bongo** (w Heneker, Norman/Wolf Mankowitz) Saville Theatre 23 April

1960 **The Golden Touch** (Gilbert) Piccadilly Theatre 5 May

1963 **The Perils of Scobie Prilt** (w Norman) New Theatre, Oxford 12 June

1967 **The Man from the West** (David Russell) Adeline Genée Theatre, East Grinstead 25 March

1969 **Quick, Quick, Slow** (w Norman/David Turner) Birmingham Repertory Theatre 20 August

1971 **Good Time Johnny** (Gilbert) Birmingham Repertory Theatre 16 December

1973 **R Loves J** (Alexander Faris/Peter Ustinov) Chichester Festival Theatre 11 July

1974 **Bordello** (Al Frisch, Bernard Spiro) Queen's Theatre 18 April

1979 **Songbook** (w Norman) Globe Theatre 25 July

1987 **Roza** (Gilbert Bécaud) Royale Theater, New York 1 October

1988 **Can-Can** revised libretto (Strand Theatre)

MORENO TORROBA, Federico (b Madrid, 3 March 1891; d Madrid, 12 September 1982)

The successful composer of orchestral ('La Ajorca de oro', 'Caprichio romantico', 'Zoraida', 'Caudros castallanos' etc) and guitar music as well as of the scores for some 80 zarzuelas, Torroba scored significant successes with his full-length musical plays *Luisa Fernanda* (Federico Romero, Guillermo Fernández Shaw, Teatro Calderón 26 March 1932) and *La Chulapona* (Romero, Fernández Shaw) Teatro Calderón 31 March 1934). He toured with his own zarzuela company in North and South America in the 1940s, and later became conductor at Madrid's Teatro de la Zarzuela.

His other stage works include: *La virgen de la Mayo* (1925), *La mesonera de Tordesillas* (1925), *La marchenera* (1928), *Monte Carmelo* (1939), *Maravilla* (1941), *Caramba* (1928), *La ilustre moza* (1943), *Polonesa* (1944), *Siera morena* (1952), *Maria Manuela* (1957) and *Ella* (1965).

MORETTI, Raoul (b Marseille, 10 August 1893; d Venice, 6 March 1954). Songwriter who turned out the scores for a number of successful French musicals of the 1920s and 1930s.

Educated in Marseille before moving to Paris for his later studies, Moretti first became known in the world of the popular song, a field in which he was to find considerable success ('Le petit dactylo', 'Tu me plais', 'En parlant un peu de Paris', 'Ce sont des choses'). He won further success with the vast amount of dance music he turned out for the voracious orchestras and gramophones of the 1920s and 1930s, with music for the theatre and with such film scores as *Sous les toits de Paris*, *Il est charmant* and *Si tu veux*. The first of these gave him an international hit with its title song, 'Sur les toits de Paris' (w René Nazelles, ad Irving Caesar, Bruce Sievier).

Gustave Quinson and Edmond Roze mounted Moretti's first stage piece, the medieval burlesque *En chemyse*, at the Bouffes-Parisiens, with a cast headed by Dranem and the heroine of *Phi-Phi*, Alice Cocéa, and then found a long-running success with a second Moretti musical, *Troublez-moi*, again starring Dranem, produced later in the same

year. Well and truly launched by these two pieces, Moretti became one of the most popular Parisian theatre composers of the 1920s and early 1930s as he followed up his first big stage hit with several others: a third Bouffes piece with Dranem, *Trois jeunes filles ... nues!* (1925, 'Est-ce je te demande?', 'Quand on ne dit rien'), *Comte Obligado* (1927, 'La Caravane', 'Les artichauts', 'You-oo, ma Caroline', 'Un petit bout de femme', 'Si maman le veut') produced at the Nouveautés with Milton at the head of the comedy, and the comical *Un soir de réveillon* ('Quand on est vraiment amoureux', 'Ninon', 'J'aime les femmes', 'Quand on perd la tête'). *Rosy*, played at the Folies-Wagram with a cast including Sim-Viva ('Quand j'ai promis, je tiens') and Mireille Perrey ('C'est un rien, mais ça fait plaisir'), *La Femme de minuit*, with Urban ('Amour sauvage') and soprano Danièle Brégis ('N'importe comment') at its head, and *Six filles à marier*, again featuring Dranem as its overwhelming star ('T'as bonne mine', 'Tout va bien, bien, bien') all added to the composer's list of well-played dance-era songs.

As the dance-era began to wane a little, Moretti's theatrical fortunes faded proportionately. *Les Soeurs Hortensia*, with Dranem yet again at the head of the comedy, did well enough without the accent being really on its songs, but *Les Joies du Capitole*, which cast Arletty as Agrippina and comedian Michel Simon as Claudius in some up-to-date Ancient Greek doings, did not succeed and *Simone est comme ça*, with a starry cast including film star Henri Garat, Duvaleix, René Koval and Davia, who had made so many Moretti (and other folk's) songs into favourites, lasted but seven weeks. Moretti's last musical, *Destination inconnu*, with Réda Caire starred, was played only in the provinces.

1924 **En chemyse** (Albert Willemetz, Cami) Théâtre des Bouffes-Parisiens 8 March

1924 **Troublez-moi** (Yves Mirande) Théâtre des Bouffes-Parisiens 17 September

1925 **Trois jeunes filles ... nues!** (Mirande, Willemetz) Théâtre des Bouffes-Parisiens 3 December

1927 **Comte Obligado** (André Barde) Théâtre des Nouveautés 16 December

1930 **Rosy** (Barde) Folies-Wagram

1930 **Six filles à marier** (René Pujol/Jean Guitton) Scala 20 September

1930 **Femme de minuit** (Barde) Théâtre des Nouveautés 11 December

1932 **Un soir de réveillon** (Paul Armont, Marcel Gerbidon, Georges Boyer) Théâtre des Bouffes-Parisiens

1934 **Les Soeurs Hortensia** (Barde) Théâtre des Nouveautés 11 April

1935 **Les Joies du Capitole** (Jacques Bousquet, Willemetz) La Madeleine 25 February

1936 **Simone est comme ça** (Willemetz/Mirande, Alex Madis) Théâtre des Bouffes-Parisiens 5 March

1940 **Destination Inconnu** (Pujol)

MORGAN, Helen (b Danville, Ohio, 2 August 1900; d Chicago, 8 October 1941).

Pretty, bright-eyed Helen Morgan appeared in the chorus of a touring company of *Sally* (1924) and on Broadway in revue, but made her name as an extraordinarily effective singer of mostly despairing and/or dejected torch songs. She won Broadway stardom when she created the rôle of Julie la Verne in *Show Boat* (1927), introducing 'Bill' and 'Can't Help Lovin' Dat Man' in what Stanley Green has called her 'tear-stained voice'. Oscar Hammerstein II and Jerome Kern subsequently wrote *Sweet Adeline* (1929) to her measure, allowing her to pour out the negative sentiments and soaring melodies of 'Why Was I Born?', 'Here Am I' and 'Don't Ever Leave Me' as the show's heroine rose to Broadway stardom with a broken heart. Thereafter, although she appeared in the *Ziegfeld Follies* of 1931 and repeated her Julie in the 1932 *Show Boat* revival, she did not again visit Broadway in a new rôle before her death at the age of 41.

Miss Morgan appeared in several films, including *Applause* (1929), in which she appeared in the rôle of a sluttish, down-at-the-hem vaudeville performer, and *Go into Your Dance* (1936) and memorably re-created her *Show Boat* part in the 1936 movie version. A film loosely based on her life was made as *The Helen Morgan Story* in 1956, with Miss Morgan played by Ann Blyth.

Biography: Maxwell, G: *Helen Morgan, Her Life and Legend* (Hawthorn, New York, 1974)

MORILLA Operette in 3 acts with text by Julius Hopp based on a tale by Wieland. Music by Hopp. Theater an der Wien, Vienna, 13 November 1868.

One of the earliest full-length native Operetten to be produced in Vienna in the wake of the vast successes of Offenbach's opéras-bouffes, Julius Hopp's *Morilla* did not follow the burlesque mode, but instead stayed in the popular area of fairytale and chivalric romance. Its libretto, set in 15th-century Spain, told of a magic wishing ring given to the peasant girl Morilla by a friendly fairy called Valida. It draws the Prince Leon from his bride to her, makes her beautiful, and summons up an army of Amazons to defeat his enemies. But when the Prince's foster-brother Amarin gets her to wish for knowledge, Morilla realizes that only the ring makes Leon love her. Sadly, she hands the talisman over to the Prince, who happily finds that he loves her without the aid of magic.

Although played only four times at the Theater an der Wien on its initial production, *Morilla* proved to have a future. It was produced at Budapest's Budai Színkör with Kornelia Mindszenti starred in 1871, had its Berlin première the following year at the Viktoria Theater and was performed in America as late as 1890 at Gustav Amberg's German-language theatre with Carola Engländer, Ernst Schütz and Carl Adolf Friese featured.

Hungary: Budai Színkör 3 June 1871; Germany: Viktoria Theater, February 1872; USA: Amberg Theater 2 May 1890

MORLET, [Louis] (d 1913). Star baritone/actor who had a fine career in the fin-de-siècle Parisian musical theatre.

At first a member of the company at the Opéra-Comique, where he made a considerable effect in his début as Harlequin in *Les Surprises d'amour*, Morlet found that he was decidedly under-used thereafter. After appearing there in his first light opera, the première of Chabrier's one-act *Une Éducation manquée* (1879), he left the Salle Favart in 1880 and took over the rôle of Brissac in *Les Mousquetaires au couvent* at the Théâtre des Bouffes-Parisiens. The part, created by the actor Frédéric Achard, was reorganized and enlarged with two strong singing solos and Morlet, who proved to be as fine an actor as he was a baritone vocalist, became the star of the show.

As a result of this personal triumph, he was cast in the lead rôle of the piece that followed *Les Mousquetaires* at the Bouffes-Parisiens, and thus created the very contrasting light comedy baritone rôle of Pippo in Audran's *La Mascotte* ('Glou Glou' duet) opposite the newly in-town Mlle Montbazon. After this second huge success, Morlet paired again with Mlle Montbazon in a third which almost approached them in Audran's *Gillette de Narbonne* (1882, Roger), and he subsequently starred as a fine run of richly baritone leading men: as Saverdy in Serpette's *Fanfreluche* (1883), as Lorenzo in Varney's *Babolin* (1884), le Comte in *Serment d'Amour* (1886) and in the piratical title-rôle of Planquette's *Surcouf* (1887). He later created rôles in *Miette* (1888), Messager's *Le Bourgeois de Calais* (1887, Duc de Guise) and *Isoline* (1888, Obéron), played the title-rôle in Lecocq's *Ali Baba*, and appeared in Planquette's *Le Talisman* (1893, Chevalier de Valpinçon) as well as re-appearing regularly in his first and most famous rôle of Brissac and other classic parts in between times.

MOROCCO BOUND Musical farcical comedy in 2 acts by Arthur Branscombe. Lyrics by Adrian Ross. Music by F Osmond Carr. Shaftesbury Theatre, London, 13 April 1893.

Poor Arthur Branscombe became the joke of theatrical London in the years around the turn of the century with his oft-repeated line 'when I invented musical comedy'. The ex-Gaiety Theatre publicity man's claim was based on the fact that he was responsible for what passed for a libretto to the highly successful mixture of comedy and variety turns that was *Morocco Bound*. This 'musical farcical comedy' followed and imitated George Edwardes's *In Town* to the extent of using the same composer and lyricist, whilst in other ways searching even further back in theatrical time for its inspiration. The result was a jolly, bright, topical, easily digestible piece of theatre which, whilst it affected to parody the music halls, was in fact compiled of material sufficiently like that purveyed by the 'halls' to allow the polite Shaftesbury Theatre public, who would not even have considered going inside a music hall, to partake of the new society craze for the kind of songs and artists that might be seen there.

Spoofah Bey (John L Shine) is an Irish conman, out, with the aid of his phoney countess sister (Jenny McNulty), to get the concession for music halls in Morocco. He takes nouveau-riche Squire Higgins (Charles Danby), his brother (Herbert Sparling), sons (Sydney Barraclough, Alfred C Seymour), sons' girlfriends (Violet Cameron, Letty Lind) and a lady journalist (Marie Studholme) out to Morocco, gets them all to do an act for the local Grand Vizier (Colin Coop) and, just when his concession looks safe, finds his plot blown apart by goofy Percy Pimpleton (George Grossmith) from the British Embassy. If the plot surfaced only intermittently, and vanished almost entirely in the second act when everyone lined up to do their 'turn' in a veritable and unvarnished variety programme, this structure did give each player in the cast the chance to perform the kind of item he or she did best. Some legitimacy was conferred on the 'musical farcical comedy' by the fact that most of these items were actually written by Carr and Ross – at least to start with. Letty Lind scored best with her song and dance about 'Marguerite of Monte Carlo' and imitated a society girl attempting the famous skirt dance (which Miss Lind had, to all intents and purposes, re-invented) and Shine had some jolly moments as he took the mickey out of Ireland's new parliament in 'The New Home Rule' and duetted with Danby through a piece called 'The Music Hall' which allowed them to impersonate favourite stars and their songs.

During the 295 performances for which the show ran at the Shaftesbury and later the Trafalgar Square Theatre, its musical content changed regularly and its cast underwent a number of changes, resulting in Savoyard Richard Temple (Vizier) and Minnie Palmer both joining the show for a period. Acts were also slipped in as required – the illusionist Hercat, Nini Patte en l'air and the quadrille dancers of the Moulin-Rouge, duettists A Nylsson Fysher and Maurice Farkoa, and two American artists, the as yet not famous Marie Cahill and the distinctly famous Loie Fuller with her tricked-up version of Letty Lind's skirt dance. When Miss Fuller moved on, Miss Lind returned to the cast and, according to *The Stage* newspaper, 'out-Fullered Fuller'.

After its London run, *Morocco Bound* toured and toured, first under Fred Harris's syndicate, which had concocted and produced the piece for town, then under Branscombe, whilst number-two and number-three companies were sub-licensed. *Morocco Bound*s were seen in South Africa and in Australia, where brother Wilfred Shine (Spoofah Bey) and William Elton (Squire) headed seasons in Sydney and Melbourne (Princess Theatre, 6 October 1894), it was toured in America by A H Chamberlyn, and taken round the Continent by Harris, Chamberlyn, Gustav Amberg and Ernest Cavour in a company in which 'the remarkably clever songs and dance of the sisters Valli' (future Broadway leading lady Valli Valli and sister Lulu) won notice. Full houses in Hamburg and Berlin applauded the songs and dances but sat stonily through the English dialogue, and the company had to wait for Amsterdam and Rotterdam to get their laughs back. The show was brought back to London in 1901 by William Greet with John Shine and Danby reappearing in their original rôles and Branscombe, who had been unable to find himself another show, directing, and in 1914 it was brought out again to follow a newer fashion, compressed into a one-act entertainment to play in variety houses, under the title *I've Seen the 'arem*.

Thus, while Branscombe, like most folk who make such claims, didn't 'invent' anything, he did provide his part of a jolly variety musical which helped just a little to encourage the shift away from the dying 'new burlesque' to Edwardesian musical comedy and, more particularly, to the kind of touring variety musical, with its first act of plot and its second act of virtual concert, which would be the joy of the British provinces and colonies in the 1890s.

Australia: Lyceum Theatre, Sydney 1 September 1894; Germany: Hamburg 2 February 1895, Theater Unter den Linden 16 February 1895; USA: Park Theater, Boston 11 January 1901

MOROSS, Jerome (b Brooklyn, NY, 1 August 1913; d Miami, 25 July 1983).

An eclectic composer of orchestral and vocal music, Moross turned out works which ranged from such stage pieces as the 1938 ballet *The Scandalous Life of Frankie and Johnny* and the three dance-song plays, *Ballet Ballads* (w Latouche) played at the Music Box Theater in 1948, to scores for a number of 1950s and 1960s films whose titles

mostly speak for themselves (*When I Grow Up*, *The Sharkfighters*, *The Big Country*, *The Proud Rebel*, *The Jayhawkers*, *The Cardinal*, *The War Lord*, *Rachel Rachel*). In 1963 he provided part of the text and the music for a minstrel-show style retelling of the events leading up to the Civil War, produced at the City Center for three performances with Dick Shawn featured, but his name in the musical theatre rests on his adventurous score for the cult musical *The Golden Apple* (1954, 'Windflowers' etc).

His other stage works include the 1935 revue *Parade* (w Paul Peters, George Sklar, Guild Theater) and a one-act opera, *Sorry, Wrong Number*.

1954 **The Golden Apple** (John Latouche) Alvin Theater 20 April
1963 **Gentlemen, Be Seated!** (w Edward Eager) City Center 10 October

MORROW, Doretta [MARANO, Doretta] (b New York, 27 January 1928; d London, 28 February 1968). Broadway soprano who scored several times in a short career.

Pretty, dark Doretta Morrow took over and toured the rôle of Gretchen in the 1946 revival of *The Red Mill* at 18 years of age, played the heroine in the flop Billy the Kid musical *Shootin' Star* (Amy) in the same year, and subsequently created three major ingénue rôles in Broadway musicals. The first of these was the part of Kitty in Frank Loesser's *Where's Charley?* (1948) in which she introduced 'My Darling, My Darling', the next Tuptim in Rodgers and Hammerstein's *The King and I* (1951) in which she teamed with Larry Douglas to sing 'I Have Dreamed' and 'We Kiss in a Shadow' and performed the narration to the Little House of Uncle Thomas ballet sequence, and the third and last was Marsinah in *Kismet* (1955) in which she introduced 'Baubles, Bangles and Beads', joined in 'And This is My Beloved' and shared 'A Stranger in Paradise' with Richard Kiley.

Miss Morrow repeated her *Kismet* rôle in London and toured America in the title-rôle of *Fanny* (1957), but when she returned to London to appear as the Princess in Cole Porter's *Aladdin* (1957) it became evident that she had for some reason utterly lost her stage confidence. She married soon after the show closed and did not perform again before her death from cancer at the age of 40.

In 1950 she appeared as Tina in a TV version of *Knickerbocker Holiday*.

MORSE, Robert (b Newton, Mass, 18 May 1931).

After supporting rôles in straight theatre and in the musicals *Say, Darling* (1958, Ted Snow) and *Take Me Along* (1959, Richard Miller), boyish, gap-toothed Morse shot to the forefront of the Broadway firmament with his Tony Award-winning performance as J Pierrepont Finch, the determinedly upwardly mobile window cleaner of *How to Succeed in Business Without Really Trying* (1961, 'I Believe in You') and its subsequent film (1967). He scored again on a return to Broadway as Jerry, the bass-player who takes to a frock and attracts himself a millionaire, in *Sugar* (1972), the musical version of *Some Like it Hot*.

In a career embracing film, television and non-musical theatre, his last musical appearances have been in the short-lived *So Long, 174th Street* (1976) and as Scooter

Malloy in the Todd biomusical *Mike* (Philadelphia, 26 March 1988).

MORSE, [Henry] Woolson (b Charleston, Mass, 24 February 1858; d New York, 3 May 1897). 19th-century Broadway composer.

Well-heeled Woolson Morse studied music at the Boston Conservatory and in Europe, and on his return made his first serious attempt at writing for the theatre with what was purported to be an adaptation of Kate Carrington's *Aschenbrödl* combined with a burlesque of Tom Robertson's play *School*, under the title of *Cinderella at School*. Unable to find a producer for his piece, the 22-year-old composer mounted it himself, in an amateur production in Springfield, Massachusetts, where somehow it attracted the attention of Augustin Daly. As a result, in March 1881 *Cinderella at School* was produced at Daly's Theater, New York, with May Fielding in the title-rôle, James Lewis in the chief comedy rôle and such Daly luminaries as Laura Joyce, Ada Rehan and Mrs Gilbert in supporting parts. It was a genuine success, was swept happily away on to the touring circuits and was even seen again if briefly on Broadway the following season, as performed by Rice's Surprise Party, and yet again in 1883.

Less prolific than most of his contemporaries, Morse turned out only four more Broadway scores in the next decade, of which a replacement for Chabrier's score to *L'Étoile* was the only one not to be given a quick exit visa from New York. However, in 1891 he teamed with his now-regular partner, Cheever Goodwin, to turn out the comical *Wang*. As played by De Wolf Hopper and his company, *Wang* became a major hit which served its star for a good many years and several returns to Broadway. A successor to *Wang*, in the same vein, cast the star as the *Panjandrum* (1893), but neither this nor a rewrite of *Cinderella at School*, rechristened *Dr Syntax* to give Hopper the title-rôle, managed to approach the success of the earlier show.

The pair were, however, to find success again when Goodwin adapted and Morse musicalized the French comedy *Le Baptême du petit Oscar* under the title *Lost, Strayed or Stolen*. Broadway success was followed by a London production, a rare thing for an American musical at the time, but that success was to be Morse's last. He died the following year before his 40th birthday.

1881 **Cinderella at School** (?w J Cheever Goodwin) Daly's Theater 5 March
1884 **Madam Piper** (w Goodwin) Wallack's Theater 5 December
1887 **Circus in Town** (Edward Holst) Bijou Theater 12 September
1890 **The Merry Monarch** (*L'Étoile*) American version with new music w Goodwin (Broadway Theater)
1890 **Pippins** (Goodwin) Broadway Theatre 26 November
1891 **Wang** (Goodwin) Broadway Theater 4 May
1893 **Panjandrum** (Goodwin) Broadway Theater 1 May
1894 **Dr Syntax** revised *Cinderella at School* Broadway Theater 23 June
1896 **Lost, Strayed or Stolen** (aka *A Day in Paris*) (Goodwin) Fifth Avenue Theater 21 September

MORTIER, Arnold [MORTJE] (b Amsterdam, 1843; d Croissy, 3 January 1885).

A prominent Parisian journalist and theatre critic ('Monsieur de l'orchestre' of *Le Figaro*) for many years, Mortier also collaborated on a number of revues and several successful libretti for the French opérette stage. If the text for *Le Manoir du Pic-Tordu* was written in more the style of the later vaudeville-opérettes, his other pieces were all in the spectacular and féerie genre. Two of these, for his friend Offenbach, were more or less based on, or suggested by, the science-fiction novels of Jules Verne (*Le Voyage dans la lune*, *Le Docteur Ox*), the remainder included the three-act, 30-scene *L'Arbre de Noël* and the four-act, 25-scene tale of *Le Petit Poucet*. Mortier also co-wrote the scenarii for several ballets.

The libretti of *L'Arbre de Noël* (*Der Weinachtsbaum*, *Der Schatzgrüber*), *Le Petit Poucet* (*Der Daumling* ad Julius Stettheim, Viktoria Theater, Berlin 25 January 1886) and *Madame le Diable* (*Des Teufels Weib*) were all re-used in Austria and/or Germany and/or Hungary, re-set to scores by local composers.

Mortier also authored a series of annuals on *Les Soirées Parisiennes* from 1874, looking at the theatrical season in a joky and gossipy fashion.

1875 **Le Manoir du Pic-Tordu** (Gaston Serpette/w Albert de Saint-Albin) Théâtre des Variétés 28 May
1875 **Le Voyage dans la lune** (Jacques Offenbach/w Albert Vanloo, Eugène Leterrier) Théâtre de la Gaîté 26 October
1877 **Le Docteur Ox** (Offenbach/w Philippe Gille) Théâtre des Variétés 26 January
1880 **L'Arbre de Noël** (Charles Lecocq/w Leterrier, Vanloo) Théâtre de la Porte-Saint-Martin 6 October
1882 **Madame le Diable** (Serpette/w Henri Meilhac) Théâtre de la Renaissance 5 April
1885 **Le Petit Poucet** (André Messager et al/w Leterrier, Vanloo) Théâtre de la Gaîté 28 October

MOSS, Hugh (b Agra, India, 30 November 1855; d London, 23 July 1926). Director of Victorian musical comedy, operetta and burlesque.

Originally engaged in the medical profession, Moss became an actor and then a stage manager and stage director for such stars as Marie Litton, Wilson Barrett, Sarah Thorne and producers Ben Greet and F R Benson. He entered the musical theatre when he directed the touring musical *The Punch Bowl* (1888) for Gilbert Tate, and followed this by staging *Gretna Green* (1890) and Luscombe Searelle's extravagant *The Black Rover* (*Isidora*) in London. He was reponsible for the direction of the original production of Sullivan's opera *Ivanhoe* (1891) and Messager's *La Basoche* (1891) at the English Opera House, and in the following decade directed a series of new musicals on the London stage. The burlesque *Blue-Eyed Susan* (1892), *La Rosière* (1893) and *The Bric-à-Brac Will* (for which he also took a co-writing credit) were less than wholly successful, but he scored a fine hit with Arthur Roberts's vehicle *Gentleman Joe* (1895) and he directed the comedian's *The White Silk Dress* the following year. His later credits included the touring *The Southern Belle* (1901) and the London production of the Laurence Housman/Liza Lehmann *The Vicar of Wakefield* (1906).

1895 **The Bric-à-Brac Will** (Emilio Pizzi/Harry Greenbank, W Sapte jr/w S J Adair Fitzgerald) Lyric Theatre 28 October

MOSTEL, [Samuel Joel] Zero (b New York, 28 February 1915; d New York, 8 September 1977).

Moon-faced, pop-eyed comic actor Mostel did not

make his first foray into the world of performing until he was in his late twenties. He began by working in cabaret before going on to appear in revue, musicals and plays, his first stage musical rôle on Broadway being as Hamilton Peachum in *Beggar's Holiday* (1946). His second, 17 years later, was as the rascally slave Pseudolus in the classical burlesque *A Funny Thing Happened on the Way to the Forum* (1962, Tony Award). In 1964 he created the rôle of the Russian-Jewish milkman Tevye in *Fiddler on the Roof* ('If I Were a Rich Man', 'Sunrise Sunset', 'Do You Love Me?'), a part which he repeated on a number of occasions thereafter and which brought him his second Tony Award from three Broadway musical appearances.

Mostel repeated his Pseudolus in the film based on *A Funny Thing*, and also appeared in the film version of *Dubarry was a Lady* (1943, Paliostro), but his most famous screen rôle remains a non-musical one: as the improbable impresario of *The Producers* (1968).

Biographies: Mostel, K and Gilford, M: *170 Years of Show Business* (Random House, New York, 1978) Brown, J: *Zero Mostel* (Athenaeum, New York, 1989)

THE MOST HAPPY FELLA Musical in 3 acts by Frank Loesser based on the play *They Knew What They Wanted* by Sidney Howard. Imperial Theater, New York, 3 May 1956.

Frank Loesser's third musical, following behind the brittle British high-jinks of *Where's Charley?* and the winning and warm New Yorkeries of *Guys and Dolls* was like neither of its predecessors. Like *Where's Charley?* it was adapted from a successful play – Howard's Pulitzer Prize-winning *They Knew What They Wanted* had been a Theater Guild hit with Richard Bennett and Pauline Lord starred in 1924–5 – and like *Guys and Dolls* it was a piece which was both set in America and peopled with a set of likeable American characters, but it was still like neither of them, either textually or, in the event, musically.

The Most Happy Fella, to which Loesser himself constructed the libretto, was not, like the two earlier shows, basically comic – it was inherently romantic, and the heart of its book was the unusual love story of the middle-aged Napa Valley winegrower, Tony Esposito. Hardworking Tony (Robert Weede) goes to town one day and is served in a restaurant by waitress Amy (Jo Sullivan) who catches his eye. In her he sees the kind of girl he would like to marry. He leaves her a note, addressed to 'Rosabella', and she writes. A correspondance grows up between them and finally 'Rosabella' asks Tony for his photo. Ashamed of being fat and fiftyish, Tony sends her a picture of his handsome foreman, Joe (Art Lund). When the correspondence culminates in an engagement and Rosabella comes to the Napa Valley to be married, the deception is bound to be uncovered. But tragedy strikes first. Tony's truck overturns on the way to pick his bride up at the station. Spurred on by a multitude of angers, Rosabella agrees to go through with the wedding, but that night she forgets her hurt in Joe's arms. As she nurses Tony back to health, however, real love grows between them only to be shattered when Rosabella finds she is pregnant with Joe's child. She is at the bus station, leaving for New York, when Tony comes to find her and take her home. Susan Johnson as Cleo, Rosabella's comical waitress chum, and Shorty Long as the unshakeably cheerful farm-worker Herman,

with whom she pairs up, provided the lighter moments, with the Italian-American folk of the valley supplying the choruses and background colour.

Loesser's music blended with the story in each of its parts. Tony laughed out his joy at being 'The Most Happy Fella' in his postal love affair, whilst city Rosabella just plain wondered that 'Somebody, Somewhere' actually cared about her, and when their love story rose to its first, happy peak their simple happiness filtered out in the silliness of an English lesson ('Happy to Make Your Acquaintance') and then poured out in one of the loveliest duets to have been written for a modern romantic operetta, 'My Heart is So Full of You'. The straightforward Joe gave out with his wandering philosophy in 'Joey, Joey, Joey' whilst Cleo wailed over her waitress's life in 'Ooh, My Feet' and found a Texas friend in Herman who also comes from 'Big D'. Herman and his pals lilted out their fondness for the small-town pastime of 'Standing on the Corner (watching all the girls go by)', whilst the farm folk provided some exuberant ensemble work ('Abbondanza').

The substantial musical values of the show were emphasised in Kermit Bloomgarden and Lynn Loesser's production by the casting of operatic baritone Robert Weede in the rôle of Tony, paired with the strong, straight young soprano of Miss Sullivan, and *The Most Happy Fella* was a substantial success. It played for 676 performances in its original Broadway run, and toured for six months. If that seemed rather less than its due, in comparison with other contemporary pieces, it was in a way due to the fact that the show was, in every way, substantial. It was a long evening in the theatre, an evening which never hastened through its action and which comprised no less than 30 musical pieces – many not slip-out songs – in its score. No matter how well it was done, it was more than many theatregoers were interested in taking.

This reasoning was behind the show's failure to travel at first. It was four years after the Broadway production before London saw the show and then it was H M Tennent Ltd, riding high on their production of *My Fair Lady*, who mounted the English *Most Happy Fella*, in association with Loesser's own Frank Productions. Another operatic bass-baritone, Inia te Wiata, played Tony, with Helena Scott (Rosabella), Libi Staiger (Cleo), Jack de Lon (Herman) and Lund in his original rôle in support, and the piece ran for 288 performances. The following year Australia also saw te Wiata in the rôle, supported by Barbara Leigh, Stella Moray and Myron Natwick for three months in Melbourne.

The Most Happy Fella has become one of those works that people talk about reviving much more often than they do it. However, Broadway saw its first return production of the show before it saw a proper repeat of *Guys and Dolls*. In 1979 Giorgio Tozzi starred in a Detroit-originated revival at Broadway's Majestic Theater (11 October) with Sharon Daniels (Rosabella), Richard Muenz (Joe), Louisa Flaningam (Cleo) and Dennis Warning (Herman) in the other main rôles. It failed to run more than 53 performances.

It seemed that, in an age when a selection of musical theatre pieces have become fodder for the opera houses of the world, *The Most Happy Fella* would be a logical contender for such a home. Its logistics (cast and orchestra size), its length and its vocal demands all had an opera-house air to them. So, it was something of a surprise to find the show return to Broadway in 1992 (Booth Theater 13 February). The logistics question had been solved in an unexpected way: the Goodspeed Opera House's production had replaced Loesser's orchestra with two pianos. This rearrangement drew a mixed reaction, and the production, with Spiro Malas and Sophie Hayden featured, lasted only 229 performances.

UK: London Coliseum 21 April 1960; Australia: Princess Theatre, Melbourne 9 June 1961

Recordings: original cast (Columbia, 3 records), London cast (HMV), selection (WRC) etc

MOUËZY-ÉON, André (b Nantes, 9 June 1879; d Paris, 23 October 1967). Librettist for everything from vaudevilles to spectaculars in a long Parisian career.

Mouëzy-Éon had his first successful play produced in 1904, and he worked for more than a decade in the straight theatre, notably in the area of the military vaudeville (*Tire-au-flanc!*, *L'Enfant de ma soeur*, *L'Amour en manoeuvres*, *Les Dégourdis de la 11ème*), before becoming more than incidentally involved in the musical theatre. In the later part of the war years he wrote a handful of vaudevillesque pieces, mainly for the little Théâtre Edouard VII, scoring a distinct success with the first, the saucy *La Folle Nuit*, but it was to be a further decade before he devoted himself to what would be the main body of his musical work.

After the First World War he began a long association with the Théâtre du Châtelet, supplying the texts for the large, spectacular shows played there under the management of Alexandre Fontanes (*Malikoko, roi nègre*, *Capoulade de Marseille*, *Mam'zelle sans peur*) and, later, of Maurice Lehmann, who favoured a programme of opérette à grand spectacle, original and imported, as the entertainment both at the Châtelet and at his Théâtre de la Porte-Saint-Martin.

Mouëzy-Éon worked frequently in tandem with lyricist Albert Willemetz on the original works which he wrote for the larger stages of Paris, combined in several cases with composers Maurice Yvain and Tiarko Richepin, and on one occasion on an original opérette à grand spectacle, *Rose de France*, with Sigmund Romberg. From amongst these highly pictorial pieces it was the splenditious north-African *Sidonie Panache* and the gipsy-romantic *Chanson Gitane* which proved the most successful, but a number of his other opérettes à (very) grand spectacle such as *Au temps des merveilleuses*, *Au soleil du Mexique*, *Venise* and *Pour Don Carlos* had long runs on their initial productions and still receive occasional revivals in regional theatres.

Mouëzy-Éon also attempted rewritten versions of several classic opérettes – *Les Cent Vierges* with considerable success, *La Grande-Duchesse* and *Le Petit Faust* without – but his most successful adaptation was that of the Viennese Strauss pasticcio *Walzer aus Wien* for the French stage. The libretto as rewritten by him was a much more comically orientated version than either the original German or the subsequent English-language ones and, backed by a lavish production, it established itself as a long-lasting favourite.

Mouëzy-Éon deputized for Lehmann at the head of the Châtelet's affairs for a period.

His 1917 opérette *La Marraine de l'escouade* was adapted from his own play *Les Fiancés de Rosalie*, whilst his play *Le Loup dans la bergerie* was unsuccessfully adapted as an opérette, *Le Joly Jeu*, by other hands at Lyon in 1933. *Le Papa du régiment* (1909 w J Durieux) was turned into a Budapest musical comedy by Jenő Heltai and Károly Stephanides (*Az ezred apja*, Vigszinház, 13 May 1911) and his famous military vaudeville *Tire-au-flanc!* (w André Sylvane), adapted by no less an author than the young Ferenc Molnár, became *Gyöngyélet* (Ferenc Békési/Adolf Mérei, Magyar Színház 21 April 1906) for the Hungarian stage. As recently as 1984 he (w Yves Mirande) served as source to another Hungarian musical comedy *Uraim, csak egymás után* (music: Szabolc Fényes) based on Adorján Stella's 1926 adaptation of one of his plays.

1906 **Monsieur Popotte** (Henry Moreau-Febvre) 1 act Théâtre Grévin

1917 **La Folle Nuit, ou Le Dérivatif** (Marcel Pollet/w Félix Gandéra) Théâtre Edouard VII 7 April

1917 **La Marraine de l'escouade** (Moreau-Febvre/w M Daveillans) Théâtre du Vaudeville 6 December

1917 **La Petite Bonne d'Abraham** (Pollet/w Gandéra) Théâtre Edouard VII 13 December

1918 **Daphnis et Chloé, ou la leçon d'amour** (Moreau-Febvre/w Gandéra) Théâtre Edouard VII

1919 **La Liaison dangereuse** (Pollet/w Gandéra) Théâtre Edouard VII 5 December

1919 **Malikoko, roi nègre** (Marius Baggers) Théâtre du Châtelet 10 December

1927 **Venise** (Tiarko Richepin/Albert Willemetz) Théâtre Marigny 25 June

1929 **Olive** (Fred Pearly, Pierre Chagnon/w Pearly/w Alexandre Fontanes) Théâtre Ambigu October

1929 **Le Renard chez les poules** (Richepin/w Alfred Machard) Théâtre Michel 31 January

1930 **Sidonie-Panache** (Joseph Szulc/Willemetz) Théâtre du Châtelet 2 December

1931 **Nina-Rosa** French libretto (Théâtre du Châtelet)

1932 **La Tulipe noire** (Richepin/Willemetz) Théâtre de la Gaîté-Lyrique 19 March

1933 **Rose de France** (Sigmund Romberg/Willemetz) Théâtre du Châtelet 28 October

1933 **La Dubarry** (*Die Dubarry*) French version (Théâtre de la Porte-Saint-Martin)

1933 **Valses de Vienne** (*Walzer aus Wien*) French libretto w Jean Marietti, Max Eddy (Théâtre de la Porte-Saint-Martin)

1934 **Le Petit Faust** revised version (Théâtre de la Porte-Saint-Martin)

1934 **Aux temps des merveilleuses** (Richepin, Henri Christiné/Willemetz) Théâtre du Châtelet 25 December

1935 **Au soleil du Mexique** (Maurice Yvain/Willemetz) Théâtre du Châtelet 18 December

1935 **Un coup de veine** (Yvain/Willemetz) Théâtre de la Porte-Saint-Martin 11 October

1936 **Un de la Musique** (Roger Dumas/w Camille François) Théâtre de la Porte-Saint-Martin 12 March

1936 **Yana** (Richepin, Christiné/Willemetz/w Henri Wernert) Théâtre du Châtelet 24 December

1936 **La Margoton du bataillon** (C Oberfeld/René Pujol, Jacques Darmont) Théâtre de la Porte-Saint-Martin 22 December

1937 **Le Chant du Tzigane** (*Forbidden Melody*) French version w Henri Wernert (Théâtre du Châtelet)

1938 **Balalaika** French version w Maurice Lehmann (Théâtre Mogador)

1939 **Billy et son équipe** (*Roxy und ihr Wunderteam*) French adaptation w Willemetz (Théâtre Mogador)

1942 **Les Cent Vierges** revised version w Willemetz (Théâtre Apollo)

1945 **D'Artagnan** ('Bétove'/w André Mauprey, Robert de

Mackiels, Maquet) Théâtre de la Gaîté-Lyrique 18 Novenber

1946 **Les Chasseurs d'images** (Roger Dumas, Georges van Parys/Jean Manse) Théâtre du Châtelet 26 October

1946 **Chanson gitane** (Yvain/Louis Poterat) Théâtre du Châtelet 13 December

1948 **La Grande-Duchesse de Gérolstein** revised version w Willemetz (Théâtre de la Gaîté-Lyrique)

1950 **Annie du Far-West** (*Annie Get Your Gun*) French libretto (Théâtre du Châtelet)

1950 **Pour Don Carlos** (Francis Lopez/w Raymond Vincy) Théâtre du Châtelet 17 December

Autobiography: *Les Adieux de la troupe* (La Table Ronde, Paris, 1963)

MOUILLOT, Frederick [Charles Arthur] (b Dublin, 31 May 1864; d Brighton, 4 August 1911).

Frederick Mouillot worked for many years as a touring actor before moving into management where, in partnership with H H Morell, for many years he put out multiple companies of the popular musical comedies of the Gaiety/Daly's era in Britain and overseas. In 1904 he presented the successful touring musical *My Lady Molly* at Terry's Theatre for a 342-performance run and accomplished an unlikely feat by opening the same show the same night in South Africa where he also held extensive touring interests. First in partnership and later alone, he presented several original musicals including *The Little Duchess* (1897) of which he was the part-author, the well-considered *The Transit of Venus* (1898) which had the top authorial names of James Tanner and Adrian Ross attached to its Napoleon Lambelet score, and *The Gipsy Girl* (1905), written by the brother of his *My Lady Molly* star, Sybil Arundale.

1897 **The Little Duchess** (Frank Congden/w F W Marshall) Stockton-on-Tees 9 September

MOULAN, Frank (b New York, 24 July 1875; d New York, 13 May 1939). Broadway comedy star of the musical stage.

Originally a church choir singer, Moulan took to the stage as a member of the Calhoun Opera Company and in 1897 joined the Castle Square Players. He appeared with them in their huge musical repertoire as Thorillière in *The Black Hussar* (*Der Feldprediger*), Jules le Meagre in Julian Edwards's *Madeleine*, Scalza in *Boccaccio*, Tuppit in *Dorothy*, Nakid in *A Trip to Africa* (*Die Afrikareise*), Major Murgatroyd in *Patience*, Paris in Gounod's *Romeo and Juliet*, Major General Stanley, Morales in *Carmen*, the Bailli in *Les Cloches de Corneville*, Alcindoro in *La Bohème*, Florestein in *The Bohemian Girl*, Baron Truenfels in *Lurline*, The Sheriff in *Martha*, Don Sancho in *The Queen's Lace Handkerchief*, Sir Joseph Porter in *HMS Pinafore*, Prince Paul in *La Grande-Duchesse*, Coquelicot in *Olivette*, The Mikado, Caius in Nicolai's *The Merry Wives of Windsor* and Figaro in *The Barber of Seville*. In 1902 he followed his old employer, Castle Square producer Henry Savage, into the commercial musical theatre in the starring rôle of Ki-Ram in *The Sultan of Sulu* (1902).

After the enormous and long-toured success of this piece, he moved on to star in *Humpty Dumpty* (1904) and as George Washington Baker in another touring musical comedy *The Grand Mogul* (1907) before taking the chief comic part of Simplicitas/James Smith in the American

production of *The Arcadians* (1910). During the craze for Viennese Operette, he starred alongside Julia Sanderson as Baron Siegfried in Leo Fall's *The Siren* (1911), as the cut-out Grand Duke Rutzimov in *The Count of Luxemburg* (1912), and as the thoroughly vamped Professor Clutterbuck in *The Queen of the Movies* (1914, *Die Kino-Königin*). He then changed genre again to feature first in the variety musical *Fads and Fancies* (1915), then in Victor Herbert's *Her Regiment* (1917, Blanquet) and in *Little Miss Charity* (1920) in which he appeared as the crook 'Fingers' Clay. His last Broadway creations were in the indifferent *Princess Virtue* (1921, Hiram Demarest) and *Just Because* (1922, Mr Cummings), and though he returned in the early 1930s to play the chief comedy rôles in several sets of Gilbert and Sullivan revivals, he did not again find the opportunities his earliest Broadway rôles had provided.

LES MOULINS QUI CHANTENT Opérette in 3 acts by Frantz Fonson and Fernand Wicheler. Music by Arthur van Oost. Galeries Saint-Hubert, Brussels, 25 March 1911.

Les Moulins qui chantent was produced at Brussels's famous Galeries Saint-Hubert, then under the management of its co-author Frantz Fonson, and it gave him and his partner Wicheler, already the writers of the hit play *Le Mariage de Mlle Beulemans* (musicalized the following year as *Beulemans marie sa fille*), a second splendid success. Their little Dutch story, set amongst the mills of Zeeland, was stirred up by a bunch of silly men trying to win an infidelity from pretty Lisabeth (Angèle van Loo). When her loving husband Claes (Armand Franck) jokingly gives her a 'ticket' permitting her a fling with any man, she uses it instead both to put the pretenders in their place and to win the pressing Parisian painter Henry (Daniel Vigneau) for her niece, Nele (Gina Féraud). The most amusing characters of the piece, however, were two local children, Kate (Yvonne Arnold) and Petrus (Alice de Tender), professional Dutch postcard and biscuit-barrel models, whose tempestuous business association and romance ran alongside the ins and outs of Lisbeth's story. They also had a good share in the song and dance of a score the solos of which fell mostly to Lisbeth, Nele and Henry.

A London version (ad Leslie Stiles) produced as *The Love Mills* was a 24-performance failure.

UK: Globe Theatre *The Love Mills* 3 October 1911

THE MOUNTEBANKS Comic opera in 2 acts by W S Gilbert. Music by Alfred Cellier. Lyric Theatre, London, 4 January 1892.

Written and produced during Gilbert's estrangement from Sullivan and D'Oyly Carte, *The Mountebanks* was composed by Alfred Cellier (although Gilbert had wanted Arthur Goring Thomas, who turned the text down) and produced by Horace Sedger. It looked back to the author's pre-Savoy period in its style and its subject matter, being more akin to such now-elderly pieces as Offenbach's *Les Brigands*, *Fra Diavolo* or *The Contrabandista* in its tale of comic-opera brigands than to the more sophisticated pieces the librettist had worked on with Sullivan. Its action centred on Gilbert's favourite 'lozenge' plot, which Sullivan had so often rejected since its use in *The Sorcerer*.

Having gathered together some inefficient bandits (Frank Wyatt, Arthur Playfair, Cecil Burt et al), some male (tenor J G Robertson) and female (prima donna Geraldine Ulmar) villagers, and a band of mountebanks (Lionel Brough, Aida Jenoure, Harry Monkhouse et al) the author has them all take a magic potion by which everything becomes what it seems to be. Love affairs go awry and one village maiden (Miss Ulmar) who has pretended to be mad really does become so, until all is finally set back to normal. The construction of the piece was very close to that of *The Sorcerer*, there were clearly recognizable repeats of other Gilbert characters and motifs and, if there was still sufficient of the Savoy esprit in his writing, *The Mountebanks* did rather seem as if its author might have written it 15 years earlier.

Cellier supplied a score in a similar vein: attractive light-opera music of the kind heard in his *Dorothy*, but in the style of an earlier period and without the inherent humour of Sullivan's scores. A rousing song for Frank Wyatt as the brigand chief ('High Jerry, Ho!') and a duo for the two mountebanks (Monkhouse, Miss Jenoure) who are turned into mechanical dolls ('Put a Penny in the Slot') were the most popular numbers of a score which was left unfinished when Cellier died before the show's production. Musical director Ivan Caryll put the music in order, but the three numbers Cellier had not composed were simply cut.

London audiences, deprived of a genuine Savoy opera, supported *The Mountebanks* well, and Sedger's production played for eight months and 228 performances at the Lyric whilst no less than three touring companies took it on the road. Early the following year T Henry French produced the show in America with Lillian Russell's company, his star appearing in Miss Ulmar's rôle alongside sculptural baritone Hayden Coffin as her fellow villager and Laura Clement and Louis Harrison as the actor-dolls. It played 47 Broadway performances and served in the company's repertoire on the road. South Africa and Australia, where J C Williamson and George Musgrove's company played *The Mountebanks* through 1893–4, also both welcomed the latest work of Gilbert and the last of Cellier. However, it did not prove the kind of piece which, like the favourite works of either collaborator, would come back to the stage in the years that followed.

USA: Garden Theater 11 January 1893; Australia: Princess's Theatre, Melbourne 1 April 1893

THE MOUSMÉ
Musical play in 3 acts by Robert Courtneidge and Alexander M Thompson. Lyrics by Arthur Wimperis and Percy Greenbank. Music by Howard Talbot and Lionel Monckton. Shaftesbury Theatre, London, 9 September 1911.

On the heels of the enormous success of *The Arcadians*, Robert Courtneidge attempted a follow-up with the same team of writers and performers. *The Mousmé* was, however, in a much less brightly comic and topically satirical vein than its predecessor, with its tale of oriental Hana (Florence Smithson) who sells herself to a geisha house to pay off the gambling debts of her beloved Fujiwara (Harry Welchman) so that he may take his honourable place in the army. The evil Yamaki (Eric Mathurin) takes credit for Fujiwara's heroic wartime deeds and dooms him to silence and disgrace by gaining Hana's indentures, but an earthquake kills the villain in time for a happy ending.

The composers supplied some lovely numbers for Miss Smithson – a temple bell song (Monckton), and a sweet song to 'My Samisen' (Talbot) which allowed the singer to show off her exquisite E in alt – and some bouncy and humorous ones for Dan Rolyat as a comical fortune-teller ('In Toki-oki-o') and Miss Courtneidge as the heroine's soubrette sister ('Honourable Jappy Bride', 'Little Japanese Mama'), whilst Courtneidge provided one of the most lavish productions seen in years, topped by an earthquake which won sighs of wonderment. Unfortunately, it also provoked vast deficits, for the running costs of *The Mousmé*, which was greeted enthusiastically all round, proved its undoing and, although it was played 209 times in London, the result was a £20,000 red figure. Henry Savage never used his American option, and the touring version which subsequently went out in Britain was cut down to a more realistic scale.

A French opérette of the same title, written by Michel Carré and Albert Acremant and composed by Marius Lambert, was staged in Paris in 1920 (Théâtre Michel 11 July).

LES MOUSQUETAIRES AU COUVENT
Opérette in 3 acts by Paul Ferrier and Jules Prével based on *Le Habit ne fait pas le moine* by Saint-Hilaire and Duport. Music by Louis Varney. Additional music by Achille Mansour. Théâtre des Bouffes-Parisiens, Paris, 16 March 1880.

A version of the successful comédie-vaudeville *Le Habit ne fait pas le moine*, produced at the Théâtre du Vaudeville in 1835, the libretto of *Les Mousquetaires au couvent* was entrusted by Bouffes-Parisiens director Louis Cantin, who had just had a splendid success with the first Paris work of one novice composer, Audran (*Les Noces d'Olivette*), to another, the conductor and son of a well-known musician, Louis Varney. The result was a success which outshone even that of *Les Noces d'Olivette* and which brought forth one of the most enduring opérettes of its period.

Two soldiers, the lovelorn Gontran (Marcelin) and his energetic pal, Brissac (Frédéric Achard), steal the garb of some mendicant monks in order to fake their way into a convent to carry off Gontran's beloved Marie de Pontcourlay (Mlle Rouvroy) who, with her sister Louise (Elise Clary), is about to be forced to take the veil. Their plan goes awry amongst a festival of comical events, but they are saved and rewarded with the girls' hands when it turns out that the monks they left unclothed were not monks at all but plotters against Cardinal Richelieu. Although the principal story of the piece is theoretically the romance of Marie and Gontran, the almost-incidental characters – best-friend Brissac, naughty Louise, Gontran's comical tutor, the Abbé Bridaine (Paul Hittemans) and an incidental innkeeper's wife, Simonne (Mme Bennati), who makes up with her feminine and soprano presence for the fact that the two girls don't get into the story until the action moves to the convent in the second act – take up the largest part of the action. This group is at the centre of a plentiful supply of comedy scenes, highlighted by Brissac's drunken cavalcade through the convent, and is endowed with a barrelful of bright songs.

The score of *Les Mousquetaires au couvent* is a remarkable first major work, full of truly melodious and catchily lilting numbers – criticized at the time by some for being insufficiently 'original', they have by and large outlasted the pieces by which they were supposed to have been influenced – surrounded by some fine ensembles. There are repeated

highlights, from the bouncy introduction of 'L'Abbé
Bridaine', the disguised soldiers' monkish 'Nous venons
de la Palestine' and Louise's all-purpose confession ('Mon
Père, je m'accuse') to Gontran's lovely 'Il serait vrai, ce fut
un songe' and a superb trio for three male voices in Act I.
Needed quickly, when Cantin's revival of *Fleur de thé* didn't
last as long as was hoped, *Les Mousquetaires au couvent* had
to be completed in a hurry, and apparently Varney – who
later always seemed to compose at great speed – was not
able to finish his last act in time. Two or three numbers of
Act III are said to be the work of Mansour, musical director of the Bouffes-Parisiens.

In spite of the enormous success it won on its production, the show did not remain frozen. When the actor
Achard was obliged to return to the Théâtre du Gymnase
after the show's spring run, Cantin recast the rôle of
Brissac with the former Opéra-Comique baritone Louis
Morlet. The part, originally laid out for an actor-who-
sings-a-bit, was now the property of a superb vocalist with
notable acting talents. Varney promptly came up with two
fine set-piece baritone numbers, the drunken 'Gris, je suis
gris' and the ringing 'Pour faire un brave mousquetaire'
which, as sung by Morlet, proved to be the hits of what
became the definitive, if musico-dramatically lopsided,
version of the show. A first run of 219 performances was
followed by regular revivals at the Bouffes-Parisiens (1883,
1896, 1906) and the Folies-Dramatiques (1886, 1887,
1888, 1891, 1909), at the Menus-Plaisirs (1896–7), the
Gaîté (1899, 1901, 1913, 1914, 1922, 1923, 1924, 1938,
1952, 1958) and at the Mogador (1940) as the piece
established itself as one of the staples of the French
opérette repertoire, regularly played in France up to this
day. In 1992 it appeared in the now operettic desert of
Paris for a season at the Salle Favart (17 December) with
Gabriel Bacquier as L'Abbé Bridaine, Michel Vasissière as
Brissac and Patricia Jumelle as Marie.

Outside France, *Les Mousquetaires au couvent* was soon
received in nearly all the main musical-theatre centres – as
well as Brussels, Geneva, Cairo, Mexico, Buenos Aires,
Madrid and Rome – but with results which, although
mostly good, did not reach the swingeing success of the
French version. In London, H B Farnie's version, with
Frank Celli (Brissac), Harry Paulton (Bridaine), Henry
Bracy (Gaston) and Alice May (Simonne) featured, was
played for a good three months, with only a brief hiccup
when Celli got a fishbone stuck in his throat and had to be
replaced by Guillaume Loredan. Budapest's production
(ad Lajos Evva, Béla J Fái), played at the Népszinház with
Pál Vidor (Brissac) and Vidor Kassai (Bridaine), was given
a fine 37 times and revived there in 1897 (11 September)
as well as on other Hungarian stages, but Vienna rejected
its version of 'musketeers in frocks' (*Die Musketiere in
Damenstift* ad Julius Hopp, Eduard Mautner) at the
Theater an der Wien after just 12 performances, in spite of
a cast including Girardi (Brissac), Felix Schweighofer
(Bridaine), Rosa Streitmann (Louise) and Karoline Finaly
(Simonne).

Maurice Grau's opéra-bouffe company introduced the
show to America with Nigri (Brissac) and Duplan
(Bridaine), and with Paola Marié choosing to play
Simonne rather than the love interest, but whilst American
audiences were going wild over *Olivette* and *La Mascotte*,
they rather overlooked the third of Cantin's great produc-

tions, and *Les Mousquetaires* only got an English-language
showing in a version produced by the Bostonians in 1882
and subsequently played at Haverly's Theater in Brooklyn
as a not very prominent part of their repertoire.

In Germany the first performances were not seen until
Mme Aubert's touring French company played *Les
Mousquetaires au couvent* in their repertoire in 1893, and a
vernacular version followed at Berlin's Alexanderplatz
Theater in 1896.

Another *Musketiere in Damenstift*, by Charles Cassman
and Fritz Baselt, was produced at the Königstadt Theater
in Cassel (21 June 1896).

UK: Globe Theatre *Les Mousquetaires* 20 October 1880; Hungary:
Népszinház *Tiszturak a sárdában* 11 February 1881; Austria:
Theater an der Wien *Die Musketiere in Damenstift* 30 Septem-
ber 1881; USA: Boston *The Musketeers* 27 February 1882,
Fifth Avenue Theater (Fr) 25 April 1882; Germany: Apollo-
theater (Fr) 13 February 1893, Alexanderplatz Theater
Musketiere in Damenstift 20 March 1896
Recordings: complete (Decca, EMI), selection (EMI-Pathé) etc.

MOZART Comédie musicale in 3 acts by Sacha Guitry.
Music by Reynaldo Hahn. Théâtre Edouard VII, Paris,
2 December 1925.

Guitry presented his wife, Yvonne Printemps, as the 23-
year-old composer and himself as the Baron Grimm, the
boy's nominal sponsor who finally sends him packing from
Paris when his amours become embarrassing and irritating, in a blank verse piece to which Reynaldo Hahn supplied the score of ten musical numbers, threaded through
with Mozartian elements, which Messager had flatly
refused to write. The hero(ine) did not have the entire
score to herself for, alongside the Letter Song ('Depuis ton
départ, mon amour'), which was, in the hands of Mlle
Printemps, the musical highpoint of the show, and
Mozart's final farewell to Paris and the woman with whom
he has fallen in love (Air des adieux), the glamorous Countess d'Épinay, as portrayed by the beautiful soprano
Germaine Gallois, was also given a chance to shine
musically.

Mozart was a considerable success through some 200
performances at the Théâtre Edouard VII, and the Guitrys
subsequently took it to London's Gaiety Theatre for a
season – in French – before repeating their performances
in America. In fact, America was treated to two versions of
Mozart in little more than a month. Allegedly E Ray Goetz
went to Paris to sign up the Guitrys for a Broadway season
only to find that he had been forestalled by fellow producer
A H Woods. He instead secured the English-language
rights from Guitry and staged the piece (ad Ashley Dukes,
prologue: Brian Hooker) with his wife, Irene Bordoni, as
the boy Mozart and Frank Cellier as the Baron von Grimm
for a Broadway season of 32 performances, shortly before
the French couple set foot in America. The Guitrys played
their French *Mozart*, with Mlle Gallois supporting in her
original rôle, 28 times before switching to *L'Illusioniste* for
their last fortnight.

In France, *Mozart* has been revived on a number of
occasions since Mlle Printemps's introduction of the piece:
Graziella Sciutti appeared in the rôle at the Théâtre
Marigny in 1952 (12 November) with considerable success
and in 1985 the show was revived at the Théâtre des
Variétés with Raphaëlle Ivery in the starring rôle.

Other musical theatre pieces on Mozart's life include the one-act *Mozart und Schikanaeder* put together to the composer's music for the Theater in der Leopoldstadt in 1845, the Theater an der Wien's 1854 *Mozart* written by Alois Wohlmuth and with music by Suppé (23 September) and a 1923 Singspiel by H Duhan, Paul Frank and Julius Wilhelm (Volksoper, 2 June). In 1873 Franz Jauner and Hermine Meyerhoff appeared at Vienna's Carltheater in a little 'Charakterstizze' by Anton Langer as *Wolfgang und Constanze*, whilst one of the highlights of Vienna's Mozart celebrations of 1991 was the Wiener Kammeroper's production of a new play with Mozartean music, *Lacrymosa 91*, written and played by English actor Michael Heath.

UK: Gaiety Theatre 21 June 1926 (Fr); USA: Music Box Theater 22 November 1926 (Eng), 46th Street Theater 27 December 1926 (Fr)
Recording: complete (Gaîté-Lyrique)

MR CINDERS Musical comedy in 2 acts by Clifford Grey and Greatrex Newman. Additional lyrics by Leo Robin. Music by Vivian Ellis and Richard Myers. Opera House, Blackpool, 25 September 1928; Adelphi Theatre, London, 11 February 1929.

Originally commissioned from Grey and Newman by Leslie Henson to star himself as a male Cinderella opposite Violet Loraine, *The Kid* (as it was then called) fell by the wayside when Henson went into London's production of *Funny Face*. It was sold instead to touring producer Julian Wylie, and a selection of second-hand songs which Grey had brought from his American collaboration with Richard Myers – a Philadelphia composer who racked up a remarkable percentage of pre-Broadway closures – were added to by Vivian Ellis. Bobby Howes and Binnie Hale were cast in the lead rôles of poor, hard-done-by Jim and Jill, the rich man's daughter with whom he falls in love in her disguise as a maid. Well-produced, the piece had a fine 13-week tour and a Glasgow Christmas season, and was taken up for London by the Australian firm of J C Williamson Ltd. Rearranged, redirected (twice, for original director Pat Malone died during rehearsals), re-choreographed, but with its two stars firmly in place, *Mr Cinders* scored a huge hit at the Adelphi Theatre. It ran there for five months, then shifted to the Hippodrome for another eight, closing only after a run of 529 West End performances.

Perhaps the most delightful musical comedy of its period, *Mr Cinders* gambolled through a succession of comical scenes filled with bright and bubbling banter as Jim was harassed by his booming stepmother (Eileen Redcott) and his grimly elegant step-brothers (Jack Melford, Basil Howes), swanned around the ball given by Jill's father (Charles Cautley) disguised as the famous Amazonian explorer Lord Ditcham, or scrambled through the countryside on a motor-bike with Jill on his pillion and a jewel-thief in his baggage. The score, too, was a winner, with Ellis's charming encouragement to 'Spread a Little Happiness', as delivered by Miss Hale, proving a long-lived favourite, alongside the frenetic, revusical rhyming of Jim's description of life 'On the Amazon' and the sweetly simple but affecting strains of such love songs as 'Every Little Moment' and 'I Want the World to Know' (by Myers, and originally heard in the very short-lived *You're Some Girl* and *Hello Yourself*) and the comical 'I've Got You'. Myers's most successful contribution was the song

'One Man Girl', transplanted, like the attractive 'True to Two', from his *Brewster's Millions* musical *Bubbling Over* (1925) where it had been introduced, before the show folded out-of-town, by Jeanette MacDonald and Cecil Lean.

Following the London run, *Mr Cinders* quickly got back on the road, where Hindle Edgar and Marjery Wyn became a perennial Jim and Jill as the piece toured Britain year in and year out. Edgar also crossed the world to star in J C Williamson Ltd's hometown production, with the Australian star of *No, No, Nanette*, Elsie Prince, following Binnie Hale's example by taking up the rôle of Jill. Frank Leighton and Sonny Ray were the ugly brothers and veteran Maidie Hope boomed out her Lady Lancaster through a Sydney season followed by a disappointing month in Melbourne (Theatre Royal 11 October 1930) in which Edgar paired with another favourite local soubrette, *Sally* star Josie Melville.

In 1930 the show turned up in Germany as *Jim und Jill* (ad Hans Adler) and the following year it was seen both for 35 performances at Budapest's Vigszinház (ad István Zágon) and in Vienna, where Irene Palasty starred in what was now a 'grosse Tanz- und Ausstatungsoperette in 7 Bildern', with special dances inserted for the star (her Jim was down below the title whilst she had 80 per cent billing above it) and the Palasty-Boys and Palasty-Girls in support. In 1934 *Mr Cinders* went into the film studio and emerged in a 70-minute version, starring Clifford Mollison and Zelma O'Neal, and with celebrated comic W H Berry as the policeman of the piece, which took the usual amount of liberties with the stage show.

In 1982 *Mr Cinders* was given a second life when, in the wake of a surprise hit-parade reappearance of 'Spread a Little Happiness', American-born, London-based producer Dan Crawford exhumed it and presented a version, which kept pretty close to the original, on the pocket-handkerchief stage of London's King's Head Theatre Club. Denis Lawson was a Jim who had, billing *oblige*, appropriated the top song. Ellis's 'She's My Lovely' was interpolated, one number was suppressed, the score was given a vivacious two-piano rearrangement and the evening, cast and staged with a wholly uncampy and unclichéd 1920s flavour, turned out to be the miniature delight of the London season. After three months the show transferred to the West End, where it continued until the total of the original run had been passed (587 performances). As a result *Mr Cinders* set off on a new round of touring and regional theatre productions as well as winning its first American performances at Metuchen, and subsequently at the Goodspeed Opera House (22 October 1988). It also, temporarily, provoked a fresh look at an era of British musicals which had been thoroughly forgotten behind the mist of better-plugged shows from other countries.

Germany: Deutsches Künstlertheater *Jim und Jill* 16 September 1930; Austria: Wiener Bürgertheater *Jim und Jill* 6 February 1931; Hungary: Vigszinház *Jim és Jill* 4 April 1931; Australia: Her Majesty's Theatre, Sydney 5 July 1930; USA: Forum Theater, Metuchen, NJ 30 April 1986; Film: BFI 1934

MR MANHATTAN Musical play in 2 acts by Fred Thompson and C H Bovill. Additional lyrics by Ralph Roberts. Music by Howard Talbot. Prince of Wales Theatre, London, 30 March 1916.

Devised by London producers Grossmith and Laurillard as a British vehicle for the American comedian Raymond Hitchcock, *Mr Manhattan* featured its star as a foolishly rich young American in England. Melville (Hitchcock) has an apartment in London and is engaged to the lovely Evelyn (Peggy Kurton). In time-honoured musical-comedy fashion, however, his valet has sub-let his absent master's flat to a flashy tenor (Robert Cunningham) with a wife (Iris Hoey) who wears very thin negligées, and his friend Bobby (Austin Melford) has simultaneously decided to 'borrow' it for a party with a lot of chorus girls. None of this impresses Evelyn's very strict papa. Harassed husbands, fathers and fiancés sweep through the apartment, and many farcical doings are the order of the day as the action gallops from London to France to a happy ending.

Howard Talbot's score was a slightly unusual one for, although it supplied its main characters with some top-notch songs – Hitchcock's recital of 'Things I Must Not Do', a winning solo for a lass on the make 'Remember, We Christened You Hope', and a male quintet about 'Man, Poor Man' and his subjugation to woman – it also included what Talbot called scenas, virtual sung scenes in which the tenor and his wife quarrelled to suitable music or a bunch of chorus girls greedily attacked their sugar-daddy, chanting in ragtime rhythms their demands for money. A couple of borrowed American songs were interpolated, and of them Silvio Hein's 'All Dressed Up and No Place to Go' proved another success for the star, who won a delighted London reception and played to full houses for four and a half months before returning to America. He was replaced by another American comedian, Robert Emmett Keane, who did not have the same effect but who took the show through to the end of its 221-performance run.

Mr Manhattan proved that it could survive without the star for whom it had been created, however, when comic Fred Duprez took it on the road in Britain for several years with considerable success, whilst Maurice Bandmann trouped it round the far East and J C Williamson's musical comedy company played Melbourne (four weeks) and Sydney (27 October 1917, five weeks) seasons with Louis Kimball as Mr Manhattan, supported by a fine cast including established London stars C H Workman, Carrie Moore (Lolotte) and Ethel Cadman (Evelyn).

Australia: Her Majesty's Theatre, Melbourne 15 September 1917

MR POPPLE [OF IPPLETON]
Comedy with music in 3 acts by Paul Rubens. Apollo Theatre, London, 14 November 1905.

Mr Popple (of Ippleton) was, if not his most long-running, probably Paul Rubens's best work for the British musical stage. This was very largely thanks to a text which abandoned the coy English antics of so many of his libretti and, very largely, the schoolboyishly suggestive dialogue and songwords of *Three Little Maids* or *Lady Madcap*, in a genuinely funny and farcical play which produced, in its title character, an endearing musical-comedy hero.

Freddy Popple (G P Huntley) comes up to London from very provincial Ippleton and, unable to find a hotel room, accepts the loan of an apartment from the actress La Boléro (Ethel Irving). In the second act, the two hopeful, bourgeois gentlemen (William Cheesman, Harold Eden) who have both leased the apartment for Boléro turn up,

followed by their wives (one booming, one lachrymose) and by a bevy of other theatrical and society folk, and poor old Freddy finds himself temporarily declared as the actress's husband. He does his best obligingly to act up the part, but he is very happy when everybody is safely paired off where they belong and he can hurry back to uneventful Ippleton.

Huntley gave a wonderfully winning portrayal of the shy, gentle 'country mouse', aided by such charming songs as 'Rabbits' ('I'm not the least bit shy with rabbits'), and Ethel Irving stopped the show with the rousing exhibition of her profession in 'Oh, la, la la!' and wooed Freddy comically with 'You're Such a Dear, Sweet, Clumsy Old Thing'. The show's very little concession to spectacle was made by edging in half-a-dozen girls in red satin as 'the Scarlet Runners' and a final act set at the Kursaal at Bexhill, but *Mr Popple* was essentially a comedy in the French style, illustrated by characterful and even plotful songs in their writer's most attractive style.

Tom Davis's production proved distinctly popular and passed its hundredth performance on 21st February 1906, but after four months *Mr Popple* was obliged to move out of the Apollo Theatre. Business was still booming, so Davis shifted to the Shaftesbury. After another seven weeks, however, the County Council ordered the closure of the dilapidated Shaftesbury and, another transfer proving impracticable, the show shut down. Charles Macdona took over the management and put *Mr Popple* on the road with Huntley starring alongside Millie Legarde and with huge success, and he continued the tour in 1907, first with Huntley and then with Arthur Longley starred, through 1908 into 1909 (with Huntley again, and then producer Macdona himself) until the piece had run more than three years around the country. Maurice Bandmann also introduced the show to India and the Eastern circuit from 1907.

Mr Popple was, however, not quite done. Almost a decade after its first production a version of the show turned up in America. By the time it reached the stage, it had suffered more than most from the heavy rewriting practised there on pieces purchased from overseas. What remained of *Mr Popple*, rechristened *Nobody Home* (20 April 1915), after Guy Bolton (book), Jerome Kern (music) and a variety of interpolaters had had a go at it, had less effect on Broadway-goers (135 performances) than the original (173 performances) had had on Londoners. Nevertheless, F Ray Comstock's production at the little Princess Theater was encouraging enough for the management to continue with more such unshowy, smallish-scale pieces, giving Bolton and Kern, in particular, the opportunity to turn out some happy comedy musicals on the same well-proven French vaudeville lines.

MR PRESIDENT
Musical comedy in 2 acts by Howard Lindsay and Russel Crouse. Music and lyrics by Irving Berlin. St James Theater, New York, 20 October 1962.

Following their successful teaming with Irving Berlin on *Call Me Madam*, Lindsay and Crouse supplied the composer with another libretto based on diplomacy and/or politics of which fictional United States President Stephen Decatur Henderson (Robert Ryan – although it is said the rôle was first offered to Ronald Reagan!) and his wife (Nanette Fabray) and daughter (Anita Gillette) were the central characters. It followed the family's personal life through, most particularly, daughter Leslie's love affair with a high-up Turk (Jack Washburn), which is responsible for ruining her father's career and losing his party the next election. This, as everyone knows, is the most cardinal sin in politics. However, the ex-President is the sort of man the United States of America needs, and even the opposition invites him back into the charmed circle of his country's representatives before the curtain falls.

Mr President was a piece with a different flavour from the comically Ruritanian political shenanigans of *Call Me Madam*, and neither its book nor Berlin's agreeable score, which waved the flag rather less happily than George M Cohan had done decades earlier, produced anything to equal the highlights of the earlier show, or caught on in the same fashion. The performances of Ryan and Miss Fabray won plenty of praise, but the piece ran for only eight months and 265 Broadway performances.

Recording: original cast (Columbia)

MR WHITTINGTON   Musical comedy in 2 acts by Clifford Grey, Greatrex Newman and Douglas Furber. Additional lyrics by Edward Heyman. Music by John W Green, Joseph Tunbridge and Jack Waller. London Hippodrome, 1 February 1934.

Grey and Newman's second musical comedy version of a favourite pantomime tale, *Mr Whittington*, was constructed on rather different lines to their earlier *Mr Cinders*, favouring an extravaganza style rather than that of musical farce. Without equalling the outsized success of its predecessor, it nevertheless proved a fine London and provincial success for the Moss' Empires circuit producing arm.

The show's tale had lad-about-town Dick (Jack Buchanan) ruined by the father of his sweetheart, Ena (Lalla Collins), so that she will have to marry fat and fatuous Lord Leatherhead (Fred Emney). His private ('there's nothing private about it') secretary, Betty (Elsie Randolph) urges Dick to persevere, like his namesake, and, when he is knocked down by a cab, the modern Whittington dreams himself through a series of revusical situations – all ending in triumph – before waking up to find the stock market has reversed, his horse has won the Derby and the girl is still unwed. The 'dream' scenes had Buchanan dancing with a bunch of policemen, riding the Derby winner, boxing for the Lonsdale belt, facing a county council made up of Christy Minstrels, and (on film) leading the scouts and guides of the nation, in a variety show which allowed Buchanan to spread himself as never before.

Green's songs, topped by a gliding duo for Buchanan and Miss Randolph, 'Oceans of Time', and by the Buchanan–Collins 'Weep No More, My Baby' (borrowed from his Broadway flop *Murder at the Vanities*), were the heart of an attractively dancing score, to which Tunbridge and Waller provided a burlesque 'Pipes of Pan' number for the policemen's dance and the music for the minstrel show.

Produced for a Christmas season at Glasgow and Manchester (30 November 1933), with Buchanan directing and co-choreographing as well as starring, the show was taken to London in February and there played out 298 performances at the Hippodrome and the Adelphi before returning to the road.

MR WIX OF WICKHAM   Musical comedy in 2 acts by Herbert Darnley. Music by Frank Seddon, George Everard, Frank E Tours and Herbert Darnley. Borough Theatre, Stratford East, London, 21 July 1902.

Conceived as a vehicle for music-hall star Dan Leno, *Mr Wix* had its hero mistaken for the descendant of a ducal family, fighting off African natives, getting arrested for going AWOL, court-martialled and finally acquitted by a female jury as part of a series of comic scenes which allowed Leno to display his talents, including the Lancashire clog dance which had originally made him famous, for three hours. When it was toured, however, the star's illness (he was going insane) forced the piece from the road after only six weeks. Although it never reached the West End, *Mr Wix* was played by William Walton in South Africa and was also taken up for Broadway. Rewritten by John Wagner, and with the name 'Jerome D Kern' appearing alongside those of Darnley and Everard as composer, E E Rice's production, with Harry Corson Clark in Leno's rôle, played 41 performances in New York.

USA: Bijou Theater 19 September 1904

MR WONDERFUL   Musical comedy in 2 acts by Joseph Stein and Will Glickman. Music and lyrics by Jerry Bock, Larry Holofcener and George Weiss. Broadway Theater, New York, 22 March 1956.

A musical play formed around the talents of the bright and youngish vocalist Sammy Davis jr and the act which he had successfully played in vaudeville with his uncle, Will Mastin, and his father, *Mr Wonderful* was the 1950s equivalent of the old variety musical, with its first act and plot existing principally to allow the performers to put in a version of 'the act as known' into the second. The billing read '*Mr Wonderful* a new musical comedy with the Will Mastin Trio starring Sammy Davis jr' (both in 80 per cent of the title type).

Mr Wonderful simply presented Davis as young performer Charlie Welch who, supported by his girlfriend Ethel (Olga James) and his pals Fred (Jack Carter) and Lil Campbell (Pat Marshall), takes the course of the evening to get out of the showbusiness small-time and into the showbusiness big-time as represented by the 'Palm Club, Miami Beach'. The piece gave Davis a fine Broadway showcase and also produced two numbers in its score which became standards, Davis's 'Too Close for Comfort' and the title-song as sung by Miss James. Chita Rivera, in a supporting rôle, had fun with 'I'm Available' and Carter and Miss Marshall were the support act with three and a half numbers.

Jule Styne and George Gilbert's production had a 383-performance Broadway run, but in spite of what seemed a reasonably sized production the show failed to recoup its outlay and ended in the red.

Recording: original cast (Decca/MCA)

MÜLLER, Adolf (i) [SCHMID, Adolf] (b Tolna, Hungary, 7 October 1801; d Vienna, 29 July 1887). Prolific composer for the 19th-century Viennese stage.

Adolf Müller first appeared in the theatre at the age of 22 for a brief career as an actor and a singer before shifting his ground and becoming a conductor and a composer. He held an early position at the Vienna Hofoper, but in 1827 became a conductor at the Theater an der Wien where, apart from one period at the Theater in der Leopoldstadt and another, much later, at the Ringtheater, he spent the bulk of his long and hugely productive career.

Müller composed his first stage music for a short comic opera and a Posse in a spectacle coupé at the Theater in der Josefstadt in 1825 and, over the next 60 years, wrote the music for more than 600 shows, mostly for the Theater an der Wien, ranging from Possen, Lebensbilder and every other kind of musical comedy, through children's shows, burlesques, vaudevilles, incidental music to dramas and comedies, ballets and a variety of spectaculars, as well as a handful of Operetten, only one of which, the latter-day *Der galante Vicomte* (1877, 5 performances) was a regular, full-sized 19th-century Operette. It has been estimated that, in all, Müller composed over 5,000 individual numbers.

His earliest work staged at the Theater an der Wien was the enormously successful burlesque of Boïeldieu's opera *La Dame blanche* (*Die schwarze Dame*/K Meisl) and he followed up with other burlesque successes in *Othellerl der lustige Mohr von Wien* (on Rossini's *Otello*/Meisl) and *Robert der Teuxel* (*Robert le Diable* 1833). He provided the original songs and scene music for Nestroy's Possen *Nagerl und Handschuh* (1832), *Der böse Geist Lumpacivagabundus* (1833), *Tritsch-Tratsch* (1833), *Eulenspiegel* (1835), *Zu ebener Erde und im ersten Stock* (1835), *Die beiden Nachtwandler* (1836), *Die verhängnisvolle Faschingsnacht* (1839), *Der Talisman* (1840), *Das Mädel aus der Vorstadt* (1841), *Einen Jux will er sich machen* (1842) and *Der Zerissene* (1844), as well as for many works by Karl Haffner, including *Therese Krones* (1854). The list of other authors with whom Müller worked included many of the Viennese theatre's writing royalty: Friedrich Hopp (*Hutmacher und Strumpfwirker*), Friedrich Blum, Julius Bittner (*Die Gefopten*, *Wiener Leben*), Alois Berla (*Zaunschlupferl*), Anton Langer (*Ein Wiener Freiwilliger*, *Die Aktien-Geissler*, *Ein Prater Wurstl*), Friedrich Kaiser (*Stadt und Land*, *Eine neue Welt*), Karl Elmar (*Paperl*, *Das Mädchen von der Spule*), O F Berg (*Die Probierenmamsell*, *An der schönen blauen Donau*), Julius Feld, Alois Blank (*Wiener G'schichten*) and Ludwig Anzengruber (*Der G'wissenwurm*).

He provided the music for Josef Böhm's parody *Die falsche Pepita* which introduced Marie Geistinger to Vienna in 1853, and for the Viennese versions of such successful French pieces as *Marie die Tochter des Regiments* (*La Fille du régiment*), the fairytale spectaculars *Schafhaxl* (*Pied de mouton*), *Die Eselshaut* (*Peau d'âne* 1865), and *Prinzessin Hirschkuh* (*La Biche au bois* 1866), Dumas's vast *Napoleon* (1868), and for such Hungarian classics as the famous *A falu rossa* (*Der Dorflump* 1879).

1825 **Wer andern eine Grube gräbt** (?) 1 act Theater in der Josefstadt 13 December

1827 **Die erste Zusammenkunft** (?) 1 act Kärntnertör-Theater 29 March

1828 **Seraphine** (*Die Kriegsgefangene*) (M Schmid) Theater an der Wien 21 October

1856 **Der Liebeszauber** (*Barbier und Pächterin*) (Adolf Bahn) 1 act Theater an der Wien ?27 November

1864 **Die Fabriksmädeln** (Julius Findeisen) 1 act Theater an der Wien 3 December

1865 **Heinrich IV** (Schröder) 1 act Theater an der Wien 14 December

1877 **Der galante Vicomte** (aka *Der galante Abenteuer*) (K Plank) Theater an der Wien 30 November

MÜLLER, Adolf (ii) (b Vienna 15 October 1839; d Vienna, 14 December 1901).

The son of the elder Müller, Adolf junior made a similar career as a conductor and composer. He worked from 1864 as a conductor in a series of provincial houses (Posen, Magdeburg, Düsseldorf, Stettin, Bonn) as well as for periods at Pest's Deutsches-Theater and at Rotterdam's German-language opera house and, on two separate occasions, spent periods at the Theater an der Wien. He made his first theatrical composing venture with an opera, *Heinrich der Goldschmied*, produced in 1867 in Magdeburg (1 February). Three years later he had a short Operette produced at the Theater an der Wien, at a time when he had briefly taken up a conducting post alongside two celebrated house musicians, his father and Richard Genée, a team which was soon joined by the young Carl Millöcker. Although he had one more large-scale comic opera (*Waldmeisters Brautfahrt*) and one more opera (*Van Dyck*, Rotterdam, 1877) produced, Müller then largely abandoned composing, and for some time concentrated on a career as a conductor.

When the fashion for Operette became established, however, he again began to compose for the stage. His first such piece, *Der kleine Prinz* lasted only one week, but the second, *Der Hofnarr*, did altogether better. With Girardi, Friese, Carl Streitmann and Ottilie Collin featured, it played 85 performances at the Theater an der Wien, and was subsequently produced throughout Germany and Hungary (*Az udvari bolond*) and in a brief Broadway season under the title *The King's Fool* (Niblo's Garden 17 October 1890). *Der Liebeshof* (13 performances) lasted but a short time, but there was further success waiting with *Des Teufels Weib*, a Viennese Operette version of Henri Meilhac and Arnold Mortier's libretto *Madame le Diable*, originally set to music in France by Serpette (51 performances). Of his later works, *Der Millionenonkel* (34 performances), *Lady Charlatan*, produced at the Carltheater (34 performances) and given just one guest showing at Müller's own base, *General Gogo* (30 performances) and *Der Blondin von Namur* (31 performances), all had respectable runs, with *Lady Charlatan* coming the closest to repeating the success of *Der Hofnarr*. *Der Blondin von Namur* and *Lady Charlatan* were both played with some success in Germany. The only one of Müller's works which has survived into the classic repertoire, however, is a pasticcio reworking of Johann Strauss music into the score for the Operette *Wiener Blut* (1899).

Amongst his other theatre work, Müller supplied the score for Ludwig Anzengruber's highly successful *Der Pfarrer von Kirchfeld*, another successful Posse in *Eine Kleinigkeit*, and music for the German production of Mór Jókai's *Az arany ember* (*Der Goldmensch* 1885). He also arranged a new score for the interminably travelling vaudeville *Le Voyage en Suisse*, contributed to the extremely successful Posse *Die Wienerstadt in Wort und Bild* (100 performances in two years) and rearranged his father's score, with other pasticcio elements, for a revised version of Nestroy's celebrated piece *Der böse Geist Lumpacivagabundus*.

1870 **Das Gespenst in der Spinnstube** (Julius Bacher) 1 act Theater an der Wien 20 August

1870 **Der Pfarrer von Kirchfeld** (Ludwig Anzengruber)

Theater an der Wien 5 November

1870 **Der Glöckelpolster** (O F Berg) Theater an der Wien 22 December

1873 **Waldmeisters Brautfahrt** (Arthur Müller) Hamburg 15 February

1882 **Der kleine Prinz** (Julius Rosen) Theater an der Wien 11 January

1883 **Auf der Rax** (Eugène Labiche, Édouard Martin ad Theodore Taube) Theater an der Wien 1 February

1885 **Eine Kleinigkeit** (Heinrich Thalboth) Theater an der Wien 7 January

1886 **Der Reise in die Schweiz** (*Le Voyage en Suisse*) pasticcio new score (Theater an der Wien)

1886 **Der Hofnarr** (Hugo Wittmann, Julius Bauer) Theater an der Wien 20 November

1887 **Die Wienerstadt in Wort und Bild** (w Julius Stern et al/Bauer, Isidore Fuchs, F Zell) Theater an der Wien 10 April

1888 **Der Liebeshof** (Wittmann, Oskar Blumenthal) Theater an der Wien 14 November

1889 **Lumpaci** revised *Der böse Geist Lumpacivagabundus* new pasticcio score arr

1890 **Des Teufels Weib** (*Madame le Diable*) (ad Theodor Herzl) Theater an der Wien 22 November

1892 **Der Millionenonkel** (Zell, Richard Genée) Theater an der Wien 5 November

1894 **Lady Charlatan** (Paul von Schönthan, Leo Stein) Carltheater 29 November

1896 **General Gogo** (Wittmann, Gustav Davis) Theater an der Wien 1 February

1896 **Der Pfiffikus** (Julius Horst, Stein) 1 act Raimundtheater 18 April

1898 **Der Blondin von Namur** (Horst, Stein) Theater an der Wien 5 October

1899 **Wiener Blut** (Johann Strauss arr/Victor Léon, Stein) Carltheater 26 October

1900 **Das Lied im Volke** (Richard Nordmann) Theater an der Wien 23 December

MÜLLER, Wenzel (b Tyrnau in Mähren, 26 September 1767; d Vienna, 3 August 1835).

Musical director of the Theater in der Leopoldstadt and one of the most prolific and popular theatre composers of the late 18th- and early 19th-century Viennese stage, Müller composed a number of scores and songs which lasted well into the latter part of the 19th century as accompaniment to various successful Singspiele, Possen, Volksstücke, Zauberspiele, burlesques and plays ranging from the works of Shakespeare and Goldoni to the Viennese masters of the time.

Several of Müller's early works were billed as Operetten – *Je grösser der Schelm, je grösser das Glück* (1786), *Die Gräfin* (1786) – or komische Oper – *Das Neusonntagskind* (1793), *Ritter Don Quixotte* (1802), *Die Bewöhner der Tükenschanze* (1804) – and others as operas – *Jawina* (1807), *Die Prinzessin von Cacambo* (1814) – but it was the various forms of musical comedy and fairytale spectaculars that made up such an important part of the theatre diet of his time which formed the bulk of his work.

Amongst his credits were included the music for Raimund's *Der Barometermacher auf der Zauberinsel* (1823), *Die gefesselte Phantasie* (1828) and *Alpenkönig und Menschenfeind* (1828), an 1800 Posse which was called *Der Bettelstudent* and a comic-opera version of Shakespeare's *Tempest* (*Der Zauberinsel*, 1798).

THE MULLIGAN GUARDS

The Mulligan Guards made their first appearance on the Chicago stage, in a song and a sketch. Ned Harrigan and Dave Braham wrote the song 'The Mulligan Guards' as part of an act which featured a marching band of two characters, the one based on a tailor called Dan Mulligan, the other on a Captain Jack Hussey, and which burlesqued the target company exercises of the time, as the two men spent their ten-minute sketch trying to master the manoeuvres in their manual. Dressed in exaggerated military costumes, Tony Hart (as the captain) and Harrigan (as his troop of one) went through some ridiculous by-play to the strains of their song, and the sketch turned out a great success. Harrigan and Hart played it to good effect both in New York and around the country in the years that followed.

In 1878, Ned Harrigan brought the Guards back for a more thorough exposure in his short farcical musical show *The Mulligan Guards' Picnic* at the Theatre Comique. His Guards, now encountered in greater number, were a pseudo-military marching, parading, slogan-shouting, song-singing, dressing-up group of immigrant Americans, who liked nothing better than to get together flag-wavingly with ex-fellow countrymen and identify themselves with the country they had abandoned, to drink as much as possible with them after the marching was over and, if possible, stir up a good fight with some other national and/or racial group. Hart this time played the Dan Mulligan whose name was given to the group.

The Mulligan Guards' Picnic was a singular success, and the Mulligan Guards and its characters remained a feature of Harrigan and Hart's shows for many seasons. After the first piece, it was Harrigan who appeared as Dan Mulligan, whilst Hart was blacked and frocked-up to play the comical negress Rebecca Allup and/or Mulligan's son, Tommy, and there was usually a Germanic or, later, a Jewish protagonist (or, rather, antagonist) somewhere to be found, as the series of shows ran through seven different titles in three years. The pair tried out other shows and other characters, but Harrigan picked up the character of Dan Mulligan and Hart returned to Rebecca again in 1883 for one of their most successful shows, *Cordelia's Aspirations*, in which Annie Yeamans, the regular portrayer of Dan's hot-mouthed, pretentious wife, attempted – obviously, with no luck – to take the Mulligan family upmarket. They repeated in the following *Dan's Tribulations* (1884) before letting go of their alter egos for good.

The plays drew from all quarters of racist humour and lively, if clichéd, nationalist-immigrant characteristics – real, idealized and wished-for. The Irishman were stage Irishmen of the deepest hue, merry, boozy, impecunious, irresponsible, scrapping; the negro characters spoke in minstrel blackface dialect, with 'de' for 'the' and many a 'gwine', and were the Irishman's natural enemy; the German-Americans indulged in the 'Dutch' comic dialect which was to grow into a feature of the comedy industry in America. From these types, Harrigan drew some fine and funny characters whom he continued and even occasionally developed from show to show, giving his audiences the thrill of recognition found in the later film serials or television soap-operas. He also gave them some very clever, if not always very original, low-comic and farcical scenes. A bonus was added to the entertainment by musical director,

Dave Braham, who turned out a series of bristling songs for the series, a number of which became popular and extractable standards. There was also, naturally, plenty of musical opportunity for the Guards to leap into displays of costumed marching which always aroused the same type of enthusiasm in the theatre as it did out of it.

Played to an audience which revelled in the music halls and farce-comedy, who identified with the characters and enjoyed seeing the opposition made fun of and/or beaten up, the Mulligan Guards series served Harrigan and Hart splendidly through the large part of their time as a team, and proved for many years one of the most successful popular entertainments on the American musical stage.

Literature: *Illustrated History of the Mulligan Guards* (Collin & Small, New York, 1874), Harrigan, E: *The Mulligans* (G W Dillingham, New York, 1901)

MUNROE, Kate [LISTER, Katherine] (b Brooklyn, NY, 1848; d London, 17 October, 1887). Well-travelled American-born prima donna of the opéra-bouffe and -comique stage.

Daughter of a Brooklyn doctor, Kate Munroe left her homeland in 1869 to go to Italy to study, and she made her first notable appearance in Milan as Norina (*Don Pasquale*). Engaged as an opera singer in Paris, she soon found that her voice was not equal to operatic stresses and strains and she moved to Britain where she entered the lighter musical theatre. She starred as Mlle Lange in *La Fille de Madame Angot* at the Gaiety and at the Philharmonic (1875), then crossed to the Alhambra where, between 1875 and 1877 she was seen in a revival of *Chilpéric* (Galswinthe), *Spectresheim* (Herminia), *Don Quixote* (Altissidora), *Le Voyage dans la lune* (Princess Fantasy), *Orphée aux enfers* (Eurydice) and as someone called Hilda in the house's version of *Die Fledermaus*. She then joined Alexander Henderson at the Folly Theatre to play Judic's rôle in *La Créole*, appeared as Dindonette in a version of *L'Oeil crevé* and was then cast as the first British Serpolette in *Les Cloches de Corneville*, a rôle which she retained for much of the show's record-breaking run.

She took time off from Planquette's piece to make an appearance in Paris in 1879, featuring in Coèdes's *Les Deux Nababs* at the Nouveautés and in a rôle which was kindly made into that of an English girl in Hervé's *La Marquise des rues* (1879, Albina) at the Bouffes-Parisiens, and then visited New York for her only theatrical appearances in her home country, starring with the Comley–Barton Company as Serpolette. Miss Munroe returned to London to star in *La Belle Normande* (1881, Eglantine), *Boccaccio* (1882, Isabella), *The Merry Duchess* (1883, Duchess) and *Gillette de Narbonne* (Rosita) before she married in 1885. She returned to the stage to appear at the Theatre Royal, Drury Lane, in *Frivoli* (1886, Marchioness de Piombino), but she died of jaundice in childbirth the following year.

MURRAY, Alfred
British librettist of the Victorian stage.

After a promising showing with the burlesque *Little Carmen*, produced at a try-out matinée in 1884, the team of Murray and composer Edward Jakobowski were commissioned to write a comic opera by the town's most active musical producer, John Hollingshead of the Gaiety

theatre. *Dick*, an enjoyable comic-opera version of the pantomime tale of *Dick Whittington*, won some success and several overseas productions. Whilst Jakobowski then went on to triumph with *Erminie*, Murray was taken up by *Erminie*'s producer Violet Melnotte, paired with the untried Belgian composer Ivan Caryll, and given the task of writing an English version of the original French libretto to which Caryll had composed what became his first full stage work, *The Lily of Léoville*. The show failed to repeat *Erminie*'s success, and although he won some runs with further French adaptations, and a veritable Broadway hit with *Nadgy*, for several years Murray drifted further and further from such a success with such works as the complicated mythological-spectacle *The Palace of Pearl*, a provincial remake of *Le Grand Duc de Matapa* (*Glamour*) and an attempt at comic opera by the respected musician Tito Mattei (*La Prima Donna*) which used as its basis the same magazine story Gilbert later used for *The Grand Duke*.

He supplied some songwords for several further shows, including the Arthur Roberts *A Modern Don Quixote* and the long-running *A Chinese Honeymoon*, and finally had his name substantially connected to a genuine hit when he wrote the dialogue for the Gaiety musical comedy *The Messenger Boy* (1900).

1881 **Gibraltar** (aka *Madame Rose*) (*La Reine des Halles*) English version (Haymarket Theatre)
1883 **Lurette** (*Belle Lurette*) English version w Frank Desprez (Avenue Theatre)
1884 **Little Carmen** (Edward Jakobowski) Globe Theatre 7 February
1884 **Dick** (Jakobowski) Globe Theatre 17 April
1886 **The Lily of Léoville** English version (Comedy Theatre)
1886 **The Place of Pearl** (Jakobowski, Frederic Stanislaus/w William Younge) Empire Theatre 12 June
1886 **Glamour** (William Hutchison/w H B Farnie) Edinburgh 30 August
1886 **La Béarnaise** English version (Prince of Wales Theatre)
1888 **Babette** (*La Grappe d'amour*) English version w T G Mosenthal (Strand Theatre)
1888 **Nadgy** (*Les Noces improvisées*) English version (Avenue Theatre)
1889 **La Prima Donna** (Tito Mattei/w Farnie) Avenue Theatre 16 October
1900 **The Messenger Boy** (Lionel Monckton, Ivan Caryll/Adrian Ross, Percy Greenbank/w James T Tanner) Gaiety Theatre 3 February

MUSGRAVE, Frank
A musical director and a composer of dance-music arrangements for publishing houses and of incidental songs and music ('composed and arranged by') for the burlesque stage, Musgrave, during his period as musical director of the old Strand Theatre under the management of the Swanborough family, unwittingly assured himself a place in the history books when he composed the score of entirely original music for F C Burnand's 1865 burlesque *Windsor Castle*. Produced at the Strand, after a long series of the pasticcio burlesques which were the norm at the time and for many of which Musgrave had organized and sometimes composed more than the usual small original part of the score, *Windsor Castle* was justifiably claimed by Burnand as the first English opéra-bouffe. Musgrave composed a burlesque of *L'Africaine* to follow *Windsor Castle* before the theatre returned to the old style of musical patchwork shows. He later cemented his connection with

opéra-bouffe when he acted as conductor for the important London production of *Chilpéric* (1870).

Musgrave later became lessee of the Theatre Royal, Nottingham and managed a number of not notably successful touring productions, including companies of *Giroflé-Girofla*, *La Fille de Madame Angot* and his own *Prisoners at the Bar*. At the same time, without again venturing a complete London score, he continued to turn out the same sort of music and arrangements as before, mostly for touring burlesque companies such as those run by Emily Duncan (*The Miller and his Men*, *Sindbad* etc), but occasionally as interpolations in major musicals, such as H B Farnie's version of Offenbach's *La Vie parisienne* ('For Thee, My Love', 'The Tout'). He was also heard briefly and for apparently the only time on Broadway in 1881 when a combination called M B Leavitt's Grand English Opera Burlesque Company staged a full-blooded *Carmen* burlesque with Musgrave's name on its music and a top-line English company headed by no less a star than Selina Dolaro.

Musgrave subsequently disappeared from sight, and the 'inventor' of English opéra-bouffe was discovered in 1887 in the Bethnal Green lunatic asylum where, it was reported, he was 'too poor to buy winter clothes'.

1865 **Windsor Castle** (F C Burnand) Strand Theatre 5 June
1865 **L'Africaine** (Burnand) Strand Theatre 18 November
1873 **Nottingham Castle, or the Crusader, the Cruel Uncle and the Children of Sherwood** (F R Goodyer) Theatre Royal, Nottingham 22 September
1873 **Lothair, or Batti-Batti and the Shah-de-doo** (Frank W Green, Robert Soutar) Theatre Royal, Liverpool 13 October
1878 **Prisoners at the Bar** (C H Ross) 1 act Royal Alexandra Theatre, Liverpool 17 June
1881 **Carmen, or Soldiers and Seville-ians** (Green) Haverley's Theater, New York 13 September

MUSGROVE, George (b Surbiton, Surrey, 21 January 1854; d Sydney, 21 January 1916). Australian producer for both the colonial and London stage.

A nephew of the Australian opera and comic-opera producer William S Lyster, Musgrove originally worked in a solicitor's office before taking a post with his uncle at the Theatre Royal, Melbourne. In 1880–1 he had a considerable success with his own first producing venture, a lavishly staged Australian production of *La Fille du tambour-major* with imported stars Pattie Laverne and Alfred Brennir, and in 1882 he joined with J C Williamson and Arthur Garner in a triumvirate (Williamson, Garner and Musgrove's Royal Comic Opera Company) which was to consolidate the foundations of Australia's most famous theatrical management.

Through the 1880s the partnership, with Musgrove very much an active element, imported shows and performers to Australia from around the world, but Musgrove then split from the firm to go on his own with such projects as the Nellie Stewart Opera Company and the importation of the Gaiety Theatre company (previously presented by Williamson) from London with their burlesques *Joan of Arc*, *Carmen Up-to-Data* and *Faust-Up-to-Date*. In 1893 he rejoined Williamson, and the partners continued to bring a flood of the most successful musical shows of the time to Australia.

From 1896 he based himself in London where he was intended to represent the partnership's interests. There he took a lease on the Shaftesbury Theatre and produced a version of Lecocq's *La Petite Mademoiselle* as a vehicle for Miss Stewart (for many years his wife in all but name) without success, but in 1898 he picked up an unlikely prospect in America, the Casino Theater musical comedy's *The Belle of New York*, and brought it to London. It proved the most successful American import Britain had ever hosted and went on to a worldwide career from the Shaftesbury Theatre, making back all the money Musgrove had lost on his earlier London ventures and more, but also causing an irreparable split with Williamson, on whose company's name he had traded without consultation.

In 1900 Musgrove returned to Australia where, in rivalry with his former partner, he continued, through perhaps more downs than ups, for more than another decade as a continuing force in the presentation of musical theatre, opera and plays.

Musgrove's sister Henrietta Hodson, a successful actress in London, appeared there in Stephenson and Sullivan's operetta *The Zoo*. She was the wife of the celebrated politician Henry Labouchère.

MUSIC IN THE AIR Musical adventure in 2 acts by Oscar Hammerstein II. Music by Jerome Kern. Alvin Theater, New York, 8 November 1932.

A second calculated attempt by Jerome Kern, following his success with *The Cat and the Fiddle*, to write a Continental-style operetta, *Music in the Air* had, unlike the earlier piece, an Oscar Hammerstein libretto, but one that was made up of nothing more than a bundle of ageing Viennese Operette clichés and characters. It was set in a picturesque Bavarian village and in Vienna, and its star characters were an operettic prima donna, her composer, and the ingénue who comes professionally and personally between them until she returns to her village lover for a chocolate-box happy ending (which, so the tale is told, Hammerstein insisted was an 'innovative' unhappy one, apparently because the lass didn't become a megastar).

Tullio Carminati played Bruno Mahler, the composer, Natalie Hall was the tempestuous Frieda, and Katherine Carrington the little Sieglinde whom Bruno decides to make his star and his lover until she turns out to have the temperament for neither. Walter Slezak was the village schoolmaster, Karl, who finally wins Sieglinde back and Al Shean (formerly of Gallagher and Shean) had an attractive rôle as her father, a 'merry peasant' music master with a village reputation as a composer who does not come up to scratch in the big city. Kern's score included a number of extremely winning pieces, the two most successful being the song written by Papa Lessing and sweetly sung into Mahler's heart by his little daughter, 'I've Told Every Little Star', and the tenor's rhapsodic love song 'The Song is You'. There were other highlights as well: the soprano's rendition of Mahler's operetta scena 'I'm Alone' and, in particular, a charming little do-you-remember piece sung by a minor character, 'In Egern on the Tegern See'.

Music in the Air had a fine Broadway run, shifting from the Alvin to the 44th Street Theater to clock up a total of 342 performances. London's version, with Mary Ellis (Frieda), Arthur Margetson (Bruno), Eve Lister

(Sieglinde) and Bruce Carfax (Karl) ran through 275 performances, a record which was better than those that such contemporary, and altogether less conventional, Continental pieces as *Mother of Pearl* (*Eine Frau, die weiss, was sie will*) and *Ball at the Savoy* managed in the same London season, and more or less the equivalent of that put up by its nearest simulacrum, the vast combination of schmaltz and spectacle which made up London's version of *Wild Violets* (*Wenn die kleinen Veilchen blühen*).

In Australia *Music in the Air* was given one of the most lavish and publicized productions of J C Williamson Ltd's long career, with local comedy favourite Cecil Kellaway starred as Dr Lessing, lovely down-under *Dubarry* Sylvia Welling as Frieda and Shirley Dale, veteran Carrie Moore and Frank Sale in support. But Australia rejected the show wholly and Williamsons incurred both one of their biggest-ever losses and a real blow to their whole musical producing policy. In spite of this knock, the company did persevere, and *White Horse Inn* arrived at the right time to restore both finances and confidence.

In America the show retained a public. It was filmed in 1934, with Gloria Swanson appearing as Frieda and Shean in his original rôle, toured briefly, played in San Francisco first with Vivienne Segal starred, and again in the 1941-2 season with John Charles Thomas. It was mounted frequently in provincial houses, and returned to Broadway in 1951 in a revised version under the direction of Hammerstein, with Dennis King (Bruno), Jane Pickens (Frieda) and Charles Winninger (Lessing) for a run of 56 performances.

UK: His Majesty's Theatre 19 May 1933; Australia: Theatre Royal, Sydney 8 July 1933; Film Fox 1934

Recording: revival cast (RCA), film extracts (JJA) London cast items (WRC), selection (WRC) etc

THE MUSIC MAN Musical comedy in 2 acts by Meredith Willson based on a story by Willson and Franklin Lacey. Majestic Theater, New York, 19 December 1957.

'If *Guys and Dolls* is the most New York of Broadway musicals, *The Music Man* is surely the most American. There is more heart-warming truth in the Iowa folk of this tale of a tricksy travelling salesman finally shamed out of his shenanigans for the love of a good but difficult woman than in all the Ruritanian farmers and cowboys of *Oklahoma!* put together.'

The Music Man was a musical which was a long time a-borning, but it was one that proved worth waiting for. As early as 1949 Frank Loesser suggested to Meredith Willson that he make up a show out of his tales and reminiscences of his Iowa childhood, but it was another eight years, many writings and rewritings, and a false start with different producers (Feuer and Martin) before Kermit Bloomgarden's production of *The Music Man* opened on Broadway. In a tale a little reminiscent of George M Cohan's 1910 *Get-Rich-Quick Wallingford*, Robert Preston played 'Dr' Harold Hill, a travelling salesman in musical instruments whose line of patter is good enough to lumber outback Americans with tubas and triangles which they only discover they have no use for, nor any manner of learning how to play, when Hill has moved safely on to the next state. But when he arrives to turn his chat onto the folk of River City, Iowa, he finds there not only his old comrade-in-charms, Marcellus Washburn (Iggie Wolfington), but an inimical mayor (David Burns) and a young music teacher-cum-librarian, Marian Paroo (Barbara Cook), who doesn't seem to fall for his line.

Harold gets the leading ladies of the town into Classical Dance and the bickering school board into barbershop harmonies, and wins over Marian when she sees the joy a shiny cornet brings to her shy little brother, but he stays in town too long, falling in love. Exposure inevitably comes: Harold Hill is no 'Dr', no music teacher, the money the folk have been bamboozled into spending on instruments and band uniforms for their children is wasted. The Mayor is victorious, but Harold Hill has brought sunshine into many lives in River City: the once-bored ladies, the school board, Marian and little Winthrop all rally to his side, and when the River City Boys Band marches in, bright and shiny and almost playing music, his case is won. The results pay for all, and Harold Hill has a right to his happy ending.

Willson's score had as much appeal as his tale. Hill's rôle was written to accommodate a limited voice, but it moved through a variety of styles from the platinum-tongued patter of 'Trouble' as he persuades River City of its need for a band, to the swinging description of 'Seventy-Six Trombones', the wry wish for 'A Sadder But Wiser Girl' and the real romance of his duet with Marian, 'Till There Was You'. Marian's other musical moment, in a strong but unshowy soprano rôle, came in her longing wish for a person to say 'Goodnight My Someone' to, whilst the Buffalo Bills, as the harmonizing quartet, had some humorously barbershop moments in 'Lida Rose' and 'Sincere', the town ladies niggled away hilariously in a 'Pick-a-Little' ensemble, little Winthrop lisped out a joyous welcome to 'The Wells Fargo Wagon' and the piece got off to a flying start with an imaginative, chanted salesmen's ensemble, battered out to the rhythms of the wheels of the train bringing Harold Hill to River City. If it was the marching 'Seventy-Six Trombones' which became the take-away hit, virtually every part of the score of *The Music Man* was a winner.

Broadway's production ran for 1,375 performances. The first touring company went on the road nine months into the run, with Forrest Tucker in the starring rôle, and was still going strong when London's version opened and when the Broadway edition finally closed down. Harold Fielding's London production starred Van Johnson alongside Patricia Lambert (Marian) and a winsome Winthrop called Denis Waterman, who 20 years later would become one of Britain's biggest TV names. The piece played for 395 performances, surviving only a little Johnson's departure, but it did not catch on in the regions, where its very American-ness appeared to be a disadvantage.

Australia's Garnet Carroll featured Ted Scott and Carolyn Maye through five months in Melbourne and a fine Australian tour including a season at Sydney's Tivoli (12 December 1960), and a film version captured Preston's once-in-a-blue-moon performance in a musical on a film which retained virtually all of the show's original music. However, following its first runs all round, the show, whilst carrying on through a steady line of regional productions in America and occasionally elsewhere, has not been given a major revival apart from a 1980 New York City Center season with Dick van Dyke starred (5 June).

UK: Adelphi Theatre 16 March 1961; Australia: Princess
Theatre, Melbourne 5 March 1960; Film: Warner Bros 1962
Recordings: original cast (Capitol), London cast (HMV), film
soundtrack (Warner Bros), selection (Telare), composer
(Capitol) etc

DAS MUSIKANTENMÄDEL Operette in 3 acts by
Bernhard Buchbinder. Music by Georg Jarno. Theater in
der Josefstadt, Vienna, 18 February 1910.

Jarno and Buchbinder's successor to the vastly successful *Die Förster-Christl* presented the composer Josef Haydn
as one of its central characters in a curious love story which
would seem to have no historical background. Whilst
working as Kapellmeister to the womanizing Fürst
Esterhazy (Ferdinand Mayerhofer), Haydn (Kurt Lessen)
takes time out to go and visit his nephew in a neighbouring
town. There, he is mightily taken with the boy's fancied
maiden, the cow-girl Resel (Hansi Niese), and he ends up
taking her back to Eisenstadt with him. There she falls
under the eye of Esterhazy, but she does the Fürst more
harm than good when she innocently exposes his affaire
with the dancer Elena Montebelli (Käthe Krenn) to the
Fürstin (Josefine Joseffy). Haydn is preparing himself to
wed the young girl, when she discovers a song he once
wrote which reveals that she is his illegitimate daughter. So
nephew Karl (Leo Bünau) gets his girl after all.

The show played a regular 57 performances at Josef
Jarno's Theater in der Josefstadt, with its central character
tactfully described in the programme as simply 'the
Kapellmeister'. It was later played at the Raimundtheater
(28 December 1913) and in Budapest (ad Adolf Mérei),

Plate 187. **Das Musikantenmädel:** *Kurt Lessen as the composer
Haydn and Hansi Niese as his country maiden.*

but it was in Germany that it won its chief popularity,
scoring a hit at Berlin's Berliner-Theater and going on to a
mass of regional productions which combined to bring it to
a place in the top 20 of Keller's up-to-1921 survey
of 20th-century Operetten, ahead of such better-known
pieces as *Zigeunerliebe*, *Herbstmanöver*, *Der tapfere Soldat*,
Der Rastelbinder and *Die Kino-Königin*.

Hungary: Budai Színkör *A muzsikus leány* 4 June 1911; Germany:
Berliner Theater 1 September 1910

MY FAIR LADY Musical in 2 acts by Alan Jay Lerner
based on *Pygmalion* by George Bernard Shaw. Music by
Frederick Loewe. Mark Hellinger Theater, New York, 15
March 1956.

My Fair Lady is, probably deservedly, considered as the
model amongst the scenes-and-songs shows that were the
regular fare in the musical theatre in the 1940s and 1950s.
An expertly adapted libretto based on an outstanding and
outstandingly successful play in G B Shaw's bitter-sweet
Cinderella tale, *Pygmalion*, is musically illustrated with a
near-classic combination of the traditional elements of the
merriest style of Operette – the soprano heroine, the light-
comedy leading man, the romantic tenor and the music-
hall-style low comedian (but no soubrets), each equipped
with the type of songs suitable to their rôle – accompanied
by spectacular and dance elements in perfectly dosed
amounts, the whole treated in the tidiest style of contemporary Broadway.

Alan Jay Lerner's libretto slimmed Shaw's play tactfully
whilst opening it out into more settings than previously,
and in spite of combining or reorganizing some scenes and,
above all, in spite of placing an emphasis on a romantic
association between Professor Henry Higgins (Rex Harrison) and the cockney flower girl, Eliza Doolittle (Julie
Andrews), whom he educates in speech and manner until
she passes for a princess – a romance Shaw specifically
denied – the adaptation excels not only as a modern musical book, but also as a very fair representation in musical-
theatre terms of Shaw's play.

The bulk of the score falls to the two principals, a mixture of the ingénue lyrical ('I Could Have Danced All
Night', 'Wouldn't it be Loverly') and the mixed-voiced
characterful/soubrette ('Just You Wait', 'Show Me') for
Eliza and some crisp, wordful patter songs ('Why Can't the
English', 'An Ordinary Man', 'A Hymn to Him') topped by
a wistfully semi-sung, semi-spoken ballad, 'I've Grown
Accustomed to Her Face', for a Higgins coming, perhaps
too late, to a realization of a dependency he would never
have admitted in the presence of another. The low-comedy rôle of dustman Alfred Doolittle (Stanley Holloway),
Shaw's philosopher of the lower classes, supports with a
pair of cockney comedy numbers ('A Little Bit of Luck',
'Get Me to the Church on Time') and Freddy Eynsford-
Hill (John Michael King), Eliza's inept aristocratic suitor,
completes the list of solo numbers with the starry-eyed,
lilting hymn to just being 'On the Street Where You Live'.

Although the piece, in the American and musical-comedy style of its time, includes little in the way of ensemble
work and no genuine duet in its score, such pieces as the
choral Ascot Gavotte (Ascot having taken the place of Mrs
Higgins's tea party as Eliza's first trial), the countermelodied 'You Did It' and the gay, jubilant triologue
'The Rain in Spain', celebrating Eliza's triumph over her

Plate 188. **My Fair Lady:** *Glyn Worsnip (Freddy Eynsford-Hill) comes face to face with Mrs Pearce (Morar Kennedy) after his vigil on 'The Street Where You Live' (Harrogate Opera House, 1972).*

vowels, provide the necessary variation to the series of solo numbers. Almost every song in the *My Fair Lady* score became individually successful outside the show, with the lyrical 'On the Street Where You Live' and 'I Could Have Danced all Night' finding particular popularity, but all, even the stand-up numbers for Doolittle, combined impeccably with the text, in a way increasingly deemed desirable at the time, in a smooth and extremely effective whole.

The idea of a musical *Pygmalion* had begun with Gabriel Pascal, the producer who had filmed the play – with Shaw's approval and the young Wendy Hiller starred – in 1938. However, Shaw refused his permission, and it was not until after the playwright's death that Pascal actively began to push the project. It was, apparently, turned down by a long list of potential adapters and composers from Coward to Porter to Rodgers and Hammerstein before Loewe and Lerner were approached, tried, gave up, and eventually came back for a second try which produced a piece that began its life under the title *My Lady Liza*. Pascal having died without seeing his idea come to fruition, producer Herman Levin took up the growing show, and it was under his management that *My Fair Lady* – a fairly flimsy title which has become honoured with success and the years but which must, at the time, have been a desperation choice – opened in New Haven. There, before moving on to Broadway and a place in that street's history, it was slimmed of two songs, the cheekily titled 'Come to the Ball' (had *The Quaker Girl*'s big hit been truly forgotten?) and Eliza's pre-ball 'Say a Prayer for Me' (later re-used in the film *Gigi*) and of an extraneous dance routine which, like the song, held up Eliza's departure for the all-important ball.

Levin's production of *My Fair Lady* ran for 2,717 performances, establishing a long-run record for a musical play on Broadway which held for nearly a decade, until the advent of *Hello, Dolly!* A year into its run it sent out its first touring company, headed by Brian Aherne and Anne Rogers (like Miss Andrews, a *Boy Friend* Polly turned Eliza), and another year later the stars of the Broadway production (Miss Andrews, Harrison, Holloway and Robert Coote as Colonel Pickering) took themselves to London where the piece opened under the unlikely management of celebrated play producers H M Tennent. It was a piece of cool action by Tennent director 'Binkie' Beaumont which had secured the British rights before anyone else had had a chance to bid. Knowing Levin was desperate to have Rex Harrison for the lead rôle, he purposely kept his failing production of *Bell, Book and Candle* running, forcing Levin to ask him to give Harrison a release. In exchange for the release, Beaumont got a bit of the action, and *My Fair Lady* came to Tennents. The show's fame was already thoroughly established by the time it reached London, where its Broadway triumph was repeated through a run of 2,281 performances. If this stopped just a few performances short of *Salad Days*' all-time long-run record, it clearly outvalued it by the size of the auditorium of the Theatre Royal, Drury Lane, as compared to that of the little Vaudeville Theatre.

The other principal English-language centres, headed by J C Williamson Ltd's first Australian production with Robin Bailey and Bunty Turner starred, soon followed on, but *My Fair Lady* went beyond that, to areas which Broadway and British musical shows had rarely penetrated in recent years. Robert Gilbert's German adaptation was mounted at Hans Wölffer's Theater des Westens with Karin Hübner and Paul Hubschmid as an agreeably youthful Higgins, and in 1963 the once-again richly successful production moved south to play Vienna's Theater an der Wien with the same stars (112 performances). Vienna subsequently produced its own version (ad Gerhard Bronner) which translated Eliza's cockney caterwaulings into a broad Viennese (Theater an der Wien, 11 November 1969) as played by Gabriele Jacoby alongside the Higgins of Josef Meinrad through two seasons totalling 148 performances.

Manolo Fabregas and Cristina Roja starred in Mexico's *Mi bella dama* (with a certain Plácido Domingo as one of Doolittle's pals), Mogens Wieth and Gerda Gilboe top-billed in Denmark's *My Fair Lady*, Delia Scala and Gianrico Tedeschi in Italy's version and Zsuzsa Lehoczky and Lajos Básti in the Fővárosi Operettszinház's Budapest production (ad Tamás Ungvári, György Dénes), all of which maintained the now-famous English-language title. Rivka Raz and Shai Ophir starred in Israel and Bibi Ferreira and Paolo Autran in Buenos Aires, as *My Fair Lady* established itself as the most thoroughly international musical comedy in decades. Only France, as ever, stayed aloof and it was not until 1977 that *My Fair Lady* finally made its way to Lille (ad Bruno Tellenne, Pierre Carrell), there to be introduced by Claudine Coster and Dominique Tirmont.

In 1964 *My Fair Lady* was put on to film. Harrison and Holloway were called on to repeat their original rôles but, with Hollywood worried at presenting a top-of-the-bill of all British names in their British story, Julie Andrews was replaced by proven film star Audrey Hepburn and the singing voice of Marni Nixon. There was little chance that any filmed *My Fair Lady* could get everything as right as the stage show had done, and so it proved. The obviously made-in-the-studio film did not become the classic its source had, and Miss Andrews went on to make exactly that kind of classic out of her first film, *Mary Poppins*, the same year.

My Fair Lady established itself as a worldwide perennial, both in the main centres and in regional theatres of innumerable languages, and it came round with unusual speed to its first major revivals. Broadway brought it back just a decade after its closure, with Ian Richardson and Christine Andreas starred (St James Theater 25 March 1976, 377 performances), and Cameron Mackintosh and Harold Fielding followed in London in 1979 when Tony Britton starred opposite Liz Robertson and Anna Neagle in the rôle of Mrs Higgins, a rôle which had been originated by another famous veteran, Cathleen Nesbitt, and first played in Britain by Zena Dare (Adelphi Theater 25 October). In 1981 Harrison took up his old rôle as a now-rather-aged Higgins with Miss Nesbitt as his extremely aged mother in a trouble-struck touring production which eventually camped at Broadway's Uris Theater (18 August) for 119 performances, in 1992 a British touring production with Helen Hobson and Edward Fox starred took the show around the main provincial houses once again, and the following year an American tour with Richard Chamberlain as Higgins was mounted. Both these last productions made an interesting point about the show and the size of its classic status. Although classic operas have suffered all sorts of denaturization by directors in recent decades, classic musicals have – a little rewrite or so apart – been largely spared 'rethought' and gimmicky stagings on the English-language stage. On the evidence of the 1990s, *My Fair Lady* is now – in advance of its fellows – becoming as fair game as *Rigoletto* or *Don Giovanni*.

Most regional productions in America and Britain have, like the London revival, shorn *My Fair Lady* of its principal piece of stage spectacle, the Embassy Ball scene, proving that *My Fair Lady* can be brought down to *Pygmalion*-size with no loss of effect, but in Europe, where *My Fair Lady* followed the ground-breaking *Kiss Me, Kate* into a prosperous and often-staged position in the German, Austrian and Hungarian Operette houses, it eventually and inevitably fell into the hands of the famous German 'Bearbeitung' merchants, the 'improvers' of classic pieces. There, amongst 60-year-old Higginses and 50-year-old Elizas, it has been already proved that even as impeccably made a piece as *My Fair Lady* can be destructible.

UK: Theatre Royal, Drury Lane 30 April 1958; Australia: Her Majesty's Theatre, Melbourne 24 January 1959; Germany: Theater des Westens 25 October 1961; Austria: Theater an der Wien 19 September 1963; Hungary: Fővárosi Operettszinház 11 February 1966; France: Théâtre Sebastopol, Lille, 8 October 1977

Recordings: original cast (Columbia), London cast (CBS), Austrian cast (Preiser), Danish cast (Philips), Israeli casts (Columbia, Acum), Italian casts (CBS), Mexican cast (Columbia), Netherlands cast (Philips), Swedish casts (Sonet, Stora Teatern), German casts (Fontana, Philips, Metronome), Japanese cast (King), Hungarian cast (Qualiton) American revival 1976 (Columbia), film soundtracks in English, French, German (CBS) etc

MY GIRL Domestic musical play in 2 acts by James T Tanner. Lyrics by Adrian Ross. Music by F Osmond Carr. Theatre Royal, Birmingham, as *The Clergyman's Daughter*, 13 April 1896; Gaiety Theatre, London, 13 July 1896.

For his successor to *The Shop Girl*, the first of his modern-dress 'musical comedies' produced at the Gaiety Theatre, George Edwardes resorted to a practice which had not previously been his, the out-of-town try-out. *The Clergyman's Daughter* was opened at Birmingham, however, for a reason. It was very definitely much more of a musical play than had been the habit at the Gaiety – much more invested with such items as plot and character, whilst still full of Gaiety songs and dances written by the *In Town* team of Adrian Ross and Osmond Carr – and its producer needed to test the water.

Theo (Ernest Snow), son of the Rev Arthur Mildreth (Charles Ryley), has come to financial grief thanks to the devious doings of the financier von Fontein (Martin Adeson), who is now swanning around the town taking in the Mayor (Percy Paul) and his jumped-up wife (Connie Ediss) with a phoney African Prince. With the help of the comical stock-jobber Alex McGregor (John Le Hay) the villain is unmasked, Theo gets his girl (Ethel Sydney) and his sister May (Kate Cutler), whose mining shares have opportunely rocketed, gets a Lord (Paul Arthur). The story was illustrated by some jolly songs which had jabs at lady cyclists, the music hall, the grenadier guards and a whole host of topical subjects, alongside such more plot-worthy pieces as 'Stocks and Shares' and, the hit of the evening, a rewritten version of May Irwin's Broadway hit 'The Bully Song' sung by Connie Ediss, drooling plumply over 'When My Husband is Sir Tom'.

My Girl had been set up with the lead rôles intended for Seymour Hicks and Ellaline Terriss, the husband and wife lead players of the latter days of *The Shop Girl*, but Hicks refused the part of Theo when the time for West End recasting came along and Miss Terriss played the rôle of May opposite Paul Arthur until Edwardes brought Louis Bradfield in. The piece was received by the Gaiety audiences with mixed reaction. Some resented their frivolous fare being laden down with 'a number of facts about banks with limited liability and the different prices of shares', others approved the principle and others, again, the result. Some newspapermen who had cried long and loud for more plot in musical entertainments recanted. Edwardes's confidence was not high and he started to prepare a new show. But *My Girl* prospered and Edwardes had to postpone the announced *The Circus Girl*. The second time he announced it *My Girl* promptly shot up again, so the producer transferred the hardy piece to the Garrick Theatre whilst *The Circus Girl* took over the Gaiety. Most of the Gaiety's stars, of course, stayed there, so it was a shadow of the original show which played out the final seven weeks of an 183-performance run its producer clearly hadn't expected. *My Girl*'s life continued through no less than five provincial seasons and the show was seen in South Africa, where it had a considerable success, as late as 1903.

Another musical under the same title was mounted in America in 1924 (Vanderbilt Theater, 24 November). Produced by Jules Hurtig and Lyle Andrews, it was Harry Archer and Harlan Thompson's successor to their hit musical comedy *Little Jessie James*, and it offered another set of lively, catchy dance songs set to a jolly, farcical book which was written this time around the popular theme of bootlegging. To the surprise of some theatre watchers, who hadn't rated Archer and Thompson as repeaters (it got only the second-string critics on its first night), *My Girl* confirmed its authors' first success very nicely with a fine run of 291 performances.

MY LADY FRAYLE   Musical play in 2 acts by Arthur Wimperis and Max Pemberton. Lyrics by Arthur Wimperis. Music by Howard Talbot and Herman Finck. Prince of Wales Theatre, Birmingham, as *Vivien* 27 December 1915; Shaftesbury Theatre, London, 1 March 1916.

My Lady Frayle was a reversed-sex version of the Faust legend, in which Lady Frayle (Irene Browne) vows her soul and that of her ward, Dick Bassett (J V Bryant) to Lucifer (Cecil Humphreys) in exchange for the youth and beauty that will allow her to win Dick away from young Virginia Desborough (Anne Croft). The dramatic central story was shot through by a comical one involving the music-hall's Miss Vera de Vere (Cicely Debenham), butler Wilcox (Arnold Richardson) and the Dean of Dorchester (Courtice Pounds). An unusually strong libretto was illustrated by a score which, at its best, was one of the finest London had heard in a long time, rising to a dramatic peak at the end of the first act as Lady Frayle cries out to Lucifer for her lost youth in Herman Finck's 'Just One Hour' (one critic, already, compared the number to the work of Puccini). The comic side was well served too, with a jolly piece on 'Married Life', a speech lesson on 'Papa, Potato, Prisms and Prunes' and a dissertation on that new phenomenon 'Flappers', as well as a ringing 'Song of the Bowl' for ageing D'Oyly Carte tenor Pounds, now in a second coming as the best singing character man in the business.

If Pounds was well cast, however, producer Courtneidge made a mess of his lead casting. He used up two Lady Frayles out of town and a third, 19-year-old Irene Browne, chosen to open in town, was so vocally under-equipped that she lost her voice in rehearsal and the opening night was played by her understudy. Nevertheless, the show won a marvellous first-night reception and superlative notices, but not a run. It closed after 129 performances, and although it went out in three touring companies in 1916 and in 1917 (one with Dina North, one with Hilda Charteris, and one with certified vocalist Phyllys LeGrand) and again in 1918, 1919 and 1920 it never found itself the place in the repertoire that it might have been expected to.

My Lady Frayle was also seen in Australia, produced under the management of Hugh D McIntosh, with a fine singer, Vera Pearce, billed as 'Australia's own beauty actress', starred alongside ex-Savoyard Claude Flemming (Lucifer), Goodie – daughter of Ada – Reeve (Virginia) and Marie La Varre (Vera), but here again it struck bad luck. Announced to open on 1 February it saw its first night cancelled when all Sydney's theatres were closed by the authorities because of an influenza epidemic. It was more than a month before the show could get on the stage and then, after a few weeks, it was closed down when the epidemic worsened again. Transferred to Melbourne (Tivoli, 26 April) it finally got six uninterrupted weeks and was brought back later in the year for a second showing.

The ever-touring Maurice Bandmann company hawked *My Lady Frayle* as part of their repertoire throughout the Orient, but in spite of its wide showing, it did not succeed in leaving a mark in the southern hemisphere any more than in the northern. Its score was heard one last time when it was broadcast in 1936 by the BBC with Edith Day singing the rôle of Lady Frayle.

Australia: Tivoli Theatre, Sydney 8 March 1919

MY LADY MOLLY   Comedy opera in 2 acts by George H Jessop. Additional lyrics by Percy Greenbank and Charles H Taylor. Music by Sidney Jones. Theatre Royal, Brighton, 11 August 1902; Terry's Theatre, London, 14 March 1903.

After Sidney Jones left Daly's Theatre, the site of his greatest successes, his first new work was a piece in a different mould from those he had written for George Edwardes's theatre. *My Lady Molly* was a 'comedy opera', a piece on the lines of *Dorothy* and classic English comic opera, with a libretto by George Jessop, the author of *Shamus O'Brien*, which busied itself with marriages, disguises and rapier-fights in 18th-century England. The score, whilst not neglecting the comic, was based largely on ballads in the classic English style and a full book of well-written ensembles. *My Lady Molly* used no Lionel Monckton, as Edwardes had done, to pop up-to-date point numbers into Jones's score.

The tale had Lady Molly Martingale (Sybil Arundale) getting into disguise as Harry Romney (Richard Green) to prevent that young man's marriage to Alice Coverdale (Decima Moore). The real Harry is imprisoned as an impostor, and ends up fighting a duel with and finally marrying the false Harry. The comedy was provided by the Irish servant of both Harrys, Mickey O'Dowd (Bert Gilbert), equipped with some fine comic songs ('Don't Whistle So Loud', 'Ballinasloe').

Jones himself produced *My Lady Molly* and he put it out on the road with himself conducting and *Florodora* director/choreographer Sydney Ellison staging. It was a splendid success, and the following year Frederick Mouillot took it over and produced it in London with the same leading players for an excellent run of 342 performances. The producer piled on four matinées a week to cope with the demand for seats, but when his lease ran out he was obliged to close. The following season *My Lady Molly* was back on the road, its fine English record topped up by productions in South Africa and in Australia where Florence Young (Molly), Carrie Moore (Alice), Harold Thorley (Harry) and George Lauri (Mickey) were featured to considerable success. However, someone in America, doubtless sparked by the girl-in-man's-clothing plot of the show, came up with the idea of starring British music-hall star Vesta Tilley, the celebrated travesty 'Burlington Bertie from Bow', as Lady Molly. Miss Tilley naturally brought her own grindingly unsuitable material to interpolate in Jones's well-made score ('Algy', 'The Seaside Sultan') and she and the show were encouraged to leave New York after 15 performances. Miss Tilley did not remain long with the show, and she was replaced by the less unlikely Ethel Levey as *My Lady Molly* went around America.

Australia: His Majesty's Theatre, Melbourne 9 May 1903; USA: Daly's Theater 5 January 1904

MY MARYLAND   Musical romance in 3 acts by Dorothy Donnelly. Music by Sigmund Romberg. Jolson's Theater, New York, 12 September 1927.

A musical version of Clyde Fitch's highly successful Civil-War romance *Barbara Frietchie*, *My Maryland* presented the historically elderly Barbara (Evelyn Herbert) as a young and lovely adherent to the Union cause – and to

Plate 189. *A dramatic moment from* **My Maryland**, *the musical play which still holds the long-run record in the Philadelphia theatre.*

the Union Captain Trumbull (Nathaniel Wagner) – in the Confederate stronghold of Frederick, Maryland. The jealous Jack Negly (Warren Hull) and his father, a colonel in the Confederate army (Louis Cassavant), try to kill Trumbull and then, when Barbara defiantly waves the Union flag before the advancing Confederate Colonel Stonewall Jackson (Arthur Cunningham), do their best to have her shot as a traitor. The girl is saved by Jackson's magnanimity. The musical did not, like the play, go on to include Barbara's murder by Negly and Negly's subsequent execution, but remained happily on an ending which brought the young folk together.

The work of the *Student Prince* team of author Dorothy Donnelly and composer Sigmund Romberg, in their first re-pairing in the three years since their great hit, the Shuberts' production of *My Maryland* was, from the first, marked out as a good thing. The fashion for romantic costume operetta was high, the tale was a dashing and respected one with opportunity not only for spectacle but for the massed male-voice choral effects that had been such a triumph in *The Student Prince*, and Romberg had written an attractive score with the stirring Connecticut

Marching Song, a choral hymn to 'Your Land and my Land', soon fingered as a big winner amongst a bookful of romantic music for Miss Herbert, Wagner and Hull. The rest of it ('familiar American airs worked into the texture of the European operetta form ... a background of Offenbach with Viennese colour and American decorations and flourishes') included a strangely Irishy number called 'Mother' for Barbara, waltz duos for her with Trumbull ('Silver Moon') and the rejected Jack ('Won't You Marry Me?') who, if he didn't get the girl, got marginally the better song, a sneezing song ('Ker-Choo!') for Berta Donn in the supporting rôle of Sue Royce, and a touch of comedy and ragtimey music for George Rosener.

The show's reception in its pre-Broadway run in a Philadelphia in the throes of the Sesquiecentennial Exposition was sensational. There had been nothing quite like it in the proud and colourful history of the Philadelphia musical theatre. Business was so great that there was no question of moving the production onwards, and *My Maryland* simply stayed in Philadelphia. And stayed, and stayed. By the time that the Shuberts decided that enough was enough, and that it was time to take their newest hit to New York, it had played for no fewer than 40 weeks in Philadelphia, a record for a musical in the town and one which, 65 years later, still stands.

My Maryland was neither the first nor the last Philadelphia hit to find a less enthusiastic reception on Broadway. Not unenthusiastic, just less enthusiastic. Romberg's score was much liked, particularly the now famous marching song, which nevertheless won some queries over its originality ('it starts out a bit like "Le Sabre de mon père", and swings by way of a German student song effect into "John Brown's Body" ... none the less does it acquire a character of its own, a real "lift" as well as a fine swing'), but the expected landslide didn't occur. However, Broadway was on a high in the later 1920s, business in general was grand, and the Shuberts had amortised their expenses thoroughly in Philadelphia, so, without provoking the interest of the season's other major musicals (*Good News, Show Boat, A Connecticut Yankee, The Three Musketeers, Funny Face* – although it had a longer run than the last-named), *My Maryland* ran through the season and closed with 312 Broadway performances to its credit. Although it subsequently toured, it was not exported in the way that each of those other pieces were, and its Philadelphia season remained its greatest achievement.

MYNHEER JAN Comic opera in 3 acts by Harry Paulton and 'Mostyn Tedde' (Edward Paulton). Music by Edward Jakobowski. Comedy Theatre, London, 14 February 1887.

Paulton and Jakobowski's follow-up to the amazing *Erminie* was a piece dogged by what might have been bad luck, but might equally have been a case of a swollen head or two. Cleverly constructed on the *Erminie* plan, with Paulton and his *Erminie* sidekick, Frank Wyatt, this time cast as a pair of rebels in the Spanish occupied Netherlands, *Mynheer Jan* had Hans (Paulton), disguised as Don Diego, the pretender to the hand of the governor's daughter (producer Violet Melnotte), with Wyatt as his servant, inveigling their way into the gubernatorial fortress in the same way the two thieves had done in the earlier play. Paulton's imitations of the Spanish grandee were the show's highlight and on a par with his *Erminie* performance as Cadeau/the Baron, and the company's new leading lady, Camille D'Arville, was well supplied with winning songs alongside the comical ones for Paulton and some quite stiff baritone music for Wyatt. A fine supporting cast included Kate Munroe, Madame Amadi in an older-lady rôle which was, for once, not a caricature, Marius as the Governor and the tenor Joseph Tapley.

The authors and producer were faced with competing with the reputation of their own great hit, but *Mynheer Jan* won a good London reception – better than that of Gilbert and Sullivan's *Ruddigore* a few weeks previously – and it looked set for a fine run, until authors and producer fell out, apparently over money. The show was closed after 35 performances, and the authors themselves put it on tour, but without Wyatt who had recently become 'Mr Melnotte' and without Miss Melnotte's business acumen. The tour lasted eight weeks. The American success of *Erminie* nevertheless encouraged a production there, but a company headed by C H Drew and William T Carleton did not make it beyond two weeks in Philadelphia.

USA: Chestnut Street Theater, Philadelphia 17 September 1888

MY ONE AND ONLY *see* FUNNY FACE

MYRTIL, Odette (b Paris, 28 June 1898; d Doylestown, Pa, 18 November 1978). French performer in mostly Broadway musicals.

At first a violinist in music hall, Mlle Myrtil appeared in revue on both sides of the Atlantic, playing in two editions of Ziegfeld's *Follies* in New York, and in such pieces as *The Bing Boys Are Here, Tabs, Tails Up* and *Bubbly* in London. At the age of 21 she was seen as the French actress Cora Merville in the London musical farce *The Officers' Mess*, before returning to revue and cabaret. She made a rare musical comedy appearance at the Paris Apollo, playing Venus in *La Ceinture de Vénus* in 1921, but in the mid-1920s, having moved definitively to America, she turned more to the musical stage and appeared on Broadway as Hortense Schneider to the Offenbach of Allan Prior in *Love Song* (1925), as the young gypsy Manja in *Gräfin Mariza*, as George Sand opposite the Chopin of Guy Robertson in another biomusical pasticcio, *White Lilacs* (1928), and created the rôle of the jealous Odette in Kern's *The Cat and the Fiddle* (1931).

During a period where she doubled her performing career with work as a dress designer, she took over from Lyda Roberti in *Roberta*, played Mrs van Dare in *The Firefly* in Los Angeles and, after more than a decade of absence from Broadway, returned to play the motoring Countess de la Fère in the 1945 revival of *The Red Mill* (equipped, as almost invariably, with her violin). After several years further playing in regional productions and nightclubs, she succeeded to the rôle of Bloody Mary in Broadway's *South Pacific* (1952). Her last Broadway appearances were as Madame Marstonne in the short-lived *Maggie* and as Belle Piquery in *Saratoga* (1959), after which she retired to run a restaurant in Pennsylvania.

Mlle Myrtil also appeared in the screen version of the Rodgers and Hart musical comedy *I Married an Angel*.

MY SON JOHN *see* RIQUETTE

THE MYSTERY OF EDWIN DROOD Musical in 2 acts suggested by Charles Dickens's novel of the same name. Book, lyrics and music by Rupert Holmes. Delacorte Theater, New York, 4 August 1985; Imperial Theater, 2 December 1985.

Billed as the 'solve-it-yourself Broadway musical', *The Mystery of Edwin Drood* took Charles Dickens's famously unfinished novel of the same name and presented it in a burlesque music-hall style up to the moment where Dickens's narrative ceased. At that point, the audience was asked both to vote as to the identity of the mysterious Dick Datchery and to nominate their choice as the murderer of Edwin Drood. The show finished in accordance with the chairman's opinion of the house's choices.

The entertainment was presented as the work of the 'Music Hall Royale' company under their chairman Cartwright (George Rose), and the rôle of Edwin Drood was played in travesty by the company's 'leading lady' Alice Nutting (Betty Buckley). Schizophrenic choirmaster John Jasper (Howard McGillin) lusts helplessly after the purer-than-pearls Rosa Bud (Patti Cohenour), the betrothed-since-birth of his nephew Edwin. She also attracts the attentions of the mysterious Singhalese Neville Landless (John Herrera), who has arrived in town with his sister, Helena (Jana Schneider). Add to the plot, amongst others, an opium-house keeper known as Princess Puffer (Cleo Laine), the curious Rev Crisparkle (George N Martin) and an enigmatic bit-part player with ambitions called Bazzard (Joe Grifasi), and when young Drood vanishes after a Christmas Eve storm, there are plenty of suspects on hand.

The score, like the libretto written by popular songster Rupert Holmes, was a winning mixture of pastiche music-hall songs for Puffer ('The Wages of Sin', 'The Garden Path to Hell') and the Chairman and company ('Off to the Races'), some adventurous character solos for such as Jasper ('A Man Could Go Quite Mad'), Rosa (the beautiful soprano 'Moonfall') and the peculiar Bazzard ('Never the Luck'), and several highly successful ensembles – a quartet with chorus about 'Ceylon', a warning pre-Christmas septet 'No Good Can Come From Bad' and the passionate face-to-face of Rosa and Jasper which brought the first act to its climax ('The Name of Love').

Following its original production at the New York Shakespeare Festival (25 performances), The Mystery of Edwin Drood moved to Broadway's Imperial Theater, gathering in the Tony Awards for the season's best musical, book, score and direction (as well as one for Rose) on its way. However, in spite of its attractions and the recognition given to them, the show did not take off as it might have. An effort to give it a snappier appeal was epitomized in a title change to the rather bald Drood, but ultimately The Mystery of Edwin Drood went the way of the majority of Broadway shows of the 1980s which favoured wit and comic content over glitter, drama and/or spectacle. It found an audience for a respectable but barely blockbusting 608 performances.

A London production, mounted at the Savoy Theatre, had vaudeville straight man Ernie Wise (Chairman) and former pop star Lulu (Puffer) awkwardly top-billed alongside David Burt (Jasper), Julia Hills (Drood), Cohenour, Marilyn Cutts (Helena) and Paul Bentley (Bazzard), but the parody of music-hall styles still current in London's Players' Theatre and provincial summer shows was no novelty for London, and the piece played to sparse houses (which nevertheless included a nub of hugely enthusiastic partisans who returned over and over again) for 68 performances.

The German première of Drood (ad Markus Weber) was given in Pforzheim in 1991 with Veit-Ulrich Kurth (Jasper), Tanja Hiller (Drood) and Lilian Huynen (Rosa) featured.

An earlier musical attempt to put an ending on The Mystery of Edwin Drood was given by T C de Leon in his Jasper. In this version Jasper turned out guiltless, and Drood was not dead but a druggie.

UK: Savoy Theatre 7 May 1987; Germany: Pforzheim Drood 31 December 1991
Recording: original cast (Polydor)

MY SWEETHEART Operatic comic drama in 3 acts by William Gill. Haverley's 14th Street Theater, New York, 18 September 1882.

A vehicle for the little-girl-style personality performer Minnie Palmer, My Sweetheart was a combination of a heavily sentimental melodrama and a good deal of traditional 'Dutch' low comedy, studded with songs, dances and any other 'turns' the star felt like interpolating. Miss Palmer played Tina Hatzell, an angelic and very juvenile German-American who is the little sweetheart of the handsome Tony Faust (Charles Arnold). When Tony becomes rich and a German Count, the fawners and filchers crowd round and the adventuress Louisa Fleeter wins his adoration, but Tina and good Doctor Oliver expose her, and Tony goes blind from shock at the second-act curtain. He has regained his sight by the time the third act begins, cared for on the Hatzell farm, but Louisa and her crooked brother return to try again, only to be defeated a second time. She sweeps out, lamenting 'I have played high, and lost, and even you, Tina, cannot pity me! Farewell!' and leaving Tony and his little sweetheart to waltz to the final curtain together. Some of the hither-and-yon collection of songs used in My Sweetheart became a popular and fixed part of the entertainment, whilst others were movable and were regularly moved and/or replaced.

Originally staged in her native America, this unsophisticated variety-show-cum-black-moustachioed-weepie, adapted for the British stage by Fred G Maeder, proved a novelty and an enormous success when the heavily publicized Miss Palmer brought it to the British provinces. It was toured both with and later even without its star for many years. Miss Palmer went so far as to venture a London season with – for such a blatantly unsophisticated piece – outstandingly good results (163 performances), and she happily trouped her show as far afield as Australia, where she toured through Melbourne, Sydney (Opera House), Adelaide, Ballarat and Sandhurst for a total of 32 successful weeks, then on to New Zealand, Japan and to India. When she attempted new pieces (My Brother's Sister, The School Girl) she found that, in spite of a faithful following, My Sweetheart without her continued to do better than she did without My Sweetheart, and she returned time and again to her trusty vehicle.

My Sweetheart was still to be seen stalking around the American outer-backs, now credited to authors R A Roberts and Thomas Reilley and composer Alfred Robyn, with no less a leading man than Charles Winninger, as late as 1908.

UK: Royal Princess's Theatre, Glasgow 4 June 1883, Strand Theatre 14 January 1884; Australia: Princess Theatre, Melbourne 31 January 1886

N

EINE NACHT IN VENEDIG Operette in 3 acts by F Zell and Richard Genée based on *Le Château Trompette* by Jules Cormon and Michel Carré. Music by Johann Strauss. Friedrich-Wilhelmstädtisches Theater, Berlin, 3 October 1883.

The zigzagging line of Johann Strauss's career as a theatrical composer followed the successes of *Das Spitzentuch der Königin* (1880) and the delicious *Der lustige Krieg* (1882) with a failure in *Eine Nacht in Venedig*. Theatrical myth has it that librettists Zell and Genée offered the composer the choice between their versions of *The Lady of Lyons* and the French comic opera text *Le Château Trompette*, previously set by François Gevaert (Opéra-Comique, 23 April 1860), and kidded him into taking the weaker of the two scripts, whilst Millöcker made *Der Bettelstudent* of the other. That myth, for all that it made a good story, has now been discredited. Strauss – who had in any case a weakness for Italian-set texts – simply accepted and set the book of *Eine Nacht in Venedig* as he had those of his earlier works. It was only later that he vilified Zell and Genée's work and, claiming not to have read the dialogue prior to production, blamed it for not fitting the moods of his music. In fact, whilst the book for *Eine Nacht in Venedig*, with its conventional story of randy nobility and tricksy ladies and wenches paraded through an actful of disguises and now-you-bed-me-now-you-don'ts to a happy ending, was no masterpiece, it was no worse – and indeed even better – than many other Operette libretti of the era.

Old Senator Delacqua (Herr Binder) has plans to send his young wife, Barbara, to an out-of-the-way aunt when the philandering Duke of Urbino (Sigmund Steiner) comes to town, but whilst the Duke's pimping barber Caramello (Jani Szika) is setting up a nice little enlèvement, Barbara is organizing a trick of her own. She arranges for the fishergirl, Annina (Ottilie Collin), Caramello's sweetheart, to take her place on the departing gondola so that she may spend the night, instead, with her young lover, Enrico. And so it is the disguised Annina who is duly lifted from the gondola as it glides towards Barbara's aunt's home and carried off to the Ducal masked ball, which Delacqua is attending with a phoney wife, the cook Ciboletta (Frln Grünfeld). As a result, both Caramello and Ciboletta's chap, the pastrycook Pappacoda, spend the evening trying to stop the Duke getting their girls in a quiet corner. After a third act of little action, all ends happily with promotion and marriage for the two boys and their signorine, as the Duke covers his tracks.

If Strauss's score had not the brilliance nor the warmth of the music of his *Der lustige Krieg*, it nevertheless included some winning ensembles – the swinging carnival ensemble 'Alle maskiert', the sweet soprano-voiced 'Die Tauben von San Marco' and the pretty apropos of nothing serenade 'Ninana' – and, amongst its solos, a charming, unfishwifely soprano entrance for Annina ('Frutti di mare'), a gondola-song for Caramello ('Komm in die Gondel') and the Duke's featured Lagunen-Walzer ('Ach, wie so herrlich').

Eine Nacht in Venedig was ill received on its Berlin production, and the authors put in some solid rewrites before the Theater an der Wien's production. One of the most notable of these was the transfer of the relyricked Lagunen-Walzer from the rôle of the Duke to that of Caramello, a part now, in the hands of *Der lustige Krieg*'s triumphant Alexander Girardi, thoroughly turned into the star rôle of the piece. Josef Joseffy (Duke), Karoline Finaly (Annina), Felix Schweighofer (Pappacoda) and Rosa Streitmann (Ciboletta) headed the rest of a very fine cast, and this time the reception was better. The show was played a fair 35 times, with a guest season at the Carltheater. Maintained in the repertoire, *Eine Nacht in Venedig* was played in 1886–7 with Karl Streitmann as Caramello, Collin (whom the admiring Strauss had had brought from Berlin to Vienna) in her original rôle, and

Plate 190. **Eine Nacht in Venedig** *The Herzog von Urbino (Hans-Josef Kasper) and Annina (Monika Starke) unmasked in the Theater Trier production of 1986.*

young Therese Biedermann making her Vienna début as Ciboletta, again in 1892–3, passing its 100th performance in the process, and in 1896–8.

In spite of the improvements, however, the show did not excite international attention in the way Strauss's previous shows had done. J C Duff ventured an English-language production at New York's Daly's Theater with a cast headed by Louise Lester and W H Fitzgerald, and Gustav Amberg later ventured a three-week German-language season of what he called *Venetianische Nächte* with the visiting Streitmann (8 January 1890), but Britain, France and Australia all passed the piece by and even the voracious Budapest theatre did not get around to trying it until several years on (ad Béla J Fái, Ferenc Reiner). The Népszinház finally played a version in 1890 and then only 12 times.

The name of Strauss on its billhead ensured that the piece reappeared occasionally in Austria, notably in a revival in 1912 at Ronacher with Grete Holm starred, but it did not ever find itself a real place in the general repertoire, until later writers latched on to the saleable Strauss name and, doubtless additionally encouraged by the picturesque setting of the show, started putting out their own 'versions' of *Eine Nacht in Venedig*. Carl Hagemann seems to have started the process with his Baden-Baden production of 1918, before the Theater an der Wien staged an Ernst Marischka rewrite, with Strauss's score done over by E W Korngold, in 1923. The main effect of this musical remake, which pasted larger and smaller bits of other Strauss works into the composer's score, was to beef up the rôle of the Duke (played by Richard Tauber) with a couple of throbbingly romantic tenor bon-bons, one ('Sei mir gegrüsst, du holdes Venezia') fabricated from the song 'Der Frühling lacht, es singen die Vöglein' from *Simplicius*, the other ('Treu sein – das liegt mir nicht') made over from one of *Eine Nacht*'s own soprano songs. Betty Fischer (Annina) and Hubert Marischka (Caramello) co-starred through 32 performances during which the show was further vulgarized by the addition of a piano concert, stuck into the second half to feature Pietro Mazzini in what now began to resemble an old-days variety musical.

However, Strauss, plus Venice, plus throbbing tenors were all definite pluses at this period, and versions of this version of the show began to appear elsewhere. The Vienna Staatsoper (1929) and the Berlin Opera (1931) took in *Eine Nacht in Venedig*, a new *Egy éj Velenceben* surfaced in Budapest (1924), Yvonne d'Arle starred in a St Louis Muny production in America (1924) and the Monte Carlo Opera House brought out a first French version. Later, another inveterate adapter, Gustav Quedenfeldt, brought out his version (1936, w Eugen Rex, Karl Tutein) which subsequently surfaced at Vienna's Raimundtheater (31 December 1944) and, in 1948, conductor Anton Paulik brought out a version at the Volksoper, where the show returned in 1975 to mark Johann Strauss's 150th birthday. Britain finally heard *A Night in Venice* when it played briefly at London's Cambridge Theatre (ad Dudley Glass, Lesley Storm) with Dennis Noble and Daria Bayan heading the cast, before moving into the Phoenix Theatre for a 433-performance run, by far the longest, in any-sized house, that the show had ever achieved. Another British version, based on Paulik's remake, but taking in non-

Strauss music, surfaced at the English National Opera in 1976.

One planned revival, sponsored in America by the Shuberts, defied previous opinion by ultimately throwing out all the music and using just the despised libretto as the basis for what ultimately became Rudolf Friml's *Annina*. Since then, the show has found its niche – in varying versions – largely as a spectacular piece for specialist theatres: the vast American Jones Beach Marine Theater hosted a huge Mike Todd production of an alarmingly adapted version in 1952, and another version was given with great effect at the Seebühne at Bregenz on several occasions. However, even without real water, gondolas and Venetian carnivals in support, *Eine Nacht in Venedig* seems to be more liked, certainly by adapters and theatre directors, in the 1980s and 1990s than it was in the 1880s and 1890s, and it has indubitably outlasted the then-more-popular *Das Spitzentuch der Königin* and *Der lustige Krieg*. And that in spite of the fact that none of the many folk who have fiddled with Zell and Genée's libretto have come up with anything better (or probably as good as) than the text Strauss so disliked.

A film version, whose Rudolf Österreicher screenplay also stuck much closer to the original script than Operette films were inclined to do, featured Hans Olden (Duke), Jeannette Schultze (Annina), Hermann Thimig (Pappacoda), Peter Pasetti (Caramello) and Lotte Lang (Ciboletta), with Nico Dostal conducting his own arrangements of Strauss's music.

Austria: Theater an der Wien 9 October 1883; USA: Daly's Theater 26 April 1884; Hungary: Budai Színkör *Egy éj Velenceben* 13 May 1887; Monaco: Théâtre de Monte-Carlo (Fr) 19 March 1930; UK: Cambridge Theatre *A Night in Venice* 25 May 1944; Film: Universal Films 1953

Recordings: complete (EMI, HMV, CBS) etc

A NAGYMAMA Enekes vigjatek (musical comedy) in 3 acts by Arpád Pásztor adapted from the play by Gergely Csiky. Music by Raoul Mader. Népszinház-Vigopera, Budapest, 11 February 1908.

Csiky's play, first produced at the Nemzeti Színház on 6 March 1891 with Cornélia Prielle in the titular rôle of the grandmother, was made into a 'musical comedy' for the Népszinhaz-Vigopera by experienced librettist Pásztor and the director of the short-lived theatre, composer Raoul Mader.

No less a star than Lujza Blaha was the Countess Szerémy, the grandmother of the musical's title, with Ferenc Pázmán as her grandson, Ernő. The Countess has arranged that her grandson should wed his beloved cousin, Márta (Olga Turchányi), and, rather than cause the old lady pain, the girl has agreed to the betrothal even though she is in love with the young baron Kálmán Örkényi (Béla Bálint). But the truth soon comes out. Then Ernő finds his affections engaged by Kálmán's sister, Piroska (Eugenie della Donna). The Countess – whose last thought was to make an unhappy match – sees the prospect of a different unhappiness, for between the Szerémy family and the Örkényi family there is a shadow. In his youth, the senior Baron Örkényi (Vince Horváth) asked for the hand of the Countess in marriage and was refused by her parents. Grandmother now takes matters in hand. She calls upon

Plate 191. **A nagymama:** *Lujza Blaha in the most famous rôle of the last part of her career, alongside Olga Turchányi.*

the Baron and tells him the old truth: she had been in love with him, but she had not been brave enough to defy her parents. She asks him to let the young folk wed as their hearts will, and the Baron agrees.

A nagymama was far and away the most successful of the seven musical shows mounted at the Népszinház-Vigopera during its year of activity, passing its 50th night on 22 April 1908, and totalling 65 nights in the repertoire (more than twice as many as *The Catch of the Season*, *Der Mann mit den drei Frauen* or *Tündérszerelem*) before the theatre's closure. The show was then taken up by the Magyar Színház (22 September 1908), which had switched from musicals to an all-play schedule, but which kept the piece in its repertoire and included it in its programme when it visited Vienna's Theater in der Josefstadt in 1912 with its Hungarian-language programme. The Király Színház followed just weeks behind, mounting its first musical *Nagymama* on 23 November 1908.

A film version was subsequently made, in which Blaha made her last film appearance.

A nagymama, stamped with Blaha's image, became a special classic of the Hungarian stage, reserved as a vehicle for other senior musical stars of special class. It was played by Lilly Berky – an operett soubrette before going on to an acting career – at the József Attila Színház, then by Hanna Honthy who appeared in a new production at the Fővárosi Operettszínház in 1964 (22 October). Another version mounted at the same house in 1991, featuring Marika Németh in the title-rôle, was an adaptation of Csiky's play by György Kardoss with music by Szabolc Fényes.

Austria: Theater in der Josefstadt (Hung) *Die Grossmama* 13 June 1912

DIE NÄHERIN Posse mit Gesang in 4 acts by Ludwig Held. Music by Carl Millöcker. Theater an der Wien, Vienna, 13 March 1880.

Produced at the Theater an der Wien under the management of Maximilian Steiner, in a season where the two old rivals Marie Geistinger and 'Pepi' Gallmeyer were featured, Ludwig Held's musical comedy *Die Näherin* fell to the lot of Geistinger, whilst Gallmeyer got *Die Böhmin* and made do mostly with her previous year's hit *Der Gypsfigur.*

Geistinger played Lotti Griessmayer, the Näherin (seamstress) of the title, and made an 'unforgettable hit' in the comical rôle of the girl who never stops talking. Alexander Girardi as Stefan Hoch, Carl Adolf Friese as Julius von Sombár and Herr Witte as Ferdinand supported the star as the show was played for 50 nights at the Theater an der Wien, before settling in as a part of Geistinger's regular repertoire. In 1881 she introduced it to America at New York's Thalia Theater, repeating the following season, only to discover that the opposition had brought Gallmeyer to America, and Gallmeyer, as well as playing her own famous rôles, was also playing *Die Näherin*. The show provoked sufficient interest in America for an English-language version to be produced by John McCaull. *Chatter*, with Mathilde Cottrelly as Lotti, De Wolf Hopper as Jeremiah Hackett (ex-Sombár), Edwin Hoff (Frederick Hackett) and Harry Macdonough (Ganymede Gurgle), topped up Millöcker's score with the hit song from the theatre's previous production *The Black Hussar (Der Feldprediger,* also by Millöcker) and ran four weeks.

Die Näherin won further productions in Austria and Germany (ad Eduard Jacobson), in Prague and throughout Central Europe following its Vienna première, but it remained always connected with Geistinger who kept it in her repertoire for the rest of her career, playing it in America as late as 1897 and as part of her last season at the Carltheater in 1898.

In 1913 a revised version by Hugo Held, with additional music by Leo Held, was seen at Vienna's Theater in der Josefstadt (13 April).

Germany: Theater am Gärtnerplatz, Munich 7 May 1880; Friedrich-Wilhelmstädtisches Theater, Berlin 4 September 1880; USA: Thalia Theater (Ger) 8 April 1881; Wallack's Theater *Chatter* 17 August 1885

DE NAJAC, Émile (b Lorient, 14 December 1828; d Paris, 11 April 1889).

A highly successful French playwright and vaudevillist, whose best-known work was his collaboration with Sardou on the international hit *Divorçons* (Palais-Royal, 6 December 1880), de Najac also produced a number of opérette libretti without striking comparative success. Several of his successful straight pieces were also subsequently turned into musical shows, notably the play *Bébé* (Gymnase 10 March 1877 w Alfred Hennequin) produced in Britain as *Oh, Don't, Dolly!* (1919), the 1878 *Les Petites Correspondences* (w Hennequin) played in Vienna as *Kleine Anzeigen* (music: Brandl, Carltheater 25 September 1880) and, inevitably, *Divorçons*, which became *Frau Lebedame* in 1907 (Anselm Goetzl/Rudolf Bernauer, Alexander Pordes-Milo, Neue Deutsches Theater, Prague 31 December) and *Cyprienne* in 1966 (Gerhard Jussenhoven/Curt Flatow, Theater am Dom, Cologne, December).

1857 **La Momie de Roscoco** (Eugène Ortolan, Émile Jonas) 1 act Théâtre des Bouffes-Parisiens 27 July

1858 **Mam'zelle Jeanne** (Léonce Cohen) 1 act Théâtre des Bouffes-Parisiens 17 February

1860 **C'était moi** (Jean-Jacques de Billemont/w Charles Deulin) 1 act Théâtre des Bouffes-Parisiens 27 March

1861 **La Beauté du Diable** (Jules Alary/w Eugène Scribe) 1 act Opéra-Comique 28 May

1864 **Bégayements d'amour** (Albert Grisar/w Deulin) 1 act Théâtre Lyrique 8 December

1865 **Les Douze Innocents** (Grisar) 1 act Théâtre des Bouffes-Parisiens 19 October

1866 **Bettina** (Cohen) 1 act Fantaisies-Parisiennes 14 June

1868 **Petit Bonhomme vit encore** (Louis Deffès) 1 act Théâtre des Bouffes-Parisiens 19 December

1870 **Calonice** (Jules ten Brinck) 1 act Théâtre de l'Athénée 19 May

1872 **Le Docteur Rose** (Luigi Ricci) Théâtre des Bouffes-Parisiens 10 February

1872 **Au pied du mur** (Ricci) 1 act Théâtre des Bouffes-Parisiens 11 February

1872 **Un garçon de cabinet** (Adrien Talexy) 1 act Folies-Marigny 4 May

1872 **La Fête des lanternes** (Talexy) 1 act Folies-Marigny 2 October

1878 **Les Noces de Fernande** (Deffès/w Victorien Sardou) Opéra-Comique 19 November

1881 **Maître Grelot** (Talexy) 1 act Folies-Bordelaises, Bordeaux 1 September

1882 **La Bonne Aventure** (Jonas/w Henri Bocage) Théâtre de la Renaissance 3 November

1882 **Ah! Le Bon Billet** (Frédéric Toulmouche/w E Bureau, F.Jattiot) 1 act Théâtre de la Renaissance 6 December

1883 **Le Premier Baiser** (Jonas/w Raoul Toché) Théâtre des Nouveautés 21 March

1885 **La Vie mondaine** (Charles Lecocq/w Paul Ferrier) Théâtre des Nouveautés 13 February

1887 **La Noce à Nini** (Hervé/w Albert Millaud) Théâtre des Variétés 19 March

1887 **Le Roi malgré lui** (Emmanuel Chabrier/w Paul Burani) Opéra-Comique 18 May

1888 **La Japonaise** (Louis Varney/w Millaud) Théâtre des Variétés 23 November

NANON, die Wirthin vom 'goldenen Lamm' Operette in 3 acts by F Zell based on the play *Ninon, Nanon et Madame de Maintenon* by Emmanuel Théaulon, Armand d'Artois and Lesguillon. Music by Richard Genée. Theater an der Wien, Vienna, 10 March 1877.

Zell and Genée's long-popular Operette was based on a comédie-vaudeville from the early part of the French century and it told the story of Nanon, the hostess at the Inn of the Golden Lamb (Bertha Olma), and of her romance with the man she thinks is a drum major. He is actually the gaily philandering Marquis d'Aubigny (Jani Szika) and as, when it comes to the point, he has no intention of marrying the little innkeeper, he arranges to disappear by getting himself arrested for duelling. In order to try to win his release, Nanon goes to beg the court beauty Ninon de l'Enclos (Caroline Bendel) to use her influence with the King. Unfortunately for all concerned, Ninon is the merry Marquis's uptown lady. Ultimately, when d'Aubigny accidentally gets into genuine hot water and Nanon's pleas to the King himself save his head, he revises his behaviour and makes her his Marquise. The chief comic rôle of the Marquis von Marsillac, master of the king's revels, was played by Carl Adolf Friese, and the smaller rôle of his nephew Hector by the rising Alexander Girardi, whilst Bertha Steinher played Gaston, Ninon's page.

Genée's musical score was a catching one, with the usual mixture of waltzes ('Beim ersten Mal, wo er sich geschlagen') and marches (Marsch de Wache, Marsch der Trommler und Pfeiffer), a minuet ('Nach diesem Intermezzo') and a polka ('Man lernt's mit der Zeit') all joined by a pretty lullaby and Nanon's lively entrance piece. Nanon also had effective duos with both Ninon and d'Aubigny, and the second soprano, Ninon, some lively second-act couplets ('Was du nicht willst, das die geschehe') which proved one of the evening's favourites. There were a whole series of bright pieces for Marsillac, one teaching Hector how to behave ('Den Kopf jetzt in die Höh'') another, and the most successful, a drinking song ('Ventre saint gris!'), a third theatrical ('Tritt man bei Ninon an'), and a fourth ('Wenn ich auch Philosoph bin') which came to the conclusion 'Der Weiseste der Weisen ist wer zeitweise die ganze Weisheit vergisst'. Alongside the comedian, d'Aubigny was rather less prominently served, his only solo being a little romanze in the first act.

Oddly, the show which was to run to many hundreds of performances in all sorts of languages over the next 40 years or so was given only a handful of showings on its original production in Vienna. Even when it was later revived at the Theater an der Wien (19 Sept 1885) with Paula Löwe (Nanon), Antonie Hartmann (Ninon), Girardi (Hector), Heinrich Thalboth (King) and Josef Joseffy (d'Aubigny), its total exposure on that stage still came to only 28 performances, and a production at the Carltheater in 1909 with Mizzi Zwerenz (Nanon), Dora Keplinger (Ninon), Hubert Marischka (Hector) and Richard Waldemar (Louis) added only another 18 nights to the tally.

Its short life in Vienna may have been the reason that it was slow to travel. Hungary's Népszinház, which had had such a success with Genée's previous *Der Seekadett* mounted a production (ad Jenő Rakosi) in 1877 which played just a few performances, and Berlin's Walhalla-Theater, the next international house to pick up the piece, did not mount its production until 1883. When it did, however, the results were staggeringly different. In the 12 months following its first Berlin showing *Nanon* played more than 300 performances, and the Operette was well and truly launched. It galloped through the houses of provincial Germany, was played in German-language theatres in Hungary and Russia, at Riga, Basle, Strasbourg, Prague, Brussels and at New York's Thalia Theater (2 January 1885) where it scored another big hit with Emmy Meffert (Nanon), Franziska Raberg (Ninon), Ferdinand Schütz (d'Aubigny) and Otto Meyer (King Louis) featured. Later, Emma Seebold took over the lead rôle and the show reappeared regularly in the Thalia repertoire thereafter till the end of Gustav Amberg's tenancy in 1888.

In the meanwhile *Nanon* had been picked up by New York's Casino Theater, where it was mounted with Sadie Martinot, a very shapely lady who had climbed the star-system since being America's original Hebe in *Pinafore*, as Nanon and another singing beauty, Pauline Hall, as Ninon de l'Enclos. William T Carleton (d'Aubigny), Francis Wilson (Marsillac), Alice Vincent (Mme de Maintenon), W H Fitzgerald (Hector) and Gustavus Levick (Louis) supported the two stars, and the show ran a superb four and a half months (152 performances), qualifying as a major hit. It was brought back in 1892 (12 January) with Marie Tempest as the lady of the title, paired with Drew Donaldson (Ninon) and Schütz now playing d'Aubigny in English. *Nanon* remained one of the most popular of all Austrian Operetten in America for many years, thoroughly outpointing most of the works of such composers as Strauss and Suppé, as it was played regularly and widely throughout the country.

Nanon was played all over Europe in the 1880s. It was adapted into Swedish, Polish, Croatian and Italian, revived at the Népszinház (as *Nanon, Ninon*) in 1892, and appeared at Berlin's Deutsches Opernhaus in 1917 in one of many productions throughout Germany, at first in its original state and latterly in adapted versions (Städtische Bühnen, Lübeck, 6 February 1938 ad A Treumann-Nette).

However, in spite of its triumphs in other countries, the show never became part of the repertoire in Austria, nor was it ever staged in France, whilst a British production failed to reach the West End. Produced at Birmingham in an indifferent adaptation with two very capable vocalists in Laura Clement (Nanon) and Esme Lee (Ninon) featured as its central ladies, it toured discreetly and closed.

A UFA film version of *Nanon* (scr: Georg Zoch, Eberhard Keindorff) used a foxtrotting musical score by Alois Melichar and Franz Baumann to illustrate the same tale (credited to Zell and Genée) for Erna Sack (Nanon), Dagny Servaes (Ninon) and Johannes Heesters (Aubigny).

Hungary: Népszinház *Nanon csaplárosné* 23 November 1877; Germany: Walhalla-Theater 30 October 1883; USA: Thalia Theater (Ger) 2 January 1885, Casino Theater (Eng) 29 June 1885; UK: Grand Theatre, Birmingham 16 September 1889

NAPIER, John (b London, 1 March 1944).

A designer at Britain's principal subsidized theatres (*Nicholas Nickelby* RSC, *Equus* National Theatre, *Lohengrin*, *Macbeth* Royal Opera House etc) over a number of years, Napier moved conspicuously into the musical theatre in the company of his Royal Shakespeare Company colleague Trevor Nunn as the designer of *Cats* (1980, Tony Award). He subsequently designed the mass of hydraulics and skating tracks on which *Starlight Express* (1984, Tony Award) was played, the atmospheric if less obviously intricate settings for *Les Miserables* (1985, Tony Award), *The Baker's Wife* (1989) and the moving mansion of *Sunset Boulevard* (1993) in further collaborations with Nunn, as well as masterminding the overwhelming space-age scenic effects for the vast Dominion Theatre's *Time*, the Creation in *Children of Eden* and the helicopter and its accessory settings featured in *Miss Saigon* (1989). Napier's early credits included the Galt MacDermot musical *Isabel's a Jezebel*, produced in London in 1970.

NAPLES AU BAISER DE FEU Opérette à grand spectacle in 2 acts by Henri Varna, Marc-Cab and René Richard. Music by Renato Rascel. Théâtre Mogador, Paris, 7 December 1957.

Continuing their series of opérettes à grand spectacle which were the joy of the Théâtre Mogador in the 1950s, the team of manager Henri Varna and librettists Marc-Cab and René Richard followed up *Les Amants de Venise* and *Les Amours de Don Juan* with a vehicle for star tenor Tino

Rossi, fresh from his triumph in Francis Lopez's *Méditerranée* at the Châtelet. *Naples au baiser de feu*, loosely based on the singer's 1937 film hit, featured Rossi as an Italian singer who temporarily leaves his village love, Sylvia d'Andia (Jenny Marlaine) for a showier lady, Costanzella (Jacqueline Mille), but comes back to her to find she has been blinded by the eruption of Mount Vesuvius. All comes right for the finale, which also brings together the soubret pair (Pierjac, Arlette Patrick) who have supplied the regular light relief. The tale allowed the Mogador stage to display the eruption of Mount Vesuvius and 19 to 22 other picturesque scenes whilst Rossi performed the bulk of a Napoli-flavoured imitation of a Francis Lopez score by Italian songwriter Renato Rascel ('Sérénade pour un ange', 'Te voglio bene tanto, tanto', 'Costanzella', Prière à San Gennaro, 'Sans toi', 'Naples au baiser de feu'), which replaced the Vincent Scotto numbers and Neapolitan standards which had illustrated the film. The Mogador lived up to its reputation for glamorous entertainment and the show ran for 15 months. It has remained on the fringe of the French regional repertoire since, and made a recent reappearance in 1990 at Rochefort.

Recording: original cast (Columbia), studio cast w Rudi Hirigoyen (CBS)

NAPOLEON UND DIE FRAUEN Singspiel in 3 acts by Heinrich Reinhardt. Volksoper (Kaiser-Jubiläums Stadttheater), Vienna, 1 May 1912.

Written and composed by the musician of *Das süsse Mädel*, *Napoleon und die Frauen* lived up to its title. Its first act, set in 1790 and subtitled *Die Frau Oberst*, presented Napoleon (Herr Leonhardt) as a young sub-lieutenant in the Lafère Regiment becoming involved with his General's wife (Frln Engel), whilst the second act, subtitled *Die Putzmacherin*, set in 1804, with Napoleon now Emperor and married to the famous Josephine (Frln von Martinowska), found him face to face with charlady Madeleine Calot (Frln Sax), a part of his past who ends the act singing and dancing with the private secretary Vauban (Herr Markowsky) instead, as Napoleon moves on to the third act, *Die Wienerin*. In 1809, during his invasion of Vienna, he meets up with little Lori 'die Gumpendorferin' (Frln Ritzinger) in whose company he can at least try to pretend that he is still the carefree little corporal of his youthful days.

The rôle of Napoleon was liberally equipped with songs, from the 'heavy lies the head'-themed second-act solo 'Selig ist, wer des Herzens Zug', to the longing 'Es war ein kleiner Korporal' of the last scenes but, if Lori was a sweetly standard juvenile heroine with a song to fit ('Über Stock, über Stein'), the ripely enjoyable Frau Oberst, her comical husband and his seamstress-on-the side, the charlady and her secretary, and a couple of incidental Wiener-folk in the final act all provided the opportunity for plenty of song and dance in Reinhardt's most lively, singable and danceable style. Rainer Simons's production at the Volksoper was played in repertoire with such pieces as *Ernani*, *Der Kuhreigen* and *Carmen*.

The great success of Reinhardt's *The Spring Maid* (*Die Sprudelfee*) in America prompted a production of *Napoleon* there. Reinhardt's neat tripartite story with its triple look at the love-life of a man in power went out the window, leaving Napoleon (Harrison Brockbank) only one girl,

Wanda (Valli Valli), with whom to wallow sentimentally, and the score was permeated with interpolations by William Frederick Peters, one of which, a pretty if reminiscent waltz song called 'The Mysterious Kiss', was plugged as the show's big number. Edward Martindel's performance of the booming 'Diplomacy', in the rôle of Colonel Stappe, was, nevertheless, the show's highlight. Produced by Joseph Gaites as *The Purple Road*, with Eva Fallon (Kathi) and Clifton Webb (Bosco) in support of the two stars, the show was well received and ran for 138 Broadway performances.

Napoleon's attraction for Viennese girls was again celebrated in a piece called *Napoleon und die Wienerin* (Heinrich Strecker/Franz Gribitz) produced at the Breslau Schauspielhaus in 1934 (16 May), on one of the many occasions that the monarch has appeared on the musical stage. The internationally successful *The Duchess of Dantzic* and several other musicals presented him as the protagonist of Sardou and Moreau's *Madame Sans-Gêne* tale, and Johannes Riemann played the emperor in Oscar Straus's *Teresina* (1925) where, as in *The Duchess of Dantzic*, he remained a dignifiedly non-singing character. In Richard Genée and Louis Roth's *Zwillinge* (1885), however, he seems to have been – as portrayed by one Herr Graselli – a dancing character. In France the 'little corporal' has been seen portrayed in such diverse vehicles as Francis Lopez's *Viva Napoli!* and popular vocalist Serge Lama's spectacular vehicle *[De Bonaparte à] Napoléon* (Théâtre Marigny, 20 September 1984, Yves Gilbert/Lama, Jacques Rosny). Like the hero of *Viva Napoli!*, comedian Francis Wilson, in Broadway's *The Little Corporal* (1898), got himself disguised as Napoleon – if for rather different reasons, and in rather more low comic style. The German musical comedy *Die Kino-Königin*, similarly, included a film section in which the leading actor portrayed Napoleon.

In Vienna, Hubert Marischka appeared as Napoleon junior in Stojanovits's *Der Herzog von Reichstadt* and as Louis Napoleon in *Mariette* without graduating to their famous forebear. The Herzog von Reichstadt was seen again in the pasticcio Operette *Die Tänzerin Fanny Elssler* and, romancing the same ballerina, in Pepöck's *Hofball in Schönbrunn*, whilst Louis Napoleon – ie Napoleon III – put in an appearance in the Hungarian operett *Offenbach*, and was portrayed in the Viennese version of that show by Karl Althoff and on Broadway by Harrison Brockbank. None of these shows, however, was of the tone to deliver one of the most enjoyable Napoleon numbers of the musical theatre, E Ray Goetz and Vincent Bryan's 'Who Ate Napoleons With Josephine When Bonaparte Was Away?' as delivered by Sam Bernard in Broadway's version of *As You Were* (1919).

Not to be outdone in the Napoleonic stakes, the ladies got in on the act as well, and Anna Held portrayed Jean Richepin's *Mam'selle Napoleon* on Broadway. Oskar Nedbal provided the score for a piece of the same title in Europe.

USA: Liberty Theater *The Purple Road* 7 April 1913

NÄSTLBERGER, Robert (b Graz, 1887; d Hanover, 9 June 1942). Leading tenor-cum-choreographer for the inter-war Viennese stage.

At first an army officer, Nästlberger exchanged his epaulettes for the garb of an operettic tenor when his singing talent was discovered. He played in supporting rôles at the Theater an der Wien in *Wenn zwei sich lieben* (1916, Agaston) and *Die Winzerbraut* (1916, Baron Bogdan Lukovac), then rose through larger to leading ones at Ronacher in *Liebe im Schnee* (1916, Gedeon von Römmler), at the Theater an der Wien in *Nimm mich mit!* (1919, Gregor Gregorowitsch), at the Raimundtheater in *Was Mädchen träumen* (1920, Fred von Emmerling Emmerling), *Zwölf Uhr nachts* (1920, Karl Hellmer) and *Der Tanz ins Glück* (1920, Fritz Wendelin), at the Apollotheater as Graf Leandro de Cavaletti in *Die Tangokönigin* (1921) and in *Indische Nächte*, and at the Stadttheater in *Die Siegerin* (1922, Alexander Mentschikoff) and *Ein Jahr ohne Liebe* (Hector von Fontenay).

He returned to the Theater an der Wien to replace Hubert Marischka in the star rôle of *Die gelbe Jacke* and subsequently appeared there opposite Fritzi Massary as Prinz Beladonis in *Die Perlen der Cleopatra*, at the Carltheater in the title rôle of *Hoheit Franzl* (1924), at the Johann Strauss-Theater as Caesar Christow in *Alexandra* (1926) and as Niki in a revival of *Ein Walzertraum*, and at the Bürgertheater in *Yvette und ihre Freunde* (1927, Rittmeister Marko Bajanescu). He starred as Murger in *Das Veilchen vom Montmartre* (1930) and Gábor Palffy in *Sisters* (1930) in Vienna, and then opposite Gitta Alpár in Berlin's *Die Dubarry* (1931), before spending the latter years of his performing career in Berlin and in the German provinces, where he ultimately became manager of Hanover's Mellini Theater.

Nästlberger doubled his performing both with choreography (*Der Tanz ins Glück, Die Tangokönigin, Was Mädchen träumen, Eine Sommernacht, Die Tanzgräfin, General d'Amour*, the film *Operette* w Hedy Pfundmayr, Franz Bauer etc) and, later, directing (Raimundtheater etc) and also wrote the libretti for a wartime Operette, *Der Reiter der Kaiserin*, and the screenplays for several musical films.

1941 **Der Reiter der Kaiserin** (August Pepöck/w A von Czibulka) Raimundtheater 30 April

NATSCHINSKI, Gerd [Joachim] (b Chemnitz, 23 August 1928).

Conductor and composer of light music for film, television and the then East German theatre, Natschinski had a success with his first musical, *Messeschlager Gisela*, but his most popular work has been *Mein Freund Bunbury*, a piece 'freely' based on Oscar Wilde's *The Importance of Being Earnest* in which the original story is swamped under scenic considerations and alarming liberties are taken with the characters. Chasuble, for example, becomes a Salvation Army Major and opens the show with the equivalent of 'Follow the Fold' on Victoria Station.

Natschinski's later pieces *Terzett* and *Casanova* have also been played beyond their first runs. In 1978 he became, for a period, the director of the Berlin Metropoltheater.

1960 **Messeschlager Gisela** (Jo Schulz) Metropoltheater, 16 October
1963 **Servus Peter** Metropoltheater, 27 October
1964 **Mein Freund Bunbury** (Helmut Bez, Jürgen Degenhardt) Metropoltheater 2 October
1974 **Terzett** (Bez, Degenhardt) Musikalische Komödie, Leipzig 15 June

1976 **Casanova** (Bez, Degenhardt) Metropoltheater, 10 September
1979 **Das Dekameronical** (Heinz Kahlow) Halle 18 November

NATZLER, Siegmund (b Vienna, 8 September 1865; d Vienna, 12 August 1913). Viennese singing comedian and stage director.

After a decade working in provincial theatres, Natzler moved up to play leading comedy rôles at the Carltheater and at the Theater an der Wien in the last part of the 19th century and the early years of the 20th century, appearing in the regular Viennese repertoire and in a variety of foreign pieces both on the musical and non-musical stage. He also worked for a period as Oberregisseur at the Theater an der Wien, directing such pieces as *Befehl des Kaisers* (1904), *Der rothe Kosak* (1904), *Der Juxheirat* (1904), *Pufferl* (1905), the 1905 revival of *Wiener Blut* and *Der Rebell*.

Amongst the rôles in which he appeared at the Carltheater were the composer Lanner in the Festspiele *Sein erster Walzer* (1894), Papillon in *Die Königin von Gamara*, Dr Graham in *Lady Charlatan* (1894), Jules César in *Olympia* (*Les Forains*), Wasulko Okinski in *Die Lachtaube* (1895), Axel in Ferron's *Sataniel*, Cheops in Victor Herbert's *Der Zauberer von Nil* (*The Wizard of the Nile*), Popolani in *Blaubart*, Siegbert in *König Chilperich*, Dr Berndorf in *Bum-Bum* (1896), Harold in W S Gilbert's *Der Herr Gouverneur* (*His Excellency*), Bum in *Die Grossherzogin von Gerolstein*, Charles Rochou in *Der Cognac-König*, Wun Hi in *Die Geisha* (1897) Chrisostoms Barriolo-Schuyder in *Die Pariserin*, Graf Falconi in *Carneval in Rom*, Balthasar Groot in *Der lustige Krieg*, Klex in Ferron's *Das Krokodil* (1898), General des Ifs in *Die kleine Michus*, Mercury in *Adam und Eva* and Jacques Grognard in *Das kleine Korporal* (1899).

He was seen as Calchas in *Die schöne Helena* at the Theater an der Wien on the 70th birthday celebration of Karl Blasel in 1901, and played that rôle along with such as Balthasar Groot and Frank in *Die Fledermaus* in repertoire when he joined the company there. In the years he spent at the Theater an der Wien he also created or introduced to Vienna such rôles as Mister Archibald Handsome in *Die Dame aus Trouville*, Weisskopf in *Der Fremdenführer* (1902), Graf Tibor Korösi in *Der Lebemann*, Schwudler in *Bruder Straubinger*, Sir Archibald Slackett in *Der Toreador* (1903), von Karseboom in *Der neue Bügermeister*, Bartolomeo Sparaducci in *Der Generalkonsul*, Corporal la Galette in *Befehl des Kaisers*, Fürst Gavrile Lupasco in *Der rothe Kosak*, the detective Tom Clip in *Die Millionenbraut*, Major Baranyi in *Das Garnisonsmädel* (1904), Stampfl in *Pufferl*, Ypsheim-Gindelbach in the revised *Wiener Blut*, Sir Pomponius in *Prinz Bob*, Tobias Stephenson in *Vergeltsgott* and Schmulos in *Der Rebell*, before winning his most outstanding creation, in his last rôle there, as Baron Zeta in *Die lustige Witwe* (1905).

His brother, **Leopold NATZLER** (b Vienna, 17 June 1860; d Vienna, 3 January 1926) also led a career as a comedian in straight and musical theatre in Marburg, Oldenburg, Berlin (1884–6), Graz, Brünn and in Vienna at the Theater an der Wien – *Die indische Witwe*, Momo in *Capitän Fracassa* (1889), Mermeros in *Das Orakel*, Flink in *Drei Paar Schuhe*, Doux-Doux in *Die Jungfrau von Belleville*, Stefan Hoch in *Die Näherin*, Zsupán, Ajax I et al – at the Theater in der Josefstadt and the Raimundtheater. He

guested at the Carltheater in *Der liebe Schatz* (1902, Fabian Müller), at the Theater an der Wien as Tympanon in *Venedig in Paris* (1903) and, most memorably, alongside his brother as the conductor Klobuschitzky in *Der Toreador*. He subsequently became the manager of the 400-seater Hölle studio theatre, attached to the Theater an der Wien, in the early years of its activity. The brothers also, at one stage, ran a music-publishing firm together, and Leopold contributed music of his own composition to the Vienna stage (*Ein kecker Schnabel* 1896, *Fräulein Stationschef* 1903).

Their sister Regine Natzler (b Vienna, 24 November 1866; d unknown) played minor rôles at the Theater in der Josefstadt and for six years at the Carltheater (Miss Grant in *Die Uhlanen*, Aline in *Das Fräulein vom Telephone*, Mary in *Lachende Erben*, Maud Palmer in *Goldland*, Filomena in *Die Brillantenkönigin* etc).

NAUGHTY MARIETTA Musical comedy in 2 acts by Rida Johnson Young. Music by Victor Herbert. New York Theater, New York, 7 November 1910.

Naughty Marietta was written as a commission from impresario Oscar Hammerstein, a transfuge from the world of opera, for a piece to feature the star members of his former opera company, the tiny, sparkling Italian prima donna Emma Trentini, the slightly portly 'little Caruso' of America, Orville Harrold, French contralto Marthe Duchêne and the tall, angular bass-baritone Edward Martindel. Mrs Young evolved a period story which cast Trentini as an Italian countess who impersonates a boy, Duchêne as a dramatic quadroon, Martindel as a colonial aristocrat and Harrold as a dashing American adventurer and, since Hammerstein also insisted on the introduction of some comedians from the variety stage to provide what was considered to be the necessary leavening to the operatic elements, she slipped in a couple of funny folk with some irrelevant scenes.

Captain Dick (Harrold), the head of a ranger band of new Americans, has sworn to track down the pirate Bras-Priqué who has been harassing the colonies of the Louisiana coast. No one knows that the marauder is, in fact, the lofty Étienne Grandet (Martindel) whose foolish father has usurped the position of Governor in New Orleans. Marietta, Countess d'Alténa (Trentini), who has hidden away on a bride ship to escape an unwanted marriage in Europe, arrives in New Orleans and Dick helps her to hide, disguised as the son of a puppeteer. Marietta has sworn that she will only marry the man who can complete a melody which came to her once in a dream, but Étienne discovers her identity and he determines to wed this profitable, high-born lady, much to the distress of his mistress, Adah (Duchêne), whom he, following the local tradition, puts up for auction at the Quadroon Ball. To Marietta's annoyance, Dick saves the girl's face by buying her but Adah repays her benefactor by betraying Étienne's secret. Dick hurries to find Marietta whom the Grandets have imprisoned, trying to force her into a marriage. Outside her window, he sings to her ... it is her dream song and he sings it all the way through. Blades flash, and a happy ending is achieved when Dick's followers march to the rescue.

Undoubtedly helped and even encouraged by the quality of the voices for which he was writing, Herbert turned out some of his best work in the score of *Naughty Marietta*. If the comic and choral numbers were unexceptional, Trentini (who complained originally that her songs were too high), Harrold and Duchêne were finely served. The dream song, 'Ah! Sweet Mystery of Life', had a quality which too many other songs which have been given such a key place in a plot have failed to achieve, and its romantic lyricism happily complemented the vigorous masculinity of Harrold's 'Tramp, Tramp, Tramp' – destined to become one of the world's most famous marching songs – his dreamy waltz 'I'm Falling in Love with Someone', and Trentini's brilliant Italian Street Song and vivacious title-number. Perhaps the most impressive musical moments, however, came in less obvious places: the quadroon's sombrely coloured lament ''Neath the Southern Moon' and the glorious second-act quartet 'Live for Today'.

Naughty Marietta underwent very little change on its way to town. Herbert stuck to his guns, and all Trentini's high notes stayed in, and only one number, an irrelevant attempt at some local colour called 'Boo, Mr Voodoo, Don't You Hoodoo Me', was dropped. When the show reached Broadway it proved to be a fine success. It played 136 New York performances before moving on to Boston and to the touring circuits under the management of Hammerstein's son, Arthur. It returned to Broadway in 1916, then again in 1929 and 1931 with Ilse Marvenga, another Continental star, as Marietta, and was played at San Francisco's Light Opera in 1941 and in 1948 with film star Susannah Foster featured. In 1955 Patrice Munsel and Alfred Drake starred in a television adaptation.

However, in spite of its success in America, the show remained relatively unknown overseas until a 1935 film version, starring Nelson Eddy and Jeanette MacDonald (with a slightly different story, which no longer required the lady to get into short pants) popularized Herbert's songs internationally. 'Tramp, Tramp, Tramp', 'I'm Falling in Love with Someone', ''Neath the Southern Moon' and the Italian Street Song became perhaps the best known of all Herbert's music outside America, amateur societies took to the show that held them, and in 1945 British touring manager James Shirvell put out a road company with Lorely Dyer and Derek Oldham starred, directed by Edward Royce, and with a banderole 'prior to West End presentation' attached. It didn't make it, and New York remains to this day the only theatrical capital to have hosted *Naughty Marietta*, most recently under the aegis of the New York City Opera (1978).

UK: Ladbroke Hall (copyright) 24 October 1910, tour 1945; Film: MGM 1935

Recording: complete (Smithsonian Institution); selections (RCA Victor, MGM, Columbia, Capitol)

THE NAUTCH GIRL, or The Rajah of Chutneypore

Indian comic opera in 2 acts by George Dance. Lyrics by George Dance and Fred Desprez. Music by Edward Solomon. Savoy Theatre, London, 30 June 1891.

Richard D'Oyly Carte, faced with a crisis when Gilbert split with Sullivan and with him after the production of *The Gondoliers*, turned to composer Teddy Solomon, hailed since his *Billee Taylor* more than a decade earlier as Sullivan's most likely rival, and to the clever if inexperienced young journalist and playwright George Dance. This pair were given the almost impossible task of providing the next new show for the Savoy Theatre while the living shades of Gilbert and Sullivan hovered over them. They were good choices, for Solomon, always supremely confident of his talent, would have no qualms, while Dance had nothing to lose, and, as it turned out, the piece they supplied to their producer was well worthy of the Savoy and certainly comparable in quality with the works of their famous predecessors.

Indru (Courtice Pounds), son of Punka, the Rajah of Chutneypore (Rutland Barrington), falls in love with dancing girl Hollee Beebee (Leonore Snyder), but he cannot wed her because – for reasons too quaintly complex to explain – her family has gone and lost their caste. Indru bravely renounces his own caste so that the two can be wed, but then, after endless years of quiproquos, Beebee's appeal against her deprivation finally comes to court and she wins! She is a Brahmin again and their marriage is illegal. The Rajah is forced to condemn his law-breaking son to death, much to the delight of his ambitious relative Pyjama (Frank Thornton) who has taken advantage of the Punka's greatest failing, irrepressible nepotism, to become Grand Vizier. Punka's failing even stops him from arresting Pyjama, who he knows has stolen the diamond eye from Bumbo, the local idol (W H Denny), but the vile Pyjama has no such family compunctions. With the throne in sight, he tries to get Punka deposed as being the father of a criminal. Bumbo descends from his shelf to administer justice, but Hollee Beebee, who has fled the country and gone on tour with a dance group, returns just in time, and around her neck is a diamond, a gift from a stage-door admirer. It is Bumbo's missing eye, and the delighted idol promptly condemns its thief and returns to his shelf accompanied by the amorous Chinna Loofah (Jessie Bond, in her most characterful Savoy rôle), who would rather be a wooden idol's bride than nobody's bride at all.

Carte's secretary, Frank Desprez, helped out on the lyrics for some songs which were Gilbertian enough without being imitations: a piece about fashionable 'Idols' for Denny, a topical carmagnole for Denny and Miss Bond describing married life ('Vive la liberté'), a vast and vastly funny patter song for Thornton about avoiding bad luck, and some much-less-ordinary-than-usual romantic songs for Pounds.

The Nautch Girl was greeted by critics and public with surprise and relief. Gilbert and Sullivan were missed, but the Savoy could survive and supply the kind of entertainment its public loved without them. The show ran through 200 performances at the Savoy and was taken on tour for the two following seasons. At a time when comic opera, even of a superior kind, was tumbling in popularity before the onslaught of new burlesque and similar entertainments, this was a considerable achievement, but the achievement ended there. *The Nautch Girl* apparently, and rather curiously, was exported only to the eastern circuits, where a touring troupe played it to genuine Indian audiences, and, sadly, Dance and Solomon did not collaborate again.

NEAGLE, Anna (Dame) [ROBERTSON, Florence Marjorie] (b Forest Gate, Essex, 20 October 1904; d London, 3 June 1986). Much-loved star of the British screen and stage.

Originally a chorus dancer for Charlot and Cochran in

50 INDRU (1st Dress)

PUNKA Act II

PYJAMA

Act I

HOLLEE BEEBEE 1st Dress (Nautch Girl)

Plate 192. **The Nautch Girl:** *Percy Anderson's designs for Courtice Pounds (Indru), Rutland Barrington (Punka), Frank Wyatt (Pyjama) and Lenore Snyder (Hollee Beebee).*

revue and then in musicals (*Rose Marie*, *The Desert Song*), Miss Neagle played her first speaking rôle in a small part in the film *The Chinese Bungalow* before being promoted to partner Jack Buchanan as the ingénue of the 1931 musical *Stand Up and Sing*. She subsequently had a distinguished career as a film actress, mostly in stalwartly heroic rôles but also in musical vehicles ranging from the film version of *Good Night, Vienna* (1932, with Buchanan) to *Bitter-Sweet* (1933), Hollywood's *No, No, Nanette* (1940) and *Sunny* (1941), and a version of *King's Rhapsody* (1956) which was reorganized to allow the by then important star to take a larger part in the action than the original Marta Karillos (Phyllis Dare) had done.

She appeared on stage in straight pieces ranging from *As You Like It* (Rosalind) and *Twelfth Night* (Olivia) to *Peter Pan* and *Emma* (opposite Robert Donat), and in the Coronation revue *The Glorious Days* in 1953 as a bevy of characters including Queen Victoria, but she had her only significant stage-musical success late in her career when she starred as Lady Hadwell throughout the seven-year run of *Charlie Girl* (1965) in Britain and then in Australia. *Charlie Girl* brought Miss Neagle back to the West End public's eye, and in 1973 she filled the rôle of Sue, remade for another dancer, Ruby Keeler, in the revised and revived *No, No, Nanette*. She made her last stage appearance, at the age of 70-plus, as the fairy in pantomime at the London Palladium.

Autobiography: *There's Always Tomorrow* (W H Allen, London, 1974)

NEDBAL, Oskar (b Tábor, 26 March 1874; d Agram, 24 December 1930).

Nedbal studied at the Prague conservatoire and worked at first as a viola player before moving on to a career as a conductor, initially with the Prague Philharmonic Orchestra and then, from 1906 to 1919, at the head of the Vienna Tonkünstlerorchester. His earliest compositions were in the field of chamber, orchestral and, in particular, ballet music (*Der faule Hans*, *Von Märchen zu Märchen*, *Prinzessin Hyazintha*, *Des Teufels Grossmütterchen*, *Andersen*), but his greatest success as a composer came when he moved into the field of Operette.

His first work, *Die keusche Barbara*, a piece set in 19th-century Britain, was originally produced in his native Czechoslovakia (*Cudná Barbara*), but it moved quickly to Vienna, Germany, and later Hungary (*Az erénycsősz*), establishing its composer in the theatrical world in the process. Of the four full-length works that he then turned out for Viennese theatres between 1913 and 1918, the outstanding piece was his second work, *Polenblut* (1913). Produced at the Carltheater, it had a remarkable first run, was played throughout central Europe and, with Emma Trentini starring, on Broadway (*The Peasant Girl*), as it confirmed itself as a staple item in the 'Silver Age' repertoire. However, Nedbal's other pieces were by no means unsuccessful. *Polenblut*'s successor *Die Winzerbraut*, a piece set partly in Agram and the Slavonic countryside, mounted at the Theater an der Wien with Betty Fischer as its heroine and a cast including Ernst Tautenhayn, Robert Nästlberger, Karl Tuschl, Karl Pfann, Margit Suchy and Gustav Werner also had a fine first run (137 performances) and later performances around Europe, whilst a second piece for the Carltheater,

Die schöne Saskia, was played there 131 times and subsequently also produced in Hungary (*A szép Saskia*, 8 November 1918 Városi Színház).

Nedbal returned enthusiastically to his homeland when the Czechoslovak republic was formed after the war and he became widely involved in the musical and theatrical affairs of the country during the 1920s. His composing output, however, shrank and only a comic opera *Sédlak Jakub* (1922) and one last operetta score for Vienna were added to his work list during years which were often disillusioned and, altogether, less than happy ones. In 1930, convinced that he was being pursued by enemies, he committed suicide by jumping from the window of the ballet room at the Agram theatre.

1910 **Die keusche Barbara** (Rudolf Bernauer, Leopold Jacobson) Theater Weinberge, Prague, 14 September
1913 **Polenblut** (Leo Stein) Carltheater 25 October
1916 **Die Winzerbraut** (Stein, Julius Wilhelm) Theater an der Wien 11 February
1917 **Die schöne Saskia** (A M Willner, Heinz Reichert) Carltheater 16 November
1918 **Eriwan** (Felix Dörmann) Wiener Komödienhaus 29 November
1919 **Mam'selle Napoleon** (Emil Golz, Arnold Golz) 1 act Hölle 31 January
1925 **Donna Gloria** (Victor Léon, Reichert) Carltheater 30 December

NEIDHART, August (b Vienna, 12 May 1867; d Berlin, 25 November 1934). All-purpose playwright and librettist of the Austrian and German stage.

Neidhart made his entry into the theatre as an actor, then moved to the Burgtheater to take up the post of prompter, and did not begin writing for the stage until he was already in his thirties. His first pieces, mostly short comedies and adaptations, were staged in minor Viennese houses, and he provided the texts for a number of mostly modest musical plays in the first decade and a bit of the new century before being employed in 1916 as dramaturg and 'artistic advisor' by Gustav Charlé at the Berlin Komische Oper.

His first musical play for that theatre turned out to be Leon Jessel's triumphant *Schwarzwaldmädel* which, even though its author was Viennese and its composer born in what is today Poland, may be accounted one of the greatest successes of the German Operette stage. It was a kind of success that he did not repeat, although he combined with Jessel on six other musicals, several of which did well enough, and also partnered Leo Fall on *Die Strassensängerin* and Leo Ascher, an ally of earlier days, on an adaptation of Nössler's comedy *Im Klubsessel* (*Baronesschen Sarah*) and *Ninon im Scheideweg* during a busy career which saw his works produced all around central Europe.

Neidhart committed suicide in Berlin in 1934.

1901 **Ein braver Ehemann** (Franz Wagner) Jantschtheater 10 May
1901 **Es ist erreicht** (Ludwig Gothov-Grüneke) Jantschtheater 6 July
1903 **Amor & Cie** (Paul Mestrozzi) Kaiser-Jubiläums Theater 11 September
1903 **Über Land und Meer** (Karl Rella) Jantschtheater 14 April
1904 **Die Praterfee** (Karl J Fromm) Jantschtheater 2 September
1904 **'s Zuckersgoscherl** (J Wolffsgruber/Jean Kren, Alfred Schönfeld ad w Carl Lindau) Carltheater 15 October

1905 **Friedl mit der Fidel** (Arthur von Henriques) Kleines Theater 10 October

1906 **Der Erste** (Richard Fronz) Bürgertheater 16 March

1906 **Der Triumph des Weibes** (Josef Hellmesberger) Danzers Orpheum 17 November

1907 **Wien bleibt Wien** (Josef Bayer) 1 act Venedig in Wien 11 June

1907 **Der Lebensretter** (F Kollmaneck/Ferdinand Korb) Lustspieltheater 20 August

1907 **Die schöne Griechin** (Max R Steiner/Lucien Boyer ad) 1 act Danzers Orpheum 20 December

1908 **Die wilde Komtesse** (Adolf Ripka von Rechthofen) Stadttheater, Brünn 25 October

1909 **Ein Belagerungszustand** (Leo Ascher) 1 act Kabarett Fledermaus 1 November

1909 **Der junge Papa** (Edmund Eysler/w Alexander Engel) 1 act Apollotheater 31 January

1911 **Sein Herzensjunge** (Walter Kollo/w Rudolf Schanzer) Thalia-Theater, Elberfeld 1 April

1913 **Freddy und Teddy** (Digby la Touche/H L Melbourne ad w Lindau) Theater am Nollendorfplatz, Berlin 23 December

1914 **Komm, deutscher Bruder** (Eysler, Lehár/w Lindau) Raimundtheater 4 October

1914 **Schürzenmanöver** (Walter Goetze/w R von Gatti ad Hans Brennert) Operettentheater, Leipzig 25 March

1915 **Die ledige Frau** (Karl Eibenschütz/w Lindau) Landestheater, Linz 3 December

1917 **Liebessport** (Eibenschütz/w Lindau) Theater am Gärtnerplatz, Munich 26 May

1917 **Schwarzwaldmädel** (Leon Jessel) Komische Oper, Berlin 25 August

1918 **Eine modernes Mädel** (Jessel) Volkstheater, Munich 28 June

1918 **Ohne Mann kein Vergnügen** (Jessel) Komische Oper, Berlin

1920 **Baronesschen Sarah** (Ascher) Komische Oper, Berlin 5 December

1920 **Die Schönen von Baden-Baden** (Hermann Beutten ad Eduard Künneke) Kurhaustheater, Baden-Baden 12 June

1920 **Die Strohwitwe** (Leo Blech) Stadttheater, Hamburg 16 June

1921 **Die Postmeisterin** (Jessel) Centraltheater, Berlin 3 February

1921 **Die Strassensängerin** (Leo Fall) Metropoltheater, Berlin 24 September

1921 **Das Detektivmädel** (*Miss Nobody*) (Jessel) Centraltheater, Berlin 28 October

1923 **Süsse Susi** (Siegfried Grzýb/w Richard Bars) Schiller Theater

1923 **Die Abenteuerin**

1923 **Der unsterbliche Kuss**

1924 **Die Frau ohne Schleier** (Byjacco/Richard Rillo/w Lothar Sachs) Theater am Zoo, Berlin 24 November

1925 **Prinzessin Husch** (Jessel) Operettenhaus, Hamburg 22 December, Theater des Westens, Berlin 11 March 1926

1926 **Yvonne** (Hugo Hirsch/w Arthur Rebner) Theater am Kurfürstendamm 1 August

1926 **Der Trompeter vom Rhein** (Viktor Nessler arr Robert Winterberg/w Cornelius Bronsgeest) Centralhalle 23 December

1926 **Ninon am Scheideweg** (Ascher) Theater am Zoo 27 December

1928 **Die Männer von Manon** (Goetze/w Robert Gilbert) Kleines Haus, Düsseldorf 30 September

1929 **Prosit, Gipsy** (R Gilbert/w Henry) Deutsches Künstlertheater 19 April

1929 **Die Luxuskabine** (Jessel) Neues Operettentheater, Leipzig 20 October

1931 **Thron zu vergeben** (Bertram Wittmann) Komische Oper 29 August

1933 **Junger Wein** (Jessel) Theater des Westens, Berlin 1 September

NELL GWYNNE Comic opera in 3 acts by H B Farnie based on the play *Rochester* by W T Moncrieff. Music by Alfred Cellier. Prince's Theatre, Manchester 17 October 1876; revised as comic opera in 2 acts by H B Farnie. Music by Robert Planquette. Avenue Theatre, London, 7 February 1884.

Following Cellier's considerable success with *The Sultan of Mocha*, his first and best musical for the Manchester theatre, he was commissioned to provide others. None of these proved, in fact, successful enough to move on from Manchester, but his score for the insufficiently well-received 1876 show *Nell Gwynne* (Pattie Laverne played the lady in question) was later adapted to become that of *Dorothy*, the most successful British musical of the century. Prior to this musical rebirth, however, librettist Farnie had withdrawn his text from the melded copyright of the show in order to have it reset by a hotter-name composer – Robert Planquette, then at the peak of his popularity with *Les Cloches de Corneville* and Farnie's musical version of *Rip van Winkle*.

The enormous London success of *Rip* made the new *Nell Gwynne* a much awaited event. Produced by Alexander Henderson with Florence St John starring as Nell, D'Oyly Carte tenor Lyn Cadwaladr as Rochester, Giulia Warwick (the original Constance of *The Sorcerer*) as Jessamine and with two outstanding comic stars, Lionel Brough and Arthur Roberts, heading the comedy, it proved to be a pretty if slightly patchy piece, with Miss St John's 'Only an Orange Girl' and Miss Warwick's little Song of the Clock more effective than the comical material of the score. The show lasted only a disappointing 86 performances in London, and though it was subsequently toured and produced in a number of other countries, it never established itself in the revivable repertoire in the way that *Rip van Winkle* had done or that *Dorothy* would.

America's Nell was Mathilde Cottrelly (38 performances) first time round, and May Baker when the Maud Daniels Opera Company brought the show back to Koster and Bials in 1901. Maurice Ordonneau and Emil André's French version simply dropped the lady from the show and called it and her, as played by Juliette Darcourt, *La Princesse Colombine* (19 performances), the Germans made her into *Prinzessin Pirouette*, whilst the Hungarians – who obviously hadn't heard of Mistress Gwynne either, but who liked her a little more – kept a touch closer to the original by calling Ilka Pálmay 'The Countess of the Stage'. However, by and large, it was India (Calcutta 20 March 1885) that seemed to like this particular piece the most, and that may have been because the Nell they got was the incisive American soprano and actress Emilie Melville. *Nell Gwynne* outdid more generally favoured pieces in the Melville repertoire and it proved the hit of her otherwise very iffy eastern tour. She subsequently introduced the piece in Australia.

All these switches of its heroine's identity came from the fact that the Farnie libretto had very little to do with even the more apocryphal details of the life of the actress and royal mistress. Her name was simply tacked on to the piece and its leading lady to give the show a nice, recognizably catchy title. The book followed the lines of Moncrieff's *Rochester*, itself an adaptation from the French *L'Exil de Rochester* and previously set to music in America under the title *Fast Men of Olden Time* for the Boston Museum in 1860. This tale simply told of the discomforting of a couple of overbold courtly gentlemen who mistake a lady for an easy country lass and suffer her revenge.

Several other musicals which have portrayed Mistress Gwyn(ne) got little closer to what historical fact exists. José Collins starred as *Our Nell* (Gaiety Theatre 16 April 1924) in a piece which had originally been called *Our Peg* and once presented her as Peg Woffington, and singer-songwriter Jackie Trent appeared as the sexy orange-seller in a *Nell!* by John Worth and Philip Mackie produced at London's Richmond Theatre in 1970 (8 April). Cabaret vocalist Dorothy Squires threatened London with her own Nell Gwynne musical at one stage, but it got no further than a demonstration of its songs at the Dominion Theatre. Other briefly lived Nells included H T Arden and W H C Nation's 'new musical extravaganza' which survived 48 performances at its wealthy composer's expense at the Royalty Theatre, London, in 1871 and a one-act burlesque *Nell Go-In* composed by A Baldwin Sloane with Mabel Fenton as Nell which was seen momentarily on Broadway in 1899 (New York Theater, 31 October).

A highly successful character on the straight stage in the hands of Julia Neilson and others (*Sweet Nell of Old Drury*), Mistress Gwynne has singularly failed to appeal as the heroine of musical plays.

USA: Casino Theater 8 November 1884; Australia: Opera House, Melbourne 17 July 1886; France: Théâtre des Nouveautés *La Princesse Colombine* 7 December 1886; Hungary: Népszínház *Komédiás hercegnő* 15 April 1887; Germany: Friedrich-Wilhelmstädtisches Theater *Prinzessin Pirouette* 7 December 1889

NELSON, Rudolf [LEWYSOHN, Rudolf] (b Berlin, 8 April 1878; d Berlin, 5 February 1960).

Pianist, accompanist and vocalist Nelson was a pioneering songs-at-the-piano performer in Berlin cabaret, composing much of his own material ('little Frenchified tunes') as well as supplying a vast number of pieces to other performers. He continued throughout his life and career to perform in cabaret and later to run his own cabaret venues, but at the same time he also composed a considerable amount of music for revue, at first for the Metropoltheater and later for his own house, as well as for musical comedies and for Operetten. One Operette, *Miss Dudelsack*, was well enough received in Berlin to later win productions not only in Austria and Hungary, but also in America. His longest-running piece on home ground, however, was the wartime *Blaue Jungens* which was played for six months at the Theater am Nollendorfplatz.

In 1914 Nelson opened his own Berlin theatre, the Nelson-Theater, where he was for many years director, author, composer and pianist, and he had a second spell as a Berlin manager in the early 1930s with a revue theatre. At the coming of National Socialism he moved to Zurich and Amsterdam, still continuing to perform through his sixties and into his seventies, and after his return to Berlin in 1949 he was seen on television and in his revue-concert 'Rudolf Nelson spielt', remaining active almost to the end of his days.

Nelson's music exported to mainly revue productions in other countries, but his name made an unaccustomed appearance on a southern-hemisphere playbill when it was writ large as the co-composer of a musical called *The Honeymoon Girl* mounted at Fuller's Theatre, Sydney (23 May) in 1925. Quite what of Nelson's music had been borrowed is unclear, for *The Honeymoon Girl* was a disguised version of the London show *Oh! Julie* of half a decade earlier, of which the nominal composers were Herman Darewski and H Sullivan Brooke.

1906 **Das bummelnde Berlin** (Benno Jacobson) Apollotheater 10 March

1908 **Principessa** (Fritz Grünbaum, Georg Burghard) Residenztheater, Frankfurt-am-Main 1 May

1909 **Miss Dudelsack** (Grünbaum, Heinz Reichert) Neues Schauspielhaus 3 August

1911 **Hoheit amüsiert sich** (Julius Freund) Metropoltheater 29 April

1912 **Schwindelmeyer & Cie** (*The Arcadians*) new score for German version w Freund Metropoltheater 27 April

1914 **Der Krümel vor Paris** (Franz Cornelius) Residenz-Theater 13 October

1915 **Neueste Nachtrichten** (Cornelius, Willi Prager) Kristall-palast, Leipzig 1 January

1915 **Mufflick und Bimse** (Julius Winckelmann) Viktoria-Theater, Breslau 1 October

1915 **Verheiratet Junggesellen** (Arthur Lippschitz) Trianon-Theater 27 December

1916 **Blaue Jungens** (Hermann Frey/Hermann Haller, Kurt Kraatz) Theater am Nollendorfplatz 25 August

1917 **Neptun auf Reisen** (Franz Arnold, Ernst Bach) Apollo-theater January

1918 **Inkognito** (*Der Damenkrieg*) (Kraatz, Richard Kessler) Berlin Kammerspiele 4 June

1921 **Das Prachtmädel** (Leo Walther Stein) Schillertheater, Berlin-Charlottenburg 10 July

1923 **Die Damen von Olymp** (Rudolf Schanzer, Ernst Welisch) Nelson-Theater May

1928 **Weisst du was? – wir heiraten!** (Franz Landry, Richard Rillo) Neues Theater am Zoo 21 December

NEMESIS, or Not Wisely But Too Well
Bouffonnerie musicale by H B Farnie based on *Les Deux Noces de M Boisjoli* by Alfred Duru. Music selected and arranged by John Fitzgerald. Strand Theatre, London, 17 April 1873.

The most successful of the many pasticcio extravaganzas expertly cobbled together by the free-stealing Farnie for the London theatre, *Nemesis* combined a version of Alfred Duru's 1872 Palais-Royal play *Les Deux Noces de M Boisjoli* with a score borrowed from various stage works by Hervé, Delibes, Lecocq, Victor Robillard, Vasseur, Jonas and Adolphe Lindheim to make up what was really an equivalent of a French pasticcio vaudeville: a genuine 'musical comedy'.

The story of the piece dealt with the aptly named Calino (Edward Terry) – the Boisjoli of Duru's original – who determines on one last flirtation before settling down to the married life that is scheduled for him. The trouble is that he gets in a little deep, and he finds that he is 'promised' – nay wed – to two ladies. Worse, the two ladies are the daughters of two neighbours, the retired butter-maker Putiphar Patoche (Harry Cox) and the fire-breathing, oath-spouting military Major Roland de Roncevaux Ramponneau (Claude Marius). And just to complicate things further, whilst he has wooed and wed Rosalie Ramponneau (Angelina Claude) under his real name, his amours with Praline Patoche (Nellie Bromley) have been conducted under the name of his friend Zidore de Filoselle (Maria Jones). Of course, it is this latter who, by the law of French farce, finally takes the spare wife off our hero's hands, but only after five scenes of bristling comedy. Sallie Turner featured as Praline's comical spinster aunt Turlurette.

Nemesis succeeded *Geneviève de Brabant* as the musical hit of the time, and its only concession to the arrival of the all-conquering *La Fille de Madame Angot* was to begin advertising itself as an opéra-bouffe. An enormous run of 262 London performances was followed by revivals in 1874, 1875, 1876 and 1878, and the publishing house of J B Cramer made bold enough to publish all but two of the 18 uncredited numbers which made up the pilfered score. The exceptions were two pieces from *La Fille de Madame Angot*.

By the time of an 1885 revival, with a cast including Arthur Roberts, Claude Marius and Lottie Venne the score had, for the benefit of the first named, been augmented with the Geographical Love Song called 'Grab', 'Troubadour', what was called Tosti's 'Goodbye and Go' and 'S'm' Other Evening'.

Tenor, director and would-be-producer Henry Bracy purchased the overseas rights to *Nemesis* and took it in his baggage to the colonies. It served him well enough on his first Australian visit in 1874 for him to repeat it in 1878 and again as late as 1890.

A Lebensbild mit Gesang also entitled *Nemesis*, written by O F Berg and composed by Adolf Müller, was produced at Vienna's Theater an der Wien 23 October 1869 for 20 performances, and a Viennese adaptation of *Les Deux Noces de M Boisjoli* was mounted at the Carltheater (5 April 1873) under the title of *Zwei Hochzeiten und ein Brautigam* (music: C F Conradin/ad Karl Treumann), with Karl Blasel as Boisjoli and Josef Matras as Quincampoix, a fortnight before *Nemesis* appeared on the stage in London.

Australia: Opera House, Melbourne 2 February 1874

NESTROY, [Nepomuc] Johann (b Vienna 7 December 1801; d Graz, 25 May 1862). Celebrated actor, playwright and producer of the mid-19th-century Viennese stage.

Nestroy made his début as an actor in 1822, and appeared at a very young age as Sarastro in *Der Zauberflöte* at the Vienna Opera. He worked in Amsterdam, Brünn and Graz and from 1831 at the Theater an der Wien where many of his most important works as a playwright were given their premières. These included a long list of musical Possen such as *Tritsch-Tratsch* (20 November 1833), *Eulenspiegel* (22 April 1835), *Zu ebener Erde und im ersten Stock* (24 September 1835), *Die beiden Nachtwandler* (6 May 1836), *Der verhängnisvolle Faschingsnacht* (13 April 1839), *Der Talisman* (16 December 1840), *Das Mädel aus der Vorstadt* (24 November 1841) and *Der Zerissene* (9 April 1844), burlesques such as *Nagerl und Handschuh* (23 March 1832), *Zamperl der Tagdieb* (22 June 1832) and *Robert der Teuxel* (9 October 1833) and Zauberspiele and Zauberpossen including his famous [*Der böse Geist*] *Lumpacivagaundus* (11 April 1833). He subsequently sup-

Plate 193. **Johann Nestroy**'s Lumpacivagaundus, *remusicalized by Robert Stolz as* Drei von der Donau, *is seen here at the Dresden Staatsoperette: Thomas Georgi (Leim), Frithjof Hoffmann (Knieriem), Werner Knodel (Zwirn) and Gottfried Neumann (Hausierer).*

plied a number of pieces to the Theater in der Leopoldstadt where his other most celebrated play, *Einen Jux will er sich machen* (15 January 1842), and his Wagner burlesque *Der fliegende Holländer zu Fuss* (4 August 1846) were both initially staged, and to other theatres (*Tannhäuser-Parodie* etc), being eventually credited with a total of more than 60 works produced on the Viennese stage.

Between 1854 and 1860 Nestroy was the director of the Carltheater where, with the collaboration of Karl Treumann, he mounted the first series of Offenbach productions to be seen in Vienna in the German language: *Die Hochzeit bei Laternenscheine, Das Mädchen von Elisonzo* (1858), *Schühflicker und Millionär, Die Zaubergeige, Die Savoyarden, Der Ehemann vor der Türe* (1859) and *Tschin-Tschin* (1860) as well as the earliest attempt by a local writer and composer to follow in the same style – Conradin's *Flodoardo Wuprahall* (1859). In 1860 he adapted, mounted and starred in the first full-length opéra-bouffe production in Vienna, *Orpheus in der Unterwelt*, appearing in the show as a Jupiter written up like a meneur de revue, with a parade of topical jokes to hand.

After giving up the Carltheater, he appeared for a season at Treumann's little Theater am Franz-Josefs-Kai, where he played the part of Pan in a specially re-arranged version of Offenbach's *Daphnis und Chloë*, and his own adaptation of *Vent du soir* as *Häuptling Abendwind* (1 February 1862) in the last months before his death.

Many of Nestroy's works, virtually all of which were originally played with the accompaniment of music and songs, have been rearranged and remusicked over the years, but it is *Einen Jux will er sich machen* which has come down to modern times the most effectively, being an ancestor of the musical *Hello, Dolly!*

Nestroy himself became the hero of a couple of bio-musicals, one written by Bruno Zappert to a pasticcio score and produced at Graz, where Nestroy had had some of his earliest stage works played in the late 1820s (*Johann Nestroy* 17 January 1885), the second a Singspiel mounted, even more aptly, at the Carltheater in 1918 (4 December). A M Willner and Rudolf Österreicher's libretto was set to an arrangement of old Viennese melodies made by Ernst Reiterer. Willy Thaller portrayed Nestroy.

NESVILLE, Juliette [LESLE, Juliette] (b Paris, ?1870; d Paris, 26 July 1900). Heroine of several Paris, London and New York musicals during a very brief career.

Daughter of a Parisian restaurateur, Mlle Lesle was convent-raised in France and in Clapham before going on to study music. Shortly after graduating from the Paris Conservatoire, she was cast in the title-rôle of the Parisian première of Lacôme's *Ma mie Rosette* (1890). She went on to appear in a revival of *La Fille de l'air* and *L'Égyptienne* and in 1891 was taken first to Brussels and then to London where she starred as the modest, teen-aged heroine of the local versions of the Paris hit *Miss Helyett* (1891, *Miss Decima*). Mlle Nesville repeated her *Ma mie Rosette* rôle at London's Globe Theatre and appeared at the Palace Musical Hall in a J M Glover musical sketch, *A Pal o' Archie's*, before being signed up by George Edwardes.

She began with Edwardes in the London and Broadway original casts of *A Gaiety Girl* (1893) playing the French maid who causes the trouble which constitutes the plot ('When Your Pride Has Had a Tumble'), took over as Madame Amélie in *An Artist's Model* (1895), and had the rôle of Juliette, the social-climbing little French interpreter in *The Geisha*, written to her measure (1896, 'If That's Not Love, What Is?'). The following year a rôle (Juliette Belleville) was written into *In Town* when she was hired as a member of the company which belatedly took this show to America, and in 1898 she starred opposite Arthur Roberts in the try-out of *Campano*.

Her career as London's favourite little musical-comedy French girl was terminated abruptly by her death at what seems to have been 30 years of age, whilst she was rehearsing for her return to the Paris stage in *Mariage Princier*.

THE NEW BARMAID Musical play in 2 acts by Frederick Bowyer and W Edwards Sprange. Music by John Crook. Opera House, Southport, 1 July 1895; Avenue Theatre, London, 12 February 1896.

Specially constructed for the British touring circuits, *The New Barmaid* was a musical comedy which told the twin tales of the reversal of the fortunes of two comical brothers (Arthur Alexander, J B Montague), and of the efforts of the aptly named Captain Lovebury (Wilfred Howard) to fend off a breach-of-promise suit from Brenda, the plotting ex-barmaid of his club (Reika Ronalds), so that he can wed her replacement (Amy Augarde) who is, so it turns out, actually a long-lost heiress.

The low comedy of the White brothers, the nice one rising from menial tasks to riches and the other not-so-nice one going the opposite way, and some lively musical numbers provided a very solid backbone for the entertainment, with the topical 'A Little Bit of Sugar for the Bird' becoming a major hit, and other pieces like 'Mother Was the Mother of Us Both', 'Just Bread and Cheese and Kisses' and the satirical 'The Lady Journalist' also proving very popular. Brought to town, and cast up with Lottie Collins, J J Dallas and John Shine in its leading rôles, *The New Barmaid* had a 138-performance run in two theatres before returning to its natural habitat on the road. There it trouped virtually non-stop for considerably more than a decade, playing thousands of performances through Britain and the colonies. One company, sent out by Alex-

ander Loftus in 1904, toured for 130 weeks with only one short break.

The New Barmaid was introduced to Australia by John F Sheridan who put aside the skirts of his famous Widow O'Brien and appeared as William White in seasons in Melbourne and Sydney (Lyceum 22 December 1900) before moving on to other frocked and unfrocked rôles.

Australia: Theatre Royal, Melbourne 3 February 1900, Criterion Theatre, Sydney *The Lady Barmaid* 31 January 1903

NEW GIRL IN TOWN Musical in 2 acts by George Abbott based on *Anna Christie* by Eugene O'Neill. Music and lyrics by Bob Merrill. 46th Street Theater, New York, 14 May 1957.

Eugene O'Neill's darkly dramatic play *Anna Christie* (Vanderbilt Theater, 2 November 1921, 177 performances) had for its heroine a young woman who has known a parentless youth, rape by a relative, and life as a prostitute before returning to New York to find her father and to doubtfully share with him his life as a bargee. She finds something cleansing in the sea, but when she meets a man she could love, and who would marry her, she has to complete that cleansing by revealing all her story to both her lover and her father. Then it is their turn to take once more to the sea, taking their thoughts with them, whilst Anna waits at home to see what will become of them all.

Highly praised, and the recipient of a Pulitzer Prize, *Anna Christie* might have been material for an operatic adaptation, but it seemed scarcely suitable as the source of a 1950s Broadway musical comedy. In fact, what became *New Girl in Town* began life trying to be a film, MGM having planned, shortly after O'Neill's death, to issue a musical version of the already twice-filmed (once with Garbo) piece with a Bob Merrill score. The film project went the way of a lot of other film projects, but the idea stayed alive, found its way to George Abbott, who found his way to producers Freddie Brisson, Hal Prince and Robert E Griffith, who found the way to get the rights out of MGM and the show on to the stage.

They were, of course, playing with critical fire in putting a set of period pastiche songs and, above all, dances into what was still a recent dramatic success, but the show that eventuated, whilst sharing little with the original play but its main storyline, was by no means incongruous to, at least, those who were not acquainted with O'Neill's play. The drama was recoloured and re-set amongst traditional musical-comedy elements and songs, Abbott and choreographer Bob Fosse were at the helm, and dancing actress Gwen Verdon, equipped with enough appeal to wow the O out of O'Neill and a rare pair of feet, played Anna. The result was a show with some considerable charms, most of which were dancing ones ('At the Check Apron Ball', 'There Ain't No Flies on Me'). The ones that weren't were in the hands of Thelma Ritter, who shared top-billing with Miss Verdon (the men were dumped below the title) in the low-comedy rôle of Anna's father's rough-and-tough mate ('Flings', 'Chess and Checkers').

New Girl in Town had sufficient attractions to run 432 performances, which was considerably more than *Anna Christie* had done on its first run, but it didn't win a Pulitzer Prize and there was no second run.

Recording: original cast (RCA)

NEWLEY, Anthony (b London, 24 September 1931). Heavily mannered British actor and vocalist who later turned to mostly nightclub and cabaret entertaining.

Newley began his career as a juvenile actor, playing a memorable Artful Dodger in the 1948 film of *Oliver Twist*, and made his first adult stage appearance in the revue *Cranks*. In the 1950s he won success in all quarters, featuring in several successful British films and finding fame as a popular vocalist as he reached the top of the hit parades with 'Why?' and 'Do You Mind' and placed three other numbers in the top ten within a space of two years. He consolidated his success on British television (*The World of Gurney Slade*) and, then, aged 29, returned to the theatre as the star and director of the musical comedy *Stop the World – I Want to Get Off*, a little fable of one man's existence which he had himself written and composed in collaboration with Leslie Bricusse. *Stop the World* gave Newley, in what was almost a solo show, a grand success both in London and on Broadway, and launched several strong songs of the heartfelt variety towards the hit parades and cabaret circuits ('What Kind of Fool Am I', 'Once in a Lifetime'). In a career where everything he attempted seemed to succeed, he also joined Bricusse in penning the title-song for the James Bond film *Goldfinger* (1964).

A second show, *The Roar of the Greasepaint, the Smell of the Crowd*, written on similar lines to the first, closed on the road in Britain (with Norman Wisdom starring) to be remounted on Broadway with Newley featured in a rôle which echoed his *Stop the World* character through a fair 232 performances. However, if the show's stage life was limited, Newley and Bricusse's score again produced more than the usual quota of durable songs, and this time the tortured ballads ('Who Can I Turn To?', 'The Joker') were complemented by the positive bounce of 'Nothing Can Stop Me Now' and by 'On a Wonderful Day Like Today', a song destined to top the repertoire of what seemed like every holiday camp and pantomime artist for the next two decades.

Newley then disappeared from the theatre into the world of night clubs, but he emerged again in 1972 as author, director and star of a third show, *The Good Old, Bad Old Days*, written on the same lines as the earlier ones. The shallowly philosophizing style which had suited the 1960s seemed rather risible in the 1970s, Newley himself had turned himself into a braying caricature of his cockily abrasive old persona, and many of the new show's songs seemed like burlesques of their predecessors. *The Good Old, Bad Old Days* was shepherded through nine months in London before Newley returned to the cabaret circuits. He later re-emerged to appear in an American musical based on the life of Charlie Chaplin which stopped short of Broadway, to briefly bring *Stop the World* back to London (1989) and to feature in a stage musical version of *Scrooge* (Birmingham, 1992).

In 1978 a compilation show made up of Newley/Bricusse numbers was unsuccessfully produced in London under the title *The Travelling Music Show* (Her Majesty's Theatre, 28 March).

1961 **Stop the World – I Want to Get Off** (w Leslie Bricusse) Queen's Theatre 20 July
1964 **The Roar of the Greasepaint, the Smell of the Crowd** (w Bricusse) Theatre Royal, Nottingham 3 August; Shubert Theater, New York 16 May 1965

1972 **The Good Old, Bad Old Days** (w Bricusse) Prince of Wales Theatre 20 December
1983 **Chaplin** (w Stanley Ross) Music Center Pavilion, Los Angeles 12 August

NEWMAN, Greatrex (b Manchester, 3 July 1892; d Eastbourne, 19 January 1984).

The writer of sketches, scenarios and lyrics for many revues from 1914 onwards (*The Passing Show*, *Joy-Bells*, *The Punch Bowl* etc) and writer for and sometime proprietor of the long-flourishing concert parties The Co-Optimists and The Fol de Rols, Newman also wrote occasionally for the book musical stage. He supplied additional lyrics for the musicals *Patricia* (1924) and *The Blue Kitten* (1925), additional scenes in *Lady Luck* (1927), had his concert-party song 'Murders' interpolated to fine effect in Broadway's and London's versions of *Tonight's the Night* and contributed to the remaking of an unspecified Arnold and Bach play and the 1912 Broadway musical *The Man from Cooks* as the short-lived *The Girl from Cook's* (1927) before scoring his major musical stage success as co-librettist and co-lyricist of *Mr Cinders* (1928). A second piece in similar vein, *Mr Whittington* (1933) also had a successful London run, but his last musical comedy, *Love Laughs – !*, was a failure.

Newman died at the age of 91 during the run of a successful revival of *Mr Cinders* (1982) for which he and composer Vivian Ellis had written an additional number.

1927 **The Girl from Cook's** (Raymond Hubbell, Jean Gilbert/w R H Burnside) Gaiety Theatre 1 November
1928 **Mr Cinders** (Vivian Ellis, Richard Myers/w Clifford Grey) Opera House, Blackpool 25 September
1933 **Mr Whittington** (John Green, Joseph Tunbridge, Jack Waller/w Grey, Douglas Furber) London Hippodrome 1 March 1934
1935 **Love Laughs – !** (ex- *Leave it to Love*) (Noel Gay/w Grey) London Hippodrome 25 June

THE NEW MOON Romantic musical play in 2 acts by Oscar Hammerstein II, Frank Mandel and Laurence Schwab. Music by Sigmund Romberg. Chestnut Street Opera House, Philadelphia, 22 December 1927; Imperial Theater, New York (revised version), 19 September 1928.

The team responsible for that overwhelming hit of 1926, *The Desert Song*, mined a similar vein for their next collaboration, *The New Moon*, a romantic operetta set in the *Naughty Marietta* precincts of 18th-century New Orleans. In contrast to *Naughty Marietta*, this time it was the leading man, Robert Misson, rather than the heroine who was on the run from Europe, having sold himself into colonial servitude to escape arrest for the murder of a royal rapist. He is engaged as steward in the home of Beaunoir family, where he falls in love with the aristocratic Marianne and where the French policeman Ribaud tracks him down. Misson pirates the ship taking him back to France and he and his anti-Royalist followers sail it to an unoccupied island where they establish a new colony where all men are equal, except him. When the French invade, however, it turns out that they now represent not the bad old King but the nice new Republic. Marianne is expediently converted to being Citizeness Misson, Ribaud, refusing to bow to the mob, is condemned, and Misson, named Governor of his island (since Kings are now not allowed), settles down for a happy ending with his men and his Marianne.

Plate 194. **The New Moon:** *the French got it right – by the time the rewrites were done, 'Robert the Pirate' was a much better title for the show.*

The show was produced in Philadelphia, which had given such a tremendous welcome to Romberg's *My Maryland* earlier the same year, with Robert Halliday as Misson, Desirée Tabor (quickly replaced by Jessie Royce Landis) as Marianne, and William O'Neal (Philippe), William Wayne (Alexander), Margaret Irving (Madame Duchêne) and Walter Brennan as Girard, supporting. *New Moon* did not win the same response that *My Maryland* had, and Schwab and Mandel decided to close the production down rather than to fiddle with it on what looked like a rocky road to town. For seven months *The New Moon* went back into the workshop. Romberg, with the five other musicals on which he had worked during 1927 finally out of the way, devoted himself to rewriting his score. Out went Julie and Alexander's 'When I Close My Eyes' and Robert and Marianne's ''Neath a New Moon' (leaving the show's title now referring only to the name of a ship!), Marianne's 'La, la, la, la' and 'A Voice in the Dark', Besace's sea shanties and 'Women, Women, Women', Robert's 'I Love You', Mme Duchêne's praises of 'Paris', 'I'm Just a Sentimental Fool' and 'Liar', leaving the stirring march 'Shoulder to Shoulder' (later rechristened 'Stout hearted Men') and the comical 'Try Them Out at Dancing' (sic) from the original set of songs to be supplemented with more than half a score of new music. The additions included the heroine's

waltz 'One Kiss' and the love song 'Lover, Come Back to Me', the soaring duet 'Wanting You' and one of Romberg's and, certainly, of Hammerstein's, most beautiful songs, 'Softly as in a Morning Sunrise', sung by neither of the stars but by the tenor Philippe, an accessory to Misson's crime who has turned 'republican' through sexual jealousy, sighing, in his American exile, over all that his foolishness has lost him.

On 27 August 1928 the producers reopened the much-altered show in Cleveland (even though they were opening *Hold Everything!* at virtually the same time in Newark), with Evelyn Herbert (Marianne), Robert Halliday (Misson), William O'Neal (Philippe) and Max Figman (Ribaud) in the dramatic rôles and Gus Shy heading the incidental comedy. Former D'Oyly Carte tenor Pacie Ripple played Beaunoir. In a few weeks *The New Moon* was on Broadway, and Schwab and Mandel's decision to stop and rewrite was fully justified. *The New Moon* effaced the disappointments of Romberg's *My Princess* and *The Love Call*, scored a splendid success and finished by totting up an even longer Broadway run than *The Desert Song* with a total of 509 performances at the Imperial Theater.

Before Broadway's production had closed, *The New Moon* was mounted at London's Theatre Royal, Drury Lane, following behind *Rose Marie*, *The Desert Song* and *Show Boat* at what had become the headquarters of the best of Broadway operetta in the West End. Howett Worster (Misson), Evelyn Laye (Marianne), Ben Williams (Philippe), Edmund Willard (Ribaud) and Gene Gerrard (Gus) headed the cast with Vera Pearce as Clotilde, but *The New Moon* proved not to have the same attractions for London as the previous pieces had had. It lasted only 148 performances. Paris, which similarly saw the show in the wake of *Show Boat* (*Mississippi*), gave a warmer welcome to a version more explicitly retitled *Robert le Pirate* (ad Albert Willemetz). Here the figures were reversed, and *Robert le Pirate*, with the rising baritone André Baugé starred alongside the striking soprano Danielle Brégis and the comic Bach, played 237 times on the Châtelet's vast stage where the disappointing *Mississippi* had been seen just 115 times.

Like Britain, Australia reacted slightly disappointingly to *The New Moon*, especially given the huge local popularity of *The Desert Song*. J C Williamson Ltd's production starring *The Desert Song*'s hero Lance Fairfax, Marie Bremner (Marianne), Frederick Bentley (Gus), Herbert Browne (Philippe) and Vera Spaull (Clotilde), played only a single Sydney season before it was replaced by a revival of *The Belle of New York*. Sydney Burchall took over as Misson for seven weeks in Melbourne (Theatre Royal, 19 July 1930).

However, *The New Moon* and, most especially, its music were still destined to be received as classics throughout the English-speaking world and, as in the case of *Naughty Marietta*, it was the cinema which was largely responsible for this. The first film version, with Grace Moore and Lawrence Tibbett starred, Adolphe Menjou as the Governor and Gus Shy, Roland Young and Emily Fitzroy at the head of the comedy, used only a little of Romberg's score attached to a wholly different story which transported the action to the Caspian sea and turned her into yet another Princess and him into yet another hussar. She got to sing 'Lover Come Back to Me'. However, a Nelson Eddy-Jeanette MacDonald movie of 1940 returned to a version much more like the stage show and found much more success. Eddy and Miss MacDonald imprinted their performances on to the material and ensured *The New Moon* regular productions – beginning with performances at Carnegie Hall (18 August 1942) and the New York City Center (17 May 1944) – which have continued, largely in regional and amateur circumstances, to the present day.

UK: Theatre Royal, Drury Lane 4 April 1929; France: Théâtre du Châtelet *Robert le Pirate* 20 December 1929; Australia: Her Majesty's Theatre, Sydney 4 January 1930; Film: MGM 1930, MGM 1940

Recordings: Selections (Decca, RCA Victor, Columbia, Capitol, World Record Club) etc

NEWTON, H[enry] Chance (b London, 13 March 1854; d London, 2 January 1931). Librettist for the Victorian burlesque stage.

After early experience as an actor, Newton became a journalist and wrote for many years for, in particular, *The Referee* (as 'Carados'), *The Sketch* and *The New York Dramatic Mirror* (as 'Gawain'). Under the pseudonym of 'Richard Henry', he collaborated with the editor of *The Referee*, Richard Butler, on the libretti for a number of burlesques, including the Gaiety piece *Monte Cristo Jr*, which was amongst the earliest successes of the new burlesque era under George Edwardes, and supplied the texts for several touring shows including vehicles for Vesta Tilley (*Cartouche & Co*, a burlesque of *Mam'zelle Nitouche*) and Marie Lloyd (*The ABC*), and later for the music halls, without ever equalling his first success.

Alongside a book of memoirs, Newton also wrote the music-hall history, *Idols of the Halls*.

1883 **Giddy Godiva, or The Girl that was Sent to Coventry** Sanger's Auditorium 13 October
1886 **Monte Cristo Jr** (W Meyer Lutz et al/w Richard Butler) Gaiety Theatre 23 December
1887 **Jubilation** (Ivan Caryll, Henry J Leslie/w Butler) 1 act Prince of Wales Theatre 14 May
1887 **Frankenstein** (Lutz/w Butler) Gaiety Theatre 24 December
1889 **Lancelot the Lovely** (John Crook/w Butler) Avenue Theatre 22 April
1892 **Opposition** (Caryll/w Butler) 1 act Lyric Theatre 28 June
1892 **Cartouche & Co, or The Ticket of French Leave** (George Le Brunn) Theatre Royal, Birmingham 22 August
1893 **Weatherwise** (Ernest Ford) 1 act Lyric Theatre 29 November
1894 **Jaunty Jane Shore** (Crook/w Butler) Strand Theatre 2 April
1895 **The Newest Woman** (Georges Jacobi) 1 act Avenue Theatre 4 April
1897 **The Maid of Athens** (F Osmond Carr/w Charles Edmund Pearson) Opera Comique 3 June
1898 **Much Ado About Something, or Beerbohm-Treelawney of the Wells** (sketch interpolated into *Dandy Dan, the Lifeguardsman*)
1898 **The ABC, or Flossie the Frivolous** (Granville Bantock et al/w Butler) Grand Theatre, Wolverhampton 21 March
1901 **The Belle of Cairo** (F Kinsey Peile/revised libretto) Grand Theatre, Birmingham 25 November
1912 **Wellington** (John Neat/J P Harrington) 1 act Oxford Music Hall 22 January

Autobiography: *Cues and Curtain Calls* (John Lane/Bodley Head, London, 1927)

NICHOLAS, Paul [BEUSELINCK, Paul] (b London, 3 December 1944). Popular ever-young English performer in all media including 25 years of musicals.

Paul Nicholas made his first appearance on the West End stage as Claude in London's production of *Hair* (1968) before being cast in the title-rôle of the first British production of *Jesus Christ Superstar* (1972) and, in succession to Richard Gere, as Danny Zuko to the Sandy of Elaine Paige in London's version of *Grease* (1974). In a career which mixed stage appearances with film (*Tommy, Stardust, Lizstomania, Sergeant Pepper's Lonely Hearts Club Band*) and recording engagements (he made the British top ten with 'Dancing with the Captain' and 'Grandma's Party' in 1976 and scored with 'Heaven on the Seventh Floor' in America), he created his first musical rôles as Talkative (and other characters) in *Pilgrim* (1975), a touring musicalization of Bunyan's *The Pilgrim's Progress*, and as the hero of the unfortunate successor to *The Rocky Horror Show, T Zee* (1976).

He had his most successful new rôle in 1981, when he created the part of the sleek, pop-singing puss, the Rum-Tum-Tugger, in *Cats*, and followed up as another pop persona, the swinging minstrel with the ghastly girlfriend in Tim Rice and Stephen Oliver's *Blondel* (1983). However, a swelling television career which would establish him as one of the most popular adorable rogues of the British small screen meant that his stage appearances were, from then on, both more demanded and more limited. In recent years he has appeared in Manchester and, later, in London as the Pirate King of *The Pirates of Penzance*, in London and in the provinces as Joe, the boyish hero of the revived *Charlie Girl*, and as P T Barnum in a revival of the musical *Barnum*.

Nicholas latterly turned to producing and co-produced (w Robert Stigwood, David Ian) the 1993 London revival of *Grease*.

NICHOLLS, Harry (b London, 1 March 1852; d London, 29 November 1926).

For many years a popular comedian and pantomime artist, Nicholls spent the bulk of his acting career at the Theatre Royal, Drury Lane, and at the Adelphi Theatre, but he had, in his early days on the stage, played in comic opera on the London stage in Selina Dolaro's *La Périchole* (Don Andres) company. Alongside his performing career, Nicholls also worked as a playwright, scoring a major hit with the comedy *Jane* (1890 w William Lestocq) and then further successes as the part-author of two of the most internationally played of the Gaiety Theatre musical comedies, *A Runaway Girl* and *The Toreador*. In a busy and eclectic career, he also wrote many lyrics for both popular and show songs and appeared at the Gaiety in the rôle of Hooker Pacha in *The Messenger Boy* (1900).

Jane was turned into a musical comedy in 1919 under the title *Baby Bunting* (Nat D Ayer/Clifford Grey/Fred Thompson, Worton David) with some success, and it may very well have also been the basis of a pasticcio musical comedy called *Oh! Jemima* which appeared in Melbourne, Australia in 1913 with Nicholls's name attached to it and Carrie Moore as its star.

1898 **A Runaway Girl** (Ivan Caryll, Lionel Monckton/Aubrey Hopwood, Harry Greenbank/w Seymour Hicks) Gaiety Theatre 21 May

901 **The Toreador** (Monckton, Caryll/Adrian Ross, Percy Greenbank/w James T Tanner) Gaiety Theatre 17 June

NICK, Edmund [Josef] (b Reichenberg, 22 September 891; d Geretsried, 11 April 1974). German Operette omposer, critic and author.

Nick studied law in Graz and music in Vienna and Dresden and, after the First World War, worked as a piano eacher, music critic and then as conductor at the Lobe-Theater in Breslau (1921 sq), where he provided the music or the company's shows, including the fairytale pieces *Die Silbermeilenstiefl* and *Pipfaxs Weltenreise*. In 1933 he moved o Berlin where he worked for two years in the Kabarett Katakomb before becoming a conductor at the Theater les Volkes (1936–40) and, during this period, he wrote a number of stage works. The first and most successful of hese was the 'musikalisches Lustspiel' *Das kleine Hofonzert* (1935), a period piece featuring an ingénue who teps in for an ailing singer and wins herself an aristocratic Lieutenant, which won several further productions following its first showing in Munich. He also contributed to the inema stage, notably with a 1936 film version of his successful Operette (*Das Hofkonzert* UFA w Johannes Heesers, Marta Eggerth).

After the Second World War Nick continued conducting (including a period at the Bavarian State Operette Theatre) and teaching, and wrote and conducted for film nd for radio, but he contributed little more to the theatre s a composer. He was, in his later years, music critic or *Die Welt* and *Süddeutsches Zeitung*, and authored a biography of Paul Lincke and the book *Vom Wiener Walzer zur Wiener Operette* (1954).

935 **Das kleine Hofkonzert** (Paul Verhoeven, Toni Impekoven) Kammerspiele, Munich 19 November
937 **Die glücklichen Tage** Bremen
938 **Xanthippe** Frankfurt-am-Main
939 **Titus macht Karriere** Theater in der Behrenstrasse, Berlin
939 **Über alles siegt die Liebe** (Bruno Hardt-Warden) Stadttheater, Troppau 25 November; Theater des Volkes, Berlin 1940
940 **Nur für Erwaschsene**
941 **Dreimal die Eine** Leipzig
941 **Karusell-Karusell!** (G Graepp, R Reith) Darmstadt
948 **Das Halsband der Königin** (Gerhard Metzner) Theater am Gärtnerplatz, Munich 1 December

NIELSEN, Alice (b Nashville, Tenn, 7 June 1876; d New York, 8 March 1943). Soprano star of 19th-century Broadway.

Alice Nielsen sang for several years as a church soloist in Kansas City and then in various light-opera productions in California, appearing as Yum-Yum and La Périchole with Pike's Opera Company and in operetta at the San Francisco Tivoli, before she joined joined the Bostonians Boston Ideal Comic Opera Company) in 1896. She layed Annabelle in *Robin Hood* and Nanette in Herbert's *Prince Ananias* with the famous Boston company, and reated leading rôles in Oscar Weil's *The Wartime Wedding* nd, more significantly, in Victor Herbert's *The Serenade* 1897, Yvonne). In *The Serenade*, however, she had to allow he centre of attention to go to the Bostonians' much-loved ontralto Jessie Bartlett Davis, and this did not fit with her mbitions. She swiftly split from the Bostonians, effectively

if not immediately destroying a company that had been built up into America's finest light-opera troupe by taking a number of its performers with her to form the Alice Nielsen Comic Opera Company.

With that company Miss Nielsen produced two new Victor Herbert works with herself in the starring rôles. She played the vast dual lead rôle in *The Fortune Teller* (1898) successfully in both America and Britain, and if *The Singing Girl* (1899) was less popular, it still served her for a good season's touring in repertoire. Miss Nielsen then quit the light musical theatre to pursue a career in opera where she found some success in the lighter areas of the soprano repertoire (Zerlina, Norina, Susanna, Gilda, Mimi, Marguerite), sharing a bill with Caruso in *Le nozze di Figaro* on one occasion in Europe, appearing at the Metropolitan Opera House in 1909, but making the bulk of her operatic career in Boston.

She returned when that career was done to appear one last time on Broadway, under her own management, in the title-rôle of the Rudolf Friml/Otto Harbach musical *Kitty Darlin'* in the 1917 season. The piece failed, and Miss Nielsen retired from the stage to be a doctor's wife.

NIESE, Hansi (b Vienna, 10 November 1875; d Vienna, 4 April 1934).

The most popular soubrette of the Viennese light comic stage for many years, the comical 'naïve' Frln Niese was equally at home in straight or musical rôles, which she mixed with considerable effect and great success during her years at the Raimundtheater (1893–8) and at the Theater in der Josefstadt (1899 sq) and between times at other Viennese houses run by her then husband, Josef Jarno.

She appeared in many musical Possen during her years at the Raimundtheater, mixing comedy and even occasionally drama with pieces such as the protean musical comedy *Das Blitzmädel* and co-starring on occasion with the visiting Girardi (*Der Schusterbub* etc), but her most successful musical play creation was the part of Christl, the heroine of the Operette *Die Förster-Christl*, composed by her brother-in-law, George Jarno, and mounted by her husband at the Theater in der Josefstadt. She followed up in the Jarno brothers' *Das Musikantenmädel* (1910, Resel) and *Das Waschermädel* (1913, Betti), as well as in such other musical productions as *Die eiserne Jungfrau* (1911, Beate Binder), the oft-revived *Drei Paar Schuhe* (Leni), and Jarno's productions of Béla Zerkovitz's *Die Wundermühle* (1914, in a dual mother-and-daughter rôle as Josefa and Fritzi) and the Hungarian operett *Die Patronesse vom Nachtcafé* (1915, Marie Gangel), but the musical part of her talent remained always an accessory to the comical, and in spite of her *Förster-Christl* success she did not venture into the world of the Viennese Operette.

In her second marriage Frln Niese became the Baroness Popper, whilst her daughter from her marriage to Jarno, Hansi Niese-Jarno, also took the stage for a small career prior to an early death.

THE NIGHT BOAT Musical comedy in 2 acts by Anne Caldwell based on *Le Contrôleur des wagons-lits* by Alexandre Bisson. Music by Jerome Kern. Liberty Theater, New York, 2 February 1920.

A light comedy, with touches of Kern's earlier *Very Good*

Eddie in its shipboard setting and the duplicated names of its plotline, *The Night Boat* took its outline from Alexandre Bisson's internationally successful *Le Contrôleur des wagons-lits* (Théâtre des Nouveautés, 11 March 1898), a piece which had been played in America in Madeleine Lucette Ryley's adaptation as *On and Off* (Madison Square Theater 17 October 1898).

John E Hazzard played the central Bob White who, in order to get a little respite from his wife's ever-present family, pretends that he is the captain of the Albany night boat (rather than the original's railway sleeping-car inspector), a ruse which allows him to get away 'to work' in the evenings. Unfortunately, his wife's monstrous mother Mrs Maxim (Ada Lewis) decides to check him out and, accompanied by Mrs White (Stella Hoban) and her sister Barbara (Louise Groody), she books a ticket on the night boat. The second-act ride up the river – on which the real captain turns out to be called ... Robert White (Ernest Torrence) – provided a regulation ration of misunderstandings, flirtations and the opportunity for a jolly concert of such favourite riverish songs as Ivan Caryll's 'By the Saskatchewan' (*The Pink Lady*), 'Congo Love Song' (*Nancy Brown*), Paul Dresser's 'On the Banks of the Wabash' (*Monte Carlo*), and Harry Tierney's 'M.I.S.S.I.S.S.I.P.P.I' (*Hitchy Koo*, *The Beauty Spot*) and a round of speciality dances. These topped up effectively Kern's new first-act successes – the charming 'Whose Baby Are You?' sung by the juvenile coupling of Miss Groody and Hal Skelly (Freddie), Miss Hoban's hit-worthy 'Left All Alone Again Blues' and the pretty ensemble 'Good Night Boat'. A melody which was later to be heard celebrating 'London, Dear Old London' in Kern's British show *The Cabaret Girl*, here declared that 'Girls Are Like a Rainbow'. An amusing novelty item had the chorus recapping the plot, some way into Act I, for the benefit of latecomers and rounding it off at the top of Act II for those who had to rush for early trains.

A splendid success through 38 weeks (313 performances) on Broadway, Charles Dillingham's production of *The Night Boat* was tumbled out of its New York home to let in the same producer's anticipated new hit, *The Half Moon*. Whilst *The Half Moon* flopped painfully, the ejected show moved on to several seasons of touring life in America. However, in spite of the announcement, in 1920, of a London production by Alfred Butt and William Boosey *The Night Boat* did not cross either the Atlantic or the Pacific.

A NIGHT OUT Musical play in 2 acts by George Grossmith jr and Arthur Miller adapted from *L'Hôtel du Libre Échange* by Maurice Desvallières and Georges Feydeau. Lyrics by Clifford Grey. Music by Willie Redstone. Additional songs by Arthur Anderson and Melville Gideon, Cole Porter, R P Weston and Bert Lee, and Philip Braham. Winter Garden Theatre, London, 19 September 1920.

The Grossmith and Laurillard producing partnership continued with their successful recipe of turning French comedies into musicals (*Theodore & Cie*, *Les Dominos roses*, *Madame et son filleul*) by musicalizing the celebrated *L'Hôtel du Libre Échange* (aka *Hotel Paradiso* and, in its 1896 London production, *A Night Out*) for Leslie Henson and the rest of their Winter Garden Theatre team. Henson was

the little Pinglet who takes his neighbour's neglected lad (Lily St John) out for the night and ends up in prison when their naughty hotel is raided. Fred Leslie (dupe), Dave Burnaby (heavy), Phyllis Monkman (maid) and Stella S Audrie (dragonistic wife) added to the essential comedy assisted by some sparky songs ('The Hotel Pimlico', the Clifford Grey/Cole Porter 'Why Didn't We Meet Before?'), a burlesque of the then-popular Russian ballet, a caveman number about 'Bolshevik Love' and some special material for Henson, through a highly successful 311 performance run prior to a three-year British and colonial touring life.

The Australian portion of that colonial life turned out to be quite a sensational one. *A Night Out* was first staged by J C Williamson Ltd in Melbourne with Maud Fane, Alfred Frith, Cecil Bradley, Cyril Ritchard and Madge Elliot featured in its cast and there it put up a remarkable run of 18 weeks, a record second only to the all-time top recently set up there by *The Maid of the Mountains*. Moving on to Sydney (Her Majesty's Theatre 3 June 1922) the show confirmed its Melbourne run with a further three months of performances, and established itself as one of the most revivable in Williamson's repertoire of revivable pieces. As long as the fashion for comedy-based musicals lasted (and here it lasted longer than in most areas), *A Night Out* was regularly revived in Australia.

In spite of all this success, however, *A Night Out* flopped when it finally got to America. But the few Americans who saw it, saw it in a heavily remade form. Laurillard and Alex Aarons's production jettisoned almost the entire score ('Bolshevik Love' and the Ragpickers Dance with its ballet burlesque remained) and replaced it with one by Vincent Youmans, freshly hot through *No, No, Nanette*. The producers imported British performers for the main rôles, but the shine was taken off this when a visiting (unemployed) English actress sniffed in print – not without some justification – that she'd never heard of Mr Aarons's transatlantic 'stars'. Norman Griffin, Henson's regular London cover, and Australian Toots Pounds were the principals, she getting to share 'Sometimes I'm Happy', the best song from the new score, with Frederick Lord in the two weeks before the show closed on the road.

Australia: Theatre Royal, Melbourne, 21 January 1922; USA: Garrick Theater, Philadelphia, 7 September 1925

NIMM MICH MIT! Operette in 3 acts by Heinrich von Waldberg and A M Willner based on the novel *His Official Wife* by Richard Henry Savage. Music by Hermann Dostal. Theater an der Wien, Vienna, 1 May 1919.

Nimm mich mit! was a Viennese musical-comedy remake of the tale related in Colonel Savage's vastly popular American spy novel, a book which had already been dramatized with great success for the German-language stage as a sensational drama by Hans Olden (*Die offizielle Frau*, Berliner Theater) and by a number of others. This version starred Mizzi Günther as the seductive 'stranger' who stands in for the stay-at-home wife of Franz Xaver Edelbrunner, President of the Society for Social Welfare in Vienna (Ernst Tautenhayn), on a trip to Russia, with all the expected complications and – given that the lady is actually a potential assassin – a few more. Luise Kartousch appeared in breeches as Baron Boris Zofimov, a guards cadet, romancing sugar-magnate's daughter Sonia (Klara

Plate 195. **A Night Out:** *It was all the maid's fault! Victorine (Phyllis Monkman) gets the pointed fingers of the police (E Graham), Mme Pinglet (Stella St Audrie), Pinglet (Leslie Henson), Matthieu (Davy Burnaby) and Maurice Paillard (Fred Leslie).*

Karry), and Robert Nästlberger was the Russian Police Chief who gets caught up with the 'official wife' both romantically and, when she turns out to be not what she seems, professionally. The title duet and Miss Günther's second-act waltz 'Frauen aus Wien' were the principal musical successes of the piece which was played 155 times at the Theater an der Wien, and gave the elder Dostal his most significant success on the Viennese stage.

His Official Wife – which became *The Passport* in Britain, *Passe la grille!* in France, *Hivatalos feleség* in Hungary and so forth, in its dramatic form – was also used as the basis for the successful American musical *The Red Widow* (1911) and for Richard Kessler and Max Jungk's German musical comedy *Die offizielle Frau* (music: Robert Winterberg) produced at Berlin's Theater am Nollendorfplatz on 23 December 1925.

NINA ROSA Musical play in 2 acts by Otto Harbach. Lyrics by Irving Caesar. Music by Sigmund Romberg. Forest Park Theater, St Louis, May 1930; Majestic Theater, New York, 20 September 1930.

A Peruvian love story in a fairly direct line of descent from *Rose Marie* and *Rio Rita*, *Nina Rosa* starred the original heroine of the latter show, Ethelind Terry (replacing Margaret Carlisle from the original St Louis open-air production), as the colourful foreigner of the title who ends up being paired off with the dashing American mining engineer Jack Haines (Guy Robertson) rather than a not-very-pleasant fellow South American called Pablo (Leonard Ceeley) at the end of a story of mining options and gold discovery, Inca ruins and horrid ambushes. Even the happier parts of Romberg's score, 'Your Smiles, Your Tears' or 'My First Love, My Last Love', were not in the same league as his previous year's *The New Moon* material, but they nevertheless provided an agreeable accompaniment to a huge 150-cast, 36-band, heavily scenic production.

Just fair runs on Broadway (137 performances) – where, once sufficient success had been established the producers' billing altered from 'Milton I Shubert presents' to 'the brothers Shubert present' – and in London (117 performances), where Lee Ephraim teamed Miss Terry (later Helen Gilliland) with Geoffrey Gwyther, and Robert Chisholm in his production at the Lyceum Theatre, were a prelude, however, to a considerable success in France (which had also liked *Rose-Marie* and, perhaps significantly, hadn't had *Rio Rita*). Staged with all the vast resources of Maurice Lehmann's Théâtre du Châtelet, the Paris production of *Nina Rosa* (ad André Mouëzy-Éon, Albert Willemetz) featured Sim-Viva, popular baritone André Baugé, comics Bach and Monique Bert, the Marche des Gauchos, 12 sets, 700 costumes, a car chase through the Andes in an LR4 Rosengart, and a vast amount of featured dances including a flamenco aux eventails, a marching drill, an exhibition rumba, a huge Inca ballet and even a children's dance. The production played no fewer than 710 performances, was brought back in 1936 (30 September) for a further 98 and established *Nina-Rosa* and such songs as 'Les Femmes sont perfides', 'Nina Rosa', 'Toutes les roses' and 'Un seul regard' in France in such a fashion that the show can still occasionally be seen or heard today whilst it remains all but forgotten in its original language.

UK: Lyceum Theatre 7 July 1931; France: Théâtre du Châtelet 18 December 1931

NINE Musical in 2 acts by Arthur Kopit based on the screenplay *8½* by Federico Fellini. Music and lyrics by Maury Yeston. 46th Street Theater, New York, 9 May 1982.

Guido Contini (Raul Julia) is a weakly macho Italian film director, a man who apparently has a sufficient reputation in his line of work for the fact that he has directed three successive failures not to prevent a producer from pursuing him to make a new movie. As the evening progresses, we see how the different sets of demands he encourages from the various women in his life allow him endlessly to postpone getting down to work and, when he is finally forced to put up or ship out, he can come up with only a facile piece of screen spectacular which goes as wrong as his relationships with those women. Indecisive to the last, he is unable even to kill himself, but finally he accepts a useful bit of advice from his young self – 'grow up'.

The show's libretto compensated for the spinelessness of its central character and the non-action of its plot by following the example of the 1966 Italian musical *Ciao, Rudy* and surrounding its 'hero' with a colourful collection of 21 variegated women which included his wife (Karen Akers), his current mistress (Anita Morris), his star (Shelly Burch), his producer (Liliane Montevecchi) and his mother (Taina Elg), and the score reflected that variety of colour in a series of character numbers of which the wife's even 'My Husband Makes Movies' and the star's admission that she loves the man 'In an Unusual Way' proved coolly extractable.

On a one-set stage, tiled white to represent a spa, Miss Morris whispered suggestive nothings down the telephone in a mixture of chest and soprano tones whilst performing an ecstatic contortion act in what Guido tried to make his wife believe is 'A Call from the Vatican', Kathi Moss recounted Contini's introduction to sex with booming exuberance ('Ti voglio bene'), Montevecchi displayed splendid legs in a pastichey piece about 'Folies Bergère' and Taina Elg reminisced gently over her son at 'Nine' in a succession of revusical highlights, which were complemented by some appreciable choral part-writing in a sung 'Overture di Donne' and a bristling introductory 'The Germans at the Spa'.

Nine was awarded the 1982 Tony Award as Best Musical of a season which also included *Dreamgirls* and the decade-old *Joseph and the Amazing Technicolor Dreamcoat*, and went on to a good Broadway run of 732 performances. In spite of a lot of announcements, however, it did not travel, and a 1987 Australian production was the only one to appear in the other main centres. Cast to the hilt with some of the country's top female performers, it won sufficient local success for its producer to spread word of an international transfer which in the end did not take place. London ultimately heard a concert performance in lieu of the promised stage one.

Australia: Her Majesty's Theatre, Melbourne, 5 March 1988
Recordings: original cast (Columbia), Australian cast (Polydor), English concert (TER)

NINETTE Opérette in 3 acts by Charles Clairville. Music by Charles Lecocq. Théâtre des Bouffes-Parisiens, Paris, 28 February 1896.

The *Ninette* of the title of Lecocq's opérette is Ninon de l'Enclos, the same historical personage who battled for a man with Nanon of the Golden Lamb in Genée's *Nanon*. In Clairville's libretto she comes out better, scoring most of the hits in a light-hearted plot that matches her with the chevalier of the nose, Cyrano de Bergerac.

The ageing Lecocq had originally intended the score of this piece as the material for a substantial *Cyrano de Bergerac* which he hoped would be staged at the Opéra-Comique with Marcelle Dartoy as its Ninon, but, having failed to convince the gentlemen of the Salle Favart that

Cyrano and/or Lecocq (who had failed there with *Plutus*) were suitable material for them, he transformed his score with a few lighter pieces into another and rather different kind of period piece. In spite of the then vogue for the 'gentille' in musical theatre, the very well-made *Ninette* was played 107 times under Georges Grisier's management at the Bouffes-Parisiens with Germaine Gallois as the *spirituelle* Ninon and Piccaluga in the rôle of Cyrano. It won a production in Budapest and then, with fashion of the times thoroughly against it, slipped from the schedules.

Hungary: Népszinház 16 January 1897

NINICHE Vaudeville-opérette (pièce) in 3 acts by Alfred Hennequin and Albert Millaud [and Émile de Najac, uncredited]. Music composed and arranged by Marius Boullard. Théâtre des Variétés, Paris, 15 February 1878.

The first, one of the most successful, and in some ways even the most successful – *Lili* and *Mam'zelle Nitouche* included – of the series of vaudeville-opérettes produced at the Théâtre des Variétés with Anna Judic as star, *Niniche* went round the world several times after its huge initial success in Paris.

Judic was 'Niniche', once a demi-mondaine, now the wife of the Polish Count Corniski. In her days in the demi-monde, one of her admirers had been the heir to the Polish throne and now, as his succession approaches, he is anxious to regain possession of some rather embarrassing letters which he once wrote to the lady. Unfortunately, the Countess left her old affairs in Paris in rather a dubious state when she vanished into the northern aristocracy, and her apartment and furniture have been seized by the bailiffs, sealed, and are about to be put up for auction. Everyone heads for Paris: the Countess, her diplomat husband (Baron), the friendly *gommeux* Anatole de Beaupersil (Lassouche) and the ambitious Grégoire (Dupuis), anxious to prove his abilities by being the one to bring back the letters. Alas, once on her old home ground, the Countess finds the urges to become 'Niniche' again irresistible, a feeling and a fact which do not help matters during the two acts of farcical ins-and-outs, disguises and delicate situations which are gone through on the way to the ultimately modest and satisfactorily face-saving ending.

Judic caused a sensation in her rôle, not only with her virtuoso playing of the 'double' part and her long-talked-about second-act entrance in a dazzling costume and toilette, transformed from the Comtesse Corniska back into 'Niniche', but most particularly by appearing on the stage in a bathing costume. Dupuis, who had a fine rôle, also indulged in a bathing suit without creating a parallel sensation, and went through a comical scene of disguise as a waiter in the final act. In the other feminine rôles, Paris's favourite 'dragon', Aline Duval, played la veuve Sillery and Augustine Leriche appeared as Georgina.

Although *Niniche* was, properly speaking, a vaudeville and thus not perhaps quite what the public normally expected to find in the way of entertainment at the theatre that had so long and well provided them with the best of Offenbach, Variétés director Eugène Bertrand had recognized when the piece was submitted to him for his consideration that it would make a fine vehicle for Judic, a star for the half-dozen years since *Le Roi Carotte* and *Le Timbale d'argent* and recently seen to advantage in

Offenbach's *Le Docteur Ox*. He duly approached Offenbach to compose some music for the songs which were needed to make Judic's rôle into a sufficiently showy one, and was refused. The composer, apparently taken aback by the huge and recent success of Planquette's *Les Cloches de Corneville* and Lecocq's *Le Petit Duc*, was determined that his next work would be an important one and he was not interested in writing vaudeville tunes. With his production already scheduled, Bertrand took the quickest way out: he asked former Variétés musical director Marius Boullard to supply the music for Judic's songs. Boullard, leaning in traditional fashion on pont-neufs, the well- and oft-used popular airs which were used and re-used as melodies for vaudeville songs, provided just the straightforward, rhythmic and tuneful material which was required – music which allowed the actress to put across her songs rather than sing them too lyrically – to make up a score of eight numbers and some bits.

Judic opened with a swim-suited shivering song, complaining (though, of course, no one else did) 'mon costume est si collant!' and brrrr!-ing through a refrain which concluded 'Baigneur, viens me prendre, j'ai froid!', followed up with a rondo, and, in the second act, another as she looked longingly over her old Parisian haunt ('Nature supérieure'). She reminisced further, dressed in her grande toilette ('Avec ce costume, Anatole'), joined in a comic duo with Dupuis ('Il faut oser') and tied up her vocal contribution with the Couplets du Commissaire of the final act. There was, of course, little space for anyone else in the music of the piece, and only Dupuis of the other stars had his musical moments. He confided, in his Couplets du baigneur in the first scene, 'Si j'avais suivi les voeux de mon père, oui, j'aurais pu faire un bon sous-préfet', concluding 'Moi, je baigne!'. He teaches the ladies swimming, an occupation which, of course, involves putting his two hands ... here! His hands and their occupation were also the subject of his second song, the Couplets du masseur, in the third act.

Niniche and Anna Judic turned out to be an enormous success together, quite able to compete with the Planquette and Lecocq triumphs at the Folies-Dramatiques and the Théâtre de la Renaissance, whilst Offenbach's 'substantial' *Maître Péronilla* was a 50-performance flop at the Bouffes-Parisiens. The first run of Bertrand's production continued through the whole season at the Variétés (275 performances) and its amazing triumph persuaded the producer to continue with a policy of mounting similarly constructed and cast vaudeville-opérettes. It was a policy which turned out to be a paying one and one which, not unnaturally, included several revivals of *Niniche*, a piece and a rôle which Judic kept in her repertoire for more than two decades. Her last Paris appearance in the part was in 1901, nearly a quarter of a century after her first appearance in the famous maillot de bain. The maillot de bain was now a few sizes larger.

Niniche was a great international success, but apart from the interminable tours made throughout Europe and America by Judic, and later by Jane Pierny, it was rarely seen outside France in the form in which it was played at the Théâtre des Variétés. Improvers were everywhere. In Vienna, the text (ad Richard Genée) was reset with new music by Josef Brandl for its production at the Carltheater. Josephine Zampa scored a huge personal success in Judic's

rôle, alongside Wilhelm Knaack (Corniski), Karl Blasel (Beaupersil) and Franz Tewele (Grégoire), for a fine 28 straight performances before the show was put into repertoire (56 performances in 1878–9) and played throughout the country in provincial theatres.

The Boullard music was performed by its original star at the Theater an der Wien in 1883 (16 November) and at the Carltheater when the Variétés company with Judic, Baron and Dupuis visited in 1889 (21 April) and Judic repeated her rôle there again in 1895, before another version with the text of the piece (in a German version by Victor Léon and Heinrich von Waldberg which made Niniche a South American princess), musically reset by Richard Heuberger as *Ihre Excellenz*, was performed at the Theater an der Wien with Ilka Pálmay starred (28 January 1899). *Ihre Excellenz* was played later the same year in Germany (Nuremberg 14 July). However, the earlier 'Possenspiel mit Gesang', in its Brandl version, had already been played widely through Germany since its first production in Dresden, and *Ihre Excellenz* did not prove able to compete.

Budapest, in spite of following on behind the Austrian and German premières, did not take up Brandl's music, but, alone of the translated versions, stuck basically with Boullard's score for the production (ad Ferenc Csepreghy) at the Népszinhaz. Gerőffyné starred alongside István Együd (Korniszky), Elek Solymossy (Boperszil) and Miklös Tihanyi (Gregoár) in a production which was a veritable hit (55 performances), resulting in a revival (9 Sept 1887) and a countrywide success, as the piece joined the other Judic shows, *Lili* and *Mam'zelle Nitouche*, in confirming an outstanding success for the family of Théâtre de Variétés vaudevilles in Hungary.

Although *Niniche* was ultimately played in America in its original state by Judic in the 1885–6 season, it had already been plundered for two American pieces prior to the French star's visit. Both emphasized the swimsuit. The first was an 1878 comedy called *Manhattan Beach, or Down Amongst the Breakers*, the second, remade version, was *Newport; or, the Swimmer, the Singer and the Cypher* (15 September 1879) which was mounted by no less an impresario than Augustin Daly, with Catherine Lewis starring in Judic's rôle. Shortly after that, *Niniche* was seen in New York in German, in the Brandl version, with Poldi Pietsch, Tewele (Grégoire) and Knaack (Corniski) starred. That version was also later remade in English and the result was produced on Broadway as *The Merry Countess*, with Brandl's music intact. The whole thing was done over yet once more in 1901 as a vehicle for Anna Held – a performer aspiring to the Judic manner – as *The Little Duchess*, this time with a Reginald De Koven score.

London saw Judic play *Niniche* in its original form and language in her repertoire season (w *Lili*) in 1883 and (w *Mam'zelle Nitouche* and *La Cosaque*) in 1884, but F C Burnand's highly successful English version, *Boulogne*, was played – in spite of being introduced by the Gaiety Theatre's greatest musical comedy star, Nellie Farren – without any musical score. Since none of the American versions ever crossed the Atlantic, London ultimately never got a musical, English-language *Niniche*.

Niniche travelled to virtually every corner of the earth in one or another of its forms, more often than not gathering local music on the way. Thus Portugal's version picked up a musical score by Sgr Alvarenga, whilst in Italy a 1916 *Niniche* produced at Milan's Teatro Carcano (18 October) bore the names of Carlo Vizzotto and Angelo Bettellini under its title.

Austria: Carltheater (Brandl score) 12 October 1878; Germany: Dresden (Brandl score) 26 November 1878; Hungary: Népszinház *Niniss* 20 December 1878; London: Gaiety Theatre (Fr) 9 June 1883; USA: Thalia Theater (Ger, Brandl score) 31 October 1882, Garrick Theater *The Merry Countess* 2 November 1895

NINI LA CHANCE Comédie musicale in 2 acts by Jacques Mareuil. Music by Georges Lifermann. Théâtre Marigny, Paris, 21 October 1976.

A vehicle for musical-comedy and popular-song star Annie Cordy who started the show as a nurse in 1939 San Francisco and, by way of the phoney war and the real war, ended up saving the life of an American colonel and becoming a Broadway star. Her manfriend Jimmy (author Mareuil) becomes a war hero, and his mate Tom (James Sparrow) gets to be a Hollywood film star. On the way, Mlle Cordy gave out with 'Un gars comme ça', 'Nini la Chance', 'Y'a des moments' and 'Ça ira mieux demain' in her inimitable style, and Sparrow declared himself fleet-footedly 'Dingue de danse'.

After a fine Paris season, *Nini la Chance* was toured through France and Belgium into 1978.

Recording: original cast (CBS)

NISIDA Comic Operette in 3 acts by Moritz West and F Zell. Music by Richard Genée. Carltheater, Vienna, 9 October 1880.

Another internationally played product of the early Viennese stage, *Nisida* was an up-to-date Cuban piece which mixed a standard romantic story, featuring Frln Klein in the title-rôle as the soubrettey niece of a Spanish impresario called Barnacle (Wilhelm Knaack) and Karl Drucker as one Don Montiel de Caragui who was apparently a spare-time buccaneer, with some showbiz jollity in which Barnacle was joined by a pair of theatrical agents (played by Franz Eppich and Müller) and the whole troupe of 'Die lustigen Nigger' who have descended on Havana for the duration. Karl Blasel played the local potentate, Don Leonida Palestro, Corregidor in Havana and father of the buccaneering Montiel, Frau Benisch was his wealthy but unwed sister Micaëla, whilst Frln Bisca as their niece Mercedes and Josef Joseffy as the military Don Rodrigo Sandoval provided the secondary and more soulful love interest.

Nisida played only a few performances at the Carltheater, but they were by no means the end of its career. The piece promptly surfaced in the German-speaking theatre in New York where Mathilde Cottrelly starred in the title-rôle alongside Adolfi as the Corregidor, Schnelle (Montiel) and Lube (Barnacle) and it had a magnificent success, playing uninterruptedly for more than a month, a rare thing at that limited-audience theatre. Thus, it was not surprising that an English-language production soon followed.

A fortnight after the end of the Thalia season – and only three months after the Viennese première – Daly's Theater opened *Zanina, or the Rover of Cambaye* billed as 'Augustin Daly's adaptation (of) a musical comedy in 3 acts with an original East Indian Interlude by Harry W French, several original musical numbers by Mr E Mollenhauer, the words of the songs by Mr Fred Williams'. Laura Joyce was Zanina, John Brand played Montiel, James Lewis was Lumlini Strakoschini Barnaco and Digby Bell was His Excellency Booma Poota, which was sufficient to show that the action no longer took place in Cuba. It had been shoved into the good old orient, and decorated with a bundle of nautch girls with a dance performed 'for the first time in the history of the world outside the confines of India', magicians who grew rice from grains of sand, transformed a rag baby into pigeons and did The Indian Basket Trick, snake charmers, a knife-thrower and so forth, all of which the management insisted had been imported from India. There was also a hurricane to bring Act II to its peak. Ada Rehan played the small rôle of Muttra, 'a native with European tendencies but with the universal craving for rupees'.

Messrs Mollenhauer and Williams's contribution wasn't defined on the bills, but they were probably not responsible for the Cuban-flavoured Smoking Duet, which insisted (already) 'Clearly smoking is annoying …'. There were solos for Montiel ('The Rover of Cambaye') and Zanina ('I'm a Cherry Sweet to Taste', Song of the Czakik, Boléro) – who also joined in a pair of duos – Captain Trafalgar (ex-Sandoval, 'Love is Made of Smiles and Tears') and Numa (ex-Mercedes, 'Love with Doubt Can Never Dwell', 'Fragrant their perfume'), and the comics were equally well supplied, the three impresarii singing their self-praises and Booma Poota avoiding the usually unavoidable 'I am' type of potentate song.

All Daly's trouble and expense, however, did not win him a hit. *Zanina* in English ran the same four weeks as the German version had done. In the meanwhile, however, that German version had been produced at Hamburg, and Berlin, Prague, Leipzig and many other central European theatres queued up to mount *Nisida* in the early 1880s. But the show nevertheless remained well in the shadow of Genée's two major hits, *Der Seekadett* and *Nanon*.

Another piece called *Nisida* (Carlo di Barbieri/Krüger) and subtitled *die Perle von Procida* was produced at Hamburg in 1852 (29 September).

USA: Thalia Theater 7 December 1880, Daly's Theater *Zanina* 19 January 1881; Germany: Carl-Schultze Theater, Hamburg 15 January 1881, Friedrich-Wilhelmstädtisches Theater, Berlin 5 March 1881

LES NOCES DE JEANNETTE Opéra-comique in 1 act by Michel Carré and Jules Barbier. Music by Victor Massé. Opéra-Comique, Paris, 4 February 1853.

Massé's little opéra-comique was one of the mid-19th-century pieces which blended over the join between the Auber/Adam/Boieldieu era of French opéra-comique and the newer, more frankly joyous style of musical play as composed by Hervé and Offenbach. Its libretto told of a young lad who takes fright for his liberty and runs off for a boozy spree when he should be getting married, only to be reconciled to his girl and to married life by her forbearance and charm. It was a book in the same vein as those that would characterize the little 'rural' opérettes of Offenbach's early years (as opposed to the crazy burlesque ones), and Massé's score, whilst more vocally demanding in places than was later normal, rendered nothing to the later works in spirit and charm. Introduced at the Opéra-Comique (where much of Offenbach's work was refused) by Félix Miolan-Carvalho (Jeannette) and Couderc (Jean) it became a perennial item there (1,000th performance 10 May 1895) and quickly found its way into the repertoire of operatic troupes throughout the world and in a multitude of languages.

Britain and America heard an English version from the Pyne-Harrison Opera Company, in an adaptation written by William Harrison in which Jeannette became Georgette, whilst Karl Treumann introduced the piece to Vienna at his Kai-Theater alongside the early works of Offenbach and such other survivors of the cross-over period as Poïse's *Bonsoir voisin*, Caspers's *Ma tante dort*, Flotow's *Madame Bonjour* and Adam's *Les Pantins de Violette*. Another German version (ad Ida Schuselka-Brüning) was later played at the Vienna Hofoper, and, a witness to the durability of this little piece, a version of that adaptation was played in 1992 at the Dresden Staatsoperette. England, however, showed a rather cavalier attitude to Massé's music: an 1861 production at the Princess's Theatre (*Jeannette's Wedding* 10 October) quite simply omitted the score and played Carré and Barbier's libretto as a one-act play.

Australia, on the other hand, got the show in two stages. The first colonial *Jeannette's Wedding* was played at the Princess Theatre in Melbourne in 1858 (11 October), but again without Massé's music. The advertisement for the night stated that it had 'music composed expressly for this theatre by S D Nelson Esq'. It was not, apparently, until 1906 that the 'Australian première' took place, thus billed in a programme given by singer Blanche Arrall at the Sydney Town Hall which, if it apparently included most of the music, does not seem to have otherwise been quite the whole piece.

Germany: Dresden 9 January 1854, Berlin 30 October 1857; USA: New Orleans 1854, Niblo's Garden, New York *The Marriage of Jeannette* 9 April 1855; UK: Theatre Royal, Covent Garden *The Marriage of Georgette* 26 November 1860; Austria: Theater am Franz-Josefs-Kai 18 October 1862; Hungary: Nemzeti Színház *Jeannette menyegzöje* 4 February 1879; Australia: Town Hall, Sydney 29 September 1906

LES NOCES D'OLIVETTE

Opérette in 3 acts by Henri Chivot and Alfred Duru. Music by Edmond Audran. Théâtre des Bouffes-Parisiens, Paris, 13 November 1879.

Having taken over the ailing Théâtre des Bouffes-Parisiens from Charles Comte, Louis Cantin took the first step towards restoring the house's popularity when he staged *Les Noces d'Olivette*. If the libretto was signed by two well-proven authors, the composer Edmond Audran was, on the other hand, unknown to Paris audiences. He had, however, had a significant success in Marseille with the delightful opérette *Le Grand Mogul*, a sufficient credential for Cantin to commission him to write a fresh piece for the Paris stage.

The text for *Les Noces d'Olivette* was one of the complex sexual-marital tales so popular at the time. Olivette (Elise Clary), the daughter of the seneschal of Perpignan, is in love with and due to be wed to Valentin (Marcelin). However, climbing up to a window he thinks is his soon-to-be bride's, Valentin instead breaks in upon the local potentate, the Countess Bathilde de Roussillon (Mlle Bennati). Although the lady is far from displeased at the handsome lad's visit, his escapade leads to Valentin ending up in prison. He escapes from his cell disguised as his uncle Merimac (Gerpré) and when Bathilde, now determined that Olivette shall not wed Valentin, forces her instead to wed 'Merimac', a curious marriage duly takes place, with Valentin having, in turn, to be both himself and his uncle. Since the truth is kept well hidden from all but the wedded pair, Bathilde still pursues Valentin, and things get even more complex when the real Merimac, taking advantage of the situation, tries to pretend that he is the legitimate husband of the heroine. However, after some local conspiring has led to the kidnapping of the Countess, all is ultimately untangled and a happy ending arrived at. Olivette's noces are clarified, and the Countess instead weds the chief conspirator, the Duc des Ifs (Alfred Jolly), to stop him conspiring any more.

If Olivette had the title-rôle of the piece, the two female parts were, in fact, of equal value, with the heroine being the soubrette rôle and Bathilde the more legitimate soprano. Olivette had her best moment in a jolly Chanson du mousse, Bathilde in the waltz 'Pays du gai soleil', and the two joined together in the Act II farandole 'Sous la tonnelle'. A boléro for the Duc, Couplets du Plongeon – a piece parallelling breaking up with a woman and overthrowing a government, which proved as pointed as it was no doubt intended to be – and a Chanson du vin de Roussillon for three supporting characters were the other musical high-points.

Les Noces d'Olivette was a clear-cut success for Cantin, running an initial 89 nights at the Bouffes, and it followed its Parisian success by carrying its composer's name around the world. Alexander Henderson took up the show for London and produced it at the Strand Theatre (ad H B Farnie) with Florence St John, the sensational star of his *Madame Favart*, as Olivette, alongside other members of that show's cast in Violet Cameron (Bathilde), Claude Marius (Merimac) and Henry Ashley (des Ifs) and with tenor Knight Aston as Valentin. Amidst accolades for its libretto 'brimming with comic situations' and its score of 'so much gaiety and liveliness', the show gave Henderson a second huge success, running through the whole of 1881 and into 1882 before closing after a remarkable 466 performances which put it straight into the top-scoring handful of London musical shows of all time. It was later revived at the Avenue Theatre in the gap between *Manteaux Noirs* and *Belle Lurette* (1883) and it also proved a long-time touring proposition in Britain.

The reception given to *Olivette* in Britain was echoed thoroughly in the United States. Produced at the Bijou Theater by the Comley-Barton troupe with a cast headed by the British star of *The Royal Middy*, soprano Catherine Lewis (Olivette) as guest, Hetty Tracy (Bathilde), Australian John Howson (Merimac), Digby Bell (Coquelicot), Marie Jansen (Veloutine) and James Barton (Ifs), it was an instant hit. The tale of the 'Torpedo and the Whale' challenged *Billee Taylor*'s 'All on Account of Eliza' for the show tune of the year as the company moved on from the Bijou to the Fifth Avenue Theater and other producers hurried to get themselves a version of *Olivette* on to the stage. John Duff took just three weeks to get his *Olivette* up at the Park Theater (17 January 1881), the Bostonians brought their version to Booth's, Maurice Grau's French company gave the piece in its original French, Emilie Melville's company featured its manageress at the Standard Theater, J Fred Zimmerman starred Selina Dolaro in his version at the Metropolitan Alcazar and the burlesque merchants proffered an *All-of-it* whilst the *Olivette* craze raged on Broadway, only to be partially extinguished by the arrival of its successor, *La Mascotte*. Australia, too, welcomed *Olivette* enthusiastically as played by the J C Williamson troupe featuring Elsa May (Olivette), Agnes Consuelo (Veloutine), Nellie Stewart (Bathilde), Edwin Kelly (Merimac) and E W Royce (Coquelicot), and the show was played in repertoire there for several seasons.

Europe was less swift to take the show up. Budapest's Népszinház did not play Lajos Evva's version until 1881, hard on the heels of the huge success in Hungary of *La Mascotte* and, if the production with Mariska Komáromi (Olivette), Aranka Hegyi (Bathilde) and Vidor Kassai (Mérimac) did not quite equal the run of the more famous piece, it was nevertheless played a fine 25 times and revived for a second run five years later (14 August 1886). Vienna, too, waited until *La Mascotte* had made Audran's name interesting, and Franz Tewele produced *Olivette* at the Carltheater in late 1881 with Antonie Schläger in the title-rôle alongside Frln Horty (Bathilde), Karl Drucker (Valentin), Josef Joseffy (Ifs), Karl Blasel (Mérimac) and Franz Eppich (Marvéjol). This time, however, it didn't go. Tewele got just 17 performances out of the show. The piece was clearly not to German tastes either, for although it finally reached Munich in 1883, it was a further 12 years before a version of the show, played for some reason under the title of *Kapitän Caricciolo*, reached Berlin and there rang no such bells as it had done in the French and English-speaking versions.

UK: Strand Theatre *Olivette* 18 September 1880; USA: Bijou Theater *Olivette* 25 December 1880; Australia: Theatre Royal, Sydney 13 August 1881; Hungary: Népszinház *Olivette lakodalma* 8 September 1881; Austria: Carltheater *Olivette* 29 October 1881; Germany: Theater am Gärtnerplatz, Munich *Olivettens Hochzeit* 4 November 1883, Theater Unter den Linden *Kapitän Caricciolo* 23 February 1895

LES NOCES IMPROVISÉES Opérette in 3 acts by Armand Liorat and Albert Fonteny. Music by Francis Chassaigne. Théâtre des Bouffes-Parisiens, Paris, 13 February 1886.

Delphine Ugalde's production of *Les Noces improvisées* at the Bouffes-Parisiens did not have a notable career, playing just 35 performances. But those 35 nights were to be the prelude to many hundreds more outside France.

Set in Hungary, the piece concerned itself with the folk-hero Rákóczi (Alexandre) who, having been exiled, sneaks back into town, disguised as a wandering minstrel, to visit his beloved Nadgy (Jeanne Thibault). In Act II Nadgy is revealed as the heiress to the Hungarian throne who was carried off by the Austrian overlord as a child, and in Act III she and Rákóczi, disguised this time as glass-vendors, make their way into Hungary in time to lead their countrymen in a contra-revolt against the Austrian Emperor. The marriage of the title referred to a union of convenience which Nadgy is forced to contract with a com-plaisant Austrian count (Paravicini) in Act I, presumably to make it decent for her to go cavalcading across Europe with a dangerous patriot in Acts II and III. The romance and rebellion were more than counterpointed by the show-stealing Mily-Meyer in the rôle of the helpful count's dancer-mistress, and chief comedian Édouard Maugé as one Bobinnrumkorff.

Chassaigne's score, occasionally tinted Hungarian (one csárdás) was topped off by the inclusion of the Berlioz march which had made the name of Rákóczi a peg to hang the action of the opérette on, made over into a song for Alexandre.

Following the exceptional success of Chassaigne's *Falka* in Britain, in particular, *Les Noces improvisées*, retitled *Nadgy* (ad Alfred Murray) was produced with great pomp and promises by Henry Watkin at London's Avenue Theatre in 1888. The libretto, although its story remained fairly intact, had undergone some severe reorientation for the occasion. Arthur Roberts (Phelix Pharagas) and Marie Vanoni (Nadgy) were star-billed, he in an introduced comic rôle as a 'professor of deportment' tagging on behind (or, more often, in front of) Rákóczi, she in the rôle originated by Mily-Meyer, now, confusingly, called by the name of the original romantic heroine. Tenor Joseph Tapley was Count Maximilien, comedian J J Dallas his uncle, the Marquis of Bobrumkoff, whilst Giulia Warwick (Princess Etelka) and Alec Marsh (Rákóczi) played the now-rather-submerged romantic rôles but still ended up crowned king and queen of Hungary. The eagerly awaited piece, though faring well enough, did not, however, live up to its blockbusting predecessor in popularity and it closed after 162 performances to go on the road.

The production of *Nadgy* in London was held up because of the long-running success of *The Old Guard* and, in consequence, Murray's adaptation was first seen on Broadway, mounted under the aegis of publishers Alfred Hays. With Marie Jansen (a last-minute replacement for Sadie Martinot as Nadgy), Isabelle Urquhart (Etelka), Mark Smith (Rákóczi), Henry Hallam (Maximilien), Fred Solomon (Marquis) and James T Powers as Pharagas in the lead rôles, and staged by Richard Barker, it was singularly successful. It notched up a run of no fewer than five unbroken months before the Casino Theater decided to pull it in favour of their newest prize: *The Yeomen of the Guard*. Hays threatened to sue, as *Nadjy* (sic) had not fallen below its $4,500-per-week guaranteed figure, and, as a result, when Gilbert and Sullivan's piece ended its run, *Nadjy* was remounted at the Casino (21 January 1889) with Lillian Russell starring, for a second run of a further three months which brought its total run to a very fine 259 performances. This record, and London's perfectly respectable one, however, did not persuade the rest of the world to have a look at the show, but *Nadjy* or *Nadgy* remained with an altogether better record than *Les Noces improvisées*.

Rákóczi got himself rather less over-imaginatively pic-tured in a native Hungarian operett, *Rákóczi*, written by Károly Bakonyi, with lyrics by Sándor Endrődi, Árpád Pásztor and Csaba Sassy, and music by Pongrác Kacsoh, produced with some success at Budapest's Király Színház 20 November 1906.

USA: Casino Theater *Nadjy* 14 May 1888; UK: Avenue Theatre *Nadgy* 7 November 1888

NOËL, Lucien (d Varenne St Hilarie, April 1930).

For many years one of the most important baritone leading men on the French musical stage, Noël was condemned, by the lack of first-class new pieces appearing on the French stage in the early years of the 20th century, to have his most successful moments in revivals of such pieces as *Les Cloches de Corneville* (Marquis), *Le Petit Duc* (Montlandry), *La Fille de Madame Angot* (Ange Pitou), *Le Grand Mogol* (Joquelet), *Rip* (Rip), *Giroflé-Girofla* (Mourzouk), *La Petite Mariée* (Podestat), *François les basbleus* (François), *Surcouf* (Surcouf), *Fanfan la Tulipe* (Fanfan), *Boccace* (Tromboli), *Les Mousquetaires au couvent* (Brissac), *Les 28 Jours de Clairette* (Vivarel), *Les P'tites Michu* (Gaston), *La Mascotte* (Pippo) and *La Fauvette du Temple* (Pierre).

He created rôles in such pieces as *Panurge* (1895, Pantagruel), *La Poupée* (1896, Père Maximin), *Les Soeurs Gaudichard* (1899, Gontran), *Les Saltimbanques* (1899, Grand Pingouin), *Le Curé Vincent* (1901, Bernard) and *La Demoiselle du tabarin* (1910, Marcel) and played la Galette in *Ordre de l'Empereur*, Philippe de Bellegarde in the French première of *Capitaine Thérèse* and Brignol in Paris's *Les Hirondelles* (1907) as well as taking a turn as Danilo in Paris's *La Veuve Joyeuse*.

NO, NO, NANETTE Musical comedy in 3 acts by Frank Mandel, Otto Harbach and Irving Caesar based on *My Lady Friends* by Mandel and Emil Nyitray (and *Oh, James!* by May Edgington). Music by Vincent Youmans. Garrick Theater, Detroit, 23 April 1923; Harris Theater, Chicago, 7 May 1923; Globe Theater, New York, 16 September 1925.

The instigator of *No, No, Nanette* was Broadway producer Harry H Frazee. In 1919 he had, in collaboration with Dan V Arthur, produced a play called *My Lady Friends* which had done decidedly well for him through 228 Broadway performances and afters. Four years was quite a lapse in these times when even the previous season's flop comedies served by the handful as the bases for the new annual crop of musicals, but *My Lady Friends* was a good property, and it had plenty of life to run through before it was ready to be remade. Composer Vincent Youmans thought it was a good property too, and he applied to Frazee for the job of composing the songs for the new musical version of the show. A sizeable production investment from the young man's mother convinced the producer that he would be an ideal composer, and Youmans became part of the new musical's team along with the play's original author Mandel and with Otto Harbach, who had adapted Frazee's biggest musical success, *Madame Sherry*.

Jimmy Smith (Richard 'Skeets' Gallagher) cannot get his careful wife Sue (Juliette Day) to spend the money his bible-publishing firm makes, so instead he gives himself a little pleasure spending some of it on a row of cuties, Winnie and Betty and Flora. When the cuties start to get a bit pressing, Jimmy decides that they will have to go, and his lawyer friend Billy (Francis X Donegan) promises to help. He helps by arranging a showdown with all three lassies at one and the same time in the safely distant Atlantic City. It is a rotten choice, and not nearly distant enough, for not only is Jimmy weekending down in Atlantic City with his ward, Nanette (Phyllis Cleveland), but both Sue

and Billy's wife Lucille (Anna Wheaton) also turn up. The due actful of understandings and misunderstandings is gone through before wedded bliss is re-established and Nanette safely proposed to by Billy's assistant, Tom. A dose of low comedy was injected into this jolly, harmless little tale in the person of a wisecracking maid (Georgia O'Ramey).

The try-out of *No, No, Nanette* started in Detroit. It started slowly, and the writers were pushed by their producer to come up with some fresh songs as the show moved on. Two of these, 'Tea for Two' and 'I Want to Be Happy', were in place before Chicago was reached. The critics were pleased, but Frazee was apparently not. Within weeks he sacked the director, E W Royce, and most of the lead players. With Louise Groody (Nanette), Charles Winninger (Jimmy), his wife Blanche Ring (Lucille) and Bernard Granville (Billy) as replacements, and the two new songs already whistling through half of Chicago's teeth, Frazee got the critics in again, and this time he hit paydirt. The show settled in for a record Chicago run of 12 months. Although *No, No, Nanette* had yet to get anywhere near Broadway (Frazee had booked his starry Chicago takeovers for New York, so New York had to wait till Chicago was done with them), other *Nanettes* were quick to follow.

Neophyte British producers Jack Waller and Herbert Clayton, visiting America in search of novelties to launch them in London, picked up four musicals, one of which was the still-young *No, No, Nanette*. When the bigger boys came hunting, once the show had blossomed, they found they had been beaten to the game. London's *Nanette* was cast to the gunwales by its new-boy producers, with Binnie Hale in the title-rôle, *Merry Widow* hero Joe Coyne as Jimmy, George Grossmith as Billy, Irene Browne as Lucille and old-time comedienne Gracie Leigh as the maid, and, equipped with a couple of fresh numbers ('I've Confessed to the Breeze', 'Take a Little One-Step'), it duly turned up West End trumps in a quite dramatic way. London's *No, No, Nanette* occupied the Palace Theatre for 665 performances.

At the same time, Frazee branched out round America, opening a second company for a long run in Philadelphia whilst a third moved into Los Angeles for an extended stay – both companies cast up with such favourite performers as Donald Brian and Julia Sanderson, or Cecil Lean and Cleo Mayfield. And, whilst New York still waited for the show, the Fullers and Hugh Ward opened their production in Melbourne, Australia. Elsie Prince was Australia's Nanette, with Jimmy Godden starred as Jimmy, and May Beatty, Madge White, Winifred Dalle and Charles Morton supported in a company which had a super four-and-a-half-month run in Melbourne – not too far behind the six-month record recently set up by *Sally* – before moving on to Sydney's new St James Theatre (26 March 1926) and another fine season which established the show as a favourite and led to a series of revivals.

Back in America, finally, the Chicago season ended, and *Nanette* moved into New York's Globe Theater with Miss Groody, Winninger and Miss O'Ramey (still there since the beginning) now teamed not with Fritzi Scheff, as had been at one stage promised, but with Josephine Whittell (Lucille), Wellington Cross (Billy) and Eleanor Dawn (Sue). New York tried to be grumpy about not seeing the show everyone else had been raving about for more than a year until everyone else had seen it for more than a year, but the two now-enormous song hits – and that was not counting Lucille's 'Too Many Rings Around Rosie', 'Where Has My Hubby Gone' blues and 'You Can Dance with Any Girl at All', the perky title-song and Billy's lively appeal to his 'Telephone Girlie' – and the show's happy, dancing ladling of pure quality meant that it stayed on Broadway for 321 performances.

If New York hadn't turned out to be the show's best tour date, Frazee wasn't complaining. But now that he was in New York, he had another local hazard to look out for: the Broadway lawsuit. With *Nanette* such a big hit, it couldn't be long coming. Sure enough, old partner Dan Arthur now surfaced with a suit claiming an interest in the source material. There were 12 companies playing *Nanette* throughout America when a court awarded him a 25% stake in the royalty which Frazee had allotted to *My Lady Friends*. Frazee fought back (after all, that royalty had presumably been his own perk), and presumably there was an end to it sometime.

In the meanwhile, *Nanette* made her dancing way through the cities of Europe. Paris was the first to take the show up, and what they took up was Waller and Clayton's London production. The Isola Brothers imported director William Mollison and musical director Percival Mackey (a white-gloved act in the pit in himself), 20 English girl dancers and ten boys ('the London Palace Boys and Girls') and their captain and soloist Rita MacLean, and staged a fairly faithful French version (ad Roger Ferréol, Robert de Simone, Georges Merry, Paul Colline) of the London version at the Théâtre Mogador. Plump-cheeked, bobbed and top-billed Loulou Hégoburu sang 'J'ai confessé à la brise' and 'Thé pour deux' with Adrien Lamy (Tom) and explained 'Vous marquez bien un temps' with Cariel (Billy) whilst principal dancer Carlos Conte (who had previously had a charleston spot in the first act) danced illustratively. Félix Oudart (Jimmy) told his girls to 'Battez-vous pour moi' and dark and perky Gabrielle Ristori triumphed as Lucile with 'On tourne trop autour de Rose', 'Pourquoi suis-je triste quand tu pars' (ie 'Where Has My Hubby Gone') and 'Tu peux danser avec toutes les femmes'. The comedy maid's rôle was reduced, the dances (both Miss Maclean and the dancer playing Winnie had solos as well as Conte) increased, the second-act setting was moved to 'Paris-Plage', and *No, No, Nanette* (the title was kept, even though the song went 'non, non, Nanette') was an enormous success all over again. It passed its 400th performance, and spurred the end-of-the-year revuists to the sort of parody titles reserved as a compliment to only the biggest hits – *Nu, nu, Nunette* (Concert Mayol, Vincent Scotto/Léo Lelièvre; Henri Varna, Deyrmon), *T'y fourre tout* (La Lune Rousse) – before the Isolas removed it to mount *Rose-Marie*. In the decades that followed, *No, No, Nanette* returned more frequently to the Paris stage (1930, 1935, 1946, 1965, all at the Mogador) than to the boards of any other musical theatre metropolis.

Germany's version (ad Hans Hellmut Zerlett, Arthur Rebner) which also followed the British version and set the action in London and the Isle of Wight (rather than New York and Atlantic City), and also for some reason rechristened Sue as Mary, was produced at the Metropoltheater with Irene Palasty as Nanette and Max Hansen

giving an answer to the 'No, no' of the title in an interpolated Shimmy-Lied by Rebner and Austin Egen which insisted 'Jawohl! Jawohl! Jawohl!' By the time this production arrived at Vienna's Bürgertheater 13 months later, it had gone past its 450th performance. Vienna added another 90 or so to the total, and the company then moved on to Budapest where Miss Palasty (in German) starred for a fortnight at the Király Színház where *Mersz-e, Mary?*, with a score attributed to Youmans, had triumphed five months previously. But Budapest, apparently, stayed loyal to *Mercenary Mary* which had got to them first (possibly with some of the *Nanette* music in it), and *Nanette* apparently got no Hungarian production.

London saw a *Nanette* revival in 1936 (Hippodrome 8 July), and film versions were produced in 1930 with Alexander Grey, Bernice Claire, Louise Fazenda and Lucien Littlefield featured in a 'Vitaphone sound film' and in 1940 with Anna Neagle top-billed (another, entitled *Tea for Two*, used only two numbers of the score), but it was not until 1971 than *No, No, Nanette* made a return to Broadway (46th Street Theater 17 January 1971). Harry Rigby and Cyma Rubin's production top-billed old-time film star Ruby Keeler in an expanded version of Sue's rôle (she was given the Nanette/Billy 'Take a Little One-Step' as a dance routine), alongside Susan Watson (Nanette), Jack Gilford (Jimmy), Bobby Van (Billy) and Helen Gallagher (Lucille), kept the comedy maid (Patsy Kelly) to her reduced proportions and ran for 861 performances. The success of this production gave the show a whole new impetus as it sent out road companies (one with June Allyson featured, another with Evelyn Keyes, Don Ameche and Swen Swensson), spawned a weakly done London copy of the production (Theatre Royal, Drury Lane, 16 May 1973) with Anne Rogers (Lucille), Teddy Green (Billy) and Anna Neagle (Sue) which folded in 277 performances, an Australian revival with Yvonne de Carlo (later Cyd Charisse), and spurred *Nanette* on to making her way back into the regional theatres of the English-speaking world.

UK: Palace Theatre 11 March 1925; Australia: Princess Theatre, Melbourne 27 June 1925; France: Théâtre Mogador 29 April 1926; Germany: Metropoltheater 7 November 1926; Austria: Wiener Bürgertheater 23 December 1927; Hungary: Király Színház (Ger) 17 March 1928; Film: Vitaphone 1930, 1940

Recordings: London cast recordings (WRC, Stanyan), 1971 revival cast (Columbia), London revival cast (CBS), selections (Fontana, Saga, WRC, EMI etc), selections in French (Pathé, CBS) etc

Literature: Dunn, D: *The Making of No, No, Nanette* (Citadel Press, Secaucus, NJ, 1972)

NORIAC, Jules [CAIRON, Claude Antoine Jules] (b Limoges, 1827; d Paris, 16 October 1882).

A prominent figure in journalistic (*Le Figaro*) and literary circles, and in the French Société des Auteurs, Noriac ventured into the theatre both as a producer and as an author. He shared the directorship of the Théâtre des Variétés with the brothers Cogniard for a period and, in the late 1860s and early 1870s, was allied with Charles Comte at the Théâtre des Bouffes-Parisiens. It was at that theatre, which knew few profitable days during their management, that he co-authored his biggest opérette success with the particularly saucy libretto for *La Timbale d'argent*, the Leon Vasseur opérette which, by its long and fruitful run, helped the Comte-Noriac management to hold up rather longer than it would otherwise have done. He had some further success with *La Branche cassée*, the first composition of another young composer, Gaston Serpette, and with another light blue piece, Vasseur's *La Cruche cassée*, produced at the little Salle Taitbout with Céline Chaumont as its chief attraction, but a collaboration with Offenbach brought little joy and his last piece with Vasseur, *La Sorrentine*, was a 40-performance failure.

1871 **Le Barbier de Trouville** (Charles Lecocq/w Adolphe Jaime) 1 act Théâtre des Bouffes-Parisiens 19 November

1872 **La Timbale d'argent** (Léon Vasseur/w Jaime) Théâtre des Bouffes-Parisiens 9 April

1873 **La Petite Reine** (Vasseur/w Jaime) Théâtre des Bouffes-Parisiens 20 May

1873 **Le Mouton enragé** (Paul Lacôme/w Jaime) 1 act Théâtre des Bouffes-Parisiens 27 May

1874 **La Branche cassée** (Gaston Serpette/w Jaime) Théâtre des Bouffes-Parisiens 23 January

1875 **La Cruche cassée** (Vasseur/w Jules Moinaux) Théâtre Taitbout 27 October

1876 **Pierrette et Jacquot** (Jacques Offenbach/w Philippe Gille) 1 act Théâtre des Bouffes-Parisiens 13 October

1876 **La Boîte au lait** (Offenbach/w Eugène Grangé) Théâtre des Bouffes-Parisiens 3 November

1877 **La Sorrentine** (Vasseur/w Moinaux) Théâtre des Bouffes-Parisiens 24 March

1892 **Eros** (Paul Vidal/w Jaime, Maxime Bouchor) Théâtre des Bouffes-Parisiens 22 April

NORMAN, Monty (b London, 4 April 1938). Songwriter who worked on several successful British shows of the 1950s and one in the 1970s.

After beginning his working life as a barber's apprentice, Norman made his first moves into the music business as a singer and songwriter. He became implicated in the musical theatre when he was brought in, as a potential leading man, to sing through the music of a show which never happened and he stayed to collaborate on its writing with the original authors, Julian More and David Heneker. The show which didn't happen did, however, result in a commission for another, and thus Norman, along with his two associates, became involved in two of the most interesting musicals of the late 1950s: as one of the adaptors of *Irma la Douce* for the English-speaking stage, and as a partner in the songs of the memorable *Expresso Bongo*. Further collaborations with *Expresso Bongo*'s librettist, Wolf Mankowitz, brought another success with *Make Me an Offer* and a failure, which nevertheless brought forth a popular song ('The Dit-Dit Song'), in *Belle*, a piece which related the story of murderer Dr Crippen in music-hall terms.

Amongst film and television work in the 1960s, his stage shows – a spoof spy thriller, a Jewish fable, and a humorous piece set in the world of competition ballroom dancing – were more discreet and there was no success to be found in a trendy 1970s version of the Jack Sheppard tale or in the small-scale *So Who Needs Marriage?* However, 20 years after his last West End success he rejoined More to turn out *Songbook*, a clever parody on the stream of so-and-so-and-his-music compilation shows which had been dampening British theatres since the Mermaid Theatre had ventured with *Cole* and *Cowardy Custard*. He subsequently supplied some humorous numbers for *Poppy*, a bitterer burlesque of Victorian British pantomime and politics, which drowned in production values at the Royal

Shakespeare Theatre and the Adelphi Theatre in two attempts at making it to the big time.

Norman's most important hit outside the theatre was his James Bond Theme, first heard in the 1962 film *Doctor No*.

1958 **Expresso Bongo** (w David Heneker, Julian More/Wolf Mankowitz) Saville Theatre 23 April

1958 **Irma la Douce** English version w Heneker, More (Saville Theatre)

1959 **Make Me an Offer** (w Heneker/Mankowitz) Theatre Royal, Stratford East 17 October

1961 **Belle** (Mankowitz) Strand Theatre 4 May

1963 **The Perils of Scobie Prilt** (w More) New Theatre, Oxford 12 June

1967 **Who's Pinkus, Where's Chelm?** (Norman/w C P Taylor) Jeannetta Cochrane Theatre 3 January

1969 **Quick, Quick, Slow** (w More/David Turner) Birmingham Repertory Theatre 20 August

1972 **Stand and Deliver** (Mankowitz) Royal Lyceum Theatre, Edinburgh 20 September

1975 **So Who Needs Marriage?** Gardner Centre, Brighton 8 May

1979 **Songbook** (w More) Globe Theatre 25 July

1982 **Poppy** (Peter Nichols) Barbican Theatre 25 September

NORTON, [George] Frederic (b Salford, Manchester, 11 October 1869; d Holford, 15 December 1946). Singer turned songwriter for one huge hit.

Originally a clerk in insurance, Norton escaped and became a professional singer, touring as an operatic chorister with Carl Rosa and making occasional appearances in the musical theatre. He also tried his hand at writing parlour songs, turned out the music for a fairy play, had the odd number interpolated in musical comedies (*The Beauty of Bath* etc) and then, through the offices of a friend, was brought together with author W Graham Robertson. The result of their union was the charming little musical fairytale *Pinkie and the Fairies* presented by no less a personage than Beerbohm Tree with Ellen Terry and Stella Patrick Campbell in the cast.

Tree subsequently recalled Norton to help with the organizing of Offenbach's score for *Orpheus in the Underground* (1912), but apart from a little revue called *What Ho, Daphne!* produced at the Tivoli music-hall and a few songs for *The Passing Show of 1915*, Norton was heard little of until his Tree connection won him the opportunity to compose the score for Oscar Asche's fairy-tale spectacular *Chu Chin Chow*. The vast, record-breaking success of that show, the popularity won by Norton's 'Any Time's Kissing Time' and 'The Cobbler's Song' and the degree of skill apparent in such pieces as 'I Long for the Sun' made it all the more strange that the composer failed utterly to follow up his one great hit. He turned out a rather pale score for the Lily Elsie musical *Pamela* the following year, before fading back into turning out just the odd interpolated number ('Rosie' in Broadway's *The Man with Three Wives*, another in London's *Flora*). He ventured back onto the stage only with a little piece called *The Willow Pattern Plate* played by amateurs and a children's Christmas piece, *Teddie Tail*.

During the run of *Chu Chin Chow*, Norton occasionally stood in for Courtice Pounds in the chief comedy rôle of Ali Baba.

1908 **Pinkie and the Fairies** (W Graham Robertson) His Majesty's Theatre 19 December

1916 **Chu Chin Chow** (Oscar Asche) His Majesty's Theatre 31 August
1917 **Pamela** (Arthur Wimperis) Palace Theatre 10 December
1920 **Teddie Tail** (Charles Folkard) Duke of York's Theatre 26 December

NO SONG, NO SUPPER   Comic opera in 2 acts by Prince Hoare. Music composed [and arranged] by Stephen Storace. Theatre Royal, Drury Lane, 16 April 1790.

One of the few 18th-century comic operas to have survived in production into the later part of the 19th century, this humorous story of the lascivious lawyer Endless and his undoing over a supper of a leg of lamb was illustrated with an attractive score which featured not only some tidy solos but, most notably, a pretty ladies' trio ('Knocking at This Hour of Day') and a quintet finale to the first act, all written in the French-flavoured opéra-comique style of the time. However, although Storace's name alone was attached to the score, the old ballad-opera influences had not yet vanished, and the composer was quite content to borrow some of his music 'from the French' – notably from the oft-plundered Grétry – without bothering to acknowledge the fact.

No Song, No Supper was a first performed at a benefit at Drury Lane with a celebrated cast, featuring Michael Kelly (the author of the famous *Reminiscences*), the concert vocalist Mr Dignum (Crop), the composer's sister Miss Storace (Margaretta, the mover of the plot) and Miss Romanzini (Dorothy Crop) in the featured singing rôles, and Bannister and Suett, two noted comedians of the day, as Margaretta's jolly sailor and the discomforted lawyer. The leg of lamb, instead of being a prop one, was genuine, and it remained a tradition in the years that followed, that for this particular opera a real piece of meat should always be used.

Widely played in the British provinces, *No Song, No Supper* was also given several major revivals in London, being staged at the Theatre Royal, Covent Garden, in 1820 with Frederick Pyne and Miss Stephens and again in 1827. In 1870 it was played at Manchester and at the Haymarket and 1871 it was introduced at the Gaiety Theatre (13 May).

USA: Philadelphia 30 December 1792, New York 15 February 1793; Germany: Hamburg 20 February 1795

NO STRINGS   Musical in 2 acts by Samuel Taylor. Music and lyrics by Richard Rodgers. 54th Street Theater, New York, 15 March 1962.

Richard Rodgers's first musical for the Broadway stage following the death of Oscar Hammerstein was built around the talents of the young vocalist Diahann Carroll. Librettist Samuel Taylor cast her as Barbara Woodruff, an American model in Paris, who meets up with a successful but dropped-out novelist called David Jordan (Richard Kiley). Although she is profitably paired with the elegant Louis de Pourtal (Mitchell Gregg), Barbara is soon sharing intimate moments with David, and encouraging him to throw over his indolent, gay life and pick up his typewriter again. After an evening of American-in-Paris-isms, amatory swip-swaps and ups-and-downs among members of a supporting cast which included Alvin Epstein as a French fashion photographer, Noelle Adam as his assistant, Jeanette, Ann Hodges as his infidelity, Gabrielle,

Don Chastain as the loose-living Mike Robinson and Bernice Massi as a filthy-rich Europe-eater, and a trip through some other French locations, David heads back to America and a less unproductive life. It is 1962, so there is no happy ending. Barbara stays behind in Paris, where a black girl apparently has better opportunities than in America, and gets on with her work as well.

Rodgers's score mirrored its little tale to a degree, with love songs for the two central lovers and bright numbers for the other folk, and it got through the evening without a single songtitle mentioning Paris: in fact the only number in praise of a place was Kiley's happy reminiscence of 'Maine'. The score of *No Strings*, however, produced one number which would find itself a place on the bottom of the long list of Rodgers and Hart's and Rodgers and Hammerstein's hits: Kiley and Miss Carroll's introductory duet 'The Sweetest Sounds' which also served to close out the show. Alongside this winning piece, Barbara delivered 'Loads of Love' and 'An Orthodox Fool', and paired with Kiley in further duos including a title-number, 'You Don't Tell Me' and 'Look No Further' in what was the more appealing side of the score.

The handouts insisted that *No Strings* was not just another boy-meets-girl-by-the-Seine story, that it had an underlying theme which was 'yet another example of how Richard Rodgers has used his great skills to push out walls of the American musical theatre so that audiences today willingly accept meaningful, adult themes in works that still provide evenings of gaiety and enchantment' and that it featured 'daring use of stagecraft and subject matter'. The tricks of the evening were, in fact, mostly orchestral: a band with no strings, to go with the title of the show, which played not from the pit but onstage (a gimmick which was far from being the innovation that was suggested) or backstage, in a staging by Joe Layton which was simple and effective, and did not use the excuse of the French settings for vistas of scenery.

The simple (white) boy-meets-(black) girl-by-the-Seine tale, which eventually turned out to be less important than Rodgers's songs and name and the attractively spare mounting, all helped *No Strings* to a good Broadway run of 580 performances, and – in a season featuring *How to Succeed in Business* and *Carnival* – half-a-Tony Award each for Rodgers's music, Miss Carroll's performance and Joe Layton's dances. Then the show ran out of steam. An American tour company stayed on the road for five months, and a London production, mounted by Rodgers's own Williamson Music, with Art Lund (David) and Beverly Todd (Barbara) featured, and future Shakespearian star Geoffrey Hutchins as Luc, folded in 135 performances. Australia (and other countries) produced *Carnival* and *How to Succeed in Business*, but passed on *No Strings*.

Rodgers's own reputation and his string of romantic operetta hits with Hammerstein meant that whatever he had written at this stage of his career was bound to be placed in a difficult situation both with the public and the critics, and the pretentious announcements with which *No Strings* was launched cannot have helped. Opinions on the piece were widely divergent from the beginning (the Tony results mirror the problem), but the verdict of time has rejected the show just as it has favoured the seductive melody of its hit song.

UK: Her Majesty's Theatre 30 December 1963
Recordings: original cast (Capitol), London cast (Decca/DRG), selection (Atlantic) etc

NOVELLO, Ivor [DAVIES, David Ivor] (b Cardiff, 15 January 1893; d London, 6 March 1951).

A matinée idol and silent-screen favourite as an actor, Ivor Novello (his nom de théâtre was borrowed from his well-known musician mother, Clara Novello Davies) led an equally successful parallel career as a writer and composer of both straight and musical plays.

His earliest single success as a writer and composer came in 1914 with the wartime song known popularly as 'Keep the Home Fires Burning', his first contribution to the theatre was a song included in the revue *The Bing Boys Are Here*, and his first full theatre credit came when, on the strength of his hit song, he replaced the ailing Paul Rubens as the basic composer of the highly successful Gaiety musical *Theodore & Co* (1916). He subsequently provided more or less music for several other book shows: C B Cochran's very considerable but successful remake of the French musical play *Arlette* (1917) in which Novello's song 'On the Staff' proved a hit for rising comedian Stanley Lupino, the romantic Harold Fraser-Simson operetta *A Southern Maid* (1917) with which José Collins confirmed her *Maid of the Mountains* hit, the long-running Pinero adaptation *Who's Hooper?* (1919) and Miss Collins's Nell Gwynne musical *Our Nell* (1924). He also contributed to several revues (*See-Saw*, *A to Z*, *Tabs*, *Puppets*, *The House That Jack Built*), and composed the whole score for the comic opera *The Golden Moth*, a new version of the *Erminie* story which ran for 281 performances at the Adelphi Theatre in 1921. At the same time, however, he was devoting increasing amounts of his time to the other areas of his high-profile career, and in the years that followed his name was absent from the musical stage.

When he returned in 1935, after a decade away, it was as a result of a lunch-time conversation with the head of the floundering Theatre Royal, Drury Lane. He found, at the end of the meal, that he had committed himself to write and star in a large-scale spectacular musical show. The success of the lush, romantic *Glamorous Night* led to a series of similar pieces of which *Careless Rapture* (1936) was the first, and *The Dancing Years* (1939), produced like the two previous pieces, on the large Drury Lane stage, the three generation tale of *Perchance to Dream* (1945) and *King's Rhapsody* (1949), all starring Novello in their non-singing lead rôle, were the most successful. They compiled long runs in the theatre and contributed a mass of richly sentimental and enduring songs ('Waltz of My Heart', 'I Can Give You the Starlight', 'We'll Gather Lilacs', 'Some Day My Heart Will Awake', 'Shine Through My Dreams', 'Love is My Reason for Living') to the concert stage. However, in spite of their large and long-lasting vogue in the British theatre, Novello's works remained staunchly ignored by the rest of the world. Even the British colonies and Dominions which normally snapped up the hit products of the West End ignored his pieces. It was not merely a case of their failing: they did not even get produced. Novello himself toured to South Africa with *Perchance to Dream*, and *The Dancing Years* – and it alone – was produced with unspectacular results in Australia. Broadway, itself floundering more than somewhat through much of

the 1930s but scarcely in a financial state to host a Novello spectacular, passed, and the only productions of Novello's works in America have been in such bulwarks of romantic operetta production as St Louis's Municipal Opera.

In his final show, *Gay's the Word*, which he wrote as a vehicle for comedienne Cicely Courtneidge whilst he was performing in *King's Rhapsody*, Novello abandoned the Ruritanian tales of his large-scale pieces and returned with no little success to the brighter, musical comedy style of his earliest days ('Vitality', 'It's Bound to Be Right on the Night'). However, he is almost entirely remembered today for his sentimental spectaculars and, particularly, for the broadly melodic and romantic songs which they produced.

1916 **Theodore & Co** (w Jerome Kern/Clifford Grey, Adrian Ross/H M Harwood, George Grossmith) Gaiety Theatre 16 September
1917 **Arlette** (w Guy Le Feuvre/Grey, Ross/ad Austen Hurgon, George Arthurs) Shaftesbury Theatre 6 September
1919 **Who's Hooper?** (w Howard Talbot/Grey/Fred Thompson) Adelphi Theatre 13 September
1921 **The Golden Moth** (Thompson, P G Wodehouse) Adelphi Theatre 5 October
1924 **Our Nell** (w Harold Fraser-Simson/Harry Graham/Reginald Arkell, Louis N Parker) Gaiety Theatre 16 April
1935 **Glamorous Night** (Christopher Hassall) Theatre Royal, Drury Lane 2 May
1936 **How Do, Princess** revised version of *Arlette* (Manchester)
1936 **Careless Rapture** (Hassall) Theatre Royal, Drury Lane 11 September
1937 **Crest of the Wave** (Hassall) Theatre Royal, Drury Lane 1 September
1939 **The Dancing Years** (Hassall) Theatre Royal, Drury Lane 23 March
1943 **Arc de Triomphe** (w Hassall) Phoenix Theatre 9 November
1945 **Perchance to Dream** (Novello) London Hippodrome 21 April
1949 **King's Rhapsody** (Novello) Palace Theatre 15 September
1951 **Gay's the Word** (Alan Melville) Saville Theatre 16 February

Biography: Noble, P *Ivor Novello, Man of the Theatre* (Falcon Press, London, 1951), Wilson, S: *Ivor* (Michael Joseph, London, 1975), MacQueen Pope, W: *Ivor* (Hutchinson, London, 1952); Harding, J: *Ivor Novello* (W H Allen, London, 1987) etc

NUITTER, Charles [TRUINET, Charles Louis Étienne] (b Paris, 24 April 1828; d Paris, 24 February 1899).

A Parisian lawyer who threw in the Bar for a career as a theatrical writer, 'Nuitter' was the author of any number of farces, ballets (notably the scenarii for *Coppélia* and *La Source*, both w Saint-Léon) and vaudevilles and, for more than 40 years, a librettist for the opérette stage.

His earliest significant musical pieces were written for Offenbach: the adaptation of Cervantes's little tale *Los Habladores* which ultimately became his first longer work as *Les Bavards*, the short pieces *Jeanne qui pleure et Jean qui rit* and *Le Soldat magicien*, the not-very-successful adaptation of de Leuven's vaudeville as the libretto for *Vert-Vert* and, the most often and internationally played of their collaborations, a comical variation on the doll-girl tale, *La Princesse de Trébizonde*. Nuitter collaborated on the French version of Émile Jonas's delightful retelling of the Cinderella tale as *Javotte* and on the turning of

Offenbach's *Whittington* into *Le Chat du Diable* for Paris, but his best and most successful original libretto, amongst a surprisingly large amount of minor work, was the sex-farcical tale set by Charles Lecocq as *Le Coeur et la main* (w Alexandre Beaumont).

Nuitter, who was employed subsequently as archivist at the Paris Opéra, also wrote a number of operatic texts (de Joncières's *Le Dernier Jour de Pompeii*, Boieldieu's *La Halte du roi* etc), without being associated with anything which became a standard, but he was also responsible, often in collaboration, for the French translations of a good number of the principal works of the operatic repertoire (*Der Zauberflöte*, *Abu Hassan*, *Preciosa*, *Oberon*, *I Capuleti e i Montecchi*, *Rienzi*, *Der fliegende Holländer*, *Tannhäuser*, *Macbeth*, *Crispino e la Comare*, *Lohengrin*, *La forza del destino*, *Aïda* etc). He also wrote several books on classic opera.

His text (w Victorien Sardou) for the 1861 play *Piccolino* was subsequently used as the source for Johann Strauss's Operette *Carneval in Rom* and for Guiraud's opéra-comique *Piccolino* (Opéra-Comique, 1876).

1855 **Une nuit à Séville** (Frédéric Barbier/w Alexandre Beaumont) 1 act Théâtre Lyrique 14 September

1855 **Rose et Narcisse** (Barbier/w Beaumont) 1 act Théâtre Lyrique 21 November

1856 **Le Nid d'amour** (Édouard Montaubry/w Nérée Desarbres) 1 act Théâtre du Vaudeville 21 October

1858 **Le Pacha** (Barbier) 1 act Théâtre des Folies-Nouvelles 24 March

1861 **La Servante à Nicolas** (Jules Erlanger/w Desarbres) 1 act Théâtre des Bouffes-Parisiens 11 March

1861 **Flamberge au vent** (Barbier/w Georges Steaune) 1 act Théâtre du Châlet des Isles 3 October

1862 **Bavard et Bavarde** (Offenbach) 1 act Bad Ems 11 June

1863 **Les Bavards** revised 2-act *Bavard et Bavarde* Théâtre des Bouffes-Parisiens 20 February

1863 **Il Signor Fagotto** (Offenbach/w Étienne Tréfeu) 1 act Ems 11 July

1863 **Un Othello** (Isidore Legouix) 1 act Théâtre des Champs-Elysées 20 June

1864 **L'Amour chanteur** (Offenbach/w Ernest L'Épine) 1 act Théâtre des Bouffes-Parisiens 5 January

1864 **Die Rheinnixen** (Offenbach/w Tréfeu) Hofoper, Vienna 4 February

1864 **Jeanne qui pleure et Jean qui rit** (Offenbach/w Tréfeu) 1 act Ems July; Théâtre des Bouffes-Parisiens 3 November 1865

1864 **Le Soldat magicien** (aka *Le Fifre enchanté*) (Offenbach/w Tréfeu) 1 act Ems 9 July; Théâtre des Bouffes-Parisiens 30 September 1868

1864 **Le Lion de Saint-Marc** (Legouix/w Beaumont) 1 act Théâtre Saint-Germain 24 November

1865 **Coscoletto** (Offenbach/w Tréfeu) Ems 24 July

1865 **Une fantasia** (Hervé) 1 act Théâtre des Variétés 12 November

1865 **Les Mémoires de Fanchette** (Nicolo Gabrielli/w Desarbres) 1 act Théâtre Lyrique 22 March

1865 **Le Roi Midas** (Émile Jonas) 1 act privately

1866 **Les Oreilles de Midas** (Barbier/w Desarbres) 1 act Fantaisies-Parisiennes 21 April

1866 **Le Baron de Groschaminet** (Jules Duprato/w Charles Garnier) 1 act Fantaisies-Parisiennes 24 September

1867 **Cardillac** (Lucien Dautresne/w Beaumont) Théâtre Lyrique 11 December

1868 **Le Vengeur** (Legouix/w Beaumont) 1 act Théâtre de l'Athénée 20 November

1869 **Vert-Vert** (Offenbach/w Henri Meilhac) Opéra-Comique 10 March

1869 **La Princesse de Trébizonde** (Offenbach/w Tréfeu) Baden-Baden 31 July

1870 **Le Kobold** (Ernest Guiraud/Louis Gallet) 1 act Opéra-Comique 26 July

1871 **Boule de Neige** (Offenbach/w Tréfeu) Théâtre des Bouffes-Parisiens 14 December

1871 **Javotte** (*Cinderella the Younger*) French version w Tréfeu (Théâtre de l'Athénée)

1872 **Der schwarze Korsar** (Offenbach/w Tréfeu) Theater an der Wien, Vienna 21 September

1874 **Les Dernières Grisettes** (Legouix/w Beaumont) Fantaisies-Parisiennes, Brussels 12 December

1875 **Amphitryon** (Paul Lacôme/w Beaumont) 1 act Théâtre Taitbout 5 April

1877 **L'Oppoponax** (Léon Vasseur/w William Busnach) 1 act Théâtre des Bouffes-Parisiens 2 May

1878 **Pépita** (L Delahaye fils/w Jules Delahaye) 1 act Opéra-Comique 13 July

1878 **Maître Péronilla** (Offenbach/w Offenbach, Paul Ferrier) Théâtre des Bouffes-Parisiens 13 March

1880 **Monsieur de Floridor** (Théodore de Lajarte/w Tréfeu) 1 act Opéra-Comique 11 October

1882 **Le Coeur et la main** (Charles Lecocq/w Beaumont) Théâtre des Nouveautés 14 October

1888 **La Volière** (Lecocq/w Beaumont) Théâtre des Nouveautés 1 February

1888 **La Demoiselle de Belleville** (*Die Jungfrau von Belleville*) French version w Beaumont (Théâtre des Folies-Dramatiques)

1888 **Oscarine** (Victor Roger/w Albert Guinon) Théâtre des Bouffes-Parisiens 15 October

1890 **L'Égyptienne** (Lecocq/w Henri Chivot, Beaumont) Théâtre des Folies-Dramatiques 8 November

1893 **Le Chat du Diable** (*Whittington*) French version w Tréfeu (Théâtre du Châtelet)

1897 **La Gaudriole** (Albert Vizentini/w Tréfeu) Aix-les-Bains 12 September

1898 **Le Soleil à minuit** (Albert Renaud/w Beaumont) Théâtre des Bouffes-Parisiens 14 October

NUNN, Trevor (b Ipswich, 14 January 1940). Royal Shakespeare Company director who moved with wide success into the spectacular musical theatre.

Nunn began his theatrical career on a directing bursary to the Belgrade Theatre, Coventry, where his early productions included a musical version of *Around the World in 80 Days*. In 1964 he joined the Royal Shakespeare Company and in 1968 he was appointed its Artistic Director, a position he held until 1986. During his tenure at the Royal Shakespeare Company, Nunn ventured, in a regular directing schedule of classic plays, towards the musical theatre with a production of *The Comedy of Errors* (1976) into which sufficient song and dance elements (ch: Gillian Lynne) were introduced for it to be given a 'Best Musical' award.

His first musical theatre directing assignment in the West End was the creation of the enormously successful Andrew Lloyd Webber musical *Cats* (1980 w Miss Lynne) from which he emerged not only with a directorial credit but also with a share in the lyric to the show's hit song, 'Memory', a number created from pieces and reminiscences of published and unpublished works of *Cats* 'librettist', T S Eliot. Nunn directed three further Lloyd Webber musicals in the songs-on-skates saga *Starlight Express* (1984) and the winningly atmospheric tale of love in warm places, *Aspects of Love* (1989), repeating his direction in each case in the American reproductions of the London stagings, and the 1993 *Sunset Boulevard*.

He joined *Cats* producer Cameron Mackintosh again to produce (under the name of, and in the theatre of, the Royal Shakespeare Company) and to direct (w John Caird) the enormously successful English adaptation of the French musical *Les Misérables* (1985) which won him awards both in Britain and America (Tony Award) and which was reproduced (sometimes by himself, sometimes by others) in most countries of the world where musical theatre is popular and in several where it isn't. In 1986 he took over the direction of the Tim Rice/Abba musical *Chess*, following the death of its intended director, Michael Bennett, and he staged two different versions of the show, the first in Britain with considerable success and a long run, and a revised one in America with little success and a short run.

In 1986 he quit the Royal Shakespeare Company to continue as a freelance director in theatre and film (*Hedda, Lady Jane*), and in 1989 he co-produced (Homevale Ltd) and directed a short-lived revival of the 1976 musical *The Baker's Wife* in his home town of Ipswich and at London's Phoenix Theatre. He subsequently directed an unsuccessful musical-play version of *The Blue Angel*.

The director of two of the world's most successful musicals of the 1980s in *Cats* and *Les Misérables*, Nunn has evinced both a sense and sensitivity in his handling of large-scale modern musical theatre and its often large-scale stories and characters, human and other, whilst rejecting the gimmickry so many other directors of his generation have employed, in all fields from classic theatre to opera, in order to win themselves notice.

NYMPH ERRANT Play with music in 2 acts by Romney Brent adapted from the novel by James Laver. Music and lyrics by Cole Porter. Adelphi Theatre, London, 6 October 1933.

The novel *Nymph Errant*, written by James Laver, keeper of the theatrical collection at the Victoria and Albert Museum, was a triumphantly funny morsel of understated sexual frivolity and a piece of eminently natural fodder for the musical stage. The nymph of the title was a lass called Evangeline, gorgeous and comical and adored by men, and the 'errant' qualification had nothing to do with a fall from purity. It referred, rather, to Evangeline's wanderings throughout all the most deliciously perilous and picturesque parts of Europe and Asia, passing from the lustful hands of one pretty potentate to another yet, to her despair, coming out at the end of a series of unforeseen circumstances just as virginal as she had set out.

The book was dramatized by the actor Romney Brent, the songs written by Cole Porter, and C B Cochran's production mounted in London, under the direction of Brent, with revue star Gertrude Lawrence as the winsome Evangeline. The supporting cast included Hella Kürty (the original Mi of *Das Land des Lächelns*), Moya Nugent, Iris Ashley, Doris Carson, Elisabeth Welch, Austin Trevor, dancer Walter Crisham and American gangster-specialist

David Burns, Doris Zinkeisen was the designer and the young Agnes de Mille supplied the dances (subsequently redone by Barbara Newberry and Carl Randall). However, what should have been a spectacular and spectacularly funny extravaganza fell flat. The adaptation was voted weak, and the songs, many of them both amusing and attractive in their own right, were a revusical lot which often had precious little to do with the show.

Amongst those numbers which survived the production were 'The Physician', a remake of a 1930 number performed by Marie Cahill in the early stages of the production of *The New Yorkers*, here put over by Miss Lawrence with a suggestiveness which led to its being banned by the BBC, a piece about mass adultery by the wives of 'Solomon' introduced by Elisabeth Welch, and Moya Nugent's advice to the heroine to 'Experiment'. The most fun, however, in what became a rather relentless, one-toned parade of not-very-wide variations on a sexual theme, came from Queenie Leonard, revusically complaining of being 'an annoyed, unemployed cocotte'. One variation of the theme didn't please, however: Doris Carson's transvestite tale of 'Georgia Sands' was dropped after the opening and replaced by a more conventional call to 'Cazanova' (sic) to 'come ova ...'.

The show foundered in four months and 154 performances and Cochran cancelled his announced Broadway production. Whilst the favourite songs continued to find performances, the show was put sufficiently away for a fresh musicalization of Brent's script, unimaginatively titled *Evangeline*, to be mounted for the benefit of Frances Day in 1946 (George Posford, Harry Jacobson/Eric Maschwitz, Cambridge Theatre 14 March). It played 32 performances.

During the fashionable free-for-all which whirled around anything and everything written by Porter during the 1980s, *Nymph Errant* was played at New York's Equity Library Theatre (11 March 1982), given a concert performance in Britain and at various stages was mumbled about as a revival prospect without, however, reappearing on the metropolitan stage.

Recording: Selection (EMI)

NYPE, Russell (b Zion, Ill, 26 April 1924). Double Tony Award winner who won few other Broadway chances.

After an early career as a club singer, Nype played on Broadway in *Regina* (1949, Oscar Hubbard) and *Great to be Alive* (1950) before creating the rôle of Kenneth Gibson, and the duet 'You're Just in Love' with Ethel Merman, in *Call Me Madam* (1950, Tony Award). He won a second Tony Award for his portrayal of the hapless bridegroom George Randolph Brown in *Goldilocks* (1958, 'Shall I Take my Heart and Go') and appeared at the New York City Center as Enoch Snow, Jeff Douglas (1967, *Brigadoon*) and Freddie Eynsford-Hill and on the road as Jimmy Smith in *No, No, Nanette*. He later succeeded to the rôle of Cornelius Hackl in *Hello, Dolly!* (1970), again alongside Miss Merman, 20 years after their more famous pairing.

O

OATES, Alice [née MERRITT] (b Nashville, Tenn, 22 September 1849; d Cincinnati, 24 February 1881). Livewire 19th-century touring producer/performer who took opéra-bouffe in English to all corners of America.

When she became the wife of actor/producer James A Oates, 16-year-old Alice Merritt abandoned an operatic training to join her husband on the stage. Amongst her early engagements, she toured with C D Hess's company in the burlesque *The Field of the Cloth of Gold*, and then mounted her own company which made its way across the country to New York to play *The Fair One in the Golden Wig* and *La Fille du Régiment* on the fringes of Broadway. The coming of opéra-bouffe found her in her element, and she quickly became one of the first and most adventurous managers to successfully produce English-language burlesque and comic operas in America.

Mrs Oates's activities and celebrity were centred largely on the west coast, but she toured indefatigably through all the main centres and made brief appearances on Broadway throughout the 1870s with her versions (often severely botched) of such pieces as *Giroflé-Girofla*, *Le Petit Duc*, *La Fille de Madame Angot*, *La Jolie Parfumeuse*, *La Princesse de Trébizonde*, *Les Bavards*, *Les Prés Saint-Gervais* and *La Grande-Duchesse*. Her style and her adaptations were found a bit obvious and 'provincial' by the sophisticates, who preferred their opéra-bouffe from Aimée or Tostée and in French, and without a bundle of music-hall songs or nigger sketches thrown into the middle, but she maintained a long and unbroken popularity with her own audiences.

Mrs Oates became the first manager to produce a Gilbert and Sullivan work in America when she staged *Trial By Jury* at Philadelphia's Arch Street Theatre in 1875, and she was quickly on the boards with a botched version of *HMS Pinafore* (with herself as a travesty Ralph Rackstraw) at the Bush Theatre in San Francisco shortly after the show's Boston première and before the piece had reached New York.

She also gave early opportunities to a number of people who later became important in the American musical theatre, notably J Cheever Goodwin who, having come to her as a performer, found his niche as an author when he was set to Alice-izing French opéras-bouffes, and the beautiful Pauline Hall of *Erminie* fame, and she also employed a number of the finest established performers of the English musical stage such as J G Taylor, E D Beverly, Edward Connell and John Howson in companies which were more than just a setting for their manageress and her performances.

After the death of her husband, she briefly married her agent, Titus Tracy, who booked her to visit Australia in 1880. However, the now divorced, re-married and rather buxom Alice fell ill and died before she had the chance to undertake her first overseas season.

DER OBERSTEIGER Operette in 3 acts by Moritz West and Ludwig Held. Music by Carl Zeller. Theater an der Wien, Vienna, 6 January 1894.

Carl Zeller never succeeded in composing another Operette which found the same enormous success as his delightfully melodious, countryside-and-court show *Der Vogelhändler*, but he nevertheless turned out several other winning scores, of which that for *Der Obersteiger*, attached to a libretto which, above all, created a large and cornucopic Girardi-rôle for the megastar of the Viennese Operette stage, was one of the most attractive.

Girardi was cast as Martin, the loose-living, work-shy foreman of a mine in a little village somewhere on the Austro-German border. Engaged to pretty Nelly (Therese Biedermann), he nevertheless chases after her cousin, Julie Fahnenschwinger (Jenny Pohlner), but he gets tetchy and openly accusing when he sees Nelly richly dressed. When he is put in charge of a mineworkers' strike for 'less work, more pay' he uses his position to his own financial profit, and he is not above making love to the overseer's wife (Lori Stubel) to get a job for his on-the-side miners' band. However, Martin gets his points when the 'enemy', the mine overseer Zwack (Carl Lindau), is made to look ridiculous: having admitted Julie as his illegitimate daughter, he sees it revealed that she is actually a Countess in disguise. Before the show is over she has paired off with the local Count Roderich (Karl Streitmann), and Martin goes back to the soft Nelly.

Der Obersteiger was a less agreeable libretto than that of *Der Vogelhändler*, even though the characters were lined up in almost a repeat of the first show: the country lad, his betrayed country girl, the aristocratic lady whom he runs after and who finally marries one of her own kind, and even two crazy mining officials as equivalents to the two professors of the earlier piece. And the rôle of Martin, whilst certainly large and equipped with one magnificent hit number, the obligatory Girardi-waltz 'Sei nicht bös', had none of the appeal of *Der Vogelhändler*'s Adam: he was a fairly despicable boor, and it needed all the charm of a Girardi to make him anything else.

Alexandrine von Schönerer's production at the Theater an der Wien was well received, and the piece was given a first run of 61 performances in two months. It was retained in the repertoire throughout the year, making regular reappearances, passing its 100th night on 21 October, and still putting in the occasional matinée performance in 1897. In 1901 it was revived at the Carltheater (15 November) with Mizzi Zwerenz as Nelly, and it remained thereafter on the fringe of the revivable repertoire, reappearing at the Theater an der Wien in 1919 and in 1953 at the Raimundtheater (18 December).

The show's Austrian success was repeated in Germany where, again without equalling *Der Vogelhändler*, it was for a number of years a highly popular piece in German houses, and also in Hungary. First produced there at the Népszinház (ad József Markus) with Pál Vidor starred as Martin, Aranka Hegyi as 'Julie', Mariska Komáromi (Nelly) and Sándor Dárdai (Roderich) it had a very fine first run of 35 performances and was played throughout the country.

If the show did not travel noticeably beyond central Europe, however, the same could not be said for its star song. 'Sei nicht bös' (aka 'The Obersteiger Waltz', aka 'Don't be Cross') went quickly round the world becoming, curiously, a concert favourite with sopranos. London's George Edwardes snapped it up, had Adrian Ross write some English words, and popped it into his *An Artist's Model* as a duet for Hayden Coffin and Marie Tempest under the title 'Music and Laughter', but he was forced to withdraw it when the publishers objected. Since *Der Obersteiger* never crossed the channel, this prohibition did them little good, but they duly made their hit with the song which is sung to this day in English.

Germany: Theater Unter den Linden 27 January 1894; Hungary: Népszinház *A banyamester* 15 September 1894

O'BRIEN, Richard (b New Zealand, 1942).

An intermittent actor who had played in the chorus of *Jesus Christ Superstar* in London, O'Brien invented and authored the show which became *The Rocky Horror Show* in which he himself featured as the spidery butler-cum-creature-from-outer-space Riff Raff ('The Time Warp'). The success of that piece encouraged producer Michael White and the Royal Court Theatre to mount a second O'Brien piece, but *T Zee* (the title's reference was to Tarzan), another Hollywoodian spoof with neither the novelty value nor the bite of the earlier show folded in 38 performances.

1973 **Rocky Horror Show** Royal Court Theatre Upstairs 19 June
1976 **T Zee** (w Richard Hartley) Royal Court Theatre 10 August

THE O'BRIEN GIRL Musical comedy in 2 acts by Frank Mandel and Otto Harbach. Lyrics by Harbach. Music by Louis Hirsch. Liberty Theater, New York, 3 October 1921.

George M Cohan brought back the team which had given him a hit show in *Mary* to attempt a repeat the following year with *The O'Brien Girl*. Once again Frank Mandel and Otto Harbach turned out plot and words on a Cinderellic line with yet another poor, Irish-American lassie singing and dancing her way into the hands, the arms and ultimately the family tree of a handsome, wealthy (or should that be wealthy, handsome?) upper-class, thoroughly-American version of a fairytale prince. This time the little heroine was a typist called Alice O'Brien (Elisabeth Hines), her reward was called Larry Patten (Truman Stanley) and the obstacles were her employer Mr Drexel (Robinson Newbold) and his not unreasonably suspicious wife (Georgia Caine) who had destined Larry as a mate for her own daughter, Eloise. Fairyland was an hotel in the Adirondacks where little Alice had gone to spend her savings on one glorious blow-out and where she

ran into the rest of the principals. One critic remarked, perhaps naïvely, that the tale seemed to be borrowed from the successful play *Diana of Dobson's* – it could, of course, have been borrowed from any one of a dozen recent musical plays, but it was none the worse nor any the less popular for that.

If Hirsch's score didn't produce anything that caught on like the big numbers of *Mary* had done, songs like 'Learn to Smile', 'The O'Brien Girl', 'I Wonder How I Ever Passed You By' and a new 'My Little Canoe' (Billie Burke's pre-war hit must have been forgotten) illustrated the story happily alongside a bevy of dance numbers (The Indian Prance, The Conversation Step, 'The Last Dance').

The O'Brien Girl ran for a more-than-respectable 164 Broadway performances and then toured, but only Australia showed any overseas interest in taking it up. It proved a good decision. Budding producer Hugh J Ward used *The O'Brien Girl* to open the New Princess Theatre in Melbourne and mounted it with Mamie Watson (Alice), Leyland Hodgson (Larry), Mark Daly (Drexel) and May Beatty (Mrs Drexel) featured, with dancer June Roberts in the rôle of Eloise and soprano Ena Dale (Miss Hope) tacked in to do their specialities. It ran for an outstanding 202 performances in five and a half months at the Princess, followed up with a hit season in Sydney (Grand Opera House 15 September 1923) where Ward went twice-daily to cash in on his show's vogue through a further three months, and became one of the longest-running hits of the 1920s on the Australian musical stage. It was brought back to Melbourne as late as 1936 when Benjamin Fuller and the young Garnet Carroll mounted a revival at the Apollo Theatre (8 August) with Charles Norman and Catherine Stewart featured.

Australia: New Princess Theatre, Melbourne 26 December 1922

AZ OBSITOS Énekes színjáték (play with songs) in 3 acts by Károly Bakonyi. Music by Emmerich Kálmán. Vigszinház, Budapest, 16 March 1910.

Produced at Budapest's Vigszinház, as Kálmán's previous piece, the internationally successful *Tatárjárás*, had been, *Az obsitos* was, like that work, a collaboration with playwright Károly Bakonyi. Unlike the earlier piece, however, it was not described as an 'operett' but as an 'énekes színjáték', and the text to the piece was indeed no Ruritanian operetta tale of soubrettes and so forth, but a period play 'part serious drama, part folk play, part tale', which – whilst far from being a fantasy – had some of the characteristics of Bakonyi's great *János vitéz* to it, and to which the musical part was a support.

In an Hungarian village a mother (a nemzetes asszony, Hermin Haraszthy) and her daughter Málcsika (Irén Varsányi) wait. They are waiting for their soldier son and brother to come home from Italy whence he went during the Hungarian uprisings of 1848. They cannot know that he will not return, for he is dead. The news of his death is to be brought to them by his friend, András Dömötör (Gyula Hegedüs). But András is very close, in physical appearance, to his dead friend, and when he arrives both the mother and, at first, the daughter mistake him for their boy returned home. András cannot undeceive the old lady, and he will not allow himself, under such conditions, to accept the fact that Málcsika is falling in love with him. But, eventually, the secret has to come out. The nemzetes asszony accepts that she has lost her son, but she has the consolation of a new son. For András will marry Málcsika.

The Budapest public, expecting another brightly operettic piece in the style of *Tatárjárás*, were rather taken aback by the new Kálmán/Bakonyi product, but the show soon found its audience and appreciation. *Az obsitos* was no *János vitéz* but, following its initial 25 performances at the Vigzinház, it nevertheless had a remarkable career. And that career was not simply in Hungary but, in a series of transformations, in a whole series of other countries.

The first of these was Austria. Librettist Victor Léon took the show up, combined with Kálmán on some alterations – one of which was the shifting of the action from its Hungarian setting to an Upper-Austrian one, in the year 1859 – and directed the resultant *Der gute Kamerad* (now described curiously as 'ein Theaterstück für Musik') under the management of Oskar Fronz, and with the composer conducting, at the Wiener Bürgertheater. Willy Strehl was Alwin von Kammerer with Viktoria Pohl-Meiser (Stanzi), Franz Mainau (Baron Martin von Schenkenbach) and Erna Fiebinger (Marlene) in support.

Der gute Kamerad had a respectable run of 53 performances, but didn't get a look-in after the end of its first run, for the Bürgertheater then began its great run of Eysler Operetten, and the Austro-Hungarian piece was forgotten. Not wholly, however, for in 1914 Wilhelm Karczag decided that *Der gute Kamerad* would be a good piece with which to reopen his theatre after the outbreak of war. Léon rewrote his text (now advertised as being 'freely based on an idea by' Bakonyi) to make this a Kriegsoperette, a frankly patriotic piece set in the present day, and retitled it *Gold gab ich für Eisen*. Karczag cast the piece up with Ernst Tautenhayn (Rabenlechner), Luise Kartousch repeating her *Herbstmanöver* travesty as the young Xaver alongside Therese Tautenhayn also in travesty as von Kammerer, Betty Fischer in her Theater an der Wien début as Marlene, and such fine veterans as Paul Guttmann and Karl Tuschl. Vienna showed only a limited interest, however, in being stirred up by a Kriegsoperette. *Gold gab ich für Eisen* passed its 50th performance on 4 December, and little more than three weeks later Karczag remounted the decidedly escapist *Der Opernball* in replacement. *Auf Befehl der Kaiserin* and, above all, *Die Rose von Stambul* soon confirmed that good-old-days entertainment and colourful, ringing Operette were what the wartime Viennese (like their brethren everywhere else) really wanted. *Gold gab ich für Eisen* ended up with a total of 82 showings, during which Frln Kartousch gave up her rôle to the very untravestied Viktor Flemming.

Germany had earlier picked up *Der gute Kamerad*, without particular enthusiasm, and although it had a veritable factory of Kriegsoperetten of its own, the revised *Gold gab ich für Eisen* was pulled in to add its weight to the war effort. What was good for one side, however, could apparently also be good for the other. Shortly after what remained of *Az obsitos* had done its new rounds in Austria and Germany, it turned up on Broadway. Done over by Rida Johnson Young, its tale was now a semi-weepie, studded with conventional musical comedy comedy (although no travesty), and with an improbable happy ending. After the soldier hero (John Charles Thomas) had pretended to

be his buddy (Frank Ridge) to save the dead man's family pain, he not only won the buddy's sister (Beth Lydy), but saw the undead buddy return safely home. Clifton Crawford and Adele Rowland were the comedy. Kálmán's score now included a bundle of Sigmund Romberg music, plus a handful of other pieces including 'Pack Up Your Troubles in Your Old Kit Bag'. The Shuberts' production of *Her Soldier Boy* bore no family resemblance at all to *János vitéz*, which probably helped it to its 204 performances on Broadway.

Kálmán's name appeared nowhere on the bills when *Soldier Boy* was produced in London, right under the nose of the self-appointed wartime guardian of the racial purity of the nation's musical stages, J M Glover, whose much boasted knowledge of music and musical shows apparently didn't reach to knowing from where this show had originally sprung. Edgar Wallace revised Mrs Johnson's book, Frederic Chapelle had his go at the score, and the combination of the heart-tugging tale and songs with titles like 'Song of Home', 'I'm Going Home', 'He's Coming Home', 'The Battle Front at Home', 'Mother', 'Lonely Princess', 'March Along' and 'The Military Stamp' ensured the show its longest run of all: 372 performances which straddled Armistice Day with great advantage to the box-office. *Az obsitos*, although barely recognizable, had the distinction of being the only 'Germanic' piece (Cuvillier's *The Lilac Domino* counted as French) to play the West End in the War years. France, however, did not play it, in any version.

Austria: Wiener Bürgertheater *Der gute Kamarad* 27 October 1911, Theater an der Wien *Gold gab ich für Eisen* 18 October 1914; Germany: *Der gute Kamerad*; Neues Operetten-Theater, Leipzig *Gold gab ich für Eisen* 28 November 1915; USA: Astor Theater *Her Soldier Boy* 6 December 1916; UK: Apollo Theatre *Soldier Boy* 26 June 1918

L'OEIL CREVÉ Folie musicale in 3 acts by Hervé. Théâtre des Folies-Dramatiques, Paris, 12 October 1867.

Hervé's second attempt, after *Les Chevaliers de la table ronde* (1866), to produce a full-length burlesque opérette to challenge the all-consuming works of Offenbach, *L'Oeil crevé* did precisely that, proving itself one of the most successful opéras-bouffes of the era.

Fleur de Noblesse (Julia Baron) is, in accordance with her name, a flower of a noble family, the daughter of the local Marquis (Berret) and Marquise d'Enface (Adèle Cuinet). However, she has taken a passion for carpentry and, not coincidentally, for the young cabinet-maker Ernest. Ernest is also a jolly archer, and he is a competitor in the archery contest which is the highlight of the piece. He hits the bullseye, but his triumph is postponed when the Robin-Hoodish forester Alexandrivoire (Marcel), the beloved of the peasant girl Dindonette (Mlle Berthal), arrives on the scene with a challenge. However, far from splitting his rival's shaft, or marking a bullseye, Alexandrivoire simply succeeds in putting his arrow in the eye of the noble maiden. The one gendarme, Géromé (Milher), who constitutes the whole of the Marquisal army, arrests the miscreant and plunges him into the dungeon tower. An actful of disguises, doctors and duets later, Dindonette effects a magical cure on Fleur de Noblesse and everything can end happily.

The tale gave the opportunities for a whole series of particular burlesques from the *Robin Hood*, *William Tell*

Plate 196. L'Oeil crevé.

and *Lucia di Lammermoor* moments of the archery contest, to musical mockeries of *Der Freischütz* (a hunters' chorus) and *Il trovatore* (a miserere duo for Dindonette and her imprisoned swain), but the favourite portions of Hervé's brightly comical score were a duo for the Marquis and Dindonette – the Légende de la langouste atmosphérique – an auvergant dialect tale about a chap who used the magic herb of brotherly love to spice his cooked lobster instead of spreading it around the world, Alexandrivoire's La Polonaise et l'hirondelle ('Un jour passant par Meudon'), the third-act tyrolienne ('Tournes, tournes, petits bâtons'), Gérôme's comical military number equipped with drum imitations, and the septet, chorus and finale of the second act which culminated in a crazy, concerted massed effect much like the first-act closing of *Chilpéric* with its umbrellas and horses.

L'Oeil crevé ran a remarkable 345 performances in its first year, and returned regularly to the Parisian stage thereafter. It was seen again at the Folies-Dramatiques in 1876, revised by Hector Crémieux for a production at the Théâtre de la Renaissance in 1881 (24 September), mounted at the Théâtre des Menus-Plaisirs in 1889, 1890 and 1892, and at the Variétés in 1896 (18 April) where Albert Brasseur (Duc d'Enface), Germaine Gallois (Fleur de Noblesse), Juliette Méaly (Dindonette), Ève Lavallière (Ernest), Paul Fugère, Jane Pernyn (Alexandrivoire), Guy (Marquis), Baron (Bailli) and Milher, repeating his original rôle, headed the starry cast. It came back to the Variétés again in 1904 (30 December), well after the vogue for genuine opéra-bouffe had faded, with Anna Tariol-Baugé playing Dindonette alongside Brasseur and Mlle Pernyn, now promoted to Fleur de Noblesse.

L'Oeil crevé was a burlesque piece in Hervé's furthest-out style, and if the Paris of 1867 found that style hilarious, it was by no means sure that other centres would – presuming that an adapter could be found who would repeat the flavour of the original in another language. Vienna gave *Das Pfeil im Auge* (ad Julius Hopp) just four hearings, and New York, which got the piece in its original French from Maurice Grau's company with Rose Bell (Dindonette), Marie Desclauzas (Fleur de Noblesse), Carrier (Alexandrivoire), Beckers (Marquis) and Gabel (Gérôme) featured also gave it the thumbs down with sufficient meaning to ensure that the show was never produced in New York in English.

England, however, which was to repeatedly prove the most receptive to Hervé's extravagant comicalities, was pleased enough with its first glimpse of his work when F C Burnand's adaptation of *L'Oeil crevé* was produced at the Olympic Theatre as *Hit or Miss, or All My Eye and Betty Martin* in 1868 ('the music puts to shame the music-hall stuff accepted in burlesque'), and after the huge success of *Chilpéric* London was happy to see the show again. It got it both in French, from the visiting Folies-Dramatiques Company (who also did *Chilpéric* and *Le Canard à trois becs* but won greatest applause for this piece), featuring Paola Marié (Dindonette), Blanche d'Antigny (Fleur de Noblesse) and Vauthier (Marquis), and then in a new H B Farnie version at the Opéra-Comique (*L'Oeil crevé or the Merry Toxophilites*) produced under the management of E P Hingston. Julia Mathews (Fleur de Noblesse), Mlle Clary (Alexandrivoire), Pattie Laverne (Dindonette), Richard Temple (Gérôme) and David Fisher (Marquis) headed the cast in which Richard Barker, the director, appeared as the Sentry, and the piece scored a fine success running through November and December and into the New Year. Yet another version of the piece – the fourth in a decade – returned to the West End in 1877 when a five-scene reduction of Farnie's text was added to Alexander Henderson's triple bill (*La Créole, Up the River*) at the Folly Theatre (*Shooting Stars*, 22 November) with Kate Munroe (Dindonette), Lizzie Beaumont (Fleur de Noblesse), Violet Cameron (Alexandrivoire), John Howson (Gérôme) and C H Drew (Marquis) featured.

Austria: Theater an der Wien *Der Pfeil im Auge* 29 February 1868; Germany: Friedrich-Wilhelmstädtisches Theater *Fleur de Noblesse* 22 May 1868; USA: Théâtre Français (Fr) 11 January 1869; UK: Olympic Theatre *Hit or Miss, or All My Eye and Betty Martin* 13 April 1868, Globe Theatre (Fr) 15 June 1872; Australia: Opera House, Melbourne 28 February 1874

OFFENBACH, Jacques [EBERST, Jacob] (b Cologne, 20 June 1819; d Paris, 3 October 1880). The 19th century's most popular musical-theatre composer.

The son of a German bookbinder, music-teacher and cantor called Eberst, but known as Offenbach, the young Jacob was given a good musical education from an early age. When he was 14 years old, his father took him to Paris where he secured a place at the Conservatoire (becoming Jacques instead of Jacob) but, after a year of studies, he left to earn a living as an orchestral cellist, ultimately in the orchestra of the Opéra-Comique. He progressed from orchestral playing to solo work and, in the 1840s, gave concert performances in several of the world's musical capitals.

1073

Offenbach began writing music almost at the same time that he began performing it, at first producing occasional pieces, orchestral dances and instrumental and vocal music before, in 1839, he was given the opportunity to compose for the stage for the first time with a song for the one-act vaudeville *Pascal et Chambord*, produced at the Palais-Royal. That commission, however, had no tomorrow and, although Offenbach began writing with serious intent for the stage in the 1840s, he found that he was unable to get his works staged. The Opéra-Comique, the principal producer of lighter musical works, rejected his efforts and although *Pépito*, a pretty if slightly self-conscious little opérette housing some parody of Rossini, was played briefly at the Théâtre des Variétés, he was obliged to mount performances of his other short pieces under fringe theatre conditions to win a hearing. Not even when he was nominated conductor at the Théâtre Français in 1850, a post which led him to be called upon to supply such scenic and incidental music and/or songs as might be required for that theatre's productions, did he succeed in getting one of his opérettes produced. Then in 1855, he launched himself on the Parisian stage from two different fronts.

On the one hand, with the help of a finely imagined and funny text by Jules Moinaux, he managed to place one of his opérettes at Hervé's Folies-Nouvelles. This piece, *Oyayaïe, ou La Reine des îles*, was in a different vein from his previous works, works which had been written rather in the style of a Massé or an Adam, with the polite portals of the Opéra-Comique in sight. *Oyayaïe* was written in the new burlesque style initiated and encouraged by Hervé, and it rippled with ridiculous and extravagantly idiotic fun. There was not a milkmaid or a Marquis in sight and the show was peopled instead by the folk of burlesque with Hervé himself at their head, in travesty, as the titular and cannibalistic Queen of the Islands.

By the time that *Oyayaïe* had found her way to the stage, however, Offenbach had already set another project on its way. The year 1855 was the year of the Paris Exhibition, and the city's purveyors of entertainment were preparing for lucratively larger audiences than were usual as visitors from out of town and overseas poured into Paris. It seemed like a good time to be in the business. Thus, Offenbach, who had managed the production of his early unwanted works himself and who now saw Hervé presenting his own works successfully at the Folies-Nouvelles, decided to become a manager. He took up the lease of the little Théâtre Marigny in the Champs-Élysées, rechristened it the Théâtre des Bouffes-Parisiens, and opened with a programme made up of four pieces by J Offenbach: a little introductory scena *Entrez Mesdames, Messieurs*, a virtual two-hander for two comics *Les Deux Aveugles*, the three-handed opéra-comique *Une nuit blanche* and a little pantomime *Arlequin barbier*. *Les Deux Aveugles* proved a major Parisian (and later international) hit, *Une nuit blanche* (which also subsequently became much favoured in English under the title *Forty Winks*) supported it happily, and Offenbach's little theatre and its programme became one of the most successful entertainments of the Exhibition season. Thus launched, the composer/producer began to vary his programme, taking in some pieces by other writers, writing himself four further opérettes and two further pantomimes and scoring a second significant success with the sentimental scena ('légende bretonne') *Le Violoneux* in which the young Hortense Schneider made her first Paris appearances.

Once the end of the summer season arrived, however, accompanied by the closing of the Exhibition, it soon became clear that the little theatre way out in the Champs-Élysées was no longer a good proposition. Offenbach needed to shift his activities to a more central location if he were to continue as he had begun. He leased an auditorium in the Passage Choiseul, gained a permit in which the limit to the number of characters allowed in his pieces was raised from three to four, and opened, still as the Bouffes-Parisiens, at the end of December with a programme which featured but one piece of his own. But that one piece was a winner. *Ba-ta-clan* was a return to the burlesque genre of *Oyayaïe*, and it gave Offenbach the producer and Offenbach the musician a fresh success comparable to that of *Les Deux Aveugles*. The new house was rocketed off to the same kind of start as the old one had been. The successes of his winter season included Offenbach's melodrama burlesque *Tromb-al-ca-zar* and an adaptation of Mozart's little *Der Schauspieldirektor* as well as the prize-winning efforts of two neophyte composers, Georges Bizet and Charles Lecocq, before the happy manager moved back to the Champs-Élysées for the summer and a programme including such new pieces as *La Rose de Saint-Flour* – a piece in the rustic opérette vein of Massé's *Les Noces de Jeannette* or of Offenbach's own *Le Violoneux* – and *Le 66*.

At the end of this second summer, Offenbach abandoned his first little home, and established himself on a full-time basis at the Passage Choiseul, now the one-and-only Théâtre des Bouffes-Parisiens. There he continued to mount an ever-changing programme of short pieces, through the year 1857 (*Croquefer* with a fifth character semi-mute, *Une demoiselle en loterie*, *Le Mariage aux lanternes* etc) and into 1858 (*Mesdames de la Halle*, with a full-sized cast at last permitted, and a musical version of Scribe and Mélesville's little vaudeville *La Chatte metamorphosée en femme*), whilst taking the company and its repertoire on tour to Britain and to Lyon, to command performances, and managing to lose money all the while.

The restrictions as to the size of his productions having finally been withdrawn, Offenbach now stretched out for the first time into a more substantial work. October 1858 saw the Bouffes-Parisiens' first production of a full-sized, two-act opéra-bouffe, a piece written in an extension of the Hervé-style which Offenbach and his librettists had carried so successfully through from *Ba-ta-clan* to *Tromb-al-ca-zar* and *Croquefer*. This style now blossomed into something on a different scale in *Orphée aux enfers*, a gloriously imaginative parody of classic mythology and of modern events decorated with Offenbach's most laughing bouffe music. The triumph of *Orphée aux enfers* put the Bouffes-Parisiens on a steady footing, and those corners of the international theatrical world which had not yet taken more notice of Offenbach than to pilfer such of his tunes as they fancied for their pasticcio entertainments began to wake up to the significance of the new hero of the Paris musical theatre and his work.

However, in spite of its great home success (228 successive performances at the Bouffes) and the wide spread of the popularity of its music, *Orphée* did not, at the time, produce the major change of emphasis in the international musical theatre that, in retrospect, might have been expected. It took a number of years, further shows (and not always the same one for every area) for the Offenbach pen to do that.

In the meanwhile, there were further successes – financial, or at least artistic – to come. The year 1859 brought two more: the short *Un mari à la porte* and Offenbach's second full-length piece, the hilarious burlesque of all things medieval *Geneviève de Brabant* which, although it was a financial loser, confirmed the triumph of *Orphée* at the Bouffes-Parisiens. But there were also some real and substantial failures. When Offenbach moved outside his usual genre and finally forced the gates not only of the Opéra-Comique (*Barkouf*, to a libretto co-written by Scribe) but also of the Opéra (the ballet *Le Papillon*), he had two thorough flops. Back at the Bouffes, however, he produced in 1861 a third triumphant full-length work, the Venetian burlesque *Le Pont des soupirs*, the shorter but no less successful *La Chanson de Fortunio* and the Duc de Morny's delightful *Monsieur Choufleuri restera chez lui le ...*, followed in 1862 by the sparkling musical comedy *Le Voyage de MM Dunanan père et fils*, the little *M et Mme Denis* and, at his preferred spa town of Ems, *Bavard et Bavarde* a little piece which he subsequently worked up into a larger one as *Les Bavards*. But, whilst the successes piled up, the money did not. The dizzily spending Offenbach was not a talented manager and the series of outstandingly popular shows which should have made his fortune instead left the Bouffes-Parisiens almost permanently in the red. After the production of *M et Mme Denis* he was obliged to give up the theatre he had begun, and in 1863 the only fresh Offenbach music premièred in Paris was a song written for a little Palais-Royal vaudeville, *Le Brésilien*, by his old collaborator, Ludovic Halévy, and the librettist's newest partner, Henri Meilhac.

Ems, again, was the venue for one of his tiniest and sweetest pieces, *Lischen et Fritzchen*, and Vienna – where his works had begun to raise interest – the chosen city for his next venture into the area that had suited him so ill in 1860: *Die Rheinnixen*, an opéra-comique produced at the Vienna Hofoper, proved as total a failure as had *Barkouf* in Paris. Offenbach returned to the Parisian theatre with *Les Géorgiennes*, less successful perhaps than his previous three-act shows but still back in his 'own' world, and then, at what was clearly a crucial point in his career, he began the collaboration which would lead him to an even more outstanding position in the musical theatre than that he had already conquered with *Orphée*, *Geneviève* et *Le Pont des soupirs*.

Halévy and Meilhac joined the composer to write his second burlesque of classic antiquity, *La Belle Hélène*. Produced by Cogniard at the Théâtre des Variétés in December 1864, the piece won its trio of authors a ringing success such as Paris had not seen in years. And now Offenbach began his real take-over of the world's stages: Vienna was conquered in 1865 with Geistinger's *Die schöne Helena*, and as Offenbach, Halévy and Meilhac swept the stage of the Variétés with further burlesque triumphs in *Barbe-bleue* (1866), *La Grande-Duchesse de Gérolstein* (1867), *Les Brigands* (1869) and the rather less burlesque but ultimately equally successful *La Périchole* (1868), London fell belatedly before Emily Soldene in *Geneviève de Brabant* and Julia Mathews's *La Grande-Duchesse*, whilst in America

Lucille Tostée's *La Grande-Duchesse* gave serious impetus to a craze for opéra-bouffe in general and for the works of Offenbach in particular. And at home, the composer continued to turn out successes: the glittering comedy-cum-opérette *La Vie parisienne* for the Palais-Royal, the frivolous *La Princesse de Trébizonde* premièred at Baden-Baden before taking over the stage of the Bouffes-Parisiens, and the little bouffonnerie *L'Île de Tulipatan*. *Les Bergers*, a sardonic three-part look at fidelity in love through the ages, and *La Diva*, a vehicle for Schneider, both staged at the Bouffes, and two further pieces for the Opéra-Comique, *Robinson Crusoë* and *Vert-Vert*, proved less popular.

Les Brigands was playing at the Variétés when the Prussian army marched into Paris. Offenbach, like his chief competitors of times before and after, Hervé and Lecocq, marched quickly out and he spent the year of the conflict capitalizing on his now-thoroughly-spread fame around the world. When he returned, however, things did not take up where they had left off. The days of opéra-bouffe were done, and so were the days when Offenbach, Halévy, Meilhac and their star Hortense Schneider reigned over the Paris musical theatre and its glittering audiences. Hervéesque burlesque with its weirdly extravagant tales was no longer the order of the day, the dazzling gaiety of the Variétés shows was of yesterday. The fashion, like the régime, had changed. Offenbach still found hits: the grand opéra-bouffe féerie *Le Roi Carotte* owed both some of its success and also its truncated run to an extravagant production which made it impossible to balance the books, *La Jolie Parfumeuse* (1873) and *Madame l'Archiduc* (1874) both found genuine international successes, and a Christmas show for London, *Whittington*, fared much better than a Vienna one, *Der schwarze Korsar* (23 performances). But none was a *Grande-Duchesse* or a *Belle Hélène*.

At the same period, however, Offenbach decided almost perversely to go back into management. He took the Théâtre de la Gaîté and there staged revivals of his two earliest Bouffes-Parisiens successes, *Orphée aux enfers* and *Geneviève de Brabant*, and of *La Périchole*, each of which he expanded to larger proportions, with mixed results: if the *Orphée* took least well to having additional songs and scenes stuck into its fabric, it did best at the box-office. However, box-office proved Offenbach's downfall once again and a distastrously expensive flop with Sardou's play *La Haine* found him once more an ex-theatre manager and financially in a parlous state.

He was also, now, for the first time for many years, not alone at the head of the French light-musical theatre. The emergence of Charles Lecocq and, above all, the younger man's triumphs in 1872 with *La Fille de Madame Angot* and in 1874 with *Giroflé-Girofla*, had rather overshadowed Offenbach's works of the same period, whilst the success of Robert Planquette's *Les Cloches de Corneville* in 1877 was the kind of success which Offenbach had not known for nearly a decade. Against these works, the long run of the spectacular opéra-bouffe féerie *Le Voyage dans la lune*, the at-best semi-successes of *La Boulangère a des écus* and *La Créole* and the utter failures of *La Boîte au lait* and *Maître Péronilla* weighed sadly light.

However, Offenbach was by no means done. In 1878, the year of Lecocq's latest triumph with *Le Petit Duc*, he found himself in tandem with one of the most efficacious and talented pairs of librettists of the day, Henri Chivot and Alfred Duru, and to their brilliant, action-packed text for *Madame Favart* he composed a score which more than did it justice. *Madame Favart* was no opéra-bouffe, and the music the 60-year-old Offenbach wrote for it had none of the brilliant fireworks of the scores of *Orphée*, *Geneviève* and *Barbe-bleue*. It was a period comic opera, a farcical tale of sexual hide-and-seek with a series of fine rôles and fine songs, and with both something of *La Fille de Madame Angot* and something of the Palais-Royal comedy about it. It was also a hit. The team repeated their success the following year with the splendid *La Fille du tambour-major*, the hit of the Parisian season, and thus Offenbach, who had known so many years at the top of his profession, was able to go out of it at the top. He died the following year of heart trouble, exacerbated by the gout and rheumatics which had dogged him all his adult life.

Following his death, his opérette *Belle Lurette* (completed by Delibes) was produced at the Théâtre de la Renaissance and overseas, and the opera *Les Contes d'Hoffmann* (completed by Guiraud) at the Opéra-Comique. This last piece finally gave him, posthumously, the success at the Opéra-Comique which he had always wanted so much, but which he had never been able to win during his lifetime.

Inevitably, after his death, and more particularly following the expiry of his legal copyrights, Offenbach's shows and his music became carrion for the compilers of pasticcio shows in the same way that they had been in his earliest years. One of these, in the wake of the huge success of the Schubert biomusical *Das Dreimäderlhaus*, even attempted to set his music to a version of his life. *Offenbach* (arr Mihály Nádor/Jenő Faragó), produced at Budapest's Király Színház (24 November 1920), fabricated a romance between the composer (song-and-dance comedy player Márton Rátkai) and Hortense Schneider (Juci Lábass) which seemed a little unnecessary, given the fact that he had allegedly had a long liaison with his other principal star, Zulma Bouffar, amongst others. It won a considerable success, racking up 150 performances in Budapest by 25 April 1921, being very soon revived (20 September 1922) and then exported in various versions to Vienna's Neues Wiener Stadttheater (ad Robert Bodanzky, Bruno Hardt-Warden), with Otto Tressler as the composer and Olga Bartos Trau as Hortense, to Germany variously as *Der Meister von Montmartre* and *Pariser Nächte* and, under the title *The Love Song*, to America (13 January 1925), where Allan Prior impersonated the composer alongside Odette Myrtil as Hortense and Evelyn Herbert as his wife, Herminie.

The English-speaking theatre, which made merry pasticcio with the composer's music in the 1860s and 1870s, to the extent of inventing a handful of Offenbach opérettes to texts the composer had never seen (including that of Lecocq's *Fleur de thé*) has, in later years, largely preferred to play the unadventurously small group of his most favoured opérettes which have been kept in their repertoire rather than manufacture its own. Broadway was, however, treated to a piece called *The Happiest Girl in the World* (Martin Beck Theater 3 April 1961) which mixed bits of Offenbach with bits of Aristophanes and little success, and London to a piece called *Can-Can* (Adelphi

Theatre 8 May 1946), another called *Music at Midnight* (His Majesty's Theatre 10 November 1950) and a new opéra-bouffe, well in the spirit of the old ones, *Christopher Columbus*.

The French musical theatre, too, even at its nadir of recent decades, has still found the space to give revivals of many of Offenbach's works rather than to paste-up 'new' ones. It is the German-speaking theatre which, by and large, has been responsible not only for the most drastic remakes of the original works but also for the largest number of pasticcio shows. From the very earliest days when Karl Treumann rewrote and had re-orchestrated Offenbach's pieces to suit the personnel of his company and local tastes in comedy, Viennese managers concocted their own Offenbach shows but, after the turn-of-the-century years, even though there were plenty of Offenbach shows to play, the new 'make-your-own-Offenbach-copyright' shows began in earnest. Amongst them may be numbered *Die Heimkehr des Odysseus* (Carltheater 23 March 1917), a version of *L'Île de Tulipatan* with a pasticcio score as *Die glückliche Insel* (1 act, Volksoper 8 June 1918), a composite of music from *Der schwarze Korsar* and elsewhere and an E T A Hoffmann tale made by Julius Stern and Alfred Zamara as *Die Goldschmied von Toledo* (Volksoper 20 October 1920), *Fürstin Tanagra* (Volksoper 1 February 1924), *Der König ihres Herzens* (Johann Strauss-Theater 23 December 1930), a remade version of *Robinson Crusoe* as *Robinsonade* (ad Georg Winckler, Neues Theater, Leipzig 21 September 1930), an *Italian Straw Hat* musical *Hochzeit mit Hindernissen* (Altes Theater, Leipzig 16 February 1930), *Das blaue Hemd von Ithaka* (Admiralspalast, Berlin 13 February 1931), *Die lockere Odette* (Edwin Burmester, Staatstheater, Oldenburg 25 February 1950), *Die Nacht mit Nofretete* (Romain Clairville, Theater am Rossmarkt, Frankfurt 13 November 1951), *Hölle auf Erden* (Georg Kreisler, Hans Haug, Nuremberg 21 January 1967), *Die klassische Witwe* (1 act, Cologne 20 June 1969) and many others.

1847 **L'Alcôve** (Pittaud de Forges, Adolphe de Leuven) 1 act Salle de la Tour d'Auvergne 24 April

1853 **Le Trésor à Mathurin** (Léon Battu) 1 act Salle Herz 7 May

1853 **Pépito** (Battu, Jules Moinaux) 1 act Théâtre des Variétés 28 October

1854 **Luc et Lucette** (de Forges, Eugène Roche) 1 act Salle Herz 2 May

1855 **Le Décameron** (Jules Méry) 1 act Salle Herz May

1855 **Entrez Messieurs, Mesdames** (Méry, Ludovic Halévy) 1 act Théâtre des Bouffes-Parisiens 5 July

1855 **Les Deux Aveugles** (Moinaux) 1 act Théâtre des Bouffes-Parisiens 5 July

1855 **Une nuit blanche** (Édouard Plouvier) 1 act Théâtre des Bouffes-Parisiens 5 July

1855 **Le Rêve d'un nuit d'été** (Étienne Tréfeu) 1 act Théâtre des Bouffes-Parisiens 30 July

1855 **Oyayaïe, ou La Reine des îles** (Moinaux) 1 act Folies-Nouvelles 7 August

1855 **Le Violoneux** (Eugène Mestépès, Émile Chevalet) 1 act Théâtre des Bouffes-Parisiens 31 August

1855 **Madame Papillon** (Halévy) 1 act Théâtre des Bouffes-Parisiens 3 October

1855 **Paimpol et Perinette** ('De Lussan' ie de Forges) 1 act Théâtre des Bouffes-Parisiens 29 October

1855 **Ba-ta-clan** (Halévy) 1 act Théâtre des Bouffes-Parisiens 29 December

1856 **Un postillon en gage** (Plouvier, Jules Adenis) 1 act Théâtre des Bouffes-Parisiens 9 February

1856 **Tromb-al-ca-zar, ou Les Criminels dramatiques** (Charles Dupeuty, Ernest Bourget) 1 act Théâtre des Bouffes-Parisiens 3 April

1856 **La Rose de Saint-Flour** (Michel Carré) 1 act Théâtre des Bouffes-Parisiens 12 June

1856 **Les Dragées du baptême** (Dupeuty, Bourget) 1 act Théâtre des Bouffes-Parisiens 18 June

1856 **Le 66** (de Forges, Laurencin) 1 act Théâtre des Bouffes-Parisiens 31 July

1856 **Le Financier et le savetier** (Crémieux, [Edmond About, uncredited]) 1 act Théâtre des Bouffes-Parisiens 23 September

1856 **La Bonne d'enfant[s]** (Eugène Bercioux) 1 act Théâtre des Bouffes-Parisiens 14 October

1857 **Les Trois Baisers du Diable** (Mestépès) 1 act Théâtre des Bouffes-Parisiens 15 January

1857 **Croquefer, ou le dernier des Paladins** (Adolphe Jaime, Tréfeu) 1 act Théâtre des Bouffes-Parisiens 12 February

1857 **Dragonette** (Mestépès, Jaime) 1 act Théâtre des Bouffes-Parisiens 30 April

1857 **Vent du soir, ou l'horrible festin** (Philippe Gille) 1 act Théâtre des Bouffes-Parisiens 16 May

1857 **Une demoiselle en loterie** (Jaime, Crémieux) 1 act Théâtre des Bouffes-Parisiens 27 July

1857 **Le Mariage aux lanternes** revised *Le Trésor à Mathurin* (Carré, Battu) 1 act Théâtre des Bouffes-Parisiens 10 October

1857 **Les Deux Pêcheurs** (Dupeuty, Bourget) 1 act Théâtre des Bouffes-Parisiens 13 November

1858 **Mesdames de la Halle** (Armand Lapointe) 1 act Théâtre des Bouffes-Parisiens 3 March

1858 **La Chatte metamorphosée en femme** (Eugène Scribe, Mélesville) 1 act Théâtre des Bouffes-Parisiens 19 April

1858 **Orphée aux enfers** (Crémieux, Halévy) Théâtre des Bouffes-Parisiens 21 October

1859 **Un mari à la porte** (Alfred Delacour, Léon Morand) 1 act Théâtre des Bouffes-Parisiens 22 June

1859 **Les Vivandières de la grande armée** (Jaime, de Forges) 1 act Théâtre des Bouffes-Parisiens 6 July

1859 **Geneviève de Brabant** (Tréfeu) Théâtre des Bouffes-Parisiens 19 November

1860 **Daphnis et Chloë** (Clairville, Jules Cordier) 1 act Théâtre des Bouffes-Parisiens 27 March

1860 **Barkouf** (Scribe, Henry Boisseaux) Opéra-Comique 24 December

1861 **La Chanson de Fortunio** (Crémieux, Halévy) 1 act Théâtre des Bouffes-Parisiens 5 January

1861 **Le Pont des soupirs** (Crémieux, Halévy) Théâtre des Bouffes-Parisiens 23 March

1861 **M Choufleuri restera chez lui le ...** ('Saint-Rémy', Crémieux, Halévy) 1 act Présidence du Corps-legislatif 31 May

1861 **Apothicaire et perruquier** (Élie Frébault) 1 act Théâtre des Bouffes-Parisiens 17 October

1861 **Le Roman comique** (Crémieux, Halévy) Théâtre des Bouffes-Parisiens 10 December

1862 **Monsieur et Madame Denis** (Laurencin, Michel Delaporte) 1 act Théâtre des Bouffes-Parisiens 11 January

1862 **Le Voyage de MM Dunanan père et fils** (Paul Siraudin, Moinaux) Théâtre des Bouffes-Parisiens 23 March

1862 **Les Bavards** (ex-*Bavard et Bavarde*) (Charles Nuitter) 1 act Ems 11 June, revised version in 2 acts Théâtre des Bouffes-Parisiens 20 February 1863

1862 **Jacqueline** (Crémieux, Halévy) 1 act Théâtre des Bouffes-Parisiens 14 October

1863 **Il Signor Fagotto** (Nuitter, Tréfeu) 1 act Ems 11 July

1863 **Lischen et Fritzchen** (Paul Boisselot) 1 act Ems 21 July, Théâtre des Bouffes-Parisiens 5 January 1864

1864 **L'Amour chanteur** (Nuitter, Ernest L'Épine) 1 act Théâtre des Bouffes-Parisiens 5 January

1864 **Die Rheinnixen** (Nuitter, Tréfeu) Hofoper, Vienna 4 February

1864 **Les Géorgiennes** (Moinaux) Théâtre des Bouffes-Parisiens 16 March

1864 **Jeanne qui pleure et Jean qui rit** (Nuitter, Tréfeu) 1 act Ems 19 July; Théâtre des Bouffes-Parisiens 3 November 1865

1864 **Le Fifre enchanté** (aka *Le soldat magicien*) (Nuitter, Tréfeu) 1 act Ems 9 July; Théâtre des Bouffes-Parisiens 30 September 1868

1864 **La Belle Hélène** (Meilhac, Halévy) Théâtre des Variétés 17 December

1865 **Coscoletto** (aka *Le Lazzarone*) (Nuitter, Tréfeu) Ems 24 July

1865 **Les Bergers** (Crémieux, Gille) Théâtre des Bouffes-Parisiens 11 December

1866 **Barbe-bleue** (Meilhac, Halévy) Théâtre des Variétés 5 February

1866 **La Vie parisienne** (Meilhac, Halévy) Palais-Royal 31 October

1867 **La Grande-Duchesse [de Gérolstein]** (Meilhac, Halévy) Théâtre des Variétés 12 April

1867 **La Permission de dix heures** (Mélesville, P Carmouche) 1 act Ems 9 July; Théâtre de la Renaissance, 4 September 1873

1867 **Le Leçon de chant electromagnétique** (Bourget) 1 act Ems August

1867 **Robinson Crusoë** (Eugene Cormon, Crémieux) Opéra-Comique 23 November

1868 **Le Château à Toto** (Meilhac, Halévy) Palais-Royal 6 May

1868 **L'Île de Tulipatan** (Henri Chivot, Alfred Duru) 1 act Théâtre des Bouffes-Parisiens 30 September

1868 **La Périchole** (Meilhac, Halévy) Théâtre des Variétés 6 October

1869 **Vert-Vert** (Meilhac, Nuitter) Opéra-Comique 10 March

1869 **La Diva** (Meilhac, Halévy) Théâtre des Bouffes-Parisiens 22 March

1869 **La Princesse de Trébizonde** (Nuitter, Tréfeu) Baden-Baden 31 July; Théâtre des Bouffes-Parisiens, 7 December

1869 **Les Brigands** (Meilhac, Halévy) Théâtre des Variétés 10 December

1869 **La Romance de la Rose** (Tréfeu, Jules Prével) 1 act Théâtre des Bouffes-Parisiens 11 December

1871 **Boule de neige** revised *Barkouf* Théâtre des Bouffes-Parisiens 14 December

1872 **Le Roi Carotte** (Victorien Sardou) Théâtre de la Gaîté 15 January

1872 **Fantasio** (Paul de Musset) Opéra-Comique 18 January

1872 **Fleurette** (*Trompeter und Näherin*) (de Forges, Laurencin) 1 act Carltheater, Vienna 8 March

1872 **Der schwarze Korsar** (Nuitter, Tréfeu) Theater an der Wien, Vienna 21 September

1873 **Les Braconniers** (Chivot, Duru) Théâtre des Variétés 29 January

1873 **Pomme d'api** (William Busnach, Halévy) 1 act Théâtre de la Renaissance 4 September

1873 **La Jolie Parfumeuse** (Crémieux, Ernest Blum) Théâtre des la Renaissance 29 November

1874 **Bagatelle** (Crémieux, Blum) 1 act Théâtre des Bouffes-Parisiens 21 May

1874 **Madame l'Archiduc** (Albert Millaud, Halévy) Théâtre des Bouffes-Parisiens 31 October

1874 **Whittington** (H B Farnie) Alhambra, London 26 December

1875 **La Boulangère a des écus** (Meilhac, Halévy) Théâtre des Variétés 19 October

1875 **La Créole** (Millaud, Meilhac) Théâtre des Bouffes-Parisiens 3 November

1875 **Le Voyage dans la lune** (Eugène Leterrier, Albert Vanloo, Arnold Mortier) Théâtre de la Gaîté 26 October

1875 **Tarte à la crème** (Millaud) 1 act Théâtre des Bouffes-Parisiens 14 December

1876 **Pierrette et Jacquot** (Jules Noriac, Gille) 1 act Théâtre des Bouffes-Parisiens 13 October

1876 **La Boîte à lait** (Grangé, Noriac) Théâtre des Bouffes-Parisiens 3 November

1877 **Le Docteur Ox** (Mortier, Gille) Théâtre des Variétés 26 January

1877 **La Foire Saint-Laurent** (Crémieux, Albert Saint-Albin) Théâtre des Folies-Dramatiques 10 February

1878 **Maître Péronilla** (Offenbach, Nuitter, Paul Ferrier) Théâtre des Bouffes-Parisiens 13 March

1878 **Madame Favart** (Chivot, Duru) Théâtre des Folies-Dramatiques 28 December

1879 **La Marocaine** (Ferrier, Halévy) Théâtre des Bouffes-Parisiens 13 January

1879 **La Fille du tambour-major** (Chivot, Duru) Théâtre des Folies-Dramatiques 13 December

1880 **Belle Lurette** (Blum, Édouard Blau, Raoul Toché) Théâtre de la Renaissance 30 October

1881 **Mademoiselle Moucheron** (Leterrier, Vanloo) 1 act Théâtre de la Renaissance 10 May

Memoirs: *Offenbach en Amérique: Notes d'un musicien en voyage* (Calmann-Lévy, Paris, 1877); Biographies: Schneider, L: *Offenbach* (Librairie Academique Perrin, Paris, 1923), Martinet, A: *Offenbach* (Dentu, Paris, 1887), Decaux, A: *Offenbach* (Pierre Amiot, Paris, 1958), Brindejoint-Offenbach, J: *Offenbach, mon grand-père* (Plon, Paris, 1940), Faris, A: *Jacques Offenbach* (Scribner, New York, 1980) etc

THE OFFICERS' MESS (and how they got out of it) Musical farce in 3 acts by Sydney Blow and Douglas Hoare. Music by Philip Braham. St Martin's Theatre, London, 7 November 1918.

One of the rarely successful attempts by revue producer André Charlot to stage a book musical, *The Officers' Mess* was a follow-up to its authors' *Telling the Tale*. Unlike that show, however, the new one was not a French farce adaptation, but an attempt at an English equivalent. Three soldiers (it was wartime, and all good musical-comedy heroes were soldiers), played by head comic Ralph Lynn, Herbert Sparling and Evan Thomas, place a newspaper advertisement devised to lure some nice girls to a 'borrowed' apartment. The advertisement attracts instead jewel robbers, police, Odette Myrtil as a French actress, the owner of the flat, and, in the second act, an ingénue for each man. Phil Braham's lively score included a ragtime version of Tchaikovsky's '1812' for Miss Myrtil, as well as songs both comical ('I am the APM', 'The Major, the Captain and the Loot') and crooning ('Float with the Tide') in the new mode, conducted by the composer of 'In a Persian Market', Alfred Ketèlby. The show ran 200 West End performances with a shift to the larger Prince's Theatre in mid-run, and its story was subsequently made into a film without its songs.

The songs were still reasonably intact, however, for an Australian season played on Hugh D McIntosh's Tivoli circuit with Vera Pearce (Kitty) delivering 'Give Me a Cosy Little Corner' and dancing the charleston alongside Claude Flemming (APM), Bert Clarke (Tony), Marie La Varre (Cora), Ellis Holland, Hugh Steyne and assorted specialities and interpolated songs. It played ten weeks in Melbourne and a fine 90 nights in Sydney (Tivoli 23

August 1919) to end its Australian life well on the credit side.

Australia: Tivoli, Melbourne 7 June 1919

OF THEE I SING Musical comedy in 2 acts by George S Kaufman and Morrie Ryskind. Lyrics by Ira Gershwin. Music by George Gershwin. Music Box Theater, New York, 26 December 1931.

George S Kaufman and the Gershwin brothers had ventured into the mirth-provoking world of national politics for the first time in 1927 with their musical *Strike Up the Band*. The show had folded on the road to New York, but a second version, with its libretto remoulded by Morrie Ryskind and remounted in 1930, did better, and the new *Strike Up the Band*'s 191 Broadway performances were sufficient to encourage the collaborators to write another piece with an off-White House tinge, to have another go at burlesquing those most popular burlesque subjects in the world – the rapacious numbskulls in political power and the system that put them there.

In fact, what the authors turned out this time around was a delicious piece of on-the-mark foolery in the best vein of such pieces as *La Grande-Duchesse de Gérolstein* or *Chilpéric*: an opéra-bouffe full of endearingly exaggerated and theatrical characters who get themselves involved in a series of almost surreal events as they struggle for wealth and/or marriage and their country's throne. The difference was, of course, that this being the United States of America, the throne in question was not that of Merovingia or Gérolstein, but that seat of power at number 1600 Pennsylvania, Washington, D C.

John P Wintergreen (William Gaxton) has been chosen to represent his party in the election for United States President at one of those hilarious mock-democratic affairs called a Convention. Convention has also given him a running mate – if anyone can remember the fellow's name. Oh yes, it's Alexander Throttlebottom (Victor Moore). In planning their man's campaign for the top job, Wintergreen's party committee sound out a Common Person and they discover that what interests the Average American most (after money, of course) is Love. So they decide to base their campaign on love. Bachelor Wintergreen must have a romance, and a wedding – these will provoke votes. To find the girl they hold a contest, and the luscious Miss Diana Devereaux (Grace Brinkley) is announced the winner. Unfortunately for the committee, Wintergreen has decided, in the meantime, that he's going to marry nice, homely secretary Mary Turner (Lois Moran) who can bake corn muffins and sew. Mary and John sweep to victory and the White House on their love-ticket, but Diana Devereaux will not be balked. She sues, then (since she is called Devereaux) she gets hold of the French ambassador and turns the whole thing into an international incident. She looks like winning, but Mary comes up with a case-breaker. She has a baby. Diplomatic relations hang on an umbilical cord until a logical answer of Gilbertian proportions is found. When the President is unable to fulfil his duty, it falls to the Vice President to deputize. Someone must find what's-his-name who will marry Diana Devereaux and allow the occupants of the White House to get on with ruling their country and eating their corn muffins in peace.

The Gershwins supplied a score for *Of Thee I Sing*

which was in the same bouffe manner as the libretto, characterized by the use of the phrase 'of thee I sing' from the American anthem, which was thrilled out before the crowds at Madison Square on election night, only to be deliciously defused: 'of thee I sing, baby ...'. The campaign zoomed to triumph on 'Love is Sweeping the Country', Mary trilled out a veritable opéra-bouffe waltz scena 'I'm Abount to Be a Mother', and Mlle Devereaux pulled off her petals in rejected despair in 'I Was a Beautiful Blossom' amongst a series of concerted pieces which bubbled with musical and textual humour, and a jolly jumble of reminiscences of everything from Gilbert and Sullivan to *Florodora* to Vienna.

Of Thee I Sing had fun with its music, but it also had fun with its subject and its characters, of whom the Vice-President whose name and face no one can ever remember (well, how many Vice Presidents do *you* remember?) proved the biggest winner, particularly as played by Moore. There was the occasional touch of personal or particular parody – various of the senatorial and political characters were made to resemble physically current incumbents in the old, traditional manner, without those people being personally parodied in the text – but mostly *Of Thee I Sing* was blossoming burlesque and not biting, or even nibbling satire. Of course, it succeeded very much better as such. The show stayed for 411 performances on Broadway, and the text was awarded a Pulitzer Prize for Drama (the first musical libretto thus to be favoured), before *Of Thee I Sing* went out on the road with Oscar Shaw, Donald Meek and Harriette Lake at the head of its cast.

Perhaps surprisingly, given its very general fun, the show did not get taken up outside America. Equally surprisingly, given the praise it won from critics and discerning audiences early on, it has had a disappointing career since. A 1952 revival (Ziegfeld Theater 5 May) with Jack Carson (John), Paul Hartman (Throttlebottom), Betty Oakes (Mary) and Lenore Lonergan (Diana) featured, and with author Kaufman as director, failed in 72 performances, and although a version of the show was seen on CBS television in 1972 with Carroll O'Connor, Jack Gilford, Chloris Leachman and Michele Lee in the leading rôles, *Of Thee I Sing*'s subsequent theatre life has been limited to intermittent productions in the regions. Even in the 1980s, with the great vogue for Gershwin productions and for anything with a whiff of politics to it, the best that *Of Thee I Sing* managed was a recorded concert performance, given in tandem with a similar performance of its sequel *Let 'em Eat Cake*.

That sequel may, in fact, have been partly responsible for the eclipse of *Of Thee I Sing*. Produced two seasons after the original piece, it went further into surreality, in a tale which had John (Gaxton), Mary (Miss Moran) and Throttlebottom (Moore) bumped from their Presidential positions and leading a revolution to get back in by force. At one stage Throttlebottom is sentenced to the guillotine, but by the end of the evening he is President, and John and Mary are working in the clothing business. Some incoherent plotting and a wholesale lack of the joyous tone that had made the first show such a treat contributed to this rather bilious piece shuttering after 90 performances, and perhaps taking something of the shine off its predecessor at the same time.

Whatever the reason, however, *Of Thee I Sing* remains more spoken-of than played in an era where the Gershwins' more lazily digestible works are all the fashion.

Recordings: revival cast (Capitol), TV cast (Columbia) Brooklyn Academy of Music concert (w *Let 'em Eat Cake*) (CBS) etc

OH, BOY! Musical comedy in 2 acts by Guy Bolton and P G Wodehouse. Music by Jerome Kern. Princess Theater, New York, 20 February 1917.

Librettist Guy Bolton and songwriter Jerome Kern, this time with the collaboration of novelist-cum-lyricist P G Wodehouse, followed up their successful small-stage ventures *Nobody Home* and *Very Good Eddie* with another piece in the same vein. *Oh , Boy!*, unlike its predecessors, was not an adaptation, but Bolton took his inspiration from the French vaudeville stage, and from such winningly translated versions of its products as *The Girl from Kays* and *Oh! Oh! Delphine*, in constructing a libretto based on well-used Continental comedy characters: the lady discovered in the rooms of the married (or almost married) man, the bride's pompous parents and the nice-but-strict wealthy relative who need to be convinced and/or placated before a happy and moneyed ending can be reached.

On this occasion the feminine intruder into the home of George Budd (Tom Powers) and his secretly new little wife Lou Ellen (Marie Carroll) is one Jackie Sampson (Anna Wheaton) who is fleeing from the law after landing one on an over-amorous gentleman (Frank McGinn) in a cabaret bar. Amongst the farcical events that follow, Jackie masquerades both as George's wife and as his Quaker aunt. Events wind up to their comic pitch when real Aunt Penelope (Edna May Oliver) turns up and knocks back a couple of courage-maintaining Bronxes intended for the phoney Aunt, Jackie's over-amorous gent turns out to have been the disapproving father of George's covert bride, and a comical policeman appears on the scene to stir and shake up all the elements of the action until they come out into a joyfully predictable dénouement. Hal Forde added to the high spirits of the piece as Jim, one of those 'amusing' best friends whom you wouldn't want for a friend in a thousand years, whilst the two most forward of the floosies whom he smuggles into George's flat for a rave-up were played by girls who would make their name in another medium: Marion Davies and Justine Johnstone. Dance pair Dorothy Dickson and Carl Hyson performed a speciality.

Kern's score for *Oh, Boy!* included some attractive numbers, of which the ringing duo 'Till the Clouds Roll By' (George/Jackie) proved the most popular, alongside a winsome waltz for Lou Ellen about being 'An Old-Fashioned Wife' and an interestingly Leslie Stuartish, long-lined number for the comic heroine about her eclectic tastes, 'Rolled into One'. The comedy was served by Jackie and Jim's dream of 'Nesting Time in Flatbush' and by one of the handful of songs popped in purely for decoration, telling the tale of 'Flubby Dub, the Caveman'.

If *Oh, Boy!* was made up of familiar elements, it was extremely well made up, and its combination of good, well worked-out comic situations and winning songs and dances were precisely what was needed for the kind of small auditorium for which it was designed. The show was greeted with delighted notices and ran in New York for a very fine 463 performances. It shifted from the little Princess to the Casino Theater in the latter days of this run to take advantage of the additional low-price seating the larger theatre offered, before setting out on a long and large series of touring productions.

Australia welcomed the show in quick time, and in July 1918 J C Williamson Ltd opened their production of *Oh, Boy!* in Sydney with Maud Fane as Jackie, William Green (Jim), George Willoughby (Judge) and London's Gaiety star Connie Ediss as Aunt Penelope. It played seven weeks before being replaced by a revival of *So Long, Letty!* then five further weeks in Melbourne (Theatre Royal, 14 September 1919) before *High Jinks* was brought back as a substitute, compiling a fair record but not one to equal those of those two established favourites.

London's Grossmith and Laurillard took up the British rights to the piece and, after having had the good idea of casting revue comedienne Beatrice Lillie as Jackie opposite Broadway's Powers, had the less good idea of housing the show in the out-of-the-mainstream Kingsway Theatre. Another rising actress, Isabel Jeans, played the obviously good-luck-bringing part of the foremost floosie, and one Harry Tierney number, 'Wedding Bells', was slipped into the show's score. The producers also rechristened the piece *Oh, Joy!*, which seemed unneccesary as, in the fashion of the time, it was just as irrelevant as the original title. A fair run of 167 performances was followed by one tour.

Oh, Boy! was revived at the Goodspeed Opera House in 1964 and again in 1984, and it was presented in New York in 1979 by the New Princess Theatre Company with Judith Blazer starred.

A 1919 film version, made by Albert Capellani, featured Creighton Haley, June Caprice and Joseph Conyers but, of course, not the songs. Or the dialogue.

Australia: Her Majesty's Theatre, Sydney 14 September 1918;
  UK: Kingsway Theatre *Oh, Joy!* 27 January 1919; Film: 1919
Recording: London cast recordings (WRC)

OH, I SAY! Musical comedy in 2 acts by Sydney Blow and Douglas Hoare based on their play of the same name and its original *Une nuit de noces* by Henri Kéroul and Albert Barré. Lyrics by Harry B Smith. Music by Jerome Kern. Casino Theater, New York, 30 October 1913.

Kéroul and Barré's play *Une nuit de noces* (Théâtre des Folies-Dramatiques, 2 February 1904) was enjoying a fine London run which would eventually total no fewer than 288 performances in Blow and Hoare's adaptation at the Criterion Theatre (28 May 1913) when those adapters engaged to musicalize the piece for the Shuberts. Jerome Kern was given the job of providing the music, and Cecil Cunningham was cast as the actress Sidonie de Mornay whose naughty maid (Clara Palmer) lets her flat to a pair of newlyweds (Charles Meakins, Alice Yorke) only to have her mistress return unexpectedly and to discover the bridegroom is her old boyfriend. Joseph Herbert was cast as the bride's father.

Kern provided some catchy numbers, notably the unusual, loping love duo 'Alone at Last' and the hammering dance-song 'Katy-Did', and *Oh, I Say!* opened at the Harmanus Bleecker Hall in Albany and then at Broadway's Casino Theater whilst the play ran on in London. It did not succeed. It closed after 68 performances and was put out on the road under the more alluring title of *Their Wedding Night.*

However, five years later the authors took up their text again, threw out the score, replaced it with some songs by the newly popular Phil Braham, then Britain's most adept practitioner of the new dance-time style of music, and had it produced in London by Gerald Kirby and John Wyndham under the title *Telling the Tale* (Ambassadors Theatre 31 August 1918). Marie Blanche played Sidonie, Lucienne Dervyle had the most successful song about 'Rin Tin Tin and Ninette', and the production was filled with wartime references and patriotic bits and pieces. It ran 90 performances before being taken into the country by a touring company which had agreed to stop touring the non-musical version of the show before *Telling the Tale* opened in exchange for the rights.

OH, KAY! Musical comedy in 2 acts by Guy Bolton and P G Wodehouse. Lyrics by Ira Gershwin. Additional lyrics by Howard Dietz. Music by George Gershwin. Imperial Theater, New York, 8 November 1926.

Although the play in question had been around for nearly a quarter of a century, and French comedies – credited and uncredited – had been the raw material for Broadway libretti for some two decades, the 1926-7 season saw the announcement and production of two musical comedies based on Maurice Hennequin and Pierre Veber's hit French comedy *La Présidente* (Théâtre des Bouffes-Parisiens 12 September 1902). One of the two musicals was called *Oh, Please!*, was produced by Charles Dillingham, and starred British revue star Beatrice Lillie, the other was called *Cheerio!*, was produced by Aarons and Freedley, and starred British revue star Gertrude Lawrence. Both had fine credits: *Oh, Please!* was the work of Anne Caldwell, and *No, No, Nanette*'s Otto Harbach and composer Vincent Youmans; *Cheerio!* was written by Bolton, Wodehouse and the Gershwin brothers.

Cheerio! opened at Philadelphia on 18 October, whilst *Oh, Please!*, already into rewrites, pitched camp at the Forrest Theater in the same city. If the battle of the *Présidentes* was on, it was soon looking like a pretty one-sided battle, for the unready *Oh, Please!* suffered a series of postponements and by the time it opened on 19 November, *Cheerio!*, with its title switched now to *Oh, Kay!* was already out of Philadelphia and on Broadway. The show had, by now, given up saying that it was based on *La Présidente* and, indeed, their resemblance between the two pieces was no longer precisely startling.

Whilst Jimmy Winter (Oscar Shaw) is away, a bunch of rum-runners have been using his Long Island home as a depôt. The chief criminals are a tax-paupered aristocratic British pair, the Duke of Durham (Gerald Oliver Smith) and his sister Lady Kay (Miss Lawrence), who are being assisted by a couple of local bootleggers, Shorty McKee (Victor Moore) and Larry Potter (Harland Dixon). When Jimmy returns, he brings a bride, the acidulous Judge's daughter, Constance (Sascha Beaumont). But Constance is not around for long, for there has been a legal hitch in the marriage and, of course, whilst she is chastely spending the night in an hotel prefatory to being properly re-married the next day, rum-running Lady Kay blunders into Jimmy's now-occupied bedroom. By the time Kay has impersonated Mrs Winter and Jane, the maid, and Shorty has done service as both a butler and a revenue officer, and the plot has taken a bundle of comic turns and back-turns, Kay rather than Constance ends up as the ultimate Mrs Winter. Harry T Shannon played a ubiquitous revenue officer who is not what he seems, whilst twins Marion and Madeleine Fairbanks were a couple of incidental twins who provided another running gag and a couple of numbers with Dixon (who had equally little to do with the plot) in what was otherwise a pretty tight-knit show.

The songs for *Oh, Kay!* included several that would became favourites. Miss Lawrence cooed over the thought of 'Someone to Watch Over Me' and duetted 'Maybe' and then 'Do, Do, Do' with Jimmy as a part of their pretence at being husband and wife in the presence of the ever-snooping revenue officer, whilst Dixon scored with his two pasted-in pieces, 'Clap Yo' Hands' and a description of his 'Fidgety Feet'. There was also a jolly title song, to which Howard Dietz supplied the late lyric in place of an indisposed Ira Gershwin.

Oh, Kay! proved a splendid vehicle for Miss Lawrence, Moore and Shaw, all of whom had delightful rôles in what was certainly one of the best musical-comedy libretti that Bolton and/or Wodehouse manufactured in their long careers. And Miss Lawrence and Shaw were also provided with some delicious musical moments. The public proved swift to appreciate both the performers and their material, and *Oh, Kay!* remained at Broadway's Imperial Theater for 256 performances, whilst the rather bedraggled *Oh, Please!* came and went in 75 nights.

The following year the producers tied up with London's Musical Plays Ltd and exported their show and its star to Britain. Harold French (Jimmy), John Kirby (Shorty), Eric Coxon (Larry) and Claude Hulbert (Duke) supported Miss Lawrence with rather less starpower than Moore and Shaw had done, and *Oh, Kay!* was rewarded with a good 214 performances in the West End, before going on the road in two companies in 1928–9 as part of a rush of musical-comedy productions which included two *Hit the Deck*s, three *So This is Love*s, two *No, No, Nanette*s, two *Lady Luck*s, a *Mercenary Mary*, an *Oh, Letty!*, a *Good News*, a *Girl Friend*, a *Tip-Toes* and a bundle of others. In the same season, First National films put out a silent film version of the plot, with Colleen Moore, Lawrence Gray, Alan Hale and Ford Sterling featured.

Although *Oh, Kay!* apparently went no further (Australia took *Queen High*, *Castles in the Air*, *Katja the Dancer*, *The Desert Song*, *Hit the Deck* and *Rio Rita* from the Broadway season's crop, but not *Oh, Kay!*), it remained a favourite in both America and Britain in the years that followed, winning regular regional productions and establishing itself, behind *No, No, Nanette*, as one of the flagbearers of 1920s musical comedy to theatre-goers of later decades. It was also mounted for a number of more metropolitan revivals, in a series of altered versions, beginning with a 1960 mounting at off-Broadway's East 74th Street Theater in 1960 (19 April). Marti Stevens (Kay), Bernie West (Shorty) and David Daniels (Jimmy) featured in a version for which Wodehouse reorganized the score, relyricking two numbers, adding two from Gershwin's early *Primrose* with fresh words attached, and others from Gershwin's film score *Damsel in Distress* and *Lady, Be Good!*. The revival played 89 performances. A 1978 revival, mounted in Toronto (Royal Alexandra Theater 20 July, ad Thomas Meehan), ended its Broadway-bound life in Washington.

A lightweight London revival played 228 times in the specially receptive surroundings of the Westminster Theater in 1974 (7 March), but another production mounted at the Chichester Festival Theatre (17 May 1984, ad Ned Sherrin, Tony Geiss), with a cast headed by Geoffrey Hutchings, Michael Siberry and Jane Carr, did not make the intended move to London. More than 60 years after Moore and Lawrence's triumph, a version of *Oh, Kay!* did return to Broadway, when David Merrick transferred an updated production (ad James Racheff, Dan Siretta) with a racially limited cast from Connecticut's Goodspeed Opera House to New York's Richard Rodgers Theater (25 October 1990). It closed after 77 performances, and an attempt at a return (2 April Lunt-Fontanne Theater) shuttered after 16 previews.

UK: His Majesty's Theatre 21 September 1927; Film: First National 1928
Recordings: original London cast (Smithsonian), off-Broadway revival cast (20th Fox/DRG), studio cast (Columbia) etc

OH, LADY! LADY!! Musical comedy in 2 acts by Guy Bolton and P G Wodehouse. Music by Jerome Kern. Princess Theater, New York, 1 February 1918.

Built to follow the same team's successful *Oh, Boy!* into the small Princess Theater, *Oh, Lady! Lady!!* (the title was a minstrel catchline which had characteristically little to do with anything) did not come up to its predecessor in anything but its number of exclamation points. After the brightly knit vaudeville-libretti of *Nobody Home* and *Oh, Boy!*, and the ingenuous good cheer of the play-based *Very Good Eddie* and *Leave it to Jane*, the new show plunged back into stage cliché with its tale of stolen jewels and temporarily broken romances. Rich Mollie (Vivienne Segal) is going to wed Willoughby Farringdon (Carol Randall) when Fanny (Florence Shirley), the girlfriend of his valet, Spike (Edward Abeles), steals the family jewels. Mollie's mum suspects Bill – whose old girlfriend (Carroll McComas) has also come on the scene – and she is keen to call the wedding off, but the valet steals the jewels back and everything is all right. Bride and groom shared the most attractive number in Kern's made-for-dancing score, a catchily scooping 2/4 duo, 'Not Yet', remade from a number previously interpolated into the out-of-town flop version of the German hit *Polnische Wirtschaft*. However, the number which eventually proved the most durable, Miss Segal's song in praise of her 'Bill', was relegated to a moment in the first-act finale on the road to town and had to wait another decade to become a favourite.

Oh, Lady! Lady!! took its time coming to town, arrived in well worked-in condition, and was well received, but its run of 219 performances in its tiny house was much less than was expected of it. Indeed, from a producer's point of view, it was a disappointment all round, for it toured unproductively and failed to win any major overseas productions beyond a season for J C Williamson Ltd in Australia. There, Dorothy Brunton, who somehow managed to find the opportunity to sing 'My Mammy' during the course of the evening, was featured above the title, with Alfred Frith and Edith Drayson supporting her for just five weeks in Melbourne and another under-par run in Sydney.

Australia: Her Majesty's Theatre, Melbourne 11 June 1921

Plate 197. **Oh! Oh! Delphine:** *Victor Jolibeau (Scott Welsh) and the ladies of the chorus.*

OH! OH! DELPHINE Musical comedy in 2 acts by C M S McLellan based on *La Grimpette* by Georges Berr and Marcel Guillemaud. Knickerbocker Theater, New York, 30 September 1912.

McLellan and Caryll had scored a grand international success with their adaptation of Berr and Guillemaud's 1907 Parisian comedy *Le Satyre* as *The Pink Lady*, and they decided to follow it with another musical based on an earlier work by the same authors, *La Grimpette* (Palais-Royal, 7 February 1906).

The plot of the show was a wife-swapping one, in which Victor Jolibeau (Scott Welsh) and his estranged wife Delphine (Grace Edmond) agree to change partners with Alphonse Bouchotte (Frank McIntyre) and his wife Simone (Stella Hoban). A Persian lady of some charms called Bimboula (Octavia Broske) was also mixed up in the swappings. However, one of those rich uncles (George A Beane) who hold power over the life and love-life of their juniors through their wallets and wills turns up and propriety has, at least, to seem to be restored. But when the two pairs get temporarily back in their old combinations they find they like it and the swap is called off. The action was set at the Hotel Beaurivage in the naval port of Brest, allowing some dashing uniforms to sweep by, and the title,

unlike most of the *Oh!* titles which littered the theatre of the time, actually had a point to it. One of the prominent characters of the piece (it was even the poster for the show) was Delphine's pet parrot, whose warning cry 'Oh! Oh! Delphine' perforated the action at the slightest hint of anything feather-raising.

Caryll supplied another delightful score, topped by a particularly bubbly title duo for Delphine and Bouchotte, assisted by the chorus and the parrot, Bouchotte's comical complaint 'Everything's at Home Except Your Wife', the husband-and-wife waltz duet 'Can We Forget?', a concerted 'Poor Bouchotte' and a broadly gliding 'The Venus Waltz' for Jolibeau and Bimboula, the last two of which would have seemed even finer had they resembled *The Pink Lady*'s 'Donny Did' and 'Beautiful Lady' just a little less clearly.

Klaw and Erlanger's Broadway production was enthusiastically received ('hit the bull's eye again') and if it ran a little less long than its predecessor (258 performances) that was perhaps partly because it came along second, and partly because it produced no new star from its ranks as *The Pink Lady* had done with Hazel Dawn. It was, in any case, the best run put up by any new show of its season. The following year Klaw and Erlanger put the show on the road prefatory to a return season on Broadway, whilst Robert Courtneidge produced a British *Oh! Oh! Delphine* in London with a cast headed by Harry Welchman (Jolibeau), Iris Hoey (Delphine), Walter Passmore (Bouchotte), Nan Stuart (Simone) and veteran Courtice Pounds as Colonel Pomponnet. Its subject matter caused a little indignant stir in London, and cries of 'censor' were heard on the first night, but the show lived up to its US reputation with an 174-performance run in the West End before two companies took it on the road.

It was a few years before *Oh! Oh! Delphine* reached Australia, and when it did it seemed to have missed its moment. Reginald Roberts (Jolibeau), Phil Smith (Bouchotte), Gladys Moncrieff (Delphine), Olive Goodwin (Simone) and Florence Young (Bimboula) headed the J C Williamson Ltd company which played four weeks in Melbourne and six in Sydney – a regular run, but nothing exciting.

Coming on the heels of *The Pink Lady, Oh! Oh! Delphine* and the success which it won confirmed the coming of the more textually substantial musical comedy of the *Die geschiedene Frau* type to the Broadway stage. It was a trend that would soon find a following, particularly in less oversized theatres of the Princess Theater type, where genuine comic plots and dialogue and lyrics which occasionally needed to be heard could be displayed.

UK: Shaftesbury Theatre 18 February 1913; Australia: Her Majesty's Theatre, Melbourne 7 September 1918

O'HORGAN, Tom   (b Chicago, 3 May 1926).

The director of shows for the off-Broadway Café La Mama Theatre Group and Stage 73, O'Horgan came into the limelight with his direction of the original production of *Hair* (1968) at the New York Shakespeare Festival. He subsequently introduced a second hit when he provided the highly coloured original production of *Jesus Christ Superstar* (1971) on Broadway, and he also directed Canada/France's attempt to follow in the *Hair* trail with the futuristic teeny-musical *Starmania* (1979).

O'Horgan directed several other musicals including Broadway's shortlived *Dude* (1972) and a number of off- and off-off-Broadway and regional pieces, both dramatic and musical.

He also put his hand to writing, composing and arranging music for several plays at La Mama, and he had a hand in the creation of several shows, including *Lenny*, Julian Barry's 1971 play on the life and works of Lenny Bruce (incidental music), and a 1989 musical about Senator Joseph McCarthy, produced by Adela Holzer, which closed after three previews.

1971 **Inner City** (Helen Miller/w Eve Merriam) Ethel Barrymore Theater 19 December
1989 **Senator Joe** (Perry Arthur Kroeger) Neil Simon Theater 5 January

OH! PAPA...   Opérette in 3 acts by André Barde. Music by Maurice Yvain. Théâtre des Nouveautés, Paris, 2 February 1933.

By the time they wrote *Oh! Papa...* in 1933, Maurice Yvain and André Barde, two of the most outstanding contributors to the jazz-age musical-comedy genre that had been the joy of the French 1920s, were approaching the end of their work together, before the composer set out to

follow newer and more expansive fashions in the musical theatre. Benoît-Léon Deutsch's production of this, their second-last piece as a partnership, ensured that they added one more full-sized hit to their already bulging records.

Nane (Jacqueline Francell) was a happy little poule with an almost-permanent sugar daddy (Carol) until the day that sugar daddy presented her with a lovely diamond, a big cheque, told her he had just got married, and goodbye. Modern young girls with their forward know-how are spoiling the market for the professional mistress these days, so Nane decides to change profession and become a 'modern young girl' instead of a 'mistress'. She frocks up, and sets off for the soci l setting of Bandol with her pal Julia (Suzanne Dehelly) pretending to be her maid and Godin (Boucot), the pianist from their dance-bar, masquerading as her industrialist papa. Nane plays her part so well that she outclasses Monique, the real industrialist's daughter (Davia), and attracts an eligible young man (Germain Champell). Of course, her old lover, Thibaudet, is there, too, with his new little wife, Danièle (Christiane Néré), and Danièle just happens to be Nane's young man's sister. But, in the third-act finale, Godin resigns his position as 'papa'...

Yvain's score was made up of the same delicious mix of sexy ballads, tongue-in-cheek romance and blatant comedy that his earlier shows had established. Boucot demonstrated his versatility as 'L'Homme orchestre', unblushingly shrugged off his tiny stature in 'Je suis petit', and told a woeful tale of mistimed love in 'Contradictions', soubrette Davia led a physical jerks number in bathing suits, mused on the values of a mature husband and declared that she was who she was ('Comme je suis'), while Mlle Dehelly provided the comedy with two music-hally numbers, 'Avec un bruit sec' and the tale of a ladies' wrestling match ('Qu'est-ce que m'a mis Mimi'). Nane and her young man waltzed sensuously to 'Rien qu'en se frôlant' and Robert Darthez sang of the useful properties of 'Le Gigolo', whilst Danièle built up a bluesy description of her 'Nuit de noces' and the orgasm that never came and joined Nane in a duo describing how to marry a man first and change his ways thereafter ('Tambour battant'). And alongside this battery of happy songs, Yvain provided some concerted finales and also a magnificent quintet ('Allons aux eaux').

The show ran through five months in Paris, and was swiftly carried off to the provinces and to Hungary (ad Adorján Stella, Imre Harmath) – the country which had shown itself most apt to appreciate France's knuckly jazz-age musicals – but, in spite of the general worldwide famine in musical theatre at the time, it went no further beyond French frontiers. Within them, however, it kept alive for some time, and it returned to Paris and the Théâtre de la République for a fresh season in 1950.

Hungary: Andrássy-uti Színház 6 January 1934

OKLAHOMA!   Musical play in 2 acts by Oscar Hammerstein II based on *Green Grow the Lilacs* by Lynn Riggs. Music by Richard Rodgers. St James Theater, New York, 31 March 1943.

Oklahoma! is one of those shows which – like *The Shop Girl* or *Orphée aux enfers* or even *The Beggar's Opera* – has, over the years since its production, become laden down with the responsibility of being labelled a 'landmark'. Like

Plate 198. **Oklahoma!**: *John Diedrich (Curley) describes to Christina Matthews (Laurey) the joys of a surrey with a fringe on the top.*

all landmarks, real or the product of a publicist's imaginings, it has became endowed with all sorts of significances, that dangerous word 'first' has been waved around a whole lot (including by some folk who ought to know better), and picked up on by the repeaters of easy phrases. But that's how a lot of theatrical 'history' (with the help of the publicists) gets made.

Oklahoma! was a first. It was the first Broadway musical which the celebrated team of composer Richard Rodgers and librettist and lyricist Oscar Hammerstein II wrote together. And that is quite enough of a landmark to be going on with. It should, in the course of things, have been a Rodgers and Hart show, for Rodgers had worked on every single one of his nearly 30 stage shows up to the time of *Oklahoma!* with his partner of 20 years and more, Lorenz Hart. However, Hart's increasing unreliability in both his private and professional lives had meant that Rodgers had seriously had to consider a new alliance, and when the Theatre Guild approached him with the proposal to turn their play *Green Grow the Lilacs* into a musical, Rodgers asked Hammerstein, a friend and colleague from his earliest days, to work with him on the project.

Green Grow the Lilacs was an unpretentious, countrified tale of romance, and Rodgers and Hammerstein kept that same tone in their musical version, a musical version that was built solidly on the classic tenets and personnel of the romantic musical theatre: one pair of strong-singing juvenile lovers, one pair of soubrets, one low (preferably accented) comic, one villain, and a tale which separated the lovers at the half-way mark, before getting them together for the Act II finale.

Laurey Williams (Joan Roberts) is keen on cowhand Curly (Alfred Drake) and is counting on him asking her to the box social at the Skidmore place, but a girl has her pride and she's not going to let him know she's keen and counting. Unfortunately, she plays her cards wrong, loses her temper, and ends up spitedly accepting the offer of the surly Jud Fry (Howard Da Silva) instead. Even though Laurey is quickly aware that she's been foolish, Jud holds to the girl's promise, and Curly drives Laurey's Aunt Eller (Betty Garde) to the dance in the buggy he'd hired for the occasion. The time comes where the lads bid for the girls' picnic hampers to get themselves a partner for the night, and when it is Laurey's turn Curly outbids Jud for the now-frightened girl's hand. But not before he's had to hock his horse, his saddle and his gun to raise the cash. Laurey has learned her lesson now, and when Curly proposes to her she is happy to accept. A few weeks later they are wed, but on the wedding night Jud Fry turns up for his revenge. A fight ensues, Curly throws Jud, and the villain falls on the knife he had been ready to use on his rival. Curly is technically guilty of killing Jud, but Aunt Eller is equal to the occasion. The local justices are all here for the festivities, so they can just declare the boy innocent right away and let him get on with his married life and the finale.

The tiny, fresh tale of country romance was counterpointed with its parallel soubret story – the off-and-on affair between cowboy Will Parker (Lee Dixon) and the bouncing, unresisting Ado Annie Carnes (Celeste Holm). Annie's father has promised the boy he can wed Annie when he's got $50 but, unfortunately, each time Will manages to earn the $50 he goes right on and spends it and he has to start again. And Annie isn't much good at waiting. As soon as Will is out of sight, she's off necking with the Jewish peddler, Ali Hakim (Joseph Buloff). Ali doesn't have weddings in mind, but Pop Carnes (Ralph Riggs) does. When Will goes mad bidding for Annie's hamper at the social, Ali has to spend all his profits outbidding him just so that Will will still have his $50 and Annie, and Ali won't have to wed her himself.

Both sides of the show were equipped with a barrel of winning songs. At the opening of the piece, Curly hailed the country sunrise with the simple, optimistic 'Oh What a Beautiful Mornin'', then described the buggy he's hired for the ball to the trotting rhythms of 'The Surrey with the Fringe on Top' and duetted, fencingly, with Laurey on the things they oughtn't to do otherwise 'People Will Say We're in Love'. She pouted and pretended not to care as she declared 'Many a New Day' would dawn before she'd worry over a boy, and then dreamed longingly of him, under the effect of too deep a sniff of sal volatile, to the strains of 'Out of My Dreams'. All these pieces came in the first act: when the fun and the action began in Act II, there was no more time for sentimental songs, and Curly's contribution to the later stages of the show came in leading the driving paean to 'Oklahoma!' – the brand new state in which the show was set, the future of which was paralleled with that of the newly-weds. Amongst the comical pieces, Annie squawked out her excuses for congenital infidelity in 'I Cain't Say No!', Will poured out a catalogue of the horrors of great big 'Kansas City' and demanded of Annie 'All er Nuthin'', whilst Curly painted a picture of Jud's funeral ('Pore Jud is Daid') as part of a curious conversation with his rival as he confronts him in the smokehouse where he lodges. The villain had a moody soliloquy

('Lonely Room') and there were some lively moments for the chorus, notably a dancing opening to the second act which centred on the rivalries between 'The Farmer and the Cowman'.

The Theatre Guild's production of *Oklahoma!* was a huge success. Once again wartime audiences flocked to see a native, good-old-days musical as they had been doing in wartime all over the world ever since there had been wars and musicals to flock to. But this all-American romantic operetta was one with an undeniable freshness to it, and it was hard to credit that its book and lyrics came from the same pen as the last American romantic operetta seen on Broadway, the Hammerstein/Romberg *Sunny River* with its over-used tale of the self-sacrificing café singer and the high-born youth. Laurey Williams certainly wasn't going to conclude *Oklahoma!* by becoming the umpteenth famous prima donna of operettic last acts.

Everything about the show was enthused over: the gay, unpretentious story with its recognizably American – if operettically idealized – setting and characters; the matching songs – so often in a vernacular that sounded almost like a real vernacular (give or take a 'rose and a glove') and neatly fitting their places in the play; Agnes de Mille's dream-sequence ballet scena; the simple opening with no chorus girls – just Aunt Eller sitting alone on stage churning butter and Curly's off-stage voice bringing his 'Oh What a Beautiful Mornin'' closer till he came swaggering on stage. Enthusiasm reigned: it was only long afterwards that enthusiasm started being expressed in 'firsts' and 'never befores', and someone somewhere picked up the deadly term 'integrated' and started proselytizing with it. Contemporary opinion was satisfied with noting that it was nice, for a change, not to have the revusical kind of low-comic plus dancing-girl-star type of show where everything stops 'for the introduction of songs and bits of funny dialogue, not to mention the complete sweeping away of the story to make way for a chorus intended to catch public fancy rather than help along the show as a whole'.

When *Oklahoma!* first arrived on Broadway it was just a vast hit, a splendid musical play, well made from top to bottom (even if Jud's revenge and death seemed just a touch tacked-on, in the 'ah-ha me proud beauty' tradition), full of entertainment – romance, comedy, song, dance, visuals – in the shapeliest of proportions. It was also, on a Broadway long starved of outstanding new works, the first really top-class romantic native musical (*Pal Joey* and *Lady in the Dark* not really fitting that bill) since the far-off days of *Show Boat*.

Oklahoma! ran at the St James Theater for 2,212 performances, becoming in the process far, far and away the longest-running musical in Broadway history – a record it held for 15 years until the coming of *My Fair Lady*. But it did more than just break a record. It gave a whole impetus to the musical theatre in America, an impetus which *Pal Joey* and *Lady in the Dark* had not – for all their qualities – given. As it sat royally in place at the St James Theater, *Oklahoma!* became the focal point for a fresh round of romantic musical plays on Broadway. Some – like *Bloomer Girl* – copied almost slavishly and were successful, others followed only in part and were also successful. For years *Oklahoma!*-style dance scenes became the sine qua non and eventually a cliché of the contemporary musical stage. Rodgers and Hammerstein themselves went on to build on

their first collaboration with a series of outstanding, colourful romantic musicals which didn't slavishly imitate their own previous work except in their tone and their quality, but *Oklahoma!* proved to be the coccyx to the backbone of the next decade and a half of Broadway operettas.

The first American touring company went out on the road little more than half a year into the run with Harry Stockwell (Curley), Evelyn Wyckoff (Laurey), Pamela Britton (Annie) and David Burns (Ali) featured, at the beginning of more than a decade of travelling the country, but it was not until the war was well and truly over that the show began to be seen in other countries. Britain came first. The Theatre Guild mounted their show at London's Theatre Royal, Drury Lane, with local firm H M Tennent Ltd managing on their behalf and a cast headed by Harold (later to be Howard) Keel (Curly), Betty Jane Watson (Laurey), Dorothea MacFarland (Annie), Walter Donahue from the American tour company (Will) and Marek Windheim (Ali). Most of London had, by now, heard of *Oklahoma!* and knew and loved its songs: pretty soon they loved the show too. The postwar musical stage in London blossomed as, within a matter of weeks, *Oklahoma!*, *Annie Get Your Gun* and *Bless the Bride* all swept into town. Enthusiasm raced as fans lined themselves up as the champions of one or other of the three great hits – but how good it was to have three such hits to champion! *Oklahoma!* ultimately had the longest run of the three (although *Annie* was housed in the biggest auditorium), even though it ran out the last of its 1,543 performances in the unloved Stoll Theatre (from 29 May 1950) after being displaced from Drury Lane by none other than Rodgers and Hammerstein's next musical: *Carousel*.

Australia did not see *Oklahoma!* until 1949, although J C Williamson Ltd had bought the show some time before. Williamson manager E N Tait was an *Annie* fan and, having purchased both shows from the Rodgers and Hammerstein office, he decided that *Annie Get Your Gun* was the better proposition. The huge success of that piece around Australia and New Zealand proved him right, but *Oklahoma!* didn't do too badly either when it came along behind nearly two years later. Robert Reeves (Curly), Carolyn Adair (Laurey) and Louise Barnhardt (Annie) headed the cast which played 231 performances in Melbourne, and seven and a half months in Sydney (Theatre Royal, 29 November 1949).

A film version was produced in 1955 which cast Gordon MacRae (Curly), Shirley Jones (Laurey), Gloria Grahame (Annie), Gene Nelson (Will), Eddie Albert (Ali), Charlotte Greenwood (Aunt Eller) and Rod Steiger (Jud) in a Fred Zinneman production of rosy cheeks and haystacks which remains the classic *Oklahoma!* for many who saw it. The score was kept largely intact, and the peremptory ending was made more dramatically satisfying by the resetting of the wedding-night high-jinks in a haystack to which Jud attempts to set fire. The film succeeded just as each and every *Oklahoma!* up to the time had done.

In the same year, *Oklahoma!* went further afield when a touring company sent out by the State Department and headed by Jack Cassidy (Curly) and the film version's Shirley Jones (Laurey) took the show to Paris and to Rome (Teatro Quattro Fontane, August 1955) but it was some time before the piece – by then a solid part of the standard repertoire in every corner of the English-language theatre

– was given foreign-language stagings. The first French version was seen in Belgium, at the Opéra Royal de Wallonie in Liège (22 December 1972), where the company has made a speciality of producing French versions of the classic works of the English-language musical stage.

Regularly played in the half-century since its first production, *Oklahoma!* had its most important round of revivals from 1979 when the piece was remounted on Broadway under the aegis of Zev Bufman and James M Nederlander (Palace Theater 13 December 1979) with Laurence Guittard (Curly), Christine Andreas (Laurey), Christine Ebersole (Annie), Harry Groener (Will) and Bruce Adler (Ali) featured and the now-revered choreography reproduced. A 301-performance run was followed by a British provincial and London mounting under the management of Cameron Mackintosh (Palace Theater 17 September 1980, 419 performances) with John Diedrich (Curly), Rosamund Shelley (Laurey), Jillian Mack (Annie), Linal Haft (Ali) and Mark White (Will) and by an especially successful Australian reproduction (Festival Theatre, Adelaide 1 May 1982) in which Diedrich teamed with Sally Butterfield, Donna Lee, Henri Szeps and Peter Bishop.

UK; Theatre Royal, Drury Lane 29 April 1947; Australia: Her Majesty's Theatre, Melbourne, 19 February 1949; Germany: Berlin 1951; France: Théâtre des Champs Élysées 20 June 1955; Film: Magna 1955

Recordings: original cast (Decca/MCA), revival cast (RCA), London revival cast (Stiff), Australian revival cast (RCA), film soundtrack (Capitol/EMI), selection in German (Ariola) etc

Literature: Wilk, M: *The Story of 'Oklahoma!'* (Grove Press, New York, 1993)

OKONKOWSKI, Georg (b Hohensalza, 11 February 1863; d Berlin, 25 March 1926).

A prolific author of plays and libretti for the German stage, Okonkowski came to the fore at the same time as composer Jean Gilbert, as the author of their long-running Posse *Polnische Wirtschaft*. Thereafter he collaborated on the writing of many of Gilbert's most successful pieces, notably his two most significant international hits of the 1910s, *Die keusche Suzanne* and *Die Kino-Königin*. In the later part of his career he also worked with Walter Bromme, and supplied the text for the manager-composer's most successful work *Mascottchen*.

Apart from his two big successes, a number of Okonkowski's other works travelled beyond Germany, *Polnische Wirtschaft* and *Die moderne Eva* being both produced in America as well as in Vienna where *Madame Serafin* (Johann Strauss-Theater, 3 Sept 1911), *Zwischen zwölf und eins* (Theater in der Josefstadt, 29 March 1914), *Das Fräulein von Amt* (Wiener Stadttheater, 1 February 1916) and *Mascottchen* (Carltheater 26 September 1924) also got a showing. Alongside *A mozitündér* (Kino-Königin), *Az ártatlan Zsuzsi* (Die keusche Suzanne), *Lengyel menyecske* (Polnische Wirtschaft) and *Ő Teréz!* (Das Fräulein von Amt), Hungary also saw versions of *Zwischen zwölf und eins* (Éjfélkor, Népopera 11 April 1914) and *Der brave Henrik* (A dérek Fridolin, Budai Színkör, 7 July 1916) and London welcomed *The Girl in the Taxi*, *The Cinema Star* and *Mam'selle Tralala*.

1897 **1842** (*Der grosse Brand in Hamburg*) (Leo Fall) Centralhallen-Theater, Hamburg 25 July

1899 **Der Brandstifter** (Fall) Ostendtheater 1 January

1899 **Der griechische Sklave** (*A Greek Slave*) German version w C M Röhr

1899 **Die Venus von der Markthalle** (Franz Wagner/w Emil Sondermann) Viktoria-Theater 4 December

1900 **Berliner Bilder** (Wagner/w Sondermann) Centraltheater 14 April

1901 **Diana im Bade** (Max Gabriel) Centralhallen-Theater, Hamburg October

1903 **Der Sonnenvogel** (Viktor Holländer/w Rudolf Schanzer) St Petersburg 22 August; Centraltheater, Berlin, April 1904

1905 **Der Strohwitwer** (Wagner/w Fritz Friedmann-Friedrich) Apollotheater, Nuremberg 27 June

1907 **Der Milliardär** (Ferdinand Gradl/w Arthur Lippschitz) Centraltheater 16 February

1908 **Doktor Klapperstorch** (Max Schmidt/Alfred Schönfeld/w Jean Kren) Thalia-Theater 28 March

1909 **Wo wohnt sie denn?** (Holländer/Schönfeld/w Kren) Thalia-Theater 12 February

1909 **Polnische Wirtschaft** (Jean Gilbert/Schönfeld/w Kurt Kraatz) Stadttheater, Cottbus 26 December; Thalia-Theater, Berlin 6 August 1910

1910 **Die keusche Susanne** (J Gilbert) Wilhelm Theater, Magdeburg 26 February; Neues Operettentheater, Berlin 6 August 1911

1910 **Madame Serafin** (Robert Winterberg/w Bruno Granichstädten) Neues Operettenhaus, Hamburg 1 September

1911 **Die Luxusweibchen** (Gabriel) Tivoli-Theater, Bremen 5 August

1911 **Königin Loanda** (Oskar Malata) Stadttheater, Chemnitz 29 October

1911 **Die moderne Eva** (J Gilbert/Schönfeld) Neues Operetten-Theater 11 November

1912 **Die elfte Muse** (J Gilbert) Operettenhaus, Hamburg 22 November

1913 **Die Kino-Königin** (revised *Die elfte Muse*) (J Gilbert/ad Julius Freund) Metropoltheater 8 March

1913 **Das Farmermädchen** (Georg Jarno) Grosses Operetten-Theater 22 March

1913 **Das Gassenmädel** (Paul Freund) Schauspielhaus, Breslau 2 May

1913 **Fräulein Tralala** (J Gilbert/w Leo Leipziger) Neues Luisen-Theater, Königsberg 15 November

1913 **Zwischen zwölf und eins** (Walter Goetze/w Max Neal, M. Ferner) Neues Operetten-Theater, Leipzig 9 February

1914 **Wenn der Frühling kommt!** (J Gilbert/Schönfeld/w Kren) Thalia-Theater 28 March

1914 **Die schöne Kubanerin** (Gabriel) Rembrandt Theater, Amsterdam 17 January

1914 **Kam'rad Männe** (J Gilbert/Schönfeld/w Kren) Thalia-Theater 3 August

1915 **Der brave Hendrik** (aka *Der brave Fridolin*) (Gabriel) Rembrandt Theater, Amsterdam 3 April

1915 **Das Fräulein von Amt** (J Gilbert/w Ernst Arnold) Theater des Westens 13 November

1916 **Die Perle der Frauen** revised *Die Luxusweibchen* Central-Theater, Magdeburg 21 May

1916 **Die stolze Thea** (Gabriel) Rembrandt Theater, Amsterdam 16 September

1917 **Der verliebte Herzog** (aka *Der verliebte Prinz*) (J Gilbert/w Hans Bachwitz) Theater des Westens 1 September

1917 **Senorita Pif-Paf** (Gabriel) Rembrandt Theater, Amsterdam 22 December

1919 **Die Schönste von allen** (J Gilbert) Centraltheater 22 March

1920 **Eine Nacht im Paradies** (Walter Bromme/w Willy Steinberg) Theater am Nollendorfplatz 30 April

1921 **Mascottchen** (Bromme/w Steinberg) Thalia-Theater 15 January

1921 **Schäm' dich Lotte** (Bromme/w Steinberg) Berliner Theater 2 September

1921 **Die Kleine aus der Hölle** (Tilmar Springfield/w Steinberg)

1922 **Madame Flirt** (Bromme/w Steinberg) Berliner Theater 15 April

1923 **Schönste der Frauen** (Bromme/w Steinberg) Metropoltheater May

1923 **Casino-Girls** (Eduard Künneke) Metropoltheater 15 September

1923 **Die blonde Geisha** (Hans Ailbout/L Czerney)

1923 **Die schöne Rivalin** (Hans Linne/w Steinberg) Theater am Nollendorfplatz 28 March

1923 **Die Tugendprinzessin** (Kurt Zorlig) Deutsches Künstlertheater ?May

1923 **Charlie** (Goetze)

1925 **Tausend süsse Beinchen** (Bromme/Steinberg) Metropoltheater 28 March

1925 **Der Stern von Assuan** (Richard Goldberger/w Ralph A Roberts) Opernhaus am Königplatz 1 July

1925 **Annemarie** (J Gilbert, Robert Gilbert/w Martin Zickel) Schillertheater 2 July

1926 **Lene, Lotte, Liese, Josefinens Tochter** (J Gilbert, R Gilbert) Thalia-Theater 14 January

1926 **Miss Amerika** (Bromme/Kurt Schwabach/w Steinberg) Berliner Theater 20 August

OLCOTT, Chauncey [OLCOTT, Chancellor John] (b Buffalo, 21 July 1860; d Monte Carlo, 18 March 1932). American tenor who turned temporarily comic, then romantic Irish, becoming the classic stage-Irish performer of his era.

Olcott began his performing career singing tenor music in minstrel shows and variety (Haverly's Minstrels, Thatcher's Minstrels, Primrose and West, Cairncross Minstrels in Philadelphia, Denman Thompson Company), and he made his first, rather stiff musical-theatre appearance only in 1886 in Teddy Solomon's *Pepita* (Pablo) alongside Lillian Russell. He later toured for two years in the play *The Old Homestead*, performing an interpolated song, but in the following years he was seen in lead tenor rôles in several Broadway productions of English works, ranging from Gilbert and Sullivan for John Duff's company (Ralph Rackstraw, Nanki Poo) to Jakobowski's *Paola* (1889, Lucien). He featured in John McCaull's productions of *Clover*, *Tar and Tartar* and Millöcker's *Die sieben Schwaben* (1890) and then, in 1891, he left for Europe to study for the operatic stage. Seasick, he got off in Britain. There he soon got himself a job playing a character tenor rôle in London's *Miss Decima* (*Miss Helyett*, Chevalier Patrick Julius O'Flannagan), then another in the burlesque *Blue-Eyed Susan* (1892, Gnatbrain), but he soon headed back to America, and landed on his feet. The American stage had recently been bereft of its favourite 'Irish' touring hero, the much-loved Scanlan, and Olcott's pudgy good looks and attractive tenor led him first to one 'Scanlan' part, touring in George Jessop's *Mavourneen*, then to a whole series of long-travelling Irish musical plays in which, although he was in no manner an Irishman, he made himself a career and a name as popular as that of his predecessor.

By 1894 Olcott was well enough established to have a first piece, *The Irish Artist*, made to measure for him, and *The Irish Artist* set the successful pattern for those to come. In a quarter of a century of indefatigable touring, he followed up in *The Minstrel of Clare* (1896, 'Olcott's Love Song', 'Love Remains the Same'), *Sweet Inniscarra* (1897, 'The Old Fashioned Mother', 'Olcott's Fly Song'), *A Romance of Athlone* (1899, 'Olcott's Lullaby', 'My Wild Irish Rose'), *Garret O'Magh* (1901, 'Paddy's Cat'), *Old Limerick Town* (1902, 'The Voice of the Violet', 'Every Little Dog Must Have His Day'), *Terence* (1904, 'My Sonny Boy', 'Tick, Tack, Toe', 'The Girl I Used to Know', 'My Own Dear Irish Queen'), *Edmund Burke* (1905, 'Your Heart Alone Must Tell', 'You Can Sail in My Boat'), *Eileen Asthore* (1906, 'For Love of Thee', 'Wearers of the Green', 'Eileen Asthore'), *O'Neill of Derry* (1907), *Ragged Robin* (1908), *Barry of Ballymore* (1910, 'Mother Machree', 'When Irish Eyes Are Smiling'), *Macushla* (1911, 'Macushla'), *The Isle o' Dreams* (1912), *Shameen Dhu* (1913), *The Heart of Paddy Whack* (1914), *Honest John O'Brien* (1916), *Once Upon a Time* (1917) and *The Voice of McConnell* (1920).

Olcott remained a favourite star of the American country circuits until he was 60 years of age, delivering annually precisely the combinations of homespun Irishy sentiment, comedy and tenorizing that were expected of him. His sometimes creaky vehicles each introduced a number of songs, and those songs produced a remarkable number of enduring hits, the most notable of which were 'When Irish Eyes Are Smiling (for which he shared writer's credit with George Graff and Ernest Ball), 'Mother Machree' (Ball/Olcott/Rida Johnson Young), and 'Macushla' (Josephine Rowe/Dermot MacMurrough).

Olcott was the subject of a Hollywood biopic, *My Wild Irish Rose* (1947) in which he was portrayed by Dennis Morgan.

Biography: Olcott, R: *A Song in His Heart* (House of Field, New York, 1939)

OLD CHELSEA Musical romance in 3 acts by Walter Ellis. Lyrics by Walter Ellis and Fred Tysh. Music by Richard Tauber. Additional numbers by Bernard Grün. Birmingham, 21 September 1942; Prince's Theatre, London, 17 February 1943.

A wartime operetta of the most florid olde-worlde kind, *Old Chelsea* was composed by and for the Austrian tenor, Richard Tauber, whose librettists for some reason cast him as a poor 18th-century British composer with an opera he longs to have produced. Australian soprano Nancy Brown played the opera singer who sings his music and falls in love with him and Carol Lynne was the little milliner who helps him through his hard days and steps in to sing the opera to triumph when the prima donna returns to her lordly lover. The light comedy was provided by young Charles Hawtrey, later to find fame in the *Carry On ...* films. The music of the piece was mostly unimpressive, but it did produce one hit in the star's big solo 'My Heart and I' to set alongside an enjoyably catty quartet ('A Little Gossip') which was part of the contribution of another expatriate European, Bernard Grün.

Originally played for three months on the road (with Tauber proving more reliable than he had in his London appearances) it was then taken to London, but it survived only 95 performances before returning to the provinces where it later found several revivals. *Old Chelsea* marked both the last West End appearance of Tauber and the first London musical production for its young producer, Bernard Delfont.

OLDHAM, Derek [OLDHAM, John Stephens] (b Accrington, 29 March 1887; d Portsmouth, 20 March 1968). Lead tenor of the D'Oyly Carte Company and a string of West End shows.

Lancashire vocalist Oldham had been a bank clerk before he made his London début as a performer in Reinhardt's one-act operetta *The Daring of Diane* (*Die süssen Grisetten*) at the Tivoli. He had his first regular West End part when he appeared in the title-rôle of a revival of *The Chocolate Soldier* in 1914 and, after the First World War, he became principal tenor with the D'Oyly Carte Opera Company for three years. He later played leading rôles in *Whirled into Happiness* (*Der Tanz ins Glück*) and a revival of *The Merry Widow* (Camille), and then starred in three major imported successes in the West End: opposite Evelyn Laye as René in Fall's *Madame Pompadour*, as Jim Kenyon to the Rose Marie of Edith Day in *Rose Marie* and in the title-rôle of *The Vagabond King*.

Oldham subsequently returned on several occasions to the D'Oyly Carte company, during which time he sang the tenor rôles in the first comprehensive recordings of the Gilbert and Sullivan repertoire, interleaving these periods with further musical theatre rôles – *Blue Eyes*, *The Song of the Drum*, *The Merry Widow* revival, *The Desert Song* tour, *Lilac Time*, *The Dancing City* (t/o from Franco Foresta as Archduke Franz), *White Horse Inn* revival, *Monsieur Beaucaire* tour, *A Waltz Dream* tour, *I Call it Love* – and some film appearances. At the age of 53, he played Dick Warrington in the British première of *Naughty Marietta* (tour), and he continued performing into the 1950s.

Oldham was married to soprano Winnie Melville who appeared alongside him in *Whirled into Happiness* (t/o Florrie), and who starred in London's *The Student Prince* (Kathie), *Princess Charming* (Elaine) and, opposite Oldham, *The Vagabond King* (Katharine) and played leading soprano rôles with the D'Oyly Carte company.

OLIAS, Lothar (b Königsberg, 23 December 1913).

Prussian-born Olias studied in Berlin, and worked as a musician and as a music publisher, before, in the years after the war, basing himself in Hamburg. There he began to supply music first for cabaret and revue, and then for the first of the many films which would make up the large part of his work. He made his first appearance as a musical-comedy composer when he wrote the score for the sailory *Heimweh nach St Pauli*, produced in Hamburg in 1954 with singing star Freddy Quinn top-billed in the rôle apparently based on himself. The show was later revised with considerable success for Berlin, played in Vienna, and ultimately filmed. Another piece, the spoof Western *Prairie-Saloon*, originally written for Hamburg, was also enlarged and rearranged for a successful Berlin production (Berliner Theater 10 November 1961) and later staged on the other side of the Wall (Erfurt 30 September 1973). In 1965 Olias provided the score for a piece loosely based on some events from Brandon Thomas's *Charley's Aunt*, and in 1967 wrote the songs for a crook musical, set in modern New York, *Millionen für Penny* (Penny being the heroine, and not a coin), which subsequently also played in Eastern Germany (Plauen, 18 May 1968).

1954 **Heimweh nach St Pauli** (Rothenburg) Operettenhaus, Hamburg 3 February (revised version Operettenhaus, Hamburg 18 October 1962)

1958 **Prairie-Saloon** (Heinz Wunderlich, Kurt Schwabach) Junges Theater, Hamburg 31 December

1965 **Charley's neue Tante** (Gustav Kampendonk) Hamburg

1967 **Millionen für Penny** (Max Colpet) Theater im Gärtnerplatz, Munich 5 February

1971 **Der Geldschrank steht im Fenster** (*Eine feine Familie*) (Colpet, Wunderlich) Niedert Theater, Bremen 6 February

OLIVER! Musical in 2 acts by Lionel Bart founded on *Oliver Twist* by Charles Dickens. New Theatre, London, 30 June 1960.

When Lionel Bart first thought of making a musical out of Charles Dickens's *Oliver Twist* he had not actually read the book, and his initial idea was that it would make a good vehicle for his rock-and-rolling friend Tommy Steele. However, the misconception was set right and, without trying to cram in every bit of the original tale, Bart fashioned a libretto out of the essentials of Dickens's narrative, following the life of little Oliver (Keith Hamshere) through his expulsion from the workhouse by the beadle (Paul Whitsun-Jones) for asking for a second helping of gruel, his hateful apprenticeship to the undertaking Sowerberrys (Barry Humphries, Sonia Fraser), his flight to London, his encounter with the Artful Dodger (Martin Horsey) and his induction into the gang of thieves run by the grim Fagin (Ron Moody) up to his ultimate discovery of his wealthy birth and comfortable family. The outline of the original story was well-adhered-to, although, given the age of the leading character, it was necessary, for female and romantic interest, to build up the prominence of the brutish love affair between the East End villain, Bill Sikes (Danny Sewell) and the kind-hearted Nancy (Georgia Brown). Sikes's murder of Nancy and his own death were included in the text in all their dark drama, but in general the colours of Dickens's tale were jollified up. *Oliver!* presented a patter-song Fagin who was a musical-comedy 'lovable' villain, on the one hand, and a set of sweet stage children doing a jolly cockney knees-up on the other.

The simple-sounding songs which Bart supplied to illustrate *Oliver!* were a standard mixture of sentimental and comic, lively and pensive, but they proved to be songs that were made of the stuff that catches and the stuff that endures. The little boy, wondering in his frail soprano 'Where is Love?' in words of touching, unashamed simplicity; the ill-treated Nancy, sticking doggedly by the man she knows may very well kill her, and pouring out her reason in 'As Long as He Needs Me'; the beadle's plump paramour simperingly threatening 'I Shall Scream' as she sits on his over-padded knee; and the Artful Dodger's walloping 'Consider Yourself (at home)' were amongst the musical highspots of a show in which almost every song was a winner.

Bart touted his show around town until producer Donald Albery took it on. Peter Coe and Sean Kenny, director and designer of Bart's previous show, *Lock Up Your Daughters*, were engaged to fulfil the same functions on this one, and the original idea of a production at East London's Theatre Royal, Stratford East, was abandoned when Kenny produced his designs: a revolving complex of multi-purpose dark platforms, stairs and arches which were to win him excited praise and to influence theatre design in Britain for a number of years. *Oliver!* opened instead at Wimbledon, prior to the West End's New Theatre. If there were problems in the suburb, however,

Plate 199. *Ron Moody as Fagin in London's* **Oliver!**.

they were all ironed out before the in-town opening and *Oliver!* had a triumphant first night in its West End home.

The show remained at the New Theatre for six years and 2,618 performances, during which time it made its first appearance in Holland, Sweden, Australia, South Africa and Israel, as well as on Broadway where it arrived, after seasons in both Los Angeles and Toronto, with several of the original London cast, including Miss Brown, featured alongside British juveniles as Oliver (Bruce Prochnik) and the Dodger (David Jones, later to be known as a Monkee) and Clive Revill as Fagin. Once again, the show opened triumphantly, proved the hit of the 1962/3 season and settled in for a 774-performance run which eclipsed the totals established by *The Boy Friend*, *Florodora* and *Erminie* and made it the longest-running British musical to have been seen on Broadway up to that time.

In Australia it found equivalent success. Mounted by J C Williamson Ltd in Melbourne with Johnny Lockwood (Fagin), Sheila Bradley (Nancy), Richard Watson (Bumble), John Maxim (Sikes) and former star of operetta and silent-screen, Nancy Brown, as Mrs Bumble, it played there for four and a half months, then for four further months in Sydney (Theatre Royal, 17 February 1962), returning for a second showing in 1966 (Her Majesty's, Melbourne 22 July, Theatre Royal, Sydney, 26 August).

In Britain, the show went on the road in 1965 with Richard Easton and Marti Webb starred and, just seven months after the original New Theatre production had closed, Miss Webb paired with Barry Humphries – promoted now from Sowerberry to Fagin – in a quick revival at the Piccadilly Theatre which added another 331 performances to the show's remarkable total.

In 1968, whilst *Oliver!* continued its life as one of the most popular new musicals of the postwar years, a film version was made, with Moody repeating his original rôle alongside Shani Wallis (Nancy), Mark Lester (Oliver), Jack Wild (Dodger), Oliver Reed (Sikes), Leonard Rossiter (Sowerberry) and Harry Secombe (Bumble), and, within a decade, it was back in the West End again. The 1977 revival, which toured for five months under the banner of Cameron Mackintosh before settling into its old home at the Albery (ex-New) Theatre, continued the show's impeccable record of success. With a cast initially headed by Roy Hudd as an outstanding Fagin and Gillian Burns (Nancy), it ran for nearly three years (1,139 performances), taking the show past its 4,000th metropolitan performance and culling appreciable royalties for the property company to which Bart, in a time of need, had sold out his interest in the show.

Mackintosh put *Oliver!* back on the road again following its London run, bringing it back for a brief Christmas season in 1983–4. Moody repeated his original rôle on the original Kenny settings under the distracted direction of original director Coe, and all three showed the signs of having been dragged out once too often. The feeling was confirmed when all three were used on a Broadway repeat *Oliver!* (29 April 1984) which also featured Patti LuPone (Nancy) and Braden Danner (Oliver) for a sad handful of performances. Australia, which was intended to receive the production, did not, when down-under unions insisted on remaking all the now-famous scenery and originally taken-from-stock but faithfully-reproduced-thereafter costumes.

These failures, however, did not dim the popularity of the piece which continued to be widely played on English-language stages. In the 1980s, as the English-language musical began to make inroads into Europe and as Mackintosh, who had now virtually adopted *Oliver!*, became established as internationally the most successful and wide-reaching producer of musicals, it also made its way into Continental houses. A German-language version (ad Wilfried Steiner) was first produced at Salzburg in 1985, and continues to win productions in central Europe, and Hungary was introduced to a local language version the following year (ad Lia Bassa, György Dénes) as *Oliver!* began a belated invasion of the European continent.

In 1990 Britain's National Youth Theatre brought the piece back to London once more and a large cash gift from Mackintosh to the Royal National Theatre for the production of musicals has apparently led to plans for *Oliver!* to be the first modern British musical (following a number of imported ones) to play at the country's most subsidized theatre.

Australia: Her Majesty's Theatre, Melbourne 23 September 1961; USA: Imperial Theater 6 January 1963; Austria: Landestheater, Salzburg 8 January 1985; Germany: Theater am Gärtnerplatz, Munich 29 May 1986; Hungary: Arany János Színház 27 November 1986

Recordings: original cast (RCA), Broadway cast (RCA), Israeli cast (CBS), Dutch cast (Philips), South African cast (RCA), Danish cast (Radius), Hungarian version (Qualiton), studio casts (Capitol, World Records, TER etc), film soundtrack (RCA) etc

ON A CLEAR DAY YOU CAN SEE FOREVER
Musical in 2 acts by Alan Jay Lerner. Music by Burton Lane. Mark Hellinger Theater, New York, 17 October 1965.

Originally intended, following the end of the Lerner/Loewe partnership, to be a collaboration between the author and Richard Rodgers entitled *I Picked a Daisy*, the retitled *On a Clear Day You Can See Forever* was rescheduled with Burton Lane as composer when the original pair found themselves incompatible. Lerner's libretto provided a novel twist on the familiar dream-sequence and through-the-generations conventions of the musical theatre. Its heroine, Daisy (Barbara Harris) suffers from extrasensory perception to a degree that arouses the fascinated attention of her psychiatric lecturer, Mark Bruckner (John Cullum, replacing the try-out's Louis Jourdan). When she agrees to be a subject for his research, she reaches back into an earlier life and brings out an alter ego called Melinda, an 18th-century damsel caught up in the gay-dog life of London and with the raffish Sir Edward Moncrieff (Clifford David). As they work, Daisy's personal interest in Mark grows, and at the same time he takes a shine to Melinda, but when she discovers that she is becoming a cause célèbre in the psychiatric world Daisy runs away. By the final curtain, however, she is back to cement her relationship with Mark. Lane's score brought up two numbers which had a considerable life outside the show, Cullum's comforting explanation of Daisy's extraordinary powers in the title-song, and his own effort at extra-sensory power as, in the final scene, he wills the vanished girl to 'Come Back to Me'.

Lerner's production of *On a Clear Day* ran for 280 performances and toured briefly, with John Raitt, with Howard Keel and with revised libretto and song list, before being adapted for a film version, produced again by its author (w Howard W Koch) who had rewritten his stage libretto to give Melinda (Barbra Streisand) multiple reincarnations and no final button with Marc (sic, because it was the Gallic Yves Montand). Miss Streisand had two new numbers to add to two of her own and two of other people's from the stage show, whilst Montand sang the three songs from his stage rôle and no one else sang anything.

Film: Paramount 1970
Recordings: original cast (RCA Victor), film soundtrack (Columbia)

ONCE UPON A MATTRESS Musical comedy in 2 acts by Jay Thompson, Marshall Barer and Dean Fuller based on *The Princess and the Pea*. Lyrics by Marshall Barer. Music by Mary Rodgers. Phoenix Theater, New York, 11 May 1959.

A burlesque fairytale of a kind, and on a scale, rarely written since the turn of the century, *Once Upon a Mattress* began its life as a rather smaller Barer–Thompson–Rodgers collaboration produced at the Tamiment resort in Pennsylvania in August of 1958. Fuller joined the team to aid in the expansion which was undertaken before *Once Upon a Mattress* was brought to New York's Phoenix Theater, under the management of Edward Hambleton, Norris Houghton and the show's designers, William and Jean Eckhart, nine months later.

This retelling of the tale of the Princess and the Pea introduced Carol Burnett as the Princess Winnifred (pet name not Winnie, but Fred), a lusty, booming nymphet from the outer swamps, who swims the moat to get to her appointment with the daunting Queen Aggravaine (Jane White) to audition for the post of wife to the royal lady's progeny, Dauntless (Joe Bova). No one else in court is allowed to wed till the prince does, so all, particularly the longing Lady Larken (Anne Jones) and her beau Sir Harry (Allen Case), are on Fred's side. When the Queen's secret test – the famous pea under the mattresses – is sussed out by the court minstrel (Harry Snow) and Jester (Matt Mattox), they provide a little extra help to make sure that Winnifred passes, and all is prepared for a happy ending in which Dauntless gets his bride and the once mute King Sextimus (Jack Gilford) is restored to connubial and royal power.

Miss Rogers's score caught the mood of burlesque neatly as Miss Burnett explained how 'Shy' she was, yodelled out a description of 'The Swamps of Home' and mused voluminously over her 'Happily Ever After', and the prevented pair of Larken and Harry promised themselves a married life 'In a Little While'. The Jester wooed the Queen's secret from the Wizard (Robert Weil) with reminiscences of showbiz in the soft-shoe 'Very Soft Shoes' and the other dance highlight of the evening came in Joe Layton's staging of 'The Spanish Panic', the exhausting dance intended by the Queen to wear Winnifred out before bedtime. The most charming moment of the night's entertainment, however, came when the mute little king decides it is his duty to tell his innocent son about the birds and the bees: his 'Man to Man Talk' has to be conducted in mime, whilst the amazed boy translates.

Once Upon a Mattress ran for 216 performances at the Phoenix Theatre and 244 more performances on Broadway, followed by a tour, with a company headed by Buster Keaton, Dody Goodman and Cy Young, a two-month Australian Christmas-season production at Melbourne's Princess Theatre, and an oversized London production. Sponsored by the Rodgers and Hammerstein organization (as Williamson Productions) in the spacious Adelphi Theatre, with Jane Connell (Winnifred), Milo O'Shea (King), Thelma Ruby (Queen) and Max Wall (Jester) featured, it proved a 38-performance failure.

Sydney saw *Once Upon a Mattress* for a couple of months at the Palace Theatre in 1962 (3 August), the piece was twice televised with Miss Burnett each time repeating her rôle, and a British revival, staged nearly 30 years later by Wendy Toye on the tiny stage of the Watermill Theatre in provincial Newbury, confirmed the small-scale delights of a piece which finally made its first incursion into Europe in 1990 in a German version.

Australia: Princess Theatre, Melbourne 4 December 1959; UK: Adelphi Theatre 20 September 1960; Germany: Stadttheater, Hildesheim *Winnifred* 30 December 1990
Recording: original cast (Kapp/MCA), London cast (HMV)

L'ONCLE CÉLESTIN Opérette-bouffe in 3 acts by Maurice Ordonneau and Henri Kéroul. Music by Edmond Audran. Théâtre des Menus-Plaisirs, Paris, 24 March 1891.

Audran followed up the splendid success of *Miss Helyett* (1890) with a similarly lively, vaudevillesque piece of musical comedy which won its composer another ringing Parisian success through a first run of 150 performances, followed by a revival in 1895 for a further 50 performances, and by productions round the world.

Ordonneau and Kéroul's story was another variation on the musical-comedy will theme. The provincial lawyer Pontaillac (Vandenne) and his wife Paméla (Yvonne Stella) are peacocking their way into Parisian society as Baron and Baronne, on the proceeds of a legacy from their despised aubergiste Uncle Célestin. Their aim is to marry their daughter Célestine (Mme Augier) to Gontran des Accacias (Ternet), son of the noble des Accacias (Vavasseur) and his lofty wife (Fanny Génat). Célestine, however, is determined to wed none but her little cousin Gustave (Verneuil). The Pontaillacs are well into their act when Célestin's will turns up. It doesn't stop them inheriting, but it obliges them to go through six months' work in Célestin's inn before doing so. Thus, whilst the 'Baron' and 'Baronne', deeply disguised as the innkeeping Lenglumés, have their mail phonily redirected from their 'holiday in Switzerland', the penniless Accacias are busy having false letters redirected from their 'holiday in Naples and Monte Carlo'. Inevitably they turn up at the inn, on the last day of the Pontaillacs' service, and all sorts of farcical scenes occur with the result that when the notary (F Constance) comes to check up on the fulfilment of the will's conditions, the Pontaillacs deny their identity and lose all. When all seems darkest, a codicil turns up which makes Célestine the heir, and allows her to get her man. Discomforture of the Accacias, reform of the foolish Pontaillacs, and all ends happily. Montcavrel played the rôle of Moreau, Célestin's old pal, who helps the action of the piece in its rebounds.

The songs of the piece fell largely to Clémentine, who had a number about her late uncle ('Il aurait fait bien pitieuse mine') and a love duo ('L'amour, o mon cousin Gustave') in the first act, delivered a Chanson de Langlois ('Langlois qu'était au clou') and a duetto des Cauchois with Gustave ('Nous sommes nés natifs tous les deux') in her disguise as a Normand serving wench, and topped off the third act with an angry Couplets du jeu de massacre, tearing the foolish Gontran to bits, and a post-codicil letter song in which she begins to bring home the truth to her parents. Gustave had a first-act air, the notary a comic song ('Vous appelez-vous Bernard?') in the midst of a situation when neither the disguised Pontaillacs nor the disguised Accacias will admit to having a name, and they all joined in moments of buffo ensemble in a score which was, although sizeable, largely an accompaniment to the comedy of the evening.

Following its Parisian success, L'Oncle Célestin took off, in the wake of Miss Helyett, for all the main musical theatre centres, but it fared rather less well than the earlier show. The German version appeared first, at Berlin's Friedrich-Wilhelmstädtisches Theater, followed by an American one (ad Georges Millet) with Jefferson de Angelis (Pontaillac), Jennie Reiffarth (Paméla), Annie Meyers (Clémentine), Harry Macdonough (Gontran) and Jennie Weathersby (Mme des Accacias) featured, and dancer Loie Fuller interpolated into the action as an additional attraction, which played through two months at Broadway's Casino Theater. London's production did little better. The score was altered with additional numbers by Meyer Lutz and Leslie Stuart and the old stars of Erminie, Harry Paulton (Marreau) and Frank Wyatt (Acacia) were joined by Gaiety stars E J Lonnen (Golosh) and Sylvia Grey (Countess Acacia) and the Savoy's Scott Russell (Gustave) and

Florence Perry (Clementine) at the head of the cast. It failed to take, and the replacement of Miss Grey with Ada Reeve and Paulton by Charles Danby, the addition of William Vokes as 'an india-rubber waiter' and the wholesale remake of the score after seven weeks could not help enough to get the show through the summer. Budapest's Celesztin apó (ad Emil Makai, Ferenc Reiner) was played just six times and, in all, L'Oncle Célestin failed to live up to its home success in its various translated and 'adapted' versions.

Germany: Friedrich-Wilhelmstädtisches Theater Onkel Cyprian 26 September 1891; USA: Casino Theater 15 February 1892; UK: Trafalgar Square Theatre Baron Golosh 25 April 1895; Hungary: Népszinház Celesztin apó Népszinház 8 January 1897

O'NEAL, Zelma [SCHROEDER, Zelma] (b Rock Falls, Ind, 29 May 1907; d unknown).

A song-and-dance girl in musical theatre and vaudeville, Miss O'Neal struck oil first time up on Broadway when she appeared as a bouncing incidental soubrette with a song in De Sylva, Brown and Henderson's Good News (1927, Flo). She repeated her rôle and 'The Varsity Drag' in the show's London production the following year before going on to play another similar rôle in the same team's Follow Thru (1929, Angie Howard) and being gratified with a second hit song in 'Button Up Your Overcoat'.

She appeared in the film version of Follow Thru (1930) and in Paramount on Parade (1930), contributed to Broadway's The Gang's All Here (1931, Willy Wilson), and in 1932 returned to Britain where, for several years, she appeared in supporting soubrette rôles in the London musical theatre. She was seen in Nice Goings On (1933, Tutti) with Leslie Henson, in Jack o'Diamonds (1935, Peggy Turner), for which she was also choreographer, and in Henson's Swing Along (1936, Miami), as well as, no small thanks to an important filmland husband, in a number of British film musicals (Give Her a Ring, Mr Cinders in Binnie Hale's rôle of Jill etc).

110 IN THE SHADE Musical in 2 acts by N Richard Nash based on his play The Rainmaker. Lyrics by Tom Jones. Music by Harvey Schmidt. Broadhurst Theater, New York, 24 October 1963.

The musical 110 in the Shade was made up of a slimmed version of Nash's enjoyable and touching 1954 play (Cort Theater, 28 October, 124 performances) and a score by the successful songwriters of The Fantasticks. Inga Swenson played Lizzie Curry, the plain and tough-tongued daughter of a country family whose livelihood is threatened by drought. The charlatan 'rainmaker' Starbuck (Robert Horton) who promises to save them, at a price, does not fool her, but she does find in his arms the regard, real or faked, that she cannot win from the divorced sheriff, File (Stephen Douglass). When rain does not come, and Starbuck is forced from town, the musical version puts Lizzie into File's arms. And then the rain comes.

The score for the piece produced no take-away number to rival the hit of The Fantasticks but Horton's set piece 'Rain Song', his Quarrel Duet with Lizzie ('You're Not Fooling Me') and a lively, incidental 'Poker Polka' all fitted the play well, which a curiously off-character piece for the sensible Lizzie about being 'Raunchy' did rather less.

David Merrick's production of 110 in the Shade ran for

331 performances on Broadway, but a London presentation by Merrick and Emile Littler with Miss Swenson and Douglass repeating their rôles and Ivor Emmanuel as File lasted only a disappointing 101 nights. However, a German version (ad Max Colpet) was premièred at Kassel in 1971, and the show, fortified by its fine leading rôles and sympathetic tale, has continued to find regional and secondary productions in America over the 30 years since its first staging. A revised version was mounted by the New York City Opera in 1992 (18 July) with Brian Sutherland, Richard Muenz and Karen Ziemba featured.

UK: Palace Theatre 8 February 1967; Germany: Staatstheater, Kassel 27 February 1971

Recording: original cast (RCA Victor), London cast (Columbia) etc

ONE TOUCH OF VENUS Musical in 2 acts by S J Perelman and Ogden Nash based on *The Tinted Venus* by F Anstey. Lyrics by Ogden Nash. Music by Kurt Weill. Imperial Theater, New York, 7 October 1943.

The whimsical 1885 *The Tinted Venus* of 'F Anstey' [Thomas Anstey Guthrie, 1856–1934], whose 1900 fantasy *The Brass Bottle*, with its magical tale of a genie, had already been made up into a musical in Britain, told the comical story of a 19th-century London hairdresser, Leander Tweddle, who brings a statue of Aphrodite to life. Statues had become coming to life regularly on the musical stage since the days of *Galathée* and *Adonis*, but the book proved nonetheless a fine basis for a spectacular musical comedy, and the use of accredited and classy humorists Perelman and Nash as authors ensured a libretto and lyrics of bristling humour for what would be Kurt Weill's most brightly comical musical play.

New York art collector Whitelaw Savory (John Boles) has bought and imported an Anatolian statue of Venus (the name must have rhymed more easily than Aphrodite) which reminds him of his long-lost love. However, when the statue (Mary Martin) comes to life she attaches herself not to her owner but to Savory's barber, Rodney Hatch (Kenny Baker), who has been the unintentional instrument of her awakening. Savory is miserable, Rodney is aghast, and his fiancée, Gloria (Ruth Bond), and her mother are simply furious, as Venus and Rodney, with a touch of classic magic to aid them, cause havoc throughout Manhattan. Venus magicks ghastly Gloria off to the North Pole when the girl gets too much to take and Rodney is suspected of murder, but when the Grecian goddess finally realizes that marriage to her awakener means a life as an American suburban housewife, she prefers to change back to stone. The little fellow has a happy ending, however, when a nice, suburban Venus-double arrives in time for the final curtain.

Weill's score produced several romantic numbers which became favourites – Venus's smooth, exploratory 'I'm a Stranger Here Myself', her seduction of Rodney to the strains of 'Speak Low' and Savory's rueful, reflective 'West Wind' – whilst the comical side of affairs was highlighted by a wordful description of the trip of Gloria and her mother 'Way Out West in Jersey' and Rodney's description of 'The Trouble with Women'. Two set-piece Agnes de Mille ballets, one illustrative of New York's midday rush ('Forty Minutes for Lunch') and the other showing Venus the delights of lower-middle-class life and tempting her

back to Olympus ('Venus in Ozone Heights') were inset into the action, along with a pageant number about 'Dr Crippen'.

Cheryl Crawford and John Wildberg's production of *One Touch of Venus*, directed by Elia Kazan, gave Weill the longest Broadway run of his career with a fine record of 567 performances, but although the show was subsequently made over into a film with a truncated and infiltrated score, and with Ava Gardner and the singing voice of Nan Wynn starring as Venus, it did not travel into a first-class production beyond America. It was televised in 1955 and revived at the Goodspeed Opera House on 22 April 1987, with Lynette Perry (Venus) and Michael Piontek (Rodney) featured.

Film: Universal 1948

Recording: original cast (Decca/MCA), film soundtrack (Ariel) etc

THE ONLY GIRL Musical farcical comedy in 3 acts by Henry Blossom based on the play *Our Wives* by Frank Mandel and Helen Craft, a version of *Jugendfreude* by Ludwig Fulda. Music by Victor Herbert. 39th Street Theater, New York, 2 November 1914.

A piece in the small-scale musical comedy genre with a book taken this time from the German rather than from the French, *The Only Girl* had three of its once relatively confirmed bachelors (Jed Prouty, Richard Bartlett, Ernest Torrence) falling into marriage quickly and happily enough to be singing a sextet on 'Connubial Bliss' in the second act, but to be already warning their surviving chum, who practises the profession of librettist (Thurston Hall), about 'When You're Wearing the Ball and Chain' in the third. Nevertheless, it is not long before he gets around to singing 'You're the Only One for Me' with his lady composer partner, Ruth (Wilda Bennett), who had been playing and singing the show's love theme in the wings since the first act.

The show's largest singing rôle (a third of the songs), however, fell to none of these reasonably plotworthy folk but to an incidental soubrette called Patsy (Adele Rowland) who opened up proceedings with what Herbert billed as 'an imitation of the present-day ragtime song' called 'The More I See of Others, Dear, the Better I Like You', delivered a piece about 'Personality', slipped in a marching song with wartime sentiments ('Here's to the Land We Love, Boys') and a theatrical song redolent of old comic-opera days ('You Have to Have a Part to Make a Hit') and joined a sextet of girls, accompanying themselves with the clash of knives, forks and plates, to open the last act. Another incidental lassie had a song and dance routine about someone called 'Antoinette', but it was Ruth's soprano solo 'When You're Away', a waltz song with a Victorian parlour-song lyric which ended on a top B-natural, which proved the best-liked piece of *The Only Girl*'s score, over and above all the composer's more modernly-made numbers.

Joe Weber's production of *The Only Girl* gave Herbert another fine success to follow up that of *Sweethearts* the previous year. It ran through 240 performances, moving up to a larger house from its tiny original theatre when success was clear, before heading to a fine life of some two years on the road.

Grossmith and Laurillard's London production of *The*

Only Girl did rather less well, notching up 107 performances in the small Apollo Theatre with Mabel Russell as Patsy and Kenneth Douglas and Fay Compton featured as the last-wed couple. It did, however, give Herbert the longest run he would achieve from the five of his shows which were played in London (*The Wizard of the Nile*, *The Fortune Teller*, *The Red Mill*, *Angel Face*).

A 1933–4 San Francisco production, with its score titivated with Herbert favourites from other shows and Guy Robertson as a star, provoked a Shubert revival on Broadway with Robert Halliday and Bettina Hall in the cast (44th Street Theater, 21 May 1934), but neither it nor a second west coast revival, put up in the mid-1940s on the strength of the success of the Broadway revival of Herbert's *The Red Mill*, and which replaced the book with a new one by Alonzo Price, managed to establish *The Only Girl* alongside the best-loved Herbert shows.

UK: Apollo Theatre 25 September 1915

ON THE TOWN
Musical in 2 acts by Betty Comden and Adolph Green based on the ballet *Fancy Free*. Music and additional lyrics by Leonard Bernstein. Adelphi Theater, New York, 28 December 1944.

The musical *On the Town* had its genesis in the ballet *Fancy Free*, a work composed (with one sung number, 'Big Stuff') by Leonard Bernstein and staged by Jerome Robbins for the Ballet Theater (18 April 1944). Under the aegis of producers Oliver Smith and Paul Feigay, Bernstein and Robbins – joined for the text by Bernstein's friends Betty Comden and Adolph Green – took the ballet's basic premise of three sailors on shore leave going out in New York in search of girls and made it into a musical.

Sailors Gabey (John Battles), Ozzie (Green) and Chip (Cris Alexander) get off their ship ready to enjoy a day off in New York but, when Gabey flips his lid over a poster of a lass billed as the subways' 'Miss Turnstiles' of the month, his pals agree to spend their day helping him to track his dream girl down. Chip gets waylaid by an extrovert lady cabdriver (Nancy Walker), Ozzie runs into a lass (Betty Comden) with unstoppable impulses and a martyrized fiancé in a museum, but Gabey finally runs his heroine (Sono Osato) to earth, only to finally find out that she is not some kind of a star but a cooch dancer at Coney Island. Then it is time for the boys to go back to their ship and, as they get ready to set off to sea again, three other bright-eyed sailors bounce onto the quay for their day 'on the town'.

Bernstein's score, which was a wholly new one and did not include the music from *Fancy Free*, mixed a series of lively, revusical songs which ranged from the sailors' leaping welcome to 'New York, New York' to the cabdriver's enthusiastic promise 'I Can Cook, Too' and Comden and Green's paroxysmically unleashed 'I Get Carried Away', with some large and distinctly superior pieces of dance music as accompaniment to the important dance sequences of the show: Gabey's fantasy of 'Miss Turnstiles', his wander through the 'Lonely Town', the second-act 'Times Square Ballet' and Gabey's imaginings of Coney Island as 'The Playground of the Rich' in which the dancing Miss Osato featured as a glamorous man-tamer.

The fresh and lively *On the Town*, with its semi-revue, semi-dance-and-laughter-show construction, its funny songs, its zippy Robbins dances and unfussy George

Abbott staging, proved an immediate success and the initial Broadway production ran through 463 performances. A 1949 film version, with a cast headed by Frank Sinatra, Gene Kelly, Jules Munshin, Vera-Ellen, Betty Garrett and Ann Miller, although it varied significantly from the original show musically (five new numbers were introduced), successfully recaptured the taking brightness and innocence of the original. The show did not, however, attract foreign takers and subsequent attempts to reproduce it in later and less innocent days in New York proved failures.

A 1959 off-Broadway production (Carnegie Hall Playhouse 15 January) with Harold Lang (Gabey), Joe Bova (Ozzie), and Joe Layton as choreographer played 70 performances and sparked a first staging (also by Layton) in London where Don McKay (Gabey), Elliott Gould (Ozzie), Gillian Lewis (Claire) and Andrea Jaffe (Ivy) featured through 53 performances. A 1971 New York revival (Imperial Theater 31 October) with a cast including Ron Husmann (Gabey), Donna McKechnie (Ivy), Phyllis Newman (Claire) and Bernadette Peters (Hildy) folded in 73 performances.

A German version (ad Rolf Merz, Gerhard Hagen) was premiered in Kaiserslautern in 1977, and in 1991, following the Stuttgart Ballet's successful production of *On Your Toes*, the Hamburg Ballet turned its attentions to classic Broadway and produced a version (ad Claud H Henneberg, John Neumeier) of *On the Town* (Hamburg Staatsoper 15 December 1991).

UK: Prince of Wales Theatre 30 May 1963; Germany: Pfalztheater, Kaiserslautern 11 September 1977; Film: MGM 1949
Recordings: selections (Columbia, Decca/MCA), London cast (CBS), film soundtrack etc.

ON THE TWENTIETH CENTURY
Musical in 2 acts by Adolph Green and Betty Comden based on *Twentieth Century* by Ben Hecht, Charles McArthur and Bruce Millholland. Lyrics by Betty Comden and Adolph Green. Music by Cy Coleman. St James Theater, New York, 19 February 1978.

The play *Twentieth Century* (the title referred to the famous luxury train linking New York and Chicago) had a successful 152-performance run at Broadway's Broadhurst Theater in 1932–3 with Moffatt Johnstone and Eugenie Leontovich in the lead rôles, was made into an even more successful film with John Barrymore and Carole Lombard as its stars, and returned to Broadway and further success in 1950 with Gloria Swanson and José Ferrer, before it was made into a musical, in 1978, with perhaps the most success of all.

The flamboyant but financially frowsy impresario Oscar Jaffee (John Cullum) books a compartment on the long-distance train from west to east. Not any compartment, but the one next to the fabulous film star Lily Garland (Madeleine Kahn), now a household name but originally his 'discovery' and once his mistress. Jaffee plans to woo Lily back to his management, and the bait he uses is the rôle of Mary Magdalene in a spectacular epic which will be financed by an elderly and religious heiress (Imogen Coca) he has encountered on the trip. He has to battle against a more conventional producer equipped with a Somerset Maugham play, against Lily's resident bit of bruisable beefcake, Bruce Granit (Kevin Kline), and the ultimate revelation that his backer is an escaped lunatic, before the two fall, laughing, into each other's arms.

Astutely slimmed, the original (male) lunatic resexed for the benefit of Miss Coca, and equipped with a volley of witty lyrics, the piece was set by Coleman as a burlesque comic opera. A series of musically dazzling and hilarious solos and ensembles was highlighted by a dilemma scene for Lily, torn between Oscar and the Magdalene on the one hand and the rôle of Somerset Maugham's 'Babette' on the other, in a musical monologue which raced from the depths of chest voice to the most distant soprano leger lines, demanding a vocal and dramatic virtuosity rare in any kind of musical theatre. Another scena, in which little Miss piano-playing Plotka, having devastated an incompetent leading lady's singing audition, is transformed by Oscar into a star in the musico-patriotico-weepie 'Véronique' helped make the rôle of Lily one of the outstanding comedy/singing vehicles in musical theatre history, whilst Oscar's extravagantly baritonic hymn of self-confidence 'I Rise Again', his fake farewell 'The Legacy', and their too-good-to-be-true duo about 'Our Private World' ensured that her co-star was never left behind. The other musical high-spots include a manic sextet in which Oscar and his allies try to get Lily to 'Sign' a contract, a burlesque death duo ('Lily, Oscar') and the plotters' harmonized glee at getting a cheque with 'Five Zeros' on it.

Hal Prince's direction heightened the burlesque fun of the script and score without ever over-exaggerating it, Robin Wagner's train sets (inside and outside, still and moving) won delighted acclaim and *On the Twentieth Century* gathered a handful of Tony Awards, including Best Musical. Its soon-in-difficulties leading lady was replaced by Judy Kaye as the piece ran through 460 performances on Broadway before going on the road with Miss Kaye starred opposite Rock Hudson. Harold Fielding's London production, with Keith Michell and Julia McKenzie starred and Mark Wynter as the maltreated Granit, took a couple of nips in the show (two numbers were cut) but, after playing to bulging houses for several months, found its audience vanish almost overnight and closed after 165 performances.

UK: Her Majesty's Theatre 19 March 1980
Recording: original cast (Columbia)

ON YOUR TOES Musical comedy in 2 acts by Richard Rodgers, Lorenz Hart and George Abbott. Lyrics by Lorenz Hart. Music by Richard Rodgers. Imperial Theater, New York, 11 April 1936.

Hollywood provided Rodgers and Hart with material for several of their musicals. *America's Sweetheart* used film-land as its subject matter, but two others of the partner's shows were developed from material which had been originally envisaged as the stuff of a film musical. One was *I Married an Angel* and the other, which found its way to the stage the first, was *On Your Toes*, a dance-based piece set around some amorous and comical situations in a ballet company, initially dreamed up as a movie vehicle for Fred Astaire.

Junior Dolan (Ray Bolger), once a vaudeville performer, is now a music teacher with a couple of promising pupils in composer Sidney Cohn (David Morris) and songwriter Frankie Frayne (Doris Carson). Sidney has composed a

jazz ballet, and when Frankie lets out that ballet Maecenas Peggy Porterfield (Luella Gear) is a family friend, Junior wangles an introduction, determined to get Sidney's piece produced. Peggy is all for something new, artistic director Sergei Alexandrovitch (Monty Woolley) is all against, and company star Vera Barnova (Tamara Geva), who has quarreled with Morrosine (Demetrios Vilan), her leading man, is all for Junior (who has just admitted love to Frankie). Peggy's money wins *Slaughter on Tenth Avenue* a production, but since Morrosine can't do the modern steps, Junior steps in to dance the lead male rôle opposite Vera. The furious Morrosine hires a gunman to shoot him down on opening night, but Junior keeps himself a moving target until the police arrive and he can relax into a fairly improbable happy ending.

The ballet choreographer Georges Balanchine was hired to do the dances which made up an important part of the show. The first act featured the ballet company's *Princess Zenobia* in which Junior, shoved on at the last minute to replace a missing member of the corps de ballet, manages to bungle every step and cause havoc with his ineptitudes, whilst the second act included a title-song and dance in which phalanxes of ballet performers and tap-dancing students faced up to each other in a confrontation of the two styles which were to be blended in Sidney's ballet. The show came to its climax with the performance of the story ballet *Slaughter on Tenth Avenue*, which began as a dramatic dance piece about a sleazy dance-hall girl (Vera) and a vaudeville hoofer (Junior) before developing into a piece of wild comedy as the hero danced exhaustingly round the stage, keeping out of the way of the killer's bullets.

In consequence of the large dance element, the song list of *On Your Toes* was shorter than usual, but it still brought out several pieces which would become Rodgers and Hart favourites. Frankie presented 'It's Got to be Love' as an example of her songwriting, and another pupil showed off his homework in 'Quiet Night', whilst Frankie and Junior slipped in the wishful 'There's a Small Hotel' as their love blossomed, and she torched wistfully that she was 'Glad to Be Unhappy' when he neglected her to make a fuss over Vera. Peggy had the stand-up numbers of the night, insisting that 'The Heart is Quicker Than the Eye' and joining Sergei in 'Too Good for the Average Man'.

If the show's plot was occasionally rather incoherent, its contents – song, dance and the large dash of comedy – were grand entertainment, and Dwight Deere Wiman's production of *On Your Toes* had a fine Broadway career of 315 performances in 1936–7. Whilst it ran on, Wiman and Lee Ephraim mounted a London production whose comedy element was emphasized in their choice of director: laughter star Leslie Henson. Jack Whiting played Junior, Vera Zorina was Vera and Gina Malo sang Frankie, with Jack Donohue (Morrosine), songwriter Eddie Pola (Sidney) and Oliver Blakeney (Peggy) amongst the support cast. The piece did not win the same popularity in London as it had in New York, and it was shuttered after six weeks and sent on the road. The producers decided, however, to have a second go, and on 19 April they re-opened the show at the London Coliseum. The original verdict was confirmed and *On Your Toes* folded a second time after 54 additional performances.

On Your Toes made its way back to Hollywood in 1939,

to be filmed with Vera Zorina (but without its songs), and it was given a second Broadway showing in 1954 when, following the success of the 1952 revival of *Pal Joey*, George Abbott mounted a new production with Zorina, Bobby Van (Junior) and Kay Coulter (Frankie) featured. Elaine Stritch played Peggy and was given an additional number, 'You Took Advantage of Me', plucked from the score of *Present Arms*. If this revival lasted only 64 performances, a further mounting in 1983 won an altogether different level of appreciation. Ballet-star Natalia Makarova was featured in a version which used much of Balanchine's original choreography for its ballet sections (add choreography Peter Martins, Donald Saddler) alongside Lara Teeter (Junior), George S Irving (Sergei), Christine Andreas (Frankie), Dina Merrill (Peggy) and another ballet name, George de la Peña, as Morrosine. The aged Abbott directed (which he had not officially done first time round in spite of being involved in the project almost from the start) and the revival had a grand New York run of 505 performances.

This revival set the show up for the future. The production was exported to London, where Makarova starred alongside Tim Flavin (Junior) and Siobhan McCarthy (Frankie), and the show more than compensated for its unimpressive first visit to the West End by winning a 539-performance run at the same Palace Theatre which it had visited so briefly in 1937. And with the rôle of Vera now established as OK for a real, live ballet name (Makarova had been followed in America by Galina Panova, and in London by Doreen Wells) new horizons opened for *On Your Toes*. Opera Houses had been making back some of the money lost on operas on productions of operettas and musical plays for some years: *On Your Toes* – even if much of its dance content was un-balletic and comic – was splendid meat for the ballet world. In 1991 the Stuttgart Ballet mounted an *On Your Toes* with choreography newly done by Larry Fuller and with Marcia Haydée and Richard Cragun starring, as Rodgers and Hart's show moved towards the 21st century looking more popular than it had at any time since the war.

UK: Palace Theatre 5 February 1937; Germany: Theater im Forum, Ludwigsburg (Eng) 16 September 1990
Recordings: Broadway 1954 revival cast (Decca/DRG), Broadway 1983 revival cast (TER/Polydor), selection (Columbia) etc

OPERETTE in 2 acts by Noël Coward. His Majesty's Theatre, London, 16 March 1938.

After the successes of *Bitter-Sweet* and *Conversation Piece*, Coward persisted in writing romantic operettas without ever again winning the same success. Having successfully imported the queen of the Parisian musical theatre, Yvonne Printemps, for *Conversation Piece*, Coward this time created a rôle for Berlin's longtime favourite Operette star, Fritzi Massary. Massary featured as a Viennese singing star dispensing song and advice alongside Irene Vanbrugh as the mother of the lovestruck Nigel Vaynham (Griffith Jones) who has to be stopped from the socially suicidal course of marrying Rozanne Grey (Peggy Wood), the chorine promoted to star of *Operette*'s show-within-a-show, *The Model Maid*. Much of *Operette*'s score was the score of *The Model Maid* in which Coward had fun with pastiches of turn-of-the-century musical styles: the

Florodora sextet, Gaiety low comedy, and a good ration of soprano solos. However, the enduring success of the score was another of Coward's revusical comedy jeux d'esprit, a male quartet about 'The Stately Homes of England'.

Operette hit trouble on the road and its author/ composer/producer/director (and, briefly, musical director after he sacked the original one) made alterations before town, but they were not sufficient and the show, which Coward later counted his least satisfactory, lasted only 133 performances in London before going out on tour with Ivy St Helier playing a remade version of Massary's rôle.

Recording: original cast (part-record) (WRC)

DER OPERNBALL Operette in 3 acts by Victor Léon and Heinrich von Waldberg based on the comedy *Les Dominos roses* by Alfred Hennequin and Alfred Delacour. Music by Richard Heuberger. Theater an der Wien, Vienna, 5 January 1898.

One of the most internationally successful comedies of its era, Hennequin and Delacour's *Les Dominos roses* (Théâtre du Vaudeville, 17 April 1876) was made over as a musical play in three languages – none of which was French – of which the most enduring has turned out to be the Viennese *Der Opernball*. The adaptation, which kept the setting a French one, was musically set by the operettic novice Heuberger, with whom co-librettist Léon had earlier collaborated on a ballet *Struwwelpeter* for Dresden, and who apparently took his time over it. *Der Opernball* was cited in the production schedules for several years before it appeared, but when it was produced by Alexandrine von Schönerer at the Theater an der Wien in 1898 it achieved the kind of success that was worth waiting for.

Georges Duménil (Karl Streitmann) offers to take his country friend Paul Aubier (Josef Joseffy) to the Opéra Ball in search of a little feminine adventure, and is delighted when the opportunity effortlessly presents itself even before the event, in the form of anonymous billets-doux arranging a ball-night rendezvous apiece with an unknown lady disguised in a pink domino. Duménil's pubescent nephew, Henri (Fr Frey), who is aching for his first experiences of the demi-monde, gets a letter too. They are not to know, of course, that the letters come from the female members of their own suspicious household. All three men meet their mystery ladies, and Beaubuisson (Karl Blasel), Mme Duménil's ageing Uncle, joins in the farcical fun on the arm of a pretty danseuse (Therese Biedermann), as the gentlemen and their pink-dominoed ladies pop in and out of 'private' boxes (the traditional place for bal masqué hanky-panky). In the course of all this 'popping' the pairings get rather mixed up and instead of the men romancing their own wives (Fr Ottmann, Fr Reichsberg), as the plotting ladies had intended, each, in turn, ends up making advances to Henri's partner, who is none other than the Duménil's obliging maid, Hortense (Annie Dirkens). When the men, having discovered the plot, make a joke of the whole business with their wives the next day, it is the ladies' turn to be hoist – each suspects her husband of having flirted perhaps too heavily with the other's wife – but all is finally assuaged when Hortense owns up, and it is chastenedly agreed all round that no harm has been done.

Plate 200. **Der Opernball:** *A little bit of feminine plotting sets up a little bit of masculine undoing in Ulmer Theater's production of the musicalized* Dominos roses.

Heuberger's score was one of dances – polka, mazurka, march and waltz – combined in three acts of music (including only a single chorus number, subsequently cut) from which one song, Hortense's waltzing invitation to little Henri, 'Geh'n wir in's Chambre separée', emerged as an enduring Operette standard.

Frau von Schönerer's production of *Der Opernball* was one of her greatest successes. It was played 56 times en suite and brought back regularly in the Theater an der Wien repertoire thereafter, passing its 100th performance on 29 March 1899, and playing on into 1900, during which time one of the cast changes brought in Ilka Pálmay as Henri. It was then taken into the Carltheater (14 April 1901) where Blasel repeated his Beaubuisson alongside Mizzi Günther (Hortense) and young Louis Treumann (Philippe, the butler) and where it passed its 200th night on 14 December 1902 with Dirkens, Blasel and Streitmann all in their original rôles. It played at the Raimundtheater (7 May 1901), made its first appearance at the Volksoper in 1908 (12 February) and in 1914 returned for a month in a starry new production to the Theater an der Wien (30 December) with Luise Kartousch (Henri), Ernst Tautenhayn (Paul), Paul Guttmann (Beaubuisson), Hubert Marischka (Duménil), Betty Fischer (Hortense) and Cordy Millowitsch (Angèle) in the cast.

In 1920 *Der Opernball* was played at the Bürgertheater, in 1922 at the Johann Strauss-Theater, whilst in 1931 the Staatsoper presented a version (ad Röhr, 24 January) with a cast including Leo Slezak (Beaubuisson), Adele Kern (Henri) and Lotte Lehmann (Angèle) which was revived in 1938, and in 1952 the Volksoper presented another revised version (ad O T Schuh), with the music done over by Anton Paulik and Rudolf Kattnigg. That version was abandoned for the most recent Volksoper production (27 October 1985) of an Operette which has remained a solid item of the Viennese repertoire, in the shadow only of the most international of favourites.

Der Opernball has twice been filmed, first by Geza von Bolvary in 1939, and in 1956 by Ernst Marischka in a version adapted by its producer and re-set in Vienna, featuring a cast including Josef Meinrad (Paul), Johannes Heesters (Georg), Sonja Ziemann (Helene), Herta Feiler

(Elisabeth) and Hans Moser, who had also appeared in the first film, in a typical Moser rôle as a comically all-arranging Oberkellner.

Although it proved as popular in Germany as in Austria, *Der Opernball* didn't do as well in the other main centres. It was not given in America until more than a decade after its first production, after the fashion for Viennese Operette had been aroused by *Die lustige Witwe*. The intial performances were played at the German-language Yorkville Theater, with Emil Berla (Beaubuisson), Minnie Landau (Angèle), Wilhelm Nikow (Duménil), Mizi Raabe (Henri) and Louise Barthel (Hortense) amongst the cast but, although a subsequent English version was originally announced as a vehicle for Lillian Russell, it ended up being produced, in a version by Sydney Rosenfeld and Clare Kummer, with Marie Cahill topbilled as Celeste (ex-Hortense) singing 'What Are We Coming To?' and dancing the Turkey Trot. Harry Fairleigh (Dumesnil), George Lydecker (Aubier), Harry Conor (Beaubuisson), Olive Ulrich (Angèle) and Burrell Barbarette in the rôle of a non-travesty Henry supported the star through just 32 performances of *The Opera Ball* on Broadway.

Shortly after, Grossmith and Laurillard brought to Broadway their English musical-comedy version of the *Pink Dominos* tale, *Tonight's the Night*. This proved altogether more to Broadway's tastes and, after a successful season in America, was duly taken back to be played for a long run in London, where *Der Opernball* had been ignored. Paris passed on both pieces, and Budapest had its own *Dominos roses* musical produced whilst Heuberger was still getting round to completing his score (*Három légyott* text and music by Jozsef Bokor 22 October 1897 Népszinház). *Der Opernball* was, nevertheless, mounted in Budapest, at the Magyar Színház (ad Jenő Faragó) in 1899, and revived at the Népopera in 1916 (16 December). In 1970 a musical version of James Albery's English adaptation *Pink Dominos* was produced at Britain's Salisbury Playhouse (music: John Gould, 17 March) under the title *Who Was That Lady?*.

Germany: Theater Unter den Linden 11 March 1898; Hungary: Magyar Színház *Az operabál* 16 May 1899; USA: Yorkville Theater 24 May 1909, Liberty Theater *The Opera Ball* 12 February 1912; Films: Geza von Bolvary 1939; Ernst Marischka 1956
Recording: selection (Philips)

ORBACH, Jerry (b New York, 20 October 1935). American actor-singer who has created several major Broadway musical rôles.

Orbach made his first notable musical appearance in succession to Scott Merrill as Macheath in the long-running 1958 revival of *The Threepenny Opera*. In 1960 he created the rôle of the adventurer, El Gallo, in *The Fantasticks*, introducing the show's hit song 'Try to Remember', and the following year created the part of the misanthropic, many-voiced puppeteer in *Carnival*, opposite Anna-Maria Alberghetti. He appeared in revivals of *The Cradle Will Rock*, *Annie Get Your Gun* (Charlie Davenport) and *Carousel* (Jigger) in the 1960s and, in 1969, created the leading rôle of the too-obliging apartment-owner, Chuck Baxter, in another highly successful musical, *Promises, Promises*.

In 1975 Orbach starred with Gwen Verdon and Chita

Rivera as the glint-toothed lawyer Billy Flynn in *Chicago* ('All I Care About is Love') and in 1980 as the magnetic Julian Marsh in the stage version of *42nd Street*, compiling an impressive list of major new musical rôles for an era where many a star artist is credited with only one or two such parts in (or as) an entire career.

THE ORCHID Musical play in 2 acts by James T Tanner. Lyrics by Adrian Ross and Percy Greenbank. Music by Ivan Caryll and Lionel Monckton. Gaiety Theatre, London, 28 October 1903.

The Orchid continued the run of world-famous musical comedies which George Edwardes had produced at the old Gaiety Theatre in the Strand when the producer moved his operation to the newly built Gaiety, further along the same thoroughfare. If the theatre was new and different, the show was not: *The Orchid* maintained the same formulae, the same writers and the same stars that had given the older house its vast vogue, and it won its reward with a 559-performance run (including an official 'second edition').

The plot concerned the precious flower of the title and the efforts of British (Harry Grattan) and French (Robert Nainby) politicians to get their hands on it. The bloom discovered by Peruvian flower-hunter Zaccary (Fred Wright jr) gets destroyed, but little Meakin (Edmund Payne), a gardener at a horticultural college, has grown another and he becomes the object of the politicians' pursuit. That pursuit became mixed up with another, of two young couples who have just been married in Paris but, through the vagueness of the registrar, to the wrong mates (Lionel Mackinder and Ethel Sydney, Gertie Millar and George Grossmith). Connie Ediss was Caroline Twining, a lady mad to marry who ended up sporting the orchid in her hat, and Gabrielle Ray was the little secretary to the British minister.

Amongst all the fun – Payne equipped with armour and broadsword (accompanied by the strains of the sabre song from *La Grande-Duchesse*) and challenged to a duel for his flower by the fire-breathing Frenchman, Grattan touching on a caricature of Joseph Chamberlain and Gabs Ray making his relationship with his secretary so pointed that it had to be rewritten – came the Gaiety songs. Miss Millar sang of 'Little Mary' in reference to Barrie's recent play, and waxed northern in 'Liza Ann', Connie Ediss in a comical get-up sang of 'Fancy Dress' and Grossmith and Payne gave their opinion of 'The Unemployed' ('It ain't much enjoyment to ask for employment and only get work instead'), but the hit of the show was, as so often in these days, an interpolated number. Grossmith popped in Blanche Ring's Broadway hit 'Bedelia' and made as big a success of it in London as she had done on the other side of the Atlantic.

The Orchid duly made its way to the other English-speaking stages of the world which had revelled in the earlier Gaiety musicals. J C Williamson Ltd promptly mounted their version in Australia, with Evelyn Scott and Florence Young playing the two young ladies, George Lauri as Meakin and Clara Clifton as Caroline, whilst the Gaiety version still ran on in London and two companies purveyed the piece to the British provinces at the beginning of a series of tours that would last for several years. In 1905 the Edwardes-Wheeler repertory company intro-duced the show to South Africa at the Cape Town Opera House (1 August), but Edwardes stepped in with an injunction to prevent *The Orchid* and a bundle of his other shows being played on the far east circuits when royalties were not forthcoming. Only after all this did *The Orchid* make its appearance on Broadway.

The Shuberts' American production hit a problem on the run into town when its top-billed star Eddie Foy (Meakin) threatened to walk out if the part of his co-star Trixie Friganza (Caroline) were not reduced. In spite of the fact that his own rôle had been beefed up with such pieces as Bryan and Goetz's hit 'He Goes to Church on Sundays' his worries proved justified, for Miss Friganza (who stayed) was a great success, but so was *The Orchid*. It put up a Broadway run of 178 performances, and proved the most popular of all the Gaiety shows that had been transported to Broadway. Indeed, so successful was it that the producers announced that they would take their version of the piece back to London and let British audiences compare Foy and Miss Friganza with Payne and Miss Ediss. Foy refused the challenge, however, and it was not for nearly another decade that a remade American version of a London musical braved (very briefly) the West End.

Australia: Her Majesty's Theatre, Melbourne 29 October 1904;
  USA: Herald Square Theater 8 April 1907

ORDONNEAU, Maurice (b Saintes, 18 June 1854; d Paris, December 1916).

A journalist and dramatic critic, Ordonneau began writing for the theatre in his early twenties, making an early appearance on a Paris playbill teamed with the established Eugène Grangé and Victor Bernard as an author of the Folies-Marigny revue *Les Cri-cris de Paris* (1876). Over the next four decades, working more often alone than was usually the case in this age of authorial pairings, he contributed liberally to both the straight and musical stage in Paris. Many of his earliest musical collaborations were with composer Edmond Audran with whom he paired on a first success with *Serment d'amour* in 1886 and again with the vaudevillesque *L'Oncle Célestin* and with *Madame Suzette* before the two produced their biggest success together in 1896 in the comical *La Poupée*. Ordonneau combined with other prominent composers such as Gaston Serpette (*Cousin-cousine*), Louis Varney (*La Falote*), Victor Roger (*L'Auberge du Tohu-bohu*) and Louis Ganne (*Les Saltimbanques*) on pieces which found success mainly in their country of origin, but he also produced several other pieces which, like *La Poupée*, found greater favour in other countries and in other languages than their original.

The most striking example of this was his text for *Madame Sherry*, a piece in a straightforward French vaudeville mode, which made a considerable hit when it was produced in Germany, with a score by the Austrian composer Hugo Felix, and was then turned into an equally successful American musical comedy with songs by Karl Hoschna and Otto Harbach. His *Les Hirondelles*, set to music by Henri Hirschmann, also had its first production in Germany, whilst his vaudeville *Le Jockey malgré lui*, played in France with a score by Victor Roger, became *The Office Boy* (Victoria Theater 2 November 1903) in America with the piece's original music replaced by some new songs by Ludwig Englander. The Henry Blossom/Raymond Hubbell musical comedy *The Man from Cook's* (New

Amsterdam Theater 25 March 1912) was said to be based on an Ordonneau piece called *Un Voyage Cook*, Vienna's Theater in der Josefstadt staged a home-made Posse mit Gesang *Wien über alles* (1 January 1901) which credited Ordonneau (w Grenet-Dancourt) as author of its source, probably *Paris, quand-même, ou les deux Bigorret* (Théâtre Cluny 31 March 1896), and Düsseldorf's Lustspielhaus staged a musical version of *Une affaire scandaleuse* (w Gavault) as *Eine kitzliche Geschichte* (31 October 1912, Hugo Hirsch/Rudolf Schanzer).

In the later part of his career Ordonneau adapted an increasing number of foreign pieces for the French stage – Spanish, English and Viennese – amongst which were *Charley's Aunt* (equipped with some songs by Ivan Caryll) and Harry Paulton's *Niobe* as well as a run of musical shows, and he had one final sizeable success with an original libretto the year before his death, with the patriotic wartime musical *La Cocarde de Mimi-Pinson*.

1875 **Les Diamants de Florinette** (Louis Desormes/w Ernest Hamm) 1 act La Pépinière 20 March

1879 **La Demoiselle de compagnie** (Francis Chassaigne) Olympia 20 March

1880 **Madame Grégoire** (Édouard Okolowicz et al/w Paul Burani) Théâtre des Arts 20 May

1882 **Au Premier Hussards** (Léon Vasseur/w Hamm) 1 act

1882 **Mimi-Pinson** (Gustave Michiels/w Arthur Verneuil) Théâtre Cluny 14 March

1886 **Serment d'amour** (Edmond Audran) Théâtre des Nouveautés 19 February

1886 **La Princesse Colombine** (*Nell Gwynne*) French version w Émile André (Théâtre des Nouveautés)

1887 **La Fiancée des verts-poteaux** (Audran) Théâtre des Menus-Plaisirs 8 November

1888 **Babette** (*La Grappe d'amour*) (Michiels/w Verneuil ad Alfred Murray, J G Mosenthal) Strand Theatre, London 26 January

1888 **Miette** (Audran) Théâtre de la Renaissance 24 September

1891 **La Petite Poucette** (Raoul Pugno/w Maurice Hennequin) Théâtre de la Renaissance 5 March

1891 **L'Oncle Célestin** (Audran/w Henri Kéroul) Théâtre des Menus-Plaisirs 24 March

1892 **La Cocarde tricolore** (Robert Planquette/Hippolyte Cogniard, Théodore Cogniard ad) Théâtre des Folies-Dramatiques 12 February

1893 **Madame Suzette** (Audran/w André Sylvane) Théâtre des Bouffes-Parisiens 29 March

1893 **Mademoiselle ma femme** (Frédéric Toulmouche/w Octave Pradels) Théâtre des Menus-Plaisirs 5 May

1893 **Cousin-cousine** (Gaston Serpette/w Kéroul) Théâtre des Folies-Dramatiques 23 December

1894 **La Plantation Thomassin** (Albert Vizentini/w Albin Valabrègue) Eden-Théâtre, Vichy 24 July

1895 **La Perle du Cantal** (Toulmouche) Théâtre des Folies-Dramatiques 2 March

1895 **La Saint-Valentin** (Toulmouche/w Fernand Beissier) Théâtre des Bouffes-Parisiens 28 March

1896 **La Gran Via** French version (L'Olympia)

1896 **La Falote** (Louis Varney/w Armand Liorat) Théâtre des Folies-Dramatiques 17 April

1896 **La Poupée** (Audran) Théâtre de la Gaîté 21 October

1896 **La Demoiselle de magasin** (*The Shop Girl*) French version (Olympia)

1897 **L'Auberge du Tohu-bohu** (Victor Roger) Théâtre des Folies-Dramatiques 10 February

1897 **La Chula** (d'Hidalgo/w Ensenat, 'G Pollonnais' [ie Hubert Desvignes]) 1 act Olympia 30 September

1898 **L'Agence Crook et cie** (Roger) Théâtre des Folies-Dramatiques 28 January

1898 **The Royal Star** (*La Petite Vénus*) (Justin Clérice/ad Francis Richardson) Prince of Wales Theatre, London 16 September

1899 **Les Soeurs Gaudichard** (Audran) Théâtre de la Gaîté 21 April

1899 **Les Saltimbanques** (Louis Ganne) Théâtre de la Gaîté 30 December

1901 **Le Curé Vincent** (Audran) Théâtre de la Gaîté 25 October

1902 **Madame Sherry** (Hugo Felix/w Paul Burani ad Benno Jacobson) Centraltheater, Berlin, 1 November

1902 **Le Jockey malgré lui** (Roger/w Paul Gavault) Théâtre des Bouffes-Parisiens 4 December

1904 **Les Hirondelles** (*Das Schwalbennest*) (Henri Hirschmann/ad Maurice Rappaport) Centraltheater, Berlin 9 January

1904 **Le Voyage de la mariée** (Clérice, Edmond Diet/w Paul Ferrier) Galeries St-Hubert, Brussels, 9 December

1905 **Les Filles Jackson et cie** (Clérice) Théâtre des Bouffes-Parisiens 29 November

1907 **Miss Zozo** (Georges A Haakman/w André Alexandre) Théâtre des Capucines 19 March

1908 **La Môme Flora** (Toulmouche/w Pradels) Scala 26 December

1910 **La Demoiselle du tabarin** (Edmond Missa, Diet, Toulmouche/w Alexandre) Nouveau Théâtre du Château d'Eau 25 March

1911 **La Marquise de Chicago** (Toulmouche/w Beissier, Louis Hérel) Enghien 26 September

1911 **Les Trois Amoureuses** (*Der Mann mit den drei Frauen*) French version (Théâtre Molière, Brussels)

1912 **Eva** French version w Jean Bénédict (Alhambra, Brussels)

1913 **Coeur de Créole** (*Kreolenblut*) French version w Bénédict (Lille)

1913 **Le Roi des montagnes** (*Das Fürstenkind*) French version w Bénédict (Théâtre Molière, Brussels)

1913 **La Petite Manon** (Hirschmann/w Henze) Théâtre Royal, Ghent 15 March

1914 **La Fauvette envolée** (Georges de Seynes/w Bénédict) Marseille

1915 **La Cocarde de Mimi-Pinson** (Gustave Goublier/w Francis Gally) Théâtre de l'Apollo 25 November

1916 **La Demoiselle du Printemps** (Goublier) Théâtre de l'Apollo 17 May

1923 **J'épouse Cendrillon** (Guy de Pierreu, A Rachet) Avignon, 17 February

ORLOB, Harold [Fred] (b Logan, Utah, 3 June 1885; d 25 June 1982). Prolific songwriter of exceedingly light material.

Orlob's first song hit 'I Wonder Who's Kissing Her Now', interpolated in the Hough-Adams-Howard Chicago production of *The Prince of Tonight* (and later in other shows – including the Australian edition of *The Balkan Princess* – and films), was long credited to Joe Howard who had purchased it from the young composer and put his own, better-known, name to it. Orlob had previously interpolated numbers in several shows on Broadway, where he had worked as a rehearsal pianist and assistant musical director, and supplied music to some minor hometown (*The Prince and the Peasants*, *The Merry Grafters*) and travelling musicals (*The Seminary Girl*, *Look Who's Here*, *Anita the Singing Girl*) without attracting much notice, but his hit song won him the chance to work further with the Chicago team. He subsequently wrote part of the score for their *The Flirting Princess* (1909) and *Miss Nobody from Starland* (1910), and, when Howard split from the group, apparently irked by the younger man's presence, he provided Hough and Adams with most of the music for their next Chicago show, *The Heartbreakers*. Around the same time he had some Broadway exposure when Orestes Utah Bean's Salt Lake City play *An Aztec Romance* (Manhattan Opera House, 19 September 1912), for which he had written incidental music some years previously, was produced in New York.

Odd Orlob numbers were heard in several Broadway revues, including an edition of *The Passing Show* and *Hitchy Koo of 1918*, several more in Ned Wayburn's *Town Topics* at the Century Music Hall (1915) and as additional material for Sigmund Romberg's score to *The Melting of Molly* (1918), and he presented a full Broadway score in 1914 with *The Red Canary*, all without arousing too much attention. However, the long-running success of the extremely light musical comedy *Listen Lester* (1918), for which he composed the songs, led to several fruitless attempts by producer John Cort and his writers to repeat their coup, before in 1923 Orlob himself turned producer to stage his own *Take a Chance (Ginger)* with a singular lack of success. Although he remained around Broadway for some time thereafter, Orlob's early promise was never confirmed. His first song hit remained his only one, and *Listen Lester* his only winning show.

Orlob's exceedingly long lifespan means that his one hit song, written in the earliest years of the 20th century, stays in copyright until a third of the way through the 21st.

1909 **The Flirting Princess** (Frank Adams, Will M Hough, Joe Howard) Princess, Chicago 1 November

1910 **Miss Nobody from Starland** (w Howard/Adams, Hough) Princess Theater, Chicago

1911 **The Heartbreakers** (w Melville Gideon/Adams, Hough) Princess Theater, Chicago 30 May

1914 **The Red Canary** (Will Johnstone/Alex Johnstone, William LeBaron) Lyric Theater 13 April

1917 **The Masked Model** (Frederick Herendeen/ H B Smith, R B Smith) Johnstown, Pa 7 April

1918 **Listen Lester** (Harry L Cort, George Stoddard) Knickerbocker Theater 23 December

1919 **Nothing But Love** (Frank Stammers) Lyric Theater 14 October

1919 **Just a Minute** (H Cort, Stoddard) Cort Theater 27 October

1923 **Take a Chance** (H I Phillips) Playhouse, Wilmington, Pa 24 January

1923 **Ginger** (revised *Take a Chance*) (Phillips) Daly's Theater 16 October

1924 **A Trial Honeymoon** (Orlob) La Salle Theater, Chicago 29 June

1926 **Suzanne** (John Hunter Booth, William Cary Duncan) National Theater, Washington 7 February

1927 **Talk About Girls** (w Stephen Jones) Waldorf Theater 14 June

1943 **Hairpin Harmony** National Theater 1 October

Other titles attributed: *The Moon Maiden, Making Mary* (1931)

DER ORLOW
Operette in 3 acts by Ernst Marischka and Bruno Granichstädten. Music by Granichstädten. Theater an der Wien, Vienna, 3 April 1925.

One of the most successful musicals to come from the Viennese theatre in the 1920s, *Der Orlow* curiously crept out of the general repertoire thereafter whilst other, less popular, lusher pieces with more fashionable names than that of Bruno Granichstädten attached to them won revivals and a regular place on the schedules.

Der Orlow is set in the Ruritanian land of modern America, where the once-Grand Duke Alexander, now just plain Alex Doroschinsky (Hubert Marischka), works as a machinist a in car factory owned by John Walsh (Richard Waldemar) and Jolly Jefferson (Fritz Steiner). The two most important elements of a fairly slim plot were the beautiful Russian ballerina Nadja Nadjakowska (Betty Fischer) and the regal diamond of inestimable value, known as Der Orlow, which the ex-Duke has smuggled out of war-torn Europe. Both ballerina and diamond are coveted by Walsh. After interludes at Walsh's mansion and at the Alhambra variety theatre, it is, of course, Alex who gets the girl. Elsie Altmann was the soubrette who gets the boss, and Hans Moser had one of his famous character cameos as a commissaire at the Alhambra.

Granichstädten's light and bright, slightly jazzy score began with a shimmy, to which it returned not only as soon as the soubrets came in sight but also after the lovers of the tale had finished romancing to more traditional rhythms. Several sections of the show's music were, in fact, scored for jazz band (alto and tenor sax, two trombones, banjo, piano and drums), but Alex still sang sentimentally over his balalaïka, Nadja moved regularly into valse lente tempo, and the men of the piece sang of love in march-time when the band was not making the most of the shimmy, the Boston, the tango or Moser's comic song in foxtrot time. The most successful single number, however, was the hero's 12/8 Cigarette Song which, joyously plugged by the Austrian State Tobacco Company, made some very dubious claims for the properties of nicotine ('Was tät das arme Herz, wenn es nicht hätte Das süsse Guft, ein kleines bissel Nikotin!').

Der Orlow was a hit of the kind of proportions that only *Die lustige Witwe* and *Die Rose von Stambul* had previously been at the Theater an der Wien. It ran through 403 performances to 25 March 1926, then, when *Die Zirkusprinzessin* took possession, moved to the Bürgertheater (5 June 1926) for a further six weeks, and then to the Raimundtheater where it passed its 600th performance on 6 May 1927 before returning to the Theater an der Wien (23 July 1927) with Anny Coty and Ernst Nadherny now in its lead rôles. It announced the 2 August performance as its 650th. The show was played again intermittently in repertoire until 1930, by which time it had done the rounds of Europe.

Az orlov was well received in its Hungarian version (ad Zsolt Harsányi) with Juci Lábass, Tibor Halmay and Jenő Nádor starred at the Fővárosi Operettszinház, but an English version, adapted by P G Wodehouse and Lauri Wylie under the not-unreasonable title of *Hearts and Diamonds*, was a disappointment in just 46 performances at London's Strand Theatre. *Hearts and Diamonds* featured a strong cast headed by Georges Metaxa, operatic star Louise Edvina and comic Lupino Lane under the direction of Theodore Komisarjevsky, and used some additional numbers by Max Darewski inserted into Granichstädten's score. In Paris the piece was produced by Victor de Cottens at the Folies-Wagram in an adaptation by Roger Ferréol and Georges Merry with André Baugé (Alex), Marthe Ferrare (Nadja) and Boucot in Moser's comic spot, but Broadway passed *Der Orlow* by and its principal success remained its stunning first run in the Austrian capital to where it returned as late as 1959 in a Raimund-theater revival with Johannes Heesters, Margit Bollmann and Rudolf Carl at the head of its cast.

Hungary: Fővárosi Operettszinház *Az orlov* 23 September 1925; UK: Strand Theatre *Hearts and Diamonds* 1 June 1926; France: Folies-Wagram *L'Orloff* 7 December 1928

ORME, Denise [SMITHER, Gertrude Jessie] (b London, 26 August 1884; d London, 20 October 1960). Edwardian ingénue who married two peers.

At the age of 22, after studying violin at the Royal Academy of Music and singing at the Royal College, Miss Orme took to the stage in the chorus of George Edwardes's production of *Les P'tites Michu* at Daly's Theatre. She was promoted to the rôle of Blanche-Marie during the run, and she followed up by creating several leading musical rôles for the famous producer, including the title rôle of *See See* (1906) and soprano parts in *Les Merveilleuses* (1906, Illyrine) and *Our Miss Gibbs* (1909, Lady Elizabeth Thanet). She also took over from Gertie Millar in the part of Franzi in *A Waltz Dream* (1908) and appeared alongside George Huntley in the less fortunate *The Hon'ble Phil* (1908, Marie Martinet). An accomplished violinist, she managed to have a display of this talent inserted into most of her musical rôles. She retired from the theatre to become the Baroness Thurston and, later, Duchess of Leinster, apparently the only ex-Edwardes employee to wed not one peer of the realm, but two.

ORNADEL, Cyril (b London, 2 December 1924).

A West End conductor of mostly Broadway musicals (*My Fair Lady*, *Kiss Me Kate*, *Call Me Madam*, *Paint Your Wagon*, *Pal Joey*, *Kismet*, *The King and I*, *The Sound of Music* etc) from the 1950s to the 1980s, Ornadel also composed and arranged much film and television music and wrote both popular songs ('Portrait of my Love' 1961 w Norman Newell) and the scores for several stage musicals. These were mostly adaptations of English classic literature, and of them *Pickwick* ('If I Ruled the World') was easily the most successful. A musical version of Robert Louis Stevenson's *Treasure Island* proved a repeatable seasonal entertainment at London's Mermaid Theatre, and was later staged in Germany, whilst an adaptation of *And So to Bed* was produced by British television as *Pepys*.

1956 **Starmaker** (David Croft/Ian Stuart Black) King's Theatre, Glasgow 13 February
1958 **The Pied Piper** (Croft) Connaught Theatre, Worthing 24 December
1963 **Pickwick** (Leslie Bricusse/Wolf Mankowitz) Saville Theatre 4 July
1969 **Ann Veronica** (Croft/Frank Wells, Ronald Gow) Cambridge Theatre 17 April
1973 **Treasure Island** (Hal Shaper/Bernard Miles, Josephine Wilson) Mermaid Theatre 17 December
1975 **Great Expectations** (Shaper/Trevor Preston) Yvonne Arnaud Theatre, Guildford, 24 December
1978 **Once More Darling** (Norman Newell/Ray Cooney, John Chapman) Churchill Theatre, Bromley 5 June

ORPHÉE AUX ENFERS Opéra-bouffon in 2 acts by Hector Crémieux [and Ludovic Halévy]. Music by Jacques Offenbach. Théâtre des Bouffes-Parisiens, Paris, 21 October 1858. Revised 4-act version Théâtre de la Gaîté, Paris, 7 February 1874.

Orphée aux enfers was Offenbach's first venture into mounting a full-scale opéra-bouffe at his blossoming little Théâtre des Bouffes-Parisiens, where it marked a significant advance on the three-, four- and five-handed short pieces which, because of legal restrictions on the size and kind of entertainments allowable under his licence, had been the house's diet since its inception. The idea of a burlesque of the Orpheus legend, particularly familiar to theatregoers of the time as the subject of Gluck's revered opera, had been nurtured some time in the brains of librettists Crémieux and Halévy, but whilst Offenbach was forced to work inside a format which allowed him a maximum of four or five characters, there was little chance of producing a piece which aspired to show Olympus and its inhabitants in all their parodied glory. The dissolution of the prohibitive restrictions in 1858 allowed the collaborators finally to go to work on their *Orphée*, although Halévy, now making advances in the diplomatic world, decided against allowing his name to go on the credits. By October *Orphée aux enfers* was on the stage.

Orpheus (Tayau) is a boring Theban music-teacher with an eye for a nymph, and his flirtatious wife, Eurydice (Lise Tautin), in her turn, makes sheep's eyes at the handsome shepherd Aristaeus (Léonce). What Eurydice doesn't know, however, is that her new boyfriend is no less than Pluto, the King of the Underworld, in earthly disguise. He wants to have her around more permanently, so he fixes it that she treads on a nasty asp in a cornfield and, having duly expired, is consigned to a comfy boudoir in his nether regions. Orpheus is rid of Eurydice, Pluto has her, and everyone would now be quite happy, were it not for that nosy, hectoring creature called Public Opinion (Mme Macé-Montrouge). She bullies the unwilling Orpheus into going up to see Jupiter (Désiré) on Olympus, to demand the return of his stolen wife. As a result, the Olympian deities, all thrilled at the thought of a bit of subterranean slumming, descend to Hades en masse and Jupiter winkles out the hiding place of Eurydice. Enchanted by her, he proposes that she swap Hades for Olympus. But there is still Orpheus to account to and, worse, the dreadful Public Opinion, who seems to have the silly musician mesmerized. When she gets the traditional story back on its rails, and forces Pluto to make Eurydice follow Orpheus back to earth, Jupiter is obliged to use a little thunderbolt to make the musician follow mythology, look back, and lose forever the wife he is longing to lose forever. But that is where mythology must stop. For, if he can't have Eurydice himself, Jupiter is not going to leave her with Pluto and so, in defiance of the classics and of Gluck, he turns her into a Bacchante. A highly suitable ending for the girl.

The music with which the composer illustrated this bouquet of comical and satirical fireworks was the most dazzling display of light, comic theatre music in the history of the genre. From the earliest moments of the score, with Eurydice mooning over her shepherd, or screeching insults at her husband's music-making, from Aristaeus' mocking entry song, and the lady's melodramatic parody of an operatic death ('La mort m'apparait souriante') the score bounced along on a bubble of laughter and melody. The Olympian scene introduced Diana with some fleet-footed hunting couplets, and a trio of godly offspring chiding their father over his amorous adventures (Rondeau des Transformations) as well as a quote from Gluck's most famous moment, the aria 'Che faro senza Eurydice?', in Orpheus' unwilling exposure of his case before Jupiter. Hades helped pile up the total of memorable moments with the solo for the lugubrious comic Bache as the dead King of Boeotia ('Quand j'étais roi de Béotie'), Jupiter's attempts to seduce Eurydice whilst disguised as a fly ('Il me semble que sur mon épaule') and the famous galop infernale which was to come to be known as 'the can-can'.

The show was quickly a major hit (although Offenbach apparently continued well after the opening to operate cuts and rewrites) and by the time it was removed in the following June it had run for no fewer than 228 nights, and its music was being played throughout the country and even beyond. The first production of the show outside France seems to have been at Breslau (ad L Kalisch) in November 1859 before Prague then Vienna took the show up. Johann Nestroy, at that time in charge of the Carltheater and already the producer of Vienna's early versions of the short Offenbach works, produced the first Vienna *Orpheus in der Unterwelt* in his own adaptation with himself playing Jupiter, equipped with enough extra satirical dialogue to make his rôle into something like a meneur de revue. Karl Treumann was Pluto, Philipp Grobecker played Orpheus, Therese Schäfer was Eurydice, Anna Grobecker Public Opinion and Wilhelm Knaack a memorable Styx. *Orpheus* was a distinct hit and it was brought back at the Carltheater again the following year, by which time Berlin and New York's German-speaking theatre had also welcomed Nestroy's version with equally happy results. In Berlin, the piece was popular enough to provoke a burlesque of its burlesque – *Orpheus in der Oberwelt* – produced at Meysels Theater. In the meantime, *Orphée aux enfers* had also continued its cavalcade around Paris where, on one famous occasion, the celebrated courtesan Cora Pearl appeared as Cupid.

Many other centres soon had their versions – more or less faithful – of *Orphée*, amongst them Stockholm, Brussels, Copenhagen, Warsaw and St Petersburg, but some places took longer than others to take up this novel kind of entertainment. Although *Orpheus in der Unterwelt* was played in German at several Budapest theatres and in Hungarian at Kassa (ad Endre Látabár) in 1862, the show was not played in the vernacular in Budapest until 1882. When it was (ad Lajos Evva) it was produced with a starry cast topling Ilka Pálmay (Eurydice), Elek Solymossy (Jupiter), János Kápolnai (Orpheus), Pál Vidor (Pluto), Vidor Kassai (Styx) and Mariska Komáromi (Cupid), scored a grand success, and quickly began to make up for lost time with revivals in 1885, 1889 and 1895.

England was even slower and, although the *Orphée* score was swiftly and thoroughly plundered to supply music for burlesque scores, it was not until seven years had gone by that the master of extravaganza J R Planché had his English version, *Orpheus in the Haymarket*, staged at Her Majesty's Theatre with a cast including Louise Keeley, William Farren and David Fisher. Well enough received, it was by no means a sensation, but bits of it got a second showing, at the Strand burlesque house where an Orphean burlesque was produced in 1871 as *Eurydice* with Harry Paulton as Aristaeus and at the Royal Surrey Gardens in 1873 when another *Eurydice* (ad by W F Vandervell) was

given a hearing for more than 50 nights before going on to the National Theatre, Holborn in November. After Hortense Schneider had played two London seasons with *Orphée* in her repertoire, and after Offenbach's later full-sized works had made a more considerable mark, it was brought back in two new versions. One, produced by Kate Santley (Royalty Theatre, December 1876), starred its manageress as a Eurydice who expanded her rôle with a few cockney music-hall songs, alongside the more conventional Pluto of Henry Hallam and the Jupiter of J D Stoyle, a second, a few months later (ad H S Leigh) was a spectacular mounting at the Alhambra (3 June 1877) in a version this time advertised as 'altered by the composer'. Kate Munroe/Cornélie d'Anka (Eurydice), W H Woodfield (Pluto) and Harry Paulton (Jupiter) starred with the rising J H Ryley as Mercury and a 'grand procession of 300' and several ballets interpolated. The piece ran almost four months and was one of the Alhambra's most successful productions to date.

Australian managers waited even longer to pick up the show, although Offenbach's score was heard there almost in toto in Pringle's and Cellier's concerts but, when *Orpheus* did finally appear on stage in the 'underworld', two different productions were mounted within 48 hours of each other. William S Lyster produced Planché's version in Melbourne with top vocalists Alice May (Eurydice), Armes Beaumont (Pluto) and Georgina Hodson (Public Opinion) and with Richard Stewart as Jupiter, whilst two nights later the burlesque actress Lydia Howard presented her production of the same adaptation at Sydney's Royal Victoria Theatre, herself playing Eurydice to the Pluto of J J Welsh and the Jupiter of W Andrews in repertoire with two contrasting pasticcio British burlesques, Byron's *Fra Diavolo* and *[The Nymph of the] Lurleyburg*.

New York, though initially quicker to see the show than Britain, had it several times in German and then at both the Théâtre Français and from Lucille Tostée's company in the original French, before it was finally played in English. That first vernacular production was seen at the Bijou Theater in 1883 with a cast including Digby Bell (Jupiter), Marie Vanoni (Eurydice), Pauline Hall (Venus) and D'Oyly Carte contralto Augusta Roche (Public Opinion).

In 1874, when Offenbach had launched himself on a new period as a theatrical manager, this time at the Théâtre de la Gaîté, he decided to mount a new production of *Orphée*. To fit it for this considerably larger stage, he remade the show, making it both more spectacular (chorus of 120, orchestra of 60, ballet of 60) but also longer and more full of 'items'. The new *Orphée* stretched to four acts and included, beyond its additional scenery and ballets, a considerable amount of new vocal material, both solo and choral, let in to the script like so many undone pleats. Eurydice (Marie Cico, who had been the original Minerva) and Pluton both got an extra song, and Mercury, Mars and Cupid all got solos to add to what virtually became a divine variety show on Olympus. The final act was extended with a piece for the Judges of the Underworld and a comical policemen's chorus. If the alterations did little for *Orphée* as a work (the piece has mostly since been played in its original rather than its expanded version) they served their purpose in giving a 'second edition' to the Paris public, who came to the Gaîté in their enthusiastic numbers, giving Offenbach a success which encouraged him to give the same treatment to several other of his early works for the same stage.

Orphée aux enfers has survived – with intermittent fallow periods – in the international repertoire through all the changes in musical theatre tastes of the past 130 years. It has moved from the commercial theatre into the subsidized theatre, and more specifically the opera houses of the world, as one of the handful of classic musical pieces which are repeatedly reprised, taking precedence virtually everywhere even over those later Offenbach pieces which, originally, had a notably greater popularity in various countries: *Die schöne Helena* in Austria and Hungary, *Geneviève de Brabant* in Britain, *La Grande-Duchesse* in America. In Germany, however, it has from the start been the favourite Offenbach work.

Orphée was regularly revived in France until it reached first the Opéra-Comique and then the Paris Opéra itself (19 January 1988) and, amongst countless other productions, was given a large and glitzy German revival under Max Reinhardt at the Grosses Schauspielhaus in 1922. It won a major fresh boost in Britain in 1960 with Wendy Toye's production of Geoffrey Dunn's hilarious if unsatirical new translation for the Sadler's Wells Opera, but that company's successor, English National Opera, did less well when (5 September 1985) they attempted a rather incoherent staging of the expanded version (ad Snoo Wilson).

Austria: Carltheater *Orpheus in der Unterwelt* 17 March 1860; Germany: Breslau 17 November 1859, Friedrich-Wilhelm-städtisches Theater 23 June 1860; USA: Stadttheater (Ger) March 1861, Théâtre Français (Fr) 17 January 1867, Bijou Theater *Orpheus in the Underworld* 1 December 1883; Hungary: Kassa (Hung) 16 March 1862, Budai Színkör (Ger) 6 May 1862, Népszinház, Budapest *Orfeuz al alvilágban* (or *Orfeuz a pokolban*) 12 May 1882; UK: Her Majesty's Theatre *Orpheus in the Haymarket* 26 December 1865; Australia: Princess Theatre, Melbourne 30 March 1872
Recordings: complete (Musidisc Festival, EMI-Pathé, Golden Age), selections (EMI-Pathé), selection in English (HMV, TER), selection in German (Philips) etc

ÖSTERREICHER, Rudolf (b Vienna, 19 July 1881; d Vienna, 23 October 1966).

Performer, author and playwright, Österreicher had a long and wide career in most areas of showbusiness, performing in cabaret, writing for both the musical and the non-musical stage, and authoring the standard biography of Emmerich Kálmán during a career in which he had some 40 musical comedies and Operetten produced in European theatres.

His first pieces to appear on the Vienna stage were the Possen mit Gesang, *Der Gummiradler* and *Bediene dich selbst!*, produced at the Raimundtheater when its author was in his early twenties, and he turned out the comic *Die Spottvogelwirtin*, with music by Ziehrer, for the same house before he had his first operettic success with the text to Winterberg's *Ihr Adjutant*, a piece which was played for 46 nights at the Theater an der Wien in 1911 with Fritz Werner starred, and subsequently in Germany and in Hungary (*Az Adjutáns*, ad Frigyes Hervay). A collaboration with Ziehrer on *Das dumme Herz* was worth 68 nights at the Johann Strauss-Theater, Reinhardt's *Die erste Frau* ran for over two months at the Carltheater, and Österreicher then followed up with wartime hits around central Europe, having his most successful moments to date with Carl Weinberger on *Drei arme Teufel*, with Eysler on *Graf Toni*, and with Dr Willner on the refitting of chunks of Kálmán's *Zsuzsi kisasszony* score with a new libretto as *Die Faschingsfee*. However, he won his first and only major international success, after nearly 20 years as a librettist, when he supplied the book to Jean Gilbert's *Katja, die Tänzerin*.

Österreicher had further home successes with his texts for Gilbert's *Das Weib in Purpur*, and Stolz's *Eine einzige Nacht*, *Mitternachtswalzer* and *Drei von der Donau*, the first beginning its career with 160 nights at the Carltheater, the second topping 100 nights at the Bürgertheater and the last, a version of Nestroy's *Lumpacivagabundus*, being produced under his own management during a period of management at the Wiener Stadttheater between 1945 and 1947. In the 1950s he collaborated with Hubert Marischka on two last stage musicals.

Österreicher also supplied the screenplays for a number of Operette films.

1903 **Der Gummiradler** (Rudolf Raimann) Raimundtheater 22 December
1905 **Bediene dich selbst!** (Arthur von Henriques) Raimundtheater 14 October
1906 **Die Spotvogelwirtin** (Carl Michael Ziehrer) Raimundtheater 30 October
1911 **Ihr Adjutant** (Robert Winterberg/w Franz von Schönthan) Theater an der Wien 3 March
1911 **Vielliebchen** (Ludwig Engländer/w Carl Lindau) Venedig in Wien 5 May
1914 **Das dumme Herz** (Ziehrer/w Wilhelm Sterk) Johann Strauss-Theater 27 February
1914 **Der Kriegsberichterstatter** (many/w Sterk) Apollotheater 9 October
1914 **Das Mädchen im Mond** (Karl Stigler/w Sterk) Carltheater 7 November
1914 **Der Durchgang der Venus** (Edmund Eysler/w A M Willner) Apollotheater 28 November
1915 **Liebesgeister** (Ernst Steffan/w Bela Jenbach) 1 act Apollotheater 1 March
1915 **Der künstlicher Mensch** (Leo Fall/w Willner) Theater des Westens, Berlin 2 October
1915 **Die erste Frau** (Heinrich Reinhardt/Willner) Carltheater 22 October
1916 **Drei arme Teufel** (Carl Weinberger/w Heinz Reichert) Theater am Gärtnerplatz, Munich 11 March
1917 **Graf Toni** (Eysler) Apollotheater 1 March
1917 **Die Faschingsfee** (Emmerich Kálmán/w Willner) Johann Strauss-Theater 21 September
1918 **Johann Nestroy** (arr Ernst Reiterer/w Willner) Carltheater 4 December
1919 **Der Künstlerpreis** (Leo Ascher/w Julius Horst) Apollotheater 1 October
1921 **Nixchen** (Oscar Straus/w Willner) Wallner-Theater, Berlin 10 September
1921 **Rinaldo** (*Gróf Rinaldo*) German version w Jenbach (Johann Strauss-Theater)
1923 **Katja, die Tänzerin** (Jean Gilbert/w Leopold Jacobson) Johann Strauss-Theater 5 January
1923 **Vierzehn Tage Arrest** (Eysler/w Horst) Raimundtheater 16 June
1923 **Das Weib im Purpur** (Gilbert/w Jacobson) Neues Wiener Stadttheater 21 December
1924 **Ein Ballroman** (Robert Stolz/w Willner, Fritz Rotter) Apollotheater 29 February
1924 **Geliebte seiner Hoheit** (Gilbert/w Bernauer) Theater am Nollendorfplatz, Berlin 30 September

1925 **[Der Abenteuer des Herrn] Meiermax** (Hugo Hirsch/w Jacobson) Lessing-Theater 31 December

1926 **Der Mitternachtswalzer** (Stolz/w Willner) Wiener Bürgertheater 30 October

1927 **Yvette und ihre Freunde** (Michael Krasznay-Krausz/w Sterk) Wiener Bürgertheater 18 November

1927 **Eine einzige Nacht** (Stolz/w Jacobson) Carltheater 23 December

1930 **Peppina** (Stolz/w Jacobson) Komische Oper, Berlin 22 December

1933 **Zwei lachende Augen** (Straus/w Ludwig Hirschfeld) Theater an der Wien 22 December

1943 **Brillanten aus Wien** (Alexander Steinbrecher) Theaterakademie

1947 **Drei von der Donau** (Stolz/w Robert Gilbert) Wiener Stadttheater 24 September

1948 **Ohne Geld war ich reich** (Karl Loubé) Raimundtheater 9 January

1955 **Liebesbriefe** (Nico Dostal/w Hubert Marischka) Raimundtheater 23 November

1958 **Deutschmeisterkapelle** (Ziehrer arr/w H Marischka) Raimundtheater 31 May

OTTENHEIMER, Paul (b Stuttgart, 1 March 1873; d Darmstadt, 1951).

Ottenheimer studied in Stuttgart and subsequently became a conductor in Augsburg, Trier, Linz, Graz, Prague, Nuremberg and then, from 1913, at the Hoftheater in Darmstadt. He had a considerable success as a theatre composer when his Operette *Heimliche Liebe* (1911) proved a highly appreciated Viennese vehicle for Alexander Girardi and ran through a first series of 200 performances at the Johann Strauss-Theater in 1911–12 before going on to be seen in Germany and in Hungary (*A kis dobos* Sopron, 1 April 1912). This success won him the chance to compose the score to another Julius Bauer text, *Der arme Millionär*, for the same theatre and the same megastar. Erich Müller's production of this second piece lasted a more modest 62 performances, but *Der arme Millionär* followed *Heimliche Liebe* on to further performances in Germany. Another star vehicle, *Hans im Glück*, written this time for Max Pallenberg, was played at the composer's home base in Darmstadt but went no further.

1911 **Heimliche Liebe** (Julius Bauer) Johann Strauss-Theater 13 October

1913 **Der arme Millionär** (Bauer) Johann Strauss-Theater 17 October

1914 **Hans im Glück** (E Rudy) Hoftheater, Darmstadt 7 June

1916 **Des Burschen Heimkehr** (aka *Der tolle Hund*) (Ernst Elias Niedergall) Hoftheater, Darmstadt 30 January

OUR MISS GIBBS Musical comedy in 3 acts by 'Cryptos' and James T Tanner. Lyrics by Adrian Ross and Percy Greenbank. Music by Ivan Caryll and Lionel Monckton. Gaiety Theatre, London, 23 January 1909.

Fifteen years after the Gaiety Theatre had launched its first modern musical comedy, *The Shop Girl*, about a little vendeuse who wins her way to wealth and social position, George Edwardes's famous and hugely successful house was still turning out tales of the same kind. And, by and large, they were still being compiled and decorated by the same team of writers who had, for more than a decade, been London's and the world's favourite purveyors of the kind of brightly comical song and dance shows in which the Gaiety specialized. *Our Miss Gibbs*, written by the famous five under the pseudonym of 'Cryptos', and again

Plate 201. **Our Miss Gibbs:** *The Gaiety front line disport themselves in front of a reproduction of the White City.*

telling the tale of a little vendeuse who wins her way to wealth and social position, turned out to be one of the best made and most popular of the series.

Gertie Millar, now the certified star of the Gaiety, played Mary Gibbs, a nice, no-nonsense Yorkshire lass (like Gertie) who sells sweets in Garrods department store, and Teddy Payne, her comical co-star, was her brother Timothy. Mary falls in love with a bank clerk who turns out to be an earl (J Edward Fraser), whilst Timothy accidentally gets mixed up with the attempt by Hughie Pierrepoint (George Grossmith), an aspiring aristocratic criminal, to pinch the Ascot Gold Cup. Robert Hale played Hughie's crook tutor, Slithers, Denise Orme was the ingénue and Hughie's ultimate partner, and Maisie Gay, Gladys Homfrey and Jeannie Aylwin had supporting rôles in which they were predictably soubrettish, dragonistic and Scottish-with-songs respectively. The Gaiety Girls got to parade about glamorously at the White City in the second act.

Caryll and Monckton's score was as lively and pretty as usual, with Monckton's solo for his leading lady wife proving the hit of the evening. Gertie sang 'Moonstruck', prettily done up in pierrot costume, apropos of very little, but probably of just slightly more than the show's other major song success, Grossmith's latest interpolation from America. 'Yip! I-addy! I-ay!' had nothing at all to do with Yorkshire, the Ascot Gold Cup or *Our Miss Gibbs*, but it was a hit for its performer as the show ran on for a London season of 636 performances, a score better than any but *The Toreador* of the 15 years of Gaiety musicals. *Our Miss Gibbs* also remained, thereafter, the best-loved and most often repeated of the group.

Soon on the road in England, it also began its overseas travels before the London run was done. Gabor Steiner transported the show swiftly to Vienna (ad Carl Lindau, Max Baer, Leopold Krenn, Julius Freund) along with the Gaiety's Fred Wright who played Timothy in German opposite the Miss Gibbs of a little, teenaged Hungarian soubrette called Mizzi Hájos. As Mitzi she was soon to find fame and a long musical comedy career in America. The supporting cast included such names as Gisela Werbezirk, Karl Tuschl (Slithers), Betti Seidl and Josef Victora (Hughie), whilst Gracia Soria from the Royal Opera of Madrid headed an interpolated 'Liebesfest' concert in the second act, in one of the four songs of which a young artist called Betty Fischer was given her chance.

From Vienna, Wright moved on to America to star in Charles Frohman's Broadway production of the show, opposite former Gaiety chorine Pauline Chase, but 57 performances were all the much-tampered-with show managed in New York. It was much better received in Australia where J C Williamson billed it, with what eventually proved to be splendid foresight, as 'the greatest musical success of our generation'. His production featured another of the Wright family, brother Bertie, as Timothy alongside Blanche Browne (Mary) and Langford Kirby (Hughie) and with an Australian dancer-actor called Fred Leslie who was in no way related to the famous Gaiety actor doubling as Slithers and choreographer. *Our Miss Gibbs* quite simply broke every long-run record in the Australian theatre. At a time when six weeks was considered a good run, it ran for a quite amazing seven-and-a-bit months at Sydney's Her Majesty's and the Theatre Royal (230 performances), smashing Sydney's long-run record before going on to seasons around Australia and regular revivals for half a dozen years. The eclipse of Gaiety musical comedy by modern Viennese and American shows led it to drop from the repertoire after the war, but its record remained good until the coming of *Rose Marie* 16 years later.

Austria: Wiener Stadttheater *Miss Gibbs* 12 November 1909; USA: Knickerbocker Theater 29 August 1910; Australia: Her Majesty's Theatre, Sydney 24 September 1910

OUT OF THIS WORLD Musical in 2 acts by Dwight Taylor and Reginald Lawrence. Music and lyrics by Cole Porter. New Century Theater, New York, 21 December 1950.

The Cole Porter successor to *Kiss Me, Kate* was allegedly based on the Amphytrion legend, but in fact it had less in common with that specific tale than with bedroom farce in general, and with the many musical plays which had happily mixed immortals and mortals in comical fantasy since the 18th-century *Midas*. The most Amphytrionic bit of the libretto had Jupiter (George Jongeyans, ie George Gaynes) lusting after and laying a young American tourist (Priscilla Gilette) whilst in the shape of her husband (William Eythe), but top-billing (with four and two shared songs) went to comedienne Charlotte Greenwood, cast in the normally peripheral part of the jealous Juno. Mercury (William Redfield) played his traditional rôle as Jupiter's pander, David Burns appeared as a Greek gangster and Barbara Ashley as an incidental nymph with a song. The song which caused the most enjoyment in the show, however, was Miss Greenwood's loose-limbed rendition of the plain girl's lament 'Nobody's Chasing Me' with its typical Porter catalogue of things that were being chased whilst she wasn't. However, the song which lasted the best was one that didn't last in the show as far as Broadway: the surging 'From This Moment On'. The show itself, under the management of *Kiss Me, Kate*'s Saint Subber and Lemuel Ayers, didn't last either, playing only 157 Broadway performances.

It did, however, get some brief later showings on stage, being seen off-Broadway in 1956, at New York's Equity Library Theatre in a revamped version (ad George

Oppenheimer) in 1973 and turning up in Australia in 1967, when a production was mounted at the Menzies Theatre Restaurant in Sydney. Rosina Raisbeck, Colin Croft and Roslyn Dunbar featured through a short season.

Australia: Menzies Theatre Restaurant, Sydney 4 January 1967
Recording: original cast (Columbia)

OVER HERE! America's big band musical by Will Holt. Music and lyrics by Richard M Sherman and Robert B Sherman. Shubert Theater, New York, 6 March 1974.

A 1940s nostalgia show which featured the two surviving members of the Andrews Sisters – Pattie and Maxene – in a tongue-in-cheek wartime story. Janie Sell made up the team as the ring-in to the act who turns out to be a rotten German spy. The Sherman brothers, better known for their contribution to filmland musicals such as *Mary Poppins*, provided a 1940s pastiche score arranged by period specialist Louis St Louis and played by a big band, which was topped by a 'best of' selection of Andrews Sisters favourites. The supporting cast included Ann Reinking and a young man called John Travolta, and *Over Here!* ran through 341 Broadway performances.

Recording: original cast (Columbia)

OVER SHE GOES Musical tantivy in 2 acts by Stanley Lupino. Additional dialogue by Arty Ash. Lyrics by Desmond Carter and Frank Eyton. Music by Billy Mayerl. Saville Theatre, London, 23 September 1936.

Continuing their series of dance-and-laughter shows, Laddie Cliff and Stanley Lupino scored a fresh success and a 248-performance run with the jollities of *Over She Goes*. The pair played a couple of vaudevillians whose chum (Eric Fawcett) inherits a title and then finds an opportunistic old fiancée (Barbara Francis) on the doormat. Lupino pretends to be the late Uncle come back to life, the Dowager (Doris Rogers) promptly appears, and complications thicken until the uncle really does turn up. Adele Dixon, Teddie St Denis and Sally Grey were the boys' partners, whilst Syd Walker and Richard Murdoch scored a supporting hit as a pair of policemen called in to help tidy up the mess. Billy Mayerl produced one of his catchiest handfuls of songs for the moments between the fun, with the three boys' version of the title song, Fawcett and Miss Dixon's bandworthy 'I Breathe on Windows' and Murdoch's silly-ass copper singing about a 'Speed Cop' proving the highlights.

The show turned out to be the highpoint of the Lupino/Cliff association and also, sadly, its end. Before the next of their shows appeared Cliff had become too ill to take part. He did, however, appear with Lupino and Murdoch in the film version of the piece alongside Bertha Belmore as the dowager, Claire Luce and Gina Malo.

Australia took a glimpse at the new-style Gaiety musical with seasons of *Over She Goes* and *Swing Along* in 1937. George Gee, Donald Burr, Valerie Hay, Percy Le Fre, Lois Green and Billie Worth were the principals of the company, and *Over She Goes* did better than its companion piece with seven-week seasons in both Melbourne and Sydney (Theatre Royal, 25 September).

Australia: Her Majesty's Theatre, Melbourne 10 July 1937; Film: Associated British Picture Corp 1937

P

PACIFIC 1860 Musical romance in 3 acts by Noël Coward. Theatre Royal, Drury Lane, London, 19 December 1946.

Coward's romantic costume operetta *Pacific 1860* reopened the Theatre Royal, Drury Lane after its reconversion from its wartime use as the headquarters of the troops' entertainment organization. Set in a fictional south seas island, it had a main storyline which followed the romance of the son of a socially striving expatriate family, Kerry Stirling (Graham Payn), and the therefore unacceptable opera singer Elena Salvador (Mary Martin) through three acts and a couple of minor hiccoughs to a happy ending. If the show's story was flimsy, its trappings were much less so and in the score to *Pacific 1860* Coward produced some of his best writing. None of it, however, was for the two leading characters. Sylvia Cecil as the heroine's duenna had a vintage Coward waltz song ('This is a Changing World') and joined two maids in a beautiful trio ('This is a Night for Lovers'), whilst the comical part of the proceedings included the young society folks' tongue-poking 'His Excellency Regrets', the tale of naughty 'Uncle Harry' who tried to be a missionary (cut, then replaced), a plump lassie's bewailing 'I Wish I Wasn't Quite Such a Big Girl', a grim lament for three uncomfortably ageing mammas ('Here in the Twilight of Our Days') and another cut number describing how 'Alice is at it Again'. The incidentals, however, were not enough to compensate for the show's very soft centre and the miscasting of Miss Martin, and *Pacific 1860* closed in 129 performances. Coward later rescued Miss Cecil's two numbers and put them into the original *Sail Away*, but they were cut out of that show when the soprano rôle was excised on the road.

Recording: original cast (TER)

PACIFICO Opérette in 3 acts by Paul Nivoix. Lyrics by Camille François and Robert Chabrier. Music by Jo Moutet. Théâtre de la Porte-Saint-Martin, Paris, 10 December 1958.

Pacifico brought back to the Paris stage the effective team of matinée-idol vocalist George Guétary and celebrated 'paysan' actor and comedian Bourvil which had triumphed in the long-running *La Route fleurie*. Guétary rejoiced in 'Reveillon à Paris', topped off the title-song, and soupily romanced 'Marilyn' (Corinne Marchand), whilst the comic crinkled his way inimitably through 'C'est du nanar', assured the world that 'C'est pas si mal que ça chez nous', and also got together with his soubrette partner, Pierrette Bruno, in a couple of duets and with Guétary in one of the less wallpapery numbers of the score, 'Casimir'. If the jolly material was far from exceptional, the performers, and Bourvil in particular, were, and they kept *Pacifico* in Paris for three seasons.

Recording: original cast (Pathé)

PACIFIC OVERTURES Musical in 2 acts by John Weidman. Music and lyrics by Stephen Sondheim. Additional material by Hugh Wheeler. Winter Garden Theater, New York, 11 January 1976.

Stephen Sondheim's successor to *A Little Night Music* swapped the earlier show's mixture of acerbic old-world tale and brilliant dance-rhythmed music for a purposely undemonstrative and stylized manner in a musical pageant which told, in a semi-revusical style and from a Japanese point of view, the tale of the forcible opening-up of Japan to the West under the initial prodding of Commodore Perry and his American 'invaders'. The show's score mixed textually and musically laconic, often formal and even opaque utterances from some of the Japanese characters, with such items as the witty poisoning of the Shogun by 'Chrysanthemum Tea', some national parodies in the invading 'Please, Hallo', a part-song for some British sailors attempting to make unwelcome advances to a 'Pretty Lady', and a final scene, 'Next', showing the more-Western-than-Western result of the outside world's interference.

Produced by Harold Prince, and staged by him in a style which took in elements of Japanese traditional theatre, *Pacific Overtures* was played by a cast of Asian performers headed by Mako as the Reciter, Sab Shimono as Manjiro, the fisherman with experience of the West who attempts to maintain the old Japan, and Isao Sato as Kayama, the samurai who rises to political power on an opportunistic pro-Western line. The production and the show failed to please and *Pacific Overtures* closed in 193 Broadway performances. It was given an off-Broadway revival by the York Players in 1984 (22 March, 20 performances) and subsequently a more determined one, with such names as the Shuberts and Nugent and McCann attached to its billhead, at the Promenade Theater (25 October, 1984) which lasted 109 performances.

In Britain, *Pacific Overtures* was first staged in Manchester with a Caucasian cast and in a production which swapped the formal style of the original staging for a much coloured-up presentation. It pleased its public much better than a subsequent, greyly plodding performance by operatic vocalists which was quickly swept from its unlikely place in the repertoire of the subsidized English National Opera, and was given a second Manchester season later the same year (1 October 1986).

UK: Forum Theatre, Wythenshawe, Manchester, 29 April 1986, London Coliseum 10 September 1987
Recordings: original cast (RCA), English National Opera cast (TER)

PADILLA [Sánchez], José (b Almeria, 28 May 1889; d Madrid, 25 October 1960).

Best known internationally as the composer of the

popular songs 'El relicario', 'La violetera' and 'Valencia', Padilla wrote a considerable number of zarzuelas for the Spanish stage as well as providing songs for Parisian revue – 'Ça, c'est Paris' (ad Lucien Boyer, Jacques-Charles, from *La bien amada*), 'Le Tango de Miss' performed by Mistinguett at the Moulin-Rouge – and the scores for two Paris opérettes. His first Parisian piece, *Pépète*, a musical-comedy tale of an aunt's attempts to arrange the devirginizing of an apparently uninterested lad, was produced by Dupont and Baudry at the Théâtre de l'Avenue, with Edmée Favart (Monique), Félix Oudart (Leblairois, director) and Robert Burnier (Gilbert) heading the cast, the second, *Symphonie Portugaise*, 25 years later, was an opérette à grand spectacle in the style of its period produced by and played by Germaine Roger at the Gaîté-Lyrique, and subsequently played in the French provinces without notable success.

Padilla's 'My Spanish Rose' was interpolated in the Broadway score of Jerome Kern's *The Night Boat*.

1906 **La mala hembra** (Ventura de la Vega) 1 act Teatro Barbieri 24 March

1907 **Las palomas blancas** (Justo Huste) Teatro Apolo, Almeria 31 October

1908 **El centurión** (Miguel Mihura, Navarro, Cumbrearas) 1 act Teatro Lux-Eden 5 October

1908 **La Titiritera** (Garcia Revenga, E Zaballos) 1 act Teatro Lux-Eden 12 October

1909 **Los tres reyes** (L Ferreiro) 1 act Teatro la Latina 5 January

1909 **La copla gitana** (w Quislant/Juan Tavares) 1 act Teatro Barbieri 8 January

1909 **De los barrios bajos** (w Franco) 1 act

1909 **Juan Miguel** (Ventura de la Vega) 1 act Teatro Barbieri 1 October

1909 **El decir de la gente** (Mihura, Ricardo Gonzáles de Toro) 1 act Teatro Martin 5 November

1909 **La presidaria** (Ventura de la Vega) 1 act Teatro Barbieri 19 November

1909 **Los viejos verdes** (Manuel de Lara, Joaquín Valverde) Teatro Barbieri 14 December

1910 **Los hombres de empuje** 1 act Teatro Benvenuto June

1910 **Pajaritos y flores** (Mihura, González de Toro) 1 act Teatro Apolo 28 September

1911 **Almas distintas** (Ventura de la Vega) 1 act

1911 **Mirando a la Alhambra** 1 act

1911 **El pueblo del Peleón** (Mihura, González de Toro) 1 act

1911 **El divino jugete** (Quiles Pastor) 1 act Teatro Novedades December

1912 **El principe celoso** (Soler Múgica) 1 act Madrid 8 November

1913 **La plebe** (M Fernández Palomero) 1 act Teatro Novedades, Barcelona 13 December

1914 **De España al cielo** (w Jéronimo Jiménez) 1 act Barcelona, February

1914 **El suspiro del moro** (Serrano Clavero) Teatro Comedia, Buenos Aires 24 December

1915 **El mantón roja** (Mihura) 1 act Teatro Barbieri 18 December

1916 **La oracion de la vida** (Fernández Palomero) 1 act Teatro Martin 24 June

1916 **La corte del amor** (Fernández Palomero) Teatro Comedia, Buenos Aires 24 June

1916 **Marcial Hotel** (Mihura, Gonzáles de Toro) 1 act Teatro Martin 4 October

1916 **Miguelin** (Armando Oliveros, José María Castellví) Teatro Tivoli, Barcelona 20 October

1917 **Judith, la viuda hebrea** (Gonzalo Jover, Juan Eugenio Morant) 1 act Teatro Victoria, Barcelona 21 September

1917 **Luzbel** (José Aguado, Miguel Nieto) 1 act Teatro Tivoli, Barcelona 7 November

1917 **Sabino el trapisondista** (*El saber todo lo puedo*) 1 act (Oliveros, Castellví) Teatro Victoria, Barcelona 21 December

1918 **El secreto de la paz** (José Ramón Franquet) 1 act Teatro Cómico, Barcelona 30 March; Teatro Prince, Madrid March 1920

1919 **Reyes, la Jerezana** (F Pérez Capo) 1 act Teatro Martin 30 January

1924 **Pépète** (Didier Gold, Robert Dieudonné, Charles-Antoine Carpentier) Théâtre de l'Avenue, Paris 3 February

1924 **Sol de Sevilla** (José Andres de la Prada) Teatro Tivoli, Barcelona 18 March

1924 **La bien amada** (de la Prada) Teatro Tivoli, Barcelona

1924 **La mayorala** (de la Prada) Teatro Tivoli, Barcelona

1933 **Con el pelo suelto** (José Silva Aramburu) Teatro Zarzuela 29 November

1934 **Las inviolables** (Aramburu) Principal Palace, Barcelona 19 July

1934 **La bella burlada** (de la Prada) Teatro Nuevo, Barcelona 9 November

1934 **El duende** (Aramburu) 1 act Teatro Cómico, Barcelona 28 December

1935 **Mucho ciudado con la Lola** (T Borrás) Teatro Comedia, Barcelona 11 March

1935 **Los maridos de Lydia** (Aramburu) Teatro de la Comedia, Barcelona 28 June

1935 **La canción del desierto** (Aramburu) Teatro Nuevo, Barcelona 8 November

1935 **La dama del sol** (de la Prada) Teatro Victoria, Barcelona 23 December

1939 **La giralda** (Serafin Alvárez Quintero, Joaquín Alvárez Quintero) Teatro Victoria, Barcelona 22 September

1939 **Lo que fue de la Dolores** (José María Acevedo) Teatro Victoria, Barcelona 2 December

1940 **Repoker de corazones** (Rafael Fernández Shaw) Teatro de la zarzuela 13 October

1941 **La Violetera** (de la Prada) Teatro Comicó, Barcelona 17 February

1943 **Nené** (de la Prada, Gonzáles de Toro) Principal Palace, Barcelona 12 March

1943 **¡Oh, Tiro liro!** (Aramburu) Principal Palace, Barcelona 7 May

1949 **Symphonie Portugaise** (aka *Romance au Portugal*) (Marc-Cab, Raymond Vincy) Théâtre de la Gaîté-Lyrique 9 October

1950 **La hechicera en Palacio** (Rigel, A Ramos de Castro) Teatro Alcázar 23 November

1952 **Peligro de Marte** (Alvaro de la Iglesia, Rigel) Teatro Lope de Vega 13 September

1956 **La chacha, Rodriguez y su padre** (José Muñoz Román) Teatro Martin 19 October

Many other titles attributed

Biography: Montero, E: *José Padilla* (Fundacion Baco Exterior, Madrid, 1990)

THE PADLOCK   Comic opera in 2 acts by Isaac Bickerstaff based on *El celoso estremeño* by Cervantes. Music by Charles Dibdin. Theatre Royal, Drury Lane, 3 October 1768.

One of the most successful of all the English-language musical plays of its era, Bickerstaff and Dibdin's little piece found itself worldwide audiences for many years after its first production.

Don Diego (Charles Bannister) is an ageing bachelor who is about to wed the 16-year-old Leonora (Mrs Arne), a penniless lass who has spent the last three months in his home, under lock and key, 'on approval'. However, on the very night that he goes out to meet the girl's father to confirm that he will take her to wife, the amorous student

Leander (Joseph Vernon) woos his way past the comic servant Mungo (Dibdin) and the key-holding duenna, Ursula (Mrs Dorman), scrambling over the garden wall to Leonora's side. Diego returns unexpectedly and, confronted with the sight of the two young people together, realizes that he is foolish to be thinking of taking a young wife. He hands over Leonora to Leander, but he is less magnanimous with the untrustworthy servants: Ursula is fired and Mungo sentenced to the bastinado. The padlock of the title was the extra lock that Diego fastened on his house's gate before leaving, a fact which arouses the indignation of the hitherto punctilious Ursula to whom he has not entrusted the key.

The thirteen musical numbers which made up the score of the show were largely the brief solos typical of the period, but there was a quartet to end the first act and a finale to the second, as well as a 'Good Night' duo for the young pair. However, the numbers which became most popular were those given to Mungo, and most particularly his opening song bemoaning 'Dear heart, what a terrible life am I led' with its catchphrase refrain 'Mungo here, Mungo there, Mungo everywhere'.

It was Mungo, in fact, who was the key to the show's success for, although notably well written and tuneful, *The Padlock* had otherwise little about it of originality. Its plot lines were vastly overused – although they still had many more years life and success in such pieces as *The Quaker* and *The Duenna* to come – and its characters: the innocent bride, the aged bridegroom, the amorous student and the duenna, wholly stock ones. But Mungo was something else. To the standard comic servant rôle, Bickerstaff added a fresh element – the West Indian negro accent, with all its potential for dialect comedy – and this proved a winner. The rôle had originally been written with actor John Moody in mind, but Moody dropped out of the show during rehearsals and composer Dibdin, suitably blacked-up, stepped in to a part which he was convinced should have been his from the start. He was proven right when he made an enormous personal hit inside the general success of *The Padlock*, and the show went on to play a remarkable 54 performances in its first season at Drury Lane.

The play and its famous part were taken up throughout the English-speaking world, and *The Padlock* was seen in every outpost of Empire which possessed anything resembling a theatre. In America, Lewis Hallam jr introduced Mungo to New York audiences. Ultimately, it also made it into other languages. A German-language version (ad Carl Bruno), apparently equipped with a different score of music by Carl Binder, was produced as a 1-act Posse mit Gesang at Vienna's Carltheater in 1857 with Karl Treumann playing Mungo and Albin Swoboda as Leander, and was later played, by Treumann's visiting company, in Budapest. An Hungarian version had previously been mounted at the Nemzeti Színház.

In Britain, America and the other colonies the show won repeated revivals, including a number with variations. The 'African Roscius', Ira Aldridge took a break from his Othellos and suchlike and appeared through Britain and Europe as Mungo in a performance rather different from that given by Dibdin, and in 1894 J C Bond Andrews and Walter Parke put out a rewritten

version under the title *The Keys of Castle* (Lyric Theatre, Hammersmith, 10 July). The show was seen in a more pristine form at London's Old Vic as recently as 1979, played in a double-bill with *Miss in Her Teens*. Nickolaus Grace appeared as Mungo.

USA: John Street Theater 29 May 1769; Australia: Emu Plains Theatre 20 November 1830; Austria: Carltheater (Eng) 19 February 1853, Carltheater *Das Vorhängeschloss* 18 April 1857; Hungary: Nemzeti Színház *A lakat* 30 August 1853, Budai Szinkör *Das Vorhängeschloss* 29 May 1857

PAGANINI Operette in 3 acts by Paul Knepler and Béla Jenbach. Music by Franz Lehár. Johann Strauss-Theater, Vienna, 30 October 1925.

The text to *Paganini* was written by Paul Knepler, the librettist and composer who had scored a fine success with his romanticized biomusical of the Viennese actress and singer Josefine Gallmeyer at Vienna's Bürgertheater in 1921. Whilst he again composed his own score for his next piece, *Wenn der Hollunder blüht* (w Ignaz M Welleminsky), for the Berlin Bundestheater, he sent a third book (which a friend persuaded him not to set himself), constructed on the same kind of showbiz biography lines, to Lehár. The artist whose name was this time tacked on to a fictional romance was the violinist Niccolò Paganini – whose putative love-life had already been plumbed in several plays including a 1915 one by Eddie Knoblock – and the lady in the case was Maria Anna Elisa, Princess of Lucca and Piombino and, for good measure, sister of the Emperor Napoléon. The lady (Emmi Kosáry) hears Paganini (Carl Clewing) playing his violin while she is having lunch in a country inn, without her husband (Peter Hoenselaers) who is off wooing the prima donna of his Court Opera (Gisa Kolbe). A romance begins, and the lady is able to use her knowledge of the Prince's little affair to stop him from expelling her violinist from Lucca and, indeed, to force him to appoint Paganini to a court position. But Napoléon gets annoyed at the international gossip over his sister's indiscreet love affair and sends a general (Felix Dombrowski) to remove Paganini. Although Anna Elisa protects him, the violinist finally convinces her that he must leave her to go to his only real love, his music.

Lehár was delighted with Knepler's offering, had Béla Jenbach, the experienced librettist of his recent *Cloclo*, help give the piece a final form, and set it with some the lushest music he had yet provided for the theatre, with the large bulk of that music contained in the two extremely showy, sentimental leading rôles. The tenor's bon-bon was the pretty 'Gern hab' ich die Frau'n geküsst' (widely known in English as 'Girls Were Made to Love and Kiss'), but the part of Paganini also had many other big musical moments including a showy entrance number, 'Schönes Italien', and the sizeable duo 'Was ich denke' shared with his soprano whose own most expansive raptures came in the aria 'Liebe, du Himmel auf Erden'. Bella, the prima donna, and Pimpinelli, the Princess's chamberlain (Fritz Imhoff) provided some slightly lighter numbers, but it was only really in a jolly rustic opening to the final act that the Operette turned very far from the staunchly romantic.

Textually and musically far in temper from Lehár's *Die lustige Witwe* style, *Paganini* laid a heavy accent on its lead tenor rôle. This is said to have been due to the composer's wish to create a star rôle for the favourite tenor Richard Tauber but, as it happened, Tauber did not create the rôle of Paganini. When it was decided to produce in Vienna rather than Berlin, Kammersänger Carl Clewing, the 40-year-old actor-turned-heldentenor of the Staatsoper Unter den Linden and Bayreuth's Walther von Stolzing (*Die Meistersinger von Nürnberg*) of the previous season, was selected for the star rôle of the production at the Johann Strauss-Theater. He was paired with the Hungarian soprano Emmi Kosáry, who had delighted Lehár with her creation of his *Wo die Lerche singt* in Budapest, as his Anna Elisa. Clewing, a rare visitor to the Operette stage, soon moved on, and when Peter Hoenselaers took over, the show's posters provided the unusual spectacle of top-billing Kosáry above the show's masculine title. Before *Paganini* reached its 138th and last performance, she too had given over her rôle to Lola Grahl.

It was a fair run rather than a fine one (less, for example, that Benatzky's *Adieu Mimi* which followed in the same year), but one which was bettered only marginally (apparently for salary reasons) in Berlin when Tauber took up the title-rôle alongside operatic soprano Vera Schwarz, Eugen Rex and Edith Schollwer in Heinz Saltenberg's production at the Deutsches Künstlertheater. In Budapest (ad Ernő Kulinyi), Jenő Nádor and the newest star of Hungarian operettic stage, Gitta Alpár, sang their way to a fine success, whilst in France baritone André Baugé – who was as popular in Paris as Tauber in Berlin – tackled the show's title-rôle when André Rivoire's version was produced at the Théâtre de la Gaîté-Lyrique a couple of years later. Louise Dhamarys (Anna-Elisa), Renée Camia (Bella) and Robert Allard (Pimpinelli) played the other principal rôles and Baugé and the show won a good Parisian season which established *Paganini* as a repertoire piece in France. Subsequent French productions have often followed Baugé's casting by using a high baritone rather than a tenor in the rôle of Paganini.

Two German-language films were made of *Paganini*, one, as *Gern hab' ich die Frau'n geküsst*, in 1926 (silent!) and a second in 1934, but *Paganini* did not make its way beyond Europe until 1937 when Tauber encouraged a C B Cochran production in London (ad A P Herbert, Reginald Arkell). The tenor starred opposite Evelyn Laye, with Charles Heslop and Joan Panter in support, and found London indifferent.

Excuses have been advanced and readvanced for this failure, just as they have been for the other fair but not fine runs of *Paganini*, but the fact remains that, like any other good but not outstanding piece with a big starring rôle, it mostly (but not always) did well enough when it was cast up with a large and fine-voiced star name, but otherwise provoked limited interest. That big starring rôle has ensured that it has won, in particular, several recordings and some revivals, although it remains most popular in its French version, seen as recently as 1988 at the Opéra de Wallonie in Liège and Verviers.

Paganini was not Lehár's first romantic Operette, nor was it Tauber's first essay into Operette, nor his first performance of a Lehár rôle, nor even did he create the part, but – with more trend-setting help from Knepler and his celebrity-based, 'unhappy-ending' libretto than is generally acknowledged – it led Lehár and Tauber into the first stages of the series of colourful, romantic Operetten – several others also tenuously attached to famous names and all, bar one remake of an old piece, with unhappy endings – with which they would be involved together in the years that followed.

Germany: Deutsches Künstlertheater 30 January 1926; Hungary: Városi Színház 7 May 1926; France: Théâtre de la Gaîté-Lyrique 3 March 1928; UK: Lyceum Theatre 20 May 1937
Recordings: complete (EMI), complete in French (Decca), selections (RCA, Eurodisc etc), selection in French (EMI-Pathé)

PAIGE, Elaine [BICKERSTAFF, Elaine Mary] (b Barnet, Herts, 5 March 1949). *Evita* star who followed up her first notable hit with a series of others.

Elaine Paige made her earliest musical theatre appearances as one of the Urchins in the pre-London cast of *The Roar of the Greasepaint ... the Smell of the Crowd* (1964), as a take-over in the West End's *Hair*, as Michelle (ie Micaëla) in *Rock Carmen* (1972), as a replacement ensemble player in *Jesus Christ Superstar*, and in *Nuts* (Theatre Royal, Stratford East). She took over from Stacey Gregg as Sandy (to the Danny of Paul Nicholas) in the West End production of *Grease* before she created her first important London musical rôle as rough-as-guts Rita to the Billy Liar of Michael Crawford in the musical *Billy* at the Theatre Royal, Drury Lane, in 1974 ('Any Minute Now').

In 1978 she rocketed into the general public's eye when, after a hugely publicized casting, she created the title-rôle in the stage production of *Evita* ('Don't Cry for Me, Argentina', 'Rainbow High') and won the kind of overnight fame that had virtually died out in the London theatre world. She compounded that fame when she stepped in during rehearsal to replace the injured Judi Dench as Grizabella, the Glamour Cat of *Cats*, creating the song 'Memory'. In a subsequent career balanced between recording and the stage, she created both on record and then in the theatre the rôle of Florence Dassy in *Chess* ('I Know Him So Well', 'Heaven Help My Heart') and appeared again at the Prince Edward Theatre (which had housed her successes in both *Evita* and *Chess*) as Reno Sweeney in the London edition of the latest Broadway adaptation of *Anything Goes*.

PAINTER, Eleanor (b Davenport [Walkerville], Iowa, 1890; d Cleveland, Ohio, 4 November 1947). Prima donna of 1910s and 1920s Broadway.

Miss Painter studied voice under Lilli Lehmann in Europe and made her début as an operatic singer in 1912 as Cio Cio San in *Madama Butterfly*. She appeared in other less expansive operatic rôles (Mignon, Micaëla etc) in Germany before Andreas Dippel brought her back to America in 1914 to star in the Broadway production of Cuvillier's *The Lilac Domino*. She subsequently created the title-rôles of Victor Herbert's *The Princess Pat* (1915) and the Catherine Cushing/Rudolf Friml *Glorianna* (1918) and starred in the play (with two songs) *Art and Opportunity* (1917) created in London by Marie Tempest, and as Dolores in the 1920 revival of *Florodora*.

Miss Painter walked out in rehearsals for the American

Plate 202. **Elaine Paige,** *the original Grizabella in* Cats.

production of Jean Gilbert's *The Lady in Ermine* on the grounds that her character spent too long off stage in the third act, but she returned to Broadway to score a further success as Vera Elizaweta in the American version of Oscar Straus's *Der letzte Walzer,* and to appear in two less memorable musicals, *The Chiffon Girl* (1924) and, after another period working in Germany, in an on-the-road

replacement, as Jenny Lind in the biomusical *The Nightingale* (1927). In later days she returned to the operatic stage in San Francisco and Philadelphia.

PAINT YOUR WAGON Musical play in 2 acts by Alan Jay Lerner. Music by Frederick Loewe. Shubert Theater, New York, 12 November 1951.

Paint Your Wagon appeared on the stage some four years after Lerner and Loewe's first big success with *Brigadoon* and, if its Broadway run did not approach that of its predecessor, it nevertheless confirmed all the good that the earlier piece had promised. The show was as far away from *Brigadoon* in feeling and in style as could be: the fantastical Scots tale of the earlier show was replaced by a rumbustious and throughly American tale of pioneering days, set with songs to match.

Ben Rumson (James Barton) discovers gold whilst burying a fellow prospector and he and his daughter Jennifer (Olga San Juan) settle down in the newly built Rumson Town as get-rich-quick miners flock in. Widower Ben takes as a wife the divorced Mormon Elizabeth and, when Jennifer gets old enough, she falls for the handsome Mexican prospector Julio (Tony Bavaar). Her father promptly decides she needs to go back east for some schooling but, soon after her departure, it becomes clear that Rumson's mines are fading. The miners start to move away to more promising grounds, Elizabeth deserts Ben, and Julio goes into the hills in search of fabled riches. When Jennifer returns, she finds Ben almost alone. He will not leave his town and neither will she, for she will wait there for the day when Julio returns. When he finally does he is a different man, with all the dreaming knocked out of him. But whilst they may not have the green future they once hoped for, at least they have a future together.

The songs included some charming ballads for Julio ('I Talk to the Trees') and for Jennifer ('How Can I Wait?'), but it was the songs of the mining men which made up the backbone of the score: the driving, crazy rush for the goldfields in 'I'm On My Way', the rough, round-the-fire landshanty 'They Call the Wind Maria' (introduced by Rufus Smith) and Ben's crumpled memories of his dead wife ('I Still See Elisa') and his reflective 'Wand'rin' Star'. The introduction of a gold-town music-hall saloon provided the opportunity for the required dance routines of the period (ch: Agnes de Mille), first in anticipation of the girls who will come to town, and then in fact.

Cheryl Crawford's production of *Paint Your Wagon* had a fair but insufficient Broadway run of 289 performances, but London gave the show a warmer welcome in a Jack Hylton production which featured Bobby Howes, long exiled from London since an unfortunate confrontation with an audience, as Ben, his real-life daughter, Sally Ann Howes, as Jennifer and Ken Cantril as Julio. It played 477 West End performances before going on the road in 1954. In Australia, Alec Kellaway, Lynne Lyons, Richard Curry and Jill Perryman played a good four months in Melbourne, followed by a Sydney season (Her Majesty's Theatre, 8 April 1955).

A 1969 film version with a curiously twisted story and a fragmented score (eight numbers, with five fresh ones by André Previn and Lerner interpolated) starred Western heroes Lee Marvin and Clint Eastwood, with Jean Seberg (dubbed by Anita Gordon) and vocalist Harve Presnell as the lovers, and launched Marvin's double-bass growled version of 'Wan'drin' Star' as hit-parade material.

UK: Her Majesty's Theatre 11 February 1953; Australia: Her Majesty's Theatre, Melbourne 27 November 1954; Film Paramount 1969

Recordings: original cast RCA), London cast (Columbia), film soundtrack (Paramount), selection (Fontana)

THE PAJAMA GAME Musical in 2 acts by George Abbott and Richard Bissell based on Bissell's novel $7\frac{1}{2}$ Cents. Music and lyrics by Richard Adler and Jerry Ross. St James Theater, New York, 13 May 1954.

Many of the names attached to *The Pajama Game*, both above and below the title, were new ones to Broadway: the producing team of Freddie Brisson, Harold Prince and Robert Griffith were mounting their first show in New York, Jerome Robbins was directing and Bob Fosse choreographing on Broadway for the first time, and songwriters Adler and Ross were offering their first score for a book musical. The wisdom of the ages was represented by veteran musical man George Abbott, who had half credits with Robbins and with Richard Bissell, the author of the novel on which the show was based, on the libretto.

Sid Sorokin (John Raitt), the new foreman in the Sleep Tite pajama factory, gets attracted to a tart little dolly bird called Babe (Janis Paige) who is boss of the Grievance Committee of the firm's union. Babe professes to return his feelings, but her priority is with fouling up production at the factory to try to blackmail the Boss into raising wages. Sid has to sack her, but her ethics have rubbed off on him and he manages to get the Boss's secretary drunk and amorous enough to give him the keys to the firm's confidential ledgers. Equipped with Sleep Tite's figures and projections, he himself moves into the blackmailing business, and gets a compromise out of the Boss which looks sufficiently like a 'win' to Babe and her pals for Sid to 'win' Babe. If Babe was motivated mostly by money, the other principal characters of the piece operated mainly on lust: the lubricious Prez of the Union (Stanley Prager) chasing after secretary Gladys Hotchkiss (Carol Haney), who is the promised preserve of Time-and-Motion man Hines (Eddie Foy jr), or alternatively after her co-worker Mabel (Reta Shaw).

The songs which illustrated the story were a particularly bright and bounding lot: Babe scornfully denying Sid's attractions in the waltzing 'I'm Not at All in Love', Gladys's burlesque description of the passion pit 'Hernando's Hideaway', the 'Once a Year Day' of the firm's picnic, Hines's impossible promise 'I'll Never Be Jealous Again' and his job description, 'Think of the Time I Save' and, at the top of the lot, Sid's winning soliloquy, sung to his dictaphone – 'Hey There (you with the stars in your eyes)'. The two second-act set dance pieces both featured Carol Haney, as Gladys, opening the half with the sexy 'Steam Heat' (introduced as an entertainment at a union meeting!) and later, in a Jealousy Ballet depicting the alarmed imaginings of Hines over Gladys's tipsy episode with Sid.

The songs and dances and the colourful, high-spirited staging served to take the distasteful edge off the plot and characters of this long-distance successor to the Garment Workers' revue *Pins and Needles* (1937) in the line of musical shows about Garment Workers, and *The Pajama Game*

had a magnificent Broadway run of 1,063 performances, as well as spending two seasons on the road with Larry Douglas and Fran Warren starring.

In London, Rodgers and Hammerstein's Williamson Music found considerable success when they joined Prince Littler to present Edmund Hockridge (Sid), Joy Nichols (Babe), Max Wall (Hines), Joan Fred Emney (Mabel) and Elizabeth Seal (Gladys) in a restaging of the Broadway production at the huge London Coliseum through a very fine 588 performances. In Australia, too, where J C Williamson Ltd took the then unusual step of casting the piece wholly with native Australians (Bill Newman, Toni Lamond, Tikki Taylor, Keith Peterson) instead of imported 'stars' (who usually weren't), *The Pajama Game* scored a fine success, beginning with a four-month initial Melbourne season, and in 1957, on the heels of *Kiss Me, Kate*, the show even reached Austria where, at that period, no other modern Broadway shows had been produced.

In the same year, a Warner Brothers film cast Doris Day as Babe alongside the principals of the original stage production in a version which used virtually all the score, the notable cut being 'Think of the Time I Save'.

The piece has had regular playing in regional American theatres since its production, and in 1973 it returned to Broadway (Lunt-Fontanne Theater 9 December) under the management of composer Adler. Hal Linden, Barbara McNair, Cab Calloway and Sharron Miller headed the cast of a version which attempted to lift the libretto into a different area by introducing a question of race into the central romance (she was black and he white), through only 65 performances. In the 1980s *The Pajama Game* was still to be found on the production schedules, and it got a couple of very different treatments on the two sides of the Atlantic: Richard Muenz, Judy Kaye, Avery Saltzman and Leonora Nemetz featured in a very thoroughly sung production sponsored by the New York City Opera (4 March 1989), whilst in Britain an undersung provincial mounting, with Paul Jones and Fiona Jane Hendley featured, did not make it to its intended berth in the West End.

UK: London Coliseum 13 October 1955; Australia: Her Majesty's Theatre, Melbourne *The Pyjama Game* 2 February 1957; Austria: Stadttheater, Klagenfurt *Herz im Pajama* 8 November 1957; Film: Warner Bros 1957

Recordings: original cast (Columbia), original London cast (HMV), film soundtrack (Columbia) etc

PAL JOEY Musical in 2 acts by John O'Hara based on his own short stories. Lyrics by Lorenz Hart. Music by Richard Rodgers. Ethel Barrymore Theater, New York, 25 December 1940.

Rodgers and Hart had been mixing their musicals with some agility since their return from Hollywood to Broadway, ranging from the elephantine spectacularities of *Jumbo* to the dance-based *On Your Toes*, the kiddie-concert tale of *Babes in Arms*, the fantasy of *I Married an Angel*, the classic burlesque of *The Boys from Syracuse* and the college high-jinks of *Too Many Girls*, and almost everywhere with success. The question: where do we go next? was answered when author John O'Hara suggested they look at his 'Pal Joey' pieces in the *New Yorker* magazine with the idea of using the character of the cheap cabaret compère as a starting point for a show. O'Hara was a different kind of writer from those the partners had worked with up till now and it was no surprise that *Pal Joey* turned out to be a different kind of show. As Rodgers later said, 'There wasn't one decent character in the entire play except for the girl who briefly fell for Joey – her trouble was simply that she was stupid'. But indecent and/or stupid, the characters of *Pal Joey* made up a tough and effective tale.

Joey Evans (Gene Kelly) is compère at a tacky nightclub in Chicago. He's also full of himself, empty-headed and -hearted, and more than eager to drop the dumb Linda English (Leila Ernst), when wealthy, randy Vera Simpson (Vivienne Segal) prowls by the club one evening and flicks her fingers at him. Vera's not interested in Joey's head or heart, her sights are rather lower down. While she's getting what she wants from the boy, she's happy enough to spend cash to let him run his own club and rig himself out like a spiv, but when blackmail rears its head, she shuts her purse, shrugs him off, and calls up a friend at the Police Department. Its over, and Joey's back where he started, still emptily talking the big time.

The show's score mixed a bundle of deliberately second-rate cabaret numbers, performed in the club, with a set of ballads which eschewed all that was in that bundle. Joey wooed Linda with the phoney sentiment of 'I Could Write a Book', Vera delightedly found herself 'Bewitched (bothered and bewildered)' by a young man all over again, and joined in a clear-headed tit-for-tat with Linda as each told the other to 'Take Him'. Pasted into the middle of all this was a revusical number for an incidental journalist, Melba (Jean Casto), 'Zip', detailing what a stripper thinks about as she does. June Havoc played club chorine Gladys Bumps who led the routines, the plotting and a bit of the comedy, and the supporting cast included Van Johnson and Stanley Donen.

Some folk found the shabby characters of *Pal Joey* and their shabby behaviour didn't make much of an evening in the theatre, but musicals with unpleasant lead characters had been successful before (remember *Der Obersteiger?*) and *Pal Joey* found plenty of fans. George Abbott's production ran for 374 performances on Broadway – more than *Jumbo*, more than *I Married an Angel* or *On Your Toes*, more in fact than any other Rodgers and Hart show in 20 years except *A Connecticut Yankee*. It followed up Broadway with a three-month tour, and then was put aside.

That might have been all, but in 1950 Columbia records put out a long-playing record of the songs from *Pal Joey*, with Vivienne Segal singing her original numbers and dancer Harold Lang as Joey. The record had a remarkably fine success, and songwriter-producer Jule Styne decided to put the show back on the Broadway stage. Miss Segal and Lang were supported by Patricia Northrop (Linda), Helen Gallagher (Gladys) and Elaine Stritch (Melba), the revival was mounted at the Broadhurst Theater (3 January 1952) and it gave Rodgers and Hart their best run ever: 542 performances. This time, other folk paid attention. Jack Hylton exported *Pal Joey* and Lang to Britain and, with Carol Bruce (Vera) and Sally Bazely (Linda) in the principal female rôles, watched his production run up a pretty fair 245 performances at London's Prince's Theatre. Hollywood came next with a film which used a large amount of the original music, supplemented by four Rodgers and Hart hits from earlier shows. It also used Frank Sinatra as a less-dancing, thoroughly convincing Joey, alongside a brace of glamorous co-stars: Rita Hayworth (Vera, sung by Jo Ann Greer) and Kim Novak (Linda, sung by Trudy Ewen).

Pal Joey's revival fixed it firmly in the American repertoire, and it won regular productions thereafter. Bob Fosse (Lang's cover in the 1952 show) played Joey in 1961 and 1963 revivals at the City Center, and in 1976 Christopher Chadman and Joan Copeland featured in a revival at New York's Circle in the Square (27 June 1976, 73 performances) but a 1978 production with Lena Horne and Clifford Davis ended its pre-Broadway life in Los Angeles. Australia got its only metropolitan *Pal Joey* to date in 1967 at a Sydney dinner theatre, and in 1980 London got a new production (25 September), brought from the small fringe Half Moon Theatre. Denis Lawson's dazzling Joey, supported by Danielle Carson (Linda) and Sîan Phillips (Vera), headed the cast of a genuinely shabby production (with genuinely shabby chorus girls for its club) through a fine 415 performances.

In 1982 the ever-enterprising Opéra Royal de Wallonie in Belgium gave the first French-language *Pal Joey* (Liège, 15 October).

One of the few musicals of its period which has survived into the 1970s and 1980s as an at least partly verismo piece, *Pal Joey* has found more partisans and productions in the years since its re-launch than it did in its first decade of life.

UK: Prince's Theatre 31 March 1954; Australia: Menzies Theatre Restaurant, Sydney June 1967; Film: Columbia 1957
Recordings: 1950 studio cast w Vivienne Segal (Columbia), part-revival cast w Jane Froman (Capitol/EMI), London 1980 revival cast (TER), film soundtrack (Capitol) etc

PALLENBERG, Max (b Vienna, 18 December 1877; d nr Carlsbad, 20 June 1934).

Regarded for many years as Germany's finest player of classic character and comedy rôles, in works by Molière, Shakespeare, Schiller, Goethe, Ibsen, Pirandello, as Molnár's Liliom or the Good Soldier Schweik, Pallenberg also made regular appearances on the musical stage.

He took his first steps to fame when he scored a great success in the Theater an der Wien's production of *Herbstmanöver* (1909) in the rôle of the comical Wallerstein, appeared as Lindoberer in Vienna's *Der fidele Bauer*, and created the parts of Peter Walperl in *Die Förster-Christl* (1907) at the Theater in der Josefstadt, Gregorio in *Der Frauenjäger* (1908), Oberst Kasimir Popoff in *Der tapfere Soldat* (1908) and of Basil Basilowitsch in *Der Graf von Luxemburg* (1909) in the years before quitting his home town to play, at first, in Munich, and later in Berlin.

During his career in Berlin he appeared in versions of several classic musical plays – as Menelaos in the chopped-around Metropoltheater *Die schöne Helena*, as Jupiter in *Orpheus in der Unterwelt*, as Ko-Ko in Charell's mashed-up *Mikado* of 1927, and as Calicot to the Pompadour of his wife, Fritzi Massary. He was also seen alongside his wife in Jean Gilbert's Posse *So bummeln wir!* (1912) at the Theater Gross-Berlin am Zoo and created the rôle of the tribune, Marc Antonius, in Massary's Oscar Straus Operette *Die Perlen der Cleopatra* (1923) at Vienna's Theater an der Wien.

Effectively exiled from Berlin by the anti-Jewish measures of 1933, Pallenberg was killed in an air crash soon after, at the age of 56.

Plate 203. **Max Pallenberg** *as Basil Basilowitsch in* Der Graf von Luxemburg.

PÁLMAY, Ilka [PETRÁSS, Ilona Pálmay] [aka SZIGLIGETINÉ, Ilka] (b Ungvár, 21 September ?1859; d Budapest, 17 February 1945).

The 18-year-old (or 13-year-old if you believe the dates given in some biographies) Ilka Szigligetiné, who had first trod the boards at Kaschau, shot to the theatrical forefront when she appeared at Budapest's Népszinház as Serpolette in the Hungarian première of *A Cornevillei harangok* (*Les Cloches de Corneville*, 1878). Over the next decade, during which she shed her first husband, József Szigligeti (1851–1889) and his name, she shared with Aranka Hegyi the major operettic rôles – prima donna, soubrette and travesty – at the Népszinház, Budapest's principal musical theatre, as well as taking leads in many of the straight plays which made up the theatre's programmes.

Amongst the 48 different musical pieces and rôles she played there were *A királykisasszony bábúi* (*Les Poupées de l'Infante*), Manola in *Nap és hold* (*Le Jour et la nuit*), Sora in *Gasparone*, Lisbeth (ie Gretchen) in *Rip*, Offenbach's Eurydice, his *Belle Hélène* and Gabrielle in *Párizsi élet* (*La Vie parisienne*), Micaela in *A kertészleány* (*Le Coeur et la Main*), Bronislawa in *Koldusdiák* (*Der Bettelstudent*), a travesty Barinkay in *A cigánybáró* (*Der Ziegunerbaron*), the title-rôle of *A béárni leány* (*La Béarnaise*), the Queen in *A királynő csipkekendője* (*Das Spitzentuch der Königin*), the title-

rôles of *Les Noces d'Olivette, La Grande-Duchesse de Gérolstein, Donna Juanita, Marjolaine, Le Petit Duc, Niniche* and *Boccaccio,* Clairette in *La Fille de Madame Angot,* both Yum Yum and Nanki Poo in different productions of *The Mikado,* Denise de Flavigny in *Nebántsvirág* (*Mam'zelle Nitouche*), Benjamine in *Jozéfa Egyiptomban* (*Joséphine vendue par ses soeurs*), Tilly in *Simplicius,* Nell Gwynne in *A komédiás hercegnő* (Planquette's *Nell Gwynne*), Phryné (apparently Phoebe) in *A gárdista* (*The Yeomen of the Guard*) and Borka (presumably Patience) in *Fejő leány* (*Patience*).

She created starring rôles in several early Hungarian operetts including the remake of *L'Étoile* as *Uff király* (1887, Lazuli) and Béla Hegyi and Szidor Bátor's *A titkos csók* (1888, Lolotte) and the musical plays *A piros bugyelláris* (1878, Török Zsófi) and *Csókon szerzett vőlegeny* (1883, Irén Abrai) and also played such non-singing rôles as that of Zola's *Nana* (1882). In 1883 she appeared with the Budapest company as Micaela, Manola and Serpolette in a season in Vienna, and she returned there in 1891 to spend more than two years as leading lady at the Theater an der Wien. During that time she created the rôle of the little postmistress Christel in Zeller's *Der Vogelhändler* (1891, 'Ich bin der Christel von der Post'), Lady Sylvia Rockhill

Plate 204. **Ilka Pálmay** *as Yum-Yum.*

in Millöcker's *Das Sonntagskind* (1892) and the title-rôle in Johann Strauss's *Fürstin Ninetta* (1893) as well as appearing as Hélène, Javotte in *Fanchon's Leyer* (*La Fille de Fanchon la vielleuse*) and in German versions of Judic's rôles of Denise de Flavigny (*Mam'zelle Nitouche*) and Princess Anna Semionowna Machinstoff (*Die Kosakin*).

After a brief retirement from the stage to become the Gräfin Eugen Kinsky, she moved on to appear at the Theater Unter der Linden in Berlin, returning to Vienna in 1895 to star in travesty as Hector in *Die Karlsschülerin* and appearing in London, with the Saxe-Coburg Company, in *Der Vogelhändler* at the Theatre Royal, Drury Lane. This visit resulted in her being offered a contract by D'Oyly Carte and in 1896–7 she created the rôles of Julia Jellicoe in Gilbert and Sullivan's *The Grand Duke* and Felice in *His Majesty* and appeared as Elsie Maynard in a revival of *The Yeomen of the Guard* at the Savoy Theatre.

In 1898–9 she played again in Vienna, starring at the Theater an der Wien in a series of largely new but not very impressive Operetten: *Die Küchen-Comtesse* (Lisa Schwarzen), von Taund's *Der Dreibund* (Lydia), Adolf Müller jr's *Der Blondin von Namur* (Blondin), Josef Bayer's *Fräulein Hexe* (Magdalene), and as the Principessa Santiago de Merimac in Heuberger's version of *Niniche, Ihre Excellenz*.

The later part of her career was spent mostly in Budapest (where in 1901 she played Belasco's *Madame Butterfly*), although she visited New York in 1905 and appeared there in the multi-parted rôle of Ilona in *Heisses Blut* in the German-language theatre. In some of her latter-day appearances in Budapest she appeared as the old Countess Irini in the local production of *Der Zigeunerprimás* (1913) and as the elder Hannerl in *Medi* (1918), the Hungarian version of *Hannerl*. She did not officially retire from the stage until 1928 after a career of 50 years in which she had compiled one of the most remarkable careers in the European musical theatre – a career which held the unusual distinction of including the creation of leading rôles for both Johann Strauss and for Gilbert and Sullivan.

Autobiography: *Meine Errinerung* (Verlag von Richard Bong, Berlin, 1911)

PALMER, Minnie   (b Philadelphia, 31 March ?1857; d East Islip [Bay Shore], Long Island, 21 May 1936). 'A great favourite, if not much of an actress'.

Diminutive Minnie Palmer made her first appearance on the stage at the age of what was probably 17, playing in *Pavillon Rouge*, and she made her Broadway début two years later when she appeared in breeches as Jimmy Loose, alongside Nat Goodwin, in the burlesque *The Pique Family*, and subsequently in several other burlesques. Profiting from her very young looks, she also appeared as Meenie to the Rip of Jefferson, featured as *The Little Rebel* at Booth's, played Dorothy in Gilbert's *Dan'l Druce* and the juvenile lead in his *Engaged*, Dot in *Dot*, Blanche in *Hurricanes* and Josephine Onyx in *Blondes and Bombshells*. She also appeared as Katharine Schulz to the Fritz of Emmet in *The New Fritz* (1878) and created the rôle of Grace Brandon in Bartley Campbell's drama *My Partner* (1879). In 1879–80 she toured America as Jessie Fairlove in a tailor-made vehicle called *Minnie Palmer's Boarding House* and in 1882 she appeared at Haverley's 14th Street Theatre as the

Plate 205. *American actress* **Minnie Palmer** *at 40, going on 12.*

good-as-gold Tina in the low-comedy-cum-sentimental drama *My Sweetheart*, a portmanteau piece of Dutch-accented 'musical comedy' which was tricked out with narrow-range songs and speciality acts, inserted to showcase its girlish star's various talents.

In 1883 (slicing eight years – but later only three – off her age for the benefit of the press) she took *My Sweetheart* and leading man Charles Arnold to Britain where she opened in Glasgow (4 June 1883) and quickly established herself as a phenomenally popular touring attraction. She easily overran the six months of her announced tour and, with publicity continually bubbling (although married to her manager, John Rogers, since 1880, she 'admitted' to the press that she was bound by a $15,000 bond not to marry and leave the stage for five years), producer H Cecil Beryl kept *My Sweetheart* and its 'juvenile' star profitably on the road and even essayed a daring visit to London (Strand Theatre 14 January 1884) without the notices being too scalding and with audiences mobbing the house for 200 performances.

Miss Palmer went back to America for 'unavoidable engagements' but she returned to Britain to play more *My Sweetheart* before, in 1886, she took her show to Australia (Princess, Melbourne 31 January 1886) for a 32-week tour. There she repeated her British success, in spite of the press remarking on the show's similarity to the J C Williamsons' celebrated *Struck Oil*. She followed up in several similar if less successful vehicles, such as Fred Maeder's *Pert and Her Stepmother* (Bush Theater, San

Francisco 15 August 1887), *My Brother's Sister* (1889 New York, 1890 London), in which Miss Palmer appeared successively as two boys and two girls, and which was ventured at a matinée at the Gaiety Theatre, and *The School Girl* (Cardiff 2 September 1895), but none held for long and she returned ultimately to *My Sweetheart*.

She made one brief appearance in a slightly more regular form of musical theatre when she took over Letty Lind's rôle of Maude Sportington in the London production of the variety musical *Morocco Bound* and interpolated her own material, and starred, on one occasion, in an almost genuine comic opera, Oscar Weil's remake of *Le Voyage de Suzette* as *Suzette*, at the Trenton Opera House (1890) and New York's Hermann's Theater, playing alongside vocalists of the calibre of Bertha Ricci. She also made what should have been a lucrative London appearance (at £75 per week and 2 per cent of the gross) as Cinderella in Henry Leslie's carelessly spectacular and financially disastrous pantomime of 1889. She remained, however, basically a personality performer whose appeal was not to audiences with any degree of sophistication.

Minnie Palmer stuck to the stage even after her large number of days playing very young girls was over, and she made her final appearance in 1918 in a supporting rôle in the Broadway play *Lightnin'* (Mrs Jordan). In 1927 she was taken into the Actor's Fund home in Long Island and died there in 1936, admitting to an age of 71.

PANAMA HATTIE   Musical comedy in 2 acts by Herbert Fields and B G De Sylva. Music and lyrics by Cole Porter. 46th Street Theater, New York, 30 October 1940.

The fourth of five teamings of songwriter Cole Porter and star Ethel Merman, *Panama Hattie* followed on behind *Anything Goes* which had cast its star as a nightclub-singer-cum-evangelist, *Red, Hot and Blue!* in which she had played a kookie millionairess, and *Dubarry Was a Lady* which had presented her as a nightclub-singer dreamed into antique France. Since the nightclub gals had done much better than the millionairess, it was not so much of a surprise that *Panama Hattie* had for its heroine a bright-as-a-button, hard-as-a-hamstring nightclub hostess. Hattie Maloney (Miss Merman), who runs a classy joint in Panama City, has pulled herself a proposal from a classy gent. Nick Bullett (James Dunn) is the real *Mayflower* type, even if he is slightly used. That is to say, he's been married before, and he has an eight-year-old daughter called Geraldine, known as Jerry (Jean Carroll), to prove it. This makes Hattie a touch uneasy, but by the end of the evening she's got the kiddie on her side and the wedding can go ahead. Betty Hutton supported as soubrette-comic Florrie, Rags Ragland (Woozy Hogan), Pat Harrington (Skat Briggs) and Frankie Hyers (Windy Deegan) were three comedy sailors out on the town looking for girls, and Englishman Arthur Treacher completed the principal cast as Florrie's opposite number, Englishman Vivian Budd.

The score of *Panama Hattie* included the usual bundle of Porterish name-dropping songs. Miss Merman's 'I've Still Got My Health' got in the Astors, Lucius Beebe, Fred Astaire, L B Mayer, Ethel Barrymore, Ina Claire and Billy Rose, and her 'I'm Throwing a Ball Tonight' plugged Monty Woolley, Clifford Odets, Grace Moore, Mae West, Bert Lahr, Fanny Brice, Gracie Allen and a few more local luminaries. But it was perhaps no coincidence that the most popular number to emerge from the set was none of these backscratchers, but the star's rueful torch song to the curative value of booze, 'Make it Another Old-Fashioned, Please'. Amongst the other songs, Miss Merman informed her chap off-puttingly 'My Mother Would Love You' and shared a 'Let's Be Buddies' with the child, Miss Hutton bounced out a couple of hunting numbers ('All I've Got to Get Now is My Man', 'They Ain't Done Right by Our Nell') and the sailors jollied forth a couple of songs.

Panama Hattie was a happy, other-folks'-wartime hit. By the time it shuttered on Broadway it had statistically outdone the initial records of *Anything Goes* and *Dubarry Was a Lady* with its 501 performances, as it headed on to the rest of the country, with Dunn and Frances Williams in the lead roles, and for Hollywood, where Ann Sothern took up the part of Hattie for celluloid alongside Red Skelton, Ben Blue, Lena Horne, Dan Dailey, Ragland and Virginia O'Brien. The film version took in half a dozen other Porter and non-Porter numbers to add to four of the original songs.

Panama Hattie brought its share of cheer to wartime London as part of what local producers voted the most prosperous theatrical year in memory. Emile Littler, Tom Arnold and Lee Ephraim's production, with Bebe Daniels as a Hattie who was costumed by Hartnell, Ivan Brandt as her man, and Richard Hearne (Loopy) and Claude Hulbert (Budd) amongst the support, ran up a bomb-bisected 308 performances at the Piccadilly and Adelphi Theatres between 1943 and 1945.

Miss Merman reprised her rôle alongside Ray Middleton in 1954 for a potted television version which used her three main songs (plus a couple from her other Porter shows), and the show has been given the occasional reshowing, notably at Equity Library Theatre in 1976 and at the Paper Mill Playhouse later the same year, but in spite of its top statistical score in the Porter-Merman stakes first time round, *Panama Hattie* has been eclipsed by *Anything Goes* as a long-term survivor.

UK: Piccadilly Theatre 4 November 1943; Film: MGM 1942
Recording: original cast (Decca/MCA)

LE PAPA DE FRANCINE   Opérette à grand spectacle in 4 acts by Victor de Cottens and Paul Gavault. Music by Louis Varney. Théâtre Cluny, Paris, 5 November 1896.

'A rattling, vulgar farce, but amusing and unpretentious' commented one usually slightly white-lipped critic after the opening of *Le Papa de Francine*, without yet mentioning all the other elements – from a hit song and a lively score, to as many lavishings of scenic and costume values as could be fitted on to the little Cluny stage – which went to make up a show, much on *Voyage de Suzette* lines, which proved a jolly Parisian hit.

Francine's Papa is an American called Burnett (Allart), whom she has never met, for after his productive little French idyll with the danseuse Palmyre Plumet (Adèle Cuinet), he nipped off back across the Atlantic into anonymity. 18 years later, having struck both oil and the melancholy remorse of middle age, he now determines to find his child (Mary Lebey). Burnett hires a secret agent, Mongrapin (Dorgat), who sets off in search of the now plump and plain Palmyre and her daughter. The spectacle of the evening is ensured by the fact that young Francine is

Plate 206. **Panama Hattie:** *Ethel Merman outfaces the fleet.*

working at the Moulin-Rouge as an 'equestrian chanteuse' and it is there that Mongrapin tracks her down. However, although Francine has support from her devoted noble lover, Gontran (Conradin), who has turned circus clown for love of her, there is opposition to the father and

daughter reunion from the masher, cousin Adhémar (Hamilton), and his mistress, Diane de Pontivy (Mlle Manuel), who stand to profit if the missing heiress is not found. Disguises and impostures abound as the baddies try to sandbag the goodies on their way to the all-important meeting point at Saint-Germain, via the rowing-club bar in Asnières, a rosière ceremony in Nanterre, the 'sinking of Mme Plumet' at Chatou, and a villa in Le Vésinet, where Adhémar and Diane impersonate Brazilians and the place becomes the scene for a confrontation between a band of burglars and the gendarmerie. Needless to say, the goodies get there just in time for the happy ending.

The hit of *Le Papa de Francine* was the burglary scene, an item inserted to feature the Price family of pantomimists as the burglars, and highlighted by a delightful waltz trio ('Faire la montre et la chaîne') in praise of pilfering, performed by the singing burglars La Puce (Mlle Norcy), Galoppe-Chopine (Prévost) and Lilas-Blanc (Houssaye), which became the number of the night. Francine rode onto the stage on a live horse (at the Cluny!) and delivered a Chanson du petit jockey; her mother had her moment in the scene in which she was dropped in the Seine and then, clad in male underwear, fought a duel; and the detective let loose with a comical madrigal ('Vous êtes la rose embaumée') amongst a whole plethora of jokes about pompiers (a speciality of Nanterre) putting out the flames evident in the local virgins. The baddies took time off from being bad to perform a strenuous boléro and a polka.

Le Papa de Francine drew the public to its little theatre for more than 200 nights in its first run, before being taken up for other centres – but without its title. In Vienna, instead of Francine's father having the title-rôle it was *Lolas Cousin*, otherwise the wicked Adhémar, who was promoted. Lola (still 'eine Sängerin zu Pferde') was played by Frau Wittels-Moser, with Viktoria Pohl-Meiser (Mme Plumet), Otto Maran (Mongrapin), Adele Moraw (Diane), Rauch (Adhémar) and Karl Pfann (Bob Smitting, ex-Gontran) in the other main rôles of a version (ad Julius Horst) which actually kept the jokes about the pompiers of Nanterre (surely not very funny outside France) but reduced the piece from seven scenes to five. Without coming near the huge totals secured by the French *Toto* and *Les Fêtards* at the Theater in der Josefstadt, *Lolas Cousin* confirmed nicely the success of Varney's *Les Petites Brebis* at the same house three years earlier with a useful season of 30 nights.

Hungary got papa back in the title, without Francine, in a version entitled *Utazás egy apa körül* (voyage around a father, ad Emil Makai) staged just a few months later at the Magyar Színház, whilst an English-language version dropped papa, and simply called Francine *A Lucky Girl* (ad Wallace Erskine, Adeline Stuart). Mounted by Erskine for a provincial tour with Miss Stuart starred as Diane to his Charles (ex-Adhémar), Edie d'Arthur as Stella (ex-Francine), C J Barber as Adolphus Raveller and the cast's only 'name', Florence Vie, as mother, it reduced the baggage by making Stella a 'descriptive vocalist', cutting the horse and setting the whole thing in England. The first scene was now 'the Winter Gardens, Brightpool', the May Queen Festival was at Cobford, and mama got dumped in Mrs Plummer's baths, Eastbourne, instead of the Seine. The famous Fred Evans troupe (without their deceased namesake) were the burglars.

Austria: Theater in der Josefstadt *Lolas Cousin* 11 January 1898; Hungary: Magyar Színház *Utazás egy apa körül* 22 April 1898; UK: *A Lucky Girl* (aka *In Search of a Father*) Grand Theatre, Derby 1 August 1898

PAPP, Joseph [PAPIROFSKY, Yosi] (b Brooklyn, NY, 22 June 1921; d New York, 31 October 1991).

Originally a theatre stage manager, then a producer, Papp was from 1956 the Director of the New York Shakespeare Festival which, progressively belying its title after its first decade of activity, was responsible for the production of a considerable number of original musicals. The enormously successful *Hair* (1967) was the first of these, but although a second Galt MacDermot musical, *Two Gentlemen of Verona*, found some success and a Tony Award, it was the 1975 production of the record-breaking *A Chorus Line* which remained Papp's most outstanding and outstandingly profitable producing achievement. A further major success was won with a lively version of Gilbert and Sullivan's *The Pirates of Penzance* (1980) which, re-orchestrated and performed by modern pop voices, totted up the longest run of any Gilbert and Sullivan work in Broadway history and gave the show a new round of international productions and even a film, whilst an effective musical retelling of *The Mystery of Edwin Drood* (1985), equipped with alternative endings, also moved to longish-running success on Broadway (Tony Award).

Other Papp/New York Shakespeare Festival musical theatre productions included *Stomp* (1969), *Sambo* (1969), *Mod-Donna* (1970), *The Wedding of Iphigenia* (1971), *Lotta, or the Best Thing Evolution's Ever Come Up With* (1973), *More Than You Deserve* (1973), *Apple Pie* (1976), *On the Lock-In* (1978), *Dispatches* (1979), a stage adaptation of the French film musical *Les Parapluies de Cherbourg* as *The Umbrellas of Cherbourg* (1979), *Leave it to Beaver is Dead* (1979), *The Haggadah* (1980), *The Death of von Richthofen as Witnessed from Earth* (1982), *Lullaby and Goodnight* (1982), *Lenny and the Heartbreakers* (1983), *The Human Comedy* (1983), a *Non Pasquale* (1983) and a *La Bohème* (1984) which attempted to take the same trail as *The Pirates of Penzance* without the same success, *The Knife* (1987), *A Stranger Here Myself* (1988), *Genesis* (1989), *Songs of Paradise* (1989), *Romance in Hard Times* (1989), *Up Against It* (1989) and *Jonah* (1990).

Biography: Little, S: *Enter Joseph Papp* (Coward, McCann & Geoghegan, New York, 1974)

PAPP, Mihály (b Makó, 22 November 1875; d Budapest, 20 September 1915).

In his short life and career, character-actor Papp worked at first in provincial theatres, before moving in 1903 from Kolozsvár to Budapest's Király Színház. After two years he left to join the company at the Vigszinház, but he returned to the Király Színház for a second period before moving on to the Magyar Színház. Although his career was made largely on a diet of non-musical plays, he did appear in a number of musical pieces, notably in the Hungarian productions of Lincke's *Lysistrata*, as Prince Paul in *La Grande-Duchesse*, as Scrop in *Die geschiedene Frau*, as Coucy-Couça in the local version of Terrasse's *Le Sire de Vergy* (*Én, te, ő*) and, in particular, created the rôle of the pathetic Bagó in Hungary's most enduring musical play, *János vitéz*.

LE PARADIS DE MAHOMET Opérette in 3 acts by Henri Blondeau. Music by Robert Planquette. Additional music by Louis Ganne. Théâtre des Variétés, Paris, 15 May 1906.

Planquette's final stage work, completed after his death by Louis Ganne, was produced by Fernand Samuel at the Théâtre des Variétés in 1906. Henri Blondeau's libretto was set in modern Trébizonde, where it took good care continually to take the mickey out of the old Turkish-set opérettes and their characters, whilst employing a plot which might well have served for one of them.

Prince Bredindin (Henri Defreyn), who fancies himself as the Don Juan of his age, wagers with the lovely and uncompliant widow Bengaline (Juliette Méaly) that she will be his within 24 hours. Having failed to stop her marriage to the young merchant Baskir (Jeanne Saulier), he resorts to spiking the reception wine and carries off the sleeping bride to his harem. There, his wives convince the 'dead' Bengaline that she is in Mahomet's paradise, and the Prince comes to the widow disguised as the spirit of her adored deceased huband, the slaver and sea-captain Musaor. 'Paradise' fills up farcically with 'deceased' folk: Baskir, Uncle Maboul (Baron), Aunt Sélika (Mme Gilberte), Baskir's little mistress Fathmé (Amélie Diéterle) and her protective brother (Lise Berty), all under the eye of the Prince's myopic secretary Radaboum (Max Dearly) who is disguised as the Turkish equivalent of Saint Peter. The Prince's trick fails in the midst of an embrace when his moustache falls off but, when the disgusted Baskir calls in the law to rid him of his unfaithful new wife, that law condemns Bredindin and Bengaline to wed.

Planquette's score gave everyone a sing: the Prince advertised his qualities ('Je fus toujours un homme aimble') did his impersonation with gusto ('Mes chers amis, e le proclame') and intimated to his beloved 'Je voudrais tre escarpolette' in order to enfold her the better, Bengaline declared unequivocally 'Il est trop dur de supporter les abstinences du veuvage', tossed off a bridal brindisi, pondered her dilemma in the presence of two 'dead' husbands ('Je dois contenter mon premier') and let rose with a 'Toast à l'amour'. Baskir celebrated his wedng day ('Ah! mes amis, quelle journée') and duetted with athmé, who was in her turn well supplied with an aubade nd a yodelling song as well as another duet with Dearly ho had his best moment in his impersonation of 'le grand uphti' sung to the accompaniment of a little dance. In trospect, however, the melody which won the most atten-on was a waltz tune which bore the most amazing resem-ance to the principal waltz from *Die lustige Witwe*, which d premièred five months earlier at the Theater an der 'ien.

The show was received with enthusiasm and played me 70 times at the Variétés. It was subsequently produ-d in Hungary (ad Andor Gábor) and in a German ver-on (ad C A Raida) at Dortmund, and in 1911 it turned up Broadway (ad H B Smith, R B Smith). Dan V Arthur's oduction, which had Planquette's music 'arranged' by lvio Hein, starred Grace van Studdiford as Bengaline d George Leon Moore as Prince Bredindin, and lasted performances. The famous copycat waltz got a wider owing, when a production which claimed it was not *Die tige Witwe* used it as its big tune.

Le Paradis de Mahomet was revived in Paris, at the ianon-Lyrique, in 1922.

An earlier *Le Paradis de Mahomet*, a three-act opéra-nique by Eugène Scribe and Mélesville, with music by

MM Kreubé and Kreutzer, was produced at Paris's Théâtre Feydeau in 1822 (23 March).

Hungary: Király Színház *Mohamed paradicsoma* 10 September 1909; Germany: Stadttheater, Dortmund *Im Paradies Mahomets* 8 February 1910; USA: Herald Square Theater *The Paradise of Mahomet* 17 January 1911

LES PARAPLUIES DE CHERBOURG

Musical comedy in 2 acts by Jacques Demy based on his film screenplay of the same name. Music by Michel Legrand. Public Theater, New York, 1 February 1979.

A sweetly romantic 1963 French film, which presented the particularity of being sung through, Jacques Demy and Michel Legrand's *Les Parapluies de Cherbourg* told the *Fanny*-like tale of umbrella-merchant's daughter Geneviève (Catherine Deneuve) who settles for marrying her mother's choice when Guy (Nino Castelnuovo), who has got her pregnant, does not return from the war in Algeria. A surprise screen success, the piece was sub-sequently adapted for the stage by its author, but its first production was given not in French but in English (ad Sheldon Harnick, Charles Burr) when it was workshopped and then produced by Joseph Papp and the New York Shakespeare Festival for a series of 78 performances in 1979.

Later the same year, the French version was mounted at Paris's Théâtre Montparnasse, directed by Raymond Gérôme, with an orchestra of 11 and a cast of 13, headed by Bee Michelin (Geneviève) and France's *Jesus Christ Superstar* star Daniel Beretta (Guy). Although it was not successful, a London production followed the next year. Susan Gene, Martin Smith and Sheila Matthews headed the cast through 12 sad performances which lost £140,000.

France: Théâtre Montparnasse 14 September 1979; UK: Phoenix Theatre *The Umbrellas of Cherbourg* 10 April 1980
Recording: original French cast (Accord)

PARÈS, Philippe

(b Paris, 3 May 1901; d Clarettes, 1979). French composer whose stage successes came in the 1920s and early 1930s.

The son of a musician, Gabriel Parès, the young Philippe began his friendship with Georges van Parys during their studies, and the pair sub-sequently composed together the scores for a number of films, including René Clair's version of Berr and Verneuil's *Le Million* and Barnoncelli's version of *La Femme et le pantin* ('Conchita'), and above all for half a dozen opérettes in the jazz-age vein played on the Paris stage within a four-year period.

Their first Parisian venture with *Lulu* resulted in a singular success and the Théâtre Daunou followed it the next year with another dancing comedy, *L'Eau à la bouche*, with a cast headed by Paris's Nanette, Loulou Hégoburu, and Fernand Graavey. A transfer of their Brussels produc-tion of *La Petite Dame du train bleu*, the comical filmland tale of *Louis XIV* with Dranem at the Théâtre de la Scala, and *Le Coeur y est* confirmed the partnership's vogue. *Couss-couss*, however, marked the end of their Parisian theatre career, and Parès's only subsequent metropolitan venture, alone, was with the postwar piece *La Bride sur le cou*.

A final collaboration with van Parys, another decade on and 30 years after their first success together, produced *Le*

Moulin sans-souci. A costume opérette which delved back in time for a plot involving a girl brought up as a boy who makes a heroic soldier, attracts a King's mistress, and finally weds a baritonic lieutenant with whom, in her male guise, she has been forced to fight a duel, *Le Moulin sans-souci* found the composers far from the foxtrots and one-steps of their most successful days. Although the show followed the newer fashion for romantic musicals adeptly, its life was limited to the French provinces.

1927 **La Petite Dame du train bleu** (*Quand y-en a pour deux*) (w Georges van Parys/Léo Marchès, Georges Lignereux) Galeries St-Hubert, Brussels, May; Eldorado, Paris 22 October

1927 **Lulu** (w van Parys/Serge Veber) Théâtre Daunou 14 September

1928 **L'Eau à la bouche** (w van Parys/S Veber) Théâtre Daunou 5 September

1929 **Louis XIV** (w van Parys/S Veber) Théâtre de la Scala

1930 **Le Coeur y est** (w van Parys/Roger Bernstein, Fernand Vimont/Raoul Praxy) Théâtre de l'Athénée 20 May

1931 **Couss-couss** (w van Parys/Jean Guitton) Théâtre de la Scala 26 February

1947 **La Bride sur le cou** (Henry Lemarchand/André Huguet, Max Eddy) Théâtre de la Potinière

1958 **Le Moulin sans-souci** (w van Parys/Marc-Cab/S Veber, Marc-Cab) Opéra, Strasbourg 24 December

A PARISIAN MODEL Musical comedy in 2 acts by Harry B Smith. Music by Max Hoffman. Broadway Theater, New York, 27 November 1906.

A libretto borrowed from the early George Edwardes success *An Artist's Model* and a few other pieces of a similar shape – not excepting the brand-new and not-yet-seen-in-New York *Die lustige Witwe* – put into shape by Harry B Smith, a basic score by the workaday Max Hoffman studded with interpolations as required, and a dazzling Florenz Ziegfeld production equipped with a host of girls marshalled by top director/choreographer Julian Mitchell provided the setting for Anna Held in her 1906 starring vehicle on Broadway. Miss Held played an artist's model whose painter lover (Henri Leoni) does not trust her rise to riches and goes off with another girl (Truly Shattuck) until just before the final curtain, and she performed two of her biggest song hits during the course of the evening – her americanized version of the Scotto/Christiné 'La Petite Tonkinoise' entitled 'It's Delightful to Be Married' and Gus Edwards and Will Cobb's 'I Just Can't Make My Eyes Behave'. Charles Bigelow provided the traditional low comedy, and the entertainment prospered through 222 performances and a tour which included a three-week return to the Broadway Theater. The two hit songs were reused for the 1989 London revue *Ziegfeld*, performed by Fabienne Guyon in the rôle of Anna Held.

PARIS, OU LE BON JUGE Opéra-bouffe in 2 acts by Robert de Flers and Gaston de Caillavet. Music by Claude Terrasse. Théâtre des Capucines, Paris, 18 March 1906.

Introduced as part of a two-part programme at the tiny Théâtre des Capucines, paired with a vaudeville by the same authors, the classical burlesque *Paris, ou le bon juge* followed, on a smaller scale (and to piano accompaniment), the style which de Flers and de Caillavet had successfully used in their earlier collaborations with composer Terrasse, *Les Travaux d'Hercule*, *Le Sire de Vergy* and *Monsieur de la Palisse*.

The libretto quite simply reversed the classical tale of the judgement of Paris. Venus (Germaine Gallois), Minerva (Mlle Derys) and Juno (Mlle Desprez), sent down from Olympus by an annoyed Jupiter to cool their heels and their ardours on the slopes of Mount Ida, terrorize the shy satyr Sylvain (Victor Henry) with their excesses of femininity, and then turn their attentions onto the very plain shepherd Paris (Charles Lamy). He gives his famous apple to Venus when, unlike the others, she makes herself irresistible by refusing herself to him, and she gives it to his wife Glycère (Alice Bonheur) whose moribund interest in her husband is reawakened by seeing him the centre of all this feminine attention.

The work, and Terrasse's score, with its waltzing music for Venus and its comical pieces for the two men (a satyr singing 'Je suis timide') won delighted responses, and the little piece was given two series of performances at the Capucines before it was picked up for a series of productions outside France. In Vienna (ad August Neidhart) it was seen firstly for a month as part of the programme at Danzers Orpheum with Flora Siding featured, later at the same house in a bill with the revue *Wien bei Nacht* (16 March 1907) and then in the smaller Hölle (29 September 1911); in Budapest (ad Adolf Merei) it was the last opérette to be produced at the Népszinház before the great theatre's closure after which it was taken up by the Royal Orfeum (*A jó biró*, 12 August 1911), and in Berlin it was produced at the little Figaro-Theater in a different German adaptation by Waldemar Westland.

In Paris, the piece was brought back to the Capucines in 1908 (21 May) with all but one of the original cast, and it was later played in an enlarged version with an orchestra and chorus and a cast headed by Mlle Gallois, Edmée Favart and the comedian Polin at the Scala in 1911 (9 April), then again at the Théâtre Michel (4 March 1922) with Germaine Huber featured alongside Lamy and Mlle Favart. Thereafter, however, like the other principal works of Terrasse, it drifted from the repertoire as first the jazz-age musical and then the opérette à grand spectacle took preference over such a small-scale and soigné burlesque as the town's preferred entertainment. It has remained, however, a connoisseur's favourite amongst the French works of its period.

Austria: Danzers Orpheum *Paris der gute Richter* 12 October 1906; Germany: Figaro-Theater *Paris* 1906; Hungary: Népszinház-Vigopera *Paris almája* 23 May 1908

PARKE, Walter (d 6 December 1922).

Following a substantial first stage success with the transmutation of Scribe's libretto for the opéra-comique *Giralda* into the text for the London piece *(Les) Manteaux Noirs*, Parke turned out books for a number of further musicals over a period of 20 years. The majority did not play London, but although the comic opera *Estrella*, which did appear briefly in both London and New York, found some favour in Australia, Parke never again approached the quality or success of his first venture.

He adapted Costé's *Les Charbonniers* as a text for Ernest Bucalossi, and Bickerstaff's *The Padlock* as *The Keys of the Castle* for Bond Andrews.

1882 **(Les) Manteaux Noirs** (Procida Bucalossi/w Harry Paulton) Avenue Theatre 3 June

1883 **Estrella** (Luscombe Searelle) Gaiety Theatre 24 May

1886 **Rhoda** (Antonio Mora) Comedy Theatre 13 November

1887 **Herne's Oak** (J C Bond Andrews) Prince of Wales Theatre, Liverpool 24 October

1887 **Gipsy Gabriel** ('Florian Pascal'/w William Hogarth) Theatre Royal, Bradford 3 November

1887 **A Shower of Blacks** (*Les Charbonniers*) (Ernest Bucalossi/ w Arthur Shirley) 1 act Terry's Theatre 26 December

1889 **The Rose of Windsor** revised *Herne's Oak* Prince's Theatre, Accrington 16 August

1890 **The Dear Departed** (Martin van Lennep) 1 act Garrick Theatre 29 May

1893 **Mr FitzW** (Bond Andrews/w Horace W C Newte) 1 act Manchester; Bijou, Bayswater 1 June 1894

1894 **The Keys of the Castle** (Bond Andrews) Lyric Theatre, Hammersmith 19 July

1895 **Daye and Knight** (L Barone) 1 act St George's Hall 4 November

1896 **En Route** (E Bucalossi/Cecil Maxwell) Parkhurst Theatre 21 September

1897 **Kitty** (Henry Parker) Opera House, Cheltenham 30 August

1901 **Carmita** (Jesse Williams/w Shirley) Victoria Theatre, Broughton, Salford 7 October

PARR DAVIES, Harry   (b Briton Ferry, Glam, 24 May 1914; d London, 14 October 1955). British revue, film and stage composer.

Before venturing into the musical theatre, the young Davies worked as accompanist to Gracie Fields and composed many songs for her use on the screen and in concert, notably and most successfully 'Mary Rose' and 'Happy Ending' for the film *This Year of Grace* (1933), the title-number from the 1934 film *Sing as We Go*, 'The Fairy on the Christmas Tree' (w Roma Campbell-Hunter), 'The Sweetest Song in the World' from *We're Going to be Rich* (1938) and 'Wish Me Luck as You Wave Me Goodbye' (w Phil Park) sung in *Shipyard Sally* (1939). He also served George Formby with his memorable 'In My Little Snapshot Album' (w Jimmy Harper, Will Haines) originally displayed in the film *I See Ice* (1938).

Parr Davies's music was heard in many revues beginning with *Black Velvet* (1939) and including *Haw Haw, Come Out to Play, Top of the World, Happidrome, Gangway, Big Top, Best Bib and Tucker, Fine Feathers* and *The Shephard Show*, but his first musical play proper was a collaboration with George Posford on the score for the successful Cicely Courtneidge show *Full Swing*. His second show, the wartime melodrama *The Lisbon Story*, not only proved a remarkable and atypical London success, but also launched his best-remembered song, the incidental 'Pedro, the Fisherman'. If Emile Littler's musical version of *When Knights Were Bold* and the Welsh romance *Jenny Jones* proved ephemeral, he found further success in a second vehicle for Miss Courtneidge, *Her Excellency*, in a charming adaptation of J M Barrie's *Quality Street* as *Dear Miss Phoebe* ('I Leave My Heart in an English Garden') and in the long-running comedy musical *Blue for a Boy*, prior to a premature death.

1942 **Full Swing** (w George Posford/Archie Menzies, Arthur Macrae, Jack Hulbert) Palace Theatre 16 April

1943 **The Lisbon Story** (Harold Purcell) London Hippodrome 17 June

1943 **The Knight Was Bold** (aka *Kiss the Girls*) (Barbara Gordon, Basil Thomas/Emile Littler, Thomas Browne) Piccadilly Theatre 1 July

1944 **Jenny Jones** (Purcell/Ronald Gow, Ronald Millar) London Hippodrome 2 October

1949 **Her Excellency** (w Manning Sherwin/Purcell/Menzies, Purcell) London Hippodrome 22 June

1950 **Dear Miss Phoebe** (Christopher Hassall) Phoenix Theatre 13 October

1950 **Blue for a Boy** (Purcell/Austin Melford) His Majesty's Theatre 30 November

PARYS, Georges van   (b Paris, 7 June 1902; d Paris, 25 June 1971). French stage and film composer.

Georges van Parys formed an early partnership with Philippe Parès which resulted in some considerable work for the screen and, most notably, a half-dozen mostly successful jazz-age musical comedies for the Paris stage in the late 1920s and early 1930s. When the two men went their separate ways after their sixth show together, van Parys notched up the more significant theatrical contribution thereafter, scoring a success with the wartime musical comedy *Une femme par jour* (subsequently played in Britain), with his contribution to the music of the Fernandel spectacular *Les Chasseurs d'images* at the Châtelet, and with the songs for *Minnie Moustache*, a spoof Western manufactured to feature the popular singing group the Compagnons de la Chanson.

He rejoined Parès once more, 30 years on, to compose a costume opérette, *Le Moulin sans-souci*, but reverted to the small-scale with *Le Jeu de dames* before signing his last Paris score to a grandiose production, *La Belle de Paris*, produced with insufficient success at the Opéra-Comique.

Van Parys also provided additional music to Hervé's score for the Fernandel film version of *Mam'zelle Nitouche*.

1922 **Madame la Comtesse** (M Mauday) Théâtre des jeunes artistes 29 April

1927 **La Petite Dame du train bleu** (*Quand y-en a pour deux*) (w Philippe Parès/Léo Marchès, Georges Lignereux) Galeries St-Hubert, Brussels, May; Eldorado, Paris, 22 October

1927 **Lulu** (w Parès/Serge Veber) Théâtre Daunou 14 September

1928 **L'Eau à la bouche** (w Parès/S Veber) Théâtre Daunou 5 September

1929 **Louis XIV** (w Parès/S Veber) Théâtre de la Scala

1930 **Le Coeur y est** (w Parès/Roger Bernstein, Fernand Vimont/Raoul Praxy) Théâtre de l'Athénée 20 May

1931 **Couss-couss** (w Parès/Jean Guitton) Théâtre de la Scala 26 February

1937 **Ma petite amie** (S Veber) Théâtre des Bouffes-Parisiens 31 January

1943 **Une femme par jour** (S Veber, Jean Boyer) Théâtre des Capucines

1946 **Virginie Déjazet** (Jean Marsan, Raymond Vogel) Théâtre des Champs-Elysées

1947 **Les Chasseurs d'images** (w Roger Dumas/Jean Manse/ André Mouëzy-Éon) Théâtre du Châtelet 26 October

1956 **Minnie Moustache** (Jean Broussolle, André Hornez) Théâtre de la Gaîté-Lyrique 13 December

1958 **Le Moulin sans-souci** (w Parès/Marc-Cab/S Veber, Marc-Cab) Opéra, Strasbourg 24 December

1960 **Le Jeu de dames** (Albert Willemetz, Georges Manoir) Théâtre Moderne 2 December

1961 **La Belle de Paris** (Jean-Jacques Etchevery, Louis Ducreux) Opéra-Comique 9 February

Autobiography: *Les Jours comme ils viennent* (Plon, Paris, 1969)

PASCAL, Florian [WILLIAMS, Joseph] (b London, 1850; d London July 1923). Victorian composer and music publisher.

The son of the important music publisher Joseph Williams, and himself a member of the board of the family firm, Florian Pascal was a fluid composer of parlour music and light theatre works in an attractive if scarcely very individual style. His theatre ventures did not earn him celebrity, in spite of his being in the right places at almost the right times. He combined with Harry Paulton on *Cymbia* in 1882, but it was Bucalossi (*Manteaux Noirs*) in the same year and Jakobowski a few years later with *Erminie* who profited by the author's best comic libretti. He was the composer of *The Vicar of Wide-awake-field*, the piece which heralded the coming of the new burlesque at the Gaiety, but when the inaugural *Little Jack Sheppard* followed, he contributed only five numbers to a score organized by Meyer Lutz, and it was Lutz who went on to score the famous series of burlesques. He did, however, have the consolation that every piece he wrote, whether produced professionally or by amateurs or not at all, and some, such as Gilbert's *Eyes and No Eyes* which he had not written, but for which he composed a fresh score, was published.

1883 **Cymbia, or the Magic Thimble** (Harry Paulton) Royal Strand Theatre 24 March
1885 **The Vicar of Wide-awake-field, or The Miss-Terryous Uncle** (Henry Pottinger Stephens, William Yardley) Gaiety Theatre 8 August
1887 **Gipsy Gabriel** (Walter Parke, William Hogarth) Theatre Royal, Bradford, 3 November
1890 **Tra-la-la Tosca, or The High-Toned Soprano and the Villain Bass** (F C Burnand) Royalty Theatre 9 January
1896 **The Black Squire** (Stephens) Torquay 5 November
1897 **The Golden Age** (Henry Byatt) 1 act Savoy Theatre 5 July

PASSIONNÉMENT! Comédie musicale in 3 acts by Maurice Hennequin and Albert Willemetz. Music by André Messager. Théâtre de la Michodière, Paris, 15 January 1926.

One of the most successful of Messager's latter-day works, the 'comédie musicale' *Passionnément!* was composed to an up-to-date libretto in which the virtual inventor of the jazz-age musical comedy, Albert Willemetz, had a half-share. It told of how the Machiavellian American millionaire William Stevenson (René Koval) yachts his way across the Atlantic to find the dissolute young gambler Robert Perceval (Géo Bury) in order to persuade him to cash in on some land that he has inherited in Colorado. Stevenson knows the land contains oil. He brings with him his pretty young ex-actress wife, Ketty (Jeanne Saint-Bonnet) but, mistrustful of the reputation of French men, insists that she disguise herself in dark glasses and a grey wig. His mistrust is well placed, for when Perceval spies Ketty without her disguise he falls in love with her. She keeps up the double rôle of aged wife and her own young niece until she falls in her turn, and warns him of her husband's intentions. That way, Perceval ends up, in the best tradition, with both the money and the girl. Renée Duler was Hélène Le Barrois, Perceval's discarded (between Acts I and II) mistress, whilst Denise Grey as Julia, Ketty's oversexed maid, spent the evening with the captain of the yacht (Lucien Baroux) before finding the ultimate satisfaction with her employer's ultimately ex-husband. Hélène's husband (who gets her back, one abandonment and three solos later) and two servants completed the cast.

Messager's 21-piece score was topped by solos for Perceval (the title-waltz 'Passionnément'), Hélène (the reconciliatory rondeau 'N'imaginez pas' with which she returns to married bliss), Julia (three, including the comical prayer for a man 'Vous avez comblé ma patronne') and Ketty, demanding in 'Ah! pourquoi les bons moments' why the peak of pleasure has to be so short. Stevenson had a comical piece crediting America's success to 'le régime sec' (teetotalism), but after discovering 'le bon vin français' and a new personality between the second and third acts, had a much more amorous solo for the final act. Duets, trios, and ensembles played their part in a soigné modern score which won the 73-year-old composer outstanding reviews and a major success.

The original production of the show, mounted by Quinson and directed by Edmond Roze – all the most experienced the city had to offer – was a grand success. After its initial Paris season it went on the road, with Bury playing his original rôle, and in 1932 it was seen again in Paris at the Trianon-Lyrique. In the meanwhile, it had made a small excursion abroad. In Hungary, which showed the most enterprise towards the French musical comedy of the 1920s, Jenő Molnár's version of *Nászéhszaka* (wedding night) was a great success at the Belvárosi Színház, running more than 100 performances in its first run. Another version, *A legszebb éjszaká* (the most wonderful night), which credited new music by Bela Csanak and a book done over by Andor Pünkösti, was played at the Markus Park Színház in 1943.

The piece travelled little otherwise, although it was seen briefly in New York as played by a visiting French repertoire company with Sonia Alny and Georges Foix featured. A René Guissart film, with Fernand Graavey as its star, was produced in 1932, and *Passionnément!* has continued to make regular regional appearances in France through to the present day.

Hungary: Belvárosi Színház *Nászéjszaka* 16 December 1927; USA: Jolson Theater (Fr) 7 March 1929; Film: 1932
Recording: complete (Gaîté-Lyrique)

PASSMORE, Walter (b London, 10 May 1867; d London, 29 August 1946). D'Oyly Carte star comic who transferred successfully to the musical-comedy stage.

Apprenticed as a piano-maker at Cramer's, Passmore left that business at the end of his indentures and appeared in concert party and comedy until he was engaged by D'Oyly Carte in 1893 to appear in a supporting rôle in *Jane Annie* at the Savoy. He stayed with Carte to create the rôles of Tarara, the public exploder in *Utopia (Ltd)*, and Bobinet in Messager's *Mirette*, and he was promoted to principal comedian with the D'Oyly Carte Company to play the part of Grigg in *The Chieftain* (1894).

Passmore remained chief comic at the Savoy for a decade, starring in the Gilbert and Sullivan repertoire (Ko-Ko, the Grand Duke, Grand Inquisitor, Jack Point, John Wellington Wells, Joseph Porter, Bunthorne, Sergeant of Police, Lord Chancellor) and also in the theatre's productions of *His Majesty* (Boodel), *La Grande-Duchesse* (General Boum), *The Beauty Stone* (The Devil), *The Lucky Star* (King Ouf), *The Rose of Persia* (Hassan), *The Emerald Isle* (Professor Bunn), *Merrie England* (Walter

Wilkins) and *A Princess of Kensington* (Puck). He remained with Carte's successor, William Greet, when he switched from comic opera, to appear as the little dog trainer, Jim Cheese, in the musical comedy *The Earl and the Girl* (1903) and he subsequently played lead comedy rôles, more often in a legitimate and farcical vein than in the old-fashioned low style, in London's *The Talk of the Town* (1904, Jerry Snipe), *The Blue Moon* (1905, Private Taylor), *The Dairy-maids* (1906, Sam Brudenell), *Lady Tatters* (1907, Seth Lewys), *The Three Kisses* (1907, Garibaldi Pimpinello) and *The Belle of Britanny* (1908, Baptiste Boubillon).

He went on the road playing his original rôle in *Merrie England* and Simplicitas in *The Arcadians* in 1909–10, and spent several periods playing in home-made musical playlets on the halls with his second wife, Agnes Fraser, but he returned to London to play in *Die Fledermaus* (1910, Frank), *Baron Trenck* (1911, Nikola), *Oh! Oh! Delphine* (1913, Alphonse Bouchotte), *Young England* (1916, Tom Moon) and *Valentine* (1918, Gastricus) before moving into the provinces for several years in *Betty* (Achille Jotte), *Petticoat Fair* (1918, Tom), *Fancy Fair* (1919), *Too Many Girls* (1920, Tim Grogan) and *The Purple Lady* (1920, Mooney).

He was seen in London again in the chief comedy rôle of the light opera *The Rebel Maid* (1921, Solomon Hooker), with José Collins in *Our Nell* (1923, Mardyke) and in *The Damask Rose* (1930, Count Theodore Volny) interspersing his town dates with tours in *Madame Pompadour* (Calicot), *Princess Charming* (Chubby), *The First Kiss* (Bené Ben) and, lastly, at the age of 63, alongside an even older-timer, Amy Augarde, in Courtneidge's tour of *Lavender* (1930).

Passmore and Agnes Fraser were the parents of vocalist Nancy Fraser.

1912 **A Queer Fish** (Dudley Powell/w Percy Bradshaw) 1 act New Cross Empire 19 August
1914 **The Soldier's Mess** (Herbert C Sargent) 1 act Nottingham 22 June

PAS SUR LA BOUCHE Opérette in 3 acts by André Barde. Music by Maurice Yvain. Théâtre des Nouveautés, Paris, 17 February 1925.

Following the huge successes of *Ta bouche* (1922) and *Là-haut* (1923), which had placed their composer alongside Henri Christiné at the top of the honours list of the new French musical comedy era, Maurice Yvain paired with André Barde (who, likewise, had joined Willemetz at the head of the librettists' ranks) to turn out another major success with the années folles story of sex and marriage called *Pas sur la bouche*.

Gilberte (Régine Flory) is happily wed to industrialist Georges Valandray (Berval), but she and her companion aunt, Mlle Poumaillac (Jeanne Cheirel), have taken care to hide the fact that she has been married before, for Georges has metallurgical theories on marriage: the first man who 'puts his mark' on a woman can never be deceived by her. Unfortunately, when Georges invites an American associate to the house, that associate turns out to be Gilberte's ex, Eric Thomson (René Koval), all anxious to resume their relationship hors mariage. Mlle Poumaillac and Gilberte plot to distract him. Thomson has a weakness – he will not allow himself to be kissed on the lips since the day, when he was aged 12, his governess did just that and aroused ungovernable passions in him – so they set every available female on to him. Two acts of dizzyingly farcical

complications later, Mlle Poumaillac is forced by circumstances to supply the kiss herself.

The jaunty score included an irrepressibly bouncing title-song, delivered by the American, a stand-up number for the low-comic concièrge (Pauline Carton) of the garçonnière where the last act takes place, describing what she sees through keyholes ('Par le trou'), Georges's topical song 'Je me suis laissé embouteiller', and Mlle Poumaillac's good advice 'Quand on n'a pas ce qu'on aime', all of which became popular, alongside a varied group of numbers for Gilberte – from the waltz 'Comme j'aimerais mon mari' to the South American strains of 'La Péruvienne' and 'Soirs de Méxique' – a pair of taking duos for the juveniles of the piece (Pierrette Madd, Robert Darthez) and a hiccoughing song for the comically sighing Faradel (Germain Champell) who completed the principal cast. The rest of the show's forces comprised five chorines and a band of a surprising 17 players.

Produced by Benoît-Léon Deutsch at the Nouveautés, *Pas sur la bouche* was a major hit. Its tunes overflowed the market and the show stayed in its Paris home for a first run of more than a year and a half. It got the supreme accolade when one of the year's topical revues gleefully picked up its title to parody as *Pas sous la douche*. The show was taken up and produced in Britain as *Just a Kiss* before that original run was done. However, *Just a Kiss* (ad Frederick Jackson) was a deodorized version of the original which reset the action in Windsor and Mayfair, and which interpolated songs by Vivian Ellis (five) and Phil Charig (two) as well as some pieces of *Ta bouche*, which had not been played in Britain, into the remnants of Yvain's score. Marjorie Gordon was wife Valerie, American soubrette Marie George played the aunt, Miss Trask, light-opera vocalist Frederick Ranalow was husband number two, and Arthur Margetson his predecessor, through a run (93 performances) at the Shaftesbury and Gaiety Theatres that was as messed about as the show.

Hungary continued its fidelity to Yvain's musicals with a production (ad Jenő Heltai) at the Magyar Színház, and the show was seen in its original form in America as played in the repertoire of a French musical-comedy company touring Canada and America. Sonia Alny and Georges Foix appeared as the married couple, with Jane de Poumeyrac as the spunky aunt.

A film version mounted by Nicolas Rimsky and Nicolas Evreïmof in 1930 starred Mireille Perrey, Alice Tissot and Rimsky, and *Pas sur la bouche* has continued an episodic life in the French regions up to the present day, marked by a return to Paris and the Théâtre des Bouffes-Parisiens in 1948 with a cast headed by Lestelly, Martina Hotine, Spinelly and Gérald Castrix.

UK: Shaftesbury Theatre *Just a Kiss* 8 September 1926; Hungary: Magyar Színház *Csókról csókra* 4 March 1927; USA: Jolson Theater (Fr) 25 March 1929; Film: Rimsky & Evreïmof 1930
Recording: selection (Decca)

PASTOR, Tony [PASTOR, Antonio] (b New York, 28 May 1837; d New York, 26 August 1908). Baron of Broadway variety.

The son of a theatre violinist, Pastor himself performed as a child of nine at Barnum's Museum, then later in minstrel shows and in circuses as a rider, tumbler, actor and ultimately ringmaster and, on occasions, clown. He made his first appearances in variety in 1860, and on the theatrical stage in a pantomime at the Bowery Theater in the same year, before starting a new career as a performer of comic songs in appearances at the Broadway Music Hall and the American Theater.

In 1865 Pastor took his own company on the road and, on returning to New York, opened a variety theatre in the Bowery with the avowed aim of running a cleaner house than the majority of dives in which he had worked, a house with less emphasis on drink and blue jokes and with the lucrative prospect of providing family entertainment. He had sufficient success that a decade later he was able to move to larger premises and, finally, in 1881, to the house on 14th Street which had once been the German-language Germania Theater and which was to become famous under Pastor's name.

At Tony Pastor's Music Hall he produced variety bills which, moving with the times, included musical playlets, parodies and later farce-comedies as part of the entertainment, and many later well-known figures of the musical-comedy stage from Lillian Russell and May Irwin to Joe Weber and Lew Fields appeared in his bills. His theatre was burnt down in early June 1888 but by the end of October a new theatre had arisen on the site and he was able to reopen for the sterling business which he continued to find for many years until new ways and new ethics in the vaudeville business pushed him to the side.

Biography: Zellers, P: *Tony Pastor: Dean of the Vaudeville Stage* (East Michigan University, 1971)

PÁSZTOR, Árpád (b Ungvár, 12 April 1877; d Budapest, 26 October 1940).

Pásztor's earliest important stage work was the translation of Sidney Jones's *A Greek Slave* for Budapest's Népszinház, but he subsequently wrote and rewrote libretti for most of the front guard of contemporary Hungarian composers, notably József Konti, for whom he adapted Alexander Dumas's *Les Demoiselles de Saint-Cyr* as the libretto for *Fecskék*, Pongrác Kacsoh and Ákos Buttykay. He adapted Harry and Edward Paulton's famous comedy *Niobe* as a libretto for an operett by Stoll, and provided the Hungarian version of De Koven's *Robin Hood*, but his greatest single musical theatre success came with his adaptation of Gergely Csiky's famous Hungarian play *A nagymama* for the Raoul Mader musical of the same name. His text for the 'legend' *A harang* was subsequently used as the basis for the libretto of Eduard Künneke's Berlin Singspiel *Das Dorf ohne Glocke*.

Pásztor also wrote and adapted several operatic libretti, notably the Hungarian version of Richard Strauss's *Salome*, and, in the second part of his career, devoted himself entirely to straight plays, of which the most widely successful, the 1912 piece *Innocent*, was played on Broadway (Eltinge Theater, 9 September 1914) for 109 performances.

1899 **A görög rabszolga** (*A Greek Slave*) Hungarian version w Emil Makai (Népszinház)
1900 **Kadétkisasszony** (Raoul Mader) Népszinház 10 January
1900 **A csillag fia** (*Bar Kochba*) Hungarian version w László Beöthy (Népszinház)
1900 **Primadonnák** (Mader) Magyar Színház 29 December
1902 **Niobe** (Károly Stoll) Népszinház 7 November
1903 **Fecskék** (József Konti) Kiraly Színház 20 January
1904 **Robin Hood** Hungarian version (Király Színház)
1904 **A kis császár** (Stoll) Népszinház 2 March
1905 **A bolygó görög** (Akós Buttykay) Király Színház 19 October
1907 **A harang** (Pongrác Kacsoh, Buttykay) Kiraly Színház 1 February
1907 **Rákóczi** (Kacsoh/Sándor Endrődi/w Károly Bakonyi) Király Színház 20 November
1908 **A nagymama** (Mader) Népszinház-Vigopera 11 February

PATIENCE, or Bunthorne's Bride

Aesthetic comic opera in 2 acts by W S Gilbert. Music by Arthur Sullivan. Opera Comique, London, 23 April 1881.

After the nautical burlesque of *HMS Pinafore* and the melodrama burlesque of *The Pirates of Penzance*, Gilbert and Sullivan turned to a more specific and up-to-date subject with which to make their fun in *Patience*. Their target was the aesthetic movement and its acolytes, the flower-power people of their day, with their wilfully refined sensibilities and other-worldly attitudes, and their professed return to the modes and manners of ancient, simple days before the debauchery of the world and its people began. Gilbert chose the more extreme end of the movement, as personifed by such devotees as Oscar Wilde, as the very easy target for his darts.

Every lass of the village is sighing medievally at the feet of the pretentious poet Reginald Bunthorne (George Grossmith), rebuffing the 35th Dragoon Guards who were their last year's delight. Only the milkmaid Patience (Leonora Braham) remains innocently aloof, equating love with the feeling one has for an aunt, until she is informed by her more experienced sisters of the sentiment's sublime unselfishness. Dutifully she determines to love, but to love her handsome childhood sweetheart Archibald Grosvenor (Rutland Barrington) cannot be considered unselfish, so she regretfully agrees to love the boring but smitten Bunthorne, who has secretly admitted to her that his persona is nothing but an attention-grabbing sham. But once he has a partner, the other maidens promptly desert him to adulate Grosvenor instead, and Bunthorne becomes morbidly miserable at being insufficiently admired. He forces the usurper to de-aestheticize and become commonplace, and he himself takes up his rival's blithely poetic and agreeable manner. Since Bunthorne is now perfectly agreeable, Patience feels duteously able to desert him for Grosvenor, and since the other girls return to the Dragoons rather than to dear Reginald, the foolish fellow is the only one left without a partner at the final curtain.

Sullivan's score included many gems: Patience's pretty soubrette solos 'I Cannot Tell What This Love May Be' and 'Love is a Plaintive Song'; the over-super-virile songs of Dragoon Colonel Calverley (Richard Temple) ('When I First Put This Uniform On', 'If You Want a Receipt for a Popular Mystery'), the ageing longings of the booming Lady Jane (Alice Barnett), accompanying herself on the violoncello in 'Silvered is the Raven Hair', and the comical pieces for the rival poets – Bunthorne's recipe for aetheticism ('If You're Anxious for to Shine'), Grosvenor's nursery-rhyme tale of 'The Magnet and the Churn', and their pairing in 'When I Go Out of Doors' – as well as Bunthorne and Jane's vengeful anti-Grosvenor duo 'So Go to Him and Say to Him'.

Owing to the loquacity of friend Freddie Clay, the

Plate 207. **Patience:** *Bunthorne (Dennis Olsen) risks a rapprochement with Lady Jane (Heather Begg) (Australian Opera, 1987).*

eternally anti-Gilbert F C Burnand discovered that the librettist was working on an 'aesthetic' piece, and he hurried *The Colonel*, his own play on the same phenomenon, into production. Its enormous success – Burnand's biggest ever – prompted Gilbert and Carte publicly to announce that their piece had been written earlier, but they need not have worried. The two shows were very different and the success of one did not harm the other. *Patience*'s London run mounted to 20 months and 578 performances. Only 170 of these, however, were in the old Opera Comique, the bedraggled house which had shot back to popularity as the home of *HMS Pinafore* and *The Pirates of Penzance*. Part way through the run, Carte shifted the show into his brand new Savoy Theatre, built on the profits of the earlier shows. As the opening attraction at the Savoy, *Patience* ran on for more than an additional year.

The show was soon on the British road and J C Williamson briskly brought it to the Australian stage with Alys Rees (Patience), Howard Vernon (Bunthorne), George Verdi (Grosvenor) and Maggie Moore (Lady Jane) in the leading rôles but, in spite of the fact that the piece had been published and, thus, made free to producers in America, few transatlantic pirates leaped in to take advantage in the way they had with *HMS Pinafore*. When Carte opened his official production on Broadway nine months after the London opening, he was the first to show New Yorkers the piece which local managers had, apparently, considered a dubious prospect. Aestheticism had not, at that stage, reached America. Not, that is, until Oscar Wilde arrived full willingly on a lecture tour ... sponsored by Carte.

J H Ryley (Bunthorne), James Barton (Grosvenor), Carrie Burton (Patience) and Augusta Roche (Jane) headed Carte's Broadway cast. New York soon caught on to the extravagances that were being parodied, as well as to the general wit and charm of the piece's words and music, and *Patience* became a decided hit. When the theatre's obligations forced a new production, they avoided having to close immediately by playing split weeks of *Patience* and the new show until 177 performances had been reached. Other managers by now had their versions of *Patience* on the go (one splashy one boasted 50 lovesick maidens instead of the regulation 20) and the comic opera made regular Broadway appearances over the next 15 years. The most substantial of these was an 1896 revival (Herald Square Theater 13 July 1896) in which Lillian Russell played the rôle of Patience, a rôle she had first played 13 years previously in Tony Pastor's burlesque of the burlesque entitled *Patience, or the Stage-Struck Maidens* (Tony Pastor's Opera House 23 January 1883). Henry Dixey was her Bunthorne and Sadie Martinot caused a déshabille sensation in the little rôle of Angela.

Carte's Englische-Opern-Gesellschaft, with Josephine Findlay as Patience and James Muir as Bunthorne, later played *Patience* in Germany and Austria (including 10 performances at the Carltheater), Hungary ventured a translated version (ad Lajos Evva, Béla J Fái) with Ilka Pálmay starred, and Spain later staged a vernacular version of the show, but by and large *Patience* stuck to the English-speaking areas of the world where it found a continued popularity and a prominent, enduring place in the D'Oyly Carte and Williamson repertoires to go alongside its American successes. After the expiry of the Gilbert and Sullivan copyrights, the piece even went opera-housewards and *Patience* was staged by London's English National Opera in 1969 and again at the Coliseum in 1984, the latter production being also played at New York's Metropolitan Opera House.

Australia: Theatre Royal, Sydney 19 December 1881; USA: St Louis 28 July 1881, Standard Theater, New York 22 September 1882; Germany: Krolls Theater (Eng) 30 April 1887; Austria: Carltheater *Patience (Dragoner und Dichter)* (Eng) 28 May 1887; Hungary: Népszinház *Fejő leány, vagy Költőimádás* 5 November 1887

Recordings: complete (Decca, HMV) etc

PATINKIN, Mandy (b Chicago, 30 November 1952). Strong-voiced American leading man of the 1980s and 1990s.

In an acting career which has included more than intermittent appearances in the musical theatre, Patinkin made his two most prominent Broadway appearances in the rôle of Che in the American production of *Evita* (1980, Tony Award) and as the artists called George in Stephen Sondheim and James Lapine's *Sunday in the Park with George* (1984). Amongst his other musical credits, he appeared in Joseph Papp's production of *The Knife* (1987, Peter), at Britain's 1990 Chichester Festival as Martin in *Born Again*, an unsuccessful musical version of Ionesco's *Rhinoceros*, and the following year, in a return to Broadway, as Archibald in the musicalized kiddie-classic *The Secret Garden*.

In 1989 he appeared at the Public Theater, and subsequently at Broadway's Helen Hayes Theater, in *Mandy Patinkin in Concert: Dress Casual* (25 July, 56 performances) which he later performed throughout America. In 1993 he took over the leading role in *Falsettos* in New York.

PAUL, Mrs Howard [née FEATHERSTONE, Isabelle] (b Dartford, Kent, ?1833; d London, 6 June 1879).

The celebrated, versatile Isabelle Paul appeared in Shakespeare at Drury Lane, in comic opera in Paris, as Macheath in *The Beggar's Opera* at the Strand (1853), in Planché's revusical *Mr Buckstone's Voyage Round the Globe* (1854) at the Theatre Royal, Haymarket, and Farnie's burlesque *Little Gil Blas* (1870) at the Royal Princess's and was credited with introducing the can-can to America in a busy career in all areas of the theatre. However, she won much of her considerable fame in the drawing-room entertainments which she performed with her equally well-known comedian husband, **[Henry] Howard Paul** (b Philadelphia, 1830; d Christchurch, UK, 9 December 1905), under the title *Patchwork*.

With the coming of opéra-bouffe, she made a speciality of the title-rôle of *La Grande-Duchesse de Gérolstein* (Olympic, London, 1868; Théâtre Français, New York, 1870), and her rich contralto voice won her the rôles of the glamorous spirit Mistigris in Dion Boucicault's spectacular *Babil and Bijou* at Covent Garden (1872) and of Lady Sangazure in the original production of *The Sorcerer* (1877). In spite of an illness during the run of that show, she was hired to create the next of Gilbert and Sullivan's dragonistic ladies, Sir Joseph Porter's fearsome cousin Hebe, in *HMS Pinafore*, but she was not sufficiently well to make it to opening night. The rôle was all but cut from the show, leaving the piece with no heavy lady and the secondary contralto rôle of Little Buttercup as prima contralto. Mrs Paul died the following year without reappearing on the stage.

PAUL JONES *see* SURCOUF

PAULSEN, Harald (b Elmshorn, 26 August 1895; d Altona, 4 August 1954).

On the stage from the age of 16 as a dancer and actor in provincial German theatres, Paulsen was engaged at the Deutsches Theater in Berlin in 1919. He played there, and later in other Berlin theatres, in a variety of productions from opera and Operette to revue and plays, as well as building a substantial career in more than 150 German films as a bonvivant and character actor (Falke in *Die Fledermaus*, Zsupán in *Der Zigeunerbaron* etc). He appeared in Hugo Hirsch's *Der Fürst von Pappenheim* with Lea Seidl, and as Tom Flips in Granichstädten's *Evelyne* in Berlin and in Vienna, was the original Macheath in *Die Dreigroschenoper* (1928) at the Theater am Schiffbauerdamm and Vienna's Raimundtheater, and played the rôle of Harald Stone, opposite Anny Ahlers, in the Berlin Metropoltheater première of Ábrahám's *Die Blume von Hawaii* (1931) and that of Leander Bill in Berlin's *Katja, die Tänzerin*.

Between 1938 and 1945 Paulsen ran the Theater am Nollendorfplatz in Berlin before moving on to take up the direction of the Schauspielhaus in Hamburg in his later years.

PAULTON, Harry (b Wolverhampton, 16 March 1842; d London, 17 April 1917).

A prominent figure as a performer in the days of opéra-

Plate 208. **Harry Paulton:** *Victorian comedian and librettist who launched* Erminie *towards international success.*

bouffe in Britain, Harry Paulton was also significantly involved as writer, actor and director in the early days of the modern British musical theatre.

After beginning as a small-time actor in his native Wolverhampton, Paulton first appeared in London in 1867 at the Surrey Theatre in the play *The Lottery Ticket*. Three years later he was engaged by the Swanborough family at the Strand Theatre and he made an immediate success as a comedian in the role of Blueskin in the burlesque *The Idle Prentice* (September 1870). The following year he made his London début as a writer at the same theatre when, in collaboration with his brother Joseph and musical director John Fitzgerald, he turned out a burlesque of Dumas entitled *The Three Musket-Dears (And a Little One In)* which he co-directed and in which he starred as Athos to the Lady de Winter of Edward Terry. He also appeared at the Strand in the burlesques *Coeur de Lion* (1870, Archduke), *Eurydice* (1871, Aristaeus), *Miss Eily O'Connor* (Danny Mann), *Ivanhoe* (Isaac of York) and *Arion* (Molasses) as well as in the comedies which ran alongside and with those pieces.

In 1872 he was engaged for the piece *Clodhopper's Fortune* at the Alhambra Theatre which, after a period running composite programmes including operetta and burlesque, was about to launch into what would be its most famous period as a theatre with the grandiose production of *Le Roi Carotte*. Paulton was cast in the title-role of Offenbach's grand opéra-bouffe féerie and quickly became a great favourite in this vast theatre where his brand of broad comedy was well suited. For the next five-and-a-half years he played in virtually every one of the Alhambra's productions, reigning supreme as chief comedian even when the battles between the Alhambra's rival prima donnas Kate Santley and Rose Bell were at their height. Between 1872 and 1877 he appeared in Offenbach's *La Belle Hélène* (Menelaos), *La Jolie Parfumeuse* (La Cocadière), *Whittington* (Sergeant of the Patrol), *Le Voyage dans la lune* (King Cosmos) and *Orpheus in the Underworld* (Jupiter), in Strauss's *King Indigo* (Indigo), in *Chilpéric* (Physician) and in several pasticcio extravaganzas (Leporello in *Don Juan*, Max Doppeldick in *Spectresheim*, Rhadamathus John in *Lord Bateman*, Kit in *Wildfire*) as well as original works including *The Demon's Bride* (Filastenish), his own imitation of the grand opéra-bouffe féerie, *The Black Crook* (Dandelion), a spectacular version of the *Biche au bois* tale in which he co-starred with Kate Santley, and the grand opéra-bouffe *Don Quixote*, written with Frederic Clay, in which he wrote for himself the very large rôle of Sancho Panza.

In 1878 he left the Alhambra to appear as Frimousse in the British production of *Le Petit Duc* and he subsequently took leading comic rôles in burlesque at the Globe (Dame Tiller in *My Poll and Partner Joe*), and in a further series of Continental pieces including *Stars and Garters* (*L'Étoile*, Zadkiel), *Les Cloches de Corneville* (Bailie), *Der Seekadet* (Don Prolixio), *Les Mousquetaires au couvent* (Abbé Bridaine), *La Belle Normande* (Épinard) and *La Boulangère* (Flam). He also made return visits to the Alhambra for *La Petite Mademoiselle* (Taboureau), the English version of *Rothomago* (Rothomago) and *Le Cheval de bronze* (Great Bamboo), before starring there in revised versions of his own *The Black Crook* and of another fairytale spectacular *Babil and Bijou* (Auricomus).

During the run of this last piece, he directed the production of the comic opera *Manteaux Noirs* (1882), which he had adapted from Scribe's *Giralda* in collaboration with Walter Parke. The success of the piece was such that Paulton took over the lead comedy rôle of Dromez at the end of his Alhambra season, but he had less luck with another writing/directing/performing combination when his *Cymbia* (1883, Arthur), an Alhambra piece in all but size, was produced at the Strand. As an author he also supplied two long-lasting pieces, *The Babes* and the short *The Japs*, to comedian Willie Edouin's touring repertoire while, as a performer, he returned to established successes to play in *Falka* (Folbach), *Chilpéric* and *Rip van Winkle* (Nick Vedder) whilst preparing his next productions, a musical play called *Lilies* in which he toured during 1885, and a comic opera version of *L'Auberge des Adrets* staged at the Comedy Theatre as *Erminie*.

Erminie proved to be the biggest success of Paulton's career, both as a writer and as a director as well as as a comedy star. He played his showy rôle as the buffoonish thief Cadeau through the London run, then travelled to America to stage the Broadway production, a production which was to prove the outstanding Broadway musical of the era. He then turned producer to bring the piece back for a second London season before taking it on tour. A successor modelled on the same lines, *Mynheer Jan*, was sabotaged by internal management wranglings and Paulton returned to America, where he was much celebrated as the author of *Erminie*, and took starring roles on Broadway in *Dorothy* (Lurcher) and in his own version of Lecocq's *La Princesse des Canaries* (*The Queen's Mate*) opposite his preferred leading lady, Camille D'Arville, and Lillian Russell.

During his American stay Paulton also premièred a comedy with music called *Dorcas*, which was toured with *Erminie* heroine Pauline Hall in its title-rôle. *Dorcas*, like the pieces Paulton had written for Edouin, was a fairly unsophisticated comic show with a score concocted from a variety of sources, made for the less highbrow out-of-town audiences and, as such, it succeeded largely. Like another similar if mostly non-musical piece, the *schöne Galathee*-like tale of *Niobe*, (which travelled the world, was played in a multitude of languages and was made into a musical, with a score by Károly Stoll in Hungary), it had a long life on the touring circuits in both America and Britain.

Back in Britain, Paulton played both *Dorcas* and *Niobe* with some success and also turned to appearing again in comedy, but the biggest moments of his multiple career were now in the past. In 1895 he made his last appearance on the West End musical stage when he appeared briefly in Audran's *L'Oncle Célestin* (Baron Golosh) equipped with a rewrite of Courtright's decidedly un-French old song 'Johnny, My Old Friend John', before taking a trip to Australia and New Zealand where he directed and appeared in the Paulton-Stanley Company with statuesque Alma Stanley playing *A Night Out*, *My Friend from India*, *Niobe*, his own *In a Locket* and *Too Much Johnson*.

He was latterly seen in London only in straight plays, latterly appearing as Sir Toby Belch in *Twelfth Night* at Her Majesty's Theatre and Grumio (*The Taming of the Shrew*) with Martin Harvey in 1913. His last writings included an adaptation of the French opérette *Les Petites Brebis* (*The Little Innocents*) for the British touring circuits and another collaboration with *Erminie*'s Edward Jakobowski on a piece for the Shuberts, Nixon and Zimmerman called *Winsome Winnie*. *Winsome Winnie* went through sackings, rewrites and failure (by which time it was credited to Kerker and Ranken but still billed as 'as great a success as *Erminie*'), and although Paulton went on to supply several further plays to both London and New York, he dipped no more into the musical theatre.

Paulton was the most consistently popular comedian of the British opéra-bouffe stage but, more significantly, he was largely responsible as a director and a writer for the success in Britain of a style of musical theatre based on the French opéra-comique with the low-comedy portion heavily emphasised for his own benefit as a performer. *Erminie* was the crowning success of this career, but *Manteaux Noirs* was also a notable achievement.

1870 **The Gay Musketeers** (pasticcio/w Joseph Paulton, Joseph Eldred) Prince of Wales Theatre, Liverpool, 1 May

1871 **The Three Musket-Dears and a Little One In** (pasticcio/w J Paulton) revised *The Gay Musketeers* in 5 scenes Strand Theatre 5 October

1872 **The Black Crook** (Frederic Clay, Georges Jacobi) Alhambra Theatre 23 December

1875 **Una** (Lecocq pasticcio) Queen's Theatre, Dublin 4 April

1876 **Don Quixote** (Clay/w Alfred Maltby) Alhambra Theatre 25 September

1881 **The Black Crook** revised version (Alhambra Theatre)

1882 **(Les) Manteaux Noirs** (Procida Bucalossi/w Walter Parke) Avenue Theatre 3 June

1883 **Cymbia** (Florian Pascal) Strand Theatre 24 March

1884 **The Babes, or Whines from the Woods** (William C Levey) Toole's Theatre 9 September

1884 **Lilies, or Hearts and Actresses** (various) Prince of Wales Theatre, Liverpool 10 November

1885 **The Japs** (Meyer Lutz/w Mostyn Tedde) Prince's Theatre, Bristol 31 August

1885 **Erminie** (Edward Jakobowski/w Claxson Bellamy) Comedy Theatre 9 November

1886 **Masse-en-Yell-oh** (pasticcio/w Mostyn Tedde) 1 act Comedy Theatre 23 March

1887 **Mynheer Jan** (Jakobowski/w Mostyn Tedde) Comedy Theatre 14 February

1888 **MD** English version w Mostyn Tedde (Theatre Royal, Doncaster)

1888 **The Queen's Mate** (*La Princesse des Canaries*) American version (Broadway Theater, New York)

1889 **Paola** (Jakobowski/w Mostyn Tedde) Grand Opera House, Philadelphia and Royalty Theatre, Chester 10 May

1894 **Dorcas** (Max Hirschfeld, Clement Locknane et al/w Edward Paulton) USA; Lyceum, Ipswich 31 December 1894, Lyric Theater, New York 28 December 1896

1899 **The Dear Girls** revised *Lilies* (Locknane et al/w Mostyn Tedde) Regent Theatre, Salford 11 September

1901 **The Little Innocents** (*Les Petites Brébis*) English version (Richmond Theatre)

1903 **Winsome Winnie** (Jakobowski) Academy of Music, Baltimore

Several of Paulton's works were written in collaboration with his son **Edward A[ntonio] PAULTON** (b Glasgow, 1866; d Hollywood, Calif, 20 March 1939), who wrote in Britain under the name of 'Mostyn Tedde' and who continued a subsequent career as a prolific author and adapter of comedy, lyrics and libretti under his given name in America. He had a hand in several reasonably successful Broadway pieces (the adaptation of Berény's *Little Boy Blue*, for which he also wrote additional songs, and of Adolf Philipp's *Adele*, *Flo-Flo*) without ever approaching a hit like *Erminie* in which he later claimed to have had an authorial hand whilst still in fairly short pants. This, like his obituary's claim that he played with the Gaiety Theatre Company in New York and collaborated on the Cohan musical *The Royal Vagabond*, is not supported by contemporary documents, and if true can only mean that the apparent pseudonym of 'Claxson Bellamy' was a further (inexplicable) effort by 'Mostyn Tedde' to hide his identity. For, unlikely as it may seem, the Count Stephen Idor Szinnyey of the latter show was a real person, buried in the Bronx in 1919, just a month after *The Royal Vagabond*'s opening.

Paulton junior formed a useful writing (or rewriting) partnership with the German actor-singer-playwright-composer-producer Adolf Philipp when that Proteus of the New York German-language stage ventured into the English-language musical theatre, and together they turned out a series of musicals and plays of which one, *Adele*, won a brief London production. He also adapted the lyrics and sometimes the libretti of a number of Continental works, including Oscar Straus's *Die schöne Unbekannte* and *Mein junger Herr* for the American stage, but without success. His last Broadway musical, *Cherry Blossoms*, was produced in 1926 with the author appearing in the cast as an elderly Chinaman nearly 40 years after starring his 22-year-old self in a touring adaptation of the German comic opera *MD*. Paulton's last eight years were spent in Hollywood as a scenarist and dialogue writer.

The libretto to Ivan Caryll's Broadway musical *Kissing Time* (1920) was based on a musical comedy, *Mimi*, written by Paulton and Adolf Philipp which had closed out of town.

1885 **The Japs** (Meyer Lutz/w Harry Paulton) Prince's Theatre, Bristol 31 August

1886 **Masse-en-Yell-oh** (Edward Jakobowski/w H Paulton) 1 act Comedy Theatre 23 March

1886 **Pepita** (*La Princesse des Canaries*) English version (Royal Court Theatre, Liverpool)

1887 **Mynheer Jan** (Jakobowski/w H Paulton) Comedy Theatre 14 February

1888 **MD** English version w H Paulton (Theatre Royal, Doncaster)

1889 **Paola** (Jakobowski/w H Paulton) Grand Opera House, Philadelphia and Royalty Theatre, Chester 10 May

1894 **Dorcas** (Max Hirschfeld, Clement Locknane et al/w H Paulton) USA; Lyceum, Ipswich 31 December

1899 **The Dear Girls** (Locknane & pasticcio/w H Paulton) Regent Theatre, Salford 11 September

1903 **All at Sea** (Wilfred Arthur) Llandudno 21 May

1904 **My Lady's Maid** (*Lady Madcap*) American version w R H Burnside, Percy Greenbank (Casino Theater)

1907 **The Princess Beggar** (Alfred Robyn) Casino Theater 7 January

1908 **The Naked Truth** 1 act Fifth Avenue Theater June

1911 **Little Boy Blue** (*Lord Piccolo*) American version w A E Thomas, Grant Stewart (Lyric Theatre)

1913 **The Midnight Girl** (*Das Mitternachtsmädel*) English version (44th Street Theater)

1913 **Adele** (Adolf Philipp/w Philipp) Longacre Theater, New York 28 August

1913 **Two Lots in the Bronx** (Philipp/w Philipp) Adolf Philipp's 57th Street Theater 27 November

1914 **Madame Moselle** (Ludwig Englander) Shubert Theater, New York 23 May

1914 **The Queen of the Movies** (*Die Kino-Königin*) American version w Glen MacDonough (Globe Theater)

1915 **The Girl of Girls** (Oreste Vessella) Columbia Theater, Washington 4 January

1915 **The Girl Who Smiles** (Philipp/w Philipp) Lyric Theater, New York 9 August, revised version Bronx Opera House 14 February 1916

1915 **Two is Company** (Philipp/w Philipp) Lyric Theatre 22 September

1917 **The Beautiful Unknown** (*Die schöne Unbekannte*) English version (Parsons' Theater, Hartford) (later played on Broadway in a rewritten version as *My Lady's Glove*)

1917 **Boys Will Be Boys** (*Mein junger Herr*) English version w Ferdinand Stollberg (Playhouse, Wilmington, Del)

1917 **Flo-Flo** (Silvio Hein/Fred de Grésac) Cort Theatre 20 December

1919 **Daly Dreams** (Hein) 1 act Lambs Gambol, Metropolitan Opera House 8 June

1920 **Lady Kitty, Inc** (Paul Lannin/Melville Alexander, Irving Caesar) Ford's Opera House, Baltimore 16 February

1920 **Mimi** (w Adolf Philipp) National Theater, Washington DC 13 March

1920 **Look Who's Here** (Hein/Frank Mandel) 44th Street Theater 2 March

1920 **It's Up to You** (ex-*High and Dri*) (Klein, John C McManus/w Harry Clarke/Douglas Leavitt, Augustus McHugh) Trenton, NJ, 8 November

1920 **All for the Girls** (revised *It's up to You*) Cincinnati 12 December

1921 **It's Up to You** new version Casino Theater 28 March

1924 **That's My Boy** (Robert Simmonds, Billy Duval/Karyl Norman) Auditorium, Baltimore 10 November

1926 **Cherry Blossoms** (Bernard Hamblen) Syracuse 18 January

rry Paulton's first burlesque and *The Black Crook* were
tten with an elder brother, Joseph Paulton (d 31
tober 1875) whose career as an actor was centred
ely on Birmingham. Another brother, Thomas G
lton (b 1838; d 25 March 1914), also wrote for the
ge (*Princess Amaswanee* Pier, Eastbourne 15 April 1895
) and was active as an actor, appearing in a touring
npany of *Erminie* in Harry's role of Cadeau. A son,
rry Paulton jr, also worked as a performer and a director
I several other members of the family were also engaged
he theatrical profession.

YNE, Edmund [J] (b London, 1865; d London 1
y 1914). Star 5ft 4ins-tall comedian of George
wardes's greatest years of Gaiety Theatre musical
nedy.

After a number of years as a youthful theatrical com-
an in the provinces, Payne got his first London break
en he was hurried on to replace Charles H Kenney as
phistopheles in a brief stop-gap season of *Faust-Up-
Date* being played by Auguste van Biene's touring com-
iy at the Gaiety Theatre. He returned to the road for
eral years of burlesque, reminded London of his
stence when van Biene played another stopgap *Faust*
son, and finally made it to town when he was brought in
second takeover to the rôle of the little call-boy Shrimp
Edwardes's musical farce *In Town*, in succession to
ny Rogers and Florence Thropp. He had his first own
t at the Gaiety in a supporting comedy rôle in the
lesque *Don Juan* (1893), but made the move to stardom
en he was featured as the little shopboy Miggles in the
t show, *The Shop Girl* (1894).

As chief comedian of the Gaiety Theatre for the next
• decades, the little man established himself as one of
ndon's most popular theatrical stars, through top-billed
es in *The Circus Girl* (1896, Biggs), *A Runaway Girl*
98, Flipper), *The Messenger Boy* (1900, Tommy Bang),
ere, in deference to his seniority, the 'girl' element of
title switched sexes, *The Toreador* (1901, Sammy Gigg),
Orchid* (1903, Meakin), *The Spring Chicken* (1905,
dle), *The New Aladdin* (1906, Tippin), *The Girls of Got-
berg* (1907, Max Moddelkopf), *Our Miss Gibbs* (1909,
nothy), *Peggy* (1911, Albert Umbles), *The Sunshine Girl*
12, Floot) and (after a brief absence during which he
mpted to become a producer) once more with *The Girl
n Utah* (1913, Trimmit).

Payne was forced out of this last show by the illness
ich led to his death at the age of 49, not long before that
his mentor, Edwardes. The two passings marked, even
re than the war and the coming of revue, the end of an
in the British musical theatre.

ARCE, Vera (b Broken Hill, Australia, 1895; d
ndon, 18 January 1966). Australian beauty turned
rus girl, turned film star, turned musical leading lady,
ned character comedienne in an eventful international
eer.

The extremely beautiful Miss Pearce was first seen in
Australian theatre as a child, appearing in a juvenile
tet in *Florodora*. She was playing in the chorus of
stralia's *Our Miss Gibbs* when she won West's Beauty
mpetition, and was soon to be seen starred in Australian
nt films (*The Shepherd of the Southern Cross*, *Nurse Edith

Cavell etc). In her twenties, with the development of a
strong, rich soprano voice, she became one of Australia's
leading musical-comedy performers, appearing in star
rôles in Hugh D McIntosh's productions of *My Lady Frayle*
(1919, Lady Frayle, billed as 'Australia's own beauty
actress'), *The Officer's Mess* (1919), *His Little Widows* (1920,
Blanche), *Maggie* (1920, Maggie) and *Chu Chin Chow*
(1920, Zahrat), at the same time as exercising another
talent in choreographing several musical shows including
Australia's production of *The Lads of the Village* (1919).

She switched from playing leading ladies when she
moved to Britain and utilized her increasingly buxom
talents in the West End in comical-vocal rôles. The first of
these was in the brief run of Poldini's light opera *Love's
Awakening* (1922, Marietta), the first successful one as the
big and bosomy Flora in London's *No, No, Nanette*. During
the 1920s she appeared with Billy Merson in *My Son John*
(1926, Clare), as the operatic Sunya Berata in Jack
Buchanan's *That's a Good Girl* (1928), as Clotilde in *The
New Moon* at the Theatre Royal, Drury Lane (1929), in the
disastrous *Open Your Eyes* (1929, Rosalie Symes), the road-
closing import *Two Little Girls in Blue*, and in the semi-
operatic *Dear Love* (Jeanette), both in London and, in her
first American appearance, in its Shubertized girly-show
version on Broadway under the title *Artists and Models*.

In the 1930s she attacked Jack Buchanan in song-and-
dance in *Stand Up and Sing* (1931, Princess Amaris),
toured as Auguste in *Wild Violets*, loomed over Bobby
Howes in *Yes, Madam?* (1934, Pansy Beresford,
'Czechoslovakian Love') and galumphed about as the
gymnastic teacher, Miss Trundle, in *Please, Teacher!*
(1935). Further monstrous ladies followed in *Big Business*
(1937, Annabelle Ray), *Wild Oats* (1938, Maria Cloppitt),
and *Sitting Pretty* (1939, Clementina Tuttle), before she
co-starred with Leslie Henson in *Bob's Your Uncle* and then
appeared one last time in the musical theatre in *Rainbow
Square* (1951) before taking a number of straight theatre
comedy rôles in Britain and in America.

She appeared on film – with sound this time – in her
original stage rôle in the screen version of *Please, Teacher!*

Her brother, Harold Pearce, also worked on the musical
stage.

THE PEARL GIRL Musical comedy in 3 acts by Basil
Hood. Music by Howard Talbot and Hugo Felix. Shaftesbury Theatre, London, 25 September 1913.

Robert Courtneidge assembled an authorial team for
The Pearl Girl which glittered with both marquee and real
value: Basil Hood, the classiest lyricist and librettist of the
Edwardian age, Howard Talbot, composer of *A Chinese
Honeymoon* and of half *The Arcadians* and Hugo Felix, com-
poser of the hit *Madame Sherry* and George Edwardes's *Les
Merveilleuses*. His reward was a fine musical play whose
254-performance London run would undoubtedly have
been greater had it been produced a few years earlier for,
although Felix turned out a company number ('Over
There!') in the newly fashionable tango rhythm, *The Pearl
Girl* was, in the early days of the rage for transatlantic
rhythms, written textually and musically staunchly in the
Edwardian style.

When the fabulously wealthy Mme Alvarez (Marjorie
Maxwell) decides to do the London season she resolves to
wear not her famous pearls, but imitation ones fabricated

by the London firm of Palmyra Pearls. Palmyra boss Jecks (Lauri de Frece) is thrilled until, with all the puff done, Mme Alvarez cancels her trip. Jecks's secretary Miranda Peploe (Iris Hoey) saves the day by taking to the salons of Mayfair as Mme Alvarez, winning the desired publicity for her boss and a Duke (Harry Welchman) for herself. Alfred Lester was a little lovelorn shopboy, Cicely Courtneidge and Jack Hulbert (who became engaged during the show's run) had a soubret romance and songs ('At the Zoo' etc) to match, and Ada Blanche played a parvenue socialite who paired off at the curtain with Mr Jecks, who had spent most of the evening disguised as a Spaniard comically shepherding his secretary through social shoals.

Fay Compton and Marie Blanche succeeded to the rôle of Miranda, but Miss Hoey took it up again for the road, succeeded by Ruby Vyvan as the tour ran into 1915. A second company took to the road for part of 1915, and *The Pearl Girl* was seen in the British provinces again in 1916 and 1917.

PEARLY, Fred

The composer of some lively and unpretentious measures for such musicals-by-committee as the long-running *Je t'veux*, Pearly kept up a presence in the Parisian theatre during the years when the dance music, which he also supplied liberally to the dance halls and revues, made up the scores of its musical plays.

1923 **Je t'veux** (w Gaston Gabaroche, René Mercier, Albert Valsien/Bataille-Henri) Théâtre Marigny 12 February

1924 **Mon Vieux** (w Gabaroche, Josef Szulc, Raoul Moretti, Pierre Chagnon, Albert Chantrier/André Birabeau, Bataille-Henri) Théâtre de la Potinière 18 December

1929 **Vive Leroy** (w Chagnon/Henri Géroul, René Pujol) Théâtre des Capucines 2 May

1932 **Babaou** (w Chagnon/Louis Boucot, Raphaël Adam) Théâtre Daunou 1 April

1932 **Azor** (w Chagnon, Gabaroche/Max Eddy/Raoul Praxy) Théâtre des Bouffes-Parisiens 16 September

1938 **J'hésite** (w Gabaroche/Praxy) Théâtre Antoine 16 February

PEGGY Musical play in 2 acts by George Grossmith jr based on *L'Amorçage* by Léon Xanrof and Gaston Guérin. Lyrics by C H Bovill. Music by Leslie Stuart. Gaiety Theatre, London, 4 March 1911.

When George Edwardes decided to re-deploy his forces and introduce a little novelty at the Gaiety Theatre, where the team of Tanner, Ross, Greenbank, Caryll and Monckton had steadily supplied him with hits for so many years, he turned to *Florodora* composer, Leslie Stuart, who had already been tried at the Gaiety with some success with *Havana*. Long-time Gaiety comedy star and *Havana* co-librettist George Grossmith adapted the French comedy *L'Amorçage* as the libretto for a piece which needed to supply good rôles for himself and Teddy Payne, but no longer for the long-time Gaiety star Gertie Millar, who had gone with her husband, Monckton, to the Adelphi and *The Quaker Girl*.

Phyllis Dare played Peggy, the little manicurist with whom rich James Bendoyle (Robert Hale) falls in love. To detach her from her little hairdresser fiancé, Albert Umbles (Payne), Bendoyle adopts the principle of ground bait: he hires an impecunious friend, Auberon Blow (Grossmith), to impersonate Albert's long-lost rich uncle

and to pour gifts and high-living on to the pair until Peggy becomes used to having nice things. When the supply is suddenly cut off, she will see the advantage of wedding Bendoyle rather than Umbles. Complications include the arrival of a real uncle (Herbert Jarman) with a gorgeous daughter (Olive May), and the fact that Auberon and Peggy fall in love. Grossmith's rôle allowed him to play the usual comic dandy, but this time also the phoney rich uncle and, to his undoubted delight, to get the girl. Auberon and Peggy duly pair off, leaving Bendoyle to the gorgeous Doris, whilst Umbles is given a French danseuse (Gabrielle Ray) as a consolation prize.

Stuart's score mixed waltzes and comical songs for his principals in standard Gaiety style with, as so often, a number for a supporting character proving the best liked. In this case it was Olive May's rope-swinging description of herself as 'The Lass With the Lasso'. Edwardes kept *Peggy* infused with new items: Grossmith was given a topical song about 'Mr Edison', Connie Ediss was written into the script and given two fine and funny Phil Braham/Arthur Wimperis numbers ('Which He Didn't Expect From a Lady', 'A Little Bit On'), but, in spite of mostly good reviews, the piece did not come up to *Our Miss Gibbs* in popularity and closed after a good-but-not-grand 270 performances.

In America, Thomas W Ryley, who had made a fortune with *Florodora*, lost what remained of it on 37 Broadway performances of a version of *Peggy* with Renée Kelly (Peggy), Charles Brown (Blow), Joe Farren Soutar (Bendoyle) and Harry Fisher as Umbles, now called Cecil Custard Carruthers, into which he popped some favourite old bits from *Florodora* and *Havana* amongst a welter of other 'improvements'. The British provinces, however, welcomed the show: in early 1912 there were three *Peggy*s on the road, the A-company richly topped by May de Souza, Millie Hylton and W Louis Bradfield, but this was apparently not a good enough result for Edwardes. He cancelled Stuart's three-play contract, ending the composer's theatrical career, and turned to Paul Rubens for the next Gaiety shows.

USA: Casino Theater 7 December 1911

PEGGY-ANN Musical comedy in 2 acts by Herbert Fields based on the libretto *Tillie's Nightmare* by Edgar Smith. Lyrics by Lorenz Hart. Music by Richard Rodgers. Vanderbilt Theater, New York, 27 December 1926.

For *Peggy-Ann*, Herbert Fields took the good old 'dream sequence' gimmick of 19th-century extravaganza, which had been re-used with great success in his father's production of the daydreamy musical comedy *Tillie's Nightmare* (1910), tricked it out with some up-to-date references to Freud, and tried to fool folk that it was daring and meaningful in an avant-garde way. Perhaps a few folk were fooled, but most just enjoyed a show whose well-proven convention meant that it was able to let itself go with joyfully unreal absurdity in a manner little seen since the days of the more unbounded burlesques had passed away.

Like the heroine of *Tillie's Nightmare*, Peggy-Ann (Helen Ford) is a slavey in a boarding-house, and her dreams take her off into glamorous and ridiculous situations in society New York, on an ocean-going yacht complete with shipwreck, and on a version of the island of Cuba. The dream was peopled by her mother (Edith

iser), Mr (Grant Simpson) and Mrs Frost (Lulu
Connell) and their daughter Alice (Betty Starbuck),
y Pendelton (Lester Cole), Arnold Small (Fuller Mel-
, jr), Patricia Seymour (Margaret Breen), Freddie
awn (Jack Thompson), 12 chorus girls, six chorus boys
l a fish (Howard Mellish).

During the musical part of the evening Peggy delivered
His Arms' and 'A Little Birdie Told Me So' and joined
y in 'A Tree in the Park' and Patricia in 'Where's That
nbow?', whilst Mrs Frost encouraged 'Give This Little
l a Hand' and Patricia and Fred sang about 'Havana'.
Fields's production had a sticky start when it hit leading
y troubles. Ona Munson and Ada Mae Weeks were
h announced, and Dorothy Dilley, star of *Kitty's Kisses*,
ually began rehearsals before being replaced by Miss
rd, the leading lady of Rodgers and Hart's first success-
musical, *Dearest Enemy*. The title, too, was changed, as
gy (perhaps because of Leslie Stuart's pre-war musical)
ame *Peggy-Ann*. The changes clearly didn't harm it, for,
spite of the fact that the score, unlike that of *Tillie's*
htmare (which had brought forth 'Heaven Will Protect
Working Girl'), produced no songs which proved take-
y hits, the show had a fine run of 333 Broadway per-
mances, a four-month post-Broadway tour and a
ndon production. Alfred Butt's London version, direc-
by the elder Fields, with Dorothy Dickson as the
amy and now anglicized heroine, did less well and
sed in 134 performances.

: Daly's Theatre, 27 July 1927

S PENSIONAT Comic opera (Operette) in 2 acts
'C K'. Music by Franz von Suppé. Theater an der
en, Vienna, 24 November 1860.

Generally quoted (in preference to Conradin's
lesque *Flodoardo Wuprahall*) as the first significant
sical play of the modern era to come out of Vienna,
opé's little 'komische Oper in zwei Bildern' followed the
del supplied by the one-act works of Offenbach and his
nch contemporaries, which the Carltheater had been so
cessfully playing for the past couple of years. The
igned libretto was assumed to be 'from the French'.
is may very well have been so, but, whether it was
owing or faking the fashion, it served its purpose well,
viding a comical little story which allowed plenty of girls
to the stage.

The law student Karl (Albin Swoboda) wants to marry
lene (Laura Rudini), but her father will only permit this
e finds a job within 48 hours. Karl has his eye on the
ninistrator's post at Helene's school, but it seems that
headmistress, Brigitte (Friederike Fischer), will give it
er cousin. With the help of his comical servant, Florian
sef Röhring), Karl lures Helene's schoolfriends to a
lnight rendezvous where they become witnesses to his
sionate declaration to the headmistress and to her not-
ifferent response. To save her good name, Brigitte is
iged to give Karl the job which ensures him his Helene.
Suppé's short score included a good dose of ensemble
l choral music – the opening Praeludium and Kirchen
or ('Mutter von deinem Bild') and a quartet ('Gute
cht') in the first scene, and the second scene's septet
ör meiner Lieder tiefen Liebslaut') and Spottchor
let schnell wir müssen sehen') – alongside a Ballade
l dance number for a schoolgirl called Amalie (Frln

Wiener), a serenade with schoolgirl accompaniment for
Karl ('Wenn des Mondes Licht durch die Büsche bricht')
and a duo for Karl and Helene ('O Pein! Ach der Gedanke
bring mich um!').

Das Pensionat was a grand success at the Theater an der
Wien where it was played for 20 nights in succession, and
34 times in all in the six months it remained in the
repertoire. It was played immediately afterwards in Hungary – first in German and then at the Nemzeti Színház in
an Hungarian translation (ad Lajos Csepreghi), with
Károly Huber, Ilka Markovits and Vilma Bognár featured
– in Germany, and in the German theatres of America,
notably at New York's Stadttheater where it was mounted
in 1867 with Richard Kaps, Herr Herrmann and Hedwig
L'Arronge supported by rather more schoolgirls than original half-dozen. In Vienna, it was soon taken up by the
Carltheater where it was given a new production in 1879
(27 December) with Karl Blasel featured as Florian, but
although the piece was occasionally reprised thereafter, it
was largely bypassed by producers in favour of Suppé's
progressively more substantial and more popular works,
beginning with *Flotte Bursche*, *Leichte Kavallerie* and *Die
schöne Galathee*.

Although the show did not, apparently, get seen in
Britain first time around, it put in an appearance there a
century and more on. An English-language version has
been played in London by the Guildhall School of Music
and Drama and, in 1993, by Morley College.

Hungary: Budai Színkör (Ger) 1 June 1861, Nemzeti Színház *A
nőnövelde* 14 April 1862; USA: Stadttheater 18 November
1867

PEPITA

A popular title in the 19th-century musical theatre, it
was given first of all to Edward A Paulton's long-touring
British adaptation of Lecocq's *La Princesse des Canaries*
(Liverpool 1886). A Broadway comic opera *Pepita* (Edward
Solomon/Alfred Thompson) in which Lillian Russell – at
that time the composer's sort-of-wife – starred in a version
of the old doll-girl tale through a fair 88 performances,
subtitled itself uncomfortably 'the girl with the glass eyes',
whilst Hungary's *Pepita* was an operett composed by the
successful local musician Béla Hegyi (Népszinház 2 January 1890) and said to be based on Théophile Gauthier's *Ne
touchez pas à la reine*.

PÉPITO Opéra-comique in 1 act by Léon Battu and
Jules Moinaux. Music by Jacques Offenbach. Théâtre des
Variétés, Paris, 28 October 1853.

The first Offenbach opéra-comique to be produced in a
regular Paris theatre, *Pépito* was a little piece part rural
light opera and part operatic parody. The Pépito of the title
does not appear, but he is the background to the action as
much as its Basque village. The pretty innkeeper
Manuelita (Mlle Larcéna) rebuffs the advances of her
Figaroesque competitor Vertigo (Leclère) as she saves up
her meagre profits for the day when her Pépito returns
from the army to wed her. Their childhood friend Miguel
(Biéval) comes back to his native village, is attracted by
Manuelita, and when (having been ill-informed by the
hopeful Vertigo as to the level of her virtue) he makes a
rude pass at her he gets soundly turned down. Repentant,
he offers to take Pépito's place in the army to allow him to

return home, but it turns out that Pépito has married a cantinière and Manuelita is not too unhappy to take the gallant Miguel instead. The parody came mostly in the rôle of Vertigo, whose Rossinian character was given some Rossini-ish music in an eight-number score which mixed pretty country strains, in the solos and duos for Manuelita and Miguel, with rather formal opera buffa moments, as in Vertigo's air bouffe, without attaining the freedom of musical expression which would later be Offenbach's trademark.

The production of *Pépito* at the Variétés was a fiasco. It lasted just one performance. Nevertheless, Offenbach staged it again himself and brought it back to the Paris boards during the first year of operation of his Bouffes-Parisiens (10 March 1856) to a rather better reception and a place in the Bouffes repertoire at home and in their 1850s travels abroad. However, the show ultimately found its main popularity not in France but in Austria. Following the great success of his first Viennese Offenbach presentation, *Hochzeit bei Laternenscheine* (*Le Mariage aux lanternes*), Johann Nestroy staged a slimmed and remade (textually by Karl Treumann, musically by Carl Binder) version of *Pépito* under the title *Das Mädchen von Elisonzo* (later *Elizondo*) on his Carltheater programme. Treumann played Vertigo, Therese Braunecker-Schäfer was Manuelita, and Anna Grobecker was a travesty Vasco (ex-Miguel) and the show gave Nestroy a second Offenbach hit which Treumann later reproduced at his Theater am Franz-Josefs-Kai. This reshaped version was soon seen in Germany and in Hungary, first in German and soon after at the Nemzeti Színház (ad Lajos Csepreghi) in Hungarian, with Ilka Markovits, Vilma Bognár and Kószeghy featured, and it won numerous repeats in both countries and in Austria over the following years.

UK: St James's Theatre 24 June 1857; Austria: Carltheater *Das Mädchen von Elisonzo* 18 December 1858; Hungary: Budai Színkör (Ger) 1 June 1859, Nemzeti Színház *Az elizondoi lány* 30 September 1861; Germany: *Das Mädchen von Elizondo* 8 November 1859

PEPÖCK, August (b Gmunden, 10 May 1887; d Gmunden, 5 September 1967). Austrian composer of vocal and choral music, of film and stage scores.

A chorister as a child, Pepöck moved to Vienna to make music his study and, after the war, he worked for a number of years as a theatre conductor in Germany and in Austria. However, he did not make his first contribution to the lyric stage until he had left the podium and returned to base himself in his home town of Gmunden. His first piece, *Mädel ade!*, originally produced at Leipzig, was subsequently picked up for the Wiener Bürgertheater. It ran there just under a month. He had more success with the 1937 German production of *Hofball im Schönbrunn*, a good-old-days Operette which dragged the poor old Herzog von Reichstadt on to the operettic stage one more time for a romance with the equally over-operetticized ballerina Fanny Elssler, and he subsequently collaborated with librettist Hardt-Warden on another Operette, on the Posse *Eine kleine Liebelei* and on a revision of Ernst Reiterer's successful *Coquin de printemps* pastiche of Josef Strauss music. Like these last two, Pepöck's *Der Reiter der Kaiserin*, a collaboration with singer Robert Nästlberger, was produced in composer-starved wartime Vienna.

1930 **Mädel ade!** (Bruno Hardt-Warden) Operettenhaus, Leipzig 14 January, Wiener Bürgertheater 5 October
1934 **Trompeterliebe** Leipzig
1937 **Hofball im Schönbrunn** (Josef Wenter, Hardt-Warden) Theater des Volkes, Berlin 4 September
1938 **Drei Wochen Sonne** (Hardt-Warden) Städtische Bühne, Nuremberg 15 November
1941 **Der Reiter der Kaiserin** (Robert Nästlberger, A von Czibulka) Raimundtheater 30 April
1942 **Eine kleine Liebelei** (Hardt-Warden, E A Iberer) Exlbühne 3 July
1944 **Frühlingsluft** revised version w Hardt-Warden
1949 **Der verkaufte Spitzbub** (A von Hamik) Exlbühne, Innsbruck 3 September
1951 **Geschichten aus dem Salzkammergut** Linz 14 December

PERCHANCE TO DREAM Musical play in 3 acts by Ivor Novello. London Hippodrome, 21 April 1945.

One of the most successful of the series of romantic musical plays written by Ivor Novello for the larger theatres of London in the 1930s and 1940s, *Perchance to Dream* followed the multiple-generation format used with such success by Bernauer and Schanzer in *Wie einst im Mai* (1913) and, more recently, by Armin Robinson and Paul Knepler in *Drei Walzer* (1935). In Novello's story the first generation were the aristocratic highwayman, Sir Graham Rodney (Novello), his mistress, Lydia (Muriel Barron), and Melinda (Roma Beaumont), the hated relative whom, in *Lilac Domino* fashion, he wagers he will bed, before falling in love with her. To pay the debt he must lose, he rides to rob one last time and is killed. The second generation are the music teacher Valentine Fayre (Novello), his wife Veronica (Barron), and Melanie (Beaumont) the passionate girl who cannot prevent herself coming between them. When Veronica discovers she is pregnant, Melanie knows that Valentine will now never leave his wife, and kills herself. In the final, modern generation, the descendants of the families of the unhappy Graham/Valentine and Melinda/Melanie finally get together. The tales were linked by their setting, the mansion called Huntersmoon where the Rodney/Fayre family live and quarrel and die, and the first two acts both featured Margaret Rutherford as the dowager of the family.

The score of *Perchance to Dream* was again, given its necessarily non-singing leading male character, written largely for the soprano (Barron) and contralto Olive Gilbert as the blowsy actress Ernestine in the first act and a stout incidental dame in the second. It produced one of Novello's biggest hits in the two women's duet 'We'll Gather Lilacs', alongside Lydia's waltz song 'Love Is My Reason for Living', the richly contralto 'Highwayman Love' and some attractive parlour music. Melanie/Melinda was supplied with some gently girlish numbers ('The Night That I Curtsied to the King', 'The Glo-Glo') made to the measure of the vocally light Miss Beaumont.

Tom Arnold's production at the London Hippodrome was a huge success. *Perchance to Dream* played in the West End for more than two and a half years (1,022 performances) before the company took the show to South Africa and then toured it through Britain whilst Novello prepared his next show. Like Novello's other shows, it was seen little outside Britain, although its favourite songs became worldwide concert pieces, but within Britain it kept up a regular presence, being played in several regional theatres in the 1980s and being taken on tour with Simon Ward and Diana Martin starred as Rodney/Valentine and Melanie/Melinda.

Recordings: original cast (Decca), selection (EMI)

LA PÉRICHOLE Opéra-bouffe in 2 acts by Ludovic Halévy and Henri Meilhac based on *Le Carrosse du Saint-Sacrement* by Prosper Mérimée. Music by Jacques Offenbach. Théâtre des Variétés, Paris, 6 October 1868. Revised 3-act version, Théâtre des Variétés, 25 April 1874.

In some ways, *La Périchole* represented a departure for Offenbach, Meilhac and Halévy, the trio of collaborators who had made themselves the world's most famous authors of the musical theatre in the five years, four enormous hits (and just one comparative failure) since their first teaming. Although it was still labelled an 'opéra-bouffe', and although it still contained some of the extravagant elements of the kind of burlesque humour displayed in the earlier pieces, *La Périchole* was inherently of a different tone to the purely bouffe *La Belle Hélène*, *Barbe-bleue* and *La Grande-Duchesse de Gérolstein*, and also to the paper-sharp comedy of mores *La Vie parisienne*. Its colourfully comical south-of-the-border tale was even based (albeit very sketchily) on someone's else work, and not as a parody of that work: *La Périchole* was, for all its appellation, a genuine comic opera.

When the penniless Peruvian busker La Périchole (Hortense Schneider) collapses at the end of a day's work and her companion Piquillo (José Dupuis) goes off to earn some food, she falls easy prey to the libidinous Viceroy, Don Andrès de Ribeira (Grenier), his offer of dinner and a place as lady-in-waiting to his deceased wife. She pens a sad farewell to Piquillo and goes where food awaits her. However, court etiquette insists that the Viceroy's 'lady-in-waiting' must for decency's sake be a married woman. After some liquid persuasion Périchole agrees to a marriage of convenience, and the Viceroy's minions bring in a convenient husband, a fellow found trying to hang himself from despair: a very drunk Piquillo.

When Piquillo finds out the next day what he has done he berates his new wife hideously (and unfairly, for she, at least, knew whom she was marrying!), gets thrown in prison, then released to perform his duty by presenting his wife at court. But at the presentation Périchole offers back all the Viceroy's rich gifts and tells her tale, and that of Piquillo, with such affecting sincerity that Don Andrès gives up his untouched new mistress to her husband and sends them richly on their way.

Offenbach's music to *La Périchole* reflected the difference in tone. There were jolly pieces, like the trio of the three innkeeping ladies ('Au Cabaret des trois cousines') and the Viceroy's description of his 'Incognito', and there was high comedy in the first-act finale, overflowing with hard liquor, with a group of wobbly notaries summoned from their supper to perform the ceremony, Périchole's replete 'Ah! quel dîner je viens de faire' and poor Piquillo's blind drunk declaration of love ('Je dois vois prévenir, madame'), but the popular highlights of *La Périchole*'s score were the simple song of the strolling minstrels ('L'Espagnol et la jeune Indienne') with its famous cockeyed refrain 'il grandira, car il est espagnol',

and the wholly sentimental and sincere letter song, in which Périchole bids her Piquillo farewell ('O mon cher amant, je te jure'). Sentimental and sincere, and just a little bouffe, for to those who knew their *Manon Lescaut*, Périchole's letter of regrets had a familiar ring.

Critics and early-come public alike refused initially to admit that Offenbach and his librettists had given them another fine, funny and melodious work, and one which was not solely crazy fun. Groups were even formed to whistle down Schneider. But *La Périchole* was stronger than them. It held its place at the Variétés through a fine run and was soon exported to every corner of the musical theatre world at the beginning of what was to be a long and strong career. America was the first foreign part to see the show when *La Périchole* was introduced to New York by H L Bateman's company with Mlle Irma starring as the street-singer alongside Aujac (Piquillo) and Leduc (Don Andrès). It had to struggle against the stiff competition offered by Marie Desclauzas and Rose Bell in *Geneviève de Brabant* up the road at the Théâtre Français, and a few days after the opening Bateman gave up and sold out his lease and company to the adventurous James Fisk. But although this first production was only a quarter-success, *La Périchole* soon established itself amongst the most popular items in the American opéra-bouffe repertoire and it became part of the baggage of all the touring French companies, making regular New York appearances during their Broadway dates. In 1895 Lillian Russell appeared in a Broadway revival at Abbey's Theater (29 April), a Shubert presentation at the Jolson in 1925 was played in Russian and featured Olga Baclanova (21 December), and in 1956 the Metropolitan Opera played a version with Patrice Munsel, Theodore Uppman and Cyril Ritchard in the leading rôles.

Just a few days after Irma's American opening, Friedrich Strampfer produced *Périchole, die Strassensängerin* (ad Richard Genée) at Vienna's Theater an der Wien. Once again, the piece did not find the triumph of the composer's earlier works and its record at the house closed at 48 performances. London saw Schneider herself as Périchole, in repertoire at the Princess's Theatre in 1870, but it was not until five years later that Selina Dolaro presented herself in what London's *Era* described as 'the racy opéra-bouffe' with Walter Fisher as her Piquillo and Fred Sullivan (brother of Arthur) as the Viceroy. 'A pity that such melody was ever united to so worthless a story' huffed the same paper, complaining that if the sex was taken out of the adaptation there would be nothing left. Dolaro played the show for a fine three months before switching to *La Fille de Madame Angot*, brought it back again in October and again in 1879, by which time Londoners had also seen Emily Soldene in the rôle in a larger production at the Alhambra (9 November 1878). In 1897 Florence St John played *La Périchole* (Garrick Theatre 14 September) and it has returned to British stages intermittently over the century since.

Oddly enough, Australia seems to have heard *La Périchole* in English before either London or New York. Lyster's opéra-bouffe company introduced it into its repertoire in May 1875 with Henry Bracy and Clara Thompson starred. Emilie Melville followed up just months behind with her version (and also with Bracy), Fannie Simonsen gave her very sung version of the heroine, and the piece was seen regularly through the 1880s as Melville with her four-act version and Gracie Plaisted (with Majeroni and Wilson's Company, then with Searelle and Harding) trouped their productions through the colonies and the orient.

The first significant revival of *La Périchole* in Paris was in 1874 (25 April), and for that revival, which featured the three stars of the original production, Offenbach and his librettists enlarged the show. Unusually, it 'enlarged' very well indeed. Unlike the remake of *Orphée*, where the expansion had consisted of sticking bits and pieces in throughout the work, the new *Périchole* left its highly satisfactory first act pretty well alone and attacked the notably weaker second part of the show. The authors, who had already made alterations and extensions to their book, introduced a whole new plot turning and took a much more burlesque tone in a preposterous new dungeon scene in which the Viceroy appeared in fantastical disguise as a jailor for a whole series of high jinks. Offenbach added no fewer than ten extra numbers to his score to suit the rearranged text, one of which was a delightful – and again unburlesquey – solo for his heroine, 'Je t'adore, o brigand'.

Other top Parisian prima donnas later took turns at *La Périchole*. In 1877 Judic made a Parisian appearance in the rôle and in 1895 Jeanne Granier was also seen as la Périchole at the Variétés, but although the show persisted in the early 19th-century and 20th-century repertoire, it did not do so with quite the vigour that its more exuberant predecessors did. However, in more recent years, as the fashion for theatrical sentimentality has won out over the old fondness for comedy, *La Périchole* has found itself progressively more popular amongst the list of Offenbach's works. In the later years of this century *La Périchole* holds a position and a popularity in the Offenbach canon greater than at perhaps any other time, a popularity witnessed by several recordings and by Paris revivals in 1969 (Théâtre de Paris), 1979 (Théâtre Mogador, 19 May) and 1984 (Théâtre des Champs-Élysées, 17 September).

Le Carrosse du Saint-Sacrement has served for several other stage pieces, including a comic opera by Henry Busser, *Der Vizekönig von Peru*, mounted at St Gallen's Stadttheater 27 March 1957.

USA: Pike's Opera House (Fr) 4 January 1869, Abbey's Theater (Eng) 29 April 1895; Austria: Theater an der Wien *Périchole, die Strassensängerin* 9 January 1869; Germany: Friedrich-Wilhelmstädtisches Theater 6 April 1870; Hungary: Budai Színkör (Ger) 12 September 1869, (Hung) 21 July 1871; UK: Princess's Theatre (Fr) 27 June 1870, Royalty Theatre (Eng) 30 July 1875; Australia: Prince of Wales Theatre, Melbourne 1 May 1875

Recordings: complete (EMI-Pathé, Erato, EMI), complete in German, complete in Russian (Melodiya), Metropolitan opera excerpts (RCA) etc

PÉRIER, Jean [Alexis] (b Paris, 2 January 1869; d Paris, 3 November 1954). Star baritone of the Parisian operatic and musical stage.

The son of an opera singer and répétiteur, and the brother of the music-hall artist known as Ram-Hill, Jean Périer soon got himself out of his earliest employment with the Crédit Lyonnais and into the Paris Conservatoire. He quickly made himself known in the Paris musical theatre as a young leading man with an exceptionally fine baritone voice, appearing at the Opéra-Comique as Monostatos,

Cantarelli (*Le Pré-aux-clercs*) and in *Le Dîner de Pierrot* before going out into the commercial theatre. He featured as Boslard in *Mam'selle Carabin* (1893) at the Bouffes-Parisiens, played alongside Mily-Meyer as Maxime Lambert in Wenzel's *L'Élève de conservatoire* (1894) and took leading rôles in the Folies-Dramatiques productions of *La Fiancée en loterie* (1896, Angelin), *La Falote* (1896, Pierre), *Rivoli* (1896), *L'Auberge du tohu-bohu* (1897, Paul Blanchard) and *La Carmagnole* (1897) as well as in revivals of such pieces as *François les bas-bleus* (François) and *Mam'zelle Nitouche* (Champlatreux).

One of Périer's most important creations came when he moved to the Bouffes-Parisiens to introduce the rôle of Florestan, the hero of Messager's *Véronique* (1898, 'Poussez l'ecarpolette', Duo de l'âne). He was seen subsequently on the commercial stage in *Shakespeare!* (1899, Brutus), *La Belle au bois dormant* (Olivier), as François again, in *Les 28 Jours de Clairette* and in the Châtelet spectacular *Les Aventures du Capitaine Corcoran* (1902), but, for a number of years from 1901 the bulk of his time was spent appearing at the Salle Favart where he created, amongst others, the rôle of Pélleas in Debussy's *Pélleas et Mélisande*, and that of Landry in *Fortunio*.

In 1906 Périer created another important musical-theatre part when he appeared in the title-rôle of Ganne's *Hans, le joueur de flûte* at Monte Carlo. In 1910 he repeated his Hans in Paris, but each time returned to the Opéra-Comique. In 1918 he played in revue with Yvonne Printemps and in 1920 he repeated his Florestan at the Gaîté-Lyrique where he also appeared as Falsacappa in *Les Brigands*, in 1921 he played the Podesta in a revival of *La Petite Mariée* at the Mogador and at the Théâtre des Champs-Élysées in *La Rose de Roseim*, before in 1923 he created one further memorable rôle as Duparquet, the ageing Rodolphe of *La Vie de Bohème*, in the Reynaldo Hahn opéra-comique *Ciboulette*.

Now well and truly into playing 'father' rôles, he spent several years appearing in Paris's more intimate musical houses, pairing with Edmée Favart in the successful *Quand on est trois* (1925) and *Mannequins* (Le Marquis), and creating the part of Cardot in Szulc's *Divin mensonge* (1926) at the little Théâtre des Capucines. He also appeared on the variety stage, and was to be seen as late as 1938 in the rôle of the aged Prince Karagin in the Théâtre Mogador's French mounting of the musical *Balalaïka*.

Périer also appeared in musical film and took a small rôle in the famous Ludwig Berger film version of *Trois Valses* (1938).

DIE PERLEN DER CLEOPATRA Operette in 3 acts by Julius Brammer and Alfred Grünwald. Music by Oscar Straus. Theater an der Wien, Vienna, 17 November 1923.

A vehicle for Fritzi Massary, Germany's favourite operettic star of the pre-Nazi era, which cast her as a more than slightly comical soubrette of an Egyptian sex-cat, alongside her celebrated comedian husband, Max Pallenberg, in the rôle of a Marc Antonius who was rather cut out by a younger Roman. The couple were supported by Robert Nästlberger (Prinz Beladonis), Richard Tauber (the Roman Victorian Silvius), Franz Glawatsch (Pampylos, Cleopatra's minister) and Mizzi Mader-Anzengruber (Charmian), and the production directed by perhaps the most skilled musical stager of his era, Miksa

Preger, not in Berlin, but on the stage of the Theater an der Wien.

Straus's score, not angled quite as violently towards its star as might have been expected, was a mixture of vaguely foreign-sounding tones and Viennoiseries. The flavour of the evening was set when Cleopatra introduced herself in song: 'Mir fehlt nicht als ein kleiner ägyptischer Flirt'. She carried on to sing about 'Der König Tutenkhamen', reminding at the end of each verse 'So war ich bin Cleopatra', and let loose in her main arietta 'Für euch allein musst es geschehen' in which the Queen of the Nile was heard to disport herself in some distinctly un-Egyptian Ländler measures. She joined in duet with her Roman officer ('Ich bring' mein Herz', 'Ja so ein Frauenherz') without being required to linger long above the stave, and the showiest music of the evening was allotted to the young Tauber, who was given a 'Ja, ja so soll es sein' which was pasted into the second act like a silver-wrapped bon-bon (it even had a gift-tag ... in the printed score the number was separately dedicated to 'mein Freund Richard Tauber').

Die Perlen der Cleopatra had only a measure of success. It played for two months (61 performances) at the Theater an der Wien, and was subsequently exported to London where Jimmy White staged it with vast splendour and some botching by Arthur Wood, at Daly's Theatre (ad J Hastings Turner, Harry Graham). Evelyn Laye was a truly fair Cleopatra with Shayle Gardner as Mark Antony, Alec Fraser as Silvius, John E Coyle as Beladonis and Jay Laurier as Pamphylos. However, all the splendour (and White ladled in more of everything when the thing refused to go) could not make *Cleopatra* a success, and she sank after just 110 forced nights.

A revised version of the piece by Erwin Straus was presented at the Stadttheater, Zürich, on 31 December 1957.

Since what seems to have been her first operatic appearance in a 1662 Venetian work by Castrovilli, Cleopatra has made a number of appearances on the musical stage, but with very limited fortune. The Hungarian theatre housed perhaps the most successful operettic tale of the Nile Queen in a *Kleopatra* composed by György Verő (6 March 1900, Magyar Színház) and played later in Germany as *Die Bettelgräfin* (which seems to suggest that it wasn't hugely about Egypt and the Ptolemys). In other parts of Europe, Adolf A Philipp and Alexander Neumann's 'Ausstatungsoperette', produced at Hamburg's Carl-Schultze Theater in 1897 (24 January), Wilhelm Freudenberg's operatic *Kleopatra* (Magdeburg 12 January 1882), and another by August Enna (Copenhagen 7 February 1894) all left little trace.

A musical version of G B Shaw's *Caesar and Cleopatra* as *Her First Roman* (ad Ervin Drake) which featured Leslie Uggams as Cleopatra was a 17-performance Broadway flop (Lunt-Fontanne Theater 20 October 1968) whilst an attempt to operaticize Shakespeare as *Antonius und Cleopatra* by the Graf von Wittgenstein (lib: Mosenthal) at Graz, 1 December 1883, seems to have gone no further. The lady presumably put in an appearance in Goetze's 1940 *Kleopatra die zweite* (*Die zwei Gesichte einer Königin*), another piece which had apparently no future.

The longest stage run which the famous Queen has achieved, however, is undoubtedly that compiled through the more than 2,000 nights of Julian Slade and Dorothy Reynolds's *Salad Days* in which, each night, the Manager of the Nightclub sang the comical praises of 'Cleopatra' marginally more grammatically than the comedienne of the evening had done in *Leave it to Jane* ('Cleopatterer').

UK: Daly's Theatre *Cleopatra* 2 June 1925

LA PERMISSION DE DIX HEURES

LA PERMISSION DE DIX HEURES Opérette in 1 act by Mélesville and Pierre Carmouche. Music by Jacques Offenbach. Bad Ems, 9 July 1867; Théâtre de la Renaissance, Paris, 4 September 1873.

A little military opérette which managed to cram enough farcical content for two pieces into its action, *La Permission de dix heures* dealt with the attempts of Larose Pompon (Grillon) and his beloved Nicole (Marie Lemoine) to pair off the girl's maiden aunt (Mme Colas) with Pompon's sergeant, Lanternick (E Gourdon), thus leaving the way free for their own wedding. A 'ten-hour leave' intended for Lanternick is issued, by Nicole's machination, to Pompon, and the sergeant, who has started wooing the niece instead of the aunt, gets whisked back to barracks. In the second part of the entertainment some in-the-dark wooing leads to proposals and beribboned tokens being exchanged, and Lanternick, who thinks he has been promised Nicole, duly ends up with Madame Jobin.

First produced, like a number of Offenbach's smaller pieces, at his preferred spa town of Ems, *La Permission de dix heures* followed another group of Offenbach opérettes by becoming more popular in its German-language version than in the original French. *Urlaub nach Zapfenstreich*, as adapted by Karl Treumann, was produced at the Carltheater the year after its première, and reprised there in 1873 with Hermine Meyerhoff as Madame Jobin, Josef Matras as Lanternik and Franz Eppich as Larose Pompon. It also went on to be seen in Hungary before finally making its appearance in Paris six years after its début. Mme Dartaux (Mme Jobin), Laurence Grivot (Nicole), Falchieri (Pompon) and Bonnet (Lanternick) headed the cast of the performances at the Théâtre de la Renaissance.

Austria: Carltheater *Urlaub nach Zapfenstreich* 13 February 1868; Hungary: Budai Színkör *Takarodo után* 13 June 1871

PERREY, Mireille [PERRET, Camille Mireille] (b Bordeaux). Parisian stage and screen soubrette.

Mlle Perrey studied at the Paris Conservatoire, made her first stage appearance at the Odéon, and went on to play leading juvenile rôles on both the Parisian musical stage (*La Térésina, Deshabillez-vous, Arthur*, the title-rôle in *Rosy*) and then in London, where she appeared in the 'French' rôle of Yvonne (created on Broadway by Lili Damita) in *Sons o' Guns* (1930), in the title-rôle of *Paulette* (1932) and in Marilyn Miller's rôle of Madelon in *The One Girl* (ex-*Smiles*, 1932). She also appeared on the non-musical stage and on musical film, notably in the screen versions of *Pas sur la bouche* and *Dédé*.

PESSARD, Émile [Louis Fortuné] (b Paris, 29 May 1843; d Paris, 10 February 1917).

The winner of the Paris Conservatoire's top composition prize, the Prix de Rome, in 1866, Pessard did not rise to the heights of some other winners. He held the post of inspector of singing tuition for Paris and included amongst his theatrical compositions the scores for a number of tidily elegant opéras-comiques, large (*Le Capitaine Fracasse, Les Folies amoureuses*) and small (*La Cruche cassée, Le Char*), a cantata, *Dalila* (1867), an opera *Tabarin* (Paul Ferrier, Opéra 12 January 1885), a féerie for the Gaîté, the incidental music for the drama *Une Nuit de Noël* (1893) and a mimodrama, *Le Muet* (1894).

In later years, he shifted his sights and composed several opérettes, of which his first venture into the commercial musical field, *Mam'zelle Carabin*, was his most successful. The others won more praise for the distinction of their music than public popularity.

1870 **La Cruche cassée** (Hippolyte Lucas, Émile Abraham) 1 act Opéra-Comique 21 February

1878 **Le Char** (Alphonse Daudet, Paul Arène) 1 act Opéra-Comique 18 January

1878 **Le Capitaine Fracasse** (Catulle Mendès) Théâtre Lyrique 2 July

1888 **Tartarin sur les Alpes** (Henri Bocage, Charles de Courcy) Théâtre de la Gaîté 17 November

1889 **Don Quichotte** (Jules Deschamps) 1 act Théâtre des Menus-Plaisirs 4 July

1891 **Les Folies amoureuses** (André Lénéka, Emmanuel Matrat) Opéra-Comique 15 April

1893 **Mam'zelle Carabin** (Fabrice Carré) Théâtre des Bouffes-Parisiens 3 November

1897 **Gifles et baisers** (Paul Barbier) 1 act Théâtre Luxembourg 16 December

1898 **La Dame de trèfle** (Charles Clairville, Maurice Froyez) Théâtre des Bouffes-Parisiens 13 May

1902 **L'Armée des vierges** (Ernest Depré, Louis Hérel) Théâtre des Bouffes-Parisiens 15 October

1903 **L'Épave** (Depré, Hérel) 1 act Théâtre des Bouffes-Parisiens 17 February

1909 **Mam'zelle Gogo** (Léon Xanrof, Maxime Boucheron) Théâtre Molière, Brussels February

PETER PAN   Musical based on the play in 2 acts by J M Barrie. Lyrics by Carolyn Leigh, Betty Comden and Adolph Green. Music by Mark Charlap and Jule Styne. Winter Garden Theater, New York, 20 October 1954.

J M Barrie's much-loved play was originally produced with a substantial score of incidental music and small songs, composed by John Crook to the author's own words. Other writers have since composed incidental scores and such songs for subsequent productions of the play, the best-known being those by Leonard Bernstein (Imperial Theater, New York 24 April 1950, with six musical pieces), but without adding numbers to a degree which necessitated the filleting of the play.

The extent of music involved in the Crook score was the musical limit for the show as far as Barrie was concerned. Although he himself wrote for the musical stage, he did not want *Peter Pan* turned into a musical and, in his lifetime, both firmly refused to do the job himself, and refused permission for an adaptation by other hands. This did not stop some producers from going ahead at least in a partial way. Charles Dillingham popped two second-hand Jerome Kern numbers (ly: B G De Sylva, Paul West) into his 1924 production with Marilyn Miller, and he was neither the first nor the last to act so.

After Barrie's death, his estate at first continued to refuse permission to musicalize *Peter Pan* but some kind of unrecorded persuasion eventually made them change their mind. After first being made into an animated musical film

(1953) with a score by Sammy Fain and Sammy Cahn ('Never Smile at a Crocodile', 'The Second Star to the Right') and a surprising degree of success, Barrie's piece was transformed from the original, oddly atmospheric fairy play into a primary-coloured song and dance show for Broadway. It was a show which used only some of the play's scenes, topped them up with a series of musical numbers in a different mode from either Crook's melodies or the film songs, and immersed then in a large amount of incidental dancing, principally for a Tiger-Lily whose transformation from the heroic huntress of the original into a tiny figure of fun characterized the spirit of the adaptation.

This production had, apparently, been originally intended by director Jerome Robbins to be a more conventional *Peter Pan*, with Mary Martin (Peter) and Cyril Ritchard (Hook) starred and a Crook-sized score by Charlap and Carolyn Leigh. The expansion into a conventionally sized and shaped musical occurred en route to and from the original west coast mounting, and on that same route a number of Charlap and Leigh's songs were replaced and/or complemented by some by Styne, Comden and Green. The first team's contribution included Peter's 'I Gotta Crow', 'I Won't Grow Up' and 'I'm Flying', the second team provided a piece about 'Never, Never Land'.

The musical comedy *Peter Pan* played only 152 performances on Broadway, but it was transmitted on television the two years following, with most of its stage cast, and it was ultimately made into a television film which, over the years, won Miss Martin America-wide identification with this version of the rôle of Peter. Thus kept alive, the musical was toured and eventually won a Broadway revival (Lunt-Fontanne Theatre 6 September 1979) with Sandy Duncan as a memorably agile Peter, George Rose perpetuating the local tradition for playing Hook as an effeminate English fop, some expertly designed and performed flying into the auditorium, and an extra song.

This highly successful revival (554 performances) prompted a British production at Plymouth's Theatre Royal, with Bonnie Langford as a very much younger and boyish Peter and Joss Ackland a Hook in the more traditional (masculine) English vein, but British audiences were less happy with such non-Barrie material as a 'Mysterious Lady' song-scene filled with pantomime business and a menagerie of peluche animals hopping through Neverland, and the show played only a 73-performance festive season in London. The following season Lulu was the song-and-dance Peter with similar results.

This *Peter Pan* was subsequently given in Germany (ad Erika Gesell, Christian Severin), and in 1991 returned to Broadway again, as part of a long nationwide tour, with former Olympic gymnast Cathy Rigby as an athletic (if, again, not very young) Peter in a version which restored some of the play and omitted the 'Mysterious Lady' double-act.

These revivals resulted in France also putting out a version of this musical comedy *Peter Pan* (ad Alain Marcel). Cast on English lines, with a Peter both young and femininely boyish (Fabienne Guyon) and a handsome, vigorous Capitaine Crochet (Bernard Alane), it also failed to run, but all the time the American company continued to tour, putting in a second stop on Broadway as part of that tour, and establishing further an image of Peter Pan which is special to America, and in considerable contrast to the more 'fairy-play' image held and preferred elsewhere.

Since the expiry of the copyright on *Peter Pan*, and in spite of a staggeringly unfair move by the British authorities to reverse that expiry, several other more or less musical versions of the play have been produced, but none under metropolitan conditions.

UK: Theatre Royal, Plymouth 7 November 1985, Aldwych Theatre, London 20 December 1985; Germany: Theater des Westens 21 December 1984; France: Casino de Paris 28 September 1991

Recordings: original cast (RCA), French cast (Carrere)

PETERS, Bernadette [LAZZARA, Bernadette] (b Ozone Park, NY, 28 February 1948). Favourite Broadway ingénue with an off-the-wall air.

After a juvenile appearance in *The Most Happy Fella* (1959) and teenage performances off-Broadway as the Cinderella heroine of the J M Barrie musical adaptation *The Penny Friend* (1966) and in the original cast of the long-running *Curley McDimple* (1967, Alice), Miss Peters played her first Broadway rôle as Josie Cohan in the biomusical *George M* ('Oh, You Wonderful Boy', 'Ring to the Name of Rose'). Her next musical *A Mother's Kisses* folded in Baltimore on its inward trail, but she won notice and some of the season's kudos with a wide-eyed Ruby Keeler parody in the super-ingénue rôle of off-Broadway's *Dames at Sea* (1968).

She appeared briefly in the ill-fated *La Strada* (1969, Gelsomina), in the five performances of the off-Broadway *Nevertheless They Laugh* (1971, Consuelo) and as Carlotta Monti in the pre-Broadway life of the oddly-titled *WC*, a musical about Fields which starred Micky Rooney and did not make it to New York, and appeared in the comedy rôle of Hildy in the 1971 revival of *On the Town* before making a second personal hit, opposite Robert Preston, as Mabel Normand in *Mack and Mabel* (1974, 'Look What Happened to Mabel', 'Wherever He Ain't', 'Time Heals Everything').

Miss Peters subsequently appeared on Broadway as the vocal soloist for the American adaptation of *Song and Dance*, created two leading rôles in Stephen Sondheim musicals – as the mistress of one George and the grandmother of the other in *Sunday in the Park with George* (1984, Dot), and as the Witch in *Into the Woods* ('The Last Midnight') – and introduced the title-rôle of *The Goodbye Girl* (1993, Paula). She also played the part of Daddy Warbucks's secretary, Grace Farrell, in the screen version of *Annie*.

LE PETIT CHOC Opérette in 3 acts by P-L Flers. Music by Josef Szulc. Théâtre Daunou, Paris, 25 May 1923.

The composer of *Flup..!* had a further success with his light, up-to-date songs for the musical comedy *Le Petit Choc*, produced by Jane Renouardt at the little Théâtre Daunou, one of the most successful of the houses specializing in the small-scale 1920s Parisian musical comedies which were the jazz-age rage. Flers's text featured Régine Flory as the virtuous music-hall star Féfé Mimosa, who is still awaiting 'le petit choc' before giving herself to a man, and Paul Villé as a young and thoroughly affianced businessman, Maurice Pardeval, off to America on a big business deal. The pair are banned from entering America by a morality official when a mix-up makes it appear they are pretending to be husband and wife and, desperate to make their respective appointments, they hurriedly marry each other. After two acts of quiproquos, they find that they like the situation. Maurice's Suzette (Christiane Dor) weds his best friend Alfred (Adrien Lamy) and the all-important American millionaire Eusebius Rubbish is charmed by Féfé into doing business with her husband.

The show's score was topped by Féfé's 'On a toujours ce qu'on ne veut pas', her description of 'Le Petit Choc' and the realization 'J'aime!', alongside the well-intentioned 'Copain-copine' (Féfé/Maurice), the masculine 'Il faut savoir prendre les femmes' (Alfred) and the tale of six little English girls in search of husbands which signalled 'L'ouverture de la pêche' as described by the very prominent Alfred.

Seven months of *Le Petit Choc* in Paris were followed by a good touring life, during which the young Gabrielle Ristori appeared as Féfé Mimosa, and a production in Hungary (ad Zsolt Harsányi), where the sexy sophistications, jazzy music and small actor-singer casts of the French 1920s musicals found their readiest and most unembarrassed export market.

Hungary: Belvárosi Színház *Le Jolly Joker* 29 September

LE PETIT DUC Opéra-comique in 3 acts by Henri Meilhac and Ludovic Halévy. Music by Charles Lecocq. Théâtre de la Renaissance, Paris, 25 January 1878.

The most successful and enduring of the highly successful series of musical plays which Lecocq composed for, and Victor Koning produced at, the Théâtre de la Renaissance in the late 1870s, *Le Petit Duc* combined a shapely and, by and large, gently comical libretto, touched with just sufficient endearing sentiment, with some of Lecocq's most ravishing soprano music, mostly dedicated to the travesty rôle of the teenaged Duc de Parthenay, devised for the theatre's enormously popular star, Jeanne Granier.

For reasons of state, and the benefit of others generally, the 'little' teenaged Duc de Parthenay is married to the ever-younger Blanche de Cambrai (Mily-Meyer), only to find that their elders, decreeing them too young for such things, will not allow them to consummate their marriage. The little Duchesse is sent off to a school at Lunéville, but the disconsolate Duc is, as a consolation, permitted to quit the tutelage of the musty Frimousse (Berthelier) and, thanks to his friendly master of arms, Montlandry (Vauthier), is put at the head of his own regiment. He may be too young for sex, but he's old enough to send men into battle. The Duc, however, has his preoccupations in order. He promptly orders his regiment to Lunéville, besieges the school, and disguises himself as a peasant girl to get inside and meet his Blanche. However, he is forced to withdraw when his regiment is called to battle. When the dallying French are almost caught unawares by an enemy attack, the Duc banishes women from the encampment only to be himself exposed when Blanche escapes from Lunéville and comes to find him. All is forgiven, however, in the following victory and the little Duc and his little Duchesse are permitted to become husband and wife for real. The comedy of the piece was enhanced by a 'rôle de Desclauzas', the comico-aristocratic headmistress of the second-act school, which was played and played to the low-comic hilt by none other than Marie Desclauzas herself.

The romantic part of Lecocq's score was of a rare delicacy, notably the first-act soprano duet for the Duc and his bride in which he tries to encourage her to exchange the formal 'vous' for the more intimate 'tu' as in 'Je t'aime' in addressing him, their no-less-innocent reunion on the battlefield in the final act ('Ah, qu'on est bien'), and the Duc's sweet explanation that 'on a l'âge du mariage quand on a l'âge d'amour' (you are old enough to be wed when you are old enough to be in love). The comical part of proceedings, topped by the Duc's peasant-girl tale ('Mes bell' madame écoutez-ça!') of the hazards of crossing the army lines (she lost her eggs, but saved her virtue), and the old tutor's creaky wooing of the disguised boy ('C'est un idylle'), was equally successful, as was the lively dash of military music that the settings permitted: Montlandry's jolly Chanson du petit bossu, the regiment's choral greeting of 'Mon colonel' in the first act finale, and the final hailing of the Duc as 'Le plus bel officier du monde'.

Le Petit Duc was a vast success. Granier found in the Duc her greatest rôle, little Mily-Meyer won her first triumph and one which would only be equalled when she turned to comedy rôles, Berthelier and Vauthier both gave anthology performances, and Desclauzas made of the Directrice, Mlle Diane de Château-Lansac, the most memorable character of her memorable career as a character lady. After a first run which took it through the season, the piece remained solidly in the Renaissance repertoire for five years, and Mlle Granier repeated her rôle at the Théâtre de l'Eden in 1888 and again at the Variétés in 1890, each time with José Dupuis as a famous Frimousse.

Marcelle Dartois (Bouffes-Parisiens, 1897), Jeanne Saulier (Variétés, 1904), Anne Dancrey (Gaîté-Lyrique, 1912), Gina Féraud (ibid, 1915), Edmée Favart (Mogador, 1921), Louise Dhamarys (Gaîté-Lyrique, 1926) and Fanély Revoil (Châtelet, 1933) succeeded to Mlle Granier's rôle on the Paris stage whilst *Le Petit Duc* kept up a regular presence in French theatres as an important part of the heart of the French opérette repertoire. Only with the decline of the Paris musical theatre did it, too, decline and become limited to occasional regional performances, the most recent of which in Grasse in 1991.

By the end of the year of its production, *Le Petit Duc* had been played in all the main centres. Uncharacteristically, Britain was the first to produce its *The Little Duke* (ad B C Stephenson, Clement Scott), perhaps because the venue was Islington's Philharmonic Theatre, the house which had been responsible for launching the vastly profitable English versions of *La Fille de Madame Angot* and *Giroflé-Girofla*. Alice May, the original prima donna of *The Sorcerer* was the Duc, Alice Burville (London's most recent Geneviève de Brabant) the Duchess, top comic Harry Paulton played Frimousse, Australian actress and singer Emma Chambers the Directrice, and Lecocq supplied a fresh entr'acte for the slightly rearranged show which opened one week before the newest local show, *HMS Pinafore*. *The Little Duke*'s success in Islington was such that a West End season at the St James's Theatre was arranged (16 June 1878) with Ethel Pierson replacing as the Duchess and J D Stoyle as Frimousse. Londoners later had a chance to see the original version when Mlles Granier, Mily-Meyer and Desclauzas played *Le Petit Duc* at the Gaiety Theatre in 1881.

Budapest gave an enthusiastic greeting to *A kis herceg* (ad Jenő Rákosi) when it was produced with the great Lujza Blaha (then Soldosné) as the Duc paired with little Mariska Komáromi and with Elek Solymossy as Montlandry, at the Népszinház (where it was revived in 1881 and again in 1889), and a month later Vienna's Carltheater produced its German version. Antonie Link (Duc), Rosa Streitmann (Duchesse) and Josef Matras (Frimousse) headed the cast for a disappointing 20 performances. The following year, however, the Carltheater remounted the piece with Frlns Klein and Streitmann and with the Austrian Desclauzas, Therese Schäfer, as Diane (6 September 1879).

In America there was no such diffidence. *Petit Duc*s descended on Broadway en masse just as soon as the performance materials were available. James C Duff's initial New York production (ad Frederick Williams, T R Sullivan), starring Florence Ellis and Louise Beaudet, played three indifferent weeks at Booth's, but before he was finished Alice Oates had got into breeches for her company's English-language production at the Lyceum (less regularly, James Meade donned skirts to take the rôle of the Directrice in this production). When Duff closed, Mlle Beaudet moved over to sing her rôle of the Duchess opposite Marie Aimée's Duke in French at the same theatre. The following year Paola Marié gave Broadway her little Duke, by which time the piece was being liberally played throughout the country in the touring opéra-bouffe companies' repertoires. It returned for a substantial revival at the Casino Theater (4 August 1884, ad H C Bunner, W J Henderson) in which J H Ryley played the rôle of Frimousse, and again in 1896 when Lillian Russell was seen as the Duke at Abbey's Theatre.

Australia got its first hearing of *Le Petit Duc* in the Williams/Sullivan version as played by Horace Lingard's company with Lingard himself playing Frimousse, his wife, Alice as the Duc and Mrs J H Hall and Alma Stanton taking turns at the Duchess. However, none of the favourite touring opéra-bouffe stars chose to include Granier's best vehicle in their repertoire, and although the show was seen at Melbourne's Alexandra Theatre in 1887 with Marion Norman starred (21 May), it got little other exposure down under.

Brussels, Amsterdam, Madrid, Turin, Stockholm and Prague all presented *Petit Duc*s in the same period, and both South America and other European centres soon followed, confirming the piece – in spite of Vienna's reaction (or translation) – as one of the great opérettes of its period.

UK: Philharmonic Theatre, Islington *The Little Duke* 27 April 1878; Hungary: Népszinház *A kis herceg* 11 October 1878; Austria: Carltheater *Der kleine Herzog* 9 November 1878; Germany: Friedrich-Wilhelmstädtisches Theater *Der kleine Herzog* 24 November 1878, Frankfurt-am-Main *Der fidele Herzog* 7 December 1878; USA: Booth's Theater 17 March 1879; Australia: Academy of Music, Melbourne *Fabrice, the Little Duke* 11 August 1879
Recordings: selection (EMI-Pathé, Decca)

LA PETITE BOHÈME Opérette in 3 acts by Paul Ferrier based on *La Vie de Bohème* by Henri Murger. Music by Henri Hir(s)chmann. Théâtre des Variétés, Paris, 19 January 1905.

Ferrier and Hirschmann's version of Murger's famous tale took an altogether different tone from that which Giacosa, Ilica and Puccini had taken less than a decade earlier in their celebrated operatic adaptation of the same piece in *La Bohème* (1896). The piece was not a burlesque (which didn't stop its authors beginning one number 'je m'appelle Mimi') but simply a conventional musical-comedy version of the tale where the main focus was on the on-again off-again romance of Musette (Jeanne Saulier) and Marcel (Alberthal) and on the comical Barbemuche (Paul Fugère), and in which Mimi (Ève Lavallière) was still well and truly alive for a finale which tried to convince its audience that the so-called bohemian life, lived on bread and water (not evident in the course of the show), was 'la terre de génie et le paradis de l'amour'. Mimi gushed 'C'est mon dada', and got into carnival travesty alongside Barbemuche who camped a coloratura Catherine the Great, Musette flirted with a vicomte (Prince) but returned to join Marcel in the lyrical 'Nous n'avons qu'un temps à vivre' in the third act, and everyone said 'vive la bohème' a lot, whether they were invading an aristocratic home and drinking its champagne (presumably as a change from all that bread and water) or galloping off to the country.

Fernand Samuel's production at the Variétés had but a 16-performance first run, but the piece (ad Benno Jacobson) was subsequently picked up by Berlin's Centraltheater, where the composer had launched his *Les Hirondelles* the year before, and by the voracious Budapest theatre (ad Jenő Heltai), as well as throughout France. The Bouffes-Parisiens brought it back for a season (3 February 1907) with Mariette Sully (Musette) and Simon-Max (Barbemuche) featured, and it was seen once more in Paris in 1921 with Mme Mathieu-Lutz as Musette and Jeanne Saint-Bonnet as Mimi.

Germany: Centraltheater *Musette* 11 November 1905; Hungary: Magyar Színház *Bohemszerelem* (*Musette*) 1 December 1905

LA PETITE MADEMOISELLE Opérette in 3 acts by Henri Meilhac and Ludovic Halévy. Music by Charles Lecocq. Théâtre de la Renaissance, Paris, 12 April 1879.

After having been le petit duc (not to mention la petite mariée), Jeanne Granier – in the hands of the same librettists and the same composer who had given her the earlier triumph – became la petite mademoiselle. The Comtesse Cameroni was the 'petite' mademoiselle, thus called in reference to the historical 'grande mademoiselle', otherwise la Duchesse de Montpensier, the 17th-century aristocrat who sided with the Condé-Bourbons and Spain in their ill-fated rebellion against Cardinal Mazarin.

The plottings of the petite mademoiselle involve her in a regulation operettic quantity of disguises. In the first act she takes on the identity of a certain Mlle Douillet, a notary's wife from Angoulême and, when one of that frequently unfaithful wife's military lovers, the young vicomte de Manicamp (Vauthier), comes to seek his old flame out, she accidentally finds true love. She does not find political success, however. In spite of spending the second act disguised, *Madame Favart*-like, as a serving wench called Trompette (Manicamp is impersonating an apprentice sausage-maker and calling himself Lambin) amongst a bevy of aristocrats all pretending to be what they are not, such contribution as she has made to the cause goes down with the victory of Mazarin's troops. A further

act is necessary for her to finally escape the 'royal' dictates and to be allowed to wed her little vicomte rather than the elderly brother of her equally elderly deceased husband. Mily-Meyer (Jacqueline Tab.oureau) and Marie Desclauzas (the tripière, Madelon) from the *Petit Duc* cast again had fine rôles as the employers of the two disguised stars, Berthelier was the inn-keeper Taboureau, and Lary (Boisvilette) and Urbain (Juvigné) were the other principals.

All the girls had good numbers – Granier describing herself as 'Arrivée dans Bordeaux' or, in her serving-maid disguise, swinging in with 'Notre patron, homme estimable', Mily-Meyer summoning 'Jeunes et vieux ...' and Desclauzas doing particularly well with her 'Quand le cervelas va, tout va!' and 'Pauvre peuple, pauvre pays'. Manicamp, disguised as Lambin, pretended 'Me v'la, j'arriv' de Normandie', whilst Taboureau had his moment in his Couplets du cabaretier ('Ces bons parisiens'). The Mazarinade and its call to arms which ended the second act, a conspiracy septet and an old 'Faridondaine' refrain all went to add to a substantial score which was amongst Lecocq's favourites of his own works.

Without in any way demeriting, *La Petite Mademoiselle*, whether because it followed a touch too closely the recipe as before, whether because of a post-Paris Exhibition kind of decompression, or simply because it just didn't tickle the public quest for novelty, did not score the same kind of long-running success as its predecessors. By the time it was withdrawn in September it had reached the total of 83 performances which was to be its Parisian career. However, this comparative disappointment did not stop it from making its way to the many other cities and countries where Meilhac, Halévy and Lecocq's names were potent theatrical attractions. But it did not become a notable hit in any of them. Even in Budapest (ad Béla J Fái), where Lujza Blaha took on another Granier rôle, it did not repeat the Hungarian successes of *La Petite Mariée*, *La Marjolaine*, *Le Petit Duc* and *La Camargo*, whilst in London (ad Robert Reece, H S Leigh), where Constance Loseby took Granier's rôle, alongside Harry Paulton (Taboureau), Alice May (Madelon), Emma Chambers (Jacqueline) and the young Fred Leslie (Manicamp) it played only a satisfactory 75 performances at the vast Alhambra before being displaced by the year's Christmas show.

Neither country had thought it worthwhile to do much about the title (which meant precious little to those who didn't know about Madame de Montpensier), but in Germany the little miss, as played by one of the Stubel sisters (it seems to have been Lori), became, more interestingly, *Die Feinden des Cardinals*, or the Cardinal's enemy. Swoboda, Schulz and Frln Kopka supported and again the show did just all right. Broadway also saw the piece in German, under the less interesting title of *Trompette*, but with no less a star than Marie Geistinger as the Countess Cameroni alongside Adolf Link (Taboureau) and Frau Haubrich (Madelon). Unlike other centres, however, it also got a second helping, six years later, when the Casino Theater mounted the piece in English under yet another title, *Madelon*. Max Freeman's version seemed to owe something to the German and to the English versions before him, but it did seem a little strange to take the title-rôle away from the prima donna and give it to the comedienne. Bertha Ricci was the heroine and Lillie Grubb

1137

played Madelon alongside James T Powers (Taboureau), Courtice Pounds (Jolivet), Isabelle Urquhart (Pompanon) and Mark Smith (Rabicamp) for a run of six weeks.

Australia, like Britain, retained *La Petite Mademoiselle* as the title of what seemed to be a revamped version of London's text – credited to Leigh and to W H Harrison. Nellie Stewart appeared in the Royal Comic Opera Company's production as the Countess Cameroni, with her sister Docy Stewart as Madelon, Emma Chambers repeating her London Jacqueline, Sgr Broccolini/W H Woodfield (Manicamp) and H R Harwood/Robert Brough (Taboureau) through a good season of six Melbourne weeks and onwards.

Hungary: Népszinház *A kis nagysám* 5 September 1879; UK: Alhambra Theatre 6 October 1879; Germany: Friedrich-Wilhelmstädtisches Theater *Die Feinden des Cardinals* 20 March 1880; USA: Germania Theater *Trompette* (Ger) 13 October 1882, Casino Theater *Madelon* 5 December 1888; Australia: Theatre Royal, Melbourne 14 April 1885

LA PETITE MARIÉE

LA PETITE MARIÉE Opéra-comique in 3 acts by Eugène Leterrier and Albert Vanloo. Music by Charles Lecocq. Théâtre de la Renaissance, Paris, 21 December 1875.

When Victor Koning went into management at the Théâtre de la Renaissance on the proceeds of his contribution to *La Fille de Madame Angot*, he made his start with the enormously successful Paris transfer of Lecocq's *Giroflé-Girofla*, and it was to his old collaborator (and, just coincidentally, the hottest composer in town), and the librettists and little star of *Giroflé-Girofla* that he turned for his first new piece. The result was another splendid success, which set the Renaissance off on a six-year, eight-show cycle of Lecocq/Koning shows.

Leterrier and Vanloo supplied a delightfully sex-farcical libretto, with a fine rôle specially made for Jeanne Granier as Graziella, the 'little wife' of the title. Graziella is secretly marrying San Carlo (Félix Puget), the great friend of the local Podesta (Vauthier). The reason for the secrecy is that, once upon a time, San Carlo and the Podesta's wife erred together and got caught, and the great man, rather than expel his friend from court, simply told him that the day that he married he would feel free to take a similar liberty with his wife. The best man for this hush-hush occasion is the bridegroom's other best friend, Montefiasco (Dailly), a man who is kept close tabs on by his wife, the congenitally jealous Lucrézia (Mlle Alphonsine) who is inclined to make her points with a horsewhip. All four are together, after the ceremony, when the Podesta turns up and – after little dissembling, a touch of lying, and a small swap of identity – the farce begins. Two acts and many twists later, the Podesta has his revenge: San Carlo is made to weep with doubt and with jealousy before he is allowed a happy ending. But the revenge has its underside, for the Podesta finds out more about his late wife than he might, for self-esteem's sake, have wished to know.

Graziella-Granier had the lion's share of the music, amongst which were included the waltz couplets of the first act as she showed off her bridal gown before her husband ('Je tenais, monsieur mon époux'), the little fable of the nightingale which she recites to and with the Podesta, her high-speed Couplets de l'enlèvement, a pretty Ronde de la petite mariée in the second-act finale and the Couplets des

reproches and sobbing duo of the final act which lead to the dénouement. Vauthier, also well served, had a fine basso rondo in the first act, teasingly reminding his friend of his promise ('Le jour où tu te marieras') and Lucrézia snapped out her Valse de la cravache, with whiplash accompaniment, as a further musical highlight.

La Petite Mariée was a full-scale success which filled the Renaissance for ten months. During this time Koning's old associate Humbert mounted it in Brussels and then exported it to London's Opera Comique with Marie Harlem starred as the little bride, before it went on to be seen in Portugal, Spain, Egypt and, in its first foreign-language production, in Hungarian in Budapest (ad Jenő Rákosi). In its initial season at the Népszinház *La Petite Mariée* became the first opérette to have a major success there without the theatre's overwhelming star, Lujza Blaha, in its lead rôle. Erzi Vidmár played Graziella, and the show did well enough to be brought back for a second season in 1880.

Marie Aimée introduced *La Petite Mariée* to Broadway, and was seen as Graziella in two successive seasons in New York in between which she purveyed the piece throughout America with her touring company, and London was also given a second showing of the piece in French when Jeanne Granier and the Renaissance company played a season at the Gaiety in 1881. However, perhaps because of the impossibility of deodorizing a plot which rested entirely on things sexual, an English version did not appear in London or New York. But Australia – not for the first or last time – did not wait for those two main centres of English-language theatre. William S Lyster produced *La Petite Mariée* in Melbourne, in a version which seems to have been done by brother Fred Lyster, with Catherine Lewis starred as Graziella. It was another Australian, George Musgrove, who 20 years later mounted Harry Greenbank's adaptation, *The Scarlet Feather*, both at London's Shaftesbury Theatre and later in his home country. Decima Moore was the little bride in London's season, but the score had been rearranged and peppered with additional numbers by Lionel Monckton and Alfred Plumpton, mostly for the benefit of Musgrove's other half, soprano Nellie Stewart, in a large inserted rôle as a page called Pippo. *The Scarlet Feather* was not a success either in Britain nor when Musgrove remounted it, with much fanfare, back home.

Berlin's production of *Graziella* was followed by several others throughout Germany, but Vienna's *Graziella* (ad Karl Treumann), in spite of a fine cast headed by Karoline Finaly, Karl Blasel (Montefiasco), Josefine Gallmeyer (Lucrézia) and Wilhelm Knaack as the bride's comical father, was played only a so-so 14 times. On the home front, however, in spite of the wash of famous Lecocq opérettes which followed it, *La Petite Mariée* remained a favourite and was brought back to Paris on a number of occasions. It returned to the Renaissance in 1877 with Jane Hading (Mme Koning) starred, and in 1880 with Granier taking up her old rôle once more, as she did again at the Menus-Plaisirs in 1887. Nearly 30 years later it was played at the Théâtre Moncey (6 August 1915) and finally, at the Mogador in 1921, with Mme Mathieu-Lutz, Jean Périer and Adrien Lamy at the head of its cast, before slipping, with most of the rest of the shows of the period, from the repertoire.

UK: Opera Comique (Fr) 6 May 1876, Shaftesbury Theatre *The Scarlet Feather* 17 November 1897; Hungary: Népszinház *A kis menyecske* 21 September 1876; Austria: Carltheater *Graziella* 11 November 1876; USA: Eagle Theater (Fr) 6 February 1877; Germany: Friedrich-Wilhelmstädtisches Theater *Graziella* 23 August 1877; Australia: Prince of Wales Theatre, Melbourne 6 December 1876, Princess Theatre, Melbourne *The Scarlet Feather* 26 November 1900

LA PETITE MUETTE Opérette in 3 acts by Paul Ferrier. Music by Gaston Serpette. Théâtre des Bouffes-Parisiens, Paris, 3 October 1877.

Ferrier's story told of pretty 17th-century Spanish Mercedes (Louise Théo), struck dumb on the day of her wedding to Don José d'Albatros (Daubray), the disgraced ex-governor of Burgos, and diagnosed by his doctor Camomillas (Alfred Jolly) as able to recover her voice only when love (or, more to the point, sex) comes along. Her husband is constitutionally unable to effect the cure, and is in despair when, as a mark of his potential recall to favour, his mute wife is given the honour of being named reader to the Infanta. Raphael (Mme Peschard), the handsome envoy who brings the appointment, not only drives Mercedes to court but also operates the necessary cure on the way there.

The comedy of the piece was accompanied by some lightsome Serpette music of which a certain amount, in spite of her plot-line inability to speak until half-way through the second act, fell to Théo. She burst forth, in the 11th number of the score, with an understandable 'Ah! que c'est bon de parler!', and promptly followed up with an eight-page duet, a trio and, in spite of doctor's orders, a waltz song ('J'accorde que c'est malaisé'). In the last act, in the course of her work, instead of reading the baby monarch the classics she sings it a kiddie song. Théo had the soubretteries, the winks and nods, and the fun, but the bravura music of the piece was the province of Mme Peschard. She entered with a love song ('Oui, je vous aime') which scooted up to high C, followed up with a virtuoso coloratura showpiece habanera ('Déjà vos mules rapides'), and negotiated a showy waltz chantée drinking song in the second act ('Plus de tristesse') and an aubade ('Réveillez-vous belle endormie') in the third. The other principal rôles were played by Mlle Luce (Casilda), the comedian Scipion (Don Gill) and the tenors Minart (Henrique, with a chanson militaire) and Jannin (Pédrille).

After 56 Parisian performances under Charles Comte's management, the piece was played both in Budapest (ad Jenő Rákosi) and in New York by Maurice Grau's opéra-bouffe company with Paola Marié in the rôle of Mercedes.

Hungary: Népszinház *A kis néma* 12 February 1878; USA: New Fifth Avenue Theater 24 March 1880

LES PETITES BREBIS Opérette in 2 acts by Armand Liorat. Music by Louis Varney. Théâtre Cluny, Paris, 5 June 1895.

Les Petites Brebis was a not-very-far-distant relation of *Das Pensionat*, which was of course just one member of the large family of French and French-derived comedies and opérettes which dealt with chaps chasing after their beloved girls inside the girls' boarding schools. The chaps in this case were the noble Christian (Moizard) and his comical pal Fifrelin Grobichon (Hamilton), the girls were Alice von Stahlberg (Mlle Azimont) and Fifrelin's sister

Fanny (Mlle Norcy), whilst Adèle Cuinet featured as Mlle Emeraldine Mouton, the headmistress of the establishment.

Of the 15 numbers in Varney's score the couplets 'Y a de la femme' for Christian and Fifrelin, the Couplets de la lecture as performed by Fanny, Alice, the headmistress and the schoolgirls, Alice's 'Dieu que c'est bon' ('lorsque je me retrouve seule') with its shivering 'brrrr' refrain, the schoolgirls' bedtime Prière des anges gardiens, and the Christian/Fifrelin rondo couplets de l'amour, celebrating the happy ending to all the gallivanting, proved the most appreciated.

Les Petites Brebis ran for more than 100 performances at the little Théâtre Cluny on its first run, and promptly set off round Europe, where it found distinct favour amongst the parade of similar French musical comedies of the 1890s and 1900s.

Heinrich Bolten-Bäckers's German adaptation was a distinct hit at Berlin's Alexanderplatz-Theater, and it was promptly picked up by Vienna's Theater in der Josefstadt, the Viennese centre of French vaudeville and the recent home of Banès's *Toto* and Varney's *Le Brillant Achille*. Karl Pfann (Christian), Rauch (Fifrelin), Viktoria Pohl-Meiser (Emeraldine), Frln Peroni (Alice) and Frln Grunert (Fanny) headed the cast through a fine 49 consecutive performances, making the show the theatre's most successful piece of the year. Two seasons later, Budapest's Magyar Színház produced their version (ad Emil Makai) with the British operetta *Weather or No* as an afterpiece.

In spite of its European popularity, however, the show did not make its way into the English-language main centres. When *The Little Innocents* was finally seen in Britain, in an adaptation by veteran comedian/author Harry Paulton, in 1901, it played only a minor tour.

Germany: Alexanderplatz-Theater *Die kleine Lämmer* 16 October 1895; Austria: Theater in der Josefstadt *Die kleinen Schäfen* 22 November 1895; Hungary: Magyar Színház *A báránykák* 10 November 1897; UK: Richmond Theatre *The Little Innocents* 17 November 1901

LE PETIT FAUST Opéra-bouffe in 3 acts by Hector Crémieux and Adolphe Jaime. Music by Hervé. Théâtre des Folies-Dramatiques, Paris, 28 April 1869.

Of Hervé's three most successful full-scale opéras-bouffes, it was *Le Petit Faust*, the only one of the three to parody another specific work (*L'Oeil crevé* more or less burlesqued *William Tell* amongst other targets and *Chilpéric* burlesqued the medieval in general) in Goethe's *Faust* and Gounod's operatic version thereof, which ultimately proved the most successful and the most enduring, both in France and beyond. Allegedly written with the Variétés company in view, with Schneider and Dupuis tagged for the rôles of Marguerite and Faust, and at one stage mooted for the Palais-Royal, where it was suggested that the vast-nosed comic Hyacinthe might play Siebel, the piece was ultimately mounted at the Folies-Dramatiques with no such starry casting.

Marguerite (Blanche d'Antigny) is brought to the academy for young persons run by Doctor Faust (Hervé) by her brother Valentin (Ange Milher) who is off to the wars. Faust is elderly and immune to girls, but the combination of Marguerite's determined teenage vamping and the interference of the cocky Méphisto (Anna van Ghell) sets the pedagogue in a whirl. Having awakened desire in Faust, Méphisto now has fun helping him assuage it, at the usual price. The artificially rejuvenated Faust, rich and handsome, goes to Paris in search of Marguerite and, having disposed of the interfering Valentin in a duel, prepares to wed the willing girl. Méphisto makes sure that Faust suffers first jealousy, then disappointment when he discovers that his beloved is only after his money, then remorse when the ghost of Valentin turns up inopportunely in the wedding soup, and at last he carries both the foresworn Faust and his ill-behaved bride off to Hell.

The extravagances of Crémieux and Jaime's libretto were not so much in the tale but in the telling of it. The authors indulged in the most far-fetched, zany scenes and speeches, highlighted by the burlesque duel between Valentin and Faust, waged with vegetable knives and won by chicanery when the devil offers the soldier a pinch of snuff in mid-fight. The craziness extended to the songs in pieces such as the gobbledegook Trio de Vaterland and Valentin's burlesque operatic death, whilst still leaving place for lashings of the suggestive, as in Marguerite's insistence on mock-childishly showing Faust her well-placed bruises (C'est tout bleu') and her trouser-dropping tale of 'Le Roi de Thuné', and even the picturesque, as in the parade of the Margarets of all nations in Faust's search for his love. Méphisto had a lively rondeau with which to introduce himself, Marguerite a winsome tyrolienne and Valentin a martial soldier-song, and echoes of the most famous elements of Gounod's score were prominently placed.

Following its highly successful Paris creation, Le Petit Faust followed the most successful works of the French opéra-bouffe stage around the world. Hervé, who had rocked London with his Chilpéric, decided not to play the follow-up season of Faust as well, and it was Thomas Maclagan who introduced the English version, done by H B Farnie after Dion Boucicault withdrew, with Marguerite Debreux as his Méphisto and Emily Soldene as a buxom Marguerite. One of the most successful elements of the London production was an interpolated scene of a waltz contest, parodying Die Meistersinger. A fine success, the production ran from mid-April to the beginning of July. By that time Doktor Faust junior (ad Richard Genée, also with the Wagnerian parody) had made its appearance on the Vienna stage with sufficient success to be repeated 40 times during the two seasons it remained in the repertoire. Budapest was given an Hungarian version (ad Endre Látabár, Solymossy), St Petersburg a Russian one and both Italy and South America were given the show in its original French, whilst New York got the most bouffe version of all when Kelly and Leon's Minstrels, who normally stuck to homespun burlesque and small French operettas, produced the piece in their inimitable fashion, with Leon in the rôle of Marguerite.

James Fisk used a more conventional staging of Le Petit Faust to introduce his newly imported set of Parisian opéra-bouffe stars to Broadway during the 1870–71 season. Léa Silly played Méphisto and Céline Montaland was Marguerite alongside the Faust of Constant Gausins and, if the stars proved not as popular as their predecessors in the opéra-bouffe line of importations, the piece, which ran three straight weeks at the Grand Opera House, pleased well. Marie Aimée followed up with her version in the same season, Coralie Geoffroy and (in English) Alice Oates and the Worrell Sisters (Little Faust) all followed suit, and finally Paola Marié appeared at the Fifth Avenue Theater in the rôle of Méphisto, which she had taken over in the original Paris production.

Le Petit Faust was brought back to the Paris Folies-Dramatiques in 1876 with Simon-Max, Coralie Geoffroy and Mlle Prelly starred, and in 1882 a revised and expanded version, which stretched the rôle of Siebel (played as a tiresomely smart schoolboy) as a vehicle for Marie Gélabert and included two chunks of ballet for spectacle's sake, was mounted at the larger Théâtre de la Porte-Saint-Martin. Cooper and Jeanne Granier starred in an 1891 reprise at the same theatre, and Guy and Juliette Méaly were featured in yet another at the Variétés in 1897. Both London and New York also mounted later and larger versions of the show during this period. In London, the Alhambra Theatre's Mefistofele II (ad Alfred Maltby) gave Lizzie St Quentin as the devil the title-rôle alongside Fred Leslie (Faust), Lionel Brough (Valentine) and Constance Loseby (Marguerite), whilst a 1897 New York version, played under the title of Very Little Faust and Much Marguerite, written by Richard Carroll and Clement King and musically souped up by Fred Eustis, was produced at Hammerstein's Olympia.

Le Petit Faust won further revivals in Paris in 1908 (Folies-Dramatiques 1 December) and 1934 (Porte-Saint-Martin 19 December with Boucot as Faust and Dranem as Valentin), and it has remained on the fringe of the played repertoire for more than a century, returning most recently in a production at Metz in 1990.

UK: Lyceum Theatre Little Faust 18 April 1870, Alhambra Theatre Mefistofele II 20 December 1880; Austria: Theater an der Wien Doktor Faust junior 4 May 1870; USA: Kelly and Leon's Le Petit Faust 29 August 1870, Grand Opera House (Fr) 26 September 1870; Hungary: Budai Színkör Kis Faust 10 June 1871; Germany: Friedrich-Wilhelmstädtisches Theater 30 June 1871; Australia: Opera House, Melbourne 15 February 1875

Recordings: complete (Clio, Rare Recorded Editions)

PETRÁSS, Sári [Gabrielle] (b Budapest, 5 November 1888; d Sainte-Anne, Belgium, 7 September 1930). Hungarian musical star of five countries' stages.

A niece of Hungary's internationally famous musical star, Ilka Pálmay, Sári Petráss began what was to be a similarly international career as a teenager when she appeared at Budapest's Vigszinház in Offenbach's Ancsi sír, Jancsi nevet (Jeanne qui pleure et Jean qui rit). She played at the Népszinház in the musicals Két Hippolit (Nanett), Sportlovagok (Böske), Külteleki hercegnő (Willibald), Izsó Barna's A mádi zsidó (Évike) and Jenő Sztojanovits's Papa lánya, then moved in 1907 to the Király Színház where, over the following years, she appeared as the original Hungarian Hélène in Straus's Ein Walzertraum, in the British Hollandi-lány (Miss Hook of Holland), the American A sogun (The Sho-Gun), as Die Dollarprinzessin, Bronislawa in Der Bettelstudent, Angèle Didier in Der Graf von Luxemburg (1910) and where she also created the ingénue rôle of Lucy in Victor Jacobi's important Leányvásár (1911).

Petráss subsequently appeared in Vienna and in Berlin, where she made a considerable success at the Neues Operettenhaus in Die keusche Suzanne, and then moved on to Britain and to the management of George Edwardes for whom she played the romantic lead of Ilona (ex-Zorika) in *Gipsy Love* (1912) and her original rôle in his production of *Marriage Market* (*Leányvásár*). Edwardes described her prior to her British début as 'a personality that fascinates you at once. She is not a great singer, but her phrasing is perfect. She speaks English well. She is quiet, demure, an Edna May with differences ...'.

Petráss returned to Hungary to star as Helena in *Polenblut* at the Király Színház before moving on again, this time to America. There she starred in the American version of the Hungarian operett *Zsuzsi kisasszony* entitled *Miss Springtime* (New Amsterdam 1916, Roszika Wenzel), and in Oscar Straus's *The Beautiful Unknown* (1917) pre-Broadway. She was replaced before it moved to Broadway and flopped as *My Lady's Glove*. She was seen again in London when she appeared as Sylva Varescu in *The Gipsy Princess* at the Prince of Wales Theatre in 1921, and then back in Hungary where she created the rôle of Örzse in Szirmai's *Mézeskalács* (1923) and played, amongst others, the title-rôle in *Marinka a táncosnő* (*Katja die Tänzerin*, 1923), in Jacobi's posthumous *Miami* (1925), in *Hamburgi menyasszony* (1926) and as Anna Baróthy in *Cigánykirály* (Városi Színház, 1927). In 1930 she was drowned in the River Scheldt, in Belgium, in a motoring accident, at the age of 41.

Petráss's second husband was the British vocalist Gordon Crocker.

PFINGSTEN IN FLORENZ
Operette in 3 acts by Richard Genée and Julius Riegen. Music by Alfons Czibulka. Theater an der Wien, Vienna, 20 December 1884.

The most generally successful of Czibulka's stage works, *Pfingsten in Florenz* was produced at the Theater an der Wien under the management of Camillo Walzel. Girardi was cast as Fra Bombardo, the dictator of the 16th-century republic of Florence, and Ottilie Collin was Rita, the daughter of the fur merchant Aldo Castrucci (Rotter) and his wife Perpetua (Katharina Herzog), on whom he casts his nasty potentate's eye. Marie Theresia Massa got into breeches to play the young Angelo Malanotti, a sculptor (and, thus, inevitably a goodie) whilst Karl Blasel as the letter-writer Sparacani and Carl Lindau as the physician Lorenzi shared the comicalities.

Pfingsten in Florenz was played 31 times at the Theater an der Wien before moving on to productions in Prague, in Dresden, in Budapest, Berlin and, most notably, in America (ad Sydney Rosenfeld, George Goldmark). For the Casino Theater's production the heroine grew from being Rita to being Amorita and, as played by ex-English-chorine, soon-to-be-authoress Madeleine Lucette, gave her name to the English version as its title. Frank H Celli was Bombardo alongside Francis Wilson (Castrucci), W H Fitzgerald (Sparacani) and Pauline Hall (Angelo) for a run of three months, prior to other productions around America.

Germany: Residenztheater, Dresden 15 February 1885, Walhalla-Theater 9 April 1887; USA: Casino Theater *Amorita* 16 November 1885; Hungary: *Pünközd Florenzben* 27 February 1886, Budai Színkör 5 May 1886

THE PHANTOM OF THE OPÉRA
Musical in a prologue and 2 acts by Andrew Lloyd Webber and Richard Stilgoe based on the novel by Gaston Leroux. Lyrics by Charles Hart. Music by Andrew Lloyd Webber. Her Majesty's Theatre, London, 9 October 1986.

Following the remarkable success of the youth-orientated spectacle of *Starlight Express*, composer Lloyd Webber changed direction thoroughly for his next stage work and entered the realm of the romantic melodrama. The impetus for this change in direction was given by a production of a stage adaptation of *Le Fantôme de l'Opéra*, Gaston Leroux's famous and much-filmed novel, written by Ken Hill, the author of a long list of happy musical plays for the British stage, illustrated by a pasticcio opera score, and produced at London's suburban Theatre Royal, Stratford East. Lloyd Webber's original thought was to have his production company mount a piece on similar lines as a vehicle for his then wife, Sarah Brightman, in whom he discerned operatic possibilities but, as the project advanced, the idea of a pasticcio score was abandoned and Lloyd Webber decided to compose original music for the piece.

Christine Daaë (Miss Brightman), a chorister at the Paris Opéra, receives inspiration and vocal coaching from an unseen 'spirit' voice which she superstitiously believes to be that of the angel of music promised to her as a guardian by her late father. The voice, however, is that of the Phantom of the Opéra (Michael Crawford), a horribly disfigured genius who has made his home deep in the sous-sols of the Opéra building and who has fallen in love with the young woman and her voice. He blackmails and frightens the lessees of the theatre (John Savident, David Firth) into giving her leading rôles at the expense of their prima donna, Carlotta (Rosemary Ashe), and into producing an unconventional opera, *Don Juan Triumphant*, which he has written for her. He cannot, however, support Christine's love for the young Raoul de Chagny (Steve Barton) and tragedy threatens to engulf both the lovers and the theatre as a result of his jealousy. But when the young aristocrat pursues the Phantom and the captured Christine to his underground home, the man is ultimately unable to harm the girl and the one she loves.

The score of the piece produced Lloyd Webber's lushest and most romantic music to date, from which three of the principal numbers, 'The Phantom of the Opéra', Raoul and Christine's duet 'All I Ask of You' and the Phantom's monologue 'Music of the Night' all made their way into the top ten of the hit parades. Alongside these pieces were ranged a series of operatic parodies, the Meyerbeerish opera *Hannibal* with its coloratura excrescences, the classical Italianate *Il Muto* which the Phantom's tricks turn into Carlotta's downfall, and the Phantom's own intermittently 'difficult' *Don Juan Triumphant* which moves into the climactic, non-operatic duet between the Phantom and Christine ('Past the Point of No Return'). The score also included some vocal ensemble music of a kind and a quality rarely attempted in the postwar British musical theatre ('Prima Donna').

Unable to occupy Lloyd Webber's own theatre, the Palace, which had been leased to the unexpectedly long-running *Les Misérables*, the Cameron Mackintosh/Really Useful Company production was mounted instead at the slightly undersized (for profitability) Her Majesty's

Plate 209 a and b. **The Phantom of the Opéra** *goes Japanese.*

Theatre. Staged with all the colourful romanticism of the 19th-century stage that its text and music encouraged, with a sea of candelabra rising from the stage to light the Phantom and Christine on their journey through the sewers of Paris to the Phantom's home, and the auditorium's central chandelier tumbling to the stage at the Phantom's command, *The Phantom of the Opéra* proved a triumphant London success and settled in for a long and, at this date, still-continuing run. Crawford and Miss Brightman repeated their rôles when the piece was produced, with equivalent success and longevity, on Broadway in 1988, and subsequently appeared at the head of the Los Angeles company as *The Phantom of the Opéra* went on to its earliest foreign-language productions at Vienna's Theater an der Wien, with Alexander Goebel and Luzia Nistler featured in the leading rôles, in Japan, in Australia (with ex-Australian opera baritone Anthony Warlowe as the Phantom) and in Hamburg where operatic vocalist Peter Hoffmann starred initially as the most Wagnerian Phantom to date. In each and every venue the show proved a major hit.

In the wake of the success of the show, Ken Hill's much less elaborate version won further productions in Britain, including an ill-judged West End season opposite the Her Majesty's Theatre production, which was still playing at a sell-out height, in America and around the Continent (including a visit to Paris's Salle Favart in 1992), whilst a number of other writers jumped swiftly on to the non-copyright Leroux tale, turning out shows under the same or very similar titles in a despairing-seeming copycat manner of a kind which had not been seen in the professional theatre for decades. Several American musicalizations of the *Phantom of the Opéra* tale were launched: one at Texas's Theatre Under the Stars (*Phantom*, 31 January 1991) with the Broadway-proven names of composer Maury Yeston and author Arthur Kopit attached to it, and another at Miami Beach's Al Hirschfeld Theater (Paul Schierhorn, Lawrence Rosen/Bruce Falstein, Stan Barber 5 February 1990). Both went on to further sites,

but neither, any more than the original Hill piece, proved likely to be genuinely mistaken for the show that was filling houses across a handful of continents.

USA: Majestic Theater 26 January 1988; Austria: Theater an der Wien 20 December 1988; Australia: Princess Theatre, Melbourne 1990; Germany: Neue Flora-Theater, Hamburg *Das Phantom der Opera* 29 June 1990
Literature: Perry, G: *The Complete 'Phantom of the Opéra'* (Pavilion, London, 1987)

PHILIPP, Adolf (b Hanover [or Hamburg?], 29 January 1864; d New York, 30 July 1936). Eclectic leading light of the German-language stage in America.

Adolf Philipp ran away from home at the age of 14, joined a German provincial stock company, and went on to make himself a career as a performer in straight and musical theatre which led him first to Vienna and then, in 1890, to New York for an engagement as principal tenor at Gustav Amberg's German-language theatre. He quickly became a local star in rôles such as Vandergold in *Der arme Jonathan*, the hero of Zeller's *Der Vagabund* and as Simon in *Der Bettelstudent*. Following Amberg's collapse, he went on to star with his own company at the Terrace-Garten, appearing in the title-rôle in *Fra Diavolo*, a German version of Herbert's *The Wizard of the Nile* and in his own Operette *Die Royalisten* (music: Josef Manas), before taking on the management of the Germania Theater in September 1893. There, he embarked on a memorable career as manager, star and author, writing and appearing in the large central rôles of a series of often long-running German-Jewish comedies (with plenty of songs for himself) which included *Der Corner Grocer aus der Avenue A* (1893, music by Karl von Wegern), *Der Pawnbroker von der East Side* (1 March 1895, von Wegern), *A New York Brewer and His Family*, *A Day in Manila*, *Dollars and Cents*, *Doktor Darkhorst* and *Der Butcher aus der erste Avenue* (1896), a series which gained him the nickname of 'the German Harrigan'. It also gained him his first mainstream Broadway credit, when *The Corner Grocer* was anglicized, stuck full of variety acts, and mounted at the Casino Theater under the title *About Town* (26 February 1894). Jacques Kruger starred in the author's rôle for the three weeks of the run.

In 1901, having now purchased the Germania on the proceeds of his successes, he produced a musical comedy, *Der Teufel ist los*, for which he added to his usual functions of producer, director, overwhelming star and author, a co-composing credit. His other productions included a piece called *Der Kartoffelkönig* which, half a century before *The King and I*, used a play-within-a-play *Uncle Tom's Cabin* to make a point.

Philipp then returned temporarily to Germany where, with his brother Paul Philipp (d New York, 21 May 1923) as administrator, himself as artistic director and Ober-regisseur and one Ludwig Stein providing the necessary, he opened the 1,000-seater Deutsch-Amerikanische Theater in Berlin (29 August 1903). There he staged a variety of pieces, with more or less music involved, including his own *New York in Wort und Bilt*, *Im wilden Westen*, *Der Teufel ist los*, *In Land der Freiheit*, *Aber, Herr Herzog!* (Lied des schwarzen Katze) and *Er und ich* (1905), and at the same time the brothers began to work on the wider exploitation of Adolf's successful New York plays, both in the German language and also in English translation. After four years they gave up the Berlin house and returned to America where they again attempted a Deutsch-Amerikanische Theater, this time in collaboration with a certain A Geller, who apparently supplied the finance for the venture.

Philipp mounted a production of *New York in Wort und Bild* – which had also been played in Berlin and Viennese versions as *Über'n grossen Teich* (Theater an der Wien 2 September 1906, music Ziegler) – as *From Across the Big Pond* (later *Across the Pond* 'w Mortimer Theise', Circle Theater 7 September 1907) without luck, but he scored a genuine hit at Geller's Wintergarten 'zum schwarzen Adler' with his musical version of the slightly scandalous *Alma, wo wohnst du?* (1909). This piece gave him a long run as author and star, got him hauled up on a delightfully publicity-worthy morals charge, and was subsequently translated into English and produced with further success on the regular Broadway stage (Weber's Theater, New York, 26 August 1910, 232 performances).

In 1912 Philipp established himself as The Adolf Philipp Company, headquartered at the newly built 500-seater 57th Street Theater (later to be better known as the Bandbox), and switched his attention to writing musical plays, at first in German and then in the more competitive English field. His first production, the musical *Auction Pinochle*, with its author starring as Harry Schlesinger, played for 150 nights, and was followed by *Die Mitternachts-mädel*, another piece which was written, like the first, in collaboration with composer 'Jean Briquet' and original author 'Paul Hervé'. Both these gentlemen may have existed – perhaps minor figures on the Paris and Berlin theatre scene – but almost certainly they served here only to hide the fact that the producer-author-star had written and composed his shows single-handed. As *Alma* had done, *The Midnight Girl* shifted to Broadway, with Philipp playing now in English, and there it notched up a run of 104 performances (44th Street Theater, 23 February 1913).

Philipp mounted and starred in a German-language revival of *Alma* (17 April 1913), followed up with another local-comic musical, *Two Lots in the Bronx*, and then brought what he tried to fool public and press was 'a French operetta' (again home-made with the English aid of Edward Paulton), called *Adele*, to the Longacre. *Adele* not only ran 196 performances on Broadway before going to the country, but it was even given a brief production at London's famed Gaiety Theatre. Philipp's style of show, genuine small-theatre musical comedies in the German Posse vein, without spectacle or choruses, and the atten-tion firmly fixed on the action, the comedy and the songs, had proven itself undeniably popular, and it was perhaps no coincidence that it was soon after followed by a local attempt in a similar vein (but with chorus girls) in a popular handful of shows at Broadway's little Princess Theater.

Philipp subsequently joined Saul Rechmann in running the Yorkville Theater as a home for German-language plays and musicals (*Wie einst im Mai*, *Die schöne vom Strande* etc) and, with the coming of the First World War, mounted a typically outspoken play called *Zabern*, which provoked the German ambassador in New York to demand its closure as being insulting to the Kaiser. He also authored, produced and starred in a patriotic American comedy-drama called *Tell it to the Marines*, whilst continu-ing with his run of allegedly adapted musicals. *The Girl Who Smiles* topped the 100-performance mark, but *Two Is Company*, which Philipp also directed, was a 29-perform-ance failure. *Mimi*, another piece built on the lines of *Alma* and produced at Washington with Chapine starred, failed to make it to town in its original production, but Philipp's play was adapted and remusicked by another specialist of the book-based comedy musical, composer Ivan Caryll, and George Hobart, and the result was later produced in New York as *Kissing Time* (Lyric Theater, 11 October 1920).

Although he thereafter went quiet on the musical front, Philipp did not remain inactive. The intriguingly titled play *Tin Pajamas* (w Paulton) closed on the road and, having insulted the Kaiser in the First World War, in 1933 the Jewish author turned out as his last Broadway effort, a very early anti-Hitler play, *Kultur*. Then he finally went into retirement. He died in New York at the age of 72.

An accurate list of Philipp's early German credits is hard to establish, as a second Adolf Philipp was, like him, operating out of Hamburg around the same time as the semi-American one was authoring his earliest Operetten. However, his claim of 'hundreds of performances' in Ger-many make it likely – even allowing for his penchant for fibbing – that he was the author of the musical shows listed below.

1885 **Die Brieftaube** (Karl Stix) Klagenfurt 21 January
1888 **Die Royalisten** (Josef Manas) Braunschweig 19 July
1889 **Der Abenteuerer** (Stix/w Emil Sondermann) Carl-Schultze Theater, Hamburg 14 September
1892 **Der arme Edelmann** (Aurel Donndorf/w Sondermann) Carl-Schultze Theater, Hamburg 29 November
1900 **Die Reise nach America** Belle-Alliance Theater, Berlin
1901 **Der Teufel ist los** (w Edward A Weber) Adolf Philipp's Germania Theater 31 December
1903 **Über'n grossen Teich** (*New York in Wort und Bilt*) Deutsch-Amerikanische Theater, Berlin 29 August
1904 **New York** Deutsch-Amerikanische Theater, Berlin 22 November

1905 **Aber, Herr Herzog!** Deutsch-Amerikanische Theater, Berlin 2 September

1906 **Im wilden Westen** Deutsch-Amerikanische Theater, Berlin 23 October

1906 **Der Sorgenbrecher** Deutsch-Amerikanische Theater, Berlin 22 December

1909 **Alma, wo wohnst du?** Wintergarten 'zum schwarzen Adler' 25 October

1912 **Auction Pinochle** 57th Street Theater

1912 **Das Mitternachtsmädel** Adolf Philipp's 57th Street Theater 1 September

1913 **Adele** (Edward Paulton/w Paulton) Longacre Theater 28 August

1913 **Two Lots in the Bronx** (Paulton/w Paulton) Adolf Philipp's 57th Street Theater 27 November

1915 **The Girl Who Smiles** (Paulton/w Paulton) Lyric Theatre 9 August

1915 **Two is Company** (Paulton/w Paulton) Lyric Theater 22 September

1920 **Mimi** (w Frank E Tours/Paulton/w Paulton) Shubert Belasco Theater, Washington 13 March

PHI-PHI Opérette légère in 3 acts by Albert Willemetz and Fabien Sollar. Music by Henri Christiné. Théâtre des Bouffes-Parisiens, Paris, 12 November 1918.

Although it was not the first small-scale modern musical comedy to visit the Paris stage of the 1910s (Barde and Cuvillier and the Théâtre des Capucines had been at it for years), *Phi-Phi* is generally accepted as the landmark show which launched the postwar craze for small-scale, snappily up-to-date, dance-melodied musical comedy in the French theatre. Once again, as with *Midas*, *Olympic Revels*, *Orphée aux enfers*, *Die schöne Galathee* and *Thespis*, the (almost) infallible classical burlesque turned up in an important position in theatre history. In a way, *Phi-Phi* was indeed the jazz-age equivalent of an *Orphée aux enfers* or a *Die schöne Galathee*, for it used its ostensibly Ancient Greek story as an often anachronistic vehicle for witty modern chat and the comical portraying of current (and, of course, eternal) social mores and preoccupations, most particularly, naturally, sexual ones. Like the earlier pieces, it also decorated its comical tale with the popular light music of the moment but, whereas for the older shows that meant waltzes and galops, in 1918 the fashion called for the fox-trot, the one-step and waltzes of a rather different flavour from those of half a century earlier.

Initially intended for production at Gustave Quinson's 210-seater, underground Théâtre de l'Abri, *Phi-Phi* was written on an economical scale: six principals, eight chorus girls, two dancers and a small band. The chief comic rôle was that of Phi-Phi (Urban), otherwise that ancient Greek marble-chipper Phidias, who brings home an ostensibly virginal little lass called Aspasie (Alice Cocéa) to serve as model for 'Virtue' in his new statue. He also has other designs for her, which his wife (Pierrette Madd) would be more concentrated on dampening were she not herself involved in sort of dissuading the attentions of a beautiful young man called Ardimédon (Ferréal) who has followed her home from the portes de Trezène. Ardimédon's presence chez Phidias is justified when – after a quick strip-off audition – he is chosen to model for 'Love' in the statue. Chlamyses and stolai drop with more ease than pants and frocks in a fury of Greek-French farce but, of course, in the end Phi-Phi has to share Aspasie (who, as our history books tell us, was no virgin but a particularly

good street-walker) with his patron, Périclès. A ménage à cinq on the best French (and probably Greek) principles (husband, wife, his mistress, her young lover, mistress's wealthy protector) brings down the curtain. The sixth character was the traditionally comic Greek servant (Dréan) who managed to get mixed up with most of the plot without indulging in anything more immoral than a touch of pandering, a lot of gambling and a little unsecured 'borrowing'.

Christiné's sparkling score was arguably the gayest, most dazzling shower of music to have decorated a French opérette since the early days of Offenbach. Phi-Phi himself gurgled rhapsodically over Aspasie's charms in general ('C'est une gamine charmante') and over her breasts in particular (Chanson des petits paiens), whilst the lady in question waltzed through a catalogue of all the lines she'd ever been spun ('Je connais toutes les historiettes'), gasped out an innocent introduction to Périclès ('Ah! cher monsieur!'), justified the importance of a good wardrobe for a woman ('Bien chapeautée'), and got topical in a description of newspaper novelettes in a number in which Douglas Fairbanks and Mabel Normand got a mention. Madame Phidias, determined to model herself for 'Virtue' rather than let the wench do so, presented her naked self in a mock operatic Prayer to Pallas, comically described her pursuit by Ardimédon ('J'sortais des portes de Trezène'), waltzed through her seduction in duo with her seducer ('Ah! Tais-toi') and then looked back on it (Duo des souvenirs), whilst her young man joined in the duets and in the delicious ensembles and finales which completed an 18-number score.

Quinson's production, ultimately shifted from the Abri to the larger Théâtre des Bouffes-Parisiens when that stage went suddenly vacant, proved at first a fair and then – in the celebratory days of 'la victoire' – a huge success. Although he removed it, at one stage, from the Bouffes and sublet it to Alphonse Franck at the Théâtre Édouard VII, in order to mount another piece, the producer quickly realized his error and hastened the little musical back to its original home, as the revue-writers acclaimed it in the only way they knew how, by parodying its title in such pieces as the Concert Mayol's *Phi-Fi-Fi-Tie* (Jules Bastin/Gibet, Devere). *Phi-Phi* passed its 1,000th performance on 24 January 1921, and it ran on for a further three months before being finally replaced. That replacement was temporary, however, and a little more than a month later *Phi-Phi* was back for a second run, and the following year for a third. In 1933 and then, in the wake of the Second War as of the First, in 1947, Urban again appeared on the Paris stage as Phi-Phi, and the Bouffes continued thereafter to host regular fresh productions (1949, 1957, 1980, 1983) of a piece whose delights and tidy proportions made it a practical proposition even in a commercial theatre which had largely renounced opérette productions. Most recently, a rather battered version was seen at Paris's Nouveau Théâtre Mouffetard in 1989 (31 October), whilst every season brings further *Phi-Phi*s in the French provinces.

However, if *Phi-Phi* were the rage of the French stage in the years following the war, its export possibilities were quite clearly very limited. How did one translate Willemetz and Sollar's pun-spiked dialogue? And if one could, how would the theatregoers and critics of certain other nationalities react to the bright blue content of the piece? Not to mention all that nudity (male and female). The British, who had already massacred Barde's much-less-demanding *Son p'tit frère* in the name of decency, needless to say, cowered out. C B Cochran produced a piece called *Phi-Phi*, but it was unrecognizable. The story (Fred Thompson, Clifford Grey) was altered, the characters were altered, the lyrics were thrown out, the tunes that were left were given to the wrong voices, and the score was larded with interpolations by Herman Darewski ('Beautiful Greece', 'There's Another One Gone', 'The Chicken'), Nat D Ayer and Cole Porter ('The Ragtime Pipes of Pan'), as well as a quintet and a trio by Chantrier, a ballet by Dvořák and a dance by Eugene Goossens. Evelyn Laye, Clifton Webb, Arthur Roberts, Stanley Lupino and June held up a mediocre show which was not *Phi-Phi* for 132 performances.

In America, things went even worse. The Shuberts' production of a version by Glen MacDonough and Harry Wagstaffe Gribble which featured Frances White as Miss Myrtle Mink, alias Aspasia, and Frank Lalor as Abel Carver (get it?) otherwise Phidias, did not even make it to Broadway. It was perhaps just as well, as the adaptors and lyricist E Ray Goetz had had a fine time with the original, sticking on a prologue and an epilogue, bringing Venus (in a Greek setting?) into the proceedings, and generally shuffling the work up alarmingly. Only one piece of music, a ballet-pantomime in Act III, was credited to musical director Arthur H Guttman, but Christiné's melodies had been made to do work other than that for which they were intended.

Hungary's Jenő Heltai clearly did a better job of adaptation than his English-speaking colleagues for Budapest's *Fi-Fi*, as produced at the Lujza Blaha Színház with Hanna Honthy starred, was a great success. In a city which revelled in the product of the French jazz-age stage throughout its decade and a bit of prominence, the show ran for more than 200 performances and earned a revival at the Király Színház in 1930. The show also, apparently, reached Germany, where it left sufficient mark to be revived in a new German version (ad Walter Brandin, Artur Maria Rabenalt) which was played at the Deutsches Theater, Munich in 1963–4.

Hungary: Lujza Blaha Színház *Fi-Fi* 7 October 1921; UK: London Pavilion 16 August 1922; USA: Globe Theater, Atlantic City ?1922

Recordings: complete (Decca), selections (EMI-Pathé, Westminster) etc

PICCALUGA, [Albert]

Baritone Piccaluga was whisked straight from his second prize at the Conservatoire to take over in *Le Bois* at the Opéra-Comique in October 1880, and he remained several years a member of the company there before turning to the commercial musical theatre. He made his first appearance on the musical-comedy stage at the Menus-Plaisirs in the rôle of Prince Doriando in a revised version of *Les Pommes d'or* in February 1883 and his fine voice and superior style swiftly won him an engagement at the Bouffes-Parisiens and leading rôles in a long series of opérettes. His most successful creations, in a career covering more than 20 subsequent years, were the parts of lubricious Annibal de Tourendor with a passion for *Madame Boniface*

(1883), the young painter, Paul, who sketches the bits of the inverted *Miss Helyett* (1890) which only a husband ought to see and the opera-singing hero Montosol in *Joséphine vendue par ses soeurs* (1893).

Piccaluga also appeared, amongst others, in the original productions of *La Dormeuse éveillée* (1883, Octave), *Le Diable au corps* (1884, Franz), *Pervenche* (1885), *Les Grenadiers de Mont-Cornette* (1887, Bel-Amour), *Mam'zelle Crénom* (1888), *La Vénus d'Arles* (1889, Prosper), *Le Mari de la reine* (1889, Florestan), *Cendrillonnette* (1890), *Sainte-Freya* (1892, Captain Ludwig), *Madame Suzette* (1893, William Robiquet), *Mam'zelle Carabin* (1893, Ferdinand), *Ninette* (1896, Cyrano de Bergerac), *Le Petit Moujik* (1896, Fleury), *Mariage princier* (1900, Médéric), *Les Petites Vestales* (1900) and *La Bouquetière du Château d'Eau*.

He also appeared in many of the classic baritone rôles, notably several times as Brissac in *Les Mousquetaires au couvent*, as Favart, Roger in *Gillette de Narbonne* and Miguel in *Le Jour et la nuit*, as well as playing Frank Abercoed in the French production of *Florodora* (1903) and Duparquet (ie Falke) in the belated French première of *La Chauve-souris*.

PICKWICK
Musical in 2 acts by Wolf Mankowitz based on Charles Dickens's *Posthumous Papers of the Pickwick Club*. Lyrics by Leslie Bricusse. Music by Cyril Ornadel. Saville Theatre, London, 4 July 1963.

In the wake of the success of *Oliver!*, the works of Charles Dickens became ripe for rifling by musical writers. In this case it was a performer, the bulky *Goon Show* comedian-cum-tenor Harry Secombe, who conceived the idea of a musical *Pickwick Papers* built all the way around himself in the rôle of Samuel Pickwick. The idea was taken up by author Mankowitz and producer Bernard Delfont (later joined by Tom Arnold), with Leslie Bricusse and Cyril Ornadel, who had written pantomime songs for Secombe, allotted the music, and *Oliver!* director and designer, Peter Coe and Sean Kenny hired for the making of more musical Dickens.

The text ran through the favourite Pickwick episodes – Mrs Bardell's (Jessie Evans) breach-of-promise suit, the Eatanswill election, the skating party, the Jingle and Rachel Wardle (Hilda Braid) business – in what one critic called 'comic-strip Dickens' style, accompanied by some jolly songs, most of the best of which were not for the star. Sam Weller (Teddy Green) sang of how he could 'Talk' his way out of things, and joined Tony Weller (Robin Wentworth) discoursing on 'The Trouble with Women', whilst Jingle (Anton Rodgers) described himself as 'A Bit of a Character' and pattered through an enjoyably concerned 'Very'. The most successful number, however, did fall to Secombe, tenoriously describing to the electors, in the Eatanswill scene, what he would do 'If I Ruled the World'. The song ran 17 weeks in the top twenty, the show for a year and a half (694 performances) in the West End. *Pickwick* subsequently got several provincial productions, and a less bulky Secombe returned to his rôle thirty years on in a production at Chichester's Festival Theatre.

David Merrick produced *Pickwick* for America, with Secombe and Rodgers repeating their rôles alongside David Jones (Sam) and Charlotte Rae (Mrs Bardell) but, after a fine pre-Broadway season in which it recouped its entire investment, it failed in only 56 performances in New York.

In 1889 a one-act musical called *Pickwick* (Edward Solomon/F C Burnand) which concentrated on the favourite Mrs Bardell episode, so often seen in John Hollingshead's little *Bardell v Pickwick* at the Gaiety (1871 sq), was produced at London's Comedy Theatre. Arthur Cecil (Pickwick), Lottie Venne (Mrs Bardwell) and Rutland Barrington (Baker) featured in the first showing of a piece later played at the Trafalgar Square Theatre (13 December 1893) with C P Little, Jessie Bond and Charles Hawtrey, and also produced both in New Zealand (City Hall, Dunedin 18 September 1890) and in Australia.

USA: 46th Street Theater 4 October 1965
Recording: original cast (Philips, WRC)

PICON, Molly (b New York, 28 February 1898; d Lancaster, Pa, 5 April 1992)

Molly Picon spent much of the first 40 years of her performing career playing in Yiddish theatre where she established herself as a considerable star, and she only subsequently turned to English-language and Broadway theatre. Although she had appeared in a number of original Yiddish musical pieces at the 2nd Avenue Theater and the Molly Picon Theater (*The Jolly Orphan* 1929, also lyrics, *The Kosher Widow* 1959 etc) and made her first regular Broadway appearance in 1940, her first musical part on Broadway was as Clara Weiss, the husbandless American tripper in Israel, in *Milk and Honey*. She scored a sizeable personal success in the rôle both on Broadway and on tour (1961–4). She later played briefly in the roadfolding *Chu Chem* (1966), in the musical *How to Be a Jewish Mother* (1967), toured in *Funny Girl* and in the title-rôle of *Hello, Dolly!* (1970), and appeared in the film version of *Fiddler on the Roof* as the matchmaking Yente.

Autobiography: w Rosenberg, E: *So Laugh a Little* (Messner, New York, 1962), w Bergantini, J: *Molly!* (Simon & Schuster, New York, 1980)

PIERNÉ, [Henri Constant] Gabriel (b Metz, 16 August 1863; d Ploujean, 17 July 1937).

As a student at the Paris Conservatoire, Pierné was the winner of the Prix de Rome of 1882. He subsequently became a celebrated conductor, notably at the head of the Concerts Colonne, and was the composer of a number of varied theatre pieces of which the earliest included the mimodrame *Le Docteur Blanc* written to a livret by Catulle Mendès and produced at the Théâtre des Menus-Plaisirs in 1893, the spectacular 'fantaisie lyrique' *Bouton d'or*, the pantomime *Salomé* (1895) and the incidental music to Rostand's *La Princesse lointaine* (1895) and *La Samaritaine* (1897).

His 'comédie-lyrique' *La Fille du Tabarin* (1901), a version of Musset's *On ne badine pas avec l'amour* (1910), the one-act opéra-comique adaptation of La Fontaine and Champmeslé's *La Coupe enchantée* (1905, *Der Zauberbecher* Stuttgart 1907) and *Sophie Arnould* (1927) were all produced at the Opéra-Comique, but his one full-scale light lyric work for the commercial theatre, *Fragonard*, produced first in Belgium and then at Paris's Théâtre de la Porte-Saint-Martin won more connoisseur's praise than performances. It was taken into the repertoire of the Opéra-Comique in 1946 for 18 performances.

1893 **Bouton d'or** (Michel Carré) Nouveau Théâtre 4 January
1895 **La Coupe enchantée** (Emmanuel Matrat) 1 act Casino, Royan 24 August; Opéra-Comique, Paris, 20 December 1905
1901 **La Fille du Tabarin** (Victorien Sardou, Paul Ferrier) Opéra-Comique 20 February
1910 **On ne badine pas avec l'amour** (Alfred de Musset ad Louis Leloir, Gabriel Nigond) Opéra-Comique 30 May
1927 **Sophie Arnould** (Nigond) 1 act Opéra-Comique 21 February
1933 **Fragonard** (André Rivoire, Romain Coolus) Théâtre de la Monnaie, Brussels; Théâtre de la Porte-Saint-Martin 16 October 1934

PIETRI, Giuseppe (b Sant' Ilario in Campo, Elba, 6 May 1886; d Milan, 11 August 1946). Composer of several of the most successful Italian operettas.

The young Pietri was sent to study in Milan under the patronage of an Elban music-lover who had heard him playing the organ in the local church, and he made his début as a composer in the theatre in 1910 with a one-act operatic scena, *Calendimaggio*. His first contribution to the light lyric stage came three years later, and his first significant success in 1915 with the score for the operetta *Addio giovinezza*. Pietri subsequently became one of the most popular Italian stage writers, through further successes with such pieces as *L'acqua cheta* (1920), a musical version of de Flers and de Caillavet's play *Primerose* (*Primarosa*, 1926), and *Rompicollo* (1928), which became one of the few Italian musical shows to win a production outside Italy when it was played at Berlin's Theater des Volkes under the title *Das grosse Rennen* (27 November 1938, ad Rudolf Frank, Rolf Sievers). He later turned back to operatic writing and had an opera *Maristella* produced with Gigli in its leading rôle in 1934.

1913 **In Flemmerlandia** (Antonio Rubino) Teatro Fossati, Milan 24 September
1915 **Addio giovinezza** (Camasio, Oxilia) Politeama Goldoni, Livorno 20 January, Teatro Diana, Rome 20 April
1916 **Il Signore di Ruy Blas** Bologna
1917 **La Modella** (Antonio Lega) Teatro Quirino, Rome 29 January
1919 **La Lucciola** (Carlo Veneziani) Politeama Goldoni, Livorno 26 March
1920 **L'acqua cheta** (Angelo Nessi/Augusto Novelli) Teatro Nazionale, Rome 27 November
1922 **L'ascensione** (Novelli) Teatro della Pergola, Florence 17 May
1923 **Guarda, guarda la mostarda** (Giovanni Colonna di Cesaro) Teatro dei Piccoli 4 April
1923 **La donna perduta** (G Zorzi, A Giannini) Teatro degli Italiani 26 September
1924 **Quartetto vagabondo** Teatro Eliseo 4 December
1926 **Namba Zaim** (Veneziani) Teatro Lirico, Milan
1926 **Primarosa** (Carlo Lombardo, Renato Simoni) Teatro Lirico, Milan 29 October
1927 **Tuffolina** (Novelli) Politeama Genovese, Genoa 26 October
1928 **Rompicollo** (Luigi Bonelli, Ferdinando Paoleri) Teatro dal Verme 29 December
1929 **L'isola verde** (Lombardo, Bonelli) Teatro Lirico, Milan 16 October
1930 **Casa mia, casa mia ...** (Nessi, Novelli) Teatro Quirino, Rome 5 October
1930 **Gioconda Zapaterra** (Giulio Bucciolini) Teatro Alfieri, Florence 10 December
1931 **La dote di Jeannette** (Rossato) Teatro Principe 4 July

1932 **Vent' anni** (Bonelli) Teatro Quirino 2 April

Biography: Carli, R.: *Giuseppi Pietri cantore dei goliardi* (Soc Ed Italiana Demetra, Livorno, 1955)

PIFF! PAFF! POUF! Musical cocktail in 2 acts by Stanislaus Stange. Lyrics by William Jerome. Music by Jean Schwartz. Casino Theater, New York, 2 April 1904.

Thomas Q Seabrooke appeared at the top of the bill for *Piff! Paff! Pouf!* as Mr Augustus Melon, a widower, and anxious to tie a second knot with the widowed Mrs Montague (Alice Fischer). However, Melon's financial situation is precarious, as he inherits his late wife's fortune only if and when he has successfully married off his four daughters, Nora (Mabel Hollins), Cora (Grace Cameron), Encora (Hilda Hollins) and Rose (Frances Gibsone). Fortunately there are pretendants at hand. Chief comedian Eddie Foy as Peter Pouffle, British baritone Templar Saxe as Lord George Piffle, John Hyams as Macaroni Paffle, and a journalist with the burlesquey name of Dick Daily (Harry Stuart).

Stanislaus Stange's low-vaudevillesque book was illustrated by a score by successful songwriters Schwartz and Jerome from which Foy pulled out a jolly success as, aided by the Pony Ballet, he described himself as 'The Ghost That Never Walked' ('Ghost of a troupe that disbanded in Peoria ...'), but out of which Seabrooke drew the most enduring number in 'Cordalia Malone'. Cordalia was represented as being the sister of 'Bedelia', the heroine of the song which had won its writers their biggest ever hit, and if she didn't quite repeat her relative's success, she nevertheless proved popular both in America (the song was reused in *Glittering Gloria*) and in Britain where it was interpolated into the Gaiety Theatre's *The Orchid*. Mabel Hollins tootsie-wootsied through 'Under the Goo-Goo Tree', Miss Cameron contributed the topically showbizzy saga 'Since Little Dolly Dimple's Made a Hit' and the Pony Ballet performed a 'Radium Dance' with luminous frocks and skipping-ropes.

The whole made up an entertainment which drew happily through 264 performances on Broadway for producer Fred C Whitney, before going into the country.

The show's title – a common enough bit of onomatopoeic French for a volley of shot which had been highlighted in song from *Les Huguenots* to *La Grande-Duchesse de Gérolstein* – was used in Paris soon after as the title of Victor de Cottens and Victor Darlay's 1906 Châtelet Christmas spectacular (*Pif! Paf! Pouf!, ou un voyage endiablé*, 6 December, music: Marius Baggers).

PINERO, Arthur Wing (Sir) (b London, 24 May 1855; d London, 23 November 1934).

In a high-profile career as a playwright, initially of comedies and later of more serious dramatic works, Pinero was only once drawn into the musical theatre, when he collaborated with Arthur Sullivan and Comyns Carr on a 'romantic musical drama' for Richard D'Oyly Carte and the Savoy Theatre. The obtrusively un-comic opera *The Beauty Stone* was bundled out of the Savoy in 50 stretched performances.

Pinero had, however, a much more profitable connection with the musical stage when, with the coming to English-speaking stages of the equivalent of the French vaudeville – a coherent and often complex comedy with songs – not only established French comedies, but also British ones, became the raw material for the musical plays of the day. The first such adaptation of a Pinero play came not in Britain but in Vienna where his 1885 *The Magistrate* was made into a musical comedy by Heinz von Waldberg and A M Willner, music by Richard Heuberger, under the title *The Baby* (Carltheater, 3 October 1909), but the most outstanding success amongst the morceaux of musicalized Pinero was *The Boy* (Adelphi Theatre, 14 September 1917), a British version of the same play adapted by Fred Thompson with songs by Lionel Monckton and Howard Talbot. After its two-year London run, it appeared in America as *Good Morning, Judge*.

This success prompted the same management to adapt the playwright's *In Chancery* (1884) as *Who's Hooper?* (ad Thompson, music Talbot, Ivor Novello, 13 September 1919), also with considerable success (349 performances), and Donald Calthrop to mount a version of *The Schoolmistress* under the title *My Nieces* (ad Percy Greenbank, mus: Talbot, Phil Braham, 19 August 1921) with slightly less. After this little splurge, there was a moratorium on Pinero for half a century until the fashion of book-strong shows returned. Michael Stewart, David Heneker and John Addison combined on a musical version of *The Amazons* (1893) produced at the Nottingham Playhouse (7 April 1971) and Julian Slade composed two Pinero pieces: *Trelawny* (Sadler's Wells 27 June 1972), a version of the author's more sentimental *Trelawny of the Wells* (1898), and a second *Schoolmistress* musical, *Out of Bounds* (Theatre Royal, Bristol 26 December 1973).

1898 **The Beauty Stone** (Arthur Sullivan/J Comyns Carr) Savoy Theatre 28 May

PINKIE AND THE FAIRIES Fairy play in 3 acts by W Graham Robertson. Music by Frederic Norton. Her Majesty's Theatre, London, 19 December 1908.

Robertson's enchantingly poetic little fantasy, first published in book form, found itself a stage production of an unlooked-for kind when Beerbohm Tree mounted it at Her Majesty's Theatre as a Christmas entertainment. It got an even more classy look to it when Ellen Terry decided that she would like to play one of the adult rôles, and Tree cast several other established and coming names as the piece's other characters. Marie Löhr was a chatty, society Cinderella, Viola Tree a dozy Sleeping Beauty, Frederick Volpé and Augusta Havilland were the other two adults, whilst Stella Patrick Campbell played teenaged Molly, who is taken off to a fairy party by her two little cousins (Iris Hawkins, Philip Tonge). An 11-year-old called Hermione Gingold made her first stage appearance as a fairy herald, but when Montesole and McLeod sent out a touring company the following year she was promoted to the title-rôle.

At a time when children's entertainments such as the very successful *Bluebell in Fairyland* were more inclined to be juvenile versions of adult shows, full of up-to-date songs and sentiments, *Pinkie* was a return to the fairyland of Victorian picture books, and it was much appreciated as such. Tree revived the show for a second Christmas, and it was subsequently seen in regular provincial productions for a number of years thereafter.

Australia: Metropolitan Theatre, Sydney 16 January 1955.

THE PINK LADY Musical comedy in 3 acts by C M S McLellan based on *Le Satyre* by Georges Berr and Marcel Guillemaud. Music by Ivan Caryll. New Amsterdam Theater, New York, 13 March 1911.

A frequent visitor to France (where he had studied and where he kept a magnificent second home), the composer Caryll had also written from time to time for the Paris stage and, in his *S.A.R.*, he had turned out the kind of substantial vaudeville/musical comedy fare which he could not give to his London employers at the Gaiety Theatre, where the shows had to be built around the stars and to the style of the house. When he quit London to settle and work in New York, it was this French style of piece, rather than the very much less coherent British kind, which he offered to a Broadway which itself had had only a little experience of such thoroughly legitimate comedies with music. If the first of his contributions in such a style, *Marriage à la Carte*, had only an indifferent run, the second, *The Pink Lady*, a musicalized version of the Parisian farce *Le Satyre*, was a different proposition. It proved to be both a classy piece of work and a major hit and helped give an important impetus towards a better book content in local musicals.

Some lightfingered fellow has been on the loose in the Bois de Compiègne, snatching kisses and pinching bottoms, and he is all the talk at 'Le Joli Coucou' restaurant where the action of the first act of the play takes place. Lucien Garidel (William Elliott) comes there to have a last little pre-marital fling with his mistress, Claudine (Hazel Dawn), but unfortunately for him his fiancée, Angèle (Alice Dovey), choses the 'Coucou' to have a quiet lunch with Maurice d'Uzac (Craufurd Kent) on the very same day. Lucien pretends that Claudine is the wife of the antique dealer Dondidier (Frank Lalor), and is busy setting up this alibi when the Countess of Montanvert (Louise Kelley) is 'got' by the hot-lipped 'satyr'. She accuses Dondidier and calls the police, but all the ladies take the funny little chap's side and, as the events of the evening wind up to their climax, he finds himself a celebrity. Amongst all the brouhaha, Lucien and Angèle are happily reunited and Claudine glides equally happily back into the demi-monde.

Caryll's score (five songs, three choruses, three concerted numbers, three finales, four duets) was as sparkling as the comedy, and its principal number, Claudine's richly romantic 'The Kiss Waltz', reintroduced in the last act as a duet with Angèle as 'My Beautiful Lady', turned out to be one of the biggest hits not only of the season but of the period. A second major hit came with the jaunty, tuneful 'By the Banks of the Saskatchewan' sung by two subsidiary characters (Flora Crosbie, Scott Welsh), whilst Dondidier, basking in his 'infamy', admitted his little escapades and admitted 'I Like It!', and the ensembles were topped by a brilliantly babbling ensemble of accusation ('Donny Didn't, Donny Did').

Klaw and Erlanger's production of *The Pink Lady* was a Broadway hit of the first order, playing 316 performances at the New Amsterdam before Charles Frohman took the entire company and production (with Jack Henderson replacing Elliott) across the Atlantic. London's production was as big a success as Broadway's had been, but unfortunately Klaw and Erlanger's economics did not work in the West End in the same way they did in New York and even full houses at the undersized Globe Theatre could not keep the books buoyant. After 124 performances the

Plate 210. **The Pink Lady,** *on each side of the Atlantic.*

1148

London season was closed down and the company transported back to Broadway where, a month after the last British performances, they reopened at the New Amsterdam Theater (26 August 1912) for a further 24 performances before taking to the road.

From there on, the show moved slowly but surely around the world. In 1917 J C Williamson produced *The Pink Lady* in Australia with Phil Smith (Dondidier), Minnie Love (Claudine) and Ethel Cadman (Angèle) starred through two months in Sydney and a month and a half in Melbourne (Her Majesty's Theatre 9 June 1917), but a scheduled French production, with the original French play somewhat revamped by Louis Verneuil and some Caryll numbers from other shows introduced, hit all sorts of problems. *La Dame en rose* was actually put into rehearsal on more than one occasion before Gustave Quinson finally got it on the stage in 1921. The 'Valse de la Dame en Rose' was now sung by Odette (Lucette Darbelle) and Garidel (Henri Defreyn), 'Saskatchewan' was allotted to Henri Vilbert as Dondidier (now called Verdousier), and *Chin-Chin*'s 'Goodbye, Girls, I'm Through' was metamorphosed into a piece called 'Charmante!' which Defreyn made the hit of the night. Unfortunately for all concerned, Quinson had removed his *Phi-Phi* from the Bouffes-Parisiens to produce *La Dame en rose* and, when it became evident that *Phi-Phi* was still performing in the manner of a big, big hit at the Édouard VII, the producer promptly took Caryll's piece off and brought *Phi-Phi* back. If one month was all the show got out of Paris, the production was nevertheless responsible for the show being spotted and taken on to one further production, in Hungary, where *A rózsalány* (ad István Zágon, from Verneuil's version) was produced in 1923.

'The Kiss Waltz', which became popularly known as 'The Pink Lady Waltz', was given a fresh whirl across the musical stage when it was prominently featured in the score of the London extravaganza *Ziegfeld*.

UK: Globe Theatre 11 April 1912; Australia: Her Majesty's Theatre, Sydney 17 February 1917; France: Théâtre des Bouffes-Parisiens *La Dame en rose* 30 April 1921; Hungary: Lujza Blaha Színház *A rózsalány* 13 October 1923
Recording: selection (AEI)

PINZA, [Fortunato] Ezio (b Rome, 18 May 1892; d Stanford, Conn, 9 May 1957).

After a highly successful international career in opera, the celebrated basso was engaged by Edwin Lester of the Los Angeles Light Opera Company to make a musical comedy début. Lester, unable to find a suitable vehicle, shared his problem with Richard Rodgers and, thus, Pinza made his first Broadway musical appearance in the specially tailored star rôle of Rodgers and Hammerstein's *South Pacific*, creating 'Some Enchanted Evening', 'This Nearly Was Mine' and a sensation. In 1954 he starred on Broadway a second time in the rôle of César in a potted musical version of Marcel Pagnol's Marseillais trilogy entitled *Fanny*.

Pinza also appeared in several films, notably as Chaliapin in *Tonight We Sing*.

Autobiography: *Ezio Pinza* (Rinehart, New York, 1959)

PIPE DREAM Musical in 2 acts by Oscar Hammerstein II based on the novel *Sweet Thursday* by John Steinbeck. Music by Richard Rodgers. Shubert Theater, New York, 30 November 1955.

After the international successes of their colourful romantic operettas, Rodgers and Hammerstein brought the rather less colourful down-and-outs of Steinbeck's *Sweet Thursday* to the stage in a musical whose central love story was between a marine biologist without a microscope (Bill Johnson) and a thieving layabout (Judy Tyler) and whose top-billed star, opera's Helen Traubel, played a good-hearted brothel-keeper. The two other principal characters of the piece were other vagrants (Mike Kellin, G D Wallace), one of whom organizes a dubious raffle to get the Doc his microscope, the other of whom breaks Doc's arm to get the girl to return to him after a squabble.

Rodgers and Hammerstein's score brought forth no numbers to help stock their big, big book of standards, and their production ran through a comparatively poor, and certainly unprofitable, 246 performances which sent them back promptly to more romantic locations and characters for their next works.

Recording: original cast (RCA)

PIPPIN Musical in 2 acts by Roger O Hirson. Music and lyrics by Stephen Schwartz. Imperial Theater, New York, 23 October 1972.

Originally produced, in an earlier version with a libretto by Ron Strauss and music and lyrics by Schwartz, at the Carnegie-Mellon University in Pittsburgh in 1967, *Pippin* was brought to Broadway in 1972 after the notable success of Schwartz's *Godspell* the previous year. Like that show, *Pippin* was a piece very much of the 1960s, sporting a hero who could have stepped out of the cast of *Godspell*, and period love and war sentiments to match, but this time, under the influence and the remaking of director-choreographer Bob Fosse, the original small piece was worked up into something decidedly larger.

The basic tale of the piece was set in a kind of frame, in the fashion which, though normally used to take the curse off unconfident material, had been successfully used a few seasons earlier by *Man of La Mancha*. Ben Vereen played a compèring character called the Leading Player, at the head of a group of white-faced utility players of the *Godspell* brand, introducing the tale of Pippin (John Rubenstein), son of King Charlemagne, who goes out looking for himself. On the way from Home, he finds War, The Flesh, Revolution, Encouragement, The Hearth (inclusive of Jill Clayburgh as Catherine) and The Finale, as well as some agreeable songs. The Players' introduction, 'Magic to Do' and Pippin's opening solo 'Corner of the Sky' both became popular out of the show, but the catchy if preachy 'Spread a Little Sunshine' (introduced by Leland Palmer as Fastrada), 'No Time at All' (sung by Irene Ryan as Berthe) and the more masculine 'War is a Science' sung by Pippin and his father (Eric Berry) also did well in situ.

Pippin proved a worthy successor to *Godspell* and, aided by some charming sets and a television advertising campaign which has gone down in Broadway history as a classic of efficacy, it established itelf as a long-running hit. Stuart Ostrow's production remained at the Imperial Theatre for 1,944 performances.

In Britain, where television advertising was unheard of, Robert Stigwood's production with Paul Jones (Pippin), Northern J Calloway (Leading Player), Patricia Hodge, Diane Langton, John Turner and Elisabeth Welch featured ran 85 performances. Popular singer Johnny

Farnham starred in Kenn Brodziak's Australian production in Melbourne and Sydney (Her Majesty's Theatre 10 August 1974), South Africa saw *Pippin* in 1985 (Her Majesty's Theatre, Johannesburg, 10 June), and a German-language version (ad Robert Gilbert) was launched at the Theater an der Wien with Joachim Kemmer as the Leading Player, Béla Erny as Pippin and Grete Keller as Berthe (75 performances). In 1982 the show was televised with Vereen repeating the rôle which had earned him a Tony Award a decade earlier, by which time it showed up already as a period piece.

Pippin had already served as subject matter for an earlier, German musical comedy, *Pippin der kleine*, produced in the 1920s with a score by Hugo Hirsch.

UK: Her Majesty's Theatre 30 October 1973; Australia: Her Majesty's Theatre, Melbourne 23 February 1974; Austria: Theater an der Wien 6 February 1974

Recordings: original cast (Motown), Australian cast (EMI), South African cast (Satbel)

THE PIRATES OF PENZANCE, or The Slave of Duty

Comic opera in 2 acts by W S Gilbert. Music by Arthur Sullivan. Bijou Theatre, Paignton, 30 December 1879; Fifth Avenue Theater, New York, 31 December 1879.

Gilbert and Sullivan's successor to the phenomenal *HMS Pinafore* proved to be another enormous international opéra-bouffe hit. Where the former piece had burlesqued things theatrico-naval, the new one, developed from an original scenario about some burglars combined with some elements of an earlier Gilbert operetta, *Our Island Home*, used the highly coloured characters and conventions of the melodrama stage as the butt of its fun.

Owing to an error by his childhood nurse, Ruth (Alice Barnett), Frederic (Hugh Talbot) was accidentally apprenticed to the Pirate King (Sgr Broccolini). Now, after having faithfully served his indentures to the age of 21, he is free, and his well-pronounced sense of duty drives him to join the police force and devote himself to the extermination of his old skull-and-crossbone-mates. Back in the unpiratical world, Frederic falls in love with the first soprano he sees: Mabel (Blanche Roosevelt), daughter of Major General Stanley (J H Ryley). Unfortunately, the pirates are out for revenge on Stanley, who has unfeelingly fibbed himself out of a confrontation with them just as they were about to wed his daughters en masse. Frederic is preparing to lead the police in a raid against the buccaneers, but he is stopped when it is revealed that by a strict reading of the wording of his indentures he is still bound in loyalty to his old master. Battle is joined between pirates and police, and, with the duty-bound Frederic helpless to prevent them, the pirates are victorious – until the police bring out their secret weapon: the name of Queen Victoria. As loyal subjects, the pirates surrender. Then Ruth comes out with the truth: they are all actually peers in disguise, so their naughtiness can naturally be forgiven and they can mass marry General Stanley's daughters after all.

Sullivan's score echoed the burlesque fun of the script, whether in a rousing song for the pirate king ('Oh, Better Far to Live and Die'), the merry parody of operatic coloratura in Mabel's 'Poor, Wandering One' or her extravagantly dramatic farewell ('Go, Ye Heroes') to the countermelodied police forces, off to die in battle. In line with

HMS Pinafore, there was a wordful self-descriptive set-piece for Stanley ('I Am the Very Model of a Modern Major General), introducing himself much as Sir Joseph Porter had done in the earlier show, a lugubrious comic number for the Sergeant of Police (Fred Clifton), a song of confession for Ruth, the successor of Little Buttercup's confession from the previous show ('When Frederic Was a Little Lad'), and some rather less parodic material for Frederic and Mabel, initiating their romance whilst Mabel's sisters gossip tactfully about the weather, or, in particular bidding each other farewell with seeming sincerity before Frederic is forced to change sides again ('Ah! Leave Me Not to Pine Alone'). The whole was topped by ensemble and chorus music in turn pretty, parodic and atmospheric.

Produced under the management of Richard D'Oyly Carte, now acting as an independent producer for the first time after his battles with his consortium of backers over *Pinafore*, *The Pirates* was mounted almost simultaneously in New York and in Britain, in order to protect the copyright of the piece in both countries. But the continuing run of *HMS Pinafore* at the London Opera Comique meant that whilst a first-class production was staged on Broadway (with the cast given above), the British end was secured by a mocked-up approximation of the show put on at Paignton, Devon, by one of Carte's touring companies. It took place, because of the time difference, slightly before the other, so Richard Mansfield (Stanley), Emilie Petrelli (Mabel), Lyn Cadwaladr (Frederic) and Federici (King), in theory, 'created' their rôles.

The Pirates of Penzance was a great hit in New York, but some uncharacteristic mismanagement by Carte meant that its Broadway run was a messy one, in three different theatres over five months. But by the time it closed and the myriad of companies around America which had coined a fortune on *Pinafore* had leaped onto the firmly in-copyright *The Pirates of Penzance*, Carte had opened his London version with a lead cast made up largely of the *Pinafore* veterans for whom the rôles in its successor had been conceived. Grossmith was Stanley, Richard Temple the Pirate King and tenor George Power played Frederic. There was a pretty new soprano called Marian Hood to play Mabel, Emily Cross stepped in to play Ruth when *Pinafore*'s Harriet Everard was injured by falling scenery in rehearsal, and Rutland Barrington, who hadn't been included in the plan, asked for and got the rôle of the Police Sergeant.

The Pirates of Penzance repeated its Broadway success in London (3 April 1880), playing exactly a year and 363 performances at the Opera Comique before giving place to the next Gilbert and Sullivan show, and thereafter it had an uneventfully successful life as a prominent part of Carte's repertoire, being toured incessantly and brought back for regular revivals by his principal London-based company. The rest of the English-speaking world also snapped up the new Gilbert and Sullivan show and Australia's J C Williamson introduced his production, without the unlawful challenges he had suffered on *HMS Pinafore*, in 1881. James South was the Major General, Armes Beaumont played Frederic and Josephine Deakin/Elsa May Mabel whilst J C Williamson himself played the Sergeant of Police, soon joined by his wife, Maggie Moore, in the rôle of Ruth. *The Pirates of Penzance*

came a huge Australian favourite and was revived
gularly over the next century.

Like the bulk of Gilbert and Sullivan's works, *The
rates of Penzance* got little exposure in any language but its
vn but, following the success of *The Mikado* in Austria,
chard Genée and Camillo Walzell did the piece over into
erman for the Theater an der Wien. It proved to have
ne of the attractions for Austrian audiences that the
iental piece had, and was played only 16 times.

The show was given a major re-lease of life in 1980
nen the New York Shakespeare Festival produced an
inhibitedly high-spirited version of the piece which, in
ite of tacking in some unfortunate outcuts and clumsily
terpolating two numbers from other shows, stayed fairly
ose to Gilbert's text. The music was partly reorchestrated
r a modern band whilst retaining the spirit of the
iginal. With Linda Ronstadt (Mabel), George Rose
tanley), Rex Smith (Frederic) and Kevin Kline (Pirate
ng) in the leading rôles, this production played 787
rformances on Broadway – the longest run anywhere
d ever of a Gilbert and Sullivan show – and was
produced at London's Theatre Royal, Drury Lane, with
mela Stephenson, George Cole, Michael Praed and
m Curry with similar success (601 performances) before
ing taken up around the world. It was also filmed, toured
itain endlessly and got a further London season, at the
lladium with Bonnie Langford (Mabel) and Paul
icholas (Pirate King) starred, whilst the original version –
th no royalties attached – continued to be played
sewhere.

stralia: Theatre Royal, Sydney 19 March 1881; Austria:
 Theater an der Wien *Die Piraten* 1 March 1889; Germany:
 Düsseldorf 1 December 1936; Film: (new version) 1982

XLEY, Frank (b Richfield, Ohio, 21 November 1867;
 San Diego, 30 December 1919). Librettist to some of
 e happiest early American comic operas.

Chicago journalist Pixley is said to have been respon-
ble, in his earliest days in the theatre, for an uncredited
nericanizing' of Owen Hall's text for *Florodora*, but he
ade his first original contribution to the musical theatre
nen he teamed with composer Gustave Luders to write
e musical comedy *King Dodo*. The pair were initially
able to find a producer for this piece, but a second
fort, *The Burgomaster*, was a major Chicago success, had a
ief Broadway run, and proved highly popular on tour,
ading to *King Dodo* being snapped up by Henry Savage to
llow a similar path.

The third Luders/Pixley work, *The Prince of Pilsen*,
rned out to be their best and their most successful. This
ne even Broadway took notice of the happily American-
ontinental comic opera with its fine 'Stein Song' and its
etty 'The Message of the Violet' and the piece, certainly
e of the best of early American comic operas, not only
ed out many years on the road but returned for revivals
d even travelled to London and to Paris with some
ccess.

This success prompted a call east from Florenz Ziegfeld
r Luders, but he continued to work with the Chicago-
sed Pixley and the pair turned out a further, if more
nited, success in the pretty fantasy *Woodland* (83 per-
rmances). The last of the team's shows, Klaw and

Erlanger's production of the old-fashioned Hawaiian tale
of the balloon-blown American who becomes *The Grand
Mogul* (40 performances), Louise Gunning's impersonation of *Marcelle* (68 performances) and the disastrous *The
Gypsy* (12 performances) which looked far enough back in
time to base its plot on a baby-swap – all built on the same
format of old-fashioned comedy and pretty straightforward
songs – did progressively less well and, after the thorough
failure of *The Gypsy*, Pixley retired from the theatre and
devoted his writing talents to cinematic screenplays. He
died in San Diego as the consequence of a fall aboard a
steamship.

1900 **The Burgomaster** (Gustave Luders) Dearborn Theater,
 Chicago 17 June; Manhattan Theater 31 December
1901 **King Dodo** (Luders) Chicago; Daly's Theater 12 May
 1902
1902 **The Prince of Pilsen** (Luders) Tremont Theater, Boston
 May; Broadway Theater 17 March 1903
1904 **Woodland** (Luders) Tremont Theater, Boston 25 April;
 New York Theater 21 November
1906 **The Grand Mogul** (Luders) Colonial Theater, Chicago 7
 December; New Amsterdam Theater 25 March 1907
1908 **Marcelle** (Luders) Casino Theater 1 October
1912 **The Gypsy** (Luders) Park Theater 14 November

PLAIN AND FANCY Musical in 2 acts by Joseph
Stein and Will Glickman. Lyrics by Arnold B Horwitt.
Music by Albert Hague. Mark Hellinger Theater, New
York, 27 January 1955.

A musical set amongst the Amish community of Pennsylvania, *Plain and Fancy* did not make foolish fun of the
virtues of the simple life as some turn-of-the-century
musicals had done with, for example, the Quaker way of
life, even if it presented it as a quaint and picturesque
contrast to modern American mores. That modern way of
life was represented by Dan (Richard Derr) and Ruth
(Shirl Conway) who come to Pennsylvania to sell Dan's
farm to Papa Yoder (Stefan Schnabel). The farm will be a
dowry for Papa's daughter Katie (Gloria Marlowe) who is
to be married to Ezra Reber (Douglas Fletcher Rodgers).
But Ezra's brother, Katie's childhood sweetheart Peter
(David Daniels), who was cast out of the community for
failing its standards, returns and, saving Ezra from a disgrace fuelled by the alcohol introduced into the house
by the outsiders, wins Katie for himself. Barbara Cook
appeared as soubrette Hilda who ventures into the 'real'
world as represented by a local fair, and returns wiser and,
fortunately, not sadder.

The show's highlight came in a representation of an
Amish barn-raising and its most successful musical
moment in Peter and Katie's duet, reminiscing over the
days when they were 'Young and Foolish'. The song
became a hit-parade success and the show played through
a fine 461 Broadway performances. A London production,
mounted under the management of music publishers
Chappell and theatre-owner Prince Littler, teamed Derr
and Miss Conway with Grace O'Connor (Katie), Malcolm
Keen (Yoder) and Jack Drummond (Peter) through a disappointing, forced run of 315 performances.

UK: Theatre Royal, Drury Lane 25 January 1956
Recordings: original cast (Capitol, EMI), London cast (part
 record) (Dot, Oriole, WRC).

PLANCHÉ, James Robinson (b London 27 February 1796; d London 30 May 1880).

The prolific author of all kinds of musical entertainments from operas (many of which were adaptations or pastiches of Continental pieces) and music dramas (sic) to operetta, burletta, musical farce and extravaganza on the one theatrical hand, and pantomimes, dramas and comedies on the other, Planché has survived as the name to grab on to in the English-language light-musical theatre of the first half of the 19th century.

His first staged work was a burlesque, *Amoroso, King of Little Britain*, but in the more than a decade following, the operatic world held most of his attention. Amongst a vast list of writings, he adapted Scott's *Guy Mannering* as the text for William Reeve's *The Witch of Derncleugh* (1821), provided texts for the 'operatic drama' *The Pirate* (1822) and Henry Bishop's *Maid Marian, or the Huntress of Arlingford* (1822), the lyrics for *Clari, or the Maid of Milan* (1823) and *Cortez, or the Conquest of Mexico* (1823), wrote the original English libretto for Weber's *Oberon* (1826, 'Ocean, Thou Mighty Monster'), did English versions of Auber's *La Neige* (*The Frozen Lake*, 1824), *Le Maçon* (*The Mason of Buda*, 1828), *L'Ambassadrice* (*Manoeuvring*, 1829), *La Fiancée* (*The National Guard*, 1830), *Le Philtre* (*The Love Charm, or the Village Coquette*, 1831) and *Gustavus III* (1833), adapted Marschner's *Der Vampyr* (1829), Rossini's *Guilliame Tell* as *Hofer or Tell of the Tyrol* (1830), Hérold's *Le Pré aux Clercs* as *The Court Masque* (1833), Marliani's *Il Bravo* as *The Red Mask*, and wrote the English versions of *The Marriage of Figaro*, Rossini's *The Siege of Corinth*, *Norma*, *The Magic Flute* and *Der Freischütz*.

Planché provided texts, original, borrowed or adapted for a series of burlettas, burlesques and extravaganzas with pasticcio scores, but made his historical mark when he co-wrote the classical burlesque *Olympic Revels* (1831 w Charles Dance) which set in motion a highly successful series of extravaganzas which, interspersed with such revues as *The Drama's Levée, or a Peep at the Past* (1838), *The Drama at Home* (1844), *The New Planet, Mr Buckstone's Ascent of Parnassus, The Camp at the Olympic* (1853), *Mr Buckstone's Voyage Round the Globe* (1854) and *The New Haymarket Spring Meeting* (1855), were mounted initially at the Olympic Theatre and later at the Haymarket and the Lyceum.

Planché's principal fame, however, was won by his poetic stage musical adaptations of classic tales and, above all, of the fairy stories of the French canon, which he also translated in book form. Pieces such as *Fortunio, or The Seven Gifted Servants, The Fair One with the Golden Locks, The Golden Fleece, The Invisible Prince, The King of the Peacocks* and *The Prince of Happy Land* were played throughout the English-speaking world and revived regularly in Britain, America and Australia, the most celebrated of them holding a place in the repertoire even through that later and great period of extravaganza and burlesque writing in the middle years of the 19th century, during which authors such as the Brough brothers, a'Beckett and, later, Byron and Burnand flooded the stage with works based on similar areas of literature.

In his later years, Planché was responsible for the original English version of Offenbach's *Orphée aux enfers* and provided the lyrics for Dion Boucicault's huge imitation of the French grand opéra-bouffe féerie, *Babil and Bijou*, at Covent Garden.

A number of his non-musical pieces were subsequently adapted to the musical stage by other writers. The 1875 Alhambra extravaganza bouffe *Spectresheim* was based on his *A Romantic Idea*, the 1892 comic opera *The Duke's Diversion* on *The Follies of a Night* and Bucalossi's 1894 light opera *Massaroni* on his *The Brigand*.

1818 **Amoroso, King of Little Britain** (arr Tom Cooke) 1 act Theatre Royal, Drury Lane 21 April

1819 **The Caliph and the Cadi, or Rumbles in Baghdad** 1 act Sadlers Wells Theatre 16 August

1819 **Fancy's Sketch, or Look Before You Leap** Adelphi Theatre 29 October

1819 **Odds and Ends, or Which is the Manager?** 1 act Adelphi Theatre 19 November

1820 **A Burletta of Errors, or Jupiter and Alcmena** Adelphi Theatre 6 November

1820 **Who's to Father Me?, or What's Bred in the Bone Won't Come Out in the Flesh** Adelphi Theatre 13 November

1820 **The Deuce is in Her, or Two Nights at Madrid** Adelphi Theatre 27 November

1821 **Giovanni the Vampire, or How Shall We Get Rid of Him?** Adelphi Theatre 15 January

1821 **Lodgings to Let** Adelphi Theatre 19 February

1821 **Half an Hour's Courtship, or Le Chambre à coucher** 1 act Adelphi Theatre 27 February

1821 **Sherwood Forest, or The Merry Archers** Adelphi Theatre 12 March

1821 **Capers at Canterbury** Adelphi Theatre 1 October

1821 **Love's Alarum** Adelphi Theatre 8 November

1822 **(Henri IV and) the Fair Gabrielle** (Barham Livius) 1 act English Opera House (Lyceum) 5 September

1823 **I Will Have a Wife** (William Reeve) English Opera House (Lyceum) 7 August

1825 **Success, or A Hit if You Like It** 1 act Adelphi Theatre 12 December

1827 **Pay to My Order, or A Chaste Salute** 1 act Royal Gardens, Vauxhall 9 July

1827 **The Rencontre, or Love Will Find a Way** (Henry Bishop) Theatre Royal, Haymarket 12 July

1828 **Paris and London, or A Trip Across the Herring Pond** Adelphi Theatre 21 January

1828 **The Green Eyed Monster** Theatre Royal, Haymarket 18 August

1829 **Theirna-na-oge, or The Prince of the Lakes** (Cooke) Theatre Royal, Drury Lane 20 April

1831 **Olympic Revels, or Prometheus and Pandora** (w Charles Dance) Olympic Theatre 3 January

1831 **Olympic Devils, or Orpheus and Eurydice** (w Dance) Olympic Theatre 26 December

1832 **The Paphian Bower, or Venus and Adonis** (w Dance) Olympic Theatre 26 December

1833 **Promotion, or A Morning in Versailles in 1750** Olympic Theatre 18 February

1833 **The Students of Jena, or The Family Concert** (*La Table et le Logement*) English version (Theatre Royal, Drury Lane)

1833 **High, Low, Jack and the Game, or The Card Party** 1 act (w Dance) Olympic Theatre 30 September

1833 **The Deep, Deep Sea, or Perseus and Andromeda** (w Dance) Olympic Theatre 26 December

1834 **The Loan of a Lover** 1 act Olympic Theatre 29 September

1834 **My Friend the Governor** 1 act Olympic Theatre 29 September

1834 **Telemachus, or The Island of Calypso** w C Dance 1 act Olympic Theatre 26 December

1835 **The Court Beauties** 1 act Olympic Theatre 14 March

1836 **The Two Figaros** (*Les Deux Figaro*) Olympic Theatre 30 November

1836 **Riquet with the Tuft** (w Dance) 1 act Olympic Theatre 26 December
1837 **A New Servant** 1 act Olympic Theatre 29 September
1837 **Puss in Boots** (w Dance) Olympic Theatre 26 December
1839 **Blue Beard** (w Dance) 1 act Olympic Theatre 2 January
1840 **The Sleeping Beauty in the Wood** Theatre Royal, Covent Garden 20 April
1841 **Beauty and the Beast** Theatre Royal, Covent Garden 12 April
1842 **The White Cat** (arr J H Tully) Theatre Royal, Covent Garden 28 March
1842 **The Follies of a Night** (Cooke) Theatre Royal, Drury Lane 5 October
1843 **Fortunio, or The Seven Gifted Servants** Theatre Royal, Drury Lane 17 April
1843 **The Fair One with the Golden Locks** 1 act Theatre Royal, Haymarket 26 December
1844 **Graciosa and Percinet** 1 act Theatre Royal, Haymarket 26 December
1845 **The Golden Fleece, or Jason and Medea** Theatre Royal, Haymarket 24 March
1845 **The Bee and the Orange Tree, or The Four Wishes** 1 act Theatre Royal, Haymarket 26 December
1846 **The Birds of Aristophanes** 1 act Theatre Royal, Haymarket 18 April
1846 **The Invisible Prince, or The Island of Tranquil Delights** 1 act Theatre Royal, Haymarket 26 December
1847 **The Golden Branch** Theatre Royal, Lyceum 27 December
1848 **Theseus and Ariadne, or The Marriage of Bacchus** Theatre Royal, Lyceum 25 April
1848 **The King of the Peacocks** Theatre Royal, Lyceum 26 December
1849 **The Seven Champions of Christendom** Theatre Royal, Lyceum 9 April
1849 **The Island of Jewels** (arr J H Tully) Theatre Royal, Lyceum 26 December
1850 **Cymon and Iphigenia** (arr Michael Arne/David Garrick ad) 1 act Theatre Royal, Lyceum 1 April
1850 **King Charming, or The Blue Bird of Paradise** Theatre Royal, Lyceum 26 December
1851 **The Queen of the Frogs** Theatre Royal, Lyceum 21 April
1851 **The Prince of Happy Land, or The Fawn in the Forest** Theatre Royal, Lyceum 26 December
1852 **The Good Woman in the Wood** Theatre Royal, Lyceum 27 December
1853 **Once Upon a Time There Were Two Kings** Theatre Royal, Lyceum 26 December
1854 **The Yellow Dwarf, and the King of the Gold Mines** 1 act Olympic Theatre 26 December
1855 **The Discreet Princess, or Three Glass Distaffs** 1 act Olympic Theatre 26 December
1856 **Young and Handsome** 1 act Olympic Theatre 26 December
1859 **Love and Fortune** 1 act Princess's Theatre 24 September
1865 **Orpheus in the Haymarket** (*Orphée aux enfers*) English version (Theatre Royal, Haymarket)
1871 **King Christmas** 1 act Gallery of Illustration 26 December
1872 **Babil and Bijou** (Hervé, Frederic Clay, Jules Rivière et al/Dion Boucicault) Theatre Royal, Covent Garden 29 August

Autobiography: *Recollections and Reflections* (Tinsley Bros, London, 1872)

PLANQUETTE, [Jean] Robert (b Paris, 31 March 1848; d Paris, 28 January 1903). One of the foremost composers of Parisian opérette in the last decades of the 19th century.

Born in Paris of Norman stock, Planquette attended the Paris Conservatoire, but he left after one year of study and, still in his teens, launched himself into the world of popular song-writing. He performed a number of his works himself, working in the cafés-concerts as a vocalist at the piano, but he had his first memorable success when Lucien Fugère introduced his march song 'Le Régiment de Sambre-et-Meuse' at the Ba-ta-clan in 1867. Over the next decade, beyond a steady supply of songs, he produced a handful of little opérettes and musical monologues (*La Confession de Rosette*, *On demande une femme de chambre* performed by Judic) for the cafés-concerts, and eased himself into a theatrical production for the first time with the production of the one-acter *Paille d'avoine* at the Délassements-Comique. Finally Louis Cantin, the manager of the Théâtre des Folies-Dramatiques, gave in to the persistent plugging of Pierre Véron, the editor of the journal *Charivari* and Planquette's sometime librettist and permanent champion, and gave the composer the opportunity to see his first full-length opérette mounted at a major theatre. *Les Cloches de Corneville*, with its lively, colourful and catchy score, won a horrified response from the more snobbish elements of the French musical establishment, glued squarely in the formalities of yesteryear, but a delighted one from the theatre-going public which gave it a long Paris run and a permanent place in the forefront of the French opérette repertoire as it went on to establish a European and overseas record which, in the 19th century, made it the most popular French work of its age.

The works with which Planquette followed his great triumph did not evoke the same extravagant response, but they did not do too badly. *Les Voltigeurs de la 32ème*, a military opérette produced amongst the series of Lecocq pieces at the Théâtre de la Renaissance, with that theatre's resident star, Jeanne Granier, in its lead rôle, racked up 73 performances and *La Cantinière*, another piece on a military theme, with Berthelier, Brasseur and Léa Silly featured, managed 80, before both pieces went on to other productions in other countries. Planquette's second major hit, however, was not long in coming. The British producer Alexander Henderson, who had made a fortune out of the record-breaking run of *Les Cloches de Corneville* in London, commissioned Planquette to write the score for a musical version of the Rip van Winkle story, which he and his inseparable librettist, Henry Farnie, were preparing as a vehicle for the young singing comedian Fred Leslie. Planquette left Paris and took lodgings in London, and there turned out the made-to-measure score for a *Rip van Winkle* which proved one of the most successful British productions of its time, both at home and abroad. A second collaboration with Farnie and Henderson produced a *Nell Gwynne* which, if its London run was a little disappointing, nevertheless went round the world, and did very much better than the composer's next Paris endeavour, a disastrous piece called *La Cremaillère* which had been co-written by Albert Brasseur, the son of the manager of the Nouveautés, and was played there for just a handful of performances.

The Parisian success of *Rip* (shorn of his van Winkle) in 1884 and an indifferent hometown run for a version of *La Princesse Colombine* (*Nell Gwynne*) preceded another fine success for the composer with a swashbuckling, comical opérette about the buccaneer *Surcouf* (1887), and

Planquette hit the target simultaneously on the other side of the Channel when Farnie, deprived of his fashionable collaborator when Planquette returned to France after *Nell Gwynne*, turned out a heavily reorganized version of *Les Voltigeurs de la 32ème*, which had never been seen in English in Britain, under the title *The Old Guard*. The remake proved enormously popular, *The Old Guard* trouped Britain and the colonies for many years, and Farnie engaged himself in doing a similar job on *Surcouf*. As he had for *The Old Guard*, Planquette supplied such extra music as was deemed necessary, and the result was an almost new opérette called *Paul Jones* which, mounted by the newly-set-up Carl Rosa Light Opera Company, proved another long-lived success for its librettist and for its composer, who was finding that his works were, in fact, more successful in Britain than they were in his home country. The run of big London successes, however, came to an end when the Carl Rosa production of *Captain Thérèse* (originally written in French, by Alexandre Bisson, and adapted not by Farnie but by the less popular-touched F C Burnand) lasted a comparatively indifferent 104 performances on its British production and failed totally in Paris.

Amongst the composer's subsequent Paris productions, *Le Talisman* (130 performances) and *Mam'zelle Quat' sous* both had good home runs and, like the posthumously completed *Le Paradis de Mahomet* (1906), found productions outside France, but they did not equal the popularity of the happiest of his previous pieces, of which *Les Cloches de Corneville*, in particular, and *Rip* and *Surcouf* less prominently, have remained in the French repertoire in the century and more since their composition.

It has been repeatedly written that Planquette's music was that of a popular songwriter (understood, as opposed to the more soigné work of his theatrical contemporaries), that he was obliged to have his orchestrations done by others, and that he borrowed melodies from and/or was reminiscent of his famous predecessors (a comment which scarcely fitted with the first accusation). Looking at his scores alongside the more successful shows of his contemporaries, in a Parisian theatre world in which many a Prix de Rome winner and star Conservatoire pupil had failed to make a memorable career, the first is scarcely obvious, unless tunefulness is regarded as the preserve of 'popular song'; the second is hardly a crime to a listening public; and the third no more provable in his case than in all the others. Planquette quite simply caught the mood of his time, wrote some of the most enjoyable show music of his era, and had the hits to prove it.

Amongst the foreign remakes of his shows, Planquette's most curious credit was undoubtedly one which came from America. The 1916 musical play *The Amber Express*, for which the score was apparently largely written by Zoel Parenteau, credited him as having composed it 'with R Planquette'. A difficult feat, 13 years after the composer's death, but *The Amber Express* didn't make sufficient impression for Planquette's contribution to be able now to be evaluated.

1872 **Méfie-toi de Pharaon** (Germain Villemer, Lucien Delormel) 1 act Eldorado 12 October
1874 **Le Serment de Madame Grégoire** (Louis Péricaud, Delormel) 1 act Eldorado 12 October
1874 **Paille d'avoine** (Lemonnier, Adolphe Jaime, Rozale) 1 act Délassements-Comiques 12 March

1875 **Le Zénith** (Adolphe Perreau) 1 act Eldorado 24 April
1875 **Le Valet de cœur** (Péricaud, Delormel) 1 act Alcazar 1 August
1875 **Le Clé du sérail** (?w Frédéric Barbier/Mathieu, Fuchs) 1 act Alcazar 1 August
1876 **Le Péage** (Émile André) 1 act Théâtre de la Porte Saint-Martin 21 October
1877 **Les Cloches de Corneville** (Clairville, Charles Gabet) Folies-Dramatiques 19 April
1879 **Le Chevalier Gaston** (Pierre Véron) 1 act Monte-Carlo 3 March
1880 **Les Voltigeurs de la 32ème** (Edmond Gondinet, Georges Duval) Théâtre de la Renaissance 7 January
1880 **La Cantinière** (Paul Burani, Félix Ribeyre) Théâtre des Nouveautés 26 October
1881 **Les Chevaux-légers** (Péricaud, Delormel) 1 act Eldorado 15 December
1882 **Rip van Winkle** (H B Farnie) Comedy Theatre, London 14 October
1884 **Nell Gwynne** (Farnie) Avenue Theatre, London 7 February
1885 **La Cremaillère** (Burani, Albert Brasseur) Théâtre des Nouveautés 28 November
1887 **Surcouf** (Henri Chivot, Albert Duru) Théâtre des Folies-Dramatiques 6 October
1887 **The Old Guard** revised English version of *Les Voltigeurs de la 32ème* by Farnie (Avenue Theatre, London)
1889 **Paul Jones** revised English version of *Surcouf* by Farnie (Prince of Wales Theatre, London)
1890 **Captain Thérèse** (Gilbert a' Beckett, F C Burnand/Alexandre Bisson ad Burnand) Prince of Wales Theatre, London 25 August
1892 **La Cocarde tricolore** (Maurice Ordonneau) Théâtre des Folies-Dramatiques 12 February
1893 **Le Talisman** (Adolphe d'Ennery, Burani) Théâtre de la Gaîté 20 January
1895 **Les Vingt-huit Jours de Champignolette** (Burani) Théâtre de la République 17 September
1895 **Panurge** (Henri Meilhac, Albert de Saint-Albin) Théâtre de la Gaîté 22 November
1896 **La Leçon de danse** (Mlle Mariquita) 1 act Théâtre de la Gaîté 9 April
1897 **Mam'zelle Quat' Sous** (Antony Mars, Maurice Desvallières) Théâtre de la Gaîté 5 November
1906 **Le Paradis de Mahomet** (completed by Louis Ganne/Henri Blondeau) 14 May Théâtre des Variétés

Other title credited: *Le Fiancé de Margot*

PLAYFAIR, Nigel (Sir) (b London, 1 July 1875; d London, 19 August 1934).

Barrister turned actor Playfair appeared, in the early part of his career, in London's ill-fated production of *Madame Sherry* and in the revue *Pell Mell* in a life otherwise conducted almost wholly in the non-musical theatre.

In 1918 he took over the management of the Lyric Theatre, Hammersmith and was there responsible for a 1920 production of *The Beggar's Opera* which won a memorable success and prompted him to mount (and often play in) further versions of ballad operas and 18th-century musical plays (*Lionel and Clarissa*, *Love in a Village*, *Polly*, *The Duenna*). He also produced several original, but less successful, musical shows (*Midsummer Madness*, *Tantivy Towers*, *The Fountain of Youth*, *Derby Day*), a badly mangled remake of *La Vie parisienne*, and the admired revue *Riverside Nights*, before retiring from management in 1932.

LEASE, TEACHER! Musical comedy in 2 acts by
R G Brown, R P Weston and Bert Lee. Lyrics by
'eston and Lee. Music by Jack Waller and Joseph Tun-
-idge. London Hippodrome, 2 October 1935.

A successor to Jack Waller's successful *Yes, Madam?*,
ease, Teacher! employed the same writers and most of the
me principal cast as its predecessor. Bobby Howes was
-oke Tommy, masquerading as the explorer brother of
hoolgirl Ann Trent (Sepha Treble) in order to get into
er school (which was once his family home) to look for
ocuments which could bring him an inheritance.
nfortunately Ann's real brother has carried off a sacred
ject from an Oriental shrine, so Tommy has to befuddle
collection of malevolent Chinese as well as headmistress
ertha Belmore, bosomy gym mistress Vera Pearce and
usic master Wylie Watson as he gambols through the
oy's Own Mag plot and jolly songs of the evening.

Former concert party man Watson scored with a self-
companied 'Song of the 'Cello', Howes told Miss Treble
ou Give Me Ideas' and instructed 'Mind How You Go
cross the Road', and there were comedy ensembles in the
urlesque Indian style and for the School Pageant. The
iece was expertly constructed around the Waller team,
d the result was a 301-performance run and a good
uring life (it was seen on the road as late as 1950). The
how was also compressed into a film musical with its four
ars teamed with juvenile girl Rene Ray.

ilm: Associated British 1937

.L.M. Opérette in 3 acts by Rip. Music by Henri
hristiné. Théâtre des Bouffes-Parisiens, Paris, 21 April
925.

The P.L.M. is the Paris–Lyon–Méditerranée – the
rench railways system – and the action of *P.L.M.* actually
kes place in a railway carriage which, when the curtain
oes up, is in Menton station. Rip's text cast the evening's
p-liner, Dranem, as the contrôleur of the train, taking
harge like a meneur de revue of a succession of the kind of
morous events and mistakes of identity that are usually set
a seaside hotel. Dranem's feminine co-star was
Iarguerite Deval, playing the sexually deprived Mme de la
imprenelle who takes advantage of a short-circuit blackout
etween stations to fall into the arms of young Candide
Georgé)...without results! However, the voyage does see
Candide deflowered – by the cocotte Cricri (Suzette O'Nil)
ho had started out the journey as the little bit of fluff of the
inister, Anatole Limacé (Jean Gabin). The youngsters of
e piece were played by Max de Rieux (Pierre Limace) and
Iarie Dubas (Madame's niece, Paule). This pair went
kinny-dipping in the Mediterranean and ended up clad in
ach other's overcoats and unable to change back because
nderneath they were 'tout nus'. Madame de la Pim-
renelle thinks Anatole is the contrôleur, he thinks she is
e cleaning lady, and Dranem nearly ... but nearly ... ends
p having ... if it weren't for an inopportune firecracker in
is pocket going off at the wrong time and bringing
veryone running thinking they have heard gunshots ...

The comicalities and the sexy imbroglios – perhaps
ightly less slick and witty than if they had come from a
3arde or a Willemetz – were accompanied by a typical
Christiné score of songs and ensembles, from which
Dranem's stand-up piece about being 'trop nerveux' (to be
ble to get it up at the right times), his 'On s'y fait' and his

lecture to Candide about his disgraceful behaviour in the
blackout ('Ça ne se fait pas') in NOT taking advantage of a
lady, Mlle Deval's deploring of her husband's lack of
amorous expertise ('J'en veux') and her amazement at her
own uncontrollable and indiscriminate desires ('Mais
qu'est-ce que j'ai?') and the Java duo for the star pair, 'Ça
changerait', all gave their performers splendid opportunities. The two youngsters admitted to being 'Tout nus!',
Dranem took the railway analogies a touch further in 'Mon
coeur est un compartiment' and Candide went on about
'Quand une femme vous court après' amongst the rest of a
jolly, dancing set of jazz-age numbers.

Produced at the Bouffes by Gustave Quinson and
Edmond Roze (also director), the show ran for more than
seven months and added to the heap of 1920s hits already
compiled by its composer and its star.

POCAHONTAS

The (Red) Indian Princess who got herself involved with
an Englishman who said he was called John Smith has
made her way onto the musical stage a number of times.
The most successful of these was a five-scene burlesque
written by American actor-playwright John Brougham,
subtitled *The Gentle Savage* and produced in New York in
1855 (Wallack's Theater, 24 December). Charles Walcot
(Smith) and Georgina Hodson (Po-ca-hon-tas) were the
principals of the tale, with Brougham himself appearing as
the Indian King, Pow-Ha-Tan. The piece was largely a
burlesque of the well-known story, with its dialogue
phrased in parody of Longfellow's 'Hiawatha', but it
served as a movable vehicle for any bits of current, topical
burlesque required. Its songs were made up from popular
tunes in the style of the time. The piece had a two-month
original run at Wallack's, and was revived regularly thereafter whilst going around the English-speaking stages of
the world in a way that no other American burlesque of the
period did.

A version of Brougham's *Po-ca-hon-tas* was given by
William S Lyster's company in Melbourne in 1862 (21
April, music arr Fred Lyster), and Emily Thorne played
the parodied Princess in Britain, but the biggest success on
that side of the Atlantic came when Mrs John Wood,
Brougham's partner on the American stage for some time,
appeared as a jolly, plumpish Indian maid in what was now
called *La Belle Sauvage* (music arr W H Montgomery) at
the St James's Theatre (27 November 1869). The show
now burlesqued the Bancrofts' hit comedy *School*, and took
swipes at various popular papers and at the current controversy on Harriet Beecher Stowe, and included one song
'The Dutchman's Wee Little Dog' (Barton Hill/W H
Montgomery), which became a distinct success as the
burlesque ran up a remarkable series of nearly 200
London performances.

Lillian Russell had the opportunity to play Pocahontas
when her 'husband', Teddy Solomon, composed a comic
opera, to a text by Sydney Grundy, under that title (subtitled *The Great White Pearl*) which she introduced in 1884
at London's Empire Theatre. Frank Celli was her John
Smith, and there was a bundle of comical characters
(Robert Brough, Alice Barnett, Herny Ashley, John L
Shine) to support the soprano and baritone. This *Pocahontas* was a 24-performance flop.

Another, more recent, Indian princess also sank swiftly

when an inept *(Princess) Pocahontas* (Goell) produced at Glasgow (8 October) and brought to London's Lyric, Hammersmith in 1963 (14 November), foundered in 12 nights.

POLENBLUT Operette in 3 scenes by Leo Stein. Music by Oskar Nedbal. Carltheater, Vienna, 25 October 1913.

The most successful of Oskar Nedbal's stage compositions, and the only one which has remained in the played repertoire, *Polenblut* was a bright, uncomplicated Operette, composed to a conventional but lively libretto by Leo Stein (alleged, though not by Stein, to be based on a bit of Pushkin) set in the present day, in city and country Poland.

The estates of the overly high-living Count Boléslaw Baránksi (Karl Pfann) are so run down that the only way for him to restore his fortunes and save his lands is to make a rich marriage. However, he refuses to even meet Hélena, (Mizzi Zwerenz) the daughter of the wealthy but unaristocratic Pan Jan Zarémba (Richard Waldemar), and carries on instead with the ballet girl Wanda (Käthe Ehren) after whom his friend Popiel (Josef König) had been sighing. With the aid of Popiel, the insulted Hélena sets out for revenge. She becomes 'Marynia', Bolo's new housekeeper, and by her sense, thrift and hard work gets him and the farms working and his worthless friends out of the house. When the truth comes out, Bolo has enough sense to realise that Hélena will make a better Countess Baránksi than the ballet girl.

Nedbal's score did not produce any hits, but a colourful set of numbers in the most popular of rhythms – the waltz duos 'Ich seid ein Kavalier' (Bolo/Hélena) and 'Hören Sie, wie es singt und klingt' (Bolo/Wanda), and the big waltz of the second-act finale, 'Mädel, dich hat mir die Glücksfee gebracht', Bolo's marching raptures over Wanda, 'Ich kenn' ein süsses Frauchen' – backed up by some mazurka and polka strains, some touches of what passed for Polish colour, and some fine ensembles of which a comical trio (Hélena/Popiel/Zarémba) in which Helena's father boasts of his tactfulness ('Ich bin ein Diplomate') proved one of the most enjoyable items of the evening.

Produced at Vienna's Carltheater by Sigmund Eiben-schütz, *Polenblut* had a fine first run of 185 performances, before going into the repertoire. It was played frequently in 1914 and 1915, passed its 250th performance on 26 January 1916, and was given regular performances, with Mizzi Zwerenz retaining her rôle of Hélena, at the Carltheater for more than a decade.

Berlin's *Polenblut*, mounted at the Theater des Westens with Käthe Dorsch starred, was also a fine success, whilst in Hungary (ad Andor Gábor) Sári Petráss returned from her overseas starring assignments to play Hélena in a Budapest production, the success of which helped the Király Színház through the difficult early days of the war. However, the same war meant that *Polenblut*, although it won returns in central Europe, did not, by and large, travel further. The one exception was America, where reaction against Germany had not, as in Britain, led to a wholesale rejection of German-language theatre. Comstock and Gest, soon joined by the Shuberts, picked up *Polenblut* and produced it, with some additional numbers by Rudolf Friml, as a vehicle for Emma Trentini. When the show set out from Albany, it was entitled *The Ballet Girl*, said to be adapted from an Hungarian source, and credited wholly to Friml. John Charles Thomas was Bolo, Clifton Crawford was Popiel and Letty Yorke played Wanda. When Trentini and Friml began a professionally disruptive affair, the producers threw out the composer and his songs, but the prima donna (having first got the duo 'The Flame of Love' and ultimately a whole half-dozen of her boyfriend's songs reinstated) had her revenge. When what was now called *The Peasant Girl* (ad Edgar Smith, Harold Atteridge, Herbert Reynolds) proved a hit and she was asked to extend her eight-week Broadway contract, Trentini refused. She was going to Japan with Friml. Her understudy went on and the show ran a further month in New York before touring. The turtle-doves didn't have time to go to Japan before they broke up.

One of the most popular pieces on the German-language stage during and after the First World War, *Polenblut* was filmed in 1934, and subsequently taken into the repertoire of the Volksoper (ad Haberland, 10 October 1954) where it was given a new production in 1986 (1 February) with Kurt Schreibmayer and Mirjana Irosch in the leading rôles.

Germany: Theater des Westens 1913; Hungary: Király Színház *Lengyelvér* 22 December 1914; USA: 44th Street Theater *The Peasant Girl* 2 March 1915; Film: Carl Lamac 1934
Recordings: selection (Ariola/Philips)

LA POLKA DES LAMPIONS Comédie musicale in 2 acts by Marcel Achard taken from the screenplay *Some Like it Hot*. Music by Gérard Calvi. Théâtre du Châtelet, Paris, 20 December 1961.

A French stage musical version of *Some Like it Hot*, produced at the Théâtre du Châtelet with Georges Guétary (Charles Courtois) and Jean Richard (Blaise Charignon) playing French versions of the two lads disguised by the necessity to earn a living as members of a ladies' orchestra, and Nicole Broissin (pianist Nicole) and Annie Duparc (conductor Marie Prévost) in the principal female rôles.

The piece went somewhat against the Châtelet's reputation for romantic costume opérette à grand spectacle, but even if the period was the unusually recent 1920s and the

Plate 211. **Polenblut:** *Gerti Gordon and Melanie Holliday in the Vienna Volksoper production.*

tting Deauville and other French venues, there was a
od Châtelet total of 20 scenes in the way of spectacle, as
ell as a lively singing and dancing score including Mlle
oissin's 'Enfin, voici l'amour', the boys' conviction that
a ira demain', their Prohibition Tango, a 'Cha-cha-
arleston' and a polka title song for Mlle Duparc, and a
gular ration of tenor numbers ('Marie et Charles',
uelle qu'elles soient' etc) for Guétary.

La Polka des lampions proved a fine success and, with a
cord of 534 performances in its vast auditorium, it outran
Broadway alter ego, *Sugar*, as it rang in the centenary of
e famous theatre.

cording: original cast (Pathé)

OLLY

The passion for using girls' names as the titles for musi-
l shows from *Dafne* to *Evita* has, not unnaturally, resulted
one or two of these names being given more than one
ow. Polly has had (at least) three. The first of these was
hn Gay's musequel to *The Beggar's Opera* which pro-
oted Miss Peachum (or Mrs Macheath as she now was)
the title. Originally banned in 1728 as being of too
tirical' a nature, *Polly* ultimately made it to the stage,
arly 50 years after it had been written, at the Haymarket
heatre in 1777, and it flopped. It was nevertheless
ought back for revivals in 1782 and in 1813 at Drury
ane and, following the great success of the 1920 *Beggar's
pera* revival in London, it was given two rival productions
1922, one at Chelsea (mus Hubert Bath, Norman Slee)
d the other at the Kingsway Theatre (ad Clifford Bax, 30
ecember) with Lilian Davies as Polly. Olde Englishe was
early fashionable, for this time the latter version of the
ece stayed 324 performances. It was subsequently given
New York's Cherry Lane Theater (10 October 1925)
ith Dorothy Brown in the name part. New York took olde
nglande's attitude and *Polly* folded in a month.

The second *Polly*, subtitled *The Pet of the Regiment*, was a
mic opera by James Mortimer, with music by Edward
olomon, produced at the Novelty Theatre, London 4
ctober 1884. Lillian Russell was Polly, orphan mascot of
regiment and, apparently, the illegitimate daughter of the
eneral's unmarried sister. When it turns out she actually
n't, she can marry her Private Mangel, who is – would
u credit it – actually a Prince. Teetering on the edge of
rlesque and of the Gilberty and Sullivanish, *Polly* (with
e help of Miss Russell's hit song, borrowed from
olomon's last flop *Lord Bateman*, 'The Silver Line') had a
-performance run in London, and played 79 Broadway
rformances for J C Scanlan and E E Rice (Casino
heater 17 April 1885).

Having hosted two foreign *Polly*s, Broadway finally
rought out its own. *Polly* Mark III was a musical version of
uy Bolton and George Middleton's successful play *Polly
ith a Past* (Belasco Theater, 6 September 1917, 315 per-
rmances). Lyrics by Irving Caesar and music by Phil
harig and Herbert Stothart, however, did nothing to
nsure Polly a future as well as a past and Arthur
lammerstein's production (Lyric Theater, New York, 8
nuary 1929) with June as Polly folded in 15 perform-
nces. Two preceding American Pollys, *Polly of the Circus*,
largaret Mayo's own adaptation of her successful 1907
lay (Liberty Theater, 23 December, 160 performances)
t with Hugo Felix music which stopped short of New

York, and *Polly of Hollywood*, another little lassie who went
into films in a Harry Cort production (Cohan Theater 21
February 1927), but only for 24 nights, didn't help to lift
the *Polly*-average.

POLNISCHE WIRTSCHAFT Vaudeville-Posse in 3
acts by Kurt Kraatz and Georg Okonkowski. Lyrics by
Alfred Schönfeld. Music by Jean Gilbert. Stadttheater,
Cottbus, 26 December 1909; Thalia-Theater, Berlin, 6
August 1910.

The first collaboration of playwright Okonkowski and
composer Gilbert, and both the playwright's and the composer's first big success, *Polnische Wirtschaft* was produced
at Cottbus at the end of 1909, scoring an enormous hit
which resulted in its making its way in the new year to
Berlin's Thalia-Theater.

The libretto bundled together many familiar and farcical
elements, from the musical-comedy will to a comedian in
women's clothes, but the mixture proved a well-made and
extremely successful one. Polish Marga Hegewaldt,
heiress to the Gross-Karschau estates, and her husband
Willy are paid an annual legacy as long as they remain
happily married. They haven't been so for five years, but
each year they go lovingly together to pick up the cash. The
Graf Kasimir Schofinsky, who stands to gain if Marga fails,
watches their every move. And he has something to watch,
for the now-liberated Marga is not only pursued by an
aviator called Fritz Sperling, she has also had a little
adventure with a certain 'Herr Krause', whilst Willy has
lined up a second wealthy wife in Erika Mangelsdorf,
whose father is actually the pretended 'Herr Krause'. In

Plate 212. **Polnische Wirtschaft**: *'Und die Clarinette spielt: Di-
didi-da ...'* Helene Ballot and Arnold Rieck in the Thalia-Theater's hit
production of Gilbert's musical comedy.

fact, though each of this pair thinks the other wealthy, neither is. Add a blackmailing photographer to the proceedings, and the legacy looks thoroughly threatened. All comes right, however, when Marga and Willy fall back in love and Erika and their funny friend Hans, who inherits a fortune in timely fashion, find they are made for each other. The second and third acts were made up largely of farcical comedy with 'Herr Krause' avoiding recognition in Polish disguise, and Hans dressed up as a girl to flirt with Willy and thus make Erika go off his rival.

Gilbert's score favoured waltz rhythms – Mangelsdorf leading a 3/4 trio in praise of Berlin ('Wie schön bist du, Berlin'), Hans and Erika's Dorfmusik waltz ('Es bläst ein Trompeter') with its imitation of orchestral instruments, and the duo for Willy and Marga 'Wer kann dafür?' – but the first act ended with a big march number as everyone decided to go off to the funfair ('Komm, mein Schatz, in den Lunapark') and Erika and Hans shared a comical last act Rheinländer-Couplet 'Männe, hak' mir 'mal die Taille auf' in contrast.

Jean Kren, manager of the Thalia and a successful playwright, added his own touches and his name to the authorial credits before *Polnische Wirtschaft* opened at his theatre, his partner Alfred Schönfeld re-staged the show, Emil Sondermann (Mangelsdorf), Arnold Rieck (Hans), Lotte Reinecken (Auguste, the maid), Helene Ballot (Erika), Eugenie della Donna (Marga), Fritz Junkermann (Fritz Sperling) and Paul Bechert (Willy) headed the cast, and among them all they turned up a major hit. *Polnische Wirtschaft* ran at the Thalia until the next Gilbert Posse, *Autoliebchen*, was ready to take its place a year and a half later. It was revived in 1918 (December 6) for a three-month season, during which time it passed its 700th Berlin performance (21 February 1919). A favourite for many years and through many productions in Germany (during which time the score became decorated with such favourite Gilbert numbers from other sources as *Puppchen*'s 'Puppchen, du bist mein Augenstern!' and *Autoliebchen*'s 'Ja, das haben die Mädchen so gerne'), the show had, considering the worldwide exposure of Gilbert's almost contemporary *Die keusche Susanne*, a curiously limited life outside that country.

Austria, of course, took the Berlin hit up quickly, and it was played (as *Tolle Wirtschaft* – the marriage was now 'mad' instead of 'Polish') first by the Thalia-Theater company at the Lustspieltheater, complete with almost all its original stars, and then in a local production at Ronacher. Frln Ballot was again Erika, alongside Käthe Krenn (Marga), Ferdinand Stein (Willy), Gustav Müller (Mangelsdorf), Karl König (Hans) and director Karl Tuschl (Graf Kasimir). Nowhere, however, did the show win the success it had found at home. In Hungary, where Jenő Farago's localized adaptation turned the hit waltz about Berlin into 'Ah, ilyen Budapest' and Willy and Marga pinched the Rheinländer, *Lengyel menyecske* caused no great stir, whilst in America a version adapted by George V Hobart, peppered with additional numbers by Jerome Kern, produced by George M Cohan and Sam Harris, and with Valli Valli (Marga), Mathilde Cottrelly (Gabrielle), Sydney Bracy (Rudolf) and Armand Kalisch (Willy) featured, made it to the Grand Opera House, Chicago (8 September 1912) but not to New York. The show was never seen in London or Paris.

Another piece under the title of *Polnische Wirtschaft* written by Richard Genée and Moritz West, with music by Hermann Zumpe, had been previously produced at Berlin's Friedrich-Wilhelmstädtisches Theater on 26 November 1891.

Austria: Lustspieltheater *Tolle Wirtschaft* 14 October 1910; Hungary: Városligeti Színkör *Lengyel menyecske* 18 November 1911; USA: Empire Theater, Syracuse *A Polish Wedding* 31 August 1912

POMME D'API Opérette in 1 act by Ludovic Halévy and William Busnach. Music by Jacques Offenbach. Théâtre de la Renaissance, Paris, 4 September 1873.

Of the handful of one-act opérettes which Offenbach wrote alongside the more substantial pieces of the last decade of his life, the pretty three-handed *Pomme d'api*, helped along by the Parisian début of Louise Théo in the title-rôle, was the most successful.

Womanizing Uncle Amilcar Rabastens (Daubray) has threatened to cut off Gustave's (Mlle Dartaux) allowance because the silly young fellow has kept the same mistress too dangerously long. He has also sacked his maid, and ordered a nice new young one. The new maid is, of course, Gustave's Pomme d'api, otherwise Catherine (Louise Théo), and the young man has to watch his Uncle making purposeful passes at her before the comedy is ended happily. Although Gustave had two numbers and Uncle one, it was Catherine to whom the bulk of the musical opportunities fell, but the highlight of the evening was the most bouffe part of the entertainment, a comical trio constructed (with a slight reminiscence of *Cox and Box*) around a grill-pan and some chops.

Played regularly in France – most recently as part of a spectacle coupé with *Mesdames de la Halle* and *Monsieur Choufleuri* in several Paris seasons – *Pomme d'api* also won productions in its earlier days in London, first at John Hollingshead's Gaiety Theatre and nearly 20 years later in a new translation (ad A Schade, Percy Reeve) as a forepiece at the Criterion, at Vienna's Theater an der Wien as *Nesthäkchen* and in a later German version as *Der Onkel hat gesagt*. It was also seen in America, played in its original French, in the repertoire of Maurice Grau's company.

UK: Gaiety Theatre *Love Apple* 24 September 1874, Criterion Theatre *Poor Mignonette* 2 August 1892; Austria: Theater an der Wien *Nesthäkchen* 22 November 1877; USA: Academy of Music 20 May 1880

Recordings: EMI, Bourg

LE POMPON Opérette in 3 acts by Henri Chivot and Alfred Duru. Music by Charles Lecocq. Théâtre des Folies-Dramatiques, Paris, 10 November 1875.

It is Palermo and carnival time, and the brigand Tivolini is going to be there, identifiable by a red and white pompon on his hat. Unfortunately, the innocent little doctor Piccolino (Mme Matz-Ferrare), the darling of the ladies and the beloved of the flower-girl Fioretta (Mlle Caillot), wears the fatal pompon, is arrested, and condemned to prison by the viceroy, Melchior (Ange Milher). Worse is to come. The viceroy's fiancée, the Duchesse Ortensia Cazadores y Florida (Mlle Toudouze), is an old flame of the little doctor, and when it gets known that she has visited the prisoner in his cell things look like getting even hotter for our hero. It takes another whole act for everything, with a little help from a blush-making fib from Fiorella, to be sorted out in time for a happy ending. Luco played Barabino, the minister of police, Didier was Castorini and Mlle Paurelle completed the principal cast as Béatrice.

Lecocq's long score, heavy in choral work and in showy vocalizing for the principal singers, included amongst its most favoured pages a brindisi for Piccolo, a barcarolle, and a virtuoso chanson de la folie for Fiorella.

After the great successes of *La Fille de Madame Angot* and *Giroflé-Girofla* and the semi-succès d'estime of *Les Prés Saint-Gervais*, *Le Pompon* gave Lecocq the first real Paris flop of his career. It was played just 14 times. This, however, was not the end of its career for, in spite of the Paris failure, Vienna's Carltheater mounted the piece as *Tivolini, der Bandit von Palermo*, and Budapest's Népszinház as *A kis doktor* (ad Lájos Tinódy, István Toldy). With Erzsi Vidmár, Emilia Sziklai, János Kápolnai, Miklós Tihanyi and Elek Solymossy at the head of its cast, the Hungarian 'little doctor' was played a highly satisfactory 29 times in its first series, and went on to a number of further performances, outrunning many of the composer's elsewhere-more-successful works in the Hungarian repertoire.

Hungary: Népszinház *A kis doktor* 18 November 1876; Austria: Carltheater *Tivolini, der Bandit von Palermo* 3 November 1877; Germany: *Tivolini* 12 January 1878

LE PONT DES SOUPIRS
Opéra-bouffe in 4 acts by Hector Crémieux and Ludovic Halévy. Music by Jacques Offenbach. Théâtre des Bouffes-Parisiens, Paris, 23 March 1861; revised version, Théâtre des Variétés, Paris, 8 May 1868.

An opéra-bouffe in the most thoroughly burlesque manner, *Le Pont des soupirs* saw Offenbach and his librettists returning to the style so successfully employed in *Orphée aux enfers* and *Geneviève de Brabant*, after the composer's abortive attempt to take the Opéra-Comique with the more sedately silly *Barkouf*. From Olympus and the French medieval world, he now turned to another favourite funspot of the spectacular-dramatic stage, the watery ways of the city of Venice with its Doges and Council of Ten and other such picturesque and easily burlesqued accoutrements. The librettists of *Orphée* fashioned another wildly extravagant tale around characters heretofore treated more dramatically in operatic pieces such as the 1841 *Katharina Cornaro, Königin von Cypern* (Franz Lachner/Alois Büssel), Halévy's *Reine de Chypre*, Balfe's *The Daughter of St Mark* (1844) or Pacini's *Regina di Cipro* (1846).

Cornarino Cornarini (Désiré), Doge of Venice in this year of 1321, has fled from his foundering fleet and, accompanied by his faithful Baptiste (Bache), arrived back home in deepest disguise and disgrace. He has to watch, powerless, as his wife, Catarina (Lise Tautin) is serenaded by her pretty pageboy, Amoroso (Lucille Tostée), and dramatically courted by the vile and powerful Malatromba (Potel), a lecherous monster who aspires to the post of Doge. Melodrama rises to farcical heights as Cornarino tries to make contact with his wife and avoid his rival, but the disguised Doge is finally dragged before a very eccentric version of the Council of Ten to give a report on his own death. Malatromba quickly gets himself elected in his place, but then the news comes – Cornarino left too

soon, and his fleet won the battle! He is reprieved and can come back to life, but who is Doge? The old or the new? There is nothing left for it but to have a contest. Since this is Venice it is a sea duel, and Cornarino comes out on top, thanks to a bit of cheating by Amoroso.

Offenbach's score was in his best bouffe manner and, even if it had not the one big hit number, such as *Orphée*'s galop infernale or the duo of the gens d'armes in *Geneviève*, there was a long list of sparkling and funny musical pieces in the new burlesque: the first-act multiple serenade under the Dogaressa's balcony ('Catarina, je chante'), the comical tale of the loss of the fleet (Complainte de Coranarino), Catarina's parody of an operatic mad scene, staged to keep Malatromba's malevolent fingers from doing fate-worse-than things to her bodice, the crazy Quattuor des poignards staged amongst the bodies and hiding-places of the boudoir-farcical second act, as well as some solos which, in typical Offenbachian fashion, verged on being too charming to be properly burlesque.

Produced by Offenbach himself at the Bouffes-Parisiens, with several of the original *Orphée* cast – Mlle Tautin, ex-Eurydice now Catarina, Désiré, formerly Jupiter now the Doge, and Bache, the lugubrious Styx now Baptiste – *Le Pont des soupirs* was not a great success, but it was by no means a failure.

Karl Treumann, now established at his Theater am Franz-Josefs-Kai, was the first foreign manager to host the show, when Offenbach's company visited Vienna in June 1861 with *Le Pont des soupirs* in its baggage, and he was also the first to mount a foreign-language version when his uncredited adaptation of *Die Seufzerbrücke* was produced, just under a year later. Treumann himself played the Doge, alongside Knaack (Baptiste), Markwordt (Malatromba), Anna Marek (Catarina) and Helene Weinberger (Amoroso). Treumann's biggest female star, Anna Grobecker, however, played Cascadetto and her rôle was enlarged by a song composed (along with a fourth-act chorus, pierrot dance and Schluss-Galoppade, 'based on original Venetian motifs') by the theatre's musical director, Franz von Suppé. Close behind Vienna, Berlin mounted its version of *Die Seufzerbrücke* and the French (Bouffes company tour) and German versions were also both played in Budapest.

In 1868 *Le Pont des soupirs* was given a major revival at Paris's Théâtre des Variétés (8 May). Mlle Tautin was again Catarina, Thiron was Cornarino, Lise Garait played Amoroso and José Dupuis himself was the mean Malatromba. For the occasion, Offenbach reorganized his score, replaced some numbers and added others, and the librettists took the opportunity to change the ending of their show. In the new version, the contest became a banal shimmy up a pole with a goblet at the end, and Cornarino is defeated. Whilst Malatromba takes over the Empire, the ex-doge, his wife and, of course, his wife's pretty page are sent off to an ambassadorial post in deepest Spain.

Although the revival did no better, as far as a run was concerned, than the original, it nevertheless sparked revivals and productions of its own. Vienna's Carltheater staged its *Seufzerbrücke* (8 February 1873) with Hermine Meyerhoff as Catarina (11 performances), Hungary now got round to an Hungarian version, Marie Aimée and her company introduced the show to America (in French), whilst in London Henry S Leigh's English version was mounted by Richard Mansell at the St James's Theatre (after a short postponement to replace an unsatisfying French Amoroso by a British one) with Edmund Rosenthal as Cornarino, Frank Celli, Augusta Thompson, J A Shaw and Annie Beauclerc. It had to be closed after six weeks when the (unpaid?) orchestra walked out, but, in a reversal of the French procedure, *The Bridge of Sighs* was brought out again in London in 1873, this time in a cut-down version.

In spite of this clumsy beginning, London persevered longer with the show than most other cities, for in 1879 another version, enlarged again, and expanding Offenbach's score with music by Hérold, Waldteufel, Campana and Georges Jacobi, was spectacularly produced at the Alhambra under the title *Venice* (ad Charles Searle). Herbert Campbell (Cornarino), Mme Zimeri (Catarina), Constance Loseby (Angelo, ex Amoroso) and Ambrose Collini (Magnifico, ex-Malatromba) headed a cast which also included such celebrities as Arthur Williams, Emma Chambers and the pantomimic Conquests, through two months. Long in the wake of this, New York had its first English-language performance in 1885 in Brooklyn where Selina Dolaro headed the cast alongside Florence Vallière, Lillie West and Harry Brown.

After many years of silence, during which it languished in the shadows of Offenbach's better-liked pieces, *Le Pont de soupirs* resurfaced intermittently in the 20th century. A new German version (ad Otto Maag) was staged at Basle (26 March 1933) and Wiesbaden (31 January 1965), and several French regional theatres, as well as the then ever-enterprising French radio, reprised the work, before a major stage and television revival was mounted in France in 1987 and played at the Théâtre de Paris (10 November 1987) with alternating casts. Directed with a truly bouffe vigour, the production was distinctly successful both in itself and in bringing *Le Pont des soupirs* back to general notice.

Austria: Theater am Franz-Josefs-Kai (Fr) 15 June 1861, *Die Seufzerbrücke* 12 May 1862; Germany: Friedrich-Wilhelm-städtisches Theater 17 May 1862; Hungary: Nemzeti Színház (Fr) 18 July 1861, Budai Színkör *Seufzerbrücke* 24 June 1865, Budai Színkör *A sóhajok hidja* 27 August 1871; UK: St James's Theatre *The Bridge of Sighs* 18 November 1872, Alhambra Theatre *Venice* 5 May 1879; USA: Lina Edwin's Theater (Fr) 27 November 1871, Grand Opera House, Brooklyn 20 April 1885

Recording: complete (Bourg)

POPPY Musical comedy in 3 acts by Dorothy Donnelly. Music by Stephen Jones and Arthur Samuels. Apollo Theater, New York, 3 September 1923.

Yet another piece in the Broadway Cinderella series of the early 1920s, *Poppy* joined *Irene*, *Mary*, *Sally* and the rest in following the fortunes of its winsome little heroine from obscurity to wealth and a wedding ring. This one had a ring of Maurice Ordonneau's *Les Saltimbanques* about it, as Poppy (Madge Kennedy) started life in a circus, only to discover, when skies seemed darkest, that her mother was an heiress. The star turn of the show was, however, not Poppy but comedian W C Fields, cast in the rôle of the little heroine's guardian.

From amongst the songs of the show two pieces, 'What Do You Do Sunday(s), Mary?' and 'Alibi Baby' (Samuels/Howard Dietz), found some success and the mixture, if

almost wearyingly the same as before, proved sweet and savoury enough to win *Poppy* a 344-performance run on Broadway, and a British production. In London, staged at the Gaiety Theatre with Anne Croft as Poppy and the town's favourite clown, W H Berry, taking Fields's rôle, *Poppy* notched up a fair run of 188 performances – which was more than her trans-Atlantic sisters *Mary* and *Tip-Toes* had managed, but significantly less than *Irene*, *Sally*, *Sunny* and, particularly, the less winsome *Mercenary Mary*.

The same title, with trendily druggy overtones, was used for a breast-beating British musical by Peter Nichols, music by Monty Norman (Barbican Theatre, London, 25 September 1982), which used British pantomime conventions and extravagant production values to preach of how the spotlessly noble Orient was debauched by the vile colonizing Victorian British. It had a much shorter life in its original Royal Shakespeare Company production than the Cinderella-with-comedy American show, was remounted with trans-Atlantic money and intent in the West End, failed a second time, but was later played again in a small-stage version on the London fringe.

UK: Gaiety Theatre 4 September 1924
Recordings: US show: radio dialogue by Fields (Columbia); UK show: London cast (WEA)

PORGY AND BESS Folk opera in 3 acts by Du Bose Heyward based on the play *Porgy* by Du Bose and Dorothy Heyward. Lyrics by Du Bose Heyward and Ira Gershwin. Music by George Gershwin. Alvin Theater, New York, 10 October 1935.

Initially produced by the Theater Guild as a commercial production on Broadway, the 'folk opera' *Porgy and Bess* has subsequently found much of its future in the opera houses of the world.

Adapted from Heyward's novel and play, itself also a Theater Guild production, the musicalized *Porgy*, set in Catfish Row, amongst low-living negro folk, centred on the love affair between the crippled Porgy (Todd Duncan) and Bess (Anne Brown), the flashy mistress of the uncouth Crown (Warren Coleman). Crown kills a man in a gambling brawl and flees the area, leaving the unlikely pair to get together in his absence, and when he manages to come out from hiding to reclaim his woman, Porgy murders him. When he gets out of prison, he finds that Bess has gone to New York with the drug peddler Sportin' Life (John W Bubbles), and he sets off in his donkey cart to find her.

George Gershwin's score illustrated this dramatic tale with great force in a range of musical pieces which brought more individual numbers to the peaks of popularity than any similar work since *Carmen*: the reaching, spun-soprano lullaby 'Summertime', Porgy's song of the satisfied vagabond, 'I Got Plenty o' Nuttin'', his proud duet with Bess, 'Bess, You is My Woman Now', the harshly comical song of the evil spiv, Sportin' Life ('It Ain't Necessarily So'), and perhaps the most beautiful piece of all, the despairing 'My Man's Gone Now' sung by the bereft Serena over her murdered husband's body.

Although its merits were quickly recognized by some (but not all), as a commercial proposition *Porgy and Bess* was a first-time failure, its initial production lasting only 124 performances on Broadway. A revival, bravely sponsored by Cheryl Crawford (Majestic Theater, 22 January 1942) with Duncan and Miss Brown again starred, did better (286 performances), and *Porgy and Bess* was picked up for a number of overseas productions, beginning with one in Denmark. However, the piece got its most significant exposure not from a regular theatre season but from two other sources. The first of these was a four-year international tour, played under the aegis of State Department, which took *Porgy and Bess* to Vienna, Berlin, London and Paris with William Warfield and Leontyne Price starred before bringing the show back to Broadway (Ziegfeld Theater, 10 March 1953, 305 performances) and then continuing on to Europe, Arabia and South America as well as through America and Canada. The other was a 1959 film version in which Sidney Poitier and Dorothy Dandridge (and the voices of Robert McFerrin and Adele Addison) were starred alongside Pearl Bailey and Sammy Davis jr.

Now thoroughly established as a classic of the American light-opera stage, inhabiting that area between opera and musical theatre most famously occupied by *Carmen* and other classics of the opéra-comique stage, *Porgy and Bess* has subsequently been given a multitude of stagings, principally in America but also throughout the rest of the world. It has played further seasons on Broadway in a Houston Grand Opera production (Uris Theater, 25 September 1976, 122 performances) and at the Radio City Music Hall, and has been produced at the Metropolitan Opera House (1985 w Grace Bumbry, Simon Estes) and at Britain's Glyndebourne Festival Opera (1986, w Willard White, Cynthia Hayman) and Royal Opera House, Covent Garden (1992), as it has become accepted as part of the modern operatic repertoire.

All the major American and British productions of *Porgy and Bess* have been played with racially limited casts and, although a New Zealand Opera Company production starring Inia te Wiata as Porgy was staged in New Zealand and Australia with mostly maori players, and some Continental houses have, forcibly, mounted productions without regard to race, even in times which can produce such events as the *Miss Saigon* casting fiasco the first colour-blind *Porgy and Bess* on an American or British stage is yet to come.

Austria: Volksoper 7 September 1952; Germany: Titaniapalast 18 September 1952; UK: Stoll Theatre 9 October 1952; France: Théâtre de l'Empire February 1953
Literature: Alpert, H: *The Life and Times of Porgy and Bess* (Knopf, New York, 1990)
Recordings: original 1935 cast selection (Mark 56), 1942 revival cast (Decca/MCA), London 1953 cast (RCA Victor), 1976 revival cast (RCA Victor), film soundtrack (Columbia), Glyndebourne cast 1988 (EMI), complete (Columbia/Odyssey), selection in Swedish (SR) etc

PORTER, Cole [Albert]   (b Peru, Ind, 9 June 1891; d Santa Monica, 15 October 1964). Broadway songwriter for a series of successful and a handful of enduring shows.

Wealthy and well-living, Cole Porter purveyed from his early writing days a kind of songwriting which reflected his lifestyle: self-aware and crisply suave (if not always so very sophisticated) lyrics blended with smoothly insinuating melodies or comical blips of tune to produce material of a kind that, particularly given its overwhelming devotion to things sexual and/or social, would frequently have seemed more suitable to the then newly popular cabaret world than to that of the theatre. However, although he turned out a number of successful single songs which were not conceived as part of any stage show, it was as a writer of songs

Plate 213. *Fame had yet to come – London's music publishers clearly hadn't heard of* **Cole Porter** *when they issued the sheet music to* The Eclipse. *But 'Col' Porter lasted a good deal longer than their show.*

and collections of songs for the musical theatre that Porter made his greatest success.

Porter seemed destined for a quick introduction to Broadway when, following several years of supplying songs to college shows and the placing of a couple of interpolations in Broadway pieces (*Hands Up*, *Miss Information*), he was signed by Elisabeth Marbury, top-flight agent and producer, along with his college chum Lawraston Riggs, to write a musical for New York. As a result, Porter had his first full-frontal exposure to Broadway at the age of 24, with the 'comic opera' *See America First*. It was not an auspicious beginning. The show lasted 15 performances, and it was to be another dozen years before Porter would again essay the score for a book musical.

The young man had other things to occupy his salad days, and most of them were not in America. He took to the society circuits of Europe, where he played gaily through the final part of the First World War and through the 1920s, living the life of the high-flying rich (and even more richly wed) and turning out, on the way, a regular supply of brisk and bright songs which found their way into such London shows as Jerome Kern's exported *Very Good Eddie*, the musical farce *Telling the Tale*, *The Eclipse*, the formerly French revue *As You Were*, *A Night Out* (ly: Clifford Grey), C B Cochran's revue *Mayfair to Montmartre* and his heavily botched version of the French 'victory' hit, *Phi-Phi*. For the American stage, he supplied the full scores for Raymond Hitchcock's revusical *Hitchy Koo of 1919* (56 performances) and the Shuberts' sequel *Hitchy-*

Koo of 1922 (which closed out of town), as well as for John Murray Anderson's longer-lived *Greenwich Village Follies* (1924, 127 performances). For Paris he composed the dance piece *Within the Quota* (1923) and supplied the songs for a 1928 revue at Les Ambassadeurs.

Porter's return to the Broadway book-musical stage was made on a reduced scale, when he provided the six songs (new and recycled) required to top up those borrowed from the Continent by producer E Ray Goetz to make up the musical part of *Paris*, his latest vehicle (w Gilbert Miller) for Irene Bordoni (Mrs Goetz). The small-scale *Paris* was a 195-performance success on Broadway, and it provided the first showcase for one of Porter's most famous songs, the mildly suggestive 'Let's Do It (let's fall in love)' which was developed into a much more pointed piece in its subsequent reincarnation as a cabaret number than it was in the theatre – even in the throat of perky Mlle Bordoni.

Porter was now in his late thirties, and, after promising so much so early, his musical comedy career had really only just begun. After the happily gallivanting dilettantism of the past decade, he now became a regular contributor to the Broadway musical stage. The 1929 C B Cochran London revue *Wake Up and Dream* (263 performances, 'I'm a Gigolo') transferred to Broadway (136 performances) later in the same year, by which time, again under the management of Goetz (who had also been the first, as producer of *Hands Up*, to use a Cole Porter song on Broadway), the composer had seen his first full-sized book musical since *See America First* produced on the New York stage. *Fifty Million Frenchmen* ('You've Got That Thing', 'You Do Something to Me'), composed to a Herbert Fields libretto, won a tidy success in 254 performances.

Goetz produced another Porter/Fields piece, *The New Yorkers* ('Love for Sale', 'I Happen to Like New York'), the following year with a cast that included Jimmy Durante, Ann Pennington, old-time stars Richard Carle and Marie Cahill and Fred Waring and his Pennsylvanians (168 performances), but a third teaming of producer and writers, on a piece called *Star Dust* (1931) with Peggy Wood slated as star, was abandoned without going into rehearsal. However if, with this abortion, Goetz's career in the musical theatre was over, Porter was only getting into his stride.

His next engagement was on the Dwight Deere Wiman/Tom Weatherly production of *Gay Divorce* in which Fred Astaire, the certified star of *For Goodness' Sake*, *Lady, Be Good!* and *Funny Face* was featured for the first time without his sister and up-to-then partner, Adele. The songs which Porter provided for Astaire and his new partner, Claire Luce, included 'Night and Day', and the show, the star and the song all won success on Broadway, in London and in Hollywood. One last show for Cochran, a musical stage version of the comic novel *Nymph Errant* (154 performances), produced several openly saucy songs ('Experiment', 'The Physician', 'Solomon'), to go with the show's innocently saucy text and *Once Upon a Time*, a commission from Gilbert Miller, went the same way as *Star Dust* when it was aborted before reaching the stage, but next time up Porter topped all his musical comedy efforts to date. *Anything Goes* (1934, 'I Get a Kick Out of You', 'You're the Top', 'Anything Goes', 'Blow, Gabriel, Blow' etc), gave him a real and international hit and one which was not just a once-around hit like *Gay Divorce*, but a show which, like few other American pieces of this period, would also become an enduring part of the revivable and revived canon.

Over the next 20 years, and in spite of a 1937 riding accident which confined the songwriter in a life of pain and disability for the rest of his days, Porter made up for his delayed start by providing regular new scores to the Broadway stage, and several more to the screen (*Born to Dance*, *Broadway Melody of 1940*, *The Pirate* etc). Not all of these stage shows were successes, but even the less successful amongst them, such as *Jubilee* (169 performances, 'Begin the Beguine', 'Just One of Those Things'), *Red, Hot and Blue!* (183 performances, 'Down in the Depths', 'It's De-Lovely'), a re-musicalization of Siegfried Geyer's already-musicalized *Bei Kerzenlicht* as *You Never Know* (78 performances, 'At Long Last Love'), the revue *Seven Lively Arts* (183 performances, 'Every Time We Say Goodbye') and the classical burlesque *Out of This World* (157 performances, 'From This Moment On') brought forth new hit songs to add to the considerable catalogue of popular Porter numbers.

Unlike this group, however, the bulk of Porter's musical shows of the late 1930s and the 1940s had extended runs on Broadway. In just half a dozen years, Vinton Freedley's second vehicle for *Anything Goes*'s comedy pair, William Gaxton and Victor Moore, *Leave it to Me!* (307 performances, 'My Heart Belongs to Daddy', 'Most Gentlemen Don't Like Love'), Fields's and Buddy De Sylva's comic fantasy *Dubarry was a Lady* (408 performances, 'Friendship', 'Katie Went to Haiti'), a follow-up vehicle for his most helpful star, Ethel Merman, *Panama Hattie* (501 performances, 'Make it Another Old-Fashioned, Please') and Freedley's musical farce *Let's Face It* (547 performances, 'Let's Not Talk About Love') with Danny Kaye starred, all had a first-rate metropolitan success, and if a further Merman vehicle, *Something for the Boys* (422 performances), and the Mike Todd spectacular *Mexican Hayride* (481 performances) produced rather less in the way of extractable song hits than the others, this series of shows each and all had fine, colourful careers on the American stage.

This period of Porter's career produced so many long-running successes, so many song hits, a number of London productions (*Dubarry Was a Lady*, *Let's Face It*, *Panama Hattie*, *Something for the Boys*) which more than made up for *Fifty Million Frenchmen*'s earlier death on the British road, and several film versions, yet the series of musicals which he and his collaborators turned out in these years in and around the Second World War were, as shows, largely ephemeral, and none of them succeeded in following *Anything Goes* into the list of standards.

In 1948, however, after more than 30 years in the business and at an age when more than 90 per cent of composers and musical-comedy songwriters have all their best successes behind them, Porter wrote the show which clinched his place in the musical theatre's pantheon. Even more than *Anything Goes*, which has always seemed the quintessential Porter show, the almost atypical backstage musical comedy *Kiss Me, Kate* proved durable, memorable and revivable – not just its songs, this time, but the show as a whole. After its initial 1,077 performances on Broadway, *Kiss Me, Kate*, with its comical script and panorama of revusical and romantic songs, returned to the stages of the world again and again. It proved an international hit of a kind that had gone out of style, a hit which even carried the

Broadway musical back into European houses which had barely taken notice of an English-language piece since the days of *The Geisha* half a century earlier. And having got there, it stayed. *Kiss Me, Kate* was the very opposite of the ephemeral.

Can-Can (892 performances, 'I Love Paris', 'C'est magnifique' etc) and *Silk Stockings* (477 performances, 'Paris Loves Lovers') were further Porter Broadway stage hits in the 1950s, *High Society* ('Who Wants to Be a Millionaire?', 'True Love' etc) and *Les Girls* gave him further film successes, and in 1958 he composed the score for a television version of *Aladdin* ('Wouldn't it be Fun (not to be famous?)'), a piece subsequently transferred to the stage. In the wake of the West End success of Rodgers and Hammerstein's *Cinderella*, *Aladdin* was produced in 1959 (with its short score, Porter's last, made up to full-length by the borrowing of numbers from *Red, Hot and Blue!*, *Out of This World* and *Mexican Hayride*) on the London stage where so much of the composer's early work had been first heard and where, in more recent decades, he had provided songs new or borrowed for the Drury Lane spectacular *The Sun Never Sets*, *The Fleet's Lit Up* ('Its De-Lovely'), the musical play *Somewhere in England* and the revue *Black Vanities*.

Porter was essentially a songwriter, and a songwriter who varied his light and apparently jokey style but little through score after score of numbers which bristle with what seems like the entire contents of his address book – from the Mayor of New York to Rin Tin Tin – catalogues of the once-famous, many of whom mean as little today as Gilbert's Captain Shaw, but who were both topical and good for a laugh and/or a rhyme in their time. However, his elegantly knowing command of words and music – the one fitted into the other as only a solo writer can do – coupled with a kind of period pout that belongs to an attractive-seeming era somewhere between the days when 'a glimpse of stocking was looked on as something shocking' and these days, when 'anything goes', have given his songs a fervent following. This following has, in its turn, resulted in his work being pushed back into the theatre in the 1980s and 1990s in varying if often unfortunate and/or unflattering forms.

An early Porter compilation, under the title *The Decline and Fall of the Entire World as Seen Through the Eyes of Cole Porter* was played at New York's Square East Theater (30 March 1965), and another patchwork show, *Cole* (ad Alan Strachan, Benny Green) was mounted at London's Mermaid Theatre (2 July 1974), with considerably more success than an attempt at a Broadway musical version of the play *Holiday* with a Porter pasticcio score (*Happy New Year*, arr Buster Davis/Burt Shevelove, Morosco Theater 27 April 1980). A remade version of *You Never Know* which re-blended Porter's songs with more than before of Robert Katscher's original Continental score for *Bei Kerzenlicht* was produced at New York's Eastside Playhouse (12 March 1973), whilst London has been given compilations of Porter material tacked loosely on to the libretti and part-scores of *High Society* (Victoria Palace 25 February 1987) and *Can-Can* (Strand Theatre 26 October 1988). Almost every production of *Anything Goes* has also, if with rather more consideration for the original, raided Porter's song-book for extra musical icing.

A Hollywood biomusical which did to Porter's life pretty much what musicals and musical films had been doing to composers for decades was issued in 1946 under the title *Night and Day*. The very much alive Porter was doubtless pleased to be played by Cary Grant, even if the story told was pretty fictional.

1916 **See America First** (T Lawrason Riggs) Maxine Elliott's Theater 28 March
1928 **Paris** (Martin Brown) Music Box Theater 8 October
1929 **Fifty Million Frenchmen** (Herbert Fields) Lyric Theater 27 November
1930 **The New Yorkers** (H Fields) Broadway Theater 8 December
1932 **Gay Divorce** (Dwight Taylor) Ethel Barrymore Theater 29 November
1933 **Nymph Errant** (Romney Brent) Adelphi Theatre, London 6 October
1934 **Anything Goes** (Guy Bolton, P G Wodehouse ad Howard Lindsay, Russel Crouse) Alvin Theater 21 November
1935 **Jubilee** (Moss Hart) Imperial Theater 12 October
1936 **Red, Hot and Blue!** (Lindsay, Crouse) Alvin Theater 29 October
1938 **You Never Know** (ad Rowland Leigh) Winter Garden Theater 21 September
1938 **Leave it to Me!** (Bella Spewack, Sam Spewack) Imperial Theater 9 November
1939 **Dubarry Was a Lady** (H Fields, B G De Sylva) 46th Street Theater 6 December
1940 **Panama Hattie** (H Fields, De Sylva) 46th Street Theater 30 October
1941 **Let's Face It** (H Fields, Dorothy Fields) Imperial Theater 29 October
1943 **Something for the Boys** (H Fields, D Fields) Alvin Theater 7 January
1944 **Mexican Hayride** (H Fields, D Fields) Winter Garden Theater 28 January
1946 **Around the World [in 80 Days]** (Orson Welles) Adelphi Theater 31 May
1948 **Kiss Me, Kate** (B Spewack, S Spewack) New Century Theater 30 December
1950 **Out of this World** (Taylor, Reginald Lawrence) New Century Theater 21 December
1953 **Can-Can** (Abe Burrows) Shubert Theater 7 May
1955 **Silk Stockings** (George S Kaufman, Leueen McGrath, Burrows) Imperial Theater 24 February
1959 **Aladdin** (S J Perelman ad Peter Coke) London Coliseum 17 December

Biography, etc: Ewen, D: *The Cole Porter Story* (Holt, Rinehart Winston, New York, 1965); Hubler, R: *The Cole Porter Story* (World, Cleveland, 1965), Eells, G: *Cole Porter: the Life That Late He Led* (Putnam, New York, 1967), Kimball, R, Gill, B: *Cole* (Holt, New York, 1971), Schwartz, C: *Cole Porter: a Biography* (Dial Press, New York, 1977); Grafton, D: *Red, Hot and Rich!* (Stein & Day, New York, 1987) etc

DIE PORTRÄT-DAME, or Die Profezeinungen des Quiribi Komische Oper in 3 acts by F Zell and Richard Genée. Music by Max Wolf. Theater an der Wien, Vienna, 1 March 1877.

One of Zell and Genée's lesser-known works, set by the lesser-known Max Wolf, *Die Porträt-Dame* was produced at Vienna's Theater an der Wien in 1877. The piece was set in the late 17th century and featured Albertina Stauber (most recently the Cunégonde of the theatre's *Le Voyage dans la lune*) as the 18-year-old Friedrich-August, future monarch of Saxony, and Bertha Steinher as Charlotte, the daughter of the schoolmaster of the little town of Plowirz (Jani Szika), who was apparently the lady in the case. Herr

Binder was Quiribi, the prophesying magician of the sub-title, Alexander Girardi played Hofmarschall Graf von Loos and Georgine von Januschowksy was his daughter Amalie, in yet another tale of the early amours of the aristocracy.

Die Porträt-Dame was only played five times at the Theater an der Wien, but it was picked up for production later the same year at Berlin's Friedrich-Wilhelmstädtisches Theater and was played widely around Germany for the next decade. During that time it was also given a German-language production in New York, with Marie König as Charlotte, Kuster as a non-travesty Friedrich-August, Frln Holzapfel as Amalia, and Max Lube and Gustav Adolfi in the other principal rôles.

Germany: Friedrich-Wilhelmstädtisches Theater 1877; USA: Thalia Theater 20 September 1880

POSFORD, [Benjamin] George [Ashwell] (b Folkestone, 23 March 1906; d Worplesdon, 24 April 1976).

Law student turned composer Posford began his musical-theatre career with some additional songs for Robert Courtneidge's touring musical *Lavender* (1930), before turning to writing for the radio. There, he hit an unexpected bonus when he collaborated with the powerfully-placed Eric Maschwitz on a radio operetta, *Good Night Vienna*. When the broadcast of his piece was delayed, Maschwitz negotiated for a film version which, with Jack Buchanan and Anna Neagle starred, gave a nationwide airing to the young composer's title-song, as sung to success by Buchanan, and score. Posford collaborated on another radio musical with Herbert Farjeon (*One Day in Summer*, 1934), but continued his work with Maschwitz on a touring stage musical *The Gay Hussar*. In the wake of the first of Novello's romantic operetta successes, that piece was remade on Novello-esque lines as *Balalaika*, and Posford's title-song ('At the Balalaika') again became a considerable song success within the success of the show itself.

A follow-up, *Paprika/Magyar Melody*, was a quick flop, as were an attempt to go where Cole Porter had failed in giving a score to Romney Brent's *Nymph Errant* libretto, as *Evangeline*, and a Maschwitz musicalization of the famous play *The Ghost Train*. However, Posford's principal score for the Cicely Courtneidge and Jack Hulbert show *Full Swing* was an adjunct to a sizeable musical-comedy success, and a further pairing with Maschwitz on the musical adaptation of the play *Brewster's Millions*, *Zip Goes a Million*, as a vehicle for comedy singing star George Formby ('I'm Saving Up for Sally') had a fine run, even after the star was forced to retire from the production.

Posford provided music for a number of British films (*The Good Companions*, *Invitation to the Waltz*, *The Gay Desperado*, *Café Colette*), and scored song successes in 1941 with 'The London I Love' and 'The Song of the Clyde'.

1933 **The Gay Hussar** (Eric Maschwitz) Manchester 2 October
1936 **Balalaika** revised *The Gay Hussar* w Bernard Grün Adelphi Theatre 22 December
1938 **Paprika** (later **Magyar Melody**) (w Grün/Harold Purcell/ Maschwitz, Fred Thompson, Guy Bolton) His Majesty's Theatre 15 September
1942 **Full Swing** (w Harry Parr Davies/Archie Menzies, Arthur Macrae, Jack Hulbert) Palace Theatre 16 April
1946 **Evangeline** (w Harry Jacobson/Maschwitz/Romney Brent) Cambridge Theatre 14 March
1946 **Goodnight Vienna** (Purcell/Maschwitz) Pavilion Theatre, Bournemouth 22 July
1951 **Zip Goes a Million** (Maschwitz) Palace Theatre 20 October
1954 **Happy Holiday** (Maschwitz) Palace Theatre 22 December

LE POSTILLON DE LONGJUMEAU Opéra-comique in 3 acts by Adolphe de Leuven and Brunswick. Music by Adolphe Adam. Théâtre de l'Opéra-Comique, Paris, 13 October 1836.

Adam's opéra-comique *Le Postillon de Longjumeau* was one of the pre-Offenbach pieces which remained in the repertoire of international light-operatic companies after the opéra-bouffe craze had wiped the majority of older pieces from their slates. Its libretto told the tale of the coachman Pierre Chappelou (Chollet) who abandons his rustic wife (Zoë Prévost) on their wedding night to go to Paris and become an operatic star. He meets trouble when he falls in love with and weds a fashionable lady, but she turns out to be his Madeleine who has used the ten years in between as profitably as he. The keystone of Adam's score is the song of the Postillon de Longjumeau, with its fabled top Ds, which causes the singing coachman to be discovered at the top of the first act but, like much of Adam's music, the remainder of the score happily straddled the gap between the operatic and the opéra-bouffe.

Hugely successful in France, the piece was given in an English-language version (ad Gilbert a'Beckett sr) in London five months after the Paris première, and it was played in several German versions in the principal central European cities before the end of the year. Thereafter it was regularly performed in all three languages (and less frequently in several others) in repertoire houses and companies. It was given a major commercial revival by John Hollingshead in London in 1886 under the title *A Maiden Wife* (Empire Theatre, August) with Henry Walsham and Mlle Devrient, was produced at the Vienna Volksoper in 1908 and again in 1964, and in 1989 was seen at the Grand Théâtre de Genève.

UK: St James's Theatre *Postillion!* 13 March 1837; Germany: 3 June 1837; Hungary: (Ger) 30 September 1837, Magyar Királyi Operaház *Longjumeau postakocsis* 29 November 1904; Austria: Hoftheater 14 October 1837; USA: Park Theater 30 March 1840

DIE POSTMEISTERIN Operette in 3 acts by August Neidhart. Music by Leon Jessel. Centraltheater, Berlin, 3 February 1921.

Following the European triumph of *Schwarzwaldmädel*, Jessel and Neidhart made several attempts to repeat that success with similarly flavoured pieces. If *Die Postmeisterin* did not quite come up to the earlier show, it nevertheless put up a good showing.

Neidhart's story – set in a Hessian village of 1806 – involved Magdalene, the postmistress (post as in carriage-post) of his story, in an adventure with Prince Louis Ferdinand of Prussia which had but little of the adventure of that more famous post-office lady, *Der Vogelhändler*'s Christel von der Post, about it, and rather more of those of all the Princes who had been busy over the past operettic decade or two falling in love with village maidens. This Prince is unusual in that he's not out gallivanting but actually running away from Napoleon's army, and the lady dresses him up as the postmaster whilst her postboy-lover Fritz pretends to be the Prince. The French Captain Virvaux – who sees the 'postmaster' making love to pretty Pauline Wiesel, and his 'postmistress' Magdalene with Fritz, and has to be put off with the excuse that the locals are practising French-style wife-swapping – finally winkles his Prince out, but the Prussians attack in timely fashion and prepare the ground for a happy ending.

If Pauline got the Prince, however, Magdalene got the bulk and best of the music including an opening solo 'Wenn ich Mädel wär', a second-act number 'Vis-à-vis von mir' with the Capitain and chorus, a Storch-duo with the Prince ('Ja, ja der Storch, das ist ein Vieh'), a Slowaken-duo with Fritz ('Röckchen fliegen') and share in the waltz Quartet (w Pauline, Fritz, Ferdinand) 'Reich mir die Lippen, reich mir den Mund' which was the evening's big tune.

Die Postmeisterin had a good Berlin career. It passed its 100th night on 13 September before being taken off to allow the production of Jessel and Neidhart's next piece, *Das Detektivmädel*, and it then moved on to Vienna, where, with Paul Kronegg (Louis Ferdinand) and Rosy Werginz (Magdalene) featured, it played nearly three months (81 performances) at Oskar Fronz's Bürgertheater.

Austria: Wiener Bürgertheater 29 September 1922

POTTER, Paul M[eredith] [McLEAN, Walter Arthur] (b Brighton, 3 June 1852; d New York, 7 March 1921).

A journalist and sometime newspaper editor, Potter worked at first in Britain and then, forced to flee the country following the Lombard Street homosexual scandal, in America. There he authored a number of successful plays, the most notable being the stage adaptations of Gerald du Maurier's *Trilby* (1895) and Ouida's *Under Two Flags* (1901), but he also supplied the libretti for several musical pieces ranging from farce comedies in the 1890s to Leslie Stuart's successful London musical comedy, *The School Girl* (1903). He also wrote the libretto for Broadway's *The Queen of the Moulin Rouge*, a piece which illustrated a prince's night spent in the Parisian underworld – complete with apache dance – when he fails to get amorous satisfaction from his princess. Lambasted by the critics – 'a conglomeration of noise, vulgarity and commonplace idiocy' (*New York Dramatic Mirror*), 'degrades the stage' (*Theatre*) – it was whispered about as being slightly scandalous, and consequently ran up a series of 163 performances.

There have been numerous attempts to musicalize *Trilby*, including unstaged pieces by Victor Herbert, Isidore de Lara, Hubert Bath and Haddon Chambers, and Malcolm Williamson, whilst an American show, *The Studio Girl* (1927, Will Ortmann/J Kiern Brennan) which made the stage with Jeanette MacDonald starred, folded pre-Broadway. Britain's Kidderminster Playhouse staged its version in 1962 and, when it again became an obvious target following the success of *The Phantom of the Opéra*, several other attempts were made to get a *Trilby* off the ground. She seems, however, to defy musicalization.

Trilby also came in for much parody at the time of its production, both in song ('Trilby Will Be True') and in stage burlesque in Britain (*A Modern Trilby*, *A Trilby Triflet*, *A Dumaur'alised Trilby*) on Broadway (*Thrilby*) and in Australia (*Trilby Burlesque* Edwin Finn, music arr George Pack Theatre Royal, Melbourne, 4 December 1897)

where Maggie Moore starred as the heroine. Another Potter stage success, *The Conquerors*, which he eventually admitted was an adaptation from de Maupassant and Sardou's *La Haine*, was also burlesqued, as *The Con-Curers* (1898), by Weber and Fields.

1890 **The City Directory** (W S Mullaly) Bijou Theater 10 February
1895 **A Stag Party, or A Hero in Spite of Himself** (Herman Perlet/w William Nye) Garden Theater 17 December
1903 **The School Girl** (Leslie Stuart/Charles H Taylor/w Henry Hamilton) Prince of Wales Theatre 9 May
1908 **The Queen of the Moulin Rouge** (Vincent Bryan/John T Hall) Circle Theater 7 December
1912 **Half Way to Paris** (Arthur J Lamb/Hall) Court Square Theater, Springfield, Mass 19 April
1913 **The Man with Three Wives** (*Der Mann mit den drei Frauen*) American version w Harold Atteridge, Agnes Morgan (Weber and Fields' Theater)

POUCHE Opérette in 3 acts by Alphonse Franck adapted from a play by René Peter and Henri Falk. Music by Henri Hir(s)chmann. Théâtre de l'Étoile, Paris, 18 February 1925.

One of Hirschmann's more successful attempts at a modern musical comedy, *Pouche* was written to a text adapted by producer Alphonse Franck, manager of the Théâtre de l'Étoile, from a comedy of two seasons earlier (Théâtre de la Potinière, 8 February 1923). Discovering that the young widowed Marquise de Poulignon (Mlle Vioricia) is planning secretly to look him over as a prospective husband, the miffed Gaston la Fajolle (Gaston Gabaroche) determines to put her off and gets his friend Jacques Bridier (Henri Defreyn) to hire a little dressmaker, Pouche (Yo Maurel), to pose as his mistress. The Marquise discovers the ruse and takes Pouche's place and the plot begins to roll towards its predestined dénouement.

Hirschmann's score included the catchy 'J'ai Pippo dans la peau' performed by the real Pouche and her Alfred (Robert Pizani) and 'Ah! les femmes, comm' ça change' delivered with ease by Gabaroche, as well as some slightly more soigné pieces which shifted *Pouche* just a little away from the most popular musical-comedy genre. The show had a good Parisian run and subsequent touring life.

The play – its original rather than Franck's musicalization – was very loosely adapted for America by Avery Hopwood as a 'romantic song-farce ... far from the French' under the title *Naughty Cinderella* (Lyceum Theater 9 November 1925) and produced by E Ray Goetz and Charles Frohman as a vehicle for Irene Bordoni (Mrs Goetz). Hirschmann's score was dispensed with, and the musical selection performed by Miss Bordoni included Paul Rubens's ageing 'I Love the Moon', Goetz's setting of Henri Christiné's 'L'Homme du dancing' as 'Do I Love You?', a Messager/Sacha Guitry song and the A L Keith/Lee Sterling 'That Means Nothing to Me'. Henry Kendall was Gerald Grey (ex-Gaston), Evelyn Gosnell played Claire Fenton (ex-Marquise) and Mlle Bordoni, in the rôle of the Cinderella who was supposed to be naughty, was called Chouchou Rouselle. The show served its star for 121 Broadway performances and for further use around America until her next vehicle was ready. It also temporarily scared the Shuberts' production of Straus's *Riquette* (which claimed to be based on the same original *Pouche* text) away from Broadway.

LA POULE BLANCHE Opérette in 3 acts by Antony Mars and Maurice Hennequin. Music by Victor Roger. Théâtre Cluny, Paris, 13 January 1899.

Chapitel (Hamilton) has just married Angèle Bardubec (Blanche Marie) when he hears he has inherited a fortune in Corsica. The newlyweds go off to honeymoon there, only to find that they have been tricked. Chapitel's mild little uncle, Tromboli (Prévost), needs his only nephew to wed Frisca (Mlle Leblanc), the daughter of his friendly neighbour Quiquibio (Gravier jr) so that they can officially end the vendetta which has been raging between their two families since a little episode over a white hen, ages and ages ago. The unhappy Chapitel is bigamously wed to the unwilling Frisca, and the complications increase when he helplessly puts Angèle in the kindly charge of a fellow (Rouvière) who just happens to be a passionate former suitor of the unbedded bride. The expert comic writing of Mars and Hennequin carried their characters through plenty of colourful quiproquos on the way to a happy ending.

In spite of playing only 32 performances at the Théâtre Cluny, *La Poule blanche* was quickly exported both to Germany where a version (ad Heinrich Bolten-Bäckers) was produced at Berlin's Viktoria Theater, and to Hungary (ad Emil Makai, Gyula P Zempléni). In 1907 a *The White Hen* (Casino Theater, 16 February) turned up on Broadway, but Roderic Penfield's piece (which had started off being called *The Girl from Vienna*) which also dealt with a man married to two women simultaneously, had a Viennese setting, a score by Gustave Kerker, Penfield and Paul West, and gave no credit to the French authors. Since 'The White Hen' was a Tyrolean hotel and the first act was set in a Viennese marriage brokery, it seems that there may have been no lien of parentage with the older piece. Ralph Herz, Louis Mann, Lotta Faust and Louise Gunning starred for a cheerful 94 New York performances.

Hungary: Népszinház *A fehér csirke* 28 April 1899; Germany: Viktoria-Theater *Die weisse Henne* 11 September 1899

POUNDS, Courtice [POUNDS, Charles Curtice] (b London, 30 May 1862; d London, 21 December 1927). Short, boyishly pudgy tenor who went from star rôles in comic opera to a career as Britian's best senior singing comedy actor.

Pounds did his first singing as a boy soprano, being a choir soloist at St Stephens, South Kensington at the age of 11. He subsequently studied at the Royal Academy of Music and had his first professional job at 19 in the chorus of D'Oyly Carte's *Patience*. He rose through the Savoy ranks, from acting as understudy to Durward Lely and Rutland Barrington and playing in forepieces in London, to being New York's first regular Nanki-Poo (*The Mikado*), Hilarion (*Princess Ida*) and Richard (*Ruddigore*). During his American stay, from 1885 to 1887, he also took the tenor rôles in the Broadway productions of Lacôme's *Jeanne, Jeannette et Jeanneton* (*The Marquis*, Prince de Soubise) and Lecocq's *La Petite Mademoiselle* (*Madelon*, Jolivet).

He returned to Britain in 1888 and replaced Durward Lely as principal tenor of the Savoy company, creating the rôles of Colonel Fairfax in *The Yeomen of the Guard* (1888, 'Is Life a Boon?'), Marco in *The Gondoliers* (1889, 'Take a Pair of Sparkling Eyes'), Indru in *The Nautch Girl* (1890), Sandford in the revised *The Vicar of Bray* and John Manners in *Haddon Hall*, before leaving Carte's company

in 1892 to appear in the London version of *Ma mie Rosette*.

In 1893 he staged three one-act operettas with a company of his own on the pier at Brighton but, after appearing as Ange Pitou in a revival of *La Fille de Madame Angot*, in the disastrous *Miami* (1893) with Violet Cameron, and as the heroic Mark Mainstay in *Wapping Old Stairs*, he returned to the Savoy to appear as Vasquez in *The Chieftain* (1894). He subsequently went to Australia for a six-month season (Louis Pomerol in *La Belle Thérèse*, Marco, Fairfax) and, on his return, now noticeably plumper, he was cast with great success in the juvenile comedy/tenor rôle of Lancelot in *La Poupée* (1896). *The Royal Star* and *The Coquette* for the same management were less successful, and a season of *Dorothy* (playing the rôle made popular by Ben Davies) was brief, and Pounds then moved away from the musical theatre to spend a period playing supporting rôles in the classics with Beerbohm Tree.

He returned to the musical theatre in 1903, as the extravagant King in a revival of *Chilpéric*, and then, over more than a decade, created a series of varying singing character rôles in a long run of popular musicals, often stealing the show from the nominal stars with his mixture of fun and fine singing: *The Duchess of Dantzic* (1903, Papillon), *The Cherry Girl* (1903, Starlight), *The Blue Moon* (1905, Major Callabone), *The Belle of Mayfair* (1906, Hugh Meredith), *Lady Tatters* (1907, Dick Harrold), *Havana* (t/o Diego de la Concha), *The Dashing Little Duke* (1909, Abbé de la Touche), *The Merry Peasant* (*Der fidele Bauer* 1909, Mattheus), *The Spring Maid* (*Die Sprudelfee* 1911, Nepomuc), *Orpheus in the Underground* (1911, Orpheus), *Princess Caprice* (*Der liebe Augustin* 1912, Jasomir), *Oh! Oh! Delphine* (1913, Ponponnet), *The Laughing Husband* (*Der lachende Ehemann* 1913, Otto Brückner) in London and on Broadway, *Oh, Be Careful* (*Fräulein Tralala* 1915, Bruno Richard), and *My Lady Frayle* (1916, Canon of Dorcaster), as well as appearing in the halls in musical sketches (*A Very Modern Othello, Charles his Friend* etc).

The biggest success of the second half of his career came in 1916 when he created the principal comic rôle of Ali Baba in *Chu Chin Chow* ('Anytime's Kissing Time', 'When a Pullet is Plump'), a part which he played throughout the whole of the show's record-breaking run. Oscar Asche provided him with a similar rôle in the successor, *Cairo*, but the third great starring success of his career awaited him at the age of 53, when he was cast as Schubert in London's *Lilac Time* (*Das Dreimäderlhaus*). His last appearance on the musical stage was in his sixties, in the Spanish musical *The First Kiss* (1924).

His youngest sister, **Louie POUNDS**, began as a chorister and understudy with George Edwardes (*Joan of Arc, Blue-Eyed Susan, In Town*) who promoted her to a tiny rôle in *A Gaiety Girl* (1893, Daisy Ormsbury) and a better one in *An Artist's Model* (1895, Amy Cripps) in the UK and America. On her return in 1896 she was given the ingénue rôle in the touring musical *The French Maid* (1897, Dorothy Travers) which subsequently came to London. She appeared in the flop *Her Royal Highness* (Prince Rollo, 1898) and then joined the D'Oyly Carte company with whom she played in *The Rose of Persia* (Heart's Desire), *The Pirates of Penzance* (Kate), *Iolanthe* (Iolanthe), *Ib and Little Christina* (Christina), *The Emerald Isle* (Molly O'Grady), *A Princess of Kensington* (Joy Jellicoe) and *Merrie England* (Jill-all-Alone) between 1899 and 1903.

Plate 214. **Louie Pounds** *with Constance Drever in* Dorothy, *and brother* **Courtice Pounds** *as Ali Baba in* Chu Chin Chow.

She continued with William Greet in *The Earl and the Girl* (1903, Daisy Fallowfield), took over as one of the 'ugly' sisters in the Cinderella story of *The Catch of the Season* (1904), created the title-rôle in Basil Hood's *The Golden Girl* (1905, Mrs Robinson) on the road, took over in *The White Chrysanthemum* (1906, Cornelia Vanderdecken) and then scored a personal success alongside her brother in Leslie Stuart's *The Belle of Mayfair* (1906, Princess Carl, 'The Weeping Willow Wept', 'Said I to Myself'). She paired again with Courtice in *Lady Tatters* (1907, Isabel Scraby), the *Dorothy* revival (1908, Lydia) and *The Dashing Little Duke* (1909, Duchesse de Burgoyne) and went to America where she appeared on Broadway as the outrageous Olga of *The Dollar Princess* (1910).

She subsequently toured in the star rôles of *The Merry Widow*, *Autumn Manoeuvres* and *The Girl in the Train* and visited South Africa and Australia, mixing straight and musical appearances, including the rôle of Alcolom in Australia's production of her brother's great hit, *Chu Chin Chow*. Her last London musical rôles were in *Toto* (1916, Madame Jollette) and *The Island King* (1922), and on the road in *The Blue Kitten* and *Lionel and Clarissa* in the later 1920s.

Another sister, Nancy, played in comic opera and musical comedy and a third sister, Lillie, was also a musical-comedy performer, who married George Mudie (1859–1918), a longtime singing comedian, and formerly the husband of comic-opera contralto Adelaide Newton.

LA POUPÉE Opéra-comique in 4 acts by Maurice Ordonneau. Music by Edmond Audran. Théâtre de la Gaîté, Paris, 21 October 1896.

A good many years on from his first great successes with *Les Noces d'Olivette*, *La Mascotte* and *Gillette de Narbonne*, composer Audran suddenly surfaced, amongst the routine of comfortable Parisian runs and not-so-comfortable failures, with another major international hit in *La Poupée*. If Maurice Ordonneau's libretto was not precisely original in its bases – the doll/girl exchange was a well-worn, but apparently not yet worn-out plot device – it did, however, create some endearing characters, most particularly its pink-cheeked monastic hero, and some amusing and charming scenes around which, and in keeping with which, Audran composed one of his prettiest scores. Times had changed since the brightly coloured and fun-packed days of *La Mascotte* and, without going into the pastel colours of some later opérette successes, *La Poupée* purveyed a kind of comical charm rather than the more vigorous humour of yesteryear.

When his monastery falls on hard times, Father Maximin (Lucien Noël) hits on a plan. The novice monk Lancelot (Paul Fugère) had been promised a vast dowry by his drunken, half-blind old Uncle (Paul Bert) on his marriage. So Lancelot shall 'marry' ... but his bride shall be one of the dolls from the shop of Maître Hilarius (Dacheux). The one the boy unwittingly chooses, however, is the doll-maker's daughter Alésia (Mariette Sully) who has been standing in for a figure she damaged in the

1167

dusting. By the time the marriage is done, and Lancelot has taken his doll-bride back to the monastery, he has grown attached enough to her that, when she turns out to be real, he prefers to give up his tonsure than his wife. The lower comedy, alongside the gentler strain in the Lancelot-Alésia scenes, was provided by Madame Hilarius (Gilles Raimbaut), sold as a job lot with her daughter, and courted by old Uncle La Chanterelle under the unsuspecting doll-maker's nose.

The music of the show was very largely the province of the two principal players. Alésia described in waltz-song the young man with whom she fell in love in church ('Mon Dieu, sait-on jamais, en somme?'), went through her paces as the automaton ('Je sais entrer dans un salon'), attacked Lancelot amorously in duo ('Je t'aime! je t'adore!'), charmed Uncle and his boozy pal in a flowing waltz trio, and the monastery in a 6/8 'Je suis un petit mannequin', whilst Lancelot put his inexperienced nose into the real world in 2/4 time ('Dans les couvents on est heureux'), discovered a liking for womanhood in the little duo 'Que c'est donc gentil', and awoke wonderingly at the touch of the 'doll's' kiss into the waltzing duo 'On dirait comme une caresse de femme' and his final profession of love ('Qui? la femme donne à l'âme'). Amongst the concerted music, the monks' choral farewell to their brother at the end of the first act was a highlight.

La Poupée had a fine first run in Paris, holding up happily through 121 performances, but it was not immediately snatched up for overseas productions. London's leading producers turned it down, and, finally, it was tyro impresario Henry Lowenfeld who took up the rights with the idea of starring comic Arthur Roberts as Hilarius. The adaptation was done by Arthur Sturgess, George Byng fashioned some new numbers from Audran's music, largely to give a good singing rôle to baritone Norman Salmond as Père Maximin, and the piece was produced at the Prince of Wales Theatre with Courtice Pounds (Lancelot), young Parisian ingénue Alice Favier (Alésia) and Willie Edouin (Hilarius). *La Poupée* turned out to be the most successful musical import to the London stage for many years. It ran in London for 576 performances, the Audran/Byng 'A Jovial Monk Am I' became a baritone party piece and Edouin scored a huge personal hit as the comical doll-maker. The show returned to the Prince of Wales in 1898 (13 December) and in 1904 with Edna May as Alésia (12 April), and was seen in London again as late as 1931 (24 December) and 1935 (21 December) with Jean Colin and Mark Lester. It also toured incessantly for many years with Mlle Favier's understudy Stella Gastelle making half a career of the rôle of Alésia. So popular, in fact, was the piece with English-speaking audiences, that it even became the subject for a 1922 five-reeler Wardour film, with Flora Le Breton starred in the rôle of a silent Alésia.

After the British success of *La Poupée* other countries began to show interest in the show. Broadway's *La Poupée* opened eight months after London's, with another French star, Anna Held, as Alésia alongside G W Anson, Trixie Friganza, Frank Rushworth and Rose Leighton. Oscar Hammerstein's production of Sturgess's version ran 46 nights and returned quickly (15 April 1898) this time with Virginia Earle at its head alongside James T Powers, Frank Celli and two famous old-timers in gangling comedian Joseph Herbert and Catherine Lewis as the doll's parents,

for a second series of 18 performances. In Budapest Klara Küry was *A baba* (ad Ferenc Rajna) to the travesty Lancelot of Aranka Hegyi and the Hilarius of József Németh when the piece was mounted at the Népszinház. This production played its 50th performance on 4 November 1899 and ultimately totalled 82 playings – a figure which put the show into the very top league of opérettic hits at Budapest's most important musical house – prior to a number of revivals at other theatres (Városligeti Színkör 1909, Esküteri Színház 1920 etc).

In Berlin, José Ferenczy followed up his Centraltheater hit with *Die Geisha* by starring little Mia Werber, who had triumphed in the English piece, as the doll-girl of his German version of *Die Puppe* (ad A M Willner), and scored a second hit (100th performance 16 April 1899). Thereafter *Die Puppe* spread through Germany's theatres at a great rate, outstripping not only all of Audran's earlier works in popularity, but quite simply establishing itself (according to Keller's 1926 tally of all-time performances) as the most played of all French works in Germany, ahead of all the favourite works of Offenbach and even of *Les Cloches de Corneville*. In 1904 Ferenczy's company took their version of *Die Puppe* to New York and played it at the Irving Place Theater in repertoire with *Das süsse Mädel* and *Die Geisha*, whilst a 1919 revival at the Theater am Nollendorfplatz proved the show's enduring popularity by running for over 100 nights.

Perversely, Vienna did not take to Willner's version of the show in the same way. Produced by Alexandrine von Schönerer with Frln von Naday/Frln Worm (Alésia), Ferdinand Pagin (Lancelot) and Franz Tewele (Hilarius), and with Josef Joseffy (Lorémois) and Therese Biedermann (Heinrich) in supporting rôles in an otherwise second-best Theater an der Wien cast, it was played 25 successive times and only a handful more thereafter. It was, however, later produced by Gabor Steiner for a season at Danzers Orpheum in 1902 (12 December) with Mizzi Zwerenz as the false doll, and at his Venedig in Wien summer theatre the following season.

La Poupée returned to the Gaîté in 1898 and was seen again on the Paris stage in 1921 when Mlle Mathieu-Lutz appeared as Alésia in a revival at the Théâtre Mogador (10 September), but it never won the extraordinary favour in its country of origin that it had done in England or, most particularly, in Germany.

UK: Prince of Wales Theatre 24 February 1897; USA: Lyric Theater 21 October 1897; Hungary: Népszinház *A baba* 13 January 1898; Australia: His Majesty's Theatre, Sydney 10 September 1898; Germany: Centraltheater *Die Puppe* 5 January 1899; Austria: Theater an der Wien *Die Puppe* 10 October 1899; Film: Wardour (Eng) 1922

LA POUPÉE DE NUREMBERG Opéra-comique in 1 act by Adolphe de Leuven and Arthur de Beauplan. Music by Adolphe Adam. Théâtre Lyrique, Paris, 21 February 1852.

One of the most popular one-act opéras-comiques in the French repertoire in the pre-Offenbach era, Adam's little piece was played throughout Europe for more than half a century, translated into a dozen foreign-language versions, and was one of the few early opérettes to survive, with regular productions, the 'modern' Offenbach onslaught.

Cornelius, the toymaker of Nuremberg, makes a wonderful doll which he believes, with the help of magic art, he can bring alive as a wife for his beloved son, Benjamin. On the night of the carnival ball, Cornelius's nephew and assistant, the ill-treated Heinrich, dresses up as the devil and 'borrows' the doll's clothes as a costume for his sweetheart, Bertha. When the toymaker comes home, and believes what he sees, Heinrich sees how he can manipulate things to his advantage. 'The doll' misbehaves so terribly that Cornelius smashes it with an axe, and Heinrich then lets him believe he has killed Bertha. With the hush money Cornelius gives him, the two will be able to wed. And Cornelius is happy just not to be a murderer.

An American comic opera, *Ardriell* (Union Square Theater 3 June 1889) which professed to be composed by a J Adahm was also professed to be based on *La Poupée de Nuremberg*.

Germany: Friedrich-Wilhelmstädtisches Theater *Die Nürnberger Puppe* 26 November 1852; Austria: Carltheater *Die Nürnberger Puppe* December 1860; UK: Theatre Royal, Covent Garden *The Toymaker* 19 November 1861, Gaiety Theatre *Dolly* 22 August 1870, Sheffield *The Miraculous Doll* 12 July 1886; Hungary: Nemzeti Színház *A Bubagyáros* (aka *Bűvös baba, A nürnbergi baba*) 16 May 1863

POUR DON CARLOS Opérette à grand spectacle in 2 acts by André Mouëzy-Éon and Raymond Vincy based on the novel by Pierre Benoît. Lyrics by Raymond Vincy. Music by Francis Lopez. Théâtre du Châtelet, Paris, 17 December 1950.

The first of the Vincy/Lopez opérettes à grand spectacle mounted at the Châtelet by Maurice Lehmann, *Pour Don Carlos* assembled, at the hôtel des Cimes at Cauterets, a group of characters who might have been borrowed from the theatre's hit of the previous year, *L'Auberge du cheval blanc*. There was the rich industrialist Pommier (Fernand Sardou) with his daughter (Colette Hérent), an anti-Carlist policeman (Jack Claret) and his nephew (Pierjac), and, of course, Don Carlos (Georges Guétary) himself, striving for the throne of Spain. The 1875 action led the star through 16 settings, a drill, a ballet lumineux, two grands ballets, the royal court of King Alfonso, the field, prison, hospital, a half dozen solos (three of which were boléros/rumbas) and duets with his gipsyish leading lady (Maria Lopez, herself equipped with four numbers, one a rumba-boléro) to flight towards America, without a crown but with the leading lady, at the final curtain.

Although some of the music was agreeable enough, and Guétary's 'Je suis un bohémien' did well outside the show, *Pour Don Carlos* was not vintage Lopez nor certainly vintage Vincy. Nevertheless, with the aid of its star and the grand spectacle, it ran through 420 performances at the Châtelet and went on to a provincial afterlife.

Recording: original cast (Pathé)

POWERS, James T [McGOVERN, James] (b New York, 22 April 1862; d New York, 10 February 1943).

A little man, with a face like a cross between a sandwich machine and a Venus flytrap with the giggles, which predestined him for comedy, 'Jimmy' Powers began his theatrical career in musical farce comedy, and toured with Willie Edouin in America and on his unfortunate venture to Britain with *Dreams* and *A Bunch of Keys*. He sub-

sequently played in Britain with the Vokes Family, in pantomime, and in John Hollingshead's revival of *Chilpéric* at the Empire Theatre, before returning to America.

Powers played for a period in comic opera at the Casino Theater, appearing in such rôles as the little Briolet in *The Marquis* (*Jeanne, Jeannette et Jeanneton*), Taboureau in *Madelon* (*La Petite Mademoiselle*), Faragas in *Nadgy*, the sighing tailor, Griolet, in *La Fille du tambour-major*, and as Cadeau to the Ravannes of Edwin Stevens in a revival of *Erminie*. He then returned to farce comedy for some years, but he came back to the more legitimate musical stage for what would be the most memorable portion of his career, playing the star comic rôles in the New York productions of a series of mostly British musical comedies in the 1890s and 1900s.

Beginning with Arthur Roberts's *Gentleman Joe* (1896), these subsequently included the orientals Wun-Hi in *The Geisha* and Li in *San Toy* (both created at Daly's Theatre by Huntley Wright), Teddy Payne's little-chap comic rôles in the Gaiety musicals *The Circus Girl*, *The Messenger Boy* and *A Runaway Girl*, Pentweazle in *The Medal and the Maid*, Walter Passmore's Moolraj (*The Blue Moon*), Henry Lytton's Jelf (*A Princess of Kensington*) and, with particular success, Alfred Lester's creation, Samuel Nix, in the Leslie Stuart musical *Havana*. He also played Hilarius in *La Poupée* (revival), and appeared in such native musical plays as Oscar Hammerstein's *Santa Maria*, *The Jewel of Asia*, and Gustave Kerker's second remake of *Two Little Brides* (*Schneeglöckchen*).

In his later career Powers appeared almost wholly in straight theatre, but without maintaining the star profile he had won through some 20 years of musical comedy. In 1922 he ventured into authorship with a musical version of the comedy *Somebody's Luggage* written with Mark Swan. He himself starred in a fine cast including Allen Kearns, Marjorie Gateson and Flavia Arcaro, under the direction of Ned Wayburn, but *The Little Kangaroo* died on the road.

Powers's wife, Rachel Booth, appeared in soubrette rôles alongside her husband in several shows.

1922 **The Little Kangaroo** (aka *Little Miss Butterfly*) (Werner Janssen/w Mark Swan) Stamford, Conn, 23 November
Autobiography: *Twinkle, Little Star* (Putnam, New York, 1939)

PRADEAU [Étienne] (b 1817; d January 1895).

The celebrated opérette comedian began his career of more than half a century on the Paris stage singing secondary tenor rôles at the Opéra-Comique, but he took his most important step to fame when he left those semi-august halls and appeared, paired with Berthelier, as one of the original 'blind men' in Offenbach's *Les Deux Aveugles* at the Bouffes-Parisiens. He remained a member of Offenbach's company for some years, playing in such pieces as *Croquefer* (Croquefer), *Le Financier et le savetier* (Belazor), *Pépito* (Vertigo), as one of *Les Deux Pêcheurs* with Gerpré, *Le Docteur Miracle*, *Tromb-al-ca-zar* (Beaujolais), *La Rose de Saint-Flour* (Marcachu), *Le Voyage de MM Dunanan* (Tympanon), *Il Signor Fagotto* (Bacolo) and *Les Bavards* (Sarmiento).

He later moved on to less musical employment at the Palais-Royal and the Gymnase (Sancho Pança in Sardou's *Don Quichotte* etc), but returned to musicals when he joined the company at the Théâtre des Variétés and there created such comic rôles as Le Commissaire in *La Boulangère a des écus* and Van Tricasse in *Le Docteur Ox* (1877), alongside a long list of plays. He was later seen at the Nouveautés in France's original production of *Fatinitza* (1879, Makouli).

PRESENT ARMS Musical comedy in 2 acts by Herbert Fields. Lyrics by Lorenz Hart. Music by Richard Rodgers. Lew Fields' Mansfield Theater, New York, 26 April 1928.

Herbert Fields followed up his naval success, *Hit the Deck*, with a marine-military piece, and for *Present Arms* he rejoined forces with his habitual partners, Richard Rodgers and Lorenz Hart. He brought with him the star of *Hit the Deck*, Charles King, who was featured in the new piece as a marine who pretends that he is a ranking officer when courting the English Lady Delphine (British supporting actress Flora Le Breton, here getting her big chance) who is also ogled by the rich foreigner Ludwig von Richter (Anthony Knilling). It was another English lass, comedienne Joyce Barbour, however, who teamed with Busby Berkeley (doubling as choreographer and hero's best friend) to put across the song that proved the highlight of an evening which was not up to *Hit the Deck*, when they joined together in 'You Took Advantage of Me'. *Present Arms* lasted 155 Broadway performances and was not exported.

London did, however, get a *Present Arms* in the form of 'a revusical comedy in 2 acts by Fred Thompson. Additional dialogue by Bert Lee. Lyrics by Frank Eyton. Music by Noel Gay' produced at the Prince of Wales Theatre, during the Second World War (13 May 1940). Wylie Watson, George Gee and Billy Bennett comicked through wartime France as three old soldiers who had fond memories of the First World War and of Babette (Phyllis Monkman) in a piece built on the lines of the first War's hit show *The Better 'Ole*. In an ephemeral score, grapeshot through with transatlantic interpolations, American soubrette Evelyn Dall and the Vincent Tildesley Meistersingers harmony group encouraged 'Dig for Victory' and Miss Dall danced with her partner, Max Wall, to 'Dancing People', Miss Monkman was 'Mademoiselle de France' and Herman Timberg's song tried to make people believe that in spite of everything it was a 'Hap-Hap-Happy Day'. Tom Arnold and Harry Foster's production provided lively, topical entertainment on a twice-daily format for 225 performances before being chased out of town by disapproving bombs.

LES PRÉS SAINT-GERVAIS Opéra-comique in 3 acts by Victorien Sardou and Philippe Gille based on Sardou's play of the same title. Music by Charles Lecocq. Théâtre des Variétés, Paris, 14 November 1874.

Following his two enormous international successes with *La Fille de Madame Angot* and *Giroflé-Girofla*, Lecocq took a turn in a more opéra-comique direction with his musical version of Sardou's play *Les Prés Saint-Gervais*, a piece originally played in 1862 at the Théâtre Déjazet by Virginie Déjazet (24 April).

The expanded (by an act) and musical version of Déjazet's rôle of the young Prince de Conti was written for and to the measure of favourite prima donna Zulma Bouffar, but before *Les Prés Saint-Gervais* could get to the stage Mlle Bouffar had crossed words with the Variétés management,

done a walk, and left the prize rôle of the latest Lecocq piece to the splendidly voiced but less charismatic Mlle Peschard.

The pubescent young Prince has a hard time getting Harpin (Berthelier), his hypocritical, lecherous old tutor, and the rest of the folks around him – notably the girls – to recognize the fact that he is becoming a man. So, on the day when the folk of the area hie to the Prés Saint-Gervais for a jolly picnic, the lad slips away and follows. But when he tries to join in the fun of the bourgeois folk, he is ridiculed for his courtly ways, and the certain success with women that Harpin has taught his royal pupil will naturally be his is made mockery of by a little flowergirl called Friquette (Paola Marié). Events come to the point where he ends up fighting a duel with La Rose (Christian), a sergeant in his own regiment. Although the experienced soldier pinks the boy, he then becomes his champion and helps him to put all his mockers in their place (and to sew his royal wild oat with Friquette) before leading him home, wiser to the ways of a world from which he has been all too shielded before. Two of the bourgeois folk, Angélique and Grégorie, provided some contrasting comedy.

Lecocq's score to *Les Prés Saint-Gervais* was written in a manner suited to its period and classic subject, without the bouffe effects of a *Giroflé Girofla*, or the entrain of an *Angot*, and although there was some fine soprano singing for the star, jolly moments for the comic folk and a good dash of military music, the *Prés Saint-Gervais* music did not produce anything like the remarkable score that Lecocq would provide, a few years later, for a similar subject in *Le Petit Duc*.

Les Prés Saint-Gervais played only 46 nights at the Variétés, but its composer's reputation ensured that it was exported in amazingly quick time. London, avid for the newest Lecocq musical, snapped it up and Robert Reece's English version was mounted at the Criterion Theatre with Pauline Rita (Conti) and Catherine Lewis (Friquette) starred and Alfred Brennir as La Rose, only a fortnight after the Paris première. One critic, outraged by opéra-bouffe and the can-can and longing for 'good taste' and the days of Planché, sighed happily '(it) might have been written twenty years ago', but it nevertheless, and in spite of a cast of 60, ran for 132 performances at its very little house. It doubtless appeared less 'good taste' when the lively Kate Santley, with her penchant for interpolating saucy songs into her shows, then took it to the provinces.

Nowhere else, however, did the piece win a run like that in London. Vienna's Carltheater production, with Hermine Meyerhoff as Conti, Karoline Finaly as Friquette, Franz Eppich as La Rose, Josef Matras (Harpin) and Therese Schäfer (Dorette), was played ten times. The uncredited translation retitled the piece *Prinz Conti*, a title retained for Germany and for Hungary where the piece found little more success. In America, the Comley-Barton troupe ventured a *Prince Conti* as well, with Catherine Lewis, now a major star, swapping the rôle of Friquette for that of the Prince, alongside Constance Lewis (Friquette). The company played only a few nights of *Prince Conti* at New York's Fifth Avenue Theater as part of their touring schedule.

UK: Criterion Theatre 28 November 1874; Austria: Carltheater *Prinz Conti* 10 March 1876; Australia: Prince of Wales

Theatre, Melbourne 10 July 1876; Hungary: Budai Színkör *Conti herceg* (*A tizenhat éves ezredes*) 19 July 1877; Germany: Aachen *Prinz Conti* 7 August 1880; USA: Fifth Avenue Theater *Prince Conti* February 1883

PRESTON, Robert [MESERVEY, Robert Preston] (b Newton Highlands, Mass, 8 June 1918; d Santa Barbara, Calif, 21 March 1987).

After a 25-year career in theatre and film, the twinkling, crushed-voiced Preston became a musical-theatre star overnight with his 1957 performance of an era as the roguish Professor Harold Hill in *The Music Man* ('Till There Was You', 'Seventy-Six Trombones', Tony Award). He subsequently starred on Broadway in the musical *Ben Franklin in Paris* (1964, Benjamin Franklin), alongside Mary Martin in the two-handed saga of American marriage *I Do! I Do!* (1966, Tony Award) and as Mack Sennett in the sorry musical tale of *Mack and Mabel* (1974, 'I Won't Send Roses'). His last musical, *The Prince of Grand Street* (1978) folded on the way to town, a fate which had earlier befallen *We Take the Town* (1962), a musical based on the Ben Hecht play *Viva Villa* in which Preston appeared as Pancho Villa.

Preston repeated his *Music Man* rôle on film and also appeared as Beauregard, the honeymooning husband of *Mame*, in the filmed version of that musical.

PRÉVEL, Jules (b Saint-Hilaire de Harcouët, 1835; d Paris, 12 September 1889).

A Parisian journalist and theatre critic, Prével is credited with having invented the theatre gossip column or 'courrier des théâtres' with the rubrique which he began at *Le Figaro* in 1865. The boyish-looking, devotedly 'investigative' journalist operated in and around the Paris theatre for nearly 25 years, penning his columns with a serious enthusiasm in which an actress's private affairs took on all the importance of affairs of state, and winning himself many enemies in the process.

Prével collaborated on the texts of a number of plays and opérettes, including several successful works in conjunction with Paul Ferrier (notably the very fine and very durable *Les Mousquetaires au couvent*) and with Armand Liorat. His part therein was, however, not accepted by all: 'Ill-natured tongues have asserted, indeed, that, if his name was attached to many plays, he seldom contributed anything else to them, and that without writing a line of the text he acquired a share of the author's dues in return for the valuable publicity at his disposal. This charge has been often repeated, but never proved ...'.

1861 **Marianne** (Theodore Bennet-Ritter) 1 act Opéra-Comique 17 June
1863 **Une paire d'anglais** (Charles Domergue/w Alexis Bouvier) 1 act
1866 **La Viperine** (Jean-Jacques de Billemont/w William Busnach) 1 act Théâtre des Folies-Marigny 19 October
1869 **La Romance de la rose** (Jacques Offenbach/w Charles Nuitter, Étienne Tréfeu) 1 act Théâtre des Bouffes-Parisiens 11 December
1869 **Tu l'a voulu** (Samuel David/w Émile Abraham) 1 act Théâtre des Bouffes-Parisiens 12 September
1874 **Le Cerisier** (Jules Duprato) 1 act Opéra-Comique 15 May
1879 **Le Grand Casimir** (Charles Lecocq/w Albert de Saint-Albin) Théâtre des Variétés 11 January

1880 **Les Mousquetaires au couvent** (Louis Varney/w Paul Ferrier) Théâtre des Bouffes-Parisiens 16 March
1882 **Attendez-moi sur l'orme** (Vincent d'Indy/Robert de Bonnières) 1 act Opéra-Comique 11 February
1882 **Fanfan la Tulipe** (Varney/w Ferrier) Théâtre des Folies-Dramatiques 21 October
1884 **Mademoiselle Réséda** (Gaston Serpette) 1 act Théâtre de la Renaissance 2 February
1884 **Babolin** (Varney/w Ferrier) Théâtre des Nouveautés 19 March
1885 **Les Petits Mousquetaires** (Varney/w Ferrier) Théâtre des Folies-Dramatiques 5 March
1887 **L'Amour mouillé** (Varney/w Armand Liorat) Théâtre des Nouveautés 25 January
1890 **Ma mie Rosette** (Paul Lacôme/w Liorat) Théâtre des Folies-Dramatiques 4 February

PRIMROSE Musical comedy in 3 acts by George Grossmith and Guy Bolton. Lyrics by Desmond Carter and Ira Gershwin. Music by George Gershwin. Winter Garden Theatre, London, 11 September 1924.

Following his productions of two Anglo-American musicals with Jerome Kern scores (*The Cabaret Girl*, *The Beauty Prize*) it was rumoured that George Grossmith and his producing partner Pat Malone would next bring out a piece on which the young Noël Coward would collaborate. However, Grossmith, in the event, opted instead for a young American called George Gershwin whose music had recently been heard in the revues *The Rainbow* and *The Punch Bowl* and who had just premièred a piece called 'Rhapsody in Blue'.

Grossmith and Guy Bolton's book had parts made to suit the Winter Garden cast of favourites. Leslie Henson was aristocratic and silly Toby Mopham who has promised more than he should to common but attractive Pinkie Peach (Heather Thatcher) and who uses the author Hilary Vane to help him get out of his commitment. As a result, Hilary's ingénue Joan (Margery Hicklin) gets upset and makes rash promises to foolish Freddie (Claude Hulbert). Toby's mum (Muriel Barnby) follows the example of the Merry Widow and turns her stately home into a nightclub to keep Toby indoors and it is there that all the pairings are finally sorted out. Grossmith, the comic who always had a yen towards romantic rôles, had the part of Hilary Vane mapped out for himself, rather than the more suitable one of Freddie, but Gershwin objected and asked for a singer. He got Percy Heming, a staunchly operatic baritone, and Grossmith limited himself to directing.

Heming got new songs, topped by a ballad 'This is the Life for a Man' which sounded as if it had come from the same parlour piano as 'Wandering the King's Highway' and other such British yo-ho ballads, Henson had three comedy songs which (particularly one regretting 'Wasn't it Terrible What They Did to Mary, Queen of Scots') were more English old-time music-hall than anything seen on the London stage in years and, if a delightfully lyricked little piece for the ill-matched heroine and Freddie, 'Berkeley Square and Kew', was one of the prettiest musical moments of the night, most of the best material came from Gershwin's trunk. He sounded much more at home in the jaunty 'Wait a Bit, Susie', the vampy 'Boy Wanted' (ex- *A Dangerous Maid*) and 'Naughty Baby' and the lilting 'Some Far Away Someone' (ex- *Nifties of 1923*) than in the rather effortfully English tones of the custom-made songs.

Primrose was a well-tailored Winter Garden show and, even without Grossmith, and soon without the clever and popular Miss Thatcher, it had a well-tailored run of 255 performances. That was just about it. It was picked up for an Australian production and mounted by J C Williamson Ltd with Maud Fane and Albert Frith featured for two-and-a-half months in Melbourne and then, with Hugh Steyne replacing Frith at eight minutes' notice on opening night, for just under two months in Sydney (Her Majesty's Theatre, 29 August 1925), but although it was announced for Broadway with Basil Durant and Kendall Lee as stars for the 1925–6 season, it never appeared.

Australia: Her Majesty's Theatre, Melbourne 11 April 1925
Recording: original cast (WRC)

PRINCE, Hal [PRINCE, Harold Smith] (b New York, 30 January 1928). Vastly successful Broadway producer turned even-more-successful director of musicals on both sides of the Atlantic.

Originally a stage-management assistant with George Abbott, Prince moved into the production of musical plays at the age of 26 in partnership with co-Abbott-worker Robert E Griffith and Freddie Brisson. The trio began with two considerable hits, *The Pajama Game* (1954) and *Damn Yankees* (1955), and drew ambivalent results with the musicalized Eugene O'Neill *New Girl in Town* (1957) before Prince and Griffith took up a project which would turn into an even more significant triumph than their two initial hits: *West Side Story* (1957).

The pair followed up with another hit in *Fiorello!* (1959) and the same authors' less attractive *Tenderloin* (1960), and following Griffith's death in 1961 Prince continued as a producer alone. His first solo venture was yet another hit: *A Funny Thing Happened on the Way to the Forum* (1962), and in an amazing run of fine shows – which only very occasionally included a mis-hit – he followed up with *She Loves Me* (1963), *Fiddler on the Roof* (1964), *Flora, the Red Menace* (1965), *It's a Bird ... It's a Plane ... It's Superman* (1966), *Cabaret* (1966), *Zorba* (1968), *Company* (1970), *Follies* (1971), *A Little Night Music* (1973), *Candide* (1973, w Chelsea Theater Group) and *Pacific Overtures* (1976).

By this stage, established as one of the most important and certainly one of the very most successful producers on the postwar Broadway musical stage, Prince had also established himself amongst the leading American directors of musicals. His close association with Abbott meant that in his early days as a producer it was the experienced and effective elder statesman of the New York theatre who had been responsible for the staging of Prince's shows, even though Prince had been a 'creative' producer, providing artistic input as well as cash. It was not until 1962 that he was responsible for the physical staging of a musical, and then it was not one of his own productions but Andrew Siff's *A Family Affair*, a piece which numbered amongst its authors the young John Kander. *A Family Affair* was a 65-performance flop, but Prince moved into the director's chair more happily the following year when he staged his own production of *She Loves Me*.

After one more step aside, to direct Alexander Cohen's Sherlock Homes show *Baker Street* (1965), Prince directed all of his own productions, creating memorable stagings for such pieces as *Cabaret*, *Company* (Tony Award), *A Little Night Music* and the new, multi-stage version of *Candide*

(Tony Award). He also took half a third Tony award for his co-staging (w Michael Bennett) of *Follies*.

In the last years of the 1970s, Prince devoted himself to directing rather than to producing, and he scored fresh success with the remarkable mountings of two pieces of widely different kinds in 1978: the operetta burlesque *On the Twentieth Century* for Broadway, and *Evita*, the record-turned-stage-show which most of theatrical London had said couldn't be put onto a stage. Both pieces of staging remain classics of the genre.

Thereafter, things went a little less well for the man who had stood so long under the shower of success. The over-sized Broadway mounting of *Sweeney Todd* (1979) proved a misjudgement, and three projects for which he again donned a co-producer's hat, *Merrily We Roll Along* (1981), *A Doll's Life* (1982) and *Grind* (1985), were swift failures. But success returned in 1986 when Prince mounted the extravagant, romantic production of London's *The Phantom of the Opéra*, a staging which was, in the manner of modern musical productions, subsequently re-created in the long series of reproductions staged all around the world.

Subsequent projects as a director, amongst a continuing series of operatic productions since 1978, have included *Roza* (1986–7) and *Kiss of the Spiderwoman* (1992).

Prince's daughter, Daisy Prince, appeared in the original cast of the musical *Merrily We Roll Along*.

Autobiography: *Contradictions: Notes on 26 Years in the Theatre* (Dodd Mead, New York. 1974). Biographies: Hirsch, F: *Harold Prince, and the American Musical Theatre* (CUP, New York, 1989); Ilson, C: *Harold Prince from Pajama Game to Phantom of the Opera* (UMI Press, Ann Arbor, 1989).

LE PRINCE DE MADRID Opérette à grand spectacle in 2 acts by Raymond Vincy. Lyrics by Jacques Plante. Music by Francis Lopez. Théâtre du Châtelet, Paris, 4 March 1967.

Favourite French tenor Luis Mariano returned to the Paris stage in 1967 to play (in his early fifties) the rôle of the painter Goya in a spectacularly staged Spanish romance which had as little to do with the real Goya as Lehár's libretti had with their nominal subjects. This Goya got involved with an ingénue called Florécita (Janine Ervil) and the amorous Duchesse d'Albe (Maria Murano), thus invoking the jealous rivalry of a basso matador (Lucien Lupi) and of the ducal Captain of Guards (Jean Chesnel) who plots to have him brought before the inquisition. Maurice Baquet and Eliane Varon were tacked into the tale as the traditional soubrets of the Vincy/Lopez opérette in a piece which, whilst sticking minutely to the formula they had so successfully established, did not, particularly in its music, rise to the level of the best of the team's previous work. However, Mariano, singing to 'España' and 'Florécita', enjoying 'La Feria de Séville', acclaimed as 'Le Prince de Madrid', or sighing 'Toi, mon seul amour' in a piece where the rest of the cast took a very secondary musical place, ensured that Marcel Lamy's production lasted 554 performances at the Châtelet prior to serving its time on the road. It became well enough established that whilst better Vincy and/or Lopez pieces are little seen it still wins regional revivals.

Goya and the Duchess of Alba had gambolled rather more briefly across the Broadway stage a couple of decades earlier in a kind of Spanish *Dubarry Was a Lady* called *The*

Duchess Misbehaves (Adelphi Theater, 13 February 1946). He was Joey Faye and she was Audrey Christie, five times.

Recording: original cast (Pathé)

THE PRINCE OF PILSEN Musical comedy in 2 acts by Frank Pixley. Music by Gustave Luders. Tremont Theater, Boston, May 1902; Broadway Theater, New York, 17 March 1903.

Luders and Pixley had established themselves amongst the most enjoyable American writers of musical comedy of their time with *The Burgomaster* and *King Dodo*; with *The Prince of Pilsen*, their best and most successful show, they confirmed themselves at the very top of their profession.

Pixley's book gave the opportunity for a jolly display of the popular low 'Dutch' comedy of the day by making its central character one Hans Wagner, a Cincinnati brewer, of a very obviously 'deutsch' background, equipped with the accent which flagged him as a comical person. At Nice's International Hotel, Wagner (John W Ransome, a comedian known for his impersonations of politico 'Boss' Crocker) is mistaken for the secretly expected and incognito Prince of Pilsen. He wins wonderful attentions from the hotel staff, the slightly disappointed attentions of the pretty and wealthy widow Mrs Crocker (Dorothy Morton) who was once rescued from a horse-riding accident by the Prince, and the enmity of Artie, the impoverished Earl of Somerset (Maurice Darcy), who is after the millions of Mrs Crocker. The real prince, Carl Otto (Arthur Donaldson), happy to keep his planned incognito, woos and wins little Nellie Wagner (Ruth Peebles), so that when Artie, after all sorts of beastly tries at discrediting Hans, exposes his uncomprehending 'pretence', Carl Otto is able to announce that Nellie will after all be, as all had thought her, the Princess of Pilsen. The genuinely funny plot also managed ingeniously to get a foxhunt (with 'Tally-ho!' chorus), a sub-plot with secret documents, a duel and the once-famous Nice Bataille des fleurs into the action.

Luders's score decorated the comedy with some delightful songs in a range of the usual styles, of which a traditionally rousing and partially unaccompanied Stein Song for the Prince and his pals, the pretty 'Tale of a Sea Shell' for Carl Otto, and another romantic piece, the waltz 'The Message of the Violet' which fell to the number-two juvenile couple (Ivey Anderson, Mabel Pierson), proved the take-away hits. The production numbers included Mrs Crocker's song about 'The American Girl', a piece sub-titled 'the Song of the Cities' which plugged various towns: Baltimore 'where the oysters thrive and the streets are alive and the lobsters are fresh and frisky', St Louis which boasted 'ginger and push and Anheuser Busch', Chicago where 'the stockyards so fair perfume the air', and New York where 'the news is so hot they're printing asbestos

Plate 215. **The Prince of Pilsen:** *A duel on the hills overlooking what is now Nice airport. Tom Wagner (Harry Fairleigh) and the incognito Prince (Arthur Donaldson) come mistakenly to blows under the eyes of Artie Shrimpton (Victor Morley), bellboy Jimmie (Eva Westcott) and Nellie Wagner (Ruth Peebles).*

papers', to the accompaniment of musical quotes from 'My Maryland', the cake-walk, *King Dodo* and 'Yankee Doodle', and a parallel parade of feminine beauty.

After a brief run-in at Malden, Mass, Henry Savage's production scored a decided success when it was introduced to Boston, but the producer showed no haste to take it to New York. It was ten months and many touring dates later that Broadway finally got *The Prince of Pilsen*. Helen Bertram was now the widow, Lillian Coleman played Nellie, and Albert Parr and Anna Lichter sang about the Violet, and *The Prince of Pilsen* ran through 143 Broadway performances before moving on. It returned during each of the next four years for further seasons, and it also travelled to London where the American company moved into the Shaftesbury Theatre, the old home of *The Belle of New York*, for a season. *The Prince of Pilsen* was a much superior piece to its predecessor, but it had not the attraction of novelty that that show had had, and a respectable 160 performances was its lot. The show was considerably boosted, however, by a different kind of novelty. One of its chorus girls, the minutely waisted Camille Clifford, who represented New York as 'the Gibson Girl' in the 'Cities' number, became a gawper's phenomenon. The stare of the season. When the rest of the cast went home, she stayed in Britain to briefly become a top-of-the-bill name, and almost an actress, before hooking her nobleman and retiring.

Having made it to London, *The Prince of Pilsen* then went on to become one of the few American musicals of the era to go into Europe when the Isola Brothers introduced it as one of a handful of foreign musical plays which they presented at l'Olympia (ad Victor de Cottens), with London's Fred Wright and American singer May de Souza starred. It also went to Australia, under the management of J C Williamson. Charles A Lorder (Hans) George Whitehead (Carl Otto), Olive Goodwin (Mrs Crocker), Myles Clifton (Artie) and Amy Murphy (Nell) featured in a six-week season in Sydney before *The Prince of Pilsen* gave way to another American musical, *The Red Mill*, in the Williamson repertoire.

The Prince of Pilsen hung on as a perennial favourite on American stages for a good many years, and it was given a brief reprise on the Broadway stage amongst the Shuberts' series of old favourites which were mounted at the Jolson Theatre in 1930 (13 January). Al Shean played the rôle of Hans.

UK: Shaftesbury Theatre 14 May 1904; France: Olympia *Le Prince de Pilsen* 14 December 1907; Australia: Theatre Royal, Sydney 30 May 1908
Recording: selection (AEI)

LA PRINCESSE DES CANARIES Opéra-bouffe in 3 acts by Henri Chivot and Alfred Duru. Music by Charles Lecocq. Théâtre des Folies-Dramatiques, Paris, 9 February 1883.

Following his split with Victor Koning and the Théâtre de la Renaissance, Lecocq had scored a double triumph at the Nouveautés with *Le Jour et la nuit* and *Le Coeur et la main*. His next show took him back to the authors of some of his earliest pieces, Chivot and Duru, now as famous as he, but with whom in the years since their early success with *Les Cent Vierges* the composer had come together only once, on *Le Pompon*, the show no one liked except the

Hungarians, for the Folies-Dramatiques. Authors and composer did decidedly better with their new effort for the same house, *La Princesse des Canaries*, a piece which presented the particularity of being a two-headed star vehicle for two young girls.

Juliette Simon-Girard had won her star's stripes several years back in *Les Cloches de Corneville*, but little Jeanne Andrée, who took the second rôle à tiroirs of *La Princesse des Canaries*, was a beginner. In a plot which offered something of the opportunities of Mme Simon-Girard's other great triumph, *Madame Favart*, multiplied by two, the girls played foster sisters, Pépita (Mme Simon-Girard) and Inès (Mlle Andrée), who, aided by Uncle General Bombardos (Lepers), cavalcaded through a series of disguises on their under-cover mission to win back the throne for whichever one of them is the real Princess of the Canaries. Their rural husbands Inigo (Simon-Max) and Pédrille (Dekernel), kept in the dark, have to be stopped time and again from scuppering the venture. When Pépita is proclaimed Queen, the incumbent General Pataquès (Delannoy) has her arrested but, of course, it is all a red herring and at the final curtain Inès (who is the ingénue and has been singing the top soprano line all evening, so we should have known) turns out to be the real monarch.

Lecocq's score was another delightful one, highlighted by its pretty duo music for the two girls, a particularly enjoyable two-faced comic encounter for the rival generals ('Bonjour, Général'), and such happy irrelevancies as the tale of Cupid and Psyche, sung as a ronde for the first-act finale, and the Toréador song which made up part of the very large soubrette rôle of Pépita. Mme Simon-Girard's rôle allowed her to run the gamut from impersonation, in the servant-girl's song 'Comm' tout's les femmes', to Grande-Duchesse-style comedy in her political declaration of intent (Chanson de la Princesse des Canaries), a plan which – a couple of years before *The Mikado*'s appearance – included a list of nuisances to be suppressed (the Chambre des Deputés, the police, and anyone who takes liberties with her), to some moments of genuine sentiment ('J'étais contente de mon sort'). Mlle Andrée, whilst not lacking sparky moments, had the corner on the loving ones, notably in her first-act romance ('De mon coeur vous êtes le maître'), and the pretty ones, as in her last-act Flowergirl's number ('Les fleurs que nous admirons').

La Princesse des Canaries was a tidy success at the Folies-Dramatiques, playing for nearly three months, returning after the summer break to pass its 100th performance on 7 September and finally totalling 139 showings in its first year. Oddly, however, it seems not to have returned to the Paris stage and, equally oddly, its career abroad was mostly undistinguished.

Germany's production of *Die Canarien-Prinzessin* aroused no particular interest, Vienna quite simply passed on Lecocq's latest work, and Budapest's Népszinház played *Kanári hercegnő* (ad Lajos Evva, Béla J Fái) a fair but scarcely outstanding 14 times. Maurice Grau introduced the piece to New Yorkers in the original French with Marie Aimée (Pépita), Mlle Angèle (Inez), Mezières (Pataquès), Duplan (Bombardos), Lary (Inigo) and Mlle Delorme (Catarina) without featuring it extensively in his repertoire, but the piece finally found an altogether more cheering success when it was produced in the English language.

A British version, *Pepita* (ad 'Mostyn Tedde', ie Edward Paulton), directed by Harry Paulton and starring Fanny Wentworth, Louis Kelleher and producer Horace Lingard, trouped the provinces for some 400 performances before venturing a season in London, starring Tillie Wadman and Frank Wyatt, and then returned to the out-of-town scene to tot up a longer British life than any other Lecocq work bar *La Fille de Madame Angot* had achieved. Paulton sr was sufficiently impressed by all this to take the show further. Four-and-a-half years after Aimée's performances, he brought what was now billed as his own version of *La Princesse des Canaries* to Broadway under the title *The Queen's Mate*. After the double-meaning original title and the prima-donna-pleasing second one, this third referred to none other than the buffeted-about Inigo, scarcely the chief character of the piece, but here played by ... Paulton. Camille D'Arville was Anita (ex-Pepita), Lillian Russell played Inez and J H Ryley was Pataquès. The anglicized show was a hit. It played for two months before moving out of town (30 June) for the height of the summer, then came right back in again (13 August) to continue its run – with Miss Russell now playing Anita – until 10 September before heading again for the country. On 7 January 1889 *The Queen's Mate* had a third Broadway season, this time with Lilly Post (Anita) and Marie Halton (Inez) starred.

Quite how much difference there was between the father's and the son's English versions of *La Princesse des Canaries*, or which was the better (if indeed they were not the same), cannot now be fathomed, but Australia opted for the younger generation and mounted *Pepita* in 1889. Nellie Stewart (Pepita), Fanny Liddiard (Inez), W H Woodfield (Inigo), Walker Marnock (Bombastes) and William Elton (Pataquès) headed the cast. It did well enough to be retained in the repertoire until 1891.

Germany: Viktoria-Theater *Die Canarien-Prinzessin* 13 May 1883; USA: Fifth Avenue Theater (Fr) 10 September 1883, Broadway Theater *The Queen's Mate* 2 May 1888; Hungary: Népszinház *Kanari hercegnő* 19 October 1883; UK: Royal Court Theatre, Liverpool *Pepita* 30 December 1886, Toole's Theatre, London 30 August 1888; Australia: Princess Theatre, Melbourne *Pepita* 9 February 1889

LA PRINCESSE DE TRÉBIZONDE Opéra-bouffe in 2 acts by Charles Nuitter and Étienne Tréfeu. Music by Jacques Offenbach. Baden-Baden, 31 July 1869. New version in 3 acts Théâtre des Bouffes-Parisiens, Paris, 7 December 1869.

Originally produced at Baden-Baden, *La Princesse de Trébizonde* proved successful enough that Offenbach and his librettists subsequently expanded it into a full evening's entertainment and, later in the same year, at the same time that *Les Brigands* was being mounted at the Théâtre des Variétés, *La Princesse de Trébizonde* Mark II was staged at the Bouffes-Parisiens. Tréfeu and Nuitter's libretto made use of the already over-used doll-girl motif, but they surrounded that motif with such jolly characters and scenes as to make it seem less stageworn. As a result, the piece survived, alongside the ballet *Coppélia* and Audran's *La Poupée*, as the happiest example of that eternal 19th-century plot on the musical stage.

Sparadrap (Édouard Georges), the eagle-eyed tutor of the pubescent Prince Raphaël (Anna van Ghell), allows him to visit the waxworks run by Cabriolo (Désiré), unaware that the mountebank's daughter Zanetta (Mlle Fonti) is standing in for a broken doll. When Cabriolo wins a château in the fair's lottery, and Raphaël's family turn out to be their neighbours, the prince's ultra-careful father, Prince Casimir (Berthelier), is delighted to see that his son's youthful passions are limited to the next-door folks' doll and he promptly takes the waxworks and their proprietors back to court. When Casimir discovers that his son has known for an act and a half that Zanetta was not made of wax, the boy brings out his dad's old and indiscreet diaries, which he has been using as guide-lines to growing up, and father is obliged to mutter away into consent. Céline Chaumont starred as Zanetta's sister, Régina, in love with the once-aristocratic servant, Trémolini (Bonnet), who becomes first the company's fair-barker and then (because of his knowledge of etiquette) their butler, and Mlle Thierret played the plum female comedy rôle of Cabriolo's sister, Paola, who suffers from delusions of royal relationships.

In line with its libretto, the score of *La Princesse de Trébizonde*, although labelled as opéra-bouffe, had a little less of the zany freedom of music of Offenbach's earliest opéras-bouffes. The burlesque was still there – the first-act finale, with Cabriolo and his family bidding farewell to their old sideshow ('Adieu, baraque héréditaire') in one of the happiest pieces of the score was a direct parody of Rossini's *Guglielmo Tell* – but the fun and Offenbachian melody in Casimir's smoke-from-the-ears description of his easily fired temper ('Me maquillé-je comme on dit'), Régina's song about her tightrope act ('Quand je suis sur la corde raide'), Zanetta's Ronde de la Princesse de Trébizonde, and in Raphaël's repeated raptures, both with and over his 'doll' was often a little less 'bouffe'.

The success of *La Princesse de Trébizonde* was barely overshadowed by that of *Les Brigands*, and it stayed at the Bouffes for some four months as a first run. It was revived there, after the interruptive Franco-Prussian War, in 1875 (14 February) with Louise Théo as Régina, again in 1876, and was given a new production at the Théâtre des Variétés in 1888 (15 May) with a cast headed by Mily-Meyer, Mary Albert, Cooper and Christian. The record thus established was a highly satisfactory one, in the terms of any other composer, yet *La Princesse de Trébizonde* remained and remains a little in the shadow of the more celebrated Offenbach works in France where it has been rarely heard from since that last Paris revival.

Something of the same thing happened in London where the show, nevertheless, had a fine first production (ad Charles Lamb Kenney) under John Hollingshead's management, at the Gaiety Theatre. Nellie Farren was Régina and J L Toole ad-libbed freely as Cabriolo, at the head of a cast which included Robert Soutar (Casimir), Constance Loseby (Raphaël) and Annie Tremaine (Zanetta) and the show stayed in the bill for a little under three months, was brought back later in the year, was toured and then played again at the Gaiety in 1872 (19 April) in Toole's repertoire. In 1879 it was given a spectacular revival at the Alhambra with Charles Collette (Cabriolo), J Furneaux Cook (Casimir), Miss Loseby (Raphaël), Alice May (Zanetta) and Emma Chambers (Régina), and an 'Automatic Ballet' of wax dolls introduced in the final act. But that was it.

La Princesse de Trébizonde was also introduced to America in Kenney's English version with a production at Wallack's Theater which presented the unusual feature of starring the famous burlesquer Lydia Thompson in a French opéra-bouffe rôle. Aimée appeared in French breeches as Prince Raphaël in 1874, but the piece prospered in America in translation rather than in the original. It was produced at the Casino Theater (5 May 1883) with a top cast including John Howson, Lillian Russell, Digby Bell and Laura Joyce, played in German at the Thalia Theater (14 December 1882), at the Casino Theatre with Marie Jansen and Francis Wilson (15 October 1883) and, in a heavily revised version, with Pauline Hall and Fred Solomon starred, at Harrigan's Theater in 1894 (5 March).

Die Prinzessin von Trapezunt also won a good reception in Germany, but it was in Austria that the piece found most particular favour. Produced at the Carltheater (ad Julius Hopp) with a very strong cast headed by Pepi Gallmeyer (Regina), Hermine Meyerhoff (Zanetta), Karoline Tellheim (Raphaël), Josef Matras (Casimir), Karl Blasel (Cabriolo), Wilhelm Knaack (Sparadrap) and Therese Schäfer (Paola) and conducted by Offenbach himself, it was immediately seen to be one of the theatre's biggest-ever successes. It was played 53 times between March and May, came back in the spring to reach its 72nd night by the new year, passed its 100th in repertoire on 24 June 1873, its 125th on 13 September 1874, and reached its 141st on 28 May 1878. It was given for ten performances at the Theater an der Wien in 1885 (17 January) with Ottilie Collin (Raphaël), Blasel, Friese (Casimir), Rosa Streitmann (Zanetta) and Marie Theresia Massa (Zanetta), it was revived at the Carltheater, with Blasel, Knaack, Anna von Boskay and Frln Tornay in 1892, played in 1899 at the Jantschtheater and in 1905 at the Theater in der Josefstadt. However, unlike elsewhere, *Die Prinzessin von Trapezunt* did not then disappear. It was played at the Berlin Opera in 1932, and has been seen in Vienna at the Theater an der Wien (12 May 1966) and at the Wiener Kammeroper in the 1980s.

In Budapest (ad Endre Latabár), where it was first seen in 1871, it was later taken briefly into the repertoire of the Népszinház (18 May 1876, 5 performances), and it was also played in many other European centres (Brussels, Naples, Copenhagen, Stockholm, Prague, Bucharest, Zagreb etc), as well as in Australia where William Lyster introduced it in 1874, but it seems to have survived best and only where the taste for the less extravagantly burlesque operettic works is the strongest.

UK: Gaiety Theatre 16 April 1870; Austria: Carltheater *Die Prinzessin von Trapezunt* 18 March 1871; Germany: Friedrich-Wilhelmstädtisches Theater 30 June 1871; USA: Wallack's Theater 11 September 1871; Australia: Prince of Wales Theatre, Melbourne 22 June 1874; Hungary; Budai Színkör *A Trapezunti hercegnő* 17 September 1871

PRINCESS FLAVIA Musical play in 2 acts by Harry B Smith based on *The Prisoner of Zenda* by Anthony Hope. Music by Sigmund Romberg. Century Theater, New York, 2 November 1925.

The Shubert/Romberg follow-up to *The Student Prince* was another romantic operetta set in a Germanic neverland and dealing with the problems of royalty. The piece was originally intended as a vehicle for tenor Walter Woolf in the rôle of Rudolf Rassendyl, the sosie of the Prince of Ruritania who doubles for the monarch and falls in love with his bride, the Princess Flavia. However, the production lost first its star, then two titles (*Zenda*, *A Royal Pretender*), and then its leading lady when Marguerite Namara, who had already walked out of *The Love Song*, dropped out of this one as well. British baritone Harry Welchman and soprano Mary Mellish took over the rôles, the latter replaced before Broadway by Evelyn Herbert who was even gratified with the title-rôle when the show became *Princess Flavia*. All the troubles proved in vain, for *Princess Flavia*, regarded as a pale imitation of *The Student Prince* both musically and textually, played for 152 performances without establishing itself as in any way memorable, and then sent one company on the road to join the nine *Student Prince*s currently touring.

Some 40 years later, the San Francisco Light Opera under Edwin Lester produced another *Prisoner of Zenda* musical, *Zenda* (Vernon Duke/Lenny Adelson, Sid Kuller, Martin Charnin/Everett Freeman, Curran Theatre, San Francisco 5 August 1963), with Alfred Drake and Anne Rogers as its leading characters. This one didn't even get as far as Broadway.

PRINCESS IDA, or Castle Adamant Respectful operatic perversion in 2 acts and a prologue (later 3 acts) of Tennyson's *The Princess*, being a revised version of *The Princess* by W S Gilbert. Music by Arthur Sullivan. Savoy Theatre, London, 5 January 1884.

Never one to waste his own (or other people's) ideas, W S Gilbert re-used parts and plots of several of his early works in later pieces, but *Princess Ida* was the only example of his taking and remaking an entire musical show. It was also the only example in his mature works of a burlesque of a specific work of literature, in this case Tennyson's poem. The original of *Princess Ida* was the 1870 burlesque *The Princess* (Olympic Theatre, 8 January 1870), a piece written in metre and affecting the fashionable wordplay of mid-19th century burlesque, equipped with a pasticcio score which included such melodies as Rossini's 'Largo al factotum', *La Périchole*'s Trois Cousines trio and Auber's *Manon Lescaut* laughing song. For the remake, Gilbert took portions of his old text and spaced them out with fresh dialogue and lyrics which, being written in the modern Gilbert style in which puns and metric dialogue had given way to the kind of stylish wit to which his name has become attached, did not always blend as happily as they might have. Similarly, on this occasion, what had become the Savoy 'team' of performers did not have rôles made to their measure, as had become their habit.

After the rehearsal-time sacking of Lillian Russell, it was ingénue Leonora Braham – originally intended for a lesser rôle – who was Princess Ida, a bluestocking who has renounced men and set up a university where the male sex is not permitted, nor anything which reeks of the masculine. However Ida's father King Gama (George Grossmith) had betrothed her at a childish age to Hilarion (Henry Bracy), the son of King Hildebrand (Rutland Barrington), and that grumpy king now threatens inconveniences if the contract is not carried out. Hilarion and his friends Cyril (Durward Lely) and Florian (Charles Ryley) get into the university in female disguise, and the whole institution soon crumbles as much under the influence of the randy laddies inside its walls as Hildebrand's armies without.

Sullivan's score for *Princess Ida* was also of a dual nature. There were the now expected 'Savoy-style' songs: two magnificently brittle, wordful patter songs for Grossmith as the misanthropic Gama – a rôle originally conceived as a direct burlesque of Tom Taylor's Tribouht in *The Fool's Revenge* – ('I Can't Think Why', 'Whene'er I Spoke Sarcastic Joke'), a delightfully clever solo for the Prince ('Ida Was a Twelvemonth Old') which argued, that, since he was two when she was one, 'husband twice as old as wife argues ill for married life', Cyril's joyously tipsy 'Would You Know the Kind of Maid', and the boys' anticipatory 'Expressive Glances'. Alongside these, there were less-expected pieces. Ida's numbers ('O Goddess Wise', 'I Built Upon a Rock') were not in the light, nigh-on soubrette style of the Savoy's usual soprano music: they were wholly serious, both lyrically and musically, whilst Richard Temple, cast peripherally as one of Hildebrand's avenging sons, had a mock-Handelian aria, 'This Helmet I Suppose', which came straight from the world of burlesque.

Princess Ida won a mixed reaction and, truth to tell, it sat a little uncomfortably at the Savoy. The performers were, by and large, not suited to their rôles as well as in the earlier shows, the comedy was less prominent, and the show's hybrid nature could not be overlooked. But the show was still Gilbert and Sullivan, with many parts which were up to their best work, and it found itself a willing audience for 246 performances. If this was short of the previous shows' totals, it was, nevertheless, superior to just about anything else around: *Princess Ida* was no failure. Not in London, anyhow. Broadway was less interested in the piece and a production with Cora Tanner (Ida) and J H Ryley (Gama) was taken off after 48 performances, although producer John Stetson did bring it back, several years later, with Geraldine Ulmar, Joseph W Herbert and Courtice Pounds, for a second brief season.

In Australia, Colbourne Baber (Ida) and William Elton (Gama) headed J C Williamson's production at Melbourne, whilst Sydney was treated to original star Leonora Braham and minstrel veteran Edwin Kelly (Hildebrand) the following year. Williamson brought out *Princess Ida* at intervals thereafter, but London did not see the piece again until it was brought back into the D'Oyly Carte repertoire in 1919 and New York saw it again for the first time only in 1925 (Shubert Theater, 13 April, 40 performances). The piece has remained a minor part of the Gilbert and Sullivan canon, but in recent years its apparently feminist (or, more accurately, anti-feminist) tale and sub-operatic star music have given it a newly fashionable air. A version was produced at Hagen (ad Stefan Trossbach) in 1986, and another – tricked out in 1960s junk-theatre gimmickry – at the English National Opera in 1992.

USA: Fifth Avenue Theater 11 February 1884; Australia: Princess Theatre, Melbourne 16 July 1887

A PRINCESS OF KENSINGTON

Comic opera in 2 acts by Basil Hood. Music by Edward German. Savoy Theatre, London, 22 January 1903.

Having proven themselves the most likely inheritors of Gilbert and Sullivan's position in the British musical theatre with their *Merrie England*, Hood and German followed that piece with one which delved into Gilbert's favourite fairyland. Teased eternally by the sprite Puck (Walter Passmore), Fairy Prince Azuriel (Ernest Torrence) has nursed jealousy for a thousand years over the love once shared by the fairy Kenna (Constance Drever) and the long-dead mortal Prince Albion. Finally – forgetting about such things as mortal men's mortality – he decides that he will force Albion to wed someone else. Puck and Kenna choose William Jelf of the *S S Albion* (Henry Lytton) and Joy Jellicoe (Louie Pounds) to perform the charade. Since he is engaged to zealous Nell Reddish (Rosina Brandram) and she to Lieutenant Brook Green (Robert Evett) there are many complications before the testy fairy is calmed and the mortals can get back to normality.

German's score was a model piece of light opera, with some rich ensembles and lovely fairy music, topped by a charming ballad for the tenor ('My Heart a Ship at Anchor Lies') and by a genuine hit song in the jolly male quartet 'We're Four Jolly Sailormen', a piece which became a favourite parlour and concert number for more than half a century. The show itself, however, was not a success. It had a highbrowish flavour to it which the more comical *Merrie England* had not, and although it was much liked by hard-core light opera-goers, it attracted the general public for only 115 performances. Manager William Greet gave up the Savoy Theatre and, after an indifferent tour, switched the company to musical comedy productions. The famous Savoy era was effectively over.

A Princess of Kensington was, nevertheless, picked up for Broadway where Dora de Fillipe (Kenna), James T Powers (Jelf) and William Stephens (Puck) featured in John C Fisher's production for a 41-performance run.

USA: Broadway Theater 31 August 1903

THE PRINCESS PAT

Comic opera in 3 acts by Henry Blossom. Music and lyrics by Victor Herbert. Cort Theater, New York, 29 September 1915.

The Princess Pat was an Irish lass, but unlike the series of her sisters who would soon take over the Broadway stage she was neither poor nor in search of a princely husband to wed at the final curtain. Patrice O'Connor (Eleanor Painter) has already got a prince, for she is wed to Prince Antonio di Montaldo (Joseph Letora) when the curtain goes up. He is, however, not as attentive as a princely husband might be, now they are married. As a little encouragement to some flattering jealousy, and in order to help out a friend (Eva Fallon), Pat pretends to elope with the ageing and comical Anthony Schmalz (Al Shean). She succeeds on both counts, and she goes back to her revived prince whilst friend Grace marries the more suitable junior member of the Schmalz family (Robert Ober).

The show suffered a nasty setback when the actress originally cast as Grace was murdered by a jealous boyfriend on the eve of the production. Miss Fallon saved the day, and John Cort's production, at the little theatre named for him, was able to open as planned. Blossom's above-average talents as a writer of dialogue and an attractive Herbert score which included the heroine's pretty 'Love is Best of All' (amongst some Irishy bits), her Italian husband's 'Neapolitan Love Song' (amongst some Italiany bits) and the comic's amusing and tuneful longing 'I Wish I

Were an Island in an Ocean of Girls', aided by the talented Miss Painter and the comical Shean, assured a Broadway run for *The Princess Pat*. The show ran for a good 158 performances and toured most profitably without, however, finding itself a significant afterlife or an export licence.

PRINCESS TOTO English comic opera in 3 acts by W S Gilbert. Music by Frederic Clay. Theatre Royal, Nottingham, 26 June 1876; Strand Theatre, London, 2 October 1876.

When Kate Santley, who had commissioned Frederic Clay's *Cattarina* as a vehicle for herself with some success, went on the road again in 1876 she ordered another new piece from the composer. This time, she got a rather superior one, as Clay collaborated on *Princess Toto* not with burlesque's Robert Reece, but with the young librettist and lyricist W S Gilbert.

Miss Santley was Princess Toto, a chronically forgetful royal with a crush on a local brigand called Barberini. When her betrothed Prince Doro (E Loredan) appears to have vanished, she agrees to wed Prince Caramel (Joseph E Beyer), but he is late for the wedding and Doro turns up so she takes him instead. Caramel disguises himself as Barberini and whisks the princess off for a jolly bandit life, but her father (John Wainwright) leads his court (including J H Ryley and W S Penley) to the rescue, all of them disguised as Red Indians, and lures her back. Finally the dizzy lady settles down with the man she has actually married.

Clay provided a fine opéra-bouffe score which gave the prima donna opportunities for the sentimental ('Like an Arrow from its Quiver (comes my love to marry me)') to the comical ('The Pig with the Roman Nose'), whilst Prince Doro had a similar combination in his apostrophe to his unknown bride ('Oh, Bride of Mine, Oh, Baby Wife') and the lightly topical 'There Are Brigands in Every Station'. There was less of the topsy-turvy humour of the libretto in the lyrics than would later become usual in Gilbert's writing, but the piece was a fine one and quickly proved the most popular item in its producer's repertoire. In October it was brought to London, with Claude Marius (Doro), J G Taylor (Caramel) and Harry Cox (Portico) supporting Miss Santley, but some backstage strife occurred which resulted in its being pulled off after just 48 performances.

Bad management hit an American production, with Leonora Braham starred as Toto, which was put on poorly prepared and ran only 22 performances, but Gilbert remained convinced of the value of his piece and, following his rise to fame with *HMS Pinafore* and *The Pirates of Penzance*, he succeeded in persuading John Hollingshead to remount a revised version of *Princess Toto*. This time, instead of the flamboyantly sexy Miss Santley, the title-rôle was cast with operatic vocalist Annie Albu and baritone Richard Temple was given the rôle of Portico. But it still ran just 65 performances and spawned a not very successful Australian production with Robert Brough repeating his London performance as Zapeter alongside Annette Ivanova (Toto), Armes Beaumont (Doro) and Edwin Kelly (Portico). In 1935 Barry Jackson exhumed the forgotten piece for a showing at the Birmingham Repertory Theatre.

USA: Standard Theater 13 December 1879; Australia: Opera House, Melbourne 12 June 1886

PRINTEMPS, Yvonne [WIGNOLLE, Yvonne] (b Ermont, 25 July 1895; d Paris, 19 January 1977). Individually styled actress and vocalist who made herself a star on every kind of stage.

Mlle Printemps began her stage career at the age of 12, and played at first largely in revue, making her earliest appearances in opérette as Prince Charmant in *Les Contes de Perrault* (1913) at the Gaîté, alongside Henri Defreyn in *Le Poilu* (1916, Suzanne Letillois) at the Palais-Royal, and in *La Petite Dactylo* (1916) at the Gymnase. She abandoned the musical stage when she joined Sacha Guitry (soon to become her husband) for a series of plays which made them one of the oustanding items in the Paris theatre, but in 1923 she appeared with Guitry in his musical play *L'Amour masqué* ('J'ai deux amants') and, thereafter, music took an important part in many of their plays: *Mozart* (1925), in which Printemps appeared as the boy composer, a revival of *Jean de la Fontaine* into which were slipped several songs by Lully and one by Gilles Durant, and *Mariette* (1928) which allowed its heroine the luxury of appearing as a 100-year-old woman (as well as a young one).

Printemps played *Mozart* in London and New York, *Mariette* in London, and then, following the break-up of her marriage, created in London the rôle of Melanie in *Conversation Piece*, written to her measure by Noël Coward, partly in English, partly in French, ('I'll Follow my Secret Heart'). She played the same rôle in New York, before returning to Paris where she appeared in a version of the German Operette *Drei Walzer* specially remade to suit her and her new partner, Pierre Fresnay. *Les Trois Valses*, which had evoked only minor interest in its original form, was an enormous success with Printemps in the three generations of its starring rôle, and she repeated it, under her own management, when she subsequently took control of the Théâtre de la Michodière, and again in Ludwig Berger's celebrated film version. Thereafter, in a long and always starry career, she confined herself to the nonmusical theatre, although she was seen on the screen as Hortense Schneider to the superb Offenbach of Fresnay in *Valse de Paris*.

An impishly winning actress with a mastery of comic timing both in her acting and in the songs which she put across in a clear, accurate and very individual soprano, she was a phenomenon of the musical stage to which, because of the non-singing men in her life, she returned only intermittently.

Biography: Dufresne, C: *Yvonne Printemps* (Perrin, Paris, 1988)

PRINZ METHUSALEM Operette in 3 acts by Karl Treumann adapted from a libretto by Victor Wilder and Alfred Delacour. Music by Johann Strauss. Carltheater, Vienna, 3 January 1877.

Franz Jauner of the Vienna Carltheater commissioned a French libretto from Victor Wilder (the co-author of the remaking of Johann Strauss's *Indigo* as *La Reine Indigo*) and Alfred Delacour to tempt Strauss to abandon the Theater an der Wien and compose an Operette for his theatre instead. Strauss, who had had a happy experience working on the French *Indigo* and considered its libretto much superior to the Viennese original, was duly tempted and, although the composer's French was minimal, much of the work was already composed before Karl Treumann, the longtime adaptor of Offenbach's works for the Vienna stage, put *Prinz Methusalem* into German.

Herzog Cyprian of Riccarac (Wilhelm Knaack) and Sigismund, Fürst von Trocadero (Josef Matras) are signing a military treaty, to be sealed dynastically by the marriage of Prince Methusalem of Riccarac (Antonie Link) and Pulcinella (Karoline Finaly), daughter of the ruler of Trocadero. The marriage has taken place, but the treaty is not yet signed when news comes that Cyprian has been deposed. Sigismund, who is offered his neighbour's crown by the revolutionaries, tries to stop the consummation of the unfortunate marriage, but the young folk are in love and they not only consummate but, by the end of the evening, end up replacing both their tricky fathers as the much-loved rulers of a coalition of both countries. Therese Schäfer was Cyprian's comical wife, Sphisteira, Franz Eppich played Trombonius, the court composer, and the tenor Ausim was the Lord Chamberlain, Vulcanio, in which rôle he inherited one of the show's happiest songs, 'Du schöner mai, du liebelei'. The hit number of the piece, however, was the comical number performed by Matras, 'Das Tipferl aus dem i'.

Jauner got 54 performances out of his Strauss Operette before the end of 1877, and another eight, with Lori Stubel as the Prince, in the first five months of 1878, before he threw in his managerial hand. When Franz Tewele took over he gave the piece another five showings, and intermittent performances took it up to its 89th on 19 September 1881. In 1904 (13 April) it appeared for a week at the Theater an der Wien with Phila Wolff starred but, although it was occasionally played thereafter, it never became a part of the generally revived Strauss canon.

Prinz Methusalem duly had a German production, at Berlin's Friedrich-Wilhelmstädtisches Theater, which was followed by a number of others (it returned to Berlin, at the Theater des Westens, as late as 1932), and New York also saw its first performances in German when the piece was mounted at the Thalia with Marie König (later Franziska Raberg) as the Prince. It was several years more before *Prince Methusalem* was played in New York in English, but when it was it appeared both at the Cosmopolitan with Catherine Lewis (Methusalem) and J H Ryley (Cyprian) starred and, a few days later, at the Casino Theater (9 July) with Mathilde Cottrelly in the title-rôle and Lilly Post (Pulcinella), A W Maflin (Cyprian) and Francis Wilson (Sigismund) in support. This latter production proved popular enough for producer John McCaull to bring it back for a second brief season at the Casino the following year (15 December 1884), and again, in 1888, to Wallack's Theater (16 July) with Marion Manola, De Wolf Hopper and Jefferson de Angelis featured. It stayed a month, apparently partly due to Hopper's interpolation, apropos of nothing, of what was to become his celebrated party piece, the recitation of the poem 'Casey at the Bat'.

If New York more or less liked *Prince Methusalem* (or just 'Casey'?), London, which had seen it a month earlier in English (ad H S Leigh), had shown very firmly that it did not. Tenor W S Rising played a non-travesty Prince, Camille Clermont and Ethel Pierson headed the ladies and Phil Day the comedy, to one of the most thundering thumbs-downs London had seen in years. The show did not last a week. It was bundled off, and the music of Strauss was replaced on the stage of the Folies Dramatiques by that of the urging New Zealander Luscombe Searelle as heard in *Estrella*. In Australia, where prima donna Emilie Melville presented herself as the Prince, alongside Gracie Plaisted (Pulcinella) and a score 'for a considerable portion of whose music Strauss is not responsible' which included music-hall songs and a Christy Minstrel quartet, the show did little better. Similarly, in Budapest (ad György Verő), where Strauss's *Die Fledermaus* had been a considerable success, *Prinz Methusalem* with the tiny Sarolta Tarnay in her first (and only) lead rôle as Pulcinella, played just seven times. Paris, never much dazzled by the Strauss name, let it pass, in spite of the piece's French genesis, and they were probably right as although the show had won many mountings, it had played remarkably few performances in most of them.

Germany: Friedrich-Wilhelmstädtisches Theater 21 January 1878; USA: Thalia Theater (Ger) 29 October 1880, Cosmopolitan Theater (Eng) 26 June 1883; UK: Folies Dramatiques *Prince Methusalem* 19 May 1883; Hungary: Népszinház *Metuzalem herceg* 5 September 1884; Australia: Princess Theatre, Melbourne 22 September 1883

PROMISES, PROMISES Musical in 2 acts by Neil Simon based on the screenplay *The Apartment* by Billy Wilder and I A L Diamond. Lyrics by Hal David. Music by Burt Bacharach. Shubert Theater, New York, 1 December 1968.

A one-and-only stage musical by popular songwriters Burt Bacharach and Hal David, whose decade of collaboration had brought forth such hit numbers as 'The Story of My Life', 'Magic Moments', 'Twenty-Four Hours from Tulsa', 'Anyone Who Had a Heart', 'There's Always Something There to Remind Me', 'What's New, Pussycat?', 'Trains and Boats and Planes', 'What the World Needs Now', 'Do You Know the Way to San Jose?' and a bookful of others, *Promises, Promises* maintained its writers' high-success profile by becoming a very large and international hit. It was, on the other hand, by no means a one-and-only hit for its librettist, Neil Simon, already the author of two splendid musicals in *Little Me* and *Sweet Charity* and here called upon, as with *Sweet Charity*, to turn a film-script into a libretto.

Chuck Baxter (Jerry Orbach) isn't noticed much at work until middle-management discover he has a bachelor apartment. Middle-management are sufficiently grateful for the use of that apartment for Chuck to get an appointment with J D Sheldrake (Edward Winter), head of personnel. Chuck gets promotion, Sheldrake gets an exclusive on the apartment, and all is well until the boy discovers that 'the branch manager from Kansas' whom Sheldrake meets at his home is Fran Kubelik (Jill O'Hara), the girl he has sighed over so long. But it has been and is a rocky affair and one night the desperate Fran inconsiderately takes an overdose in Chuck's apartment. Fortunately the next-door-neighbour is a doctor, and by the end of the act a happy ending has been arranged. At the final curtain it is clear that the apartment won't be available to anyone any more except its two inhabitants.

The show's set of songs duly turned out a Bacharach/David hit in the simple, guitar-accompanied promise of the recovering Fran, 'I'll Never Fall in Love Again' (an on-the-way-in addition to the score), and its highlight was a jolly office party scene where the tiddly truths and sexual jockeyings were contrasted with a memorably zippy Michael Bennett song-and-dance routine to 'Turkey Lurkey Time' for three girls (Adrienne Angel, Barbara Lang, Donna McKechnie) who had lost their second number when the hit solo was added.

David Merrick's production of *Promises, Promises* was a 1,281-performance hit on Broadway, and the show repeated its success when it was reproduced in London by Merrick and H M Tennent Ltd whilst Broadway's version ran on. Tony Roberts (later to take over on Broadway), Betty Buckley and James Congdon featured, and the show ran 560 performances in the West End. Australia followed quickly behind, with a production featuring Orson Bean, Ann Hilton, Bruce Barry and Nancye Hayes through a rather disappointing ten weeks in Melbourne and a short season in Sydney.

A German version, which returned to the film title (aka *Das Schlusselkarussell*) was later produced at Munich and Berlin's Theater des Westens (ad Werner Wollenberger, Charly Niessen), and in localized version (ad Gerhard Bronner) at Vienna's Theater an der Wien where, with Peter Fröhlich as Willy Draxler and Marianne Mendt as Franzi Kubelik, and the song 'She Likes Basketball' transmuted into 'Sie hat Fussball gern', it played a season of 72 performances. Italy hosted *Promesse, Promesse* and Switzerland played *Das Appartment*, as the musical got worldwide coverage. Perhaps, however, because of a period flavour which has not yet become nostalgiable, it has not remained a standard piece in the repertoire in the way that its initial success suggested it might.

UK: Prince of Wales Theatre 2 October 1969; Germany: Theater des Westens *Das Appartment* 16 April 1970; Australia: Her Majesty's Theatre, Melbourne 15 August 1970; Austria: Theater an der Wien *Das Appartment* 3 November 1973
Recordings: original cast (UA), London cast (UA), Italian cast (CGD/FGS) etc

PRUETTE, William (b Washington DC, ?1863; d Liberty, NY, 15 July 1918).

Baritone Pruette made his first ventures on to the stage singing grand opera at McVicker's Theater in Chicago under the name Signor Pruetti and subsequently sang in Paris, and on tour with Emma Abbott's Opera Company, before making his first appearance in opéra-bouffe as Mourzouk in *Giroflé-Girofla*. In 1891 he sang the rôle of Alfio in some of the first American performances of *Cavalleria rusticana* and then appeared with the Bostonians as Pippo to the Bettina of Camille D'Arville in *La Mascotte*, and at the Casino Theater as Picasso in *The Lion Tamer* (*Le Grand Casimir*), in *The Child of Fortune* (*Das Sonntagskind*), as King René in Julian Edwardes's *King René's Daughter* (1893) and as Mars in *Prince Kam* (1894). In 1894 he also created the title-rôle in De Koven's highly successful *Rob Roy*. Later Broadway rôles included the Duc du Bouillon in Julian Edwardes's *The Wedding Day* (1897) alongside Jeff de Angelis and Lillian Russell, Admiral Hi Lung in *A Chinese Honeymoon* (1902), an appearance with De Wolf Hopper and Madge Lessing in a revival of *Wang* (1904) and Henry VIII to the Mary Tudor of Lulu Glaser in *A Madcap Princess*.

Now established as one of the musical stage's best 'fathers', he won his finest rôle to date when he appeared as the grouchy Comte de Saint Mar in Victor Herbert's *Mlle Modiste* (1905), introducing 'I Want What I Want When I Want It'. He appeared as The Rajah in *The Tourists* (1906), as the Governor General in *Algeria* (1908) and found himself in his element with the arrival in America of the fashion for Viennese Operette. He scored another great success as Colonel Popoff in *The Chocolate Soldier* (1909) and subsequently appeared as Pish Tush in the Casino Theater's star-studded *Mikado* of 1910, played in *The Kiss Waltz* (*Liebeswalzer*, 1911) and, in his last Broadway appearances, in *The Red Petticoat* (1912, Big Regan) and Oscar Straus's *My Little Friend* (*Die kleine Freundin*, 1913, Barbasson).

LES P'TITES MICHU Opéra-comique in 3 acts by Georges Duval and Albert Vanloo. Music by André Messager. Théâtre des Bouffes-Parisiens, Paris, 16 November 1897.

In a busy, varied career in which his musical theatre writings had often received more connoisseur's praise than profitable runs, Messager had not succeeded in being party to a genuine, full-scale hit of international proportions since his very first opérette venture, completing the score of the late Firmin Bernicat's *François les bas-bleus*, 14 years earlier. With *Les P'tites Michu* not only was that omission thoroughly remedied, but the show's combination of a gently charming libretto, full of enjoyable characters, and a musical score of refinement and beauty as well as of considerable gaiety, produced one of the most elegantly attractive opérettes of the pre-war French theatre.

The little Michu sisters, Blanche-Marie (Odette Dulac) and Marie-Blanche (Alice Bonheur), are not really sisters. One of them was confided to Madame Michu (Mme Vigoureux) and her shopkeeping husband (Regnard) as a baby, and is really the aristocratic child of General des Ifs (Barral). However, as Michu once bathed the babes, they now have no idea which is which. When des Ifs returns to claim his child from the foster-mother, so that she may wed his handsome lieutenant, Gaston Rigaud (Manson), Blanche-Marie insists that her more extrovert sister, who has fallen madly for Gaston, must be nominated. Blanche-Marie will marry the Michu's shop-boy, Aristide (Maurice Lamy). But Marie-Blanche finds the proprieties of aristocratic life unbearably constricting and Blanche-Marie is just hopeless in the shop. It is clear that blood will

Plate 216. **Les P'tites Michu:** *London's Michu twins – who aren't twins – were Mabel Green and Adrienne Augarde.*

out. When the positions are reversed, everyone is much happier.

The gems of Messager's score began with the little sisters' introductory duo 'Blanche-Marie et Marie-Blanche', the bouncing trio 'Michu, Michu, Michu' of their first schoolgirlish meeting with Gaston, and Marie-Blanche's frank appreciation of his qualities ('Sapristi, le beau militaire'), they continued with Aristide's puzzled light tenor attempt to make his choice between the two girls ('Blanche-Marie est douce et bonne'), and with the girls' second-act discovery of their position ('Ah quel malheur') and their double prayer to Saint-Nicolas: each sister praying she isn't the one picked to wed the unknown lieutenant and, after they've realized who the bridegroom is, each praying that she is. The jolly appearance of the senior Michus, the General's explosive nonsense, Gaston's smooth baritonic vocalizing and some superior ensembles all went with these to make up a model opérette score.

Les P'tites Michu was a fine Paris success. It ran for more than 150 nights in its first series, was briskly taken up by the theatres of France and was soon exported first to Hungary (ad Ferenc Rajna), then to Germany (ad Heinrich Bolten-Bäckers) and then to Vienna's Carltheater. Franz Jauner's production cast Betty Stojan and Aurélie Révy as the two sisters, Louis Treumann was Aristide, and Siegmund Natzler the General through 24 performances before the arrival of Mme Sarah Bernhardt removed them from the stage. In Paris, Mariette Sully and Mary Lebey appeared in an 1899 revival at the Folies-Dramatiques, but although the show appeared in Lisbon and in Prague in the following years, its record outside France was a disappointing one and it seemed that the perhaps rather too wink-and-nodless *Les P'tites Michu* would go no further. But it did.

George Edwardes had decided, after the evident drop in quality of his Daly's Theatre entertainments with *The Cingalee*, that a change was needed at that theatre. Given the great success of his recent production of Messager's *Véronique*, he reached back for the composer's earlier piece and produced an English adaptation of *The Little Michus* (ad Henry Hamilton, Percy Greenbank) at Daly's Theatre. The choice proved a fine one. With Adrienne Augarde and Mabel Green as the two little girls, Willie Edouin as the General, Amy Augarde stealing a scene as Madame Michu, the ever-versatile W Louis Bradfield as Aristide and Bobbie Evett as a tenor Gaston, the show took off for a splendid run of 401 London performances, a run in line with what a Daly's show expected and even intrinsically better than the slightly longer life secured by *Véronique* at the smaller Apollo Theatre. The piece moved on from there not only to the provinces but to the colonies, and Florence Young and Margaret Thomas were featured as the little semi-lost Michus, supported by Reginald Roberts (Gaston), George Lauri (Ifs), W S Percy (Aristide) and Clara Clifton (Mme Michu), in an Australian production which played a fine seven weeks in Sydney before moving on to the rest of the country.

Last of all, *The Little Michus* got its showing in America. But J C Duff's production, with Alice Judson and Ruth Julian as the girls, and British comedian George Graves splattering excesses all over the stage as a General des Ifs with a wooden leg, flopped in 29 performances.

The show returned to Paris's Trianon-Lyrique in 1909 (27 September), but whilst *Véronique* prospers to this day, this piece – arguably better, if less thoroughly romantic – has been seen only spasmodically since.

Hungary: Magyar Színház: *Michu lányok* 19 February 1898; Germany: Metropoltheater *Die kleinen Michu's* 25 December 1898; Austria: Carltheater *Die kleinen Michu's* 16 September 1899; UK: Daly's Theatre *The Little Michus* 29 April 1905; Australia: Her Majesty's Theatre, Sydney 2 June 1906; USA: Garden Theater 31 January 1907
Recording: complete (Gaîté-Lyrique), selection (EMI-Pathé)

PUFFERL Operette in 3 acts by Ignaz Schnitzer and Sigmund Schlesinger. Music by Edmund Eysler. Theater an der Wien, Vienna, 10 February 1905.

On a hint from Girardi as to the sort of rôle and scene(s) that he, the biggest star of the Viennese Operette stage, would like to play in his next piece, Schnitzer and Schlesinger built up a piece around the character of the hairdresser, Pufferl, a figure taken from a set of old Vienna tales.

Pufferl's hairdressing shop on the Graben is a great place for gossip and intrigue and the hairdresser gets the usual kind of confidences from his clients. The Graf Dreyschatten (Adalbert Minnich) is anxious to get his hands on some land owned by the family of Ewald, Fürst von Limenau (Karl Meister), and Pufferl suggests to him that he get the young man to make an unsuitable marriage, thus forfeiting his property. Dreyschatten enlists Pufferl to his aid with the promise of promotion to 'Hoffriseur' and the crafty fellow decides to entrap Limenau into an alliance with the singer Poldi, a wench who is the perfect double of the eccentric Countess Christine Rottek (Gerda Walde) with whom Ewald fell in love when rescuing her from a carriage accident. Although Pufferl thinks the Countess is on his side, she falls for her 'prey' during the course of the events, and when Pufferl and Dreyschatten think they have tricked Limenau into marrying Poldi, it turns out that it wasn't Poldi, but her 'double'. A third act sorts everything out, gets Pufferl his title and his girl, Mali (Mila Theren), pairs his hopeful housekeeper, Kathi (Sarolta von Rettich-Birk) off with his assistant (Franz Glawatsch), and gets Dreyschatten out of a sticky spot. Director Siegmund Natzler completed the principal cast as Mali's father.

Eysler's typically Viennese score supplied Girardi with his obligatory hit number, the waltzing Kirschenlied (on the forbidden-fruit theme), at the head of a catchy score also marked by a lively dialect march trio 'Gehn ma Freunderl'. Leading lady Gerda Walde, however, had her best number cut at the star's behest after she scored altogether too well with it on the opening night.

Pufferl clearly had the making of a good success in it, but it was not to be allowed to run. Girardi's jealousies went beyond his fellow actors, and he could not bear being directed by Karl Wallner, once a supporting actor and now in charge at the Theater an der Wien. He was as troublesome as possible, and as soon as his minimum contract was up, he abandoned the Theater an der Wien and *Pufferl* which, as of 31 March, had played just 51 performances.

Pufferl later turned up in Italy under the title of *Amor di Principi* and the Italian version was briefly played in New York by a touring company, but at home it had committed suicide, leaving just its Kirschenlied behind.

PUGNO, Raoul (aka 'Franz [or Max] Richard') (b Montrouge (Seine), 23 June 1852; d Moscow, 3 January 1914).

After a notable career at the Paris conservatoire (first prize in organ etc), Pugno began his career as a composer with classic works, including an oratorio *La Résurrection de Lazare* (1879). He later wrote the scores for several opérettes as an adjunct to a more appreciable career as a virtuoso pianist and organist and, from 1862, a professor at the Conservatoire.

His stage pieces had mostly a limited success, although his first opérette, *Ninetta* (16 performances), was staged with a brilliant cast featuring Jeanne Granier, Mily-Meyer, Daubray and Marie Desclauzas, and with much hope and hype. The two vaudeville-opérettes *La Vocation de Marius* and *La Petite Poucette* (a spectacular vehicle allowing Mily-Meyer to play a female Tom Thumb) each had something of a run, with the latter being subsequently produced in Hungary (*Hüvelyk Kató* ad Adolf Mérei, Magyar Színház 26 March 1904), but Pugno never established himself in the world of light music-theatre in the way that he did as a classic performer.

Pugno's other stage works included an opera *Tai-Tsoung* (Marseille 1894), the ballets *Viviane (1886)* and *Le Chevalier aux fleurs* (1897 w Messager), a mimodrama *Pour le drapeau* (1895) and the music for Xavier Roux's short comedy *Trop tard* (1893).

1877 **À qui la trompe?** (as 'Max Richard'/Hans de Sartem) 1 act Asnières 13 December

1881 **La Fée Cocotte** (w Léon Bourgeois/Gaston Marot, Édouard Philippe) Palace Théâtre 26 January

1882 **Ninetta** (Alexandre Bisson, Alfred Hennequin) Théâtre de la Renaissance 26 December

1887 **Le Sosie** (Albin Valabrègue, Henri Kéroul) Théâtre des Bouffes-Parisiens 8 October

1888 **Le Valet de coeur** (Paul Ferrier, Charles Clairville) Théâtre des Bouffes-Parisiens 19 April

1889 **Le Retour d'Ulysse** (Fabrice Carré) Théâtre des Bouffes-Parisiens 1 February

1890 **La Vocation de Marius** (Carré, Émile Dehelly) Théâtre des Nouveautés 29 March

1891 **La Petite Poucette** (Maurice Ordonneau, Maurice Hennequin) Théâtre de la Renaissance 5 March

PUPPCHEN Musical comedy (Posse mit Gesang und Tanz) in 3 acts by Kurt Kraatz and Jean Kren. Lyrics by Alfred Schönfeld. Music by Jean Gilbert. Thalia-Theater, Berlin, 19 December 1912.

Puppchen followed on behind *Autoliebchen* in Jean Gilbert's run of Berlin hits at the Thalia-Theater and rendered nothing to its predecessor in the way of success or of song hits. Comedian Arnold Rieck played Hänschen Schulze-Bosdorf, the 'little doll' of the title, a fellow who pretends to be still a young boy and takes advantage of the liberties this allows him with the ladies. The ladies in this case are the four Briesekorp nieces: Hortense (Eugene della Donna), Lore (Elsa Grünberg), Marie (Ellen Dalossy) and Hilde. Hortense is married to lawyer Blankenstein (Paul Beuchert) but it is her flirtation with the pilot Egon von Hallersdorf (Fritz Junkermann) which sets off many of the complexities of the action. By the end of the evening, Puppchen and Hortense have both reformed, and all four sisters are neatly mated. Theodore Stolzenberg was American Fred William Black, at one

Plate 217.

stage taken for Puppchen's guardian and ultimately paired with Marie, whilst Emil Sondermann and Lotte Reinecker supplied the rest of the comedy.

Gilbert's score was made up largely of waltzes ('Das kann ein Herz nur, welches liebt') and marches, of which the two-steppable duet 'Puppchen, du bist mein Augenstern' was the show's oversized hit. The ensemble 'Gehn wir mal zu Hagenbeck!' and a gavotte ('Lorchen, wo hast du deine Ohrchen?') were amongst the other favourite numbers.

Puppchen passed its 250th performance and had almost reached the 300th when it was replaced on 4 October by Gilbert's next piece, *Die Tangoprinzessin*. The Thalia-Theater was, however, only a starting point nowadays for Gilbert's works, for *Autoliebchen* had followed *Die keusche Susanne* and *Die Kino-Königin* onto the international musical stage, and *Puppchen* was set to do the same. *Buksi* (ad Zsolt Harsányi), with the young Juci Labáss as its female star, opened with more than a little success in Budapest before the Berlin run was done, and George Edwardes bought up the British rights. London was set to be the take-off point to the rest of the world. But then there was war. Edwardes junked all his German shows, *Puppchen* (for which he had paid out £1000 in advance) the first, for its march tune had quickly become a German troop song.

Hungary: Király Színház *Buksi* 16 August 1913

DAS PUPPENMÄDEL Vaudeville in 3 acts by Leo Stein and A M Willner based on the play *Miquette et sa mère* by Robert de Flers and Gaston de Caillavet. Music by Leo Fall. Carltheater, Vienna, 4 November 1910.

The doll girl of *Das Puppenmädel* was not, like so many of her predecessors, a stand-in for a doll herself, but merely a little lass who finds her doll better company than the local boys. The librettists turned the 'Miquette' of de Flers and de Caillavet's successful Paris comedy (Théâtre des Variétés, 2 November 1906) into an Yvette, Yvette Prunier (Lisa Weise), who is whisked off from her country home in Picardy to Paris by a kindly, middle-elderly but definitely amorous Marquis (Richard Waldemar) who equates love with 'a mansion, buttons like millstones, a 60-horse-power car, a pretty house in Trouville, dresses from Worth and a bank account'. But Yvette, like Miquette, has a mother (Dora Keplinger) who is soon hot-foot on the train to Paris, as is her friend, the Marquis's love-struck nephew Tiborius (Hubert Marischka), who ultimately wins the girl after sending her flowers and verses under the pseudonym of René Brion. The Marquis has to resign himself to being loved 'wie ein Papa'. Mizzi Zwerenz featured (heavily) as a phoney Spanish danseuse called Rosalillja, Josef König was theatre director Romuald Talmi, and the aged Karl Blasel appeared in a non-singing rôle as Buffon.

Fall's score was written, in vaudeville style, practically wholly for the play's six principals and it contained some charming music. Yvette sang a little Ländler to her doll confiding 'look at every man twice before you count on him, thrice before you trust him, four times before you love him, and five before you wed', yodelled out a Picard song, joined Tiborius in a clever railway number ('Es war am fünfzehnten Mai') and gave out with the brisk tale of 'Die kleine Adele', whilst Tiborius sang forth his love in waltz time in 'Du kleine Fee im Pavilion' and, jubilantly, in the final act's 'Sie liebt den, der ihr Blumen schickt', and Rosalillja spread unconvincing Spanish through her 'Ach, wie bist du süss, Amigo' and her seductive dance duo with Talmi.

Sigmund Eibenschütz's production (with 'architect Joseph Urban' co-credited on the designs) was well received and played for 104 performances at the Carl-theater, but, oddly, the piece did not receive the overseas attention that might have been expected for a successor to the enormously successful *Die geschiedene Frau*. Budapest's *Babukska* (ad Andor Gábor) was played some 30 times, but in Britain, which had stormed to *The Girl in the Train*, and in France, which loved *La Divorcée*, the show remained unproduced. When Charles Frohman mounted *The Doll Girl* (ad H B Smith) in America, he gave the Marquis's rôle to comedian Richard Carle, cast Hattie Williams as an Irish-Spanish Rosalilla, alongside Dorothy Webb and London's Robert Evett as the lovers, and filled up the score with additional bits of music from all over the place: one number from Eysler's *Der Frauen-fresser*, another by Henri Christiné, a thumping Walter Kollo song insisting 'Come on, Over Here', and several Jerome Kern numbers of which a wistful 'Will it All End in Smoke' was, at least, not incompatible with Fall's melodies. *The Doll Girl* played 88 performances on Broadway and, if that was more than such other imports of the season as *Der liebe Augustin*, *Leányvásár*, *Filmzauber*, *Der lachende Ehemann* and *Das Fürstenkind*, it was still something of a disappointment.

Germany: Theater des Westens 26 November 1910; Hungary: Király Színház *Babuska* 24 February 1911; USA: Globe Theater *The Doll Girl* 25 August

PURCELL, Charles (b Chattanooga, 1883; d New York, 20 March 1962).

Purcell was the creator of many richly singing baritonic heroes in American musicals between 1908 and 1933 – Count Androssy in *The Golden Butterfly*, Forest Smith in *The Pretty Mrs Smith*, Prince Nicholas in *Flora Bella*, Captain Poildeau in *My Lady's Glove*, John Moore in *The Melting of Molly*, Edmond Dantès in *Monte Cristo Jr*, Beppo Corsini in Romberg's *The Magic Melody*, Bill Pemberton in *Poor Little Ritz Girl*, Victor in *The Rose Girl*, Jack Lethbridge in *Judy*. However, the bright-eyed and boyish singing star had his most successful moments as the hero of Romberg's *Maytime* (1917), introducing 'Will You Remember' with Peggy Wood, as John Copeland in Rodgers and Hart's *Dearest Enemy* ('Here in My Arms' w Helen Ford) and in the title-rôle of several reproductions of *The Chocolate Soldier*. He also appeared opposite Beatrice Lillie in Vincent Youmans's *Oh, Please!*, took over the leading rôles in *The Right Girl* (1921) and *Sky High* (1925), played opposite Helen Kane in *Shady Lady* (1933, Richard Brandt) and made his last Broadway appearance, in 1946, in a character rôle in Arthur Schwartz's short-lived *Park Avenue*.

PURCELL, Harold (b London, 9 December 1907; d London, 28 May 1977).

A schoolmaster and journalist, Purcell made his first contribution to the musical stage by supplying some lyrics to Eric Maschwitz's megaflop *Magyar Melody*. Undaunted by this unpromising beginning, he subsequently wrote lyrics for a long list of London revues (*Diversion*, *Rise Above It*, *The New Ambassadors Revue*, *Orchids and Onions*, *Apple Sauce*, *Hulbert Follies*, *Big Top*, *Here Come the Boys*, *The Shephard Show*, *The Glorious Days*) and also for the series of very successful and long-running musical comedies starring Cicely Courtneidge (*Full Swing*, *Something in the Air*, *Under the Counter*, *Her Excellency*).

Purcell had his biggest success when he provided both book and lyrics for wartime musical melodrama *The Lisbon Story*, a piece which also produced his major song success, 'Pedro, the Fisherman'. He subsequently worked on the highly successful musical farce *Blue for a Boy* as well as supplying lyrics for a short-lived Offenbach pastiche, for an equally unfortunate remake of *The Red Mill* and the spectacular but unsatisfactory *Rainbow Square*.

Purcell also worked for film, writing lyrics for *Spring in Park Lane* and the screenplay for *The Lady is a Square*.

1939 **Magyar Melody** (George Posford, Bernard Grün/w Eric Maschwitz/Maschwitz, Fred Thompson, Guy Bolton) Her Majesty's Theatre 20 January
1942 **Full Swing** (Posford/Arthur Macrae, Archie Menzies, Jack Hulbert) Palace Theatre 16 April
1943 **Something in the Air** (Manning Sherwin/w Max Kester/Macrae, Menzies, Hulbert) Palace Theatre 23 September
1943 **The Lisbon Story** (Harry Parr Davies) London Hippodrome 17 June
1944 **Jenny Jones** (Parr Davies/Ronald Gow) London Hippodrome 2 October
1944 **Under the Counter** (Sherwin/Macrae) Phoenix Theatre 22 November
1949 **Her Excellency** (Sherwin, Parr-Davies/w Kester/w Menzies, Kester) London Hippodrome 22 June

1950 **Music at Midnight** (Offenbach arr/Guy Bolton) Her
Majesty's Theatre
1950 **Blue for a Boy** (Parr Davies/ad Austin Melford) Her
Majesty's Theatre 30 November
1951 **Rainbow Square** (Robert Stolz/w Bolton) Stoll Theater
21 September

PURLIE Musical comedy in 2 acts by Ossie Davis,
Peter Rose and Peter Udell based on the play *Purlie Victorious* by Ossie Davis. Lyrics by Peter Udell. Music by
Gary Geld. Broadway Theater, New York, 15 March
1970.

A musical version of Davis's successful and winning
1961 play, *Purlie* (the 'Victorious' part was his middle
name, as well as the result of the play's action) followed
its hero (Cleavon Little) in his battles to hornswoggle
some cash he is sort of owed out of the double-
hornswoggling old Cap'n Cotchipee (John Heffernan) so
that he can rebuild the Big Bethel Chapel and take up
preaching there. Little Lutiebelle (Melba Moore),
Purlie's girl, is the secret weapon with which they intend
to trick the old man, but she blows it and, ultimately, it
is the Cap'n's own son, the gormless Charlie (C David
Colson), who double-crosses his father and secures the
church for Purlie.

The story was accompanied by some vibrant and often
moving musical pieces, from the stirring opening sounds of
the church choir and its soloist (Linda Hopkins) singing
the soul of the Cap'n – who dropped dead at his son's
treachery – up to Heaven ('Walk Him Up the Stairs') to
Lutiebelle's all-stops-out recital of her love for 'Purlie' in
'I Got Love', the man's jaunty description of himself as 'A
New Fangled Preacher Man', and the joyously wry comedy
of 'The Bigger They Are, the Harder They Fall'. Purlie's
weaselly brother's procrastinating '(There's more than
one way of) Skinnin' a Cat' and Charlie's running-joke
attempts to write a folksong, ending, after his momentous
betrayal, in success with 'The World is Comin' to a Start',
were other unthumpingly funny moments.

Purlie marched victoriously through 689 Broadway performances, was toured, and later televised (1981), all
without convincing any other musical-theatre centres to
share its enjoyments.

Recording: original cast (Ampex/RCA)

Q

THE QUAKER Comic opera in 2 acts by Charles Dibdin. Theatre Royal, Drury Lane, London, 7 October 1777.

One of the few 18th-century 'ballad farcical operas' which survived into productions in the mid-19th century, *The Quaker* was seen as late as 1870 (5 September) in the repertoire of London's Gaiety Theatre, with Nellie Farren starring as Lubin, the village lad who returns from finally getting himself well-enough-established to marry pretty Gillian, only to find that her parents have betrothed her to the Quaker, Mr Steady. While the wise and kindly Quaker does all he can to win sulky Gillian's love, Lubin plots to make use of that kindness to make his rival humiliate himself before the whole village. Mr Steady, however, is way ahead of him, but instead of turning the situation against the boy he sagely resigns the lass. The action was decorated with 14 musical numbers, mostly solo songs but including a quintet and two duets, written and arranged by the author.

USA: Charleston Theater *The Quaker, or the May Day Dower* 13 February 1793; Australia: Albert Theatre, Hobart 29 March 1842

THE QUAKER GIRL Musical play in 3 acts by James T Tanner. Lyrics by Adrian Ross and Percy Greenbank. Music by Lionel Monckton. Adelphi Theatre, London, 5 November 1910.

When George Edwardes took over the Adelphi Theatre to add to his Gaiety and Daly's at the centre of the musical-comedy activity of London, he delegated James Tanner, the constructor-in-chief of Edwardes's musicals through their palmiest years, and Lionel Monckton, co-composer of so many Gaiety shows, to write the first musical for the new house in his string. Monckton's wife, Gertie Millar, the star of the Gaiety, insisted on going where her husband went, and in consequence *The Quaker Girl* was written to feature Miss Millar in its title-rôle.

The star played Prudence Pym who, whilst helping the runaway marriage of the Bonapartist Princess Mathilde (Elsie Spain) and the English Captain Charteris (Hayden Coffin), is caught sipping a little celebratory champagne and thrown out of the Family by the uncompromising elders of the Quaker group. Mathilde's friend Madame Blum (Mlle Caumont), a Paris couturier, takes her up and before the second act is long under way, Prudence's little grey dress and bonnet have become the Parisian rage, and she has attracted the attention of the lupine Prince Carlo (Georges Carvey). This doesn't please her American admirer, Tony Chute (Joe Coyne), but Tony is handicapped by an old and jealous mistress, Diane (Phyllys LeGrand), who gives Prudence a bundle of what she thinks are his old love-letters. They turn out to be love-letters from a Parisian Minister and, when Prudence tactfully returns them to him, she earns the safety of Mathilde and Charteris and a final curtain with Tony.

Miss Millar's Prudence had some of the prettiest songs Monckton had made for his wife over the years: the dainty title-song, her wide-eyed appreciation of 'Tony from America' and, later, a sweet solo about her 'Little Grey Bonnet' as well as the shared tale of 'The Good Girl and the Bad Boy' with Coyne, whose light-comedy rôle was not overweighted with singing. Jimmy Blakeley as a comical Quaker and Gracie Leigh, as a jokey maid, had the humorous moments, and Miss Spain had a delightful soprano waltz song, 'Time', but the gem of the score fell to Carvey, the libidinous Prince, as he tried to persuade the little Quaker girl to 'Come to the Ball'.

The Quaker Girl was the biggest hit of a season which included *The Chocolate Soldier* and *The Girl on the Train* amongst its other big successes. It played 536 performances at the Adelphi, was swiftly on the road, and, in June 1911 played 13 guest performances at Paris's Théâtre du Châtelet (which had, the previous week, been scandalized by the première of *L'Après-midi d'un faun*) with Phyllis Dare as Prudence. This little season provoked a delighted response and, as a result, in 1913 *La Petite Quaker* (ad Paul Ferrier, Charles Quinel) was produced in French at the Olympia with Alice O'Brien starred and the young Alice Delysia as Diane. It was later also played at Brussels' Théâtre de la Gaîté with Marthe Lenclud as its star, and brought back in 1920 to Paris's Ba-ta-clan.

In the meanwhile, Broadway had also welcomed the show enthusiastically. Ina Claire (Prudence), Clifton Crawford (Tony) F Pope Stamper (Charteris), Percival Knight (Jeremiah), Maisie Gay (Mme Blum) and May Vokes (Phoebe) headed the cast of Henry B Harris's production which stayed on Broadway for an exceptionally good run of 246 performances. J C Williamson's Australian production was another singular success: Blanche Browne (Prudence), Leslie Holland (Tony), Bertie Wright (Jeremiah) former Gaiety starlet Grace Palotta (Mme Blum) and Jessie Lonnen (Phoebe, from the British touring company) featured, Miss Vera Pearce performed a champagne dance, and the show played 90 performances in Sydney before moving on for its next date.

The Quaker Girl remained a favourite in English theatres for many years and returned to London in a barely professional production in 1934, and then in an Emile Littler 'revised' version in 1944. This production, intended to star Jessie Matthews, was instead mounted with Celia Lipton (Prudence), Billy Milton (Tony) and Ivy St Helier (Mme Blum), and it turned out such a success that, despite being interrupted by bombs, it was given two London seasons of two months apiece as well as a long tour.

France: Théâtre du Châtelet (Eng) 20 June 1911, L'Olympia *La Petite Quaker* 1913; USA: Park Theater 23 October 1911; Australia: Her Majesty's Theatre, Sydney 13 January 1912

QUATRE JOURS À PARIS Opérette in 2 acts by Raymond Vincy. Music by Francis Lopez. Théâtre Bobino, Paris, 28 February 1948.

Whilst Vincy and Lopez established the standards for postwar Parisian opérette à moyen to grand spectacle with *La Belle de Cadix* and *Andalousie*, they also collaborated on some pieces for smaller stages, of which *Quatre Jours à Paris* was one of the most successful. It also boasted far and away the best libretto that Vincy ever wrote, in the hilariously complex and farcical story of what happens as the result of Gabrielle Montaron (Ginette Catriens) spending four days in Paris.

Whilst in town, Gabrielle steals the heart of dashing Ferdinand (Andrex), the star attraction of the beauty parlour run by Monsieur Hyacinthe (Orbal), and Ferdinand abandons his hairdriers to follow her to her home in the country. This maddens both Hyacinthe, who needs Ferdinand to 'look after' the fiery Brazilian chanteuse, Amparita Alvarez (Nelly Wick), and the manicurist Simone (Marguette Willy) who has her own feelings about Ferdinand, and these three, along with the singer's husband (René Bourbon), Simone's adoring little Nicolas (Henri Gènes) and the vast Clémentine (Wally Winck), who is mad about Nicolas, all end up tracking Ferdinand down at the rural home of chicken-loving Montaron (Duvaleix). There, amongst pretences, disguises, chickens, a game of chess and a fair amount of unsuccessfully lustful cavalcading, in which Montaron's exceedingly plain maid Zenaïde (Jeannette Batti) manages to get herself involved, the farce begins. It carries on when the characters troop back to Paris and, ultimately, to an incredibly de-complicated happy ending.

Lopez's jolly score illustrated the comedy effectively with numbers such as Ferdinand's work-song ('Un petit coup par-ci'), the reminiscence of what can be done in 'Quatre jours à Paris', Zenaïde's comical admission of seeing things ('J'ai des mirages'), and, most successfully, a Samba Brésilienne which brought the first act to its curtain in a display of lively inconsequentiality.

Quatre Jours à Paris played for a year at the Bobino, after which a version was filmed (ad Vincy, André Berthomieu) with Luis Mariano taking top billing and the central rôle (rechristened Mario for the occasion) alongside Roger Nicolas (Nicolas), Geneviève Kervine, Orbal, Fernand Sardou, Gisèle Robert, Jackie Rollin and Jane Sourza. Four songs survived from the score alongside a couple of drearies staged in a revue theatre (Mario's abandoned love was now a revue star rather than a working girl) and several more for the star. Mlle Sourza was a comical rather than a fatale Mme Alvarez and original star Andrex, who was tacked in as a local policeman who helped to tie up the ends of a plot which was cut off at about Act one-and-a-half and thus missed almost all Vincy's cleverest complexities, provided a touch of comic class.

The show returned to the Paris stage in 1960 (Théâtre de l'ABC, 19 February) in a 'revised version' in which Andrex and Orbal from the original cast, back in their original rôles, teamed with Mlle Kervine from the screen, Ginette Baudin (Mme Andrex) and Jean-Marie Proslier.

Thoroughly played in the provinces, and televised in 1979 in a now heavily distorted version with Georges Guétary featured, it remains – in its pristine version – one of the slickest French comedy musicals of the postwar period.

Film: Lyrica 1955
Recording: television version (Festival)

QUEEN HIGH Musical comedy in 2 acts by Lawrence Schwab and B G De Sylva based on Edward Peple's play *A Pair of Sixes*. Lyrics by De Sylva. Music by Lewis E Gensler. Ambassador Theater, New York, 9 August 1926.

A lively comedy musical, based on a 1914 play and illustrated with songs in the style of the period, *Queen High* told the tale of two unhappy business partners who no longer see eye-to-commercial-eye. One of them has to go. A game of cards decides that George Nettleton (Frank McIntyre) gets to run the firm, whilst T Boggs Johns (Charles Ruggles) has to act as his butler for the duration. Johns is not a very adept butler, and the conflict and the comedy increase until little Miss Nettleton (Mary Lawlor) and little Master Johns (Clarence Nordstrom) bring about a reconciliation by finding that the younger generation of the warring dynasties are made for each other. Gensler's score, which included a nod to Anita Loos in a song called 'Gentlemen Prefer Blondes', threw up one number, a loping little piece called 'Cross Your Heart', which became a hit.

Mounted in Providence in April, *Queen High* was not taken straight to Broadway. As Schwab's previous year's piece, *Captain Jinks*, had done, it went instead to Philadelphia and there it won the same sort of enthusiastic reception as its predecessor. Adjectives like 'sensational' were flung about, and London's Alfred Butt, mindful of the way Clayton and Waller had snapped up *No, No, Nanette* out of town, quickly bought up the British rights to *Queen High*. The show's Philadelphia summer season stretched to 21 weeks and 'Cross Your Heart' made its way into the best-seller list, before Schwab, perhaps mindful of the Broadway disappointment of *Captain Jinks*, announced it would go on to Chicago and not to New York.

In the event, it did both. A new company, headed by Julia Sanderson and Frank Crumit, opened *Queen High* in Chicago, whist the Philadelphia company moved to Broadway. This time there was no disappointment. *Queen High* was a fine success, continuing the rise of producer-librettist Schwab – for whom it was the first of five consecutive Broadway hits – and giving composer Lewis Gensler his one moment of success. It ran for 378 Broadway performances.

Meanwhile, Alfred Butt had got his London production on to the stage. Joseph Coyne (Johns) and A W Baskcomb (Nettleton) played the partners, Sonnie Hale and Anita Elson the youngsters, and Joyce Barbour (Florence) and Hermione Baddeley (Coddles) supported. *Queen High* did not give him a *No, No, Nanette*, but it ran through 198 performances in the little Queen's Theatre then toured in 1927–8, and ensured that Butt was first in line to import Schwab's next piece to London. *The Desert Song* did better.

In Australia, however, *Queen High* turned out an unmitigated flop. J C Williamson Ltd's production – with R Barrett-Lennard (Johns) and Cecil Kellaway (Nettleton) heading the comedy and Josephine Read and Alfred Hugo 'the famous dancers from the Folies-Bergère' in support alongside Irene North (Polly) and Leyland Hodgson – played a forced five-week season in Melbourne and was left there.

UK: Queen's Theatre 2 November 1926; Australia: Theatre Royal, Melbourne 24 December 1927

QUINSON, Gustave (b Marseille, ?1867; d Paris, 1943). Dominating Parisian producer of the years between the wars.

In his early working years Quinson practised as a photographer in Marseille before moving to Paris in 1900 where he operated in turn the Théâtre de la Tour Eiffel and the tiny Théâtre Grévin before making his fortune by inventing the 'billet Quinson'. This was a fashion of selling cheap theatre tickets for plays in difficulty in a city in which such things were normally done only in obvious desperation – a system almost identical to the modern cut-price ticket booths. The 'billet Quinson' was, however, available to Quinson's 'subscribers' only, and he thus touched not only 10 per cent on his ticket sales but also his subscriptions.

In 1910 Quinson took over the Palais-Royal and he succeeded in making it pay handsomely enough for him to become involved singly or in partnership in several other Paris theatres. In 1913 he paired with Alphonse Franck at the Théâtre du Gymnase, then with Porel at the Vaudeville, and he took over the Bouffes-Parisiens on his own before spreading to another half-dozen venues during the war years. In 1921 he built the Théâtre Daunou and in 1925 the Théâtre de la Michodière, becoming, in the process, probably the most influential single person in the Parisian theatre.

The vast level of production needed to fill all of these houses meant that Quinson soon moved from producing only plays to including musical pieces in his output. One of these was *Phi-Phi* (1918) which launched the fashion for the small-scale jazz-age musical in France, a fashion which Quinson maintained with his subsequent productions of pieces such as *Ta bouche* and *Là-haut*. Discovering late in life the desire to be considered a dramatist, Quinson came to agreements with several prominent authors, notably Albert Willemetz and Yves Mirande, which effectively guaranteed his name on their shows (for a greater or, inevitably, much lesser contribution) as co-author and which in turn guaranteed those shows house room in the Quinson theatres.

In later years, he gradually decreased his enormous activity, taking on partners at the Bouffes-Parisiens (Edmond Roze, Willemetz, Meucci) and ultimately ceding it to Willemetz, but he continued to direct the Palais-Royal, his mascot theatre, alone until the end of his life.

R

RAIMANN, Rudolf (b Veszprém, Hungary, 7 May 1861; d Vienna, 26 September 1913).

A child performer as pianist, Raimann studied in Vienna and, after beginning a career as a conductor at Oldenberg, Graz, Cologne and at Gróf Eszterházy's personal theatre (the job had once and long been held by Haydn), he was occupied over an extended period as conductor and musical director at a series of Viennese theatres, including the Carltheater, the Theater an der Wien, the Venedig in Wien summer theatre in the Prater and, most notably, at the Theater in der Josefstadt.

Raimann wrote all kinds of theatre music from an early age, including, at the age of 20, a comic-opera version of *The Three Musketeers* played in Germany and at Pest's German Theatre, an operatic *Szinán basa* (*Haroun el Raschid*) produced in Tata in 1890, and a pair of one-act operas, *Imre Király* and *Enoch Arden*, produced at Budapest's Magyar Királyi Operaház in 1894 and subsequently played in several Austrian cities.

He provided part of the score, with his compatriot Béla Szabados, for the vaudeville *Die Küchenkomtesse* (a botched version of Szabados's 1897 *A kuktakisasszony*) at the Theater an der Wien (18 performances) and for a number of Possen, mostly at the Theater in der Josefstadt, before scoring a fine success with his Operette *Das Wäschermädl*. Produced at the Theater in der Josefstadt in 1905 (38 performances), with producer's wife and musical-comedy megastar Hansi Niese in the title-rôle, it was subsequently played in Germany, as *A szoknyahős* at Budapest's Városligeti Nyári Szinház (15 June 1906), and was performed by the Josefstädter company in 1913 in a Gastspiel at the Johann Strauss-Theater. Amongst the other vehicles he provided for Frln Niese, *Die Tippmamsell* (played in Hungary as *A gepirókisasszony*, ad Aurél Föld, Városligeti Színkör 15 May 1908), provided a second success, whilst *Der Schusterbub* (1906) paired the favourite soubrette with the town's most celebrated comic, Alexander Girardi.

1881 **D'Artagnan** (*Die drei Musketiere*) (Victor Léon) Carl-Schultze Theater, Hamburg 18 September
1887 **Das Ellishorn** (Bernhard Buchbinder, Felix Philippi) Theater am Gärtnerplatz, Munich 7 May
1898 **Die Küchenkomtesse** (*A kuktakisasszony*) additional music to Béla Szabados's score/ad Buchbinder, Theater an der Wien 15 March
1900 **Unsere Gustl** (Franz von Radler) Theater in der Josefstadt 9 February
1900 **Der schönste Zeitvertreib** (*Joli Sport*) (ad Otto Eisenschitz) Theater in der Josefstadt 9 October
1901 **'s Muttersöhnerl** (Theodore Taube) Theater an der Wien 7 November
1902 **Tarok** (Léon) Raimundtheater 8 February
1902 **Er und seine Schwester** (Buchbinder) Theater in der Josefstadt 11 April

1902 **Der Burengeneral** (Emil Norini, Ernst Baum) Jantsch-theater 10 May
1903 **Der Verwandlungskünstler** (Emil Golz, Arnold Golz) Jantschtheater 9 January
1903 **Der Musikant und sein Weib** (Buchbinder) Theater an der Wien 12 April
1903 **Der Gummiradler** (Rudolf Österreicher) Raimundtheater 22 December
1904 **Wie du mir ...** (Friedrich Eisenschitz, Siddy Pal) Raimund-theater 16 February
1904 **Port Arthur** (w R Laubner/Julius Wilhelm) Venedig in Wien 1 June
1904 **Der kleine Märchen haus** (Emil Görg) Theater in der Josefstadt 11 December
1905 **Das Wäschermädel** (Buchbinder) Theater in der Josef-stadt 31 March
1906 **Der Schusterbub** (Buchbinder) Theater in der Josefstadt 16 January
1906 **Zur Wienerin** (Richard Skowronek, Leo Walther Stein ad Ottokar Tann-Bergler) Lustspieltheater 7 April
1907 **Sie und ihr Mann** (Buchbinder) Raimundtheater 5 April
1907 **Der Eintagskönig** (Buchbinder, Hans Liebstöckl) Lustspieltheater 15 May
1908 **Die Tippmamsell** (Wilhelm Frieser, Karl Georg Zwerenz) Danzers Orpheum 28 January
1909 **Paula macht alles** (Buchbinder) Theater in der Josefstadt 23 March
1910 **Chantecler in Wien** (*G'schichten aus dem Hühnerhaus*) ('Fanfaron') 1 act Carltheater 24 February
1911 **In Frauenparlament** (Julius Horst) 1 act Apollotheater 1 March
1911 **Die Frau Gretl** (Buchbinder) Theater in der Josefstadt 7 April
1912 **Der Jungfraubrunnen** (Oskar Friedmann) 1 act Wiener Colosseum 1 February
1912 **Unser Stammhalter** (Buchbinder) Lustspieltheater 15 November

Other titles attributed: *Der Pauakönig, Das Damenregiment* (1890)

THE RAINBOW GIRL Musical comedy in 3 acts by Rennold Wolf based on *Fanny and the Servant Problem* (aka *The New Lady Bantock*) by Jerome K Jerome. Music by Louis A Hirsch. New Amsterdam Theater, New York, 1 April 1918.

Jerome K Jerome had shown little talent as a librettist for the musical stage, but his luck changed when his internationally popular play, *Lady Fanny and the Servant Problem*, was given a Broadway going-over to serve as a libretto for the musical *The Rainbow Girl*.

Mollie Murdock (Beth Lydy) is starring in *The Rainbow Girl* at the Frivolity Theatre when she meets and marries Robert Dudley (Harry Benham) – in the theatre green room. It turns out that her new husband is Lord Wetherell, and Mollie is transported to Wetherell Hall (near Manchester, England) where a curious surprise awaits her. The staff of her new stately home, from the butler (Sydney

Greenstreet) to the laundry and scullery maids, are all from one family. Hers. She tries to get rid of the embarrassment by sacking them, by getting the comedian from the Frivolity (Billy B Van) to pretend to be her uncle, but ultimately the truth has to come out: Lord Wetherell has married his butler's niece. It takes a third act to straighten things out happily.

Louis Hirsch's score was one which had all the attractions of his *Going Up* music. The central number was the prettily lilting 'I'll Think of You (and maybe you will think of me)', introduced in the second act by Harry Delf and Leonora Novasio, as the footman and the house maid, meaningfully reprised by Mollie as a farewell at the end of the act, and by everyone as half of the finale. The other half of the finale was the show's title-song, a swinging paean to 'The Rainbow Girl' which had been plugged as early as the show's opening, sung there by Mollie as part of the show-within-a-show, before getting a more expansive performance as a love song for the star pair. Their other big duet, 'Just You Alone', was a more conventional waltz, whilst 'Love's Ever New' was backed by angel voices. Robert had a curious, cavalier piece telling a bunch of girlies 'Call Around Again (in a month or two)' when he might have tired of monogamy, and Mollie begged his ancestress's picture, in waltz time, to give her some advice. Alongside these pieces there were several novelty numbers: 'The Alimony Blues' ('I've got the alimony blues from paying matrimony dues ...') as sung by Van, a second duo for Delf and Novasio, 'Soon We'll Be Upon the Screen' which dropped the names of Pickford, Bushman and Chaplin, and took some digs at the 'amateurs engaged in faking' in a business where 'talent cuts no ice', and a pyjama number for the soubrette (Laura Hamilton) and ladies' chorus.

Klaw and Erlanger's production was well received, but somehow, in spite of all its charms, *The Rainbow Girl* did not take off in the way that *Going Up* had done. It ran for 160 performances at the New Amsterdam Theater without establishing itself as a prospect for a trip around the world in the way the earlier piece had.

A German musical comedy based on Jerome's play and entitled *Lady Fanny* (Theo Mackeben/Erik Ernst, P Holl) was produced in Berlin (Deutsches Künstlertheater 16 February 1934) and, following the composer's expatriation, in London (Duke of York's Theatre 1939, ad A Dyer, H Risseley, Reginald Long) where it collapsed messily in its first week.

RAISIN Musical in 2 acts by Robert Nemiroff and Charlotte Zaltzberg based on the play *A Raisin in the Sun* by Lorraine Hansberry. Lyrics by Robert Brittan. Music by Judd Woldin. 46th Street Theater, New York, 18 October 1973.

The musical *Raisin* featured Virginia Capers in the rôle, originally played on the straight stage by Claudia McNeil, of Lena Younger ('Mama') the Chicago ghetto dweller whose longings to move up a neighbourhood are threatened by her self-centred son, who spends most of her insurance windfall on trying to be a big man in business. Joe Morton took the part of the selfish son, Walter Lee (portrayed in the original play by Sidney Poitier), Ernestine Jackson played his unfortunate wife, Ruth, and

Debbie Allen his more intelligent and striving sister, Beneatha.

Mama gave forth with her dreams for a better life in 'A Whole Lotta Sunlight' and made excuses for her son in 'Measure the Valleys', whilst Beneatha and her boyfriend (Robert Jackson) headed a sort of African Dance ('Alaiyo') which was the highlight of the entertainment.

Co-author Nemiroff (the husband of the play's late author) produced *Raisin* on Broadway, and the musical and its leading lady were both awarded the season's Tony Award in a season which included *Candide*, *Seesaw* and *Gigi*. *Raisin* went on to run for 847 performances. It was later produced in Germany, and toured in Europe.

Recording: original cast (Columbia); European tour cast (Stadttheater St-Gallen)

RAITT, John [Emmet] (b Santa Ana, Calif, 19 January 1917). Broadway baritone leading man who won a brace of top rôles.

Raitt made his first stage appearances in the chorus of the Los Angeles Civic Light Opera Company and subsequently played several operatic rôles before entering the musical theatre as the first takeover of the rôle of Curly in the national tour of *Oklahoma!* (1944). The following year he found stardom when he created the rôle of the shiftless carnival barker Billy Bigelow in Rodgers and Hammerstein's next musical, *Carousel*, introducing the celebrated Soliloquy and 'If I Loved You'.

In 1948 he appeared as the leading man of Wright and Forrest's Villa-Lobos musical *Magdalena*, and subsequently played regionally as the heroes of *Rose Marie* and *A New Moon*, and created the rôles of Jamie in *Three Wishes for Jamie* (1952) and The Duke in the quickly departing *Carnival in Flanders* (1953) on Broadway, but it was not until nearly a decade after his first great success that he found himself a second fine starring rôle, with a long run as Sid Sorokin in *The Pajama Game* ('Hey There').

Raitt subsequently appeared around America in a number of productions of *The Pajama Game* (which he also filmed with Doris Day in 1957), *Oklahoma!* and *Carousel* as well as in *Destry Rides Again*, *On a Clear Day You Can See Forever*, *Zorba*, *Annie Get Your Gun*, *Camelot*, *Seesaw* and *Kismet*, but returned to Broadway only for the folksy and fast-gone *A Joyful Noise* (1966).

He was seen in television productions of *Knickerbocker Holiday* (ABC 1950, Broem Broeck) and of *Annie Get Your Gun* (NBC 1957).

LE RAJAH DE MYSORE Opéra-comique in 1 act by Henri Chivot and Alfred Duru. Music by Charles Lecocq. Théâtre des Bouffes-Parisiens, Paris, 21 September 1869.

One of the most popular of Lecocq's short works, *Le Rajah de Mysore* told of a dissatisfied Rajah, Madapolam (Désiré), who, desiring immortality, is given a brew by his court physician which is supposed to do the trick. He wakes to find himself apparently 18 years on, bereft of wife and friends, and promptly wishes himself back as he was. Nothing is easier than for the physician to undo the deception.

First played in Paris at the Bouffes-Parisiens, *Le Rajah de Mysore* was later seen in Vienna under Geistinger and Steiner (ad Josef Weyl) at the Theater an der Wien, and at London's Gaiety Theatre, played on a programme with the burlesque of *Little Don Caesar de Bazan*. The plot of the piece was largely taken over for the British comic opera *The Punch Bowl* (Novelty Theatre 18 June 1887).

Austria: Theater an der Wien 9 July 1871; UK: Gaiety Theatre 13 May 1878

RÁKOSI, Jenő (b Acsád, 12 November 1842; d Budapest, 8 February 1929).

Celebrated Hungarian journalist, political editor, poet and dramatist, theatrical producer and director, the author of the hugely successful *Aesopus* (1866), the tragedy *Magdolna* (1883) and *Endre és Johanna* (1885) and the translator of Shakespeare into Hungarian, Rákosi also began and maintained a long connection with the musical theatre from the time that he took up the management of the newly-built Budapest Népszinház (15 October 1875). Under his management, in the first six years of its operation, the theatre became the most important musical house in Budapest, without in any way compromising its eminent position in the production of non-musical plays.

Amongst the 158 productions mounted during Rákosi's management were included many of the works of the French opéra-bouffe and -comique stage (a number of which he adapted himself) of which *La Fille de Madame Angot* (48 performances), *La Boulangère a des écus* (28 performances), *Le Pompon* (29 performances), *La Petite Mariée* (35 performances), *Kosiki* (41 performances), *La Marjolaine* (56 performances), *Les Cloches de Corneville* (205 performances), *Le Petit Duc* (42 performances), *Niniche* (55 performances), *La Camargo* (25 performances), *Madame Favart* (34 performances), *Les Mousquetaires au couvent* (37 performances), *La Mascotte* (62 performances) and *Les Noces d'Olivette* (25 performances) all did well. He also mounted a number of Austrian pieces of which *Boccaccio* (129 performances) and *Der Seekadett* (48 performances) were the big successes, as well as Sullivan's *HMS Pinafore* (4 performances) and a number of original Hungarian works including the famous play with music *A falu rossza*, Elek Erkel's *Székely Katalin* (1880) and Ferenc Puks's *Titilla hadnagy* (1880), for which he authored the libretto.

When Rákosi resigned from the Népszinház in favour of his sometime collaborator Lajos Evva in order to devote himself more fully to his other activities, he continued to write occasionally for the house, supplying both adaptations and original texts for Hungarian operetts, amongst which were a musical version of Shakespeare's *Pericles, Prince of Tyre* under the title *A fekete hajó* (the black ship), and another based on a Labiche source (*Az első és a második*).

1876 **A talléros pékné** (*La Boulangère a des écus*) Hungarian version (Népszinház)

1876 **A kis menyecske** (*La Petite Mariée*) Hungarian version (Népszinház)

1877 **Kapitánykisasszony** (*Der Seekadett*) Hungarian version (Népszinház)

1877 **Kosiki** Hungarian version (Népszinház)

1877 **Kisasszony feleségem** (*La Marjolaine*) Hungarian version (Népszinház)

1877 **Nanon csaplárosné** (*Nanon*) Hungarian version (Népszinház)

1878 **Ancsi sír, Jancsi nevet** (*Jeanne qui pleure et Jean qui rit*) 1 act Hungarian version (Népszinház)

1878 **Szenes lány, szenes legény** (*Les Charbonniers*) 1 act Hungarian version (Népszinház)

1878 **A kis néma** (*La Petite Muette*) Hungarian version (Népszinház)

1878 **A Cornevillei harangok** (*Les Cloches de Corneville*) Hungarian version (Népszinház)

1878 **A kis herceg** (*Le Petit Duc*) Hungarian version (Népszinház)

1878 **A csillag** (*L'Étoile*) Hungarian version (Népszinház)

1879 **A zengő angyalok** (Elek Erkel/Roderich Fels ad) Népszinház 19 April

1879 **Koko** (Coèdes et al/Clairville, Eugène Grange, Alfred Delacour ad) Hungarian version of French play with added songs Népszinház 16 May

1880 **Titilla hadnagy** (Ferenc Puks) Népszinház 27 February

1880 **Fatinitza** Hungarian version (Népszinház)

1880 **Az utszéli grófkisasszony** (*La Marquise des rues*) Hungarian version (Népszinház)

1880 **A kétnejü gróf** (*Der Graf von Gleichen*) Hungarian version (Népszinház)

1881 **Dragonyosok** (*Les Dragons de Villars*) Hungarian version w Lajos Evva (Népszinház)

1881 **Apajune, a vizitündér** (*Apajune der Wassermann*) Hungarian version w Evva (Népszinház)

1881 **Az üdvöske** (*La Mascotte*) Hungarian version (Népszinház)

1881 **A Pannifor kapitánya** (*HMS Pinafore*) Hungarian version (Népszinház)

1881 **Szép Ilonka** (Erkel) 1 act Népszinház 22 May

1882 **Szélháziak** (Erkel) Népszinház 16 March

1883 **A fekete hajó** (György Bánffy) Népszinház 26 January

1883 **Tempefői** (Erkel) Népszinház 16 November

1883 **Az Afrikautazó** (*Die Afrikareise*) Hungarian version w Evva (Népszinház)

1884 **A kék madár** (*L'Oiseau bleu*) Hungarian version w Arpad Berczik (Népszinház)

1886 **A Mikádó** (*The Mikado*) Hungarian version w Jenő Molnár (Népszinház)

1887 **Világszépasszony Marcia** (Lajos Serly) Népszinház 25 February

1887 **Uff király** (revised *L'Étoile*) (Szidor Bátor, Béla Hegyi) Népszinház 21 May

1890 **A négy király** (Béla Szabados) Népszinház 10 January

1891 **Az első és a második** (Szabados) Népszinház 8 April

1892 **A koronázás emléknapja** (Szabados) 1 act Népszinház 6 June

1893 **Indigo** (*Indigo und die vierzig Räuber*) Hungarian version (Népszinház)

1898 **A bolond** (Szabados) Magyar Színház 29 December

RALEIGH, Cecil [ROWLANDS, Abraham Cecil Francis Fothergill] (b Nantyglo, Monmouthshire, 27 January 1856; d London, 10 November 1914). British playwright and librettist.

At first a performer, Raleigh began his theatrical life touring in an opéra-bouffe chorus, before moving from the stage to front-of-house as acting manager at the Royalty Theatre in the 1880s, and then out of the house to journalistic jobs with *Vanity Fair*, *The Lady*, and as drama critic of *The Sporting Times*. He then began writing for the stage, often in collaboration with another journalist, George R Sims, and the pair scored a fine musical theatre success with the burlesque *Little Christopher Columbus*. However, Raleigh found his principal fame in a series of dramas for Augustus Harris and later Arthur Collins at the Theatre Royal, Drury Lane (*The Derby Winner*, *Cheer Boys Cheer*, *White Heather*, *The Great Ruby* w Henry Hamilton, *Hearts are Trumps*, *The Great Pink Pearl*, *The Pointsman* etc). He returned to the musical stage with an inept vehicle for *Little Christopher Columbus* star May Yohé as *The Belle of Cairo* and to collaborate with Seymour Hicks on the book for his alleged adaptation of the Armenian comic opera *Leblebidii Hor-Hor* as *The Yashmak*, but only the latter-day Gaiety musical *The Sunshine Girl*, on which he shared a book credit with Paul Rubens, approached his first musical hit in success.

1889 **The New Corsican Brother** (Walter Slaughter) Royalty Theatre 31 December

1893 **Little Christopher Columbus** (Ivan Caryll/w George Sims) Lyric Theatre 10 October

1896 **The Belle of Cairo** (F Kinsey Peile) Court Theatre 10 October

1897 **The Yashmak** (Napoleon Lambelet et al/w Seymour Hicks) Shaftesbury Theatre 31 March

1912 **The Sunshine Girl** (Paul Rubens/Arthur Wimperis, Rubens/w Rubens) Gaiety Theatre 24 February

RANDOLPH, Elsie (b London, 9 December 1904; d London, 15 October 1982). Dancing comedienne who starred in several musicals with Jack Buchanan.

Miss Randolph appeared on the stage as a chorister in *The Girl for the Boy* (1919), *The Naughty Princess* (1920), *My Nieces* (1921), *His Girl* (1922) and *Battling Butler* (1923) before being given her first supporting rôle as the comic soubrette, Folly, in Jack Buchanan's *Toni* (1924). She succeeded to the rôle of Madeleine in *Madame Pompadour* at Daly's Theatre and then followed up in further light comedy rôles in *Boodle* (1925, Clematis Drew), *Sunny* (1926, Weenie) and *Peggy-Ann* (1927, Alice Frost) before cementing the dance-and-comedy partnership with Buchanan, begun in *Toni* and *Boodle*, in the first of a series of musical comedies, *That's a Good Girl* (1928, Joy Dean).

In a Jack-and-Elsie musical, the ingénue was swept to the side as Buchanan and Miss Randolph took the stage for their song-and-dance routines and their wisecracking dialogue, and she returned only in time to lead the leading man to the altar before or after the final curtain. Miss Randolph appeared in *Follow Through* (1929, Ruth Vanning) and *The Wonder Bar* (1930, Inez) without the otherwise-engaged Buchanan, but they came together again for *Stand Up and Sing* (1931, Ena), *Mr Whittington* (1934, Betty Trotter) and *This'll Make You Whistle* (1936, Bobbie Rivers) in a pairing which, in just over a decade of stage performances, and two films, *That's a Good Girl* (1933) and *This'll Make You Whistle* (1935), captured the public's imagination.

After some subsequent appearances in comedy, she appeared in the soubrette rôle of Vittoria in the 1942 revival of *The Maid of the Mountains* at the London Coliseum and came back together one last time with Buchanan for *It's Time to Dance* (1943, Marian Kane), her last appearance on the London musical stage.

RANKEN, Frederick (b Troy, NJ, ?1870; d New York, 17 October 1906).

Originally a salesman and partaker of amateur theatricals, Ranken had his first taste of the professional stage when he joined Frank Perley on rewriting a piece called *The Sporting Duchess* which the pair then mounted and managed themselves. He joined Kirk La Shelle to write the libretto and lyrics for the musical *The Ameer*, and soon became a popular choice as a play doctor, working on such pieces as *The Runaways*, *The Smugglers* and *Nancy Brown*, and rewriting Harry Paulton's *Winsome Winnie* to such an extent that by the time it got to town Paulton's name had been replaced on the bill by Ranken's. He also wrote text and lyrics for several shows of his own. Ranken had been signed by Henry Savage to work on a series of musicals with Reginald De Koven when he died at the age of 36.

1899 **The Ameer** (Victor Herbert/w Kirk LaShelle) Wallack's Theater 12 April

1902 **The Chaperons** (Isidore Witmark) New York Theater 5 June

1903 **The Jewel of Asia** (Ludwig Englander/Harry B Smith) Criterion Theater 16 February

1903 **Winsome Winnie** (Gustave Kerker/Harry Paulton ad) Casino Theater 1 December

1905 **Happyland** (Reginald De Koven) Lyric Theater 2 October

1905 **The Gingerbread Man** (A Baldwin Sloane) Liberty Theater 25 October

1906 **The Student King** (De Koven/Stanislaus Stange) Garden Theater 25 December

RANZATO, Virgilio (b Venice, 7 May 1883; d Como, 20 April 1937). One of the handful of Italian composers who made a significant contribution to a brief flowering of musical plays in the Italian theatre of the early 20th century.

Ranzato spent the earliest part of his career as a concert and chamber-music violinist, but the bulk of his career as a composer was directed towards the light musical theatre and he had two enduring successes with operettas written in collaboration with the liveliest bricoleur of the Italian musical stage, Carlo Lombardo. The pretty, rustic 'navy-in-town' musical *Il paese dei campanelli*, with its mixture of traditional elements and tango and foxtrot rhythms and, above all, his version of Lombardo's version of another oft-used subject, the East-meets-West tale of *Cin-ci-là*, both became oft-played parts of the small basic Italian operetta repertoire.

1911 **Velivolo** Teatro Balbo, Turin 28 January

1912 **Yvonne** Teatro Apollo, Rome 16 November

1916 **La Leggende delle arance** Teatro Diana, Milan March

1919 **Quel che manca a sua altezza** (Gioacchino Forzano) Teatro Quirino, Rome 8 May

1923 **Il paese dei campanelle** (Carlo Lombardo) Teatro Lirico, Milan 23 November

1924 **Luna Park** (Lombardo) Teatro Lirico, Milan 26 November

1925 **Cin-ci-là** (Lombardo) Teatro dal Verme, Milan 18 December

1927 **Zizi** (Carlo Ravasio) Teatro Lirico, Milan 13 April

1927 **La Città rosa** (w Lombardo/Ravasio) Teatro Lirico, Milan 13 April

1928 **Cri-cri** (Lombardo) Teatro dal Verme 28 March

1928 **La danze del globo** Politeama, Genoa 30 October

1928 **I Merletti di Burano** (w Lombardo/Lombardo, Ravasio) Teatro Lirico, Milan 22 December

1929 **Lady Lido** (D Marchi) Teatro Nazionale 31 July

1930 **Fuoco fatuo** Teatro Savoia, Messina 16 March

1930 **I Monelli fiorentini** (Luigi Bonelli) Teatro Nazionale, Palermo 13 July

1930 **La Duchessa di Hollywood** (Lombardo) Teatro dal Verme, Milan 31 October

1932 **Re Salsiccia** (Giulio Bucciolini) Politeama, Florence 29 January

1932 **Prigioni di lusso** (Lombardo, Ravasio) Odeon, Milan 26 March

1936 **A te vogliar torne** (Giovanni Maria Sala) Teatro Municipale, Alexandria 24 February

1936 **Briciolina** (M Tibaldi-Chiesa) Teatro Arcimboldo, Milan 7 December

Other title attributed: *Valentina* (G M Sala, 1936)

RASCH, Albertina (b Vienna, 1896; d Woodland Hills, Calif, 2 October 1967). Broadway choreographer with leanings to the balletic.

Miss Rasch trained and worked as a dancer in Austria before going to America in 1911. There she danced at the Hippodrome, with the Century and Chicago Opera and in vaudeville at the Capitol before beginning a career as a choreographer in revue, notably for *The George White Scandals of 1925*.

Her training predisposed her to a ballet-based style of dance, now less current on the Broadway stage after many years of popular dance routines, both solo and chorus, set to modern ballroom-dance music. This solid ballet background was in evidence in her dances for the spectacular *Rio Rita* (1927, 'Spanish Shawl' etc), dances which scored her a major success within the show's success. She was subsequently engaged for the dances of a number of other Broadway revues (*Three's a Crowd*, *The Band Wagon*, two editions of the *Ziegfeld Follies* etc) and for a long list of musical plays amongst which were included *The Three Musketeers* (1928), *Sons o' Guns* (1929), *Princess Charming* (1930), *The Pajama Lady* (1930), *The Cat and the Fiddle* (1931), *The Great Waltz* (1934), *Jubilee* (1935), *Very Warm for May* (1939), *Lady in the Dark* (1941) and Kálmán's *Marinka* (1945). She visited Britain to choreograph Hassard Short's Theatre Royal, Drury Lane production of the hugely spectacular *Wild Violets* (*Wenn die kleinen Veilchen blühen*) and she also worked in the Paris theatre.

From 1929 Miss Rasch choreographed a number of film musicals including the celluloid versions of *The Cat and the Fiddle* (1934), *Rosalie* (1936), *The Firefly* (1937) and *Sweethearts* (1938), *Rogue Song, The Girl of The Golden West* and *The King Steps Out*.

DER RASTELBINDER Operette in a Vorspiel and 2 acts by Victor Léon. Music by Franz Lehár. Carltheater, Vienna, 20 December 1902.

The first major success of Franz Lehár's career, *Der Rastelbinder*, opened at the Carltheater just a month after his début piece *Wiener Frauen* had been staged at the Theater an der Wien so that, briefly, the two maiden Operetten of the young composer held the boards at the same time in Vienna's two principal musical houses. *Der Rastelbinder* was in a different vein from the other piece, being a Volksstück or peasant-piece in its subject matter and presenting as its main characters a Slovakian tinker and an old Jewish onion-seller, both strongly delineated and accented rôles which gave fine opportunities to the theatre's principal character actor/singers.

The 12-year-old orphan Janku, who has been raised by tinkers, is about to set out on the road to begin to earn his living selling mouse-traps. Before he goes, he must by tradition become betrothed and the girl chosen is eight-year-old Suza, the daughter of his 'parents'. Suza must send him on his way with the gift of a silver gulden, but her family have no money and, finally, she borrows it (at 5 per cent) from the poor Jewish onion-seller Wolf Bär Pfefferkorn (Louis Treumann). A dozen years pass, and hardworking Janku (Willy Bauer), no longer a tinker, has risen to a good job in Vienna. He is betrothed to his employer's daughter Mizzi (Therese Biedermann) and his future is

Plate 218. **Der Rastelbinder:** *Herta Freund, Erich Donner and Toni Niessner in the Raimundtheater revival of Lehár's first big hit.*

assured. Suza (Mizzi Günther) is in love with the rich farmer's son, Milosch Blacek (Karl Streitmann), now a soldier in Vienna, and she persuades the ambulant Pfefferkorn to take her with him on his next visit. Pfefferkorn, believing she is going to the capital to find Janku, delivers her to his door and the old betrothal is remembered. In the final act, they all go to the Uhlan camp in search of Milosch. The girls end up disguised in uniforms, and Janku and Pfefferkorn – his beard and hair shorn and forced on to a horse – are taken as reservists before everything is sorted out and the juvenile betrothal annulled in favour of grown-up preferences.

The book was a strong one, the cast included many of the city's best performers, and both profited from a Lehár score made up of waltzes and polkas and other dancing music – including a quadrille and a duo-gavotte – tinted with Slavonic tones. Louis Treumann – a few years later to be Lehár's Danilo – had a superb rôle as Pfefferkorn, a comic rôle which was musically topped by his introductory number in the show's prologue ('Jeder Mensch, was handeln thut'), an episode to which he also provided the summing-up (Die einfache Rechnung) which would return as the curtain piece of the main part of the show. He also led a Remembrance Trio with Janku and Suza in the first act and joined Suza in the four-part quadrille. The lyric music was in the hands of the young people, and it was from here that the show's favourite number emerged in the shape of a second-act duettino for Milosch and Suza, 'Wenn zwei sich lieben ...'. In the short list of solos, Janku declared 'Ich bin ein Wiener Kind' and told the tale of 'Die beiden Kamaraden' whilst Suza looked forward to her reunion with Miloch in 'Ach endlich, endlich heut''.

Der Rastelbinder was a big success for the Carltheater. It ran up its 100th performance before the summer break (13 April 1903), passed the 150th in September and the 225th just before it was replaced on the bill by Lehár's next work, *Die Göttergatte*, a few weeks more than a year after its première. In the meanwhile, it had been widely played in central Europe. It became highly popular in Germany and had another great success in Budapest (ad Adolf Mérei, György Ruttkay) with Kornel Sziklay in the rôle of Pfefferkorn, playing a magnificent 150 performances in its first year at the Magyar Színház, but it did not attract takers in English-speaking areas where theatrical attention was taken up with such pieces as *Florodora* and *A Chinese Honeymoon*, nor in France. America saw the show only in a German-language production played at Irving Place Theater.

In Vienna, however, *Der Rastelbinder* remained a frequently played favourite. It was maintained in the repertoire – and played every year – at the Carltheater for more than 20 years, with Friedrich Becker and Ernst Rollé supplementing Treumann in the star rôle. It was played for the 300th time on 2 December 1908, the 400th time on 13 April 1918 with Treumann again in his great rôle, and on 28 June 1920 it played its 500th performance at the Carltheater under Lehár's baton with Karl Blasel still in his original rôle of Gloppler alongside Willy Bauer, now playing Pfefferkorn, Hubert Marischka, Dora Keplinger and Viktor Robert. Treumann played his rôle again in a handful of performances at the Theater an der Wien in 1923, and there was a new Hungarian production at the Fővárosi Operettszinház the following year (19 September) but, in spite of the great popularity the piece enjoyed in central Europe during the first decades of the century, it subsequently slipped from the repertoire in favour of Lehár's later and more fulsomely romantic works.

A burlesque of *Der Rastelbinder* written by C Karl and Carl Strobl and composed by Karl Josef Fromm was produced at the Jantschtheater (23 April 1904) under the title *Wolf Bär Pfefferkorn auf Reisen*.

An earlier *Der Rastelbinder*, subtitled 'oder Zehntausend Gulden', a Posse in 3 acts written by Friedrich Kaiser and composer by Adolf Müller, was produced at the Carltheater 12 April 1858.

Germany: ?1903; Hungary: Magyar Színház *A Drótostót* 21 April 1903; USA: Irving Place Theater (Ger) 1909

RÁTKAI, Márton (b Budapest, 18 October 1881; d Budapest, 18 September 1951).

One of the mainstays of the company at Budapest's Király Színház from 1905 through some three decades, Rátkai created during that period comic rôles in a large number of the most important new Hungarian musicals. Amongst these were included, in the earlier years, the parts of the eunuch Zülfikár in Huszka's *Gül Baba* (1905), Nurza in Jacobi's *Tüskerózsa* (1907), Fritz in his *Leányvásár* (1911) and Poire in his *Szibill* (1914), Roth in Aladár Rényi's *A kis gróf* (1911) and the title-rôle in Zsigmond Vincze's *Limonádé ezredes* (1912), and later Manó Csollán in Károly Komjáthy's *Pillangó főhadnagy* (1918), Alois Stühlmüller in Mihály Nádor's *Fanny Elssler* (1923), the comedy lead of Zerkovitz's *Árvácska* (1924), Ribizli in Vincze's *Aranyhattyú* (1927) and Rudolf Rezeda in Zerkovitz's *A legkisebbik Horváth lány* (1927). He also played in many of the operetts of Albert Szirmai – *A Mozikirály* (*Filmzauber*), the title-rôle of *Mágnás Miska* (1916), Gróf Kereszthy in *Gróf Rinaldo* (1918), Buhu in *Mézeskalács* (1923), Achilles Kelemen in *Éva grófnő* (1928), Károly in *Alexandra* (1925), in *A Ballerina* (1931) – as well as such overseas-Hungarian works as those of Kálmán (Pali Rácz in *Cigányprimás* (1913), Bóni in *Csárdáskirálynő* (1916), Napoleon in *Die Bajadere* (1922), Zsupán in *Gräfin Mariza* (1924), Toni in *Die Zirkusprinzessin* (1926) etc) and of Lehár (Pfefferkorn in *Der Rastelbinder* (1908), Basil Basilowitsch in *Der Graf von Luxemburg*, Dagobert Millefleurs in *Eva* etc).

Rátkai also appeared in the very many other musical and non-musical works produced at the Király Színház or reprised in the house's repertoire, ranging from rôles such as Ménélas (*Belle Hélène*), Célestin (*Mam'zelle Nitouche*) and Gaspard (*Les Cloches de Corneville*) to Dom Gil de Tenorio in *Die ideale Gattin* (1913), Fridolin in *Die Rose von Stambul* (1917), Rettenetes Tamás (ie Hard-Boiled Herman) in *Rose Marie* (1928), and Kristóf in *Mersz-e-Mary?* (1927), and to the aged comicalitites of the French King in *János vitéz*, but also in Shakespeare and the rest of the comic and dramatic repertoire. In 1920 he appeared as Offenbach in the successful *Dreimäderlhaus*-style pasticcio operett on the French composer's life and works.

In the 1930s and early 1940s he continued as a major musical-comedy star through increasingly characterful and/or 'older' rôles in such pieces as *A csalódott Szerelmesek klubja*, *Vihar a Balatonon*, *Hajrá Hollywood*, *Őfelsége frakkja* (1931), as Giesecke in Hungary's *Im weissen Rössl* (1931), as Jim-Boy in *Die Blume von Hawaii* (1932), *Éjféli tangó* (1932), *Amikor a kislányból nagylány lesz*, *Manolita*, *Zsákmabamacska* (1932), *A Sok szerencsét*, *Sültgalamb* (1933), *Kék Duna*, *Ördöglovas* (1934, *Der Teufelsreiter*), *Montmartrei ibolya* (1935, *Das Veilchen vom Montmartre*), *A fenséges asszony* (*Eine Frau von Format*), Benatzky's *Párizsi nő* (1937), *Legyen úgy, mint régen volt* (1938), *Kavé habbal*, *Ki gyereke vagyok én?* (1939), *Tokaji aszú* (1940) and *Angóramacska*.

Latterly Rátkai played more in drama and less in musical theatre, and in his sixties, having created a sensation with his performance as Tartuffe, had a second starring career as a senior comedy actor in classic plays with the National Theatre in Budapest.

He was married at one stage to the star operett soubrette Juci Lábass.

Biography: Szomory, G: *Rátkai, Márton* (Muzsák, Budapest, 1988)

RAY, Gabrielle [née COOK] (b Stockport, 28 April 1883; d London, 21 March 1973). Postcard beauty who had supporting rôles in a number of London musicals.

'Gabs' Ray made her first stage appearance as a child, in John Hollingshead's production of *Miami* (1893), and graduated to touring companies of *The Belle of New York* and *The Casino Girl* before being brought to London by George Edwardes to understudy in *The Toreador* at the Gaiety Theatre. She was given a small rôle in the next Gaiety musical, *The Orchid* (1903, Thisbe), then was moved across to the Prince of Wales Theatre to take over the number-three female rôle in *Lady Madcap*, performing 'La Maxixe' with Dorothy Craske, but by the time of *The Little Cherub* (1906, Lady Dorothy Congress) she had become one of the most popular picture-postcard beauties of the day, and her rôle in that piece reflected her new status.

She had good supporting rôles in *See See* (1906, So-Hie) and *Les Merveilleuses* (1906, Egle) and headed the grisettes as Frou-Frou in *The Merry Widow* (1907) before Edwardes cast her up a notch as the soubrette, Daisy, in *The Dollar Princess* (1909). She next appeared alongside Phyllis Dare and Olive May as the feminine portion of the Gaiety Theatre *Peggy* (1911, Polly Polino) before she temporarily took her leave of the stage. However, she returned four years later to play in Edwardes's production of *Betty* (1916, Estelle) and in revue at the Hippodrome before fading away into variety and pantomime and a long-lived real retirement.

RAYMOND, Fred[y] [VESELY, Raimund Friedrich]
(b Vienna, 20 April 1900; d Öberlingen, Germany, 10 January 1954). German songwriter who scored some musical-theatre success under National Socialism.

Vesely began his musical career writing songs and performing them himself in amateur cabaret under the fashionably foreign-sounding name of Fredy Raymond, whilst working daytime in a bank for his living as plain Vesely. Just before his 24th birthday, however, he decided to throw in his 'proper' job and to become a full-time performer. He made his first professional appearance at Dresden's Regina-Palast, singing and accompanying himself at the piano and, for the next few years, he remained in Germany, where his employment situation was greatly eased by the fact that he had, after a genial success with the song 'Ich hab' das Fräulein Helen baden 'sehn', produced a veritable hit song for himself. 'Ich hab' mein Herz in Heidelberg verloren' (1925 w Ernst Neubach) became an international song success under the title 'I Left My Heart in Heidelberg'. Having sold his song to its publishers outright, Raymond cashed in on his biggest success by using its title as that of his first stage work, a semi-pasticcio Singspiel staged in 1927 at the Vienna Volksoper, with some considerable success.

Nevertheless, in spite of turning out several more songs which found success in Germany and Austria ('In einer kleinen Konditorei', 'Im Mainz am schönen Rhein'), several revues (*Damals in Jean*, *Die Welt um Mitternacht*) and a regular amount of film music, Raymond had no further stage success until he was hired by Heinz Hentschke, the director of Berlin's Metropoltheater, to provide the scores to Hentschke's libretti for what turned out to be a series of popular revusical pieces at that theatre.

The most successful of these was the 1937 *Maske in Blau*, a jolly hotch-potch of a piece which boasted some exotic settings and some bouncy melodies which became popular favourites – 'Die Juliska aus Budapest' and 'Ja das Temprament' – and which has found ready acceptance on other stages over the subsequent half-century.

A split with Hentschke led Raymond to have his next work staged at Kiel. The charming *Salzburger Nockerln* (aka *Saison in Salzburg*, 1938) benefited greatly from a more adept and attractive libretto than Hentschke had ever been able to concoct, and also from the most attractive score of all Raymond's works, mixing foxtrots and a splendid march with polka, waltz and even Ländler rhythms, and with some easy flowing love songs in a delightfully unpretentious mélange. The 1941 *Die Perle von Tokay* also found a measure of success, but the remainder of Raymond's wartime and postwar work produced little beyond the song 'Es geht alles vorüber, es geht alles vorbei' (1942) which came up to the popularity of his favourite works.

He died at the age of 54, at his home on Bodensee, leaving his pair of successful pre-war works as two of the most popular German-language pieces of the last 50 years, on the fringe of the standard repertoire.

1927 **Ich hab' mein Herz in Heidelberg verloren** (Ernst Neubach/Bruno Hardt-Warden, Fritz Löhner-Beda) Volksoper, Vienna 29 April

1928 **Es kam ein Bursch gezogen** (Neubach, Ernst Wengraf) Neue Wiener Bühne, Vienna 20 January
1929 **Die Jungfrau von Avalon** (Paul Franck, Peter Herz) Zentraltheater, Dresden 16 June
1933 **Der Königsleutnant** (Gutzkow ad Frank, Herz) Neues Operetten-Theater, Leipzig 27 February
1934 **Lauf ins Glück** (Paul Beyer) Metropoltheater 24 September
1935 **Ball der Nationen** (Hentschke, Beyer) Metropoltheater 27 September
1936 **Aus grosser Fahrt** (Schwenn/Hentschke) Metropoltheater 21 August
1936 **Marielu** (Hentschke, Theo Halton) Centraltheater, Dresden 19 December
1937 **Maske in Blau** (Günther Schwenn/Hentschke) Metropoltheater, Berlin 27 September
1938 **Saison in Salzburg** (aka *Salzburger Nockerln*) (Max Wallner, Kurt Feltz) Stadttheater, Kiel 31 December
1939 **Das Bett der Pompadour** (Wallner, Feltz)
1941 **Die Perle von Tokay** (Wallner, Feltz) Theater des Volkes, Dresden 7 February
1948 **Konfetti** Theater am Nollendorfplatz 5 November
1949 **Flieder aus Wien** (Hannes Reinhardt) Staatsoper, Kassel 8 November
1951 **Geliebte Manuela** (Just Scheu, Ernst Nebhut) Mannheim 12 July

Other titles attributed: *Liebling schwindel' nicht* (1934), *Christian mit Herz* (1946), *Wohin mit der Frau?* (1949)

RAYMOND, Hippolyte (b Valréas, Vaucluse, 1844; d Paris, August 1895).

The author of many successful Parisian comedies and vaudevilles, Raymond at first doubled his theatrical work with employment as a clerk, and later sous-chef de bureau at the Crédit Lyonnais. He wrote several plays for the Théâtre du Gymnase, collaborated with Alfred Duru in one of that author's rare ventures without his usual partner, Chivot (*Fille du clown*), and his early ventures into the musical theatre included the text for the Châtelet's spectacular *Le Prince Soleil* and a revised version of the Cogniard brothers' féerie *La Fille de l'air*. The one enduring hit with which he provided the musical stage, however, was not in the field of the musical spectacular, but in that of vaudevillesque comedy: the hilarious military piece *Les 28 Jours de Clairette* (1892). Following this major success, he essayed several other pieces with Antony Mars and Victor Roger, his collaborators on that show, but without approaching the results won by their first work together. Raymond committed suicide in 1895, before the production of his last musical piece, a reconstitution of his highly successful play *Le Cabinet Piperlin* accompanied by the Hervé music which was originally commissioned for it but not previously used.

Several of Raymond's works were remade as musical shows in other countries. His vaudeville *Les Deux Nababs* (w Alphonse Dumas) was produced at the Vienna Carltheater as *Der Kukuk* with a fresh score by Josef Brandl (24 April 1880), *Cocard et Bicocquet* (w Maxime Boucheron) was the basis for F Zell's Viennese Posse mit Gesang *Wolf und Lampel* (Julius Stern/Hoffman) produced at the Theater an der Wien in 1888 (13 October), and *Le Cabinet Piperlin* was given another musical score, in an English version, as *The Antelope* (Hugo Felix/Adrian Ross) for an unsuccessful London production (Waldorf Theatre 28 November 1908). The text for the indifferently successful

Clary-Clara, however, was turned into a hit when it was borrowed by Hungarian composer Béla Zerkovitz as the text (ad László Szilágyi) for his *A csókos asszony* (Várósi Színház 27 February 1926).

1873 **Rallye-Champdouillard** (de Polignac) 1 act Palais-Royal 20 June

1877 **La Goguette** (Antonin Louis/w Paul Burani) Théâtre de l'Athénée-Comique 13 April

1879 **Les Deux Nababs** (Auguste Coèdes/w Alphonse Dumas) Théâtre des Nouveautés 9 February

1880 **Le Voyage en Amérique** (Hervé/w Maxime Boucheron) Théâtre des Nouveautés 16 September

1889 **Le Prince Soleil** (Léon Vasseur/w Burani) Théâtre du Châtelet 11 July

1890 **La Fille de l'air** revised version w Armand Liorat, Paul Lacôme Théâtre de Folies-Dramatiques 20 June

1892 **Les Vingt-huit Jours de Clairette** (Victor Roger/w Antony Mars) Théâtre des Folies-Dramatiques 3 May

1892 **La Bonne de chez Duval** (Gaston Serpette/w Mars) Théâtre des Nouveautés 6 October

1893 **Catherinette** (Roger/w Mars) Lunéville 17 July

1894 **Clary-Clara** (Roger/w Mars) Théâtre des Folies-Dramatiques 20 March

1895 **Nicol-Nick** (Roger/w Mars, Alfred Duru) Théâtre des Folies-Dramatiques 23 January

1895 **Mam'selle Bémol** (Louis Varney/w Alfred Delilia) Théâtre Cluny 7 September

1896 **Le Cabinet Piperlin** (Hervé/w Burani) Théâtre de l'Athénée-Comique 17 September

RAYNER, Minnie (b London, 2 May 1869; d London, 13 December 1941).

Minnie Rayner first appeared on the stage as a child, making her musical-theatre début in the original production of Planquette's *Rip van Winkle* (1882) before, at the age of 17, taking over the rôle of the little rustic bride, Phyllis Tuppitt, in *Dorothy*, and playing it for several years of the show's record-breaking run. For a long while thereafter she toured in plays and musicals in South Africa, England (Mitsu in *The Mousmé* etc) and on Maurice Bandmann's Eastern circuits, finally graduating to the character rôles which brought her back to the West End. The creations of the second half of her London career included

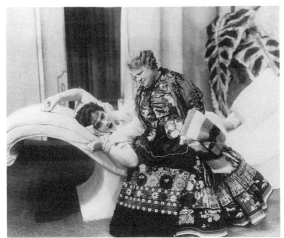

Plate 219. **Minnie Rayner** *was a big lady by the late stage in her career when Ivor Novello cast her in a series of character rôles, beginning with the part of the prima donna's duenna in* Glamorous Night.

the part of Clara the dresser in Coward's *Hay Fever*, and subsequently, after nearly half a century away from the London musical stage, a series of non-singing rôles in Ivor Novello's musicals: Phoebe, the fat ex-chorus-girl dresser to the star of *Glamorous Night*, Mrs Ripple in *Careless Rapture*, the heroine's mother, Mrs Wortle, in *Crest of the Wave* and Hattie, the jolly innkeeper, in *The Dancing Years* (1939).

READER, Ralph (b Crewkerne, Somerset, 25 May 1903; d Bourne End, Bucks, 13 May 1982). Choreographer and dance-driller who marshalled the choruses of two decades of musicals.

After an early non-theatrical working life spent in America, Reader performed as a dancer in several New York shows (*The Passing Show of 1924*, *Big Boy*, *June Days*). He also choreographed several others including *Artists and Models*, *The Greenwich Village Follies*, *Yours Truly* with Leon Errol and the Tiller girls and *Sunny Days* (1928), as well as a number, such as *Cynthia* (1926, in which he also appeared as a last-minute replacement), *Miss Happiness* (1926) and *Take the Air* (1927) which didn't get to town, before returning to his native Britain for the large part of his career. His first job there was as a performer, touring as Tom Marlowe in *Good News*, but thereafter he worked almost wholly as a choreographer and later also a director. He choreographed *Virginia*, *Merry Merry*, *Hold Everything!*, *Dear Love* (UK and USA), *Sons o' Guns*, the spectacular *Silver Wings* and *Little Tommy Tucker* for Herbert Clayton and/or Jack Waller and the large and military *The Song of the Drum* and *Three Sisters* (1934) for Alfred Butt at the Theatre Royal, Drury Lane, and he made his West End début as a director with the London version of *Viktória* (1931) at the Palace Theatre.

Reader returned to Waller to direct and choreograph the highly successful Binnie Hale/Bobby Howes musical *Yes, Madam?* (1934), its sucessor *Please, Teacher!* (1935), and the less successful *Certainly Sir* (1936) and *Big Business*, and continued his association with Drury Lane when he provided the massed dances for Ivor Novello's *Glamorous Night* and for the unfortunate Robert Stolz musical *Rise and Shine*. He returned to the stage in the London Hippodrome musical *The Fleet's Lit Up* (1938) for which he also shared the choreographic credit with Frederick Ashton and Harry Dennis, but by this stage his attention had begun to be diverted from the professional theatre by the enormous success which he had had in writing, producing and staging the boy-scout movement's *Gang Show*s. He remained involved with these young people's spectaculars, throughout the world, up until the mid-1970s.

In 1950 he returned to the theatre at the head of his own National Light Opera Company which toured *Merrie England*, *The Lilac Domino* and *Chu Chin Chow* for a season, and in 1956 he came back together with Waller to write (under a pseudonym) and stage the musical *Wild Grows the Heather*. Sabotaged at what should have been a successful opening night by hordes of over-applauding boy scouts, the piece failed. Reader subsequently wrote another musical, *Summer Holiday*, produced in Scarborough, but he had more success as a songwriter, notably with the number 'Strolling', the anthem of the Flanagan and Allen comedy team. Again, however, he was not named on the bill, for Flanagan took the writing credit.

1956 **Wild Grows the Heather** (Jack Waller, Joseph Tunbridge/Ralph Reader) London Hippodrome 3 May
1960 **Summer Holiday** Open Air Theatre, Scarborough

Autobiographies: *It's Been Terrific* (Laurie, London, 1954), *Ralph Reader Remembers* (Bailey & Swinfen, Folkestone, 1974)

REDHEAD Musical comedy in 2 acts by Herbert and Dorothy Fields, Sidney Sheldon and David Shaw. Lyrics by Dorothy Fields. Music by Albert Hague. 46th Street Theater, New York, 5 February 1959.

The prototype of *Redhead* was originally conceived by Herbert and Dorothy Fields (under the title *The Works*) as a mystery tale about a waxworks woman and envisaged as a vehicle for Beatrice Lillie. Having been shelved, the scenario was brought out again in the mid-1950s to be adapted for a rather younger star, Gwen Verdon, and as the piece developed it picked up co-librettist Sidney Sheldon (not yet a best-selling mystery writer), *Plain and Fancy* composer Albert Hague, and then another co-author and two producers who had been working on another piece for the same star.

The result was a period musical murder mystery cum love story with a London setting which presented Miss Verdon, who had recently starred at the same theatre in *Damn Yankees* and *New Girl in Town*, as Essie Whimple, an ordinary little Victorian girl who makes waxwork figures for a living but who keeps on seeing things. It is thus that she gets mixed up with murder. Essie falls in with music-hall strongman Tom Baxter (Richard Kiley) whose stage partner has been the victim of a mysterious Jack-the-Ripperish strangler and she even goes on the stage as a dancer at the ill-starred Odeon Music Hall herself, at great risk to her throat, before the murderer is run to ground. The criminial is not the rather obviously red-bearded Sir Charles Willingham (Patrick Horgan), but George Poppett (Leonard Stone), another act on the music hall's bill, who has availed himself of a false red beard to spread a red herring. The audience might have guessed for, after the two sleuths, Mr Stone had third billing.

The show's score featured Miss Verdon in 'Merely Marvelous' and ''Erbie Fitch's Twitch', Kiley in 'My Girl is Just Enough Woman for Me' and 'I'm Back in Circulation' and the pair together in 'Look Who's in Love', 'I'll Try' and 'Just for Once' with Stone, but, under the direction and choreography of Bob Fosse, at the helm for the first time on Broadway, it was not the songs but the dances which were the outstanding feature of *Redhead*: 'The Uncle Sam Rag', the 'Pick-Pocket Tango', Essie's Vision (Dream Dance) and a Final Chase in the Keystone Kops vein.

Robert Fryer and Lawrence Carr's production of *Redhead* swept the board at the Tony Awards with Miss Verdon, Kiley, the authors, composer and choreographer all taking first prize. It remained on Broadway for over a year for a run of 455 performances, but its success remained there. It did not travel to London (where its version of stage cockney and music hall would have doubtless fitted ill) and – unlike most Tony laureates of those times – it did not secure itself a regular future.

Recording: original cast (RCA)

RED, HOT AND BLUE! Musical play in 2 acts by Howard Lindsay and Russel Crouse. Music and lyrics by Cole Porter. Alvin Theater, New York, 29 October 1936.

A thorough-going attempt at a repeat by the authors and composer of *Anything Goes*, Vinton Freedley's production of *Red, Hot and Blue!* was apparently constructed for and scheduled to feature the original stars of the earlier show, Ethel Merman, Victor Moore and William Gaxton. Ultimately (after names from Eddie Cantor to Willie Howard had been 'mentioned' by the kind of guessing press that 'mentions' such things) it was not Moore but the much more up-front comedian Jimmy Durante who shared the top-billing, and while Gaxton went off to yodel sweet nothings to Kitty Carlisle in *White Horse Inn* the rôle that would have been his was taken by a funny young man called Bob Hope who had till recently been duetting 'I Can't Get Started' with Eve Arden in *The Ziegfeld Follies of 1936*.

Miss Merman, the only relict of *Anything Goes*, was cast as the widowed 'Nails' O'Reilly Duquesne, a former manicurist risen to wealth and social position in Washington, Durante was 'Policy' Pinky, an ex-(but only just)-convict, and Hope played a young lawyer called Bob Hale who has been spoiled for women by the memory of the lost love of his extreme youth. In a plot which managed, in the 1930s let's-play-political mode, to bring both the Senate and the Supreme Court into the action, the search for the missing lass (Polly Walters), identifiable by the imprint of a hot waffle-iron on her posterior, took pride of place. When she is found, however, she proves to be nothing like the little girl of the waffle-iron days and Hale, his mental blockage cleared, is left free to stop 'Nails' being a widow any longer. This time, after having to take second prize in *Anything Goes*, Miss Merman got to have a Happy Ending with the juvenile man.

The score did not turn up the list of perennials that the earlier show had done, but it nevertheless produced one major hit in the duet 'It's De-lovely', performed by Miss Merman and Hope, which proved to be a regular successor to 'You're the Top', became a Porter standard, and survived beyond *Red, Hot and Blue!* to be heard in the theatre in London's *The Fleet's Lit Up* and both on film and in later, popped-up stage adaptations of *Anything Goes*. Merman had two other fine numbers, the rousing 'Ridin' High' which closed out the first act in 'Blow, Gabriel, Blow'-style and the comically down-in-the-dumps 'Down in the Depths on the 90th Floor'. This number had been written and put into the show in double-quick time during the Boston try-out when it was decided that the delicately lovely 'Goodbye, Little Dream' (which Porter had salvaged from his *Born to Dance* film cutouts) did not fit the bill. Another number, 'You're a Bad Influence on Me', was dropped after opening and replaced by the burlesque hillbilly 'The Ozarks Are Calling Me Home'. Durante introduced the crazy saga of a pregnant sea-captain who admits to being a girl in 'A Little Skipper from Heaven Above', Merman asked for melodies that were 'Red, Hot and Blue!', and supporting couple Dorothy Vernon and Thurston Crane sang 'Ours' and 'What a Great Pair We'll Be' while Grace and Paul Hartman danced.

In spite of its star values, its enjoyably over-the-top book and a score which, if it was not *Anything Goes*, contained many good things, *Red, Hot and Blue!* did not score a hit.

After 183 Broadway performances it closed, while *White Horse Inn* ran on, and in spite of the general success overseas of the earlier show it found no takers for foreign productions. Perhaps it was the waffle iron.

Recording: original cast recordings (part record) (AEI)

THE RED HUSSAR Comedy opera in 3 acts by Henry Pottinger Stephens. Music by Edward Solomon. Lyric Theatre, London, 23 November 1889.

After his record-breaking success with *Dorothy* and a good run from its successor *Doris*, the now-very-rich Henry Leslie purchased *The Red Hussar* from composer Solomon as a third vehicle for his star and mistress, Marie Tempest. *The Red Hussar* had much of the layout of Stephens and Solomon's first (and only) big success, *Billee Taylor*, about it with its heroine Kitty Carroll (Miss Tempest) who follows her lover Ralph Rodney (Ben Davies) to war in men's clothes, being a close relative of the earlier piece's Phoebe. As in *Billee Taylor*, Kitty sees her beloved tempted by rank and wealth, in the person of Miss Barbara Bellasys (Florence Dysart), but rather than following the comical twist which had given such a lift to the first show's ending, *The Red Hussar* stuck to the romantic and had Kitty discover rank and title and win her man in the most conventional fashion.

The rest of the *Dorothy* team were given rôles to suit: comic Arthur Williams was a private soldier and baritone Hayden Coffin made an heroic ultimate partner for Miss Dysart, whilst director Charles Harris, choreographer Johnnie D'Auban, costumier Lucien Besche and conductor Ivan Caryll all repeated their functions on the new show. Amongst the minor players were principal dancer 'Birdie' Irving (later to call herself Ethel) and the young Ellis Jeffreys as 'a vivandière'.

Miss Tempest, naturally, had the largest share of Solomon's attractively straightforward comic-opera score, varying from march rhythms ('Song of the Regiment') to waltzes ('Only Dreams', 'The Glee Maiden') in a showy rôle which demanded considerable vocal resources, and Coffin was supplied with two ballads with which to attempt a follow-up to his huge hit with 'Queen of My Heart'. However, as in *Doris*, it was the tenor, Davies, who turned out to have the top songs in 'When Life and I' and 'Guides of the Night'. Williams had a comical number called 'Variations' which, in an age where the topical and the ad lib were rife, presented the particularity of using no anachronisms to cut across the period story.

The Red Hussar had a fine London run of 175 performances, went on the road with Effie Chapuy starring, and was exported to America where Miss Tempest scored a great success in 78 performances on Broadway and the first part of a tour which gave out when her voice did. In the meanwhile, however, the show had stayed in the news in England. A piece called *The White Sergeant* had been part of Solomon's assets during a recent bankruptcy and the receiver now claimed that *The Red Hussar* was that same piece and that the royalties belonged to the creditors. There were other claims too, for it seemed that Solomon had sold both *The White Sergeant* and a piece called *The Blue Hussar* at least once, and on one occasion to his own cousin, but the composer somehow survived all the suits as *The Red Hussar* went on to productions in South Africa (Edgar Perkins Co) and on the Eastern circuits. In Britain it continued to surface over the years, being reproduced for touring in a revised version in 1918, played by the Poluskis in 1919, and ultimately put out in a chopped-up version under the title *Soldier Girl* under the management of the cousin who had claimed all along that it was his.

USA: Palmer's Theater 5 August 1890

THE RED MILL Musical play in 2 acts by Henry Blossom. Music by Victor Herbert. Knickerbocker Theater, New York, 24 September 1906.

Written by Blossom and Herbert and produced by Charles Dillingham as a vehicle for the comedy team of Montgomery and Stone, *The Red Mill* presented the pair as Kid Conner (Montgomery) and Con Kidder (Stone), a couple of outrageous and impecunious Yankees loose amongst the tulips and windmills of the Netherlandish town of Katwyk-ann-Zee. The two comical fellows get involved in the love-affair between Burgomaster's daughter Gretchen van Borkem (Augusta Greenleaf) and a sailor called Doris (Joseph M Ratcliff), and they take the side of the lovers against her father (Edward Begley) in a farago of comic events which had them mixed up in moonlit doings in a theoretically haunted mill, and disguised, for a part of the time, as Sherlock Holmes and Dr Watson. Stone had a pretty soubrette called Tina (Ethel Johnson) as a love interest, there was a sub-plot involving Gretchen's intended husband, the Governor of nearby Zeeland (Neal McCay), with her auntie Bertha (Allene Crater), and a second one sparked off by a car crash between a motoring Countess (Maxine Verande) and a British lawyer (Claude Cooper) with a carful of daughters, both of which were unusually neatly tied in to the final dénouement of the show.

Blossom's lively libretto gave good opportunities to all the characters, and not just his two nevertheless overwhelming stars, and Victor Herbert's score was a versatile mixture of the music-hally and the light operatic. The two comedians sang of 'The Streets of New York' and ragged their way through 'Go While the Goin' is Good', Miss Johnson sparkled out a handful of bright songs ('Mignonette', 'Whistle It', 'I Want You to Marry Me'), Doris joined his lady-love in 'The Isle of Our Dreams' and Miss Crater gave point to 'A Woman Has Ways', but the popular gems of the score went to Miss Greenleaf and to McCay. The first-act closing had Gretchen locked up in

Plate 220. *The hero of* **The Red Mill** *is under arrest on the very steps of the titular mill. And not simply because his name is Doris.*

the haunted mill to await her unwilling marriage, taking the moment – which seemed as good as any – to serenade 'Moonbeams' in a ballad that was to become a long-time favourite. Only when she was done did the act come to its climax as the two heroes staged the moonlit rescue of the sung-out soprano, Stone dangling from the sails of the mill in an acrobatic attempt to bring Miss Greenleaf down to earth. The other hit came in the second half when the jolly governor bounced out his creed in 'Every Day is Ladies' Day with Me' prior to settling for the comfy Bertha in 'Because You're You'.

The Red Mill was a big success, and audiences flocked to the show which Dillingham made sure everyone knew about by constructing a moving red mill sign with electric lights on it outside the Knickerbocker Theater. Montgomery and Stone played their rôles for 274 performances on Broadway before taking the show on the road for a long stint of touring with most of the cast in their original parts. The run of *The Red Mill* remained a record for a Victor Herbert show on Broadway until 1945 when Stone's daughter, Paula, and Hunt Stromberg jr sponsored a revival of the same piece (Ziegfeld Theater 16 October) in the wake of successful revivals at the San Francisco Light Opera. The libretto was tactfully revised, with new lyrics by Forman Brown, Eddie Foy jr and Michael O'Shea took the comedy rôles, Stone's daughter Dorothy was the soubrette, Odette Myrtil and her violin were the motoring Countess (now called Madame La Fleur) and the sailor was understandably rechristened Hendrik instead of Doris. *The Red Mill* was a grand success all over again, and it played for 531 performances before once more heading successfully around the country.

First time round, the show created only a little interest outside America. J C Williamson Ltd picked up *The Red Mill* for Australia, and it was played there in 1908 with Fred Leslie and John Ford featured alongside Fanny Dango as Tina, but it was another decade before the show was seen in Britain. Alfred Butt eventually took the show up for the Empire Theatre and featured the dwarfish variety-comedian Little Tich in Montgomery's rôle alongside the gangling Ray Kay, Ivy Tresmand (Tina) and Amy Augarde (Bertha). The lead pair failed to attract to a poorly-staged production and the show folded in 64 performances. The success of the Broadway revival prompted a second London attempt with the piece in 1947 with variety comedians Jimmy Jewel and Ben Warriss starred, but Emile Littler's £15,000 production lasted only two weeks.

A 1927 film entitled *The Red Mill*, with Marion Davies and Owen Moore starred, had virtually nothing to do with the show, but a 1958 television edition featuring Donald O'Connor, Nichols and May and Shirley Jones had rather more.

UK: Empire Theatre 26 December 1919; Australia: Theatre Royal, Sydney 11 July 1908

Recordings: selections (Capitol, Turnabout, RCA), 1945 revival cast selection (Decca)

REDSTONE, Willie [ROTTENSTEIN, Wilhelm] (b Paris, ?1883; d Sydney, Australia, 30 September 1949). Conductor and composer for stages on both sides of the world.

The son of a half-sister of Charles Gounod and a cousin of Albert Carré, Redstone was born into a Strasbourgeois family whilst they were taking refuge in Paris from the German attacks of the latest Franco-Prussian warring. He studied at the Paris Conservatoire for six years from the age of 17 and it was during that time that he anglicized his name, allegedly to hide from the authorities the fact that he was breaking the rules by working professionally during his studies.

He began writing short opérettes in 1905, and he had some early success with a larger piece, *Mik 1er*, which ran for more than three months in Paris, before striking up a connection with the famous British ballet master John Tiller for whose school and whose northern-England productions he supplied an amount of musical material. Redstone wed a Tiller pupil and remained in Britain, fathering two children and working at the Alhambra until the outbreak of war took him into the French army. Wounded before the Battle of the Marne, he returned home and to his musical activities, taking the baton for the London productions of *Tonight's the Night* (1915), *Theodore & Co* (1916) and *Yes, Uncle!* (1917) and supplying music to such pieces as Sybil Arundale's *All Women* revue (1915), before returning to the front. At the end of the war, he picked up where he had left off, acting as musical director for the highly successful Winter Garden production of *Kissing Time* (1919), supplying music for revue *Now's the Time*, and composing the principal score for the next Winter Garden show, the internationally successful musical comedy *A Night Out*.

In 1922 he was hired by Hugh J Ward to go to Australia as musical director for his production of *The O'Brien Girl*, and he remained in the southern hemisphere to conduct *Tangerine*, *The Honeymoon Girl*, *Little Nellie Kelly*, *The Rise of Rosie O'Reilly*, *The Film Girl*, *Princess Charming*, *Whoopee* for Ernest Rolls, *The Vagabond King* and many other shows.

As his *A Night Out* settled in to a series of revivals as one of Australia's favourite 1920s musical comedies, he also continued to compose, providing the score for a musical version of the farce *Tons of Money* produced by Ward which ran long and strong around Australia (New Palace Theatre, Melbourne 27 October 1923), and individual numbers for pantomimes and other productions. He also composed the score for First National Films's *The Sea Hawk*.

Redstone spent the rest of his life in Australia, where he latterly became a music editor for the Australian Broadcasting Corporation.

1907 **Le Trou d'Almanzor** (Rip, Wilned) 1 act Théâtre des Arts 9 February; Théâtre des Bouffes-Parisiens 6 April 1908
1907 **Fleur de pétun** (Rip, G P Lafargue) 1 act Tréteau Royale 14 May
1907 **Midas** (Louis Marsolleau, Henri Géroule) 1 act Comédie Royale 22 November
1908 **Le Planteur de Connecticut** (Rip, Georges Arnould) Théâtre Marigny 1 September
1908 **Chanteclairette** (Lafargue, Jean Roby) Scala 9 September
1909 **Nuit sicilienne** (Lucien Meyrargue) mimodrama Théâtre Michel 18 May
1910 **Le Costaud de l'Olympe** (Georges Nanteuil, Léon Miral) La Cigale 11 May
1910 **Baby Pepper** (Lucien Boyer, Max Boyer) 1 act Concert Mayol 2 December
1911 **Baby** (w Adolf Stanislas/L Boyer, Jean Boyer, A Monfred) revised *Baby Pepper* tour

Plate 221. The Red Widow: *Chief comic Raymond Hitchcock comes under inspection from the suspicious 'red widow' (Sophie Barnard) in Broadway's version of the much-musicalized* His Official Wife.

1911 **Mik 1er** (Charles-Antoine Carpentier) Scala 28 September

1912 **Berlingot** (L Boyer, M Boyer, Mlle Mazier) Concert Mayol December

1913 **Les Petits Crevés, ou Henri III et son petit cour** (Rip, Jacques Bousquet) Théâtre des Capucines 24 December

1919 **Aladin, ou La Lampe merveilleuse** (Rip) Théâtre Marigny 21 May

1920 **A Night Out** (Clifford Grey/George Grossmith, Arthur Miller) Winter Garden Theatre 19 September

1921 **Faust on Toast** (w Melville Gideon/Firth Shephard, Adrian Ross) Gaiety Theatre 19 April

1924 **Tons of Money** (Vaires Louis) Grand Opera House, Sydney 1 March

THE RED WIDOW Musical play in 3 acts by Channing Pollock and Rennold Wolf based on *His Official Wife* by Richard Henry Savage. Music by Charles J Gebest. Astor Theater, New York, 6 November 1911.

Colonel Savage's enormously successful novel *His Official Wife* was leaped upon by a horde of theatrical adapters, filmed by Hollywood and, with its dramatic ending suitably revamped, successfully musicalized both in Europe and, as *The Red Widow*, in America.

In Pollock and Wolf's version, Raymond Hitchcock appeared as Cicero Hannibal Butts, 'manufacturer of CHB Corsets and a Colonel in the New York State National Guard, USA', who gets himself into trouble abroad. At London's Alcazar Music Hall he encounters the glamorous Anna Varvara (Sophye Barnard) who persuades him to let her take his wife's place on a trip to see relatives in St Petersburg. Anna is, however, the nihilist Red Widow of the title, out to shoot the Czar and pursued by the Russian Secret Police, headed by Ivan Scorpioff (John Hendricks) and Baron Maximilian Scareovich (Joseph Allan). The big dénouement is due to come during the White Fête in the Gardens of the Winter Palace, but by then Anna has fallen in love with Captain Basil Romanoff of the Imperial Bodyguard (Theodore Martin) and, when the crucial moment comes, she decides, amongst a plethora of top B naturals, that love comes before politics and she ends up joining in a chorus in praise of the 'Soldiers of the Czar'.

Hitchcock described himself as 'A Wonderful Man in Yonkers (but in London nothing at all)' and schottisched to the rueful 'I Shall Never Look at a Pretty Girl Again', whilst Miss Barnard had romantic moments both alone, in the waltz song 'Just for You', and in duet with her Basil in the show's effort to duplicate the *Merry Widow* waltz, 'I Love Love'. The stars were supported by lighter romancing from Butts's son Oswald (Harry Clarke) and his danseuse Yvette (Gertrude Vanderbilt) ('You Can't Pay the Landlord with Love'), and George Mack had a comical number in the part of a striving nihilist called Popova equipped with some lyrics which yielded some approximate but amusing rhymes ('... when a King starts out to be a Cromwell, we buy a little bombshell').

George M Cohan and Sam Harris presented Hitchcock in *The Red Widow* through a highly successful tour and a season of 128 performances at Broadway's Astor Theatre between 1911 and 1912, after which the show was taken up by J C Williamson Ltd and produced in Australia and New Zealand with Florence Young (Anna), Phil Smith (Butts) and Reginald Roberts (Basil) featured, beginning its down-under career with three weeks in Melbourne and four in Sydney (Her Majesty's Theatre, 3 December 1917). It was later played in South Africa in 1917 by Wybert Stanford's London Gaiety Company headed by Blanche Browne. However, a copyright performance staged in London failed to encourage anyone to produce the piece there and elsewhere folk manufactured their own more-or-less comic versions of *His Official Wife*, notably in Vienna where Hermann Dostal's *Nimm mich mit!* had a successful run at the Theater an der Wien.

UK: Ladbroke Hall 31 August 1911; Australia: Her Majesty's Theatre, Melbourne 4 August 1917

REECE, Robert (b Barbados, 2 May 1838; d London, 8 July 1891). One of the busiest writers for the British burlesque stage.

Educated at Balliol College, Reece began his working life as a clerk in the emigration branch of the Colonial office. He first came to theatrical notice with the texts for a handful of burlesques and operettas written for Fanny Reeves and her husband Eliot Galer and played during their seasons at the Royalty Theatre and went on from there to become one of the most popular writers in the burlesque theatre in the late 1860s and early 1870s.

Reece's Royalty burlesques *Prometheus* and *Ulf the Minstrel* were sufficiently successful, but he aroused livelier interest with his parody of Kotzebue's drama *The Stranger*, *The Stranger – Stranger Than Ever*, which not only had a fine first run at the Queen's Theatre but was reprised two years later at the Royalty. The most enduring of his burlesque works, however, was *Brown and the Brahmins*, an extravaganza based on Kenney's old musical farce *The Illustrious Stranger* (1827), a tale suggested in its turn by the Arabian Nights story of Sindbad, and involving the notion of the burying-alive of a relict spouse which was later reprised with equal humour by Gilbert in *The Mikado*. The piece ran a remarkable 100 consecutive performances at the Globe Theatre.

With the coming of opéra-bouffe and opéra-comique Reece began adapting French works for the English stage, writing the libretto for the famous first London production of *Chilpéric* and providing the difficult translation of Lecocq's sexy *Les Cent Vierges* for the Gaiety, and he also authored one of the earliest English attempts at the new-style comic opera when Kate Santley commissioned him to supply her with the text for the show which became *Cattarina*.

In 1877 Reece began a partnership with Henry Farnie with whom he subsequently wrote a number of extravaganzas, burlesques and further translations from the French and German musical theatre, their most outstanding successes coming with the record-breaking English version of *Les Cloches de Corneville* and the adaptation of *La Mascotte*, two of the longest-running musicals of the early Victorian period. He was at different times chief text-writer for the Alhambra and for John Hollingshead at the Gaiety, wrote several of Lydia Thompson's successful pieces, and there was little time during the 20 years of his playwriting career when he was not represented on the London stage.

A sometime composer and songwriter, Reece also supplied individual songs which were used from time to time in his burlesques and in the Alhambra's extravaganzas.

1865 **Castle Grim** (G B Allen) 1 act Royalty Theatre 2 September

1865 **Prometheus, the Man on the Rock** (pasticcio) Royalty Theatre 23 December

1865 **The Quiet Château** (Virginia Gabriel) 1 act Gallery of Illustration

1866 **Love's Limit** (J E Mallandaine) 1 act Royalty Theatre 16 February

1866 **Ulf the Minstrel** (pasticcio arr Hermann) Royalty Theatre 30 March

1866 **The Lady of the Lake, plaid in a new tartan** (pasticcio) Royalty Theatre 8 September

1866 **Guy Mannering** (pasticcio) Edinburgh, December

1868 **Agamemnon and Cassandra, or The Prophet and Loss to Troy** Prince of Wales Theatre, Liverpool 13 April

1868 **The Stranger – Stranger Than Ever** (pasticcio arr Schöning) Queen's Theatre 4 November

1868 **The Last of the Paladins** (*Croquefer*) English version (Gallery of Illustration)

1869 **Brown and the Brahmins, or Captain Pop and the Princess Pretty-Eyes** (pasticcio arr George Richardson) Globe Theatre 23 January

1870 **Chilpéric** English version w Richard Mansell, F A Marshall (Lyceum Theatre)

1870 **Undine** (pasticcio arr John Winterbottom) Olympic Theatre 2 July

1870 **Whittington Jr and His Sensation Cat** (pasticcio) Royalty Theatre 23 November

1870 **Faust in a Fog** (pasticcio) King's Cross Theatre 7 December

1871 **Little Robin Hood, or Quite a New Beau** (pasticcio) Royalty Theatre 19 April

1871 **In Possession** (Frederic Clay) 1 act Gallery of Illustration 22 June

1871 **Paquita, or Love in a Frame** (Mallandaine) Royalty Theatre 21 November

1872 **The Very Last Days of Pompeii** (pasticcio arr Arthur Nicholson) Vaudeville Theatre February

1872 **The Vampire** (pasticcio) Strand Theatre 15 August

1872 **Ali Baba à la Mode** (Clay, Mallandaine, Richardson, pasticcio) Gaiety Theatre 14 September

1872 **Romulus and Remus** (pasticcio arr Nicholson) Vaudeville Theatre 12 December

1873 **Don Giovanni in Venice** (pasticcio) Gaiety Theatre 17 February

1873 **Martha** (pasticcio) Gaiety Theatre 14 April

1873 **Richelieu Redressed** (pasticcio) Olympic Theatre 27 October

1873 **A Lesson in Love** (Pede) 1 act Alexandra Theatre, Camden Town 10 November

1873 **Moonstruck** (T Thorpe Pede) 1 act Alexandra Theatre 24 November

1874 **Ruy Blas Righted** (pasticcio) Vaudeville Theatre 3 January

1874 **Plucky Parthenia** (pasticcio) Portsmouth 26 February

1874 **Cattarina** (Clay) Manchester 17 August, Charing Cross Theatre, London, 15 May 1875

1874 **Les Prés Saint-Gervais** English version (Criterion Theatre)

1874 **The Island of Bachelors** (*Les Cent Vierges*) English version (Gaiety Theatre)

1874 **Green Old Age** (pasticcio) 1 act Vaudeville Theatre 31 October

1875 **Spectresheim** (pasticcio arr Georges Jacobi) Alhambra Theatre 14 August

1875 **The Half Crown Diamonds** (pasticcio) Mirror Theatre 27 September

1875 **Toole at Sea** (pasticcio) Gaiety Theatre 3 December

1876 **Coming Events** (Procida Bucalossi) 1 act Royalty Theatre 22 April

1876 **Young Rip van Winkle** (pasticcio) Gaiety Theatre 18 May

1876 **William Tell Told Again** (pasticcio) Gaiety Theatre 21 December

1877 **Oxygen** (pasticcio/w H B Farnie) Folly Theatre 31 March

1877 **The Lion's Tale and the Naughty Boy who Wagged It** (pasticcio arr Nicholson) Globe Theatre 16 June

1877 **Champagne** (pasticcio arr Henry Reed/w Farnie) Strand Theatre 29 September

1877 **Sea Nymphs** (*Les ondines au champagne*) English version (Folly Theatre)

1877 **Up the River** English version (Folly Theatre)

1877 **La Créole** English version w Farnie (Folly Theatre)

1877 **Wildfire** (pasticcio/w Farnie) Alhambra Theatre 24 December

1878 **Madcap** (*La Chaste Susanne*) (pasticcio arr A J Levey/ad w Farnie) Royalty Theatre 7 February

1878 **Pom** (Procida Bucalossi) revised text Park Theatre 2 April

1878 **Les Cloches de Corneville** English version w Farnie (Folly Theatre)

1878 **Stars and Garters** (*L'Étoile* ad w Farnie) Folly Theatre 21 September

1879 **Carmen, or Sold for a Song** (pasticcio arr Michael Connelly) Folly Theatre 25 January

1879 **Babiole** English version (Prince's Theatre, Manchester)

1879 **The Marionettes** (pasticcio/w J F McArdle) 1 act Haymarket Theatre 16 June

1879 **La Petite Mademoiselle** English version w H S Leigh (Alhambra Theatre)

1880 **Le Voyage en Suisse** English version (Gaiety Theatre)

1880 **The Forty Thieves** (pasticcio) Gaiety Theatre 24 December

1881 **Jeanne, Jeannette et Jeanneton** (aka *The Marquis*) English version (Alhambra Theatre)

1881 **The Half Crown Diamonds** revised version (pasticcio arr Lutz) Gaiety Theatre 14 May

1881 **Herne the Hunted** (pasticcio/w Henry Pottinger Stephens, William Yardley) Gaiety Theatre 24 May

1881 **La Mascotte** English version w Farnie (Comedy Theatre)

1881 **Aladdin** (pasticcio) Gaiety Theatre 24 December

1882 **Boccaccio** English version w Farnie (Comedy Theatre)

1882 **Little Robin Hood** revised version (pasticcio arr Lutz) Gaiety Theatre 15 September

1882 **On Condition** (Lutz) 1 act Opera Comique 9 October

1882 **The Merry War** (*Der lustige Krieg*) English version (Alhambra Theatre)

1882 **Valentine and Orson** (pasticcio) Gaiety Theatre 23 December

1882 **The Yellow Dwarf** (pasticcio) Her Majesty's Theatre 30 December

1883 **The Flying Dutchman** (pasticcio) Prince of Wales Theatre, Liverpool March

1883 **Our Cinderella** (pasticcio) Gaiety Theatre 8 September

1884 **Our Helen** (pasticcio) Gaiety Theatre 8 April

1884 **Out of the Ranks** (pasticcio) Strand Theatre 3 June

1884 **The Lady of Lyons Married and Claude Unsettled** Royalty Theatre, Glasgow 27 September

1885 **Kenilworth** (pasticcio arr Michael Connelley/w Farnie) Avenue Theatre 19 December

1886 **Lurline** (pasticcio arr Connelley/w Farnie) Avenue Theatre 24 April

1886 **Robinson Crusoe** (pasticcio/w Farnie) Avenue Theatre 23 December

1886 **The Commodore** (*La Créole*) new English version w Farnie (Avenue Theatre)

1889 **La Girouette** English version (Avenue Theatre)

REED, Mrs German [née HORTON, Priscilla] (b Birmingham, 1 January 1818; d London, 18 March 1895). The multi-talented mainstay of the German Reed company and entertainment.

Miss Horton made her début at the age of ten at the old Surrey Theatre under Elliston, playing a gipsy girl in *Guy Mannering*, but from the beginning of her adult career she rose swiftly up to important rôles in important houses. In 1834 she played at the Victoria Theatre as Kate in Sheridan Knowles's *The Ballad of Bethnal Green*, the following year as at the English Opera House in the ballad opera *The Covenanters* and in *Monsieur Jacques*, in 1838 she was seen at Covent Garden as Ariel in *The Tempest* and in 1840 she appeared as Ophelia to the Hamlet and Laertes of Phelps and Macready at the Haymarket. Later the same year she created the rôle of Georgina Vesey in *Money*, and she subsequently continued a round of Shakespearian engagements with Charles Kean at the Haymarket Theatre.

What was described as 'the finest contralto on the English stage' was employed in Purcell's *King Arthur* (1842) and in a long series of the famous extravaganzas written for the Haymarket Theatre, in which she supplemented and/or replaced the celebrated Madame Vestris, mainly in breeches rôles: Fortunio in *Fortunio* (1843), Graceful in *The Fair One with the Golden Locks* (1843) Ariel in *The Drama at Home* (1844), Percinet in *Graciosa and Percinet* (1844), Jason in *The Golden Fleece* (1845) to the Medea of Vestris, Princess Linda in *The Bee and the Orange Tree* (1845), The Nightingale in *The Birds of Aristophanes* (1846), Don Leander in *The Invisible Prince* (1846), the title-rôle of *The New Planet* (1847), Rebecca in *The Last Edition of Ivanhoe* (1850), Thaddeus in *Arline* (1851), Fancy in *Camp at the Olympic* (1853) and many others.

In 1854 she virtually put an end to what was potentially a memorable stage career, and she and her husband went on tour with a drawing-room entertainment in which she sang comic songs and performed impersonations to German Reed's piano accompaniment. Successful in the provinces, they expanded the entertainment and presented it as 'Miss Priscilla Horton's Illustrative Gatherings', at the St Martin's Hall in Longacre (12 March 1855). The mixture of character sketches and songs gradually developed into more substantial performances, with other artists being engaged to support Mrs Reed, and the solo items being replaced by original sketches and one-act more-or-less-musical plays as the entertainment moved, gathering in popularity, to more permanent premises at the Gallery of Illustration (1856) and then to the larger St George's Hall. The layout for a programme consisted most frequently of two short musical plays supplemented by a humorous monologue at the piano, performed in the earlier days by John Parry and, after his retirement, by Corney Grain who, along with Mr and Mrs Reed and their son Alfred (b 1840; d 10 March 1895) made up the backbone of the German Reed company.

Mrs Reed herself was the centrepiece of the early operettas at the house, creating, amongst other rôles, Maggie McMotherly in *Ages Ago*, Mrs Bumpus in *Charity Begins at Home* and Daphne in Gilbert and Clay's *Happy Arcadia* and becoming, arguably, Gilbert's model for the subsequent series of comical elderly contraltos of the Savoy operas. She retired from performing in the entertainment in 1879, but continued for many years to take part in its organization alongside first her husband and later her son.

In a curious hecatomb, Mrs Reed turned out to be the last survivor of the group. Her son Alfred died on March 10, followed just a few days later by his friend Grain, and just two days after that Mrs Reed also passed away.

Memoirs: ed Williamson, D; *The German Reeds and Corney Grain* (A D Innes, London, 1895)

REED, Michael [Campbell] (b Belstone, 30 April 1953). Conductor, orchestrator and composer for the modern musical stage.

Reed entered on a career as a musical-theatre conductor direct from the Royal College of Music, beginning with the off-West End *Let My People Come* and then, after the rehearsal-time sacking of the original conductor, taking over the baton for Harold Fielding's London Palladium production of *Hans Andersen* (1974). He subsequently conducted 15 years of musicals in the West End (*Irene, On the Twentieth Century, Barnum, Singin' in the Rain* etc) before becoming Musical Associate to Andrew Lloyd Webber's Really Useful Group for the original productions of *The Phantom of the Opéra* and *Aspects of Love*, the revival of *Joseph and the Amazing Technicolor Dreamcoat* and the series of 'Music of Andrew Lloyd Webber' concerts.

Reed composed additional material for several London musicals (*Irene, The Biograph Girl*), arranged the scores of *Mr Cinders, Bitter-Sweet* and *Wonderful Town* for 1980s revivals and that of *The Beggar's Opera* for a touring production with Edward Woodward starred. He also composed the songs for London's only-ever two-evening musical, *Six for Gold*, and for a small-scale piece about J M Barrie played at the Edinburgh Festival.

1984 **Six for Gold** (Warner Brown) King's Head Theatre 5 July
1990 **The House on the Corner** (Brown) Edinburgh Festival, August

REED, Thomas German (b Bristol, 27 June 1817; d Saint-Croix, Surrey, 21 March 1888). Founder of the famous Gallery of Illustration, and godfather to a whole era of English operetta.

Thomas German Reed became musical director at the Theatre Royal, Haymarket, at the age of 22 and he spent the bulk of his theatrical career, there and later at the Olympic Theatre, conducting the orchestra and composing and arranging music for their various plays and pasticcio entertainments. The most notable such products at these two houses, both of which were amongst the most important producers of musical extravaganzas in London, were the long series of bi-annual burlesques written by J R Planché, and the pieces of Charles Mathews.

In 1844 Reed married vocalist and actress Priscilla Horton with whom he later established a company playing drawing-room operetta at the Gallery of Illustration, an establishment which prided itself on giving clean parlour-style entertainments to a middle-class of music- and theatre-lovers for whom a visit to the regular theatre held too many moral perils. At the Gallery, Reed was instrumental in giving early opportunities to some of the most important English composers and librettists of the time – Frederic Clay, Arthur Sullivan, Edward Solomon, Alfred Cellier, Charlie Stephenson, W S Gilbert – as well as to several artists of distinction including Leonora Braham, Fanny Holland, Alice Barth, Alfred Bishop, Arthur Cecil, Richard Mansfield and Wallace Brownlow.

Reed had particular success with the productions of Sullivan's short *Cox and Box* and the Clay/Gilbert *Ages Ago* and, as a result, he attempted a season of larger works in which he presented Auber's *L'Ambassadrice*, Offenbach's *La Chatte metamorphosée en femme* and *Bata-clan* and Sullivan's first full-length work, *The Contrabandista*. However, the economics of the enterprise beat him and he returned to staging chamber musicals. The German Reed entertainments, presenting whimsical, character-based comic operettas which gave their performers plenty of opportunity for impersonations and songs of the drawing-room variety, were enormously popular with their regular audiences for many years. They moved from the Gallery of Illustration to the larger St George's Hall in 1874 and later the works which were played stretched first to two acts and finally to full length. They only declined in popularity with the retirement of Mrs Reed, the death of her husband and a general acceptance of at least certain areas of the theatre by middle-class audiences.

Reed performed in the entertainment for several years, and also composed the music for a number of the operettas produced.

1864 **Too Many Cooks** (*La Rose de Saint-Flour*) English version (Gallery of Illustration)
1869 **No Cards** (W S Gilbert) 1 act Gallery of Illustration 29 March
1870 **Our Island Home** (Gilbert) 1 act Gallery of Illustration 20 June
1873 **Mildred's Well** (F C Burnand) 1 act Gallery of Illustration 6 May
1874 **He's Coming** (Burnand) 1 act St George's Hall 17 May
1874 **The Three Tenants** (Gilbert a' Beckett) 1 act St George's Hall 26 December
1875 **Eyes and No Eyes** (Gilbert) 1 act St George's Hall 5 July
1875 **Ancient Britons** (a' Beckett) 1 act St George's Hall 25 January
1875 **A Spanish Bond** (a' Beckett) 1 act St George's Hall 1 November
1876 **An Indian Puzzle** (a' Beckett, Arthur a' Beckett) 1 act St George's Hall 28 February
1876 **The Wicked Duke** (a' Beckett) 1 act St George's Hall 9 June
1876 **Matched and Mated** (Burnand) 1 act St George's Hall 6 November
1877 **A Night Surprise** (Arthur Law) 1 act St George's Hall 12 February
1877 **Number 204** (Burnand) 1 act St George's Hall 7 May

REEVE, Ada [ISAACS, Amy Mary Adelaide] (b London, 3 March 1874; d London, 25 September 1966). Music-hall and musical comedy soubrette of the turn of the century.

Miss Reeve began performing regularly at the age of six and won her first notice in musical comedy playing a little boy in a touring melodrama with variety turns called *Jack in the Box*. She had some considerable success as a singing, wisecracking music-hall artist before making her first appearance in the musical theatre as Haidee, alongside Teddy Payne and Katie Seymour, in the touring company of the Gaiety burlesque *Don Juan*. In 1894 George Edwardes brought her to London to create the title-rôle of his celebrated musical comedy *The Shop Girl*, but she quit the show soon after its opening to take up a pantomime engagement and did not return. She subsequently interleaved other up-front, top-billed musical theatre performances (*All Abroad*, Julie Bon-Bon in *The Gay Parisienne*) into a career which was operated with a music-hall mentality, a mentality which made her a favourite partner of the unsoberly ad-libbing Arthur Roberts (*Milord Sir Smith*) to whom she was able to respond, when necessary, with wholly off-the-cuff scenes of not necessarily new material which returned to the cues only to lead in the songs. She appeared in the burlesque *Great Caesar* in 1899 and had her biggest success at the turn of the century when she created the rôle of Lady Holyrood ('Tact', 'An Inkling', 'When I Leave Town') specially tacked into the original production of *Florodora* (1899) to feature her.

She returned to Edwardes's management for *San Toy*, the successor to his all-conquering *The Geisha*, but walked out in rehearsal when bested by Marie Tempest over pecking order. She later went back to the show to play not her original comic rôle but her own music-hally version of Miss Tempest's part, and subsequently appeared for Edwardes in Evie Greene's rôle of *Kitty Grey*, and in succession to Madge Crichton as Ada (for the rôle was intended originally for Miss Reeve) in Paul Rubens's *Three Little Maids*. She had less luck in the star comedy rôle of *The Medal and the Maid* (1903) and with two touring musicals which she commissioned and produced for herself (*Winnie Brooke, Widow*, *The Adventures of Moll*), but she had one further London success with the charming remake of Locke's *The Palace of Puck* as *Butterflies* (1908, Rhodanthe). Thereafter she devoted herself largely to music-hall, revue and overseas touring, especially in Australia (where she played in *Winnie Brooke, Widow* in 1918) and South Africa, for the latter part of a long career. Her last appearance in the musical theatre was in 1947 when she appeared at the Prince's Theatre as Madame Sauterelle to the *Dubarry* of Irene Manning.

One of her husbands, Bert Gilbert, was a comedian and dancer in the musical theatre in Britain and Australia, another, Wilfred Cotton, went bankrupt producing her shows. Her daughter, Goodie Reeve, also appeared briefly on the musical stage, notably as Suzette in *The Better 'Ole* (1917) in London, and in the soprano rôle of Virginia in *My Lady Frayle* (1919) in Australia.

She must have had her tongue firmly in her aged cheek when she titled her autobiography *Take it for a Fact*.

Autobiography: *Take it for a Fact* (Heinemann, London, 1954)

REICHE MÄDCHEN Operette in 3 acts by Ferdinand Stollberg. Music by Johann Strauss. Raimundtheater, Vienna, 30 December 1909.

When Alfred Cellier and H B Farnie's *Nell Gwynne* closed out of town, it reproduced, amoeba-like. The libretto went one way and got attached to a Planquette score and became *Nell Gwynne* Mark II, whilst the now left-over score went another way, joined up with a new book, and became the record-breaking *Dorothy*.

Virtually the same thing happened in Vienna. Alfred Maria Willner, Bernhard Buchbinder and Johann Strauss's Operette *Die Göttin der Vernunft* was, however, seen in town. It was produced by Alexandrine von Schönerer at the Theater an der Wien (13 March 1897) with Annie Dirkens (Mathilde), Therese Biedermann (Susette), Julie Kopácsi-Karczag (Ernestine), Karl Blasel (Bonhomme), Josef Joseffy (Oberst Furieux) and Carl Streitmann (Capitaine Robert) heading its megastarry cast, and played there for 32 consecutive performances and four later matinées before going on to be seen at the Bellevue-Theater, Stettin (15 July 1897) and Berlin's Theater Unter der Linden (20 January 1898). It was, undoubtedly, a flop but its bits lived on.

Both halves of *Die Göttin der Vernunft* later reappeared on the Vienna stage within weeks of each other. The libretto, revised by Willner and Robert Bodanzky, appeared on the Theater an der Wien stage on 12 November 1909, now attached to a Lehár score and called *Der Graf von Luxemburg* (sic). It was the Raimundtheater, however, which had pulled the big names. It had Strauss's score, now attached to a libretto called *Reiche Mädchen*, and the star of the piece was Alexander Girardi, who was to introduce the new Strauss Operette during a Girardi Gastspiel which also included performances of his most famous plays (*Der Verschwender, Mein Leopold*) and Operetten (*Der Zigeunerbaron, Bruder Straubinger*).

Girardi played Michael Karinger, a millionaire manufacturer with a social-climbing wife and a pair of daughters with aristocratic marital ambitions. Karinger had hoped that one of his children would marry Stefan, the son of his business associate Falkenberg, but the title-crazy women are not interested – they are busy being taken in by the gold-digging Marquis de los Puntos-Torrenos and his ally Countess Ramsatoff. Stefan has to pretend to be a Count to get near to his beloved Marie. When Michael loses his money, and thus his wife, second daughter Fanni – who had won herself the Baron Bronninger – helps him to start over, and there is a happy ending when Marie finds that Stefan, if not an aristocrat, is at least a helpfully wealthy husband.

The score featured the regulation amount of waltz-music – 'Hand in Hand', 'Kein Vergnügen diesem gleicht' – whilst Blasel's best number from *Die Göttin der Vernunft* became 'Geh' zahl!, geh' zahl!' for Girardi. The duo 'Liebe allein macht nicht satt' and the song 'Das liebe Geld' were the other principal numbers of the score.

Gerda Walde, Genie von Grössl, Luise Lichten, Ludwig Herold and Gustav Werner supported the star through 82 performances of *Reiche Mädchen* to 18 March, and Girardi threw in a few more performances on his next visit (14 October 1910), before the show went on to win itself a goodly number of performances around Germany, but *Reiche Mädchen*, for all its productions, never looked like becoming the enduring hit that the show built on the libretto – that libretto originally blamed for all of *Die Göttin der Vernunft*'s woes – did. Just as in the case of *Nell Gwynne*, it was the less-prized half of the collaboration which made up into the great hit, and not the one with the more shining name attached to it.

Germany: Theater am Gärtnerplatz, Munich 28 August 1910

REICHERT, Heinz [BLUMENREICH, Heinrich] (b Vienna, 27 December 1877; d Hollywood, 16 November 1940). Viennese librettist whose most far-reaching hits came with the pasticcii *Dreimäderlhaus* and *Walzer aus Wien*.

Heinz Reichert was educated in Vienna, but left his home city to become an actor in Berlin. He soon threw in acting and became for a while a journalist with the *Ullstein Verlag* before returning to Vienna in 1906 and turning his attention to writing for the stage. He had his first taste of success in his new career with a Berlin piece, Rudolf Nelson's Scottish musical comedy *Miss Dudelsack* (1909), which went on from Germany to productions in several other countries, and in the next decade he turned out a regular stream of musical scripts, at first in collaboration with Fritz Grünbaum and subsequently with two other choice partners – A M Willner and Victor Léon – to various stages throughout Germany and Austria. He found regular success, particularly in Vienna, and it was there in 1916 that he scored the greatest triumph of his career with his text (w Willner) to the international hit of the era: *Das Dreimäderlhaus*.

Das Dreimäderlhaus's enormous success was, however, seconded by a number of others, lesser but nevertheless significant, on the Vienna and central European stages. *Drei arme Teufel* (1916) was played in Vienna a number of years after its original German production (Bürgertheater 1923, 51 performances), *Die schöne Saskia* (1917) ran through 131 performances at the Carltheater, the *Dreimäderlhaus* follow-up *Hannerl* (1918) totted up a better run than most such musequels, and the adaptation from its Hungarian original of Lehár's *Wo die Lerche singt* (*A pacsirta*) scored a genuine hit at the Theater an der Wien. The Posse *Hol mich der Teufel* which ran up 159 nights at the Bürgertheater and *Der Herzog von Reichstadt* (1921) which counted 183 performances in two seasons at the Carltheater, gave him two further successes.

During the same period, Reichert collaborated on the text for Puccini's venture into light opera with *La Rondine* (1917), which was premièred in an Italian translation, but, unlike most writers, he had the rest of his most important successes in the final part of his career.

In 1922 he collaborated on the making of Pierre Louÿs's *La Femme et le pantin* into the Spanish tale of *Frasquita* for Lehár, then worked on the confection of the Russian lost-love story of *Der Zarewitsch* from Gabryela Zapolska's piece of the same name, and finally on the texts for Leo Fall's posthumously completed and staged *Rosen aus Florida* and for the extremely successful Johann Strauss pasticcio *Walzer aus Wien*, the starting point for all the *Great Waltz*-style Strauss biomusicals of subsequent stage and screen.

With the rise of Hitler, Reichert left Europe and in 1938 settled in America, finishing his days soon after, in Hollywood.

Reichert was for some years a director of the Austrian performing rights society.

1908 **Madame Flirt** (Anselm Götzl/w Fritz Grünbaum) Neues Operetten-Theater, Hamburg 25 December
1909 **Das Himmelbett** (Fritz Lehner/w Franz Wagner) Jantschtheater 27 March
1909 **Miss Dudelsack** (Rudolf Nelson/w Grünbaum) Neues Schauspielhaus, Berlin 3 August
1910 **Don Quixote** (Richard Heuberger/w Grünbaum) 1 act Hölle 1 December
1910 **Der ledige Gatte** (Gustav Wanda/w Grünbaum) Residenz-Theater, Dresden 28 October
1910 **Die teuerste Frau von Paris** (Leo Schottländer/w Grünbaum) Bellevue-Theater, Stettin 13 November
1912 **Der Frechling** (Carl Weinberger/w Grünbaum) Wiener Bürgertheater 21 December
1913 **Der Prinzenjagd** (Ludwig Friedmann/w Grünbaum) Residenztheater, Dresden 4 April
1915 **Man steigt nach!** (Oscar Straus/w Victor Léon) Carltheater 2 May
1915 **Papa wider Willen** (Ernst Pfau/Wagner) Stadttheater, Zurich 2 December
1916 **Das Dreimäderlhaus** (Franz Schubert arr Heinrich Berté/w A M Willner) Raimundtheater 15 January
1916 **Drei arme Teufel** (Weinberger/w Rudolf Österreicher) Theater am Gärtnerplatz, Munich 11 March
1917 **Die schöne Saskia** (Oskar Nedbal/w A M Willner) Carltheater 16 November
1917 **La Rondine** (Giacomo Puccini/w Willner ad G Adami) Monte Carlo 27 March
1917 **Wiener Kinder** (Josef Schrammel arr Oskar Skalla/w Léon) Johann Strauss-Theater 16 May
1918 **Hannerl** (Franz Schubert arr Karl Lafite/w Willner) 8 February
1918 **Wo die Lerche singt** (*A pacsirta*) German version w Willner (Theater an der Wien)
1918 **Eine einzige Rettung** (Gustav Benedict/w Grünbaum) Bellevue-Theater, Stettin 30 July
1920 **Hol mich der Teufel** (Leopold Reichwein/w Léon) Bürgertheater 29 October
1921 **Der Herzog von Reichstadt** (Peter Sztojanovits/w Léon) Carltheater 11 February
1922 **Frasquita** (Lehár/w Willner) Theater an der Wien 12 May
1923 **Glück bei Frauen** (Bruno Granichstädten/w Léon) Carltheater 4 December
1925 **Donna Gloria** (Nedbal/w Léon) Carltheater 30 December
1927 **Der Zarewitsch** (Lehár/w Bela Jenbach) Deutsches Künstlertheater, Berlin 21 February
1928 **Ade, du liebes Elternhaus** (Oskar Jascha/w Willner) Volksoper 5 January
1929 **Rosen aus Florida** (Fall arr E W Korngold/w Willner) Theater an der Wien 22 February
1930 **Walzer aus Wien** (Johann Strauss arr Julius Bittner, Korngold/w Willner, Ernst Marischka) Wiener Stadttheater 30 October
1933 **Ein Liebestraum** (Károly Komjathy/Ferenc Martos, Laszló Szilágyi ad) Theater an der Wien 27 October

LA REINE JOYEUSE Opérette in 3 acts by André Barde. Music by Charles Cuvillier. Théâtre des Variétés, Marseille, 31 December 1912; L'Olympia, Paris, 6 February 1913 (as *La Reine s'amuse*); revised version Théâtre Apollo, Paris, November 1918.

The first version of the opérette which made its name as *La Reine joyeuse* was initially produced by Charles Montcharmont at Marseille in 1912, under the title *La Reine s'amuse*, with Angèle Gril featured in the title-rôle. It won a considerable success there, and Montcharmont brought it to his Théâtre des Célestins at Lyon (20 January 1913) for a further showing before launching it on Paris the following month. There, with Mlle Gril sharing the limelight with revue artist Régine Flory, comedian Polin, Mme Martens, Dorville and Morton, it was housed in the Olympia music hall and given a production by glamour-revue specialist Jacques-Charles which used such revusical staging tricks as the passerelle over the front stalls and entrances through the auditorium. Even under these odd (for a reasonably book-based show) conditions it still confirmed its provincial promise. *La Reine s'amuse* then returned to the touring circuits where (without a passerelle) it passed the war, but its career was far from finished. In November 1918 it was reproduced in Paris in a revised version, under its new *joyeuse* title, not at a music-hall but at the Théâtre Apollo, Parisian home of the *Veuve joyeuse*. Jane Marnac starred alongside Albert Brasseur, Aimé Simon-Girard and Beauval, and this time the show was more thoroughly noticed amongst the celebrations of the armistice.

Barde's lively Ruritanian libretto was set in the Kingdom of Panoplie where the ageing King (Sulbac/Polin), realizing that his young wife (Mlle Gril) is ripe for a love affair, orders his nephew Boléslas (Armand Franck/Max Capoul) to fill the bill ... up to a point. Boléslas 'carries off' the Queen to Paris – chaperoned by the Countess Katisch (Lucy Blémont/Mme Martens) and followed incognito by the king and his court – and after the young pair have danced through the Cabaret du Perroquet and the Quat'z'Arts Ball, got involved with the soubret pair (Mary-Hett, Fabert/Régine Flory, Dorville) and gone as far as the first horrifyingly revelatory kiss, the King decides magnanimously that perhaps it is time for him to head for the divorce court and a consolatory Parisienne.

Cuvillier's score mixed the comical and the romantic in classic doses. The King worried about his people's habit of dethroning their monarchs with a 'Ping, Pan, Vlan!', Katisch pointedly wondered when the Queen was going to get a 'Coquerico!' out of her royal husband, and recommended her mother's recipe of a pretty aide de camp as a remedy for frustration ('Voilà ce que faisait ta mère'), but the hit of the evening came when the heroine moved into waltz rhythm with the aroused 'Ah! la troublante volupté'. As in so many cases before and after, this waltz was not in the original show, but made up part of Cuvillier's revisions: it proved a revision well done and gave him the biggest single song hit of the French part of his career.

At the height of Cuvillier's popularity in Britain, following the enormous success there of *The Lilac Domino*, Grossmith and Laurillard picked up *La Reine joyeuse/s'amuse* and, re-angling its title and text once again as *The Naughty Princess* (for British consumption, the heroine was no longer a married woman, which made it all right to be naughty), produced it at London's Adelphi Theatre in a version by J Hastings Turner and Adrian Ross. Played by star comedian W H Berry (Michel), Grossmith (who cast himself as the hero, Ladislas), Lily St John (Sophia) and Amy Augarde (Kittisch), with young Yvonne Arnaud as soubrette, and featuring a front line including Heather Thatcher, Elsie Randolph and Sylvia Leslie in the bit-part created by the young Alice Delysia, it ran for seven and a half months. *The Naughty Princess* was subsequently produced in Australia, with Gladys Moncrieff starring alongside Jack Cannot (King), George Gee (another comical Ladislas), Ethel Morrison (Kittisch), Hugh Steyne and Gracie Lavers through six weeks in Melbourne. However, before its Sydney season it was again rearranged. The lighter-voiced Kitty Reidy replaced Moncrieff as the Princess and certified operettic baritone Howett Worster took over from

comic Gee as Ladislas in a line-up much more like that of the French original as the piece duly ran through its six weeks.

La Reine s'amuse was revived at the Théâtre Marigny under the management of Léon Volterra in 1929 with a cast headed by Mlle L Welcome (Sophia), Charles Prince (Michel), Louis Arnoult (Boléslas) and with former Cuvillier prima donna Anna Tariol-Baugé moving into duenna rôles as Katisch.

UK: Adelphi Theatre *The Naughty Princess* 7 October 1920; Australia: Her Majesty's Theatre, Melbourne 29 July 1922

REINHARDT, Heinrich (b Pressburg, 13 April 1865; d Vienna, 31 January 1922). The composer of sizeable hits on both sides of the Atlantic without actually making himself a rememberable name.

Reinhardt studied music in Pressburg and at the Gesellschaft der Musikfreunde in Vienna and his earliest compositions, in the field of piano and vocal music, were written whilst he ran a parallel career as a musical journalist. His first attempts at theatre work, in collaboration with author Hans Koppel, were in opera (*Die Göldner*) and in ballet-pantomime (*Kunst und Co*), but in 1901 he produced the score to Landesberg and Stein's light-hearted and happily folksy Operette *Das süsse Mädel*, a pretty, dancing piece of uncomplicated musical writing in a style far from that of the Suppé, Millöcker and Strauss Operetten of the declining 'golden era' of Viennese musical theatre. *Das süsse Mädel* won a very considerable success at Vienna's Carltheater and through Europe and confirmed its composer in a career in the light musical theatre.

The success of *Das süsse Mädel* was followed by another in the same genre, *Der Generalkonsul* (1904), and in 1909 by his most widely played overseas success, the pretty, spa-town tale of *Die Sprudelfee*. As played in a 1910 American version written by the Smith brothers and titled *The Spring Maid*, *Die Sprudelfee* made a great hit on Broadway and around America, and although its London life was considerably shorter, Reinhardt was brought brightly to the attention of the English-speaking world. Broadway welcomed a second Reinhardt piece, under the title *The Purple Road*, in 1913, in which the original score for the composer's shapely *Napoleon und die Frauen* had been dotted with extra numbers by the unexceptional William Frederick Peters, and London's Tivoli music hall staged what it called a 'leap-year comedy Operette in one act', *The Daring of Diane* (*Die süssen Grisetten*, ad Arthur Anderson, 22 January 1912) in the period during which it was fashionable to feature Viennese operettas on variety bills. *The Daring of Diane*, in fact, went further afield than any other Reinhardt work, for it was played by Hilda Vining in Australia (Her Majesty's Theatre, Melbourne, 12 July 1913) as part of an Adeline Genée 'Imperial Russian Ballet' programme.

The 1913 *Prinzess Gretl* proved more popular than any of these nevertheless well-received works in Germany, whilst Hungary, which had welcomed both *Das süsse Mädel* (*As édes lanyka*) and *Der Generalkonsul* (*A fökonsul*, Király Színház), as well as *Prinzess Gretl* (*Diákhercegnő*, Fövárosi Nyari Színház) showed its preference for the 1915 *Die erste Frau* (*Az első feleseg*, Budapesti Színház 1917).

Most of Reinhardt's Operetten earned a pleasing reception in Vienna – *Prinzess Gretl* (156 performances) and *Die erste Frau* (101 performances) being the most long-running after *Das süsse Mädel* – and a representation elsewhere in Europe, but the coming of *Die lustige Witwe* and the brightest of the early Lehár, Eysler, Fall and Oscar Straus pieces rather submerged the composer's agreeable and always light-handed work, and *Das süsse Mädel*, which had not had to put up with such tough concurrence, remained Reinhardt's single most successful work in his home country and in the rest of central Europe.

1895 **Die Minnekönigin** (Hans Koppel) 1 act
1901 **Das süsse Mädel** (Alexander Landesberg, Leo Stein) Carltheater 25 October
1902 **Der liebe Schatz** (Landesberg, Stein) Carltheater 30 October
1904 **Der Generalkonsul** (Landesberg, Stein) Theater an der Wien 29 January
1906 **Krieg im Frieden** (Julius Wilhelm) Carltheater 24 January
1907 **Die süssen Grisetten** (Wilhelm) 1 act Hölle 1 December
1908 **Ein Mädchen für Alles** (Heinz von Waldberg, A M Willner) Theater im Gärtnerplatz, Munich 8 February
1909 **Die Sprudelfee** (Willner, Wilhelm) Raimundtheater 23 January
1909 **Die siamesischen Zwillinge** (Louis Windhopp, Ernst Ress) 1 act Hölle 16 March
1910 **Studentenhochzeit** (Reinhardt) 1 act Kleines Schauspielhaus 1 October
1910 **Miss Exzentric** (Alexander Engel, Armin Friedmann) 1 act Apollotheater 31 October
1912 **Napoleon und die Frauen** (Reinhardt) Volksoper 1 May
1913 **Prinzess Gretl** (Willner, Robert Bodanzky) Theater an der Wien 31 January
1915 **Die erste Frau** (Willner, Rudolf Österreicher) Carltheater 22 October
1916 **Der Gast des Königs** (Friedmann) Volksoper 9 January
1922 **Der Glückstrompeter** (Gustav Beer, Friedmann) Apollotheater 7 December
1928 **Grisettenliebe** (Wilhelm) Rolandbühne 23 March

RÉNYI, Aladár (b Kolozsvár, 9 September 1885; d in a concentration camp, 1944).

Rényi studied at the Budapest Zeneakadémia and had his first operett produced at the Király Színház at the age of 26. *A kis gróf* had a great success and it went on to be produced the following year at the Carltheater in Vienna under the title *Susi*, returning to the Király Színház in its German version during the Carltheater company's visit to Budapest in 1913. *Susi* was successfully played in Germany and staged on Broadway (Casino Theater, 1914) before Rényi's second work, *Tiszavirág*, was produced in Budapest. He wrote two further operetts, as well as chamber music, songs and piano music, but without again finding the success of his first stage work.

1911 **A kis gróf** (Ferenc Martos) Király Színház 9 September
1915 **Tiszavirág** (István Brody, László Vajda) Király Színház 27 March
1917 **Vandergold kisasszony** (Sándor Hevesi, Zsolt Harsányi) Városi Színház 24 October
1926 **Kitty és Kati** (Martos) Király Színház 30 April

REVILL, Clive [Selsby] (b Wellington, New Zealand, 18 April 1930).

Revill's early career was in the non-musical theatre, including a period at Britain's Ipswich Repertory Theatre and another at the Shakespeare Memorial Theatre, Stratford-on-Avon. His first musical appearances were in children's pieces – Pearson in *Listen to the Wind* (1955) and

Ratty in Fraser-Simson's *Toad of Toad Hall* – and his first great success in that area his portrayal of the bar-owner/narrator Bob le Hotu in the English and American productions of *Irma la Douce* (1957–61). He appeared with the opera company at Sadler's Wells Theatre as a memorable Ko-Ko in their production of *The Mikado* (1962) and returned to Broadway to take the rôle of Fagin in the American production of *Oliver!* (1963). He subsequently starred as Sheridan Whiteside in *Sherry!*, the unsuccessful musical version of *The Man Who Came to Dinner* (1967), but has devoted himself since to the non-musical theatre and to film.

REVOIL, Fanély (b Marseille, 25 September 1910).

A charming ingénue, with an attractive and accurate soprano voice, Mlle Revoil was one of the principal stars of the French opérette theatre of the 1930s.

She had her earliest experience at Nimes, at Mulhouse (where in 1930 she played Lisa in the French première of *Comtesse Maritza*) and at the Théâtre du Havre where, the following year, she created the the title-rôle of the French version of Lehár's *Frasquita*. She was hired by Maurice Lehmann for the Théâtre de la Porte-Saint-Martin in 1933, made her Paris début as Lecocq's *Petit Duc* and, a few months later, stepped in as a late replacement for the star of the Paris première of *La Dubarry*. She was seen over the next three seasons as the Countess in *Valses de Vienne*, la Guimard in Pierné's *Fragonard*, in *Véronique* (Hélène), *Les Mousquetaires au couvent* (Louise), *Le Domino noir*, *Chanson d'amour* (Carlina), *Mam'zelle Nitouche* (Denise), *La Mascotte*, *Gillette de Narbonne* (Gillette), *Le Petit Faust* (Méphisto), *La Fille de Madame Angot* (in each of the lead rôles), *Rêve de valse*, *La Fille du tambour-major* (Stella), *Les Dragons de Villars* (Rose Friquet), and as Sonia in a made-over version of *Der Zarevitsch* played in Paris as *Rêve d'un soir*.

Mlle Revoil appeared alongside Mistinguett in Yvain's *Un coup de veine* (1935) and, again under Lehmann's direction, at the Théâtre du Châtelet in *Au soleil du Mexique* (1935, Juanita). She was seen in *La Belle Traversée* at the Alhambra (1936), and then moved to the Opéra-Comique where she played in *Le Testament de Tante Caroline* and *La Chambre bleu*, in the rôle of Lazuli when Chabrier's *L'Étoile* was admitted to the Salle Favart, as Hahn's *Ciboulette* and as la Guimard in *Fragonard*. After the Second World War she again appeared on the commercial stage, playing *Rose-Marie* at the Châtelet (1945), and creating the title-rôles of a 1946 opérette based on the life of the actress *Virginie Déjazet* and of a Châtelet spectacular on *Madame Sans-Gêne* (1948). Thereafter she appeared largely in concert and on radio before turning to teaching, ultimately spending more than a decade at the head of the opérette class of the Paris Conservatoire.

LA REVOLTOSA Zarzuela in 1 act by Guillermo Fernández Shaw and José Lopez Silva. Music by Ruperto Chapí y Llorente. Teatro Apolo, Madrid, 25 November 1897.

The most successful of Chapí's 'genero chico' zarzuelas, *La Revoltosa* was a typically colourful little picture of everyday Madrid and its characters, the chief of which was the unruly lass of the title, Maria-Pépa (Isabel Brú). Maria-Pépa puts herself around amongst the men in her apartment block, and even the policeman Candelas (José Mesejo) falls for her when he should be keeping her from causing trouble. The women of the block get their revenge on festival night when, taking a leaf out of the book of the ladies of *Les Dominos roses*, they fake invitations to each of their men to meet Maria-Pépa after the dancing. When they all end up knocking at her door at midnight, the women spring their trap and the frightened girl takes refuge in the arms of the genuine Felipe (Emilio Mesejo), her lesson learned.

The music accompanying the tale was spread amongst both principal and subsidiary characters and featured a seguidilla for one of the men which proved the evening's favourite musical moment.

Recordings: complete (Alhambra/Columbia, Montilla/Zafiro, EMI, Hispavox, Edigsa)

REYNOLDS, Dorothy (b Birmingham, 26 January 1913; d 1977).

Miss Reynolds joined the Bristol Old Vic company as an actress in 1952 and during her engagement there collaborated with another company member, Julian Slade, in writing revue and small-scale musical comedy for their colleagues. Their first efforts, the Christmas revue *Christmas in King Street* (the Bristol Theatre Royal is situated in King Street) and *The Merry Gentleman* (ie Santa Claus), were genuine local successes, and their third seasonal piece, the ingenuous, revusical *Salad Days*, became a theatrical phenomenon when it transferred to London's Vaudeville Theatre for a record-breaking run, with Miss Reynolds herself appearing in one of the most comical of the show's revusically composite rôles and introducing the mock-cabaret song 'Sand in My Eyes'.

She wrote four further works with Slade, appearing in *Free as Air* (1957, Miss Catamole), *Hooray for Daisy* (1959, Georgina Cosens) and *Wildest Dreams* (1960, Harriet Gray) but not in the revised *Christmas in King Street* which played London as *Follow That Girl* (1960). In 1962 she played the rôle of Elinor Spencer-Bollard in the London version of Noël Coward's *Sail Away* before returning to exclusively straight theatre.

1953 **The Merry Gentleman** (Julian Slade) Theatre Royal, Bristol 24 December
1954 **Salad Days** (Slade) Vaudeville Theatre 5 August
1957 **Free as Air** (Slade) Savoy Theatre 6 June
1959 **Hooray for Daisy** (Slade) Theatre Royal, Bristol 23 December; Lyric Theatre, Hammersmith 20 December 1960
1960 **Follow that Girl** (Slade) Vaudeville Theatre 17 March
1960 **Wildest Dreams** (Slade) Everyman Theatre, Cheltenham 20 September; Vaudeville Theatre 3 August 1961

RICE, E[dward] E[verett] (b Brighton, Mass, 21 December 1848; d New York, 16 November 1924).

Busy American producer/songwriter of the 19th century whose troupes covered the country with the kind of fare which pulled 'em in, yet who also manufactured several large Broadway hits.

Originally an actor, and then an advertising printer and copywriter in Boston, the 23-year-old Rice made his first profitable connection with the theatre when he wed Clara Rich, the daughter of one of Boston's principal theatre managers. Two years later, however, whilst earning his daily bread in the Cunard Company office in Boston, he found theatrical success in a wholly different way when he combined with the young librettist Cheever Goodwin to compose the songs for an extravagant burlesque of Longfellow's *Evangeline*. Previewed musically in Boston, then produced on the stage at Cambridge, Massachusetts, *Evangeline* found sufficient success to be moved along to other venues and, in July 1874 it opened at New York's Niblo's Gardens, beginning a career which would make it one of the most popular and successful American burlesques of all time.

Rice continued to write and produce loose-limbed entertainments for the popular touring circuits. He turned out text, lyrics and music for the easy-going *Pop*, put his name to a ripped-off version of George Fawcett Rowe and John Sheridan's *Fun on the Bristol* (it included burlesques of *Il Trovatore* and *The Lady of Lyons* and was billed as 'revived after two years of success in Britain') for his Rice's Travestie Company and, when he jumped on the *HMS Pinafore* bandwagon and put out a company which played the Lyceum in 1879, he made Gilbert's sophisticated burlesque into an unsophisticated one by casting George Fortescue as Buttercup and Lizzie Webster as Ralph.

Rice then founded a group which he called Rice's Surprise Party, taking on board a number of players from Lydia Thompson's famous burlesque company, and he toured this 'Party' successfully for many years playing a repertoire of burlesques, extravaganza and the kind of low-comedy-with-variety-items shows which became known as 'farce comedy'. Amongst the early and long-lived successes played by the troupe were *The Babes in the Wood*, *Horrors, or the Maharajah of Zogobad* (aka *Prince Achmet*), *Hiawatha*, *Robinson Crusoe* and *Revels*.

Raising his sights a notch, Rice took on New York's Fifth Avenue Theater (w Jacob Nunnemacher) to produce a version of Genée's Operette *Der Seekadett*, and moved throroughly upmarket when he joined D'Oyly Carte to produce Solomon's *Billee Taylor* under the 'Rice-Goodwin Lyric Company' banner in New York, but although he ventured with further touring Carte productions (*Billee Taylor*, *Patience*, *Iolanthe*) and produced Solomon's *Polly* (w J C Scanlan) on Broadway, he mainly stuck to the area he knew best. He produced, directed and/or composed music for the burlesque *The Corsair*, the farce comedies *A Bottle of Ink* and *Circus in Town*, the extravaganzas *1492* and *The Seven Ages* and a badly battered version of Lecocq's *Fleur de thé* mounted burlesque-fashion and with some success as *The Pearl of Pekin*, but he had his greatest successes as a producer with Willie Gill's burlesque extravaganza *Adonis* (1884), one of the longest-running Broadway shows of its era (603 performances), and with a virtual variety-show version of the British burlesque *Little Christopher Columbus* (1894).

In 1895 he produced another spectacular extravaganza, *Excelsior Jr*, which scored another vivid Broadway success, but Rice's Broadway seasons were only a showcase part of his activity, for his companies toured extensively throughout America and even at times both to Britain (with *Adonis*) and to Australia (*Adonis*, *The Corsair*) and it was in those companies that he found his steadiest success.

With the displacing of burlesque by English musical comedy, Rice shifted with the fashion and imported several pieces of the kind from Britain, having successes with *The*

Girl from Paris (1896, *The Gay Parisienne*) and *The French Maid* (1897), less with *Monte Carlo* (1898) and very little with *The Ballet Girl* (1897) and *Mr Wix of Wickham* (1904). Into several of these he interpolated additional or replacement songs of his own writing, and he continued throughout his producing career to pen the kind of material in which he had specialized in his earlier days for touring stars and companies (*Captain Kidd USN* for Ernest Hogan, etc). Some of his numbers even turned up in such unlikely places as Seymour Hicks's London musical comedy *The Yashmak*.

After *The French Maid*, however, success became harder to find. He produced the little negro musical *Clorindy, or the Origin of the Cakewalk* (1898) at the Casino Theater roof garden, winning a small summertime success, but two other Broadway ventures with un- or little-tried material, *The Show Girl* (aka *The Cap of Fortune*, 1902) and *King Highball* (1902) were quick failures, and in the years that followed Rice's name slipped out of sight.

1873 **Evangeline** (J Cheever Goodwin) Niblo's Gardens 27 July 1874
1880 **Hiawatha** (Nathaniel Childs) Standard Theater 21 February
1882 **Pop** (Rice) San Francisco; 14th Street Theater 21 May 1883
1884 **Adonis** (William Gill) Hooley's Theater, Chicago 6 July, Bijou Theater, New York 4 September
1887 **The Corsair** (w John Braham) Bijou Theater 18 October
1889 **The Seven Ages** (w Braham) Standard Theater 7 October
1893 **1492** (Carl Pflueger/w R A Barnet) Boston; Palmer's Theater, New York, 15 May
1895 **Excelsior Jr** (w A Baldwin Sloane, George Lowell Tracy/Barnet) Hammerstein's Olympia 29 November
1899 **Little Red Riding Hood** (w Fred Eustis/Harrison Ward/ Charles Dennee) Casino Theater 8 January
1899 **Around New York in 80 Minutes** (w John Braham/ Goodwin/James T Waldron, Edward Fales Coward) Koster and Bial's Music Hall 27 September

RICE, Tim[othy Miles Bindon] (b Amersham, 10 November 1944). Innovative British lyricist of the rock-opera era whose short list of credits has nevertheless produced some of the most appreciable shows of the last 20 years.

In the early 1970s, in collaboration with composer Andrew Lloyd Webber, lyricist Rice pioneered a breakaway from the long popular scenes-and-songs style of musical show which had, in the postwar years, rarely shaken off the classic operetta-without-ensembles layout represented most prominently and recently in the works of Rodgers and Hammerstein and their followers. Rice and Lloyd Webber returned to a cantata form, a sung-through text with no intervening dialogue, scarcely used in the musical theatre since Gilbert and Sullivan's *Trial By Jury*, for their first work, the little *Joseph and the Amazing Technicolor Dreamcoat* (1968–72). The composer's mixture of modern popular and classical elements was blended with Rice's individual and contemporary verse style, part speech-patterned, part lyrical and combining everyday language with occasional more fanciful flights and an enjoyable and youthful comic sense in a style that was new to the modern British stage. This combination was developed further in the pair's more serious *Jesus Christ Superstar* (1972), subtitled a rock opera, and in *Evita*

(1978), two works which became internationally the most successful musical stage shows of the 1970s.

By and large, other writers failed to encompass the style and method of these shows, which could have been expected to encourage a rich generation of sung-through, dramatic modern musical shows, but Rice, in a disappointingly rare return to the theatre, secured a further London success in the same mode with *Chess* (1986) written in collaboration with Björn Ulvaeus and Benny Andersen, former members of the Swedish pop group Abba. He has subsequently adapted the French/Canadian teeny-musical *Starmania* for an English-language recording under the title *Tycoon*, and found a different kind of success when his song 'A Whole New World' (w Alan Menken) in the Disney film *Aladdin* took the 1992 Academy Award.

1971 **Jesus Christ Superstar** (Andrew Lloyd Webber) Mark Hellinger Theater, New York 12 October
1972 **Joseph and the Amazing Technicolor Dreamcoat** (Lloyd Webber) Edinburgh Festival 21 August. Young Vic 26 October
1973 **Jacob's Journey** (Lloyd Webber) 1 act Albery Theatre 17 February
1978 **Evita** (Lloyd Webber) Prince Edward Theatre 21 June
1984 **Blondel** (Stephen Oliver) Old Vic 9 November
1986 **Chess** (Björn Ulvaeus, Benny Andersen) Prince Edward Theatre 14 May

RICHEPIN, Tiarko (b Paris, 9 March 1884; d 1973).

The younger son of Jean Richepin, author and librettist (*Le Chemineau*, *Le Carilloneur*, the 1907 féerie *La Belle au bois dormant* w Henri Cain, and apparently of the source for Anna Held's Broadway show *Mamselle Napoléon*), Tiarko Richepin made his earliest theatre ventures in an eclectic variety of areas: incidental music for Paul Vérola's four-act dramatic poem *Nirvana* and for the five-act tragedy *Dalila* (1908), a little burlesque opérette with another son of a famous father, Sacha Guitry, for the tiny Théâtre Mévisto, a one-act Bohemian ballet *Rômi-Tchâvé* for the opening programme at the newly reconstructed Folies-Bergère (1909), incidental music for the verse play *Le Minaret* (1913) written by his elder brother, Jacques (author of the successful play *Xantho et les courtisanes*) and, in 1914, a three-act 'conte lyrique' *La Marchande d'allumettes*, written by Mme Edmond Rostand and produced by the Isola brothers at the Opéra-Comique.

Wounded during the First World War, he returned to the lyric stage in 1919, but there was to be no return to the Opéra-Comique. Several conventionally sized opérettes were failures and, in a career which included songwriting ('Il n'y a qu'un Paris', 'Si tu reviens' etc) and film music, he ultimately found his only success in the theatre with the scores or part-scores for a series of opérettes à grand spectacle of which *Venise*, originally composed with the Opéra-Comique in mind, and a collaboration with Henri Christiné on the Châtelet spectacular *Au temps des merveilleuses* proved the most successful.

1909 **Tell père, Tell fils** (Sacha Guitry) 1 act Théâtre Mévisto 17 April
1914 **La Marchande d'allumettes** (Rosemond Gérard) Opera-Comique 25 February
1919 **Rapatipatoum** (Albert Willemetz) Théâtre Edouard VII 7 April
1927 **Venise** (Willemetz/André Mouëzy-Éon) Théâtre Marigny 25 June

1929 **Le Renard et les poules** (Mouëzy-Éon, Alfred Machard) Théâtre Michel 31 January
1932 **La Tulipe noire** (Willemetz/Mouëzy-Éon) Théâtre de la Gaîté-Lyrique 19 March
1934 **Au temps des merveilleuses** (w Henri Christiné/Willemetz, Mouëzy-Éon) Théâtre du Châtelet 25 December
1936 **Yana** (w Christiné/Willemetz, Mouëzy-Éon, Henri Wernert) Théâtre du Châtelet 24 December
1941 **L'Auberge qui chante** (Georges Hirsch, André de Badet) Théâtre de la Gaîté-Lyrique

Other title credited: *Le Jolly Joker* (?1920, Willemetz)

RIDEAMUS [OLIVEN, Fritz] (b Breslau, 10 May 1874; d Porto Alegre, 30 June 1956). German lyricist and librettist whose work was blessed with an occasional enjoyably unconventional touch.

Oliven moved to Berlin as a child and studied there until he became a practising doctor of law. At the same time, he doubled as a writer of revue material, song lyrics and plays, under the gently learned pseudonym of 'Rideamus' (Lat: let us laugh).

'Rideamus' made an early venture into the musical theatre as the author of the burlesque *Die lustigen Nibelungen*, and collaborated with composer Oscar Straus on a second and equally imaginative piece for the Carltheater, *Hugdietrichs Brautfahrt*, but he found his most considerable success when, abandoning this kind of high-comic opéra-bouffe, he joined author/producer Hermann Haller as lyricist to a series of romantic musical plays and revues at the Theater am Nollendorfplatz. In the years during and after the Great War, Haller produced such pieces as Kollo's *Quality Street* musical *Drei alte Schachteln*, which ran for nearly 500 performances, and a series of five Operetten composed by Eduard Künneke of which *Der Vetter aus Dingsda* was the highlight and which filled the theatre, with only one interruption, for more than three years.

'Rideamus' later provided the German adaptations of the French *Ta bouche* and of the American *Rose Marie*, and wrote revue material for Haller for his Admiralspalast revues before joining the exodus of virtually all that was talented (and some that was not) in the German theatre in the early 1930s.

1904 **Die lustigen Nibelungen** (Oscar Straus) Carltheater 12 November
1906 **Hugdietrichs Brautfahrt** (Straus) Carltheater 10 March
1917 **Drei alte Schachteln** (Walter Kollo/Haller) Theater am Nollendorfplatz 6 October
1919 **Die Vielgeliebte** (Eduard Künneke/w Haller) Theater am Nollendorfplatz 27 October
1920 **Wenn Liebe erwacht** (Künneke/w Haller) Theater am Nollendorfplatz 3 September
1921 **Der Vetter aus Dingsda** (Künneke/w Haller) Theater am Nollendorfplatz 15 April
1921 **Die Ehe im Kreise** (Künneke/w Haller) Theater am Nollendorfplatz 2 November
1922 **Verliebte Leute** (Künneke/w Haller) Theater am Nollendorfplatz 15 April
1922 **Dein Mund** (*Ta bouche*) German version w Haller (Theater am Nollendorfplatz)
1928 **Rose Marie** German version (Admiralspalast)
1930 **Majestät lässt bitten** (Kollo) Komische Oper 5 April
1933 **Die Männer sind mal so** (Kollo/w Theo Halton) Schillertheater 4 January

RIEGEN, J *see* BOHRMANN, HEINRICH

RIGBY, Harry (b Pittsburgh, 21 April 1925; d New York, 17 January 1985).

Co-producer of *Make a Wish*, *John Murray Anderson's Almanac*, the Broadway version of *Half a Sixpence*, *Hallelujah, Baby!* and *I Love My Wife*, Rigby is remembered mostly as the guiding genius behind the brief series of 1970s revivals of classic American musicals which resulted in *No, No, Nanette* (not very altered) and *Irene* (considerably altered) being given a fresh lease of life and a fresh trip round the world's stages. A third attempt with *Good News* failed to make the same sort of impact. In 1982 Rigby also mounted the Schmidt/Jones *Colette* with Diana Rigg, Robert Helpmann and John Reardon heading a starry cast to closure out of town.

RING, Blanche (b Boston, 24 April 1877; d Santa Monica, Calif, 13 January 1961). One of the brightest Broadway stars of the first decades of the 20th century.

Born into a theatrical family – her grandfather had been for 30 years manager of the Boston Museum – Blanche Ring began performing at an early age. After a number of teenage years touring with James Hearne, Nat Goodwin, Chauncey Olcott (*Mavourneen*) and other barn- and region-storming companies, Miss Ring introduced her mega-watt personality and bright, permeating singing voice to Broadway in the 1902–3 season. She opened her metropolitan career in *The Defender*, performing the interpolated 'In the Good Old Summertime', and made herself a name which guaranteed her spots, later the same season, in *Tommy Rot* (introducing 'The Belle of Avenue A'), *The Jewel of Asia* and *The Blonde in Black*. The following year, she was back, equipped with another hit song (Jerome and Schwartz's 'Bedelia'), in *The Jersey Lily* and she then visited England where she appeared in variety, and caused a sensation singing Lotta Faust's Broadway hit 'Sammy' in George Grossmith's youthful but otherwise unremarkable musical *The Lovebirds*.

In 1905 she played the sprightly Lady Bickenhall in Broadway's version of Liza Lehmann's London musical *Sergeant Brue*, fitted out with another interpolated and soon-to-be-hit number, 'My Irish Molly O' and, in an unlikely piece of casting, she succeeded Marie Cahill in the lead of Victor Herbert's *It Happened in Nordland*. Like Cahill, she was ultimately asked to leave for interpolating her own songs into Herbert's score. She appeared in the Chicago musical *The Pink Hussars* (1905, Katrinka), in a short-lived vehicle called *His Majesty* (1906, Mrs Brown), and, obviously forgiven by Herbert for her *Nordland* vagaries, on the road in an 'improved version' of Lulu Glaser's rôle in *Miss Dolly Dollars* (1906) scoring a hit 'especially in the musical numbers that had been re-arranged to suit her personality'.

She reprised *His Honor the Mayor* (1906, which had started life as *The Pink Hussars*) performing her latest song success, 'Waltz Me Round Again, Willie' to considerable success, played in the revusical *About Town* (1906), the burlesque *The Great Decide*, and *The Great White Way* (1907) and took over the title-rôle in the burlesque of *The Merry Widow and the Devil* (1908) for Joe Weber, bringing another of her most successful numbers, 'Yip-I-Addy-I-Ay', to add to the piece's musical part.

Plate 222. **Blanche Ring**: *Longtime star of the American musical stage, as* The Yankee Girl.

In 1909 she played in *The Midnight Sons* (Mrs Carrie Margin), performing 'I've Got Rings on My Fingers', which she also popped into the following year's *The Yankee Girl*, and followed up in *The Wall Street Girl* ('I Want a Regular Man') and in a virtual pasticcio called *When Claudia Smiles* (1913–14, Claudia Rogers) into which she inserted several of her old hit numbers. In the following seasons, she played Adele Rowland's rôle of 'Tony' Miller in *Nobody Home* in Los Angeles, starred as Madame Nadine (otherwise Jane O'Day) in A H Woods's production of *Broadway and Buttermilk* (aka *Jane O'Day from Broadway*) and appeared in the unsuccessful tryout of the Harry Tierney musical *What's Next?* (1917, Angie).

In the war years she played in revue, in classic comedy (Mistress Quickly) and in regional shows, one of these last being the out-of-town try-out of *No, No, Nanette* in which she was brought in to play Lucille ('Where Has My Hubby Gone Blues') in the Chicago company which established the show. Her husband, Charles Winninger, was cast as

Jimmy Smith, a rôle he retained when Blanche 'moved on' to another job (after some acrimony) and thus missed the show's delayed, triumphant Broadway transfer.

She appeared with John E Hazzard in his *The Houseboat on the Styx* and, in 1930, trouping on, though no longer the big-drawing star she had been, she played a character rôle in the Broadway production of Gershwin's *Strike Up the Band* (Mrs Grace Draper). In 1938 she returned one last time to appear in the Sammy Fain musical *Right This Way* (Josie Huggins) at the age of nearly 70.

One of the great musical-comedy personalities of her period, Blanche Ring combined an attractive star presence and a brazen, attacking delivery which were responsible for making many of the songs she performed into durable hits.

THE RINK Musical in 2 acts by Terrence McNally. Lyrics by Fred Ebb. Music by John Kander. Martin Beck Theater, New York, 9 February 1984.

A small-cast musical play following the ups and, mostly, downs of the lives of Anna Antonelli (Chita Rivera, Tony Award) and her daughter, Angel (Liza Minnelli). After a life of drudgery running a seaside fairground skating-rink, Anna is finally selling up and getting out to relax for the first time in memory. Then her daughter, who walked out years ago to enjoy sex, marijuana and no responsibility in the west-coast 1960s, turns up, expecting things to be all coloured lights and childhood again. A confrontation develops, the self-centred Angel holding it over her mother that she pretended the girl's father was dead when he was only departed, but by the end, aided by the fact that Angel finally reveals that she has a fatherless child of her own to bring up, the two come together in some kind of reconciliation. The characters (male and female) who featured in the flashbacks which made up much of the piece were all played by a gang of a half-dozen men, the wrecker's men sent to pull down the rink, who were put on roller skates.

Kander and Ebb's songs included Anna's recital of her life as 'Chief Cook and Bottle Washer' and her youthful encouragement to her cracked-up husband ('We Can Make It'), a piece for Angel dreaming of the 'Colored Lights' that represent the childhood where everything is done for you, and a piece in which the two paired in a druggy decision that they have something in common ('The Apple Doesn't Fall Very Far from the Tree').

The Broadway production of *The Rink*, sponsored by a half-dozen producers, played for only 204 performances, but in spite of this failure the reputations of its writers and its economical size made it a candidate for further productions. In Britain, the Manchester Library Theatre's *The Rink* featured Josephine Blake and Diane Langton in a staging which was sent on, without success, to the West End, but in Germany the piece, rolling in on the increasing fashion for English and American musical plays, followed up its initial German-language showing at Bielefeld with a number of others, at first in Germany and then also in Austria.

Germany: Bielefeld 1986; UK: Forum Theatre, Wythenshawe, Manchester, 29 September 1987, Cambridge Theatre, London 17 February 1988; Austria: Landestheater, Salzburg 8 April 1990

Recordings: original cast (TER), London cast (TER)

RIO RITA Musical comedy in 2 acts by Guy Bolton and Fred Thompson. Lyrics by Joseph McCarthy. Music by Harry Tierney. Ziegfeld Theater, New York, 2 February 1927.

Rio Rita was the show with which Florenz Ziegfeld opened the new Broadway theatre named after himself, and it was produced with all the extravagance and style for which the showman and his designer Joseph Urban were celebrated. The libretto was a conventional romantic-swashbuckling one with echoes of Hollywood to it, but its south-of-the-border setting and its high-country heroics were well adapted to the spectacular treatment for which it was constructed. Texas Ranger Captain Jim Stewart (J Harold Murray) is simultaneously pursuing a bandit who is known as the Kinkajou and the love of the fair Rio Rita Ferguson (Ethelind Terry). His enemy on both accounts is General Romero Joselito Esteban (Vincent Serrano), who not only tries to alienate Jim from Rita by telling her that the ranger suspects her brother (Walter Petrie) of being the bandit, but who is actually the chief criminal himself. Bert Wheeler as Chick Bean and Robert Woolsey as lawyer Ed Lovett were the comedy and Ada May in the rôle of Dolly, a cabaret girl, provided the soubretteries which aerated the romantic plot.

The score of the show was by the writers of *Irene*, but it bore little resemblance to the charmingly up-to-date set of songs which had scored them their biggest success. *Rio Rita* was written in a wholly different range of colours, designed for the very different set of voices which were used in a piece which was laid out more on the *Rose Marie* plan than that of *Irene*. The South American rhythms of the baritone title-song, the distinctly operettic sentiments of 'If You're in Love You'll Waltz', and the Rangers' Song, a direct descendant of its equivalents in *Naughty Marietta* and *Rose Marie*, were all housed in strong pieces, each soon to be popular, which were well made for the needs of an opérette à grand spectacle. One of the more unlikely moments of the evening had the villain's nickname (apparently actually a small but vicious local rodent) turned into the cue for a Charlestonny dance routine, 'The Kinkajou', which was clearly a challenge to 'Totem Tom-Tom' in its scope rather than to the 'Tickle-Toe' of *Going Up*.

Rio Rita's colourful production, tale and score won it a year-long Broadway success (494 performances) and a quick sale to RKO for whom it became one of the earliest sound musical films. The 'radio picture screen operetta' had Bebe Daniels as Rita, John Boles her Captain and Wheeler and Woolsey repeating their comedy of the stage version alongside '1,000 others' and two new Tierney/McCarthy numbers ('Sweetheart, We Need Each Other', 'You're Always in My Arms'). The film was seen in London early in 1930, and soon after Lee Ephraim opened his stage version of *Rio Rita*, with Edith Day and Geoffrey Gwyther (who interpolated a song written by himself) and comics George Gee and Leslie Sarony featured, at the Prince Edward Theatre. It was poorly received, and Ephraim called in popular playwright and novelist Edgar Wallace to effect running repairs, but after 59 performances the show was taken off and replaced by the film *Song of My Heart*. The effects of films in general – and the film of the show in particular – on shows in general and *Rio Rita* in particular, became a hot topic for a few weeks, but it

Plate 223. **Rio Rita**: *Guy Robertson and Leonard Ceeley starred in the St Louis Muny production of Guy Bolton and Fred Thompson's South-American tale of skull-thuggery.*

seemed to have little relevance to this case as the film version of *Rio Rita* had proved no more to London's taste than the stage one. The show was toured in Britain later in 1930 and into 1931.

If London didn't like *Rio Rita* on celluloid or stage, Australia conversely took to it with all the will in the world. It took to the lavish production the Fuller management gave the show, to its eight little Gringos, to the black and white dance and the lovely Spanish Shawl routine choreographed originally by Albertina Rasch, but mostly it took to the country's favourite prima donna, Gladys Moncrieff – Our Glad – in her first appearance back in Australia after some time in London. Glad was known and loved for her gypsyish heroines of *The Maid of the Mountains* and *A Southern Maid* and *Rio Rita* gave Australia the chance to again see her as it preferred her. With Charley Sylber, Janette Gilmore and John Valentine/Les Pearce in support, Gladys and *Rio Rita* made their way from a season of more than six months in Sydney to four months in Melbourne (Princess Theatre 22 December 1928) and then around Australia and New Zealand for a total of some two years, popularizing the show's songs in those areas more than in perhaps any other part of the world. When the film arrived, the ground was prepared. But the film came and went, and the stage version of *Rio Rita* remained a revivable feature of the Australian theatre scene, mostly with Gladys but occasionally even without her in its lead rôle. And there are still many Australians of a certain age who can hum you 'The Kinkajou'.

In 1942 the piece was brought to the screen a second

time, as a vehicle for the comedy team of Abbott and Costello whose fun became more important than Kathryn Grayson's Rita.

Australia: St James Theatre, Sydney 28 April 1928; UK: Prince Edward Theatre 3 April 1930; Films: RKO 1929, MGM 1942

Recordings: selections (WRC, RCA Victor)

RIP [THENON, Georges] (b Neuilly-sur-Seine, 28 February 1884; d Paris, 25 May 1941).

The busiest and the most successful Parisian revue author of the peak years of the 20th-century French revue theatre, the former cartoonist 'Rip' began his career in the genre with *Le Cri de Paris* at the Théâtre des Capucines in 1907 and thereafter wrote or, more often, co-wrote over 100 such pieces – part-evenings or full evenings – for the Paris stage. At the same time, he also penned a regular supply of plays and of opérettes, as well as a number of pieces which straddled the line between revue and opérette, though usually tending more to the former.

His *Plus ça change* (1915) was adapted for the British and American stages as *As You Were*, whilst his *Les Fils Touffe sont à Paris* (billed as an opérette-revue) was adapted, with fresh music, into the British revue hit *The Bing Boys Are Here*. His most successful musical plays, the comical trainboard *P.L.M.* and the romantic *Brummell*, found favour, however, only in France.

1907 **Le Trou d'Almanzor** (Willie Redstone/w Wilned) 1 act Théâtre des Arts 9 February
1907 **Fleur de pétun** (Redstone/w G Lafargue) 1 act Tréteau Royal 14 May
1908 **Le Coq d'Inde** (Claude Terrasse) Théâtre des Capucines 6 April
1908 **Le Planteur de Connecticut** (Redstone/w Arnould) 1 act Folies Marigny 2 September
1912 **Les Fils Touffe sont à Paris** (Fernand Malet/w Jacques Bousquet, Lucien Richemond) Théâtre Fémina 10 April
1912 **Le Cochon qui sommeille** (Terrasse/w Robert Dieudonné) Théâtre Michel 24 December
1913 **Les Petits Crevés, ou Henri III et son petit cour** (Redstone/w Bousquet) Théâtre des Capucines 24 December
1915 **Plus ça change** (Édouard Mathé) 1 act Théâtre Michel 7 September
1919 **Aladin, ou La Lampe merveilleuse** (Redstone) Théâtre Marigny 22 May
1920 **Gigoletto** (Albert Chantrier/w Dieudonné) La Cigale February
1924 **Spartagas** (Léo Pouget/w Paul Briquet, Yoris de Hansewick) Pie qui chante 15 February
1925 **P.L.M.** (Henri Christiné) Théâtre des Bouffes-Parisiens 21 April
1927 **Comme le temps passe** (w Alfred Savoir) Théâtre des Capucines 10 October
1931 **Brummell** (Reynaldo Hahn/w Dieudonné) Folies-Wagram 17 January
nd **Le Roi Bobard** (arr Xavier Rogé/w Régis Gignoux) tour

RIP VAN WINKLE Comic opera in 3 acts by H B Farnie, Henri Meilhac and Philippe Gille based on *Rip van Winkle* by Washington Irving and the play taken therefrom by Dion Boucicault, and *The Legend of Sleepy Hollow*. Music by Robert Planquette. Comedy Theatre, London, 14 October 1882.

The overwhelming success of Planquette's *Les Cloches de Corneville* in Britain had made the composer famous there, and when Alexander Henderson, the London producer of

the earlier show, and his favourite librettist H B Farnie envisaged an adaptation of Dion Boucicault's *Rip van Winkle* as a comic-opera vehicle for the young comedian Fred Leslie, the French composer was approached to write the score. Farnie, known more as an adapter than an original author, was teamed with the experienced French librettists Meilhac and Gille who, it is reasonable to suppose, would have laid out the scenario on which Farnie then wrote the English dialogue and lyrics. The plot differed slightly from the original 1829 Washington Irving tale and the play which Joseph Jefferson had made famous.

When the layabout Rip van Winkle (Leslie) and his wife Gretchen (Violet Cameron) are to be thrown out of their home by their creditor, the burgomaster Derrick von Hans (W S Penley), Rip suddenly returns from the mountains with pocketsful of gold. Suspected by the townsfolk of having betrayed them to the British, he flees their anger back into the mountains and during the stormy night that ensues he goes through a terrible encounter with the ghostly Captain Henrik Hudson whose long-hidden hoard of gold he has plundered. Returning to his home on what he thinks is the next day, Rip finds that 20 years have passed overnight, he is forgotten, and Gretchen has wed Derrick. But all is a dream and when Rip really awakes and returns home, he finds that Gretchen is still his lovely, young wife and has sold their home for a vastly inflated price to the British. Worked into this tale, there were comical rôles for the landlord Nick Vedder (Lionel Brough) and his adored serving wench Jacintha (Constance Lewis), and romantic ones for young Peter van Dunk (Louis Kelleher) and Katrina Vedder (Sadie Martinot).

Planquette moved to London and installed himself at the home of expatriate French costumier Charles Alias, and there wrote the score of *Rip van Winkle* to order for the chosen stars of Henderson's production. Leslie sang 'O Where's My Girl', appeared with two little children to sing 'These Little Heads Now Golden' and the composer even supplied him with some musical yodelling when he learned that the actor had such a talent. The bulk of the lyric music fell to Miss Cameron, the Germaine of London's *Cloches de Corneville*, who had the musical highlights of the evening in 'The Legend of the Katskills', a Letter Song and the pretty 'Twilight Shadows'. Planquette also provided a varied and lengthy divertissement for the central dream sequence which included a basso chanty for Hudson (S H Perry), a travesty soprano Ninepins number (Miss Lewis), a duo serenade for two other sailors (W S Rising, Clara Graham), a ballet suite with a Rhine Fay's dance which became the show's most popular take-out musical items, and a choral finale.

Rip van Winkle was a major success in London and established Leslie as a regular star whilst giving the composer his best references since *Les Cloches de Corneville*. It played at the Comedy Theatre for over a year (328 performances) at a time when such runs were rare, and only closed when Leslie left the cast after being unable to negotiate himself a large enough raise to renew for a second year. Without him, the show no longer had the same attraction, even though his replacement was J A Arnold, who had made himself a name playing the non-musical *Rip van Winkle*. The musical was snapped up by Richard D'Oyly Carte for America where it bowed on Broadway as part of a Carte season with *Manteaux Noirs* and *Iolanthe* shortly after its London opening. It boasted a cast almost as starry as the London one: William T Carleton (Rip), Selina Dolaro (Gretchen), Richard Mansfield (Nick), J H Ryley (Peter), Arthur Wilkinson (Hugh) and Lyn Cadwaladr (First Lieutenant), but it had but a four-week life, as it had to be removed to allow *Iolanthe* to open simultaneously with its London opening.

Shortly after the end of the London season, as the piece began a decade of provincial touring, *Rip van Winkle* began to show itself around Europe. Camillo Walzel presented *Rip-Rip* (ad Eduard Jacobsen, Ferdinand Gumbert) at the Theater an der Wien with Josef Joseffy playing Rip, Frln Grünner as Lisbeth (ex-Gretchen) and Carl Adolf Friese (Derrick) and Carl Lindau (Nick) in the principal comic rôles. It ran for a month, before its initial run was broken by the production of *Gasparone*. It was later revived and eventually totalled 48 Viennese performances. This total was far outrun in Budapest where the Népszinház version (ad Lajos Evva, Béla J Fái) with Pál Vidor (Rip) and Ilka Pálmay (Lisbeth) starring, was a great hit. It had 53 performances in its first year, was revived 22 October 1886 and passed its 100th performance on 5 September 1888, by which time most of the principal provincial theatres of Hungary had taken it up. Thereafter it became a Budapest regular, playing again at the Népszinház (28 May 1903), at the Népopera (7 February 1914 with Gáspár Szántó and Ilona Szoyer), at the Városi Színház (26 April 1919), at the Revü-Szinház (14 May 1921) and at the Fővárosi Operettszinház (22 April 1949).

The first German performance was given in Dresden, and there were productions in Prague (14 April 1884), Stockholm and Australia before the show was finally given in its composer's homeland. Australia's production, mounted under the management of Alfred T Dunning, presented the British comedian Thomas Bilton Appleby as Rip, with Annette Ivanova (Gretchen), Annie Leaf (Katrina) and Howard Vernon (Vedder) in support, and it too found success, being featured by Dunning's company through several repertoire seasons.

For its French production, the show which had had so much international success was heavily rewritten. Meilhac did over the libretto, making the piece less of a comedy and more of a light opera, and Planquette gave his score a heavy rewrite, making the lead rôle into a big-singing romantic baritone part instead of the light comic one it had been originally. Some of the music was redistributed – the Katskills Legend became a number for Rip called 'Vive la Paresse', which was one of the hits of the new *Rip!*, and, in return, the leading lady got a new version of 'Oh, Where's My Girl' called 'Quel chagrin, hélas!' – and some, including much of the splendid dream divertissement, was cut. Planquette also supplied some fresh pieces including a Chanson de Jeunesse which, set alongside the echo song and drinking song of the second act, became one of the highlights of Rip's rôle and the show. Brémont (Rip), Mme Scalini (Nelly, ex-Gretchen), Simon-Max (Ichabod, ex-Hans) and Mily-Meyer (Kate) were amongst the cast, and the new, more vocal *Rip!* proved to be as much to the taste of French audiences as the lighter original had been to London, Sydney and Budapest. It entered the basic repertoire, much as the piece had done in Hungary, and was reprised at its original house in 1889, given a major

revival at the Gaîté-Lyrique with Soulacroix starring and repeated there in 1900, 1902 and 1915, each time with Lucien Noël, in 1913 with Dezair and in 1924 with Robert Jysor. In 1920 Ponzio appeared as Rip at the Théâtre Mogador, and André Baugé played the rôle in 1933 at the Porte-Saint-Martin and again at the Gaîté-Lyrique in 1938. Over a century after its première, *Rip* is still to be seen on occasions in the French regions.

Amongst the other works to have used the tale of Rip van Winkle on the musical stage, an 1855 operatic version by American composer George F Bristow produced by the Pyne-Harrison company at Niblo's Gardens, New York (27 September) seems to have been the first. It was followed by three British burlesques – a *Rip van Winkle, or Sonnambulistic Knickerbockers* (Newcastle, 13 June 1866), *Young Rip van Winkle* by Robert Reece (Gaiety Theatre 18 May 1876) and *Rip van Winkle, or A Little Game of Nap* by H Savile Clarke (Portsmouth, 29 March 1880) – and by several American pieces: a vehicle for Henry Dixey (1890), a version by Jules Jordan played by the Bostonians with Henry Barnabee as Rip (Providence, RI, 1897) and a three-act folk opera by Percy Mackaye (text) and Reginald De Koven (music) (Chicago, 2 January 1920) all of which stopped short of Broadway. Another romantic operatic version written by Franco Leoni was played at London's His Majesty's Theatre in 1897 (4 September). Mr van Winkle was also featured in two much-used if incidental musical-theatre hit songs: 'Rip van Winkle Was a Lucky Man' (Jean Schwartz/William Jerome, *The Sleeping Beauty and the Beast, The Cherry Girl*) and 'Who Paid the Rent for Mrs Rip van Winkle (when Rip van Winkle was away)?' (Alfred Bryan/Fred Fisher sung by Al Jolson in *The Honeymoon Express*, in *The Belle from Bond Street* and in the *Ziegfeld Follies*).

Washington Irving's works have been used as the bases for several other musical theatre works. His *The Legend of Sleepy Hollow* was made into a light opera by Max Maretzek (25 September 1879) and a short-lived 1948 musical *Sleepy Hollow* (St James Theater 3 June) and his *Tales from the Alhambra* went into the making of the Ladislaw Tarnowksi opera *Achmed der Pilger der Liebe*, as well as Albert Smith's British burlesque *The Alhambra, or The three Moorish Princesses* (Princess's Theatre 1851) and H J Byron's often-played *The Pilgrim of Love*, first produced at the London Haymarket Theatre in 1860, and subsequently seen in America, Australia and other English-language theatres. The piece was also credited as a source for the Chicago musical *The Rose of the Alhambra* (Lucius Hosmer/Charles Emerson Cook, Majestic Theater 4 February 1907).

USA: Standard Theater 28 October 1882; Austria: Theater an der Wien *Rip-Rip* 22 December 1883; Hungary: Népszinház 28 December 1883; France: Théâtre des Folies-Dramatiques *Rip!* 11 November 1884; Germany: Residenztheater, Dresden 3 May 1884, Walhalla-Theater 13 November 1886; Australia: Opera House, Melbourne 1 January 1884
Recording: selection in French (EMI-Pathé)

RIQUETTE Operette in 3 acts by Rudolf Schanzer and Ernst Welisch. Music by Oscar Straus. Deutsches Künstlertheater, Berlin, 17 January 1925.

First produced by Heinz Saltenburg at the Berlin Deutsches Künstlertheater, *Riquette* starred Käthe Dorsch as the Parisian telephone-girl of the title. Riquette is a poor lass with a young brother to support, so when she gets a proposition from well-off young Gaston, she says 'yes'. The proposition is, however, an odd one. Riquette is to be his mistress only in appearance, to cover up his affair with the married Clarisse. Clarisse sets off for a holiday in colourful parts (a second act must take place in colourful parts, and this time it is a spa in the Pyrénées) and Gaston and Riquette follow at an almost discreet distance, but the lady's husband is not wholly fooled. He hires the little telephone attendant Picasse to follow Madame. Picasse disguises himself as an Albanian Prince for the purpose, only to discover, as the fun starts to fizz, that there is a vengeful real Albanian on his heels. Needless to say, by the end of the evening, Riquette has replaced Clarisse in Gaston's affections.

Riquette had a goodish Berlin run of three and a half months before giving over the Deutsches Künstlertheater stage to Hugo Hirsch's *Monsieur Trulala* and then to Straus's *Teresina* with the other major star of the Berlin musical stage, Fritzi Massary, at its head, but thereafter it had a rather curious career. It doesn't seem to have headed right away for the more obvious centres of Vienna or Budapest, yet it was promptly produced in both Britain and in America, albeit with rather strange results.

The American version (ad Harry B Smith) was originally announced to star Stanley Lupino and June, but in the event it was Vivienne Segal who was in the title-rôle when the show opened at Detroit, only to be replaced by Mitzi as the show wended towards Broadway. It wended slowly, for E Ray Goetz was taking the same route with *Naughty Cinderella* (a version of the French musical comedy *Pouche*) and the two pieces were said (although it is difficult to see any more than the already well-used fake-girlfriend motif in common) to be based on the same original. Since the musical content of *Naughty Cinderella* was limited to Irene Bordoni's usual handful of songs, however, it was adjudged a play and the 'musical' rights held by the Shuberts were apparently not infringed. The Shuberts retorted by making their *Riquette* into *Naughty Riquette*, but they kept her away from Broadway, playing lucrative dates such as Philadelphia, until more than a year had passed. Once the now 'naughty' show arrived in New York, with Straus's score by this stage decorated with extra numbers by Al Goodman and Maurie Rubens, it played for 11 weeks.

In Britain, Jimmy White produced the show (ad Gertrude Jennings, Harry Graham) with Annie Croft in the title-rôle and Jay Laurier heading the comedy, with a run at Daly's Theatre in view. Unconvinced by a pre-London Christmas season in Scotland, he abandoned *Riquette*, but comedian Billy Merson picked it up, chopped it up, and put such pieces of it as he fancied into a show which he called *My Son John* (ad Graham John, Desmond Carter, Graham, add nos Vivien Ellis) which, with Croft again featured, played 255 performances at the Shaftesbury Theatre (17 November 1926).

USA: Detroit 17 August 1925, Cosmopolitan Theater 13 September 1926; UK: Kings Theatre, Glasgow 21 December 1925; Austria: Raimundtheater 1927

RISCOE, Arthur [BOORMAN, Arthur] (b Shelburne-in-Elmet, Yorks, 19 November 1896; d London, 6 August 1954). Comic actor on the postwar London musical stage.

A concert-party player before the First World War, Riscoe served through the war in the Australian army before making his stage début touring Britain in *The Lilac Domino* (Norman) and *Irene* (Madame Lucy). He covered Joe Coyne in the London production of *Dédé* and, though he made several other London appearances (the revue *Sky High*, as a take-over in *The Bamboula*), it was in the British provinces that he became a firm favourite as seen in Jack Buchanan's starring rôle of *Battling Butler*, in *No, No, Nanette* (Billy), *Princess Charming* (Albert Chuff), *The Girl Friend* (Jerry), *Virginia* (Nicholas), *Hold Everything!* (Spike) and *Follow Through* (Jack Martin).

With *Nippy* (1930, Albert Crumpet) he began a London career which continued with *For the Love of Mike* (1931, Conway Paton) and leading comic rôles in *Out of the Bottle* (1932, Tom Oakland), *The One Girl* (1933, Slick Sam) and, with the greatest success, in *Jill, Darling* (1934, Jack Crawford). He mixed star rôles in comedy musicals (Freddy Bax in *Going Places*, Willie Cloppitt in *Wild Oats*, Jeremiah Tuttle in *Sitting Pretty*) and revue during the war years, appearing, notably, opposite his *Jill, Darling* partner, Frances Day, in the comic lead of the London production of *Dubarry Was a Lady* (Louis/King), as Madame Lucy in the 1945 revival of *Irene*, and, under his own management, in a moderately successful revival of his biggest success, *Jill Darling* (1944). He was touring in *And So to Bed* when his final illness took him.

Riscoe put his name to several songs, amongst which the popular 'Goodbye Sally' (w J Borelli) featured in the London revue *Shephard's Pie*, and he also appeared in several films, notably as Chitterlow in the 1941 *Kipps*.

RISQUE, W[illiam] H[enry] (b Chorlton-upon-Medlock, 25 August 1860; d Oxford, 17 August 1916).

At first engaged in the theatre on the production and managerial side, Billy Risque made his début as a lyricist with the songs to *All Abroad*, one of the first attempts to copy the new Gaiety Theatre style of musical comedy by an outside management. *Shop Girl* star Ada Reeve sang his tale of 'The Business Girl', alongside some interestingly adventurous pieces such as a legal document delivered to music ('In re the Trespass') and a musicalized piece of land agent's chat ('This Desirable Residence'). His career thereafter curiously failed to take off. He was involved with success when he wrote the lyrics to Leslie Stuart's follow-up to *Florodora*, *The Silver Slipper*, but with failure when he turned librettist for the flop *Miss Wingrove*, co-authored the revue *Pot-Pourri* and supplied additional words for George Edwardes's *The New Aladdin* and *The Little Cherub*, and in later days was limited to occasional musical sketches for the music halls.

Risque was married to musical-comedy soubrette Susie Nainby.

1895 **All Abroad** (Frederick Rosse/Owen Hall, James T Tanner) Criterion Theatre 8 August
1901 **The Thirty Thieves** (Edward Jones) Terry's Theatre 1 January
1901 **The Silver Slipper** (Leslie Stuart/Owen Hall) Lyric Theatre 1 June

1905 **Miss Wingrove** (Howard Talbot/Henry Hamilton) Strand Theatre 4 May

1907 **The Zuyder Zee** (Carl Kiefert) 1 act London Hippodrome June

1914 **Lucky Miss** (Howard Talbot) 1 act Pavilion 13 July

RISTORI, Gabrielle (b Paris, 26 July 1899; d April 1988). Bright-eyed, big-nosed and beautiful leading lady of the French musical stage between the wars.

Mlle Ristori began her theatrical career at Lyon under the management of Charles Montcharmont and there, amongst rôles in a series of revivals and post-Paris productions, she took part in several of Montcharmont's premières of imported works, playing Ketty in the French version of *Leányvásár*, *Le Beau Voyage* (1923) and Mariette in *La Bayadère* (1925). Whilst playing at Lyon in a production of Yvain's *Ta bouche* she caught the eye of the composer who later cast her in her first Parisian rôle in *Bouche à bouche* (1925, Micheline), and whose long-term mistress she subsequently became.

She repeated her *Bayadère* performance in the show's metropolitan production at the Théâtre Mogador, and took her most notable early part, at the same theatre, as a delightfully young Lucille Early in the French première of *No, No, Nanette* (1926, 'Rose', 'Faites danser', 'Dis-le moi?'). This success was a prelude to a long series of musical-comedy leads through the 1920s and into the 1930s in such Yvain pieces as *Elle est à vous* (1929, Monique, 'Son Doudou') and *Kadubec* (1929, tomboy Edith Rabourdin singing 'Ouagadougou', 'J'aurais voulu être un garçon'), in *Pépé* (1930, Jacqueline), Yvain and Christiné's *Encore cinquante centimes* (1931, La Reine Stasia), Marcel Lattès's *Xantho chez les courtisanes* (1932, Xantho), and opposite André Baugé in *Le Chant du tzigane* at the Châtelet (1937). She scored her greatest success, however, in another imported musical when she created the rôle of Josépha in the enormously successful French production of *L'Auberge du cheval blanc* (1932).

After a Second World War effort which involved resistance, arrest and internment, she appeared throughout France in various starring rôles, including that made famous by Yvonne Printemps in *Les Trois Valses*, returning in between times to Paris for such revivals as *Le Grand Mogol* (Bengaline) and *Mozart* (Madame d'Épinay) and new pieces such as Louis Beydts's *L'Aimable Sabine* (1947, Olympe). In the 1950s and 1960s she moved on to play character rôles, notably at the Opéra-Comique.

RITA, Pauline (b ?1842; d ?July 1920).

For half-a-dozen years a prima donna of the British opéra-bouffe stage, Miss Rita was sometimes criticized (by the same journalists who criticized Kate Santley for being too forward) for being too aloof a performer. None, however, criticized her singing. Originally a concert vocalist, she was first seen on the stage in 1874 in the travesty rôle of Jean in the London production of Serpette's *The Broken Branch*, and later the same year starred as Prince Conti in Lecocq's opéra-comique *Les Prés Saint-Gervais*, before going on to play Mlle Lange in the Opera Comique production of *La Fille de Madame Angot* and creating the leading rôle of Barbara in Alfred Cellier's comic opera *Tower of London* (1875).

In 1876 she starred as Gustave Müller in *The Duke's Daughter* (*La Timbale d'argent*), but withdrew through illness and was not seen on the London stage again until she was featured as the Plaintiff in the huge, starry production of *Trial By Jury* mounted for the Compton benefit (1877). The following year she was hired by Carte to lead the first touring company of *The Sorcerer* (Aline), and she succeeded to the rôle of Josephine in the rebel *HMS Pinafore* at the Imperial Theatre, but she held neither rôle long, and disappeared thereafter from the theatrical scene. In the early 1880s she was seen on the Pacific circuits, billed as 'prima donna of the Criterion Theatre, London', touring with her flautist husband in 'Radcliff and Rita's entertainment' and later in a musical lecture, *Pan to Pinafore*, to which she contributed a song or two.

Several years later it was reported that her ill-health had finally sent her blind, but she survived to the age of 78.

RITCHARD, Cyril [TRIMNELL-RITCHARD] (b Sydney, Australia, 1 December 1898; d Chicago, 18 December 1977). Dancer and light comedian who formed a famous partnership with his wife on British and Australian stages.

Ritchard joined the theatre at the age of 19, playing in the chorus of J C Williamson's Australian production of *A Waltz Dream*, and for the next seven years he appeared continuously in dancing, light comedy and juvenile rôles in a series of British and American musical comedies produced in Australia (*Oh Lady!, Lady!!*, *The Pink Lady*, *Yes, Uncle!*, *You're in Love*, *The Cabaret Girl*, *So Long, Letty*, *Kissing Time*, *Going Up* etc). He then left Australia for America and Britain where, after early appearances in revue, he became a feature of the dance-and-comedy musicals of the 1920s and 1930s, appearing with his partner, Madge Elliott, as an elegant juvenile dancing, sort-of-singing and intermittently (and un-Australian) acting duo in Laddie Cliff's successful productions of *Lady Luck* (1927, Tommy Lester), *So This is Love* (1928, Peter Malden), *Love Lies* (1929, Jack Stanton), *The Love Race* (1930, Harry Drake) and *The Millionaire Kid* (1931, Aubrey Forsythe).

Ritchard and Miss Elliott then returned to Australia and appeared there for several seasons playing in *Blue Roses*, *Hold My Hand*, *Our Miss Gibbs*, *The Quaker Girl*, the Australian musical *Blue Mountain Melody*, *Roberta* (also director), *Gay Divorce* and *High Jinks*, and getting married to each other, before making a second visit to Britain in 1936. This time Ritchard appeared largely in revue and comedy but in 1943 he and Miss Elliot paired in a production of *The Merry Widow* and in 1945 he partnered Ruth Naylor as the Eisensteins of *Gay Rosalinda*.

In 1946 the pair appeared in Australia in Noël Coward's *Tonight at 8.30*, and in 1954 Ritchard appeared on Broadway as Captain Hook and Mr Darling to the Peter Pan of Mary Martin in the American musical adaptation of Barrie's play (Tony Award). After Miss Elliott's death, he remained in America where, in his sixties, he appeared characterfully as Don Andrès in the Metropolitan Opera's version of *La Périchole*, in the Offenbach pasticcio *The Happiest Girl in the World* (1961, Pluto), the St Louis Muny's *Around The World in 80 Days* (1962, Phineas Fogg), and as Sir in Anthony Newley's *The Roar of the Greasepaint ... the Smell of the Crowd* (1965). In his seventies he was seen in *Lock Up Your Daughters* in Florida and as the lovestruck Osgood Fielding jr in the Broadway production of *Sugar* (1972). He subsequently toured as Jimmy in *No, No, Nanette* (1973) and in the narrator's rôle in the compilation show *Side by Side by Sondheim* (1977).

Ritchard's activities in these American years also extended to directing, and he was responsible for the staging of the Metropolitan Opera's production of *Der Zigeunerbaron* and a revival of *La Périchole*, and the national tour of *Where's Charley?* He also appeared as an extravagant Chitterlow in the film version of *Half a Sixpence* (1967) and on musical-theatre-based television (*Peter Pan*, *Dearest Enemy* etc).

RITCHIE, Adele [PULTZ, Adele] (b Philadelphia, 21 December 1874; d Laguna Beach, Calif, 24 April 1930). Leading lady of the early 20th-century Broadway stage.

Born in Philadelphia of French Quaker parents, Adele Ritchie made early stage appearances in *The Isle of Champagne* (1893) and *The Algerian* (Suzette, and u/s Marie Tempest as Celeste) before, at 20 years of age, winning her first major rôle as the ingénue of Francis Wilson's production of Jakobowski's *The Devil's Deputy* (1894, Princess Mirane). She played Madge in *The District Attorney* (1895), Little Willie in a Broadway burlesque of *Trilby* (*Thrilby*), appeared in De Koven's *The Mandarin* (1896, Ting Ling) and visited Britain to play in Victor Herbert's *The Wizard of the Nile* (1897, Cleopatra), then took a turn in vaudeville before launching on a series of lead rôles in mostly successful musical comedies on Broadway: *A Runaway Girl* (1898, in Ethel Haydon's rôle of Dorothy), the ex-Boston Cadets show *Three Little Lambs* (1899, Beatrice Jerome), *The Cadet Girl* (1900, Marguerite), *The King's Carnival* (1900), *The Toreador* (1902, Dora Selby), as Mrs Pineapple in Nixon and Zimmerman and Shubert's Broadway production of *A Chinese Honeymoon* (1902), as leading lady to Vesta Tilley's leading 'man' in *My Lady Molly* (1904, Alice Coverdale), in *Glittering Gloria* (1904, Gloria) and in the Chicago success *Fantana* (1904–5, Fanny Everett).

She moved away from ingénues and up to spunkier material to star as Lady Holyrood in a revival of *Florodora* (1905), as the dashing heroine of *The Social Whirl* (1906, Violet) and as the Flora of *Fascinating Flora* (1907) at the Casino Theater but, thereafter, her Broadway appearances were few, although she appeared away from New York in Planquette's *Le Paradis de Mahomet* (1909), *The Girl in the Taxi* (1910) and *The Motor Girl*. Her last Broadway musical, an adaptation of a French farce called *All for the Ladies* (1912, Nancy Paturel), in which she supported the comedian Sam Bernard, came two years after a messy bankruptcy and, shortly after, she announced that she was marrying the wealthy Charles Nelson Bell 'for money'. She subsequently toured in variety singing wartime songs before her career and marriage both faded away.

Adele Ritchie's biggest headlines, however, were made not in her life but in her death. Having married (1916) and then divorced the successful actor Guy Bates Post, she quit their home in Hollywood for Laguna Beach and its high-society 'bohemian' (the then euphemism for homosexual) colony, where she was active in directing local dramatics. She also became involved with another divorcée, the well-off Mrs Palmer. Their bodies were found at her home. Adele had shot Mrs Palmer in the back before turning the gun on herself. It was at first suggested in court that the killing was due to jealousy over Mrs Palmer supplanting Ritchie at the helm of playhouse, then a suicide pact was promoted as motive instead, but when the women's wills and some 'intimate letters' were introduced into the mystery the court and newspaper reports faded pinkly away on what seems to have been nothing but a crime passionel.

RIVERA, Chita [del RIVERO, Dolores Conchita Figueroa] (b Washington, DC, 23 January 1933). Striking star dancer-singer for whom Broadway found a worthwhile rôle only once a decade.

Miss Rivera made her earliest musical-theatre appearances as a chorus dancer in *Call Me Madam* (1952), *Guys and Dolls* (1953) and *Can-Can* (1954) and took a very visible part in *The Shoestring Revue* (1955) before playing her first named rôle as Fifi in *Seventh Heaven*. She moved quickly up the bill to appear alongside Sammy Davis jr in *Mr Wonderful* (1956, Rita Romano) and, after standing in for Eartha Kitt in *Shinbone Alley* the following year, broke through to stardom when she created the rôle of the stormy Puerto-Rican Anita in *West Side Story* ('America', 'A Boy Like That').

Miss Rivera repeated her *West Side Story* rôle on the London stage before winning a second success as 'Spanish Rose', otherwise Rose Grant – who is not Spanish and who wants her ambitious man to be 'An English Teacher' – in *Bye Bye Birdie* (1960) both on Broadway and in London. After these two sizeable and personal successes she had to wait curiously long for another. She appeared with Alfred Drake and Anne Rogers in *Zenda*, which died before making it to New York, and top-billed as Anyanka in the less-than-successful *Bajour* (1964), but thereafter played away from Broadway for a number of years, appearing in a mixture of straight and musical stage pieces including *Sweet Charity* (in the film of which she appeared as Nicky), *Zorba* and *Kiss Me, Kate*, the west-coast production of Meredith Willson's *1491*, and in nightclub and cabaret dates, before coming back, 15 years after her last Broadway hit, to score a third immense success as Velma, the dazzling dancing murderess of *Chicago* (1975, 'When Velma Takes the Stand', 'I Can't Do it Alone', 'Cell Block Tango', 'My Own Best Friend').

The musequel *Bring Back Birdie* (1981) was a quick Broadway flop, but Rivera had a fine run as a partner to the magic tricks of Doug Hemming in *Merlin* (The Queen) and a rather less long but more visible one when she paired as mother and daughter with Liza Minnelli in Kander and Ebb's *The Rink* (1985). In 1992 she appeared again in London when she top-billed in the Live Entertainment Corporation of Canada's production of *Kiss of the Spider Woman* (Spider Woman/Aurora) prior to repeating that performance in the show's Broadway edition.

RIVIÈRE, Jules (b Aix-en-Othe, 6 November 1819; d Colwyn Bay, 26 December 1900).

Rivière was an orchestral player turned conductor and composer whose long career very rarely brought him into contact with the musical theatre. After he had fled to Britain during the Franco-Prussian War he, nevertheless, turned out one of the biggest song hits the young British musical theatre had had to that time when he supplied the treble chorus 'Spring, Gentle Spring' as part of his portion of the music for the Dion Boucicault spectacular *Babil and*

Bijou. If the song, which was an international hit and interpolated into shows on Broadway (the Kiralfy's *The Naiad Queen*) and in Europe, is now forgotten, the aged Rivière's book of memoirs remains to provide a colourful glimpse into musical life in the mid-19th century.

Autobiography: *My Musical Life and Recollections* (Sampson Low, Marston & Co, London 1893)

RIVOIRE, André (b Vienne, 5 May 1872 ; d Paris, 19 August 1930).

Poet, playwright and adapter, Rivoire was responsible for the French versions of Frederick Lonsdale's *Monsieur Beaucaire* and Paul Knepler's *Paganini*, both of which have remained part of the occasionally revived repertoire in France. His only original musical libretti, produced after his death, included the posthumous Messager work *Sacha* and that for the much-admired but little-played *Fragonard*. He also wrote the texts for Samuel-Rousseau's operas *Le Hulla* (1923) and *Le Bon Roi Dagobert* (1927), the latter based on his own play of the same title.

1913 **Il était une bergère** (Marcel Lattès) 1 act Opéra-Comique 16 April
1925 **Monsieur Beaucaire** French version w Pierre Veber (Théâtre Marigny)
1928 **Paganini** French version (Théâtre de la Gaîté-Lyrique)
1930 **Frédérique** (*Frederika*) French version (Théâtre de la Gaîté-Lyrique)
1930 **Sacha** (André Messager, Marc Berthomieu) Monte Carlo
1933 **Fragonard** (Gabriel Pierné/w Romain Coolus) Théâtre de la Monnaie, Brussels; Théâtre de la Porte-Saint-Martin 16 October 1934
1934 **Mandrin** (Joseph Szulc/w Coolus) Théâtre Mogador 12 December

THE ROAR OF THE GREASEPAINT ... THE SMELL OF THE CROWD Musical in 2 acts by Anthony Newley and Leslie Bricusse. Theatre Royal, Nottingham, 3 August 1964.

The successor to the highly successful *Stop the World – I Want to Get Off*, *The Roar of the Greasepaint* followed the earlier piece both in its style and in its content. Another small-cast piece with a large central character to its pantomime-style fable, it pitted little Cocky (Norman Wisdom) the epitome of the have-not, against the vast and powerful Sir (Willoughby Goddard), the representative of the 'haves' who artfully stay on top by continually pulling the rules of the game from under the opposition's feet. If the text proved rather more naïve this time, the songs were almost as successful as the hit-parading lot from the previous show.

Bernard Delfont's production, which Newley directed but did not appear in, closed down in the provinces without braving London, but the songs survived. The innocent, bright 'On a Wonderful Day Like Today' became a holiday-camp and club classic as a cabaret-opening number, and the throbbing torch song 'Who Can I Turn To?' followed it on to the nightclub circuits, whilst the confidence-filled 'Nothing Can Stop Me Now' and the self-pitying 'The Joker' also had a longer life out of the show than in it.

The Roar of the Greasepaint's career was not, however, limited to the abortive British production. David Merrick visited the show on the road in Britain and picked it up for Broadway where Newley himself starred as a rather less

victimish little chap, pitted against a rather less vastly imposing rival in Cyril Ritchard. It had a 232-performance run. The chorus of the British show included Elaine Paige, whilst the New York production introduced choreographer Gillian Lynne to Broadway.

USA: Shubert Theater 16 May 1965; Australia: Marian Street Theatre, Sydney 11 November 1975
Recording: Broadway cast (RCA)

ROBBINS, Jerome [RABINOWITZ, Jerome] (b New York, 11 October 1918). Choreographer and director of several major musicals of Broadway's bonanza years.

Robbins began his theatre career as a dancer, appearing in the chorus of *Great Lady* (1938), *Stars in Your Eyes* and *The Straw Hat Revue* (1939) before joining the Ballet Theatre where he established himself as a choreographer as well as a performer. He returned to Broadway when he choreographed the Leonard Bernstein musical *On the Town* (1944), a piece which had originated in the ballet *Fancy Free* which the two men had composed and performed and choreographed respectively for the Ballet Theatre the previous year. Thereafter, he devised the dances for a number of musicals (*Billion Dollar Baby, Look, Ma, I'm Dancin', Miss Liberty, Call Me Madam*), winning particular praise for a comic routine parodying the silent films in *High Button Shoes* (1947, Tony Award) and the narrated pantomime 'The Small House of Uncle Thomas' in *The King and I* (1951), before sharing the direction (w George Abbott), but not the choreography, of *The Pajama Game* (1954).

He acted as both director and choreographer for a musical comedy version of *Peter Pan* (1954) and subsequently first for *Bells are Ringing* (1956), and then for a remarkably variegated trio of musicals: the contemporary drama of *West Side Story* (1957, Tony Award ch) with its exciting, youthful dancing, the megawoman star-vehicle *Gypsy* (1959), and the warmly characterful tale of a changing world that is *Fiddler on the Roof* (1964, Tony Awards dir and ch). He also co-directed yet another hit in the Fanny Brice biomusical *Funny Girl* (w Garson Kanin).

Robbins's work for the hugely successful *West Side Story*, on the dramatic form of which he had a considerable influence, epitomized his skill at expressing contemporary action in a strong combination of dance and drama, and also showed that – against strong proofs to the contrary throughout the history of the musical theatre – there are possibilities and advantages in the creative pairing of the functions of director and choreographer when neither function is made subsidiary to the other.

For the next 25 years he then devoted himself exclusively to the world of dance before, in 1989, taking a twist on the endless run of songwriter compilation shows of recent years, he returned to the musical theatre and Broadway to mount a musical entertainment which was compiled largely of clips from his earlier shows (*Jerome Robbins' Broadway* Imperial Theater, 26 February). It was perhaps a compliment to his style of work that routines which had been memorable examples of musical-theatre dance in their time and in their correct context now seemed very much less so out of both the one and the other. For a Broadway looking nostalgically backwards to its finest hours, however, the evening was a marvellous one. In what was, admittedly, a no-contest season, *Jerome*

Robbins' Broadway was awarded Best Musical and direction (by the rules it was not eligible for its recreated choreography) 1989 Tony Awards and, in spite of its large overheads (including what must be the longest rehearsal period for a recent musical show) the compilation played for 634 performances in New York.

Robbins co-directed and choreographed the screen version of *West Side Story* and choreographed the film of *The King and I*.

ROBERTA Musical comedy in 2 acts by Otto Harbach based on the novel *Gowns By Roberta* by Alice Duer Miller. Music by Jerome Kern. New Amsterdam Theater, New York, 18 November 1933.

Abandoning his Continental Operette streak after *The Cat and the Fiddle* and *Music in the Air*, Jerome Kern turned for the inspiration for his 1933 musical *Roberta* to a novel by American authoress Alice Duer Miller, whose *The Charm School* had earlier been the basis for the 1925 Shubert musical *June Days* (Fred J Coots/Clifford Grey/Cyrus Wood, Astor Theater 6 August). *Gowns By Roberta* bore, in fact, a certain similarity to *The Cat and the Fiddle* in that it once again had for its central characters a group of Americans set down in that modern equivalent of the crazy foreign islands of early comic opera, the up-to-date Ruritania of glamorous Europe, on this occasion Paris, France.

American footballer John Kent (Ray Middleton) inherits a Parisian modiste's shop from his old Aunt Minnie (Fay Templeton) and, with the help of her assistant Stephanie (Tamara), he sets himself to trying to run the business. His American ex-girlfriend (Helen Grey) comes to Paris to make up with him, but by this time he is on his way to a final curtain with Stephanie, even though (and this in 1933!) she turns out to be no shop-girl but a real live Princess. A large helping of incidental comedy was provided by popping into this tale a couple of theatrical folk, played by Bob Hope (Huck Haines) and Lyda Roberti (Clementina Scharwenka).

The score for *Roberta* was altogether less conventional than its story. The heroine's song 'Smoke Gets in Your Eyes' (made up from a melody Kern had half-used a couple of times) proved to be one of the most internationally popular and successful songs of the composer's long theatrical career. Alongside it, another remade number, 'You're Devastating' (formerly 'Do I Do Wrong?' from *Blue Eyes*), was manhandled by Hope before getting a more sincere treatment from Tamara, the aged Fay Templeton crackled out her gentle memories of 'Yesterday(s)' to another lovely melody and one of Harbach's most tortured rhymes, Tamara joined William Hain in 'The Touch of Your Hand' and Miss Roberti provided a flamboyant contrast as she insisted in jaunty style 'I'll Be Hard to Handle' (lyric: Bernard Dougall). There were also two dance set-pieces, a bundle of impersonations (Fred MacMurray did Rudy Vallee and Allan Jones was Morton Downey), and a fashion parade.

Max Gordon's production of *Gowns By Roberta* (as it began its life) had problems from the start, problems not lightened when Gordon sacked the director and brought in spectacle-merchant Hassard Short as a replacement. The original director had been Kern. Its patently feeble book – some of Harbach's weakest-ever work – was slammed, and

Plate 224. *Fay Templeton, as Aunt Minnie, and Sydney Greenstreet in the Broadway production of* **Roberta**.

all the fashion parades in the world couldn't compensate. Gordon kept the show running, however, and the popularity of 'Smoke Gets in Your Eyes' (and some salary cuts) helped him to stretch its run to 295 Broadway performances before taking it on the road with Tamara, Templeton, Odette Myrtil (Clementina), Middleton and Marty May (Huck) featured. Unsurprisingly, it toured only once, and of the other main theatrical centres, only Australia showed any interest in taking it up. With local megastars Cyril Ritchard (Huck and director) and Madge Elliott (Stephanie) at the top of the bill and Australia's best musical character lady, Ethel Morrison, as Aunt Minnie, it played two months in Melbourne and another two in Sydney (Theatre Royal, 16 March 1935) before being replaced, in each city, by the indefatigable *High Jinks*.

Roberta had not long departed from town when Sydney folk got another version of it. For if theatres and theatre audiences had not cared greatly for the show, Hollywood did. In 1935 RKO put out a film version which had Irene Dunne as its heroine and Fred Astaire and Ginger Rogers for the dances and jollies, five of the original songs plus the newly written 'Lovely to Look At' and 'I Won't Dance' (salvaged from Kern's flop show *Three Sisters*). The new numbers proved as popular as the very best of the old ones, but even they and their famous performers could not give *Roberta* new stage life. They simply gave it an extended screen life, for in 1952 MGM put out another film version of the show, this time under the title *Lovely to Look At*. Kathryn Grayson was romanced by Howard Keel, Red Skelton was funny, and Gower and Marge Champion danced to a score which brought back a couple of numbers dropped last time round, retained the two new ones and added two new ones which didn't rate.

The show was twice televised with Hope in his old rôle

(1958, 1969) and regular stock productions – with varying libretti – were seen before efforts were made, in the 1980s, to find a first-class theatre production for a revised version of *Roberta*, but the libretto (which has proved less of a problem at film-length than at stage-length) remained an insuperable barrier to its revival. *Roberta* joins such pieces as *Mack and Mabel* and *Great Day* on the list of shows that long-remembered songs come from, rather than a piece for the stage.

Australia: Her Majesty's Theatre, Melbourne 22 December 1934; Films: RKO 1935, *Lovely to Look At* MGM 1952
Recordings: selections (Columbia, Decca, Capitol), film soundtrack 1952 (MGM)

ROBERT AND ELIZABETH Musical in 2 acts by Ronald Millar based on *The Barretts of Wimpole Street* by Rudolph Besier. Music by Ron Grainer. Lyric Theatre, London, 20 October 1964.

One of the most outstanding British musical plays of the postwar period, *Robert and Elizabeth* came into being only because of the insufficiencies of an unproduced show. An American legal gentleman with writing aspirations had secured the rights to Besier's famous stage play, *The Barretts of Wimpole Street*, concocted a script, and succeeded (with the help of letters sent out on New York Supreme Court headed paper) in convincing the Associated British Picture Corporation of its potential as a movie musical. The filmmakers – ignoring or ignorant of the fact that MGM held the film rights in the play – arranged for *The Third Kiss* to be tried in the theatre first. Stage producer Martin Landau, realizing that the show as written was embarrassingly unproduceable, called in a playwright (Ronald Millar), who called in a director (Wendy Toye) who called in a composer (Ron Grainer) and, by the time they had finished, not a phrase of the original adaptation remained. They had written a fresh and fine new *Barretts of Wimpole Street* musical.

Elizabeth Barrett (June Bronhill), an invalid bound to a bed in a house where her widowed father (John Clements) rules his large, young family with a formidable sternness, has established a correspondence with the poet, Browning (Keith Michell). When he, all ebullience and life, walks into her room and her palely loitering life and speaks of love to her, she finds the strength to get up from her bed for the first time in years. However, her father, prey to feelings which border on the incestuous, intervenes. Elizabeth's dream of love and her confidence in her ability to lead a normal life are shattered and she returns to her invalid's bed. The furious Barrett now plans to shift his family out of London, but Browning encourages Elizabeth to hope again, and finally to marry and elope with him to Italy and a new life together.

The deft remake of Besier's play focused firmly on the three central characters, and the bulk of the music was written for the two lovers. The rôle of Elizabeth, tailored to the extraordinary talents of operetta soprano Bronhill, was demanding and dazzling to a degree rarely seen in the musical theatre, skating from one end of the voice to the other as she longed for 'The World Outside', soliloquized sanely but desperately (Soliloquy) over her position, or faced up to her father in a triumphal expression of the right to love ('Woman and Man') which took the soprano up to an all-vanquishing D in alt to finish. Browning joined his

Plate 225. **Robert and Elizabeth**: *Robert Browning (Mark Wynter) encourages Elizabeth Barrett (Gaynor Miles) to try to walk (Chichester Festival Theatre).*

beloved in the less extreme love duet 'I Know Now', which became the show's take-away tune, and bounded through the joyous 'The Moon in My Pocket', but top-billed Clements's vocal limitations meant that one of his numbers had to be cut. He was still left with the powerful, parlando 'What the World Calls Love'. Some lighter moments were provided by the young Barretts, equipped with one of the most charming of the piece's songs in their daydreaming over 'The Boys That Girls Dream About', and by the parallel romance of Elizabeth's sister, Henrietta (Angela Richards) with the military Surtees Cook (Jeremy Lloyd).

Robert and Elizabeth was a major hit in London. It ran for 948 performances, a total which put it into London's top ten all-time scorers, went on the road (shorn of its top notes, for actresses with a top D in alt are not legion), was produced in Australia with Miss Bronhill starring opposite Denis Quilley and Frank Thring for almost six months in Melbourne prior to a season in Sydney (Tivoli 19 November 1966), and in South Africa, but not on Broadway. The author of the original adaptation, livid over the success of the show he had not written, went to court to stop *Robert and Elizabeth* playing in America. Given his connections with the judiciary, this was not difficult (or expensive) for him, but the British end of the operation were, as he doubtless intended, frightened out of their rights by the thought of an expensive (for them) American court action.

However, there were those in America prepared to brave the legalistic threats, amongst them the Forum Theater in

Chicago, Victoria Crandall's Brunswick Music Theater, and, in 1982, the Paper Mill Playhouse in New Jersey, which mounted the show to open their new theatre. This time, when puffing noises came from the New York courts, the authors decided, at last, to take a stand. They won.

In spite of the multiple acting and singing demands of its female lead rôle, *Robert and Elizabeth* has continued to find productions. In 1987 the Chichester Festival Theatre staged a revival of a slightly rewritten version into which Millar restored some pieces cut, for cast reasons, in the original, and which eliminated almost completely the dance element, making the piece into an ever-tighter musical play. Gaynor Miles (Elizabeth, with the top D), Mark Wynter (Robert) and John Savident (Barrett) featured through a highly successful season.

Australia: Princess Theatre, Melbourne 21 May 1966; USA: Forum Theater, Chicago 1974

Recordings: original cast (EMI), Chichester Festival cast (First Night)

ROBERTS, Arthur (b London, 21 September 1852; d London, 27 February 1933). Star comedian of the British burlesque and musical comedy stage.

After an early career as a music-hall comic, Roberts moved into the musical theatre in his early thirties when he toured with Emily Duncan in the burlesques *The Miller and his Men* (1883, Ravina) and *Sinbad* (Mrs Sinbad), and then appeared in a version of *La Vie parisienne* (1883, Joe Tarradiddle) at the Avenue Theatre. He followed up with important comedy rôles in *Nell Gwynne* (1884, Weasel), *Black-Eyed Susan* (1884, Captain Crosstree), *Le Grand Mogol* (1884, Jugginsee-Lal), *Barbe-bleue* (1885, Bobêche), the pasticcio *Nemesis* (1885, Calino), *La Mascotte* (1885, Laurent), *Boccaccio* (1885, Pietro) and several plays, and appeared at the Gaiety Theatre in the burlesque *The Vicar of Wide-awake-field* (1885, Vicar) and *Billee Taylor* (1885, Ben Barnacle), by which time he had become established as one of the foremost musical comedians in London. He confirmed his reputation in several more burlesques (Sir Rupert the Reckless in *Lurline*, Sir Richard Varney in *Kenilworth*, Crusoe in *Robinson Crusoe*, Lancelot in *Lancelot the Lovely*) and comic operas (Frontignac in *The Commodore*, Matt o' the Mill in Audran's *Indiana*, Polydore Poupart in *The Old Guard*, Faragas in *Nadgy*), and then made the transition first to new burlesque and then to musical comedy with ease.

He hit rare trouble when he played Scarpia in *Tra-la-la-Tosca*. Not bothering to learn his rhymed and metred lines, he ad-libbed his way through the entire script, instead of merely taking time out in the course of the show, as he had mostly done before, to do his 'off-the-cuff' turn. The show was a flop, and he took his next burlesque *Guy Fawkes* to the provinces where this free-and-easy 'instant theatre' (little of which, of course, was original stuff, but simply tipsy rechauffé whose charm was in the telling rather than the material) was less frowned upon. He returned to London in the George Edwardes burlesques *Joan of Arc* (1891, de Richemont) and *Blue-Eyed Susan* (1892, Crosstree), but took a different version of this latter (*Too Lovely Black-Eyed Susan*) on tour in order to pay less royalties, on the grounds that he didn't speak the lines as written anyway.

Plate 226. **Arthur Roberts** *as Polydore Poupart in* The Old Guard.

In 1892 he was top-billed as the society pimp Captain Coddington in George Edwardes's early variety musical comedy *In Town*, but he returned to more burlesque parts (Pedrillo in *Don Juan*, Claude in *Claude Du-val*) before taking on the title-rôle in his best-ever musical comedy vehicle, as the cockney cab-driver in Basil Hood and Walter Slaughter's *Gentleman Joe*. Several attempts to repeat this impressive success under his own management were failures (John Jenkins in *Biarritz*, Jack Hammersley in *The White Silk Dress*, Smith in *Campano/Milord Sir Smith*) and only *Dandy Dan the Lifeguardsman*, another Hood/ Slaughter piece written to formula, around Roberts, had an appreciable London life.

Roberts's alcohol-aided gagging had, by now, become repetitive and tiresome rather than inventive, but the provinces welcomed him gladly in such made-to-measure pieces as *The Cruise of the HMS Irresponsible* (1900, Jim Slingsby) and *Bill Adams, the Hero of Waterloo* (1903, Bill Adams). His last major West End rôle was in *The School Girl* (1903, Sir Ormesby St Leger) when he took over the comedy rôle previously played by G P Huntley and George Grossmith, but he continued to appear for another 20 years, mostly in variety and revue, making his last musical stage appearances in a sadly amateurish piece called *Society Ltd* (1920, Count Solomon Dupont) and in C B Cochran's unfortunate version of the French musical comedy *Phi-Phi* (1922). In an attempt to make ends meet, Roberts was still to be found touring with a company called Veterans of Variety in his late seventies.

Autobiography: *Fifty Years of Spoof* (Bodley Head, London, 1927)

ROBERTSON, Guy (b Denver, Colo, 26 January 1892; d unknown). Dashing leading man of two decades of Broadway musicals.

Originally trained as an engineer, Robertson served in the Great War and made his first stage appearance only at the end of hostilities, playing in Henry Savage's production of *Head over Heels*. His handsome physique and fine baritone voice very quickly opened the way to principal rôles and to Broadway, and he appeared at the George M Cohan Theater later the same year in another Savage show, *See-Saw* (1919, Billy Meyrick), and in the Ed Wynn show *The Perfect Fool*. He then spent five years as a juvenile leading man under Arthur Hammerstein's management, creating the rôles of Kenneth Hobson in *Daffy Dill* (1922) and Guido in *Wildflower* (1923, 'Wildflower'), touring as Jim Kenyon in *Rose Marie*, and pairing with Tessa Kosta as the romantic Russian protagonists of *The Song of the Flame* (1925). He was then hired to create the rôle of Gaylord Ravenal in Ziegfeld's new musical *Show Boat*, but the postponement of the production led him to take up another romantic lead, as Mister X to the Fedora Palinska of Desirée Tabor in *The Circus Princess* (1927) instead.

Robertson followed up in the Frenchified *Lovely Lady* (1927, Paul de Morlaix) and as Chopin to the Georges Sand of Odette Myrtil in the Broadway version of the Hungarian biomusical *White Lilacs* (1928), was the hero successively of Busby Berkeley's production of *The Street Singer* (1929), of Romberg's South American spectacular *Nina Rosa* (1930, Jack Haines), the Shuberts' Harry Revel/Mack Gordon musical *Arms and the Maid* (1931), of the St Louis Municipal Opera's *Show Boat* – where he finally got to play the rôle intended to be his first time round – and of the German musical *Marching By* (1932, Franz Almassy). He visited Chicago to star in a revised version of the *Circus Princess* now called *The Blue Mask*, played both there and in New York opposite Nancy McCord in *All the King's Horses* (1933), in a West Coast revival of *The Only Girl* and as Johann Strauss jr in the pasticcio *The Great Waltz*, both in San Francisco and New York.

He was later seen regionally in *The Three Musketeers* (D'Artagnan), *Glamorous Night* (in Ivor Novello's rôle of Anthony Allen), *Music in the Air*, *Wild Violets* (Paul Gutbier), *Rio Rita* and as Allen Phillips in Frederick Loewe's prematurely killed *Salute to Spring* (St Louis, 1937). His last Broadway appearances were in *Right This Way* (1938) and as a replacement in *Very Warm for May* (1939).

ROBESON, Paul [Leroy Bustill] (b Princeton, NJ, 9 April 1898; d Philadelphia, 23 January 1976).

Bass-baritone Robeson appeared as a singer in *Shuffle Along* (1921) and in the chorus of the 1922 *Plantation Revue* before making his reputation as an actor both on stage (*The Emperor Jones*, *Othello*) and on film. Although he performed as a vocalist in concert and on record, his one and only stage musical rôle was the part of *Show Boat*'s Joe, created by Jules Bledsoe, which Robeson played at London's Theatre Royal, Drury Lane, and in the Broadway revival of 1932. He played the same rôle in the *Show Boat* film of 1936, introducing 'I Still Suits Me', and appeared in several other films with music, notably the 1933 *Sanders of the River* ('My Little White Dove', Canoe Song), which was later adapted to the stage (with different songs) as *The Sun Never Sets*.

Autobiography: *Here I Stand* (Beacon, Boston, 1971); Biographies: Seton, M: *Paul Robeson* (London, 1958), Hoyt, E: *Paul Robeson, the American Othello* (World, Cleveland, 1967), Gilliam, D: *Paul Robeson: All American* (New Republic, Washington DC, 1976) etc

ROBIN, Leo (b Pittsburgh, Pa, 6 April 1900; d Los Angeles, 24 December 1984).

Lyricist Robin made an early contribution to Broadway's *Greenwich Village Follies of 1925* and collaborated with the young Philadelphia composer Richard Myers on a musical adaptation of *Brewster's Millions* mounted in that city. With Cecil Lean, Cleo Mayfield and the young Jeanette MacDonald starring, *Bubbling Over* was well worked over in Philadelphia, but failed to make it to Broadway and songs such as 'Red Hot Cradle Snatchers', 'It's All Right with Me', 'Snap Out of the Blues' and 'Bubbling Over' went down with it. However, two songs, 'True to Two' and 'I'm a One Man Girl', did not. They later turned up in the London musical *Mr Cinders* (1928) where they found a deserved success.

Robin worked on an adaptation of A E Thomas's *Just Suppose* as *Just Fancy* ('You Came Along' w Joseph Meyer and Phil Charig, later used in London's *Lady Mary*) and another of Mark Swan's play *Judy Forgot*, which forgettably became just *Judy*, the Chicago revue *Allez-Oop!* (1927, w Phil Charig), and another Myers effort, *Hello Yourself*, a musical comedy built around Fred Waring's Pennsylvanians, and he scored a major Broadway hit in his collaboration with Vincent Youmans on *Hit the Deck* before, in 1929, moving to Hollywood.

There, he teamed with Richard Whiting on such films as Maurice Chevalier's *The Innocents of Paris* (1929, 'Louise') and *The Playboy of Paris* (1930), *Monte Carlo*, featuring Jeanette MacDonald and Jack Buchanan and the song 'Beyond the Blue Horizon' (w Franke Harling); then with Ralph Rainger for the scores of such films as *The Big Broadcast* (1932), *She Loves Me Not* (1934), *Here is My Heart* (1934, 'June in January', 'Love is Just Around the Corner', 'With Every Breath I Take'), *The Big Broadcast of 1936*, *Waikiki Wedding* (1937, 'Blue Hawaii') and *Paris Honeymoon* (1939). In 1938 he and Rainger won an Academy Award for 'Thanks for the Memory' performed by Bob Hope and Shirley Ross in *The Big Broadcast of 1938*.

After Rainger's death, Robin worked with a variety of composers on such films as *The Girls He Left Behind*, *Centennial Summer*, *The Time, the Place and the Girl* (1946), *Something in the Wind* (1947), *Casbah* (1948), *Just for You* (Bing Crosby and Jane Wyman's 'Zing a Little Zong' w Harry Warren), *Meet Me After the Show* (1950), *My Sister Eileen* (1955) etc. Whilst in Hollywood he also contributed to film versions of several stage musicals: the 1930 Paramount film *The Vagabond King* ('If I Were King' w Sam Coslow, Newell Chase), the 1936 film of *Anything Goes* ('Sailor Beware' w Richard Whiting) and 1955 film of *Hit the Deck* (extra song w Youmans).

In 1949, after almost two decades in which his only contribution to the musical stage had been with a quick flop version of *Sailor Beware* entitled *Nice Goin'* for Lawrence Schwab, Robin returned to Broadway to the same kind of success which he had tasted with *Hit the Deck*, when he supplied the sparkling lyrics for Anita Loos's famous characters in *Gentlemen Prefer Blondes* ('Diamonds

Are a Girl's Best Friend', 'Little Girl from Little Rock', 'Bye Bye Baby' etc). He lyricked the Jule Styne score for a television musical *Ruggles of Red Gap*, but his only subsequent Broadway venture was with the less-successful Sigmund Romberg piece *The Girl in Pink Tights*.

1926 **Bubbling Over** (Richard Myers/Clifford Grey) Garrick Theater, Philadelphia 2 August
1927 **Judy** (Charles Rosoff/Mark Swan) Royale Theater 7 February
1927 **Just Fancy** (Joseph Meyer, Phil Charig) Casino Theater 11 October
1927 **Hit the Deck** (Vincent Youmans/w Clifford Grey/Herbert Fields) Belasco Theater 25 April
1928 **Mr Cinders** (Vivian Ellis, Richard Myers/w Grey, Greatrex Newman) Opera House, Blackpool 25 September; Adelphi Theatre 11 February 1929
1928 **Hello Yourself** (Myers/Walter de Leon) Casino Theater 30 October
1939 **Nice Goin'** (Ralph Rainger/Lawrence Schwab) New Haven 21 October
1949 **Gentlemen Prefer Blondes** (Styne/Anita Loos, Joseph Fields) Ziegfeld Theater 8 December
1954 **The Girl in Pink Tights** (Romberg/Jerome Chodorov, Joseph Fields) Mark Hellinger Theater 5 March

ROBIN HOOD   Comic opera in 3 acts by Harry B Smith. Music by Reginald De Koven. Opera House, Chicago, 9 June 1890; Standard Theater, New York, 28 September 1891.

The most generally successful comic opera of the 19th-century American musical theatre, *Robin Hood*, like so many other musical shows, had only a little to do with the accepted events belonging to its hero's 'history'. The libretto to the show was made up by writer Harry B Smith from a series of scenes and comic turns which were borrowed rather from the basic characters and plot elements of the classic comic-opera stage than from the famous British folk tale of the chap who robbed his enemies to fund his pals.

The Sheriff of Nottingham (Henry Clay Barnabee) has settled that his ward, Lady Marian Fitzwalter (Marie Stone), is to marry his protégé, Guy of Gisbourne (Peter Lang), whom he intends to elevate to the Earldom of Huntingdon, at the expense of its young heir, Robert (Edwin Hoff). Robert runs off to Sherwood forest and there, under the alias of Robin Hood, joins a merrie band of outlaws. Amorous complications arise when, thinking himself deserted by Marian, he flirts with Annabel (Carlotta Maconda), the sweetheart of Allan-a-Dale (Jessie Bartlett Davis) who, as a result, Judasly betrays his captain to the Sheriff. When Act III gets under way, Marian and Annabel are to be forcibly wed to Guy and the Sheriff, but with the help of a trunkful of disguises Robin is freed, the weddings stopped, and King Richard turns up in time for a pageant of an ending.

Although these outlines were not unfamiliar (and there actually was an archery contest in the first act), their content was less so. The comic rôle of the Sheriff was all-important: in the first act, after an introductory song on regular comic-opera principles ('I Am the Sheriff of Nottingham') he machinated over the winning of the Huntingdon earldom and gave Guy a musical lesson in how to woo ('When a Peer Makes Love to a Damsel Fair'), in the

second, disguised as a tinker (Tinker's Song), he entered the forest for an encounter with the outlaws which left him drunk and in the clutches of the husband-hunting Dame Durden (Josephine Bartlett), was taken prisoner by the outlaws, stuck in the village stocks, and rescued by Guy in time for the third act. Marian, too, had a versatile rôle, appearing first in disguise as a page boy ('I Come as a Cavalier'), then as a milkmaid, then in lincoln green ('Forest Song') and then as Annabel, before actually spending the last act as herself. Amongst the other solos, Allan-a-Dale, disguised as a monk, sang a contralto 'Song of the Bells', Will Scarlet (Eugene Cowles), disguised as the forger of Robin's chains, had a fine basso Armourer's Song, Robin serenaded Annabel-Marian with 'A Troubadour Sang to his Love' and Little John (W H MacDonald) counselled 'Brown October Ale' for lovesickness, alongside a full book of concerted finales, choruses and ensembles.

Produced by the Bostonians in Chicago, with a top-flight cast taken from their fine list of vocalists, *Robin Hood* instantly became a key part of their repertoire. However, New York being only one stop on the company's rota, the show actually appeared in London's West End before it arrived on Broadway. Produced under the title of *Maid Marian* (in order not to be mistaken for a pantomime) it was again given a top-line cast including baritone Hayden Coffin (Robin), Harry Monkhouse (Sheriff), American soprano Marion Manola (Marian), John Le Hay (Guy), Violet Cameron (Allan), Canadian Attalie Claire (Annabel) and Gaiety veteran Madame Amadi (Dame) as well as a chorus of 60. That casting required some little rejigging of the score, including the beefing-up of the rôle of the slightly underparted Robin for Coffin, and the star duly got an extra number, a 'romanza' replacing a quintet in the last act. It was a wedding song, with lyrics by London theatre critic Clement Scott, and its title was 'O Promise Me'. It has, in the century since, been sung at countless millions of weddings throughout America.

Maid Marian had a run of more than two months in London – a little disappointing given the artillery mustered for the occasion – and dropped a sizeable £6,000. Soon after it made its appearance, under its rightful title, in New York. There are various tales related about 'O Promise Me', its genesis and its arrival in the show, most, if not all, not mentioning Coffin, but only Miss Davis and her tantrum over not having a song (which she, surely, did have – see above), and some versions crediting her with having introduced the number prior to the London production. No positive proof to the contrary seems to have emerged, unless it be the unlikelihood of London's very popular and powerful Violet Cameron allowing herself to be deprived of the show's hit number even for Coffin's sake, but neither does there seem to be any affirmative proof. Miss Davis did, in any case, manage to get 'O Promise Me' transferred from being Robin's song in London to being Allan-a-Dale's song in New York, and it was she who made it famous (and it did as much for her).

Robin Hood's New York season was the first of many that the show would have, both in the repertoire of the Bostonians and, after their dissolution, in a series of revivals, the last to date in 1944, as it carved itself a classic niche in the American musical theatre. De Koven and Smith subsequently wrote a sequel, *Maid Marian* (Garden

Theater 27 January 1902), which suffered the fate of virtually all other musequels.

Robin Hood itself was later produced in Australia, by J C Williamson, with Charles Kenningham (Robin), Carrie Moore (Marian), George Lauri (Sheriff), Viola Gillette (Allan), Clara Thompson (Dame Durden), Florence Perry (Annabel) and Howard Vernon (Little John) in the cast, for a season. It also eventually appeared in Hungary (ad Árpád Pásztor), and Smith related in his memoirs that it was similarly scheduled for Vienna's Theater an der Wien, where it ought to have followed the quick flop of Fall's *Der Rebell*. He asserts that owing the unavailability of an unnamed artist, it was put aside in favour of *Die lustige Witwe*. The truth probably reads something like this: it was one of a number of pieces which had been optioned and was thus available to Karczag when *Der Rebell* failed, but he chose to produce Lehár's. In any case, Vienna never did see *Robin Hood*.

The story of Robin Hood has, in various guises, been long played on the stage since Adam de la Halle's 13th-century *Le Jeu de Robin et Marion* introduced one of his forebears to an early form of musical theatre. In England, Robin Hood was used as the subject for an opera by William Shield (Covent Garden, 17 April 1784) and another by Macfarren (Her Majesty's Theatre 11 October 1860), and there were a number of *Robin Hood* burlesques or extravaganzas produced in Victorian times including those by Shirley Brooks et al (Lyceum, 1846), F C Burnand (1862), and Robert Reece whose *Little Robin Hood* was produced at the Royalty in 1871 and revived at the Gaiety in 1882. Another version, played in America, allowed Lydia Thompson to show off her form in lincoln green tights. In 1894 Stanley Rogers and Henry May's *Robin Hood Esq* toured Britain and, in 1907, Herbert Shelley and Ernest Bucalossi authored a *Robin Hood* burlesque which was played by Arthur Roberts at the Tivoli. In 1965 Lionel Bart was responsible for the last British *Robin Hood* burlesque to date, the dark-doomed *Twang!!*

The German-language theatre also had its *Robin Hood*s, including one by Reinhard Mosen and Albert Dietrich (Kassel, 17 March 1883) and another with a score by Moritz Fall, father of Leo, whilst France saw a *Robin des bois*, subtitled an 'opéra fantastique', from the pens of Castil-Blaize and Theodore Sauvage in the mid-19th century. In 1978 a Czechoslovakian *Robin Hood* (Petr Zdeněk/Jiři Aplt) was produced in Prague.

Quite early, the character of Robin, often played in travesty and supported by his Maid Marian and a long-legged chorus of merrie 'men', appeared as the titular hero of a run of British pantomimes, but today he has become most widely seen tacked, slightly curiously, into the tale of another traditional pantomime, *The Babes in the Wood*.

UK: Prince of Wales Theatre *Maid Marian* 5 February 1891; Australia: Her Majesty's Theatre, Sydney 25 November 1899; Hungary: Király Színház 29 October 1904
Recording: Radio broadcast, selection (AEI)

ROBINSON CRUSOE

Daniel Defoe's shipwrecked hero (1719) and his man Friday seem to have made their first appearance on the musical stage as the subject of a pantomime, *Robinson Crusoe, or Harlequin Friday* (1781), written by no less an author than Richard Brinsley Sheridan. Since that time,

Mr Crusoe has remained an intermittently popular feature of the British pantomime season, whilst also serving to animate a number of other musical stage pieces of which the best known is probably Offenbach's opéra-comique version of 1867, written to a text by Hector Crémieux and Eugène Cormon. In spite of being a 32-performance failure at Paris's Opéra-Comique (23 November 1867), the piece was subsequently played in New York (6 September 1875), in a much-altered version as *Robinsonade* in Leipzig (21 September 1930), in Zurich and Prague, and ultimately in London (ad Don White, Camden Festival, 1973).

An earlier Paris opérette, written by William Busnach and composed by Jean-Francis Pillevestre, was played at the Fantaisies-Parisiennes in 1866 (21 February), but Italy had got off the mark much more swiftly with a *Robinson Crusoe*, music by Vincenzo Fioravanti, produced at the Naples Teatro Nuovo in 1828. A German musical *Robinson Crusoe* appeared at Berlin's Belle-Alliance Theater on 11 November 1881, Ernest Blum and Pierre Decourcelle produced a pasticco spectacular on the famous castaway for the Théâtre du Châtelet in 1899 (mus: Marius Baggers, 20 October), Adolf Philipp and Wilhelm Hock, with music by Hans Lowenfeld, supplied a similar piece for Hamburg's Stadttheater (10 December 1901) and Karl Josef Fromm and Alexander Ludwig were responsible for a four-act spectacular produced at Vienna's Kaiser-Jubiläumstheater in 1904 (3 April). Spain's *Robinson Crusoe* (Teatro Circo, 18 March 1870), again an opéra-bouffe and following as so often where France led, was composed by Francisco Asenjo Barbieri to a text from José F Godoy and Rafael Garcia Santisteban, and lasted a little better than most – it was on display in Madrid in 1992.

In Britain, outside the pantomime productions, *Robinson Crusoe* appeared in burlesque as *Crusoe the Second* (Lyceum, 1847), H J Byron's *Robinson Crusoe* (Princess's, 1860), a multiple-authored piece, in which W S Gilbert had a hand (Haymarket, 1867), an Alfred Thompson piece about *How I Found Crusoe (or a Flight of Imagination from Geneva to Cosmopolis)* which burlesqued Stanley's much-publicized trip to 'find' Livingstone (1872), H B Farnie's *The Very Latest Edition of Robinson Crusoe* (Folly, 1876) in which Lydia Thompson was the hero and Willie Edouin Man Friday, and a second piece by the same author and Robert Reece (Avenue, 1886). In 1894 a *Crusoe the Cruiser* was seen on the touring circuits.

In Hungary, the Népszinház mounted a spectacular piece taken from the Blum/Decourcelle show, with a musical accompaniment composed and arranged by Jósef Bokor (2 June 1900), in Paris Victor de Cottens, Robert Charvay, Harry Fragson and Maurel combined to turn out a punning *Robinson n'a pas cru Zoé* (22 December 1899) for the Boîte à Fursy, whilst, in America, an extravaganza, *Robinson Crusoe Jr*, was produced at the Winter Garden Theater 17 February 1916 (Romberg, James Hanley/Atteridge, Edgar Smith) with Al Jolson starred. This last show included perhaps the most memorable bit of Crusoeiana: the popular song in which George W Meyer, Sam M Lewis and Joe Young demanded 'Where Did Robinson Crusoe Go (with Friday on Saturday Night)?' The song was given to Londoners in the revue *Follow the Crowd* (1916) as sung by Ethel Levey.

Recording: Offenbach version (Opera Rara)

ROB ROY, or The Thistle and the Rose Comic opera in 3 acts by Harry B Smith. Music by Reginald De Koven. Herald Square Theater, New York, 29 October 1894.

In his mostly ill-rewarded efforts to produce another *Robin Hood*, De Koven's most successful work was another comic opera based on (or, at least, titled for) a British folk hero, this time one from north of the border, *Rob Roy*. Harry B Smith provided the book in which the chief comedian, the Mayor of Perth (Richard F Carroll), was as much the hub of the action as the Sheriff of Nottingham had been in the first show. Whilst Rob Roy (William Pruette) and his lieutenant Lochiel (W H McLaughlin) connive at the escape of Bonnie Prince Charlie (Baron Berthald) and his inamorata Flora MacDonald (Lizzie McNichol), the Mayor is busy imitating the more famous Vicar of Bray – changing sides with expediency and promising his daughter Janet (Juliette Cordon) in marriage to representatives of whichever team he thinks looks like winning. Janet does not only end up, but has secretly been from the beginning, Mrs Rob Roy.

The score, if it did not turn out anything which would achieve the popularity of *Robin Hood*'s 'Brown October Ale' or 'O Promise Me', nevertheless featured some persistently heather-flavoured music which was well adapted to the style of things, topped by the military 'Prince Rupert's Cavaliers' and Grenadier's Song, a splendidly basso Turnkey's song ('In Darkness Deep') which was every bit as good as the previous show's Armourer's Song, and Janet's catchy cautionary tale of 'The Merry Miller' who married a wild coquette.

The Broadway production of *Rob Roy* was a fine success, running up 253 performances during the 1894–5 season and, in that area at least, easily topping the record of *Robin Hood*. It was played around the country, taken into the repertoire of the Bostonians where Henry Barnabee, the original Sheriff of Nottingham, appeared as the Mayor, returned very briefly to Broadway for a second run of two weeks with Jefferson de Angelis starred (15 September 1913) and was reprised at the St Louis Muny in 1925 with Leo de Hierapolis and Yvonne d'Arle starred. It did not, however, follow *Robin Hood* beyond American stages and across to Europe.

Britain made do with its own depiction of Rob Roy MacGregor as seen in the highly successful opera *Rob Roy MacGregor*, written by Pocock and composed by J Davy and often revived after its first production at Covent Garden (12 March 1818), and in burlesque as *Robbing Roy* (F C Burnand, Gaiety Theatre, 1879 etc) where Edward Terry played the hero to the Francis Obaldistone of Nellie Farren. France, in its turn, saw the Scots hero translated to the musical stage in an 1837 opéra-comique with a score by the young Flotow.

UK: (copyright performance) Morton's Theatre, Greenwich 29 September 1894

ROBYN, Alfred G (b St Louis, 29 April 1860; d New York, 18 October 1935).

Musician, composer of songs and also of a handful of theatrical scores, Robyn worked as a pianist with Emma Abbott's opera company and as a church organist before making his début on the Broadway stage with a comic opera, *Jacinta*. Produced at the Fifth Avenue Theater by Fred Whitney with Louise Beaudet cast in the title-rôle opposite Signor Perugini and Edwin Stevens as chief comic, it lasted but 16 performances, and it was a further decade before Robyn was again represented on Broadway.

This time, however, the result was much more positive. *The Yankee Consul*, with its bristling Henry Blossom book, proved a first-rate vehicle for comedian Raymond Hitchcock, and a second piece in the same vein, *The Yankee Tourist*, was also a long-touring success. Robyn's last Broadway show, *All for the Ladies*, was produced by A H Woods as a vehicle for another star comedian, Sam Bernard, and also had a respectable Broadway stay. Robyn continued to compose (a revue, *Let's Go*, was played in Baltimore in 1919) but the latter part of his musical career was spent as a cinema organist at the Rialto and other movie houses.

1894 **Jacinta** (William H Lapere) Fifth Avenue Theater 26 November
1904 **The Yankee Consul** (Henry Blossom) Broadway Theatre 22 February
1907 **The Princess Beggar** (Edward Paulton) Casino Theater 7 January
1907 **The Yankee Tourist** (Max Figman, Joseph Blethen) Astor Theater 12 August
1908 **My Sweetheart** new music for revised version by Thomas Reilly, R A Roberts
1911 **Will o' the Wisp** (Walter Percival) Studebaker Theater, Chicago 8 May
1912 **All for the Ladies** (Blossom) Lyric Theater 30 December
Other titles credited: *The Gipsy Girl* (1905), *Fortune Land* (1907)

THE ROCKY HORROR SHOW Rock musical by Richard O'Brien. Theatre Upstairs, Royal Court Theatre, London, 19 June 1973.

An innocently winning musical fantasy made up from elements of the less ambitious kind of science fiction and horror movies, some fashionable post-*Hair* intimations of sex, drugs and violence, and a group of simple 1950s-style pop songs, *The Rocky Horror Show* began its life in a tiny studio theatre, from where it stretched out not only into a very long initial run in London but also into a feature film and a continuing life, around the world, as a novelty show.

Toothpaste-clean Brad (Christopher Malcolm) and Janet (Julie Covington) take refuge on a nasty night in a castle in the American countryside (a castle in America ... wouldn't you have been suspicious?) where they meet the spidery Riff-Raff (O'Brien), peculiar Magenta (Patricia Quinn) and tap-dancing Columbia (Little Nell), and the transvestite lord of the manor, Frank'n'Furter (Tim Curry). Frank has built himself a perfect man, Rocky (Rayner Bourton), to assuage his desires, but he takes time off to indulge in Brad and Janet (separately), before their tutor, Dr Scott (Paddy O'Hagan), trundles to the rescue in his wheelchair. Dr Scott knows that all the castle's inhabitants are Creatures-from-Outer-Space, and he helps Brad and Janet escape as internecine warfare erupts, Frank and Rocky are gunned down, and the other aliens saucer off home. The accompanying songs included Frank's introduction as a 'Sweet Transvestite from Transexual, Transylvania', a dance routine called 'The Time Warp', a hymn to the 'Science Fiction, Double Feature' and an incidental rock 'n' rolling 'Whatever Happened to Saturday Night?'.

The show emerged as a thoroughly entertaining 80 minutes, endearing in its half-attempts to outrage, innocently unsexy with its black suspenders, cross-dressing, tap-dancing and silhouetted grunting, always keeping to the comic-strip and avoiding the campy, and inspiring the same enjoyment as the ghastly-funny films which were its inspiration. Michael White's production moved from its tiny nest to first one and then a second atmospherically decrepit cinema in the then trendy King's Road, and there it developed into a long-running if not highly profitable operation. White foresaw the dangers of moving the piece from its suitable home into a genuine theatre but, finally, in its sixth year and after 2,358 Chelsea performances, *Rocky* was taken out of its natural habitat and transferred to the West End's Comedy Theatre. It undoubtedly lost something of its special atmosphere in the shift, but nevertheless ran another 600 performances in its midtown home before closing down.

In the meanwhile, *Rocky* productions had sprung up all round the world. An American production was launched in a nicely scruffy Hollywood ex-nightclub, but when it was moved to Broadway's Belasco Theater it proved totally out of its area and failed quickly. In Australia, producer Harry M Miller caught the then still unconfirmed appeal of the piece when he opened his 1974 production with a midnight showing at an elderly cinema in the Sydney suburb of Glebe. The epicene Reg Livermore made a hit and a name as Frank'n'Furter, and the show had long runs both in Sydney and, with Max Phipps succeeding to the star rôle, through 19 months in Melbourne, prior to regular revivals in the years that followed.

A film version, *The Rocky Horror Picture Show*, with Curry, O'Brien, Quinn and Little Nell featured alongside Susan Sarandon and Barry Bostwick, was also a quick failure, but only a temporary one. It later became a late-night campus favourite and, as the show had done in the King's Road, began to attract regulars. A cult grew up, complete with little audience rituals performed with matches, rice, water and frozen peas and with chanted responses to the dialogue, as the film found itself a semi-permanent home in a number of cinemas. In Britain, would-be cultists could not find the film, but regional theatres and then the touring circuits took up the stage show and British youngsters transferred the American film liturgy to the stage show. It proved so popular, that soon – in contrast to the lesson learned earlier – the show was playing some of the vaster provincial houses to accommodate the audience demand. Fortunately, they also had the staff to clean up the water, the matches, the unfrozen peas and the soggy rice.

In the process, of course, the original character of the show had been lost. It had become like a game, with many of the performers having lost the innocently winning tone of the original, which was now replaced by a pantomime silliness. At one stage the essentially masculine Frank'n'Furter was played by a female impersonator. But the *Rocky* craze blossomed through the 1980s and it was in those years that the show reached its greatest heights of popularity as an audience participation activity. The boom, however, was past its peak when it was decided to bring the show back to the West End. Produced at the Piccadilly Theatre with television comedy actor Adrian Edmondson featured as Frank, it found less audience than it might have

done five years earlier at the Windmill or some other Soho dive, but nevertheless held up for a 412-performance run before going back on the road.

Australia: New Art Cinema, Glebe, Sydney 19/20 April 1974; USA: Roxy, Sunset Strip, Los Angeles, 1974; Belasco Theater, New York 10 March 1975; Germany: Theater der Stadt, Essen (Ger) 20 January 1980; France: Théâtre de l'Union 14 February 1984; Film: Twentieth Century-Fox 1976

Recordings: original cast (UK), American cast (Ode), Australian casts (Elephant, Festival), London revival cast 1990 (Chrysalis), film soundtrack (Ode), Mexican recording (Orfeon), German recording (Ariola) etc

RODGERS, Richard [Charles] (b Hammel's Station, 28 June 1902; d New York, 30 December 1979). Pre-eminent Broadway composer who won fame twice over, in two seemingly separate careers, one each side of the war, as half of Rodgers-n-Hart and then of Rodgers-n-Hammerstein.

The young Rodgers served his musical-theatre apprenticeship writing songs for amateur and college shows, coming together early on in a partnership with lyricist Lorenz Hart which would survive virtually up to the latter's early death. The pair had their first Broadway exposure with a song, 'Any Old Place with You', which was interpolated into the already sizeable Malvin Franklin/Robert Hood Bowers score of Lew Fields's production of *A Lonely Romeo* (1919), and a more substantial one the following year when seven of their numbers survived into the Broadway version of the semi-successful *Poor Little Ritz Girl*. This youthful start, however, did not produce further opportunities, and it was not until 1925, when the pair supplied the score for the revue *Garrick Gaieties* ('Manhattan'), mounted by some of the younger members of the Theater Guild company, that they got the impetus of genuine success behind them. That success set Rodgers and Hart off on a steady and prolific Broadway career that would last for 23 shows (plus a small handful for London) over 16 years of a virtually exclusive partnership.

The earliest Rodgers and Hart book musicals did extremely well. *Dearest Enemy* ('Here in My Arms'), a piece with a libretto in a kind of period operetta style to which Rodgers would not return until his collaboration with Hart had ended, and for which the pair had had no success in finding a home until their revue had boosted their profile, was the first. Its 286-performance Broadway run was followed by a tour, and before that was over they had done even better with a thorough song-and-dance comedy, *The Girl Friend* ('The Blue Room'). *The Girl Friend* ran up 301 performances in New York and bequeathed part of its score to a London show, which, under the same title, played 421 nights in the West End.

A commission to write a vehicle for Cicely Courtneidge and Jack Hulbert for the London stage brought forth an unexceptional piece called *Lido Lady* which nevertheless did duty for 259 performances at the Gaiety Theatre and productions in Australia and France, and an updated rewrite of that grand old hit *Tillie's Nightmare* called *Peggy-Ann*, in spite of including nothing to equal the earlier piece's song hit 'Heaven Will Protect the Working Girl', also had a fine Broadway life (333 performances) and a London production (134 performances). A 1927 revue for C B Cochran, produced in London as *One Dam Thing After*

Plate 227. **Richard Rodgers** *watches rehearsal for the stage version of his* State Fair *at St Louis Muny.*

green ('Dancing on the Ceiling') which was played for 254 performances in London before heading for screendom.

It was at this stage that Hollywood, avid for the best of Broadway talent to feed the newly popular musical film, called Rodgers and Hart, and the pair spent four mildly unforthcoming years in and out of filmland from which the score of *Love Me Tonight* ('Isn't it Romantic?', 'Lover', 'Mimi') emerged as the chief product. Finally, the writers found the will to extract themselves from their celluloid quicksand, returned to the theatre, and, with their return to a Broadway which had passed the worst Depression years, they found once again the kind of success that they had known in their earliest days.

Their first assignment was the score for a grandiose circus spectacular, *Jumbo* ('The Most Beautiful Girl in the World'), mounted by Billy Rose with such magnificence as to fold in 233 expensive performances, but in 1936 they turned out the dancing tale *On Your Toes* ('There's a Small Hotel', Slaughter on 10th Avenue, 'Glad to Be Unhappy' etc), for which they had themselves invented the book, and scored a fine New York success (315 performances). In London, however, where Rodgers had not been represented on the stage since *Evergreen*, seven years earlier, *On Your Toes* was a failure and, although their songs were used in several revues (*All Clear, Funny Side Up, Up and Doing*) in the years that followed, no further Rodgers and Hart show was played in the London theatre until 17 years later when the Broadway revival of *Pal Joey* sparked a London production.

In America, however, between 1937 and 1940 Rodgers turned out a run of successful scores. First came the let's-do-a-show show par excellence, *Babes in Arms* (289 performances, 'The Lady is a Tramp', 'Where or When', 'My Funny Valentine'), then one in the series of singing-President shows of the era, *I'd Rather Be Right*, with George M Cohan occupying the White House through 290 performances, the Hungarian fantasy *I Married an Angel* (338 performances), a Shakespearian burlesque *The Boys From Syracuse* (235 performances, 'Falling in Love With Love', 'This Can't be Love'), a less-than-wholly-winning college musical, *Too Many Girls* (249 performances, 'I Like to Recognise the Tune', 'I Didn't Know What Time it Was', 'Give it Back to the Indians') and the lowlife off-the-beaten-track *Pal Joey* (374 performances 'Bewitched'). And in this time the partners had just one real failure with the misconceived *Higher and Higher*.

In 1941, under the influence of the multi-active George Abbott, Rodgers extended his theatre interests by going into partnership with Abbott as a producer on the musical *Best Foot Forward* and, on his own next musical, *By Jupiter*, he again shared the producing duties. It proved a good move, for *By Jupiter*, a burlesque of antiquity, had the longest Broadway first run of any of the Rodgers and Hart musicals (427 performances). But it was also the last new show the pair would write. Hart's irregular personal habits had put the partnership in peril repeatedly and with increasing frequency, and Rodgers had needfully looked elsewhere for a more professional lyricist. Nevertheless, he worked with Hart on a revamp of their old success *A Connecticut Yankee* ('To Keep My Love Alive') which he himself produced before the partnership was naturally dissolved by Hart's death.

In the meanwhile, Rodgers had not only extended his

Another, had a satisfactory run, partly thanks to the success of the song 'My Heart Stood Still', and that song also proved one of the hits of the most Broadway-successful of all the team's early shows, a fantasy musical comedy based on Mark Twain's tale of *A Connecticut Yankee* ('Thou Swell').

In less than three years, Rodgers and Hart had had four successes on Broadway, two and a bit in London, and had made themselves into one of the foremost and most audible forces in the American musical theatre, and by that token in London, where the shows of Hirsch, Youmans, Gershwin, Romberg, Kern and Tierney – not to forget *Mercenary Mary* – had induced and developed a craze for all that was theatrically and musically trans-Atlantic, and even further afield.

Then the pudding sank. The pair had tasted failure when, in the midst of their successes, they had succumbed to the siren song of Florenz Ziegfeld and turned out songs for a weak piece called *Betsy* which even the interpolation of Irving Berlin's 'Blue Skies' and Gershwin's 'Rhapsody in Blue' could not boost beyond 39 performances. But now, after three good years, came three very indifferent years in which, if their shows turned out a regular stream of durable songs, the shows themselves proved anything but durable. The Beatrice Lillie vehicle *She's My Baby* flopped in 71 performances, a piece about a potential eunuch called *Chee-Chee* winced through 31, London's production of *A Connecticut Yankee* fell in 43, and a musical called *Heads Up!*, which had managed 144 performances on Broadway, crumbled in just 19 in England. There were better runs for *Present Arms* (155 performances, 'You Took Advantage of Me'), *Spring is Here* (104 performances, 'With a Song in My Heart'), the Ed Wynn vehicle *Simple Simon* (135 performances, 'Ten Cents a Dance') and a spoof of the silent films, *America's Sweetheart* (135 performances), but the only show which achieved a really decent run was a revusical piece for Cochran entitled *Ever-*

producing activities (*Beat the Band*, 1942), but had also made a momentous entry onto Broadway with his old friend and new partner, Oscar Hammerstein II. For the same Theatre Guild with which Rodgers and Hart had made their mark as a team with *The Garrick Gaieties*, Rodgers and Hammerstein supplied the score for a musical version of the Guild's play *Green Grow the Lilacs*. It was a period costume piece of Americana not unlike in flavour to Rodgers and Hart's début musical, *Dearest Enemy*, a naïve, romantic tale built on traditional comic-opera lines, full of simple charm and immensely singable songs ('The Surrey with the Fringe on Top', 'I Cain't Say No', 'People Will Say We're in Love' etc), a show of a type which had become rather forgotten amongst the dancing President shows and very light, comedy-and-chorus-girl-based spectaculars of the past decade. *Oklahoma!* proved as welcome as lilacs that bloom in the spring and made such a hit as to break Broadway's long-run record with its run of 2,212 performances whilst going on to conquer London and the rest of the English-speaking world.

The traditional style of Broadway songwriting which Rodgers had practised to good effect in his years with Hart was replaced, in his collaboration with Hammerstein, by a more romantic or operettic kind of writing. The slick, smart take-away song was replaced by a variety of number which proved every bit as take-awayable, but which was musically more substantial, vocally more demanding, and made for a rather different kind of performer, whether romantic or comic, than its predecessor. It was a style to which the pair would largely stick with remarkable results. The flood of popular songs that came out of *Oklahoma!* was followed by another heap from Rodgers and Hammerstein's next show, and next important hit, the musicalized Molnár play *Carousel* (Soliloquy, 'You'll Never Walk Alone', 'If I Loved You' etc) a piece which followed *Oklahoma!* from Broadway triumph on to the international circuits. *Carousel* was produced, like its predecessor and like its rather less colourful and less successful successor, *Allegro* ('The Gentleman is a Dope'), under the aegis of the Theatre Guild, but Rodgers had by no means renounced producing and, whilst *Oklahoma!* and *Carousel* reigned on Broadway, he was responsible for producing the show that would prove their greatest rival for popularity, *Annie Get Your Gun*.

Rodgers joined the functions of producer and author for the first time since the revival of *A Connecticut Yankee* for the fourth Rodgers and Hammerstein musical, *South Pacific* ('Younger than Springtime', 'Some Enchanted Evening', 'Bali H'ai', 'Once Nearly Was Mine') and, with that piece and with the following *King and I* ('Hello, Young Lovers', 'Shall We Dance?', 'Something Wonderful', 'Getting to Know You') the team scored two further enormous successes to set alongside the vast hits of *Oklahoma!* and *Carousel*. That the writers were not, however, infallible was seen when they abandoned the romantic operetta for a rather humdrum backstage tale in *Me and Juliet* ('No Other Love') or for the downlife characters and unromantic happenings of *Pipe Dream*. There was altogether more success to be found in the Oriental sweet-and-not-very-sourness of *Flower Drum Song* ('I Enjoy Being a Girl', 'A Hundred Thousand Miracles') but, 16 years after their first epoch-making success, Rodgers and Hammerstein combined on what was to be their last work together and produced what

was to be perhaps their most widely and wholly successful work: *The Sound of Music* ('Climb Every Mountain', 'Do-Re-Mi', 'The Sound of Music', 'My Favorite Things' etc).

Hammerstein's death ended Rodgers's second long and fruitful collaboration, but their years of work together had produced a body of nine musical shows from which five won worldwide popularity both as stage shows and in the cinema and became established both as an essential part of the American classic repertoire, and as the outstanding representatives of the musical theatre of their time.

Rodgers continued to write for the stage, if with less regularity than in his younger days, but the same kind of success would not come again. He provided his own lyrics for his first post-Hammerstein show, *No Strings*, which had a 580-performance run on Broadway (and 135 performances in London). The show added the song 'The Sweetest Sounds' to his standards catalogue, but it did not have the same appeal nor the same propensity to endure as his best works of the 1940s and 1950s. The composer nevertheless proved excitingly that he had lost none of his writing talent when, at 63 years of age, in collaboration with lyricist Stephen Sondheim, he turned out one of the most appealing romantic-comic scores of his career for *Do I Hear a Waltz?* This time, however, Rodgers the producer did not do his job as well as Rodgers the composer, for *Do I Hear a Waltz?* underwent some wrong-headed decisions on its way to the stage and did not become a success in the theatre.

The shows which followed were not in the same class: a television musical version of G B Shaw's *Androcles and the Lion* (1967) and a Noah's ark musical, *Two by Two*, which featured Danny Kaye as the floating refugee of the floods, were followed by a dispiritingly uninviting musical version of the play *I Remember Mama* which Rodgers had himself mounted, without music and with great success, in his early days as a producer, and which now marked his farewell to Broadway more than half a century since his first appearance there.

Rodgers's screen scores for *State Fair* (film) and Cinderella (television) were both subsequently used as the musical part of stage musicals put together by other hands.

Rodgers's career in the musical theatre, principally as a composer, but also as a producer, was the most important in the American theatre of his time. During his years of collaboration with Hart, he was one of the most effective of the peloton of popular and successful musical theatre composers then working on Broadway, and from their partnership a good number of popular songs have survived as standards. However, in spite of the immensely saleable names of their writers, only two shows – *Pal Joey* and *On Your Toes* – have lasted into the stage repertoire of the latter part of the century. It is the group of five famous and substantial musical plays written and, later, produced in tandem with Hammerstein which have survived as the enduring part of Rodgers's work as a theatre composer. In their time, these works encouraged and confirmed a return to the basic tenets of the British and Continental operettas of the late 19th and early 20th century, to their classic combination of the sentimental and the comic, their music orientated towards vocal values rather than dance rhythms or Tin Pan Alley, and dance which came from balletic roots rather than from the ballroom, the gymnasium or the parade ground. Since then, their appeal has never weakened. They have held their place as five of the most popular and frequently played works of their period, a body of work as impressive as any in the history of the Broadway musical and as memorable as the kernel of the opus of Gilbert and Sullivan, of Offenbach or Lecocq, of Franz Lehár or Emmerich Kálmán.

A Hollywood musical biography of Rodgers and Hart called *Words and Music* (1948) featured Tom Drake as Rodgers to the Hart of Mickey Rooney.

Rodgers's daughter, **Mary RODGERS** (b New York, 11 January 1931), had a notable success as a composer for the musical stage with the score for the fairytale burlesque *Once Upon a Mattress*. She also composed the music for *Hot Spot* (Martin Charnin/Jack Weinstock, Willie Gilbert, Majestic Theater 19 April 1963), *The Mad Show* (1966) and contributed to the score of *Working* (1978).

1920 **Poor Little Ritz Girl** (w Sigmund Romberg/Lorenz Hart/Lew Fields, George Campbell) 28 July
1925 **Dearest Enemy** (Hart/Herbert Fields) Knickerbocker Theater 18 September
1926 **The Girl Friend** (Hart/H Fields) Vanderbilt Theater 17 March
1926 **Lido Lady** (Hart/Guy Bolton, Bert Kalmar, Harry Ruby) Gaiety Theatre, London 1 December
1926 **Peggy-Ann** (Hart/ad H Fields) Vanderbilt Theater 27 December
1926 **Betsy** (Hart/Irving Caesar, David Friedman) New Amsterdam Theater 28 December
1927 **She's My Baby** (Hart/Kalmar, Ruby) Globe Theater 3 January
1927 **A Connecticut Yankee** (Hart/H Fields) Vanderbilt Theater 3 November
1928 **Present Arms** (Hart/H Fields) Lew Fields Mansfield Theater 26 April
1928 **Chee-Chee** (Hart/H Fields) Lew Fields Mansfield Theater 25 September
1929 **Spring is Here** (Hart/Owen Davis) Alvin Theater 11 March
1929 **Heads Up!** (Hart/John McGowan, Paul Gerard Smith) Alvin Theater 11 November
1930 **Simple Simon** (Hart/Bolton, Ed Wynn) Ziegfeld Theater 18 February
1931 **America's Sweetheart** (Hart/H Fields) Broadhurst Theater 10 February
1935 **Jumbo** (Hart/Ben Hecht, Charles McArthur) Hippodrome Theater 16 November
1936 **On Your Toes** (Hart/Rodgers, Hart, George Abbott) Imperial Theater 11 April
1937 **Babes in Arms** (Hart/Rodgers, Hart) Shubert Theater 14 April
1937 **I'd Rather Be Right** (Hart/Moss Hart, George S Kaufman) Alvin Theater 2 November
1938 **I Married an Angel** (Hart/ad Rodgers, Hart) Shubert Theater 11 May
1938 **The Boys from Syracuse** (Hart/Abbott) Alvin Theater 23 November
1939 **Too Many Girls** (Hart/George Marion jr) Imperial Theater 18 October
1940 **Higher and Higher** (Hart/Gladys Hurlbut, Joshua Logan) Shubert Theater 4 April
1940 **Pal Joey** (Hart/John O'Hara) Ethel Barrymore Theater 25 December
1942 **By Jupiter** (Hart/Rodgers, Hart) Shubert Theater 2 June
1943 **Oklahoma!** (Oscar Hammerstein II) St James Theater 31 March
1945 **Carousel** (Hammerstein) Majestic Theater 19 April
1947 **Allegro** (Hammerstein) Majestic Theater 10 October
1949 **South Pacific** (Hammerstein/Hammerstein, Logan) Majestic Theater 7 April
1951 **The King and I** (Hammerstein) St James Theater 29 March
1953 **Me and Juliet** (Hammerstein) Majestic Theater 28 May
1955 **Pipe Dream** (Hammerstein) Shubert Theater 30 November
1958 **Flower Drum Song** (Hammerstein/Hammerstein, Joseph Fields) St James Theater 1 December
1958 **Cinderella** (Hammerstein) London Coliseum 18 December
1959 **The Sound of Music** (Hammerstein/Russel Crouse, Howard Lindsay) Lunt-Fontanne Theater 16 November
1962 **No Strings** (Rodgers/Samuel Taylor) 54th Street Theater 15 March
1965 **Do I Hear a Waltz?** (Stephen Sondheim/Arthur Laurents) 46th Street Theater 18 March
1969 **State Fair** (Hammerstein/Lucille Kallen) Municipal Opera, St Louis 2 June
1970 **Two By Two** (Martin Charnin/Peter Stone) Imperial Theater 10 November
1976 **Rex** (Sheldon Harnick/Sherman Yellen) Lunt-Fontanne Theater 25 April
1979 **I Remember Mama** (Charnin, Raymond Jessel/Thomas Meehan) Majestic Theater 31 May

Autobiography: *Musical Stages* (Random House, New York, 1975); Biographies: Green, S: *The Rodgers and Hammerstein Story* (Day, New York, 1963), Ewen, D: *With a Song in His Heart* (Holt, New York, 1957), Deems Taylor: *Some Enchanted Evening: the Story of Rodgers and Hammerstein* (Harper, New York, 1953), Marx, S & Clayton, J: *Rodgers and Hart: Bewitched, Bothered and Bedevilled* (Putnam, New York, 1976), Nolan, F: *The Sound of Their Music* (Dent, London, 1976), *Richard Rodgers: Letters to Dorothy (1926–1937)* (NY Public Library, 1988), Mordden, E: *Rodgers and Hammerstein* (Abrams, New York, 1992) etc

ROGER, Germaine   (d 1975).

Soprano Germaine Roger appeared on the Paris stage in a number of opérettes from the end of the 1920s (*Un soir de réveillon, Un coup de veine, L'Auberge du chat coiffé, Un petit bout de femme, Ma petite amie*, the revamped *Les Cent Vierges, Moineau, Phi-Phi* etc). After the Second World War, her husband, actor and sometime musical performer Henri Montjoye (né Barbero) took over the management of the large Théâtre de la Gaîté-Lyrique and, in 1950, on his death, Mme Roger-Montjoye succeeded him. Through the 1950s and part of the 1960s she produced a programme consisting of a mixture of classic revivals (*Les Mousquetaires au couvent, Les Cloches de Corneville, La Chaste Susanne*), reprises of more modern favourites (*Andalousie, Trois Valses, Le Pays du Sourire, La Belle de Cadix, Chanson gitane*) and a number of new works including *Colorado, Minnie Moustache*, the long-running *Chevalier du ciel* with Luis Mariano, José Padilla's *Romance au Portugal, Pampanilla*, the unfortunate *Premier Rendez-vous* and the musical comedy *Visa pour l'amour* in which Bourvil and Annie Cordy danced the twist. In a number of these productions, notably *Pampanilla, Trois Valses* and, eternally as the teenaged heroine of *Mam'zelle Nitouche*, the fair proprietress herself took a leading rôle.

ROGER, Victor   (b Montpellier, 22 July 1853; d Paris, 2 December 1903). Composer of a long list of mostly vaudevillesque scores for the French musical-comedy stage.

Victor Roger studied music at the École Niedermeyer, and thereafter spread his young writing talents through every available area of music-related work: vocal and piano music, dance music for the theatre, musical criticism and a number of small scenes and opérettes for the cafés-concerts, notably the Eldorado. One of these, *Mademoiselle Louloute*, was well enough regarded to be revived, 14 years after its initial production, at the Moulin-Rouge (29 September 1896), by which time Roger had thoroughly established himself as a popular composer for the light musical stage.

His first major success came when he provided the score to the particularly clever Paul Ferrier-Fabrice Carré libretto for the vaudeville-opérette *Joséphine vendue par ses soeurs*, which won a long first run (245 performances) in Paris and went on to a list of foreign productions and adaptations. A repeat success of the kind, however, was not swift to follow, although Roger supplied some typical light-hearted and often charming and comical music for a series of shows over the next decade. Only one emerged as the legitimate successor to *Joséphine*, the military vaudeville *Les 28 Jours de Clairette* which, like its predecessor, had a long Parisian season (236 performances) and a clutch of foreign performances and has remained, even more prominently than the earlier piece, a feature of the French musical theatre repertoire.

Of Roger's other works, *Cendrillonnette* found the most home town success (124 performances), with *Mademoiselle Asmodée* (88 performances), *La Dot de Brigitte* (73 performances) and *Le Voyage de Corbillon* (72 performances) all putting up respectable runs, but *Oscarine* (45 performances), *Le Fétiche* (37 performances), *Samsonnet* (29 performances), *Les Douze Femmes de Japhet* (31 performances, and revival), *Le Coq* (43 performances), *Clary-Clara* (8 performances), *Nicol-Nick* (35 performances) and *Sa Majesté l'amour* (10 performances) did not establish themselves in the French repertoire.

In spite of this, a good number of this group of pieces were taken up outside France, and a number of them (not always with Roger's music still attached) became successful in other centres. Vienna saw *Japhet und seine zwölf Frauen*, *Le Voyage de Corbillon* (as *Das rothe Parapluie*) and *La Dot de Brigitte* (as *Frau Lieutenant*) at the Theater in der Josefstadt, Berlin's Thalia-Theater also played the latter piece, and Hungary staged *Klari* (*Clary-Clara*), *Brigitta* (*La Dot de Brigitte*), *Jafet 12 felesége* (*Les Douze Femmes de Japhet*), *A babona* (*Le Fétiche*), *Vegye el a lányomat!* (*Nicol-Nick*) and *Corbillon utazása/Az orleansi szúzek* (*Le Voyage de Corbillon*).

The year 1897 proved a vintage one for Roger, bringing him two more fine international successes, the jolly, comical *L'Auberge du Tohu-bohu* and the very superior musical comedy *Les Fêtards*. If, in Paris, the former (231 performances) won much longer consideration than the latter (72 performances), that verdict was by and large reversed by the rest of the world, even if some of the rest of the world found it preferable to replace much or all of Roger's *Fêtards* score with home-written songs. Vienna's Theater in der Josefstadt, Berlin's Thalia-Theater (*Tohu-Bohu*, *Wie man Männer fesselt*), London and Broadway (both for the first, but not the second) and the appreciative Budapest (*A biblias asszony*, *Óssze-vissza fogadó*) welcomed the shows more or less as written.

Of his remaining shows, those written in the last half-dozen years of the composer's life, none reached the same

popularity. *La Poule blanche* was played in both Berlin (*Die weisse Henne*) and in Budapest (*A feher csirke*) after 32 Paris performances, but *L'Agence Crook et Cie* was a four-performance flop, *La Petite Tache* was played just 12 times and, although his last work, *Le Jockey malgré lui*, after 33 performances in its initial production, was picked up for an American production (it was produced there as *The Office Boy*), it, like America's *Les Fêtards*, replaced Roger's score with one with a more local flavour.

Provided, during the 16 effective years of his career, with some exceptionally fine and funny libretti, Roger decorated them with the kind of light, dancing music, often with an amusingly apt burlesque touch, which was most suitable to this brand of comedy-with-songs. If *Les 28 Jours de Clairette* with its popular military setting and antics has survived the best of these on the French stage, *Les Fêtards*, in particular, *Les Douze Femmes de Japhet* and *Joséphine* render it nothing in pure, comic enjoyment and almost certainly owe their comparative eclipse to the modern preference for the romantic and spectacular over the witty and farcical in musical theatre.

1880 **L'Amour quinze-vingt** (Laurencin [ie Paul-Aimé Chapelle]) 1 act Eldorado 10 August

1882 **Mademoiselle Louloute** (Louis Péricaud, Lucien Delormel) 1 act Eldorado 9 September

1882 **La Nourrice de Montfermeuil** (Péricaud, Delormel) 1 act Eldorado November

1883 **La Chanson des écus** (Armand de Jallais) 1 act Eldorado 19 May

1883 **Mademoiselle Irma** (Fabrice Carré) 1 act Casino, Trouville 18 August

1886 **Joséphine vendue par ses soeurs** (Paul Ferrier, F Carré) Théâtre des Bouffes-Parisiens 19 March

1888 **Le Voyage en Écosse** (Cottin, Maurice Lecomte) 1 act Lille 17 May

1888 **Oscarine** (Charles Nuitter, Albert Guinon) Théâtre des Bouffes-Parisiens 15 October

1890 **Cendrillonnette** (w Gaston Serpette/Ferrier) Théâtre des Bouffes-Parisiens 24 January

1890 **Le Fétiche** (Ferrier, Charles Clairville) Théâtre des Menus-Plaisirs 13 March

1890 **Samsonnet** (Ferrier) Théâtre des Nouveautés 26 November

1890 **Les Douze Femmes de Japhet** (Antony Mars, Maurice Desvallières) Théâtre de la Renaissance 16 December

1891 **Le Coq** (Ferrier, Ernest Depré) Théâtre des Menus-Plaisirs 30 October

1891 **Mademoiselle Asmodée** (w Paul Lacôme/Ferrier, C Clairville) Théâtre de la Renaissance 23 November

1892 **Les Vingt-huit Jours de Clairette** (Hippolyte Raymond, Mars) Théâtre des Folies-Dramatiques 3 May

1893 **Catherinette** (Mars) 1 act Lunéville 17 July

1893 **Pierre et Paul** (Mars) 1 act Lunéville 17 July

1894 **Clary-Clara** (Raymond, Mars) Théâtre des Folies-Dramatiques 20 March

1895 **Nicol-Nick** (Raymond, Mars, Albert Duru) Théâtre des Folies-Dramatiques 23 January

1895 **La Dot de Brigitte** (w Serpette/Ferrier, Mars) Théâtre des Bouffes-Parisiens 6 May

1896 **Le Voyage de Corbillon** (Mars) Théâtre Cluny 30 January

1896 **Sa Majesté l'amour** (Mars, Maurice Hennequin) Eldorado 24 December

1897 **L'Auberge du tohu-bohu** (Maurice Ordonneau) Théâtre des Folies-Dramatiques 10 February

1897 **Les Fêtards** (Mars, M Hennequin) Palais-Royal 28 October

1898 **L'Agence Crook et Cie** (Maurice Ordonneau) Théâtre des Folies-Dramatiques 28 January

1898 **La Petite Tache** (F Carré) Théâtre des Bouffes-Parisiens 26 March

1898 **Les Quatre Filles d'Aymon** (w Lacôme/Liorat, Albert Fonteny) Théâtre des Folies-Dramatiques 20 September

1899 **La Poule blanche** (Mars, Hennequin) Théâtre Cluny 13 January

1901 **Le Jockey malgré lui** (Ordonneau, Paul Gavault) Théâtre des Bouffes-Parisiens 4 December

ROGERS, Anne (b Liverpool, 29 July 1933).

Nineteen-year-old Anne Rogers won her first success in novelettish style when she was promoted from the small rôle of Fay ('It's Never too Late to Fall in Love') to principal girl in the original club theatre production of *The Boy Friend*, creating 'I Could Be Happy with You', 'A Room in Bloomsbury' and 'The Boy Friend'. She repeated the rôle of Polly Browne in the next year's expanded version of the show and again when it moved to the West End.

In 1957 she went to America to head the first national tour of *My Fair Lady* and she repeated her Eliza Doolittle, in succession to Julie Andrews, at London's Theatre Royal, Drury Lane in 1959–61. She starred as Princess Flavia alongside Alfred Drake in a musical version of *The Prisoner of Zenda* (*Zenda*) which failed to reach Broadway and as Amalia Balash in the short-lived London production of *She Loves Me*, played Clarissa in Bickerstaff's *Lionel and Clarissa* at Guildford, toured America opposite Dick Kallman as the tough little heroine of *Half a Sixpence* (1966) and replaced Louise Troy as Maggie Hobson in the musical version of *Hobson's Choice* (*Walking Happy*) at Broadway's Lunt-Fontanne Theatre the following year.

Back in London, she paired with Ian Carmichael for the British production of *I Do! I Do!* and several years later with Teddy Green, delivering 'You Can Dance with Any Girl at All' and the 'Where Has My Hubby Gone?' blues as Lucille Early in the Theatre Royal, Drury Lane, revival of *No, No, Nanette*. She has subsequently appeared as Guinevere in *Camelot* in San Francisco, succeeded to the rôle of Dorothy Brock in Broadway's *42nd Street* and appeared as The Ghost of Christmas Past in the Long Beach Light Opera's musical *A Christmas Carol*.

ROGERS, Ginger [McMATH, Virginia Katherine] (b Independence, Mo, 16 July 1911). The musical screen's most popular dancing heroine, particularly as seen in the arms of Fred Astaire.

After early appearances in vaudeville and as a dancer, Miss Rogers began her musical-comedy career appearing on Broadway in *Top Speed* (1929, Babs Green) and in *Girl Crazy* (1930, Molly Gray) in which she introduced George Gershwin's 'Embraceable You' and 'But Not for Me'. Later the same year she began a film career in *Young Man of Manhattan* and, for the next 30 years, had an oustanding career as a dancing-singing light comedienne in musical and comedy films. She played in *Golddiggers of 1933* and *42nd Street* before being teamed for the first time with Fred Astaire in *Flying Down to Rio* (1933). Thereafter the pair appeared together in a series of 1930s films (*The Gay Divorcee, Roberta, Top Hat, Follow the Fleet, Swing Time, Shall We Dance, Carefree, The Story of Vernon and Irene Castle*) which made them into the foremost representatives

Plate 228. **Ginger Rogers** *as Auntie Mame makes a stab at a job as a manicurist and gets herself a southern aristocrat (Barry Kent) as a husband.*

of the Hollywood musical film. Her later films were largely in the non-musical sphere, although she starred, notably, in the 1943 movie version of *Lady in the Dark*. She won an Academy Award in 1940 for her performance in *Kitty Foyle*. In 1959 (May 18) she starred on British television, alongside tenor David Hughes, as Lisa Marvin in a version of the Hans May musical *Carissima*.

Miss Rogers returned to the musical stage in 1959 in a Vernon Duke musical *The Pink Jungle* (Tess Jackson) which closed on the road, toured in *Annie Get Your Gun* and *The Unsinkable Molly Brown*, and retook to the Broadway stage in 1965 to succeed to the rôle of Dolly Levi in *Hello, Dolly!* which she subsequently toured. In 1969 she recreated the rôle of *Mame* for its British production at London's Theatre Royal, Drury Lane, and she subsequently toured in the rôle created by Katharine Hepburn, as Coco Chanel in *Coco* (1971), as part of a continuing performing life which has latterly included little theatre work. In 1985 she directed a revival of *Babes in Arms*.

Autobiography: *Ginger, My Story* (Harper Collins, New York, 1991); Biographies: Richards, D: *Ginger Rogers* (Clifton, London, 1969), McGilligan, P: *Ginger Rogers* (Pyramid, New York, 1975), Croce, A: *The Fred Astaire and Ginger Rogers Book* (Galahad, New York, 1972) etc

THE ROGERS BROTHERS
ROGERS, Gus [SOLOMON, Augustus] (b New York, 1869; d 19 October 1908).
ROGERS, Max [SOLOMON, Max] (b New York, 1873; d Far Rockaway, 26 December 1932).

A song-and-dance act from their earliest teens, the brothers subsequently switched to playing German-accented knockabout comedy. They appeared at Tony Pastor's in 1889, toured in variety for four years and then formed a company of their own playing, at first, variety bills and then dipping occasionally into something a tiny bit more vertebrate. In 1897 they appeared alongside Richard Carle as Boomps (Gus) and Schrumm (Max) in *A Round of Pleasure*, and in 1899 played in the John McNally variety farce *A Reign of Error*, before far-reaching producers Klaw and Erlanger then set them up in a series of musical comedy shows with which they sought to break, or at least shake, the popularity of the rival and highly successful Dutch-comedy performers and renegade producers, Weber and Fields. The brothers appeared on Broadway successively in *The Rogers Brothers in Wall Street*, *The Rogers Brothers in Central Park*, *The Rogers Brothers in Washington*, *The Rogers Brothers at Harvard*, *The Rogers Brothers in London*, *The Rogers Brothers in Paris*, *The Rogers Brothers in Ireland* and *The Rogers Brothers in Panama*.

The younger brother, Max, was generally acknowledged as the strong half of the act. However when Gus, the elder brother who had been the business brains of the combination, died during the post-Broadway tour of *The Rogers Brothers in Panama*, Max was never able to again reach the heights that he had achieved during their partnership. He appeared in the same kind of rôles that he had played in the series in the mediocre Max Hoffman/Harry H Williams/Aaron Hoffman piece *The Young Turk* (1910, Howe Swift jr), in Lew Fields' *Hanky Panky* (1912, William Rausmitt) and in *The Pleasure Seekers* (1913, Heinrich Brobscloff) before fading out of the musical theatre.

LE ROI CAROTTE Grand opéra-bouffe féerie in 4 acts by Victorien Sardou. Music by Jacques Offenbach. Théâtre de la Gaîté, Paris, 15 January 1872.

Le Roi Carotte, for which Offenbach temporarily left his habitual text-partners to collaborate with the successful, popular (and younger) playwright Victorien Sardou, had little in common either with his great opéras-bouffes or with the hugely successful opéras-comiques with which he would end his career. In both of those areas, Offenbach's scores held an important and even predominant place, but in *Le Roi Carotte* the music was an adjunct not only of a pointedly politico-satirical text but also of a vast physical production, in the vein of *La Biche au bois* and *La Chatte blanche*, the like of which even Paris had rarely seen.

Sardou's libretto, apparently based on an idea from one of E T A Hoffman's tales, and played in four acts and 22 (later 17, later even fewer) spectacular scenes, had been written before the Franco-Prussian War and the horrors of the days of the Commune, and it warned only too accurately of the fate that awaited the Second Empire. However, it required few alterations in view of the events of the past years' hostilities before it was put on the Paris stage in 1872.

The text told the allegorical tale of penniless Prince Fridolin (Masset) who sells his ancestral armour to pay for his wedding to the rich Princess Cunégonde (Anna Judic). The suits rise up magically against him and tell him that his sacrilege means that he will be dispossessed. The evil fairy Coloquinte (Mlle Mariani) brings to life the vegetables of the kitchen garden, headed by the hideous King Carotte (Vicini), and under her enchantment the court and

Cunégonde all fall under the vegetable monarch's sway. Fridolin goes into exile, along with the faithful Robin Luron (Zulma Bouffar), the court sorcerer Truck (Alexandre) and pretty Rosée du Soir (Mlle Seveste), and seeks out the magician Quiribibi, who sends him off in quest of a magic ring which is hidden in the ruins of Pompeii. Whilst he is making his way there, via such spectacular venues as the Kingdom of Insects and Monkey Island, the people realise that the new rule is much worse than the old and revolt. The vile Carotte, defeated, goes back to being just a vegetable whilst Fridolin is restored to power with Rosée du Soir at his side.

The spectacle and the scenes of the show were supported by a score from which an Air des Colporteurs, 'Nous venons du fin fond de la Perse', an ants chorus and a Fridolin/Cunégonde duo proved the best-liked moments.

There was little doubt that, if not exactly an opérette à clef, *Le Roi Carotte* was making a specific political stand. The exiled Napoleon III in particular and the Empire in general were obviously represented by Fridolin and his friends (the foreign marriage pointed at Napoleon's union with Eugénie), and those characters were drawn markedly more sympathetically than the proletarian vegetable (Lat: radix = radical etc) rabble and their demagogue King Carotte, who was just as clearly meant to represent the left-wing speechifier Léon Gambetta, who had declared the overthrow of the Empire in 1870. Some committed critics, however, preferred to encourage the readers of their newspapers to believe the reverse.

The show had attracted great attention before its opening as much because of this pointed political content and the whisper that it actually represented the Emperor on stage as for the figures that were being touted about as to its extravagant staging. However, in a way to which Offenbach had shown himself prone in the past, producer Bouvet who had, with the composer's encouragement, spent the equivalent of nearly £14,000 on the gorgeous production at the Gaîté – a production on which the first-night curtain fell at 2.30 am – had calculated his running costs ill and, although he insisted that he could break even on a 65 per cent house, he found, after some time, that even 65 per cent of an audience was hard to come by. The piece which had been puffed as the glory of the season was barely making ends meet. Bouvet reduced his tickets to half-price, but it was not enough and *Le Roi Carotte* closed after 149 performances with certainly no profit and, if the truth were known, probably a sizeable loss.

Le Roi Carotte was nevertheless regarded as a success, or enough of a success to be given a number of productions outside France. London's large Alhambra Theatre was the first (ad H S Leigh), with a production which lost nothing in spectacular comparison with Paris. Harry Paulton (Carotte), Cornelie d'Anka (Cunégonde), Frank Celli (Fridolin), Elisa Savelli (Rosée du Soir) and Anetta Scasi (Robin Wildfire) headed a large principal cast backed up by a chorus of 50, an orchestra of 50 and a ballet of 200 which performed a sabatière, a farandole, the grand ballet of insects and a monkey divertissement, through 184 performances up to the Christmas production of its successor, *The Black Crook*, another piece based on a French grand opéra-bouffe féerie. This production of *Le Roi Carotte* was said to have lost the theatre £37,000, but it was given a revival, of nearly two further months, two years later (2 November 1874, with Paulton and Rose Bell as Robin) when a flop left a gap in the Alhambra's programme.

Augustin Daly's New York production cut out the bulk of the political allusions and the satire and made do with the fairytale and the spectacle. Mrs John Wood (Robin), John Brougham (Carotte), Rose Hersee (Rosée du Soir), Robert Craig (Fridolin), Emma Howson (Cunégonde) and Stuart Robson (Truck) headed a stellar cast, supported by the Lauri family of pantomimists and the acrobatic Majiltons, and the show played for nearly three months on Broadway, even though, as in Paris, Daly found it hard to make ends meet. It was enough of an event on Broadway, however, to spawn several burlesques: Kelly and Leon's minstrels came up with a *King Karrot* and the Theatre Comique played *King of Carrots*, without the benefit of extravagant scenery. Both of these parodies were more metropolitan than Britain's burlesque: George Thorne's *Le Raw Carrot* was produced at Margate's Theatre Royal (19 September 1873).

In Vienna (ad Julius Hopp), with a reduced visual content of 12 scenes, *König Carotte* played as a Christmas entertainment at the Theater an der Wien with Felix Schweighofer (Carrot), Jani Szika (Fridolin), Alexander Girardi (Truck), Bertha Steinher (Princess Abendroth) and Hermine Meyerhoff (Rubin) for 37 performances under the management of Maximilian Steiner – rather less than the other main Offenbach spectacular *Le Voyage dans la lune* had totalled earlier the same year.

Although neither the piece nor any portion of its score has endured as a generally popular item in the 20th century, *Le Roi Carotte* has nevertheless survived into intermittent productions and was most recently revived in Amsterdam in October 1990.

UK: Alhambra Theatre 5 June 1872; USA: Grand Opera House 26 August 1872; Austria: Theater an der Wien *König Carotte* 23 December 1876

LE ROI DE CARREAU

Opérette in 3 acts by Eugène Leterrier and Albert Vanloo. Music by Théodore de Lajarte. Théâtre des Nouveautés, Paris, 26 October 1883.

When Leterrier and Vanloo, the preferred librettists of Jules Brasseur at the Théâtre des Nouveautés, presented their *Le Roi de carreau* to the producer, they might have expected to see it confided to Planquette or to Lecocq, but Brasseur chose to commission the score from Théodore de Lajarte. Lajarte (1826–1890), a composer of much dance and march music and a number of short comic operas, including a little piece called *Le Portrait* which had recently been received at the Opéra-Comique, was not precisely a young talent, but he was new to the world of the opérette and his setting of *Le Roi de carreau* proved to be elegantly acceptable. A top-notch cast including Brasseur himself as the aged aristocrat La Roche Trumeau, and his son Albert as the comical Mistigris, Vauthier and Mlle Vaillant-Couturier in the principal singing rôles, Berthelier in the plum part of the thief-king, Tirechappe, and the favourite soubrette Mily-Meyer starred in this tale of a lost aristocratic child picked up by a vagabond and necromancer and trailed through some 18th-century risings before being restored to her rightful place.

The piece was played 88 times in its first run and revived in 1885 for several further weeks after the flop of

Planquette's *La Cremaillère* left the theatre at a temporary loss. It was subsequently played in Hungary and in Germany, but it did not achieve a wide acceptance there any more than a remusicked version did in America. Harry B Smith adapted Leterrier and Vanloo's story as *Half a King* (Knickerbocker Theater, 14 September 1896), Ludwig Englander replaced Lajarte's music, and Francis Wilson starred as Tirechappe alongside Peter Lang (Mistigris) and Lulu Glaser (Pierette) amongst much more low comedy and much less operettic singing than had been heard in the original.

Hungary: Népszinház *Tökfilkó* 14 November 1885; Germany: Friedrich-Wilhelmstädtisches Theater *Der Carreau-König* 18 February 1887

RÖKK, Marika [RÖKK, Marie Karoline Ilona] (b Cairo, 3 November ?1913). Durable Hungarian soubrette whose greatest success came in German films.

Born in Egypt of Hungarian parents, somewhen between 1906 and 1913, Rökk began her working life as a dancer in a touring circus. She made her first theatrical mark in Budapest where she took the principal soubrette rôle at the Király Színház in *Sültgalamb* (1931), as the jazz-composer Daisy (created by Rózsi Bársony in Berlin) in Hungary's production of *Ball im Savoy* (1932) and then at the Pesti Színház as the leading lady of Eisemann's highly successful modern musical comedy *Zsákbamacska* (1932). Over the next years, she moved into films, both in Hungary (*Csókolj meg édes* 1932) and in Germany, whilst still appearing from time to time on the stage in such pieces as Komjáthy and Eisemann's *A cirkusz csillaga* (Vigsinház, 1934) and Benatzky's *Egy lány, aki mindenkié* (*Wer gewinnt Colette*, Muvesz Színház 1936), but by the mid-1930s she was thoroughly established as a star of Berlin's UFA musical and revusical films (Rosika in *Leichte Cavallerie* 1935, *Heisses Blut* 1936, *Der Bettelstudent* 1936, *Und Du, mein Schatz, fährst mit* 1936, *Gasparone* 1937 etc).

When others were fleeing Germany, Rökk was moving in. She became the favourite film soubrette of the Hitler era and an important part of the German film industry through such pieces as *Hallo Janine* (1939), *Kora Terry* (1940), *Tanz mit dem Kaiser* (1941), *Hab' mich Lieb* (1942) and *Frau meiner Träume* (1944), and in the postwar years, now based in Austria, in *Das Kind der Donau* (1950), *Die Csárdásfürstin* (1951), *Die geschiedene Frau* (1953), *Maske in Blau* (1953), *Nachts im grünen Kakadu* (1957), *Bühne frei für Marika* (1958), *Die Fledermaus* (1962), *Hochzeitsnacht im Paradies* (1962) and others.

In later years, Rökk returned to the stage, appearing at Vienna's Raimundtheater in her old rôle in *Ball im Savoy* and in *Maske in Blau*, playing Dolly Levi in the German production of *Hello, Dolly!* (1968) and appearing at the Theater an der Wien in the Damon Runyon musical *Die Gräfin vom Naschmarkt* (1978). In 1992 she returned to the Budapest stage to take the rôle originally constructed for another Hungarian veteran, Hanna Honthy, in *Gräfin Mariza*.

Rökk was married in 1940 to film director Georg Jacoby (b Mainz, 23 July 1882; d Munich, 21 February 1965), the director of many operetta films through a long career, and is the mother of Gabriele Jacoby (b 1944), the Eliza Doolittle of Vienna's *My Fair Lady* and the Raina of *Helden, Helden*.

ROLYAT, Dan [TAYLOR, Herbert] (b Birmingham, 11 November 1872; d London, 10 December 1927). Acrobatic comedy star of several early 20th-century London musicals.

After an insignificant provincial beginning to his stage career, the young Rolyat was spotted by the George Edwardes organisation and put to tour in Teddy Payne's lead comedy rôle in *The Toreador*. However, Rolyat went no further in that organization and instead he went touring with Fred Karno's comedians and played in variety before being discovered a second time, by Robert Courtneidge, and given a comedy rôle in his London production of *The Dairymaids* (1906).

Courtneidge then cast him in his two most memorable rôles, as the pattering barber, Benjamin Partridge, in *Tom Jones* (1907) and as John Smith, alias Simplicitas, the comical hero of *The Arcadians* (1909, 'All Down Piccadilly'). He subsequently played the chief comic rôle in Courtneidge's *The Mousmé*, toured for him in *Princess Caprice*, and returned to London to play the professionally unemployed Slinks in a revival of *Miss Hook of Holland*, but by this time had become a depressive, suffering from the sequels of a series of stage accidents – a fall from a chandelier in *The Dairymaids* and from his horse in *The Arcadians*. He never re-established himself at his *Arcadians* level, attempted suicide, and finally died after some years away from the stage.

Rolyat was married to his *Arcadians* co-star, soprano Florence Smithson, who went through the odd bottled problem herself.

ROMBERG, Sigmund (b Nagykanizsa, Hungary, 29 July 1887; d New York, 9 November 1951). Composer of several of Broadway's most successful romantic musicals of the first decades of the 20th century.

Romberg studied the violin in his youthful years in Hungary, but he was set at first towards an adult career in engineering. However, during his technical studies in Vienna he doubled as a member of the house staff at the Theater an der Wien and the attraction of the musical theatre won out over the more practical career. He moved to London and then, in 1909, to New York where he took work as a pianist and an orchestra leader in a city restaurant whilst making his first attempts at breaking into the songwriting world. His first theatrical song was interpolated into Adolf Philipp's English version of his *Das Mitternachtsmädel* in 1913.

Romberg's earliest published works caught the eye of Jake Shubert and the young composer joined the Shubert staff to take over from the resigning Louis Hirsch the task of providing the musical piece-work the management required for their heavy turnover of revues and musical plays. He made his entrée on to Broadway as the composer of the score for the 1914 revue *The Whirl of the World* and then in quick succession sputtered out several years' worth of melodies for the splendiditious Shubert revues at the Winter Garden Theatre (*The Passing Show, Dancing Around, Maid in America, A World of Pleasure, The Show of Wonders, The Passing Show* of 1917, 1918 and 1919, *Doing Our Bit*), as well as for a bundle of soi-disant book musicals which had more than a little of revue about them (*Hands Up,* Al Jolson's *Robinson Crusoe Jr*, Justine Johnstone's *Over the Top,* Jolson's *Sinbad,* and the cheekily titled *Monte Cristo*

Jr). He also contributed to the odd play with occasional songs (*Ruggles of Red Gap*) and, more and more frequently as the fashion turned, supplied made-to-order interpolations – often considerable enough to leave little place for the melodies of the original composer – to be stuck into American versions of such Continental musical shows as Eysler's *Ein Tag im Paradies*, Leo Ascher's *Was tut man nicht alles aus Liebe*, Winterberg's *Die schöne Schwedin*, Kálmán's *Der gute Kamarad*, Straus's *Die schöne Unbekannte* and Kollo's *Wie einst im Mai*, or even a home-made piece, such as Zoel Parenteau's *Follow the Girl.*

A number of these shows were distinctly successful and in several it was Romberg's part of the music which produced the tunes that Broadway's audiences favoured. *Wie einst im Mai,* rewritten thoroughly as *Maytime,* produced the composer's first significant hit song, 'Will You Remember?' (better known by its first line, 'Sweetheart, sweetheart, sweetheart', as performed by Jeanette MacDonald), but it brought him no improved commissions as a composer from the Shuberts and he therefore departed their employ and attempted to produce his own work himself. Teamed with Max Wilner, he offered as his first production a very *Maytime*ish work called *The Magic Melody* at the Shubert Theater. It lasted 143 performances, displayed little of enduring character, and did not make money, but it had at least the merit of bringing its composer forward as having the potential to be more than the virtual hack he had been used as heretofore. The venture, however, did not bring sufficiently immediate fruits of the green and pocket-sized kind, and the partners got deeper into problems with a non-starter called *Oh! Pat* designed for Pat Rooney and another musical, *The Three Kisses,* which went into rehearsal with Vivienne Segal as star and Hassard Short directing, but which was abandoned without even opening in Springfield (January 1921).

While they tried their hand at producing rather less expensive non-musical plays, Romberg took a composing assignment, from Lew Fields, to provide some interpolations into an apparently only partly satisfactory score for a show called *Poor Little Ritz Girl* by two young writers called Rodgers and Hart. He returned to producing his own work with *Love Birds,* but the show (105 performances) did not even come up to *The Magic Melody* and Romberg found himself obliged to fold up his managerial activities and turn back to the Shuberts and to hack work.

His first adaptation during part two of his Shubert career turned out to be his most successful to date. The Franz Schubert pasticcio biomusical *Das Dreimäderlhaus* had been hugely successful wherever it had been played, and the version which Romberg and Dorothy Donnelly concocted from the dismembered parts of the previous versions and named *Blossom Time* confirmed that success in America, becoming a hardy annual of the touring circuits and a Broadway regular. *Bombo,* the new Al Jolson vehicle, for which Romberg provided the basic score, was also a fine success, and even the rag-bag revusical *The Blushing Bride* won a run and some praise for the composer, who had replaced the show's songs between its tryout and its Broadway outing. However, when the Shuberts went as far as to water down Leo Fall's outstanding score for *Die Rose von Stambul* with gobbets of Romberg, the limits of that praise were displayed.

More revusical pieces followed – *The Passing Show*s of

1923 and of 1924, *Artists and Models*, the Winter Garden shows *The Dancing Girl* and *Innocent Eyes* (for Mistinguett), and musicals such as the slim-booked *Marjorie*, but, apart from *Springtime of Youth*, an americanized version of Walter Kollo's *Sterne, die wieder leuchtet*, the Shuberts took a reef in their production of botched Continental shows. In fact, they would shortly have no need of imported operetta, for by the end of 1924 they had at last discovered that they had an American, or at least a naturalized American, operetta composer very near to hand who was capable of turning out scores which there was no excuse for botching. Romberg, who had just knocked off a considerable part of the score for Ziegfeld's production of *Annie Dear*, a musical version of Clare Kummer's *Good Gracious Annabelle*, for November, supplied the Shuberts with *The Student Prince in Heidelberg* in December. It had taken a decade, but was swiftly evident that the producers finally had that original operetta hit that Romberg had been trying so long to provide. *The Student Prince* was an enormous success and its songs 'Golden Days', 'The Drinking Song', 'Deep in My Heart, Dear', 'Just We Two', 'Come Boys, Let's All Be Gay, Boys' and the celebrated Serenade became a part of the heart of the American classic operetta repertoire.

Of Romberg's 1925 pieces, neither the musical comedy *Louie the 14th*, a vehicle for Leon Errol, nor the Ruritanian operetta *Princess Flavia*, based on *The Prisoner of Zenda* and all too obviously intended to be as much like *The Student Prince* as possible, came up to the expectations aroused by *The Student Prince* and further whetted by Friml's *The Vagabond King*, but with his next work Romberg confirmed thoroughly. *The Desert Song* teamed him with Otto Harbach and Oscar Hammerstein, who had been responsible for the libretto to Friml's *Rose Marie*, under the management of Frank Mandel and Lawrence Schwab and the result was a second huge and enduring hit and a second bundle of classic songs ('The Desert Song', 'The Riff's Song', 'One Alone', 'Romance').

The next year's bundle of shows were less successful. *Cherry Blossoms* mixed reminiscences of *Die schöne Galathee*, *The Geisha*, *David Garrick* and *Madame Butterfly* with a utilitarian score; the Barbara Frietchie musical *My Maryland* was a huge hit in Philadelphia but, in spite of a 312-performance Broadway run, left little mark on the musical world beyond the patriotic song 'Your Land and My Land'; whilst the too-routine *My Princess* and *The Love Call* (an adaptation of Augustus Thomas's *Arizona*) both went under thoroughly.

However, Romberg had proven once that he could turn out the most mechanical of music and then follow it up with a truly fine score. He did it again the following year when, whilst supplying Ziegfeld with some unexceptional numbers to set alongside some rather better Gershwin ones for *Rosalie*, he joined with Oscar Hammerstein for a third grand show and a third great score in *The New Moon* ('Lover, Come Back to Me', 'Softly, as in a Morning Sunrise', 'The Girl on the Prow', 'One Kiss', 'Stout-hearted Men'). This third great hit was, however, to be his last of real and enduring value. A further collaboration with Hammerstein produced the by no means unsuccessful South-American-romantic *Nina Rosa*, whilst *Rose de France*, a piece written for Paris, where Romberg's works had proven highly popular as fodder for the kind of opérette à grand spectacle stagings then beloved in the

French capital, had a good career at the Théâtre du Châtelet. At the same huge house, a French adaptation of *Forbidden Melody*, played as *Le Chant du Tzigane*, subsequently proved more popular than its American original. There was success, too, with the 1945 Broadway production of *Up in Central Park*, but the piece was not on the same level as the three works for which Romberg had become famous, and its 504-performance run did not preface the same kind of afterlife those shows have enjoyed.

Romberg proved his considerable worth with the scores of his trio of outstanding shows, a threesome which, along with Friml's *Rose Marie* and *The Vagabond King* and Kern's *Show Boat*, made up the nucleus of the Broadway-bred romantic operettas of the 1920s. Although his music was solidly founded in the Continental Operette tradition, it yet had a flavour to it which marked it out as being distinctly not of Hungary nor of Vienna. As early as *The Blue Paradise*, Romberg's interpolated pieces, set alongside of those of Edmund Eysler, showed a manner and a tone which identified them from those of that most warmly Viennese of Viennese composers. It was, perhaps, a measure of his knowledge of his audiences that, although his numbers had not the quality of Eysler's, it was one of his which turned out the popular success of the show. After his and its peak in the 1920s, the fashion for the American romantic operetta passed, and Romberg duly had less success. He attempted to adapt to contemporary tastes in some of his later works, but he was never as happy as in the richly lyrical Americo-European idiom which he had employed in the three shows by which his name endures.

1915 **Little Mary Mack [of Hackensack]** (w Newton Ashenfelder/Delbert E Davenport) Scranton, Pa, 19 April

1915 **Hands Up** (w E Ray Goetz/Goetz/Edgar Smith) 44th Street Theater 22 July

1915 **The Blue Paradise** (*Ein Tag im Paradies*) part-score for revised American version (Casino Theater)

1915 **Ruggles of Red Gap** (Harold Atteridge/Harrison Rhodes) Fulton Theater 24 December

1916 **Robinson Crusoe Jr** (Atteridge) Winter Garden Theater 17 February

1916 **The Girl from Brazil** (*Die schöne Schwedin*) part-score for revised American version (44th Street Theater)

1916 **Follow Me** (*Was tut man nicht alles aus Liebe*) part-score for revised American version w Robert B Smith (Casino Theater)

1916 **(Her) Soldier Boy** (*Az obsitos*) part-score for revised American version w Rida Johnson Young (Astor Theater)

1917 **My Lady's Glove** (*Die schöne Unbekannte*) part score for revised American version w Edward Paulton (Lyric Theater)

1917 **Maytime** (*Wie einst im Mai*) new score for revised American version w Young, Cyrus Wood (Shubert Theater)

1918 **Sinbad** (Atteridge) Winter Garden Theater 14 February

1918 **The Melting of Molly** (Wood/Marie Thompson Davies, Edgar Smith) Broadhurst Theater 30 December

1919 **Monte Cristo Jr** (w Jean Schwartz/Atteridge) Winter Garden Theater 12 February

1919 **The Magic Melody** (Frederic Arnold Kummer) Shubert Theater 10 November

1920 **Poor Little Ritz Girl** (w Richard Rodgers/Alex Gerber, Lorenz Hart/George Campbell) Central Theater 28 July

1921 **Love Birds** (Ballard MacDonald/Edgar Allan Woolf) Apollo Theater 15 March

1921 **Blossom Time** (*Das Dreimäderlhaus*) new arranged score for revised American version w Dorothy Donnelly (Ambassador Theater)

1921 **Bombo** (Atteridge) Jolson Theater 6 October

1922 **The Blushing Bride** (Wood/Edward Clark) Astor Theater 6 February

1922 **The Rose of Stamboul** (*Die Rose von Stambul*) part score for revised American version w Atteridge (Century Theater)

1922 **Springtime of Youth** (*Sterne, die wieder leuchtet*) part score for revised American version w Wood, Woodward (Broadhurst Theater)

1923 **The Dancing Girl** (Atteridge) Winter Garden 24 January

1923 **The Courtesan** (w Jean Schwartz/Atteridge/Atteridge, Harry Wagstaffe Gribble) Parsons' Theater, Hartford 17 October

1924 **Marjorie** (w Herbert Stothart, Stephen Jones, Philip Culkin/Clifford Grey/Fred Thompson, Atteridge) Shubert Theater 11 August

1924 **Annie Dear** (Grey/Clare Kummer) Times Square Theater 4 November

1924 **The Student Prince (in Heidelberg)** (Donnelly) Jolson Theater 2 December

1925 **Louie the 14th** (Arthur Wimperis) Cosmopolitan Theater 3 March

1925 **Princess Flavia** (ex-*A Royal Pretender*) (Harry B Smith) Century Theater 2 November

1926 **The Desert Song** (ex-*My Lady Fair*) (Otto Harbach, Oscar Hammerstein, Frank Mandel) Casino Theater 30 November

1927 **Cherry Blossoms** (H B Smith) 44th Street Theater 28 March

1927 **My Maryland** (Donnelly) Jolson Theater 12 September

1927 **My Princess** (Donnelly) Shubert Theater 6 October

1927 **The Love Call** (ex-*Bonita, Love Song, My Golden West*) (H B Smith/Edward Locke) Majestic Theater 24 October

1928 **Rosalie** (w George Gershwin/P G Wodehouse, Ira Gershwin/Guy Bolton, William Anthony McGuire) New Amsterdam Theater 10 January

1927 **The New Moon** (Hammerstein, Mandel) Chestnut Street Opera House, Philadelphia 22 December; Imperial Theater 19 September 1928

1930 **Nina Rosa** (Irving Caesar/Harbach) Majestic Theater 20 September

1931 **East Wind** (Hammerstein) Manhattan Theater 27 October

1933 **Melody** (Caesar/Edward Childs Carpenter) Casino Theater 14 February

1933 **Rose de France** (Albert Willemetz/André Mouëzy-Éon) Théâtre du Châtelet, Paris 28 October

1935 **May Wine** (Hammerstein/Mandel) St James Theater 5 December

1936 **Forbidden Melody** (Harbach) New Amsterdam Theater 2 November

1941 **Sunny River** (Hammerstein) St James Theater 4 December

1945 **Up in Central Park** (Herbert Fields, Dorothy Fields) Century Theater 27 January

1948 **My Romance** (Rowland Leigh) Shubert Theater 19 October

1954 **The Girl in Pink Tights** (Leo Robin/Jerome Chodorov, Joseph Stein) Mark Hellinger Theater 5 March

Biography: (fictionalized) Arnold, E: *Deep in My Heart* (Duell, Sloane & Pearce, New York, 1949)

ROME, Harold [Jacob] (b Hartford, Conn, 27 May 1908). Songwriter who scored several good postwar Broadway runs.

An architectural draftsman, then a summer-camp officer, Rome won his way into Broadway's eye when he provided the songs for an amateur revue, *Pins and Needles* ('Sing Me a Song With Social Significance'), which, as presented by members of the Garment Workers' Union, proved a novelty hit in a series of ever-largening theatres through more than two seasons. A second, and this time professionally produced, revue *Sing Out the News* ('Franklin D Roosevelt Jones') did not have the same novelty and lasted but four months.

A period in the wartime army, during which he contributed to the servicemen's revue *Stars and Gripes* (1943), convinced Rome to find his fun in military life and its consequences rather than in 'social signifiance' and the result – helped by an (almost) all-troops cast – was a two-year success for a further revue, *Call Me Mister* ('South America, Take it Away'). A return to the socially significant for a book musical *That's the Ticket* ('The Money Song'), produced by Joe Kipness, resulted in an out-of-town closure.

Rome found success again with the love-in-a-summer-camp show *Wish You Were Here* which sported a swimming pool on the stage and a hit-parade ballad in its croony title song, and in the following decade he turned out three more shows which posted up fine to fair runs in New York. A pulpy condensation of Marcel Pagnol's Marsellais trilogy into *Fanny* didn't offend those who hadn't heard of Pagnol, and kept on not offending them for 888 performances, a musical version of the endearing film story of *Destry Rides Again* with Andy Griffith as a memorable Destry marked up 472 performances, and *I Can Get it for You Wholesale* returned to the garment business which had started its composer on the road to success for a 300-performance run, which nevertheless landed it in the red.

In 1965 Rome provided the lyrics for the short-lived American version of the French revue *La Grosse Valise* (1965), and saw what would be his last Broadway book show, the South African-Jewish musical play *The Zulu and the Zayda*, played through an indifferent run. However, several years later, he was invited to compose the score for a Japanese production of a version of the celebrated novel *Gone With the Wind* and the resultant piece, produced in Tokyo as *Scarlett*, was sufficiently successful for an English version to be produced at London's Theatre Royal, Drury Lane. Atlanta burned convincingly and Clarke Gable and Vivien Leigh were made to sing, altogether less convincingly, through a profitable London engagement. An attempt to brave Broadway was, however, aborted on the west coast, and a second burned out in Atlanta.

At his best in the gentle fun of *Destry* or the soupy foolishness of *Wish You Were Here*, Rome was unfortunate elsewhere in being assigned subjects which required much more substantial writing, both musically and lyrically, than he provided. But if *Fanny* and *Gone with the Wind* emerged trivialized from the musicalizing process, they nevertheless found stage room through a good number of performances.

1940 **The Little Dog Laughed** (w Joseph Schrank) Garden Pier Theater, Atlantic City 14 August

1948 **That's the Ticket** (Julius Epstein, Philip Epstein) Shubert Theater, Philadelphia 24 September

1952 **Wish You Were Here** (Arthur Kober, Joshua Logan) Imperial Theater 25 June

1954 **Fanny** (S N Behrman, Logan) Majestic Theater 4 November

1959 **Destry Rides Again** (Leonard Gershe) Imperial Theater 23 April

1962 **I Can Get it for You Wholesale** (Jerome Weidman) Shubert Theater 22 March

1965 **The Zulu and the Zayda** (Howard Da Silva, Felix Leon) Cort Theater 10 November

1970 **Scarlett** (Kasuo Kikuta) Imperial Theatre, Tokyo 3 January

1972 **Gone with the Wind** revised *Scarlett* (Horton Foote) (Theatre Royal, Drury Lane)

ROSALIE Musical comedy in 2 acts and 11 scenes by Guy Bolton and William Anthony McGuire. Lyrics by P G Wodehouse and Ira Gershwin. Music by Sigmund Romberg and George Gershwin. New Amsterdam Theater, New York, 10 January 1928.

A Florenz Ziegfeld vehicle for dancing ingénue Marilyn Miller, *Rosalie* had its star playing a Princess called Rosalie from a Ruritanian country called Romanza (a not-very-subtle reference to Marie of Romania?) who falls in love with a nice American lad-in-uniform called Fay (Oliver McLennan) who airplanes to her side across the Atlantic. Her rank being the obstacle between them, it was obvious that Rosalie's father (Frank Morgan) would have to abdicate before the final curtain. Lieutenant Fay is quite within his rights to wed ex-Princess Rosalie.

Gershwin popped a couple of outcuts from *Funny Face*, one of which was 'How Long Has This Been Going On?' (performed by Bobbe Arnst as soubrette Mary), into a hurriedly compiled score which also included 'Oh, Gee! Oh, Joy!' and 'Everybody Knows I Love Somebody', as well as some not top-drawer and rather reminiscent bits of Romberg. Staged with lavish splendour, Ruritanian hussars, a ballroom with a ballet (by Urban and Seymour Felix respectively) and any other production value available, *Rosalie* drew for 335 performances on Broadway. It did not export, but MGM subsequently decided that the book was worth filming and a cinematic piece which went under the title of *Rosalie* was produced with a wholly different score (by Cole Porter) and a cast headed by Eleanor Powell, Nelson Eddy, and Morgan repeating a version of his original rôle.

ROSE, Billy [ROSENBERG, William Samuel] (b New York, 6 September 1899; d Montego Bay, 10 February 1966). Broadway showman.

After a ten-year career as a songwriter which included a lyric credit on such theatrical numbers as 'A Cup of Coffee, a Sandwich and You' (*Charlot's Revue of 1926*), 'More Than You Know', 'Great Day!', 'Without a Song' (*Great Day*) and others – some of which were ghosted for him by other less pecunious writers – Rose ventured as a Broadway producer.

He staged several revues, but is largely remembered for his extravagant production of Rodgers and Hart's circus musical *Jumbo* which became *Billy Rose's Jumbo* when filmed. He also produced Oscar Hammerstein's *Carmen Jones* (1943), named the old National Theatre after himself, rescued the famed Ziegfeld Theater and, after accepting the plaudits, sold it to developers, and was flamboyantly in charge of the Diamond Horseshoe club in the late 1930s and 1940s.

Rose was married for a period to the revue comedienne Fanny Brice.

1929 **Great Day** (Vincent Youmans/w Edward Eliscu/William Cary Duncan, John Wells) Cosmopolitan Theater 17 October

Autobiography: *Wine, Women and Words* (Simon & Schuster, New York, 1948); Biographies: Gottlieb, P: *The Nine Lives of Billy Rose* (Crown, New York, 1968), Conrad, E: *Billy Rose: Manhattan Primitive* (World, Cleveland, 1968), Nelson, S: *Only a Paper Moon: The Theatre of Billy Rose* (UMI Research Press, Michigan, 1987)

ROSE, George (b Bicester, 19 February 1920; d Dominican Republic, 5 May 1988). British character actor who became Broadway's standard Englishman.

For a number of years a member of the Old Vic Company and the company at the Shakespeare Theatre at Stratford-on-Avon, Rose made his first musical appearance in 1959 in the Royal Court Theatre's revue *Living for Pleasure*. He made his Broadway début in a musical as Henry Horatio Hobson in the *Hobson's Choice* musical *Walking Happy* (1966) and thereafter became a favourite choice for senior English rôles in America. He appeared at the City Center as Doolittle in a revival of *My Fair Lady* and at the Eugene O'Neill Theatre in a combination of English character rôles in the British musical of the *Canterbury Tales* (1969), and later the same year had a non-English assignment when he appeared as Louis Greff in *Coco*, a rôle which he also later toured.

Subsequent musical assignments, interleaved with non-musical rôles, included Lutz in *The Student Prince* (1973, tour), a repeat season as Doolittle in a Broadway revival of *My Fair Lady* (1976, Tony Award), Captain Hook to the *Peter Pan* of Sandy Duncan in the Broadway revival of the American musical-comedy version of Barrie's play, the Major General in Broadway's bounced-up *Pirates of Penzance* and the principal comic rôle in the music-hall mystery *(The Mystery of Edwin) Drood*.

Rose was murdered in the Dominican Republic in 1988.

ROSE, L Arthur (b Edinburgh, 27 September 1887; d 1958). Scots playwright who wrote four British musical-comedy successes.

An actor, and for a period a minor producing manager, Rose began writing plays and sketches for the variety stage in 1911. He had his first experience of the musical theatre when he wrote *Pretty Peggy*, a musical play which was in the nature of an extended variety sketch, with and for comedian Charles Austin. Instead of touring the halls, as originally intended, *Pretty Peggy* was taken up by C B Cochran and shown at the Prince's Theatre for a very respectable and surprising 168 performances.

In spite of this success, Rose's name did not appear on a musical-theatre bill again for 16 years, but when it did he garnered an even greater success than the first time, with a racing farce written to feature another comic, Lupino Lane, as a little chap called Bill Snibson. *Twenty to One* ran 383 performances at the London Coliseum and became a perennial vehicle for Lane. As a result, Rose, in collaboration with Douglas Furber, brought the star out a new Bill Snibson adventure. In fact, Snibson-Lane merely remained the same cheeky cockney character, and the events of the new piece, *Me and My Girl* (1937), were in no way a sequel to the earlier one. *Me and My Girl* had an extended wartime run, was regularly revived thereafter, and ultimately won Rose a posthumous Tony Award for the Broadway reproduction of a British revival half a century on.

Rose did not contribute to the Lane musicals which followed *Me and My Girl*, but returned principally to writing for revue and variety, and collaborated only on one further musical, a vehicle for Jack Buchanan, *It's Time to Dance*, which kept his hundred per cent success record intact.

1919 **Pretty Peggy** (Archie Emmett Adams/Douglas Furber/w Charles Austin) Kilburn Empire 25 August

1935 **Twenty to One** (Billy Mayerl/Frank Eyton) London Coliseum 12 November

1937 **Me and My Girl** (Noel Gay/w Furber) Victoria Palace 16 December

1943 **It's Time to Dance** (Kenneth Leslie-Smith et al/several/w Furber) Winter Garden Theatre 22 July

ROSE DE FRANCE Opérette à grand spectacle in 2 acts by André Mouëzy-Éon. Lyrics by Alfred Willemetz. Music by Sigmund Romberg. Théâtre du Châtelet, Paris, 28 October 1933.

The great success of the works of Sigmund Romberg in France, and notably at the Châtelet where the 237 performances of *Robert le Pirate* (*The New Moon*) had been followed by some 700 of *Nina Rosa*, inspired the theatre's director Maurice Lehmann to commission a new work from the composer, especially for the Châtelet. The libretto, with a title that nicely recalled another American hit in *Rose-Marie*, was provided by Lehmann's faithful Mouëzy-Éon and was constructed with a wise eye on the spectacular demands of the big Châtelet stage.

Princess Marie-Louise of France (Danielle Brégis) escapes from the strictures of the court and encounters a young sculptor called Beauval (Roger Bourdin). However, her idyll is betrayed by her lady-in-waiting Athénaïs (Simone Faure) and Beauval, caught in a duel, is condemned to the galleys. When Marie-Louise is sent to Spain, where she is to be diplomatically wed to the King (Pierre Morin), she finds that Beauval is a slave on her ship. The Princess helps him to escape, but he is wounded whilst protecting her in a skirmish in the mountains and, when she steals away from her escort to go to her beloved's side, the King arrives at Burgos to meet his bride. Athénaïs takes her place and, since the King seems content, Marie-Louise lets things remain that way. The ambitious lady-in-waiting will be Queen of Spain and the Princess will wed her sculptor in anonymity.

Whether Romberg's score for *Rose de France* was new, or whether at least some of it was taken from some of the many of his scores unknown in France, it proved more than apt for the occasion. The hits of the show were Mlle Brégis's Marche Militaire 'Quand les soldats vont au pas' and the big baritone/soprano waltz duet of the evening 'Pour vivre auprès de vous', which was supplemented by two other duos, one in tango time ('Rose de France') and the other another waltz ('Frivolette'). The baritone sang a galley-slave solo and insisted 'Je vous aimerai dans l'ombre', the soprano had a letter song, and the light-comedy content was supplied by Bach and Monique Bert, as faithful servants of the Princess, with a couple of one-steps ('Pour fair' le tournedos', 'Le Baron de Ragotin').

Rose de France had all the extras expected in a Châtelet show in plenty: the 15 scenes began with a vista of the Pont Neuf with a lacemakers' ballet, moved to the kitchens where a childrens' little chef ballet was danced, then to

'une fête de nuit au Château de Versailles' where the première danseuse and her partner performed a divertissement. The royal galley, a storm in the Pyrénées and a Spanish gipsy encampment with a suitable gipsy ballet succeeded each other in supplying the visuals, and the crowning of the Spanish monarch brought the spectacle to its peak. One of the less common features, however, also proved one of the most popular: the performance of the comedian Arnaudy in the travesty rôle of the Princess's old duenna the Duchesse de Terra-Nova.

Rose de France proved all that could have been wished and remained at the Châtelet for 476 performances before going into the provinces but, in an era when Romberg was decidedly short on Broadway successes, it did not appear in America.

ROSE DE NOËL Opérette à grand spectacle in 2 acts by Raymond Vincy. Music by Franz Lehár adapted by Paul Bonneau and Miklos Rekaï. Théâtre du Châtelet, Paris, 20 December 1958.

At his death, Franz Lehár allegedly left an unused and undated score which had been intended to illustrate a libretto by Károly Kristof which had curiously never got further than an outline. When this score was brought to light in Budapest, the music and its discoverer, Professor Rekaï, were taken to Paris by Maurice Lehmann of the Théâtre du Châtelet and the 17 pieces of 'exhumed' music worked into a score around a libretto written by Raymond Vincy and based on the old scenario.

The plot showed up the age of the scenario. Gadabout Count Michael Andrássy (André Dassary) is ordered to a distant provincial post by an Emperor tired of his excesses. Since Michael is gadding and cannot be found, his friend Sándor (Henri Chananon) takes his place to avoid the imperial thunders. When Michael finally gets to his exile, he lets Sándor carry on his aristocratic masquerade while he falls in love with local Vilma (Nicole Broissin). When all comes out, the girl rejects the well-known rake in horror, but all ultimately turns out all right on the Christmas eve of the show's title. Rosine Brédy was the soubrette, Dominique Tirmont the heroine's father, and Henri Bédex (Popelka) provided the comedy.

The score (which may, or as many believe, may not be genuine Franz) was topped up with several Lehár bon-bons including the 'Gold and Silver Waltz' for dance music, but tenor Dassary made much of 'Déjà' (with violin accompaniment), 'Rose de Noël' (with Mlle Broissin), 'Mon ciel et ma chanson' and 'Rendez-vous d'amour' and *Rose de Noël*, produced with the Châtelet's usual splendour, ran for 415 performances in Paris before going on to a kind of enduring provincial life which had been denied to most of Lehár's other, more legitimate but less glamorously mounted works.

Recording: Original cast (Véga, Decca)

LA ROSE DE SAINT-FLOUR Opérette in 1 act by Michel Carré. Music by Jacques Offenbach. Théâtre des Bouffes-Parisiens, Paris, 12 June 1856.

One of the most generally successful of Offenbach's early rural operéttes, the three-handed *La Rose de Saint-Flour* centred on pretty auvergnate Pierrette (Hortense Schneider) and her two lodgers, the shoemaker Charpailloux (Charles Petit) and the potmaker Marcachu

(Pradeau), both of whom sigh after their landlady. On her fête day, each gives her a gift of something that he has made: a pair of dancing shoes from Charpailloux and a stout iron cooking pot from Marcachu. Pierrette puts the pot to good use to make the traditional local cabbage soup, but when the two men begin to fight over her, she takes the side of the shoemaker. The disappointed Marcachu breaks all the crockery and runs off with his pot, full of soup, but finally he returns apologetically bringing some new dishes and the soup and the three dance and eat together. The score consisted of an overture and seven straightforward musical pieces sung in jolly auvergnat dialect: Pierrette's dilemma 'Entre les deux mon coeur balance', the practical gift of Marcachu ('Chette marmite neuve') and the frivolous one of Charpailloux ('Pour les petits pieds'), two duos and two pieces for all three, the list ending in a lively bourrée which meant happily ever after.

Helped on its way in its first performances by the young Hortense Schneider's portrayal of Pierrette, *La Rose de Saint-Flour* confirmed itself as a happy little favourite in Paris before being shown in foreign parts. In London, J A Shaw (Michele), Mme d'Este Finlayson (Lisette) and Thomas Whiffen (Potatou) appeared in *Too Many Cooks* (ad T German Reed) at the Gallery of Illustration, but the first regular theatre performance was at the Gaiety Theatre where, as *The Rose of Auvergne* (ad H B Farnie) the piece was the second short Offenbach work, in the wake of the success of *Lischen et Fritzchen*, to be produced by John Hollingshead. Annie Tremaine played Fleurette, with Charles Lyall and Edward Perrini as her lovers, and the opérette was reprised regularly for a number of years as an opening item on the Gaiety bill. It was subsequently played in another English version as *Spoiling the Broth* – a version which was even played on the vast stage of the Alhambra – and was also seen in its original French at the Charing Cross Theatre (1870, w *Les Pompiers de Nanterre*).

The New York Théâtre Français performed the original French version of *La Rose de Saint-Flour* a number of times during the 1860s, and it was also played regularly by Bateman's and by Grau and Chizzola's opéra-bouffe companies, amongst others, in the 1870s. The little English operetta company headed by Susan Galton played *Too Many Cooks* in America in their bills during the late 1860s, whilst Kelly and Leon's Minstrels performed their own English-language version, with Leon as a travesty Lisette to the Brown of Kelly and the Smith of S S Purdy, and Henri Laurent's company also travelled *The Rose of Auvergne* in its repertoire. Kelly and Leon later played their version in Australia (Queen's Theatre 9 March 1878) and New Zealand as well, but the piece had already been seen in the colonies as early as 1871.

In Vienna, again, the piece was first introduced in its French original, played by the Bouffes-Parisiens company during their visit to the Theater am Franz-Josefs-Kai in 1861 with Lucille Tostée, Desmonts and Marchand as its cast, but it was also later produced in a German version at the Strampfertheater. An Hungarian version (ad Ferenc Toldy) was first seen in 1875, but central Europe had different favourites in the Offenbach repertoire and *La Rose de Saint-Flour* did not win the same strong popularity there as it did in its French and English versions.

Austria: Theater am Franz-Josefs-Kai (Fr) 6 July 1861, Strampfertheater 19 February 1872; USA: Théâtre Français

14 February 1863, Washington Hall, Williamsburgh *Too Many Cooks* 22 September 1868, Kelly and Leon's (Eng) 24 October 1870; UK: Gallery of Illustration *Too Many Cooks* 1 September 1864, Gaiety Theatre *The Rose of Auvergne* 8 November 1868; Australia: Princess Theatre, Melbourne 30 August 1871; Hungary: Népszinház *A saint-fleuri rósza* 12 November 1875.

ROSE MARIE Musical play in 2 acts by Otto Harbach and Oscar Hammerstein II. Music by Rudolf Friml and Herbert Stothart. Imperial Theater, New York, 2 September 1924.

Although the Broadway musical theatre had established itself worldwide with its light-handed song-and-dance shows – *Going Up, Irene, Mercenary Mary, No, No, Nanette, Sally* and their kind – American producers had largely gone for imported shows or composers when the more musically substantial, romantic type of operetta was required. Since the days of Victor Herbert and *Mlle Modiste* and *Naughty Marietta*, there had been few local successes in the operettic vein, but the enormous triumph of *Blossom Time* (*Das Dreimäderlhaus*) had shown postwar producers that there was certainly an audience for a robustly sentimental show on classic light-opera lines. The show which gave the Broadway musical its first major international success of the kind was *Rose Marie*.

Rose Marie was commissioned by Arthur Hammerstein from his nephew, Oscar II, and from Otto Harbach and composer Rudolf Friml with both of whom the younger Hammerstein had worked regularly since the pair's first collaboration a dozen years earlier on *The Firefly*. *The Firefly*, built for an operatic diva, had been the last example of a memorable Broadway operetta, since which Harbach and Friml had concentrated on following the fashion for light comedy and dancing musicals, from the well-named *High Jinks* to the jaunty *Blue Kitten* of two seasons previously. Harbach and Hammerstein had also collaborated, under Arthur Hammerstein's management, on three musicals: Herbert Stothart's *Tickle Me* and *Jimmie* and the previous year's colourfully Ruritanian Youmans/Stothart success *Wildflower*.

Using the producer's suggested Canadian setting as a backdrop, the authors put together a plot which was, perhaps, rather more dramatic than was standard and

Plate 229. *Wanda (Mira Nirska) stabs her drunken lover, Black Eagle (P Parsons) to death under the gaze of the machinating Hawley (Brian Gilmour) in London's* **Rose Marie***.*

which had a distinct air of Willard Mack's 1917 play *Tiger Rose* to it. The plot turned on a murder, the murder of a drunken villain by his mistress, and the use of that murder by the woman's ex-lover to entrap his rival for the love of the show's heroine. If the terms in which that tale was told were less than precisely powerful, if the dramatic facts were rather drowned in romantic considerations and low comedy, and if the murderess in the case was also the entertainment's principal dancer, the killing nevertheless remained as a dramatic spine for what producer Hammerstein referred to mouthfillingly as 'an operatic musical play'.

Rose Marie la Flamme (Mary Ellis), the sister of a French Canadian trapper (Edward Cianelli), is in love with miner Jim Kenyon (Dennis King) rather than the well-off city man Edward Hawley (Frank Greene) whom her brother would have her wed. When Hawley's half-caste ex-mistress Wanda (Pearl Regay) stabs her drunken Indian concubine (Arthur Ludwig) to death, Hawley engineers it that the suspicion falls on Kenyon, and the miner is forced to flee before the Mounties. Blackmailed by her brother, who agrees not to reveal Kenyon's escape route if she will agree to marry Hawley, Rose Marie is gradually persuaded that Jim really is a killer, but Kenyon's comical little friend Hard-Boiled Herman (William Kent) tricks the truth from Wanda. When the guilty girl realizes, rather late, that she is going to lose Hawley to Rose Marie, she interrupts their wedding with her dramatic revelation. With the air now cleared, Rose Marie and Jim can finally get together. The comic element of the piece was provided by another triangle in which both Herman and the Mountie Captain Malone (Arthur Deagon) battled for the hand of soubrette Lady Jane (Dorothy Mackaye).

The music of *Rose Marie*, and most particularly the romantic music, was one of the show's principal assets. Rose Marie and Kenyon joined together in the Indian Love Call, a song which in later decades would become mocked – for its words rather than its melody – as the representative of old-fashioned musical theatre. The song had nothing of the old-fashioned or even the conventional about it in 1924 and it won an outstanding success as sung by King and Miss Ellis. King had a strong, lilting song (w Deagon) in praise of 'Rose Marie', Herbert Stothart combined with Friml on a ringing ensemble for 'The Mounties' and a pounding stage-Indian ballet ('Totem Tom-Tom') both of which backed up set pieces with unusual strength, and, in contrast, Friml provided a delicately dancing melody for the heroine's song about the 'Pretty Things' that money and Hawley can buy her, a piece which proved much more popular than the waltz 'Door of my Dreams' which the composer had thought would be the hit of the evening. Stothart was also responsible for some of the comic numbers, of which Herman's profession of faith, 'Hard-Boiled Herman', stood up the best in front of the tidal wave of success that attended the lyric part of the score.

The producer extended his determination that the production was 'operatic' by announcing that he would not list the numbers separately in the programme (a determination echoed 60 years later by Andrew Lloyd Webber's refusal to individually track his cast recordings) as they were part of the action. Of course, the comedy pieces in particular were nothing of the kind. The action surrounding them was as often as not there only to justify the songs and a piece such as 'Totem Tom-Tom' with its balletic murderess at its head was inserted solely as incidental spectacle. However, for anyone who cared, many of the numbers were indeed solidly linked to the characters or tale, just as they had been in musical theatre since the days of such 'realistic' musicals as *Le Mariage aux lanternes* and well before.

Hammerstein also posted up his serious intentions by his lead casting. Rose Marie was played not by an established star, from either the opera or musical stage, but by the young Mary Ellis who had played supporting rôles alongside Chaliapin and Caruso at the Metropolitan Opera at a very young age before quitting opera for the straight theatre. *Rose Marie* was her only musical rôle in America. Leading man King, like Miss Ellis, had abandoned a lyric career begun in Britain for Shakespeare on Broadway, but it was Miss Ellis who got the big billing, even if it were under the title.

The spectacular part of *Rose Marie* was also contributory to its success. Arthur Hammerstein's Canadian settings as given shape by Gates and Morange were dazzling, the towering cliffs and mountains adding, *Maid of the Mountains*-style, both to the dramatic moments and to the long-distance moments of the romance, the 'gowns and costumes' of Charles Le Maire no less attractive and very numerous on the backs of the large company, whilst David Bennett's arrangment of the dance of the massed ranks of Red Indian girls who featured in 'Totem Tom-Tom' was a show-stopper. If Hammerstein had operatic pretensions with *Rose Marie*, he certainly did not allow that to stop him taking out an insurance on success with a lavishly spectacular stage production.

Rose Marie was a huge hit on Broadway. One of the biggest of all time, even if, in cold figures, in the ultimate tot-up its run came to just 557 performances, a figure inferior to those chalked up by *Irene* and such old-time favourites as *Erminie*, *Adonis* or *A Trip to Chinatown*, and on a par with *Florodora* and *Sally*. The first touring companies were on the road before the Broadway run was six months old. They were joined soon after by others, and these tours continued way beyond the end of the New York run. Alfred Butt took up the piece for London and produced it at the venerable Theatre Royal, Drury Lane, which had been struggling along on a mixture of spectacular drama, pantomime and even films. Another young American performer, Edith Day (the original Broadway and London star of *Irene*), starred opposite Derek Oldham and comedian Billy Merson and, once again, the piece found a huge following which resulted in an 851-performance, two-year run and the definitive re-orientation of the famous house to musical productions.

In Britain, as in America, the touring companies were on the road whilst the metropolitan production ran on, but London, unlike New York, also subsequently welcomed *Rose Marie* back on several occasions. Miss Day starred in a 1929 revival at Drury Lane (100 performances) and Raymond Newell played Kenyon at the Stoll Theatre in 1942, but a 1960 revival at the Victoria Palace done with neither the conviction nor the means of the original only reinforced the prejudices of those for whom such pieces were by then 'old-fashioned'.

The show was produced by J C Williamson Ltd in Australia with Harriet Bennett (Rose Marie), Reginald

Dandy (Jim) and Frederick Bentley (Herman) in the leading rôles, and once again it scored a major success through nine months in Sydney and a further six in Melbourne (Her Majesty's Theatre 26 February 1927), but *Rose Marie*'s longest run of all came, wholly surprisingly, in Paris. The Isola brothers who ran the Théâtre Mogador visited London and saw *No, No, Nanette* and *Rose Marie*. They bought both and staged *Nanette* first with such success that they were obliged, eventually, to cut short the show's run in order to stage *Rose-Marie* (ad Roger Ferréol, Saint-Granier, and with a hyphen) within their option period. But this time the success was even greater, and by the time *Rose-Marie* closed, the production had created a Parisian long-run record with 1,250 consecutive performances.

Two young performers, Cloé Vidiane and Madeleine Massé, alternated in the title-rôle, the baritone Robert Burnier was Jim, Félix Oudart was Malone and the comic Boucot appeared as Herman whilst the world-travelling American dancer June Roberts led 'Totem Tom-Tom' (choreography credited to co-director J Kathryn Scott). The piece was luxuriantly staged, with the individually credited mountain scenes, the Totem Pole Hotel, a maison de couture (with a mannequin parade) and a Quebec ballroom commissioned from four different designers, decorated by hundreds of costumes, and the music played by an orchestra of 50. There had been spectacular musical plays in Paris for decades and decades, but *Rose-Marie* set off a new fashion for opérette à grand spectacle which would last for many years until it ultimately destroyed itself and the musical theatre in Paris.

The Mogador brought back *Rose-Marie* in 1930 (20 January), 1939 (1 June), 1963 (23 November with Marcel Merkès and Paulette Merval) and in 1970 (19 December, starring Bernard Sinclair, Angelina Cristi), it was played at the Châtelet in 1940 (19 December with no less a Rose-Marie than Fanély Revoil) and 1944 (21 October, with Madeleine Vernon), at the Théâtre de l'Empire in 1947 and 1950 (12 May with Merval) and most recently at the Théâtre de la Porte-Saint-Martin (18 February 1981) confirming itself as one of the staples of the musical theatre repertoire in France.

The show opened almost simultaneously with its Paris production both in Germany (ad Rideamus) where, in spite of Hammerstein's personal supervision, operatic tenor Aagard Oestvig and soprano Margarethe Pfahl Wallerstein did not succeed in making the conventions of the Broadway operetta appeal, and in Hungary where Irén Biller and Glenn Ellyn starred at Budapest's Király Színház (ad Adorján Stella, Imre Harmath) with rather more in the way of response. The German version was introduced at the Brussels Stadttheater in 1933 (28 January).

In 1928 *Rose Marie* was also made into a film with Joan Crawford starred as a silent Rose-Marie (apparently with a hyphen!). If the tale without the songs was good enough in 1928, 1936 preferred it the other way round and the libretto was rewritten for a second MGM film in which Jeanette MacDonald, Nelson Eddy, Allan Jones and James Stewart participated. The score was also punctuated with bits of opera, 'Dinah', 'Some of These Days' and two extra Stothart songs. A third version, again rewritten, featured Ann Blyth, Howard Keel, Bert Lahr and Fernando Lamas and four additional songs dubiously credited to the aged

Friml (who sat in an office at MGM and magically produced songs without a pen) as well as 'The Mountie That Never Got His Man'.

The question of the hyphen in Rose(-)Marie has become a cause celèbre amongst those to whom such things matter. Stanley Green and Gerald Bordman, who must be considered the arbiters in such matters of life and death, finally reached the compromise shortly before Stanley's death that the stage show had no hyphen (except in France), whilst the film did. So why not.

UK: Theatre Royal, Drury Lane 20 March 1925; Australia: Her Majesty's Theatre, Sydney 29 May 1926; France: Théâtre Mogador 9 April 1927; Germany: Admiralspalast 30 March 1928; Hungary: Király Színház 31 March 1928; Films: MGM 1928 (silent), 1936 and 1954

Recordings: London cast recordings (WRC), selections (Columbia, Capitol, Decca, RCA, WRC etc), film soundtrack 1936 (Hollywood Soundstage), film soundtrack 1954 (MGM), French version (Pathé, CBS etc), Russian version (Melodiya) etc

ROSEN AUS FLORIDA Operette in 3 acts by A M Willner and Heinz Reichert. Music by Leo Fall arranged by Erich Wolfgang Korngold. Theater an der Wien, Vienna, 22 February 1929.

Rosen aus Florida was an Americo-Ruritanian musical with a score put together from music left by Leo Fall at his death, and produced by Hubert Marischka at the Theater an der Wien for a run of 216 performances. Set in New York and Palm Beach with a third act in a Paris cabaret of 'Zum lustigen Emigranten' where titled Russian émigrés work as barman, vocalist and liftboy (a situation 'borrowed', shortly after, for the better-known musical *Balalaika*), *Rosen aus Florida* took three acts to bring together the self-made millionaire Goliath Armstrong (Hubert Marischka), who hasn't got time to fall in love, and the lady who makes him change his mind when it is almost too late. She is the Russian Princess Irina Natyschkin (Rita Georg) and she supplies the romantic music in solo (a first-act 'Heimatlied', a second-act 'Mir ist, als lag' mein ganzes Glück') and in duet with Goliath ('Rote Rosen', 'Das Schönste der Wunder auf Erden'). It was, however, he who was given the show's catchiest number, 'Wer kann die Frauen je ergründen?'. Dorrit (Ossi Oswalda), the girl Goliath didn't quite wed, helped supply the lighter moments alongside his secretary Tommy (Fritz Steiner) and another émigré, Fürst Nikifor Wladimirowitsch Urusoff (Fritz Imhoff).

The show's satisfactory run in Vienna didn't encourage any exportation at a time when Fall's name had become a little forgotten in the rage for more up-to-date things.

ROSENFELD, Sydney (b Richmond, Va, 26 October 1855; d New York, 13 June 1931). Broadway 'character' who got himself involved in several decades of theatrical projects.

Journalist, magazine editor, playwright, adapter, an unembarrassed cobbler-together of plays and musical libretti, on occasions both producer and director, and even, at one stage, briefly the proprietor of his own classical drama company, the Century Players (1904), Rosenfeld began his career in the theatre by writing one-act pieces for minstrel shows. His first Broadway script was a burlesque of the play *Rose Michel* (1874), and a stream of all kinds of other pieces followed it on to the New York stage.

An early attempt at the regular musical theatre with an adaptation of Genée's *Der Seekadet* as *The Sea Cadet* fared poorly when a much superior version (*The Royal Middy*) beat it to town, but other adaptations from the German, such as versions of Millöcker's *Der Feldprediger* (*The Black Hussar*) and Genée's *Nanon*, were considerable successes. His theatrical activities ended him in prison when he pirated Gilbert and Sullivan's *The Mikado* and produced it at the Union Square Theatre (1885), and he returned to wreaking his will on the less protesting German works, supplying versions of such as *Der Zigeunerbaron* and *Prinz Methusalem* to the Broadway stage. When he attempted a version of Audran's *Serment d'amour* he again struck a rival production, and this time both sank, but he did very much better with Lecocq's *La Jolie Persane* whose new title, *The Oolah*, highlighted the different emphases given such shows on Broadway – the girl lost the title to the all-important low comedian. But Rosenfeld's emphases ensured the opérette its longest run anywhere in the world.

Rosenfeld ventured with an original libretto for the first time when he turned the famous short story *The Lady or the Tiger* into a musical for John McCaull's comic-opera company and, with a certain bravado, arranged simultaneous premières in New York and London – the latter a matinée at the roughish suburban Elephant and Castle Theatre. It was typical of Rosenfeld that he provided an ending for the celebrated endless piece, but even that was not enough to make the show more than a half-success. He continued his producing efforts, combining episodically with the marginally more reliable George Lederer, an association which led him to becoming the author of the script for the Casino's *The Passing Show*, generally quoted as being the first genuine American revue. Many of his subsequent pieces, nominally musicals, also had much of the revue about them (*The Giddy Throng*, *A Round of Pleasure* etc), dissolving away into concerts halfway through in the manner of the old British variety musicals, but some, like the romantic southern-American comic opera *The Mocking Bird*, proved that Rosenfeld could, when he wished, turn out material that was better than run-of-the-mill.

For all his easy-going prolificity, his often hurried and shoddy work, Rosenfeld was not wholly devoid of ability, as his adaptations of such straight pieces as *Dr Clyde* and *At the White Horse Tavern* (*Im weissen Rössl*) proved, but eventually his theatrical cheek proved insufficient to get him work and his later years were spent rather pathetically attempting to drum himself up engagements with out-of-date showbizzy extravagance.

Rosenfeld's brother, Monroe H Rosenfeld, also tried his hand in the musical and theatrical world, turning out songs with such titles as 'Those Wedding Bells Shall Not Ring Out!' and 'With All Her Faults I Love Her Still'.

1876 **Rosemishell, or Oh! My Daughter** (pasticcio) Eagle Theater 24 January
1876 **The Pique Family** (pasticcio) Eagle Theater 13 March
1879 **The Sea Cadet, or The Very Merry Mariner** (*Der Seekadet*) American version (Fifth Avenue Theater)
1882 **Apajune the Water Sprite** (*Apajune, der Wassermann*) American version (Bijou Theater)
1885 **Ixion** all-female version adapted from Burnand's burlesque 4 February
1885 **Amorita** (*Pfingsten in Florenz*) American version w George Goldmark (Casino Theater)

1885 **The Black Hussar** (*Der Feldprediger*) American version (Wallack's Theater)
1885 **Nanon** American version (Casino Theater)
1886 **The Mystic Isle** (John B Grant) Philadelphia 2 October
1886 **The Gipsy Baron** (*Der Zigeunerbaron*) American version (Casino Theater)
1886 **The Bridal Trap** (*Serment d'amour*) American version (Bijou Theater)
1888 **The Lady or the Tiger** (Julius J Lyons) Bijou Theater, New York and Elephant & Castle Theatre, London 7 May
1888 **Prince Methusalem** American version (Bijou Theater)
1889 **The Oolah** (*La Jolie Persane*) American version (Broadway Theater)
1893 **The Rainmaker of Syria** (aka *The Woman King*) (Rudolf Aronson) Casino Theater 25 September
1893 **Fritz in Prosperity** Grand Opera House 23 October
1895 **The Twentieth Century Girl** (Ludwig Englander) Bijou Theater 25 January
1898 **A Dangerous Maid** (*Heisses Blut*) English version (Casino Theater)
1898 **Lili Tse** 1 act English version (Daly's Theater)
1901 **The King's Carnival** (A Baldwin Sloane) New York Theater 13 May
1901 **The Supper Club** (various) Winter Garden Theater 23 December
1902 **The Mocking Bird** (Sloane) Bijou Theater 10 November
1902 **The Hall of Fame** (Sloane/George V Hobart) New York Theater 3 February
1905 **The Rollicking Girl** revised version of *A Dangerous Maid* (W T Francis) Herald Square Theater 1 May
1906 **The Vanderbilt Cup** (Robert Hood Bowers/Raymond Peck) Broadway Theater 16 January
1908 **Mlle Mischief** (*Ein tolles Mädel*) English version (Lyric Theater)
1911 **The Happiest Night of His Life** (Albert von Tilzer/w Junie McCree) Criterion Theater 20 February
1911 **Jumping Jupiter** (Karl Hoschna/w Richard Carle) Criterion Theater 6 March
1912 **The Opera Ball** (*Der Opernball*) American version w Clare Kummer (Liberty Theater)
1912 **The Rose of Panama** (*Kreolenblut*) English version fr trans Maurice Hageman w John L Shine (Daly's Theater)
1913 **Hop o' My Thumb** American version w Manuel Klein (Manhattan Opera House)

THE ROSE OF PERSIA, or The Story Teller and the Slave Comic opera in 2 acts by Basil Hood. Music by Arthur Sullivan. Savoy Theatre, London, 29 November 1899.

The sticky patch through which the Savoy Theatre and Richard D'Oyly Carte had passed in the years since the collapse of the Gilbert and Sullivan partnership finally got a little less sticky when Sullivan teamed up with Basil Hood, the experienced librettist and lyricist of such popular successes as *Gentleman Joe*, to write *The Rose of Persia*. Hood had begun his career writing in a literary and 'Gilbertian' style before finding his biggest successes with the more popular brand of musical comedy, and now he returned to the comic-opera manner of his early works with a script for Sullivan which was based on the Arabian Nights tale of Abu Hasan.

The eccentric, rich Hassan (Walter Passmore) holds open house to the scroungers of Baghdad, and one night his uninvited guests include the disguised Sultana Rose-in-Bloom (Ellen Beach Yaw) who has sneaked out for a look at the world and then been unable to get back into the palace. When the Sultan Mahmoud (Henry Lytton) arrives at his door, Hassan drugs himself up to the eyeballs in expectation of immediate execution and, under the influence, declares himself the equal of any Sultan. When he comes to, he finds that he apparently is Sultan. It is Mahmoud's little joke. Hassan's ear-crushing wife Dancing Sunbeam (Rosina Brandram), the trouble-making Abdallah (George Ridgewell), the poor story-teller Yussuf (Robert Evett) and the Sultana's maid Heart's Desire (Louie Pounds) are all mixed up in the divorces, marriages and executions which are bandied about before Hassan uses a little bit of semantics to force the Sultan to pardon everyone and put everything back as it was – even to the devastating extent of giving him back Dancing Sunbeam.

Sullivan's score was not in quite the same merry burlesque vein as those he had written for the best of the Gilbert shows. It was comic-opera music rather than opéra-bouffe music, music which happily illustrated both the superior romantic poetry which Hood composed for numbers such as Yussuf's 'Our Tale is Told' and the comical songs performed by Passmore in something like regular Savoy style, and also the specialist numbers which Sullivan was obliged to write for his prima donna. Miss Beach Yaw was an American soprano with a famed top register, and her rôle was written to include some of the top Fs in alt in which she specialized. The experiment proved a bad idea, Miss Beach Yaw soon left the cast to be replaced by her understudy Isabel Jay, the upper extremities were written out of the songs, and both the music and the show gained.

The Rose of Persia was a fine critical success and Hood was quickly hailed as the successor of Gilbert (who was doubtless not at all pleased to be seen as needing a successor), but even so, at the height of the fashion for Gaiety musical comedy, the show was only able to last for a fair-to-unprofitable seven months and 220 performances at the Savoy. Carte sent *The Rose of Persia* on tour, and it was duly produced in both Australia and in America. J C Williamson mounted Australia's version with two genuine Savoyards, Wallace Brownlow and Charles Kenningham, appearing as the Sultan and Yussuf alongside George Lauri (Hassan), Dorothy Vane (Dancing Sunbeam) and, in a role which seemed to attract double-barreled names, Ada Winston-Weir as the stratospheric sultana. It did better in Australia than in America where John Le Hay and Ruth Vincent crossed the Atlantic to star in Carte's Broadway production and remained only a sad 25 performances.

Hood and Sullivan continued their partnership, and were part-way through their next work, *The Emerald Isle*, when the composer died, leaving the author to continue a partnership with Edward German that would carry their style of comic opera through into the earliest part of the 20th century. *The Rose of Persia* was, however, revived in 1935 in the wake of a successful revival of German's *Merrie England*. Helene Raye and Joseph Spree featured, with Desiree Ellinger (Heart's Desire) and Amy Augarde (Dancing Sunbeam) supporting, in a production which again managed only 25 performances.

Australia: Her Majesty's Theatre, Sydney 21 July 1900; USA: Daly's Theater 6 September 1900
Recording: Amateur cast recording (RRE)

THE ROSE OF THE RIVIERA Musical comedy in 2 acts by Reginald Bacchus and George Sheldon. Music by F Osmond Carr. Eden Theatre, Brighton, 25 May 1903.

A farcical made-for-the-provinces piece in which comic Harry Dent featured as a silly Englishman who photographs French bathing belles and gets arrested on suspicion of snapping military installations, *The Rose of the Riviera* had music by Osmond Carr, 20 years earlier the young hero of the West End as the composer of *In Town* and *Morocco Bound* and now turning out ditties for minor tours. The show flopped, losing its producer £12,000, but he somehow persuaded a sporting gentleman from Christchurch, New Zealand, who wanted to tinker with professional theatre to purchase the show for the colonies where it proved – helped by a bundle of interpolated songs and comical bits – a distinct success as played by Edward Lauri and May Beatty.

Australia: Lyceum Theatre, Sydney 28 May 1904

DIE ROSE VON STAMBUL Operette in 3 acts by Julius Brammer and Alfred Grünwald. Music by Leo Fall. Theater an der Wien, Vienna, 2 December 1916.

Although the Turkish potentate Kemal Pascha (Karl Tuschl) is very European in some ways, he is still traditional enough to have made a dynastic marriage for his daughter, Kondja Gül (Betty Fischer), with Achmed Bey (Hubert Marischka), the son of his Prime Minister. Kondja Gül has been given much freedom and a European education and she has struck up a warm correspondence with the writer André Lery, an outspoken supporter of Western liberties for Turkish women. However, she cannot stop the marriage her father has arranged for her. To delay and discourage the union, she imposes a drawn-out, traditional courtship on Achmed while she continues a growingly romantic exchange with Lery. What she does not know is that the two are one and the same man. When Achmed finally breaks his silence she will not believe him, but, finally, under the spell of a Swiss honeymoon hotel, she realises that the man she has been made to marry is, in fact, then man she would have chosen to marry.

The score of *Die Rose von Stambul* was one of Fall's most outstanding achievements. Richly romantic in its tenor and soprano music, deliciously dancing and laughing in the soubret numbers with which the contrasting comic characters leavened the sentimental main plot, it was a classic example of the Viennese Operette of its period – the period prior to the fashion for the unhappy ending and Big Gloomy Operettes. The rôle of Achmed Bey was one of the great romantic tenor rôles written for the Viennese stage, and his music gave him three ringing solos of wide range: the ecstatic waltz song 'O Rose von Stambul' as he anticipates meeting the beautiful woman who is to be his wife, his sweet-toned greeting of his wife's handmaidens ('Ihr stillen, süssen Frau'n') and the third act 'Heut' wär ich so in der gewissen'. Along with two duets with Kondja, of which the sweeping 'Ein Walzer muss es sein', in which he introduces her to the romantic joys of Western dancing in a sort of *The-Princess-and-I* scena, is another highlight in a score of highlights, these tenor numbers form the backbone of the star rôle and of the Operette.

A third-act solo for the heroine and some fine ensemble music support the main romantic pieces, but it is the light comic portion of the score which is its other great joy. Fridolin Müller (Ernst Tautenhayn), the little Hamburg million-heir, and his veiled sweetheart Midili (Luise Kartousch) meet in duet ('Als fromme Tochter des Pro-

further. Wartime conditions and attitudes forbade it to English and French audiences and, later, when England imported other such wartime Operetten as *Das Dreimäderlhaus* and *Die Csárdásfürstin*, *Die Rose von Stambul* was ignored. In France the music-publishing firm of Max Eschig had a translation done by Léon Uhl, Jean de Letraz and Jean Marietti, but the show failed to find a producer. America ultimately took *Die Rose von Stambul*, but the Shuberts handed it over to house remakers Harold Atteridge and Sigmund Romberg and the piece that appeared on Broadway as *The Rose of Stambul* with baritone Marion Green and prima donna Tessa Kosta in its leading rôles proved to have been sadly mangled. The bits of Fall which remained were sufficient to win a three-month run but the lesson that botching very rarely worked – particularly on such a major hit as *Die Rose von Stambul* – still didn't sink in.

This ill-managed production undoubtedly killed the future of *Die Rose von Stambul* in America as stone dead as the war had done for its propects in Britain and France and, to this day, the show has never become established outside central Europe. There, however, it remains amongst the still-performed but secondary pieces of the repertoire, even though it has curiously not yet been taken into the Volksoper where Fall's works seem to be little favoured. In 1953 a second, sound film was produced, featuring some very scantily clad Turkish girls and a rather different text (ad Walter Forster, Joachim Wedekind). Herbert Ernst Groh supplied the tenor voice to Albert Lievin's Achmed Bey, Ursula Ackermann sang Kondja Gül for Inge Egger, Hans Richter pranced as Lili von Ballett and Paul Hörbiger appeared as the 106-year-old Pascha. Stage productions, too, have taken some trendy liberties with Brammer and Grünwald and one recent production modernized the tale to the extent of making André Lery not a poet, but a pop singer.

Germany: Metropoltheater 29 September 1917; Hungary: Király Színház *Sztambul Rózsája* 27 June 1917; USA: Century Theater *The Rose of Stambul* 7 March 1922; Films: 1919, Karl Anton 1953

Recordings: selections (RCA, Eurodisc, EMI, Polydor) etc

ROSS, Adrian [ROPES, Arthur Reed] (b Lewisham, 23 December 1859; d London, 10 September 1933). The British stage's senior lyricist through several eras of musical theatre.

A King's College, Cambridge, history graduate who had won the Chancellor's Medal for verse, and subsequently a fellow and a lecturer at Cambridge, Ross made his first attempt at stage writing with the libretto and lyrics for a burlesque, *Faddimir*. *Faddimir* got itself a showing at a showcase matinée and won sufficient praise for its author and his fellow Cambridge man, Frank Osmond Carr, who had composed the music, to be commissioned to write a burlesque for George Edwardes. Edwardes did, however, take the precaution of pairing his new writer with the experienced comedian John Shine on his first outing. *Joan of Arc* ('I Went to Find Emin', 'Round the Town', 'Jack the Dandy-O') was a big success, and Ross and Carr were promptly put to work – this time unaided – on another, slightly different kind of piece for Edwardes. *In Town*, with its cocky tale of backstage and society doings, broke away

Plate 230. **Die Rose von Stambul:** *Henrike Hoffmann and Hartmut Schneider try out a step that she never learned in the harem in the Bremerhaven Stadttheater's production of 1986.*

pheten'), discuss smoking in duet ('Ihr süssen Zigaretten') get engaged and have their first moustachy kiss in duet ('Fridolin, ach wie dein Schnurrbart sticht'), get a little more familiar in duet (Schnucki-Duett), and calm Hamburger papa with thoughts of grandchildren in a trio ('Papachen, Papachen'), each a sprightly song-and-dance. The rôle of Fridolin was as comical as the star rôle was romantic, and Tautenhayn had particular success in a scene in which he dressed up in feminine garb in order stay in the Palace near his Midili and then paraded about pretending to be 'Lilli vom Ballett'.

It was, in fact, Tautenhayn and Frln Kartousch who made the biggest personal successes of *Die Rose von Stambul*, but although Fall's demanding score stretched both Marischka and Frln Fischer to their vocal utmost, the Theater an der Wien's two star vocalists came through well, and all four contributed to the greatest success that the Theater an der Wien had had since *Die lustige Witwe*. The show played for 15 virtually unbroken months and 422 performances before moving on to other theatres and other countries. At Berlin's Metropoltheater Fritzi Massary starred as Kondja Gül for just under a year, whilst Budapest's Király Színház presented the Hungarian version (ad Andor Gábor) with Emmi Kosáry and Ernő Király in the romantic rôles and Juci Lábass and Árpád Latabár in the comic to splendid success.

The piece continued around Central Europe and was filmed in 1919 with Massary starred, but it did not go

from the burlesque pattern and helped set the up-to-date style for the famous series of Gaiety musicals which followed. For these early works, Ross worked on both libretto and lyrics but, as from his next piece, *Morocco Bound* ('Marguerite from Monte Carlo'), he limited himself almost entirely to writing lyrics, and his few subsequent ventures into original book-writing were the less successful side of a remarkable career.

During the great days of the Gaiety Theatre, Ross contributed many lyrics to virtually all of that theatre's shows from *The Shop Girl* ('Brown of Colorado') onwards, sharing in all the greatest international hits of the Edwardes 'Gaiety' era of musical comedy. Edwardes also put him to writing additional numbers for the shows at Daly's Theatre and, after small contributions to *An Artist's Model* and *The Geisha*, he became a fixed part of the Daly's 'team' from *A Greek Slave* onwards, a function increased on the premature death of Daly's Theatre's lyricist-in-chief, Harry Greenbank. He remained in 'the Guvnor's' service through the whole Daly's Theatre era of British musicals and, when Edwardes switched to importing Continental shows, he took over the function of adapting the lyrics of those shows into English. His first assignment was *Die lustige Witwe*, and his songwords to *The Merry Widow* ('Vilja' etc) became the standard English version of that piece, performed throughout the world for many decades and rarely equalled by subsequent adaptors. Amongst the other Continental musicals which Ross anglicized were *The Girl on the Train*, *The Marriage Market*, *The Dollar Princess* and *The Count of Luxemburg*, all of which had a wide and enduring success in their English versions.

After writing songwords for Edwardes's shows, both original works and adaptations, through more than 20 years, Ross continued, after the producer's death, to supply his successors at the Gaiety, Daly's and the Adelphi, whilst also working for other managements on other successful shows. With the advent of the revue, he even ventured into that area, working with Herman Darewski on *Three Cheers* (1917) and with Monckton on *Airs and Graces*, but revue was no more his field than it was that of Monckton or Jones or Stuart, and he worked only once more on a major London revue, much later, when he wrote the lyrics for the Palladium's *Sky High*.

In the postwar years, he nevertheless kept up the extremely heavy schedule of his earlier days, collaborating on such hit shows as the musicalized French comedy *Theodore & Co*, the Pinero musical *The Boy*, the memorable musicalization of Booth Tarkington's *Monsieur Beaucaire* ('Philomel') and, in 1922, supplying both the libretto and the lyrics for the enormously successful English version of *Das Dreimäderlhaus*, produced in Britain as *Lilac Time*. In his late sixties and his seventies he eased his work-load, and contributed his last original work to the London stage in 1927 when he collaborated with Australian composer Dudley Glass on a musical version of W J Locke's *The Beloved Vagabond*. His final farewell came three years later, with the English version of Ludwig Herzer and Fritz Löhner-Beda's libretto to the Lehár Operette *Friederike* and a musical version of Austin Strong's *The Toymaker of Nuremberg* played as a Christmas entertainment at the unfavoured Kingsway Theatre.

Ross wrote regularly and extensively with all of the most successful British-based composers of his time, from Caryll, Monckton, Lutz and Stuart at the Gaiety to Sidney Jones at Daly's and, in later days, Howard Talbot and André Messager, through more than 40 busy years which included uncountable hit shows and hit songs in and beyond the theatre. If, in the manner of the day, much of what he wrote was ephemeral and banal in its subject and sentiments, it was nevertheless tailored precisely to its producer's needs. Ross never wrote a Gaiety song for Daly's, or vice versa, and the result was a personal success inside the general success of, in particular, the Edwardes shows. His many adaptations were literate and to the point and, in spite of the vast changes in speech patterns during the 20th century, those for the most popular shows are still performed today.

1889 **Faddimir, or The Triumph of Orthodoxy** (F Osmond Carr) Vaudeville Theatre 29 April

1891 **Joan of Arc** (Carr/w John L Shine) Opera Comique 17 January

1892 **The Young Recruit** (*Les Dragons de la Reine*) English lyrics w Harry Greenbank, Harry Nicholls (Newcastle)

1892 **In Town** (Carr/w 'James Leader') Prince of Wales Theatre 15 October

1893 **Morocco Bound** (Carr/Arthur Branscombe) Shaftesbury Theatre 13 April

1893 **Don Juan** (Meyer Lutz/James T Tanner) Gaiety Theatre 28 October

1894 **Go-Bang** (Carr) Trafalgar Square Theatre 10 March

1894 **The Shop Girl** (Ivan Caryll, Lionel Monckton/w Henry J Dam/Dam) Gaiety Theatre 24 November

1894 **Mirette** revised English version (Savoy Theatre)

1895 **Bobbo** (Carr/w Tanner) 1 act Prince's Theatre, Manchester 12 September

1896 **Biarritz** (Carr/w Jerome K Jerome) Prince of Wales Theatre 11 April

1896 **My Girl** (ex-*The Clergyman's Daughter*) (Carr/Tanner) Gaiety Theatre 13 July

1896 **Weather or No** (Luard Selby/w W Beach) 1 act Savoy Theatre 10 August

1896 **The Circus Girl** (Caryll/w Harry Greenbank/Tanner, Walter Palings) Gaiety Theatre 5 December

1897 **His Majesty, or The Court of Vignolia** (Alexander MacKenzie/w F C Burnand, Rudolf C Lehmann) Savoy Theatre 20 February

1897 **The Ballet Girl** (Carl Kiefert/Tanner) Grand Theatre, Wolverhampton 15 March

1897 **The Grand Duchess** (*La Grande-Duchesse de Gérolstein*) new English lyrics (Savoy Theatre)

1898 **The Transit of Venus** (Napoleon Lambelet/Tanner) Dublin 9 April

1898 **Billy** (Carr/w G Cooper) Tyne Theatre and Opera House, Newcastle 11 April

1898 **A Greek Slave** (Sidney Jones/w H Greenbank/Owen Hall) Daly's Theatre 8 June

1898 **Milord Sir Smith)** (ex-*Campano*) (Edward Jakobowski/ad Arthur Roberts etc) Comedy Theatre 15 December

1899 **The Tree-Dumas-Skiteers** addition to *Milord Sir Smith* (Comedy Theatre)

1899 **The Lucky Star** (*L'Étoile*) (Caryll/w Aubrey Hopwood/ad J Cheever Goodwin et al) Savoy Theatre 7 January

1899 **San Toy** (Jones/w H Greenbank/Edward Morton) Daly's Theatre 21 October

1900 **The Messenger Boy** (Caryll, Monckton/w Percy Greenbank/Tanner, Alfred Murray) Gaiety Theatre 3 February

1901 **The Toreador** (Caryll, Monckton/w P Greenbank/ Tanner, Harry Nicholls) Gaiety Theatre 17 June

1901 **Kitty Grey** (Monckton, Talbot etc/w Paul Rubens/ J Smyth Piggott) Apollo Theatre 7 September

1902 **A Country Girl** (Monckton/w P Greenbank/Tanner) Daly's Theatre 18 January
1903 **The Girl from Kays** (Cecil Cook, Caryll etc/w Claude Aveling/Hall) Apollo Theatre 15 November
1903 **The Orchid** (Monckton, Caryll/w P Greenbank/Tanner) Gaiety Theatre 26 October
1904 **The Cingalee** (Monckton/w P Greenbank/Tanner) Daly's Theatre 5 March
1905 **The Spring Chicken** (Monckton, Caryll/w P Greenbank/ad George Grossmith) Gaiety Theatre 30 May
1906 **The Little Cherub** (Caryll/Hall) Prince of Wales Theatre 13 January
1906 **Naughty Nero** (Augustus Barratt) 1 act Oxford Music Hall March
1906 **See-See** (Jones/w P Greenbank/C H E Brookfield) Prince of Wales Theatre 20 June
1906 **Les Merveilleuses** (Hugo Felix/Victorien Sardou ad Basil Hood) Daly's Theatre 27 October
1907 **The Girls of Gottenberg** (Caryll, Monckton/w Basil Hood/Grossmith, L E Berman) Gaiety Theatre 15 May
1907 **The Merry Widow** (*Die lustige Witwe*) English lyrics (Daly's Theatre)
1908 **A Waltz Dream** (*Ein Walzertraum*) English version (Globe Theatre)
1908 **Havana** (Leslie Stuart/w George Arthurs/Graham Hill, Grossmith) Gaiety Theatre 25 April
1908 **The King of Cadonia** (Jones/Frederick Lonsdale) Prince of Wales Theatre 3 September
1909 **The Antelope** (Felix) Strand Theatre 28 November
1909 **Our Miss Gibbs** (Caryll, Monckton/w P Greenbank/Tanner, 'Cryptos') Gaiety Theatre 23 January
1909 **The Dashing Little Duke** (Frank E Tours/Seymour Hicks) Globe Theatre 17 February
1909 **The Dollar Princess** (*Die Dollarprinzessin*) English lyrics (Daly's Theatre)
1910 **Captain Kidd** (Stuart/Hicks) Wyndham's Theatre 12 January
1910 **The Girl in the Train** (*Die geschiedene Frau*) English lyrics (Vaudeville Theatre)
1911 **The Quaker Girl** (Monckton/w P Greenbank/Tanner) Adelphi Theatre 5 November
1911 **Castles in the Air** (*Frau Luna*) English lyrics (Scala Theatre)
1911 **The Count of Luxemburg** (*Der Graf von Luxemburg*) English lyrics w Hood (Daly's Theatre)
1912 **Gipsy Love** (*Zigeunerliebe*) English lyrics (Daly's Theatre)
1912 **The Wedding Morning** (Lachlan McLean) 1 act Tivoli 30 September
1912 **Tantalising Tommy** (Felix/w Michael Morton) Criterion Theater, New York 2 October
1912 **The Dancing Mistress** (Monckton/w P Greenbank/Tanner) Adelphi Theatre 19 October
1913 **The Girl on the Film** (*Filmzauber*) English lyrics (Gaiety Theatre)
1913 **The Marriage Market** (*Leányvásár*) English version (Daly's Theatre)
1913 **The Girl from Utah** (Jones, Rubens/w Rubens, P Greenbank/Tanner) Adelphi Theatre 18 October
1914 **The Belle of Bond Street** revised *The Girl from Kays* (Shubert Theater, New York)
1915 **Betty** (Rubens/w Rubens/Lonsdale, Gladys Unger) Daly's Theatre 24 April
1915 **The Light Blues** (Talbot, Hermann Finck/Mark Ambient, Jack Hulbert) Prince of Wales Theatre, Birmingham 13 September; Shaftesbury Theatre 14 September 1916
1916 **The Happy Day** (Rubens, Jones/w Rubens/Hicks) Daly's Theatre 13 May
1916 **Theodore & Co** (Ivor Novello, Jerome Kern/w Clifford Grey/Grossmith, H M Harwood) Gaiety Theatre 19 September

1916 **Oh! Caesar** (Nat D Ayer, Arthur Wood/Alexander M Thompson, Max Pemberton) Royal Lyceum, Edinburgh 23 December
1916 **The Happy Family** (Cuthbert Clarke/w Arthur Aldin) Prince of Wales Theatre 18 December
1917 **Arlette** English version (Shaftesbury Theatre)
1917 **The Boy** (Talbot, Monckton/w P Greenbank/Fred Thompson) Adelphi Theatre, 14 September
1919 **Monsieur Beaucaire** (André Messager/Lonsdale) Prince's Theatre 19 April
1919 **The Kiss Call** (Caryll/w Grey, P Greenbank/Thompson) Gaiety Theatre 8 October
1919 **Maggie** (Marcel Lattès/Thompson, H F Maltby) Oxford Theatre 22 October
1919 **The Eclipse** (Herman Darewski, Melville Gideon/w Davy Burnaby/E Phillips Oppenheim, Thompson) Garrick Theatre 12 November
1920 **Medorah** English lyrics (Alhambra Theatre)
1920 **The Love Flower** (Herman Finck/w James Heard/Robert Marshall) Theatre Royal, Brighton 8 March
1920 **A Southern Maid** (H Fraser Simson/w Harry Graham/Graham) Daly's Theatre 15 May
1920 **The Naughty Princess** (*La Reine s'amuse*) English lyrics (Adelphi Theatre)
1921 **Faust on Toast** (Willie Redstone, Gideon/w Firth Shephard) Gaiety Theatre 19 April
1921 **Love's Awakening** (*Wenn Liebe erwacht*) English book and lyrics (Empire Theatre)
1922 **Lilac Time** (*Das Dreimäderlhaus*) English book and lyrics (Lyric Theatre)
1922 **The Cousin from Nowhere** (*Der Vetter aus Dingsda*) English lyrics w Furber, Robert C Tharp (Prince's Theatre)
1923 **Head Over Heels** (Fraser-Simson/w Graham/Hicks) Adelphi Theatre 8 September
1927 **The Beloved Vagabond** (Dudley Glass) Duke of York's Theatre 1 September
1930 **Frederica** (*Friederike*) English version (Palace Theatre)
1930 **The Toymaker of Nuremberg** (Glass/w Austin Strong) Kingsway Theatre 20 December

ROSS, Jerry [ROSENBERG, Jerrold] (b New York, 9 March 1926; d New York, 11 November 1955).

A keen theatre participator from a young age, Ross began writing songs before his college years, but he made no breakthrough until he met up with and began to collaborate with Richard Adler in 1950. The pair attracted the attention of Frank Loesser, had a hit song with 'Rags to Riches', broke into Broadway with *John Murray Anderson's Almanac* in 1953 and, in quick time, brought out the scores for two hit musicals, *The Pajama Game* ('Hey There') and *Damn Yankees* ('Whatever Lola Wants', 'Heart'). Ross, who had suffered from serious bronchiectasis for many years, died from the infections caused by that illness at the age of 29.

1954 **The Pajama Game** (w Richard Adler/George Abbott, Richard Bissell) St James Theater 13 May
1955 **Damn Yankees** (w Adler/w Abbott, Douglass Wallop) 46th Street Theater 5 May

ROSSE, Frederick (b Jersey, 1867; d Brighton, 20 June 1940).

A very versatile music-comedy man, Frederick Rosse took the juvenile lead in the 1894 musical comedy *Go-Bang*, composed the music for the song 'Hands Off' which Hayden Coffin featured in *An Artist's Model* (1895), wrote the basic score for James Tanner and Owen Hall's musical farce *All Abroad* (1895), and was conductor for the West

End production of *The Gay Pretenders* (1900), for Rutland Barrington's version of *The Water Babies* (1902) for which he also composed the score, for *Sergeant Brue* (add music), *Miss Wingrove* (1905) and for the 1908 revival of *Dorothy*.

1895 **All Abroad** (W H Risque/Owen Hall, James T Tanner) Criterion Theatre 8 August

1898 **At Zero** (T Hughes) Reading, 4 July

1902 **The Water Babies** (Rutland Barrington) Garrick Theatre 18 December

1904 **Little Black Sambo and Little White Barbara** (w Wilfred Bendall/Barrington) Garrick Theatre 21 December

ROSSI, Tino [ROSSI, Constantin] (b Ajaccio, 29 April 1907; d Neuilly, 27 September 1983). Favourite singing star of postwar French screen and, later, stage.

Rossi began his career in southern France as a singer of the songs of his native Corsica, and subsequently made himself a reputation in the music halls and as a recording artist. His first stage appearance was in revue, the 1934 Casino de Paris *Parade de France*, but he was 48 years old, with a long career as a star of film and radio behind him, before he made his début in the musical theatre. With Luis Mariano and *The Belle of Cadix* having made the romantic opérette topped by a popular tenor the latest rage, Rossi appeared at the Châtelet in the rôle of a Corsican singing star in *Méditerranée*, written and composed by the authors of Mariano's piece, and scored a success no less ringing than his younger and svelter rival had done.

He subsequently played in a stage version of his old film *Naples au baiser de feu* (1957) as an amorous Italian, in another Lopez opérette, *Le Temps des Guitares* (1963), and as an eccentric millionaire in *Le Marchand de Soleil* (1969), each of which owed a substantial part of its good run to the presence at the top of its bill of Rossi's name. On the screen, he played Schubert in Marcel Pagnol's version of the *Dreimäderlhaus* tale, *La Belle Meunière* (1948), and starred in the film version of the Alibert/Scotto *Au Pays du soleil* (1951).

Literature: Trimbach, G: *Tino Rossi* (Delville, Paris, 1978)

ROTHOMAGO, or The Magic Watch Grand opéra-bouffe féerie in 4 acts by Adolphe d'Ennery, Clairville and Monnier adapted into English by H B Farnie. Music by Procida Bucalossi, Edward Solomon, Gaston Serpette and Georges Jacobi. Alhambra Theatre, London, 22 December 1879.

A spectacular pasticcio féerie in the line of the perennially popular *Les Pilules du Diable* and *La Biche au bois*, the original *Rothomago* (mus: A de Groot) was first played at the Paris Cirque (1 March 1862) and subsequently used to open the new Parisian Théâtre du Châtelet (19 August 1862). Although it was given only a handful of performances on that occasion, it was acclaimed as 'one of the masterpieces of its kind', and it went on to be played around France, remounted at the Châtelet again in 1863, revived spectacularly by Castellano in 1877 (171 performances) with a cast headed by Anna van Ghell (Rothomago fils), Tissier (Rothomago), Henri Cooper (Blaisinet) and Mlle Donvé (Princesse Miranda), and yet again in 1878. As a result of this last production, staged at the height of London's infatuation with grandiose fairytale productions, the piece was picked up by the inveterate 'adapter' H B

Farnie, rewritten, fitted out with an original and rather fuller score by Bucalossi, Serpette, Jacobi and Solomon (one act apiece) and presented on London's large Alhambra stage.

Harry Paulton played the inefficient court sorcerer Rothomago, and Constance Loseby his son of the same name who is supposed to marry Princess Allegra (Mlle Julic), daughter of reigning monarch Impecunioso (Louis Kelleher). Édouard Georges was the rustic Dodo (the Blaisinet of the French version) who gets hold of the magic watch which gives him power and the princess until – after everyone has spent the evening trying to distract him – he finally forgets to wind it up and loses all. Hetty Tracy was the good fairy Anisette and Annie Bentley the nasty Angostura. The chase after the watch went via bear-infested Freezeland, an escape by balloon, the French countryside (cue for a Wine Ballet) and Egypt (mummies' dance, plus real camels and an elephant) and the happy ending was celebrated in a Porcelain ballet which was one of the evening's highlights. Special effects, broad comedy, not too much dialogue, and a spectacle which lasted four hours kept London entertained for nearly four months.

The Châtelet remounted its version in 1897.

THE ROTHSCHILDS Musical in 2 acts by Sherman Yellen based on a book by Frederic Morton. Lyrics by Sheldon Harnick. Music by Jerry Bock. Lunt-Fontanne Theater, New York, 19 October 1970.

Harnick and Bock, who had triumphed with the Russo-Jewish tale of *Fiddler on the Roof*, tackled a second Jewish subject with a biomusical of the Rothschilds, another family struggling against the problems of being Jewish in period Europe. If the 18th- to 19th-century Rothschilds were a rather less appealing bunch than Tevye and his daughters, it might have been that their aims – financial gain, power and an invitation, even an unwilling one, to the ball – were less sympathetic than those of the famous milkman, but their stage potential was proven: the family, and notably the dowager mother, Gutele Rothschild, had earlier made the subject of an enormously successful straight play, Karl Rössler's *Die fünf Frankfurter*.

In this musical, Mamma was not the central figure. Hal Linden played Mayer Rothschild, the father of the five sons who help him build up his banking empire and, after his death, get the Frankfurt ghetto and its laws abolished. Leila Martin was his wife, Gutele, and Jill Clayburgh provided a love interest for Nathan Rothschild (Paul Hecht), whilst Keene Curtis had a good time in a multiple rôle as Prince William of Hesse, Fouché and Metternich. The subject meant that there was no place for the endearing warmth of *Fiddler* in the show's score, which instead leaned towards songs of striving, lightened by some sentimental moments and a touch of comedy, as in the young Mayer's spiel ('He Tossed a Coin') in selling some antique coins, a sale which makes him early money and rich contacts.

Lester Osterman and Hillard Elkins's production played 507 performances on Broadway and won Linden a Tony Award, and, although the show did not follow *Fiddler on the Roof* overseas, it was later revived at New York's American Jewish Theater in 1990 (25 February) and played at off-Broadway's Circle in the Square Downtown (27 April 1990) with Mike Burstyn featured as Meyer Rothschild.

An earlier musical on the Rothschilds was produced in

Hungary, when an 1860 play *Rothschild ház titka* (the secret of the Rothschild house) openly subtitled 'how to get rich', was followed by a successful 1932 operett entitled *A Rotschildok* (Lajos Lajtai/Istaván Békeffy/Ferenc Martos, 25 November Fővárosi Operettszinház) in which Gyula Kabos and Vilma Medgyasszay (Mama Rothschild) starred. This version, whilst keeping Mama prominent, took more interest in Jacob (Gábor Kertész), the son who went to Paris and (in this version, at least) got mixed up with the actress Lageorges (Hanna Honthy) and things Napoleonic, than it did in Nathan and the ghettos.

Recording: original cast (Columbia)

ROTT, Matthias [KOCH, Carl Matthias] (b Vienna, 23 February 1807; d Vienna, 10 February 1876). Viennese comic actor who played important rôles in the earliest modern musicals in his home town.

A teenaged organist at the Church of Maria Geburt, a choirboy at the Vienna Hofoper, a theatre chorister at the old Kärntnertor Theater, a cellist in the theatre orchestra at Pressburg, a sometime composer who is said to have written the music to accompany Nestroy's first play, and eventually a comedy actor, Rott spent a decade at the Theater in der Josefstadt, and a short period in Pest, before joining the company at the Theater an der Wien. There, more than two decades later, he was one of the principal comic players in Vienna's early productions of opéra-bouffe, a form which he tasted at its very beginnings with some performances at Karl Treumann's Theater am Franz-Josefs-Kai (Herr Boudinet in *Apotheker und Friseur*, Sarmiento in *Die Schwätzerin von Saragossa* etc) in one of his rare excursions away from the Theater an der Wien.

Rott was Vienna's original Calchas (*Die schöne Helena*), Frangipani (*Coscoletto*), Alphecibdus (*Die Schäfer*), Pompery (*Die Reise nach China*), Popolani (*Blaubart*), Grabuche, paired with Blasel as the gens d'armes in *Genovefa von Brabant*, the Mandarin Wau-Wau in *Theeblüthe*, General Bum-Bum to Geistinger's *Grossherzogin von Gerolstein*, Pietro (*Die Banditen*), Carol von Calabrien (*Fantasio*), Meister Fulbert in Litolff's *Heloise und Abälard*, Tokuwaka in Jonas's *Die Japanesin*, Themistocles in *Madame 'Herzog'* and also appeared as König Klingerlinging in *Prinzessin Hirschkuh*, the Viennese adaptation of *La Biche au bois*.

He also played in some of the earliest Viennese Operetten, as Jonas in Hopp's *Das Donauweibchen* and Herr von Varoshazy in Millöcker's version of *Drei Paar Schuhe* and he created the title-rôle of Johann Strauss's first Operette *Indigo und die vierzig Räuber*, before retiring at the age of nearly 70 after the scenery of *Madame 'Herzog'* fell on his head.

His wife also appeared in minor rôles in opéra-bouffe at the Theater an der Wien.

ROUNSEVILLE, Robert [Field] (b Attleboro, Mass, 25 March 1914; d New York, 6 August 1974).

Tenor Rounseville appeared on Broadway in *Babes in Arms*, *The Two Bouquets*, *Knickerbocker Holiday* and *Higher and Higher*, took the rôle of Jolidon (Camille) in the 1943 revival of *The Merry Widow* and played in a 1944 *Robin Hood* before creating his first major musical rôle as Andrew Munroe in *Up in Central Park* (1945). In a career which

ranged from the operatic to the nightclubby, he appeared in Gilbert and Sullivan, as Ravenal in the City Center's *Show Boat* and Charlie in their *Brigadoon* and regionally in such rôles as Karl-Franz, Camille, Charlie Dalrymple, Danilo, Bumerli, Eisenstein, Nordraak, El Gallo and Macheath, and returned to Broadway in 1956, to create the title-rôle in *Candide*, and again in 1965 to introduce 'To Each His Dulcinea' in the rôle of the Padre in *Man of La Mancha*.

Rounseville was also seen on film as Hoffman in *The Tales of Hoffman* (1951) and as Mister Snow in the 1956 film version of *Carousel*.

LA ROUSSOTTE Comédie-vaudeville in 3 acts and a prologue by Henri Meilhac, Ludovic Halévy and Albert Millaud. Music by Charles Lecocq, Hervé and Marius Boullard. Théâtre des Variétés, Paris, 28 January 1881.

La Roussotte followed *La Femme à papa* in the hugely successful series of made-for-Judic vaudevilles produced by Eugène Bertrand at the Variétés and, if it were not quite the outsized hit that *Niniche* or *Mam'zelle Nitouche* was, it nevertheless proved to be a grand success, playing through over 100 performances on its first run and being toured through the world as an oft-played part of Mme Judic's repertoire. For this occasion, Albert Millaud was joined in creating the star's vehicle by none less than Meilhac and Halévy who created an amusing tale and, most importantly, a first-class rôle for the lady as the 'readhead' of the title.

The gambling Comte Dubois-Toupet (Baron) once had a fling with the English wife (Anna Judic) of a sea captain and of that fling were born a pair of little red-headed children who were tactfully brought up by a foster-priest (Léonce). But one day the Comte over-gambled and was obliged to set out to refill his purse by selling opium to the Chinese. By the time he returned home, re-enriched, both the priest and the English lady were dead, and his children had vanished. The devious quasi-lawyer Gigonnet (Lassouche), whom he employs to find them, tracks down la Roussotte (Mme Judic again) working in an inn, and he determines to wed her and her fortune before she is aware she has a fortune. When she turns him down in favour of his assistant, Médard (José Dupuis), Gigonnet revengefully announces that Médard is her lost brother. Back at the Dubois-Toupet château the two find co-existence as brother and sister unbearable, but a happy ending arrives when the real Édouard (Didier), a red-headed gambling chip off the old green baize, turns up.

The score for *La Roussotte* was to have been written by Lecocq, but his illness prompted Bertrand to turn first to Hervé and then to the reliable Marius Boullard who had obliged under similar circumstances on *Niniche* and who finished off the half-done music. Most of the 11 numbers of the score were, of course, for the star who had three songs in Act I, three in Act II and the only one in Act III, alongside a little romance for Dupuis, plus a jolly introduction for Léonce and one song and a fragment for Baron in the prologue. The star opened with an unblushing reminiscence of her first meeting with her man ('Attendez, je m'rappelle maint'nant'), threw off the story of her love-life in Boullard's Couplets des amoureux, and tossed a warning at the would-be compromising Gigonnet ('Ah! n'fait's pas ça!'). She comically depicted a waitress's life ('Un peu d'silence'), pleaded with her papa against wedding a toff ('Sans Médard') and, finally, showed off her new aristocratic talents as a horsewoman in waltz time, admitting, alas!, to riding astride. Her big song success of the piece, however, was popped in as a 'come on, la Roussotte, give us a song' number. Hervé's cheeky Chanson de la Fille du Peintre en Bâtiment, better known by its chorus noise 'Piiii-ouit!', gave Judic another big, saucy hit, to follow the famous Chanson du Colonel from *La Femme à papa*.

Like *La Femme à papa* and *Niniche*, *La Roussotte* was seen in its original state virtually only when Judic took it around the world, with Paris reprises in 1885 and 1889. Elsewhere, it seemed deemed obligatory to replace the French score with locally written music. Vienna's Theater an der Wien produced the piece as *Ein süsses Kind* (ad Franz von Schönthan, 1 April 1882) with a score by Millöcker attached, Rosa Streitmann as Anne Marie (no longer doubling as her own mother), Girardi as Médard and Friese as Gigonnet, Berlin saw *Rotkäppchen*, described as a Vaudeville-Posse, with book and music both credited to Genée (Thomas-Theater 6 February 1882), whilst Budapest's version was played as *Pirók és Piróska* (ad Emil Kürthy, Népszinház 22 Feb 1890) with music by Oskar Feith.

Conversely, 'Piiii-ouit!' went travelling without its play, and it was heard in America as part of Louise Théo's performance in *La Jolie Parfumeuse* in the 1882–3 season, before Broadway had had a chance to hear Judic and *La Roussotte*.

USA: Star Theater (Fr) 6 April 1885; Austria: Theater an der Wien (Fr) 19 December 1900

LA ROUTE FLEURIE Opérette in 2 acts by Raymond Vincy. Music by Francis Lopez. Théâtre de l'ABC, Paris, 19 December 1952.

Written by the pair of the moment of the Parisian musical theatre, Vincy and Lopez, who had lined up the successes over half a dozen years with *La Belle de Cadix*, *Andalousie*, *Le Chanteur de Mexico* and *Quatre Jours à Paris*, *La Route fleurie* was a piece more in the mode of the last-named of the group rather than in the opérette à grand spectacle style of the other three. It was, however, like the bigger pieces, and in contrast to the more book-orientated and farcical *Quatre Jours à Paris*, written around a star tenor rôle, which was taken in the original production by Georges Guétary.

Guétary played a Montmartre composer called Jean-Pierre who writes a film-score and then gallivants pennilessly off to the Côte d'azur to stay in a rich aunt's house with his friends Raphaël (Bourvil), Lorette (Annie Cordy) and the mannequin Mimi (Claude Arvelle) for whom he sighs, in order to write a screenplay which will satisfy the powers that produce to go with his songs. Unfortunately the servants, who are used to letting the house on the side whilst madame is away, have booked in a crazy scientist called Poupoutzoff, and Jean-Pierre has also double-booked the place to his incipient film-producer and his star (Annie Dumas). The comic and romantic ins-and-outs of the preparations, the trip and the house party made up an evening's entertainment and, in the dénouement, also the material for the plot's required screenplay. The whole was illustrated by some lively Lopez songs of which Mlle Cordy's soubrette/comic 'Tagada-Tsoin-Tsoin', Bourvil's

Plate 231. *Annie Cordy and Bourvil set off for a happy song and danc. on the Côte d'azur via* **La Route fleurie**.

poeticizing over 'Les Haricots', a pretty rhapsody 'Un dinette' which recalled Guétary's London hit with 'A Table for Two' (*Bless the Bride*) and the tenor's tale of th 'Jolie Meunière' were amongst the happiest.

Producers Mitty Goldin and Léon Ledoux lined up bill which proved to be a real winner. Guétary's value wa known (and valued at F100,000 a performance), but that o the other two stars was not. Bourvil was in the doldrum after some successful years playing gormless peasant rôles mostly on film, and the young Mlle Cordy was playing third on a music-hall bill when they were cast – and value at F15,000 and F5,000 respectively. Mlle Arvelle, beauty-contest winner, was scarcely in the same league with a trio which turned out to be the most remarkabl team on the Paris musical stage in years. *La Route fleuri* was a major hit, filling its smaller house for three and a hal years until mid-1956 and remaining a success even after it three stars had moved on to other successes. It was sub sequently played liberally through France and was revive in 1980 at the Théâtre de la Renaissance (25 October).

Recordings: original cast (Pathé), revival cast (Vogue), selectio (TLP)

ROUTLEDGE, Patricia (b Birkenhead, 17 Februar 1929). Atlantic-hopping character lady of the straight an musical stages through 35 years in search of a memorabl new musical rôle.

After an early career in repertory theatre, Mis Routledge made her first London appearances in musica plays – the Bristol Old Vic's Julian Slade version of *Th Duenna* (1954, Carlotta) and the same composer's comi opera version of *A Comedy of Errors* (1956). In 1957 sh appeared in the short-lived *Zuleika* (Aunt Mabel), in 195 the even-shorter-lived Molière with music, *The Love Docto* (Henrietta), and in 1960 played Susan Hampshire' mother in Slade's charming *Follow that Girl* ('Waiting fo

Our Daughter'). In 1962 she appeared in the title-rôle of the British production of *Little Mary Sunshine* and the following year played Berinthia in the musical version of *The Relapse*, *Virtue in Danger* (1963), before returning to the non-musical theatre for several years.

Amongst a list of stage and television (Megaera in Richard Rodgers's *Androcles and the Lion*, 1967) credits which produced some memorably characterful performances as the years went by, Miss Routledge returned regularly to the musical stage. She gave London a Grande-Duchesse de Gérolstein which was spoken of with enthusiasm for decades after and, in 1968, she starred as Alice Challice in the unsuccessful Broadway musical *Darling of the Day*, a performance which nevertheless won her a Tony Award. She played Queen Victoria in a musical tale of that monarch's *Love Match* with Prince Albert which closed pre-Broadway, and in 1976 visited America again to play the President's wives in Leonard Bernstein's short-lived *1600 Pennsylvania Avenue*. In 1981 she appeared as Veta Louise Simmons in *Say Hello to Harvey*, an unsuccessful musical version of *Harvey* in Canada, in 1989 succeeded to the rôle of the Old Lady in Scottish Opera's production of *Candide* for its London season, and in 1992 appeared as Nettie Fowler in Britain's National Theatre mounting of *Carousel*.

ROXY UND IHR WUNDERTEAM
Vaudeville-Operette in 3 acts by Alfred Grünwald adapted from an original by Lázsló Szilágyi and Dezső Kellér. Lyrics by Grünwald and Hans Weigel. Music by Pál Ábrahám. Theater an der Wien, Vienna, 25 March 1937.

Composed by a Pál Ábrahám who was on the run from Nazism and already falling away from the finest moments he would know as a composer with *Viktória*, *Die Blume von Hawaii* and *Ball am Savoy*, this Vaudeville-Operette was a jolly, up-to-date, flag-waving show about a Scots girl – the titular Roxy – who goes mad over the Hungarian national football team. All things considered, this is fairly natural, for in the Operette the Hungarians hand out a thrashing to the once almighty English team.

Produced by Artur Hellmann at a Theater an der Wien also in the days of its decline, with Rószi Bársony starred as Roxy alongside her partner Oszkár Dénes and Max Brod, *Roxy und ihr Wunderteam* lasted 59 performances. However, portions of it resurfaced in Paris, to where Ábrahám had continued his flight, two years later and two months before the outbreak of war. Maurice Lehmann staged a piece at the Théâtre Mogador under the title *Billy et son équipe* 'opérette à grand-spectacle en 10 tableaux' credited to Mouëzy-Éon and Albert Willemetz for the text and to Michel Emer and 'Jean Sautreuil' (ie Maurice Yvain) for the music. Ábrahám was noted as having supplied 'airs additionels', but Urban, who starred alongside Coecilia Navarre, Félix Paquet and Arnaudy, apparently performed the 'Lambeth Walk'. The new football show did no better than its Hungaro-Viennese prototype, leaving America's sporting musicals alone at the top of the medal-list.

THE ROYAL VAGABOND
Cohanised opera comique in 3 acts by Stephen Idor Szinnyey and William Cary Duncan. Lyrics by Duncan. Music by Anselm Goetzl. Cohan and Harris Theater, New York, 17 February 1919.

The Cohanised element of *The Royal Vagabond* (for which the canny gentleman pulled a royalty of 5 per cent) was the element that made it into a novelty success. *Cherry Blossoms* was the work of the expatriate mid-European Anselm Götzl, who had been responsible, amongst others, for the score of Prague's *Frau Lebedame* (1907). This time, however, he did not have a Sardou libretto to work with, but the most conventional tale of Prince and milliner and Ruritanian antics concocted by William Cary Duncan and one Count Stephen Szinnyey.

Cohan took the conventional work, redid most of the lyrics, popped in a couple of his own, and the result was an operetta in which Frederic Santley as Prince Stephan of Bargravia and Tessa Kosta as Anitza Chefcheck, the milliner, still sang their hearts out about 'When the Cherry Blossoms Fall', but did it after an opening chorus which has confided 'tra-la-la, the lyric would make you laugh, ha-ha, for that we pay the royalties, they sing it in fifty different keys ...' and introduced each of the main characters and their conventionalities. When the heroine then sang that her heart was bleeding and his lips had thrilled her it was difficult, without looking at the programme, to know whether one was listening to Cohan or Duncan (it was Duncan). Cohan and Harris produced, Julian Mitchell and Sam Forrest directed, Dorothy Dickson and Carl Hyson danced, the audiences laughed, and *The Royal Vagabond* (as the piece had been renamed) ran 208 Broadway performances. Only a few of them had played when the 48-year-old Szinnyey was buried in the Bronx, presumably not as a result of a broken heart.

Goetzl and Duncan later tried again for success with a piece called *The Rose Girl* which travelled from Wilkes-Barre, Pa, to Broadway (11 February 1921). Un-Cohanised, it nevertheless gave them a second good, if more modest, run.

LE ROYAUME DES FEMMES
Opérette à grand spectacle in 3 acts by Hippolyte Cogniard and Desnoyers, adapted by Ernest Blum, Paul Ferrier and others. Music composed and arranged by Gaston Serpette. Eldorado, Paris, 24 February 1896.

One of the earliest of the run of highly successful musical spectaculars originated by the Cogniard brothers in the mid-19th century, *Le Royaume des femmes* was first produced in 1833 in a version by Hippolyte Cogniard and Desnoyers. For some reason, it was banned during the reign of Louis-Philippe and the Empire, but it resurfaced in 1866, in a new version, done over by Cogniard and Ernest Blum, and was mounted at the Variétés with considerable success. In 1889, Blum and the habitual collaborator of his later years, Raoul Toché, revised the piece once more, and staged it at the Théâtre des Nouveautés during the Exhibition, and in 1896 it was given a final going-over, this time by Blum and Paul Ferrier, for a fourth production, in a fourth version, at the Eldorado. The piece had now come quite a way from its origins, but the bones of the tale, now decorated with a half-new/half-old score from Gaston Serpette, who had proven his skill at musicking grandiose scenic pieces, were much as they had been originally.

Baron Frivolin (Juliette Simon-Girard) and Vicomte Citronnet (Berthaut) are carried away in a balloon, and land on an island where women rule. They not only rule, but they behave like Parisian men, particularly in their affairs with the opposite sex. Queen Suavita (Marie de l'Isle) takes a fancy to Frivolin, whilst General Trombolinette (Mlle Simier) treats Citronnet like a grisette, which upsets the gentlemen's macho-Parisian amour-propre something proper. Meanwhile the Commanderess-in-Chief, Xéressa (Mily-Meyer), is pursuing the gentle Alcindor (Sulbac), who has been kept to the virtuously straight path by his aunt, Prudhomma (Mme Mathilde), and when he proves sexually shy she simply has him carried off to her apartments. Ultimately, the visiting men provoke a revolt and everything in this upside-down world is turned back to 19th-century normal.

The island of women, with its topsy-turvy habits, gave the opportunity for much spectacle, not least the parade of the women's army, clad in suitably 'active' clothing.

Le Royaume des femmes made its way through Europe, several times, in its various forms and under varying titles such as 'the topsy-turvey world' and 'the island of women'. Berlin took it twice, both in its 1889 version (*Das Paradies der Frauen*, Metropoltheater, 3 September, mus: Einödshofer, B Sänger, ad Julius Freund) and then again in its 1896 version (*Die verkehrte Welt*, Metropoltheater, 25 December 1899, add mus Einodshöfer, ad Freund). Vienna's Danzers Orpheum (22 February) and Venedig in Wien both played a *Die verkehrte Welt* (1901) credited to Lindau and Krenn with Karl Kappeller for music, but the *Paradies der Damen* (30 January 1901) mounted at the Theater an der Wien was not a rip-off of the Parisian spectacular, but a wholly different show: in this case the 'women's Heaven' was a couturier's shop called the Salon Frippon. In Hungary the 1866 version was played at the Deutsches Theater, Pest, in 1869 with a musical score by the young Karl Millöcker under the title *Die Fraueninsel*, and the Blum/Ferrier version with Serpette's music still attached was played as *Felfordult világ* (ad Ferenc Molnár, Emil Makai) at the Fővárosi Nyari Színház (22 August 1900).

ROYCE, E[dward] W[illiam] (b Eversholt, 11 August 1841; d London, 24 January 1926). Burlesque star of the Gaiety days.

Royce was a dancer and comic actor in the provinces until John Hollingshead spotted him and brought him to the Gaiety Theatre in 1873. At first he was seen largely in comedy, playing both at the Gaiety and at other theatres, and he also directed both plays and musicals, staging amongst others London's perversion of *La Timbale d'argent*, *The Duke's Daughter*, but in 1877 he became one of the four-cornered star group of Gaiety burlesque players (with Nellie Farren, Edward Terry and Kate Vaughan) who were to be the triumph of the first great era of Gaiety burlesque. Over the next years he played at Hollingshead's theatre in *Don Caesar de Bazan* (Don José), *The Bohemian G'yurl* (Count Smiff), *Little Doctor Faust* (Valentine), *Il Sonnambulo* (Elvino), *Young Fra Diavolo* (Giacomo), *Pretty Esmeralda* (Quasimodo), *Gulliver* (Smuggins), *Robbing Roy* (The Dougal Creature), *Very Little Hamlet* (Claudius), *Mazeppa* (Laurinski), *The Forty Thieves* (Hassarac), *Bluebeard* and many others such pieces, until his health broke down and he was forced to leave both the theatre and the country.

Plate 232. **Edward Royce**: *choreographer and/or director for a generation of British and American musicals.*

In 1886 he made his way to the more sanitary climate of Australia where he worked at first for Brough and Boucicault and later for other managements, appearing in comedy (Medway in *Turned Up* etc), burlesque (*Young Fra Diavolo*, Blueskin in *Little Jack Shepperd*, Hassarac in *The Forty Thieves* etc), drama (*The Silver King*, *The Silver Falls*, *Human Nature*, *The Pointsman*, *Formosa* etc) and comic opera (Jack Joskins in *Dick*, Coquelicot in *Olivette*) and adapting, directing and playing in pantomime for Sam Lazar at Sydney's Theatre Royal.

Restored by his stay in the colonies, he returned to Britain in 1892, and returned also to the London stage, playing in the burlesque *Atalanta*, at the Gaiety in *Don Juan* and the 1894 revival of *Little Jack Sheppard* and in the comic opera *The Bric-à-brac Will* (1895, Barnaba) as well as appearing on the road in *The Black Squire* (1896, Septimus P Chipmunk) and intermittently directing and choreographing (*The Ballet Girl* etc). As late as 1908 he appeared on the West End stage, as Old Jacques in *The Belle of Brittany*, and he survived to a ripe 84.

His son, **Edward ROYCE** (b Bath, 14 December 1870; d London, 15 June 1964) was originally trained as a scenic artist, and then as a dancer, but made himself a memorable career as a choreographer and a director on both sides of the Atlantic.

His earliest West End credits, for producer William Greet, included the dances for the original production of *Merrie England* at the Savoy Theatre, for *A Princess of Kensington* (1903), *The Earl and the Girl* (1903), *Little Hans Andersen* (1903) and *The Talk of the Town* (1905) and for the Charles Frohman/Seymour Hicks shows *The Catch of the Season* (1904), *The Beauty of Bath* (1906), *My Darling* (1907) and *The Gay Gordons* (1907). Royce directed and choreographed for the first time on the 1905 revival of *Bluebell in Fairyland*, and he fulfilled the same double function on the tour of *The Girls of Gottenberg* and the Gaiety Theatre's *Havana* (1908) for George Edwardes. He subsequently served Edwardes on *Our Miss Gibbs* (1909), *The Dollar Princess* (1909), *The Girl in the Taxi* (1910), *A Waltz Dream*, *Peggy*, *The Count of Luxemburg* (1911), *Gipsy Love* (1912) and *The Marriage Market* (1913).

Royce visited America to work for Frohman on his production of *The Doll Girl* (1913), following which he repeated his *Marriage Market* for Broadway and mounted the American version of *The Laughing Husband*, before returning to London for *The Country Girl* and the revue *Bric-à-Brac*. In 1916 he went to America a second time to direct the Gaiety Theatre musical *Betty* for Charles Dillingham, and this time he remained there, becoming one of the most sought-after and successful directors and choreographers on Broadway. He was put under contract by F Ray Comstock and Morris Gest for whom in the years that followed he staged *Oh, Boy!* (1917 w Robert Milton), *Leave it to Jane* (1917), *Oh! Look* (1918 w Milton), *Oh, Lady! Lady!!* (1918, w Milton), *Oh My Dear* (1918, w Milton) and *See You Later* (1919), but he was loaned out regularly to mount such pieces as Louis Hirsch's highly successful *Going Up* (w James Montgomery) with its famous 'Tickle Toe' dance, *Kitty Darlin'* (1917), *Have a Heart* (1917), *Rockabye Baby* (1918), *The Canary* (1918, w Fred Latham), *Come Along* (1919 w Frank Jackson), *She's a Good Fellow* (1919, w Latham), *Apple Blossoms* (1919), *Irene* (1919), *Honeymoon Town* (1919) and *Lassie* (1919–20). His popularity ultimately became such that Elisabeth Marbury sued him for abandoning A H Woods's sinking Avery Hopwood musical *Dodo/I'll Say She Does* to hurry on to assignments on *The Ziegfeld Follies*, *Kissing Time* (1920) and *Sally* (1920).

In the 1920s he had a slightly less demential schedule. In 1921 he directed and choreographed a second *Ziegfeld Follies*, *The Love Letter* and Jerome Kern's successful *Good Morning, Dearie*, and the following year he turned producer to stage *Orange Blossoms*. Its so-so career was followed by a genuine flop for a second production, *Cinders*, and Royce abandoned producing and returned solely to staging. He mounted the comedy musicals *Kid Boots* and *Louie the 14th*, *Marjorie* (1924), the musical comedy *Annie Dear*, and was the original stager of *No, No, Nanette*, until Harry Frazee took a bottle in both hands and fired him. Thing went less well thereafter. *Ziegfeld's Palm Beach Girl* wandered through several titles in a disappointing life and the *Brewster's Millions* musical *Bubbling Over* (1926 also producer) failed to make it to town, and Royce slipped away to Australia where he staged the hugely successful local production of *Katja, the Dancer*. Back in America he had Broadway flops with *She's My Baby* (1928) and *Billie* (1928), mounted Los Angeles's *The Rose of Flanders* and San Francisco's *Bambina*, choreographed a couple of 1929 movies (*Married in Hollywood*, *Words and Music* w Frank Merlin) and then, after 20 years' absence, went back to London.

There, he directed a revival of *A Waltz Dream* at the Winter Garden, and the following year his name was attached to the libretto of a romantic musical called *Fritzi* (of which he was not connected with the staging). The end of his 30-year career seems to have been marked by his arrangement of the dances for a 'musical-comedy travelogue' *George Ahoy*, mounted by Tom Arnold as a vehicle

for provincial comic George Clarke and Dan Leno jr in 1936.

ROYSTON, Roy [CHOWN, Roy] (b London, 5 April 1899; d unknown). Durable juvenile leading man of the song-and-dance stage.

Royston made his first appearances on the stage as a child performer in London, in Liverpool and in Birmingham where he took part in Basil Dean's production of the fairy musical *Fifinella* (1912, Olly). He made his London musical début as the dude boy David in *Betty* at Daly's Theatre, and he subsequently appeared in plays and in revue before going into active service in the war. He returned to the stage in 1919, taking over the rôle of the boy Hughie in *The Boy* at the Adelphi Theatre, then appeared in the London production of *Fifinella* in an adult rôle and starred opposite Evelyn Laye as the hero of the Gaiety Theatre's revival of *The Shop Girl* (1920).

There followed a series of lead juvenile rôles in the musicals *Now and Then* (1920, Henry Bablock-Hythe), *The Lady of the Rose* (1922, Adrian Beltramini), *The Cousin from Nowhere* (1923, Adrian van Piffel) and *Little Nellie Kelly* (1923, Jack Lloyd) and a season in the revue *Snap!* before Royston crossed to America to take up a similar line of juvenile leads in rather less appreciable shows: *Peg o' My Dreams* (Jerry), *Marjorie* (Brian Valcourt) and *June Days* (Austin Bevans). Back in London in 1925 he took the lead juvenile rôles in three American musicals, *The Blue Kitten* (Armand du Velin), *Happy-Go-Lucky* (ex- *When You Smile*, Wally King) and the *Kitty's Kisses* version of *The Girl Friend* (Robert Mason) and, thereafter, he hopped backwards and forwards between Broadway and Britain playing *Ups-a-Daisy* (Roy Lindbrooke) in America, *Lucky Girl* (King Stephan) and *Meet My Sister* (René Fleuriot) on the road in England, *Cochran's Revue* and *Blue Roses* (Jimmy Mallowes) in London, and then the Fred Stone *Smiling Faces* (Robert Bowington) in America.

Back in London once more he took the juvenile lead in the American import *The One Girl* (ex- *Smiles*) and played in revue and in pantomime, and then joined the company at the Gaiety Theatre where between 1935 and 1939 he was to create his best run of rôles, paired with American dancer Louise Browne as the straight love interest of the comedy musicals which featured the Leslie Henson, Fred Emney and Richard Hearne comedy team: *Seeing Stars* (Ken Carraway), *Swing Along* (Paul Jerome), *Going Greek* (Leander) and *Running Riot* (Richard Vane). He went once again into uniform for the duration of the Second World War, and emerged in 1943 to return to the stage as Billy in a tour of *No, No, Nanette*. He subsequently appeared in London and Australia (1950) alongside Arthur Askey in *The Love Racket*, in the West End as Stanislaus in *The Bird Seller* (*Der Vogelhändler*) and on the road in *No, No, Nanette*, *The Quaker Girl* and *The Chocolate Soldier*, until well after his juvenile days.

ROZE, Edmond

A little, round-faced character actor, Roze appeared in Paris before the First World War in comedy, in revue and in musical pieces (*Florodora* etc) and took his first steps as both a stage director (*Cocorico* at the Apollo etc) and an administrator under the wing of the all-powerful Gustave Quinson who appointed him as administrator/secretary general – whilst continuing as an actor – at the Palais-Royal. After his demobilization, he continued his multiple career as a performer, mostly in supporting parts but occasionally in sizeable rôles, director and administrator. He was, however, never considered an outstanding actor, and it was as a director that he made his mark on the post-war Paris stage.

After staging the opening revue at Quinson's little wartime L'Abri, Roze directed the original production of the show which had been scheduled to follow it. The vast success of *Phi-Phi* – ultimately mounted at the Bouffes-Parisiens – set him off on a busy career as a director, and thereafter he staged many of the most important Parisian musical comedies of the era including *Dédé, Ta bouche, Madame, Là-haut, Gosse de riche, Troublez-moi, En chemyse, Nonnette, P.L.M., Passionnément, J'aime, Lulu, J'adore ça!, L'Eau à la bouche, Yes, Trois jeunes filles ... nues!, Zou!* and *Rosy*. He also directed such imported musical comedies as *Tip-Toes* and *Mercenary Mary* (in which he appeared as Christophe) and latterly also directed some less book-based, more visual shows such as the period piece *Brummell* and Ralph Benatzky's extravagant *Deux sous de fleurs*.

He was, at various periods, co-manager of Théâtre des Nouveautés with Benoît-Léon Deutsch, co-director with Quinson at the Bouffes-Parisiens, and later sole director of the Folies-Wagram.

RUBENS, Paul [Alfred] (b London, 29 April 1875; d Falmouth, 25 February 1917). Songwriter and scribe of the very lightest kind of material for the Victorian and Edwardian musical stage.

The younger son of an exceedingly wealthy and social London family, Rubens had no musical training, but began as a student by composing a score (w Nigel Playfair) for an Oxford production of *Alice in Wonderland* on which Lewis Carroll himself collaborated. He took part in university dramatics, continued to write songs and music, and at the age of 19 saw his 'The Little Chinchilla' performed in *The Shop Girl* at the Gaiety Theatre by Ellaline Terriss. He persevered in the field, providing songs for Arthur Roberts in *Dandy Dan the Lifeguardsman*, the revised version of *A Modern Don Quixote* (1898, 'There's Just a Something Missing') and *Milord Sir Smith*, for *Little Miss Nobody* ('Trixie of Upper Tooting' 'A Wee Little Bit of a Thing Like That' with his stockbroker brother, Walter, 'We'll Just Sit Out', 'The People All Come to See Us') and for George Edwardes's *San Toy* (1899, 'Me Gettee Outee Velly Quick'). At the same time he made his first but unsuccessful venture as a dramatist with the play *Young Mr Yarde* (1898, w Harold Ellis) and another, equally shortlived, as the co-author and co-composer of a burlesque, *Great Caesar*, which was produced in the West End with a fine cast but a feeble reception.

Rubens continued songwriting with contributions to two Tom Davies productions, *L'Amour mouillé* (again with brother Walter and with Landon Ronald) and, most importantly, to *Florodora* where he managed to get not only lyrics but a number of tunes tacked into the angry Leslie Stuart's score ('Inkling', 'Tact', 'When I Leave Town', 'I Want to Marry a Man', 'When an Interfering Person', 'Queen of the Philippine Islands', 'When We're on the Stage'). After this success, George Edwardes put Rubens under contract as an 'additional material' writer, and he

used further of his numbers in *The Messenger Boy* (1900, burlesque 'Tell Me Pretty Maiden', 'How I Saw the CIV' 'A Perfectly Peaceful Person'), *The Toreador* (1901, 'Everybody's Awfully Good to Me'), *A Country Girl* (1902, 'Two Little Chicks', 'Coo'), *The Girl from Kays* (1902, 'I Don't Care') and *The Cingalee* (1904, 'Sloe Eyes', 'Make a Fuss of Me' 'She's All Right', 'You and I and I and You', 'Gollywogs', 'Somethings Devilish Wrong'), many with considerable success. The prolific young songwriter also interpolated pieces during the same period in Tom Davis's *The Medal and the Maid* (1902, 'Consequences') and *The School Girl* (1903). At the same time Rubens not only provided incidental music for the 1901 His Majesty's Theatre *Twelfth Night* but finally authored a musical all his own, a piece in which most of the book as well as lyrics and music were his work.

Three Little Maids was a breeze-weight piece of thoroughly English material, written to order for Edwardes to feature Ada Reeve, Edna May and Hilda Moody. Like its heroines, it was alternately music-hally, pretty, pale, mildly suggestive and also successful. It ran 348 performances in London prior to an international career. A second piece in a similar vein, *Lady Madcap*, also did well, as did *The Blue Moon* for which Rubens supplied some catchy little numbers with which to contrast Howard Talbot's more substantial songs and ensembles.

In spite of their success, both *Three Little Maids* and *Lady Madcap* were pieces of little substance or sense, but in 1905 Rubens turned out the musical which, if not his most generally successful, was almost certainly his best. *Mr Popple of Ippleton* had a genuine libretto, which gave every sign of being modelled on the style if not the substance of a French vaudeville, it had delightful characters and much less of the schoolboy-sniggery tone for which Rubens always showed such a wearying propensity in his lyrics. Bedevilled by theatre arrangements, *Mr Popple* had only a medium London career (173 performances), but it left behind a couple of Rubens's most adult and delightful songs.

A merry hotchpotch called *The Dairymaids* and the happy Dutch 'musical incident' *Miss Hook of Holland*, decorated with what the composer/author disarmingly but nonetheless accurately called his 'jingles and tunes', gave him further successes, the latter proving ultimately to be the most enduring of all his works. There was less success with a musical version of Tristan Bernard's *La Soeur*, made over as *The Hoyden* for Elsie Janis on Broadway – where Rubens's songs had been already heard as interpolations in several shows including Anna Held's *A Parisian Model* as well as productions of his British shows – and similarly little with attempts at French Riviera and Danish follow-ups to *Miss Hook* (*My Mimosa Maid, Dear Little Denmark*) and a 'song comedy', *The Genius*, written by the De Mille brothers and mounted in America by Mort Singer. However Frederick Curzon's production of *The Balkan Princess*, a Ruritanian imitation of the successful *King of Cadonia*, gave the composer a rather surprising success in an area – the costume romantic musical – which seemed far from his most likely area.

The departure of Ivan Caryll to America and the unreliability of Leslie Stuart as a chief composer gave Rubens the opportunity to take over as the main musical supplier to George Edwardes. Thereafter, the Edwardes houses and their stars helped the composer, as he helped them, to further successes and semi-successes with *The Sunshine Girl*, *The Girl from Utah* (w Sidney Jones), *After the Girl*, *Tina* and *Betty*. His best and most enduringly popular piece from this period, however, was Fred Thompson's adaptation of the famous farce *Les Dominos roses*, *Tonight's the Night*. Supplied, as he had been in *The Balkan Princess*, with an infinitely better libretto than those which he confected for himself, and limited to melodies (this was all he supplied musically, the rest had to be written for him) and some of the lyrics, Rubens proved, with a singular success, that this kind of illustration of a sound comic text was what he did best. However, just as an era of such pieces was beginning in the British theatre, Rubens, who had suffered severe ill-health through virtually his whole career, died at the age of 41.

His songs were still to be heard, interpolated into shows in London and New York, for several years theraafter, and in 1924 his 'The Gondola and the Girl' was used, alongside pieces by Padilla, Gershwin and E Ray Goetz as part of the score of Irene Bordoni's *Little Miss Bluebeard* (1924).

1899 **Great Caesar** (w Walter Rubens/w George Grossmith jr) Comedy Theatre 29 April

1902 **Three Little Maids** (w Howard Talbot/w Percy Greenbank) Apollo Theatre 20 May

1904 **Lady Madcap** (w P Greenbank/N Newnham-Davis) Prince of Wales Theatre 17 November

1904 **The Blue Moon** (w Talbot/P Greenbank/Harold Ellis) Theatre Royal, Northampton 29 February; Lyric Theatre, London 28 August 1905

1905 **Mr Popple of Ippleton** Apollo Theatre 17 March

1906 **The Dairymaids** (w Frank E Tours/w Arthur Wimperis/Robert Courtneidge, A M Thompson) Apollo Theatre 14 April

1907 **Miss Hook of Holland** (w Austen Hurgon) Prince of Wales Theatre 31 January

1907 **The Hoyden** (w Tours, John Golden, Robert Hood Bowers/ad Cosmo Hamilton et al) Knickerbocker Theater, New York 19 October

1908 **My Mimosa Maid** (w Hurgon) Prince of Wales Theatre 21 April

1909 **Dear Little Denmark** Prince of Wales Theatre 1 September

1910 **The Balkan Princess** (w Wimperis/Frederick Lonsdale) Prince of Wales Theatre 19 February

1911 **The Genius** (Vincent Bryant/William de Mille, Cecil de Mille)

1912 **The Sunshine Girl** (w Wimperis/Cecil Raleigh) Gaiety Theatre 24 February

*1912 **A Mix-Up at Newport** (Lew Kelly, Fred Wyckoff, Lon Hascall) 1 act Columbia Theater, New York 21 October

*1912 **A Rube in Chinatown** (Lew Kelly, Fred Wyckoff, Lon Hascall) 1 act Columbia Theater, New York 21 October

?1912 **The Boss of the Show** (Wimperis) 1 act

1913 **The Girl from Utah** (w Sidney Jones/w Ross, P Greenbank/Tanner) Adelphi Theatre 18 October

1914 **After the Girl** (w P Greenbank) Gaiety Theatre 7 February

1914 **Tonight's the Night** (w P Greenbank/Fred Thompson) Shubert Theatre, New York 24 December

1915 **Betty** (w Adrian Ross/Lonsdale, Gladys Unger) Daly's Theatre 24 April

1915 **Tina** (w Haydn Wood/w Harry Graham, P Greenbank) Adelphi Theatre 2 November

1915 **The Miller's Daughters** revised *Three Little Maids* (w P Greenbank) Prince's Theatre, Manchester 24 December, London Opera House 1916)

1916 **The Happy Day** (w Sidney Jones/w Ross/Seymour Hicks) Daly's Theatre 13 May

* The publicity for these pieces insists that Paul Rubens is 'a bandmaster from Schenectady'. If there were indeed two of them, *The Genius* may also belong to this mysterious bandmaster.

RUBY, Harry [RUBENSTEIN, Harold] (b New York, 27 January 1895; d Los Angeles, 23 February 1974).

Initially a composer, Ruby had his name appear on a musical theatre bill for the first time in Chicago, bracketed in fourth place behind Ted Koehler, William Mills and Paul Church as the supplier of music to the Marigold Gardens revue *Arabian Knights* (3 April 1922). His lyricist for the occasion was Bert Kalmar with whom he would be linked throughout a career which saw them active not only as Broadway and Hollywood songwriters, but also as librettists for musical comedy, and sketchwriters for revue.

Their early Broadway experience included the songs for the unfortunate Kaufman and Connelly *Helen of Troy, New York*, sketches for *The Music Box Revue* (1924, 1925), three cracks at a piece which, ultimately called *No Other Girl*, went under in 52 performances, and a rush job rewrite on the libretto of Will Ortmann's Continental Operette *Frühling im Herbst* to star Orville Harrold and his daughter Patti. They also supplied songs for a much longer-running comedy vehicle for Bobby Clark and Paul McCullough, *The Ramblers* (289 performances), which produced them a hit number in 'All Alone Monday', some additional scenes and songs for Louis Werba's production of *Twinkle Twinkle*, and had a share in the scenes and songs of *Lucky*, a musical collaboration with Jerome Kern and Otto Harbach which did not live up to its name (71 performances). At the same time, a libretto which they had written but not used was picked up by Jack Hulbert and Paul Murray and, after some remaking, became the basis for the London musical *Lido Lady*. The songs, on this occasion, were mostly by Rodgers and Hart.

Philip Goodman, the producer of *The Ramblers*, engaged Kalmar and Ruby as songwriters for *The Five o'Clock Girl*, which found considerably more success around the world than Charles Dillingham's Beatrice Lillie vehicle *She's My Baby*, on which they joined Guy Bolton as librettists to the songs of Rodgers and Hart, but *Good Boy*, on which they shared instead the songwriting with Herbert Stothart, had a good run and launched one of their biggest song successes in the squeakily delivered 'I Wanna Be Loved by You'. The Marx Brothers show *Animal Crackers* gave them another good run, but their own production of *Top Speed*, for which they provided both songs and, with Bolton, the text, arrived just as New York was teetering on the edge of its Wall Street window-sills, and its run was an indifferent one.

This was a good moment to leave town, and Ruby and Kalmar did just that. They went to Hollywood where the film of *Animal Crackers* prefaced the Marx Brothers *Horse Feathers* and *Duck Soup*, as well as *The Kid from Spain* ('What a Perfect Combination' w Harry Akst), *Do You Love Me?* and, in 1946, *Wake Up and Dream* ('Give me the Simple Life' w Rube Bloom). They returned only once to Broadway, for the nostalgic *High Kickers* in 1941.

Hollywood put out a Kalmar and Ruby biopic called *Three Little Words* in which Ruby was portrayed by Red

Skelton (to the Kalmar of Fred Astaire) whilst he himself appeared in the film in a small rôle.

A revue of Kalmar and Ruby songs was staged at the Manhattan Theater Club 9 June 1981 as *Harry Ruby's Songs My Mother Never Sang* (Michael Roth, Paul Lazarus).

1923 **Helen of Troy, New York** (w Bert Kalmar/George S Kaufman, Marc Connelly) Selwyn Theater 4 September

1924 **The Town Clown** (w Kalmar/Aaron Hoffman) Chicago 6 January

1924 **The Belle of Quakertown** revised *The Town Clown* Stamford, Conn, July

1924 **No Other Girl** revised *The Belle of Quakertown* Morosco Theater, 13 August

1925 **Holka Polka** (*Frühling im Herbst*, ex-*Spring in Autumn*) American version w Kalmar, Gus Kahn, Raymond Egan (Lyric Theater)

1926 **The Fly-by-Nights** (w Kalmar/Guy Bolton) Werba's Theater, Brooklyn 30 August

1926 **The Ramblers** (ex-*The Fly-by-Nights*) (w Kalmar/Guy Bolton) Lyric Theater 30 September

1926 **Lido Lady** (Richard Rodgers/Lorenz Hart/w Guy Bolton, Kalmar, Ronald Jeans) Gaiety Theatre, London 1 December

1927 **Lucky** (w Jerome Kern/w Otto Harbach) New Amsterdam Theater 22 March

1927 **The Five o'Clock Girl** (Bolton, Fred Thompson) 44th Street Theater 10 October

1928 **She's My Baby** (Rodgers/Hart/w Bolton) Globe Theater 3 January

1928 **Good Boy** (w Herbert Stothart/Oscar Hammerstein II, Harbach, Henry Meyers) Hammerstein's Theater 5 September

1928 **Animal Crackers** (Kaufman, Morrie Ryskind) 44th Street Theater 23 October

1929 **Top Speed** (w Bolton) 46th Street Theater 25 December

1941 **High Kickers** (w George Jessel) Broadhurst Theater 31 October

RUDDIGORE, or The Witch's Curse Supernatural comic opera in 2 acts by W S Gilbert. Music by Arthur Sullivan. Savoy Theatre, London, 22 January 1887.

The Savoy Theatre's successor to *The Mikado* reverted to the burlesque of melodrama which Gilbert and Sullivan had so successfully practised in *The Pirates of Penzance* and, like that piece, it slipped in a recyclable piece of material borrowed from its author's Gallery of Illustration days, in this case a scene taken from the long-running short piece *Ages Ago*.

Ruthven Murgatroyd (George Grossmith) has run away from a baronetcy which, because of a witch's curse, obliged him to commit a crime every day, and he lives a happy life disguised as a pure and blameless village lad called Robin Oakapple. Unfortunately, when he falls in love with Rose Maybud (Leonora Braham), his jealous foster brother Richard Dauntless (Durward Lely) feels moved to reveal his true identity. Sir Despard Murgatroyd (Rutland Barrington), who has inherited the horrid baronetcy, is freed from his obligation to daily crime and weds his victim, Mad Margaret (Jessie Bond), but Ruthven, hoist to his rightful place, squeamishly finds every way he can to avoid his doomful duty. His angry ancestors descend from their picture hooks and demand that he honour his responsibilities, but Ruthven emerges with a spotless piece of complex logic which allows him to baffle the old curse and tie up a happy ending with his Rose.

Sullivan produced a delightful melodrama-burlesque score, from which Richard Temple's sub-operatic solo as the chief of the ghostly ancestors, 'The Ghost's High Noon', nautical Richard's breezy 'I Shipped y'see in a Revenue Sloop' and Magaret's burlesque mad scene stood out alongside an *Il Trovatore*-ical legend for Rosina Brandram as the ghost's aged sweetheart, several pretty soprano pieces and some typically nifty patter from which a truly dazzling flat-out trio for Grossmith, Barrington and Miss Bond was the outstanding moment.

Ruddigore had all the elements necessary for success, but it also had one fault: most of the brilliance came in the first act, which was followed by a second which, apart from the picture-gallery scene, was rather uneventful. The show was generally compared unfavourably with *The Mikado* by a press not averse to seeing Gilbert have a failure. The paper-men also squealed maidishly over the title (originally *Ruddygore*, but hypocrisy was silenced by replacing the 'y') and accused the author of cribbing pieces of his piece from places ranging from John Brougham's *The Crimson Mask* to J H Ryley's old 'quaker' musical-hall act. The public, however, supported *Ruddigore* through 288 West End performances.

Although Carte then sent it on tour, *Ruddigore*'s life thereafter was less happy. Carte's Broadway production, with Courtice Pounds (Richard), Geraldine Ulmar (Rose) and George Thorne (Ruthven) played only 53 performances, and *Ruddigore* then vanished from the Carte repertoire. It was 1920 before it was reintroduced and, in the following years, it was played again in America and, for the first time, in Australia with Charles Walenn and Strella Wilson featured, but in spite of sporadic productions thereafter, and in spite of its undeniable if uneven merits, it never became a favourite member of the Gilbert and Sullivan canon.

A revival at London's Sadler's Wells Theatre in 1987 which featured Marilyn Hill Smith (Rose), Harold Innocent (Despard) and Gordon Sandison (Robin) gave London a fresh look at *Ruddigore* and, in an age when *The Crimson Mask* and J H Ryley were long forgotten, the piece showed no obvious lack of originality – merely a saggy second act.

In spite of the much-less-than-usual popularity of *Ruddigore* compared to other works of the Savoy canon, it was one of the very few Gilbert and Sullivan works to provoke a home-town burlesque, and even a burlesque in the West End. John L Toole was the culprit, the piece was called *Ruddy George* (Toole's Theatre 19 March 1887) and it found little favour.

USA: Fifth Avenue Theater 21 February 1887; Australia: Theatre Royal, Adelaide 23 June 1927

RUFFELLE, Frances (b London, 29 August 1965).

Daughter of a stage-school family, Frances Ruffelle began her theatre and television career as a juvenile, appearing on the West End stage in *Gavin and the Monster* (1981, Debbie) and as the narrator in the incessantly touring *Joseph and the Amazing Technicolor Dreamcoat* (1982). In 1984 she created the rôle of Dinah, the dining car, in *Starlight Express* ('U.N.C.O.U.P.L.E.D'), before going on to an international success in the rôle of Eponine ('On My Own') in the English-language version of *Les Misérables* (1985, London, New York, Tony Award). She subsequently had leading rôles in two less successful pieces: *Apples* (1989, Delilah) and *Children of Eden* (1991, Yonah).

Miss Ruffelle is married to former Royal Shakespeare Company director **John CAIRD** (b Edmonton, Canada, 22 September 1948), the co-director and -adapter of *Les Misérables* (Tony Award), director of London's *Song and Dance* (1982) and the author and director of *Children of Eden* (mus: Stephen Schwartz, Prince Edward Theatre, London, 8 January 1991).

RUGANTINO Musical by Pietro Garinei and Sandro Giovannini. Additional scenes by Festa Campanile and Massimo Franciosa. Music by Armando Trovaioli. Teatro Sistina, Rome, 15 December 1963.

The only Italian musical of recent times to have been seen on Broadway, *Rugantino* was one of the most successful of the long series of shows written and produced in Italy by Garinei and Giovannini. Set in 1830s Italy, it presented Nino Manfredi as Rugantino, a cocky layabout who prides himself on his sex appeal and pimps for his basic mistress Eusebia (Bice Valori) to keep himself in food and comforts. Gallivanting through a series of picturesque situations, he chases after one Rosetta (Lea Massari) and, when her spy husband Gnecco is murdered, finds himself convicted and condemned to death. The aristocratic Marta Paritelli (Franca Tamantini) who could give him an alibi prefers not to become involved, and Maestro Titta (Aldo Fabrizi), Eusebia's latest touch, but also the local executioner, has the job of ridding the world of Rugantino.

Rugantino had two fine seasons in Rome, and was taken to America by Alexander H Cohen where Manfredi, Ornella Vanoni and Fabrizi played the show in its original Italian with surtitles. It then went on to South America and, finally, was revived at the Sistina 15 years after its first staging with Enrico Montesano in the title rôle, Fabrizi and Bice Valori repeating and Alida Chelli as Rosetta.

USA: Mark Hellinger Theater 6 February 1964
Recordings: original cast (Orizzonte), American cast (Warner Bros), revival cast (Cam, 2 records)

A RUNAWAY GIRL Musical comedy in 2 acts by Seymour Hicks and Harry Nicholls. Lyrics by Aubrey Hopwood and Harry Greenbank. Music by Ivan Caryll and Lionel Monckton. Gaiety Theatre, London, 21 May 1898.

George Edwardes followed up the great success of *The Circus Girl* at the Gaiety Theatre with an even more successful piece in *A Runaway Girl*, a slip of a show written by Harry Nicholls and by Seymour Hicks, an ex-Gaiety star himself and the husband of ingénue Ellaline Terriss for whom the piece's title-rôle was constructed. The other favourite players of the Gaiety team were also well fitted out. Winifred Grey (Miss Terriss) is a 'runaway' from her Corsican convent and she has run so that she won't have to wed the unseen nephew of old Lord Coodle (Fred Kaye). In her flight, she joins up with a band of wandering minstrels-cum-bandits where other temporary recruits include handsome Guy Stanley (W Louis Bradfield), and Coodle servants Flipper (Edmund Payne) and Alice (Katie Seymour). Intrigues and disguises intervene as the 'minstrels' turn nasty, but finally all the English escape back to England where it turns out that Guy is Lord Coodle's nephew and Winifred can stop running. Harry Monkhouse shared the comedy as Lay Brother Tamarind,

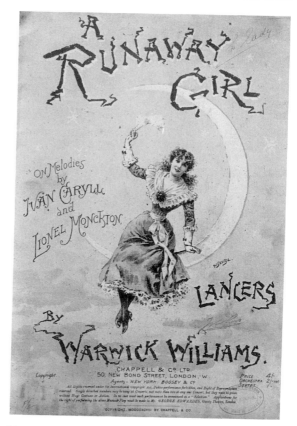

Plate 233.

and infringed occasionally on the story line.

The songs were in the now-established Gaiety tradition. Miss Terriss waltzed to an admission to a craving for nicotine ('The Sly Cigarette') and scored a hit with Monckton's 'The Boy Guessed Right', Connie Ediss, cast as a Corsican brigand from London's East End, sighed glutinously over her dreams of being in 'Society' and gave her phoney version of being Spanish in 'Barcelona', Teddy Payne and Katie Seymour performed their expected duet, this time in blackface (a disguise to escape the Corsicans) as 'Piccaninnies', operatic vocalist John Coates as the chief brigand had a ringing ballad in praise of 'My Kingdom' and Ethel Haydon, Willie Warde, Fred Wright, Robert Nainby, Grace Palotta, Lawrance d'Orsay, Fritz Rimma and others, all cast as a group of Cooks tourists, wandering in and out of the story, joined together to explain why one should 'Follow the Man from Cooks'. The hit of the night, however, fell to Miss Haydon, with the merry 'Soldiers in the Park', a march melody which has turned out to be the most surviving number from any of the original group of Gaiety musical comedies.

The show ran on, with new songs being constantly added, and even an official 'second version' being announced, until it had reached 593 performances and taken the Gaiety Theatre into the 1900s. In the meanwhile, it had already set out on its travels. Augustin Daly, who had done a superior job with the Gaiety's previous *The Circus Girl* on Broadway, took up the new show and produced it at his New York Daly's Theater, without subjecting the piece to the low-comedy rewrites and local interpolations which had marred so many imports in the hands of other producers. Virginia Earle was Winifred with James T Powers (Flipper), Mabelle Gilman (Alice), Paula Edwardes (Carmenita), Herbert Gresham (Tamarind) and Cyril Scott (Guy) in support, and the tasteful producer was rewarded with a very fine 216 performances before heading for the road. The show was even revived in 1900, by Daniel Frohman, for a return season on Broadway (40 performances).

In Vienna, *Ein durchganges Mädel* (ad Carl Lindau, Leopold Krenn) starred American soubrette Marie Halton alongside such eminent locals as Karl Streitmann as the bandit leader, Josef Joseffy as Tamarind, Karl Blasel as Jaromir Spindel (ex-Flipper) and Therese Biedermann as Pampeluna (ex-Carmenita), and adapter Lindau appeared as the heroine's father through 37 performances, whilst in Budapest *A kis szökevény* (the little runaway, ad Geza Kacziány, Emil Makai) scored a major hit at the Népszinház. Klara Küry played Winifred, accompanied by Aranka Hegyi, József Németh, Imre Szirmai, Mihály Kovács, Sári Blaha and Mihály Kiss through an excellent 79 performances. In Berlin, where the heroine and title became *Daisy* in C M Roehr's adaptation for his Lessing-Theater, the young Lina Abarbanell starred through 41 consecutive performances before *Daisy* was replaced on the Lessing-Theater stage by a revival of another Edwardes show, *The Geisha*.

Back in Britain the show was quickly on the road, and the colonial companies soon followed – South Africa in 1901, Australia in 1902 with Florence Young running away from Charles Kenningham, and George Lauri (Flipper), Carrie Moore (Alice), May Beatty (Carmenita), and Grace Palotta from the London cast (Dorothy) amongst the pursuers – as *A Runaway Girl* established itself as the most internationally successful of all the Gaiety Theatre musical comedies.

USA: Daly's Theater 25 August 1898; Austria: Theater an der Wien *Ein durchganges Mädel* 2 April 1899; Hungary: Népszinház *A kis szökevény* 11 November 1899; Germany: Lessing-Theater *Daisy* 19 May 1900; Australia: Her Majesty's Theatre, Melbourne 15 February 1902

RUND UM DIE LIEBE Operette in 3 acts by Robert Bodanzky and Friedrich Thelen. Music by Oscar Straus. Johann Strauss-Theater, Vienna, 9 November 1914.

A wartime hit at Vienna's Johann Strauss-Theater, *Rund um die Liebe* ran up a fine sequence of 375 consecutive performances in just over a year in its initial production, and it remained in the repertoire at the Johann Strauss-Theater until 1924 by which time it had been seen more than 450 times.

The journey 'all around love' to which 'marriage is the terminus' didn't take any unusual routes in Thelen and Bodanzky's book. Fritz Werner was the Baron Hans, travelling incognito whilst his chauffeur Vincenz (Josef König) temporarily borrows his title, Mizzi Günther was Countess Stella von Hempel-Heringsdorf with whom he spends a slightly tipsy night in the garden of the Four Seasons restaurant, and Käte Ehren was Steffi Bachmayer, daughter of the enthusiastically nouveau-riche Florian (L Strassmeyer) who thinks he is getting a Baron for a son-in-law when Vincenz and Steffi fall for each other. Florian is disabused in the second-act finale, leaving the third act for

the pairs to get tidily together with their socially right partner.

Straus's attractive score gave fine chances to the soprano, topped by a tipsy waltz-song, 'Ein Schwipserl', and a buffo-duo with Vincenz which was a patent follow-up to that of *Ein Walzertraum* with its musical intrumental imitations. She also duetted in less staunchly romantic fashion than some with her Baron in 'Schau mein Schatz', and 'Es gibt Dinge, die muss man vergessen', saving the real moment of musical romance for their final clinch. Hans was equipped with a pair of tidy waltzing tenor solos: 'Ich weiss schön, was ich möcht'' and 'Sie red't nichts, Sie sagt nichts' and partook of a march trio ('Kinder, so ein Mädel'), whilst the soubret pair of Vincenz and Steffi had a choice of soubret numbers, alongside a jolly introduction for Florian, a topical piece about being a reservist performed by Max Brod, and a set of finales that simply rattled with reprises.

In spite of its Vienna success and a good life in Germany, *Rund um die Liebe* had, however, little exposure elsewhere. Hungary welcomed a version (ad Andor Gábor) to the Király Szinház for 40 performances but, probably at least partly because of wartime conditions, it did not travel west. It was seen again in Vienna in 1945, but has slipped from the repertoire sufficiently for the Volksoper to scalpel out 'Ein Schwipserl' and tack it fairly incongruously into its production of *Ein Walzertraum*.

Germany: ?1915; Hungary: Király Színház *Legénybucsu* 23 September 1915

RUNNIN' WILD Musical comedy by Flournoy Miller and Aubrey Lyles. Lyrics by Cecil Mack. Music by James P Johnson. Additional numbers by Jo Trent and Porter Grainger. Colonial Theater, New York, 29 October 1923.

A successor to the successful *Shuffle Along* which represented Miller and Lyles in their characters of Steve Jenkins and Sam Peck through a further series of scenes of low comedy and high spirits and a handful of songs and dances. The piece played 213 performances at the out-of-the-mainstream Colonial Theater, and introduced the dancing world to 'The Charleston' for the first time.

Recording: instrumental selection (Columbia)

RUPERT, Michael [RUPPERT, Michael] (b San Marino, Calif, 23 October 1951)

Rupert began in the theatre as a young teenager and appeared on Broadway as the boy Bibi Bonnard in *The Happy Time* at the age of 16. He worked as a young adult as a singer and a television actor, and returned to Broadway to take over the title-rôle of *Pippin* (1976). He appeared in *Shakespeare's Cabaret* in New York, *Damn Yankees* and *Working* regionally, and made a particular success in creating the rôle of Marvin in *March of the Falsettos* in New York (1981) and Los Angeles (1982). He subsequently played on Broadway in the *Sweet Charity* revival of 1986 (Oscar, Tony Award), as Alex in his own musical *Mail* (1988), and succeeded to the rôle of Stine in *City of Angels* before reprising his Marvin in *Falsettoland* (1990) and then in the Broadway double-header of Marvin musicals produced in 1992 as *Falsettos*.

Alongside his acting career, Rupert has also composed the scores for two musicals, the first of which, *Three Guys Naked from the Waist Down*, was mounted off-Broadway in

1985. *Mail*, originally produced at the Pasadena Playhouse, was brought to Broadway in 1988 (48 performances).

1985 **Three Guys Naked from the Waist Down** (Jerry Colker) Minetta Lane Theater 5 February
1988 **Mail** (Colker) Music Box Theater 14 April

RUSSELL, H[arold] Scott (b Malvern, 25 September 1868; d Malvern, 28 August 1949). Vocalist and actor, who took part in several eras of the musical theatre.

After an early career as an engineer, Russell made his first appearance on the stage at the age of 22 in the chorus of *Paul Jones* with Agnes Huntington. Three years later, having visited America with Miss Huntington in *Captain Thérèse* (Marquis), he joined the D'Oyly Carte company at the Savoy Theater where he appeared in the Gilbert and Sullivan repertoire and created the rôles of Lord Dramaleigh in *Utopia (Ltd)*, Bertuccio in both versions of Messager's *Mirette*, Pedro Gomez in *The Chieftain*, Dr Tannhäuser in *The Grand Duke* and Count Cosmo in *His Majesty*, taking time out from the Savoy to appear as Gustave in *Baron Golosh* (*L'Oncle Célestin*) at the Trafalgar Theatre.

He took over Charles Ryley's rôle in *The Yashmak* after that actor died on stage, and then joined George Edwardes's company at Daly's Theatre where he succeeded to the tenor rôle of Katana in *The Geisha* before going on to play in *A Greek Slave* (Archias), *A Gaiety Girl* (revival, in Hayden Coffin's original rôle) and *San Toy* (Fo Hop). After a further period with the D'Oyly Carte company, touring in the principal tenor rôles, he returned to Edwardes to play in *Véronique*, *The Geisha* (revival) and *Les Merveilleuses*, appeared with Thomas Beecham's Light Opera Company, played in some of the earliest pre-war London revues (*Everybody's Doing It*, *All the Winners*) and took the rôle of Gilfain in a wartime revival of *Florodora* before moving on to war duties.

In 1920 he appeared as Lockit in the celebrated Lyric, Hammersmith revival of *The Beggar's Opera*, a part he reprised on several occasions, whilst taking several other rôles, musical and straight, under the same management. The musical rôles included parts in *Lionel and Clarissa* (Colonel Oldboy), a hacked-up *La Vie parisienne*, *The Fountain of Youth* (Mark Mugwort) and *Derby Day* (John Bitter). During the 1930s he played in Ann Croft's comic opera *Prudence*, took the burlesque rôle of The Bloody Pirate with George Robey in *Jolly Roger*, and played Rocco in Herbert Farjeon's pasticcio *An Elephant in Arcady* (1938) at the age of 70 before retiring from the stage after nearly half a century of activity.

RUSSELL, Lillian [LEONARD, Helen Louisa] (b Clinton, Iowa, 4 December ?1861; d New York, 5 June 1922). America's queen of comic opera in the last decades of the 19th century, and the buxom beauty of early 20th-century Broadway burlesque.

The daughter of printer Charles E Leonard and of Cynthia Leonard, a well-known women's rights campaigner, the young Miss Russell was convent-educated in Chicago and went to New York at the age of 16 to study singing with Madame Rudersdorff. Before long she was appearing in the chorus of E E Rice's *HMS Pinafore* (with which she played a single week on Broadway) and

Evangeline companies and was married (briefly) to Harry Braham, the musical director. The shapely young soprano soon won engagements as a solo vocalist, and appeared at Tony Pastor's variety theatre as a ballad singer with a considerable success which soon merited her the leading rôles in the house's burlesque production of *Olivette*, *The Pie-Rats of Penn Yann* (Mabel) and his potted *Patience*.

She left Pastor to go on tour with Willie Edouin's farce company and when she returned to New York it was under the management of John McCaull, newly launched at the Bijou Theater with the intention of becoming the city's only and/or best musical theatre producer. McCaull starred the 19-year-old Miss Russell as the snake-charming Irma (here called Djemma) opposite Selina Dolaro in his production of Audran's *Le Grand Mogol* (*The Snake Charmer*) and she compounded this success as Bathilde in a revival of *Les Noces d'Olivette* (*Olivette*) before organizing her own production of *Patience* (1882) with McCaull, hot on the heels of the D'Oyly Carte production which had just left town. *Patience* was a 92-performance success for the popular young star, already hailed as 'The Queen of the Dudes', and she and her producer followed it with another good run with *The Sorcerer* (Aline, 1882). However, just when she should have been ready to follow up her English operetta sucesses with a piece written specially for her by the composer of *Billee Taylor*, the dashing Teddy Solomon, she fell ill. The illness caused a furore, and the newspapers daily chronicled the fair prima donna's slow progress to health whilst *Virginia*, without its prima donna, sank in five weeks.

Miss Russell made her return to the theatre in breeches as Prince Raphael in *La Princesse de Trébizonde* (Casino Theatre), but she walked out after three weeks in an early example of the cavalier attitude to contracts which was to speckle and damage her career, to follow Solomon to Britain and escape some contractual obligations to the Standard Theater. After some characteristic lack of legal co-operation between the British and American courts, she was permitted to appear in *Virginia* (retitled *Paul and Virginia*) at the Gaiety Theatre, but although she won some nice personal notices, the show was quickly over. She then signed to appear in comic opera for Alexander Henderson but was released by him to create the rôle of Princess Ida for Carte. However, her unwillingness to rehearse and her generally unprofessional attitudes resulted in her being dumped by the Savoy.

This time it was she who squealed 'contract', but to no avail, and before long she and Solomon were off to Europe with a tour of *Billee Taylor*. They dropped out after a few weeks, leaving the tour to wander on and become stranded, and came back to Britain where, later in the year, they had success together at last as star and composer of *Polly, the Pet of the Regiment*. When Lillian played Solomon's version of *Pocahontas* they were less successful, and the duo promptly switched their field of action back to America. There they did rather better with *Polly* and another new piece, *Pepita*, before the dramatic break between them when it was revealed that the composer – whose attitude to contracts was pretty much the same as that of his 'wife' – was a bigamist.

Solomon went back to face charges in Britain, Lillian remained in America to play for John Duff, appearing in *The Maid and the Moonshiner*, in the title-rôle of *Dorothy*, as

Inez (and later Anita) in *The Queen's Mate*, as Princess Etelka in *Nadgy*, Fiorella in *The Brigands*, in the title-rôle of *The Grand-Duchess*, as Harriet in Broadway's version of *Poor Jonathan* and Pythia in *Apollo* (*Das Orakel*). She starred in the American production of Audran's *La Cigale* and as Teresa in *The Mountebanks*, and took out her own touring company with these last two pieces, before returning to Broadway to play *Giroflé-Girofla* and the rôle of Rosa in the American comic opera *Princess Nicotine*.

Miss Russell made her first return to England since her 'divorce' to play at the Lyceum in a specially organized production of Edward Jakobowski's Austrian success *Die Brillantenkönigin* (*The Queen of Brilliants*) which was using London as a springboard to Broadway, but the show was a failure and she returned to the safety of Offenbach to star on Broadway in another Hortense Schneider rôle as *La Périchole*. Over the next few years she also appeared in revivals of *Le Petit Duc*, *Patience* and *La Belle Hélène*, but a series of new home-made musicals (*The Tzigane*, *The Goddess of Truth*, *An American Beauty*, *The Wedding Day*) did not find her the original vehicle which had eluded her throughout a long and otherwise remarkable career.

After appearing in a revival of *Erminie* she turned, with the century, back to burlesque and the last part of her career, with the exception of a 1904 sally forth to appear as Lady Teazle in a comic opera of that name, was spent at Weber and Fields's place of entertainment, appearing in the revusical concoctions produced there (*Whirl-i-gig*, *Fiddle-Dee-Dee*, *Hoity-Toity*, *Twirly Whirly*, *Whoop de doo*, *Hokey Pokey*). If these naturally did not produce the elusive rôle, *Twirly Whirly* did produce the only song since Solomon's 'The Silver Line' (which she had not created) to which Miss Russell's name would stay attached, John Stromberg's 'Come Down Ma Evenin' Star'.

Lillian Russell has been portrayed on stage and film a number of times. A London rewrite of *Sally* (1942) managed to introduce her into the proceedings in the person of the buxom Linda Gray (soon after to be Queen Elizabeth I in *Merrie England* and later London's Domina in *A Funny Thing* ...), but Hollywood devoted an entire 1940 film to her in which she was portrayed by Alice Faye. Andrea King (*My Wild Irish Rose*) and Binnie Barnes (*Diamond Jim*) were other screen Lillians.

Biography: Morell, P: *Lillian Russell: The Era of Plush* (Random House, New York, 1940)

RUY BLAS AND THE BLASÉ ROUÉ Burlesque in 2 acts by 'A C Torr' (Fred Leslie) and Herbert F Clark. Music by W Meyer Lutz. Gaiety Theatre, London, 21 September 1889.

Constructed for the Gaiety Theatre's overwhelmingly popular star team of Fred Leslie and Nellie Farren by Leslie himself, *Ruy Blas and the Blasé Roué* continued the almost unbroken run of first-rate successes which the house had produced since the innovation of the 'new burlesque' and the partnership between the two performers. Victor Hugo's 1838 verse drama about the phoney Prime Minister who wins the love of the Queen of Spain underwent the usual kind of perversion, ending up as a jolly romp in which Ruy (Nellie Farren), Don Caesar (Leslie) and Donna Cristina (Sylvia Grey) spent their time plotting to get back some incriminating papers and the Queen's jewels in the midst of a mass of songs and dances

for the two stars and for such other principals as Marion Hood (Queen), Letty Lind and Fred Storey.

The songs had been written, bit by bit, as Fred and Nellie toured their previous burlesques in America, and had been posted back to Edwardes to be set by a variety of composers. The result (with interpolations) was a bevy of contrasting numbers. If there was no resounding hit, the score nevertheless turned up its ration of popular songs from Fred's advice to 'Stick to the Whisky You're Used To', to his dressed-up duos with Nellie as a silly sister act ('Ma's Advice'), in a parody of the Christy Minstrels ('Johnny Jones and his Sister Sue') or with a range of topicalities ('I've Just Had a Wire to Say So', 'Don't Know'). There was also a Whistling Lullaby, Fred Bowyer's encouragement to 'Razzle Dazzle', Marion Hood's soprano 'Españita' (mus: Antonio Mora) and a shoeful of dances. One of these last was a burlesque of the Gaiety's own great success, the *Faust Up-to-Date* pas de quatre performed by four men made up as famous actors. One of the four burlesques, Henry Irving, called in the Lord Chancellor to forbid Leslie to thus ridicule him. Edwardes inherited some splendid publicity and the actor more ridicule than if he had simply kept quiet.

Ruy Blas filled the Gaiety for 282 performances before it had to be taken off to go on the road. That road stretched as far as Australia, where the Gaiety Company presented their show with Leslie, Farren, Grey and Storey supplemented by Grace Pedley as the Queen, Florence Levey in Letty Lind's dance spot, and the young Sidney Jones conducting. Back home, the show continued round the touring circuits for two years where it did well even without the stars around whom it had been constructed, before being put away in favour of the next Gaiety burlesque.

The *Ruy Blas* story had been previously burlesqued in *Ruy Blas Righted* (Vaudeville Theatre 3 January 1874), as well as being given serious musico-dramatic treatments in operas by such as William Glover (Covent Garden 24 October 1861) and Filippo Marchetti (La Scala, Milan 3 April 1869).

Australia: New Princess Theatre, Melbourne 27 June 1891

RYLEY, J[ohn] H (b England, ?1841; d London, 28 July 1922). America's pre-eminent Gilbert and Sullivan comedian of the 19th century.

Ryley began his performing life in the music halls where he formed a successful partnership with Marie Barnum in a mock-serious routine as the 'Dancing Quakers'. However, he found significant and sustained success when he switched, in his mid-thirties, to the musical theatre and after a busy and sought-after few years performing in Britain, established himself as an outstanding comic opera comedian in America.

Ryley made his earliest appearances in the musical theatre with Kate Santley in *Cattarina* (1875, Fernando), Lecocq's *Le Prés Saint-Gervais* (Nicole), Gilbert and Clay's *Princess Toto* (Zapeter) and alongside W S Penley and Florence Trevallyan in *Madame l'Archiduc* (1876). He then appeared at Manchester in pantomime with Mrs John Wood, in *The Sultan of Mocha* (Flint), as Amen Squeak in Cellier's *Nell Gwynne* and as the Foreman in *Trial By Jury*, before taking over as Flint in the London production of *The Sultan of Mocha* (St James's Theatre 1876). He appeared through 1877 at the Alhambra in *Orpheus in the Underworld* (Mercury), *King Indigo* (Babazouk) and *Wildfire* (Baron Hey Derry Downe) and then joined D'Oyly Carte (1878) to play the principal comic rôles (John Wellington Wells, Judge, Joseph Porter) in his company in the British provinces. After a Christmas spent playing Dame at Leeds, he was taken across to America with Carte's company to play Porter in the 'official' Broadway production of *HMS Pinafore* (1879).

Ryley then remained in America, performing frequently as Carte's principal comedian, and introducing such British characters as the Major General (*Pirates of Penzance*, 1879), Flapper (*Billee Taylor*, 1881, 1885), Blood-Red Bill (*Claude Duval*, 1882), Bunthorne (*Patience*, 1882), Lord Chancellor (*Iolanthe*, 1882), The King then Don José (*Manteaux Noirs*), King Gama (*Princess Ida*, 1884), Ko-Ko (*The Mikado*), General Bangs (*Polly*, 1885) and Jack Point (*The Yeomen of the Guard*, 1888) to Broadway. He also appeared as Laurent (*La Mascotte*, 1882), Cyprian (*Prince Methusalem*, 1883), as the King in both Broadway versions of *Le Coeur et la main*, *Micaëla* and *Hand and Heart* (1883), von Folbach in *Falka* (1883), Frimousse in *Le Petit Duc* (1884), Fanfani Pasha in *A Trip to Africa* (1886) Chow-Vhow in *The Arabian Nights* (1887) and General Pataquès in *The Queen's Mate* (1887).

Ryley was seen less frequently in the 1890s, playing in Broadway's version of Messager's *La Basoche* and in the 1895 'romantic comic opera' *Leonardo* before drifting into a long retirement.

His wife **Madeleine Lucette [Ryley]** (b London, 26 December 1858; d London, 17 February 1934) had a career in the musical theatre both in Britain – appearing with Ryley as a teenaged chorister with Kate Santley, at the Alhambra in *Orpheus in the Underworld* (Vesta) and *King Indigo* (Zobeide) and with D'Oyly Carte – and, with much more success, in America where she was seen as Susan in *Billee Taylor*, Constance in *The Sorcerer*, Regina in *La Princesse de Trébizonde*, in *Princess Toto*, as Hilaria in McCaull's production of *The Lady or the Tiger* and in the leading feminine rôle of Amorita in the American version of *Pfingsten in Florenz* at the Casino. She then turned her attention wholly to a highly successful career as a playwright, during which she adapted Messager's *La Basoche* for the American stage.

RYSKIND, Morrie (b New York 20 October 1895; d Washington, DC, 24 August 1985). One of the main instigators of Capitol-Hillarity in the Broadway musical of the 1930s.

Ryskind made his first entrance into the theatre writing sketches for the revues *The 49ers* (1922), *The Garrick Gaieties* (1925) and both sketches and lyrics for *Merry Go Round* (1927) before his first musical-comedy assignment, on the words for an out-of-town flop called *Pardon Me* with music by Charles Rosoff (composer of 'Don't Let 'em Take the Blue and White Out of the Red, White and Blue') and Harold C ('This Little Piggie Went to Market') Lewis. He did better next time up, in collaboration with George S Kaufman, on the libretto of the Marx Brothers musical *Animal Crackers*, which (like the brothers' earlier *The Cocoanuts* and their *A Night at the Opera*) he later wrote into a screenplay.

He provided further revue material to *Americana* and *Ned Wayburn's Gambols* (1929) and rejoined Kaufman for three musicals without the Marx Brothers, but with George Gershwin and a political tinge: *Strike Up the Band* (rewrite), *Of Thee I Sing* and *Let 'em Eat Cake*. A fourth piece which found its characters in the world of politics brought him into partnership with another famous name when he scripted the successful *Louisiana Purchase*, set to songs by Irving Berlin.

Ryskind directed the musical *The Lady Comes Across* (1942).

1927 **Pardon Me** (Charles Rosoff, Harold C Lewis/Ralph Murphy/w Murphy)
1928 **Animal Crackers** (Bert Kalmar, Harry Ruby/w George S Kaufman) 44th Street Theater 23 October
1930 **Strike Up the Band** (George Gershwin/Ira Gershwin/w Kaufman) Times Square Theater 14 January
1931 **The Gang's All Here** (Lewis Gensler/w Russel Crouse, Oscar Hammerstein II) Imperial Theater 18 February
1931 **Of Thee I Sing** (G Gershwin/I Gershwin/w Kaufman) Music Box Theater 26 December
1933 **Let 'em Eat Cake** (G Gershwin/I Gershwin/w Kaufman) Imperial Theater 21 October
1940 **Louisiana Purchase** (Irving Berlin) Imperial Theater 28 May

S

SACKS, Joseph L[eopold] (b Russia, 17 February 1881; d Johannesburg, South Africa, 19 May 1952).

Born in Russia, buried in South Africa, Joe Sacks wreaked most of his theatrical career on the London theatre where he produced several outstanding hits, more than once took advantage of the laws of bankruptcy, was banned from business, but bounced back irrepressibly from the depths of disgrace to the brink of dishonesty in a couple of decades of activity.

Sacks began his connection with the theatre as a fruit-seller in a circus and, ever unable to read or to write English, he launched himself first upon some theatrical ventures in South Africa before appearing in London during the First World War (allegedly rich from staging shows for the troops) to mount a revue called *Three Cheers*. It was, however, his unlikely second choice, his first musical play, which launched him to prominence and temporary prosperity, when the up-to-then only mildly successful *The Lilac Domino* scored a huge London success. He confirmed that success with another import, *Going Up*, in the same year before burning his fingers badly on two further transatlantic imports – a spectacular piece by music publisher Isidore Witmark called *Shanghai* and an inane *Nobody's Boy*, neither of which had been tried at home.

Sacks had a further block-busting success, however, with one more import, *Irene*, and he also invested significantly in Jimmy White's fine production of *Sybil*, but had less luck with two other quality pieces: Broadway's pretty *Mary*, and a version of Kálmán's *Das Hollandweibchen* with no less a star than Maggie Teyte. He took a thorough tumble, however, with his attempt to create his own *Irene*, a feebly imitative piece called *Jenny*. A second attempt at an original piece, *The Bamboula*, also flopped and when Friml's *Katinka* (108 performances) and a version of Lehár's *Libellentanz* (*The Three Graces*, 121 performances) also disappointed, Sacks ended up in the bankruptcy court.

Thereafter his appearances on the London theatre scene were sporadic, and (although he admitted to 'an interest' in *The Blue Kitten* and the super-flop *The Girl from Cooks*) his only further musical attempts with *The One Girl* (ex-*Smiles*) in 1932 and a feeble piece called *Royal Exchange*, which attempted to give film star Ramon Novarro a stage musical vehicle, were as fast and hefty failures as his three big hits had been winners.

SADDLER, Frank (b Pennsylvania; d 1921). Classic orchestrator of the dance-age Broadway musical.

Originally a musical director for touring shows, Saddler subsequently became an arranger and orchestrator for the publishing firm of Witmark. Working, for the most part, neither as a composer nor as a theatre conductor like the majority of his most important orchestrating colleagues, but as a full-time orchestrator and arranger, he became, at a time when virtually all composers did not or could not write full scores for their music, very largely responsible for the orchestral sound of the Broadway musical comedies of the 1910s. It was a sound which, making use of a more limited number of players than had mostly been the case before, provided a closely textured accompaniment both attractive and, when necessary, sufficiently expansive-sounding in itself and which was, in the pre-amplification age, also supportive to the singer.

Amongst the shows for which Saddler supplied the scoring were Jerome Kern's *Very Good Eddie* (1915), *Oh, Boy!* (1917), *Oh, Lady! Lady!!* (1918), *The Night Boat* (1920) and *Sally* (1920), Gershwin's maiden *La La Lucille* (1919), Dillingham's Hippodrome extravaganzas, and other Dillingham shows such as *Watch Your Step* (1914), *Stop! Look! Listen!* (1915), *Jack o' Lantern* (1917) and *Tip Top* (1920).

SAGAN, Leontine (b Austria, 1889; d Pretoria, South Africa, May 1974).

A former actress, the South African-bred Sagan made her name with her direction of the cult play *Mädchen in Uniform* and, in the musical theatre, as the director of Ivor Novello's romantic musical spectaculars (*Glamorous Night, Careless Rapture, Crest of the Wave, The Dancing Years, Arc de Triomphe*) and their Eric Maschwitz spinoffs *Balalaika* and *Paprika*. She directed the British production of Stolz's *Venus in Seide* and the 1940s remakes of Strauss's works as *A Night in Venice* and *Gay Rosalinda*, and travelled to Australia to direct *The Dancing Years*. In spite of her successes, she is largely recalled today as a bullish, militaristic director who took an apparent pleasure in reducing actresses to tears.

SAGER, Carole Bayer (b New York, 8 March 1946)

Lyricist Sager made her first appearance on a Broadway bill with the four performances of the 1970 musical *Georgy*, but returned a little short of a decade and a good many hit songs ('Nobody Does It Better', 'Through the Eyes of Love' etc) later to write the songs, with Marvin Hamlisch, for *They're Playing Our Song*, an enormously successful musical play apparently based on the relationship between herself and the composer. Which must make her the only lyricist to have authored an autobiographical musical comedy hit.

1970 **Georgy** (George Fischoff/Tom Mankiewicz) Winter Garden Theater 26 February
1979 **They're Playing Our Song** (Marvin Hamlisch/Neil Simon) Imperial Theater 11 February

SAIDY, Fred [SAIDY, Fareed Milhelm] (b Los Angeles, 11 February 1907; d Santa Monica, Calif, 14 May 1982).

Originally a journalist, Saidy wrote revue sketches, a pair of film scripts (w Sig Herzig) and television material

Plate 234. **Sail Away:** *Elaine Stritch as cruise hostess Mimi Paragon digs out some 'Useless Useful Phrases' from one of those books.*

before entering the musical theatre with the libretto for one of the earliest attempts to clone an *Oklahoma!* in *Bloomer Girl*. It cloned exceedingly happily through 652 performances, but it was topped by a second collaboration between the librettist and lyricist Yip Harburg on the fantasy *Finian's Rainbow* (725 performances).

When Saidy went into production with the comedy musical *Flahooley* the results were less happy, but a fourth collaboration with Harburg produced yet another good run when the pair manufactured a vehicle for Lena Horne which, as *Jamaica*, played more than 500 Broadway performances. Like his earlier hits, however, *Jamaica* found its success only at home and no takers outside the United States. His final Broadway offering (for a remake of the flop *Darling of the Day* which he authored did not come to the stage) was *The Happiest Girl in the World*, a piece which did unkind things to the works of Aristophanes and Offenbach simultaneously, and which played 97 performances in 1961.

1944 **Bloomer Girl** (Harold Arlen/E Y Harburg/w Sig Herzig) Shubert Theater 5 October

1947 **Finian's Rainbow** (Burton Lane/Harburg/w Harburg) 46th Street Theater 10 January

1951 **Flahooley** (Sammy Fain/Harburg/w Harburg) Broadhurst Theater 14 May

1952 **Jolly Anna** revised *Flahooley* (Philharmonic Auditorium, Los Angeles)

1957 **Jamaica** (Arlen/Harburg/w Harburg) Imperial Theater 31 October

1961 **The Happiest Girl in the World** (Offenbach arr/ Harburg/w Henry Myers) Martin Beck Theater 3 April

SAIL AWAY Musical comedy in 2 acts by Noël Coward. Broadhurst Theater, New York, 3 October 1961.

Sail Away was the nearest thing Noël Coward ever wrote to the witty, revusical kind of musical play which his enormous success as an author of comedies and revue material might have led public and producers to expect from him, rather than the romantic musical plays with which he persisted, following his success with *Bitter-Sweet*. But it was not originally designed as such. *Sail Away* was constructed for the American stage. Named for a song tacked into the new score from his earlier London musical *Ace of Clubs*, the show was set on a Cunard cruise liner and its action followed the *Love Boat*-style amours of the passengers, most especially those of middle-aged Verity Craig (Jean Fenn, equipped with two numbers from another London failure, *Pacific 1860*) and the younger John van Mier (John Hurst). It didn't follow them for long, for soon after the Boston opening major revisions were put into action and Verity Craig and all her miserable love-life and her lovely songs went under the knife. A secondary character, the comical cruise hostess Mimi Paragon (Elaine Stritch, who had won the best of the applause in Boston), became John's new love, and she and the bevy of comically drawn Coward characters who peopled the cruiser became the centre of the piece. With no soprano, no love duets, no soul-searching, the accent was now very largely on comedy and the *Sail Away* that reached Broadway was a very different show from the one that had opened in Boston.

The comedy songs provided many funny moments: Miss Stritch doing things to one of those books that dispense 'Useless Useful Phrases' or bewailing 'Why Do the Wrong People Travel (and the right people stay back home)?', or Charles Brasewell in uniform instructing the ship's stewards that 'The Passenger's Always Right' and later as an Arab pimp repeating, to the same tune, instructions to a horde of guides on how to please and skin the arriving hordes ('Compel him, sell him anything from sex to dynamite ...'). The romantic songs took a definite second place, as in all the best revues.

The show opened strongly on Broadway and looked set for success but, suddenly, its audience ran out. It closed after 167 performances. But Miss Stritch, who had had a definite personal success, was not finished with Mimi

Paragon. Three months later she opened in *Sail Away* in Britain. Harold Fielding's production included several of the Broadway cast and also one new number: 'Bronxville Darby and Joan', which had been cut out of town in America. The ageing star of *Irene*, Edith Day, paired with Sydney Arnold to bicker 'We're a dear old couple, and we *hate* one another ...' and grumble another classic into the Coward song book. However, once again *Sail Away*, after a brilliant opening, found that its audience, if enthusiastic, was limited. From fine houses the attendance vanished to a half virtually overnight. The production closed after 252 performances. The following year Maggie Fitzgibbon gave her Mimi Paragon to Melbourne and Sydney (Her Majesty's Theatre 19 July 1963), after which *Sail Away* was folded away, having given a tantalizing glimpse of the musical Coward didn't feel inclined to write.

UK: Savoy Theatre 21 June 1962; Australia: Her Majesty's Theatre, Melbourne 24 May 1963

Recordings: original cast (Capitol), London cast (HMV), composer performing (Capitol)

SAINT-ALBIN, Albert de (b Paris, 1843; d Paris, 1901).

Journalist (*Figaro*, sometime editor of *Jockey*) and playwright (*Le Train de plaisir*, *Monsieur l'Abbé*, *Leurs gigolettes*, *Les Grandes Manoeuvres*) Saint-Albin managed, in just a handful of musicals, to collaborate with each of Offenbach, Planquette, Lecocq and Hervé, albeit not on their greatest successes. His single most successful piece was the vaudevillesque *Le Grand Casimir* in which Céline Chaumont encouraged the mode for the vaudeville-opérette instigated by Judic and *Niniche*, but Planquette's *Panurge* was a fine Parisian success and Hervé's *La Belle Poule*, a Judic vehicle, also won some overseas attention. Both Serpette's *Le Manoir du Pic-Tordu* and Offenbach's *La Foire Saint-Laurent*, in spite of quick failures at home, were also exported. His *Mam'zelle Gavroche*, a vehicle for Jeanne Granier, played 56 Parisian performances.

Saint-Albin also put his name to both revues and ballet scenarii.

1872 **Le Ruy Blas d'en face** (w Émile Blavet, Henri Chabrillat) Théâtre des Folies-Dramatiques 13 April
1875 **Le Manoir du Pic-Tordu** (Gaston Serpette/w Arnold Mortier) Théâtre des Variétés 28 May
1875 **La Belle Poule** (Hervé/w Hector Crémieux) Théâtre des Folies-Dramatiques 29 December
1877 **La Foire Saint-Laurent** (Jacques Offenbach/w Crémieux, Ernest Blum) Théâtre des Folies-Dramatiques 10 February
1879 **Le Grand Casimir** (Charles Lecocq/w Jules Prével) Théâtre des Variétés 11 January
1885 **Mam'zelle Gavroche** (Hervé/w Blum, Edmond Gondinet) Théâtre de la Renaissance 24 January
1895 **Panurge** (Robert Planquette/w Henri Meilhac) Théâtre de la Gaîté 22 November

SAINT-BONNET, Jeanne. Lovely Parisian leading lady of the jazz-age musical comedy.

Mlle Saint-Bonnet, who worked early on under the name of Jane Fréda, began her career in small theatres in her native Lyonnaise region playing the classic theatre repertoire. Montcharmont engaged her at the Lyon Théâtre des Célestins in 1907 and she appeared both there and the following season in Brussels in comedy and drama. She made an early Paris appearance at the Capucines in *Yette* and a revue, played at the Gaîté-Rochechouart, at the Cigale, and in 1913 at l'Olympia in the cast of the French version of *Les Arcadiens*. During the First World War, she appeared in Britain (*High Jinks* etc), and she played further English pieces in Paris (Prudence in *La Petite Quaker*, Kate in *Rip* for the opening of the Théâtre Mogador in 1920) as well as in such local pieces as *Le Roi de l'air* (1917) at the Variétés, *Béguin des dames* (1918, l'Abri), *La Folle Escapade* (1919, Cecily Palmer) alongside Polin, Victor Alix's *Princesse Lily* and various classic revivals including *La Petite Bohème* (1921, Mimi) and *La Mascotte* (Fiametta). However, she came to the fore thoroughly when she created the rôle of Eva, the lass with a penchant for pre-practising for her wedding night, in *Ta bouche*.

She starred thereafter in the juvenile leading rôles of several other 1920s musicals – *Elle ou moi* (1925, Conrad), as Lotte in *Trois jeunes filles ... nues!* (1925, 'Quand on ne dit rien') and as Ketty, who is both herself and her grandmother, in *Passionnément* (1926, 'Ah! pourquoi les bons moments'), whilst also being seen in more classic rôles, such as Diana in the Mogador's starry *Orphée aux enfers* revival (1931) and Pauline in their *La Vie parisienne* (1931).

Mlle Saint-Bonnet was the wife of star musical comedian and director Max Dearly.

SAINT-GRANIER [de GRANIER de CASSAGNAC, Jean] (b Paris, 1890; d Paris, 1976). Highly popular songwriter/performer of the Parisian revue, cabaret and musical-comedy stages.

Saint-Granier studied for the Government service exams, but he threw it in before the day and instead dabbled at first in the stock exchange, and then in journalism. During this time, he began to write and privately perform songs and ultimately provided and directed a full revue for the Little Palace, *Tais-toi, c'est fou*. During the rehearsals for this piece, his own 'performance' was sufficiently noted for him to cross the footlights and take to the stage as a performer, at the Porc-épic at Saint-Mandé and then at the Parisian Moulin de la Chanson where he found himself top-billed in *La Revue des Folies-Bergère*. Thereafter, he made himself a successful career as a performer in music hall and revue ('Attends moi sous l'horloge', 'Pardon mam'selle', 'Ma p'tite canne à la main', 'J'ai fait ça', 'Pour t'écrire que je t'aime', 'Je vous fais mes voeux', 'Marchéta', 'Dinah', 'Ah! Suzanne', 'Ça, c'est bien français', 'So Blue', 'Pour une chanson d'amour' ie 'In a Little Spanish Town' etc) at the Pie-qui-chante, the Théâtre Michel (*Plus ça change*), Le Perchoir, the Scala, the Folies-Bergère, the Théâtre Réjane etc until it could be claimed, at the end of the 1920s, that he was 'second to Chevalier in popularity' on the Parisian variety stage. Saint-Granier mixed an attractive light baritone singing voice and an elegant appearance with a knowingly sophisticated style which eventually proved equally as usable on the book-musical stage (*Katinka*, Christiné's *La Madone du promenoir* etc) and on the screen as in revue.

Alongside this career as a performer he had an even more active and successful one as a revuist and lyricist, writing more than 40 revues in the first decade of his career, as well as a long list of popular songs, a number of which were heard on the Parisian large-scale revue stage.

These were often concocted in collaboration with such fellow-lyricists as Albert Willemetz and Jean le Seyeux and with composers of the ilk of Christiné ('Avec mes lunettes' for Chevalier) and Scotto ('C'est bête de faire ça' etc), or in the form of French adaptations of foreign hits by writers from Walter Kollo ('Quand on revient') to De Sylva, Brown and Henderson ('So Blue').

In 1916 Saint-Granier was responsible, with Jean Bastia, for founding 'Le Perchoir', and in 1919 he built and, for its first unprofitable 15 months of operation, managed the 250-seater Théâtre de la Potinière. There he made some early essays, teamed with Gaston Gabaroche and Rip, in both writing and producing revue (*Danseront-ils?*, *Vas-y-voir* etc), but he made his first substantial effort as a writer for the book musical theatre in collaboration with Christiné and Willemetz on the successful musical comedies *J'adore ça* and *J'aime*. However, as could be seen by his frequent choice of trans-Atlantic songs as performance material, Saint-Granier had a decided lean to the west, and his biggest theatrical triumphs as an author came with his adaptations of Broadway musicals for the Paris stage – *Rose-Marie*, *The Desert Song*, *Hit the Deck* and whatever it was of De Sylva, Brown and Henderson's work that was turned into *Miami* for Paris.

1920 **Je t'adore** (Gaston Gabaroche) 1 act Théâtre de la Potinière 1 December

1925 **J'adore ça** (Henri Christiné/w Albert Willemetz) Théâtre Daunou 14 March

1926 **J'aime** (Christiné/w Willemetz) Théâtre des Bouffes-Parisiens 23 December

1927 **Rose-Marie** French version w Roger Ferréol (Théâtre Mogador)

1929 **Boulard et ses filles** (Charles Cuvillier/w Jean le Seyeux/ Louis Verneuil) Théâtre Marigny 8 November

1929 **Le Chant du désert** (*The Desert Song*) French version w Ferréol (Théâtre Mogador)

1930 **Au temps des valses** (*Bitter-Sweet*) French version (Théâtre Apollo)

1930 **Miami** French lyrics (Théâtre des Ambassadeurs)

1931 **Halléluia** (*Hit the Deck*) French version w Ferréol (Théâtre Mogador)

1933 **Deux Sous de fleurs** (Ralph Benatzky/Paul Nivoix) Théâtre de l'Empire 6 October (?)

1948 **Les Pommes d'amour** (Louiguy/w Pierre Varennes) Théâtre des Variétés 27 March

ST HELIER, Ivy [AITCHISON, Ivy] (b St Helier, Jersey, ?1890; d London, 8 November 1971).

The diminutive actress, singer and songwriter made her first appearance on the West End musical stage in a comedy rôle in the Seymour Hicks/Ellaline Terriss flop *Captain Kidd*. She toured South Africa and the wartime front with the Hickses, played in comedy and in variety houses in such short musical pieces as *The Model and the Man* and Leo Fall's *Darby and Joan* (*Brüderlein fein*), and featured in revue, notably in one of the earliest of the American influenced pieces *Everybody's Doing It*, at the Empire and the Apollo, in *Samples*, *Three Cheers* and *Johnny Jones and His Sister Sue*.

In 1921 St Helier appeared in *Ring Up* at the Royalty, for which she had also supplied the songs, in 1925 took a comedy rôle in the musical *Patricia*, and in 1929 she created the part of her career when she was cast as the little cabaret vocalist Manon la Crevette in Noël Coward's *Bitter-Sweet*, introducing 'Bonne Nuit, Merci' and 'If Love

Were All'. She subsequently played in the Ralph Benatzky circus musical *The Flying Trapeze* (1935) with Jack Buchanan, toured in 1938 in the rôle written for Fritzi Massary in *Operette* and played Madame Blum in Emile Littler's revival of *The Quaker Girl* (1944) in between engagements in revue and the straight theatre.

As a composer, she supplied additional material for a number of book shows including *His Girl* (1922), Harold Fraser-Simson's *The Street Singer* (1924) and the London versions of Friml's *The Blue Kitten* and Robert Stolz's *Mädi* (1927, *The Blue Train*) as well as for many a revue. In *The Quaker Girl* she interpolated a number of her own making, 'It's the Profit That Makes It Dear'. Her most successful single number was 'Coal Black Mammy' written with Laddie Cliff for *The Co-Optimists* (1921).

St Helier also appeared on film, notably repeating her Manon la Crevette alongside Anna Neagle and Fernand Graavey in the British film version of *Bitter-Sweet*.

ST JOHN, Florence [GRIEG, Margaret] (b Tavistock, 8 March 1854; d London, 30 January 1912). London's unchallenged 'queen of comic opera' throughout the Victorian era.

Florence St John, equipped with a splendidly strong and true soprano and all the taste and talent needed to use it to best effect, had a career of 40 years in the musical theatre during which she was unflaggingly the darling of the public and the critics through a royal register of the musical shows of the time. Married at the age of 14 to a naval officer, the young Mrs St John was thus able to take early professional employment as an adult and she began her career touring as a vocalist with a diorama. She moved on to join an operetta company run by a certain Dr Hodges, touring in Offenbach's *The Rose of Auvergne* and *Breaking the Spell*, and appeared on music halls as a ballad singer. When she played the Oxford Music Hall (as Florence Leslie) in 1875, her singing of Sullivan's 'Meet Me Once Again' won her a six-week engagement.

She was next hired by the Durand Opera Company as contralto and made her first operatic appearance as one of the ugly sisters in Rossini's *La Cenerentola*. She subsequently sang with the Blanche Cole Opera Company, the Rose Hersee Company and Henry Walsham's Company in a selection of rôles ranging from Cherubino, Maritana and Arline to Azucena, before making her musical theatre début as Germaine in *Les Cloches de Corneville* in 1878. She made a veritable sensation the following year when Alexander Henderson presented her at the Strand Theatre in the title-rôle of Offenbach's *Madame Favart* and, from then on, one star rôle followed another: the title rôle in *Olivette* (*Les Noces d'Olivette*), more *Madame Favart* at the Avenue Theatre, where she subsequently appeared as Girola in *Manteaux Noirs*, Olivette, Lurette in Offenbach's posthumous *Lurette* (*Belle Lurette*), Boulotte in *Barbe-bleue* and Nell Gwynne in Planquette's piece of that name. *Nell Gwynne* transferred to the Comedy Theatre and its star remained there at the end of the run to play Bettina in a revival of *La Mascotte* and Djemma in *The Grand Mogul* (accompanied by a live snake). She went briefly to the Empire Theatre to star in the spectacular *The Lady of the Locket* (1885), but returned to the Comedy Theatre and there created the title-rôle of Jakobowski's *Erminie* and its famous lullaby in 1885.

Plate 235. **Florence St John**: *Victorian London's 'queen of comic opera' as the Carmen of the Gaiety Theatre's* **Carmen Up-to-Data**.

'Jack' St John appeared as Jacquette in the London version of Messager's *La Béarnaise*, repeated her *Madame Favart* and, after a period out through illness, returned to the stage in burlesque at the Gaiety Theatre where she appeared as Marguerite in the hugely successful *Faust Up-to-Date* (1888). She toured with this piece to America for a season and returned to the Gaiety to appear in the showcase of *Dick Turpin II* (1889) and to create the rôle of Carmen in *Carmen Up-to-Data* (1890). She played her Carmen in London and on the road before taking a quick turn at the slightly unlikely title-rôle of the teenage *Miss Decima* (*Miss Helyett*). She then toured opposite Auguste van Biene in *Rip van Winkle*, returned to the Gaiety for a season of *Faust Up-to-Date* and, in October 1892, was top-billed there alongside Arthur Roberts in George Edwardes's new kind of Gaiety entertainment, the musical comedy *In Town*.

She subsequently played further revivals of *Madame Favart* and *La Mascotte* and appeared for a while in the burlesque *Little Christopher Columbus* but, with her voice sounding if anything better than ever, she tended back towards more substantial singing and, rather than heading on into more musical comedy with Edwardes, she went instead to the Savoy Theatre where she starred in the title-rôle of Carte's Messager musical *Mirette* and as Rita in *The Chieftain*. She went lucratively into the insufficient comic opera *The Bric-à-Brac Will* at the request of a failing management but refused to allow the management to transfer her contract when the piece closed and, instead of going into the musical comedy *The New Barmaid*, she succeeded Annie Dirkens as *The Little Genius* (*Der Wunderknabe*) before returning to opéra-bouffe to appear

as *La Périchole* and as *La Grande-Duchesse* in a major revival sponsored by Carte.

In 1900 she took over from Evie Greene in the starring rôle of *Florodora* and thereafter she began playing regularly in non-musical vehicles, although she re-appeared on the musical stage in 1902, at the closure of the old Gaiety Theatre, to play Marguerite in *Faust Up-to-Date* once more, at nearly 50 years of age. The straight theatre scene seemed to suit her less well, but when she returned to singing, as Catherine in *Madame Sherry*, the piece was a failure. She appeared on the music halls with a piece called *My Milliner's Bill*, and in 1909 returned for the last time to play the supporting rôle (with the show's favourite song) of Red Lizi in *The Merry Peasant* at the Strand Theatre as a full-stop to a remarkable career which had taken in opéra-bouffe, Savoy comic opera, musical comedy and burlesque all with equivalent success.

Mrs St John was married four times, the second of her husbands being the six-foot-four musical-comedy actor Lithgow James and the third the Frenchman Claude Marius.

ST LOUIS WOMAN   Musical play by Arna Bontemps and Countee Cullen based on Bontemps's novel *God Sends Sunday*. Lyrics by Johnny Mercer. Music by Harold Arlen. Martin Beck Theater, New York, 30 March 1946.

When the jockey Little Augie (Harold Nicholas) hits a winning streak he also succeeds in attracting the attentions of Della Green (Ruby Hill), the easy-going, self-pleasing St Louis woman of the title. But Della is the woman of the local bar-owner, Biglow Brown (Rex Ingram), and Brown takes his revenge for this betrayal by beating Della up. Augie goes for his gun, but he is beaten to the shot by Lila (June Hawkins), Brown's rejected mistress. The villain dies cursing Augie. The curse hangs over the jockey and he begins to lose races, and Della, who believes she is handicapping him, decides to leave. Finally both Augie's racetrack touch and Della return.

Harold Arlen and Johnny Mercer provided the score for *St Louis Woman*, a score which was one of the most remarkable of its time and which won a remarkable performance from its cast. The number which proved to be the most popular outside the show was 'Come Rain or Come Shine' delivered by Augie and Della during their first blissful thoughts of marriage, but there were half a dozen others of equal power and beauty: Della's loping, off-handed, yet red-hot 'Any Place I Hang My Hat Is Home', the two cheerfully comical songs of the barmaid Butterfly (Pearl Bailey in her Broadway début), the one demanding that her man (Fayard Nicholas) 'Legalize My Name' before getting his way with her, the other reminding him that 'It's a Woman's Prerogative (to change her mind)', Augie's whoopingly joyous 'Ridin' on the Moon' and the two dramatic pieces performed by Lila, the despairing 'I Had Myself a True Love' and the revengeful, hopeless 'Sleep Peaceful (Mr Used-to-Be)'. On top of this exceptional string of numbers came equally powerful ensembles, the lively closing to the first act with 'Cakewalk Your Lady' and the second act funeral scene 'Leavin' Time', both whipped up vocally as well as visually under the direction of *Porgy and Bess* director Rouben Mamoulian.

In spite of such advantages, *St Louis Woman* played only

113 performances on Broadway. The libretto took the blame. Countee Cullen had died before the show reached town, and the text had never been satisfactorily completed. After its closure Arlen reworked his music, making it up into a more substantial folk-opera style of piece which he called *Blues Opera* and, subsequently, into an orchestral suite which was premièred by the New York Philharmonic Orchestra in 1957. After further false starts, the show was metamorphosed into a 'blues opera' now called *Free and Easy* and produced in Amsterdam (December 1959) and in Paris, but the experiment was not considered worth pursuing, and *St Louis Woman* did not make it back to Broadway, as it had been hoped it would. It remains one of that handful of musicals which have left a spectacular legacy of individual songs without leaving a stageworthy show in which to display them.

Recording: original cast (Capitol), *Blues Opera* suite (Columbia/EMI)

SAISON IN SALZBURG
Revue-Operette in 2 acts and 5 scenes by Max Wallner and Kurt Feltz. Music by Fred Raymond. Kiel, 31 December 1938.

The jolly story of *Saison in Salzburg* follows the efforts of Toni Haberl, owner of the 'Blaue Enzian' inn, to buy up the failing old 'Salzburger Nockerln' as well and there to instal little Vroni, the waitress who cooks the best nockerln in town as manageress and, hopefully, his wife. Opposition emerges in the shape of the old owner's daughter, Steffi, and an incognito millionaire, Frank Rex, who has fallen for her. When it turns out that Steffi is an even better cook than Vroni, things get all muddled up. Half-way through the evening, everyone is engaged to the wrong person for all the wrong reasons, but Steffi gives Vroni her recipe and things ultimately come to a happy ending amongst ribbons and gingerbread in the joyful atmosphere of a little country fête.

Raymond's score mixed the lively and countrified melodies of pieces such as the rousing hymn to 'Salzburger Nockerln', the hopeful little love duet 'Wenn der Toni mit der Vroni' and the rhythmic march of the 'Blaue Enzian' with some slightly more towny pieces, notably the smoothly tuneful romancing of Frank and Steffi in 'Warum denn nur bin ich dich verliebt?', and some up-to-date dance melodies as featured in Toni and Vroni's 'Und die Musik spielt dazu', in a score of winning charm.

Saison in Salzburg, which had – undoubtedly intentionally – something of the tuneful and picturesque ingenuousness of *Im weissen Rössl* in it, was a splendid success both in Germany (Theater am Rudolf-Wildeplatz, Berlin 8 June 1946) and then in Austria where it played an enthusiastically received initial season at the Raimundtheater and was subsequently revived (Titania-Theater 1 July 1946). A first film version was made the year after the première under the title of the song hit *Und die Musik spielt dazu* whilst a second, unsuccessful, one made by Ernst Marischka in 1952 attached some of the music to a completely different story which had an out of work actor (Adrian Hoven) romancing a Salzburger inn-keeper (Gretl Schörg) amongst the Austrian scenery.

The show was subsequently played in Belgium in a French translation (*Vacances au Tyrol* ad André Mouëzy-Éon, Henri Wernert 1 April 1967) and its music is still featured in record-shop windows in Salzburg where, without reaching the same international renown, it is to Salzburg what *Im weissen Rössl* is to the neighbouring Salzkammergut.

Austria: Raimundtheater *Salzburger Nockerln* 20 December 1940; Films: *Und die Musik spielt dazu* 1939, Sascha Films/Ernst Marischka 1952
Recordings: selection (Polydor, Elite Special, Amadeo)

SALAD DAYS
Musical entertainment in 2 acts by Julian Slade and Dorothy Reynolds. Music by Julian Slade. Theatre Royal, Bristol, 1 June 1954; Vaudeville Theatre, London, 5 August 1954.

The modern repertory theatre system in Britain (which, in fact, was not based on companies with a repertory of pieces but only on permanent acting companies with a series of plays) originally concentrated entirely on performing straight theatre pieces but, during the 1950s, several enterprising repertory theatre directors began to include small-scale musical productions in their schedule. The most notable of these was the Bristol Old Vic Company under Denis Carey which produced, at first, versions of Shakespeare's *Two Gentlemen of Verona* and Sheridan's *The Duenna* with original music by company member Julian Slade, as well as a Christmas revue (*Christmas in King Street*) and a festive musical, *The Merry Gentleman*, before launching a revusical end-of-term romp called *Salad Days* written by another company member, Dorothy Reynolds, and by Slade.

Topical and localized, the lightweight framework of *Salad Days* followed the progress of two young Bristol University Students, Timothy (John Warner) and Jane (Eleanor Drew), from graduation into the real world of work, reponsibility and marriage. Urged by his parents, Timothy visits a series of Uncles trying to find himself a congenial job, whilst Jane is pushed vivaciously towards marriage at all costs by her mother. The results of all these efforts made up the series of scenes of the entertainment with, in revue fashion, each of the dozen actors playing several of the many rôles involved. Miss Reynolds was a wordless beautician battering Yvonne Coulette (Jane's mother) into shape whilst her customer carries on a non-stop telephone conversation in the most unlikely positions, later a sultry night-club singer ('Sand in My Eyes') seducing the beastly Minister of Pleasures and Pastimes, and then a hopeless model displaying clothes at danger to limb if not life. Eric Porter was a deeply 'Hush, Hush' Diplomatic uncle and a night-club manager with revusical tendencies, Alan Dobie a tramp who gives Timothy a job looking after a piano called Minnie which sets the world dancing, Norman Rossington a PC with ballet shoes in his back pocket, Bob Harris (in a rôle custom-fitted to his mime talents) was an appealing comic mute, and Pat Heywood a crotchety Aunt one minute and a perky soubrette the next.

The songs which Slade composed for the piece were necessarily musically unambitious, for only Miss Drew of the Bristol company had any skill as a singer. She was in consequence given the whole lyric part of the piece, singing sweetly 'I Sit in the Sun' as she mulled over her mother's list of eligible gentlemen, duetting with her Tim that 'We Said We Wouldn't Look Back', and celebrating adulthood in the show's loveliest melody '(I'm having) The Time of My Life', whilst the other members of the company enjoyed the light comedy of such pieces as 'We Don't Understand Our Children', the nightclub number

Plate 236. **Salad Days**: *Dorothy Reynolds complains torchily of 'Sand in My Eyes'.*

'Cleopatra', and the simple tunefulness of 'It's Easy to Sing a Simple Song' or 'Look at Me, I'm Dancing'.

The Bristol production won a fine reception and, before its three-week run was over, it had won itself a transfer to London's Vaudeville Theatre under the management of the firms of Linnit and Dunfee and Jack Hylton. Although some cast changes had intervened, the piece was largely what had been seen in Bristol, and London, which according to *The Times* was 'reacting sharply against the hard-hitting, hard-boiled American musical' gave it a welcome if anything more enthusiastic than Bristol had done. Certainly, its mixture of fantasy, revue, youthful and innocent fun and jovial tunefulness proved to be the apt combination for the time and place. *Salad Days* remained at the Vaudeville Theatre for five-and-a-half years (2,283 performances), becoming in the process the longest-running West End musical to date, before going on to be played in virtually every provincial theatre in Britain and in several overseas venues.

Australia saw *Salad Days* in the slightly larger (than the Vaudeville) Princess Theatre in Melbourne for ten weeks before it was bundled off to Sydney's Elizabethan Theatre (30 January 1958). It was bundled back again when *Bells Are Ringing* didn't go, and played two more Melbourne months, before being moved on again to allow *Free as Air*, the next Slade/Reynolds show, to move in. Through all this curious management, it nevertheless established itself as a success. The same could not quite be said for an attempt to interest New York in *Salad Days*. A Canadian production was played at the off-Broadway Barbizon-Plaza for 80 performances in 1958.

Back in Britain, however, *Salad Days* proved that it was not just a one-run hit. After that first huge run, and a thorough provincial exposure, it returned to London on several occasions: for seasons at the Prince's Theatre (26 December 1961) and the Lyric, Hammersmith (18 August 1964) and, in a production transferred from the Theatre Royal, Windsor, for 113 performances at the Duke of

York's Theatre (14 April 1976). A badly cut television version was produced in 1983.

The first adult musical comedy to move to London from the now virtually vanished British repertory theatre system, *Salad Days* still remains, more than 35 years later, the most successful.

Australia: Princess Theatre, Melbourne 13 November 1957; USA: Barbizon-Plaza 10 November 1958; France: Théâtre en Rond 1957

Recordings: original cast (Oriole), studio cast with members of 1976 revival (TER), Australian cast (Planet 45 rpm) etc

SALLY Musical comedy in 3 acts by Guy Bolton. Lyrics by Clifford Grey. Additional lyrics by P G Wodehouse, B G De Sylva and Anne Caldwell. Music by Jerome Kern. Ballet music by Victor Herbert. New Amsterdam Theater, New York, 21 December 1920.

One of the line of popular Cinderellery musicals which followed the success of *Irene*, *Sally* was ordered by Florenz Ziegfeld as a vehicle for Marilyn(n) Millar, the lovely blonde dancing star of his 1918 and 1919 *Follies*. Originally to have been a collaboration between Bolton, Kern and P G Wodehouse and based on a piece called *The Little Thing* on which the three had worked together several years previously, it was ultimately written by Bolton alone, when Wodehouse preferred to spend the time on another project, and another British lyricist, Clifford Grey, replaced him for the show's lyrics.

Little orphan Sally (Miss Miller) is a dishwasher in Greenwich Village, but like all orphaned blonde dishwashers she harbours the ambition to become a star in the Follies. Her co-worker, Connie (Leon Errol), is the exiled Grand Duke Constantine of Czechogovinia who carries on a high social life on the one hand and earns a living as a waiter on the other. Theatrical agent Otis Hooper (Walter Catlett) has been engaged to supply the entertainment for a party given by the father of wealthy Blair Farquar (Irving Fisher) and, when he loses his exotic foreign dance star, Sally is disguised to take her place. The party ends in disaster and quarrels, but between the end of Act II and Act III Sally makes it to the star dressing room at the Follies in record time and by the end of that act she has netted Blair as well.

Although the part of Connie had been specially written in to feature Errol, Miss Miller was the show's consuming star and her dancing talents in particular were extensively displayed. She performed two first-act numbers, including a solo routine plotworthy enough to bring her to Otis's notice as a danseuse, a slavic dance at the party, and a Follies Butterfly Ballet in the last act, but she also had a voice in the two most enduring songs in the show, 'Look for the Silver Lining', which she shared with Fisher in the first act, and her admission in the second act that she is 'The Wild Rose' (as opposed to a primrose). She also had a share in another pretty duo 'Whip-poor-Will' (ly: De Sylva). Errol had a comical number about the thankless and naked courtesan who leapt from his palace bedroom window and swam the river 'Schnitza-Komisski', leaving him to be deposed alone, and Catlett joined with Mary Hay (Rosalind) in the one piece brought forward from *The Little Thing*, 'The Church 'Round the Corner'. A second piece from that unfinished show also intended for *Sally* did not make it to opening night, but 'Bill' would surface half-a-

Plate 237. **Sally**: *The Butterfly Ballet, the apotheosis for the orphaned dishwasher (Dorothy Dickson) – she is starring in the Ziegfeld Follies.*

dozen years on and make itself famous in another setting. Other, produced shows provided fodder for *Sally*'s score as well: 'The Lorelei' (ly: Anne Caldwell) had been in *The Night Boat* and the title-song, sung by Fisher, was a remake of a number Kern had inserted into the British musical *King of Cadonia* many years previously.

Given truly Ziegfeldian production values, *Sally* was an immediate and great Broadway success. Miss Miller starred for a run of 570 New York performances and then took the show on tour where it continued to collect handsomely. And whilst the Broadway version continued to run, Grossmith and Laurillard opened the show at London's Winter Garden with the theatre's resident stars Leslie Henson (Connie) and Grossmith himself (Otis) featured alongside American dancer Dorothy Dickson as Sally. Once again it was a splendid success (387 performances) and became a touring circuit regular. Proportionately, however, perhaps the biggest success that this hugely popular piece found was in Australia. Dancer Josie Melville was starred as Sally alongside George Lane (Connie, equipped with a variation on George Graves's old routine, 'Olga the Hen'), George Baker (Blair), George Gee (Otis), Gracie Lavers (Rosalind) and William Valentine (Jimmy). It opened to a dazzling reception – it cannot wholly have been a coincidence that Ada Reeve, star of neighbouring *Spangles*, suffered a nervous breakdown the same night and abandoned her show – and it established itself at Her Majesty's Theatre for a run of 26 weeks, topping all but the monster Australian record held by *Our Miss Gibbs*. In Melbourne (Theatre Royal 15 September 1923), its success was equally remarkable – another 26 weeks, fairly qualifying the show as the most popular production to have ever played in Australia.

The show returned to the Australian circuits and also both to Broadway and to London. A 1948 Broadway revival featuring Bambi Linn, Willie Howard and Jack Goode blew up the score with a couple of extra numbers from *Leave it to Jane* and a baker's half-dozen of other Kern pieces and the text with some low comedy and was gone after 36 performances, but a London revamp (ad Richard Hearne, Frank Eyton), produced as *Wild Rose* (Prince's Theatre 6 August 1942) with Jessie Matthews in a rare musical comedy appearance as Sally did rather better (205 performances). Hollywood, too, tried *Sally*, originally as a silent film with Colleen Moore and with Errol repeating his stage creation (and the music played as an accompaniment) and then again in 1930 when Miss Miller put her part on screen to rather better effect with the help of sound and Joe E Brown at the head of the comedy.

An Eddie Dowling vaudeville sketch which burlesqued the rather overused Cinderella theme in the musical theatre of the time was, in 1922, turned into a full-length musical by its author and presented on Broadway by the Shuberts under the title *Sally, Irene and Mary* (4 September Casino Theater). The joining-together of the names of Broadway's three favourite little heroines of recent years persuaded the public to give the show, which had little or no merit, a 112-performance run. Jean Brown was the not-very-burlesqued Sally.

UK: Winter Garden Theatre 10 September 1921; Australia: Her Majesty's Theatre, Sydney 6 January 1923; Films: First National 1925, Warner Brothers 1930
Recordings: London cast (WRC/Monmouth Evergreen), studio cast (WRC)

LES SALTIMBANQUES Opéra-comique in 3 acts by Maurice Ordonneau. Music by Louis Ganne. Théâtre de la Gaîté, Paris, 30 December 1899.

The most commercially successful of Louis Ganne's opérettes, *Les Saltimbanques*, with its picturesque circus atmosphere, is one of the few French pieces of its period which have remained in the repertoire in its native country where it is regularly played in the provinces to this day.

Nasty Malicorne (Vauthier) and his wife (Mme de Mérengo) run a little circus in which strongman Grand Pingouin (Lucien Noël), the sad, amorous clown Paillasse (Paul Fugère), Suzon (Jeanne Saulier) and Marion (Lise Berty) are engaged. Little Suzon, the Malicorne's foster-child, is particularly hard done by and, after an episode involving the handsome soldier André de Langéac (Émile Perrin), she runs away. She and her circus friends roam the country pursued by the now rather circus-less Malicornes until Suzon finds her wealthy if unmarried parents, André, and a happy ending.

Ganne's score was in the basic and colourful strain of Ordonneau's text, which was one of much less craft and literary merit than usual on the part of an author with some fine credits to his name. It rang with the march music which the composer always handled with especial felicity (notably André's 'Va, gentil soldat') and also included some pretty sentimental moments, such as Paillasse's plea of love to Suzon, 'La nature a pour ses élus', Marion's gentle reply, 'Mon pauvre Paillasse', and a catchy waltz introduced by Marion and Pingouin ('C'est l'amour') to close the first act, alongside a predominance of lively and bouncy pieces.

Les Saltimbanques was played for more than 100 performances at the Théâtre de la Gaîté in 1899–1900, and was thereafter regularly reprised there: in 1902 with Jeanne Petit starring, with Angèle Gril in 1913, 1914 and 1915, in 1921 and 1922 and once more in 1945. It was also performed at the Apollo in 1911, at the Mogador in 1941 with André Baugé as Pingouin and at the Théâtre de la Porte-Saint-Martin in 1968. Its principal and enduring career, however, has been in the provinces.

Outside France, the piece was played in several other languages, notably in Italian, in which language it made its only American appearance in a guest performance by an Italian troupe, but with lesser effect. In Vienna, where Louis Treumann appeared as Paillasse, Mizzi Günther as

Suzon and Therese Biedermann as Marion, it was a four-performance disaster, and Emil Makai's Hungarian version had an indifferent career at the Magyar Színház.

Austria: Carltheater *Circus Malicorne* 20 April 1901; Hungary: Magyar Színház *A csepűrágók* 28 December 1901; USA: Majestic Theater *I Saltimbanchi* 24 April 1911
Recordings: complete (Decca, EMI), selection (EMI-Pathé) etc

SAMUEL, Fernand [LOUVEAU, Fernand] (d Cap d'Ail, 22 December 1914). Celebrated straw-hatted French producer and director of the turn-of-the-century decades.

When Fernand Louveau decided to go into the theatre he decided to change his name. In a reversal of the usual procedure, he swapped his gentile name (to which, apparently, he had no more claim than that it was the name of his mother's husband ... who was not his father) for a Jewish one, on the theory that it would help him to get on. He got his first footing in Paris when he ran the Cercle Pigalle, and soon moved upmarket when in 1884 (14 October) he took over the once-great Théâtre de la Renaissance which had been stumbling along through short-lived and inexperienced managements. He presented a programme of almost entirely non-musical productions through his years at the Renaissance (*Miette, La Gardeuse d'oies, Les Douze Femmes de Japhet, La Petite Poucette*), but when he moved on to take over from Eugène Bertrand at the head of the Théâtre des Variétés on 1 January 1892 that changed. Baron, Brasseur, Vauthier, Dupuis, Guy, Prince, Max Dearly, Anna Judic, Jeanne Granier, Marguerite Ugalde, Ève Lavallière, Marie Magnier, Anna Tariol-Baugé, Juliette Méaly, Jeanne Saulier, Germaine Gallois, Mariette Sully, Henri Defreyn, Paul Fugère and other stars of the period played a mixed series of new and classic plays, opérettes and revues, mounted in a vastly splendid fashion under his own stage direction as Samuel brought back to the Variétés something like the glory it had known in the heyday of Offenbach. The musical portion of his programmes included: *Un lycée de jeunes filles, La Vie parisienne* (1892), *Les Brigands* (1893), *Lili* and *Mam'zelle Nitouche* with Judic and Dupuis (1894), *Le Carnet du Diable, La Femme à papa* with Judic, *Chilpéric, La Chanson de Fortunio, La Périchole* with Granier (1895), *Le Carillon, L'Oeil crevé, La Vie parisienne* (1896), *Le Pompier de service, Le Petit Faust* (1897), *Les Petites Barnett* (1898), *La Belle Hélène* (1899), *Le Carnet du Diable, Les Brigands, Mademoiselle Georges* (1900), *Niniche* with Judic (1901), a famous production of *Orphée aux enfers* (1902), *Le Sire de Vergy, Chonchette* (1903), *La Chauve-Souris, Barbe-bleue, La Fille de Madame Angot, Monsieur de la Palisse, L'Oeil crevé* (1904), *La Petite Bohème, Les Dragons de l'Impératrice, L'Age d'or, Miss Helyett* (1905), *Le Paradis de Mahomet* (1906) and *Geneviève de Brabant* (1908).

With the passing of classic French opérette in favour of *La Veuve joyeuse* and her sisters, Samuel rather abandoned musical productions in favour of plays and the inevitable end-of-year revue, and in the final five years of his famous management, up to his death in 1914, only further revivals of *La Vie parisienne* (1911) and *Orphée aux enfers* (1912) and a Paris production of London's *Les Merveilleuses* (1914) were played at the Variétés.

SANDERSON, Julia [SACKETT, Julia] (b Springfield, Mass, 20 August 1887; d Springfield, 27 January 1975).

The delicately beautiful Julia Sanderson was one of the most durable stars of the American musical theatre in the 1910s and 1920s, and her china-doll features, pretty but never pale personality and fine light soprano saw her through more than 15 years of starring in what were mostly soubrette rôles.

Daughter of an actor, she began in the theatre very young and made her first adult appearances on the musical stage at the age of 15 in the chorus of *A Chinese Honeymoon* and, later the same year, in the chorus rôle of Lady Monde whilst understudying Paula Edwardes as *Winsome Winnie* (1903). She played a couple of out-of-town dates deputizing in Adele Ritchie's leading rôle in *A Chinese Honeymoon* (Mrs Pineapple) the following year, played a season in breeches alongside De Wolf Hopper in a Broadway revival of *Wang*, and then joined the Chicago cast of *Fantana* in a minor rôle as cover to Miss Ritchie. She soon moved on to improving Broadway rôles in *The Tourists* (1906) and in Carrie Moore's soubrette rôle of Peggy in the Broadway version of *The Dairymaids* (1907) before she made a first trip to Britain to play opposite G P Huntley in the shortlived *The Hon'ble Phil*. The journey, however, proved worth the making for, when the show failed, producer Charles Frohman promptly exported both Miss Sanderson and Huntley to Broadway as the stars of a production of the established hit *Kitty Grey*, giving 21-year-old Julia, as Kitty, her first regular star rôle in New York.

She was hurried back to Britain to try (unsuccessfully) to boost the Ellaline Terriss musical *The Dashing Little Duke* by replacing Coralie Blythe in the soubrette rôle, but her next Broadway rôles confirmed her new star status: Eileen, the 'girl with the brogue' in *The Arcadians*, Lolotte, opposite Donald Brian, in Frohman's production of Leo Fall's *The Siren*, and principal soubrettes in two musicals from London's Gaiety Theatre, *The Sunshine Girl* and *The Girl from Utah*, in which she introduced respectively 'Honeymoon Lane' and 'They Didn't Believe Me', Jerome Kern interpolations which Phyllis Dare and Ina Claire had not performed in the same rôles in London.

Miss Sanderson toured America in *The Girl from Utah*, and then returned to Broadway in 1916 in a very different rôle, the romantic-comedy and strongly singing title-rôle of Victor Jacobi's Hungarian operett *Sybil*. Another less fine Jacobi piece, *Rambler Rose*, followed and in 1918 she paired for the last time with Joseph Cawthorn (her regular comic co-star for the past five years) in Ivan Caryll's *The Canary*. After a long period touring with that show, she ventured into revue in *Hitchy Koo* (1920), then went on to Broadway and touring assignments as the still-juvenile star of the highly successful *Tangerine* (1921, Shirley Dalton) and of *Moonlight* (1924, Betty Duncan).

Now rising 40, she went on the road in *No, No, Nanette* (1925, Lucille), *Oh, Kay!* (Kay) and *Queen High* (1926, Florence), and saw out the last years of her career in revue (*Crazy Quilt*, *Sweet and Low*) and vaudeville before retiring from the stage after some 30 active years to a new kind of stardom, hosting a popular radio series with her husband, Frank Crumit, through more than a decade.

In private life, Miss Sanderson was for a period wife to the famous jockey Tod Sloane, before her marriage to Crumit with whom she appeared in a number of her later shows.

SANTLEY, Joseph [MANSFIELD, Joseph] (b Salt Lake City, 10 January 1889; d Los Angeles, 8 August 1971). Longtime leading man of American musicals.

A member of a family of actors, Santley went on the stage as a young child and as a youth played in stock companies and toured as a juvenile star in melodrama before turning to musical comedy. He made his first Broadway appearance in *The Queen of the Moulin-Rouge* (1909) and the following year played the juvenile lead, Dick Allen, alongside De Wolf Hopper in *A Matinée Idol*. He continued with a long series of light song-and-dance lead rôles, starring with Marie Cahill in *Judy Forgot* (1910, Dixie Stole), in Lew Fields's *The Never Homes* (1911, Webster Choate), the Broadway version of Eysler's *Der Frauenfresser* (*The Woman Hater*, 1912, Camillo) and top-billed in the unexceptional *When Dreams Come True* (1913, Kean Hedges). Appearances in vaudeville and revue intervened before he returned to semi-musical comedy as Van Courtland Parke in Irving Berlin's *Stop! Look! Listen!* (1915) and in the rôle of Gerard in the Broadway version of the Daly's Theatre musical *Betty* (1916) opposite his wife, Ivy Sawyer.

He toured in the lead rôle of *Oh, Boy!*, returning to New York for *Oh! My Dear* (1918, Bruce Allenby) at the Princess Theater, and the Jerome Kern/Anne Caldwell *She's a Good Fellow* (1919, Robert McShane) at the Globe, in which he introduced 'The First Rose of Summer' with Miss Sawyer. After two further musicals in a similar light vein, *The Half Moon* (1920, Charlie Hobson) and the out-of-town part of *It's Up to You* (1921, Ned Spencer), he moved into the *Music Box Revue* with which he played in New York and London for two years, before returning to the musical theatre for a further series of rôles in his established line: the Shuberts' Eduard Künneke musical *Mayflowers* (1925, Billy Ballard), Friml's *The Wild Rose* (1926, Billy Travers) opposite Desirée Ellinger, the impressive flop *Lucky* (1927, Jack Mansfield), and in the part of the Prince of Wales in *Just Fancy*, for which he also took a part-author's credit.

At this stage, with 17-year-old stardom starting to wear just a little thin, Santley moved to Hollywood where he began writing and directing films, including such musical pieces as the Marx Brothers' *The Cocoanuts*, *Treasure Girl* and *Swing High*. However, after a few years, he returned to the theatre, playing in New York in *Heigh Ho, Everybody* and taking over Fred Astaire's rôle in *Gay Divorce* for the road. He subsequently backtracked to Hollywood where he worked as a director through the 1940s (*Swing, Sister, Swing, Brazil, Make Believe Ballroom, Yokel Boy* etc), bringing his screen musical tally to some 30 films.

Santley seems to have had a hand in the writing of several unsuccessful musicals, but the co-existence of songwriter Joseph H Santly, composer of the successful song 'Hawaiian Butterfly', can lead to a little confusion over credits.

Santley's wife **Ivy SAWYER** began her career as a London child starlet. She appeared for several years as *Alice in Wonderland*, played in Seymour Hicks's *My Darling* and for George Edwardes as the midshipman in *The Marriage Market* before, aged 20, she went to America to

1269

appear in the title-rôle of Edwardes's *Betty*. She married her co-star, stayed, and they became an on-stage as well as off-stage pair appearing together in the *Oh, Boy!* tour (Mrs Budd), *Oh! My Dear* (Hilda Rockett), *She's a Good Fellow* (Jacqueline Fay), *The Half Moon* (Grace Bolton), *It's Up to You* (Harriet Hollister), three *Music Box Revues*, *Mayflowers* (Elsie Dover), *Just Fancy* (in which she played an American girl, Linda Lee Stafford, whilst her American husband played the English Prince), and *Lucky* (Grace Mansfield), in which Miss Sawyer appeared for once with, but not opposite, her husband.

Santley's elder brother, **Frederic SANTLEY** (b Salt Lake City, 20 November 1887; d 14 May 1953) also had a kiddie-onward stage career, playing in nearly two decades of musicals (*Queen of the Moulin-Rouge*, *Jumping Jupiter*, *When Dreams Come True*, *Have a Heart*, *The Royal Vagabond*, *Glorianna*, *Poor Little Ritz Girl*, *Two Little Girls in Blue*, *Up She Goes*, *Topsy and Eva*, *Dew-Drop Inn*, *Sitting Pretty*, *Kiss Me, Happy*, *Present Arms*, *Funny Face*, *Hello, Daddy*) on the road and in New York.

1915 **All Over Town** (Silvio Hein/Harry B Smith) Shubert Theater, New Haven 26 April

1925 **The Daughter of Rosie O'Grady** (Cliff Hess/Edgar Allen Woolf) Walnut Street Theater, Philadelphia 14 September

1926 **Shamrock** (Hess) 1 act RKO/Keith Vaudeville circuit

1927 **Just Fancy** (Phil Charig, Joseph Meyer/Leo Robin/A E Thomas ad) Casino Theater 11 October

SANTLEY, Kate [GAZINA, Evangeline Estelle] (b Charleston, Va, 29 August 1837; d Hove, 18 January 1923). One of the great and influential personalities of the early days of the modern British musical theatre.

Born in Virginia and educated in South Carolina, Miss Santley went on the stage in early childhood as a fairy queen in pantomime, but later claimed only to have considered the stage as a career when her parents lost their all in the Civil War. She next popped up far from home, in Scotland, as juvenile lady in a stock company, in which capacity she apparently played Ophelia and Jessica with the visiting Charles Kean. However, she came to general notice for the first time in a rather different field when she appeared at London's Oxford Music Hall, under the name of Eva Stella, and won a considerable success performing the song 'The Bells Go a-Ringing for Sarah' and a sketch called 'Good-for-Nothing Nan' in which she displayed her talents as a pianist.

Soon after 'Kate Santley' made her first regular theatre appearance in London, in burlesque at the Queen's Theatre, playing in breeches as Peter in Reece's *The Stranger – Stranger Than Ever*, and in skirts in the Christmas entertainment *The Gnome King* (Princess Beatrix). The following year she appeared with the Vokes family in the Drury Lane pantomime *Beauty and the Beast*, but her career in the theatre got regularly under way when she was hired by the Swanboroughs at the Strand Theatre in 1870 and appeared there as Princess Sabra in *Sir George and a Dragon*, in *Loving Hearts* and in leading rôles in the burlesques *Kenilworth*, *The Field of the Cloth of Gold*, *The Idle Prentice* (with Harry Paulton) and *Coeur de Lion* (with Paulton and Edward Terry).

It was while she was at the Strand that the operatic manager Colonel Mapleson took an interest in her and is said to have arranged for her to have singing lessons with Pauline Viardot-Garcia. However, the experiment proved a failure, the young woman cracked, and returned to America. Her confidence returned, however, and she had not long ventured again into provincial theatre before she was given the chance to appear at Niblo's Garden as Stalacta in a revival of *The Black Crook* (December 1871). She had sufficient success to follow up in the title-rôle of *The Naiad Queen* (February 1872), winning herself a small following and pushing 'the Santley girdle', a black velvet belt pointed at the waist and embroidered with a matching sash, to popularize her name as she moved on to play Stalacta in Boston (March 1872).

She then returned to Britain and took over the rôle of Cunégonde in *Le Roi Carotte* at the Alhambra, winning a significant popularity which was only increased when she was starred in the chief soubrette rôle of the British version of *The Black Crook*, introducing the popular 'Nobody Knows as I Know'. She remained at the Alhambra, where she consolidated her new stardom as Hélène in *La Belle Hélène* (1873), Haidée in the extravaganza *Don Juan* (1873) and Rose Michon in *La Jolie Parfumeuse* (1874), playing in each case opposite Rose Bell. The juxtaposition of these two very different ladies – the soubrette and the soprano – provoked street-fights between their partisans which culminated in a court case brought by Miss Santley against her rival's claque.

Kate left the Alhambra to make her début as a producer with an original English comic opera which she commissioned for herself from Robert Reece and the composer of part of *The Black Crook*, the young Frederic Clay. She toured as *Cattarina* in the later part of 1874 and, after returning to the Alhambra to star in the title-rôle of Offenbach's specially commissioned *Whittington* (1874) for Christmas, introduced her musical to London. It did very well and, with the cachet of a London season behind her, Miss Santley promptly toured it again, in repertoire with *Les Prés Saint-Gervais*, before returning to town to appear in breeches alongside Emily Soldene's *Madame l'Archiduc* (1876, Fortunato) and in *La Fille de Madame Angot* (Clairette) at the Opéra Comique.

In the summer she again went touring, taking with her a repertoire including a rather battered *Orphée aux enfers*, *Cattarina*, *Madame l'Archiduc* – which Soldene was also touring – and another new English comic opera commissioned from Freddie Clay. This one was called *Princess Toto* and it starred its manageress as a forgetful little royal invented by the young librettist W S Gilbert. Miss Santley's commission gave its author the opportunity to write his first full-length comic opera. *Princess Toto* was successful enough to be brought to London's Strand Theatre, but strife of some kind arose between those involved and it was closed prematurely.

Kate left the Strand and moved to the Royalty Theatre where she produced her version of *Orphée aux enfers*, a version with, as was her wont, interpolated cockney point numbers for herself in the rôle of Eurydice, topped by her all-time favourite number 'Awfully Awful'. She then took a long lease on the Royalty and, in the years that followed, she presented herself in a series of often broadly staged musical pieces – Lecocq's saucy *La Marjolaine* (1877), the pasticcio *Madcap*, *La Belle Hélène*, *La Jolie Parfumeuse*, *Little Cinderella*, *Tita in Thibet* (1878) – in the seasonal months, whilst taking herself and her shows to the country in the summer. She let her theatre to others whilst she went to the Globe to take over as Serpolette in *Les Cloches de Corneville*, played principal boy in the pantomime at the Theatre Royal, Drury Lane, or toured in *La Mascotte* (1882), but she took up residence again to present her third new Clay musical, *The Merry Duchess*, in 1883.

With Kate starring as the (ultimately reformed) villainess of the piece, *The Merry Duchess* found a pretty success and a Broadway production, but her subsequent productions, versions of Audran's *Gillette de Narbonne* and Hervé's *La Cosaque*, were less fortunate. She persisted with French works and staged Bernicat's *François les bas-bleus* (*François the Radical*) but that too failed, and once again she let the Royalty and took to the road, first in another commissioned musical, the English comedy with songs *Chirruper's Fortune*, and then in a piece called *Vetah* for which she herself claimed an authorial credit and Bernicat (who was dead) was credited with the score. She toured again, in 1887, in *Vetah* and in Audran's *Indiana*, but her performing career was entering its final stages and her producing life was virtually at an end.

In the meanwhile, her Royalty Theatre hosted a hotchpotch of shows of which the best were the regular visits of French dramatic companies, but the controversy which Kate seemed to court struck again when she let her theatre to the Independent Stage Society to produce Ibsen's *Ghosts* (1891). It caused a small scandal. Shortly after making her last appearance on stage in *A Night on the Town* (1894), she sublet the theatre to Arthur Bourchier, but although she retired to Hove and a very long retirement as Mrs Lieutenant-Colonel Lockhart Mure Hartley Kennedy, she maintained the lease on the Royalty Theatre up to her death at the age of 86. In 1902 she produced her own version of Sardou and de Najac's play *Divorçons* (already performed in a more safely adapted version) under the title *Mixed Relations*.

One of the great figures of the British musical stage during the earliest years of its modern period, Miss Santley was adored by the public (if often lambasted for vulgarity by the press) as a performer, whilst as a producer she was amongst the earliest and most important to encourage British authors and composers to challenge the might of Offenbach and the French opéra-bouffe, and an expert discoverer of new acting talent.

SAN TOY, or The Emperor's Own Chinese musical comedy in 2 acts by Edward A Morton. Lyrics by Harry Greenbank and Adrian Ross. Music by Sidney Jones. Additional music by Lionel Monckton. Daly's Theatre, London, 21 October 1899.

Following the success of *The Geisha* and that, slightly lesser, of *A Greek Slave*, at Daly's Theatre, George Edwardes continued with more of the same in *San Toy* – an exotically set costume piece which, like *The Geisha*, set picturesque Eastern and nattily dressed Western civilizations up against each other to the tune of some richly romantic love songs and a barrage of comic scenes, songs and dances. For *San Toy*, instead of sticking with the extremely reliable Owen Hall, Edwardes accepted a libretto written by 'Edward Morton', a well-known and influential journalist who had not succeeded in breaking through into the theatre. Sidney Jones was again composer, but Harry Greenbank who had written the lyrics for

the earlier Daly's successes died, aged only 33, with the work incomplete and was replaced by the experienced Adrian Ross. If it did not have the same team as before, *San Toy* was, by the time it reached the stage, much the mixture as before.

Mandarin's daughter San Toy (Marie Tempest) has been brought up as a boy to avoid the draft in a country where the Emperor's troops are female. In time, this brings problems, especially when she falls in love with English Captain Bobby Preston (Hayden Coffin) and then when a new and horrider law drafts mandarin's sons. San Toy goes to court as a girl, joins the Emperor's guard, fends off his passes and finally comes to a happy ending amongst a barrage of misunderstandings and comedy scenes. What was left of Morton's rather substantial and uncomic book by the time Edwardes's comedy stars had also been fitted with rôles – Rutland Barrington as Yen How, the heroine's father, with his six little wives; Huntley Wright as another comical Chinee, Li; and Ada Reeve as the comedy maid Dudley in place of Letty Lind who had left Daly's for solo stardom – made up into a distinctly jolly if rather wandering text.

It was illustrated by some fine Sidney Jones songs, of which Barrington's description of his 'Six Little Wives' and his topical 'I Mean to Introduce it into China' stood alongside Wright's comparison of soldiers of different nations, told in Daly's Theatre pidgin ('Chinee Sojeman'), and Lionel Monckton's soubrette tale of 'Rhoda and Her Pagoda' at the head of the fun. In the more lyrical moments Coffin scored with the pretty 'Love Has Come from Lotus Land' and the lilting 'The One in the World' and Miss Tempest sang of 'The Petals of the Plum Tree', all with considerable success.

San Toy had a famously hard birth. Whilst Morton's libretto was being to all intents rewritten in rehearsal to sound more like Owen Hall, it became clear that Ada Reeve and Marie Tempest did not combine as the latter had so happily done with Letty Lind, and sparks flew until Reeve cried enough and walked out. Gracie Leigh replaced her and began a career as a star comedienne. Then, during the show's run, Miss Tempest engineered a crisis by cutting up one of her costumes to make it more revealing and, to a shower of publicity, walked out when reprimanded, conveniently breaking her long contract with Edwardes and her connection with the musical theatre in order to begin a second career on the straight stage. *San Toy* survived all the dramas unshakeably. It was one of the greatest successes of the Victorian musical stage, whether with Tempest or with Florence Collingbourne as San Toy or, later, with Reeve who returned to take up the rôle she had wanted all the time and then promptly altered it to be a more music-hally one, in line with her talents, with three new songs ('It's Nice to Be a Boy Sometimes', 'All I Want is a Little Bit of Fun', 'Somebody'). Other artists also got fresh songs, notably Coffin, the specialist of the interpolated song, who patriotically gave both 'Tommy Atkins' and Lionel Monckton's 'Sons of the Motherland' as the Boer War raged, and Wright, who had an almost-plot song 'Me Gettee Outee Velly Quick', by young Paul Rubens added to his part.

San Toy ran 14 months and 778 performances at Daly's Theatre, the longest tally of any of the great group of musicals which made that theatre's fame, and, well before

Plate 238. **San Toy** *was one of the handful of English-language musicals of the 19th and early 20th centuries to be widely played through Europe. It made it from Leicester Square to Russia.*

that run was over, it set off round the world. New York proved particularly welcoming, hosting four seasons of the show in a five-year period: an original run of 65 performances with James T Powers (Li) and Marie Celeste (San Toy) starring, a quick revival (4 March 1901) by the same Daniel Frohman company for a further 103 performances, and short return seasons in 1902 (Daly's Theater 7 April) with Sam Collins replacing Powers, and in 1905 (Daly's Theater 17 April).

In Vienna, Louis Treumann, soon to be famous as the hero of *Die lustige Witwe*, played Li in a version translated by composer Hugo Felix for a fine first run of 53 performances alongside Therese Biedermann (Dudley), Franz Glawatsch (Yen-How) and America's remarkable international soubrette Marie Halton who continued her multilingual triumph on the world's musical stages by going on to appear in the show's title-rôle in both Berlin and Budapest. If it did not score the overwhelming Continental success that *The Geisha* had, *San Toy* nevertheless did as well as or better than any other English-language musical of the 19th century, barring its famous predecessor and *The Mikado*, winning hundreds of performances all around central Europe.

Australia echoed the British success when the piece was mounted there in 1901 with Carrie Moore in the title-rôle, George Lauri (Li), Grace Palotta (Dudley) and Charles Kenningham (Bobby), and *San Toy* followed its Melbourne introduction with visits to Adelaide, Perth, Brisbane and Sydney (Palace Theatre 9 August 1902). In Britain, meanwhile, the piece was toured solidly, at one stage in multiple companies, then more intermittently for several decades,

and it even returned to London for a brief season in 1932 (Daly's Theatre 22 February) with Jean Colin starring and Leo Sheffield as Yen How.

USA: Daly's Theater 1 October 1900; Hungary: Népszinház 10 October 1900; Austria: Carltheater *San Toy (Der Kaisers Garde)* 9 November 1900; Germany: Centraltheater 2 March 1901; Australia: Her Majesty's Theatre, Melbourne 21 December 1901

S.A.R. (*Son Altesse Royale*) Comédie musicale in 3 acts by Léon Xanrof and Jules Chancel taken from their play *Le Prince Consort*. Music by Ivan Caryll. Théâtre des Bouffes-Parisiens, Paris, 11 November 1908.

Xanrof and Chancel's 'comédie fantaisiste' *Le Prince Consort* (Théâtre de l'Athénée, 25 November 1903) had a fine success in the first decade of the century in France, where Augustine Leriche and Lefaur introduced its memorable comedy rôles in Abel Deval's original production of a piece decorated vaudeville-style with songs by Paul Marcelles. The play, without songs, had further success in England where it played at the Comedy Theatre under the title of *His Highness My Husband* (ad William Boosey, Cosmo Gordon-Lennox) and in Germany, but rather less in Liebler and Co's American mounting (*The Prince Consort*, New Amsterdam Theater 1905, 28 performances) with Henry E Dixey and Kate Phillips starred. The authors made their own book revisions and added a more extended and very happy lyrical contribution of some wit for Ivan Caryll's full-scale musical version – an early one in the composer's long and important series of musical comedies manufactured from French stage plays – which was produced at the Théâtre des Bouffes-Parisiens in 1908.

The government ministers of her country are anxious that young Queen Sonia of Concornie (Suzanne Dumesnil) should be married as quickly as possible to assure the dynasty and thus dampen a nasty republican movement which is threatening their privileged positions. Sonia's exuberant maiden aunt Xénofa (Marguerite Deval) selects the excessively male Prince Cyrill (Henri Defreyn), son of the ex-King of Ingra (Tournis) for the purpose, and all goes splendidly when the two young folk fall in love at first sight. After the marriage, however, Cyrill cannot take the court routine which prevents him having a private life with his wife, nor her protocolic duties and position above him. He gets moody and tetchy and ends by withdrawing the only thing he can withdraw. Things go from bad to worse, divorce is threatened, and Sonia finally forces the government to offer her decorative husband a share of the throne – for the sake of the child she is bearing. The principal love story was adeptly paralleled by the comical and unsuccessful efforts of Xénofa to add a pretty virgin soldier called Sandor (Robert Hasti) to her long list of military bedmates before being herself checkmated by the charming, opportunist ex-King.

Although greater than Gaiety-weight in its music, Caryll's score was certainly more in the vein of his more substantial works for the London stage than in the traditional and now slightly tired French opérette mould, with both Deval and Defreyn, who were the effective stars of the piece, working through their amusing numbers in an unforcedly sung and light-comically played style whilst the principal lyrical music was entrusted to the rôle of Sonia. *S.A.R.* scored a fine success at the Bouffes-Parisiens and was later reprised at the Trianon-Lyrique, in 1924 (12 March), with Jane Ferny starring as Xénofa alongside René Rudeau and Marcelle Evrard.

Its career outside France, at least, was undoubtedly handicapped by the fact that Oscar Straus's highly successful *Ein Walzertraum* (1907) shared (some would say had pilfered) its main plot premise, but this did not prevent it from being seen and published in Germany (ad Erich Moss) nor from having its plot, if not the score, taken up by Hollywood for the 1930 Ernst Lubitsch musical film *The Love Parade* (Victor Schertzinger/Clifford Grey/ad Ernst Vajda, Guy Bolton) in which Jeanette MacDonald, Lilian Roth, Lupino Lane and Maurice Chevalier starred. Xanrof and Chancel got some recognition from the *Walzertraum* folk by being allotted the task of doing the French version of the work which was specifically stated to be based on a much older source.

Le Prince Consort was given another musical treatment in Hungary in 1904 when *A királynő férje* (László Kun/Jenő Heltai) was produced at the Vigszinház (8 April) for a good run of 23 performances.

Germany: Altes Stadttheater, Leipzig *Die kleine Königin* 27 August 1910

SARDOU, Victorien (b Paris, 7 September 1831; d Paris, 9 November 1908).

In a long and successful career as a playwright which led to his being regarded as the doyen of the French stage, Sardou wrote comparatively little deliberately for the musical stage. His forceful and satirical libretto for Offenbach's *Le Roi Carotte*, an adaptation of the play *Les Prés Saint-Gervais* – which he had written for Virginie Déjazet – into a comic opera composed by Lecocq, and the preparation of the libretto to *Les Merveilleuses*, based on his 1873 play, for George Edwardes (played only in Basil Hood's English version and, in France, in a re-translation by Paul Ferrier), were his main contribution to the lighter end of the musical theatre. These were complemented by the libretti for such more operatic pieces as Paladilhe's opera *Patrie* based on his own play (Opéra 20 December 1886), Pierné's *La Fille du Tabarin* (Opéra-Comique 20 February 1901), Saint-Saëns's *Les Barbares* (Opéra 23 October 1901) and Webber's one-act *Fiorella* (London 1905).

A number of his other stage works were, however, adapted by other writers both for the operatic and the lighter musical stage. On the operatic front, *La Haine* became the Russian opera *Kordeliya* (P K Bronnykow, St Petersburg 24 November), *Fédora* became Giordano's successful opera of the same name (Milan 17 November 1898) and another by Xavier Leroux (Monte Carlo 1907), whilst *La Tosca* was the stuff of the even more successful Puccini work (14 January 1900). An operatic version of *Gismonda* composed by Février was produced in Chicago in 1919.

In a lighter vein, his *Piccolino* (w Charles Nuitter) became the basis for Mme de Grandval's opera (Italiens 5 January 1869), Strauss's *Carneval in Rom* and subsequently for Guiraud's opéra-comique *Piccolino* (Opéra-Comique 11 April 1876), whilst his delightful dramatic-comic *Madame Sans-Gêne* (w Émile Moreau) proved enormously popular worldwide as a source for musical pieces. It was used as the basis for Ivan Caryll's highly successful musical *The Duchess of Dantzic* (Lyric Theatre, London, 17 October 1903), for an Operette by Bernhard Grün, an Italian piece called *Cri-Cri* (1928), a Bulgarian *Madame Sans-Gêne* by Paraskev Chadziev, Paris's Châtelet spectacular *La Maréchale Sans-Gêne* (Pierre Petit/Albert Willemetz/Maurice Lehmann, 17 February 1948) and for a Czech musical by Eugen Drmola and Milos Vacek. It was also given in an operatic version with a score by Giordano (New York, 1915).

The comedy *Divorçons* (w Émile de Najac) was made into a musical play in 1907 by Anselm Goetzl, Rudolf Bernauer and Alexander Pordes-Milo as *Frau Lebedame* (Neues Deutsches Theater, Prague, 31 December) and again in 1966 by the German author/composer Gerhard Jussenhoven as *Cyprienne* (Theater am Dom, Cologne, 2 December), whilst Sardou's *Fernande* shared with Bulwer Lytton's *The Lady of Lyons* (and, according to some sources, 'an old French vaudeville') the distinction of being the basis for one of the best Viennese Operette libretti, *Der Bettelstudent*. Victor Léon's libretto to Oscar Straus's 1909 Operette, *Didi*, was credited as based on Sardou's play *La Marquise*, whilst another Viennese piece, *Schottenfeld und Ringstrasse* (Theater an der Wien, 1869, Millöcker/Berla), acknowledged an unnamed piece by Sardou as its source.

The success of Sardou's plays also led to a number of them being used as the butt of burlesques. In Paris *Fernande* was done over as *Fernandinette, ou la rosière d'en face* at the Palais-Royal and as *Ferblande, ou l'abonneé de Montmartre* at the Variétés, London's F C Burnand burlesqued *Theodora* in *The O'Dora, or the wrong accent* (Toole's 1885), *Dora* as *Dora and Diplunacy or a Woman of Uncommon Scents* (Strand 1878), the Bancrofts' production of *Fédora* as *Stage-Dora* (Toole's 1883) and *La Tosca* as *Tra-la-la Tosca* (Royalty 1890), whilst Broadway hit *Fédora* even lower with an 1884 piece called *Well-Fed Dora* (5th Avenue Theatre). The Kiralfys staged a short-lived but spectacular musicalish version of the serious *La Patrie* at Niblo's Gardens in 1888 which was not intended as a burlesque.

Sardou actually made as appearance on the Operette stage – as a character – when he managed to get mixed up in the storyline of the *Dreimäderlhaus*-like piece made up around the love and life of *Offenbach* when it was turned from its original Hungarian into Shubertian for Broadway by Harry B Smith. J W Hull portrayed the writer.

1863 **La Bataille d'amour** (Auguste Vaucorbeil/w Charles Dalin) Opéra-Comique 13 April

1864 **Le Capitaine Henriot** (François Gevaert/w Gustave Vaëz) Opéra-Comique 29 December

1865 **Les Ondines au champagne** (Charles Lecocq/ as 'Jules Pélissié' w Hippolyte Lefèbvre, Merle) 1 act Folies-Marigny 5 September

1872 **Le Roi Carotte** (Jacques Offenbach) Théâtre de la Gaîté 15 January

1874 **Les Prés Saint-Gervais** (Charles Lecocq/w Philippe Gille) Théâtre des Variétés 14 November

1878 **Les Noces de Fernande** (Louis Deffès/w Émile de Najac) Opéra-Comique 19 November

1906 **Les Merveilleuses** (Hugo Felix/w Basil Hood) Daly's Theatre, London 27 October

SARI *see* DER ZIGEUNERPRIMÁS

SAVAGE, Henry W[ilson] (b New Durham, NH, 21 March 1859; d Boston, 29 November 1927).

Harvard-educated Savage was a real-estate operator in Boston when a combination of circumstances led him to take over the proprietorship of the failing Castle Square Opera Company, a company playing a repertoire of comic and light opera in English. He turned the group's fortunes around, and in 1897 installed their principal company at New York's American Theater for an extended and highly successful run.

The company's repertoire included, on the one hand, operas such as *Aida*, *The Barber of Seville*, *Rigoletto*, *Carmen*, *Il trovatore*, *Cavalleria Rusticana*, *Romeo and Juliet*, *The Merry Wives of Windsor*, *Martha*, *I Pagliacci*, *Mignon*, *La Gioconda*, the English-language staples *Lurline*, *Maritana*, *The Bohemian Girl* and *The Lily of Killarney* and pieces as diverse as *Die Meistersinger* and *Lohengrin* or *La Fille du régiment* and *Fra Diavolo*. On the other hand, they also performed an interesting mixture of English versions of lighter Continental works (*Die Afrikareise*, *Boccaccio*, *Der Feldprediger*, *Der Zigeunerbaron*, *Nanon*, *Das Spitzentuch der Königin*, *La Grande-Duchesse*, *Les Cloches de Corneville*, *Les Noces d'Olivette*), British comic opera (*Dorothy*, *Billee Taylor*, *Patience*, *The Mikado*, *The Pirates of Penzance*, *Iolanthe*, *HMS Pinafore*, *Paul Jones*) and a handful of home-grown pieces including De Koven's *The Fencing Master*, Julian Edwards's *Madeleine* and Harry B Smith's burlesque *Sinbad*. Amongst the company, for varying periods, such musical-theatre artists as young comedians Raymond Hitchcock and Frank Moulan, tenor Charles Campbell and sopranos Marie Celeste and Attalie Claire played a sometimes surprising range of rôles.

Savage's success at the American Theatre encouraged him to venture further in the theatre and over the following two decades he introduced to Broadway a number of successful plays (*The County Chairman*, *The College Widow*, *Madame X* etc) and some fine musicals. His first musical-comedy venture was Luders and Pixley's previously shunned *King Dodo*, for which he made the most effective bid following the team's success with *The Burgomaster*, and his subsequent productions included some of the happiest early American comic operas: *The Sultan of Sulu* (1902), in which he starred his Castle Square comedian Moulan, the highly successful Luders/Pixley *The Prince of Pilsen* (1903), George Ade's *Peggy from Paris*, his successful collaboration with Luders on *The Sho-Gun* (1904), and *The Yankee Consul* (1904) starring Savage's other Castle Square favourite, Raymond Hitchcock. Luders and Pixley's *Woodland* (1904), the revusical science-fiction musical *The Man from Now* (1906) and Reginald De Koven's Ruritanian *The Student King* (1906) were less impressive, but Hitchcock's follow-up to his *Yankee Consul* success in *The Yankee Tourist* (1907) did better.

Savage had his biggest success, however, when in 1907 (now, curiously, calling himself 'Colonel' Savage) he introduced *The Merry Widow* to Broadway. Its enormous success led him virtually to abandon the American musicals which he had so diligently fostered up to this time, and most of his subsequent productions were imports. Unlike London's *Merry Widow* man, George Edwardes, however, he failed to pick the right ones – whilst other producers snapped up *Die Dollarprinzessin* and *Der tapfere Soldat*, Savage had mixed fortunes with Edward German's *Tom Jones*, Kálmán's *Tatárjárás* (*The Gay Hussars*), a piece fabricated from the scores of Eysler's *Johann der Zweite*, *Das Glücksschweinchen* and *Künstlerblut* (*The Love Cure*) which he announced as a second *Merry Widow* and Henri Bereny's *Lord Piccolo* (*Little Boy Blue*) which, at least at the time, went much further towards being so, but he notched up a full-sized disaster with the one-week run of Luders and Pixley's last work, *Somewhere Else*.

Europe at last gave him a second significant hit when he presented the little Hungarian soubrette Mitzi Hajós in a version of Kálmán's *Der Zigeunerprimás*, played on Broadway as *Sari* (1914), but thereafter success proved harder to find. Lehár's *Das Fürstenkind* (*The Maids of Athens*), Hugo Felix's remake of Hungary's *Csibéskirály* as *Pom-Pom* (1916) and the homegrown musicals of Jerome Kern (*Have a Heart*, *Toot-Toot!*, *Head over Heels* with Mitzi Hajós) and Louis Hirsch (*See-Saw*), and yet a further vehicle for the tenacious Mitzi called *Lady Billy* (Harold Levey/Zelda Sears) did, at best, adequately and, at worst, very badly, and although he got a six-month run out of a gently feminist piece called *The Clinging Vine* (1922) by Sears and Levey, a further show *The Magic Ring* (again with Mitzi) failed.

His final musical production, on which Miss Sears teamed with Vincent Youmans, was *Lollipop* (1924) a show which allowed the man who had produced so many fine pieces in his early days, and two enormous successes in *The Merry Widow* and *Sari* in his middle years, to go out with at least a respectable run.

SAY, DARLING Comedy about a musical in 2 acts by Richard and Marian Bissell and Abe Burrows. Lyrics by Adolph Green and Betty Comden. Music by Jule Styne. ANTA Theater, New York, 3 April 1958.

A comical backstage musical of some novelty, *Say, Darling* was co-written by Richard Bissell, the author of the novel *7½ Cents* and co-author of the musical libretto *The Pajama Game* which was based on that novel. It was based on a subsequent novel which he had written about the turning of the other/another novel into a hit musical and all the trials and tribulations that went with it. Jule Styne and Lester Osterman produced the piece, which called itself 'a comedy about a musical' and eschewed an orchestra which was instead replaced by two pianos to accompany the songs, many of which represented the score of the fictitious musical of which *Say, Darling* followed the creation. A cast, which was as à clef as you liked it to be, headed by David Wayne, Vivian Blaine, vocalist Johnny Desmond and Robert Morse as Ted Snow (who either was or wasn't *Pajama Game* producer Hal Prince, depending on whether you were a lawyer or a musical-theatre buff) had a lot of fun with a lot of theatrical in-jokes and out-jokes and, with some help from the two pianos, *Say, Darling* played for ten months and 332 performances on Broadway, followed by a three-week revival at the New York City Center the next season.

Recording: original cast (RCA)

THE SCARLET FEATHER *see* LA PETITE MARIÉE

SCHÄFER, Therese [née BRAUNECKER] (b Vienna, 3 April 1825; d Iglau, 8 March 1888).

One of the most important Viennese prima donnas of the earliest days of the opéra-bouffe and Operette period, Therese Braunecker-Schäfer (later known simply as Frau Schäfer) began her career as a popular vocalist and then as an actress and singer at the German theatres in Pest and Prague. She was a leading member of the Johann Nestroy company at the Carltheater during the period in which Karl Treumann masterminded his first and influential Vienna productions of the works of Offenbach and other French composers and she appeared as Annemarie (ie Fanchette) in the Carltheater's landmark production of *Hochzeit bei Laternenschein* (1858). She was Marguerite in *Das Mädchen von Elisonzo* (1858), Susette in *Der Ehemann vor der Tür* (1859) and the first German-language Eurydice in *Orpheus in der Unterwelt* (1860) at the Carltheater, and then moved with Treumann to his Theater am Franz-Josef-Kai where she played Fé-an-nich-ton in *Tschin-Tschin* (*Ba-ta-clan*), Magellone (ie Geneviève) in *Die schöne Magellone* (1861, *Geneviève de Brabant*), Madame Fortunio in *Meister Fortunio und sein Liebeslied*, Madame Balandard in *Salon Pitzelberger* (*Monsieur Choufleuri*) etc.

In the late 1860s she began a second and even more prominent career as a low-to-lowish comedy singer/actress in Operette, appearing at the Carltheater in, at first, a mixture of good comic character and not-too-juvenile soubrette rôles and some which bordered on being bit parts: *Die schöne Weiber von Georgien* (Zaida), *Tulipatan* (Aloë), *Pariser Leben* (Madame Quimper-Karadec), now as Babette in *Meister Fortunio*, *Kakadu* (Mademoiselle Paturelle), *Die Jungfrau von Dragant* (Gertrude), *Die Prinzessin von Trapezunt* (Paola), *Angot die Tochter der Halle*

(the lusty market-woman Amaranthe with her swingeing expository song), *Cassis Pacha*, *Die schöne Bourbonnaise* (Gervaise), Delibes's *Confusius IX* (Frau von Moppeldorf), Suppé's ill-fated *Die Frau Meisterin* (the nurse, Petronella), *Hundert Jungfrauen* (Kaca), *Schönröschen* (Julienne), *Prinz Conti* (Dorette) etc. She moved smoothly from this series of rôles into a major career as Vienna's foremost Operette 'komische Alte', playing mostly at the Theater an der Wien as the voluminously bossy Aurore in *Giroflé-Girofla* (1875), the storyteller Wassildschi in *Fatinitza* (1876), Madame de Parabès in *Margot die reiche Bäckerin* (1877), Sphisteira in *Prinz Methusalem* (1877), as man-hungry Peronella in *Boccaccio* (1879), Donna Olympia in Suppé's *Donna Juanita* (1880), the Marquise von Villereal in *Das Spitzentuch der Königin* (1880), Heloise in *Apajune, der Wassermann* (1880), Javotte Bergamotte in *Die Jungfrau von Belleville* (1881), Sister Opportune in *Musketiere in Damenstift* (1881), the battle-chief Countess Artemisia Malaspina in *Der lustige Krieg* (1881), Madame Victor in Millöcker's *Ein süsses Kind* (1882), Hermine von Tricasse in Offenbach's *Doctor Ox*, the grotesque Buccametta of *Die Afrikareise*, the splendidly comico-aristocratic Palmatica, Gräfin Nowalska in *Der Bettelstudent* (1882), Agricola Barbaruccio in Vienna's revised *Eine Nacht in Venedig* (1883), the duenna Zenobia in *Gasparone* (1884), the housekeeper Barbara in *Der Feldprediger* (1884), Mirabella in *Der Zigeunerbaron* (1885), introducing Strauss's happily comical description of feminine fate in wartime, 'Just sind es vier und zwanzig Jahre', written particularly for her, and Donna Candida de Quesada y Mendizabal in *Der Viceadmiral* (1886). She also appeared in Brandl's *Die Mormonen* (Mutter Snow), *Zwillinge* (Pomponne Sarazin) and several other less successful pieces, and reprised her rôle of Paola in *La Princesse de Trébizonde* at the age of 60.

In the course of this decade and more of comic rôles she established herself as one of the town's most popular musical players, and, as noted in the case of *Der Zigeunerbaron*, her presence in the Theater an der Wien company influenced the writing-in of suitably substantial comic dame rôles and songs into the new shows of her time. Frau Schäfer was forced by illness to retire from the stage in 1886 after a remarkable career of some 30 years in which she had an important hand in the emergence of Operette in Vienna and, above all, established the low-comedy female rôle in 19th-century Viennese Operette in the same way that Marie Desclauzas had in France and Priscilla German Reed had in Britain.

SCHANZER, Rudolf (b Vienna, 12 January 1875; d Fiume, 1944). Librettist and lyricist of a number of standard German Operetten.

Vienna-born Schanzer spent his early working years as a journalist and was for a number of years based in Paris where he became secretary to a well-off gentleman. When gentleman and secretary moved to Berlin, Schanzer began to contribute to several newspapers and then tried his hand at writing for the theatre. His first full-sized piece was an adaptation of H G Wells's *The Time Machine* entitled *Der Sonnenvogel* on which he collaborated with Georg Okonkowski and composer Holländer. It was toured by Julius Spielmann's Wiener Operetten Ensemble, and subsequently seen at Berlin's Centraltheater, but although this piece was a by no means negligible start, his first real success came with the internationally played *Lord Piccolo* (1910), with whose composer, Henri Berény, Schanzer then went on to write two further Operetten.

Later the same year he successfully collaborated with the Berliner Theater's director Rudolf Bernauer to turn out an adaptation of the classic Posse *Auf eigenen Füssen* as *Bummelstudenten* and they again teamed with considerable success on other pieces for Bernauer's theatre, the burlesque *Die Grosse Rosinen* and the musical comedy *Filmzauber*, before Schanzer became installed as dramaturg and stage director at the Berliner. Beginning with the highly successful *Wie einst im Mai*, Bernauer, Schanzer and principal composer Walter Kollo turned out a five-year series of musical plays which entertained wartime Berlin and, occasionally, other countries staunchly.

In 1918 Schanzer teamed up with another Berliner Theater man, Ernst Welisch, and the two quickly became Berlin's most successful librettists, turning out texts for Jean Gilbert (*Die Frau im Hermelin*), Leo Fall (*Madame Pompadour*), Oscar Straus (*Riquette*, *Die Teresina*) and Ralph Benatzky (*Casanova*, *Die drei Musketiere*) with considerable national and international success. In the early 1930s this pair moved on, along with most of the rest of Jewish and/or operettic Germany, and in the years that followed they wrote for Vienna and Switzerland rather than Berlin, but Schanzer did not flee Hitler sufficiently fast or far. He ended his own days when he committed suicide in the face of the Gestapo.

1900 **Der schwarze Mann** (Oscar Straus/Gustav von Moser, Thilo von Trotha ad) 1 act Colberg; Secession-Bühne, Berlin 28 December 1901

1902 **Der Sonnenvogel** (Viktor Holländer/w Georg Okonkowski) St Petersburg (Wiener Operetten Ensemble); Central-theater, Berlin April 1904

1903 **Atelier Edgar** (Robert Leonhard) 1 act Kurtheater, Bad Liebenstein 4 August

1908 **Der Sterndeuter** (Leonhard) Neues Operetten-Theater, Leipzig 16 May

1910 **Lord Piccolo** (Henri Berény/w Carl Lindau) Johann Strauss-Theater, Vienna 1 September

1910 **Bummelstudenten** (Bogumil Zepler, Willi Bredschneider/Emil Pohl, Heinrich Wilken ad w Rudolf Bernauer) Berliner Theater 31 December

1911 **Das Mädel von Montmartre** (Berény) Neues Theater 26 October

1911 **Sein Herzensjunge** (Walter Kollo/w August Neidhart) Thalia-Theater, Elberfeld 1 April

1911 **Der verbotene Kuss** (*Tilos a csók*) German version w I Pasztae (Centraltheater, Dresden)

1911 **Die grosse Rosinen** (*Berlin hat's eilig*) (Leon Jessel, Zepler, Bredschneider et al/w Bernauer) Berliner Theater 31 December

1912 **Filmzauber** (Kollo, Bredschneider/w Bernauer) Berliner Theater 19 October

1912 **Eine kitzliche Geschichte** (Hugo Hirsch/w Erich Urban) Lustspielhaus, Düsseldorf 31 October

1913 **Mein Mäderl** (Berény/w Eugen Burg, Lindau) Raimund-theater, Vienna, 21 January

1913 **Die beiden Husaren** (Leon Jessel/w Wilhelm Jacoby) Theater des Westens 6 February

1913 **Wie einst im Mai** (Kollo, Bredschneider/w Bernauer) Berliner Theater 4 October

1914 **Tangofieber** [*Tanzfieber*] (Hirsch/w Max Heye, Theo Halton/Urban) Walhalla-Theater 15 January

1914 **Extrablätter** (Kollo, Bredschneider/w Heinz Gordon) Berliner Theater 24 October

1915 **Wenn zwei Hochzeit machen** (Kollo, Bredschneider/w Bernauer) Berliner Theater 23 October

1916 **Auf Flügeln des Gesanges** (Kollo, Bredschneider/w Bernauer) Berliner Theater 9 September

1917 **Die tolle Komtess** (Kollo/w Bernauer) Berliner Theater 21 February

1918 **Blitzblaues Blut** (Kollo/w Bernauer) Berliner Theater 9 February

1918 **Sterne, die wieder leuchtet** (Kollo/w Bernauer) Berliner Theater 6 November

1919 **Die Frau im Hermelin** (Gilbert/w Ernst Welisch) Theater des Westens 23 August

1919 **Bummelstudenten** revised version (Zepler, Bredschneider/w Bernauer) Berliner Theater 2 October

1920 **Der Geiger von Lugano** (Jean Gilbert/w Welisch) Thalia-Theater 25 September

1920 **Die spanische Nachtigall** (Leo Fall/w Welisch) Berliner Theater 18 November

1921 **Die Braut des Lucullus** (Gilbert/w Welisch) Theater des Westens 26 August

1921 **Prinzessin Olala** (Gilbert/w Bernauer) Berliner Theater 17 September

1922 **Madame Pompadour** (Fall/w Welisch) Berliner Theater 9 September

1923 **Die Damen von Olymp** (Rudolf Nelson/w Welisch) Nelson-Theater May

1923 **Der süsse Kavalier** (Fall/w Welisch) Apollotheater, Vienna 11 December

1925 **Riquette** (Oscar Straus/w Welisch) Deutsches Künstler-theater 17 January

1925 **Die Teresina** (Oscar Straus/w Welisch) Deutsches Künstlertheater 11 September

1925 **Das Spiel um die Liebe** (Gilbert/w Welisch) Theater des Westens 19 December

1926 **Jugend im Mai** (Fall/w Welisch) Zentraltheater, Dresden 22 October; Städtische Oper, Berlin, 1927

1927 **Eine Frau ohne Format** (Michael Krasznay-Krausz/w Welisch) Theater des Westens 22 September

1928 **Casanova** (Johann Strauss arr Benatzky/w Welisch) Grosses Schauspielhaus 1 September

1929 **Die drei Musketiere** (Benatzky/w Welisch) Grosses Schauspielhaus, Berlin 28 September

1929 **Die erste Beste** (Straus/w Welisch) Deutsches Theater Prague 19 October

1930 **Das Mädel am Steuer** (Gilbert/w Welisch) Komische Oper 17 September

1932 **Der Teufelsreiter** (Emmerich Kálmán/w Welisch) Theater an der Wien, Vienna 10 March

1932 **Der Studentenprinz** (*The Student Prince*) German version w Welisch (Grosses Schauspielhaus)

1933 **Die Lindenwirtin** (Krasznay-Krausz/w Welisch) Metropoltheater 30 March

1935 **Maya** German version w Welisch (Theater an der Wien, Vienna)

1936 **Dreimal Georges** (Paul Burkhard/w Welisch) Stadttheater, Zurich 3 October

SCHEFF, Fritzi [JÄGER, Anna Friederike] (b Vienna 30 August ?1879; d New York, 8 April 1954). Ex-opera soprano who became a Broadway leading lass.

The daughter of an opera singer, Hortense Scheff, the young Fritzi was trained as a vocalist in Dresden and Frankfurt and made her operatic début at 19 as Flotow's Martha, as Juliette in Gounod's *Roméo et Juliette* and as *La Fille du régiment* in Munich. She remained in Munich appearing in a variety of operatic rôles (Marguerite, Santuzza, Mimi, Mignon), before going to America in 1901 on contract to Maurice Grau for the Metropolitan Opera House. There she took the lighter soprano rôles of the operatic repertoire (Marzelline, Musetta, Zerlina, Cherubino, Nedda, Papagena) over a period of some two years, before abandoning opera to make her first appearance on the light musical stage, under the management of Charles Dillingham, in the title-rôle of Victor Herbert's *Babette* (1903).

Miss Scheff subsequently created the part of Rose in *Two Roses* (a musical version of *She Stoops to Conquer*) and appeared at the Broadway Theater, New York, during 1905 in the starring rôles of a series of classic Continental Operetten: *Fatinitza*, *Giroflé-Girofla* and *Boccaccio*, but she had her most significant success when she introduced the rôle of the tiny, sparkling hat-shop demoiselle, Fifi, in Herbert's *Mlle Modiste* ('Kiss Me Again'), a vehicle which served her for several seasons on the road. She had less success when cast in another Herbert piece whose title insisted fatally (it has always been unlucky) that she was *The Prima Donna* (1908).

She appeared as a suitably tiny Yum-Yum to Sam Bernard's Ko-Ko and the Pitti Sing of Lulu Glaser/ Christie MacDonald in the Casino Theater's starry 1910 revival of *The Mikado*, but her fourth Victor Herbert vehicle *The Duchess* (1911) was a quick Broadway failure. It was also her last Herbert vehicle, as the lady's notoriously difficult temperament got the better of the composer in the same way as that of his other operatic star, Emma Trentini, had done and he wrote for her no more.

The Love Wager (1912) a piece adapted from an Hungarian play and featuring its star as the fourth of its titular *Seven Sisters* – inevitably called Mitzi – to a score by Charles J Hambitzer did not make it to Broadway, but *The Pretty Mrs Smith* (1914) did, even though the nominal star had to battle for her laurels with the up-and-coming Charlotte Greenwood's comical dancing. Several years of vaudeville, (silent!) film work (*The Pretty Mrs Smith* etc) and an out-of-town closure in *Husbands Guaranteed* (1916) intervened before Miss Scheff returned to success in the musical theatre, touring for John Cort in the rôle created by Eleanor Painter in *Glorianna* (1919 ... 'Miss Scheff is wearing auburn hair this season'). She disappeared from the casts of *The O'Brien Girl* and *Bye Bye Bonnie* before those shows made Broadway, was announced to lead the Broadway cast of *No, No, Nanette* following the sacking of Blanche Ring, but didn't, and she was not seen in New York again in a singing rôle until she repeated her one genuine Broadway hit, *Mlle Modiste*, in a 1929 revival, at the age of 50.

Scheff continued to perform, however, appearing in musicals in regional theatres (Frieda in *Music in the Air* etc), and often in supporting rôles, for a number of years thereafter. In 1946 she was seen at the Diamond Horseshoe in cabaret, and as late as 1948 was still to be seen on the stage.

DER SCHELM VON BERGEN

DER SCHELM VON BERGEN Operette in 3 acts by Carl Loewe and Carl Lindau. Music by Alfred Oelschlegel. Theater an der Wien, Vienna, 29 September 1888.

Heinrich Heine's narrative poem *Der Schelm von Bergen* is better known for the Operetten it didn't become than for that which it did. At the suggestion of Johann Strauss,

Ignaz Schnitzer, the author of *Der Zigeunerbaron*, wrote him a libretto based on this tale of the rogue of Bergen, which was intended to allow the composer, who had jealously noticed the recent success of Nessler's *Der Trompeter von Säkkingen*, to sneak a little further away from the operettic genre with what he regarded as its insufficient singers, and a little closer to the romantic opera which he was now anxious to write. However, having prematurely accepted the libretto and, indeed, written music for much of one act, Strauss finally reneged on the excuse that the central character of the tale bore too close a resemblance to Ko-Ko, the comic executioner of Gilbert's *The Mikado* which had recently premièred in Austria. Strauss went to work instead on Victor Léon's *Simplicius*, taking over some of the *Schelm von Bergen* music for use in that piece, and Schnitzer subsequently handed his orphaned libretto to the young and unproduced Edmund Eysler. Eysler composed a full score, *Der Hexenspiegel*, to it which won the interest of publisher Josef Weinberger, but which was never staged and Eysler, like Strauss, then cannibalized his score for his hugely successful *Bruder Straubinger* whilst Schnitzer's text once again went back on the shelf.

Although Schnitzer's adaptation was never produced, Heine's Bergen-scamp did make it to the stage. The Theater an der Wien clearly did not share Strauss's worries about *The Mikado*, and they produced an operettic version of *Der Schelm von Bergen* composed by Alfred Oelschlegel in October 1888, the same year in which they played a significant series of performances of ... *The Mikado*. It was played 17 times. Subsequently another *Schelm von Bergen* by A Camillo Grans and Gustav Niehr was produced at Dessau (13 March 1900) and Ignaz M Welleminsky and Oskar Ritter wrote an operatic libretto on the same tale, set by Kurt Atterberg, and produced at Stockholm under the title *Fanal* (27 January 1934).

Author Heine also eventually got his operettic 'due' when his fictionalized life was decorated with a pasticcio score taken from the works of Mendelssohn and put on the musical stage under the title *Dichterliebe* (arr Ernst Stern/Julius Brammer, Alfred Grünwald). In Vienna, Heine was impersonated by Hubert Marischka, owner and director of the Theater an der Wien.

SCHMIDSEDER, Ludwig

SCHMIDSEDER, Ludwig (b Passau, 24 August 1904; d Munich, 21 June 1971). Composer for the wartime German and postwar Austrian theatre.

After a youth spent playing as a pianist in a trio, first in South America and then around the world, Schmidseder returned in 1930 to his native Germany and worked as a bar pianist whilst beginning a career as a songwriter. He turned out a series of popular songs which soon led the way into both the theatre and the film worlds. He wrote three Operetten for the Berlin Metropoltheater of which *Die – oder keine* proved the most successful, and after the war combined with Hubert Marischka on a biomusical of Marie Geistinger, produced in Vienna under the title *Die Walzerkönigin*, and a romantic period piece called *Abschiedswalzer*, again set in the Viennese good old days, both of which, with their librettist starring, had good runs. *Die Walzerkönigin*, with its Viennese star Elfie Meyerhofer repeating, was played in Paris in 1949 (*La Reine des valses*, Théâtre des Champs Elysées) and subsequently in the French provinces.

1937 **Die verliebte Frau, Viola** (Günther Schwenn/Paul Beyer) Neues Operetten-Theater, Leipzig 22 January

1938 **Melodie der Nacht** (Schwenn/Heinz Hentschke) Metropoltheater 21 September

1939 **Die – oder keine** (Schwenn, Hentschke) Metropoltheater 20 September

1940 **Frauen im Metropol** (Hentschke) Metropoltheater 27 September

1942 **Heimkehr nach Mittenwald** (Günther Resee) Landestheater, Linz 26 August

1943 **Vorsicht Diana** (Resee) Fürth 19 March

1944 **Linzer Torte** (Ignaz Brantner, Aldo Pinelli/Hans Gustl Kernmayer) Landestheater, Linz

1948 **Die Walzerkönigin** (Hubert Marischka, Pinelli) Bürgertheater 11 October

1949 **Abschiedswalzer** (Marischka, Rudolf Österreicher) Bürgertheater 8 September

1952 **Mädel aus der Wachau** (Jorg Bartner, Pinelli) Landestheater, Linz 26 April

Other titles attributed: *Glück in Monte Carlo* (Salzburg, 1947), *Arm wie eine Kirchenmaus* (1947)

SCHMIDT, Harvey [Lester] (b Dallas, Tex, 12 September 1929).

Schmidt made up a team with songwriting partner Tom Jones during university days and the pair made their earliest stage ventures in college shows. He then began a career as a commercial artist in New York whilst simultaneously carrying on his writing efforts, and the pair placed songs in such revues as Julius Monk's *Demi-Dozen* and *Pieces of Eight*, *The Portfolio Revue* and *Shoestring '57* before their first stage musical *The Fantasticks* ('Try to Remember') was brought to the stage. The immense success of this little piece won Schmidt and Jones the opportunity to work on a very much larger show, the adaptation of the play *The Rainmaker* into the musical *110 in the Shade*, but, although the piece had a certain success, they intelligently returned to what they recognized they did best and produced another intimate piece, the two-handed musical adaptation of Jan de Hartog's *The Fourposter* as *I Do! I Do!* The result was another long-running hit, not in a tiny house like that which housed *The Fantasticks*, but on a regular Broadway-sized plateau. Thereafter, however, success deserted the pair and several attempts at a biomusical on the French writer and music-hall artist Colette, a small-scale allegoric piece with multiple echoes of *The Fantasticks* and many more of its 1960s era entitled *Celebration*, a classical burlesque, *Philemon*, and a musical version of Thornton Wilder's *Our Town* failed to confirm their popularity as established by their first three shows.

1960 **The Fantasticks** (Tom Jones) Sullivan Street Playhouse 3 May

1963 **110 in the Shade** (Jones, N Richard Nash) Broadhurst Theater 24 October

1966 **I Do! I Do!** (Jones) 46th Street Theater 5 December

1969 **Celebration** (Jones) Ambassador Theater 22 January

1970 **Colette** (Jones/Elinor Jones) Ellen Stewart Theater 6 June

1975 **Philemon** (Jones) Portfolio Studio 8 April

1982 **Colette** revised version 5th Avenue Theater, Seattle 9 February

1983 **Colette Collage** revised version of *Colette* York Players 31 March

1987 **Grovers Corners** (Jones) Marriott Lincolnshire Theater, Chicago 29 July

SCHNEIDER, Hortense [Catherine] (b Bordeaux, 30 April 1833; d Paris, 5 May 1920).

The six-year shooting star of Offenbach's Théâtre des Variétés series whose dazzling career declined at the same time as that of the French Empire of which she was such a feature.

Hortense Schneider made her first theatrical appearance in her native Bordeaux in the play *Michel et Christine* at the age of 15, and then moved on to play in Agen where she appeared in everything from farce to opera, as ingénue or pageboy or 'amoureuse'. She was out of her teens by the time she got to Paris, where she soon got to know the comedian Berthelier and, with his help, auditioned for Hippolyte Cogniard (unsuccessfully) and for Offenbach, with whom Berthelier had scored a great hit a few weeks earlier in *Les Deux Aveugles*. Offenbach, at that stage still running his first little summer Bouffes-Parisiens house, was obviously more impressed by the pretty little actress than Cogniard had been, and she was given the female rôle, opposite her useful boyfriend, in the next Offenbach one-acter, *Le Violoneux* (31 August 1855). Offenbach's regular soprano, Marie Dalmont, created *Ba-ta-clan* later in the year, but the new little starlet, fresh from her personal success in the distinctly successful little rustic opérette, moved with Offenbach's company to the new house in the Passage Choiseul and there created the more lively part of the actress of *Tromb-al-ca-zar* (1856, Simplette), appeared in Adam's *Les Pantins de Violette* (reportedly to the delight of the composer), and triumphed in the delightful little three-cornered battle of *La Rose de Saint-Flour* (1856, Pierrette).

Cogniard now changed his mind about the young actress who was winning such delighted reviews for her charming performances and he whisked Hortense off to his Théâtre des Variétés where she opened a few weeks later in *Le Chien de garde*. From the Variétés she moved on to the Palais-Royal and over the next years, through a long series of vaudevilles à couplets and the other varied entertainments which made up the programmes of that house (Hervé's *Les Toréadors de Grenade* etc) her reputation, both on-stage and off-, grew apace.

It was nearly a decade since her first appearance in Paris in *Le Violoneux* when Schneider, now something of a star, returned to Offenbach to create the title-rôle of *La Belle Hélène* at the Variétés (1864). The success of the piece, and of Hortense Schneider in the piece, were only equalled by those of its successors as the star followed up her burlesque Helen of Troy with the rough-and-tough but infinitely sexy last wife of *Barbe-bleue* (1866, Boulotte), as the pubescent teenaged *Grande-Duchesse de Gérolstein* (1867) with her famous Sabre Song and her insinuating 'Dites-lui', and (in spite of difficult beginnings) the street-singer heroine of *La Périchole* (1868, Letter song). The series filled the Variétés for the best part of four seasons and, during the off-season Hortense, at the height of her enormous fame, took her vehicles and 'her' company to other venues, notably across the channel to London where she appeared in several seasons with great popularity.

Always difficult, perpetually walking out and usually returning, avid over salary even though her royal and rich off-stage admirers made such cares unneccesary, Schneider became only more so as she became more successful. She was persuaded to appear as little more than her famous self in Offenbach's *La Diva* (1869), but the piece turned out a failure and even her popularity could not save it. She turned down *Les Brigands* and left the Variétés, having created her last Offenbach rôle. Several years later, after the Franco-Prussian War and after another truncated run in Hervé's *La Veuve du Malabar* (1873, Tata-Lili), she agreed to return to the Variétés to appear in an enlarged version of her old rôle in *La Périchole* and again to play Margot, the titular baker's wife in *La Boulangère a des écus*, the newest piece written by the authors of her greatest successes, but before the first night of this delicious new vehicle she had walked out (or been dropped, depending which version you believe). Instead, she played Hervé's *La Belle Poule* (1875, Poulette) with only mediocre results, and several tart comments about playing her age.

Schneider had no intention of playing her age. She had been the reigning queen of the Paris stage for a good half-dozen years, and she had no intention of now being its queen mother. She had seriously threatened, more even than just threatened, to quit the theatre before and she had no compunction about doing so now. With *La Belle Poule* the curtain came down on one of the most dazzling – if not extended – careers of the musical stage, and for the 45 years of life remaining to her, Hortense Schneider lived a life of respectability at utter odds with the gay and gallivanting years of her theatrical heyday when she had been known, not with a little admiration as 'le passage des Princes'.

A character bearing little resemblance to Schneider but given her name and even a love affair with Offenbach was portrayed on the screen by Yvonne Printemps in the film *Valse de Paris*. A different romance for the composer – apparently with Empress Eugénie! – was proposed by the Hungarian author of the composer's biomusical *Offenbach* (1920), but both real-life wife Herminie and Hortense appeared in the piece, the diva originally played by Juci Labáss. In the Vienna production she was portrayed by Olga Bartos-Trau, on Broadway by Odette Myrtil.

SCHNITZER, Ignaz [Manuel] (b Pest, 20 December 1839; d Vienna, 18 June 1921). Author of one major Viennese hit in each century of his activity.

A Budapest journalist who, after a late beginning, made a theatrical career in Vienna, Schnitzer was given his earliest exposure on the operatic stage when his text to Bachrich's *Muzzedin* was heard at the Vienna Opera in 1883. He had, however, already cast his eyes in the direction of the lighter musical theatre and, in 1882, had sent an Operette synopsis to Johann Strauss. This had led to a collaboration on a piece about *Salvator Rosa* (already in 1874 the subject of a fine opera by Gomez) being announced. *Salvator Rosa* never appeared, but it was in collaboration with Strauss that, three years later, Schnitzer wrote his first Operette to make it before the Viennese footlights: the musical stage adaptation of fellow Hungarian Mór Jókai's *Sáffi* as *Der Zigeunerbaron* (1885). Schnitzer later prepared a second libretto for Strauss, based on Heinrich Heine's *Der Schelm von Bergen*, but part way through setting it Strauss abandoned the work.

In 1885 Schnitzer also adapted Jókai's *Az aranyember* for the Theater an der Wien as *Der Goldmensch* and in 1889 he had another operatic piece, *Der Königsbraut* (music: Fuchs) produced, as well as a second Operette, a piece of classical antiquity called *Das Orakel*, based on the work of another famous Hungarian author, Gergely Csiky, and set to music by Hellmesberger. Produced at the Theater an der Wien it lasted only 13 performances, but nevertheless won a production in America as *Apollo*. He turned Csiky's famous *Nagymama* into *Die Grossmama* for the German-language stage without music, but yet another Hungarian-based Schnitzer libretto, taken from Csepreghi's equally celebrated play *A piros bugyelláris*, was set to music by Hugo Felix. It was played just 20 times.

A second attempt to get his *Schelm von Bergen* script produced, this time with a score by the young Edmund Eysler (*Der Hexenspiegel*), also failed but the connection with Eysler proved highly fruitful, for a further collaboration between the two on *Bruder Straubinger* not only made the stage at the Theater an der Wien but also turned out to be a major hit. The pair, and Schnitzer's new writing partner Siegmund Schlesinger, subsequently provided a second fine vehicle for *Bruder Straubinger* star Alexander Girardi as the olde Viennese hairdresser *Pufferl*, but the piece's run was decapitated by the star's departure from the theatre.

Three subsequent Operetten, all written with Schlesinger, found less success. *Zur Indischen Witwe*, set musically by Oscar Straus, struck no sparks in Berlin, a piece called *Der Elektriker*, with Ferdinand Pagin in the title-rôle, played just eight performances at the Carltheater, and *Tip-Top*, a musical based on the stories of Bret Harte and with a cast including Louis Treumann and Luise Kartousch, foundered in 25 nights at the Theater an der Wien. A collaboration with Emmerich von Gatti on the text for *Kreolenblut* was a little more profitable, for Heinrich Berté's Operette went on from its Hamburg première to be seen, albeit not for long, on Broadway and in the French provinces.

1884 **Raffaela** (Max Wolf/Eugène Scribe ad w Adolf Schirmer) Theater am Gärtnerplatz, Munich March
1885 **Der Zigeunerbaron** (Johann Strauss) Theater an der Wien 24 October
1889 **Das Orakel** (Hellmesberger) Theater an der Wien 30 November
1891 **Hand in Hand** (Franz Roth/w Friedrich Gustav Triesch) Deutsches Volkstheater 7 April
1894 **Husarenblut** (Hugo Felix) Theater an der Wien 10 March
1903 **Bruder Straubinger** (Edmund Eysler/w Moritz West) Theater an der Wien 20 February
1905 **Pufferl** (Eysler/w Siegmund Schlesinger) Theater an der Wien 10 February
1905 **Zur Indischen Witwe** (Oscar Straus/w Schlesinger) Centraltheater, Berlin 30 September
1906 **Der Elektriker** (Karl-Josef Fromm/w Schlesinger) Carltheater 23 February
1907 **Tip-Top** (Josef Stritzko/w Schlesinger) Theater an der Wien 5 October
1910 **Kreolenblut** (Heinrich Berté/w Emmerich von Gatti) Neues Operetten-Theater, Hamburg 25 December
1914 **Anno 1814** (Paul Eisler/w Hugo H Regel) Festspieltheater im Kaisergarten 1 May

SCHÖNBERG, Claude-Michel (b Vannes, 6 July 1944). Composer of the operettic version of *Les Misérables*.

A popular music producer at Pathé-Marconi for a number of years, Schönberg had his first contact with the musical theatre when he composed the score for *La Révolution française*, a musical pageant of the events surrounding that well-publicized event, which was issued as a double-disc recording. The piece followed the *Jesus Christ Superstar* path by transferring subsequently from disc to a stage production at Paris's Palais des Sports in 1973, with Schönberg himself appearing as Louis XVI.

Two years later, Schönberg issued his own first recording as a performer, and went on to find considerable succes purveying his own material to the hit parades of France. A second alliance with *Révolution française* writer Alain Boublil and with the poet Jean-Marc Natel then resulted in the production of a second recorded musical, *Les Misérables*. This piece, too, found its way to the Paris stage in a spectacular Robert Hossein production. However, it then went further. It was taken up by British producer Cameron Mackintosh and, after considerable rewriting by both adapter and composer, it was produced first in London and then around the world as it became one of the most oustandingly successful musical plays of the 1980s and 1990s.

In 1989 Schönberg composed a second, this time made-to-order, musical for Mackintosh and the West End and Broadway stages, to a libretto resituating the *Madame Butterfly* story in the Vietnam War. Although it lacked disappointingly the vigorously exciting musical score which had been such a solid part of the success of his first two works, *Miss Saigon*, given an opérette-à-grand-spectacle mounting, profited from the backing of the most successful production organization in the world to win itself runs in Britain, America and Japan.

A composer in the mode established by the musicals of Andrew Lloyd Webber, blending popular music strains with a solid operettic and classic foundation in sung-through scores, Schönberg proved in his first two record-to-stage works that he had abilities second to none amongst modern writers for the musical theatre, treating dramatic, romantic and comic situations with equal effectiveness.

1973 **La Révolution française** (w Raymond Jeannot/Jean-Max Rivière, Alain Boublil) Palais des Sports
1980 **Les Misérables** (Boublil, Jean-Marc Natel) Palais des Sports 17 September
1985 **Les Misérables** revised English version ad Herbert Kretzmer Barbican Theatre, London 8 October
1989 **Miss Saigon** (Boublil, Richard Maltby jr) Theatre Royal, Drury Lane, London 20 September

DIE SCHÖNE GALATHÉE Comic mythological opera in 1 act by 'Poly Henrion'. Music by Franz von Suppé. Meysels Theater, Berlin, 30 June 1865.

The most enduringly successful of the early short Operetten written for the Viennese stage under the influence of the French opéra-bouffe.

One of the moving forces behind the making of the *Die schöne Galathée* was the actor and producer Karl Treumann, who had been largely reponsible for bringing the works of Offenbach to the German-speaking public, but also for encouraging the composer, von Suppé, whose *Zehn Mädchen und kein Mann* and *Flotte Bursche* he had produced during his management of the Theater am Franz-Josefs-Kai, to write this kind of piece for the theatre. The other was the favourite actress Anna

Plate 239. **Die schöne Galathee**: *A very schöne Galathee hits the bottle in the Wiener Kammeroper's production of 1990.*

Grobecker who had been a huge success in the earlier Suppé pieces, and for whom a fine and typical 'boy' part was prepared in the new work.

The text, by 'Poly Henrion', otherwise actor and author Leopold Karl Dietmar Kohl von Kohlnegg (b 13 December 1814; d 1 May 1876), was very closely modelled on that written by Jules Barbier and Michel Carré for Victor Massé's successful French opéra-comique *Galathée*. It had the same four characters and a chorus, and it not only followed the same plot but even copied situations, scenes and song ideas. The Cypriot sculptor Pygmalion (Telek) has made a statue of a lovely woman, Galatea (Amilie Kraft), which bewitches the art critic Midas (Treumann) by its beauty and prompts the longing sculptor to pray to the gods to bring her to life. When they do, however, Galatea proves to be a liability. She over-indulges in food and wine, prefers the attentions of the studio-boy Ganymede (Anna Grobecker) to those of the passionate Pygmalion and the rich Midas, and finally Pygmalion has to beg Venus to turn her safely back to stone.

Suppé's score was a delightfully light-hearted one, from its set-piece overture with its broad waltz theme, through Midas's comic relating of his pedigree ('Meinem Vater

Gordios'), Ganymede's ancient Greek topical song ('Wir sind Griechen'), Galatea's tipsy aria ('Hell im Glas') and her kissing duet with the boy ('Ach, mich zieht's zu dir').

The piece got its first showing not in Vienna, but in Berlin, on the occasion of Grobecker's Benefit during her summer season at Woltersdorff's little Meysels Theater, sharing a spectacle coupé programme with Zaytz's *Fitzliputzli* and the comedy *Ein Gläschen Tokayer*. Two months later, the star and her producer mounted the show back at home base. It won a fine success, remained more than a decade in the Carltheater repertoire, and was later played at many other Viennese theatres, entering the Theater an der Wien in 1872 and the Volksoper in 1909, whilst spreading itself thoroughly through German-speaking houses including those in Hungary and in America, where Theodore and Hedwig L'Arronge, Friedrich Herrmann and Laura Haffner first introduced the piece in 1867. An Hungarian version (ad Endre Latabár) quickly followed the first German performances in Budapest and it won repeated productions, but it was not until 1872, following a performance of the show by a visiting German company in London, that an English-language version was produced. John Hollingshead staged an anonymous adaptation at the Gaiety Theatre with Constance Loseby (Galatea), Nellie Farren (Ganymede), Frank Wood (Pygmalion) and Fred Sullivan (Midas) in the principal rôles. America waited another decade before Tony Pastor mounted an English version at his music hall with Pauline Hall and Pauline Canissa featured. In the meanwhile, however, Australia had been treated to its first *Galatea* by the enterprising American minstrel team of Kelly and Leon. Female impersonator Leon played Galatea (apparently with music quasi-complete), whilst Kelly played Midas, his son Edwin Lester was Ganymede and the minstrel known as 'Japanese Tommy' made an appearance as Bacchus.

Unsurprisingly, the piece did not venture to France, where Massé's work was still popular, but in spite of the virtual disappearance of the short Operette from the musical stage, it has remained a perennial in Austrian and German houses where, mostly in altered and expanded versions made to turn it into a full-length entertainment, it is regularly produced to the present day.

Austria: Carltheater 9 September 1865; Hungary: Budai Színkör *Die schöne Galatea* 15 July 1867, Budai Népszinház *A szép Galathea* 24 August 1867; USA: Stadttheater (Ger) 6 September 1867, Tony Pastor's Music Hall *The Beautiful Galatea* 14 September 1882; UK: Opera Comique (Ger) 6 November 1871, Gaiety Theatre *Ganymede and Galatea* 20 January 1872; Australia: Queen's Theatre, Sydney *Galatea* 2 March 1878
Recordings: RCA, Saga

SCHÖNERER, Alexandrine von (b Vienna, 5 June 1850; d Vienna, November 1919).

From 1 September 1884 to 30 April 1900, Frau von Schönerer was the owner and, either in partnership or alone, the manager of the Theater an der Wien, at that stage one of the two most important and productive of Vienna's musical houses. In 1884 she joined Camillo Walzel, Franz Jauner (director of the Carltheater) and, briefly, the actor Girardi, as a 23 per cent part of a consortium to run the theatre which had for the previous decade been run by Maximilian Steiner and his son Franz.

When Walzel, who had been the active artistic director, also withdrew in 1889, she continued as 'Eigenthümerin und Direktorin' in partnership with Jauner (to 1895) and then, for the last five years of her management, alone.

Amongst her musical productions during the decade in which she actively ran the theatre were Dellinger's *Capitän Fracassa* and Hellmesberger's *Das Orakel* (1889), two considerable successes in *Der arme Jonathan* and *Mam'zelle Nitouche* as well as *Die Gondoliere* in 1890, the triumphant *Der Vogelhändler*, *La Cosaque* and *Miss Helyett* in 1891, Millöcker's *Das Sonntagskind*, the long-running musical Posse *Heisses Blut*, *La Fille de Fanchon la vielleuse*, *Der Millionen-Onkel* and Czibulka's *Der Bajazzo* (1892), Strauss's *Fürstin Ninetta* and the Posse *Ein armes Mädel* (1893), *Der Obersteiger*, *Jabuka* and *Der Probekuss* (1894), Dellinger's *Die Chansonette*, *Die Karlsschülerin* and *Waldmeister* (1895), von Taund's *Der Wunderknabe*, *Nordlicht*, Weinberger's *Der Schmetterling* and Verő's Hungarian operett *Der Löwenjäger* in a poor 1896, Strauss's *Die Göttin der Vernunft* and Weinberger's *Die Blumen-Mary* in an even less profitable 1897, redeemed by the 1898 production of Heuberger's *Der Opernball*. In 1899 she mounted another Heuberger work, *Ihre Excellenz* without equivalent success, and won fair runs with the British pieces *Ein durchgeganges Mädel* (*A Runaway Girl*) and *Der griechische Sklave* (*A Greek Slave*) and the French *Die Puppe* (*La Poupée*) as well as lesser ones with the home-made *Fräulein Präsident* and *Die Strohwitwe*. Her final productions, another Heuberger piece *Der Sechs-Uhr-Zug* and Messager's *Véronique* (rechristened *Brigitte*), did not improve matters and she renounced her managership, the latter days of which had, unfortunately, coincided with the fading days of the first prime period of Viennese Operette which had so profited her earlier years. She, nevertheless, sold the theatre for almost double what she had paid for it.

During her period of management, Frau von Schönerer latterly directed a number of the pieces staged at her theatre. Theatre-bills began only in the 1890s to credit directors, but she is credited with the original staging of *Der Opernball* as well as of *Die Blumen-Mary*, *La Poupée* and *Der griechische Sklave* amongst others.

DIE SCHÖNE RISETTE Operette in a Vorspiel and 3 acts by A M Willner and Robert Bodanzky. Music by Leo Fall. Theater an der Wien, Vienna, 19 November 1910.

When the 11th-century King of Burgundy's courtiers drowned his shepherdess mistress, Risette, as a witch so that he would marry and beget an heir, the monarch had his 'democratic' revenge by enacting a law whereby, every 17 years, seventeen 17-year-old maidens from the village of Beauséjour could come to court and choose themselves an aristocratic 'husband'. After three months' trial, during which the men had to live on the land, the marriage could be confirmed. Fifteenth-century King Pierre (Adolf Lussmann), full of himself and fresh from university, ignores the tradition and goes off hunting on 'Schöne Risette-Day', so to palliate his absence his friend Edgar de la Tourelle (Max Willenz) stands in as King. The shepherdess Jeanette (Grete Holm) chooses the handsome huntsman, and Princess Margot (Luise Kartousch) of neighbouring Aquitaine, having cheated a little to become a Risette, looks at the 'king' to whom she is betrothed and takes him. The men find life on the land hard, but both fall in love with their 'brides' before King Thomasius II of Aquitaine (Ernst Tautenhayn) comes in search of his daughter and all is exposed. When Jeanette hears that Philippe is the King, she runs away, but after an act of song and suffering, returns for a happy royal ending.

Fall's score was composed very largely in march and waltz rhythms (although the first genuine waltz did not come till part way through the first-act finale) and had the peculiarity that, amongst its 14 musical numbers, it included only one song for its hero ('Wisst Ihr, was Grisetten sind?'), a bright 3/8 number illustrating his preference for city grisettes over country maids, and one for its heroine – an entry song about 'Schöne Risette', both early in the first act. Thereafter the score was made up of duets and ensembles and a substantial first-act finale all featuring the two lead pairs, plus a comic duet for Thomasius and his Adjutant (Franz Glawatsch). The final act featured only a march quintet and the little musical scene in which Jeanette/Risette returns to her King.

Die schöne Risette had a fine run in Franz Glawatsch's production at the Theater an der Wien, being played 100 times in the 12 months following its première (as well as a Gastspiel at the Raimundtheater) and lifting Ernst Tautenhayn into the star bracket. It went on to be produced with indubitable success in Germany, in Spain (*La bella Riseta* Teatro de la reina Victoria 8 November 1916), and it was also played in Paris by the Theater an der Wien company during their 1911 guest season at the Théâtre du Vaudeville.

Germany: ?1911; France: Théâtre du Vaudeville (Ger) 1911

DIE SCHÖNE SCHWEDIN Operette in 3 acts by Julius Brammer and Alfred Grünwald. Music by Robert Winterberg. Theater an der Wien, Vienna, 30 January 1915.

The Stockholm banker Sven Liverstol (Ernst Tautenhayn) is in secret money troubles and anxious to marry his beloved daughter Hilma (Luise Kartousch) to the apparently rich young German Baron Heinz von Reedingen (Hubert Marischka). He is offered a large loan by Torkel (Karl Tuschl) and Schnorkel (Kurt Mikulski) on condition that the marriage takes place, but he is flung into desperate straits when his biggest customer, a dazzling lass from Brazil called Edith Lloyd (Betty Fischer), turns up and won't wait to withdraw her funds. No marriage, no money, and Edith goes back to Brazil with the actually underfunded Heinz as her secretary, leaving the Liverstols in the Swedish soup. In Act III, however, Edith finds her business in trouble through growing competition from one Sr Camberito. It turns out that Camberito is none other than the financially recovered Liverstol, and all can end with Hilma and Heinz at last together and Edith and Liverstol joining hands and fortunes.

Die schöne Schwedin proved a disappointment at the Theater an der Wien and it was withdrawn after its 50th performance (16 March) to be replaced by Granchistädten's *Auf Befehl der Herzogin*, a good-old-days piece which proved much more to the wartime public's taste than this unromantic tale of financial dealings. Nevertheless, it went on to other productions. It was produced in Germany, Budapest was given Vilmos Tihanyi's Hungarian

version, *A szöke csoda* (the marvellous blonde), it was foreseeably snapped up by Albert Ranf for the Stockholm Opera House and the Shuberts took the American rights. In its American production the piece started out from New Haven under the title *A Brazilian Honeymoon* (perhaps a reference to the very first Shubert success, *A Chinese Honeymoon*), and by the time New York was reached, the lovely Swedish lass (played by Beth Lydy) had given place to *The Girl from Brazil* (statuesque Frances Demarest) as the show's title. Hal Forde was Liverstol, John H Goldsworth played Heinz, and George Hassell had an enlarged comedy rôle as Torkel (Schnorkel had vanished). The American version was the work of Edgar Smith (book) and Matthew Woodward (lyrics), and Winterberg's 'above average' score was supplemented by the inevitable Shubert interpolations from the pen of Sigmund Romberg ('Bachelor Girl and Boy', 'The Right Brazilian Girl', 'Señorita', 'Come Back, Sweet Dream'). In spite of agreeable notices the piece remained only 61 performances on Broadway.

Germany: ?1915; Hungary: *A szöke csoda* Budai Színkör 22 May 1915; USA: 44th Street Theater *The Girl from Brazil* 30 August 1916

DIE SCHÖNE UNBEKANNTE Operette in 2 acts and an epilogue by Leopold Jacobson and Leo Walther Stein. Music by Oscar Straus. Carltheater, Vienna, 15 January 1915.

A brightly conventional story of flirtations, secrets and mistakes, *Die schöne Unbekannte* (the fair unknown) was set in a garrison town, allowing its hero to be a philandering soldier – Oberleutnant Leopold von Höllriegl (Franz Felix) – and composer Straus to introduce a healthy slice of martial music into his score. The ladies of the piece, both of whom seem to be the fair unknown to whom he commits himself, were Elly (Mizzi Günther), the daughter of the local count (Richard Waldemar), and the exotic Lydia Petrowska (Martha Kriwitz) who doesn't put in an appearance until the second act. The young Robert Nästlberger was the number-two man. Alongside the marches 'Servus Kamerad' and 'Mit Trommeln, Pfeifen and Tschinellen', came the requisite amount of waltzes – notably the song of the 'schöne Unbekannte' introduced in the first-act finale and 'Der Walzer von heute Nacht', but also a polka quartet, a brilliant entrance song for Lydia ('Ausverkauft'), Poldi's 'Der letzte Frist', Tanz-Duetten for Elly and Emil Lampl, a salesgirls' chorus and some pantomime and burlesque.

Produced by Sigmund Eibenschütz at the Carltheater, *Die schöne Unbekannte* had a good run of 103 performances and was taken up by those countries who, in this time of war, were willing to look at the product of the Vienna stage. Thus, whilst England and France were out, the show was still seen in Germany, in Budapest where Sári Petráss, recently returned from Broadway starred as Elly, and in America. The Shuberts' production proved unsatisfactory in its out-of-town tryout as *The Beautiful Unknown* and by the time the show reached town the action had been resituated in France, the score peppered with Romberg and the title changed to *My Lady's Glove*. Vivienne Segal and Charles Purcell played the leads for 16 Broadway nights.

Germany: ?1915; Hungary: Király Színház *A bajós ismeretlen* 29

May 1915; USA: Parsons' Theater, Hartford, Conn, *The Beautiful Unknown* 29 January 1917, Lyric Theater, New York *My Lady's Glove* 18 June 1917

SCHÖNFELD, Alfred (b Breslau, 30 March 1859; d Berlin ?9 December 1916). The most prolific and successful lyricist of the German stage in the years prior to the First World War.

Schönfeld began his theatrical life writing Possen, musical and not-so-musical for various German theatres, before becoming dramaturg at Berlin's Centraltheater under the management of Richard Schultz. It was in that post that he first collaborated with actor-turned-playwright Jean Kren. When Schultz began regularly to use librettists Julius Freund and Wilhelm Mannstädt for his shows, the pair decided to move on and ultimately they took on their own house, the old Adolf-Ernst-Theater, rebuilt and rechristened the Thalia-Theater, where they began a successful run of musical comedies. By and large, Kren became the bookwriter and Schönfeld specialized in the writing of the lyrics, whilst also turning his hand to the job of stage director.

Julius Einödshofer and Max Schmidt were their earliest musical collaborators, and Paul Lincke and Victor Holländer both provided them with scores for several years, but their greatest successes came when they brought Jean Gilbert to the Thalia-Theater to musically illustrate such musical comedies as *Autoliebchen*, *Puppchen*, *Die Tangoprinzessin* and *Blondinchen*, a list of hits which lifted the Thalia into the international league whilst also giving lyricist Schönfeld a bevy of song hits. The success of the Thalia allowed Kren to spread himself managerially, and the pair had one of their greatest authorial successes when he produced their *Der Soldat der Marie* (mus: Leo Ascher) at the Neues Operettenhaus. This was also their last great success together, for Schönfeld died, at the height of their prosperity, in 1916.

Schönfeld was also the principal of Thalia-Theater Verlag, the publishing company which printed the music and texts of the theatre's pieces.

1892 **Das grosse Los** (Johann Döbber/w Jean Kren) Tivoli Theater, Bremen 6 August

1892 **Das Sportmädel** (Max Lustig) Alexanderplatz-Theater 12 November

1893 **Berliner Vollblut** (Julius Einödshofer/w Kren) Centraltheater 31 August

1894 **Falstaff** (Georg Schönfeld) Apollotheater 15 July

1894 **Ein gesunder Junge** (Einödshofer/w Kren) Centraltheater 6 March

1894 **Der neue Kurs** (Einödshofer/w Leopold Ely, Kren) Centraltheater

1899 **Leuchtkafer** (Moritz Fall/w Ludwig Fernand) Wilhelm-Theater, Magdeburg, 18 February

1899 **Im Himmelshof** (Max Schmidt/Kren) Thalia-Theater 23 December

1899 **Der Platzmajor** (Gustav Wanda/w Kren) Thalia-Theater 9 September

1900 **Der Liebesschlüssel** (Schmidt/Kren) Thalia-Theater September

1900 **Der Amor von heute** (Wanda/w Kren) Thalia-Theater 30 November

1901 **Der Cadetten-Vater** (ex- *Lucinde vom Theater*) (Conradi, Schmidt/Emil Pohl ad Kren) Thalia-Theater 9 March

1901 **Ein tolles Geschaft** (Einödshofer/Kren) Thalia-Theater 7 September

1901 **Die Badepuppe** (Einödshofer/Kren) Thalia-Theater 26 November

1902 **Seine kleine** (Einödshofer/Kren, Ely) Thalia-Theater 18 January

1902 **Die bösen Mädchen** (Einödshofer/Kren, Leopold Ely) Thalia-Theater 23 December

1903 **Der Posaunenengel** (Einödshofer, Schmidt/Kren) Thalia-Theater 24 March

1903 **Der reicheste Berliner** (Einödshofer, Schmidt/Kren) Belle-Alliance-Theater 23 December

1904 **'s Zuckersgocherl** (Josef Wolffsgruber/Kren ad August Neidhart) Carltheater, Vienna 15 October

1904 **Freut euch des Lebens** (Einödshofer/Wilhelm Jacoby, Robert Stein ad Kren) Belle-Alliance-Theater 8 April

1904 **Kam'rad Lehmann** (Einödshofer, Julius Stern/F Zell ad Kren, Ely) Belle-Alliance-Theater 7 May

1904 **Der Weiberkönig** (Einödshofer/Kren) Thalia-Theater 15 September

1904 **Der grosse Stern** (Einödshofer/Kren) Thalia-Theater 23 December

1905 **Der beste Tip** (Schmidt/Kren) Thalia-Theater 9 February

1905 **Noch einmal so leben** (Schmidt/Kren) Belle-Alliance-Theater 1 April

1905 **Bis früh um Fünfe** (Lincke/Kren, Arthur Lippschitz) Thalia-Theater 26 August

1906 **Hochparterre-Links** (Lincke/Kren, Lippschitz) Thalia-Theater 7 April

1906 **Wenn die Bombe platzt** (Lincke/Kren, Lippschitz) Thalia-Theater 25 August

1906 **Eine lustige Doppelehe** (Lincke/Kraatz) Thalia-Theater 27 November

1907 **Wo die Liebe hinfallt** (Schmidt/Kren, Lippschitz) Thalia-Theater 20 April

1907 **Ihr sechs-Uhr Onkel** (Lincke/ad Kren) Thalia-Theater 25 August

1908 **Doktor Klapperstorch** (Schmidt/Kren, Georg Okonkowski) Thalia-Theater 28 March

1908 **Die Brunnennymphe** (uncredited/Heinrich Stobitzer, Max Neal) Thalia-Theater 18 April

1908 **Immer obenauf** (Lincke/ad Buchbinder) Thalia-Theater 22 January

1908 **Das Mitternachtsmädchen** (Viktor Holländer/Kren, Lippschitz) Thalia-Theater 14 August

1909 **Meister Tutti** (Holländer/w Kren) Thalia-Theater 15 January

1909 **Wo wohnt sie denn?** (Holländer/Kren, Okonkowski) Thalia-Theater 12 February

1909 **Prinz Bussi** (Holländer/Kren) Thalia-Theater 13 August

1909 **Die ewige Lampe** (Schmidt/Kren) Thalia-Theater 30 October

1909 **Die süsse Cora** (Holländer/Kren, Lippschitz) Thalia-Theater 11 December

1910 **Polnische Wirtschaft** (Gilbert/Okonkowski, Kraatz ad Kren) revised version (Thalia-Theater)

1910 **Die lieben Ottos** (Jean Gilbert/Xanrof ad Kren) Thalia-Theater 30 April

1911 **Die moderne Eva** (Gilbert/Okonkowski) Neues Operetten-Theater 11 November

1912 **Autoliebchen** (Gilbert/Kren) Thalia-Theater 16 March

1912 **Puppchen** (Gilbert/Kren, Kraatz) Thalia-Theater 19 December

1913 **Die Millionenbraut** (Döbber/Kren, Kraatz) Wilhelm-Theater, Magdeburg 17 February

1913 **Die Tangoprinzessin** (Gilbert/Kren, Kraatz) Thalia-Theater 4 October

1914 **Wenn der Frühling kommt!** (Gilbert/Kren, Okonkowski) Thalia-Theater 28 March

1914 **Kam'rad Männe** (Gilbert/Kren, Okonkowski) Thalia-Theater 3 October

1915 **Des Kaisers Rock** (Döbber/Kren, Kraatz) Residenz-Theater 19 February

1915 **Drei Paar Schuhe** (Gilbert/Carl Görlitz ad Kren) Thalia-Theater 10 September

1916 **Blondinchen** (Gilbert/w Kraatz, Kren) Thalia-Theater 4 March

1916 **Der Soldat von Marie** (Leo Ascher/w Kren, Buchbinder) Neues Operettenhaus 2 September

1916 **Das Vagabundenmädel** (Gilbert/Kren, Buchbinder) Thalia-Theater 2 December

SCHÖN IST DIE WELT Operette in 3 acts by Fritz Löhner-Beda and Ludwig Herzer, a revised version of *Endlich allein* by A M Willner and Robert Bodanzky. Music by Franz Lehár. Metropoltheater, Berlin, 3 December 1930.

The first version of Lehár's 'mountain musical' *Endlich allein* (Theater an der Wien 10 February 1914) had had a reasonably successful and even international career during the Great War, but this did not prevent the composer, who never showed any reticence to reprocess his older scores in lesser or greater remakes, from bringing its music out again. Having already successfully re-done *Die gelbe Jacke* as *Das Land des Lächelns* as a vehicle for Richard Tauber, he handed Willner and Bodanzky's text over to Fritz Löhner and Ludwig Herzer to be similarly made over into a new piece for the popular tenor's benefit.

The 'in the present' story of the piece was modernized with motor cars and radios, but otherwise there wasn't too much that was modern about the text of *Schön ist die Welt*: the principals were the royal families of the most conventional of Operetten. Tauber was cast as Georg, prince of a significant but unwealthy country, the Hungarian soprano Gitta Alpár was Elisabeth von und zu Lichtenberg, his intended bride and source of finance. They meet without knowing who each other is, and spend the second act together out in the mountains where they are trapped overnight by an avalanche. Love blossoms and, as in all the best old tales, the Prince and the Princess end up wanting to marry the very one they are supposed to marry. Leo Schützendorf as the Prince's penniless father, Kurt Vespermann as his adjutant Sascha, and Lizzi Waldmüller, as the latinate dancer he has culpably wed without his monarch's permission, provided the rest of the entertainment in the first and third acts.

The two stars had plenty of music, and Tauber's rôle included a swingeing title-song, the whole of the two-handed second act with its 'Liebste, glaub' an mich', and the lighter moment of 'In der kleinen Bar' in the final act, whilst his partner had her solo moments in the anticipatory 'Sag', armes Herzchen, sag'' and her lovestruck 'Ich bin verliebt'. The latinate dancer got to be latinate in a song and dance about 'Rio de Janeiro'.

Tauber, still in fine voice but physically impossible, was less well suited as the young Ruritanian prince than he had been as the impassive Chinese one of the previous show, but Alpár was an enormous success as his princess, and the fact that the show's central novelty (which, nevertheless, had an inkling of *Miss Helyett* in it) was elsewhere swathed in happy old clichés did not seem to matter. The Rotter brothers' Berlin production did well enough, and the show was duly picked up for Vienna where Hans Heinz Bollmann and Adele Kern headed a cast which featured Gustav Charlé as the King and Kálmán Latabár as the adjutant. It played only a disappointing 93 times.

Hungary's version with László Szűcs and Irma Patkós was produced at the Szeged Városi Színház and subsequently played for two weeks by that company at the Király Színház, whilst France gave a version nebulously entitled *La Chanson du bonheur* (ad André Mauprey) with only a modicum of success. André Burdino (Georges), Georgette Simon (Elisabeth), Roger Tréville (Sacha), Lyne Clevers (Mercedès), Félix Oudart (King) and Nina Myral (Duchesse Marie de Brankenhorst) topped the bill of an 'opérette in 8 tableaux' which featured a selection of 'attractions choréographiques sur glace' performed by ten apparently Hungarian lady skaters, a series of dances by 16 English girl dancers, and 12 French 'boys' choreographed by June Roberts and Max Revol. On the whole, *Schön ist die Welt* went rather less far and less well than its original had done 15 years earlier, but the tenor bon-bons and the second-act duo survived well enough to make the odd recording.

Austria: Theater an der Wien 21 December 1931; Hungary: Városi Színház, Szeged *Szép a világ* 23 November 1934, Király Színház (Szeged company) *Szép a világ* 24 December 1934; France: Théâtre de la Gaîté *La Chanson du bonheur* 2 November 1935

Recordings: selections (Philips, Eurodisc, EMI Electrola)

THE SCHOOL GIRL Musical play in 2 acts by Henry Hamilton and Paul M Potter. Lyrics by Charles H Taylor. Music by Leslie Stuart. Prince of Wales Theatre, London, 9 May 1903.

A well-made musical comedy of the Edwardian era, *The School Girl* featured all the favourite elements of the genre, beginning with a star ingénue in the person of *The Belle of New York*, Edna May, continuing with a mass of popular comedy and comedians (G P Huntley, George Graves, James Blakeley), a score by the man of the moment, *Florodora* composer Leslie Stuart, and a production by George Edwardes and Charles Frohman, the most liberal and tasteful of London's managers.

The suitably merry and nonsensical plot had Miss May running away from school to a job as a temp at the stock exchange in Paris. There she unmasks a swindle and saves everyone from ruin. The score gave her a trio of pretty numbers of which her invitation to the chorus boys to 'Call Around Again' was the most fetching. However, it could not compare for popularity with the catchy 'My Little Canoe' sung by 17-year-old Billie Burke, making her West End début as an American chorus girl, nor with the more musically substantial 'When I Was a Girl Like You' sung by the Mother Superior of the convent in the show's prologue. For this rôle the producers had lured Violet Cameron, the great star of *Les Cloches de Corneville* and *La Mascotte* a quarter of a century earlier, back to the stage for a final and hugely appreciated appearance.

The School Girl was a fine London success, playing for 11 months and 333 performances at the Prince of Wales Theatre before moving on to the provinces and to New York where it marked Miss May's return home as an established star. The score was decorated, to Stuart's annoyance, with some additional ditties mostly by Paul Rubens (and including a 'Japanese Medley' which ended up with 'Auld Lang Syne') and Miss May appropriated

'My Little Canoe' and duly did well with it, but the strong plotlines were maintained along with a number of the London cast. It was some of these – the comic trio of George Grossmith, Fred Wright and Blakeley – who, in fact, proved the most popular part of Broadway's *The School Girl* and helped it to a fine run of 120 performances.

The same title had previously been used by the diminutive (if at least 35-year-old) actress Minnie Palmer for a vehicle (Albert Maurice et al/George Manchester, Grand Theatre, Cardiff 2 September 1895) which cast her as the teenaged Little Miss Loo in what was largely a stand-up performance by its star who got all the songs and, in spite of competition from her mother, the man. It was played in the British provinces, but not in London, and was also briefly seen in one of its star's brief Broadway seasons (Bijou Theater 30 December 1895). The show, which was apparently a version of *Pert and Her Stepmother* given as written by Fred Maeder, later appeared credited to Willie Gill (for whom it seems 'Manchester' may have been a pseudonym) and with the score announced as being by Maurice Denham-Harrison and others.

USA: Daly's Theater, 1 September 1904

SCHRÖDER, Friedrich (b Näfels, Switzerland, 6 August 1910; d Berlin, 25 September 1972).

Educated in Münster and Berlin, the Swiss-born Schröder quickly found himself a career writing song and dance music and, at the age of 20, the first of what would ultimately total 43 film scores (*Sieben Ohrfeigen* (1937), *Immer nur du* (1941), *Des Teufels General*, *Charley's Tante* (1952), the arrangement of Fall's *Die geschiedene Frau* (1953) etc). In 1934 he became assistant conductor to Werner Schmidt-Bölke at the Berlin Metropoltheater, a post which he held through 1937.

Schröder made his first mark on the musical stage with the production of his 1942 musical comedy *Hochzeitsnacht im Paradies* which was played for more than 500 performances at the Metropoltheater, then throughout central Europe before, in its turn, going on to become the basis for two films. His second stage work, *Nächte in Shanghai*, produced at the Metropoltheater after the War, brought forth the popular song 'Komm mit mir nach Tahiti' to add to the successes he had had with various single and film songs (the most famous being the 1937 'Ich tanze mit dir in den Himmel hinein') but none of his subsequent shows came near to sharing the success of the first.

1942 **Hochzeitsnacht im Paradies** (Günther Schwenn/ Heinz Hentschke) Metropoltheater 24 September
1947 **Nächte in Shanghai** (Schwenn/Waldemar Frank, Leo Lenz) Metropoltheater
1947 **Chanel Nr 5** (Schwenn/B E Lüthge) Corso Theater, Berlin
1947 **Lucrezia in Stockholm** Berlin
1949 **Isabella** (Schwenn/Frank, Eduard Rogati) Nuremberg
1955 **Die grosse Welt** (Schwenn) Staatstheater, Wiesbaden
1955 **Das Bad auf der Tenne** (Schwenn/Rolf Meyer) Nuremberg-Fürth 26 March
1969 **Die Jungfrau von Paris** (Schwenn) Raimundtheater 19 December

SCHUBERT, Franz [Peter] (b Lichtenthal, 31 January 1797; d Vienna, 19 November 1828).

Schubert's connection with the musical stage in his own lifetime was an eclectic one, ranging from the operatic

Alfonso und Estrella and *Fierrabras* to music for the 'grand romantic Schauspiel mit Musik' *Rosamunde, Fürstin von Cypern* (1823), the melodrama *Die Zauberharfe*, the one-act Georg von Hoffmann Singspiel *Die Zwillingsbrüder* mounted at Vienna's Kärtnertor-Theater, and the comic opera *Der Verschworen, oder der häusliche Krieg* (1823), subsequently played in French as *La Croisade des dames* and as *Les Conjurées, ou la guerre au foyer* and in Hungarian as *Cselre cselt* on a programme with a one-act, six-scene ballet-pantomime made up from the 'moments musicales' by Ernő Dohnányi.

From soon after the composer's death, however, his music became the raw material for pasticcio pieces compiled by other hands. In 1834 Adolf Müller arranged a Schubert score for *Der Erlkönig* (Theater an der Wien 21 February), whilst in 1864 the first Schubert biomusical, the Singspiel *Franz Schubert* written by Hans Max and with a score arranged by Franz von Suppé, was produced at the Carltheater (10 September) with Karl Treumann playing the rôle of the composer. A grand success, it was revived in 1886, at the Theater an der Wien in 1897 and at the Volksoper in 1922, and played at Budapest's Budai Színkör in 1867 (28 June). Other pieces such as the Dresden Singspiel *Die vierjährige Posten* (1 act, Robert Hirschfeld, Theo Körner 23 September 1895) followed, but Schubert's greatest success as an operettic composer came in another biomusical, the famous *Das Dreimäderlhaus* (arr Heinrich Berté, 1916) and its derivatives the British *Lilac Time* (arr G H Clutsam), and the two pieces entitled *Blossom Time* (Sigmund Romberg and G H Clutsam – again – respectively).

Following the vast success of *Das Dreimäderlhaus*, Schubert musicals flooded the world's stages. In 1917 Vienna saw *Anne-Marie* (ad Max Egger, lib: Fritz Löhner-Beda, Singspiel 1 act, Ronacher), Magdeburg produced *Fernando* (Albert Stadler, Singspiel 1 act Viktoria Theater, 1 August) and Budapest *Tavasz és szerelem* (*Liebe und Lenz*, Berté, Bruno Hardt-Warden, Ignaz M Welleminsky, Városi Színház), whilst in 1918 the Raimundtheater launched a musequel to *Das Dreimäderlhaus* under the title *Hannerl*. Stuttgart put out *Der treue Soldat* (arr Fritz Busch, F D Tovey/Theo Körner, Rolf Lauckner Landestheater, 2 July 1922), the Volksoper staged *Der unsterbliche Franz* (Ernst Decsey, Julius Bittner, Julius Bauer, 1928) and Basle saw *Die Freunde von Salamanka* (ad Hermine Moerike, Josef Rainer, 10 May 1934). The little Viennese Theater Auges-Gottes had a Schubert revue-Operette in 1946, *So war's einmal* (Deutsch, E Limé, 1 October), whilst in 1954 Britain's Liverpool Playhouse turned out a new Schubert biomusical, *Spring Quartet* (Willard Stoker), with tenor Carlos Montes starred.

Schubert's life and putative loves have also made it to the musical screen, with Germany's Karlheinz Böhm (*Das Dreimäderlhaus*, Sascha Films, 1958) and France's Tino Rossi (*La Belle Meunière*, 1948) amongst the celluloid Franzes, all equipped with various degrees of fuzzy hairdos and the obligatory little spectacles.

DIE SCHÜTZENLIESEL Operette in 3 acts by Leo Stein and Carl Lindau. Music by Edmund Eysler. Carltheater, Vienna, 7 October 1905.

When Alexander Girardi decided to part company with the Theater an der Wien, the theatre where he had become a star and lived through years of idolized successes, he did not part company with the composer who had provided him with the substance of his latest hits. Edmund Eysler was, in fact, part of the package which was richly paid to bring Girardi and his newest vehicle to Andreas Aman's Carltheater, long the chief rival of the Theater an der Wien and much in need of a new musical comedy success. Eysler was paid 2,000 kronen, and his two librettists the same sum, for *Die Schützenliesel* – sums which, since the departure of such star authorial names as Strauss, were no longer current in the Viennese theatre. But in spite of this expense, *Die Schützenliesel* turned out to be a good buy for the Carltheater.

Girardi starred as Blasius Nestel, fresh out of the army and the winner of the local shooting contest, with Mizzi Zwerenz as his Liesel, the daughter of the Bürgermeister and landlord Mooshammer (Friedrich Becker), of the 'zur Schützenliesel' inn, in a little countrified tale set at Gegend-am-See in the Königssee area. Tenor Max Rohr was the intrusive love interest – the forester Konrad Wille – whilst Artur Guttmann and soprano Flora Siding played the beer-brewer Hippolit Zillinger and his daughter Wilhelmine. Venerable comedian Karl Blasel took the part of the old landowner Daszewski, the key to the evening's troubles and to its happy ending. For the rich old man promises a fine sum of money to his young relatives, Blasius and Wilhelmine, when they wed each other. Their parents are, of course, anxious for the match to go ahead, and although the young folk wish to follow their hearts, they decide to wed, get the money and then, with their fortunes assured, divorce and wed their right partners. The foreseeable misunderstandings and mishaps intervene when Blasius starts setting up the divorce evidence, but (unlike the usual operettic ending which has the forced pairs coming to like their situation) old Daszewski comes along in time to give his blessing to a rematching in time for the final curtain. Richard Waldemar (Schlehreba) and Therese Löwe as the star's mother and the cue for his principal song headed the supporting cast.

Once again, Eysler turned out the hit numbers that were needed for his star and the rest of the cast, numbers that challenged even his *Bruder Straubinger*'s 'Küssen ist keine Sünd' as all-time favourites. Girardi's 'Mutterl-lied', a slow and sentimental waltz lullaby ('Schlaf, mein liebes Büberl, schlaf') which was a contrast to his livelier and more comical hits, was a no-dry-eye-in-the-house sensation, whilst his Letter Song 'Du süsse, süsse..!' gave him a second severe hit. Originally this latter piece had not been pointed up as a likely winner, but on the insistence of the singer Willy Bauer, who was present at the dress rehearsal, Eysler made a last-minute rewrite and, cutting a chunk of his carefully built concerted second-act finale, inserted there a big reprise of the Letter Song. Bauer proved right, and 'Du süsse, süsse..!' became a favourite. There were, of course, further waltz-songs – one for the tenor in praise of 'Wilhelmine', one for Blasel ('Keine Angst, ich bitte sehr') and a lilting 'Ist jung man wie schäumender Wein' as well as a popular march number ('Heut' fahr ich aus der Haut') in a score which lived up to the tuneful and appealing standards Eysler had set in his earlier shows.

In spite of the competition of the all-conquering *Die lustige Witwe* at the Theater an der Wien, *Die Schützenliesel* had a fine run. It passed its 100th performance on 15

January 1906 and played its 105th before Girardi left the Carltheater to go to play in *Der Schusterbub* at the Theater in der Josefstadt. It was played again for a few performances when the star returned to the Carltheater in October of the same year, until the next Eysler/Stein/Lindau piece, *Künstlerblut*, was ready. *Die Schützenliesel* passed its 120th performance on 6 January 1907, was played again in 1908 and was later seen at the Raimundtheater in 1910 (27 August) with Ernst Tautenhayn playing Blasius. It reappeared at the Carltheater in 1913, with many of its original cast, as a 60th birthday tribute to author Lindau, then at the Johann Strauss-Theater in 1915, at the Carltheater again in 1920 with Blasel repeating his original part and once more in 1924 with Fritz Imhoff starred. Mizzi Zwerenz was still to be seen in her original rôle 20 years after its creation, but Girardi found others of the Eysler pieces – *Bruder Straubinger* and *Künstlerblut* – more to his revivable liking. The show was also exported with great success to Germany as well as to Italy.

In 1954 a Rudolf Schündler/Central-Europa film called *Schützenliesel*, allegedly based on the piece (ad Ernst Nebhut, Fritz Böttger, ly: Günther Schwenn, add mus: Herbert Trantow) was produced with Paul Hörbiger, Herta Staal, Gretl Fröhlich and Peter W Staub taking the principal singing rôles, backed by the Four Ping-Pongs, Egon Kaiser and his orchestra and zither-player Anton Karas.

Another musical comedy (Posse mit Gesang) with the same title, written by Leon Treptow and set to music by Ludwig Gothov-Grüneke, was produced at the Carltheater (24 September 1882) and again, adapted by G Görss with music by Gustave Steffens, at Berlin's Central-theater (25 December 1882).

Germany: ?1906; Film: 1954 Central-Europa

SCHWAB, Laurence (b Boston, 17 December 1893; d Southampton, NY, 29 May 1951). Author and producer of some of the top Broadway shows of the 1920s.

Harvard-educated Schwab worked with the Alf Wilton agency and, after the First World War, with the Floyd Stoker agency before he made his first venture into producing for the musical stage at the age of 28, in collaboration with Daniel Kussell, with a piece called *Love and Kisses* (1922). An elaboration of a vaudeville act called *A Man of Affairs*, the show was tried out at Atlantic City in June, and finally made its way into New York under the title *The Gingham Girl* three months later. There, with Helen Ford starring in the title-rôle, it proved a sweet little success.

Schwab then went out on his own to write and produce another piece with a dear little country girl for a heroine in the following season. Publishers Harms provided him with some rising young collaborators in playwright Frank Mandel and composer George Gershwin, but *Sweet Little Devil* did not catch on as the earlier piece had done and the most significant thing to come out of the show was the partnership between Schwab and Mandel. It soon developed into more than a writing partnership, for Mandel joined Schwab as a producer and, although Schwab presented the successful 1926 show *Queen High* alone, in six years of collaboration the pair produced eight musical shows together, as well as a number of plays, a body of work which included a number of memorable pieces.

If their promising *Captain Jinks* disappointed slightly on

Broadway after being hailed as a major hit on its way to New York, *The Desert Song* (which Schwab did not help write), *Good News*, *The New Moon* and *Follow Thru* (all of which he did) were all great successes, taking Schwab and Mandel quickly to the forefront of the producing establishment. After five years of success, however, things turned sour in the year of 1931. The partnership's production of the film burlesque *America's Sweetheart* did not come up to their previous successes, *Free for All*, a weak piece which Schwab co-wrote with Oscar Hammerstein and which purported to be about socialism and free love, flopped in just 15 performances (and even the cast turned down the offer to buy it for just its $5,100 a week running costs), and an attempt to create another *The Desert Song* with a romantic piece called *East Wind* foundered in 23 performances.

Mandel then abdicated from the partnership, wisely, as it turned out, for the handful of pieces Schwab presented after his departure were decreasingly successful: *Take a Chance* (1932) which managed 243 performances, Romberg and Mandel's preposterous *May Wine* (1935) which lasted 213 nights and an attempt at a Gilbert and Sullivan biomusical called *Knights of Song* (1938), which survived two weeks on Broadway, were his last representatives in New York, whilst an English version of Robert Stolz's attractive *Venus in Silk* (1935) and a musical version of the play *Sailor Beware* produced as *Nice Goin'* (1939 w Lee Dixon) folded without reaching town.

Towards the end of his career as a producer, Schwab also worked for a while in films (*You Can't Have Everything, Ali Baba Goes to Town*, 1937).

1924 **Sweet Little Devil** (George Gershwin/w Frank Mandel) Astor Theater 21 January

1925 **Captain Jinks** (Lewis E Gensler, Stephen Jones/B G De Sylva/w Mandel) Martin Beck Theater 8 September

1926 **Queen High** (Gensler/De Sylva) Ambassador Theater 8 September

1927 **Good News** (Ray Henderson/De Sylva, Lew Brown/w De Sylva) 46th Street Theater 6 September

1928 **The New Moon** (Sigmund Romberg/Oscar Hammer-II/w Hammerstein, Mandel) Imperial Theater 18 November

1929 **Follow Thru** (Henderson/De Sylva, Brown/w De Sylva) 46th Street Theater 9 January

1931 **Free for All** (Richard Whiting/w Hammerstein) Manhattan Theater 9 September

1932 **Take a Chance** (ex-*Humpty Dumpty*) (Nacio Herb Brown, Whiting/De Sylva) Apollo Theater 26 November

1935 **Venus in Silk** (aka *Beloved Rogue*) (*Venus im Seide*) English version w Lester O'Keefe (Municipal Opera, St Louis)

1939 **Nice Goin'** (Ralph Rainger/Leo Robin) New Haven, Conn 21 October

DAS SCHWALBENNNEST

A twice-used title. The first 'swallows' nest' appeared in Berlin in 1904 when an Operette in 3 acts by Maurice Ordonneau adapted into a German version by Maurice Rappaport, with music by Henri Hirschmann, was mounted at the Centraltheater on 9 January 1904. A tale of 18th-century Versailles, with one of those stories which involved a fellow in disguise in a girls' school in search of his sweetheart, it was subsequently rewritten and reproduced as *Les Hirondelles* (Galeries Saint-Hubert, Brussels, 17 November 1906) and had a reasonable life thereafter. However, it did not equal the record of its successor, an Alt Wiener Singspiel in 3 acts by Ernst Marischka and

Bruno Granichstädten, with music by Granichstädten, produced by Hubert Marischka and Rudolf Beer at the Raimundtheater, Vienna, on 2 September 1926. This *Das Schwalbennest* was set in the Viennese Schloss Rohnsdorff, but it interested itself in the servants of the house rather than the nobles: Franz Glawatsch played the butler, Franz Rettenbacher, with Luise Kartousch and Margit Künl as his daughters, and Ernst Tautenhayn was the coachman, Ferdinand Brakl. However the evening's tenor was to be found upstairs: Prince Karl was played by Victor Flemming.

The original production of the piece was a fine success, playing four-and-a-half months and 134 performances en suite (to 17 January 1927), swapping stages with *Die Zirkusprinzessin* to go through a 30-performance Gastspiel at the Theater an der Wien in January 1927, and returning to base to finally run to its 208th night. It was later seen in Hungary in a version by István Zágon (Király Színház *A fecskefészek* 23 September 1927).

SCHWARTZ, Arthur (b Brooklyn, NY, 25 November 1900; d Pennsylvania, 3 September 1984). Revue and film songwriter who dipped intermittently into the book musical without comparative success.

The son of a lawyer, Schwartz had his first contact with show business playing piano for the silent films. He passed through college and law school and worked both as a high school teacher and as a lawyer whilst writing songs, at first for college shows and later with professional publication and performance in mind. He placed several numbers in revues (*The Grand Street Follies*, *The New Yorkers*) and in Broadway musicals (*Good Boy*, *Queen High* 'Brother, Just Laugh it Off' ly: E Y Harburg, Ralph Rainger) without notable success, before in 1928 he joined forces with lyricist Howard Dietz, already the veteran of a Broadway show with no less a composer than Jerome Kern (*Dear Sir*, 1924) but, like Schwartz, looking for the elusive song hit that would fuel a career.

After further similar contributions to *Ned Wayburn's Gambols* and *Wake Up and Dream*, the pair had a first success with their part of the score for the revue *The Little Show* (1929). Dietz successfully relyricked a melody Schwartz had written a number of years before to a Lorenz Hart lyric ('I Love to Lie Awake in Bed') as 'I Guess I'll Have to Change My Plan' alongside four other numbers including 'I've Made a Habit of You'. Schwartz had recently been given his first opportunity to write at least part of a score for a book musical when he combined on the songs for a musical by *Potash and Perlmutter* author, Montague Glass, called *Well, Well, Well*. A version of the show did reach Broadway in 1929 as *Pleasure Bound*, but with a rather different book and score from that with which it had started out. By then, Muriel Pollock and Maurie Rubens had the music credit. He had a happier experience later that year, when he combined with lyricist Desmond Carter and with Dietz on the songs for Julian Wylie's production of the touring British musical *Here Comes the Bride* (1930). It was a fairly functional score, subordinate to the highly farcical libretto, but it turned up one prettily lilting piece in 'High and Low', which Schwartz later reused in the Broadway revue *The Bandwagon* (1931).

The composer supplied songs to several other London shows of 1930s (*The Co-Optimists*, *Little Tommy Tucker*)

and back in America he contributed to the revue *Three's a Crowd* ('Something to Remember You By') and to the musical montage which Szirmai's *Princess Charming (Alexandra)* had become, but it was the revue *The Bandwagon* ('Dancing in the Dark', 'New Sun in the Sky', 'I Love Louisa') which established Schwartz – who had now renounced law for the theatre on a full-time basis – and Dietz as coming men.

The pair had further success with another Broadway revue *Flying Colors* ('A Shine on Your Shoes', 'Louisiana Hayride', 'Alone Together', 'Smokin' Reefers', 'Two-Faced Woman', 'Fatal Fascination') the following season, but Schwartz's next book musical was again for London. He provided nine songs to illustrate the German musical farce *Nice Goings On* ('The Devil and the Deep, Blue Sea', 'What a Young Girl Ought to Know') which starred Leslie Henson through 221 performances. A first Broadway musical score, *Revenge with Music* (1934) lasted less time on the stage (158 performances) but housed a more enduring hit number in 'You and the Night and the Music' as well as the attractive 'If There is Someone Lovelier Than You'. In between times, 1933 Schwartz teamed with Edward Heyman to supply a pair of songs for Dwight Deere Wiman's production of the Howard Lindsay play *She Loves Me Not*, and the following year set a Morrie Ryskind lyric for use in Ryskind and Kaufman's play *Bring on the Girls*.

Schwartz's real successes in the 1930s came in revue, both on Broadway with *At Home Abroad* (1935, 198 performances) in which Eleanor Powell introduced 'Gotta Brand New Suit' and Beatrice Lillie performed 'Get Yourself a Geisha' and in London with *Follow the Sun* (1936, 204 performances) where Jessie Matthews made a success with 'Love is a Dancing Thing', as well as contributions to *Stop Press* and *At Home Abroad*. The book musicals fared less well. Of the two premièred in 1937 *Between the Devil*, with Evelyn Laye, Jack Buchanan and Adele Dixon starred, lasted but 93 performances at Broadway's Imperial Theater, but nevertheless introduced 'Triplets' (popular ever since as a novelty and benefit item) and 'I See Your Face Before Me', whilst *Virginia* survived 60 performances and left nothing more memorable than 'You and I Know'.

When Dietz went to Hollywood as a publicist for MGM, Schwartz began working with lyricist Dorothy Fields. Their first Broadway show was *Stars in Your Eyes* which, disembowelled on the road, lasted only marginally longer than the 1937 pieces (127 performances) in spite of a cast headed by Jimmy Durante and Ethel Merman ('This is It', 'The Lady Needs a Change', 'Okay for Sound'), after which Schwartz followed Dietz to Hollywood. There he produced the Rita Hayworth film *Cover Girl* and the much less satisfactory Cole Porter biopic *Night and Day*, as well as providing songs for a number of films, most notably *Thank Your Lucky Stars* (1943, 'They're Either Too Young or Too Old'), *The Time, the Place and the Girl* (1946, 'A Gal in Calico') and also including *Navy Blues*, *All Through the Night*, *Crossroads*, *Cairo* and *Princess O'Rourke*.

Back on Broadway, Schwartz paired with Ira Gershwin on the score for the short-lived *Park Avenue* (72 performances) and came together again with Dietz for the successful 1948 revue *Inside USA* ('Rhode Island is Famous for You' 'Haunted Heart'), which he also produced, before teaming again with Miss Fields for two vehicles for star

comedienne Shirley Booth. Both *A Tree Grows in Brooklyn* ('I'm Like a New Broom', 'Look Who's Dancing', 'He Had Refinement') and *By the Beautiful Sea* ('I'd Rather Wake Up By Myself', 'Alone Too Long') ran through 270 performances and both found some fond adherents.

The film version of *Bandwagon* (1953) produced Schwartz's most widely famous song, 'That's Entertainment', and the screen's *You're Never Too Young* included 'Relax-ay-voo' (w Sammy Cahn), but two subsequent stage musicals with Dietz, the uncomfortable Broadway-Viennesy *The Gay Life* (113 performances) – which it has since become fashionable to claim as a petit chef d'oeuvre – and *Jennie*, which featured Mary Martin and one catchy song called 'Before I Kiss the World Goodbye' (82 performances), failed.

Schwartz subsequently shifted to Britain, but none of the pieces on which he worked there came to fruition. He withdrew his score for *Nickelby and Me* before production, and a revised English-set version of *By the Beautiful Sea* (for which he composed a number encouraging 'Come to Blackpool' to add to a pot-pourri score of Schwartz/Dietz hits) remained unproduced. Schwartz's success remains chiefly as a writer of revue material and of individual songs for, in spite of the number of his song successes, he did not manage to compose a show score which showed qualities of endurance.

1929 **Well, Well, Well** (w Muriel Pollock/Max and Nathaniel Lief/Montague Glass, Jules Eckert Goodman, Harold Atteridge) Chestnut Street Opera House, Philadelphia 7 January

1929 **Here Comes the Bride** (Desmond Carter/Robert P Weston, Bert Lee et al) Opera House, Blackpool 7 October; Piccadilly Theatre, London 20 February 1930

1933 **Nice Goings On** (Doulas Furber, Frank Eyton/Furber) Strand Theatre, London 13 September

1934 **Revenge with Music** (Dietz) New Amsterdam Theater 28 November

1937 **Virginia** (Albert Stillman/Laurence Stallings, Owen Davis) Center Theater 2 September

1937 **Between the Devil** (Dietz) Imperial Theater 22 December

1939 **Stars in Your Eyes** (Dorothy Fields/J P McEvoy) Majestic Theater 9 February

1946 **Park Avenue** (Ira Gershwin/Nunnally Johnson, George S Kaufman) Shubert Theater 4 November

1951 **A Tree Grows in Brooklyn** (D Fields/Betty Smith, George Abbott) Alvin Theater 19 April

1954 **By the Beautiful Sea** (D Fields/Herbert Fields, D Fields) Majestic Theater 8 April 1954

1961 **The Gay Life** (Dietz/Fay Kanin, Michael Kanin) Shubert Theater 18 November

1963 **Jennie** (Dietz/Arnold Schulman) Majestic Theater 17 October

SCHWARTZ, Jean (b Budapest, 4 November 1878; d Sherman Oaks, Calif, 30 November 1956). Multi-hit songwriter whose numbers often proved the takeaway tunes of other fellows' shows of the early 20th century.

Schwartz had his earliest musical education from his sister, a sometime pupil of Liszt, during his youthful days in Hungary. He moved to America with his family at the age of ten and was soon on the work market, holding jobs in a cigar factory and a turkish bath, amongst others, before his earliest musical engagements as a band pianist at Coney Island, a song-plugger at the Siegel-Cooper store on Sixth Avenue and for the music-publishing house of

Shapiro-Bernstein, and later as a rehearsal and pit pianist for Broadway shows.

Schwartz formed a songwriting partnership with lyricist William Jerome and the young team ('who have risen from the obscure variety halls') soon succeeded in getting their songs placed in Broadway shows, notably in Weber and Fields's *Hoity-Toity* (1901, 'When Mr Shakespeare Comes to Town'), a show for which young Schwartz was employed as an on-stage pianist. Their first big song successes came with 'Rip van Winkle Was a Lucky Man' sung on Broadway in J J McNally's *Sleeping Beauty and the Beast* (1901) and in London's *The Cherry Girl* (1903), 'Mr Dooley', one of several songs interpolated in the Broadway production of *A Chinese Honeymoon* (USA), and 'Bedelia' as sung first by Blanche Ring in the short-lived *The Jersey Lily* (1903) on Broadway and in London by George Grossmith jr (who had done well with 'Mr Dooley' on the halls) in the very much more successful *The Orchid*.

The pair provided fresh material for the americanized version of the English musical *An English Daisy* (1904), they wrote the songs (one of which was 'Bedelia') for a vehicle for the Ellmore Sisters, Kate and May, called *Mrs Delaney of Newport* and, shortly after, the now established songwriters were able to show off their first full Broadway score in Fred C Whitney's production of *Piff! Paff! Pouf!*, billed as 'a musical cocktail', at the Casino Theater. *Piff! Paff! Pouf!* had a fine run of 264 performances, and its composer and his partner were set up to such an extent that they provided or contributed largely to the scores for no less than five musicals – principally the vaudeville-style shows or spectaculars that their frankly popular songs suited best – over the next year. Their biggest song success of that year, however, was again an interpolation: 'My Irish Molly O', one of several their numbers performed by Blanche Ring in *Sergeant Brue*.

Over the next 20 years a vast stream of numbers issued from Schwartz's pen – 'Sit Down, You're Rocking the Boat', 'I Love the Ladies' etc – but his main and most successful activity was still in the theatre. He wrote a large amount of revue material, including the basic musical scores for such pieces as *The Passing Shows* of 1918, 1919, 1921, 1923 and 1924, *The Shubert Gaieties of 1919*, the Shuberts' *The Midnight Rounders* and its 1921 edition, *The Whirl of the Town*, *The Mimic World of 1921*, *Make it Snappy* (1922), *Artists and Models* (1923), *Topics of 1923* and *A Night in Spain* (1927) as well as providing odd numbers for shows such as the *Ziegfeld Follies* of 1907 ('Handle Me With Care' w William Jerome) and 1908 ('When the Girl you Love is Loving').

Over the same period Schwartz also supplied scores both for regular musicals and for shows which ran a fine line between revue and musical comedy for Blanche Ring (*When Claudia Smiles*), Eddie Foy (*Up and Down Broadway* in which 'Chinatown, My Chinatown' was first heard, and *Over the River*), Eddie Cantor (*Make it Snappy*), Julian Eltinge (*The Fascinating Widow*) and Mistinguett (the 1924 revue *Innocent Eyes*), and in collaboration with J J McNally, author of the successful Rogers Brothers series of variety musicals, he also wrote the songs for vehicles for the popular blackface duo McIntyre and Heath (*The Ham Tree*, *In Hayti*) and for Lulu Glaser (*Lola From Berlin*). However, he found the most effective successor to Blanche Ring as champion purveyor of his songs when Al Jolson introduced

his 'Rum Tum Tiddle' (ly: Edward Madden) in *Vera Violetta* (1911). Schwartz subsequently wrote the basic score of the 'spectacular farce with music' *The Honeymoon Express* for Jolson but, more notably, he supplied him with four songs for the hit-filled *Sinbad* (1918), including the durable 'Rockabye Your Baby with a Dixie Melody' and 'Hello Central, Give Me No-Mans Land' (ly: Joe Young, Sam Lewis).

He also, throughout, continued to supply individual numbers and special material for use as interpolations in musicals both imported and native, amongst which were *The Prince of Pilsen* (1903, 'In Cincinnati'), *The Little Cherub* (1906, 'My Irish Rose'), *The Rich Mr Hoggenheimer* (1906, 'Any Old Time at All'), *The Silver Star* (1909), *The Echo* (1909), *The Wall Street Girl* (1912, 'Whistle It' for Blanche Ring), *Oh, My Dear!* (1918) and *Tangerine* (1921). In the 1920s, although he continued to turn out happy songs for the Shuberts and others, Schwartz generally fared less well, and in 1923 all three musicals for which he provided the score closed during their out of town tryout. His last Broadway score was written in 1928 for the musical *Sunny Days*, in which some of it was favoured by the fresh voice of the young Jeanette MacDonald.

Schwartz also paired with Jerome as a music publisher, and, for a period, with the Hungarian artist Roszika (Rosie) Dolly of the Dolly Sisters as a husband.

1903 **Mrs Delaney of Newport** (William Jerome) Grand Opera House 3 November

1904 **Piff! Paff! Pouf!** (Jerome/Stanislaus Stange) Casino Theater 2 April

1905 **The Athletic Girl** (George V Hobart) 1 act Colonial Musical Hall 15 February

1905 **A Yankee Circus on Mars** (w Manuel Klein/Jerome/ George V Hobart) New York Hippodrome 12 April

1905 **Lifting the Lid** (Jerome/J J McNally) New Amsterdam Theater 5 June

1905 **The Ham Tree** (Jerome/Hobart) New York Theater 28 August

1905 **Fritz in Tammany Hall** (Jerome/McNally) Herald Square Theater 16 October

1905 **The White Cat** (w Ludwig Englander/Harry B Smith, Jerome/ad H B Smith) New Amsterdam Theater 2 November

1907 **Lola from Berlin** (Jerome/McNally) Liberty Theater 16 September

1908 **Morning, Noon and Night** (Jerome/Joseph Herbert) Yorkville Theater 5 October

1909 **In Hayti** (Jerome/McNally) Circle Theater 30 August

1910 **Up and Down Broadway** (Jerome/Edgar Smith) Casino Theater 18 July

1912 **Over the River** (w John Golden/Hobart, H A Du Souchet) Globe Theater 8 January

1912 **The Fascinating Widow** (w F A Mills/Otto Harbach) Chestnut Street Opera House, Philadelphia 3 April

1913 **The Honeymoon Express** (Harold Atteridge) Winter Garden Theater 6 February

1913 **When Claudia Smiles** (Jerome/Leo Ditrichstein) Illinois Theater, Chicago 13 April

1914 **When Claudia Smiles** (revised version by Anne Caldwell) 39th Street Theater 2 February

1918 **See You Later** (*Loute*) new score w William F Peters/ad Guy Bolton, P G Wodehouse Academy, Baltimore 15 April

1919 **Monte Cristo Jr** (w Sigmund Romberg/Atteridge) Winter Garden Theater 12 February

1919 **Hello Alexander** (revised *The Ham Tree*) (Alfred

Bryan/Edgar Smith, Emily Young) 44th Street Theater 7 October

1920 **Page Mr Cupid** (Blanche Merrell/Owen Davis) Shubert Crescent Theater, Brooklyn 17 May

1923 **The Bal Tabarin** (w Fred J Coots/McElbert Moore/ Moore, Edward Delaney Dunn) Apollo Theater, Atlantic City 30 April

1923 **The Courtesan** (w Romberg/Atteridge/Harry Wagstaffe Gribble, Atteridge) Parsons' Theater, Hartford, Conn 17 October

1923 **That Casey Girl** (Jerome/Hobart, Willard Mack) Lyceum, Paterson, NJ 22 October

1926 **Nancy** (William H Clifford) Mission, Long Beach 16 May

1928 **Headin' South** (A Bryan et al/Edgar Smith) Keith's Theater, Philadelphia 1 October

1928 **Sunny Days** (w Eleanor Dunsmuir/Clifford Grey/ William Cary Duncan) Imperial Theater 8 February

1942 **Full Speed Ahead** (Irving Actman, H Leopold Spitany/Rowland Leigh) Philadelphia 25 December

SCHWARTZ, Stephen [Lawrence] (b New York, 6 March 1948).

The writer of songs for two long-running musical shows of the early 1970s, *Godspell* ('Day By Day') and *Pippin* ('Magic To Do', 'Corner of the Sky'), which mirrored the attitudes and preoccupations of American youth of the 1960s.

Schwartz had his earliest work – including revue material, title-songs to the plays *Butterflies Are Free* and *Little Boxes*, and a first version of *Pippin* – produced whilst still studying theatre and music at college. By the time he was 25 years old, *Godspell* and the revised Broadway version of his early *Pippin* were both playing successfully, he had written additional lyrics (w Leonard Bernstein) to the Roman mass for the composer's *Mass* and become a recording company executive and producer.

Schwartz had a further long run with the musical score for magician Doug Hemming's vehicle *The Magic Show*, but a musical adaptation of the French classic *La Femme du boulanger* as *The Baker's Wife*, in spite of containing Schwartz's most substantial and adult work to date, folded without making its Broadway opening. He subsequently contributed to the score of the musical *Working*, and then ventured once more and with distaste into the large-scale commercial theatre as the lyricist of the short-lived *Rags*.

In 1988, on the initiative of director Trevor Nunn, who had been impressed with songs from *The Baker's Wife* which he had heard in auditions, the show was exhumed, rewritten and produced by Nunn in Britain. But the very long new version seemed to have more faults than the first and the piece failed again. It was, however, followed by a second London enterprise, a collaboration with Nunn's Royal Shakespeare Company colleague John Caird on another biblical musical, *Children of Eden*. Extravagantly staged, it proved to lack the attractions of the simpler *Godspell* and folded quickly.

1971 **Godspell** (John Michael Tebelak) Cherry Lane Theater 17 May

1972 **Pippin** (Roger O Hirson) Imperial Theater 23 October

1974 **The Magic Show** (Bob Randall) Cort Theater 28 May

1976 **The Baker's Wife** (Joseph Stein) Dorothy Chandler Pavilion, Los Angeles 11 May

1978 **Working** (many inc Schwartz) 46th Street Theater 14 May

1986 **Rags** (Charles Strouse/Stein) Mark Hellinger Theater 21 August

1991 **Children of Eden** (John Caird) Prince Edward Theatre, London, 8 January

DER SCHWARZE HECHT *see* Feuerwerk

SCHWARZWALDMÄDEL Operette in 3 acts by August Neidhart. Music by Leon Jessel. Komische Oper, Berlin, 25 August 1917.

Hans and Richard, two Viennese lads-about-town, come to the little Black Forest town of St Christoph so that Hans can escape the overwhelming attentions of Malwine von Hainau. Amidst the lively dancing, boozing and scrapping of the festivities of St Cecilia's Day, Malwine (who has arrived in hot pursuit) transfers her attentions to Richard, whilst Hans finds happiness with Bärbele, the orphan maidservant of old Blasius Römer (Gustav Charlé), the town organist, who had almost got around to foolishly proposing to her himself.

Jessel's score is a bright and infectious one, full of dancing country melodies of which the most winning, a little waltz called 'Erklingen zum Tanze die Geigen' and a pretty shadow dance ('Schöner Tänzer, du entschwindest'), both fall to the ingénue playing Bärbele. Richard wins the best of the men's numbers with the bouncy title-song 'Mädel aus dem schwarzen Wald' and his uncomplicated wooing of 'Malwine, ach, Malwine' whilst that lady and Hans soup things up with their contrasting big, lyrical tongue-in-cheek duo 'Muss denn die Lieb' stets Tragödie sein'.

As so often happens in troubled times, this piece of good-old-days simplicity with its delightful folksy music proved a singular success when mounted by Gustav Charlé at his Komische Oper in wartime Berlin. Only *Das Dreimäderlhaus*, another piece of simply sentimental and romantic musical theatre, did better than *Schwarzwaldmädel* which passed its 500th performance on 30 December 1918, and then its second anniversary before it finally closed on 1st September 1919. The show's success, however, did not limit itself to the war years. Although it was oddly ignored outside its homeland – a production in Buenos Aires and another in the German-language theatre in New York being isolated non-European productions – *Schwarzwaldmädel* went on to play thousands of performances throughout Germany, proving itself there probably the most popular piece ever premièred in Berlin prior to *Im weissen Rössl*, and establishing itself as part of the standard repertoire. It also found its way on to film four times. The first, in 1920, featured a silent Uschi Elleot in its central rôle, whilst Victor Janson's version of 1929 starred Liane Haid, Walter Janssen, Fred Louis Lerch, Georg Alexander and Olga Limburg.

The show's career was halted when the Jewish Jessel was declared persona non grata by the Nazis, but after the war and the death of the composer at the hands of the régime, *Schwarzwaldmädel* made its way ineluctably back to the screen in a 1950 filmed version, onto television, to the stage, where it remains regularly performed to this day, and onto a number of recordings.

Austria: Neues Wiener Stadttheater 1923; USA: Irving Place Theater October 1924; Films: Luna Film/Arthur Wellin (1920), Victor Jansson (1929), Georg Zoch (1933), Hans Deppe (1950)

Recordings: Selections (EMI-Electrola, Ariola-Eurodisc) etc

SCHWEIGHOFER, [Karl] Felix (b Brünn, 22 November 1842; d Blazewitz nr Dresden, 28 January 1912). Comic star of the Viennese musical stage through the peak of the 'golden age'.

The young Schweighofer spent a colourful decade in theatres of mostly a lower level throughout central Europe, playing everything from comedy and Possen to the rôles normally played by travesty sopranos in Operette, in theatres from Odenburg to Odessa and Bucharest or on tour before graduating to good comic rôles and the Stadttheater in Graz.

He was engaged briefly at the Theater an der Wien under Strampfer, but after one season he moved on to Brünn and then to Berlin's Friedrich-Wilhelmstädtisches Theater. He guested in leading comic rôles at several houses in company with Josefine Gallmeyer whom he also joined for a period at the Strampfertheater when she and the author Rosen went into management there. He played there in the Offenbach opérettes *Dorothea* and *Paimpol und Perinette* and in Jonas's *Der Ente mit drei Schnabeln* (*Le Canard à trois becs*), and introduced the rôle of Hammlet in the Strampfertheater burlesque of that title, but in the following years he again trod the stages of Europe, this time in lead rôles. At the same time, however, he also began to make himself a place back at the Theater an der Wien, now under the management of Maximilian Steiner.

In the mid- and late 1870s he appeared in many Possen on that house's programme and also in a long list of opérettes and Operetten: *Die Perle der Wascherinnin* (1875,

Plate 240. **Felix Schweighofer**: *the great Viennese comedian dressed for an unidentified rôle.*

van der Pruth), *Die Creolin* (1876, De Feuillemorte), *Luftschlosser* (Kasimir Staarl), *Der Seekadett* (Don Januario), *König Carotte* (Carotte), as Frank in the 100th performance of *Die Fledermaus*, in *Königin Indigo* (1877, Romadour), *Ein Blitzmädel* (Leo Brüller), *Der galante Vicomte* (Desfontains), *Der Jahrmarkt von St Laurent* (Ramolini), *Die Glocken von Corneville* (1878, Gaspard), *Madame Favart* (1879, Pontsablé), *Gräfin Dubarry* (Novailles), *Blindekuh* (Kragel), *Die hübsche Perserin* (1880, Moka), *Ein Schotte* (*L'Écossais de Châtou*, Hippolyte), *Musketiere in Damenstift* (1881, Abbé Bridaine) and *Lili* (St Hypothèse).

In the early 1880s Schweighofer created a memorable series of comic rôles in some of the most important Austrian shows of the time: Graf Villalobos y Rodriquez in Strauss's *Das Spitzentuch des Königin* (1880), the lubricious Prutschesko in *Apajune, der Wassermann* (1880), little lost tulip-grower Balthasar Groot in *Der lustige Krieg* (1881), the vengeful Colonel Ollendorf in *Der Bettelstudent* (1882, introducing the great waltz song 'Ach ich hab' sie ja nur auf die Schulter geküsst'), Pappacoda in the Viennese version of *Eine Nacht in Venedig* (1883) and the pompous Podesta Nasoni in *Gasparone* (1884) as well as Troupeau in Millöcker's *Der Jungfrau von Belleville* and Oppini in Müller's *Der kleine Prinz*, before quarrelling with the management of the Theater an der Wien and quitting it for the rival Carltheater. His one important new rôle there was that of Don Ranucio di Colibrados in Dellinger's *Don Cesar* (1885). He then left Vienna to make his second home in Dresden and to once more run the circuits of the European houses, now as a fully qualified star.

He returned occasionally for guest appearances in Vienna, and in 1899 he visited New York, appearing for Hans Conried in several popular Possen including *Das Blitzmädel*. He retired from the stage in 1904.

Autobiography: *Mein Wanderleben* (Heinrich Minden, Dresden, 1912)

SCOTT, Clement [William] (b London, 6 October 1841; d London, 25 June 1904).

The most celebrated theatre critic of the British Victorian era, Scott turned out detailed and informative first-night reports in the *Daily Telegraph* between 1871 and 1898 which remain models of the genre. His journalistic career was effectively ended when he cast doubts on the perfect moral purity of members of the theatrical profession in an interview, and was attacked with hypocrital fervour by the theatrical establishment.

Scott wrote a number of stage pieces, having considerable success with an adaptation of Sardou's *Dora* as *Diplomacy* and with the long-touring musical comedy drama *Jack in the Box* (w George Sims), and he also penned the lyrics to some highly successful songs including the patriotic 'Here Stands a Post' interpolated by contralto Adelaide Newton in *Wildfire* (Alhambra Theatre) and 'O Promise Me' an additional number inserted in the London and New York productions of De Koven's *Robin Hood* which became an American wedding-day standard. His 'Sixty Years Ago, Boys' (w J M Glover) was sung in the musical *The Yashmak* (1897).

1878 **The Little Duke** (*Le Petit Duc*) English version w B C Stephenson (Philharmonic Theatre)
1881 **Many Happy Returns** (Lionel Benson/w Gilbert a' Becket) 1 act St George's Hall 28 March

1885 **Jack in the Box** (William C Levey, James Glover/w George Sims) Theatre Royal, Brighton 24 August

1886 **The Lily of Léoville** (Ivan Caryll/Félix Remo ad Alfred Murray) Comedy Theatre 10 May

1898 **Oh, What a Night** (*Eine tolle Nacht*) English lyrics to new score by John Crook (Wakefield)

SCOTTO, Vincent (b Marseille, 20 April 1876; d Paris, 15 November 1952).

The teenaged Vincent Scotto, Marseille-born of Neapolitan stock, operated as an amateur songwriter and performer in his home town until the famous chansonnier Polin picked up his song 'Le Navigatore' and, having had it set to fresh lyrics by the established Henri Christiné, made it famous throughout France as 'La Petite Tonkinoise'.

The 19-year-old composer moved to Paris, and there became one of the favourite songwriters of the new century, supplying, in partnership with such lyricists as Albert Willemetz, René Sarvil, Lucien Boyer, Phylo, Geo Kogler, Audiffred, Léo Lelièvre and many others, what – in a long career – eventually totalled thousands of songs to such stars as Josephine Baker ('J'ai deux amours', 'Mon coeur est un oiseau des Îles'), Maurice Chevalier ('Si j'étais papa', 'C'est mon petit doigt'), Perchicot ('Mon Paris', 'Viva Mussolini' ly: Lucien Boyer), Milton ('Le Beau Navire') Raquel Meller ('Adieu, mon rêve'), Damia, Tino Rossi ('Le Marin veille', 'Soirs d'Espagne', 'Corsica bella', 'Dans la nuit, j'entends une chanson', 'Le Pousse Pousse', 'Si votre coeur vagabonde', 'Je vous aime sans espoir') and Alibert ('Catherine', 'Mon Bateau', 'Toute la ville danse', 'C'est pas mal ... c'est bien mieux'). A number of his songs made their way beyond France: 'La Petite Tonkinoise' became 'It's Delightful to Be Married' as performed by Anna Held in America (and subsequently by Fabienne Guyon as Anna Held in London's *Ziegfeld*) and 'Angelina' was sung in Britain's *Our Miss Gibbs*.

Scotto also wrote songs and music for nearly 200 films including *Naples au baiser de feu*, *Le Roi de la couture*, *Marseille tire-au-flanc*, *Embrassez-moi*, *La Douceur d'aimer*, *Pomme d'amour*, as well as the scores for the majority of the Marcel Pagnol films and, over a period of some 40 years, also turned out a regular supply of stage opérettes. The earliest of these were played in the provinces or in cafés-concerts and other smaller Paris venues without exciting much attention but in 1931, in collaboration with two other southerners, Henri Alibert and René Sarvil, he launched *Au pays du soleil*, the first of what would become a series of seven Marseillais revue-opérettes which, with their cheerful, regional flavour, accented comedy dialogue and lively songs, proved to be the popular musical equivalent of the Pagnol plays. The best of these simple, happy shows – *Au pays du soleil*, *Trois de la marine*, *Arènes joyeuses* and *Un de la Canebière* ('Le plus beau tango du monde') – remained favourites for a number of years, during which time they were toured, filmed, revived and toured again, and they remain part of the French regional repertoire to the present day.

In 1948 Scotto stepped away from the jolly, locally coloured style of these small-scale pieces to supply the score for what was to be his most substantial and long-running stage show, the Théâtre Mogador's romantic and glamorous *Violettes impériales*, and, as a result of its success,

he ventured two further spectacular pieces for the same theatre: the period romance *La Danseuse aux étoiles* (1949) and the posthumously-produced *Les Amants de Venise* (1953) which won a run of more than 500 performances.

One of the most memorable French songwriters of his age, he proved with his large-stage works that he could adapt effectively to a lusher style.

In 1983 a compilation show of the *Dreimäderlhaus* kind, loosely based on the composer's (love-) life, was played at the Théâtre de la Renaissance under the title *Vincent et Margot*, whilst a Scotto pasticcio, *Le Curé de la Canebière* (ad Michel de Carol) was produced at Sanary 25 July 1986.

1910 **Hugues**

1912 **Suzie** (Mareil) Toulouse 6 April

1919 **Charlot de la Chapelle** (Armand Foucher) Bouffes-Concert 24 January

1920 **L'Amour qui rôde** (Michel Carré fils, Albert Acremant) Eldorado 30 April

1922 **Zo-Zo** (Bertal, Maubon, Hérault) Eldorado 2 May

1922 **Pan-Pan** (Carré, Acremant) Ba-ta-clan 19 April

1924 **La Princesse du Moulin-Rouge** (Émile Codey, Denis) Excelsior-Concert 1 February

1924 **Coeur d'artichaut** Limoges

1925 **La Poule des Folies-Bergère** (Codey) Gaîté-Rochchouart 9 October

1925 **La Famille Banaste** Tarascon

1931 **Au Pays du soleil** (Alibert/René Sarvil) Moulin de la Chanson 22 October

1933 **Trois de la marine** (Alibert/Sarvil) Nouvel Ambigu 20 December

1934 **Zou, le Midi bouge** (aka *Arènes Joyeuses*) (Alibert) Alcazar

1935 **Un de la Canebière** (Alibert/Vincy) Théâtre des Célestins, Lyon 14 October; Théâtre des Variétés 3 April 1936

1936 **Les Gangsters du Château d'If** (Alibert/Sarvil) Théâtre des Célestins, Lyon 10 November; Théâtre des Variétés 22 January 1937

1938 **Le Roi des Galéjeurs** (Alibert) Théâtre des Célestins, Lyon; Théâtre des Variétés 16 September

?1946 **Les Gauchos de Marseille** (Scotto/Sarvil) Théâtre des Variétés

1948 **Violettes impériales** (Paul Achard, René Jeanne, Henri Varna) Théâtre Mogador 31 January

1949 **La Danseuse aux Étoiles** (Varna, Guy des Cars) Théâtre Mogador 18 February

1953 **Les Amants de Venise** (Marc-Cab, René Richard, Varna) Théâtre Mogador 28 February

SCRIBE, [Augustin] Eugène (b Paris, 24 December 1791; d Paris, 20 February 1861).

The most important librettist to the international musical stage of the first half of the 19th century, Scribe authored or co-authored 120 operas and opéras-comiques, long and short, including 37 for Auber (*La Muette de Portici*, *Les Diamants de la couronne*, *Fra Diavolo*, *Leicester*, *Léocadie*, *Le Maçon*, *La Fiancée*, *Le Philtre*, *Gustave III*, *Le Cheval de bronze*, *Le Domino noir*, *La Sirène*, *La Part du Diable*, *Haydée*, *Marco Spada*, *Manon Lescaut*, *La Circassienne* etc), and others for Meyerbeer (*Robert le Diable*, *Les Huguenots*, *Le Prophète*, *L'Étoile du nord*, *L'Africaine*), Verdi (*Les Vêpres siciliennes* and an adapation of his earlier *Gustave III* as *Un Ballo in Maschera*), Donizetti (*Betly*), Adam (*Le Chalet*, *Giralda*), Boieldieu (*La Dame blanche*), Balfe (*Le Puits d'amour*), Halévy (*La Juive*, *La Tempesta* based on Shakespeare) and Rossini (*Le Comte Ory*). Several of his opéras-comiques, particularly those with such composers as Hérold or Auber, or those which treated such subjects as Cherubini's *Ali Baba, ou Les Quarante Voleurs*, ran very close to the imaginary line between the ancient and modern musical theatre, a modern theatre to which his direct contribution was limited only by the fact that he died in 1861. He had, however, strayed across the line in collaborating twice with Offenbach, once on a version of his 1827 vaudeville *La Chatte metamorphosée en femme* (already musicalized in Austria by Hauptner) and again on the full-length tale of a dog called *Barkouf*.

The absent Scribe had, however, a strong indirect influence on what followed his era, both as the most important forefather of the late 19th-century opérette libretto, but also more concretely, through the multiple adaptations of his plays and libretti made not only by countless contemporaries but also by later writers. Undoubtedly the most important of these, in the modern musical theatre, was the remaking of his text to *La Circassienne* as the libretto for von Suppé's highly successful *Fatinitza* (1876). The widow Scribe's objections to this re-use did not stop other Austrian writers and composers from plundering the bottomless Scribe catalogue.

Max Wolf set two remade Scribe libretti: *Césarine* (lib: Adolf Schirmer), produced in 1878 at Berlin's Komische Oper and the Vienna Ringtheater, admitted to being based on an unspecified Scribe piece, but the 1884 *Raffaela* (lib: Ignaz Schnitzer) was announced as based on *Le Duc d'Olonne*. Charles Cassmann and Willi Wulff's text for Zumpe's successful *Farinelli* (1888) was based on Scribe's text for Auber's comic opera *La Part du Diable* (already borrowed for a Vienna vaudeville *Carlo Bracci, oder der Antheil des Teufels* by Emil Titl and Franz Xaver Told) mixed with parts of a play called *Farinelli* (Teigmann), whilst Bernhard Buchbinder's book to Alfred Zamara's *Der Sänger von Palermo* was a version of *Ne touchez pas à la Reine*, a piece already musicalized in 1847 (mus: Boisselot) as *Die Königin von Leon* (Theater an der Wien, 15 July). *Der Liebesbrunnen* with music by Paul Mestrozzi (Fürsttheater, 21 April 1889) was a fresh version of *Le Puits d'amour*, Ludwig Held and Benjamin Schier's libretto for the Eduard Kremser Operette *Der Schlosserkönig* (1889) admitted to being 'nach ein Idee des Scribe' and Zell and Genée's *Die Dreizehn* (Carltheater, 6 Feb 1887) and *Die Piraten* (Walhalla-Theater, Berlin, 9 October 1886) also came from unspecified Scribe sources.

The borrowing did not let up in the 1890s. The text for Franz Wagner's Operette *Der Cognac-König* (Carltheater, 20 February 1897) was taken by Held and Léon from *La Frontière de Savoie, Katze und Maus* by the younger Johann Strauss (1898) was based on the famous *La Bataille de dames* (w Ernest Legouvé), *Der Husar* (1898, Ignaz Brüll/Victor Léon) was taken from 'Scribeschen Stoffe' and *Leuchtkäfer* (Ludwig Fernand, Alfred Schönfeld), composed by Moritz Fall – father of Leo – and produced at the Wilhelm-Theater, Magdeburg (18 February 1899), also nodded towards Scribe without being more precise. A comic opera, *Offizier der Königin*, composed by Otto Fiebach and produced at Dresden (3 May 1900), was based on *Le Verre d'eau* and the Hirschberger/Pohl libretto to Dellinger's *Jadwiga* (Dresden, 1901) again noted that it was 'frei nach Scribe'. The author's name was also mentioned in connection with Karl Stix's 1861 one-acter *Ein*

Kapitalist, der einen Dienst sucht (mus: Suppé, Theater an der Wien 1 June).

Undoubtedly there were many more 'Scribeischen' borrowings hidden under the admissions (in various forms) that libretti were 'from the French', but again some of these nebulous credits were undoubtedly due to the fact that at certain periods it was considered fashionable (and critic-warning) to be announced as a version of an unspecified Paris success.

In Hungary Scribe's *La Déesse* became *Az istennó* (Miklós Forrai, Népszinház, 6 March 1896) and *La Bataille de dames* got a second musicalization as *Nők harca* (Pesti Színház, 19 November 1942, István Zágon/Tibor Hegedüs), whilst in Britain *Le Philtre* was reused by Macfarren as the basis for his operetta *Jessy Lea* (1863), *Giralda*, already made over as a play by Dion Boucicault, was most successfully remade into *Manteaux Noirs* and that show's composer Bucalossi commandeered a second Scribe piece, *La Frileuse* (ad Frank Desprez), to set as *Delia* (Bristol, 11 March 1889). However, by the 20th century both countries had moved on to a different style of show and Scribe material was no longer useful as raw stuff.

Nevertheless, Künneke's opera *Coeur-As* (Emil Tschirsch, Carl Berg, Dresden, 31 October 1913) declared itself based on something by Scribe and even the 1920 Broadway musical *Betty Be Good* insisted that its wisp of a plot was 'from a French vaudeville by Scribe'. Musical versions of *La Bataille de dames* continued to appear, the younger Strauss's version and an Italian operatic one being followed by a pair of Italian operettas (*Battaglia di dame*, Mario Bona/Gigi Mecheletti, La Spezia, 19 September 1914 and *Battaglia di dame*, Gea della Garisenda/Luigi Michelotti Teatro Fossati, Milan, 1915), a German one, *Inkognito*, (Rudolf Nelson/Kurt Kraatz, Richard Kessler, Kammerspiele, 4 June 1918) and mostly recently an Austrian one (Hans Pero/Arthur Kendall, Kammerspiele, Innsbruck, 15 September 1961). *Ein Glas Wasser* got a fresh musicalization as 'ein Stück mit Musik' by Helmut Käutner at the Dresden Staatsoperette in 1978 (8 November).

Scribe's little *L'Ours et le pacha* (1820, w J X B Saintine) was made over many times as a musical piece – Hervé and Audran both cut their composing teeth on versions and Bazin's setting was played at the Opéra-Comique (21 February 1879), whilst in Austria (1820) and Germany (1821), in different musical versions, it became *Der Bär und der Bassa* and in Britain it was made up into the little *Bears not Beasts*.

Scribe's texts, and the successful operas made from them underwent much burlesquing in the age of burlesque. In Britain, *Les Diamants de la couronne* (*The Half-Crown Diamonds*), *La Muette de portici* (*Mass-en-yelloh* etc), *Fra Diavolo* and *L'Africaine* all came under the burlesque-merchants' punny hands, whilst in Vienna *La Dame blanche* became *Die schwarze Frau* (Adolf Müller, 1826).

1853 **La Lettre au bon dieu** (Gilbert Duprez/w Frédéric de Courcy) Opéra-Comique 28 April
1858 **Broskovano** (Louis Deffès w Henri Boisseaux) Théâtre Lyrique 29 September
1858 **Les Trois Nicolas** (Louis Clapisson/w Bernard Lopez, Gabriel de Lurieu) Opéra-Comique 16 December

1858 **La Chatte metamorphosée en femme** (Jacques Offenbach/w A H J Mélesville) 1 act Théâtre des Bouffes-Parisiens

1860 **Le Nouveau Pourcegnac** (Aristide Hignard/w Charles Gaspard Delestre-Poirson) 1 act Théâtre des Bouffes-Parisiens 14 January

1860 **Barkouf** (Offenbach/w Boisseaux) Opéra-Comique 24 December

1861 **La Beauté du Diable** (Giulio Alary/w Émile de Najac) 1 act Opéra-Comique 28 May

[LA] SCUGNIZZA Operetta in 3 acts by Carlo Lombardo. Music by Mario Costa. Teatro Alfieri, Turin, 16 December 1922.

One of the most successful Italian operettas of its period, the light-footed *La scugnizza* used for its libretto some of the most hard-worked plot and character elements of the past decades, joined to an attractive dance-based score. The tale introduced an American millionaire called Toby, his daughter Gaby and his secretary Chic into a nice, normal Italian town where Toby takes a fancy to pretty little Salomè. By the time there has been a costume ball and Gaby has taught Salomè how to do the shimmy, the signorina sensibly decides to stick to her local Toto, Gaby can pair off with Chic, and Toby has to make do with the embraces of Auntie Maria Grazia.

Mario Costa's score duly took in the fashionable dance rhythms of the foxtrot in Salomè's Fox-Trott della Scugnizza ('Napoletana! come canti tu') and the shimmy in the duetto comico 'Schimmy!', and there were sizeable dance breaks to be found in most of the other main numbers of the score – the Quartetto degli Scugnizzi ('Ombre son che nella notte') for the four young people, the duetti

Plate 241.

1294

comici 'Salomè' and 'I capelli bianchi!' – with only the occasional pause for a more romantic moment, such as the soprano romanza 'La giovinezza non ritorna più!'.

La scugnizza has remained a part of the small list of (intermittently) revivable Italian shows through the 70 years since its production.

Recording: selection (EDM) etc

SEABROOKE, Thomas Q[uigley] [QUIGLEY, Thomas James] (b Mount Vernon, NY, 20 October 1860; d Chicago, 3 April 1913). Comic star of the 19th-century American musical stage.

Originally a bank clerk, Seabrooke went on the stage at the age of 20 and had his early experience touring as a juvenile man in all kinds of pieces from drama to farce comedies and burlesques (*Aphrodite*, *A Tin Soldier* etc). He toured in the principal comic rôle of General Knickerbocker in *The Little Tycoon*, visited Broadway as Deacon Tidd in Charles Hoyt's farce comedy *A Midnight Bell* (1889) and in *The Stepping Stone* (1890) and then established himself thoroughly as a Broadway musical comic when he shared the comedy of *Castles in the Air* with De Wolf Hopper (1890, Cabalastro). He ran through a series of leading comic rôles in musicals in the years that followed: the title-rôle in *The Cadi* (1891), King Pommery in the popular extravaganza *The Isle of Champagne* (1892), Francis in another Orientalish bit of nonsense called *Tabasco* (1894) and the title-rôle of a Fred Gagel/Edgar Smith sequel called *The Grand Vizier* (1895) which he produced himself. He subsequently appeared in a couple of plays and then visited Britain where he appeared in George Musgrove's production of a rehash of Lecocq's *La Petite Mariée* under the title *The Scarlet Feather* (1897, Dr Alphonse).

Back in America, having parted company with the musical *Papa Gougou* on the road, he took a fresh turn in the insistent *The Isle of Champagne* before joining the company at the Casino Theater where he appeared in their 1897 revue *Yankee Doodle Dandy*, as Calchas in the Lillian Russell revival of *La Belle Hélène* (1899) and as Ravannes to the Cadeau of Francis Wilson and the Erminie of Miss Russell in a revival of *Erminie* (1899). He stayed at the Casino to play in the American version of *Les Fêtards*, here called *The Rounders* (1900), playing the rôle of the roguish and sexually striving King of Illyria, which was turned for his benefit into an low-comic oriental Irish potentate called Maginnis Pasha. In 1902 he appeared at the Winter Garden in a short musical show called *The Belle of Broadway*, and later the same year scored his biggest success when he returned to the Casino Theater to star as Mr Pineapple the unfortunate bridegroom of the British musical comedy *A Chinese Honeymoon* for the up-and-zooming Shubert brothers.

He followed up as Baron Bulverstrass in the Casino Theater's less successful *The Red Feather* (1903) and Augustus Melon in *Piff! Paff! Pouf!* (1904) and toured as John Doe in the Gustave Kerker musical *The Billionaire*, before taking a turn in vaudeville. He had just one further big rôle on Broadway, as chief comic Johnny Rocks in *Mexicana* (1906), but although his starring days were done he continued to work in the theatre virtually up to his death.

SEAL, Elizabeth [Anne] (b Genoa, Italy, 28 August 1933). British soubrette who scored a major success as *Irma la Douce*.

After appearing in the chorus of *Gay's the Word* and *Glorious Days*, Elizabeth Seal made her first significant London appearance as Gladys in the London Coliseum production of *The Pajama Game*. She then replaced the miscast Belita as Lola in *Damn Yankees* before being cast in the rôle of Irma in the English version of *Irma la Douce*. She had a great success in that part, both in London and in New York (Tony Award), but, like the rôle's French originator, failed to find another part in which to confirm, and her career disintegrated.

When *A Chorus Line* was taken to London, she was cast as Cassie, but she was replaced in rehearsals and the subsequent outcry in the acting profession resulted in a serious change in the Equity standard contract, preventing a management from altering a cast during the preparatory stages of a production. Her only appearance in a West End musical after *Irma la Douce* was in a revival of *Salad Days* (1976). She subsequently became involved with teaching and directing young performers.

SEARELL[E], [William] Luscombe (b Kingsteignton, Devon, 13 September 1853; d East Molsey, Surrey, 18 December 1907).

One of the most colourful characters of the Victorian musical theatre scene, British-born and New Zealand-bred Searelle began his career as a pianist, a conductor and a composer in Christchurch, NZ. He left there in the tow of another colourful fellow, Horace Lingard, conducting a pirated version of *HMS Pinafore* and a self-composed 'sequel' to Gilbert and Sullivan's show, *The Wreck of the Pinafore*, which had been produced in Dunedin.

The pair made their way to Australia on a wave of court cases, and Searelle began a career as composer and self-publicist which eventually took him from Australia to America – where he apparently talked someone into giving a performance of another of his stage works – and to Britain, where he succeeded in getting not only *The Wreck of the Pinafore* (4 performances), but another comic opera, *Estrella* (37 performances) exceedingly brief showings in London. Searelle did not give up, however. He got *Estrella* staged in America, only to have it burned out almost immediately (3 performances) but, in spite of great announcements as to his forthcoming productions sprayed through whatever newspapers he could charm into printing them, he ended up returning to Australia.

There, at last, he found his success. British comedian Phil Day made *Estrella* a small hit with his low-comic antics, and Searelle – now working as a musical director and co-producer with Majeroni and Wilson and/or singer-manager Charles Harding – won productions for his Arabian Nights musical *Bobadil*, which made its own success, and also for *Isidora*, a vastly melodramatic piece of *Flying Dutchman*nery which did less well. He pushed, chivvied and publicized himself and others into further productions, went loudly bankrupt in 1886, and eased his way on again to America and to South Africa. There he paused. Having seen what had happened to property and to entertainments in Australia with the discovery of gold, he bought up large, invested in theatre buildings and made (so he said) a fortune. In 1889 he was reported to be

proprietor of the Theatre Royal, Johannesburg, and four or five more of the principal theatres in South Africa (although the *Era* had to retract Searelle's exaggerations after printing his freely distributed self-advertising).

He now set out to try again to conquer London, and managed to get *Isidora* produced at the Globe Theatre under the title *The Black Rover*. It didn't conquer. From that time on, neither did he. After a few years, alongside his brother Ernest, importing all kinds of artists to South Africa, he lost his South African holdings and – in spite of his 'good friend Cecil Rhodes' for whom he had written a national anthem – was chased from the country, allegedly because the rebels found he was hiding guns for the enemy under his theatre's stage. His missionary sister was murdered by the Boxers in China, his brother went to the Klondyke and never recovered, and his announcements, whilst not lessening in bravado, came less and less to fruition. Yet, with typical style, the last Searelle work to appear on the stage was a sacred verse drama with music and songs entitled *Mizpah* written in collaboration with no less a personality than Ella Wheeler Wilcox and produced at Baltimore (22 January 1906). It did not make it to Broadway, but its text was published ... with each author's contributions printed in a different colour.

Searelle's other works included an opera, *The Kisses of Circe*, which he had mounted in South Africa, a cantata *Australia*, a published verse epic *The Dawn of Death*, and a selection of *Tales from the Transvaal*. His music was eclectic and apparently run-of-the-mill, but he was a master at getting his shows seen and himself into the public eye, and if London rejected its first New Zealand composer with scorn, the Southern hemisphere gave his pronouncements and his works much more credence. In the end, he probably fooled posterity as well, for almost everything we know about Searelle comes from newspaper paragraphs, and there is little doubt as to who supplied those.

In 1885 Searelle married a Sydney architect's daughter and amateur singer, Blanche Ella Fenton Spencer (aka Blanche de Fontaine) who then took leading rôles in several of his works in Australia, South Africa and also in the London production of *The Black Rover*. She proved insufficient to this last task and was quickly replaced.

1880 **The Wreck of the Pinafore** (W H Lingard) Prince of Wales Theatre, Dunedin, New Zealand 29 November
1881 **The Fakir of Travancore** Tivoli Garden Theater, San Francisco 7 June
1883 **Estrella** (Walter Parke) Prince's Theatre, Manchester 14 May; Gaiety Theatre, London 24 May
1884 **Bobadil** Opera House, Sydney 22 November
1885 **Isidora** (aka *The Black Rover*) Bijou Theater, Melbourne 7 July

SECOMBE, Harry (Sir) (b Swansea, 8 September 1921). Greatly popular barrel-chested Welsh comedian and vocalist, best known for his contribution to radio's *The Goon Show* and for having placed a recording of 'Vestia la giubba' on the British hit parades.

After appearing in revue, straight theatre and in variety, Secombe moved into the musical theatre for the first time when, in the wake of the success of *Oliver!*, he conceived and starred in the London musical *Pickwick* (1963, introducing 'If I Ruled the World'), which he later also played in America (1965). He subsequently starred as D'Artagnan in a Dumas burlesque, *The Four Musketeers* (1967), with rather less success, the strains of the piece leading him to have to – on occasions – mime his singing to a taped track. Thereafter, although he was announced in 1972 to star in a biomusical on anti-Americanist Sydney Smith, he restricted his musical-theatre appearances to pantomime where he was for many years a great favourite, returning only in 1993 to repeat his Pickwick at the Chichester Festival.

Secombe appeared as Mr Bumble in the screen version of *Oliver!* (1968) and of *Song of Norway* (1970).

LE SECRET DE MARCO POLO Opérette à grand spectacle in 2 acts by Raymond Vincy. Music by Francis Lopez. Théâtre du Châtelet, Paris, 12 December 1959.

Luis Mariano, backed by 17 of the Châtelet's most magnificent scenes and a cast including Janine Ribot, Pierjac, Rosine Brédy, Claude Daltys and Robert Pizani, and equipped with a scoreful of what by this time had become very routine Francis Lopez songs ('Marco Polo', 'Belle', 'Viens', 'Tiki Tiki Chou', 'Cavaliers' etc) and duets, played Marco Polo through a series of unlikely and Oriental adventures. He played it for ten months (268 performances) but both he and it left a general taste of disappointment. The piece was apparently subsequently played in Romania, making it one of the few (if not the only) Lopez piece to have been seen in translation.

Recording: original cast (Philips)

DER SEEKADETT Operette in 3 acts by F Zell adapted from *Le Capitaine Charlotte* by Jean-François Bayard and Philippe Dumanoir. Music by Richard Genée. Theater an der Wien, Vienna, 24 October 1876.

Der Seekadett shared its title with the popular 1835 comic opera by Labarr and Kupelwieser, but Zell's version of Bayard and Dumanoir's well-known story for the newer piece had, in fact, little enough to do with the sea. The soubrette Fanchette Michel (Hermine Meyerhoff) comes to Lisbon in search of her lover, Lambert de Saint-Querlonde (Jani Szika), who has been secretly married to the Queen of Portugal (Bertha Steinher). To escape the Queen's jealousy she disguises herself as a sea-cadet, and when she, in turn, arouses the Queen's interest and is cleverly caught in the royal quarters, she takes the opportunity to save the situation by changing back into a girl. Leaving Lambert to his consort's position and the Queen to her red cheeks, Fanchette finally goes off into the sunset with a wealthy Peruvian called Don Januario de Sonza-Silva e Pernambuco (Felix Schweighofer). The lightest moments were the province of Alexander Girardi, cast as Don Domingos Borgos de Barros, the royal Master of Ceremonies, paired with Georgine von Januschowsky as Donna Antonia, the Queen's lady-in-waiting.

Der Seekadet was a decided success on its production at Maximilian Steiner's Theater an der Wien and it was played 48 times before dropping from the repertoire in 1878. In 1882 it was taken up by Strampfer at the rival Carltheater with Jenny Stubel appearing as Fanchette Michel and Karl Drucker as Don Januario. The Vienna production was swiftly followed up in Berlin, Chemnitz, Riga, Munich and many other German venues as well as, with outstanding results, in Budapest (ad Jenő Rákosi) where Lujza Blaha starred as Fanchette Michel alongside

Erzsi Vidmar (Queen), János Kápolnai (Lamberto) and Elek Solymossy (Don Januario) for 48 performances at the top of a long career in Hungarian theatres.

America, as it was to do so many times and particularly whilst the reasonably unprincipled Sydney Rosenfeld was active, turned out two separate English-language versions, but the law stepped in to stop a duplication of the original German version. The Thalia-Theater mounted *Der Seekadett* with Mathilde Cottrelly as Fanchette alongside Frln Fiebach (Queen), Schnelle (Lamberto) and Gustav Adolfi (Januario), and they scored such a vast success that the opposition Germania Theater promptly announced their production of *Der Marine-Kadett*. They were summonsed and stopped, whilst the Thalia production ran an unprecedented two months. Augustin Daly's production of the English version, *The Royal Middy*, was also a fine success and, after a good two-month season on Broadway with Catherine Lewis wearing the breeches, it proved a fine touring prospect both in America and on the Pacific and oriental circuits where Emilie Melville played the very grateful leading rôle for some years. Rosenfeld's version, *The Sea Cadet, or the Very Merry Mariner*, with Blanche Chapman starred in E E Rice and Jacob Nunnemacher's production, went under in less than a week in town, which didn't stop Rosenfeld from pirating happily round the country with it.

London picked up news of the American success and Alexander Henderson staged an H B Farnie version of *The Naval Cadet* to follow his record-breaking production of *Les Cloches de Corneville* at the Globe. Selina Dolaro was called Cerisette but still dressed up as a boy, Violet Cameron played the Queen, Loredan was a new version of Lamberto called Florio, and Harry Paulton had the largest comic rôle, but the piece had a hard act to follow and, after a month and a half, Henderson brought back *Les Cloches*. A few months later the conductor of *The Naval Cadet*, Edward Solomon, broke through as a composer with the much-more-successful *Billee Taylor*, a tongue-in-cheek tale of a girl who disguises herself as a sea-cadet to go in search of her lover. *The Naval Cadet*, in spite of its less-than-momentous London season, nevertheless went to the British provinces, and Emily Soldene was seen starred in Farnie's version around the country later the same year.

A French-language version (ad Gustave Lagye) was first heard at Brussels' ever enterprising Fantaisies-Parisiennes (25 January 1880) but, in a period where Germanic works aroused limited interest in Paris, it never reached the French capital.

An Italian operetta, *Il capitano Carlotta* (Raffaele Mazzoni), also based on Bayard and Dumanoir's play, was produced at Città delle Pieve in 1891 (22 April).

Hungary: Népszinház *Kapitánykisasszony* 13 January 1877; Germany: Friedrich-Wilhelmstädtisches Theater 3 March 1877; USA: Thalia Theater 27 October 1879 (Ger), Daly's Theater *The Royal Middy* 28 January 1880, Fifth Avenue Theater *The Sea Cadet* 7 June 1880 (Eng); UK: Globe Theatre *The Naval Cadets* 27 March 1880; France: *Le Cadet de Marine* 19 April 1881; Australia: Prince of Wales Theatre, Melbourne *The Royal Middy* 1 October 1880

SEESAW Musical in 2 acts originally written by Michael Stewart based on *Two for the Seesaw* by William Gibson, subsequently revised by, and wholly credited to, Michael

Bennett. Lyrics by Dorothy Fields. Music by Cy Coleman. Uris Theater, New York, 18 March 1973.

Gibson's 1958 two-handed play *Two for the Seesaw* (Booth Theater, 16 January 1958) was a major Broadway success with Henry Fonda starring as the besuited out-of-towner Jerry Ryan, who finds a long-term relationship with the determinedly bohemian New Yorker Gittel Mosca (Anne Bancroft) impossible for more than two acts. The musical version of the play padded out this central story with a second introduction for its hero (Ken Howard): not only did he come to town and find Gittel (Michele Lee), he found New York itself and a whole lot of trendy 1960s–70s theatrical people who are put forward as representative of the city and its good life. Choreography was assured by making the most visible of this group a rising young choreographer (Tommy Tune) and period ethnics by popping in a Puerto Rican troupe (Giancarlo Esposito et al).

The pre-Broadway troubles of *Seesaw* make up one of 1970s show business's longer and less sympathetic sagas. After an unsatisfactory start, the original director was sacked and director-choreographer Michael Bennett was brought in to restage the piece. The result was some severe rewriting and the departure of librettist Michael Stewart, mostly new and up-front choreography, many sackings including star Lainie Kazan, and even a hatful of alterations to the score which had become and would remain the backbone of the show. By the time *Seesaw* opened on Broadway, it was a very different show from that which had begun in try-out, but its dual nature remained: Gibson's warmly intimate tale on one side, and the glitzy, revusical Broadway extras on the other.

The best of the Coleman/Fields songs belonged, significantly, to the love story: Gittel's 'Nobody Does it Like Me', soon to become a cabaret standard, 'He's Good for Me' and 'Welcome to Holiday Inn', but the glitz department also came up trumps with the energetic company song 'It's Not Where You Start (it's where you finish)' which was another number to survive beyond the 296 Broadway performances and subsequent (and again altered) touring version in which Lucie Arnaz and John Gavin starred. The Broadway establishment's kudos, however, went to the show's decorative part. Bennett was awarded a Tony for his choreography and Tune, who had also had a hand in that choreography, took a Best Supporting performance award.

The same title – though with a gap between the See and the Saw – had previously been used for another Broadway musical (Louis Hirsch/Earl Derr Biggers), based on Biggers's novel *Love Insurance*, and produced by Henry Savage at the Cohan Theater in 1919 (23 September). A clever plot had a Lord (Charlie Brown) whose rival in love is an American insurance man (Guy Robertson) taking out a policy with that rival against the lady (Elizabeth Hines) refusing him, and the piece ran for 89 performances.

Australia: Marian Street Theatre, Sydney 2 November 1979; UK: Theatre Royal and Opera House, Northampton 3 April 1987
Recording: original cast (Buddah/DRG)

SEE SEE Chinese comic opera in 2 acts by Charles H E Brookfield adapted from the play *La Troisième Lune* by Fred de Grésac and Paul Ferrier. Lyrics by Adrian Ross. Music by Sidney Jones. Additional material by Frank E Tours and Percy Greenbank. Prince of Wales Theatre, London, 20 June 1906.

See See was a 1906 attempt by producer George Edwardes and composer Sidney Jones, in the wake of the success of Edwardes's production of *Les P'tites Michu*, to put a little more 'comic opera' substance back into home-made contemporary musical comedy. The libretto, taken from a Parisian play which had originally included a score of incidental music by Cuvillier, was set, like Jones's two big hits *The Geisha* and *San Toy*, in the Orient but it did not follow the standard Daly's patterns in plot and layout.

Wise and beautiful See See (Denise Orme) teams with comical Hang-Kee (Huntley Wright, chief comic of *The Geisha* and *San Toy*) and Mai Yai (Amy Augarde of *Les P'tites Michu*) to disgust Cheoo (Bill Berry) so that he will not allow his son Yen (Maurice Farkoa) to wed unwilling little Lee (Adrienne Augarde, one of the *P'tites Michu*). Things go wrong, and See See herself ends up as Yen's wife, leading to a second act in which the bridegroom tames and woos his horrified partner into happiness. This highly starry cast was supplemented by the queen of the postcard girls, Gabrielle Ray, in a travesty rôle, young Lily Elsie as See See's maid, Fred Emney and Kitty Hanson for some low comedy, and a set of comical wives for Berry which included Sybil Grey, one of Gilbert and Sullivan's original three maids (*The Mikado*).

The plot gave Wright a bagful of disguises in which to display himself, Miss Orme (a *Les P'tites Michu* take-over) plenty of pretty songs, and Miss Ray lots of exposure including the show's most popular number, a sweet little duo with Wright in which they dressed as and sang about 'Chinese Lanterns'. The vastly experienced Edwardes had seemingly done everything right, the papers could find no criticisms except to say it was too lush and too long and too full of good things, but *See See* simply refused to catch on. After 152 performances it was closed, leading to one of those periodic floods of newspaper articles declaring the imminent death of the musical (or any other) theatre.

SEGAL, Vivienne [Sonia] (b Philadelphia, 19 April 1897; d Los Angeles, 29 December 1992). Star musical ingénue who made a second career as a wisecracking character lady.

Miss Segal had studied music and appeared in operatic productions in her native Pennsylvania before her début in the professional musical theatre. The Shuberts, who were producing an americanized version of Eysler's *Ein Tag im Paradies* under the title of *The Blue Paradise*, had engaged Chapine for the important rôle of the ingénue who turns out a shrew and it quickly became evident that the lady was not up to the rôle. Miss Segal's father offered to invest substantially in the show if his daughter was made the replacement. The ring-in leading lady was the hit of the highly successful production and began her career where she would stay – at the top.

She toured with *The Blue Paradise* and then went on to play leading rôles in *My Lady's Glove* (Oscar Straus's *Die schöne Unbekannte*, 1917, Elly), the revue *Miss 1917*, Jerome Kern's *Oh, Lady! Lady!!* (1918, Molly Farrington), Friml's *The Little Whopper* (1919, Kitty Wentworth), in the tryouts of *Tangerine* (February 1921) and Ivan Caryll's *Little Miss Raffles* (1921) and, most substantially, as Odette Darimonde in the americanization of Kálmán's *Die*

Bajadere as *The Yankee Princess* (1922). She appeared in the title-rôle of *Adrienne*, played in *The Ziegfeld Follies of 1924*, and took the title-rôle of Oscar Straus's *Riquette* pre-Broadway until the Shuberts decided to use Mitzi instead, and then took up instead the lead in Earl Carroll's publicity musical, *Oh, You!* (it was backed by and plugged a real-estate corporation) which came to Broadway as *Florida Girl* (1925, Daphne). After its quick closure, she went to Chicago to play the lead rôle in Percy Wenrich's *Castles in the Air* (1925, Evelyn Devine).

Castles in the Air was a huge success through a run of almost a year in that city and Miss Segal later played her rôle when the show moved to New York. *Castles in the Air* was reaching its latter days on Broadway when the cast were asked to take salary cuts. Miss Segal refused, but generously tore up her contract, thus allowing the management to recast more cheaply and her to take the job she had been offered in the tryout of *Lady Fair*. Her judgement proved sound when *Lady Fair* came into town as *The Desert Song* (1926) with Miss Segal as Margot Bonvalet creating 'Romance' and 'One Kiss'. She followed up as Constance Bonacieux in Friml's *The Three Musketeers*, appeared throughout the country as Nadina in a revival of *The Chocolate Soldier* (1931), and subsequently appeared in regional productions of *Music in the Air*, *The Three Musketeers*, *No, No, Nanette*, and at Jones Beach as Rosalinde in *A Wonderful Night*, as Ottilie in *Maytime* and Fedora Palinska in *The Circus Princess*.

Ten years after her last Broadway creation as a romantic lead, Miss Segal began a second career as a character lady. She appeared as the wordly-wisecracking Peggy Palaffi of *I Married an Angel* and followed up for the same authors with a memorable performance (aged 43) as man-nibbling Vera Simpson in *Pal Joey*, creating 'Bewitched (bothered and bewildered)' and 'Take Him'. A revival of the Rodgers and Hart *A Connecticut Yankee* (1943) cast her as Morgan Le Fay, equipped with a new number, 'To Keep My Love Alive', which was destined to become an anthology piece.

From these wryly comical ladies, it was something of a volte face to the romanticism of the Tchaikovsky pasticcio *Music in my Heart* (1947), and a step down to the weak and unsuccessful *Great to be Alive*, but another Rodgers and Hart revival – a repeat of her original rôle in *Pal Joey* – closed out a memorable pair of Broadway careers covering nearly 40 years with a hole in the middle.

Miss Segal also appeared in a handful of musical films, including the cinema versions of *Golden Dawn* (1930, Dawn) and *The Cat and the Fiddle* (1934), and *Viennese Nights* (1930).

SEIDL, Lea [MAYRSEIDL, Caroline] (b Vienna, 22 August 1894; d London, 4 January 1987). Viennese diva who finished her career in London.

Lea Seidl began her career as a young teenager in juvenile rôles at the Vienna Carltheater, and subsequently played adult rôles in Zurich, Berlin (*Das Mädel von Davos*, Princess Stefanie in *Der Fürst von Pappenheim*, *Die vertauschte Frau*, *Tausend süsse Beinchen*) and in Vienna (Dorine in the Berlin Neues Theater production of *Dorine und der Zufall*, *Der Fürst von Pappenheim*, Mara Beltramini in Julius Bittner's *Die silberne Tänzerin*) before appearing as *Friederike* to the Goethe of Richard Tauber in the Vienna version of Lehár's Singspiel. She was also seen in Vienna

as 'Sie' in the German version of *L'Amour masqué*, paired with Joseph Hislop in the British production of the *Friederike* and created the rôle of Josefa in the English version of *Im weissen Rössl* at the London Coliseum.

Seidl remained in Britain, but apart from a revival of *A Waltz Dream*, a short-lived version of May's *Der tanzende Stadt* and the flop *No Sky So Blue* was not seen in the musical theatre thereafter, restricting her appearances to plays and film.

THE SENTIMENTAL BLOKE Musical play in 2 acts by Nancy Brown and Lloyd Thomson based on the poems of C J Dennis. Lyrics by Nancy Brown, Albert Arlen, Lloyd Thomson and C J Dennis. Music by Albert Arlen. Comedy Theatre, Melbourne, 4 November 1961.

C J Dennis's Australian narrative poems *The Songs of a Sentimental Bloke* (1915) went through adaptation into films both silent (1918) and spoken (1932) and as a stage play (1922) before becoming a stage musical in the hands of Sydney husband-and-wife team Albert Arlen and Nancy Brown (one-time leading lady to Richard Tauber and the star of the 1932 film of *The Maid of the Mountains*) and Canberra diplomat Lloyd Thomson.

Originally produced by the amateur Canberra Repertory Company, *The Sentimental Bloke* was subsequently taken up by the then all-powerful J C Williamson Theatres Ltd and, after a try-out and some considerable rewrites to make it a more conventional 1950s musical show, it was given a professional production. The original Canberra leading man, Edwin Ride, repeated his performance as Bill, 'the sentimental bloke', opposite Patsy Hemingway as his beloved Doreen, and comedy from Frank Ward (best friend Ginger Mick), Alton Harvey (the rival Stror 'At Coot) and Gloria Dawn (his girl Rosie), all re-creating the familiar (to Australians) characters of Spadger's Lane. The tale was illustrated by some pleasant songs, which mostly escaped being stage-ocker (the Australian equivalent of stage-cockney) and *The Sentimental Bloke* became the most successful Australian musical of its time. It was (and still occasionally is) played throughout that country but, in spite of efforts to find it a production overseas, it was not exported any further than New Zealand.

Recordings: original cast (Talent City), radio cast (RCA Camden)

THE SERENADE Comic opera in 3 acts by Harry B Smith. Music by Victor Herbert. Knickerbocker Theater, New York, 16 March 1897.

After having tried repeatedly, with a considerable adventurousness but little luck, to find another work with which to repeat the success of their famous production of *Robin Hood*, The Boston Ideal Comic Opera Company (The Bostonians) got perhaps the nearest that they ever would with *The Serenade*. The piece was written by *Robin Hood* librettist Harry Smith and composed by Victor Herbert to whom, three years earlier, the company had given his first stage opportunity with the flop *Prince Ananias*. The basic story of *The Serenade* was barely a fresh one and Smith, aware that his plotline carried uncomfortable resemblances to those of several other recent comic operas, used the time-honoured critic-baffling trick of announcing that the libretto was an adaptation of a piece by Goldoni.

The baritone of the Madrid Opera, Alvarado (W H

MacDonald) is in love with Dolores (Jessie Bartlett Davis), and he woos her with the serenade of the title, in spite of the efforts of the Duke of Santa Cruz (Henry C Barnabee) to prevent him. Since Dolores was written as a contralto for the Bostonians' senior lady, Miss Davis, it was the other woman in the affair who had to be the soprano. Yvonne (Alice Nielsen), pursuing Alavardo as having jilted her, finally pairs off much more suitably with Lopez (William Philp, tenor) the secretary of the President of the Royal Madrid Brigandage Society, Romero (Eugene Cowles). Romero is an uncomfortable brigand: on alternate days he puts aside thieving and becomes a monk. Harry Brown appeared as Colombo, a former primo tenore now reduced to playing pantomime devils and giving singing lessons, and another Bostonians stalwart, George Frothingham, played the tailor Gomez, a hopeless suitor for Dolores's hand.

The feature of the score was, of course, the plotworthy serenade itself, 'I Love Thee, I Adore Thee', introduced by Dolores and Alvarado in the first act, and reprised lyrically, chorally by a group of monks and even comically (Colombo trying to teach it to the anxious Gomez) through the course of the evening. Romero had a baritone 'Song of the Carbine' and the tale of 'The Monk and the Maid', Yvonne gave out a bolero ('In Fair Andalusia') and a waltz ('Cupid and I'), Dolores sang of 'The Angelus' and the tenor Lopez a romance, 'I Envy the Bird', alongside a good ration of concerted music.

First played in Cleveland, Ohio (17 February), *The Serenade* came to Broadway a month later and played for 79 performances before being taken on the road as a popular part of the Bostonians' repertoire. *The Serenade* did not, however, follow *Robin Hood* to Europe. Alice Nielsen chose to tour her own production of *The Fortune Teller* with its large double-soprano lead rôle when she went to Britain, and *The Serenade* was seen only in Australia, where it was produced by George Musgrove, along with *The Fortune Teller*, in 1903. Like its fellow comic opera it starred Lillian Slapoffski in its soprano prima donna rôle whilst May Beatty (Dolores), J C Piddock (Alvarado), Edward Lauri (Duke), Jack Leumane (Colombo) and Lemprière Pringle (Romero) completed the principal cast of a production which left little mark.

Portions of *The Serenade* were later used, along with some of *The Fortune Teller*, to make up a 1946 portmanteau piece called *Gypsy Lady* (aka *Romany Love*, Robert Wright, George Forrest/Henry Myers) which went from its original production at the San Francisco and Los Angeles Light Opera to short runs on Broadway and in London.

Another piece, originally from Scandinavia, produced as *Serenade* (without the article) in England and advertised as 'the Swedish *Oklahoma!*' did not behave at all like *Oklahoma!* and folded on the road.

Australia: Princess Theatre, Melbourne 18 July 1903

SERGEANT BRUE

Musical farce in 3 acts by Owen Hall. Lyrics by J Hickory Wood. Music by Liza Lehmann. Additional music by James Tate and Ernest Vousden. Strand Theatre, London, 14 June 1904.

Producer Frank Curzon had scored a record-breaking success with his production of *A Chinese Honeymoon* at the Strand Theatre and, after that show had finished its run of more than 1,000 performances, he needed a follow-up piece which would continue to attract the audiences who had been wooed back to the old Strand Theatre. He hired top librettist Owen Hall and, in a surprising decision, paired him with Liza Lehmann, best known as a composer of drawing-room music (*In a Persian Garden* etc), and the result was a fine musical comedy of a certain quality.

Willie Edouin, the star of *Florodora*, made a memorable character of the amiable but not very crookworthy Sergeant Brue who needs to win promotion to the rank of Inspector before he can inherit a fine legacy. He gets a friendly burglar (Arthur Williams) to help him fake a capture and gets caught out but, when he accidentally stumbles upon the magistrate in charge of his case involved in illegal gambling, promotion arrives like lightning, bringing Brue both money and the hand of pretty Lady Bickenhall (Ethel Irving).

Miss Lehmann's songs imitated the popular models classily in pieces like 'The Twopenny Tube' and 'So Did Eve', but to her fury Curzon diluted her score with American popular songs ('The Sweetest Girl in Dixie', 'Under a Panama') and even British interpolations. It was not, however, any individual song which was the hit of *Sergeant Brue* but the performance of Edouin, and with him at its head the show quickly became a popular success. Unfortunately, Owen Hall was not content. He demanded that the show be transferred to a 'first class theatre' and Curzon was apparently contractually obliged to respond. *Sergeant Brue* moved to the Prince of Wales Theatre where he remained for the five months the theatre was available and then, in spite of Hall, moved back to the Strand. The show lasted 280 performances which might, without the vanity-salving moves, have been very many more.

A Broadway production with Frank Daniels in the title-rôle and Blanche Ring interpolating 'My Irish Molly O' (J Schwartz/W Jerome) into the rôle of Lady Bickenhall had a fair run of 93 performances; Rupert Clarke and Clyde Meynell introduced the show to Australia with Edwin Brett (Brue) and Ruth Lincoln (Lady Bickenhall) starred, and *Sergeant Brue* went on to be played throughout the other English-speaking outposts of the musical theatre to good effect.

USA: Knickerbocker Theater 24 April 1905; Australia: Criterion Theatre, Sydney 29 January 1910

SERMENT D'AMOUR

Opéra-comique in 3 acts by Maurice Ordonneau. Music by Edmond Audran. Théâtre des Nouveautés, Paris, 19 February 1886.

With the far-reaching successes of *La Mascotte* and *Gillette de Narbonne* and, most recently, the Paris production of *Le Grand Mogol*, composer Audran had secured a position on the heels of, if not quite alongside, Lecocq at the head of the list of the musical theatre's most fashionable composers of the 1880s. *Serment d'amour*, without ever becoming a major success, confirmed those pretensions thoroughly.

Ordonneau's libretto used some well-worn plot parts. A marquise with money in her sights tries to prevent her nephew from wedding the lowly Rosette by deceitfully marrying the girl off to Grivolin, a local peasant. But Grivolin's girlfriend, Marion, substitutes herself under the wedding veil and all ends happily. The score was bright, tuneful and often graceful, with the most popular number being the lively, ingenuous peasant rondo ('Holà, vertinguette! Holà, vertingué!') sung by the heroine in the first act (on the cue from the hero to 'sing one of the good old songs of our childhood'). Marguerite Ugalde and the baritone Morlet created the rôles of the lovers whose 'serment d'amour' is so tested, with Juliette Darcourt in the soprano rôle of the machinating Marquise and Albert Brasseur (Grivolin), Mlle Lantelme (Marion) and Berthelier as the comical marquisal steward, caught in an unwanted duel or drunkenly courting the heroine unwares, providing the comedy.

The show was well received and ran for a very respectable 104 performances in a season where the first run of *Joséphine vendue par ses soeurs* put up strong competition. By and large, however, it drew little attention from other centres, with the notable exception of America. American producers moved enthusiastically for *Serment d'amour*, with the result that two productions, differerently translated as *The Bridal Trap* (by Sydney Rosenfeld) and *The Crowing Hen* (John McCaull's Company) opened on Broadway within two days of each other. The two producers waged a battle across the street separating the their theatres, projecting unfavourable criticisms onto each others' façades with stereopticons. Rosenfeld, who had been involved in a similar fiasco not long before over *The Mikado*, and his producers went under first, but *The Crowing Hen*, in spite of a cast starring Mathilde Cottrelly, Bertha Ricci and De Wolf Hopper, was not far behind. Maurice Grau's opéra-bouffe company subsequently gave New Yorkers the French original at the Star Theater with Mary Pirard featured as Rosette.

USA: Bijou Theater *The Bridal Trap* May 31 1886, Wallack's Theater *The Crowing Hen* 29 May 1886

SERPETTE, [Henri Charles Antoine] Gaston (b Nantes, 4 November 1846; d Paris, 3 November 1904). Able and prolific French composer who never struck the big time.

Gaston Serpette originally studied for the law and qualified as a barrister but at the age of 22 he put aside barristering and enrolled at the Paris Conservatoire where he studied under, amongst others, Ambroise Thomas. He was awarded the prestigious Prix de Rome for his scène lyrique *Jeanne d'arc* (lib: Jules Barbier) in 1871 but, on his return to France following his scholarship period, he found, like other and more celebrated composers, difficulty in getting his stage works accepted by the moguls of the Opéra-Comique. When his first proper opérette, *La Branche cassée* (1874), was produced and played for more than 40 performances at the Bouffes-Parisiens and then in London, he decided to continue in the field of the light musical theatre and, over the next 30 years, he composed the scores for some 30 full-sized and one-act stage pieces. A number of these had some success in Paris, others were seen throughout central Europe, and a handful even made it further afield, but, unlike such of his comparable contemporaries as Vasseur and Varney, Serpette did not manage to produce one outstanding work which would find itself a place in the permanent repertoire.

Serpette's career and the careers of the shows which he composed were both curiously erratic. Amongst his early pieces, the vaudevillesque *Le Manoir du Pic-Tordu* failed in 14 performances in Paris, yet it went on to be seen in Berlin (*Schloss Pictordu*) and *La Petite Muette*, after an indifferent run in Paris, was played in both America and in Hungary. There was a considerable success for the spectacular London version of the old féerie *Rothomago* for which Serpette was invited to compose one act and the grandiose *Madame le Diable* (1882) had a fine run at the Théâtre de la Renaissance but, in the manner of the time, when it was adapted for the German-language stage (*Des Teufels Weib*), a fresh score by a local composer was substituted for the original.

A little one-acter called *La Princesse* proved popular, and was adapted into both German and Hungarian, but *Fanfreluche*, a rewrite of a piece originally produced in Brussels, disappointed in 46 Parisian performances. The 'opérette fantastique' *Le Château de Tire-Larigot*, which found Serpette back amongst devils and magic and lashings of stage effects brought another good Paris run which, in spite of its attractive score, cannot have been said to be wholly due to the show's musical attractions, whilst a further collaboration with authors Blum and Toché produced another picturesque piece in *Adam et Ève* which, helped by Louise Théo's appearance in the costume of Ève, was another to have a fairly good Paris run (80 performances) and an export to Budapest. *La Gamine de Paris* (75 performances) also did respectably at the Bouffes-Parisiens whilst the fairytale *Cendrillonnette* played 120 performances at the same theatre.

In the long run, the most successful of Serpette's works came, a little surprisingly, not in the area of the féerie or the spectacular, which had served him best in the first part of his career, but in the field of the vaudeville. Antony Mars and Maurice Desvallières's musical-comedy tale of *La Demoiselle du téléphone* was not only a Parisian success, but it travelled throughout Europe and (with its musical score being more and more replaced en route) to Britain, Australia and America. If the large part of the triumph went to his authors rather than to the composer, Serpette nevertheless had his share in the original success.

There was further success and progress to foreign productions for two other musical-comedy pieces, *Cousin-cousine* and *La Dot de Brigitte*, and for the spectacular devil-piece *Le Carnet du Diable* (*Das Scheckbuch des Teufels*), whilst the ancient Roman opérette *Le Capitole* was seen in Germany (*Metella*) and Hungary (*Az erenyes Metella*) and the latest rewrite of the spectacular girlie-show *Le Royaume des femmes*, for which he provided new music, played throughout Europe (*Das Paradies der Frauen*, *Die verkehrte Welt*, *Felfordult vilag*). Once again, however, as so often in the case of both spectacular pieces and vaudevilles, Serpette's score was often diluted or wholly replaced by local music.

A composer of undoubted skill, Serpette composed much music of unfailing taste and charm, finely orchestrated and apt, and he won a steady livelihood from the productions of his works in a solid and respectable career. It was perhaps the lack of a dash of individuality or imagination, of comic esprit, that prevented him from turning out one particular work which would be remembered beyond his lifetime.

1870 **Lucrèce Orgéat** Le Gaulois 5 April

1874 **La Branche cassée** (Adolphe Jaime, Jules Noriac) Théâtre des Bouffes-Parisiens 23 January

1875 **Le Manoir du Pic-Tordu** (Albert de Saint-Albin, Arnold Mortier) Théâtre des Variétés 28 May

1876 **Le Moulin du Vert Galant** (Eugène Grangé, Victor Bernard) Théâtre des Bouffes-Parisiens 10 April

1876 **La Petite Muette** (Paul Ferrier) Théâtre des Bouffes-Parisiens 3 October

1877 **Les Poupées parisiennes** (Gaston Marot, Henri Buguet) Théâtre Taitbout 7 February

1879 **Rothomago** (w Georges Jacobi et al/H B Farnie) Alhambra Theatre, London 22 December

1880 **La Nuit de Saint-Germain** (Gaston Hirsch, Raoul de Saint-Arroman) Théâtre des Fantaisies-Parisiennes, Brussels 20 March

1882 **Madame le Diable** (Henri Meilhac, A Mortier) Théâtre de la Renaissance 5 April

1883 **La Princesse** (Raoul Toché) 1 act Casino de Trouville 25 August, Théâtre des Variétés 22 October

1883 **Steeplechase** (Pierre Decourcelle) 1 act St Gratien 22 July

1883 **Tige de lotus** (Toché) 1 act Hôtel de la Rochefoucauld May, Casino de Contrexéville 26 July

1883 **Insomnie** (de Mayréna, Félix Cohen) 1 act Casino, Deauville 17 August

1883 **Fanfreluche** (Paul Burani, Hirsch, de St-Arroman) revised *La Nuit de Saint-Germain* Théâtre de la Renaissance 16 December

1884 **Mam'zelle Réséda** (Jules Prével) 1 act Théâtre de la Renaissance 2 February

1884 **Le Château de Tire-Larigot** (Ernest Blum, Toché) Théâtre des Nouveautés 30 October

1885 **Le Petit Chaperon Rouge** (Blum, Toché) Théâtre des Nouveautés 10 October

1886 **Le Singe d'un nuit d'été** (Édouard Noël) 1 act Théâtre des Bouffes-Parisiens 1 September

1886 **Adam et Ève** (Blum, Toché) Théâtre des Nouveautés 6 October

1887 **La Lycéenne** (Georges Feydeau) Théâtre des Nouveautés 23 December

1887 **La Gamine de Paris** (Eugène Leterrier, Albert Vanloo) Théâtre des Bouffes-Parisiens 30 March

1890 **Cendrillonnette** (w Victor Roger/Ferrier) Théâtre des Bouffes-Parisiens 24 January

1891 **La Demoiselle du téléphone** (Antony Mars, Maurice Desvallières) Nouveautés 2 May

1892 **Mé-na-ka** (Ferrier) 1 act Théâtre des Nouveautés 2 May

1892 **La Bonne de chez Duval** (Mars, Hippolyte Raymond) Théâtre des Nouveautés 6 October

1893 **Cousin-cousine** (Maurice Ordonneau, Henri Kéroul) Théâtre des Folies-Dramatiques 23 December

1895 **Pincette** (Raoul) 1 act Théâtre de la Bodinière 4 January

1895 **Chiquita** (Charles Clairville) 1 act Théâtre des Nouveautés 4 February

1895 **La Dot de Brigitte** (w Victor Roger/Mars, Ferrier) Théâtre des Bouffes-Parisiens 6 May

1895 **Le Carnet du Diable** (Blum, Ferrier) Théâtre des Variétés 23 October

1895 **Le Capitole** (Ferrier, Clairville) Théâtre des Nouveautés 5 December

1896 **Le Royaume des femmes** (Cogniard ad Ferrier, Blum) Eldorado 24 February

1896 **Le Carillon** (Ferrier, Blum) Théâtre des Variétés 7 November

1898 **Le Tour du bois** (Jules Oudot, Henri de Gorsse) Théâtre des Variétés 3 June

1899 **Shakespeare!** (Paul Gavault, P-L Flers) Théâtre des Bouffes-Parisiens 23 November

1903 **Amorelle** (1810) (Barton White/Ernest Boyd-Jones) Kennington Theatre, England 8 June

SEVENTEEN Musical in 2 acts by Sally Benson based on the play by Stanislaus Stange and Stannard Mears and the novel by Booth Tarkington. Lyrics by Kim Gannon. Music by Walter Kent. Broadhurst Theater, New York, 21 June 1951.

Booth Tarkington's 1916 novel of very young and quite catastrophic love between wide-eyed Willie Baxter (Gregory Kelly) and fluffy, appalling Lola Pratt (Ruth Gordon) was a considerable success as a Broadway stage play (Booth Theater, 22 January 1918, 225 performances), was made up into a silent movie (Jack Pickford, Louise Huff, 1917) and later into a 1925 musical, *Hello, Lola* (Broad Street Theater, Newark, 16 November; Eltinge Theater, 12 January 1926) in an adaptation by Dorothy Donnelly with music by William Kernell. Edythe Baker and Richard Keene starred for some 60 performances. The well-loved tale made it to the cinema screen again in 1940 (Jackie Cooper, Betty Field) and it was then given a second chance in a musical adaptation, produced on Broadway by Milton Berle, Sammy Lambert and Bernie Foyer. Another well-established lady writer, Sally Benson, author of the successful magazine tales which became the play *Junior Miss*, was responsible for the adaptation, with songs by Kim Gannon, the lyricist of a number of 1940s Hollywood songs ('Moonlight Cocktail', title-song of *Always in My Heart* w Ernesto Lecuona, 'The Lady who Didn't Believe in Love' w Jule Styne, 'It Can't Be Wrong' in *Now Voyager* etc) and Walter Kent, the composer of Vera Lynn's anthem 'The White Cliffs of Dover' (w Nat Burton).

Kenneth Nelson starred as Willie, desperate for a dress suit and for the fluttering eyes and tortured consonants of Lola (Ann Crowley), with Frank Albertson and Doris Dalton as his parents, Harrison Muller as the slick, Yale competition for Lola's favours and Maurice Ellis as the family handyman, in a version which kept the play's homey, sentimental atmosphere whilst topping it up with some more conventional musical-comedy elements and a score which included such titles as 'Things Are Gonna Hum This Summer', 'Summertime is Summertime', 'After All, it's Spring' and 'If We Could Only Stop the Old Town Clock'. The musical *Seventeen* ran 182 performances in a disappointing Broadway season.

Recording: original cast (RCA)

1776 Musical in 7 scenes by Peter Stone based on an idea by Sherman Edwards. Music and lyrics by Sherman Edwards. 46th Street Theater, New York, 16 March 1969.

The musical tale of *1776* follows the efforts of the secessionist bloc in the American Continental Congress to progressively persuade or purchase each of the undecided or opposing members of the house into signing his name to the Declaration of Independence. The abrasive and unpopular John Adams (William Daniels), the unquestioned leader of the movement, is persuaded by the more reasonable Benjamin Franklin (Howard da Silva) to let Virginia's high-spirited Richard Henry Lee (Ron Holgate) put forward the motion for Independency, ultimately formulated into a document by the young Thomas Jefferson (Ken Howard). The voting begins, the tally swings one way and then the next, and the anti-secessionists under John Dickinson (Paul Hecht) lose ground until the whole game is thrown open by the decision that the vote must be unanimous. But, by the final curtain, the document that

Plate 242. *1776: Cheryl Kennedy (Martha Jefferson) whirls between David Kernan (Edward Rutledge) and Ronald Radd (Benjamin Franklin).*

creates the independent United States of America is being signed.

With little suspense possible about the outcome of the musical's action, the interest of the show resided in the way the famous characters were depicted, how they retained their credibility in spite of bursting into song, and how the long lucubrations of 18th-century politicians could be made both dramatic and interesting. Adams, irascible and unpersuasively bigoted in politics, kept his impatience in check in a series of letters to his wife Abigail (Virginia Vestoff), Jefferson piaffed with impatience to get away from Congress and back to his bright young bride (Betty Buckley), Lee was represented as gauchely enthusiastic, Dickinson as severely dignified and honourable, Franklin – equipped with the bald patch and flowing locks – as a crinkly paterfamilias, amongst a Congress in which each member was individually characterized. The ins and outs of their plotting and voting were contrasted with a handful of outside scenes, notably Jefferson's reunion with Martha and a glimpse of the war against the British as described by a little messenger ('Momma, Look Sharp').

The show's musical part moved rarely into conventional song in what was, naturally, a male-voice dominated score. Adams soliloquized ('Till Then', 'Is Anybody There?'), Lee exuberated ('The Lees of Old Virginia'), Rutledge of Southern Carolina (Clifford David) fulminated against the North's selfish attempt to abolish slavery ('Molasses to Rum'), Congress chattered ('Piddle, Twiddle and Resolve') and harmonized, whilst Martha Jefferson made the most extractable contribution to the score with the dancing waltz song 'He Plays the Violin', describing her husband's attractions with only a twinkle of double meaning.

1776 was a long time coming to the stage. It had originally been written wholly by Edwards, a former history major and teacher, in the early 1960s, and it had since gone through a long series of 'developments', but by the time it reached Broadway it was clear that the authors had succeeded in surmounting all and any of the odds against them, and *1776* was in the shape to win a run of 1,217 performances, followed by more than two years of tours, a film in which Daniels, da Silva, Howard and Miss Vestoff repeated their stage performances, and a London

reproduction by the Broadway team. Lewis Fiander (Adams), Ronald Radd (Franklin), John Quentin (Jefferson) and Cheryl Kennedy (Martha) were featured, but the subject matter did not have the same interest for Britain and the piece ran for only 168 performances. That did not stop Australia from trying its hand at the show, but a ten-week season in Melbourne, followed by just four weeks in Sydney (Theatre Royal, 11 September 1971), proved its appeal limited there, too.

The title *1776* had previously been used for an 1884 Broadway musical (Ludwig Englander/Leo Goldmark) produced in German at the Thalia Theater (26 February) with Austria's top musical-comedy star, Marie Geistinger, starred. It was later played under the title *Adjutant James* and in 1895 revised and revived at the Broadway Theater, in English, as *The Daughter of the Revolution* (27 May).

UK: New Theatre 16 June 1970; Australia: Her Majesty's Theatre, Melbourne 26 June 1971; Film; Columbia 1972
Recordings: original cast (Columbia), London cast (Columbia), film soundtrack (Columbia)

70, GIRLS, 70 Musical in 2 acts by Fred Ebb and Norman J Martin based on the play *Breath of Spring* by Peter Coke as adapted by Joe Masteroff. Lyrics by Fred Ebb. Music by John Kander. Broadhurst Theater, New York, 15 April 1971.

Coke's comical play about a group of naughty geriatrics who turn to crime was produced at London's Cambridge Theatre in 1958 with Athene Seyler as Dame Beatrice Appleby and Elspeth Duxbury in memorable support. It had a 430-performance run, was regularly revived, and filmed as *Make Mine Mink* (1959) with the same two stars featured before being adapted as a Broadway musical.

Resituated in a New York City venue, its characters declassed, and illustrated with some lively, revusical Kander and Ebb songs ranging from a spiritual ('Believe') to a topical 'Coffee in a Cardboard Cup' and a regulation New York number ('Broadway, My Street'), the now confusingly re-titled *70, Girls, 70* was produced by Arthur Whitelaw with Mildred Natwick and David Burns starring. Burns died before the show reached town, and *70, Girls, 70* survived only a month on Broadway. The popularity of Kander and Ebb's best works meant, however, that it had further chances. *70, Girls, 70* was subsequently played regionally in America and in 1990 was seen for the first time in Britain in the tented studio theatre adjoined to the Chichester Festival Theatre, with Dora Bryan starred. That production, with Miss Bryan playing merry Oldham with the text in what became virtually a stand-up comedy show, later played a short run in the West End and toured.

UK: Chichester Festival Theatre 27 June 1990, Vaudeville Theatre, London 17 June 1991
Recordings: original cast (Columbia), London cast (TER)

SEYMOUR, Katie [SEYMOUR, Catherine Phoebe Mary Hollorand] (b London, ?1870; d London, 7 September 1903).

The pretty dancing soubrette Katie Seymour appeared on the stage as a child, worked in the music halls and pantomime from the age of 12 and appeared for C J Abud in *Blue-Eyed Susan* (1892, Rosy Morn) and for George Edwardes in *Joan of Arc* (1891, Blanche d'Arc) and *Don Juan* (1893, Zoë, t/o Donna Julia) before she became a

West End favourite in her partnership with the Gaiety's chief comic, Edmund Payne. They scored a great hit together in the song and dance 'Love on the Japanese Plan' in *The Shop Girl* (1894, Miss Robinson), and Miss Seymour became the Gaiety's principal soubrette-dancer through *My Girl* (Phoebe Toodge), *The Circus Girl* (Lucille, the wire walker) and *The Messenger Boy* (Rosa), in each of which she was paired with enormous success with Payne. She made a sole Broadway appearance when she was added to the cast of *The Casino Girl* after its rewrite, and toured to South Africa with a musical comedy company including John Le Hay and Frank Celli shortly before her death at the age of 33-ish.

SHAKESPEARE! Opérette-bouffe in 3 acts by Paul Gavault and P-L Flers. Music by Gaston Serpette. Théâtre des Bouffes-Parisiens, Paris, 23 November 1899.

The Shakespeare of the title of Serpette's opérette-bouffe was not William, but a dog. A specifically English dog, for the English were both the villains and the buffoons of Gavault and Flers's libretto, and also a dog who had only a little, if crucial, part to play in what was a piece of standard operettic high jinks, of disguises and amorous combinations, set on the island of Gibraltar.

The travelling salesman Brutus (Jean Périer), his wife Éponine (Mariette Sully) and the Spanish dancer Consuéla (Anna Tariol-Baugé) go to Gibraltar to rescue Consuéla's lover, Miguel (Alberthal), who has attempted to retake the island for Spain, been captured by the Governor (Régnard) but spared extinction through the intervention of his amorous wife (Léonie Laporte). The conspirators impersonate Lord Winning-Post (Vavasseur), his niece (Maud d'Orby) who is coming to Gibraltar to wed Jack (Maurice Lamy), and her maid (Evelyne Janney), and when the real English turn up chaos and counter-accusations reign until the real English are recognized by their dog, Shakespeare. A little amorous blackmail, however, secures everyone's release in time for the final curtain.

Serpette provided Mme Tariol-Baugé with several Spanish-flavoured pieces ('Fleur d'Andalousie'), Périer and Mlle Sully with vivacious numbers to suit their vivacious rôles, and the comical pair of Régnard and Mlle Laporte with opportunities to play the low heavies in a score which also offered a good ration of concerted music and which didn't bother standing around singing love songs when there was comedy to be mined.

Shakespeare! was produced at the Bouffes-Parisiens by MM Coudert and Berny and found a ready audience for its gaiety and its starry cast, the principals of whom had recently been the darlings of the town as the stars of the same theatre's triumphant *Véronique*. *Shakespeare!*, however, did not have the same future as *Véronique*. It closed after 65 performances, and with that closure its 53-year-old composer exited from the Parisian theatre to which he had supplied much happy and successful music without securing the one important hit which might have helped his name endure.

SHAKESPEARE, William (b Stratford-upon-Avon, 26 April ?1564; d Stratford-upon-Avon, 23 April 1616)

The most famous of English-language dramatists borrowed the source material for a large number of his plays from the works of earlier writers, and his own body of work, in its turn, was incessantly plundered both for the operatic and light musical stage of later years.

The most successful operas based on his works included Gounod's *Roméo et Juliette*, Ambroise Thomas's *Hamlet*, Verdi's versions of *Othello*, *Macbeth* and *Falstaff*, Berlioz's *Béatrice et Bénédict*, Otto Nicolai's *Die lustige Weiber von Windsor*, Vaughan Williams's *Sir John in Love*, Charles Villers Stanford's *Much Ado About Nothing* and Benjamin Britten's *A Midsummer Night's Dream*. *The Taming of the Shrew* was operaticized in half-a-dozen languages, Spain produced an *Otello y Desdemona* (Manuel Nieto, 1883), Ambroise Thomas and Leoncavallo both tackled *A Midsummer Night's Dream*, and *Twelfth Night* went from being metamorphosed into a *Cesario* in Düsseldorf to a swatch of *Viola*s in various other parts of Germany and a *Malvolio* in Melbourne, Australia. However, the adaptation of Shakespeare to the lighter stage, an exercise practised mostly outside his native Britain (which has limited itself to vivisecting his texts and/or gussying them up in gimmicky productions), has by and large proven much less effective.

The very bare skeleton of *Romeo and Juliet*, set in different times and places, was the basis for two hit musicals in *The Belle of Mayfair* and *West Side Story*, whilst a production of a musical version of *The Taming of the Shrew* made up the play-within-a-play of *Kiss Me, Kate* and its parallel framework. *A Comedy of Errors* was used as the raw material for the Rodgers and Hart musical *The Boys from Syracuse*, Julian Slade's London comic opera *A Comedy of Errors* (Arts Theatre, 28 March 1956), and the up-dated *Oh, Brother!* (Michael Valenti/Donald Driver ANTA Theater, New York 1981). In Britain, a fine musical adaptation of *The Merchant of Venice* produced as *Shylock* at the Edinburgh Festival was destroyed when glossied up into *Fire Angel* for the West End and the play's casket episode was used for the Players' Theatre *The Three Caskets, or Venice re-Served* (Peter Greenwell/Gordon Snell 5 November 1956), whilst another *Romeo and Juliet* derivative, *R Loves J* was launched at the Chichester Festival in 1973 and also produced in Germany.

A rash of mod-musicalized Shakespeare in 1960s–70s America turned out a *Twelfth Night* variant called *Your Own Thing* (1968), and a John Guare/Mal Shapiro/Galt MacDermott *Two Gentlemen of Verona* (1971) on the credit side, and very much more on the debit. There were two further *Twelfth Night*s in *Love and Let Love* (S J Gelber/John Lollos, Don Christopher Sheridan Square Playhouse 1968, 14 performances) and *Music Is* (Richard Adler/Will Holt/George Abbott St James Theater, 1976); *A Midsummer Night's Dream* was metamorphosed into *Babes in the Wood* (Rick Besoyan, Orpheum Theater, 1964) and there were a risible Canadian *Rockabye Hamlet* (aka *Kronborg, Something's Rockin' in Denmark*, Cliff Jones, Charlottetown Festival, Canada, 1974), a one-performance *As You Like It* (John Balamos/Dran Seitz, Tani Seitz) played at the Theater de Lys, yet another shaken-and-stirred *Romeo and Juliet* under the title *Sensations* (Wally Harper/Paul Zakrzewski, New York, 1970), *The Tempest* served up as *Dreamstuff* (Marsha Malamet/Dennis Green/Howard Ashman, WPA Theater, New York, 1976), *A Musical Merchant of Venice* (Jim Smith/Tony Tanner, Roundabout Theater 1975) which lasted 13 performances and a *King Lear* made, presumably with a straight face, into *Pop* (Donna Cribari/Larry Schiff, Chuck Knull, New York,

Plate 243. **Shakespeare**'s The Merchant of Venice *became a musical as* Shylock. *Author Paul Bentley was Shylock in the 1982 production at Manchester's Library Theatre.*

1974) which also survived one performance. In spite of its obvious bankruptcy, the trend crept into the 1980s with a piece called *Ta-Dah!* (1981) which quoted *Much Ado About Nothing* as its source. A Los-Angeles-initiated version of *Othello* (*Catch My Soul*, Ahamson Theater 5 March 1968) went further than any of this group, being later seen in both London and Paris.

In earlier times, Shakespeare was offered as being at the basis of the plots of the successful French opérette *Gillette de Narbonne* and, more surprisingly, the British song-and-dance low-comedy *The Dairymaids* (in the latter case a microscope was necessary to find a similarity with *As You Like It*, but Shakespeare's name doubtless looked good in the publicity), whilst in Hungary one of the more unlikely candidates for a musical treatment, *Pericles*, was made into a operett under the title *A fekete hajó* (György Banffy/Jenő Rákosi Népszinház, 1883) and in Germany *Twelfth Night* was used as the basis for *Viola*, a 'comic opera with ballet' by Richard Genée, music by Adolf Arensen (Stadttheater, Hamburg, 16 March 1893) and again in 1963 for *Was ihr wollt, oder Die Schiffbrüchigen von Illyrien* (Klaus Fehmel/ Günther Deicke, Theater der Freundschaft, Berlin, 4 October 1963). *The Taming of the Shrew* was musicalized in 1896 for the Spanish stage by J Lopez Silva and Ruperto Chapí under the title *Las bravias*.

Other 20th-century derivatives have included a disastrous attempt at *Swingin' the Dream* (1939) in which Erik Charell had a glossy hand, a British provincial piece which decided that the characters of *The Merchant of Venice* were *The Gay Venetians*, a rock opera which insisted there were *Drei Herren aus Verona* (H C Artmann, Nicolas Brieger

Städtische Bühnen, Nuremberg, 16 June 1972), a French-language version of *Love's Labours Lost* mounted at the Brussels Théâtre de la Monnaie, another *Shylock* which appeared off-Broadway at the York Theater (23 April 1987, Ed Dixon) and *The Merry Wives of Windsor, Texas*, a western musical produced by a clutch of writers at Houston's Alley Theater (1 December 1988).

In 1989 a TV-space-age pastiche of the plot of *The Tempest* and aged pop tunes was brought into London's West End (Cambridge Theatre, 18 September) as *Return to the Forbidden Planet*. It caught the upswing of 1950s/1960s nostalgia, and scored surprise British success before going on to be played in America, Australia and Germany (as *Shakespeare und Rock 'n' Roll*).

Given his domination of the serious stage, Shakespeare's works were not too often maltreated by the makers of 19th-century burlesque. *Hamlet* was the play which was given the most attention, beginning with Poole's landmark *Hamlet Travestie* (1810) which made the Dane's celebrated soliloquy into a song. There followed *Hamlet à la mode* (G Lash Gordon, G W Anson, Liverpool, 1877) and William Yardley's *Very Little Hamlet* (Gaiety Theatre, 1884) and, in Vienna, a successful Strampfertheater *Hammlet* (Richard Genée/Julius Hopp) in which Felix Schweighofer appeared as the hero. Most of the other principal Shakespeare parodies belonged to the earlier age of burlesque. Poole's burlesque of Hamlet was followed by Maurice Dowling's highly successful *Othello Travestie* (Strand Theatre 1834), Gilbert a' Beckett tried his hand with *King John* (St James's Theatre, 1837), Dowling followed up with a *Romeo and Juliet* (Strand, 1838) and

Andrew Halliday did the same some 20 years later at the same theatre (*Romeo and Juliet Travestie, or The cup of cold poison*, 1859) with Marie Wilton as Juliet. *Richard III* was 'done' twice, by Charles Selby and Stirling Coyne in 1844, and again by F C Burnand (*The Rise and Fall of Richard III, or A new front to an old Dicky*, Royalty 1868), Francis Talfourd did *Macbeth, somewhat removed from the Text of Shakespeare* (Strand 1848) and the Brough brothers turned *The Tempest* into a popular extravaganza, *The Enchanted Isle, or raising the wind on the most approved principles* (Adelphi Theatre, 1848). This piece, introduced by Mr Stewart in the character of the ghost of Shakespeare, featured Priscilla Horton as Ariel and Buckstone as Caliban, burlesquing Lablache, the star of Halévy's operatic version of *The Tempest*, and managed to slide in a parody of *Hamlet* amongst its various burlesques.

F C Burnand later gave his version of the same piece in *Ariel* (with Nellie Farren as the sprite introducing electric light to the Gaiety stage) and also tackled *Antony and Cleopatra* (Haymarket 1866, Gaiety Theatre 1873). In 1853 the Strand Theatre mounted a *King Queer and his Daughters Three* whilst Talfourd initiated *The Merchant of Venice* to the burlesque stage in *Shylock* (Olympic, 1853), but perhaps the most successful of the Shakespeare burlesques of this period was William Brough's *Perdita, or the Royal Milkmaid* (Lyceum, 1856) taken from *A Winter's Tale*. From the 1870s onwards, burlesques of Shakespeare were largely limited to the more unsophisticated circuits, and pieces like *Romeo the Radical and Juliet the Jingo* (1882) kept to the touring lists, but in 1899 George Grossmith and Paul Rubens perpetrated a West End piece called *Great Caesar* (Comedy Theatre, 29 April 1899) which had as much to do with Shakespeare's play as previous parodies of the tale of the favourite military dictator of ancient Rome had done.

Shakespeare was also the victim of what may have been the earliest example of a compilation show in the modern musical theatre. London was treated to an Easter show in 1853 which billed itself as 'an historical, musical and illustrated entertainment', *Leaves from the Life and Lays from the Lyre of William Shakespeare. Will!* might have been more inviting. Or not.

The playwright himself has appeared only occasionally on the musical stage, but oddly enough not in the only musical which was called, simply, *Shakespeare!* The Shakespeare of Gaston Serpette's 1899 opérette was not an author, but a dog. An English dog, though. Nor, in spite of being a moving element in the plot, was Will an on-stage character in the 1948 musical comedy *The Kid from Stratford*. In Britain, Martin Adeson played Shakespeare in George Edwardes's *The Merry-Go-Round* (1899) which stayed shy of the West End, Miles Malleson was a plump Shakespeare alongside Beatrice Lillie in *Now and Then* (1921), Conway Dixon a baritonically intrusive one in Eddie Knoblock's remake of *Merrie England* (1946), and Derek Godfrey was the burlesqued Bard in *No Bed for Bacon* (1959), whilst in America William Castle was a 19th-century Shakespeare to the Queen Elizabeth I of Emilie Melville in the 1877 *A Summer Night's Dream* (Fifth Avenue Theater 15 October). The Broadway musical's most enduring Shakespearean reference, however, remains a passive one: *Kiss Me, Kate*'s instruction to 'Brush Up Your Shakespeare'.

SHAMUS O'BRIEN, a story of Ireland 100 years ago Romantic comic opera in 2 acts and 3 tableaux by George H Jessop based on the poem by Joseph Sheridan Le Fanu. Music by Charles Villiers Stanford. Opera Comique, London, 2 March 1896.

The Irish-American writer George Jessop had turned out a long run of pieces for the American theatre, including some with an Irish flavour, but nothing that presaged the agreeable and touching libretto with which he provided the well-considered British composer Charles Villiers Stanford (*The Canterbury Pilgrims* etc) for the latter's one attempt at writing for the lighter lyric stage. *Shamus O'Brien* was described as a romantic comic opera, but its central story was a dramatic one. The rebel Shamus O'Brien (Denis O'Sullivan) is betrayed to the British by Mike Murphy (Joseph O'Mara) who then courts his wife, Nora (Kirkby Lunn), with promises of securing her husband's release. When O'Brien escapes, Murphy is killed trying to stop him. That drama was thinned with a heavy dose of flirting and singing from the soubrette, Kitty (Maggie Davies), who chases the English Captain (William Trevor) while he unwillingly pusues Shamus. Stanford's music steered a course between the operatic and folk-music styles in a score in which the patriotic songs of Shamus ('I've Sharpened the Sword for the Sake of Ould Erin') and the pert soubrette melodies ('Where is the Man Who is Coming to Marry Me?') were contrasted with some truly dramatic moments for the contralto rôle of Nora, and which did not shrink from quoting genuine Irish folk airs.

Produced by its authors in collaboration with the publishers Boosey & Co, *Shamus O'Brien* was cast with students from the Royal College of Music. All three leading players went on to memorable careers, Miss Lunn in the operatic world, O'Sullivan on the musical stage until an early death, and O'Mara at the head of his own touring opera company. The production was largely well-received and, at the height of the craze for musical comedy, was played 82 times in London before going on to New York where O'Sullivan and O'Mara were teamed with Annie Roberts and G B Shaw's sister, Lucy Carr-Shaw (Kitty), for a 56-performance Broadway season. In 1897 it was toured through Ireland, under the management of Ben Greet with Eone Delrita starred, and the following year in England with the Savoy Theatre's Leonora Braham as Nora, Avalon Collard as Mike and Frank E Tours conducting.

In 1910 *Shamus O'Brien* was played in repertoire by the Beecham Opera Company with Albert Archdeacon, Edith Evans and O'Mara, and it was for many years also seen in the repertoire of O'Mara's own company. In 1930 it was broadcast by the BBC, but in spite of its composer's respected name, it has since been ignored professionally. In 1960 it was played by the BBC Club Operatic Society at St George's Hall (6 October).

USA: Broadway Theater 5 January 1897

SHARMAN, Jim [SHARMAN, James David] (b Sydney, 12 March 1945).

Australian-born director Sharman entered the musical theatre in his own country when he was hired to direct Harry M Miller's Australian versions of *Hair* and *Jesus Christ Superstar*. The success of the latter resulted in his being asked to stage the subsequent record-breaking London version of the show, and he followed this by mounting the original production of another of the 1970s' most enduring London successes, *The Rocky Horror Show*. He repeated his *Rocky Horror Show* assignment in America and on the subsequent cult film, but was thereafter seen rarely in the musical theatre until he directed a partially rewritten version of *Chess* in Sydney in 1989.

SHAW, George Bernard (b Dublin, 26 July 1856; d Ayot St Lawrence, 2 November 1950).

In spite of the fact that his mother was a singer and music teacher and that his sister, Lucy Carr-Shaw, had a respectable career, mostly as a provincial leading lady, in the musical theatre, G B Shaw professed a lofty disdain for the genre. In his career as a critic, he rarely had a good word to say for even the most successful musical plays, he rejected an 1895 offer to write a libretto with the comment that star Arthur Roberts was 'better at inventing lines than speaking other folks' (Jerome K Jerome took the job), and he insisted that it was impossible for any of his own works to be made into an example of the despised genre. By the time *My Fair Lady* demonstrated posthumously what a perfect musical-comedy style of writing he had, Shaw had already been healthily proven wrong, in his own lifetime, by librettists Rudolf Bernauer and Leopold Jacobson and composer Oscar Straus with their 'unauthorized' adaptation of *Arms and the Man* as *Der tapfere Soldat*. It must indeed have hurt the snooty dramatist's feelings to see his plot and dialogue, re-Englished from the German by Liverpudlian American Stanislaus Stange as *The Chocolate Soldier*, piling up long and successful runs both on Broadway and in London, runs which far outdid those established by his original play.

The success of *My Fair Lady* provoked surprisingly few attempts to musicalize other Shaw works. After a British musical on *Caesar and Cleopatra* (1899), written by Kitty Black and Michael Flanders and composed by Manos Hadzidakis, had failed to get off the drawing board in 1961, another version entitled *Her First Roman* (Lunt-Fontanne Theater, 20 October 1968) made it to Broadway for 17 performances. A musical *Androcles and the Lion* composed by Richard Rodgers (1967) was restricted to television, whilst a version of *The Admirable Bashville* (1903) slimmed to *Bashville* (Denis King/Benny Green) was produced at London's Regent's Park Open Air Theatre (2 August 1983). The same team of King and Green also musicalized Shaw's *You Never Can Tell* under the title of *Valentine's Day* (lib: Green, David Williams, Queen's Theatre, 17 September 1992).

The German-language stage followed up *Der tapfere Soldat* with a comic-opera version of *Great Catherine* (*Die grosse Katharine* Ignaz Lihén/Trebitsch, Maril Staatstheater, Wiesbaden, 8 May 1932), and a second successful version of *Arms and the Man* called *Helden, Helden* (Udo Jürgens/Eckart Hachfeld, Walter Brandin, Hans Gmür, Theater an der Wien, 23 October 1972), whilst *Mrs Warren's Profession* became *Frau Warrens Gewerbe* (Charles Kálmán/Peter Goldbaum) at the Theater am Dom, Cologne (23 December 1974).

Shaw was portrayed on the musical stage by John Neville when Britain's Nottingham Playhouse mounted a biomusical of the playwright (Johnny Dankworth/Benny Green) under the title *Boots with Strawberry Jam* (28 February 1968).

SHAW, Oscar [SCHWARZ, Oscar] (b Philadelphia, 1889; d Little Neck, NY, 6 March 1967).

After beginning his career as a chorus boy in revue, dapperly handsome Shaw had a career of nearly 20 years as a Broadway leading man. Early credits in *The Girl and the Wizard* (1909, Max Andressen), *The Kiss Waltz* (1911, Albert), *Two Little Brides* (1912, Deschamps) and in London in revue, prefaced his first important assignments as Dick Rivers, the love-smacked straight man of *Very Good Eddie* (1915, 'Some Sort of Somebody', 'If I Find the Girl') and Stub Talmadge, the football-mad fun of *Leave it to Jane* (1917, 'The Sun Shines Brighter', 'A Peach of a Life'). There was less success for him in 47 performances as Tommy Tilson, forced to wed *The Rose of China* for having seen her unveiled (1919), and just one night more as Bradford Adams whose self-made papa doesn't want him to wed society in *The Half Moon* (1920), but he had successes in both Youmans's *Two Little Girls in Blue* (1920, 'Oh Me! Oh My!') and as socialite hero Billy van Courtlandt in Kern's *Good Morning Dearie* (1920, 'Blue Danube Blues', 'Kailua').

What remained of the rôle of Bastien in *One Kiss* (1923, ex-*Ta bouche*) and *Dear Sir* (1924, Laddie Munn) were less productive jobs, but 1926 brought him his most memorable creation of all as the beleaguered bridegroom Jimmy Winters in *Oh, Kay!* introducing 'Do, Do, Do' and 'Maybe' alongside Gertrude Lawrence's Kay. He followed up as Gerald Brooks, the hero of *The Five O'Clock Girl* (1927, 'Thinking of You'), as Tom Addison in *Flying High* (1930, 'Thank Your Father') and, finally, as Steve Addison in *Everybody's Welcome* (1931) before, now in his forties, being forced by nature to drop out of the line of juvenile-to-lead men he had played for a decade and a half. He toured alongside Harriette Lake (aka Ann Sothern) in the rôle of Wintergreen in *Of Thee I Sing* in 1932, but thereafter faded from the scene.

On the musical screen, he appeared as the Brylcreemy juvenile man to the antics of the Marx brothers in *The Cocoanuts*.

SHEAN, Al [SCHÖNBERG, Albert] (b ?Dornum, Germany, 12 May 1868; d New York, 12 August 1949).

A popular 'dutch' vaudeville comedian, who found fame in partnership with Ed Gallagher, Al Shean also appeared in a number of musicals. The first of these (pre-Gallagher) was Harry von Tilzer's inept *The Fisher Maiden* (1903), the second, the touring *The Isle of Bong Bong*, and the first of consequence (with Gallagher), was the highly successful American version of Granichstädten's *Bub oder Mädel?* (1912), *The Rose Maid*, in which they appeared (with Eugene Redding and Arthur Laceby) as a quartet of iffy 'loan brokers and bankers' who have the show's extravagant hero in their comical grip. He later appeared (post-Gallagher) in Victor Herbert's *The Princess Pat* (1915, Anthony Schmalz) and the surprise success *Flo-Flo* (1917, Isidor Moser).

A reconstitution of the team brought the famous song

'Mr Gallagher and Mr Shean' to light and gave the pair the most prominent moment of their careers, performing in the *Ziegfeld Follies of 1922*. After a second split, Shean later returned to the musical comedy stage in the shortlived *Betsy* (1926, Stonewall Moskowitz), starred in one of the best of all Broadway 'dutch' rôles as Hans Wagner in a revival of *The Prince of Pilsen* (1930) and as the genuinely and only gently comical Austrian Dr Walther Lessing in the Broadway strudel-operetta *Music in the Air* (1932). As late as 1946 he appeared on the musical stage as Gramps O'Brien in *Windy City*.

Shean was seen on the musical screen in such films as *San Francisco* (1936), *The Great Waltz* (1938) and *Ziegfeld Girl* (1941).

SHE LOVES ME   Musical by Joe Masteroff based on the play *Illatszertár* by Miklós László. Lyrics by Sheldon Harnick. Music by Jerry Bock. Eugene O'Neill Theater, New York, 23 April 1963.

László's 1937 play *Illatszertár*, a piece about two perfume shopworkers who cordially dislike each other but who are unknowingly engaged in a lonelyhearts correspondence which leads them to a happy ending, was first produced at Budapest's Pesti Színház (20 March) and was subsequently made into a Hollywood film (*The Shop Around the Corner*, 1940) with James Stewart and Margaret Sullavan starred. A second film version entitled *In the Good Old Summertime* (1949) was equipped with songs.

In 1963 the piece was made into a stage musical. Barbara Cook played Amalia Balash, warm and wonderful, and Daniel Massey was Georg Nowack, quiet and capable. But apparently incompatible. Alongside them were their gleamingly plastic co-worker, Steve Kodály (Jack Cassidy), who is currently knocking off both the wife of the boss (Ludwig Donath) and another perfumery clerk Ilona Ritter (Barbara Baxley), the more straightforward Ladislaw Sipos (Nathaniel Frey) and the boy Árpád László (Ralph Williams) with longings to rise to be a clerk. As Amalia and Georg head through the usual misunderstandings towards their happy ending, the boss tries to shoot himself because of nasty Steve, who is ultimately sacked and vanishes from the story leaving Ilona free to become more decently attached. Árpád gets the vacant job.

The songs which accompanied everyone's progress to happiness were a curious mixture, ranging from gentle, pastelly pieces of charm for the heroine ('Ice Cream', 'Dear Friend') and equally ingenuous if neatly brighter ones for her partner ('She Loves Me') to some harsh and almost crude numbers for Steve and Ilona. There was not a large amount of ensemble music and the show's chorus intruded little.

Harold Prince's production of *She Loves Me*, directed by its producer and advertised slightly curiously or even ungrammatically as 'the happiest new musical', played 302 performances on Broadway and it was subsequently produced in London where Anne Rogers (Amalia), Gary Raymond (Georg), Gary Miller (Steve) and Rita Moreno (Ilona) featured through an indifferent 189 performances. It was later telefilmed by Britain's Channel 4 with Gemma Craven as Amalia.

UK: Lyric Theatre 29 April 1964
Recordings: original cast (MGM/DRG), London cast (HMV)

SHENANDOAH   Musical in 2 acts by James Lee Barrett, Peter Udell and Philip Rose based on Barrett's screenplay of the same title. Lyrics by Peter Udell. Music by Gary Geld. Alvin Theater, New York, 7 January 1975.

Based not on the successful Bronson Howard play of 1889, but on the equally successful 1965 film featuring James Stewart, the musical *Shenandoah* told the story of Charlie Anderson (John Cullum), a mind-my-own-business farmer in the Shenandoah Valley who is determined not to allow the warmongers of the Confederacy and the Union to drag him and his family – six sons and one daughter – into their civil war. But the warmongers and those they have infected, the young men of each army who yell for their side as if they were at a football match, do not allow anyone not to play their game. Charlie's determinedly neutral family is attacked and his youngest son carried off by the Union soldiers, and the Anderson family have to get involved. It is a long and cruel time before they can creep, battered and scarred, back to the Shenandoah Valley to rebuild their lives.

The score of the show, written in a warmly countrified vein, had for its backbone a series of soliloquies for Charlie from which his fierce, anti-war 'I've Heard it All Before' and the 'Meditation' over the grave of his wife stood powerfully alongside the happy songs of his young family, topped by a delightful country duo for Anne (Penelope Milton) and Jenny (Donna Theodore), 'We Make a Beautiful Pair', and a heart-rending solo of a young soldier (Gary Harger) wending his way back in the aftermath of the war to 'The Only Home I Know'.

Originally produced at the Goodspeed Opera House, and staged without glitz or grandeur, *Shenandoah* was greeted by the more sophisticated Broadway critics with a gentle sneer, yet its sincere, wholesome characters and their straightforward and moving story put across their anti-war message far more effectively than any of the trendier love-not-war musicals of the era, and its songs (even if one did generalize on that sadly overworked period word 'Freedom') illustrated their story most effectively. The public soon made up their own mind about the show, and continued to support it for 1,050 performances and a tour.

In 1989 Cullum reprised the rôle he had created, and which had earned him the 1975 Tony Award, for a touring production. Launched in Canada, it played a brief return Broadway season (Virginia Theater, 8 August, 31 performances) during its tour under the management of Howard and Sophie Hurst and Peter Ingster.

Recording: original cast (RCA)

SHEPHARD, [F] Firth [SHEPHARD, Frederick Edward] (b London, 27 April 1891; d London, 3 January 1949). London producer of the 1920s and 1930s.

Shephard began his working life in an insurance office, but he renounced his desk to become a whistler in a concert party at Clacton. He wrote songs and sketches for the concert party and, during the First World War, began contributing to London and provincial revues. His first connection with the musical theatre came when he was entrusted with the adaptation of Rida Johnson Young's tale of mormon marriage, *His Little Widows*, for Bernard Hishin's London production. He subsequently collaborated on the construction of a musical-comedy vehicle for Ethel Levey, *Oh! Julie*, and on the disastrous Gaiety Theatre burlesque *Faust on Toast* before taking his first turn into management, in partnership with Laddie Cliff, on the dance-and-laughter musical *Dear Little Billie* (1925).

Although he authored Cliff's subsequent musical comedy *Lady Luck* (a libretto which was filched fairly straight from *His Little Widows*), Shephard's own producing ventures for the next few years were in the revue field. However, at the end of the 1920s he teamed with comedian Leslie Henson on the presentation of a series of successful comedies, amongst which the London production of Broadway's *Follow Through* (1929), the musicalized German farce *Nice Goings On* (1933) and the remake of Broadway's *Little Jessie James* as *Lucky Break* (1934), each with Henson starred, represented the musical portion.

Thereafter Shephard once again went it alone, with Henson remaining as star if not co-producer of a run of musicals which relit the sadly tenebrous Gaiety Theatre in no uncertain manner: *Seeing Stars* (1935), *Swing Along* (1936), *Going Greek* (1937) and *Running Riot* (1938). The very loose-limbed *Wild Oats* (1938, for which, like *Running Riot*, Shephard was credited with 'from a plot by') and *Sitting Pretty* (1939) also contributed to the comedy-musical gaiety of the pre-war years.

The war effectively put an end both to the Gaiety series and to the budding Prince's Theatre series begun by *Wild Oats* and *Sitting Pretty*. In 1941 Shephard produced *Wild Rose*, a revamped version of *Sally* as a vehicle for filmland's Jessie Matthews, but he then returned to producing plays (*Arsenic and Old Lace*, *My Sister Eileen* etc) until the end of his career.

1919 **His Little Widows** English adaptation (Wyndham's Theatre)
1920 **Oh! Julie** (aka *The Honeymoon Girl*) (H Sullivan Brooke, Herman Darewski/Harold Simpson/w Lee Benson) Shaftesbury Theatre 22 June
1921 **Faust on Toast** (Willie Redstone, Melville Gideon/w Adrian Ross) Gaiety Theatre 19 April
1925 **Dear Little Billie** (H B Hedley, Jack Strachey/Desmond Carter) Shaftesbury Theatre 25 August
1927 **Lady Luck** (Hedley, Strachey/Carter/w Greatrex Newman) Carlton Theatre 27 April

SHERIDAN, J[ohn] F[rancis] (b USA, ?1848; d Newcastle, Australia, 25 December 1908). Famous American dame comedian.

Sheridan began his career in minstrel shows and music hall, touring early on in the sketch *Rum* in his native America, but he made his mark on the musical stage when he invented the travesty rôle of the Widow O'Brien and the musical comedy cum variety show *Fun on the Bristol* (1880) of which she was the central character and had both it and her written around his talents by George Fawcett Rowe. After a considerable tour in America, he took this 'musical comedy oddity' to Britain (1882) where he scored a singular success in the provinces and more than safely braved a London season at the Olympic Theatre, before setting off again in 1884 to introduce the Widow O'Brien to Australia and the Eastern circuits. In 1887 he again presented himself at London's Gaiety Theatre and the Opera Comique in the eternal *Fun on the Bristol* and also brought out a sequel to his now-celebrated vehicle, *Bridget O'Brien Esq* ('Bright Little Glass'), which served him well

in the southern hemisphere without ever coming up to its fellow in popularity.

Sheridan found himself a second splendid frock part when he took over from heavy lady Adelaide Newton as the Second Mrs Block in London's *Little Christopher Columbus* (1894). He worked the originally minor rôle up into a major showpiece with above-the-title billing and then, in an age where travesty performances outside pantomime were becoming rare, moved on to appear as the lion-taming Lady Fitzwarren (to whom 'I love' is pronounced 'je tame') in the same authors' *Dandy Dick Whittington* (1895). He toured his own company through Britain with a repertoire including *An Artist's Model*, *Dandy Dick Whittington*, *The Shop Girl*, *The New Barmaid* and *A Trip to Chinatown* before he returned once more to South Africa and to Australia, where he had become a particular favourite, a fact perhaps not unconnected with his reputation as the man who 'wears the tightest trousers in Australia'.

During his time in Australia, Sheridan continued to appear regularly as the Widow O'Brien and as Mrs Block and also attempted a new travesty vehicle *Mrs Goldstein*. He again toured a selection of musicals under his own management, including *Naughty Nancy* (which allowed him three rôles, one female), a version of the British touring extravaganza *A Trip to Chicago* written by himself and Fred Lyster, and personal versions of *The New Barmaid*, *The Lady Slavey* (Roberts), *King Dodo* (Dodo) and *The Earl and the Girl* (Cheese). He was also seen in further male comedy rôles in such more traditional pieces as *Dorothy* (Lurcher), *Erminie* (Cadeau), *Rip van Winkle* (Rip), the Gilbert and Sullivan repertoire and Boucicault's *The Shaughraun*. He remained in Australia, still taking the Widow O'Brien around the country, until his death at the age of 61. He was buried in his adopted homeland under a stone bearing his catchphrase 'It's sorry I'm here, I am'.

Sheridan collaborated on the authorship of several theatre pieces, including his last vehicle, and undoubtedly less officially on most of his variety musicals.

1887 **Bridget O'Brien Esq** (J A Robertson et al/Bert Royle/w Fred Lyster) Opera Comique 29 October
1902 **Mrs Goldstein** (aka *Mrs Dooley's Joke*) (F Weiterer/w Pat Finn) Criterion Theatre, Sydney 29 September

SHERWIN, Manning (b Philadelphia, 4 January 1903; d Hollywood, 26 July 1974).

Journeyman composer Sherwin had songs used in the *Bad Habits of 1926*, *Merry-Go-Round* (1927), *Crazy Quilt* (1931) and *Everybody's Welcome* (1931) before moving to Hollywood where he worked as a songwriter for the early sound films for some six years. In 1938 he moved again, this time to London, where his first West End song was interpolated into the Eric Maschwitz flop *Magyar Melody*. Over the next decade he provided the scores for a series of revues including *Shephard's Pie* ('Who's Taking You Home Tonight?' w Tommy Conner), *Up and Doing*, *Rise Above it II*, *Fun and Games*, *Fine and Dandy* (w Eric Blore), *Magic Carpet* and *Here Come the Boys*, as well as for a number of musical comedies. The first of these, *Sitting Pretty* was cut short by the outbreak of war, but he had successes with George Black's long-running cabaret-mystery musical *Get a Load of This* ('Wrap Yourself in Cotton Wool') and with three sturdy comedy vehicles for Cicely Courtneidge, each of which had a fine London run and one of which, *Under the Counter*, was taken to America and to Australia as well. His most successful single song was the revue number 'A Nightingale Sang in Berkeley Square' (Eric Maschwitz, Jack Strachey), introduced by Judy Campbell in the revue *New Faces*.

1939 **Sitting Pretty** (Douglas Furber) Prince's Theatre 17 August
1941 **Get a Load of This** (Val Guest/James Hadley Chase, Arthur Macrae) London Hippodrome 19 November
1943 **Something in the Air** (Harold Purcell, Max Kester/Macrae, Archie Menzies, Jack Hulbert) Palace Theatre 23 September
1945 **Under the Counter** (Purcell/Macrae) Phoenix Theatre 22 November
1948 **The Kid from Stratford** (Barbara Gordon, Basil Thomas) Prince's Theatre 30 September
1949 **Her Excellency** (w Harry Parr Davies/Kester, Purcell, Menzies) London Hippodrome 22 June

SHEVELOVE, Burt[on George] (b Newark, NJ, 19 September 1915; d London, 8 April 1982).

Shevelove made his first appearance in the theatre as the co-lyricist and director of the revue *Small Wonder* (Coronet Theater 15 September 1948) and three years later combined again with composer Albert Selden on a musicalization of Victor Wolfson's play *Excursion* as *A Month of Sundays*. With Nancy Walker topbilled, it folded pre-Broadway. He directed a revival of *Kiss Me, Kate* at the City Center and finally hit success when he co-authored the Plautian pastiche *A Funny Thing Happened on the Way to the Forum* with Larry Gelbart.

He subsequently found Broadway success also as a director with *Hallelujah, Baby!* and the 1971 revival of *No, No, Nanette*, but was unable to rescue disaster from disaster when he took over the staging of London's *Twang!!* (1965) from Joan Littlewood. As a writer he again went to classic literature when he teamed with Stephen Sondheim for a novelty on-the-water piece, *The Frogs*, but met with an unhappy ending when he arranged Philip Barry's play *Holiday* as a musical with a selection of second-hand Cole Porter numbers as its musical part.

1951 **A Month of Sundays** (Albert Selden/w Ted Fetter) Shubert Theater, Boston 25 December
1962 **A Funny Thing Happened on the Way to the Forum** (Stephen Sondheim/w Larry Gelbart) Alvin Theater 8 May
1974 **The Frogs** (Sondheim) New Haven, Conn, 20 May
1980 **Happy New Year** (Cole Porter arr Buster Davis) Morosco Theater 27 April

SHINE, John L[loyd Joseph Aloysius] (b Manchester, 28 May 1856; d New York, 17 October 1930). Comic actor and would-be producer of the British musical stage.

John Shine began his career as an actor in Manchester and toured in stock before reaching London in 1880. He made his first appearance there with the Hanlons in their pantomime *La Voyage en Suisse*, played in several plays at the Gaiety and then went into management for the first time, touring a company with a repertoire including the burlesque *Don Juan*. He then made his initial attempt at West End management with Sydney Grundy's play *The Glass of Fashion*. The piece failed utterly, dropping £10,000, but Shine continued, in partnership with the Gaiety manager John Hollingshead, with the production of the comic opera *Dick* (1884) at the Globe. The piece, in

which he himself took the chief comic rôle (Fitzwarren), had a certain success but, along with Hollingshead and the money of financier Henry O'Hagan (who had also been behind the financing of much of the Gaiety's early production), he had also taken on the management of the new Empire Theatre, and it proved a difficult house to make viable.

An opening with a lavish revival of *Chilpéric* was followed by a transfer of *Dick*, another of Lillian Russell in Teddy Solomon's *Polly*, the production of a new Solomon work *Pocahontas* and of the super-lavish *The Lady of the Locket*, followed by a revival of Solomon's *Billee Taylor* before the management went under. Impoverished, Shine had, however, done well as an actor with principal rôles in *Pocahontas* (Sir Hector Van Trump), *The Lady of the Locket* (Oblivio) and *Billee Taylor* (Ben Barnacle).

The following year he produced a rewritten version of the old extravaganza *Piff Paff* (ex- *Le Grand Duc de Matapa*) under the title of *Glamour* and toured it with himself and his brother in the lead comic rôles, but management again proved his downfall and at one stage he ended up in Holloway jail for a debt of £12 to Allen's, the poster-printers.

Shine finally threw in his manager's hand and returned instead to acting in plays. In 1891, however, he co-authored a burlesque of *Joan of Arc*, otherwise commissioned by George Edwardes from a promising new pair called Adrian Ross and Osmond Carr. He was unable to join in the management side this time, as his previous producing activities had brought him face to face with the bankruptcy courts, and, of course, *Joan of Arc* was a singular hit. He had not even the consolation this time of the lead comic rôle, for Edwardes had cast Arthur Roberts at the top of the bill and Shine had to be content with playing the Dauphin.

The coming of musical comedy brought Shine a number of juicy star comedy rôles including Spoofah Bey in *Morocco Bound* (1893 and 1901), Dam Row in *Go-Bang* (1894) and William White in *The New Barmaid* (1896), but he could not help himself getting mixed up in production again, and he suffered his worst battering yet when getting involved with a feeble burlesque called *All My Eye-van-hoe* (1893) in which he starred and which ended him up once more in the debtors' courts.

The larger part of his later career was spent in the straight theatre where in 1904 he created the rôle of Larry Doyle in Shaw's *John Bull's Other Island* at the Court Theatre. He ventured not again as a producer, although as a writer he adapted Berté's *Kreolenblut* as *The Rose of Panama* (aka *Jacinta*) for John Cort in America, where he spent the last of his years, apparently much to the relief of his relations.

His brother **Wilfred E[dwin] SHINE** (b Manchester, 12 July 1862; d Kingston-on-Thames, 14 March 1939) appeared from 1879 on both the musical and straight stages, spending a period touring with the D'Oyly Carte companies (Bunthorne, Major General, Judge, Wells) and playing in London for his brother in *Dick* (Alderman Fitzwarren) and *Polly* (t/o Pipeclay). He toured in burlesque for George Edwardes, in John's production of *Glamour* (1886, Count Inferno do Penseroso), with Horace Lingard in *Falka* and *Pepita*, and made further musical appearances in London in the try-out of Adrian Ross and Osmond Carr's first musical *Faddimir* (1889), and in *Miss*

Decima (t/o Flannagnan). However, he had his most considerable success in Australia and on the Eastern circuit, particularly in his brother's rôle of Spoofah Bey in *Morocco Bound*. He later toured Britain in the title-rôle of Harry Monkhouse's *Pat* and played in the musical comedy *Nana* (1902) at Birmingham.

A second brother, Harry Shine [William Henry SHINE] (b Manchester, 24 May 1870; d Australia, 11 October 1909), also had a successful career, mostly in Australia, as a musical comedian. The companion of Australian music-hall star Florrie Forde, he died – apparently from persistent liquid intake – before they could legalize their attachment.

Wilfred's son, Bill Shine [Wilfred William Dennis SHINE] (b London, 20 October 1911), has carried on in the family business, making a handful of musical appearances (Squeezum in *Lock Up Your Daughters*, Boganovich in *The Merry Widow*, Lord Littlehampton in *Maudie!* etc) in a very long career as an actor.

1891 **Joan of Arc** (F Osmond Carr/Adrian Ross) Shaftesbury Theatre 17 January
1911 **The Rose of Panama** (*Kreolenblut*) English version (Daly's Theatre, New York)

THE SHO-GUN Comic opera in 2 acts by George Ade. Music by Gustave Luders. Studebaker Theater, Chicago 4 April, 1904; Wallack's Theater, New York, 10 October 1904.

The Sho-Gun was a musical show in a strict line of descent from half a century of such successful Oriental pieces as *Ba-ta-clan*, *Dick*, *The Mikado* and *A Chinese Honeymoon*, combining all kinds of comical high-jinks with a cast of the sort of colourful barbarians with burlesquey names who get you mixed up with their royals and then either put you on a throne or do unspeakable things to you with an axe or a stake. In George Ade's version of the tale the intruder was one William Henry Spangle (Christopher Bruno), an American chewing-gum magnate, who makes his way to Kachoo, 'an imaginary and secluded island in the Sea of Japan, between Japan and Corea ... untouched by modern civilisation' to introduce his wares and his American ways (including labour unions and advice on how to treat them) to the Sho-Gun, Flai-Hai (Edward Martindel). There he becomes involved with as many complications as the entire cast of *A Chinese Honeymoon* put together, as well as with Princess Hunni-Bun (Anna Wilson), little Moozo-May (Adeline Sharp), lusty Omee-Omi (Trixie Friganza) and the aptly named Hi-Faloot (Florence Morrison), not to mention ballad-singing Tee-To (Clyde McKinley) and the royal astrologer, Hanki-Pank (Etienne Girardot). By the end of it all, yankee enterprise has won Spangle both girl and crown.

Gustave Luders's score was in a photo-fit Victorian musical-comedy vein, with Spangle heading affairs describing himself in march rhythms as 'The Irrepressible Yank' ('a regular touring board of trade, and a two-legged sort of a bank ...') and wooing Omee-Omi with a number about ill-matched couples ('Love, You Must Be Blind') and an anthropomorphic piece about bunny-rabbits ('She's Just a Little Different from the Others That I Know'). The girls sang the pretty numbers, Tee-To provided the tenor romancing, one Ensign Beverly (N E Daignault) turned out the stirring stuff with a nautical song

about 'The Jackie', and the Sho-Gun described himself ('The Sho-Gun of Kachoo') in the same way that every English comic-opera potentate had done for more than two decades.

First produced in Chicago by Henry Savage – after the traditional run-in at Milwaukee's Davidson Theater (31 March) – *The Sho-Gun* was a splendid success and it quickly found its way east. New Yorkers were as little worried as their western neighbours over the piece's derivative nature, and they gave an equally warm welcome to its fooleries and melodies and to a mostly new cast including Charles E Evans (Spangle), Georgia Caine (Omee-Omi) and Christie MacDonald (Hunni-Bun). The show played for 120 performances at Wallack's Theater, proving itself one of the most popular home-bred shows of its time, before taking again to the road. It did not return to Broadway nor did it ever appear in Britain but, by a combination of circumstances which are now sadly undecipherable, *A Sogun* appeared in 1906 on the stage of Budapest's Király Színház (which had hosted *Robin Hood* two years previously), oddly billed as 'an Amerikai operett by Clyde McKinley'. 'Flutter, Little Bird' became 'A gyönge pillanat' and 'Wistaria, My Bride' was delivered as 'Köszöntelek bájos holdvilág' and, curious billing or not, it proved well-liked. It ran for nearly two months, a run given something of a boost three weeks in when Maud Allen arrived in town and, with little care for geography, inserted her 'Greek dance' and 'Salomé' into the second act.

In November 1990 a musical spectacular based on the successful novel *Shogun* by James Clavell, and using that title (with 'the musical' added in explanation) was mounted briefly on Broadway.

Hungary: Király Színház *A Sogun* 15 December 1906

THE SHOP GIRL Musical farce in 2 acts by H J W Dam. Music by Ivan Caryll. Additional numbers by Adrian Ross and Lionel Monckton. Gaiety Theatre, London, 24 November 1894.

The Shop Girl is one of those shows which has been lumbered, in the past, by being dubbed 'the first musical comedy' by some of the theatre's more facile commentators. It was, of course, nothing of the kind, any more than were George Edwardes's earlier productions *A Gaiety Girl* and *In Town* or Fred Harris's *Morocco Bound* – whose author, Arthur Branscombe, became a figure of fun with his conversational gambit 'when I invented musical comedy ...' – and *Go-Bang*, or even the touring phenomenon *The Lady Slavey* which also preceded it. *The Shop Girl* merely marked a change in style at London's Gaiety Theatre where it was the first of a series of successful modern-dress musical productions (many retaining the 'girl' element of the title) which confirmed that theatre as the most popular light musical house in the West End during the turn-of-the-century years.

The death of Fred Leslie and the illness of Nellie Farren, the two most important Gaiety stars, helped to put an end to the era of New Burlesque which George Edwardes had fostered with such huge international success at his theatre, and the success at other theatres of his *In Town* and *A Gaiety Girl*, up-to-date pieces full of smart, topical chat and dressed in fashionable modern clothes, led him to commission a like piece for the Gaiety to follow the indifferent burlesque *Don Juan*. He went for his text not to

A Gaiety Girl's Owen Hall but to an obscure American journalist and small-time playwright, Henry Dam, and for his score to Ivan Caryll, recently triumphant with *Little Christopher Columbus*, rather than to the Gaiety's house composer, Meyer Lutz, the writer of so many celebrated burlesque scores for him. He also put together an almost wholly fresh company, with only comic Edmund Payne, dancers Katie Seymour, Topsy Sinden and Willie Warde and character-lady Maria Davis remaining from the *Don Juan* principals.

The book which Dam concocted was not precisely original in its plot elements. John Brown (Colin Coop) is searching for a lost heiress and it seems she is to be found amongst the girls employed at the store run by Mr Hooley (Arthur Williams). When it seems that plumply pouting Ada Smith (Lillie Belmore) is she, Hooley swiftly proposes and Ada dumps her little fiancé, shopwalker Miggles (Payne), for a quick tie-up with the boss, only for the pair to discover that the real heiress is not Ada but soubrette Bessie Brent (Ada Reeve). Bessie marries her upper-class Charlie (Seymour Hicks) and Miggles consoles himself with duets with the pretty Miss Robinson (Katie Seymour). If the content of the libretto was old hat, it was, however, told in the style of the moment – crisp, modern dialogue with none of the wordplay or pantomime jokes of burlesque. Hicks and the music hall's Miss Reeve played their juvenile rôles with bantering comedy and without one of those soulful duetting moments that were usually the province of the 'romantic leads' of a musical play, and the whole piece came out as decidedly smart and up-to-date.

The show's score gave all the artists a chance to shine: Payne and Miss Seymour came out perhaps the best with a little oriental duo called 'Love on the Japanese Plan', George Grossmith in the incidental rôle of a mashing dude described himself in a Lionel Monckton number as 'Beautiful, Bountiful Bertie', Coop narrated his rise to millionaire status in the soon-popular 'Brown of Colorado', Lillie Belmore comically invented an early life for herself as 'The Foundling' and American soubrette Marie Halton, in a wholly incidental rôle called Dodo, supplied a slightly more sentimental moment with the soprano waltz song 'Over the Hills'. The most successful single song, however, was one interpolated by Seymour Hicks. Felix McGlennon's 'Her Golden Hair Was Hanging Down Her Back' had been sung in the British music halls by Alice Leamar and subsequently pirated in America where Hicks heard it and, given the copyright laws of the time, annexed it for himself. Adrian Ross wrote new lyrics, and Hicks scored a great hit with the slyly suggestive song. The hit cost, however, for when 'Her Golden Hair' turned out be a British and not a 'free' American song, McGlennon and Miss Leamar had to be heavily paid off for the privilege of its use. During the run the ever-changing cast interpolated many other successful songs (Leslie Stuart's 'My Lousiana Lou', Fay Templeton's 'I Want Yer My Honey', Paul Rubens's début song 'The Little Chinchilla') but 'Her Golden Hair' and 'Love on the Japanese Plan' remained the two biggest song successes of the evening.

The Shop Girl was an enormous success at the Gaiety. It ran for 18 months and 546 performances and established itself as the model for the next decade of internationally popular Gaiety musicals. *The Shop Girl* itself remained a favourite in spite of the popularity of its successors, touring long and late in the British provinces, and playing virtually every English-speaking theatre town from Calcutta to Johannesburg to Sydney and New York. Edwardes sent his own company to America – a very starry affair with Hicks, Grossmith, Ethel Sydney and his new discovery, Connie Ediss (Ada), at its head – where it played 72 performances on Broadway, and another to Australia where Harry Monkhouse, Louis Bradfield, Fred Kaye and Decima Moore played the show in a Gaiety repertoire season. *The Shop Girl* found sufficient success in this visit for J C Williamson to mount his own Australian production a decade later. Florence Young played Bessie and helped herself to 'Over the Hills', leaving soprano Margaret Thomas (Dodo) to re-equip with a Teresa del Riego number called 'The Man in the Moon', whilst George Lauri (Miggles), Rose Musgrove (Miss Robinson) and W S Percy (Bertie) supplied the fun and Clara Clifton as Ada borrowed 'Class' from *The Silver Slipper* in a score which was something of a paste-up job of hits from London musical comedies.

The Shop Girl, however, went further than the round of English-speaking stages. *La Demoiselle de magasin* accomplished the rare exploit for an English-language show of being produced in France, at the Olympia Music Hall, where café-concert diva Mdlle Micheline starred as Bessie alongside Messieurs Berville (Houley), Maréchal (Migles) and Danvers (Charley) in a spiced-up version by Maurice Ordonneau which gave 'Love on the Japanese Plan' to Bessie and Charley, and introduced a 'Chrysanthemum Dance' divertissement for the big 16 of the Olympia's ballet. This production was followed by a *Die Ladenmamsell*, at Vienna's Theater in der Josefstadt (ad Carl Lindau). Frln Dworak was Bessie, Herr Rauch played Miggles, Otto Maran was Hooley, Viktoria Pohl-Meiser was Ada (now called Eva), Karl Pfann was rich Charley and there were a Puppenlied, a Cancan-Duette and a ten-part Tanz-Ensemble all composed by musical director Karl Kappeller to add to the entertainment.

The most sizeable subsequent production of *The Shop Girl*, however, was back in London, at the new Gaiety Theatre. After Edwardes's death, Seymour Hicks and Alfred Butt produced a revised *Shop Girl* (25 March 1920, ad Arthur Wimperis) with the score infiltrated by a bundle of new Herman Darewski songs and with Evelyn Laye (Bessie) and Alfred Lester (Miggles) starring. The show proved popular all over again, a quarter of a century and many, many more musicals in the same vein after its first appearance, and added another 327 performances to the show's West End tally.

USA: Palmer's Theater 28 October 1895; Australia: Princess Theatre, Melbourne, 25 May 1895; France: L'Olympia *La Demoiselle de magasin* 4 June 1896; Austria: Theater in der Josefstadt *Die Ladenmamsell* 5 February 1897

SHORT, [Hubert] Hassard (b Edlington, Lincs, 15 October 1877; d Nice, France, 9 October 1956). British actor turned director with a flair for the musical spectacular.

Originally an actor, at first, from the age of 18 in Britain and then from 1901 in America, Short created the rôles of Alaric in *Peg o' My Heart* and James Potter in *East is West* and also made just one musical appearance as Teddy

Bacon in the 1911 *Betsy*. He retired from performing in 1919 and moved into directing.

His earliest productions included several revues, notably the *Music Box Revue* series, but also an indifferent set of book musicals – *Honeydew* (1920), Nora Bayes's *Her Family Tree* (1920), Anselm Goetzel's self-produced *The Rose Girl* (1921), the musicalized *Peg o' My Heart* known as *Peg o' My Dreams* (1924) and Harold Levey and Zelda Sears's *The Magnolia Lady* (1924) – before he struck seriously lucky as the director of Charles Dillingham's production of the Jerome Kern musical *Sunny* (1925).

An announced move into management with a version of Reynaldo Hahn's *opérette Ciboulette* did not materialize, and in the next years, although Short turned out some successful revue productions (*Three's a Crowd*, *The Band Wagon*), he did not again find the same fortune in his musical plays (*Oh, Please!*, *Lucky*). However, he had a fresh upturn in fortune when he returned to London to direct the vast, double-cast challenge to the movies that was Sir Oswald Stoll's London production of the Viennese Strauss pasticcio *Walzer aus Wien* (*Waltzes from Vienna*) at the Alhambra. He took a 'scenario by' credit along with Desmond Carter which did not interfere with Carter's bookwriting credit, and was also billed above the title in larger letters than Stoll, Strauss or anyone else connected with the production. The next year he took a double credit as director and co-adaptor on London's vast Drury Lane production of Robert Stolz's *Wenn die kleinen Veilchen blühen* (*Wild Violets*) before returning to America and a series of substantial musical shows.

In 1933 he directed the revue *As Thousands Cheer* and a third Kern musical, *Roberta*, in 1934 the American version of *Walzer aus Wien* (*The Great Waltz*), in 1935 Cole Porter's *Jubilee*, in 1937 the American versions of Lehár's *Frederika* and Oscar Straus's *Drei Walzer* and the home-made *Between the Devil* and, in 1939, Mike Todd's bowl of souped-up Gilbert and Sullivan, *The Hot Mikado*, and Jerome Kern's last musical, *Very Warm for May*. *Lady in the Dark* (1941) gave him one of his most memorable successes, but the same season's *Banjo Eyes* had only a short run.

There followed further successes with the Ethel Merman vehicle *Something for the Boys* (1943), Oscar Hammerstein's Bizet rehash *Carmen Jones* (1943), Cole Porter's *Mexican Hayride* (1944), the revue *Seven Lively Arts* (1944) and the 1946 revival of *Show Boat*, which overshadowed the failure of the Ruritanian *Marinka* (1945) and a Tchaikovsky pasticcio, *Music in My Heart* (1947), which did not do for the composer what *Das Dreimäderlhaus* had done for Schubert. He had further revue successes with *Make Mine Manhattan* (1948) and *Mike Todd's Peep Show* (1950) but his last musicals, produced when he was well into his seventies, were not as successful. The musical version of *Seventeen* (1951) had a fairish run, but an americanized *Aida* called *My Darlin' Aida* (1952) tied up a long and effective career with one of the director's few real flops in the later part of his career.

SHOW BOAT Musical play in 2 acts by Oscar Hammerstein II based on the novel by Edna Ferber. Lyrics by Oscar Hammerstein II. Music by Jerome Kern. Ziegfeld Theater, New York, 27 December 1927.

One of the most successful romantic musical plays of the 1920s, *Show Boat* has endured into the quasi-sophisticated 1990s much better than librettist Hammerstein's other memorable successes of the period, *Rose Marie* and *The Desert Song*, to be acclaimed as the masterpiece of the American musical theatre. A large amount of that enduring power has been derived from the show's very basis, Edna Ferber's successful novel, the outline of which Hammerstein and composer Kern followed fairly closely in their construction of the show, whilst eschewing some of its darker and more unpleasant endings.

Unlike *Rose Marie* and *The Desert Song*, the musical play *Show Boat* – although it held to many of the basic tenets of operetta – was not laid out with a traditional cast of predictable romantic comic-opera characters, a soprano and baritone/tenor destined to be mated at the final curtain, a villain thwarted, a couple of soubrets with a romance pursued in parallel to the vocalists' one, and so forth. *Show Boat* had no real 'villain', the soprano and baritone were wedded at the end of the first act (and the soubrets in the first interval), the 'hero' – probably the most anti-heroic hero in a major musical since *Billee Taylor* and *Ange Pitou* – fell to his own weakness, and the heroine suffered misery that was not just temporarily losing her boyfriend, even if she did, like *Sally* and her sisters, rise conventionally to join the vast number of musical-play heroines crowding out the star dressing-rooms of Broadway. It also had two further unconventional elements to its libretto: the genuinely dramatic sub-plot of the mixed-blood actress whose life is ruined by the laws of miscegenation, and the colourful background to the Mississippi scenes provided by a group of negro principals and choristers who were not just mammy-lingoed minstrels and comic relief.

Cap'n Andy Hawkes (Charles Winninger) and his wife, Parthy Ann (Edna May Oliver), run a show boat on the Mississippi river. Amongst their employees are leading lady Julie La Verne (Helen Morgan) and her husband Steve Baker (Charles Ellis), soubrets Frank Schultz (Sammy White) and Ellie May Chipley (Eva Puck), and negro maid Queenie (Aunt Jemima). Whilst the boat is berthed at Natchez, the exposure of Julie's mulatto blood forces her and Steve to flee the state and the Hawkes's daughter Magnolia (Norma Terris) and the handsome riverboat gambler Gaylord Ravenal (Howard Marsh) take their places in the company. Soon the young pair are wed, and leave the river. But Ravenal's luck as a gambler is intermittent and he is unwilling or unable to find a stabler employ. The good days soon pass, and the gambling husband, knowing himself a burden to his wife and young daughter, finally leaves them. Thanks to an abnegating gesture from Julie, Magnolia finds work and success as a singer in a club and goes on to Broadway fame. In the years that follow, daughter Kim follows her mother's steps to stardom and Frank and Ellie, too, end up rich and happy, but Julie dwindles to a sad off-stage end. Nothing is heard of Ravenal until he runs into Magnolia's father one day and is persuaded to return to the show boat, where his wife has taken her retirement, and there – where nothing ever changes – 30 years after their first meeting, the pair are reunited in time for the final curtain.

The score which illustrated this tale was very more substantial musically than the song-and-dance scores which Kern had been supplying for the musical comedies of the previous decade. It mixed the tones of comic opera, in the romantic music for the lovers ('Make Believe', the waltz

Plate 244. *Roland Friederich (Cap'n Andy), Bianca Fink (Ellie) and Michael Greif (Frank) entertain in the Coburg Landestheater production of* **Show Boat**.

duet 'You Are Love') and some dashingly insouciant solos for Ravenal ('Where's the Girl for Me?', 'Till Good Luck Comes My Way') with the regular soubret style of numbers for Frank and Ellie ('I Might Fall Back on You', 'Life on the Wicked Stage') in classic style and added a variety of negro-flavoured pieces from a beautiful baritone hymn to the Mississippi, 'Ol' Man River', sung by Queenie's shiftless man, Joe (Jules Bledsoe), to a searing ballyhoo ('C'mon Folks') and the superb ensemble 'Can't Help Lovin' That Man'. This all in the first act. The second, rather in the style of the old variety musicals, rather tailed away in so far as important new songs were concerned. It consisted principally of a number of acts, some of which used Kern's own material, others of which (in the manner which he had shown himself effectively willing to use in earlier shows) were selected from the successes of an earlier period, the period in which the show was set. Amongst these were Charles K Harris's *A Trip to Chinatown* hit, 'After the Ball', performed by Magnolia as her nervous club début, and Joe Howard's infectious 'Goodbye, My Lady Love' given as an item by Frank and Ellie. Julie's stand-up song, however, was an older number by Kern himself which he had been unsuccessfully trying to place in a show for some time. 'Bill' found itself a home worth waiting for in the second act of *Show Boat*. The other 'variety' items included a variable selection illustrating the entertainment at the World's Fair, several dances, and a series of impersonations performed by Miss Terris in the character of Kim. Apart from 'Bill', only the jaunty 'Why Do I Love You?' and Queenie's 'Hey, Feller!' added to the list of new Kern 'numbers' in the show's second half.

Show Boat was produced by Florenz Ziegfeld. It had a false start when, with leading players Elizabeth Hines (Magnolia), Guy Robertson (Ravenal) and Paul Robeson (Joe) announced, it had to be postponed to allow its authors more time to complete their work, but it ultimately opened (without those three players), directed by Hammerstein, at Washington's National Theater on 15 November 1927. It was instantly successful, but there were nevertheless alterations made in the half-dozen weeks prior to the Broadway opening. Several pieces of music were removed and 'Why Do I Love You?' was added. The Broadway opening confirmed the out-of-town reception and the production went on to play 575 performances on its first New York run.

London's production, under the management of Alfred Butt and the Theatre Royal, Drury Lane, starred Edith Day (Magnolia), Howett Worster (Ravenal), Marie Burke (Julie), Leslie Sarony (Frank), Dorothy Lena (Ellie), Cedric Hardwicke (Hawkes) and Paul Robeson in the rôle of Joe for which he had been originally slated. In spite of the difficulties engendered by the mixed-race cast (blacks and whites had to dress on opposite sides of the stage, Robeson not excepted) it had a good run of 350 performances. Australia's J C Williamson production of *Show Boat* also had a good, if unexceptional, run. Glen Dale (Ravenal), Gwynneth Lascelles (Magnolia), Muriel Greel (Julie), Bertha Belmore (Parthy Ann), Leo Franklyn (Frank), Frederick Bentley (Andy), Madge Aubrey (Ellie) and the blacked-up Colin Crane (Joe) and June Mills (Queenie) played 80 nights in Melbourne and rather less in Sydney (Her Majesty's Theatre, 2 November 1929). This was rather more than the disappointing 115 nights achieved by a French adaptation (ad Alexandre Fontanes,

Lucien Boyer) mounted by Fontanes and Maurice Lehmann in the vastness of the Théâtre du Châtelet with British soprano Désirée Ellinger as Magnolia and American baritone Harvey White as Joe alongside locals Bourdeaux (Ravenal) and Jacqueline Morrin (Julie).

If *Show Boat* did not follow *Rose Marie* further into Europe, it nevertheless established itself firmly at home. In spite of the iffy financial conditions of the early 1930s, it was toured, filmed in 1929, and brought back to Broadway at the Casino Theater (19 May 1932) with Dennis King (Ravenal) and Robeson alongside Misses Terris and Morgan and Winninger (180 performances) prior to another tour and a second film, with Winninger, Robeson and Miss Morgan featured alongside Irene Dunne (Magnolia) and Allan Jones (Ravenal). London reprised the show during the Second World War (Stoll Theater, 17 April 1943, 264 performances) with a cast headed by Gwynneth Lascelles (Magnolia), Bruce Carfax (Ravenal), Pat Taylor (Julie), Leslie and Sylvia Kellaway (Frank, Ellie) and blacked-up basso Malcolm McEachern (Joe), and three years later it again played Broadway's Ziegfeld Theater (5 January 1946, 418 performances) with Jan Clayton (Magnolia), Charles Fredericks (Ravenal) and Carol Bruce (Julie) and toured yet again.

In 1951 a third film version (Kathryn Grayson, Howard Keel, Ava Gardner, Joe E Brown, Marge and Gower Champion, William Warfield) made its way to the screen, in 1954 the show was taken into the New York City Opera, in 1970 it made its first appearance on the German-language stage, and in 1971 had its longest-running production of all time, in London. Harold Fielding's mounting (29 July) starred Frenchman André Jobin (Ravenal) alongside Americans Lorna Dallas (Magnolia), Thomas Carey (Joe) and Kenneth Nelson (Frank) and locals Cleo Laine (Julie) and Jan Hunt (Ellie) and played 910 performances at the Adelphi Theatre. In 1990, on the heels of the issue of a major EMI recording, it appeared once more in Britain and in London (London Palladium 25 July) in a production sponsored by Opera North and the Royal Shakespeare Company (but including barely a member of either company) and featuring Karla Burns (Queenie) and Bruce Hubbard (Joe) of the recording's cast.

Show Boat is now generally accepted as the foremost American musical-theatre work of its period. In the modern English-speaking world (if not elsewhere) it is surely the most performed. It has had an entire book devoted to it, commentators write of it with awe and never a pejorative adjective. There is little question that its canonization is justified, and that there is nothing to be pejorative about. There is, however, less justification for investing the show with 'significance'. Certainly it has more breadth, depth and verisimilitude than a *Rose Marie* or a *Desert Song*, but these qualities were not innovations. In the same way, its avoidance of many of the more popular operettic clichés of its era is a quality, but those clichés had been avoided many times before. Bordman (*Jerome Kern, His Life and Music*, OUP) calls the show 'the first truly, totally American operetta ... identifiable American types sang American sentiments in an American musical idiom'. There is no question over any word there except 'first' and, even then, the 'truly', the 'totally' and the 'operetta' narrow the field, but something like the same comments could surely have been applied in their time to such older period

American musical plays as *Naughty Marietta*, *The Mocking Bird* or the Civil War piece *Johnny Comes Marching Home*, in spite of the Irish, German and English blood in the pedigree of their writers. *Show Boat* stood (and stands) out from its fellow shows not because it was innovatory (for a poor show may be innovatory), but because it was excellent, with the kind of excellence which endures.

UK: Theatre Royal, Drury Lane 3 May 1928; France: Théâtre du Châtelet *Mississippi* 15 March 1929; Australia: Her Majesty's Theatre, Melbourne 3 August 1929; Germany: Städtische Bühne, Freiburg 31 October 1970

Recordings: complete (EMI, 3 records London cast recordings (WRC), 1946 revival (Columbia), 1966 revival (RCA), London revival (Stanyan), film soundtrack ASI (CBS/MGM), selections (TER, Columbia, RCA Victor, HMV, Decca), selection in Swedish etc

Literature: Kreuger, M: *Show Boat: The Story of a Classic American Musical* (OUP, New York, 1977)

SHOW GIRL Musical by William Anthony McGuire based on the novel of the same title by J P McEvoy. Lyrics by Gus Kahn and Ira Gershwin. Music by George Gershwin. Ziegfeld Theater, New York, 2 July 1929.

Ruby Keeler played Dixie Dugan, the 'show girl' heroine of Florenz Ziegfeld's 1929 production, struggling like so many of her contemporaries towards that nirvana: a star dressing room in a Ziegfeld show. On the way, she sang 'Liza (all the clouds'll roll away)', and stood aside whilst Jimmy Durante (equipped with three songs written by himself) and Eddie Foy jr purveyed the comedy of the evening. However, neither this starry line-up (with the intermittent assistance of Al Jolson, singing 'Liza' from the audience to 'help' his wife), nor a sumptuous Ziegfeld production featuring an Albertina Rasch ballet to Gershwin's 'American in Paris' music could make *Show Girl* into a success. It lasted just 111 performances.

An earlier piece under almost the same title (it had a *The* attached), produced by E E Rice with Frank Lalor and with Paula Edwards starred, was a 1902 adaptation of a Boston Cadets show originally called *The Cap of Fortune* and written by the unstoppable Boston pair of R A Barnet and H L Heartz. It was added to by Edward Corliss and interpolated into by Jerome and Schwartz ('In Spotless Town') before it got to Broadway where it remained for 64 performances. A later piece, which sent the title round once again, was a vehicle written by Charles Gaynor to feature Carol Channing. It played 100 nights at the Eugene O'Neill Theater in 1961 (12 January).

SHUBERT, Messrs [SZEMANSKI]
SHUBERT, J J [SZEMANSKI, Jacob] (b Shervient, Lithuania, 15 August 1878; d New York 26 December 1963).
SHUBERT, Lee [SZEMANSKI, Levi] (b Shervient, Lithuania, 15 March ?1873; d New York, 25 December 1953).
SHUBERT, Sam S [SZEMANSKI, Samuel] (b Shervient, Lithuania, ?1876; d Pennsylvania, 11 May 1905).

The most productive and powerful musical-theatre managers of the first half of Broadway's 20th century.

Brought from their native Lithuania to Syracuse, NY, in 1882, the Shubert boys began their connection with the theatre as youngsters, working in the local houses in various jobs. Sam, who was professedly the youngest, became a box-office manager and before long he and his brother Lee began their careers as theatrical producers, with a touring company of the successful Charles Hoyt farce comedy *A Texas Steer* (1894).

It took them half a dozen years to make it from Syracuse to Broadway. There, as independent producers, they leased the Herald Square Theater and slowly – at first with a small man's alliance with the giant Theatrical Syndicate – began to make their way with a schedule of plays and musicals. Their first production was a play, *The Brixton Burglary* (1901), their first musical the record-breaking London hit *A Chinese Honeymoon* (1902). Although the masthead credited Sam Shubert and Nixon and Zimmerman as producers, *A Chinese Honeymoon* was, in fact, the production of Sam and Lee Shubert. Nixon and Zimmerman were the representatives of the Syndicate who controlled this independent production on the organization's behalf.

A Chinese Honeymoon was a fine success, running 376 performances at Broadway's Casino Theater and going on to a profitable life on the road. It was the beginning of great things. Over the 40 years that followed, the Shubert name would be attached to some 200 musicals on Broadway and a vast number which didn't make it that far. The team, however, did not remain the same through those four decades. Third brother Jacob (known as J J – although the second J apparently had no meaning) soon joined Sam and Lee, but in 1905 Sam, the most active of the team, was killed in a train crash, effectively leaving Lee to guide his firm's destiny through the decades of their greatest success.

Having succeeded in securing the rights for London's biggest-ever hit in *The Chinese Honeymoon*, Sam Shubert followed up by securing those for the latest of the Savoy operas. If the kudos was there, however, he was a little late this time. *The Emerald Isle* was the tail end of the Savoy product, and there was no *Mikado* type of run to be had from it. Billed as the production of 'the Jefferson de Angelis Opera Company', it played 50 nights at the Herald Square before moving on to the country.

In 1903 Sam Shubert produced his first native-bred musical when he imported the Chicago Orpheum's burlesque extravaganza *Chow Chow* (w Nixon and Zimmerman) to Broadway, under the title *The Runaways*. It ran for 167 performances, and Shubert pursued the line of home-made musicals a little further when he launched his first own such pieces later the following year. *Winsome Winnie*, a new musical by the English authors of the famous *Erminie*, hit trouble on the road to town. Sam had it remade by Frederick Ranken and Gustave Kerker before it reached Broadway, and ushered it out again after 56 nights. The 'Sam Shubert and Nixon and Zimmerman' production of the semi-pasticcio *The Girl from Dixie*, for what was intended to be a musical stock company, did even less well, not helped by ending up in the centre of a confrontation between Shubert and Zimmerman and the Syndicate's Abe Erlanger.

The continued backward-looking part of Sam's policy followed the work of the *Erminie* men with a revival of *Wang* and a comic opera on *Lady Teazle* for old-time star Lillian Russell: his forward looking led him to take a trip to scout out a theatre in London where, with no 'Syndicate'

to provoke eternal battles, he might produce in profitable peace. Sam Shubert's last Broadway musical production was one of his most successful. Launched in Chicago under the 'Jefferson de Angelis Company' banner, *Fantana*, which billed Sam Shubert as co-author (much to the fury of real author Robert Smith, who had been forced to use Sam's 'ideas'), was a firm success, and Sam announced it to open the new London Waldorf Theatre which he had leased. But, by then, he was dead.

With Lee at the firm's head, fighting a continuing and ultimately victorious war against Erlanger and his allies for control of as large a slice of the American theatrical action as was possible, the schedule of musical productions continued at the rate of a regular half-dozen or so per year: a mixture of imports and new shows. The year 1905 continued with the American fantasy *Happyland*, the London hit *The Earl and the Girl*, and an English pantomime *The Babes and the Baron* on Broadway and a tour of the Chicago *The Royal Chef* amongst touring operations; the year 1906 brought the home-made *Mexicana* and *The Tourists*, the British *My Lady's Maid* (ex- *Lady Madcap*) and *The Blue Moon* and the revusical *The Social Whirl* as well as *Pioneer Days*, the first Shubert production at the vast New York Hippodrome which Lee had taken over as the brothers' sphere of influence grew.

Their 1907 list included *The Orchid* and *The Girl from Kays* from London, the Stanislaus Stange/Julian Edwards comic opera *The Belle of London Town* and Reginald De Koven's *The Snowman/The Girls of Holland* from home, and a new spectacular for the Hippodrome; their 1908 productions of the operetta *Marcelle*, the children's show *The Pied Piper*, Eddie Foy's *Mr Hamlet of Broadway* and – having missed *The Merry Widow* – a first attempt with a Continental Operette with *Miss Mischief* (*Ein tolles Mädel*) with Lulu Glaser. Although the Shuberts stuck a little longer with the old habit of importing shows from the once-rich supply made in Britain – *Havana* and *The Belle of Brittany* in 1909, *King of Cadonia* in 1910 and *The Balkan Princess* in 1911 – their regular diet soon switched to being a mixture of home-made musical comedies, revusical spectaculars and Operetten imported from the Continent. By the time these last made their appearance on the Broadway stage, however, they were often barely recognizable. Frequently – but oddly not always – souped up with spectacle, girls and low comedy and their musical scores sprayed with 'easy' songs, they were usually very different in character from the pieces they had begun as, and very many of them failed. Yet in spite of this failure rate the policy of 'botching' was apparently never questioned.

Amongst the new musicals which the Shuberts produced before and during the First World War were included *The Girl and the Wizard* starring Sam Bernard, *Old Dutch* with and starring Lew Fields (1909), the Rida Johnson Young/William Schroeder *Just One of the Boys, He Came from Milwaukee* with Bernard (1910), Victor Herbert's *The Duchess* with Fritzi Scheff starred, the Julian Edwards *The Wedding Trip* (1911), *The Red Petticoat*, another Bernard vehicle *All for the Ladies* (1912), Jolson's *The Honeymoon Express*, the musical version of the Anglo-French farce *Oh, I Say* (1913), Mrs Young's *Lady Luxury* (1914), *Hands Up* (1915), Jolson in *Robinson Crusoe Jr*, Bernard's remade *The Girl from Kays, Step This Way* (1916), *Love o' Mike* (1917), the Philip Bartholomae/Frank Tours *Oh Mama!/Girl o'*

Mine, Jolson's *Sinbad*, *Little Simplicity*, *The Melting of Molly* and a musical version of Daly's old hit *A Night Off* (1918).

It was a list which included little that was durable, little outside the Al Jolson and Bernard vehicles which was notably successful, and it was much less interesting than the list of bought-in and botched shows mounted by, or partly by, the Shuberts in the same period: *Madame Troubadour*, *Die Förster-Christl* (*The Girl and the Kaiser*), *Liebeswalzer* (*The Kiss Waltz*), *Vera Violetta*, *Schneeglöckchen* (*Two Little Brides*), *Die Fledermaus* (*The Merry Countess*), *Der Mann mit den drei Frauen* (*The Man with Three Wives*), *Der liebe Augustin*, *Filmzauber* (*The Girl on the Film*), *Polenblut* (*The Peasant Girl*), *Ein Tag im Paradies* (*The Blue Paradise*), *Endlich allein* (*Alone at Last*), *Die schöne Schwedin* (*The Girl from Brazil*), *Was tut man nicht alles aus Liebe* (*Follow Me*), *Az obsitos* (*Her Soldier Boy*), *Die schöne Unbekannte* (*My Lady's Glove*), *Wie einst im Mai* (*Maytime*) and *Der Sterngucker* (*The Star Gazer*). If this was an impressively long list, it was nevertheless one which was the result of significant weeding. In one season, the Shubert office announced such mostly provincial German pieces as Robert Leonhard's *Der Sterndeuter*, Berté's *Der Glücksnarr* (*The Fortunate Fool*), Gustav Wanda's *Der ledige Gatte*, Weinberger's *Die Primaballerina*, Albini's *Die Barfüsstanzerin*, Kollo's *Die Königin der Nacht*, Karl Kappeller's *Der blaue Klub*, Anselm Goetzl's *Madame Flirt*, the Millöcker pasticcio *Cousin Bobby* and a number of other pieces which never found their way onto the American stage. And some, such as Fritz Korolanyi's Leipzig piece *Der Liebesschule* (1909), which did, did not get further than such try-out venues as Wilkes-Barre, Pa.

The big successes of the Shubert production arm (as opposed to their ever-growing theatre-owning arm) in the wartime period were *The Blue Paradise* and *Maytime*, and the Continental stage was to bring them further hits in the 1920s, the greatest of which was their remake of *Das Dreimäderlhaus* as *Blossom Time*. Other great European hits – and by now the Shuberts, who had missed out on most of the best early German, Austrian and Hungarian hits, were culling virtually all the cream – fared rather less well. Of *Der letzte Walzer*, *Drei alte Schachteln* (*Phoebe of Quality Street*), *Die Rose von Stambul*, *Die Frau im Hermelin*, *Sterne, die wieder leuchtet* (*Springtime of Youth*), *Der Vetter aus Dingsda* (*Caroline*), *Der Tanz ins Glück* (*Sky High*), *Riquette* (*Naughty Riquette*), *Gräfin Mariza*, Hungary's *Offenbach* (*The Love Song*) and *Chopin* (*The Charmer/White Lilacs*), *Katja* (*die Tänzerin*), *Die Zirkusprinzessin*, France's *Un bon garçon* (*Luckee Girl*), *Musik im Mai* and in the 1930s *Drei arme kleine Mädchen*, *Das Land des Lächelns*, *Meine Schwester und ich* (*Meet My Sister*), *Die Wunder-Bar*, Benatzky's *Cocktail*, *Hotel Stadt-Lemberg* (*Arms and the Maid/Marching By*), *Liebe im Schnee* and the last Shubert imports to Broadway, *Friederike*, *Drei Walzer* and *Bei Kerzenlicht*, more, much more, or in some cases less tampered with, barely a single one lived up to the run or the reputation that it had gained in Europe, even though some served reasonable periods in New York and longer ones on the American road.

Alongside this heavy schedule of Continental operetta productions, the Shuberts also staged a large number of revue productions in the years between the wars, and their quota of home-bred book shows lowered a little. Jolson's later shows, *Bombo* and *Big Boy*, verged on being revue, *The Blushing Bride* – when it finally got to Broadway – verged on being a variety musical, *Sally, Irene and Mary* was little more than an up-to-date burlesque, and the genuine musical comedies, such as the Ivan Caryll *The Hotel Mouse* (*Little Miss Raffles*), *June Days*, *Hello Lola*, *Ain't Love Grand/Lovely Lady* or *The Madcap* didn't actually do so very well. The biggest hit that the firm found during this period was one which followed frankly in the *Wie einst im Mai/Das Dreimäderlhaus* tradition of European operetta: *The Student Prince (in Heidelberg)*. Given this, it was understandable that they persevered with their versions of Continental hits, revivals of classic successes and, now, with home-made romantic operetta: *Princess Flavia*, *Mayflowers* (mus: Eduard Künneke), *Cherry Blossoms*, *My Maryland*, *The Love Call*, *Nina Rosa*, *Cyrano/Roxane*. However, another *Student Prince* was not forthcoming.

From 1938 on the Shubert brothers' musicals became fewer and the handful of book shows produced amongst the revues and revivals did not bring any successes. Pieces like the unrecognizably altered *Bei Kerzenlicht* (*You'll Never Know*), the mock-European *Night of Love* or Romberg's unhappy *My Romance* were quick failures.

Dominant as producers and theatre-owners on the Broadway stage for four decades, the Shubert brothers nevertheless initiated only a small handful of worthwhile new American musicals, and only one – *The Student Prince* – which has stood the test of time and entered the basic repertoire of Broadway shows. All the best and most internationally successful of the flood of both the romantic musicals – *The Desert Song*, *Rose Marie*, *New Moon*, *Show Boat* and their like – and the dancing musical comedies of the age – *Irene*, *No, No, Nanette*, *Mercenary Mary*, *Sally*, *Going Up* and their fellows – which flowed from America during the years between the wars came from other managements. And yet the Shuberts mounted 200 musical shows. And flourished.

The Shubert organization continued after the deaths of the two brothers who ran it for so long. Today it exists principally as a theatre-owning company, although it also operates as a producing interest, often in order to supply product – or to secure the best product amongst what is currently available – for its theatres. Thus, the Shubert name which has topped so many playbills and fronted so many theatre marquees across America since the beginning of the century is still very much in evidence as the end of that century approaches.

Biographies: Stagg, J: *The Brothers Shubert* (Random House, New York, 1968), McNamara, B: *The Shuberts of Broadway* (OUP, New York, 1990)

SHUFFLE ALONG Musical comedy in 2 acts by Flournoy Miller and Aubrey Lyles. Lyrics by Noble Sissle. Music by Eubie Blake. 63rd Street Theater, New York, 23 May 1921.

Nearly 20 years after *In Dahomey*, another negro musical entertainment, effectively mixing cheerfully un-hung-up, high-energy comedy and 'coon' vaudeville turns in a similar style to its predecessor, was produced on Broadway. Again, like *In Dahomey*, much of the material for the show was provided by members of the cast.

In a tale which was an expansion of an old variety sketch, vaudeville team and authors Flournoy Miller (Steve

Jenkins) and Aubrey Lyles (Sam Peck) featured themselves as a couple of untrusting partners in a small-town grocery store. Both of the men are running for the post of Mayor of Jimtown, and each suspects the other of rifling the till to finance his campaign. Each hires a private detective to catch the other out. The show's choreographer, Larry Deas, played Jack Penrose – the detective hired, unwittingly, by both competitors. Lyricist Noble Sissle appeared as Tom Sharper, campaign manager to Jenkins, equipped with an impressive box of dirty tricks which help to win the day, especially as Peck's suffragette wife (Mattie Wilks) proves a right handicap to him. Sharper ends up with the job of Chief of Police, until both the scallywags are routed and regular Harry Walton (Roger Matthews) takes over at the head of Jimtown's affairs. Lottie Gee was fitted in as the show's leading lady, Gertrude Saunders was soubrette, the local Board of Aldermen supplied the close harmony singing (shades of *The Music Man*), and composer Eubie Blake, the other half of Sissle's act, climbed up from his position in the pit to join his partner in a singalong in the second act.

Sissle and Blake's score threw up one thoroughly enduring number, 'I'm Just Wild About Harry', alongside such pieces as 'Bandana Days', 'If You've Never Been Vamped by a Brownskin', 'Love Will Find A Way' (a very different number to that of the same title heard just a few years previously in *The Maid of the Mountains*), 'The Baltimore Buzz' and the piece's title-song. The second enduring piece of the score, however, was an interpolation: during their act, Sissle and Blake performed Walter Donaldson's razzly 'How Ya' Gonna Keep 'em Down on the Farm' amongst a series of what were otherwise mostly their own numbers (w James Reese Europe).

If Broadway had rejected *In Dahomey*, it had other ideas about *Shuffle Along*. The verve, energy and enthusiasm of the players zipped the show to popularity in New York just as it had done for the earlier show in London and *Shuffle Along* remained on Broadway for 504 performances.

An attempt to repeat the success with a *Shuffle Along of 1933* (note the revusical title) was not a success, and a revival of the original show (Broadway Theater, 8 May 1952) with fresh added material written by Sissle and Blake and additional numbers by Joseph Meyer, Floyd Huddlestone and Dean Elliot, foundered in just four performances.

A number of the songs from *Shuffle Along*, however, got almost as long a showing as they had first time around when they were included in a successful compilation show made from the songs of composer Blake and entitled *Eubie!* (Ambassador Theater, 23 September 1978).

Shuffle Along has, like a number of other shows, suffered in recent years from being burdened with 'significance', such extravagant tags as 'a record-breaking, epoch-making musical comedy' (what record? what epoch?) and such silly claims as 'the first negro show on Broadway'. What it was was simply a particularly lively New York hit of its moment, which provided one spanking new candidate for the standards song-list, without going out into the international theatre or proving the stuff of which revivals are made.

Recordings: compilation with original cast members (New World Records); selection with 1952 revival cast members (RCA Victor)

SIDONIE PANACHE Opérette à grand spectacle in 2 acts by Albert Willemetz and André Mouëzy-Éon. Music by Joseph Szulc. Théâtre du Châtelet, Paris, 2 December 1930.

Alexandre Fontanes and Maurice Lehmann presented *Sidonie Panache* at the Châtelet with all the splendour which was both the trademark of that theatre and the key to the success of the series of pieces played there. Nevertheless, the management took care to go for quality in the other values of their shows. It was no less a star than Edmée Favart who top-billed in the title-rôle of *Sidonie Panache* as a little blanchisseuse who goes to the Arab wars, in male disguise, in place of the artist Armand des Ormeaux (Géo Bury). After some dramatic complications, during which Sidonie is captured, then saved by an Arab spy to whom she had shown kindness, she leads the French general to the Arab camp and thus sets up the victory which wins Algeria for France. The star of Paris's *No, No, Nanette*, Loulou Hégoburu (Rosalie), was chief soubrette opposite the Châtelet's favourite comic, Bach (Chabichou).

The score was the work of Joseph Szulc and, although it maintained the dancing rhythms of his small-scale musical comedy scores in such pieces as Mlle Hégoburu's fox-trot 'C'est Rosalie', it also allowed itself moments both more romantic, as in Mlle Favart's charming 'A quoi bon aimer', or military, as in her Marche des Zouaves. However, although all its elements were at least satisfactory, the key to the year-long run of *Sidonie Panache* was to be found in its production values, 16 scenes of grand spectacle including the bal Mabille, a panorama of 'les grands boulevards 1840' and a series of desert scenes highlighted by a cavalry charge of soldiers, on live horses, galloping at full tilt towards the footlights.

In spite of these demands – and presumably with them reduced – *Sidonie Panache* found itself a home in the French provinces after its 500 Paris nights.

Film: Henry Wuschleger 1935

DIE SIEBEN SCHWABEN Volksoper (Operette) in 3 acts by Hugo Wittmann and Julius Bauer. Music by Carl Millöcker. Theater an der Wien, Vienna, 29 October 1887.

Die sieben Schwaben (the title taken from a Brothers Grimm fairy-tale) was a mixture of politics, magic and romance set in medieval Stuttgart which followed the efforts of the war-hero Junker Otmar von Mannsperg (Karl Streitmann) to win the heart and hand of Käthchen (Ottilie Collin), the daughter of his political opponent, the Burgermeister Stickel (Herr Adam) and with his other hand defeat the Swabian Alliance. Aided and abetted by Dr Theophrastus Bombastus Paracelsus (Siegmund Stelzer), he sets up a helpfully heroic manifestation at the tower of the witch, Die schwarze Grete (Frln Stein), to whom the girls go for advice on their love lives, but when Käthchen finds him out it takes a whole act of heroics and politics and a timely appearance by the seven Swabians of the title for Otmar to win both his bride and the war. The prominent comedy element of the piece was largely provided by Alexander Girardi, in the rôle of Spätzle, Paracelsus's servant, who romanced his Hannerl (Therese Biedermann), made a mess of being a magician's apprentice, and performed the show's two most popular numbers

'Um halber Neune' and the heftily dialected 'Wart a bissele, halt a bissele, sitz a bissele nieder'.

The piece, written by the authorial team of Wittmann and Bauer who had successfully supplied the Theater an der Wien with *Der Hofnarr* earlier in the year, was described as a Volksoper without musically differing largely from Millöcker's earlier works. It had a reasonable success at the Theater an der Wien, where it was well enough considered to be brought back a dozen years later during the last year of the management of Alexandrine von Schönerer, with Streitmann repeating as Otmar, Marie Ottmann as Käthchen, Josef Joseffy as Paracelsus, Seibold (Spätzle) and Guste Zimmermann (Hannerl), to top up its total to 63 performances. It was performed with some success in Germany, at St Petersburg, Prague and in many other middle European venues, returning to Vienna in 1910 when Ernst Tautenhayn appeared as Spätzle in a production at the Raimundtheater (30 September).

An American German-language production with Streitmann (Otmar) and Frln Zimmermann (Käthchen) starred was well-received and, in consequence, a translated version was produced by John McCaull's Comic Opera Company starring Chauncey Olcott and Mathilde Cottrelly. It got no closer to Broadway than the Harlem Opera House.

Germany: Friedrich-Wilhelmstädtisches Theater 22 December 1887; USA: Amberg Theater 12 February 1890, Harlem Opera House *The Seven Swabians* 1 September 1890

DIE SIEGERIN Musikalische Komödie in 3 acts by Oskar Friedmann, Fritz Lunzer and Bela Jenbach. Music by Josef Klein arranged from the works of Piotr I Tchaikovsky. Neues Wiener Stadttheater, Vienna, 7 November 1922.

The most successful of the line of attempts at a Tchaikovsky pasticcio musical, Herbert Trau's production of *Die Siegerin* not unreasonably took an early 18th-century Russian subject as its basis. The 'siegerin' of the show was Catherine (the first, not the Great), although when she is first seen she is simply a serf called Marta (Erika Wagner). She sings all her duets with Fieldmarshal Alexander Mentschikoff (Robert Nästlberger) but she nevertheless ends up as the Empress of Peter the Great (Rudolf Teubler). Josef König as Wassili Bronin and producer-director's wife Olga Bartos-Trau (Sonja) were the soubrets, and the production went after a little deep-north authenticity by engaging the Russian Wassilow-Truppe as a speciality.

Following its successful Vienna run (150th performance 23 March 1923), *Die Siegerin* was produced in Budapest (ad Zsolt Harsányi) and was secured by London's Robert Evett as a vehicle for José Collins with which to follow her first success under his management as Vera Lisaweta in *The Last Waltz* (*Der letzte Walzer*). The original makers of the piece were barely mentioned, the libretto being credited to adaptors Reginald Arkell and Fred de Grésac, and the score worked over by Evett himself with Klein's name tacked limply on to the end of the credits. Miss Collins sang 'I Am but a Simple Maid' and scored the success of the show with 'Star of Fate' as she made her way to the throne of all the Russias. Robert Michaelis (Mentschikoff) shared three duets with the star, and sang about 'The Life of a Soldier', Amy Augarde and Billy Leonard supplied the light relief with a duo in each of the three acts,

and Bertram Wallis played the non-singing Czar through a good run of six months and 217 performances.

Although Emmi Kosáry apparently sang a performance of *Die Siegerin* somewhere in America, Broadway never saw it. F C and B C Whitney fabricated what they claimed as their own Tchaikovsky musical called *Natja* (Knickerbocker Theater 16 February 1925) with a different-Catherine script by Harry B Smith and a score arranged by Hungarian conductor Karl Hajós. Madeleine Collins was the lassie of the title who gets dressed up as a pretty boy to win the attention of Catherine the Great and, having thus got her ear, air the griefs of Crimea. Since she was pleading to a woman, Natja was spared the fate of Marta of having to wed where her heart was not, and was thus able to be paired off with Smithian conventionality to her tenor. This may or may not have had something to do with the fact that *Natja* lasted only four weeks.

In an era where, in the wake of *Das Dreimäderlhaus*, romantic biomusicals of composers had become fashionable, European writers seem to have shied off subjecting Tchaikovsky's equivocal love-life to such a treatment, but America didn't. A San Francisco piece, *Song Without Words*, written by Frederick Jackson and musically adapted by Franz Steininger for a production in the 1945–6 season, starred Margit Bokor and John Maxwell Hayes and invented the composer a romance with a French singer. The piece was subsequently rewritten and presented on Broadway as *Music in My Heart* (ad Franz Steininger/Forman Brown/Patsy Ruth Miller, Adelphi Theater 2 October 1947) for a run of 124 performances. Robert Carroll was Tchaikovsky and Martha Wright his putative beloved.

Hungary: Városi Színház *A diadalmas asszony* 27 April 1923; UK: Gaiety Theatre *Catherine* 22 September 1923

IL SIGNOR FAGOTTO Opérette in 1 act by Charles Nuitter and Étienne Tréfeu. Music by Jacques Offenbach. Bad Ems, 11 July 1863.

A pointed little burlesque of musical styles, *Il Signor Fagotto* had the pretentious Bertolucci (Désiré) and the overblown Caramello (Édouard Georges) put in their places by the valet Fabricio (Lucille Tostée) who, disguised as the sort of Italian by whose music-making they swear, knocks spots off their overblown trilling with something more lively. Zulma Bouffar was the leading lady, Moschetta, and Pradeau completed the comical cast of five as Bacolo. First produced at Offenbach's preferred spa-town of Ems, *Il Signor Fagotto* was staged at the Bouffes-Parisiens the following year and a few weeks later by the Vienna Carltheater.

France: Théâtre des Bouffes-Parisiens 13 January 1864; Austria: Carltheater 11 February 1864

SILK STOCKINGS Musical comedy in 2 acts by George S Kaufman, Leueen McGrath and Abe Burrows based on the screenplay *Ninotchka* by Charles Brackett, Billy Wilder and Walter Reisch and suggested by *Ninotchka* by Melchior Lengyel. Music and lyrics by Cole Porter. Imperial Theater, New York, 24 February 1955.

Having got into Paris with a certain success in *Can-Can*, Cole Porter – this time aided by Mr and Mrs George S Kaufman – remained there for his next musical, *Silk Stockings*. The libretto was based on Ernst Lubitsch's 1939 comedy film *Ninotchka*, in which Greta Garbo had appeared as the ice-cube, hard-line Russian of the title, melted ('Garbo Laughs!') by her contact with Melvyn Douglas and Paris. Hildegarde Neff took Garbo's rôle in the musical, travelling to Paris to remove the happily defecting composer Peter Boroff (Philip Sterling) from the comfy arms of capitalism and movie star Janice Dayton (Gretchen Wyler). Boroff's agent, Steve Canfield (Don Ameche), and the sights of Paris weaken her resolve, but she duly takes her composer back home. Not for long, though. By the end of the evening not only have Ninotchka and Boroff closed the iron curtains behind them, but the heroine's boss, the Commissar of Art (George Tobias), and his lady friend have followed them.

Porter's songs were in his by-now-traditional mould although, in the final score, there were only three names dropped (all in the same song) and the references to sex were both fewer and more romantic than nudgy. Ameche suggestively hymned the effects of the French capital in 'Paris Loves Lovers' whilst Miss Neff dropped succinct showerlets of cold water on his warmth, dismissing human attraction as 'It's a chemical reaction, that's all' before they got to the genuine sentiment of 'All of You' (him), 'Without Love' (her) and 'As on Through the Seasons We Sail' (them). The title-song had Ameche reminiscing over the silk stockings Ninotchka leaves behind, the symbol of her lapse from doctrine, when she returns to Russia. Three thoroughly lapsed Russians (Leon Belasco, David Opatoshu, Henry Lascoe), agents unsuccessfully sent out on the same quest before Ninotchka, indulged in several swipes at the restrictions of communism ('Siberia', 'Too Bad') whilst the revue numbers of the show fell to Miss Wyler, happily detailing the necessity of the latest inventions, including 'Stereophonic Sound', to the movie industry, and of 'Satin and Silk' underwear for a girl's morale, as well as relating in oddly coarse tones the attractions of 'Josephine'.

Feuer and Martin's production of *Silk Stockings* had a sticky start, and *Can-Can* librettist Abe Burrows moved in to make major changes in the text on the road to Broadway. Large amounts of the original score were dropped and replaced, so that there was ultimately as much of Porter's material not used in the show as finally remained to make up the definitive score. By the time *Silk Stockings* got to New York, however, it was in condition to stay there for 478 performances.

The musical was later made into a movie, with Cyd Charisse and Fred Astaire featured, and, although London did not take the show up, it did make it overseas, surfacing at the Landestheater in Linz and the Staatstheater in Kassel (ad Johanna von Koczian) following the great success of *Kiss Me, Kate* in German-language theatres.

Austria: Landestheater, Linz *Seidenstrumpfe* 5 October 1974; Germany: Staatstheater, Kassel 5 November 1975; Film: MGM 1957

Recordings: original cast (RCA), film soundtrack (MGM/CBS)

SILLY, Léa

Tall, dark and suggestively handsome Mdlle Silly began her career in the Parisian theatre as a chorus girl at the Théâtre des Variétés at a time when choristers were choristers and principals, even in their early teens, began as principals. She nevertheless, with a little help from her apparently not-uninfluential gentlemen friends, managed the exploit of getting out of the chorus and into an employ as a principal at the very same theatre. Silly established herself as a Parisian personality by sporting a monocle and smoking cigars, thus making herself an obvious choice for the travesty rôles of the period which, in comparison to the feminine leads, allowed the performer to appear in costumes which were low above and short below, and of which she took advantage to considerable effect. She also established a fierce and public rivalry with Hortense Schneider, the Variétés leading lady, and was said to have been the one to have acidly if aptly christened that queen of opéra-bouffe 'la passage des Princes' because of her numerous royal 'visitors'.

Silly had her first rôle at the Variétés as the slave-girl Busa in Hervé's *Le Joueur de flûte* (1864) and later the same year had her most memorable success when she created the part of Oreste in *La Belle Hélène* ('Au cabaret du Labyrinthe'), a part from which she was ultimately sacked when the battle between herself and Schneider got too hot. Schneider proved powerful enough to keep her rival off the Variétés stage thereafter, but Silly continued a top-billed career, which included a New York season in 1870 (Méphisto, Grande-Duchesse etc) and a tour under James Fisk's management in tandem with Marie Aimée, as well as an engagement at Saint Petersburg at the announced salary of 25,000 francs a month in 1872. She kept at it usefully to the end of the decade and beyond (*Les Bibelots du Diable*, *La Reine Indigo*, *Fleur d'Oranger*, *Les Deux Nababs*, *La Cantinière*) without ever getting near another new rôle of the quality of Oreste.

SILVERS, Phil [SILVER, Philip] (b Brooklyn, NY, 11 May 1911; d New York, 1 November 1985).

A confident, old-style comedian with a face like a surprised sausage, Silvers appeared on the Broadway musical stage in his youth as Punko Parks in the unimpressive *Yokel Boy* (1939). Later in his career, after garnering success in the film world, he returned to the musical theatre to appear in star rôles as the fast-talking fall-about Harrison Floy in *High Button Shoes* (1947) and as Jerry Biffle in the variety-based telly-mocker *Top Banana* (1951). With his famous creation of television's Sergeant Bilko behind him, he came back once more to Broadway in 1960 to play get-rich-quick Hubie Cram in *Do Re Mi*, helping to stretch the show's run considerably but, as in the case of *Top Banana*, not long enough to get it into the black.

In 1966 he appeared as Marcus Lycus in the film version of *A Funny Thing Happened on the Way to the Forum*, and six years later made his last Broadway appearance playing the rôle of Pseudolus in revival of the same show (Tony Award).

Autobiography: w Saffron, R: *The Laugh is on Me* (Prentice-Hall, Englewood Cliffs, NJ, 1973)

THE SILVER SLIPPER
New modern extravaganza in 2 acts by Owen Hall. Lyrics by W H Risque. Additional lyrics by Leslie Stuart, Charles H Taylor and George Rollitt. Music by Leslie Stuart. Lyric Theatre, London, 1 June 1901.

Producer Tom Davis, author Owen Hall and composer Leslie Stuart combined on *The Silver Slipper* in the wake of their enormous worldwide success with *Florodora*. Hall provided a libretto which was notably different from that for the earlier work – a fantasy in which a young Venusian maiden (Winifred Hare) slyly drops her slipper from the skies and is bound to descend to earth to retrieve it. There she meets *Florodora* star Willie Edouin as a dubious bookmaker, Gaiety star Connie Ediss as his housekeeper, matinée-idol vocalist Henri Leoni, all-purpose leading man Louis Bradfield and Coralie Blythe as a girl in boy's clothes. Stuart's score had, on the other hand, many reminiscences of *Florodora* – notably a double sextet 'Come, Little Girl and Tell Me Truly' which was a colourable imitation of 'Tell Me, Pretty Maiden' and a piece called 'A Glimpse-impse-impse' which was a close relative of 'An Inkling' – even though it attempted fresh things elsewhere, as in a light operatic 'Invocation to Venus' for the ladies' chorus and soprano solo. It was, however, Connie Ediss's comical musings on 'Class' and Leoni's parlour ballad 'Two Eyes of Blue' which proved the most popular pieces of *The Silver Slipper*'s score.

The show was received indifferently on opening night, with Owen Hall's sometimes vicious society cracks often missing their mark, and Davis hurried into action. The piece was pruned and patched and before the advance engendered by *Florodora* was gone, it had established itself nicely. *The Silver Slipper* played six and a half months (197 performances) at the Lyric Theatre, went briskly into the provinces, and the following year was staged on Broadway. By the time it opened in New York, it had undergone some further changes since its Shaftesbury Avenue season. The book had been 'adapted' by Clay Greene, and Stuart, who loathed foreign interpolations, had provided some new songs. However he was still unable to stop Arthur Weld grabbing his conductor's perk of slipping in several pieces of his own. Sam Bernard played the bookmaker, Edna Wallace-Hopper his boyish daughter and Josie Sadler sang 'Class', but it was Harry B Burcher from the London sextet who restaged Sydney Ellison's choreography who was responsible for the show's success, for a dance routine, 'The Champagne Dance', in which the girls danced with waiters with little trick tables between them, caused a sensation. *The Silver Slipper* and its Champagne Dance became as big an attraction as Ellison's arrangement of the *Florodora* double sextet had been, and *The Silver Slipper* ran for 165 New York performances.

The Silver Slipper also travelled in the opposite direction, being played in Berlin at the Neues Königliches Opernhaus (ad Wilhelm Mannstädt) in repertoire with no less classics than *Der Zigeunerbaron* and *Der Bettelstudent*, and it was also mounted in Budapest (ad Jenő Heltai) with the town's favourite musical star Klara Küry in the lead. It did well enough, but did not find extended success in either venue.

Germany: Neueliches Königliches Opernhaus *Der silberne Pantoffel* 1 July 1902; USA: Broadway Theater 27 October 1902; Hungary: Népszinház *Az ezüstpapucs* 8 January 1904

SIMON, [Marvin] Neil (b New York, 4 July 1927).

The most successful comic playwright of the postwar Broadway era, Simon has intermittently contributed a libretto to the musical stage. Each of his first four essays in the field, all comic-based and yet all different, was an international success, and his work has combined with that of writers like Larry Gelbart to keep alive and prominent the genuinely comic element of a genre which used to be called 'musical comedy' before classy comic writing became too difficult for librettists.

Simon began writing for radio and television and made contributions to the revues *Catch a Star* (1955) and *New Faces of 1956* before scoring a major success with his first Broadway play, *Come Blow Your Horn*. The following year he succeeded in translating the orange-flavoured witticisms of Patrick Dennis's tale of Belle Poitrine to the musical stage in the crisply funny libretto to *Little Me*, and he combined again with that show's composer, Cy Coleman, on a second outstanding piece when he adapted the screenplay *Nights of Cabiria* as the libretto for the composer's warmly and kookily funny 1966 hit *Sweet Charity*. Another screenplay, *The Apartment*, was the basis for the hit Burt Bacharach-Hal David musical *Promises, Promises*, but the virtually two-handed *They're Playing Our Song*, a triumph of realistic and contemporary comedy writing, was an original script, which had for its bases, apparently, only the relationship between its songwriters, Hamlisch and Bayer Sager.

1962 **Little Me** (Cy Coleman/Carolyn Leigh) Lunt-Fontanne Theater 17 November
1966 **Sweet Charity** (Coleman/Dorothy Fields) Palace Theater 29 January
1968 **Promises, Promises** (Burt Bacharach/Hal David) Shubert Theater 1 December
1979 **They're Playing Our Song** (Marvin Hamlisch/Carol Bayer Sager) Imperial Theater 11 February
1993 **The Goodbye Girl** (Hamlisch/David Zippel) Marquis Theater 4 March

SIMON-GIRARD, Juliette [née GIRARD] (b Paris, 8 May 1859; d Nice, 1954).

Juliette Girard was the daughter of theatrical parents – the actor/author Lockroy (Joseph Philippe Simon, 1803–91), co-author of *Les Dragons de Villars*, and the Opéra-Comique dugazon soprano Caroline Girard who had created the rôle of Georgette in *Les Dragons de Villars* and played in *Robinson Crusoe* and *Vert-Vert* – and she was trained at the Conservatoire as an actress. She apparently made her debut at the age of 18 – though announced as being 16 – at the Théâtre des Folies-Dramatiques in the rôle of Carlinette in Offenbach's short-lived *La Foire Saint-Laurent*, allegedly after only a few weeks of singing lessons. She scored a personal success and was promptly given the rôle of Serpolette in the theatre's next new show, *Les Cloches de Corneville*. This second performance made her a star, a status thoroughly confirmed when she subsequently created the large title-rôle à tiroirs of *Madame Favart* (1878) and then that of Stella in *La Fille du tambour-major* (1879) for Offenbach.

Having wed her *Cloches de Corneville* co-star, Simon-Max, she was now known as Mme Simon-Girard (which, given her father's name, she would seem to have had a right to do all along) and she continued to be so known even after her divorce in 1894 and her remarriage to another star of the Paris stage, Félix HUGUENET. Huguenet, best known as a straight actor (L'ami Fritz, Monsieur Bretonneau, Dartez in *L'Animateur*, Le Roi, Denis Roulette in *Sire* etc) nevertheless spent many years on the musical stage, making a famous success as Puycardas in *Miss Helyett* and often playing alongside Mme Simon-Girard (Briancourt in *La Duchesse de Ferrare*, *Le Brillant Achille*, Antonio in *L'Enlèvement de la Toledad*, *La*

Plate 245. **Juliette Simon-Girard** *in the title-rôle of Messager's* La Fauvette du Temple.

Femme de Narcisse, Les Trois Devins, Riquet in *Riquet à la Houppe,* Colonel in *La Dot de Brigitte,* Paul Vaubert in *Les Forains,* Adolphe in *Mam'zelle Carabin,* Lieutenant du police in Berger's *Le Chevalier d'Éon* etc).

A long list of starring rôles followed Mlle Simon-Girard's brilliant beginnings, but few would come near to the three great parts which the young diva had created before the age of 21. Over the next 20 years she created leading rôles in *La Mère des compagnons* (1880, Francine Thibault), *Le Beau Nicolas* (1880, Camille), *Fanfan la Tulipe* (1882, Pimprenelle), *La Princesse des Canaries* (1883, Pépita), *La Vie mondaine* (1885, Georgette), *La Fauvette du Temple* (1885, Thérèse), *Le Dragon de la reine* (1888), *La Petite Fronde* (1888, Madame Jabotin), *Le Voyage de Suzette* (1890, Suzette), *Mademoiselle Asmodée* (1891), *Cendrillon* (1891, Cendrillon), *La Femme de Narcisse* (1892, Estelle), *Miss Robinson* (1892, Eva), *Mam'zelle Carabin* (1893, Olga), *Le Bonhomme de neige* (1894), *Les Forains* (1894, Olympia), *L'Enlèvement de la Toledad* (1894, la Toledad), *La Duchesse de Ferrare* (1895, Nadège), *La Belle Épicière* (1895, Nicette), *La Dot de Brigitte* (1895, Brigitte), *La Biche au bois* (1896, Prince Souci), *Le Royaume des femmes* (1896, Frivolin), *Les Soeurs Gaudichard* (1899, Cécile and Clara), *Mademoiselle George* (1900, Mademoiselle George) and *Le Chien du régiment* (1902, Jacquotte), as well as playing the classic repertoire (both Clairettes, Hélène, Thérèse in *La Cigale* etc), reappearing in her own great rôles – including a Serpolette as late as 1908 – and latterly playing in straight theatre. She was also seen on the London stage in 1886 when she appeared at Her Majesty's Theatre as Wanda to the Grande-Duchesse of Mary Albert.

Her son, **Aimé SIMON-GIRARD** (b Paris, 1889; d 1950), after starting life as a lawyer's clerk and the author of several amateur revues, also made a career in the musical theatre, in French and British revue and in both silent and spoken films from 1913 on. His musical-theatre appearances included *Les Petits Crevés* at the Capucines (1913, Raoul de Trémouillac), *Mam'zelle Boy Scout* (1915, the English soldier Tommy, billed as Aimé Simon), *L'Archiduc des Folies-Bergère* (1916), *Carminetta* (1917, Don José to the Carminetta of Lavallière), *La Reine joyeuse* (1918) at the Apollo, *Hello!! Charley* (1919), *Princesse Carnaval* (1920), *La Belle du Far West* (1920), Cuvillier's *Annabella* (1922), *Épouse-la!* (1923, André Montrachet), *Le Diable à Paris* (1927), *Un soir de réveillon* (1933), *Erosine* (1935) and London's *No Sky So Blue* (1938, the French Count Paul Ravel). On film, the dapper, dark moustachioed actor was, notably, the silent d'Artagnan of *Les Trois Mousquetaires* (1921).

SIMON-MAX (b Reims, 1852; d Paris, 1923). Light-comic vocalist who created a long series of rôles in 19th-century French opérettes.

Simon-Max began his career in cafés-concerts before moving from the Alcazar to join the company at the Théâtre des Folies-Dramatiques under Louis Cantin. He made his first appearance there as Quillenbois in a revival of *Les Cent Vierges* and created his first important stage rôle as the gently comic and tenorious Poulet, opposite the Poulette of Hortense Schneider in her last stage performances in *La Belle Poule* (1875). He took character tenor rôles in *Fleur de Baiser* (1876) and a *Le Petit Faust* revival (1876–7, Faust) and at 24 created his best rôle to date as Briolet, the comical little sweetheart (eventually) of the Jeanne of *Jeanne, Jeannette et Jeanneton* (1876).

He later took over as Janio in *La Reine Indigo* at the Renaissance (1876) but returned to the Folies-Dramatiques for Offenbach's indifferent *La Foire Saint-Laurent* (1877, Nicolas Curtius) before winning a run of three memorable shows and rôles, cast alongside Juliette Girard – soon to be Mme Simon-Girard – which would be the highlights of his career. He created, in succession, the part of the rural wide-boy Jean Grénicheux in *Les Cloches de Corneville* (1877, 'Va, petit mousse'), the young Hector in *Madame Favart* (1878) and the longing little tailor, Griolet, in *La Fille du tambour-major* (1879).

Other fine new rôles, more often than not alongside his wife, followed in *La Mère des compagnons* (1880, Gaston de Champrosé), *Le Beau Nicolas* (1880, Criquet), *Fanfan la Tulipe* (1882, Michel), *La Princesse des Canaries* (1883, Inigo), *Rip* (1884, Ischabod), *Les Petits Mousquetaires* (1885, Planchet), *La Fauvette du Temple* (1885, Joseph Abrial), *Le Voyage de Suzette* (1890, Pinsonnet) the Châtelet's *Cendrillon* (1891), *La Femme de Narcisse* (1892, Saint-Phar) and *Miss Robinson* (1892, Capédiou), and he also made regular appearances in both his famous rôles and other classic parts (Pomponnet etc).

By the time the pair divorced, Simon-Max was leaning away from the tenor-with-comic-flair rôles to the stocky-to-plump comedian-who-sings parts, and he spent the next decade in such pieces as *Rivoli* (1896), *L'Auberge du Tohu-Bohu* (1897, Bel-Oeil), *Les Quatre filles d'Aymon* (1898), as Smithson in *Miss Helyett* (1900), *Madame la Présidente* (1902, Don Géranios), *L'Armée des vierges, Le Jockey malgré lui, Florodora* (1903 Plum-Quick, ie

Tweedlepunch), Berény's *Miss Chipp*, Lecocq's late *Rose Mousse* (1904, Gilbert Duterroir) and as Barbemuche in a *La Petite Bohème* revival, without ever again finding a rôle quite like those of his youthful character tenor days.

SIMONS, Moïses (b Havana, 24 August 1888; d Madrid, 28 June 1945).

Songwriter Simons, the son of a Spanish musician, made his fame with the song 'El Manisero' (known in L Wolfe Gilbert and Marion Sunshine's English version as 'The Peanut Vendor') and was partly responsible for the spread of the craze for South American rhythms, particularly the rumba, in the postwar years. Simons also wrote for the theatre, composing zarzuelas for the Barcelona theatre and later winning a major Parisian success with the musical comedy *Toi c'est moi* ('Sous les palétuviers') the second act of which, set in his native Caribbean, allowed the composer to indulge in a festival of rumba, samba and conga rhythms. In *Le Chant des Tropiques*, two years later, he returned to the same part of the world as the setting for a tale of hidden treasure, ultimately discovered by the island's Irish pastor, O'Patt (Morton), after a score of rumbas, blues, a fire dance, a paso doble, and something called a Cubanacan, and songs from stars romantic – Hélène Regelly ('Mon coeur est un oiseau perdu'), Roger Bourdin and Jean Sablon – and comic ('Ah! y'en a bon le doudou'), without hitting the same kind of lightning rod that he had first time up.

1934 **Toi c'est moi** (Henri Duvernois/Bertal, Maubon, Chamfleury) Théâtre des Bouffes-Parisiens 19 September
1936 **Le Chant des Tropiques** (Sauvat, Chamfleury) Théâtre de Paris 4 October

SIMPLE SIMON Musical entertainment by Ed Wynn and Guy Bolton. Lyrics by Lorenz Hart. Music by Richard Rodgers. Ziegfeld Theater, New York, 18 February 1930.

A Florenz Ziegfeld vehicle for comedian Ed Wynn – 'the perfect fool' – *Simple Simon* followed the kind of fairytale layout of which Montgomery and Stone had made such a success, introducing Wynn as a newspaper-seller with a passion for fairytales whose daydreams took him off into all sorts of adventures with characters such as Cinderella and Snow White, amongst a dazzling series of Joseph Urban stage pictures. The more successful of Rodgers and Hart's songs for the piece included two made-over pieces from their recent flop *Chee-Chee* ('Send for Me', 'I Still Believe in You') as well as one based on Wynn's lisped catchphrase 'I Love the Woods' and another encouraging (as London's *Mr Cinders* had done just shortly before) 'On with the Dance'. Two other songs, 'He Was Too Good for Me' and 'He Dances on My Ceiling', were cut by the producer before the show reached town. The second of them the writers subsequently remodelled for use in the London revue *Evergreen* where it became a hit for Jessie Matthews. The big song success of the night was, conversely, a number written and inserted during the show's pre-Broadway weeks to fit into a comedy scene Wynn had devised. He pedalled onstage on a novelty piano-bicycle with a girl perched on top and accompanied her on his keyboard as she delivered a piece called 'Ten Cents a Dance'. When the song's original performer was sacked for being drunk on stage, Ziegfeld hired the young Ruth Etting to replace her. The artist made a personal success with her unusually low-life number, launching it on a career as a standard.

In spite of Wynn's proven drawing power, *Simple Simon* turned out to be slow to take off. Ziegfeld made further alterations and cuts in the piece (including the removal or replacement of four more numbers) but finally took the show off after 135 performances and sent it on the road.

SIMPLICIUS Operette in a Vorspiel and 2 acts by Victor Léon taken from Hans Jakob Christoffel von Grimmelhausen's novel *Der abenteuerliche Simplicissimus* (*Simplicius Simplicissimus*). Music by Johann Strauss. Theater an der Wien, Vienna, 17 December 1887.

The musical version of Grimmelhausen's 1669 novel was cannily written by the young Léon with every appearance of providing a splendid vehicle for the reigning king of the Viennese musical theatre, Alexander Girardi. The part of Simplicius, a seeming peasant boy caught picaresquely up in the Thirty Years War and in one of those identity crises which were standard operettic fare at the time, gave him a useful series of guises and complications to go through before turning out to be the long-lost son of the equally long-lost Graf von Grübben.

For, in fact, the nub of Léon's plot had little enough to do with the War. It concerned the identity of this Graf von Grübben, a young man who is supposed to be getting married to Hildegard von Bliessen-Wellau, daughter of the Colonel of the regiment in which Simplicius has, through slightly *Candide*-type circumstances, become enrolled. The apparent heir, Melchior, and Hildegard's beloved Arnim, who impersonates him awhile, are eventually both displaced by Simplicius, but since it turns out that his father is actually still alive, and has been lurking about on the fringes of the show's plot most of the night disguised as a hermit, the boy is still able to wed his beloved Tilly and let Hildegard pair off with her Arnim. Melchior is left with the danseuse with whom he started out.

Strauss displayed an enormous enthusiasm for this project, which he saw as providing him with some moments in which he could write music of a less frivolous kind than that with which he had his greatest triumphs, but this enthusiasm for writing something more resembling a light opera than an Operette did not prevent him from using bits of music left over from *Der Zigeunerbaron* and from his recently aborted comic opera on another respected piece of German literature, *Der Schelm von Bergen*, in making up his score.

Simplicius, as is signalled in its overture, did include some more serious musical moments, but it was nevertheless presented at the Theater an der Wien with a cast of the finest Operette performers in Vienna: Girardi, in the rôle destined for him, playing alongside Josef Joseffy (Hermit), Karl Streitmann (Arnim), Ottilie Collin (Tilly), Antonie Hartmann (Hildegard), Therese Biedermann (Lisbeth), Alois Pokorny (Wellau) and Siegmund Stelzer.

Strauss's score did best when it stayed staunchly in waltz time, and the two most liked pieces from *Simplicius* turned out to be the obligatory Girardi waltz – here shared with his Tilly – 'Dummer Bub' and, even more so, Joseffy's last-act waltz romance 'Ich denke gern zurück'.

The show was not a success. It played but 29 performances at the Theater an der Wien and an attempt to remount it in Budapest, with its libretto, which had – as ever when a Strauss Operette was in trouble – taken the bulk of the brickbats, revised by Lajos Dócsi (ad Sándor Lukácsy, Ferenc Rajna), lasted only 12 nights at the Népszinház. *Simplicius*, however, proved to be one of those pieces which, in spite of repeated failures, folk will try to revise and revive over and again. It was given a hopeful third try at the Theater an der Wien in 1894 with the libretto revised by Karl Lindau, and Fraulein Stein cast as a travesty Simplicius alongside Streitmann, Joseffy, Frln Pohlner (Tilly), Therese Biedermann, Frln Frey (Hildegard) and the adaptor himself as Melchior. It lasted for a meagre 11 showings.

A fourth and happier revision was not just a revision but a thorough rewrite done by Léon himself. He junked the book. The new piece, produced under the title *Gräfin Pepi*, interleaved bits of the *Simplicius* score with numbers from another of Strauss's less-than-long-running works *Blindekuh* (arr Ernst Reiterer) and the resulting piece was staged by Gabor Steiner at the Venedig in Wien summer theatre on 5 July 1902 with Mizzi Zwerenz in the rôle of Pepi. This version was subsequently played in Germany (Centraltheater 27 February 1903).

The various Strauss pasticcio musicals have helped themselves to such bits of *Simplicius* as they fancied, the best-known being the remake of 'Der Frühling lacht, es singen die Vöglein ein' as 'Sei mir gegrüsst, du holdes Venezia' in one of the souped-up versions of *Eine Nacht in Venedig*.

Hungary: Népszinház (revised version by Dócsi) 7 February 1889

SIMS, George R[obert] (b London, 2 September 1847; d London, 4 September 1922). Journalist and stage author with a winning touch for the popular.

Educated in Eastbourne and Bonn, Sims found fame as a journalist (Lunatic Laureate in *Fun*, Dagonet of *The Referee*), a crusading pamphleteer (*How the Poor Live*), a poet ('The Dagonet Ballads', 'Ballads of Baylon') and as a dramatist. His first play, an adaptation, *One Hundred Years Old*, was produced at the Olympic Theatre in 1875 and he had his first big success with the comedy *Crutch and Toothpick* (1879), following up with a series of successful plays including *The Mother-in-Law* (1881), *The Member for Slocum* (1881) and *The Gay City* (1881) before launching with *The Lights of London* (1881) and *The Romany Rye* (1882) on the run of dramas which were to bring the best of his theatrical fame.

His name first appeared on a London burlesque bill in 1881 when his *The Of-Course-Akin-Brothers, Babes in the Wood* was mounted at the Royalty Theatre, and he made his first serious venture into the musical theatre with the comic opera *The Merry Duchess* produced by and starring the inimitable Kate Santley at that same house. *The Merry Duchess* won a fine London run, a tour and productions in America and Australia. A second happy collaboration with composer Frederic Clay on the fairy-tale spectacular *The Golden Ring*, a Christmas show for the Alhambra, indicated that the composer – W S Gilbert's pre-Sullivan partner – had very likely found the new book-and-lyrics collaborator he needed. When Clay suffered a stroke that ended his career shortly after, Sims effectively abandoned the made-for-London comic-opera style they had shared, and the run of musical theatre successes which he produced over the next 15 years in parallel with such straight theatre hits

as *Harbour Lights* (1885), *The Trumpet Call* (1891) and *Two Little Vagabonds* (1896) fell into two different and separate areas. On the one hand, he co-authored some of the most successful examples of the 'new burlesque' genre instituted by George Edwardes at the Gaiety Theatre, whilst on the other he wrote book and lyrics for several of the most successful touring musicals of the time.

The earliest Gaiety burlesques (*The Vicar of Wideawake-field*, *Little Jack Sheppard*) of the new era had been co-written by Sims's cousin and fellow journalist William Yardley, and both the team of 'Richard Henry' and the Gaiety's star Fred Leslie had then taken their turns at constructing the new kind of song-and-dance shows which were the rage of the town. Sims and his *Harbour Lights* colleague Henry Pettitt, however, brought the new burlesque to its peak with two shows for Edwardes – *Faust Up-to-Date* and *Carmen Up-to-Data* – which not only brought the expression 'up-to-date' into the language as a synonym for modernity, but which gave all concerned two worldwide hits. Both these pieces retained the old burlesque notion of a parody of their subject – the operas of Gounod and Bizet respectively – but a third burlesque hit, *Little Christopher Columbus*, followed the way of fashion and had very little to do with its nominal subject. It did, however, fit public tastes to a nicety and its Ivan Caryll/Sims score produced several hit songs ('Lazily, Drowsily', 'Oh Honey, My Honey') which helped long runs in London and New York.

These three large-sized hits were more than equalled by three provincial Methusalems. The tuppence-coloured 'musical variety drama' *Jack-in-the-Box* written with another respected critic, Clement Scott, was a hugely popular piece of sentimental drama decorated with songs and dances for its personality heroine which had years of touring life; *Skipped by the Light of the Moon* was a musical adaptation of his early touring comedy *A Gay City* which trouped virtually non-stop through the three English-speaking continents for a decade and more, whilst *The Dandy Fifth* was an old French hearts-and-uniforms comic opera which contained some of the best songwords of Sims career ('Tommy's Tournament', 'The Sprig o' Horringe Blossom').

The Dandy Fifth was a regular feature of the British touring scene for many years, and Sims tried two more musicals with its composer, Clarence Corri: a Spanish piece, *Miss Chiquita*, which did fairly well, and a vehicle for Dan Leno, *In Gay Piccadilly*, which didn't. In his elderly days Sims continued to write for the stage, and he supplied the text for the Drury Lane pantomime of 1911 as well as a number of songs and musical playlets for the music halls and variety theatres. His success owed much to his ability to judge aright the level at which to pitch his pieces, both musical and non-musical, without any condescension, to appeal to the large popular audience.

Sims also authored one of the most readable and apparently accurate books of theatrical memoirs to have come from the British stage.

1879 **A Dress Rehearsal** (Louis Diehl) 1 act Langham Hall 30 October
1881 **The Of Course-Akin-Brothers, Babes in the Wood** Theatre Royal, Hull 19 March; Royalty Theatre, London
1881 **The Girl He Left Behind Him** (Max Schröter) 1 act Vaudeville Theatre 29 November

1883 **The Merry Duchess** (Frederic Clay) Royalty Theatre 23 April

1883 **The Golden Ring** (Clay) Alhambra Theatre 3 December

1885 **Jack-in-the-Box** (William C Levey, James Glover et al/w Clement Scott) Theatre Royal, Brighton 24 August; Strand Theatre 7 February 1887

1886 **Skipped by the Light of the Moon** (various composers) USA; Bijou Theatre, Melbourne 23 April 1887

1888 **Faust Up-to-Date** (Meyer Lutz/w Henry Pettitt) Gaiety Theatre 30 October

1890 **Carmen Up-to-Data** (Lutz/w Pettitt) Gaiety Theatre 4 October

1892 **Blue-Eyed Susan** (F Osmond Carr/w Pettitt) Prince of Wales Theatre 6 February

1893 **Little Christopher Columbus** (Ivan Caryll/w Cecil Raleigh) Lyric Theatre 10 October

1894 **The Yaller Girl** (Caryll) 1 act Moore and Burgess Minstrels 31 December

1895 **Dandy Dick Whittington** (Caryll) Avenue Theatre 2 March

1897 **The Dandy Fifth** (Clarence C Corri) Prince of Wales Theatre, Birmingham 11 April

1899 **A Good Time** revised *Skipped by the Light of the Moon* Opera Comique 27 April 1899

1899 **Miss Chiquita** (later *Dancing Girl of Spain*) (Corri) Prince of Wales Theatre, Birmingham 7 August

1899 **In Gay Piccadilly** (Corri) Theatre Royal, Glasgow 9 October

1906 **In Sunny Spain** (Herman Finck/w Charles Fletcher) Blackpool July

Autobiography: *My Life: Sixty Years Recollections of Bohemian London* (Eveleigh Nash, London, 1917)

SIM-VIVA [VIVA, Simone] (b ?1903; d 1982). Bobbed, pretty-voiced and unforced ingénue of the 1920s and 1930s.

Sim-Viva made early appearances on the musical stage in revivals of Planquette's posthumous *Le Paradis de Mahomet* and Terrasse's *Cartouche* (1922) at the Trianon-Lyrique and subsequently played there in *Sylvie* (1923), but her career was largely made in the jazz-age musical comedies which were the joy of the Parisian musical theatre of the 1920s. She introduced the rôles of Lilette, one of the ladies referred to in the title of *Trois jeunes filles ... nues!* (1925), Nicole in Henri Christiné's *J'aime* (1926, 'C'est pas ça le bonheur'), Jenny in the French version of *Mercenary Mary* (1927), Magali who gets the man from soubrette Christiane Dor in Szulc's *Zou!* (1930, 'J'aime') and the title-rôle of *Rosy* (1930, 'Quand j'ai promis, j'y tiens'). She moved into a slightly different area when she appeared as Peggy, the little lost laundress love of the British Beau in Reynaldo Hahn's *Brummell* (1931) and when she took the title-rôle of the vast production of *Nina Rosa* (1932) at the Châtelet, but she returned to musical comedy in Christiné's *La Madone du promenoir* (1933), *Miss Cocktail* (1934), *L'Auberge du chat coiffé* (1935) and *Un p'tit bout de femme* (1936). Through the more-than-a-decade that she starred in jeune fille rôles, she never changed her publicity and programme photograph, but the ingénue rôles nevertheless finally stopped coming.

Her husband **Géo BURY** began a career as a bright-eyed singing juvenile man in a tiny featured rôle in *Dédé* (1921, Le Commissaire), took the lead rôle in *Le Beau Voyage* (*Leányvásár*) at Lyon (1923, Jack Grims) and came to light in *Trois jeune filles ... nues!* (1925), before going on to create the rôle of Robert Perceval, the American hero of

Passionnément, lending a ringing baritone to Messager's title waltz. He paired with his wife again as Gaston in Christiné's *J'aime* (1926, 'Quand on est 'de''), took over as Jim Kenyon in *Rose-Marie* (1927), shared 'Je suis tour à tour' ('Sometimes I'm Happy') with Coecilia Navarre in *Hallelujah!* (*Hit the Deck*, 1929, Bill Smith), played the jeune premier rôle of the artist, Armand, in *Sidonie Panache* with Loulou Hégoburu and Edmée Favart ('Le jour de la blanchisseuse') and appeared at the Théâtre de l'Étoile in *Érosine* (1935). Between times he was seen in lead juvenile rôles in musical comedy on the roads of France.

SINBAD Musical extravaganza in 2 acts and 14 scenes with dialogue and lyrics by Harold Atteridge. Music by Sigmund Romberg. Additional numbers by George Gershwin, Irving Caesar, B G De Sylva, Jean Schwartz, Joe Young, Walter Donaldson, Gus Kahn, Sam Lewis, Al Jolson et al. Winter Garden Theater, New York, 14 February 1918.

If the Messrs Shubert's production of *Sinbad*, which ran for 164 performances at the Winter Garden Theater in 1918, goes down as statistically the most successful of the musical theatre's tales of the Arabian Nights sailor, it must be admitted that this was not because of the old tale, to which this extravaganza's resemblance was fairly incidental. In this Sinbad, Al Jolson performed in his regular blackface, down on one knee on a thrust stage, and gave forth with 'Swanee', 'Rock-a-Bye Your Baby with a Dixie Melody', 'My Mammy', 'Chloe', 'Dixie Rose', 'Hello, Central, Give Me No-Man's-Land' and others of the same un-Arabian ilk in the middle of Sigmund Romberg and Harold Atteridge's attempts to be at least reasonably eastern with 'A Thousand and One Arabian Nights', 'The Raglad of Baghdad' and 'A Night in the Orient'.

The story of Sindbad or Sinbad the Sailor was a less popular theatrical one in Victorian times than its companions *Aladdin*, *Ali Baba* and *Prince Camaralzaman*, but it nevertheless found its way with reasonable frequency to the spectacular and musical stages. Sinbad seems to have made his first stage appearance as the hero of a pantomime in 1814 (*The Valley of Diamonds, or Harlequin Sinbad*), and returned as such regularly afterwards, affubled with a variety of subtitles such as *Sinbad the Sailor, or Old Bob Ridley and Davy Jones Locker*, but he did not so much as rate a major burlesque in Britain (although a minor one was toured in the early 1880s by Emily Duncan). In America, he did a little better, becoming the hero of *Sinbad, or the Maid of Balsora* written by Harry B Smith and played by the Castle Square Opera Company. Having almost wholly disappeared from the stage in the 20th century, *Sinbad* has made a slight comeback as a British pantomime subject in recent years, in a tiny reaction against the sad shrinkage of the repertoire to a half dozen over-and-over-repeated titles.

SINGIN' IN THE RAIN Musical in 2 acts by Tommy Steele adapted from the screenplay by Adolph Green and Betty Comden. Songs by Arthur Freed and Nacio Herb Brown. London Palladium, 30 June 1983.

A Chicago lawyer named Rosenfeld, having persuaded from MGM the rights to use the story and songs of the milestone movie musical *Singin' in the Rain* in a stage show, took the package to Britain and to producer Harold

Fielding to get it made up into a stage musical and put into the theatre. Fielding called in the cockney musical star Tommy Steele who penned the stage adaptation, whilst his office organized replacement songs for some from the film which had suddenly – when it came to the point – become 'unavailable', and the resultant piece was produced at the London Palladium, with Steele not only starring as movie star Don Lockwood, but also directing. Roy Castle (Cosmo) performed 'Be A Clown' (instead of 'Make 'em Laugh') and tapped out 'Fit as a Fiddle' and 'Moses Supposes' with the star, soubrette Danielle Carson played, sang and danced the rôle which Debbie Reynolds had danced and mimed ('Would You', 'Good Morning' and 'I Can't Give You Anything But Love' replacing 'All I Do is Dream of You') and planted a cream-cake in the face of glamorous Sarah Payne (Lina Lamont) who, in this version, got to sing a corncrake version of 'Temptation', which had been only briefly heard, unsung, in the movie. Steele, attempting neither an American accent nor any kind of Gene Kelly imitation, scored on all fronts whether pounding out the low comedy, tapping with Castle, duetting with Carson, crooning 'You Are My Lucky Star' or flinging himself into a very individual and very wet reproduction of the famous rain scene and title-song.

Singin' in the Rain broke all records for a musical at the London Palladium, closing only when Steele finally cried enough after 894 nights of being drenched to the skin. It was then only a matter of time before the show went to Broadway. However, without reference to his British partners, Rosenfeld announced a Broadway production solo, simultaneously slapping out diversionary Broadway lawsuits in the direction of even peripheral members of the London team which kept them busy too long to fight back. And so, *Singin' in the Rain* opened on Broadway in a different stage version and a very different production (Gershwin Theater, New York 2 July 1985). It closed after appalling notices, a very forced run of 367 performances, and what was rumoured, following an amazingly – even for the musical theatre – masochistic determination to throw good backers' money after bad, to be the biggest deficit in Broadway history. A touring production which followed hired the London production's choreographer and stayed alive a little longer and less painfully.

Fielding, having subsequently succeeded in recouping the songs his lawyer colleague had 'lost' and replacing them in the show's score, promptly revived his London version with Steele for two British provincial seasons, a season in Tokyo, and a return to the London Palladium (1989, 156 performances), whilst sub-licensing the first foreign-language production in Hungary (ad György G Dénes, Mihály Bátkai) and another in South Africa.

Hungary: Fővárosi Operettszinház *Ének az esőben* 24 March 1989
Recording: original cast (Safari)

SIRAUDIN, Paul (b Paris, 18 December 1812; d Enghien, 8 September 1883).

The author, or normally co-author (for he was reputedly an ideas man rather than a dialoguist) of examples of every kind of theatrical piece, Siraudin ended up with his name attached to two of the most memorable pieces of his time: the drama *Le Courrier de Lyon* (w Eugène Moreau, Alfred Delacour) and the Charles Lecocq opéra-comique *La Fille de Madame Angot* (w Clairville, Victor Koning).

His other credits ranged from drama at the Châtelet (*Le Deluge universal* w Clairville) or the Ambigu (*Canaille et cie* w Clairville), to the Thérésa féeries for the Menus-Plaisirs (*La Cocotte aux oeufs d'or*, *La Reine Carotte*), to revue (Hervé's *La Revue pour rien* with its burlesque *Roland à Rongeveaux*, *Paris Revue* at the Châtelet, *La Revue en ville*, *La Revue n'est pas au coin du quai* at the Variétés) and burlesque (*Paul faut rester!*, burlesque of *Paul Forestier*), to vaudevilles, large and small, comedy and the opérette where, alongside his one huge success, he also teamed with Jules Moinaux on the splendidly comical tale of *Le Voyage de MM Dunanan père et fils* for Offenbach.

In spite of these two memorable successes, however, he contributed little to the regular operettic stage after *La Fille de Madame Angot*, collaborating only on the enjoyable *La Marquise des rues* and on the vaudevillesque *Fla-Fla*, both with Gaston Hirsch and composer Hervé.

1846 **Le Veuf du Malabar** (Alexandre Doche/w Adrien-Robert Basset) 1 act Opéra-Comique 27 May
1861 **Le Jardinier galant** (Ferdinand Poïse/w Adolphe de Leuven) Opéra-Comique 4 March
1862 **Le Voyage de MM Dunanan père et fils** (Offenbach/w Jules Moinaux) Théâtre des Bouffes-Parisiens 23 March
1862 **La Fanfare de Saint-Cloud** (Hervé/w Ernest Blum) 1 act Delassements-Comique 30 May
1866 **Le Barbier de Molarido** (Victor Robillard) Palais-Royal 5 April
1867 **Malborough s'en va-t-en guerre** (Georges Bizet, Léo Delibes, Isidore Legouix, Émile Jonas/w William Busnach) Théâtre de l'Athénée 15 December
1868 **Paul faut rester!** (Robillard/w Marc Leprévost) 1 act Palais-Royal 22 February
1871 **El Señor Inigo** (Robillard) 1 act Folies-Bergère 24 December
1872 **La Fille de Madame Angot** (Charles Lecocq/w Clairville, Victor Koning) Fantaisies-Parisiens, Brussels 4 December
1879 **La Marquise des rues** (Hervé/w Gaston Hirsch) Théâtre des Bouffes-Parisiens 23 February
1879 **Jean qui pleure et Jean qui rit** (Franz) 1 act Ba-ta-clan 15 March
1886 **Fla-Fla** (Hervé/w Hirsch) Théâtre des Menus-Plaisirs 4 July

LE SIRE DE VERGY Opéra-bouffe in 3 acts by Robert de Flers and Gaston de Caillavet. Music by Claude Terrasse. Théâtre des Variétés, Paris, 16 April 1903.

The production of *Le Sire de Vergy* under the management of Fernand Samuel at the Théâtre des Variétés in 1903 marked the most substantial and successful staging of a genuine opéra-bouffe since the palmy days of Hervé and Offenbach three decades earlier. The team of authors de Flers and de Caillavet and composer Terrasse had already embarked into the burlesque area with the classical *Les Travaux d'Hercule* (1901), and this time they followed the same path taken by Offenbach (*Orphée* to *Geneviève de Brabant*) and moved from Ancient Greece to medieval France – an area which Terrasse had already visited in his recent *Au temps des croisades* – with a burlesque of the savage tale of Gabrielle de Vergy, operaticized in all its horror by Carafa (1816) and Mercadante (1828) and previously burlesqued, although only in one act, by Hector Monréal and Henri Blondeau, to music by Demarquette, in 1871 (Folies-Marigny 11 November).

Whereas the original Vergy killed his wife's lover and served up his heart for her dinner, the opéra-bouffe Vergy

(Guy) lives quite contentedly with his philandering lady (Anna Tariol-Baugé) and her boyfriend, Coucy (Albert Brasseur). Coucy, however, is embarrassed at being such a comfy cuckolder, so he persuades Vergy to leave his nice home and go off to the crusades with his energetic neighbour Millepertuis (Claudius), entrusting the key of Mme Vergy's chastity belt to him. By the time Vergy returns, the Coucy-Gabrielle affair is on the rocks, but the absent husband has had a grand time. Like his *Geneviève de Brabant* forebears, he stopped off on the way to the crusades and has been having a ball with the sumptuous Mitzy (Ève Lavallière) whom he has brought home, disguised as a Saracen captive, along with her friends (Prince, Max Dearly). Millepertuis, however, seems determined that the story shall have its proper ending. All is dramatically revealed, but Coucy has no more wish to be eviscerated than Vergy has to carry out the operation and all ends as cosily as it started, with a bit of beef from the butcher replacing the fatal dinner.

Terrasse's score supported the burlesque brio of the book happily, with Brasseur reaping one of the comic highlights with his 'Je suis l'sire de Coucy-Couça' and Prince and Dearly, ludicrous and laden down with chains, scoring with a comical prisoners' duo, whilst Mlle Lavallière knocked all eyes out with her version of a belly dance which moved every part of her anatomy.

Produced in a period when the French musical theatre was in a veritable trough of despond, *Le Sire de Vergy* brought forth not only a good deal of critical enthusiasm but also of public interest. It was played for 110 performances at the Variétés, and thereafter in the provinces, but it failed to travel very effectively. In 1904 it was produced at Budapest's Király Színház (as 'Me, You, He'), with József Németh in the rôle of Vergy, and in Milan, and the following year, rather surprisingly, it appeared under the management of Tom Davis, in the West End of London. Arthur Sturgess had the unenviable job of making the wholly sexual tale acceptable for the moral dragons of the British press and letters-to-the-editor columns, and musical director Theo Wendt was allowed to botch the score. John Le Hay (Vergy) starred opposite the French actress Aurélie Révy (Gabrielle), Aubrey Fitzgerald (Coucy) and comedienne Gracie Leigh (Mitzy) in what was one of the quickest failures of the era (7 performances).

The piece has continued to be well thought of by commentators and that-kind-of-music lovers, and a successful small-scale revival was staged in Paris in 1952 (Théâtre Labruyère 31 October) with comedians Roger Pierre and Jean-Marc Thibault starred and without the expensive orchestra.

Hungary: Király Színház *Én, te, ő* 13 May 1904; UK: Apollo Theatre *The Gay Lord Vergy* 30 September 1905

DIE SIRENE Operette in 3 acts by A M Willner and Leo Stein. Music by Leo Fall. Johann Strauss-Theater, Vienna, 5 January 1911.

The famous police-chief Philippe Aristide Fouché (Max Brod) sets Lolotte Boncourt, the siren of the title (Mizzi Günther) and a member of his private band of feminine spies, to entrap Armand de Ravaillac (Louis Treumann) who has been writing satirical letters against the Emperor. Lolotte succeeds, by the end of the second act, both in fulfilling her mission and in falling in love with her victim,

but Fouché's jubilant unmasking of Armand gives away his spy's identity and she thus loses her love for the length of the third act.

Die Sirene played 67 times at Vienna's Johann Strauss-Theater and, although it did not follow *Der fidele Bauer*, *Die Dollarprinzessin* and *Die geschiedene Frau* to major international triumph, it was nevertheless successfully staged in Germany and in America. Charles Frohman's Broadway production was mounted in style. Donald Brian, hero of *The Merry Widow*, was Armand, lovely Julia Sanderson played Lolotte and Frank Moulan (Baron Bazilos, ex-Fouché) headed the comedy with Elizabeth Firth from the cast of London's *Merry Widow* as his errant wife. The 14 numbers of Fall's score were, inevitably, augmented with extraneous songs, a list which included the Arthurs/David music-hall song 'I Want to Sing in Opera' made famous by Wilkie Bard, and pieces by Howard Talbot, Egbert van Alstyne and Jerome Kern. America's *The Siren* ran for a very respectable 113 performances before touring.

USA: Knickerbocker Theater *The Siren* 28 August 1911; Germany: Carl-Schultze Theater, Hamburg 25 October 1911

SISSY Singspiel in 2 acts by Ernst and Hubert Marischka based on a play by Ernst Decsey and Gustav Holm. Music by Fritz Kreisler. Theater an der Wien, Vienna, 23 December 1932.

The celebrated violinist Fritz Kreisler had ventured successfully into the world of the musical theatre with a share of the score for the 1919 Broadway musical *Apple Blossoms* (Globe Theater, 6 October, 256 performances) during the decade, during and following the War, which he had spent in America. It was more than another decade, however, before he wrote his only other theatre score, for Hubert Marischka and the Theater an der Wien.

Marischka and his brother, Ernst, adapted their libretto from a play which had embroidered a conventional fictionalized version of the lead-up to the historical marriage of the Empress Elisabeth ('Sissy') and the Emperor Franz Josef. The monarch had originally been – in this version of the 'facts' – intended as the husband of Sissy's sister, Helena, who in any case preferred the Prince von Thurn und Taxis. To this piece of period romance, Kreisler provided a score which was worked partly around the themes of some of his most successful compositions, principally for the violin. The Caprice Viennoise was turned into 'Ich glaube das Glück hält mich heute in Arm', the Liebeslied became another duet 'Dein Küss hat mir den Frühling gebracht', whilst the melody which was to become 'Stars in Your Eyes' (and which had already done duty in *Apple Blossoms*) this time made up into Sissy's solo 'Ich wär so gern einmal verliebt'.

Paula Wessely starred as the young Empress-to-be, with Hans Jaray as Franz Josef, Hubert Marischka in the rôle of Herzog Max of Bavaria, Maria Tauber as Helena, and Erika Wagner (Erzherzogin Sophie), Charlotte Waldon (Ludovika, Max's wife), Otto Maran (Thurn und Taxis), Fritz Imhoff (von Kempen) and Irene Ziláhy (Ilona Varady, ballet-dancer) amongst the other principals. Ludwig Itznegg, Hanns Schöbinger and Egon von Jordan succeeded to the rôle of the Emperor, Hilde Schulz and Anny Coty to that of Sissy and Ernst Tautenhayn, Kurt Lessen and Imhoff all played Max as the show compiled a straight 289-performance run, followed by a quick reprise three years later (25 October 1935) of a further 24 performances (300th, 7 November), all making up the best record of any new piece produced at the Theater an der Wien in the last decade of Hubert Marischka's management. It went on from that success to periodic revivals in Austria up to the present day.

Although *Sissy* was not played on Broadway, it was picked up by Hollywood where it was used as the basis for the film *The King Steps Out*, a version which again used a partial Kreisler score and allowed Grace Moore to sing 'Stars in your Eyes'. It was a different film, however, that got *Sissy* its most considerable exposure. A series of non-musical films about Elisabeth of Austria made in the 1950s with Romy Schneider starring were (and are) highly popular in France, and as a result Henri Varna of Paris's Théâtre Mogador ventured a production of *Sissy*, turned into an opérette à grand spectacle in the habitual style of the house. Varna himself, publisher Jean Marietti, librettist Marc-Cab and René Richard all had book credits whilst Gil Vidal and Françoise Doué appeared as hero and heroine for a slightly forced 11-month run which, nevertheless, established the piece in France.

Sissy appeared on the opérette à grand spectacle stage again, this time at the Théâtre Mogador, when she was portrayed by Raymonde Devarennes as a supporting character to a fictional romantic pair (Marcel Merkès, Paulette Merval) in the 1967 musical *Vienne chante et danse*, whilst in 1991 a *Sissi* with music by Francis Lopez was produced at Paris's Eldorado (Nadine Rotschild, Claude Dufresne, Daniel Ringold 28 September), and in 1992 Vienna turned out yet another variation on the theme (*Elisabeth*, Sylvester Levay/Michael Kunze Theater an der Wien 3 September) confirming the Empress Elisabeth, this time impersonated by Pia Douwes, as a well-established cliché of the romantic operettic stage.

An Austrian musical entitled *Sissi und Romy*, produced at the Mörbisch lake theatre in 1991 (Roland Baumgartner/Daniel Pascal 13 July), was based on the films and attempted to point parallels between the life of the Empress and the life of the actress who played her on film. Claudia Dallinger portrayed the actress/empress.

France: Théâtre Mogador *Sissi, futur imperatrice* 14 March 1959
Recording: *Sissi und Romy* original cast members (Polydor)

SISTERS Operett in 3 acts and 7 scenes by István Békeffy. Music by Lajos Lajtai. Király Színház, Budapest, 10 January 1930.

Rózsi Bársony and Ilona Titkos played the parts of Rosi and Anni, two little orphan girls from Pest who are taken in by the Müller family, father Miska (Árpád Latabár sr), mother (Ella Gombaszigi) and daughter Ildiko (Magda Kun). The girls follow in their departed mother's footsteps and take up dancing. They dance so well that by act two, spurred on by Anni's disappointment at the engagement of her farmer swain Gábor (József Sziklai) to Ildiko, they have left Pest behind, and become a sister act at the Paris Moulin-Rouge. Gábor follows, and sees Anni courted by the rich and easy Parisians, and almost wed to the Baron Radványi (Kornél d'Arrigó), before she listens to his professions of love, snaps out of her Parisian daydream and flees from the bright lights and barons back to Hungary. Rosi and her Tommy (Oszkar Dénes) follow close behind and, as the temptations of an American tour

swirl round the 'Sisters', they sit back to take count of what happiness is.

The show's score was very dance-heavy. In the first scene Anni and Rosi's schoolgirl chums set things rolling, and the sisters, deciding to be 'like mama', launched into an up-to-date foxtrot as an extension to each of two duets. In the second act, the sister-act allowed the girls to go through a Hawaiian routine, an English dance and an Hungarian csárdás, and the tango. The foxtrot, the slow-foxtrot, and a good old-fashioned march were all featured in the finale of a piece where every number was stretched by a considerable dance break. In the final act, Anni had a little song and dance with a bundle of kiddies.

Sisters proved a decided success in Budapest, and within months it had moved up to Vienna (ad Béla Jenbach) where it was produced at Erich Müller's Johann Strauss-Theater with Irén Biller and Grete Hornik starred as the two girls, Robert Nästlberger (Gábor) and Ernst Tautenhayn (Tommy) as their boys, Richard Waldemar (Müller), Felix Donbrowski (Radvány) and Daisy Solms (Ildiko) amongst the other principals. It stayed for a good run of two months.

Austria: Johann Strauss-Theater 22 October 1930

LE 66 Opérette in 1 act by Philippe Pittaud de Forges and 'Laurencin' (Paul Aimé Chapelle). Music by Jacques Offenbach. Théâtre des Bouffes-Parisiens, Paris, 31 July 1856.

A three-handed piece in the warmly rustic vein of *Le Mariage aux lanternes* and *Le Violoneux*, *Le 66* told the tale of tyrolean Frantz (Gertpré) who wins 100,000 florins in a lottery with the ticket number 66. He promptly borrows money from the pedlar Berthold (Guyot) and goes on a fatuous spending spree until he discovers with horror that his ticket is actually number 99. But the pedlar turns out to be a long-lost and wealthy relation, so all ends happily for Frantz and his pretty cousin Grittly (Mlle Maréchal). The score, which began unusually with a duo sung offstage, included a particularly popular tyrolienne ('Dans mon Tyrol') and romance ('En apprenant cette détresse') for Grittly, a jolly air for the pedlar ('Voilà le colporteur') and a happy trio in which the three discover that they are all related ('Ah! quel bonheur se trouver ensemble').

Le 66 was one of nine one-act pieces which Offenbach produced at the Bouffes-Parisiens during the year 1856, whilst still bound by the laws limiting the number of characters which could be used in his opérettes, and along with *La Rose de Saint-Flour*, *Tromb-al-ca-zar*, *La Bonne d'enfants* and *Le Savetier et le financier* it won a fine success. It remained in the Bouffes repertoire, and was played by the company on their 1862 summer visit to Vienna, where it had, by that time, already been seen in Karl Treumann's Carltheater version as *Die Savoyarden* (1859). That German version was also played in Budapest before a Hungarian one (ad Pál Madarassy) was produced.

An English version was first seen at London's Oxford Music Hall in 1865, toured by Susan Galton in a double-bill with *Les Noces de Jeannette*, and later played in the West End by Albert Brennir, Edith Percy and Norman Kirby as a curtain-raiser to *The Marble Heart* (Charing Cross Theatre, 4 July 1876). Miss Galton subsequently introduced it to America, in 1868–9, at Woods Museum and the Williamsburg Theater in her repertoire of short pieces, which also included *Lischen and*

Fritzchen, *Le Mariage aux lanternes*, *Too Many Cooks* (ie *La Rose de Saint-Flour*) and MacFarren's *Jessy Lea*.

Its most recent appearance on the Paris stage was in 1984, played in a double bill with Offenbach's *Pépito* (Studio Bertrand 24 July).

Austria: Carltheater *Die Savoyarden* 24 November 1859; Theater am Franz-Josefs-Kai (Fr) 4 June 1862; Hungary: Budai Színkör *Die Savoyarden* 29 June 1860, Budai Népszinház *A 66-os szám* 7 December 1863; Germany: *Loterielos No 66* np nd; UK: Oxford Music Hall July 1865; USA: Woods Museum 31 August 1868

SKIPPED BY THE LIGHT OF THE MOON

Musical farcical comedy in 2 acts adapted from *A Gay City* by George R Sims. Lyrics by Percy Marshall. Music by George Pack and Henry W May. United States of America, date and place unknown.

Skipped By the Light of the Moon was a latter-day farce-comedy, in the line of the American shows of Charles Hoyt and his contemporaries, which toured incessantly and with singular success in English-speaking countries in the last part of the 19th century. The history of its development is now rather obscure, but it began in 1881 when Charles Majilton commissioned a play for his famous family troupe from the master of the provincial comedy, George Sims. The resulting piece, *A Gay City* (Nottingham, 8 September 1881), a lively imbroglio of husbands on the loose, mistaken identities, and pursuing wives, with a lost baby thrown in for good measure, proved absolutely to the taste of the kind of unsophisticated rural and provincial city dates in which the Majiltons prospered and it remained in their repertoire for many years. One night, at Carlisle, two gentlemen sat in the front row with hats on their laps. As the play progressed, they scribbled the dialogue onto a pile of visiting cards, dropping the filled cards into the hats, and finally walked out of the theatre with *A Gay City* on, rather than in, their heads.

The two gentlemen went to America and, not long after, a pirated version of *A Gay City*, decorated with popular songs, and entitled *Skipped By the Light of the Moon*, appeared on the American circuits. It proved as popular as the parent show had been in England and it trouped solidly for a decade through America and onto the Pacific circuit with an ever-varying musical content, songs being pilfered with the same abandon that the original play had been. In Australia, John Gourlay introduced *Skipped By the Light of the Moon* in 1887 and he played it there for many years, being joined in 1893 by Harry Shine and George Walton (both members of well-known British families of comedians) who had come out to Australia to play opéra-bouffe with Soldene. Walton and Gourlay kept the piece going for a number of years, in repertoire with such pieces as *Milky White* and George Sims's *Corsican Brothers* burlesque.

It was Walton who took *Skipped By the Light of the Moon* back to Britain. Billed as 'the electrical musical comedy', with Sims given his author's due and the music credited to the Australian musical director George Pack and to Walton's own conductor Henry W May (but including numbers by such composers as Ivan Caryll, R G Knowles, Milton Wellings and the ballad composer Harry Trotère), it opened at Reading and set off on a very long and lucrative career in the provinces. Both the book and score were regularly updated with topicalities and new tunes, and its

success was such that in 1899 an inexperienced producer brought it into London under the title *A Good Time* (27 April). The piece was certainly not London fodder, and it quickly returned to the provinces to see out its second decade of prosperity in its natural habitat.

Australia: Bijou Theatre, Melbourne 23 April 1887; UK: Reading 24 August 1896, Shaftesbury Theatre *A Good Time* 27 April 1899

SKYSCRAPER Musical comedy in 2 acts by Peter Stone based on the play *Dream Girl* by Elmer Rice. Lyrics by Sammy Cahn. Music by James van Heusen. Lunt-Fontanne Theater, New York, 13 November 1965.

Based rather distantly on the 1945 play *Dream Girl* (the leading character rather than the plot survived), *Skyscraper* was a musical made up largely of a series of daydream sequences, the escapist musings of antique-shopkeeper Georgina Allerton (Julie Harris) who is refusing to sell her home to Bert Bushman (Dick O'Neill), a chap who wants to demolish it to build a skyscraper. She does, however, accept an invitation to dinner with his architect brother, Tim (Peter L Marshall), who tries to explain modern urban beauty to her. Georgina's shop-assistant Roger (Charles Nelson Reilly), who has been bought by the Bushmans, proposes to her to get her to leave the building but she snaps out of her dreaming and opts instead for Tim and demolition.

Cahn and van Husen's score had the advantage of being able to spread itself over reality and dreamland, but it was reality which brought up the most successful song of the score, Tim's 'Everybody Has the Right to Be Wrong', and also the most amusing production number, an incidental piece choreographed by Michael Kidd in which a construction foreman forces two indifferent site workers to keep up the uncouthly macho image of their genre by whistling and jawing at passing girls.

Feuer and Martin's production of *Skyscraper* went through a fair if slightly forced run of 248 performances without becoming a genuine success.

Recording: original cast (Capitol)

SLADE, Julian (b London, 28 May 1930). Composer of several fresh and unpretentious musical scores for the English stage of the 1950s and 1960s, amongst which was one record-breaking hit.

Julian Slade studied at the Bristol Old Vic drama school and joined the Old Vic company at that city's Theatre Royal in 1951. He appeared briefly on the stage, but soon turned his attention to writing and, in collaboration with two other company members, supplied the Old Vic with the highly successful Christmas revue *Christmas in King Street* (1952). He provided the incidental music for a production of *The Duenna*, which subsequently transferred to London, for local productions of *Love for Love* and *She Stoops to Conquer*, and for *The Merchant of Venice* at Stratford-on-Avon (1953), and collaborated with Dorothy Reynolds on a first musical play, *The Merry Gentleman*, as a successor to the previous year's seasonal revue. A comic-opera version of *The Comedy of Errors* was produced on BBC-TV in 1954, but it was a second Slade/Reynolds musical, *Salad Days* ('I Sit in the Sun', 'We're Looking for a Piano', 'The Time of My Life'), written later the same year as an end-of-term romp for a company who had been playing largely more serious things, which hit the jackpot. Following its brief Bristol season, it moved to London where it became the longest-running musical play in the West End's history up to that time.

Slade co-wrote and composed four further works with Miss Reynolds, the slightly more substantial *Free as Air* (1957), another seasonal piece, *Hooray for Daisy* (1959), a version of *Christmas in King Street* stiffened with a libretto and entitled *Follow That Girl* (1960, 'Follow That Girl') and *Wildest Dreams* (1960), before teaming with playwright Robin Miller and Alan Pryce-Jones on his largest venture to date, a musical adaptation of *Vanity Fair*. This was not a success, and Slade returned to writing for smaller stages with incidental music for Shakespeare plays at Bristol and London's Regents Park Open Air Theatre, and musical play adaptations of *The Knight of the Burning Pestle* as *Nutmeg and Ginger*, of Nancy Mitford's *The Pursuit of Love*, and of Pinero's *The Schoolmistress* under the title *Out of Bounds*. He also arranged Fraser-Simson's *The Hums of Pooh* with some additional music of his own into a children's musical (*Winnie the Pooh*) which was played a number of times as a seasonal entertainment in London and also in Germany.

Another Pinero adaptation, a musical version of the romantic *Trelawny of the Wells* (*Trelawny*), initially staged at Bristol, followed the *Salad Days* trail into the West End but, although it showed up as perhaps Slade's most substantial and accomplished piece, it had a reasonable rather than a fine run there. This was perhaps partly because *Trelawny* appeared in London in the same year as *Jesus Christ Superstar*. The passing of an era which that 'meeting at the crossroads' represented meant that Slade's style of work was thereafter less in demand than before. Although *Salad Days* continues to be revived, and 1991 saw a reprise of *Nutmeg and Ginger* at London's Orange Tree Theatre, the composer's most recent work, a féerique musical version of J M Barrie's *Dear Brutus*, remains, to date, unproduced.

1953 **The Merry Gentleman** (Dorothy Reynolds) Theatre Royal, Bristol 24 December

1954 **Salad Days** (Reynolds) Vaudeville Theatre 5 August

1956 **The Comedy of Errors** (Lionel Harris, Robert McNab) Arts Theatre 28 March

1957 **Free as Air** (Reynolds) Savoy Theatre 6 June

1959 **Hooray for Daisy** (Reynolds) Theatre Royal, Bristol 23 December; Lyric Theatre, Hammersmith 20 December 1960

1960 **Follow That Girl** (Reynolds) Vaudeville Theatre 17 March

1960 **Wildest Dreams** (Reynolds) Everyman Theatre, Cheltenham 20 September, Vaudeville Theatre 3 August 1961

1962 **Vanity Fair** (Robin Miller, Alan Pryce-Jones) Queen's Theatre 27 November

1963 **Nutmeg and Ginger** (Slade) Everyman Theatre, Cheltenham 29 October

1967 **The Pursuit of Love** (Slade) Theatre Royal, Bristol 24 May

1970 **Winnie the Pooh** (Harold Fraser-Simson ad/Slade) Phoenix Theatre 17 December

1972 **Trelawny** (w Aubrey Woods, George Rowell) Theatre Royal, Bristol 12 January, Sadler's Wells Theatre 27 June

1973 **Out of Bounds** (Slade) Theatre Royal, Bristol 26 December

SLAUGHTER, Walter [Alfred] (b London, 17 February 1860; d London, 2 March 1908). Successful Victorian composer of musical comedy, comic opera and children's shows.

Brought up in London, Slaughter studied music under Georges Jacobi, musical director of the Alhambra, and was both organist at St Andrews Church and a cellist and pianist in the music halls prior to becoming a musical director in a series of West End theatres. He spent three years at the Theatre Royal, Drury Lane, under Sir Augustus Harris (1887–90), and also held engagements at the Prince's, the St James's under George Alexander (1890), the Avenue, the Vaudeville and, in his last days, as the first musical director for Oswald Stoll at the London Coliseum (1904–6).

After composing some ballet music for the South London Theatre and some individual songs, including the popular 'The Dear Homeland', he found his first theatre success as a lyric composer with the score for the little all-women operetta *An Adamless Eden* (1882), played in Britain and America by Lila Clay's ladies' company, and he confirmed with a pretty score for what is, a century and many shows later, still the most successful musical version of *Alice in Wonderland* to have been produced (1886).

He had some more substantial success with the score to the medieval comic opera *Marjorie* produced by the Carl Rosa Light Opera Company (1890), and contributed to the Gaiety Theatre's *Cinder-Ellen Up-too-Late* (1891), but he achieved his greatest success when he paired with Basil Hood to produce the outstanding musical comedy *Gentleman Joe* as a vehicle for low comic Arthur Roberts. Of his further collaborations with Hood, *The French Maid*, gave him a second and even longer-lived international success, *Dandy Dan the Lifeguardsman* proved a second happy vehicle for Roberts and *Orlando Dando* did similar if less long service for for Dan Leno. *An English Daisy*, written with Seymour Hicks, won a Broadway production (if not a London one), but the most successful of his subsequent works was another children's piece, *Bluebell in Fairyland*, produced by Charles Frohman and played by Hicks and Ellaline Terriss. Slaughter provided the basic score, subsequently riddled through with interpolations, for what was to turn out to be the most popular Christmas entertainment of its time. One more show written with the visiting American comedian and playwright Richard Carle under the title *Little Miss Modesty* seems to have remained unproduced.

Slaughter also composed much incidental music, notably for the plays produced at the St James's during his employment there – Walter Frith's *Molière*, Quinton and Hamilton's *Lord Anerley*, Haddon Chambers's *The Idler* (1891), the original production of Wilde's *Lady Windermere's Fan* (1892), Henry James's *Guy Domville* (1895) and *The Prisoner of Zenda* (1896).

His wife Luna Lauri (Mlle Luna) was one of the two famous dancing daughters of John Lauri, ballet-master at the Alhambra Theatre, who, as Mlles Stella and Luna, appeared as featured soloists in many of the Alhambra spectaculars. Her brother, **George LAURI** (d 4 January 1909), made himself a fine career in Australia, being for many year's the colony's foremost comic star of musical comedy before cutting his throat when he feared his fame was faltering. Slaughter's daughter Marjorie Slaughter, the composer of a number of songs, also wrote the score for the operetta *The Constable and the Pictures* (1 act Devonshire Park Theatre, Eastbourne 1907) and supplemented her father's music for a two-act comic opera *A Tangerine*

Tangle, staged for one copyright performance after his death at the age of 48 from dropsy.

1880 **Change Partners** ('Lewis Clifton', Joseph J Dilley) 1 act tour
1882 **An Adamless Eden** (Henry Savile Clarke) 1 act Opera Comique 13 December
1882 **His Only Coat** (J J Dallas) 1 act Gaiety Theatre 22 May
1883 **Sly and Shy** (A R Phillips) 1 act Princess Theatre, Edinburgh 21 May
1885 **The Casting Vote** (Walter Helmore) 1 act Prince's Theatre 7 October
1886 **Sappho** (Harry Lobb) 1 act Opera Comique 10 February
1886 **Alice in Wonderland** (Savile Clarke) Prince of Wales Theatre 23 December
1889 **The New Corsican Brothers** (Cecil Raleigh) Royalty Theatre 20 November
1890 **Marjorie** (Dilley, Clifton) Prince of Wales Theatre 18 January
1890 **The Rose and the Ring** (Savile Clarke) Prince of Wales Theatre 20 December
1892 **Donna Luiza** (Basil Hood) 1 act Prince of Wales Theatre 23 March
1893 **The Crossing Sweeper** (Hood) 1 act Gaiety Theatre 8 April
1893 **Peggy's Plot** (Somerville Gibney) 1 act St George's Hall 20 December
1894 **A Big Bandit** (T Malcolm Watson) 1 act St George's Hall 30 April
1894 **Melodramania** (Watson) 1 act St George's Hall 27 December
1895 **Gentleman Joe** (Hood) Prince of Wales Theatre 2 March
1896 **The French Maid** (Hood) Theatre Royal, Bath 4 April; Terry's Theatre 24 April 1897
1896 **Belinda** (B C Stephenson, Hood) Prince's Theatre, Manchester 5 October
1897 **Dandy Dan the Lifeguardsman** (Hood) Belfast 23 August, Lyric Theatre, London 4 December
1897 **The Duchess of Dijon** (Hood) Portsmouth 20 September
1897 **Hans Andersen's Fairytales** (Hood) Terry's Theatre 23 December
1898 **Orlando Dando** (Hood) Grand Theatre, Fulham 1 August
1898 **Her Royal Highness** (Hood) Vaudeville Theatre 3 September
1901 **You and I** (Aubrey Hopwood/Seymour Hicks) 1 act Vaudeville Theatre 24 April
1901 **Bluebell in Fairyland** (Hopwood, Charles H Taylor/Hicks) Vaudeville 18 December
1902 **An English Daisy** (Hicks) Royal County Theatre, Kingston 11 August
1903 **Little Hans Andersen** (Hood) Adelphi Theatre 23 December
1906 **S'Nero, or a Roman Bank Holiday** (Roland Carse/Christopher Davis) 1 act London Coliseum January
1907 **Lady Tatters** (Carse/Herbert Leonard) Shaftesbury Theatre 31 August
1909 **A Tangerine Tangle** (w Marjorie Slaughter/Norman Slee) Vaudeville Theatre 2 July (copyright performance)

Other titles attributed: *Marie's Honeymoon* (1885), *The King and the Abbot* (1904), *The Cruise of the Great Britain*

SLEEP, Wayne (b 17 July 1948).

For a number of years a principal dancer with Britain's Royal Ballet, the diminutive Sleep moved into the musical theatre to create the rôle of Mister Mistofolees/Quaxo in *Cats* (1980). He subsequently created the principal rôle in the 'Dance' half of the entertainment *Song and Dance* (1982), played in pantomime, toured and televised with his own dance show (*The Hot-Shoe Show*), and appeared in London as the MC in a revival of *Cabaret* (1986).

SLEZAK, Walter (b Vienna, 3 May 1902; d New York, 22 April 1983).

The son of the celebrated opera tenor Leo Slezak (who ventured into opéra-bouffe as Offenbach's *Barbe-bleue*), Walter Slezak came to the theatre after false starts in medicine and as a bank clerk. He began his career in Berlin where, in his twenties, he appeared as juvenile man in several musical plays. He visited Vienna in December 1928 to play Teddy Vandermeere in Oscar Straus's *Hochzeit in Hollywood* and Weyland in *Friederike* at the Johann Strauss-Theater and succeeded to the rôle of Roger in *Meine Schwester und ich* in Berlin. Allegedly, he was hired to repeat his rôle in *Meine Schwester und ich* on Broadway by error – one Shubert brother saw original cast star Oskar Karlweis, the other hired replacement Slezak – but he went and made a fine impression, laying the foundations for what would be the main part of his career, on the American stage and screen.

After *Meet My Sister* (1930), he went back to Europe and played alongside Fritzi Massary in her return to the musical stage in *Eine Frau, die weiss, was sie will* at the Berlin Metropoltheater. However, he soon joined the exodus from Germany and returned to America where he created the rôle of village schoolmaster Karl Reder (who ultimately gets the ingénue) in *Music in the Air* and, after a brief experience in the road-folding *Love! Out of the Window*, was cast in further mittel-European rôles as the psychoanalyst Professor Volk in the unfortunate *May Wine* (1935) and the angel-marrying banker Harry in *I Married an Angel* (1938).

After a number of years in Hollywood, Slezak came back to the Broadway musical stage to star alongside Ezio Pinza as Panisse in the homogenized Pagnol show, *Fanny* (Tony Award). When the Metropolitan Opera House dipped into Operette with a version of *Der Zigeunerbaron* he appeared as Zsupán, and he later played regionally as Fagin in *Oliver!* and as Frosch in *Die Fledermaus*. Slezak committed suicide at the age of 80.

Amongst his musical film credits are *The Pirate* (1948), and the screen version of *Call Me Madam* (1953, Tantinnin).

Autobiography: *What Time's the Next Swan?* (Doubleday, Garden City, 1962)

SLOANE, A[lfred] Baldwin (b Baltimore, 28 August 1872; d Red Bank, NJ, 21 February 1925). Supplier of mostly utilitarian music to a generation of Broadway shows.

Interested by the musical theatre at a young age, Sloane was instrumental in the formation of an amateur musical group, the Paint and Powder Club, in his home town, and nominated himself as the composer of their 1894 show, *Mustapha*. This show was seen by producer Edward Rice who promptly offered the amateur composer his first professional stage work, a commission to compose some songs for the score for his extravaganza *Excelsior Jr*. The extravaganza was a considerable success on Broadway, and the facile and versatile young composer soon found opportunities coming from other sources. He subsequently composed the whole score for two further pieces by *Excelsior's* prolific librettist, R A Barnet, the juvenile extravaganza *The Strange Adventures of Jack and the Beanstalk*, produced by Klaw and Erlanger at the Casino Theater, and another piece in the same vein, *Simple Simon*, which was introduced by the enterprising Boston group the Cadets. He contributed several numbers to Anna Held's *Papa's Wife*, and in the course of one year supplied much of the music for the revusical-spectaculars *Broadway to Tokio* and *A Million Dollars* and for *The Giddy Throng* which had a 'burlesque review' and a 'musical sketch' enclosed in its meanderings, and composed a burlesque of *Nell Gwynne* and the score for the farce-comedy *Aunt Hannah* ('Ma Tiger Lily').

Over the following years Sloane wrote or contributed to a large number of further such half-revue, half-musical comedy pieces, had a song success with 'When You Ain't Got No Money, Well, You Needn't Come Around' (ly: Clarence Brewster) as performed by May Irwin in America and Annie Wünsch in Vienna ('Wer Kein Gelt hat, der bleibt z' Haus'), yet also turned out the appreciable and charming score for the comic opera *The Mocking Bird* and for an old-fashioned girl-goes-to-war piece called *Sergeant Kitty*, hailed by one journal as 'a capital example of a real comic opera of the Strauss-Suppé-Millöcker school'. However, George R White's production lasted but 55 performances on Broadway. Sloane's most memorable credit – although the show's success cannot truthfully be said to be attributable to its score – was his composing credit on the fairytale spectacular *The Wizard of Oz* for which he supplied half the basic score ('In Michigan', 'Niccolo's Piccolo' etc).

With *Lady Teazle*, a comic-opera vehicle for Lillian Russell as Sheridan's *School for Scandal* heroine, Sloane reached the high point of his ambitions. After its 57-performance failure, he devoted himself to turning out a stream of unexceptional musical scores for light entertainments of a mostly easygoing structural nature. He supplied the score for Chicago's advertisedly first-ever local revue, *All Round Chicago* (McVickers Theater 1905), provided Weber and Fields with music for their revusical *Hokey Pokey* (8 February 1912), *Hanky Panky* (5 August 1912) and *Roly Poly* (21 November 1912 w Goetz/Edgar Smith), including the songs for the little set-piece burlesques featured in those shows, and later wrote for Lew Fields's series of successful 'summer musicals'. He wrote another musical for the Paint and Powder Club (*Dear Dorothy*, 1916), contributed to John Murray Anderson's revue *Venus on Broadway* (Palais Royal 1 October 1917), to *The Greenwich Village Follies* in 1919 and 1920, and to something called *Fantastic Fricassee* produced in Greenwich Village in 1922. Amongst all this forgettable material, he did however turn out one hit song, 'Heaven Will Protect the Working Girl', as sung by Marie Dressler in the fantasy comedy *Tillie's Nightmare*.

For his last work, Sloane returned to what was labelled 'operetta', in the company of two of the more prolific junk librettists of his time, Harry Cort and George Stoddard, but although the show's Broadway run was short its composer did not see its last night, having died shortly after the opening. Lambasted right and left, virtually from the beginning of his career, as a hack, Sloane rarely won critical appreciation for his music, but he nevertheless seems to have held the confidence of producers, for his output was huge and his presence on Broadway, with at least one show at any time, fairly continuous over nearly two decades. He proved, in the best of his pieces, that he was not without ability, but by and large he worked as a journeyman musician without much ambition.

1895 **Excelsior Jr** (w E E Rice, George Lowell Tracy/R A Barnet) Olympia Theater 29 November

1896 **The Strange Adventures of Jack and the Beanstalk** (Barnet) Casino Theater 2 November

189? **Simple Simon** (Barnet) Boston

1900 **Broadway to Tokio** (George V Hobart) New York Theater 23 January

1900 **Aunt Hannah** (Clay Greene/Matthew J Royal) Bijou Theatre 22 February

1900 **A Million Dollars** (Hobart, Louis Harrison) New York Theater 27 September

1900 **Nell-Go-In** 1 act New York Theater 31 October

1900 **After Office Hours** (Hobart) sketch in *The Giddy Throng* (Sydney Rosenfeld) New York Theater 24 December

1901 **The King's Carnival** (Hobart/Sydney Rosenfeld) New York Theater 13 May

1901 **The Liberty Belles** (w others/Harry B Smith) Madison Square Theater 30 September

1902 **The Hall of Fame** (Hobart/Rosenfeld) New York Theater 3 February

1902 **The Belle of Broadway** (w others/Hobart/W H Post) 1 scene Winter Garden Theater 17 March

1902 **The Mocking Bird** (Rosenfeld) Bijou Theater 10 November

1903 **The Wizard of Oz** (w Paul Tietjens/Glen Macdonough/Frank Baum) Majestic Theater 20 January

1904 **Sergeant Kitty** (R H Burnside) Daly's Theater 18 January

1904 **Lady Teazle** (John Kendrick Bangs, Roderic Scheff) Casino Theater 24 December

1904 **Cupid and Co** (E Tracy Sweet) Wilkes-Barre, Pa, 14 November

1905 **Mama's Papa** (Joseph Hart) Grand Opera House, Salem 1 February

1905 **The Gingerbread Man** (Frederick Ranken) Liberty Theater 25 December

1906 **Comin' Thru the Rye** (w J Sebastian Heller/Hobart) Herald Square Theater 9 January

1906 **Seeing New York** (Joseph Hart/Hart, Clifton Crawford) 1 act New York Roof Garden 5 June

1907 **The Mimic and the Maid** (Allen Lowe) Bijou Theater 11 January

1907 **Happy Days** (Al Leech/H Hilbert Chalmers) Atlantic City 8 August

1907 **Cupid at Vassar** (Owen Davis, George Totten Smith) Waterbury, Conn, 23 August

1908 **Li'l Mose** (Charles H Brown/Fred Nixon Nirdlinger) Atlantic City 20 April

1909 **Lo** (Franklin P Adams/'O Henry') Davidson Theater, Milwaukee 29 August

1909 **The Girl from the States** (w Raymond Hubbell/Glen MacDonough) Adelphi Theater, Philadelphia 11 October

1910 **Tillie's Nightmare** (Edgar Smith) Herald Square Theater 5 May

1910 **The Summer Widowers** (MacDonough) Broadway Theater 4 June

1910 **The Prince of Bohemia** (E Ray Goetz/J Hartley Manners) Hackett Theater 14 June

1911 **The Henpecks** (Goetz/MacDonough) Broadway Theater 4 February

1912 **Bunty Bulls and Strings** (Goetz/E Smith) 2 scenes Broadway Theater 9 February

1912 **Without the Law** (Goetz/E Smith) 1 act Weber and Fields Music Hall 21 November

1912 **The Sun Dodgers** (Goetz/E Smith) Lew Fields Broadway Theater 30 November
1917 **We Should Worry** (Charles Hoyt ad Henry Blossom) Apollo, Atlantic City 26 October
1918 **Look Who's Here** (H B Smith) Trenton, NJ 30 August
1918 **Ladies First** (H B Smith) Broadhurst Theater 24 October
1925 **When Summer Comes** (Jack Arnold) Poli's Theater, Washington 15 February
1925 **The China Rose** (Harry L Cort, George Stoddard) Martin Beck Theater 24 December

SMILES Musical comedy in 2 acts by William Anthony McGuire (with others). Lyrics by Harold Adamson and Clifford Grey. Additional lyrics by Ring Lardner. Music by Vincent Youmans. Ziegfeld Theater, New York, 18 November 1930.

Florenz Ziegfeld commissioned *Smiles* (originally entitled *Tom, Dick and Harry*) as an extravagant vehicle for his preferred but slightly passée star Marilyn Miller, whom he wished to team up with the Astaires, brother and sister, who had had such fine successes on both sides of the Atlantic in *Stop Flirting*, *Lady, Be Good!* and *Funny Face*. From a storyline allegedly suggested by Noël Coward, McGuire produced a text in which Smiles (Miss Miller), a French war orphan brought back to America and godfathered by four soldiers, grows up to be a Salvation Army lassie, equipped with a song photocopied from Edna May's famous 'They All Follow Me', and meets up with rich, bored Bob Hastings (Fred Astaire) and his sister Dot (Adele Astaire). In McGuire's original script she married him, but in rehearsal Ziegfeld changed the ending so that she paired instead with dashing doughboy Dick (Paul Gregory).

The show hit trouble and lawsuits on the road, Youmans suing Ziegfeld to stop him sacking his selected conductor, Paul Lannin, and threatening to walk out with the music. Ziegfeld won the court case and opened *Smiles* on Broadway to largely negative notices from which the Astaires emerged better than Miss Miller who, in turn, emerged better than either the book or the music. Ziegfeld ordered changes, but relations with Youmans still being sticky, he ultimately inserted two replacement numbers by Walter Donaldson. It was in any case too little and too late, and *Smiles* closed in failure after 63 performances.

Oddly enough, that was not the end of the show nor its scorned score. Fred Astaire occasionally re-used his 'Say, Young Man of Manhattan', but it was another *Smiles* song which was responsible for the show's getting a second opportunity. The Prince of Wales took a fancy to 'Time on My Hands', sung in the original show by Paul Gregory, and began asking dance bands to play it. The New Mayfair Dance Orchestra, Eddie Duchin, Ray Noble and the Mills Brothers recorded it, and finally someone thought to look up the show that it came from. And so in 1933 a revised version of *Smiles* adapted by Frank Eyton, Clifford Grey and Herbert Sargent, with additional songs by Melville Gideon and entitled *The One Girl*, opened at the London Hippodrome under the management of Joe Sacks. It had a fine cast including Gaiety dancing ingénue Louise Browne and her habitual partner Roy Royston in the rôles created by the Astaires, French musical comedy star Mireille Perrey as the heroine, hero Dennis Noble (replaced by Guy Middleton), and a bevy of comics including Lupino Lane, Robert Hale and Arthur Riscoe. Apart from 'Time on My

Hands', 'Say, Young Man of Manhattan', 'Be Good to Me', 'Carry on, Keep Smiling' and the Chinese ballet music, the *Smiles* score seemed to have disappeared under a welter of new and nearly new numbers of which Youmans's title-tune (salvaged from the flop *Rainbow*) proved most popular. The show did not, and folded on April Fools' Day after a five-week run.

UK: London Hippodrome *The One Girl* 24 February 1933

SMITH, Edgar [McPhail] (b Brooklyn, NY, 9 December 1857; d Bayside, NY, 8 March 1938). Actor turned all-purpose penman through a long career in the musical theatre.

Educated at Pennsylvania Military Academy, Edgar Smith began his association with the theatre as an actor at the age of 21, and had his first experience as a dramatist when he wrote a comedy-drama to be played by a touring company of which he was a member. His first musical piece was a burlesque, *Little Lohengrin*, written for the Chicago theatre, but he was soon plunged into the very centre of America's musical theatre activity when he was engaged as resident dramaturg and sometime supporting actor at the Casino Theater. He held this position for more than six years, assisting German-born house director Max Freeman and others in the adaptation of the French opéras-comiques and Austrian Operetten which were the theatre's main fare, and intermittently appearing in them (Dimoklos in *Apollo*, Grog in *La Grande-Duchesse*, Clampas in *The Drum Major*, *The Talisman*, Nowalksy in *Der arme Jonathan* etc).

After leaving the Casino, Smith appeared with Thomas Q Seabrooke in *Tabasco*, as a result of which he authored a sequel to that successful vehicle for its star under the title *The Grand Vizier*. He also provided the text for the Casino Theater's successor to its revusical *Passing Show*, a part-revue part-burlesque called *The Merry World*, and for an extravaganza, *Miss Philadelphia*, staged with great success in Philadelphia, before taking on a new position as dramaturg – far from the refinements of Continental comic opera – as house writer to the Weber and Fields organization.

Over the next six and a half years, Smith turned out outlines, sketches and scenes for the part-revue, part-burlesque entertainments which were the characteristic productions of Weber and Fields. The basic entertainment was one which allowed for movable parts and regularly, during the run of a piece, an entire one-act or two-scene burlesque of a currently popular play would be inserted. These, too, Smith was more often than not called upon to write, in collaboration with composer John Stromberg (*Onions* on *Carrots*, *Sapolio* on *Sappho*, *Waffles* on *Raffles*, *Trilby*, *Arizona* etc). Amongst the songs which emerged from the collaboration was one that lasted: 'Ma Blushin' Rosie'.

At the same time Smith continued to work for other producers, adapting – or rather americanizing – Ivan Caryll's *The Gay Parisienne* as *The Girl from Paris* with lyrics to new songs by Nat D Mann, the enormously successful English musical *The French Maid* and Harry Greenbank's *Monte Carlo* for the voluminously importing E E Rice, and doing what seems to have been a major rewrite on the French vaudeville-opérette *L'Auberge du Tohu-bohu* for American consumption. He also worked on two original musicals, *The Little Host* and *Sweet Anne Page*, which, in spite of starring Della Fox and Lulu Glaser respectively, failed to catch on.

In 1903, at the break-up of the association of Weber and Fields, Smith went with Weber, and for two seasons performed his old job for Weber's Music Hall, a job which included a collaboration with Victor Herbert on *The Dream City* and, 20 years after the first time, a second *Lohengrin* burlesque, *The Magic Knight*. However, he did not give up the connection with Fields for whom he re-manufactured one of his finest rôles, Henry Pecksniff in the americanized version of the British musical *The Girl Behind the Counter* (1907). Smith worked at a great rate on a long list of revues and musical comedies, and in 1910 turned out what would remain his most famous lyric: the words to Baldwin Sloane's 'Heaven Will Protect the Working Girl' as performed by Marie Dressler in *Tillie's Nightmare*.

When Weber and Fields came back together again, Smith resumed his old position and supplied them with *Hokey-Pokey*, *Hanky-Panky* and *Roly Poly*, but the bulk of the work of his latter days was for the Shuberts for whom he ended his career as he had begun it, adapting Continental musical shows for the American stage with the same kind of hand with which he had written for Weber and Fields. The last work to which his name was attached, 45 years after his first show, was an American version of *Das Land des Lächelns* which closed out of town.

1886 **Little Lohengrin** Chicago
1887 **Madelon** (*La Petite Mademoiselle*) American version (Casino Theater)
1888 **Nadgy** (*Les Noces improvisées*) American version of English version (Casino Theater)
1889 **Les Brigands** American version w Max Freeman (Casino Theater)
1889 **The Drum Major** (*La Fille du tambour-major*) American version w Freeman (Casino Theater)
1890 **Poor Jonathan** (*Der arme Jonathan*) American version (Casino Theater)
1890 **The Brazilian** (Francis Chassaigne ad Gustave Kerker) American version (Casino Theater)
1890 **Apollo** (*Das Orakel*) American version w Helen F Tretbar (Casino Theater)
1890 **The Grand-Duchess** (*La Grande-Duchesse de Gérolstein*) American adaptation of C H Kenney's English version (Casino Theater)
1891 **Fleurette** (Emma Steiner/w Mrs C Doremus) Standard Theater 24 August
1895 **The Grand Vizier** (Frederick Gagel) Harlem Opera House 4 March
1896 **Miss Philadelphia** (Herman Perlet) Park Theater, Philadelphia 27 April
1896 **The Girl from Paris** (*The Gay Parisienne*) American version (Herald Square Theater)
1897 **Under the Red Globe** (John Stromberg) 1 act Weber and Fields' Music Hall 18 February
1897 **Poussé-Café** (Stromberg/w Louis de Lange) 1 act Weber and Fields' Music Hall 2 December
1897 **The French Maid** American version (Herald Square Theater)
1898 **The Con-Curers** (Stromberg/w de Lange) 1 act Weber and Fields' Music Hall 17 March
1898 **Monte Carlo** American version (Herald Square Theater)
1898 **Hurly Burly** (Stromberg/w H B Smith) Weber and Fields' Music Hall 8 September

1898 **Hotel Topsy Turvy** (*L'Auberge du Tohu-bohu*) American adaptation of Arthur Sturgess's English version (Herald Square Theater)
1898 **Cyranose de Bric-à-Brac** (Stromberg) 1 act Weber and Fields' Music Hall 3 November
1898 **The Little Host** (W T Francis, Thomas Chilvers/w de Lange) Herald Square Theater 26 December
1899 **Catherine** (Stromberg/w H B Smith) Weber and Fields' Music Hall 19 January
1899 **Onions** (Stromberg) 1 act Weber and Fields' Music Hall
1899 **Helter Skelter** (Stromberg/H B Smith) Weber and Fields' Music Hall 6 April
1899 **Zaza** (Stromberg) 1 act Weber and Fields' Music Hall
1899 **Mother Goose** (Gagel, Fred Eustis/w de Lange) 14th Street Theater 1 May
1899 **Whirl-I-Gig** (Stromberg/H B Smith) Weber and Fields' Music Hall 21 September
1899 **Barbara Fidgety** (Stromberg/H B Smith) 1 act Weber and Fields' Music Hall 7 December
1900 **Fiddle Dee Dee** (Stromberg) Weber and Fields' Music Hall 25 July
1900 **Quo Vass Is!** (Stromberg) 1 act Weber and Fields' Music Hall 6 September
1900 **Arizona** (Stromberg) Weber and Fields' Music Hall 18 October
1900 **Sweet Anne Page** (W H Neidlinger/w de Lange) Manhattan Theater 3 December
1901 **Exhibit II** (Stromberg) 1 act Weber and Fields' Music Hall 10 March
1901 **Hoity Toity** (Stromberg) Weber and Fields' Music Hall 5 September
1901 **The Curl and the Judge** (Stromberg) 1 act Weber and Fields' Music Hall
1902 **Twirly Whirly** (Stromberg, Francis) Weber and Fields' Music Hall 11 September
1903 **Whoop-Dee-Doo** (Francis) Weber and Fields' Music Hall 24 September
1904 **An English Daisy** American version (Casino Theater)
1904 **Higgledy Piggledy** (Maurice Levi) Weber's Music Hall 20 October
1905 **The College Widower** (Levi) 1 act Weber's Music Hall 5 January
1906 **Twiddle Twaddle** (Levi) Weber's Music Hall 1 January
1906 **The Squaw Man's Girl of the Golden West** (Levi) 1 act Weber's Music Hall 26 February
1906 **The Dream City** (Victor Herbert) 1 act Weber's Music Hall 25 December
1906 **The Magic Knight** (Herbert) 1 act Weber's Music Hall 26 December
1907 **The Girl Behind the Counter** American version (Herald Square Theater)
1907 **Hip! Hip! Hooray!** (Gus Edwards) Weber's Music Hall 10 October
1908 **The Merry-Go-Round** (G Edwards/Paul West) Circle Theater 25 April
1908 **The Mimic World** (Ben Jerome, Seymour Furth) Casino Theater 9 July
1908 **Mr Hamlet of Broadway** (Jerome/Edward Madden) Casino Theater 23 December
1909 **Philpoena** (part of *Higgledly Piggledy*) (Levi) Aldwych Theatre, London 27 February
1909 **Old Dutch** (Victor Herbert/w George V Hobart) Herald Square Theater 22 November
1910 **Tillie's Nightmare** (A Baldwin Sloane) Herald Square Theater 5 May
1910 **Up and Down Broadway** (Jerome Schwartz) Casino Theater 18 July
1911 **La Belle Paree** (Jerome Kern, Frank Tours) Winter Garden 20 March

1911 **A Certain Party** (Robert Hood Bowers) Wallack's Theater 24 April

1911 **The Kiss Waltz** (*Liebeswalzer*) American libretto (Casino Theater)

1912 **Hokey-Pokey** (Sloane, Francis) Broadway Theater 8 February

1912 **Bunty Bulls and Strings** (Sloane/E Ray Goetz) 2 scenes Broadway Theater 8 February

1912 **Hanky-Panky** (Sloane/Goetz) Broadway Theater 5 August

1912 **Roly Poly** (Sloane/Goetz) Weber and Fields' Music Hall 21 November

1912 **Without the Law** (Sloane/Goetz) 1 act Weber and Fields' Music Hall 21 November

1912 **The Sun Dodgers** (Sloane/Goetz) Broadway Theater 30 November

1913 **Lieber Augustin** (aka *Miss Caprice*) (*Der liebe Augustin*) American version (Casino Theater)

1913 **The Pleasure Seekers** (Goetz/Goetz) Winter Garden Theater 3 November

1915 **The Peasant Girl** (*Polenblut*) American adaptation w Herbert Reynolds, Harold Atteridge (44th St Theater)

1915 **Hands Up** (Romberg, Goetz/Goetz) 44th Street Theater 22 July

1915 **The Blue Paradise** (*Ein Tag im Paradies*) American version w add music by Sigmund Romberg (Casino Theater)

1915 **Alone at Last** (*Endlich Allein*) American version w Joseph W Herbert, Matthew Woodward (Shubert Theater)

1916 **Robinson Crusoe Jr** (Romberg, James Hanley/Atteridge) Winter Garden Theater 17 February

1916 **Step This Way** revised *The Girl Behind the Counter* w Goetz, Bert Grant (Shubert Theater)

1916 **The Girl from Brazil** (*Die schöne Schwedin*) American version w Matthew Woodward, Sigmund Romberg (44th Street Theater)

1916 **Lieutenant Gus** (*Wenn zwei sich lieben*) American version w Woodward (44th Street Theater)

1917 **My Lady's Glove** (ex-*The Beautiful Unknown*) (*Die schöne Unbekannte*) American version w Edward Paulton, Romberg (Lyric Theater)

1917 **The Golden Goose** (Silvio Hein/Herbert Reynolds, Schuyler Green) Apollo, Atlantic City 29 November

1918 **Fancy Free** (Augustus Barratt/w Dorothy Donnelly) Astor Theater 11 April

1918 **The Melting of Molly** (Romberg/w Cyrus Wood) Broadhurst 30 December

1919 **Oh! What a Girl** (ex- *Oh! Uncle*, ex- *The Wrong Number*) (Charles Jules, Jacques Presburg/w Edward Clark) Shubert Theater 28 July

1919 **Hello, Alexander** revised *The Ham Tree* (Jean Schwartz/Alfred Bryan) 44th Street Theater 7 October

1921 **The Whirl of New York** revised *The Belle of New York* w Sidney Mitchell, Al Goodman, Lew Pollock, Leo Edwardes (Winter Garden Theater)

1922 **Red Pepper** (Albert Gumble, Owen Murphy/Howard Rogers, Murphy/w Emily Young) Shubert Theater 29 May

1928 **Headin' South** (J Schwartz/A Bryan et al) Keith's Theater, Philadelphia 1 October

1929 **The Street Singer** (Niclas Kempner, Sam Timberg/ Graham John) Shubert Theater 17 September

1930 **Hello Paris** (aka *So This is Paris*) (Charles D Locke, Frank Bannister/Russell M Tarbox, Michael Cleary) Shubert Theater 15 November

1930 **Prince Chu Chang** (*Das Land des Lächelns*) American adaptation w Henry Clarke (Shubert Theater, Newark)

Other Weber and Fields burlesque scenas include *The Girl from Martins, Sapolio, Trilby, Waffles, The Other Way*

SMITH, Harry B[ache] (b Buffalo, NY, 28 December 1861; d Atlantic City, NJ, 2 January 1936). The most prolific librettist, lyricist and adapter of the Broadway stage over nearly half a century of writing in the decades round the turn of the century.

The name of Harry Bache Smith permeates the American musical theatre from the late 1880s until the early 1930s. Intelligent, prolific, though rather too often facile, he was able swiftly to turn his hand to anything from comic-opera plots and song-words to the Weber and Fields style of burlesque, music-hall material or a Rogers Brothers song, from the kind of adaptations from the English, the French or the German (as the importing fashion turned) which were thought to be what the American public wanted (and that 'thought' was often fairly insulting to its public's tastes) to the modern postwar style of revue and musical comedy. He rarely attempted anything which smacked of originality, being content to rework familiar elements in more or less new guises and in a variety of different dresses, helping himself, in the manner of H B Farnie and the other most successful bricoleurs of musical theatre texts of the past, to plot-pieces and characters from the multitude of sources which his wide theatrical experience and even wider reading exposed him. Few of Smith's principal original libretti were credited with being direct adaptations: most preferred to take a familiar name or title and decorate it with a lively mixture of traditional comic opera doings. Thus his list of early comic opera credits included a Begum, a Caliph, a Mandarin, a Tzigane, a Highwayman, a Fencing Master, a Student King and so forth as well as such ear-catching names as Robin Hood, Don Quixote, Rob Roy, Ali Baba, Peg Woffington and their well-used fellows.

From early on, Smith teamed with composer Reginald De Koven, and their first effort together, the *Mikado*-ish *The Begum*, was soon followed by a considerable success in *Robin Hood*. It was a success in which Smith's neatly constructed libretto – which had little enough to do with *Robin Hood*, but involved a great deal of the disguises, mistaken identities and low comedy traditional in British and French comic opera – played a considerable part. Thereafter, he was established at the head of his profession, and in the decades that followed he collaborated with the best Broadway had to offer in the way of comic-opera composers. By the time he was done – and that kind of comic opera was done as well – he had provided 16 libretti to De Koven (of which *Rob Roy* was the next most successful), worked on 14 shows with Victor Herbert, as well as others with Julian Edwards, Ludwig Englander and on one occasion Sousa, and he was still around when the new, romantic style of comic opera surfaced in the 1920s to supply texts to Sigmund Romberg.

From the earliest years of his career, Smith also engaged in adaptations of foreign works. Suppé's *Die Jagd nach dem Glück* and Dellinger's *Capitän Fracassa* were amongst the earliest, but when the fashion abandoned French and Austro-German Operette in favour of the product of the British stage, he was still at hand to 'americanize' such London products as *The Toreador, The Belle of Mayfair, The Girl from Kays* and *The Sunshine Girl*, and when the first French vaudevilles were borrowed as the texts for Broadway shows, Smith was there to cobble together *Mam'zelle Nitouche* and *La Femme à papa* to make up an Anna Held show, to take the dazzling comic shower of *Les Fêtards* and turn it into *The Strollers* with Ludwig Englander or transform the vaudeville *Le Jockey malgré lui* into *The Office Boy*.

However, it was the coming of the modern Viennese Operette which set him on his most solid swag of adapting. Something like half of his work from 1910 onwards was in compiling American versions of Continental hits, and the final assignments of his long career included two attempts to make Benatzky's *Hotel Stadt-Lemberg* into a Broadway piece, and a short-lived try at making Rudolf Lothar's *The Phantom Ship* into a musical for George Lederer as *The Pajama Lady*.

Smith's contribution to the lighter forms of musical theatre was less than that to the 'comic-opera' style of piece, but it was by no means negligible. In his early days he wrote burlesque and pantomime scripts and songs, he supplied lyrics to John Stromberg for Weber and Fields and to Maurice Levi for the Rogers Brothers, and he authored the Casino Theater's attempt to write its own Gaiety Theatre musical with *The Casino Girl* and did it well enough that the show did very nicely in London. He wrote a children's fairytale spectacular with Herbert, material for the *Ziegfeld Follies*, the revusical sketch *Gaby* for after-dinner roof-garden entertainment, revamped a couple of Charles Hoyt plays as libretti, took part in the writing of musical comedies of a more or less vertebrate nature with such composers as Ivan Caryll, Jerome Kern and Irving Berlin, and supplied Ned Wayburn with the texts for revue at the Century Music Hall. On one occasion he even wrote a musical comedy script which he asserted was based on no less venerable a source than Eugène Scribe. And all this time, he kept steadily turning out romantic operetta texts, original or, latterly, more often adapted.

One thing, however, emerges from the long list of Smith's credits. Although a number of his adaptations did extremely well – *Die Sprudelfee*, *Der lila Domino*, *Szibill* – and many of his pieces served their purpose through a month or two on Broadway and a solidly profitable touring life, virtually only the best pieces of his earliest years – *Robin Hood*, *The Wizard of the Nile*, *The Serenade* and *The Fortune Teller* – proved to be of the stuff that revivals and exports are made. In the 35 years of constant writing that followed this group, only *The Casino Girl* (1900) and the revusical Irving Berlin piece *Watch Your Step* (1914) were given much wider life, and only the Victor Herbert operetta *Sweethearts* (1913) with its incoherent Ruritanian libretto was judged worthy of revival at home. From being one of the flag-bearers of the American musical theatre in the first decade of his writing career, at a period when the products of America's musical theatre were just reaching out towards giving rather than taking on the international scene, Smith faded into being a utilitarian writer. Whilst others were writing the musical comedies and operettas of the 1910s and 1920s which would establish the American musical theatre around the world, Smith, still producing texts and lyrics at a great rate, turned out only a mass of material for home consumption, quickly consumed.

When his theatrical writing days were all but done, Smith turned out one of his most enjoyable pieces of writing in the form of a friendly, amusing – if occasionally factually forgetful – set of memoirs, which has sadly now become a rarity.

Smith was married to the actress and singer **Irene Bentley** (b Baltimore, 1870; d 3 June 1940) who appeared on the Broadway stage as a chorus girl in *Little Christopher* (1895), *The Merry World* (1895) and *The Belle of New York*

(1898 and London, Gladys Glee, a bridesmaid) before being upped to better rôles by George Lederer in *The Rounders* (1900) and *The Belle of Bohemia* (1900, Geraldine McDuffy), then paired at the top of the comedy with Francis Wilson as Bertha Lump in Smith's adaptation of *Die Landstreicher* as *The Strollers* (1901). She had lead rôles in *The Wild Rose* (1902), *The Girl from Dixie* (1903, Kitty Calvert), *The Belle of Mayfair* (1906, Princess Carl) and *The Mimic World* (1908). Her brother, Wilmer Bentley, worked in the theatre as a striving performer (Mucki in *The Strollers*), director and sometime writer, for some nine years on the staff on George Lederer's office, and in the early 1920s in Australia.

Smith's brother, Robert Bache Smith, followed Harry into the theatre and also had a long career there as, principally, a lyricist.

A collected edition of Harry Smith's lyrics was published by R H Russell in 1900 under the title *Stage Lyrics*. He seems to have been the first musical-theatre lyricist thus to have been honoured.

1884 **Rosita, or Cupid and Cupidity** (George Schlieffarth/ Matthew C Woodward) Chicago March; Park Theater, Brooklyn 30 April
1884 **Amaryllis**
1887 **The Begum** (Reginald De Koven) Fifth Avenue Theater 21 November
1888 **The Crystal Slipper, or Prince Prettywitz and Little Cinderella** (Fred J Eustis/w Alfred Thompson) Chicago; New York 26 November
1889 **Don Quixote** (De Koven) Boston Theater, Boston 18 November
1889 **Clover** (*Die Jagd nach dem Glück*) English version (Palmer's Theater)
1890 **Captain Fracasse** (*Capitän Fracassa*) American version
1891 **The Tar and the Tartar** (Adam Itzel jr) Palmer's Theater 11 May
1891 **Robin Hood** (De Koven) Chicago 9 June; Standard Theater, New York, 28 September
1892 **Ali Baba, or Morgiana and the Forty Thieves** (W H Batchelor/w Franklyn W Lee, John Gilbert)
1892 **Jupiter, or The Cobbler and the King** (Julian Edwards) Palmer's Theater 2 May
1892 **Sinbad** (W H Batchelor) Garden Theater 27 June
1892 **The Fencing Master** (De Koven) Boston; Casino Theater 14 November
1892 **The Knickerbockers** (De Koven) Boston; Garden Theater 29 May 1893
1893 **The Algerian** (De Koven) Garden Theater 26 October
1894 **Rob Roy** (De Koven) Herald Square Theater 29 October
1895 **The Tzigane** (De Koven) Abbey's Theater 16 May
1895 **Little Robinson Crusoe** (Gustave Luders) Schiller Theater, Chicago 21 June
1895 **The Wizard of the Nile** (Victor Herbert) Casino Theater 4 November
1896 **The Caliph** (Ludwig Englander) Broadway Theater 3 September
1896 **Half a King** (*Le Roi de carreau*) American version w music by Englander Knickerbocker Theater 14 September
1896 **The Mandarin** (De Koven) Herald Square Theater 2 November
1897 **The Serenade** (Herbert) Knickerbocker Theater 16 March
1897 **Gayest Manhattan, or Around New York in Ninety Minutes** (Englander) Koster and Bial's 22 March
1897 **The Paris Doll** (De Koven) Parsons' Theater, Hartford, Conn, 14 September
1897 **Peg Woffington** (Herbert) Lyceum Theater, Scranton, Pa 18 October

SMITH, Harry B

1897 **The Idol's Eye** (Herbert) Broadway Theater 25 October

1897 **The Highwayman** (De Koven) Broadway Theater 13 December

1898 **Hurly Burly** (John Stromberg/w Edgar Smith) Weber and Fields' Music Hall 8 September

1898 **The Little Corporal** (Englander) Broadway Theater 19 September

1898 **The Fortune Teller** (Herbert) Wallack's Theatre 26 September

1898 **Cyranose de Bric-à-Brac** (Stromberg/w E Smith) 1 act Weber and Fields' Music Hall 3 November

1899 **Catherine** (Stromberg/w Edgar Smith) 1 act Weber and Fields' Music Hall 19 January

1899 **The Three Dragoons** (De Koven) Broadway Theater 30 January

1899 **Helter-Skelter** (Stromberg/E Smith) Weber and Fields' Music Hall 6 April

1899 **The Rounders** (*Les Fêtards*) American version with score by Englander Casino Theater 12 July

1899 **Cyrano de Bergerac** (Herbert) Knickerbocker Theater 18 September

1899 **Whirl-i-Gig** (Stromberg/w E Smith) Weber and Fields' Music Hall 21 September

1899 **Barbara Fidgety** 1 act (in *Whirl-i-gig*) Weber and Fields's Music Hall 21 September

1899 **The Singing Girl** (Herbert/Stanislaus Stange) Casino Theater 23 October

1899 **Papa's Wife** (De Koven) Manhattan Theater 13 November

1900 **The Casino Girl** (Englander) Casino Theater 19 March

1900 **The Viceroy** (Herbert) Knickerbocker Theater 30 April

1900 **The Cadet Girl** (*Les Demoiselles de Saint-Cyriens*) American version w Cheever Goodwin and new music by Englander Herald Square Theater 25 July

1900 **The Belle of Bohemia** (Englander) Casino Theater 24 September

1900 **Foxy Quiller** (De Koven) Broadway Theater 5 November

1901 **The Prima Donna** (Aimé Lachaume) Herald Square Theater 17 April

1901 **The Strollers** (*Die Landstreicher*) American version with new music by Englander Knickerbocker Theater 24 June

1901 **The Rogers Brothers in Washington** (Maurice Levi/J J McNally) Knickerbocker Theater 2 September

1901 **The Liberty Belles** (A Baldwin Sloane, John Bratton et al) Madison Square Theater 30 September

1901 **The Little Duchess** (*Niniche*) American version with new score by De Koven Casino Theater 14 October

1902 **Maid Marian** (De Koven) Garden Theater 27 January

1902 **The Wild Rose** (Englander/w George V Hobart) Knickerbocker Theater 5 May

1902 **The Billionaire** (Gustave Kerker) Daly's Theater 29 December

1903 **The Jewel of Asia** (Englander/Frederick Ranken) Criterion Theater 16 February

1903 **The Blonde in Black** (Kerker) Knickerbocker Theater 8 June

1903 **The Office Boy** (*Le Jockey malgré lui*) American version with new score by Englander Victoria Theater 2 November

1903 **Babette** (Herbert) Broadway Theater 16 November

1903 **The Girl from Dixie** (C F Dodgson et al) Madison Square Theater 14 December

1904 **The Madcap Princess** (Englander) Knickerbocker Theater 5 September

1904 **A China Doll** (Alfred Aarons) Majestic Theatre 19 November

1904 **Fatinitza** new American version (Broadway Theater)

1905 **Miss Dolly Dollars** (Herbert) Knickerbocker Theater 4 September

1905 **The Belle of the West** (Karl Hoschna) Chicago 29 October; Grand Theater 13 November

1905 **The White Cat** (Englander/Arthur Collins, Arthur Wood ad) (American version) New Amsterdam Theater 2 November

1906 **The Three Graces** (Stafford Waters) Chicago Opera House 2 April

1906 **The Free Lance** (John Philip Sousa) New Amsterdam Theater 16 April

1906 **The Rich Mr Hoggenheimer** (Englander) Wallack's Theater 22 October

1906 **The Parisian Model** (Max Hoffman) Broadway Theater 27 November

1907 **The Rogers Brothers in Panama** (Hoffman) Broadway Theater 2 September

1907 **The Tattooed Man** (Herbert/w A N C Fowler) Criterion Theater 18 February

1908 **The Soul Kiss** (Levi) New York Theater 28 January

1908 **Nearly a Hero** (several) Casino Theater 24 February

1908 **The Golden Butterfly** (De Koven) Broadway Theater 12 October

1908 **Little Nemo** (Herbert) New Amsterdam Theater 20 October

1908 **Miss Innocence** (Englander) New York Theater 30 November

1909 **The Silver Star** (Robert Hood, Bowers, Raymond Hubbell, Hoschna, Jean Schwartz et al) New Amsterdam Theater 1 November

1909 **The (Hot) Air King** (Hubbell) Star Theater, Buffalo 26 November

1910 **The Girl on the Train** (*Die geschiedene Frau*) American version (Globe Theater)

1910 **The Bachelor Belles** (Hubbell) Globe Theater 7 November

1910 **The Spring Maid** (*Die Sprudelfee*) American version w R B Smith (Liberty Theater)

1911 **The Paradise of Mahomet** (*Le Paradis de Mahomet*) American version w R B Smith (Herald Square Theater)

1911 **Little Miss Fix-It** (various/w William J Hurlbutt) Globe Theater 3 April

1911 **Gaby** (Bowers/w R B Smith) Folies-Bergère 27 April

1911 **The Red Rose** (Bowers/w R B Smith) Bijou Theater 22 June

1911 **The Siren** (*Die Sirene*) English version (Knickerbocker Theater)

1911 **Gypsy Love** (*Zigeunerliebe*) American version w R B Smith (Globe Theater)

1911 **The Duchess** (Herbert/w Joseph Herbert) Lyric Theater 16 October

1911 **The Enchantress** (Herbert/w Fred de Grésac) New York Theater 19 October

1911 **The Wedding Trip** (De Koven/w de Grésac) Broadway Theater 25 December

1912 **Modest Susanne** (*Die keusche Susanne*) American version w R B Smith (Liberty Theater)

1912 **A Winsome Widow** (Hubbell/Charles Hoyt ad) Moulin Rouge 11 April

1912 **The Rose Maid** (*Bub oder Mädel*) English version w R B Smith (Globe Theater)

1912 **The Girl from Montmartre** (*Das Mädel von Montmartre*) English version (Criterion Theater)

1912 **The June Bride** (*Johann der Zweite*) English version (Majestic Theater, Boston)

1913 **My Little Friend** (*Die kleine Freundin*) English version w R B Smith (New Amsterdam Theater)

1913 **The Doll Girl** (*Das Puppenmädel*) English version (Globe Theater)

1913 **Sweethearts** (Herbert/R B Smith/w de Grésac) New Amsterdam Theater 8 September

1913 **Oh, I Say!** (Jerome Kern/Sydney Blow, Douglas Hoare) Casino Theater 30 October

1914 **The Lilac Domino** (*Der lila Domino*) American version w R B Smith (44th Street Theater)

1914 **Papa's Darling** (Ivan Caryll) New Amsterdam Theater 2 November

1914 **The Debutante** (Herbert/w R B Smith) Knickerbocker Theater 7 December

1914 **Watch Your Step** (Irving Berlin) New Amsterdam Theater 8 December

1915 **All Over Town** (Silvio Hein/Joseph Santley) Shubert Theater, New Haven 26 April

1915 **90 in the Shade** (Kern/Guy Bolton) Knickerbocker Theater 25 January

1915 **Stop! Look! Listen!** (Berlin) Globe Theater 25 December

1916 **Sybil** (*Szibill*) American version from Harry Graham's English version (Liberty Theater)

1916 **Molly O!** (Carl Woess/R B Smith) Cort Theater 20 May

1917 **Love o' Mike** (Kern/Thomas Sydney) Shubert Theater 15 January

1917 **The Masked Model** (Woess, then Harold Orlob/ Frederick Herendeen/w R B Smith) Johnstown, Pa 17 April

1917 **Rambler Rose** (Victor Jacobi) Empire Theater 10 September

1918 **Look Who's Here** (Sloane) Trenton, NJ 30 August

1918 **Ladies First** (Sloane/Hoyt ad) Broadhurst Theater 24 October

1919 **A Lonely Romeo** (Franklin, Bowers/w R B Smith, Lew Fields) Shubert Theater 19 January

1919 **Angel Face** (Victor Herbert/R B Smith) Knickerbocker Theater 30 December

1920 **Betty Be Good** (Hugo Riesenfeld) Casino Theater 4 May

1922 **The Springtime of Youth** (*Sterne, die wieder leuchtet*) American version w Cyrus Wood (Broadhurst Theater)

1923 **Caroline** (*Das Vetter aus dingsda*) (ex- *Virginia*) American version w Edward Delaney Dunn (Ambassadors Theater)

1923 **Peaches** (Max R Steiner/w R B Smith) Garrick Theater, Philadelphia 22 January

1925 **Sweetheart Time** (Walter Donaldson, Joseph Meyer/ Ballard MacDonald) Imperial Theater 19 January

1925 **The Love Song** (*Offenbach*) American version (Century Theater)

1925 **Natja** (Tchaikovsky arr Karl Hajós) Knickerbocker Theater 16 February

1925 **Princess Flavia** (Sigmund Romberg) Century Theater 2 November

1926 **Naughty Riquette** (*Riquette*) American version (Cosmopolitan Theater)

1926 **Countess Maritza** (*Gräfin Mariza*) American version (Shubert Theater)

1927 **Cherry Blossoms** (Romberg) 44th Street Theater 28 March

1927 **The Circus Princess** (*Die Zirkusprinzessin*) American version (Winter Garden Theater)

1927 **Half a Widow** (Shep Camp/w Frank Dupree) Waldorf Theater 12 September

1927 **The Love Call** (ex-*Bonita* et al) (Romberg) Majestic Theater 24 October

1928 **White Lilacs** (*Chopin*) American version (Shubert Theater)

1928 **The Red Robe** (*Das Weib im Purpur*) American version w Edward Delaney Dunn Shubert Theater 25 December

1930 **Three Little Girls** (*Drei arme kleine Mädels*) American lyrics (Shubert Theater)

1930 **Prince Chu Chang** (*Das Land des Lächelns*) American lyrics (Shubert Theater, Newark)

1930 **Arms and the Maid** (*Hotel Stadt-Lemberg*) American version w Ernest Clark (Walnut Street Theater, Philadelphia)

1930 **The Pajama Lady** (Phil Charig, Richard Myers/w John Mercer/R B Smith, George Lederer) National Theater, Washington 6 October

1932 **Marching By** (*Hotel Stadt-Lemberg*) revised American version (46th Street Theater)

Autobiography: *First Nights and First Editions* (Little, Brown, Boston, 1931)

SMITH, Oliver [Lemuel] (b Wawpawn, Wis, 13 February 1918).

The set designer for a long list of important Broadway musicals from the mid-1940s to the mid-1960s (*On the Town, Brigadoon, Gentlemen Prefer Blondes, Pal Joey* revival, *My Fair Lady, Candide, West Side Story, The Sound of Music, Camelot, Hello, Dolly!* etc), gathering in the process a clutch of Tony Awards, Oliver Smith was also for a time active as a musical-theatre producer, notably on the original productions of *On the Town* and *Gentlemen Prefer Blondes*, as well as the less-successful *Billion Dollar Baby, Juno, Show Girl*, and *Bonanza Bound* (w Paul Feigay, Herman Levin), a number of non-musical plays and a signifcant amount of dance productions.

SMITH, Queenie (b New York, 8 September 1902; d Burbank, Calif, 5 August 1978). Button-bright dancing star of the dance-age musical comedy.

Originally a member of the corps at the Metropolitan Opera House, the little dancer left the ballet at the age of 17 to go on the musical-comedy stage where she had featured dancing rôles in John Cort's production of *Roly Boly Eyes* (1919, Ida Loring), the Shuberts' first attempt to get what became *The Blushing Bride* off the ground as *The Girl in the Private Room* (1920) and in Friml's indifferent *June Rose* (1920, Tiny Golden). Carrying on an end-to-end schedule, she played in an Earl Carroll mounting of a musical called *Just Because* (1922, Syringa) written by two lady amateurs and backed by their society friends to the tune of $75,000, in *Orange Blossoms* (1922, Tillie), *Cinders* (1923, Tillie Olsen) and in George S Kaufman and Marc Connelly's *Helen of Troy, New York* (1923, Maribel). She then appeared as Gertrude Bryan's twin sister in *Sitting Pretty*, singing 'Shufflin' Sam', and in a second Kaufman/ Connelly musical, *Be Yourself* (1924, Tony Robinson), before winning the rôle of her career as the titular lassie of Gershwin's *Tip-Toes* (1925), creating 'Looking for a Boy', 'These Charming People' and 'That Certain Feeling'.

She followed up in the title-rôle of the flop *Judy* (1927), succeeded Louise Groody as the star of *Hit the Deck* (1927) and toured in that part the following season, before taking the leading rôle of Busby Berkeley's production of *The Street Singer* (1929). The Shuberts' *Hearts in Repair* (Brighton Beach, 17 August 1931) went down the drain, and her last musical appearance on Broadway was in 1932 as Dixie in *A Little Racketeer*, but from 1935 she found herself a second career as a film actress – memorably as a delicious Ellie Mae in *Show Boat* – and she remained active for 30 further years in often sizeable film and television rôles as a character and comedy actress.

SMITH, Robert B[ache] (b Chicago, 4 June 1875; d New York, 6 November 1951). Lyricist to a long era of Broadway musicals.

Originally a reporter on the Brooklyn *Eagle*, Robert Smith soon followed his brother, Harry B Smith, into the theatre, initially as a press representative for the Casino Theater. His first writings were in the form of sketches for vaudeville and burlesque houses, but his career was given its direction when he supplied the lyrics for the Weber and

Fields burlesque *Twirly Whirly* and came out with one of the biggest song hits of the period, Lillian Russell's 'Come Down, Ma Evenin' Star'. Although his principal activity over the next two decades was as an enormously prolific lyricist, he also worked on libretti and adaptations for a number of shows, often in collaboration with his brother. Amongst the songs for which he wrote the words are included Victor Herbert's 'Sweethearts' for the show of the same name and 'I Might Be Your Once in a While' (*Angel Face*).

1900 **The Casino Girl** revised version Casino Theater 6 August
1902 **Twirly Whirly** (John Stromberg/Edgar Smith) Weber and Fields' Music Hall 11 September
1904 **A China Doll** (Alfred Aarons/w H B Smith) Majestic Theatre 19 November
1905 **Fantana** (Raymond Hubbell) Chicago; Lyric Theater, New York 14 January 1905
1905 **When We Were Forty-One** (Gus Edwards) New York Roof Garden 12 June
1905 **Breaking into Society** (various/w Lee Arthur) West End Theater 2 October
1905 **The Babes and the Baron** (Herbert E Haines et al/Alexander M Thompson, Robert Courtneidge et al) Lyric Theater 25 December
1906 **Mexicana** (Hubbell/w Clara Driscoll) Lyric Theater 29 January
1906 **Mam'selle Sallie** (Hubbell) Grand Opera House 26 November
1907 **[The Girl from] Yama** (Aarons/George Totten Smith) Walnut Street Theater, Philadelphia 4 November
1907 **Knight for a Day** revised *Mam'selle Sallie* Wallack's Theater 16 December
1908 **The Hotel Clerk** (Aarons) Walnut Street Theater, Phialdelphia 27 April
1908 **The Girl at the Helm** (Hubbell) La Salle Theater, Chicago 30 August
1909 **The Girl and the Wizard** (Julian Edwards/J Hartley Manners) Casino Theater 27 September
1910 **The Spring Maid** (*Die Sprudelfee*) American version w H B Smith (Liberty Theater)
1911 **The Paradise of Mahomet** (*Le Paradis de Mahomet*) American version w H B Smith (Herald Square Theater)
1911 **Gaby** (Robert Hood Bowers/w H B Smith) (Folies-Bergère) 27 April
1911 **The Red Rose** (Bowers/w H B Smith) Bijou Theater 22 June
1911 **Gypsy Love** (*Zigeunerliebe*) American version w H B Smith (Globe Theater)
1912 **Modest Susanne** (*Die keusche Susanne*) American version w H B Smith (Liberty Theater)
1912 **The Rose Maid** (*Bub oder Mädel*) English version w H B Smith, Raymond W Peck (Globe Theater)
1912 **The Girl from Montmartre** (*Das Mädel von Montmartre*) English version w H B Smith (Criterion Theater)
1913 **My Little Friend** (*Die kleine Freundin*) English version w H B Smith (New Amsterdam Theater)
1913 **Sweethearts** (Herbert/H B Smith, Fred de Grésac) New Amsterdam Theater 8 September
1914 **The Lilac Domino** (*Der lila Domino*) American version w H B Smith (44th Street Theater)
1914 **The Debutante** (Herbert/w H B Smith) Knickerbocker Theater 7 December
1916 **Molly O!** (Carl Woess/H B Smith) Cort Theater 20 May
1916 **Follow Me** (*Was tut man nicht alles aus Liebe*) American version w Romberg (Casino Theater)
1917 **The Masked Model** (Woess then Harold Orlob/Frederick Herendeen/w H B Smith) Johnstown, Pa 17 April

1919 **A Lonely Romeo** (Malvin Franklin, Bowers/w H B Smith, Lew Fields) Shubert Theater 19 January
1919 **Angel Face** (Victor Herbert/H B Smith) Knickerbocker Theater 30 December
1920 **Oui, Madame** (Herbert/w 'G M Wright') Little Theater, Philadelphia 22 March
1920 **The Girl in the Spotlight** (Herbert/Richard Bruce) Knickerbocker Theater 12 July
1923 **Peaches** (Max R Steiner/w H B Smith) Garrick Theater, Philadelphia 22 January
1923 **Sunbonnet Sue** (G Edwards) Illinois Theater, Chicago 7 October
1930 **The Pajama Lady** (Phil Charig, Richard Myers/w John Mercer/H B Smith, George Lederer) National Theater, Washington 6 October

SMITHSON, Florence [Annette] (b Leicester, 13 March 1884; d Cardiff, 11 February 1936). Soprano star whose career wasted away too soon.

The elfin-pretty, dark-eyed little daughter of Will Smithson, manager of the Theatre Royal, Merthyr, was bundled on to the stage for the first time at the age of three, and had an early 'education' in pantomime, drama and farce-comedy before attending the London College of Music and graduating to a minor touring opera company. She made her first appearance in the musical theatre in Robert Courtneidge's tour of *The Cingalee*, created the rôle of the Indian singing maid Chandra Nil in *The Blue Moon* at Northampton and repeated that rôle in London when the intended 'name' dropped out of the production prior to opening. The wispy 21-year-old with the sweet, high soprano voice won fine notices, and Courtneidge cast her next as the ingénue of *The Dairymaids* and sent her on tour as Sophia in *Tom Jones* before allotting her the creation of the rôle of Sombra in his production of *The Arcadians* ('The Pipes of Pan').

Plate 246. **Florence Smithson.**

The composers of that piece wrote the star rôle of its successor, *The Mousmé* ('My Samisen'), to suit her exceptional voice, but thereafter her career (marred by a drinking problem) was spent largely in variety and in pantomime in Britain, Australia and South Africa. She was married for a period to another Courtneidge star, the ill-fated comedian Dan Rolyat.

SNAGA, Josef (b Branitz, Silesia 3 June 1871; d unknown).

The composer of a dozen Operetten in the years around the First World War, Snaga had a fine success throughout Germany with his first piece, *Der Rodelzigeuner*, and later with the Singspiel *Frau Bärbel*, a piece untypically premièred in the metropolis of Berlin, and *Der Hutmacher seiner Majestät*. His works were seen regularly in the German provinces, but did not travel further afield.

1910 **Der Rodelzigeuner** (Leo Kästner) Altes Theater, Leipzig 15 May

1912 **Der Lumpenprinz** (Kästner) Schauburg, Hanover 25 May

1913 **Die Bretteldiva** (Rudolf Lothar, Alexander Engel) Stadttheater, Magdeburg 21 February

1913 **Die ledige Ehefrau** (Theo Halton, Alexander Pordes-Milo) Schauburg, Hanover 31 December

1914 **Das kleine Mädel** (*Das Leutnantsmädel*) (Halton, Arthur Lippschitz) Wilhelm Theater, Magdeburg 31 October

1915 **Der Hutmacher seiner Majestät** (Gustav Quedtenfeldt, Halton) Schauburg, Hanover 26 January

1915 **Fürst Xanderl** (Halton, Erich Urban) Neues Operetten-Theater, Leipzig 20 November

1917 **Hanuschka** (Kästner) Neues Operetten-Theater, Leipzig 29 September

1919 **Der Glücksschloss** (Walter Grabenitz) Stadttheater, Bromberg 5 March

1920 **Die Perle von Mexico** (Karl Rodemann) Stadttheater, Bromberg 23 February

1920 **Frau Bärbel** (Halton, Fischer) Centraltheater, Berlin 10 September

1935 **Wenn Liebe befiehlt** (Julius Werth ad Quedtenfeldt, Eugen Rex) Stadttheater, Fürth 9 February

1935 **Die Weltmeisterin** (Christian Decker, Hans Decker) Stadttheater, Fürth 1 September

Other title attributed: *Lolas Rache* (?1919)

DER SOLDAT DER MARIE Operette in 3 acts by Bernhard Buchbinder, Jean Kren and Alfred Schönfeld. Music by Leo Ascher. Neues Operettenhaus, Berlin, 2 September 1916.

Along with *Hoheit tanzt Walzer*, *Der Soldat der Marie* was the most successful of all Ascher's Operetten, and the best of his pieces to have been premièred in Berlin.

Buchbinder and Kren's libretto told the rakish tale of the philandering Prince Kurt von Hansendorf who courts two of the three daughters of the dispossessed dancer-turned-miller Theodor Mumme at one and the same time: in his lordly guise he makes love to Mariann whilst he worms his way into the heart of Marie (Käthe Dorsch) dressed as a simple soldier. When he is discovered, the sensible Marie realizes that she is much better off with the sincere Hans Wonneberger leaving the Prince, suddenly aware of the depth of his feelings, to offer title and marriage to Mariann. Amongst this plethora of Ms, the littlest sister, Mariett, goes off and becomes a famous dancer as ... Maria Mirabelli.

Ascher's score was dominated by dance rhythms: the broad waltzes 'Ach liebste ich halt dich' and the mirror song ('Spieglein, Spieglein in meiner Hand'), the March-gavotte 'Mit Parapluie und Pompadour', the polka 'Ach Theo – Theo – Theodor!', the marching Trommellied ('Ja, ja im jeden Städtchen') and 'Wenn die Veilchen wieder spriessen' all of which together, along with the romantic serenade 'Du bist meine Freunde', made up the most popular part of the music.

Produced as Jean Kren's initial offering as manager at Berlin's Neues Operettenhaus (ex-Montis Operetten-Theater), the sweetly old-fashioned *Der Soldat der Marie* scored a considerable success with a typical wartime public avid for good-old-days entertainment, and it was soon being staged throughout central Europe. In Oscar Fronz's Vienna production, Otto Storm (Kurt), Ida Russka (Marie), Grete Holm (Mariann), Ludwig Herold (Hans) and Leopold Strassmeyer (Mumme) headed the cast for a season of 112 performances, whilst in Budapest *A Marcsa katonaja* was played happily at the Városi Színház for a good run. However, any wider life the show might have had was stifled by the very wartime conditions which had first helped it to success.

Austria: Wiener Bürgertheater 19 January 1917; Hungary: Városi Színház *A Marcsa katonaja* 28 December 1918

SOLDENE, Emily [?LAMBERT, Emily] (b Clerkenwell, 30 September 1840; d London, 8 April 1912). One of the most memorable characters of the English and international opéra-bouffe stage.

Emily Soldene, happily equipped with a generous rounded figure and a fine mezzo to soprano voice, began her career singing ballads and arias and an occasional potted opéra-bouffe (*Orphée aux enfers*) or opérette (*Le 66*) in the music halls under the name of Miss Fitz-Henry, whilst performing in more sedate concert and oratorio surroundings under her own name. She made her first appearance on the opéra-bouffe stage deputizing for Julia Mathews as *La Grande-Duchesse* and she followed up as Offenbach's Boulotte (*Barbe-bleue*, 1869) before replacing the composer Hervé in the extravagantly burlesque title-rôle of the London production of his *Chilpéric*. She followed this by appearing as Marguerite in the subsequent season of his *Le Petit Faust* (1870) before shooting to stardom in the rôle of the little pastrycook, Drogan, in the enormously popular English version of *Geneviève de Brabant* (1871).

After appearing in tights again in a season of Delibes's *Fleur-de-Lys* (*La Cour du Roi Pétaud*, Prince Hyacinth), she had a further major London success as Mlle Lange in *La Fille de Madame Angot* and, now established at the top of her profession, turned manager and presented herself at the Lyceum in *La Grande-Duchesse* before taking the 'Soldene Opéra-Bouffe Company', under the management of Messrs Grau and Chizzola, off to America. The repertoire which she played there included her inevitable *Geneviève de Brabant*, *La Fille de Madame Angot*, *Chilpéric*

Plate 247. **Emily Soldene**.

and the new Offenbach *Madame l'Archiduc* of which the title-rôle of Marietta became another Soldene regular.

The success of this experiment meant that in the following years Soldene was continually on the move, playing both in London and on Broadway, touring in Britain and in America before, in 1877, making a first trip to Australia and New Zealand. She was rapturously received there ('... a fine actress in comic opera. She never loses a point and all her by-play is telling, while she takes care that the idea of the character is carried consistently through the opera') and her company, especially the distinctly buxom and lightly clad supporting ladies whom their manageress chose with particular care, became legends. Her now celebrated basic repertoire was supplemented, at various times, by *La Belle Poule*, *La Jolie Parfumeuse*, *La Belle Hélène*, *Trial By Jury*, *La Grande-Duchesse*, *Barbe-bleue*, *La Périchole*, *Carmen* and *Giroflé-Girofla*, but Drogan, Lange (into which rôle she was not above inserting her rendition of 'Silver Threads Among the Gold') and, a notch below, Marietta long remained her staple rôles.

She played pantomime in Glasgow, toured comic opera in Britain and was forced to disband her company after a one disastrous season in San Francisco in 1881, but she was up and going again the following year, trouping around Britain with Alice May and that lady's husband's comic opera *The Wicklow Rose* as well as her hardy annuals. Finally, in 1883, she stopped racing round the world and took first to the music halls and then to the management of the Gaiety Theatre, Hastings, where she settled down with her family. However, before long the theatre produced cash-flow problems and Soldene was quickly back playing Drogans and Langes and singing opéra-bouffe arias on the music halls to raise money. There is little doubt that she

was one of those artists to whom money will not stick, and as a result she stuck to the stage.

In 1886, now decidedly buxom, she abandoned her traditional rôles and appeared in London in an unfortunate piece called *Frivoli*, and then for McCaull on Broadway as Madame Jacob in *Joséphine vendue par ses soeurs* and in *Lorraine* (1887, Oudarde). She stayed a while in America, playing in variety and theatre (Broken Arrow in *Dovetta* etc), and celebrated her 25 years on the stage with a jubilee at London's Terry's Theatre to which Fred Leslie and Nellie Farren sent a recorded message which was played on a phonograph.

She adapted and directed the French melodrama *La Porteuse de pain (Jeanne Fortier, the Bread Carrier)* and saw it produced in New York in 1889, she went on tour with the Mestayer-Vaughan company in *The Tourists*, and in 1890–91 was seen yet again at San Francisco's Tivoli Theatre in her old rôle in *Geneviève de Brabant*, at the Alcazar playing another travesty rôle in *The Red Bird*, at the Orpheum as the Gipsy Queen in *The Bohemian Girl* and at the Bush Theatre as the old Princesse de Gramponeur in *Erminie*. A benefit mounted for her at the Tivoli at the end of her season featured a sparring bout between Jim Corbett and McCord.

Soldene was not able, however, to keep out of business problems. She was declared bankrupt before, in 1892, she took up the reins of management again and left San Francisco for Australia where she announced productions of *La Fille de Madame Angot* (now playing the supporting rôle of Amaranthe herself), *Geneviève*, *The Merry War* and *The Black Hussar*. The planned seasons did not run their course, and Emily switched to exercising another of her talents, as a journalist, writing columns for Sydney's *Sun* and *Evening News*.

On her return to Britain, she brought with her her memoirs, a book which remains one of the classic theatre books of all time, the most outstanding and warming (and, for a theatre book, remarkably accurate – if personally discreet) picture of the theatre of her age. Finally, now, she renounced performing and management but when, in 1906, a benefit matinée was given for her at London's Palace Theatre, the crisp result proved that Madame Soldene was still fondly remembered by Victorian musical theatregoers.

Soldene's much younger sister, **Clara VESEY** [Clara Ann SOLDEN], (b St Luke's, 8 May 1850; d unknown) appeared in the Soldene company for many years, mostly playing rôles which allowed her to show off her legs rather than her voice (Riccardo in *Madame l'Archiduc*, Oswald in *Geneviève de Brabant*, Bacchis in *La Belle Hélène*, Hermia in *Barbe-bleue*, Plaintiff in *Trial By Jury*, Wanda in *La Grande-Duchesse* etc) and her daughter later appeared on the variety and musical comedy stage in Britain and Australia under the name of **Kate Vesey** [née Hoffmeister] (solo dancer in *The Lucky Star* (1899), *The Messenger Boy* (1900) at the Gaiety, Miss Enid Gibson in *The Catch of the Season* (1904), *The Golddiggers* (1906) etc). Soldene's son Edward, who worked under the name E Soldene-Powell, also had a career as a minor actor and stage manager in Britain and America (*Miss Dynamite*, *The Sunshine Girl* etc).

Autobiography: *My Theatrical and Musical Recollections* (Downey & Co, London, 1897)

Plate 248. **Edward Solomon**.

SOLOMON, Edward (b London, 25 July 1855; d London, 22 January 1895). Victorian composer whose irresponsibilites eventually won him more notice than a rather wasted musical gift.

The son of a small-time music-hall pianist, Charles Solomon, Edward was brought up in the rough-and-ready atmosphere of the Winchester music hall where both he and his brother, Fred, gained a colourful and varied early musical experience and where the young Edward officiated as an accompanist to the variety of singers and other acts from an early age. He was still a teenager when he won his earliest position as a theatre musical-director at the Alexandra Palace, and he moved on to the St James's Theatre, and the Royalty before, in March 1876, he took over the desk at the Globe Theatre, where he became musical director of Alexander Henderson's record-breaking production of *Les Cloches de Corneville*. During this period, he provided incidental music and arrangements for the plays and burlesques at these theatres and made his first attempts at composing original scores with some small operettas which won favourable notice.

In 1879 he won his most important commission to date when he supplied the whole of the music to the first act of the Alhambra's spectacular opéra-bouffe féerie *Rothomago* – the other three acts being written by Procida Bucalossi, Gaston Serpette and musical director Georges Jacobi – and his first solo full-length work came the following year when a collaboration with journalist Henry Pottinger Stephens resulted in the comic opera *Billee Taylor*. *Billee Taylor* combined a neatly written, tongue-in-cheek libretto with attractive and catchy songs ('All on Account of Eliza') and, as staged by Charles Harris, proved both a critical and a popular success, favourably compared by some critics with Sullivan's contemporaneous *The Pirates of Penzance*.

After this success, Solomon continued to work with Stephens on a series of comic operas based on ballad subjects but although *Claude Duval* (1881) won some success, the successors of *Billee Taylor* did not live up to the hopes, too easily kindled, that the pair would become a combination to rival Gilbert and Sullivan, and ultimately their partnership broke up.

Over the years which followed, the darkly dashing Solomon was a colourful figure in theatrical circles both in Britain and in America and his gaudily irresponsible private life, which led him frequently into the courts for both debt and also once for bigamy, often overwhelmed his professional life. His bigamous marriage to the American singer Lillian Russell led to her appearing in several of his works in Britain, America and on the Continent but, following Solomon's arrest and trial, she kept the Atlantic Ocean between them and, when his divorce was finally settled, he married instead another musical-comedy actress, Kate Everleigh.

The half-success of *Claude Duval* and the failures of *Lord Bateman* (1882) and the original version of *The Vicar of Bray* (1883) in London led Solomon to try his luck in America, where *Billee Taylor* had been even more successful than in Britain. His *Virginia* (1883) was staged in New York by John McCaull without adding to his reputation, but Solomon brought both the piece and Miss Russell back to Britain. When *Virginia* was staged at the Gaiety Theatre, the actress had more success than the piece, but Solomon and James Mortimer supplied her with a more efficient vehicle in *Polly* the following year at the Novelty and Empire Theatres. A third vehicle which featured the Iowa-born star as the Indian maiden *Pocahontas* was a failure, and the pair, having now gone through a form of marriage, left Britain to take their shows to America. *Polly* proved a fair success on Broadway, but of two new pieces, *Pepita* did only moderately well and *The Maid and the Moonshiner*, with Tony Hart in its starring rôle, was a failure.

Only a few weeks after the production of *The Maid and the Moonshiner* Solomon was back in Britain and in jail. The bigamy case took some time to be cleared up and Solomon suffered badly from his spell in prison. His health never wholly recovered, but his theatrical fortunes were soon on an improving bent. Henry Leslie, who had made his fortune with Cellier's comedy opera *Dorothy*, bought Solomon's *The Red Hussar*, a comic opera which he had originally written in happier times to be played by Lillian, as a vehicle for *Dorothy* star Marie Tempest and the piece proved a fine success in both Britain and America. However, much of the fire seemed to have gone out of the little composer and, although he turned out several handfuls of songs, including some for the Gaiety Theatre new burlesques, and music for a few short theatre pieces, it seemed as if the ebullient composer of *Billee Taylor* had seen his day.

The break-up of the Gilbert and Sullivan partnership, however, proved Solomon's chance for a second coming. When D'Oyly Carte, bereft of his standard authors, was left at a loss for a new show for the Savoy Theatre in 1891 he chose to produce Solomon's *The Nautch Girl*. *The Nautch Girl* was a fine piece and a fine success, and once again Solomon found himself being compared to Sullivan and on the edge of a second career. Carte followed the 200 performances of *The Nautch Girl* with a revival of Solomon's 1882 piece, *The Vicar of Bray*, and subsequently sent both pieces on the road in repertoire, but when Sullivan supplied him with *Haddon Hall* the Savoy once again billed its favourite composer and Solomon's moment was over.

Although he continued to work, in spite of serious bad health, and his bottom drawer piled up collaborations with F C Burnand and with Bill Yardley, he had no more London productions. He had individual numbers included in a whole array of musicals and continued to work, from time to time, as a theatre conductor over the next few years, but his career as a composer was virtually done. In January 1895 he was working as conductor of a dreadful piece called *The Taboo* when he was taken seriously ill and died at the age of 39.

Teddy Solomon had no formal musical training. He was a product of a musical background wholly different from that of Arthur Sullivan, yet he produced music which in its time was considered by some to be comparable in value to that of the Savoy operas, and Sullivan himself went on record as saying that Solomon had it in him to have been the British Bizet. In the versatile manner of the day, he was able to switch from writing a comic song, like his famous 'All on Account of Eliza' in *Billee Taylor*, to a complicated piece of ensemble work or a finale, but his more substantial work held the same catchiness which made his comedy songs so popular and his comedy songs had something of the substance which characterized his ensemble writing, to the advantage of both.

If most of Solomon's works did not live on after their original productions, it was not largely the fault of the composer. It was perhaps a weakness in him that he suffered so clearly and so often from poor libretti but, in the wake of *Billee Taylor*, although he had successes with *Polly* (1884), *The Red Hussar* (1889) and above all *The Nautch Girl* (1891), George Dance's highly humorous book for the last-named gave him his only really satisfactory libretto and lyrics since *Billee Taylor*. The work proved wholly worthy of the famous theatre which played it.

Solomon's first wife, Jane Isaacs, was a music-hall artist under the name of Lily Grey, and their daughter, Clara (b London, 21 December 1873; d 21 December 1964), became a musical stage and variety performer in her turn. As Carrie or Claire Solomon she played Eliza Bangs in her father's *Polly* at the age of 11 (1884) and in *Erminie* at 12, and later appeared at the Gaiety in the chorus of *Cinder-Ellen Up-too-Late* and as an understudy to Cissie Loftus and Katie Seymour in *Don Juan* (1893). She also took over the rôle of the call-boy, Shrimp, in *In Town* on tour (1894) and later played it in Broadway's season (1897), and understudied Ada Reeve in the title-rôle of *The Shop Girl*. She became **Claire ROMAINE** after her marriage to Edgar Romaine Keddie and went on to play in *The Maid of Athens* (1897, Ina), the title-rôle in the successful touring musical *The Gay Grisette* (1898, Babette) and was taken back to the Gaiety to deputize for Connie Ediss as the heavy lady of *The Messenger Boy* (1901, t/o Mrs Bangs) and *The Toreador* (Mrs Malton Hoppings). On the verge of the big-time, she blew it when her husband chose to have a row with George Edwardes over his wife's material. She only played once in a London musical after that: in the heavy-lady rôle of the short-lived *Amorelle* (1904). She visited Australia where she billed herself as the 'idol of London' on the Australian halls, and ended up a useful touring character lady in revue and in such pieces as *Toni* and *Peggy-Ann*. Her last chance of a return to the West End was poleaxed when the British production of Vincent Youmans's *Two Little Girls in Blue*, in which she was

cast as Hariette Neville, closed on the pre-London road.

1876 **Crotchets** (Frederick Hay) 1 act Strand Theatre 7 June
1876 **A Will With a Vengeance** (Hay) 1 act Globe Theatre 27 November
1877 **Contempt of Court** (Arthur Matthison) 1 act Folly Theatre 5 May
1879 **Another Drink** (Henry Savile Clarke, Lewis Clifton) 6 scenes Folly Theatre 12 July
1879 **The Happy Man** (Tyrone Power) new score 1 act Globe Theatre 6 September
1879 **Venus, or the gods as they were and not as they should have been** (aka *Vulcan*) (pasticcio arr/Edward Rose, Augustus Harris) Royalty Theatre 27 June
1879 **Balloonacy** (pasticcio arr/H Pottinger Stephens, F C Burnand) Royalty Theatre 1 December
1879 **Rothomago** (H B Farnie) 1st act of four Alhambra Theatre 22 December
1880 **Billee Taylor** (Stephens) Imperial Theatre 30 May
1880 **Popsy Wopsy** (Sydney Grundy) 1 act Royalty Theatre 4 October
1881 **Claude Duval** (Stephens) Olympic Theatre 24 August
1881 **Quite an Adventure** (Frank Desprez) 1 act Olympic Theatre 7 September
1882 **Lord Bateman** (Stephens) Gaiety Theatre 29 April
1882 **The Vicar of Bray** (Sydney Grundy) Globe Theatre 22 July
1883 **Virginia** (aka *Virginia and Paul*) (Stephens) Bijou Theater, New York 9 January
1884 **The Little Cricket** (James Mortimer) Avenue Theatre 24 May
1884 **Polly, the Pet of the Regiment** (Mortimer) Novelty Theatre 8 November
1884 **Pocahontas, or the Great White Pearl** (Grundy) Empire Theatre 26 December
1886 **Pepita, or the Girl with the Glass Eyes** (Alfred Thompson) Union Square Theater, New York 16 March
1886 **The Maid and the Moonshiner** (Charles Hoyt) Standard Theater, New York 16 August
1888 **Penelope** (Stephens) Star Theatre, New York 15 October
1889 **The Real Truth About Ivanhoe, or Scott Scotched** (E C Nugent) Theatre Royal, Chelsea Barracks 1 February
1889 **Pickwick** (F C Burnand) 1 act Comedy Theatre 7 February
1889 **Penelope** (G P Hawtrey) 1 act Comedy Theatre 9 May
1889 **Tuppins & Co** (Malcolm Watson) 1 act St George's Hall 24 June
1889 **The Red Hussar** (Stephens) Lyric Theatre 23 November
1890 **Domestic Economy** (Burnand) 1 act Comedy Theatre 7 April
1890 **The Tiger** (Burnand) 1 act St James's Theatre 3 May
1890 **A Swarry Dansong** (Barrington) Criterion Theatre 5 June
1890 **In and Out of Season** (Watson) 1 act Lecture Hall Ipswich
1891 **Incompatibility of Temper** (Barrington) 1 act private performance
1891 **Killiecrumper** (Watson) 1 act St George's Hall 30 March
1891 **Robinson Crusoe Esq** (William Yardley) Theatre Royal, Chelsea Barracks 11 April
1891 **The Nautch Girl** (Desprez/George Dance) Savoy Theatre 30 June
1892 **The Vicar of Bray** (revised version) Savoy Theatre 28 January
1893 **Crusoe Up-to-Date** revised *Robinson Crusoe Esq* Preston 16 October
1893 **Sandford and Merton** (Burnand) 1 act Vaudeville Theatre 20 December
1895 **The Professor** (Barrington) 1 act St George's Hall 15 July
1896 **On the March** (w John Crook, Frederic Clay/Yardley, B C Stephenson, Cecil Clay) Prince of Wales Theatre 22 June

SOLOMON, Fred[erick Charles] (b London, 31 August 1853; d New York, 9 September 1924).

Fred Solomon ultimately had a career in the musical theatre which was no less notable, and both longer and more varied, than his brother Edward's. He, too, benefited from the eclectic show business upbringing which their father's life imposed on them, becoming adept on a multiplicity of musical instruments during his life around the Winchester music hall. During a colourful career of nearly half a century in the theatre he worked as an author, director, composer and musical director, on Broadway and in London, but the heart of his work was in a highly successful career as a comic-opera comedian.

In the early part of his working life Fred followed in his brother's traces, appearing at the Royalty in 1879 (Remy in *Nicette*, Jupiter in *Venus*, Charley Maloni in *A Will with a Vengeance*) and made his first hit when he played the rôle of Ben Barnacle in *Billee Taylor* (1880), introducing the show's top song 'All on Account of Eliza'. Over the years that followed, he reprised this rôle around Britain and in 1884 through Europe. He also created the comic rôles of Edward's *Quite an Adventure* and *Claude Duval* (Blood-Red Bill) and appeared with Lotta at the Royalty Theatre, conducting her performances as *Nitouche* and appearing as a performer in the musical afterpiece *Wagnermania*. He also spent a period with the band of the Royal Marines, and composed the music for some musical stage pieces.

In 1886 he emigrated to America where he made a good Broadway career as a comic actor in musicals, beginning with a six-year stint at the Casino Theater. He took over as Cadeaux in *Erminie* from Francis Wilson (1886, and a reappearance in 1915), was the original American Shadbolt in *The Yeomen of the Guard* (1888) and appeared, amongst others, in *Nadgy* (Margrave), *Les Brigands* (Pietro), *The Brazilian* (Daniel), *La Fille de Madame Angot* (Larivaudière), *La Grande-Duchesse* (General Boum), *The Tyrolean* (Baron Weps), *Nanon* (Abbé La Plâtre), *Puritania* (John Smith), *La Tzigane* (General Buguslav Schlemvitchkoff) and *Le Petit Duc* (Frimousse). He toured as Jonathan in *Der arme Jonathan*, played Baton Blanc in E E Rice's production of *The Ballet Girl* (1897) and, as late as 1900, was seen as Yellowplush in *The Belle of Bohemia* (1900). Directly prior to this last engagement, however, he had been seen, with his other hat on, wielding the baton for the Casino Theater's production of *The Cadet Girl*.

Solomon wrote and composed burlesques for Koster and Bial's Music Hall and appeared in them as lead comedian, alongside a third brother, Sol Solomon [né Bowers SOLOMON] (b London, 9 September 1858; d unknown), who later played comic rôles in such musicals as *The Belle of Bohemia*, *The Chaperons* and *The Little Cherub*. He also composed a number of popular songs, additional material for a variety of Broadway shows (*The Man in the Moon*, *Three Million Dollars* etc) and even a full-scale Broadway musical, *King Kalico*, as well as adapting the musical part of several British pantomimes for their Broadway productions. He latterly acted for some 14 years as head of music for Klaw and Erlanger's productions, and took a Broadway baton on *The Pink Lady* and others of their shows.

Fred Solomon married a chorus lady from the Casino Theater, who was called either Miss Sutton or Miss Nathan (unless he married two of them), and his daughter went on the stage under the name of Justine Grey.

1881 **The Good Young Man Who ...** 1 act Aberdeen 30 May
1883 **Captain Kidd** (Charles Harrie Abbott) Prince of Wales Theatre, Liverpool 10 September
1885 **The Fairy Circle** 1 act Grand Theatre, Islington 27 May
1886 **A-Donis** Koster & Bial's Music Hall 8 February
1892 **King Kalico** (w R L Scott/Frank Dupree) Broadway Theater, New York 7 June
1901 **The Sleeping Beauty and the Beast** (w J M Glover/J Hickory Wood, Arthur Collins ad Cheever Goodwin, J J McNally) Broadway Theater 4 November
1903 **Mr Bluebeard** (Wood, Collins ad Goodwin) Knickerbocker Theater 21 January
1903 **Mother Goose** (w others/George V Hobart/Wood, Collins ad McNally) New Amsterdam Theater 2 December
1904 **Humpty Dumpty** (w Bob Cole, J Rosamund Johnson et al/Wood, Collins ad McNally) New Amsterdam Theater 14 November

SO LONG, LETTY Musical farce in 2 acts by Oliver Morosco and Elmer Harris, based on Harris's play *Your Neighbour's Wife*. Music and lyrics by Earl Carroll. Morosco Theater, Los Angeles, 3 July 1915; Shubert Theater, New York, 23 October 1916.

After the success won by comedienne Charlotte Greenwood in his production of *Pretty Mrs Smith*, producer Oliver Morosco soon had the actress bundled into a star-billed rôle as Letty Robbins in *So Long, Letty*. Miss Greenwood had been Letitia (Letty) Proudfoot in *Pretty Mrs Smith*, but *So Long, Letty* was the first of what would become a series of comical 'Letty' musicals fabricated around her. This one, written by Morosco and Elmer Harris on the bones of Harris's 1911 *Your Neighbour's Wife* (Lyceum, Los Angeles), had her involved in a bit of husband-swapping. Tommy Robbins (Sydney Grant) and Harry Miller (Walter Catlett) covet the comfy and sensual qualities, respectively, of each other's wives, Letty (Miss Greenwood) and Grace (May Boley). They swap spouses and go through an evening of comedy before going back to the status quo. Vera Doria was Mrs Cease, a wealthy aunt, caught up in the whole affair in the way that wealthy aunts always are in such affairs. Earl Carroll provided a lightweight score, topped by its title duo, 'Here Come the Married Men', 'All the Comforts of Home' and 'On the Beautiful Beach' as an accompaniment to the comedy.

The show was a considerable success when Morosco mounted it at his base in Los Angeles, but the producer did not hurry it east. Whilst Miss Greenwood was deployed into a damply splashy Ned Wayburn revue *Town Topics*, the musical moved to San Francisco's Cort Theater (11 October) and then to the rest of the country. It was another year before *So Long, Letty* touched down – complete with its original star – in New York.

The show played but 96 performances on Broadway, but it was soon back on the road to continue a long touring life, as Morosco readied the next of the series of like shows which would follow, and it also found itself a really appreciative home in Australia. The show was first produced there as a wartime Christmas entertainment in Sydney before it had even made its way from its original American west-coast production to Broadway. It was advertised by the banner 'when husbands exchange wives they sing 'So Long, Harry, Gracie, Tommy, Letty'!'. Dot Brunton was Australia's Letty (equipped with the interpolated 'They Didn't Believe Me'), the Gaiety star Connie Ediss was Grace, and ex-Savoyard C H Workman (Tommy), Alfred

Frith (Harry) and Ethel Morrison as the aunt completed a strong cast which played an outstanding 113 performances in Sydney before going on to two months in Melbourne (Her Majesty's Theatre 22 April 1916). Its success encouraged the Williamson firm to pick up the next Morosco/Carroll piece, the less worthy *Canary Cottage*, but what was lost on that venture was more than made up by repeat seasons of *So Long, Letty* which remained an Australian favourite for many years.

In 1928 the piece was finally taken up for Britain by producer Laddie Cliff. Rewritten by Austin Melford, equipped with a new and equally weightless score by Billy Mayerl and Frank Eyton, it was set on the road with the producer's wife, Phyllis Monkman, starred as Letty (Theatre Royal, Birmingham 22 October). When it proved ineffective, it was again rewritten by Stanley Lupino as *Oh, Letty!* and failed again. Producer H Wellesley Smith took up the now-orphaned show, had it done over yet again as *Change Over* (8 April 1929), and put it out yet again with Renée Reel starred. It toured for two and a half months and left it at that. Wife-swapping didn't get to the West End musical stage until *I Love My Wife* came along more than half a century later.

Australia: Her Majesty's Theatre, Sydney 26 December 1915

SOMETHING FOR THE BOYS Musical comedy in a prologue and 2 acts by Herbert and Dorothy Fields. Music and lyrics by Cole Porter. Alvin Theater, New York, 7 January 1943.

A wartime musical put together by producer Mike Todd for the frequently proven *Anything Goes* combination of Ethel Merman (star) and Cole Porter (songwriter), *Something for the Boys* featured its leading lady as Blossom Hart, a chorus girl become war-worker who inherits a share in a broken-down ranch. She and her cousins (Paula Laurence, Allen Jenkins) fit the place out as a rendezvous for the wives of men at a nearby base but, when Blossom gets too matey with airman Rocky Fulton (Bill Johnson), his girl Melanie Walker (Frances Mercer) casts doubt on the morals of the place and gets it closed down. Blossom becomes a heroine when she turns out to be a human radio-receiver and saves an aeroplane from disaster, so her house is rehabilitated and she, of course, gets her Rocky.

The zany final twist redeemed a script that was more like a wartime film scenario than anything else, but the rôle of Blossom gave Miss Merman sufficient to get her energetic teeth into and she lit into Porter's 'Hey, Good Lookin'' with Johnson, 'He's a Right Guy', 'The Leader of a Big-Time Band', and a revusical Indian duo with Miss Lawrence about bigamous doings 'By the Mississinewa' with her usual all-conquering vibrancy. But Porter's score was, in fact, a little disappointing. Johnson had an attractive ballad in 'Could it Be You?' but there was little else to compare with the songwriter's more popular work. Nevertheless, Miss Merman, a splendid physical production and that wartime effect which encourages long runs for happy shows proved more than sufficient to keep *Something for the Boys* at the Alvin Theater for 422 performances.

A British Bernard Delfont production was opened in Glasgow in December 1943 with Evelyn Dall (Blossom),

Jack and Daphne Barker, and Leigh Stafford (Rocky) starring and, in March 1944, it came into the London Coliseum. There it ran for three months until an onslaught of enemy bombs compounded the effect of already less-than-full houses and Delfont called it a day.

UK: London Coliseum 30 March 1944
Recording: selection (AEI)

SOMETHING IN THE AIR Musical play in 2 acts by Arthur Macrae, Archie Menzies and Jack Hulbert. Lyrics by Max Kester and Harold Purcell. Music by Manning Sherwin. Palace Theatre, London, 23 September 1943.

A successor to the two hugely successful Cicely Courtneidge-Jack Hulbert musical comedies *Under Your Hat* and *Full Swing*, *Something in the Air* was very much cooked to the same recipe as before: the two comical stars, here called Jack Pendelton and Terry Porter, spent the evening chasing about in a series of disguises trying to foil the machinations of a German spy. This time a third comedian, Ronald Shiner, took part in the fun as an upstart officer who, under war conditions, is the superior of the wealthy Jack in his own co-opted house. The fun and the stars were the thing, but on this occasion the Manning Sherwin-Purcell-Kester score also came up with a couple of numbers which were superior to anything from the previous episodes of the Cis-and-Jack-beat-the-Germans series of shows. Both went to the lady, who announced comically 'The Airforce Didn't Want Me (but they got me)' and crackled warmly through the heart-strung 'Home is the Place Where Your Heart Is'. Hulbert also scored with a war-orientated piece, as he looked forward to the outbreak of peace in 'It'll Take a Lot of Getting Used To'.

Something in the Air was quickly established as a hit and by the time of the bombing excesses which closed down the other *Something* – *Something for the Boys* – in the first week of July 1944 it had been played 336 times at the Palace Theatre. *Something in the Air*, however, didn't close. It moved out of London to take in some provincial dates and, three months later when things had calmed down, it returned to its London home. It happily achieved the difficult task of starting over again, and played another four and a half months and 163 performances.

SOMETHING'S AFOOT Musical in 2 acts by James MacDonald, David Vos and Robert Gerlach. Additional music by Ed Linderman. Lyceum Theater, New York, 27 May 1976.

A small-scale burlesque of the Agatha Christie murder-mystery genre, *Something's Afoot* took the tale of the 'Queen of Crime's enormously successful novel and play *Ten Little Niggers* and pummelled it into an hilariously exaggerated series of unlikely deaths perpetrated in a storm-bound English country house under the beady little eyes of the bemused Miss Tweed. As the audience tried to guess which of the guests was the murderer through a preposterous series of 'accidents', the characters took time off to confide their thoughts in such songs as the sleuthly lady's 'I Owe It All to Agatha Christie', the dastardly-seeming nephew's claim to be 'The Legal Heir', the suspiciously awakened title-song or some moon-in-June romancing for a pair of chocolate-box juveniles.

First produced at the Goodspeed Opera House (20

August 1973) and then at Los Angeles' Huntingdon Hartford Theater (19 February 1975), the show was given a Broadway production the following year with bulky British variety performer Tessie O'Shea brought in to appear as Miss Tweed in a cast made up mostly of members of the west-coast production: Neva Small (Lettie), Gary Beach (Nigel Rancour), Willard Beckham (Geoffrey), Barbara Heuman (Hope), Liz Sheridan (Grace Manley Prow), Sel Vitella (Clive), Gary Gage (Col Gillweather), Marc Jordan (Flint) and Jack Schmidt (Dr Grayburn). *Something's Afoot* lasted only 61 performances at the Lyceum Theatre, but a West End production in London's little Ambassador's Theatre with a cast featuring a number of performers from the Player's Theatre, Britain's home of Victorian burlesque productions, did altogether better (232 performances) and helped establish *Something's Afoot* as a favourite piece in small and limited-resources theatres.

Australia: Marian Street Theatre, Sydney 3 February 1977; UK: Ambassador's Theatre 17 June 1977

SOMETIME Musical comedy in 2 acts by Rida Johnson Young. Music by Rudolf Friml. Additional lyrics by Ed Wynn. Shubert Theater, New York, 4 October 1918.

Henry Vaughan (Harrison Brockbank) was engaged to marry actress Enid (Francine Larrimore), his now wife, when the exuberantly voluptuous Mayme (Mae West), who had other ideas, got Henry in a situation which caused Enid to call the wedding off. Or, rather, to postpone it for five years with Henry on a good-behaviour bond. The story, in line with its title (which purposely tried to recall that of mega-hit *Maytime*), was told in a flashback as Enid related the story of her love-life to her girlfriends, and it went in for some film-style switchbacks in the plot before reaching the point where the lovers were reunited and Mayme left to vamp alone. The love story was supplemented by comedy from top-billed Ed Wynn who had been brought in to the show in try-out (Atlantic City, 26 August) as a replacement for Herbert Corthell in order to give the piece some star value. Wynn had rewritten the libretto, supplied some (very weak) lyrics for himself, but basically swanned through the evening doing his own thing in the characters, variously, of the props man of Enid's show or a theatrical landlord.

The musical part included a 'Baby Doll' for Enid, a title-waltz, 'Picking Peaches' for Vaughan, and a 'Keep on Smiling' and 'The Tune You Can't Forget' for Frances Cameron as supporting Sylvia. Wynn gave out with his own 'Oh, Argentine' and a Spanish singer delivered 'Spanish Maid' in a set of Southern American songs and dances during a plot-turn which took everyone to the Argentine. Mae West did the 'Shimmy Schwabble' and 'bowled them over with her dance after "Any Kind of a Man" ... with the assistance of a well-placed claque'.

Sometime did well, but it hit a problem when it had to shift from the Shubert to the Casino. Wynn was given the star dressing room and Miss Larrimore objected. When producer Arthur Hammerstein sided with Wynn and he installed himself, the lady took all the comic's things, turfed them out on to the stage, and moved in. Not for long, as Hammerstein sacked her. The show, nevertheless, totted up a fine 238 performances before going on the road.

A London production with Desirée Ellinger and Joe Farren Soutar triumphing over Bibi Delabere and without a star comedian lasted for just 28 performances.

UK: Vaudeville Theatre 5 February 1925

SONDHEIM, Stephen [Joshua] (b New York, 22 March 1930).

Stephen Sondheim had an early connection with the musical theatre through a family friendship with the Oscar Hammersteins, and began his own contribution by writing college shows. He studied music, but had his first show-business work writing scripts for television's *Topper* before providing incidental music for plays *The Girls of Summer* (1956) and *Invitation to a March* (1961).

It was, again, not as a composer that he broke through into the Broadway musical establishment. As a result of Arthur Laurents hearing some lyrics he had written for a non-start show called *Saturday Night* he was brought in to work on *West Side Story*, supplying the lyrics the now too-busy Leonard Bernstein was originally to have done. The vigour and variety of the show's 'Something's Coming', 'America', 'I Feel Pretty', 'A Boy Like That', 'Officer Krupke' and 'Tonight' gave the young writer a memorable launch. He followed up by combining with Laurents again, and with composer Jule Styne, on a second assignment as a lyricist on *Gypsy* ('Everything's Coming Up Roses', 'All I Need is the Girl', 'Let Me Entertain You', 'If Mama Was Married', 'You Gotta Have a Gimmick', Rose's Turn'), before, in 1962, offering his first score – lyrics and music – to Broadway in the classical burlesque *A Funny Thing Happened on the Way to the Forum*. The show's inherently comic nature gave endless possibilities for lyric wit, if little for expansive musical writing, and those possibilities were hilariously fulfilled in a set of songs which helped the piece to a position alongside the great classical burlesques of the past, from *Orphée aux enfers* to *Phi-Phi*: 'Comedy Tonight', 'Lovely', 'Everybody Ought to Have a Maid', 'Impossible', 'I'm Miles Gloriosus' etc.

A third collaboration with Laurents on a sour, extravagant piece called *Anyone Can Whistle* proved a curious misfire all round, but Sondheim returned to form with a vengeance in a collaboration with Richard Rodgers on the score to Laurents's adaptation of his own *The Time of the Cuckoo* as *Do I Hear a Waltz?* Composer and lyricist combined to produce a musically and lyrically rangy score which was as good as anything they had ever or would (to date, in the case of the lyricist) ever write. 'Someone Woke Up', 'This Week Americans' 'Take the Moment', 'Moon in My Window', 'Here We Are Again', 'We're Gonna Be All Right', 'Stay' and their fellows made up a remarkable and remarkably shapely score in the traditional Broadway mould. But *Do I Hear a Waltz?*, manhandled in production, was not a success.

It was also the last time (to date) that Sondheim would supply lyrics to another composer's show score. In the more than 25 years and nine shows that have followed – apart from a lyrical contribution to the 1974 revisions of Leonard Bernstein's *Candide* – he has written both lyrics and music, although oddly enough never a libretto, to each of the shows with which he has been involved.

The first of these was *Company*, a revusical piece which

paraded through a sharply observed series of sketches and songs which exposed the little pretensions, vanities and impossibilities of a group of married, middle-class New Yorkers. 'Another Hundred People', 'Barcelona', 'Getting Married Today', 'You Could Drive a Person Crazy', 'The Little Things You Do Together' and 'The Ladies Who Lunch' each sketched a story or personality to fine revusical effect, and *Company* won its songwriter the first of what would become a bundle of Tony Awards in the years to come, a good Broadway run, and the first of the fervent followers who would soon become legion.

Company was followed by another piece on similarly revusical lines. *Follies*, however, exchanged the everyday New Yorkers for a parade of everyday ex-*Follies* girls. Once again, as in *Company*, the audience had to look hard to find a warmly drawn or sympathetic character amongst the mostly foolish, egotistical folk who peopled the evening's parade of characters, but those people gave the songwriter fine opportunities to display his talents in a number of fairly friendly parodies of the song-styles of past days: the pattering of the comedian's 'The God-Why-Don't-You-Love-Me-Oh-You-Do-I'll-See-You-Later Blues', the charming old Vienna 'One More Kiss', the dance routine of overgrowing-up 'Who's That Woman?', the sweetie-pie duo 'Rain on the Roof', and the creaky self-serenade of an elderly 'Broadway Baby'. Some of the burlesques ran close enough to the real thing to be taken for the real thing, and the blowtorch song 'Losing my Mind' went on to join the show's catalogue of a tough life, 'I'm Still Here', as a nightclub favourite. But the Broadway production of *Follies*, like *Do I Hear a Waltz?* was not a genuine success, although it played over 500 nights on Broadway, gave Sondheim its second successive Tony award, and produced several enduring numbers.

An adaptation of the Ingmar Bergman film *Smiles of a Summer Night* was a different kind of project to the two previous pieces on which Sondheim had worked. For the first time since *Do I Hear a Waltz?* he was dealing with 'real' people set in a story with a beginning, an end and a development, characters who, for all that many of them were again foolish folk, were without exception likeable and interesting. It was a piece which required painting in different colours, and this time Sondheim the composer surfaced with as many trumps as the previously superior Sondheim the lyricist. The waltzing score of *A Little Night Music* was both an homogenous score, rather than a collection of songs, and as melodious as it was witty, and it remains for many the most appreciable achievement of Sondheim the composer-lyricist. The score produced a hit song in 'Send in the Clowns', but that piece was only one high spot of a score which mixed the wryly funny, the wordfully funny and the musically funny, but never the harshly or cruelly funny in such pieces as the three-part dilemma expressed in 'Soon', 'Now', and 'Later'; in the characters' horrid premonition about a 'Weekend in the Country' which they wouldn't miss for the world; in the aged ex-plaything of a king reminiscing about the devalued status of 'Liaisons'; in a husband telling his ex-mistress 'You Must Meet My Wife'; or in two rivals for a lady's bed joining (separately) in regretful wishes ('It Would Have Been Wonderful').

A Little Night Music found fond friends from one end of the world to the other as it went on to a round of continu-

ing productions in a multitude of languages. In the meantime, however, Sondheim had switched dramatically from Sweden, warmth and waltzes, to Japan, cardboard cut-out figures and a slow-paced tale of exploitation in *Pacific Overtures*. There were moments that were recognizably the Sondheim of *A Little Night Music* or of *A Funny Thing* in the new show, but by and large *Pacific Overtures* was a piece apart, from which such 'items' as a Gilbert and Sullivan parody ('Hello, Hello') and a plotfully witty murder ('Chrysanthemum Tea') emerged to remind the listener of the author's earlier work. Some of its lyrics seemed to have taken of the succinct opaqueness of the haiku style: they were difficult to comprehend and the show and its songs were, all in all, not made to appeal to those who had loved the sweet and worldly sophistication of *A Little Night Music*.

Pacific Overtures was a failure. But with that show the composer reached a position from which he was rarely to retrench. There were to be no more *A Little Night Music*s. Having proved the qualities of warmth and wit were not only compatible but hugely effective in his hands, Sondheim put aside subjects which called for such treatment. And, bit by bit, he began what can only have been an intentional series of attempts to stretch various parameters of the established style and structure of the contemporary musical play, both textually and musically, as he had done in *Pacific Overtures*. The literate lyrical style, both comic and sentimental, which he had developed in his earlier shows with a skill unequalled in the modern musical theatre became refined in such a fashion that it often led to a lack of accessibility or clarity that was incompatible with general popularity. But if that general popularity was frankly renounced, a fervent minority following of the kind and strength usually reserved for the works of the best-plugged dead composers quickly became his.

This following was given an early boost by the production, in Britain, of a compilation show of songs from Sondheim's musicals under the title *Side By Side by Sondheim*. Britain, which had given Sondheim's works a limited appreciation, suddenly discovered the wit and wonder of his songwords in this evening which displayed the numbers naked, without the often irritating characters who had originally delivered them in their various plays. The entertainment was a major London success, and its pocket-size (five characters, no scenery) helped it to be toured and produced throughout the country in regional theatres, spreading the composer's work far and wide in a way that London's productions of *A Funny Thing* and *Company* or, latterly, *Gypsy* had not done. With *Side By Side by Sondheim* Britain suddenly woke up to the works of Stephen Sondheim. The little show then went on to Broadway and round the English-speaking world, continuing its missionary work, and creating happy zealots wherever it went.

Sondheim's next Broadway work was another curious one. It was not that it was in any way recherché – it was, rather, a musical melodrama of mostly two-dimensional grand guignol, grandly dressed up. *Sweeney Todd* was peopled with almost burlesque characters, allowing the songwriter to have much fun with the broad humour of songs describing the meat in a human pie or burlesquing a British parlour ballad, but also to include a mixture of the powerful, the high-romantic and the hyper-dramatic in a score which sometimes teetered on the verge of the tongue-in-cheek. Sunk by over-production on its original mounting on Broadway and in London, *Sweeney Todd* nevertheless earned yet another Tony for its composer/lyricist and became a perennially revived piece in a cut-down version which placed heavier emphasis on the grand guignol and less on the scenery, as it angled for the same audiences who once patronized Tod Slaughter and now wallow in *The Texas Chain-Saw Massacre* or *Carrie*.

An attempt to musicalize George S Kaufman and Moss Hart's bitter tale of youth disillusioned, *Merrily We Roll Along* (1981), was a failure, but there was, on the other hand, a reasonable Broadway run and some special kudos for Sondheim's next work, *Sunday in the Park with George* (1984). This time, both librettist and songwriter purposefully went once again down the path established in *Pacific Overtures*. The former supplied a two-part text which followed what was virtually a one-act operetta about the artist Seurat with an actful of dissertation on artistic matters. The latter illustrated it with a meandering, impressionistic score from which, as in *Pacific Overtures*, only the occasional set piece of wit or charm emerged. Those who had mumbled 'pretentious' at *Pacific Overtures* now said it out loud, those who had enthused over the former work now enthused doubly. Many a theatre-goer was on the first list, the second list included the Pulitzer Prize committee and Britain's National Theatre. The Sondheim legend was now becoming well fixed in place, and it was being orientated towards the refined rather than towards the popular.

Into the Woods (1988) proved a little more generally popular than its predecessor, largely because its once-more sour and sombre tale was dressed up in the clothes of a fairytale burlesque, encouraging the composer to variants on his early burlesque material which showed up clearly his change in style: the clear and clever humour of his early song lyrics was now largely replaced by something much more in a vein of contemporary poetry. It was a style which sometimes fitted well (when, like much modern poetry, it could be comprehended) and on other occasions was less effective. And it was paired with a musical style which took the same track, rarely going in for frank melody in the traditional style of the musical theatre on the one hand, nor yet for the kind of ensemble work, so effectively achieved in *A Little Night Music*, which might have taken the piece into the light operatic area. It was quite clear, however, that established 'areas' were of little interest to Sondheim and his collaborators and, as a result, these works remain of interest largely to connoisseurs.

At the time of writing, Sondheim's latest show is on the try-out trail. This time the sour and the sombre and perhaps the grand guignolesque are all on show again. In an age when a graphic movie about a serial killer is one of the American establishment's most successful films, *Assassins* is a revusical piece about murderers: the murderers whose victims have been American presidents. After a short, small-house season in London, where it was the second American-made show to open in a month, in preference to a Broadway whose ground rules have become too distorted to risk millions on, it has been seen swiftly on the Continent, and even if it does not ultimately attack the Big Time, it will undoubtedly win further showings in those areas where Sondheim's work is prized above all other.

In 35 years of contributing to the musical stage, in an era when the popular mainstream has gone from the well-made musical plays of Rogers and Hammerstein to the musically lush romantic and speciality shows of Andrew Lloyd Webber, Sondheim has moved steadily away from that mainstream. In doing so he has disappointed many who were thrilled by his pre-*Pacific Overtures* work, but he has established a firm and truly enthusiastic following for his new styles which have ensured even his commercially unsuccessful works repeated productions throughout the world in non-commercial circumstances.

1957 **West Side Story** (Leonard Bernstein/Arthur Laurents) Winter Garden Theater 26 September
1959 **Gypsy** (Jule Styne/Laurents) Broadway Theater 21 May
1962 **A Funny Thing Happened on the Way to the Forum** (Burt Shevelove, Larry Gelbart) Alvin Theater 8 May
1964 **Anyone Can Whistle** (Laurents) Majestic Theater 4 April
1965 **Do I Hear a Waltz?** (Richard Rodgers/Laurents) 46th Street Theater 18 March
1970 **Company** (George Furth) Alvin Theater 26 April
1971 **Follies** (James Goldman) Winter Garden Theater 4 April
1973 **A Little Night Music** (Hugh Wheeler) Shubert Theater 23 February
1974 **The Frogs** (Shevelove) New Haven, Conn, 20 May
1976 **Pacific Overtures** (John Weidman, Wheeler) Winter Garden Theater 11 January
1979 **Sweeney Todd** (Wheeler) Uris Theater 1 March
1981 **Merrily We Roll Along** (Furth) Alvin Theater 16 November
1984 **Sunday in the Park with George** (James Lapine) Booth's Theater 2 May
1987 **Into the Woods** (Lapine) Martin Beck Theater 5 November
1991 **Assassins** (Weidman) Playwrights Horizons 27 January; Donmar Warehouse, London 22 October 1992

Biographies: Zadan, C: *Sondheim & Co* (Macmillan, New York, 1974 and 1986), Gordon, J: *Art isn't Easy* (Southern Illinois University Press, 1990)

SONG AND DANCE   Concert for the theatre in 2 parts with music by Andrew Lloyd Webber. Lyrics by Don Black. Palace Theatre, London, 26 March 1982.

This 'concert for the theatre' consisted of a semi-staged and slightly expanded version of Lloyd Webber's 50-minute solo song-cycle 'Tell Me on a Sunday', originally sung, televised and issued as a top-ten record by vocalist Marti Webb, and a performance of his 'Variations' (on a theme of Paganini), written for and recorded by his cellist brother, Julian, and now re-orchestrated and used as the basis for a series of dance scenes.

The song cycle, which followed a middle-ageing English woman in New York through a series of unfortunate love affairs with wry optimism and melodious humour, was played by Miss Webb on a small stage-within-a-stage set between the two halves of the orchestra and in front of an effective series of projections of American skylines. The ups and (mostly) downs of her relationships brought forth some unexaggerated and highly effective modern songs, peaking in 'The Last Man in My Life' and 'Nothing Like You've Ever Known', dipping into humour in 'Capped Teeth and Caesar Salad' and linked throughout by recurring fragments of the hopeful 'It's Not the End of the World'. The dance part, choreographed by Anthony van Laast, formerly of the London Contemporary Dance Theatre, brought together an eclectic team of eight dancers including ballet's Wayne Sleep, jazz dancer Jane Darling, contemporary dance's Linda Gibbs and acrobatic Paul Tomkinson in a dance entertainment which mixed technical brilliance with a stylish sense of fun and a kaleidoscope of styles in a colourful and audience-pleasing piece.

Originally envisaged as a limited-season production, John Caird's mounting of *Song and Dance* soon proved to have the potential to be more than that. The Cameron Mackintosh/Really Useful Group production ultimately ran for two years (781 performances) at the Palace Theatre, was toured, re-televised (BBC 27 August 1984 with Sarah Brightman) and later returned to London for a second season at the Shaftesbury Theatre with its original stars (25 April 1990, 149 performances). An Australian production, with Gaye Macfarlane at its head as an Australian girl abroad, won fine notices but failed to catch on in seasons in Sydney and Melbourne (Her Majesty's Theatre 21 October 1983), whilst a German one (ad Michael Kunze) turned its heroine (Angelika Milster) into a German girl and did rather better.

For Broadway, the 'Dance' section was re-choreographed and the 'Song' part rewritten to an extent which no successful foreign musical had suffered since the bad old days of botching, three-quarters of a century earlier. The whole immensely believable character of the little piece's deeply ordinary and real heroine was metamorphosed into a campy kook, several numbers were excised and a linking piece, written to the theme of the 'Dance' part and unhappily inserted late in the London run, made prominent. Bernadette Peters and Christopher d'Amboise were featured, and the resulting show ran 474 performances without ever looking like repeating the London success.

Australia: Theatre Royal, Sydney 4 August 1983; USA: Royale Theater 18 September 1985; Germany: Deutsches Theater, Munich 10 October 1987

Recordings: original song cycle (Polydor), original cast (Polydor), television cast (RCA), American cast (RCA), German cast (Global) etc

SONGBOOK   A tribute to Mooney Shapiro in 2 acts by Monty Norman and Julian More. University of Warwick Arts Centre, Warwick, 2 May 1979; Globe Theatre, London, 25 July 1979.

A burlesque of the endless stream of composer-based compilation shows which had engulfed British theatres since the production of *Cole* and *Cowardy Custard*, *Songbook* followed the musical and personal fortunes of the fictitious Mooney Shapiro (Bob Hoskins/David Healey) through a life and career of endless opportunity and professional mediocrity, illustrated by songs which gleefully parodied various musical clichés of the century. Diane Langton out-Ciceli'ed Miss Courtneidge in a cheery wartime 'Bumpity-Bump' and joined Gemma Craven in demolishing the socio-political musical comedy in 'I Accuse', whilst Anton Rodgers smoked his way through a parody of the French chanson and the full cast of five joined in a selection from *Happy Hickory*, a winsomely identifiable musical full of outback innocence which umpteen years later provides Shapiro with his biggest hit when its ghastliest song is revamped as a blazing pop number.

Originally conceived as a small-theatre cabaret-style piece, allegedly for the National Theatre, *Songbook* was first presented by the Cambridge Theatre Company before being brought to London by Stoll Moss Theatres. It won a fine reception, but was taken off after only 208 performances in a climate of boardroom battling at Stoll Moss. Its future was downhill thereafter. A New York version produced by Stuart Ostrow as *The Mooney Shapiro Songbook* was criticized as too unsophisticated for Broadway and folded after one performance, and the show failed to find the place it might have expected in small and provincial theatres.

USA: Morosco Theater *The Mooney Shapiro Songbook* 3 May 1981
Recording: original cast (PYE)

SONG OF NORWAY   Operetta in 2 acts by Milton Lazarus adapted from a play by Homer Curran and based on the life of Edvard Grieg. Lyrics and musical adaptation from the works of Edvard Grieg by Robert Wright and George Forrest. Imperial Theater, New York, 21 August 1944.

Song of Norway was a biomusical in the *Das Dreimäderlhaus* tradition, illustrating a romantic incident allegedly taken from the life of a famous composer – this time Grieg rather than Schubert – with a score fabricated from his own melodies.It proved one of the happier examples of its kind and succeeded in its aims much better than most of the slather of such pieces which had tumbled such composers as Offenbach, Chopin, Tchaikovsky and Johann Strauss onto the world's stages in the nearly 30 years since Schubert's story and songs had set the band-wagon careering.

Initiated by San Francisco theatre-owner and writer Homer Curran, and musically created by filmland's Robert Wright and George Forrest, the piece had the young Grieg (Walter Cassel) plucked from his homely Norwegian hills by the man-eating diva Louisa Giovanni (Irra Petina) and carried off towards fame and fortune, leaving behind him Nina (Helena Bliss), the girl he was to have wed, and Nordraak (Robert Shafer), the poet friend with whom he had dreamed one day of writing the great Norwegian work. Louisa promotes Grieg in the high places of the musical and social world, and it takes Nordraak's death to bring him to the realization that he has been led away from his real purposes. He returns to Norway, to Nina and to his friend's text, and finds both fame and happiness.

Amongst the musical items, the theme of the A-minor piano concerto (the setting of the Nordraak poem) and 'Ich liebe dich' both got a virtually straight performance, whilst a Norwegian Dance was twinklingly turned into 'Freddy and His Fiddle', and 'Wedding Day at Troldhaugen' and a nocturne were melded together into the expressive 'Strange Music'. The comic moments were provided by Louisa and her little husband, and she had an enjoyably extravagant soprano moment in another piece made up from two Grieg sources, 'Now'.

The show was lavishly produced by Edwin Lester for the Los Angeles and San Francisco Civic Light Opera (July 1944), with the Ballet Russe de Monte Carlo choreographed by Georges Balanchine providing the dance element alongside the strong legitimate vocal part of the show. It won a fine west-coast success and was duly transferred to Broadway's Imperial Theater, with Lawrence Brooks replacing Cassel in the rôle of the composer. Once again it won a splendid reception, as well as an 860-performance run. Emile Littler's 1946 London production did almost as well. Splendidly staged with a singing cast featuring John Hargreaves (Grieg), Halina Victoria (Nina), Janet Hamilton-Smith (Louisa) and Arthur Servent (Nordraak), and with Robert Helpmann and Pauline Grant in charge of the dances, it notched up a very fine 526 performances at the Palace Theatre. Australia saw *Song of Norway* in 1950 with Charles Dorning (Grieg), Marjorie Cooke (Nina), Doreen Wilson (Louisa) and Henrik de Boer (Nordraak) featured for four months in Melbourne and for three and a half in Sydney (Theatre Royal, 15 December).

A large-scale revival was mounted at Jones Beach in 1958, and in 1970 a version of the show, with considerable rewriting by Wright and Forrest, was filmed by Cinerama with Toralv Maurstad, Florence Henderson, Frank Poretta and Christina Schollin featured. In 1981 *Song of Norway* was played by the New York City Opera.

UK: Palace Theatre 7 March 1946; Australia: Her Majesty's Theatre, Melbourne 17 July 1950; Film: Cinerama 1970

Recordings: original cast (Decca/MCA), Jones Beach cast (Columbia), film soundtrack (ABC) etc

SONG OF THE FLAME Romantic opera in a prologue, 2 acts and an epilogue by Oscar Hammerstein II and Otto Harbach. Music by George Gershwin and Herbert Stothart. 44th Street Theater, New York, 30 December 1925.

Russian upper-class Aniuta (Tessa Kosta) takes the side of the local revolutionaries against her own people, and goes into action dressed in a dramatic red dress which earns her the soubriquet 'the flame'. Without suspecting that Aniuta and 'the flame' are one and the same person, Prince Volodyn (Guy Robertson) falls in love with her, but it is not until the fall of Russia that the two can come together as émigrés in Paris.

After the fleeting melodies of *Lady, Be Good!* and *Tip-Toes*, which had opened just two nights before *The Song of the Flame*'s première, it was something of a surprise to find Gershwin's name attached to the score of what was a distinctly Rombergian romantic operetta, even in a collaboration with that operettic sturdy Herbert Stothart. However, the score of *Song of the Flame* turned out to be thoroughly in the spirit of the tradition which had in that same season turned out *The Vagabond King* and *Princess Flavia*, even if it produced none of the enduring numbers which Friml's show did. The richly voiced Miss Kosta had the score's best moments in the title-song and the Cossack Love Song ('Don't Forget Me') whilst a group called the Russian Art Choir performed a selection of interpolated Russian folk songs.

Lavishly produced by Arthur Hammerstein, *Song of the Flame* had a 219-performance run on Broadway and, though not exported, was later used as the basis for a First National technicolor film starring Bernice Claire, Alexander Grey and Noah Beery. It was billed as 'The talking screen's answer to *The Volga Boatmen*' and supplied with the warning 'children not admitted', which was doubtless not because the remnants of the original score were supplemented by new songs by Grant Clarke and Harry Akst.

Film: First National 1930

DAS SONNTAGSKIND Operette in 3 acts by Julius Bauer and Hugo Wittmann. Music by Carl Millöcker. Theater an der Wien, Vienna, 16 January 1892.

A Viennese piece with a British setting, *Das Sonntagskind* began at the Schloss Rockhill in Scotland, and ended up in the dungeons of Damkirk. Ilka Pálmay was Lady Sylvia Rockhill, Frln Stein her sister Betty Parnell (known as 'Miss Droll'), and they were teamed with the royal register of the Theater an der Wien's male staff: Alexander Girardi as Tristan Florival, Siegmund Stelzer as Rolf Butterfield, Rudolf del Zopp as the guardsman Sir Edgar Lanimor, Josef Joseffy as his colleague, Sir Lothar, and Carl Lindau as the Sheriff Plumkett. The complex amorous and political doings of these Austro-tartan folk were illustrated by an attractive Millöcker score from which an Echo Song proved the plum.

Das Sonntagskind was a fine success, running for 62 performances between January and 17 March at the Theater an der Wien, and establishing itself thoroughly before going on to productions in Germany and in Hungary (ad Béla J Fai, Ferenc Rajna) and in America, where an initial two-month season in English (ad Helen F Tretbar) at the Casino Theater with Lilly Post, Annie Meyers, Jennie Reiffarth, Henri Leoni, Harry Macdonough, William Pruette and Jefferson de Angelis featured was followed by a German-language production by Hans Conried's company at the Amberg Theater.

Although it did not establish itself in any of those countries, *Das Sonntagskind* nevertheless got a fresh showing in Vienna. A major revival was mounted at the Johann Strauss-Theater on 17 March 1922 with Fritz Werner starred, and it actually played longer than the original production had done, running through until 24 May.

A fairytale piece by Albert Dietrich and Heinrich Bulthaupt under the same title had been previously given at Bremen in 1886.

Germany: ?1892; USA: Casino Theater *The Child of Fortune* 18 April 1892; Amberg Theater (Ger) 2 March 1893; Hungary: Népszinház *A serencsefia* 20 September 1892

SON P'TIT FRÈRE Opérette légère in 2 acts by André Barde. Music by Charles Cuvillier. Théâtre des Capucines, Paris, 10 April 1907.

This nine-handed libretto by the young, and as yet unknown, Barde was – a decade before *Phi-Phi* – a comically and classically Grecian one in which, like its more famous successor, the accent was firmly on wit and on sparkling sexual comedy, leavened with a good deal of puns and jokes on classical words and names. Barde's story centred on the fading Ancient-Greek courtesan Laïs (Marguerite Deval), abandoned by her lover and become unfashionable, who inveigles the prettiest, richest and most innocent newcomer in town, the aptly named Agathos (Henri Defreyn), to her house by pretending to be his long-lost sister. Before too long she is very happy to admit to her 'little brother' that she lied. Polin appeared as the comical and grubby parasite of Laïs's household, Eukratès, and Lucienne Delmay had the other principal rôle as Xantho.

Cuvillier's score, written to be accompanied only by a piano (the pianist at the Capucines at this stage was none other than composer Albert Chantrier), echoed Barde's intimate and tongue-in-cheek comicality in the dancing rhythms of the pre-*thé dansant* age, and if his melodies were scarcely deathless, his music had the merit of holding up and cleanly displaying the cleverest lyrics the Parisian theatre had heard in years. Eukratès lauded the virtues of having a Parasite round the house ('Être parasite, ah! le bon métier!') – a house philosopher is a family luxury, like having a mother but less expensive and 'cela remplace un petit chien' – and encouraged Laïs towards the cult of pleasure ('Laïs laicisons!') apparently for the pure joy of the song's opening pun. The lady began affairs by justifying letting herself go, after years of keeping her figure and athleticism for her customers – 'à quoi bon soigner les décors, puisqu'il n'y a plus de spectacteurs ...', before lurching into a big burlesque love duo on her meeting with Agathos and launching her little deception in the Couplets du petit frère. Faced with real love, however, the courtesan loses all her amorous skills and tells us about it in song ('Oui j'ai tout appris auprès d'Aphrodite'). The Duo du frisson saw Agathos – introduced in the first act protesting, like Aspasie in *Phi-Phi* (not to mention Meïlhac and Halévy's Baronne Gondremarck), 'je suis encore tout étourdi' - go, via fear and madness, to 'amour' and, in the second-act finale to alarm: 'j'étais si vertueux, et je deviens incestueux!' Eukratès, always there with a bon mot, is around to comment 'L'inceste c'est comme le pal, ça commence bien et finit mal'. Another jolly moment of the second act was a musical ancient-Greek tea-party with distinctly modern Parisian overtones ('les ten o'clock c'est vraiment bien moins toc et mieux assorti que le five o'clock tea ...').

The production of *Son p'tit frère* at the little Théâtre des Capucines was a fine small-house success and the show went on to have a substantial provincial life, was played in Brussels by its two original stars, and was revived at the Théâtre Édouard VII a decade later (18 January 1917). In 1930 it was enlarged into a three-act opérette and played on tour by the singer Geneviève Vix, Guy Ferrell and Julien Carette under the title *Laïs, ou la courtisane amoureuse*.

After the successes of *The Lilac Domino* and *Afgar*, Cuvillier was a name to reckon with in London, and what purported to be a version of *Son p'tit frère* was produced by André Charlot at the Comedy Theatre in 1920 as *The Wild Geese*. It had a text by Ronald Jeans which involved neither courtesans nor ancient Greece. Jack Buchanan and Phyllis Monkman were amongst the cast, Amy Augarde played one Dame Agatha Boot, and it ran for 112 performances whilst bigger shows, led by *Irene*, prospered more thoroughly in the public favour.

UK: Comedy Theatre *The Wild Geese* 12 February 1920

SONS O' GUNS Musical comedy in 2 acts by Fred Thompson, Jack Donahue and Bobby Connolly. Music and lyrics by Fred J Coots, Benny Davis and Arthur Swanstrom. Imperial Theater, New York, 26 November 1929.

A spectacular Connolly and Swanstrom production with Urban sets, Charles le Maire costumes, a Connolly mounting, Albertina Rasch dances and a Hollywood leading lady (Lili Damita), *Son o' Guns* followed the fortunes of co-author Jack Donahue in the rôle of devil-may-care Jimmy Canfield, ill-fittingly drafted into the wartime army with his peacetime manservant (William Frawley). Dona-

hue gambolled with 'rough-hewn grace' through a serious of low-comic adventures to accidental heroism and to Mlle Damita (as a mademoiselle called Yvonne), winning the war in the traditional Old Bill style which *The Better 'Ole* had so happily exploited a decade earlier. The score was made up of lightly reminiscent numbers with titles such as 'Why?', 'It's You I Love', 'Cross Your Fingers' and 'I'm That Way Over You' which served their purpose in the show, became dance-band fodder, and were otherwise not remembered.

A reviewer announced that 'the war has been refought with spendthrift prodigality' as *Sons o' Guns* and its 'pawky, homespun humours' found itself a cheerful and light-hearted Broadway success for 295 performances. It was subsequently and elaborately produced in London by Jack Waller and Herbert Clayton with equally happy results. Bobby Howes and Robert Hale took the comedy rôles, the Parisian musical-comedy star Mireille Perrey played French Yvonne, and the piece lasted 211 performances at the London Hippodrome before going on the road.

Australia, too, enjoyed the show with Gus Bluett (Jimmy), Leo Franklyn (Hobson), Bertha Riccardo (Yvonne) and Elsie Prince (Bernice) featured in a J C Williamson Ltd production which resituated the events of the evening in Australia. It played through ten weeks in Sydney and nine in Melbourne (Theatre Royal 5 February 1931).

UK: London Hippodrome 26 June 1930; Australia: Her Majesty's Theatre, Sydney 4 October 1930; Film: 1929

THE SORCERER Comic opera in 2 acts by W S Gilbert. Music by Arthur Sullivan. Opera Comique, London, 17 November 1877.

The first full-length comic opera from the Gilbert and Sullivan partnership, following their collaborations on *Thespis* and *Trial By Jury*, *The Sorcerer* was produced in London by budding manager Richard D'Oyly Carte who, as business manager for Selina Dolaro, had been responsible for the first staging of *Trial By Jury*. Carte formed the Comedy Opera Company with investors' capital and took a lease on the unpopular old Opera Comique to stage the new work by the pair who had caused such a stir with their one-act dramatic cantata. He advertised the piece as a well-mannered English comic opera, in the vein of the pieces played at the German Reeds' Entertainment, in a deliberate contrast to the colourful but suspiciously naughty opéras-bouffes which were currently filling London theatres.

Like *Trial By Jury*, *The Sorcerer* was based on a magazine story which Gilbert had written for the *Graphic*, but it was less straightly satirical than its predecessor. It told the story of one John Wellington Wells (George Grossmith), a professional sorcerer, who is hired by philanthropic young Alexis (George Bentham) to distribute a love potion to the inhabitants of his rural home-town on the occasion of his betrothal to lovely Aline (Alice May). The potion has unintended effects, throwing Alexis's aristocratic father (Richard Temple) into the arms of the common pew-opener Mrs Partlett (Harriet Everard), separating her daughter Constance (Giulia Warwick) from the curate she adores (Rutland Barrington), and setting the dragonistic Lady Sangazure (Mrs Howard Paul) onto Wells himself.

The sorcerer has to give himself up to the spirits of the underworld to undo the effects of his necromancing.

Sullivan's music followed the vein set up at the German Reeds' establishment and in *Trial By Jury*, eschewing the extravagant gaiety and big burlesque effects of opéra-bouffe and remaining merrily and wittily melodious within the normal bounds of English operetta. The score included several pieces which became drawing-room favourites, notably the comedian's patter song 'My Name is John Wellington Wells', Barrington's reminiscences of the days when he was 'A Pale Young Curate' and the soprano solo 'Happy Young Heart', and Gilbert turned out some sharply funny lyrics for pieces such as the duo in which Temple manfully resisted the amorous advances of Mrs Paul ('Hate Me!').

The Sorcerer was well received and well attended, but Carte had to fight with his investors who, having quickly recouped, were soon anxious to close the show before they lost what they had won. They were, apart from anything else, having to pay Gilbert and Sullivan six guineas' royalty a performance, and that on top of the £200 the writers had earned on delivering the script and score. Carte fought hard enough to keep the show on for 175 performances, closing only in time to stage the new piece which Gilbert and Sullivan had written to follow it, *HMS Pinafore*. The new piece would be much more, and much more widely, successful, but *The Sorcerer* had not only laid the foundations for that success by both putting the production structures in place and introducing the public to the brand of show they would see at the Opera Comique, but also by putting together the basis of the company – Grossmith, Miss Everard, Temple, Barrington – which would help make the Gilbert and Sullivan operas what they became.

The Sorcerer did not attract attention outside Britain until later, when *HMS Pinafore* had made Gilbert and Sullivan internationally famous. Then it was played for 20 performances at the Broadway Theater with Horace Lingard in the rôle of John Wellington Wells, and it was later seen again on Broadway as played by the company from Philadelphia's Arch Street Theater. However, *The Sorcerer* had its principal New York run in 1882 when John McCaull produced a version with John Howson (Wells), Laura Joyce (Sangazure), Digby Bell (Daly) and Lillian Russell (Aline) featured which played for 92 performances at his Bijou Theater and returned for three further weeks at the Casino the following year. In 1892 it was again played at Palmer's Theater by Henry Dixey's Company.

Five months after the first Broadway performances, Lingard and his wife Alice Dunning (Aline) introduced Australia to *The Sorcerer* in a version in which the music was boasted as having been 'specially arranged' by conductor Charles van Ghele.

The Sorcerer returned to London in 1884 when Carte staged a major revival of the piece, revised by its authors for the occasion, at the Savoy Theatre. Temple, Barrington and Grossmith repeated their original rôles with Rosina Brandram, Mrs Paul's erstwhile understudy, as Sangazure and tenor Durward Lely and soprano Leonora Braham as the lovers. It played for 150 performances in a bill with *Trial By Jury*. The Savoy Theatre hosted a further 102 performances in 1898 (still with Temple and Miss Brandram) and the piece subsequently became an undeservedly minor part of the repertoire of the D'Oyly Carte Company, perching slightly politely alongside its writers' later and often more colourful shows, through the remaining part of the company's existence.

USA: Broadway Theater 21 February 1879; Australia: Academy of Music, Melbourne 28 July 1879
Recordings: complete (Decca)

SO THIS IS LOVE Musical play in 2 acts by Stanley Lupino and Arthur Rigby. Lyrics by Desmond Carter. Music by 'Hal Brody'. Winter Garden Theatre, London, 25 April 1928.

The first solo production of producer-performer Laddie Cliff, *So This is Love* crystallized the dancing-comedy format which he had successfully used in the recent *Lady Luck* and *Dear Little Billie*. Comedian Leslie Henson directed, ubiquitous choreographer Max Rivers did the dances, Australian dancers Cyril Ritchard and Madge Elliott were given the romantic leads, acrobatic Australian Reita Nugent (as a character called Cherry Carleton, with a number called 'Dance') was in support, the chorus was the John Tiller Girls, and eccentric dancer-comedian Cliff paired with co-author and comedian Lupino at the head of the fun.

Ritchard was rich Peter who pretends to be poor to woo his proud and penniless secretary, Pamela (Miss Elliott), Cliff played a brash and bespectacled Yankee called Hap J Hazzard, who got the rich and rejected Kitty (Sylvia Leslie), and Lupino was Potiphar Griggs, a newly married man with a buxom and suspicious wife, Minnie (Connie Emerald). The comedy was fairly continuous, the dancing bright and varied and accompanied by suitable music which was not, as Cliff tried to pretend, by a fashionably transatlantic composer but by a bundle of English ones including H B Hedley and Jack Strachey hidden under a portmanteau pseudonym. Amongst the rare occasions on which the music was not meant to be danced to, Sylvia Leslie had a pretty ballad, 'Lazy Father Time (can't you see I'm finding you too slow)', and Lupino had a go at the craze for thrillers in 'Hats off to Edgar Wallace'.

So This is Love hit the mood of the moment precisely and racked up 321 performances at the Winter Garden before going on the road for the next three seasons whilst Cliff and his team carried on turning out more successful shows on the same lines.

In spite of its lively success, the show scarcely seemed like an export prospect, but that was reckoning without the world's most cosmopolitan musical-theatre cities. Budapest, having gone through the products of the new French musical-comedy genre and dipped briefly into Broadway, cast a glance at London and *Ez hát a szerelem!* (ad István Békeffy) turned up at the Fővárosi Operett-színház the year after the London production. The following year Melbourne and, a year further on, Sydney (Grand Opera House, 7 November 1931) also welcomed *So This is Love*. The White-Edgeley production company featured Clem Dawe (Potty), Betty Eley (Pamela), Rita McLean (Minnie) and Bobby Gordon (Hap) in a pairing of *So This Is Love* and the later *Love Lies*, and George Marlow presented the former piece in Sydney where Eric Edgeley renounced his producing credit but instead starred as Hap Hazzard alongside his partner, Dawe, and John Wood as Peter.

Hungary: Fővárosi Operettszinház *Ez hát a szerelem!* 24 September 1929; Australia: King's Theatre, Melbourne 10 May 1930

THE SOUND OF MUSIC Musical in 2 acts by Howard Lindsay and Russel Crouse. Lyrics by Oscar Hammerstein II. Music by Richard Rodgers. Lunt-Fontanne Theater, New York, 16 November 1959.

The Sound of Music was the last and arguably the greatest success of the famous team of Rodgers and Hammerstein. It put the button on the memorable set of five romantic musical plays which the pair turned out in their 16 years as the most successful musical theatre writers and producers on Broadway, and with which they marked not only American stages, but the rest of the English-speaking theatre and musical cinema world as well.

The story of Maria von Trapp and her step-children who together formed the singing group known as the Trapp Family Singers and the episode of the family's escape from Nazi Germany were originally used as the subject for a German film. It was a proposal to make a Hollywood film based on that film which tossed the subject into currency in America in the 1950s. The idea was taken to Mary Martin, the project furthered by her husband, Richard Halliday, and Leland Hayward, and Howard Lindsay and Russel Crouse signed by them to write a libretto into which it was primitively intended to introduce examples of the material sung by the Trapp Family Singers. When it was decided to supplement that material with some more up-to-date songs, Rodgers and Hammerstein were approached and the result was that the original idea went out the window and *The Sound of Music* became a Rodgers and Hammerstein project with the pair both writing the show's score and acting as co-producers.

Maria Rainer (Miss Martin) is a fledgeling nun in the abbey at Nonnberg, but her natural exuberance seems to fit her ill for a life of walled devotion and the Abbess (Patricia Neway) decides to send her as governess to the widowed Captain von Trapp (Theodore Bikel). Maria wins the confidence and friendship of the seven von Trapp children, but when she awakens romantic feelings in the Captain – and something she does not quite understand in herself – she flees back to Nonnberg. The children are distressed, the more so as von Trapp is to wed the wealthy and not very lovable Elsa Schräder (Marion Marlowe), but the Abbess, refusing to let Maria hide from life behind a wimple, orders her to return to her duties and, as a result, she shortly becomes the Baroness von Trapp. When von Trapp's aggressively nationalist and anti-German stance threatens to make trouble for his family, they are obliged to flee Austria and, with the help of the nuns, they make their way over the mountains of Maria's youth to Switzerland and safety.

The score for the piece fell largely to Maria, beginning with a rhapsodic hymn to the hills in 'The Sound of Music', continuing with a set of tuneful and sweet numbers with, since most of them were addressed to children, a suitably innocent air to them ('My Favourite Things', 'Do-Re-Mi', 'The Lonely Goatherd'), and returning to things adult to sing with the Captain of being 'An Ordinary Couple'. The singing of the children was displayed in 'So Long, Farewell' and of the Captain in the folky 'Edelweiss', whilst eldest daughter Liesl (Lauri Peters) and her teenage boyfriend (Brian Davies) romanced in-

genuously to 'Sixteen Going on Seventeen'. Elsa and the parasitic but plotworthy impresario Max Detweiler (Kurt Kasznar) supplied the more sophisticated/cynical element ('How Can Love Survive', 'There's No Way to Stop It') and a quartet of sub-operatic nuns discussed the problems posed by 'Maria' in a delightfully comic number, but the evening's hit number proved to be the most substantial bit of singing in the score, the last in the series of throbbing feminine hymns which had been a feature of the Rodgers and Hammerstein shows. After 'Bali H'ai', 'You'll Never Walk Alone' and 'Something Wonderful' came 'Climb Every Mountain', the soaring homily with which the Abbess sent Maria from the Abbey to face life, and which returned to head the escaping family on their way at the play's end.

The Sound of Music, directed by Vincent Donehue – the man who had brought the idea to Miss Martin in the first place – initially won a few dismissive critical comments for its pink-ribboned ingenuity, but the public made its positive feelings felt in no uncertain way, driving the show to a 1,443-performance Broadway run, parallel to a long tour in which Florence Henderson was the first Maria. Fine though that record was, however, it was only the beginning. London's edition, in spite of being cast without any of the star values of the Broadway version, proved to be the most successful production of a Broadway musical ever to have played London. Jean Bayless (Maria), Roger Dann (von Trapp) and opera's Constance Shacklock (Abbess) headed a reproduction which played for 2,385 performances in the West End. Australia's production, with June Bronhill as a Maria with much more substantial vocal qualifications than the usual soubrette casting, followed, before *The Sound of Music* moved into another dimension with the issue of its film version in 1965.

It was a film version with a difference, for whereas the earlier Rodgers and Hammerstein filmed musicals had been slimmer but fairly faithful versions of the stage shows, on this occasion the score underwent significant changes between stage and screen. Rodgers (Hammerstein was now dead) wrote two fresh songs – the bubbling, characterful 'I Have Confidence' and the sublimely and foolishly happy 'Something Good' – with which to give Maria's rôle a little more breadth and a little less of the soubrette, and 'An Ordinary Couple' and the Max/Elsa pieces were cut. One of the triumphs of modern-day musical-film casting – that of Julie Andrews (soubrette neither in personality nor voice) as Maria – compounded by shots of some of the world's most beautiful mountain scenery helped turn *The Sound of Music* into what must be, in real terms, the most successful motion-picture version of a stage musical ever made. Christopher Plummer (von Trapp, with the voice of Bill Lee), Peggy Wood and the singing voice of Margery McKay (Abbess) and Eleanor Parker (Elsa) took the other principal rôles.

The vast success of the film had a dual effect on the show. It turned its songs into even greater hits than they already were and it was ultimately responsible for the show being adapted into both German and French (and probably other languages), but it presented a problem for a major revival. How to cast Julie Andrews and how to reproduce those mountains? It was a challenge that Broadway declined to pick up, but London's Ross Taylor was less chary. Using a neatly revised text and score which incorporated 'I Have Confidence', a design which went remarkably far towards reproducing the main pictorial elements of the film, and with former child actress and pop vocalist Petula Clark as a pleasingly gentle, folksy Maria – quite different from, but just as appealing as, Miss Andrews – he produced a version (Apollo Victoria Theatre, 17 August 1981) which satisfied almost everyone. It ran 444 performances, prompted a decade of fresh touring and provincial productions, an Australian revival (Princess Theatre, Melbourne, 25 May 1983) with Julie Anthony (Maria) and Anthea Moller (Abbess) featured, and proved that there is still a life on stage for *The Sound of Music* without Julie Andrews and those mountains. The show visited London once again, in 1992, when a touring production featuring Christopher Cazenove and Liz Robertson stopped off at Sadler's Wells Theatre as part of its tour.

Unlike most of the Rodgers and Hammerstein opus, *The Sound of Music* also made some headway in Europe. The Opéra Royal de Wallonie, Belgium's specialists in French-language versions of American musical plays, introduced *La Mélodie de bonheur* in Liège in 1973 (22 December) with Pierrette Delange as Maria, Guy Fontagnère as von Trapp, Maria Murano (Abbess), Madeleine Vernon (Eva) and Hubert Meens (Max). It had a great success, and was regularly reprised there (1974, 1977, 1981, 1986), whilst making its way thence into the provincial theatres of France. The first German production (ad Ute Horstmann, Eberhard Storch) followed in 1982, but the piece did not establish itself in its German-language version in the same way that it did in the French and the only sighting of the piece on the Vienna stage has been a clever-dick mounting (the children played by adults, etc) shoestrung together at the Schauspielhaus in 1993.

The Sound of Music continues to flourish around the world, and the piece has also received repeated revivals at home, even though it has yet to make a full-scale return to Broadway. New York's most recent *Sound of Music* was seen under the aegis of the New York City Opera (8 March 1990, 54 performances) with Debby Boone starred as Maria alongside Laurence Guittard (von Trapp) and Claudia Cummings (Abbess).

UK: Palace Theatre 18 May 1961; Australia: Princess Theatre, Melbourne 20 October 1961; Germany: Stadttheater, Hildesheim *Die Trapp Familie* 9 March 1982; Austria: Schauspielhaus 27 February 1993; Film: Twentieth Century-Fox, 1965

Recordings: original cast (Columbia), London casts (HMV, Epic), Australian casts (HMV, EMI), Mexican cast (Orfeon), Netherlands cast (Philips), Israeli Cast (Disneyland), film soundtrack in English, French and Spanish (RCA), selection (Telarc) etc

SOUSA, John Philip (b Washington, DC, 6 November 1854; d Reading, Pa, 6 March 1932).

The American march king was still a touring musical director when he made his first produced attempt to break into the theatre as a comic-opera composer. His *The Smugglers*, written to a libretto patently pinched from F C Burnand's book for *The Contrabandista* (which he had recently been conducting), had a short life, but several tries and more than a decade later, allied with a good, professional librettist in Charles Klein, he produced what would be his one genuine musical-theatre hit in *El Capitan*.

Having written some of his own lyrics to *El Capitan*, Sousa ventured to write his own libretto for his next piece, *The Bride Elect*, but the negative results encouraged him to go back to Klein and then to such favourite Broadway librettists as Glen MacDonough and Harry Bache Smith for his later comic operas. *The Charlatan* (1898), a vehicle for favourite musical comedian De Wolf Hopper, had a short Broadway life (40 performances), but served its star well on the road and as far afield as London (as *The Mystical Miss*, 13 December 1899), whilst *Chris and the Wonderful Lamp*, an *Aladdin* derivative, proved happier through 57 performances than his earlier attempt at a children's piece with *The Queen of Hearts*.

However, in spite of *El Capitan*'s success, Sousa's career as a composer of comic opera did not flourish. Several other pieces remained unproduced, and on another occasion he priced himself out of a job. When Francis Wilson wanted the libretto of the French opérette *Babolin* reset, Sousa's financial demands proved too much for him and it was Edward Jakobowski who wrote *The Devil's Deputy*. The handful of Sousa scores which did make it to the stage in the 20th century did so for very short and unprofitable seasons and *El Capitan* and, to a lesser extent, *The Charlatan* remained Sousa's sole musical-theatre references.

In 1987 his music was used as the basis for the score of a musical about the American presidential Roosevelt family entitled *Teddy and Alice* (arr Richard Kapp/Hal Hackady/Jerome Alden, Minskoff Theater 12 November 1987 77 performances).

1882 **The Smugglers** (Wilson J Vance) Washington DC, 25 March
1884 **Desirée** (Edward M Taber) Washington DC, 1 May
1886 **The Queen of Hearts, or Royalty and Roguery** (Taber) 1 act Washington DC, 12 April
1896 **El Capitan** (w Tom Frost/Charles Klein) Broadway Theater 20 April
1898 **The Bride Elect** (Sousa) Knickerbocker Theater 11 April
1898 **The Charlatan** (Klein) Montreal 29 August
1900 **Chris and the Wonderful Lamp** (Glen MacDonough) New Haven 23 October
1906 **The Free Lance** (Harry B Smith) New Amsterdam Theater 16 April
1913 **The American Maid** (Leonard Liebling) Broadway Theater 3 March

Autobiography: *Marching Along* (Hale, Cushman, Boston, 1928); Biography: Bierley, P E: *John Philip Sousa: American Phenomenon* (Prentice Hall, Englewood Cliffs, NJ, 1973)

SOUTAR, J[oseph] Farren (b Greenwich, 17 February 1870; d Cookham, 23 January 1962).

The son of the famous Nellie Farren and her husband, Gaiety Theatre actor and director Robert Soutar, J Farren Soutar (as he was billed) went on the stage at the age of 16. He became a successful musical-comedy leading man in the prewar part of a long and varied stage career, which effectively began under George Edwardes at Daly's Theatre (t/o Bobbie Rivers in *A Gaiety Girl*, Algernon St Alban in *An Artist's Model*) and, subsequently, included the early revue *Pot Pourri* (1899), the Broadway production of *The Girl from up There* and its London transfer, and the juvenile leads of London's *A Chinese Honeymoon* (1902, t/o Tom Hatherton), *Sergeant Brue* (1904, Michael Brue) and

The Belle of Mayfair (1906, Raymond Finchley), in which he was Romeo to the Juliet of Edna May.

He toured in America, played in music-hall, straight theatre, revue and the short-lived musical play *The Antelope* (1908) in Britain but, after his appearance in the juvenile rôle of *Peggy* (1912, Bendoyle) on Broadway and war service, he had less luck with his choice of musicals (Sydney Heap in *The Eclipse*, Amarak el Deeb in *Almond Eye*, Hank Vaughan in *Sometime*, Dodo in *Riki-Tiki*) until he appeared as Baron Chamard in *The Dubarry* (1932) in the twilight of his career.

Soutar was married to the statuesque **Maud HOBSON** (d 6 January 1913), an Australian-born niece of John Hollingshead, who appeared for George Edwardes as a showgirl in *Faust Up-to-Date* (1888, Donner and u/s Faust), *Ruy Blas and the Blasé Roué* (1889, t/o Major-domo) and *Carmen Up-to-Data* (1890, Intimidad) before marrying for the first time and going off to Honolulu. She soon came back, and took slightly better parts in *Cinder-Ellen Up-too-Late* (1891, Lord Taplow) and *In Town* (1892, Bob) before being promoted to create the title-rôle of *A Gaiety Girl* (1893, Alma Somerset). She then moved up to playing aristocratic Ladies, succeeding to the part of Lady Cripps in *An Artist's Model* at Daly's and creating the rôle of Lady Constance Wynne – like that of Alma a virtually non-singing star rôle – in *The Geisha* (1896). She later moved to the Gaiety, taking over the part of Lady Coodle in *A Runaway Girl* and creating that of Lady Punchestown in *The Messenger Boy* (1900).

A SOUTHERN MAID Musical play in 3 acts by Dion Clayton Calthrop and Harry Graham. Lyrics by Harry Miller. Additional lyrics by Adrian Ross. Music by Harold Fraser-Simson. Additional music by Ivor Novello. Prince's Theatre, Manchester, 24 December 1917; Daly's Theatre, London, 15 May 1920.

A Southern Maid was commissioned by Robert Evett for Daly's Theatre, and designed as a follow-up to the enormously successful *The Maid of the Mountains*. Its title-rôle was made to measure for the darkly dramatic heroine of the earlier piece, Daly's Theatre's adored new prima donna, José Collins. *A Southern Maid's* Dolores was as like as could be to *The Maid of the Mountains's* Teresa, but this time the brigand beauty's alliance was on the opposite side. Dolores was in love with the apparently cruel governor, Sir Willoughby Rawdon (Claude Flemming), and she helped him to escape the assassination planned by her gipsy lover (Frederick Ross). If the score did not have a basketful of songs destined for the popularity of *The Maid of the Mountains's* music, it nevertheless turned up one genuine hit, Miss Collins's sultry hymn to nicotine, 'Love's Cigarette', which outpointed what was billed as 'The Great Waltz Song', 'Dark is the Sky', a number clearly intended to be the 'Love Will Find a Way' of the new show.

The Maid of the Mountains had been running for ten months when Evett took Miss Collins out of the cast, put understudy Dorothy Shale on, and sent his star to Manchester for a Christmas tryout season of *A Southern Maid*. He intended to follow the same plan which had worked so well with the first piece – Christmas in Manchester, then in to Daly's in February – but, in spite of the overwhelming reception that Manchester gave to the new piece, it was obvious that *The Maid of the Mountains*

still had too much life left in it to be removed. Miss Collins was re-routed back to *The Maid of the Mountains* and *A Southern Maid* was sent on tour, with Gracie Sinclaire starring, to await its moment. It waited for two further years, returning for a second Manchester Christmas season the following year, before Miss Collins had finally had more than she could take of *The Maid of the Mountains* and demanded a change. *A Southern Maid* moved into Daly's two and a half years after its original try-out with Flemming and *Maid* stars Bertram Wallis (Francesco) and Mark Lester (Wex) teaming with Miss Collins. If its quality was something less than its predecessor, it nevertheless had all of 'the mixture as before' in the right doses and it proved a first-class vehicle for its star, running through 1920 (306 performances) until, while Miss Shale again held the fort, the star had been back to Manchester to prepare its successor, *Sybil*.

A Southern Maid continued its already-long touring life during and after the London production, and it was produced in Australia with Miss Collins's down-under double, Gladys Moncrieff, scoring as big a success there as her model had done in London. The initial Melbourne run, with Claude Flemming back home repeating his original rôle, Arthur Stigant, Robert Chisholm and Reginald Purdell supporting and Daly's Theatre's other Australian, Asche, directing, topped 100 consecutive Melbourne performances – a rare feat at this time – and a Sydney season later the same year (Her Majesty's Theatre, 27 October) added another two and a half months to its fine record.

In 1933 *A Southern Maid* was made into a film starring Bebe Daniels, Harry Welchman, Clifford Mollison and comedian Lupino Lane.

Australia: Theatre Royal, Melbourne 27 January 1923; Film: BIP 1933

SOUTH PACIFIC Musical play in 2 acts by Oscar Hammerstein II and Joshua Logan adapted from *Tales of the South Pacific* by James Michener. Lyrics by Oscar Hammerstein II. Music by Richard Rodgers. Majestic Theater, New York, 7 April 1949.

Director Joshua Logan was pointed towards Michener's *Tales of the South Pacific* by a filmland friend, and he tied up successively with producer Leland Hayward and with Rodgers and Hammerstein in adapting a combination of the book's stories for the musical stage. Logan's original idea was to centre on the story 'Fo' Dolla', the love-story of American officer Joseph Cable and the island girl Liat, but in his scenario Hammerstein made this tale a secondary one and focused the main attention on another love-story, as related in 'Our Heroine', featuring the middle-ageing French planter Émile de Becque and a bright little nurse from Arkansas. Other elements were taken in from other stories to make up the actual plotline of the libretto.

Nellie Forbush (Mary Martin) is quite enjoying being away from Little Rock and stationed out on a wartime Pacific island. She knows how far she has come from Little Rock when she falls in love with the older, foreign De Becque (Ezio Pinza). However, she has not come far enough, for when she finds out that he is not just a widower, but that his wife was a Polynesian and he is the father of two half-caste children, she is revolted. But if Nellie cannot throw off the effects of her upbringing, the young lieutenant Cable (William Tabbert) can. Inveigled

Plate 249. *Gemma Craven as Nellie Forbush touts the charms of her 'Honey Bun' (Johnny Wade) in London's revival of* **South Pacific**.

by the venal Asian peddler Bloody Mary (Juanita Hall) into the arms of her lovely young daughter, Liat (Betta St John), he quickly finds both love and the determination to drop his old values. The disappointed De Becque agrees to join a dangerous American spying mission to a neighbouring island, and only when she realizes that she may not see him again does Nellie realise the depths of her feelings. Émile escapes the Japanese attack and returns to a final-curtain happy ending, but there is no such happy ending for Joe Cable and his island girl. Cable is killed in the attack, and Liat is left alone. The love stories of the evening were flavoured with comedy from Bloody Mary, and from her equally venal American counterpart, the sailor Luther Billis (Myron McCormack), a sticky-fingered gob who is always trying to get a bit of business going amongst the boys, and his lively pals.

The rôle and the soubrette songs of Nellie Forbush were written with Mary Martin in mind – her declaration of intent 'A Cockeyed Optimist', the bouncing hymn to her 'Wonderful Guy', her later determination that 'I'm Gonna Wash That Man Right Out of My Hair', her amateur-dramatics number describing the mincing Billis as 'Honey Bun' – and the casting of the rôle of Émile de Becque had an even more important effect on the score. Edwin Lester at the San Francisco and Los Angeles Light Opera Company had contracted the Metropolitan Opera's Ezio Pinza for a two-year stint, and had nothing to put him into. *South Pacific*'s producers took over that contract, and Rodgers and Hammerstein wrote Émile's songs around the voice of the great basso. The falling-in-love 'Some Enchanted Evening', the glorious deep-toned waltz of regrets 'This Nearly Was Mine', and the Twin Soliloquies between Émile and Nellie (the nearest they got to a duet, as Miss Martin not unwisely didn't fancy doing battle with that voice) were some of the finest pieces that the composer and lyricist would ever write.

The hits of the evening were not, however, channelled only into the star rôles. Cable fell in love to 'Younger Than Springtime' (a melody taken from an *Allegro* outcut), the sailors declared raucously that 'There Is Nothing Like a

Dame' and serenaded 'Bloody Mary', and that lady wove her matchmaking between Cable and Liat in the delicate 'Happy Talk', but it was another big, romantic number rather than one of the comic or lively pieces which proved to be, with 'Some Enchanted Evening', the most enduringly favourite part of this enduringly favourite score. Little Bloody Mary took up where Nettie Fowler of *Carousel* had left off, with one of Rodgers's big-voiced, sweeping feminine solos, singing the praises of the island of 'Bali H'ai'.

South Pacific put Rodgers and Hammerstein back on the romantic musical play trail they had begun to follow with *Oklahoma!* and *Carousel*, but strayed from in *Allegro*, and it also put them back on the trail of oversized success. The show settled in for a 1,925-performance run on Broadway, as the first national tour (April 1950) with Janet Blair, Pinza's erstwhile understudy Richard Eastham and Ray Walston (Billis) at its head, went out for what would be more than four years of travelling. Miss Martin left the Broadway production to open the show in London, where it arrived at the Theatre Royal, Drury Lane, dressed out with more pre-publicity than had ever before been seen in the West End. Betta St John from the original cast and Walston from the tour were teamed with American baritone Wilbur Evans (Émile), Muriel Smith (Mary) and Peter Grant (Cable) and the show effortlessly bucked its advance oversell, going on to become another fine hit through 802 performances in the theatre which had already housed *Oklahoma!* and *Carousel* through a combined total of some 2,000 performances.

Australia's J C Williamson Ltd followed up the next year with a production which, similarly, imported its leading players – Swede Richard Collett (Émile), Americans Mary La Roche (Nellie), Leonard Stone (Billis) and Virginia Paris (Mary), Briton David Welch (Cable) – and similarly scored a massive success: 333 performances in Melbourne alone, before going on to Sydney (Empire, 9 July 1953).

In 1958 *South Pacific* followed *Oklahoma!* and *Carousel* into the film studios. Logan, who had directed both the original and the London productions was again at the helm. In contrast to the earlier Rodgers and Hammerstein films, *South Pacific* was not made with singer-actors. Although film soubrette Mitzi Gaynor was cast as a bubbling little Nellie, and Walston repeated his tour and London Billis, the rest of the cast were dubbed. Handsome Rossano Brazzi was given the voice of Giorgio Tozzi, Miss Hall got to play her original rôle but when she sang it was London's Miss Smith who was heard, and John Kerr's Cable gave over 'Younger Than Springtime' to the voice of Bill Kerr. The film also had the unfortunate luck to arrive at the time that one of those periodic bigger-n-better size-shape-and-colour processes was going on in Hollywood, and in consequence some of the visual results – such as the infamous rainbow-sky accompaniment to 'Bali H'ai' – were a little curious.

South Pacific, like the rest of its fellows, made its impression almost entirely and solely on the English-speaking theatre, but in that area it was a major hit. Its songs became entrenched in the classic show-song repertoire, and it was given regular regional productions over the decades that followed. The show was seen at New York's State Theatre in 1967 with Giorgio Tozzi and

Florence Henderson featured (12 June, 104 performances), and the New York City Opera mounted a *South Pacific* in 1987, but it has yet to have a regular Broadway revival. London, on the other hand, welcomed the show back in 1988 when a touring production moved into the Prince of Wales Theatre, with a cast headed by Emile Belcourt, Gemma Craven and Bertice Reading (Mary) for a fine run of 413 performances, and Australia followed suit with its first major revival, starring Bernard Alane and Paige O'Hara, in 1993.

A French-language version (ad Marc-Cab, André Hornez) was launched in 1974 by the ever-Broadway-orientated Belgian Opéra de Wallonie (*Sud-Pacific*, Verviers, 8 November) with Guy Fontagnère (Émile), Caroline Dumas (Nellie), Line May (Mary) and Willy Fratellini (Billis) featured.

UK: Theatre Royal, Drury Lane 1 November 1951; Australia: His Majesty's Theatre, Melbourne, 13 September 1952; Film: Twentieth Century-Fox 1958

Recordings: original cast (Columbia), London cast (Columbia EP), revival cast 1967 (Columbia), London revival 1988 (First Night), film soundtrack (RCA), studio casts (CBS, Warner Bros, Decca, WRC etc)

SPENSER, Willard (b Cooperstown, NY, 7 July 1852; d St David's, Pa, 16 December 1933).

The son of a wealthy New York family, Spenser studied music with serious intent and, settling in Philadelphia, there began writing for the musical theatre. Beginning with the merrily very long-running *The Little Tycoon* (1886), which credited Spenser only as composer and which he insisted had been written and copyrighted some three years before *The Mikado* gave a new impulse to things oriental, his shows were highly successful in his adopted home town and also in other parts of the United States. When the first two were, in spite of good records, scornfully attacked by the New York press – intolerant of successes brewed anywhere else but hometown – Spenser not only hit back at the jealous journalists; he took the simple way out and happily excluded New York thereafter from the healthy and profitable itinerary of his shows.

In fact, Spenser's musicals, if fairly conventional comic operas in their substance, were as good as or better than most of what New York had to offer in the way of original musical-theatre entertainment at the time, and *The Little Tycoon*, introduced by comic R E Graham and later played by more famous names, *Princess Bonnie*, originally directed by no less a luminary than Richard Barker and starring Frank Daniels, and *Miss Bob White*, which featured top comic Raymond Hitchcock and Merry Widow-to-be Ethel Jackson at the head of its cast, racked up amongst them several thousands of performances on the American circuits around the turn of the century.

1886 **The Little Tycoon** Temple Theater, Philadelphia 4 January; Standard Theater, New York 29 March
1894 **Princess Bonnie** Chestnut Street Theater, Philadelphia 26 March; Broadway Theater, New York 2 September 1895
1901 **Miss Bob White** Chestnut Street Theater, Philadelphia 15 April
1906 **Rosalie** (w Helen Louise Burpee) Chestnut Street Theater, Philadelphia 23 April
1912 **The Wild Goose** Lyric Theater, Philadelphia 22 April

SPEWACK, Sam[uel] (b Bachmut, Russia, 16 September 1899; d New York, 14 October 1971)

Continental-born, but American-educated, Sam Spewack and his wife **Bella SPEWACK** (b Bucharest, 25 March 1899; d New York, 27 April 1990) both ran careers in journalism, including a four-year stint in Europe as foreign correspondents for the *New York World* (1922–6), prior to beginning a play- and screenwriting collaboration which produced several successful Broadway shows (*Boy Meets Girl*, *My Three Angels* etc). They made their first musical venture when adapting their 1932 play *Clear All Wires* as a libretto for Cole Porter's *Leave it to Me!*, and in their only other foray into that field, paired with the same composer, scored their biggest single hit with the internationally successful *Kiss Me, Kate*.

Sam, who also directed *Leave it to Me!* and the London production of *Kiss Me, Kate*, later teamed with Frank Loesser to manufacture the libretto for Loesser's unsuccessful period piece *Pleasures and Palaces*, a musical based on an equally unsuccessful Spewack play, *Once There Was a Russian*. Catherine the Great hired John Paul Jones to help her fight the Turks, but not on Broadway.

1938 **Leave it to Me!** (Cole Porter/w Bella Spewack) Imperial Theater 9 November
1948 **Kiss Me, Kate** (Porter/w B Spewack) New Century Theater 30 December
1965 **Pleasures and Palaces** (Frank Loesser/w Loesser) Fisher Theater, Detroit 11 March

DAS SPITZENTUCH DER KÖNIGIN Operette in 3 acts by 'Bohrmann-Riegen' and Richard Genée. Music by Johann Strauss. Theater an der Wien, Vienna, 1 October 1880.

Following the notable success of *Die Fledermaus*, Johann Strauss had fared less well with *Cagliostro in Wien* and *Prinz Methusalem* and disastrously with *Blindekuh* and he was constantly on the lookout for a winning libretto for, although he had been enthusiastic about each when setting it, it was inevitably the libretto that was ultimately blamed for his half- or whole-failures. The secretary of the Stadttheater unter Laube, Heinrich Bohrmann who, with his partner Julius von St Albino Nigri, *dit* Riegen, had ambitions as librettists, had written a piece around a supposed adventure of the poet Cervantes which they hoped to have set by Suppé. But Strauss, hearing of this, summoned Bohrmann to his presence and, having listened to him read his play, took it for himself. Aware that it was not wholly stageworthy, he passed it to the Theater an der Wien's Richard Genée (and also, apparently, to a number of other folk, judging by the legal wrangles which later arose) for improvements, and the finished piece appeared on that theatre's stage in October 1880.

The under-aged King of Portugal (Eugenie Erdösy) is kept away from both affairs of state and from his young Queen (Karoline Tellheim) by the regent Villalobos (Felix Schweighofer) who is plotting a coup, but the poet Cervantes (Ferdinand Schütz) and his sweetheart Irene (Hermine Meyerhoff) secretly prepare the King to announce his majority and thus end the hated regency. Villalobos uses the handkerchief of the title, dangerously but innocently inscribed by the lonely Queen with the words 'A Queen loves you, though you are not a King', to turn the King against his wife and Cervantes, and back to reliance on himself, but a bit of disguise and a few opportune explanations round off the final act and the action happily. Therese Schäfer played the Marquise de Villareal, the Queen's duenna, and Alexander Girardi supported as the King's tutor, Don Sancho d'Avellaneda.

The similarities of Bohrmann's starting point with the very recent *Le Petit Duc* and the handful of reminiscences of *La Grande-Duchesse* seemed to worry no one, and *Das Spitzentuch der Königin* was well received. Strauss's score turned in several numbers which became popular, the King's waltzing Trüffel-Couplet 'Stets komm mir wieder in die Sinn' remembering – with further Offenbachian reminiscence, this time of *Geneviève de Brabant* – the delicious pie his new wife served him on their wedding night, and the waltz poem 'Wo die wilde Rosen erblüht', sung by Cervantes to open the second act, winning special favour. Although neither is now remembered as a song, their melodies are well known as the principal themes of Strauss's concert piece 'Rosen aus dem Süden'.

Franz Steiner's production at the Theater an der Wien played through the month of October, and the piece was subsequently brought back for additional performances in repertoire, playing its 55th night on 13 February 1883. It was revived by Wilhelm Karczag in 1901 with Julie Kopácsi-Karczag as the King and Carl Streitmann as Cervantes, and again in 1911 with Ida Russka (King), Poldi Rizek (Queen) and Max Rohr (Cervantes), at both the Theater an der Wien and the Raimundtheater, ultimately bringing its tally up to 100 performances at its original home.

Berlin followed the original production of what looked like being Strauss's most successful piece since *Die Fledermaus* quickly, but although the Friedrich-Wilhelmstädtisches Theater had the rather uninspiring libretto revised by Julius Rosen, the show did not prove overly successful. Similarly, Gyorgy Verő's Hungarian version, with Ilka Pálmay (King) and Célia Margó (Irene) starring, was only reasonably received in a delayed Budapest production, where it had the misfortune to open just after the highly successful local piece *Az eleven ördög*. Neither Paris nor London took the piece on and, in spite of an unpromising start, the show ultimately had its best career of all in America.

The Queen's Lace Handkerchief was selected by Rudolf Aronson and John McCaull to initiate their grand new musical theatre, the Casino Theater. It opened, with John Perugini (Cervantes), Lilly Post (the Queen), Louise Paullin (the King), Joseph Greenfelder (Villalobos), Jennie Reiffarth (Marquise) and Mathilde Cottrelly (Irene) in the leading rôles, only to be met by a storm of protest. The theatre was not sufficiently finished to be comfortable. The producers closed at the end of the week, sent the company off to Philadelphia's Broad Street Theatre and to Chicago, and brought them back (with William Carleton now Cervantes and the young Francis Wilson in Girardi's rôle) a month later (30 December). This time, in a new and well-appointed house, they were a hit, running 113 consecutive performances followed by a quick return (11 June 1883) when a following production, *La Princesse de Trébizonde*, was sabotaged by one of Lillian Russell's contract-breaking walk-outs. The piece was subsequently produced at the Thalia Theater (1 October 1883) in its original German with Schütz playing his original rôle

alongside Frlns Seebold (King), Engländer (Queen) and Schatz (Irene). It did well in the country, was revived in the German theatres and when all was said and totted up, actually played more performances in America than in any other area.

The English-language version was also seen, though much more briefly, in Australia where it was introduced by soprano Clara Merivale (Irene) and her English Comic Opera Company, featuring Knight Aston (a tenor King), W H Woodfield (Cervantes), Katharine Hardy (Queen) and Edwin Kelly (Villalobos) through a short season.

In 1931 a revised version of the show written by Rudolf Österreicher and Julius Wilhelm, which kept the title but replaced the characters and the plot with a tale which was now set in Vienna, Salzburg and Munich in 1842, was played at the Johann Strauss-Theater in Vienna. Hans Heinz Bollmann was Nikolaus von Tomba, Mizzi Zwerenz the Fürstin-Mutter, Anny Coty played Rosette Falcari and the music was 'für die Bühne musikalisch neuarbeitet' by Karl Pauspertl. But things didn't go any better with a conventional new libretto than they had with a conventional old one.

Germany: Friedrich-Wilhelmstädtisches Theater 24 November 1880; USA: Casino Theater *The Queen's Lace Handkerchief* 21 October 1882; Hungary: (Ger) 21 February 1881, Népszinház *A kiralyné csipkekendöje* 29 December 1885; Australia: Theatre Royal, Melbourne *The Queen's Lace Handkerchief* 12 August 1893

SPORTING LOVE Musical horse play in 2 acts by Stanley Lupino. Additional dialogue by Arty Ash and Arthur Rigby. Lyrics by Desmond Carter and Frank Eyton. Music by Billy Mayerl. Gaiety Theatre, London, 31 March 1934.

The fourth in the successful series of Laddie Cliff/ Stanley Lupino shows staged at the Gaiety Theatre in the 1920s and 1930s, *Sporting Love* followed the other three happy comedy musicals at a distance of three years and did as well as they (and better than anything else around) with a ten-month, 302-performance town run, a good touring life and a film (which omitted the songs) in which Cliff and Lupino repeated their stage rôles with great success.

Lupino's libretto was a farcical hotch-potch of well-used musical comedy elements ranging from mistaken identities and impersonations to rich aunts and the inevitable curtain-time pairing-off, and settings including the Derby (being used as a scene for the third time in a year in a London musical) and a shipboard scene, which served merely to give Cliff and Lupino as many comic opportunities as possible and to introduce some dance-and-song pieces by pianist-composer Billy Mayerl mostly written for the no fewer than four pairs of dancing-singing young folk in the cast ('Have a Heart', 'You're the Reason Why').

Film: Hammer 1936

THE SPRING CHICKEN Musical play in 2 acts by George Grossmith based on the play *Coquin de printemps* by Adolphe Jaime and Georges Duval. Lyrics by Adrian Ross and Percy Greenbank. Music by Ivan Caryll and Lionel Monckton. Gaiety Theatre, London, 30 May 1905.

The Gaiety musical comedy, as exemplified by the very lightly-plotted, song-and-dance filled pieces which had reigned supreme in London over a dozen years and more

Plate 250.

from *The Shop Girl* to *The Orchid*, underwent something of a change in character with the advent of *The Spring Chicken*. George Edwardes had sensed that change was due, and had turned – as he would do several times – to France for inspiration. Daly's Theatre, the bulwark of the English musical play, now held his production of Messager's *Les P'tites Michu*, the same composer's *Véronique* was a hit at the Apollo, and on top of all this Gallic entertainment Edwardes announced a new English musical comedy for the Gaiety which would be 'based on' an established French farce, part-written by Georges Duval, one of the librettists of the two Messager works. It was the first time that a Gaiety musical had been genuinely based on the text of a modern farce with all that meant in the way of problems – those same problems encountered by the old opéra-bouffe adapters, trying to translate French 'indecencies' into English 'seeming decencies' – as well as of unaccustomed plot intricacy and vertebracy.

Every year the lawyer Babori (librettist George Grossmith), a faithful husband for most months, gets wanderlusty when spring arrives. This year his attack of below-the-belt fever sets him making eyes and passes at one of his clients, the Baronne Papouche (Kate Cutler), whose divorce he is handling. Just to complicate things, the parents of his English wife Dulcie (Olive Morrell) choose this moment to arrive in Paris. Papa Girdle (Edmund Payne) promptly experiences the same kind of fever – a little more indiscriminately – but the enterprising Mama Girdle (Connie Ediss) leaps into action and leads the ladies in getting everyone back, undamaged and almost uncompromised, to the status quo by the final curtain.

If the construction and the workings of even this thinned-down version of Jaime and Duval's sprightly farce was rather more substantial than usual fare for the Gaiety's audiences, there was no stinting on the Gaiety's

accompanying specialities: the spectacle, the girls, the fun and the songs and dances. The fun was headed by Payne, a ludicrous little Englishman abroad trying to chat up the countrified French Rosalie (Gertie Millar), reminiscing over 'The Delights of London', swapping thoughts with Grossmith over whether it was better to be 'Under or Over Forty' or disserting blithely on the eternally ghastly attributes of 'The British Tourist', and by Connie Ediss who had the hit of the show with her plump and pointed accusations of family philandering in 'I Don't Know, But I Guess'. Caryll and Monckton's songs and dances, if producing no standards, were nevertheless as bright and apt as ever, and the girls and dances were legion. Miss Millar, in the evening's principal soubrette rôle, had a number of songs by her husband, Monckton, and a little interpolated march, named after her character, by Jerome Kern.

The extra bit of substance in *The Spring Chicken* dismayed the Gaiety patrons not a whit. The piece spent a splendid 14 months in London (401 performances) before heading out to the provinces and overseas. Richard Carle snapped the piece up for America and he presented himself on Broadway in the rôle created by Payne as 'americanized' by himself with Bessie McCoy in Miss Millar's rôle and Emma Janvier as Connie Ediss. He also interpolated several songs partly or wholly his own ('A Lemon in the Garden of Love', 'All the Girls Love Me', 'Marching', 'No Doubt You'd Like to Cuddle Up to Baby') and billed the show 'Richard Carle presents himself and his songs in George Edwards (*sic*) success of two London seasons'. The American *Spring Chicken* succeeded splendidly, chalked up 91 performances in town and returned for a repeat season (24 performances) the following year during the long touring run which was Carle's most lucrative activity.

Coquin de printemps served as the bases for two other musical plays, the Josef Strauss pasticcio *Frühlingsluft* produced with considerable success in Vienna (Venedig in Wien, 9 May 1903) before going on to be played in Germany, Hungary and America, and the French musical *Coquin de printemps* (Guy Magenta/Fernand Bonifay/Jean Valmy, Marc-Cab, Théâtre de l'Européen 30 January 1958) which, with a cast headed by Henri Gènes, Brigitte Mars, Orbal and Jeannette Batti and Fernand Sardou, ran up an excellent initial run in Paris, soon followed by a second season (September 1959, Théâtre de l'ABC) with Luc Barney, Padquaim, Aglaë and Mathé Altéry in the cast and a long touring life.

USA: Daly's Theater 8 October 1906; Australia: Her Majesty's Theatre, Melbourne 3 November 1906

SPRING IS HERE Musical comedy in 2 acts by Owen Davis adapted from his play *Shotgun Wedding*. Lyrics by Lorenz Hart. Music by Richard Rodgers. Alvin Theater, New York, 11 March 1929.

A commission from producers Alex Aarons and Vinton Freedley, *Spring is Here* paired Pulitzer Prize-winning author Owen Davis, whose comedy *The Nervous Wreck* had been made into the successful musical *Whoopee* the previous year, with songwriters Richard Rodgers and Lorenz Hart, whose most recent Broadway shows (*She's My Baby, Present Arms, Chee-Chee*) had not been too successful, but who had had a fine run with their musical version of *A Connecticut Yankee* in 1927.

The show's tiny story covered the attempts of its heroine, Betty Braley (Lilian Taiz), to get herself wed to a fellow called Stacy Haydon (John Hundley) of whom her father disapproves. Daddy wins out and bone-headed Betty realizes that there has been better in the person of Terry Clayton (Glenn Hunter) around all the time. Since the Hollywooden Hunter (*Smilin' Through*, *Merton of the Movies*) had a negligible singing voice, the score's big ballad, 'With a Song in My Heart', was taken away from the show's hero and given to Hundley, who thus got the hit if not the girl, leaving Hunter to tiptoe his way parlando through the letter-song 'Yours Sincerely' with Miss Taiz and to effuse 'What a Girl!'. Miss Taiz joined with Inez Courtney, in the rôle of her sister, Mary Jane, in the show's other favourite song 'Why Can't I?'

Spring Is Here was well enough received, but it survived only 104 performances on Broadway before going on to be made into a film with Frank Albertson, Lawrence Grey and Bernice Claire featured and Miss Courtney repeating her original rôle. 'With a Song in My Heart', however, survived to be heard in London's Cochran revue of 1930, and in a long series of musical films which culminated in the Jane Froman biopic which used the song's title as its own (Twentieth Century-Fox, 1952)

Film: First National 1930

DIE SPRUDELFEE Operette in 3 acts by A M Willner and Julius Wilhelm. Music by Heinrich Reinhardt. Raimundtheater, Vienna, 23 January 1909.

Wilhelm Karczag and his partner, Karl Wallner, had taken over the ailing Raimundtheater in 1908, and there they found themselves obliged to fight a battle against a lease which bound them to stage only the classic German-language repertoire – and no musical pieces. It was not long before they had that discriminatory clause struck out, and their second new Operette production, following Ziehrer's *Liebeswalzer*, was the latest work of Heinrich Reinhardt, still haloed with the success of *Das süsse Mädel*.

Die Sprudelfee (the mineral-water fairy) was set at the Carlsbad springs in the year of 1830 and followed the flirtations of Fürst Aladar von Marosházy (Ludwig Herold), a nobleman whose taste in ladies leads him towards the girls who serve at the water-fountains rather than towards Princess Bozena (Betty Seidl), daughter of the lofty but ill-financed Fürst Nepomuk Wrzbrzlicky (Franz Glawatsch). Bozena temporarily puts her rank away and becomes a Sprudelfee until she has hooked her Hungarian. The comedy of the piece was boosted by Karl Göstl as a matinée idol, sighed after by a married lady (Gisela Wurm) and pursued by a policeman (Karl Matuna), the romance profited from the gallivantings of pretty Annamirl (Rose Karin-Krachler) daughter of the local innkeeper (Luise Lichten) and the other Sprudelfeen who paired off neatly in number with a male chorus of more Barons and Grafs than there would seem to have been room for even in Carlsbad in the summer.

Reinhardt's score was in the same catchingly sweet and unpretentious style as that of his biggest success and the piece's principal waltz once again proved the hit of the evening, but *Die Sprudelfee*, in a post-*Die lustige Witwe* era brimming with new hits, did not pull the same reaction in Vienna as *Das süsse Mädel* had done. However, if the show was overwhelmed by the competition on its home ground,

it was that very competition which finally resulted in it having a success ... in America. American producers, frantically searching for another *Merry Widow*, were snatching up Austrian and German musicals by the often fairly indiscriminate handful and the young partnership of Louis F Werba and Mark Luescher got *Die Sprudelfee* as part of their booty. Adapted by Harry and Robert Smith as *The Spring Maid* (spring as in fountain, not as in season), musically fiddled with by Robert Hood Bowers, expanded with a danced 'divertissement depicting the legend of the discovery of Carlsbad Springs', and cast with Christie Mac-Donald (Bozena), Lawrence Rea (Aladar), William Burress (Nepomuk) and Tom McNaughton (Roland, a famous English tragedian, equipped with a music-hall recitation 'The Three Trees') it turned out a singular hit. Whilst versions of Continental mega-hits *Die Förster-Christl* and *Die geschiedene Frau* did only fairly, the pretty *The Spring Maid* ran through 194 performances on Broadway and saw its waltz (now called 'Day Dreams') become a top-notch hit, before going triumphantly on to the road with Mitzi now starring in its title-rôle.

F C Whitney, revelling in the riches brought to him by *The Chocolate Soldier*, introduced an anglicized version of the show (ad C H E Brookfield) to London the following year at his Whitney (ex-Waldorf) Theatre with Tom McNaughton repeating his rôle alongside Paris's Marise Fairy (Bozena), Walter Hyde (Aladar), Julia James (Annamirl) and Courtice Pounds (Nepomuk). London was less enthusiastic than Broadway, and the show's 64 performances put an end to Britain's *The Spring Maid* and to the Whitney Theatre.

USA: Liberty Theater *The Spring Maid* 26 December 1910; UK: Whitney Theatre *The Spring Maid* 30 September 1911.

STAND UP AND SING Musical play in 2 acts by Douglas Furber and Jack Buchanan. Lyrics by Douglas Furber. Music by Vivian Ellis and Phil Charig. London Hippodrome, 5 March 1931.

Stand Up and Sing was constructed as a vehicle for the favourite comedy-with-dance team of Jack Buchanan and Elsie Randolph, returning to the London stage where they had triumphed in 1928–9 with *That's a Good Girl*. As with the previous show, Douglas Furber was the author and American composer Phil Charig shared the musical score, this time with local composer Vivian Ellis, and once again the accent was on the fun and the dancing. These were set in a minimal tale which had Buchanan as layabout Rockingham Smith taking employment as a valet in order to gain the good graces of his young lady and, as a result, being put in a position to win back some frightfully important papers for her originally disapproving father. Buchanan's partner, Miss Randolph – firmly labelled comedienne, and thus unable to play the heroine – instead appeared as her maid, whilst a chorus dancer called Marjorie Robertson was given the ingénue rôle. She changed her name to Anna Neagle and from there moved on to an impressive career on film and stage.

A fine display of scenery included one of the currently inevitable shipboard scenes, an English country house and a visit to Cairo, the songs followed the established patterns from the earlier Buchanan shows, featuring a new tipsy song for the star, a ballad 'There's Always Tomorrow' as performed by Buchanan and Miss Neagle, and a comedy number 'It's Not You' for him to sing and dance with Miss Randolph, as well as a jolly title-song. There was also a big, bright dance finale tacked on to the end of the show, apropos of nothing at all, to climax the routines, straight and comical, which Buchanan performed with his respective ladies and with the lushly comical Vera Pearce, here cast as an Egyptian Princess. When the stars were not on, handsome Richard Dolman did his number-two song-and-dance spot, Anton Dolin performed more classical dance, the Seven Hindustanis did acrobatics and soprano May Tomlinson performed a Vivian Ellis vocalize called 'Cairo', all adding their bit to to the highly revusical entertainment.

Stand Up and Sing was, unusually, produced out of town and played in several provincial cities, including a six-week Christmas season in Glasgow (without Miss Randolph, who didn't tour), before coming to London. There it remained for eight and a half months (325 performances) before rounding off in the suburbs after a total of some 600 performances.

STANGE, Stanislaus   (b Liverpool, 1862; d New York, 2 January 1917).

English-born Stange, originally an actor, made his career from 1881 in America where, for more than a decade, he turned out comic-opera libretti for pieces designed by and large for the more musically ambitious end of the market. Although several of these – notably an adaptation of Garrick's *The Country Girl* as *Dolly Varden* and the not-unoriginal American Civil War musical *When Johnny Comes Marching Home*, both written with his habitual musical partner, fellow expatriate Englishman Julian Edwards – did well enough, he had rather more success when he dropped his sights a little. The extravaganza *The Man in the Moon* and the farcical-comical *Piff! Paff! Pouf!* were both long-running Broadway hits alongside their author's successful (non-musical) dramatization of the novel *Quo Vadis?* (1900).

Stange's musical version of *She Stoops to Conquer* (*Two Roses*) starred Fritzi Scheff, *The Singing Girl* had Alice Nielsen singing Stange's lyrics to Victor Herbert's music and *Love's Lottery* boasted the operatic diva Ernestine Schumann-Heink as its star, but none of these more ambitious pieces performed as well in New York as his two more 'popular' shows. His greatest success, however, came when the new fashion for Continental Operetten hit America and Stange was given the job of turning the Germanized George Bernard Shaw of *Der tapfere Soldat* back into English. It was reported that he had 'evolved a book of subtle humour, literary nicety and consequential interest' for the piece that became known through thousands of performances as *The Chocolate Soldier* (what Shaw thought is not reported). In the process, he invented the lyric to 'My Hero', the song which remained his most enduring contribution to the musical theatre and, compounding his success, also directed Broadway's production of the show for F C Whitney.

Stange subsequently adapted Anthony Mars's play *Fils à papa* for a semi-musical Broadway production as *The Girl in the Taxi* (not to be confused with the British production of the same title), but in the remaining half-dozen years before his death provided no more texts to the Broadway musical stage. His stage adaptation (w Stannard Mears) of

Booth Tarkington's novel *Seventeen* became the basis for the musicals *Hello, Lola* (1925) and *Seventeen* (1951).

1893 **Friend Fritz** (Julian Edwards) Herrmann's Theater 26 January
1895 **Madeleine, or The Magic Kiss** (Edwards) Bijou Theater 25 February
1896 **The Goddess of Truth** (Edwards) Abbey's Theater 26 February
1896 **Brian Boru** (Edwards) Broadway Theater 19 October
1897 **The Wedding Day** (*La Petite Fronde*) English version w new music by Edwards (Casino Theater)
1898 **The Jolly Musketeer(s)** (Edwards) Broadway Theater 14 November
1899 **The Man in the Moon** (Ludwig Englander, Gustave Kerker, Reginald De Koven/w Louis Harrison) New York Theater 24 April
1899 **The Singing Girl** (Victor Herbert) Casino Theater 23 October
1902 **Dolly Varden** (Edwards) Herald Square Theater 27 January
1902 **When Johnny Comes Marching Home** (Edwards) New York Theater 16 December
1904 **Piff! Paff! Pouf!** (Jean Schwartz/William Jerome) Casino Theater 2 April
1904 **Love's Lottery** (Edwards) Broadway Theater 3 October
1904 **The Two Roses** (Englander, Kerker) Broadway Theater 21 November
1906 **The Student King** (De Koven) Garden Theater 25 December
1907 **The Belle of London Town** (Edwards) Lincoln Square Theater 28 January
1907 **The Girls of Holland** (ex-*The Snowman*) (De Koven) Lyric Theater 18 November
1909 **The Chocolate Soldier** (*Der tapfere Soldat*) American version (Lyric Theater)
1910 **The Kissable Girl** (Harry von Tilzer/Vincent Bryan) 8 March
1910 **The Girl in the Taxi** (various) Astor Theater 24 October

STANISLAUS, Frederic   (b ?1844; d London, 22 November 1891). Conductor and composer for the 19th-century British stage.

Originally an operatic conductor, Stanislaus subsequently worked as a theatrical musical director in Dublin, Manchester and London. In a very full and top-flight career at the baton, he toured with Julia Mathews in America, conducted Broadway's *Pirates of Penzance* for Carte, *Princess Toto* for Kate Santley and *Dick* for Hollingshead in London, new burlesque in Australia for Brough and Boucicault (1886), the Carl Rosa company in *Paul Jones* and *Marjorie*, and *Joan of Arc* for George Edwardes, supplying such occasional songs and music as was needed.

His one major stage work as a composer was the comic opera *The Lancashire Witches*, produced in Manchester to some considerable praise. In spite of this success, however, Stanislaus did not follow it up with any further pieces of equal significance.

Stanislaus was married to burlesque actress and principal boy **Fanny ROBINA** (b 1862; d 13 February 1927) who appeared in a number of musicals both in Britain (notably as the original Faust in the Gaiety's *Faust Up-to-Date*) and in Australia (*Young Fra Diavolo*, *Dick*, *Little Jack Sheppard*, Ganem in *The Forty Thieves*).

1873 **Tom Tug** (comp and arr/F C Burnand) Opera Comique 12 November

1879 **The Lancashire Witches** (R T Gunton) Theatre Royal, Manchester 20 October

1884 **Called There and Back** (comp and arr/Herman C Merivale) Gaiety Theatre 15 October

1884 **Im-Patience** (Walter Browne) Prince of Wales Theatre, Liverpool 25 August

1886 **The Palace of Pearl** (w Edward Jakobowski/Alfred Murray) Empire Theatre 12 June

STARLIGHT EXPRESS Musical in 2 acts with lyrics by Richard Stilgoe. Music by Andrew Lloyd Webber. Apollo Victoria Theatre, London, 27 March 1984.

Composer Andrew Lloyd Webber and director Trevor Nunn followed up their success with *Cats* (1981) with another musical show which, like its predecessor, presented a set of anthropomorphic characters in a series of loosely linked songs and choreographic routines. Where *Cats* had presented felines, *Starlight Express* featured trains, and the characters of the piece – the macho-mechanical Greaseball (Jeff Shankley), the country-and-western dining car called Dinah (Frances Ruffelle), the two-faced little red caboose (Michael Staniforth), soul-singing Poppa (Lon Satton) and the androgynous electric train – were brought together around a simplistically improbable plot line in which a good old steam train called Rusty (Ray Shell) beats all modern opposition in some kind of railway challenge and wins himself a coupling with a pretty carriage called Pearl (Stephanie Lawrence).

Lloyd Webber's score for *Starlight Express* was a purposefully youth-orientated one with the songs mostly written and orchestrated in a forceful, modern pop idiom varied occasionally with some burlesques of older song styles, and Nunn's production – which put all the performers on roller skates – was equally youthful and also probably the most technically complex and spectacular ever seen on the West End stage. To accommodate this wheelie concept and John Napier's settings for the series of races which comprised the backbone of the show's action, the entire interior of the Apollo Victoria Theatre, an ugly big cinema of the 1920s, was gutted and rebuilt with a network of wooden tracks, encircling the auditorium, rising to the level of the dress circle, and meeting at a mobile, hydraulically-operated bridge suspended high above the stage area. In order that the public could watch the races, minutely timed to a musical accompaniment, even when they were taking place above or behind them, pop-concert style television screens were installed at the front of the auditorium.

Unlike *Cats*, *Evita* and *Jesus Christ Superstar*, *Starlight Express* produced no hit parade singles. The principal ballad 'Only He Has the Power to Move Me' and the electric train's 'AC/DC' performed by the pop world's Jeffrey Daniels did not catch on and, in the show, it was the burlesques, such as Frances Ruffelle's plaintive country version of 'U.N.C.O.U.P.L.E.D' and the droopily comical 'One Rock and Roll Too Many' which proved the most popular individual pieces, alongside such lively skated ensembles as 'Freight'. In spite of some adverse criticism from journalists who belonged to another world and/or time and/or entertainment industry to *Starlight Express*, the show itself caught on decidedly. At the time of writing it has been playing for more than eight years and some 3,000 performances in London, notching itself into second place on London's 'all-time' list of runs. On 23 November 1992,

the show broke a record all of its own: without being taken from the London stage it was given a £½m overhaul, with all its original creative team returning to restage and rechoreograph a revised version of the show in the kind of 'second edition' not seen on the London stage since the days of George Edwardes's running remakes of his Gaiety Theatre hits. Several new songs ('Crazy', 'Next Time You Fall in Love') were added, several others remade, two characters vanished (with their numbers), the plot was slimmed vigorously, the music re-orchestrated in line with 1990s sounds, and the now dated pop references and styles updated, as the 'new' *Starlight Express* rolled on towards its first decade on the London stage.

A Broadway production, with the show slightly reorganized with several new musical pieces and the addition of a clever explanation of the piece's naïve action as taking place on a child's train-set layout, played for 761 performances in 1987–9 prior to touring America, whilst a highly successful German production and another, less successful, played in Japan and Australia both opened the piece up as something more approaching an arena entertainment rather than a stage show. The German production has, like the London one, proved to be a long-running fixture and is running on into its fifth year at its custom-made Starlighthalle at the time of writing.

USA: Gershwin Theater 15 March 1987; Australia: Sydney Showground 24 January 1988; Germany: Starlighthalle, Bochum 12 June 1988

Recordings: original cast (Polydor), German casts (Stella, Polydor), touring cast (EMI), American selection (MCA), new London version

STARMANIA Rock opera by Luc Plamondon. Music by Michel Berger. Palais des Congrès, Paris, 16 April 1979.

A Franco-Canadian attempt at an answer to everything from *Jesus Christ Superstar*, *West Side Story* and *Hair* to *Batman*, *The Rocky Horror Show*, *Metropolis* and the less imaginative American comic strips, *Starmania* is a strange compound which hovers between being a burlesque and a calculated aim at a pre-puberty crowd weaned on TV, computer games and comics and a belief in the power of 'naughty' words. If its writing tends, *Rocky Horror Show*-style, towards being a parody of the sci-fi strip material that is its content, its performance has tended to indicate that it is actually taken for real by those who play it and watch it.

Starmania is a kind of science-fiction melodrama, illustrated by songs whose titles point up the level of its ambition: 'Sex shops, cinéma pornos', 'Ce soir on danse à Naziland', 'Un enfant de la pollution', 'Le Monde est stone'. It takes place in a futuristic city called Monopolis, and its chief characters are the black-leather clad Sadia (Nanette Workman), head of the terrorist 'Black Stars' who are actively led by one Johnny Rockfort (Daniel Balavoine) in trying – unsuccessfully – to stop the millionaire businessman Zéro Janvier (Étienne Chicot) becoming President of the Western World on a law-and-order ticket. In the course of affairs Johnny falls in love with the TV-child's equivalent of the Princesses of operetta, a television presenter called Cristal (France Gall). She dies in his arms during a bombing attack on Janvier's offices. The other main characters include filmstar Stella Spotlight (Diane Dufresne), the fiancée of Janvier, Marie-Jeanne (Fabienne Thibeault) the waitress at the automat which the Black

Stars use as their rendezvous, and Ziggy (Grégory Ken), the androgynous young person over whom she sighs.

First produced, *Superstar*-style, as a two-record concept disc, the piece threw up one number – Janvier's 'Les Blues du Business-Man' – which found its way to the pop charts, and the show was duly put on stage in Paris, under the management of Roland Manuel and the direction of *Superstar* and *Hair* director Tom O'Horgan, in a vast, colourful, gimmicky production sponsored by the radio station Europe 1 and, of all unlikely backers, Perrier mineral water. France's *Superstar* star Balavoine was the leading man, alongside some of the choicer French/Canadian female pop vocalists. *Starmania* played a season of 25 performances but, if its Parisian stage life was short, it outdid even *Superstar* by spawning a four-record cast album.

Starmania, however, continued to be energetically pushed and promoted. It was played in Montreal, toured in Canada and in 1988 a new version of the piece, revised into a very much reduced size physically, orchestrally and in all personnel departments (the original had boasted a cast of 70, the new a dozen) was remounted in Paris (Théâtre du Paris 15 September) with a cast headed by Norman Groulx (Johnny), Maurane (Marie-Jeanne), Martine St-Clair (Cristal) and Renaud Hantson (Ziggy). Directed this time by its writers, without the frills and sillies of the first mounting, and with the comic-strip humour replaced by a certain earnest belief (or pretended belief) in the material, it won sufficient success to transfer to the Théâtre Marigny (14 January 1989) for a further five months, returning after the summer for a further season of six weeks before going on tour.

In 1992 a German-language version (ad Jürgen Schwalbe, Gerulf Pannach) was mounted at Essen with Andrea Weiss (Marie-Jeanne), Erwin Brühn (Janvier), Paul Kribbe (Johnny) and Annika Bruhns (Cristal) featured and, at the time of writing, an English-language *Tycoon* (ad Tim Rice) has been issued as a recording and is on trial at Andrew Lloyd Webber's Sydmonton Festival.

Germany: Aalto Theater, Essen 14 February 1992
Recordings: pre-production recording, original cast recording (Warner Brothers), revival cast recording (Apache), English recording (Epic)

STARS IN YOUR EYES Musical play in 2 acts by J P McEvoy. Lyrics by Dorothy Fields. Music by Arthur Schwartz. Majestic Theater, New York, 9 February 1939.

Originally conceived as a satire on left-wing doings in Hollywood, *Stars in Your Eyes* was intended to feature Ethel Merman as Jeanette Adair, a filmstar pursuing a lefty, boy-wonder screenwriter called John Blake (Richard Carlson) with the aid of a union man (Jimmy Durante) and a bookful of nibbling songs lyricked by Dorothy Fields. However, bit by bit, through the planning stages, the politics went out the window, dancer Tamara Toumanova was inserted as a rival for Merman in her chase after the now-apolitical Blake and, under the guidance of director Joshua Logan, the piece finally turned into a sex-and-films one instead of a politics-and-films one, even though odd traces of the original orientation remained in the songs.

Without the political focus, which had not been replaced by anything else, the show lacked much in the way of individuality, and even its starry credits could not keep

Plate 251. **Tommy Steele** *as Hans Andersen in his own musical-play version of the Frank Loesser film.*

Dwight Deere Wiman's production on Broadway more than 127 performances. Amongst the songs provided for the star were 'This is It', 'It's All Yours', 'A Lady Needs a Change' (replacing the union-ridiculing 'My New Kentucky Home') and 'Just a Little Bit More', none of which feature amongst either Schwartz's or Miss Merman's enduring credits.

Recording: selection (AEI)

STEELE, Tommy [HICKS, Thomas] (b London, 17 December 1936).

Seaman turned Britain's first and foremost rock idol, Steele was re-orientated towards the musical stage when he was starred as Buttons in a stage version of Rodgers and Hammerstein's television musical *Cinderella* in 1958. His success in this piece encouraged producer Harold Fielding to commission a musical play vehicle for him, and the resultant *Half a Sixpence* (1963), in which Steele played H G Wells's Artie Kipps ('Half a Sixpence', 'If the Rain's Got to Fall', 'Flash, Bang, Wallop'), established him as one of Britain's top musical theatre names.

He repeated *Half a Sixpence* on Broadway (1965) and for the screen but it was a decade before, in a carefully dosed career, he returned to the West End in a second Fielding production, the stage adaptation of Frank Loesser's *Hans Andersen* (1974, 'The Ugly Duckling' etc). This piece served him for a year's run, two tours and a second London run before, once again, he returned to television, concert and a record-breaking West End one-man (with dancers) show at the Prince of Wales Theatre. In 1983 he appeared in his third West End musical, again under

Fielding's management, playing Don Lockwood in a stage version of *Singin' in the Rain* which he had himself adapted and for which he also acted as director. It gave him a third success, with a two-year run, two tours, a Japanese season and another return to London.

In 1991 he authored, directed and starred in another film-based musical, *Some Like it Hot*, using elements of the film script and (of contractual necessity) much of its earlier musical adaptation, *Sugar*. After an extensive British tour, the show was taken to London in March 1992, but it failed to give its star a fourth consecutive musical hit.

In 1978 Steele appeared as Jack Point in the production of *The Yeomen of the Guard* mounted in the moat of the Tower of London on the occasion of the building's 900th anniversary. The production was later reproduced in a television film (ATV, 1978).

STEIN, Joseph (b New York, 30 May 1912). Librettist of several Broadway hits of the 1950s and 1960s.

Stein's earliest contributions to the stage were made in the world of revue where he supplied material for such pieces as *Inside USA*, *Lend an Ear*, *Alive and Kicking* and the *Ziegfeld Follies of 1956*. His first venture into writing for a musical play, in collaboration with Will Glickman, was on *Plain and Fancy*, a piece which brought him a considerable success with its tale of the results of the interference of some worldly folk into the well-ordered lives of the Amish community. The pair had a further good Broadway showing with *Mr Wonderful*, a showbusiness tale without a difference set up as a vehicle for the young Sammy Davis jr. After three less-than-successful shows in the years that followed, Stein then turned out two of the most impressive libretti of 1960s Broadway with his adaptation of Sholem Aleichem's tales as the book for *Fiddler on the Roof* (Tony Award) and the remaking of the warmly passionate tale of *Zorba the Greek*, already famous on the screen, as the musical play *Zorba*.

A rewrite of a rewrite of the libretto to the classic musical comedy *Irene*, whilst going rather far from the original, provided a winning text for a 1970s 1919 musical and it was rewarded with a long run, but an adaptation of his own 1963 play *Enter Laughing* as the musical *So Long, 174th Street* was a failure. Several further adaptations, the Pagnol/Giono *La Femme du boulanger* as *The Baker's Wife*, another screenplay as *King of Hearts*, and yet another, *Buona Sera, Mrs Campbell*, as *Carmelina* failed to bring another success, and Stein's most recent libretto, to the Charles Strouse/Stephen Schwartz musical *Rags*, was seen for only four nights on Broadway. While it came and went, *Fiddler on the Roof* and *Zorba* continued to be played worldwide.

1955 **Plain and Fancy** (Albert Hague/Arnold B Horwitt/w Will Glickman) Mark Hellinger Theater 27 January
1956 **Mr Wonderful** (Jerry Bock, Larry Holofcener, George Weiss/w Glickman) Broadway Theater 22 March
1958 **The Body Beautiful** (Bock/Sheldon Harnick/w Glickman) Broadway Theater 23 January
1959 **Juno** (Marc Blitzstein) Winter Garden Theater 9 March
1959 **Take Me Along** (Bob Merrill/w Robert Russell) Shubert Theater 22 October
1964 **Fiddler on the Roof** (Bock/Harnick) Imperial Theater 22 September
1968 **Zorba** (John Kander/Fred Ebb) Imperial Theater 17 November

1973 **Irene** adaptation w Harry Rigby, Hugh Wheeler (Minskoff Theater)
1976 **So Long, 174th Street** (Stan Daniels) Harkness Theater 27 April
1976 **The Baker's Wife** (Stephen Schwartz) Dorothy Chandler Pavilion, Los Angeles 11 May
1978 **King of Hearts** (Peter Link/Jacob Brackman/w Steve Tesich) Minskoff Theater 22 October
1979 **Carmelina** (Burton Lane/Alan Jay Lerner/w Lerner) St James Theater 8 April
1986 **Rags** (Charles Strouse/Stephen Schwartz) Mark Hellinger Theater 21 August

STEIN, Leo [ROSENSTEIN, Leo] (b Lemberg, 25 March 1861; d Vienna, 28 July 1921).

A railway official turned playwright and librettist, Stein collaborated – at first mostly with Alexander Landesberg, Julius Horst or Alexander Engel, and later with Victor Léon, Carl Lindau and Béla Jenbach – on a large number of successful plays and, most particularly, of Operetten during the most fruitful years of the Viennese theatre.

His first piece, *Lachende Erben*, produced with a cast headed by Wilhelm Knaack and Karl Blasel, was played 32 times at the Carltheater and was subsequently produced both at Berlin's Theater Unter den Linden (15 January 1893) and as *A Nevető örökösök* in Budapest (Budai Színkör 2 April 1893). Two further pieces for the Carltheater, *Die Königin von Gamara* (27 performances) and *Lady Charlatan* (37 performances), did only fairly, but his first piece for the Theater an der Wien, *Der Wunderknabe* (36 performances), topped its Vienna run by making it to the London stage (*The Little Genius*). *Die Blumen-Mary* (41 performances), *Der Dreibund* (23 performances) and *Der Blondin von Namur* (31 performances) all performed just adequately, but Stein's first major success came with a first collaboration with Victor Léon on the libretto for the slow-starting but eventually popular Johann Strauss pasticcio *Wiener Blut* (1899).

Two seasons later, Stein scored an even more considerable hit with the Heinrich Reinhardt Operette *Das süsse Mädel*, and thereafter the hits began to come with more regularity. He combined again with Léon on the text for the so-so classical burlesque *Der Göttergatte* for Franz Lehár, teamed with Carl Lindau and Edmund Eysler on the highly successful rustic *Die Schützenliesel* as a vehicle for Girardi, but returned to Léon and Lehár for his greatest hit of all, the adaptation of the French play *L'Attaché d'ambassade* as the text for *Die lustige Witwe*.

The partnership with Eysler also continued fruitfully, bringing forth further international hits in *Künstlerblut*, *Vera Violetta*, *Der Frauenfresser* and *Ein Tag im Paradies*, but Stein, haloed with his success as the author of the most successful Operette of the age in *Die lustige Witwe*, supplied texts to virtually all of the outstanding composers of his period and harvested hits, national and/or international, with each of them. His name appeared on Leo Fall's *Das Puppenmädel* and *Die Sirene*, Oskar Nedbal's *Polenblut* and *Die Winzerbraut*, Oscar Straus's *Die kleine Freundin*, Kálmán's vastly successful *Die Csárdásfürstin* and *Das Hollandweibchen*, Lehár's long-running Vienna hit *Die blaue Mazur* (curiously, his only subsequent work with the composer of *Die lustige Witwe*), and Robert Stolz's *Mädi*.

Stein's body of work, which ranged from such featherlight pieces as the delightful *Das süsse Mädel* and the sentimental musical comedies written for Girardi to Operetten more richly romantic than comic, gave him a place amongst the most important of all the Operette writers of his age. If *Die lustige Witwe* and, to a lesser extent, *Die Csárdásfürstin* are largely responsible for his continuing presence on the world's stages, *Das süsse Mädel*, *Künstlerblut*, *Ein Tag im Paradies*, *Polenblut* and others were major successes of their time, and both the last-named and *Wiener Blut* also continue to be performed nearly a century after their initial performances.

Stein was active, much of his career, with an almost homonym: **Leo Walther Stein** (b Gleiwitz, 10 August 1866; d Berlin, 3 January 1930) whose libretto and lyrics credits included *Zur Wienerin* (1906, Rudolf Raimann/w Richard Skowronnek), *Der blaue Reiter* (1914, Friedrich Bermann/w Ludwig Heller), *Die schöne Unbekannte* (1915, Oscar Straus/w Leopold Jacobson), *Die Dose seiner Majestät* (1917, Jean Gilbert/w Presber), *Der Hoflieranten* (1917, Hugo Hirsch), *Der Liebesdiplomat* (1921, Franz Dorffe/w Presber), *Ein Prachtmädel* (1921, Rudolf Nelson), *Die beiden Nachtigallen* (1921, Bredschneider/w Presber), *Die Scheidungsreise* (1922, Hugo Hirsch), *Der Gauklerkönig* (Gilbert/w Presber, Hans Hellmut Zerlett), *Sonja* (1925, Leo Ascher/w Presber) and the Singspiel *Chopin* (w Presber), as well as a source credit (w Oskar Walther) in the 1920 musical *Zwei tipp-topp Mädel* (Friedrich Schmidt/Curt Lauermann). Following his suicide in 1930 he had a posthumous credit on a musical version of the British farce *Tons of Money* produced as *Geld wie heu* at Berlin's Neues Theater am Zoo in November of that year.

1892 **Lachende Erben** (Karl Weinberger/w Julius Horst) Carltheater 24 October
1893 **Münchener Kind'l** (Weinberger/w Alexander Landesberg) Theater Unter den Linden 7 November
1894 **Die Königin von Gamara** (Alexander Neumann/w Julius Nigri, Richard Genée) Carltheater 27 October
1894 **Lady Charlatan** (Adolf Müller jr/w Paul von Schönthan) Carltheater 29 November
1895 **Der Lachtaube** (Eugen von Taund/w Landesberg under ps 'Otto Rehberg') Carltheater 14 April
1896 **Der Pumpmajor** (Neumann/w Horst) Theater in der Josefstadt 11 January
1896 **Der Wunderknabe** (von Taund/w Landesberg) Theater an der Wien 28 March
1896 **Der Pfiffikus** (Müller/w Horst) 1 act Raimundtheater 18 April
1896 **Der Löwenjäger** (*Az oroszlánvadász*) German version (Theater an der Wien)
1897 **Die Blumen-Mary** (Weinberger/w Landesberg) Theater an der Wien 11 November
1898 **Der Dreibund** (von Taund/w Landesberg) Theater an der Wien 28 April
1898 **Frau Reclame** (Louis Roth/w Horst) Venedig in Wien 6 August
1898 **Der Blondin von Namur** (Müller/w Horst) Theater an der Wien 25 October
1899 **(Die) Gräfin Kuni** (*Der Minnesänger*) (F Baumgartner/w Paul von Schönthan) Theater an der Wien 11 March
1899 **Wiener Blut** (Johann Strauss arr/w Victor Léon) Carltheater 26 October
1899 **Der griechische Sklave** (*A Greek Slave*) German version (Theater an der Wien)
1899 **Die wahre Liebe ist das nicht** (Fritz Skallitzky/w Horst) Raimundtheater 9 November
1900 **Der Sechs-Uhr-Zug** (Richard Heuberger/w Léon) Theater an der Wien 21 January

1900 **Man lebt nur einmal** (w Horst) Raimundtheater 14 November
1901 **Das süsse Mädel** (Heinrich Reinhardt/w Landesberg) Carltheater 25 October
1902 **Das gewisse Etwas** (Weinberger/w Léon) Carltheater 15 March
1902 **Der liebe Schatz** (Reinhardt/w Landesberg) Carltheater 30 October
1902 **Clo-Clo** (Ferdinand Pagin/w Landesberg) Danzers Orpheum 23 December
1904 **Der Göttergatte** (Franz Lehár/w Léon) Carltheater 20 January
1904 **Der Generalkonsul** (Reinhardt/w Landesberg) Theater an der Wien 29 January
1904 **Das Garnisonsmädel** (*Huszarver*) (Raoul Mader/w Landesberg) Theater an der Wien 29 October
1904 **Eduard, der Herzensdieb** (w Alfred Schick von Markenau) Raimundtheater 17 December
1905 **Der Schnurrbart** (*A bajusz*) German version w Carl Lindau (Carltheater)
1905 **Die Schützenliesel** (Edmund Eysler/w Lindau) Carltheater 7 October
1905 **Die lustige Witwe** (Lehár/w Léon) Theater an der Wien 30 December
1906 **Tausend und eine Nacht** (Johann Strauss arr Reiterer/w Lindau) Venedig in Wien 15 June
1906 **Künstlerblut** (Eysler/w Lindau) Carltheater 20 October
1907 **Der selige Vincenz** (Mader/w Landesberg) Carltheater 31 January
1907 **Vera Violetta** (Eysler) 1 act Apollotheater 30 November
1907 **Weiberlaunen** (*Leányka*) German version (Frankfurt am Main)
1908 **Das Glücksschweinchen** (Eysler/w Lindau) Sommer Theater Venedig in Wien 26 June
1908 **Johann der Zweite** (Eysler/w Lindau) Carltheater 3 October
1910 **Lumpus und Pumpus** (Eysler) 1 act Apollotheater 21 January
1910 **Das Puppenmädel** (Leo Fall/A M Willner) Carltheater 4 November
1911 **Die Sirene** (Fall/w Willner) Johann Strauss-Theater 5 January
1911 **Die kleine Freundin** (Oscar Straus/w Willner) Carltheater 20 October
1911 **Der Natursänger** (Eysler/w Jenbach) 1 act Apollotheater 22 December
1911 **Der Frauenfresser** (Eysler/w Lindau) Wiener Bürgertheater 25 December
1912 **Die Premiere** (Josef G Hart/w Bela Jenbach) 1 act Apollotheater 10 August
1912 **Der fliegende Rittmeister** (Herman Dostal/w Jenbach) 1 act Apollotheater 5 October
1913 **Polenblut** (Oskar Nedbal) Carltheater 25 October
1913 **Der Nachtschnellzug** (Leo Fall/w Léon) Johann Strauss-Theater 20 December
1913 **Ein Tag im Paradies** (Eysler/w Jenbach) Wiener Bürgertheater 23 December
1915 **Die – oder keine** (Eysler/w Jenbach) Wiener Bürgertheater 9 October
1915 **Die Csárdásfürstin** (Emmerich Kálmán/w Jenbach) Johann Strauss-Theater 13 November
1916 **Die Winzerbraut** (Nedbal/w Julius Wilhelm) Theater an der Wien 11 February
1918 **Bloch und co** (Robert Stolz/w Ernst Wengraf) 1 act Budapester Orpheum 5 April
1920 **Das Hollandweibchen** (Kálmán/w Jenbach) Johann Strauss-Theater 30 January
1920 **Der blaue Mazur** (Lehár/w Jenbach) Theater an der Wien 28 May

1923 **Mädi** (Stolz/w Grünwald) Berliner Theater, Berlin 1 April

Biography: Herz, P: *Die Librettisten der Wiener Operette: Leo Stein* (Weinberger, Vienna, 1973)

STEINER, Max[imilian] (b Buda, 27 August 1830; d Vienna, 29 May 1880).

At first a shopworker, then an actor and stage director in the German theatres at Temesvár, Arad and Hermanstadt under Friedrich Strampfer, Max Steiner was one of those who followed their director to Vienna when he took over the management of the Theater an der Wien. When Strampfer moved on, Steiner, who had already taken a secretarial rôle in the running of the house, took over and became lessee and manager of the theatre. He remained at the house's head, in partnership with Marie Geistinger, from 1869 up to 1875, and then alone, until his death in 1880.

During his management the fashion for French opéra-bouffe, which had been fostered at the theatre by Strampfer, continued, and Steiner produced the Viennese versions of such pieces as *Les Brigands* (*Die Banditen*), *Le Petit Faust* (*Doktor Faust Junior*), *Fantasio*, *Les Braconniers* (*Die Wilderer*), *La Créole* (*Die Creolin*), *Le Voyage dans la lune* (*Die Reise in den Mond*), *Le Roi Carotte* (*König Carotte*), *La Foire Saint-Laurent* (*Der Jahrmarkt Saint Laurent*), *Madame Favart*, *La Fille du tambour-major* (*Die Tochter des Tambour-Majors*) and, most successfully of all, *Die Glocken von Corneville*, as well as Offenbach's original Viennese piece *Der schwarze Korsar*. It was, however, his productions of local musical comedies and Operetten with which he left his mark. He introduced Johann Strauss to the musical stage with *Indigo und die vierzig Räuber* (on which he took a book credit to cover the mass of contributors), and subsequently produced his *Carneval in Rom*, *Die Fledermaus* and *Cagliostro in Wien*. He staged Genée's *Der Seekadett* and *Nanon*, and Millöcker's most important early venture into Operette, *Das verwunschene Schloss*, as well as such successful musical plays as *An der schönen blauen Donau*, *Schottenfeld und Ringstrassen*, *Der deutsche Bruder*, *Der Pfarrer von Kirschfeld*, *Drei Paar Schuhe*, *Abenteuer in Wien*, *Durchgegangene Weiber*, *Ihr Korporal*, *Der barmherzige Bruder*, *Ein Blitzmädel*, *Der Gypsfigur* and *Die Näherin*.

The eldest of Steiner's four sons, **Franz STEINER** (b Temesvár, 1855; d Berlin, February 1920) took over the running of the theatre during his father's final illness and succeeded him as manager through four further successful seasons, during which time he produced Strauss's *Das Spitzentuch der Königin*, *Der lustige Krieg* and the revised *Eine Nacht in Venedig*, Millöcker's *Apajune, der Wassermann*, *Die Jungfrau von Belleville*, *Der Bettelstudent* and *Gasparone*, Suppé's *Die Afrikareise* and the German versions of *La Mascotte*, *Rip van Winkle* and the French spectacular *L'Arbre de Noël* remusicked with a new local score. In 1884, when the lessee of the theatre, Franz Jauner, sold out to Alexandrine von Schönerer, Steiner was replaced as artistic director of the house and left Vienna for Berlin, accompanied by the former Frau Lili Strauss with whom he had been all too obviously linked for the theatre's good relations with Vienna's most famous composer. In Berlin, he took over the running of the Walhalla-Theater, where he successfully mounted Dellinger's *Don Cesar* (1885), but he returned two seasons later to Austria to take over the Carltheater from Carl Tatartzy. His productions there

(*Rikiki*, *Die Dreizehn*, *Der Glücksritter*, *Der Sänger von Palermo*, *Don Cesar*, *Ein Deutschmeister*, *Der Freibuter*, *Farinelli*, *Colombine*, *Die Jagd nach dem Glück*) were not particularly successful, and after three years he handed over the house to Carl Blasel. He ultimately returned to Berlin where for some dozen years he managed the Wintergarten.

Another son **Gabor [Christian] STEINER** (b Temesvár, 1858; d Hollywood, 9 September 1944) spent a career in the theatre world in almost every kind of activity, being at one time an agent, another a publisher and, ultimately, a director specializing in extravagant and spectacular productions with a variety element. He worked as secretary to Carl Tatartzy during his mangagement of the Carltheater, ran the Residenztheater in Hanover, the Residenztheater in Dresden, and supported his brother during his reigns at both the Theater an der Wien and the Carltheater, before, in 1895, setting up the Summer Theater Venedig-in-Wien in the 'Englischer Garten im Praterstern', the pleasure gardens at the Prater with their celebrated Riesenrad, or ferris-wheel (1897). There he produced a programme which included a good percentage of the foreign imports which always appealed to him, including the German versions of Broadway's *The Belle of New York* and *The Girl from Up There*, of Britain's *Miss Hook of Holland*, Berlin's *Venus auf Erden*, Paris's *La Poupée*, Madrid's *La gran vía* and also an original Operette *Der Reise nach Cuba* composed by London's Ivan Caryll. He also mounted a number of successful pasticcio shows based on the music of favourite composers, including *Jung Heidelberg*, *Gräfin Pepi*, *Der schöne Rigo*, the highly successful *Frühlingsluft* and *1001 Nacht*. His most notable production, however, was an original piece, Carl Michael Ziehrer's *Die Landstreicher*, which he both produced and directed.

The success of the Summer Theater led him to open a winter counterpart, Danzers Orpheum, in 1900 and he ran the two houses together, sometimes sharing productions, and continuing with his bias to the imported with such pieces as *Trial By Jury*, the Gaiety Theatre's *The Circus Girl* and *The Messenger Boy*, a visit by the Berlin Apollo Company (*Frau Luna*, *Lysistrata*, *Im Reiche des Indra*), Paris's *Le Carnet du Diable*, *Le Fils prodigue* and *Paris ou le bon juge* as well as burlesque, revue and semi-variety programmes. In 1908 he moved to the rebuilt 3,000 seater Établissement Ronacher, an entertainment house built and run with a purposely Parisian air, which he operated until 1912. Once again, he favoured English productions (*Our Miss Gibbs*, *A New Aladdin*, *The Arcadians* etc), which he himself directed, often surrounded with variety items. He also took an author's credit on a revamped version of Offenbach's *La Belle Hélène* (*Die schöne Helena von heute* [Offenbach arr Ludwig Gothov-Grüneke/w Leopold Krenn] Ronacher, 1911).

His son, **Max[imilan Raoul] STEINER** (b Vienna, 10 May 1888; d Hollywood, 28 December 1971) ventured into the musical theatre from his earliest days, and produced an amount of music which got a hearing in the provinces (*Ein Kosestündchen*, 1903) or at his father's houses – additional music for the Viennese versions of Serpette's *Das Scheckbuch des Teufels* (*Le Carnet du Diable*, 1906) and a Berlin burlesque of *Die lustige Witwe* (*Der lustige Witwer*, 1907) the mime scene *Bei Ihr* (1906), and the score for the two-act Lucien Boyer vaudeville *Die schöne Griechen* (20 December 1907) which played for three weeks at Danzers Orpheum on a double-bill with the burlesque *Eine Sensation*. He won intermittent jobs conducting variety programmes in Britain and France before, in 1914, moving on to try his luck in America. There he continued his theatrical activity not as a composer but as an arranger and orchestrator of other folks' music and as a conductor for mostly touring musical shows. In 1929 he moved on again, this time to the newly sound-conscious Hollywood, and there he finally found success. He became at first a screen conductor and then a highly successful composer of film music (*Gone with the Wind, A Star Is Born, Now Voyager, Since You Went Away, Mildred Pierce* etc, 3 Academy Awards). Steiner impinged intermittently on the musical theatre with scores for such piece as the flop George Lederer musical production *Peaches* (1923 w R B Smith, H B Smith) without ever finding a success comparable to that which he found in the film world.

A third of the four sons of the elder Max Steiner, Alexander Steiner, familiarly known as 'Doc', was for a long time employed on the American Keith vaudeville circuit.

STEPHENS, Henry Pottinger [Lygon] (aka Henry Beauchamp) (b Barrow-on-Soar, Leicestershire, 1851; d London, 11 February 1903).

A journalist (*Daily Telegraph, Tit Bits* etc) and the first editor of *Topical Times*, 'Pot' Stephens made his first appearance as a dramatic author under the aegis of the German Reed management at St George's Hall. He subsequently wrote lyrics for F C Burnand's *Robbing Roy* burlesque at the Gaiety and collaborated with Burnand on a couple of other burlesques before, in the wake of *HMS Pinafore*, joining up with composer Teddy Solomon on a comic opera. Their *Billee Taylor* appeared the same year as *The Pirates of Penzance*, won a major success and favourable comparison with Gilbert and Sullivan's piece, and caused its authors to be hailed briefly as the equals of Carte's prized writers. Carte had his associate, Michael Gunn, get the pair under contract, but they failed to come up with a second piece at the same level. Stephens returned to burlesque, and he had an important effect on London theatre when his *The Vicar of Wide-awake-field* and *Little Jack Sheppard* set in motion George Edwardes's management at the Gaiety Theatre and the fashion for the 'new burlesque'.

However, other authors provided the later scripts for the Gaiety, and Stephens had just one more success, like the first in tandem with Solomon, when a piece they had written several years before was produced under the title *The Red Hussar*. Since Solomon was involved, law suits were also the order of the day, but the show had a good international career, giving Stephens his third major stage hit. He also authored novels, plays, a revue (*A Dream of Whittaker's Almanack* w Walter Slaughter, Florian Pascal, Georges Jacobi, Walter Hedgecock, Crystal Palace 5 June 1899), and pantomimes, in one of which he was appearing at Brighton at the time of his death.

1879 **Back from India** (Cotsford Dick) 1 act St George's Hall 25 June
1879 **Robbing Roy, or Scotched and Kilt** (pasticcio arr Meyer Lutz/F C Burnand) Gaiety Theatre 11 November

1879 **Balloonacy, or A Flight of Fancy** (pasticcio arr Edward Solomon/w Burnand) Royalty Theatre 1 December
1880 **Cupid, or Two Strings to a Beau** (pasticcio arr Barrow/w Charles Harris [uncredited]) Royalty Theatre 26 April
1880 **The Corsican Brothers & Co Ltd** (pasticcio w Burnand) Gaiety Theatre 25 October
1880 **Billee Taylor** (Solomon) Imperial Theatre 30 October
1881 **Herne the Hunted** (pasticcio/w William Yardley, Robert Reece) Gaiety Theatre 24 May
1881 **Claude Duval** (Solomon) Olympic Theatre 24 August
1882 **Lord Bateman, or Picotee's Pledge** (Solomon) Gaiety Theatre 29 April
1882 **Through the Looking Glass** (Solomon) 1 act Gaiety Theatre 17 July
1883 **Virginia and Paul, or Changing the Rings** (aka *Virginia*) (Solomon) Bijou Theater, New York, 8 January
1883 **Galatea, or Pygmalion Re-Versed** 1 act Gaiety Theatre 26 December
1885 **Hobbies** (George Gear/w Yardley) 1 act St George's Hall 6 April
1885 **The Vicar of Wide-awake-field, or the Miss-Terryous Uncle** (Florian Pascal/w Yardley) Gaiety Theatre 8 August
1885 **Little Jack Sheppard** (Meyer Lutz et al/w Yardley) Gaiety Theatre 26 December
1889 **The Red Hussar** (Solomon) Lyric Theatre 23 November
1896 **The Black Squire, or Where There's a Will There's a Way** (Pascal) Torquay 5 November

STEPHENSON, B[enjamin] C[harles] (aka Bolton Rowe) (b 1838; d Taplow, 22 January 1906).

The nephew of General Sir Frederick Stephenson, 'Charlie' Stephenson began his working life in government service whilst simultaneously turning out some little dramatic texts. He collaborated with the young composer Frederic Clay on three pieces played by amateurs – *The Pirates Isle, Out of Sight* and *The Bold Recruit* – the last of which was picked up to be played at a benefit at the Gallery of Illustration in 1870. His first professional success came at the same venue, two years later, when he provided the text for Alfred Cellier's little operetta *Charity Begins at Home*, and another short comic piece, *The Zoo*, set by Arthur Sullivan, brought his name further to the front.

Stephenson's first full-scale successes came when he collaborated with Clement Scott on the English versions of Sardou's plays *Nos intimes* (as *Peril*) and *Dora* (*Diplomacy*) and the text for Lecocq's opérette *Le Petit Duc*, but his most notable was his first full-length musical, the comedy opera *Dorothy*, manufactured around Alfred Cellier's second-hand *Nell Gwynne* score. Much criticized on its first production, Stephenson's libretto was subjected to all sorts of scholarly analysis after *Dorothy* became the hit of the century, and its initially despised plot was traced seriously back to the Restoration playwrights, Garrick and Aphra Behn. Although the pair – bohemian, chattery Cellier and the fussy, health- and money-conscious Stephenson – made up an unlikely pair, together they continued to prosper and another Cellier remake, *Doris*, had a good run. However a collaboration with Arthur Goring Thomas on another staunchly period comedy piece, *The Golden Web*, in spite of some appreciative critical nods, was short-lived and Stephenson did not again find a musical-theatre success.

1868 **The Bold Recruit** (Clay) 1 act Theatre Royal, Canterbury 4 August

1872 **Charity Begins at Home** (Alfred Cellier) 1 act Gallery of Illustration 7 February

1875 **The Zoo** (Arthur Sullivan) 1 act St James's Theatre 5 June

1878 **The Little Duke** (*Le Petit Duc*) English version w Clement Scott (Philharmonic Theatre)

1886 **Dorothy** (Cellier) Gaiety Theatre 25 September

1888 **Warranted Burglar Proof** (Ivan Caryll, H J Leslie) 1 act Prince of Wales Theatre 31 March

1889 **Doris** (Cellier) Lyric Theatre 20 April

1892 **The Young Recruit** (*Le Dragon de la reine*) English version w Augustus Harris et al (Newcastle)

1893 **The Golden Web** (Arthur Goring Thomas/w Frederick Corder) Lyric Theatre 11 March

1893 **The Venetian Singer** (aka *The Improvisatore*) (Edward Jakobowski) 1 act Court Theatre 25 November

1896 **On the March** (John Crook, Edward Solomon, Clay/w William Yardley, Cecil Clay) Prince of Wales Theatre 22 June

1896 **Belinda** (Walter Slaughter/w Basil Hood) Prince's Theatre, Manchester 5 October

STEPPING STONES

STEPPING STONES Musical comedy in 2 acts by Anne Caldwell and R H Burnside. Lyrics by Anne Caldwell. Music by Jerome Kern. Globe Theater, New York, 6 November 1923.

The seventh in the series of Fred Stone children-of-all-ages shows staged by Charles Dillingham, *Stepping Stones* was an ingenuous piece based not very heavily on the Red Riding Hood story. Prince Silvio (Roy Hoyer) is in love with little Rougette (Dorothy Stone), but that villainous robber of the woods, Otto de Wolfe (Oscar Ragland), wants his daughter Lupina (Evelyn Herbert) to have the royal title. Stone was Peter Plug, a plumber, whose various comic machinations helped the lovers to a happy ending.

Jerome Kern's functional score included little to rate amongst his best music, but the pretty trio 'Once in a Blue Moon' and the jaunty 'Raggedy Ann' emerged as enjoyable numbers. Another lilting tune, 'In Love with Love', was reused after *Stepping Stones* was gone, reappearing in the London musical *Lady Mary* (1928) set to a fresh Graham John lyric as 'If You're a Friend of Mine'. Alongside the songs, there was plenty of dance music for the Tiller Sunshine Girls and the first act highlighted a selection of old 'Rose' favourites (as Kern's score to *The Night Boat* had done with 'river' songs) ranging from 'Ma Blushin' Rosie' to 'The Last Rose of Summer'. Stone's daughter Dorothy, making her stage début billed above the title as Rougette, performed a duet, 'Wonderful Dad', with Fred, the connotations of which went clearly beyond the show's context. Another famous man's daughter was seen in the smaller rôle of Radiola – Primrose Caryll, daughter of the late Ivan who had composed the earlier Fred Stone shows.

Stepping Stones was immediately popular, and it had reached its 241st Broadway performances (in spite of higher than usual ticket prices) when it was closed by an actors' strike. Stone later took it on the road with equal success.

STERK, Wilhelm

STERK, Wilhelm (b Budapest, 28 June 1880; d during 1943–4).

A prolific writer of Operetten and revues for Austrian and German theatres for 30 years, Sterk provided material for a number of smaller and provincial theatres, but also intermittently and particularly in his later days for some of the principal houses. His most successful piece was the small-scale musical comedy *Dorine und der Zufall*, set to music by Jean Gilbert, and he also had several productions out of Robert Stolz's *Der Favorit* and Jessel's *Des Königs Nachbarin*. He was deported to Theresienstadt during the war and not seen again.

1907 **Odysseus Heimkehr** (Hans Albert Cesek) 1 act Hölle 1 October

1907 **Ein tolles Mädel** (Carl Michael Ziehrer/Kurt Kraatz, Heinrich Stobitzer) Walhalla-Theater, Wiesbaden 24 August

1908 **Die Wunderquelle** (Heinrich Berté/w Emmerich von Gatti) 1 act Hölle 1 November

1909 **Herr und Frau Biedermann** (Ziehrer pasticcio) 1 act Lustspielhaus, Munich 10 January; Kleine Bühne 5 October 1910

1910 **Die schlaue Komtesse** (Béla Laszky) 1 act Kleine Bühne 18 November

1910 **Champagner** (Karl Stigler) 1 act Wiener Colosseum 1 December

1911 **Ball bei Hof** (Ziehrer) Stadttheater, Stettin 22 January

1911 **Der Flotte Bob** (Stigler/w A M Willner) Altes Theater, Leipzig 8 April

1912 **Die klingende Mühle** (Cesek) 1 act Hölle 1 October

1914 **Der Märchenprinz** (Berté/w Willner) Schauburg, Hanover 28 February

1914 **Das dumme Herz** (Ziehrer/w Rudolf Österreicher) Johann Strauss-Theater 27 February

1914 **Der Gott der Kleinen** (Laszky) 1 act Künstlerspiele 1 January

1914 **Der Kriegsberichterstatter** (many/w Österreicher) Apollotheater 9 October

1914 **Das Mädchen im Mond** (Stigler/w Österreicher) Carltheater 7 November

1916 **Der Favorit** (Robert Stolz/w Fritz Grünbaum) Komische Oper, Berlin 7 April

1916 **Mein Annerl** (Georg Jarno/w Grünbaum) Carltheater 7 October

1916 **Servus, Mädel** (Stolz) 1 act Wintergarten, Budapest December

1919 **Wiener Leut – einst und heut'** (Arthur M Werau) 1 act Künstlerspiele Pan 30 December

1920 **Das verbotene Fräulein** (Werau) 1 act Künstlerspiele Pan January

1920 **Wer hat's gemacht** (Eysler) 1 act Variété Reclame 1 October

1920 **Der Filmstern** (Fritz Lehner) Lustspieltheater 21 July

1920 **Eine tolle Sache** (Werau) Künstlerspiele Pan 1 October

1920 **Der Herr Oberst** (Károly Hajós) 1 act Hölle 1 November

1920 **Ein nobler Herr** (Werau) Rolandbühne 1 November

1921 **Die 1000ste Jungfrau** (Lehner) Femina 1 January

1921 **Eine feine Nummer** (Hajós) 1 act Olympia Variété 1 February

1923 **Dorine und die Zufall** (Jean Gilbert/w Grünbaum) Neues Theater am Zoo, Berlin 15 September

1923 **Pusztaliebchen** (Michael Krasznay-Krausz) Johann Strauss-Theater 19 December

1924 **Agri** (Ernst Steffan/w A M Willner) Wiener Bürgertheater 30 January

1923 **Des Königs Nachbarin** (Leon Jessel/w Grünbaum) Wallner-Theater, Berlin 15 April

1926 **Ich hab' dich lieb...!** (Leo Ascher) Raimundtheater 16 April

1926 **Ich und Du** (Lamberto Pavanelli/w Grünbaum) Prague 28 November

1927 **Meine Tochter Otto** (Jessel/w Grünbaum) Rolandbühne 5 May

1927 **Rosen aus Schiras** (Frank Stafford/w Grünbaum) Johann Strauss-Theater 24 June

1927 **Yvette und ihre Freunde** (Krasznay-Krausz/w Österreicher) Wiener Bürgertheater 18 November
1929 **Der lustige Krieg** revised libretto (Johann
Strauss-Theater)
1930 **Eine Woche Glück** (Max Niederberger) Opernhaus, Graz
25 January
1930 **Die verliebte Eskadron** (Ziehrer arr Karl Pauspertl)
Johann Strauss-Theater 11 July
1930 **Der König ihres Herzens** (Offenbach arr Pauspertl)
Johann Strauss-Theater 23 December
1933 **Tango um Mitternacht** (*Éjféli tangó*) German version
(Volksoper)
1933 **Die Schönste im Dorf** (Friedrich Smetana arr J Orel)
Volksoper 24 March
1934 **Wiener G'schichten** (Josef Hellmesberger ad Oskar
Jascha) Volksoper 27 October
1937 **Die goldene Mühle** (Jessel/Hugo Wiener, Karl Costa ad)
Johann Strauss-Theater 21 April

STERN, Ernst (b Bucharest, 1876; d London, 28
August 1954). Set designer whose name became
synonymous with large and lavish in Germany, then
wherever *Im weissen Rössl* was staged.

In 1906 Stern joined the staff of Max Reinhardt at
the Deutsches Theater in Berlin and there, over a
period of 15 years, designed a variety of productions,
mostly of classic plays, but also (in spite of being described by one journal as 'Reinhardt's spare set designer',
with the 'spare' certainly not describing his style) his
versions of *Orphée aux enfers* and *La Belle Hélène*. He
subsequently designed for Ernst Lubitsch for film and
for Hermann Haller at the Theater am Nollendorfplatz
(*Wenn Liebe erwacht* etc) before being picked up by Erik
Charell to design his spectacular Berlin musical productions. He contributed much, by his elaborate stage pictures, to such productions as Charell's expanded
Madame Pompadour, the disastrously jazzed-up *The Merry
Widow* with its purposely grotesque design, his
mincemeat *Mikado*, to the much happier productions of
Benatzky's *Casanova* and *The Three Musketeers* ('the most
exceptional dictator of colour and line in the international theatre'), and, most famously, to the first production of *Im weissen Rössl*. Versions of his designs were
repeated for *White Horse Inn* and *L'Auberge du cheval
blanc*, spreading Stern's reputation for everything-that-
moves design throughout the world.

Stern subsequently left Germany and moved to London
where his musical credits included *Bitter-Sweet* (1929 w
Gladys E Calthrop), *White Horse Inn* (1931) and *The Song
of the Drum* (1931, scenery and costumes), *The Lilac
Domino* revival (1944) and *The Bird Seller* (1947, *Der
Vogelhändler*).

Autobiography: *My Life, My Stage* (Gollancz, London, 1951)

DER STERNGUCKER *see* LIBELLENTANZ

STEWART, Michael [RUBIN, Michael Stewart] (b
New York, 1 August 1929; d New York, 20 September
1987). Librettist for some sizeable hits of Broadway's postwar heyday.

Stewart made his way into the musical theatre by way of
writing for summer shows and for revue, supplying lyrics
and sketches for such pieces as the *Shoestring Revue* (1955)
and comedy material for Sid Caesar before joining song

writers Strouse and Adams, who had followed a similar
route to Broadway, as the librettist of the rock-and-roll
parody musical *Bye Bye Birdie*. The piece gave its writers a
highly successful introduction to the musical stage, and
Stewart soon built on that success with two fine adaptations, teaming with songwriter Bob Merrill on the
delightful and successful *Carnival*, a musical based on the
film *Lili* and its original story by Paul Gallico, and then
with Jerry Herman on the blockbusting triumph of *Hello,
Dolly!*, a musical version of *The Matchmaker* and its German-language model.

After this memorable start to his career, things
quietened down for a decade. *How Do You Do, I Love You*
pulled up before Broadway, and if a pasticcio biomusical
on George M Cohan had a good Broadway run, an adaptation of Pinero's play *The Amazons*, produced in Britain,
also failed to find a metropolitan showing and Stewart's
original adaptation of the play *Two for the Seesaw* as the text
for the Cy Coleman musical *Seesaw* (1973) was dollied up
and around by Michael Bennett and a handful of other folk
before the show's New York presentation. The following
year, a second collaboration with *Hello, Dolly!* composer
Herman, on a vaguely biographical musical on silent filmland's Mack Sennett and Mabel Normand (*Mack and
Mabel*) folded in 66 performances.

The indifferent results of Stewart's post-*Hello, Dolly!*
years gave way to renewed success with the small-scale
musical comedy *I Love My Wife*, a piece based on a Continental on-the-verge-of-sex farce, for which Stewart provided this time both text and lyrics. A fine metropolitan
success in New York and in London, the show found a
lively life thereafter. In 1979 Stewart paired with fledgling
writer Mark Bramble to adapt the successful play
Jacobowsky and the Colonel to the musical stage and though
neither this nor their musical version of Maxwell Anderson's *Elizabeth the Queen* proved successful, the pair had a
major success third time around with the circus-filled biomusical *Barnum*, on which Stewart was credited with lyrics
and Bramble with the libretto.

A second substantial hit followed when the pair adapted the celebrated film *42nd Street* to the musical stage,
but the show was to be Stewart's last success. An attempt
at a musequel to his first hit, *Bring Back Birdie* failed to
connect, a Harrigan and Hart pasticcio biomusical on
George M! lines, and a new musical version of Robert
Louis Stevenson's *Treasure Island* were failures, and his
last work, a fresh musicalization of the famous farce
Nothing But the Truth (w Coleman, Bramble), remained
unproduced at the time of his death, in the wake of an
operation, in 1987.

A writer of great freshness and vigour, his great successes, after the original *Bye Bye Birdie*, were with adaptations
(*Carnival, Hello, Dolly!, I Love My Wife, 42nd Street*) but his
infrequent excursions into lyric-writing (*I Love My Wife,
Barnum*) encouraged regrets that he had not ventured
more frequently into that field.

1960 **Bye Bye Birdie** (Charles Strouse/Lee Adams) Martin
Beck Theater 14 April
1961 **Carnival** (Bob Merrill) Imperial Theater 13 April
1964 **Hello, Dolly!** (Jerry Herman) St James Theater 16 January
1967 **How Do You Do, I Love You** (David Shire/Richard
Maltby jr) Shady Grove Music Fair, Gaithersburg 19
October

1968 **George M!** (George M Cohan/w John and Fran Pascal) Palace Theater 10 April

1971 **The Amazons** (John Addison/David Heneker) Playhouse, Nottingham, UK 7 April

1974 **Mack and Mabel** (Herman) Majestic Theater 6 October

1977 **I Love My Wife** (Cy Coleman) Ethel Barrymore Theater 17 April

1979 **The Grand Tour** (Herman/w Mark Bramble) Palace Theater 11 January

1980 **Elizabeth and Essex** (Doug Katsaros/Richard Engquist/w Bramble) South Street Theater 24 February

1980 **Barnum** (Coleman/Bramble) St James Theater 30 April

1980 **42nd Street** (Harry Warren, Al Dubin pasticcio/w Bramble) Winter Garden Theater 25 August

1981 **Bring Back Birdie** (Strouse/Adams) Martin Beck Theater 5 March

1985 **Harrigan and Hart** (Max Showalter, David Braham/Peter Walker, Edward Harrigan) Longacre Theater 31 January

1985 **Pieces of Eight** (Jule Styne/Susan Birkenhead) Citadel Theater, Edmonton 27 November

STEWART, Nellie (b Sydney, 20 November 1858; d Sydney, 18 June 1931).

The daughter of a well-known touring actor and actress – father Richard [Richard Stewart TOWZEY] had been Australia's first Jupiter in *Orphée aux enfers* and mother, Theodosia, under the name of Mrs Geary, had been the first star of *The Bohemian Girl* in Australia – the young Nellie performed with her half-sisters, Maggie and Docie, children of Theodosia's marriage to lace-maker James Guerin, in the Stewart family's entertainments. These included a specially written programme called *Rainbow Revels*, which Richard took as far afield as London's Crystal Palace in 1866, a hotch-potch entitled *If, or an old gem reset* and a pirate production of *HMS Pinafore* (1878) with Nellie as Ralph Rackstraw to Docie's Josephine, which tactfully became a burlesque, *HMS Pinnacle*, with Nellie playing Jack Jackstraw, when legal furies threatened.

Hired as a replacement by George Musgrove during the run of his record-breaking Australian production of *La Fille du tambour-major*, she made a personal success when she succeeded Jessie Grey to the normally tenor rôle of the little tailor Griolet, and subsequently went on to play such parts as Suzanne (*Madame Favart*), Bathilde (*Les Noces d'Olivette*) and Serpolette (*Les Cloches de Corneville*) before the sudden departure of prima donna Emilie Melville allowed her to take over the star parts in the company's repertoire.

Over the next five years she became Australia's favourite native musical star, appearing for Musgrove (with whom she developed what was to be a lifelong liaison) and with his partners J C Williamson and Arthur Garner in a long series of comic operas: *Olivette* (Bathilde, Olivette), *Madame Favart* (Suzanne, Mme Favart), *La Fille du tambour major* (Stella), *Les Cloches de Corneville* (Serpolette), *La Petite Mademoiselle* (Countess Cameroni), *The Merry Duchess* (Duchess), Searelle's *Estrella* (Estrella), *Billee Taylor* (Phoebe), *La Mascotte* (Fiametta), *The Sorcerer* (Aline), *HMS Pinafore* (Josephine), *The Pirates of Penzance* (Mabel), *Patience* (Patience), *Iolanthe* (Phyllis), *The Mikado* (Yum-Yum), *La Fille de Madame Angot* (Clairette), *Pepita* (*La Princesses des Canaries*, Pepita), *Dorothy* (Dorothy), *Ma mie Rosette* (Rosette), *Mam'zelle Nitouche* (Denise) etc. In 1888 Alfred Cellier persuaded her to attempt *Faust*, and in 1890 Musgrove financed the Nellie Stewart Comic Opera

Company which played successfully, around its star, in Australia and New Zealand.

Miss Stewart made several trips overseas, appearing in New York in *An Artist's Model* (Adèle) and in London in the title-rôle of *Blue-Eyed Susan* (1892) and for two weeks as a replacement in the lead rôle of Princess Micaëla in the English version of *Le Coeur et la main* (*Incognita*), but Cellier's attempts to persuade D'Oyly Carte to take her on foundered when she walked out on a rôle in *The Nautch Girl* after having a number cut. Later, during an extended London stay whilst Musgrove was running the Shaftesbury Theatre, she starred in a specially made new boy-rôle in his *The Scarlet Feather* (*La Petite Mariée*) and also played principal boy in the 1899 Drury Lane pantomime, but she never achieved the same success outside Australia that she did at home.

From 1902 she renounced the musical stage and found new success, most notably as *Sweet Nell of Old Drury*, on the straight stage.

Docie (Theodosia) Stewart also played for many years on the musical stage, before retiring to married life as Mrs Pierre Chamboissier of the Savoy Hotel, Market Street, Sydney.

Autobiography: *My Life's Story* (John Sands, Sydney, 1923)

STIGWOOD, Robert (b Adelaide, 15 April 1934). Highly successful musical theatre and film producer who made his pile then shot off to spend it.

A pop-music man with a career with as many downs as ups to his career – one of the principal ups being his management of the Bee Gees – Robert Stigwood zoomed to the forefront in London's musical theatre when his cleverly calculated purchase of the English rights of *Hair* (he guessed that the censor was about to be abolished) gave him a long-running London hit. He hit the gold again when he mounted the American and British productions of *Jesus Christ Superstar*, followed up with the less-successful London seasons of *Pippin*, *Joseph and the Amazing Technicolor Dreamcoat* (w Michael White), *Jeeves* (w White) and an Off-Broadway *Sergeant Pepper's Lonely Hearts Club Band* (1974), and then put a full-stop to his theatre career with another vast hit, *Evita*.

He did not yet get out of the business, but instead moved on into the film world. He had already been responsible for the films of *Jesus Christ Superstar* (1973) and *Tommy* (1975), now he followed up with *Bugsy Malone* and then with the two oversized teeny-hits of their age – *Saturday Night Fever* and *Grease* – *Sergeant Pepper's Lonely Hearts Club Band* (1978) and *Times Square* (1980).

Then, with a common-sense which few producers have been able to show, he folded up his account books and went off to enjoy himself on the proceeds of so much intelligently run entertainment business.

STOJANOVITS, Péter [Lázár] (b Budapest, 6 September 1877; d Belgrade, 12 September 1957). Composer of two Operette hits from two tries in a career devoted to other areas of music.

Stojanovits studied composition and violin in Hungary, Vienna and Bonn, and subsequently first taught violin, then became an inspector of violin teaching in both Vienna and Budapest, before establishing his own school for violinists in Vienna in 1913. Parallel to his teaching and to some performing, he also composed for the concert hall (violin music, sonatas, chamber music) and for the stage, and his one-act opera *A tigris* was produced at Budapest's Magyar Király Operaház when he was 18 years of age. However, he found his most important success as a theatrical composer, a dozen years on, with a pair of Operetten produced at the Vienna Carltheater.

Liebchen am Dach, written and directed by Victor Léon, had an excellent first run of 183 performances and was subsequently produced in Hungary (*Padlásszoba*, Varósi Színház 30 November 1917) and in Germany, and its successor, *Der Herzog von Reichstadt*, a period piece with Hubert Marischka and Mizzi Zwerenz starred as the son of Napoleon and ballerina Fanny Elssler, was played 111 times in its initial season and brought back later in the year for a further 75 performances before going on to a like career (*A reichstadti herceg* Városi Színház 14 October 1921).

In 1925 Stojanovits became director of the Belgrade conservatoire, and although he continued a career as a concert violininst, in spite of the success of his two Vienna Operetten, he did not again return to the lyric stage.

1917 **Liebchen am Dach** (Victor Léon) Carltheater 19 May
1921 **Der Herzog von Reichstadt** (Léon, Heinz Reichert) Carltheater 11 February

STOLZ, Robert [Elisabeth] (b Graz, 25 August 1880; d Berlin, 27 June 1975). The composer of three-quarters of a century of music for the Viennese operettic stage.

Robert Stolz began his theatrical career as a répétiteur and a conductor in his home town, then worked as Kapellmeister in Marburg (Maribor), Salzburg and Brünn before being engaged at the Theater an der Wien in 1907. There he conducted the premières of such pieces as *Tip-Top* (1907) and *Der schöne Gardist* (1908), and performances of some of the most important European Operetten of the time – *Die lustige Witwe*, *Der tapfere Soldat*, *Der Graf von Luxemburg*, *Ein Herbstmanöver* – which made up part of the theatre's repertoire at that time.

During this period Stolz composed both Viennese songs ('Servus Du') and theatre scores, and his first Viennese première, with *Die lustigen Weiben von Wien*, took place at the Colosseum in 1908, followed by a Budapest first with an Hungarian version, *A trabuói herceg*, 12 months later. His first full-sized metropolitan Operette *Das Glücksmädel*, produced in 1910 at the Raimundtheater, played 52 performances with no less a star than Alexander Girardi in its central rôle, *Die eiserne Jungfrau* made some 40 nights with another favourite local star, Hansi Niese, at the top of the bill, whilst *Der Favorit*, first produced in Berlin, was later played at Vienna's Apollotheater and in Budapest (ad Zsolt Harsányi) and brought forth, if not a long run, a popular song in 'Du sollst der Kaiser meiner Seele sein'.

During the war years and after, Stolz produced a mixture of short stage pieces and musical plays, popular songs ('Im Prater blühn wieder die Bäume', 'Salomé', 'Hallo, du süsse Klingelfee') and a one-act opera *Die Rosen der Madonna* (1920), before he had his first significant international success with the Operette *Der Tanz ins Glück*. *Der Tanz ins Glück* was played for 200 performances at the Raimundtheater before being exported to a widespread series of foreign productions (*Whirled into Happiness*, *Sky*

Plate 252.

High, *Szerencsetánc*, *La Danza di fortuna*) in a variety of remade shapes and musical forms.

Die Tanzgräfin, first produced in Berlin, went on to play a splendid 204 performances at Vienna's Johann Strauss-Theater (but flopped pre-Broadway when lavishly produced in America as *The Dancing Duchess*), and if *Eine Sommernacht*'s two-month run and the 68 performances of *Die Liebe geht um!* were not in the same league, the pretty tale of *Mädi*, produced at the Berliner Theater for a fine run and later at the Vienna Apollotheater and London's Prince of Wales Theatre (*The Blue Train*) gave him a third success to round off this most productive period of his stage-writing life.

A costly divorce and the equally costly failure of an attempt to become a theatre director led him to leave Vienna, but he resurfaced with the coming of the film musical, scoring a hit with his score for *Zwei Herzen im Dreivierteltakt* (1930) near the beginning of more than a decade of pre-war film writing which included such movie musicals as *Das Lied ist aus* (1930, 'Adieu, mein kleiner Gardeoffizier'), a screen version of his *Der Hampelmann* (1931) with Max Hansen starred, *Liebeskommando* (1931), *Sein Liebeslied* (1931), Geza von Bolvary's *Die lustigen Weiber von Wien* (1931), *Der Liebling von Wien* (1933), *Frühjahrsparade* (1934), *Der Himmel auf Erden* (1935), *Herbstmanöver* (1935) and *Husaren, heraus* (1938) in Germany and *Spring Parade* (ex-*Frühjahrsparade*, 'Waltzing'), *My Heart is Calling* (1935), *The Night of the Great Love* (1937) and *It Happened Tomorrow* (1943) in Hollywood.

At the same time that this second career was beginning, Stolz also turned out what were to be his most famous stage songs, two of the many interpolations inserted in Ralph Benatzky's score for *Im weissen Rössl* ('Mein Liebeslied muss ein Walzer sein', 'Die ganze Welt ist Himmelblau'), later supplemented by the song from *Das*

Lied ist aus, made over famously by Harry Graham as 'Goodbye' and by 'Auch du wirst mich einmal betrügen' ('You Too'), borrowed from *Zwei Herzen im Dreivierteltakt*, when the show's score was expanded in London. Parallel to his film career, he continued to produce Operetten, making a success with the pretty *Wenn die kleinen Veilchen blühen*, initially produced in the Netherlands, with the romantic period piece, *Venus in Seide*, and *Grüezi*, both mounted in Zürich, and a stage version of *Zwei Herzen im Dreivierteltakt*.

Stolz's musical hand subsequently moved far and wide as he provided additional music for Paris's *Balalaika* and Yves Mirande's *Saisissez-moi*, had a fast London flop with the Drury Lane production of the very indifferent *Rise and Shine* (44 performances) and, during a six-year stay in America, contributed rather less happily to the stage than to the screen. *Night of Love*, an operetta about operetta folk taken from the successful 1930 play *Tonight or Never*, lasted just one week on Broadway for the Shuberts, whilst an umpteenth attempt to write an operetta about Johann Strauss, decorated this time not with a pasticcio score but one by Stolz, had a life of just 12 performances.

Back in Vienna, after the Second World War, Stolz turned out further pieces for the stage, including a remake of Nestroy as *Drei von der Donau*, and for the screen (*Die Deutschmeister* etc), and in his eighties saw *Frühjahrsparade* transferred to the stage and several other earlier pieces remade for the modern Operette theatre as he continued a career as a conductor in concert and the recording studio. In the still remarkably active years up to his death at the age of 94, Stolz, who had throughout his life composed music in the lightest and most Wienerisch style, became the epitome of old-world Vienna and its waltzing music, not only to the world in general, but to Vienna itself where his monument, in the heart of Vienna, is today as prominent as that of that of Johann Strauss.

His music was used by Italian pasticcio writer Carlo Lombardo as the basis for a score illustrating Hennequin and Veber's Parisian farce *La Présidente* (*La Presidentessa*).

1901 **Studentenulke** (Theodor Haller) Marburg 21 March

1902 **Schön Lorchen** (A Moisson [ie Hans Kleindienst]) Stadttheater, Salzburg 3 March

1906 **Manöverliebe** (Karl Waldeck, Gustav Bondi) Stadttheater, Brünn 15 April

1908 **Die lustigen Weiber von Wien** (Julius Brammer, Alfred Grünwald) 1 act Wiener Colosseum 16 November

1909 **Die Commandeuse** (Egon Horn) 1 act Wiener Colosseum 1 September

1910 **Grand Hotel Excelsior** (Fritz Friedmann-Friedrich) Auenkeller-Theater, Erfurt 28 August

1910 **Das Glücksmädel** (Robert Bodanzky, Friedrich Thelen) Raimundtheater 28 October

1911 **Der Minenkönig** (Ernst Marischka, Gustav Beer) 1 act Apollotheater 3 October

1911 **Die eiserne Jungfrau** (Léon) Raimundtheater 11 November

1913 **Du liebes Wien** (aka *Komm, Mädel und tanze ...!*) (Otto Hein, Kurt Robitschek) 1 act Intimes Theater 24 January

1913 **60 Meilen in 60 Minuten** (Fritz Schönhof/Herbert Emmerson) 1 act Ronacher 1 September

1914 **Das Lumperl** (revised *Die eiserne Jungfrau*) Hoftheater, Stuttgart 31 July

1915 **Die Variété-diva** (revised *Du liebes Wien*) 1 act Ronacher 1 December

1916 **Die schöne Katharin** (Ludwig Hirschfeld, Hein) 1 act Ronacher 11 January

1916 **Pension Schraube** (Hein, Ernst Wengraf) Ronacher 27 February

1916 **Der Favorit** (Fritz Grünbaum, Wilhelm Sterk) Komische Oper, Berlin 7 April

1916 **Mädel, küsse mich!** (Hardt-Warden, Emil Schwarz) Lustspieltheater 29 April

1916 **Servus Mädel** (Sterk) 1 act Wintergarden, Budapest December

1916 **Die anständige Frau** (Hein) 1 act Budapester Orpheum 16 December

1917 **Die Bauernprinzessin** (Anton Aldermann, Fritz Lunzer) Volkstheater, Munich 3 March

1917 **Eine einzige Nacht** (Jacobson, Österreicher) 1 act Budapester Orpheum 15 March

1917 **Lang, lang ist's her** (Bruno Hardt-Warden) Lustspieltheater 28 March

1917 **Dolores** (Robitschek) 1 act Budapester Orpheum 1 September

1917 **Die Familie Rosenstein** (Hein, Wengraf) 1 act Budapester Orpheum 12 October

1918 **Die Hose des Tenors** (Willy Berg, Hein) 1 act Budapester Orpheum 1 January

1918 **Muschi** (aka *Die Kuckucksuhr*) (Fritz Löhner-Beda) Gartenbau 1 January

1918 **Brautersatz** (Gutbach) 1 act Gartenbau 1 March

1918 **Bloch und Co** (aka *Die schöne Maske*) (Wengraf, Hein) 1 act Budapester Orpheum 5 April

1918 **Leute von heute** (w Eysler, Arthur M Werau/Lunzer, Arthur Rebner) Bundestheater 22 June

1918 **Das Busserl-schloss** (Grünbaum) 1 act Ronacher 1 August

1918 **Muzikam** (Hein, Wengraf) 1 act Budapester Orpheum 2 September

1919 **Dagobert, wo warst du?** (Hein) 1 act Wintergarten, Budapest 19 January, Rolandbühne, Vienna, 8 August

1919 **Funserls Entdeckung** (Hein) 1 act Rolandbühne 1 November

1920 **Ein toller Tag** (Robitschek) 1 act Rolandbühne 1 January

1920 **Das Sperrsechserl** (Robert Blum, Grünwald) Komödienhaus 1 April

1920 **Das Mädel vom Variété** Hölle April

1920 **Das Haus des Schreckens** (Hein, Wengraf) 1 act Künstlerspiele Pan 1 May

1920 **Die fidele Pension** (Hein, Wengraf) 1 act Hölle May

1920 **Die schönste Frau** (Hein) 1 act Variété Reclame 1 October

1920 **Der Tanz ins Glück** (Bodanzky, Hardt-Warden) Raimundtheater 23 December

1921 **Kirikiri** (Hein, Fritz Löhner-Beda) 1 act Rolandbühne 1 January

1921 **Das Vorstadtmädel** (Hein, Adolf Klinger, Otto Taussig) 1 act Hölle February

1921 **Die Tanzgräfin** (Jacobson, Bodanzky) Wallner-Theater, Berlin 18 February

1921 **Eine fesche Landpartie** 1 act Rolandbühne 1 March

1921 **Eine tolle Nacht** (Hein) 1 act Hölle 1 October

1921 **Eine Sommernacht** (Bodanzky, Hardt-Warden) Johann Strauss-Theater 23 December

1922 **Die Liebe geht um!** (Bodanzky, Hardt-Warden) Raimundtheater 22 June

1923 **Mädi** (Alfred Grünwald, Leo Stein) Berliner Theater, Berlin 1 April

1923 **Der Hampelmann** (Gustav Beer, Fritz Lunzer) Komödienhaus 9 November

1924 **Ein Ballroman** (*Der Kavalier von zehn bis vier*) (Fritz Rotter, Österreicher/Karl Wallner) Apollotheater 29 February

1924 **Das Fräulein aus 1001 Nacht** (*Ein Rivieratraum*) (Karl Farkas, Hardt-Warden, Rotter) Robert Stolzbühne 6 October

1925 **Märchen im Schnee** (Robitschek, Morgan) 1 act Kabarett der Komiker 1 December

1926 **Der Mitternachtswalzer** (Willner, Österreicher) Wiener Bürgertheater 30 October

1927 **Eine einzige Nacht** (expanded 3-act version) (Leopold Jacobson, Österreicher) Carltheater 23 December

1928 **Prinzessin Ti-Ti-Pa** (Beer, Lunzer) Carltheater 15 May

1930 **Peppina** (Österreicher) Komische Oper, Berlin 22 December

1932 **Wenn die kleinen Veilchen blühen** (Hardt-Warden) Princess Theater, The Hague 1 April

1932 **Venus in Seide** (Grünwald, Ludwig Herzer) Stadttheater, Zurich 10 December

1933 **Zwei Herzen im Dreivierteltakt** (aka *Der verlorene Walzer*) (R Gilbert/Paul Knepler, Ignaz M Welleminsky) Stadttheater, Zurich 30 September; revised version Zentraltheater Dresden 26 December

1934 **Grüezi** (aka *Servus, Servus, Himmelblaue Träume*) (Robert Gilbert/'Georg Burkhard' ie Gilbert, Armin Robinson) Stadttheater, Zurich 3 November

1935 **Zum goldenen Halbmond** (Fritz Koselka) Deutsches Nationaltheater, Osnabrück 21 March

1936 **Rise and Shine** (aka *Darling You*) (w others/Gilbert ad Desmond Carter/Franz Arnold ad Harry Graham) Theatre Royal, Drury Lane, London 7 May

1936 **Gloria und der Clown** (Julius Horst, R Gilbert) Stadttheater, Aussig 31 December

1937 **Der süsseste Schwindel der Welt** (Weys) Scala Theater 21 December

1937 **Die Reise um die Erde in 80 Minuten** (R Gilbert, H Gilbert, Wiener Volksoper 22 December

1941 **Night of Love** (Rowland Leigh) Hudson Theater, New York 7 January

1944 **Mr Strauss Goes to Boston** (Robert B Sour/Leonard L Levinson) Century Theater, New York 6 September

1946 **Schicksal mit Musik** (Farkas) Apollotheater 24 November

1947 **Drei von der Donau** (Johann Nestroy ad Österreicher, R Gilbert) Wiener Stadttheater 24 September

1948 **Lied aus dem Vorstadt** (Dora Maria Brandt, Georg Fraser) Deutsches Volkstheater 19 April

1949 **Frühling im Prater** (Ernst Marischka) Wiener Stadttheater 22 December

1949 **Fest in Casablanca** (Günther Schwenn, Waldemar Frank) Städtische Bühnen, Nuremberg 27 March

1951 **Das Glücksrezept** (Hugo Wiener/Raoul Martinée, Wiener) Wiener Bürgertheater 1 May

1951 **Rainbow Square** (Guy Bolton, Harold Purcell) Stoll Theatre, London 21 September

1953 **Mädi** revised version (Stadttheater, Zurich)

1955 **Signorina** (Per Schwenzen, R Gilbert) Städtische Bühnen, Nuremberg-Fürth 23 April

1956 **Die kleine Schwindel in Paris** revised *Die süsseste Schwindel der Welt* (R Gilbert) Theater in der Josefstadt 25 December

1958 **Hallo! das ist die Liebe?** (revised *Der Tanz ins Glück* Wiener) Raimundtheater 4 January

1959 **Kitty und die Weltkonferenz** (aka *Die kleine und die grosse Welt*) (R Gilbert/Kurt Nachmann, Peter Preses) Theater in der Josefstadt 4 February

1960 **Joie de vivre** (Paul Dehn/Terence Rattigan) Queen's Theatre, London 14 July

1960 **Wiener Café** revised *Zum goldenen Halbmond* ad Willy Werner Gottig Städtische Bühnen, Dortmund 15 October

1962 **Trauminsel** revised *Signorina* Seebühne, Bregenz 21 July

1963 **Ein schöner Herbst** (Hans Weigel) Theater in der Josefstadt 5 June

1964 **Frühjahrsparade** (Marischka, H Wiener) Volksoper 25 March

1968 **Wohl dem, der lügt** (Weigel) Theater in der Josefstadt 4 June

1969 **Hochzeit am Bodensee** revised *Grüezi* Seebühne, Bregenz 23 July

Biographies: Holm, G: *Im Dreivierteltakt durch die Welt* (Ibis Verlag, Linz, 1948), Brümmel, W and van Booth, F: *Robert Stolz, Melodie eines Lebens* (Marion von Schröder Verlag, Hamburg, 1967), Herbrich, O: *Robert Stolz: König der Melodie* (Amalthea Verlag, Vienna, 1975), Stolz, R, Stolz, E ed Bakashian, A: *Servus Du* (Blanvalet Verlag, Munich, 1980) *The Barbed Wire Waltz* (1983)

STONE, Fred [Andrew] (b Denver, Colo, 19 August 1873; d Hollywood, 6 March 1959). Long-loved comic star of the American musical-comedy stage.

Topeka-raised Fred Stone first appeared on stage at the age of 11 and worked as a teenager at first in variety, then along with his brother, Edwin, as an acrobat, clown and general all-purpose lad with the Sells-Renfrew Circus before he took his first steps in the theatre, making an early appearance as Topsy in a touring production of *Uncle Tom's Cabin*. In 1894 Stone teamed up with another young comedian, David Montgomery, and the pair began working the variety theatres as a double act. During this time they crossed to London for an engagement at the Palace Theatre (1900).

They made their musical theatre débuts when they were engaged by Charles Frohman to appear as a pair of comical pirates in his production of *The Girl from Up There*, both at New York's Herald Square Theater (1901) and again in the London transfer of the show (Duke of York's Theatre, 1901), but they achieved their first memorable success when they were featured as the Scarecrow (Stone) and the Tin Man (Montgomery) in Fred Hamlin's spectacular production of *The Wizard of Oz* (1903).

The pair confirmed themselves as public favourites with their extravagant clowning in Charles Dillingham's production of *The Red Mill*. In the rôles of Con Kidder (Stone) and Kid Connor (Montgomery), two cocky, loud-mouthed, down-in-the-pocket Yankees, stranded in the land of windmills and tulips amongst a plotful of plots and a handful of girls, the two men indulged in a festival of fall-about, broadly cracking, full-of-disguises comedy which took time off only for some bright Victor Herbert songs of which their most successful number, 'The Streets of New York', almost out-Cohaned George M Cohan.

After three years milking the fun and profit from this great success all around America, the pair came back to Broadway with their 1909 touring piece *The Old Town* (1910). This time they were presented as a pair of circus performers in an elastic libretto which allowed them to ease in their versions of popular low-comedy routines and dances, and although neither the characters, the text nor the score came up to the *Red Mill*, the piece served the now-famous pair as a vehicle through two seasons on the road. They got the next two seasons and 232 performances at the Globe Theatre out of a version of the Cinderella tale called *The Lady of the Slipper*. Stone was Spooks, Montgomery was Punks and together they helped the little lady of the title (Elsie Janis) to get to the ball to the accompaniment of a Victor Herbert score which threw them no lasting songs but which served its purpose as an adjunct to the comedy and to a lavish Dillingham production.

Another fairytale subject, Aladdin, served as a basis for their 1914 vehicle, *Chin-Chin*, in which the pair, served up with their best vehicle since *The Red Mill*, cavorted through a story which hadn't too much to do with the traditional one as a pair of loopy coolies, Chin Hop Hi (Stone) and Chin Hop Lo (Montgomery), in various disguises and unchanging style, singing about 'Ragtime Temple Bells' and 'A Chinese Honeymoon'.

After Montgomery's death in 1917, Stone continued on alone in custom-built shows of the same kind which they had played together. Producer Dillingham and the writing team of *Chin-Chin* (Ivan Caryll, Anne Caldwell, R H Burnside) had confected the pair another of the semi-pantomime, semi-comedy spectacular shows which had been their speciality ever since *The Wizard of Oz*, and it was revised to allow Stone to star at the Globe (1917) in a vaguely *Babes in the Wood*sical piece as the good assassin *Jack o' Lantern*. The show turned out Stone's most successful single song hit, 'Wait Till the Cows Come Home', and gave him three further seasons of touring.

Tip Top (1920, Tip Top), in which he appeared as a little handyman, supported by the variety duo the Duncan Sisters, and *Stepping Stones* (1923, Peter Plug) which featured him in a similar character mixed up in a version of the *Little Red Riding Hood* tale, alongside his daughter Dorothy, both served for good seasons on Broadway and similar touring lives. *Criss-Cross* (1926, Christopher Cross), another piece built on the now very familiar model, also obliged if with a little less éclat than before, but illness obliged Stone to drop out of his next piece, *Three Cheers* (1928), before its opening on Broadway. He was back again in 1930 teamed with his daughter as Rip and Ripples van Winkle in *Ripples*, but this time the surely overripe formula went wrong. The show had only a short Broadway season before being turned out into the country.

For *Smiling Faces* (1932, Monument Spleen) the recipe was changed, and the old fantasy-comedy line exchanged for a straighter musical comedy which cast Stone – now nearly 60, and no longer as limberly acrobatic as before – as a curious old movie director. This piece proved even less successful than its predecessor, and Stone gave up the round which he had followed for 30 years. He appeared on the stage intermittently thereafter, but his outstanding decades as the most durably popular comedian of America's musical theatre were over.

Stone's wife, **Allene CRATER**, seen on Broadway as early as 1897 in a supporting rôle in E E Rice's *The Ballet Girl* (Violette) and then in Oscar Hammerstein's *War Bubbles* (1898, Niblette), appeared alongside him in a number of his shows (Bertha in *The Red Mill*, Romnyea in *The Lady of the Slipper*, Widow Twankey in *Chin-Chin*, Vilanessa in *Jack o' Lantern*, Mrs Hood in *Stepping Stones* etc), whilst his elder daughter **Dorothy STONE** (b Brooklyn, NY, 3 June 1905; d Montecito, Calif, 24 September 1974) made her first appearance on the stage, with above-the-title billing, opposite her father (and playing her mother's daughter) as Rougette Hood in *Stepping Stones* (1923). She paired with him a second time in *Criss-Cross* (Dolly Day), played with his replacement, Will Rogers, in *Three Cheers* (Princess Sylvia), and herself replaced Ruby Keeler in *Show Girl* (1929), before again teaming with Fred for *Ripples* and *Smiling Faces*. After his retirement she appeared in a number of shows outside New York, and on Broadway in the revue *As Thousands Cheer* (vice Marilyn Miller), in *Sea Legs* (1937, with her husband, Charles Collins) and as Tina in a

1945 revival of *The Red Mill* co-produced by her sister **Paula STONE**.

Paula, who had in earlier days also worked as a performer with her father and who appeared with Dennis King in his shortlived *She Had to Say Yes*, later also produced (w Mike Sloane) a revival of *Sweethearts* (1947), the 1951 *Top Banana* and the 1957 musical *Rumple*, a piece reminiscent of her father's old vehicles (Alvin Theater, 45 performances).

Autobiography: *Rolling Stone* (Whittlesey House, New York, 1945)

STONE, Peter [H] (b Los Angeles, 27 February 1930).

Playwright Stone had his first stage work produced in St Louis in 1958 and made his début in the musical theatre with the libretto to Wright and Forrest's musicalization of the Jean-Paul Sartre play *Kean*, before going on to make a mark in the film world with the screenplays for such movies as *Charade* (1963) and *Father Goose* (1964, Academy Award).

In a career embracing film, television and stage he adapted a number of other well-known works to the musical theatre. Elmer Rice's *Dream Girl* became *Skyscraper*, Clifford Odets's *The Flowering Peach* was made into *Two By Two* for a run of 343 Danny-Kaye-oed performances, whilst two shows adapted from screenplays also had long and international lives: *Some Like it Hot* under the title of *Sugar*, and *Woman of the Year*. He combined with Sherman Edwards on the final, highly successful version of Edwards's Declaration of Independence musical, *1776*, and 30 years after his first entrance onto Broadway he had a further stage success with the libretto to the Tony Award-winning musical show *The Will Rogers Follies*.

Stone also adapted *Sweet Charity* (1968) and *1776* (1972) for the screen, and his musical version of *Androcles and the Lion*, with a score by Richard Rodgers, was produced for television.

1961 **Kean** (Robert Wright, George Forrest) Broadway Theater 2 November
1965 **Skyscraper** (James van Heusen/Sammy Cahn) Lunt-Fontanne Theater 13 November
1969 **1776** (Sherman Edwards) 46th Street Theater 16 March
1970 **Two by Two** (Richard Rodgers/Martin Charnin) Imperial Theater 10 November
1972 **Sugar** (aka *Some Like it Hot*) (Jule Styne/Bob Merrill) Majestic Theater 9 April
1981 **Woman of the Year** (John Kander/Fred Ebb) Palace Theater 29 March
1983 **My One and Only** (Gershwin pasticcio/w Timothy S Mayer) St James Theater, 1 May
1991 **The Will Rogers Follies** (Cy Coleman/Betty Comden, Adolph Green) Palace Theater 1 May

STOP FLIRTING *see* FOR GOODNESS' SAKE

STOP THE WORLD – I WANT TO GET OFF
Musical in 2 acts by Anthony Newley and Leslie Bricusse. Queen's Theatre, London, 20 July 1961.

In 1961 impresario Bernard Delfont hired successful pop-singer and actor Anthony Newley for a summer season at the Brighton Hippodrome but, when he was subsequently offered the potentially more lucrative Max Bygraves for the same date, he approached Newley to stand down. Newley agreed to do so, and made it a condition that, in return, Delfont produce a small-scale musical which he had written for himself. The bargain was struck and, for an outlay of £2,000, Delfont staged *Stop the World – I Want to Get Off* at the Queen's Theatre.

Stop the World told the story of the life of Littlechap (Newley) in a revusical journey from his birth to his death via ambition, accomplishment, marriage, infidelity, fatherhood and disillusion. A kind of a biographical harlequinade with a strong flavour of the 1960s to it, the piece mixed brief, spiky sketches with broad ballads in which Newley, intermittently supported by one actress (Anna Quayle) playing his wife, Evie, and all his other incidental women, and very occasionally by a pair of indentical twins (Baker twins) as his daughters and a small group of choristers dressed as clowns, performed what was virtually a stand-up routine in the middle of a circus-ring.

The naïvety and the rather pretentious simplicity of the piece and its production were counterbalanced by the curious, appealing character that Newley created at its centre, and also by a score which produced an enduring group of successful hit singles. Newley sang strivingly of how 'I'm Gonna Build a Mountain' as he set off to turn his boss's most unpromising area office into a model of successful enterprise, launched emotionally into 'Just Once in a Lifetime', and looked back sadly and selfishly, demanding 'What Kind of Fool Am I? (who never fell in love)'. Each number fitted its place in the show, but each also became hit-parade and cabaret material par excellence. The star howled out a youthful 'I Wanna Be Rich', bewailed getting 'L.U.M.B.E.R.E.D' with a pregnant girlfriend-wife, and later gently wondered how a creep like him had been lucky enough to be paired with 'Someone Nice Like You', whilst Miss Quayle made a personal success with Evie's 'Typically English' (later repeated by her as each of Littlechap's multi-national concubines in her own national character).

The show proved a popular success and, aided by its reasonable break-figure and costs, ran through 16 months and 478 performances at the Queen's Theatre. Shortly before its end, Newley, Miss Quayle and the Bakers departed the cast to repeat their assignments in David Merrick's New York production and, again, *Stop the World* proved to have an undeniable appeal. Newley, and subsequently Joel Grey, headed the piece through 555 performances. In Australia, however, without Newley and with Jackie Warner and Evelyn Page featured, it had uneven fortunes, playing three months in Melbourne, but only five weeks in Sydney (Theatre Royal 13 May 1964).

The piece's manageable size, hit songs and vast leading rôle won it not only a good touring life but also numerous productions in regional theatres and further international showings in both English and in translation. Vocalist Sammy Davis jr, who particularly affectioned the show and the rôle, played it on a number of occasions including on a brief visit to Broadway (State Theater, 3 August 1978) and in an unreleased film, whilst in 1989 Newley made a short-lived return to London (Lyric Theatre, 21 August) with a piece which, although it remained his most successful show, proved to be too marked by its era to succeed for a second time.

A German version was produced in Berlin (ad Mischa Mleinek) with Harald Juhnke and Violetta Ferrari starred and the boast of 1,000 London performances attached to its advertising.

A 1966 Warner Brothers film which starred London take-over Tony Tanner and Millicent Martin was released, but was not a success.

USA: Shubert Theater 3 October 1962; Australia: Tivoli, Melbourne 7 February 1964; Germany: Der Komödie *Halt die Welt an – ich mochste aussteigen*; Film: Warner Bros 1966
Recordings: original cast (Decca), Broadway cast (AM), Broadway revival cast w Sammy Davis (Warner Bros), German cast (Philips), film soundtrack (Warner Bros) etc

THE STORKS Musical fantasy in 2 acts by Richard Carle and Guy F Steely. Lyrics by Steely. Music by Frederic Chapin. Dearborn Theater, Chicago, 18 May 1902.

Written and directed by rising comedian Richard Carle, in the style of the recently successful Chicago musicals of Gustave Luders and Frank Pixley, *The Storks* starred its author in the comic role of The Bungloo of Baktaria who is turned into a stork by a miffed magician (Henry Norman). The poundmaster's daughter, Violet (Harriet Standon) is made an owl for trying to help him turn back, but all eventually ends happily after some picturesque fantasy and merry songs. Steely's lyrics ran through such titles as 'Tootsie Wootsie', 'Flirty Little Gertie', 'The Cuckoo and the Pussy Cat' and 'The Terrible Puppy Dog', whilst Chapin's pleasantly ordinary score included a jolly patter song for the magician declaring 'I Did It!', some romantic parlour-ballady pieces for the magician's son (Edmund Stanley) and Violet ('Sorrow is Mine'), and a picnic ensemble which was faintly reminiscent of the era's biggest hit song, 'Tell Me, Pretty Maiden'.

The Storks was a great success in Chicago, running right through the summer months (traditionally, at this era, empty of touring companies) and beyond, and helped encourage the burgeoning Chicago theatre to continue to develop a highly successful musical tradition of its own. It also encouraged Carle, soon a major star, to base himself there artistically. *The Storks* did not bother to take in New York, which, given the mostly unappreciative attitude taken to Chicago shows there in later days, probably saved its producers some of the profits they made in 17 Chicago weeks and a road tour.

STOTHART, Herbert P (b Milwaukee, Wis, 11 September 1885; d Los Angeles, 1 February 1949). Musical director, arranger and composer for the stage and screen.

Stothart left a teaching career to try his luck as a composer and conductor of musical plays and he had his first contact with the musical theatre in Chicago – where he combined with Joe Howard on the songs for a 1912–13 Christmas production – and in St Louis – where his name appeared on a musical bill as co-composer of the local *The Manicure Shop*. However, he moved on to become a Broadway musical director and to supply songs for a decade of Broadway musicals, all but one mounted under the management of Arthur Hammerstein, whose own attempts at lyric writing he set to music when the producer's 1918 show *Somebody's Sweetheart* needed some hurried pre-town revamping. His first four works for the New York stage, including three in one year and all sponsored by Hammerstein, were composed alone, but although *Tickle Me*, with the help of the antics of popular comedian Frank

Tinney, lasted 207 performances on Broadway, they were indifferent pieces, notable in retrospect only for having introduced Oscar Hammerstein II to the Broadway stage for the first time.

Thereafter, Stothart worked musically in a series of partnerships, being teamed with Vincent Youmans, Rudolf Friml, Emmerich Kálmán and George Gershwin on further shows for Hammerstein, often in collaboration with the young Oscar Hammerstein and Otto Harbach as librettist(s) and/or lyricist(s). He contributed six numbers (though not the hits) to the score of the successful Vincent Youmans piece *Wildflower*, 'Hard-Boiled Herman', 'Why Shouldn't We?', 'Only a Kiss' and much of the incidental and concerted music to what has become generally thought of as Friml's *Rose Marie* (although Stothart had equal billing), to Gershwin's atypical *Song of the Flame*, and shared an all-in credit with Kalmar and Ruby on *Good Boy* with its boop-de-doop song 'I Wanna Be Loved By You'.

In 1930 Stothart joined MGM as a staff composer and conductor and, during the years that followed, he supplied songs for a long list of films including additional and/or replacement numbers for the screen versions of *I Married an Angel* (w Wright and Forrest), *New Moon*, *Rose Marie* and *Sweethearts* ('Summer Serenade'), supervised the musical devastation of *Zigeunerliebe* as *Rogue Song* for Lawrence Tibbett and scored his most particular successes with the title song for *Cuban Love Song* (w McHugh, Fields), also for Tibbett, and 'Sweetheart, Darling' (w Gus Kahn) in the film *Peg o' my Heart*. He remained at MGM, as musical director, until shortly before his death.

1912 **Frivolous Geraldine** (w Joe Howard/Theodore Stempfel) Olympic Theater, Chicago 22 December
1914 **The Manicure Shop** (w Howard/Stempfel) Suburban Garden, St Louis 29 June
1920 **Always You** (ex-*Joan of Ark-ansaw*) (Oscar Hammerstein II) Central Theater 5 January
1920 **Tickle Me** (Otto Harbach, Hammerstein, Frank Mandel) Selwyn Theater 17 August
1920 **Jimmie** (Harbach, Hammerstein, Mandel) Apollo Theater 17 November
1922 **Daffy Dill** (Hammerstein/Guy Bolton, Hammerstein) Apollo Theater 22 August
1923 **Wildflower** (w Vincent Youmans/Harbach, Hammerstein) Casino Theater 7 February
1923 **Mary Jane McKane** (w Youmans/William Cary Duncan, Hammerstein) New Imperial Theater 25 December
1924 **Marjorie** (w Sigmund Romberg, Stephen Jones, Philip Culkin/Clifford Grey, Fred Thompson) Shubert Theater 11 August
1924 **Rose Marie** (w Rudolf Friml/Harbach, Hammerstein) Imperial Theater 2 September
1925 **Song of the Flame** (w George Gershwin/Harbach, Hammerstein) 44th Street Theater 30 December
1927 **Golden Dawn** (w Emmerich Kálmán/Harbach, Hammerstein) Hammerstein Theater 30 November
1928 **Good Boy** (Kalmar, Ruby/Harbach, Hammerstein, Henry Meyers) Hammerstein Theater 5 September
1929 **Polly** (w Phil Charig/Irving Caesar/Guy Bolton, George Middleton ad Isobel Leighton) Lyric Theater 8 January

STRACHEY, Jack (b London, 25 September 1894; d London, 27 May 1972). Composer for a handful of the dancing musicals of the London 1920s.

An education at Marlborough and Oxford University led Jack Strachey to an early career as a pianist in seaside concert parties before he won his first London credits as the composer of revue material for such shows as *The Punch Bowl*, *Charlot's Revue* and *The Nine O'Clock Revue*. He entered the musical theatre in the early days of the craze for dance-and-comedy shows, sharing the musical credit on Laddie Cliff's early musicals *Dear Little Billie* and *Lady Luck* and then, along with H B Hedley, Stanley Lupino et al under the pretendedly American umbrella-name of 'Hal Brody', on the highly successful *So This is Love* and *Love Lies*.

He continued to write principally material for revue (*Shake Your Feet*, *The Bow Wows*, *Charlot's Masquerade*, *The Chelsea Follies*, *The Savoy Follies*, *Spread it Abroad*, *All Wave*, *Moonshine*, *Swinging the Gate*, *Apple Sauce*, *New Ambassadors Revue*, *Sky High*, *Sweet and Low*, *Flying Colours*, *The Boltons Revue*, *Pay the Piper* etc) and had his most notable single song hit in 1940 when 'A Nightingale Sang in Berkeley Square' (w Eric Maschwitz, Manning Sherwin) was featured in *New Faces*.

Two decades after his last West End dance-and-laughter musical, Strachey returned to the musical stage with a rather different type of score for the costume operetta *Belinda Fair* (131 performances) which, although not disgraced, did not find the same success as those light-footed shows of the 1920s.

1925 **Dear Little Billie** (w H B Hedley/Desmond Carter/Firth Shephard) Shaftesbury Theatre 25 August
1926 **Lady Letty** (w Ernest Longstaffe/Sydney Blow, Douglas Hoare) Empire Theatre, Glasgow 18 January
1927 **Lady Luck** (w Hedley/Carter/Shepard) Carlton Theatre 27 April
1928 **So This is Love** (w Hedley et al/Carter/Stanley Lupino, Arthur Rigby) Winter Garden Theatre 25 April
1929 **Love Lies** (w Hedley et al/Carter/Lupino, Rigby) Gaiety Theatre 20 March
1932 **The Compulsory Wife** (w Carter, Collie Knox/C Bailey Hick) tour
1949 **Belinda Fair** (Eric Maschwitz, Gilbert Lennox) Saville Theatre 25 March

STRAMPFER, Friedrich (b Grimma, 23 May 1827; d Graz, 8 April 1890). One of the most influential personalities of the Austrian stage in the infancy of the Operette.

The son of an actor, Strampfer began his theatrical career in Weimar, but when he – a protestant – wed the catholic prima donna of the theatre, they were forced out of town. He ran a touring theatre company for a number of years and, during the 1850s, moved his operations from Trieste to Temesvár to Hermannstadt, in the early 1860s to Laibach, and then back to Temesvár. Then, in May 1862, he took on the lease of Vienna's Theater an der Wien. There, at a period when the first stirrings of the new style of musical theatre were beginning, he put together a remarkable troupe of performers – a number of whom had worked with him in his previous theatres – and quickly made his theatre into one of the most important purveyors of musical plays in Vienna. In the wake of Karl Treumann's success with Offenbach's pieces, he made a deal with the French composer which got him a three-year contract for three one-acters and one full-length opéra-bouffe per year and thus creamed off much of the best of the famous composer's works from his principal rival's theatre. In 1863 he played Offenbach's *Der Brasilianer* and Suppé's *Flotte Bursche*, in 1864 *Eine Kunstreiterin* and *Ritter*

Eisenfrass (*Croquefer*), but his first major acquisition was *La Belle Hélène*. After having gone to see it in Paris, he cast the leading rôle in masterly fashion with the young, Berlin-based Marie Geistinger and produced *Die schöne Helena* in 1865 with enormous success for the theatre and the new star.

Coscoletto, *Die Schäfer*, *Blaubart*, *Der Zaubergeige* (1866), *Orpheus in der Unterwelt*, *Die Grossherzogin von Gérolstein* (1867), *Genovefa von Brabant* (1868) and *Périchole, die Strassensängerin* (1869) were amongst the Offenbach pieces which followed alongside such other imports as *Die Reise nach China* (1866), a version of the Cogniards' immense féerie *La Biche au bois* as *Prinzessin Hirschkuh* (1866), Grisar's *Les Douze Innocents* as *Ein dutzend Naturkind* (1866), Frédéric Barbier's *Les Oreilles de Midas*, Jonas's *Les Deux Arlequins* (1867) Hervé's *L'Oeil crevé* (1868) and Lecocq's *Fleur de thé* (1869) and home-made pieces including *Das Donauweibchen und der Ritter von Kahlenberg* (1866) and Genée's comic opera *Der schwarze Prinz*.

Strampfer left the Theater an der Wien in 1869, after seven years, and the following year turned the old Musikvereinsaal into a theatre as the Strampfertheater. He operated there with the same kind of material he had promoted at the Theater an der Wien, but luck seemed to have left him and he did no better when he moved on to try his hand at the Pest Deutsches Theater nor, later, when he took on the Komische Oper in Vienna with his sister Frau Völkl (1878). He returned to Pest (1881), then for a short period took on the management of his old rival establishment the Carltheater (16 September 1882). Under his direction there were produced there Jonas's *Javotte* (*Cinderella the Younger*), the English comic opera *Drei Schwarzmäntel*, Lecocq's *Kosiki*, and a revival of *Der Seekadett*.

He later tried his luck in America where he took to the boards as an actor and reciter and, finally, set up as a backwoods farmer. He returned to Europe in 1888 and tried to set up a theatre school in Graz, before he died, in poverty, two years later.

STRAUS, Oscar [Nathan] (b Vienna, 6 March 1870; d Bad Ischl, 11 January 1954). One of the most important composers for the 20th-century Viennese and Berlin stages.

The young Oscar Straus spread his interest and his composing and conducting activity through all areas of musical and theatrical life, but he soon centred himself on a career as a theatre conductor and worked in several houses in Berlin and the German provinces in the 1890s. In the earliest years of the 20th century, when he began to concentrate more on composing for the theatre than conducting in it, he turned out, amongst other pieces, such diverse works as the comic opera *Der schwarze Mann*, the pantomime *Pierrots Fastnacht* (w Leo Held, Secession Bühne, Berlin 13 Jan 1901) and a one-act opera, *Colombine*, produced at the Theater des Westens in 1904, some 500 Überbrettlgesänge and duets with such collaborators as Rudolf Volker and Paul von Schönthan ('Krabbel-Krabbel', 'Der Piccolo', 'Lied von der höhern Tochter', 'Wiener Corso' etc) and, most importantly, the Wagnerian burlesque *Die lustige Nibelungen*, his first step towards the mainstream world of Operette.

In the wake of the success of *Die lustige Witwe*, Straus

Plate 253.

was one of the first and most effective composers to follow Lehár into the new era of Viennese Operette, and the first to win a comparable triumph. The piece which won him that triumph was *Ein Walzertraum*. Produced at Vienna's Carltheater, where his *Die lustige Nibelungen* had previously been introduced to Vienna and his imaginative *Hugdietrichs Brautfahrt* had played 88 times the previous year, it turned out to be a huge success, running virtually uninterrupted for more than 450 performances in its first series, launching the duo 'Leise, ganz leise klingt's durch den Raum' as one of its composer's most popular ever melodies, and establishing itself there as one of the classic pieces of its time before setting off to play other areas of the world.

His next full-length Operette, an adaptation of G B Shaw's *Arms and the Man* as *Der tapfere Soldat* (1908), played only 60 performances at the Theater an der Wien, but it more than solidified Straus's international fame when, adapted in Stanislaus Stange's English-language version under the title *The Chocolate Soldier*, it proved more popular in America and Britain than in Europe, introducing the popular waltz song 'My Hero' into the canon of Operette standards and ultimately becoming the basis of a Hollywood film.

Straus's next efforts were less successful. An adaptation of Sardou's *La Marquise* (a plot perhaps rather too reminiscent of *Der Graf von Luxemburg*) as *Didi*, with Mizzi Zwerenz starred, failed at the Carltheater (26 performances), *Mein junger Herr*, with Girardi featured, lasted only some 30 nights at the Raimundtheater, *Die kleine Freundin*, also with Zwerenz top-billed, was gone in 55 performances, and if the richly written *Das Tal der Liebe* provoked considerable praise from musicians, the show itself did not turn out to be a success on the scale of his two earliest triumphs. All the last three pieces were tried in America, in the wake of the success of *The Chocolate Soldier* (*Boys Will Be Boys*, *My Little Friend*, *Das Tal der Liebe*) but none took.

Straus ventured two pieces on the London stage, one, *Eine vom Ballet* being played at first by a German touring company in German, then recast to be played in English, and neither time with success, the other (*Love and Laughter*, 65 performances) composed to a British libretto, with disappointing results, but he encountered some kind of success once more when, in wartime Vienna, he took up the kind of good-old-days libretto which inevitably succeeds at such times, and told the tale of the much theatrically maltreated ballet dancer Fanny Elssler in the Operette *Die himmelblaue Zeit*.

Major success, however, soon came once more with a second wartime Operette. *Rund um die Liebe* gave him an even longer first run than had been achieved by *Ein Walzertraum*, tenanting the Johann Strauss-Theater for a year and a half and 533 performances. The same wartime circumstances which boosted its run also lopped off its overseas prospects, and the show did not ever establish itself in the standard repertoire, but it remains nominally Straus's longest-running show in Vienna. At the Carltheater the Operette *Die schöne Unbekannte* played 103 performances prior to going on to foreign productions, but the Posse mit Gesang *Man steigt nach!* saw Straus abandon the regular Operette format which had been his since *Ein Walzertraum* with a piece which included a 2-act film parody (*Opfer der Sünde*) and 'sensationelle Naturaufnahme *Strasse in Bombay*', described as 'a glimpse at deepest India'. It ran for five weeks.

After the fair run of the more conventional *Liebeszauber* at the Bürgertheater (77 performances), Straus turned briefly to management and took on the running of the Établissement Ronacher where he produced a revival of his own *Die lustige Nibelungen* with Mizzi Freihardt as Brünnhilde and his newest piece, the Singspiel *Nachtfalter* (later played at the Theater an der Wien, to its 99th performance), as well as Ralph Benatzky's *Liebe im Schnee*, both with Mizzi Günther starred, before getting out of his producer's shoes and handing over the management to Egon Dorn.

Another new piece composed at this time, *Die Marmorbraut*, received its first performance in Budapest prior to being given in its original German, as Straus continued to turn out a regular supply of agreeable and often successful Operetten. Both *Eine Ballnacht* and *Dorfmusikanten* (166 performances), tuneful if now perhaps rather conventional, pleased Vienna and Berlin for good runs, but it was Berlin which mounted the composer's next major success, *Der letzte Walzer*, a mixture of power politics and sex illustrated by one of the composer's most outstanding musical scores. *Der letzte Walzer* gave Straus his first truly international showing, and his first truly international success since his two initial hits more than a decade earlier.

Straus subsequently based himself in Berlin and there he turned out several further scores for Fritzi Massary, the beloved star of *Der letzte Walzer* – *Die Perlen der Kleopatra*, *Die Königin*, *Teresina* – and one for Berlin's other major Operette star, Käthe Dorsch, as *Riquette*, in a continuing and regular list of mostly successful pieces. But from the late 1920s he led a peripatetic existence which was reflected in his credits. He composed the score for Sacha Guitry's successful *Mariette*, a vehicle for Yvonne Prin-temps which was first produced in Paris before being souped up with extra sentiment and songs for Berlin and Vienna productions, he turned an eye to the filmland fashion of the time with *Hochzeit in Hollywood* which played eight weeks at Vienna's Johann Strauss-Theater and was duly metamorphosed into a Hollywood film, and he had pieces produced in Magdeburg and in Prague, at the Theater an der Wien and, for the last time, in Berlin, with a final and highly successful vehicle for Fritzi Massary, an adaptation of a Louis Verneuil play entitled *Eine Frau, die weiss, was sie will* (which became an equally fine vehicle for Alice Delysia in the English language), whilst also supplying Hollywood with film music for such celluloid pieces as *One Night with You* (1932) alongside screenic versions of *Hochzeit in Hollywood* (*Married in Hollywood*), *Ein Walzertraum* (*The Smiling Lieutenant*) and *Der tapfere Soldat* (*The Chocolate Soldier*).

In 1935 he assembled and composed the best of the many Strauss pasticcio shows with which the stages of Europe had been invested even before the waltzing Johann's death, the nostalgic *Drei Walzer*, before he pointed his definitive departure from Germany and from Austria by taking out French nationality. It was in France that *Trois Valses* established itself as an enduring favourite, and in France, in his 70th year, that Straus composed the score for one of his last musical plays, *Mes amours*, a musical version of Edward Childs Carpenter's successful play *Bachelor Father*, but he returned, after the Second World War, to Austria where, in his eighties, he worked on revised versions of *Drei Walzer*, *Eine Frau* and *Ein Walzertraum* and added one more memorable credit to a list stretching back half a century, with the theme song for the film *La Ronde*.

As skilled and tuneful a writer of light theatre music as any of his contemporaries, Straus's quality is evidenced by the way his original music stands up alongside the Strauss melodies which comprise the rest of the *Drei Walzer* score, and his versatility by the way different countries have retained different of his works as favourites – *Ein Walzertraum* still goes best in Vienna, *The Chocolate Soldier* is still the favourite of the English-speaking world, whilst *Trois Valses* holds pride of place in France. Until the day when someone listens again to *Hugdietrichs Brautfahrt*, *Der letzte Walzer* or *Das Tal der Liebe*, or dips into the original *Mariette*.

1894 **Die Waise von Cordova** (Max Singer) 1 act Pressburg 1 December

1900 **Der schwarze Mann** (Rudolf Schanzer) 1 act Colberg 24 August, Secession Bühne, Berlin 28 December 1901

1904 **Die lustige Nibelungen** (Rideamus) Carltheater 12 November

1905 **Zur indischen Witwe** (Ignaz Schnitzer, Siegmund Schlesinger) Centraltheater, Berlin 30 September

1906 **Hugdietrichs Brautfahrt** (Rideamus) Carltheater 10 March

1906 **Mam'zell Courasch** (Erich Korn) 1 act Lustspieltheater 16 March

1907 **Ein Walzertraum** (Felix Dörmann, Leopold Jacobson) Carltheater 2 March

1907 **Der Frauenmörder** (Victor Léon) 1 act Danzers Orpheum 8 November

1908 **Der tapfere Soldat** (Rudolf Bernauer, Jacobson) Theater an der Wien 14 November

1909 **Little Mary** (Léon ad Auguste Germain, Robert Trébor) 1 act Comédie-Royale, Paris 9 January

1909 **Didi** (Léon) Carltheater 23 October

1909 **Der tapfere Kassian** (Arthur Schnitzler) 1 act Stadttheater, Leipzig 30 October

1909 **Venus in Grünen** (Rudolf Lothar) 1 act Stadttheater, Leipzig 30 October

1909 **Das Tal der Liebe** (Lothar) Kaiser-Jubiläums-Stadttheater (Volksoper) and Komische Oper, Berlin 23 December

1910 **Mein junger Herr** (Ferdinand Stollberg) Raimundtheater 23 December

1911 **Der andere Herr war nicht so** (Léon) 1 act Hölle 1 February

1911 **Die kleine Freundin** (Leo Stein, A M Willner) Carltheater 20 October

1912 **Eine vom Ballet** (Julius Brammer, Alfred Grünwald) London Coliseum 2 June

1913 **Love and Laughter** (Frederick Fenn, Arthur Wimperis) Lyric Theatre, London 3 September

1914 **Die himmelblaue Zeit** (Paul Wertheimer, Richard Batka) Volksoper 21 February

1914 **Rund um die Liebe** (Robert Bodanzky, Friedrich Thelen) Johann Strauss-Theater 9 November

1915 **Die schöne Unbekannte** (Jacobson, Leo Walther Stein) Carltheater 15 January

1915 **Man steigt nach** (Léon, Heinz Reichert) Carltheater 2 May

1916 **Liebeszauber** (Léon) Bürgertheater 28 January

1917 **Der Nachfalter** (Jacobson, Bodanzky) Wiener Stadttheater (Ronacher) 13 January

1917 **Die Marmorbraut** (*A márványmenyasszony*) (Oskar Blumenthal ad Jenő Heltai) Vigszinház, Budapest 19 April; as *Niobe* Lessing-Theater, Berlin 1 June

1918 **Eine Ballnacht** (Jacobson, Bodanzky) Johann Strauss-Theater 11 October

1919 **Die galante Markgräfin** revised *Das Tal der Liebe* (Dörmann) Volksoper 24 January

1919 **Dorfmusikanten** (Jacobson, Bodanzky) Theater an der Wien 29 November

1920 **Der letzte Walzer** (Brammer, Grünwald) Berliner Theater, Berlin 12 February

1921 **Das Nixchen** (Willner, Rudolf Österreicher) Wallner-Theater, Berlin 10 September

1923 **Die törichte Jungfrau** ('Florido' ie Heinz Saltenburg) Grosses Schauspielhaus, Berlin 13 January

1923 **Die Perlen der Kleopatra** (Brammer, Grünwald) Theater an der Wien 17 November

1924 **Der Tanz um der Liebe** (Jacobson, Saltenburg) Deutsches Künstlertheater, Berlin 25 September

1925 **Riquette** (Schanzer, Ernst Welisch) Deutsches Künstlertheater, Berlin 17 January

1925 **Teresina** (Schanzer, Welisch) Deutsches Künstlertheater, Berlin 11 September

1926 **Die Königin** (Ernst Marischka, Bruno Granichstädten) Deutsches Künstlertheater, Berlin 4 November

1928 **Mariette, ou comment on écrit l'histoire** (Sacha Guitry) Théâtre Édouard VII, Paris 1 October

1928 **Hochzeit in Hollywood** (Jacobson, Hardt-Warden) Johann Strauss-Theater 21 December

1929 **Herzdame** (Richard Kessler, Willi Steinberg) Centraltheater, Magdeburg 26 February

1929 **Der erste Beste** (Schanzer, Welisch) Neues Deutsches Theater, Prague 19 October

1931 **Der Bauerngeneral** (Brammer, Gustav Beer) Theater an der Wien 28 March

1932 **Eine Frau, die weiss, was sie will** (Grünwald) Metropoltheater, Berlin 1 September

1933 **Zwei lachende Augen** (Österreicher, Ludwig Hirschfeld) Theater an der Wien 22 December

1935 **Das Walzerparadies** (Grünwald) Volksoper 15 February

1935 **Drei Walzer** (Paul Knepler, Armin Robinson) Stadttheater, Zurich 5 October

1940 **Mes amours** (Leopold Marchand, Albert Willemetz) Théâtre Marigny, Paris 2 May

1948 **Die Musik kommt** (Knepler, Robinson) Stadttheater, Zurich 6 November

1950 **Ihr erster Walzer** (revised *Die Musik kommt* ad Robert Gilbert) Bayerische Staatsoper, Munich 31 March

1952 **Bozena** (Brammer, Grünwald) Theater am Gärtnerplatz, Munich 16 May

Biographies: Grün, B: *Prince of Vienna* (W H Allen, London, 1955), Mailer, F; *Weltbürger der Musik* (Österreichische Bundesverlag, Vienna, 1985)

STRAUSS, Johann [Baptist] (b Vienna, 25 October 1825; d Vienna, 3 June 1899). The Viennese 'Waltz King' of the middle years of the 19th century whose ventures into the musical theatre produced several major hits and much more frustration.

For the first 25 years of his career as a composer and conductor of the orchestral dance music which was the chief entertainment of his time, Johann Strauss had little to do with the theatre. He composed a set of dance variations on themes from Offenbach's *Orphée aux enfers* following the piece's production at the Vienna Carltheater in 1860 (Orpheus-Quadrille op 236) and in 1862 he married Henriette Chalupetzky, otherwise known as Jetty Treffz, a successful singer. It was probably she, who for the rest of her days organized much of her husband's life, who was foremost in encouraging him to write for the musical stage. His beginnings were halting. A *Die lustigen Weiber von Wien*, composed to a text by Josef Braun – the author of Suppé's popular *Flotte Bursche* – which was destined as a vehicle for Josefine Gallmeyer at the Theater an der Wien did not come to fruition. Not for the last time, Strauss failed to get to grips with a score. It was several years and several subjects later that the first Strauss Operette finally made it to the stage, and then only with a struggle. It was a fairytale piece, based on the Arabian Nights story of Ali Baba, and theatre-manager Maximilian Steiner's name on the librettist's side of the bill only veiled the fact that the text of the show had gone through all kinds of writers and rewriters in an effort to get the composer to complete his work. There is little doubt, however, that the main midwife to *Indigo und die vierzig Räuber* was not so much Steiner, nor indeed Jetty Treffz, but Richard Genée, the multi-talented resident author and composer at the Theater an der Wien.

Indigo had an indifferent reception and an indifferent career in Vienna, but its music went round the town, and the show was nevertheless picked up for productions in many of the other musical centres where Strauss's name was a potent one. When it ultimately reached France, the libretto was given a major rewrite rather than just an adaptation and Strauss wrote some additional music to fit the remodelled text. He liked *La Reine Indigo* (Théâtre de la Renaissance ad Victor Wilder, Adolphe Jaime 27 April 1875) better than *Indigo und die vierzig Räuber* and, thus, it was put back into German and reproduced in Vienna as *Königin Indigo* (ad Josef Braun, Theater an der Wien 9 October 1877). It was the first of many attempts, both in the composer's lifetime and after, to make a theatrical success out of an unremarkable libretto and a Strauss score which sounded better out of a show than in one.

Strauss persevered in his new career and two years later the Theater an der Wien produced his second Operette, *Carneval in Rom*. There was nothing wrong with the libretto of this one. And it was a text much more suited to the composer's style of writing. Braun had come up with a lively adaptation of Victorien Sardou's *Piccolino* – a piece which was successfully set just three years later in French by Guiraud – which mixed country scenes and Roman festive gaiety with both a genuine and a frisky love story. *Carneval in Rom*, again with the theatre's co-director and star, Marie Geistinger, in the lead rôle, did somewhat better than the muddly *Indigo* but it certainly didn't set the Danube alight.

It was the trusty Genée who supplied the text for the piece that did. Another French play, the comedy *Le Réveillon*, provided the starting-point for the libretto of *Die Fledermaus*, a piece which was all women, wine and frivolity. No longing love story such as that of the little Swiss maiden and her untrue painter in *Carneval in Rom*, just fickle, bright comedy from end to end to end. Here Strauss found himself in his element, and the result was the triumph that the world had been expecting from him since his first piece. *Die Fledermaus* went round the world, beginning the career which would ultimately (if slightly unfairly) lead it to be the one really great survivor of the 19th-century Viennese Operette stage, the familiar representative of its era to the later part of the 20th century.

Having hit the tone so rightly with *Die Fledermaus*, Genée and Strauss then missed it with their next collaboration. *Cagliostro in Wien* abandoned the French gaiety of the earlier piece for a lumpen tale of chicanery and romance which its Viennese carnival-time setting could not alleviate. Once again, the music was glued to the piece rather than going with it, and once again the results were indifferent. Strauss later cannibalized *Cagliostro in Wien*'s music and used his favourite bits, along with more of *Die Fledermaus*, to make up the score of his Paris pasticcio piece *La Tzigane* (lib: Wilder, Alfred Delacour, Théatre de la Renaissance 30 October 1877).

The Carltheater's Franz Jauner, anxious to challenge the Theater an der Wien with his own Strauss Operette, commissioned a libretto from Victor Wilder, the author of the French *Reine Indigo* which Strauss had so liked, with which to tempt the composer. If he succeeded in tempting, the piece he got – *Prinz Methusalem* – proved to be another indifferent one, although its composer's fame once again ensured that it got both a certain run and a certain, if not very happy, overseas life. *Prinz Methusalem* was, however, a triumph compared to Strauss's next stage piece, *Blindekuh*. This one played just 16 performances.

After some eight years in the musical theatre, Johann Strauss had composed six original Operetten and he had had just one genuine success. Compared with Offenbach – and people insisted on making the comparison – it was a feeble average. However, the next few years brought a singular improvement: between 1880 and 1885 the composer produced four more Operetten, a group of four which – after his monumental hit with *Die Fledermaus* – would comprise the principal valuable bulk of his stage opus. *Das Spitzentuch der Königin*, an apparently so-so tale of amorous high-jinks in period Spain, nevertheless worked reasonably well in the theatre, and Strauss's score

worked pretty well with it, but *Der lustige Krieg* was a different matter altogether. Genée and his co-writer 'F Zell', turned out another French-borrowed text which was fun from top to bottom – barely a pause for a lush, romantic moment, although some charming ones for a little pathetic sentiment – and Strauss pulled out some of his most magical melodies to fit this 'merry war' and its laughable characters. The piece was a stinging success, and Strauss was able once more to taste – after more than a half-dozen years of trying – the kind of success he had found with *Die Fledermaus*.

For *Eine Nacht in Venedig* Zell and Genée dug up another French text, and one with the composer's apparently preferred Italianate setting. If the result was not an Operette as thoroughly good as its predecessor, the show produced some charming numbers and, after some revisions on its way from its Berlin première to Vienna, it did well enough to establish itself as one of the favourite targets for Strauss-remakers of the future. It was the fourth of the set, however, which brought Strauss the biggest and most enduring triumph. Having split with Zell and Genée over what he regarded as the insufficient libretto of *Eine Nacht in Venedig*, Strauss turned instead to a novel by Hungary's respected Mór Jókai, which was adapted into a libretto by Hungarian-born librettist Ignaz Schnitzer, an author with whom he had had one of his false starts on another project several years previously.

Der Zigeunerbaron was a piece of a different colour altogether from anything the composer had yet tackled. Based on a thoroughly romantic Hungarian tale of gipsies and lost treasures and princesses, it had not a champagne-bubble in sight. It was a text seemingly suited to one of the more vigorous Hungarian composers than to the Viennese waltz king. Yet the composer whose talent had always seemed to be in the gay, in the comic, in the frivolous found an inspiration in the highly coloured sentimental melodrama of this tale, and produced a score, which was enough to override the wandering banalities of the story. *Der Zigeunerbaron*, with its rangy, powerful musical score gave the composer the third major hit of his career.

Strauss now became determined to compose further stage pieces in a musically more substantial manner. Whether it was because of that decision or not, because of his dissatisfaction with the musical voice of *Die Fledermaus* and *Der lustige Krieg* and his wish to write operatic music, in the ten years and six more musical plays that remained of his career Johann Strauss never had another success.

Five Operetten and his one attempt at an operatic piece, a show based on another Hungarian original, *Ritter Pásmán* (lib: Lajos Dóczi, Opernhaus, 1 January 1892), were all failures, even though *Fürstin Ninetta* was played 76 times at the Theater an der Wien, *Jabuka* 57 and *Waldmeister* 88, and all were given further productions. The libretti got the blame each time: yet Victor Léon and A M Willner, two of the 'culprits', were to become two of Vienna's finest musical stage writers who would each total many more hits than the composer. And Willner later took back the unloved libretto to the final flop, *Die Göttin der Vernunft*, remade it, presented it to Lehár and got no less a hit than *Der Graf von Luxemburg* from it. What was more likely as a reason for Strauss's failure was that text and music were out of sympathy with each other. Strauss – whose music was often, in any case, vaguely 'untheatrical' – did not have, or could not retain interest and/or enthusiasm in his texts. He considered, and so many people told him, that they had let him down so often.

If Strauss wrote no more for the Operette stage after the quick failure of *Die Göttin der Vernunft*, he did at least concur in the making of the first of what would later became an avalanche of pasticcio shows fabricated from his music. *Wiener Blut*, written to a libretto by Léon and Stein, its music arranged by the younger Adolf Müller, did not get to the stage, however, until a few months after the composer's death. On its production at the Carltheater on 25 October 1899 it did not prove popular, and it was soon put away, but it was later remounted at the Theater an der Wien, and this time it won a rather different reaction. The success of *Wiener Blut*, and the magic of the name of Strauss which survived whilst the *Blindekuh*s and *Simplicius*es were forgotten soon led to many, many more such paste-ups and a number of remakes. Julius Hopp arranged a Strauss score for a *Das Narrenhaus* (Centraltheater, Berlin 3 May 1906), Gabor Steiner mounted two remakes amongst his series of pasticcio works, *Gräfin Pepi* (Venedig in Wien, 5 July 1902) with music from *Blindekuh* and *Simplicius* arranged by Ernst Reiterer, and *Tausend und eine Nacht* (Venedig in Wien, 15 June 1906, arr Reiterer), yet another piece trying to make something out of the *Indigo* score, whilst the *Die Göttin der Vernunft* score was put to a new text by Ferdinand Stollberg under the title *Reiche Mädchen* (mus arr Reiterer, Raimundtheater 30 December 1909).

In 1928 Ralph Bentazky turned a bit of *Blindekuh* into the Nuns' Chorus as part of a Strauss pasticcio score to the Berlin spectacular *Casanova* (lib: Schanzer, Welisch, 1 September 1928) and in 1930 the Wiener Stadttheater, launched a *Dreimäderlhaus*-style biomusical of the composer. Willner, Reichert and Marischka's libretto to *Walzer aus Wien* (arr Julius Bittner, E W Korngold, Stadttheater, 30 October) had a Johann Strauss struggling against his father's wishes that he become a composer, wooing a local maiden, winning his musical spurs with the aid of a sexy countess, and indulging a little bedroom-farcery before heading on to fame and fortune. In its essentials their book crystallized the Johann Strauss myth that would be handed down through many a remake of this almost wholly fictional, conventional operettic tale. Others would have a go at the pasticcio, but by and large the tale stuck through a series of *Great Waltz*es, *Valses de Vienne* and a bevy of other such stage and screen soft-soap Strauss-stories with music.

Walzer aus Wien also pulled out the stopcock on a gusher of homogenized Strauss musicals. Another Korngoldized piece, *Das Lied der Liebe*, mounted at the Berlin Metropoltheater later the same year (23 December 1931) with Richard Tauber proved an expensive flop, but the Volksoper followed up with a *Freut euch das Lebens* (arr Grün/Wilhelm, Herz 22 December 1932), Nuremberg mounted an *Eine Nacht am Bosporus* (arr Ernst Schlieppe/ Gustav Heidrich, 30 August 1936), Hanover produced a *Ballnacht in Florenz* (Eugen Müri, Edwin Burmester, Mellni Theater 21 January 1939) which went on to be seen at Berlin's Theater des Volkes (24 January 1941), and the Neues Wiener Stadttheater hosted a Strauss Revue-Operette *An der schönen blauen Donau* (arr Tiller, 21 December 1939).

The Strausses' family life got another going over in a piece called *Die Straussbuben* which used music by both Johann Strauss and his brother Josef for its score (arr Stalla/Marischka, Weys Raimundtheater 20 October 1946), but it was another shared score which produced the best of all the Strauss remakes, Oscar Straus's three-eras tale, *Drei Walzer* (arr Oscar Straus/Paul Knepler, Armin Robinson Stadttheater, Zurich, 5 October 1935) which used Johann Strauss I music for its first act, Johann II for the second act and Straus's own for the third in a wholly winning combination.

Father Strauss, in fact, also supplied the entire score for another successful Operette, a biomusical on the actress Therese Krones who, as portrayed by Betty Fischer at the Raimundtheater in 1913 (21 November) was called *Die tolle Therese* (ad Otto Römisch/Krenn, Josef von Ludaffy). The piece ran for more than 150 nights. The same Römisch later arranged the score for a piece called *Lanner und Strauss* (1937) which gave theatre-goers a chance to see father Strauss depicted as something other than the spoil-sport of the *Walzer aus Wien* story.

Perhaps surprisingly, it was brother Josef, who never wrote a note for the musical stage, who proved to be a real musical-theatre winner years after his death. The ever-arranging Ernst Reiterer organized a pasticcio of his music as the score to an adaptation of the famous French play *Coquin de printemps* and, produced at Venedig in Wien under the title *Frühlingsluft* (lib: Lindau, Wilhelm, 9 May 1903), it became a serious hit. Josef was made to serve again for Steiner's 1905 *Frauenherz* (*Die kleine Milliardärin*) (Danzers Orpheum, Lindau 29 September), the Raimundtheater's *Das Schwalberl aus dem Wienerwald* (ad Fritz Sommer/E Berger, Louis Taufstein (31 March 1906) and the little *Das Teufelsmädel* (arr Siebert/J S Chifford, Apollotheater, 2 March 1908), before having his life done over again in the 1942 Singspiel *Walzerträume* (ad Bruno Uher/Tilde Binder, Ernst Friese).

From 1908 onwards Vienna had a theatre in the Favoritenstrasse which devoted itself to Operette and which was named after the composer of *Die Fledermaus*, *Der lustige Krieg* and *Der Zigeunerbaron*. The Johann Strauss-Theater opened with *Tausend und eine Nacht*, and played each of the composer's main works, as well as versions of *Eine Nacht in Venedig* and *Das Spitzentuch der Königin* during its some 25 years of existence. It later became first shabby and second-class and then the Scala Theater.

Portrayed on both stage and screen interminably in various versions of *Walzer aus Wien* by such performers as Hubert Marischka, Robert Halliday, Esmond Knight, André Baugé, Guy Robertson, Fernand Graavey and Edmund Schellhammer, Johann Strauss has become a cliché of the old-days-Vienna storytelling of the 20th century, his name attached to all sorts of dashing juvenile men with a waltz to play and a girl to win. The fact is that, even though he and his music can fairly be considered a major representative of the Viennese world of entertainment in the second part of the 19th century, it was in entertainment in general – the world of balls and concerts and so forth – that he shone brightest. His work for the theatre was neither the happiest nor the most successful part of his musical life, and he was never a comfortable man of the theatre. But he still left to posterity the scores of *Die Fledermaus*, *Der lustige Krieg* and *Der Zigeunerbaron* – a musical-theatre contribution greater than that produced by many nevertheless talented writers who spent the whole of their lives and all their efforts on a career in Operette.

1871 **Indigo und die vierzig Räuber** (Maximilian Steiner) Theater an der Wien 10 February

1873 **Der Carneval in Rom** (Josef Braun) Theater an der Wien 1 March

1874 **Die Fledermaus** (Carl Haffner, Richard Genée) Theater an der Wien 5 April

1875 **Cagliostro in Wien** (F Zell, Richard Genée) Theater an der Wien 27 February

1877 **Prinz Methusalem** (Wilder, Delacour ad Karl Treumann) Carltheater 3 January

1878 **Blindekuh** (Rudolf Kneisel) Theater an der Wien 18 December

1880 **Das Spitzentuch der Königin** (Bohrmann-Riegen, Richard Genée) Theater an der Wien 1 October

1881 **Der lustige Krieg** (Zell, Genée) Theater an der Wien 25 November

1883 **Eine Nacht in Venedig** (Zell, Genée) Friedrich-Wilhelm-städtisches Theater, Berlin 3 October

1885 **Der Zigeunerbaron** (Ignaz Schnitzer) Theater an der Wien 24 October

1887 **Simplicius** (Victor Léon) Theater an der Wien 17 December

1893 **Fürstin Ninetta** (Hugo Wittmann, Julius Bauer) Theater an der Wien 10 January

1894 **Jabuka** (*Das Apfelfest*) (M Kalbeck, Gustav Davis) Theater an der Wien 12 October

1895 **Der Waldmeister** (Gustav Davis) Theater an der Wien 4 December

1897 **Die Göttin der Vernunft** (A M Willner, Bernard Buchbinder) Theater an der Wien 13 March

Biographies: Kemp, P: *The Strauss Family* (Baton Press, Tunbridge Wells, 1985), Eisenberg L: *Johann Strauss: Ein Lebensbild* (Breitkopf & Härtel, Leipzig, 1894), Decsey, E.: *Johann Strauss: ein Wiener Buch* (Deutsche Verlag-Anstalt, Stuttgart, 1922), Loewy, S: *Johann Strauss, der Spielmann der blauen Donau* (Wiener Literarische Anstalt, Vienna, 1924), Jacob, H E: *Johann Strauss und das 19 Jahrhundert* (Querido Verlag, Amsterdam, 1937), Prawy, M: *Johann Strauss: Weltgeschichte in Walzertakt* (Veberreuter Vienna, 1975), Mailer, F.: *Das kleine Johann Strauss Buch* (Residenz Verlag, Salzburg, 1975), *Johann Strauss (Sohn): Leben und Werk in Briefe und Dokumenten* (Hans Schneider, Tutzing, 1983) etc

STREET SCENE Broadway opera in 2 acts by Elmer Rice taken from his play of the same name. Lyrics by Langston Hughes. Music by Kurt Weill. Adelphi Theater, New York, 9 January 1947.

Street Scene, advisedly described as a 'Broadway opera', was an attempt to straddle the apparent gap between the operatic form and the popular theatre in the same style that such pieces as *Porgy and Bess* had done, and as Gian-Carlo Menotti would do regularly with such pieces as *The Medium* and *The Telephone* later the same year, *The Consul* (1950), and other works.

Elmer Rice's 1929 play, a memorable Broadway success (Playhouse Theater, 10 January, 601 performances), was closely adapted by its author, retaining the many characters who make up the atmospheric population of the street where the adulterous Mrs Maurrant is murdered by her husband one hot afternoon. The lyrics were written by Langston Hughes, poet and the successful author of the play *Mulatto* (1935), and the score composed by Kurt Weill, recently successful on Broadway with *Lady in the*

Dark and *One Touch of Venus*. The natural yet stark drama of the text and the mostly colloquial poetry of the song-words were matched by the composer with music which was in the same mode – darkly and operatically dramatic in Mrs Maurrant's aria 'Somehow I Never Could Believe', warmly light-operatically chatty in such pieces as the young father to-be's 'When A Woman Has a Baby', and ranging from the lyrical-gossipy to the almost burlesque operatic in the chatter of the folk on the block ('Ain't it Awful the Heat', 'The Woman Up There', 'Get a Load of That'). The darker moments of the piece were contrasted with plenty of lighter ones – an ice-cream septet, the jitterbugging 'Moon-faced, starry-eyed' – and only in the lightly jazzy 'Wouldn't You Like to Be on Broadway?' does the musical mix falter a little as the 'Broadway' dominates the 'opera' rather than combining with it as elsewhere.

The piece was purposely aimed for the Broadway market rather than for an opera-house production. Weill insisted that opera houses were museums, and that living, popular theatre should be seen under commercial-theatre conditions. It also, of course, stood to make considerably more money under such conditions. After some tergiversation, the show was produced by the Playwrights Company and Dwight Deere Wiman. Polyna Stoska from New York's City Center Opera played Mrs Maurrant, operatic vocalist-turned-Hollywood-actress Ann Jeffreys and Joseph Sullivan, recently come to Broadway from opera, were the juveniles, and Metropolitan Opera basso Norman Cordon was the murderer in a cast where legitimate singing was foremost.

Street Scene had a disastrous out-of-town tryout, but its reception on Broadway was much more encouraging and for a while there was hope that a commercial-theatre audience might accept the sombrely ending local tragedy as a complement to the newly opened and definitely successful fantasies of *Brigadoon*. However, with the first fine flush of enthusiasm over, *Street Scene*'s audience began to dwindle. In spite of protests from the authors who had, after all, wanted a commercial production, Wiman began to advertise, but it was in vain and after 148 performances the show closed in failure.

Aided by the cast recording of its original production, *Street Scene* continued, after its closure, to have strong partisans and, aided by the strong promotion of Weill's works in the 1970's and 1980s, ultimately it found its way back to the stage in the very opera houses to which Weill had originally insisted it did not belong. The New York City Opera produced *Street Scene* in 1978 (State Theater, 27 October 1979) and, after its first British stage presentation in a single performance benefit in 1987, it was seen at both the Scottish Opera (1989) and the English National Opera (12 October 1989).

Germany: Düsseldorf 1955; UK: Palace Theatre 26 April 1987
Recordings: original cast (Columbia), studio casts (Decca, TER)

THE STREET SINGER Musical play in 3 acts by Frederick Lonsdale. Lyrics by Percy Greenbank. Music by Harold Fraser-Simson. Additional numbers by Ivy St Helier. Lyric Theatre, London, 27 June 1924.

A romantic costume piece from the pens of Freddy Lonsdale and his *Maid of the Mountains* partner Harold

Fraser-Simson, the old-fashioned *The Street Singer* was a splendid West End success in an era full of revue hits, Viennese musicals and of up-to-date dancing melodies which, before *The Street Singer* had ended its run, would find their most successful expression in the production of *No, No, Nanette*. Phyllis Dare, no longer the youngest of ingénues, purchased *The Street Singer* from the authors and arranged for Daniel Mayer to produce the show for her. It opened at Birmingham in February 1924 with Miss Dare starring as the Duchess of Versailles who anonymously buys her beloved Bonni's garret paintings on the one hand, and woos and is wooed by him (Arthur Pusey) disguised as a little street singer on the other. Sam Wilkinson headed the comedy as misogynistic François, tracked down to marriage by a merry little widow (Julie Hartley-Milburn).

The show played 16 weeks on the road before opening in London, with Harry Welchman now taking the romantic lead and A W Baskcomb the comedy one, and there it was greeted with critical bouquets for the well-written book – which had, after all, been provided by the author of some of the town's most popular light comedies – and for its merrily romantic Fraser-Simson score, of which Baskcomb's furious 'Ow I 'ate Women' and the love duet 'Just to Hold You in My Arms' were the most popular single pieces. These were topped off by three songs by Ivy St Helier which contrasted with the main music as effectively as Jimmy Tate's songs had done in *The Maid of the Mountains*, but a misguided attempt to pop George Gershwin's 'Virginia' into the score of this period French romance later in the run was quickly reversed.

The Street Singer played for ten months and 360 performances in London to such effect that Lee Shubert made an offer to Mayer to export the whole production and cast bodily to New York. But leading man Welchman was preparing one of his periodic ventures as producer/star of a fourth-rate light opera, and that and other factors sunk the proposal. *The Street Singer* headed, instead, for the British provinces and there over the next half-dozen years it kept up a fairly constant presence in the face of the first famous barrage of Broadway musicals, a barrage which had probably already helped shorten its town life. It also followed the bulk of the most successful shows from both sides of the Atlantic to Australia where Gladys Moncrieff was starred as Yvonne alongside Arthur Stigant (François), Noël Leyland (Bonni) and Claude Flemming (Armand). It moved out of Sydney after a good seven weeks to make way for Gershwin's *Primrose*, and made its way to Melbourne (Theatre Royal, 24 October 1925) where it played for two months as part of a satisfactory Australian life.

In America the show was not seen, only its title. The title *The Street Singer* had been previously used for a 1905 touring musical drama of the sentimental type, and it was now used again, in 1929, for a musical written by Edgar Smith, Graham John and composers Niclas Kempner and Sam Timberg (Shubert Theater, New York 17 September 1929) in which the heroine of the title (Queenie Smith) ended up at – guess where – the Folies-Bergère. The Busby Berkeley production emphasized dancing and glamour in a show which, like its English equivalent, was rather after its time but which nevertheless had a good run of 191 performances.

Australia: Her Majesty's Theatre, Sydney 4 July 1925

STREISAND, Barbra [STREISAND, Barbara Joa (b Brooklyn, NY, 24 April 1942). Protean woman of entertainment world whose early career included stage a film musicals.

First seen on the New York revue stage in the 1961 o Broadway *Another Evening with Harry Stoones* and on musical-comedy stage as the secretary, Miss Marmelste in the musical *I Can Get it for You Wholesale*, the soon-t be-celebrated recording star had a major Broadway playing the rôle of comedienne Fanny Brice in *Funny G* ('People', 'I'm the Greatest Star' etc). A London repe cut short by pregnancy, marked Miss Streisand's la musical-stage appearance.

She subsequently appeared on film in the starring rô of *Funny Girl* (1968, Academy Award), *Hello, Dolly!* (196 and *On a Clear Day You Can See Forever* (1970), followed a series of both comedy films (*Funny Lady* etc) and mo dramatic rôles (*A Star is Born*, *Yentl*) featuring some mus prior to turning her hand with notable success to fil directing.

Biographies: Jordan, R: *I'm the Greatest Star* (Putnam, New Yo 1975), Spada, J: *Barbra: The First Decade, the Films and Car of Barbra Streisand* (Citadel, Secaucus, NJ, 1974), Zec, D a Fowles, A: *Barbra* (St Martin's Press, New York, 1981), Co sidine, S: *Barbra Streisand* (Delacorte Press, New York, 198 Carrick, P: *Barbra Streisand* (Hale, London, 1991) etc

STREITMANN, Carl (b Vienna, 8 May 1858; Vienna, 29 October 1937). Strapping-voiced tenor sing and actor who had a memorable career in the music theatre.

Carl Streitmann studied medicine before turning to th stage and becoming an actor at Pressburg, at the Wien Stadttheater and in small musical rôles at the Carlthea (Affaroth in Suppé's *Der Teufel auf Erden*, de Mérignac *Der kleine Herzog* (1878), t/o Pomponnet in *La Fille Madame Angot* (1878), Josef, Casimir's butler in *Der gro Casimir* (1879), Scharbel in *La Marjolaine* (1879), t Briddidick in *Hundert Jungfrauen* (1879), Riflos in *D Gaskogner* (1881) etc). He had a further engagement Meiningen before ultimately being engaged as an ope singer in Prague at the age of 24.

The operatic episode did not last. In August 188 Streitmann made his début at the Theater an der Wie taking over as Caramello in *Eine Nacht in Venedig*. H quickly became the theatre's leading tenor, creating handful of new rôles in each of the next three seasor (Sándor Barinkay in *Der Zigeunerbaron*, Henri de Vill neuve in *Der Viceadmiral*, Prinz Julius in *Der Hofna* Armin in *Simplicius*), to add to star parts in the reprises the theatre's most successful pieces (Eisenstein from 188 when still in his twenties, Umberto in *Der lustige Krie* Symon in *Der Bettelstudent* etc). In 1888 he left the Theat an der Wien and moved once more to the Carltheater appear as Rudolf in Suppé's *Die Jagd nach dem Glück*, ar he played there as Baron Hellborn in *Ein Deutschmeiste* Oscar de Morande in *Colombine*, Nanki-Poo in *D Mikado*, the Brazilian in *Pariser Leben* and Azalea *Tulipatan* before moving on to make an extended visit America.

There, between 1889 and 1891 he was starred at th German-language Amberg Theater where he was seen Barinkay, Symon, Eisenstein, de Villeneuve, Caramell

Rudolf and Nanki-Poo as well as in *Mignon*, *Die sieben Schwaben* (Otmar), Julius Hopp's *Morilla*, Zamara's *Der Doppelgänger* et al. In 1891–2 he made a single appearance on the English-language stage when he took the rôle of Chevalier Franz von Bernheim in the highly successful Broadway production of Audran's *La Cigale et le fourmi*.

On returning to Vienna he once again joined the company at the Theater an der Wien and, apart from a period spent at the Carltheater between 1902 and 1905, he played there and at the same management's Raimundtheater for virtually all of the next 20 years, repeating his famous rôles and playing such other or new parts as Fodor in *Der Millionen-Onkel* (1892), Ferdinand in *Fürstin Ninetta* (1893), Bryk in a revival of *Carneval in Rom*, Armin in the revised *Simplicius*, Fürst Roderich in *Der Obersteiger* (1894), Mirko von Gradinaz in *Jabuka* (1894), Prinz Dietrich von der Pfalz in *Der Probekuss* (1894), Rodolfo in *Die Chansonette* (1895), Jim in *Der goldene Kamerad* (1895), Botho von Wendt in *Waldmeister* (1895), Gaston Catusse in *General Gogo* (1896), Graf Edward in *Der Wunderknabe* (1896), Emile Prévillier in Verő's *Der Löwenjäger* (1896), Egon in Leo Held's *Die Schwalben*, Erwin von Sleiwitz in *Die Blumen-Mary*, Capitaine Robert in *Die Göttin der Vernunft* (1897), Graf Julius Hardt in *Die Küchen-Comtesse* (1898), Dr Oskar von Pendl in *Der Dreibund* (1898), Otmar in a revival of *Die sieben Schwaben*, St Raymond in *Der Blondin von Namur* (1898), Georges Duménil in *Der Opernball*, Henri in *Katze und Maus* (1898), Anatole de Beaupersil in *Ihre Excellenz* (1899), Leonello in *Ein durchgeganges Mädel* (*A Runaway Girl*), Raleigh in *Die Strohwitwe* (1899), Prinz von Cypern in *Die Stiefmama* (1900), Hermann in a revival of *Leichte Kavallerie*, and Florestan in *Brigitte* (*Véronique*, 1900).

In his period at the Carltheater his new rôles included Milosch in *Der Rastelbinder* (1902), Meridan in *Der Glückliche* (1903), Manolle Ritschano in the revived *Apajune der Wassermann* (1903), Léonardo y Gomez in *Madame Sherry* (1903), Metello in *Der Mameluck* (1903), Amphytrion in *Der Göttergatte* (1904), Fred in *Der Schätzmeister* (1904) and Rafael Garrucci in *Der Polizeichef* (1905), before he returned to the Theater an der Wien, picking up as Jimmy Blackwell in *Vergeltsgott* and Nicola in *Der Rebell* (1905).

He succeeded for a long period to the rôle of Camille de Rosillon (*Die lustige Witwe*) and later to Louis Treumann's part of Fredy in *Die Dollarprinzessin*, introduced Adhemar Ricardon in *Der Mann mit den drei Frauen* (1908) and Major Alexius Spiridoff in *Der tapfere Soldat* (1908) and appeared at the Raimundtheater and/or Theater an der Wien as Eisenstein, Barinkay, Symon and Pluto (*Orphée aux enfers*) as well as playing repeats of his Camille and Fredy. In 1909, past the age of 50, he celebrated his 1,000th performance of the rôle of Barinkay at the Raimundtheater, and he continued there in *Die arme Lori*, *Jabuka* (Mirko), *Die schöne Galathee* (Pygmalion) and *Das süsse Mädel* (Hans), before moving to the Bürgertheater to take over the part of Hubertus von Murner in *Der Frauenfresser* from Fritz Werner at its 148th night.

He continued through the following years to play Barinkay, Camille de Rosillon and Eisenstein, took a turn at playing Schubert in *Das Dreimäderlhaus* (1916) during the long run of that piece, created *Bruder Leichtsinn* (1917, Graf Fabrice Dunoir) and *Die schöne Mama* (1921) at the Bürgertheater, took over in *Die Herzogin von Chicago* in

1928 and celebrated his 74th birthday by appearing as Eisenstein at the Raimundtheater. The Theater an der Wien marked his 80th birthday with a performance of *Die Fledermaus*, but this one was posthumous.

His sister **Rosa STREITMANN** (b Vienna, 21 February 1857; d Vienna, 30 July 1937) made her début in the theatre as a ballet dancer, but her small well-produced voice and attractive personality soon won her principal rôles and she went on to establish herself as one of the most important soubrette performers of her time. She made her début as a singing actress in 1876 as Rose Michon in a revival of *Schönröschen* (*La Jolie Parfumeuse*) at the Carltheater, then played in *Flotte Bursche* (Brand), *Leichte Kavallerie* (Dorothea), *Margot die reiche Bäckerin* (1877, the page Ravannes), as Spadi in *Prinz Methusalem*, Isabella in Suppé's *Der Teufel auf Erden*, Jeannette in *Jeanne, Jeannette et Jeanneton* and Hanne in Brandl's short comic opera *Der verfallene Mauer* (1878). Her status as 'principal girl' was confirmed when she was featured in Gallmeyer's rôle of Regina in a revival of *La Princesse de Trébizonde* (1878), as Caroline in *Niniche* (1878) and as the Herzogin von Parthenay in *Der kleine Herzog* (1878) and she appeared as Ninetta in *Der grosse Casimir*, as Aveline in *Marjolaine*, created the leading juvenile rôles of Fiametta in *Boccaccio* (1879) and René Dufaure in *Donna Juanita* (1880) and starred in Judic's rôle of Anna in *Papas Frau* before departing to join the opposition Theater an der Wien.

There, she was given some fine rôles (in mostly fine shows) including Louise in *Musketiere in Damenstift*, Else in *Der lustige Krieg*, Virginie in *Die Jungfrau von Belleville* (1881), Beatrix in *Tag und Nacht*, Anne Marie in *Ein süsses Kind* (1882), Ciboletta in the Viennese production of *Eine Nacht in Venedig* (1883), Sora in *Gasparone* (1884), the page, Jerome in *Der Marquis von Rivoli* (1884), Rosette in *Der Feldprediger* (1884), Clapotte in *Zwillinge* (1885), Rosita in *Gillette de Narbonne* and Regina in the 1885 revival of *La Princesse de Trébizonde* before disappearing from the Viennese playbills.

STRIKE UP THE BAND Musical play in 2 acts by Morrie Ryskind based on a libretto by George S Kaufman. Lyrics by Ira Gershwin. Music by George Gershwin. Times Square Theater, New York, 14 January 1930.

Strike Up the Band was a preliminary attempt by Kaufman and the Gershwins to get into the openly burlesque-political stride which they hit more accurately soon after in *Of Thee I Sing*. An anti-war, anti-politics, anti-business, anti-anyone-rich-or-in-power saga, it followed what happens when Switzerland and America go to war over import duties on cheese: everyone makes such a nice profit on both sides that, when it is all over, the Americans arrange another fun war against Russia. The score included lots of comic-bitter and eye-pecking pieces – including the martially mocking title-song – as well as the re-used and very contrasting 'The Man I Love', originally included in the out-of-town score of *Lady, Be Good!* and subsequently dance-band fodder around the world.

The show was produced at Long Branch, New Jersey, under the management of Edgar Selwyn on 27 August 1927, directed by R H Burnside, designed by Norman Bel Geddes with a company including Herbert Corthell (Fletcher), Vivian Hart (Joan), Roger Pryor (Jim), Lew Hearn (Colonel Holmes), Jimmie Savo (George Spelvin),

Edna May Oliver (Mrs Draper), and Max Hoffman jr leading the title-number as Timothy Harper. After two weeks it was abandoned.

Selwyn, however, did not give up on the show and in the 1929–30 season he remounted a rewritten version, still under the title of *Strike Up the Band*. Kaufman's libretto had had its bitterest bits sandpapered down with comedy by Morrie Ryskind, who had framed the whole piece as a dream, and it now pinpointed the rather more frivolous product of chocolate as the cause of war. Half a dozen numbers retained from the old score (including the title march, but not 'The Man I Love' which had by now become too well known) were supplemented by a baker's dozen of new ones by the brothers Gershwin, including 'I've Got a Crush on You' rescued from the flop *Treasure Girl*.

Chocolate manufacturer Horace J Fletcher (Dudley Clements) tries to persuade America to go to war with Switzerland to boost his business, and even offers to pay for the war as long as it is named after him. Jim Townsend (Jerry Goff) who is engaged to Joan Fletcher (Margaret Schilling) finally blackmails the businessman into turning pacifist, but America is already at war and, with the Swiss defeated, is happily preparing to have a caviar war against Russia as the curtain falls. Popular comedian Bobby Clark as 'The Unofficial Spokesman' (a faceless politician who prefigures Throttlebottom in *Of Thee I Sing*), singing gleefully about 'If I Were President' and a megastar of earlier days, Blanche Ring, were included in the cast in less plotworthy rôles, Doris Carson and Gordon Smith sang 'I've Got a Crush on You' and the principal juveniles did prettily with 'Soon', a number developed from a couple of lines in *Strike Up the Band* Mark 1, whilst Red Nichols's Band, including a line-up of jazz royalty from Benny Goodman and Gene Krupa to Glenn Miller, Jimmy Dorsey and Jack Teagarden, gave their all to the title number.

Strike Up the Band lasted 191 performances and then called it a day, but it is regularly recalled memory by those commentators who go mad for a mention of anything just a whiff political in their musical theatre. Its title-song remains the one original piece of the score in the current repertoire where it is now performed, like Gilbert's 'When Britain Really Ruled the Waves', with every ounce of its satiric intent washed away, as a genuine, patriotic march.

Recording: complete (Elektra-Nonsuch)

STRITCH, Elaine (b Detroit, Mich, 2 February 1925). Comico-musical belter who belted herself into an interesting rasp in later years.

Miss Stritch had her first Broadway assignments in the revue *Angel in the Wings* (1947, 'Civilization') and as the newspaperwoman, Melba, in the 1952 revival of *Pal Joey* before she took over the rôle of Mrs Sally Adams in the national tour of *Call Me Madam*. She returned to New York to play Peggy Porterfield in the 1954 revival of *On Your Toes*, played her first straight Broadway rôle in *Bus Stop* (1955), and created her first Broadway musical rôle as musical-comedy star-turned-film actress Maggie Harris in *Goldilocks* (1958).

She had a personal success when she was upped from second lead to star as part of the on-the-road rewriting of Noël Coward's *Sail Away* (1961), and she delivered 'Why Do the Wrong People Travel?' and 'Useless Useful Phrases' to Broadway and London in the character of cruise-hostess Mimi Paragon. She subsequently appeared in America as Anna Leonowens (*The King and I*), Ruth (*Wonderful Town*, City Center 1967) and Vera Charles and later Mame Dennis in *Mame*, in a schedule which mixed musical- and straight-theatre appearances, before creating her next major rôle as the loud, nailfile-tongued Joanne in *Company* (1970), performing 'The Ladies Who Lunch' in what were now becoming corncrake tones.

Ms Stritch settled for some time in London, appearing in the West End theatre in Neil Simon's *The Gingerbread Lady* and Tennessee Williams's *Small Craft Warnings* and top-billed with Donald Sinden in a successful British television series, *Two's Company*, but she introduced no further musical rôles to add to the three she had created in America, before returning there in 1985. She appeared as Hattie in the gala concert performance of *Follies* in New York in 1985, and was seen in Canada in 1993 as Parthy Ann in *Show Boat*.

STROUSE, Charles [Louis] (b New York, 7 June 1928). The most prolific musical stage composer of the modern age who hit it good and even very good on several occasions.

After a thorough schooling in classical music, Strouse began a song-writing collaboration with lyricist Lee Adams in 1950, a collaboration which led first to a series of published songs as well as special material for television and nightclub performers and, from 1954, for revue. From writing for a summer resort in the Adirondacks, they progressed to supplying their efforts to New York where they placed additional material in Ben Bagley's *The Littlest Revue* (1956) and *Shoestring '57*, in *The Ziegfeld Follies of 1956* and *Catch a Star* before joining a third young habitué of summer camp and the off-Broadway revue, Michael Stewart, to write a full-scale musical.

Bye Bye Birdie (1960), which kidded the newish rock-'n'-roll craze, won its authors a Tony Award, racked up a 607-performance Broadway run, and proved a sizeable and enduring international success ('Kids', 'Put on a Happy Face', 'A Lot of Livin' to Do'). Strouse and Adams followed up with the scores for seven further musicals over the next two decades or so. Of these, *Applause*, a musicalization of the film *All About Eve* and its source novel, which starred Lauren Bacall in a first-rate Broadway-Big-Momma rôle, proved the most generally successful (Tony Award), whilst New York also welcomed a musical version of the play *Golden Boy* with Sammy Davis jr featured as a black singing version of Clifford Odets's ill-fated Italian boxer.

All American (1962), with a libretto by Mel Brooks and a cast headed by Ray Bolger, and a musical version of the Superman comic strips (predating the widely publicized modern films of the same subject) both found some adherents but insufficient audiences, but an effort to bring a singing, dancing Queen Victoria to the London stage in *I And Albert* (something that the censor had forbidden Rodgers and Hammerstein to do) foundered nastily. Their later shows, including an attempt to mount a sequel to *Bye Bye Birdie*, were first-week failures.

In the meanwhile, however, Strouse had provided the music to the lyrics of Martin Charnin for what would turn out to be his most successful show and score to date, the musical version of the *Little Orphan Annie* comic-strip, *Annie* ('Tomorrow', 'You're Never Fully Dressed Without a Smile', 'Easy Street', 'Little Girls'). Niftily pitched at just the right level between ahhh! and yrrchh!, *Annie* proved to be one of the most internationally successful musical plays of its period, but in spite of a regular series of new shows (and several pieces, such as a musical about Bojangles Robinson and a new piece based on Anouilh's *Thieves' Carnival*, which were announced but which did not make it to the stage) in the years that followed, Strouse did not succeed in finding another success.

An affecting musical version of the Daniel Keyes novel *Charlie and Algernon*, originally mounted in Edmonton, Canada, failed to find appreciation either in Britain or America, a collaboration with Alan Jay Lerner on an awkwardly updated musical version of *Idiot's Delight* was a quick failure, whilst a 'cabaret musical' based on the life and the autobiography of New York mayor Ed Koch played 198 performances off-Broadway and 70 on. Another full-sized Broadway musical, *Rags*, lasted but four performances. There was no more success for a children's piece about a crocodile called *Lyle*, based on Bernard Waber's already musicalized *The House on 88th Street*, which faded away in disarray at London's Lyric, Hammersmith. The same house had earlier given an almost metropolitan home to a little Strouse operetta, *The Nightingale*, a version of the Hans Andersen *The Emperor's Nightingale*, previously produced at Buxton and in a juvenile theatre in New York.

Undeterred by the failure of *Bring Back Birdie*, Strouse also collaborated on a musequel to his other principal success, *Annie*, which was christened movie-style as *Annie 2*. It failed to reach Broadway at its first attempt and was later brought back, rewritten bootlessly to try again. In the meanwhile he had seen yet another piece with all the right names attached to it, a musical based on the *Thin Man* films, *Nick and Nora*, also go down as a quick flop.

In 1978 Strouse mounted a compilation show of his own material at off-Broadway's Ballroom-off-Broadway under the title of *By Strouse* (1 February) which played for a run of 156 performances.

1960 **Bye Bye Birdie** (Lee Adams/Michael Stewart) Martin Beck Theater 14 April
1962 **All American** (Adams/Mel Brooks) Winter Garden Theater 19 March
1964 **Golden Boy** (Adams/Clifford Odets, William Gibson) Majestic Theater 20 October
1966 **It's a Bird ... It's a Plane ... It's Superman** (Adams/David Newman, Robert Benton) Alvin Theater 29 March
1970 **Applause** (Adams/Adolf Green, Betty Comden) Palace Theater 30 March
1971 **Six** Cricket Playhouse 12 April
1972 **I And Albert** (Adams/Jay Presson Allen) Piccadilly Theatre, London 6 November
1977 **Annie** (Martin Charnin/Thomas Meehan) Alvin Theater 21 April
1978 **Flowers for Algernon** (David Rogers) Citadel Theater, Edmonton, Canada 12 December; Queen's Theatre, London 14 June 1979
1978 **A Broadway Musical** (Adams/William F Brown) Lunt-Fontanne Theater 21 December
1981 **Bring Back Birdie** (Adams/Stewart) Martin Beck Theater 5 March
1982 **The Nightingale** First All Childrens Theater 25 April

1983 **Dance a Little Closer** (Alan Jay Lerner) Minskoff Theater 11 May
1985 **Mayor** (Warren Leigh) Top of the Gate 13 May
1986 **Rags** (Stephen Schwartz/Joseph Stein) Mark Hellinger Theater 21 August
1988 **Lyle** (Bernard Waber ad) Lyric Theatre, Hammersmith, London 3 December
1989 **Charlotte's Web** Wilmington, Del 17 February
1990 **Annie 2** (Charnin/Meehan) Kennedy Center, Washington 4 January
1991 **Nick and Nora** (Richard Maltby jr/Arthur Laurents) Marquis Theater 8 December
1992 **Annie Warbucks** (revised *Annie 2*) Marriott's Lincolnshire Theater, Chicago 6 February

STUART, Leslie [BARRETT, Thomas Augustine] (aka Lester Thomas) (b Southport, 15 March 1864; d Richmond, Surrey, 27 March 1928). British songwriter who made himself a musical comedy mark as the composer of *Florodora*.

Leslie Stuart spent some of his earliest professional musical moments as a pianist at Manchester's Ship Inn and then, from the age of 14, as church organist for seven years at St John's Roman Catholic Cathedral in Salford and a further seven at the Church of the Holy Name in Manchester. At the same time, he gradually became known as a writer of popular songs, ranging from such heroic stuff as 'The Bandolero' for the popular baritone who called himself Signor Foli, to a veritable flood of the then-popular coon songs, many of which were introduced by Eugene Stratton, the supreme blackface singer of the time. The most successful and enduring of these was 'Lily of Laguna', but Stuart had notable successes with 'Little Dolly Daydream', 'Sweetheart May', 'Is Your Mamie Always with You?' and with a song fabricated from a march which he had written to celebrate the opening of the Manchester Ship Canal and later re-lyricked under the title 'Soldiers of the Queen'. Stuart also became for a while a concert impresario in the Manchester area, presenting Paderewski in his first British appearances and opera's Fanny Moody in concert.

Stuart's earliest theatrical writing was done for the Manchester theatre, where he provided songs and incidental music in particular for the local pantomimes which boasted some of the biggest British names in their bills. In the 1896 Liverpool *Aladdin* he supplied Lottie Collins with 'The Girl on the Rand-dan-dan', 'I Went with Papa to Paris' and 'Is Your Mamie Always with You?'. Stuart also had individual numbers interpolated in a number of West End and touring musicals in the late 1890s, beginning with the highly successful 'Lousiana Lou', which had already been published by Francis, Day and Hunter (who would remain Stuart's publishers throughout his career) and performed on the music halls before being picked up by Ellaline Terriss and inserted into the original production of *The Shop Girl* at the Gaiety Theatre alongside Stuart's 'The Little Mademoiselle'.

When the *Trilby* craze hit London during the run of George Edwardes's *An Artist's Model* (1895, 'The Military Model'), Stuart wrote (though the lyrics are credited to his brother, Lester Barrett) and composed 'Trilby Will Be True' for Maurice Farkoa to perform at Daly's Theatre, and he subsequently had songs used in *Baron Golosh*, *The Circus Girl* (1896, 'She May Not Be That Sort of a Girl'

1385

Plate 254. **Leslie Stuart**.

for Louis Bradfield), the London version of the American musical *A Day in Paris* (1897, 'The Goblin and the Fay'), Kiefert's *The Ballet Girl* (1897, 'She's an English Girl', 'I Never Saw a Girl Like That', 'De Baby am Crying, Mommer Come') and *The Yashmak* (1897, 'The Silly Old Man in the Moon'), but it was not until 1899 that he completed his first full musical-comedy score.

Florodora, written in collaboration with London's most fashionable librettist, Owen Hall, and produced by neophyte producer Tom Davis at the Lyric Theatre in Shaftesbury Avenue, was a musical-comedy sensation. Its famous double sextet, 'Tell Me Pretty Maiden', became the most successful show tune of its time and the show itself, for which Stuart had provided a score ranging from the most traditional and beautiful of waltzes ('The Silver Star of Love', 'The Fellow Who Might') to the more quirkily rhythmic and long-lined numbers which were his trademark, was a worldwide success, earning its composer an international theatrical reputation to add to that already secured by his songs.

Davis followed *Florodora* at the Lyric Theatre with a second Stuart/Hall musical *The Silver Slipper*. If its musical content seemed to be moulded rather closely on the *Florodora* score, it nevertheless fulfilled the 'more of the same' requirements opened by the extravagant success of the earlier show and *The Silver Slipper* had good runs in the West End and on Broadway, as well as being played in Hungarian in Budapest and in German in Berlin, where it played at the Neues Königliches Opernhaus in repertoire with no less pieces than *Der Zigeunerbaron* and *Der Bettelstudent*. The composer had further show-successes in London, New York and on the national and international touring circuits with *The School Girl* (1903, 'My Little Canoe'), *The Belle of Mayfair* (1906, 'Come to St George's', 'In Montezuma') and *Havana* (1908, 'Hello, People, Hello') and George Edwardes, always on his toes to keep one step ahead of public taste, decided that Stuart was the

man to replace the well-loved and well-used Ivan Caryll/Lionel Monckton combination at the Gaiety Theatre.

However, Stuart did not turn out a Gaiety musical to follow *Havana*, but instead wrote the score for *Captain Kidd*, a Seymour Hicks piece which the scavenging actor had adapted from the American farce *The Dictator*. His undistinguished songs added nothing to a weak piece which lasted but a month on the stage, in spite of the drawing power of Hicks and his wife, Ellaline Terriss, and Stuart was faced with his first and only flop, a flop so complete that his publishers did not even print up the score.

1911 saw his return to the Gaiety with the reasonably successful *Peggy*, and in the same year he finally composed his one and only Broadway score – something which had been announced by American managers on a number of occasions since *Florodora* had become the hottest hit on the New York stage – with a useful if undistinguished vehicle for Elsie Janis as *The Slim Princess*, an anorexic lass who goes to America for a husband because slim girls are fashionable there. The score to *The Slim Princess* was, in true Broadway fashion, dotted with non-Stuart interpolations, but by this stage the composer was no longer in a position to object to a practice which he had fought energetically and sometimes legally throughout the ten years of his time at the theatrical top, ever since he had discovered Paul Rubens's songs being shovelled into his very first show, *Florodora*, at an early stage of preparation.

Sometimes, when he had the weight of his *Florodora* fame behind him, Stuart had succeeded in stopping this time-dishonoured practice – a practice which was not simply dictated by artistic motives but by financial ones, as publishers and wealthy second-rate songwriters would pay for exposure for their songs, especially in a show by a 'hot' composer like Stuart. Similarly, he had succeeded from time to time in parts of his fight in Britain and in America against music piracy and on behalf of firmer national and international copyright laws. But by 1911 his personal and, most particularly, his financial life were in the doldrums and later the bankruptcy courts, the days of his style of music were rapidly coming to an end under the influence of modern dance rhythms and, at the age of 45, his career in the musical theatre had effectively come to an end.

Stuart interpolated a number into Broadway's *The Queen of the Movies* (*Die Kino-Königin*) and composed some unexceptional songs for a 1915 revival of *Florodora*, but his last contributions seem to have been, against all his expressed principles, songs for the provincial management of Mark Blow to interpolate into their tour of *Toto* (1919), and for the short-lived *Jenny* (1922) at the Empire Theatre. In his later years he continued to write, and although he would not show his final work, *Nina*, to anyone, both it and *The Girl from Nysa* were mooted for production both before and after his death without ever coming to the stage. When his gambling debts outweighed his royalties from the still-lively *Florodora*, Stuart appeared in variety performing his most famous songs at the piano.

Stuart's stage works fell somewhere between the very light song-based shows of the Gaiety Theatre and the more substantial fare played at Daly's, but although the concerted music – in which he was aided by the West End's master journeyman musician, Carl Kiefert – was highly effective, the greatest success of all his shows was in their individual songs, many of which became widely and enduringly popular.

His daughter May Leslie Stuart appeared on the musical stage as Beauty in *Pinkie and the Fairies* (1909) and as a last-minute replacement for Ada Reeve as Lady Holyrood in the 1915 *Florodora*.

1899 **Florodora** (Ernest Boyd-Jones, Paul Rubens/Owen Hall) Lyric Theatre 11 November

1901 **The Silver Slipper** (W H Risque/Hall) Lyric Theatre 1 June

1903 **The School Girl** (Charles H Taylor/Henry Hamilton, Paul Potter) Prince of Wales Theatre 9 May

1906 **The Belle of Mayfair** (Basil Hood, C H E Brookfield) Vaudeville Theatre 11 April

1908 **Havana** (Adrian Ross/Graham Hill, George Grossmith jr) Gaiety Theatre 25 April

1910 **Captain Kidd** (Ross/Seymour Hicks) Wyndham's Theatre 12 January

1911 **The Slim Princess** (Henry Blossom) Globe Theater, New York 2 January

1911 **Peggy** (C H Bovill/Grossmith) Gaiety Theatre 4 March

A STUBBORN CINDERELLA Musical comedy in 3 acts by Frank R Adams and Will M Hough. Music by Joseph E Howard. Princess Theater, Chicago, 1 June 1908; Broadway Theater, New York, 25 January 1909.

Adams, Hough and Howard, the most successful purveyors of musical comedy to the turn-of-the-century Chicago stage, carried on their run of unbroken success with this curiously straggly piece in which an aristocratic Scots lady (Sallie Fisher) gets together with a sculptor called Mac (John Barrymore) who tells her the tale of Cinderella whilst their train is landlocked by a slip. Howard and his clever lyricists provided several pretty and imaginative songs including the waltz finale 'When You First Kiss the Last Girl You Love', an Anna Held-ish piece declaring 'Don't Be Cross with Me, (for I'm having lots of trouble with my smile)', another in which the hero addressed the heavens with 'Don't Be Anybody's Moon But Mine', booking the moon to shine on his smooching, and a comical 'What's the Use (of sleeping, when there's things to do instead)'. There were several incidental ballets, scenes set in California and including an orange fête, and a lot of pre-production buzz about the new young leading man, and the Princess Theatre company kept the piece on stage for more than 300 performances in their home town before producer Mort Singer took them east. *A Stubborn Cinderella* ran 88 performances on Broadway, the most New York would ever allow one of the 'foreign' musicals from the Chicago team, but it toured happily enough thereafter to compensate for Broadway's disdain of its charms and of the young John Barrymore.

STUBEL, Lori (b Vienna; d Vienna, 21 June 1922). Well-travelled Viennese soubrette who matured into a good character lady.

The career of Lori Stubel is a little hard to decipher in retrospect, principally due to the fact that she had a sister, **Jenny STUBEL** (b Vienna; d Kierling, 19 August 1893) who led a parallel career in often similar rôles, and who had a similar penchant for travel. It seems, however, that it was Lori who worked as a dancer in the corps de ballet of the Hofoper, then from 1867 as a dancer and singer at the Harmonietheater, and subsequently became a member of the company at the Carltheater where she won good soubrette rôles, taking over from Gallmeyer as Regina in *Die Prinzessin von Trébizonde* (1872), playing Clairette in *Cannebas* and Prinz Leo in *Confusius IX* (1872), Eglantine in *Hundert Jungfrauen* (1873), Cascadetto in *Der Seufzerbrucke* (1873) and Annette in *La Jolie Parfumeuse* (1874). She then, apparently, began her travels, playing in Germany (Countess Cameroni in *La Petite Mademoiselle*) and with her own company throughout Italy (Florence, Rome, Genoa, Naples, Milan, Venice, Trieste), returning (it seems) to Vienna to take over the title-rôle in *Prinz Methusalem* at the Carltheater, and in 1882 turning up in London (this was definitely her) where she was cast alongside Constance Loseby, Henry Walsham and Allen Thomas in what was claimed to be 'her original rôle' as Else in *The Merry War* (it wasn't). Her comedy proved a little near the knuckle for the Alhambra audience, and when they shouted her 'vulgar' antics down she thumbed her nose at them. She vanished 'ill' from the Alhambra cast list shortly afterwards and a few weeks later the theatre burned down. 'Frln Stubel' next turned up in 1884 playing Possen at the Theater in der Josefstadt, but she was soon on the move again, and in 1885 she made her first appearance in America playing the title-rôle in *Boccaccio*, Pauline in Brandl's Posse *Der Walzerkönig* and Fanchette Michel in *Der Seekadett*. All pieces from Jenny's repertoire at the Carltheater.

Eventually both the soubretting and the travelling came to an end, and in 1894 Lori Stubel (the playbills had, at last, started giving full names – unnecessarily in this case, for Jenny was now dead) joined the Theater an der Wien company as a character lady. Over the next four years she appeared in *Der Obersteiger* (1894, Elfriede, announced as her house début), *Husarenblut* (1894, Frau Kendler), *Kneisl & Co* (1894, Frau Stowasser), *Der Probekuss* (1894, Die Obersthofmeisterin), *Die Chansonette* (1895, Miss Box), *Der Bettelstudent* (t/o Palmatica), *Die Karlsschülerin* (1895, Generalin von Papperitz), *Waldmeister* (1895, t/o Malvine), *General Gogo* (1896, Miss Kopkins), *Der Löwenjäger* (1896, Dorothée), *Die Blumen-Mary* (1897, Bessie Thomson), *Die Schwalben* (1897, Emitschka), *Die Küchen-Comtesse* (1898, Miss Nelly), *Der Dreibund* (1898, Sabine von Drachenfels) and *Der Opernball* (1898, Madame Beaubuisson), before retiring from the stage.

Jenny Stubel had the shorter but seemingly better-quality career of the two sisters. It is probably she who is the 'Frln Stubel' who appeared in what were simply chorus tights-rôles as Fernand in *Die Wilderer*, Sigefroi in *Heloïse und Abälard* (1873) and as a Japanese chorine, Cili, in *Die Japanesin* (1874) before winning promotion to the title-rôle of Wilhelmine in *Die Perle der Wascherinnen* (1875). It is undoubtedly she who was – several years before her elder sister – playing at New York's Thalia Theater in 1881–2 as Haiderose (Serpolette) in *Die Glocken von Corneville*, Bettina in *La Mascotte*, Natalitza in *Apajune der Wassermann*, Reger in *Das verwunschene Schloss*, *Die Fledermaus*, Fanny Rehborstl in *Der Chevalier de San Marco* and the vocally demanding Violetta in *Der lustige Krieg*. Jenny Stubel then went home to the Carltheater as principal soubrette and between 1882 and 1883 she played title-rôles in *Javotte* and *Kosiki*, Girola in *Drei Schwarzmantel*, Boccaccio and Fanchette Michel in *Der Seekadett* under the short management of Friedrich Strampfer, before she went off with her boyfriend, tenor Karl Drucker, to Germany. She was engaged as lead soubrette at the Walhalla-Theater for a couple of seasons, then appeared back at the Carltheater to play Danilowna in *Der Jagdjunker* and Eurydice in *Orphée aux enfers* (1886), before returning to take up a post at the head of the female company at the Friedrich-Wilhelmstädtisches Theater. There she played Berlin's *Madame Favart*, Arsena in *Der Zigeunerbaron* and other leading rôles until 1892, her final illness and death the following year.

Just to make things even more indecipherable, there was a third singing Stubel sister, Ludmilla or Emilie (known as Milly), who also went on the operettic stage. She made a career apparently entirely in Berlin (unless, that is, she was the 'Frln Stubel' with the legs at the Theater an der Wien in the early 1870s) but she outdid her sisters thoroughly in newsworthiness. She was the companion of 'Johann Orth', otherwise Johann Nepomuk Salvator the abdicated Archduke of Austria and Prince of Tuscany, when he set out from Hamburg on a post-abdicatory yacht-trip around the world in 1890. They were never seen or heard from again.

A fourth sister, Marie, apparently stuck to the non-musical stage before becoming wardrobe mistress at the Theater an der Wien.

THE STUDENT PRINCE [IN HEIDELBERG]
Musical play in 2 acts by Dorothy Donnelly based on *Old Heidelberg* by Rudolf Bleichmann, a version of *Alt-Heidelberg* by Wilhelm Meyer-Förster. Lyrics by Dorothy Donnelly. Music by Sigmund Romberg. Jolson Theater, New York, 2 December 1924.

The Student Prince was the second musical piece to be based on Meyer-Förster's 1901 Studentenstück *Alt Heidelberg* – the first, written by Alberto Collantuoni and composed by Ubaldo Pacchierotti, having been produced in Milan in 1908 (*Eidelberga mia!*) and subsequently played at Vienna's Kaiser-Jubiläums-Stadttheater (Volksoper, 12 February 1909). The original play had been an international success, notably in America where, in spite of having a very limited Broadway life both as *Old Heidelberg* (1902) and as *Prince Karl* (1903), it became a long-touring vehicle for popular actor Richard Mansfield as the Prince Karl-Heinrich who was to become 'the student prince'.

Dorothy Donnelly's American musical version stuck closely to the lines of the well-known play as the Prince, now called Karl-Franz (Howard Marsh), accompanied by his tutor Dr Engel (Greek Evans) and his pompous valet Lutz (George Hassell), left the cloistered life of his home court and headed off to Heidelberg University for an education in Latin and in life. We see little of the Latin, but his life quickly includes pretty Kathi (Ilse Marvenga), a waitress at his lodgings, to whom he vows eternal love before a term is over. But Karl-Franz has presumed on his liberty. He is recalled home to the death-bed of his grandfather and ordered, for reasons of state, to wed Princess Margaret (Roberta Beatty). He tries desperately to hold off the end of the only brief period of youthful freedom he has known, but in the end he has to bid farewell to Kathi and follow his duty.

This Leháresque plot provided Romberg with many opportunities for romantic music, but the setting also gave him the chance to include any amount of virile Continental student songs and marches, and, indeed, the score of *The Student Prince* was made up almost entirely of these two

styles of music, the traditional comic element of operetta being relegated to a very subsidiary place. It was, in fact, the masculine music of the piece which was its greatest triumph: Dr Engel reminiscing soaringly over the 'Golden Days' of youth, Karl-Franz serenading the skies in what was to become perhaps the best-known Serenade since Schubert's ('overhead the moon is beaming...'), and the students raising their voices in the equally famous Drinking Song ('Drink, drink, drink'). Kathi had a lively showpiece, trilling above the massed male voices in 'Come Boys, Let's All Be Gay, Boys' and joined with Karl-Franz in the evening's big duet 'Deep in My Heart, Dear', a piece which was echoed in the gentler strains of the duo 'Just We Two' shared by Margaret and Tarnitz, the man she would really have liked to marry had dynastic considerations not interfered.

The Student Prince had a difficult road to the stage. The Shuberts, for whom most of Romberg's previous work had been on flimsily built revusical pieces and botchings of foreign shows, had not expected their house composer to turn their old play into a big, florid operetta which featured a sad ending and a big, singing male chorus instead of wedding bells, a walk-down and a female and dancing chorus. At first Romberg got his way. The show went into production with his score intact, the unhappy ending intact and with the 40-strong male chorus he had demanded, all in matching costumes. It also went into production with Patti Harrold, a former *Irene* star, as its female lead.

Miss Harrold caused the first problem. One day she came to rehearsal and heard some other soprano singing her music. She apparently didn't wait to find out that Elsa Ersi was both Austrian and unavailable; she said her bit and she walked. The next contretemps came the moment the piece went on stage at the Apollo, Atlantic City, and Jake Shubert could see and hear those men, that music and the ending without a clinch. He started to try to fiddle with the show. When Romberg protested, a row ensued which ended with Shubert taking the composer's name off the billing and Romberg going to law. He won his suit in time to get back on the billboards before *The Student Prince* opened on Broadway to become not only the biggest success the Shuberts had had in years, but far and away the most important original musical they had or would ever produce.

The original production of *The Student Prince* ran for 608 performances and, before it closed, the show was already on the road with the first of what would become multiple, long-running touring companies. For some 20 years *The Student Prince* was permanently on tour in America and it remained a perennial favourite for decades thereafter. It reappeared on Broadway in 1931 (Majestic Theater, 29 January) and again in 1943 (Broadway Theater, 8 June) and in 1980 it was produced by the New York City Opera (29 August).

In spite of its enormous success, however, the piece failed to export in the same way that the other two comparable hits of the era, *The Desert Song* and *Rose Marie*, did. France, where Meyer-Förster's *Vieil Heidelberg* had for many years been a favourite in the repertoire at the Odéon and which welcomed the other two pieces largely, did not take up this work by a composer who otherwise found a wide welcome in the Paris theatre. A production at Berlin's Grosses Schauspielhaus in 1932 left little trace, whilst

England rejected the show not once but twice. Produced at His Majesty's Theatre in London with several of the original cast, including Miss Marvenga who was starred opposite Allan Prior as Karl-Franz, it was poorly received and closed after three months and 96 performances whilst *Rose Marie* continued its triumphant progress at Drury Lane. A road tour convinced producer Edward Laurillard that the show had been unlucky, and he brought it back to the Piccadilly Theatre (7 November 1929) with Donald Mather now starring. It lasted 60 performances.

Australia, however, gave *The Student Prince* a much warmer welcome than Britain had done. The show played for nearly three months in Sydney, after which the Dutch soprano Beppi de Vries (Kathy) and James Liddy (Karl-Franz) featured in a splendid four-month Melbourne run (Her Majesty's Theatre, 5 November 1927) before the show returned for a revival season in Sydney the following year (Her Majesty's Theatre, 15 September 1928). It got a further showing in Melbourne in 1929 when it shared the public's attention with a concurrent run of a film version starring Ramon Novarro and Norma Shearer, and it was brought out again in 1940 by the 'New Royal Comic Opera Company', confirming a success which the show had found nowhere else outside America.

In 1944 *The Student Prince* was tried yet again in the West End (Stoll Theatre 23 May), but England, like the rest of the world, got its most significant glimpse of *The Student Prince* via the medium of film – the 1954 MGM picture in which the dashing Edmund Purdom and the voice of Mario Lanza at its peak established Romberg's score (botched with three numbers by Nicholas Brodszky) internationally.

Endless and often cheap tours of the popular operetta slightly tarnished the title of *The Student Prince* in America, much in the same way that they did with *Blossom Time* and *The Desert Song* and the works of Ivor Novello in Britain. But John Hanson, the darkly tenor hero of many such British tours, had proved he could be a draw in the West End with a 1967 stop-gap revival of *The Desert Song*, and he selected *The Student Prince* as his next vehicle. This sadly botched 1968 revival gave *The Student Prince* (with additional songs by Hanson) its longest London season, but confirmed a creak-and-tat image for it which effectively finished it off as a revival prospect.

In 1974 the Heidelberg Festival produced a version of *The Student Prince*, with American tenor Erik Geisen starring, in the courtyard of Heidelberg castle, overlooking the well-preserved streets of the University city where the action of the play takes place. It has subsequently been performed regularly there, during the summer months.

Although it let such obvious libretto material as *Alt-Heidelberg* slip past, the Austrian musical theatre did, however, provide a before-the-Romberg-event musical-play sequel to *The Student Prince*. *Jung Heidelberg*, with a text by Carl Lindau and Leopold Krenn and a pasticcio score taken from the works of Carl Millöcker by Ernst Reiterer, followed the son of Karl-Franz to a happier ending with a suitable Princess in a production which top-billed Mizzi Zwerenz and Max Brod at Gabor Steiner's Venedig in Wien (9 July 1904). *Jung Heidelberg* was seen the following season both in Germany (Neues Königliches Opernhaus, Theater des Westens) and in America, where it was played in the German-language theatre with Curt

Weber and Mariesa Verena in the lead rôles and Lina Abarbanell in breeches as Lieutenant Vogel.

UK: His Majesty's Theatre 3 February 1926; Australia: Empire Theatre, Sydney 16 July 1927; Germany: Grosses Schauspielhaus *Der Studentenprinz* 1932; Films: MGM 1927, 1954
Recordings: British tour/revival cast (Philips), Heidelberg cast recording (Kanon), film soundtrack (RCA), complete (TER), selections (Columbia, Capitol, RCA, Pye, Philips, WRC etc)

STUDHOLME, Marie [LUPTON, Marion] (b Eccleshill, 10 September 1875; d London, 10 March 1930). Postcard beauty who played 20 years of musical-comedy juveniles.

After early appearances in *La Cigale*, *The Mountebanks* and *Haste to the Wedding* (1892, Anna Maria Maguire), pretty teenaged Marie Studholme rose up the cast list to take, take over and/or tour in good rôles in some of the earliest Victorian musical comedies. She played Rhea Porter and covered Jenny McNulty as the Comtesse before taking over Violet Cameron's rôle of Ethel Sportington in *Morocco Bound* (1893) and took the tiny rôle of Gladys Stourton in *A Gaiety Girl* (1893) before being promoted to succeed Maud Hobson in the show's title-rôle. She continued under George Edwardes's management, creating the small rôle of Jessie, and succeeding star soubrette Letty Lind as Daisy in *An Artist's Model* (1895), toured as Molly in Edwardes's number one *Geisha* company (1896–7), played Gwendoline in *In Town* on the road and on Broadway (1897), toured as Dora in *The Circus Girl* (1898) and as Iris in *A Greek Slave* (1899) and returned to London to repeat her Alma in his *Gaiety Girl* revival (1899). She then succeeded Violet Lloyd as the soubrette (Nora) of *The Messenger Boy* at the Gaiety, and had her first major London creation there in the leading juvenile rôle of Dora Selby in *The Toreador* (1901).

During the course of the run, she was succeeded by the rising Gertie Millar, which may have been why she ended up back on the road playing the title-rôle of *San Toy* (1903), but she returned to London to create the second juvenile rôle of Cicely Marchmont, alongside Edna May, in *The School Girl*, replaced Ethel Sydney as Josephine Zaccary in *The Orchid*, repeated her Molly in *The Geisha* revival and succeeded to the title-rôle of *Lady Madcap* (Lady Betty). In 1906 she appeared as Alice in *Alice in Wonderland* and then starred in *My Darling* in place of Ellaline Terriss (1907, Joy Blossom). She later played the title-rôles in such pieces as *Miss Hook of Holland* (1907–8 and 1909) and *My Mimosa Maid* (1908–9) on the road and appeared in South Africa before the approach of her fortieth year ended an ingénue career which had spawned a vast number of picture postcards.

STYNE, Jule [STEIN, Julius Kerwin] (b England, 31 December 1905).

British-born Styne, who moved to America with his family at the age of eight, had a juvenile career as a classical pianist, but in his young adult years he switched his attention to dance-band music, playing piano and, during his university years in Chicago, leading his own group. He later worked as a vocal coach and arranger in New York and then in Hollywood, and gradually began placing songs in films. He had his first success, still as Julius Stein, with the number 'Sunday' (w Chester Conn, Ned Miller, Benny Krueger) in 1927, but his next decade was spent largely as a piano player, both accompanying and coaching the new stars of Hollywood's singing films, rather than in writing.

His songwriting career did not take off until he had given up the piano playing and taken a post, first with Republic Pictures and then with Paramount, specifically as a composer. Now metamorphosed into Jule Styne, he teamed with lyricist Frank Loesser to produce a series of songs including 'Since You' (*Sailors on Leave*, 1941) and 'I Don't Want to Walk Without You' as sung by Betty Jane Rhodes in *Sweater Girl* (1942), and then with Sammy Cahn for a prolific period which produced, amongst other successful numbers, 'I've Heard That Song Before' (*Youth on Parade* 1942), 'The Victory Polka' (*Jam Session*, 1944), 'Thinking About the Wabash', 'There Goes That Song Again' (*Carolina Blues*, 1944), 'I'll Walk Alone' (*Follow the Boys*, 1944), 'And Then You Kissed Me', 'Come Out, Come Out Wherever You Are' (*Step Lively*, 1944), Frank Sinatra's 'Saturday Night is the Loneliest Night of the Week' (1944), 'Can't You Read Between the Lines', 'I Fall in Love Too Easily', 'What Makes the Sunset' and 'The Charm of You' (*Anchors Away*, 1945), 'Let it Snow!' (1945), 'It's Been a Long, Long Time' (*I'll Get By*, 1945), 'Five Minutes More' (*Sweetheart of Sigma Chi*, 1946), 'The Things We Did Last Summer' (1946), Sinatra's 'Time After Time' and 'It's the Same Old Dream' (*It Happened in Brooklyn*) and 'It's Magic' (*It's Magic*).

Cahn and Styne made a first attempt at a theatre show with the songs for David Wolper's production of *Glad to See You*, a 1944 musical which starred Eddie Foy jr and Jane Withers, but they had more success with a second venture, *High Button Shoes*, three years later. A jolly, old-fashioned piece of musical comedy with a cast headed by top comedian Phil Silvers and set alight by some energetic dancing, *High Button Shoes* ran for some two years and put in evidence such numbers as 'I Still Get Jealous' and 'Papa, Won't You Dance with Me?' as performed by Nanette Fabray and Jack McCauley.

From this time on, Styne devoted most of his attentions to the theatre. He followed *High Button Shoes* with another successful musical comedy, *Gentlemen Prefer Blondes* (1949), which, if its score was not necessarily its most attractive attribute, nevertheless produced 'Diamonds Are a Girl's Best Friend' and 'A Little Girl from Little Rock', and in 1951 he turned producer to collaborate with Alexander H Cohen and Harry Rigby on the Hugh Martin musical *Make a Wish* (Winter Garden Theater, 18 April 102 performances). In the same year he underwent a first stage collaboration with lyricists Betty Comden and Adolph Green on the revue *Two on the Aisle*, a collaboration which would be repeated often, although only surprisingly occasionally with success, over the following 15 years.

Through the 1950s Styne continued to mix composing and producing on Broadway, whilst still turning out single songs, of which the title-song to the film *Three Coins in a Fountain* (Academy Award, 1954) was the most memorable. His productions included the 1952 revival of Rodgers and Hart's *Pal Joey* (w Leonard Key, Anthony Brady Farrell), Jerry Bock's *Mr Wonderful* (1956 w George Gilbert, Lester Osterman), a vehicle for the young Sammy Davis jr,

and his own 1958 musical about the making of a musical, *Say, Darling* (w Osterman), all of which found success, and finally a musical version of *Pride and Prejudice*, *First Impressions* (1959), which did not, and folded in 84 performances.

The composing front, too, brought mainly success for, if *Hazel Flagg* (1953) had only a mild career (190 performances) and a collaboration with Comden, Green and Moose Charlap on a musical version of *Peter Pan* (152 performances) had to wait until a 1979 revival to win a substantial stage run, the lively *Bells Are Ringing*, the love-story of an answer-service girl, produced a long run (924 performances), overseas performances, a film and two hit songs, 'Just in Time' and 'The Party's Over'. Another musical written around an overwhelming central female rôle also proved successful, if not quite as long-running, when Styne composed the music to Stephen Sondheim's lyrics for *Gypsy* (1959). Ethel Merman made 'Everything's Coming Up Roses' into a hit, whilst other pieces of the score ('All I Need is the Girl', 'If Momma Was Married', 'Some People') also found popularity.

Do Re Mi, another vehicle for Phil Silvers, had a 400-performance run in 1960–1, and *Subways Are for Sleeping* (1961) lasted a little more than half of that time, but Styne had one further hit show to come. A return to the vehicle for a big female star, an area for which he had proven himself particularly adept at writing, brought forth *Funny Girl* (1964) in which Barbra Streisand played a version of the life story of comedienne Fanny Brice, and for which Styne composed the melodies to Bob Merrill's lyrics for 'People', 'Don't Rain on My Parade', 'I'm the Greatest Star', 'If a Girl isn't Pretty' and 'You Are Woman'. *Funny Girl* gave Styne his longest Broadway run as well as a highly successful film.

The year 1964 also saw Styne's début as a director in the musical theatre when he helmed the short-lived *Something More* (Sammy Fain/Marilyn and Alan Bergman/Nate Monaster) for his old partner Lester Osterman, but it also marked the peak of his career in the musical theatre. He continued to compose theatre scores for 15 further years, teaming again with Cahn on *Darling of the Day* and finding a limited success with *Hallelujah, Baby!* (Tony Award) and a good run with a musical version of *Some Like it Hot* entitled *Sugar* which topped 500 Broadway performances in spite of its score rather than because of it, but there were no more *Funny Girl*s or *Gypsy*s, no more megastars and no more successful songs. Styne's last works, a disastrous musical adaptation of a successful television play, *Barmitzvah Boy*, for London and the 1980 *One Night Stand* which closed on Broadway without playing its opening night were too feeble shows to come from a man who was not chary of going into print to rubbish other people's works.

In the composer's 84th year a 'new' Styne musical was produced off-off-Broadway: *The Dangerous Games of Red Riding Hood* was an adaptation of a 1965 television score of an updated version of the fairytale (*The Dangerous Christmas of Red Riding Hood*). A further television musical (w Comden, Green) entitled *I'm Getting Married* was broadcast in 1967.

Styne's other credits include the 1964 World's Fair revue *Wonder World*, and a score of incidental music for the very brief 1963 Broadway revival of *Arturo Ui*.

1944 **Glad to See You** (Sammy Cahn/Fred Thompson, Eddie Davis) Shubert Theater, Philadelphia 13 November

1947 **High Button Shoes** (Cahn/Stephen Longstreet) New Century Theater 9 October

1949 **Gentlemen Prefer Blondes** (Leo Robin/Anita Loos, Joseph Fields) Ziegfeld Theater 8 December

1953 **Hazel Flagg** (Bob Hilliard/Ben Hecht) Mark Hellinger Theater 11 February

1954 **Peter Pan** (w Moose Charlap/Betty Comden, Adolph Green, Carolyn Leigh) Winter Garden Theater 20 October

1956 **Bells Are Ringing** (Comden, Green) Shubert Theater 29 November

1958 **Say, Darling** (Comden, Green/Richard and Marian Bissell, Abe Burrows) ANTA Theater 3 April

1959 **Gypsy** (Stephen Sondheim/Arthur Laurents) Broadway Theater 21 May

1960 **Do Re Mi** (Comden, Green/Garson Kanin) St James Theater 26 December

1961 **Subways Are for Sleeping** (Comden, Green) St James Theater 27 December

1964 **Funny Girl** (Bob Merrill/Isobel Lennart) Winter Garden Theater 26 March

1964 **Fade Out – Fade In** (Comden, Green) Mark Hellinger Theater 26 May

1967 **Hallelujah, Baby!** (Comden, Green/Laurents) Martin Beck Theater 26 April

1968 **Darling of the Day** (E Y Harburg/Nunnally Johnson, Keith Waterhouse, Willis Hall) George Abbott Theater 27 January

1970 **Look to the Lilies** (Sammy Cahn/Leonard Spiegelgass) Lunt-Fontanne Theater 29 March

1971 **Prettybelle** (Merrill) Shubert Theater, Boston 1 February

1972 **Sugar** (aka *Some Like it Hot*) (Merrill/Peter Stone) Majestic Theater 9 April

1974 **Lorelei** revised *Gentlemen Prefer Blondes* (ad Kenny Solms, Gail Parent) Palace Theater 27 January

1978 **Barmitzvah Boy** (Don Black/Jack Rosenthal) Her Majesty's Theatre, London 31 October

1980 **One Night Stand** (Herb Gardner) Nederlander Theater 20 October (previews only)

1985 **Pieces of Eight** (Michael Stewart/Susan Birkenhead) Citadel Theater, Edmonton 27 November

1989 **The Dangerous Games of Red Riding Hood** (Merrill) TADA Theater December

Biography: Taylor, T: *Jule* (Random House, New York, 1979)

SUBWAYS ARE FOR SLEEPING

SUBWAYS ARE FOR SLEEPING Musical in 2 acts by Adolph Green and Betty Comden adapted from a novel of the same name by Edmund G Love. Music by Jule Styne. St James Theater, New York, 27 December 1961.

An uneventful musical about people who do nothing, *Subways Are for Sleeping* saw two professional drifters (Sydney Chaplin, Orson Bean) court a journalist who is doing an article on drifters (Carol Lawrence) and a down-and-out dolly (Phyllis Newman) respectively in a modern New York atmosphere which just occasionally, in its more revusical moments, recalled the zany joys of *On the Town* (not the least in a museum scene). Comden and Green's lyrics sparked best when Bean serenaded Miss Newman, clad in nothing but a bath towel to avoid eviction, with 'I Just Can't Wait (to see you with your clothes on)'.

When the show reaped poor notices, producer David Merrick published quotes from members of the public with the same names as the critics, winning outraged publicity that helped his show to a nevertheless largely insufficient 205 performances.

Recording: original cast (Columbia)

SUGAR Musical in 2 acts by Peter Stone based on the screenplay *Some Like it Hot* by Billy Wilder and I A L Diamond. Lyrics by Bob Merrill. Music by Jule Styne. Majestic Theater, New York, 9 April 1972.

The 1959 film *Some Like it Hot*, an all-time favourite as interpreted by Jack Lemmon, Tony Curtis, Marilyn Monroe and Joe E Brown, was an adaptation of an original story by Robert Thoeren made by Wilder and Diamond, the authors who would come up with *The Apartment* the following year. Like their later screenplay, *Some Like it Hot* was natural fodder for a transfer to the musical-comedy stage, and a French version of the tale, *La Polka des Lampions*, came out in 1961 (Théâtre du Châtelet, Paris, 20 December). However, after the splendid and successful results achieved by Neil Simon, Hal David and Burt Bacharach on the transformation of *The Apartment* into *Promises, Promises*, another *Some Like it Hot* musical appeared, this time on Broadway.

Musicians Joe (Tony Roberts) and Jerry (Robert Morse) witness a gangland killing and are obliged to 'disappear'. They do this by getting themselves dressed up in frocks, and joining an all-girl band run by Sweet Sue (Sheila Smith) which is heading out of town for an engagement in the summer sunspots. Their travesty leads the boys into all sorts of troubles. Joe – or Josephine – gets sweet on a fellow band-member called Sugar (Elaine Joyce), whilst Jerry – otherwise Daphne – attracts the attentions of millionaire Osgood Fielding jr (Cyril Ritchard). Morse and Roberts sang about the attractions of 'Sugar' and of themselves in 'The Beauty That Drives Men Mad' and Ritchard had a 'November Song', but the score did not bring out anything that looked like eclipsing the screenic memories of Miss Monroe singing 'I Wanna Be Loved By You'.

Produced by David Merrick, directed by Gower Champion, *Sugar* simply wasn't in the same class as *Promises, Promises* and it didn't raise a blink at the Tony Award prize-giving, but that didn't stop it running through 505 performances on Broadway and netting itself not only regional productions but a number of overseas ones, especially in South America and Mexico and in central Europe. However, the show had to wait 20 years to reach London. British star Tommy Steele, who had had a singular success with his adaptation of *Singin' in the Rain*, lit on *Some Like it Hot* as a next vehicle for himself. He then discovered it had two stage scores already. Rejecting strong advice to take the French one, he instead went for the English-language one, only to find that – unlike on *Singin' in the Rain* – the songwriters had the power to forbid interpolations. They did – particularly of 'I Wanna Be Loved By You' – and the score was instead bolstered with several songs taken from others of their own shows. With the libretto reorganized and the original film title restored (at a price, although the Hungarians had done it without even asking), *Some Like it Hot* was played with some success in the British provinces and with considerably less in London (108 performances).

A further, Australian musicalization of *Some Like it Hot* saw stagelight at Sydney's Bankstown Town Hall Theatre Restaurant in 1983 (8 February).

The title *Sugar* was earlier used for a little piece (Louis Jerome/George Arthurs/Lauri Wylie, Alfred Parker) produced at London's Oxford Theatre in 1917 (15 July).

Hungary: Vidám Színpad *Van aki forrón szereti* 19 March 1987;
   UK: Prince Edward Theatre *Some Like it Hot* 17 March 1992
Recordings: original cast (United Artists), Mexican recording
   (Daff), London cast (First Night)

SULLIVAN, Arthur [Seymour] (Sir) (b London, 13
May 1842; d London, 22 November 1900). The most
successful composer of the English opéra-bouffe and
-comique stage.

Educated at the Chapel Royal, the Royal Academy of
Music and Leipzig Conservatory, Arthur Sullivan was
intended for a serious musical career. Indeed he was
regarded, after his earliest orchestral, choral and
instrumental compositions – including a first theatrical
venture with incidental music to Shakespeare's *The
Tempest* – as one of the white hopes of the British musical
establishment. However, even early on he had expressed a
liking for lighter forms of music, and had also looked
towards the musical stage, making an attempt at an
unstaged piece – probably a light opera – called *The
Sapphire Necklace* when in his earliest twenties.

It was Sullivan's friendships in musical and theatrical
London that ultimately led him to take his first steps in the
world of the musical theatre. An acquaintance with draper
and amateur actor/singer Arthur Lewis, the leading light
in a group called 'The Moray Minstrels' which had
recently performed Moinaux and Offenbach's *Les Deux
Aveugles*, resulted in Sullivan being asked if he would compose another, similar piece for the group's members to
play. F C Burnand, another acquaintance, was seconded
for the text and, to his adaptation of Maddison Morton's
favourite farce *Box and Cox*, Sullivan wrote his first musical
comedy score. At first played privately, then at a memorial
benefit, *Cox and Box* was taken up by Thomas German
Reed two years later and given a long run at his Gallery of
Illustration.

By this time, however, Sullivan had stepped fully into his
new career. He and Burnand went on to compose a full-
length comic opera for the enterprising Reed, whose
entertainments had been successful enough that he was
preparing to launch himself onto more substantial things.
He took the St George's Hall for a season, hired a full
orchestra and chorus and, amongst his Offenbach and
Auber productions, he produced *The Contrabandista, or The
Law of the Ladrones*. *The Contrabandista* was an interesting
piece: a full scale comic opera with more than a touch of
the new French 'bouffe' flavour which the experienced
Burnand, an inveterate and vastly successful burlesque
writer since his earliest days in the theatre, had
encountered as recently as the previous year in adapting
Meilhac and Halévy's text to Offenbach's *La Belle Hélène*
for the British stage. Sullivan, who might have been expected to compose in the style of those English classics *The
Bohemian Girl*, *Maritana* and *The Lily of Killarney*, instead
turned out a matching score which had a decided quantity
of the bubble of the old French musical theatre amongst its
English strains. The buffo song 'From Rock to Rock' gave
the composer his first show-song success as it headed for
parlour pianos on the one hand, and was also 'borrowed'
by the makers of overseas pasticcio entertainments on the
other.

The Contrabandista was played 72 times, a very fine
record for a contemporary comic opera, and it went on to

Plate 255. **Arthur Sullivan**.

be played in America, pilfered – textually and even musically – in both America and Australia and, many years
later, actually revised and revived in London. It was not, a
has been so many times written, a failure. It was remove
to allow the other part of Reed's advertised season to b
played, and only dropped from his repertoire when h
found the finances of a full-scale company beyond hi
means and returned to the piano/harmonium and one-ac
operetta formula and to the Gallery of Illustration. Ther
Reed took up *Cox and Box*, played on a double-bill with
piece composed by Reed himself and entitled *No Cards*
The author of *No Cards* was barrister and burlesque-write
W S Gilbert.

Actively advertised by Messrs English and Blackmore
agents, *Cox and Box* went the rounds while Sulliva
returned to his more serious work. A couple of month
after the closure of *Cox and Box* at the Gallery, th
Philharmonia was performing his *In Memoriam* and *Th
Prodigal Son*. It was not too long, however, before Sulliva
ventured back into the musical theatre. This time – after
parlour operetta and an English comic opera – he venture
with the score for a Christmas extravaganza for the Gaiet
Theatre. *Thespis, or The Gods Grown Old* was the work o
Gilbert, who had supplied the opening-night burlesque fo
the Gaiety's manager, Hollingshead, and although it wa
only part of the Gaiety programme it was indeed a full-
length work. The first performance ran over three hours
The score that Sullivan ('our most distinguished Englis
composer') provided included some fine comical pieces
and also a ballad, 'Little Maid of Arcadee', which foun
some popularity as a single. *Thespis* was played 64 time
before the Gaiety moved on to its next change o
programme.

More than three further years passed, however, befor

the collaboration between Sullivan and Gilbert was repeated. Richard D'Oyly Carte, searching for a filler piece to go with Selina Dolaro's production of *La Périchole*, got the pair to get up a 'dramatic cantata' which Gilbert had prematurely intended as a vehicle for the late Mme Parepa Rosa. As *Trial By Jury* the little piece, with its witty words and laughing score, proved a sensation. A second little piece ('after the pattern of the agreeable entertainments given by Mrs German Reed...'), *The Zoo*, written to a text by B C Stephenson, followed ('recollections of Mozart, Auber and Donizetti, blended with Mr Sullivan's own ideas'), but, although it was reported in June 1876 that Sullivan and Gilbert 'have been engaged in arranging as a comic opera *The Wedding March* of LaTour Tomline' (ie Gilbert's version of *Le Chapeau de paille d'Italie*) and then that Arthur's brother, Fred Sullivan was taking the Globe Theatre to produce a new work by the pair, the nearest the musician got to another stage work was the interpolation of his song 'Once Again' into J A Cave's Christmas production, *Lord Bateman*, at the Alhambra for contralto Adelaide Nelson. It was left to Carte, launching himself as a producer after a number of years managing for others, to bring Sullivan and Gilbert firmly together on their first full-length comic opera.

The Sorcerer put the first seal on the British comic opera tradition which had been developing in the decade since *The Contrabandista*, and Sullivan swiftly placed himself alongside and even ahead of his friends Cellier and Clay who had been leading the field in the production of local musical plays up to this time. But it was left to the writers' second work together for Carte to confirm worldwide what *The Sorcerer* had shown only to those able to believe their ears. *HMS Pinafore* was the international musical hit of its era in the English-speaking theatre, and the Gilbert and Sullivan partnership was launched.

Eight further Sullivan and Gilbert comic operas followed *HMS Pinafore* on to the stage in the next decade or so, and almost all were major international successes, establishing the partnership as the English-speaking world's most important and popular writers of musical theatre. However, ceaselessly chivvied by a section of the press, who had never forgiven Sullivan for becoming merely the country's most popular writer of light theatre music, the composer still hankered after writing an opera. Carte, too, was not indifferent to the plan, and between them they nurtured an *Ivanhoe* into production at Carte's newly built Royal English Opera House. Though *Ivanhoe* was no disgrace, it was no *Iolanthe* either. It failed, the Opera House failed, and Carte and Sullivan ended up back at the Savoy. But they ended up back there without Gilbert. Whether because of the fact that the other two had been off playing operas without him, or whether because of some other reason, a breach had grown between the author and his producer and composer. Gilbert departed the Savoy, and Carte, after filling in with some non-Sullivan works, instead teamed the composer with the author of one of these, the respected playwright Sydney Grundy. Their *Haddon Hall* reeked more of old English not-very-comic opera than the joyous burlesques which Sullivan had composed with Gilbert, but it had a fair run in town and country.

The breach between author and composer was mended, and Gilbert and Sullivan came back together for two more

comic operas. *Utopia (Limited)* and, especially *The Grand Duke* were not up to their earlier works and, after the last-named, the collaboration lapsed once again. Gilbert moved away, Sullivan stayed with Carte. An attempt to pair the composer with Pinero and J Comyns Carr on *The Beauty Stone*, a curious medievally fantasy with undertones of *Ivanhoe* to it, which was all too painfully an effort not to compete with or copy the style of the Gilbert comic operas, was a failure. But although the Victorian age was coming to an end, there was still a place for Victorian comic opera and Sullivan was still as well- if not better-equipped than anyone else to provide it. The answer was, however, not a medieval romantic opera.

The answer turned out to be a librettist from the lowly world of musical comedy. Apparently there was at one time question of Sullivan writing a work with 'Owen Hall', the most successful author of contemporary musical libretti from *A Gaiety Girl* to *The Geisha* and *A Greek Slave*, but temporarily displaced at Daly's Theatre by Edwardes's need to humour a powerful journalist by using his text for what became *San Toy*. A Daly's Theatre musical by Arthur Sullivan and Owen Hall? It would have been a curious combination, worth hearing, the only problem being that the pair – both super-extravagant gambling men – might have spent their time playing cards rather than writing. As it turned out, Sullivan got the second most successful musical-comedy librettist of the time, the author of *Gentleman Joe* and *Dandy Dan, the Lifeguardsman*, Basil Hood. Hood provided his composer with the best libretto he had seen in years: a spendidly crafted version of the Arabian Nights Abu Hasan tale, written in a witty comic-opera style which differed from Gilbert's only in eschewing that ultimate air of cockeyed burlesque. Sullivan rose to the script with a score in the same style, and *The Rose of Persia* was a splendid success, scoring a fine run of 213 performances in a London where comic opera had definitely given over its place as a favourite entertainment to the products of the Gaiety and Daly's Theatres and their ilk.

Sullivan and Hood began work on a second piece together, an Irish musical comic opera called *The Emerald Isle*. It was clever, it was fun, it was tuneful – not quite as attractive as its predecessor perhaps – but it was also unfinished. Sullivan died in November 1900 with *The Emerald Isle* still in the writing, and it was completed by Edward German for its production and a thoroughly respectable run at the Savoy Theatre.

During his life as Britain's most popular composer of comic opera, Sullivan did not wholly neglect the areas of more serious music in which it had been originally thought that he would make his career. Although the flow of individual songs, hymn tunes and orchestral and instrumental works which he had composed in the 1860s and 1870s largely dried up once he became devoted to the theatre, he composed two important choral works (*The Golden Legend, The Martyr of Antioch*), several sets of incidental stage music (*Macbeth, King Arthur, The Foresters*) and a ballet for the Alhambra Theatre (*Victoria and Merrie England*), as well as continuing a celebrity conducting career.

Sullivan's music for the Victorian British theatre struck precisely the right note for its time and place. It was a little less extravagant than that of the overly French Offenbach, just as Gilbert's text held back from the extreme burlesque of a Hervé, but it mixed grace, melody and sufficient, but never low or vulgar, humour in almost the same measure as the author did with his texts. Sullivan's comic-opera scores were not only good music and attractive music, they were nice. They could be played and sung in any decent household, and they have been now for well over a century whilst almost every other bit of British writing of the period has slipped away into oblivion or rarity. And their composer stands up today in his home country as the only representative of the Victorian musical theatre, and in popular terms – give or take a music-hall song or two – of Victorian music to have stood the test of time with an almost undiminished appeal.

Sullivan's brother, **Fred[eric Thomas] SULLIVAN** (b 25 December 1837; d 18 January 1877) was for many years an architect and surveyor, but he turned to the stage late in his short life for a brief but high-profile career ended by his death at the age of 39.

Fred appeared on the stage under his brother's baton as Cox in *Cox and Box* and Punch in W C Levey's operetta *Punchinello* (July 1871), repeated *Cox and Box* at the Alhambra Theatre (October 1871), and took a supporting rôle in Arthur's next work, at the much more demanding Gaiety Theatre, as Apollo in *Thespis* (1871) with sufficient success to be cast with the theatre's stars, Nellie Farren and Connie Loseby, as Midas in the four-handed *Ganymede and Galatea* (*Die schöne Galathee*).

He played *Cox and Box* at the Gaiety and on the road, the operetta *Fleurette* at the Gaiety (1873, Marquis Beaurivage) and both *Cox and Box* and *Die schöne Galathee* at Crystal Palace (1874) before he tried his hand at management, presenting *Cox and Box* and *The Contrabandista* for fortnights at the Prince's, Manchester (11 May) and Birmingham (25 May) with Cellier as conductor and a cast including Ella Collins, Adelaide Newton, Frank Wood, Edward Connell and himself as Grigg and Cox. When things went poorly he added Fred Evans's comic ballet *Fra Diavolo* and Offenbach's *Lischen and Fritzchen*. The agent for the season was one Mr D'Oyly Carte.

Fred returned to performing in *Ixion* at the Opera-Comique (1874), played the principal comic rôle of the Viceroy in London's first *La Périchole* (1875) and had his biggest success when he created the rôle of the Judge in *Trial By Jury* (Royalty Theatre 1875) and played it at the Royalty, on the road and at the Opera-Comique (1876) with no less than three different main pieces. During this run he was taken ill and *Trial By Jury* was suspended till his return. It was announced that he would further his producing activities by staging the first full-length work by his brother and W S Gilbert the following season at the Globe Theatre, but his illness worsened and *The Sorcerer* was ultimately produced by Richard D'Oyly Carte at the Opera Comique some months after his death.

He is largely remembered today through the song 'The Lost Chord' which Sullivan composed in mourning for his brother.

1867 **Cox and Box, or The Long Lost Brothers** (F C Burnand) 1 act Adelphi Theatre 11 May, Gallery of Illustration 29 March 1869

1867 **The Contrabandista** (Burnand) St George's Hall 18 December

1871 **Thespis, or The Gods Grown Old** (W S Gilbert) Gaiety 26 December

1875 **Trial by Jury** (Gilbert) 1 act Royalty 25 March

1875 **The Zoo** (B C Stephenson) 1 act St James's Theatre 5 June

1877 **The Sorcerer** (Gilbert) Opera Comique 17 November

1878 **HMS Pinafore, or The Lass That Loved a Sailor** (Gilbert) Opera Comique 25 May

1880 **The Pirates of Penzance, or The Slave of Duty** (Gilbert) Fifth Avenue, New York 31 December

1881 **Patience, or Bunthorne's Bride** (Gilbert) Opera Comique 23 April

1882 **Iolanthe, or The Peer and the Peri** (Gilbert) Savoy Theatre 25 November

1884 **Princess Ida, or Castle Adamant** (Gilbert) Savoy Theatre 5 January

1885 **The Mikado, or The Town of Titipu** (Gilbert) Savoy Theatre 14 March

1887 **Ruddigore, or The Witch's Curse** (Gilbert) Savoy Theatre 22 January

1888 **The Yeomen of the Guard, or The Merryman and His Maid** (Gilbert) Savoy Theatre 3 October

1889 **The Gondoliers, or The King of Barataria** (Gilbert) Savoy Theatre 7 December

1892 **Haddon Hall** (Sydney Grundy) Savoy Theatre 24 September

1893 **Utopia (Limited), or The Flowers of Progress** (Gilbert) Savoy Theatre 7 October

1894 **The Chieftain** revised *The Contrabandista* Savoy Theatre 12 December

1896 **The Grand Duke, or The Statutory Duel** (Gilbert) Savoy Theatre 7 March

1898 **The Beauty Stone** (Arthur Wing Pinero, J Comyns Carr) Savoy Theatre 28 May

1899 **The Rose of Persia, or The Storyteller and the Slave** (Basil Hood) Savoy Theatre 29 November

1901 **The Emerald Isle, or The Caves of Carric-Cleena** (w Edward German/Hood) Savoy Theatre 27 April

Biographies: Jacobs, A: *Arthur Sullivan, a Victorian Musician* (OUP, Oxford, 1984), Lawrence, A H: *Sir Arthur Sullivan* (James Bowden, London, 1899), Findon, B W: *Sir Arthur Sullivan, His Life and Music* (James Nisbet, London, 1904) revised as *Sir Arthur Sullivan and His Operas* (Sisley's, London, 1908), Sullivan H and Flower, N: *Sir Arthur Sullivan* (Cassell, London, 1927), Young, P M: *Sir Arthur Sullivan* (Dent, London, 1971), Dunhill, T: *Sullivan's Comic Operas* (Edward Arnold, London, 1928), Saxe Wyndam, H: *Arthur Seymour Sullivan (1842–1900)* (Kegan Paul, Trench, Trubner, London, 1926) etc, etc

SULLIVAN, Jo [SULLIVAN, Elizabeth Josephine] (b 28 August).

A bitingly pert little ingénue with a strong soprano voice (and something to hide about her birth?), Miss Sullivan made her most notable musical theatre appearances in off-Broadway's *Threepenny Opera* (Polly Peachum) and as 'Rosabella', the waitress heroine of Frank Loesser's *The Most Happy Fella* ('My Heart is So Full of You'). Rosabella, however, surprisingly turned out to be her only Broadway rôle. She played at the City Center as Julie in *Carousel*, Eileen in *Wonderful Town* and Magnolia in *Show Boat* and regionally as Dorothy in *Wizard of Oz*, Sharon (*Finian's Rainbow*), Kathie (*Student Prince*) and Kitty (*Charley's Aunt*) and appeared in the musical version of *Of Mice and Men* at the Provincetown Playhouse (1958). In later years she administered the musical legacy of her late husband, Frank Loesser, and appeared in a show – *Perfectly Frank* – compiled from his works.

SULLY, Mariette (b Belgium 9 December 1878; d unknown).

Mlle Sully was first seen on the Paris stage in 1894 as Kate in Planquette's *Rip*, and she subsequently appeared in leading opérette rôles at most of Paris's principal musical houses in a career of more than 40 years. During this period, which was far from the most productive of the French musical stage, she created several of the most important new prima donna rôles available: the doll-girl Alésia in Audran's *La Poupée* (1896), the title-rôle of Messager's *Véronique* (1898), and another doll-girl, Lisbeth, in Louis Ganne's *Hans, le joueur de flûte* (1906).

Amongst her other creations were included *Panurge* (1895, Caterina), *Le Bonhomme de neige*, *Les Forains* (Clorinde), *Shakespeare!* (Éponine), *Le Petit Chaperon rouge*, *Princesse Bébé* (1902, Maia), *La Bouquetière du Château d'Eau*, *Les Dragons de l'Imperatrice* (1905, Cyprienne), *Oeil de Gazelle*, *Madame Marlborough*, *Rhodope*, *Les Maris de Ginette* (1916, Ginette), *La Fiancée du lieutenant* (1917) and, as late as 1935, *La Nuit est belle*. At the same time she appeared on the Paris stage in such classic rôles as Miss Helyett, Serpolette, Rose Michon, Marie-Blanche, Suzette (*Le Voyage de Suzette*), Musette (*La Petite Bohème*) and Missia (*La Veuve joyeuse*).

Mlle Sully appeared in the French version of *A Country Girl* in Paris, and in London both as Pervenche in *Les Merveilleuses* (1906) and as Juliette – the rôle created for another *Miss Helyett*, Juliette Nesville – in George Edwardes's revival of *The Geisha* (1906). She played in the zarzuela *La Rose de Grenade* at the Olympia, appeared in a number of opérettes, both new and revived, in Monaco, and repeated her most famous rôle of Véronique for over 20 years.

THE SULTAN OF MOCHA   Comic opera in 3 acts by Albert Jarret (? uncredited) and others. Music by Alfred Cellier. Prince's Theatre, Manchester, 16 November 1874; St James's Theatre, London, 17 April 1876.

The Sultan of Mocha was one of the earliest British musicals of the modern era to have a significant career at home and also to win overseas productions. It was first produced at the Prince's Theatre, in Manchester, by Charles Calvert, the actor-manager who with his wife had become known for their superior productions of Shakespeare, and who accepted a text supplied by 'a local gentleman of some literary attainment' which he had set to music by the young musical director of his theatre, Alfred Cellier.

Dolly (Bessie Emmett) is in love with handsome sailor Peter (Robertha Erskine), but she is whisked away from such nautical temptations by her horrid slave-trading uncle, Captain Flint (Henry M Clifford), and carried off to Mocha where she is pounced upon by the amorous Sultan (John Furneaux Cook). Rescued by Peter, recaptured by the falsity of another jealous suitor, Sneak (Fred Mervin), Dolly finally escapes becoming a Sultana by disguising a more ambitious member of the Sultan's harem in her wedding veil.

Well in the tradition of such popular nautical yarns as *Black-Eyed Susan* and of pantomime extravaganza, with its staunchly British hero and heroine, comical villains and exotic second-act location, the tale was told in some naïve and sometimes punning dialogue which nevertheless supported a well-made and tuneful score in a similar tradition.

Plate 256.

Cellier's music took little or no notice of the French opéra-bouffe style which had been dominant in Britain's musical theatres for the past years and which had featured in such French-composed British musicals as *Aladdin II* (Hervé), *Cinderella the Younger* (Jonas) and *Whittington* (Offenbach) and the spectacular *The Black Crook* and *Babil and Bijou*. Following instead the tones of Sullivan's *Contrabandista* and Clay's *The Gentleman in Black* and *Cattarina*, Cellier's music for *The Sultan of Mocha* helped establish the kind of English comic-opera score which would find its apogee in the Savoy operas and his own *Dorothy*.

Amongst the solos, Peter had a delightful ballad in an old English mode ('Twas Sad When I and Dolly Parted'), and a Yawning Song which, like Dolly's Slumber Song, became a popular recital piece. Dolly also had a number which made no bones about 'Women's Rights' ('woman strongminded is not to be bullied by man when he's minded to make her his slave'), Sneak listed the contents of his shop ('The Telescope') to dazzle the heroine and the Sultan described himself ('Sultan am I') in multiple rhymes alongside a series of lively choruses of which the finale 'We'll Sail Away with Peter' was particularly well received.

In the manner of the time, the piece was produced first, and worked on after, and it was worked up and added to with new jokes and songs to such effect that it was still running after five weeks when it was time for Calvert to mount the annual pantomime. As soon as Christmas was over it was hurried back to the Prince's Theatre stage with London star Catherine Lewis now as Dolly and a tenor instead of a travesty Peter, and it was brought back again after another pre-booked season had intervened, and again the following year. Finally Manchester's musical was produced in London by Mrs John Wood, 18 months and five series after its first appearance. Constance Loseby (Dolly), Alfred Brennir (Peter) and Henri Corri (Sultan) headed the cast, the book was sharpened up (and its Mancunian references cut), and a chorus of 70 engaged to boom out Cellier's finale, but in spite of some good notices 47 performances were its lot.

The Sultan of Mocha continued to win provincial productions, however, and it was allegedly given a San Francisco showing by the indefatigable Alice Oates in 1878 before, two years later, Blanche Roosevelt, who had encountered Cellier whilst singing Josephine (*HMS Pinafore*) at the Opera Comique, got John McCaull to stage it for her 'Blanche Roosevelt Comic Opera Company' in New York. Poorly and hastily produced, it folded quickly. After the vast success of Cellier's *Dorothy*, *The Sultan of Mocha* was given a brush-up, a fresh book and a new production under the management of Lydia Thompson (Strand Theatre, 21 September 1887). Violet Cameron and Henry Bracy starred, and the piece won a fine reception and 114 performances, following which Bracy took up the Australian rights and produced the show in Melbourne in 1889 and at Sydney's Criterion Theatre the following March. The producer again played Peter to the Dolly of Lilian Tree, with John Forde (Sneak), Knight Aston (Sultan), Flora Graupner (Lucy) and William Stevens (Flint) supporting. After 15 colourful years of life from one side of the globe to the other *The Sultan of Mocha* was then left at rest.

USA: Union Square Theater 14 September 1880; Australia: Alexandra Theatre, Melbourne 9 November 1889

THE SULTAN OF SULU Comic opera in 2 acts with lyrics by George Ade. Music by Alfred G Wathall. Additional music by Nat D Mann. Studebaker Theater, Chicago, 11 March 1902; Wallack's Theater, New York, 29 December 1902.

The Islamic Philippine island domain of Ki-Ram, Sultan of Sulu (Frank Moulan), is an idyllic place where 'we have no daily papers to tell of Newport capers, no proud four hundred to look down on ordinary folk, no French imported liquors, no stock exchange and tickers, to fill one full of rosy hopes and someday land him broke'. One day Sulu is annexed by America which, in the persons of Arkansas Colonel Budd (William C Mandeville), baritonic Lt William Hardy (Templar Saxe) and the bigoted Judge Jackson (1870s Gilbert and Sullivan star Blanche Chapman), promptly decides to that it is time to civilize – that is to say, americanize – both island and Sultan.

Thirty years before Ira Gershwin won fulsome praise for equating war with trade in musical-comedy terms in *Strike Up the Band*, Englishman Templar Saxe marched on to the stage singing George Ade's softly stinging backhander 'But though we come in warlike guise and battle-front arrayed, It's all a business enterprise, we're seeking foreign trade'. Education arrived in the shape of four schoolma'ams 'from the land of the cerebellum where clubs abound and books are plenty we come to teach this new possession all that's known to a girl of twenty', and new experience in the disastrous form of cocktails which led poor, innocent Ki-Ram to end up intoning a splendidly comical post-drinking song of 'R.E.M.O.R.S.E.'. After a busy evening of song and dance in which the blithely satirical was mixed with such

popular items as a hoe-down for the Colonel ('Ol' Ja Bird'), a Irish number ('Rosabella Clancey'), a topical tri ('Oh, What a Bump!'), several marching routines, fashionably croony Nat Mann two-step ('My Sulu Lu Loo'), a coon song ('Delia') for Gertrude Quinlan a Number One Wife and some jolly ensembles, Ki-Ram an Sulu escape their dreadful fate on a legal technicality.

Commissioned by Henry Savage from the well established journalist and author Ade and from a 22-year old English musician, Alfred Wathall, who was a teacher a Chicago's North Western School of Music, *The Sultan Sulu* was produced in Chicago under the auspices Savage's Castle Square Opera Company, which had bran ched out from several successful years playing operatic an light-operatic repertoire seasons. After a sticky start, became a major success. With a score constantly growin ('The Puzzled Man', 'Money, Money, Money', 'Th Cuckoo and the Clock'), and a libretto perked up wit fresh topicalities for the occasion, the show moved t Broadway. Perhaps because the Castle Square compan had so long been installed in New York, the piece wa apparently not regarded as a Chicago musical and it wa both well reviewed and a fine success. It ran up 200 per formances at Wallack's Theater and put the final stardu on Frank Moulan's reputation before continuing a stron career around the country for a number of seasons.

The Sultan of Sulu was a jolly mixture of plot notion which had done duty for years on the English comic oper stage (with 'americanization' here replacing the 'angliciza tion' of such pieces as *Dick* and *Utopia Ltd*), and some c which had had a particularly happy recent showing i Britain, America and around the world in the record breaking *A Chinese Honeymoon*. But Ade had done hi librettist's and lyricist's jobs with skill and humour and th piece's singular success was no accident. That succes helped revive the favourite old musical-theatre hometown boy-in-exotic-foreign-places theme with its preposterou Rurarabian monarchs and harum-scarum plots for the jo of another generation of Americans, but it did not encour age this particular show to travel beyond its native borders

SUMMER SONG Story of the new world in 2 acts b Eric Maschwitz and Hy Craft. Lyrics by Eric Maschwitz Music arranged from the works of Anton Dvořák b Bernard Grün. Prince's Theatre, London, 16 Februar 1956.

Yet another in the series of romantic biomusicals alleg edly based on the life and works of a composer, *Summe Song* invented an American episode for Dvořák in order t inspire him to the New World Symphony. Laurenc Naismith portrayed Dvořák, and since the composer' rather stolid life gave no opportunity to invent a love affai it gave the singing and love-making to opera star Davi Hughes (Shaun) and Sally Ann Howes (Karolka). Th New World Symphony, the Slavonic Dances and *Rus salka*'s beautiful 'Song to the Moon' were amongst th pieces of music put to the mill in an unsuccessful attemp to produce another *Dreimäderlhaus*.

Recording: original cast (Philips)

SUNDAY IN THE PARK WITH GEORGE Musica in 2 acts by James Lapine. Music and lyrics by Stephe Sondheim. Booth Theater, New York, 2 May 1984.

Sunday in the Park with George presents the peculiarity of being a musical drawn not from a text, but from a painting: Georges Seurat's well-known pointilliste *Un dimanche d'été à l'île de la Grande Jatte.* The libretto that James Lapine constructed around, or rather drew from, the work of art fell into two loosely linked halves, which gave the impression of being a one-act musical play followed by a modern commentary on that play.

In the first act the artist, George (Mandy Patinkin), is seen gathering together the material and the people who will ultimately make up the subject matter of his painting, and the audience gets to know who the soldiers, the girls, the boatman, the child, and the memorably straight-backed couple with a monkey are, before they are all frozen onto canvas together in the artist's imaginative, rather than factual, rearrangement at the end of the act. Parallel to the construction of the painting, the act follows the ups and (mostly) downs of the failing relationship between George and his mistress, Dot (Bernadette Peters). The second act moves on from the period setting of the first to modern times. The modern George (Patinkin again) is the illegitimate great-grandson of the first, and Marie, the child borne to the first George by Dot (and played by the same actress), is now an elderly woman. This George is an artist as well, and in contrast to his ancestor's painting, he produces a Chromolume, a piece of mechanical performance art, the display of which is used by the authors to give the audience their comments on art patronage and criticism.

The musical score illustrating this pair of acts is not made up of 'numbers' in the traditional sense, but rather seems to take on the flavour of the artistic techniques the show deals with, building up its 'modern art' score from repeated fragments and conversational pieces rather than extended solo pieces. Its most generally accessible parts come in the first act, notably in a monologue for Dot where Sondheim the lyricist produces some amusing moments as he collects the thoughts going through her brain as she models uncomfortably for her artist, and the act comes effectively to an end in its picture to the strains of 'Sunday'.

Highly regarded in some quarters, and the recipient of several awards, *Sunday in the Park with George* – and in particular its second act – nevertheless proved incomprehensible and/or uninteresting to the bulk of theatre-goers and it finished its New York run of 604 performances in the red. The show was subsequently played for a season at Britain's Royal National Theatre with Philip Quast (Georges) and Maria Friedman (Dot) in the principal rôles. A German version was premièred in 1989 at Kaiserslautern, but a French production announced for 1992 at the Opéra-Comique was ultimately cancelled and replaced by an evening of zarzuelas.

Germany: Kaiserslautern *Sonntags im Park mit George* 1989; UK: Lyttelton Theatre 15 March 1990

SUNNY Musical comedy in 2 acts by Oscar Hammerstein II and Otto Harbach. Music by Jerome Kern. New Amsterdam Theater, New York, 22 September 1925.

Sunny was commissioned by producer Charles Dillingham as a vehicle for ex-Ziegfeld star Marilyn Miller, and it was built around her and a series of scenic considerations with rather less expertise than might have been expected, given the famous names which were attached to the show's book. Since a circus setting had been decided

Plate 257. **Sunny**: *The sheet music got to Europe, where Jerome Kern was billed as 'the composer of "Who?"', but the show didn't go further east than London.*

upon, Miss Miller was cast as Sunny Peters, the daughter of a lovable old German-accented circus man (written to type for ageing star comic Joseph Cawthorn), and herself a circus rider. The circus element had nothing to do with what little plot there was, but it allowed Dillingham to fill the stage with circus acts. Similarly, the circus was situated in Britain, which allowed that little plot to step sideways for a hunting scene even more ridiculously unsuitable than the infamous one tacked into *Dorothy* 40 years earlier. The second act (apparently not written when rehearsals began) got the principals on an ocean liner – a fashionable setting of the time – heading for America, and the plot had Sunny married, because of American entry laws (in one version), to the wrong man (in one version) before, ultimately, getting the right one (in one version). Jack Donahue (Jim), Paul Frawley (Tom) and Clifton Webb (Harold) were the men in the piece, Mary Hay (Weenie) the soubrette, and – for a while – Ukelele Ike, who had gone down so well in *Lady, Be Good!* the previous season, was another item on the bill.

Jerome Kern's songs for *Sunny* – which also underwent heavy overhauling pre-Broadway – shared its most popular pieces amongst the principals. Miss Miller and Frawley joined together in 'Who (stole my heart away)?', Frawley serenaded his 'Sunny' who, in turn, demanded 'Do You Love Me?', and Webb and Miss Hay soubretted in song and dance about 'Two Little Bluebirds' (which had begun life, less romantically, as 'Two Total Losses'). All these soon-to-be-favourites came in the first act, and the second, which introduced only three fresh (or made-over) Kern songs, plus a lot of dances, Ukelele Ike's spot, another for Pert Kelton and George Olsen and his Music, was less productive.

Sunny's run-in to New York was hair-raising. Whilst frantic writes and rewrites went on, Dillingham announced to the press that the problem was simply that they had discovered that their plot was very similar to that of a Raymond Hubbell/Anne Caldwell piece called *Miss Liberty* which Abe Erlanger was producing. The same excuse was able, at a pinch, to cover the wholesale replacement of the second act by a fresh one, but not the sacking of choreographer Julian Alfreds, replaced by veteran Julian Mitchell. Rumour was floated that the show was costing $250,000, Miss Miller being on a vast guarantee of $2,000 per week and Donahue and Webb on $1,000 apiece, and it looked like a bad investment. However, in just two weeks between opening at Philadelphia's Forrest Theater and bowing on Broadway, *Sunny* was turned into a hit. Miss Miller, Donahue, the spectacle and Kern's successful and singable songs earned the show some splendid reviews, 517 Broadway performances, a tour, and a London production under the auspices of Moss' Empires, Lee Ephraim and Jack Buchanan. *Miss Liberty* didn't ever show, but Dillingham's excuses and cover-ups were soon forgotten.

Binnie Hale (Sunny), Jack Buchanan (Jim), Jack Hobbs (Tom) and Elsie Randolph (Weenie) featured in the London *Sunny* which ran up a fine 363 performances of a version that took in four additional numbers, did without Ike and his 'Paddlin' Madelin' Home', and even altered the ending to give the heroine her final curtain with the other young man of the piece. Australia, too, proved fond of *Sunny*, as produced by Rufe Naylor at Sydney's Empire Theatre with Wyn Richmond in the little heroine's rôle supported by Fred Heider (Jim), Queenie Ashton (Weenie), Fred Bluett (Siegfried) and Jack Morrison (Tom). A good Sydney run was followed by a Melbourne season (Princess Theatre 15 July 1927) of three months, the whole accompanied by some of the most over-the-top advertising of the period. The advertising did not, however, encourage Australia to support *Sunny* to the grand extent it had done *Sally*.

Sunny was metamorphosed twice into a film. The first starred Miss Miller repeating her original rôle alongside the Tom of Lawrence Grey and the papa of O P Heggie, whilst Jim Donahue, brother of her recently deceased partner, Jack, was given the rôle of Jim. A decade later, a second *Sunny* featured Anna Neagle in the title-rôle. Each time the three principal numbers of the stage show's score were retained.

UK: London Hippodrome 7 October 1926, Australia: Empire Theatre, Sydney 27 February 1927; Films: First National 1930, RKO 1941

Recording: London cast compilation (WRC, Stanyan) (part-record)

SUNNY RIVER   Musical in 2 acts by Oscar Hammerstein II. Music by Sigmund Romberg. St James Theater, New York, 4 December 1941.

First produced at the St Louis Muny under the title of *New Orleans*, the show headed for Broadway with its title altered to the less precisely geographical *Sunny River*. That river was the Mississippi, and the show's tale was a period

piece (1806) set in New Orleans and stretched over the ten years between the first attempt of the little singer Marie Sauvinet (Muriel Angelus) to win lofty Jean Gervais (Robert Lawrence) away from his intended Cécile Marshall (Helen Claire) and her return, now a famous prima donna, for a second and equally unsuccessful try.

Marie got the main part of the musical action both in solo ('Call it a Dream', 'Can You Sing?') and duo with Jean ('Along the Winding Road', 'Let Me Live Today', 'Time is Standing Still') whose own principal solo was in praise of 'My Girl and I'. The show's title-song fell to a supporting character.

The Mississippi did not yield another *Show Boat* nor New Orleans another *Naughty Marietta* and Max Gordon's Broadway production drew only enough public to last for five weeks. However, London's Emile Littler ('by arrangement with Max Gordon of New York City') picked the piece up for Britain and produced it with a strong cast headed by Evelyn Laye (Marie) and Dennis Noble (Gervais) and with older stars Edith Day (Lolita, with the title-song) and Bertram Wallis (George Marshall) amongst the character players. It was many years since Romberg's music had been heard in the West End, but *Sunny River* could not interest a wartime public who preferred Jack Buchanan, Cicely Courtneidge, Palladium revue or, for heavier stuff, the topical romance of *The Lisbon Story*. The show closed after little more than two months.

UK: Piccadilly Theatre 18 August 1943; Film: 1946

THE SUNSHINE GIRL   Musical comedy in 2 acts by Paul Rubens and Cecil Raleigh. Lyrics by Paul Rubens and Arthur Wimperis. Music by Paul Rubens. Gaiety Theatre, London, 24 February 1912.

In the twilight of the great musical-comedy years at the Gaiety Theatre, a new (or, rather, new-old) team of writers took a turn at supplying the famous house with what they thought the contemporary theatre-goer, whisked along on the brand new wave of syncopated rhythms and revue, might best appreciate. Far from taking anything resembling a turn for the modern, however, Rubens, Raleigh and Wimperis moved in a distinctly backward direction. They threw out the noticeably more vertebrate musical-comedy form which the theatre's previous piece, the George

Plate 258. **The Sunshine Girl:** *George Grossmith fends off the embraces of Connie Ediss whilst Teddy Payne and the juveniles of the piece look on unamused and/or bemused.*

Grossmith/Leslie Stuart *Peggy*, had ventured and, far from constructing their musical play on an established comedy as that piece had done, they simply put together a show to the very old Gaiety days formula of minimal plot and maximum star exposure.

The Sunshine Girl had a skeletal story in which soap-factory worker Delia Dale (Phyllis Dare) wins the heart and hand of her workmate Vernon (Basil Foster) who is – in good 19th-century fashion – really the factory's owner in disguise. George Grossmith was the hero's best friend, Teddy Payne and Connie Ediss were an East End pair who spot the deception, Mabel Sealby was soubrette and the beautiful Olive May, soon to quit the stage to join the British peerage, paired with Grossmith at the head of the usual line of Gaiety belles.

The piece was staged in the habitually attractive Gaiety style and illustrated with a bundle of the simplistically suggestive but catchy songlets which Rubens purveyed so successfully. Miss Ediss pulled the best of these, describing 'Brighton' and relating how 'I've Been to the Durbar', Miss Dare simpered pinkly 'Take me for – !' and Grossmith clipped out a jaunty and decidedly catching 'Little Girl, Mind How You Go' alongside the score's rare tentative try at things new in the form of Miss Dare and Grossmith performing 'a new dance from South America' called the tango, and the show filled the bill very well. The favourite stars had plenty to do (the unimportant Vernon was quickly pushed aside to allow the top-of-the-bill folk to do their thing) and they did it with gusto for a 12-month run (336 performances), confirming the fact that Grossmith's attempts to turn Gaiety musicals into something more substantial were not really necessary.

The Sunshine Girl even proved capable of existing without Payne, Grossmith, Connie Ediss and their fellows. It had a fine life in the British provinces, and Charles Frohman took it to Broadway where Gaiety stage manager Pat Malone directed the equally potent local stars Julia Sanderson and Joseph Cawthorn (who interpolated a song of his own, 'You Can't Play Every Instrument in the Orchestra'), Eva Davenport (who didn't go to the Durbar, but instead insisted 'I've Been to America') and Vernon Castle (who tangoed with Miss Sanderson) in a suitably americanized version which played for a fine 101 nights in New York before going on the road. Amongst the supporting cast was one Edward Soldene Powell, the son of the great London prima donna of opéra-bouffe days.

J C Williamson Ltd, continuing their association with the Gaiety Theatre, duly took *The Sunshine Girl* to Australia, where she was seen in seasons in Sydney and in Melbourne (Her Majesty's Theatre, 17 May 1913) with Jessie Lonnen – daughter of the former Gaiety star E J – in the soubrette rôle, and the following year the show was mounted in Budapest, where the product of the London stage had been, for a number of years, receiving unusual attention. The Gaiety had furnished *A Runaway Girl* and *The Circus Girl* to Hungarian stages some while previously, and Edwardes had memorably provided the oft-revived *The Geisha* and *San Toy* to Europe at the turn of the century, but recently it was Paul Rubens who had been winning the most attention from Budapest. Both *Miss Hook of Holland* (1908) and *The Balkan Princess* (1910) had been produced at the Király Színház, and now *Napsugár kisasszony* (ad Jenő Heltai) followed them. It evidently did well enough, for the same theatre also subsequently purchased Jones and Rubens's *The Girl from Utah* from the Gaiety.

Australia: Her Majesty's Theatre, Sydney 19 January 1913; USA: Knickerbocker Theater 3 February 1913; Hungary: Király Színház *Napsugár kisasszony* 3 June 1914

SUPPÉ, Franz von [SUPPÉ, Francesco Ezechiele Ermenegildo von] (b Spalato, 18 April 1819; d Vienna, 21 May 1895). The first major composer to emerge in the budding Viennese Operette tradition.

A descendant of a Belgian family who had settled in Italy, von Suppé was born in Spalato, Dalmatia (the modern Split) where his parents were civil servants. After the death of his father in 1835, his mother left Italy and moved her family to her native Vienna where the young Suppé continued the general musical and composition studies which he had already pursued in Italy and, at the age of 21, took up his first professional post as third conductor at the Theater in der Josefstadt, under the management of Franz Pokorny. There, in the manner of the time, the young Kapellmeister helped supply such songs and incidental music as the theatre's productions required, and his first full score appeared the following year, attached to a Volksstück called *Jung lustig, im Alter traurig*. It was well received, and quickly followed by a second fine success in Schickh's *Die Hammerschmiedin* which went on to be seen in Budapest (14 April 1844) and later at the Theater an der Wien (23 September 1846). Thereafter Suppé provided regular full scores for the Theater in der Josefstadt – including one for the same vaudeville *Marie, die Tochter des Regiments* (*La Fille du régiment*) which Donizetti had used as the basis for his opera four years previously – as well as for the other suburban and provincial theatres which Pokorny managed.

When Pokorny took over the Theater an der Wien in 1845, his young conductor and composer moved with him. He provided an original occasional overture for the opening programme under the new régime, and then moved into the same conducting/composing routine that he had pursued in the Josefstadt, between 1846 and 1848 alongside Albert Lortzing of *Waffenschmied* and *Zar und Zimmermann* fame, and then, for the rest of his long period at that theatre, with Adolf Müller as a colleague. In the first year, of the half-dozen pieces for which he was called on to supply music and songs, one ran just a single performance and only Kaiser's Charakterbild *Sie ist verheiratet* (43 performances) compiled a good run. The following year two pieces cleared the 20-performance mark, but the overture which Suppé composed for one of these, Karl Elmar's *Dichter und Bauer* (*Poet and Peasant*), was to have a much longer life than the 22 performances the play lasted, and it went on to become a concert classic with a century and a half of life in it.

In 1847 Suppé covered seven new shows, but he also posted up his ambition to write something more substantial when he combined with Elmar to write an opera, *Das Mädchen vom Lande*. It was Suppé's third completed opera, but his first to be produced (Theater an der Wien 7 August) and it was played just eight times. Opera for the moment put behind him, he returned to the normal run of his duties and provided the scores the following year for the usual run of comedies with songs as well as for a full-scale Alois Berla burlesque of von Flotow's *Martha* and incidental music for a five-act drama.

In his years at the Theater an der Wien, the most immediately successful pieces with which he was involved were the long-running Possen *Des Teufels Brautfahrt*, *Gervinus* and *Wo steckt der Teufel?*, but the most noteworthy was the little one-act Operette *Das Pensionat*, produced in 1860 with considerable success and played for a series of 34 performances. *Das Pensionat* is generally regarded as the first significant local attempt to follow the Offenbachian operettic fashion which had been imported to Vienna in the last few years, and its success set first Suppé, and then Millöcker, Strauss and others on the road to building what would become the 19th-century tradition of Viennese Operette.

The success of *Das Pensionat* encouraged Suppé to go where his career as a composer of such pieces would be best appreciated and, in consequence, he left the Theater an der Wien after more than 15 years in residence and took up the position of conductor and composer at the little Theater am Franz-Josefs-Kai, run by Karl Treumann, the most moving spirit in the production of Offenbach and other musical theatre of the kind in contemporary Vienna. Treumann mounted several Suppé Operetten and, after an initial flop with *Die Kartenschlägerin*, the composer scored two further successes with the little *Zehn Mädchen und kein Mann* and the part-fresh, part-pasticcio *Flotte Bursche*.

After the destruction of the Kai-Theater, Suppé moved with Treumann back to the producer's old base at the Carltheater. There, whilst still turning out scores for the usual run of Possen, including the musical biography *Franz Schubert* (with Treumann as Schubert), and burlesques such as *Dinorah* (on Meyerbeer's opera), he produced a line of further short Operetten of which *Die schöne Galathee*, in 1865, proved the high-water-mark of the new Viennese tradition up to that time. His other principal pieces at this time included *Leichte Kavallerie* – another piece which used some existing popular music in its score but which rendered up an original overture to posterity which would be no less popular than his *Dichter und Bauer* – and *Banditenstreiche*.

In 1868 Suppé first ventured with a three-act Zauberposse, *Die Frau Meisterin* (also briefly seen in Germany) which was produced with a stellar cast including Pepi Gallmeyer, Franz Tewele, Josef Matras, Wilhelm Knaack and Therese Braunecker-Schäfer, followed in 1870 by a full-length opéra-bouffe, *Die Jungfrau von Dragant*, which benefited from Matras, Karl Blasel, Knaack, Albin Swoboda, Frau Schäfer and Anna Grobecker as its leading players. Neither was successful, and they were put away after a handful of performances whilst the little *Die schöne Galathee*, *Leichte Kavallerie* and *Flotte Bursche* were brought back on a regular basis. However, Strauss's triumph in 1874 with *Die Fledermaus* convinced Suppé to have another try. Utilizing a well-proven French libretto written by no less a playwright than Eugène Scribe, a libretto already once used by Auber for his opera-comique *La Circassienne*, he turned out, to the words of Zell and Genée, the Operette *Fatinitza* (1876), which was produced by Franz Jauner, by this time the manager of the Carltheater.

The enormous success of *Fatinitza* re-placed Suppé alongside Strauss at the forefront of the Viennese Operette. Now able to put aside forever the virtual ha[ck] composing that had been so long his lot, Suppé co[n]centrated from that time on a ten-year series of full-size[d] Operetten, almost all staged at the Carltheater, from whi[ch] he was able comfortably to take retirement as a conduct[or] in 1882. *Der Teufel auf Erden* had only a limited success (2[?] performances) but his next work, *Boccaccio* (1879), not on[ly] confirmed but topped the success of *Fatinitza* and, in t[he] opinion of Suppé and of most of posterity, marked t[he] acme of his career as a theatre composer.

There was further, if not quite equivalent, success wi[th] his third Zell-Genée piece *Donna Juanita* (1880) and, to [a] lesser extent, with the Eugène Sue-based *Der Gascogn[er]* (1881) and his one piece written for his old house, t[he] Theater an der Wien, the lively, jolly *Die Afrikareise* (188[3]) which had a fine worldwide career, but his other wor[ks] were not immune from lesser or greater degrees of failur[e]. *Herzblättchen*, which came between *Der Gascogner* and D[ie] *Afrikareise*, proved the most ephemeral. In spite of a ca[st] headed by Pepi Gallmeyer, Josef Joseffy and Karl Blasel, [it] survived only four performances. His two last works als[o] had limited first runs. *Bellman* lasted two and a half wee[ks] at the Carltheater whilst *Die Jagd nach dem Glück* played f[or] just a month and, although both won further and overse[as] productions and the latter's music was as substantial stu[ff] as his best, neither was a success in the image of *Fatinitz[a]*, *Boccaccio*, *Donna Juanita* or *Die Afrikareise*. The posth[u]mous *Das Modell* (completed by Alfred Zamara and Juli[us] Stern) did somewhat better, beginning with a six-and-a[-]half week run at the Carltheater, followed by a brief reviv[al] and a very reasonable career in Germany and Hungary, b[ut] it was far from finding a place in the permanent repertoir[e].

Suppé shared his life in later years between Vienna an[d] a little estate in Kampthal in Lower Austria where h[e] worked on a regular plan – writing from 6.30 am to 1 p[m,] sleeping till 5pm, and relaxing in the evening. It was und[er] these agreeable conditions that the now-famous an[d] courted composer turned out the last items of a half-cen[tury] tury of writing life in which he had composed the scores f[or] more than 200 Operetten, Possen, burlesques, Singspiel[e] and other stage pieces, including several further unsuc[cessful] cessful operas (*Paragraph drei*, *Des Matrosens Heimkehr*, th[e] unproduced *The Corsican*), as well as over a thousand oth[er] musical works ranging through church music, overture[s,] symphonies, orchestral music, and songs and choral piece[s] both in the serious and light vein.

Boccaccio and *Die schöne Galathee* alone remain t[o] represent Suppé in the very limited 'Golden Ag[e'] repertoire that is still played, often in a sadly savaged stat[e] today, even though his overtures fill many a gramophon[e] record. *Donna Juanita* has retained some place in Easter[n] Europe but, amazingly, *Fatinitza*, in particular, has disap[-] peared. However, in spite of this limited appreciation of hi[s] work in the late 20th century, Suppé's reputation and posi[-] tion as 'the father of the Viennese Operette' remains intac[t.]

Although he has not yet had the misfortune to have hi[s] life and loves transmogrified into an operette à grand spec[-] tacle, Suppé has crept onto the musical screen alongsid[e] his contemporaries, Strauss and Millöcker. In Will[i] Forst's film *Operette* he was portrayed by no less an artis[t] than Leo Slezak, and in 1953 he was given the gloriou[s] technicolor treatment in a Schönbrunn/Farbe film, *Hab ic[h] nur deine Liebe*, in which Johannes Heesters, Gretl Schörg[?]

Margit Saad, Helmut Qualtinger and Pepi Glöckner featured and his music was 'arranged' by Rudolf Kattnigg.

1841 **Jung lustig, im Alter traurig** (*Die Folgen der Erziehung*) (C Wallis) Theater in der Josefstadt 5 March

1841 **Die Wette um ein Herz** (*Künstlersinn und Frauenliebe*) (Karl Elmar) Theater in der Josefstadt 10 March

1841 **Stumm, beredt, verliebt** (Franz Xaver Told) Ödenburg 1 May, Theater an der Wien 15 July 1856

1841 **Die Bestürmung von Saida** (w Carl Binder, Anton Emil Titl/Told) Theater in der Josefstadt 10 September

1841 **Der Pfeilschütz im Lerchenfeld** (Josef Kilian Schickh) Theater in der Josefstadt 27 October

1841 **Der Komödiant** (*Eine Lektion in der Liebe*) (Elmar) Theater in der Josefstadt 14 December

1842 **Das grüne Band** (Elmar et al) Theater in der Josefstadt 2 July

1842 **Das Armband** Theater in der Josefstadt 8 September

1842 **Die Hammerschmiedin aus Steiermark** (*Folgen einer Landpartie*) (Schickh) Theater in der Josefstadt 14 October

1844 **Ein Morgen, ein Mittag und ein Abend in Wien** Theater in der Josefstadt 26 February

1844 **Die schlimmen Buben** (*Der Teufel in allen Ecken*) (w Witt/ Anton von Klesheim) Theater in der Josefstadt

1844 **Nella, die Zauberin** (*Der Maskenball auf Hochgiebel*) (Elmar) Theater in der Josefstadt 11 May

1844 **Marie, die Tochter des Regiments** (ad Friedrich Blum) Theater in der Josefstadt 13 June

1844 **Ein Sommernachts-Traum** (Straube) Theater in der Josefstadt 31 August

1844 **Der Mörder in Einbildung** (aka *Der Kramer und sein Kommis*) (Friedrich Kaiser) Theater in der Josefstadt 28 September

1844 **Dolch und Rose** (*Das Donaumädchen*) (Told) Theater in der Josefstadt 5 November

1844 **Zum ersten Mal im Theater** (Kaiser) Theater in der Josefstadt 31 December

1845 **Die Champagner-Kur** (*Lebenshass und Reue*) (K Gruber) Theater in der Josefstadt 20 February

1845 **Die Müllerin von Burgos** (Josef Kupelwieser) Theater in der Josefstadt 8 March

1845 **Der Preussische Landwehrmann und die französischen Bäuerin** (Kaiser) 1 act Theater in der Josefstadt 22 April

1845 **Die Preussen in Österreich** (*Landmädchen, Volontair und Trompeter*) (Elmar) Theater in der Josefstadt 29 April

1845 **Der Nabob** (Karl Haffner) Theater in der Josefstadt 9 May

1845 **Die Industrie-Ausstellung** (*Reise-Abenteuer in London*) (Kaiser) Theater in der Josefstadt 1 August

1845 **Des Wanderers Ziel** (Karl Meisl) 1 act Theater an der Wien 30 August

1845 **Reich an Gelt und arm an Schlaf** (Told) Theater an der Wien 17 September

1845 **Das Lustspiel in Hietzing** (Blum) Theater an der Wien 26 September

1845 **Sie ist verheiratet** (Kaiser) Theater an der Wien 7 November

1846 **Die Gänsehüterin** (ad G Ball) Theater an der Wien 11 February

1846 **Der Sohn der Haide** (Kaiser) Theater an der Wien 15 June

1846 **Dichter und Bauer** (Elmar) Theater an der Wien 24 August

1847 **Die Karikaturen** (Kaiser) Theater an der Wien 8 February

1847 **Die Reise nach Grätz mit dem Landkutscher** (*Die Räuber auf dem Semmering*) (Schickh) Theater in der Josefstadt 24 February

1847 **Das Menschenherz** (Lang) Theater an der Wien 15 March

1847 **Liebeszauber, oder Ein Wunder in den Bergen [in der Schweiz]** (Elmar) Theater an der Wien 21 April

1847 **Zwei Pistolen** (Kaiser) Theater an der Wien 8 May

1847 **Ein Feemärchen** (Kupelwieser) Theater an der Wien 25 May

1847 **Das Mädchen vom Lande** (Elmar)Theater an der Wien 7 August

1847 **Tausend und eine Nacht** (w Anton Storch/Told) Theater in der Josefstadt 20 August

1847 **Die Schule des Armen, oder Zwei Millionen** (Kaiser) Theater an der Wien 26 October

1847 **Was eine Frau einmal will, oder der Friedrichsdor** (w Heinrich Proch/Heinrich Börnstein) Theater an der Wien 23 November

1847 **Hier ein Schmidt, da ein Schmidt, noch ein Schmidt und wieder ein Schmidt** (Elmar, Heinrich Mirani) Theater an der Wien 30 December

1848 **Männer-Schönheit** (Kaiser) Theater an der Wien 6 February

1848 **Unter der Erde, oder Freiheit und Arbeit** (*Arbeit bringt Segen*) (Elmar) Theater an der Wien 30 May

1848 **Ein Petition der Bürger einer kleinen Provinzstadt, oder Theolog, Jurist und Techniker** (aka *Bauer, Bürgermeister, Gutsherr*) (Josef Böhm) Theater an der Wien 12 July

1848 **Wie die Reaktionäre dumm sind!** (Elmar) 1 act Theater an der Wien 3 August

1848 **Ein Traum – kein Traum, oder Der letzte Rolle eine Schauspielerin** (Kaiser) Theater an der Wien 2 December

1848 **Martl** (*Der Portiunculatag [or Der Tanzboden] in Schnabelhausen*) (Alois Berla) Theater an der Wien 16 December

1848 **Nacht und Licht** (Kaiser) 1 act Theater an der Wien 31 December

1849 **Des Teufels Brautfahrt, oder Böser Feind und guter Freund** (Elmar) Theater an der Wien 30 January

1849 **Ein Fürst** (Kaiser) Theater an der Wien 17 March

1849 **Gervinus, der Narr vom Untersberg** (*Ein patriotischer Wunsch*) (Berla) Sommer-Theater in Fünfhaus/Theater an der Wien 1 July

1849 **Der Edelstein** (Berla) Sommer-Theater in Fünfhaus

1849 **Ein Blatt von Weltgeschichte** (Beethoven arr/Otto Prechtler) Theater an der Wien 3 October

1849 **Unterthänig und unabhängig** (*Vor und nach einem Jahre*) (Elmar) Theater an der Wien 13 October

1849 **'s Alraunl** (Klesheim) Theater an der Wien 13 November

1850 **Die Philister-Schule** (Elmar) Theater an der Wien 17 January

1850 **Die Kunst zu lieben** (*Gentil Bernhard*) (w Adolf Müller/ Ida Schuselka-Brüning) Theater an der Wien 26 February

1850 **Liebe zum Volke** (Elmar) Theater an der Wien 18 March

1850 **Die Assentirung** (aka *Bürger und Soldat, oder Liebe zum Vaterland*) (w Adolf Müller/V W Niklas ad Böhm) Theater an der Wien 26 April

1850 **Die beiden Fassbinder** (*Reflexionen und Aufmerksamkeiten*) (Leopold Feldmann) Sommer-Theater in Fünfhaus 16 May

1850 **Der Dumme hat's Glück** (*Er muss tolle Streiche machen*) (Berla) Sommer-Theater in Fünfhaus 29 June

1850 **Der Mann an der Spitz, oder Alles aus Freundschaft** (Anton Bittner) Sommer-Theater in Fünfhaus 19 August

1850 **Der Vertrauensmann, oder Wahrheit und Lüge** (Berla) Theater an der Wien 19 September

1851 **Dame Valentine, oder Frauenräuber und Wanderbursch** (Elmar) Theater an der Wien 9 January

1851 **Fliegende Blätter** (pasticcio comp and arr w Müller) Theater an der Wien 22 May

1851 **Waldmärchen** (Berla) Sommer-Theater in Fünfhaus 30 July

1851 **Angeplauscht** (L Wysber) Sommer-Theater in Fünfhaus 20 August

1852 **Die Jungfer Mahm von Gmunden** (Nikola) Sommer-Theater in Fünfhaus 20 May

1852 **Ein Filz als Prasser** (Leopold Feldmann, Theodor Flamm) Sommer-Theater in Fünfhaus 30 June

1852 **Pech!** (Berla) Sommer-Theater in Fünfhaus 31 July

1852 **Das Beispiel** (Nissl, Sigmund Schlesinger) Theater an der Wien 2 October

1852 **Der Grabsteinmacher** (Wysber) Theater an der Wien 6 November

1853 **Die Heimkehr von der Hochzeit** (Feldmann) Theater an der Wien 8 January

1853 **Der Baum des Lebens, oder Österreichs Eiche** (Feldmann) 1 act Theater an der Wien 13 March

1853 **Hansjörge** (Karl von Holtei) Theater an der Wien 20 April

1853 **Die Irrfahrt um's Glück** (Elmar) Theater an der Wien 24 April

1853 **Die weiblichen Jäger** (*Die Jägermädchen oder Eine moderne Diana*) (Feldmann) Sommer-Theater in Fünfhaus 30 July

1854 **Die Bernsteinhexe** (Heinrich Laube) Theater an der Wien 6 January

1854 **Durcheinander** (pasticcio arr/Wilhelm Grüner) Theater an der Wien 5 February

1854 **Trommel und Trompete** (Elmar) Theater an der Wien 1 April

1854 **Im Bauernhaus – im Herrenhaus** (J L Deinhardtstein) 1 act Theater an der Wien 25 April

1854 **Der Biberhof** (Feldmann, Märzroth) Sommer-Theater in Fünfhaus 28 June

1854 **Wo steckt der Teufel?** (Eduard Breier ad Johann Grün) Sommer-Theater in Fünfhaus 28 June

1854 **Mozart** (Alois Wohlmuth) Theater an der Wien 23 September

1854 **Nur romantisch!** (Kaiser) Theater an der Wien 18 November

1854 **Bum! Bum!, oder Zwei Schlauköpfe und ein Dummkopf** (Bittner) Theater an der Wien 9 December

1855 **Das Bründl [Schuster] bei Sievring** (*Ein Blick in die Zukunft*) (Hugo Merlin) Theater an der Wien 14 April

1855 **Der Teufel hol die Komoedie** (Merlin) Sommer-Theater in Fünfhaus 17 May

1855 **Der Höllenross** (Karl Bruno) Sommer-Theater in Fünfhaus 23 May

1855 **Die G'frettbrüder** (Bittner, Berla) Theater an der Wien 28 June

1855 **Märchenbilder und Geschichten für kleine und grösse Kinder** (*Prinz Lilliput und das Schneiderlein*) (Klesheim) Theater an der Wien 20 October

1855 **Judas im Frack** (*Ein Judas von Anno neune*) (w Müller/Langer) Theater an der Wien 20 December

1856 **Nur keine Verwandten** (Feldmann) Theater an der Wien 12 April

1856 **Ein Musikant, oder Die ersten Gedanken** (Ludwig Gottsleben) Theater an der Wien 7 June

1856 **Die Wahrheit auf Reisen** (Berg) Sommer-Theater in Fünfhaus 22 June

1856 **Die Weingeister** (Alois Blank, J Bernhofer) Sommer-Theater in Fünfhaus 10 August

1856 **Eine ungarische Dorfgeschichte** (Bittner, Berla) Sommer-Theater in Fünfhaus 31 August

1856 **Die schöne Leni** (Julius Findeisen) Theater an der Wien 4 October

1856 **Die Kreuzköpfeln** (Berg, Grün) Theater an der Wien 22 October

1856 **Vertrauen** (Moritz A Grandjean) Theater an der Wien 22 November

1856 **Ein gefährlicher Mensch** (*Der Bücher-Hausirer*) (Wilhelm Tesko) Theater an der Wien 7 December

1857 **Der Faschingsteufel** (Berla) Theater an der Wien 23 February

1857 **Eine Schlange** (Karl Gründorf) Theater an der Wien 18 April

1857 **Kopf und Herz** (Flamm) Theater an der Wien 9 May

1857 **Der Komet vom Jahre 1857** (Feldmann, Weyl) Theater an der Wien 23 May

1857 **Ein desparater Kopf** (Karl) Sommer-Theater in Fünfhaus 20 June

1857 **Die Waschermädeln** (*Ritter Bomsen und seine schauderliche Mordthau*) (aka *Die Hellseherin von Thury*) (Berg) Theater an der Wien 29 June

1857 **Eine Landpartie** (Findeisen) Sommer-Theater in Fünfhaus 17 July

1858 **Die Mozart-Geige, oder Der Dorfmusikant und sein Kind** (Elmar) Theater an der Wien 27 February

1858 **Das tägliche Brot** (Berla) Theater an der Wien 13 March

1858 **Der Werkelmann und seine Familie** (Langer) Theater an der Wien 11 May

1856 **Die Firmgold** (Elmar) Sommer-Theater in Fünfhaus 21 May

1858 **Die Kathi von Eisen** (Berla) Sommer-Theater in Fünfhaus 15 August

1858 **Nach der Stadterweiterung** (Gans, Schlesinger) Theater an der Wien 11 December

1859 **Ein Faschings-Gugelhupf** (w Müller/Langer) Theater an der Wien 5 March

1859 **Etwas zum lachen, oder Keine Politik** (Feldmann) Sommer-Theater in Fünfhaus 9 July

1859 **Eine Wienerin** (Flamm) Sommer-Theater in Fünfhaus 23 July

1859 **Über Land und Meer** (w Müller/Blank) Sommer-Theater in Fünfhaus 21 August

1859 **Eine Judenfamilie** (Mirani) Theater an der Wien 22 October

1859 **Die Zauberdose, oder Um zehr Jahr zu spät** (Elmar) Theater an der Wien 19 December

1860 **Meister Winter** (Berla) Theater an der Wien 13 March

1860 **Das Pensionat** (C K) 1 act Theater an der Wien 24 November

1860 **Mein ist die Welt** (Kaiser) Theater an der Wien 16 December

1861 **Ein Loch in der Hölle** (Johann Schönau) Theater an der Wien 1 February

1861 **Ein Faschingsdonnerstag in Venedig** (J Golinelli) (pantomime divertissement) Theater an der Wien 9 March

1861 **Ein Kapitalist, der einen Dienst sucht** (aka *Ein Ratzelhafter Freund, oder Kapitalist und Kammerdiener*) (Scribe ad Carl F Stix) 1 act Theater an der Wien 26 May

1861 **Der politische Schuster** (Berg) Sommer-Theater in Fünfhaus 1 June

1861 **Der Höllen-Kandidat** (Bernhofer, Blank) Sommer-Theater in Fünfhaus 26 July

1861 **Wiener Nachtfalter** (Gottsleben) Theater an der Wien 3 October

1861 **Ein Schwindler** (Mirani) Theater an der Wien 12 October

1861 **Die Wunderkinder aus California** (Elmar) Theater an der Wien 29 November

1862 **Ein Mann dreier Weiber, oder Ein alter Tarockspieler** (w Müller/Blank, J L Harisch) Theater an der Wien 22 April

1862 **Die Kartenschlägerin** 1 act Theater am Franz-Josefs-Kai 26 April

1862 **Zehn Mädchen und kein Mann** (W Friedrich) 1 act Theater am Franz-Josefs-Kai 25 October

1862 **Baedeckers Reisenhandbuch** (w C F Conradin/G Belly) 1 act Theater am Franz-Josefs-Kai 27 December

1862 **Werners Vergnügungszügler** 1 act Theater am Franz-Josefs-Kai 27 December

1863 **Der Herr Vetter** (Berla) Theater am Franz-Josefs-Kai 28 February

1863 **Flotte Bursche** (Josef Braun) 1 act Theater am Franz-Josefs-Kai 18 April

1863 **Überall Geister** (Langer) 1 act Carltheater 23 September

1864 **Das Corps der Rache** (Harisch) 1 act Carltheater 5 March

1864 **Franz Schubert** (Schubert arr/Hanns Max) 1 act Carltheater 10 September

1864 **Der Schweigerpapa aus Krems** (Langer) Carltheater 19 November

1864 **Das Christkindl** (Langer) Carltheater 26 December

1865 **Dinorah, oder Die Turnerfahrt nach Hütteldorf** (Friedrich Hopp) Carltheater 4 May

1865 **Die schöne Galathee** ('Poly Henrion') 1 act Meysels Theater, Berlin 30 June

1865 **Der Ehemann in der Baumwolle** 1 act Carltheater 4 November

1865 **Die alte Schachtel** (Berg) 1 act Carltheater 2 December

1866 **Leichte Kavallerie** (Karl Costa) Carltheater 21 March

1866 **Die Tochter der Puszta** 1 act Carltheater 24 March

1866 **Der letzte Gulden** (Berg) Carltheater 18 August

1866 **Ein patriotische Dienstbote** Carltheater 18 August

1866 **Theatralische Ausverkauft** Carltheater 25 August

1866 **Es wird annektiert** 1 act Carltheater 20 September

1866 **Die Freigeister** (Costa) Carltheater 23 October

1867 **Banditenstreiche** (B Boutonnier) 1 act Carltheater 27 April

1868 **Die Frau Meisterin** (Costa) Carltheater 20 January

1868 **Schlechte Mittel, gute Zwecke** (Kaiser) Carltheater 5 March

1868 **Tantalusqualen** 1 act Carltheater 3 October

1869 **Isabella** (J Weyl) 1 act Carltheater 6 November

1870 **Vineta, oder Die versunkene Stadt** Theater im Gärtnerplatz, Munich 10 February

1870 **[Lohengelb, oder] Die Jungfrau von Dragant** (Nestroy ad [Costa], M A Grandjean) Stadttheater, Graz 23 July; Carltheater 30 November

1871 **Centifolie** (Langer) Carltheater 9 February

1871 **Eine schöne Wirtschaft** (Flamm) Carltheater 15 November

1872 **Ein weibliche Dämon** (Langer) Carltheater 13 April

1872 **Cannebas** (Josef Doppler) 1 act Carltheater 2 November

1873 **Tricoche und Cacolet** (Henri Meilhac, Ludovic Halévy ad Treumann) Carltheater 3 January

1873 **Wolfgang und Constanze** (Mozart arr/Langer) Carltheater 3 May

1875 **Fräulein Schwarz** (Langer) Carltheater 11 March

1875 **Die Reise um die Erde in 80 Tagen** (Jules Verne, Adolphe d'Ennery ad Karl Treumann) Carltheater 28 March

1876 **Fatinitza** (F Zell, Richard Genée) Carltheater 5 January

1876 **Zahnarzt und Magnetiseur** (A Reichenbach) 1 act Carltheater 4 February

1876 **Nach dem Mond und unterm Meer** (Verne ad Adolphe L'Arronge, Zell) Carltheater 25 March

1876 **Die Frau Baronin vom Ballet** (Berg) 1 act Carltheater 2 December

1876 **Die treulose Witwe** (Berg) 1 act Carltheater 2 December

1877 **Unsere Handwerk** (Berg) 1 act Carltheater 1 April

1878 **Der Teufel auf Erden** (Julius Hopp, Carl Juin) Carltheater 5 January

1879 **Boccaccio** (Zell, Genée) Carltheater 1 February

1880 **Donna Juanita** (Zell, Genée) Carltheater 21 February

1880 **Die Schwestern** (Held) Carltheater 19 October

1881 **Der Gascogner** (Zell, Genée) Carltheater 21 March

1882 **Das Herzblättchen** (Karl Tetzlaff) Carltheater 4 February

1883 **Die Afrikareise** (Moritz West, Genée) Theater an der Wien 17 March

1887 **Bellman** (West, Ludwig Held) Theater an der Wien 26 February

1887 **Joseph Haydn** (Haydn arr/Franz von Radler) Theater in der Josefstadt 30 April

1888 **Die Jagd nach dem Glück** (Genée, Bruno Zappert) Carltheater 27 October

1895 **Das Modell** (Victor Léon, Held) Carltheater 4 October

1898 **Die Pariserin** (Léon, Held) revised *Die Frau Meisterin* Carltheater 26 January

Biographies: Keller, O: *Franz von Suppé, der Schöpfer der deutschen Operette* (Richard Wöpke, Leipzig, 1905), Schneidereit, O: *Franz von Suppé: ein Wiener aus Dalmatien* (VEB, Berlin, 1977)

SURCOUF Opéra-comique in a prologue and 3 acts by Henri Chivot and Alfred Duru. Music by Robert Planquette. Théâtre des Folies-Dramatiques, Paris, 6 October 1887.

The tale of *Surcouf* was (very) loosely based on that of the Captain Kidd of French popular history, the sea captain Robert Surcouf (1773–1827) who plied the Indian Ocean at the turn of the 18th century, pillaging English trading vessels, before settling down in his native Saint-Malo to become a rich commercial shipowner and, eventually, a Baron under the Empire. Chivot and Duru's libretto built upon this well-known personality a traditional comic tale of misunderstandings and revelations, topped up with a romance and a particularly colourful dose of stage spectacle. If the libretto occasionally took a breath for some slightly laboured exposition, it nevertheless turned up a very superior bunch of comical characters of whom the two slangy Breton mariners, big papa Gargousse and his little friend Flageolet, were classics of the genre.

The action begins with a prologue, in which young Robert (Louis Morlet) is sacked by businessman Kerbiniou (Montrouge) and joins up with a corsair ship, vowing to return rich within four years and wed Kerbiniou's niece, Yvonne (Mlle Darcelle). The four years pass, the war with England is over, but Surcouf, who has been rumoured dead, does not come, and the new Madame Kerbiniou (Juliette Darcourt) makes plans for Yvonne to wed the English Captain Thompson (Marcellin). But Robert, who has only been injured, arrives in time to foil the marriage, just as war with the English breaks out once more. Mme Kerbiniou is visiting her uncle MacFarlane (Duhamel) in seaside England when Surcouf is captured, but she realizes that he is the man who once saved her from a crocodile, and so she bullies her husband into 'admitting' that he is himself the real corsair. Finally, Surcouf escapes and, with Gargousse (Gobin), Flageolet (Guyon fils) and Yvonne – who have all come to the rescue disguised as Italian nobility – and the Kerbinious, heads back to France pursued by MacFarlane and Thompson. By cunning and bravery his little ship defeats them both and all ends with a vive la France!

Planquette's score was tuneful, stirring and comical in turn, with 'père Gargousse' particularly well served with a joyous opening duo with his little companion 'Moi, j'suis Gargousse', 'Et moi, Flageolet', another comical duo in their Italian disguise which contained some frenetic above-the-stave falsetto (to A in alt), and a jauntily martial 6/8 song ('Dedans l'Inde') in the last act. The fun was also well served by Mme Kerbinou's history of her encounter with the crocodile (Couplets du Caïman), whilst the romance was highlighted by a lovely prayer for Yvonne ('En ce jour, avec confiance') and her duets with Surcouf, and the patriotic fervour by the hero's final, poundingly triumphant Air de la navire ('Mon navire si beau').

Surcouf was produced by Henri Micheau and Jules Brasseur at the Folies-Dramatiques and was an instant success. It was played for 135 consecutive nights in its first season and brought back for a further showing in the next two seasons, quickly passing its 200th performance. In the meanwhile, it travelled promptly to Hungary (ad Béla J Fai, Andor Kozma) and to Austria (ad Richard Genée, Bruno Zappert) where Adolf Brackl played the title-rôle and Flageolet was played by a girl in travesty, but it paused before making its début on British soil. There was, of course, a problem with the libretto, in which the British were depicted as the baddies and, if not necessarily cowardly, at the best both buffoonish and as being sunk by a Frenchman outnumbered ten to one. The problem, however, soon disappeared. Planquette, who had found an audience for his works even greater in Britain than in France, was too much in demand and too anxious to be demanded to allow something of this nature to stand in the way of success. In H B Farnie's version, Robert Surcouf simply became Paul Jones, a swashbuckling Britisher, and the enemy was Spain.

Paul Jones was produced by the newly formed Carl Rosa Light Opera Company, an outfit with which the endlessly touring operatic group hoped to capitalize on the lucrative fashion for comic opera. Planquette went to Britain to remodel his score on 'English' lines (as he had done with enormous success with Farnie on *The Old Guard/Les Voltigeurs de la 32ème*), adding a considerable amount of new music for the benefit of Rosa's cast. The show opened in Bolton with ten new numbers included in its score. By the time it reached London, even more was new, but it was effective and so was its new leading 'man'. Paul Jones was played by the Errol-Flynnish American contralto Agnes Huntington, whose performance caused the biggest musical theatre sensation in years, Harry Monkhouse and Albert James were the comical Bouillabaisse and Petit-Pierre (with an interpolated number by md Frederic Stanislaus), with another American singer Tillie Wadman as Yvonne and Phyllis Broughton as the crocodile lady.

If anything, *Paul Jones* proved even a bigger hit even than *Surcouf*. The London production ran for a year (370 performances) and toured widely and long, and Farnie's version was also produced in both America where Miss Huntington starred alongside Marguerite van Breydell (Yvonne), Fanny Wentworth, Hallen Mostyn and James for a month at the Broadway Theater, and, with great success, in Australia where it launched the Nellie Stewart Opera Company with that lady playing Yvonne to the pirate of Mme Marion Burton and the comicals of G H Snazelle and George Leitch.

In France, *Surcouf* was revived at the Théâtre de la Gaîté in 1893 (20 December) in a more spectacular version with the baritone Jacquin as the show's hero, and again at the Château d'Eau in 1901, and it remained on the provincial schedules for some time thereafter. During the Second World War the German administration decided to revive the show, with its anti-British sentiments, in Paris, but the publisher claimed that he had accidentally mislaid the scores and scripts (they had apparently been hastily buried in someone's garden) and the revival did not take place.

Robert Surcouf (Jean Maugendrez), another opérette having Surcouf as its hero, was produced in Mauritius on 22 August 1978.

Hungary: Népszinház *A kalózkirály* 28 February 1888; Austria: Carltheater *Der Freibuter* 1 September 1888; UK: Prince of Wales Theatre *Paul Jones* 12 January 1889; USA: Broadway Theater *Paul Jones* 6 October 1890; Australia: Opera House, Melbourne *Paul Jones* 27 March 1890

SUSI *see* A KIS GRÓF

DAS SÜSSE MÄDEL Operette in 3 acts by Alexander Landesberg and Leo Stein. Music by Heinrich Reinhardt. Carltheater, Vienna, 25 October 1901.

Graf Balduin Liebenburg (Karl Blasel) comes to town to take his nephew Hans (Willy Bauer) back to the family estate to wed his niece, Lizzi (Helene Schupp). He finds him in the gaudy company of what the boy insists is a charity committee, and so the old man invites Lola Winter (Mizzi Günther), the *süsse Mädel* of the title, who is really Hans's girlfriend, and the artist Florian Lieblich (Louis Treumann) to join them in the country. Florian's jealous little Fritzi (Therese Biedermann) follows secretly. Neither Hans nor Lizzi wishes to wed the other and, after some antics at a ball, an intempestive interruption by Fritzi – who Liebenburg becomes convinced is his illegitimate child – and various other quiproquos, everyone weds whom they wish. To put the icing on the ending, Balduin's long-lost lovechild turns out to be not a girl-child at all, but Lizzi's boyfriend, Prosper Plewny (Ferdinand Pagin).

Reinhardt's first attempt at a full-length Operette score produced a bundle of light, dancing Viennesey melodies, strong on waltzes and country rhythms, from which Lola's opening number 'So g'waschen wie a Damerl' (Lied vom süssen Mädel) turned out to be a huge popular hit. Hans's waltz 'Launische Dame, Glück ist dein Name' and several pretty duets – Lola and Hans's 'Geh' sag mir nicht, dass du mich liebst', a farewell duo, 'Warum verziehst du deinen Mund' (which had the particularity of a gramophone accompaniment), and Florian and Lizzi's burlesque of an English musical-comedy duet also stood out, and helped the show to – to the surprise of some – a great success.

In spite of criticisms, particularly of its 'unsubstantial' music, from those who regretted the passing of the 'Golden Age' style of Operette, director Andreas Aman's production of *Das süsse Mädel* was the most successful piece to have been turned out by a Viennese composer in years. It was played 140 times in succession and eventually ran up its total to more than 200 performances at the Carltheater (200th performance, 18 April 1905) before returning at the Raimundtheater in 1909 with a cast headed by Genie von Grossl (Lola), Gerda Walde (Fritzi), Marie Trethan (Lizzi), Carl Streitmann (Hans) and Franz Glawatsch (Prosper). The show found a similarly enthusiastic response in Germany (Otto Keller's survey of 1925 rated it all-time number 30 amongst Viennese Operetten for the number of performances given in Germany) and went on to productions in Hungary (ad Gyula Komor) and throughout central Europe. A German-language production by José Ferenczy's Berlin company which played at New York's Irving Place Theater, with Mia Werber as Lola, Edmund Loewe as Florian, Sigmund Kunstadt as Hans, Therese Delma (Lizzi), Henny Wildner (Fritzi), Rudolf Ander (Balduin) and Carl Knaack (Prosper), was again a great hit, lasting for over a month in its first run and being reprised in 1910 with Lucie Engelke starred (19 April) without, curiously, finding the piece a vernacular production. Britain's 1906 English-language production (ad A Demain Grange, William Caine, Herbert Cottesmore, add mus K Ernest Irving), mounted by one Charles Hamilton (apparently the London agent for the Shuberts) to feature leading lady Claudia Lasell and mooted for the Shaftesbury Theatre, did not make London.

The success of *Das süsse Mädel* has been pointed up as a turning point in the Viennese musical theatre, one which signalled the end of that 'Golden Age' which had been marked by the works of such composers as Suppé, Strauss and Millöcker. By turning in a direction which followed and embraced the more folksy elements of works such as Zeller's *Der Vogelhändler* and *Der Obersteiger*, but which yet lightened them into an up-to-date and frothy musical score and story, Reinhardt and *Das süsse Mädel* helped lay the first foundations for the 'Silver Age' of 20th-century musical theatre in Vienna.

Germany: Centraltheater ?1902; Hungary: Fővárosi Nyari Színkör *Az édes lányka* 26 April 1902; USA: Irving Place Theater (Ger) 10 March 1903; UK: Theatre Royal, Nottingham *The Sweet Girl* 27 August 1906

SWANBOROUGH Family

The Swanborough family was a prominent and important one in the world of the London musical theatre in the third quarter of the 19th century. For years they ran the old Strand Theatre as a home for some of the best and brightest burlesque entertainments in town, launching many pieces which went on from their initial London runs to performances all round the English-speaking theatre world, and taking the technical honour of being the producers of the 'first English opéra-bouffe' when F C Burnand and house musical director Frank Musgrave wrote, and they staged, the original musical burlesque *Windsor Castle*.

Their era began when William Swanborough took up the lease of the decrepit and out-of-favour Strand Theatre in 1858. He overhauled it and, intermittently putting variously the name of his wife – the soon-to-be-'famous' Mrs Malaprop of the West End theatre establishment – or his elder daughter, known simply as 'Miss Swanborough' and already established as a burlesque actress at the Olympic (Alphonse in *Masaniello*, Princess Young and Handsome in *Young and Handsome* etc), at the head of the bill as proprietor, for reasons which apparently had something to do with financial liabilities, launched it on a diet of multiple-bill burlesque and comedy productions.

The musical pasticcio burlesques played a major part in the entertainment at the Strand and many of them – at first largely from the pen of H J Byron (author of the house's two previous burlesques, and who was said to be 'behind' and well as 'with' the Swanborough régime), later from other top burlesque authors including Burnand and Farnie – were major successes. The list of their original productions, which continued through the death of father Swanborough without any change in policy, included *Fra Diavolo Travestie* (5 April 1858), *The Bride of Abydos* (31 May 1858), *The Maid and the Magpie* (11 October 1858), *The Very Latest Edition of the Lady of Lyons* (11 July 1859), *The Miller and His Men* (9 April 1860), *Cinderella* (26 December 1860), *Aladdin, or the Wonderful Scamp* (1 April 1861), *Esmeralda or the Sensation Goat* (28 September 1861), *Puss in a New Pair of Boots* (26 December 1861), *Pizzaro, or the Leotard of Peru* (21 April 1862), *Ivanhoe* (26 December 1862), *Ali Baba, or the 39 Thieves* (6 April 1863), *The Motto* (16 July 1863), *Patient Penelope* (25 November 1863), *Orpheus and Eurydice* (26 December 1863), *Mazourka* (27 April 1864), *The Grin Bushes* (26 December 1864), and *Windsor Castle* (5 June 1865).

These shows proved to be successful enough that in 1865 the Swanboroughs were able to upgrade their theatre, reopening with further bills in the same style on which featured such burlesques as *L'Africaine* (18 November 1865), *Paris, or Vive Lemprière* (2 April 1866), *The Latest Edition of Kenilworth* (revival), *Der Freischutz* (8 October 1866), *Guy Fawkes* (26 December 1866), *Pygmalion and the Statue Fair* (20 April 1867), *William Tell with a Vengeance* (5 October 1867), *The Caliph of Baghdad* (26 December 1867), *The Field of the Cloth of Gold* (11 April 1868), *Joan of Arc* (29 March 1869), *The Pilgrim of Love* (revival, 30 August 1869), *Ino* (30 October 1869), *The Flying Dutchman* (2 December 1869), *Sir George and a Dragon* (31 March 1870), *The Field of the Cloth of Gold* (revival, May 1870), *The Idle Prentice* (10 September 1870), *Coeur de Lion* (December 1870), *Eurydice* (24 April 1870), *My Poll and Partner Joe* (6 May 1871), *The Three Musket-Dears* (1871), *Arion* (20 December 1871), *The Vampire* (15 August 1872) and *The Lady of the Lane* (31 October 1872).

Keeping within reach of the same kind of entertainment, the theatre moved on in the 1870s to play a mixture of pasticcio musical comedies, extravaganzas which only occasionally put themselves up as regular burlesques, and revivals of old favourites. Amongst the new pieces were the hugely successful *Nemesis* (17 April 1873), *Eldorado* (19 February 1874), *Loo* (28 September 1874), *Intimidad* (8 April 1875), *Flamingo* (18 September 1875), *Antarctica* (26 December 1875), *The Lying Dutchman* (21 December 1876), *Champagne* (29 September 1877), *An Ambassador from Below* (1878), *Dora and Diplunacy* (14 February 1878) and *The Desperate Adventures of the Baby* (1878). Mrs Swanborough then sublet the house to Alexander Henderson, the newly rich producer of *Les Cloches de Corneville*, for his French opéra-comique productions. In 1882 the Strand Theatre was once again rebuilt, but by 1887 the Swanboroughs were in financial difficulties, Mrs Swanborough was adjudged bankrupt, and the theatre was finally ceded to J S Clarke, thus ending the most famous era of its existence.

Alongside the Swanborough parents, William (d 1863) and his wife Mary Ann – always billed just as **Mrs (H V) SWANBOROUGH** (b 1804; d London 6 January 1889), five of their offspring worked at the Strand Theatre, of whom the youngest **[Marianne] Ada SWANBOROUGH** (b ?1845; d London, 12 December 1893) was the most prominent. The 'handsome, tall and graceful' actress took leading rôles in the theatre's burlesque productions from her teens – William in *Puss in a New Pair of Boots*, Hardress Cregan in *Eily O'Connor*, Lady Rowena in *Ivanhoe*, Eurydice to the Orpheus of Marie Wilton in *Orpheus and Eurydice*, Amy Robsart in *The Latest Edition of Kenilworth*, Geraldine in *The Grin Bushes*, Agnes in *Der Freischutz*, Penelope in *Patient Penelope*, Venus in *Paris*, William Tell in *William Tell with a Vengeance* – but latterly left the burlesque plums to others and appeared more in the comedy parts of the bill.

The team initially included her sister, who starred in leading rôles at the Strand until her marriage and retirement in 1860, and her brothers, William H Swanborough (b ?1828; d Liverpool, 17 December 1886), Arthur [Henry K] Swanborough (b ?1837; d London, 22 December 1895) and Edward Swanborough (d 21 December 1908). William appeared on the stage, playing Beppo in the *Fra Diavolo* burlesque and other such rôles, was 'acting manager' of the house and also directed a number of the shows (a job which was later taken by his mother), before expanding his theatrical interests at other London houses and in the provinces (Prince of Wales Theatre, Birmingham etc); Arthur was treasurer at the Prince of Wales, Birmingham, manager of the Royalty, and held the post of front-of-house manager at the Strand for a number of years before becoming manager of the Royal Music Hall in Holborn, and Edward managed the box-office and, after the collapse, ended up as manager of the London Pavilion.

The two younger brothers also married prominent actresses of the burlesque stage. Arthur was the husband of Eleanor Bufton (b ?1840; d London, 9 April 1893) and Edward of Fanny Hughes (b ?1842, d London, 12 January 1888).

SWEENEY TODD, the Demon Barber of Fleet Street Musical thriller in 2 acts by Hugh Wheeler based on a play by Chris Bond. Music and lyrics by Stephen Sondheim. Uris Theater, New York, 1 March 1979.

Sweeney Todd, the demon barber of Fleet Street, first saw daylight in Chapter One of a tale called *The String of Pearls*, written by one Fred Hazleton Esq ('author of *Edith the Captive, Charley Wag* etc') and published in a magazine called *The People's Periodical and Family Library* in 1846. The character of the barber who 'tilted his customers out of the shaving chair through a trap-door into a cellar, where he pickled them and made them into pork pies' quickly caught the public imagination and it appeared on the stage at the Britannia Theatre early the next year (*Sweeney Todd, or the Fiend of Fleet Street* by George Dibdin Pitt 8 March 1847). Hazleton's name was attached to a rival version played at the Bower Saloon as *Sweeney Todd, the Barber of Fleet Street, or The String of Pearls*, the Grecian mounted a *The String of Pearls* in 1861, a Whitechapel melodrama subtitled *The Life and Death of Sweeney Todd* was produced the following year and a Matt Wilkinson drama came out in 1870. *Sweeney Todd* was repeated regularly on the British stage for more than half a century, and other versions, including one by Andrew Melville, gave the early ones concurrence in the period where the bloody barber came to the height of his fame on the British stage, in the person of grand guignol specialist Tod Slaughter.

Although the demon barber might have seemed obvious meat for the operatic stage, he apparently did not ever make it there. On the other hand, he did make several appearances with musical accompaniment on the British stage, notably in 1959 when Donald Cotton and Brian Burke's *The Demon Barber* was mounted at the Lyric, Hammersmith (10 December) with Roy Godfrey as Todd and one Barry Humphries, né Dame Edna Everage, as Jonas Fogg. Todd's musical apotheosis came, however, as the result of a 1973 mounting of a version of *Sweeney Todd* written and staged by Chris Bond at London's suburban Half Moon Theatre. This version's difference was that it presented Todd not as a twisted maniac, but as a cruelly-done-by fellow whose murders were part of/a result of his

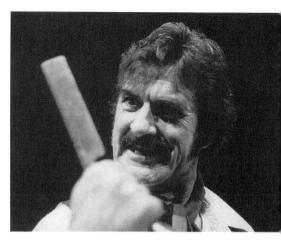

Plate 259. *Leon Greene as the demon barber of Fleet Street in th Manchester Library Theatre's 1985 production of* **Sweeney Todd**.

revenge against his (upper-class) oppressor(s), and there fore either all right, or at the worst comprehensible. Th Sweeney was the hero rather than the villain of his piec and this production, in its turn, inspired another, mor substantial, and musical *Sweeney Todd*.

Sweeney Todd (Len Cariou) returns to London cit after 15 years of prison exile, with nothing but revenge i his heart. For once upon a time he was a barber with pretty young wife and a little daughter, but a lecherou judge lusted after the barber's wife and so he had he husband transported on a trumped-up charge, raped th woman and kept her child. Todd sets up shop in Flee Street, above a pie-shop run by a common widow calle Mrs Lovett (Angela Lansbury) who soon becomes his all He establishes a reputation for his skill and determines t lure the hated Judge Turpin (Edmund Lyndeck) to h barber's chair and blade. His plans go wrong when th efforts of his young friend Anthony (Victor Garber) to ru off with Todd's daughter Johanna (Sarah Rice), a pal little prisoner whom the Judge has planned to wed himsel are exposed.

His prey escaped, Todd sets off instead on a mindles round of murders. And the corpses of his victims go t make the fillings for Mrs Lovett's pies. Eventually th Judge's turn comes, but the horror is not at an end ye Todd discovers that a crazed beggar-woman who ha fallen to his blade was his wife – not dead as Mrs Love had pretended, but witless from her rape. In revenge h hurls the widow into her own oven before he himself i cut down by her brain-addled shop-boy, Tobias (Ke Jennings). After a hecatomb to challenge *Hamlet* only th juveniles are left standing to provide a happy ending c sorts.

The melodrama was illustrated by a large score, frame in the broadsheet-style 'Ballad of Sweeney Todd', a scor which was threatening in colour, dissonant in tone on moment, and grotesquely comical the next, with the comi moments sometimes proving the most truly horrid. Mr Lovett admitted to selling 'The Worst Pies in London chuckled with Todd over the prospect of much tastie man-meat ones in the music-hally 'A Little Priest' an sang horribly flirtatious parlour music at Todd ('By th

Sea') between murders, whilst Todd duetted with the judge over 'Pretty Women' as he prepared to slit his victim's throat. Elsewhere the barber thundered out his maddened 'Epiphany', Anthony serenaded his 'Johanna', a rival Italian barber (Joaquin Romaguera) – soon to be Todd's first victim – vaunted his wares in burlesque operatic tones ('Pirelli's Miracle Elixir'), and in a rare moment of sensibility Mrs Lovett cuddled her frightened little shopboy to assure him '(No one's going to harm you) Not While I'm Around'.

Hal Prince's original production of *Sweeney Todd* encased this fairly straightforward grand guignol story in a welter of meaningful scenery in the most extravagant opérette à grand spectacle style. There were looming grey walls and a roof representing an industrial-revolutionized British factory, all heavy with implications of social (dis)order. There was a pipe organ on the proscenium arch. There was also a razor which spurted blood in the best traditions of the grand-guignol stage as each victim's throat was sliced. The production provoked mixed reactions, but for many the verdict was that somewhere the amongst the scenery, and underneath the sometimes rather pretentious sentiments that had been pasted on top of the story, there was a fine show.

Sweeney Todd took its season's Tony Award as Best Musical and played 557 performances at Broadway's Uris Theater, but a reproduction of the New York staging at London's Theatre Royal, Drury Lane, with Denis Quilley (Todd), Sheila Hancock (Mrs Lovett), Austin Kent (Judge), Andrew C Wadsworth (Anthony) and Michael Staniforth (Tobias) proved a quick failure (157 performances). The show was taken on tour in America, with Lansbury and Lyndeck repeating their original performances alongside take-over Todd, George Hearn, and this production was filmed for television (1982) before, in 1984, *Sweeney Todd* was produced by the New York City Opera.

However, whilst the musical headed for what had always seemed its story's natural home on the operatic stage, it also began to find itself a second life on another level, in another area. It was produced in Britain in a severely cut-down version – no factory, no pipe-organ, no large chorus and orchestra, just the savage story of Sweeney Todd, told in music (and with the Judge's rôle musically restored to its full length after having been cut in New York previews). Bond mounted this stark and spare version back at the Half Moon, with Leon Greene as Todd, and the piece began to find an audience in Britain which it had not attracted at Drury Lane. Provincial productions proliferated, and *Sweeney Todd* became established in the repertoire in a manner which had looked wholly unlikely after its unfortunate first London production.

In 1988 the show was mounted in Australia by the Melbourne Theatre Company with Peter Carroll and Geraldine Turner featured, subsequently playing a season in Sydney (Her Majesty's Theatre, 6 January 1988, 28 performances), and in 1989 a similarly reduced-size version (length and breadth) was mounted at New York's Circle in the Square with Bob Gunton and Beth Fowler in the featured rôles (14 September, 189 performances). Gathering impetus all the time, an impetus fuelled by the growing cult for Sondheim's works, particularly in the subsidized sector of the theatre, *Sweeney Todd* appeared in 1992 on the Hungarian stage, and in 1993 on the studio stage of Britain's National Theatre.

UK: Theatre Royal, Drury Lane 2 July 1980; Australia: Melbourne Theatre Company 1987; Hungary: Erkel Theater *Nyakfelmetsző* 5 June 1992; TV film: RKO/Nederlander 1982
Recording: original cast (RCA)

SWEET ADELINE Musical in 2 acts by Oscar Hammerstein II. Music by Jerome Kern. Hammerstein's Theater, New York, 3 September 1929.

Sweet Adeline was evolved by Hammerstein and Kern as a vehicle for the talents of Helen Morgan, who had recently created the rôle of Julie in *Show Boat* for them. An historical setting was chosen – 1890s Hoboken – and Miss Morgan was cast as the daughter of a beer-garden-proprietor who is unlucky in love (an uncomplicated romantic tale for the deliciously suffering Miss Morgan would have been entirely inept) but instead becomes a Broadway star, with a different man (Robert Chisholm) at her side. Her sister Nellie (Carly Bergman) gets the much-loved sailor (Max Hoffman jr) who caused Addie's misery.

The enduring song from this score, performed first by Miss Morgan and subsequently outside the show by more torchy vocalists, is the broadly broken-hearted 'Why Was I Born?'. Miss Morgan's other numbers ('Here Am I', 'Don't Ever Leave Me') shared the same flavour, leading Gerald Bordman in his biography of Kern to catalogue them nicely as 'three sweet, long-faced sisters'. This tendency to misery gave the carefully constructed period operetta a rather downbeat feeling which was only partially alleviated by such pieces as the bright, waltzing 'The Sun About to Rise' and the interpolations written and/or performed by Irene Franklin as an incidental Hoboken starlet.

Arthur Hammerstein's production of *Sweet Adeline* made a fine start on Broadway, but had its prospects shattered when the Wall Street Crash occurred just a few months into the run. 234 performances in such an ambiance were better than most shows managed. But in spite of this the show did not travel beyond America. It did however make it to celluloid. Kern went to Hollywood to supply extra numbers for a Warner Brothers film version, starring Irene Dunne, which bore more resemblance to its original than many other such films. Alongside seven of the show score songs, one number ('Lonely Feet') taken from his London failure *Three Sisters*, and three fresh ones, there was however also found place for the well-known von Tilzer/Bryan 'Down Where the Wertzberger Flows'.

Sweet Adeline was given a revival at the Goodspeed Opera House in 1977 (26 April).

Film: Warner Bros 1935
Recording: film soundtrack (part-record) (JJA)

SWEET CHARITY Musical comedy in 2 acts by Neil Simon based on the screenplay *Nights of Cabiria* by Federico Fellini, Tullio Pinelli and Ennio Flaiano. Lyrics by Dorothy Fields. Music by Cy Coleman. Palace Theater, New York, 29 January 1966.

The adaptation of Federico Fellini's film *Nights of Cabiria* into what eventually became *Sweet Charity* was originally done by director/choreographer Bob Fosse in the form of a one-act, half-of-an-evening musical comedy. However, the other half of the project eventually faded away and Neil Simon came in to develop the *Sweet Charity* half into a full-length musical comedy. In the process, he considerably softened down the cruel and rather gaudy colours of the original dramatic film. The heroine of that film had been a prostitute, Charity Hope Valentine (as her name suggested) was a dancing hostess in a seedy New York ballroom where you got the impression that some of the girls 'did' and some of them 'didn't'. Not unless they were in love, anyway. Cabiria, as created by Guilietta Masina, was a simple, willing girl who cannot keep a 'protector', who is the unkind joke of her fellow workers, and who is so unhappy that she attempts to drown herself. When Charity Hope Valentine falls into the water, it is accidentally and for laughs.

Falling is Charity's problem – or, rather, falling in love. She seems to do it every moment that she's not already done it, but always with the wrong kind of feller. She gets dumped as regularly as she is picked up, but she always comes back, hopeful as ever, and falls in love with the next man who asks. Her adventures during the course of the show include an accidental encounter with a Continental filmstar, Vittorio Vidal (James Luisi), who has had a stormy bust-up with his girl and who just uses Charity until the bust is mended, and an encounter with shy, deeply sincere Oscar (John McMartin) whom she meets in a stuck lift in the 92nd Street YMHA. Oscar actually gets round to proposing, but although he says that the equivocal nature of Charity's employment and the unequivocal nature of her past don't worry him, they do, and at the end of the evening Charity is back to picking herself up and starting over again.

The rôle of Charity was created by Gwen Verdon, accredited star of Fosse's productions of *Damn Yankees*, *New Girl in Town* and *Redhead*, and star and character came together perfectly in one of Broadway's most memorable performances of the era. Charity dreamed and hoped her way through a series of songs: the self-deluding 'You Should See Yourself', a jubilant 'If My Friends Could See Me Now' as she found herself in the company of the film star, an encouraging 'I'm the Bravest Individual' to the lift-shy Oscar, a dizzy 'Where Am I Going?' as she quit her dance-hall job, and an explosive 'I'm a Brass Band' on her receipt of her first proposal. The show's biggest single song successes, however, came not from the star's solo line-up but from two rather tongue-in-cheek numbers. Charity's sisters-in-work, Nickie (Helen Gallagher) and Helene (Thelma Oliver) led a tartily over-the-top encouragement to a 'Big Spender' to be their partner for the evening, and a visit to Oscar's 'church', the Rhythm of Life Church, turned up a parody of such institutions as the leader of the group, Johann Sebastian Brubeck (Arnold Soboloff), let rip with his creed in song and dance ('The Rhythm of Life'). Both songs, taken from their context, suffered the 'When Britain Really Ruled the Waves' fate of being later taken at face value and performed without the slightest satirical intent.

If the presence in the season's lists of *Man of La Mancha* and *Mame* limited the show's Tony Award takings to just a prize for Fosse's choreography, *Sweet Charity* was nevertheless a first-class Broadway hit, playing 608 performances before setting off on the road with Chita Rivera in the rôle of Charity. Australia was quickly off the mark with a production of the show and *Sweet Charity*, with Nancye Hayes as Charity supported by Peter Adams (Oscar),

Plate 260. *Juliet Prowse as London's* **Sweet Charity**.

Judith Roberts (Nickie) and Alec Novak (Vidal), opened there 12 months into the Broadway run. It played four months in Sydney and two and a half in Melbourne (Her Majesty's Theatre 6 May 1967). Harold Fielding and Bernard Delfont mounted London's version of *Sweet Charity* later the same year with Juliet Prowse as its leading lady alongside Rod McLennan (Oscar), Josephine Blake (Nickie), Paula Kelly (Helene) and Fred Evans (Brubeck), and the show marked up another hit through a run of 476 performances.

A film version of the show put out in 1969 featured Shirley Maclaine as Charity, alongside McMartin, Miss Rivera, Ricardo Montalban (Vidal) and Sammy Davis jr (Brubeck). It included the main numbers from the original score, but added a couple more and replaced the original title-song with another under the same title. And *Sweet Charity* continued its way around the world. In 1970 the piece was seen in Paris, traditionally shy of Broadway material, where Arthur Lesser mounted a version (ad Albert Husson, Jacques Plante) at the Théâtre de la Gaîté-Lyrique with Magali Noël playing Charity alongside Jacques Duby (Oscar), Sidney Chaplin (Vidal), Dominique Tirmont (Brubeck), Florence Arnell and Corinne Marchand, and in Germany. Germany's first *Sweet Charity* (the title survived, as in France) production was at Wiesbaden (ad Victor Bach, Marianne Schubart) with Dagmar Koller as Charity, and the following year this version made its first appearance on the other side of the then Wall when it was mounted at the Dresden Staatsoperette (29 April 1971).

Sweet Charity maintained a place in the standard repertoire through the years after its first productions, and in 1986 it made a return to Broadway. Fosse again directed and choreographed a version which had been slightly fiddled with musically – the Mark II title-song held its place – and Debbie Allen, the heroine of television's series *Fame*, starred as Charity alongside Michael Rupert (Oscar), Bebe Neuwirth (Nickie), Allison Williams (Helene), Mark Jacoby (Vidal) and Irving Allen Lee (Brubeck). Produced at the Minskoff Theater by the now-normal clutch of producers (four were billed) on 27 April, it this time picked up four Tony Awards from the now rather more extended selection available to be shared amongst many less and lesser contenders, and it ran for 386 performances. In 1992 another major revival was mounted at Berlin's Theater des Westens (24 January) with Michelle Becker starred, as *Sweet Charity* passed her first quarter-century as a hardy perennial.

Australia: Her Majesty's Theatre, Sydney, 21 January 1967; UK: Prince of Wales Theatre 11 October 1967; France: Théâtre de la Gaîté-Lyrique 1970; Germany: Staatstheater, Wiesbaden, February 1970; Film: Universal 1969

Recordings: original cast (Columbia), London cast (CBS), French cast (CBS), German cast (Decca), New York revival cast (EMI), Dutch cast (Philips), film soundtrack (Decca) etc

SWEETHEART MINE Musical comedy in 2 acts by Lauri Wylie and Lupino Lane based on the play *My Old Dutch* by Albert Chevalier. Lyrics by Frank Eyton. Music by Noel Gay. Victoria Palace, London, 1 August 1946.

The fourth and last of the long-running series of Lupino Lane 'little cockney chappie' musicals produced at the Victoria Palace, *Sweetheart Mine* did not find the same success as *Twenty to One* or *Me and My Girl*, but it nevertheless filled the house which he had made his own through eight months and 323 performances in the year after the war.

In a tale taken from Albert Chevalier's successful play (based in its turn on the famous song of the same title), Lane, surrounded by mostly the same company of family and friends as had worked with him in the earlier shows, starred as the layabout 'Arry 'Awkins whose 'old dutch' Liza (Barbara Shotter) wins a fortune and spends it trying vainly to make something of her husband. The score, in the jolly drop-your-aitches cockney vein, featured such Noel Gay numbers as the 'The Missus, the Moke and Me', "Appy 'Ampstead' and 'It's all a Blooming Lot of La-di-da', but the highlight of the musical part was Lane's eleven o'clock performance of Chevalier's original song: 'We've been together now for forty years, and it don't seem a day too much ...'.

SWEETHEARTS Operetta in 2 acts by Harry B Smith and Fred de Grésac. Lyrics by Robert B Smith. Music by Victor Herbert. New Amsterdam Theater, New York, 8 September 1913.

Victor Herbert wrote a great deal of highly attractive music in his career, Fred de Grésac wrote the delicious light comedy *La Passerelle* and Harry B Smith the neat comic opera libretto of *Robin Hood*, amongst a long list of others. They also got together and wrote *Sweethearts*.

Princess Sylvia of Zilania (Christie MacDonald) has been stolen away from her home as a baby to keep her safe from a revolution, and boarded with an unobtrusive family of working folk in a far-off country. (No, this is not *The Gondoliers*, it is not burlesque ... it is for real, and it's 1913.) Sylvia's foster-family aren't gondoliers, however, because they live in Bruges and she's a girl. They are laundry-folk.

Dame Paula (Ethel Du Fre Houston) runs a washing-shop called 'The White Geese'. Back home in Zilania, with the Princess given up for lost, a distant cousin called Prince Franz (Thomas Conkey) is more or less about to ascend the throne, but he comes to Belgium, just happens to wander into the washing shop, falls in love with the laundry-maid, and after a couple of acts of ups and downs they get round to true love and half-a-crown apiece. Tom McNaughton played Mikel Mikelovicz, the Prime Minister who originally stole the princess and brought her to Bruges and left her gaily prattling, Hazel Kirke was soubrette Liane who disguises herself as one of the White Geese girls to fake a disappearance and gets mistaken for the Princess, and Edwin Wilson was Karl, over whom Sylvia sighed even for a little while after she knew he was a rotter, before getting round to falling for Franz.

Herbert's score was not up to those for most of his comic operas. There was a dainty little number, 'Cricket in the Hearth', for the heroine, who also had a more soulful one singing about 'The Angelus' and a title-duo to share with her Prince, whilst he in his turn had a stridingly baritonic number declaring that 'Every Lover Must Meet His Fate'. Perhaps strangely, the prettiest moment of the score came in a nicely silly little Belgian number for the soubrette all about 'Jeanette and Her Little Wooden Shoes'.

Louis Werba and Mark Luescher's production of *Sweethearts* did very nicely. If it did not come up to their last production with Miss MacDonald, *The Spring Maid* (*Die Sprudelfee*), or to their second Smith brothers adaptation, *The Rose Maid* (*Bub oder Mädel*), in terms of its first run of Broadway performances, it nevertheless totted up 136 nights in New York before going on the road. And, unlike the two Continental shows, it came back. The Shuberts produced *Sweethearts* as part of their revival series at the Jolson Theater in 1929 with Gladys Baxter as Sylvia (21 September), it gave its title and a handful of its songs to a 1938 Jeanette MacDonald and Nelson Eddy film (for which, understandably, it was thought wiser to scrap the libretto entirely), and it returned to Broadway in 1947 in a production co-sponsored by Paula Stone and Michael Sloane, by which time its songs had become familiar and, ergo, 'favourites'.

Miss Stone had done splendidly with a revival of her father Fred's old vehicle *The Red Mill*, starring comedian Bobby Clark, two years earlier. She now looked around for another Victor Herbert piece for Clark and, of all the jolly comical musicals available she chose *Sweethearts* ... and had a comedy rôle written in (ad John Cecil Holm). Or, rather, up. Clark played Prime Minister Mikel, and when the second act arrived the hoary old plot went out of the window in the good old 19th-century fashion and the comedian got to do his thing. Gloria Story as Sylvia also profited, as the soprano ballad 'The Land of My Own Romance' was lifted from Herbert's score for *The Enchantress* and added to the score, along with *Angel Face*'s 'I Might Be Your Once in a While'. June Knight was Liane, Marjorie Gateson played Dame Paula, Mark Lawson was Franz, and *Sweethearts* comedy-model stayed a fine 288 performances at the Shubert Theater (21 January). Which seemed to signify, in statistical terms that it was twice as good without half its plot. Regional companies in America have, however, preferred not to take this reductio ad logicam to its end, and versions of *Sweethearts* still appears from time to time on amateur and professional stages. Some shows are simply survivors.

Recording: selections (RCA, MMG etc), 1944 radio broadcast (Pelican)

SWEET YESTERDAY Musical romance in 3 acts by Philip Leaver. Lyrics by Leaver, James Dyrenforth and Max Kester. Music by Kenneth Leslie-Smith. Adelphi Theatre, London, 21 June 1945.

A musical with a message, *Sweet Yesterday* was written and composed for BBC Radio (26 January 1941 Home Programme) to push home to the public that 'careless talk costs lives'. It was subsequently enlarged to stage size and produced by Lee Ephraim with radio vocalists Anne Ziegler and Webster Booth starring in a tale of love and sacrifice set in the Napoleonic wars and leading up to the British victory at Trafalgar.

The tale was set with an attractive if unexceptional romantic operetta score of the kind which gave Miss Ziegler and Booth plenty of legato things to sing and Doris Hare and Mark Daly, in the chief comedy rôles, some light relief, and *Sweet Yesterday* found some success in the atmosphere prevailing in immediately postwar London. But if the War in Europe was over, war backstage was not. *Sweet Yesterday*'s preparation had been full of sackings and unpleasantness and, after 196 West End performances, the stars refused to renew their contracts and the show was withdrawn.

SWING ALONG Musical show in 2 acts by Guy Bolton, Fred Thompson and Douglas Furber. Lyrics by Graham John. Music by Martin Broones. Gaiety Theatre, London, 2 September 1936.

Following the success of the revusical *Seeing Stars* at the Gaiety Theatre, producer Firth Shephard ordered another vehicle for Leslie Henson and company from the team which had written the earlier show. This time Henson was cast as little Maxie Mumm, stranded in nasty foreign Europe, and mixed up in the fearsome war between the 'Yellow Shirts' and the 'No Shirts'. In disguises which ranged from an impersonation of the Yellow Shirt leader to a Gainsborough hat and party frock, frog-faced Henson and his confederates – big, monocled, cigar-chomping Fred Emney and gangling, acrobatic Richard Hearne – went through a number of routines including a burlesque of radio broadcasting, a parodied can-can, and a ladies' trio (for which Emney retained his monocle and cigar), whilst juveniles Roy Royston and Louise Browne repeated their song-and-dance assignment, she danced an interpolated ballet scena, and London's most esoteric baddie, Gavin Gordon, stalked and bullied little Maxie through the various phases of the plot.

A merry, ephemeral score featured 'Another Dream Gone Wrong' for Miss Browne, the more lively 'Like a Tin Can Tied to a Puppy Dog's Tail' performed by Zelma O'Neal in one of the incidental soubrette rôles in which she specialized, and the grotesque, revusical trio 'Let's Be Ladies' performed by the three stars.

The layout, one not too distant from the old-style Gaiety entertainments of the turn of the century, worked well. *Swing Along* proved even more successful than *Seeing Stars*, played 311 performances at the Gaiety, and then toured, whilst the company began the next in the series of musicals in the same vein with which they would enliven London during the late 1930s.

Swing Along was also mounted in Australia where a cast headed by George Gee, Valerie Hay, Donald Burr, Percy Le Fre, Lois Green and John Dobbie played four weeks at Sydney's Theatre Royal and five in Melbourne (Her Majesty's Theatre 19 February 1938).

Australia: Theatre Royal, Sydney 13 November 1937

SWOBODA, Albin (b Neustrelitz, 13 November 1836; d Dresden, 4 August 1901).

The son of opera singers, Swoboda first appeared on the stage in the chorus at the Theater in der Josefstadt at the age of 16. He later played parts in provincial and suburban theatres and in 1857 joined Nestroy's company at the Carltheater where, playing alongside such stars as Karl Treumann, Wilhelm Knaack and Therese Braunecker-Schäfer, he soon began to make himself popular. He moved to the Theater an der Wien in 1859 and there his youth, handsome looks, large and rich performance and fair tenor voice won him good rôles in comedy and Operette. After making his début in the little French opérette *Singspiel am Fenster* (4 February 1859), he created the jeune premier rôle of Karl in *Das Pensionat* (1860), appeared in Conradin's *Liebchen am Dach* (1861, Serafin), played Raimund to the Therese Krones of Gallmeyer, and introduced many of Offenbach's tenor rôles to Vienna: Paris opposite *La Belle Hélène* of Geistinger, *Blaubart* to her Boulotte, Piquillo to her *Périchole*, Policarpo (*Coscoletto*), Pyramus (*Die Schäfer*) and Siegfried (*Genovefa von Brabant*) as well as Henri in *Die Reise nach China* and Pinsonnet in *Theeblüthe*.

Swoboda left the Theater an der Wien and teamed with Knaack and Röhring as the three red knights in Suppé's short-lived *Die Jungfrau von Dragant* at the Carltheater (1870, 5 performances) but he returned as a guest artist to create the rôle of Janio in Strauss's *Indigo und die vierzig Räuber* (1871), to play Ugolino in Offenbach's *Fantasio* (1872) and Kipfelbäck in *Die Theaterprinzessin* (1872) and to create Millöcker's *Abenteuer in Wien* (Friedrich Bendel, 1873). He introduced a further Strauss rôle when he appeared as Arthur Bryk in *Carneval in Rom* (1873) and also appeared as Marasquin in Vienna's version of *Giroflé-Girofla* (1874). In 1878 he was Vienna's first Henri in *Die Glocken von Corneville*, in 1879 he created Nauticus in Genée's *Die letzten Mohikaner* and Hellmuth Forst in Strauss's *Blindekuh*, and played Falkenbach in Offenbach's *Der Brasilianer*. In a career that latterly leaned ever away from singing rôles, he played in Russia, in Berlin and in Dresden before largely retiring from the stage in 1888.

Swoboda made two attempts to move into theatrical management, first at the ill-fated Vienna Komische Oper (Ringtheater), and later, with barely better results, at Budapest's German-speaking theatre.

SYLVANE, André [GÉRARD, Paul Emile] (b Laigle, Orne, 27 March 1850; d 1932).

A commissaire-priseur by profession and a playwright and play doctor as a hobby, Sylvane wrote or collaborated on many plays with such authors as Alexandre Bisson (*Disparu*), Maurice Ordonneau (*L'Article 214*) and later André Mouëzy-Éon (*Tire-au-flanc!*) as well as on the texts of a number of musical plays, mostly in the vaudevillesque vein, often without his name appearing on the bill. He apparently had an uncredited hand in Bisson's highly successful *Un lycée de jeune filles* (1881) and in the Antony Mars-Maurice Desvallières libretto for the even more widely-travelled *La Demoiselle du téléphone* (1891), and his name was attached to the texts for Audran's *Madame Suzette* (74 performances), *Mon prince!* (85 performances) and *Les Petites Femmes*, as well as to the vaudeville *Patatart, Patart et Cie* (48 performances), which was later produced at the Theatre an der Wien as *Kneisl & Co* (ad Theodor Taube, Isidor Fuchs).

Tire-au-flanc!, adapted as a libretto by no less an author than the young Ferenc Molnár, became *Gyöngyélet* (Ferenc Békési/Adolf Mérei, Magyar Színház 21 April 1906) on the Hungarian musical stage.

1889 **Mam'zelle Pioupiou** (William Chaumet/w Alexandre Bisson) Théâtre de la Porte-Saint-Martin 31 May

1892 **Nini Fauvette** (Edmond Missa/w Charles Clairville) Théâtre des Nouveautés 16 January

1893 **Madame Suzette** (Edmond Audran/w Ordonneau) Théâtre des Bouffes-Parisiens 28 March

1893 **Patatart, Patatart et Cie** (Louis Gregh/w C Clairville) Théâtre des Folies-Dramatiques 9 October

1893 **Mon prince!** (Audran/w C Clairville) Théâtre des Nouveautés 18 November

1897 **Les Petites Femmes** (Audran) Théâtre des Bouffes-Parisiens 11 October

SZABADOS, Béla (b Budapest, 3 June 1867; d Budapest, 15 September 1936).

The younger brother of the composer and conductor Károly Szabados (1860–1892), Béla Szabados studied from the age of 14 at the Budapest Zeneakadémia and had his first symphonic and stage music (including the incidental music for Béla Hetényi's *Csicsóné*, 18 July 1884) played whilst he was still a student. He subsequently became a professor of music, and had his first operetts, to texts by Jenő Rákosi, played at the Népszinház in 1890 and 1891. However, in spite of being favoured with this conjunction of one of the country's best librettists and its most important musical theatre on his very first stage works, his first important success came only several years later, after he had taken up a teaching post at the Zeneakadémia, when the same theatre presented his 1895 operett *Rika* (25 performances).

The musical plays *A három Kázmér* (41 performances) and *A kuktakisasszony* (27 performances), which was later played in a revised version at Vienna's Theater an der Wien as *Die Kuchenkomtesse* (15 March 1898), the 'song legend' *A bolond* and *Szép Ilonka* gave him further successes, during a period in which he also composed both operatic scores (the one-act comic opera *Alszik a nagynéni*, 1895, *Mária* w Árpád Szendy/Géza Béri Magyar Király Operaház 28 February 1905) and incidental theatre music, as well as symphonic and chamber works.

Szabados subsequently held several high posts in the Budapest musical establishment, and returned only rarely to the musical theatre.

1890 **A négy király** (Jenő Rákosi) Népszinház 10 January

1891 **Az első és második** (Labiche ad Rákosi) Népszinház 8 April

1895 **Rika** (József Márkus) Népszinház 23 November

1896 **A három Kázmér** (László Béothy) Népszinház 25 January

Plate 261.

1897 **A kuktakisasszony** (J Márkus) Népszinház 23 November

1898 **A bolond** (Rákosi) Magyar Színház 29 December

1904 **Felsőbb asszonyok** (Károly Lovik) Népszinház 26 March

1904 **A múmia** (Vilmos Kaczér) Magyar Színház 9 April

1905 **Sportlovagok** (Gyula Déry) Fővárosi Nyari Színház 19 May

1906 **Szép Ilonka** (Gyula Szávay, Géza Vágó) Király Színház 20 October

1922 **Bolond Istók** (Ede Sass, Ákos Bihari) Városi Színház 22 December

1923 **Menyasszonyháború** (Sass) Városi Színház 7 December

1927 **Fanni** (Jenő Mohácsi) Magyar Király Operaház 16 February

SZIBILL Operett in 3 acts by Miksa Bródy and Ferenc Martos. Music by Viktor Jacobi. Király Színház, Budapest, 27 February 1914.

Szibill, first produced in Budapest at the dawn of the War years, was the peak achievement of the short career of composer Viktor Jacobi. The young musician, who had known little but success from the very beginning of his composing career, had made an international hit with *Leányvásár* (*The Marriage Market*) in 1911, and *Szibill* followed up some three years later, his last work for Budapest before leaving for America, disillusion and a premature death.

Lieutenant Petrov (Jenő Nádor) has deserted his regiment for love of the diva Sybil Renaud (Sári Fedák) and is in hiding in her hotel at provincial Bomsk. The local Governor, charged with capturing the runaway, mistakes Sybil for the Grand-Duchess Anna Pavlovna and, to give her lover the chance to escape, she takes up the pretence. Before the pair can get away, however, Sybil is forced to attend a reception in the Duchess's honour and there she finds herself faced with – the Duke (Ernő Király). He, delighted with the possibilities offered by this new 'wife', amusedly goes along with her deception, but both are taken aback when the real Grand-Duchess (Mici Haraszti) arrives and announces herself as Mme Renaud. Jealousies flare back and forth until Sybil is able to explain all to the angry Duchess, reunite her with her husband, and win a pardon for Petrov.

Jacobi's score mixed the romantic and the comic in impeccable measures. The romantic music rises to its height with the long-lined, pregnantly pausing duet between the Duke and Sybil as he, only half teasingly, asks her to imagine a sentimental idyll for two ('Illúzió a szerelem'), whilst Sybil's opening letter-song, as she writes to her Petrov, little knowing he is on his way to her, proved another highlight. The comic side of affairs is provided by Sybil's manager Poire (Márton Rátkai) and his wife Sarah (Juci Lábass), and Jacobi served them with some outstandingly lively duos in well-accented dance rhythms, topped by the energetic mazurka 'Gombhaz, sej, hogyha leszakad' and the light-footed 'Van valami', whilst Poire's bouncing duo with Sybil provided another memorably rhythmic moment ('Félre csapom a kalapom').

The First World War prevented *Szibill* from following its Budapest triumph with what would normally, in the wake of the success of *Leányvásár*, have been a quick appearance on international stages. However, war or none, America soon picked up the show that was the rage of in-fashion Budapest, and *Sybil* was produced on Broadway with Julia Sanderson and Donald Brian as the diva and the duke and Joseph Cawthorn as Poire paired with British revue comedienne Maisie Gay (Margot). Jacobi, who had seen *The Marriage Market* plugged full of mostly sub-standard interpolated songs, was on hand to provide new numbers as and when required, to fit with Harry Graham and Harry B Smith's version of the book.

The most successful of these was a solo for Sybil herself, 'The Colonel of the Crimson Hussars'. A blatantly simple and march-rhythmically sticking number, made to measure, it was not, however, of the same quality as the piece it replaced ('Volt egy hercegnő'). Several of Jacobi's best lighter, rhythmic numbers also went under the knife, and Cawthorn performed a number ('I Can Dance with Everybody But My Wife') which he had himself written with John Golden. But *Sybil* proved indestructible enough to be a considerable success in Charles Frohman's production at Broadway's Liberty Theater (168 performances), on the road, and in a quick revival at the Empire (28 August 1916).

After Fedák and Sanderson, another of the most outstanding stars of the contemporary musical theatre took up the rôle of Sybil when the first German-language performances (ad Robert Bodanzky) appeared after the war. Fritzi Massary and Guido Thielscher introduced the piece in Berlin and the diva then took it to Vienna, where it was performed for a successful season at the Wiener Stadttheater with Massary (and later Ida Russka) playing alongside Hubert Marischka as the Duke, Viktor Flemming as Petrov and Emil Guttmann as Poire. The show was later given a further 26 performances at the Theater an der Wien.

If Britain was slow in producing *Sybil*, it was not wholly because of anti-Germanic feeling in the wake of the war, but also because of a log jam of success. Robert Evett had bought the rights to the piece early on in order to star José Collins as Sybil, and Harry Graham had duly prepared his adaptation, but the continuing popularity of Miss Collins's current vehicles, *The Maid of the Mountains* and *A Southern Maid*, retarded the show's production in London, and thus Graham's version was seen on Broadway long before Evett was able to find it stage room in England. When *Sybil* did finally arrive at Daly's Theatre, in what now looked like a revised version of the American version, some seven years after the original Budapest production, it showed it had been worth the waiting for. It proved a magnificent vehicle for Miss Collins and ran from February to Christmas (347 performances) being removed only to allow a farewell season of *The Maid* prior to Evett and Miss Collins's departure from Daly's.

Miss Collins's Australian 'double', Gladys Moncrieff, was Sybil in her native country, with Claude Flemming, Leslie Holland, Robert Chisholm, Arthur Stigant (performing Cawthorn's song), Ethel Morrison and Clarice Hardwick supporting through an excellent original run of 11 weeks in Melbourne and a further ten in Sydney (Her Majesty's Theatre 8 February).

In Hungary, *Szibill* has remained in the standard repertoire and has been produced at the Fővárosi Operettszinház in 1932 (23 April), 1945 (21 December) and, most recently, in 1972 (21 January).

USA: Liberty Theater *Sybil* 10 January 1916; Austria: Wiener Stadttheater 12 February 1919; Germany: Metropoltheater October 1919; UK: Prince's Theatre, Manchester 26 December 1920, Daly's Theatre, London 19 February 1921; Australia: Theatre Royal, Adelaide 9 June 1923, Her Majesty's Theatre, Melbourne 23 June 1923
Recording: selection (Qualiton)

SZIKA, János (b Pest, 7 February 1844; d Vienna, 20 October 1916). The original Eisenstein of *Die Fledermaus* and the star of a long run of Viennese musicals.

After being originally destined for a medical education, Jani Szika began his stage career at the age of 18 at the Deutsches Theater in his native Pest. In 1864 Friedrich Strampfer hired him for the Theater an der Wien as an actor, but soon after he found himself cast in Bazin's *Die Reise nach China* (Maurice Fréval), in the spectacular *Prinzessin Hirschkuh* (La Biche au Bois, Mesrour), and as Prince Saphir in Offenbach's *Blaubart*. During the run of *Die Grossherzogin von Gerolstein* Szika stepped in to substitute for Albin Swoboda in the lead tenor rôle of Fritz, and coped so admirably with the part that his career from then on took a quite different turning, and he became a leading man in opéra-bouffe and Operette.

In 1868 Szika appeared as Charles Martell in *Genovefa von Brabant*, in 1871 as Flink in *Drei Paare Schuhe* and, in the same year, he created the lead light-comedy rôle of Ali Baba in Johann Strauss's maiden work, *Indigo und die vierzig Räuber*, as well as playing Marzas in Lecocq's *Le Rajah de Mysore* and Falsacappa in Offenbach's *Die Banditen*. In 1872 he was Spark in Offenbach's *Fantasio* and Emil Falkner in *Die Theaterprinzessin* (La Diva), in 1873 Benvenuti Raphaeli in Strauss's *Carneval in Rom*, Abälard in Litolff's *Abälard und Heloise* and Marcassou in Offenbach's *Die Wilderer* (Les Braconniers). In 1874 he appeared as Gstettner in Jonas's *Die Japanesin* and took time out briefly to attempt to run the ill-fated Komische Oper (later the Ringtheater, and the site of Vienna's worst ever theatre fire) before returning to the Theater an der Wien to create the most famous rôle of his career as Gabriel von Eisenstein to the Rosalinde of Marie Geistinger in *Die Fledermaus*.

In the following years he played in Offenbach's *Madame 'Herzog'* (1875, Giletti), created Graf Stefan Fodor in Strauss's *Cagliostro in Wien* (1875), played Albert von Graff in Varney's *Die Perle der Wascherinnen* (1875, *La Blanchisseuse de Berg-op-Zoom*), Frontignac in *Die Creolin* (1876, *La Créole*), Prinz Qui-Passe-Par-La in *Die Reise in den Mond* (1876, *Le Voyage dans la lune*), created the part of Lambert de Saint-Querlonde in *Der Seekadett* (1876), was the Fridolin of *König Carotte* (1876), Cornelius in *Die Porträt-Dame* (1877) and the first Marquis d'Aubigny in *Nanon* (1877) before ending his ten-year tenure with the Theater an der Wien.

In 1878 he returned as a guest artist to create the rôle of Sepp in *Das verwunschene Schloss* and in 1879 he appeared as Loisl in *Das Versprechen hinter'n Herd* with Geistinger, but he was engaged in Berlin in 1880 and he made his career during the 1880s largely in Germany. There he created the rôle of Caramello in Strauss's *Eine Nacht in Venedig* in 1883, but he spent an increasing amount of time acting in non-musical plays. In 1891 he went to Frankfurt where he completed his re-transformation back to being the straight actor he had begun as, and he spent his later years playing in classic drama and comedy, from Shakespeare to Schiller.

SZILÁGYI, László (b Budapest, 2 October 1898; d Budapest, 6 September 1942).

One of the foremost librettists of the Hungarian stage of his era, Szilágyi wrote the texts for a considerable body of successful shows for the Budapest musical theatre, notably in collaboration with the composers Béla Zerkovitz and Mihály Eisemann. Few of them, however, were seen outside Hungary.

His first full-length piece, the musical comedy *Levendula*, was played more than 75 times at the Várszínház and the Lujza Blaha Színház, the operett *Régi jó Budapest* ran over 125 performances, both his adaptation of the French *Clary-Clara* as the text for *Csókos asszony* and the even further westward-looking *Miss Amerika* passed the 75 performance mark first time up, and his Hungarian version of Broadway's *Good News* also topped 100 performances – a figure which marked a major success at the time. Amongst his later pieces, collaborations with the young Eisemann on the up-to-date musical comedy *Zsákbamacska*, which played some 250 performances at the Pesti Színház in 1932-3 with the young Marika Rökk as soubrette, and with the elderly Jenő Huszka on *Mária főhadnagy* both brought major local successes, whilst such pieces as Zerkovitz's *Eltörött a hegedüm*, Buday's *Csárdás* and several other Eisemann musicals also had good runs.

Zsákbamacska was produced in Vienna as *Katz im Sack* with Trude Berliner, Magda Kun and Steve Geray starred, and also seen briefly in Britain as *Happy Weekend* (1934), whilst Zerkovitz's *Csókos asszony* was played in Prague, *Miss Amerika* in Germany and Vincze's *Aranyhattyú* is said to have been played on the New York stage. His libretto to another successful piece, *Eltörött a hegedüm*, was later used

as the basis for an early Hollywood sound film. The Komjáti operett *Ein Liebestraum* was produced in Vienna in a German translation, with Marta Eggerth starred, for 49 performances.

Szilágyi's output also included both non-musical plays and screenplays.

1923 **Levendula** (Frigyes Friedl/Sandor Somló) Várszinház 16 February

1923 **A kék póstakocsi** (Dénes Buday) Várszinház 27 December

1924 **Amerika lánya** (Gyula Kiszely/Zsolt Harsányi) Városi Színház 17 May

1925 **Régi jó Budapest** (József Radó) Király Színház 20 May

1926 **Csókos asszony** (Béla Zerkovitz) Városi Színház 27 February

1926 **Muzsikus Ferkó** (Zerkovitz) Budai Szinkör 18 June

1927 **Aranyhattyú** (Zsigmond Vincze) Király Színház 15 January

1927 **A legkisebbik Horváth lány** (Zerkovitz) Király Színház 21 May

1928 **Eltörött a hegedüm** (Zerkovitz) Király Színház 3 November

1929 **Miss Amerika** (Mihály Eisemann) Fővárosi Operettszinház 12 January

1929 **Pesti család** (József Radó/Adorján Stella) Király Színház 5 September

1929 **Tommy és Társa** (Pál Tamássy/Ernő Anday) Király Színház 11 October

1929 **Diákszerelem** (*Good News*) Hungarian version (Király Színház)

1930 **Alvinci huszárok** (Eisemann) Király Színház 9 April

1931 **Gróf Romeo** (Tividar Szántó) Fővárosi Operettszinház 28 January

1932 **Zsákbamacska** (Eisemann) Pesti Színház 3 September

1932 **Pillangó** (József Kóla/w Andor Kardos) Fővárosi Operettszinház 25 September

1932 **Kadétszerelem** (Pál Gyöngy/w István Békeffy) Fővárosi Operettszinház 23 December

1933 **Ein Liebestraum** (Károly Komjáti/w Ferenc Martos ad Heinz Reichert) Theater an der Wien 27 October

1934 **Én és a kisöcsém** (Eisemann) Fővárosi Operettszinház 21 December

1935 **Ezüstmenyasszony** (Eisemann) Royal Színház 20 December

1936 **Meseáruház** (Eisemann) Fővárosi Operettszinház 11 April

1936 **Pármai ibolya** (Béla Dolecskó) Városi Színház 9 April

1936 **Csárdás** (Buday) Budai Szinkör 16 June

1937 **Gólyaszanatórium** (Eisemann/w Dezső Kellér) Márkus Park Színház 25 June

1937 **Éva a paradicsomban** (Tamás Bródy/w Kellér) Városi Színház 22 October

1938 **Nem leszek hálátlan** (Alfred Márkus) Andrássy-uti Színház 19 March; Magyar Színház 3 May

1938 **Szomjas krokodil** (Márkus/Imre Harmath) Márkus Park Színház 21 June

1939 **Erzsébet** (Jenő Huszka) Magyar Színház 5 January

1939 **Pusztai szerenád** (Szabolcs Fényes/w Istvan Békeffyú) Fővárosi Operettszinház 29 September

1939 **Pozsonyi lakodalom** (Miklós Beck) Fővárosi Operettszinház 17 November

1940 **Handa-Banda** (revised *Macskazene*) (Eisemann/Gyula Halász, Károly Kristóf ad) Fővárosi Operettszinház 26 January

1940 **Három huszár** (Buday/w Gyula Hálasz) Fővárosi Operettszinház 12 April

1940 **Tokaji aszu** (Eisemann) Magyar Színház 15 March

1940 **Angóramacska** (Eisemann) Vigszínház 26 April

1941 **Gyergyói bál** (Huszka) Magyar Színház 4 January

1942 **Vén diófa** (Fényes) Magyar Színház 26 March

1942 **Mária főhadnagy** (Huszka) Fővárosi Operettszinház 23 September

1943 **Die verliebte Station** (Dolecskó) Nuremberg 6 March
1943 **Egy boldog pesti nyár** (Buday, Eisemann, Fenyes/w Atilla Orbók) Fővárosi Operettszinház 14 April

SZIRMAI, Albert [aka SIRMAY] (b Budapest, 2 July 1880; d New York, 15 January 1967). Top-flight Hungarian composer whose career faded when he left home.

Szirmai studied at the Budapest Zeneakadémia and subsequently worked as musical director at the Modern Színpad whilst producing all types of music for Hungarian theatres, concert halls and cabaret houses. His output included instrumental music, ballet scores, chamber music, a pair of so-called comic operas (*Bálkirálynő*, 1908, *Harangvirág*, 1918), a large number of songs and, most notably, a long string of operetts and musical comedies, the first of which, *A sárga dominó*, was produced by Raoul Mader at the Népszinház-Vigopera in 1907 (18 performances).

Szirmai had several fine early successes, amongst which were included the musical comedy *Naftalin* (still to be seen on the Budapest stage in 1990) and the operett *Táncos huszárok* (played in Austria as *Tanzhusaren*, Venedig in Wien, 30 April 1909), and he got a wider exposure for the first time when the local version of the German musical comedy *Filmzauber* (*A mozikirály*) for which he had supplied a fair amount of additional music, went on to an international career as *The Girl on the Film*. He had his greatest success to date with the wartime operett *Mágnás Miska*, later played in the German-speaking world as *Der Pusztakavalier* and subsequently regularly revived in Hungary, repeated successfully with *Gróf Rinaldo* (*Rinaldo* at Vienna's Johann Strauss-Theater 1 March 1921) and with *Mézeskalács* which ran over a 100 nights in its first season in Budapest, and scored his most international hit with the 1925 Ferenc Martos operett *Alexandra* (played in English as *Princess Charming*).

Szirmai wrote the basic scores for two musical plays produced on the London stage, of which the old-fashioned Ruritanian *The Bamboula* was a failure but *Lady Mary*, for which the remainder of the score was put together from a mixture of American sources (Kern, Charig, Richard Myers), won a respectable run at Daly's Theatre through 181 performances in the wake of the London success of *Princess Charming*. Sirmay (as he now spelled himself) then moved on from Britain to America where he settled in the late 1920s. There he contributed to the score for the disappointing Fred Stone musical comedy *Ripples* (w Oscar Levant), but his appealing Hungaro-French style of writing apparently made little mark on a Broadway more tuned to up-to-date dance music, and, although his *A ballerina* (which sported a touch of American influence – it included a song called 'Óh Zsuzsánna') played successfully in Budapest the following year, Sirmay never again recaptured the success he had known in his earlier days. Like Victor Jacobi, he seemed to have had his spark extinguished by his self-chosen, ambitious exile.

In New York, Szirmai became a backroom musical man, administering and arranging rather than composing, and he spent most of his American years as chief music editor at the firm of Chappell. Few of those who encountered the delightfully dutiful 'Doc' Sirmay, as he pursued his job of putting often less able men's music into sellable shape,

were aware that, as Albert Szirmai, he had been one of the most successful Hungarian operett composers of the most prosperous period of that country's musical theatre.

In his old age he visited Budapest on a number of occasions and wrote two further scores which were produced in Budapest theatres.

1907 **A sárga dominó** (Adolf Merei) Népszinház-Vigopera October
1908 **Naftalin** (Jenő Heltai) Vigszinház 6 June
1909 **Táncos huszárok** (Ferenc Rajna) Király Színház 7 January
1911 **A Ferencvárosi angyal** (Ferenc Molnár, Heltai) Royal Orfeum 31 December
1912 **A mexikói lány** (Andor Gábor/Ferenc Rajna) Király Színház 11 December
1912 **Filmzauber** (w Willi Bredschneider, Walter Kollo/Rudolf Bernauer, Rudolf Schanzer) additional music
1914 **Az ezüst pille** (Franz Arnold, Ernst Bach ad Andor Gábor) Vígszinház 9 May
1916 **Mágnás Miska** (Károly Bakonyi) Király Színház February
1918 **Kék orgonak** (Gábor) 1 act Belvárosi Színház
1918 **Gróf Rinaldo** (Bakonyi, Gábor) Király Színház November
1919 **Kutyuskám** (Ferenc Martos) 1 act Andrássy-uti Színház 12 December
1922 **Breton legenda** (Tamás Emöd) 1 act Andrássy-uti Színház 10 September
1923 **Mézeskalács** (Tamás Emöd) Király Színház 15 December
1925 **La Bamboula** (w Harry Rosenthal/Douglas Furber, Irving Caesar/Harry M Vernon, Guy Bolton) His Majesty's Theatre, London 24 March
1925 **Alexandra** (Ferenc Martos) Király Színház 25 November
1928 **Éva grófnő** (Martos) Király Színház 3 February
1928 **Enyém az első csók** (Heltai) Andrássy-uti Színház 16 May
1928 **Lady Mary** (Harry Graham/Frederick Lonsdale, J Hastings Turner) Daly's Theatre, London 23 February
1930 **Ripples** (w Oscar Levant/Caesar, John Graham/William Anthony McGuire) New Amsterdam Theater, New York 1 February
1931 **A ballerina** (Martos) Király Színház 7 March
1957 **Tabáni legenda** (Károly Kristóf) Déryné Színház January
1964 **A tündérlaki lányok** (Jenő Heltai ad Ernő Innocent Vincze) Fővárosi Operettszinház 29 January

Other title attributed: *A kalóz* (1933)

SZTOJANOVITS, Jenő (b Pest, 4 April 1864; d Pest 28 January 1919).

Organist, maître de chapelle, teacher, administrator and critic, Sztojanovits also covered a wide area in his composing activities which ranged from religious music to several ballets (*Uj Romeo* (1889), *Csárdás* (1890), *Tous les trois* (1892), operas (*Ninon* (1898), *Othello mesél* (1917)) and other theatre music, as well as the scores for several operetts and musical plays. The first of these, the successful *Peking rózsája*, was based on the *Turandot* tale, nearly 40 years before Puccini's operatic version, and the second, *A kis molnárné*, on Scribe's libretto for Adolphe Adam's *Giralda*, previously used for the successful British show *Manteaux Noirs*. The most successful of the remainder of the group was the 1908 fairytale piece *A csókkirály*. None, however, seems to have been played outside Hungary.

1888 **Peking rózsája** (Carlo Gozzi ad Miksa Ruttkay) Népszinház 7 April
1892 **A kis molnárné** (Antal Radó) Népszinház 29 January
1903 **A kis kofa** (*Phryné*) (Richard Falk) Magyar Színház 20 November

Plate 262.

1905 **A portugál** (Adolf Mérei) Magyar Színház 3 January
1906 **A papa lánya** (Gyula Molnár) Népszinház 4 October
1908 **A csókkirály** (Dezső Orbán) Fővárosi Nyári Színház 16 July
1910 **A sziámi herceg** (Pál Péter) Fővárosi Nyári Színház 27 July
1915 **Karikagyürü** (Dezső Urai, László Zsoldos) Király Színház 13 November

Other titles attributed: *Családi szentély* (1895, Ede Sas), *Lengyel legionarius*

SZULC, Joseph [SZULC, Józef Zygmunt] (b Warsaw, 4 April 1875; d Paris, 10 April 1956). One of the happiest musical contributors to the French musical-comedy stage between the wars.

Born of a musical family which boasted three generations of eminent Polish musicians, Szulc studied piano and composition at the Warsaw conservatory and at first attempted a career as a concert pianist. He moved to France to further his studies in 1899, and remained there, eking out a living as a piano teacher, whilst he concentrated on making a career in composition and conducting. His work as a theatre conductor took him to Stuttgart, then in 1903 back to Paris, to the Théâtre de la Monnaie in Brussels and finally once more to Paris in 1908, but his first attempts at composition, both with pieces in a serious vein and lighter works for the theatre, failed for a long time to find homes.

He placed a ballet, *Nuits d'Ispahan*, in Belgium and in 1913 the tide finally – if painfully slowly – began to turn for him when the Brussels Alhambra mounted his musical comedy *Flup..!*. Slowly, *Flup..!* made its way first to Lyon (1917) and finally, seven years on, to Paris (1920). In the meanwhile, the composer had provided the music for only one other piece which had succeeded in getting a showing, an adaptation of Pierre Veber's hit comedy *Loute* which was produced in Marseille. *Loute* moved more quickly than *Flup..!*, for although it did not make it to Paris, it was taken up by producer A H Woods for America (where *Loute* the play had done well under the title *The Girl from Rectors*) and, done over by P G Wodehouse and Guy Bolton, produced under the title *See You Later*. It opened at Philadelphia, was soon seen to be in trouble and Woods dropped it amongst a welter of lawsuits from Veber and London would-be-producer G B McLellan. *See You Later* ultimately resurfaced in Chicago (La Salle Theater 16 January 1919) in a production by Elliot, Comstock and Gest with Victor Moore starred and with a score credited to Jean Schwartz and William Peters (although a bit of Szulc seems to have remained). It did not, however, move east and New York thus narrowly missed what might have been the only example of a French provincial musical which never played Paris making its way to the Broadway stage.

The Parisian success of *Flup..!* at the Théâtre Ba-ta-clan finally launched Szulc on a career as a popular theatrical composer, and he followed it up with a second lively musical comedy full of dance melodies later the same year at the same theatre. After Dranem as Flup, the new piece featured Polin as *Titin*, a comical nouveau-riche Marseillais who purchases a Pacific Island and, if the second show did not outshine the earlier one, it certainly confirmed it. Szulc had another major hit in 1923 with *Le Petit Choc*, contributed to the six-handed score of the Potinière's successful *Mon Vieux* and scored further long-running hits with the up-to-date comedy musical *Quand on est trois* and the delightful *Mannequins* at the little Théâtre des Capucines. He also produced two more happy comical pieces, *La Victoire de Samothrace* and *Vivette*, for the Belgian stage in tandem with his *Flup..!* collaborator, Dumestre, as the rage for dancing musical comedies continued. In 1929 he scored yet again with the featherweight *Flossie* before being tempted, like such other stars of the small-scale jazz-age musical comedy as Christiné and Yvain, into writing for the larger houses with their larger potential for income.

Szulc made his very-big-stage début with the score for the Théâtre du Châtelet's production of the military spectacular *Sidonie Panache* and found himself connected with a fine success which was not unconnected with the theatre's hugely lavish staging of the piece. He supplied some or all of the score for two further opérettes à grand spectacle (*Mandrin*, *Le Coffre-fort vivant*), but he nevertheless continued to write for the smaller stages which had seen the bulk of his real success. If he had been slow to start, he compensated by staying on late, and his last piece was mounted in his 70th year.

Like most of his French contemporaries, Szulc found that his success was limited almost entirely to France and Belgium, but he also found a vogue in Hungary where, in the mid-1920s *Le Petit Choc* was mounted as *Jolly Joker* (Belvarosi Színház, 29 September 1928), *Mannequins* as *Párisi kirakat* (Magyar Színház, 9 April 1926) and *Quand on est trois* as *Hármacskán!* (Vigszinház, 4 September 1925).

Plate 263. **A szultan**: *Sári Fedák and Grete Freund in Verő's first and most famous operett.*

Mannequins also (apparently) got a showing in Vienna and Italy's Carlo Lombardo, in habitual fashion, borrowed much of the score of *Flup..!* for the score to his successful *La Duchessa della Bal Tabarin*, but after the *Loute* episode Broadway left Szulc alone.

1913 **Flup..!** (Gaston Dumestre) Théâtre de l'Alhambra, Brussels 19 December

1914 **Loute** (Pierre Veber, Maurice Soulié) Théâtre du Châtelet, Marseille February

1918 **See You Later** revised English version of *Loute* by P G Wodehouse, Guy Bolton Adelphi Theater, Philadelphia 13 May

1920 **Titin** (Dumestre, Roger Ferréol) Ba-ta-clan 5 October

1923 **Le Petit Choc** (P-L Flers) Théâtre Daunou 25 May

1924 **Mon vieux** (w others/André Birabeau, Battaille-Henri) Théâtre de la Potinière 5 January

1924 **La Victoire de Samothrace** (Dumestre) Forum, Liège

1925 **Quand on est trois** (P Veber, Serge Veber, Willemetz) Théâtre des Capucines 20 April

1925 **Mannequins** (Jacques Bousquet, Henri Falk) Théâtre des Capucines 30 October

1926 **Vivette** (Dumestre) Forum, Liège

1926 **Divin Mensonge** (Hugues Delorme/Alex Madis, P Veber) Théâtre des Capucines October

1929 **Couchette No 3** (Albert Willemetz/Madis) Théâtre des Capucines 6 February

1929 **Flossie** (Marcel Gerbidon, Charles L Pothier) Théâtre des Bouffes-Parisiens 9 May

1930 **Zou!** (Jean Boyer/Félix Gandera) Folies-Wagram 2 May

1931 **Sidonie-Panache** (Willemetz, Mouëzy-Éon) Théâtre du Châtelet 2 December

1933 **Le Garçon de Chez Prunier** (André Barde, Michel Carré) Théâtre des Capucines 19 January

1934 **Mandrin** (André Rivoire, Romain Coolus) Théâtre Mogador 12 December

1935 **L'Auberge du chat coiffé** (Alfred Lavauzelle) Théâtre Pigalle 18 December

1938 **Le Coffre-fort vivant** (w 'Jean Sautreuil'/Georges Berr, Louis Verneuil, Henri Wernert) Théâtre du Châtelet 17 December

1945 **Pantoufle** (Willemetz, Léopold Marchand) Théâtre des Capucines 28 February

A SZULTÁN Operett in 3 acts (prologue and 2 acts) by György Verő based on *Les Trois Sultanes* by Charles Favart. Népszinház, Budapest, 19 October 1892.

Thirty-five-year-old Verő, a conductor at the Népszinház and a sometime playwright, had had a busy career in the musical theatre, principally as a translator of Viennese Operetten for the Hungarian stage, when he was given the opportunity, in the wake of the success of such local composers as József Konti, to write the score for an operett for his theatre.

His first work, for which he wrote not only the music but also the book and the lyrics, was *A szultán*, a piece based on Charles Favart's verse comedy *Les Trois Sultanes, ou Soliman II*, originally played in Paris with a musical score by Gilbert (Italiens, 9 April 1761). Since then, *Les Trois Sultanes* had been through the musical mill, being set to original scores by several Italian operatic composers (*Le tre sultane*, *Solianno II*), by Vienna's Sussmayer (*Soliman II*, Kärntnertor Theater 5 October 1799), by Swedish and Danish composers, and being played in Paris, London (Bickerstaff's *The Sultan, or a Peep in the Seraglio*, 1775) and in New York in forms of its various operatic forms. Amongst a further bevy of adaptations and musicalizations it was also produced as a Singspiel under the title *Roxelane* (*Die drei Sultaninnen*) in a version by J Perinet at Vienna's

Freyhaus-Theater (18 July 1799) and was given in a new version by Lockroy at Paris's Théâtre des Variétés in 1853, with Delphine Ugalde starred as Roxelane.

Verő's version of the famous tale of a travelling mademoiselle who accidentally gets caught up in a sultan's harem was illustrated by a delightful if vocally demanding score which mixed the rhythms and harmonies of the Viennese Operette with some more particularly Hungarian ones and also with a definite but unclichéd flavour of the East. If the Sultan's waltz rondo 'Szeretlek Roxelánom' proved the hit of the show, there were plenty of other fine and funny musical moments – a delicious laughing song, with nothing but 'ha-ha-ha' lyrics, which twittered up to rows of top B-natural acciacaturas, a lively galop trio, a splendidly unsoppy romance for the number-two lady, a drinking song in waltz time, littered with trills and cadenzas, the Sultan's tricky Oriental Serenade and some flavourful ensembles, all of which made repeated use of the area above the stave in their vocal writing.

The Népszinház's established musical star Aranka Hegyi created the trousers rôle of Selim, the Sultan, whilst the newest addition to Budapest's stellar register, plumply pretty Klára Küry who had just made a hit as the heroine of Varney's *La Fille de Fanchon la vielleuse*, was cast as little French Roxeláne, with Népszinház comedians Vidor Kassai, József Németh, József Ferenczy and Adolf Tollagi and the composer's wife, Célia Márgo (Délia), in support. Helped just a little by the newfound popularity of Küry, *A szultán* was a major success. It was played no fewer than 84 times, almost equalling the record of Konti's *A suhanc*, the Népszinház's most successful local piece to date. If this was not the equal in terms of run to such all-time Budapest favourites as *Les Cloches de Corneville*, *Der Vogelhändler*, *Mam'zelle Nitouche*, *Der Zigeunerbaron*, *Boccaccio* or *Rip*, it nevertheless allowed *A szultán* to place itself firmly on the second rung alongside *The Mikado*, *Le Petit Duc* and *Der Bettelstudent* in the Népszinház's annals and, like them, it remained for many years a favourite in Hungary, being given a major revival at the Király Színház in 1911.

Later, when Verő ventured abroad, *Der Sultan* (ad Verő, Carl Lindau) was staged in Vienna – an achievement shared by few other Hungarian operetts of the period – with Sári Fedák starred in the title-rôle and Grete Freund as Roxelane (46 performances).

Austria: Johann Strauss-Theater *Der Sultan* 27 March 1909

T

TABBERT, William [Henry] (b Chicago, 5 October 1921; d New York, 19 October 1974).

After early appearances with the Chicago Civic Light Opera Company, Tabbert made his Broadway début as Sergeant Dick Benham in *What's Up?* (1943). He appeared in *Follow the Girls* and *The Seven Lively Arts* (1944), played Rocky Barton in *Billion Dollar Baby* (1945) and toured in *Three to Make Ready* before winning the rôle of his career as Lieutenant Joseph Cable in *South Pacific* ('Younger Than Springtime'). In 1954 he paired again with *South Pacific* co-star Ezio Pinza, playing singing version of Pagnol's Marius to the older man's César in the musical *Fanny*.

He subsequently had his own show on ABC-TV and led the remainder of his career in television and the nightclub world appearing only occasionally in regional musical theatre.

TA BOUCHE Opérette in 3 acts by Yves Mirande. Lyrics by Albert Willemetz. Music by Maurice Yvain. Théâtre Daunou, Paris, 1 April 1922.

One of the first and most frothily delightful of the French jazz-age musical comedies, this spicy nine-hander takes the form of a three-part serial about sex, money and sex at second-best seaside resorts. Whilst the unmoneyed Monsieur Pas de Vis (Guyon fils) and the phoney Countess (Jeanne Cheirel) prowl about in search of married wealth for their children – and, not incidentally, themselves – those starry-eyed children, her daughter Eva (Jeanne Saint-Bonnet) and his son Bastien (Victor Boucher), are out practising pre-marital sex together. Just to make sure that they will be compatible when they are married. Circumstances lead the two pairs and their pragmatic servants (Mary-Hett, Gabin) through an hilariously farcical series of unfortunate marriages and multi-coloured affairs before Eva and Bastien finally arrive at the wedding night they've been rehearsing for for three acts.

Maurice Yvain's irrepressible title-song, the comical duo in which the parents explain their lack of ready cash by assuring the other that their fortune is bound up in 'Des terres et des coupons', the heroine's wish for 'Un petit amant' for every girl in the world, La Comtesse's roguishly reminiscing 'De mon temps', young Bastien's ruefully jaunty 'Ça c'est une chose' and his admission that he takes his life, and especially his love-life with his rich wife, 'Machinalement', the backbiting ensemble 'Puisqu'un heureux hasard', and the young people's discovery that 'La seconde étreinte' is even better than the first, were all unqualified hits. In fact, they became popular to such an extent that the old British pantomime trick of dropping a song sheet from the flies to allow the audience to join the players in the refrains was finally put into action at the Théâtre Daunou.

Ta bouche had a first run of over a year in Paris and its composer was launched, alongside Henri Christiné, as one of the heroes of the new style of Parisian musical theatre as his rhythmic, up-to-date show tunes became some of the most popular dance melodies of the années folles. The show also set in motion a series of opérettes which used 'bouche' in their titles to show that they were in a similar vein (*Pas sur la bouche, Bouche à bouche, Eau à la bouche* etc). *Ta bouche* itself returned to Paris on several occasions: in 1924 at both the Ba-ta-clan (14 January) and the Variétés (18 June), at the Théâtre de la Michodière, in 1944 at the Mogador (12 August) with Daniel Clérice, Marcelle Garnier, Edmond Castel and Germaine Charley, and at the Théâtre Antoine in 1980 (29 May) with Daniel Demars, Arièle Semenoff, Caroline Cler, Bernard Lavalette, Patrick Préjean and Perette Souplex.

Its extremely French style and its irreverently enjoyful attitudes to sex and marriage limited the show's overseas

Plate 264. Ta bouche *was a 'grand succès' in Paris, a 'legnagyobb sikere' in Budapest and would have gone on to other such triumphs had not the moral pretensions of the age meant that it got emasculated as it travelled.*

productions. C B Cochran had his proposed London production banned by the Lord Chamberlain, but Charles Dillingham ventured a 1923 Broadway production with Louise Groody, Oscar Shaw, Ada Lewis and John E Hazzard featured amongst the cast of a deeply sanitized version (ad Clare Kummer) with a new and less sexy story made up of 'conventional bits of old musical comedy plot', and an expanded principal cast and chorus. It ran 95 performances. However, French-speaking New Yorkers had a change to see the unexpurgated version in 1929 when a French touring musical comedy company headed by Servatius (Pas de Vis), Jane de Poumeyrac (Countess), Georges Foix (Bastien) and Sonia Elny (Eva) played the piece in its repertoire during a season at the Jolson Theater (14 March).

Herman Haller and Rideamus adapted *Dein Mund* for an 109-performance run at Berlin's Theater am Nollendorfplatz, and Budapest's Vigszinház mounted a fearless Hungarian version (ad Jenő Heltai) for a splendid 80 performances prior to a 1930 revival (3 May) and *Ta bouche* has been regularly revived in the French provinces, both before and after its Paris revivals, remaining one of the most popular and representative shows of its era.

Germany: Theater am Nollendorfplatz *Dein Mund* 30 August 1922; Hungary: Vigszinház *Cserebere* 8 September 1922; USA: Fulton Theater *One Kiss* 27 November 1923; Film: nd
Recording: Selection (Decca)

EIN TAG IM PARADIES Musikalische Posse in 3 acts by Leo Stein and Béla Jenbach [and Carl Lindau]. Music by Edmund Eysler. Wiener Bürgertheater, Vienna, 23 December 1913.

A cheerful and cosily unpretentious musical play illustrated with the joyously tuneful kind of Viennesey score for which Eysler had become known and loved, *Ein Tag im Paradies* gave the composer his fourth major hit (after *Der unsterbliche Lump*, *Der Frauenfresser* and *Der lachende Ehemann*) in as many years at the pre-war Bürgertheater. The musical was played for 167 performances on its first run, passed its double century on 16 April 1916, and was played again to open the 1916–17 season, finally totalling some 220 nights in its initial production.

The libretto by Stein and Jenbach and, apparently, the uncredited Carl Lindau gave a fine, almost Girardiesque central rôle to Louis Treumann as Tobby Stöger, an expatriate Viennese who comes back home after 20 years away and parks himself at the Ringhotel, determined to have a wonderful time, cost what may. Things turn out to be not quite what they were 20 years ago. The fondly remembered Mizzi of his youth is married and has turned out something of a shrew. But by the end of his holiday he has attracted the attentions of an American widow, Gladys Wyne (Emmy Petko), who serenades him with 'Ahoy, my boy, reich mir die Hand, und komm mit mir in Dollarland...!' Mizzi Eisenhofer played young Gaby, the girl who makes him think of what Mizzi was, and tenor Vincenz Bauer was Hans Walther, a painter, who is destined – when fantasy time is over – to be her young and logical partner.

The most popular individual numbers in a score which brimmed over with waltz music were the waltzes 'Im Herzen da klingt eine Saite so fein' and '(Das ist) der Walzer der Saison', the march quartet 'Servus Wien' which returned repeatedly through the night and finally brought down the third-act curtain, the title-song Das Lied vom blauen Paradies ('Im Liebhartstal am Garterl') and the duo 'Nur eine Witwe' – a piece expressing the 'widows are wonderful' sentiment. There was also a merry burlesque scena in the second act which was made up of a Viennese duet, a Berliner song and an 'English-Wienerische G'stanzeln', a jolly entrance number for Gladys explaining 'Mein father war Amerikanische, meine mother war aus Wien' and insisting that American women 'haben die Hosen an', as well as much in the way of dance music, from an Alt Wiener Tanz to a parody Polka.

Following its splendid success in Vienna, *Ein Tag im Paradies* pursued its career happily through central Europe, being produced with equal success in Germany and in Hungary (ad Andor Gábor), but the outbreak of war rather clipped its prospects further afield. An American version appeared, however, produced by the Shuberts at the Casino Theater under the title *The Blue Paradise* (ad Edgar Smith, Herbert Reynolds) with Cleo Mayfield (Hazel Jones), Cecil Lean (Rudolph Stöger), Frances Demarest (Mrs Gladys Wynne) and the young Vivienne Segal (Mitzi/Gaby, replacing Chapine pre-Broadway) in the cast. It had, of course, undergone the usual kind of Shubertization. The play had gained a flashback start, and Eysler's 13-and-some-bits number score was bulked up and watered down with local interpolations, including three numbers by Leo Edwards and one 'up-to-date' little dance piece by leading man Lean. Fortunately, the remainder of the new numbers were by a Sigmund Romberg who was much more at home imitating Eysler than writing songs to order for the usual Shubert compilations and the result was a pretty and reasonably homogenous score which contributed much to a super run of 360 Broadway performances. But if Eysler's 'The Waltz of the Season' and 'I'm Dreaming of a Wonderful Night' still stood out as the gems of the musical part of the entertainment, it was little Miss Segal and Romberg's interpolated 'Auf Wiederseh'n' number which got the public's vote as the hit of the show.

The Blue Paradise was one of the most successful of all the botched Continental Operetten to appear on the Broadway stage in the history of Continental Operetten and botching, but even a success on this scale did not encourage the Shuberts to pay their bills. Counting on the War to protect them, they sent not a cent to Eysler and his producer, Oscar Fronz, until the Austrians were able to mount a lawsuit against them, at which they shruggingly settled. They had, however, given Eysler – after the indifferent record of Henry Savage's well-considered but untriumphant *The Love Cure* (*Künstlerblut*), the short-lived *The June Bride*, their own fairly successful production of a very botched version of *Vera-Violetta*, and the flop of *Der Frauenfresser* (*The Women Haters*) – his most successful American show. Even if it wasn't quite all his.

Germany: ?1914; Hungary: Király Színház *Cserebogár* 11 December 1914; USA: Casino Theater *The Blue Paradise* 5 August 1915

TAKE A CHANCE Musical in 2 acts by Laurence Schwab. Lyrics by B G De Sylva. Music by Nacio Herb Brown and Richard Whiting. Additional music by Vincent Youmans. Apollo Theater, New York, 26 November 1932.

Author-producer Schwab, cold from the quick failures of

East Wind and *Free for All* and the break-up of his once-triumphant partnership with Frank Mandel, produced a conventional backstage musical comedy called *Humpty Dumpty* at Pittsburgh in September 1932. In spite of a score by co-producer Buddy De Sylva and Nacio Herb Brown, and the casting of the rising Ethel Merman and Eddie Foy jr, it was taken off after its first awful week. Schwab, who had rescued *The New Moon* after a similarly unpromising beginning, pulled in Vincent Youmans to do seven extra songs (five of which made it to opening night), revamped and rewrote his book, and the piece resurfaced less than two months later as *Take a Chance*.

Jack Haley and Sid Silvers played two comically crooked gents who back a revue, Jack Whiting was their less worldly-wise associate and June Knight their girl-pal who proves to be really straight enough to be allowed to get the handsome Whiting at the final curtain. Miss Merman was still there, playing Wanda Brill, a performer in the revue-within-a-musical and, if she had nothing much to do with the plot, she had the most durable number of the evening in the walloping 'Eadie Was a Lady', a piece expressing similar sentiments to the later 'Cabaret'. She also delivered two other numbers which went on after the show had finished: Youmans's 'Great Day'-ish 'Rise 'n' shine' which subsequently appeared in, and gave its title to, a short-lived London musical (Theatre Royal, Drury Lane, 7 May 1936) and, with Whiting, 'You're an Old Smoothie', later re-used in London's *Nice Goings On*.

Even if the show was no *New Moon*, Schwab and De Sylva undoubtedly pulled off their rewrite, for *Take a Chance* proved decidedly popular fare, ran for 243 performances on Broadway and was then metamorphosed into a Paramount film with original cast member June Knight starred alongside Cliff Edwards, James Dunn and Lillian Roth. Only two of the show's numbers survived in this new transformation ('Eadie' was one), but one of the replacements was Harold Arlen's 'It's Only a Paper Moon'.

Film: Paramount 1933

TAKE ME ALONG Musical comedy in 2 acts by Joseph Stein and Robert Russell based on Eugene O'Neill's play *Ah, Wilderness!* Music and lyrics by Bob Merrill. Shubert Theater, New York, 22 October 1959.

The musical version of Eugene O'Neill's popular play (Guild Theater, 2 October 1933, 289 performances), a work acclaimed by George Jean Nathan as 'the tenderest and most amusing comedy of boyhood in the American drama', followed the lines of the original play closely. Its focus was, however, by reason of star values, shifted somewhat from the tale of the painful growing-up of young Richard Miller (Robert Morse), his pangs of political naïveté and his passions for classic prose and capitalist's daughter Muriel McComber (Susan Luckey), towards the subsidiary romance of the drink-sodden Sid (top-billed Jackie Gleason) and Auntie Lily (Eileen Herlie). The third above-the-title star of the musical was Walter Pidgeon as Nat Miller, the small-time newspaper proprietor who is father to the young non-hero of the piece, whilst Una Merkel completed the principal line-up as Mrs Goodwin.

Merrill was seemingly on more promising musical-theatre ground with O'Neill's one and only comic play than he had been with his previous adaptation from the author's dramatic opus (*New Girl in Town*, 1957, from the drama

Plate 265. **Take Me Along**: *Gene Kelly in the St Louis Muny production.*

Anna Christie) but oddly, in spite of the songwriter's practically permanent residence in the hit-parades of the period, *Take Me Along* did not produce any individual numbers which became generally popular. Amongst the most enjoyable moments were a comic duet for Gleason and Miss Herlie, 'I Get Embarrassed', a piece about 'Staying Young' for Pidgeon (at first refusing to admit he needs to, and in reprise acknowledging he can't) and a duo version for Pidgeon and Gleason of the show's title-song. The conventional musical-comedy dance quota of the period was satisfied by Onna White's nightmare ballet ('The Beardsley Ballet') which put young Richard's pubescent problems into dance.

David Merrick's production of *Take Me Along* (a title in the vein of the meaningless catchphrase names so favoured two decades earlier) was played for 448 performances over more than a year at New York's Shubert Theater. However, the box-office collapsed when Gleason left the cast and, in the summing-up, the show did not either make money for its Broadway investors, nor provoke any overseas productions. It did win a revival at East Haddam's Goodspeed Opera House some 25 years on, and that revival was taken to New York's Martin Beck Theater where it opened on 14 April 1985. Like the same company's recent Broadway transfer of the very different *Little Johnny Jones*, it played just one performance before shipping out.

Recording: original cast (RCA)

TALBOT, Howard [MUNKITTRICK, Richard Lansdale] (b New York, 9 March 1865; d Reigate, England, 12 September 1928). The composer of two of the new century's greatest hits.

Born in New York of an Irish family and brought up and educated from the age of four in London, Talbot originally studied medicine at King's College before switching to the Royal College of Music to pursue a musical education and career. He had a slow and difficult start to his life as a composer and musician, succeeding in the first years only in placing the occasional song, and, although it was reported as early as 1890 that the young man was 'collaborating with Fred Broughton on a piece for New York', his first staged work was a musical setting of a complex little piece, diligently based on a game of chess by its authoress, the Hon Albinia Brodrick, which was produced by amateurs at King's Lynn. King's Lynn, however, ultimately provided the venue for his first professional production, the comic opera *Wapping Old Stairs*, which was well enough received locally to earn it a London season in 1894 with a cast including D'Oyly Carte stars Jessie Bond, Courtice Pounds and Richard Temple. The show had, however, only 35 performances in London, and Talbot had further ill fortune when his contribution as composer and musical director to the quick-flop burlesque *All My Eye-van-hoe* led him to court, suing the producers for non-payment of his earned dues of £42 1s 10d.

Talbot did his principal work in these early days of his career as a musical-theatre conductor, notably of the long-touring *The Lady Slavey*, but his next produced show, *Monte Carlo* (1896), did considerably better than the first, both in Britain and in America. It did not, however, lift him into the top category of London writers, and he continued to be just a supplier of additional material here and there whilst conducting a series of London shows: the play *The Sorrows of Satan* at the Shaftesbury (1897), both *Dandy Dan the Lifeguardsman* (1897, into which he interpolated the successful 'Someone Ought to Speak to Millie Simpson') and *Milord Sir Smith* (1898) for Arthur Roberts, *Great Caesar* (1899), and George Edwardes's *Kitty Grey* (1900–1), a show which included another charming Talbot song, 'Mademoiselle Pirouette', in its score. But, during this time, a little provincial touring show for which he had composed the bulk of the music came to town, and Talbot at last found very genuine success.

A Chinese Honeymoon, equipped with a list of songs including Talbot's popular 'Martha Spanks the Grand Pianner' and 'The à la Girl', became the first musical in theatre history to run up 1,000 consecutive metropolitan performances and, as it went round the world, its composer's name and fortune were made. He continued to work as a conductor, spending a short time at the Gaiety with *The Toreador*, and then helming *Three Little Maids* for which, although Paul Rubens took sole music credit, he also composed the whole of the concerted music, and as a composer he turned out the scores for six further musicals over the next eight years, most of which he also conducted. He scored comfortable West End successes with *The Blue Moon*, *The White Chrysanthemum*, *The Girl Behind the Counter* and *The Belle of Brittany*, each of which went on to be played throughout the English-speaking theatre world, and had unmitigated flops with *Miss Wingrove* and *The Three Kisses*. He also contributed regular individual numbers to other composers' scores including the coon song 'Smiling Sambo' sung by Ella Snyder and 'Bob and Me' in *The Girl from Kays* and numbers for pieces ranging from Leslie Stuart's *The School Girl* ('One of the Boys') and Ada Reeve's *Winnie Brooke Widow* to the Gaiety Theatre's *The Sunshine Girl* ('You and I Together') and the London piece that passed for Kálmán's *Tatárjárás* (*Autumn Manoeuvres*).

In 1909 he had the second major success of his career when he combined with Lionel Monckton on the score of *The Arcadians*. Ten years after his first major triumph, he again hit the international heights with his contribution ('I've Got a Motter', 'I Like London', 'Half Past Two', the

beautiful ensemble 'The Joy of Life' and the quintet 'Truth is So Beautiful') to the most successful musical of the Edwardian era. Although its successor, *The Mousmé*, proved an over-produced failure, its music, notably Talbot's pretty high soprano 'My Samisen', moulded to the talents of the show's star Florence Smithson, was not at fault. There was also much of quality in *The Pearl Girl* and in the interesting but unlucky *My Lady Frayle*, but both of these pieces were written and composed in an idiom which was on its way out, and it was noticeable that the song success of Talbot's sprightly modern musical comedy *Mr Manhattan* was not one of his numbers, but a lively second-hand American number interpolated for the show's American star.

Talbot supplied music for several of the newly popular musical playlets produced in the variety theatres but, at a time when it might have been thought that he would gently fade away along with the other composers of his era who were unable or unwilling to adapt to the new rhythms and styles invading the musical theatre, Talbot put his name on his third long-running hit. In 1916 the composer contributed some additional material to the London wartime production of the American musical *High Jinks* which Alfred Butt was pretending wasn't by Rudolf Friml as he revamped it as a vehicle for comedian Bill Berry at the Adelphi, and he and Monckton were subsequently hired to write the full score for the comedian's next musical. *The Boy*, an adaptation of Pinero's *The Magistrate*, was a major hit, and even if the bulk of the favourite numbers were Monckton's, Talbot once again fulfilled more than a supporting rôle. The pair repeated with the score for another Pinero musical, *Who's Hooper?*, which proved almost as big a success at the first, but when Talbot went it alone on a third, *My Nieces* – not only without Monckton but, perhaps more importantly, without Berry as its very box-officeable star – it proved less happy.

My Nieces was his last West End show. Talbot retired to the south of England and, although he continued to compose, his last works were for amateur companies, for whom he had previously written *Athene* (King's Lynn 6 February 1911): *His Ladyship* (w Percy Greenbank, Dorothy Langton, Scala Theatre, 24 April 1928) and *The Daughter of the Gods* (1929).

1892 **A Musical Chess Tournament** (Albinia Brodrick) New Theatre, Oxford 28 October

1894 **Wapping Old Stairs** (Stuart Robertson) Theatre Royal, King's Lynn 4 January; Vaudeville Theatre 17 February

1896 **Monte Carlo** (Harry Greenbank) Avenue Theatre 27 August

1899 **A Chinese Honeymoon** (George Dance) Theatre Royal, Hanley 16 October; Strand Theatre, London 5 October 1901

1900 **Kitty Grey** (w Augustus Barratt, Lionel Monckton et al/Adrian Ross/J Smyth Piggott) Bristol 27 August; Apollo Theatre, London 7 September 1901

1902 **Three Little Maids** (w Paul Rubens/Percy Greenbank/Rubens) Apollo Theatre 20 May

1904 **The Blue Moon** (w Rubens/P Greenbank, Rubens/Harold Ellis) Theatre Royal, Northhampton 29 February; Lyric Theatre, London 28 August 1905

1905 **Miss Wingrove** (W H Risque) Strand Theatre 4 May

1905 **The White Chrysanthemum** (Arthur Anderson/Leedham Bantock, Anderson) Criterion Theatre 31 August

1906 **The Girl Behind the Counter** (Anderson/Bantock, Anderson) Wyndham's Theatre 21 April

1907 **The Three Kisses** (P Greenbank/Bantock) Apollo Theatre 21 August

1908 **The Belle of Brittany** (P Greenbank/Bantock, Percy J Barrow) Queen's Theatre 24 October

1909 **The Arcadians** (w Lionel Monckton/Arthur Wimperis/Mark Ambient, Alexander M Thompson, Robert Courtneidge) Shaftesbury Theatre 28 April

1911 **The Mousmé** (w Monckton/Wimperis, Greenbank/ A Thompson, Courtneidge) Shaftesbury Theatre 9 September

1913 **The Pearl Girl** (w Hugo Felix/Basil Hood) Shaftesbury Theatre 25 September

1913 **A Narrow Squeak** (F J Whitmarsh) 1 scene Hippodrome, Manchester, London Coliseum 16 June

1913 **Simple 'Earted Bill** (Barrow, Huntley Wright) 1 act London Coliseum 1 December

1914 **Lucky Miss** (Risque) 1 act London Pavilion 13 July

1915 **Vivien** (w Herman Finck/Wimperis/Max Pemberton, Wimperis) Prince of Wales Theatre, Birmingham 27 December

1916 **My Lady Frayle** (ex-*Vivien*) Shaftesbury Theatre 1 March

1916 **Mr Manhattan** (w Philip Braham, Frank E Tours)/C H Bovill, Fred Thompson) Prince of Wales Theatre 30 March

1915 **The Light Blues** (w Finck/Adrian Ross/Ambient, Jack Hulbert) Prince of Wales Theatre, Birmingham 13 September; Shaftesbury Theatre 14 September 1916

1917 **The Boy** (w Monckton/Ross, Greenbank/F Thompson) Adelphi Theatre 14 September

1919 **Who's Hooper?** (w Ivor Novello/Clifford Grey/F Thompson) Adelphi Theatre 13 September

1921 **My Nieces** (Greenbank) Queen's Theatre 19 August

DAS TAL DER LIEBE Musical play in 3 acts by Rudolf Lothar taken from *Das Tal des Lebens* by Max Dreyer. Music by Oscar Straus. Volksoper, Vienna, 23 December 1909.

The folk of the 'valley of love' are famed as wet-nurses, and when the elderly Markgraf Waldemar (Herr Aschner), piqued by his failure to produce an heir, appoints a chastity officer and decrees that only married couples may pursue such a calling, the young folk of the valley rebel. Hans Stork (Herr Zigler), elected their representative, gets himself a post as a castle guard, eventually at the young Markgräfin's (Frl Ritzinger) bedroom door. Nine months later the Markgraf has his heir, the chastity commission is forgotten, and Hans – the King Nurse – settles down with his Lisbeth (Emmy Petko) for a happy ending.

Straus's score was a most musicianly one, much more tuneful and catching than some he had recently turned out. The evening began well, with a melodious overture filled with rural refrains, and these jolly tones were echoed in the opening duo for Hans and Lisbeth ('Komm! Komm! der Pfarrer wartet schöne') and brought back repeatedly throughout the evening in what proved to be the show's most appealing musical moments. Little Lisbeth disappeared after her first duet until the last act, when her part was graced with a doleful, high tessituraed little lay about having lost her husband ('So lacht nur eine') but Hans went on to share the lushest part of the music with the Markgräfin, a part from which their duet 'Ei, ei wie sonderbar' was the principal morceau. The Markgräfin, the prima donna of the piece, led a tuneful waltz ensemble ('Wir haben gesagt'), joined a canzone and bolero with the contralto and a minuet of sterile formality with her husband, and delivered a wishful little romanze about a Princess who went out into the world disguised as a peasant girl and had a good time.

In spite of its many attractions, *Das Tal der Liebe* was not a genuine success either in Vienna or in a simultaneous production in Berlin, and an attempt to get a production off the ground in America went no further than Cincinnati. But the show's music was, in particular, praised and, over the following years, regretted in print a number of times, so it was little surprise when the piece was ultimately revised and reproduced in 1919 as *Die galante Markgräfin* (Volksoper 24 January ad Felix Dörmann). The new version, however, did not succeed in making its way into the repertoire any more than the old one had, and some of Straus's most charming music went to waste.

An earlier *Das T(h)al der Liebe* by Karl Haffner, music by Anton Titl, was produced at Vienna's Theater an der Wien 20 April 1846.

Germany: Komische Oper 23 December 1909; USA: Grand Opera House, Cincinnati 9 October 1913

TALFOURD, Francis N[oon] (b 1827; d Menton, 9 March 1862). Popular burlesque writer of the mid-19th century.

Educated at Eton and Oxford, Talfourd began his working life as a barrister on the Oxford circuit, but his first attempt at a burlesque, a parody of *Macbeth* initially produced at the Henley regatta, was picked up for transfer to the professional theater and thereafter he quickly made himself a reputation as an author of burlesques through a fine career ended by his premature death at the age of 35. A number of his favourite pieces were on the classical themes with which his education had made him familiar (*Alcestis*, *Thetis and Peleus*, *Atalanta*, *Pluto and Proserpine*, *Electra*), but he also mined Shakespeare, English legends, faërie and the *Arabian Nights* in the tradition established by Planché, and proved one of that author's most effective followers. His versions of *Ganem*, *Shylock* and *Atalanta*, in particular, proved revivable over a number of seasons, and were seen in several English-language countries.

1847 **Macbeth, somewhat removed from the Text of Shakespeare** (pasticcio) Henley-on-Thames; Strand Theatre 1848

1848 **Sir Rupert the Fearless** (pasticcio) Strand Theatre 24 April

1849 **Hamlet**

1850 **Alcestis, the Original Strong Minded Woman** (pasticcio) Strand Theatre 4 July

1850 **The Princess in the Tower, or A Match for Lucifer** (pasticcio) Olympic Theatre 2 September

1850 **La Tarantula, or The Spider King** (pasticcio/w Albert Smith) Adelphi Theatre 26 December

1851 **Godiva, or Ye Ladye of Coventrie and Ye Exyle Fayre** (pasticcio/w William P Hale) Strand Theatre 7 July

1851 **Thetis and Peleus** (pasticcio/w Hale) Strand Theatre 27 October

1851 **The Mandarin's Daughter, or The Story of the Willow Pattern Plate** (pasticcio/w Hale) Punch's Playhouse 26 December

1852 **The Bottle Imp, or Spirits in Bond** (pasticcio/w Hale) Grecian Saloon 12 April

1852 **Ganem, the Slave of Love** (pasticcio) Olympic Theatre 31 May

1852 **Leo the Terrible** (pasticcio/w Stirling Coyne) Haymarket Theatre 26 December

1853 **Shylock, or The Merchant of Venice Preserved** (pasticcio) Olympic Theatre 4 July

1854 **Abon Hassan, or The Hunt after Happiness** (pasticcio) St James's Theatre 26 December

1857 **Atalanta, or The Three Golden Apples** (pasticcio) Haymarket Theatre 13 April

1858 **Pluto and Proserpine, or The Belle and the Pomegranate** (pasticcio) Haymarket Theatre 5 April

1859 **Electra in a New [Electric] Light** (pasticcio) Haymarket Theatre 25 April

1859 **King Thrushbeard, or The Little Pet and the Great Passion** (pasticcio) Lyceum Theatre 26 December

1859 **Tell!, and the Strike of the Cantons, or The Pair, the Meddler and the Apple** (pasticcio arr Ferdinand Wallerstein) Strand Theatre 26 December

1860 **The Miller and his Men** (w H J Byron) Strand Theatre 9 April

LE TALISMAN Opéra-comique in 3 acts by Adolphe d'Ennery and Paul Burani. Music by Robert Planquette. Théâtre de la Gaîté, Paris, 20 January 1893.

A lavishly produced Versailles opérette, in which an elderly Louis XV (Lacressonière), having been served up the pretty peasant Michelette (Juliette Méaly) as a replacement for Madame Dubarry by the ambitious Valpinçon (Louis Morlet), is checked in his libertine designs by the talisman of the title. The ring in question has been given by Renée de Chavannes (Armande Cassive) to her superstitious favourite cousin Georges (Émile Perrin) in an attempt to get him to believe in his prospects, but it was originally a gift from the King to the beloved of his youth, who turns out to have been the youngsters' grandmother. Paul Fugère was the rustic swain of the rustic maid, heading the comedy which was the highlight of the piece before pairing off with his lass at the final curtain, at the same time as Renée and her loving cousin. Planquette's score decorated the tale and its scenery with his habitual charm and Le Talisman proved a 133-performance success at the Gaîté.

Oscar Hammerstein produced an English version of The Talisman at his Manhattan Opera House with Bianca Lescaut (Michelette), Max Freeman (Louis XV), Richard F Carroll (Nicolas), Marguerite La Mar (Renée) and J Aldrich Libby (Valpinçon) heading the cast. It was not a success, and proved the last blow to Hammerstein's tottering enterprise which was promptly metamorphosed into Koster and Bial's Music Hall. Budapest, on the other hand, gave a warm welcome to A varázsgyürü (the magic ring, ad Gyula Komor) which was played 36 times at the Népszinház in spite of immediate competition from the Hungarian version of La Poupée.

The title The Talisman (Il talismano, Le Talisman) has been much-used over the years, notably for operas by Salieri (1788) and Balfe (1874), and the opéra-comique by Josse (1850).

USA: Manhattan Opera House 21 June 1893; Hungary: Népszinház A varázsgyürü 17 December 1897

TAMIRIS, Helen [née BECKER, Helen] (b New York, 24 April 1905; d New York, 4 August 1966).

Miss Tamiris began her theatrical career as a dancer, originally with the Metropolitan Opera Company and ultimately with her own company, before coming to the musical theatre for the first time, in 1944, as the choreographer of the short-lived Marianne. She was subsequently responsible for the dances for Up in Central Park (1945 w Lew Kessler), the 1946 revival of Show Boat, the original production of Annie Get Your Gun (1946) and the revue Inside USA (1948), and less successfully for Park Avenue (1946), Bless You All (1950), Great to Be Alive (1950), Flahooley (1951) and Carnival in Flanders (1953). Her choreography for the revue Touch and Go (1950) won her a Tony Award, and she had further successes in the book musicals Fanny (1954), By the Beautiful Sea (1954) and Plain and Fancy (1955). In 1947 she staged the London production of Annie Get Your Gun.

TANGERINE Musical comedy in 2 acts by Guy Bolton and Philip Bartholomae, adapted from a play by Bartholomae and Lawrence Langner. Lyrics by Howard Johnson. Music by Monte Carlo and Alma Sanders. Casino Theater, New York, 9 August 1921.

In the midst of the craze for the Irene and Sally style of musical show, Guy Bolton and Philip Bartholomae suddenly and surprisingly presented 1921 Broadway with a theoretically out-of-style piece with which they had been fiddling about on the road for half a year since it had set out from Atlantic City with the young Vivienne Segal in its central rôle. Tangerine was surprising in that was a violent quarter-century throwback to such 19th-century French entertainments as Le Royaume des femmes, or to the earliest days of the modern musical comedy when such shows as Go-Bang and Morocco Bound ruled the stage and South Seas monarchs turned out to be hometown gents (as they had been doing at least since Ba-ta-clan) and their islands the setting for unbridled hi-jinks and song-and-dance concerts.

The island in this latter-day 19th-century show, which its authors saw fit to dub 'a satire of the sexes', was actually called Tangerine, and its King (John E Hazzard) was an ex-sailor called Joe Perkins who rules a society where women go to work and men stay home. A bundle of exported Americans with marital problems finds this inversion of what they consider the natural order not at all to their taste and, after the American women – obliged by law to support their husbands – have caused chaos by setting up fashion shops and salons and finally going into rebellion and deposing King Joe, everyone is returned to the status quo and the US of A at the end of the evening.

Carlo and Sanders's blow-away score included pieces with titles like 'Tropical Vamps', 'It's Great to Be Married (and lead a single life)' and 'There's a Sunbeam for Every Drop of Rain', but it was the interpolated 'Sweet Lady' (David Zoob, Frank Crumit), performed by Julia Sanderson and Crumit, which proved the nearest thing to a popular success in the show's musical part. Tangerine did not depend on its songs, however, and the old-fashioned fun of the book, Hazzard's comicalities, and the delicious Miss Sanderson were much more responsible than the tunes for the unexpected run of 337 Broadway performances which the production racked up prior to going back on to the road and to further success.

Tangerine's success was not even limited to America. Although London did not join the takers, the piece did splendidly in Australia where Hugh J Ward chose it to follow his initial venture with the hugely successful The O'Brien Girl at Melbourne's New Princess Theatre. It ran precisely half as long as its predecessor, but still managed a decidedly non-negligible 101 performances in Melbourne.

In 1925 Ward showed it in Sydney (Grand Opera House 28 March) with Mark Daly starred as Joe, and Mamie Watson, May Beatty and dancer June Roberts amongst the ladies, for a fine eight weeks.

Australia: New Princess Theatre, Melbourne 9 June 1923

DIE TANGOKÖNIGIN *see* DIE IDEALE GATTIN

DIE TANGOPRINZESSIN Posse mit Gesang und Tanz in 3 acts by Jean Kren and Kurt Kraatz. Lyrics by Alfred Schönfeld. Music by Jean Gilbert. Thalia-Theater, Berlin, 4 October 1913.

The outbreak of the new fashion for the tango in Europe in the years before the First World War was spurred on by its performance in the Paris revue theatres and then by its featuring on the London stage, notably as performed by George Grossmith jr and Phyllis Dare in the Gaiety musical comedy *The Sunshine Girl* and shown off in the glitzy Albert de Courville dance revue *Hullo, Tango* (Hippodrome, 23 December 1913, with Ethel Levey singing 'My Tango Girl'). Tangos flooded the dance-floors and sheet-music market throughout Europe, and the dance soon made its way not only into musical-comedy scores, but into their titles.

Germany surfaced with Jean Gilbert's *Die Tangoprinzessin*, a piece which featured the obligatory dance in a number called 'Ich tanz so gern den Tango'. However, the novelty number was backed up by a solid score of tried-and-true song-styles: the waltzes 'Das Glück kommt über Nacht', 'Ich bin verrückt' and 'Komm' doch bloss mal runter schatz', the two-step 'Ja, wenn das Petrus wüsste', and a whole series of marches ('In Hi-Ha-Hellerau', 'Ja das war früher mal', 'Willst du mein Kind?' etc).

Die Tangoprinzessin followed the two splendidly successful Jean Gilbert musical comedies *Autoliebchen* and *Puppchen* into Berlin's Thalia-Theater in late 1913. It played through the winter and spring, a regular season of nigh on six months, before giving way to the next Gilbert piece, *Wenn der Frühling kommt!*, in March. The show was purchased for a London production by George Edwardes, but the outbreak of the war led to all German-tainted plans being abandoned and *Die Tangoprinzessin*'s international progress was stopped short.

The tango hung around for a while, as a vaguely exotic symbol of South-Americanness, and song titles such as 'A Tango Dream' (*The Girl Who Didn't*) or 'A Tango Melody' (*The Cocoanuts*) were legion. It also snuck into the titles of such shows as the South American rewrite of Lehár's *Die ideale Gattin* as *Die Tangokönigin* (Apollotheater, Vienna, 1921) and Komjáti's Budapest operett *Éjféli tangó* (1932) later seen in Leipzig (1932) and Vienna as *Tango um Mitternacht* (Volksoper, 1933). In later days, however, the dance became associated with exaggerated vampery and was more often than not presented on the musical stage as a parody of sexuality rather than anything near to the real thing.

TANNER, James T[olman] (b London, 17 October 1858; d London, 18 June 1915). Architect-in-chief of the George Edwardes musical comedies.

In his earliest years in the theatre Tanner worked with Alice Dunning-Lingard as a scene-painter and actor, and toured with Horace Lingard and Auguste van Biene's companies, first as an actor (Volteface in *The Old Guard* etc), then as company manager and stage director. In 1892 he added the function of playwright by appointment to this list when he provided the dramatically inclined cellist who was his employer with a vehicle which would allow him to wring withers and to play his instrument in the same evening. The play Tanner turned out, *The Broken Melody*, was an enormous success on the touring circuits, and van Biene trouped his musical weepie for many years from Blackpool to Broadway to Brisbane.

By the early 1890s van Biene had gone up in the world. He was touring the major road versions of the Gaiety Theatre's burlesque productions and, in 1892, his *Faust Up-to-Date* company (directed by Tanner) was popped briefly into the Gaiety to fill a gap in the house schedule. George Edwardes's eye fell on the obviously useful Tanner, who soon exchanged touring for a place with Edwardes's organization. He retained that place through two decades, becoming one of the most important members of the Edwardes establishment as constructor of the libretti for his shows, stage director, and all-round ally and confidant to the great producer.

Tanner's first West End directing credit was on the shortlived *The Baroness*, but soon after Edwardes entrusted him with the construction (billed as 'James Leader') and the staging of his new-style musical play *In Town* (1892). He next had Tanner provide the outline on which Owen Hall would construct *A Gaiety Girl* (1893), and gave him the unfinished burlesque of *Don Juan*, which the late Fred Leslie had begun, to complete and stage as a vehicle for Arthur Roberts. Tanner directed the original Gaiety production of *The Shop Girl* (1894) and Daly's Theatre's *An Artist's Model* (1895) as well as *A Modern Trilby* (1895) for Nellie Farren, but thereafter, although he directed his own *The Ballet Girl* for Broadway (w Frederick Leon) in 1898, he mostly left the staging to Edwardes's other principal aide, J A E ('Pat') Malone, and concentrated largely on evolving the outlines and libretti of the shows with which Edwardes conquered the theatrical world in the Victorian and Edwardian eras.

1892 **In Town** (F Osmond Carr/w Adrian Ross) Prince of Wales Theatre 15 October
1893 **Don Juan** (Meyer Lutz/Ross) Gaiety Theatre 28 October
1895 **All Abroad** (Frederick Rosse et al/w Owen Hall) Portsmouth 1 April
1895 **Bobbo** (F O Carr/Ross) 1 act Prince's Theatre, Manchester 12 September
1896 **The Clergyman's Daughter** (F O Carr/Ross) Theatre Royal, Birmingham, 13 April
1896 **My Girl** revised *The Clergyman's Daughter* Gaiety Theatre 1 December
1896 **The Circus Girl** (Caryll, Monckton/Ross, Harry Greenbank/w Walter Palings) Gaiety Theatre 5 December
1897 **The Ballet Girl** (Carl Kiefert/Ross) Grand Theatre, Wolverhampton, 15 March
1898 **The Transit of Venus** (Napoleon Lambelet/Ross) Dublin, 9 April
1900 **The Messenger Boy** (Caryll, Monckton/Ross, H Greenbank/w Alfred Murray) Gaiety Theatre 3 February
1901 **The Toreador** (Caryll, Monckton/Ross, Percy Greenbank/w Harry Nicholls) Gaiety Theatre 17 June
1902 **A Country Girl** (Monckton/Ross, P Greenbank) Daly's Theatre 18 January

1903 **The Orchid** (Caryll, Monckton/Ross, P Greenbank) Gaiety Theatre 26 October

1904 **The Cingalee** (Monckton/Ross, P Greenbank) Daly's Theatre 5 March

1906 **A New Aladdin** (Caryll, Monckton/Ross, P Greenbank et al/w W H Risque) Gaiety Theatre 29 September

1909 **Our Miss Gibbs** (Monckton, Caryll/Ross, P Greenbank/w 'Cryptos') Gaiety Theatre 23 January

1910 **A Quaker Girl** (Monckton/Ross, P Greenbank) Adelphi Theatre 5 November

1912 **The Dancing Mistress** (Monckton/Ross, P Greenbank) Adelphi Theatre 19 October

1913 **The Girl on the Film** (*Filmzauber*) English libretto (Gaiety Theatre)

1913 **The Girl from Utah** (Sidney Jones, Paul Rubens/Ross, P Greenbank, Rubens) Adelphi Theatre 18 October

TANNHÄUSER-PARODIE Zukunftsposse in 3 acts (mit vergangener Musik und gegenwärtigen Gruppirungen) by Johann Nestroy (after H Wollheim). Music by Karl Binder. Theater in der Leopoldstadt (Carltheater), Vienna, 31 October 1857.

Produced just two months after Wagner's opera had been given its Viennese première at the Thalia-Theater, Nestroy's *Tannhäuser-Parodie* was one of the most successful of Vienna's regular supply of popular operatic burlesques. The newest work by the 'composer of the future' was parodied in a rhyming-coupletted 'play of the future ... with music from the past and staging from the present' which presented Venus as a Weinkeller temptress, and Elisabeth as the daughter of the Landgraf Purzel, an over-the-top Musikenthusiast who loathes the 'music of the future'. The second act, which takes place in a Wartburg where all the furniture is made in the shape of musical instruments, features a musical contest at which all the greats of classical opera, from Robert le Diable and Norma to Figaro and la muette de Portici, appear. In the contest, however, Tannhäuser shows himself up as a disciple of the dreaded modern music, and he is banished, and told not to come back until he's lost his voice. But even though the hero keeps on singing modern music, it doesn't ruin his voice, so, when Elisabeth commits suicide, he decides he might as well go back to Venusburg. The 'goddess' appears to bring the dead to life and tie up a happy ending. Alongside Nestroy's parody of the text, pieces of the Wagnerian score also got the burlesque treatment, with Wolfram delivering a song to the evening star which began 'Guter Mond, du goldene Zwiebel' and Elisabeth's greeting at the opening of the second act being paralleled by a 'Dich Harfenisten Kampplatz grüsse ich'.

The *Tannhäuser-Parodie* was played throughout the German-speaking theatre world and it was revived on a number of occasions over the years, a performance being given at the Theater an der Wien 19 March 1927 and a short season of new production mounted at the Wiener Bürgertheater 2 June 1928.

Given the often scornful attitude taken to Wagner's works on their first productions, and their eminently burlesquable subject matter and style, the 'music of the future' did not come in for as much parody as might have been expected. Alongside Nestroy's *Tannhäuser* came several French burlesques launched hot on the heels of Paris's first showing (*Panne-aux-airs* Frederic Barbier/Clairville 30 March 1861, *Ya-mein-herr* Clairville, Dela-cour, Thiboust, 6 April 1861) whilst *Lohengrin* became *Lohengelb* in the hands of Nestroy in Austria and America (Franz von Suppé/M A Grandjean 30 November 1870), *Die Jungfrau von Dragant* (Germania Theater 30 March 1874) in Vienna and *Little Lohengrin* in both London (Frederick Bowyer, Holborn Theatre, 1884) and in America (ad Edgar Smith, Chicago, 1886). *Der fliegende Holländer* was done over in Vienna as *Der fliegende Holländer zu Fuss* (Müller/Nestroy Theater in der Leopoldstadt, 4 August 1846) and in Britain as *The Flying Dutchman* (William Brough, Royalty Theatre 1869) and *The Lying Dutchman* (Alfred Lee/Arthur Clements, Frederick Hay, Strand Theatre, 21 December 1876) whilst *Die Meistersinger von Nürnberg* and its musical contest were parodied during the action of Hervé's *Le Petit Faust*. It is, however, Rideamus and Oscar Straus's 20th-century Viennese version of a bit of the Ring cycle, *Die lustigen Nibelungen*, which shares with the *Tannhäuser-Parodie* the record of being the most memorable of the Wagnerian burlesques.

Hungary: Budai Színkör (Ger) 1 June 1863

TANTIVY TOWERS Comic opera in 3 acts by A P Herbert. Music by Thomas F Dunhill. Lyric Theatre, Hammersmith, 16 January 1931.

The best of the group of original light operas produced under Nigel Playfair's management at London's Lyric, Hammersmith, *Tantivy Towers* was an enjoyable attempt at a sung-through comic opera which aspired to lines of wit – and often achieved them – in a ridiculous little story of love not levelling all ranks. Chelsea's pretentiously artistic Hugh Heather (Trefor Jones) comes to grief when he moves out of his natural habitat and tries to outshine aristocratic Captain Bareback (Harvey Braban) for the hand of Lady Ann Gallop (Barbara Pett-Fraser) on her home ground at Tantivy Towers. He is damned for all time when he shoots the fox during a hunt and has to settle for joining the Savage Club whilst the aristocrat gets the girl.

The respected serious composer Thomas Dunhill provided a suitably and strongly English score to illustrate a piece which, in spite of some happy moments, lacked the crazy sparkle of the Gilbert and Sullivan genre, but still found sufficient audience to run through two and a half months at the Lyric before transferring to the West End's New Theatre for another two months. It was revived at the Lyric by Claud Powell in 1935 with Maggie Teyte starred as Ann alongside Steuart Wilson (Hugh) and Frank Philips (Bareback).

DIE TÄNZERIN FANNY ELSSLER Operette in 3 acts by Hans Adler. Music taken from the works of Johann Strauss, arranged by Oskar Stalla and Bernard Grün. Deutsches Theater, Berlin, 22 December 1934.

The dancer, Fanny Elssler, whilst furthering her career, sidesteps the lascivious and devious statesman von Gentz and the Herzog von Reichstadt, the son of Napoleon, through three acts, postponing a reunion with her childhood friend, Baron Franz Fournier, only until she has conquered the world with her dancing. The score for the piece was made up of clips from the works of Johann Strauss.

First produced in Berlin, the show was also played with some success in Italy where it proved one of the more popular Strauss pasticcii, but elsewhere had to give way to such pieces as the superior *Drei Walzer* or the biomusical *Walzer aus Wien*.

Fanny Elssler (b Vienna, 23 June 1810; d Vienna, 27 November 1888) was a real person, an Austrian ballerina who had a notable career both in Europe and in America, but in the hands of the central-European mythmakers she became simply the archetypal 19th-century star and her name was given – like poor Nell Gwynne and Empress Elisabeth and other mythologized ladies of history – to the heroines of several stage pieces with more or less to do with her real story and character. Having at first been the 'subject' of an Hungarian play, succinctly titled 'Viennese dancer' (*Bécsi táncosnő* 8 January 1916), she later served as the title and heroine for the Hungarian musical *Fanny Elssler* or, since it was in Hungarian, *Elssler Fanny* (Mihály Nador/Jenő Faragó, Király Színház, 20 September 1923) in which Hanna Honthy played Fanny. She also got involved with the Herzog von Reichstadt a second time in August Pepöck's successful Operette *Hofball in Schönbrunn* and appeared, played by Fräulein Engel, as a character in Oscar Straus's Operette *Die himmelblaue Zeit* (Volksoper, 21 February 1914). As enduring as Mistress Gwynne and Empress Sissi and the rest of the operettic cliché ladies, she has come back for more right up to the present day and was most recently seen on the Viennese stage as the heroine of a very unfortunate new ballet at the Volksoper (1990).

DER TANZ INS GLÜCK Operette in 3 acts by Robert Bodanzky and Bruno Hardt-Warden. Music by Robert Stolz. Raimundtheater, Vienna, 23 December 1920.

The most internationally successful of Robert Stolz's extremely long list of Operetten, *Der Tanz ins Glück* was played around the world in some very diverse versions after its highly successful Viennese première at the Raimundtheater at Christmas 1920. Franz Glawatsch played Sebastian Platzer, a former music-hall attendant turned valet, who ends up accidentally unmasking the high-society charade of his employer, Fritz Wendelin (Robert Nästlberger), a hairdresser who, with the help of an identifying blue edelweiss, has been masquerading as a count in order to win the hand of hatmaker's daughter Lizzi Mutzenbacher (Anny Rainer). But Fritz is the evening's tenor, so all ends happily and conjugally when he wins a hairdressing championship. The real Count Hans-Joachim von Bibersbach (Eduard Fritsch) can go back to the arms of glamorous music-hall star Desirée Viverande (Klara Karry), who has been the object of the extra-marital desires of Lizzi's socially ambitious father (Josef Egger).

Stolz's score for this comedy musical tripped along in the popular dance rhythms of the world's theatres of the time. The one-step ('Halloh, was das für Mädeln sind!', 'Ich hab' kein Geld', 'Kakadu' quintet) and the foxtrot ('Guter Mond, schau uns nicht zu!') were mixed in with some Viennesey songs (the waltz 'Einmal im Mai', 'Brüderlein, Brüderlein!') and the usual dose of catchy marches ('Heut' geht's los!', 'Wenn es zehn wird, geht man nicht zu Bett!') in a pleasing combination which added to the evening's gaiety.

Karczag's production of *Der Tanz ins Glück* ran for a straight 200 performances, but then it had to be removed when the Raimundtheater struck its eternal problem and its stage had to be ceded for an equitable amount of time to co-manager Rudolf Beer and his serious plays. So the Raimundtheater lost its big hit which was brought back in the autumn at the Komödienhaus (18 October 1921) instead. It reappeared briefly at the Bürgertheater in 1927 with Glawatsch featured alongside Hilde Schulz (Lizzi) and Walter Swoboda (Fritz), was seen for a handful of performances at the Theater an der Wien between 1928 and 1930, and was revived at the Raimundtheater in 1949. In 1951 a Viennese film version was made (scr: Fritz Koselka, Lilian Belmont) with Waltraut Haas, Fritz Imhoff, Johannes Heesters, Josef Egger and Ursula Lingen amongst the cast, and three of the show's songs in its score.

An Hungarian version (ad Miksa Bródy) opened before the Vienna run was done, playing first at the Városi Színház and later (29 May 1922) at the Fővárosi Nyari Színház, by which time Berlin's Theater des Westens had also produced the show and a London version (ad Harry Graham, add ly: Graham John) had been mounted by James White as a 'George Edwardes production'. Billy Merson starred in *Whirled into Happiness* as valet Matthew Platt, Tom Walls was Horridge, the hatmaker, whose daughter Florence (Winnie Melville) duetted with Derek Oldham as hairdresser Horace Wiggs, and Mai Bacon was Delphine de Lavallière of the music-halls. Conductor Arthur Wood and Archie Emmett Adams supplied an extra number apiece, and the show ran a useful 244 performances (only the lavish *Wild Violets* of Stolz's shows did better in Britain) before going on the road.

It also went on to Australia where Alfred Frith (Platt), Kitty Reidy (Florence), Madge Elliott/Winnie Collins (Delphine), Harry Pearce (Wiggs) and Cecil Kellaway (Horridge) featured in 'a pot-pourri of drollery and dancing' performing 'Robinson Crusoe's Isle' (ex- 'Kakadu'), an unfamiliar 'Somebody's Wrong' and 'Once in a While I Love You' ('Einmal im Mai') and apparently not very much more of Stolz through two months in Melbourne and a fine ten weeks in Sydney (Her Majesty's Theatre 6 September 1924).

The basics of *Der Tanz ins Glück* or, more accurately, of *Whirled into Happiness* went into the making of the Shuberts' Broadway show *Sky High*, a piece put together by Harold Atteridge (the billing read, 'a new musical play by Harold Atteridge and Captain Harry Graham') to feature the talents of the much-loved fun-maker Willie Howard as the comical valet/hero, who was now called Sammy Myers. Plenty of spectacle, some impersonations, ballet specialities, two spots for a chorus girl called Marjorie Whitney, a section called 'Broadcasting' in which Howard, Ann Milburn (Aggie), Vannessi (Delphine) and John Quinlan (Horace) all got to do their thing, and a Shubert-sized chorusline (35 girls, 12 boys, 3 speciality girls and 6 ponies) all went to build up a show which featured 'added numbers' by Alfred Goodman, Maurie Rubens and Carlton Kelsey, James Kendis and Hal Dyson, additional lyrics by Clifford Grey, and 'Give Your Heart in June', advertised as 'music by Victor Herbert – his last waltz' as performed by the juveniles. Of Stolz's score there apparently remained just Florence's two solos, 'Hello, the Little Birds Have Flown' ('Halloh, was das für Mädeln sind') and 'Somewhere in Lovers' Land' which had been 'Somewhere in Fairyland' in London and 'Sonntag komm' ich zu dir', lyric by Fritz Grünbaum, and not in Vienna's *Tanz ins Glück* originally, the duo Letter Song and some concerted and orchestral moments. Whatever *Sky High* was, however, it was still a descendant of *Der Tanz ins Glück* – if perhaps a slightly distant one – and it kept up the show's good record by running for 220 performances on Broadway before going out to tour.

Der Tanz ins Glück was revised as a 33-scene spectacular (ad Hugo Wiener) and produced in 1958 at the Vienna Raimundtheater under the title *Hallo, das ist die Liebe*. The principal numbers of the original score ('Einmal in Mai', 'Ich hab' kein Geld', 'Guter Mond', 'Wenn es zehn wird') were supplemented by several new pieces with lyrics by Wiener. But this time their music was by Stolz.

Hungary: Városi Színház *Szerencsetánc* 14 May 1921; Germany: Theater des Westens 18 January 1922; UK: Lyric Theatre *Whirled into Happiness* 18 May 1922; Australia: Theatre Royal, Melbourne *Whirled into Happiness* 24 June 1924; USA: Shubert Theater *Sky High* 2 March 1925; Film: Mundus-Film/Farb-film 1951

DIE TANZGRÄFIN
Operette in 3 acts by Leopold Jacobson and Robert Bodanzky. Music by Robert Stolz. Wallner-Theater, Berlin, 18 February 1921.

Coming hard on the heels of Robert Stolz's Viennese triumph with *Der Tanz ins Glück*, *Die Tanzgräfin*, first mounted in Berlin, helped to make 1921 into the most memorable year of the composer's career.

The Gräfin Colette Planterose goes out to fête the Mardi Gras in Montmartre in disguise, gets acclaimed the festive queen of the affair, and then vanishes, leaving a lovestruck Marine-Lieutenant Octave Dupareil behind her. She is supposed to marry the unpleasant Marquis Philippe Villacroix in Act II, but Act III sees her sailing off with her sea captain on the aptly named 'Porte-bonheur' at the final curtain.

The tale was accompanied by a scoreful of dance-rhythmed music – waltzes ('Irgendwas ist mit mir heut' los', 'Mädelchen von Montmartre' etc), one steps ('Du, nur du' etc), foxtrots (including the evening's top tune 'Faschingsnacht, du Zeit der Liebe'), a polka and even a paso doble which encouraged 'Zieh an den seidenen Pyjama'.

Die Tanzgräfin played for six months at Berlin's Wallner-Theater, and it was reprised for further performances between the end of the run of its successor, Straus's *Nixchen*, and the opening of the next new piece, Goetze's *Die Spitzenkönigin*. This success was more than repeated in Vienna, where *Die Tanzgräfin* was produced by Erich Müller at the Johann Strauss-Theater, with Ida Russka (Colette), Karl Bachmann (Octave) and Max Ralf-Ostermann (Villacroix) featured. This production gave Stolz one of his most substantial Viennese successes, with a run of 204 performances in seven months, before the show moved on to score a further success in Budapest where the 'dancing countess' became the 'little grisette' in Miksa Bródy's adaptation. Emmi Kosáry and Ernő Király headed the romance through a fine initial 53 performances, and the production was later restaged at the Fővárosi Operett-színház (8 April 1923).

With the Broadway success of *Sky High* (*Der Tanz ins Glück*) fresh in memory, Paul M Trebitsch gave his American production of *The Dancing Duchess* (ad J J Garren) a hugely lavish production at Boston's Wilbur Theater. Gertrude Land and Glen Dale starred alongside a workforce of 150 personnel (including a male chorus of 24), but a weekly nut of $28,000 proved much too much for it to recoup and the show folded after five weeks without moving out of Boston.

The heroine became *La Contessa delle danze* in Angelo Nessi's Italian adaptation, mounted in Milan in 1924.

Austria: Johann Strauss-Theater 13 May 1921; Hungary: Vigszinház *A kis grisett* 11 June 1921; USA: Wilbur Theater, Boston: *The Dancing Duchess* 6 September 1926

DER TAPFERE SOLDAT
Operette in 3 acts by Rudolf Bernauer and Leopold Jacobson based on George Bernard Shaw's play *Arms and the Man*. Music by Oscar Straus. Theater an der Wien, Vienna, 14 November 1908.

Der tapfere Soldat (the brave soldier) was based on the main plotline of G B Shaw's *Arms and the Man*, with much of the subsidiary action cut away, the almost too-operetta-to-be-true character of the maid, Louka, eliminated in favour of a family cousin called Mascha, who was inserted to allow the rejected Alexius (ex-Sergius) a suitably operettic pairing off at the final curtain.

The Swiss soldier Bumerli (Gustav Werner), a mercenary in the Serbian army, takes refuge in flight in the bedroom of Nadina (Grete Holm), the daughter of the enemy Bulgarian Colonel Kasimir Popoff (Max Pallenberg). Nadina is engaged to wed the exorbitantly dashing Alexius Spiridoff (Karl Streitmann), whom she perceives as everything that is heroic, but the practical Bumerli undeceives her over the glories of war and wins not only her heart but those of the other lonely ladies of the house: Frau Oberst Aurelia Popoff (Mizzi Schütz) and cousin Mascha (Luise Kartousch). When the men come home from the war, a bit of business with some lovingly signed photographs and an overcoat stirs up feelings, and Alexius threatens a duel before all is calmed over and Nadina is promised to her 'Praliné-Soldat'.

Straus's score was a delightful one, with Nadina's waltz-song 'Komm', komm'! Held meine Träume' sighed starrily over the portrait of her long-absent 'hero', being the evening's solo gem. Amongst the ensembles, however, there were several other charming numbers: Nadina and Bumerli's duo 'Ach, du kleiner Praliné-Soldat', a first-act finale trio for the three women ('Drei Frauen sassen am Feuerherd') and a comic sextet over the wretched overcoat, a garment which each of the women wants to get back from Popoff in order to rescue the incriminatingly dedicated photo of herself, and the Colonel just wants to put comfortably on to his back ('Ach, es ist doch ein schönes Vergnügen').

Karczag and Wallner's original production of *Der tapfere Soldat* at the Theater an der Wien was, in spite of its very fine cast, a disappointment. It played just 60 initial performances before being removed from the evening bill two weeks into the new year to allow what was to be the triumphant production of Kálmán's *Tatárjárás* (*Ein Herbstmanöver*). A German production was mounted six weeks after the Vienna one at Berlin's Theater des Westens with Gustav Matzner (Bumerli), Marie Ottmann (Nadina), Julius Donath (Popoff), Albert Kutzner (Alexius), Vilma Conti (Mascha) and Fr Gaston (Aurelia), and Miksa Preger's German company introduced the piece to Budapest, in German, during a guest season of three weeks and nine shows at the Vigszinház in 1912 before the show was

Plate 266. *Gustav Matzner (Bumerli) climbs through the bedroom window of buxom Marie Ottmann (Nadina) in Berlin's* **Der tapfere Soldat**.

eventually given an Hungarian showing at the Népopera in 1916, with Ilona Dömötör as Nadina. Its title showed where the impetus had come from, for it was called *A csokoládé-katona*.

If central Europe showed no particular liking for *Der tapfere Soldat*, the English-speaking world, on the contrary, gave it a huge welcome. An adaptation by the Anglo-American writer Stanislaus Stange was produced on Broadway by Fred C Whitney, one of the many American producers who had joined the frantic grabbing for new Continental musicals, both successful and unsuccessful, in the dollar-green euphoria created by *Die lustige Witwe*. Whitney proved to have grabbed either more cleverly or more luckily than most. With J E Gardner (Bumerli), Ida Brooks Hunt (Nadina), William Pruette (Popoff), George Tallmann (Alexius) and Flavia Arcaro (Aurelia) featured, *The Chocolate Soldier* proved a splendid success through 296 performances at Broadway's Lyric Theatre, and Nadina's waltz song, anglicized as 'My Hero', was launched as an all-time soprano bon-bon.

As *The Chocolate Soldier* set off round America to reap its rewards in the first of many tours, Whitney went into partnership with London's Philip Michael Faraday to mount a production of his hit in the West End. Britain brought forth an even more enthusiastic reaction to the show. Ex-Savoyards C H Workman and Constance Drever (France's *veuve joyeuse*) played Bumerli and Nadina with Roland Cunningham as Alexius and veteran Amy Augarde as Madame Popoff and *The Chocolate Soldier* played no fewer than 500 performances at London's Lyric Theatre before going on the road and out to the other English-speaking parts of the Empire. It was quickly back, playing a further London season in 1914, and was seen again in the West End in 1932 and 1940. New York, however, solidly topped that record by welcoming the show back to Broadway in 1921, 1930, 1931, 1934, 1942 and 1947 (ad Guy Bolton, Bernard Hanighen). None of these revivals, however, had the kudos of a Los Angeles Light Opera production, which boasted – as well as John Charles Thomas as its hero – 'four new Oscar Straus songs' in its score.

Australia kept up the impressive record of Stange's version of the piece when Clarke and Meynell's production of *The Chocolate Soldier* was mounted in Melbourne. Winifred O'Connor sang 'My Hero' for 52 nights before its pro-

ducers merged their company with the great white shark of Australian entertainment, J C Williamson Ltd. Thus *The Chocolate Soldier* played its Sydney season the following year under the new banner, with Florence Young and J Talleur Andrews – who were also paired as Karel and Gonda in *Die keusche Susanne* and René and Angèle in *Der Graf von Luxemburg* – in the leading rôles. The show did well enough, playing in repertoire alongside these two fine favourites, and *The Chocolate Soldier* established itself in Australia in the same way it had done on the other side of the world, being revived as late as 1954 with Nancie Grant and Desmond Paterson featured.

Similarly spurred on by the Broadway and then the London successes of *The Chocolate Soldier*, Charles Montcharmont soon followed up with productions of *Le Soldat de chocolat* (ad Pierre Veber) at Brussels (8 September 1911) and at his Théâtre des Célestins in Lyon. Raoul Villot, Angèle van Loo and Fabert introduced the French version, before Alphonse Franck at the Théâtre Apollo – the home of *La Veuve joyeuse* and *Le Comte de Luxembourg* – took the show up for Paris. His Danilo, Henri Defreyn, was cast in the rôle of Bumerli alongside Brigitte Régent and Villot repeated his Popoff through a run of two and a half months. This was neither a record to challenge Franck's other Viennese imports, nor the kind of success the piece had had in its English version, but *Le Soldat de chocolat* nevertheless got a Parisian re-hearing more than 20 years later when it was played in the repertoire of the Trianon-Lyrique (1 March 1935).

Behind the success of *The Chocolate Soldier* there was a bitter little twist. A tale of a gesture which rebounded on the author of *Arms and the Man*, who had had to suffer the indignity of seeing the unconsidered Stange's re-Englished version of his work far outrun not only the original play but any and all of his plays to date. Shaw, who had sneered consistently at the musical theatre through his life and his career as a critic, had always insisted that it was not possible to musicalize his works. When permission was sought for the making of an Austrian musical of *Arms and the Man* he consented, but refused to take any royalties and postulated that a disclaimer be printed apologizing for the liberty taken in 'burlesquing' his play. His principles were clearly hurt when he saw the money made by *The Chocolate Soldier* and he discarded them in typical fashion when permission was sought to make the show into a film. This time he demanded big money. But he didn't get it. All MGM needed was the title and 'My Hero', neither of which belonged to Shaw, and they took these and pasted them into a version of Ferenc Molnár's *A testőr* instead. Nelson Eddy and Risë Stevens starred in a 1941 film which had virtually nothing of *Der tapfere Soldat* or *The Chocolate Soldier* about it. But no one knew that till they got into the cinema.

There had actually been a previous *Chocolate Soldier* film which also lacked part of the theatrical show, but this time it was the music. Whitney – who lacked no enterprise in cashing in on his hit – and the Daisy Film Company turned out a silent-film called *The Chocolate Soldier*, featuring Tom Richards (Bumerli), William H White and the producer's sister-in-law Alice Yorke (Nadina). Hopefully, Shaw didn't know about it.

Germany: Theater des Westens 23 December 1908; USA: Lyric Theater *The Chocolate Soldier* 13 September 1909; UK: Lyric Theatre 10 September 1910; France: Théâtre des Célestins,

Plate 267. **Anna Tariol-Baugé**

Lyon *Le Soldat de chocolat* 1911, Théâtre de l'Apollo, Paris 7 November 1912; Australia: Theatre Royal, Melbourne *The Chocolate Soldier* 26 August 1911; Hungary: Vigszinház (Ger) 24 May 1912, Népopera *A csokoládé-katona* 7 October 1916; Film: Daisy Film Co (silent)
Recordings: complete in English (RCA), selections in English (RCA, Columbia, World Records)

TARIOL-BAUGÉ, Anna (b Clermont Ferrand, 28 August 1872; d Asnières, 1 December 1944). Favourite prima donna of the Paris stage.

Anna Tariol-Baugé made her stage débuts at Bordeaux playing opéra-comique, and worked in the provinces and in Russia before making her first appearances in Paris. There she became one of the most popular opérette stars in the last years of the old century and the first decades of the new, appearing in many of the great rôles of the classic repertoire (Boccaccio, Fiorella, Gabrielle, Boulotte, Dindonette, Serpolette etc) and, in a career of over 30 years, creating a long list of new parts, of which the most important were the flighty Agathe in *Véronique*, the tempestuous Spaniard, Manuela, in *Miss Helyett*, and Gabrielle, the wife of Claude Terrasse's *Le Sire de Vergy*. Amongst the other new pieces in which she introduced rôles were *La Dame de trèfle* (1898), *Shakespeare!* (1899, Consuélo), Lecocq's *La Belle au bois dormant* (1900, Aurore), *L'Age d'or* (1905, Reine Margot) and *Les Rendez-vous Strasbourgeois* (1908, Berthe). She also played on a number of occasions at the Parisiana (*Les Poupées americaines*, *Cabriole* etc), at the Folies-Bergère and at the Moulin-Rouge in both opérette and in revue, sharing a bill with Liane de Pougy and other luminaries of the variety stage.

In 1908 she appeared in London in the title-rôles of *La Fille de Madame Angot* and *La Fille du tambour-major*, but soon after this she began to orientate her career towards the straight theatre. She returned to the musical stage in the 1920s to repeat her Agathe and then to appear in character rôles in several other musical shows (*Le Mariage de Pyramidon*, *La Reine joyeuse*, as the Directrice in *Le Petit Duc*), including a group (*Le Diable à Paris*, *Venise*, *Vouvray*) alongside her son, André Baugé, himself one of the most prominent opéra-comique and opérette leading men of the period.

TATÁRJÁRÁS Operett in 3 acts by Károly Bakonyi. Lyrics by Andor Gábor. Music by Emmerich Kálmán. Vigszinház, Budapest, 22 February 1908.

The military operett *Tatárjárás* revealed to the world in general for the first time the talents of the 25-year-old Imre (soon to be Emmerich) Kálmán, strikingly displayed in a refreshingly tuneful scoreful of Hungarian-flavoured waltzes and marches which illustrated what was to be the most internationally successful Hungarian musical play up to its time.

The regiment of Fieldmarshal Lohanyay (Ferenc Vendrey) is on manoeuvres near the castle of the widowed Baroness Riza (Juliska Keleti) who duly entertains the officers at her home. Lieutenant Lőrenthy (Gyula Hegedűs) does not join them, for not only was the castle where the baroness is installed once the home of his family, but in earlier and blither days he had himself been in love with Riza. By the end of the play's three acts, enlivened by the Jewish fooleries of the reservist Wallerstein (Aladár Sarkadi) and the chase of the little volunteer Mogyoróssy (Berta Kornai) after the Fieldmarshal's daughter, Treszka (Ilonka Komlóssy), a lass who had been intended by her father as a bride for Lőrenthy, the operettically expected happy ending has been tied up all round.

The romantic leads were supplied, as was only normal, with waltz music, and it was waltz music of a specially flavoured strain. The principal waltz theme of the piece, originally introduced by Lőrenthy ('War einst verblendet') and then duetted by tenor and soprano, by the soprano and ingénue, and finally given as a serenade by the chorus in the last act, needed no such plugging to remain irresistibly in the mind. It was a winner. Riza had a second superb waltz, 'Mir is so bang', and a third, 'Tanzen sich wiegen', with which to score in a rôle which was a prima donna's delight. But in spite of this *Tatárjárás* was not Riza's show, any more than it was Lőrenthy's show. It was the travesty soubrette rôle of the lovelorn little volunteer and that of the foolish, comical Wallerstein which proved the plum parts of the evening. Mogyoróssy made his entrance with the bright little 'Ich bin ein kernig fester Soldat', marched with the chorus to 'Ziehen die Husaren ein', won a triumph with his Küsslied ('Die kleine Gretl') and danced a lightly comical love duo with his Treszka. There were two comical numbers for the foolish Wallerstein as well, but his moments came in his comedy rather than in his numbers.

The original production of *Tatárjárás* at Budapest's Vigszinház was a fine success, running up 100 performances in the house's repertoire by 1 October 1909 and being revived there on 11 January 1913. The piece went on to be played throughout the country, the Népopera mounted a new production in August 1916 and in 1923 the Vigszinház production was played at the newly opened Fővárosi Operettszinház (14 January). In the meantime, however, *Tatárjárás* had already made the tour of the world, beginning with a phenomenally successful production under the

Plate 268. **Tatárjárás**: *Luise Kartousch made a huge hit as the little cadet Márosi in Vienna's production of* Herbstmanöver, *alongside Grete Holm as the leading lady of the piece.*

management of Wilhelm Karczag and Karl Wallner at Vienna's Theater an der Wien where Robert Bodanzky's German-language version, *Ein Herbstmanöver*, replaced the disappointing *Der tapfere Soldat* on the theatre's schedule. Grete Holm, who had just introduced 'Held meine Träume' and now got Riza's rôle full of waltzes, and Otto Storm took the romantic rôles, Max Pallenberg put aside the Bulgarian Colonel Popoff to take up the Jewish comedy of Wallerstein and Luise Kartousch got one of the most outstanding rôles of her outstanding career as the little Mogyoróssy (now called Marosi).

Ein Herbstmanöver was an immediate and enormous success – the biggest the theatre had had since *Die lustige Witwe* three years earlier – and the show ran on at the Theater an der Wien, with guest performances at the Raimundtheater, through to the close of the season in late June (150 performances). It reopened the new season and continued to its 226th performance before giving way to *Der Graf von Luxemburg* in November. It was seen again at both theatres the following year, passing its 300th performance on 8 November 1910 with Holm still in her original rôle alongside Alexander Haber (Lorenty), Mizzi Parla (Marosi) and Kurt Mikulski (Wallerstein), and being reprised in the repertoire at one or both theatres in 1914, 1916, 1920, in 1924 with Richard Tauber, Holm and Storm, and again in 1934.

Bodanzky's version was produced two months after the Vienna première in Hamburg and foreign-language versions subsequently appeared such cities as Moscow (30 April 1909), Stockholm (6 September 1909), Copenhagen (17 February 1910), Trieste (1 March 1910) and in Rome at the Teatro Apollo (25 September 1910) as the piece spread through Europe with huge success. The English-language versions, however, did not come up to the mark. Henry Savage, the American producer of *The Merry Widow*, took what he called *The Gay Hussars* (ad Maurice Brown Kirby, Grant Stewart) to Broadway with a cast including Muriel Terry (Marosi), Edwin Wilson (Lorenty), Anna Bussert (Risa), Bobby North (Wallerstein) and Florence Reid (Treszka). One critic praised 'saner, livelier music and more jollity with a basis of reason than any number of our native hodge-podges', but worried that 'the element of humorous satire on army conditions in Hungary could hardly be conveyed'. It was, apparently, more the under-par casting and staging of the piece which led to its leaving town after just 44 performances.

George Edwardes's London production of *Autumn Manoeuvres* (ad Henry Hamilton, Percy Greenbank) was anglicized into a setting at 'Ambermere Park' with Huntley Wright playing comical Captain Withers of the Broadshire Territorials, Gracie Leigh replying to him as Lady Larkins, and Robert Evett (Captain Frank Falconer) and Phyllys LeGrand (Alix Luttrell) singing the romantic bits of a co-operative score which included only two and a half Kálmán numbers. Herbert Bunning (three pieces), Howard Talbot (four and the other half), Carl Kiefert, Hamish MacCunn and Lionel Monckton (one apiece) contributed music to a show which was scarcely *Tatárjárás* and would probably have run more than its 75 performances if it had been.

Manoeuvres d'automne became the first Hungarian operett to be produced in France when Pierre Veber's version, an odd hybrid which had half British characters and half Hungarian ones not to mention an Irish servant called Pat, was staged by Montcharmont at Lyon in 1914. Maguy Warna and Claude Arnès shared the rôle of Risa alongside Edmond Tirmont (Lorenty), Marthe Lenclude (Marosi) and Urban as Waltebled (ex-Wallerstein), but the career of the show was hobbled by the outbreak of war: Paris of 1914–15 was not about to welcome a joyous musical about the enemy's military.

Austria: Theater an der Wien *Ein Herbstmanöver* 22 January 1909; Germany: Neues Operetten-Theater, Hamburg *Ein Herbstmanöver* 20 March 1909; USA: Knickerbocker Theater *The Gay Hussars* 29 July 1909; UK: Adelphi Theatre *Autumn Manoeuvres* 25 May 1912; Australia: Her Majesty's Theatre, Sydney *Autumn Manoeuvres* 26 June 1913; France: Théâtre des Célestins, Lyon, *Manoeuvres d'automne* 24 March 1914

TATE, James W (b Wolverhampton, 30 July 1875; d London, 5 February 1922). Songwriter and conductor for revue and musical theatre of the early 20th century.

The brother of Margaret Tate, who later became opera and operetta singer Maggie Teyte, Jimmy Tate was also the third husband of Lottie Collins, the famous singer of 'Ta-ra-ra-boom-di-ay', and thus stepfather to her three daughters. The eldest, José Collins, was to have a career to more than rival her mother's.

Tate began his career as a musician with ambitions in the operatic field but he soon turned himself rather towards popular songwriting and to intermittent work in the musical theatre. In 1898 he went on tour as conductor with Miss Collins in the musical comedy *The White Blackbird*, and he later went into management to stage the only subsequent musical in which his wife appeared, an adaptation of the

Parisian hit play *Coralie et Cie*, briefly staged at the Islington Grand in 1902 as *The Dressmaker*. In 1903 he toured with the musical *All at Sea*, but his principal activity over the two following decades was as a popular songwriter. He had numbers interpolated in shows from *Sergeant Brue* (1904, 'Instinct', 'And So Did Eve') to *High Jinks* (1916), scored song hits with 'If I Should Plant a Tiny Seed of Love' (1909, ly: Ballard MacDonald) and the enduring 'I Was a Good Little Girl Till I Met You' (1914, w Clifford Harris), and found his theatrical métier with the arrival of the fashion for the variety revue just before the First World War.

Tate put together the scores for the Palladium revue *I Should Worry* (1913) and the Victoria Palace's *A Year in an Hour* (1914), shared the musical credit for the more successful *Samples* (1916) with Herman Darewski and Irving Berlin and came out of this show with the evening's hit song, 'Broken Doll'. The Vaudeville Theatre revue *Some* produced another successful song, 'Ev'ry Little While', but a revue built around his variety theatre act with his new wife, Clarice Mayne, *This and That* (1916) ('That' was Tate, off-handedly referred to at his seat at the piano by his comedienne spouse), lasted only 48 performances.

His biggest success came about almost by accident. During the pre-London run of *The Maid of the Mountains* at Manchester he happened to be on hand when Robert Evett decided that Harold Fraser Simson's score needed some strengthening. Thus, Tate was called in to provide, firstly, the waltz song 'My Life is Love' for his ex-step-daughter José and the duet 'A Paradise for Two' for Miss Collins and Thorpe Bates. After the notable success of these two pieces a third song, for Bates – 'A Bachelor Gay Am I' – followed them into the show's score. These comic-operatic numbers, far distant in style from 'Broken Doll' and 'I Was a Good Little Girl', proved to be Tate's biggest successes, and 'A Bachelor Gay Am I' became one of the most popular baritone songs in the British concert repertoire.

He subsequently wrote the score for the revusical wartime piece *Lads of the Village* and another revue-musical, *The Beauty Spot*, created for Régine Flory and produced by Parisian revue specialist P-L Flers at the Gaiety Theatre, without any of his material winning equivalent notice. He continued, however, to turn out popular songs ('Somewhere in France with You' w Arthur Anderson and Valentine, 'Give Me a Cosy Little Corner' w Clifford Harris, etc) and provided the scores for his most successful revues, *Peep Show* and *Round in 50* (w Herman Finck) at the London Hippodrome, in the postwar years, but the musical which it was persistently paragraphed that he would write for his famous sister never eventuated. He did not venture again into the field of the book musical where his memorable contribution to *The Maid of the Mountains* remains his only real reference.

1904 **The Belle of the Orient** (w Paul Knox/Clifford Harris, George Arthurs, J B Peterman) 3 scenes Islington Empire 18 July
1915 **Very Mixed Bathing** (Clifford Harris, Lawrence Wright/P T Selbit) 3 scenes Palace Theatre, Bath 26 April
1915 **Kiss Me, Sergeant** (Harris/Laurie Wylie, Alfred Parker) 1 act Leicester Palace 2 August
1917 **Lads of the Village** (Harris, Valentine) 1 act Oxford Theatre 11 June
1917 **The Beauty Spot** (Harris, Valentine/Arthur Anderson, P-L Flers) Gaiety Theatre 22 December
1921 **Swindells Stores** (Valentine) 1 act Finsbury Park Empire

TAUBER, Richard [SEIFFERT, Ernst] (b Linz, 16 May 1891; d London, 8 January 1948). Much-loved tenor singer whose voice was the inspiration for some of the main romantic rôles of postwar Viennese Operette.

The son of the manager of the Stadttheater, Chemnitz, tenor Richard Tauber was orientated at first towards an operatic career, but although he found considerable success at the lighter end of the operatic repertoire, it was as the hero of a line of romantic Operetten that he was to win his greatest fame.

He made early appearances in Operette when he appeared at Berlin's Komische Oper in the German version of Ubaldo Pachetti's pre-*Student Prince* musicalization of *Alt-Heidelberg* and at the Theater an der Wien opposite Betty Fischer as Barinkay in *Der Zigeunerbaron* (1921) and, in succession to Hubert Marischka and Harry Bauer, in the tenor rôle of *Frasquita* (1922). He subsequently took over Marischka's rôles in both *Der Bacchusnacht* and *Der letzte Walzer*, teamed with Marischka and Fischer in a version of *Eine Nacht in Venedig* (1923), and appeared opposite Fritzi Massary as Victorian Silvius in *Die Perlen der Cleopatra* and alongside Grete Holm in a revival of *Ein Herbstmanöver* (1924).

After this run of Viennese engagements, Tauber based himself in Berlin where he played in Benatzky's *Ein Märchen aus Florenz* and in another revival of *Eine Nacht in Venedig* before taking up the rôle of the romantic violinist *Paganini*, originally played in Vienna by Carl Clewing, for the German production of Lehár's Operette. He continued a fruitful collaboration and friendship with the show's admiring composer thereafter, creating his first Lehár hero in the title-rôle of *Der Zarewitsch* (1927), and drawing both an adoring public and the kind of notices which would beset his career ('Richard Tauber is one of the best tenors Germany possesses today, and perhaps the best voice found in operetta anywhere. Unfortunately he looks like a butcher'). He then introduced the rôle of Goethe in the romanticized tale of the poet's love for *Friederike* (1928) equipped with Lehár's first Tauber bon-bon, the lilting 'O Mädchen, mein Mädchen', and made a fine success with a third Lehár hero, the rewritten version of the Chinese Prince Sou-Chong originally played by Marischka in *Die gelbe Jacke*, in the show's remake as *Das Land des Lächelns* (1929). He drew delighted applause for his performance of Lehár's tenorious 'Dein ist mein ganzes Herz' and rather less for his 'ponderous attempts at matinée idol mannerisms'. Another rewritten piece of Lehár cast him somewhat improbably opposite the beautiful Gitta Alpár as a dashing mountain-climbing princeling in *Schön ist die Welt* (1931). As ever, he deliverered the show's (re)made-to-measure music superbly but proved dramatically unconvincing with his 'heavy trunk on limbs twisted with gout'.

Tauber played his Sou Chong at the Theater an der Wien on the occasion of Lehár's 60th birthday celebrations, but he had an unaccustomed flop when he appeared again at the Berlin Metropoltheater in *Das Lied der Liebe* (1931), a pasticcio piece with a Korngoldized Strauss score which was quickly done away with. He had further disappointments with two attempts to establish *The Land of Smiles* in London, where he also played Schubert in a version of *Das Dreimäderlhaus* in German at the Aldwych Theatre in 1933, before he returned to Vienna and the stage of the Staatsoper

TAUBER
1431

to create perhaps the most demanding of Lehár's custom-made series of overwhelming tenor rôles in the short-lived first run of *Giuditta* (1934). Later the same year he appeared in some of the 89 performances of his own Operette, *Der singende Traum*, at the Theater an der Wien.

Soon after, Tauber joined the exodus from Germany and Austria, settled in Britain and in 1940 he became a British subject. In this period he interleaved concert work with occasional ventures into both opera (Tamino, Belmonte, Don Ottavio etc) and into the musical theatre, where his appearances included English versions of *Paganini* and *Das Land des Lächelns*, an unsuccessful *Dreimäderlhaus* remake called *Blossom Time* (Schubert), and a determinedly romantic period piece called *Old Chelsea* for which he again composed much of the score. Although in his fifties and seemingly squatter than ever, he also cast himself in a juvenile romantic lead through 95 London performances. If the show was not quite a success, it did, however, produce one of his best-known songs as a composer, the soaring ballad 'My Heart and I'. In 1946 he was seen briefly on Broadway in a version of *Das Land des Lächelns*, and he made his last stage appearance the following year.

Tauber also appeared in a number of musical films including *Blossom Time* (1934), *Heart's Desire* (1935), *Land Without Music* (1936) and *I Pagliacci* (1936) and performed solo spots in the screen versions of the British musicals *Waltz Time* (1946) and *The Lisbon Story* (1946, 'Pedro, the Fisherman').

Tauber's memorable singing career was, of course, the main part of his professional life, but his broad musical education led him both into composing and also an intermittent career as a conductor. He led several performances at the Bürgertheater in 1924, conducted matinée performances of *Marietta* at the Theater an der Wien at the same time that he was appearing in his *Der singende Traum*, and later conducted performances of both *Gay Rosalinda* and *The Bird Seller* in London.

Tauber had an important influence on the course of the German-language musical theatre in the late 1920s and early 1930s, the kind of influence rarely wielded to such an extent by a performer. His voice and his popularity encouraged Franz Lehár to develop the whole line of lush, romantic Operetten with large leading tenor rôles in which Tauber starred with such considerable success in Berlin and/or Vienna and which became the enduring classics of their time. But if the star served his composer well, that service was mutual, for nowhere else did Tauber find such music and such shows. His non-Lehár vehicles were, by and large, poor stuff and quickly gone, and outside the German and Austrian theatre, although his concert work was highly appreciated, he did not find the same success as an operettic hero.

Tauber was portrayed on the screen by Rudolf Schock in the film *Du bist die Welt für mich*.

1934 **Der singende Traum** (Ernst Marischka, Hermann Feiner) Theater an der Wien 31 August
1942 **Old Chelsea** (w Bernard Grün/Fred Salo Tysh, Walter Ellis/Ellis) Birmingham 21 September; Prince's Theatre, London 17 February 1943

Biographies; Napier, D: *Richard Tauber* (Arts & Educational Publishers, London, 1949), Korb, W: *Richard Tauber* (Vienna, 1966), Castle, C: *This Was Richard Tauber* (W H Allen, London, 1971) etc

TAUND, Eugen von (b Hausmannstetten, Steiermark, 17 July 1856; d unknown).

Eugen von Taund, whose principal occupation seems to have been in the retail trade, did not appear on the operettic scene until he was in his mid-thirties, when he had two Operetten mounted in Graz, and he flourished as a musician in his forties, in the later 1890s, when he had three further Operetten produced with some success in Vienna's principal theatres.

Die Lachtaube, played for 51 performances at the Carltheater with Julie Kopácsi-Karczag and manager Karl Blasel topping the bill, was also produced at Berlin's Theater Unter den Linden (20 August 1895) and at New York's Irving Place Theater (4 November 1898) with Kopácsi-Karczag in her original rôle, whilst *Der Wunderknabe*, mounted at the Theater an der Wien with Annie Dirkens and Girardi for 36 performances, also progressed to the Theater Unter den Linden (5 May 1897) and to London's West End, where it was played under the title *The Little Genius*. *Der Dreibund*, with Ilka Pálmay starred, was the least successful of the three, being played 23 times at the Theater an der Wien, and marking von Taund's last appearance on a Viennese playbill.

1890 **Der Gouverneur** Stadtparktheater, Graz 18 October
1891 **Die Murnixen** Stadtparktheater, Graz 18 February
1895 **Die Lachtaube** ('Otto Rehberg' ie Alexander Landesberg, Leo Stein) Carltheater 14 April
1896 **Der Wunderknabe** (Landesberg, Stein) Theater an der Wien 28 March
1898 **Der Dreibund** (Landesberg, Stein) Theater an der Wien 28 April

TAUSEND UND EINE NACHT Fantastic Operette in a Vorspiel and two acts by Leo Stein and Carl Lindau. Music by Johann Strauss arranged by Ernst Reiterer. Venedig in Wien, Vienna, 15 June 1906.

One of the series of remakes and pasticcio Operetten mounted by Gabor Steiner at his summer theatre Venedig in Wien, in Vienna's Prater, *Tausend und eine Nacht* was the house's third raking over of the Strauss family oeuvre following *Gräfin Pepi* (a musical mix of *Simplicius and Blindekuh*) and the highly successful *Frühlingsluft* (music from Josef Strauss). Unlike the latter, *Tausend und eine Nacht* did not take an established and successful play as its backbone, but instead simply tacked much of Strauss's *Indigo und die vierzig Räuber* score on to a suitably *Arabian Nights*-like dream-tale of romance and mistaken identity. Willy Bauer played Prince Suleiman who, in the dream-within-an-Operette, swaps places for a day with a fisherman so that he can romance the fisherman's wife, Leila (Phila Wolff). Fella Schreiter was Viennese Wally, the flirtatious representative of things Western, equipped with the evening's most successful musical piece, the waltz 'Ja, so singt man', and paired with Adolf Rauch as the Prince's secretary.

The show did well enough in its summer season to be taken up the following year by the Volksoper (27 October) and then by the Johann Strauss-Theater (1908 with Karl Grünwald and Therese Krammer) and to be played in both Germany and Hungary. It has been revived at the Volksoper on several occasions, and its potential for spectacular staging has made it a favourite at the Bregenz Seebühne where it has been mounted as part of several seasons.

An English version was played at London's Rudolf

Plate 269. *Light comedian* **Ernst Tautenhayn** *donned skirts for his imitation of a harem-girl in* Die Rose von Stambul.

Steiner Hall in 1936 (29 January) by the amateur Alan Turner Opera Company.

Germany: Centraltheater ?1907; Hungary: Népszinház-Vigopera *1001 éj* 8 May 1908

Recording: two-record set (Urania)

TAUTENHAYN, Ernst (b Vienna, 3 April 1873; d Zlabing, 30 August 1944).

One of the most outstanding light comedians of the Viennese musical stage of the 1910s and 1920s, Tautenhayn created a long run of rôles, mostly at the Theater an der Wien, and often in a hugely popular partnership with soubrette Luise Kartousch.

He began his metropolitan career at the Carltheater in the mid-1890s, creating small-to-supporting rôles in such pieces as *Das Modell* (Emmanuel Foresti, an officer), *Bum-Bum* (Edgar) and *Der Cognac-König* (Lt Dorn), playing Landry in *König Chilperich*, Prinz Saphir in *Blaubart*, Pedro in *Die Schwätzerin von Saragossa* (*Les Bavards*) and Ein Schildwache in *Herr Gouverneur* (W S Gilbert's *His Excellency*) before moving on to take larger rôles in provincial theatres.

In 1910 he returned to the big time when he joined the company at the Theater an der Wien and appeared there first of all in *Schneeglöckchen* (Polycarp Wasiliewitsch) before making a personal hit in the rôle of Thomasius II, the comical King of Aquitania, in *Die schöne Risette*. Over the following years he appeared in leading rôles in a number of classic pieces at that house and its companion Raimundtheater (Blasius in *Die Schützenliesel*, Spätzel in *Die sieben Schwaben*, Matthaeus in *Der fidele Bauer*, Orpheus in

Orpheus in der Unterwelt, Paul Aubier in *Der Opernball*, Fleck in *Flotte Bursche* etc) and at the same time created a decade-long series of new rôles and works: *Ihr Adjutant* (Trendelberg), Dagobert to the Pipsi of Kartousch in *Eva*, Jonny Burns in *Die keusche Barbara* (1911), *Der blaue Held* (Enzerich), *Der kleine König* (1912, Huck), *Prinzess Gretl* (Felix Hirschfeld), *Die ideale Gattin* (1913, Don Gil Tenorio de Sevilla), *Endlich allein* (Graf Willibald Splenningen), *Gold gab ich für Eisen* (1914, Rabenlechner), *Die schöne Schwedin* (Sven Liverstol), *Auf Befehl der Herzogin* (Toni) *Wenn zwei sich lieben* (1915, Baron Geza von Steinbach), *Der Sterngucker* (Franz Höfer), *Die Winzerbraut* (Franjo Svecak), the memorable Fridolin to the Midlili of Kartousch in the very long run of *Die Rose von Stambul* (1916), the Austrian *Wo die Lerche singt* (1918, Török Pál), *Nimm mich mit!* (1919, Franz Xaver Edelbrunner), *Die blaue Mazur* (Adolar), *Dorfmusikanten* (1920, Peterl) and *Die Frau im Hermelin* (1921, Suitangi).

He then left the Theater an der Wien and later in 1921 he created the plum rôle of the comical Marquis Napoleon St Cloche in *Die Bajadere* at the Carltheater. He played there again in *Die Brasilianerin* (Tobias Taube), as Calicot to the *Madame Pompadour* of Fritzi Massary, as Matthaeus in *Der fidele Bauer* and in *Glück bei Frauen* (1923, Jakob Vollaczek), before going on to play at the Wiener Stadttheater in the Anton Profès Operette *Glück muss man haben* (1923, Bacherer). He created the parts of Severin to the Cloclo of Kartousch in *Cloclo* (1924) and Tomasoni in *Revanche* (1924) at the Bürgertheater, was Abilio in *Donna Gloria* (1925) at the Carltheater, and played star comedy rôles in

Ich hab' dich Lieb (1926, Emil Schick), *Das Schwalbennest* (1926, Ferdinand Brandl), *Riquette* (1927) and *Musik in Mai* (1927) at the Raimundtheater and alongside Kartousch in *Eine einzige Nacht* (Wolfgang Schöbel) at the Carltheater. He paired with Kartousch again in *Die Lady vom Lido* (1927, Pfefferminz) at the Johann Strauss-Theater where he went on to repeat his St Cloche and to star in a revival of *Der lustige Krieg* and also took part in the premières of *Das Veilchen vom Montmartre* (1930) – in the rôle of the composer Hervé – *Der verliebte Eskadron* (1930, Dr Siegfried Apfelbaum), the Viennese version of *Sisters* (1930, Thomas Pirk) and the pasticcio *Der König ihres Herzens* (1930, Don Rodrigo del Carmona). He later succeeded to the rôle of Herzog Max in *Sissy* at the Theater an der Wien and in 1933 returned to the Johann Strauss-Theater to play President Philippe Peron in the musical comedy *Dame Nr 1 rechts*.

In 1937 Tautenhayn ill-chose his moment to try to turn manager and open a 'Deutsche Bühne' at the Raimundtheater. The project was a disastrous failure, and the adored comic of two generations of musical-theatregoers eventually committed suicide at the age of 71.

TAUTIN, Lise (b Paris, 1836; d Boulogne-sur-mer, ?1874). Leading lady of Offenbach's earliest large-scale opéras-bouffes.

The teenaged Lise Tautin made her first appearance on the Paris stage at the Théâtre des Bouffes-Parisiens as Aspasie in Offenbach's *Une demoiselle en loterie*, and she spent virtually all of her short career and life playing under the composer's aegis. She created the rôles of Catherine in the original production of *Le Mariage aux lanternes* (1857), Minette in *La Chatte metamorphosée en femme* (1858), Croûte-au-pot in *Mesdames de la Halle* (1858), Rosita in *Un mari à la porte* and Les Bouffes-Parisiens in *Le Carnaval des revues* (1860) and she found substantial fame as the original Eurydice of *Orphée aux enfers* (1858).

Mlle Tautin also created three other major Offenbach rôles in the years that followed: the outstanding travesty rôle of Drogan in the original two-act version of *Geneviève de Brabant*, the dramatically beset Catarina Cornaro of *Le Pont des soupirs* (1861) and the vocally florid Ernestine, who pretends to be Henriette Sontag, in the one-act *Monsieur Choufleuri restera chez lui le ...* (1861).

She visited Vienna and Budapest with the Bouffes-Parisiens troupe in the summer of 1861, appearing in *Le Pont des Soupirs*, *Un mari à la porte*, *Orphée aux Enfers* and the rest of the repertoire, and she subsequently created further Offenbach rôles in *Les Bergers* (1865, La Sincère) and the new version of Catarina in the extended four-act version of *Le Pont des soupirs* at the Variétés in 1868.

TAYLOR, Charles H[enry] (b Manchester ?1860; d Derby, 27 June 1907). Lyricist for a busy few years on the London stage.

Taylor began his working life alongside his father in the silk trade, but a friendship with producer Robert Courtneidge led him to supply some topical verses for pantomimes at Courtneidge's Prince's Theatre in Manchester and, eventually, for other Courtneidge ventures. He finally gave up silk and moved to London to pursue a career as a lyricist and there, after at first concentrating on songs for the popular market, he made his first incursion into the world of West End musical comedy with some additional lyrics for

Tom B Davis's production of fellow-Mancunian Leslie Stuart's *The Silver Slipper* (1901).

Taylor quickly became one of the most sought-after lyricists of the London stage and, in the two years that followed, he contributed to Sidney Jones's comedy opera *My Lady Molly* and to George Edwardes's production of *The Girl from Kays*, shared the lyric-writing credit of Seymour Hicks's extremely successful *Bluebell in Fairyland*, and wrote the entire songwords for Davis's disappointing *The Medal and the Maid* and for Leslie Stuart's *The School Girl*. Following the success of *Bluebell*, he became lyricist-in-chief to the Seymour Hicks/Charles Frohman organization, and between 1904 and 1907 he supplied the lyrics to Herbert Haines's music for the four shows that the team wrote and produced, scoring a major success with *The Catch of the Season* ('Cigarette', 'The Charms on My Chain') and a fine run with *The Beauty of Bath*. His most enduring work, however, came in his one London show with Courtneidge, *Tom Jones* (1907).

To an Edward German musical score of more lasting substance than those written by Haines, Taylor provided the words for such pieces as the celebrated waltz song 'For Tonight', the charming tale of 'The Green Ribbon' and the lusty 'West Country Lad'. *Tom Jones* proved, however, to be his last show. He was working on his first musical comedy libretto when he died at the age of 47. His last song had been played very shortly before, as a special addition to the score of *Tom Jones* for the 100th night of its run. It is that song, 'Dream o' Day Jill', which has survived through nigh on a century as his most popular single number.

1901 **A Busy Day** (Herbert E Baker/w W A Brabner) Theatre Royal, Blackburn 22 April
1901 **Bluebell in Fairyland** (Walter Slaughter/w Aubrey Hopwood/Seymour Hicks) Vaudeville Theatre 18 December
1902 **My Lady Molly** (Sidney Jones/w Percy Greenbank, G H Jessop/Jessop) Theatre Royal, Brighton 11 August; Terry's Theatre, London 14 March 1903
1903 **The Medal and the Maid** (Jones/Owen Hall) Lyric Theatre 25 April
1903 **The School Girl** (Leslie Stuart/Henry Hamilton, Paul M Potter) Prince of Wales Theatre 9 May
1904 **The Catch of the Season** (Herbert Haines, Evelyn Baker/Hicks, Cosmo Hamilton) Vaudeville Theatre 9 September
1905 **The Talk of the Town** (Haines/Hicks) Lyric Theatre 5 January
1906 **The Beauty of Bath** (Haines/Hicks, Hamilton) Aldwych Theatre 19 March
1907 **My Darling** (Haines, Baker/Hicks) Hicks Theatre 2 March
1907 **Tom Jones** (Edward German/Alexander M Thompson, Robert Courtneidge) Apollo Theatre 17 April

TELLHEIM, Karoline [BETTELHEIM, Karoline] (b Vienna, 1842; d ?Vienna, 13 December 1925).

Karoline Tellheim first appeared at the Carltheater at 19 years of age and made a success in J B Klerr's one-act operetta *Das war ich* (1862). She then played in Berlin and again at the Carltheater before joining the company at the Vienna Hofoper where for nine years she sang soubrette rôles in opera (Zerlina, Ännchen, Papagena etc). In 1871 she returned to the Operette stage to play Prince Raphael in *La Princesse de Trébizonde* at the Carltheater, and she later introduced the travesty rôle of Fortunato in the German version of *Madame l'Archiduc* at the Theater an der Wien, created the parts of Mirzl in *Das verwunschene Schloss* and of the Queen in *Das Spitzentuch der Königin* (1880) and appeared as Adele in *Die Fledermaus*. She then left the stage for the international concert platform where she saw out her career.

TELL HER THE TRUTH   Musical play in 2 acts by R P Weston and Bert Lee based on *Nothing But the Truth* by James Montgomery. Music by Jack Waller and Joseph Tunbridge. Saville Theatre, London, 14 June 1932.

One of the successful series of comedies with songs produced at the Saville Theatre by Jack Waller and starring little-chap comic Bobby Howes, *Tell Her the Truth* followed closely the tale of the well-known farcical play *Nothing But the Truth* in which the hero is bound by a bet to tell no lies, no matter how white, for 24 hours. Telling the truth about an ugly hat or frock is minor as compared to facing up to his boss's wife about her husband's attachment to a chorus girl or to a demanding client over an iffy business deal, but after hoursful of humorous situations all ends happily and little Bobby wins both his gamble and his girl.

In the very short score (six numbers) supplied by Waller and Tunbridge, Howes joined in duet with the girls of the piece, and again with the bullet-headed character actor Alfred Drayton in the rôle of his challenger and employer ('Hoch! Caroline'), but the favourite musical moments came from the bristling Wylie Watson as the innocent Yorkshireman ('I'm a child in business') on whom Bobby's firm has palmed off some dud land. He stole the song honours with his comical exhortation to 'Sing, Brothers' and in the mock oratorio scena 'Horrortorio', a pastiche of favourite oratorio bits in which he vents his fury at having been robbed.

Tell Her the Truth was closed after 239 West End performances when Howes decided he preferred the high life of the South of France to work, and a Broadway production starring Jack Sheehan jr was a quick flop, but the show had a good British touring life, still appearing on the schedules more than a decade after its production.

Nothing But the Truth was also used as the basis for the Broadway musical *Yes, Yes, Yvette* and for a musical by Michael Stewart, Mark Bramble and Cy Coleman, at the time of writing unproduced.

USA: Cort Theater 28 October 1932

TELL ME MORE!   Musical in 2 acts by Fred Thompson and William K Wells. Lyrics by Ira Gershwin and B G De Sylva. Music by George Gershwin. Gaiety Theater, New York, 13 April 1925.

Prolific librettist Fred Thompson and his partner Wells didn't trouble their heads too much about the libretto for *Tell Me More!*. The tale was just about as significant as the title. But that didn't matter: what mattered was the content – the dancing, the fun, the girls and, hopefully, the songs. Veteran producer Alfred Aarons, whose son Alex had produced the last George Gershwin musical, *Lady, Be Good!*, with such success, provided most of those ingredients and the Gershwins and Buddy De Sylva gave him a useful if not memorable score from which he was able to get a 100-performance run on Broadway.

The plot was the usual mixture of everyday amours. Jeune premier Kenneth Dennison falls for the once wealthy shopgirl Peggy Vandeleur, goofy Monty Simpkin falls for the wealthy Jane Wallace, and simple Billy falls for the passion-ate shopgirl Bonnie. And (in 1925) there was even the next best thing to a baby-swap. Peggy turns out to be Billy's long-lost sister. From the 14 numbers of the score, the lively intimation that one should be 'Kickin' the Clouds Away' surfaced as the evening's jolliest musical moment in a set of songs which weren't marked out as memorable. One song had a title that would become memorable, however: it was called 'My Fair Lady'.

Oddly enough, *Tell Me More!* had a better life outside America than it did at home. George Grossmith, who had given Gershwin one of his earliest chances as a stage writer with *Primrose*, picked up *Tell Me More!* and mounted it at his Winter Garden Theater when *Primrose* closed, just a few weeks after the New York opening. He added a couple of extra songs with local lyrics, cast the show up with Leslie Henson (Monty), Claude Hulbert (Billy), Arthur Margetson (Kenneth), Vera Lennox (Bonnie), Heather Thatcher (Jane) and Elsa MacFarlane (Peggy) and the piece even overran *Primrose*'s already good record by totalling 263 West End performances. Such a run ensured that *Tell Me More!* followed *Primrose* to the colonies.

J C Williamson Ltd's Australian production featured George Gee (Monty), Leyland Hodgson (Kenneth), Gus Bluett (Billy), Marjorie Hicklin (Peggy) and Dorothy Lena/Maud Fane (Jane) with Freddie Carpenter as principal dancer and Harry Woods's 'Paddlin' Madelin' Home', which had somehow got out of its second-hand spot in Broadway's *Sunny* and into the score of this show on the way, as the evening's musical highlight. The piece ran a good three months in Melbourne and six weeks in Sydney.

UK: Winter Garden Theatre 26 May 1925; Australia: Theatre Royal, Melbourne 17 July 1926

TEMPEST, Marie (Dame)   [ETHERINGTON, Marie Susan] (b London, 15 July 1864; d London, 15 October 1942). Singer and actress who was London's favourite comic-opera soubrette until she decided she preferred not to sing.

Convent-educated in Belgium, the young Miss Etherington studied music in Paris and at London's Royal Academy of Music and made her first professional stage appearance at the age of 21 in the rôle of Fiametta in a revival of *Boccaccio*. She was next hired by hopeful singer-manageress Agnes de la Porte to appear alongside that lady in the juvenile rôle of the dramatic *The Fay o' Fire* and, after making a personal success, followed the piece's quick closure by taking over the title-rôle of *Erminie* from Florence St John for the last part of that show's run at the Comedy Theatre.

Miss Tempest appeared as Rosella opposite Rose Hersee (and alongside prima donnas of the quality of Soldene and Kate Munroe) in a short-run piece called *Frivoli* at the Theatre Royal, Drury Lane, and took the second lead (to Miss St John) in a finely cast production of Messager's *La Béarnaise* at the new Prince of Wales Theatre, but it was a further take-over, in the title-rôle of *Dorothy*, which finally established the young vocalist as a star. When Henry Leslie took over the management of the unwanted show and transferred it to the Prince of Wales Theatre, he replaced the coolly elegant Marion Hood with the more personality-laden Miss Tempest, from the cast of the outgoing *La Béarnaise*, and the piece and its new star helped each other to memorable success through a very long run.

The new star's personal life hit the headlines when her husband divorced her, naming Leslie as co-respondent, but her popularity only increased as she continued on to play the title-rôles of *Doris* and *The Red Hussar* for the producer of the moment, repeating the latter rôle with great success in New York where one journal acclaimed her as 'a Lotta with a prima donna voice'. After dropping out of the tour of *The Red Hussar* with vocal problems (it was a big sing) and breaking up with Leslie under dramatic circumstances, she took further engagements in America. Over a period of several years, she toured with J C Duff's comic-opera company (Dorothy, Carmen, Mignon, Mabel in *Pirates of Penzance*, Arline in *The Bohemian Girl*), then appeared as a travesty Adam in a version of *Der Vogelhändler* (1891), as the girl raised as a boy in De Koven's *The Fencing Master* (1892), as the heroine of Genée's *Nanon* and as the operatic Countess of De Koven's *The Algerian* (1893) before returning to Britain in 1895.

On her return, George Edwardes hired her as prima donna for Daly's Theatre and had a rôle specially written into *An Artist's Model* (1895, Adèle) for her. She scored her biggest London success yet as the enriched model whose artist ex-lover is now chary of resuming their relationship, and confirmed dazzlingly as the heroine of *The Geisha* (1897, O Mimosa San) in which she introduced 'The Amorous Goldfish', 'Love, Love' and 'A Geisha's Life', *A Greek Slave* (1898, Maia) and *San Toy* (1899, San Toy), the series of shows which established Daly's Theatre as the bulwark of substantial modern musical theatre.

During the run of *San Toy* she brought about a situation which allowed her to break her contract with Edwardes, calculatedly ending her career in the musical theatre in order to begin what turned out to be a second and equally outstanding career as a light-comedy actress. She sang little thereafter, appearing in concert and, in 1906, for what she insisted was a lot of money, at the Palace Music Hall. She sang a little in the 1912 *Art and Opportunity*, and the last instance of her appearing in a musical show was the 1924 play *Midsummer Madness* which mixed some fragments of Clifford Bax music with its sentimental harlequinade of a story.

In spite of the fact that her musical career lasted only some 15 years, compared with the lifelong activities of such as Florence St John, the combination of a strong unaffected soprano and a superior acting talent made Tempest arguably the finest of all the musical theatre's leading ladies of the Victorian era.

Biography: Bolitho, H: *Marie Tempest* (Cobden-Sanderson, London, 1936)

TEMPLE, Richard [COBB, Richard Barker] (b London, 2 March 1847; d London, 19 October 1912). Longtime member of the original Savoy Theatre company.

Temple made his early career as a baritone vocalist in opera and comic opera, appearing in Manchester in Levey's *Punchinello* (1871, Marquis) and in London in *Ixion* (1870, Jupiter), *Le Roi Carotte* (1872, t/o Pippertrunk), *L'Oeil crevé* (1872, Gérome) and the one-act *The Wager* (1872). In 1873 he played Larivaudière in the original English *La Fille de Madame Angot* and in the operetta *Potacatapetl* (Paulo) and the following year stepped in to take over as Ange Pitou (from the tenor Edward Beverley) in an emergency in another production of the same piece. He subsequently

played Rhododendron Pasha in the Islington production of Offenbach's *Les Géorgiennes* (1875), directed and played in Sullivan's *The Zoo* on the same programme, appeared as the Sultan in *The Sultan of Mocha* at Liverpool (1876), as Buckingham in Cellier's *Nell Gwynne* at Manchester and as Carlo Maloni in Solomon's *A Will with a Vengeance* (1876) at the Royalty, and toured with Francois Cellier's Opera Company performing *Geneviève de Brabant* and *Cox and Box* (1877).

The Cellier connection was doubtless no small help in winning Temple his job with the Comedy Opera Company for whom he created the rôle of Sir Marmaduke Pointdextre in Gilbert and Sullivan's *The Sorcerer* (1877). He remained with the company to create the part of Dick Deadeye in *HMS Pinafore*, was London's first Pirate King in *The Pirates of Penzance* ('The Pirate King') and Colonel Calverly in *Patience* ('When I First Put This Uniform On'), but when Carte moved his operations to the new Savoy Theatre he remained at the Opera Comique to play for Hollingshead in his revival of Gilbert's *Princess Toto* (1880, Portico) and at the Gaiety in Solomon's *Lord Bateman* (Ephraim MacDallah).

He returned to Carte's company, however, to create further Gilbert and Sullivan rôles as Strephon in *Iolanthe* (1882), as Arac, with his mock Handelian aria, in *Princess Ida* (1884), to play the title-rôle of *The Mikado* (1885, 'A More Humane Mikado'), the ghostly Sir Roderic in *Ruddigore* ('The Ghosts' High Noon') and Sergeant Meryll in *The Yeomen of the Guard* (1888). When it came to *The Gondoliers*, however, he declined the limp rôle of Luis which had been written for him and, after more than a decade of playing little else than the works of Gilbert, attempted, with no more success than other departing members of the company, to take his Savoy popularity into other fields.

He appeared in the operetta *The Silver Trout* (1889, Jack Lacy) at a benefit, then made an attempt at management with a tour of Gounod's *The Mock Doctor* starring Effie Chapuy in 1890. It was an expensive failure, and his later ventures as a performer and director held few highlights: he played in the disastrous *Miami* (1893), succeeded Colin Coop as Sid Fakah in the musical *Morocco Bound* (1893), directed and played Dick Fid in Howard Talbot's maiden *Wapping Old Stairs* (1894) and performed in *The Geisha* in St Petersburg. He later directed the touring musical *The Red Spider* (1898), appeared as Henry VII in the unfortunate *The Gay Pretenders* (1900) and played in the children's musical *Little Hans Andersen* (1903). Temple made his final West End appearance in 1906 as Mr Burchell in Liza Lehmann's comic-opera version of *The Vicar of Wakefield*.

TEMPLETON, Fay (b Little Rock, Ark, 25 December 1865; d San Francisco, 3 October 1939). Buxom comedienne and vocalist of the burlesque and musical-comedy stage.

An actor's daughter, Miss Templeton first appeared on the stage as a small child and was seen in rôles ranging from Shakespeare's Puck (at eight) to Sullivan's Ralph Rackstraw (aged 14), Serpolette (*Les Cloches de Corneville*), *Giroflé-Girofla*, *La Mascotte*, *Patience* and *La Grande-Duchesse* in a juvenile musical company.

She graduated to adult status in a touring production of *Billee Taylor*, toured her own company with *Giroflé-Girofla*, *La Belle Coquette* and a piece called *Rosita, or Cupid and*

Cupidity by the untried Harry Bache Smith, and at the age of 20 had her first Broadway rôle as Gabriel in a revival of the favourite burlesque *Evangeline*. She played in further burlesques (*The Corsair*) and comic operas (Fanchette Michel in *Der Seekadett*, Drogan in *Geneviève de Brabant*) on the road, at first in America and then in London, where she was hired at the not inconsiderable salary of £15 per week for a supporting part in *Monte Cristo Jr* at London's Gaiety Theatre performing the song 'I Like It, I Do'. She was sacked from this job for impenitently lowering the neckline and raising the trunks of her costume, sued in a blaze of publicity, and lost. She did not play the Gaiety again, but nearly a decade later she nevertheless had a success there when the coon song 'I Want Yer My Honey' which she had written was introduced by Ellaline Terriss into *The Shop Girl*.

Back in America, whilst playing on the road in such pieces as the Russel's Comedians *Miss McGinty of the Comédie Française* (1890), she returned to the kind of burlesque which encouraged low necks and short trunks, appearing, during well-spaced Broadway visits, in the breeches title-rôles of the short-lived *Henrik Hudson* (1890) and the much more successful *Excelsior Jr* (1895). By this stage, the once well-built performer had grown extremely buxom, but this proved to be no bar to an increasing popularity and she won herself further following when she moved for two seasons to Weber and Fields' burlesque house, appearing as a revived Cleopatra in *Hurly Burly* (1898), as the hard-done-by heroine of *Catherine* (1899) and the sleepwalking star of *Helter Skelter* (1899). For *Broadway to Tokio* (1900) she repeated her impersonation of Cleopatra before she returned to Weber and Fields to share starry billing with Lillian Russell, De Wolf Hopper and David Warfield in *Fiddle-dee-dee* (1900), in which she introduced 'Ma Blushin' Rosie', and in *Hoity-Toity* (1901).

Miss Templeton appeared on Broadway in *The Runaways* (1903), co-starred with Peter F Dailey as Mrs Aurora Daye Knight in the loose-limbed vaudeville *A Little Bit of Everything* (1904) and took the top of the bill again as Mamselle Fleurette in *In Newport* (1904) before making her biggest success, teamed with Victor Moore and Donald Brian, as the devoted Mary Jane Jenkins ('Mary' [it's a grand old name], 'So Long Mary') in George M Cohan's *Forty-Five Minutes from Broadway* (1905–6). But this piece, in which she toured for a long period, was her last major stage appearance, for at the end of the tour she announced her retirement from the theatre. She returned, however, for several special occasions, appearing in the Weber and Fields reunion show *Hokey-Pokey* in 1912, as Little Buttercup in a spectacular *HMS Pinafore* and, finally, at nearly 70 years of age, played Aunt Minnie in *Roberta* (1933) introducing Jerome Kern's enduring ballad 'Yesterdays'.

She was seen on film in the 1933 *Broadway to Hollywood*, and was impersonated in the Cohan biopic *Yankee Doodle Dandy* by Irene Manning.

Beyond her *Shop Girl* song, Miss Templeton wrote and composed a number of other numbers, mostly of the coon variety, several of which found their way into musical comedies ('My Oneliest One' etc).

LA TEMPRANICA

LA TEMPRANICA Zarzuela in 1 act (3 scenes) by Julián Romea. Music by Geronimo Giménez. Teatro de la Zarzuela, Madrid, 19 September 1900.

The tale of 'la tempranica', the precocious girl, moved away from the favourite setting of many of the other most successful zarzuelas, the suburbs of the city, to the Spanish countryside and to a tale slightly more in the conventions of the rest of European musical theatre. The noble Andalucian Don Luis, Count of Santa Fe (Pepe Sigler), once had a hunting accident in the mountains and was nursed back to health by the peasant girl María (Concha Segura). During the days of his recovery a strong feeling grew up between the two young people, but Don Luis returned to his home and his own way of life. The two meet again when Luis is leading an English guest through the mountains, but María finally agrees to marry her village Miguel. When Don Luis turns up at the celebrations she is tempted to renounce Miguel, but her little brother, Grabié, brings her the news – Luis is married. María has to see for herself. She and Grabié go to Granada and, watching outside Luis's home, she sees him, his wife and his child together. Then she returns to her home, her people and to Miguel who will be her husband.

Although the music of the show included some colourful ensembles, including the village betrothal fête, and a virtual stand-up solo for the boy ('La tarantula é un bicho mu malo'), presented as such, the backbone of the score was in the romantic music for the two central characters, their duo of reminiscence 'Te quiero ... poque eres güeno', and María's showpiece 'Sierras de Granada'.

Recordings: complete (Columbia/Alhambra, Montilla/Zafiro)

THE TENDERFOOT

THE TENDERFOOT Musical play in 3 acts by Richard Carle. Music by Harry L Heartz. Dearborn Theater, Chicago, 12 April 1903; Daly's Theater, New York, 22 February 1904.

Richard Carle's self-made vehicle of 1903 presented him as Professor Zachary Pettibone LLD, BA, wandering the wildspots of the West from the ranch of heiress Marion Worthington (May de Sousa) to the Indian camping ground presided over by Big Bluff (William Russell). Honest John Martin (gambler and soubret), Reckless Reddy (cowboy), White Pill (medicine man), Abe Splicer (parson), Flora Jane Fibby (authoress and soubrette), a bunch of Texas Rangers headed by hero Paul Winthrop (Edmund Stanley) and number-two comic Bill Barker (Gilbert Gregory), and a gaggle of Gibson Girls were included in the personnel of an entertainment which rolled up 20 weeks in Chicago before the Dearborn management sent it on the road.

Carle made a hit everywhere singing about 'My Alamo Love' whose eyes outshone the rising moon, described himself as 'A Peaceable Party' and joined in trio to sing about 'The Tortured Thomas Cat', whilst the girls' chorus imitated Gilbert and Sullivan's policemen with a 'tantara' chorus, the rangers chorused to 'rataplan', the hero baritoned an 'Adios' and the heroine serenaded 'Fascinating Venus' (the planet). A New York season of what was noted as being little more than a series of variety sketches, linked by 'song and dance specialities and knockabout galore' lasted a good (for a 'foreign' show) 81 performances.

Perhaps a little suprisingly, *The Tenderfoot*'s afterlife included, beyond its touring seasons in America, a production in Australia. A producer called George Willoughby launched a company in Sydney in 1914 with Carrick Major in Carle's rôle supported by Booby Woolsey, Don Hancock, Myrtle Jersey, Eva Olivotti, George M Bogues, Grace Ellsworth and J Monte Crane, and a repertoire of *The Tender-*

foot (11 April) and *The Mayor of Tokio* (2 May). Of the two, *The Tenderfoot* did better, but the enterprise was not a lengthy one.

Australia: Adelphi Theatre, Sydney 11 April 1914

TENDERLOIN Musical comedy in 2 acts by George Abbott and Jerome Weidman based on the novel by Samuel Hopkins Adams. Lyrics by Sheldon Harnick. Music by Jerry Bock. 46th Street Theater, New York, 17 October 1960.

Following the success of their *Fiorello!*, the team of writers Jerome Weidman, George Abbott, Sheldon Harnick and Jerry Bock, and producers Robert E Griffith and Harold S Prince followed up with another New York period piece, this one set in the dirty underbelly of the city known as the Tenderloin. Maurice Evans starred as the Reverend Andrew Brock, out to wipe up and out the worst immoralities and corruptions of the area. Those immoralities are headed and personified by prostitute Nita (Eileen Rodgers), the corruption by police lieutenant Schmidt (Ralph Dunn), and the minister's ally of circumstance is a reporter Tommy Howatt (Ron Husmann) who is out to win the church choir belle, Laura (Wynne Miller). It is Tommy's court evidence which wins the day and stonkers Schmidt. Nita marries church choirman Joe (Rex Everhart), and the other girls of the Tenderloin go off to set up the best little whorehouse in the west.

A jolly score, topped by a first-rate burlesque of the damper kind of Victorian ballad, 'Artificial Flowers', sung by Tommy as his audition for Brock's choir, and a singalong exposé of 'How the Money Changes Hands' (a relation of *Fiorello!*'s 'Little Tin Box'), illustrated the costume girlie tale happily, if unprofitably, through a Broadway run of 216 performances. The show was played for a season at the Equity Library Theater in 1975 (6 November).

Recording: original cast (Capitol) etc

TENNENT, H[enry] M[oncrieff] (b 1879; d London, 10 June 1941). London play producer whose organization also imported a number of successful musicals.

After working for piano manufacturers and music publishers Broadwood, Harry Tennent moved to the managerial side of the theatre business and ultimately became General Manager of Moss' Empires and Howard and Wyndham's Tours and of the Theatre Royal, Drury Lane. In this position, he was responsible for booking many musicals into the chain of theatres under his control, and was credited by Ivor Novello with having commissioned *Glamorous Night* for Drury Lane over a luncheon table.

In 1936, in partnership with **Hugh ('Binkie') BEAUMONT** [Hughes Griffiths MORGAN, b London, 28 March 1908; d London, 23 March 1973], he founded his own theatrical management firm H M Tennent Ltd. The pair scored an early major success with the play *French Without Tears* (1936) and, from then until Beaumont's death 37 years later, H M Tennent Ltd held a place as the dominant play-producing organization in London. Although Tennent had produced a number of revues in the 1910s, and had even written songs, including the successful 'My Time is Your Time', for them, the firm did not become involved in producing musicals until well after his death.

In 1945 Noël Coward persuaded Beaumont to produce his revue *Sigh No More*, and its comparative success led to

Beaumont venturing into a number of other successful revues (*The Lyric Revue, The Globe Revue, At the Lyric*). He also made rare incursions into the musical theatre with Coward's ill-fated *After the Ball*, and, more successfully, Sandy Wilson's *The Buccaneer* and the London production of Frank Loesser's *Where's Charley?* (1958).

Beaumont secured an option on the British rights of *My Fair Lady* as part of canny piece of showbusinessmanship over the availability of Rex Harrison. When Harrison was eagerly wanted for the rôle of Higgins, he was playing for Tennent's in *Bell, Book and Candle*. Beaumont purposely kept the fading play resolutely on (and Harrison, thus, resolutely unavailable) until he had won himself a splendid deal which included London's *My Fair Lady*. Following the enormous success of this production, he had a second success with the French musical *Irma la Douce* and a third with a musical which nobody wanted and which its publishers had to virtually pay him to produce – *West Side Story*.

Amongst a heavy schedule of play production, Tennent's staged and/or managed a number of other imported musicals, some like *A Most Happy Fella, Bye Bye Birdie, Promises, Promises, Godspell* and, after a very sticky start, *Hello, Dolly!*, with success, others (*Do Re Mi, Carnival, I Do! I Do!, On the Town, No, No, Nanette* revival) with less or none. Beaumont, who was not particularly interested in the musical theatre, made little attempt to produce untried musicals after the musical version of Terence Rattigan's *French Without Tears*, produced as *Joie de Vivre* (1960), folded in four performances, and otherwise backed only a West End transfer of another classic adaptation, the richly cast *Virtue in Danger* from the Mermaid Theatre, again without success.

The one success which the firm had with an original musical came shortly after Beaumont's death, before Tennent's had begun to seriously decline from its predominant position in the West End, when the company produced the musical version of *Billy Liar, Billy*, at the Theatre Royal, Drury Lane, with Michael Crawford (succeeded by Roy Castle) starring for 904 performances.

[DIE] TERESINA Operette in 3 acts by Rudolf Schanzer and Ernst Welisch. Music by Oscar Straus. Deutsches Künstlertheater, Berlin, 11 September 1925.

Schanzer and Welisch's libretto for *Teresina* brought out that favourite operettic hero, Napoléon Bonaparte, one more time. This time he started off in Fréjus, on his way to take power in Paris, gathering on his way the allegiance of the ci-devant Comte de Lavarennes who has engaged to wed a little theatre girl, Terésa, to comply with the 'equality' decrees of the Directoire. But he is called suddenly to the road and she is abandoned. By Act II Napoléon is in power, Lavarennes is a Maréchal and Teresa has become the fabulous diva, La Térésina, sighed after by the whole male world, including the emperor. It takes till the end of the third act for Lavarennes' mysterious disappearance from Fréjus to be cleared up and the pair to be reunited. The comic characters of the piece were Terésa's barber brother, Daniel, taken up by the foolish Prince Borghese to supply him with healthy, son-producing blood transfusions, and by the Princess Borghese for altogether more agreeable reasons. The bulk of the score fell to the prima donna, played by Fritzi Massary in the Berlin première, and to her Count, with the Borgheses and Daniel providing the lighter musical moments. The rôle of Napoléon (Johannes Riemann) was a non-singing one.

A useful success through four months in Berlin, *Teresina* was subsequently given in the provinces and exported to Budapest (ad Zsolt Harsányi) where Sári Fedák took the title-rôle and Hanna Honthy played Pauline Borghese, to Vienna at Ronachers Operetten-Theater where Luise Kartousch starred as Terésa, and in Nantes and subsequently Paris (ad Léon Uhl, Jean Marietti) with Léo Bovy (Terésa), Harlé (Lavarennes) and Davenay (Napoléon).

Hungary: Fővárosi Operettszinház *Terezina* 30 December 1925; Austria: Ronacher 6 March 1926; France: Théâtre Graslin, Nantes 19 November 1927, Folies-Wagram, Paris 25 May 1928

TERRASSE, Claude (b L'Arbresle, 27 January 1867; d Paris, 30 May 1923). The musical illustrator of de Flers and de Caillavet's much-admired pre-war opéras-bouffes, whose works seem to be more talked-of than played.

Terrasse studied at the Conservatoire de Lyon and the École Niedermeyer and, after periods spent as an orchestral trumpeter, a provincial piano teacher and a church organist in Paris, he found his way into the theatre through his friendship with Alfred Jarry, for whose play *Ubu Roi* (1896) he composed the incidental music. He provided scores for a handful of plays and short opérettes, as well as for Courteline's 'fantaisie' *Paris-Courcelles* at the Grand Guignol, and the sparkling and burlesque extravagance of his composing talent, helped by an equal talent for attracting first-class friends and collaborators, ensured him early success in a genre – the genuine opéra-bouffe – which had been largely submerged since the days of Hervé, Nuitter, Meilhac and Halévy.

La Petite Femme de Loth (1900), written to a libretto by Tristan Bernard, and *Les Travaux d'Hercule* (1901), a collaboration with Robert de Flers and Gaston de Caillavet, provoked connoisseurs, in a fallow period for French opérette, to hopeful comparisons with the greatest writers of 19th-century burlesque. Those comparisons were fuelled by the successes of the same team's crazily risqué *Le Sire de Vergy* (1903) and *Monsieur de la Palisse* (1904), the topsy-turvy classicisms of *Paris, ou le bon juge* (1905) and even the tiny and non-burlesque *Chonchette* (1902). Terrasse had a further success with another little classical burlesque, *Eglé*, a piece whose heroine was the baby born of Jupiter's bovine dalliance with the nymph Io, who here somehow here got mixed up with the Golden Fleece and Jason's famous quest.

Terrasse went apparently upmarket with *Le Mariage de Télémaque* (1910), written to a text by two Academicians, produced by Albert Carré at the Opéra-Comique, and revived there in 1913. The piece called itself simply a 'comédie' and, indeed, it lacked the bouffe spirit of the earlier works. Its post-Trojan-War tale of Telemachus' infatuation with Helen, and her rather unimaginative plot to disillusion him, compared poorly with Meilhac and Halévy's *La Belle Hélène*, but the now celebrated team with de Flers and de Caillavet was not reformed and the composer never again found the same level of praise or popularity. The musical comedies *Les Transatlantiques*, which mixed Americanisms with old-world aristocracy, and *Miss Alice des PTT* were at best half-successes, and of his later full-scale works only the costume opérette *Cartouche* (1912), produced at the

Trianon-Lyrique, came near equalling the quality and success of the works of the composer's best years. His last shows returned to the one-act formula, which he had earlier practised with more success. They also inclined to lesser venues, and the composer's last full-scale piece, *Frétillon*, a period opérette written to an Albert Carré libretto based on *Les Chansons de Béranger*, was produced posthumously in Strasbourg.

Terrasse's other works included a number of revues (*Paris tout nu* at the Ambassadeurs 1908 etc), such pieces as the ballet-pantomime *La Mariée de la Rue Brisemiche* (1909, Courteline, Marsolleau) and the ballet *Strella* (1911) both produced at the Folies-Bergère, and the little divertissement *Les Lucioles* played at a matinée at the Opéra-Comique 28 December 1910.

The composer's principal opéras-bouffes were given a good number of showings in other languages and other countries, and several of his little pieces also travelled – *Chonchette* did the rounds, *La Fiancée du scaphandrier* was seen in Germany under the title of *Elisa, die Taucherbraut* (ad Maurice Rappaport, Intimes Theater, Berlin 3 September 1902) and the one-act vaudeville *Le Tiers porteur* was exported to Vienna's Apollotheater (1914, *Checkvekehr*) – but his best works were always handicapped by the 'neccessity' of making considerable alterations in the happily scabrous de Flers and de Caillavet libretti to suit the standards of the early years of this century. However, Terrasse and his best works have always enjoyed a high reputation amongst commentators in his own country and his opéras-bouffes have won several revivals there, often under non-commercial circumstances.

1900 **L'Heure du berger** (Rosenval) 1 act Théâtre Aphration 23 May
1900 **L'Amour en bouteille** (Bonis-Charancle) 1 act Folies-Parisiennes 19 June
1900 **La Petite Femme de Loth** (Tristan Bernard) Théâtre des Mathurins 10 October
1901 **On demande des chanteurs** 1 act Royan 6 March
1901 **Les Travaux d'Hercule** (Gaston de Caillavet, Robert de Flers) Bouffes-Parisiens 7 March
1902 **La Fiancée du scaphandrier** (Franc-Nohain) 1 act Théâtre des Mathurins 8 January
1902 **Chonchette** (de Caillavet, de Flers) 1 act Théâtre des Capucines 11 April
1902 **Au temps des croisades** (Franc-Nohain) Pavillon de Flore, Liège 21 December
1903 **La Botte secrète** (Franc-Nohain) 1 act Théâtre des Capucines 27 January
1903 **Le Sire de Vergy** (de Caillavet, de Flers) Théâtre des Variétés 16 April
1903 **Péché véniel** (Franc-Nohain) 1 act Théâtre des Capucines 14 November
1904 **Monsieur de la Palisse** (de Caillavet, de Flers) Théâtre des Variétés 2 November
1905 **Le Manoir de Cagliostro** (aka *Le Manoir enchanté*) (Alfred Jarry, Eugène Demolder) 1 act (privately) 10 January
1906 **Paris, ou le bon juge** (de Caillavet, de Flers) Théâtre des Capucines 18 March
1907 **Le Chant de muezzin** (Franc-Nohain) Monte-Carlo January
1907 **Eglé, ou l'enfant de la vache** (Emmanuel-Philippe Moreau, Clairville, Dupré) Théâtre du Moulin-Rouge 7 May
1907 **L'Ingénue libertin** (Louis Artus) Théâtre des Bouffes-Parisiens 11 December
1908 **Le Coq d'Inde** (Rip) Théâtres des Capucines 6 April

1908 **Le Troisième Larron** (Gauthier-Villars) 1 act Folies-Pigalle 13 April

1910 **Le Mariage de Télémaque** (Jules Lemaître, Maurice Donnay) Opéra-Comique 4 May

1911 **Pantagruel** (Jarry, Demolder) Grand Théâtre, Lyon 30 January

1911 **Le Relai** (Jarry, Demolder) Salle Rostand March

1911 **Les Transatlantiques** (Abel Hermant, Franc-Nohain) Théâtre de l'Apollo 20 May

1912 **Cartouche** (Hugues Delorme, Francis Gally) Trianon-Lyrique 9 March

1912 **Le Tiers porteur** (Jean Kolb, André de Fouquières) 1 act Théâtre Michel 27 April

1912 **Miss Alice des PTT** (Maurice Vaucaire/Bernard) La Cigale 14 December

1913 **L'Amour patriote** (Gally, Jean Kolb) 1 act Royan 12 August

1916 **La Farce du poirier** (Ferdinand Hérold) 1 act Théâtre des Bouffes-Parisiens 29 July

1918 **Le Cochon qui sommeille** (Rip, Robert Dieudonné) Théâtre Michel 24 December

1919 **Le Muphti** (Paul Millet) 1 act Monte-Carlo 10 April

1920 **Un Mari sans sa femme** (Edouard Adénis) 1 act Alhambra 1 November

1923 **Chamouche** (de Féraudy) 1 act Alhambra 23 March

1924 **Faust en ménage** (Albert Carré) 1 act Théâtre de la Potinière 5 January

1927 **Frétillon** (A Carré) Théâtre Municipal de Strasbourg 5 March

TERRIS, Norma [ALLISON, Norma] (b Columbus, Kans, 13 November 1904; d Lyme, Conn, 15 November 1989). Singing actress whose one major rôle was never followed up.

Miss Terris first appeared on the stage at the age of 15 as a dancer in *The Midnight Frolics*, and had her first speaking rôle in the musical comedy *Queen o' Hearts* (1922, Grace). She toured in vaudeville with her first husband, Max Hoffman jr, in the title-rôle of George M Cohan's *Little Nellie Kelly* and again in the George S Kaufman/Marc Connelly musical *Be Yourself*, and returned to Broadway in the revues *A Night in Paris* and *A Night in Spain*.

In 1927 the pretty, dark performer won the rôle of her career when she created the part of Magnolia Hawkes in *Show Boat*, introducing 'Why Do I Love You', 'Make Believe' and 'You Are Love' in partnership with leading man Howard Marsh (Gaylord Ravenal). She made her greatest success, however, in the final part of the show in which she returned as Magnolia's modern-day daughter, Kim, performing a series of vaudevillesque impersonations of celebrities.

The success was to remain an isolated one. Although Miss Terris again played Magnolia in a revival of *Show Boat* in 1932, she appeared only in two further Broadway musicals, both of which counted their runs in days: as the heroine of the naïve 1930 *The Well of Romance* and in the 1938 *Great Lady*. She later appeared at the St Louis Muny in her *Show Boat* rôle as well as in the star rôles of *Bitter-Sweet*, Ivor Novello's *Glamorous Night* and Fall's *Madame Pompadour*, and in various stock companies in both straight and musical rôles.

Miss Terris also appeared on the musical screen alongside J Harold Murray and Reginald Dandy as the heroine of *Married in Hollywood*, the Hollywood film version of Oscar Straus's *Hochzeit in Hollywood*.

The Goodspeed Opera House in Connecticut named its second, smaller house in Chester for Miss Terris, a long-time resident of the area.

TERRISS, Ellaline [LEWIN, Ellaline] (b Stanley, Falkland Islands, 13 April 1871; d Richmond, Surrey, 16 June 1971). Sweetheart of London's turn-of-the-century musical comedy stage.

Miss Terriss, daughter of the favourite actor William Terriss (né Lewin), made her teenaged appearances on the stage in non-musical pieces with Beerbohm Tree and, over a period of three years, with Charles Wyndham. In 1892 she took an engagement at the Court Theatre which brought her both her first singing rôles, in the little operettas *A Pantomime Rehearsal* and *His Last Chance*, and a husband in the person of fellow actor, Seymour Hicks. Over the years that followed, Hicks and Miss Terriss were to become the most famous married couple in the West End musical theatre.

The pair were taken to the Gaiety Theatre by George Edwardes for a stop-gap revival of *Little Jack Sheppard* in 1894, Hicks to fill the lead comedy rôle, and his wife to play the ingénue rôle created by Marion Hood, with whose cool elegance and coloratura soprano the prettily voiced light-comic actress had nothing in common. Edwardes next cast her as Jessie Bond's sister in Gilbert's *His Excellency* (1894) where she also played in the forepiece, *Papa's Wife*, for which she composed the little bit of accompanying music, and, after Ada Reeve, Kate Cutler and Eva Moore had all done their time as the heroine of *The Shop Girl*, he brought her back to the Gaiety to take over the rôle of Bessie Brent.

When the next Gaiety musical was prepared, Hicks refused his rôle and parted company with Edwardes, but Mrs Hicks stayed and starred as May, *The Clergyman's Daughter*, in a piece which was renamed for town *My Girl* (1896). She followed up – opposite her returned husband/partner – as the sparkily ingénue heroine of *The Circus Girl* (1896, Dora Wemyss) and here she introduced her first major hit song with Lionel Monckton's 'A Little Bit of String'. *A Runaway Girl* (1898) was another huge success for the Gaiety Theatre and for musical comedy's favourite ingénue, cast here as Winifred Grey, chased around Europe, and equipped with another popular song, 'The Boy Guessed Right'. Miss Terriss then left the Gaiety for a brief return to comedy before moving on with her husband to take up a long and lucrative association with Charles Frohman.

In the years that followed, Miss Terriss played no more musical-comedy ingénues. She had a notable success in the play *Quality Street* and also played in several juvenile musicals which had a wider than juvenile appeal, notably as Alice in *Alice in Wonderland*, as Bluebell in the 1901 *Bluebell in Fairyland*, in which she performed 'The Honeysuckle and the Bee' and 'The Sunflower and the Sun', jaunty up-to-date versions of the kind of song popularized by Letty Lind at Daly's in the previous decade, and in an attempt to repeat this same formula in 1903 as *The Cherry Girl*.

Hicks and Frohman next organized a piece intended to present the star pair in musical comedy once more, as a modern Cinderella and Prince Charming but, before *The Catch of the Season* (1904) made it to the stage, its intended heroine had become pregnant. Zena Dare was given the part until Miss Terriss was fit to return to take over, after which she toured the piece throughout Britain before returning to London to revive *Bluebell* and to open the pair's new vehicle, *The Beauty of Bath* (1906, 'My Little Hyacinth'). During the run of the show they transferred to the new Hicks Theatre, named in their honour by Frohman.

After *The Beauty of Bath* came another fine success with *The Gay Gordons* (1907, 'Humpty and Dumpty') before Hicks conceived the odd idea of putting his wife into breeches as the young hero of *The Dashing Little Duke* (1909) in a style which had long gone out of fashion, and now reeked somewhat of pantomime time. *The Dashing Little Duke* worked much less well than the previous shows, but when Hicks returned to pair with his wife in a musical adaptation of the play *The Dictator* called *Captain Kidd* (1910) they were faced with an utter and unprecedented flop. The pair left musical comedy and took to the lucrative music halls for several years and their subsequent vehicles were more often comedy than musical. Miss Terriss took over the juvenile rôle of Elphin Haye in a wartime revival of *The Earl and the Girl*, repeated *Bluebell in Fairyland* under family management at Prince's Theatre in 1916 and, in a final West End musical appearance, featured in Hicks's indifferent *Cash on Delivery* at the Palace Theatre.

During the Hickses' heyday in the musical theatre, Miss Terriss composed a number of fairyweight songs which were interpolated into London shows including *The Yashmak* (1897), *The Merry-Go-Round* (1899) and *The Talk of the Town* (1905).

1895 **Papa's Wife** (Seymour Hicks, F C Phillips) 1 act Lyric Theatre 26 January

Autobiography: *Ellaline Terriss, By Herself and Others* (Cassell, London, 1928), *A Little Bit of String* (Hutchinson, London, 1955), Biography: Hicks, S: *Me and My Missus* (Cassell, London, 1939)

TERRY, Ethelind (b Philadelphia, 14 August 1900; d unknown). Darkly lovely musical-theatre soprano whose voice and career did not last.

Miss Terry made her first Broadway appearance at the age of 20 when she took over from Eleanor Painter in the leading soprano rôle, as the Latin Dolores, in Jake Shubert's revival of *Florodora*. She subsequently appeared in Ephraim Zimbalist's musical *Honeydew* (1920, Muriel) and in two editions of *The Music Box Revue* before, in 1923, creating the part of Carmen Mendoza in *Kid Boots*. After touring the country in this rôle for several years, she was cast as yet another South Americanate lady, again equipped with songs by Harry Tierney and Joseph McCarthy, when she created the title-rôle in their *Rio Rita*. Amongst the songs which she introduced in the part were 'Rio Rita' and Tierney's own favourite of his works, 'If You're in Love, You'll Waltz'.

This second success was followed by an unsuccessful attempt at a musical film (*Lord Byron of Broadway*) and by a slightly more mitigated success as the heroine of Romberg's *Nina Rosa*, a show and a rôle which she repeated at London's Lyceum Theatre. She subsequently toured America as French Yvonne in *Sons o' Guns* in 1931–2, took part in a purée of Lehár's *Zigeunerliebe* perpetrated in Boston (*The Moon Rises*), and in 1935 visited Australia to play in Ernest Rolls's home-made musical *Flame of Desire*. Her voice was noted as being in a shabby state and she was quickly replaced by local star Strella Wilson. Back in America, she closed out of town in *Cocktail Bar* (1937, Princess Pierotti), and was not seen again on Broadway.

TÊTE DE LINOTTE Opérette in 2 acts by Raymond Vincy. Music by Francis Lopez. Théâtre de l'ABC, Paris, December 1957.

A first top-of-the-bill vehicle for comedienne Annie Cordy, who starred opposite Jean Richard and Pierre Miguel as the 'featherbrain' of the title, singing 'Jojo la fleur bleue', 'Tête de linotte', 'C'est estraordinaire' and 'Le Rhythme des tropiques' for three seasons at Paris's Théâtre de l'ABC.

Recording: Annie Cordy selection (Pathé-Marconi)

TEWELE, Franz (b Vienna, 29 July 1843; d Bad Ischl, 10 September 1914). Celebrated Viennese musical comedian of the 19th century.

The son of a Viennese court official, Tewele abandoned technical college for acting studies and worked in theatres in Brünn, Pressburg and Graz, appearing in sometimes heavy dramatic rôles, before being engaged in 1864 at the Hoftheater in Munich. There he was first cast in the kind of comedy rôles – with or without music, but always with ad-libbing and burlesque effects – for which he would become famous. In 1865 he joined the company at the Vienna Carltheater under Karl Treumann where his parts included the first Viennese Gardefeu in *Pariser Leben*, and during the rest of his almost 50 years on the stage played largely in the principal Viennese theatres, including three periods at the Carltheater (between 1878 and 1882 as the manager of the house), two substantial periods at the Wiener Stadttheater (1872–8, 1883 sq) and, at the end of his career, at the Deutsches Theater. His two significant periods away from Austria came in 1882, when he toured America and appeared at New York's Thalia Theater with Josefine Gallmeyer and Wilhelm Knaack, and later a stay of three years in Berlin.

Tewele's one important musical creation was the part of Pietro in *Boccaccio*, but amongst his other musical rôles were included comedy parts in such pieces as *Niniche* (Gregoire), *Der grosse Casimir* (Casimir), *Die Mormonen*, *Der Kukuk* (Theobald von Falibourde), *Papas Frau* (Aristides/Florestan), *Die Puppe* (Hilarius), *La Prima Ballerina* (Tamponin), *Die Pariserin* (Karl Dürer), *Die Näherin* and *Der griechische Sklave* (Heliodorus). Under his management of the Carltheater the productions included *Der kleine Herzog*, *Der grosse Casimir*, *Papas Frau*, *Marjolaine*, *Die Mormonen*, *Der Kukuk*, *Olivette*, *Die Carbonari* and Genée's *Nisida* and *Rosina*.

Tewele also won a different kind of renown as one of Vienna's first intrepid bicyclists, apparently becoming the city's first cycle casualty when he broke his leg in an accident in 1869.

TEXAS, LI'L DARLIN' Musical comedy in 2 acts by John Wheldon and Sam Moore. Lyrics by Johnny Mercer. Music by Robert Emmett Dolan. Mark Hellinger Theater, New York, 25 November 1949.

An American state for a title and a title-song, a tale of politics and shenanigans (not to mention love), a GI hero and a big business villain – all these favourite elements of the moment went into the making-up of the musical comedy *Texas, Li'l Darlin'*.

Publisher Harvey Small (Loring Smith) chooses Texan senator Hominy Smith (radio megastar Kenny Delmar) to be moulded into a candidate for high and helpful office. The opposition, headed by a group of ex-GIs, puts up one of their own, Easy Jones (Danny Scholl), against Smith. After an act and a half of in-fighting, Small sees the way things – including his daughter Dallas (Mary Hatcher) – are going, and he switches his backing to what is clearly going to be the winning team. Smith walloped out the praises of his state in the title-song and duetted with his sponsor on 'Politics' whilst Jones stuck to the more nice 'n' homely with 'Hootin' Owl Trail' and the quasi-revivalist 'The Big Movie Show in the Sky' and duetted with his Dallas over 'A Month of Sundays'.

The show provided 293 performances of easy, prejudice-patting entertainment for Studio Productions and Anthony B Farrell without ever looking like going any further.

Recording: original cast (Decca/Columbia)

TEYTE, Maggie [TATE, Margaret] (b Wolverhampton, 17 April 1889; d London, 27 May 1976).

Sister of the songwriter James W Tate, Miss Teyte made the most important part of her career in opera where she won particular fame as Debussy's Mélisande (*Pelléas et Mélisande*) whilst still in her twenties. In 1910 she appeared with the Beecham Opera Company as Melka in Edmond Missa's opéra-comique *Muguette* but it was in her thirties that she turned towards the lighter musical theatre and made a notable appearance in London as Lady Mary Carlisle in Messager's *Monsieur Beaucaire* (1919, 'Philomel'). She subsequently played Princess Julia in Kálmán's *A Little Dutch Girl* (1920, *Das Hollandweibchen*) at London's Lyric Theatre and appeared as Mrs Fitzherbert in an unfortunate and short-lived piece called *By Appointment* (1934). In 1935 she took part in a revival of Dunhill's *Tantivy Towers* at the Lyric, Hammersmith.

Biography: O'Connor, G: *The Pursuit of Perfection* (Gollancz, London, 1979)

THAT'S A GOOD GIRL Musical comedy in 2 acts by Douglas Furber. Music by Phil Charig and Joseph Meyer. London Hippodrome, 5 June 1928.

That's a Good Girl set in motion the series of dance-and-laughter musicals in which Jack Buchanan and Elsie Randolph starred over a period of 15 years as one of London's favourite musical comedy teams. On this occasion, what there was of a plot had her as a detective called Joy Dean pursuing Bill Barrow (Buchanan) from the Royal Opera House, Covent Garden, to the South of France, with the employment of a succession of disguises and predictable results. On the way, they encountered baritone Raymond Newell, soubrette Maidie Andrews, the comical and operatic Sunya Berata (Vera Pearce), Victorian musical star Kate Cutler playing rich Aunt Helen, speciality dancers from the modern to the balletic, Debroy Somers and his band, and every kind of topical rhythm and dance-step imaginable.

The music to which all this was set was a last-minute affair, ordered by Buchanan shortly before rehearsals started from the New York office of Chappell. The fashionably American score which resulted was a self-effacing one from which the happiest tune was the pretty duo for the leads, 'Fancy Our Meeting'. The same pair also sang and danced (in slow motion) together about 'The One I'm Looking For' and Newell scored with a contrastingly straight baritone 'A Marching Song'. However, the principal elements of the show were its fun (directed by Buchanan) and its dances (choreographed mostly by Buchanan), and these went down splendidly. *That's a Good Girl* ran for 363 performances in London and toured widely, establishing the Buchanan-Randolph partnership at the top of the heap, before they moved on to their next vehicle. In 1933 they filmed a version of the show, with original cast members Kate Cutler and Vera Pearce repeating their stage rôles.

Film: British and Dominion 1933

THATCHER, Heather [Mary] (b London, 3 September ?1897; d London, January 1987). Tall, attractive comedienne-who-sang who briefly took the limelight in 1920s London.

After working first as a walk-on in films and as a take-over in a London comedy, Miss Thatcher moved into the musical theatre in the small rôle of Katie Muirhead in the Adelphi Theatre production of *The Boy* (1917). She won quick promotion to a considerably larger rôle in the revue *Buzz Buzz* before running up a series of progressively better comedy rôles in London musicals of the 1920s. She played Salome in *The Naughty Princess* (*La Reine joyeuse*), and a travesty Valentine in the short-lived attempt at a return to burlesque with *Faust on Toast* (1921) before joining Grossmith and Laurillard at their Winter Garden Theatre where, between 1921 and 1925, she played a run of musico-comical rôles which lifted her to almost-star status: Rosalind Rafferty in *Sally*, Little Ada in *The Cabaret Girl*, the common Lovey Toots in *The Beauty Prize*, Victoria in the revival of *Tonight's the Night*, Pinkie Peach in *Primrose* (introducing 'Boy Wanted' to London) and Jane Wallace in *Tell Me More!*

Over the next decade she appeared largely in non-musical pieces, but she returned to the musical stage in the mid-1930s to play the colourful gossip Sophie Otford in Coward's *Conversation Piece* (1934) and to appear once more with former Winter Garden star Leslie Henson in *Lucky Break* (1934), the farcical anglicization of Broadway's *Little Jessie James*. Her subsequent career in films and straight plays faded away without her re-reaching the heights of her Winter Garden days.

THÉO, Louise [PICCOLO, Cécile] (b 1854; d Paris, 24 January 1922). One of Offenbach's most successful discoveries.

Little, blonde Louise Théo worked as a teenager in Parisian cafés-concerts before being spotted by Offenbach and taken to the Bouffes-Parisiens to create the title-rôle in the little opérette *Pomme d'api* (1873) at the age of 19. She shot to stardom when she created the rôle of the rabidly pursued little shopkeeper, Rose Michon, in *La Jolie Parfumeuse* (1875) and thereafter, in spite of never getting another rôle as good, she held a firm place at the top of her profession. She played Régina in the revival of *La Princesse de Trébizonde* (1875), but flopped, alongside Paola Marié and Lucien Fugère, when she appeared as the gallantly helpful Francine in Offenbach's *La Boîte au lait*, even though she caused something of a sensation by her ability to

Plate 270. **Louise Théo**.

genuinely handle a rapier. Neither *Le Moulin du Vert-Galant* nor Coèdes's *Fleur d'oranger* (1878) did her any better service, and she missed a third flop when she rejected the title-rôle of Vasseur's *La Sorrentine* (1877), but she had better luck when she created the titular Mercedès, the lass who loses her voice without sex, in Serpette's *La Petite Muette*. She then put aside new rôles, essayed Judic's famous parts in *La Timbale d'argent* and *Madame l'Archiduc* in Paris revivals, and moved on to play the established repertoire in Russia and further afield.

In 1883 she visited America for Maurice Grau. She was scheduled as the opening attraction for the new Casino Theater but, since the theatre was not ready, she played instead at the Fifth Avenue Theater before going on to tour America with considerable success, carrying a proven repertoire including *La Jolie Parfumeuse*, *Madame l'Archiduc*, *Les Cloches de Corneville*, *La Marjolaine*, *La Périchole*, *La Mascotte*, *La Fille de Madame Angot* and *Le Grand Casimir*.

Back in Paris, Théo finally found herself another fine new rôle as the heroine of Paul Lacôme's *Madame Boniface* (1883, Friquette) – a piece and character almost too like *La Jolie Parfumeuse* to be true – and she included that show in her repertoire when she returned to America for a second season in 1884 along with *François les bas-bleus*, *Le Jour et la nuit*, *La Fille du tambour-major*, *Giroflé-Girofla*, *La Petite Mariée*, *La Timbale d'argent* et al.

In 1886 she created the rôle of Ève in Serpette's *Adam et Ève* (her appearance in 'the costume of Eve' did more for the box-office than her rapier-duel), and she subsequently appeared at the Gaîté in Varney's *Dix Jours aux Pyrénées* (1887, Zoë Chaudillac), starred in revivals of *La Mascotte* and *Le Droit du seigneur*, and featured in the production of Pugno's *La Vocation de Marius* (1890) and alongside Félix Huguenet as Rose in the vaudeville *Le Brillant Achille* (1892).

Théo ultimately went into retirement as the wife of a well-off art dealer in New York.

THEODORE & CO Musical play in 2 acts by H M Harwood and George Grossmith taken from the play *Théodore et Cie* by Marcel Nancey and Paul Armont [here credited to Paul Gavault]. Lyrics by Adrian Ross and Clifford Grey. Music by Ivor Novello and Jerome Kern. Gaiety Theatre, London, 19 September 1916.

Producers Grossmith and Laurillard, having established themselves at the Gaiety Theatre of the post-Edwardes era with the highly successful *Tonight's the Night*, followed up by using the same company on an adaptation of another French farce, Armont and Nancey's *Theodore et Cie* (Théâtre des Nouveautés, 29 September 1909). Pony Twitchin (Leslie Henson), Theodore Wragge (George Grossmith), Fudge Robinson (Peggy Kurton) and their friends convince Bompas, the Earl of Shetland (Davy Burnaby), that it was not his daughter Pansy (Madge Saunders) who was photographed in compromising company by having Pansy dress up and pretend to be an actress who is supposed to be her double. Henri Leoni played an incidental Continental vocalist and Julia James the Hon Sapphire Blissett.

The score, originally to have been written by the dying Paul Rubens, was instead shared between the young composer of the hit song 'Keep the Home Fires Burning', 23-year-old Ivor Novello, and the experienced Jerome Kern. The honours were fairly even. Novello's share was topped by the comedy song 'My Friend John' with which Henson scored the success of the evening, but the other top number, a jaunty comic waltz duo called '365 Days', performed by Henson and Burnaby, was Kern's. Alongside the nominal authors and composers, several of the performers apparently had a hand in the text and Melville Gideon, Phil Braham, Eric Blore, Burnaby and others including Rubens (one song) contributed to the score. The pot pourri which resulted – no little thanks to the great and growing popularity of Henson, and to Grossmith's all-round expertise as performer and producer – proved a 15-month and 503-performance success, sharing the limelight in the second half of the war years with two pieces of a very different kind, the romantic spectaculars *Chu Chin Chow* and *The Maid of the Mountains*.

An Australian production was mounted for a two-month season in Melbourne in 1919 with a cast including Maud Fane (Fudge), Reginald Roberts (Legallos), Gladys Moncrieff (Pansy), Leslie Holland (Theodore), Sidney Sterling (Earl), Theodore Leonard (Pony) and Florence Young (Sapphire), but the show did not win the same kind of extreme popularity as in Britain and did not get a Sydney showing until 1921 (Theatre Royal, 22 October) with Maud Fane and W S Percy featured.

Australia: Theatre Royal, Melbourne 29 November 1919
Recording: original cast recordings on *Jerome Kern in London* (WRC)

THÉRÉSA [VALADON or VALLANDON, Emma] (b La Bazoche-Gonnet, 25 April 1837; d Neufchâtel-en-Saônois, May 1913).

Already in her mid-thirties and more than a little portly, the bosomy, bulldog-featured Mlle Thérésa had made herself into one of the biggest names in the world of the café-concert with her often more-than-risqué songs ('La Femme à la barbe', 'Rien n'est sacré pour un sapeur', 'C'est dans l'nez qu'ça m'chatouille', 'Le bon gîte' etc) before she ventured back onto the musical stage where she had taken her first, unnoticed steps as a teenaged chorister years before. Most of her appearances on the musical stage were made in the field of the spectacular féerie where, more often than not, she was able to simply insert a selection of her own material. Pieces like the Théâtre de la Gaîté's production of *La Poule aux oeufs d'or* (1872) and Armand de Jallais's production of *La Reine Carotte* (1872) at the Menus-Plaisirs, in which she delivered no fewer than eight numbers amongst the festival of scenic effects which made up the backbone of the entertainment, were typical Thérésa engagements.

However, she later starred opposite Paulin Ménier at the head of Vasseur's disappointing *La Famille Trouillat* (1874), appeared in the expanded five-act version of Offenbach's *Geneviève de Brabant* (1875) in which a new rôle, Briscotte, was specially added for her, and in the title-rôle of the revamped version of the same composer's *La Boulangère a des écus* (1876) where her boundless personality almost succeeded in making the piece into a first-class success. She returned to the féerie to play Regaillette in *Les Sept Chateaux du Diable* (Théâtre du Châtelet, 1876-7), equipped, as in her earliest appearances, with her repertoire of café-concert songs, and played in other spectaculars such as *La Cocotte aux oeufs d'or* and *La Chatte blanche*, but she also played in revue at the Menus-Plaisirs, and in 1880 took the title rôle of the vaudeville *Madame Grégoire* at the former Menus-Plaisirs (now the Théâtre des Arts) equipped with a selection of songs by such composers as Planquette, Serpette and Coèdes. In 1881 she starred in the title-rôle of Varney's *La Reine des Halles* at the Comédie Parisien.

She retired from performing in 1893 and spent the last 20 years of her life in respectable retirement in the Sâone.

Memoirs: Blum, Wolff: *Mémoires de Thérésa* (1865), Morel, H: *Nouveaux Mémoires de Thérésa* (1868)

THESPIS, or The Gods Grown Old Original grotesque opera in 2 acts by W S Gilbert. Music by Arthur Sullivan. Gaiety Theatre, London, 26 December 1871.

The first collaboration of Messrs Gilbert and Sullivan, this two-act 'grotesque opera' was produced as the 1871 Christmas entertainment at the Gaiety Theatre, where manager John Hollingshead had the previous year initiated the practice of staging an operatic extravaganza with an original score of music for the festive season with his production of Alfred Thompson and Hervé's highly successful *Aladdin the Second*.

Gilbert's tale (apparently borrowed from the old Viennese Posse *Die Schauspieler-Gesellschaft in Olymp*, Theater in der Josefstadt 13 December 1825) had the aged Gods of Olympus temporarily giving over their places to an Athenian troupe of actors whilst they descend to earth for a quick look-around. The mortals make a real mess of their mountain-sitting job, and after many jollities they are sent

scurrying back to earth. The previous year's stars were well in evidence again: last year's Aladdin, Nellie Farren, played Mercury the 'celestial drudge', and Johnnie Toole was Thespis, the manager of the theatricals, whilst Connie Loseby (Nicemis), the composer's brother Fred Sullivan (Apollo), Annie Tremaine (Daphne), Mlle Clary (Sparkeion) and the Payne family of pantomimists were also featured in a part-extravaganza, part-burlesque, part-fairy play, part-pantomime entertainment which – even if it was occasionally a touch sophisticated for some of the Gaiety audience – was just the ticket for Christmas.

Of Sullivan's score, the ballad 'Little Maid of Arcadee' proved the take-away song, whilst Nellie Farren scored roundly with a number describing her job, 'It's the Way of the World', and Toole launched patteringly into a cautionary tale which asserted 'I once knew a man who discharged a function on the North South East West Diddlesex Junction' and had as little to do with Ancient Greece as most of the entertainment.

Thespis ran to almost three hours at its first performance, but it was subsequently cut to more like two – a necessity, as it shared the programme with other pieces, including, at one stage, Suppé's *Die schöne Galathee*. It proved less successful than *Aladdin II*, but nevertheless played 63 times and was revived for an extra benefit performance in April the following year. The show was never given a full-scale revival, although D'Oyly Carte considered remounting it as a Christmas piece in 1875, and the musical score was at some stage lost, so that Sullivan's assertion that he plundered it for tunes for his later works cannot be substantiated.

Literature: Rees, T: *Thespis: A Gilbert & Sullivan Enigma* (Dillons University Bookshop, London, 1964)

THEY'RE PLAYING OUR SONG Musical comedy in 2 acts by Neil Simon. Lyrics by Carol Bayer Sager. Music by Marvin Hamlisch. Imperial Theater, New York, 11 February 1979.

A virtually two-handed musical play, allegedly based on the relationship between its composer and lyricist, *They're Playing Our Song* was one of the few musicals of its era which put the comedy back into the genre that had once been freely called musical comedy, favouring a high-class comic libretto as its basis rather than the extravaganza of visual elements emphasized in many contemporary shows.

The highly successful songwriter Vernon Gersch (Robert Klein) is in need of a new lyricist, and what he gets is Sonia Walsk (Lucie Arnaz). She sweeps crazily into his life and turns out to be the most neurotic, unreliable, impossible little collaborator he could have chosen. But she can write lyrics. By the end of Act I they are lovers, and she has sent her even more neurotic ex, Leon, on his way. By the beginning of Act II she has moved in with Vernon and they actually get down to some work. But Leon keeps ringing up whenever he has one of his crises, and his omnipresence eventually results in Vernon and Sonia's partnership – professional and personal – breaking up. But Leon (who is never seen) finally gets his life in order and, by the final curtain, Vernon and Sonia are back together again.

A number of the show's nine songs were displayed as the product of Vernon and Sonia's work together – the ballad 'I Still Believe in Love', the lively 'Workin' it Out', 'Fallin'' – and, thus, they were written in a style which adapted popular music tones and conventions (including the half-dozen backing singers who made up the rest of the cast as the hero and heroine's alter egos) to stage considerations. The remainder, topped by the rhythmic and gently tongue-in-cheek title song, a pensive and plotworthy 'If (S)He Really Knew Me' and the romantic 'When You're in My Arms' and 'Just for Tonight' took up the same tone, in a short score which illustrated the endlessly comic dialogue and action of the piece to a nicety.

They're Playing Our Song was a first-class Broadway success, running for 1,082 performances in New York before setting out for an overseas career which included productions in places that few other recent English-language musicals had got anywhere near. John Waters and Jacki Weaver starred in an extremely successful Australian production, which spawned both revivals and tours, Tom Conti and Gemma Craven were featured in a slightly undercooked London staging which nevertheless played 667 performances before the show was taken up by provincial venues, Gaby Gasser and Harald Juhnke introduced a German version of *Sie spielen unser Lied* in Berlin and Michaela Rosen and Peter Fröhlich starred in a Viennese production (ad Jurgen Wöffler, Christoph Busse). Luigi Proietti and Loretta Goggi featured in Italy's production of *Stanno suonando la nostra canzone* at Milan's Teatro Nuovo (11 November 1981 ad Roberto Lerici, Carla Vistarini), Mauricio Herrera and Macaria played *Están tocando nuestra canción* (ad Sanchez Navarro-Fresan) in Mexico's Spanish-language version, and Marianne Weber and Jachen Janett introduced the piece to Switzerland at St Gallen (Keller-bühne, 29 December 1990).

The show's economic size, allied to its ubiquitous success, encouraged a proliferation of productions in theatres and on circuits with limited resources (although the original production effortlessly encompassed a large stage and a by no means inexpensive setting), and *They're Playing Our Song*'s mixture of bright, modern comedy and music meant that its crazy but lovable pair of rib-squeezingly real Jewish New Yorkers, their comical lines and their songs, went down a treat all round the world. Few theatres felt obliged to sink to the gimmickry of one sad German-language production which desperately piled all the campy clichés and accessories this musical so refreshingly avoided back in, and pictured Vernon as Groucho Marx and Sonia as Marilyn Monroe.

Australia: Theatre Royal, Sydney 23 August 1980; UK: Shaftesbury Theatre 1 October 1980; Germany: Theater am Kurfürstendamm *Sie spielen unser Lied* 1981; Hungary: Fővárosi Operettszinház *A mi dalunk szól* 26 October 1984; Austria: Wiener Kammerspiele *Sie spielen unser Lied* 1985

Recordings: original cast (Polydor), London cast (TER), Australian cast (Festival), Italian cast (Polydor), Austrian cast (Stage), Mexican cast (Polydor) etc

THIS'LL MAKE YOU WHISTLE Musical show in 2 acts by Guy Bolton and Fred Thompson. Music and lyrics by Maurice Sigler, Al Goodhart and Al Hoffman. King's Theatre, Southsea, 16 December 1935; Palace Theatre, London, 15 September 1936.

The third Jack Buchanan-Elsie Randolph star vehicle, following the successes of their pairings in *That's a Good Girl* and *Mr Whittington*, *This'll Make You Whistle* relied, as had the first of their pieces, very largely on some farcical and

Plate 271. **This'll Make You Whistle:** *Jack Buchanan and Jean Gillie did – on stage as well as off.*

funny scenes (directed by Buchanan) and the dancing of the two favourites (choreography: Buddy Bradley). Buchanan played Bill Hopping, who pretends to be a dreadfully unproper person in order to disgust the rich and puritanical Uncle Sebastian (Charles Stone) of his now unwanted fiancée Laura (Sylvia Leslie) into forcing her to break off the engagement. Uncle, however, is not so puritanical and it is Bill's beloved Joan (Jean Gillie) who gets upset, until all comes right for the final curtain. Miss Randolph was featured as Bobbie Rivers, encouraged into disguise as a French tart as part of the plan.

It was a well-used plot, illustrated by a bundle of unexceptional songs (one of which, apparently straight-faced, actually rhymed 'spoon', 'June' and 'moon'), and when the show was produced out of town Buchanan decided that it was not ready for a London showing. He toured it for four months, closed, cut and rewrote, and relaunched the piece at Blackpool in September of the following year. A week later it came to town, spit-and-polished by its touring experience, and won a happy reception for its favourite pair and their routines. After four months at the Palace Theatre it transferred to Daly's for its last weeks, and closed after 190 performances. During that time, the stars had taken time off to record a film version and that film actually opened in London during the last week of the show's stage run, so that Jack and Elsie were visible simultaneously in the West End on celluloid (79 minutes) and in the flesh (full-length) for a short while.

Film: 1936

THOMAS, John Charles (b Meyerdale, Pa, 6 September 1887; d Apple Valley, Calif, 13 December 1960). A tall, fair, blue-eyed and rich-voiced American baritone, best remembered for his recordings of ballads and devotional songs.

Thomas came to the stage via church choirs, Baltimore's medical school and Peabody College to begin his career as a musical-theatre singer touring in Gilbert and Sullivan with De Wolf Hopper. He made his first appearance on Broadway in *The Passing Show of 1913* at the age of 25, and soon rose to take good rôles alongside Emma Trentini in *The Peasant Girl* (1915, *Polenblut*, Bolo Baranski), as the mountain-climbing Baron Franz von Hansen wooing Marguerite Namara in the successful American production of *Alone at Last* (1915, *Endlich Allein*), in the revusical *Step This Way* (1916, Charles Chetwynd), *Her Soldier Boy* (1916, *Az obsitos*, Alain Teniers), Lehár's *The Star Gazer* (1917, *Der Sterngucker*, Arthur Howard) and in the title-rôle of a revival of De Koven's *The Highwayman* (1917, Dick Fitzgerald). He toured in the principal rôle of Romberg's *Maytime* (Richard Wayne) played on Broadway by Charles Purcell, and then returned to New York to score his biggest stage success opposite Wilda Bennett as the hero of the Jacobi/Kreisler musical *Apple Blossoms* (1919, Philip Campbell, 'You Are Free'). He also starred in Victor Jacobi's last work *Love Letters* (1921), the unsuccessful musicalization of Molnár's celebrated *A farkas*.

Thomas spent several years at Brussels' Théâtre de la Monnaie (1925–8) and later sang at Covent Garden and the Metropolitan Opera, making his career largely in opera, concerts, recording and broadcasting but he ultimately returned, after 15 years' absence, to the musical theatre and made a series of appearances on the American west coast where he appeared as Shubert in *Blossom Time*, Barinkay in a badly perverted version of *Der Zigeunerbaron* which presented him as a strolling lion-tamer, in *HMS Pinafore*, as Bumerli in *The Chocolate Soldier*, and in *Music in the Air* during the late 1930s and early 1940s.

THOMPSON, Alexander M[attock] (b Karlsruhe, 9 May 1861; d London, 25 March 1948). British librettist of the early 20th century.

Socialist writer and journalist and founder of the left-wing journal *Clarion*, Thompson also worked as a theatre critic under the pseudonym 'Dangle'. He came to the theatre slowly, making his first notable stage appearances with the texts for pantomimes for his crony Robert Courtneidge, manager of the Prince's Theatre in Manchester. Courtneidge was, thereafter, the supplier of virtually all of Thompson's theatrical work, to which his own name was also sometimes appended as co-writer.

Thompson began his connection with English musical comedy when he reorganized the text of Walter Ellis's *The Blue Moon* before Courtneidge brought it to town after its author's death, and he then supplied the hotch-potch of a libretto (allegedly, but not evidently, based on Shakespeare's *As You Like It*) for Courtneidge's successful musical piece *The Dairymaids*. In real contrast to this piece of jobbery, he next fulfilled the task of expertly slimming and resituating Henry Fielding's *Tom Jones* as the libretto for the enduring comic opera of the same name, but he had his biggest success in fleshing out Mark Ambient's ideas for a fantastical musical as *The Arcadians*.

His first all-original text, the comic and romantic Japanoiseries of *The Mousmé*, was a costly failure for his producer friend, but Thompson and Courtneidge had

another success together with the London version of Leo Fall's *Der liebe Augustin*, adapted and produced as *Princess Caprice*. Having enjoyed Courtneidge's high days with him, Thompson continued to supply scripts for his later and less-fortunate ventures. A revusical piece of Ancient Roman foolery called *Oh, Caesar!* failed to make it to town, whilst the cloak-and-swashbuckle *The Rebel Maid* with its durable paean to 'The Fishermen of England' survived largely with choral societies after 114 London performances.

1897 **Toto and Tata** (*Toto*) English version w J J Wood, E Boyd Jones (Grand Theatre, Leeds)

1903 **Chilpéric** new English version w Richard Mansell (Coronet Theatre)

1905 **The Blue Moon** revised version Lyric Theatre 28 August

1906 **The Dairymaids** (Paul Rubens, Frank E Tours/Rubens, Arthur Wimperis/w Robert Courtneidge) Apollo Theatre 14 April

1907 **Tom Jones** (Edward German/Charles H Taylor/w Courtneidge) Apollo Theatre 17 April

1909 **The Arcadians** (Howard Talbot, Lionel Monckton/Wimperis/w Ambient) Shaftesbury Theatre 28 April

1911 **The Mousmé** (Talbot, Monckton/Wimperis, Percy Greenbank/w Courtneidge) Shaftesbury Theatre 9 September

1912 **Princess Caprice** (*Der liebe Augustin*) English version (Shaftesbury Theatre)

1916 **Oh, Caesar!** (Nat D Ayer, Arthur Wood/Adrian Ross/w Max Pemberton) Royal Lyceum Theatre, Edinburgh 23 December

1921 **The Rebel Maid** (Montague Phillips/Gerald Dalton/w Bertrand Davis) Empire Theatre 12 March

Autobiography: *Here I Lie* (Routledge, London, 1937)

THOMPSON, Alfred [JONES, Thompson E] (b England, ?1831; d Barnegat Park, NY, 31 August 1895). Librettist and designer for some of the best-written and -designed early British musicals.

Tall, elegant and handsome Alfred Thompson began a military career in the Eniskillen Dragoons but, having risen to the rank of Captain, he renounced the army to take up journalism, becoming sometime co-editor of *The Mask* with Leopold Lewis of *The Bells* fame. He also studied art in Munich and Paris and there 'caught the continental style of illustration, associated with the name of Grévin'. He got his first chance in the theatrical world when John Hollingshead took him on as a design co-ordinator and house author at the Gaiety Theatre. His contribution to the theatre's opening bill was an adaptation of *L'Escamoteur* as *On the Cards* and the design of the costumes for Gilbert's burlesque *Robert the Devil*.

Over the next three years, Thompson took charge of the costume designing at the Gaiety, giving a care to the costuming of burlesques such as Gilbert's *Thespis* and Offenbach's *La Princesse de Trébizonde* not usually associated with that form of entertainment – 'for delicate and harmonious combinations of colours, mostly half-tints, he was quite unrivalled ... the old coarse costume combinations – strong reds, strong greens, strong blues and strong yellows – were doomed from the hour that Thompson's dresses appeared before the footlights'. Hollingshead wrote 'Alfred Thompson was very clever and tricky with his costumes. He was the first man to utilize upholstery cretonnes for dresses, and this cheap material, at a distance, under the glamour of stage lights, looked like the most expensive tapestry products of Lyons. His embroideries, to use the theatrical slang, were "faked". On a groundwork of white satinette he stencilled patterns, with brown "smudge", rubbed across a perforated piece of paper. When the paper was removed the pattern was visible on the satin and had the appearance on the stage of elaborate needlework ... Alfred Thompson could not only design a dress, but like M Worth of Paris, if necessary, he could "fit" and make one. He ought to have started a fancy millinery business, and made a fortune'.

Thompson's talents, however, were not limited to those of a dressmaker, or even a watercolourist. He also supplied the scripts for the Gaiety burlesques *Columbus* and *Linda di Chamouni*, translated Hérold's opéra-comique *Zampa* into a new English version for Hollingshead and provided the texts for the Gaiety's two original opéras-bouffes, *Aladdin II* and *Cinderella the Younger*, which he also designed. Although Hollingshead seems to have considered him a better artist than a writer, his scripts for *Aladdin II* and for *Cinderella the Younger*, in particular, were as good as anything of their kind produced in the English language up to the time, and both his burlesques were subsequently revived.

Thompson's success at the Gaiety led to his services, notably as a costume designer, becoming called for elsewhere and he was summoned by Boucicault to design the multitude of clothes for the spectacular *Babil and Bijou* at Covent Garden, and by the Alhambra to outfit their newly commissioned, very own Offenbach spectacular *Whittington*, their English-French *The Demon's Bride* and a number of other productions, whilst the go-ahead Kate Santley had him both design her *Cattarina* (1874) and write her a forepiece. As *The Three Conspirators* that little piece of quick-change foolery proved a hugely successful vehicle for the fair manageress. Thompson also designed the grandiose Covent Garden pantomime *Sleeping Beauty* and Lydia Thompson's version of *Le Grand Duc de Matapa*, *Piff-Paff* (1876), Lauro Rossi and Frank Marshall's production of their five-act opera *Bjorn* (1877) and a long list of other productions ranging from Shakespeare to burlesque.

In the late 1870s Thompson became for a time the manager of the Manchester Prince's Theatre and Theatre Royal and under his management were produced there Cellier's *Belladonna* (for which he authored the libretto), Stanislaus's *The Lancashire Witches* (1879) and John Crook's *The King's Dragoons* (1879). In the mid-1880s he moved on to America, and there his monocled figure became a popular one in theatrical circles. He had several 'English' pieces staged in America, most notably the comic opera *Pepita*, composed by Teddy Solomon for his 'wife', Lillian Russell. He also worked with considerable success as a director, mounting a number of spectacular pieces, notably the opening of the Madison Square Garden Amphitheater in 1890. However, in his last years he fell into financial problems, and shortly before his death the profession mounted a benefit for him.

His son worked as an actor under the name of Ernest Tarleton.

1867 **The Lion's Mouth** (Virginia Gabriel) privately produced
1869 **Columbus, or The Original Pitch in a Merry Key** (arr Meyer Lutz) Gaiety Theatre 17 May
1869 **Linda of Chamouni, or Not a Formosa** (arr Lutz) Gaiety Theatre 13 September
1870 **Zampa** English version (Gaiety Theatre)

1870 **Aladdin II, or An Old Lamp in a New Light** (Hervé) Gaiety Theatre 23 December
1871 **Cinderella the Younger** (aka *Javotte*) (Emile Jonas) Gaiety Theatre 23 September
1872 **How I Found Crusoe, or A Flight of Imagination from Geneva to Crusopolis** (pasticcio arr Frederic Stanislaus) Olympic Theatre 28 December
1874 **Calypso** (pasticcio) 1 act Royal Court Theatre 6 May
1874 **The Three Conspirators** (pasticcio) 1 act Belfast 16 October, Charing Cross Theatre 12 July 1875
1878 **Belladonna, or The Little Beauty and the Great Beast** (Alfred Cellier) Prince's Theatre, Manchester 27 April
1882 **The Yellow Dwarf** (pasticcio/w Robert Reece) Her Majesty's Theatre 30 December
1886 **Pepita, or The Girl with the Glass Eyes** (Edward Solomon) Union Square Theater, New York 16 March
1888 **The Arabian Nights** (various) Opera House, Chicago; Standard Theater, New York 12 September
1888 **The Crystal Slipper, or Prince Prettywitz and little Cinderella** (Fred Eustis/w Harry B Smith) Chicago; New York 26 November

THOMPSON, Fred[erick James] (b London, 24 January 1884; d London, 10 April 1949). Prolific librettist for the musical stage on both sides of the Atlantic.

Thompson began his working life articled to an architect before taking his draftsmanship to the *London Opinion* and a job as a theatrical caricaturist. He moved on to work on several other newspapers before throwing drawing in altogether and taking employment for a while as an actor. It was at this stage that he made his first attempts at writing for the theatre. He made his first significant inroad when he contributed to George Grossmith's script for the revue *Eightpence a Mile*, and it was Grossmith again who gave him his first opportunity to work on a major musical by entrusting him with the adaptation of the famous farce *Pink Dominoes* as the libretto for the successful musical comedy *Tonight's the Night*.

Thompson subsequently wrote the text for Phil Braham's little pieces *Alice Up-to-Date* (w Eric Blore), *Violet and Pink* and *Sugar and Spice*, and for the Frank Tours revue *The Merry-go-round*, for Nat Ayer's *Pell Mell* (w Morris Harvey) and *Look Who's Here*, and worked with Grossmith first on the adaptation of the French revue *Les Fils Touffe sont à Paris* into the highly successful *The Bing Boys Are Here* and later on its successors *The Bing Girls are There* (w Grossmith), *The Other Bing Boys* and *The Bing Boys on Broadway* (w Howard Vernon), but his later work was largely in the way of libretti for book musicals.

Following his fine début, metamorphosing a French farce into a musical, Thompson moved on to an even greater triumph with a similar operation on a couple of English ones, adapting Pinero's plays *The Magistrate* and *In Chancery* as *The Boy* and *Who's Hooper?* for the Adelphi Theatre and comedian Bill Berry. He also accomplished the adaptation of the tricksy French sex tale of *Afgar* into an English version for Cochran with such skill that the British version clearly outran the original, but the same skill deserted him on the even more tricksy/sexy text of *Phi-Phi* and the piece as staged by Cochran had the fun quite murdered out of it. In the year 1919, Thompson dominated the West End musical theatre, being billed with a share in the credits of no less than six libretti.

In 1924 he moved his base to America and there furthered his success working on the libretti of a string of musicals, the large number of which were significant successes – *Lady, Be Good!, Tip-Toes, Rio Rita, Funny Face, The Five o'Clock Girl, Sons o' Guns* – before returning to Britain at the dawn of the 1930s. His most significant contribution to the West End musical stage in the following years was, in collaboration with his frequent Broadway partner Guy Bolton, in constructing the comical vehicles with which Leslie Henson, Fred Emney and Richard Hearne brought the Gaiety Theatre back to its former place at the head of London's musical theatre – *Seeing Stars, Swing Along, Going Greek* – but he also worked on vehicles for the other top teams of the musical-comedy moment: Jack Buchanan and Elsie Randolph's *This'll Make You Whistle, Hide and Seek* for Bobby Howes and Cicely Courtneidge, and *Going Places* for Arthur Riscoe and company.

Thompson subsequently spent a second period in America, and had his last hit at the age of 60 when he worked on the libretto for the comical, if old-fashioned *Follow the Girls*. He was last represented on Broadway when an original story of his went into the making of the very shortlived 1945 musical *The Girl from Nantucket* (mus: Jacques Belasco, Adelphi Theater).

One of the very best comic librettists of the inter-wars period when light and often farcical comedy rather than sentiment or spectacle was the keynote of the most popular musical plays, Thompson had considerable successes on both sides of the Atlantic, and over 30 years lined up a list of hit credits which few other bookwriters equalled.

1911 **Freddie's Flat** (Cecil Cameron/H E Garden) 1 act Alhambra 4 September
1914 **Tonight's the Night** (Paul Rubens/Rubens, Percy Greenbank) Shubert Theater, New York 24 December
1915 **The Lady Birds** (J M Glover) 3 scenes Theatre Royal, Plymouth 9 August
1915 **The Only Girl** English adaptation (Apollo Theatre)
1916 **Mr Manhattan** (Howard Talbot/w C H Bovill) Prince of Wales Theatre 30 March
1916 **Houp-La!** (Talbot, Nat D Ayer/Greenbank, Hugh E Wright/w Wright) St Martin's Theatre 23 November
1917 **The Boy** (Talbot, Lionel Monckton/Adrian Ross, P Greenbank) Adelphi Theatre 14 September
1919 **Who's Hooper** (Talbot, Ivor Novello/Clifford Grey) Adelphi Theatre 13 September
1919 **Afgar** English version w Worton David (Adelphi Theatre)
1919 **Baby Bunting** (Ayer/Grey/w David) Shaftesbury Theatre 25 September
1919 **The Kiss Call** (Ivan Caryll/Adrian Ross, P Greenbank, Grey) Gaiety Theatre 8 October
1919 **Maggie** (Marcel Lattès/Ross/w H F Maltby) Oxford Theatre 22 October
1919 **The Eclipse** (Herman Darewski, Melville Gideon et al/Ross/w E Phillips Oppenheim) Garrick Theatre 12 November
1921 **The Golden Moth** (Novello/w P G Wodehouse) Adelphi Theatre 5 October
1922 **Phi-Phi** English version w Grey (London Pavilion)
1923 **The Cousin from Nowhere** (*Der Vetter aus Dingsda*) English libretto (Prince's Theatre)
1924 **Marjorie** (Sigmund Romberg, Herbert Stothart, Stephen Jones/Grey, Harold Atteridge) Shubert Theater, New York 11 August
1924 **Lady, Be Good!** (George Gershwin/Ira Gershwin/w Guy Bolton) Liberty Theater, New York 1 December
1925 **Tell Me More** (G Gershwin/I Gershwin, B G De Sylva/w William K Wells) Gaiety Theater, New York 13 April

1925 **Tip-Toes** (G Gershwin/I Gershwin/w Bolton) Liberty Theater, New York 28 December
1927 **Rio Rita** (Harry Tierney/Joseph McCarthy/w Bolton) Ziegfeld Theater, New York 2 February
1927 **The Five o'clock Girl** (Harry Ruby/Bert Kalmar/w Bolton) 44th Street Theater, New York 10 October
1927 **Funny Face** (G Gershwin/I Gershwin/w Paul Gerard Smith) Alvin Theater, New York 22 November
1928 **Here's Howe** (Roger Wolfe Kahn, Joseph Meyer/Irving Caesar/w Gerard Smith) Broadhurst Theater, New York 1 May
1928 **Treasure Girl** (G Gershwin/I Gershwin/w Vincent Lawrence) Alvin Theater, New York 8 November
1929 **Sons o' Guns** (Fred Swanstrom et al/w Jack Donahue, Connolly) Imperial Theater, New York 26 November
1931 **The Song of the Drum** (Vivian Ellis, Herman Finck/Desmond Carter/w Bolton) Theatre Royal, Drury Lane 9 January
1932 **Out of the Bottle** (Ellis, Oscar Levant/w Grey) London Hippodrome 11 June
1935 **Seeing Stars** (Martin Broones/Graham John/w Bolton) Gaiety Theatre 31 October
1936 **Swing Along** (Broones/John/w Bolton, Douglas Furber) Gaiety Theatre 2 September
1936 **This'll Make You Whistle** (Maurice Sigler, Al Goodhart, Al Hoffman/w Bolton) Palace Theatre 14 September
1936 **Going Places** (Ellis/w Bolton) Savoy Theatre 8 October
1937 **Going Greek** (Sam Lerner, Goodhart, Hoffman/w Furber, Bolton) Gaiety Theatre 16 September
1937 **Hide and Seek** (Ellis, Lerner, Goodhart, Hoffman/w Bolton, Furber) London Hippodrome 14 October
1938 **The Fleet's Lit Up** (Ellis/w Bolton, Bert Lee) London Hippodrome 17 August
1938 **Bobby Get Your Gun** (Jack Waller, Joe Tunbridge/Grey, Lee, Carter/w Bolton, Lee) Adelphi Theatre 7 October
1939 **Magyar Melody** (George Posford, Bernard Grün/Harry Purcell/w Eric Maschwitz, Bolton) His Majesty's Theatre 20 January
1940 **Present Arms** (Noel Gay/Frank Eyton) Prince of Wales Theatre 13 May
1942 **The Lady Comes Across** (Vernon Duke/John Latouche/w Dawn Powell) 44th Street Theater, New York 9 January
1944 **Follow the Girls** (Phil Charig/Dan Shapiro, Milton Pascal/w Bolton, Eddie Davis) Century Theater, New York 8 April
1944 **Glad to See You** (Jule Styne/Sammy Cahn/w Davis) Shubert Theater, Philadelphia 13 November
1945 **The Girl from Nantucket** (Jacques Belasco/Kay Twomey/w Bern Giler) Forrest Street Theater, Philadelphia 9 October

THOMPSON, Harlan (b Hannibal, Mo, 24 September 1890; d New York, 26 October 1966). Librettist to some happy little Broadway shows of the 1920s.

A chemistry teacher, a reporter for the *Kansas Star*, a drama critic, a First World War artillery lieutenant and air force commanding officer, Thompson did not get around to writing significantly for the theatre until he returned from overseas service at the end of the War. He essayed at first in the field of vaudeville, but he found success with his first real venture in the musical theatre, paired with songwriter Harry Archer on the farcical musical comedy *Little Jessie James* ('I Love You').

The pair became hailed as the natural successors to the team of Kern, Bolton and Wodehouse in the production of an intimate, book-based style of musical comedy, as they turned out a four-year, four-show series of similar pieces for the Broadway stage. *Little Jessie James* proved to be the

most widely successful, being played in varying versions all around the world, but Thompson's libretto to *Merry, Merry* also found its way to Britain, where, adapted by Bert Lee and R P Weston, it was attached to a new score by Jack Waller, Joe Tunbridge and Harris Weston for a reasonable West End run (Carlton Theatre 28 February 1929, 131 performances) under the same title.

Thompson subsequently went on to Hollywood where, over a decade, he wrote screenplays and lyrics for a number of Paramount films (the lyrics to Oscar Straus's music for *Married in Hollywood*, *The Phantom President*, *I'm No Angel*, *Here is My Heart*, *Rose of the Rancho* etc), and also worked as a film producer (*College Holiday*, *The Big Broadcast of 1938*, *Romance in the Dark*, *Paris Honeymoon*, *The Road to Singapore*).

In 1940 he returned to the theatre, but his first attempt at a play closed on the road, and he was never to make it back to Broadway.

1923 **Little Jessie James** (Harry Archer) Longacre Theater 15 August
1924 **My Girl** (Archer) Vanderbilt Theater 24 November
1925 **Merry, Merry** (Archer) Vanderbilt Theater 24 September
1926 **Twinkle Twinkle** (Archer) Liberty Theater 16 November

THOMPSON, Lydia (b London, 19 February ?1836; d London, 17 November 1908).

Lydia Thompson has become one of the theatre's legends, and like other such legendary figures, the truth of her life and career has become fictionalized to a stage where it is rather difficult now to exhume the truth. It would appear probable that she was born in 1836 rather than the later dates sometimes given (by herself and others) and that her stage début as a dancer at Her Majesty's Theatre in 1852 took place at the age of 16 (rather than 10 or 11). Although 14 is by no means impossible.

She first won notice playing Little Silverhair (with pieces of silver thread woven into her hair) in the pantomime *Harlequin and the Three Bears* at the Haymarket Theatre the following year, and in 1854 featured there as a solo dancer in the Grand Oriental Spectacle of *Mr Buckstone's Voyage Round the Globe*, before going on to play a season at the St James's Theatre where her appearances included the burlesques *Ganem, the Slave of Love* and Thomas Selby's *The Spanish Dancers* in which she caused a small sensation with her imitation-cum-parody of the extraordinary Spanish dancer Perea Nina. She appeared in *The King's Rival*, danced some more in *Beauties of the Harem*, and at Christmas played at the Haymarket in the title-rôle in the pantomime *Little Bo Peep*, before returning to finish the season at the St James's (*Cupid's Ladder*, *The Swan and Edgar*).

In 1855 she crossed to Europe and for more than three years performed her dances before audiences which, if the reports are to be believed, included both Russian and German students who pulled her unhorsed carriage through the streets of Moscow and Berlin respectively in homage to her talent and/or sex appeal. She appeared, billed as 'first danseuse of the Drury Lane Theatre, London', with obvious success both as an act and also as an interpolated item in such theatre pieces as Karl Gross's *Eine kleine Kur* in Hungary (Budai Színkör), France and Scandinavia, before eventually returning to London.

Plate 272. **Lydia Thompson**, *the famous burlesque actress in her costume for* Robinson Crusoe.

There she was re-engaged at the St James's Theatre under Chatterton, where her rôles included 'a Mysterious Stranger' in Lester Buckingham's *Virginus* burlesque, Valentine, the magician's son ('who will introduce a Sailor's Hornpipe, les Juinea, grand Pas Seul, and Pas Demon') in the ballet-farce *Magic Toys*, Dolly Mayflower in the drama of *Black-Eyed Susan* and Young Norval in the ballet-burlesque *My Name is Norval*, and in 1860 she appeared at the Lyceum where she played again in *Magic Toys*, as Abdallah, Captain of *The Forty Thieves* in the Savage Club burlesque, in the farce *The Middy Asthore* ('in the course of which she will dance her famous sailor's hornpipe'), as Fanchette in George Loder's *The Pets of the Parterre* (*Les Fleurs animées*) and at Christmas as Mephisto in the fairy extravaganza *Chrystabelle, or the Rose Without a Thorn*. In 1861 the Lyceum cast her in the drama *Woman, or Love Against the World* and in *The Fetches*, but soon after she took time off from the stage to give birth to the daughter who was to become the actress Zeffie Tilbury.

When she returned to the stage, Lydia Thompson made her career very largely in burlesque, and there she made herself the reputation which she would carry from Britain to her greatest fame in America. She played at Liverpool's Prince of Wales Theatre as Brough's *Ernani* alongside the Iago of Lionel Brough (1865) and as Mercury in *Paris* (1866), she played *Ixion* at Cambridge, appeared at the famous Prince of Wales Theatre with Marie Wilton performing a 'Rifle Dance' as Max in the burlesque of *Der Freischütz* (1866), at the Strand Theatre in *The Field of the Cloth of Gold* and *Blue-Beard*, and then crossed the ocean to make her first appearances in America under the management of Samuel Colville and Alexander Henderson in 1868. She opened her American career at Wood's Theater on 28 September in Burnand's burlesque *Ixion*.

Lydia was given a well-publicized arrival, made an enormous effect with her extremely sexy performances, and what had been intended to be a six-month tour eventually developed into one of more like six years. Lydia Thompson became the unquestioned burlesque queen of her period, leading her company of 'British Blondes' (many of whom were neither) around the country playing pieces such as *Ixion*, *The Forty Thieves*, *Bluebeard*, *Aladdin*, *Robin Hood*, *Kenilworth*, *Mephisto*, *Lurline*, *Sinbad*, *La Sonnambula*, *Robinson Crusoe* and even the opéra-bouffe *La Princesse de Trébizonde*. If the blondes' trademarks were short trunks and shapely thighs, many of them were, however, by no means devoid of talent and several, including Pauline Markham, Alice Atherton, Camille Dubois, Eliza Weathersby, Alice Burville and Rose Coghlan went on to fine careers. From the male members of her company emerged such top comic talents as Willie Edouin and Lionel Brough. Nevertheless, the company thrived on a slightly scandalous reputation which Lydia fostered finely, winning nationwide publicity with the tales of her 'lesbian attacker' and of her horse-whipping of an ungentlemanly critic.

In 1874 she returned with her company to Britain and played in London and the provinces in *Bluebeard*, *Robinson Crusoe*, *Piff-Paff* (*Le Grand Duc de Matapa*), *Oxygen*, *The Lady of Lyons*, *Pluto!*, *Carmen* and other burlesque entertainments, but in the years to come she made regular return trips to America, where she remained a popular figure in the musical theatre.

Her days of playing in burlesque were done when in 1887 she took a turn in direction and mounted a revival of Alfred Cellier's comic opera *The Sultan of Mocha* in London, but her voice proved far from up to the task when she starred in the French vaudeville-opérette *Babette* (1888, Antonio) and in later days she found herself in no position to produce, and jobs harder to come by. Although she appeared in America in 1894 as actress in *The Crust of Society*, and George Edwardes, hearing of her plight, used her briefly the following year in *An Artist's Model*, she was badly enough off in 1899 for a benefit to be staged for her at the Lyceum Theatre. She made her last stage appearance in 1904.

A phenomenon in the American theatre, where she has been credited with giving general popularity to a superior brand of girlie show with comedy which has remained popular ever since, at home she was just one of a number of fine burlesque actresses of the period. However, her skilful management, her adept casting of her troupe, her knack for publicity, her own charms and talents, and the fact that she spent the most blooming of her blooming years on the American stage, built a special place for her in American theatre history.

Miss Thompson's first husband was J C Tilbury, and her second was her sometime business manager and later successful London impresario Alexander Henderson (she was his fourth wife) from whom she was subsequently divorced. Her sister, Clara Thompson, made a very considerable career as a vocalist and actress both under her own name and under her married name of Mrs Bracy (she was the wife of tenor Henry Bracy), in Britain, Australia and America. Daughter Zeffie Tilbury played mostly in the non-musical theatre, but can be seen in a supporting rôle as the Princess in the Hollywood version of *Balalaika* (1939).

THREE LITTLE MAIDS   Musical play in 3 acts by Paul Rubens. Additional music by Howard Talbot. Additional lyrics by Percy Greenbank. Apollo Theatre, London, 20 May 1902.

The first full show to be written by the rising Paul Rubens, *Three Little Maids* was originally conceived as a vehicle in an old English light-operatic vein for three top West End leading ladies: soprano Evie Greene, pretty Edna May and comedienne Ada Reeve. However, the choice of Rubens as author and composer meant that the light operatic was wholly improbable, and what he turned out was a whisper-light piece of froth set with the most simple of songs (Talbot supplied the ensembles), often catchy and only occasionally – in the manner which would blight his whole career – in a rather childish bad taste. Only Miss May of the three stars made it to opening night. Miss Greene, starring for producer Edwardes in *A Country Girl* and *Kitty Grey*, was deputized for by Hilda Moody and Miss Reeve was replaced in rehearsal by Madge Crichton as the third of the countrified Branscombe sisters who win partners (Bertram Wallis, Maurice Farkoa, G P Huntley) away from a trio of town ladies (Millie Legarde, Betty Belknap, Ruby Ray). Tiny George Carroll was the comedy and Lottie Venne the class.

Rubens's numbers included a pretty piece for the six ladies about 'The Town and Country Mouse', Huntley had a nifty comic number about 'Algy' who was 'simply, awfully good at algebra' and the three girls danced and sang the 'Tea and Cake Walk' to good effect, but there were also some shabby pieces that, perversely, were the ones which became popular: 'She Was a Miller's Daughter' of whom, like so many of Rubens's boringly two-faced country maidens, it was said 'there were flies on the water, but she was flier still', a witless tirade against 'Men' and an inanity called 'Sal'.

The show's muslin-and-cherries simplicity, in an era of highly coloured and up-to-date shows, aided by the star and production values supplied by Edwardes and Charles Frohman, won *Three Little Maids* an excellent London life of 348 performances at the Apollo, and later the Prince of Wales, Theatres. The show proved distinctly popular on the road, and even scored a success on Broadway, to where the producers exported a British cast including Miss Crichton, Huntley, Farkoa, Carroll and London take-over Delia Mason for a broken run of 129 performances. These stars continued further south to appear in an Australian season of the show the following year, as *Three Little Maids* covered the English-speaking world, making money for all and setting its author-songwriter on his way to a substantial career.

USA: Daly's Theater 1 September 1903; Australia: Princess Theatre, Melbourne 14 May 1904

THE THREE MUSKETEERS Musical play in 3 acts by William Anthony McGuire based on *Les Trois Mousquetaires* by Alexandre Dumas. Lyrics by P G Wodehouse and Clifford Grey. Music by Rudolf Friml. Lyric Theater, New York, 13 March 1928.

Alexandre Dumas's famous musketeers and their cavaliering quest to save the honour of the barely naughty Queen of France have been the subject of a long list of stage and musical adaptations since they first appeared on the printed page in 1844 and in the theatre the following year (Théâtre l'Ambigu, Paris, 27 October 1845 w Auguste Maquet).

Amongst their musical stage appearances have been included operatic ones in works by Reginald Somerville (Edinburgh, April 1899) and Isidore de Lara (*Les Trois Mousquetaires*, Cannes 3 March 1921 and subsequently played in Britain), and a number of operettic ones. A spectacular *D'Artagnan* ('Bétove'/Mouëzy-Éon) was produced at Paris's Théâtre de la Gaîté-Lyrique (18 November 1945) under Henri Montjoye with some success, and others of the same title in Italy (Romeo Simonesi, Genoa, July 1888), and in Germany where Victor Léon supplied the text for a Rudolf Raimann Operette, *D'Artagnan [und die drei Musketiere]* mounted at Hamburg's Carl-Schultze Theater (18 September 1881).

The musketeers were Francis Lopezzed in a *Les Trois Mousquetaires* curiously described as an 'opérette western' (Théâtre du Châtelet, February 1974, Daniel Ringold/René Jolivet), whilst Ralph Benatzky composed and arranged the score ('[he has] collected some American hits and sandwiched in a sentimental waltz or two of his own') for a spectacular-comical *Drei Musketiere* produced at Berlin's Grosses Schauspielhaus in 1929 (libretto 'nach Motiven des Dumas' by Ernst Welisch, Rudolf Schanzer, 28 September). Alfred Jerger as D'Artagnan, Max Hansen (Aramis) and Sig Arno (Porthos) were the 'three' of the title (Athos had been done away with on the principle that the title always has been misleading) featured alongside Gosta Ljungberg (Queen), Trude Hesterberg (Leona, a spy) and one Josef Schmidt, in a story which forgot all about the Queen's jewels, and instead concentrated on a plot about a marriage with the Infanta of Spain and on no less than ten ballets. The show did well enough to be taken to Vienna's Theater an der Wien (16 October 1931) with Jerger teamed with Anny Coty (Queen), Max Brod (Porthos), Max Willenz (Aramis) and Rosl Berndt (Leona). There have been further versions of the tale in recent decades from Russia and again from Germany (*Die drei Musketiere* Jaro Dlouhy/Ursula Damm-Wendler, Horst-Ulrich Wendler, 17 June 1966).

In Britain, a jolly musketeers-in-the-round was produced at the Royal Exchange, Manchester (Derek Griffiths/Braham Murray 25 June 1979) with Robert Lindsay as its athletic hero, but British musketeers have normally been burlesque ones, ranging from the days of Joseph and Harry Paultons's *Three Musket-Dears and a Little One In* (Strand Theatre 1871, mus arr John Fitzgerald) which featured

Tilly Wright as D'Artagnan, with two equally feminine fellow musketeers, Paulton as Athos and Edward Terry as Lady de Winter, up to a large-scale *The Four Musketeers* (Laurie Johnson/Herbert Kretzmer/Michael Pertwee, Theatre Royal, Drury Lane 5 December 1967) in which bulky Harry Secombe frolicked through 462 performances as Dumas's young Gascon.

Broadway had its first *The Three Musketeers* in the form of a light opera by Richard W Temple, produced by its author at the Manhattan Opera House for five performances in 1921 (19 May), but it was its second one, produced just shortly before the Grosses Schauspielhaus extravaganza, which has been the only really successful attempt at turning Dumas's flamboyant foursome into the heroes of a romantic musical play. Following on behind the romantic success of *Rose Marie* and the swashbuckling triumph of *The Vagabond King*, Willam Anthony McGuire and Rudolf Friml's *The Three Musketeers* (all four of them) romanced and swashbuckled simultaneously whilst keeping pretty much to both the central story and the characters of the original book. D'Artagnan (Dennis King) supported by his companions-in-arms, Athos (Douglass Dumbrille), Porthos (Detmar Poppen) and Aramis (Joseph Macauley) set off for England to recover the jewels embarrassingly given to the Duke of Buckingham (John Clarke) by the Queen of France (Yvonne d'Arle), whilst the romance was supplied by innkeeper's daughter and royal lady-in-waiting, Constance Bonacieux (Vivienne Segal) and the baddies were represented by Reginald Owen (Richelieu) and Vivienne Osborne (Milady). The score was in a suitably stirring light operatic vein, but The March of the Musketeers did not come up to The Song of the Vagabonds in public favour, and although the virile 'My Sword (and I)' and the romantic 'Ma Belle' (Aramis), 'My Dreams' (Queen) and 'Your Eyes' (D'Artagnan and Constance) did well enough in the show, none of them survived to the popularity gained by Friml's two earlier successes.

Florenz Ziegfeld's lavishly staged production, with settings by Urban, ballets by Albertina Rasch and, rather curiously, a brigade of Tiller Girls in support, ran for a good but untriumphant 319 performances. In London, where the show followed *Show Boat* and *The New Moon* on to the stage of the Theatre Royal, Drury Lane, the result was much the same. A very fine cast, headed by King, Raymond Newell (Aramis), Robert Wollard (Porthos), Jack Livesey (Athos), Adrienne Brune (Constance), Webster Booth (Buckingham), Lilian Davies (Queen), Arthur Wontner (Richelieu) and Marie Ney (Milady) played the piece for 240 performances under Alfred Butt's management, without approaching the grand totals achieved by Friml's two big successes. *The Three Musketeers* remained a relative success.

In 1984 a revised version of the show (ad Mark Bramble) was produced on Broadway. Michael Praed was the D'Artagnan of an all-action *Three Musketeers* which failed to please for more than a handful of nights (Broadway Theater 11 November).

UK: Theatre Royal, Drury Lane 28 March 1930
Recording: London cast recordings on *Rudolf Friml in London* (WRC)

THE THREEPENNY OPERA *see* DIE DREIGROSCHEN-OPER

Plate 273.

(THE) THREE TWINS Musical comedy in 2 acts by Charles Dickson (and Isidore Witmark) based on *Incog* by Mrs R Pacheco. Lyrics by Otto Harbach. Music by Karl Hoschna. Herald Square Theater, New York, 15 June 1908.

The play *Incog*, written by the wife of the Governor of California, Mrs Pacheco, and played in Britain by Charles Hawtrey as *Tom, Dick and Harry*, was brought to publisher Isidore Witmark with the suggestion that he might like to have it turned into a musical comedy. Witmark took the 'suggestion' and, having himself reorganized the play into a libretto form, set a team of writers to work on completing the transformation. He allotted the musical side to his young employee, Karl Hoschna, who had written the scores for three touring musicals without breaking into Broadway, and he accepted Hoschna's suggestion that he bring in as lyricist an advertising man called Hauerbach with whom he had been working on an unproduced show. Hauerbach was paid $100 for the opportunity to have his lyrics heard on Broadway.

The title that they gave to Mrs Pacheco's story had rather more significance than its original. Tom Stanhope (Clifton Crawford), the disinherited heir to the fortune of his dyspeptic General father (Joseph Allen), disguises himself as one of the Winters twins, Harry (Willard Curtiss) and Dick (George S Christy), to the deep confusion of the former's sweetheart (Bessie McCoy) and the latter's wife (Frances Kennedy) until, after two acts of mistaken identities, problems, songs and dances, things are sorted out and he can be restored to parental favour and his own sweetheart, Kate (Florence Willarde).

The nine songs (plus two opening choruses and two finales) which illustrated the piece included two which became first-class favourites, Miss Willarde's encourage-ment to her beloved to 'Cuddle Up a Little Closer, Lovey Mine' (a piece originally written for a vaudeville act and transported into the show by its writers) and a jaunty, naïve little number about the child-scaring 'Yama-Yama Man', a number very much in the line of, the famous 'Hush, the Bogie' which had been added to the score during rehearsals for the benefit of Miss McCoy. A pretty, swooping waltz duo, 'Good Night, Sweetheart, Good Night' for Crawford and Miss Willarde, the waltzed praises of 'The Little Girl Up There', a novel laughing and crying duet for Misses Kennedy and McCoy, and a rouser claiming 'We Belong to Old Broadway' also contributed to an enjoyable musical part and to the splendid success of Joseph M Gaites's Broadway production.

Three Twins stayed in New York for 288 performances, in spite of being burned out of the Herald Square Theater and being forced to take a break before re-establishing itself at the Majestic. Victor Morley (Tom), Bessie Clifford (Molly) and Eva Fallon (Kate) led out a west-coast company, and *Three Twins* was toured healthily thereafter throughout America. In spite of a showcase presentation mounted by Witmark in London, it did not succeed in finding itself a production there, but it was picked up for an Australian season. Dorothy Brunton (later Maud Fane) was Kate and Harry Wooton (later director Harry B Burcher) played Harry, with Alfred Frith (Dick), William Greene (Tom) and the Gaiety star Connie Ediss as Mrs Dick. The show, however, met some indignant opposition, its 'travesty of mourning and grief' in wartime being considered 'ill-timed' and 'disfiguring', and an illumination showing an apparently nude lady as an accompaniment to the song 'Bachelor Days' objectionable. *Three Twins* was bumped from Melbourne after only a fortnight, and played just four weeks in Sydney (Her Majesty's 1 June 1918) the following year.

UK: Victoria Hall, Westbourne Grove 3 March 1908; Australia: Her Majesty's Theatre, Melbourne 26 May 1917

TIERNEY, Harry [Austin] (b Perth Amboy, NJ, 21 May 1890; d New York, 22 March 1965). Broadway songwriter whose music accompanied both the comic and romantic-spectacular.

Born into a musical family, Tierney studied music in New York before appearing on the concert stage in both America and Europe as a juvenile pianist. He subsequently became a song-plugger in England, notably at Harrod's department store in London, and it was apparently through his playing of other people's songs in this capacity that he came in contact with C B Cochran and was ultimately given the opportunity himself to write for the stage.

Tierney contributed numbers to the pot-pourri scores of the Alhambra revues *Keep Smiling* (1913) and *Not Likely* (1914) for André Charlot along with other fashionably foreign composers such as France's Willie Redstone and American Melville Gideon, and apparently also to some numbers for Cochran before he returned to America. There he had his first significant show assignment when, with lyricist Alfred Bryan, he supplied a half-dozen songs for what had once been a Leo Ascher musical, *Was tut man nicht alles aus Liebe*, but had been metamorphosed into the Shuberts' Anna Held vehicle *Follow Me* (1916). His contribution included 'The Girls are Getting Wiser Every Day', 'Happyland', 'It's a Cute Little Way of My Own', 'It's the Little Things That Count', 'How Would You Like to Bounce a Baby on Your

YOU'RE ALWAYS IN MY ARMS

From the R.K.O. Production

RIO RITA

The
RADIO PICTURE
SCREEN OPERETTA

Starring
BEBE DANIELS
JOHN BOLES
and
1,000 OTHERS

Music by
HARRY TIERNEY
Lyrics by
JOSEPH McCARTHY

Book by
GUY BOLTON and
FRED THOMPSON

'Rio Rita'
'You're Always In My
Arms' (But Only In My Dreams)
'Sweetheart, We Need
Each Other'
'Following The Sun
Around'
'If You're In Love,-
You'll Waltz'
'The Kinkajou'
'The Rangers Song'

2'6 NET

LEO. FEIST, INC., NEW YORK

ALLAN'S

Plate 274.

Knee?' and Miss Held's memorable 'I Want to Be Good (But my eyes won't let me)'. He interpolated 'Sometime' into *Betty*, the score for *Hitchy-Koo* (1917) included his hit number 'M.I.S.S.I.S.S.I.P.P.I' (ly: Bert Hanlon, Benny Ryan), later used in London's Gaiety Theatre musical *The Beauty Spot*, *The Passing Show of 1917* used 'My Yokohama Girl', and in the same year he turned out his first full-scale musical score for the American stage. However, *What's Next?*, produced in Los Angeles by Oliver Morosco, with no less a star than Blanche Ring topping the bill, stopped short of a Broadway opening.

Tierney continued over the years that followed to provide additional numbers for the other folks' musicals, including the anglicized French musical *Afgar* ('Why Don't You?' etc) and the 'Cohanised' comic opera *The Royal Vagabond*, as well as for the revue *The Broadway Whirl* and the *Ziegfeld Follies* ('They're So Hard to Keep When They're Beautiful', 'Where Do the Mosquitos Go?', 'Take, Oh Take Those Lips Away') between 1919 and 1924 when he and his partner Joseph McCarthy, supplying seven numbers, were credited for the basic score. In the meantime, however, Tierney had achieved that one stage hit necessary to shift a composer into the classic class. The musical comedy *Irene*, produced on Broadway in 1919, introduced the most memorable of the mostly subsequent gaggle of mostly Irish Cinderella-type heroines to the New York musical stage, equipped with Tierney and McCarthy's 'Alice Blue Gown' and two handfuls of other charming songs. The show was a major international hit, scoring from Sydney to Budapest to London, and establishing its writers at the forefront of their craft.

Tierney had another, if less than international, success with a musical version of Frank Craven's *Too Many Cooks*, produced by William A Brady under the title *Up She Goes*. On this occasion, the comedy was more important than the agreeable if not particularly outstanding score, but the combination was good for 256 Broadway performances. The same success did not attend a second go at a Cinderella piece with *Irene*'s author, James Montgomery. *Glory* failed to take, and closed after 64 performances leaving behind only 'The Saw Mill River Road' as a briefly popular number.

The following year Tierney and McCarthy provided the songs for the comedy musical *Kid Boots*, and once again found a by no means first-rate score carried to success by a lively comedy and a popular star, not to mention an interpolated number ('Dinah') which gave the piece the genuine song hit they had not turned up. For their next musical, however, the pair did not go for another comedy libretto, but instead supplied the songs for the spectacular romance *Rio Rita*. The spectacle undoubtedly had as much to do with *Rio Rita*'s fine Broadway success as the comedy and the star had with that of *Kid Boots*, but this time the score – including 'Following the Sun Around', 'Rio Rita', The Rangers' Song, 'If You're in Love You'll Waltz' and 'The Kinkajou' – more than did its bit towards that success.

Thereafter, however, Tierney's career faltered and faded. A 1928 musical *Cross My Heart* played itself out in eight weeks, a period in Hollywood, which included the film version of *Rio Rita* and such movies as *Dixiana* and *Half Shot at Sunrise*, was unproductive and a subsequent return to the musical stage did not reach out as far as Broadway.

1917 **What's Next?** (Alfred Bryan/Oliver Morosco, Elmer B Harris) Majestic Theater, Los Angeles 24 June

1919 **Irene** (McCarthy/James Montgomery) Vanderbilt Theater 18 November

1922 **Up She Goes** (McCarthy/Frank Craven) Playhouse 6 November

1922 **Glory** (McCarthy/Montgomery) Vanderbilt Theater 25 December

1923 **Kid Boots** (McCarthy/William Anthony McGuire, Otto Harbach) Earl Carroll Theater 31 December

1927 **Rio Rita** (McCarthy/Guy Bolton, Fred Thompson) Ziegfeld Theater 2 February

1928 **Cross My Heart** (McCarthy/Daniel Kusell) Knickerbocker Theater 17 September

1933 **Beau Brummell** (Edward Eliscu, Raymond Egan/Gladys Unger) Municipal Opera, St Louis 7 August

TILLEY, Vesta [POWLES, Matilda Alice] *see* DE FRECE, LAURI

LA TIMBALE D'ARGENT Opéra-bouffe in 3 acts by Adolphe Jaime and Jules Noriac. Music by Léon Vasseur. Théâtre des Bouffes-Parisiens, Paris, 9 April 1872.

Jaime and Noriac's 'timbale d'argent' is the prize in a rustic singing contest. The village of Grog-et-l'eau-de-seidlitz is desperate to beat the neighbouring village of Feldkirch, and the local judge, Raab (Désiré), has offered his daughter's hand to the man who can bring off a victory. Young Müller (Mme Peschard) from over Feldkirch way crosses villages to win the prize and the girl, but the choirmaster and local gaoler, Pruth (Edouard Georges), who has had designs on Molda (Anna Judic) first on behalf of his nephew Fichtel (Debreux) and then on his own, discovers that the invincibility of the Feldkirch vocalists comes from an oath of sexual abstinence and calls Müller to hold to his troth, even on his wedding night. The men of Grog-et-l'eau-de-seidlitz take to abstinence and winning trophies, there is a women's rebellion, and Molda seduces her husband from his vow in time for a lively and happy ending.

Vasseur's happily lightsome score was largely shared between the artists playing Molda and Müller. The soprano hero introduced himself with a showy serenade ('Pendant que sur la nappe blanche') and won his timbale in jolly tyrolienne, but it was the piece's leading lady who turned *La Timbale d'argent* and its music into a major success. The 22-year-old Judic opened proceedings with the not entirely unsuggestive Couplets de la Timbale ('V'la qu'ça glis-se!'), enlivened the wedding scene with the Chanson du Postillon with its 'clic! clac! hop! hop!' refrain and seduced her husband in the Couplets de Coquetterie with a winsome sexuality, making the simple lyrics into songs of swingeing but sweet suggestiveness which took away the breath of even the delighted Paris public of 1872. Judic and *La Timbale d'argent* both became the hottest things in town – thanks to it, she was hoisted to instant stardom, and, thanks very largely to her, the show proved almost as popular as *La Fille de Madame Angot* as it totted up 300 Parisian performances in just two seasons.

Inevitably, such a hit was soon exported. Brussels quickly got not one but two productions when, in spite of the fact that the Galeries St-Hubert had paid out 5,000 francs for the rights, *Angot* producer Eugène Humbert at the Alcazar ignored what he claimed as the invalid copyright and got in first with his version. However, outside France, *La Timbale d'argent* never seemed likely to challenge the success of Lecocq's work nor even to equal the popularity it had found at home. America took its *Timbale* in French and was treated to Marie Aimée not in the rôle created by Judic, which was played by Léontine Minelly, but as Müller. Produced in the Grau and Chizzola opéra-bouffe season in 1874 it earned more pursed lips than untied purses, even in French, and it was not persevered with. However, several years later when Louise Théo visited America, she featured *La Timbale d'argent* prominently in her repertoire for several years.

In Britain the only way the piece which *The Era* gasped was 'so saturated with indecent suggestions' could be staged was to rewrite it severely. G M Layton used the score and as much as he dared of the original text to make up a piece called *The Duke's Daughter, or Sold for a Song*, still set in the village of Grogandseidlitz in the Duchy of Duffendorff, in which Pauline Rita was leading man, Alice Burville principal girl and Rachel Sanger, in a lesser role, was billed in the programme as having 'kindly consented to play the part'. Various rehashings and recastings were tried as the cleaned-up piece moved to the Globe and the Charing Cross in search of a popularity which did not come and after a peripatetic two-month life it closed.

More regular versions were staged in Italy and South America (in French), in Vienna in German (for just three nights) and St Petersburg in Russian (1874), but the real success of *La Timbale d'argent* remained in France where the show was reprised at the Bouffes-Parisiens in 1876 and 1878 (this time with Louise Théo starring), in 1888 with Mlle Gilberte, at the Théâtre des Menus-Plaisirs in 1893 and at the Folies-Dramatiques in 1897 when Blanche-

Marie (Molda), Jane Pierney (Müller) and Gardel (Raab) topped the bill.

Austria: Theater an der Wien *Der Silberbecher* 16 November 1872; USA: Lyceum Theater (Fr) 24 August 1874; UK: Royalty Theatre *The Duke's Daughter* 10 January 1876

THE TIME, THE PLACE AND THE GIRL Musical comedy in 3 acts by Will M Hough and Frank R Adams. Music by Joseph E Howard. La Salle Theater, Chicago, 20 August 1906; Wallack's Theater, New York, 5 August 1907.

The most successful of the bundle of successful musical comedies written by the team of Hough, Adams and Howard for the Chicago theatre of the earliest years of the 20th century, *The Time, the Place and the Girl* was a jolly romp which thoroughly fulfilled its description of 'musical comedy'. The tale on which the fun and the songs were draped had dashing young hero Tom Cunningham (George Anderson) and his comical pal Johnny Hicks (Cecil Lean/Arthur Deagon) fleeing from Boston after having done some damage to the cranium of a card-cheat with a bottle. They choose for their hideout a sanatorium in the nearest mountains and there Tom meets up with his old sweetheart, Margaret Simpson (Florence Holbrook/Violet McMillan). Johnny falls for the pretty nurse, Molly Kelly (Georgia Drew Mendum/Elene Foster) whose name shows quite clearly that she is none other than the sister of the belligerent chap (Thomas Cameron) with the dented cranium. Revenge is kept at bay, however, when the sanatorium is close-quarantined. By the time the all clear is given, the only bells to be heard are wedding ones.

The songs which the team provided to illustrate their tale were as lively and well-made a lot as was being produced anywhere on the east coast. The waltz 'The Waning Honeymoon' ('Honeymoon, honeymoon, why do you set so soon?') proved the favourite and enduring part of the score, alongside the winning 'Blow the Smoke Away', a jaunty 'Dixie, I Love You', 'Thursday is My Jonah Day' and 'I Don't Like Your Family', all of which did the rounds in Chicago and further afield for many years.

Chicago welcomed *The Time, the Place and the Girl* for a vast run of some 400 performances, and with that success attached to its title it set out, in the tracks of the earlier Hough-Adams-Howard hits, to tour the country. Like its predecessors, it did splendidly, and did it long. Experience might have told the managers to skip New York, but they didn't. *The Time, the Place and the Girl* not only braved New York, but braved it in the heat of the summer. One journal reported 'Chicago liked it last season, Boston accorded it a welcome last spring, and New York may grow to be fond of it, if New York can be brought to liking anything it has not conceived itself' before going on to opine that it might prove 'a little too heavy for a hot weather show', which was a slightly strange thought, given that the Chicago musicals were usually attacked as being spineless and weightless. New York, however, could not be persuaded to like it, and Ned Wayburn and Arthur Evans's production went back on the road after four weeks at Wallack's to continue its long touring life.

Time eventually saw it peep into Broadway again, in 1942, when it was brought back – with the aged Howard actually appearing himself – for a brief run at the Mansfield Theatre (21 October).

A Hollywood film which used the title *The Time, the Place and the Girl* was a campus affair which used nothing else of the stage piece but its name.

TINA   Musical play in 3 acts by Paul Rubens and Harry Graham said to be based on a play called *Kitty*. Lyrics by Paul Rubens, Percy Greenbank and Harry Graham. Music by Paul Rubens and Haydn Wood. Adelphi Theatre, London, 2 November 1915.

The play *Kitty* on which *Tina* was said to be based remains a mystery, but there were fragments of a number of other favourite shows, ranging from Rubens's own *Miss Hook of Holland* to *Ein Walzertraum* and back, to be found in the make-up of the very slim book of *Tina*. Phyllis Dare was Tina, a little Dutch cocoa heiress (the show was prematurely titled *Cocoa-Tina*) anxious to make a romantic runaway match with a dashing violinist. The one she chooses, however, turns out to be the impecunious Duke of Borgolese (Godfrey Tearle) in disguise, and she is disappointed for a whole act before the obvious ending is firmed up. Bill Berry played Tina's wealthy manufacturing father, delighted at getting a Duke in the family and also at flirting with a lady musician (Yvonne Reynolds) and there was supporting comedy from Mabel Sealby and George Gregory.

If the libretto was minimal, however, the songs which decorated it were some of Rubens's most attractive. The Violin Song, in which Tina throbbed over her lover's playing with a vocal imitation of the sound of a fiddle, proved a popular hit, and there were several other attractive pieces ('Something in the Atmosphere', 'Let Me Introduce You to My Father', 'A Self-Made Man') to support it. The romance and the comedy, too, were supported by a dance feature from Jan Oyra and Dorma Leigh ('Billstickers' Dance') and by a fine production so that *Tina* won a run of 277 London performances before going on the British road. But it didn't go further. Australia, that yardstick of international taste, showed why: it was busy around this time with *High Jinks*, *So Long, Letty*, *Tonight's the Night* and *The Pink Lady* — book-strong shows with dancing tunes. *Tina* belonged to yesterday rather than to today and tomorrow.

TIP-TOES   Musical comedy in 2 acts by Guy Bolton and Fred Thompson. Lyrics by Ira Gershwin. Music by George Gershwin. Liberty Theater, New York, 28 December 1925.

Another musical comedy in the Cinderella-superstar series of which *Sally*, *Mary* and *Irene* had been the favourite examples, *Tip-Toes* was, like them, named after its heroine (Queenie Smith), a little lady from the lesser ranks of the music-halls. Having, all unawares, captured the heart of a glue millionaire called Steve Burton (Allen Kearns) who has gone slumming in search of true love, then forfeited his regard by being so rash as to appear in a beauty contest to win money to pay an hotel bill, she sticks by her man when it seems he is ruined and Society and rich Sylvia (Jeannette MacDonald *sic*) shun him, and earns herself a happy ending. The dozen songs which made up the Gershwins' score did not include any of their biggest and/or best travelling hits, but Tip-Toes's pretty confidence that she is 'Looking for a Boy', the lovers' description of 'That Certain Feeling', the jaunty enquiry 'When Do We Dance? put out by Steve and a couple of accompanying damsels (Gertrude McDonald, Lovey Lee), the lilting 'These Charming People' as delivered by Tip-Toes and her music-hall partners (Andrew Tombes, Harry Watson jr) and the up-to-date 'Sweet and Low-Down' all proved at least locally popular, and enduringly pleasing.

Pretty *Tip-Toes* appeared in the same Broadway season as her sisters *No, No, Nanette*, *Sunny* and *The Girl Friend* and, although she had a lesser stay in town they they did, she notched up a respectable 192 performances before moving on to the road. In London, the show was presented at the Winter Garden Theatre with Dorothy Dickson starring opposite Kearns and with a supporting cast including Laddie Cliff and Vera Bryer. Its lifespan did not come up to the runs of Gershwin's earlier pieces in London, nor indeed to *Lady, Be Good!*, simultaneously on stage at the Empire, but it played a more than respectable 182 London performances before moving out of the Winter Garden and leaving it to the more resonant tones of *The Vagabond King*.

Australia's *Tip-Toes* was Elizabeth Morgan, and her pals were played by Gus Bluett, Ole Olsen and Chick Johnson through fair showings in Sydney and Melbourne (Theatre Royal, 13 August 1927) and the show was also honoured with a Parisian production (ad André Mauprey, Robert de Mackield, Serge Veber) with Loulou Hégoburu and Adrien Lamy, the juvenile stars of France's hugely successful production of *No, No, Nanette*, in the leading rôles.

Having had her moment, *Tip-Toes* tiptoed on, but she came briefly to life again when a 1978 revival was staged at the Goodspeed Opera House with Georgia Engel and Russ Thacker featured (11 April), followed by a short tour and a season in Brooklyn.

UK: Winter Garden Theatre 31 August 1926; Australia: Her Majesty's Theatre, Sydney 7 May 1927; France: Folies-Wagram 27 April 1929

Recording: London cast recordings on *George Gershwin in London* (WRC)

TOCHÉ, Raoul   (b Bougival, 1850; d Chantilly, 17 January 1895). Comic playwright and librettist to the Parisian fin-de-siècle stage.

Son of a familiar Parisian first-nighter, Toché – 'mince, elégant, assez timide, a qui son nez un peu long donnait un air à la fois étonné et narquois' – eagerly put himself about in theatrical circles until he became a happy member of the Parisian literary and musical late-nighters of his time. He began his own writing career on the one hand as a theatrical columnist under the pen-name 'Frimousse', and on the other as a revuist, providing the texts for a number of such pieces – notably the *Revue des Variétés* and the extremely successful *Paris en actions* staged by Brasseur at the Théâtre des Nouveautés. Before long he moved on to more ambitious areas, and turned out a series of highly successful and widely-played comedies and vaudevilles including *La Maison Tamponin*, *Le Parfum*, *Madame Mongodin* and *Monsieur Coulisset*, as well as the famous *Le Voyage en Suisse* (Théâtre des Variétés 30 August 1879), long toured throughout the world by the Hanlon Lees group of pantomimists, and also a number of opérettes, many of which were written in collaboration with Ernest Blum. In the journalistic world, he moved on simultaneously to pen the 'Soirées Parisiennes' of *Le Gaulois*.

The first of Toché's full-length musical works was set with a score by the aged Offenbach, the last work of the celebrated composer, but thereafter the larger and easily the most significant part of his musical theatre work was written with Gaston Serpette. If none of their works became a standard, the little *La Princesse* and the saucy *Adam et Ève* found several overseas productions, *Le Château de Tire-Larigot* won undeniable success in Paris, and his adaptation of the latest adaptation of the Cogniard *Le Royaume des femmes* attracted the lovers of a saucy spectacle during the Paris Exhibition before going on to be staged throughout Europe. He also contributed to the texts of the Châtelet spectaculars *Le Testament de M Crac* and *Madame L'Amiral*.

However, although his professional life was going well, the 'gay, inoffensive' Toché messed up his private life. He inherited money, married – apparently unwisely – more money, and embarked on a crazy spree of extravagant, away-from-home living. When he had run through his own cash, he borrowed. When the usurers became too pressing, he put a bullet through his head, in a field near Chantilly, at the age of 44.

Toché's non-musical works extended his list of musical theatre credits quite considerably in the hands of other folk. His play *La Maison Tamponin* (Palais-Royal, 22 March 1893 w Blum) was used as the basis for the Charles Weinberger/Hugo Wittmann Operette *Prima Ballerina* (Carltheater 23 November 1895) and its revised version as the same composer's 1901 *Auch so eine* (Theater in der Josefstadt 18 October), whilst their *Madame Mongodin* (Théâtre du Vaudeville, 17 December 1890) was turned into the American musical comedy *Mary's Lamb* by actor-author-manager Richard Carle (New York Theater 25 May 1908). The vaudeville, *Le Parfum* (Palais-Royal 20 October 1888 w Blum), was also given a German-language musical version at the Theater in der Josefstadt under the title *Im Pavillon* (ad Ludwig Fischl, Alexander Landesberg, mus: Karl Kappeller, March 1896).

Between 1882 and 1892 Toché put out seven volumes of *Soirées parisiennes*.

1877 **Chanteur (chanteuse) par amour** (Paul Henrion/w Georges Vibert) 1 act Casino d'Étretat 20 August, Théâtre des Variétés 1 September
1880 **Belle Lurette** (Jacques Offenbach/w Ernest Blum, Édouard Blau) Théâtre de la Renaissance 30 October
1882 **La Princesse** (Gaston Serpette) 1 act Théâtre des Variétés 22 October
1883 **Le Premier Baiser** (Émile Jonas/w Émile de Najac) Théâtre des Nouveautés 21 March
1883 **Tige de lotus** (Serpette) 1 act Casino de Contrexéville 26 July
1884 **Le Diable au corps** (Romuald Marenco/w Blum) Théâtre des Bouffes-Parisiens 19 December
1884 **Le Château de Tire-Larigot** (Serpette/w Blum) Théâtre des Nouveautés 30 October
1885 **Le Petit Chaperon-Rouge** (Serpette/w Blum) Théâtre des Nouveautés 10 October
1886 **Adam et Ève** (Serpette/w Blum) Théâtre des Nouveautés 6 October
1888 **[La] Divorcée** (Louis Varney) 1 act Cabourg 11 August
1889 **Le Royaume des femmes** (Serpette/Cogniard, Blum ad w Blum) Théâtre des Nouveautés
1893 **Madame Satan** (pasticcio/w Blum) Théâtre des Variétés 26 September
1896 **La Biche au bois** revised version w Blum (Théâtre du Châtelet)

TODD, Michael [GOLDBOGEN, Avrom Hirsch] (b Minneapolis, 22 June 1907; d New Mexico, 22 March 1958).

American showman who, after cashing-up large in real estate and in the sale of sound-proofing for movie sound stages, switched his attention to theatrical production where he specialized in the flamboyant and the spectacular much in the same way that he did in his way of life.

Todd produced *The Hot Mikado* (1939), *Star and Garter* (1942), *Something for the Boys* (1943), *Mexican Hayride* (1944), *Up in Central Park* (1945), *As the Girls Go* (1948) and *Mike Todd's Peep Show* (1950), finding some success, some good runs, some distinctly forced good runs but mounting nothing of enduring quality. At the same time, he continued his interest in whatever was most oversized and spectacular in the film world: he was behind the development and promotion of the wide-screen Todd-AO and Cinerama processes and he married Elizabeth Taylor. He was killed in an airplane crash in New Mexico.

In 1988, amidst the continuing passion for biomusicals, a musical (Mitch Leigh/Lee Adams/Thomas Meehan) was made out of his life, and produced by Cyma Rubin under the title *Mike* (without an exclamation point) at the Walnut Street Theater, Philadelphia 26 March. Todd was impersonated by Michael Lembeck. It did not go any further until 1993 when, retitled *Ain't Broadway Grand* and with Mike Burstyn portraying Todd, it was set for Broadway.

Autobiography: *The Nine Lives of Mike Todd* (Random House, New York, 1958); Biography: Todd, M Jr and Todd, S: *A Valuable Property* (Arbor House, New York, 1983)

TOI C'EST MOI Opérette in 2 acts by Henri Duvernois (and Albert Willemetz and André Mouëzy-Éon). Lyrics by Bertal-Maubon and Chamfleury. Music by Moïse Simons. Théâtre des Bouffes-Parisiens, Paris, 19 September 1934.

Bob Guibert (Jacques Pills) has been leading an extravagantly debauched life in the night-spots of Paris, sponsored by the cheque book of indulgent and not-fully-comprehending Aunt Honorine (Pauline Carton). But Aunt Honorine finally does comprehend, cries enough and banishes penniless, dependent Bob to her plantation in the Antilles, equipped with a sealed letter to the director, Pedro Hernandez (René Koval), ordering him to overwork the young cretin into something resembling a man. The cretin is smart enough to steam open the letter, and takes with him on the ship his inseparable, bludging pal, Pat Duvallon (Georges Tabet), whom he convinces to change places with him. Hernandez puts Pat to back-breaking work in the sugar fields, whilst Bob, pretending to be the 'unstable' heir's doctor, is free to romance the director's child-of-nature daughter, Maricousa (Simone Simon). Lyne Clevers played Viviane, daughter of the colonial official Robinet (Duvaleix), whose close relationship with the Colonial Minister gets her father transferred anywhere she wants to chase a man, Numès fils was Honorine's crooked secretary, and Ginette Leclerc doubled as a Parisian vamp and her smart Caribbean equivalent, all mixed up in a tale which had most of the cast getting laid and engaged (in that order) in the final act amongst such good-humoured dialogue and scenes that it didn't even seem conventional.

The show's score, written by Cuban composer Simons, had a genuine Caribbean tone to it, introducing the rumba

('À l'ombre calme des grandes palmes'), the samba and even the unheard-of conga ('C'est ça, la vie, c'est ça l'amour'), alongside a series of light-comic numbers in a more conventional style which included Bob and Pat's 'Toi c'est moi' and the hit of the evening, Honorine and Pedro's loopy duet 'Sous les palétuviers'.

Toi c'est moi was produced by Albert Willemetz and Louis Meucci at the Bouffes-Parisiens, after Willemetz and Mouëzy-Éon had (without credit) revamped the original libretto and, cast by Willemetz with some of the most attractive comic names of the period, headed by the popular double act of Pills and Tabet, the musical turned out a great success. It played a full year in Paris and was subsequently exported and translated into both English and Hungarian.

In London (ad Reginald Arkell), Charlotte Greenwood starred as Aunt Isabel alongside David Hutcheson (Bob), Clifford Mollison (Pat), Gina Malo (Vivienna) and Clare Luce (Maricousa), and the remnants of Simons's score were peppered with other folks' music, amongst which James Hanley's 'Zing, Went the Strings of My Heart' and Martin Broones's (Mr Charlotte Greenwood) 'It Happened in the Moonlight'. However it was Miss Luce's demonstration of the rumba that remained the highlight. The show was well received, but after two months producer Lee Ephraim shifted it from the Gaiety to the vastness of the London Coliseum – almost twice as large both in stage and auditorium – and after eight weeks' further run it withered away. In the same year the Hungarian version (ad János Vaszary, Andor Szenes) was produced at Budapest's Andrássy-uti Színház.

In 1936 a French film version was made, with Pills and Tabet playing their original rôles alongside Claude May and Junie Astor.

UK: Gaiety Theatre *The Gay Deceivers* 23 May 1935; Hungary: Andrássy-uti Színház *Egyszer vagyunk fiatalok* 20 February 1935; Film: 1936 René Guissart

LA TOISON D'OR
Opérette à grand spectacle in 2 acts by Raymond Vincy based on the novel by Pierre Benoît. Music by Francis Lopez. Théâtre du Châtelet, Paris, 18 December 1954.

An opérette about oil, or rather about the once opérette-worthy romantic lands of the East which have now suddenly become financially desirable property. Stanislas Monestier (André Dassary) has to fight to retain his Middle-Eastern lands in the face of some comical plotting bankers, an unhelpful basso priest (Lucien Lupi) and a power-crazy Regent. When his beloved turns out to be the local Princess (Colette Riedinger) in disguise, Stanislas helps out in a revolt against the Regent and ends up as Prince Consort of Asterabad.

The show's 'à grand spectacle' physical production – including a scene in which Stanislas blows up a burning oil-well – and Lopez's agreeably illustrative score, in which a basso title prayer for the Priest and the romantic 'L'Étoile bleue' and 'Jamais je n'aurais d'autre amour' were the most notable numbers, were elements in ensuring the show a solid run of 419 performances in Paris and an occasional provincial afterlife.

Recording: original cast (Pathé)

DIE TOLLE KOMTESS
Operette in 3 acts by Rudolf Bernauer and Rudolf Schanzer. Music by Walter Kollo. Berliner Theater, Berlin, 21 February 1917.

One of the most successful of the series of Walter Kollo Operetten produced at the Berliner Theater in the seven-year period surrounding the First World War, *Die tolle Komtess* did not, partly because of that war, find the same international success as *Filmzauber* (*The Girl on the Film*) or *Wie einst im Mai* (*Maytime*). It did, however, have a fine run of 350 performances in Berlin during the War, and was revived at the Berliner Theater in 1919.

The crazy countess of the title was a 17-year-old whose husband-seeking mama passes her off for 13. The girl revenges herself by getting up to all sorts of childish mischief, and finally gets herself engaged to the butler. Fortunately, the butler turns out to be a nice young nobleman who was just fulfilling his wealthy uncle's orders that he prove himself capable of holding down a job for three months.

Kollo's score again favoured the march rhythms featured in his previous pieces ('Edelweiss-Marsch', 'Die Kinderchen, die braven'), but there was also a regular helping of waltz music ('Du ahnungloser Engel'), a brisk polka, and the hero and heroine sang staunchly of being 'Dein auf ewig' (yours forever) in time-dishonoured fashion. The lighter musical moments included the tale of Aunt Carola who played the pianola.

EINE TOLLE MÄDEL
Vaudeville Operette in 2 acts and a Vorspiel by Kurt Kraatz and Heinrich Stobitzer. Lyrics by Wilhelm Sterk. Music by Carl Michael Ziehrer. Walhalla-Theater, Wiesbaden, 24 August 1907.

A piece in the vaudevillesque tradition exemplified by such musicals as *Les 28 Jours de Clairette* and *Toto, Eine tolles Mädel* existed largely to allow the show's female star, as the 'madcap maid' of the title, to gallivant through the evening in a rôle which got her into masculine garb, into the army, and into as many comical situations as possible, all as the result of a bet that she can get away with impersonating a soldier for a day. These antics were accompanied by a brightly tuneful Carl Ziehrer score from which the waltzes 'Manderl' and 'Gib acht!' and the just-a-kiss-in-the-dark number 'Küsse im Dunkeln' proved the favourites.

First produced at Wiesbaden, the show moved quickly on to be seen at Dresden and in other German houses and then to Austria. Wilhelm Sterk adapted the libretto for Vienna, where veteran Karl Tuschl, the former stage director/comedian of Danzers Orpheum who had taken over the management from Gabor Steiner, mounted the show on a programme with Léon and Straus's 'melodramatische szene' *Der Frauenmorder*. With Gerda Walde starred as the all-consuming Rosette alongside Rauch, Mizzi Gribl, Greissnegger, Frau Berger and Josef König, the bill played 42 straight performances and a handful of subsequent matinées. The Austrian version was then picked up both for Budapest (ad Adolf Merei) and for New York (ad Sydney Rosenfeld). In the post-*Merry Widow* era on Broadway, Lulu Glaser starred as Rosette in the Shubert brothers' production of *Mlle Mischief* for 66 performances at the Lyric Theater, then transferred to the Casino for a further three weeks, before heading on to a good life on the road and in the suburbs.

Austria: Danzers Orpheum 8 November 1907; Hungary: Fővárosi

Nyari Színház *Fuzsitus kisasszony* 15 August 1908; USA: Lyric Theater *Mlle Mischief* 28 September 1908

TOLLE WIRTSCHAFT   *see* POLNISCHE WIRTSCHAFT

TOM JONES   Comic opera in 3 acts by Alexander M Thompson and Robert Courtneidge based on the novel by Henry Fielding. Lyrics by Charles H Taylor. Music by Edward German. Apollo Theatre, London, 17 April 1907.

The comic opera version of Fielding's famous novel was brought out by producer Robert Courtneidge on the occasion of the 200th anniversary of its author's birth. Courtneidge and Alexander Thompson slimmed the original novel wisely, not attempting to take in the whole panorama of town and country depicted by Fielding, but simply following the amorous adventure of the apparently orphaned and obviously attractive Tom (Hayden Coffin) with the rampant Lady Bellaston (Dora Rignold) on his way to the finding of a family, social acceptance, and the hand of his truly beloved Sophia (Ruth Vincent). The character of the village schoolmaster, Benjamin Partridge, was rewritten to make it a traditional star comedy rôle (Dan Rolyat) and Sophia's canny maid, Honor (Carrie Moore), was the soubrette, teamed with yokel Gregory (Jay Laurier), all of them involved in the amorous goings-on gathered together by the librettists and effectively set in a wayside inn on the London road.

Edward German was an ideal choice of composer for this most English of old English subjects, and his score for *Tom Jones* turned out to be one of the best ever written for a British period light opera. Sophia's waltz song 'For Tonight', a soprano showpiece par excellence, has become a standard in the concert repertoire, Rolyat had a fine pattering piece describing himself as 'Benjamin Partridge, person of parts' and Miss Moore a delightful piece telling what a girl will do 'all for a green ribbon to tie in her hair'. Coffin had a handful of stout baritone songs, the yokels drank to the 'Barley Mow', and Ambrose Manning as the Somerset Squire Western rousted along 'On a Januairy Morning in Zummerzetshire'. During the run, the score was stiffened with several further numbers, including Sophia's long-since popular 'Dream o' Day Jill' and Honor's delicious 'I Knew That He Looked at Me', but in spite of a delighted reception the show played only 110 performances in London before being sent on the road. It was musical comedy time, and a comic opera, beautifully made though it might be, with no pretty, scanty girls, no glitz, no dance and no glamour had the same limited audience then as now. *Tom Jones* did not even make it to the total of its fellow light opera *The Rose of Persia*, a few years earlier.

Henry Savage mounted a production of *Tom Jones* in New York, with Van Rensslaer Wheeler (Tom), Louise Gunning (Sophia), Gertrude Quinlan (Honor) and William Norris (Partridge) starred, and a score expanded with 'King Neptune' from *Merrie England* and even an interpolated

Plate 275. *Many chapters of Fielding's novel* **Tom Jones** *are reduced into one scene in the inn at Upton. Hayden Coffin (Tom Jones, far right), Dan Rolyat (Partridge) and Ambrose Manning (Squire Western) (both centre) and Dora Rignold (Lady Bellaston, up centre).*

number 'The Road to Yesterday' (Clare Kummer). As in London, the show won superb reviews but failed to find sufficient audience for more than 65 performances. In spite of these disappointing first runs, however, *Tom Jones* and its favourite songs became and remained a firm part of the English repertoire whilst the less substantial shows which prospered around it disappeared.

Several other *Tom Jones*es have been written to libretti bearing more or less relation to Fielding's novel, easily the most successful being Philidor's 1765 French comic opera (Versailles, 20 March) which was subsequently played throughout Europe. Again in France, at the Théâtre de Paris, André Jobin played Tom and Georges Guétary Squire Western in a 1974 piece entitled *Les Aventures de Tom Jones* (Jacques Debronckart/Jean Marsan) which included rather more 'belles dames volcaniques' in its tale than even Fielding or certainly Edward German imagined ... and omitted Miss Western entirely!

In Britain, a comic-opera version written by Joseph Reed, imitating Philidor and using some small parts of his libretto, was produced at the Theatre Royal, Covent Garden, in 1769 (14 January) whilst in America a version was played at Stamford, Connecticut in 1976 (Barbara Damaschek/Larry Arrick, Hartman Theater), and another, billed as 'the musical version of *Tom Jones*' (as if there were no other), appeared in record form.

USA: Astor Theater 11 November 1907; Australia: Theatre Royal, Melbourne 1 October 1910
Recording: selection (EMI)

TOMMY
Rock opera with music and lyrics by Pete Townshend, John Entwhistle, Keith Moon and Sonny Boy Williamson. Derby Playhouse, England, 15 May 1975; Queen's Theatre, London 6 February 1979.

A dramatically incoherent piece with a score of contemporary rock music, *Tommy* has a deaf and dumb (but singing) hero who suffers all sorts of humiliations and interferences at the hands of the little people in his young life before temporarily becoming a 1960s pop messiah. The songs 'Pinball Wizard' and 'I'm Free' both made it to the hit parades.

Performed by The Who in a concert form, issued on record, lavishly praised by some who (erroneously, as it turned out) saw here the musical theatre/theatre music of the future, it was subsequently made into a film (1975, with Roger Daltrey, Elton John, Tina Turner, Ann-Margret, Jack Nicholson et al). Highly popular for many years, *Tommy* was played in various versions as a staged concert or a stage show before a first genuine theatre version was mounted at Derby in 1975. It was played at several British provincial theatres thereafter before a production from the Queen's Theatre, Hornchurch, was brought to London in 1979. In spite of the popularity of both the disc and the film, the rather-too-late-coming show – which boasted none of the starry names of the two earlier manifestations of the piece – failed in 118 performances.

At the time of writing, with nostalgia for the 1960s now raging hilariously, a new version of the piece is scheduled for a Broadway production.

USA: St James Theater 22 April 1993; Film: Columbia 1975
Recording: original concept recording (Polydor) etc

TONIGHT AT 8.30
Plays in 1 act by Noël Coward. Phoenix Theatre, London, 9 January 1936.

Of the group of nine (and one reject) one-act playlets which made up the three 'nights' of this entertainment, four included musical numbers. Noël Coward and Gertrude Lawrence sang 'We Were Dancing' as the victims of an ephemeral mutual attraction under the tropical moon in the play of the same name, gave out with 'Then', 'Play, Orchestra Play' and 'You Were There' in the fantastical half-dream of divorce that is *Shadow Play*, and performed the music-hall 'Has Anybody Seen Our Ship' and 'Men About Town', as a declining variety act called *The Red Peppers*, and the melodies from a music box in the post-funeral scene of *Family Album*. Several of the plays have been revived either as a group or singly since the show's first production, and two of the non-musical ones were made into films.

USA: National Theater 24 November 1936; Australia: Theatre Royal, Sydney 2 July 1938
Recordings: Songs included on HMV, WRC, RCA Victor etc

TONIGHT'S THE NIGHT
Musical play in 2 acts by Fred Thompson based on *Les Dominos roses* by Alfred Hennequin and Alfred Delacour. Lyrics by Paul Rubens and Percy Greenbank. Music by Paul Rubens. Shubert Theater, New York, 24 December 1914.

Tonight's the Night was a new musical version of the enormously successful French comedy *Les Dominos roses*, which had already been turned into a musical comedy in both Austria (*Der Opernball*) and in Hungary (*Három légyott* József Bokor, Népszinház 22 October 1897). The show was written and cast in Britain, but probably as a result of some theatrical infighting between George Grossmith and Alfred Butt – who was anxious to squeeze his rival out of the Gaiety Theatre – rather than to the war, it was not produced there. Producers George Grossmith and Edward Laurillard linked up with the Shubert brothers and transported the show, which had been originally intended and announced for the Gaiety, across to New York. George Grossmith (Hon Dudley Mitten), Davy Burnaby (Robin Carraway), James Blakeley (Montagu Lovitt-Lovitt) and Lauri de Frece (Henry) headed the men out for a spree at a masked ball, and Emmy Wehlen (June), Iris Hoey (Beatrice), Fay Compton (Victoria) and Gladys Homfrey (Angela Lovitt-Lovitt) played their respective partners. Miss Compton scored with the jolliest song of the evening, 'I'd Like to Bring My Mother', Grossmith encouraged 'I Think I Could Love You if I Tried', whilst Blakeley launched into the show's title song and joined de Frece and Grossmith in going 'Dancing Mad'. Maurice Farkoa as a spivvy tango teacher crooned over 'Pink and White' and Burnaby and Emmy Wehlen joined in 'Round the Corner' in the other main musical moments of the evening.

The show had a fine run of 112 Broadway performances and the producers then took it back to London, opening at the Gaiety in April 1915. Grossmith, Blakeley and Miss Homfrey were now teamed with Vernon Davidson, promoted understudy Leslie Henson, Haidée de Rance (briefly, then Madge Saunders), Julia James and Moya Mannering, and Max Dearly was the tango teacher. Henson joined Miss Mannering in 'I'd Like to Bring My Mother' and scored the hit of the evening, Grossmith slipped in a concert-party number by Greatrex Newman – a tipsy confession of a mass of unlikely 'Murders' with which Leslie

Henson had bolstered his little part in New York – and joined in two freshly added Jerome Kern songs brought back from America: 'They Didn't Believe Me' (from Broadway's version of *The Girl from Utah*) and 'Any Old Night' (ex- *Nobody Home*). *Tonight's the Night* was a major hit in London, staying at the Gaiety for 460 performances as it headed to the country and to productions throughout the English-speaking world.

In 1924 (21 April) Grossmith and his new partner, J A E Malone, revived the show at the Winter Garden. Since he was now a major star, Henson had his rôle as the schoolboy, Henry, enlarged to put him on a par with Grossmith, the score was remade (a good half of the original survived with 'additional lyrics by Desmond Carter'), and, with a cast including Heather Thatcher (Victoria) and Adrienne Brune (June), the old piece ran for another 139 performances. The show was still to be seen touring the British provinces in the 1940s.

In 1916 J C Williamson Ltd produced *Tonight's the Night* in Australia. Charles Workman (Montagu), Alfred Frith (Dudley), Connie Ediss (Victoria), Dorothy Brunton (June), Daisy Yates (Beatrice), Maud Fane (Angela), Fred Maguire (Henry) and Field Fisher (Robin) headed the cast which played six weeks in Melbourne and seven in Sydney (Her Majesty's Theatre 23 September 1916) in what was basically a repertoire season.

UK: Gaiety Theatre 28 April 1915; Australia: Her Majesty's Theatre, Melbourne 8 July 1916

TOOLE, J[ohn] L[aurence] (b London, 12 March ?1830; d London, 30 January 1906).

One of the greatest British comic actors of the Victorian era, 'Johnnie' Toole, like most of the other top comedy performers of his time, moved happily in and out of the musical productions which were often staged as one part of a two-or three-part programme. In 1866 he was London's first Agamemnon in *La Belle Hélène* and Popinoff in *Jeanne qui pleure et Jean qui rit*, and whilst engaged at the Gaiety Theatre in the early 1870s he introduced the rôle of Cabriolo in the English première of *La Princesse de Trébizonde*, played Ko-kil-ko in *Aladdin II* and the title-rôle in *Thespis* and appeared in such burlesques as *Guy Fawkes* (Fawkes), *Ali Baba à la Mode* (Ali Baba) and *Don Giovanni* (Giovanni). He later included the one-act operetta *Mr Guffin's Elopement* with its comical song 'The Speaker's Eye' in his repertoire and produced and played in the extravaganza *The Great Taykin* and a number of burlesques (*Paw Claudian*, *The O'Dora*, *Stage Dora*, *Faust and Loose* et al) during his tenancy of Toole's Theatre.

Autobiography: w Hatton, J: *Reminiscences of J L Toole Related by Himself* (Hurst and Blackett, London, 1889)

TOO MANY GIRLS Musical comedy in 2 acts by George Marion jr. Lyrics by Lorenz Hart. Music by Richard Rodgers. Imperial Theater, New York, 18 October 1939.

Too Many Girls was, in spite of its title, a college musical set – like all good college musicals – around that most important element of college life, a football game. Its footballing leading lad (Richard Kollmar), however, was not what he seemed: he was really one of the four bodyguards (Desi Arnaz, Eddie Bracken, Hal LeRoy) infiltrated into Pottawatomie College by rich and influential Harvey Casey

to keep an eye on his wayward student daughter, Consuelo (Marcy Westcott). When Consuelo finds she has fallen in love with her father's stool-pigeon, she threatens to leave town on the day of the big match duly followed, in the course of their bodyguarding duty, by four all-important parts of the school's team. True love and Pottawatomie are, naturally, finally triumphant.

Rodgers and Hart's bookful of songs for this unpretentious and lightweight show brought up a handful of winners including the leading pair's pretty 'I Didn't Know What Time it Was', the comical-topical rubbishing of New York in 'Give it Back to the Indians' and an enduring cry against those so-called 'arrangers' who tear a composer's work to ribbons, 'I'd Like to Recognize the Tune'.

Too Many Girls ran 249 Broadway performances and was subsequently filmed with Bracken, Arnaz and LeRoy backing up Richard Carlson, Lucille Ball and Ann Miller but, in spite of using seven of the show's songs, without 'Give it Back to the Indians' or 'I'd Like to Recognize the Tune'.

Film: RKO 1940
Recording: selection (Painted Smiles)

TOP BANANA Musical comedy in 2 acts by Hy Kraft. Music and lyrics by Johnny Mercer. Winter Garden Theater, New York, 1 November 1951.

Phil Silvers was the 'top banana' (American burlesque lingo for chief comedian) of this musical show about show-business, which was constructed around, and existed in order to feature, a series of tried and true variety and burlesque routines. The tiny story which framed these routines cast Silvers as Jerry Biffle, burlesque star turned television comedian, who loses the girl (Judy Lynn) picked to star alongside him in the Blendo Soap show to the handsome young singer of the affair (Lindy Doherty), and (temporarily) also drops his top spot to the appealing young couple.

Johnny Mercer supplied the songs, allowing Silvers to explain what it was to be a 'Top Banana', to encourage his new partner that 'You're OK for TV', to vaunt the advantages of a snappy sell for Blendo (Slogan Song) or burble cheerfully through the speciality number 'A Word a Day'. The romantic musical moments fell to the juvenile pair ('Only if You're in Love', 'That's for Sure') and there was a heroine's-best-friend (Rose Marie) to wallop out a comical 'I Fought Every Step of the Way' and head the production number 'Sans Souci'.

Paula Stone and Mike Sloane's production ran for 350 performances on Broadway, but the show did not prove to be a money-maker. A film version of a reduced version of the stage show was made, but the made-for-Silvers *Top Banana* did not have a theatre afterlife beyond regional revivals with Silvers (1964) and Milton Berle (1963) featured.

Film: United Artists 1954
Recording: original cast (Capitol)

TOPOL [Chaim] (b Tel Aviv, Israel, 9 September 1935).

The Israeli actor known simply as 'Topol' had a considerable success in the rôle of Tevye in the London production of *Fiddler on the Roof* (1967) and later in the film version (1971) of the same musical, but his subsequent ventures into the musical theatre (Aimable in *The Baker's Wife*, *R Loves J*, and, improbably, replacing Len Cariou in the title-rôle of *Ziegfeld*) were less successful. He reprised his *Fiddler* rôle on the stage on a number of occasions, making a late Broadway début as Tevye in 1990.

In 1974 Topol directed the Israeli musical play *Dominos* at London's Shaw Theatre (30 April).

THE TOREADOR   Musical comedy in 2 acts by James T Tanner and Harry Nicholls. Lyrics by Adrian Ross and Percy Greenbank. Music by Ivan Caryll and Lionel Monckton. Gaiety Theatre, London, 17 June 1901.

The last musical to be produced at the original Gaiety Theatre, *The Toreador* was also one of the most successful. Constructed by the tried and hugely successful Gaiety team of writers (plus newcomer Percy Greenbank, having his first full Gaiety credit with this show) for the tried and hugely successful Gaiety team of performers, *The Toreador* featured top comic Teddy Payne as Sammy Gigg, a little 'tiger' who gets mixed up with a luscious señora (Queenie Leighton) and a Carlist conspiracy in deepest Spain. Also on the Spanish roads were juvenile lady Dora Selby (Marie Studholme) and the fake husband (Florence Collingbourne as best friend Nancy) she sports to avert a blind marriage to Augustus Traill (Lionel Mackinder), the voluminous Mrs Malton Hoppings (Claire Romaine) with her toreador fiancé (Herbert Clayton) and his angry rival for her charms, animal dealer Pettifer (Fred Wright), not to mention man-about-town Sir Archie Slackitt (George Grossmith), soubrette Susan (Violet Lloyd) and a massed force of Gaiety Girls.

Payne got into toreador costume to help Donna Teresa in her naughty political mission and ended up facing bulls and bombs as the plot thickened dramatically between the songs. Amongst the musical numbers, Grossmith scored well with a couple of typical dude-y numbers, 'Everybody's Awfully Good to Me' and 'Archie', Clayton had a baritonic Toreador's Song, Miss Romaine sighed comically 'I'm Romantic' and Miss Collingbourne sang the wry soprano 'The Language of the Flowers', but the hit of the evening was a little character number given to the young Gertie Miller, in a tiny rôle, telling the boys to 'Keep Off the Grass'.

Miss Miller's rôle soon expanded to take in other songs ('Captivating Cora' et al) as the show rolled on to success, and the score underwent further alterations when Connie Ediss arrived back at the Gaiety and took over the rôle of Mrs Malton Hoppings which had been made to her measure. In April 1902, Edwardes even announced a 'new edition' and, by the time the show and the famous old theatre closed down *The Toreador* had been played 675 times. The Gaiety run was, however, only the beginning of the success of what would ultimately be one of the most internationally successful of all the Gaiety musicals. The show was quickly out into the provinces and the colonies, and London's triumph was repeated on Broadway when Nixon and Zimmerman mounted a version of *The Toreador* with Francis Wilson in Payne's rôle alongside Adele Ritchie (Dora), Melville Ellis (Traill), Christie MacDonald (Nancy) and Joseph Coyne (Archie), and little in the way of interpolated music, for a season of 121 performances prior to touring. In Australia J C Williamson presented the piece with George Lauri starred in the principal comic part and Carrie Moore (Susan), Lulu Evans (Nancy) and Maud Chetwynd (Dora) heading the female team, in South Africa

Myles Clifton and Victor Gouriet featured, and *The Toreador* even made it to Gibraltar.

Gabor Steiner's Viennese successes with the Gaiety's *The Circus Girl* and *The Messenger Boy* undoubtedly encouraged Karczag and Wallner at the Theater an der Wien to snap up *The Toreador* ahead of him. Their production of Richard Wilde's version – advertised as a 'spectacular Operette' – featured Siegmund Natzler as Archie, Franz Glawatsch as the Governor of Villaya, Dora Keplinger (Dora, provided with a Siegmund Eibenschütz 'English' number called 'Shoking!'), Louise Robinson (Nancy, equipped with a real English interpolation, W Wesley Wells's 'Singe, singe, Vöglein') and Carlo Böhm (Gigg, interpolating a Will Marion Cook song, 'Liebesabentuer'). However, *Der Toreador* proved no match for the theatre's other main novelty of the season, Eysler's *Bruder Straubinger* with Girardi starred in its title-rôle, and the English piece was played only 25 times. It nevertheless continued on to Hungary (ad Andor Letzkó) where it was mounted at Budapest's Király Színház.

In France, however, the show had a triumph on a par with its English one. The enormous success of *The Belle of New York* at the Moulin-Rouge prompted the management to stage further foreign musical comedies there and, amongst those which followed, *Le Toréador* (ad Arnold Fordyce, Jacques Bousquet) was the most successful, outdoing even its famous predecessor in popularity. With comics Prince and Claudius heading the fun, it ran for half the year and was brought back again the following season (9 April 1905) for a second run.

Back home, *The Toreador* toured happily for a number of seasons after its London run but, like all its fellow Gaiety musical comedies since *The Shop Girl*, it was never taken back to London.

USA: Knickerbocker Theater 6 January 1902; Australia: Her Majesty's Theatre, Melbourne 11 October 1902; Austria: Theater an der Wien 19 September 1903; Hungary: Király Színház *A Toreador* 26 February 1904; France: Théâtre du Moulin-Rouge 18 June 1904

TOSTÉE, Lucille   French opéra-bouffe star who led the export of the genre to America.

Although Lucille Tostée was to make the most famous part of her career in America, she began her life on the stage in France, becoming one of Offenbach's principal interpreters at the Théâtre des Bouffes-Parisiens at a young age. Amongst her assignments at the Bouffes, she was the original Amoroso of his *Le Pont des soupirs* (1861), donned skirts to play Béatrix in the Parisian version of *Les Bavards* (1863) and went back into travesty in the rôle of Fabricio in *Il Signor Fagotto* (1864). She appeared with the Bouffes company at Vienna's Theater am Franz-Josefs-Kai in 1861 (Croute-au-pot in *Mesdames de la Halle*, Fanchette in *Une nuit blanche*, Pierrette in *La Rose de Saint-Flour*, Atala in *Vent du soir*) and in 1862 (Dorothée in *La Bonne d'enfants* etc). After the advent of Zulma Bouffar, Tostée apparently found less favour in Offenbach's eyes, but her career did not by any means go downwards as a result.

In 1867 Lucille Tostée headed a troupe exported from Paris under the management of H L Bateman to play French opéra-bouffe at New York's Théâtre Français. On 24 September she opened in America as Offenbach's *Grande-Duchesse de Gérolstein* and she took the town by storm, launching at the same time the craze for opéra-bouffe which was to sweep the country over the following years. She appeared through that season and the next in a variety of such pieces including *La Belle Hélène*, *Lischen et Fritzchen*, as Eurydice in *Orphée aux enfers*, and in her original rôle from *Les Bavards*, sharing the star billing in later days with Mlle Irma, who had been starring in an opposition production of *Barbe-bleue* and who amalgamated her forces with Bateman's to reinforce a company which was by that time being challenged for opéra-bouffe supremacy by a team brought out by Jacob Grau and headed by Rose Bell, Marie Desclauzas and Gabel.

Equipped with some fairly dubious advertising – Tostée's Eurydice was described as 'her original rôle played by her 300 nights in Paris' – the pair continued, increasing their repertoire with such pieces as *Monsieur Choufleuri* (with Tostée in the vocally demanding rôle of Ernestine), *Le Mariage aux lanternes*, *La Chanson de Fortunio* (Valentin) and Maillart's *Les Dragons de Villars*. When Tostée left America after less than two years, the flood that she and *La Grande-Duchesse* had begun continued in the hands of artists such as Irma, Marie Aimée, Léa Silly, Céline Montaland and Marie Desclauzas.

TOTO Opérette in 3 acts by Paul Bilhaud and Albert Barré. Music by Antoine Banès. Théâtre des Menus-Plaisirs, Paris, 10 June 1892.

Banès's one great international success, *Toto* was a vaudevillesque piece with a splendid dual-sex lead rôle to its tale of an identical (well, presumably not quite identical) twin brother and sister, Toto and Tata Bernard, who find it useful to swap places temporarily. Tata (Rosalia Lambrecht) elopes with her preferred gentleman, Gaston Ferrier, disguised in Toto's army uniform, whilst Toto (also Mlle Lambrecht), dressed up in Tata's skirts, takes it under his charge to get rid of the unwanted suitor, Cabestan, who has been wished on her by the interfering director of his military academy, Dupalet, and his sister Aurélie. Toto stands in for Tata at her betrothal as the girl takes flight. Everyone winds up in a Railway hotel in the final act – Gaston and Tata waiting for their train to safety, Cabestan with Césarine Bassinet, the little bit of fluff whom he had got a job as nurse at the academy, Dupalet and papa Bernard chasing the runaways, as well as a lubricious old Academy inspector called Blanchart, and, of course, Toto who presides over a happy ending. Mlle Derly, Fanny Génat, Charpentier, André Simon, Vandenne and Saint-Léon completed the cast and *Toto* found a real success in Paris, running through 130 performances in its initial run at the Théâtre des Menus-Plaisirs, before going on to the provinces and to productions around the world.

In Vienna, *Tata-Toto* was the first opérette staged under the management of J Wild at the Theater in der Josefstadt (ad F Zell, Victor Léon) and, with Frln Dworak starring, supported by such performers as Carl Adolf Friese (Bernard), Otto Maran (Blanchard) and Viktoria Pohl-Meiser (Aurelie) it proved an enormous success, running up a quite outstanding 100 successive nights, 16 further performances in repertoire, and encouraging the management to repeat the experiment of, in particular, French vaudeville-opérettes over a number of years. *Les Petites Brebis*, *Le Voyage de Corbillon* and *Le Papa de Francine* were further successes, but only the vast and international

triumph of the Josefstädter Theater's *Les Fêtards* ever outdid the record set up there by the hugely popular *Toto*.

The Vienna version was smartly picked up for a German production at Hamburg's ever-interesting Carl-Schultze Theater whose company subsequently took the show to Berlin, and also for the German-language Irving Place Theater in New York, whilst Budapest's Népszinház followed on with a good 30-performance season of Klara Küry playing *Toto és Tata* (ad Emil Makai) in an Hungarian adaptation.

The show did less well, however, in what appear to have been some underpowered English-language versions. A first British adaptation (ad A M Thompson, J J Wood, E Boyd-Jones) was produced by Willie Edouin in Leeds in 1897 with Marie Montrose starred alongside E J Lonnen (Cabestan), Roland Cunningham (Gaston) and Alys Rees (Cezarine). It fizzled out on the road, but nine years later Edouin tried again. He had the piece revised, and mounted it under the unfortunate pantomime-sounding title of *Jack and Jill* (ad Barton White) at Manchester's Gaiety Theatre with Stella Gastelle starred. Again, it did not find its way to London. In America a heavily revised version, with Banès's score replaced by some pieces by the ex-Austrian Alfred Müller-Norden, was produced by Nathaniel Roth in 1904 (Princess Theater 30 September) under the title *The West Point Cadet*. Della Fox featured in the dual lead rôle, suported by Joseph Herbert in the rôle of Washington Graft (a name which gives some idea of the style of the adaptation) for four Broadway performances of a show which was ultimately a rip-off, rather than a production, of *Toto*.

Another musical play called *Toto* was produced in Britain in 1916 (Duke of York's Theatre, 19 April). Written by Gladys Unger with lyrics by Arthur Anderson and music by Archibald Joyce and Merlin Morgan, it was a musical adaptation of Alfred Capus's *Les Deux Écoles* and its Toto (Mabel Russell) was a little Parisian person who set married men in a whirl. She lasted only 77 performances in London, but she toured happily for several years and the show even got itself produced in Budapest (Lujza Blaha Színház, 7 April 1922, ad Zsolt Harsányi).

The title *Toto* was also used in Austria for the local adaptation of Meilhac, Halévy and Offenbach's *Le Château à Toto*, produced at the Carltheater in 1869.

Austria: Theater in der Josefstadt *Tata-Toto* 28 September 1894; Germany: Carl-Schultze Theater, Hamburg 25 December 1894, Neues Theater, Berlin 18 May 1895; Hungary: Népszinház *Toto és Tata* 5 April 1895; USA: Irving Place Theater 4 February 1896; UK: Grand Theatre, Leeds *Toto and Tata* 23 August 1897, Gaiety Theatre, Manchester *Jack and Jill* 29 October 1906

TOULMOUCHE, Frédéric [Michel] (b Nantes, 3 August 1850; d Paris, 20 February 1909).

A composer for his own pleasure rather than with any career thoughts in mind, Toulmouche studied music under Massé in Paris and thereafter contributed scores to the opérette stage for some 30 years, winning some agreeable success with some attractive work, but without ever penning the one major work which might have brought him full-scale success. His first full-length opérette, *Le Moutier de Saint-Guignolet*, was produced in Belgium with sufficient success for it to be taken up for Paris where, revised, and produced under the title of *La Veillée de noces*, it had a good run of over

50 nights at the Menus-Plaisirs. It was subsequently produced in London as *The Wedding Eve* (Trafalgar Square Theatre September 1892). His *Mademoiselle ma femme* was played for 72 Parisian performances with Rosalia Lambrecht in the central rôle, whilst *Tante Agnès*, first seen at the Paris Olympia, was later played in Budapest as *Ágnes Néni* (ad Dezső Vidor, Magyar Színház September 1899).

Toulmouche's other stage works included the ballets *Les Deux Tentations* (1895) for the Nouveau Théâtre, *Pierrot au Hammam* (1897) for the Olympia and *Madame Malbrouck* (1898 w H José) for the Casino de Paris.

He was, for a period, director of the Théâtre des Menus-Plaisirs.

1882 **Ah! le Bon Billet** (Bureau-Jattiot [ie E Bureau, F Jattiot]) 1 act Théâtre de la Renaissance 6 December

1885 **Le Moutier de Saint-Guignolet** (Bureau-Jattiot) Galeries Saint-Hubert, Brussels 5 May

1888 **La Veillée de noces** revised *Le Moutier de Saint-Guignolet* ad Alexandre Bisson Théâtre des Menus-Plaisirs 27 November

1892 **La Belle au coeur dormant** 1 act Le Clou 25 January

1892 **L'Âme de la patrie** (Lionel Bonnemère) 1 act St Brieuc 9 July

1893 **Mademoiselle ma femme** (Maurice Ordonneau, Octave Pradels) Théâtre des Menus-Plaisirs 5 May

1894 **La Chanson du roi** (Bonnemère) 1 act Fougères 7 January

1895 **La Perle du Cantal** (Ordonneau) Théâtre des Folies-Dramatiques 2 March

1895 **La Saint-Valentin** (Ordonneau, Fernand Beissier) Théâtre des Bouffes-Parisiens 28 March

1896 **Le Lézard** (Armand Liorat, William Busnach) 1 act Scala 29 August

1896 **Tante Agnès** (Maxime Boucheron) Olympia 27 October

1899 **La Rêve de Madame X** (Louis Lagarde, Georges Montignac) 1 act Carillon 25 March

1899 **Les Trois Couleurs** (Georges Arnould, H de Vrécourt) 1 act Olympia 29 March

1904 **Auto-Joujou** (Félix Puget) 1 act Théâtre des Capucines 24 September

1908 **La Môme Flora** (Ordonneau, Pradels) Théâtre de la Scala 26 December

1909 **Chez la sonnambule** (Bisson) 1 act Théâtre Grévin 24 March

1910 **La Demoiselle du Tabarin** (w Edmond Diet, Edmond Missa/Ordonneau, André Alexandre) Théâtre du Château d'Eau 25 March

1911 **La Marquise de Chicago** (Ordonneau, Beissier, Louis Hérel) Enghien 26 September

THE TOURISTS Musical comedy in 2 acts by R H Burnside. Music by Gustave Kerker. Daly's Theater, New York, 25 August 1906.

In the course of 24 hours in Rangapang in the Hindustan, a young American, John Duke (Alfred Hickman), who has escaped the not-very-eagle eye of his hopeless tutor, Timothy Todd (Richard Golden), gets mixed up with a rajah (William Pruette) and a princess (Vera Michelena), a Yankee multi-millionaire called Benjamin Blossom (Phil Ryley) toting five marriageable daughters headed by Dora (Julia Sanderson), all of whom he destines for titled gentlemen, their governess (Della Niven), and a bandit (Albert Froom) impersonating the Boojam of Bangalore. Since John is a 'Duke' it is safe betting that the eldest Blossom daughter will be his by the time the comical complications of two acts have been ironed out. The Princess, who was supposed to marry the (real) Boojam of Bangalore gets the Captain of the Guard (Howard Chambers) with

whom she has been singing about 'A Game of Hearts'. W H Denny, formerly of D'Oyly Carte's Savoy Theatre company and the original Grand Inquisitor of *The Gondoliers*, played Loofah, the owner of the Hotel Oriental, and George A Schiller was the ex-court physician.

Both the book and the score of *The Tourists* showed that their writers had studied – and borrowed from – many of the more successful musical comedies of the recent years as well as a few comic operas from further back. Kerker's score included a traditional entry song for the Rajah, some pattering pieces for Timothy Todd, a waltz declaring 'Love is a Wonderful Thing', a *Florodora*-style double quartet ('Which One Shall We Marry?'), the latest in the line of songs hymning 'Dear Old Broadway' (with a verse for Philadelphia as well), and a dance speciality called 'The Gnomes'.

If originality was not precisely rife, the combination was nevertheless jolly enough to please, and Sam and Lee Shubert's production of *The Tourists* ran for a more than useful 124 performances on Broadway before continuing its life on the road.

TOURS, Frank E[dward] (b London, 1 September 1877; d Los Angeles, 2 February 1963). Conductor, arranger, orchestrator and sometime composer to the musical stage on both sides of the Atlantic.

The son of the well-known conductor, composer and arranger Berthold Tours, Frank Tours studied music at the Royal College of Music in London and was employed thereafter, for many years, as a theatre conductor. At the age of 21 he was musical director for Marie Lloyd's tour of Granville Bantock's musical comedy *The ABC*, and over the next 20 years he conducted shows in a series of London theatres (*Lady Madcap*, *The Little Cherub*, *The Gay Gordons*, *The Dashing Little Duke*, *Captain Kidd*, *Irene* et al) and, latterly and increasingly, in American houses (*The Kiss Waltz*, *Tonight's the Night*, *Follow Me*, *Irene*, *Love o' Mike*, *Rock-a-Bye Baby*, *The Lady in Red*, *Mecca*, several editions of the *Ziegfeld Follies*, *Smiles*, *Face the Music*, *As Thousands Cheer*, *Jubilee*, the *Music Box Revues*, *Red, Hot and Blue* etc). He was also, for a period, musical director at the Plaza picture theatre in London.

As a composer, he made an early attempt at comic opera with a musical version of *The Lady of Lyons*, but he was best known as an adept at the additional number, composing songs or part-scores for such pieces as *Mr Wix of Wickham*, *The Dairymaids*, *The Little Cherub*, *See See*, *The New Aladdin*, Broadway's semi-British *The Hoyden*, and *The Gay Gordons*. He turned down the opportunity to write the full score for the last-named piece, but he did write the whole music for Seymour Hicks's subsequent *The Dashing Little Duke*, only to find it perforated with Jerome Kern numbers in the course of the run. After the limited success of this piece, he returned to composing piece-work and wrote individual songs for a number of further shows, including *Mr Manhattan* (1916), *Follow Me* (1916), *Mayflowers* (1925) and *Blue Eyes* (1928) as well as for the music halls ('Beyond the Sunset', 'Red Rose', 'In Flanders Fields'). His only other full score was that for the musical comedy *Girl o' Mine* (including a song 'Silver Lining'), produced by Elisabeth Marbury and the Shuberts for 48 performances in 1918 and then taken around America as *The Victory Girl*. He later adapted the British adaptation of *Walzer aus Wien* for

Broadway and spent six years working for Paramount Pictures in Britain and in America.

In spite of his long period as a contributor to the musical stage, Tours's most successful single song was not a show number but his setting of Rudyard Kipling's 'Mother o' Mine' as performed by Richard Crooks et al.

1901 **Melnotte, or The Gardener's Bride** (Arthur Anderson/Herbert Shelley) Coronet Theater 30 September

1902 **Mr Wix of Wickham** (w Frank Seddon, George Everard, Herbert Darnley/Darnley) Borough Theatre, Stratford East 21 July

1906 **The Dairymaids** (w Paul Rubens/Rubens, Arthur Wimperis/Alexander M Thompson, Robert Courtneidge) Apollo Theatre 14 April

1907 **The Hoyden** (w Rubens/Tristan Bernard ad Cosmo Hamilton) Knickerbocker Theater, New York 19 October

1909 **The Dashing Little Duke** (Adrian Ross/Seymour Hicks) Hicks Theatre 17 February

1910 **Little Johnnie Jones** (Preston Wayne/H M Vernon) 1 act Tottenham Palace 9 May

1911 **La Belle Paree** (w Jerome Kern/Edward Madden/Edgar Smith) Winter Garden, New York 20 March

1912 **O-Mi-Iy** (w Herman Finck/Hicks) 1 act London Hippodrome 25 March

1918 **Girl o' Mine** (aka *Oh Mama!*) (w Augustus Barrett/Philip Bartholomae) Bijou Theater, New York 28 January

1918 **The Victory Girl** revised *Girl o' Mine* (ad Alex Sullivan, Lynn Cowan) Syracuse, 16 November

1920 **Mimi** (w Adolf Philipp/Edward Paulton/Paulton, Philipp) Shubert Belasco Theater, Washington 14 March

TOVARICH Musical comedy in 2 acts by David Shaw based on the play by Jacques Deval as adapted by Robert E Sherwood. Lyrics by Anne Crosswell. Music by Lee Pockriss. Broadway Theater, New York, 18 March 1963.

A musical adaptation of the successful 1933 French play (subsequently played widely in translation and filmed with Claudette Colbert and Charles Boyer in its lead rôles), *Tovarich* featured Vivien Leigh (Tony Award) and Jean-Pierre Aumont as the Russian émigré couple Grand Duchess Tatiana Petrovna and Prince Mikhail Alexandrovitch Ouratieff who are reduced to taking jobs as servants in the Parisian household of Pennsylvania businessman Charles Davis (George S Irving). The younger members of the Davis household (Byron Mitchell, Margery Gray) are very taken with their new servants, but the pair are of even more substantial interest to the financial community as they are caretaking a vast sum of money entrusted to them by the murdered Czar. By the end of the play that trust has been betrayed: they have not taken the cash for themselves, but they have been conned by communist Commissar Gorotchenko (Alexander Scourby) in giving it to him to help 'feed the starving peasants in Russia'. The Grand-Ducal pair remain servants.

The musical part of *Tovarich* was provided by Anne Crosswell and Lee Pockriss, a pair who had earlier made an off-Broadway musical out of *The Importance of Being Earnest*, and the piece was produced on Broadway by Abel Farman and Sylvia Harris for a 264-performance run, a run largely boosted by Miss Leigh's presence and performance. A German adaptation by Gert Wilden sr and jr was produced at Aachen in 1981.

Germany: Stadttheater, Aachen *Towarischtsch* 23 February 1981
Recording: original cast (Capitol/EMI)

TOYE, Wendy (b London, 1 May 1917).

Originally a dancer, Miss Toye appeared in the musical theatre as the child, Marigold, in Fraser-Simson's *Toad of Toad Hall* (1930), in the spectacular *The Golden Toy* (1934), *Tulip Time* (1935) and *Follow the Girls* (1945) and played the rôle of Winnie in the London production of *Annie Get Your Gun* (1948). She had, by this time, already developed a considerable career as a choreographer and a director, arranging the dances for a long list of revues and for such musicals as *The Lisbon Story*, *Panama Hattie*, *Jenny Jones*, *Gay Rosalinda* and *Follow the Girls*, and staging C B Cochran's productions of *Big Ben* and *Bless the Bride*.

She subsequently directed a long series of London musical productions including *Tough at the Top*, *And So to Bed*, *Wild Thyme*, *Lady at the Wheel*, the famous Sadler's Wells production of *Orpheus in the Underworld* and its fellow versions of *La Vie parisienne* and *Die Fledermaus*, *Virtue in Danger*, the long-running *Robert and Elizabeth*, *On the Level*, the Theatre Royal, Drury Lane version of *The Great Waltz* and the 1971 revival of *Show Boat*, as well as the Chichester Festival musicals *R Loves J* and *Follow the Star*, the revue *Cowardy Custard*, and musicals, operas and light operas from Newbury to Turkey in a continuing career of more than 60 years in the theatre.

LES TRAVAUX D'HERCULE Opéra-bouffe in 3 acts by Gaston de Caillavet and Robert de Flers. Music by Claude Terrasse. Théâtre des Bouffes-Parisiens, Paris, 7 March 1901.

Following Terrasse's first opéra-bouffe success with *La Petite Femme de Loth* (1900), the composer joined with the playwriting couple who were generally agreed to be the most 'spirituel' of all Parisian comic writers, de Flers and de Caillavet, on another burlesque of things ancient in *Les Travaux d'Hercule*. In their version of mythology, we learn that it was not the lazy, cowardly, barely potent demi-god Hercules (Abel Tarride), after all, who accomplished the famous twelve labours, but the owner of those infamous stables which were the object of one of the labours, Augias, King of Elis (Colas). This extravagantly physical and energetic fellow not only zooms around doing labours, he also borrows Hercules's neglected wife, Omphale (Amélie Diéterle), and labours over her. But in the end, she finds all this energy and enthusiasm rather more than she can take and, labours or no labours, goes back to her more passive demi-god who has somehow ended up with all the credit for everything. Amongst the supporting cast Victor Henry played Palémon, a demi-demi god, and Léo Demoulin was the amazonian Erichtona.

Produced by André Lénéka and Tarride at the Bouffes-Parisiens, *Les Travaux d'Hercule* won delighted praise from those who welcomed the return of 'Offenbachian' opéra-bouffe, but its first run was limited to little more than 80 performances. It was subsequently produced in Hungary (ad Adolf Merei, Ernő Keszthelyi) and in Germany and was revived in Paris in 1913 (3 October), at the Théâtre Féminа with Gabriel Signoret (Hercule), Henri Fabert (Augias) and Edmée Favart (Omphale) featured, in a version revised by the composer which provided the female star with a new Laughing Song. Like the bulk of the Terrasse/de Flers and de Caillavet works, however, it remains more talked-about than performed.

The same title was used for a piece with music and text by Antoine Duhamel produced at the Opéra de Lyon in 1981.

Hungary: Király Színhâz *Herkules Munkái* 25 April 1902; Germany: Neues Operetten-Theater, Leipzig *Die Arbeiten des Herkules* 28 March 1908

Recording: complete (Gaîté-Lyrique)

A TREE GROWS IN BROOKLYN

Musical play in 2 acts by Betty Smith and George Abbott based on the novel of the same name by Betty Smith. Lyrics by Dorothy Fields. Music by Arthur Schwartz. Alvin Theater, New York, 19 April 1951.

A highly successful novel, then a film, then a stage musical, Betty Smith's gentle, downbeat tale of unexceptional Brooklyn folk, as remade with songs, followed the amorous misfortunes of sisters Katie (Marcia van Dyke) and Cissy (Shirley Booth) through a decade and a half of the early years of the 20th century. Sincere, faithful Katie is unlucky enough to put her trust in the charming but weak and downfallen-by-drink Johnny Nolan (Johnny Johnston) who is unable to keep a job and brings her little but sorrow, whilst flippant Cissy goes from one beau to another, christening each one Harry after the fondly remembered first (Albert Linville) until he returns and turns out a disappointment. By the finale, widowed Katie has put her hopes in daughter Francie (Nomi Mitty) and Cissy has settled for a back-number beau (Nathaniel Frey). The score of the show ranged from the comical, as in Cissie's memories of her first love ('He Had Refinement') to the lively in Johnny's 'I'm Like a New Broom' and the polka-ed wedding ensemble 'Look Who's Dancing', to Katie's heartfelt 'Make the Man Love Me', set alongside a group of ballads and a rather pasted-in (but, for the period, obligatory) Halloween ballet.

George Abbott and Robert Fryer's production won many friends, Miss Booth and her endearingly comic performance, which had become (in contrast to book and film) the centre of the evening, won more, but *A Tree Grows in Brooklyn* failed to establish itself and its 270 Broadway performances and a tour, led by Joan Blondell (who had been Sissy in the novel's 1945 film version), did not encourage anyone else to take it up.

Recording: original cast (Columbia)

TRÉFEU [DE TRÉVAL], Étienne [Victor]

(b Saint-Lô, 25 September 1821; d Paris, June 1903).

A prolific songwriter for the Parisian cafés-concerts, Tréfeu moved into the musical theatre with the rise of the small comic opérette in the mid-1850s. He wrote or co-wrote the texts for a large number of such little pieces, amongst the earliest of which the crazy medieval *Croquefer*, set by his friend Offenbach, and *Les Petits Prodiges* with a score by Émile Jonas, were successfully played at Offenbach's Théâtre des Bouffes-Parisiens. It was, however, his first full-length work, a further but much more substantial piece of medieval burlesque, *Geneviève de Brabant*, which gave Tréfeu his first big international success, a success which was repeated a few years later when, after the unsuccessful *Die Rheinnixen*, *Coscoletto* and some further happy one-act pieces (*Jeanne qui pleure et Jean qui rit*, *Il Signor Fagotto*, *Le Soldat magicien*), he again combined with Offenbach and with Charles Nuitter on the greatly successful comic opera *La Princesse de Trébizonde*.

Thereafter, although he adapted the libretti of *Javotte* (from Alfred Thompson's English original), *Boule de neige* (with music from the unsuccessful *Barkouf*) and *Le Chat du Diable* (from H B Farnie's original *Whittington*), he co-authored only one further original full-length work of any significance, the Émile Jonas *Goldchignon/Chignon d'or* which, although produced in Vienna in translation and in Brussels, was never played in Paris. His output in these later years of his writing life was mainly limited to little pieces for the cafés-concerts where he had begun his writing career and for the salons of Paris.

Tréfeu apparently also had a hand in the first draft of the text for Offenbach's *Le Violoneux*, but he received no credit alongside MM Chevalet and Mestépès on the finished work.

1854 **Les Echos de Rosine** (Alphonse Thys) 1 act Paris Salon 13 October

1855 **Le Rêve d'une nuit d'été** (Jacques Offenbach) 1 act Théâtre des Bouffes-Parisiens 30 July

1855 **Les Trois Troubadours** (Julien Nargeot) 1 act Folies-Nouvelles 19 December

1857 **Croquefer, ou Le Dernier des paladins** (Offenbach/w Adolphe Jaime) 1 act Théâtre des Bouffes-Parisiens 12 February

1857 **Les Petits Prodiges** (Émile Jonas/w Jaime) Théâtre des Bouffes-Parisiens 19 November

1859 **Geneviève de Brabant** (Offenbach) Théâtre des Bouffes-Parisiens 19 November

1863 **Il Signor Fagotto** (Offenbach/w Charles Nuitter) 1 act Ems 11 July

1864 **Die Rheinnixen** (Offenbach/w Nuitter) Hofoper, Vienna 4 February

1864 **Jeanne qui pleure et Jean qui rit** (Offenbach/w Nuitter) 1 act Ems July

1864 **Le Soldat magicien** (aka *Le Fifre enchanté*) (Offenbach/w Nuitter) 1 act Ems 9 July

1865 **Coscoletto** (Offenbach/w Nuitter) Ems 24 July

1868 **En manches de chemise** (Étienne Ettling/w Émile Mendel) 1 act Alcazar 2 April

1868 **Un bal à la Sous-Préfecture** (A de Villebichot) 1 act Alcazar

1868 **L'Invalide à la tête de bois** (Maximilien Graziani) 1 act Odéon, 3 April

1869 **La Princesse de Trébizonde** (Offenbach/w Nuitter) Baden-Baden 31 July

1869 **La Romance de la rose** (Offenbach/Jules Prével) 1 act Théâtre des Bouffes-Parisiens 11 December

1871 **Javotte** (*Cinderella the Younger*) French version w Nuitter (Théâtre de l'Athénée)

1871 **Boule de neige** revised *Barkouf* w Nuitter Théâtre des Bouffes-Parisiens 14 December

1872 **Le Nain** (Ettling) 1 act Café Tertulia 19 November

1873 **Le Tigre** (Ettling) 1 act Café Tertulia 5 April

1873 **Der Goldchignon** (*Chignon d'or*) (Émile Jonas/w Eugène Grangé) Strampfertheater, Vienna 20 May; Théâtre des Fantaisies-Parisiennes, Brussels 17 October 1874

1874 **L'Oeil de M Expert** (Ettling) 1 act Eldorado 21 November

1880 **Monsieur de Floridor** (Théodore de Lajarte/w Nuitter) 1 act Opéra-Comique 11 October

1889 **Le Marché aux domestiques** (Luigi Bordèse) 1 act Le Creuzot

1892 **Chien et chatte** (G Bornier/de Forges ad w Hubert) 1 act Eden-Concert 21 May

1893 **Le Chat du Diable** (*Whittington*) French version w Nuitter (Théâtre du Châtelet)

1897 **La Gaudriole** (Albert Vizentini/w Nuitter) Aix-les-Bains 12 September

TRELAWNY Musical in 2 acts by Aubrey Woods, George Rowell and Julian Slade taken from *Trelawny of the Wells* by Arthur Wing Pinero. Book by Aubrey Woods. Music and lyrics by Julian Slade. Theatre Royal, Bristol, 12 January 1972; Sadler's Wells Theatre, London, 27 June 1972.

Pinero's pretty period tale told of actress Rose Trelawny (Hayley Mills) who leaves her profession to move to Cavendish Square and become affianced to Arthur Gower (John Watts), the son of the lofty Sir William Gower (Timothy West). Stiflingly unhappy in this new world, she runs back to the theatre only to find that her acting abilities have deserted her. But in the new, naturalistic play written by the ever-faithful Tom Wrench (Ian Richardson), Rose is cast opposite a new actor – Arthur has come to join his beloved Rose in her world. Slade's score turned out some truly touching numbers – Rose's thoughts of 'The One Who isn't There', Arthur's letter to his sympathetic aunt, the old ballad 'Ever of Thee I'm Fondly Dreaming' and the rapprochement scene between Rose and Sir William ('Two Fools') – as well as some, like Wrench's philosophy of 'Life', forceful and some – particularly the joyous pantomimic 'The Turn of Avonia Bunn' – colourfully theatrical, and all illustrating the filleted Pinero book effectively.

Originally produced at Bristol, *Trelawny* was taken up by Veronica Flint-Shipman and the young Cameron Mackintosh and brought to London's Sadler's Wells Theatre with Richardson and Watts joined by Gemma Craven (Rose), Max Adrian (Sir William) and Joyce Carey (Miss Gower) at the head of the cast. It did well enough there to be taken to the West End proper (Prince of Wales Theatre, 3 August 1972) but after four months it was obliged to quit the house and, no other theatre being available, closed after an all-in total of 177 London performances.

Recording: original cast (Decca)

TRENTINI, Emma (b Mantua, 1878; d Milan, 12 April 1959). Diminutive operatic soprano who zoomed into the musical theatre, then pouted her way out.

Trentini made her first stage appearances in opera in her native Italy before she was taken to America by Oscar Hammerstein in 1906. There she appeared in the lightest rôles of the soprano repertoire (Nedda, Frasquita, Musetta, Antonia etc) until Hammerstein's operatic endeavour collapsed and he transferred her to the starring rôle in his venture into the musical theatre. The rôle was that of 'naughty' Marietta d'Altena in Victor Herbert's *Naughty Marietta* (1910) and Trentini scored an outstanding success with the character of the Italian countess disguised as a casket girl and then as a boy, as she introduced Herbert's 'Naughty Marietta', the Italian Street Song and, with Orville Harrold, 'Ah! Sweet Mystery of Life'. When Herbert refused to write again for the ill-behaved soprano Rudolf Friml was given the opportunity to write the score for *The Firefly* (1912), another piece that allowed the star to play an Italian and to get into boy's clothes for a good part of the evening before emerging as a full-blown prima donna. Trentini scored a second major hit, notably with the Neapolitanate serenade 'Giannina Mia' and 'Love is Like a Firefly'.

She took the rôle of Helena in a made-over Broadway version of the Austrian hit *Polenblut* called, at first, *The Ballet Girl* and then *The Peasant Girl*, and seemed to be in line for a third hit. However, anxious to go off and pursue a love-affair with Friml, she refused to extend her Broadway contract beyond its initial eight weeks and had to be replaced. In spite of her skills and attractions, her frequent displays of unprofessionalism finally rendered her all but unemployable and, although she played in vaudeville and appeared in London in the revue *The Whirligig* (1919), she ultimately went back home to Italy and oblivion.

TRESMAND, Ivy (b London, 15 December 1898; d Worthing, 2 November 1980). British soubrette of the 1920s and 1930s.

After early appearances in the chorus of the revue *Shell Out* (1915) and in small parts in the musical *Houp-La!* and the revue *Bubbly*, Ivy Tresmand was cast in the rôle of Tina in London's version of *The Red Mill* (*see* page 1467) at the age of 21. She appeared in the revue *Just Fancy*, took over the comic rôle of Margot in *Sybil* from May Beatty and featured as Sophie Lavalle in *The Lady of the Rose* (*Die Frau im Hermelin*) both at Daly's Theatre, played Frou Frou in a revival of the *Merry Widow* and Patricia in *Katja the Dancer* prior to starring in a series of late 1920s West End musical comedies at what proved the peak of her career: Yvonne in *Yvonne*, Looloo in the British version of *Hit the Deck*, Lora Moore in *Follow Through* and Thomasina Tucker in *Little Tommy Tucker* (1930).

She later toured as Bobby Carr in *The Compulsory Wife*, flopped out of town in *On the Air* (1934), played with the Co-Optimists and toured Britain in the leading rôle of *Careless Rapture* (1936) and then South Africa with Leslie Henson (*Going Greek*, *Swing Along*). She remained some time in South Africa, appearing in concert parties and plays, and did not return to the London stage.

TREUMANN, Karl (b Hamburg, 22 July 1823; d Baden bei Wien, 18 April 1877). Midhusband to the Viennese Operette tradition.

Born in Germany, while his father was working at the Stadttheater in Hamburg, Karl Treumann began his own theatrical career at the age of 18, alongside his brother Franz, in the chorus at the Deutsches Theater in Pest. He soon rose to be a popular member of the company, playing major rôles, until the theatre was destroyed by fire in 1847. However, thanks to a recommendation from a fellow singer (one story says it was Suppé) who had found an engagement at the Theater an der Wien, Franz Pokorny engaged Treumann for that theatre as first comedian for comedies and musical pieces. In 1851, unhappy under the management of Pokorny's son and successor, Treumann moved on to the Carltheater. There he was cast in often supporting comedy rôles in all kinds of musical and non-musical pieces, forming with Nestroy and Scholz a memorable comic trio.

The visit of Levassor, the French actor, in 1856 suggested to him a new direction in which he might strike out. The Palais-Royal comedian played the Carltheater with a repertoire including musical vaudeville, burlesque and the first Offenbach piece, *Les Deux Aveugles*, to be seen in Vienna. Treumann set out to imitate his style of performance – a performance not unlike those purveyed by the Howard Pauls or the German Reeds in Britain – in German. He performed in programmes made up of comic songs ('Der Jungg'sell', 'Les Deux Gendarmes') and scenes (*Der Wiener Poldl vom Burgtheater*, *Die Leiden eines Choristen*,

Plate 276. **Ivy Tresmand** *trips across a decreasing row of chairs with Ray Kay in London's* The Red Mill.

D'Froschmirl, Der Hans und sein Basle, Wiener Sommer-vergnügen, Schicksal einer Böhmischen Köchin etc), sometimes with such partners as Gallmeyer or Frln Zergraf. Then in October 1858, as part of his benefit bill he translated, adapted, directed and starred as Peter in *Die Hochzeit bei Laternenschein*, a Viennesed version of *Le Mariage aux lanternes* and the first Offenbach work to be played in Vienna in German. Offenbach protested at the unauthorized adaptation, but soon went quiet when it proved a considerable success. Treumann then adapted and/or appeared in a number of other Offenbach pieces for the Carltheater and its manager Johann Nestroy and he also introduced Offenbach's works to Hungary with German-language performances of *Hochzeit bei Laternenscheine*, *Das Mädchen von Elisonzo* and *Die Zaubergeige* at the Budai Színkör in May/June 1859.

In October 1860 Nestroy ended his management of the Carltheater, and Treumann moved on. He had previously applied for permission to build a theatre of his own and, no little thanks to some friends in high places, he had been granted royal permission to construct and operate a sixth Vienna theatre. Unfortunately he found the time too short to raise sufficient cash to build the solid edifice he had in mind, and the Theater am Franz-Josefs-Kai which resulted was a fairly flimsy building. That didn't stop it from it quickly becoming decidedly popular. Treumann opened his house the day after Nestroy handed over the Carltheater to Gustav Brauer, with many of the old Carltheater company, including Wilhelm Knaack and Anna Grobecker, amongst his players and Franz von Suppé from the Theater an der Wien as musical director. He staged mostly spectacles coupés consisting of heavily adapted versions of the opérettes of Offenbach and other French composers such as Caspers, Adam, Massé and Poise and including *Tschin-Tschin* (Peter Gix), *Meister Fortunio und sein Liebeslied*, *Daphnis und Chloë*, *Herr und Madame Denis* (Sergeant Bellerose), *Salon*

Pitzelberger, *Tromb-al-ca-zar*, *Häuptling Abendwind* (*Vent du Soir*), *Die Damen vom Stand* (*Mesdames de la Halle*), *Die verwandelte Katze*, *Zwei arme Blinde*, *Herr von Zuckerl* (*MM Dunanan*) and a variety of short comedies, also often taken from the French. In many cases the adaptations were uncredited, in other cases (*Daphnis und Chloë* etc) Treumann's name eventually appeared as author ... even though someone else had sometimes been originally credited.

Treumann also ventured into larger works with the production of *Die schöne Magellone*, his version of Offenbach's original *Geneviève de Brabant* (played Sifroy), *Die Seufzerbrücke* (*Le Pont des soupirs*, Cornarino, with 'original melodies by Franz von Suppé' inserted) and *Die Schwätzerin von Saragossa* (*Les Bavards*, Roland). Even more enterprisingly, he initiated performances of home-brewed musical theatre, producing the first performances of *Zehn Mädchen und kein Mann*, Suppé's follow-up to his successful *Das Pensionat* in which the manager appeared as Herr von Schönhahn, the father of the ten titular maidens, and the same composer's equally successful *Flotte Bursche* (Fleck), and *Die Kartenschlägerin*. He thus earned himself in retrospect the honour of being the principal assistant at the birth of what was to become the Viennese Operette tradition.

The Theater am Franz-Josefs-Kai (familiarly known as the Treumanntheater or Kaitheater) got the Offenbach seal of approval when the company of the Théâtre des Bouffes-Parisiens introduced their Parisian repertoire (*Le Pont des soupirs*, *Vent du soir*, *Un mari à la porte* etc) there to such Viennese as could comprehend them in 1861 and 1862, and the composer himself conducted several of his works. He also gave a 'cello concert on the Kaitheater stage. Nestroy played several good seasons in Treumann's little theatre as well, scoring a notable hit as Pan in *Daphnis und Chloë*. In mid-1863, after three lively and successful years of operation, Treumann was able to make plans, as he was obliged to, to replace his wooden theatre with a stone one. But one June night the Theater am Franz-Josefs-Kai was struck by fire, and overnight Treumann and his company were homeless. There was no time to rebuild and yet carry on the season, so Treumann moved his operations to the Carltheater, which was again empty. He continued as before, playing the most successful items of his repertoire and introducing new Offenbach pieces (*Der Regimentzauberer, Hanni weint* etc), but his position as unofficial Vienna agent and adapter for Offenbach was dented when Strampfer at the Theater an der Wien made a lucrative contract with Offenbach which secured him not only a great success with *La Belle Hélène* but also a regular supply of the works over which Treumann had previously held sway.

In 1866 Treumann handed over the direction of the Carltheater to Anton Ascher, but he continued to play there from time to time, taking part in what was now a share of the Offenbach goldmine: whilst Ascher produced Treumann's version of *Pariser Leben* (1867, Prosper/ Frick/Brazilian) and Julius Hopp's of *Die Prinzessin von Trapezunt* (1871), the opposition played *Blaubart* (1866) and *Die Grossherzogin von Gerolstein* (1867). Amongst the local pieces in the house's repertoire, Treumann also played Piffard in Zaytz's successful *Mannschaft an Bord*, the old balletmaster in Suppé's *Das Korps der Rache*, Schubert in the pasticcio Operette *Franz Schubert* (1864), and created the rôle of the comical art-critic, Midas, in Suppé's *Die schöne Galathee* (1865).

In parallel to his acting career, which was progressively hampered by ill health in later years, he continued to write, turning out many further adaptations from the French, including the Viennese versions of Offenbach's *La Jolie Parfumeuse*, Hervé's *Le Joueur de flûte*, Lecocq's *La Petite Mariée* and *Kosiki* and the Parisian spectacle made of Jules Verne's *Reise um die Erde in 80 Tagen*, as well as turning the French libretto prepared by Victor Wilder and Alfred Delacour for the Carltheater into the German *Prinz Methusalem* for Johann Strauss.

An all-round man of the theatre of wide and considerable talents and great enthusiasms, Treumann, particularly by virtue of his imaginative venture at the Theater am Franz-Josefs-Kai, established himself as one of the major characters of the earliest part of the modern history of Viennese theatre, which he helped to shepherd through the years which led its musical theatre from its first experience of Offenbach, through Suppé's ground-breaking Operetten, to the days of Johann Strauss and the 'Golden Age' of Austrian Operette.

1858 **Die Hochzeit bei Laternenscheine** (*Le Mariage aux lanternes*) German version wirh music ad Karl Binder (Carltheater)

1858 **Das Mädchen von Elisonzo** (*Pépito*) German version (Carltheater)

1859 **Jungfer Nachbarin** (*Bonsoir Voisin*) German version w music ad Carl Krottenthaler (Carltheater)

1859 **Schuhflicker und Millionär** (*Le Savetier et le financier*) German version (Carltheater)

1859 **Die Zaubergeige** (*Le Violoneux*) German version (Carltheater)

1859 **Die Savoyarden** (*Le 66*) German version (Carltheater)

1859 **Der Ehemann vor der T(h)üre** (*Un Mari à la porte*) German version (Carltheater)

1860 **Tschin-Tschin** (*Ba-ta-clan*) German version (Carltheater)

1860 **Magister und Zögling** (*Le Savetier et le financier*) German version

1861 **Die Schwätzerin von Saragossa** (*Les Bavards*) German version (Theater am Franz-Josefs-Kai)

1861 **Die Tante schläft** (*Ma tante dort*) German version (Theater am Franz-Josefs-Kai)

1861 **Ein Nase für 1000 Pfund** (Carl Binder) 1 act (Theater am Franz-Josefs-Kai)

1864 **Die schöne Weiber von Georgien** (*Les Géorgiennes*) German version (Carltheater)

1867 **Pariser Leben** (*La Vie parisienne*) German version (Carltheater)

1868 **Urlaub nach Zapfenstreich** (*La Permission de dix heures*) German version (Carltheater)

1869 **Der Flötenspieler von Rom** (*Le Joueur de flûte*) German version (Carltheater)

1872 **Der Dorfadvokat** (Robert von Hornstein) 1 act Munich

1873 **Zwei Hochzeiten und ein Brautigam** (*Les Deux Noces de M Boisjoli*) German version with music by Carl Ferdinand Conradin (Carltheater)

1873 **Fünfundzwanzig Mädchen und kein Mann** expanded version of *Zehn Mädchen und kein Mann* (Suppé) Hofoper 15 April

1873 **Tricoche und Cacolet** German version w music by Franz von Suppé (Carltheater)

1874 **Schönröschen** (*La Jolie Parfumeuse*) German version (Carltheater)

1875 **Reise um die Erde in 80 Tagen** (*Le Voyage autour du monde en 80 jours*) German version w music by Suppé

1876 **Graziella** (*La Petite Mariée*) German version (Carltheater)

1877 **Prinz Methusalem** German version of unproduced libretto by Victor Wilder and Alfred Delacour (Johann Strauss) Carltheater 3 January

1882 **Kosiki, der Sohn der Sonne** (*Kosiki*) German version (Carltheater)

TREUMANN, Louis [POLLITZER, Ludwig] (b Vienna, 1 March 1872; d Theresienstadt, during 1942). Versatile light-comic leading man who became a major star of the Vienna stage.

Treumann began his working life in business rather than the theatre, his main connection with the dramatic art being his membership of the claque at the Carltheater. He used this connection to make useful acquaintances and finally the chorus-leader of the theatre helped him to get a job in a minor theatre in Budapest. He moved on to Laibach and Trieste, singing in choruses, then graduated to light comedy-light baritone rôles in the German, Swiss and Austrian provinces. In 1899 he ended up back at the Carltheater, this time on the stage playing Josef in *Wiener Blut*, the sweetly gormless Aristide in *Die kleinen Michus*, Izzet Pacha (*Fatinitza*), the comical Wun Hi (*Die Geisha*), Menelaus (*Schöne Helena*), Li (*San Toy*) and Lambertier in the flop musical *Die Primadonna*.

In 1901 he played alongside top-billed Mizzi Günther in Ziehrer's *Die drei Wünsche*, as Paillasse to her Suzon in a version of *Les Saltimbanques* and Philippe to her Hortense in *Der Opernball*, and he appeared thereafter as Der Marchenkönig in *Die verwunschene Prinzessin*, Jan in *Der Bettelstudent*, Geiersberg in *Das verwunschene Schloss*, in the title-rôle of *Der Damenschneider* and in the rôle of Florian alongside the Lola of Günther in the hugely successful *Das süsse Mädel*. The following season he played alongside another choice prima donna in Ilka Pálmay as Aristide Limonard in *Das gewisse Etwas* and as Sylvester Morelli in *Der liebe Schatz* before winning his most significant rôle to date as the onion-

Plate 277. Louis Treumann: *The original Danilo of* Die lustige Witwe.

seller Wolf Bär Pfefferkorn in Lehár's *Der Rastelbinder*. This time he was not only the equal of his leading lady, but rated star billing on his own, and when (after a 3-performance flop called *Der Glücklichste*) the two came together as a genuine star pair in a revival of *Apajune, der Wassermann* (Prutschesko), the partnership which had been hovering for the two years they had been together at the Carltheater gelled.

The Carltheater schedule meant that each still played without the other: Treumann played Anatole McSherry to the *Madame Sherry* of Marie Halton and Poldl in *Das Marktkind* whilst Günther appeared on between nights with Karl Streitmann in *Der Mameluck*, but they came back together again in Lehár's *Der Göttergatte* (Sofias), as husband and wife in Hellmesberger's successful *Das Veilchenmädel* (Stiebel) and again in the German musical comedy *'s Zuckersgoscherl* (Amadeus Herzig) and Ziehrer's *Der Schätzmeister* (John Botterbroad). The Hungarian operett *Der Schnurrbart* (Graf Otto Plechnitz) and Ujj's *Kaisermanöver* (1905, Czapás) were failures and, as the Carltheater took in Alexander Girardi following his walkout from the Theater an der Wien, Treumann, soon followed by Günther, abandoned the Carltheater and went the opposite way – to the Theater an der Wien.

The pair's first vehicle there was Leo Ascher's *Vergeltsgott* (Bogumil, Graf Karinsky) and Treumann then appeared alone in Leo Fall's *Der Rebell* (Franzl Obrowitsch) before

they were cast as the lightly comic hero and heroine of the newest Lehár Operette *Die lustige Witwe*. Treumann played Danilo Danilowitsch for the large part of *Die lustige Witwe*'s immense run, and then took his now megastardom on to the rôle of Top in Stritzko's short-lived Bret Harte musical *Tip-Top* before pairing with Günther again as the hero of *Die Dollarprinzessin* (Fredy Wehrburg). *Der schöne Gardist* (Peter) was less successful, but *Der fidele Bauer* gave Treumann another fine rôle as the old peasant Matthaeus Scheichelroither before he moved on to the newly opened Johann Strauss-Theater to star in Granichstädten's successful *Bub oder Mädel?* (Fürst Fritz Ragan), in the title-rôle of a revival of *Der arme Jonathan* and, joined once more by Günther, as Hadschi Stavros in Lehár's next, *Das Fürstenkind*. In 1910 Treumann and Günther brought out *Apajune* again, Treumann starred as the detective Arsène Dupont in *Lord Piccolo*, and the pair came back together for the 74 performances of *Das erste Weib* (Alphonse, Graf Dyllenau von Dyllendorf), the 67 nights of Fall's *Die Sirene* (Fouché) and the 73 of Weinberger's *Die romantische Frau* (Fürst Egon) to end their Johann Strauss-Theater interlude.

They returned to the Theater an der Wien for the 1911–12 and 1912–13 seasons, starring together in *Der Graf von Luxemburg* (René), *Das Fürstenkind*, *Die schöne Helena* (Menelaus), the 500th *Die lustige Witwe*, *Pariser Leben* (Frick/Brasilien) and *Der Rastelbinder* and introducing Lehár's *Eva* (Octave Flaubert), the Strauss pasticcio *Der blaue Held* (Prince Balthasar) and Kálmán's *Der kleine König* (der König). Treumann then departed to the Bürgertheater to take on the star rôle of Tobias Stöger in Eysler's *Ein Tag im Paradies*, to play Célestin to the *Mam'zelle Nitouche* of Annie Dirkens, and to lead the cast of Eysler's newest and less-successful *Frühling im Rhein* (Moritz Frühling).

In 1916 he went to the Carltheater for 106 performances of *Der Weltenbummler* (Hans Holle) and 131 of *Die schöne Saskia* (Adrian von Rudder) as well as a major revival of *Der Rastelbinder* in which he once more took up his famous rôle. He re-paired with Mizzi Günther for the first time in several years for *Der Millionendieb* (1918, Tangua) at Ronacher and in 1920 directed and starred in a revival of *Der Hofnarr* (Carillon) and reprised *Das Fürstenkind* at the Apollotheater. He had further starring rôles in the successful *Die Frau im Hermelin* (1921, Oberst Paltitsch) and as the romantic Prince Radjami in *Die Bajadere* (1921), in the title-rôle of the biomusical of *Offenbach* (1922) and in *Mädi* (1923, Anatole), played more *Rastelbinder*s and appeared as Lord Durham in *Agri* (1924), but from this stage, after a solid quarter of a century almost non-stop in front of the Viennese public, most of it as a major star, his schedule slowed down.

In 1927 he took over as President Mikola Tontscheff in *Die Königin* at the Theater an der Wien where in 1931, at nearly 60 years of age, he repeated the rôle of the Ambassador, John Cunlight, which he had played in the German production of *Viktoria und ihr Husar* the previous year, alongside Rita Georg and Ernst Nadherny in the piece's Viennese production. In 1933 he directed the Vienna production of *Rosen im Schnee*.

A singing, dancing, light-comic leading man of elegance and charm, Treumann had a remarkable career as a musical comedy star of the 'Silver Age'. If it is as the creator of Lehár's Danilo that he is best remembered today, it was his Pfefferkorn in *Der Rastelbinder* which nevertheless remained his most outstanding, and more-often-repeated rôle amongst the many successful parts which he created in successful and memorable shows.

TRIAL BY JURY Dramatic cantata in 1 act by W S Gilbert. Music by Arthur Sullivan. Royalty Theatre, London, 25 March 1875.

Pretty, greedy Angelina (Nellie Bromley) is suing Edwin (Walter Fisher) for breach-of-promise before an all-male jury and a drooling Judge (Frederic Sullivan) who are not at all interested in the defendant's admirable explanations of how a fellow can change his mind. He tries to show what a rotten husband he would make, she weeps prettily to influence the award and objects when it is suggested he is got drunk to see if he would, in fact, beat her when in his cups. The Judge solves the whole affair by deciding to marry the clever little creature himself.

The libretto for *Trial By Jury* was developed by Gilbert from a comic ballad he had written for the magazine *Fun* and was originally submitted to manager-composer Carl Rosa as a possible vehicle for his wife and company. Madame Parepa Rosa died, and the libretto sat in a drawer until D'Oyly Carte asked Gilbert and Sullivan for a forepiece for Selina Dolaro's production of *La Périchole*. Sullivan quickly produced the comical score which was to be the forerunner of so many others, with its pattering number for the Judge ('When I, Good Friends, Was Called to the Bar') and its singing tenor solos ('When First My Old, Old Love I Knew', 'Oh, Gentlemen Listen, I Pray') encased in the body of a sung-through little cantata.

An instant hit, *Trial By Jury* was given for two seasons by Dolaro's company, and soon snapped up by dozens of other companies, notably by Emily Soldene who took it through Britain, America and the colonies, and the Swanboroughs who mounted it on burlesque territory at the Strand Theatre. When the length of Offenbach's *Madame l'Archiduc* meant that audiences for its London production were unable to stay to hear the afterpiece, *Trial By Jury*, the management was forced, by complaints, to cut a chunk out of Offenbach's piece.

America's Alice Oates soon had the piece on the stage in Philadelphia, and several weeks later it made its first appearance in New York. Henry Bracy and his wife Clara Thompson appeared as defendant and plaintiff at Melbourne's Opera House, Lydia Howard's troupe took the show round New Zealand and it became a thoroughgoing favourite throughout the English-speaking world.

It had an important revival at the Opera Comique as an afterpiece to *The Sorcerer* (1878) when George Grossmith appeared as the Judge, and it was paired again with that piece on its first revival by Carte at the Savoy Theatre in 1884 with Rutland Barrington playing the chief comic rôle and again in 1898 when Henry Lytton featured, remaining thereafter a fixture in the D'Oyly Carte company's repertoire. It was also a favoured piece on the programme of benefit performances, and was featured at the Theatre Royal, Drury Lane, on the programmes for Nellie Farren (1898) and for Ellen Terry (1906) with Gilbert himself playing the Associate on each occasion alongside juries and bridesmaids composed of the theatrically famous.

USA: Arch Street Theater, Philadelphia 22 October 1875, Eagle Theater, New York 15 November 1975; Australia: Prince of Wales Theatre/Opera House, Melbourne 24 June 1876; Germany: Wallner-Theater 14 June 1886; Austria: Carltheater *Im Schwurgericht* 14 September 1886, Danzers Orpheum *Das Brautpaar vor Gericht* 5 October 1901

Plate 278. **Trial By Jury**: *Anthony Warlowe (Defendant) comes face-to-face with the court Usher (John Germain) in the Australian Opera's 1984 production.*

A TRIP TO CHINATOWN Idyll of San Francisco (musical trifle) in 3 acts by Charles H Hoyt. Music written and arranged by Percy Gaunt. First produced in 1890; Madison Square Theater, New York, 9 November 1891.

A Trip to Chinatown rates arguably as the most popular American-made show of the 19th century. As far as statistics go, it had the longest single Broadway run of any home-bred musical show – 657 straight performances in its initial run in 1891–3, not counting a return visit of seven weeks in 1894 (Madison Square Theater, 12 February) – but it was its additional and widespread life as a touring piece, both in America and abroad, which made it such a phenomenon. In fact, the show took its time to come to Broadway. It was produced a whole year prior to arriving at the Madison Square Theater, and it made its real first New York appearance as part of those 12 months of pre-Broadway touring when it was played, as a stop on a regular road schedule, at the combination house known as the Harlem Opera House (8 December 1890) with Anna Boyd and Harry Conor in its featured rôles.

A Trip to Chinatown was one of those loose-limbed farcical comedies with often haphazardly introduced, and intermittently replaced, songs and dances which had become highly successful in the popular American theatre in the second half of the 19th century. Its author, Hoyt, the most generally skilful practitioner of this chimeric kind of entertainment, had a series of successes with like pieces, but in *A Trip to Chinatown* he brought together a splendid bunch of comical characters in a simple and hilarious, if derivative, plot which, decorated with several very successful songs, made the entertainment into something more than the run-of-the-mill farce comedy.

The basic story of the show (much embroidered upon as the years went by) had two young men and their girls ostensibly going out on a 'trip to Chinatown'. As in Labiche and Delacour's famous *Voyage en Chine*, they don't actually go there at all. This cultural(!) trip is a blind for the benefit of strict papa, Ben Gay, and the young folk are really off to have a high old time at a dance. They are, however, nice young people (in spite of the boys being called Rashleigh Gay and Norman Blood) and they are taking a chaperone with them, a pretty widow called Mrs Guyer (Anna Boyd). Unfortunately Mrs Guyer's letter arranging to meet the young folk at a restaurant goes to Ben by mistake, and the old fellow hurries off excitedly for this unlooked-for rendezvous with a charming lady. At the restaurant he ends up both lady-less and then unable to pay his bill as the comedy gambols on towards a forgiving and happy ending.

The other, incidental characters of the piece were headed by another variant of a favourite character, the imaginary invalid, here called Mr Welland Strong (Harry Conor), 'a man with one foot in the grave'. Strong's rôle developed, eventually, into the major comic rôle of the show, but there were humorous vignettes from such supporting characters as the regularly crushed servant, Slavin Payne, (pronounced 'slayv-in', of course), Flirt the maid, the lad Willie Grow ('proposed at the Bohemian Club' ... and played by a girl) and Noah Heap, the waiter at the Riche Restaurant.

The songs were, in the tradition of such shows, movable and changeable, but a number of those in *A Trip to Chinatown* became such favourites that they remained a fixed part of the show over the many years of its life. Percy Gaunt's 'Reuben and Cynthia', 'The Pretty Young Widow' and 'On the Bowery', all originally written and/or arranged from familiar melodies for the show, were the backbone of a score which, towards the end of the show's third year read: Act I: 'The Pretty Widow', 'Out for a Racket', African Cantata: 'Love Me Little, Love Me Long', 'Crisp Young Chaperone' (mus: Barton); Act II: Trio – burlesque of Italian opera; Medley including 'There Will Never Be Another Like You', 'Naughty Sporty Boys', 'I Will Be True', 'Reuben and Cynthia', 'Amorita Waltz', 'Whistling Extraordinary', 'You Did That'; Act III: Toe dance and Flower girl by première danseuse, 'On the Bowery'.

'Push Dem Clouds Away' was another popular early addition to the score, but it was a slightly later one, a number already seen in another production, which proved the biggest success. Charles K Harris's 'After the Ball' became, along with 'The Bowery' (which Hoyt, who claimed to have written 400 to 500 extra verses for it, averred had been 'heard in America, England and Australia ... translated and sung in German, French, Italian, Danish and Swedish [and] now the rage in St Petersburg') and 'Reuben and Cynthia' ('Reuben, Reuben, I've been thinking...'), one of the enduring elements of the show.

Hoyt covered his show with a programme note attempting to defuse any attempt to see sense in the entertainment: 'In extenuation, the author begs to say that whatever the play may be, it is all that is claimed for it'. He also claimed, second time into major dates that 'playwright Hoyt has made many alterations to his skit, adding new and witty lines here, and unique business there, until the *Trip* is almost a new play'. Whilst undoubtedly an exaggeration, it is certain that alterations and additions came with a will. The largest alteration came after Hoyt's death when a whole new version of the piece entitled *A Winsome Widow* was produced by Florenz Ziegfeld in 1912.

In Britain, the show was pre-empted by a copycat compilation of American songs and scenes calling itself *A Trip to Chicago* (Vaudeville Theatre 5 August 1893) but, nevertheless, when the real thing arrived its pitch was not spoiled. Played with a local cast headed by R G Knowles, Herman de Lange and Edith Bruce, *A Trip to Chinatown* had a good 125-performance run at Toole's and the Strand Theatres and a very long touring life around the British provinces. Australia did not, on the other hand, cast the piece locally and in fact saw the show with some of its original creators when Hoyt sent a company to the south Pacific in 1896. Harry Conor, J Aldrich Libby (Rashleigh), Frank Lawton, Amelia Stone and Bessie Clayton, played the show in repertoire with *A Milk White Flag* in Sydney, Adelaide and Melbourne (Princess Theatre, 29 August 1896). Australia later got what claimed to be the *Trip to Chicago* piece as well, billed as the work of Fred Lyster and its star John F Sheridan (Theatre Royal, Melbourne, 15 September 1900) who trouped it a while in his repertoire alongside his more favoured pieces.

UK: Toole's Theatre 29 September 1894; Australia: Lyceum, Sydney 27 June 1896

TROIS DE LA MARINE Opérette-revue in 2 acts by Henri Alibert. Lyrics by René Sarvil. Music by Vincent Scotto. Théâtre Nouvel Ambigu, Paris, 20 December 1933.

The second of the series of successful Marseillais-flavoured opérettes written and played by Henri Alibert in the 1930s, *Trois de la marine* was as good as its title. Its heros were three sailors, jeune premier Antonin (Alibert) and his comical mates Papillotte and Favouille (Rellys), and the plot – when it wasn't being amorous – concerned a spy and some mysterious stolen papers. The suspect is the gorgeous Dorah who has been casting her spell over impressionable Antonin, but Dorah turns out to be a French agent chasing the real spy and, after the exposures have all been made, Antonin comes back to his little local Rosette (Gabys Sims) in time for the final curtain.

Scotto's jolly score was topped by the three men's rousing valse-musette 'Sur le plancher des vaches' and the march 'À Toulon'. Papillotte had fun with the chanson arabe 'Viens dans ma kasbah', Rosette foxtrotted a pretty piece about being a laundress with 'De l'eau, du savon, du soleil' and joined her man in a tango declaring 'L'amour est une étoile', whilst Alibert got romantic over a pair of slow foxtrots ('Je ne sais pas ce qui m'attire', 'Depuis ... j'ai peur de tout').

Trois de la marine repeated the success won by *Au pays du soleil*, and after a fine Paris season set out for a long life on the road. It was filmed with Alibert and Mlle Sims in their original rôles, reprised at the Théâtre des Variétés in 1945, and still wins provincial productions in France to the present day.

Film: Metropa Films 1934
Recording: selection (TLP)

TROIS JEUNES FILLES ... NUES!

TROIS JEUNES FILLES ... NUES! Comédie musicale in 3 acts by Yves Mirande and Albert Willemetz. Music by Raoul Moretti. Théâtre des Bouffes-Parisiens, Paris, 3 December 1925.

The three nice, well-brought-up jeunes filles in Mirande and Willemetz's libretto (like the musketeers, there are, in fact, four) do not quite go naked, but they take part in a revue which is just about as shocking. Modest, Cinderella-like Lotte (Jeanne Saint-Bonnet) and her sisters Lilette (Sim-Viva), Lola (Eliane de Creus) and Lulu (Renée Varville) live in the country under the care of their aunt, Mme Duclos (Mlle Allems), and their good tutor, Hégesippe (Dranem). But Lotte's sisters decide that sitting sweetly in Garches isn't going to get them a husband in these up-to-date days, and in order to show off their advantages to three attentive marine officers (Géo Bury, Gustave Nellson, Adrien Lamy) they decide to take part in a show at the Folies-Bocagères. After they (and Hégesippe and Lotte who have gone in pursuit) have all been seen in rôles lightly clad enough to justify the show's title, they are all transported to the battleship *Espadon* where they are happily paired off, Lotte with the rich Lord Cheston (Raymond de Boncour) and her sisters with their trio of officers. Director Edmond Roze played Patara, a comic sailor, Jean Gabin sr was the commander of the ship in question, whilst his soon-to-be-celluloid son also appeared in the show, succeeding to Nellson's rôle.

The musical's score was in the modern dancing mode, fox-trots to the fore, as Dranem demanded comically 'Est-ce que je te demande (si ta grand'mèr' fait du vélo?)' in a lecture against curiosity which proved the hit of the evening, Mlle Saint-Bonnet delivered 'Quand on ne dit rien', Roze mused on 'Quand on n'en a pas' and Colette Etcherry (later Christiane Dor) as Miss Tapsy hurtled forth 'Raymonde'. During the course of affairs, the Charleston also found its way into the entertainment.

Trois jeunes filles ... nues! scored a bullseye, had the La Cigale end-of-season revue frantically declaring that it housed *Cent jeunes filles ... nues!*, and ultimately played for a few weeks over a year at the Bouffes-Parisiens. It thoroughly confirmed the composer of the previous season's *Troublez-moi!* as a man of the musical moment, and it took to the road with Pauley and Ginette Winter featured, with vigour. One of the many roads the show took in the following years led to Canada and then to New York where a repertoire company headed by Servatius (Hégesippe) played the piece in French during a season at the Jolson Theater.

A film version of the piece was subsequently made, and the opérette has maintained itself in the sometimes-seen category in France up to the present day.

USA: Jolson Theater 4 March 1929; Film: Robert Boudrioz 1929

TROMB-AL-CA-ZAR, ou Les Criminels dramatiques Bouffonnerie musicale in 1 act by Charles Dupeuty and Ernest Bourget. Music by Jacques Offenbach. Théâtre des Bouffes-Parisiens, Paris, 3 April 1856.

Tromb-al-ca-zar was one of the earliest short pieces written by Offenbach after the widening of his licence allowed him to present one-act comic operas with up to four speaking/singing characters. Tromb-al-ca-zar is a famous brigand, and it is with fear of his horrid depredations that the actress Gigolette and her two friends, Beaujolais and Vert-Panné, suitably and ludicrously disguised, come revengefully to taunt the cowardly Ignace, her innkeeper cousin who abandoned her as a child. The piece, bristling with extravagant parodies both of specific (and more serious) musical works and of the brigand element in opera and comic opera generally, included some merry burlesque numbers, notably Gigolette/Simplette's super-Spanish boléro 'La gitana, ah! croyez bien' and the comic Trio du jambon de Bayonne.

The show was given a choice first production with the young Hortense Schneider as Simplette teamed with top comedians Pradeau (Beaujolais) and Léonce (Vert-Panné) and Rubel as Ignace, and it won a considerable success leading to a regular continuing life in France, its most recent performance in Paris being in 1985 (Espace Marais 15 June).

Outside France the show was at first regularly musically disembowelled to provide melodies for pasticcio burlesques, but it also received several proper productions. Paul Juignet played it in his French theatre season in New York in 1864 and Jacob Grau included it alongside pieces by such as Adam, Auber and Massé in his New York opéra comique season of 1866, Karl Treumann staged a German version at his Vienna theatre with himself, Louis Grois and Helene Weinberger as the theatricals and Wilhelm Knaack as the innkeeper, and John Hollingshead played the piece (ad Charles Henry Stephenson) on a programme with *La Poupée de Nuremberg* and *Bluebeard*, and later with *Zampa*, at London's Gaiety Theatre where Julia Mathews, John Maclean and Charles Lyall did the frightening of J D Stoyle.

Austria: Theater am Franz-Josefs-Kai *Tromb-al-ca-zar, oder Die dramatischen Verbrecher* 19 March 1862; USA: Théâtre Français (Niblo's Saloon) 12 January 1864; UK: Gaiety Theatre 22 August 1870
Recording: TLP

LE TRÔNE D'ÉCOSSE [et la difficulté de s'asseoir dessus] Opéra-bouffe in 4 acts by Hector Crémieux and Adolphe Jaime. Music by Hervé. Théâtre des Variétés, Paris, 17 November 1871.

Following their burlesques of Goethe's *Faust* (*Le Petit Faust*) and Racine's *Bajazet* (*Les Turcs*), the Crémieux/Jaime/Hervé team switched to things Scottish (always popular in France) as the subject for their next extravagantly ridiculous burlesque opera.

There is a conspiracy going on in Scotland, under the leadership of one MacRazor, to replace Queen Jane (Anna van Ghell) with a descendant of Robert the Bruce. Since one can't be found, the conspirators light upon a certain Robert Mouton (José Dupuis), a commercial traveller in wines, who apparently bears a certain resemblance to the all-but-deified Bruce, as their candidate. Mouton duly ends up marrying the Queen, but when the French envoy arrives and finds his ex-wine-merchant is now King of Scotland he is livid. Things wind up to a furious and farcical height – with Queen Jane winding up the highest in a flamboyant parody of an operatic mad scene – before, finally, a genuine Bruce is found hidden in a cupboard and brought out to claim the throne and the lady. Léonce played a flashy, sexy Duke of Buckingham, Baron was the lofty Baron des Trente-six Tourelles and Céline Chaumont featured as Flora. Alice Regnault was a character called Julia Good-Morning in a cast list where the other ladies included Fanny

Hyde-Park, Ann Charing-Cross and Eva Thank-You.

Hervé's score, written whilst he sheltered in appreciative London from the problems of the Franco-Prussian War across the channel, quoted happily and humorously from other operas – notably and naturally Boïeldieu's Scottish *La Dame blanche* – as it made its bubbling burlesque way through the tale. Flora's song 'Dans mes chimères les plus sottes', the Queen's mad scene and her third-act song, and the comical gentlemen's numbers were all as lively as the best of Hervé, but *Le Trône d'Écosse* proved less popular than *Le Petit Faust* and it never established itself for any more than its initial run in Paris. Hervé promptly recycled one number for his next show in London, *Babil and Bijou*, where it appeared as the decidedly un-burlesque tenor solo 'To Her Who Owns My Heart's Devotion' as performed by Joseph Maas.

TROUBLEZ-MOI! Opérette-vaudeville in 3 acts by Yves Mirande. Music by Raoul Moretti. Théâtre des Bouffes-Parisiens, Paris, 17 September 1924.

Following his first, if limited, success with *En chemyse*, the composer Moretti provided another bright, dancing score as an adjunct to an Yves Mirande libretto called *Troublez-moi!* which, like the earlier show, featured the comedian Dranem at the top of its bill. Here the star was cast as the nouveau-riche Picotte whose little secrets from the taxman, Goulichon (Gabin), can apparently only be resolved by allowing his daughter, Suzy (Renée Duler), to wed Goulichon fils, who is unfortunately christian-named Pollux (Adrien Lamy). Suzy, however, has other ideas, and he is called Robert (Jean Poc). As for the naughty Picotte, in good Parisian middle-class fashion, he has not only a wife (A Beylat) but a mistress who goes by the give-away name of Cri-cri (Christiane Dor) and whose mother (Louise Danville) is a concièrge. He also, fortunately, has a second daughter, Arlette (Mlle Davia), to whom the dashing, comical Pollux has more appeal.

Dranem gallivanted through the comedy of the show, appearing now in a toreador's outfit (on the excuse of a visit to the Bal de l'Opéra), now in night-clothes for his night of extra-marital pleasure – taken whilst Cri-cri is deputizing for her mama and interrupted incessantly by the clanging of the concièrge's bell – and performing a series of songs including 'Ernestine', 'J'ai eu tort', 'Cordon, s'il vous plaît', 'Le petit revenez-y' and 'Ah! les p'tits poissons'. Alongside some fine ensembles, the two girls culled the best of the rest of the solo music, with Davia explaining 'Ce sont des choses qu'on dit, mais on ne fait pas', describing the efforts made to make herself beautiful 'Pour un homme' whom she has never met, and, after the coup de foudre, assuring naïvely 'Je sais ce que c'est maintenant' as she bewailed her first 20 years, passed without a grand passion. Mlle Duler sang sweetly of 'La jolie bêtise' and joined Poc in the waltz duo 'Peut-être'.

A splendid musical-comedy success, *Troublez-moi!* played seven months in Paris before going on the road, and confirmed Moretti as one of the musicians to be reckoned with in the dance-age of the French musical comedy.

TRUEX, Ernest (b Kansas City, Mo, 19 September 1889; d Fallbrook, Calif, 26 June 1973). Little character man who had some fine rôles through more than half a century in the theatre.

Truex went on the stage as a five-year-old 'prodigy', at the beginning of a busy theatre, film and television career in which the dapper little actor embraced a variety of comic and character rôles including a number in musical shows. He appeared on Broadway in *Girlies* (1910, Billy Murray) and *Dr De Luxe* (1911, Dennis) before creating his most successful musical rôle as the diminutive Eddie Kettle in *Very Good Eddie* (1915) introducing 'When You Wear a Thirteen Collar' and 'Babes in the Wood' (w Alice Dovey).

In 1919 he had star billing in the Shubert's *Page Mr Cupid*, which closed after one week's tryout, but he subsequently appeared on musical Broadway in *Pitter Patter* (1920, Dick Crawford) and as wealthy George Wimbledon in Romberg's *Annie Dear* (1924) before going on to score London successes as Johnnie Quinlan in the play *The Fall Guy*, as P G Wodehouse's Bill Paradene in *Good Morning Bill*, and in the rôle of Gerald Brooks, created on Broadway by Oscar Shaw, in the London Hippodrome production of *The Five o'Clock Girl* (1929). Truex later co-starred with Beatrice Lillie in the revue *The Third Little Show*, played the part of Lenz in Broadway's version of Lehár's *Frederika* (1937), was a mini-Menelaus in *Helen Goes to Troy* (1944) and the business mogul B G Bigelow in the brief run of *Flahooley* (1951) as part of a career largely spent in the non-musical theatre.

TUCKER, Sophie [KALISH, Sonia] (b Russia, 13 January 1884; d New York, 9 February 1966).

A vaudeville, burlesque and cabaret performer ('Some of these Days', 'My Yiddishe Momma'), who billed herself from early in her career as 'the last of the red hot mamas', Miss Tucker appeared on the Broadway stage in *The Ziegfeld Follies* in 1909, but made her first musical-theatre appearances in Chicago where she played in *Merry Mary* (1911) and Ben Jerome's *Louisiana Lou* (1912). She returned to Broadway in *The Shubert Gaieties* in 1919, and in the same year made her first appearance there in a book musical playing Aunt Kitty in the long touring McIntyre and Heath show *Hello Alexander* (ex-*The Ham Tree*). In an international career of which only a small part was spent in the theatre, she starred in London in a custom-built piece called *Follow a Star* (1930) which cast her as a cabaret vocalist and in which she spent much of the second act performing the act as known, and on Broadway as the pushy wife of the deliberately clumsy diplomat in Cole Porter's *Leave it to Me!* (1938), returning only to play herself in Kalmar and Ruby's vaudeville musical *High Kickers* in 1941.

In 1963 she was the subject of a fictionalized biomusical (*Sophie* Winter Garden Theater 15 April Steve Allen/ Philip Pruneau) in which she was portrayed by Libi Staiger for a run of one week.

Autobiography: w Giles, D: *Some of These Days* (Doubleday, New York, 1945)

TULIP TIME Musical comedy in 2 acts based on the play *The Strange Adventures of Miss Brown* by Robert Buchanan and Charles Marlowe (ie Harriet Jay) by Worton David and Alfred Parker. Lyrics by Bruce Sievier. Music by Colin Wark. Alhambra Theatre, London, 14 August 1935.

Vocalist-turned-manager Anne Croft was the force behind the musical *Sweet Seventeen*, produced at the Theatre Royal Brighton in 1933 (31 July) but quickly abandoned. The abandonment was only temporary, however, for after some rewrites Miss Croft put the show back on the stage in her home town of Hull and the rechristened *Tulip Time* finally made its way to the West End's Alhambra as a cheap-price, twice-daily entertainment. Bernard Clifton, George Gee and Hungarian comic Steve Geray played airmen disguised in frocks looking for the first-named's young wife (Jean Colin) in a girl's school to the accompaniment of a brightly coloured production (including three practical windmills), some simple songs and a lot of energy, all aimed at a music-hall audience. The aim was good, for *Tulip Time* ran 427 performances and toured for three seasons thereafter.

TUNBRIDGE, Joseph A (b London, 21 January 1886; d London, 27 December 1961). Musical director and amanuensis to Britain's producer/songwriter Jack Waller.

The young Joe Tunbridge worked originally as a pianist, accompanist and as a member of a pierrot show, whilst at the same time editing and arranging music for the Star Music Company, a purveyor of cheap printed popular music, and subsequently for the more upmarket B Feldman Ltd. The first of his own compositions to get exposure were heard in pierrot shows, concert parties and touring revues, the most long-lasting of which were those long-running minor circuit shows produced by Harry Day (*Sparkles, Rockets, Jingles* etc). He had his greatest single song success in 1919 with 'Mademoiselle from Armentières' (w Harry Carlton), and moved definitively into the theatre in 1926 when he conducted and composed the basic score (which was more interpolations than score) for C B Cochran's musical version of the famous farce *Turned Up*. Soon after, he teamed up with another graduate of the pierrot and concert party world, Jack Waller, the neophyte producer of London's *No, No, Nanette*. From then on, for more than 20 years, Tunbridge worked with Waller and his organization as musical director, amanuensis and as part-composer of many of the long list of musical plays which the producer mounted, both in partnership and alone.

The musical *Virginia* (1928) had a good West End run and produced the song 'Roll Away Clouds', written in imitation of 'Ol' Man River' and actually recorded by Paul Robeson, and others of their shows such as the spectacular *Silver Wings*, the farcical series of Saville Theatre musicals (*For the Love of Mike, He Wanted Adventure, Tell Her the Truth*) and the highly successful Hippodrome shows (*Mr Whittington, Yes, Madam?, Please, Teacher!*) had good-to-splendid successes in Britain without proving particularly exportable.

Tunbridge continued to tour as a musical-theatre conductor into his sixties, but in the 1940s his composing activity decreased and his later work was limited to additional music for Waller's productions of such pieces as *The Kid from Stratford* (1948) and *Caprice* (1950). The score of the musical version of *The Little Minister*, mounted as *Wild Grows the Heather* in 1956, was largely put together from Waller's trunk of their unused music.

1926 **Turned Up** (Stanley Lupino/Arthur Rigby) New Oxford Theatre 11 January
1928 **Billy Blue** (w Fred Elkin/Harold Dayne) Empire Theatre, Newcastle 6 August
1928 **Tipperary Tim** (w Max Miller/Arthur Field, George Arthurs) Alhambra Theatre, Bradford 6 August

1928 **Virginia** (w Jack Waller/Herbert Clayton, Douglas Furber, R P Weston, Bert Lee) Palace Theatre 24 September
1929 **Merry Merry** (w Waller, Harris Weston/Weston, Lee et al) Carlton Theatre 28 February
1929 **Dear Love** (w Waller, Haydn Wood/Clayton, Dion Titheradge, Lauri Wylie) Palace Theatre 14 November
1930 **Silver Wings** (w Waller/Titheradge, Furber) Dominion Theatre 14 February
1931 **For the Love of Mike** (w Waller/Clifford Grey, Sonny Miller/Grey) Saville Theatre 8 October
1932 **Tell Her the Truth** (w Waller/Weston, Lee) Saville Theatre, 14 June
1933 **He Wanted Adventure** (w Waller/Weston, Lee) Saville Theatre 28 March
1933 **Command Performance** (w Waller/Grey/C Stafford Dickens) Saville Theatre 17 October
1934 **Mr Whittington** (w Waller, John W Green/Grey, Greatrex Newman, Furber) London Hippodrome 1 February
1934 **Yes, Madam?** (w Waller/Weston, Lee, K R G Browne) London Hippodrome 27 September
1935 **Please, Teacher!** (w Waller/Weston, Lee, Browne) London Hippodrome 2 October
1936 **Certainly, Sir!** (w Waller/Weston, Lee) London Hippodrome 17 September
1937 **Big Business** (w Waller/Lee, Browne, Desmond Carter) London Hippodrome 18 February
1938 **Bobby Get Your Gun** (w Waller/Grey/Guy Bolton, Fred Thompson, Lee) Adelphi Theatre 31 December
1943 **Hearts Are Trumps** (w Waller, Leon Carroll/Ian Grant, Robert Fyle/Fyle) Theatre Royal, Birmingham 19 October
1956 **Wild Grows the Heather** (w Waller/Ralph Reader/Hugh Ross Williamson) London Hippodrome 3 May

TUNE, Tommy [TUNE, Thomas James] (b Wichita Falls, Tex, 28 February 1939). Award-winning performer, choreographer and director who has been instrumental in leading Broadway back towards a revusical and dance-based style of staging in the 1980s and 1990s.

The very tall and slim dancer studied at the universities of Texas and Houston, and subsequently led a dual career as a performer and a choreographer. His earliest major performing assignments were as a chorus dancer in *Baker Street* (1965), *A Joyful Noise* (1966) *How Now Dow Jones* (1967) and *State Fair* (1969, St Louis Muny) and his earliest choreographic credits in regional productions of classic musicals.

In 1973, having joined the production of *Seesaw* as assistant choreographer, he ended up having his first significant rôle when he took over the part of David during the Detroit try-out. He created the number 'It's Not Where You Start, it's Where You Finish' and collected his first Tony Award for his performance.

Tune's first New York directorial assigment was with the 'musical diversion' *The Club* produced in 1976 at the Circle in the Square, and he subsequently choreographed and co-directed (w Peter Masterson) the expanded version of *The Best Little Whorehouse in Texas* (1978) with its memorable Aggie Dance for its productions on Broadway and in London's West End. His choreography for the New York edition of the British revue *A Day in Hollywood – A Night in the Ukraine* (1980) won particular praise.

He won further praise when he directed *Nine* (1982), decorating the piece's inactive libretto with a lively series of character pieces and song-and-dance routines, and he took a Tony Award when he both starred in and co-choreographed the 1983 Gershwin pasticcio *My One and*

Only. Brought in to try to salvage *Grand Hotel* (1989) on the road, he enlivened it with some picturesque dances, including a genuine show-stopping spot for one character, which earned him further awards, before going on to confirm himself as the modern master of glamorous staging in 1991's *The Will Rogers Follies* (Tony Award). At the same time, he continued the other side of his high-profile career by leading out a highly successful touring revival of *Bye Bye Birdie*, and launching a *Tommy Tune Tonite!* at Broadway's Gershwin Theater (27 December 1992).

Tune was seen on the musical screen in the film version of *The Boy Friend*.

LES TURCS Opéra-bouffe in 3 acts by Hector Crémieux and Adolphe Jaime. Music by Hervé. Théâtre des Folies-Dramatiques, Paris, 23 December 1869.

A burlesque of Racine's *Bajazet* written by the authors who, earlier in the same year, had given Hervé the libretto for his enormously successful *Le Petit Faust*, *Les Turcs* was produced at the same house which had been so successful with the former piece, under the management of Moreau Sainti, the producer of *L'Oeil crevé*.

Augustine Déveria, a French diva who had been successful in St Petersburg, returned home to play the lovely Roxane, in love with Bajazet (Marcel), who saves him from being murdered by his beastly brother. They run away from Stamboul to Babylon where Roxane turns out to be the long-lost daughter of the King and everything can conclude happily. Needless to say, in the hands of Hervé and the librettists of *Le Petit Faust* the tale was neither as simple nor as seriously flavoured as that, but *Les Turcs*, all the same, was not quite as 'bouffe' as its predecessors. At the head of the comedy, Milher, the Gérôme of *L'Oeil crevé* and the Valentin of *Le Petit Faust*, was back to play Ababoum. Hervé's score included a Marche Turc, a Valse des houris and ... a chorus of mutes!

Although it was well received by press and public, *Les Turcs* did not go on to equal the runs of its predecessors. It was, however, taken on tour by Eugène Meynadier's company with Mme Matz-Ferrare as Roxane, Juteau as Bajazet and Christian as Ababoum, a tour which found its way as far afield as Vienna. Quite why and how *A törökök* finally turned up in Budapest (ad Gyula Zempléni) in 1901 – years after it had last been played anywhere else – remains to be explained. But it did.

Austria: Theater an der Wien 27 June 1872; Hungary: Városligeti Színkör *A törökök* 23 August 1901

TURNED UP Musical farcical comedy in 2 acts by Arthur Rigby (and Stanley Lupino) adapted from the play of the same title by Mark Melford. Lyrics by Stanley Lupino, Stanley J Damerell, Robert Hargreaves, Eric Valentine, R P Weston and Bert Lee. Music by Joseph Tunbridge. Additional numbers by Isham Jones and Jack Melton, Lupino, Sydney Clare and Cliff Friend. New Oxford Theatre, London, 28 January 1926.

Willie Edouin's famous old touring farce *Turned Up* (Vaudeville Theatre, 27 May 1886), long a feature of the British provincial circuits, was given music 40 years on by a battery of folk under the eye of producer C B Cochran and musical director Joe Tunbridge. Lupino Lane was starred as young George Medford, anxious to organize the vital meeting between his mother (Ruth Maitland) and his

beloved (Nancie Lovat) whilst all hell is breaking loose around their home. The cause of the problem is that, since the death of her husband, Mrs Medway has married the prospecting undertaker Carraway Bones (Leo Franklyn) – but now Medway (Henry N Wenman) has 'turned up'! The hotch-potch score, of which the basic music was the first West End show for provincial revue composer Tunbridge turned up nothing more memorable than a piece called 'My Castle in Spain' delivered by a female character stuck irrelevantly into the tale for nothing more then girlie value and the song.

Turned Up was shunted out of the Oxford Theatre when the building was sold during its run, and after 87 performances it went off to the provinces. It also went to Australia, where Australian Franklyn repeated his rôle alongside Gus Bluett (George), Bertha Belmore (Mrs Medway), Edwin Brett, Mary Lawson, Molly Fisher and Cecil Kellaway for six Christmas weeks in Melbourne, and the following festive season in Sydney with Franklyn now replacing the ill Bluett as George, Phil Smith as Bones and Maidie Hope as Mrs Medway (Her Majesty's Theatre 20 December 1930).

Broadway also saw a musical version of *Turned Up* when Nat Goodwin mounted his production of what was, in theory, the play, but decorated it liberally with songs and dances (Bijou Theater 11 December 1887). Goodwin played Bones, with Jeannie Weatherby as Mrs Medway.

Australia: Theatre Royal, Melbourne 26 December 1929

TURNER, J[ohn] Hastings (b London, 16 December 1892; d Norfolk, 29 February 1956).

The author of a considerable list of successful plays and revues (*Bubbly*, *Tails Up*, *Hullo! America*, *Jumble Sale*, *The Fun of the Fayre*, *Mayfair and Montmartre*, *Wake Up and Dream*, *Follow the Sun* etc) in the years between the wars, Turner also adapted several Continental musicals to the English stage. However, he had his principal musical theatre success with the well-regarded *Betty in Mayfair*, a musical adapted from his own play *The Lilies of the Field*, which played 193 performances in the West End with Evelyn Laye starred in its title-rôle. *Merely Molly*, a second self-adaptation, taken from his novel *Simple Souls* and produced by the same Daniel Mayer management with the same star, was less successful (85 performances), but the musical *Lady Mary*, on which he collaborated with another highly rated writer of the period, Freddie Lonsdale, had a satisfactory 181-performance run in London.

1920 **The Naughty Princess** (*La Reine s'amuse*) English version (Adelphi Theatre)
1921 **Now and Then** (Philip Braham/Reginald Arkell/w George Graves) Vaudeville Theatre 17 September
1925 **Cleopatra** (*Die Perlen der Cleopatra*) English version (Daly's Theatre)
1925 **Betty in Mayfair** (Harold Fraser-Simson/Harry Graham) Adelphi Theatre 11 November
1926 **Merely Molly** (Herman Finck, Joseph Meyer/Graham) Adelphi Theatre 22 September
1928 **Lady Mary** (Albert Szirmai/Graham/w Frederick Lonsdale) Daly's Theatre 23 February
1937 **Venus in Silk** (*Venus in Seide*) English version (tour)

TWAIN, Mark [CLEMENS, Samuel Langhorne] (b Florida, Mo, 30 November 1835; d Redding, Conn, 1910)

The works of American novelist Mark Twain have been regularly delved into as a source of musical libretti over the years and all over the world. Perhaps unsurprisingly, the most successful results have been achieved in his native America where the 1985 adaptation of *The Adventures of Huckleberry Finn* as *Big River* (Eugene O'Neill Theater, 25 April), and the Fields, Rodgers and Hart musical version of his *A Connecticut Yankee* (at King Arthur's Court) (Vanderbilt Theater, 3 November 1927) both became considerable successes. A third success came when *The Diary of Adam and Eve* (Jerry Bock/Sheldon Harnick) was used as one of the three one-act pieces which made up the entertainment *The Apple Tree* (Shubert Theater, 18 October 1966).

As early as 1872, Augustin Daly made what seemed like an early attempt at presenting musical Twain, when he presented an extravaganza called *Roughing It* (18 February). The Twain elements – the title apart – were apparently fairly limited. Other attempts to musicalize the Mississippi novels have included *Livin' the Life* (Jack Urbont/Bruce Geller, Dale Wasserman Phoenix Theater, 27 April 1957), the off-Broadway *Downriver* (John Braden/Jeff Tamborino, 1975) and London's *Tom Sawyer* (Tom Boyd, Theatre Royal, Stratford East, 26 December 1960). Off-Broadway also hosted a version of *The Prince and the Pauper* (George Fischoff/Verna Tomasson, 1963) and a 1963 *The Man Who Corrupted Hadleyburg* (Daniel Paget/Lewis Gardner) was produced at New York's Minor Latham Playhouse (6 August).

In France the 1925 Albert Chantrier/Jean Bastia musical comedy *Elle ou moi*, which had definite echoes of *L'Île de Tulipatan* and *San Toy* in its tale of children brought up as the opposite sex, was subtitled in English 'the right man in the right place' and given out as based on 'une nouvelle de Mark Twain' (Théâtre Daunou, 29 August 1925), whilst in Hungary *The Million Pound Note* became *Egymillió fontos bankjegy* (1962, Zdenkó Tamássy/István Kállai/János Erdődy), described as a 'revü komédia', and Otto Vincze supplied the score for another piece of Hungarian Twain, Miklós Vidor's radio musical *Szűzek városa*.

In 1992 Twain even got a biomusical when Walt Stepp's *Lightin' Out* was produced at off-Broadway's Judith Anderson Theater (3 December).

Autobiography: ed Paine, A B: *Mark Twain's Autobiography* (New York, 1924), Biography: Paine, A B: *Mark Twain: a Biography* (Harper, New York, 1912).

TWENTY TO ONE   Musical sporting farce in 2 acts by L Arthur Rose. Lyrics by Frank Eyton. Music by Billy Mayerl. London Coliseum, 12 November 1935.

Twenty to One was the musical which marked the move into management by comedian Lupino Lane, a racing farce which cast him as a cocky little chap called Bill Snibson who helps one Timothy Quaintance (Clifford Mollison), a member of the anti-gambling league, to settle his affairs and win his Mary (Betty Norton) by the helpful measure of getting him on a cert a 20 to 1. Joyce Barbour featured as Miss Lucretia Harbottle, head of the aforementioned league.

First produced at Glasgow with Lane supported by Barry Lupino, Rita Cooper and Renée Reel, the piece had a tour of a half-dozen dates before Lane took it off and had it done over and worked up into a twice-nightly vehicle for himself for the London Coliseum. The juveniles sang and danced to 'How Do You Like Your Eggs Fried?', Miss Harbottle got tipsy and fell all over the comedian gushing 'I've Never Felt Like This Before', Lane went through the acrobatic, cheeky comicalities that were his trademark and the piece proved worthy of 383 performances in six months in the West End. When *Twenty to One* ended, and began what was to be a long provincial life, the persona and name (if not the character) of Bill Snibson moved on with Lane into his next musical play, *Me and My Girl*.

Following the great success of that piece, Lane brought *Twenty to One* back to London (Victoria Palace, 10 February 1942) and, again reorganized and with new numbers by *Me and My Girl*'s Noel Gay added to the score, it did even better than it had first time round, playing for ten months and 408 performances. The show remained a provincial favourite for many years and Lane himself played *Twenty to One*'s Bill Snibson, as well as the more famous one of *Me and My Girl*, on into the 1950s.

TWO BY TWO   Musical in 2 acts by Peter Stone based on *The Flowering Peach* by Clifford Odets. Lyrics by Martin Charnin. Music by Richard Rodgers. Imperial Theater, New York, 10 November 1970.

Clifford Odets's 1954 play *The Flowering Peach* was a sincere and wilfully meaningful retelling of the legend of the devout Noah and his deluge. The musical version, which cast Danny Kaye in the rôle of Noah (from 90 to 600, or the other way round), had a rather different flavour, as the comedian plugged his part full of home-made and borrowed vaudeville tricks and ad libs which did nothing to maintain the flavour which the authors had tried to impart to their show. However, the low-comedy festival which resulted (Kaye even played in a wheelchair after an accident) proved popular enough to keep Rodgers's production of *Two By Two* on the stage for 343 performances, a total it is questionable that it would have reached if it had been played straight. The show's best musical moment came in a number for youngest son, Japheth (Walter Willison), telling his brother's wife, Rachel (Tricia O'Neil), 'I Do Not Know a Day I Did Not Love You'.

The piece was given a provincial production in Britain in 1991, a deluge-orientated year which had aleady seen a Noah musical, *Children of Eden*, go under in the West End. Colin Farrell (Noah) and Geoffrey Abbott (Japheth) featured in the older show.

UK: Wolsey Theatre, Ipswich 1991; Germany: Staatstheater, Bielefeld, 23 January 1993
Recording: Original cast (Columbia)

TWO GENTLEMEN OF VERONA   Rock musical by John Guare and Mel Shapiro based on the play by William Shakespeare. Lyrics by Guare. Music by Galt MacDermot. Delacorte Theater, New York, 27 July 1971; St James Theater, 1 December 1971.

Two Gentlemen of Verona (1971) was Shakespeare metamorphosed into a 1970s post-*Hair* American musical play with post-*Hair* music by the composer of *Hair* and some for-the-people chunks of look-how-naughty-we-little-boys-can-be vulgarity mixed in with bits of Bard. This otherwise unaggressively modern and rather long version of *Two Gentlemen of Verona* developed from what was intended as a reasonably normal production of the play for the New York Shakespeare Festival. Withdrawn after a fortnight of free performances at the Delacorte Theater, it was transferred to Broadway later in the year where, in a season which included *Follies* amongst its novelties, it picked up the Tony Awards for Best Musical and Best Libretto that the same voters hadn't been game to give to *Hair*. They weren't the only ones who liked it either for, although no longer free, *Two Gentlemen of Verona* proved itself a worthy successor to its famous predecessor on Broadway, totting up a run of 614 performances before going out on the road.

Raul Julia played Proteus, who betrays both his friend Valentine (Clifton Davis) and his lady, Julia (Carla Pinza/Diana Davila), in chasing after Silvia (Jonelle Allen), daughter of the Duke of Milan (Norman Matlock), whilst the comic element was, as in Shakespeare, in the hands of the servant, Launce (Jerry Stiller/John Bottoms). On the road, Larry Kert played Proteus alongside Davis and Miss Allen.

A London production under the management of Michael White and Robert Stigwood, with Ray C Davis as Proteus and Brenda Arnau making a personal success as Silvia, played 237 performances at the Phoenix Theatre without finding enough folk interested simultaneously in Shakespeare and pop music to make it profitable. Australia's production did not make the normal move from Melbourne to Sydney.

UK: Phoenix Theatre 26 April 1973; Australia: Her Majesty's Theatre, Melbourne 31 March 1973

Recordings: original cast (ABC/MCA), London cast (Polydor), Swedish cast *Tva gentleman fran verona* (CAM)

U

UDELL, Peter (b Brooklyn, NY, 24 May 1934).

Udell worked in a songwriting partnership with composer Gary Geld which produced such 1960s hits as 'I Ain't Gonna Wash for a Week', 'Ginny Come Lately' and 'Sealed with a Kiss' before the pair moved into the musical theatre. Geld provided the music and Udell the lyrics and, in collaboration, the libretti for two fine musical plays of the 1970s, an upliftingly vigorous musical version of Ossie Davis's play *Purlie Victorious* ('I Got Love', 'Purlie', 'Walk Him Up the Stairs', 'The Bigger They Are' etc) and a movingly unpretentious piece based on the Civil-War screenplay *Shenandoah* ('We Make a Beautiful Pair') featuring some warmly written soliloquies for its leading man. Both pieces had long Broadway runs, but a third adaptation, a version of Ketti Frings's successful but downbeat play *Look Homeward, Angel* (Ethel Barrymore Theater, 28 November 1957, 564 performances), proved a failure when put to music.

Udell then collaborated with Philip Rose, his co-writer on each of the other shows, and composer Garry Sherman on two further musicals. A sort of Harlemized *A Christmas Carol* produced under the title *Comin' Uptown* with Gregory Hines as a modern Scrooge failed in 45 performances, and a musical *Amen Corner*, based on the play by James Baldwin, went under in 29 performances in spite of a roof-raising score of gospelly music.

1970 **Purlie** (Gary Geld/w Ossie Davis, Philip Rose) Broadway Theater 15 March
1975 **Shenandoah** (Geld/w James Lee Barrett, Rose) Alvin Theater 7 January
1978 **Angel** (Geld/w Ketti Frings, Philip Rose) Minskoff Theater 10 May
1979 **Comin' Uptown** (Garry Sherman/w Rose) Winter Garden Theater 20 December
1983 **Amen Corner** (Sherman/w Rose) Nederlander Theater 10 November

UFF KIRÁLY *see* L'ÉTOILE

UGALDE, Delphine [née BEAUCÉ] (b Paris, 3 December 1829; d Paris, 19 July 1910). Star Parisian vocalist turned producer and teacher.

Delphine Ugalde made her début at the Opéra-Comique at the age of 19 in *Le Domino noir* and became a major star at the Salle Favart, creating the rôle of Massé's *Galathée* (1852) and playing in such pieces as Adam's *Le Toréador*, *La Fée aux roses* and *Le Songe d'un nuit d'été*. In 1862, with her voice just slightly used by a dozen years of lead rôles, she left the Opéra-Comique and turned her attention to opérette. She played Eurydice in *Orphée aux enfers* at the Bouffes-Parisiens, and followed this by creating the rôle of the chattering Roland at Baden and in the full-sized Paris edition of *Les Bavards*. She later created another major Offenbach rôle as Feroza in *Les Géorgiennes* (1864).

When Offenbach was obliged to give up the Bouffes-Parisiens, Varcollier, whom Madame Ugalde had married after Ugalde's death in 1858, took up the lease on the theatre, and for the next two years his wife effectively ran the house. The Varcolliers produced Hervé's *Les Chevaliers de la table ronde* with Mme Ugalde starred and Frédéric Barbier's *Légendes de Gavarni*, then revived *Orphée* with Mme Ugalde as Eurydice and the famous bit of casting of courtesan Cora Pearl as Cupid. Their production played with great success (but without Ms Pearl) through the Exposition.

Mme Ugalde went back to the Opéra-Comique in 1870 but she departed again in the following year, and made further appearances on the opérette stage, notably in the title-rôle of Jonas's *Javotte* (otherwise London's *Cinderella the Younger*) at the Théâtre de l'Athénée at Christmas 1871. However, she largely devoted herself to a third career as a singing teacher.

In 1885 she once again went into management at the Bouffes and produced Messager's *La Béarnaise*, had a triumph with *Joséphine vendue par ses soeurs* and featured her daughter in Lecocq's *Les Grenadiers de Mont-Cornette* and Serpette's *La Gamine de Paris* (1887) before handing over the direction to Chizzola.

Mme Ugalde composed an opérette, *La Halt au moulin*, (lib: Constant Jarry, Théâtre des Bouffes-Parisiens, 11 January 1867) and played in it herself, and later a one-act opéra-comique, *Le Page de Stella* (Charly, Théâtre Bodinière, 4 January 1895).

Her daughter, **Marguerite UGALDE** [Marie VARCOLLIER, b Paris, 30 June 1862; d Paris, 6 July 1940], taught by her mother, made her Parisian début at the Opéra-Comique 19 April 1880 as Marie in *La Fille du régiment* and appeared there as Mnazile in *Le Bois*, Nicklausse in *Les Contes d'Hoffmann* etc. She soon found her way into the more congenial world of the light musical theatre and there she became one of the favourite leading ladies of her era.

Her first venture was perhaps her most successful of all, for she went straight to Brasseur's Théâtre des Nouveautés to create the rôle of Manola in *Le Jour et la nuit* (1881). Amongst the new shows that followed were *Le Droit d'aînesse* (1883) in which she created the rôle of Falka, *Le Premier Baiser* (1883, Suzel), *L'Oiseau bleu* (1884, Stenio Strozzi), *Le Nuit aux soufflets* (1884, Hélène), *Les Petits Mousquetaires* (1885, D'Artagnan), *Le Petit Chaperon rouge* (1885) and *Serment d'amour* (1886, Rosette). She left the Nouveautés to star for her mother in *Les Grenadiers de Mont-Cornette* (1887, Tonio) and *La Gamine de Paris* (1887).

She later played in Russia and in Brussels, appeared in the 1889 version of the spectacular *Le Royaume des femmes*, starred in the French production of Suppé's *Donna Juanita*, and had the most successful new rôle of her career since *Le Jour et la nuit* when she created the very different part of Clairette, who gets herself into military disguise and all sorts of comic situations in the vaudeville-opérette *Les 28 Jours de Clairette* (1892). Thereafter, when she appeared on the musical stage it was largely in revivals of the classic repertoire (Fragoletto, Frédégonde, Clairette), although she appeared, still in comely travesty, as the Prince of Styria in Hennequin and Mars's *Sa Majesté l'amour* as late as 1897.

UJJ, [Adalbert Franz Maria] Bela von (b Vienna, 2 July 1873; d Vienna, 1 February 1942).

The son of a Major in the Hungarian lifeguards, von Ujj (the von came simply from the Austrian habit of sticking them onto perfectly ordinary Hungarian names) lost virtually all his sight at the age of seven, but this handicap did not prevent him from first studying and then practising music as a career.

He made his débuts in the theatre with two shows, the opera *Der Bauernfeind* (1897) and the musical play *Die beiden Truminger* (1898) written for the theatre at Baden bei Wien, and a revised version of the second piece gave him a more substantial credit when it transferred the following year to the uptown Jantschtheater. His next work, *Der Herr Professor*, written to a text by Victor Léon which was calculatedly built around a rôle for Alexander Girardi, the star of the Theater an der Wien, was produced there in 1903 with the famous comedian starred (37 performances).

Over the following decade, the blind composer, with his extravagantly waxed moustaches and sporting a dramatic black eye-patch over his left eye, cut an unmissable figure in the Viennese music and theatrical world, where he produced regular if rarely very successful scores for the stage. The Operette *Kaisermanöver* was played just 16 times at the Carltheater in spite of being led by Mizzi Günther and Louis Treumann and *Die kleine Prinzessin* was outshone by *Miss Hook of Holland* and *Frühlingsluft* in the 1907 season at Venedig in Wien, but *Der Müller und sein Kind*, first produced in Graz, was well enough considered to be later given a showing at the Volksoper. He supplied the music for the 'Wiener Stück' *Der Dumme hat's Glück* produced at the Raimundtheater in 1911 and in 1914 collaborated with Carl Lindau on *Teresita*, a pastiche Operette for which he arranged melodies by Waldteufel as a score.

1898 **Die beiden Truminger** (Reitler) Stadttheater, Baden bei Wien
1899 **Die Stellvertreterin** revised *Die beiden Truminger* (M A Reitter [ie Emil Arter]) Jantschtheater 26 October
1903 **Der Herr Professor** (Victor Léon) Theater an der Wien 4 December
1905 **Kaisermanöver** (Léon) Carltheater 4 March
1907 **Die kleine Prinzessin** (Carl Lindau, F Anthony) Venedig in Wien 5 May
1907 **Der Müller und sein Kind** (Karl Schreder, Robert Prosl) Stadttheater, Graz 1 November; Volksoper, Vienna 30 October
1907 **Eine Sensation** (Lindau, Anthony) 1 act Danzers Orpheum 20 December
1909 **Drei Stunden Leben** (Lindau, Anthony) 1 act Apollotheater 1 November

1910 **Die schwarze Mali** (*Ma gosse*) (w pasticcio arr Maurice Jacobi) 1 act Apollotheater February
1910 **Chantecler, oder Die Sehnsucht nach dem Hahn** (Leopold Krenn, Lindau) Ronacher 25 October
1910 **Der Dumme hat's Glück** (Krenn, Lindau) Raimundtheater 10 September
1912 **Der Türmer von St-Stephan** (H Roffan, Prosl) 1 act Intimes Theater 13 September
1914 **Teresita** (Waldteufel arr/Lindau) Venedig in Wien 27 June

ULMAR, [Annie] Geraldine (b Boston, 25 June 1862; d Merstham, England, 13 August 1932).

The daughter of a Boston jeweller, pretty, dark-eyed young Geraldine Ulmar was a touring leading lady in comic opera whilst still in her teens, and she became a prima donna with the Boston Ideal Company in 1879, appearing throughout the country with them in rôles as diverse as Bettina in *La Mascotte*, the title-rôle in *Giroflé-Girofla* and Susanna in *The Marriage of Figaro*. In 1885 she played Yum-Yum in D'Oyly Carte's Broadway production of *The Mikado* and subsequently appeared in New York in the title-rôle of *Princess Ida* and as Rose Maybud in Carte's *Ruddigore* (1887). When Leonora Braham left the London cast of the latter show to go to Australia, Miss Ulmar was moved to Britain to take over at the Savoy, and she remained there as leading lady for the subsequent revival of *HMS Pinafore* and to create the rôles of Elsie Maynard in *The Yeomen of the Guard* (1888, ''Tis Done, I Am a Bride', 'I Have a Song to Sing, O') and Gianetta in *The Gondoliers* (1889).

Although she then left the Carte company, she spent the rest of her career in Britain. In 1890 she starred as Marton in the highly successful London version of Audran's *La Cigale et la fourmi*, in 1892 she introduced the leading feminine rôle of Teresa in Gilbert and Cellier's *The Mountebanks* and took over the title-rôle in Haydn Parry's light romantic opera *Cigarette* when it was recast for a first-class London run, then made a surprise shift to lighter things when she appeared for a while as the juvenile heroine of the burlesque *Little Christopher Columbus* (1894). In 1896 she starred as O Mimosa San in George Edwardes's first tour of *The Geisha*, but she was not seen again in the West End until she was persuaded out of retirement in 1904 for a disastrously amateurish piece called *Ladyland*.

In later life she became a singer teacher at the Wigmore Hall, numbering among her pupils such coming stars as José Collins, Binnie Hale and Evelyn Laye, but finally went blind before her death at the age of 70.

Married, between 1891 and 1903, to Ivan Caryll, she later wed Jack Thompson, a less high-profiled performer and composer.

ULVAEUS, Björn (b Gothenburg, 15 April 1946).

A member of the Swedish singing group, Abba, Ulvaeus collaborated with fellow-member Benny Andersson on the composition of the group's many hit songs ('Waterloo', 'Dancing Queen', Take a Chance On Me', 'The Winner Takes All' etc) during Abba's decade at the forefront of the popular-music scene. Their music was first heard as a musical-theatre score when *Abbacadabra*, a pasticcio children's show based on their songs, was transferred from a concept disc to the stage, and Ulvaeus and Andersson subsequently collaborated with Tim Rice on the successful musical *Chess* ('I Know Him So Well', 'One Night in Bangkok', 'Heaven Help My Heart').

1983 **Abbacadabra** (w Andersson/Don Black/Alain Boublil, Daniel Boublil ad David Wood) Lyric Theatre, Hammersmith 8 December

1986 **Chess** (w Andersson/Tim Rice) Prince Edward Theatre 14 May

THE UMPIRE Musical comedy in 2 acts by Will M Hough and Frank R Adams. Music by Joseph E Howard. La Salle Theater, Chicago, 2 December 1905.

One of the earliest great successes of Chicago's Hough-Adams-Howard combination, *The Umpire* had a record-breaking first season run of more than 300 performances at the little La Salle Theatre, helping to launch a decade of splendid prosperity in the musical theatre there. It then toured merrily round America for several seasons, without visiting Broadway, establishing itself as a jolly regional favourite.

The show's text took an enjoyably original turn on the musical-comedy formulae then in use, using for its hero the baseballing umpire of the title (Cecil Lean) who gets himself into trouble by making a bad on-field decision. Fleeing town, he then ends up in the picturesque Oriental locations beloved of contemporary musical-comedy second acts, where he finds not only football but also love when the local team's star player takes off his helmet, shakes out his hair and turns out to be called Maribel Lewton (Florence Holbrook, the real-life Mrs Lean).

Hough, Adams and Howard's songs included several with plotful baseballing and footballing references – 'The Umpire's a Most Unhappy Man', 'The Quarterback' – as well as a lively run through the gamut of popular styles from coon song ('The Sun That Shines on Dixie', 'Clorinda Jackson') to military ('The Drums of the Fore and Aft'), to the 'Hush the Bogie' style ('The Big Banshee'), the jolly ('Let's Take a Trolley') and the brightly romantic ('I Want a Girl Like You', 'Cross Your Heart').

UN DE LA CANEBIÈRE Opérette in 2 acts by Henri Alibert. Lyrics by René Sarvil. Music by Vincent Scotto. Théâtre des Célestins, Lyon, 14 October 1935; Théâtre des Variétés, Paris, 3 April 1936.

One of the most popular of the successful group of opérettes marseillaises produced by Alibert, Sarvil and Scotto in the early 1930s, *Un de la Canebière* once again had three joyful southern lads – fishermen, this time – as its central characters. These fishermen, Toinet (Alibert), Pénible (Rellys) and Girelle (Gorlett), spend the evening chasing Francine (Mireille Ponsard), Malou (Marguette Willy) and Margot (Mlle Gerlatta) and the dream of a factory where they can can their own fish. A few amorous fibs, the odd contretemps and a series of catchy, dancing songs headed by Alibert's enduring tango chanté 'Le plus beau tango du monde', his slow-fox declaration that 'J'aime la mer comme une femme', the foxtrotted 'Les Pescadous' and the men's hymn to the 'Cane-, Canebière' made up an entertainment which began its success in Lyon, made its way to Paris's Théâtre des Variétés for an eight-month season, was put on to film, then took itself back to the provinces where it is still happily played more than half a century later. It returned to Paris for fresh

seasons in 1952 (Théâtre Bobino) and in 1980 (Théâtre de la Renaissance 14 June).

Film: René Pujol 1938
Recordings: selections (Véga, TLP etc)

UNDER THE COUNTER Comedy with music in 3 acts by Arthur Macrae. Lyrics by Harold Purcell. Music by Manning Sherwin. Phoenix Theatre, London, 22 November 1945.

A flimsy but funny vehicle for the West End's favourite auntie-comedienne, Cicely Courtneidge, who appeared as actress Jo Fox, an enterprising Englishwoman-in-wartime, dipping her fingers into government postings and the black-market whilst simultaneously rehearsing her new show (in her living room, to save on *Under the Counter*'s wartime budget for scenery). The five songs used in the show, numbers from the show-within-the show, included a winning ballad, 'The Moment I Saw You', a fashion parade and an opening chorus for the girls, a ballad for leading man Thorley Walters, and a burlesque song and dance for the star.

A huge hit in end-of-the-wartime London, Emile Littler, Tom Arnold and Lee Ephraim's production of *Under the Counter* ran for 665 West End performances (Florence Desmond briefly spelling the holidaying star) and, whilst a British touring company went on the road, Miss Courtneidge took a company including Walters and Wilfrid Hyde White to Broadway – the first such cross-Atlantic venture in a decade. Broadway wasn't interested, and after three weeks Miss Courtneidge packed up and headed for Australia. There, the tale was very different, for in spite of a very sticky beginning when weeks of performances had to be cancelled through her illness, the star, accompanied by Walters, Aileen Bilton (Zoe) and Claude Horton (Mike), trouped her show through the antipodes for an entire year.

USA: Shubert Theater 3 October 1947; Australia: Theatre Royal, Sydney 3 January 1948

UNDER YOUR HAT Musical comedy in 2 acts by Archie Menzies, Arthur Macrae and Jack Hulbert. Music and lyrics by Vivan Ellis. Palace Theatre, London, 24 November 1938.

Under Your Hat brought Jack Hulbert and Cicely Courtneidge back to the West End stage, starred as a pair of film stars, Jack Millet and Kay Porter, chasing after a carburettor which was apparently absolutely vital to national security. Jack sets out on the track of the glamorous thief-spy Carol Markoff (Leonora Corbett), and Kay follows on the track of Jack, until nasty Russian Boris (Frank Cellier) is thoroughly outwitted and Britain triumphs. Disguises were legion, from Kay's impersonation of an extravagantly red-headed waitress to the pair's portrayal of the Rajer-than-Raj Colonel and Mrs Sheepshanks from Poona, and Vivian Ellis's score gave the pair all the musical opportunities they needed, whether singing about being 'Together Again' or rehearsing for a film in 'Rise Above It'. Miss Courtneidge burlesqued the French cabaret in 'La Danse, c'est moi!' and scored the hit of the evening delivering the hooting 'The Empire Depends on You' in her guise as the lady of the colonial East.

Quickly hailed as the biggest West End hit in a decade, Lee Ephraim's production of *Under Your Hat* was hit by the

Plate 279. **Die ungarische Hochzeit:** *Anneliese Mücke as Frusina and Sigi Kurzweil as Stuhlrichter in the Kaiserslauten Pfalztheater production of 1985.*

war and after ten months it had to be taken off when London's theatres were closed. Ephraim remounted the show out of town and brought it back to the Palace Theatre when things quietened down a bit (31 October 1939). It lasted another six months and more, closing after 512 West End performances. It was later produced by J C Williamson Ltd in Australia with Marjorie Gordon and Edwin Styles taking the lead rôles, filmed in Britain with its stage stars, and sent on the road, but some of the larger and more transatlantic plans originally announced for it did not eventuate.

Australia: Her Majesty's Theatre, Melbourne 9 September 1939; Film: Grand National 1940

DIE UNGARISCHE HOCHZEIT

DIE UNGARISCHE HOCHZEIT Operette in a Vorspiel and 3 acts by Hermann Hermecke based on the novel by Koloman Mikszáth. Music by Nico Dostal. Staatstheater, Stuttgart, 4 February 1939.

Following the success of his *Monika* at the Stuttgart Staatstheater, Dostal wrote this second Operette for the same house. Its story dealt with what was superficially the same topic as Lecocq's long-loved *Les Cent Vierges* – the organization of a supply of brides to a group of settlers. However, this being 1939, there was not a hint of the crazy fun of the older show in Hermecke's libretto, which was firmly in the conventional operettic style of its time. When the lush-living Count Stefan Bárdossy (Karl Mikoray) is ordered by his Empress to take charge of the affair, he off-handedly sends his valet Árpád to do the work instead, and the complications grow thick and fast. Etelka, who thinks she is wedding a Count, gets a valet, and Bárdossy, who falls in love with Janka (Paula Kapper), daughter of the local President, is tricked by her into marrying a maid-servant. The Empress herself arrives in the third act to annul virtually everything and to pair off tenor and soprano. The Hungarian flavours of the piece and of Dostal's music were very much more convincing than the cowboy-South American ones of his first success, *Clivia*, and the score of *Die ungarische Hochzeit* contained some of his better writing.

Die ungarische Hochzeit was played in a number of German provincial theatres, produced in Czechoslovakia and, in 1981, mounted at the Vienna Volksoper with Kurt Schreibmayer (Stefan), Mirjana Irosch (Janka), Kurt Huemer (Árpád) and Elisabeth Kales (Etelka).

Austria: Volksoper 6 March 1981
Recordings: selections (Eurodisc, Philips, EMI, Telefunken)

UNGER, Gladys B[uchanan] (b San Francisco, 1884; d New York, 25 May 1940).

After first studying art in Paris, Miss Unger changed direction and, for some 30 years from the production of her first play, *Edmund Kean*, in 1903, she became a prolific stagewriter and, particularly, adapter of French and German originals (*Inconstant George*, *The Goldfish*, *The Werewolf* etc) for the American and British theatre. She made her first incursion onto the musical stage in Britain with an adaptation of Johann Strauss's *Die Fledermaus*, under the odd title *Nightbirds*, an adaptation which had respectable runs in London (138 performances), on Broadway (retitled even more curiously as *The Merry Countess*, Casino Theater 20 August 1912, 129 performances), and in Australia (Criterion Theatre, Sydney 13 June 1912).

She had two fine successes at London's Daly's Theatre in the years before the First World War, the first when she adapted the Hungarian musical *Leányvásár* for George Edwardes as *The Marriage Market* and then in collaboration with Freddie Lonsdale on the libretto for the long popular *Betty*. The musical comedy *Toto*, adapted from her own version (*Better Not Enquire*) of Alfred Capus's French play *Les Deux Écoles*, had a reasonable touring life, but an attempt at an original Persian musical with composer-of-the-moment Charles Cuvillier produced only a short run and a short-lived marriage to her Persian co-author K K Ardaschir.

Miss Unger's last musical credits were her only ones in her native land. The first was an adaptation of Régis Gignoux and Jacques Théry's saucy *Le Fruit vert* musicalized as a vehicle for diminutive Hungarian star Mitzi under the title *The Madcap*, the second a version of André Birabeau's *Un Dejeuner de soleil* (which she had already adapted for the screen) made over for the Shuberts under the title *Ain't Love Grand* to star filmland's Edna Leedom. By the time it reached town it was called *Lovely Lady*. Miss Leedom jumped ship to marry a brewery millionaire, but Mitzi came in to save the situation and the show ran up 164 performances on Broadway.

A musical version of Elinor Glin's notorious *Three Weeks* commissioned by the Shuberts did not eventuate, and thereafter, except for a version of the *Beau Brummell* tale mounted at the St Louis Muny, Miss Unger concentrated on non-musical pieces and seven Hollywood years as a screenwriter (*Daughter of Shanghai*, *The Mystery of Edwin Drood*, *Marianne*, *Madam Satan*, *Music is Magic*, *Rendezvous at Midnight* etc).

1911 **Nightbirds** (aka *The Merry Countess*) (*Die Fledermaus*) English version w Arthur Anderson (Lyric Theatre)
1913 **The Marriage Market** (*Leányvásár*) English version (Daly's Theatre)
1915 **Betty** (Paul Rubens/Adrian Ross, Rubens/w Frederick Lonsdale) Daly's Theatre 24 April
1916 **Toto** (Archibald Joyce, Merlin Morgan/Anderson) Duke of York's Theatre 19 April
1920 **The Sunshine of the World** (Charles Cuvillier/James Heard/w Kai Kushrou Ardaschir) Empire Theatre 18 February
1927 **The Madcap** (Fred J Coots, Maurie Rubens/Clifford

Grey/w Gertrude Purcell) Royale Theater, New York 31 January

1927 **Lovely Lady** (ex-*Ain't Love Grand*) (Harold Levey, Dave Stamper/Cyrus Wood/w Wood) Sam H Harris Theater, New York, 29 December

1933 **Beau Brummell** (Harry Tierney/Edward Eliscu, Raymond Egan) Municipal Opera, St Louis 7 August

THE UNSINKABLE MOLLY BROWN Musical in 2 acts by Richard Morris. Music and lyrics by Meredith Willson. Winter Garden Theater, New York, 3 November 1960.

The heroine of *The Unsinkable Molly Brown* (Tammy Grimes) – a lass who actually existed in real life – was a brassy little pre-war broad from out-of-town, determined to make herself wealthy and social. Marrying the attractive young miner Johnny Brown (Harve Presnell) doesn't seem too promising a start, but Johnny proves to have a habit of digging up silver. However, even when she gets seriously rich, Molly finds social position can't be bought in Denver. So she tries Europe instead, and finds she goes down much better in translation. But unfortunately Johnny is only happy back home. When she finds that he is more important to her than her social position, she catches the ship back to America. The ship is the *Titanic*. In the disaster she turns out a heroine and after that society and Johnny both love her.

Like the show's characters and tale, Willson's score had rather less light and shade about it than his great hit *The Music Man*. Molly howled forth her ambitions in 'I Ain't Down Yet', headed a rousing cry to a saloonful of miners to 'Belly Up to the Bar, Boys', went fund-raising with the revivalist 'Are You Sure?' and turned polyglot in 'Bon Jour', whilst Johnny wooed her baritonically in 'I'll Never Say No'. Mitchell Gregg played Prince de Long, one of the attractive faces of Europe with a title to offer the heroine, whilst Edith Meiser (Mrs McGlone) headed the rejecting battalions of Denver society and Oliver Smith was responsible for putting the sinking of the *Titanic* on the stage.

The Theatre Guild and Dore Schary (who also directed) mounted the piece for a fine Broadway run of 532 performances. However, although the show found subsequent productions around America, and also proved to be well suited for transformation into a lively and colourful film, in which Presnell starred alongside Debbie Reynolds, it did not follow *The Music Man* to productions further afield.

Film: MGM 1964
Recording: original cast (Capitol), film soundtrack (MGM/CBS)

DER UNSTERBLICHE LUMP Altwiener Stück in 3 acts by Felix Dörmann based on a novel by Jakob Wassermann. Music by Edmund Eysler. Wiener Bürgertheater, Vienna, 15 October 1910.

Oskar Fronz, manager of the Vienna Bürgertheater, had always avoided producing musicals at his theatre, on the grounds that they were far too costly. In 1910 he allowed himself to be convinced by publisher Josef Weinberger to change this policy and to produce the Felix Dörmann/Edmund Eysler musical *Der unsterbliche Lump*. Fronz hired an orchestra and chorus, brought in three guest principals in Otto Storm, Mimi Marlow and Gisela Marion for the chief singing rôles, himself directed the show with his brother, Richard, conducting and was rewarded with a hit

which resulted in the Bürgertheater becoming, for a period, one of Vienna's most prosperous musical houses. *Der unsterbliche Lump* played 192 consecutive performances in its first run and returned to pass its 250th performance on 25 May 1913 alongside two further Eysler hits which had since made the fortune of the house – *Der Frauenfresser* and *Der lachende Ehemann*. The show was given further performances in 1914, and brought back again in a fresh production in 1920 with Josef Viktora starred alongside Vinzenz Bauer and Rosa Koppler (17 September).

The young village schoolteacher Hans Ritter (Storm) dreams of fame as a composer, but he knows he must stay at home and teach the children of Burghausen and forget such dreams. Hans is also in love with local Anna Reisleitner (Gisela Marion), but he has for rival the Bürgermeister's son, Florian (Vinzenz Bauer). Hans goes off to Vienna to make fame and fortune, but whilst he is away Anna's parents marry her to Florian. The distraught Hans becomes a vagabond, wandering the world until he finds friendship and redemption working, under a new name, as a pianist at the 'Blaue Flasche' coffee house. The singer there is a girl called Luisl Freitag (Mimi Marlow), the same girl to whom, with her old wandering harpist father, he had given shelter in the Burghausen schoolhouse years before. Slowly Hans puts his life back together, and when he revisits the village he goes unrecognized – Hans Ritter, the vagabond, is dead, and the new Hans Ritter is ready to start a new life.

Eysler's score was full of Wienerische melodies, waltzes and marches to the fore as ever. The waltzes included a Hans/Anna duet, 'Ja nur du', and a solo for the travel-weary Luisl ('Blätter rauschen') in the first act, a jolly piece for Viktoria Pohl-Meiser, the komische Alte of the piece, to introduce the second ('Sich so im Tanz zu drehn') and Hans and Luisl's duo 'Das ist das Glück', whilst the march melodies were headed by the rousing 'Blaue Flaschen-Marsch' and Luisl's Brettellied ('Tröpferl zum trinken'). Other features of the score included a childrens' chorus ('Lieber guter Sonnenschein') and Hans's principal solo Trutzlied ('Weise dem Leben die Zähne').

The libretto of *Der unsterbliche Lump* was used as the basis for two films, neither of which used Eysler's music. The first had a score by Ralph Benatzky, the second by Bert Grund and Robert Gilbert.

UP IN CENTRAL PARK Musical play in 2 acts by Herbert and Dorothy Fields. Lyrics by Dorothy Fields. Music by Sigmund Romberg. Century Theater, New York, 27 January 1945.

Mike Todd's wartime production of *Up in Central Park* bore some fine names on its bills: his own, guaranteeing your money's worth of spectacle, and those of Sigmund Romberg, Herbert Fields and Dorothy Fields, each of which had been attached to some of the happiest shows of the past decades. Only Todd truly lived up to the promise of the marquee, turning out a splendid physical production which was highlighted by a skating ballet routine (Currier and Ives ballet) set in Central Park and choreographed by Helen Tamiris in the image of a period print. The show's story was yet another featuring an all-American hero gallantly exposing the crimes of a nasty politician whilst simultaneously getting himself a girl.

The hero, in this case, was an ambitious young 'investigative' journalist called John Matthews (Wilbur Evans), the villains were the historical Boss Tweed Gang and Tammany Hall, and the girl was Rosie Moore (Maureen Cannon), daughter of one of our hero's victims. When John starts attacking her father in print, Rosie goes off and marries one of Moore's friends, but she has weakened enough by the time that she discovers her 'husband' is already married to go back to John in time for the final curtain. Romberg's period-flavoured score featured a romantic duo for John and Rosie, 'Close as Pages in a Book', which won particular popularity alongside a pretty 'April Snow' but, in spite of the show's fine run of 504 performances, none of the numbers joined the old Romberg favourites in his list of standards.

A 1947 film version featured Deanna Durbin and some of the stage score.

Film: 1947
Recording: selection (Decca, RCA)

URBAN [André] [URBAIN, Antoine André] (b Bouscat, Gironde, December 1884; d unknown). Light comedy leading man of the French musical comedy stage.

At first an employee in the contributions indirectes office at Bordeaux, Urban made his first attempts as a performer in a local café-concert and left town playing a servant in a touring company of *Ruy Blas*. In 1903 he reached Paris and, after an early career as a singer of comic songs (Bousquet-Concert, la Grande Roue, l'Epoque, Petit Casino, and from 1904 to 1909 at the Pépinière), he switched first to revue at La Cigale and then to the musical stage under the management of Charles Montcharmont at the Théâtre des Célestins at Lyon. His first big stage success, however, came when he was engaged in Belgium to play the principal comic rôle in Josef Szulc's new opérette, *Flup..!* He subsequently appeared in the French première of Kálmán's *Tatárjárás* at Lyon, playing the rôle of the Jewish volunteer which had helped launch Vienna's Max Pallenberg to fame, at the Marseille Gymnase, in *L'Orgie à Babylone* at the Olympia, in the wartime revival of *The Belle of New York* at the Variétés, reprised his rôle in *Flup..!* at Lyon and – after a period in uniform – appeared in revue at the Vaudeville and in *La Fausse Ingénue* at the Théâtre Fémina (1918, Sageret). However, his next big success came as the War ended, when he created the title rôle of the naughty Greek sculptor in the memorable *Phi-Phi* ('Les petits païens', 'C'est une gamine charmante', 'Vertu, Verturon, Verturonette'). Along with the show, Urban triumphed in a rôle which he would repeat at intervals for some 30 years.

Thus placed at the forefront of the modern musical comedy, he featured in Goublier's *La Sirène* (1920, Le Vicomte de Kernichet), in *Titin* in Brussels (1921) and then took the title-rôle of Christiné's next opérette, *Dédé* ('Elle porte un nom charmant', 'Tous les chemins mènent à l'amour'), sharing top billing with Maurice Chevalier. After playing the comical Baron, alongside Sacha Guitry and Yvonne Printemps, in Guitry's exquisite musical play *L'Amour masqué* (1923, 'Tango chanté', 'La Chanson des Bonnes'), appearing alongside Yvette Guilbert in *Les Amants légitimes* (1924), and making a return visit to Lyon to play Napoléon to the Marietta of Gabrielle Ristori in the

French première of Kálmán's *La Bayadère* (1925), he followed up with leading rôles in a series of successful Parisian musical comedies: *Un bon garçon* (1926, Pontavès), *Comte Obligado* (1927, 'Mio Padre', 'Le petit oiseau des îles'), *Elle est à vous* (1929, Jouvencel 'Elle est à vous'), *Louis XIV* (1929, Le Comte) and *Bégonia* (1930, 'Simplement', 'Que l'amour est traître').

With the passing of the best of the musical comedies of the era, his opportunities also declined. He appeared in the less successful *Femme de minuit* (1930, Verdurier), played the rôle of the Commandant in the 1934 Josephine Baker revival of *La Créole*, appeared in the Johann Strauss *Les Jolies Viennoises* (1938) and in the Paul Ábrahám remake, *Billy et son équipe*, at the Mogador performing the Lambeth Walk (1939). In the 1940s, he appeared in the revival of *Les Cent Vierges* (1942) and in 1945 took up his old part in *On cherche un roi* (ex- *Louis XIV*). But he returned, always, to Phidias and *Phi-Phi*, reappearing in his famous rôle at the Bouffes-Parisiens as late at 1947.

URBAN, Joseph (b Vienna, 26 May 1872; d New York, 10 July 1933).

Austrian architect, decorator and theatrical designer, whose eclectic career in his homeland ranged from town planning and constructing and decorating castles to illustrating fairy-tales. His work appeared on the Viennese stage in such pieces as the Carltheater *Das Puppenmädel* (1910, billed as 'architect Joseph Urban') and the 1911 *Alt-Wien*, in Berlin, Munich and Hamburg – mostly in opera houses – before he moved definitively to America in 1911. He was engaged at the Boston Opera Company for several years and later designed scenery for James Hackett's Shakespeare productions, but he became best known in the musical theatre where his name remains particularly attached to the spectacular settings he designed for Florenz Ziegfeld and his series of *Follies* (from 1915).

Amongst the Broadway musicals for which he designed scenery were Henry Savage's production of *Pom Pom* (1916), *Sally* (1920), *Sunny* (1925), *Rio Rita* (1927), *Show Boat* (1927), *The Three Musketeers* (1928), *Rosalie* (1928), *Whoopee* (1928) and *Music in the Air* (1932). He was also the designer of New York's Ziegfeld Theater and several other theatres in a parallel career as an architect.

URGEL, Louis

Madame Urgel, a comfortably-off amateur musician and composer who chose to take a male pseudonym so as not to have to write in the polite, parloury fashion considered apt for lady writers, composed the scores for three period opérettes which were played in Paris during the 1920s at the height of the fashion for jazz-age musical comedy. If her music won little in the way of appreciation from the professionals, being criticized for looking too reminiscently back to the world of Lecocq and Audran at the same time that certain critics were bemoaning the passing of traditional opérette, it nevertheless proved pleasing enough to the public who gave her works a more than respectable hearing.

The first piece, the Louis XVIII era *Monsieur Dumollet*, had Edmée Favart as a royalist spy engaged in helping a conspirator (Félix Oudart) to escape from the house of her father (Vilbert) who is faced with the problem of explaining this pre-marital child to his new wife (Mme Cébron-Norbens). After some 200 Parisian performances, it continued on to the provinces with Andrée Le Dantec and Javerzac starred whilst Mme Urgel's second piece, *Amour de princesse*, was produced in town. Vilbert again starred alongside comic Morton, baritone Robert Jysor, Germaine Gallois, Germaine Charley and Flore Mally and the show won another critically cool reception and a reasonable run amongst the Théâtre de la Gaîté-Lyrique's programme of classic revivals.

The most successful of the three pieces was, however, the third. *Qu'en dit l'abbé?* was an 18th-century 'opérette galante' of potential musical beds which had ambitious Rose Pinchon (Mlle Vioricia), to whom a title is the price of a tumble, wed off to the young and excessively innocent Vicomte de Castel-Bidon (Robert Burnier) for the carnal purposes of the lecherous Duc de Roquelaure (Harry Baur/Abel Tarride). Honorine de Pompignan (Nina Myral), the Duc's mistress, battles trick for trick with him to prevent him claiming his prize until the young spouses end up in each other's arms and the curtain comes down. The Abbé (Gaston Gabaroche/Paul Villé) was reasonably incidental, the title a catch phrase, and the music strove occasionally away from the period of the play towards more modern dance rhythms. *Qu'en dit l'abbé?* topped 150 performances at the Théâtre de l'Avenue, was subsequently revived at the Théâtre Édouard VII later the same year, and had a lively life in the French provinces.

Mme Urgel wrote a considerable number of songs ('Le Poulailler', 'Trois petits garçons' etc) and also several ballets, the first, *Lumière et Papillons*, produced at the Opéra-Comique in 1916, the second, *Le Loup et l'agneau*, at Monte Carlo and subsequently at the Paris Gaîté.

1922 **Monsieur Dumollet** (Hugues Delorme/Victor Jeannet) Théâtre du Vaudeville 25 May
1923 **Amour de princesse** (Delorme/Jeannet) Théâtre de la Gaîté-Lyrique 25 October
1925 **Qu'en dit l'abbé?** (Battaille-Henri) Théâtre de l'Avenue 22 May
1931 **Vieux Garçons** (Michel Carré) 1 act Théâtre de la Gaîté-Lyrique 21 February

UTOPIA (LIMITED), or The Flowers of Progress
Comic opera in 2 acts by W S Gilbert. Music by Arthur Sullivan. Savoy Theatre, London, 7 October 1893.

The reunification of the Carte-Gilbert-Sullivan team, some three years after its angry dissolution, for a new comic opera at the Savoy Theatre brought forth *Utopia (Limited)*, a piece more brittle and harsh in tone than its authors' earlier works. Gilbert's targets – Parliament, the ridiculous institution of government by party, big business, and British traditions in general – were hammered in a much less subtle and humorous fashion than before, and much of Sullivan's music also strayed from the old opéra-bouffe mode.

King Paramount of Utopia (Rutland Barrington), a monarch kept under the little fingers of his advisers Scaphio (W H Denny) and Phantis (John Le Hay), has sent his daughter Zara (Nancy McIntosh) to be educated amid what he believes to be the utter perfection of the institutions of Britain. When she returns, she brings with her the Flowers of Progress, a group representing those institutions: the army (Charles Kenningham), the navy (Lawrence Gridley), the law (H Enes Blackmore), local government (Herbert Ralland), big business (R Scott Fishe) and the woolsack (H Scott Russell). Their reforms threaten the smooth and natural running of Utopia with a painful perfection, but this is avoided by introducing party politics, thus allowing the re-introduction of interest, graft and squalor. Rosina Brandram played an English governess, and Walter Passmore was Utopia's Exploder, a mixture of executioner and heir to the impotent crown.

Several individual pieces of the score were on Gilbert's cleverest level: a dissertation on Company practice from businessman Mr Goldbury ('Some seven men form an Association ...'), a comic song in a music-hall vein for the army's Captain Fitzbattleaxe describing the disastrous effects of love on a tenor's top notes ('A tenor, all singers above') and a funny piece for Barrington, in the vein of its author's earliest Bab Ballads ('First you're born').

Utopia (Limited) won a fine reception and ran for 245 performances at the Savoy, longer than any other West End comic opera since the pair's last collaboration on *The Gondoliers*. It went on the road in four companies, and was restaged on Broadway by director Charles Harris, whilst the London production still ran, with J J Dallas (Paramount), Clinton Elder (Fitzbattleaxe), John Coates (Goldbury) and Isabel Reddick (Zara) featured (55 performances). After 1902, however, *Utopia Limited* (the parentheses disappeared from the title) was dropped from the Carte repertoire. In 1906 J C Williamson Ltd in Australia, which had not picked up the show originally, mounted it, with Kenningham in his original rôle alongside Howard Vernon (Paramount), Frank Wilson (Goldbury) and Dolly Castles (Zara), but the show did not establish itself amongst the Gilbert and Sullivan favourites in Australia any more than it did elsewhere.

USA: Broadway Theater 26 March 1894; Princess Theatre, Melbourne 20 January 1906
Recording: complete (Decca) etc

V

THE VAGABOND KING Musical play in 4 acts by W H Post and Brian Hooker based on the romance *If I Were King* by Justin McCarthy. Lyrics by Brian Hooker. Music by Rudolf Friml. Casino Theater, New York, 21 September 1925.

One of the many variants on the *Abu Hasan* 'king for a day' tale, Justin McCarthy's play *If I Were King* (Garden Theater, 14 October 1901) was – in spite of the cold statistics of its first run of just 56 Broadway performances – a considerable success, with Edward Sothern starred as the historical ruffian poet François Villon who, in McCarthy's version (based on R H Russell's novel), is made king for a week, defeats Burgundy and wins a royal bride.

In 1922 the young Richard Rodgers and Lorenz Hart wrote a musical version of *If I Were King* which was produced in an all-girl amateur performance with Dorothy Fields as Villon. It evoked the interest of producer Russell Janney, but he was unwilling to take a chance with these unknown writers and he subsequently hired a better-known composer to write a score for a version of the play as adapted by W H Post and Brian Hooker. The composer he chose was Rudolf Friml, basking in the enormous success of the previous season's *Rose Marie*.

Dennis King played Villon, a swaggering thief and versifier, who has been sending love-poems to the courtly Katherine de Vaucelles (Carolyn Thompson), and who boasts in the presence of the disguised King of France (Max Figman) that he would make a more effective monarch. To take a personal revenge on haughty Katherine, the King gives the arrested Villon 24 hours as Grand Marshal of France, and the mission to make good his boast to win his lady as a bride by the morrow or lose his life. Villon has the court make ostentatious revelry and simultaneously organizes the beggars and vagabonds of Paris into an army which defeats the besieging Burgundians. He is saved from the gallows when Katherine freely gives her hand to the man she now knows is only a vagabond. A traditional comic element, represented by Villon's little friend Guy Tabarie (Herbert Corthell), was tacked in alongside the main plot, but the dramatic character of Huguette (Jane Carroll) who sacrifices her life to save Villon from a plotter's dagger was retained, helping to keep a thoroughly dramatic core to the piece.

Friml's score was in the most vigorously romantic vein, more richly coloured than his *Rose Marie* music and ideally suited to the subject in hand. Villon's virile call to the people of Paris, the Song of the Vagabonds, was one of the most stirring marches to have come from the Broadway theatre, his duet with Katherine, 'Only a Rose', one of the most thoroughly romantic of love songs. The star was well equipped with further romantic numbers ('Tomorrow', 'Love Me Tonight') to place alongside his martial song, and these were supported by two fine numbers for Huguette ('Love for Sale', Huguette Waltz), an atmospheric Scotch Archer's Song which set the scene for the second act with great effect, and a comic serenade featuring Tabarie.

The Vagabond King ran for 511 performances on Broadway and it confirmed this appeal on the other side of the Atlantic when Janney mounted his show at London's Winter Garden Theatre with Derek Oldham starred as Villon alongside Winnie Melville (Katherine), Mark Lester (Tabarie) and Norah Blaney (Huguette). It ran for 480 London performances before touring and later returned to London on three occasions: in 1929 Alec Fraser played Villon (Adelphi Theatre, 14 October), in 1937 Harry Welchman starred (London Coliseum, 18 March) and in 1943 Webster Booth and Anne Ziegler featured back at the Winter Garden (22 April). In Australia, J C Williamson Ltd's production starred Strella Wilson, James Liddy, Arthur Stigant and Mabel Gibson for a season of more than 100 nights in Sydney, but although it proved less popular than *The Desert Song* which preceded it and *The Student Prince* which was brought back to replace it in Melbourne, it did well enough to cement the show's popularity, and the popularity of its songs, in another area of the English-speaking world.

In spite of the fact that it was indubitably a better made piece than its famous predecessor, *The Vagabond King* did not, however, follow *Rose Marie* to the long list of more distant, foreign-language stages which had made the earlier piece such a remarkable musical theatre phenomenon. It did, however, turn up at Amsterdam's Theater Carré in 1932 where Johannes Heesters, Mimi Lebrat, Nelly Gerritse and Oscar Tournaire featured in a rare foreign-language production.

A Paramount film was released in 1930 with King repeating his original rôle alongside Jeanette MacDonald. O P Heggie was the King, Lilian Roth played Huguette and Warner Oland the treacherous Thibault and a song entitled 'If I Were King' was interpolated. A second attempt was made at filming the show in 1956 when Maltese tenor Oreste Kirkop and Kathryn Grayson were paired in a version which used four new pieces, credited to Friml and Johnny Burke, alongside half a dozen pieces of the original score.

François Villon was earlier the eponymous hero of a French opera written by Foussier and Got, composed by Edmond de Membrée, and produced at the Paris Opéra in 1857 (20 April).

UK: Winter Garden Theatre 19 April 1927; Australia: Her Majesty's Theatre, Sydney 27 October 1928; Films: Paramount 1930, 1956
Recordings: London cast recordings on *Rudolf Friml in London* (WRC), 1956 film soundtrack (RCA), selections (RCA, WRC, Pye etc)

DER VAGABUND Operette in 3 acts by Moritz West and Ludwig Held based on a theme of Émile Souvestre. Music by Carl Zeller. Carltheater, Vienna, 30 October 1886.

Although the title of the piece was a singular one, the tale of *Der Vagabund* dealt, in fact, with the stories of two vagabonds, Alexis (Herr Detschi) and Ossip (Adolf Brackl). These wandering fellows are in Tiflis – in 1812 under Russian domination – where Alexis has cast his eyes on the lovely Marizza (Frl Peschi), daughter of the crooked local Russian police-chief, Ivan the Ghastly (Wilhelm Knaack). When the pair interfere in the plans of General Gregor Gregorovitch (Alexander Guttmann) and Gräfin Prascowia (Fr Hart) to take Marizza to the Grand Ducal court as a lady-in-waiting, they end up in prison but, since Ivan thinks Alexis is his illegitimate son, only Ossip gets sentenced. The influential fortune-teller, Dyrsa (Marie Schwarz), gets into the act too and it finally turns out, after two acts of red herrings, that Ossip is Prascowia's lost child and Alexis the by-blow of none other than the Grand Duke himself. He gets Gregor's generalship and the girl whilst Ossip pairs off with the fortune-teller.

Produced by Carl Tatartzy at the Carltheater, *Der Vagabund* was, like the rest of his productions, not a big success. It played 34 performances through November, but it nevertheless carried on. A week after its Vienna closure it opened under the management of Franz Steiner at Berlin's Walhalla-Theater. The following month Budapest's Budai Színkör mounted Lajos Makó's Hungarian version, other German language productions followed and, in 1887, the show was seen as far afield as America, played by a cast including Max Lube, Sophie Offeney, Cora Cabella, Ferdinand Schütz and Adolf Link at the Thalia Theater. It was later revived in repertoire at Amberg's Terrace Garten with a cast including Adolf Philipp.

Germany: Walhalla-Theater 10 December 1886; Hungary: Budai Színkör *A Csavargó* 23 January 1887; USA: Thalia Theater (Ger) 3 February 1887

VAILLANT-COUTURIER, Mlle

Mlle Couturier started her young career with much publicity when it was discovered that, in spite of the rule stating that Conservatoire pupils must hold themselves ready to be directed into employment as a form of payment for their study (a much-breached rule), she had signed a contract to go direct from her studies to Brussels and the Théâtre de la Monnaie. She went to Belgium and caused quite a stir there, before returning to Paris to appear at the Opéra-Comique (where she made the short list for the creations of the title-rôles of both *Carmen* and *Manon*) and in opérette where she created the vocally demanding rôle of Princess Micaëla in *Le Coeur et la main* (1882, 'Un jour, Pérez le capitaine') as well as prima-donna rôles in *Le Roi de carreau* (1883, Benvenuta) and *Babolin* (1884, Elvérine). On the last occasion it was remarked that her acting was rather 'provincial' and that she was perhaps not suited to opérette. She seems to have taken the remark to heart and went back to the Opéra-Comique where 'provincial' (by which the critic presumably meant unsophisticated) acting was apparently all right.

VALLI, Valli [née KNUST] (b Berlin, 11 February 1882; d London, 3 November 1927).

Brought up in London, with her two sisters Lulu Valli and Ida Valli, Valli Valli had a career as a child performer which included an appearance (with Lulu) at Berlin's Theater Unter den Linden in a British production of *Morocco Bound* (1895; 'a notable feature was the remarkably clever song and dance of two talented children, the sisters Valli') and another as Alice in *Alice in Wonderland*, amidst a number of other straight dramatic engagements. Although she continued to play in non-musical pieces, her adult career favoured the musical theatre, beginning with a small rôle in *Véronique* in London (replacing sister Lulu) and in New York (1905–6) and continuing through London take-overs in *A Waltz Dream* (Franzi) and *The Merry Widow* (Sonia) to another George Edwardes rôle, this time in New York, the part of Lady Binfield created for Edna May in *Kitty Grey* (1909).

She appeared in further Edwardes pieces in America (Alice in *The Dollar Princess*) and in Paris (title-rôle in *La Veuve Joyeuse* revival) and also in vaudeville and the British music-halls (*After the Honeymoon* w Seymour Hicks), but, having married music publisher Louis Dreyfus, made the later part of her career in America where she was seen in a botched version of Jean Gilbert's *Polnische Wirtschaft* called *The Polish Wedding* (1912, Marga) which failed to make it to Broadway, in Weber and Fields's *Roly-Poly* (1912), *The Purple Road* (1913, Empress Josephine, later Wanda), *The Queen of the Movies* (*Die Kino-Königin* 1914, Celia Gill), *The Lady in Red* (*Die Dame in Rot*, 1915, Sylvia Stafford) and *Miss Millions* (1919, ingénue Mary Hope).

Sister Lulu appeared as Miss Yost and deputized for Marie Studholme as Cicely in *The School Girl* (1903) and later took over Billie Burke's rôle of Mamie and played it on Broadway (without its big song 'My Little Canoe' which had been appropriated by the star) as well as appearing in such diverse pieces as *The Silver Slipper* (1902, tour), *The Maid and the Motor Man* (1907) and *Véronique*.

As for little Ida, who had done so well as a child when she appeared as Mr Hook in Frank Curzon's children's production of *Miss Hook of Holland* and in the Gaiety Theatre *Two Naughty Boys* (1906, Agnes), she apparently didn't make it as an adult.

VALMOUTH Musical in 2 acts by Sandy Wilson adapted from the works of Ronald Firbank. Lyric Theatre, Hammersmith, 2 October 1958; Saville Theatre, London, 27 January 1959.

Commissioned from the author-composer of *The Boy Friend* by Oscar Lewenstein and the Royal Court Theatre as a vehicle for American actress and vocalist Bertice Reading, the musical *Valmouth* was ultimately not produced by the English Stage Company, but by the young Michael Codron. Miss Reading starred as the ambivalent and outrageous negro masseuse of Ronald Firbank's *Valmouth* at the centre of a libretto crafted with great skill from the somewhat diffuse elements of the novellaist's quirky and esoteric universe.

At the English spa town of Valmouth we meet the eccentrically papist and centenarian lady of the manor, Mrs Hurstpierpoint (Barbara Couper), the unquenchably lustful and equally aged Lady Parvula Panzoust (Fenella

Plate 280. **Valmouth**: *Doris Hare, Fenella Fielding, Bertice Reading, Peter Gilmore and Barbara Couper caricatured by Keith Mackenzie.*

Fielding), the plebeian 120-year-old Granny Tooke (Doris Hare), and Mrs Thoroughfare (Betty Hardy) whose seafaring son, Captain Dick (Alan Edwards), provokes the events of the evening by abandoning his bosom pal, Lieutenant Whorwood (Aubrey Woods), for the charms of the dusky Niri-Esther (Maxine Daniels). Nemesis falls on the arcane mysteries of Valmouth when the defrocked and debauched Cardinal Pirelli (Geoffrey Dunn) is summoned to celebrate the young pair's nuptials and from the ensuing cataclysm only Mrs Yaj, Niri-Esther and her now illegitimate baby escape.

Wilson, having arranged these recondite folk into a shapely story, equipped them with some suitably special songs, which were eased into more natural English than Firbank's greenly jewelled prose. Lady Parvula sighed brazenly over the thighs of a teenaged shepherd (who had just been naïvely querying 'What Do I Want With Love?'), preparing to leap into the hay 'Just Once More', and apostrophized her late husband's shade apologetically with a history of her indiscretions ('Only a Passing Phase'), an incidental nun (Marcia Ashton) under a vow of silence for 364 days of the year burst forth with a veritable ejaculation of ecstatic chatter on 'My Talking Day', the Cardinal described the joys of 'The Cathedral of Clemenza', the two sailors sang (with rather different feelings) of 'Niri-Esther' and the three old beldames looked back in creaking harmony to their far-off youth when 'All the Girls Were Pretty (and all the men were strong)'. Mrs Yaj's songs glittered just a little less than these, but her bouncy 'Big Best Shoes' proved the show's easier-to-eat take-away number.

On its production in Hammersmith, *Valmouth*, not unexpectedly, drew some outraged reviews and customers and some which and who were simply thrilled. A West End transfer was delayed and, as a result, when *Valmouth* opened at the Saville Theatre, Cleo Laine deputized for the otherwise engaged Miss Reading. The show got a similarly bipartite reception, but even the enthusiasm of its fans could not win it more than 102 West End performances to add to the 84 clocked up in Hammersmith.

Gene Andrewski mounted the show at New York's York Playhouse the following year with Miss Reading starred alongside Anne Francine (Hurstpierpoint), Constance Carpenter (Parvula) and Alfred Toigo (Dick) but there the show died away in just 14 performances. For many years

after, *Valmouth* remained remembered by connoisseurs of its generation as a lost masterpiece of the musical theatre, and the next generation were given their opportunity to agree when the Chichester Festival mounted a revival of the show in 1982 (17 May). Misses Reading, Fielding, Ashton and Hare repeated their original rôles alongside Judy Campbell (Hurstpierpoint), Jane Wenham (Thoroughfare), Mark Wynter (Dick) and Sir Robert Helpmann (Cardinal) in a memorable production by John Dexter which started all the discussions over again. The show's evident minority appeal, however, meant that it did not transfer from its festival location to the commercial theatre of London.

USA: York Playhouse 6 October 1960
Recordings: original cast (Pye), Chichester Festival cast (TER)

VALMY, Jean (b Bordeaux; d 1989).

Valmy began his theatrical career writing for intimate revue in the south-west of France and then in Paris, and his earliest work in the field of the book musical was on a similarly smaller scale. The musical comedy *Baratin* (1949), a star vehicle for comedian Roger Nicolas, was a long-running comedy hit at the little Théâtre l'Européen, whilst *Les Pieds nickelés*, staged at the Bobino with Jacques Pills, Irène Hilda and the Frères Jacques heading the cast, also held the stage for some two years.

Valmy's most important play success, *J'y suis, j'y reste*, was produced for the first time in 1950, but he returned to the musical theatre with a second comic vehicle for Nicolas, *Mon p'tit pote* (1954), which proved yet another long-running success, remaining at the Européen for three and a half years, after which it was succeeded by a musical version of the classic play *Coquin de printemps*. This piece had neither Nicolas (who returned in 1961 to play *À toi de jouer* without creating the same kind of extended run) or the same very long Parisian life, but it was successful enough to have a number of out-of-town revivals over the following 20 years.

In 1958 Valmy collaborated with the aged Maurice Yvain on the composer's last work, *Le Corsaire noir*, and in 1969 moved to the opposite end of the theatrical scale to that in which he had found his greatest successes to collaborate on the indifferent Châtelet spectacle *La Caravelle d'or*. His last new work, an adaptation of Tristan Bernard's *Le Petit Café* (previously musicalized for Broadway by Ivan Caryll as *The Little Café* and by Ralph Bentazky for Vienna), returned to the musical-comedy genre.

1943 **Les Debrouillards de la Garonne** (Guy Lafarge/w Robert Valaire) Trianon, Bordeaux
1947 **On a volé une étoile** (Georges Ulmer/w Yves Bizos) Bobino 22 March
1949 **Baratin** (Henri Betti/André Hornez) Théâtre l'Européen 18 March
1949 **Les Pieds nickelés** (Bruno Coquatrix/w Hornez, Jean Lanjin) Eldorado 23 December
1951 **Le Leçon d'amour dans un parc** (Lafarge/w Lafarge/w André Birabeau) Théâtre des Bouffes-Parisiens 20 December
1954 **Les Chansons de Bilitis** (Joseph Kosma/w Marc-Cab) Théâtre des Capucines 30 January
1954 **Mon p'tit pote** (Jack Ledru/w Cab) Théâtre l'Européen 29 September
1958 **Coquin de printemps** (Guy Magenta/Fernand Bonifay/w Cab) Théâtre l'Européen 31 January

1958 **Le Corsaire noir** (Maurice Yvain) Opéra, Marseille 23 February
1959 **Bidule** (Ledru/w Cab) Théâtre l'Européen 27 November
1961 **À toi de jouer** (Ledru/w Cab) Théâtre l'Européen 24 November
1962 **Farandole d'amour** (Ledru/w Cab) Casino, Enghien 21 July
1968 **L'Auberge du cheval blanc** new French version w Marcel Lamy (Théâtre du Châtelet)
1969 **La Caravelle d'or** (Francis Lopez/w Jacques Plante) Théâtre du Châtelet 19 December
1980 **Le Petit Café** (Lafarge, Ledru/w Lafarge) Opéra du Rhin 14 December
1982 **Balalaïka** new French version (Saint-Étienne)

VALVERDE, Joaquín (b Badajoz, 27 February 1846; d Madrid, 17 March 1910).

The elder Joaquín Valverde and his son **Joaquín Quirito VALVERDE** [y San Juan] (b Madrid, 1875; d Mexico, 6 November 1918) between them kept the name of Valverde to the forefront on the zarzuela stage and, more than any other composer(s) of the Spanish musical theatre, on the international musical stage during some four decades.

Valverde sr had his most considerable success with the internationally played and enduringly popular *La gran vía*, composed in collaboration with Federico Chueca (lib: Martinez Felipe Perez, Teatro Felipe 2 July 1886) and the pair worked together on the music for a number of other pieces including *Las ferias* (1878), *La cancion de Lola* (1880), *Fiesta nacional* (1882), *De la noche a la mañana* (1883), *Caramelo* (1884), *Vivitos y coleando* (1884), *Cadiz* (1886), *Le magasin de musique* (1889), *Majas y torero* (1901) and *El bateo* (1901).

His other works for the stage included *El centenario en la aldea* (1881), *Los Puretanos* (1885, w Tómas Lopez Torregrosa), *Pasar la raga* (1886, w Julian Roméa y Parra), *Niña Pancha* (1886, w Romea), *Las grandes potencias* (1890, w Roméa/Burgos), *La paraja francesa* (1890), *El director* (1891), *Retolondron* (1892), *La de vámonos* (1894 w Felipe Perez y Gonzales), *Los coraceros* (1896), *Padre Benito* (1897), *La obra de la temporada* (1904), *Sangre moza* (1907), *El gallo de la pasión* (1907, w Joaquín Quirito Valverde y San Juan) and *La Chanteuse* (w Torregrosa).

La gran vía was seen throughout the world in various guises, whilst others of his works also got a hearing further afield, notably *Majas y toreros* which was played at Vienna's Danzers Orpheum by a visiting zarzuela company in 1902.

The younger Valverde made his first appearance on a playbill at the age of 21, turning out *Y de la niña 'que?'*, *La Zingara*, *La fuente de los milagros*, *La fantasia de Carmen* and *La marcha de Cadiz* all in 1896, and in the 22 remaining years of his life a vast number of scores for the theatre, mostly in Spain, but also abroad. He was represented on Broadway by the revusical pasticcio *The Land of Joy* (Park Theater, 1 November 1917) and a second, less successful revusical piece *A Night in Spain* (6 December 1917), and also supplied several pieces for the French-language theatre including *L'Amour en Espagne* (Alévy, Eugène Joullot, Mareil, Parisiana, 20 August 1909; Moulin-Rouge, 21 October 1910), *La Rose de Grenade* (Hanneaux, Frédoff, Théâtre des Variétés, Brussels March 1911; Olympia, Paris, 1912), *La Reluquera* (Eugène Joullot, Adams, Théâtre l'Européen, 17 November 1911) and *La Belle Cigarière* (Joullot, Benjamin Rabier, Moulin-Rouge, 20 March 1913).

His list of zarzuela credits included *La torre de babel* (1897), *El primer reserva* (1897, w Torregrosa), *El alcade de Corneja* (1898) *Los novicios* (1898), *Las niñas de Villagarda* (1898, w Torregrosa), *Toros del saltillo* (1898), *La Castafieras picadas* (1898, w Torregrosa), *La batalla de Tetuan* (1898), *Las campesina* (1898) *La chiquita de najera* (1898), *El sueno de una noche de verano* (1898), *La estatua de Don Gonzalo* (1898), *La magra negra* (1898, w Caballero), *Los tres gorriones* (1898), *Bettia* (1899), *Le Mari-Juana* (1899), *Citrato? der ver serà* (1899, w Caballero), *El trabuco* (1899, w Torregrosa), *Concurso universal* (1899, w Calleja), *Los camarones* (1899, w Torregrosa), *Los cocineros* (1899, w Torregrosa), *Instantáneas* (1899, w Torregrosa) *Las buenas formas* (w Rubio, 1899), *Los flamencos* (1899, w Torregrosa), *La reina de la fiesta* (1899), *El ultimo chulo* (1899, w Torregrosa), *Los besugos* (1899), *La señora capitana* (1900, w Tómas Barrera), *El fondó del bául* (1900, w Enrico Cleto, Marcellino Barrera y Gomez), *La tremenda* (1901), *Los niños Llorones* (1901, w Barrera, Torregrosa), *El genero infimo* (1901 w Tómas Barrera), *El debut de la Ramirez* (1901, w Torregrosa) *Plantas y flores* (1901, w Torregrosa), *Chispita* (1901 w Torregrosa), *La casta Susana* (1902), *San Juan de Luz* (1902, w Torregrosa), *El trébol* (1904, w Serrano), *La inclusera* (1904, w Caballero), *Las estrellas* (1904, w Serrano), *Pasa-calle* (1905) *La mulata* (1905), *La Galerna* (1905), *Y no es noche de dormir* (1905) *El Perro chico* (1905, w Serrano), *La reya de la Dolores* (1905, w Serrano), *El iluso Cañizares* (1905, w Calleja), *El vals de las sombras* (1906), *El moscón* (1906), *La peña negra* (1906, w Toregrosa), *El gallo de la pasión* (1907, w Joaquín Valverde), *La isla de los suspiros* (1910), *La suerta loca* (1910, w Serrano), *El principe casto* (1912), *El fresco de Goya* (1912), *La ultima Pelentia* (1913, w Torregrosa) *Las mujeres guapas* (1914, w Luis Foglietti), *Feria de Abril* (1914, w Foglietti), *La gitanada* (1914, w Foglietti), *Caralimpia* (1914, w Foglietti), *El tango argentino* (1914), *Serafina la Rubiales, o una noche en el juzgao* (1914, w Foglietti), *A versicuidas de Amalia* (1914, w Foglietti), *El potro salvaje* (1914, w Pablo Luna), *El amigo Melquiades* (1914, w Serrano), *Las pildoeas de Hercules* (1914, w Foglietti), *El principe carnaval* (1920), *El estuche de monerias*, *La guitarra*, *El Paraíso de los niños*, *La chanteuse* (w Torregrosa), *El pobre Valbuena* (w Torregrosa), *El Recluta* (w Torregrosa), *San Juan de Luz* (w Torregrosa), *Los Granujas* (w Torregrosa), *Los chicos de la escuela* (w Torregrosa), *Colorin colorao* (w Torregrosa), *El terrible Pérez* (w Torregrosa), *El puesto de flores* (w Torregrosa), *La muerte de Agripina* (w Torerosa), *La Cocotero* (w Torregrosa), *Congreso feminista*, *La grandes cortesanas*, *Los nenes*, *Viva Córdoba*, *El corenta de la partida*, *El Pollo Tejada* (w Serrano), *El noble amigo* (w Calleja), *Biblioteca popular* (w Calleja), *La ola verde* (w Calleja) and *La casa de la juerga* (w Gay).

VAN BIENE, Auguste (b Holland, 16 May ?1845; d Brighton, 23 January 1913). Performer, conductor, producer and a colourful contributor to Victorian musical theatre.

Auguste van Biene studied music in Brussels and played in the Rotterdam Opera House orchestra at the age of 15 before moving to Britain where, for lack of connections, he found himself forced to go busking with his cello in the streets of London. He related frequently how he played for nine or ten weeks in this way, in order to keep body and soul together, before he was noticed by the celebrated conductor Sir Michael Costa and given a job at the Covent Garden Theatre. Aided by an extravagant personality, his musical skills were in any case sufficient for him to rise quickly through the orchestral ranks to become a concert soloist.

He subsequently began a second career as a musical director and was engaged by D'Oyly Carte as conductor on the first *HMS Pinafore* tour (1878) before defecting to the 'rebel' production of *HMS Pinafore* staged by the Comedy Opera Company after their dispute with Carte (1879) and to their following production *Marigold* (Vasseur's *Le Droit du seigneur*, 1879). Having burnt his bridges as far as the D'Oyly Carte organization was concerned, in 1881 he joined Alexander Henderson at the Comedy Theatre and acted as musical director for his productions of *La Mascotte*, *The Grand Mogul*, *Rip van Winkle* and *Falka*, but he picked the wrong horse again when he left Henderson and went off to Europe with the ill-fated *Billee Taylor* tour of 1884. He returned to a job the Comedy Theater under Violet Melnotte's management, however, and there conducted the original London productions of *Erminie* (1885), *The Lily of Léoville* and *Mynheer Jan*, before again shifting on to take the baton for Julia Woolf's comic opera *Carina*.

In 1881 he began a career as a theatrical manager, touring opera in the British provinces with a company including such top performers as Blanche Cole, Annette Albu, Michael Dwyer and Arabella Smythe and the young Julian Edwards as chorus master and assistant conductor. He later moved into musical comedy, at first in partnership with Horace Lingard, touring *Falka*, to which Henderson had ceded him the provincial rights, and later *Rip van Winkle*. From 1890 to 1895 was given the number one touring rights on George Edwardes's enormously popular Gaiety burlesque productions, a right which made him one of the most significant musical-comedy impresarii in the country. Amongst the Gaiety pieces which he toured were the burlesques *Faust Up-to-Date*, *Carmen Up-to-Data*, *Ruy Blas and the Blasé Roué*, *Cinder-Ellen Up-too Late*, *Blue-Eyed Susan* and the musical comedy *In Town*.

Van Biene always had a yen to perform as an actor, and on one emergency occasion he took over the star rôle in *The Old Guard* on the road, calling himself 'Henri Tempo' for the occasion. He later featured himself in the title-rôle of a tour of *Rip van Winkle* and in 1892 he commissioned the sentimental musical drama *The Broken Melody*, and starred himself overwhelmingly as the dramatically weepie-effective old cellist that James Tanner had concocted for him. He played this piece with enormous success in the British provinces, at the Prince of Wales Theatre, and on overseas touring circuits, for more than 6,000 performances before commissioning a sequel, *The Master Musician*. He played this second piece in theatres and then on the halls literally up to his death, for this most flamboyant of showmen died on stage at the Brighton Hippodrome in mid-performance.

VAN GHELL, [Céline] Anna (b ?1844; d Paris, January 1926).

Recognized as one of the best vocalists amongst the leading ladies of the opéra-bouffe stage, Anna van Ghell created a number of important rôles in Paris in her twen-

ties and thirties. She made her first successes in Brussels, and came to notice in Paris when she became prima donna at William Busnach's striving Théâtre de l'Athénée, making her début in de Rillé's *Le Petit Poucet* (October 1868) and playing in *Les Horreurs de la guerre* (1868) and Legouix's *Le Vengeur* (1868). Her performances in these less-than-memorable pieces did not, however, go unnoticed and the shapely young soprano was soon creating much better rôles.

Her first big success came when she introduced the rôle of Méphisto in Hervé's *Le Petit Faust* (1869), and she compounded that with another travesty rôle, as the original Raphaël in Offenbach's *La Princesse de Trébizonde* (1869). She reprised the rôle of the chattering Roland, famously created by Delphine Ugalde in *Les Bavards* (1870), returned to Hervé to create the part of the extravagantly zany Queen Jane of Scotland, equipped with a burlesque operatic mad scene, in *Le Trône d'Écosse* (1871) and was the first Parisian Gabrielle in *Les Cent Vierges* (1872).

She played the rôle of Alaciel in *La Fiancée du roi de Garbe* at the Folies-Dramatiques (1874), was Gabrielle in the 1874 revival of *La Vie parisienne*, and had a further fine creation, again in travesty, when she played René in the first production of Offenbach's *La Créole* (1875), but she found less joy with Vasseur's *La Blanchisseuse de Berg-op-Zoom* and Offenbach's *La Foire Saint-Laurent* (1877, Bobêche). Later in 1877 she appeared at the Châtelet as Young Rothomago in the féerie *Rothomago*, after which her name seems to slip from the Parisian bills.

She died in the Baron Taylor Foundation Home for old artists in Paris at the age of 81.

VANLOO, Albert [Guillaume Florent] (b Brussels, 10 September 1846; d Paris, 4 March 1920). One of Paris's top librettists of classic opérette through a long and productive career.

Vanloo was at first destined for the law, but during his legal studies he fell in with another young man, the four-years-older Eugène Leterrier, who shared his ambitions to write for the stage, and the pair began to immerse themselves in the Parisian theatre world. They succeeded in placing several of their short pieces in various Paris houses (including the Bouffes-Parisiens) and one full-length opérette, the Tom Thumb musical *Le Petit Poucet*, which was produced by William Busnach at the Théâtre de l'Athénée, but, in spite of incursions into the straight theatre in collaboration with such celebrated writers as Labiche and Eugène Grangé, it was some years before the pair finally struck up genuine success. Thanks to a friendship struck up with Lecocq in everyone's struggling days at the Athénée, Vanloo and Leterrier got the opportunity to write the libretto for the successor to the composer's enormously successful *La Fille de Madame Angot*. Their sparklingly funny *Giroflé-Girofla* turned out a triumph, and its librettists were thoroughly launched.

The pair collaborated on a long series of subsequent opérettes with Lecocq, turning out the texts for a number of the composer's series of works mounted at the Théâtre de la Renaissance – the exceptionally classy comic book of *La Petite Mariée*, the sexy and successful *La Marjolaine*, and the rather more conventional but nevertheless joyous *La Camargo* and *La Jolie Persane* – as well as the spectacular féerie tale of *L'Arbre de Noël* for the Porte-Saint-Martin, and the complex and comical imbroglio of *Le Jour et la Nuit* for the Nouveautés, all in a period of just six seasons. Later, Vanloo provided another successful script (w Busnach) for Lecocq with his version of the *Ali Baba* tale and, as late as 1900, the librettist and composer worked together on a version of *La Belle au bois dormant* for the great stage of the Gaîté.

During their Lecocq years, Vanloo and Leterrier also produced the text for Offenbach's fantasy spectacular *Le Voyage dans la lune* and the libretto of *L'Étoile*, which was set by the young Emmanuel Chabrier in a style that did not appeal as it might have to the audiences of its time. However, the libretto was found so superior that it was later re-used throughout the world set by other composers. It became *The Merry Monarch* in America (mus: Woolson Morse), *The Lucky Star* in Britain (mus: Ivan Caryll) and *Uff király* in Hungary (mus: Béla Hegyi and Szidor Bátor), and has still survived to the present day as *L'Étoile*. Their libretto to *La Gardeuse d'oies*, set in France to a score by Paul Lacôme, underwent a similar borrowing process when it was turned into the musical play *Papa Gougou* (*A Normandy Wedding*) in the hands of American composer William Furst, whilst the book of *L'Arbre de Noël*, stripped of Lecocq's music, was reset by Louis Roth in Austria (Theater an der Wien *Der Weihnachtsbaum*), Germany and in Hungary (Népszinház, *A karácsonyfa*), and their libretto *Le Roi de carreau*, deprived of its Lajarte score in favour of one by Ludwig Englander, became *Half a King* in America.

The pair provided libretti for several other, if less notable successes, such as Chassaigne's *Le Droit d'aînesse* (a huge hit in English as *Falka*) and Messager's *La Béarnaise*, as well as for the occasional revue, and won a percentage rate of hits to failures that was quite remarkable given the size of their output.

After Leterrier's death, Vanloo worked with several different collaborators, producing the texts for all kinds of stage pieces including a handful of spectacular musical shows on the lines of *L'Arbre de Noël* of which *Le Bonnhomme de neige* (w Chivot), musically set by Antoine Banès in its Parisian version and subsequently taken up for Britain (*The Snowman*), was the most successful. Major success had to wait, however, until he found himself a real replacement for Leterrier and that replacement turned out to be a neighbour. Georges Duval had an apartment in the same block as Vanloo, and they were able to communicate from window to window.

It was with Duval that Vanloo confected the texts for André Messager's two great fin-de-siècle opérettes, *Véronique* and *Les P'tites Michu*. These pieces were more sweetly conventional than the best and most farcically funny of the Vanloo/Leterrier opérettes – decidedly different in flavour from such as *La Petite Mariée* and *Le Jour et la nuit* – but they were a stylish mixture of sentiment and gentle comedy which suited their composer ideally and the result was a pair of notable and international hits. Vanloo's last Parisian opérette libretto, *Les Dragons de l'Impératrice*, was also written with Duval and for Messager, letting him end a career of nearly 40 years during which he had been one of the brightest stars of two eras of Parisian and international musical theatre in the best company.

Amongst the other adaptations of Vanloo's works was a German piece called *Frau Lohengrin*, apparently taken from his vaudeville *L'Oncle Bidochon* (w Chivot, Roussel

Théâtre Cluny, 2 March 1894), written by Eduard Jacobson and Wilhelm Mannstädt, with lyrics by G Görss and music by Gustav Steffens, and produced at Berlin's Adolf Ernst Theater on 21 December 1895.

In his retirement, Vanloo authored a book of memoirs, *Sur le plateau*, which gives a highly enjoyable look at the Paris stage of the later years of the 19th century and which has repeatedly been mined as source material by 20th-century theatre writers.

1868 **Le Petit Poucet** (Laurent de Rillé/w Eugène Leterrier) Théâtre de l'Athénée 8 October

1869 **Madeleine** (Henri Potier/w Leterrier) 1 act Théâtre des Bouffes-Parisiens 10 January

1869 **La Nuit du 15 Octobre** (Georges Jacobi/w Leterrier) 1 act Théâtre des Bouffes-Parisiens 25 October

1871 **Nabucho** (A de Villebichot/w Leterrier) Folies-Nouvelles 13 September

1874 **Giroflé-Girofla** (Charles Lecocq/w Leterrier) Théâtre des Fantaisies Parisiennes, Brussels 21 March

1875 **Le Voyage dans la lune** (Jacques Offenbach/w Arnold Mortier, Leterrier) Théâtre de la Gaîté 26 October

1875 **La Petite Mariée** (Lecocq/w Leterrier) Théâtre de la Renaissance 21 December

1877 **La Marjolaine** (Lecocq/w Leterrier) Théâtre de la Renaissance 3 February

1877 **Madame Clara sonnambule** (Isidore Legouix/w Leterrier) 1 act Palais-Royal 15 March

1877 **L'Étoile** (Emmanuel Chabrier/w Leterrier) Théâtre des Bouffes-Parisiens 28 November

1878 **La Camargo** (Lecocq/w Leterrier) Théâtre de la Renaissance 20 November

1879 **La Jolie Persane** (Lecocq/w Leterrier) Théâtre de la Renaissance 28 October

1880 **Le Beau Nicolas** (Paul Lacôme/w Leterrier) Théâtre des Folies-Dramatiques 8 October

1880 **L'Arbre de Noël** (Lecocq/w Leterrier, Mortier) Théâtre de la Porte-Saint-Martin 6 October

1881 **Mademoiselle le Moucheron** (Offenbach/w Leterrier) 1 act Théâtre de la Renaissance 10 May

1881 **Le Jour et la nuit** (Lecocq/w Leterrier) Théâtre des Nouveautés 5 November

1883 **Le Droit d'aînesse** (Francis Chassaigne/w Leterrier) Théâtre des Nouveautés 27 January

1883 **Le Roi de carreau** (Théodore de Lajarte/w Leterrier) Théâtre des Nouveautés 26 October

1883 **Juanita** (*Donna Juanita*) French version w Leterrier (Galeries Saint-Hubert, Brussels)

1885 **Le Petit Poucet** (w Leterrier, Mortier) Théâtre de la Gaîté 28 October

1885 **La Béarnaise** (André Messager/w Leterrier) Théâtre des Bouffes-Parisiennes 12 December

1887 **La Gamine de Paris** (Gaston Serpette/w Leterrier) Théâtre des Bouffes-Parisiens 30 March

1887 **Ali-Baba** (Lecocq/w William Busnach) Alhambra, Brussels 11 November

1888 **La Gardeuse d'oies** (Lacôme/w Leterrier) Théâtre de la Renaissance 26 October

1890 **L'Oeuf rouge** (Edmond Audran/w Busnach) Théâtre des Folies-Dramatiques 14 March

1890 **La Fée aux chèvres** (Louis Varney/w Paul Ferrier) Théâtre de la Gaîté 18 December

1892 **Le Pays de l'or** (Léon Vasseur/w Henri Chivot) Théâtre de la Gaîté 26 January

1894 **Le Bonhomme de neige** (Antoine Banès/w Chivot) Théâtre des Bouffes-Parisiens 19 April

1897 **Les P'tites Michus** (Messager/w Duval) Théâtre des Bouffes-Parisiens 16 November

1898 **Véronique** (Messager/w Duval) Théâtre des Bouffes-Parisiens 10 November

1900 **La Belle au bois dormant** (Lecocq/w Duval) Théâtre des Bouffes-Parisiens 19 February

1905 **Les Dragons de l'Impératrice** (Messager/w Duval) Théâtre des Variétés 13 February

Memoirs: *Sur un plateau* (Ollendorf, Paris, nd)

VAN PARYS, Georges   *see* PARYS, GEORGES VAN

VAN STUDDIFORD, Grace [née QUIVE] (b North Manchester (Lafayette), Ind, 8 January 1873; d Fort Wayne, Ind, 29 January 1927). Vocally superior Broadway prima donna of the American stage of the early 20th century.

After making early appearances in *The Black Hussar* (*Der Feldprediger*) in Chicago, with the Bostonians and on tour with Jefferson de Angelis in *The Jolly Musketeer* (1889), Miss van Studdiford moved on to opéra-comique and appeared at the Metropolitan Opera House in the soprano rôles of the lighter repertoire: *Martha* (Lady Harriet), *Carmen* (Micaëla), *Faust* (Marguerite), *Esmeralda* (Fleur-de-Lys), *HMS Pinafore* (Josephine) and as Leonora in *Il trovatore*. She played with the St Louis Opera and the Schiller organization, and then returned to the musical theatre to create the title-rôle of De Koven's musequel to *Robin Hood*, *Maid Marian* (1903). She was subsequently seen in the comic operas *The Red Feather* and *Lady Teazle* before making her first appearances as a vocalist in variety.

She was back on Broadway in 1908 as the star of *The Golden Butterfly* (Ilma Walden), toured in *The Bohemian Girl* (1909) and played Bengaline in the Broadway version of *Le Paradis de Mahomet* (aka *The Bridal Trap* 1910) and Mimi in Jerome Kern's *La Belle Paree* at the Winter Garden (1911). She later toured in the title-rôle of *Oh! Oh! Delphine* and alongside Howard Marsh in *Maytime* and, during the war years, visited military camps playing Mrs Guyer in a version of *A Trip to Chinatown*. She died after an operation at the age of 54.

VARNA, Henri [VANTARD, Henri] (b Marseille, 1887; d Paris, 10 April 1969). Parisian manager and director with a special flair for the revusical and spectacular in the musical theatre.

After studies at Aix-en-Provence and Marseille, Varna worked as an actor, playing at the Théâtre des Célestins at Lyon in 1909 and continuing in supporting rôles at various Paris theatres. He soon found his vocation as a director and producer and from 1910 when he directed a revue at the Château d'Eau he expanded his career in that direction, writing and staging the starry variety shows at the Ambassadeurs and the Concert Mayol, and then producing and directing the spectacles at the Bouffes du Nord, the Palace, the Empire and, from 1929, at the Casino de Paris which he was to head for 40 years.

In 1939 Varna took over both the famous Théâtre de la Renaissance, menaced with demolition, and the Théâtre Mogador, which he re-opened as a home for revivals of the classics of opérette, staged in the luxurious manner with which his name had become synonymous in the world of variety. Beginning with *Les Cloches de Corneville* in March 1940 (in which he took to the stage as Gaspard), he continued with *Les Mousquetaires au couvent*, *Les Saltimbanques* (also playing Malicorne), *La Fille de Madame Angot*, *La*

Veuve joyeuse, *Véronique*, *La Mascotte* and after the end of the war *Ta bouche*, *No, No, Nanette* and *Rêve de valse* as well as mounting the Paris première of Georges Sellers's *La Vie de château* (1945) which ran for more than 12 months.

From 1948, with the modern opérette now finding its feet in the wake of the success of *La Belle de Cadix*, Varna began to produce a good ration of new works, most of which bore his own name as co-author. Over the next decade, in between periodical revivals of *La Veuve joyeuse*, he gave spectacular productions to Scotto's *Violettes impériales* (1948), *La Danseuse aux étoiles* (1949) and *Les Amants de Venise* (1953) for long runs, made over the elderly *The Belle of New York* as *Belle de mon coeur* and Fritz Kreisler's *Sissy* as *Sissi, futur Impératrice*, and starred Merkès and Merval in *Les Amours de Don Juan* (1955) and Tino Rossi in *Naples au baiser de feu* (1957). He presented Géori Boué as *La Belle Hélène*, Merval as *Rose-Marie*, and featured Merkès and Merval again in a scenic musical version of the old Châtelet favourite *Michel Strogoff* (1964), a reprise of *Les Amants de Venise* in which he took to the stage one last time to play the aged Cardinal, and in *Vienne chante et danse* (1967), his last production before his death in 1969.

In his early café-concert days, Varna co-authored a number of small pieces for such houses as the Concert Mayol and the Folies-Belleville (*Le Mariage de Pépita* (1915), *Le Voyage du Prince M'Amour* (1916), *Le Droit de la cauchage* (1919), *Le Couvent des caresses* (1920), *Le Coucher de la Pompadour* (1921), *Vive la femme!*, *Yo t'aime* (Palace, 1925) etc).

VARNEY, Louis (b New Orleans, 30 May 1844; d Paris, 20 August 1908). Composer of one major hit and many other works for the 19th-century opérette stage.

Louis Varney was the son of **[Pierre Joseph] Alphonse VARNEY** (b Paris, 1 February 1811; d Paris, 7 February 1879), conductor at and sometime manager of the Théâtre des Bouffes-Parisiens, director of the Bordeaux conservatoire and composer of a number of short opérascomiques and opérettes (*Le Moulin joli*, *La Quittance de minuit*, *La Ferme de Kilmour*, *L'Opéra au camp*, *La Polka des sabots*, *Un fin de bail*, *Un leçon d'amour*). The younger Varney was born in America during his father's engagement there with a French opéra-comique company, and lived there until the age of seven.

He ultimately followed his father into the musical side of the theatre and in 1876 became musical director at Paris's Théâtre de l'Athenée-Comique, under the management of Montrouge, conducting and supplying the various music required for such of the theatre's productions as the revues *De bric et de broc* (Clairville, Armand Liorat 5 February 1876) and *Babel Revue* (Paul Burani, Édouard Philippe 10 January 1879) or the drame-bouffe *Il Signor Pulcinella* (Beauvallet, Marc Le Prévost 26 September 1876). Following these several years of first essays at composing for the stage, he won his best opportunity to date when the ever-adventurous Louis Cantin of the Théâtre des Bouffes-Parisiens commissioned from him a full-length score to a libretto by Paul Ferrier and Jules Prével. The resulting opérette, *Les Mousquetaires au couvent*, proved an outstanding success, playing more than 200 performances in its first run and establishing itself as one of the most popular of contemporary Parisian favourites through regular revivals over the succeeding seasons. It also won itself a wide series of international productions and hoisted the 36-year-old neophyte composer immediately to the top of his profession.

If his appearance as a noticeable composer had been rather a tardy one, Varney more than made up for that tardiness by a very high rate of productivity in the years that followed. In the 25 years after the first production of *Les Mousquetaires au couvent* he composed the scores for nearly 40 opérettes and vaudevilles. If he did not ever repeat the enormous triumph of his first work, a good percentage of his pieces had successful initial runs in Paris and in the 1890s when, with the age of Offenbach and Lecocq over, French works were becoming less fashionable on the international stage, Varney was one of the few French composers to find a regular market for his shows both elsewhere in Europe and even overseas.

The first of his post-*Mousquetaires* shows were not very successful, even though the composer's new reputation found them occasional further productions: *La Reine des Halles* was a flop in London as *Gibraltar* and as *Madam Rose* (Haymarket Theatre, 6 August 1881) and *Coquelicot* was produced briefly, after its 40 Paris performances, at Budapest's Népszinház as *A pipacs* (ad Lajos Evva). The composer found more success, however, with a musical version of the tale of *Fanfan la Tulipe* and with a little piece for Anna Judic called *Joséphine* which she played as a forepiece or part-programme on her tours in Austria and America as well as at home.

Between 1884 and 1887, on the other hand, Varney had a good run of success, with four consecutive pieces reaching the 100 performances mark which, in the Paris of that time, guaranteed success. The success of the comical *Babolin* (100 performances), the picturesque and farcical *Dix Jours aux Pyrénées* (128 performances) and, above all, the perversion of Dumas written – with care to its title – by the same authors as his first great hit as *Les Petits Mousquetaires* (150 performances), was contained in France, but the saucy *L'Amour mouillé* followed its Paris run by winning productions in London, Vienna and Budapest.

La Japonaise (13 performances), *La Vénus d'Arles* (21 performances) and *Riquet à la houppe* (40 performances) were failures, but the more farcically comical *La Fille de Fanchon la vielleuse* went on from its 110-performance run at the Folies-Dramatiques to be seen in both Austria and Hungary. The vaudevillesque *Le Brillant Achille*, less successful at home (48 performances), also travelled, playing in Austria and Germany as *Die eiserne Jungfrau* (Theater in der Josefstadt, 7 April 1895; Centraltheater, 7 November 1894), as did the circus musical *Les Forains* (*Olympia die Muskelvenus* in Austria, *Olympia* in Germany, *Komédiások* in Hungary) and, above all, another comical musical *Les Petites Brebis*, which was played throughout Europe and in Britain (*Die kleine Schäfen*, *A bárányak*, *The Little Innocents*) and proved a particular hit in its German adaptation. Other pieces, like *Miss Robinson* (116 performances) and *Cliquette* (93 performances), did well at home without being seen elsewhere.

The year 1896 brought Varney's two most successful works since his first big success. The two were quite different in character, the ghost-story *La Falote* being in the old-fashioned *Cloches de Corneville* comic-opera style, whilst *Le Papa de Francine* was a thorough musical comedy piece with a touch of the spectacular revue to it. Both had fine Paris runs of nearly 200 performances, and both were produced in other countries in a series of languages and adaptations. These two pieces represented the last peak in Varney's career for although *Le Pompier de service*, *Les Demoiselles de Saint-Cyriens*, *Les Petites Barnett* and, in particular, the 1902 piece *La Princesse Bébé* of his later works found audiences in and beyond France, none were in the same league as his greatest hits.

The composer of much delightfully melodious and happy music, including several further revues and a ballet, *La Princesse Idéa* (1895), produced at the Folies-Bergère, Varney proved himself able to illustrate all the types of musical pieces – from classic opérette to musical comedy – which came and went in and from fashion in the last two decades of the 19th century. His first and most famous piece assured him a place in the very narrow repertoire of 19th-century pieces which have survived as standards a century later and, if his other works – particularly those which were based on comic and vaudeville libretti – have proven more ephemeral, the same can be said for all but a few of his contemporaries' works.

1879 **Les Amoureux de Boulotte** (P Albert, P Calixte) 1 act Folies Marigny 1 October

1879 **Les Sirènes de Bougival** (Armand de Jallais) 1 act Alcazar 8 November

1880 **Les Mousquetaires au couvent** (Paul Ferrier, Jules Prével) Théâtre des Bouffes-Parisiens 16 March

1881 **La Reine des Halles** (Alfred Delacour, Victor Bernard, Paul Burani) Comédie Parisienne 4 April

1882 **Coquelicot** (Cogniards ad Armand Silvestre) Théâtre des Bouffes-Parisiens 2 March

1882 **La Petite Reinette** (William Busnach, Clairville) Galeries St Hubert, Brussels 11 October

1882 **Fanfan la Tulipe** (Ferrier, Prével) Théâtre des Folies-Dramatiques 21 October

1883 **Joséphine** (Albert Millaud) 1 act Casino, Trouville August, Paris 15 March 1884

1884 **Babolin** (Ferrier, Prével) Théâtre des Nouveautés 19 March

1885 **Les Petits Mousquetaires** (Ferrier, Prével) Théâtre des Folies-Dramatiques 5 March

1887 **L'Amour mouillé** (Prével, Armand Liorat) Théâtre des Nouveautés 25 January

1887 **Dix Jours aux Pyrenées** (Ferrier) Théâtre de la Gaîté 22 November

1888 **Divorcée** (Raoul Toché) 1 act Cabourg 11 August

1888 **La Japonaise** (Emile de Najac, Millaud) Théâtre des Variétés 23 November

1889 **La Vénus d'Arles** (Ferrier, Liorat) Théâtre des Nouveautés 30 January

1889 **Riquet à la houppe** (Ferrier, Clairville) Théâtre des Folies-Dramatiques 20 April

1890 **La Fée aux chèvres** (Ferrier, Albert Vanloo) Théâtre de la Gaîté 18 December

1891 **La Fille de Fanchon la vielleuse** (Liorat, Busnach, Albert Fonteny) Théâtre des Folies-Dramatiques 3 November

1892 **La Femme de Narcisse** (Fabrice Carré) Théâtre de la Renaissance 14 April

1892 **Le Brillant Achille** (Clairville, Fernand Beissier) Théâtre de la Renaissance 21 October

1892 **Miss Robinson** (Ferrier) Théâtre des Folies-Dramatiques 17 December

1893 **Cliquette** (Busnach) Théâtre des Folies-Dramatiques 11 July

1894 **Les Forains** (Maxime Boucheron, Antony Mars) Théâtre des Bouffes-Parisiens 9 February

1894 **La Fille de Paillasse** (Liorat, Louis Leloir) Théâtre des Menus-Plaisirs 20 April

1895 **Les Petites Brebis** (Liorat) Théâtre Cluny 5 June

1895 **Mam'zelle Bémol** (Alfred Delilia, Hippolyte Raymond) Théâtre Cluny 7 September

1895 **La Belle Épicière** (Pierre Decourcelle, Henri Kéroul) Théâtre des Bouffes-Parisiens 16 November

1896 **La Falote** (Liorat, Maurice Ordonneau) Théâtre des Folies-Dramatiques 26 April

1896 **Le Papa de Francine** (Victor de Cottens, Paul Gavault) Théâtre Cluny 5 November

1897 **Le Pompier de service** (de Cottens, Gavault) Théâtre des Variétés 31 January

1897 **Pour sa couronne** (Arnold Fordyce) 1 act Théâtre des Bouffes-Parisiens 17 April

1898 **Les Demoiselles de St-Cyriens** (de Cottens, Gavault) Théâtre Cluny 28 January

1898 **Les Petits Barnett** (Gavault) Théâtre des Variétés 8 November

1900 **Le Fiancé de Thylda** (de Cottens, Robert Charvay) Théâtre Cluny 26 January

1900 **Frégolinette** (de Cottens) 1 act Théâtre des Mathurins 25 April

1900 **Mademoiselle George** (de Cottens, Pierre Veber) Théâtre des Variétés 1 December

1902 **La Princesse Bébé** (Decourcelle, Georges Berr) Théâtre Cluny 18 April

1902 **Le Chien du Régiment** (Decourcelle) Théâtre de la Gaîté 24 December

1905 **L'Age d'or** (Georges Feydeau, Maurice Desvallières) Théâtre des Variétés 1 May

VASSEUR, [Félix Augustin Joseph] Léon (b Bapaume, Pas-de-Calais, 28 May 1844; d Paris, 25 May 1917). Successful and prolific Parisian 19th-century composer.

The son of an organist, Vasseur moved to Paris at the age of 12 to study music at the École Niedermeyer and he subsequently began his musical career, aged 20, as organist at the Cathedral of Saint-Symphorien in Versailles. In 1872 he made his début in the world of opérette with an unsuccessful one-act piece produced at the Alcazar, but later the same year his first full-length piece, *La Timbale d'argent*, hastily composed to a Jaime and Noriac libretto to fill a gap in the schedule at the Théâtre des Bouffes-Parisiens, propelled him into the limelight. After an enormous Parisian success, the show's overseas career was limited by the fact that its libretto was based entirely on matters explicitly sexual, but it established Vasseur as a popular composer – or at least as the composer of a popular hit – in his home country.

An attempt to repeat the formula with another musical for *Timbale d'argent* starlet Anna Judic with *La Petite Reine* was not a success, but over the next quarter of a century the composer kept up a steady stream of pleasantly characteristic stage scores for the Paris theatres. He scored a couple of solid successes with another pair of saucy opérettes, *La Cruche cassée* at the little Théâtre Taitbout, and *Le Droit du seigneur* at the Fantaisies-Parisiennes, and he won several other respectable runs with both legitimate opérettes such as *Le Billet de logement* and *Mam'selle Crénom* (110 performances) and with his scores to a number of spectacular productions such as the adaptation to the musical stage of Dumas's *Le Mariage au tambour*, the partly fresh-composed and partly pasticcio *Le Voyage de Suzette*, the

Châtelet's *Le Prince Soleil* (173 performances) and the Gaîté's globe-trotting *Le Pays de l'or* (126 performances). None of these won him the kind of success and notoriety that his first great hit had done, but they served him as the basis for a well-furnished career with sufficient substantial runs to earn him a good rank amongst 19th-century French opérette composers.

That rank and reputation were, however, made and held virtually entirely in France. Following the disappointing career of *La Timbale d'argent* in other centres, those of Vasseur's later pieces to win productions beyond home territory did not do particularly well. *La Famille Trouillat*, a failure in Paris in spite of a cast headed by Paulin Ménier and Thérésa, was produced in London by Alexander Henderson as *La Belle Normande* (ad Alfred Maltby, Richard Mansell, add mus Grevé, Globe Theatre, 26 January 1881) for 40 performances, *La Blanchisseuse de Berg-op-Zoom* appeared at the Theater an der Wien (14 November 1875) as *Die Perle der Wäscherinnen* (ad Julius Hopp) for 17 performances and later at Essegg, *La Cruche cassée* became *Der zerbrochene Krug* at Vienna's Ringtheater (2 February 1881), *Mam'selle Crénom* played Budapest's Népszinház eight times as *Szedtevette nagysám* (ad Lajos Evva, Béla J Fái, 27 September 1888), *Le Droit du seigneur* failed in London's three weeks at London's Olympic Theatre as *Marigold* (ad Arthur Matthison, 29 October 1879) whilst an English version of *Madame Cartouche*, produced at Leicester (21 September 1891), did not make it to London.

The spectaculars fared better than the sauce, with *Le Mariage au tambour* being played in Germany and in Hungary and varying versions of *Le Voyage de Suzette* (not always with Vasseur's music attached) seen in several countries, but the composer did not establish himself away from home in the same fashion that, strongly aided by regular revivals of *La Timbale d'argent*, he did in the Paris theatre.

1872 **Un fi, deux fi, trois figurants** (Adolphe Jaime) 1 act Alcazar 1 April

1872 **La Timbale d'argent** (Jaime, Jules Noriac) Théâtre des Bouffes-Parisiens 9 April

1872 **Mon mouchoir** (Jaime) 1 act Théâtre des Bouffes-Parisiens 9 May

1873 **La Petite Reine** (Jaime, Noriac) Théâtre des Bouffes-Parisiens 9 January

1873 **Le Grelot** (Victor Bernard, Eugène Grangé) 1 act Théâtre des Bouffes-Parisiens 20 May

1873 **Le Roi d'Yvetot** (Henri Chabrillat, Émile Hémery) Galeries Saint-Hubert, Brussels 25 October; Théâtre Taitbout, Paris 3 April 1876

1873 **Les Parisiennes** (Jules Moinaux, Victor Koning, [Ernest Blum]) Théâtre des Bouffes-Parisiens 31 March

1874 **La Famille Trouillat** (Hector Crémieux, Blum) Théâtre des Folies-Dramatiques 19 September

1875 **La Blanchisseuse de Berg-op-Zoom** (Henri Chivot, Alfred Duru) Théâtre des Folies-Dramatiques 21 January

1875 **La Cruche cassée** (Moinaux, Noriac) Théâtre Taitbout 27 October

1877 **La Sorrentine** (Moinaux, Noriac) Théâtre des Bouffes-Parisiens 24 March

1877 **L'Oppoponax** (William Busnach, Charles Nuitter) 1 act Théâtre des Bouffes-Parisiens 2 May

1878 **Le Droit du seigneur** (Paul Burani, Maxime Boucheron) Fantaisies-Parisiennes 13 December

1879 **Le Billet de logement** (Burani, Boucheron) Fantaisies-Parisiennes 15 November

1882 **Le Petit Parisien** (Burani, Boucheron) Théâtre des Folies-Dramatiques 16 January

1884 **Royal Amour** (P Lagrange, Christian de Trogoff) 1 act Alcazar d'Hiver 10 November

1885 **Le Mariage au tambour** (Burani) Théâtre du Châtelet 4 April

1886 **Madame Cartouche** (Pierre Decourcelles, Busnach) Théâtre des Folies-Dramatiques 19 October

1887 **Ninon** (Émile Blavet, Burani, Émile André) Théâtre des Nouveautés 23 March

1888 **Mam'zelle Crénom** (Jaime, Georges Duval) Théâtre des Bouffes-Parisiens 19 January

1889 **Le Prince Soleil** (Hippolyte Raymond, Burani) Théâtre du Châtelet 11 July

1890 **Le Voyage de Suzette** (Chivot, Duru) Théâtre de la Gaîté 20 January

1891 **La Famille Vénus** (Charles Clairville, R Bénédite) Théâtre de la Renaissance 2 May

1892 **Le Pays de l'or** (Chivot, Albert Vanloo) Théâtre de la Gaîté 26 January

1892 **Le Commandant Laripète** (Armand Silvestre, Burani, Albin Valabrègue) Palais-Royal 3 March

1893 **La Prétentaine** (Paul Ferrier, Bénédite) Nouveau Théâtre 10 October

1894 **La Corde** (Lucien Puech) Théâtre des Célestins, Lyon June

1896 **Au premier hussards** (?Maurice Hennequin) 1 act Casino, Saint-Malo 6 August

1896 **Le Royaume d'Hercule** (Charles Quinel, Ernest Dubreuil) 1 act La Cigale 20 November

1897 **La Souris blanche** (w de Thuisy/Chivot, Duru) Théâtre Déjazet 9 November

1897 **Au Chat qui pelote** (Jules Oudot, de Gorsse) 1 act Scala 28 August

1898 **Dans la plume!** (Pierre Kok) 1 act Eldorado 17 November

1898 **Excellente Affaire** (w de Thuisy/Clairville, Henri Bocage, C Worms) Théâtre des Folies-Dramatiques 18 February

VAUCAIRE, Maurice (b Versailles, 2 July 1865; d February 1918).

The author of a variety of plays and libretti, Vaucaire turned out such pieces, alone or in collaboration, as *Le Carrosse du Saint-Sacrement*, *Valet de coeur* (1893), *La Petite Famille*, *Petit Chagrin*, *L'Amour quand même* (1899), *Le Fils surnaturel*, *Amoureuse Amitié* (1901) and *Souper d'adieu* (1902) as well as a number of operatic texts. He wrote a new version of Leoncavallo's *Chatterton* and an adaptation of *La Femme et le pantin* – the piece which served Lehár as libretto to *Frasquita* – as a libretto for Zandonai's *Conchita* (1911 w Carlo Zangarini), and supplied the French libretti for Puccini's *Manon Lescaut* and *La fanciulla del West*, Mascagni's *Iris* and Zandonai's *Il grillo del focolare* and *Francesca da Rimini*. He also combined with 'J Burgmein', otherwise Giulio Ricordi of the publishing firm, on a piece called *Tapis d'orient*.

In the musical theatre he scored two significant successes, the first as the author of the popular Pied Piper musical *Hans, le joueur de flûte*, and the second as the French adaptor of *Die geschiedene Frau* as *La Divorcée*. His play (w Ernest Grenet d'Ancourt) *Le Fils surnaturel* was used as the basis for Ivan Caryll's Broadway musical comedy *Papa's Darling* (2 November 1914) and for the Hungarian *A törvénytelen apa* (Király Színház, 14 October 1904), whilst *Petit Chagrin* (Gymnase, 13 November 1899) became *L'Amante ideal* in the hands of Italy's Alberto Randegger.

1905 **Au temps jadis** (Justin Clérice) Monte-Carlo 16 April

1906 **Hans, le joueur de flûte** (Louis Ganne/w Georges Mitchell) Monte-Carlo 14 April

1910 **Malbrouck s'en va t'en guerre** (Ruggiero Leoncavallo/w Angelo Nessi) Théâtre Apollo 16 November

1911 **La Divorcée** (*Die geschiedene Frau*) French version (Théâtre Apollo)

1912 **Pavillion de fleurs** Liège 7 December

1912 **Miss Alice des PTT** (Claude Terrasse/w Tristan Bernard) La Cigale 14 December

VAUGHAN, Kate [CANDELIN, Kate Alice] (b London 16 August 1855; d Braamfontein, 21 February 1903). Victorian London's graceful dancer, the 'reviver of the skirt dance' and star of the Gaiety burlesques.

Daughter of James Matthias Candelin, an orchestral musician from the old Grecian Theatre, and trained from her earliest childhood as a dancer, Kate Vaughan played in the music halls and in pantomime before making her theatrical début at the Royal Court Theatre in 1872, under Marie Litton, in burlesque. Shortly after, she was engaged by Hollingshead for the Gaiety Theatre and in 1876, after a season in Paris, featured alongside Léonce and Pradeau in the 'folie-vaudeville' *Le Dada* at the Variétés, she began the series of burlesque performances which culminated in her becoming one-quarter of the most famous contemporary foursome of British burlesque players. In a virtual end-to-end parade of shows she appeared alongside 'boy' Nellie Farren, Edward Terry and E W Royce in such principal girl rôles as Maritana in *Little Don Caesar de Bazan*, Pretty Polly of Plymouth in *Gulliver*, Arline in *The Bohemian G'yurl*, Margaret in *Little Doctor Faust*, Fatima in *Bluebeard*, Amina in *Il Sonnambulo*, Zerlina in *Young Fra Diavolo*, Esmeralda in *Pretty Esmeralda*, Morgiana in *The Forty Thieves* and Diana Vernon in *Robbing Roy*.

In 1883 she left the Gaiety in order to play in comedy, but although her name value won her good rôles, particularly on the road, she proved to be less adept and less popular in her new career. She toured to Australia and, in particular, to South Africa and made an ill-starred attempt to return to the West End alongside Terry in the 1894 musical comedy *King Kodak* before going back to the touring circuits. Thereafter, life went sour for the woman who had been the darling of London's young men for so many years, and who had briefly hit the very top of the scandal pages when she won, and later wed, Colonel Wellesley, the heir to the title of the Duke of Wellington. By 1896 she was ill and poor enough for a theatrical benefit to be mounted, raising £1,000 to send her on a restorative sea voyage, and in 1897 she was in the divorce courts. She left Britain for South Africa, but she survived only another half-dozen years and died on the very day that *The Linkman*, a piece put together by George Grossmith reviving the great days of the Gaiety, was produced at that theatre, with the young Gertie Millar performing Miss Vaughan's most famous number, Morgiana's skirt dance from *The Forty Thieves*.

Her sister **Susie VAUGHAN** [Susan Mary Charlotte CANDELIN, b Hoxton, 21 February 1853; d 17 April 1950] appeared first with Kate and later alone, in pantomime and provincial burlesque, before moving into character rôles – mostly as heavy ladies – at an unusually early age. Her principal musical credits in a long career which also included the creation of rôles in such plays as Burnand's *The Colonel* (1887, Lady Tompkins) and Jerome K Jerome's *Miss Hobbs* (1899, Susan Abbey), included grande dame rôles in such pieces as *Polly* (1884, Lady

McAsser), *Lallah Rookh* (1884, Plumjhama), *The Lady of the Locket* (1885, Cantancarina), *The Palace of Pearl* (1886, Queen Amaranth), *Glamour* (1886, Queen Palmyra Jane), *Babette* (1888, Countess Iphigenia), *Airey Annie* (1888), *Incognita* (*Le Coeur et la main*, 1892, Doña Inesilia), *The Magic Opal* (1893, Olympia then Martina) and *The Bric-à-Brac Will* (1895, Chiara). She returned to the West End musical stage in later years in *The Cinema Star* (1914, Mrs Clutterbuck) and toured in *Tonight's the Night* (1915, Mrs Lovitt Lovitt). She also spent time in Australia both with Brough and with Williamson, appearing there in such rôles as Miss Pyechase in *The Dairymaids* and the Duchess in *King of Cadonia*, and in 1924 in *The Cabaret Girl*, and also toured for a period on the oriental circuits in the middle part of a life of 97 years in length.

A second sister, who worked simply as 'Miss Vaughan' and, later, as Florence Vaughan, also appeared also appeared in burlesque and opéra-bouffe, including the original London *Geneviève de Brabant* (1871, Brigette).

VAUTHIER   (d Cassis, ?November 1910).

One of the most popular male stars of the Parisian musical theatre of the last decades of the 19th century, the vocalist and actor known simply as Vauthier used his fine and strong bass-baritone singing voice to great effect in what were, from the beginning, mostly younger character rôles. In 1872 he featured as Merlin in Hervé's *Les Chevaliers du table ronde* and as the Marquis in *L'Oeil crevé* at the Folies-Dramatiques and in 1873 he played at the Athénée in *Monsieur Polichinelle*, but it was in 1874, when he joined the company at the Théâtre de la Renaissance, that he came seriously to the fore. He made a splendid success as the rampaging moorish Morzouk in *Giroflé-Girofla* (1874), took the rôle of Romadour in one Strauss rewrite, *La Reine Indigo* (1875), and shared that of Mathias in another, *La Tzigane* (1877). He created the part of the revengeful Podesta, Rodolfo, in Lecocq's *La Petite Mariée* (1875), played in the Paris version of *La Filleule du roi* (1875) and created further Lecocq rôles in *La Marjolaine* (1876, Annibal) and *Kosiki* (1876, Namitou). He scored another major hit as the rough-and-ready soldier Montlandry in *Le Petit Duc* (1877, Chanson du petit bossu), starred opposite Jeanne Granier as the brigand, Mandrin, who kidnaps *La Camargo* (1878) and as the disguised Manicamp who gets *La Petite Mademoiselle* (1879), played the comical Moka in *La Jolie Persane* (1879) and Latignasse in the disastrous *Janot* (1881) as well as appearing in Offenbach's posthumous *Belle-Lurette* (1880, Campistrel).

Vauthier followed Lecocq from the Renaissance to the Nouveautés and was rewarded with one of his most successful rôles when the composer made the jeune premier of his *Le Coeur et la main* (1882, Gaetan) a baritone rather than a tenor, and he remained at the Nouveautés to appear in *Le Droit d'aînesse* (1883, Boléslas), *Premier Baiser* (1883, Johann), *Le Roi de carreau* (1883, Agénor de la Cerisaie), *L'Oiseau bleu* (1884, César) and *La Nuit aux soufflets* (1884, Candolle). He then moved on to create further rôles in such pieces as *Le Mariage au tambour* (1885, Sergeant Lambert), *La Béarnaise* (1885, Perpignac), *Madame Cartouche* (1886, Labretèche), *Dix Jours aux Pyrénées* (1887, Piperlin) the title-rôle of Grisart's *Le Bossu* (1889, Lagardère) and *La Fée aux chèvres* (1890, La Crémade).

By the later 1890s his voice was not quite the stentorian instrument it had been at the peak of his career but, in spite of apparently limited acting abilities, he continued a steady career for many more years, creating important character rôles in such pieces as *La Cocarde tricolore* (1892), *Les 28 Jours de Clairette* (1892, Gibard), *Miss Robinson* (1892, Robinson Crusoe), *Jean Raisin* (1893, Francoeur), *Patatart, Patatart et cie* (1893, Patatart), *La Fille de Paillasse* (1894, Paillasse), *La Fiancée en loterie* (1896, Lopez), *Madame Putiphar* (1897, Pharaon) and *Les Soeurs Gaudichard* (1899, Gaudichard), playing Athos in a revival of *Les Petits Mousquetaires* and Siegebert in the Variétés revival of *Chilpéric* (1895), as well as reviving some of his early successes (Montlandry etc) and taking the older rôles in some of the classic repertoire (Louchard, Monthabor, Pontcourlay etc). Vauthier worked on into the 1900s, playing Sombrero in Paris's *Capitaine Thérèse* and creating rôles in *La Bouquetière du Château d'Eau* and in Varney's *L'Age d'or* at the Variétés, his last appearance before a retirement after more than 30 famous years of Parisian opérettes.

His niece, Aline Vauthier, also had a good career on the musical stage.

VEBER, Pierre [Eugène]   (b Paris, 15 May 1869; d Paris, 21 August 1942).

An eclectic and eminently successful Parisian novelist, playwright and journalist, Veber was editor of and/or a contributor to papers and revues ranging from *Le Journal* and *La Vie parisienne* (editor) to *The New York Herald* and *The New York Times* (critic). Beginning in 1897, he also produced a regular supply of plays for the French stage, sometimes solo, sometimes with collaborators such as Courteline, Victor de Cottens or Léon Xanrof and, later, most often with Maurice Hennequin. Amongst these were included *Que Suzanne n'en sache rien*, *La Main gauche*, *La Dame du Commissaire*, *Mariette*, *Loute*, *L'Amourette*, *Chambre à part*, *Florette et Patapon*, *Qui perd gagne*, *La Gamine*, *Madame et son filleul*, *Vingt jours à l'ombre* and, his biggest successes, *La Présidente* and *Vous n'avez rien à déclarer?*, as well as the occasional revue and also a handful of musical theatre pieces.

The most substantial of Veber's early musicals were *Mademoiselle George*, composed by Louis Varney and played at the Théâtre des Variétés, and Henri Hirschmann's *Les Petites Étoiles*, the most extravagant was a fantaisie-opérette called *Son Altesse l'amour* which featured Gaby Deslys and the British comedian Fred Wright at the Moulin-Rouge, but perhaps the most widely-played was *La Plus Belle*, a little piece written for the Casino de Paris which had a subsequent life in German-speaking venues as *Die schöne Vestalin* (ad Heinrich Bolten-Bäckers, Apollotheater, Berlin, 22 December 1906; Apollotheater, Vienna, 31 October 1907). His musical play *Le Poilu* (w Hennequin) also got overseas exposure, being played in America, in its original French, under the Shubert management (Garrick Theater, 9 October 1916).

Latterly, Veber won longer runs with the jazz-age musical comedies *Épouse-la!* and *Quand on est trois*, and joined with his son Serge on the musical tale of the ruined banker who sold his soul to the devil (*L'Homme qui vendit son âme au Diable*), and then, with the help of little Lola the stenographer, had to spend the evening working out how to avoid the consequences of his deal. He also had a considerable success with his translations of foreign successes for the French stage. In this field he was responsible, notably, for the French versions of *Der tapfere Soldat*, *Die Bajadere* and of Frederick Lonsdale and Adrian Ross's text to the enduring *Monsieur Beaucaire*.

In France, his play *La Gamine* (1911 w Henri de Gorsse) was later used as the source for the opérette *Sans tambour ni trompette* (1931) with music composed by Henri Casadesus, and the 1902 *Loute* (highly popular in Paul Potter's American version as *The Girl from Rectors*) was given a musical score by Josef Szulc and played in France as *Loute* and in America as *See You Later*. *Madame et son filleul* (1916, w M Hennequin, de Gorsse) was made into *The Girl Behind the Gun* for Broadway and *Kissing Time* for the English stage (Ivan Caryll/ad Guy Bolton, P G Wodehouse) whilst the farce *Le Monsieur de cinq heures* (w Hennequin, Palais Royal 1 October 1924), successfully played in America as *A Kiss in a Taxi*, was musicalized for Broadway's Hassard Short under the title *Sunny Days* (Jean Schwartz/Clifford Grey/William Cary Duncan Imperial Theater, 8 February 1928) with Jeanette MacDonald starred.

Problems arose when two Broadway-bound musicals which were announced as being based on his *La Présidente* both surfaced in 1926. In fact, the source was not very evident in either case, but *Cheerio*, later renamed *Oh, Kay!*, with Gertrude Lawrence starred, went on to Broadway and success whilst *Oh, Please!*, featuring Beatrice Lillie, stayed on the road a while longer, allegedly to try and iron away the announced similarities. Italy's musical version of the play, *La Presidentessa* (Robert Stolz arr/Carlo Lombardo), had no such concurrence.

Another of his works became the 1938 Budapest musical *A hölgy hozzám tartozik*, adaptation by Adorjan Stella and István Békeffy and music by Mihály Eisemann (Andrássy Színház 29 January), whilst the German musical *Angst vor der Ehe* (Emil Reznicek/Erich Urban, Louis Taufstein, Frankfurt, 28 November 1913) was similarly announced as based on one of Veber and Hennequin's plays.

1900 **Mademoiselle George** (Louis Varney/w Victor de Cottens) Théâtre des Variétés 1 December
1901 **Les Puits d'amour** (Louis Gibaux/w L Bannières) Théâtre Cluny 26 December
1906 **La Plus Belle** (Victor Holländer/w Léon Xanrof) 1 act Casino de Paris
1908 **Son altesse l'amour** (Maurice Jacobi, pasticcio/w de Cottens) Théâtre du Moulin-Rouge 24 March
1909 **Léda** (Antoine Banès/w Lucien Augé de Lassus) Monte-Carlo 17 April
1911 **Le Soldat de chocolat** (*Der tapfere Soldat*) French version (Galeries Saint-Hubert, Brussels)
1911 **Les Petites Étoiles** (Henri Hirschmann/w Xanrof) Théâtre Apollo 23 December
1914 **Manoeuvres d'automne** (*Tatárjárás*) French version (Théâtre des Célestins, Lyon)
1914 **Loute** (Joseph Szulc/w Maurice Soulié) Théâtre du Châtelet Marseille February
1916 **Le Poilu** (Maurice Jacquet/w Maurice Hennequin) Théâtre du Palais-Royal 14 January
1916 **La Charmante Rosalie** (Hirschmann) 1 act Opéra-Comique 18 February
1923 **Épouse-la!** (Hirschmann) Théâtre Fémina 15 February

1925 **Quand on est trois** (Joseph Szulc/Albert Willemetz/w Serge Veber) Théâtre des Capucines 20 April
1925 **Monsieur Beaucaire** French libretto (Théâtre Marigny)
1925 **La Bayadère** (*Die Bajadere*) French version w Bertal, Maubon (Lyon)
1925 **Le Péché capiteux** (René Mercier) L'Étoile 18 September
1926 **L'Homme qui vendit son âme au Diable** (Jean Nouguès/w S Veber) Théâtre de la Gaîté March
1926 **Divin mensonge** (Szulc/Hugues Delorme/w Alex Madis) Théâtre des Capucines October

VEBER, Serge (b Paris, 2 September 1897; d Paris, 1975).

The son of Pierre Veber, Serge Veber also ventured into most fields of the theatre – from the grand guignol to revue – but, unlike his father, he made his principal mark in the musical comedy theatre. He formed a profitable team with the songwriters van Parys and Parès which produced several Paris successes and later supplied several long-running comedy musicals to smaller houses.

Amongst his works, *Quand on est trois* and *Lulu* were given a showing in Hungary, whilst *Une femme par jour* was produced in Britain (ad Ray Allen, Guy Elmes, add ly Stanley Lloyd, add mus Frederick Chapelle) by Morris Chalfen, in a largely remusicked version which stopped short of London.

1925 **Quand on est trois** (Joseph Szulc/Albert Willemetz/w Pierre Veber) Théâtre des Capucines 20 April
1926 **L'Homme qui vendit son âme au Diable** (Jean Nouguès/w P Veber) Théâtre de la Gaîté March
1927 **Lulu** (Georges van Parys, Philippe Parès) Théâtre Daunou 14 September
1928 **L'Eau à la bouche** (van Parys, Parès) Théâtre Daunou 5 September
1929 **Tip-Toës** French version w André Mauprey, Robert de Mackiels (Folies-Wagram)
1929 **Louis XIV** (*On cherche un roi*) (van Parys, Parès) Théâtre de la Scala
1937 **Ma petite amie** (van Parys) Bouffes-Parisiennes 31 January
1943 **Une femme par jour** (van Parys/Jean Boyer) Théâtre des Capucines
1946 **La Bonne Hôtesse** (Bruno Coquatrix/Jean-Jacques Vital) Théâtre Alhambra 26 December
1947 **Le Maharadjah** (Coquatrix/Vital) Théâtre Alhambra 19 December
1950 **Il faut marier maman!** ... (Guy Lafarge/Lafarge, Marc-Cab/w Marc-Cab) Théâtre de Paris 15 September
1950 **L'École des femmes nues** (Henri Betti/J Boyer) Théâtre de l'Étoile 22 September
1951 **Trois faibles femmes** (Coquatrix) Bobino 22 December
1953 **Mobilette** (Betti/w André Hornez) Théâtre l'Européen
1958 **Le Moulin sans souci** (van Parys, Parès/w Marc-Cab) Strasbourg 24 December

DAS VEILCHENMÄDEL Operette in a Vorspiel and 2 acts by Leopold Krenn and Carl Lindau. Music by Josef Hellmesberger. Carltheater, Vienna, 27 February 1904.

Hellmesberger's most successful Operette, *Das Veilchenmädel* was first produced by Andreas Aman at the Carltheater in the wake of the indifferent runs of *Madame Sherry*, *Das Marktkind* and *Der Mameluck* and the half-success of *Der Göttergatte*, and, in a production directed by co-author Lindau, it turned the house's luck back to good.

Krenn and Lindau's libretto featured Louis Treumann as Stiebel, a wandering prestidigitator, and tenor Willy Bauer and Ernst Greisnegger as his performing companions, singer Hans Muck and acrobat Rovelli. Sheltering overnight in an hotel, courtesy of a kindly housemaid (Therese Biedermann) who has taken a shine to the acrobat, they see the ghost of the miser Flaps (Rudolf Hofbauer) counting and hiding his gold. In the morning, the gold is there, hidden just where the dead man left it, and with it is a note proving it has been left in his care for one Hänschen Mühlbach. Hänschen turns out, after two acts of plot, not to be a little boy but a little girl – the very little flower-girl, Johanna (Helene Merviola), over whom Hans has been sighing since the prologue. Events were enlivened by the antics of Stiebel's newly rediscovered wife, Flora (Mizzi Günther), a lively piece of soubrettery who gets herself mixed up with the old Graf Willy Sickendorf (Karl Blasel). Sickendorf pays the conjurer a vast sum to divorce her and then finds his wedding with 'an artiste' vetoed by his even-more-aged Papa (Theodore Männel). Friedrich Becker played the agent Siebenschein who is mixed up in all these money businesses.

The prettiest moment of Hellmesberger's score was the violet-maiden's longing waltz 'Einmal möcht' ich mich schwingen im Tanz', and the tenor had his happiest music in the first-act song 'Ich hab' ihr in's Auge, in's dunkle geblickt' and its ensuing waltz duo with the heroine ('Für dich will gern ich betteln geh'n'), but the stars of this show were not the juveniles but Treumann and Günther and they were not surprisingly the best supplied when it came to songs. Flora bounced out 'Ein Ball ist ein schönste Vergnügen', played a comedy duet with the old Graf ('Ach, liebste Flora') and topped the last act with a song-and-dance duo with Treumann, 'Es liebt den Hugo Melanie', whilst he, apart from joining with his two compères in some lovely ensembles, had a show-off song with a waltz tag at the end of the first act ('Ich sehne mich nach Bühnenluft'). The show's Schlussgesang, instead of being the usual jolly reprise, in this score ended up with a merry couplet refreshingly agreeing that 'money is the great cure-all'.

Das Veilchenmädel played 63 consecutive performances up to the end of the season, re-opening the theatre after the summer break for a further 21 nights, and then being played in repertoire with the Posse *'s Zuckersgoscherl* and Straus's *Die lustigen Nibelungen* to the end of the year. It was reprised intermittently thereafter, passing its 100th performance at the Carltheater on 4 October 1906. Two nights later an Hungarian adaptation (ad Adolf Merei) opened in Budapest. A tongue-in-cheek brother-show, *Der Veilchenkavalier*, written by Krenn with music by Hellmesberger, was played at Ronacher in a double-bill with *Im Schilderhaus*, directed by and featuring Karl Tuschl, in 1911, but the original piece re-appeared in Vienna as late as 1925 when it was revived at the Johann Strauss-Theater.

Hungary: Magyar Színház *Az Ibolyáslány* 6 October 1904

DAS VEILCHEN VOM MONTMARTRE Operette
in 3 acts by Julius Brammer and Alfred Grünwald. Music by Emmerich Kálmán. Johann Strauss-Theater, Vienna, 21 March 1930.

Brammer and Grünwald, the author of so many bright libretti, supplied Kálmán with a rather curious, not to say clichéd, text for *Das Veilchen vom Montmartre*. It was a sort of sub-*La Bohème* affair, set in the everybody-be-jolly-in-poverty Paris of belle époque Montmartre attics and cafés and featuring as its characters no less personalities than the composer Hervé (portrayed by Ernst Tautenhayn), the *La Vie de Bohème* poet Henri Murger (Robert Nästlberger) and the painter Delacroix (Walter Jankuhn) alongside a Musetta-ish model called Ninon (Annie Ahlers), and the inevitable street-singer, Violetta Cavallini (Adele Kern), who ends up in the third act starring at the Théâtre du Vaudeville in a strictly unhistorical opérette written by Murger and Hervé. Eugen Neufeld played the Baron Jacob Rothschild who, of course, finds that Violetta is a long-lost child of the aristocracy. Needless to say, she also gets the artist, over whom she has sighed since Act I when he was preoccupied with Ninon. Ninon herself has tied up with a useful government minister.

Kálmán did his best to swap his vibrant Hungarian-to-Austrian tones for something approaching what he perceived as the French, but the result was more than a touch Kálmán and rose-water (one critic complained: 'it swims languidly along in lukewarm internationalism'). The three friends jollied along in march-time ('Warum sollen wir nicht fröhlich sein', Künstlermarsch: ''raus aus dem Quartier'), Violette introduced herself floridly in traditional style ('Ich sing' mein Lied im Regen und Schnee'), indulged in a bootblack number (Schuhputzerlied), adopted more romantic tones for numbers both alone ('Warum weiss dein Herz nicht von mir?') and with Delacroix, joined Hervé for the duo 'Ein Kuss im Frühling', and had her happiest moment in the Moon Song 'Du, guter Mond, schaust zu' of the Act I finale. In contrast, Ninon tossed off a 'Carrambolina-Carramboletta!' and also duetted with Hervé and Delacroix in turn, if in a rather different tone.

Vienna's production of *Das Veilchen vom Montmartre*, mounted under the management of Erich Müller at the less than spick-and-span Johann Strauss-Theater, did well enough. Marta Eggerth succeeded the Staatsoper's Frln Kern in the title-rôle as the show ran up 109 performances to the end of the season (10 July). The authors, who apparently thought their piece deserved better, had further and more upmarket plans for it, however. Two weeks after closing at the Johann Strauss-Theater (25 July), *Das Veilchen vom Montmartre* resurfaced at the Theater an der Wien, re-cast and restaged with Otto Maran (Raoul), Ado Darian (Murger), Paula Brosig (Ninon), Grete Philipsty (Violette) and Ernst Nadherny (Jacob Rothschild) featured, and this second production proved to have another two months and 61 further performances in it.

The newest Kálmán show was naturally picked up with an international enthusiasm, but although it was mounted in most of the main centres the results were not what might have been hoped. Gitta Alpár appeared as Violette and Karl Jöken as Raoul in a production at the Berlin Metropoltheater which broke no records, whilst in America a version produced by Lilian Albertson and her husband Louis Owen McLoon in San Francisco as *Paris in Spring* did not win sufficient success to encourage it to make its way eastwards. A second English version (ad L du Garde Peach) sprinkled with musical additions by one Herbert Griffiths was mounted at London's Alhambra as *A Kiss in Spring*. Billy Milton (Hervé), Eric Bertner (Delacroix), Kenneth Kove (Murger), Eileen Moody (Violette) and Sylvia Welling (Ninon) all had their historical names replaced with simple forenames and Rothschild became the Baron Goldstein in an Oswald Stoll production which featured danseuse Alicia Markova in a full-sized Ballet of Spring as part of its operetta within an operetta. London couldn't be persuaded to patronize it for more than seven weeks.

France witnessed Max Eddy and Jean Marietti's adaptation first at Marseille, with Marthe Ferrare and André Gaudin starred, before Maurice Lehmann took it up for the troubled Théâtre de la Porte-Saint-Martin. Lotte Schoene and Miguel Villabella headed his cast but, once again, the show failed to take and the Porte-Saint-Martin became even more troubled than before. Budapest saw *Montmartrei ibolya* in 1949 when Marika Németh, Judith Hódossy, Zoltán Szentessy, József Antalffy and Róbert Rátonyi appeared in a production at the Fővárosi Operett-színház. However, it seems that the piece found its best reception behind the iron curtain where it has been preferred to some of Kálmán's more typical and virile works.

Germany: Stadttheater, Karlsbad 31 May 1930, Metropoltheater, Berlin 1930; UK: Alhambra Theatre *A Kiss in Spring* 28 November 1932; France: Théâtre des Variétés, Marseille *Violette de Montmartre* 1932, Théâtre de la Porte-Saint-Martin 20 December 1935; USA: San Francisco *Paris in Spring* 1930–31 season; Hungary: Fővárosi Operettszinház *Montmartrei ibolya* 24 November 1949

Recording: complete in Russian (Urania)

VENISE   Opérette à grand spectacle in 3 acts by André Mouëzy-Éon based on a story by Paul de Musset. Lyrics by Albert Willemetz. Music by Tiarko Richepin. Théâtre Marigny, Paris, 25 June 1927.

A piece set in the richly picturesque and theatrically popular venue of 18th-century Venice, *Venise* was spectacularly staged at Léon Volterra's Théâtre Marigny by director Paul Clerget and designers Deshayes and Arnaud (sets) and Jean le Seyeux (costumes) and, in spite of the competition provided by the overwhelming popularity of *Rose-Marie*, it proved a fine success.

Mouëzy-Éon's libretto mixed a touch of humour with its colourful romance as the musician Gianetto (André Baugé) strove, against the enmity of the self-seeking Marcantonio (Jean Deiss), to win the consent of the unkind notary (Raimu) to the hand of his daughter Stella (Danielle Brégis). When the honest Gianetto returns a jewel that an old man has dropped in the street he is given a seal which he is promised will fulfil all his desires. Aladdin-like, he uses the seal to win the palace, fortune and jewels demanded by Stella's father as prerequisite to marriage, only to find out in Act IV, after losing both the seal and Stella in Act III, that the talisman is not magic but the signet of the rich Turk Ali-Mahmud (Gilbert Moryn) whose money helps put all to right by the final curtain. Jane Pierly (Jacomina) played Marcantonio's thieving accomplice, the ageing diva Anna Tariol-Baugé (Marietta), mother to the leading man, had a substantial rôle as the leading man's foster-mother, and the most famous of all Parisian dance captains, Elsie Skidmore, headed 16 (English) Marigny Girls in some not very Venetian dances.

Richepin had had little theatrical success in nearly 20 years of composing and *La Marchande d'allumettes*, produced at the Opéra-Comique 13 years earlier, still remained his best credit. He had originally intended *Venise* as a piece of the same genre and ambitioned its production at the

Salle Favart but, finding his seriously crafted work rejected at the Opéra-Comique, he took it back and rearranged it, removing some of the more obviously opéra-comique elements and replacing them with something more purely popular in appeal to make up the score of the piece as staged at the Marigny. The mixture proved the right one, and *Venise* turned out to be the greatest success the composer would have. The romance 'Un beau soir' as sung by the bass-baritone Moryn was the take-away hit, but several other numbers – Gianetto's first-act Serenade and Chanson de l'étoile, Marietta's Chanson du Bambino and 'C'est si bon', and the duo Barcarolle du Rialto (Gianetto/Jacomina) – also won favour and lasted better than almost anything else of their composer's work.

Venise played through the season at the Marigny, was revived in 1929 at the Trianon-Lyrique (24 May) and was thereafter consigned to the provinces where it has been intermittently played since, and as recently as 1989 (Rochefort, 28 May).

Successful and/or significant works with Venetian settings have come from virtually all the principal countries where musical theatre is created. Amongst the most notable have been included Offenbach's *Le Pont des soupirs*, Gilbert and Sullivan's *The Gondoliers*, Johann Strauss's *Eine Nacht in Venedig* and pasticcio *Casanova*, Arthur Laurents and Richard Rodgers's *Do I Hear a Waltz?* and the British musical comedy *Grab Me a Gondola* alongside such mostly less favoured pieces as *The Lady of the Locket*, *Estrella*, *The Gay Venetians*, *Fioretta*, *The Venetian Twins*, *Les Amants de Venise* and *The Bric-a-Brac Will*. Other works have used the city of canals as a romantically picturesque venue for the traditional last-act visit to somewhere with a colourful setting (Serge Veber's *Lulu*, *Hochzeitsnacht im Paradies*, *Carissima* etc) or even, as in *Kiss Me, Kate* for a show-within-a-show, and, as in *Le Voyage de MM Dunanan*, for a phoney Venice within a show. All in all, Venice has had more than its share of operettic visitors.

The title, *Venice*, was also used in London for a Charles Searle version of *Le Pont des soupirs* produced at the Alhambra Theatre (5 May 1879), and a German *Venezia* written by Herman Hermecke and composed by Arno Vetterling was produced in 1934 (Grenzland-Theater, Görlitz, 18 November).

VENNE, Lottie [VENN, Charlotte]   (b London, 28 May 1852; d London, 16 July 1928). One of Victorian London's favourite comedy and musical-comedy players.

Lottie Venne made her first stage appearance at the Gallery of Illustration in Tom Robertson's *A Dream in Venice* (1867) and she soon established herself in the provinces (Nottingham, Cheltenham etc) as a popular soubrette in comedy and burlesque, before winning herself an even greater reputation in London. She made her first metropolitan appearances in comedy at the Theatre Royal, Haymarket, and as Cupid in Talfourd's burlesque *Atalanta* (1870), toured in Farnie's *The Idle Prentice*, and returned to town to play Polly Twinkle in the same author's anglicized version of *La Vie parisienne* and Franz in *Dr Faust* (*Le Petit Faust*) at Holborn. In two seasons at the Court Theatre she was seen in the burlesques of *Christabel* (1872, t/o) and *Zampa* (1872), as Zayda in Gilbert's controversial *The Happy Land* (1873) and as principal boy in his *Creatures of Impulse* (1872, Peter). She then moved on from the Court and appeared as Zerlina in the Christmas extravaganza *Don Juan* at the Alhambra (1873).

In 1874 Lottie Venne joined the Swanboroughs' famous burlesque outfit at the Strand Theatre and she remained there for more than four years, appearing in the title-rôle of Louisa in the highly successful *Loo* (1874, *Le Carnaval d'un merle blanc*), in *Intimidad* (1875, Cachuca), a revival of *Nemesis* (1875, Rosalie Ramponneau), *Patient Penelope* (Penelope), *Flamingo* (1875), *Antarctica* (1875, Madeleine Bastille), revivals of *The Field of the Cloth of Gold* (1877, Lady Constance) and *The Maid and the Magpie* (1877), the prose burlesque *Champagne* (1877, Bobinette), *The Latest Edition of the Red Rover* (1878), *Dora and Diplunacy* (1878, Countess Zicka) and *The Baby* (1879, Dodlinette), as well as in a long list of plays and in the several musicals produced there. She played the soubrette rôle of Jelly in Gilbert and Clay's *Princess Toto* (1876), the Plaintiff in *Trial By Jury* and featured as Coraline Coalscuttle in Alfred Lee's *The Lying Dutchman* (1876).

In 1879 the Swanboroughs and burlesque gave place to Alexander Henderson and comic opera and when Henderson mounted *Madame Favart* Miss Venne moved on. In the following decade she found her best rôles in comedy, creating the rôle of Amy in *Crutch and Toothpick*, the title-rôle of the long-running *Betsy* and later appearing as Agatha Poskett in *The Magistrate* and Honour in *Sophia*, but she also made several musical appearances, notably in Sullivan's *The Zoo* (1879), as Fiametta in *La Mascotte* (1882 t/o), at the Avenue in *Lurette* (Marcelline) and *Barbe-bleue* (Fleurette), and she played Katrina in first provincial tour of Planquette's *Rip* (1883). She also appeared as Mrs Bardell in Solomon's operetta *Pickwick* and returned to musical comedy in the 1885 revival of *Nemesis*.

The musical portion of her career seemed as if it were in the past when Lottie Venne returned and made her biggest-ever hit in the musical theatre. In 1893 she created the star rôle of Lady Virginia Forrest in George Edwardes's *A Gaiety Girl* and she followed this personal triumph with a second equivalent part as Madame Amélie in *An Artist's Model* (1895). However, she did not remain with the Daly's Theatre company, and she did not better these rôles when cast as similarly attractive middle-aged ladies in *Monte Carlo* (1896, Mrs Carthew), *The Royal Star* (1898, Lady Horton), *Three Little Maids* (1902, Lady St Mallory) or *The Love Birds* (1903, Fatima Wilson West). In another two decades of distinguished career she appeared rarely on the musical stage, returning only in 1911 to play Mrs Grundy (*L'Opinion Publique*) in Tree's revival of *Orphée aux enfers* and, in her final appearance, in the Lyric, Hammersmith production of *Lionel and Clarissa* in 1925.

VENT DU SOIR, ou L'Horrible festin
Opérette bouffe in 1 act by Philippe Gille. Music by Jacques Offenbach. Théâtre des Bouffes-Parisiens, Paris, 16 May 1857.

The Parisian coiffeur Arthur (Tayau), who has been shipwrecked on a cannibal island, is served up by chief Vent du Soir (Désiré) as a meal for his neighbour Chief Lapin Courageux (Léonce), in spite of his having a distinct and non-comestible appeal for the Princess Atala (Mlle Garnier). She is fascinated by Arthur's chiming watch which plays the national hymn of Lapin Courageux's tribe. There is, of course, a reason for this. Arthur is the Chief's

long absent son, sent off to study hairdressing in London – and Vent du Soir has just served him up to his papa in a pie. Actually, he hasn't, for although the watch can be heard chiming patriotically in Lapin's stomach, Arthur has swapped places with the Sacred Bear of the tribe.

Offenbach's musical accompaniment to this extravagant tale comprised a fine storm overture and seven numbers – four of which are trios – and a finale, amongst which Atala's couplets 'Petit bébé', Arthur's couplets 'Je suis coiffeur' and the plotworthy national anthem of the Papa-Toutou tribe were the highlights.

Written in the thoroughly 'bouffe' style of a *Ba-ta-clan*, *Vent du Soir* did not find quite the same kind of success as its crazy predecessor. It nevertheless remained in the Bouffes-Parisiens repertoire for some years, and was introduced to Vienna by Offenbach's company during their 1861 visit to the Kai-Theater with Désiré repeating his original rôle alongside Lucille Tostée (Atala), Jean Paul (Arthur) and Duvernoy (Lapin Courageux). Johann Nestroy subsequently provided the same theatre with a German version in which he starred alongside Karl Treumann, Louis Grois and Helene Weinberger in one of his last appearances. It did not find the same popularity as his earlier efforts, such as *Daphnis und Chloë*, and its curiously disappointing career apparently ended there.

Austria: Theater am Franz-Josefs-Kai (Fr) 22 June 1861, *Häuptling Abendwind* 1 February 1862

VENUS AUF ERDEN
Operette in 1 act by Heinrich Bolten-Bäckers. Music by Paul Lincke. Apollotheater, Berlin, 6 June 1897.

The first of the short but showy Operetten written by Bolten-Bäckers and Lincke to be played on the programme at the Berlin variety house the Apollotheater, *Venus auf Erden* was designed as a mixture of spectacle, girls, comedy and song in the best big-variety-house style. The story on which all this entertainment was tacked had an every-dreamaday Berliner called Fritz Leichtfuss, who fancies a fling with Venus, being summoned to Olympus where his description of the jollities and pleasures of Berlin encourages the Olympian family to come down and see for themselves. Fritz takes them to a masked ball where everyone has a good naughty time, and he himself chats up Venus when he can get the local lechers out of the way. Of course, in the end he wakes up.

The piece did well enough that, when Lincke returned to Berlin and the Apollotheater after his two-season interlude at the Paris Folies-Bergère, the series was continued, producing such similarly constructed pieces as the highly successful *Frau Luna* and *Lysistrata*.

Venus auf Erden's popularity in Berlin won it a showing in similar circumstances in Vienna, where it was produced as the opening attraction at Gabor Steiner's Danzers Orpheum. It was 'freely adapted' for Vienna by Carl Lindau with musical interpolations by Ernst Reiterer and Karl Kappeller, and lavishly mounted by Steiner with Flora Siding as Venus, Eduard Lunzer as Jupiter and Karl Tuschl as Theodor (ex-Fritz). It ran for 77 straight performances before Steiner took it on to his summer theatre, Venedig in Wien, where with Frln Carena and Lunzer featured it passed its 100th performance 15 July 1901. Only the huge success of Steiner's second production, *Die Landstreicher*, kept it from being brought back to Danzers for more than 11 further performances. *Venus auf Erden* remained in Steiner's repertoire and was given by his company for a handful of performances at the Theater an der Wien in 1902. The show was given a Budapest production, several years later, under similar circumstances, following *Frau Luna* and *Nakiris Hochzeit* on to the programme at the Royal Orfeum.

Immortals on earth was one of the oldest themes in the dramatic book, even if Venus was not the most frequent visitor. However, a Venusian maiden visited earth just a few years later in London in search of *The Silver Slipper* whilst the lady herself turned up to cause havoc on Broadway in *One Touch of Venus* a few decades further on.

Austria: Danzers Orpheum 30 October 1900; Hungary: Royal Orfeum *Vénusz a földön* 1 November 1905

VENUS IN SEIDE Operette in 3 acts by Alfred Grünwald and Ludwig Herzer. Music by Robert Stolz. Stadttheater, Zurich, 10 December 1932.

Grünwald and Herzer's 'Venus in silk' was the Princess Jadja Milewska-Palotay whose intended fiancé is kidnapped on his way to their wedding and whose castle is visited instead by two fine strangers. One is the prince Stefan Teleky, the rightful heir to Jadja's castle, and the other is the famous bandit Sandór Rósza. The first is after Jadja's heart, the second is more interested in her heirlooms, and it is only after the pair have spent two acts conveniently mistaken for each other that Teleky, at least, succeeds in his aims.

Stolz illustrated this romantic comic opera text with a more unpretentiously melodic score of light music than it might have been given by other hands, thus taking some of the mostly chocolatey Ruritanianism off the tale, and the resultant Operette, produced in Zurich, was one of his most artistically successful works. It did not, however, prove very happy when produced further afield. An American version (ad Laurence Schwab, Lester O'Keefe) was produced at the St Louis Muny with Nancy McCord and Robert Halliday starred, and the piece was subsequently toured by Schwab (1 October 1935) with Miss McCord and J Harold Murray starred, without braving Broadway. Similarly, in Britain, Lee Ephraim and Carl Brisson's production of another version (ad John Hastings Turner, Graham John), advertised as a 'world première', and starring Brisson opposite Helen Gilliland, started out from Glasgow but also failed to make it to the metropolis.

In 1970 the Vienna Volksoper produced a version which introduced *Venus in Seide* to Austria.

USA: Municipal Opera, St Louis 22 July 1935; UK: Alhambra Theatre, Glasgow 26 October 1937; Austria: Volksoper 4 March 1970
Recording selection (Eurodisc)

VERA VIOLETTA Vaudeville in 1 act by Leo Stein. Music by Edmund Eysler. Apollotheater, Vienna, 30 November 1907.

The first venture by composer Eysler in writing a piece for a variety house, *Vera Violetta* was a little piece of amorous nonsense set in a Paris palais de glace. Polly Koss starred as the lady of the title, alongside Flora Siding and Carlo Böhm (who found the opportunity during the proceedings to get into a frock and impersonate a music-hall lady) and a bundle of typically tuneful Eysler melodies including the Vera Violetta waltz, the Adele Polka, 'Sapristi! Ein Käfer' and 'Paris, Paris wie bist du süss!'.

Written for and produced by Ben Tieber at the Vienna Apollotheater, the piece was played there as an important part of the bills of the 1907–8 season, running up 128 performances in its first year, being brought back again the following autumn to run up its 200th and yet again in the autumn of 1909. When it came back for a further run in 1913 it was billed as having passed its 350th night on the Viennese stage. The Paris Olympia produced a French version (ad Jacques Redelsperger) with a cast including Baron, Féréal, Sinoël, Girier, Marion Winchester, Maud d'Orly and Mathilde Gomez, whilst in America (ad Leonard Liebling and Harold Atteridge) *Vera Violetta* was featured on a Shubert Winter Garden programme, sharing the bill with the swimmer Annette Kellerman and a comedy. Amongst bits of Eysler and Stein, Gaby Deslys and Harry Pilcer did Louis Hirsch's 'Gaby Glide', José Collins as Mme von Grünberg performed her mother's old hit 'Ta-ra-ra-boom-de-ay', and Al Jolson as the waiter, Claude, gave Schwartz and Madden's 'Rum Tum Tiddle' and George M Cohan's 'That Haunting Melody' through a run of 112 performances. Like most of Eysler's music, a young lady called Mae West was replaced before opening night.

France: Olympia 7 November 1908; USA: Winter Garden 23 November 1911; Hungary: Royal Orfeum 31 December 1914

LA VERBENA DE LA PALOMA, o El Boticario y las chalupas (y celos mal reprimidos) Sainete lirico in 1 act by Ricardo de la Vega. Music by Tomas Bretón. Teatro Apolo, Madrid, 17 February 1894.

One of the most popular of the 'genero chico' zarzuelas, *La verbena de la paloma* has been regularly performed in Spanish-language theatres in the century since its production, and has, like few others of its species, also been given occasional performances in translation.

The piece's little contemporary slice-of-life tale centred on lovelorn print-worker Julián (Emilio Mesejo) who is moping because his beloved Susana (Luisa Campos) has said she cannot go with him to the last-night celebrations of the Festival of the Dove. But Julián has seen Susana and her sister Casta (Irene Alba) driving with the flirtatious old chemist Don Hilarion (Manuel Rodriguez) – it is he who is taking the girls and their Aunt Antonia (Pilar Vidal) out for the night. That evening the boy causes a scene at the dance, and things get to a state where the police are called, but Susana ultimately leaves her old beau for her young lover and all ends happily amongst the sounds of the Festival.

The story wound its way through three scenes which were, in the best zarzuela tradition, peopled by folk of the area who were quite incidental to the plot-line and to whom a number of the evening's musical pieces were allotted: the innkeeper's wife Rita (Leocadia Alba), Hilarion's compère Sebastián and his wife Mariquita, their niece Teresa and some of their friends, the janitor and his wife ('El niño está dormido'), a nightwatchman ('¡Buena está la política!') and a flamenco singer in a café ('En Chiclana me crié'). The bulk of the little piece's music, however, was the portion of Julián sighing over Susana ('También la gente del pueblo'), wondering how to win his suit with her ('Y escucha, que hablo yo') or confronting her on her doorstep on the arm of Hilarión ('¿Donde vas con mantón de Manila?'), whilst Don Hilarión sang with light comicality of his profession ('Hoy las ciencias adelantan') and of his prospects for the evening ('Una morena y una rubia').

A two-act piece called *Fiesta in Madrid* (ad Tito Capobianco), produced at New York's City Center in 1969 (28 May), admitted to being based on *La verbena de la paloma*, but it included in its score numbers lifted from the works of Chapí, Chueca and Valverde, Lleo, Serrano and Gimenez which made up some 50 per cent of its considerable score, whilst an entertainment toured in France in 1992 as *Zarzuela: historia de un patio* also quoted Bretón's zarzuela as its basis.

Recordings: complete (Philips, Alhambra/Columbia, EMI, Montilla/Zafiro, Hispavox, Edigsa)

VERDON, Gwen [VERDON, Gwyneth Evelyn] (b Culver City, Calif, 13 January 1926). One of the Broadway musical's most attractive stars of the postwar era.

Miss Verdon studied dance with choreographer Jack Cole and she later assisted him on several assignments in the theatre. She made early musical comedy appearances dancing in the choruses of *Bonanza Bound* (1947) and *Magdalena* (1948), appeared in the short-lived revue *Alive and Kicking* (1950) and worked as a dancer in four films between 1951 and 1953 (*The Merry Widow* etc). She broke through to stardom with her performance as the dancer Claudine in *Can-Can* (1953) when, in spite of her rôle being aggressively slimmed when she threatened to run away with the show, her mixture of dance and comic talents let her run away with it anyhow. Those talents found an even more effective vehicle when she was next cast as the devil's ultimate seductress, Lola, in *Damn Yankees* (1955, Tony Award) singing and dancing her way through 'Whatever Lola Wants' on Broadway and the screen.

Miss Verdon subsequently worked with (and married) choreographer/director Bob Fosse, starring for him in the musicalized version of Eugene O'Neill's *Anna Christie* as *New Girl in Town* (1957, half a Tony Award), in the mystery music-hall musical *Redhead* (1959, Tony Award) and in her two most memorable rôles, mixing an irresistible vulnerability and swingeing dancing as *Sweet Charity* (1966, 'If My Friends Could See Me Now', 'Where Am I Going?') and as the kookie, butter-melting murderess Roxie Hart in *Chicago* (1975).

VERGELTSGOTT Operette in 2 acts and a Nachspiel by Victor Léon. Music by Leo Ascher. Theater an der Wien, Vienna, 14 October 1905.

Like the recent *Der arme Jonathan* and *Der Schätzmeister*, Leo Ascher's first full-scale Operette presented the peculiarity (for the time) of being set in New York, though given its action and its carnival opening – so reminiscent of other closer-to-home pieces – it might just as easily have been set anywhere. Its tale, however, was rather more original than was usual. Bogumil, Graf Karinsky (Louis Treumann), has gone through his patrimony and now, stranded in New York, is about to put a bullet through his head when he falls in with a band of beggars headed by Slippel (Oskar Sachs) and his daughter Jessie (Mizzi Günther) and discovers that he has a lucrative talent after all – as a beggar! When Bogumil falls in love with Malona (Phila

Wolff), daughter of Police Inspector Stephenson (Siegmund Natzler), jealous Jessie and the journalist Jimmy Blackwell (Karl Streitmann) of the *New Yorker Stundenblatt* get together to fake a newspaper article exposing the 'beggar count' and the horrified Malona sends him away. Six years and a child intervene before she herself turns beggar, to beg him to return for a happy ending.

The favourite moment of Ascher's score was the march duo 'Es kommt nicht jeder reich zur Welt' sung by Jessie and Bogumil in the second act and reprised at the Schlussgesang of the evening. Elsewhere, Bogumil came out the best-served, with a comical entrance, revolver to his head ('Das ist ein Revolver'), and a song which took him through the gamut of rhythms from waltz to march ('Ist denn ein Wunder da geschehn') as well as duets with each girl and a final scene with his six-year-old son ('Fang mich, Bübchen'). Jimmy had a tenor waltz song ('Hab' nur Geduld'), Malona a soprano one ('Tage gehen, Tage kommen') and the police chief had a scene and song with a bunch of kiddies, but somewhat surprisingly apart from her March duo the star soubrette rôle of Jessie was limited to duos and a comical trio with Jimmy and Slippel imitating poor Quakers.

Vergeltsgott ran 42 performances at the Theater an der Wien before being removed to allow the production of Leo Fall's *Der Rebell* and, after the quick flop of that piece, it came back to run through to its 60th night (26 December) whilst a new replacement was prepared. When that replacement turned out to be *Die lustige Witwe*, *Vergeltsgott* didn't get much more of a look-in.

A month later it was mounted in Budapest (ad Adolf Mérei) with its title changed to *A koldusgróf* or the beggar count, and there it proved very much of a hit. It ran past its 100th night (25 August 1906) as it proved itself the most popular new piece mounted on the Magyar Színház programme for some time. In May 1907, whilst the Lessing-Theater company occupied their stage, the Theater an der Wien company presented the show in Berlin under the Hungarians' more obvious title, *Der Bettelgraf*.

Hungary: Magyar Színház *A koldusgróf* 26 January 1906; Germany: Lessing-Theater *Der Bettelgraf* 9 May 1907

VERNE, Jules (b Nantes, 8 February 1828; d Amiens, 24 March 1905).

The celebrated science-fiction author wrote 63 novels between *Five Weeks in a Balloon* in 1863 and his death more than 40 years later. A number of these were adapted for the spectacular stage in his lifetime, often by the author himself in collaboration with Michel Carré and composer Aristide Hignard, and Verne's name duly appeared on the programmes for a good number of often long-running pieces, both very large and sometimes less large (*Le Colin-Maillard*, *Les Compagnons de la Marjolaine*, *M de Chimpanzé*, *Le Page de Mme Malborough*, *L'Auberge des Ardennes*, *Le Voyage à travers l'impossible* etc).

The most famous of these, a spectacle with musical accompaniment rather than an opérette, was the adaptation the author made of his *Le Tour du monde en 80 jours* (w Adolphe d'Ennery, music: Marius Baggers) produced at the Théâtre de la Porte-Saint-Martin on 7 November 1871 and played for 415 performances there, thousands more later in a long series of revivals at the Châtelet, as well as in Hungary (Népszinház *Utazás a föld körül 80 nap alatt* 27 December 1875), Germany (Viktoria-Theater, Berlin 350 performances by 1876), Britain and in America, where it was a regular production of the spectacle specialists, the Kiralfys. In each of these versions, the physical production and the action it contained were shot through with various amounts of musical scenes and pageants, speciality acts, songs and massed dance routines.

Julius Freund and Jean Gilbert cut the time delay in half when they produced a *Die Reise um die Erde in 40 Tagen* at Berlin's Metropoltheater (13 September 1913), but it is more recent times which, with the overwhelming return of the fashion for the spectacular stage, have led to a flood of musical shows based on Verne's work. Orson Welles and Cole Porter collaborated on one which appeared at New York's Adelphi Theater on 31 May 1946 for 75 performances with Welles himself starred as 'Dick Fix' to the Fogg of Arthur Margetson and, after the 1956 film with its famous title-song and David Niven's Fogg, came a St Louis Muny version (11 June 1962), with Sammy Fain supplying additional music to Victor Young's film score and a libretto arranged by Sig Herzig. It was subsequently staged as a Jones Beach Marine Theater epic (22 June 1963) with Fritz Weaver and Dom de Luise starred and repeated there the following season. The subsequently famous directorial name of Trevor Nunn was attached to a piece produced in Coventry, England, in 1963, and a New Zealand *Around the World in 80 Days* spectacular was announced as part of a Christchurch Commonwealth Games better remembered for its mile race between Filbert Bayi and John Walker.

The tale has continued right up to the present day to appeal to producers with more thought for scenic considerations than anything else, and versions of Verne's novel have continued to flow. Jerome Savary mounted a version with music by Joachim Kuntzch at Hamburg (Deutsches Schauspielhaus, 26 November 1978), whilst in France, following a television musical (1975) composed by Gerard Calvi and written by Jean Marsan and Jean Le Poulain, there came a stage version written by Jean-Marie Lecoq and Louis Dunoyer de Segonzac and mounted at Chambéry on 10 October 1987. This was followed by further efforts in America (*80 Days* by Snoo Wilson, music and lyrics by Ray Davies, La Jolla Playhouse, San Diego, 1988) and Britain (Chris Walker/Mary Stewart-David/Roberta Hamond, Buxton, 1990). Like the earlier musicals, none looked like approaching the success of Verne's original.

Offenbach's *Le Docteur Ox*, based on Verne, spawned the H B Farnie pasticcio *Oxygen* (1877) which was played through Britain and America by Lydia Thompson, but whilst the same composer's *Le Voyage dans la lune* shared some ideas with Verne's work it was not an adaptation – the moon had, after all, long been a favourite fairyland of stage writers. Versions of his *Les Enfants du Capitaine Grant*, on the other hand, appeared on the spectacular musical stage with regularity. Following Verne and d'Ennery's Parisian mounting of their own version, local remakings turned up in Spain (*Los sobrinos del Captain Grant*), on Broadway (*Voyages in the Southern Seas* Booth's Theater 21 March 1881), and above all in Vienna where *Die Abenteuer des Seekapitäns* (Julius Hopp/Arendt Theater in der Josefstadt, 27 September 1878) and the rival *Die Kinder des Kapitän Grant*, (Kleiber/Bayer Fürsttheater, 26 September 1878) were followed the next year by yet another, under

the same title, with music by Louis Roth at the Theater an der Wien (25 September 1879).

Amongst other Verne derivatives may be numbered an Hungarian *Kin-Fu, vagy egy kinai ember kalandjai* (Jenő Farago/Géza Márkus, mus Izso Barna, 31 May 1902 Népszinház), a Viennese *Die Reise nach Sibirien* set to music by Millöcker (Theater an der Wien, 21 April 1877), a *Michel Strogoff*, following another enormously successful non-musical Parisian spectacular dating from 1880, composed by Jack Ledru and written by Henri Varna, Marc-Cab and René Richard and produced at the Théâtre Mogador in 1964 (5 December), and a German *Der Kurier des Zaren* (Döbeln, 2 November 1940, ad Ernst Hans Richter).

VERNEUIL, Louis [COLLIN du BOCAGE, Louis Jacques Marie] (b Paris, 14 May 1893; d Paris, 3 November, 1952). Parisian playwright, occasional librettist and effective source of material for the musical stage.

Louis Vernueil began his theatre career writing small-house revues before going on to establish himself as one of Paris's most successful playwrights (*Monsieur Beverley*, *Pour avoir Adrienne*, *Ma cousine de Varsovie* etc). He wrote several more substantial revues in tandem with the Parisian master of the genre, Rip (*1915*, *La Nouvelle Revue 1915* etc), and subsequently made his first entry into the world of the musical theatre in collaboration with his friend Ivan Caryll, who had successfully adapted the play *Le Satyre*, written by Verneuil's sometime collaborator, Georges Berr, for Broadway as *The Pink Lady*. Their first effort together, *Le Coffre-Fort Vivant*, an adaptation of a novel by Frédéric Mauzens, was produced in America as *The Canary* and topped 150 nights before going on the road. Verneuil subsequently adapted *The Pink Lady* for the French stage, and later collaborated on a fresh version of *Le Coffre-Fort Vivant* for Paris (mus: Szulc, 'Sautreuil').

Verneuil's stage works were the source for two highly successful musicals during a decided flush of adaptations in the late 1920s and the early 1930s. Alfred Grünwald's libretto for Oscar Straus's *Eine Frau, die weiss, was sie will* (1932), based on his 1923 play *La Fauteuil*, proved a major international hit, whilst Ralph Benatzky's *Meine Schwester und ich* (1930), a musical version of his *Ma soeur et moi* (1928, w Berr), also found success around the world. The rest did a little less well. Vienna's *Das Walzerparadies* (Oscar Straus/Grünwald, Johann Strauss-Theater 15 February 1935, then Bürgertheater), based on an uncredited Verneuil play, did not prove up to *Eine Frau*, whilst in America, where one of his plays had inspired *Oh Mama!/Girl o' Mine* aka *The Victory Girl* as early as 1917, a Shubert brothers version of his *Mademoiselle ma mère* (Théâtre Fémina, 24 February 1920), made over as *Boom Boom* (Casino Theater 28 January 1929, Werner Janssen, Mann Holiner, J Kiern Brennan/Fanny Todd Mitchell) and played by Jeanette MacDonald and Cary Grant, was a Broadway failure (72 performances). His *Ma cousine de Varsovie* was musically played as *One More Night* (1931), a 'new intimate musical divertissement' fabricated for Irene Bordoni by Russell Medcraft and composer Herman Hupfeld, but didn't make it to New York and, if his 1924 *Pile ou face*, remade for Broadway under the title *First Love* in a version illustrated with interpolated songs (Booth Theatre, 8 November 1926), did make it, it was hardly a hit. Another unidentified Verneuil piece was adapted to the

Hungarian musical stage as *Megcsallak, mert szeretlek* (ad Istvan Zagon, mus Ralph Ervin, Andrássy-uti Színház, 1930), and *Mademoiselle ma mère* was again musicalized in Germany as *Fräulein Mama* (Hugo Hirsch/Kessler).

Verneuil left Paris in 1940, three days before the German army invaded the city, and settled in America where he wrote one successful Broadway play, *Affairs of State*, adapted *La Vie parisienne* for a new American production, and authored a splendid volume of reminiscences. Very sadly, the announced second and third volumes did not appear, for Verneuil returned to Paris and, at the age of 59, slit his throat in his bath.

1918 **The Canary** (Ivan Caryll) Globe Theatre, New York 4 November
1921 **La Dame en rose** (*The Pink Lady*) French version (Théâtre des Bouffes-Parisiens)
1929 **Boulard et ses filles** (Charles Cuviller/Saint-Granier, Jean Le Seyeux) Théâtre Marigny 8 November
1938 **La Féerie blanche** (Mitty Goldin, Oberfeld) Théâtre Mogador 5 January
1938 **Le Coffre-Fort vivant** revised version of *The Canary* (Joseph Szulc, Maurice Yvain ps Sautreuil) Théâtre du Châtelet 17 December
1941 **La Vie parisienne** new American version w Felix Brentano (City Center, New York)

Autobiography: *Rideau à neuf heures* (Editions des Deux-Rives, Paris, 1943)

VERNO, Jerry (b London, 26 July 1895; d London, 29 June 1975). British comic who spent half a century on the variety and musical comedy stages.

Verno made his first stage appearances as a child vocalist in vaudeville and thereafter mixed variety and touring revue with comedy. After the war he joined Maurice Bandmann's company touring musical comedy on the oriental circuits and he did not make his first London appearance until 1925 when he appeared as the comical Alf in the play *Alf's Button*. He appeared in the musical *Song of the Sea* at His Majesty's Theatre (1928, Wilkins) and thereafter spent much of his stage career playing comedy rôles in such musical pieces as *The Three Musketeers* (1930, Planchet), *Eldorado* (1930, the crooked Mr Budwell), *The Maid of the Mountains* revival (1930, Tonio), *Wild Violets* (1932, Hans Katzen), *That's a Pretty Thing* (1933, Billy Blake), the 1940/1 revival of *Chu Chin Chow* (Ali Baba), *A Night in Venice* (1944, Pappacoda), *The Dubarry* (1947, de la Marche), *Belinda Fair* (1949, Peregrine), *The Merry Widow* (1952, Popoff) and *The Water Gipsies* (1955, Albert Bell). He toured in 1954 in George Formby's rôle of Percy Piggott in *Zip Goes a Million* and appeared as late as 1968 in the British provinces in a musical *Lysistrata* perversion called *Liz*.

His film credits included the 1932 English-language version of *Der Bettelstudent*.

Plate 281. *Comic* **Jerry Verno** *and hero Donald Mather in* El Dorado.

VERŐ, György [HAUER, Hugó] (b Igal, 31 March 1857; d Budapest, 12 March 1941).

Successful as a playwright, composer, author, conductor and director, György Verő was one of the outstanding and most versatile men of the Budapest theatre in the period when a significant native musical theatre tradition was beginning to blossom in Hungary.

Verő had originally studied law, but at the age of 23 he turned his attentions to the theatre, at first briefly as an actor and then as a writer. He made his earliest ventures translating some of the Viennese Operetten which were currently all the rage for the Hungarian stage, but at the same time he began another career, as a conductor, at the theatre in Miskolc. It was there that his first original play, *A mükedvelők*, was produced. In 1885 he supplied some translations to Budapest's principal musical theatre, the Népszinház, and the following year he joined the staff there as musical director and conductor, a position he held for the next 15 years.

In 1892, after a period in which he devoted himself to conducting rather than writing, he turned out an operett written and composed to a text taken from Favart's old opéra-comique *Les Trois Sultanes*. *A szultán* (1892) was a first-class success at the Népszinház and it quickly assured itself a place at the top of the Hungarian native repertoire, a landmark between the earlier works of such composers as József Konti and the real opening-out of the Hungarian musical theatre which would soon follow. He had a second success at the Népszinház with *Virágcsata* which merited his third operett, *Der Löwenjager*, the opportunity of being taken up for production by Alexandrine von Schönerer at the Theater an der Wien even before it had been staged in

Plate 282.

Hungary. If it lasted but 17 performances there, it won a better reception on its return to the Népszinhaz (1897). Verő wrote and composed one further operett, *Kleopatra* (later staged by Max Reinhardt at Berlin's Deutsches Theater as *Die Bettelgräfin*, 8 June 1908), as well as the scores for several musical spectaculars (*Ezer év*, *Hadjak útja*, *A pesti ucca*), before moving to the Nemzeti Színház and, for two seasons, exchanging his baton for a pen in the post of dramaturg.

In the years that followed, he wrote pieces of all kinds ranging from full-scale tragedy to cabaret material and revue, not only for the Nemzeti Színház but for many of the other principal Budapest houses. His output included the tragedy *Kain* (1902), the allegorical *Bölcső és koporsó* (1902), the play *A nép* (1907), the Singspiel-revue *Göre Gábor Budapesten* (1907) and three one-act musicals played at the Népszinház under the title *Menyecskék* (1903), as well as three full-scale musical pieces: the Hungarian musical comedy *A bajusz* (the moustache, 1903), the operett *Doktor kisasszony* (1903) and the musical comedy *Leányka*. All three were successful, and the production of *A bajusz* (*Der Schnurrbart*) at Vienna's Carltheater and Berlin's Neues Königliches Opernhaus in 1905 was followed a few years later by a Vienna production of *Der Sultan* (1909) which was also revived in Budapest in 1911. *Leányka* was played in a German version as *Weiberlaunen* (ad Carl Lindau, Leo Stein) at the Schumann-Theater, Frankfurt-am-Main in July 1907.

Following the production of the musical comedy *Falusi madonna* in 1907, Verő returned largely to playwriting with pieces such as the one-act comedy *Leánynéző* (1914), *A mennyország* (Király Színház, 1915) and *Az ellenség* (Vigszinház, 27 Feb 1915) but he also collaborated on the libretto for a German Operette, *Das geborgte Schloss*, composed by Herman Dostal, before turning full circle to end as he had begun with the translation of Robert Stolz's *Mädi* for the Hungarian stage.

In 1926 Verő authored the history of the Népszinház (*Blaha Lujza és a Népszinház*).

Verő's wife was the prominent musical-theatre contralto **Celia Margo** (1865–1942) who played at the Várszinház and then at the Népszinház where she appeared, amongst others, in *Das Spitzentuch der Königin* (Donna Irene), *Gasparone*, *The Mikado* (Katisha), *Der Gascogner* (Cascarita), *Nell Gwynne* (Margot), *Der Ziegunerbaron* (Czipra), as the Vicomte de Letorrières in Konti's *Az eleven ördög* and variously as Delia and Roxelane in her husband's most continuously popular piece, *A szultán*. She retired from the stage in 1904.

1881 **Mathuzsálem herceg** (*Prinz Methusalem*) Hungarian version (Budai Szinkör)

1883 **A gascognei nemes** (*Der Gascogner*) Hungarian version w Ivan Relle (Budai Szinkör)

1883 **Ördög a földön** (*Der Teufel im Erden*) Hungarian version w Viktor Rakósi (Budai Szinkör)

1885 **Tökfilkó** (*Le Roi de carreau*) Hungarian version (Népszinház)

1885 **A királyné csipkekendője** (*Das Spitzentuch der Königin*) Hungarian version (Népszinház)

1886 **Esketés dobszóval** (*Le Mariage au tambour*) Hungarian version w Béla J Fái (Népszinház)

1886 **Szazszorszép** (*La Jolie Parfumeuse*) Hungarian version w Fái (Népszinház)

1887 **Bellman** Hungarian version (Népszinház)

1892 **A szultán** (Verő) Népszínház 19 November
1894 **A virágcsata** (Verő) Népszínház 28 April
1896 **Ezer év** (Verő) Népszínház 17 April
1896 **Az oroszlánvadász** (*Der Löwenjager*) (Verő ad Paul Schönthan, Leo Stein) Theater an der Wien, Vienna 1 November
1898 **Hadak utja** (Verő) Népszínház 15 March
1900 **Kleopatra** (Verő) Magyar Színház 6 March
1900 **A pesti ucca** (Ferenc Rajna) Magyar Színház 14 November
1903 **Menyecskék** (Verő) three 1-act musical plays Népszinház 27 November
1903 **A bajusz** (Verő) Magyar Színház 6 February
1903 **Doktorkisasszony** (Verő) Magyar Színház 19 December
1904 **Csak tréfa** (Adolf Merei) Magyar Színhaz 10 September
1906 **Leányka** (Verő) Népszínház 17 January
1907 **Göre Gábor Budapesten** (w Zsigmond Vincze, Imre Kálmán, Béla Zerkovitz) Király Színház 25 May
1907 **Falusi Madonna** (Verő) Király Színház 6 November
1911 **Das geborgte Schloss** (Hermann Dostal/w Carl Lindau) Altes Theater, Leipzig 14 May
1924 **Huncut a lány** (*Mädi*) Hungarian version (Király Színház)

VÉRONIQUE Opéra-comique in 3 acts by Albert Vanloo and Georges Duval. Music by André Messager. Théâtre des Bouffes-Parisiennes, Paris, 10 December 1898.

The most enduring of Messager's opérettes, *Véronique* also gave its composer the largest international success of his long career as a composer of light musical theatre in the years immediately following its first production.

As in *Les P'tites Michu*, their previous very happy collaboration with the composer, Vanloo and Duval's libretto used well-worn plot elements in its construction but treated them with the slightly genteel elegance which was now fashionable in opérette. The aristocratic Hélène de Solanges (Mariette Sully) is to be wed, by royal command, to the wild-oat-sowing Vicomte Florestan de Valaincourt (Jean Périer). Florestan takes the grim news of this dowdy-sounding match to his mistress, the florist Agathe (Anna Tariol-Baugé), and he is overheard by Hélène who just happens to be in that very shop, shopping for flowers. She disguises herself as a flower-girl, Véronique, and, during a jolly lunch party at Romainville, completely wins her intended husband's heart. When Agathe spills the beans, Florestan pretends to proudly refuse Hélène for love of Véronique, but the pretence only serves to stretch the third act to a little more length. The comedy of the affair was provided by Agathe's pouter-pigeon of a husband, Coquenard (Regnard), Hélène's sporty aunt, Ermerance (Léonie Laporte), who joins her in her escapade, the impecunious aristocrat Loustot (Maurice Lamy), who has been royally deputized to get Florestan to his betrothal in one piece, and the principals of a rural wedding (Brunais, Madeleine Mathyeu, Mme Bonval) laid waste by Florestan's pursuit of his 'Véronique'.

If the material was not new, the librettists nevertheless deployed it with a great deal of charm and refined humour, and Messager set their lyrics with some of his most delightful and elegant music. Two pieces, in particular, became worldwide favourites: the little duet sung by Florestan and Hélène on their way, by donkey, to Romainville ('De ci, de là' or, in English, 'Trot Here, Trot There') and their idyllic Swing Song, 'Poussez, poussez l'escarpolette'. Agathe led a lively hymn to the country

pleasures of Romainville ('Au Tourne, Tourne, Tournebride'), Ermerance plucked a harp in soulful romance ('De magasin la simple demoiselle'), Hélène spat out her indignation at hearing her future husband calling her a 'Petite Dinde!' and Loustot rambled on about what life was like 'Quand j'étais Baron des Merlettes' in some of the score's varied highlights.

Véronique was a fine success, running for some 200 performances at the Bouffes-Parisiens, and following up with a number of productions outside France. The Theater an der Wien mounted the piece (ad Heinrich Bolten-Bäckers) with the heroine's nom-de-bataille changed to *Brigitte*. Frln Worm and Carl Streitmann headed the romance, with Frln Milton and Josef Joseffy as the floral couple, but they did it for just 11 performances. Budapest got *Veronka* and, two years later, Bolten-Bäckers's version was seen in Berlin, but Britain, in spite of the success of George Edwardes's production of *Les P'tites Michu*, seemed disinterested in the piece. However, Messager had influential friends in Britain from his days at the head of the Covent Garden Opera House and one of them, Lady Gladys de Grey, promised the composer she would find him a production. When she failed, she and her brother put up the money for a showcase performance by a Parisian cast headed by Mlle Sully, Adolphe Corin and Regnard.

The performance was well enough liked that, when the surefire *Madame Sherry* flopped horribly, George Edwardes decided to put a version of *Véronique* (ad Henry Hamilton, Lilian Eldée, Percy Greenbank) into the unexpectedly empty Apollo Theatre. Ruth Vincent (Hélène), Lawrence Rea (Florestan), Kitty Gordon (Agathe), George Graves (Coquenard) and Rosina Brandram (Ermerance) headed the cast, and the show turned out a major hit, playing 495 performances in London prefatory to a long touring and colonial life, and a wartime West End revival (Adelphi Theatre, 3 April 1915, 59 performances). Misses Vincent and Gordon and Rea later headed a company which took the piece to America, but *Véronique*'s pretty elegance appealed more to the New York press than its public and the show ran only 81 performances on Broadway before being put on the road under the title *The Flower Girl* with Louise Gunning starred as its heroine. Australia, on the other hand, proved quite partial to the piece when J C Williamson's company presented it in Melbourne with Margaret Thomas (Hélène), Florence Young (Agathe), Clara Clifton (Ermerance), John Doran (Florestan), George Lauri (Coquenard) and Claude Flemming (Octave) in the cast, and the piece was brought back a number of times in the Williamson repertoire thereafter.

Véronique was revived in Paris in 1909 (Folies-Dramatiques, 30 January) with Mlle Sully and many of the original cast, and again in 1920 (Gaîté-Lyrique, 1 March) with Edmée Favart featured alongside Périer and Mlle Tariol-Baugé, repeating yet again more than 20 years after their creation of their rôles. These revivals confirmed and even increased the popularity of the show in France, and it subsequently became a member of the basic repertoire of opérettes, even being played at the Opéra-Comique in 1925 with Mlle Favart and André Baugé as Florestan whilst his mother repeated her Agathe (thus playing his mistress!). It was remounted in Paris in 1936 and 1943, filmed in 1949 with Giselle Pascal and Jean Desailly, and played at the Opéra-Comique again in 1978 and 1980.

Austria: Theater an der Wien *Brigitte* 10 March 1900; Hungary: Magyar Színház *Veronka* 21 April 1900; Germany: Stadttheater, Cologne 28 October 1900, Krolls Theater 13 September 1902; UK: Coronet Theatre (Fr) 5 May 1903, Apollo Theatre (Eng) 18 May 1904; USA: Broadway Theater 30 October 1905; Australia: His Majesty's Theatre, Melbourne 11 November 1905; Film: 1949

Recordings: complete (EMI, Decca), selection (EMI-Pathé etc)

VERT-VERT Opéra-comique in 3 acts by Henri Meilhac and Charles Nuitter. Music by Jacques Offenbach. Opéra-Comique, Paris, 10 March 1869.

One of the rare Offenbach works to be accepted by the musically lofty gentlemen of the Opéra-Comique, *Vert-Vert* was not a success in its production there.

Meilhac and Nuitter's story, based on a deLeuven and Desforges vaudeville which had been played by Déjazet some years before, was set in a girls' school and the characters included Mlle Paturelle (Mlle Revilly), a deputy-headmistress secretly wed to the dancing master Baladon (Couderc), and a couple of pupils (Mlle Moisset, Mlle Tual) more or less affianced to a couple of dragoons (Sainte-Foy, Ponchard). The Vert-Vert of the title (Capoul) is the headmistress's nephew, thus christened after the popular parrot of the establishment, recently deceased. He is amorously pursued by another pupil, Mimi (Marie Cico), who disguises herself as a dragoon and follows him out of bounds to an inn where he is seen drinking with the singer La Corilla (Caroline Girard). With the help of the real dragoons, she gets him drunk, back to school and, having uncovered her teacher's secret marriage, she has no qualms about using that knowledge to get the required permission for a little wedlock of her own.

Vert-Vert's song 'Oui l'oiseau reviendra dans sa cage' and the Air du coche proved to be the best-liked numbers of Offenbach's score, but, even when the piece was revised by its composer after a sticky start it still didn't go and *Vert-Vert* had to be written off as a flop. However, it was still an Offenbach flop and that meant that it still found foreign theatres willing (or pre-committed) to take it up. The show was produced in German at the Carltheater (ad Julius Hopp) in 1870 with the richest of Carltheater casts – Therese Schäfer, Hermine Meyerhoff, Karl Blasel, Josef Matras and Wilhelm Knaack – and was played 21 times in that season and two more the following year. The German version was played in Berlin the same year and an Hungarian version appeared several years later. Offenbach played pieces of the show's score in his concerts when he visisted America in 1875, announcing the performance as the 'first time in this country'. It wasn't – the German *Kakadu* had been given a performance at the Stadttheater in 1870.

A piece produced in London as *Vert-Vert* (ad Henry Hermann, Richard Mansell) was an under-rehearsed, ill-cast and cut-about fiasco, apparently flung together in 48 hours and sporting Offenbach music culled from half a dozen of his works. It got sufficient scandalous notice for an under-dressed dance called the Riperelle to win it an eight-week run. When the journal *Vanity Fair* was sued by the management for announcing 'the worst orchestra, some of the flattest singing and one of the most indecent dances in London', they won their case. An altered and recast version tried again at the Globe Theatre later the same year (26 September) and somehow added another seven London weeks to the run of a show which was scarcely Offenbach's *Vert-Vert*.

Austria: Carltheater *Kakadu* 3 February 1870; Germany: Friedrich-Wilhelmstädtisches Theater *Kakadu* 4 June 1870; USA: Stadttheater *Kakadu* 31 October 1870; UK: St James's Theatre 2 May 1874; Hungary: Budai Színkör *A Papagáj* 7 August 1875

DAS VERWUNSCHENE SCHLOSS Comic Operette in 3 acts by Alois Berla. Music by Carl Millöcker. Theater an der Wien, Vienna, 30 March 1878.

The folk of the Tyrolean village situated alongside the estate of the Graf von Geiersburg (Carl Adolf Friese) keep well away from his castle, for strange lights and noises have convinced them it is inhabited by the devil. When the young dairyman Sepp (Jani Szika) says he doesn't believe in ghostly things, the farmer Grosslechner (Liebwerth), to whose daughter Mirzl (Karoline Tellheim) he is engaged, throws him out for impiety. Sepp and his goasbua Andredl (Alexander Girardi) take to the hills, and from the hut of old Traudl (Frl Herzog) and her mahm, Regerl (Josefine Gallmeyer), they look down on the lights in the castle. When they go to investigate, it turns out that the Count is simply having a bawdy party, but the devilishly masked guests are enough to curdle Andredl's blood. When the attractive Sepp is drugged and taken back to the castle, Andredl leads Regerl to the rescue. The Count's naughty excesses are displayed to the village, and he is only saved from the anger of the locals when his little mistress, Coralie (Berthe Olma), assures them that it is their wedding they are celebrating. The gratitude of the new Countess earns Sepp a fine reward to add to the hand of Mirzl, whilst Andredl and Regerl make up a third final-curtain pair.

Of the musical numbers written for the piece – described as a 'komische Operette' – it was the heavily accented dialect-comedy pieces performed by the top-billed Gallmeyer (the second act opener 'Schirlingskraut beim Mondschein g'hohlt', the hit 'S' is a Bisserl Liab' und a Bisserl Treu') and by Girardi (the hugely popular 'Dalkata Bua!'), and the tacked-in Lied in Österreichisches Mundart ('O, du himmelblauer See') performed by Andredl and Sepp, as entertainment for the Count's party, which proved the most popular items. The comic folk also had one of the most substantial ensembles, the trio 'Wie glänzt der grüne Wald', as well as a ghostly 'Gespenster, gespenster'. Mirzl was given a ballad with which to open the proceedings, but the rôle of Coralie proved rather the more grateful of the soprano rôles with its solo 'Ihr edlen Cavaliere' and some showy coloratura in the third-act trio and finale which rocketed her up to D in alt.

Berla and Millöcker's friendly, jolly piece was a lively success in a season which also featured several other hits: Gallmeyer's introduction of the Costa/Millöcker *Ihr Korporal*, Berla and Millöcker's *Plausch net Pepi* and the first performances of *Die Glocken von Corneville* with Girardi as Grénicheux. If *Das verwunschene Schloss*'s initial performance figures were limited, as a result, the show and its songs nevertheless proved their popularity by an extraordinary durability. The piece was played at the Theater an der Wien again in 1881, given a full-scale revival there in 1893 with Girardi teamed with Therese Biedermann in Gallmeyer's rôle, Lili Lejo (Coralie), Josef Joseffy (Geiersberg) and Julius Spielmann (Sepp) (19 performances), and seen again in 1894, 1901 and 1909. It had meanwhile found its way into other Viennese theatres being played, notably, at the Carltheater in 1901 (27 May) with Franz Glawatsch and Biedermann, Mizzi Günther as Coralie and Louis Treumann as Geiersberg, and in 1910 with Streitmann again as Sepp. The Johann Strauss-Theater mounted *Das verwunschene Schloss* in its first months of operation in 1908 and again in 1913, the Bürgertheater in 1916 with Gerda Walde as Coralie and again in 1924, and it was also seen at the Raimundtheater in 1921.

The success which the show found in Austria was repeated in Germany, where *Das verwunschene Schloss* compiled a record second only to *Der Bettelstudent* amongst Millöcker's works, but the show did not run very much further afield. Marie Geistinger was not averse to picking up her great rival's fine rôle, and she introduced Regerl to American audiences (in German) on several occasions between 1881–3. The German version was repeated at the Amberg Theater as late as 1890, but the show does not appear to have ever been translated into English. It was, however, put into Hungarian (ad Béla J Fai, Ferenc Rajna) for a late production in Budapest. Mounted in 1890 after the huge success of *Der arme Jonathan*, it did even better than the composer's big latter day success with a run of 55 performances at the Népszinház.

A revised version by Gustav Quedtenfeldt and Walther Brügmann was produced at the Nationaltheater, Munich 4 February 1934.

Germany: Brünn 13 September 1878; USA: Thalia Theater 3 November 1881; Hungary: Népszinház *A Boszorkanyvár* 3 October 1890

VERY GOOD EDDIE

VERY GOOD EDDIE Musical comedy in 2 acts by Philip Bartholomae and Guy Bolton based on Bartholomae's play *Over Night*. Lyrics by Schuyler Greene. Music by Jerome Kern. Princess Theater, New York, 23 December 1915.

Following their first venture at a non-girlie, non-glossy and comparatively intimate musical comedy with their adaptation of the British musical play *Mr Popple of Ippleton*, Bessie Marbury and F Ray Comstock purchased the rights to the successful comedy *Over Night* (Hackett Theater, 2 January 1911, 162 performances) and commissioned its author, Philip Bartholomae, to adapt it as a similar kind of musical comedy for the little Princess Theater. Miss Marbury's client Jerome Kern, who had provided the songs for the earlier *Nobody Home*, was booked for the music in tandem with his most recent lyric-writing partner, Schuyler Greene. The show was mounted at Schenectady, with a cast headed by Ernest Truex and Florence Nash, but the producers were unhappy with the result and it was taken off, revamped by *Nobody Home* librettist Guy Bolton, and fitted out with some additional Kern songs taken from his bottom drawer. Two and a bit of these had even been used in Broadway's *Miss Information* earlier the same year. Alice Dovey, heroine of *Nobody Home*, took over the top feminine rôle and just a fortnight after the out-of-town

closure the piece re-opened in Cincinnati prior to moving to New York.

Very Good Eddie (the title was a current Fred Stone catchphrase, and the leading comic character was named accordingly) took place on and along the Hudson River. When circumstances lead to Georgina, the hectoring new wife (Helen Raymond) of little Eddie Kettle (Truex) and Percy (John Willard), the new husband of tiny Elsie Darling (Miss Dovey), missing the honeymoon steamer, their partners are forced, for reasons explained, to pretend to be husband and wife and to pass the night almost together in the honeymoon hotel. At the end of the night little Eddie proves able to handle his suspicious wife with unsuspected firmness. Parallel to this little adventure ran the efforts of Dick Rivers (Oscar Shaw) to win himself Elsie Lilly (Anna Orr), whilst extra comedy was the lot of Ada Lewis as that young lady's eccentric singing teacher, Madame Matroppo, and of patented comedian John E Hazzard (Al Cleveland).

The show's songs included several which would become popular, notably Truex and Miss Dovey's naïve little 'Babes in the Wood', the warm duo for Shaw and Miss Orr, 'Some Sort of Somebody' (which hadn't clicked in *Miss Information* but now did), and a delightful piece of comedy material for Truex called '(When You Wear a) Thirteen Collar'. Shaw (who dominated the evening's singing quotient) also joined Miss Orr in hula rhythm to sing about 'On the Shore at Le Le Wei' (another *Miss Information* cut-out) and in waltz time for 'Nodding Roses'.

Very Good Eddie did very nicely for its producers. Between its run at the Princess and subsequent tactical transfers first to the larger Casino Theater (more cheap seats for a show which had run its first fine flush), then to the 39th Street Theater, followed by a brief return to base, it ran up 341 New York performances, prior to setting out on a touring schedule which extended its life for a further couple of seasons after which, like a number of its contemporaries, it was potted into a 45-minute version and sent out on the vaudeville circuits. It was also smartly picked up by the rising young Tait Brothers for an Australian production, and it was mounted, as the first of what would be their very many musical comedy productions, at Sydney's Palace Theatre. Barry Lupino was cast as Eddie alongside Fayette Perry (Elsie), Emily Fitzroy (Georgina), Andrew Higginson (Dick) and Lillian Rucker (Elsie Lilly) through ten weeks in Sydney and five further at Melbourne's King's Theatre (21 April 1917).

A British production in 1918 did less well. Produced under the management of André Charlot and Guy Bragdon, it featured diminutive revue actor Nelson Keys as Eddie, Nellie Briercliffe as Elsie Darling and Walter Williams as Dick Rivers, and it opened in the same week as the local version of another Broadway success, *Going Up*. London audiences gave their vote to the latter in no uncertain terms: by 574 performances to 46.

A 1975 revival, produced at the Goodspeed Opera House (8 July), dropped a handful of pieces of the original score and replaced them with eight numbers taken from other of Kern's shows. Two of the best ('Good Night Boat', 'Left All Alone Again Blues') came from the equally river-based *The Night Boat* and the sparky 'Katy-Did' was plucked from *Oh, I Say!* David Christmas and Cynthia Wells played Dick and Elsie, whilst Charles Repole and

Virginia Seidel profited from the increased score as Eddie and the other Elsie. A Broadway transfer of this made-over version played 304 performances at the Booth Theater (21 December 1975) and provoked a new London run (Piccadilly Theatre 23 March 1976). Robert Swann, Mary Barrett, Richard Freeman and Prue Clarke featured in a production which profited from a theatre anxious to stay lit to stretch its run to 411 performances.

Australia: Palace Theatre, Sydney 10 February 1917; UK: Palace Theatre 18 May 1918
Recording: 1975 revival cast (DRG)

VESTRIS, Madame [Eliza] [BARTOLOZZI, Lucy Elizabeth] (b London, ?1797; d London, 8 August 1856).

Madame Vestris (she had married into the famous dancing family) was a vocalist and actress in London and Paris before she made her name in the title-rôle of the extravaganza *Don Giovanni in London* at the Theatre Royal, Drury Lane, in 1817. Over the following decade she established herself as a public favourite in opera (Fatima in *Oberon* and many male rôles), ballad opera (Macheath), comic opera (Adela in *The Haunted Tower* etc), burletta (Apollo in *Midas*) as well as in all kinds of drama and comedy often decorated with interpolated songs for her benefit.

In 1831 she became manageress of the Olympic Theatre and there she launched what was to become a famous series of extravaganzas and burlesques authored by J R Planché and beginning with *Olympic Revels*, a burlesque of the Pandora myth with herself starred as the over-curious nymph. During nine years at the Olympic, and subsequently, with her second husband Charles Mathews, at Covent Garden and the Lyceum, Madame Vestris (no little aided by a sexually scandalous gutter press) fostered a highly popular line in burlesque and extravaganza as an important part of her repertoire, a line which provided a backbone for the freer kind of musico-comical theatre of the time and which led directly to the burlesque tradition of the later part of the 19th-century British stage.

Biographies: Pearce, C E: *Madame Vestris and Her Times* (Paul, London, 1923), Williams, C J: *Madame Vestris: a Theatrical Biography* (Sidgwick & Jackson, London, 1973)

DER VETTER AUS DINGSDA Operette in 3 acts by Herman Haller and 'Rideamus' based on a comedy by Max Kempner-Hochstädt. Music by Eduard Künneke. Theater am Nollendorfplatz, Berlin, 15 April 1921.

If *Der Vetter aus Dingsda* was far from the longest-running piece to play Berlin's Theater am Nollendorfplatz under Herman Haller's management in the 1910s and 1920s – its 200 performances paled beside the more than 650 of the wartime *Immer feste druff!* and the nearly 500 of *Drei alte Schachteln* – it was, nevertheless, qualitatively the best of the series of Operetten which Eduard Künneke composed for the house and the most enduring amongst all of Haller's musical-theatre ventures. Whilst the other Haller pieces are forgotten, it has survived through more than half a century into the repertoire of modern European theatres in a way that very few other German Operetten have done.

Pretty Dutch Julia (Lori Leux) longs for the day when her beloved cousin Roderich will come home from 'nowhere' in the East Indies. As a result, she refuses the attentions of local Egon and is not inclined to fall in with

Plate 283. **Der Vetter aus Dingsda**: *Uncle and Auntie (Horst Schäfer, Elvira Beitler) settle down to their supper unaware of the shock to their daily routine that is on its way from 'nowhere' (Stadttheater, Darmstadt, 1986).*

the plans of her Uncle Josse (Gottfried Huppert) that she should wed his brother's son, August. One day a handsome stranger (Johannes Müller) arrives at the house, and Julia is delighted when, in response to her hopeful prodding, he says he is Roderich, and then devastated when it eventuates that he is not. When the real Roderich (Eugen Rex) does come, however, he is aghast to find that Julia has kept a candle alight for him all the years since their childhood, and she, in her turn, regrets having turned the false Roderich away. But she will keep her dream: to her, August – for the stranger is none other than he – will take the place of the Roderich she dreamed of, and best-friend Hannchen (Ilse Marvenga) will be very happy with a Roderich she never dreamed of.

Künneke's score to this little, 24-hour-span, nine-handed Operette ranged from some sweetly natural scenes set around the family table, to a beautiful spun-soprano 'Strahlender Mond' in which Julia asks the moon to carry her love to her cousin on the other side of the world, to the plaintive musical line of the stranger's mysterious answer to the girl's persistent questioning: 'Ich bin nur ein armer Wandergesell', and to such up-to-date strains as the boston, the tango and the foxtrot.

Haller's production of *Der Vetter aus Dingsda* played at the Theater am Nollendorfplatz from April to its 200th night on 24th October, before making way for the next Haller-Künneke piece *Die Ehe im Kreise* and then headed out to other German-language houses. It reached Vienna the following October, playing at the Johann Strauss-Theater under the management of Erich Müller for a little under three months with Lola Grahl (Julia), Karl Bachmann (August), Fritz Imhoff (Roderich), Gisa Kolbe (Hannchen) and Georg Kundert (Josse) in the leading rôles.

The show was taken up for America by the Shuberts but, before it was seen by Broadway, it underwent a most curious transformation. It was now, thanks to Harry B Smith, called *Caroline* (after having tried out at Wilmington as *Virginia*), it was set in the American Civil War, and Künneke's svelte score had been dotted with extra bits by Al Goodman. Tessa Kosta played the eponymous heroine, whilst Harrison Brockbank and J Harold Murray were the men in the affair, and the mixture pleased for 151 performances. London's version (ad Douglas Furber, Adrian Ross, Fred Thompson, R C Tharp) which opened a few weeks later treated the original more kindly. But the Prince's Theatre production, with Helen Gilliland (Julia), Walter Williams (August), Cicely Debenham (Hannchen) and Roy Royston (Egon, worryingly renamed Adrian van Piffel) did not win the favour it might have hoped for in the West End. It closed after three months and 105 performances prior to what nevertheless turned out to be a good tour.

J C Williamson Ltd's Australian production also went through a few vicissitudes. The management decided to make a star out of a local amateur vocalist whom they renamed 'Jill Manners' and cast her as Julia alongside Claude Flemming (Stranger), Arthur Stigant (Josse), Marie La Varre (Wimpel), Gus Bluett (Adrien ie Egon), Charles Brooks (Roderich) and 'the twelve tulips, a dozen of Australia's most beautiful girls' who were dressed in white, blue and pink in successive acts. Jill Manners was a dreadful disappointment, and Marie Burke had to be hurried in to replace her for two months in Sydney. When Miss Burke went on to make a huge hit in *Wildflower*, *The Cousin from Nowhere* was put away, but it re-emerged at Christmas two years later to play a two-month Melbourne season with Maud Fane in the lead rôle (Her Majesty's Theatre, Melbourne 18 December 1926).

If the show's overseas record was just a little disappointing, however, *Der Vetter aus Dingsda* remained a strong favourite on home ground where, helped by the reasonable size of its cast, it has remained a regularly produced item in German-language houses to this day. It was twice filmed, first by Georg Zoch in 1934 and a second time in 1954 in a version where Künneke was credited as co-musical director, and one of the screenplay authors was a (but not the) Haller. Vera Molnár (Julia), Gerhard Riemann (Hans), Joachim Brennecke (Roderich) and Ina Halley (Hannchen) featured.

Austria: Johann Strauss-Theater 13 October 1922; USA: Ambassador Theater *Caroline* 31 January 1923; UK: Prince's Theatre *The Cousin from Nowhere* 24 February 1923; Australia: Theatre Royal, Sydney *The Cousin from Nowhere* 27 September 1924; Films: Georg Zoch 1934, Central-Europa/Karl Anton 1953

Recordings: complete (RCA), selections (Eurodisc, Fontana etc)

THE VICAR OF BRAY English comic opera in 2 acts by Sydney Grundy. Music by Edward Solomon. Globe Theatre, London, 22 July 1882.

The successful playwright Sydney Grundy turned librettist and lyricist for the first time on *The Vicar of Bray*, inventing a story around the character of the famous vicar of song and fable, whose byword was 'expediency' and who changed his denomination as quickly as circumstances demanded it. He mixed this character with Thomas Day's almost as well known nursery-tale pair of idealized 18th-century schoolboys – rich and horrid Tommy Merton and angelic farmer's lad Henry Sandford – and came out with a libretto in which the two fellows (the latter now a curate rather than a farmer, and both grown up) court vicar's daughter, Dorothy (Lizzie Beaumont). The vicar (W J Hill) scares off impecunious Henry (Walter H Fisher) by turning high-church, suffers along with his chorus of students the celibacy such a change incurs, but hurriedly

goes 'low' again when the bishop intervenes, allowing Dorothy to have her Henry and himself to take to wife the wealthy widowed Mrs Merton (Maria Davis). Tommy (H Cooper Cliffe) is paired off in good aristocratic fashion with danseuse Nellie Bly (Emma D'Auban). Gently Gilbertian, though set firmly in the Britain which encouraged composer Solomon to his most natural style of music, *The Vicar of Bray* seemingly suffered from its lack of demonstrativeness. It was revised and partly recast after an indifferent opening, but ended after 69 performances, and one week on Broadway in an ill-staged production with Marie Jansen (Dorothy), Harry Allen (Vicar) and the D'Oyly Carte's Lyn Cadwaldr (Sandford) in the leading rôles.

However, a decade later, after Solomon's *The Nautch Girl* had very much more than satisfactorily filled the gap left by the Gilbert–Sullivan split at the Savoy Theatre, D'Oyly Carte revived *The Vicar of Bray*. Savoy stars Rutland Barrington (Vicar), Courtice Pounds (Sandford) and Rosina Brandram (Mrs Merton) headed the cast and the show ran through five months and 143 performances before going on to tour merrily throughout Britain in the Carte repertoire companies for several seasons. On the wings of this classy revival, *The Vicar of Bray* also won a production in Australia with Joseph Tapley (Sandford), George Lauri (Vicar), Sydney Deane (Merton) and Clara Thompson (Mrs Merton) at the head of its cast.

USA: Fifth Avenue Theater 2 October 1882; Australia: Princess Theatre, Melbourne 20 May 1893

DER VICEADMIRAL Operette in a Vorspiel and 3 acts by F Zell and Richard Genée. Music by Carl Millöcker. Theater an der Wien, Vienna, 9 October 1886.

Henri, Comte de Villeneuve (Karl Streitmann), who is viceadmiral of the French-Spanish fleet fighting against Britain in the year of 1804, is obliged to get wed within 48 hours or lose a large inheritance. He heads for Cadiz to the home of Don Mirabolante, Count of Miraflores y Villalar Bermudez (Siegmund Stelzer) dressed, by his admiral's orders, as a simple sailor, to take his pick between the Don's daughters Serafina (Antonie Hartmann) and Sybillina (Frln Stein). But Henri disdains the disguise, and whilst the foolish 'prewarned' Mirabolante and his daughters make a great fuss of the common sailor, Punto (Alexander Girardi), the nobleman gets to know the family Cinderella, Gilda (Ottilie Collin). When Punto chooses Sybillina, Serafina plots with the interfering Donna Candida (Therese Schäfer) to upset things, replacing the mayor and notary with the old lady's disguised sons (Carl Lindau, Herr Horwig). Then the English capture the phoney viceadmiral, the Spanish come to his rescue, and the plotters are aghast when the ultimately victorious Henri, revealed in his true position, chooses Gilda as his bride, leaving the sisters to pair off with Candida's sons.

Millöcker's score was marked by some particularly happy ensembles: the wooing trio of the two daughters and Punto ('Geh'n wir in den Garten, atmen Blumenduft'), the introduction of Henri and Gilda in duet, a song and dance for Punto and Sybillina in the second act, and a sextet amongst the four plotters and the unwittingly unmarried bride and her father in the final act being among the evening's choice pieces.

Der Viceadmiral did not have a dazzling Viennese career.

It played its 25th performance on 3 November, then appeared intermittently in the repertoire up to its 30th on 26 March 1887, but in the meanwhile it had been taken up widely in other European cities. Berlin's production at the Friedrich-Wilhelmstädtisches Theater launched the show on a successful career in German houses, Budapest saw it first in German and subsequently (ad Emil Makai, Albert Kövessy) in Hungarian, St Petersburg (8 Dec 1886) and later Sweden, Finland, Switzerland, Romania, Mexico, Yugoslavia, Italy and Spain all saw productions, but Britain (perhaps because the British were the 'enemy' in the tale, or perhaps just continuing its general ignoring of Millöcker's works) did not mount the show.

Der Viceadmiral did, however, get an English-language production. New York's Amberg Theater introduced the show in German with a cast headed by Streitmann in his original rôle, Carl Adolf Friese and the Fräuleins Engländer and von Varndal, and some three years later the Casino Theater followed their two months of Millöcker's *Das Sonntagskind* with a version of the earlier *The Viceadmiral*. Jefferson de Angelis (Punto), Annie Meyers, Villa Knox, Jennie Reiffarth (Candida), Harry MacDonough, Henri Leoni and Charles Bassett — mostly from the earlier show's cast — got almost another three months out of Millöcker.

Der Viceadmiral remained around. It was revived in Hungary in 1903 (Budai Színkör, 22 August) and played for a few performances at Vienna's Johann Strauss-Theater from 13 February 1909, but in more recent years it has been seen only in botched versions, such as those produced in Germany as *Der Herzog von Mirenza* (ad F Giblhauser, F Neupert, Fürth, 4 January 1936) and *Das Heiratsnest* (A Mette-Neumann, Regensburg, 25 January 1936).

The most durable portion of *Der Viceadmiral*, however, turned out to be the waltz 'Geh'n wir in den Garten' which was metamorphosed from a gently comic trio into a robustly romantic solo as 'Dunkelrote Rosen', the hit number of the rehashed, and still performed, version of Millöcker's *Gasparone*.

Germany: Friedrich-Wilhelmstädtisches Theater 29 October 1886; Hungary: (Ger) 29 November 1886, *A Viceadmirális*; USA: Columbia Theater, Chicago 18 October 1888, Amberg Theater, New York (Ger) 24 October 1889; Casino Theater *The Viceadmiral* 18 June 1892

DER VIELGELIEBTE Operette in 3 acts, based on an old work, by Herman Haller. Lyrics by 'Rideamus'. Music by Eduard Künneke. Theater am Nollendorfplatz, Berlin, 17 October 1919.

One of the number of musical adaptations of the celebrated French play *Le Vicomte de Letorrières*, earlier set with considerable success as *Az eleven ördög* by Hungarian composer József Konti, this German version shifted the tale into a Germanic setting. The hero became Hans, Graf von Liebenstein (Eduard Lichtenstein), a penniless but sexy aristocrat, struggling against his horrid cousin Nicodemus for the hand of pretty Annette and the family money. In the course of a party at the home of the lofty Graf von Wildammer, Hans lives up to his reputation as 'der Vielgeliebte' (the much-loved one), wooing and manipulating the ladies and, through them their men, and after swords have been drawn, wine flowed, and flirtations succeeded flirtations, Hans gets money and girl. Claire Waldoff took the principal soubrette rôle as the tailor's daughter, Kläre, who is Hans's companion in poverty and who ends up wedding his servant, Franz.

Künneke's score featured – not surprisingly – a 'Frauen-Walzer' and a 'Lieblich und hold ist die Nacht' alongside a Vogelstellerlied, 'Ein kleines bisschen so' and 'Ach, ich tat's nur für dich' amongst its favourite moments.

Produced at the Theater am Nollendorfplatz by adapter Haller, *Der Vielgeliebte* was the first of a series of musical plays on which the director/author collaborated with lyricist 'Rideamus' and composer Künneke. It ran for six months, to 29 April 1920, before ceding place to Bromme's *Eine Nacht im Paradies*, then to its Haller/Künneke successors *Wenn Liebe erwacht* and *Der Vetter aus Dingsda*. It was subsequently produced around Germany without attracting attention in the other main centres.

Virtually the same title (but in the feminine) was given to an Operette produced in Stralsund, and also to another piece which found success in Germany – Rudolf Köller, F Maregg and Nico Dostal's 1934 *Die Vielgeliebte* (Centraltheater, Leipzig 23 December 1934; Schillertheater, Berlin 5 March 1935). On this occasion the 'much-loved' heroine was the Garboish filmstar Dena Darlo, portrayed by composer's wife Lillie Claus. Precisely the same title had also been given to another piece mounted just a few months previously at Königsberg (Manfred Nussbaum, Erich Walter/Karl Winter 1 March).

LA VIE PARISIENNE Opéra-bouffe in 4 (originally 5) acts by Henri Meilhac and Ludovic Halévy. Music by Jacques Offenbach. Palais-Royal, Paris, 31 October 1866.

In the midst of Meilhac, Halévy and Offenbach's dazzling successes with the earliest of their famous opéras-bouffes – *La Belle Hélène* (1864), *Barbe-bleue* (1866), *La Grande-Duchesse de Gérolstein* (1867) – the team collaborated on an equally successful non-burlesque work (which they, nevertheless, on the wings of the current fashion described as an 'opéra-bouffe'), which was produced by Plunkett at the Palais-Royal. That house and its company were not in the business of producing opérette, the resident company (only slightly reinforced for the occasion) were not experienced singers, only actors, and the piece – a farcical comedy of manners which did not make extravagant vocal demands on most of its performers – was written (and re-written, for it was reduced from five acts to four shortly after its première) accordingly.

Bobinet (Gil-Pérès) and Gardefeu (Priston) are a pally pair of men-about-Paris who have suffered some amour-properly bruising treatment in their affairs with the women of the demi-monde, notably the saucy Métella (Mlle Honorine). As a result they have decided to opt for an affair with a femme du monde instead. Gardefeu poses as a tour guide and picks up the visiting Swedish Baron (Hyacinthe) and Baroness (Céline Montaland) de Gondremarck and, in his attempt to seduce the lady, takes the pair to his own home, pretending it is an hotel. The Baron is hoping for a good Parisian time, and indeed has a letter of introduction to Métella, so Gardefeu gets Bobinet to arrange a jolly party – with all his servants and their friends dressed up as cavorting aristocratic guests – to keep the husband happy whilst he chats up the Baroness. However, the Baron has no luck with Métella who instead provides him with a masked friend as company whilst she turns her charms back on to Gardefeu. When the mask finally comes off, the Baron finds he has been charmed by his own wife.

Jules Brasseur had a triple rôle as an extravagant Brazilian (Acts I and IV) out to spend a fortune on a fling in Paris, as a bootmaker, disguised as an army major for the Act II party, and as a butler (Act III), Elvire Paurelle was the pretty maidservant, Pauline, who catches the Baron's eye at the party, and Zulma Bouffar – added to the cast at Offenbach's insistence to give some vocal values – played Gardefeu's little glove-maker, Gabrielle, who partakes of all the fun and impersonations and ends up on the arm of the Brazilian as everyone prepares to live it up at the final curtain.

Offenbach provided a glitteringly light-fingered musical score to go with the wittily concocted high-jinks of the text. The Brazilian gabbled out his joy at being back in Paris all over the railway station ('Je suis brésilien'), the Baron declared gluttonously 'Je veux m'en fourrer jusque-là!', Gabrielle trilled into her upper-class disguise ('Je suis veuve d'un colonel') and described sexily how 'Sa robe fait frou, frou', whilst Métella had a showpiece letter song – the letter in question being the 'recommendation' of the Baron's once-lucky friend to show the hungry Swede an extremely good time ('Vous souvient-il, ma belle'), all as part of a score which never left off laughing from beginning to end.

In spite of a lack of confidence prior to opening, *La Vie parisienne* – soon shorn of a fourth act showing what the Baroness gets up to whilst her husband is partying with Bobinet – was an enormous success, occupying the Palais-Royal for an entire year whilst the show began to spread itself to other parts of the world. Vienna's Carltheater was first off the mark, opening its version of the five-act version (ad Karl Treumann) three months to the day after the Palais-Royal première. Josef Matras (Bobinet), Franz Tewele (Gardefeu), Wilhelm Knaack (Gondremarck), Karl Treumann (Brazilian/Prosper/Frick), Josefine Gallmeyer (Gabrielle), Anna Grobecker (Pauline), Marie Fontelive (Baroness) and Anna Müller (Métella) took the leading rôles, and the piece became an instant favourite. It remained in the theatre's repertoire for many years, being played 126 times (to 11 August 1876) in its first decade, and was brought back in a new production in 1889, with Knaack in his original rôle alongside Emma Seebold (Métella) and Karl Streitmann (Brazilian), which was played for the next four seasons. A major Viennese revival was mounted at the Theater an der Wien in 1911 (28 October) with Louis Treumann (Brazilian etc), Mizzi Günther (Gabrielle), Luise Kartousch (Pauline), Paul Guttmann (Baron), Victor Flemming (Bobinet), Ludwig Herold (Gardefeu) and Ida Russka (Métella) featured through 43 performances.

New York first saw the piece, in French, two years after Vienna, with Rose Bell, Marie Desclauzas and Paul Juignet heading the cast of the four-act version, and *La Vie parisienne* was subsequently played by Marie Aimée and by other opéra-bouffe companies throughout the country, but the first English-language version (ad F C Burnand) was seen not in New York but in London. Burnand had considerably altered, resituated and generally anglicized the script and the result, in spite of being played by such actors

as Lionel Brough (Baron), Harriet Coveney (Baroness) and Lottie Venne (Polly Twinkle), was not long-lived. But the lesson of the flop was not learned. H B Farnie turned out another English adaptation which called itself simply *La Vie* (all things Parisian having been again deleted), which was mounted by Alexander Henderson with great fanfare at the Avenue Theatre in 1883 (3 October) with Brough again starred alongside Arthur Roberts, Camille D'Arville and Lillian La Rue. It again proved to be a hamfistedly anglicized and altered version and, again, it was a failure although the production was kept doggedly on for 116 performances. This version was later produced on Broadway – duly americanized and its comedy roundly lowered – with Richard Mansfield as Baron von Wienerschnitzel (the name more or less typified the tone of the adaptation) and Fannie Rice as Gabrielle. However, even more disastrous than these was an effort by A P Herbert and A D Adams to 'improve' Meilhac and Halévy (and Offenbach) with a feeble patchwork mounted at the Lyric, Hammersmith, in 1929 (29 April) and England had to wait until 1961 (24 May) and Geoffrey Dunn's witty version for the Sadler's Wells Opera Company to hear an English *La Vie parisienne* which approximated the original French one.

Budapest first saw *Pariser Leben* in its German version, but Endre Latabár's *Parizsi élet* followed and it won much the same success that the French and German versions had. Swedish, Spanish, Polish, Russian, Danish and Czech versions were amongst those that followed. However, it was in France that *La Vie parisienne* won and maintained its greatest popularity. The show was taken into the repertoire at the Théâtre des Variétés in 1875 (25 September) where Mlle Bouffar repeated her creation alongside such seasoned musical performers as José Dupuis (Baron), Berthelier (Brazilian etc), and Cooper (Gardefeu), and Paris saw regular performances thereafter. The Opéra-Comique received the piece in 1931, the Jean-Louis Barrault and Madeleine Renaud company revived it at the Palais-Royal in 1958, with its principals appearing as the Brazilian (etc) and the Baroness respectively, a revised version (ad Jean Marsan, Raymond Vogel) was produced at the Opéra-Comique in 1974 whilst, in the desert of musical productions that Paris became in the 1980s, it was nevertheless produced twice (Théâtre du Châtelet 4 November 1980, Théâtre de Paris 16 October 1985). In 1990 further performances were given at the Opéra-Comique (4 December).

An important vertebra of the French musical theatre repertoire, the show is played regularly and still retains popularity throughout the world in varying forms – the German-language theatre, for example, still favours the five-act version and now, apparently, others are also casting eyes towards it – but in the English-language theatre *La Vie parisienne* has never wholly recovered from its initial poor adaptations and the unfavourable impression they left behind.

Austria: Carltheater *Pariser Leben* 31 January 1867; Germany: Friedrich-Wilhelmstädtisches Theater *Pariser Leben* 22 May 1867; USA: Théâtre Français (Fr) 29 March 1869, Bijou Theater (Eng) 18 April 1884; Hungary: (Ger) 25 May 1867, Budai Színkör *Parizsi élet* 1 July 1871; UK: Holborn Theatre 30 March 1872, Avenue Theatre *La Vie* 3 October 1883

Recordings: complete (EMI), complete in German (Philips), revival cast 1974 (Carrere), revival cast 1958 (Paris), selections (Pathé, Philips etc), English cast recording (HMV)

Plate 284. **Viktória:** *Janczi (István Mester) chats up the French maid, Riquette (Klára Krasznói) – only to find she isn't French at all, but a good Hungarian girl from Budapest! (Pécs, 1978).*

VIKTÓRIA Operette in a prologue and 3 acts by Emmerich Földes. Lyrics by Imre Harmath. Music by Pál Ábrahám. Király Színház, Budapest, 21 February 1930.

The first and most successful of Pál Ábrahám's three hit operetts of the early 1930s, *Viktória* relied a little less than the two later pieces – *Die Blume von Hawaii* and *Ball im Savoy* – on the composer's characteristic mixture of traditional Operette and jazzy up-to-date dance elements. This was partly due to the show's story, which was a particularly strong-backed and dramatic one, flavoured with some of the easternness of the recent *Das Land des Lächelns* but using a more measured exotism in its settings and also eschewing the other piece's trendy unhappy ending.

The Hungarian hussar captain Stefan Koltay (Ferenc Kiss) and his batman Janczi (József Sziklai), who have been sentenced to death for their part in the Russian counter-revolution, bribe their way to escape and flee from Siberia to Tokyo where they are given refuge in the American Embassy. When it turns out that the wife of Ambassador John Cunlight (Dezső Kertész) is Viktoria (Juci Labáss), the woman he had loved before the war came between them, Koltay accepts Cunlight's offer to accompany them to his new posting in St Petersburg, in spite of the danger he runs in returning to Russia. Viktoria tries to put her feelings behind her and remain faithful to her kindly husband, but when Cunlight discovers the truth he both protects Koltay from the Russians who surround the Embassy and, ultimately, steps out of the picture so that Viktoria can be reunited with the lover she had thought dead in the wars. The romantic story was thoroughly filled out by the more lightly-coloured romances of two other couples: Viktoria's brother, Count Ferry Hegedűs (Oszkár Dénes) and his little Japanese bride Lia San (Rózsi Bársony), and Janczi and Riquette (Teri Fejes), the extremely 'French' maid who is actually not French at all, but Hungarian.

Both the romantic and soubret sides of the score produced a bundle of attractive and popular numbers. Cunlight and Viktoria remember his first proposal to her in

'Pardon, Madame', Viktoria reflects on her days in Japan as epitomized by 'Rote Orchideen', and first Koltay ('Reich mir zum Abschied noch einmal die Hände') and then Cunlight take their leave of the lady with a gentle 'Good Night'. In a brighter vein, Lia San explains her international personality – she is half-Japanese but half-French – in the sprightly 'Meine Mama war aus Yokohama' and Riquette and Janczi sing of the Hungarian charms of the big, brass 'Honvéd-Banda' and of compatibility ('Ja, so ein Mädel, ungarisches Mädel'). However, by far the biggest hit of the evening came in Lia San and Ferry's giggling little song and dance duo 'Mausi, süss warst du heute Nacht', a piece which would go on to become an international favourite.

Within months of the production at the Király Színház, the wheeler-dealing impresario-director Miksa Preger, who had picked up the German-language rights, found a home for *Viktoria und ihr Husar* (the gentleman got into the title in Alfred Grünwald and Fritz Löhner-Beda's German version) at Leipzig. The show caused a sensation and instantly the Berlin houses, which had previously turned Preger and his production away, began to court the man who owned this new and red-hot Hungarian musical. Preger was able to choose his terms as he brought his show to the Rotter brothers and the Metropoltheater where Anny Ahlers starred as Viktoria alongside Fritz Steiner (Koltay) and Louis Treumann, and Dénes paired with Lizzi Waldmüller for the famous duet. *Viktoria und ihr Husar* triumphed all over again in Berlin. It was hailed as 'an undeniable success ...' its book praised as being 'as water-tight as its music' and its Metropoltheater career launched it as a classic of the German-language musical stage. Later the same year, it was mounted by Preger at the Theater an der Wien with Rita Georg (Viktoria), Treumann (Cunlight), Otto Maran (Koltay) and with Dénes and Waldmüller repeating their duet. It played a three-month season and was later reprised with Betty Fischer as Viktoria, bringing its Viennese total to 121 performances.

The Hussar stayed in the title when *Viktória* made her first appearance on the English-language stage (ad Harry Graham), and Dénes gave his Ferry and 'Mausi' in a third different language as he paired with the Lia San of Barbara Diu, alongside Margaret Carlisle (Viktoria), Harry Welchman (Cunlight) and Roy Russell (Koltay) in Alfred Butt's production at London's Palace Theatre. The show was greeted as 'a musical comedy with a melodramatic plot rather than an Operette' as it played 100 performances before going out to tour. This and the German success were, oddly, not enough to provoke a production on Broadway, although America ultimately did see *Viktória* a decade later when a productions were mounted in St Louis, with Helen Gleason (Viktoria), Lansing Hatfield (Koltay) and Robert Chisholm (Cunlight), and in Los Angeles. However, Australia's J C Williamson Ltd took up both *Victoria and her Hussar* and the ubiquitous Dénes. The Hungarian actor – actually taken to Australia to play in *Ball at the Savoy* – notched up his fourth major production of *Viktória* when he took over his earlier part from Cecil Kellaway for *Viktória*'s Melbourne season, teaming this time with local soubrette Sylvia Kellaway, alongside Sylvia Welling (Viktoria), John Mayer (Stefan), Jack Kellaway (Janczi), Sydney Burchall (Cunlight) and Nellie

Barnes (Riquette). Sydney's six week season and seven weeks in Melbourne (Her Majesty's Theatre 20 April 1935) were not, however, the only chance Australians had to see *Viktória*. Although there was some critical grumbling over the fact that – most unoperettically – you didn't know which of the two chaps you were supposed to side with, the show proved a solid success and it was later brought back to the Australian circuits as a vehicle for the country's musical-comedy megastar, Gladys Moncrieff (1945).

The show's French version (ad André Mauprey, René Coëns) was staged at the rather unlikely venue of the Moulin-Rouge, which had for many years devoted itself to revue before sinking into cinema. Grazia del Rio, Lilli Palmer, Colette Fleuriot, Mercier, Péraldi and Marcel Lamy featured in Maurice Catriens's production and, although that initial production was not a success, *Victoria et son hussard* was still to be seen on the French stage in 1991.

The Hungarian and German *Viktórias* have been maintained in the repertoire since their creation and both are still regularly played to this day. Versions of the show were also put twice on to film. The first (1931) produced by Richard Oswald, adapted by Fritz Friedmann Friedrich and featuring Michael Bohnen, Friedel Schuster and Iwan Petrovich, stayed fairly close to the story, but introduced some Ábrahám dance numbers not used on the stage ('Du bist mein Glück, du bist mein Frühling!', 'Da sag' ich sehr gern: Igen!'), the second, some 20 years later (International-Films 1954), had poor Viktoria becoming 'ein Revuestar des Broadway' and went ludicrously on from there. Eva Bartok was the 'Revuestar', Frank Felder her hussar and that was about all – apart from the title – of the original which remained.

Germany: Stadttheater, Leipzig *Viktoria und ihr Husar* 7 July 1930; Austria: Theater an der Wien *Viktoria und ihr Husar* 23 December 1930; UK: Palace Theatre *Victoria and Her Hussar* 17 September 1931; France: Théâtre du Moulin-Rouge *Victoria et son hussard* 16 December 1933; Australia: Theatre Royal, Sydney, *Victoria and Her Hussar* 22 December 1934; USA: Municipal Opera, St Louis *Victoria and Her Hussar* 21 August 1937; Film: Richard Oswald 1931

Recordings: selection (Eurodisc, Telefunken, Fontana etc), selection in French (TLP), selection in Swedish (Telestar) etc

VINCENT, Ruth [BUNN, Ruth] (b Great Yarmouth, 22 March 1877; d London, 8 July 1955). D'Oyly Carte soprano who went on to further successes on the musical and operatic stages.

Miss Vincent began her career at the Savoy Theatre as a small-part player and leading lady understudy in *The Chieftain* and *The Grand Duke* (Gretchen) and she fulfilled similar functions in *His Majesty* (1897), *The Yeomen of the Guard* revival (1897) and *The Grand Duchess* (1897) before being cast as Casilda in the company's 1898 revival of *The Gondoliers*. She then played Princess Laoula in *The Lucky Star* (1899), took the lead juvenile soprano rôle in the production of Sullivan's *The Beauty Stone* (Laine) and played Aline (*Sorcerer*) and Josephine (*HMS Pinafore*) before walking out of *The Rose of Persia* in rehearsals and retiring to marriage.

Miss Vincent returned to the stage in 1903 to play in the unfortunate musical comedy *The Medal and the Maid* (Merva Sunningdale), but she found the rôle she needed to make her a star the following year when George Edwardes

cast her in the title-rôle of the London production of *Véronique* (1904). Having made her name in London she then went on to repeat her success in the same rôle in America. She appeared for Edwardes again in the indifferent *The Girl on the Stage* (1906, Molly Montrose) but then had her two most memorable new rôles as the comic opera Princess of *Amasis* ('Little Princess, Look Up') and as Sophia Western in Edward German's *Tom Jones* ('For Tonight', 'Today My Spinet'). These two parts established her as the reigning queen of London comic opera, but after further London appearances as the star of *The Belle of Brittany* (1908, Babette) and the unsuccessful *A Persian Princess* (1909, Princess Yolene), she departed the light musical stage and moved into the opéra-comique, creating Vrenchen in Delius's *A Village Romeo and Juliet* (1910) at Covent Garden and appearing in such lighter rôles of the operatic repertoire as Gretel, Micaëla, Antonia (*Tales of Hoffmann*), Missa's Muguette, Dorabella and Zerlina. In later years she performed in variety, retiring in 1930.

Her sister Madge Vincent was also a member of the D'Oyly Carte Company from 1899 and had small rôles in such musical comedies as *San Toy*, *The Toreador*, *Three Little Maids*, *The Medal and the Maid*, *Véronique*, *Amasis*, *The Gay Gordons* and *The Merry Peasant* in Britain, and larger ones in the Far East with Maurice Bandmann's company.

VINCY, Raymond (b Marseille; d 1968). The librettist of the most important successes of the postwar French musical stage.

Marseillais librettist and songwriter Vincy made his first incursions into the musical theatre on the jolly wave of Alibert/Scotto opérettes before the Second World War, but his career in the Parisian musical theatre took off in 1945 when he was invited to dig in his bottom drawer in a hurry and supply a libretto for a six-week filler opérette for the Casino Montparnasse. *Mariage à l'essai* became *Mariage gitane* which became *La Belle de Cadix* which became the hit of its time, and Vincy began a 20-year collaboration with composer Francis Lopez which, at its beginning, produced some of the best postwar French musicals, both in the field of romantic opérette à grand spectacle (*Andalousie*, *Méditerranée*, *Le Chanteur de Mexico*) and occasionally and especially in the vaudevillesque line (*Quatre Jours à Paris*).

Vincy, more than any other author, set the style of the French musical theatre of the postwar period, supplying many shapely libretti not only to the service of composer Lopez but also to such singing stars as Luis Mariano, Tino Rossi and Georges Guétary, and – more demandingly – to such comic ones as Annie Cordy and Bourvil. He crystallized the layout of the French romantic musical, with its overwhelmingly central male singing star, its often somewhat discreet soprano heroine and its supportive light comic couple, all mixed up in mildly dramatic and amorous events in colourful places, and he kept that kind of musical play fresh for a surprisingly long time before it sombred into rather repetitive formulae and less imaginative shows in later days. When Lopez and others attempted to follow his lines after his death, the genre plummeted into absolute vacuity and the quality of Vincy's work became all the more evident.

Vincy also scripted a number of the Alibert/Scotto musicals for the screen, and remade a number of his own

(*La Belle de Cadix, Andalousie, Quatre Jours à Paris* et al) as film musicals.

1935 **Un de la Canebière** (Scotto/w René Sarvil/Henri Alibert) Théâtre des Célestins, Lyon 14 October; Théâtre des Variétés 3 April

1945 **La Belle de Cadix** (Francis Lopez/Maurice Vandair/w Marc-Cab) Casino Montparnasse 24 December

1947 **Andalousie** (Lopez/Albert Willemetz) Théâtre de la Gaîté-Lyrique 25 October

1948 **Quatre Jours à Paris** (Lopez) Théâtre Bobino 28 February

1949 **Symphonie portugaise** (aka *Romance au Portugal*) (Jose Padilla/w Marc-Cab) Théâtre de la Gaîte-Lyrique 9 October

1949 **Monsieur Bourgogne** (Lopez/w Jean-Jacques Vital) Théâtre Bobino 12 March

1950 **Pour Don Carlos** (Lopez/w André Mouëzy-Éon) Théâtre du Châtelet 15 December

1951 **Le Chanteur de Mexico** (Lopez/w Henri Wernert/w Félix Gandéra) Théâtre du Châtelet 15 December

1952 **La Route fleurie** (Lopez) Théâtre de l'ABC 30 December

1953 **Le Soleil de Paris** (Lopez/as 'Henri Villard') Théâtre Bobino 7 March

1954 **La Toison d'or** (Lopez) Théâtre du Châtelet 18 December

1954 **À la Jamaïque** (Lopez) Théâtre de la Porte-Saint-Martin 24 January

1955 **Méditerranée** (Lopez) Théâtre du Châtelet 17 December

1957 **Maria-Flora** (Lopez, Henri Betti) Théâtre du Châtelet 18 December

1957 **Tête de linotte** (Lopez) Théâtre de l'ABC December

1958 **Rose de Noël** (Franz Lehár arr Miklos Rekaï, Paul Bonneau) Théâtre du Châtelet 23 December

1959 **Le Secret de Marco Polo** (Lopez) Théâtre du Châtelet 12 December

1960 **Dix millions cash!** (Lopez) Théâtre de la Porte-Saint-Martin 10 December

1961 **Visa pour l'amour** (Lopez) Théâtre de la Gaîté-Lyrique December

1963 **Cristobal le Magnifique** (Lopez) Théâtre de l'Européen December

1963 **Le Temps des guitares** (Lopez/w Marc-Cab) Théâtre de l'ABC October

1967 **Le Prince de Madrid** (Lopez/Jacques Plante) Théâtre du Châtelet 4 March

1967 **Pic et pioche** (Darry Cowl/Jacques Mareuil) Théâtre des Nouveautés

VINCZE, Zsigmond (b Zombor, 1 July 1874; d Budapest, 30 June 1935).

Trained in Budapest, Vincze subsequently led a successful career as a theatre conductor and composer in his own country. In the first of these capacities he was, in turn, musical director at Debrecen, at Budapest's Király Színház (where he conducted the première of *Gül Baba*) and Vigszinház, at Szeged and at the metropolitan Belvárosi Színház. As a composer, he made a memorable success with his first full-scale operett, *Tilos a csók* (the forbidden kiss), which was produced at the Király Színház in 1909 and subsequently played in Germany as *Der verbotene Kuss* (ad Rudolf Schanzer, I Pasztae, Centraltheater, Dresden, 24 June 1911). *Limonádé ezredes*, a musical version of a German comedy by Julius Horst and Arthur Lippschitz, confirmed this first success, scoring a big success at the Király Színház, getting an airing at the Vienna Carltheater (11 May 1913), and being regularly revived thereafter.

Vincze composed the incidental music for the Hungarian adaptation of Frances Hodgson Burnett's *Little Lord Fauntleroy* and musicalized Kéroul and Barré's play *Le Portrait de ma tante* as *Léni néni*, but he was not heard from again until after the First World War when he added to his list of hit shows with *A cigánygrófné* (the gypsy countess), played for over 100 consecutive nights at the Király Színház in 1920.

A hamburgi menyasszony, a musical version of Gyula Pekár's 1914 *A kölcsönkért kastély* which was produced at the Városi Színház a couple of years later proved equally popular, giving Vincze his biggest single song success with 'Szép vagy, gyönyörű vagy Magyarország', and running through its first 100 performances in two years in the repertoire before going on to revivals at the Várszinház (1922) and the Fővárosi Operettszinház (1926). Another adaptation of a Pekár work as *A gárdista* was less successful and Vincze then moved sideways to compose a one-act opera, *Az erősebb*, produced at the Magyar Királyi Operaház (1924), to arrange the music for the posthumous Jacobi operett *Miámi* and for a piece based on the music of Robert Volkmann, whilst also, at the other end of the musical scale, contributing to revue. When he returned to operett, however, it was to add yet another success to his list with *Aranyhattyú*, played more than 50 times at the Király Színház and reprised thereafter.

Amongst his later stage works, which ranged from musical plays to operett, only *Huszárfogás* proved to be as substantial as his most successful works of which, in a career of some 15 effective years, he had achieved a high hometown percentage without winning an international reputation. His music was heard in London's West End, however, when Eric Maschwitz and his composers posthumously borrowed one of his songs to give a little verisimilitude to their disastrous Hungarian-set *Paprika* (aka *Magyar Melody*) in 1939. It proved the show's most successful number.

1909 **Tilos a csók** (Miksa Bródy, József Pásztor) Király Színház 8 October

1912 **Limonádé ezredes** (Julius Horst, Arthur Lippschitz ad Zsolt Harsányi) Király Színház 5 September

1914 **Léni néni** (*Le Portrait de ma tante*) Hungarian version with songs Magyar Színház 2 May

1920 **A cigánygrófné** (Ferenc Martos, Ernő Kulinyi) Király Színház 13 March

1922 **A hamburgi menyasszony** (Kulinyi) Városi Színház 31 January

1923 **A gárdista** (Kulinyi) Városi Színház 15 February

1925 **Anna-bál** (Robert Volkmann arr/Kulinyi/Martos) Király Színház 30 September

1927 **Aranyhattyú** (László Szilágyi) Király Színház 15 January

1927 **Kiss és kis** (László Bús-Fekete, Kulinyi) Városi Színház 22 January

1927 **Az aranypók** (Imre Harmath) Andrássy-uti Színház 14 October

1929 **Az aranyszőrű bárány** (Ferenc Móra) Szeged 15 November

1930 **Huszárfogás** (Rezső Török, Imre Harmath) Fővárosi Operettszinház 4 April

1930 **Jobb, mint otthon** (Adorján Stella, Harmath) Nyári Operettszinház 5 July

LES VINGT-HUIT JOURS DE CLAIRETTE
Vaudeville-opérette in 4 acts by Hippolyte Raymond and Anthony Mars. Music by Victor Roger. Théâtre des Folies-Dramatiques, Paris, 3 May 1892.

One of the most successful examples of the endlessly popular (in France) military vaudeville, here given an opérettic turn, *Les 28 Jours de Clairette* (the 28 days were the government military-service requirement) was a major hit in Paris in the 1890s and won revivals for several decades.

Clairette Vivarel (Marguerite Ugalde) is going to visit her aunt whilst her husband (Guyon fils) does his 28 days, unaware that his old flame, Bérénice (Mlle Stelly) – who has no idea that he has married – has pursued him to the barracks. Auntie is not home, so Clairette goes instead to the barracks where she is met by her husband's helpful friend, Gibard (Vauthier), who assumes that – since the obviously loving Bérénice must be the new wife – she is Vivarel's mistress. The arrival of everyone's superior officer forces the out-of-bounds Clairette into disguise in a missing soldier's uniform and, while Vivarel stews horribly, she gets into a duel with the dumb recruit Michonnet (Guy), into all sorts of complexities with sleeping arrangements, and is finally arrested for insubordination for punching a superior ... her husband, whom she suspects of irregularities with Bérénice. Michonnet helps her escape, and the fourth act winds up to farcical heights until the truth comes out and marital bliss is restored. Gibard gets Bérénice as consolation.

The bulk of the numbers fell to the star, displaying the martial arts taught to her by a father who wanted a boy ('En tierce, en quarte, en quinte, en prime'), going on menacingly about infidelity ('Avec moi, c'est tout ou rien'), doing her imitation of a recruit ('Je suis Benoît, le réservisse') and topping the second-act finale with a famous call to the saddle ('Trotte, trotte, trotte, cocotte'), another sporting art at which she is an adept. The star did not have the whole musical evening to herself, however. There were first-rate songs for each of the other principals as well as a cameo for a gormless peasant girl who brought low comedy to the sleeping-quarters episode ('Eh! donc, si le coeur vous en dit'), and some lively choruses and ensemble music.

Les 28 Jours de Clairette had a splendid first run of 236 Parisian performances, with Mlle Ugalde triumphant in the big star rôle. It was brought back the following year for another 92 (during which Juliette Simon-Girard was seen as Clairette), produced at the somewhat larger Théâtre de la Gaîté (5 September 1895) in a suitably expanded form with lots of dancing and Mariette Sully top-billed, and at the Bouffes-Parisiens with Mily-Meyer (1900). It was thereafter repeated regularly in Paris, into the 1920s, before making itself a home in provincial theatres. In 1935 Mireille was starred in a film version. The show was more recently mounted at Grand Théâtre, Bordeaux in 1988 (18 March) with Mireille Laurent featured.

The military vaudeville being perhaps less enjoyed in other countries than in France, *Les 28 Jours de Clairette* did not travel as it might have. However, its inviting central rôle won it a production in London (ad Charles Fawcett) where it was produced by Willie Edouin as a vehicle for his wife, Alice Atherton. It played just over a month. A German version was produced at Berlin's Adolf-Ernst-Theater with Gisela Fischer and Alexander Klein featured, but in America, where a local adaptation was mounted to feature the waning star Della Fox, *The Little*

Trooper (ad Clay Greene) was given a new musical score by conductor William Furst (Casino 30 August 1894).

UK: Opera Comique *Trooper Clairette* 22 December 1892; Germany: Adolf-Ernst-Theater *Lolottes 28 Tage* 8 September 1894; Film: 1935

VIOLETTES IMPÉRIALES Opérette à grand spectacle in 2 acts by Paul Achard, René Jeanne and Henri Varna based on the screenplay by Henri Roussel. Music by Vincent Scotto. Théâtre Mogador, Paris, 31 January 1948.

The romantic period tale of the successful film *Violettes impériales* was adapted to the Théâtre Mogador's musical stage in the wake of the success of *La Belle de Cadix*, and composer Vincent Scotto, rather better known for his popular songs and, theatrically, for his cheerful music for the marseillais opérettes of the years between the wars, supplied a suitably romantic-spectacular score, dotted with conventional soubretteries, which followed at least partly in the style that the earlier show had made de rigeur.

Don Juan, Comte d'Ascaniz (Marcel Merkès) is in love with Seville flower-girl Violetta (Lina Walls) but his mother intends that he shall wed Eugénie de Montijo (Raymonde Allain). Violetta is devastated when she sees the two have been betrothed, but Eugénie, discovering the truth of the situation, roundly renounces her new fiancé. She wins not only the girl's tearful thanks, but an Hispanic prophecy: by losing this fiancé she has gained a throne. Two years later, Eugénie is the wife of Napoléon and Empress of France. She brings the lovers back together, but there is Spanish conspiracy in the air and Don Juan is almost involved. Violetta impersonates the Empress and attracts a conspirator's bullet before all ends happily. The lighter moments of the evening were provided by the heroine's mother, Sérafina (Marcelle Ragon), the girl's elderly suitor, Picadouros (Fernand Gilbert), a comic detective called Estampillo (Robert Allard) and a soubret couple (Pierjac, Annie Alexander) whose love affairs and interferences popped in and out of the main story.

Violette's rôle featured a soprano 'Mélancolie', two numbers about violets ('Qui veut mon bouquet de violettes', Valse des violettes) and a song set around a Spanish shawl. The hero serenaded his beloved with 'Ce soir, mon amour' and swore his faith in the first act in 'Il n'y a pas de Pyrénées' and all over again, two acts later, in 'Tu peux croire à mon amour'. The bright songs were topped by Sérafina's lusty 'Quand on a de c'sang là' and a silly spy ensemble, 'C'est un secret d'état'.

Violettes impériales proved to be what the public wanted. It ran for just over two years at the Mogador and was reprised in 1952 (28 June) with largely the same cast, and again in 1961 when Merkès teamed with Rosita, each time with further success. In 1952 the musical which had been made from a film was turned back into a film – a musical one this time. However, Scotto's score was discarded and at the behest of the star, Luis Mariano, who was cast as Don Jose alongside the Violetta of the beautiful Carmen Sevilla, a new supply of distinctly tenor songs was provided by Francis Lopez. The resultant film, distinctly popular, was thus more a fresh musical film than an adaptation of the stage show.

On the stage, *Violettes impériales* continued its life into and around the French and Belgian provinces, where it is still to be seen from time to time, and from where it emerged to pay return visits to Paris in 1981 (Théâtre de la Porte-Saint-Martin, September) and 1991 (Casino de Paris, 18 January).

Recordings: selections (Véga, Odéon, CBS), film soundtrack (HMV)

LE VIOLONEUX

LE VIOLONEUX Légende bretonne (opérette) in 1 act by Eugène Mestépès and Émile Chevalet [and Étienne Tréfeu uncredited]. Music by Jacques Offenbach. Théâtre des Bouffes-Parisiens, Paris, 31 August 1855.

Rustic Pierre (Berthelier) and Reinette (Hortense Schneider) would like to marry, but he has been called up for the army and they are too poor to pay a substitute. Reinette asks the poor fiddler Père Mathieu (Capoul/ Darcier) to help them but, when he goes off to try to find the money, the superstitious Pierre, who suspects the old man of witchcraft and his violin of harbouring black magic, breaks the instrument. When Mathieu comes back, bringing the money he has persuaded from the daughter of the local overlord, he finds in the belly of the broken instrument a letter telling him that he is the rightful heir to the surrounding lands. But his masters have proved their goodness, and Mathieu prefers to remain what he has always been, a poor fiddler. The foolish, repentant Pierre promises to mend the violin.

The little seven-piece score to the tale included songs for each of its three actors. Pierre cursed over his call-up in the Couplets du conscrit, Reinette proposed to the boy in a jolly duettino ('J' sais bien que ce n'est pas l'usage'), and Mathieu sang of his life in the village in the ronde 'Le violoneux du village', and cried sadly and angrily over his smashed fiddle ('Je t'apportais ta délivrance') before the evening finished on the hopeful couplet 'Donnons-leur la richesse, et gardons les bons coeurs'.

Le Violoneux was produced two months after the opening of Offenbach's first little Bouffes-Parisiens, on the second change of programme. It was the occasion of Hortense Schneider's début under his management and her success and the piece's success were happily mingled. The little opérette became one of the most favoured of the rural – as opposed to the burlesque – one-acters of Offenbach's early years, and it has been revived regularly since.

Le Violoneux was one of the earliest Offenbach works to be exported around Europe. Vienna had never seen one of the composer's works when, in 1856, Levassor, the comedian from the Paris Palais-Royal, visited the Carltheater with four colleagues and appeared as Père Mathieu to the Reinette of Mlle Teissière and the Pierre of M Fauvre in *Le Violoneux*, and in *Les Deux Aveugles*. Again, when Karl Treumann began staging his versions of Offenbach's works at the same theatre, *Der Zaubergeige* – with himself as Mathieu – was fourth on his list of productions. It was played there as late as 1914. Treumann also played his version at his own Theater am Franz Josefs-Kai, with Anna Grobecker appearing in breeches as the lad, Antoine, to the Georgette of Anna Marek, and later on tour in Hungary. Another German-language version was played under the title *Martin der Geiger* in Germany and in the German theatre in New York, whilst an Hungarian version (ad Kálmán Szerdehelyi) came out two seasons later, being first played at the Nemzeti Színház with Ida Huber and Ilka Markovics featured. It was played widely thereafter throughout the country and it was revived at the

Magyar Színház in 1902 (16 September) and the Duna-parti Színház in 1920 (6 March).

Offenbach's Bouffes-Parisiens company played *Le Violoneux* in London during their visit in 1857 with Guyot (Mathieu), Mesmacre (Pierre) and Mlle Maréschal (Reinette) in its three rôles, but it was not until 1870 that an English version, *Breaking the Spell* (ad H B Farnie), was first played, as a forepiece to the London production of *Le Petit Faust* at the Lyceum. It subsequently did duty on a number of occasions as a part-programme or curtain raiser. Australia first saw this English version as a part of a programme in Fannie Simonsen's entertainment, with the prima donna teaming with Messrs Daniels and Barry O'Neill, and it was played there thereafter on several other occasions in the 1870s, 1880s and 1890s. Another English version, entitled *The Chelsea Pensioner* was played at Melbourne's People's Theatre 15 January 1881 with C Florence (Peter), Maud Walton (Jenny Wood) and T R Brown (Old Matthew).

Louisville, Kentucky, apparently saw the first American *Le Violoneux* – in French – in 1860, whilst New York got it both in French, as one of the earliest items played by Paul Juignet's company at Niblo's Saloon, and later in German (*Martin der Geiger*) as played by Minna von Berkel, Hübsch and Klein at the Stadttheater. *Breaking the Spell* also got American performances at a later date, including one from Fred Zimmerman's company with Fanny Wentworth (Jennie), Paul Vernon (Peter Bloom) and J H Poulette (Matthew) at the Metropolitan Alcazar in 1882.

Austria: Carltheater (Fr) 17 April 1856, Carltheater *Der Zaubergeige* 30 April 1859; Germany: *Der Zaubergeige, Martin der Geiger*; Hungary: Budai Színkör *Der Zaubergeige* 8 June 1859, Nemzeti Színház *A varázshegedű* 14 March 1861; USA: Niblo's Saloon (Théâtre Français) 11 February 1864, Stadttheater *Martin der Geiger* 19 May 1865, Metropolitan Alcazar *Breaking the Spell* 25 September 1882; UK: St James's Theatre (Fr) 27 May 1857, Lyceum *Breaking the Spell* 2 May 1870; Australia: St George's Hall, Melbourne *Breaking the Spell* 18 November 1871.

VIRGINIA

VIRGINIA Musical comedy in 2 acts by Herbert Clayton, Douglas Furber, R P Weston and Bert Lee. Music by Jack Waller and Joseph Tunbridge. Palace Theatre, London, 24 October 1928.

In the midst of the craze for the dance-and-laughter musical comedies of the 1920s, Jack Waller and Herbert Clayton bucked the trend and produced a picturesque-to-spectacular musical play. The buck wasn't all that great, for *Virginia* (which was both the heroine's name and the setting of Act II), although its producers loudly denied it, was clearly aimed at copying as much of *Show Boat* as was delicate. Its plot, which Waller long insisted was of fashionably American composition, was actually not comparable, relying on the eons-old tale of a rich American (John Kirby) trying to marry his daughter (Emma Haig) to an English lord (Harold French). He doesn't know that she has secretly wed the little comic (George Gee) and the lord is already paired off with the soprano (Marjorie Gordon, replacing Ursula Jeans before London). It was the incidentals which bore the similitudes, notably the tacking-in of two black characters, Lizzie (Cora le Redd) and Uncle Ned (Walter Richardson), the latter of whom led the number which was clearly intended to be *Virginia*'s 'Ol' Man River', 'Roll Away, Clouds'. If it didn't reach that level, the song nevertheless provided a huge spectacular centrepiece to the show, with its lavishly staged representation of cotton-pickin' darkies slogging under a spectacular display of thunder, lightning and clouds, and went on to become a hit outside it. It was even recorded by Paul Robeson.

Jolly songs and dances for Gee and Miss Haig ('I Love You More Than You Love Me', 'All Mine'), more soulful ones for the baritone and soprano ('Dreams of Yesterday'), some more spectacle, and a Ralph Reader chorus drilled into the kind of parade ground manoeuvres popular in large-stage musicals at the time, all made *Virginia* into a perfectly good show (especially if you hadn't seen *Show Boat*) which remained 227 performances in the West End and toured for two seasons thereafter.

The title *Virginia* had already been used several times on the musical stage. Edward Solomon and 'Pot' Stephens's English musical *Virginia, or Ringing the Changes* was produced in America in 1883 (8 January), but its title had to be changed to *Virginia and Paul, or Changing the Rings* when it went home to Britain (16 July), because of the existence of a recent opera called *Virginia* by the Welsh composer Joseph Parry. Both pieces were well and truly forgotten by the time the Shuberts launched a *Virginia* at Wilmington in December 1922. Since this remake of the German *Der Vetter aus Dingsda* switched to being *Caroline* before hitting Broadway, no-one had to forget it to make way for Waller and Tunbridge. Virginia, the state, was the star of yet another American musical, again called *Virginia*, a further decade on. This time Laurence Stallings, Owen Davis and Arthur Schwartz were the writers, but the period romantico-dramatic piece, mounted at the City Center, fizzled out in 60 performances.

VISA POUR L'AMOUR

Comédie musicale (opérette gaie) in 2 acts by Raymond Vincy taken from an original by Louis Sapin. Music by Francis Lopez. Théâtre de la Gaîté-Lyrique, Paris, December 1961.

A vehicle for a pair of Paris's top musical-comedy stars, tenor Luis Mariano and comedienne Annie Cordy, *Visa pour l'amour* presented him as an over-advanced Paris architect and her as an Italian diplomat's daughter whose social position means she cannot marry him. However, she accompanies papa to Paris for an international peace conference and uses the occasion to elope. The eloping pair end up in the American Embassy and on the front pages of the papers before the happy ending. Constructed as a lively and up-to-date entertainment, it had its heroine going in for 'Le genre américaine', taking part with her man in 'Twist, contre twist!', and joining him in several other jolly numbers, whilst he revelled in the tenor ballading of such numbers as a serenade to a 'Fontaine romaine' and 'Juliette et Roméo'. The show proved accurately tailored to the public's taste and, no little thanks to its two stars, stayed at the Gaîté-Lyrique for some 600 performances.

Recording: original cast (Pathé)

VIVA NAPOLI

Opérette à grand spectacle in 3 acts by René Jolivet. Lyrics by Daniel Ringold. Music by Francis Lopez. Lille, 20 December 1969; Théâtre Mogador, Paris, 4 September 1970.

Probably the best of the later musical shows written by the already fading Francis Lopez, *Viva Napoli* was produced in Lille and subsequently made its way to Paris's Théâtre Mogador for a season of 100 performances before going back to the provinces and well-earned popularity.

The piece starred Rudi Hirigoyen as Gino, a Neapolitan water-seller, who is the double of Napoléon Bonaparte and who stands in for the emperor in a diversionary kind of I-was-Monty's-double situation, to allow him to beat the English and head on to fame and ill-fortune. The love interest was Maria Scarlettina (Angelina Cristi), an attendant of Queen Caroline of Naples, plotting to assassinate Bonaparte but falling in love with him in his plebeian disguise, whilst the good-for-little Beppo (Jean-Louis Blèze/Henri Gènes) and his bossy Pépina (Arta Verlen) provided the usual ration of comical and song-and-dance moments.

A score which had as many reminiscences of every other Lopez opérette as the plotline had of the early work of his late librettist, Vincy, nevertheless produced some fine songs: a stirring march for Bonaparte ('Soldats, je suis content de vous'), a pretty entrance song for Maria ('Les fleurs d'Italie'), some lively duos for the comics ('Les Italiennes', 'La Mandoline a du bon') and a comical scaredy-cat 'Aie! Mamma mia!' for Beppo, as well as an interpolated waltz for the Queen of Naples, written by Madame Lopez in perfect imitation of her husband's style.

Recording: original cast (Philips)

VIVES, Amadeo (b Collbató, 18 November 1871; d Madrid, 1 November 1932).

Spanish teacher and the composer of a long list of musical pieces for the theatre, ranging from the tragic and operatic in such pieces as the early operas *Artus* and *Don Lucas de Cigarral* to the 'ecloga lirica' *Maruxa* (lib: Luis Pascual Frutos) and André Bisson's commedia dramatica *El rosario* on the one hand, and to the most folky of zarzuelas on the other. Vives's most considerable success on the zarzuela stage came with the full-length *Doña Francisquita*, (lib: Federico Romero, Guillermo Fernández Shaw, Teatro Apolo 17 October 1923), written in the latest stages of his career, whilst the most important of his shorter works proved to be *Bohemios* (lib: Guillermo Perrín, Miguel Palacios, Teatro de la Zarzuela 24 March 1904), a piece which he later re-arranged and enlarged.

His other musical theatre credits included *La preciosilla* (1899), *La luz verde* (1899), *Frutta del tiempo* (w Mateos, 1899), *El rey de la Apujurra* (1899), *El Escalo* (1900), *Viage de instrucción* (1900), *La balada de la luz* (1900), *Polvoriela* (1900), *Eude d'uriach* (1900), *La Buenaventura* (1901), *La Gitaniela* (1901), *Doloretes* (w Quislant, 1901), *El coco* (1901), *La nube* (1902), *Él tivador de palomas* (1902), *Lola Montes* (1903), *El General* (w Jéronimo Jimenez, 1903), *La cancion del naufrago* (1905), *La mascera duende* (1905), *La Veladura* (1905), *La libertad* (w Jimenez, 1905), *La favorita del rey* (1905), *El alma de pueblo* (1905), *La marche Real* (w Jimenez, 1906), *¡El golpe de estado!* (w Jimenez, 1906), *El guante amarillo* (w Jimenez, 1906), *El arte de ser Benita* (w Jimenez, 1906), *Sangre torera* (*La caprichiosa*, 1906), *La rabalera* (1907), *Las tre cosos de Jerez* (1907), *El Róllo de la perla negra* (1908), *Pepe Botella* (1908), *Episodios nacionales* (w Vicente Lléo, 1908), *La orden del dia* (1908), *El talisman prodigioso* (1908), *La mujer de Boliche* (1908), *Abreme la puerta* (1909), *La muela del rey Fanfan* (1910), *Juegos malabares* (1910), *Agua de Noria* (1910), *La casa de los duendes* (w Joaquín Serrano, 1911), *Anita la risveña* (1911),

Los viajes de Gulliver (1911), *La cancion española* (w Barrera, 1911), *La generala* (1912), *La veda del amor* (1912), *El Pretendiente* (1913), *Miss Australia* (1914), *La cena de los husares* (1915), *Los pendientes de la Trini, or No hay mal que por bien no venga* (1916), *El señor Pandolfo* (1917), *El tesoro* (1917), *Todo el mundo contra mia* (1918), *Trianerias* (1919), *Balada de carnaval* (1919), *Pepe conde* (1920), *El Duqesido* (*La corte de Versailles*, 1920), *El parque de Sevilla* (1921), *El sinverguenza* (1921, w Pablo Luna) and *La Vilana* (1927).

DER VOGELHÄNDLER Operette in 3 acts by Moritz West and Ludwig Held based on the comedy *Ce qui deviennent les roses* by Charles Varin and de Biéville [ie C H Edmond Desnoyers]. Music by Carl Zeller. Theater an der Wien, Vienna, 10 January 1891.

The most outstanding and enduring product of the Viennese stage of the 1890s, Carl Zeller's warmly endearing and melodious musical play carried on the local Operettic tradition established in the best works of Strauss, Suppé and Millöcker to great effect. The libretto developed by West and Held, if not bristling with original ideas, gave fine opportunities both to the composer and to the star comedian Alexander Girardi, cast in the title-rôle of Adam, the little bird-seller from the Rhineland Pfalz.

Jolly, boyish Adam is anxious to marry the village postmistress, Christel (Ilka Pálmay), who would be able to give up her job at the post (the changing post, not the stamps-and-letters kind) if he could land the secure position of Royal Menagerie Keeper. When the Prince comes to town, on a hunting trip, Christel boldly goes to his private pavilion to speak to him about the job, but the circumstances arouse Adam's jealousy and, believing his sweetheart untrue, he impulsively promises himself to a pretty stranger called Marie (Ottilie Collin). In fact, the Prince is not the Prince but one fairly shabby Count Stanislaus (Rudolf del Zopp) masquerading as royalty, and Marie is not a villager but the real Prince's wife, out enjoying the Pfalz without her crown on. When she gets back to court, she is able to tax her husband with naughty behaviour, until she hears the innocent truth of the encounter from Christel. The deceptions are unmasked, but Adam takes a whole act to come round to believing that if Christel gave his betrothal bouquet to Stanislaus, it was only to win him a steady royal job, so they might be able to marry.

Zeller's score was the most consistently melodious to have been heard in Vienna in years, and hit followed hit as the show progressed. Girardi, who had a marvellously sympathetic rôle as the sincere, bruised, innocent, and only slightly silly bird-seller, entered to a vigorously tenor, country-accented 'Grüss enk Gott, alle miteinander', wrung hearts with his waltzed description of the serious significance of a gift of roses to a Tyrolean ('Schenkt man sich Rosen in Tirol') in the first-act finale, had a jolly time describing the amorous antics of an ancestor ('Wie mein Ahnl zwanzig Jahr') and gave forth with a heartfeltly homesick little 'Kom' ih iazt wieder ham'. Christel's introductory song ('Ich bin die Christel von der Post') proved to be the soubrette number of the century, and Princess Marie was blessed with two outstanding numbers, her fiendishly difficult, driving waltz in praise of 'Fröhlich Pfalz' and the warm, long-lined reminiscing of 'Als geblühte der Kirschenbaum'. There were numbers, too, for Stanislaus and his comical Uncle Weps (Sebastian

Stelzer) as well as an incidental comedy routine par excellence for two crazy, harmonizing examiners, sent to test Adam for aptitude for the menagerie post ('Ich bin der Prodekan').

Der Vogelhändler was played 50 times at the Theater an der Wien in January and February before Girardi went off for a month's holiday. When he returned on April 1, *Der Vogelhändler* went back into the repertoire and it passed its 100th performance on 26 November with Frln Baviera now playing Marie. The 125th was played 4 November 1892 and the show was maintained in the repertoire until 1898. It was subsequently seen for more or less performances in the basic repertoire of the other main Viennese musical houses including the Carltheater (1900), the Bürgertheater (1917–20), Johann Strauss-Theater (1910–12), the Raimundtheater (1909, 1927, 1933 revival w Josef Graf, Lizzi Holdschuh and Lya Beyer) as well as at the Theater an der Wien (1902 w Edmund Loewe, Betty Seidl, Mary Hagen, 1904, 1935 w Karl Ziegler), and more recently at the Volksoper in 1974 (21 October) as it became established throughout the German-speaking world as one of the favourite pieces from its era.

Introduced to Germany at the Friedrich Wilhelmstädtisches Theater whilst the original Viennese production was still in its first run, *Der Vogelhändler* won as many friends there as it did in Austria, to such effect that Keller's survey of 1925 rated it all-time fifth amongst 19th-century Operetten in the count-up of the number of performances played in Germany (behind *Die Fledermaus*, *Die Geisha*, *Der Zigeunerbaron* and *Der Bettelstudent*). In Hungary, the Népszinház production of *A madarász* (ad Béla J Fái) proved the biggest hit the theatre had had since *Mam'zelle Nitouche* four years earlier, and it played for 106 performances with Pál Vidor as Adam and Julie Kopácsi-Karczag as Christel prior to becoming a regular part of the repertoire in theatres throughout the country.

Several German-language film versions of the Operette have also been made, amongst which an E W Emo version (scr Max Wallner) with Wolf-Albach-Retty, Maria Andergast and Lil Dagover, a version by Geza von Bolvary (scr Ernst Marischka, music composed and arranged by Franz Grothe) featuring Hans Holt (Adam), Elfriede Datzig (Christel) and Marte Harell (Countess) with Johannes Heesters and Leo Slezak in support, another, directed by Rabenalt (scr Curt Johannes Braun) including Gerhard Riemann, Eva Probst and Ilse Werner in its cast, and a fourth, 'freely adapted' by Geza von Cziffra to include views of the Bavarian castles of Linderhof and Nymphenburg and the town of Alsfeld, top-billing Albert Ruprecht, Conny Froboess and Maria Sebalt.

Away from central Europe *Der Vogelhändler* prospered rather less. Perhaps it was simply that the name of Zeller was less fashionable than a Strauss or a Millöcker, but only America really gave the show a full-scale contemporary production. And then Helen F Tretbar's American version had – of all things – Marie Tempest cast as a travesty Adam alongside Annie Meyers (Christel), Anna Mantel (Marie) and Fred Solomon (Weps) with Jeff de Angelis playing one of the professors. *The Tyrolean* compiled a run of 100 performances before the show was mounted by the usually nippier German-language Amberg Theater with Carl Schultz as Adam. The German theatres of New York repeated the show several times thereafter.

It was a long time before Britain saw *Der Vogelhändler* in anything but its original language. Its first German glimpse came when the visiting Saxe-Coburg company played the show at the Theatre Royal, Drury Lane (with Pálmay repeating her original Christel), and it was 50 years before Bernard Delfont, Tom Arnold and Emile Littler introduced an English *The Birdseller* (ad Austin Melford, Rudolf Bernauer, Harry S Pepper) at the Palace Theatre. James Hetherington was Adam, Irene Ambrus and Adele Dixon his two ladies, and Richard Tauber conducted through a brief run.

The indifference of the English- (and French-) speaking world, however, has not dented the popularity of *Der Vogelhändler* in the German and Hungarian languages and a century after its first run, the show remains a regularly produced part of the central European repertoire – the only Viennese 'Golden Age' work apart from the Operetten of the 'top' trio of Suppé, Strauss and Millöcker so to be.

Germany: Friedrich-Wilhelmstädtisches Theater 20 February 1891; Hungary: Népszinház *A madarász* 12 September 1891; USA: Casino Theater *The Tyrolean* 5 October 1891, Amberg Theater (Ger) 26 December 1892; UK: Theatre Royal, Drury Lane (Ger) 17 June 1895, Palace Theatre *The Birdseller* 29 May 1947; Belgium: Brussels 21 October 1896 and subsequently in France as *L'Oiseleur*; Films: Majestic Films/E W Emo 1935; Geza von Bolvary *Rosen in Tirol*; Berolina/Arthur Maria Rabenalt 1953; Gloria films 1962.

Recordings: 2-record set (EMI), complete (Philips), selections (Telefunken, Eurodisc, Philips etc)

VOKES FAMILY

The celebrated Vokes family of Victorian musical-comedy performers were the children of costumier F M T Vokes (d 4 June 1890) and included Fred[erick Mortimer] Vokes (b 1846, d 3 June 1888) who married Bella Moore, the daughter of 'Pony' Moore of the Moore and Burgess Minstrels, his sisters Jessie (b 1851; d 7 August 1884), Victoria (b 1853; d 2 December 1894) and Rosina (b 1854; d 27 January 1894) and Herbert Fawdon (d 1904), who took the name Vokes on joining their act.

The family played a broad, swift mixture of comical scenes, songs and dances made up into such pieces as the famous below-stairs *The Belles of the Kitchen* and the equally celebrated *In Camp*, a tale of amateur dramatics and soldiery, which won them a vast following all around the English-speaking theatre world, and which were the fore-runners of the more substantial musical comedies of later years. All the four Vokeses died in their prime and, after their deaths, *In Camp* (credited somewhat tactically to Victoria as author) was expanded into a full-length 'legitimate' musical called *On the March* (Prince of Wales Theatre 22 June 1896) which played 77 performances in London. Part of the music for this piece was taken from the trunk of Frederic Clay, whose brother, Cecil Clay, had been the husband of Rosina Vokes.

VOLGA

Opérette à grand spectacle in 2 acts by Claude Dufresne. Lyrics by Jacques Plante. Music by Francis Lopez. Additional music by Anja Lopez. Théâtre du Châtelet, Paris, 26 November 1976.

Volga was 18 scenes of Châtelet Russian spectacle arranged around a story about Colonel Boris Gorsky (José Todaro) who goes off to crush some anti-Tsarist rebels but falls in love with the pretty innkeeper (Maria Candido) who is the head of the rebellion. The jealous local Governor (Claude Calès) gets the pair condemned to death, but they escape through the best bits of the scenery and, thanks to a friendly Tsarina (Léna Oliviera), all ends happily.

The show's musical axis was heavily towards the principal tenor (six solo numbers) singing to his 'Anja', to 'Ma troïka', 'Volga' and 'Ma Russie' all in similarly throbbing tones, whilst the soprano gave 'Les Cloches de St Petersbourg' and 'J'ai pleuré' in what had become traditional Lopez style. There was also the regular baritone number, but there was one distinctly pleasant variation to the usual Lopezzery in the inclusion of a quintet ('La loi du destin').

The show ran for 18 months at the Châtelet and was subsequently seen in the provinces.

Recordings: original cast (CBS), replacement cast (Ibach)

LES VOLTIGEURS DE LA 32ÈME

Opéra-comique in 3 acts by Georges Duval and Edmond Gondinet. Music by Robert Planquette. Théâtre de la Renaissance, Paris, 7 January 1880.

Les Voltigeurs de la 32ème had a difficult start to life, and a long road to follow before it marched ultimately to a large and long success. After the by-and-large failure of Lecocq's *La Jolie Persane* at the Théâtre de la Renaissance, Victor Koning decided that a military opérette was the thing that would catch the public and he dug out a script which had been previously submitted by the young Georges Duval which he handed to the experienced Edmond Gondinet for rubbing-up, and to Planquette, a hot property after *Les Cloches de Corneville*, for its music. He found himself legally pursued by Cantin of the Folies-Dramatiques who claimed to have first option on both the piece and the composer, but he won out and got *Les Voltigeurs de la 32ème* to the stage, only to find that in spite of largely favourable reactions it was unable to hold up for more than 73 performances.

When Napoléon Bonaparte decides to set up an artificial new class by ordering the mixture by marriage of the old aristocracy and his parvenu class, the Marquis des Flavignolles (Ismaël) decides to trick him. He has the goatherd, Nicolette (Jeanne Granier), pose as his daughter and plans to marry her off to the bourgeois Lieutenant Richard (Marchetti). However, his real daughter Béatrix turns up, decides the choice is indeed to her taste, and Nicolette is able to go back to her country César (Lary). Marie Desclauzas played Dorothée, the oversized and comical village May queen, and the young Mily-Meyer a travesty officer.

Following its disappointing Paris run, the show was seen in Budapest (ad Lajos Evva, Ferenc Nemes) as 'the goatherd marchioness', and the Renaissance company, which had played a handful of further perfomances during 1881, exported it for some performances in their season at London's Gaiety Theatre, but it then faded away. It was, however, not gone. Six years later, following the London success of *Rip van Winkle*, librettist H B Farnie combined with Planquette to do a remake on *Les Voltigeurs*. The resultant piece, *The Old Guard*, which contained a certain amount of fresh Planquette music, was constructed to English tastes, featuring a large (and expandable) principal comic rôle – Polydore Poupart – in which Arthur Roberts, recently so successful in a similar part in Farnie's *Indiana*, could woo the public.

Otherwise the bones of much of the tale were the same, with J J Dallas as the Marquis d'Artemac, Marion Edgecumbe playing the phoney daughter, now called Fraisette, Joseph Tapley the beloved Gaston de la Rochenoir, Wilford Morgan the marriageable Marcel, Fanny Wentworth as Murielle (ex-Béatrix), and with Phyllis Broughton largely featured in what seemed to be a reductio ad feminam of Mily-Meyer's part as a vivandière called Follow-the-Drum. Roberts sang of being 'The Dashing Militaire' and joined with Dallas in a topical duet about 'When We Were Young', whilst Gaston's 'The Lover's Hour', Marcel's 'Only a Moment Love Was Mine', and Fraisette's 'Fare Thee Well!' proved the pick of the romantic numbers.

Things went quite the reverse to what they had in Paris. *The Old Guard* got mediocre reviews for everything except its comic performances, and it ran for an outstanding 300 performances plus a quick revival (1 October, 1888) at the Avenue Theatre whilst Farnie and Planquette went to work on a similar adaptation of the composer's *Surcouf*. Auguste Van Biene and Horace Lingard took up the touring rights and, with Lingard taking Roberts's rôle, the show began what was to become a very long life in the British provinces and colonies. Australia launched its production four years later, with William Elton playing Poupart alongside Ida Osborne (Fraisette), Flora Graupner (Follow-the-Drum) and Jack Leumane (Gaston) and the show was revived there as late as 1915 when Ethel Cadman appeared as Fraisette. Similarly, 20 years on in Britain, *The Old Guard* was still to be seen trouping the British provinces, long after France had forgotten all about *Les Voltigeurs de la 32ème*.

Hungary: Népszinház *A kecskepásztor markiné* 28 May 1880; UK: Gaiety Theatre (Fr) 23 July 1881, Avenue Theatre *The Old Guard* 26 October 1887; Australia: Princess Theatre, Melbourne *The Old Guard* 11 April 1891

LE VOYAGE DANS LA LUNE Opéra-féerie in 4 acts by Eugène Leterrier, Albert Vanloo and Arnold Mortier. Music by Jacques Offenbach. Théâtre de la Gaîté, Paris, 26 October 1875.

Three years and eight major shows after the splenditious production of *Le Roi Carotte*, Offenbach returned to the world of the grand opéra-bouffe féerie with the spectacular *Le Voyage dans la lune*. Allegedly suggested to and planned by its librettists after a revue at the Théâtre du Château d'Eau had featured the moon as a venue, but nevertheless helping itself to an idea or two from the works of Jules Verne and several more from the brothers Cogniard, the show – for all that the novelist was said to be cross about it – really did have much more of the revusical and the fantastical than the science-fiction to it.

Prince Caprice (Zulma Bouffar), bored with earthly things, decides he wants to go to the moon. The court sage, Microscope (Grivot), makes a cannon which shoots the prince, his father King V'lan (Christian), and himself to the lunar surface, and there they encounter their equivalent in the way of royal families, King Cosmos (Tissier), Queen Popotte (Adèle Cuinet) and Princess Fantasia (Mlle Marcus). On the moon, everything is the reverse of that which it is on earth and, amongst other reversals, love

is considered a malady. That malady is spread by some apples the travellers have brought with them, and love and its physical expressions wreak havoc on the moon, ultimately leading the cosmonaughty earth-folk to be entombed in a lunar volcano from which they only escape thanks to an eruption. Finally, when all the spectacular incidents and scenes are done, the union of earth and moon occurs – Caprice weds Fantasia.

As in *Le Roi Carotte*, Offenbach's score played second fiddle to the glories of the stage-machinist's and painter's art, and to the ballets – above all the evening's most admired moment, a Snow Ballet with a corps of little snowflakes and a featured quartet of petit-sujet swallows. However, there were many attractive numbers for the Gaîté stars, headed by Mlle Bouffar who cried melodiously for the moon ('Papa, je veux la lune!') and ran through both waltz and madrigal moments, whilst her father introduced himself in comical style ('V'lan, v'lan, je suis V'lan') and the Princess ran from coloratura to boléro, alongside a staunch scoreful of choruses and ensembles.

Although Offenbach had originally refused to stage *Le Voyage dans la lune* at his Théâtre de la Gaîté, or even to compose the score for what he regarded as too costly a piece to succeed, the show was mounted at that very theatre by musical director Albert Vizentini who had taken over the management of the house from Offenbach. It was a distinct success, played for 185 performances – regularly spruced up and, in its later days, even benefitting from an appearance by café-concert queen, Thérésa, for whom Offenbach composed some additional music. When it closed the Gaîté closed too, reopening in the autumn as the Théâtre Lyrique. Vizentini was still in charge, but the fare was somewhat loftier. In the meanwhile, *Le Voyage dans la lune* began its trips abroad, being quickly seen in both London and Vienna.

The big Alhambra Theatre which had produced Britain's *Le Roi Carotte* mounted the new spectacle in London (ad H S Leigh) with all its usual lavishness. Rose Bell (Caprice), Kate Munroe (Fantasy), J D Stoyle (King Clashbang), Emma Chambers (Popette), Edmund Rosenthal (Microscope) and Harry Paulton (Cosmos) headed the company, the snow ballet danced by Mlle Pitteri and some imported Parisian swallows again turned out to be the highlight of the night, and the piece again proved elastic enough to allow the insertion of the odd music-hall act, such as the Girards acrobatic speciality (mus: Georges Jacobi), into the final act. *Le Voyage dans la lune* was ideal Alhambra fare, and it ran there for an initial five and a half months, being brought back after the failure of the following piece (11 November) to play five additional weeks until the London première of *Die Fledermaus* was ready.

In Vienna, Maximilian Steiner directed his own production (ad Julius Hopp) of 12 scenes of phantastisch-burlesk Ausstattungs-Operette at the Theater an der Wien with Bertha Steinher (Caprice), Albertina Stauber (Fantasia), Carl Adolf Friese (Vlan), Herr Grün (Cosmos), Alexander Girardi (Microscope) and Frln Zimmermann leading the two grand ballets. It proved a regular success through 67 performances and prompted Steiner to try (less happily) *Le Roi Carotte* later in the year. On the other hand Budapest, which had apparently less taste for the spectacular, passed on *Le Voyage dans la lune* as it had done on *Le Roi Carotte*, and America, which had given a good hearing to *Le Roi*

Carotte, could just not be persuaded to be interested in *A Trip to the Moon*. The Kiralfys gave the piece their inevitably glamorous production and the show still closed after ten performances.

The show was well enough liked to come around again in its most favoured venues. London saw *A Trip to the Moon* again in 1883 (26 March) when F C Leader produced a revival at Her Majesty's Theatre with a cast headed by Anna Barnadelli (Caprice), Annie Albu (Fantasy) and Lionel Rignold (Cosmos). Consuelo de la Bruyère headed the snow ballet, in which a spot was made for the famous aerialist Mlle Ænea as 'the flying dove' amongst the swallows. A Paris revival was mounted 21 March 1891 at the Théâtre de la Porte-Saint-Martin with Jeanne Granier (Caprice) and Germaine Gallois (Fantasia) in the leading rôles. However, the heavy and costly scenic content of the show militated against it thereafter until the return, in the 1970s, of the fashion for spectacular theatre. A version of the show (ad Jerome Savary) was mounted in 1979 in Berlin, repeated at Geneva's Grand Théâtre in 1985 (12 December) with Joseph Evans as a male Caprice, Michel Trempont as Vlan and Marie McLaughlin as Fantasia, and was subsequently seen in Belgium (7 February 1986).

UK: Alhambra Theatre 15 April 1876; Austria: Theater an der Wien *Die Reise in den Mond* 16 April 1876; Germany: Viktoria-Theater *Die Reise in den Mond* 1876; USA: Booth's Theater 14 March 1877

LE VOYAGE DE MM DUNANAN PÈRE ET FILS
Opéra-bouffe in 2 acts by Paul Siraudin and Jules Moinaux. Music by Jacques Offenbach. Théâtre des Bouffes-Parisiens, Paris, 23 March 1862.

Le Voyage de MM Dunanan père et fils, composed and produced by Offenbach during the period of his triumph with his series of full-length works in the genuinely burlesque opéra-bouffe mould, was something of an oddity. It was a piece set in the present, with up-to-date protagonists in modern dress, farcical in a vaudevillesque manner in its action and, in spite of taking in some parodies in its musical part and some extravagances in its tale, neither a burlesque proper nor – in the manner of so many of the composer's shorter pieces – a rural romance. In the vein of *La Vie parisienne*, produced four years later, it was a full-scale modern musical comedy in the true sense of those words, individually and together, and as such something of a novelty.

The parallel with *La Vie parisienne*, in fact, went further, for the story of the Messrs Dunanan – father Adolphe (Désiré) and son Patrocle (Léonce) – who are whipped away from their provincial home in Macon to visit the romantic fleshpots of Venice, took something of the same turn as the adventurous awaydays of the Baron and Baroness Gondremarck in the later piece. The wayfaring Tympanon (Pradeau), Astrakan (Duvernoy) and Lespingot (Potel) fool father and son into thinking they have made the trip to Italy, although they have actually got no further than Paris. There with the assistance of their disguised friends – a group of cleaning ladies – the jolly fellows present the Dunanans, in a virtual revue or variety show, with a Venice equipped with barcarolles, romances, masks and murderers, not to mention a children's ballet, much scenery and a massed cast of extras, all of which is as phoney but as temporarily effective as Raoul de Gardefeu's

house-turned-hotel – and all without leaving France. The excuse for the whole charade is that the fellows want to stop Dunanan junior being engaged to the lady that one of them loves, and they succeed in their aim when not only does Patrocle pair off with Paméla (Mme Geraldine), the most soprano of the cleaning ladies, but papa recognizes in Léocadie (Mlle Beaudoin), who has been deputized to impersonate the intended bride, an old and distinctly recyclable flame of his own.

The phoney Venice gave Offenbach, just ten months after the première of *Le Pont des soupirs*, the occasion for a goodly amount of fake Venetian music. The burlesque barcarolle 'O Venezia la bella' with its refrain of 'Youp, la Catarina!' (to be used with equal effect many years later in Hugo Felix's *Madame Sherry*), a four-part Sérénade des Guitares, a valse-mazurka 'La Perle de l'Adriatique' boasting a cadenza full of high Cs for Paméla and a quartet in which Lespingot and Tympanon pretend to be assassins ('J'escoffie') were amongst the jolly moments of the pseudo-Italian scenes, whilst Tympanon also had a stand-up number about being a one-man band and Dunanan and his Léocadie joined in a pleasingly sincere little duo ('C'était en l'an de grâce 1839'), safely 'home' after all the hurly burly was done.

Offenbach introduced *Le Voyage de MM Dunanan* at the Bouffes-Parisiens where it passed its time happily, but without causing too much stir, and three months later, during the summer break, the Bouffes company played the piece to Vienna at the Theater am Franz-Josefs-Kai. Manager Karl Treumann promptly produced a German version, *Herr von Zuckerl, Vater und Sohn*, the following year. It had little chance to prosper, as five weeks later the Kaitheater burned. By this time, the first Hungarian production, in a version by Pál Tarnay, and starring Károly Simonyi as father Dunanan alongside József Szép, Béla Szilágyi, József Vincze, Emma Harmath and Sarolta Krecsányi, had already been mounted at the Budai Népszinház. This time, the bull's-eye was hit. The piece was an enormous success. It ran for over 100 nights, a vast run for the time and place and one which broke all records in Budapest, leading to a whole series of further stagings for the piece in its Hungarian version. It was played at the Budai Színkör in German (*Zuckerl und Sohn* 4 June 1865) and in Hungarian (14 July 1867) and it was the first Operette to be produced at Budapest's new centre of musical theatre, the Népszinház, on 5 November 1875. An Hungarian company even took their production to Vienna in 1866. Another German-language version, entitled *Venedig in Paris* (ad Georg Ernst), was produced first in Germany and played subsequently at the Theater an der Wien in 1903.

Although it was long popular in central Europe, where it was periodically revived over a long period, the show had a more uneventful reception at home and it did not officially reach English-speaking territories. However, in 1874 F C Burnand turned out a piece called *The Great Metropolis, or The Wonderful Adventures of Daddy Daddles and His Son in Their Journeying from Stoke-in-the-Mud to Venice (via London)* at the Gaiety Theatre (6 April), decorated with a pasticcio score arranged by Meyer Lutz. Its origins were not difficult to trace, although no one seems to have done so at the time and, certainly, no one gave MM Siraudin and Moinaux any credit. Interestingly enough, producer

John Hollingshead in his memoirs claimed this 'burlesque in plain clothes' as 'a pioneer' almost two decades before *In Town* and its ilk set off the fashion for modern-dress musicals in the London and international theatre. He may have had a point. *Le Voyage de MM Dunanan* certainly belongs to the vaudeville and musical-comedy tradition, rather than to that of the burlesque or the romantic opéra-comique, and as such it would, in 1862, have been able fairly to be accounted, at least, one of the earliest genuine 'musicals' of the modern era of musical theatre.

Austria: Theater am Franz-Josefs-Kai (Fr) 25 June 1862, *Herr von Zuckerl Vater und Sohn* 21 March 1863, Theater an der Wien *Venedig in Paris* 5 September 1903; Hungary: Budai Népszinház *Dunanan apó és fia utazása* 17 January 1863; Germany: *Herr von Zuckerl und Sohn* (aka *Zuckerl Vater und Sohn*)

LE VOYAGE DE SUZETTE Pièce à grande spectacle in 3 acts by Henri Chivot and Alfred Duru. Music by Léon Vasseur. Théâtre de la Gaîté, Paris, 20 January 1890.

A piece of musical-theatre spectacle, signed nevertheless by a pair of top-rank authors in Chivot and Duru, *Le Voyage de Suzette* passed through 11 different tableaux during the course of its evening of visual display: from a Persian palace to a Barcelona hovel, to a Spanish sea-port, to Athens, a brigand camp, a mountain fiesta, the harem of Omar Pacha, and an English pantomime-style display called 'the butcher's shop', ending its round of scenic art and variety acts in the 'grand cirque américain'.

The linking story for the scenery and the acts had Suzette (Juliette Simon-Girard), the daughter of the poor Verduron (Mesmaecker), travelling to wed André (Alexandre), son of her father's now vastly rich foster-brother, Blanchard (Fournier), via many perils, much spectacle and plenty of musical numbers – some of which were written by Vasseur, some selected from amongst the works of other composers. Marie Gélabert was Suzette's maid, and Simon-Max (Pinsonnet) André's servant, whilst Don Giraflor (Bellot) and the amorous slave Cora (Mlle Burty) represented the opposition to the marriage. The scenery, songs and a whole series of costumed parades did duty for a good run on the big Gaîté stage, and the piece followed in the successful line of French spectacular entertainments to other areas of the world.

Vienna's Carltheater saw a ten-scene *Susette, oder zweihundert Millionen* (ad Zell, Richard Genée) reproduced from the Paris staging by régisseur Epstein with Marie Schwarz (Susette, with an interpolated 'Blaue Auge' by A Krakauer), Karl Blasel (Pinsonnet) and Wilhelm Knaack (Verduron) and ballerina Rosa Hrozsy 'from the Royal Opera of Budapest' featured for a splendid 61 performances in 1890, whilst New York (ad C A Byrne, Louis Harrison), had voluptuous Sadie Martinot as Suzette for one month at the American Theatre three years later. Chivot and Duru's book was later borrowed by American composer and author Oscar Weil and made up into a piece which he called *Suzette*. Originally produced by the Bostonians in their 1889–90 season, and played with the vocally valid Marie Stone in its title-rôle, it went on to further productions, one of which (Hermann's Theater 11 October 1891) saw the not very vocal but exceedingly popular Minnie Palmer taking the show's title-rôle alongside George Lauri and vocalist Bertha Ricci (Marchioness de Tollebrache).

Austria: Carltheater *Zweihundert Millionen* (*Susette*) 6 September 1890; USA: American Theater 23 December 1893

Plate 285.

LE VOYAGE EN CHINE Opéra-comique in 3 acts by Eugène Labiche and Alfred Delacour. Music by François Bazin. Opéra-Comique, Paris, 9 December 1865.

Like the heroes of *Le Voyage de MM Dunanan* on their trip to Venice, and like the folk of *A Trip to Chinatown* and other later shows, the characters of *Le Voyage en Chine* didn't actually go there. Marie Pompéry (Marie Cico) has secretly married the marine officer Henri de Kernoisan (Montaubry), and now the young people have to persuade her father (Couderc) to give his consent to their union, without telling him of the fait accompli. Unfortunately, Henri and Pompéry are involved on the opposite sides of a carriage accident, and the pig-headed Pompéry takes an unmoving stance against the young man, proposing instead to wed Marie to the stuttering Alidor de Rosenville (Sainte-Foy). Things come to a head when Henri follows the Pompéry family to their holiday hotel in Cherbourg. Pistols and épées are drawn, and Alidor tries to trick Henri away by a false telegram ordering him to sail for China. It is another trick, however, which works – and it is Henri who is behind it. When the Pompérys go to pass an instructive morning looking over a ship in Cherbourg harbour they suddenly find themselves at sea, under Henri's captaincy, headed for China! Pompéry ultimately gives in, but only after he has staged an abortive mutiny and his son-in-law has condemned him to hang on the high seas. Then the old man finds that the ship has never left Cherbourg. Ponchard as Maurice Frével courted the younger Pompéry sister, Berthe (Mlle Gontier), whilst Prilleux appeared as a ubiquitous comical notary, Bonneteau, and Mme Révilly completed the principal cast as mother Pompéry.

The libretto, by confirmed comic playwrights Labiche and Delacour, was illustrated with a series of ballads (several presented as drawing-room numbers) and ensembles composed by the successful composer of *Maître Pathelin* and the show, like *MM Dunanan* a veritable musical comedy, was produced with very considerable success at the Opéra-Comique. Thereafter, it was quickly mounted throughout Europe. The Theater an der Wien staged a German version (ad J C Grünbaum, uncredited) with Albin Swoboda (Henri), Matthias Rott (Pompéry), Jani Szika (Maurice), Friederike Fischer (Marie), Wilhelm Knaack (Alidor) and Carl Adolf Friese (Bonneteau) featured, which was played 21 times in half a dozen years in the repertoire, Berlin's Wallner-Theater followed suit and in 1870 an Hungarian version (ad Endre Latabár) appeared at Budapest's Budai Színkör.

The 'first complete adaptation in English' was billed at London's newly upmarketed Garrick Theatre in White-chapel in June 1879 (ad William Yardley) and again in November of the same year, but America seems to have seen the piece only in the French original, as played by Quercy (Henri), Debeer (Alidor) and Mlle Minelli (Marie) at the Park Theater in 1875. Versions of *Le Voyage en Chine* were played in Scandinavia, variously in Swedish and Danish, in the Netherlands and in South America, but its chief and enduring popularity was in France, where it continued to be played for many decades after its original production.

Le Voyage en Chine proved the inspiration, both stylistically and in its story, for a number of later shows, and the London paste-up piece *The Black Prince* even lifted a large chunk of Labiche and Delacour's tale for its libretto.

Austria: Theater an der Wien 12 May 1866; Germany: Wallner-Theater 2 July 1867; Hungary: Budai Színkör *Utazás Kínába* 12 May 1870; UK: Royalty Theatre (Fr) 13 February 1873, Garrick Theatre *A Cruise to China* 5 June 1879; USA: Park Theater (Fr) 11 January 1875

W

WALDBERG, Heinrich von (Baron) (b Jassy, ?2 March 1860; d Theresienstadt, ?1942). The co-author of one major Viennese hit and several other musical-theatre successes in an appreciable career as a librettist.

In the late 1880s and 1890s Waldberg collaborated on a number of plays, adaptations and libretti for German and Austrian theatres, largely in tandem with the highly successful Victor Léon. After beginning with a Schwank, *Die Rheintochter*, for Teplitz (1886), they found a modest success with the vaudeville *Die Chansonette*, played after its Dresden première in both Vienna (Theater an der Wien 16 February 1895) and Berlin (Theater Unter den Linden 22 August), and then a major one with an adaptation of the famous farce *Les Dominos roses* as a libretto for the Operette *Der Opernball*.

Waldberg subsequently adapted a number of other French plays as libretti without the same success. He teamed with Léon to remake *Niniche* as *Ihre Excellenz* and the vaudeville *La Dot de Brigitte* as *Frau Lieutnant*, and later with A M Willner to transform *Le Mari de la débutante* into *Die Debütantin*, first produced in Munich and then at Vienna's Carltheater (4 October 1901, 10 performances), as well as making over the English farce *The Magistrate* as *Das Baby* (17 performances). It was another adaptation, however, this time from the American, which brought him his other principal success. *Nimm mich mit!*, a light-hearted adaptation of Colonel Savage's famous *His Official Wife* produced at the Theater an der Wien at the end of the First World War, had a fine Viennese run. Edmund Eysler's *Die schöne Mama*, first produced in Italy and later for 111 performances in Vienna, gave him further success. The Baron von Waldberg's career in the theatre had been some years ended when he joined the long list of musical-theatre authors declared missing and presumed dead during the Second World War.

1890 **Der bleiche Gast** (Alfred Zamara, Josef Hellmesberger/w Victor Léon) Hamburg 6 September
1890 **Erminy** (*Erminie*) German version w Léon, F Zell (Carltheater)
1892 **Der Bajazzo** (Alfons Czibulka/w Léon) Theater an der Wien 7 December
1894 **Die Chansonette** (Rudolf Dellinger/w Léon) Residenztheater, Dresden 16 September
1895 **Die Doppelhochzeit** (Hellmesberger/w Léon) Theater in der Josefstadt 21 September
1896 **Toledad** (*L'Enlèvement de la Toledad*) German version w Léon (Theater in der Josefstadt)
1898 **Der Opernball** (Richard Heuberger/w Léon) Theater an der Wien 1 May
1899 **Ihre Excellenz** (aka *Die kleine Excellenz*) (Heuberger/w Léon) Centraltheater, Berlin 17 January; Theater an der Wien 28 January
1899 **Die Strohwitwe** (Albert Kauders/w Léon) Theater an der Wien 4 November
1900 **Frau Lieutnant** (*La Dot de Brigitte*) German version (Theater in der Josefstadt)
1901 **Die Debütantin** (Zamara/w A M Willner) Theater am Gärtnerplatz, Munich 17 January
1902 **Das Baby** (Heuberger/w Willner) Carltheater 3 October
1908 **Ein Mädchen für alles** (Heinrich Reinhardt/w Willner) Theater am Gärtnerplatz, Munich 8 February
1908 **Die Frauenjäger** (Zamara/w Hans Liebstöckl) Theater an der Wien 16 October
1911 **Die vertauschte Braut** (Zamara/w Felix Ujhély) Theater am Gärtnerplatz, Munich 20 January
1913 **Dorette** (Bruno Hartl/Julius Wilhelm) Theater am Gärtnerplatz, Munich 7 February
1919 **Nimm mich mit!** (Hermann Dostal/w Willner) Theater an der Wien 1 May
1921 **Die schöne Mama** (*La bella mamina*) (Edmund Eysler/w Bruno Hardt-Warden) Teatro Nazionale, Rome 9 April; Wiener Bürgertheater 17 September
1922 **Fräulein Frau** (Max Niederberger/w Hardt-Warden) Wiener Bürgertheater 23 December
1926 **Das Amorettenhaus** (Leo Ascher/w Hardt-Warden) Carl-Schultze Theater, Hamburg January

WALDMEISTER Operette in 3 acts by Gustav Davis. Music by Johann Strauss. Theater an der Wien, Vienna, 4 December 1895.

The least unsuccessful of Johann Strauss's later Operetten, *Waldmeister* was composed to a feather-light libretto which might have been written half a century earlier, had it not been that it was actually set in the present, albeit in a little provincial town in Saxony. The plot, such as it was, hinged on the favourite old magic-potion trick. This one was a concoction made with something called 'Waldmeister' (apparently the herb woodruff), which was administered to the guests of the lofty Christof Hessele (Herr Kernreuter) in the place of a linden-blossom brew, and resulted in a happy ending for the juveniles of the piece: Hessele's daughter Freda (Frln Pohlner) gets the woodsman, Botho von Wendt (Karl Streitmann), she wanted, instead of having to marry the head forester, Tymoleon von Gerius (Josef Joseffy). Alexander Girardi had the chief comic rôle as the John Wellington Wells-ish botanist responsible for the drink, Annie Dirkens played a prima donna caught in the rain and mistaken, in her borrowed dry clothes, for a miller's wife, and Therese Biedermann played her companion, pairing off with Girardi for the final-curtain round-up. The 70-year-old Strauss wrote an attractive light score, topped by the waltz 'Trau', schau', wem!' of the under-the-influence second-act finale, the march 'Es war so wunderschön' and Botho's waltz song 'Im Walde, wo die Buchen rauschen', without drawing forth a hit number.

Waldmeister was played 55 successive times under Alexandrine von Schönerer's management during December and January, and it put in an occasional appearance in the

Theater an der Wien's repertoire during 1896 and 1897, passing its 75th performance on 14 April 1897. It re-appeared on the schedule in 1908 for a few performances, to bring its performance total there to 88, although it had, in between times, had another Viennese showing at the Jantschtheater in 1901. Berlin's Lessing-Theater hosted a production in 1896, New York's German-language Irving Place Theater mounted the piece the following year, and an Hungarian version (ad Ferenc Reiner, Zsigmond Sebők) was produced, under the more comprehensible title of 'May Wine' at the Népszinház for ten performances in the same year.

Germany: Lessing-Theater 2 May 1896; Hungary: Népszinház *Májusi bor* 15 May 1897; USA: Irving Place Theater 29 November 1897

WALKER, George W (b Lawrence, Kansas; d Centre Islip, NY, 6 January 1911). The more sharply comical and well-dressed half of the Williams and Walker cakewalk-dancing team which became a popular musical-theatre pairing of the turn-of-the-century American stage.

Walker worked at first in western minstrel companies and joined up with the tall, gaunt Williams when he was 18 years old to perform in variety and minstrelsy as 'The Two Real Coons'. The duo first appeared on the Broadway stage when they were interpolated into a few performances of the quick-folding Victor Herbert musical *The Gold Bug* (1896), but they went on to increase their audiences play-ing in variety at Koster and Bial's Music Hall before they returned to the musical theatre to tour unsuccessfully in the summer musical *Clorindy (The Senegambian Carnival)*. After more variety appearances, they took another turn into the book-musical show when they appeared under the Hurtig and Seamon management in the musical comedies *The Policy Players*, *Sons of Ham* and *In Dahomey*. In this last and most successful of their shows, which they played with happy notoriety in Britain, Williams was characteristically cast as 'Shylock Homestead' ('Shy, to his friends') misused and misdirected by the natty, close-to-the-wind Rareback Pinkerton (his personal friend and adviser) as portrayed by the slicker Walker. During the run of their next show, *Bandana Land*, Walker was forced to retire, suffering from the onset of the paresis from which he died the following year.

A biomusical show, *Williams and Walker*, was played at off-Broadway's American Place Theater 9 March 1986.

WALKER, Nancy [SWOYER, Anna Myrtle] (b Philadelphia, 10 May 1921; d Studio City, Calif, 25 March 1992). A favourite Broadway comedienne in the musical and non-musical theatre.

The small-sized, funny-faced Nancy Walker made her earliest New York musical appearance in a supporting rôle in *Best Foot Forward* (1941) before she created the part of the energetic cab-driver Brunhilde Esterhazy in *On the Town*, insisting that her passenger 'Come Up to My Place' and, once there, that 'I Can Cook Too'. She appeared in the 1947 *The Barefoot Boy with Cheek* (Yetta Samovar) and starred as Lily Malloy, the brewery lady who goes ballet, in *Look Ma, I'm Dancin'* (1948), but she closed on the road with *A Month of Sundays*, a musical version of Victor Wolf-son's *Excursion* (1951, Shirley Harris). Walker then re-placed Helen Gallagher as Gladys in the successful 1952

revival of *Pal Joey* and was briefly seen in police-force low comedy in *Copper and Brass* (1957, Katie O'Shea) before she co-starred as the wife of Phil Silver's Herbie Cram in *Do Re Mi* (1960). It was her last rôle on a Broadway which, with its general abandonment of the comic musical in favour of the romantic and/or spectacular one, no longer seemed to have a place for a genuine low comedienne.

Although she played Domina in the 1971 revival of *A Funny Thing Happened on the Way to the Forum* on the west coast she did not move east with the production and made her latter-day success largely in television, notably as the mother of Valerie Harper's *Rhoda*.

WALKING HAPPY Musical comedy in 2 acts by Roger O Hirson and Ketti Frings based on the play *Hobson's Choice* by Harold Brighouse. Lyrics by Sammy Cahn. Music by James van Husen. Lunt–Fontanne Theater, New York, 26 November 1966.

Following the success of their musicalized *Charley's Aunt*, *Where's Charley?*, producers Feuer and Martin turned to another British classic, Harold Brighouse's celebrated English north-country comedy *Hobson's Choice*, which had been a 143-performance success on its Broad-way production in 1915 and a 246-performance hit the following year in London, as musical-mix.

Like its predecessor, *Hobson's Choice* underwent some surprising changes in both plot and character in its trans-formation into the curiously titled *Walking Happy*, which featured Norman Wisdom, London star of *Where's Charley?*, as the exceedingly simple shoemaker, Will Mossop, who is taken in marriage by his boss's daughter, Maggie (Louise Troy), as a business proposition. When Maggie's boozy father (George Rose) objects, the pair set up in competition to him, but all is sweetness and light by the end of the evening, and Will is set to become a proper husband. Ed Bakey appeared as George Beenstock, a temperance man opposed to Hobson, but who nevertheless lets his sons (James B Spann, Michael Berkson) tidily wed the bootmaker's remaining two daughters (Gretchen van Aken, Sharon Dierking) by the end of the show.

The largest part of the score fell to the two principals. He pondered 'How D'Ya Talk to a Girl?' after the surprise order to wed, she determined that 'I'll Make a Man of the Man' and they concluded 'I Don't Think I'm in Love' before he decided that a wife is a wife and 'It Might as Well Be You'. There was also a title-song. The musical comedy Maggie and Mossop played 161 performances on Broad-way, and toured briefly to the west coast where Anne Rogers was seen as Maggie.

Recording: original cast (Capitol/EMI)

WALLER, Jack (b London, 2 April 1885; d London, 28 July 1957).

Producer, songwriter and all-round showman-of-the-theatre, Waller began his life in the business working the music halls. In 1910 he formed the concert party 'The Butterflies' (whose members included Wylie Watson) and he toured the company for many years around the Pacific circuits. In Southern parts, he also ventured for the first time as an impresario and presented the revue *Look Who's Here* (1917), in conjunction with Sydney James, at Syd-ney's Palace Theatre, 'Jack Waller's Company of Comedians' in *Vanity Fair* at the Tivoli (1918) and a new edition of *Look Who's Here* the following year.

Soon afterwards he returned to Britain, the concert party broke up, and Waller went on to play in several revues (*Robey en Casserole*, *The Little Revue Starts at Nine*) before starting up a managerial partnership with Herbert Clayton, whom he had met when Clayton had booked the remaining Butterflies for the Chelsea Palace in 1920. The pair began writing and touring revues and musical comedies like those Waller had purveyed to the Australians on the minor British theatre and music-hall circuits (*Archie*, *Tilly*), but they were shot to the forefront of the big league soon after in fairytale style. On a trip to America's out-of-town venues to pick up some fashionably American pieces to mount on the British circuits, the pair purchased the British rights to *So Long, Letty*, *The Kiss Burglar* and *Canary Cottage*. Their fourth purchase was the first to be staged, however, and they eventually mounted it not on the road but in London. *No, No, Nanette*, their first West End production, gave them the hit of the era.

They didn't get the other three purchases to the London stage, but Waller and Clayton followed up with several other and more tried-and-tested American musical comedies – *Mercenary Mary*, *Kitty's Kisses* (as *The Girl Friend*), *Hit the Deck* and *Good News* – as well as the Hungarian *Princess Charming* (*Alexandra*) and a number of plays (including *Abie's Irish Rose*) before they launched their own, home-made *Virginia* (1928), a piece which Waller tried to pretend was not home-made at all, but fashionably American. It did very nicely, but thereafter neither their imports (*Merry, Merry*, *Hold Everything!*, *Sons o' Guns*) nor their original shows (the sub-operatic *Dear Love*, the expensively spectacular *Silver Wings*) came financially good, and their partnership fizzled out in 1930.

Waller, however, continued. He co-composed and mounted a series of musical comedies featuring comedian Bobby Howes (*For the Love of Mike*, *Tell Her the Truth*, *He Wanted Adventure*, *Yes, Madam?*, *Please, Teacher!*) which proved highly successful, and he even contributed half a score to another hit musical, the Jack Buchanan vehicle *Mr Whittington*, in a period in which, of all his productions, only a further attempt at a romantic musical with the adaptation of C Stafford Dickens's *Command Performance*, and a George Robey show, *Certainly, Sir!*, proved flops. After this last piece, however, things again went rather more consistently less well: *Big Business*, *Oh! You Letty* and *Bobby Get Your Gun* all failed, and a London staging of the Broadway success *Let's Face It*, produced in collaboration with Tom Arnold, didn't do sufficiently well to compensate. Waller went uncharacteristically quiet, and when he re-emerged it was with a provincial adaptation of the play *The Best People* which he had produced in London in 1925.

This *Hearts Are Trumps* stayed intentionally in the provinces, but Waller's attempt at a major comeback with a production of Broadway's *By Jupiter*, which also stopped short of London, had not been supposed to. Waller, nevertheless, battled on. He mounted a revival of *Merrie England*, a new musical called *The Kid from Stratford* with Arthur Askey (1948) and a tour of the first musical by the young Sandy Wilson, *Caprice* (1950), but it was a play picked up from a repertory theatre, the Worthing-mounted *Sailor Beware*, which restored his fortunes and his credibility for his last years in the theatre. Those years

included only one musical, a last attempt at a romantic piece with his own name and that of his musical helpmate, Joe Tunbridge, hidden under a pseudonym as the composers of a score taken piecemeal from the vast tin trunk of un- or under-used music that the producer kept in his office. *Wild Grows the Heather*, an adaptation of J M Barrie's *The Little Minister*, was not a success, but Waller kept going and he was still talking and planning productions up to the day of his death.

A *monstre sacré* of the West End theatre, sailing often near to the wind of legitimacy, and a familiar of the bankruptcy courts in the best tradition of the theatrical impresario, Waller was nevertheless responsible for many fine West End productions and hits. As a composer, he turned out much lively music – his imitation of 'Ol' Man River', 'Roll Away, Clouds', from *Virginia* being perhaps his most successful number – all of it written in collaboration with efficiently trained musicians such as Haydn Wood or Tunbridge.

1923 **Our Liz** (w Pat Thayer/Herbert Clayton, Con West) Hippodrome, Southampton 13 August

1923 **Suzanne** (w Haydn Wood/Clayton, West) Palace Theatre, Plymouth 31 December

1924 **Tilly** (w Wood/Bert Lee, R P Weston/Clayton, West) Empire, Leeds 21 July

1924 **Archie** (w Wood/George Arthurs, Worton David) Grand Theatre, Hull 28 July

1928 **Virginia** (w Joseph A Tunbridge/Lee, Weston, Clayton, Douglas Furber) Palace Theatre 24 October

1929 **Dear Love** (w Tunbridge, Wood/Dion Titheradge, Lauri Wylie, Clayton) Palace Theatre 14 November

1930 **Silver Wings** (w Tunbridge/Titheradge/Titheradge, Furber) Dominion Theatre 9 December

1931 **For the Love of Mike** (w Tunbridge/Clifford Grey, Sonny Miller/Grey) Saville Theatre 8 October

1932 **Tell Her the Truth** (w Tunbridge/Weston, Lee) Saville Theatre 14 June

1933 **He Wanted Adventure** (w Tunbridge/Weston, Lee) Saville Theatre 28 March

1933 **Command Performance** (w Tunbridge/Grey/C Stafford Dickens) Saville Theatre 17 October

1933 **Mr Whittington** (w Tunbridge, John W Green/Grey, Furber, Greatrex Newman) London Hippodrome 1 February

1934 **Yes, Madam?** (w Tunbridge/Weston, Lee, K R G Browne) London Hippodrome 27 September

1935 **Please, Teacher!** (w Tunbridge/Weston, Lee, Browne) London Hippodrome 2 October

1936 **Certainly, Sir!** (w Tunbridge/Weston, Lee) London Hippodrome 17 September

1937 **Big Business** (w Tunbridge/Carter, Lee, Browne) London Hippodrome 18 February

1938 **Bobby Get Your Gun** (w Tunbridge/Carter, Lee, Grey/Guy Bolton, Fred Thompson, Lee) Adelphi Theatre 7 October

1943 **Hearts Are Trumps** (w Tunbridge, Leon Carroll/Ian Grey, Robert Fyle/Fyle) Theatre Royal, Birmingham 19 October

1956 **Wild Grows the Heather** (w Tunbridge/Ralph Reader/Hugh Ross Williamson) London Hippodrome 3 May

WALLIS, Bertram (b London, 22 February 1874; d London, 11 April 1952). Handsome actor and singer who became a longtime London leading man.

Wallis began his career playing in classical drama, but he soon shifted to George Edwardes's management, playing the Hayden Coffin baritone rôles on tour before being brought to town to cover the same star in *The Country Girl* and to play one of the beaux to Paul Rubens's *Three Little Maids* (1902, Lord Grassmere). He appeared in *The Love Birds* (1904, Alec Rockingham) in London, and then visited Broadway where he created rôles in *A Madcap Princess* (1904, Charles Brandon) and *The Princess Beggar* (1907, Prince Karl) and played in the American editions of *The Little Cherub* (1906, Lord Congress) and *Miss Hook of Holland* (1907, Adrian Papp) before returning to Britain.

Frank Curzon starred him in the title-rôle of the successful *King of Cadonia* alongside Isabel Jay in London and then with Alice Venning on the road, and he followed this up by teaming with the same leading lady (Miss Jay) and the same management in *Dear Little Denmark* (1909, Conrad Petersen) and *The Balkan Princess* (1910, Sergius). In 1911 he moved back to George Edwardes's management to star with Lily Elsie in the title-rôle of London's *The Count of Luxemburg* (René), and he later appeared as leading man in Oscar Straus's unsuccessful *Love and Laughter* (1913, King Carol) and the British version of *Autoliebchen* (1914, *Joy Ride Lady*, Edouard Morny). He played for a period in pantomime, plays and revue before returning to the musical theatre to take over as the non-singing hero, Baldasarre, opposite José Collins in *The Maid of the Mountains* for a large part of that show's long run and he later starred opposite Miss Collins in *A Southern Maid* (1920, Francesco del Fuego) and in two other vocally limited rôles in *The Last Waltz* (1922, Prince Paul) and *Catherine* (1923, Peter the Great). He subsequently returned to Daly's Theatre to play King Louis to the *Madame Pompadour* of Evelyn Laye, appeared in the short-lived *Nicolette* (1925, Pan Fulano), in London's *The Blue Mazurka* (1927 Clement, Baron von Reiger) and as the Duke of Cumberland to Miss Laye's *Blue Eyes* (1928).

Wallis toured as Baldasarre and King Louis, and his transition from handsome leading man to handsome older gentleman continued in the musical comedy *Lucky Break* (t/o William J Pierce), alongside Leslie Henson, as King Joachim in a revival of *A Waltz Dream* (1934) and Count Hédouville in *Paganini* (1937). At 70 he played in *Blossom Time* (1942, Pierre) and the Chopin pasticcio *Waltz Without End* (1942, The Stranger), and he went on to appear in the London version of *Sunny River* (1943, George Marshall) and on the road in *Betty* (1945) before ending a career of over 50 almost non-stop years in the theatre.

WALLS, Tom [Kir(k)by] (b Kingsthorpe, Northants, 18 February 1883; d Ewell, Surrey, 27 November 1949).

Best known for his appearances in the series of farces produced at the Aldwych Theatre in the 1920s and early 1930s – and as the owner-trainer of a Derby winner (April the Fifth) – Walls had spent most of his previous stage career in musical theatre. He began in pantomime and concert parties, played principal comedy rôles in musicals in Australia (Doody in *The Arcadians*, Marquis in *The Belle of Brittany*, Mr Hook etc), and then took a number of supporting comedy rôles under George Edwardes's management in England: *The Sunshine Girl* (1912, Hodson), *The Marriage Market* (1913, Bald-Faced Sandy), *A Country Girl* revival (1914, Sir Joseph), *Véronique* revival (1915, Coquenard). He subsequently replaced George Huntley in the principal comedy part of Edwardes's production of *Betty* (Lord Playne), played in London's version

of *High Jinks* (1916, Colonel Slaughter), created rôles in *The Beauty Spot* (1917, Paul Prince) at the Gaiety and *Kissing Time* (1919, Colonel Bollinger) at the Winter Garden, succeeded Davy Burnaby as General Zonzo in *Oh! Julie* (1920) and appeared as Mephistopheles in the ill-fated *Faust on Toast*, before the production of the comedy *Tons of Money* changed his career. His last musical appearance was in the central rôle of *Whirled into Happiness* (Albert Horridge) in 1922, but he also dabbled briefly in the production of provincial musicals (*Our Liz*, *Suzanne*) with the emerging Jack Waller and Herbert Clayton before turning his attention full-time to farces and films.

WALZER AUS WIEN Singspiel in a Vorspiel and 3 acts by A M Willner, Heinz Reichert and Ernst Marischka. Music taken from the works of Johann Strauss I and II arranged by Julius Bittner (and/or Erich Wolfgang Korngold uncredited). Wiener Stadttheater, Vienna, 30 October 1930.

One of the many Operetten manufactured from the music of the Johann Strausses, *Walzer aus Wien* was constructed on *Dreimäderlhaus* lines, as a fictionalized biomusical of its composer. The young Johann Strauss (Hubert Marischka) wants to follow in his father's footsteps and become a conductor and composer, but the elder Strauss (Willy Thaller) will not hear of it. However, the seductive Countess Olga Baraskaja (Betty Fischer) takes an interest in the young man, and arranges it so that he gets a chance to conduct his father's orchestra in one of his own waltzes before a packed house at Dommayers. His name is made and, as Olga sweeps on from Vienna on the arm of Prince Gogol (Ludwig Herold), and whilst his beloved Resi (Paula Brosig), the daughter of the baker Ebeseder (Fritz Imhoff), is promised instead to the tailor's son Leopold (Karl Göttler), Johann junior is reconciled with his father and heads on to fame and, presumably, the three wives he really had. Amongst the show's supporting cast was former star soubrette Mizzi Zwerenz, now playing character rôles, as Frau Kratochwill.

The selection and arrangement of the score – which did not shrink from using some of the more obvious Strauss bon-bons that other pasticheurs had modestly side-stepped – was credited to Julius Bittner. However, it has been said that it was in fact Korngold (billed only as 'musical director') who was responsible for assembling and revamping the music, and that he allegedly had his out-of-luck friend's name included in the credits so that he might share the royalties in the work. Those royalties, indeed, were to turn out to be considerable, for although *Walzer aus Wien* did not establish itself in the repertoire of its country of origin as the earlier and slightly less musically naïve pasticcio *Wiener Blut* had done, it was used as the basis for a whole series of Strauss biomusicals around the world.

Hubert Marischka's Vienna production – which originally ran some four hours in length – played a regular season at the Stadttheater and was later seen for 19 performances at the Theater an der Wien (17 May 1931) before it was done, without attracting the attention of its nearest neighbours. However, if Germany and Hungary bypassed the piece, it was picked up by Oswald Stoll and presented at London's Alhambra Theatre (ad Hassard

Short, Desmond Carter, Caswell Garth) under the title of *Waltzes from Vienna*, 'a love story of music'. The Strausses were credited, but Bittner and Korngold's names only appeared on the programme in minuscule letters alongside the rather larger credit for G H Clutsam and Herbert Griffiths who had, it seems, done a new arrangement of a score which now started off with the Radetzky March and ended on the 'Blue Danube'. *Waltzes from Vienna* was lavishly staged (spectacle-director Hassard Short's name was splashed above the title in larger type than the Strausses) and presented as a twice-daily entertainment with Robert Halliday and Esmond Knight alternating the rôle of young Strauss, Evelyn Herbert, Adrienne Brune and Borghild Bodom sharing Resi, Marie Burke as Olga, Dennis Noble as Leopold, and C V France as Strauss sr. It played for almost a year, alongside the spate of early 1930s mega-productions that were crowding London's stages (*White Horse Inn*, *Helen!*, *Cavalcade*, *Nina Rosa* etc), totting up 607 performances at its double-paced rate prior to closing. Soon after, an English film version was made with Knight featured alongside Edmund Gwenn, Fay Compton and Jessie Matthews. In Australia, the Alhambra/Clutsam version was mounted with John Moore (Strauss), Shirley Dale (Resi), Miriam Sabbage (Olga) and Aubrey Mallalien (Strauss sr) in the lead rôles and it played three months in Melbourne prior to a season in Sydney (Her Majesty's Theatre 15 April 1933).

A French version (ad André Mouëzy-Éon, Max Eddy, Jean Marietti) put considerable further changes, both textual and – via Eugène Cools – musical, into a piece which had now gone further from its original than even the various versions of *Dreimäderlhaus* had done. For *Valses de Vienne* it was decided to add the conventional soubret element which had been avoided in the original. A baker's assistant called Pepi was added to the script, supplied with a subplot and a duet, and allowed to pair off with Leopold at the final curtain whilst – all history thrown to the winds – Strauss for-goodness-sake married Rési! But, history or no history, it was the jolly *Valses de Vienne* which proved the most durable version of the Strauss family musical. Maurice Lehmann's production with André Baugé (Strauss jr), Pierre Magnier (Strauss sr), Fanély Revoil and Lucienne Tragin starred and settings by the famous artist Marie Laurencin was a thorough success, prefatory to a long line of Parisian large-stage revivals (Théâtre du Châtelet 1941, 1947, 1957, 1958, 1964, 1974, Théâtre Mogador 1975, 1977) and an unceasing presence in French provincial houses to the present day.

In America, Moss Hart took his turn at the libretto (a revision of the London one) and Frank E Tours and Robert Russell Bennett put their hands into the score for what was now called *The Great Waltz*. Guy Robertson and H Reeves Smith played the Strausses, Marion Claire was the baker's daughter and Marie Burke repeated her London performance as the sexy Maecenas of the piece, the vast Center Theater was filled with Short's Viennesey spectacle, and the show clocked up 298 Broadway performances. Four years later, Hollywood contributed its version of the Strauss story with Fernand Graavey, Miliza Korjus and Luise Rainer in the principal rôles and a slim new score of Strauss pieces (lyrics: Oscar Hammerstein) which turned *Der Zigeunerbaron*'s Dompfaff duo into 'One Day When We Were Young' alongside the 'Blue Danube',

'Tales from the Vienna Woods' and 'I'm in Love with Vienna'.

Whilst France – understandably, given its success – stayed true to its original version, in America those bits that remained of *Walzer aus Wien* were recycled interminably. A freshly fabricated Strauss-purée piece called *The Waltz King*, masterminded by Paramount pictures music-man Boris Morros, was mounted twice on the west coast – in 1943 (13 September) with Richard Bonelli and Irra Pettina starred and, revised, in 1944 (28 August) – and flopped twice, but when, in the wake of the success of *Song of Norway*, pasticcio was all the rage on the west coast, and that show's authors, Robert Wright and George Forrest, took a turn at a Strauss show, they returned to the basis established in *Walzer aus Wien*. Film star Korjus featured as Jetty Strauss in a less improbable *The Blue Danube* in 1949, but the Los Angeles Light Opera brought out their version of *Walzer aus Wien* (lib re-adapted by Milton Lazarus, add ly: Forman Brown) the same year with Walter Slezak as the older Strauss, and again in 1953, and it was dusted off and given yet another rewrite (lib re-re-adapted by Jerome Chodorov) for a revival in 1965 (14 September) as *The Great Waltz* with Giorgio Tozzi starred. By this time, the complicated credits included no less than 13 different writers' names. The 13-handed mixture, however, proved a successful one, for the production was exported to London's Theatre Royal, Drury Lane, where, under the management of Harold Fielding and Bernard Delfont, and with Operette star Sári Barábás (Olga) featured, it rolled up a fine 706 performance run. The success prompted a further MGM film, based on this version, with Kenneth McKellar and Mary Costa featured, which was not a success.

UK: Alhambra Theatre *Waltzes from Vienna* 17 August 1931; Australia: Theatre Royal, Melbourne 24 December 1932; France: Théâtre de la Porte-Saint-Martin *Valses de Vienne* 21 December 1933; USA: Center Theater 22 September 1934; Films: Gaumont *Waltzes from Vienna* 1934, MGM *The Great Waltz* 1938, 1972
Recordings: 1970 London cast recording (Columbia) etc

EIN WALZERTRAUM Operette in 3 acts by Felix Dörmann and Leopold Jacobson based on the story *Nux der Prinzgemahl* from Hans Müller's *Buch der Abenteuer*. Music by Oscar Straus. Carltheater, Vienna, 2 March 1907.

The first major Operette success to follow *Die lustige Witwe* out of Vienna, with all that meant in the way of impetus behind it, Oscar Straus's *Ein Walzertraum* had already won an enormous pre-export success on home ground. Unlike its famous predecessor, it did not then go on to sweep the world's stages with success, but it nevertheless established itself firmly in both the German- and French-speaking repertoires for the rest of the century.

Viennese Lieutenant Niki (Fritz Werner) has been married to Princess Helene of Flausenthurm (Helene Merviola), but he quickly finds the strictures of court etiquette and his consort's position impossible to take. On his wedding night he slips out with friend Montschi (Rudolf Kumpa) to relax at a local restaurant where a Viennese ladies' band is playing, and there he falls romantically in with pretty Franzi Steingrüber (Mizzi Zwerenz), the conductor of the orchestra. King Joachim (Karl Blasel) and his cousin Lothar (Arthur Guttmann), anxious that

Plate 286. **Ein Walzertraum**: *The lights are glistening, the ladies' band is playing, and the café seems a much more welcoming place to homesick Niki than his new wife's palace* (Volksoper, Vienna).

Niki is not thinking about perpetuating their dynasty on his wedding night, follow him, and soon Helene and her lady-in-waiting Friederike (Therese Löwe) arrive worriedly on the spot too. Franzi goes to fight the newcomer for her man, but then she realizes who she is. It is Franzi, however, who saves the apparently doomed royal marriage. She helps Helene reorganize her quarters Viennese-style, with everything that might make Niki feel more at home and at ease, before heading off home with her orchestra leaving the Flasenthurm dynasty to perpetuate itself in the approved fashion.

Straus's score glittered with good things, from which the longing waltz duet for Niki and Montschi, 'Leise, ganz leise klingt's durch den Raum', tempting the new Prince from the castle to the place where the orchestra is playing, proved to be the major hit. A comic duo for Franzi and cousin Lothar with him tootling on a piccolo and her accompanying him on the violin ('Piccolo! Piccolo! Tsin-tsin-tsin') was another musical highlight, alongside the comical trio in which the future of the dynasty is debated ('Ach der arme Dynastie'), another for the three ladies on 'Temperament! Temperament!' and the lively chorus march 'Mädel, sei net dumm!'.

Ein Walzertraum was the biggest hit the Carltheater had ever had. It played 261 consecutive performances in 1907 and provoked the Wiener Colosseum to a burlesque, *Polkatraum*, before running on unbroken to the end of the next season, 15 June the following year, by which time it had been seen 427 times and the cast was now headed by Willie Strehl (Niki), Dora Keplinger (Franzi), Frln Mödl (Helene) and Richard Waldemar (Joachim). It remained in the Carltheater's repertoire for almost two decades thereafter, passing its 600th performance there on 24 May 1913, and was subsequently taken up in other Viennese houses, playing its 1,000th Viennese performance during a revival (20 January 1927) at the Johann Strauss-Theater on 15 February 1927 with Robert Nästlberger and Gisela Kolbe in the leading rôles.

Whilst the original run was still playing, most of the other major musical-theatre centres brought *Ein Walzertraum* to the stage. Budapest was the first (ad Adolf Mérei) with a production at the Király Színház which featured Ákos Ráthonyi, hero of the Hungarian *Die lustige Witwe*, as Niki alongside Gitta Ötvös (Franzi), Sári Petráss (Helene), József Németh (Joachim) and Sándor Pápi (Lothar). The piece repeated its Viennese success and passed its 100th night on 26 February 1908 before going out to other theatres and regular revivals (Városi Színház 1926, Király Színház 1 February 1936 etc). Berlin's Theater des Westens followed suit soon after.

It was in the English-language sector that the piece was to prove something of a disappointment. In America, actor-author Joseph W Herbert made the English version and took the rôle of Lothar in a production which was mounted at Philadelphia's Chestnut Street Opera House in January 1908. Sophie Brandt (Franzi), Edward Johnson (Niki), Magda Dahl (Helene) and Charles A Bigelow (Joachim) were the other principals in Frank McKee's Interstate Amusement Co production. Three weeks later it opened on Broadway. Vera Michelena and Frank Rushworth took over as Helene and Niki and the show did well enough without ever looking like approaching the status of *The Merry Widow*.

In London, however, even though the show was given a star-sprinkled production under George Edwardes and Charles Frohman's management, *A Waltz Dream* (ad Adrian Ross) was frankly a flop. Gertie Millar (Franzi), Robert Evett (Niki), George Grossmith jr (Lothar) and the great comic Arthur Williams (Joachim) starred, and there was a piece, featuring the members of the ladies' band alongside Joachim and Lothar, about 'The Big Bass Drum' which allowed the girls the extra opportunities Lehár had provided for his grisettes in London's *Die lustige Witwe*, but *A Waltz Dream* just didn't appeal. It closed after 146 determined performances (Miss Millar had already gone, being replaced by Denise Orme) whilst such pieces as *Butterflies*, *Havana* and *The Gay Gordons* prospered. All sorts of excuses were advanced to account for its poor showing, and Edwardes remained convinced the show had been unlucky, so in 1911 he remounted it (ad Basil Hood) at Daly's Theatre (7 January), the home of *The Merry Widow*, with the 'widow', Lily Elsie, starred alongside Robert Michaelis and W H Berry. But once again, with all the trumps on its side, it failed to go. Edwardes closed it after 106 performances and produced *Der Graf von Luxemburg* instead. In 1934 Lea Seidl, Bertram Wallis, Carl Esmond and Berry starred in a three-weeks revival at the Winter Garden (20 December).

In spite of the less than happy results won in Britain and America, Australia's J C Williamson duly produced *A Waltz Dream* (English version) in 1910. The Sydney season lasted but a month, and the show did not become a favourite, but it was nevertheless brought out again in 1917 with Dorothy Brunton as Franzi, William Green as Niki, C H Workman as Joachim and Connie Ediss as drummer Fifi, again in 1936 with Strella Wilson and Marie Bremner featured, and yet again in 1939. Williamson's, you see, had the costumes and the band parts.

If France was slower than other countries to stage its version of the show which was supposed to be the best thing out of Vienna since *La Veuve joyeuse*, *Rêve de valse* (ad Léon Xanrof, Jules Chancel) – in spite of the noted similarities of its libretto to the adapters' *Le Prince Consort* and Ivan Caryll's musical version thereof – did very much better there than anywhere else. Produced by *La Veuve joyeuse*'s producer, Alphonse Franck, at the same Théâtre

Apollo with Paris's Danilo, Henri Defreyn, as Niki alongside Alice Bonheur (Franzi), Alice Milet (Hélène), Saturnin Fabre (Joachim) and Paul Ardot (Lothar), it was played with great success for three months and was subsequently revived both there and later also at the Folies-Dramatiques (8 December, 1922), the Porte-Saint-Martin (11 June 1934), and on several occasions at the Mogador (22 March 1947, 24 February 1962, 31 July 1976), remaining to this day one of the most frequently seen of the short list of Viennese Operetten still played in the French provinces.

A regular part of the German-language repertoire, *Ein Walzertraum* has also been revived on a number of occasions in Vienna, notably at the Stadttheater in 1945, at the Raimundtheater in 1954, and at the Volksoper (9 February 1974) where the lesson of the English productions has not been taken and the script and score have both been uncomfortably and incongruously tinkered with to boost the rôle of Helene (notably with the addition of *Rund um die Liebe*'s 'Ein Schwipserl') above that of Franzi in importance.

A Hollywood film, *The Smiling Lieutenant*, developed by Ernst Vajda and Samuel Raphaelson from *Ein Walzertraum* and, allegedly, from Müller's novel, featured Maurice Chevalier (Niki), Claudette Colbert (Franzi) and Miriam Hopkins (Anna) in a tale where the Princess was a frumpish creature, Niki's marriage to her forced, and Franzi was behind turning the royal lady into a pretty person.

Hungary: Király Színház *Varázskeringő* 26 November 1907; Germany: Theater des Westens 21 December 1907; USA: Broadway Theater *A Waltz Dream* 27 January 1908; UK: Hicks Theatre *A Waltz Dream* 7 March 1908; Australia: Her Majesty's Theatre, Sydney *A Waltz Dream* 18 February 1910; France: Théâtre Apollo *Rêve de valse* 3 March 1910

Recordings: 2-record set (EMI), in Italian (RAI), selections (Period, Telefunken, Fontana, EMI-Electrola) in English (HMV), in French (EMI-Pathé, CBS, Véga, Decca etc)

WANDA, Gustav (b Germany, 1870; d London, December 1916).

The composer of a half-dozen musical plays, Gustav Wanda had his first success with the vaudeville *Die Dame aus Trouville*, a musicalized version of the French *La Turlutaine de Marjolin* (Théâtre Déjazet 30 November 1898) which was played after its Berlin run in Vienna (Theater an der Wien 20 September 1902), with its score decorated with a couple of American songs and one by the young Lehár which was subsequently cut, and later in Budapest (*Trouville gyönge*, Magyar Színház 23 January 1903), and a second with *Der ledige Gatte*, produced at Dresden in 1910. Wanda subsequently moved to England, where he was engaged as musical director for *After the Girl* at the Gaiety Theatre and for the imported American show *The Belle of Bond Street*, but he died soon after at the age of 46.

1897 **Leben und Lieben** (Oskar Klein) Ostende Theater 1 December
1899 **Der Platzmajor** (Alfred Schönfeld, Jean Kren) Thalia-Theater 9 September
1900 **Der Amor von heute** (*A Modern Cupid*) (Kren, Schönfeld) Thalia-Theater 30 November
1901 **Die Dame aus Trouville** (w others/Louis Péricaud, Maurice Soulié, Charles Darantière ad) Belle-Alliance-Theater 27 December

1904 **Liebeshandel** (Richard Wilde, Paul Stark) Elysium Theater, Stettin 5 June
1910 **Der ledige Gatte** (Fritz Grünbaum, Heinz Reichert) Residenztheater, Dresden 28 October
1913 **Die Nordseekrabbe** (Bruno Decker, Robert Pohl) Bellevue-Theater, Stettin 12 October

WANG Comic opera by J Cheever Goodwin. Music by Woolson Morse. Broadway Theater, New York, 4 May 1891.

Described more than a little loosely as a comic opera, *Wang* mixed elements of burlesque and extravaganza with a tale which showed the influence of, yet contrasted starkly with, its author's previous piece: an adaptation of Vanloo and Leterrier's libretto to *L'Étoile*. Once again the tale was set in picturesque faraway lands – this time, Siam – where the crafty, comical regent Wang (De Wolf Hopper) is plotting to lay his hands on the missing fortune left by his late royal brother. The young prince Mataya (Della Fox) is more interested in making love to Gillette (Anna O'Keefe), the daughter of the late French consul, but Gillette's mother (Marion Singer) suspects that the boy is really after the mysterious chest that his father left to her deceased husband's care. Mother is less careful when it comes to finding herself a second husband, and Wang gets the widow and the money and the throne before the evening is out. The favourites amongst Morse's songs included 'The Man with an Elephant on his Hands' and the topical trio 'Ask the Man in the Moon'.

Wang proved a hot-weather favourite in the summer of 1891, running 151 performances through the season and providing itself with fine credentials for the touring circuits, whilst at the same time giving both Hopper – a comical sensation as the excessively tall, plumbingly basso regent – and pretty Miss Fox the last boost to above-the-title stardom. Hopper toured *Wang* for two seasons, bringing it back to Broadway for a month in May 1892, another from 15 August (when its '450th performance' was announced) and a week in November. He revived what became his perennial warhorse in New York as late as 1904 (Lyric Theater 18 May, 57 performances) under the Shubert management with Madge Lessing and later Julia Sanderson as his leading lady, and was still playing Wang on the road as much as 20 further years on.

An Australian season of *Wang* was played by Josephine Stanton's company which toured to the South Pacific with that piece and another American comic opera, Richard Stahl's *Said Pasha*, in 1901. Miss Stanton was Mataya to the Wang of George Kunkel, with Henry Hallam as Boucher.

Australia: Criterion Theatre, Sydney 9 November 1901

WARDE, Willie [WARDE, William J] (b Great Yarmouth, 1857; d London, 18 August 1943).

Willie Warde was the son of William Warde sr and brother of John Warde, members of the celebrated dance and pantomime team of D'Auban and Warde, which in its mid-19th-century generation produced, in Willie jr and John D'Auban, the two most successful choreographers of the Victorian and Edwardian musical theatre.

Willie made his earliest stage appearances as a dancer in the music-halls before being engaged by John Hollingshead at the Gaiety in 1877. He spent some 30 years there as ballet master and then as choreographer under the managements of Hollingshead and Edwardes, whilst spreading his work around other managements and theatres as well. In latter years he designed the dances for the large part of Edwardes's productions. He also appeared frequently in character rôles and/or special dancing spots in both Gaiety and Daly's musicals.

In an age where the organizer of a show's dances was not always credited on the programme, Warde's confirmed choreography credits included *Dick* (1884), *Little Jack Sheppard* (1885), *The Lily of Léoville* (1886), *Lancelot the Lovely*, *La Prima Donna*, *The Gondoliers* (1889), *Captain Thérèse* (1890), *Joan of Arc, Cinder-Ellen Up-too-Late (1891)*, *Blue-Eyed Susan* (1892), *Don Juan* (1893), *Claude Du-val, The Shop Girl* (1894, 'Love on the Japanese Plan'), *Gentleman Joe, Dandy Dick Whittington. A Model Trilby* (1895), *My Girl, The Geisha* (1896, 'Chon-kina'), *In Town* (USA, 1897), *The Circus Girl* (1896), *A Runaway Girl, A Greek Slave* (1898), *The Lucky Star* (1899), *San Toy, The Rose of Persia* (1899), *The Messenger Boy, Kitty Grey* (1900), *The Toreador, Bluebell in Fairyland* (1901), *A Country Girl, Three Little Maids, An English Daisy, The Girl from Kays* (1902), *The School Girl, The Duchess of Dantzic, The Cherry Girl* (1903), *The Cingalee, Lady Madcap* (1904), *The Little Cherub* (1906), *Butterflies* (1908), *The Quaker Girl* (1910), *The Sunshine Girl* (1912), *The Pearl Girl, The Girl from Utah* (1913) and *After the Girl* (1914).

The London shows in which he played rôles included *Il Sonnambulo* (the clerk who dances attendance), *Gulliver* (the gorilla), *Mazeppa* (Rudzoloff), *Little Jack Sheppard* (Kneebone), *Billee Taylor* (Black Cook, ie principal dancer), *Dick* (Hassan), *Don Juan* (Cecco), *The Shop Girl* (Mr Tweets), *My Girl* (Weeks), *The Circus Girl* (Auguste), *A Runaway Girl* (Mr Creel), *The Messenger Boy* (Professor Phunkwitz), *The Toreador* (Bandmaster), *A Country Girl* (Granfer Mummery), *The Cingalee* (Myamgah), *Les Merveilleuses* (Des Gouttières), *Butterflies* (Paul), *The Dollar Princess* (Sir James McGregor). *The Count of Luxemburg* (waiter), *A Waltz Dream* revival, and the 1914 *Country Girl* revival in which he repeated perhaps his happiest rôle as old Mummery. He also made a visit to Australia for Brough and Boucicault for whom he choreographed and performed in burlesque and comic opera for a season (1886, Ben Zouatte in *The Forty Thieves*, Blobbs/choreography in *Dick* etc).

DAS WÄSCHERMÄDEL Operette in 3 acts by Bernhard Buchbinder. Music by Rudolf Raimann. Theater in der Josefstadt, Vienna, 31 March 1905.

A musical-comedy vehicle for the popular soubrette Hansi Niese, here cast as Betti, the youngest of three washergirls (the other two are called Wetti and Netti!) in a tale of 1835 Vienna which involved its heroine with the Fürst Josef von Kleben and his son, Prinz Karl, and a whole lot of other lofty folk, not to mention the obligatory lady of the theatre (Irene Leitner, a singer). *Das Wäschermädel* played 38 performances at the Theater in der Josefstadt, but it remained in the company's and in Niese's repertoire, and was seen again in Vienna in 1913 when the Josefstädter company played a season at the Johann Strauss-Theater (4 October) with Niese featured along-

side Emil Guttmann (Josef), Paul Olmühl (Karl) and Adele Baum (Irene).

The show was also seen in Germany and in Hungary, but its most significant effect was that it persuaded Josef Jarno of the Theater in der Josefstadt to mount further Buchbinder musical plays for his wife's benefit. In 1906 he supplied *Der Schusterbub* in which Niese and Alexander Girardi played 52 performances, and then in 1907 he turned out Niese's all-time greatest musical-comedy vehicle, *Die Förster-Christl*.

Germany: ?1905; Hungary: Városligeti Nyari Színház *A szoknyáshös* 15 June 1906

THE WATER GIPSIES Play with music in 2 acts by A P Herbert based on his novel of the same name. Music by Vivian Ellis. Winter Garden Theatre, London, 31 August 1955.

The musical *The Water Gipsies* was an updated version of Herbert's successful 1930 novel, which had previously been filmed with the interpolation of one song written by Ellis and performed by Dora Labette. The central characters were Jane (Pamela Charles) and Lily (Dora Bryan), the daughters of old Albert Bell (Jerry Verno), who live on a barge on the River Thames. Jane is the innocent one who gets engaged to the local communist (Wallas Eaton), falls for a dashing artist (Peter Graves) but ends up, after an innocuous adventure in an hotel room, with her childhood sweetheart (Laurie Payne). Lily is the wise and wisecracking one who doesn't expect more than is available from her flashy chap (Roy Godfrey).

The song 'Little Boat' was taken from the film score and sung by Payne, but the most successful moments of the evening came when Miss Bryan let loose with her comedy numbers, bewailing her unsuitable name ('Why Did You Call Me Lily?'), damping her beau's proposals ('It Would Cramp My Style') or helping her sister through her adventure ('You Never Know with Men'). In spite of poor general notices, Miss Bryan's performance proved a draw, so that when she got pregnant and had to leave the cast, Peter Saunders's production foundered and was ultimately withdrawn after 239 performances.

Recording: original cast (HMV, WRC)

THE WATERMAN, or The First of August Ballad opera in 2 acts by Charles Dibdin. Music composed, compiled and arranged by Dibdin. Little Haymarket Theatre, London, 8 August 1774.

The most successful and enduring of the works of Charles Dibdin, *The Waterman* was a little story of Thameside love and nagging with a salutory ending. Wilhelmina, the daughter of the simple, hag-ridden gardener Mr Bundle and his pretentious wife, is sought in marriage by the waterman, Tom Tug (Mr Bannister), and the dandified Robin, whose claims are supported by father and mother respectively. Robin relies on flowery words, but Tom goes out and wins the Thames watermen's rowing race and dedicates his victory to the girl who is, in the end, sensible enough to prefer deeds to words. Since Bundle finally squashes his ever-nagging wife, the evening can end in a happy quartet.

Dibdin's ballad score, much of it original but partly arranged from popular sea songs, went mostly to the three young folk, with Tom's tenor song 'And Did You Not

Hear of a Jolly Young Waterman?' being the most substantial song in a rôle which was decorated ad-lib with nautical numbers ('The Bay of Biscay' became a traditional feature of the part). Tom Tug was a part which proved a favourite with many famous performers – notably John Braham, Sims Reeves and Charles Santley – in the more than a century that the show enjoyed a popularity second to none (not even *The Beggar's Opera*) amongst English ballad operas.

Played endlessly through Britain and its colonies as one part of the multiple-bill theatre programmes of the 18th and 19th centuries, *The Waterman* was given its last major revival at the Gaiety Theatre in 1870 (19 November) with Santley as a baritone Tom.

The piece was burlesqued in F C Burnand's 1873 *Little Tom Tug* (Opera Comique 12 November) in which Pattie Laverne starred as Tom to the Wilhelmina of Emily Muir, with Emily Thorne, Charles Lyall and J A Shaw supporting and a score 'composed and selected' by Frederic Stanislaus.

USA: Northern Liberties Theater, Philadelphia 8 April 1791, New York 22 May 1793; Australia: Theatre Royal, Sydney 24 May 1834

WATSON, Susan [Elizabeth] (b Tulsa, Okla, 17 December 1938). Top Broadway ingénue of the 1960s.

After playing in regional productions as a teenager in America, Miss Watson appeared in London in the imported company playing *West Side Story* (Velma), and then at Mildred Dunnock's Barnard Summer Theater as the girl in the original short version of *The Fantasticks* (1959). She made her first Broadway appearances in revue and had her initial metropolitan musical-comedy rôle as the teen-dreaming Kim McAfee, the under-aged heroine of *Bye Bye Birdie* ('One Boy'). She subsequently toured as Lili in *Carnival*, then replaced Anna Maria Alberghetti in the same rôle in the show's Broadway production, and took leading ingénue rôles in *Ben Franklin in Paris* (1964, Janine Nicolet), *A Joyful Noise* (1966, Jenny Lee) and *Celebration* (1969, Angel), whilst playing in more successful shows away from Broadway (Louise in *Gypsy*, Carrie in *Carousel*, Laurey in *Oklahoma!*, Amy in *Where's Charley?*).

She returned to Broadway in 1971 as Nanette in the highly successful revival of *No, No, Nanette* and saw out her ingénue days in regional productions of *Funny Face*, *Gigi*, *Promises, Promises*, *The Music Man* before moving West and into married life and more intermittent adult rôles.

WATSON, Wylie [ROBERTSON, John Wylie] (b Scotland, 1889; d 3 May 1966). Scots variety performer who found late fame as a character man in musical comedy.

Watson worked for many years as a versatile vocalist, instrumentalist and comic in Jack Waller's 'Butterflies' concert party in the more far-flung parts of the Empire, and he was already in his forties when Waller, now a successful producer, cast him in a supporting character rôle in the musical comedy *For the Love of Mike* (Rev Archibald James, 1931). He made a personal hit when he played the comical little Yorkshireman Mr Parkin, 'fourteen years tenor with the Ilkley Parish Church', in *Tell Her the Truth* ('Sing, Brothers!', 'Horrortorio') and confirmed himself as a star comedy name as the sour-faced, long-shorted scoutmaster, Eustace Didcott in *He Wanted Adventure* ('Smile

and Be Bright'), as button manufacturer Peabody in *Yes, Madam?* (Cat's Duet, 'Laugh!') and as the cello-playing schoolteacher Mr Clutterbuck in *Please, Teacher!* (Song of the 'Cello). He later played in Waller's less-successful *Big Business*, *Oh! You Letty* and *Bobby Get Your Gun*, in the wartime *Present Arms* (Syd Pottle) as his 'usual picture of lugubrious dejection' and on tour in a showy rôle in Waller's *Hearts Are Trumps* (1943, Mr Mosscockle).

Most of Watson's later career was angled towards the cinema where he repeated his stage rôles in the film versions of *For the Love of Mike*, *Yes, Madam?* and *Please, Teacher!*, appeared as Mr Memory in the 1935 film of *The Thirty-Nine Steps*, in the 1945 movie musical *Waltz Time*, *Whisky Galore* and, in his seventies, *The Sundowners*.

WAYBURN, Ned [WAYBURN, Edward Claudius] (b Pittsburgh, 30 March 1874; d New York, 2 September 1942). Ubiquitous choreographer and director of the early 20th-century Broadway stage.

Wayburn began his working life in his father's manufacturing business in Pittsburgh and Atlanta before becoming an assistant hotel manager in Chicago. Out of hours, he also worked as an amateur entertainer, playing ragtime piano and writing his own songs. An introduction to May Irwin resulted in her taking up one of his songs and also its composer as her sometime accompanist. Thus, Wayburn began his life in the theatre as a performer – appearing on Broadway with Miss Irwin in *The Swell Miss Fitzswell* (1897) and, billed as 'the man who invented ragtime', in *At Gay Coney Island* and *By the Sad Sea Waves* (1899). It was not long, however, before he took the first steps towards making himself a name as a choreographer and stage director. From staging the routines for a group called 'The Minstrel Misses' on the New York Theater Roof, he moved on to an engagement as stage director with Klaw and Erlanger, and then with the Shuberts. Often working in collaboration at first with book-wise Herbert Gresham and later with other stagers a touch more libretto-conscious than he, he remained widely in evidence through more than 20 heavily packed years of musical shows in America and also, during the revue-time fashion for things American, in London.

Wayburn's earliest productions, including such pieces as *Star and Garter*, *The Night of the Fourth*, *The Hall of Fame*, *Miss Simplicity*, *Mother Goose*, *Humpty Dumpty*, the Eddie Foy *Mr Bluebeard*, three of the *Rogers Brothers* musicals, *In Newport* and *The Ham Tree* were in the farce comedy, extravaganza and/or variety musical style, but he had a significant success with Chicago's comical, song-filled *The Time, the Place and the Girl* (w Arthur Evans) in 1907, following which he worked on some more substantial book shows such as Lulu Glaser's protean Viennese *Mlle Mischief*, the Gaiety Theatre imports *Havana* and *Peggy*, and Victor Herbert's operetta *The Rose of Algeria*. His list nevertheless included a predominance of more free and easy pieces: the Eddie Foy show *Mr Hamlet of Broadway*, a string of the loose-limbed dance and comedy shows that were played as 'summer musicals' by producer Lew Fields, and such road pieces as the Gus Edwards/Aaron Hoffman *Schooldays* (1908).

In 1913 Albert de Courville took Wayburn to Britain to stage the short-lived Leoncavallo musical comedy *Are You

There?, but his brash and vigorously precise style proved much better suited to revue and he mounted several successful such shows in London between 1913 and 1919 (*Hullo, Tango!*, *Zig-Zag*, *Box o' Tricks*, *Joy Bells*) whilst scoring equal success back home with half a dozen editions of the *Ziegfeld Follies* and even mounting – with pocket-painfully less success – his own revue *Town Topics* (1915). He did not, for all that, wholly abandon the book musical. He was called in to work over Fields's *Poor Little Ritz Girl* after an unpromising Boston opening and, in the 1920s, he directed several further musical plays, notably the highly successful *The Night Boat* (1920) and *Two Little Girls in Blue* (1921). However, he also suffered several quick failures, failing to reach Broadway with James T Powers's *The Little Kangaroo* (1922) and, most dangerously to his already dented bank-balance, his own *Town Gossip* (1921), which he billed questionably as a 'musical comedy'.

It took Wayburn several years to pay off the debts incurred on this unfortunate production, but he surfaced again with *The Maiden Voyage* (1926) only to have the show fold on the road amongst all kinds of recriminations. He was back in 1929 with *Ned Wayburn's Gambols*, but his show could not compete with *George White's Scandals*, *Earl Carroll's Sketch Book*, *John Murray Anderson's Almanac* and the other proprietorially named shows of the time and flopped in 31 performances. His last Broadway assignment was on Ziegfeld's unhappy *Smiles* (1930).

Wayburn founded a school of theatrical dance under his own name (Ned Wayburn Studios of Dancing) in 1905, drawing many of his dancers from its classes, in time-dishonoured fashion ('Every man or woman who wishes to reach prominence – in the shortest time – needs the training of the wonderful producer ... in the new *Follies* are ... 97 Ned Wayburn-made chorus girls'), to perform the energetic physical-jerks-in-stage-patterns style of choreography which he favoured and which subsequently became much used in early cinema musicals. The 'studios' later became the Ned Wayburn Institutes of Dancing and went for a wider catchment ('You wouldn't think of neglecting your child's education. How about their bodies? Are you willing to let them grow up physically undeveloped, shy, lacking in personality?'). In 1925 he also authored a book, *The Art of Stage Dancing*.

Like most choreographer-directors before and after him, Wayburn's emphasis was ever on the visual and musical side of his productions rather than on the text. But in many of the shows on which he worked, that text was organized either by his collaborator or, when he had none, by the comedians of the show themselves.

Alongside his claim to have 'invented' ragtime, Wayburn also claimed to have invented tap-dancing, by replacing the clogs of the traditional clog-dancer with shoes equipped with little metal thingummyjigs nailed upside-down to the soles. History – and particularly theatre history – has usually shown that folk who make such claims are fibbing but, even though the pretty ludicrous ragtime statement makes Wayburn stand up as a fairly dubiously veracious claimant, no one else seems to have put in a bid for the title of the creator of claquettes. So maybe he really did do it.

The first of his wives, Agnes Saye Wayburn, was a dancer who really did appear as Lottie Chalmers, a member of the first famous sextette, in Broadway's original *Florodora*.

1921 **Town Gossip** (Harold Orlob/w George Stoddard) Ford's Theater, Baltimore, 4 September

WEATHER OR NO in 1 act by Adrian Ross and W Beach. Music by B Luard Selby. Savoy Theatre, London, 10 August 1896.

Weather or No was a tiny one-act piece about a flirtation between the man and the lady on a weather-house which was first produced at London's Savoy Theatre and played by Emmie Owen and H Scott Russell as a forepiece to six months of *The Mikado*'s original run. With the fashion for such little forepieces rapidly dying away, it did not prove one of the theatre's more durable such sketches, so it was all the more surprising to find it picked up by Continental houses, and played with considerable popularity in Berlin, Hamburg, Vienna and a number of other cities in its German version (ad Hermann Hirschel) and in Hungary in a version by Jenő Faragó.

Germany: Thalia-Theater *Das Wetterhäuschen* 19 November 1896; Austria: Theater an der Wien *Das Wetterhäuschen* 23 January 1897; Hungary: Magyar Színház *Derül-borul* 10 November 1897

WEBB, Clifton [HOLLENBECK, Webb Parmalee] (b Indianapolis, 19 November 1891; d Beverly Hills, 13 October 1966). A slimly elegant juvenile man of stage and screen.

'Encouraged' by one of the most (in)famous stage mothers of history, the very presentable Webb survived years as a child-actor and an operatic aspirant and put his song-and-dance talents to use in a list of Broadway musicals. He had his first metropolitan rôle in the American production of Reinhardt's *Napoleon und die Frauen* (*The Purple Road*, 1913, Bosco), then played in several revues, appeared discreetly in the Princess Theatre productions of *Nobody Home* and *Very Good Eddie* (t/o), in *See America First* (1916, Percy) and was upped to a supporting dance-and-charm rôle in *Love o' Mike* (1917, Alonzo Bird, 'Look in the Book'). He was the juvenile gentleman in the successful *Listen Lester* (1918, Jack Griffin), played on Broadway in the revue *As You Were* (1920) and the following year in London in the revue *The Fun of the Fayre* before being cast in the title-rôle of the show that C B Cochran called *Phi-Phi* (1922).

He played and danced the rôle of the other man in Broadway's *Jack and Jill* (1923, Jimmy Eustace) and, after a loop into some non-musical pieces, returned for a similar rôle in *Sunny* (1925, Harold Wendell Wendell), introducing 'Two Little Bluebirds'. He subsequently played in *She's My Baby* (1928, Clyde Parker) and *Treasure Girl* (1928, Nat McNally, 'I've Got a Crush on You') and in a further series of Broadway revues (introducing 'Easter Parade' in *As Thousands Cheer*), and made one final Broadway musical appearance as Gaston in the revamped musical version of *Bei Kerzenlicht* (*You Never Know*) in 1938 before moving on to some elegant and often English rôles in comedy, and to Hollywood and a second successful career of some 20 years as a character actor in films. In the 1952 film *Stars and Stripes Forever* he portrayed composer John P Sousa.

Plate 287. **Lizbeth Webb** *in* Bless the Bride.

WEBB, Lizbeth (b Reading, 30 January 1926). The outstanding ingénue of the British 1950s stage.

A teenage band- and radio-vocalist, Miss Webb was hired by C B Cochran as a trainee star and put initially into the cover of the lead rôle of his production of *Big Ben* (1946). Stardom came earlier than intended, when motherhood overtook the leading lady and the very attractive young soprano succeeded to the rôle of Grace Green. She subsequently took the lead rôle of Lucy Veracity Willow in Cochran's next production, the highly successful *Bless the Bride* creating 'I Was Never Kissed Before' and 'This is My Lovely Day' with George Guétary, then starred alongside Cicely Courtneidge as the juvenile heroine of *Gay's the Word* (1949) and played Sarah Brown in London's production of *Guys and Dolls* (1953). She departed from the unfortunate *Jubilee Girl* (1956) on the road, appeared as Giulietta in the televised version of the musical *Carissima* (1959) and subsequently retired to married life as Lady Campbell. She was seen once more in the West End when she played a season as *The Merry Widow* in 1969.

Her son, **Rory [Charles Fitzgerald] Campbell** (b 17 August 1961) has appeared on the musical stage as Growltiger in *Cats* in Zurich, London and the British provinces, as Nigel in *Salad Days* in Britain and as Freddie in *My Fair Lady* and Sigismund in *Im weissen Rössl* in Switzerland.

WEBER, [Morris] Joseph (b New York, 11 August 1867; d Los Angeles, 10 May 1942). The other half of the Weber and Fields vaudeville and burlesque team.

Weber's career as a music-hall comedian was long linked with that of Lew Fields with whom he worked in a Dutch-dialect duo and alongside whom he became the manager of the celebrated Weber and Fields burlesque house and the Broadway Theater. The pair produced and appeared in a long list of burlesque/variety musical comedy pieces in which they inevitably played rôles which allowed them to perform their heavily accented Germanic low comedy.

When the partnership broke up in 1904, Fields moved on, and Weber continued to run their theatre, producing several shows on the lines of the old Weber and Fields pieces as well as Victor Herbert's *Dream City* and a burlesque of *The Merry Widow*, in which he appeared as Disch to the widow of Lulu Glaser and of Blanche Ring with considerable success. However, the best had been had from the house and its tradition and Weber soon gave up his theatre and went into independent production, mounting the play *The Climax* (1909) and an English version of Adolf Philipp's *Alma wo wohnst du?*, a slightly scandalous hit at the German-language Terrace Garten the previous year. It was a slightly scandalous hit all over again in English.

Weber joined forces with Fields again in 1912, and the pair attempted to set their old style of show going once more, but the effort was not prolonged and Weber returned to producing regular musical plays. He had a fine success with Victor Herbert's *The Only Girl*, won esteem with the same composer's Irish operetta *Eileen* and little with his *Her Regiment* (both 1917), and after an even briefer second attempt at getting *Back Again* with Fields, mounted two last musical plays. The 'gay, girly, glad musical farce' *Little Blue Devil* (1919), an adaptation of the hit German play *Der blaue Maus*, was a disappointment, and Weber hedged by producing the Efrem Zimbalist musical *Honeydew* (1920) – this one based on a French play, *Les Surprises du divorce* – on the earlier show's sets. When the piece showed up strong in try-out he built a lavish new production for it and was rewarded with a final Broadway musical success (192 performances).

As late as 1940 Weber and Fields appeared performing one of their routines in the film *Lillian Russell*.

Biography: Isman, F: *Weber and Fields* (Boni & Liveright, New York, 1924)

WEEDE, Robert (b Baltimore, 22 February 1903; d Walnut Creek, Calif, 9 July 1972).

Operatic baritone Weede made his name in broadcasting before joining the Metropolitan Opera in 1937. He performed there until 1945, but reached his widest audience when, in 1956, he made his first appearance on Broadway, creating the rôle of Tony, *The Most Happy Fella* in the title of that show ('The Most Happy Fella', 'My Heart is So Full Of You' etc). He had a second Broadway success when he paired with another operatic vocalist, Mimi Benzell, for the middle-aged romance of the Jerry Herman musical *Milk and Honey* (1961), but thereafter made only one more Broadway appearance, in the rather less successful *Cry for Us All* (1970, Edward Quinn).

WEHLEN, Emmy (b Mannheim, 1887; d unknown).

Emmy Wehlen began her career in musical theatre in Munich and Berlin before going to London to take over the title-rôle in George Edwardes's production of *The Merry Widow*. She appeared next as the gold-digging Olga in Edwardes's version of *The Dollar Princess* in London and in the British provinces, then crossed to America to star in Ivan Caryll's *Marriage à la Carte* (1910, Rosalie) and as another fairly merry widow, Mrs Guyer, in Ziegfeld's remake of *A Trip to Chinatown* as *A Winsome Widow* (1912). She took the rôle of Winifred in the German musical comedy *The Girl on the Film* both in London and then in New York, replaced Isobel Elsom as the heroine of *After the Girl* at the Gaiety Theatre and then returned to America with the British company which played *Tonight's the Night* there in 1914. Feeling her German nationality, she remained behind when the company returned to wartime Britain, and she abandoned the musical stage for the screen where she became a favourite leading lady of silent films between 1916 and 1921, appearing in such slightly daring pieces as *The Amateur Adventuress* ('the story of a girl who wanted to know the meaning of the word *life*!'), the serial *Who's Guilty?*, *Fools and Their Money* and *The Outsider* ('she determined to become an adventuress ... she succeeded beyond her wildest dreams!'). Then she vanished from showbusiness annals.

DAS WEIB IM PURPUR Operette in 3 acts by Leopold Jacobson and Rudolf Österreicher. Music by Jean Gilbert. Wiener Stadttheater, Vienna, 21 December 1923.

The 'lady in purple' is Catherine II of Russia (Margit Suchy) who affirms that royalty cannot afford to fall in love until she meets the Lieutenant Michael Michailowitz (Hubert Marischka). She courts him in disguise as the peasant Marinka, until a birthmark gives her away. The lighter moments were provided by the Austrian Ambassador Graf Aladar Gombaty (Fritz Werner) and his wife Stanzi (Olga Bartos-Treu), a happily married pair who gambolled through happy duets ('Liebling, du hast was', 'Jedes neue Jahr') whilst the Tsarina – in her disguise as 'ein strammes Bauernmädel' (a strapping peasant lass) – and her lieutenant joined together more expansively to insist 'Bleib' bei mir die heutige Nacht'.

Produced at Wiener Stadttheater, which a year earlier had been watching *Die Siegerin* rise to power at the side of Tsar Peter the Great, *Das Weib im Purpur* had a reasonable if not memorable run. The show was subsequently played in Hungary (ad Ernő Kulinyi) and a new Viennese production was mounted at the Bürgertheater in 1929 (31 October) and played for three weeks with Ida Russka in the star rôle.

What started out to be a Broadway production of *Das Weib im Purpur* was barely recognizable as such by the time it arrived in New York. If Edward Delaney Dunn and Harry B Smith's title *The Red Robe* (Shubert Theater 25 December 1928) still had a savour of the original, the savour was all. The 'red robe' referred to Cardinal Richelieu, and their story was a *Three Musketeers* wannabe. Stars Walter Woolf and Helen Gilliland performed some

of Gilbert's tunes – and some others – for 167 Broadway nights.

Hungary: Városi Színház *A bíborruhás asszony* 3 March 1927

WEIDMAN, Jerome (b New York, 4 April 1913).

After the success of his first book, *I Can Get it for You Wholesale*, at the age of 22, Weidman abandoned thoughts of a career in the law and instead authored a long list of further novels before making his first venture into the musical theatre as the co-author of the libretto for the long-running Broadway hit *Fiorello!* (1959). He teamed with Jerry Bock, Sheldon Harnick and George Abbott for a second New York costume musical in the music-hally tale of the *Tenderloin* (1960), and scored again with a stage musicalization of his maiden novel, *I Can Get it For You Wholesale* (1962). Two subsequent musicals were, however, failures – a Faustian piece called *Cool Off!*, which featured the post-*My Fair Lady* Stanley Holloway in a multiple rôle, closed out of town, and a New Orleans version of the *Blue Angel* story set to Duke Ellington music under the title *Poussé-Café*, played just three Broadway performances. On film he took a screenplay credit on *The Eddie Cantor Story*.

His son, **John WEIDMAN**, was the author of the libretto for the 1976 musical *Pacific Overtures* (music and lyrics: Stephen Sondheim, Winter Garden Theater 11 January), co-adapted the text of *Anything Goes* for its successful revival at the Vivian Beaumont Theater and in lands beyond, and supplied the text to a second Sondheim work, *Assassins* (1991).

1959 **Fiorello!** (Jerry Bock/Sheldon Harnick/w George Abbott) Broadhurst Theater 23 November
1960 **Tenderloin** (Bock/Harnick/w Abbott) 46th Street Theater 17 October
1962 **I Can Get it for You Wholesale** (Harold Rome) Shubert Theater 22 March
1964 **Cool Off!** (Howard Blankman) Forrest Theater, Philadelphia 31 March
1966 **Poussé-Café** (Duke Ellington/Marshall Barer, Fred Tobias) 46th Street Theater 18 March

WEILL, Kurt [Julian] (b Dessau, 2 March 1900; d New York, 3 April 1950). German musician who adapted his style to the American commercial and uncommercial stage with some success in a veritable two-part career.

Kurt Weill studied music in Berlin and began his professional life in the theatre as a répétiteur at Dessau and as a conductor in Ludenscheid. At the same time he made his earliest attempts at composition and in 1922 his first stage work, a children's piece called *Zaubernacht*, was produced at Berlin's Theater am Kurfürstendamm. However, he concentrated his composing efforts at this stage principally on orchestral and instrumental writing, and his first adult theatre-piece, the one-act opera *Der Protaganist*, written to a text by the celebrated playwright Georg Kaiser, was not produced until 1925. The two collaborated on another piece of similar proportions, *Der Zar lässt sich photographieren* (1928), before Weill made his first entry into the world of the musical comedy with the music for Elisabeth Hauptmann and Bertolt Brecht's purposefully harsh revision of *The Beggar's Opera*, *Die Dreigroschenoper*. He matched the tone of the show's text with a series of numbers written in tinny, jazzy contemporary tones in which there was rarely place for sentiment or grace, or for humour of any but the bitterest kind ('Seeräuber Jenny', 'Moritat', Salomon-Lied, Barbara-Lied etc) and the show found a considerable and commercial success throughout Germany, as well as a number of productions abroad.

Hauptmann, Brecht and Weill combined on a second show for the same Theater am Schiffbauerdamm in *Happy End* ('Surabaya Johnny', 'Bilbao'), but, lacking the solid dramatic structure that had been provided by Gay's durable play for their earlier success, this attempt to paste some simplistic politicizing onto a curiously naïve little story folded in chaos in just three performances leaving some fine songs orphaned. Weill returned to the opera with the little *Der Jasager* (1930), with *Aufstieg und Fall der Stadt Mahagonny*, first played in its completed state later the same year, *Die Bürgschaft* and, again with Kaiser, in his most substantial work, *Der Silbersee* (1931), before in 1933, with the rise of the Nazi party, he and his wife, Lotte Lenya, joined the mass exodus of Jewish theatrical writers and artists from Germany, ending permanently his connection with the German theatre.

The composer stopped at first in Paris, where his sung dance piece (ballet-chanté) *Die sieben Todsünden* was given its first production, and briefly visited London where his musical play *A Kingdom for a Cow*, composed to a text by Robert Vambery, dramaturg at the Schiffbauerdamm, was produced at the Savoy Theatre. Another politically orientated piece of whimsy, it folded in two weeks. Before the end of the year Weill had continued on to America.

His first work for the American stage was the score for Paul Green's musical play *Johnny Johnson*, a mildly surrealistic anti-war parable written in a Singspiel style, which was produced by the Group Theatre at Broadway's 44th Street Theater (68 performances), and his second, a collaboration with the respected playwright Maxwell Anderson on a purposefully fictional reworking of early American history, *Knickerbocker Holiday*. Although it survived rather longer than the earlier less uncompromising, and less traditionally 'commercial' *Johnny Johnson*, *Knickerbocker Holiday* did not become a Broadway success (168 performances). The show's score, however, brought forth the wistful 'September Song' which, notably as recorded by Bing Crosby, became one of Weill's most enduring show songs.

Theatrical success, which had avoided Weill since *Die Dreigroschenoper*, returned with his next Broadway piece. *Lady in the Dark* abandoned the political posturings of the previous works and took a further step towards the standard musical play or, in this case, extravaganza in a piece which included a set of 'dream sequences' in its brightly well-written text. The musical part of the show was largely contained in those dream sections, which thus took the form of extended, operatic-style musical scenas, and some of the plangent tones of Weill's first hit could be occasionally heard interbred with operatic strains and with traditional Broadway music ('My Ship', 'Jenny') in a score which was none the less attractive for being unusual and interesting. Another fantasy, *One Touch of Venus* ('Speak Low'), which moved even closer to the traditional American musical-comedy style, confirmed the success of *Lady in the Dark*, but a period piece about sculptor Benvenuto Cellini, which insisted that he was *The Firebrand of Florence*, failed in 43 performances.

In 1947 Weill composed the score for a version of Elmer Rice's successful play *Street Scene*, which was purposely announced under the description of a 'Broadway opera', in the vein of *Porgy and Bess*. Here, Weill found himself in the area which clearly suited him best and, given a substantial, dramatic and purely personal story to illustrate he produced an excitingly pictorial modern theatre-score which richly bestrode the musical and operatic idioms. If *Street Scene* was unable to encourage the kind of audiences that *Lady in the Dark* or *One Touch of Venus* had done (148 performances) it was, years later, to find itself and its level of composition in the height of fashion, and, whilst other shows of the era were forgotten, to find itself a home in the very opera houses from out of which Weill had hoped to bring this form of musical theatre.

Street Scene was succeeded by two further musicals – a whimsical panorama of *Love Life* (1948) which played an insufficient 252 Broadway performances, and an adaptation of Alan Paton's South African novel *Lost in the Stars* (1949, 273 performances), neither of which proved to have a wide appeal, and by a one-act folk opera, *Down in the Valley*, originally played at Indiana University and subsequently broadcast and televised on several occasions as well as being played professionally in a German stage version (*Drunten im Tal* Staatstheater, Karlsruhe 22 October 1960).

However, Weill's final and most resounding success in his adopted homeland was a posthumous one. Following his death during the run of *Lost in the Stars*, a new version of *Die Dreigroschenoper* – originally unsuccessful in America – was produced at off-Broadway's Theatre de Lys (1954). The production and the piece appealed to the striving anti-establishment feelings of its times much in the same way that *Hair* would do more than a decade later, and it played for more than 2,600 performances, firmly establishing the work and its songs in the English-speaking world where it has since remained by far the most popular and the most frequently produced of its composer's works.

Weill's other theatrical work included incidental music for several plays and he also composed the songs performed in the film *Where Do We Go from Here?* (w Ira Gershwin).

The composer proved his versatility in successfully matching his music to styles of lyrics and libretti as diverse as the deep, allegorical *Der Silbersee*, the comic-strip retelling of the tale of *Die Dreigroschenoper*, the wholesale fantasy of *One Touch of Venus* and the three-dimensional drama of *Street Scene*. Most of his theatrical failures came when he teamed with authors whose political and/or social preoccupations infringed unhelpfully on their theatrical ones – but it is those same political/social preoccupations which have subsequently been responsible for several of these pieces continuing to find a place on the world's stages, sometimes in preference to their composer's better and initially more successful shows.

Since the 1970s, powerfully encouraged by a foundation set up in the composer's name by his widow, Weill's music has become both hugely fashionable and seemingly more widely performed than at any time in his life. In particular, those of his show songs which were previously identified with the performance of his wife, on whose scorched-soubrette voice many of them were modelled, have become favourite meat for a 1980s–90s stream of torch-singers. These, and others of his songs, have gone into a number of concert and compilation shows, notably the 1972 *Berlin to*

Broadway with Kurt Weill (Theatre de Lys, 1 October 1972).

1928 **Die Dreigroschenoper** (Elisabeth Hauptmann, Bertolt Brecht) Theater am Schiffbauerdamm, Berlin 31 August

1929 **Happy End** (Brecht/Hauptmann [and Brecht uncredited]) Theater am Schiffbauerdamm, Berlin 2 September

1935 **A Kingdom for a Cow** (*Der Kuhhandel*) (Desmond Carter/ Robert Vambery ad Reginald Arkell) Savoy Theatre, London 28 June

1936 **Johnny Johnson** (Paul Green) 44th Street Theater, New York 19 November

1938 **Knickerbocker Holiday** (Maxwell Anderson) Barrymore Theater 19 October

1941 **Lady in the Dark** (Ira Gershwin/Moss Hart) Alvin Theater 23 January

1943 **One Touch of Venus** (Ogden Nash/S J Perelman) Imperial Theater 7 October

1945 **The Firebrand of Florence** (I Gershwin/Edwin Justus Mayer) Alvin Theater 22 March

1947 **Street Scene** (Langston Hughes/Elmer Rice) Adelphi Theater 9 January

1948 **Down in the Valley** (Arnold Sundgaard) 1 act University of Indiana 15 July

1948 **Love Life** (Alan Jay Lerner) 46th Street Theater 7 October

1949 **Lost in the Stars** (Anderson, Alan Paton) Music Box Theater 30 October

Biographies etc: Kowalke, K: *Kurt Weill in Europe* (UMI Research Press, Ann Arbor, Michigan, 1979), (ed) *A New Orpheus: Essays on Kurt Weill* (Yale University Press, New Haven, Conn, 1986), Sanders, R: *The Days Grow Short* (Holt, Rinehart & Winston, New York, 1980), Jarman, D: *Kurt Weill* (Bloomington, Ind, 1982), Drew, D: *Kurt Weill: A Handbook* (University of Berkeley, California, 1987), Schebera, J: *Kurt Weill: Eine Biographie in Texten, Bildern und Dokumenten* (Deutsche Verlag für Musik, Leipzig, 1990)

WEINBERGER, Carl [Rudolf Michael] (b Vienna, 3 April 1861; d Vienna, 1 November 1939).

Although his pieces have long dropped from the schedules, even in central Europe, Carl Weinberger's attractive dance-rhythmed scores were heard not only in Vienna, but in Germany, in Hungary, in Italy and as far afield as America, during the last decade of the 19th century and the earliest years of the 20th, and he continued to produce music for the theatre until well after the First World War. If none of his Operetten scored the kind of success which would make it last for half a century, he regularly found respectable runs and only a handful of genuine failures.

His first piece, *Pagenstreiche*, an adaptation of Kotzebue's comedy (set with rather more success in Hungary by József Konti as *A kopé*), was produced by Camillo Walzel at the Theater an der Wien when the composer was 27 years of age, and it won only a dozen performances before being withdrawn, but the second, *Die Uhlanen*, was played 34 times at the Carltheater and again at Berlin's Thomastheater (30 April 1892), whilst the third, *Lachende Erben*, won a genuine success. It followed 33 performances in Vienna with a production at Berlin's Theater Unter den Linden (15 January 1893), another at Budapest's Budai Színkör (*Nevető örökösök* 2 June 1893) and was played at New York's German-language Irving Place Theater (25 December 1893) by Jose Ferenczy's touring Operette company.

Weinberger had a further success with *Die Karls-schülerin*, played 59 times at the Theater an der Wien with

Ilka Pálmay adding not a little to its attractions in the rôle of the leading boy, and again at Budapest's Népszinház (*Hektor kisasszony* 16 May 1903), but two efforts to make an Operette out of Toché and Blum's French vaudeville *La Maison Tamponin* (Palais-Royal, 22 March 1893) were less happy: *Die Prima Ballerina* was played 25 times at the Carltheater and again at Berlin's Thalia-Theater (24 October 1896) whilst *Auch so eine!*, produced six years later at the Theater in der Josefstadt (18 October 1901), managed only 27 nights. However, with *Der Schmetterling* he found another fair success. Produced at the Theater an der Wien, with Julie Kopácsi-Karczag top-billed, it was played 57 times there and was later seen at Berlin's Theater des Westens (29 November 1906) as well as in Italy.

Die Blumen-Mary, the following year, had Ilka Pálmay playing a New York florist, Carl Blasel an American umbrella manufacturer, and a respectable Vienna run (41 performances) before crossing the border, whilst *Adam und Eva*, which featured Girardi and American divette Marie Halton in four scenes of love through the ages (Josef and Mme Putiphar, Quixote and Dulcinea etc) up to the present day, was played 52 times at the Carltheater. Annie Dirkens was *Die Diva* (the title had been unlucky for Offenbach, too) just 22 times, and Ilka Pálmay showed that she had *Das gewisse Etwas* (otherwise 'it') for 25 nights before the piece went on to Hungary (*Az izé*, Népszinház ad Jenő Heltai, Miksa Márton, 26 April 1902) where it won a distinct popularity through 31 performances.

Weinberger's name then slipped from the schedules for a number of years, but he returned to the forefront with an adaptation from Wichert called *Die romantische Frau* which was played by Vienna's *Die lustige Witwe* stars Treumann and Mizzi Günther through a run of 73 nights. However, the composer had his longest Vienna run of all when Oscar Fronz produced *Der Frechling* with Fritz Werner starred for 86 performances at the Bürgertheater. *Drei arme Teufel*, produced in Munich, subsequently came to the Bürgertheater as well (15 June 1923, 51 performances), but after this the composer contributed little more to the metropolitan musical stage, his few remaining theatre pieces being either on a small scale or for regional houses.

Weinberger's other works included an opera, *Das Sonnenkind* (1929), songs, dance music and pantomimes.

1888 **Pagenstreiche** (Hugo Wittmann) Theater an der Wien 28 April

1889 **Der Adjutaut** (A Rupprecht) 1 act Baden bei Wien 13 July; Carltheater 24 September

1890 **Angelor** (Julius Horst) 1 act Troppau 15 January

1891 **Die Uhlanen** (Wittmann) Carltheater 5 December

1892 **Lachende Erben** (Horst, Leo Stein) Carltheater 24 October

1893 **Münch(e)ner Kind** (Alexander Landesberg, Stein) Theater unter den Linden, Berlin 7 November

1895 **Die Karlsschülerin** (Wittmann) Theater an der Wien 21 March

1895 **Die Prima Ballerina** (later *Auch so eine!*) (Wittmann) Carltheater 23 November

1896 **Der Schmetterling** (A M Willner, Bernhard Buchbinder) Theater an der Wien 7 November

1897 **Die Blumen-Mary** (Landesberg, Stein) Theater an der Wien 18 November

1899 **Adam und Eva** (*Die Seelenwanderung*) (Wittmann, Julius Bauer) Carltheater 5 January

1900 **Die Wundertrank** (Horst, Benjamin Schier) 1 act Hotel Continental 17 March

1900 **Die Diva** (Buchbinder, Josef Wattke) Carltheater 12 October

1902 **Der Spatz** (Buchbinder) Deutsches Volkstheater 14 January

1902 **Das gewisse Etwas** (Victor Léon, Stein) Carltheater 15 March

1904 **Schlaraffenland** (Mathilde Schurz) Neues Deutsches Theater, Prague 27 March

1911 **Die romantische Frau** (Karl Lindau, Bela Jenbach) Johann Strauss-Theater 17 March

1912 **Der Frechling** (Fritz Grünbaum, Heinz Reichert) Wiener Bürgertheater 21 December

1914 **Die Nachtprinzessin** (Feydeau ad Weinberger) Operetten-Theater, Hamburg 4 April

1916 **Drei arme Teufel** (Rudolf Österreicher, Reichert) Theater am Gärtnerplatz, Munich 11 March

1919 **Paragraph 88** (Edmond Gondinet, P Giffard ad Richard Wilde, M Günther) Stadttheater, Zurich 28 December

1926 **Ein Nachtmanöver** (Buchbinder, M Schulz) Bolzano March

1928 **Die Liebesinsel** (Wilde, M Schulz) Baden bei Wien 27 November

1936 **Der alte Silbergulden** (Fred Angemeyer-Höft) 1 act Stadttheater 5 April

WELCH, Elisabeth (b New York, 27 February 1904). Vocalist who featured in a handful of musicals.

After an early career in supporting rôles in New York black musical comedy (*Runnin' Wild*, *The Chocolate Dandies*) and revue (*Blackbirds*), appearances in cabaret in America and Europe, and a take-over of the rôle of May in *The New Yorkers* (1931) on Broadway, Miss Welch went to Britain where she had her first engagement in a revue, *Dark Doings* (1933). She was subsequently cast as Haidée Robinson in C B Cochran's production of *Nymph Errant*, scoring a particular success with the song 'Solomon', and then as an incidental stowaway with a couple of incidental songs in Ivor Novello's first Drury Lane spectacular, *Glamorous Night* ('The Girl I Knew', 'Shanty Town'). Thereafter, the theatrical portion of her career was largely in revue, but she had another plot-incidental rôle in a Novello musical in *Arc de Triomphe* (1943, Josie, 'Dark Music') and returned to the book-musical stage to play the Soho low-life Sweet Ginger in the 1959 *The Crooked Mile* and again as the aged Berthe in London's brief run of *Pippin* (1973). She has subsequently been seen in compilation shows and in concert into the 1990s, becoming London's most popular I-can-still-do-it artist and the darling of critics and theatricals.

WELCHMAN, Harry (b Barnstaple, 24 February 1886; d London, 3 January 1966). Handsome baritone who became the epitomic operetta leading man for several decades of London shows.

Welchman was first employed by Ada Reeve, at the age of 18, for the chorus of her touring musical *Winnie Brooke, Widow*, and he toured the British provinces in several musicals and plays before making his first appearance in London in a non-musical play. He entered London's musical theatre as understudy to Hayden Coffin in Edward German's *Tom Jones* and, after he had toured the piece in the title-rôle, producer Courtneidge subsequently cast him

between 1909 and the War in the baritone hero rôles of *The Arcadians* (Jack Meadows, 'Half Past Two', 'Charming Weather'), *The Mousmé* (Captain Fujiwara), *Princess Caprice* (Augustin Hofer), *Oh! Oh! Delphine* (Victor Jolibeau), *The Pearl Girl* (Duke of Trent) and *The Cinema Star* (Victor de Brett). He continued to play staunchly singing heros, after the war starring opposite Alice Delysia as Don Juan jr in C B Cochran's production of the saucy *Afgar* (1919), in the feather-light *Oh! Julie* with Ethel Levey (1920), as the Grand Duke Constantine to the *Sybil* of José Collins (1921), as Colonel Belacour to *The Lady of the Rose* of Phyllis Dare (1922) and as Bonni to her *The Street Singer* (1924) – four and a half long-running hits in five successive productions.

That average was soon to be spoiled, for Welchman nurtured a continual determination to present himself in a romantic operetta, and over the years he turned down fine London rôles as he tried to set up a series of invariably awful pieces under his own steam. *Love's Prisoner* (1925) was the first of these to get to London, but not for long. An attempt in a musical comedy with *The Bamboula* (1925, Jimmy Roberts) did only a little better before he switched back to other folks' romantic operettas. He appeared on Broadway as Rudolf Rassendyl in the musical version of *The Prisoner of Zenda* (*Princess Flavia*, 1925), a rôle and a show which had actually been written for Walter Woolf, toured Britain as Karl-Franz in *The Student Prince*, and then starred at Drury Lane in *The Desert Song* (1927, Pierre) and, replacing the original Howett Worster, in *The New Moon* (t/o Robert Misson). In between, however, he had another go at actor-management with the ineffectual *The White Camellia* (1929).

Welchman starred in Jack Waller's spectacular *Silver Wings* (Pablo Santos, 1930), toured in *Nina Rosa* and appeared as both leading men – in turn – in London's version of *Viktória* (Victoria and Her Hussar). He toured again as *Casanova*, found other weak vehicles as *Beau Brummell* (1933) and as the hero of the touring *Hearts Are Trumps* (1935), returned to London as the star of reprises of *The Desert Song* and *The Vagabond King* and toured in similar vehicles (*The Student Prince*, *The Maid of the Mountains*, *Chu Chin Chow*) through the later 1930s and early 1940s.

In 1944 he was seen in London as Macheath in *The Beggar's Opera*, but thereafter his musical appearances were in character rôles, and his remaining London shows, *Lucky Boy* (1953) and *The World of Paul Slickey* (1959) were both unmitigated failures.

Welchman appeared on film alongside Nancy Brown as Baldasarre in the 1932 film of *The Maid of the Mountains* and opposite Bebe Daniels as Francesco del Fuego in the 1933 *A Southern Maid*. In 1946 he appeared in the film version of *The Lisbon Story*.

WELISCH, Ernst (b Vienna, 27 February 1875; d Vienna, 26 March 1941).

Playwright, longtime dramaturg at the Berliner Theater and stage director, Welisch made an early venture into the musical theatre with the libretto for the young Leo Fall's first Operette *Der Rebell* (1905). The show was a quick flop, but Welisch had a hand in its subsequent rewriting as *Der liebe Augustin*, providing him with a success which he followed up with a series-of major Operetten written over a period of some 20 years with co-author Rudolf Schanzer and with some of the era's most important composers: Fall, Straus, Jean Gilbert, Kálmán and Ralph Benatzky.

His first significant hit after *Der liebe Augustin* was the Jean Gilbert Operette *Die Frau im Hermelin*, a romantic costume piece which, after a good Berlin run, became one of London's longest-running hits of the 1920s, and, following the respectable showings of the parallel Berlin runs of *Der Geiger von Lugano* (162 performances) and *Die spanische Nachtigall* with Fritzi Massary in its title-rôle (143 performances) and the nearly five months of *Die Braut des Lucullus* at the Theater des Westens, he saw his name attached to another major international hit, this time alongside the music of Leo Fall, with the comical tale of the putative love life of *Madame Pompadour*.

There were further Berlin successes with Straus on *Riquette* and the Napoleonic tale of *Teresina* and with Benatzky on the spectaculars *Casanova* and *Die drei Musketiere* (which, nevertheless, drew less-than-favourable mentions for its text), whilst Fall's *Der süsse Kavalier*, with a flashback libretto that took in the Chevalier d'Éon and the Queen of England, Gilbert's *Spiel um die Liebe*, produced at Berlin's Theater des Westens and Vienna's Stadttheater in 1925–6, and Krasznay-Krausz's *Eine Frau von Format* all had at least respectable careers in central Europe. Kálmán's *Der Teufelsreiter*, played 148 times at the Theater an der Wien after Welisch had left Berlin to return to his native city in the early 1930s, also did well in its initial showing.

1905 **Der Rebell** (Leo Fall/w Rudolf Bernauer) Theater an der Wien, Vienna 29 November

1912 **Der liebe Augustin** revised *Der Rebell* Neues Theater 3 February

1914 **Jung England** (Fall/w Bernauer) Montis Operetten-Theater 14 February

1919 **Die Frau im Hermelin** (Jean Gilbert/w Rudolf Schanzer) Theater des Westens 23 August

1920 **Frau Ministerpräsident** (Fall/w Bernauer) Residenztheater, Dresden 3 February

1920 **Der Geiger von Lugano** (Gilbert/w Schanzer) Wallner-Theater 25 September

1920 **Die spanische Nachtigall** (Fall/w Schanzer) Berliner Theater 18 November

1921 **Die Braut des Lucullus** (Gilbert/w Schanzer) Theater des Westens 26 August

1922 **Madame Pompadour** (Fall/w Schanzer) Berliner Theater 9 September

1923 **Der süsse Kavalier** (Fall/w Schanzer) Apollotheater, Vienna 11 December

1925 **Riquette** (Oscar Straus/w Schanzer) Deutsches Künstlertheater 17 January

1925 **Das Spiel um die Liebe** (Gilbert/w Schanzer) Theater des Westens 18 December

1926 **Teresina** (Straus/w Schanzer) Deutsches Künstlertheater 11 September

1927 **Eine Frau von Format** (Michael Krasznay-Krausz/w Schanzer) Theater des Westens 22 September

1928 **Casanova** (Johann Strauss arr Ralph Benatzky/w Schanzer) Grosses Schauspielhaus 1 September

1929 **Die drei Musketiere** (Benatzky/w Schanzer) Grosses Schauspielhaus 31 August

1929 **Die erste Beste** (Straus/w Schanzer) Deutsches Theater, Prague 19 October

1930 **Das Mädel am Steuer** (Gilbert/w Schanzer) Komische Oper 17 September

1932 **Der Teufelsreiter** (Emmerich Kálmán/w Schanzer) Theater an der Wien, Vienna 10 March

1932 **Der Studentenprinz** (*The Student Prince*) German version w Schanzer (Grosses Schauspielhaus)

1933 **Die Lindenwirtin** (Krasznay-Krausz/w Schanzer) Metropoltheater 30 March

1935 **Maya** German version w Schanzer (Theater an der Wien, Vienna)

1936 **Dreimal Georges** (Paul Burkhard/w Schanzer) Stadttheater, Zurich 3 October

1939 **Die Sacher-Pepi** (Rudi Gfaller) Operetten-Theater, Leipzig 16 September

1941 **Venedig in Wien** (Gfaller) Centraltheater, Chemnitz 29 March

WELLEMINSKY, I[gnaz] M[ichael] (b Prague, 7 December 1882; d Luschetz, 11 December 1941). Librettist to the German stage between the wars.

Originally involved principally in the operatic world, where he found some success as the co-librettist (w Bruno Hardt-Warden) of such pieces as Brandt-Buys's *Glockenspiel* (1912) and *Der Schneider von Schönau* (1916), and of Max Oberleithner's *Der eiserne Heiland* (1917), *La Vallière* (1918) and *Cäcilie* (1920), Welleminsky authored his first Operette script in 1915. By the time it reached the stage, it was in an Hungarian version, set by the violinist and composer Ludwig Gruber as *A főnyeremény-kisasszony*, but the piece and its 'jackpot girl' were later seen in Hamburg in the original German. In 1920, he wrote, in tandem with the composer, the libretto to Ralph Benatzky's Operette *Apachen*, and although he subsequently wrote several further opera texts both with Hardt-Warden (Dahn's *Fredegundis*, Brandt-Buys's *Carnevals Ende*) and with Oskar Ritter (an adaptation of *Der Schelm von Bergen* as *Fanal* for Kurt Atterberg), Welleminsky was from then on more prominent in the Operette world, where he developed a profitable partnership with author-composer Paul Knepler. Their *Die Glocken von Paris* played for over two months at the Carltheater, and they had an international hit with their new libretto and lyrics to an arranged version of Carl Millöcker's *Gräfin Dubarry* which, as *Die Dubarry*, followed Berlin success with a worldwide career. They subsequently found further success when they adapted the filmscript *Zwei Herzen im Dreivierteltakt* to the Operette stage and provided Eduard Künneke with the backstage libretto for his *Die lockende Flamme*.

1915 **A főnyeremény-kisasszony** (Ludwig Gruber/w Hardt-Warden ad Zsigmond Rajna) Pressburg, March; Hamburg 9 November 1920

1917 **Tavasz és szerelem** (*Liebe und Lenz*) (Heinrich Berté) Hungarian version Városi Színház 15 September; German version w Hardt-Warden Hamburg 1918

1920 **Apachen** (Ralph Benatzky/w Benatzky) Apollotheater, Vienna 20 December

1921 **A korhely gróf** (Gruber/w Hardt-Warden ad László Fodor) Budai Színkör, Budapest 18 June

1924 **Wenn der Hollunder blüht** (Paul Knepler/w Knepler) Bundestheater (Metropoltheater) 1 July

1927 **Die Glocken von Paris** (Richard Fall/w Knepler) Carltheater, Vienna 14 October

1929 **Die Liebesinsel** (Hans Pero/w Hardt-Warden) Stadttheater, Hamburg 12 March

1931 **Die Dubarry** (Carl Millöcker arr Mackeben/w Knepler) Admiralspalast, Berlin 14 August

1932 **Heirat aus Liebe** (Ernst Deloe/w Oskar Ritter) Stadttheater, Krefeld 5 November

1932 **Tanz durchs Leben** (R Düringer/w Paul Knepler) Stadt-theater, Danzig 13 November

1933 **Zwei Herzen in dreivierteltakt** (*Der verlorene Walzer*) (Robert Stolz/w Knepler) Opernhaus, Zurich 30 September

1933 **Die lockende Flamme** (Eduard Künneke/w Knepler) Theater des Westens, Berlin 25 December

1938 **Die Dubarry** revised version w Martin Cremer (Städtische Bühnen, Breslau)

WENN DIE KLEINEN VEILCHEN BLÜHEN Sing-spiel in 6 scenes by Bruno Hardt-Warden based on *Als ich noch in Flügelkleide* by Albert Kehm and Martin Frehsee. Music by Robert Stolz. Princess Theatre, The Hague, 1 April 1932.

Father Katzensteg (Fritz Hirsch) and his wife Auguste (Elly Krasser) reminisce in three scenes over a little incident that occurred when Frau Katzensteg was a maid-servant in the school run by Frau Gutbier years before. The headmistress's nephew Paul (Paul Harden) disguised himself as a new teacher and got inside the school to claim a kiss from his sweetheart, Liesl (Friedl Dotza), and boys and girls ended up having a champagne party together before being caught. Back in the present (the two scenes which top and tail the show), the Katzenstegs' daughter uses this tiny tale to force the now lofty Paul to let her wed his son. The sixth scene was a ballet.

The songs of this good-old-days piece (set at the turn of the century) were in the good-old-days mode, with such pieces as the scene-setting 'In Bacharach am Rhein', the praises of earlier years ('Servus, du gute alte Zeit'), and the student song 'Ich hab' gern ein Mädel' all getting several repeats throughout the evening. The young folk had some pretty, very light and less-plugged songs – schoolgirl Trude gave out the title number, and Liesl joined in duo with her Paul in 'Du, du, du, schliess' deine Augen zu', whilst Auguste and Katzen-steg peeped in Trude's juvenile diary with wonderment in 'Kleine Fee, süsse Fee'.

Produced at the Hague, *Wenn die kleinen Veilchen blühen* went neither to Vienna nor to Berlin, but it turned up later the same year in London, its puffball of a story adapted by Reginald Purdell, Desmond Carter and director Hassard Short ('entire production, including scenic and lighting effects devised and staged by') as a vast, spectacular musi-cal show for the Theatre Royal, Drury Lane. The six scenes had evolved into 15 – now set in picturesque Switzerland with its opportunities for snow and skating scenes rather than homely Bacharach-am-Rhein – there was a chorus of 55 including a half-dozen Albertina Rasch dancers and the cast was headed by Jerry Verno (Katzen), Charlotte Greenwood (Augusta), John Garrick (Paul), Adele Dixon (Liesl), Esmond Knight (Otto) and Jean Cadell (Mme Hoffmann). 'You, Just You' (recorded by no less than Heddle Nash) and 'Don't Say Goodbye' became popular singles as *Wild Violets* ran through 291 perform-ances, giving Stolz his longest West End run, before going on the road. It was later revived, at the Stoll Theatre by Prince Littler (February 1950) with a cast including Ian Carmichael (Otto), Verno (Katzen), Stella Moray (Augusta) and Doreen Duke (Liesl), for a brief season.

Plate 288. **Wenn die kleinen Veilchen blühen:** *Robert Stolz's Operette became a large-scale spectacular on the London stage, with a skating scene being featured amongst the extras.*

Wild Violets also appeared in Australia where 'the great revolving stage' manipulated by director Frederick Blackman was billed larger than Marie La Varre (Auguste), Cecil Kellaway (Algernon), Dorothy Dunkley (Mme Hoffman) and juveniles Lloyd Lamble, Phillia Dickinson and Diana du Cane.

It was also played in America, at St Louis, with Guy Robertson (Paul), Wilbur Evans (Otto), Violet Carlson (Auguste) and George Meader (Hans) without inspiring a New York showing. A tardy French-language première (ad Marc-Cab, André Hornez), based on the normal-sized original rather than the big British version, was seen at Liège in 1973.

UK: Theatre Royal, Drury Lane *Wild Violets* 31 October 1932; Australia: Her Majesty's Theatre, Melbourne *Wild Violets* 26 December 1936; USA: Municipal Opera, St Louis *Wild Violets* 23 August 1937

Recordings: selection (Eurodisc), selection in French (part-record) (TLP)

WENN LIEBE ERWACHT Operette in 3 acts by Hermann Haller based on *Renaissance* by Franz von Schönthan and Franz Koppel-Ellfeld. Lyrics by Rideamus. Music by Eduard Künneke. Theater am Nollendorfplatz, Berlin, 3 September 1920.

One of the run of successful Berlin musicals from the Haller-Künneke combination, *Wenn Liebe erwacht* had a fine run of 218 performances on its original production, but it did not prove to have the same travelling or staying-power as its more attractive companion, *Der Vetter aus Dingsda*.

The show's story, set in 19th-century Italy, centred on the reclusive and religious Countess Francesca da Costa (Lori Leux) who brings up her son, Tonio (Grete Freund), away from worldly things, under the tutelage of the well-named Dr Pedantius (Carl Geppert) and the more friendly Chaplain Philippo (Gottfried Huppertz). The household is upset when the painter Lorenzo (Erik Wirl) comes to decorate and obliges with a fresco depicting Venus and Bacchus. By the time Francesca has agreed to pose for the painter as the face of Venus, reclusion and religion have altogether taken a back seat and her son has, at the same time, learned about kissing and so forth from the apprentice artist, Marietta (Agni Wilke).

In Künneke's accompanying score, Francesca had the main waltz number of the evening, 'Es war ein Traum', Marietta shared the soubrette moments ('Komm' her, du süsser Lummerl') with the second soubrette, Nella (Claire Waldoff), and Philippo had the religious but pro-sexual pieces ('Ein Zauber ist ...').

The Operette reached its 200th night at the Theater am Nollendorfplatz on 22 March and closed on 12 April, before going on to productions throughout Germany but, like most of the rest of Künneke's shows, found few takers abroad. It did, however, find one in Britain where *Love's Awakening* (ad Adrian Ross) was produced at the Empire Theatre by Edward Laurillard. Juliette Autran and Harry Brindle, from the world of opera, were cast in the leading rôles with musical-comedy players Amy Augarde, Vera Pearce, Billy Leonard, Marjorie Gordon and Betty Chester in support for an unsuccessful 37 performances.

UK: Empire Theatre *Love's Awakening* 19 April 1921

WENRICH, Percy (b Joplin, Mo, 23 January 1880; d New York, 17 March 1952). Hit songwriter who rarely hit it in the theatre.

A popular music pianist from an early age, then for 15 years in an act with his wife, Dorothy Connolly, Wenrich doubled his night-club and vaudeville performing with a career as a songwriter which produced a considerable list of hit songs including 'Red Rose Rag', 'Silver Bell', 'On Moonlight Bay', 'Goodbye Summer, So Long Fall, Hello Wintertime' (ly: Edward Madden), 'Put on Your Old, Gray Bonnet' (Stanley Murphy), 'When You Wore a Tulip' (Jack Mahoney), 'By the Campfire' (Mabel Girling), 'The Shores of Minnetonka' (Gus Kahn) and 'Sail Along Silvery Moon' (Harry Tobias).

He made his entry into the musical theatre with some replacement songs for female impersonator Julian Eltinge's touring *The Fascinating Widow* (1912) and thereafter he contributed songs to Eltinge's later *The Crinoline Girl* (1914) and *Cousin Lucy* (1915) and to a number of revues (*Everything*, *The Greenwich Village Follies*, *Some Party* etc) before going into partnership with writer Raymond Peck, with whom he turned out four musical plays. Of the first three, two died on the road and one after a single week on Broadway, but number four, *Castles in the Air*, became a major hit when produced in Chicago, ran up exceptional stays in several centres and finally gave the composer his one Broadway success. A revue, *Who Cares?* (1930), lasted a month at Broadway's 46th Street Theater and marked the end of Wenrich's curiously unproductive Broadway career.

1914 **The Crinoline Girl** (Julian Eltinge/Otto Hauerbach) Knickerbocker Theater 16 March
1916 **The Bride Tamer** (Edgar Allan Woolf) 1 act Colonial Theater 12 June
1920 **Maid to Love** (Raymond Peck) Academy of Music, Baltimore 31 May
1921 **The Right Girl** (Peck) Times Square Theater 15 March
1922 **And Very Nice Too** (Peck) His Majesty's Theater, Montreal May 9
1925 **Castles in the Air** (Peck) Olympic Theater, Chicago, 22 November; Selwyn Theater, New York 6 September

WENZEL, Leopold (b Naples, 31 January 1847; d Asnières, August 1925).

Educated from the age of nine at the Naples Conservatoire of San Pietro Majella, Wenzel was obliged to leave school after four years when his mother died and he made his living thereafter as a violinist. He wandered around musical Africa, Asia and Europe and, in 1865, arrived in Marseille having – so it is said – hitched a ride from Cyprus with a friendly sea-captain. By 1870 he was working as chef d'orchestre at the Alcazar in Marseille. He subsequently became a naturalized Frenchman, moved to Paris and was engaged as musical director of the Alcazar there. During this period he wrote a large amount of ballet music, notably an 1884 piece, *La Cour d'amour*, for the Théâtre de l'Éden which, lavishly staged, was played some 400 times in spite of indifferent reviews, and a couple of short opérettes for the Alcazar.

In the same year that *La Cour d'amour* brought him good fortune, Wenzel's first full-scale opérette, *Le Chevalier Mignon*, was produced at the Bouffes-Parisiens with a cast headed by Edouard Maugé, Marie Grisier-Montbazon, Marguerite Deval and Paola Marié. It played an indifferent

38 performances. However, with his second such piece, *Le Dragon de la reine*, he did very much better. Produced at Brussels and then, less memorably, in Paris (36 performances), it went on to be played as *Die Dragoner der Königin* at the Viktoria-Theater, Berlin, in the British provinces as *The Young Recruit* and in Budapest as *Kiralyné dragonyosa*.

Soon after the show's production Wenzel left France for London to take up the post of musical director at the Empire Theatre. He retained that position from 1889 to 1894, during which time he composed ten ballets for the London house (Katti Lanner's *Brighton* was exported back to Paris and played at the Olympia) whilst also contributing individual songs to several West End musicals (*Cinder-Ellen Up-too-Late*, *Manola* etc) and the score for one further Parisian musical show, a vehicle for the favourite soubrette Mily-Meyer as *L'Élève de Conservatoire*, produced at the Menus-Plaisirs in 1894.

Wenzel remained in Britain, where he subsequently worked for George Edwardes as conductor and occasional songwriter at Daly's Theatre on *An Artist's Model* (1896) and *The Geisha* (1896), at the Gaiety in 1903 on *The Orchid* ('Le Promenade des Anglais') and in 1911 as the original musical director of *Peggy* and of *The Sunshine Girl* (1911–12). He returned to France in his later years.

1875 **Le Neveu du colonel** (w C Wansinck/Paul Burani) 1 act Alcazar 30 September
1876 **Une nuit à Skyros** (de Voisin) 1 act Alcazar 28 October
1884 **Le Chevalier Mignon** (Clairville ad Charles Clairville, Ernest Depré) Théâtre des Bouffes-Parisiens 23 October
1888 **Le Dragon de la reine** (Pierre Decourcelle, Frantz Beauvallet) Théâtre de l'Alhambra, Brussels, 25 March; Théâtre de la Gaîté, Paris 31 May
1894 **L'Élève de Conservatoire** (Burani, Henri Kéroul) Théâtre des Menus-Plaisirs 29 November

WEST, Moritz [NITZELBERGER, Moritz Georg] (b 1840; d Aigenschlägel, Upper Austria, 15 July 1904).

In more than 25 years as a librettist/lyricist in the musical theatre, Moritz West contributed to the authorship of a number of the most successful Operetten of his time. He began an early association with the composer Carl Zeller in the 1870s and, if their first collaboration, *Joconde*, had an indifferent Viennese life (20 performances), the pair progressed together through the two versions of *Die Carbonari* (later played in Germany and America as *Capitän Nicol*), to the more successful *Der Vagabund* and finally to their most important works, *Der Vogelhändler* and *Der Obersteiger*, and to Zeller's last, posthumously-produced *Der Kellermeister*.

West also worked, in the early part of his career, with both members of Vienna's most famous libretto-manufacturing team, Richard Genée and 'F Zell' (Camillo Walzel). The three collaborated on the Operette *Nisida*, whilst West and Genée provided the comical libretto, set by Suppé, for Franz Steiner's production of *Die Afrikareise*. West subsequently provided Suppé with a second text, the almost-operatic tale of the Swedish poet *Bellman*, written with the collaborator with whom he would go on to his biggest successes, the playwright and librettist Ludwig Held. It was, however, West's last work, written in the year before his death in collaboration with Ignaz Schnitzer, the librettist of *Der Zigeunerbaron*, which gave him his most important success apart from *Der Vogelhändler*. *Bruder Straubinger*, which launched the young Edmund Eysler as an Operette composer, brought to a close a particularly consistent and successful career on a particularly high note.

1876 **Joconde** (Karl Zeller/w Moret) Theater an der Wien 18 March
1880 **Nisida** (Richard Genée/w F Zell) Carltheater 9 October
1880 **Die Carbonari** (Zeller/w Zell) Carltheater 27 November
1881 **Capitän Nicol** revised *Die Carbonari* w Hermann Hirschel Friedrich-Wilhelmstädtisches Theater, Berlin 5 November
1883 **Die Afrikareise** (Franz von Suppé/w Genée) Theater an der Wien 17 March
1886 **Der Vagabund** (Zeller/w Ludwig Held) Carltheater 30 October
1887 **Bellman** (Suppé/w Held) Theater an der Wien 26 February
1891 **Der Vogelhändler** (Zeller/w Held) Theater an der Wien 10 January
1891 **Polnische Wirtschaft** (Hermann Zumpe/w Genée) Friedrich-Wilhelmstädtisches Theater, Berlin 26 November
1891 **Die Kosakin** (*La Cosaque*) German version w new score by Brandl (Theater an der Wien)
1894 **Der Obersteiger** (Zeller/w Held) Theater in der Wien 5 January
1897 **Die Schwalben** (Leo Held/w Held) Theater an der Wien 12 February
1901 **Der Kellermeister** (Zeller) Raimundtheater 21 December
1903 **Bruder Straubinger** (Edmund Eysler/w Ignaz Schnitzer) Theater an der Wien 20 February

WESTON R[obert] P[atrick] (b London, 7 March 1878; d London, 6 November 1936).

Songwriter, lyricist, author and adapter, Weston had several song hits to his credit ('What a Mouth', 'I'm Henery the Eighth' w Fred Murray, 'When Father Papered the Parlour' w F J Barnes, 'I've Got Rings on My Fingers' w Barnes, Maurice Scott, 'Sister Susie's Sewing Shirts for Soldiers' w Herman Darewski) before he teamed with Bert Lee to write a long list of hit songs, monologues and, variously, texts and/or songs for an extensive series of often highly successful musical plays.

1924 **Mr Tickle MP** (various/w Lee) Grand Theatre, Blackpool 29 September
1926 **King Rags** (Harry Lee/w Lee) Empire Theatre, Leeds 23 August
1927 **The Girl Friend** English adaptation of the libretto *Kitty's Kisses* w Lee (Palace Theatre)
1928 **Billy Blue** (w Joseph A Tunbridge, Fred Elkin, Lee/Harold Dyne) Empire Theatre, Newcastle 6 August
1928 **Virginia** (Waller, Tunbridge/w Furber, Lee/Clayton, Waller) Palace Theatre 24 October
1928 **Lucky Girl** (Phil Charig/w Douglas Furber, Lee) Shaftesbury Theatre 14 November
1929 **Merry, Merry** English adaptation and new lyrics w Lee (Carlton Theatre)
1929 **Hold Everything!** English adaptation w Lee (Palace Theatre)
1929 **Here Comes the Bride** (Arthur Schwartz/Desmond Carter, Howard Dietz/w Lee) Piccadilly Theatre 20 February 1930
1930 **Sons o' Guns** English lyrics w Lee (London Hippodrome)
1930 **Little Tommy Tucker** (Vivian Ellis/w Desmond Carter, Caswell Garth, Lee) Daly's Theatre 19 November
1932 **Tell Her the Truth** (Waller, Joseph Tunbridge/w Lee) Saville Theatre 14 June
1933 **He Wanted Adventure** (Waller, Tunbridge/w Clifford Grey, Lee/w Lee) Saville Theatre 28 May

1933 **Give Me a Ring** (Martin Broones/Graham John/w Guy Bolton, Lee) London Hippodrome 22 June

1934 **Yes, Madam?** (Waller, Tunbridge/w K Browne/w Lee) London Hippodrome 27 September

1935 **Please, Teacher!** (Waller, Tunbridge/w Browne, Lee) London Hippodrome 2 October

1936 **Certainly, Sir!** (Waller, Tunbridge/w Lee) London Hippodrome 17 September

WEST SIDE STORY Musical in 2 acts by Arthur Laurents. Lyrics by Stephen Sondheim. Music by Leonard Bernstein. Winter Garden Theater, New York, 26 September 1957.

Loosely based on the outlines of Shakespeare's *Romeo and Juliet* and set in the urban slums of New York, *West Side Story* used for its modern equivalents of Montagues and Capulets the juvenile gangs of local whites and immigrant Puerto Ricans, battling with a deadly childish seriousness over the streets that they claim as their 'territories'. The Romeo of the tale is Tony (Larry Kert), once the leader of the white group who call themselves the 'Jets', but now in a regular job and on his way to adulthood. It is when he allows himself to be dragged back to help the gang by its new young leader, Riff (Mickey Calin), that he meets his Juliet in the person of Maria (Carol Lawrence), sister of Bernardo (Ken LeRoy), the leader of the rival 'Sharks' gang. Their games turn to tragedy when Bernardo provokes a knife-fight, kills Riff, and is then murdered himself by the revenging Tony. Maria prepares to flee the city with Tony, but when Bernardo's girl, Anita (Chita Rivera), tries to help their rendezvous, she is nastily manhandled by the Jet boys, and in revenge tells them that Maria has been shot dead by Chino, the Puerto Rican man Bernardo had intended her to marry. Wild with grief, Tony runs from his hiding place into the streets and is shot down by the marauding Chino. As the play ends, Jets and Sharks join together as they follow Maria behind the corpse of the third victim of their immature foolishness.

The idea of developing the *Romeo and Juliet* theme in such a young, modern and American setting had first been mooted by director/choreographer Jerome Robbins some eight years earlier. Laurents and Bernstein had taken the first steps to following the idea up (at one stage, the working title was *East Side Story* and the conflict was a Jewish-Catholic one), but other projects had intervened. When it was taken up again, the same three collaborators were still involved but a fourth, the young lyricist Stephen Sondheim, joined the team to provide the words which Bernstein had originally intended to supply himself.

Bernstein gave the show a score that was not quite like any other. Whilst there were conventional love songs for Tony and Maria, and comic numbers of varying degrees, the show also included some of the vocal ensemble work already seen to such advantage in the composer's *Candide* and, most particularly, a large body of the substantial dance music, both orchestral and sung, at which he excelled and which the staging concept of director Robbins called for. If it was the love songs — Tony's hymn to 'Maria', Maria's joyously simple declaration that 'I Feel Pretty', their rapturously innocent looking-forward to their meeting 'Tonight', sung in the show over the fateful bragging of the two gangs and over Anita's less innocent thoughts, and the wishful 'Somewhere' — which proved the hit songs outside the show itself, it was the ensemble work and the dance music which gave the show its character and its climaxes.

The boy members of the Jets, dancing their way with finger-clicking energy through their Jets' Song, edgily on their toes through their captain's instructions to stay 'Cool' and facing up to their 'enemy' in the choreographed 'rumble' which turns to fatality; Anita and her friends dancing with saucy abandon to their praise of the way of life in

Plate 289. **West Side Story**. *Tony (Larry Kert), shot down by Chino, dies cradled in the arms of Maria (Carol Lawrence), as the children of the rival street gangs see their games produce one more fatality.*

'America', and the dance-hall scene which moved from a whirling contest in dance between Jets and Sharks to a dreamy slow-motion for the lovers' first meeting, worked the first act up to its climax in a dynamic display of ever-increasing energy. In the second act, with the reality of two deaths hanging over the children, the hectic, youthful tempo of the show takes a pull as the drama rises to its musical climax in the duet scene between Maria and Anita ('A Boy Like That'/'I Have a Love') before moving on to its last fatal pages.

Mounted with a young cast of dancer-actors, who were directed and choreographed by Robbins to enormous effect, Harold Prince and Robert Griffith's production of *West Side Story* had a fine 732-performance run on Broadway before going on the road. It had, in the meanwhile, opened in London, but not without some difficulty. Though there was no quarrel about the quality of the piece, there seemed some difficulty in finding a producer interested in mounting a West End musical with three deaths in it. Finally Bernstein's publisher, Louis Dreyfus of Chappell & Co, himself put up the money to stage the show and hired H M Tennent Ltd to manage it. His faith in his composer was more than justified. With a cast of young Americans headed by Marlys Watters (Maria), Don McKay (Tony), George Chakiris (Riff) and Miss Rivera and LeRoy of the original cast, the show created rather more of a sensation in London than it had in New York, and the result was a run of 1,039 performances. The same initial resistance was found in Australia, where the country's principal producer of musicals, J C Williamson Ltd, would not take the show on and Garnet Carroll mounted it in 1960 with a cast headed by Wendy Waring (Maria), Bob Kole (Tony), Rita Tanon (Anita) and Ben Vargas (Bernardo). It managed only three months in Melbourne, however, prior to a season in Sydney (Tivoli, 8 February 1961).

The New York production returned to Broadway after its initial tour and played another 249 performances at the Winter Garden Theater, and a further American company was sent out to Europe, but the seal was set on the celebrity of *West Side Story* when the film version of 1961 began its travels. Robbins and Robert Wise's transfer of the show to the screen worked dazzlingly, and Richard Beymer (Tony), Natalie Wood (dubbed by Marni Nixon, Maria), Rita Moreno (dubbed by Betty Wand, Anita), George Chakiris (Bernardo) and Russ Tamblyn (Riff) took *West Side Story* and its songs to a new and very wide audience.

New York saw *West Side Story* again in 1968 when, now accepted as a classic, it was produced at the State Theater (24 June) with Kurt Peterson and Victoria Mallory featured, and in 1980 when the original staging was reproduced for a production at the Minskoff Theater (14 February), whilst London saw a small-budget version brought from the Collegiate Theatre to the Shaftesbury in 1974 (19 December) before it welcomed back the original staging in 1984 (Her Majesty's Theatre 16 May) with Stephen Pacey and Jan Hartley in the leading rôles for a run of 589 performances. Australia saw a full-scale revival in 1983 (Her Majesty's Theatre, Sydney 19 May).

Outside English-speaking areas, the piece has had a slightly curious career. Although *West Side Story* is one of the most appreciated of all Broadway musicals in the Europe of the 1990s, and constantly on display throughout the Continent, the majority of its performances there seem to have been in English. A German-language version (ad Marcel Prawy) was produced at the Vienna Volksoper in 1968 and an Hungarian (ad Zoltán Jékely, István Remyi Gyenes) one appeared the following year – neither of which attempted to translate the title – but the continuing presence of *West Side Story* on Continental stages has been assured by companies playing one- or few-night stands in English, and suggesting in their advertising with more or with (much) less accuracy that they have something to do with Broadway and/or the original staging.

UK: Her Majesty's Theatre 12 December 1958; Australia: Princess Theatre, Melbourne 29 October 1960; France: Alhambra (Eng) 30 March 1961; Austria: Volksoper 25 February 1968; Hungary: Parkszínpad 3 July 1969, Fővárosi Operettszinház 27 September 1969; Film: Mirisch/United Artists 1961

Recordings: original cast (Columbia), Austrian cast (CBS), Japanese cast (Toshiba), Australian revival cast (K-Tel), film soundtrack (Columbia), complete (DGG) etc

WHAT MAKES SAMMY RUN? Musical in 2 acts by Budd and Stuart Schulberg based on the book of the same title by Budd Schulberg. Music and lyrics by Ervin Drake. 54th Street Theater, New York, 27 February 1964.

Another in the run of the 'how to succeed in business by stepping on other folk's faces' musical shows, *What Makes Sammy Run?*, based on a 1941 novel about 1930s filmland, followed two seasons behind the similarly flavoured *I Can Get it for You Wholesale*. The tunnel-visioned hero of the show was Sammy Glick (Steve Lawrence) who bluffs, plagiarizes and threatens his way up via the newpaper industry into a place in Hollywood, uses producer Sidney Fineman (Arny Freeman), fellow writers Kit Sargent (Sally Ann Howes), Julian Blumberg (George Coe) and Al Manheim (Robert Alda) and anyone else available to his own ends and weds the tarty daughter (Bernice Massi) of the studio boss on his way to almost the top. Fineman is dead, Kit, Julian and Al departed, and his wife faithless when we leave Sammy with one more step to run up, all on his own.

Nightclub and recording star Lawrence won plenty of radio play for the seductive 'A Room Without Windows' and his hymn to back-stabbing Hollywood as 'My Hometown', and the show ran longer (540 performances) than its predecessor had done although, like it, to insufficient audiences.

Recording: original cast (Columbia)

WHEELER, Hugh [Callingham] (b Northwood, Mddx, 19 March 1912; d Pittsfield, Mass, 26 July 1987).

At first a writer of detective fiction under the noms de plume of Patrick Quentin and Q Patrick, Wheeler had a success with his first Broadway play *Big Fish, Little Fish* (ANTA Theater, 1961) and, more than a decade later, with his first Broadway musical, the adaptation of Ingmar Bergman's screenplay to *Smiles of a Summer Night* as the libretto for *A Little Night Music* (Tony Award). He subsequently worked on a number of further adaptations, including the highly successful remakes of the 1919 musical *Irene* and the rather more recent *Candide* (Tony Award), and on the development of the London play *Sweeney Todd* as the libretto for the musical of the same title, as well as remaking *A Little Night Music* for the screen.

Reputed as an excellent play doctor, he provided sometimes uncredited assistance on several musical projects for both stage and screen, including *Pacific Overtures* (1976) on which he was credited with 'additional material', and the film version of *Cabaret* where the credit was given as 'research consultant'. He turned out the severe rewrite of Georg Kaiser's atmospheric script for the New York City Opera production of *Der Silbersee* (20 March 1980, State Theater), and also authored a musical version of Saint-Exupéry's *The Little Prince and the Aviator* which folded before opening.

A similar fate befell his one attempt at an original libretto in the 1973 *Truckload*, which did not make it past its Broadway previews.

1973 **A Little Night Music** (Stephen Sondheim) Shubert Theater 25 February
1973 **Irene** revised version w Joseph Stein, Harry Rigby Minskoff Theater 13 March
1973 **Candide** revised version w Stephen Sondheim Chelsea Theater Center 18 December; Broadway Theater 8 March 1974
1975 **Truckload** (Louis St Louis/Wes Harris) Lyceum Theater 6 September
1979 **Sweeney Todd, the Demon Barber of Fleet Street** (Sondheim/Chris Bond ad) Uris Theater 1 March
1982 **The Little Prince and the Aviator** (John Barry/Don Black) Alvin Theater 1 January (preview)

WHEN JOHNNY COMES MARCHING HOME
American (military) spectacular comic opera in 3 acts by Stanislaus Stange. Music by Julian Edwards. New York Theater, New York, 16 December 1902.

The success of Stange and Edwards's *Dolly Varden* gave the encouragement to producer Fred Whitney to mount another of the pair's light operas and in 1902 the Whitney Opera Company came out with *When Johnny Comes Marching Home*. Stange's script was unusual in that, up to that time, it had not been normal to deal with national historical events in a romantic – rather than burlesque or comic – fashion on the light musical stage. However, otherwise this Civil-War musical was barely adventurous, its tale being in the vein of sentimental melodrama and the score – to lyrics of the most thee-and-thouing kind – mixed the military-patriotic and the romantic with local colour and some polite comic pieces in standard light-operatic fashion.

In a Civil War where the two sides seem to mix rather freely socially, southern belle Kate Pemberton (Zetti Kennedy) marries Union Colonel John Graham (William G Stewart). When a stolen wallet of army dispatches is found in Graham's possession he allows himself to be condemned as a spy rather than incriminate Kate and her brother Robert (Julia Gifford). At the end, all is cleared up and John proves himself to be the long-lost son of a southern gentleman (Albert McGuckin). The temporary and phoney son, one Jonathan Phoenix (Fred H Perry), is a deserter who sings comic songs. Homer Lind as General William Allen headed the army and was given a middle-aged romance with Kate's aunt Constance (Lucille Saunders), whilst the soubrette moments were assured by the General's daughter, Cordelia (Maude Lambert).

John sang staunchly to the 'Flag of My Country' and of 'My Own United States' and serenaded 'Katie – My Southern Belle', Kate had a couple of incidental soprano ballads with cadenzas, Phoenix gave the tale of 'Sir Frog and Mistress Toad' and Constance had a ballad of the drawing-room kind musing that 'Time Leaves No Wrinkle on the Heart'. The local colour was provided by a second act opening with a cotton-picking chorus and dance of darkies 'Heah in de Land ob Coon and Chicken' and by a character called Uncle Tom (Will Bray) singing of 'My Honeysuckle Girl'. Edwards also included bits of 'Swanee River', 'John Brown's Body', 'Good Night Ladies' and 'I Wish I Was in Dixie' in his first-act finale.

When Johnny Comes Marching Home received some appreciative notices and Whitney played it 71 times on Broadway before taking it on the road where it proved a good touring prospect. The show was considered by many to be the best of Edwards's often rather stiff light-operatic output, and it was well enough thought of to be given a revival at the New Amsterdam Theater in 1917 (7 May). Although it was never exported, England heard two of the show's songs when *Dolly Varden* was produced in London. 'Katie – My Southern Belle' switched nationalities and became 'Dolly, My English Rose' whilst the soubrette duo 'It Was Down in the Garden of Eden' was shifted from Civil-War America to Restoration Britain without a word of change being needed.

WHERE'S CHARLEY?
Musical comedy in 2 acts by George Abbott based on the play *Charley's Aunt* by Brandon Thomas. Music and lyrics by Frank Loesser. St James Theater, New York, 11 October 1948.

Frank Loesser's first full Broadway score was written to what surprisingly seems to have been the first attempt to make a musical out of Brandon Thomas's celebrated 1892 farce, *Charley's Aunt*. The play, however, underwent some considerable alterations in the process of becoming George Abbott's libretto, the most far-reaching being the combining of two of the three principal male rôles to make one top-billable star part. The romantically involved Charley Wykeham – he of the aunt – was rolled into one with the main comic rôle of Lord Fancourt Babberley – he who impersonates the aunt – and, if the result allowed the artist involved to revel in both the romantic and comical sides of the evening's entertainment, the actual construction of the play and the mass of credible farcical moments which had originally helped win it its fame went very largely out of the window.

In this version, Charley (Ray Bolger) gets dressed up as his wealthy aunt, who has been delayed in her expected visit, so that Amy (Allyn McLeerie) and Kitty (Doretta Morrow), who were to lunch with him and his friend Jack (Byron Palmer), won't refuse a chaperoneless invitation. When Kitty's uncle (Horace Cooper) arrives he woos the phoney aunt, and Charley is ultimately able to get him to agree to the marriages of the two young couples before the deception is revealed. The real Donna Lucia d'Alvadorez, who has allowed the masquerade to continue, has meanwhile been happily duetting with Jack's father, Sir Francis (Paul England). Into this now rather anodine outline were fitted – in the fashion of the time – the opportunities for a Balanchine ballet scena telling of Donna Lucia's doings in Brazil, a ball scene, and a parade by 'The New Ashmolean Marching Society and Conservatory Band'.

However, if the adaptation did – in the cause of things spectacular and starry – some rather fatally painful things

Plate 290. *Brandon Thomas's* Charley's Aunt *has undergone a number of musicalizations. Here Heinz Zimmer stars as Lord Fancourt Babberley in* Die Tante aus Brasilien *at the Dresden Staatsoperette.*

to the previously durable *Charley's Aunt*, Loesser decorated it with some pretty and (the Ashmolean Band apart) suitably English-pastiche songs, few of which, however, showed of what the future composer of *Guys and Dolls* and *The Most Happy Fella* was capable. A straightforward little love duet, 'My Darling, My Darling', for Jack and Kitty, proved popular, whilst Bolger's song-and-dance performance of the equally simple but more catchy 'Once in Love with Amy' was a highlight of a singular performance which thoroughly caught the public's imagination. The ensembles 'Better Get Out of Here Quick' and 'The Gossips' allowed the songwriter a little more latitude for humour.

Feuer and Martin's Broadway production of *Where's Charley?* and, most particularly, their star (Tony Award), were both an undoubted success. *Where's Charley?* ran for 792 performances on Broadway, visited Boston and then returned to New York (Broadway Theater 29 January 1951) for a further 48 performances before Bolger went on to put his performance down on film in a version which retained the larger part of the musical's score. The show later reappeared on the New York stage at the City Center (1966 w Susan Watson as Amy) and the Circle in the Square (1974 w Raul Julia).

When *Where's Charley?* was mounted in London by Bernard Delfont and H M Tennent Ltd a decade later, with Norman Wisdom as Charley and Terence Cooper, Pamela Gale and Pip Hinton as his partners, it again had a good run (404 performances). In between, however, a production in Australia, featuring Tommy Fields ('brother of Gracie'), had foundered expensively after some two months in Melbourne. A French-language version pro-

duced in Antwerp a further 20 years on demanded 'Who is Charley?' rather than 'where?', which seemed to indicate that someone French had seen the original play.

Other musicals based on *Charley's Aunt* have included a number of German adaptations, three produced as *Charleys Tante* – the first by Arthur Rebner and Hugo Hirsch, the next by Robert Gilbert and Max Colpet, with music by Ralph Maria Siegel (Deutsches Theater, Munich 9 March 1967) in which Hans Clarin starred as Fancourt Babberley, and the third by Hertha Roth and Erwin Amend (Staatsheater, Mainz 17 February 1968) – whilst another *Charley's Tante* (Len Praverman, John Hawkins/ Ida From, Bent From) was produced in Denmark and found considerable success there. In 1965 Hamburg got a *Charleys neue Tante* (Lothar Olias/Gustav Kampendonck) which, unlike *Where's Charley?*, admitted that it was 'loosely based on some events from' Thomas's play.

Australia: Tivoli, Melbourne 4 May 1950; UK: Palace Theatre 20 February 1958; Belgium: Anvers *Qui est Charley?* 28 January 1978; Film: Warner Brothers 1952

Recordings: London cast (Columbia, EMI, Monmouth Evergreen)

WHITE, James A (b Rochdale, 1878; d London, 29 June 1927). Millionaire who tried, not without some success, to be a George Edwardes but eventually killed himself instead.

Colourful poor-boy-made-good financier White caused some shock waves in theatrical circles when he acquired the control of London's Daly's Theatre in 1922 and straight away showed his intention of keeping artistic control in his own hands. Robert Evett, who had saved the George Edwardes estate's investment from bankruptcy and who had run the theatre since he had put it back on its feet with *The Maid of the Mountains*, soon departed, taking with him the theatre's *Maid of the Mountains* star José Collins. White carried on without them, presenting *The Lady of the Rose* with Phyllis Dare for 514 performances, a revival of *The Merry Widow* with Evelyn Laye and Carl Brisson, Miss Laye as Leo Fall's *Madame Pompadour* (469 performances), a revival of *The Dollar Princess*, and *Katja the Dancer* which moved to Daly's from White's production at the Gaiety (501 performances). He also did well with *Whirled into Happiness* (*Der Tanz ins Glück*), produced at the Lyric Theatre for 244 performances, and kept a number of companies – billed under the banner 'George Edwardes presents', the formula Evett had used – on the road, but Daly's Theatre was his pride and joy.

A spectacular version of Straus's *Die Perlen der Cleopatra* with Evelyn Laye as Cleopatra flopped (110 performances), a new mounting of Edwardes's *A Greek Slave* with José Collins starred closed on the road, and neither a rehash of Jean Gilbert's *Uschi* and *Wenn zwei sich lieben* as *Yvonne* (280 performances) nor Lehár's *The Blue Mazurka* (140 performances) helped refloat the situation at a time when White's dealings in general were at a sticky impasse. He went bankrupt and committed suicide by taking poison in his office at the theatre whilst *The Blue Mazurka* struggled on, leaving behind him a long and explanatory testament which the papers published in full. Sneered at for years by theatre and newspaper folk as the man who merely provided the money, and who couldn't be expected to know anything about 'the theatre, darling', he got his best press from them – including a whole page in *Variety* – in his death.

WHITE, Michael [Simon] (b Scotland, 16 January 1936). London producer with an early taste for the youth-orientated or off-centre who later switched to importing proven Broadway hits.

After a period as assistant to producer Peter Daubeny, White began producing on his own account at the beginning of the 1960s, often, particularly in earlier days, choosing plays of a striving avant garde or provocative nature. Amongst others, he introduced London to *Cambridge Circus, The Paper Bag Players, Oh! Calcutta, The Dirtiest Show in Town* and, a little too later, a follow-up erotic-ish revue called *Carte Blanche*.

His musical-theatre ventures, on the whole more mainstream, began with a piece called *The Man from the West* which played only in East Grinstead and later included a revival of *The Threepenny Opera* (ad Hugh Mac-Diarmid), the initial West End showing of *Joseph and the Amazing Technicolor Dreamcoat* (w Robert Stigwood), Lloyd Webber's subsequent *Jeeves* (w Stigwood) and Galt MacDermot's contemporary musicalization of *Two Gentlemen of Verona*. It was, however, his production of *The Rocky Horror Show*, which made its way through several theatres and many more years to win itself the status of an institution which gave him his first memorable musical success to set alongside such long-running straight productions as *Sleuth*.

A second piece by *The Rocky Horror Show*'s author, *T. Zee* (1976), was a fast flop and another small-scale venture, *Censored Scenes from King Kong*, produced on Broadway in 1980 (w Eddie Kulukundis) also failed. White subsequently became film-maker to produce *The Rocky Horror Picture Show* and, parallel to a subsequent career much angled towards cinema (*Monty Python and the Holy Grail, The Life of Brian* etc), he has since been responsible for London's reproductions of several major Broadway musicals: *A Chorus Line* (1975), the long-running *Annie* (1978), the New York Shakespeare Festival staging of *The Pirates of Penzance* (1982), *On Your Toes* (1984) and *Crazy for You* (1993). All of these did well, which was not the case with a curious derrière-garde Continental mish-mash of variety acts called *Y* to which he loaned his name as producer.

Autobiography: *Empty Seats* (Hamish Hamilton, London, 1984)

WHITE, Onna (b Nova Scotia, Canada, 24 March 1922).

After a career as a chorus dancer in ballet and in Broadway shows (*Finian's Rainbow, Guys and Dolls, Silk Stockings*) during which she acted as assistant to Michael Kidd, Miss White reproduced Kidd's dances for the City Center's 1955 revival of *Guys and Dolls*, choreographed the 1956 revival of *Carmen Jones* and established herself at the front of her profession with her dances for the original production of *The Music Man* (1957). Her subsequent credits include *Whoop Up!* (1958), *Take Me Along* (1959), Broadway's version of *Irma la Douce* (1960), *Let it Ride!* (1961), *I Had a Ball* (1964), Broadway's *Half a Sixpence* (1965), *Mame, Ilya Darling* (1967), *A Mother's Kisses* (1968), *1776* (1969), *Gantry* (1970, also director), *70, Girls, 70* (1971), *Gigi* (1973), London's *Billy* (1974), *Goodtime Charley* (1975), *I Love My Wife* (1974), *Working* (1978), *Home Again, Home Again* (1979), *Elizabeth and Essex* (1984) and the London revival of *Charlie Girl* (1986, w Mike Fields).

She also provided the dances for the screen versions of *The Music Man, Bye Bye Birdie, Oliver!, 1776* and *Mame*.

THE WHITE CHRYSANTHEMUM Lyrical comedy in 3 acts by Leedham Bantock and Arthur Anderson. Lyrics by Anderson. Music by Howard Talbot. Criterion Theatre, London, 31 August 1905.

An unusual venture for its time, *The White Chrysanthemum* was the nearest thing London's West End had seen to an intimate musical since the explosion onto its stages of Gaiety Theatre-style musical comedy, more than a decade previously. *The White Chrysanthemum* was considerably shorter than usual, it had virtually no spectacle nor dancing, and a principal cast of just seven, supported by a chorus of half a dozen girls and half a dozen boys (a *Florodora* double sextet), made up the onstage personnel of Frank Curzon's production at the little Criterion Theatre. Otherwise, however, the show differed little from standard fare, with its tale of Reggie Armitage R N (Henry Lytton) who has to free himself from the wish of his father (Rutland Barrington) that he wed American heiress Cornelia Vanderdecken (Marie George) so that he can pair himself up with his Sybil (Isabel Jay). Sybil is biding her time close at hand, disguised as a little Japanese lady, whilst best-friend Betty (Millie Legarde) helps events on. Lawrence Grossmith was Reggie's mate who takes over Cornelia when Reggie gets Sybil and father pairs off with Betty, and M R Morand was the seventh principal of a very Savoy Theatre-flavoured cast, playing a comical oriental.

Equipped with a score which was charmingly well-written in its sentimental parts, but rather imitative and verging on the vulgar when it tried to supply up-to-date material for Miss George, in particular, *The White Chrysanthemum* nevertheless proved itself to be a well-made little piece. It drew for six months at the Criterion (179 performances) before going on the road, where it featured for several years.

An American version, which featured Ethel Jackson/Lina Abarbanell (Sybil), Lawrence Grossmith (Chippy) and Edna Wallace Hopper (Betty) in its cast and the name of Jerome Kern (which hadn't been there before) in its song list, folded without reaching Broadway, but the piece's dimensions made it a good touring prospect. Thus, it was all the more surprising that when it was later produced by John and Nevin Tait in Australia, with a cast including Barry Lupino and Florence Perry, the little piece was dolled up with 'a chorus and ballet, superb costumes and magnificent scenic effects' so that it resembled any and every other piece of the time. *The White Chrysanthemum* was also played throughout Asia and the rest of the eastern circuits by Maurice Bandmann's endlessly touring musical comedy company.

USA: Garrick Theater, Philadelphia 25 March 1907; Australia: King's Theatre, Melbourne 2 June 1917

WHITING, Jack (b Philadelphia, 22 June 1901; d New York, 15 February 1961). Durable Broadway juvenile song and dance man who didn't manage to draw too many hits from his long list of original rôles.

Young Whiting, whom a Philadelphia paper noted was

'of a socially prominent local family', worked as a stenographer before getting a job in the 1922 edition of *The Ziegfeld Follies*. He quickly moved on to rôles in musical plays – *Orange Blossoms* (1922, Frank Curran), *Cinders* (1923, Bruce), *Stepping Stones* (1923, Captain Paul), *Annie Dear* (1924, Alfred Weatherly), *When You Smile* (1925, Larry Patton), *Rainbow Rose* (1926, Tommy Lansing) – and returned to his home town to appear as the live-wire young salesman hero of *Cynthia* at the Walnut Street Theater. *Cynthia* folded after a fortnight, but Whiting went on to the juvenile lead in the successful comedy show *The Ramblers* ('All Alone Monday') and the plum leading rôle of Bobby Bennett, fated to tell 'nothing but the truth' in *Yes, Yes, Yvette* (1927).

A long series of leading juvenile rôles followed: alongside Beatrice Lillie and Irene Dunne in *She's My Baby* (1928, Bob Martin), as the boxer Sonny Jim Brooks in *Hold Everything!* (introducing 'You're the Cream in My Coffee'), as coastguardsman Jack Mason in *Heads Up!* (1929), as filmstar Michael Perry in *America's Sweetheart* (1931), and as amateur producer-cum-love-interest Kenneth Raleigh in *Take a Chance* (1932). He visited London in 1934 to star as Billy Crocker to the Reno Sweeney of Jeanne Aubert in the West End's *Anything Goes* and, following that success, was more briefly seen on the London stage in the flop *Rise and Shine* (1936) and as the hero of the unliked West End production of *On Your Toes* (1937).

Back on Broadway, he appeared in *Hooray for What!* (1937), as Johnny Graham in *Very Warm for May* (1939) and as Kitty Carlisle's love interest in *Walk with Music* (1940), got a longer run out of *Hold on to Your Hats* (1940) in which he appeared alongside the ageing Al Jolson, and a brief one out of the rôle of bandleader Damon Dillingham in *Beat the Band* (1942). In his forties, he appeared on Broadway replacing Michael O'Shea in the low-comedy rôle of Con Kidder in the 1945 revival of *The Red Mill* and toured in both that rôle (1947) and as Henry Longstreet in *High Button Shoes*, in his fifties he played the supporting rôle of the Chief Justice in the 1952 revival of *Of Thee I Sing* and the Mayor of New York in *Hazel Flagg* (1953), and his last Broadway appearance was as a soft-shoeing Charybdis in *The Golden Apple* (1954). The 1956 *Strip for Action* (Jack) in which he featured as a song-and-dance man turned soldier, closed out of town, but he was seen in 1958 playing Charlie in the City Center's *Annie Get Your Gun*.

WHITNEY, Frederick C (Detroit, ?1865; d Los Angeles, 4 June 1930).

The son of producer and theatre-owner C J Whitney of the Whitney Opera House in Detroit and later of theatres in Toronto and Chicago, Fred Whitney himself began producing in 1892, some of his earlier efforts including tours of the Chicago-based shows produced by his brother, Bert C Whitney. In his early years, Fred Whitney was a staunch supporter and producer of native comic opera, and in his first seasons as a producer he launched such pieces as Reginald De Koven's *The Fencing Master*, a Broadway success with Marie Tempest starred, and that lady's next vehicle *The Algerian* (1893) which did less well. Alfred Robyn's *Jacinta* (1894) played only 16 times, but De Koven's *Rob Roy*, produced in the same season, gave the composer his best result since *Robin Hood* and the pro-

ducer one of the longest Broadway runs (253 performances) that he would achieve in a decade of trying.

Julian Edwards's Irish light opera *Brian Boru* (1896) and a William Furth rewrite of Vanloo and Leterrier's *La Gardeuse d'oies* as *A Normandy Wedding* (ex-*Papa Gougou*) (1897) were not hits, but two other Edwards pieces, *Dolly Varden* and *When Johnny Comes Marching Home*, both achieved respectable runs in New York and good lives on the road. Edwards's *Love's Lottery* which featured the opera star Ernestine Schumann-Heink in a single venture into light opera, a Broadway staging of the London success *A Greek Slave*, and Lucius Hosmer's *The Rose of the Alhambra* all failed, but Whitney had a fine success when he left comic opera for musical comedy and mounted the nonsensical *Piff! Paff! Pouf!* for a splendid 264 performances on Broadway. If other Chicago and road ventures were sometimes less successful (*The Belle of Newport* (1903), *A China Doll (1904)*, *The Pink Hussars* (1905) etc) he did well enough with Chicago's *The Isle of Spice* and the *The Land of Nod* and he finally hit the jackpot with a vengeance when he joined the post-*Die lustige Witwe* rush for Continental musicals and staged the Broadway version of *Der tapfere Soldat* (*The Chocolate Soldier*) in 1909.

Whitney later took a hand in the very successful London reproduction of his show and, on the wings of that success, took the West End's Waldorf Theatre and, renaming it the Whitney Theatre, opened it with another Continental piece, Felix Albini's substantial *Baron Trenck*. When that flopped he replaced it with the American hit version of *Die Sprudelfee* (*The Spring Maid*). When that, too, failed to run he was forced to withdraw from London in disarray.

Things went less well thereafter. The Oscar Straus *My Little Friend* (1913) did only fairly, a 1919 musical called *Suite 16* apparently got no further than Syracuse, and his last Broadway production was a not-very-memorable Tchaikovsky pasticcio called *Natja*, mounted in partnership with Bert in 1925. Whitney nevertheless continued to be active on the west coast and his final production there was a Los Angeles mounting of Shaw's *Saint Joan*.

His brother, **Bert[ram] C WHITNEY** (d October 1929), operated theatres in Chicago, Toronto, Ann Arbor, Ypsilanti, Owosso and Battle Creek as well as, for 30 years, in his native Detroit. Amongst the musical plays and extravaganzas which he mounted or co-mounted, mostly from Chicago, were the successful *A Knight for a Day* (ex-*Mam'selle Sallie*), *The Isle of Spice*, *The Isle of Bong Bong*, *Piff! Paff! Pouf!*, *The Show Girl*, *The Broken Idol*, *They Loved a Lassie*, Clifton Crawford's *Captain Careless*, *My Little Friend*, Ed Wynn's *Carnival*, *The Perfect Fool*, *The Chocolate Dandies* and *The Head Waiters*.

WHITTINGTON Grand opéra-bouffe in 3 acts by H B Farnie. Music by Jacques Offenbach. Alhambra Theatre, London, 26 December 1874.

The history of London's very own made-to-order Offenbach opéra-bouffe has become befuddled over the years. Some French commentators have insisted that the libretto to the piece was a French one, written by Nuitter and Tréfeu and subsequently translated for the English stage by Farnie. However, these same commentators (one copying from the other, perhaps?) insist on calling the work variously *Wittington et son chat* or *Whittington et son chat*, so maybe they are not to be taken too seriously.

Contemporary English accounts reported that the favourite composer of the period was signed by the publishers Wood & Co of Regent Street to compose an original score for which he was to be paid a total of 75,000 francs, apparently then the equivalent of £3,000, the money to be paid to the composer at a rate of £1,000 as each act was handed, completed, to the copyist. The newspapers of the period noted that it was the first time that the composer would set a text in the English language. As it eventuated, the script of *Whittington* as constructed by H B Farnie to fit into the spectacular production designed by Alfred Thompson (he who had authored the splendid book to *Cinderella the Younger* for Jonas and the Gaiety) for the vast Alhambra stage was not one for which the credit was really worth squabbling over (which is possibly one reason more for denying Nuitter and Tréfeu as its authors). The traditional tale of Dick (Kate Santley) and Alice Fitzwarren (Julia Mathews) was squeezed to one side to allow three comical suitors (Harry Paulton, John Rouse, W M Terrott) to vie for the hand of Dorothy, the Cook (Lennox Grey) in Act I, and to try to run the country of Bambouli on 'perfect' English lines much in the manner later re-proposed by W S Gilbert in *Utopia (Limited)* in Act II, before the bit with the cat and the rats intervened, almost as an afterthought, in time to tie up proceedings.

The score, too, proved disappointing, and the highlight of the evening turned out to be a Grand Barbaric Ballet invented, arranged and produced by ballet-master Dewinne and danced by him with Mlles Pertoldi, Pitteri and Sidonie and the massed forces of the Alhambra corps de ballet. *Whittington* survived through 112 performances, largely on the attractions of the Alhambra's staging and was then put away.

Eighteen years later, it was disinterred, adapted (ad Nuitter, Tréfeu) and mounted at Paris's equally spectacle-orientated Théâtre du Châtelet where it was now billed as a 'féerie'. No longer was there a leggy travesty Dick, but the hero was played by Alexandre fils, whilst Gardel, the son of Hervé, was cast as King Lallali and Juliette Darcourt played his daughter. The cook (Blanche Miroir) and her suitors were still there and the cat had made it to the title as *Le Chat du Diable*. It was played 86 times.

France: Théâtre du Châtelet *Le Chat du diable* 28 October 1893

WHOOPEE Musical comedy in 2 acts by William Anthony McGuire based on the comedy *The Nervous Wreck* by Owen Davis. Lyrics by Gus Kahn. Music by Walter Donaldson. New Amsterdam Theater, New York, 4 December 1928.

Owen Davis's play *The Nervous Wreck* (Sam H Harris Theater, 9 October 1923) had been a 279-performance hit on Broadway and the basis for a silent film before comedian Eddie Cantor took it to Florenz Ziegfeld as the material for a musical comedy vehicle for himself. The musical was put together by the producer's currently favourite stagewriter, McGuire, and the songwriters Donaldson and Kahn who had provided Cantor with several big song hits in the past. Stanley Green reported 'By the time he was finished, McGuire had managed to turn an 11-character, three-set play into a 35-character, 11-set song-and-dance spectacle with room enough for cowboys, cowgirls, showgirls, ballet dancers, Indians, gipsies, two automobiles, a heifer, a kitchen stove, Eddie Can-

tor's blackface routine, and five nude girls on horseback'. The songwriters had done their bit too: Cantor had a joyously cynical number describing 'Makin' Whoopee!', and a blackface spot full of jolly numbers, the juveniles had a fine romancing duet in 'I'm Bringing a Red, Red Rose', and an incidental movie star called Leslie Daw (Ruth Etting), wandering through the plot, insisted that someone who wasn't in the play should 'Love Me or Leave Me'. Cantor's blackface spot, needless to say, did not remain static throughout the run and he introduced several more popular numbers into it as time went on.

The story centred on Sally Morgan (Frances Upton) who is about to be made to marry Sheriff Wells (Jack Rutherford) even though she is in love with the Indian Wanenis (Paul Gregory). Since her father harbours anti-Indian sentiments, she runs away. Henry Williams (Eddie Cantor), a professional hypochondriac, is kidded into being her companion in flight and they gallop through a series of adventures, characters and sets before it turns out that the leading man isn't really and truly an Indian after all, so Sally is allowed to wed him. Henry, most suitably, is left paired with his nurse, Mary Custer (Ethel Shutta).

Whoopee ran for more than seven months, took a break, and returned, with movie person Ruth Morgan now paired with Cantor, to run another three and a half months before Ziegfeld took it off to allow United Artists to film a movie version with Cantor, Ethel Shutta, Gregory and Rutherford, with Eleanor Hunt as Sally and with some fresh songs.

The show did not travel to Britain, but it was taken up for Australia by Ernest G Rolls and George Marlow who produced it at Sydney's Empire Theatre with what they advertised as 'a huge star cast of 100' topped by comic Charley Sylber (Henry), Genevieve McCormack (Mary), baritone Forest Yernall (Wanenis), Palmer Stone (Wells) and American comedienne Beulah Benson (replaced by Mary Gannon) as Sally, not long after *The Nervous Wreck* had passed across the Sydney stage. The Indians and a Hallowe'en sequence proved the most popular bits of the evening and the show managed 69 performances after being bumped from the Empire to Frank Neil's Grand Opera House after three weeks of its season. When Neil took it to Melbourne (Kings Theatre 31 August 1929) he was gratified with a run of nearly three months.

The show was televised by NBC in 1950 with Johnny Morgan and Nancy Walker featured, and a made-over version was produced at the Goodspeed Opera House in 1978 (20 July) and subsequently taken to Broadway's ANTA Theater for 204 performances. Charles Repole starred as Henry in a version which mixed half a dozen numbers from the original score with one of the additional film numbers, and half a dozen other Donaldson/Kahn pieces.

Australia: Empire Theatre, Sydney 15 June 1929; Film: United Artists 1930

Recording: archive collection (Smithsonian Institution)

WHO'S HOOPER? Musical comedy in 2 acts by Fred Thompson founded on *In Chancery* by Arthur Pinero. Lyrics by Clifford Grey. Music by Ivor Novello and Howard Talbot. Adelphi Theatre, London, 13 September 1919.

Plate 291. Who's Hooper?: *Star comedian Bill Berry tackled Pinero with music and found himself a fine success. Here, the amnesiac Hooper finds himself with – apparently – two wives (Violet Blythe, Cicely Debenham).*

The huge success of the musicalized *The Magistrate*, *The Boy*, at the Adelphi Theatre naturally suggested more Pinero-with-songs as the next vehicle for the earlier piece's town-drawing comedian W H Berry. The adapter of the former musical, Fred Thompson, chose this time to remodel the old Edward Terry hit *In Chancery* (Gaiety Theatre, 24 December 1884) for producer Alfred Butt and his star.

Berry was Vincent Hitchens who has been in a rail accident and has lost his memory. Because of the initials on his bag he is taken for one Vincent Hooper, a chap who is on the run from the law for having wed a ward-in-chancery. The plot thickens when the owner of the pub where he is taken (W H Rawlins) all but inveigles him into matrimony with his daughter (Cicely Debenham), it re-thickens when the real newly-weds (Robert Michaelis, Marjorie Gordon) turn up, and thickens all over again when they all run off to hide at a little boarding house in Portsea which turns out to be none other than Hitchens' own home. Each twist gave more opportunities to the comedian, who was also well supplied with songs: a topical drinking song, a burlesque of Tennyson's 'What Are the Wild Waves Saying?', and the explanatory 'It Must Be Very Trying to Be Mad'. Miss Debenham bounced through a Novello-ized version of *Lohengrin*'s 'Wedding March' and cooed with the star over 'Wonderful Love', but the prettiest piece of the evening went to Violet Blythe as the real Mrs Hitchens, singing of 'Day Dreams', the theme of which floated through the play, tugging poor, befuddled Vincent's memory back to reality.

Who's Hooper? had a fine run, but after seven and a half months it was given a thorough revamp, the whole last act rearranged and seven numbers replaced. The alterations did not give the show anything additional, and it ran on for two further months, closing after 349 performances.

WIE EINST IM MAI Posse mit Gesang (musical comedy) in four scenes by Rudolf Bernauer and Rudolf Schanzer. Music by Walter Kollo and Willy Bredschneider. Berliner Theater, Berlin, 4 October 1913.

The most enduring of Bernauer, Schanzer, Bred-

schneider and Walter Kollo's run of musicals for the Berliner Theater, *Wie einst im Mai* used the triple-header love-through-the-generations layout that had been so effectively foreshadowed in such pieces as *Lili* and was later to be regularly re-used in other successful stage musicals (*Drei Walzer*, *Perchance to Dream* etc) and films, allowing the authors and their designers to travel through a sentimental panorama of Berlin from the late days of the Biedermeier era to what turned out to be – although its authors could not have suspected it would be so – the last days of the Kaiser's Germany.

In the first scene, Colonel's daughter Ottilie (Lisa Weise) is prevented by convention from marrying the locksmith Fritz Jüterbog (Oscar Sabo); in the second, 20 years on, she goes to a night-spot to catch out the 'suitable' husband her family forced her to take in a dalliance and, instead, meets Fritz again. They part for a second time and, by the third scene, Fritz is rich, successful, a grandfather and living in the very house from which the Colonel had turned him out in scene one. Ottilie comes to see him on behalf of her daughter, Vera, who has attracted the unwelcome attentions of his married son. The old pair share their fond memories of their youth, and part for the last time. In the fourth scene, Vera's daughter, Tilla, and Fritz's grandson, Fred, finally bring the two families together. The four scenes were also linked by the comical exploits of the aptly named Stanislas von Methusalem, flirting and dancing his way through the generations from his youth to his 100th year.

The love story was carried musically through from 1838 to 1913 to the melody of 'Das war in Schöneberg im Monat Mai', Ottilie and Fritz's recollection of their first kiss, whilst the comical part was connected by Methusalem's sung and danced 'Heissgeliebtes Firlefänzchen', a piece which shifted into a different dance mode for each era of the play. In the other foremost minutes of the score, Ottilie scorned her faithless husband in 'Die Männer sind aller Verbrecher' and reminisced over Fritz's little grandson that, had things been different, she might have been his 'Grossmama, Grossmama'.

By the time authors and stagers had finished, *Wie einst im Mai* came out as a wholly romantic costume piece, rather than the slightly social-commenting 'Posse mit Gesang' which had been originally envisaged, and as such it proved to be wholly to its audience's tastes. It had a splendid run at the Berliner Theater, outdoing even the success of the team's previous hit, *Filmzauber*, as it held the stage for nearly a year before being taken off to be replaced by the team's more patriotic and wartimely *Extrablätter*.

The First World War virtually destroyed the international career of *Wie einst im Mai*. Adolf Weisse produced it at Vienna's Deutsches Volkstheater with Kamilla Eibenschütz (Ottilie/Tilla), Anton Edthofer (Fritz/Fred) and Hans Junkermann (Methusalem) starred, and Budapest saw *Egyszer volt* (once upon a time) in Zsolt Harsányi's version, but the other important paths opened up to the team's works by *The Girl on the Film* (*Filmzauber*) were now closed. Britain and its colonies never saw *Wie einst im Mai* as such. America, however, half-did. The Shubert brothers took up the show, but in a manner which they had made particularly their own, they threw out Bredschneider and Kollo's score (which nevertheless got a hearing at the city's German-language Irving Place Theater) and instead decorated Rida Johnson Young's fairly faithful version of Bernauer and Schanzer's tale with nine numbers composed by Sigmund Romberg.

The resultant piece, *Maytime* (Shubert Theater 16 August 1917), now set in New York rather than Berlin, kept much of the feeling and flavour of the original even though Peggy Wood and Charles Purcell as the long-term lovers were allowed to flush rather more (and more often) romantic than before alongside William Norris (Matthew, ex-Methusalem) and his succession of wives. *Maytime* was a resounding success, and the number which did duty for 'Das war in Schöneberg im Monat Mai', the duet 'Will You Remember?' (better known, perhaps, by its opening line 'Sweetheart, sweetheart, sweetheart'), became an all-time Romberg favourite. Amongst the other numbers, a 'Jump Jim Crow' replaced the Caribbean polka danced by Methusalem's wife in the second act, the lovers got two further duets ('In Our Little Home Sweet Home', 'The Road to Paradise') and the aged Matthew insisted 'Dancing Will Keep You Young'. The main Broadway production of the piece ran for 492 performances and *Maytime* proved to be one of the Shubert brothers' most successful productions ever.

The American version of *Maytime* was produced in Australia in 1919 (Criterion Theatre, Sydney 8 March 1919, Her Majesty's Theatre, Melbourne 22 August) with Gladys Moncrieff as Ottilie, Reginald Roberts as her Richard Wayne, and Leslie Holland as Matthew for a season disturbed by an influenza epidemic and later for seven weeks at Melbourne's Her Majesty's (22 August 1919). It did fairly rather than finely. But if Australia was not hugely enthusiastic and Britain didn't even take a look, *Maytime* toured for a number of years on the American circuits, and its fame was considerably increased and even spread abroad to those countries where neither *Wie einst im Mai* nor *Maytime* had previously gone when a 1937 film version starring Jeanette MacDonald and Nelson Eddy engraved 'Will You Remember' into the consciousness of a generation. This huge and happy success had only one shadow over it: it encouraged the Shuberts in particular and other American managements in general to continue to botch (invariably rather less well than Miss Young and Romberg had done here) an ever-increasing list of further overseas hits, almost always with disappointing results. But *Maytime* was there for a long, long time to prove that it was not impossible to do it and make it work.

Wie einst im Mai was brought back in Berlin as a spectacular piece of good-old-days entertainment for the next war (Theater des Volkes, Berlin 1943, w Edith Schollwer and Hubert von Meyerinck). For this occasion, it had been revised into a more scenic eight sections, with an updated final episode, by the composer's son Willi Kollo and Walter Lieck, and the score had been stripped of Bredschneider's contribution which was replaced by some additional music composed by each of the Kollos. A second update and revision was practised on the piece for a 1966 production at Braunschweig, starring grandson René Kollo, which was subsequently seen at Berlin's Theater des Westens, and the piece was given yet another all-Kollo overhaul for a Munich production in 1992.

Austria: Deutsches Volkstheater 23 April 1915; Hungary: Fővárosi Nyári Színház *Egyszer volt* 26 May 1916; USA: Irving Place Theater (Ger) 1916

Recording: 1966 version (RCA)

WIENER BLUT Operette in 3 acts by Victor Léon and Leo Stein. Music taken from the works of Johann Strauss and arranged by Adolf Müller jr. Carltheater, Vienna, 26 October 1899.

One of the earliest of the long list of scissors-and-paste Strauss Operetten, *Wiener Blut* has survived nearly a century in the German-language repertoire. Whilst other countries have preferred other Strauss pasticcii, such as *Drei Walzer/Trois Valses*, *Valses de Vienne/The Great Waltz*, *Casanova* or *Die Tänzerin Fanny Elssler*, and whilst other such shows won considerably more popularity on their original production in Vienna, it is *Wiener Blut* which has established itself – in Austria and Germany, at least – as the most frequently played semi-Strauss show, to such an extent that only *Die Fledermaus* and *Der Zigeunerbaron* of the composer's original, untouched-up shows are more often seen.

Wiener Blut had the particularity of being a pasticcio made with the composer's knowledge and even blessing, although he did not at any time attempt to take part in its making. It was originally intended for the Theater an der Wien, and that theatre's musical director, Adolf Müller jr, was given the job of selecting and adapting the Strauss tunes which would make up the score. Finally, however, it was the Carltheater under the management of Franz Jauner which mounted the show, but in the meantime Strauss himself had died.

The libretto to *Wiener Blut* centred on Balduin, Count Zedlau (Julius Spielmann), who has a wife, Gabriele (Frln

Plate 292. **Wiener Blut**: *Sabine Rössert (Gräfin) and Peter Branoff (Ypsheim) in the Salzburg Landestheater production of 1986.*

Marker) who has gone home to mother, a mistress, the dancer Franziska Cagliari (Ilonya Szoyer), as well as a potential bit on the side in the seamstress Pepi (Betty Stojan). His wife left him because he was dull and provincial but now she finds that he has become a veritable and thus, apparently, attractive Viennese rake, whilst he in the course of the evening suddenly rediscovers a preference over the others for the woman he actually married. The Count's last evening-out before returning to married life, booked to be devoted to the seduction of Pepi, goes awry amongst a barrage of mistaken identities and misconceived rendezvous, before Franzi is paired off with the interfering Prime Minister of Reuss-Schleiz-Greiz, Prince Ypsheim-Gindelbach (Eduard Steinberger), and Pepi goes undeflowered(?) back to her Josef (Louis Treumann).

The musical part of the show was composed almost entirely of dance music, preponderantly waltzes – including the popular 'Geschichten aus dem Wienerwald', 'Morgenblätter' and 'Wein, Weib, Gesang' – and polkas ('Wildfeuer', 'Stadt und Land', 'Leichtes Blut'), some presented as dances at the second-act ball, but otherwise transformed into vocal numbers and into finales to each of the show's three acts.

Wiener Blut was a failure. After 30 performances Jauner was forced to remove it and hurry back his successful production of *Die Geisha* with American soubrette Marie Halton starred until he could get his next new piece, the American operetta *Der kleine Korporal* ready. When both that and his next production, *Rhodope* failed, Jauner put a bullet through his head in his Carltheater office. *Wiener Blut* was given a half-dozen extra performances during the runs of these two pieces, and put away. However, it got a second chance when the precipitate departure of megastar Girardi from the Theater an der Wien in 1905 left that theatre with a hole in its schedule. After a handful of performances of Strauss's *Die Fledermaus* and *Prinz Methusalem*, Karczag and Wallner decided to try a revised version of *Wiener Blut*. Mounted with a cast headed by Karl Meister (Balduin), Dora Keplinger (Franziska), Phila Wolff (Gabriele), Siegmund Natzler (Gindelbach), Gerda Walde (Pepi), Carlo Böhm (Josef) and Oskar Sachs (Kagler), the show did rather better than it had first time round. It played three weeks to end the season, came back to open the new season in September, and was played again to launch the following season. Without ever running up a series, it was brought back regularly in the repertoire (1912, 1923, 1925, 1934 etc) and in 30 years perched on the edge of the repertoire it was played 134 times at the Theater an der Wien as well as at the companion Raimundtheater (1910 w Betty Fischer as Franziska, Franz Glawatsch as Kagler, 1911, 1913 etc). This was sufficient to establish it, and in 1928 it was taken into the repertoire at the Volksoper (13 June) where it has been played to this day.

Elsewhere, the reaction to the show was less receptive. Rudolf Aronson took it for Broadway, in spite of its initial failure, and mounted it as *Vienna Life* (ad Glen MacDonough) with Ethel Jackson (Gabriele), Charles H Drew (Prince), Thomas Persse (Zedlau), Amelia Stone (Franzi), Raymond Hitchcock in the chief comic rôle of Franzi's father, and with Prince Bitowski played Orlofsky-like in travesty. Some hurried rewrites and recasting after a nega-

tive opening couldn't keep the show afloat more than 35 performances.

Paris first saw the piece in 1911, played by a visiting company, but in 1934, following the enormous Paris success of *Valses de Vienne*, the enterprising Trianon-Lyrique tried to jump on the bandwagon with *Les Jolies Viennoises* (ad André Mauprey) with a cast headed by Jeanne Guyla, Coecilia Navarre, Janine Delille, Max Moutia and Morton. It did not succeed in approaching the success of its sister piece and *Les Jolies Viennoises* did not make the revivable repertoire. Another version, *Sang viennois* (ad Marc-Cab), later found its way to the stage without provoking any more attention.

London saw the show in 1955 during the visit of a Viennese company headed by Karl Terkal, Christine von Widmann, Tony Niessner and Fritz Imhoff, but has not yet witnessed an English version.

A film version was produced in 1942 with Willy Fritsch and Maria Holst in the central rôles.

USA: Broadway Theater *Vienna Life* 23 January 1901; France: Théâtre du Vaudeville (Ger) 1911, Trianon-Lyrique *Les Jolies Viennoises* 22 December 1934; UK: Stoll Theatre (Ger) 16 August 1955; Film: 1942

Recordings: complete (Urania, EMI, Eurodisc etc), selections (Fontana, Saga, Philips etc)

WIENER FRAUEN Operette in 3 acts partly 'based on a French original' by Ottokar Tann-Bergler and Emil Norini. Music by Franz Lehár. Theater an der Wien, Vienna, 21 November 1902.

Although the first entry of the young Franz Lehár into the world of the Operette was initially announced for Berlin's Centraltheater, and the title of his piece as *Der Klavierstimme*, the work in question was ultimately mounted as *Wiener Frauen*, and produced under the management of Lehár's fellow-Hungarian Wilhelm Karczag and his partner Karl Wallner at the Theater an der Wien.

The piano-teacher of the abandoned title is Willibald Brandl (Alexander Girardi) who not only played divinely but also sang a mean waltz song. He is in the past tense, for he went off to America, was rumoured lost at sea, and his romantically inclined former pupil, Klara Schwott (Lina Abarbanell), went and married the wealthy confectioner Philipp Rosner (Karl Meister) and more or less forgot about her music master. But one day, when the piano tuner was in, Klara heard that waltz. Willibald was not drowned nor in America, but in her house. Finally, marriage lines prevail, and Willibald is paired off with Klara's maid, Jeannette (Betty Seidl). Oskar Sachs played Johann Nepomuc Nechledil, head of the Musikinstitut Nechledil and the possessor of three daughters called Lini, Tini and Fini, whilst the theatre's resident komische Alte, Sarolta von Rettich-Birk played Klara's mother. The key number of the score was, of course, the plotworthy waltz (Paradies Walzer), which shared the honours of the evening with the so-called Nechledil-Marsch.

Mounted at a theatre which had gone four years without initiating a hit, *Wiener Frauen* came nearer than any piece since *Der Opernball* to fulfilling Karczag's hopes and needs. It ran for 50 straight performances over the Christmas and New Year period and, if it was little seen after the producer at last found his elusive hit in its successor, Edmund Eysler's *Bruder Straubinger*, it was nevertheless played intermittently in the repertoire up to its 75th performance on 14 September 1905, 'helped' by the interpolation into its second act of 'Mlle Celia Galley of the Paris Nouveautés in her imitations of Bernhardt, Otéro, Guilbert, Réjane etc'.

In Aurel Föld and Adolf Merei's Hungarian version the Viennese ladies became *Pesti nők* (Women of Pest) and, later, in a revival at the Varosligeti Színkör (15 May 1907), they were rejuvenated as *Pesti asszonyok* (Girls of Pest).

Lehár's first Operette was also the first of his works to undergo what was to become his habitual process of remaking. In October 1906 – less than four years after *Wiener Frauen*'s initial run – the Leipzig Stadttheater produced a rewritten version of the piece entitled *Der Schlüssel zum Paradies*.

Hungary: Budai Színkör *Pesti nők* 15 August 1903

WILDCAT Musical in 2 acts by N Richard Nash. Lyrics by Carolyn Leigh. Music by Cy Coleman. Alvin Theater, New York, 16 December 1960.

The Broadway début of composer Cy Coleman, *Wildcat* was a vehicle for film and television comedy megastar Lucille Ball in the rôle of a bright and brassy little lady by the name of Wildcat Jackson who is out to make good amongst the oilfields of the American south. With nothing but her natural advantages to her name, she bluffs and fibs herself the services and the glances of Joe Dynamite (Keith Andes) – the best foreman around – as well as a drilling crew and a plot of ten acres for them to drill in. Inevitably at least one lie is found out, and her whole tale starts to topple. When it seems she will lose all of Joe's services, she sadly tips his belongings down the dry well-hole. But those belongings include dynamite. In the resulting panic, Joe's feelings for 'Wildy' finally come to the top round about the same time the dynamite proves that the well-hole wasn't dry after all.

The score of *Wildcat* came up with a take-away hit in Wildcat's cheer-up song to her beloved, lame sister (Paula Stewart), 'Hey, Look Me Over'. Elsewhere, the star leaped into a hoe-down over 'What Takes My Fancy' and took a quieter tone to reason out her ambitions in 'That's What I Want for Janie', Joe's assistant, Hal (Clifford David), coaxed lame Janie to forget her handicap in 'One Day We Dance', and the star's faded, foolish-elegant landlady (Edith King) tried to instal some ladylikeness into this Annie Oakley of the oilwells in 'Tippy, Tippy Toes'. An invitation to 'Give a Little Whistle' had different connotations to the song of the same title made popular in the cartoon film *Pinocchio*.

Wildcat, produced by director/choreographer Michael Kidd and librettist N Richard Nash, did good business until Miss Ball left the cast when it closed after 171 performances. An attempt to mount the show in Australia, with Toni Lamond and Stephen Boyd starred, played two months in Melbourne and did not move on to Sydney.

Australia: Princess Theatre, Melbourne 19 July 1963
Recording: original cast (RCA Victor)

WILDE, Oscar [Fingal O'Flahertie Wills] (b Dublin, 15 October 1854; d Paris, 30 November 1900).

Although, unlike such of his contemporaries as Barrie and Conan Doyle, Oscar Wilde wrote nothing for the musical theatre, other writers have, in recent years, seemed determined to mend the omission. The plays of the celebrated playwright have been grist to the mill of many an adapter-librettist of the 20th century, and it is probably more a comment on the unsuitability of the wordful Wildean style of comedy as the basis for musicalization than a reflection on the abilities of the adapters that the results have been almost entirely, if not egregiously, unsuccessful.

Unsurprisingly, Wilde's most popular play, *The Importance of Being Earnest*, has come under musical attack the most frequently. Broadway was first given *Oh, Ernest!* in 1927 (Robert Hood Bowers/Francis de Witt, Royale Theater 9 May) with Marjorie Gateson as Gwendolen, Hal Forde as John and Flavia Arcaro as Lady Bracknell, whilst Britain saw its first attempt at a musical *Importance of Being Earnest* in 1957 when *Found in a Handbag* (Allan Bacon, Margate 18 November 1957) was played in the provinces. A Vivian Ellis version, *Half in Earnest*, originally mooted for production by C B Cochran on the verge of the play's copyright expiry in 1950 with a stellar cast, instead found its way to the stage at America's Bucks County Playhouse, also in 1957, with Anna Russell starred as Lady Bracknell and Jack Cassidy as Worthing, and that version was played in Britain in 1958 (Coventry, 27 March) with Marie Löhr as Lady Bracknell, and later in Australia (Independent Theatre, 6 November 1974).

Earnest in Tune (John de Grey/Humphrey Tilley, Patricia Lawrence) was played at Canterbury the same year (4 August), *Ernest* (Malcom Sircom/Neil Wilkie/Henry Burke) at Farnham the next (18 May), and *Ernest in Love* (Lee Pockriss/Anne Croswell Grammercy Arts Theater, New York, 4 May 1960) kept the limp list growing the next year. A wave of Wilde adaptations in Germany brought forth a *Mein Freud Bunbury* (Gerd Natschinski/Bez, Degenhardt Metropltheater, 2 October 1964) which did alarming things to Wilde – it opened on Victoria station with Chasuble leading a Salvation Army choir in something like 'Follow the Fold', moved on to party at Algy Moncrieff's where everyone dances the 'Black Bottom' before trotting off to a music hall, and continued in Wilder and Wilder disarray – but nevertheless turned out to be East Germany's most successful musical comedy up to that time. Another *Bunbury* (Paul Burkhard/Hans Weigel) was played, close on its heels, at the Stadttheater, Basel (7 October 1965). The most recent adaptation, probably because most of the title variations had been already used, called itself simply *The Importance* (Sean O'Mahoney, Ambassador's Theatre, London, 23 June 1984) and was the first to make it to London's West End. It played 29 regular performances.

Lady Windermere's Fan was given several thoroughly professional adaptations, most notably in Noël Coward's *After the Ball* (Globe Theatre, London 10 June 1954). There was also an early burlesque *The Babble Shop, or Lord Wyndhamere's Fun* (Edward Rose, Trafalgar Square Theatre, 1898), and an Italian version, and Karl Farkas and Peter Kreuder turned out a piece in which Zarah Leander as 'Odette' Erlynne was supposed to be the *Lady aus Paris* opposite co-star Paul Hörbiger's Augustus Lorton (Raimundtheater, Vienna 22 October 1964, Theater des Westens, Berlin 19 March 1965).

If *An Ideal Husband* did nor seem ideal libretto-fodder, the German interest in Wilde-musicals provoked its use as such not once but twice in *Der Ideale Gatte* (Franz Grothe/ Hermann Mostar, Hamburger Kammerspiele 3 December 1963) and again in the curiously-titled *Piccadilly Circus* (Hary Osterwald, Curt Prina/Hans Schachner, Dick Price, Städtische Bühne, Munster 2 May 1975). Also in Germany, *Lord Arthur Saville's Crime* became *Lord Arthurs pflichtbewusstes Verbrechen* (Bernd Wefelmeyer/Gerd Hornawsky, Theater der Stadt, Plaunen, 10 January 1975).

Possibly the first Wilde musical, however, was a version of *The Canterville Ghost* which became *Das Gespenst von Matschatsch*, a burlesque opera by 'Simplizissimus' produced at the Munich Theater am Gärtnerplatz on 18 January 1905. Eleven months later Richard Strauss's opera of *Salome*, based on Wilde's text, was given its première in Dresden, followed in 1908 by Mariotte's French version of the same tale. Zemlinsky's operas *Eine florentinische Tragödie* (1917) and *Der Zwerg* (1922, on *The Birthday of the Infanta*) and Kika's Czech *Bílý pán* (1929, on *The Canterville Ghost*) later played in Germany as *Spuk im Schloss* (Breslau, 1931) were other operatic works with Wildean origins, whilst Jenő Hubay's Hungarian opera *Az őnzo óriás* (1 act, L Markus, J Mohácsi, 26 February 1936) was written around *The Selfish Giant*.

The central European preoccupation for musicalized Wilde continued in 1990 when an Hungarian 'rock opera' version of *The Picture of Dorian Gray* (previously operaticized in a more traditional way by Leonid Kreutzer) was successfully mounted at Budapest's Vigszinház (Mátyás Várkonyi/Gunar Braunke ad János Acs, 16 July) and subsequently adapted for the German stage. Another musical based on this same play had been announced – without coming to fruition – as an early project of the young producer Cameron Mackintosh, but by and large Wilde musicals were less frequent on English-language stages. American television, however, put out a 1966 musical version of *The Canterville Ghost*, written by Sheldon Harnick and Jerry Bock.

Sent on a lecture tour to America by D'Oyly Carte in order that Americans might the better appreciate the burlesque of the aesthetic movement (if not originally of Wilde personally) in Gilbert and Sullivan's *Patience*, Wilde ultimately found himself parodied by John Howson, the Bunthorne of one Broadway production. His notoriety made him an easy target for comedians, and he was subsequently burlesqued in a number of London shows. He was, however, actually portrayed on the Broadway stage in *Knights of Songs* (a piece which proposed itself as a Gilbert and Sullivan biomusical) where Robert Chisholm 'was' Wilde and sang numbers from *Patience*. The playwright, however, suffered a greater indignity when piece called *Dear Oscar* (Playhouse, 16 November 1972) was swept off Broadway in five nights. How he would have hated it.

WILDER, Victor (b Wetteren, Belgium, 21 August 1835; d Paris, 8 September 1892).

A journalist and theatrical author in Paris, Wilder contributed mostly to the operatic stage, adapting Wagner's *Ring des Nibelungen* into French and gallicizing Schubert's *Der häusliche Krieg* as *La Croisade des dames* (3 February 1868, Fantaisies-Parisiennes) as well as Mozart's *L'Oie de Caire*, Schumann's *Le Paradis et la Péri*, Paisiello's *Il barbiere di Siviglia*, Ricci's *La Fête de Piedigrotta* and *Une Folie à Rome*, Händel's *Judas Maccabaeus* and *The Messiah*, and supplying the text (w Mestépès) for Weber's *Sylvana* and Rubenstein's *Le Tour de Babel*. However, he was called upon by Victor Koning to work on the replacement libretto for the French production of Johann Strauss's *Indigo*, and as a result he was allotted two other Strauss assignments – the supply of a fresh text to go with a mixture of *Fledermaus* and *Cagliostro in Wien* music to make up another Strauss piece for Koning (*La Tzigane*) and an original tale commissioned by the Vienna Carltheater as a bait to Strauss to compose a work for them (*Prinz Methusalem*).

1875 **La Reine Indigo** (Johann Strauss/w Adolphe Jaime) Théâtre de la Renaissance 27 April

1877 **Prinz Methusalem** (Strauss/w Alfred Delacour ad Karl Treumann) Carltheater 3 January

1877 **La Tzigane** (Strauss/w Delacour) Théâtre de la Renaissance 30 October

1879 **Fatinitza** French version w Delacour (Théâtre des Nouveautés)

WILDFLOWER Musical play in 3 acts by Oscar Hammerstein II and Otto Harbach. Music by Vincent Youmans and Herbert Stothart. Casino Theater, New York, 7 February 1923.

The most successful show of Broadway's 1922–3 season, *Wildflower* was intended by its authors to take the currently fashionable 'Cinderella and her dancing chorus' kind of musical, epitomized by such pieces as *Irene* and *Sally*, and give it a more substantial, operettic dimension. They began by setting their show not in a mixture of high- and low-life New York, but in the Lombardy sunshine, and continued by picking up that favourite old theatrical theme the musical-comedy will, beloved of authors since the days of London's German Reed establishment and the 19th-century French vaudevillists (and probably other folk before), and mixing it with a good dose of the recently succesful play *Nothing But the Truth*. Their Cinderella, the ever-simmering farmgirl Nina Benedetto (*Irene* star Edith Day), is to inherit a fortune if she can keep her temper for six months. Nasty cousin Bianca (Evelyn Cavanaugh), who is next in line to inherit, naturally pursues Nina from farmyard to fancy villa on the banks of Lake Como and back, intent on irritating her to explosion-point, but she doesn't succeed and Nina ends up happily rich and wed to her peasant Guido (Guy Robertson).

The show's 13 songs plus two finales – written about half and half by the two composers – turned out one piece which won huge popularity in the heroine's lively 'Bambalina', 'a piquant little staccato melody with a refrain to which the singer stepped with rhythmical sounds, much as in the sabot dances of Holland' (the Bambalina of the title was actually an old man who played the fiddle for dancing). The hero's apostrophe to his 'Wildflower' – written, like the hit piece, by Youmans, although all were credited jointly – ran it a good second. The comedy was headed by Olin Howard and Esther Howard singing about 'The World's Worst Women'.

Arthur Hammerstein's production of *Wildflower* fulfilled all the hopes placed in it. It ran for 477 performances on Broadway and subsequently toured for more than two seasons whilst going on to productions in both London and Australia. London's version – which arrived in town on the peak of the Broadway-in-London wave as represented by *No, No, Nanette*, *Rose Marie* and *Mercenary Mary* – featured

Kitty Reidy (Nina), Evelyn Drewe (Bianca) and Howett Worster (Guido) with Mark Daly and Julie Hartley-Milburn heading the comedy. It had a bumpy ride, being transferred first to the Adelphi (3 April), then to His Majesty's Theatre (15 May), but it never looked like coming up to the level of the earlier shows in popularity. It closed after 114 performances.

In Australia, however, *Wildflower* was a hit, no little thanks to the young and darkly soprano Marie Burke, plucked from touring variety and cast by J C Williamson Ltd in the leading rôle. Herbert Browne (Guido), Marjorie Dawe (Bianca), Gus Bluett and Marie La Varre (Lucrezia) completed the team which – again in spite of having to shift theatres in both main centres – made *Wildflower* an all-Australian favourite. The show ran almost five months in its initial Sydney season and two and a half in its first stint in Melbourne (Her Majesty's 7 August 1925), and it was still to be seen in a revival under the Williamson banner as late as 1954.

Australia: Theatre Royal, Sydney 29 November 1924; UK: Shaftesbury Theatre 17 February 1926
Recording: London cast recordings (part-record) (WRC, Monmouth-Evergreen)

WILHELM [PITCHER, William John Charles] (b Northfleet, 21 March 1858; d London, 2 March 1925).

One of the most celebrated of British theatre designers, Wilhelm was prominent in the London theatre for some 40 years, for 25 of which he designed the costumes for the famous pantomimes at the Theatre Royal, Drury Lane. He both devised and designed a large number of the ballets at the Empire Theatre (including a *La Camargo* for Adeline Genée), from soon after its opening until the First World War, provided the costumes for many major spectaculars and pantomimes, and was one of the regular designers of clothes for the musical theatre over nearly half a century.

Amongst his credits were included a long run of the most famous Gaiety Theatre shows (*Cinder-Ellen Up-too-Late*, *In Town*, *Don Juan*, *The Shop Girl*, *My Girl*, *A Runaway Girl*, *The Messenger Boy*, *The Toreador*, *The Orchid*, *The Spring Chicken*, *The New Aladdin*), the original Savoy Theatre productions of *The Mikado* and *Ruddigore*, such early British musicals as *Manteaux Noirs*, *Rip van Winkle*, *The Vicar of Bray*, *Cymbia*, *The Golden Ring*, *Marjorie* and *Jane Annie*, and early 20th-century musical comedies including *The Girl from Kays*, *The Cherry Girl*, *The Blue Moon*, *The Dairymaids*, *Tom Jones*, *The Gay Gordons*, *The Arcadians* and *The Mousmé*. Amongst his last assignments were the clothes for J M Barrie's modern musical *Rosy Rapture*, with its clothes-horse star Gaby Deslys, and, in complete contrast, the period comic opera *Young England*.

WILHELM, Julius (b Vienna, 22 February 1871; d Hinterbrühl, 20 March 1941).

For 30 years a librettist for the musical stage, Julius Wilhelm contributed texts and lyrics to several internationally successful Operetten, as well as to a number more which had fine runs on home ground without going further. He had an early and very genuine success when Gabor Steiner mounted *Frühlingsluft*, his adaptation of the French comedy *Coquin de printemps* (w Carl Lindau) to a pasticcio Josef Strauss score, at his summer theatre, and

he confirmed that beginning with the text to the little entertainment *Wien bei Nacht*, 'ein Episode aus der Grossstadt', a second summer theatre success which, like the earlier one, was played for many seasons in Vienna, right into the 1920s.

He supplied the texts for two highly successful short pieces, Heinrich Reinhardt's *Die süsse Grisetten* and Leo Fall's *Brüderlein fein*, both of which subsequently travelled far (*The Daring of Diane*, *Darby and Joan*) from their productions at the Theater an der Wien's studio theatre, Hölle, but his first full-length pieces for the major Vienna theatres, an adaptation of Schönthan and von Moser's famous *Krieg im Frieden* (27 performances) and the unfortunate *Mutzi* (6 performances), both failed when mounted at the Carltheater. A further collaboration with Heinrich Reinhardt on *Die Sprudelfee* at the Raimundtheater in 1911 gave him his biggest international success to date, and another pasticcio piece, *Alt-Wien*, this time to the music of Josef Lanner, was a hit at the Carltheater, but it was the creation of the rôle of the old violinist, Racz, for Alexander Girardi in Kálmán's *Der Zigeunerprimás* which earned Wilhelm his biggest and best single credit, both at home and abroad.

Die Winzerbraut (137 performances at the Theater an der Wien), Hermann Dostal's little *Urschula*, which was played for two seasons on the bill at the Apollotheater and later in Hungary, and a fresh libretto manufactured to go with the music of Suppé's *Donna Juanita* score and played under the title *Die grosse Unbekannte* for 101 performances at the Johann Strauss-Theater were further Viennese successes for the librettist.

Wilhelm also collaborated with A M Willner on the 1914 opera *Der Schuster von Delft* (mus: Benito von Berra, Nationaltheater, Zagreb 26 January) and with Paul Frank on the libretto for Leo Fall's 1920 opera *Der goldene Vogel* (Dresden 21 May).

He was also the author (w Paul Frank) of the comedy *Ludwig XIV* (Theater des Westens, 15 March 1918) on which the Broadway musical *Louie the Fourteenth* was based.

1902 **Die ledige Frau** (Richard Haller/w Josef Sigmund) Neues Königliches Opernhaus 29 September
1902 **Was ein Frauenherz begehrt** (Ernst Reiterer/w Louis Gundlach) 1 act Danzers Orpheum 2 October
1903 **Frühlingsluft** (Johann Strauss arr Reiterer/w Carl Lindau) Venedig in Wien 9 May
1904 **Port Arthur** (Rudolf Raimann, R Laubner) Venedigin Wien 1 June
1904 **Spiritus** (Philipp Silber)
1904 **Wien bei Nacht** (Josef Hellmesberger/w Lindau) 1 act Venedig in Wien
1904 **Die Eisjungfrau** (*The Girl from Up There*) German version w Lindau, M Band (Venedig in Wien)
1906 **Krieg im Frieden** (Heinrich Reinhardt) Carltheater 24 January
1906 **Mutzi** (Hellmesberger/w Robert Pohl) Carltheater 15 September
1907 **Die süsse Grisetten** (Reinhardt) 1 act Hölle 1 December
1908 **Die Paradiesvogel** (Silber/w A M Willner) Theater am Gärtnerplatz, Munich 6 June
1908 **Drei kleine Mädel** (Béla Laszky) 1 act Hölle 18 November
1909 **Die Sprudelfee** (Reinhardt/w Willner) Raimundtheater 23 January
1909 **Brüderlein fein** (Leo Fall) 1 act Hölle 1 December

1910 **Eine gottliche Nacht** (Hermann Dostal) 1 act Hölle 1 March

1910 **Schneeglöckchen** (Gustave Kerker/w Willner) Theater an der Wien 14 October

1911 **Alt-Wien** (Josef Lanner arr/Gustav Kadelberg) Carl-theater 23 December

1912 **Susi** (*A kis grof*) German version (Carltheater)

1912 **Der Zigeunerprimás** (Emmerich Kálmán/w Fritz Grünbaum) Johann Strauss-Theater 11 October

1913 **Dorette** (Bruno Hartl/w Heinrich von Waldberg) Theater am Gärtnerplatz, Munich 7 February

1916 **Die Winzerbraut** (Oskar Nedbal/w Leo Stein) Theater an der Wien 11 February

1916 **Urschula** (H Dostal/w Bela Jenbach) Apollotheater 1 September

1919 **Die Verliebten** (Ralph Benatzky) Raimundtheater 29 March

1919 **Die Blume von Tokio** (Laszky) 1 act Hölle 1 July

1923 **Mozart** (Hans Duhan/w Paul Frank) Volksoper 2 June

1925 **1001 Freier** (Hans Zomack/w Frank) Stadttheater, Meissen 7 February

1925 **Die grosse Unbekannte** revised *Donna Juanita* w Gustav Beer Johann Strauss-Theater 8 April

1926 **General d'amour** (Julius Bittner/w Frank) Volksoper 3 March

1928 **Grisettenliebe** (Reinhardt) Rolandbühne 23 March

1929 **Pariser Blut** (H Reichart) Rose-Theater, Berlin 23 November

1930 **Böhmische Musikanten** (Bernhard Grün/w Peter Herz) Neues Operettenhaus, Leipzig 30 October; Wiener Bürgertheater 18 December 1931

1931 **Das Spitzentuch der Königin** new version w Rudolf Österreicher (Johann Strauss-Theater)

1931 **Der Hochstapler** (Richard Schwarz/w Gustav Heim) Volksoper, Hamburg 18 February

1932 **Freut euch das Lebens** (Josef and Johann Strauss arr Grün/w Herz) Neues Operetten-Theater, Leipzig 24 October

1933 **Tango am Mitternacht** (*Éjféli tangó*) German version (Volksoper)

WILKINSON, C[olm] T[homas] (b Dublin, 5 June 1944). Tenor/actor who has introduced or played several of the most substantial musical-dramatic rôles of the modern musical theatre on both sides of the Atlantic.

At first a member of the cabaret group 'The Witnesses', the Irish singer-songwriter made his earliest musical-theatre appearance as Judas in Dublin's production of *Jesus Christ Superstar* (1972), a rôle he later took over in the show's long running London production in 1974. Wilkinson initially mixed his theatre performances with periods in variety and cabaret, appearing on the one hand as Barach in the West End musical *Fire Angel* and as Herod in *Rock Nativity* at Reading, and, on the other, representing Ireland in the 1978 Eurovision song contest.

He sang Che on the pre-production recording of *Evita*, repeated the rôle of Judas in *Jesus Christ Superstar* on tour in Britain (1981), and starred as The Witness in the Irish musical *Voices* (1984), before moving on to create the English-language version of the rôle of Jean Valjean in *Les Misérables* in London (1985). He subsequently appeared in the same rôle in New York (1987) and as the *Phantom of the Opéra*, a rôle which he had initiated in its Sydmonton try-out, in Canada.

WILLEMETZ, Albert (b Paris, 14 February 1887; d Marnes-la-Coquette, 6 October 1964). The dominant librettist and lyricist – in quality and quantity – of the

French musical stage for several decades between and beyond the wars.

The young Albert Willemetz studied law and, after his graduation, took employment in the offices of the French Ministry of the Interior. During the War years he was attached to the cabinet office of President Clemenceau's government, whilst at the same time using another and rather different pen to supply sketches and, most particularly, song words to the revue stage.

The reputation which he built up in the world of the revue and the chanson was, however, eventually equalled and even overtaken by a fame second to none as the virtual inventor of, and, with André Barde, the most outstanding practitioner of the postwar jazz-age musical comedy. Theatre owner and producer Gustave Quinson, who had mounted Willemetz's very first stage piece, the one-act *Le Renseignement*, at the Palais-Royal as early as 1905, and who had since tied the young author to him in one of those 'collaborations' for which he was notorious, commissioned and produced the small-scale opérette-bouffe *Phi-Phi*, ultimately on the stage of the Théâtre des Bouffes-Parisiens. *Phi-Phi* ('C'est une gamine charmante', 'Les petits païens', 'Bien chapeau-tée', 'Ah! tais-toi' etc etc) became the hit of an era. The intimate, wittily sexy tone of its well-constructed farcical text, and of lyrics which were both revusically pointed and unashamedly but unclichédly saucy in a style that had nothing to do with the opérettes of pre-war years, proved wholly to the taste of the audiences of a liberated France, well and truly ready for the good time the 'années folles' of one-steps and foxtrots promised. Willemetz's style became the joyously fashionable style of the French postwar musical stage.

Willemetz followed up the triumph of *Phi-Phi* with another, barely lesser, in *Dédé* ('Dans la vie faut pas s'en faire', 'Je m'donne', 'Si j'avais su' etc), but for the next two pieces in his triumphant series he left the task of the libretto to another of Quinson's team, Yves Mirande, and himself concentrated on the lyrics which were his favourite area of work. With Maurice Yvain he supplied the songs to the dazzling *Ta bouche* ('Ta bouche', 'Des terres et des coupons', 'Ça, c'est une chose', 'La seconde étreinte', 'Non, non, jamais les hommes', 'Machinalement', 'De mon temps' etc) and the Maurice Chevalier-Dranem fantasy *Là-haut* ('C'est Paris', 'Si vous n'aimez pas ça' etc), but when allied once more with *Phi-Phi* and *Dédé*'s composer, Henri Christiné, he again provided both book and lyrics for a further success in the delicious little tale of *Madame*.

Thereafter, the successes – in various degrees – rolled out in sequence, rarely interrupted by failure, as Willemetz supplied unfailingly clever song-words and, from time to time, libretti or part-libretti to many of the 1920s most popular shows. *En chemyse* returned to the historical burlesque style so successfully practised in *Phi-Phi*, if without the same triumph, the little *Ri-Ri*, a vehicle for *Le Fruit vert* star Maud Loty, ran for more than 100 nights at the Théâtre Daunou, *Trois jeune filles ... nues!* ('Est-ce que je te demande?') was a copper-bottomed hit, and the intimate comedy musical *Quand on est trois* had a fine run at the little Théâtre des Capucines. *J'aime*, a further piece with Christiné, followed the now-normal course of events, and Willemetz's collaboration with André Messager, the opérette hero of the pre-war French musical stage, on an up-to-date musical comedy proved a singular success, with first *Passionnément* and then *Coups de roulis* proving to be enduring hits.

When the fashion for his kind of musical comedy, a species based on a witty farcical text and modern songs and dances, gave way to that for the romantic opérette à grand spectacle, Willemetz went with the tide. He adapted a number of foreign successes to the French stage (*New Moon*, *Good News*, *Madame Pompadour*, *The Dubarry* etc) and authored or co-authored Richepin's spectacular *Venise* and such large-stage Châtelet shows as *Sidonie Panache* and *Au temps des merveilleuses* to scores by his erstwhile partners in the area of the intimate musical.

In 1927, without decreasing his workload as a writer, Willemetz also joined Quinson in the management of the Théâtre des Bouffes-Parisiens, the scene of his first great hit (and a great many since), and there he was involved in the production of such pieces as *Les Aventures du Roi Pausole*, *Flossie* and *Arsène Lupin banquier*. In 1929, with Quinson's era of dominance beginning to come to an end, he took over the famous theatre and, subsequently partnering with Louis Meucci, continued to run it for some years, scoring a success with the comical *Un soir de réveillon*, winning critical bouquets, at least, for Sacha Guitry's *O mon bel inconnu*, more substantially financial ones for the rumba-musical *Toi c'est moi* and, above all, for his own greatest success of the period, the adaptation (w Leopold Marchand) of the German musical play *Drei Walzer* as a vehicle for Yvonne Printemps and Pierre Fresnay. For two seasons he also joined Quinson at the head of the affairs of the Palais-Royal.

By the Second World War, though still enormously active on both the stage and screen, Willemetz had done most of his best work for the theatre, but he still had a few cartridges to expend. He expanded the libretto of Lecocq's *Les Cent Vierges* for the Théâtre de la Gaîté-Lyrique and disproved the fairly water-tight theory that adaptations are necessarily destructive when he produced a book which quite simply outshone the original. A similar attempt on the *Grande-Duchesse* was, however, not successful. Proving his continual adaptability, he joined the newly prominent Vincy-Lopez school of musical theatre and supplied the lyrics for one of the most successful of their shows, *Andalousie*, and he also adapted Irving Berlin's songwords for *Annie du Far-West* (*Annie Get Your Gun*) for the French stage.

In spite of his long and important career, however, it is as the man of the 1920s that Willemetz made his mark. But it was a mark which was almost entirely confined to France, for the 'outrageous' sexual comedy of his lyrics and libretti made them deeply unsuitable for the polite ears of the English-speaking world, in particular. *Phi-Phi*, *Dédé* and *Ta bouche* all underwent severe bowdlerization (amongst other operations) for their English-language productions and, not surprisingly, failed. Only in Hungary, beyond the borders of France, did his work find the kind of reception that it won at home.

Various figures have been given over the years as to Willemetz's output. It is said that he wrote the lyrics to over 3,000 songs ('Valentine', 'Mon homme', 'J'en ai marre' etc), contributed more or sometimes less to 150 revues and wrote the text and/or lyrics to some hundred operettes.

Even if some or all of these figures have been rounded (severely?) upwards – and the figures are never accompanied by lists – Willemetz still remains one of, if not the most important and enjoyable writers for the musical theatre of his era. Of any era. Anywhere.

Willemetz was for a number of years President of SACEM, the French copyright authority.

1918 **Phi-Phi** (Henri Christiné/w Fabien Sollar) Théâtre des Bouffes-Parisiens 13 November

1919 **Rapatipatoum** (Tiarko Richepin) Théâtre Édouard VII 7 April

1921 **Dédé** (Christiné) Théâtre des Bouffes-Parisiens 10 November

1922 **Ta bouche** (Maurice Yvain/Yves Mirande) Théâtre Daunou 1 April

1923 **Là-haut** (Yvain/Mirande, Gustave Quinson) Théâtre des Bouffes-Parisiens 31 March

1923 **Madame** (Christiné) Théâtre Daunou 14 December

1924 **En chemyse** (Raoul Moretti/w Cami) Théâtre des Bouffes-Parisiens 7 March

1925 **J'adore ça** (Christiné/w Saint-Granier) Théâtre Daunou 14 March

1925 **Quand on est trois** (Joseph Szulc/Pierre Veber, Serge Veber) Théâtre des Capucines 20 April (sic)

1925 **Ri-Ri** (Charles Borel-Clerc/Mirande, Quinson) Théâtre Daunou 6 November

1925 **Trois jeunes filles ... nues!** (Moretti/w Mirande) Théâtre des Bouffes-Parisiens 3 December

1926 **Passionnément** (André Messager/w Maurice Hennequin) Théâtre de la Michodière 15 January

1926 **J'aime** (Christiné/w Saint-Granier) Théâtre des Bouffes-Parisiens 22 December

1927 **Venise** (Richepin/w André Mouëzy-Éon) Théâtre Marigny 25 June

1927 **Le Diable à Paris** (Marcel Lattès/w Robert de Flers, Francis de Croisset) Théâtre Marigny 27 November

1928 **Coups de roulis** (Messager) Théâtre Marigny 29 September

1929 **Couchette No 3** (Szulc/Alex Madis) Théâtre des Capucines 6 February

1929 **Good News** French version (Palace Théâtre)

1930 **Madame Pompadour** French version w Eddy and Marietti (Théâtre Marigny)

1930 **Robert le pirate** (*The New Moon*) French version (Théâtre du Châtelet)

1930 **Les Aventures du Roi Pausole** (Arthur Honegger) Théâtre des Bouffes-Parisiens 12 December

1931 **Sidonie Panache** (Szulc/w Mouëzy-Éon) Théâtre du Châtelet 2 December

1932 **Nina Rosa** French version w Mouëzy-Éon (Théâtre du Châtelet)

1932 **La Tulipe noir** (Richepin/Mouëzy-Éon) Théâtre de la Gaîté-Lyrique 19 March

1933 **Rose de France** (Sigmund Romberg/Mouëzy-Éon) Théâtre du Châtelet 28 October

1933 **Florestan 1er, Prince de Monte Carlo** (Werner Richard Heymann/w Sacha Guitry) Théâtre des Variétés 8 December

1933 **La Dubarry** (*Die Dubarry*) French lyrics (Théâtre de la Porte-Saint-Martin)

1934 **Le Bonheur, mesdames!** (Christiné arr/Francis de Croisset, Fred de Grésac ad) Théâtre des Bouffes-Parisiens 6 January

1934 **Au temps des merveilleuses** (Christiné, Richepin/w Mouëzy-Éon) Théâtre du Châtelet 25 December?

1934 **La Créole** new libretto w Georges Delance (Théâtre Marigny)

1935 **Les Joies du Capitole** (Moretti/Jacques Bousquet) Théâtre de la Madeleine 25 February

1935 **Pour ton bonheur** (Marcel Lattès/Léopold Marchand) Théâtre des Bouffes-Parisiens 20 September

1935 **Un coup de veine** (Yvain/w Mouëzy-Éon) Théâtre de la Porte-Saint-Martin 11 October

1935 **Au Soleil du Mexique** (Yvain/w Mouëzy-Éon) Théâtre du Châtelet 18 December

1936 **Yana** (Christiné, Richepin/w Mouëzy-Éon, Henri Werner) Théâtre du Châtelet 24 December

1936 **Simone est comme ça** (Moretti/Mirande, Madis) Théâtre des Bouffes-Parisiens 5 March

1937 **Trois valses** (*Drei Walzer*) French version w Leopold Marchand (Théâtre des Bouffes-Parisiens)

1938 **Le Flirt ambulant** (Christiné/w Tristan Bernard) Théâtre Michel 13 January

1938 **Les Petites Cardinal** (Jacques Ibert, Honneger/w Paul Brach) Théâtre des Bouffes-Parisiens 12 February

1939 **Billy et son équipe** (Michel Emer, 'Jean Sautreuil'/w Mouëzy-Éon) Théâtre Mogador 6 March

1940 **Mes amours** (Oscar Straus/w Marchand) Théâtre Marigny 2 May

1942 **Valses de France** (pasticcio arr Henri Casadesus/Eddy Ghilain) Théâtre du Châtelet 23 December

1942 **Les Cent Vierges** new libretto w Mouëzy-Éon (Théâtre Apollo)

1945 **Pantoufle** (Szulc/w Marchand) Théâtre des Capucines 28 February

1947 **Andalousie** (Francis Lopez/w Raymond Vincy) Théâtre de la Gaîté-Lyrique 25 October

1948 **La Maréchale Sans-Gêne** (Pierre Petit/Maurice Lehmann) Théâtre du Châtelet 17 February

1948 **La Grande-Duchesse de Gérolstein** new libretto (Théâtre de la Gaîté-Lyrique)

1949 **Annie du Far-West** French lyrics (Théâtre du Châtelet)

1956 **La Quincaillère de Chicago** (Louiguy/w Jean Le Seyeux) Théâtre de l'ABC 4 October

1961 **Le Jeu de dames** (Georges van Parys/w Georges Manoir) Théâtre Moderne 2 December

Autobiography: *Dans mon retroviseur* (La Table Ronde, Paris, 1967)

WILLIAMS, Arthur (b London, 9 February 1844; d London, 15 September 1915). Top British musical comedian of the Victorian era.

Arthur Williams began his professional life as a legal stationer, and first performed in 'booths, fit-ups and ghost shows'. He graduated to the theatre in 1861, and spent seven years in the provinces before making his London début at the St James's Theatre. It was, however, yet another decade before he became prominent in the musical theatre. After appearing in a supporting part in *Venice* (*Le Pont des soupirs*) at the Alhambra he was cast in the rôle of the comico-nasty Sir Mincing Lane in the Solomon/Stephens *Billee Taylor* (1880), and he followed up in the same team's next musicals, playing Sir Whiffle Whaffle in *Claude Duval* (1881) and Robinson Brownjones in *Virginia and Paul* (1883). His success in the title-rôle of the burlesque *Oliver Grumble* (1886) won him a contract from John Hollingshead at the Gaiety Theatre and his first engagement there was the part of the comic bailiff, Lurcher, in *Dorothy*.

Dorothy made Williams a star. He remained with the show through its two-and-a-half-year run, continued on into the management's follow-up *Doris* (1889, Dinniver) and as Corporal Bundy in *The Red Hussar*, before returning to the Gaiety to play in the later new burlesques. He

Plate 293. **Arthur Williams** *as Lurcher in* Dorothy.

appeared as Zuniga ('The Villain of the Day') in *Carmen Up-to-Data*, as Sir Ludgate Hill in *Cinder-Ellen Up-too-Late*, and as Doggrass in *Blue-Eyed Susan* (1892) before Edwardes's change of policy brought musical comedy to the Gaiety. Williams went on to play more comical nasties as Mr Hooley in *The Shop Girl* (1894), and the ringmaster, Drivelli in *The Circus Girl* (1896), before moving on to a career which mixed more straight comedy with the musical comedy. He had further major successes on the musical stage, however, when he took over as Mr Pineapple, the hapless hero of *A Chinese Honeymoon* and played the amenable convict Crookie Scrubbs to the *Sergeant Brue* of Willie Edouin (1904), less when he appeared briefly as Topping in *Miss Wingrove* (1905), and found yet another hit playing Edna May's father as Sir John Chaldicott in *The Belle of Mayfair*.

Williams returned to Edwardes management in 1908 to take his place in the next new style of musical theatre, and was cast as the comical King Joachim in *A Waltz Dream*. He repeated the rôle that had made his fame in a revival of *Dorothy*, and then returned to play comedy parts in two further Viennese works: Lopf in *The Merry Peasant* and the naughty train conductor Scrop in *The Girl in the Train*. This last was his final musical theatre performance, but he remained on the stage until his death in 1915.

Williams was married to the actress and burlesque player Emily Spiller and was uncle to the comedian Fred Emney, who replaced him briefly in *Dorothy*.

WILLIAMS, [Eg]Bert [Austin] (b Antigua, West Indies, 12 November 1874; d Detroit, 4 March 1922).

During his early years in the San Francisco minstrel world, Bert Williams made up a partnership with fellow minstrel George Walker. Their cakewalk act won them a Broadway spot in the short-lived Victor Herbert musical *The Gold Bug*, and they moved on to play their mixture of comedy, song and dance in variety and, quickly at the top of the bill, in a series of musical plays. They toured in *Clorindy* (*The Senegambian Carnival*), then joined the management of Hurtig and Seamon which produced the musical comedies *The Policy Players*, *The Sons of Ham*, the pair's most successful show *In Dahomey* and *Bandana Land* before the dying Walker dropped out of the business.

Williams went on to star alone in *Mr Load of Koal* (1909) and then joined *The Ziegfeld Follies* where he became famous through a decade of stand-up comedy performances and songs ('Nobody' etc). He appeared in *Broadway Brevities* and took once more to the musical theatre in *Under the Bamboo Tree* (ex- *The Pink Slip*) in 1922, but he collapsed during a performance at Detroit and died in a town hospital 11 days later. *Under the Bamboo Tree* switched its title to *In the Moonlight* and finally struggled to Broadway with James Barton in Williams's rôle as *Dew Drop Inn* in 1923.

A *Williams and Walker* biomusical was produced at off-Broadway's American Place Theater in 1986 (9 March).

Biography: Charters, A: *Nobody: The Story of Bert Williams* (New York, 1970)

WILLIAMS, Hattie (b Boston, 1870; d New York, 17 August 1942). Broadway star soubrette of comedy and musical comedy.

Hattie Williams first appeared on the stage in her native Boston, in E E Rice's extravaganza *1492*, and she moved from the chorus to a small named rôle for the Broadway transfer. She subsequently played in several Hoyt farce comedies, appeared with the Rogers Brothers, and made her mark in musical comedy when she starred in the Broadway version of *The Girl from Kays* (1903, Winnie Harborough). In the next few years, she took the large and versatile title-rôle of *The Rollicking Girl* (*Heisses Blut*), was starred above the title as the actress Molly Montrose in *The Little Cherub* and played the title-rôle of *Fluffy Ruffles*, a musical based on the *New York Herald*'s cartoon. She then spent several seasons in the straight theatre before returning to play the naughty Praline in Berény's Operette *The Girl from Montmartre*, a rôle which she had long played in the original play, *The Girl from Maxim's*, earlier in her career. She made a last Broadway musical appearance as Rosalilla in *The Doll Girl* (1913), America's version of Leo Fall's *Das Puppenmädel*, before retiring from the stage.

WILLIAMSON, J[ames] C[assius] (b Mercer, Pa, 26 August 1845 (1844?); d Paris, 6 July 1913). Australia's principal producer of musical theatre during and, through the company he founded, long after his lifetime.

A successful character comedian on the New York and San Francisco stages, Williamson, with his wife Maggie Moore, scored a particular success in Australia where, from 1874, their Dutch-dialect comedy melodrama *Struck Oil* became an enormous hit. In 1879 Williamson legally secured the rights to the all-pervading *HMS Pinafore* for Australasia, and he appeared as Sir Joseph Porter in the region's 'official' production, whilst bringing the law to bear on pirated versions. As a result, Gilbert, who had previously had cause to be struck by the man's honesty amid wide and otherwise uncontrollable piracy, ensured that he was allotted similar rights for the other Gilbert and Sullivan comic operas, and his highly successful and high-class productions of these works provided the basis for what was to become Australia's most powerful production company for a period of almost 100 years.

Williamson's Royal Comic Opera Company (operated at various periods in partnership with Arthur Garner and/or George Musgrove) presented a large part of the most successful musical shows from the world's stages to Australia during the 1880s and 1890s and, as opposition companies came, went or were swallowed up by 'the firm', his business developed into J C Williamson Ltd which continued to introduce the largest part of the world's musical theatre to 20th-century Australia and New Zealand. Variously run by Sir George Tallis and the four Tait brothers with continuing success, the firm finally fell to pieces in the 1970s.

Biography: Dicker, I G: *J.C.W.* (Elizabeth Tudor Press, Sydney, 1974)

WILLNER, A[lfred] M[aria] (b Vienna, 11 July 1859; d Vienna, 27 October 1929). One of the busiest and most successful authors for the 20th-century Viennese Operette stage.

Journalist Willner came late to the theatre, and made his first appearances on Viennese theatre-bills as the author of ballet scenarii: Josef Bayer's *Rund um Wien* (Hofoper 1894) and Harry Berté's 1895 *Amor auf Reisen* (w Gaul, Hassreiter). It was in collaboration with Berté that he essayed his first libretto, the one-act comic opera *Die Schneeflocke*, produced in Prague and later at Berlin's Neues Königliches Opernhaus and the Budapest Operaház (March 1899) and, whilst still lingering intermittently in related areas with such pieces as Forster's one-act opera *Tokayer*, he quickly moved on to larger things in the light musical theatre, collaborating with Bernhard Buchbinder on libretti for Carl Weinberger, Josef Bayer and for Johann Strauss.

Success was not immediate. Weinberger's *Der Schmetterling* had a fair career after a 57-performance first run, Bayer's *Fräulein Hexe* folded in 11 showings, and the Strauss Operette *Die Göttin der Vernunft* played 32 successive performances and a handful of subsequent matinées in Vienna and was seen in several other central European cities without establishing itself. In fact, Willner's first real success as a librettist came, ultimately, as an adapter when he remade Maurice Ordonneau's libretto for *La Poupée* for its enormously popular German production.

Adaptations of a pair of celebrated comedies, *Le Mari de la débutante* (*Die Debütantin*) and *The Magistrate* (*Das Baby*), as distinctly uncelebrated musicals, and the translation of Planquette's operétte *Mam'selle Quat' Sous* for Girardi and the Theater an der Wien did not bring further success, but it was the latter house which gave the librettist his first major hit with an original text when it produced Leo Fall's musicalization of the dotty American tale of *Die Dollarprinzessin*.

The author's most fruitful and busy period then followed as Albini's *Baron Trenck* found its way from Leipzig to the stages of the world, and the singular international success of Lehár's *Der Graf von Luxemburg* – a rewrite of the unloved *Die Göttin der Vernunft* libretto – set in motion a series of collaborations with the composer which included the more dramatic *Zigeunerliebe, Eva, Endlich allein* and the adaptation of *La Femme et le pantin* as *Frasquita* as well as the German versions of his Hungarian operett *A Pacsirta* (*Wo die Lerche singt*) and his Italian revue-operetta *La danza delle libellule* (*Libellentanz*).

In the same period Willner and his collaborators provided Leo Fall with the texts for *Das Puppenmädel, Die schöne Risette* and *Die Sirene*, authored Oscar Straus's *Die kleine Freundin*, Reinhardt's *Die Sprudelfee* and *Prinzess Gretl* (156 performances), Eysler's *Wenn zwei sich lieben* (110 performances) and Kálmán's *Die Faschingsfee*, all with success. He adapted the famous *Official Wife* tale as the libretto for Herman Dostal's *Nimm mich mit!* and supplied Oskar Nedbal with the text for *Die schöne Saskia* for 131 performances at the Carltheater, but his greatest success came when he was teamed once more with the composer of his débuts, Harry Berté, and Heinz Reichert on the Schubert pasticcio *Das Dreimäderlhaus*. This fictional Schubertian love story turned out to be one of Vienna's greatest hits in decades, went round the world thereafter, and even provoked a musequel, *Hannerl*, from the same authors' pen.

The 1920s were mildly less productive. *Frasquita* and *Libellentanz* both had appreciable lives, Ernst Steffan's *Das Milliarden-Souper* had a six-month run at Berlin's Berliner Theater before failing in 28 performances in Vienna, Oscar Straus's *Nixchen* topped 100 performances at the Wallner-Theater and Leo Fall's posthumous *Rosen aus Florida* had a good 244 performances at the Theater an der Wien, but there was one more major success awaiting the librettist. After the success of *Das Dreimäderlhaus*, he had been tempted into another pasticcio show telling the life of *Johann Nestroy* as portrayed by Willy Thaller at the Carltheater, and now, a dozen years on, he turned his attention to Johann Strauss and, in collaboration with the most habitual partner of his later years, Heinz Reichert, embroidered a love-and-fame story onto the bones of the history of Vienna's most celebrated composer. The posthumously produced *Walzer aus Wien* did not outdo *Das Dreimäderlhaus* on home ground but, like it, it became the starting point for a long list of foreign versions, each of which maintained the fictitious romantic situations invented by the Viennese authors.

Amongst Willner's other stage works were three operatic libretti for composer Carl Goldmark: the adaptation of Charles Dickens's *A Cricket on the Hearth* as *Das Heimchen am Herd*, the 1902 version of Goethe's *Götz von Berlichingen*, and the Shakespearian *Ein Wintermärchen* (1908). His *Der Eisenhammer* and *Der Schuster von Delft*, set by Benito von Berra, were produced in Zagreb in 1911 and 1914 respectively, whilst the libretto written for Puccini by Willner and Reichert was translated into Italian before being set as *La Rondine*. His name was also attached very posthumously to the Operette *Die kleine Schwindlerin* (mus: Jára Beneš) produced at Vienna's Theater Auges Gottes in 1949 (1 March).

1896 **Die Schneeflocke** (Heinrich Berté) 1 act Prague 4 October

1896 **Der Schmetterling** (Carl Weinberger/w Bernard Buchbinder) Theater an der Wien 7 November

1897 **Die Göttin der Vernunft** (Johann Strauss/w Buchbinder) Theater an der Wien 13 March

1898 **Fräulein Hexe** (Josef Bayer/w Buchbinder) Theater an der Wien 19 November

1899 **Die Puppe** (*La Poupée*) German version Centraltheater, Berlin

1901 **Die Debütantin** (Alfred Zamara/w Heinrich von Waldberg) Theater am Gärtnerplatz, Munich 17 January; Carltheater 4 October

1902 **Das Baby** (Richard Heuberger/w Waldberg) Carltheater October

1903 **Die beiden Don Juans** (*Mam'selle Quat' Sous*) German version w Robert Pohl (Theater an der Wien)

1904 **Die Millionenbraut** (Berté/w E Limé) Theater am Gärtnerplatz, Munich 3 April

1907 **Der schöne Gardist** (Berté/w Alexander Landesberg) Neues Operetten-Theater, Breslau 12 October

1907 **Die Dollarprinzessin** (Leo Fall/w Fritz Grünbaum) Theater an der Wien 2 November

1907 **Der kleine Chevalier** (Berté) 1 act Centraltheater, Dresden 30 November

1908 **Baron Trenck** (Felix Albini/w Robert Bodanzky) Leipzig, Kaiser-Jubiläums Stadttheater 29 October 1909

1908 **Der Glücksnarr** (Berté/w Landesberg) Carltheater 7 November

1908 **Ein Mädchen für alles** (Heinrich Reinhardt/w Waldberg) Theater am Gärtnerplatz, Munich 8 February

1908 **Die Paradiesvogel** (Philipp Silber/w Julius Wilhelm) Theater am Gärtnerplatz, Munich 6 June

1909 **Der Graf von Luxemburg** (Franz Lehár/w Bodanzky) Theater an der Wien 12 November

1909 **Die Sprudelfee** (Reinhardt/w Wilhelm) Raimundtheater 23 January

1910 **Zigeunerliebe** (w Bodanzky/Lehár) Carltheater 8 January

1910 **Schneeglöckchen** (Gustave Kerker/w Wilhelm) Theater an der Wien 14 October

1910 **Das Puppenmädel** (Fall/w Leo Stein) Carltheater 4 November

1910 **Die schöne Risette** (Fall/w Bodanzky) Theater an der Wien 30 November

1911 **Die Sirene** (Fall/w Stein) Johann Strauss-Theater 5 January

1911 **Die kleine Freundin** (Oscar Straus/w Stein) Carltheater 20 October

1911 **Eva** (Lehár/w Bodanzky) Theater an der Wien 24 November

1911 **Casimirs Himmelfahrt** (Bruno Granichstädten/w Bodanzky) Raimundtheater 25 December

1911 **Der Flotte Bob** (Karl Stigler/w Wilhelm Sterk) Altes Theater, Leipzig 8 April

1913 **Prinzess Gretel** (Reinhardt/w Bodanzky) Theater an der Wien 31 January

1914 **Endlich allein** (Lehár/Bodanzky) Theater an der Wien 30 January

1914 **Der Märchenprinz** (Berté/w Sterk) Schauburg, Hanover 4 March

1914 **Der Durchgang der Venus** (Edmund Eysler/w Rudolf Österreicher) Apollotheater 28 November

1915 **Der künstliche Mensch** (Fall/w Österreicher) Theater des Westens, Berlin 2 October

1915 **Die erste Frau** (Reinhardt/w Österreicher) Carltheater 22 October

1915 **Wenn zwei sich lieben** (Eysler/w Bodanzky) Theater an der Wien 29 October

1916 **Das Dreimäderlhaus** (Franz Schubert arr Berté/w Reichert) Raimundtheater 15 January

1917 **Die Faschingsfee** (Emmerich Kálmán/w Österreicher) Johann Strauss-Theater 21 September

1917 **Die schöne Saskia** (Oskar Nedbal/w Reichert) Carltheater 16 November

1918 **Hannerl** (Schubert arr Karl Lafite/w Reichert) Raimundtheater 8 February

1918 **Wo die Lerche singt** (*A pacsirta*) German version w Reichert (Theater an der Wien)

1918 **Johann Nestroy** (arr Ernst Reiterer/w Österreicher) Carltheater 4 December

1919 **Nimm mich mit!** (Herman Dostal/w Waldberg) Theater an der Wien 1 May

1921 **Das Milliarden-Souper** (Ernst Steffan/w Hans Kottow) Berliner Theater, Berlin 16 April

1921 **Nixchen** (Straus/w Österreicher) Wallner-Theater, Berlin 10 September

1921 **Der heilige Ambrosius** (Fall/w Arthur Rebner) Deutsches Künstlertheater, Berlin 3 November

1922 **Frasquita** (Lehár/w Reichert) Theater an der Wien 12 May

1923 **Libellentanz** (*La danza delle libellule*) revised *Der Sterngucker* German version (Stadttheater)

1924 **Agri** (Steffan/w Sterk) Bürgertheater 30 January

1924 **Ein Ballroman** (Robert Stolz/w Österreicher, Fritz Rotter) Apollotheater 29 February

1926 **Der Mitternachtswalzer** (Stolz/w Österreicher) Wiener Bürgertheater 30 October

1928 **Ade, du liebes Elternhaus** (Oskar Jascha/w Reichert) Volksoper 5 January

1929 **Rosen aus Florida** (Fall arr Korngold/w Reichert) Theater an der Wien 22 February

1930 **Walzer aus Wien** (Strauss arr Korngold/w Reichert, Marischka) Wiener Stadttheater 30 October

WILLSON, Meredith [REINIGER, Robert Meredith] (b Mason City, Iowa, 18 May 1902; d Santa Monica, Calif, 15 June 1984). Author and composer of one of Broadway's most memorable postwar musicals.

A flautist in bands and orchestras, including the Sousa band (1921–3) and the New York Philharmonic (1924–9), a musical director for NBC and other radio networks, a songwriter ('May the Good Lord Bless You and Keep You', 'I See the Moon') and composer of band, piano, orchestral and film music (*The Great Dictator* 1940, *The Little Foxes* 1941), Willson was pointed towards the musical theatre by the ever-on-the-ball Frank Loesser when already well into his musical career. His first stage musical, *The Music Man* (1957), was a huge and international success, and he followed up with two other successful pieces, the jolly tale of *The Unsinkable Molly Brown* and the little fantasy, *Here's Love*, a stage musical adaptation of *The Miracle on 34th Street*, both of which had good runs on Broadway (532 and 338 performances respectively) without looking likely to equal the admittedly virtually unequalable appeal of his first show.

A 1969 piece, *1491*, produced by the San Francisco and Los Angeles Civic Light Opera with a cast headed by John Cullum, Jean Fenn and Chita Rivera, did not move east.

1957 **The Music Man** (Willson) Majestic Theater 19 December

1960 **The Unsinkable Molly Brown** (Richard Morris) Winter Garden Theater 3 November

1963 **Here's Love** (Willson) Shubert Theater 3 October

1969 **1491** (w Morris, Ira Barmak) Dorothy Chandler Pavilion, Los Angeles 2 September

Autobiographies: *And There I Stood With My Piccolo* (Doubleday, Garden City, 1948), *Eggs I Have Laid* (Holt, New York, 1955), *But He Doesn't Know the Territory* (Putnam, New York, 1959)

WILSON, Francis (b Philadelphia, 7 February 1854; d New York, 7 October 1935). Broadway musical low comic of the 19th century.

Wilson first appeared in New York in farce-comedy (*Our Goblins* etc) and played in several straight plays before fixing his career as a comedian in musical theatre. He was engaged by John McCaull for the comic opera company at the new Casino Theater where he was given increasing comedy rôles in *The Queen's Lace Handkerchief* (t/o Don Sancho), *The Princess of Trébizonde* (t/o Trémolini), *Prince Methusalem* (Sigismund), *The Merry War* (Balthazar Groot), *Falka* (Folbach), *Nanon* (Marquis de Marsillac), *Apajune* (Prutchesko), *Amorita* (Castrucci) and in *The Gipsy Baron* (Zsupán) before being cast in the British comic opera *Erminie* in the rôle of Cadeau invented by Harry Paulton for himself and here recreated in an americanized version under the direction of the author/original star.

The record-breaking success of *Erminie* lifted Wilson into the star class and, for a while thereafter, his vehicles were presented under the banner of 'the Francis Wilson Comic Opera Company'. These included versions of the French *La Jolie Persane* (*The Oolah*, Hoolah Goolah), *L'Étoile* (*The Merry Monarch*, King Anso IV) and *Le Grand Casimir* (*The Lion Tamer*, Casimir), Sullivan's *The Chieftain* (Grigg), an American comic opera *The Little Corporal* (Petipas) in which he impersonated Napoléon, and remusicked versions of France's *Babolin* as *The Devil's Deputy* (Melissen) and *Le Roi de carreau* as *Half a King* (Tireschappe), as well as frequent revivals of *Erminie*.

Wilson appeared in the title-rôle of Victor Herbert's unsuccessful *Cyrano de Bergerac* (1899), took the chief comic rôles of *The Monks of Malabar* (1900, Boolboom), and George Lederer's production of *The Strollers* (1901, August Lump), a version of the Austrian hit *Die Landstreicher*, and played Teddy Payne's rôle of little Sammy Gigg in the Broadway version of the London musical *The Toreador* (1902), in the most successful of his ventures since *Erminie*. He signed off his career as a musical star with a reprise of the inevitable *Erminie* in 1903, but returned in 1921 to play the rôle which had made his name one last time.

He subsequently authored a book of memoirs which showed if not a tendency to distort the truth for the sake of a good story or a good plug, then a distinctly iffy memory.

Memoirs: *Francis Wilson's Life of Himself* (Houghton Miflin, Boston, 1924)

WILSON, Sandy [WILSON, Alexander Galbraith] (b Sale, 19 May 1924). Versatile British author/songwriter who was able to write both a major international hit and a connoisseur's delight before wit and charm went out of fashion.

Wilson made his first impact as a writer and composer in the early 1950s, in the heyday of the small club-theatres into which British revue and musical-theatre writers had retreated under the post-war barrage of big Broadway musicals which were dominating the major West End venues of the period. A youthful venture into lyric-writing for a latter-day Jack Waller production aside, his early experiences came principally in the revues staged at the Watergate Theatre (*See You Later*, *See You Again*) but it was his first musical comedy, *The Boy Friend* ('A Room in Bloomsbury', 'It's

Never Too Late to Fall in Love', 'I Could Be Happy With You' etc), produced at the tiny Players' Theatre in 1953, which secured his fame. An affectionate pastiche (without ever being a burlesque) of the *No, No, Nanette* brand of 1920s musical, *The Boy Friend*, for which Wilson wrote book, lyrics and music, was eventually transferred to the West End Wyndham's Theatre where it became one of the longest running shows of London theatre history, before going on to a vast and worldwide succession of productions which have continued to the present day at a rate that barely any genuine 1920s musical has achieved.

Before *The Boy Friend* reached the big time, Wilson had written and composed another small-scale piece for the Watergate. Like its predecessor, *The Buccaneer*, a little tale of sculduggery and youth and virtue triumphant set in the world of kiddie comics, moved from its little home into the West End, but it was a further piece, the highly skilful 1958 musical play *Valmouth*, based on the esoteric works of Ronald Firbank, which confirmed its author-composer at the top of his profession. *Valmouth* won as much success with the cognoscenti as *The Boy Friend* had with the public, and although its West End and off-Broadway runs were comparatively brief, it remained and remains a connoisseur's delight such as few exist in the musical theatre.

An attractive 1930s musequel to *The Boy Friend*, *Divorce Me, Darling* (1964) again progressed from the Players' Theatre to the West End, but Wilson's other works, including two further musicals, a seasonal version of *Aladdin*, and songs for the play *Call It Love*, were confined to the small theatres which best suited his intimate style.

The unaffected simplicity of the *Boy Friend* text and lyrics and the brittle brilliance of those for *Valmouth* indicate Wilson's range as a writer, and the accompanying tuneful, light musical scores throw those words into prominence in the same way that was achieved by and for the best French and American writers of the 1920s.

Wilson has also authored an autobiography (up to and including *The Boy Friend*), and a book on *Ivor Novello* (London 1975).

1950 **Caprice** (Geoffrey Wright/Michael Pertwee) Alhambra Theatre, Glasgow 24 October
1953 **The Boy Friend** (Wilson) Players' Theatre 14 April
1953 **The Buccaneer** (Wilson) New Watergate Theatre 8 September
1958 **Valmouth** (Wilson) Lyric Theatre, Hammersmith 2 October
1964 **Divorce Me, Darling** (Wilson) Players' Theatre 15 December
1971 **His Monkey Wife** (Wilson) Hampstead Theatre Club 20 December
1978 **The Clapham Wonder** (Wilson) Marlow Theatre, Canterbury 26 April
1979 **Aladdin** (Wilson) Lyric Theatre, Hammersmith 27 December

Autobiography: *I Could Be Happy* (Stein & Day, New York, 1975)

WIMAN, Dwight Deere (b Moline, Ill, 8 August ?1891; d Hudson, NY, 20 January 1951)

Independently wealthy Wiman followed his dramatic studies at Yale by venturing first into films and then, as a producer, into the theatre. His early productions (w William A Brady jr) were all straight, and often serious, plays until, in 1929, the pair ventured into the area of revue with their production of *The Little Show*. Amongst a regular schedule of play productions in the 1930s, Wiman made his first ventures into the musical theatre. The very first, the Cole Porter/Fred Astaire *Gay Divorce*, was a distinctly successful one, and he followed it up with a version of *Die Fledermaus* which was entitled *Champagne, Sec* before, in 1936, he began an association with Rodgers and Hart. During that association he produced five of their shows in six years, almost always with some considerable success: *On Your Toes*, *Babes in Arms*, *I Married an Angel*, *Higher and Higher* and, the longest-running of the group, *By Jupiter* (w Rodgers, Richard Kollmar).

Wiman did less well when he mounted a piece called *Great Lady* (1938) with a score by neophyte composer Frederick Loewe, little better with the indecisive *Stars in Your Eyes* (1939) with Ethel Merman and Jimmy Durante, and disastrously with the Jay Gorney piece *They Can't Get You Down* (w Jack Kirkland) mounted in Hollywood in 1941, and if his adventurous 1947 Broadway production of the Elmer Rice/Kurt Weill 'Broadway opera' *Street Scene* won more kudos than cash, his final musical offering, the revue *Dance Me a Song*, mounted in the year before his death, was a simple 35-performance failure.

WIMPERIS, Arthur (b London, 3 December 1874; d Maidenhead, 14 October 1953). Lyricist and librettist for a quarter of a century of London shows.

Wimperis began his working life as a black-and-white artist, and it was not until after the Boer War, in which he served with Paget's Horse (1899–1902), that he began a writing career. He made his theatrical mark at first as a lyricist, contributing to Robert Courtneidge's production of *The Dairymaids* and to the Seymour Hicks and Ellaline Terriss musical *The Gay Gordons*, before he found major success with his songwords for a second Courtneidge show, *The Arcadians* ('The Pipes of Pan', 'I've Got a Motter', 'Arcady is Always Young', 'Half Past Two' etc). He next supplied some replacement lyrics to a rewrite of the in-trouble *The Mountaineers* at the Savoy Theatre (1909) but, with the coming of the Viennese musical, he found a new area of activity. He adapted a number of such pieces to the English stage, winning a major success with *The Girl in the Taxi* (*Die keusche Susanne*) and a second good run with the Hungarian musical *Princess Charming* (*Alexandra*), and he also adapted Julius Wilhelm and Paul Frank's German original as the libretto for the lavish American musical *Louie the Fourteenth*.

Several attempts at an original musical libretto, with the clever, Faustian *My Lady Frayle* (130 performances), the pretty *Pamela* (172 performances) and a vehicle for Binnie Hale as a tea-shop *Nippy* (137 performances), did well enough without establishing themselves as genuine hits.

Wimperis provided musical burlesques and lyrics for *The Follies* pierrot show during its period in London, scored two of his most memorable song hits with 'Gilbert the Filbert' and 'I'll Make a Man of You' in *The Passing Show* (1914) and contributed scenarios, scenes and songwords to a large number of other revues including *By Jingo If We Do ...*, *Bric à Brac*, Irving Berlin's *Follow the Crowd*, *Vanity Fair*, the French *As You Were*, *Buzz Buzz*, *Just Fancy*, *London, Paris and New York*, *The Curate's Egg* and *Still Dancing*. He also put out a number of plays, most of which were adaptations from French or German originals.

In 1932 Wimperis both made his last contribution to the

musical stage with a disastrous version of a piece by *Girl in the Taxi* composer, Jean Gilbert (*Lovely Lady*, 3 performances) and had his first great success in the film world with the screenplay for *The Private Life of Henry VIII*. Thereafter, filmland became his chief occupation and his subsequent screen credits included *Sanders of the River* (1935), *The Four Feathers* (1939), the wartime *Mrs Miniver* (Academy Award) and *Random Harvest*.

1906 **The Dairymaids** (Paul Rubens, Frank E Tours/w Rubens/Alexander Thompson, Robert Courtneidge) Apollo Theatre 14 April

1907 **The Gay Gordons** (Guy Jones/w others/Seymour Hicks) Aldwych Theatre 11 September

1909 **The Arcadians** (Lionel Monckton, Howard Talbot/Mark Ambient, Alexander M Thompson) Shaftesbury Theatre

1910 **The Balkan Princess** (Rubens/w Rubens/Frederick Lonsdale, Frank Curzon) Prince of Wales Theatre 19 February

1910 **Our Little Cinderella** (Herman Löhr) Playhouse December

1911 **The Mousmé** (Talbot, Monckton/w Percy Greenbank/Thompson, Courtneidge) Shaftesbury 9 September

1912 **The Sunshine Girl** (Rubens/w Rubens/Rubens, Cecil Raleigh) Gaiety 24 February

1912 **The Girl in the Taxi** (*Die keusche Susanne*) English version w Frederick Fenn (Lyric Theatre)

1913 **Love and Laughter** (Oscar Straus) English version w Fenn (Lyric Theatre)

1913 **The Laughing Husband** aka *The Girl Who Didn't* (*Der lachende Ehemann*) English version (New Theatre)

1914 **Mam'selle Tralala** aka *Oh! Be Careful* (*Fräulein Tralala*) English version w Hartley Carrick (Lyric Theatre)

1914 **The Slush Girl** (Herman Finck) 1 act Palace Theatre 14 September

1916 **My Lady Frayle** (ex-*Vivien*) (Talbot, Finck/w Max Pemberton) Shaftesbury Theatre 1 March

1917 **Pamela** (Frederic Norton) Palace Theatre 10 December

1920 **The Shop Girl** revised version (Gaiety Theatre)

1925 **Louie the Fourteenth** (Sigmund Romberg/Julius Wilhelm, Paul Frank ad) Cosmopolitan Theater, New York 2 March

1926 **Princess Charming** (*Alexandra*) English version w Lauri Wylie (Palace Theatre)

1928 **Song of the Sea** (*Lady Hamilton*) English version w Wylie (His Majesty's Theatre)

1930 **Nippy** (Billy Mayerl/w Frank Eyton/w Austin Melford) Prince Edward Theatre 30 October

1932 **Lovely Lady** (?*Die grosse Sünderin*) English version Phoenix Theatre 25 February

WINDSOR CASTLE Operatic burlesque in 5 scenes by F C Burnand based on W Harrison Ainsworth's historical romance of the same title. Music by Frank Musgrave. Royal Strand Theatre, London, 5 June 1865.

Claimed by its author, with seemingly every justification, as 'the first English opéra-bouffe', *Windsor Castle* differed from its burlesque predecessors, and followed the way led

Plate 294. *'The first English opera-bouffe'* – the playbill and the star, Ada Swanborough.

by the Offenbachs and Hervés across the channel, in one vital area. Whereas previous British burlesques had been decorated with musical scores made up from the melodies of popular songs and borrowed arias, the Swanborough family's 1865 production had a purpose-composed original score as its musical part. The capers evolved by Burnand around King Henry VIII (Miss Raynham), Anne Boleyn (Thomas Thorne), the Dukes of Richmond (Fanny Hughes) and Surrey (Elise Holt), jester Will Somers (David James), evil Morgan Fenwolf (J D Stoyle), poet Thomas Wyatt (Maria Simpson) and the heroine of the piece, Miss Mabel Lyndwood (Ada Swanborough), were of an almost Hervé-style extravagance, and the tunes written by the theatre's musical director, Musgrave, simple and catchy. Anne Boleyn's baritone arietta 'La Chevalier et sa belle', a farrago of nonsense French, proved a distinct success as did a jolly 'Tiddley Wink' piece for Herne the Hunter and the jester. The critics were a little taken aback at the exercise, and several pondered as to whether original music was a thing to be desired in a musical comedy entertainment, but *Windsor Castle* played a very respectable 43 performances before being sent to the provinces.

Musgrave's music and the occasion were considered of sufficient interest for the music publishers Metzler & Co to print up a vocal score, so that both the text and the music of the piece which can make a fair claim to be regarded as the earliest original English-language musical of the modern era have survived.

WINNINGER, Charles [WINNINGER, Karl] (b Athens [?Wausau], Wis, 26 May 1884; d Palm Springs, Calif, 19 January 1969). Favourite character man of the musical stage and film who got two of the best rôles 1920s Broadway had to give.

Winninger began his career at the age of five, playing in vaudeville as one of the 'Five Winninger Brothers'. He later worked as a trapeze artist in a circus and on a show boat, before making his first appearance on the legitimate stage in 1908 in a village-storming version of the old warhorse *My Sweetheart*. In the first part of a career which moved amongst all areas of stage and screen performing, he took part in several musicals including *The Yankee Girl* (1910, Rudolf Schnitzel), *The Wall Street Girl* (1912, John Chester and co-director w Gus Sohlke) and *When Claudia Smiles* (1914, Charles D Farnham) opposite his wife, Blanche Ring. He also appeared, in his thirties, in a number of Broadway revues, but his biggest musical-comedy successes came as a character actor, beginning with his performance in Chicago, again alongside Miss Ring, and on Broadway as the generous bible-publisher, Jimmy Smith, in the original production of *No, No, Nanette* ('I Want to Be Happy').

Winninger followed this hit with major rôles in *Oh, Please!* (1925, Nicodemus Bliss) and *Yes, Yes, Yvette* (1927, S S Ralston) before creating the other most memorable rôle of his musical theatre career as Cap'n Andy Hawkes, father to the heroine and the proprietor of Oscar Hammerstein's *Show Boat* (1927). He reappeared as Cap'n Andy in the show's 1932 revival and again in the 1936 film version, and it was on film that he subsequently made most of his musical appearances – *Babes in Arms* (1939, Joe Moran), *Little Nellie Kelly* (1940, Michael Noonan), *Ziegfeld Girl* (1941), *State Fair* (1945, Abel Frake), *Give*

My Regards to Broadway (1948) etc. He returned to Broadway only to appear as Don Emilio in *Revenge with Music* in 1934 and as Dr Walter Lessing in the 1951 revival of *Music in the Air*.

WINTERBERG, Robert (b Vienna, 27 February 1884; d Berlin, 23 June 1930). Successful tunesmith of the central-European theatre in the 1910s and 1920s.

Vienna-born Winterberg had his first pieces played on the musical stages of his home town whilst he was in his mid-twenties and scored a tidy early success with the Operette *Ihr Adjutant*, produced by Karczag and Wallner at the Theater an der Wien with a cast headed by Fritz Werner, Grete Holm, Luise Kartousch and Ernst Tautenhayn. The piece's run was cut short after six weeks when the great Girardi and the Raimundtheater company moved in to the theatre for a season, and the Theater an der Wien company departed their home stage taking *Ihr Adjutant* and the rest of their repertoire with them for a month at the Raimundtheater. The piece went on to play in Germany and, in Frigyes Hervay's Hungarian version (*Az adjutáns*), at Nagyvárad (22 October 1911) and Budapest's Fővárósi Nyari Színház (23 May 1914).

Winterberg had a second sizeable success when Berlin's Theater des Westens produced his *Die Dame in Rot* later the same year and, as that piece went on to productions around Germany and in Hungary and America, the composer left Vienna to settle in Berlin. An Operette, *Hoheit der Franz*, produced at Magdeburg did well, *Die schöne Schwedin* was mounted for 50 nights at the Theater an der Wien and subsequently played in America, Hungary, Germany and, of course, Sweden, but it was a series of musical comedies, composed to texts by Jean Kren and his collaborators, that gave Winterberg his most substantial successes in Germany. *Graf Habenichts* did well enough to be snapped up (but not produced) by Broadway's Henry Savage, *Die Dame von Zirkus* played for eight months and more than 200 performances at the Thalia-Theater and was revived within a year, and *Die Herren von und zu* also clocked up some 200 Berlin performances in a run of over seven months.

Although he was a melodist by nature, a composer who wrote down a single line and passed it on to an arranger to fill out and orchestrate, Winterberg attempted a rather more substantial piece in the 1921 *Der Günstling der Zarin*. He was gratified by a good reception, but he did not linger in such an area and returned to musical comedy with the tale of *Anneliese von Dessau*, seen after its Berlin run at New York's Yorkville Theater in 1926, with a musical version of Feydeau's *Un fil à la patte* entitled *Der letzte Kuss*, and with a musicalization of the much-adapted American novel *His Official Wife*, *Die offizielle Frau*.

At one stage, Winterberg doubled his writing with producing, and went into management variously at Berlin's Centraltheater (1926) and at the Residenztheater, but neither venture proved fruitful. In his mid-forties his health gave way, and he retired to his country estate where he died, aged 46, from pulmonary tuberculosis.

1909 **Die Frau des Rajah** (Paul Wertheimer) Deutsches Volkstheater, Vienna 18 May
1910 **Fasching in Paris** (H Vigny, Louis Windhopp) 1 act Venedig in Wien, Vienna 13 May

1911 **Ihr Adjutant** (Franz von Schönthan, Rudolf Österreicher) Theater an der Wien, Vienna 3 March

1911 **Madame Serafin** (Georg Okonkowski, Bruno Granich-städten) Operetten-Theater, Hamburg 1 September

1911 **Die Dame in Rot** (Julius Brammer, Alfred Grünwald) Theater des Westens 16 September

1912 **Die Frauen von Monte-Carlo** (Alfred Deutsch-German) 1 act Colosseum 11 March

1913 **Hoheit der Franz** (Artur Landesberger, Willy Wolff) Wilhelm-Theater, Magdeburg 27 September

1914 **Unsere Feldgrauen** (Alfred Müller-Förster, Josef Bendiner) Friedrich-Wilhelmstädtisches Theater 13 October

1915 **Die schöne Schwedin** (Brammer, Grünwald) Theater an der Wien, Vienna 30 January

1916 **Die Blume der Maintenon** (Reinhard Bruck) Königliches Schauspielhaus 19 August

1917 **Der sanfte Hannibal** (Müller-Förster, Arthur Lokesch) Bellevue-Theater, Stettin 10 August

1918 **Graf Habenichts** (Jean Kren, Berhard Buchbinder) Wallner-Theater, 4 September

1919 **Circe und die Schweine** (Max Brod) Neues Operetten-haus 4 January

1919 **Der dumme Franzl** (Bruck) Tivoli-Theater, Bremen 16 March; Thalia-Theater 17 October 1920

1919 **Die Dame vom Zirkus** (Kren, Buchbinder) Neues Operetten-Theater 31 May

1921 **Der Günstling der Zarin** (Hermann Feiner, Richard Kessler) Operettenhaus, Hamburg 3 March

1921 **Der blonde Engel** (Kessler, Arthur Rebner) Komödien-haus 18 June

1922 **Die Herr(e)n von un zu ...** (Kren, Richard Bars) Thalia-Theater 3 January

1924 **Anneliese von Dessau** (Kessler) Berliner Theater 23 December

1925 **Der letzte Kuss** Komödienhaus

1925 **Die offizielle Frau** (Kessler, Max Jungk) Theater am Nollendorfplatz 23 December

1926 **Der alte Dessauer** (Kessler) Thalia-Theater 13 February

1926 **Der Trompeter vom Rhein** (Viktor Nessler arr/August Neidhart, Cornelius Bronsgeest) Centralhalle 23 December

Other titles attributed: *Ehe auf Befehl, Der Schauspieler des Kaisers, Ausser Betrieb*

DIE WINZERBRAUT   Operette in 3 acts by Leo Stein and Julius Wilhelm. Music by Oskar Nedbal. Theater an der Wien, Vienna, 11 February 1916.

Oskar Nedbal followed up his well-spaced successes with *Die keusche Barbara* and the splendid *Polenblut* with a third colourful and popular Operette in *Die Winzerbraut*.

The first act of Stein and Wilhelm's tale was set at a gathering in the castle of Baron Bogdan Lukovac (Robert Nästlberger) in Zagreb. The actress Julia Lella (Betty Fischer), who has arrived straight from the first night of her new play, *Der Schirokko*, relates to her long-time lover Count Milan Mikolic (Karl Pfann) and the rest of the company the story of the show. Once upon a time there was an actress who had never married her long-time lover. Then, one day, when the sirocco blew, he gave a young woman shelter in the actress's car. And thus she lost him. Fact quickly starts to follow fiction when the nubile Viennese Lisa Müller (Margit Suchy) appears amongst them under very similar circumstances. The second act shifts to a vine-festival at Mikolic's estates (where Julia is the titular 'vine-harvest queen') and the third to Vienna, as the various romantic pairings – including Micolic's son Nikola (Gustav Werner), the light-comical Franjo Svecak (Ernst

Tautenhayn) and prima ballerina Mizzi Müller (Mizzi Schürz) – work themselves out.

The show's music was in the same colourful strain as the composer's earlier pieces, with the waltz duet for Milan and Lisa, 'Einmal noch erklingt es', proving the gem of the evening. The pair shared a second piece, 'Du kleine Fee vom Donaustrand', whilst Julia teamed three times with Franjo ('Kind, Ich bin so musicalisch', 'Romeo et Julie', 'Liebe, kleine Wurstelmann') in a score where double-handed dance numbers dominated.

Produced at the Theater an der Wien by Wilhelm Karczag, *Die Winzerbraut* ran through 108 consecutive performances before giving way to the spring Gastspiele of the Berlin Lessing-Theater's production of *Die Troierinnen* of Euripides and the hit *Die Dreimäderlhaus* from the Raimundtheater. When the autumn season began, however, *Die Winzerbraut* was put back on the programme and ran through to its 137th performance (24 September).

In Germany, the show proved the most popular of Nedbal's works after the all-conquering *Polenblut*, and it was played throughout central Europe in the years following its Viennese première without following its predecessor further afield.

Germany: 1918
Recording: selection in Czech (Supraphon)

WISDOM, Norman   (b London, 4 February 1920).

The favourite British little-fellow comic of his time and the star of many popular films, Wisdom appeared on the stage top-billed in three musicals. He starred in the rôle of Charley, created on Broadway by Ray Bolger, in London's 1958 edition of the *Charley's Aunt* musical *Where's Charley?*, a rôle made over from the play in a fashion which allowed him both the romance and the female impersonation, and in 1966 he went to Broadway to play the leading rôle of Willie Mossop in another musicalized classic, the *Hobson's Choice* musical *Walking Happy*, mounted by *Where's Charley?* producers Feuer and Martin.

When *The Roar of the Greasepaint ... the Smell of the Crowd* (1964) was first produced in the British provinces, pre-London, Wisdom created the central rôle of Cocky and the songs 'Nothing Can Stop Me Now', 'The Joker' and 'What Kind of Fool Am I?'. The piece was, however, abandoned on the road, and when it did re-open, on Broadway, co-author Anthony Newley himself took the starring rôle. Although he appeared thereafter in panto-mime and featured as Androcles in the 1967 TV musical of *Androcles and the Lion*, Wisdom did not return to the musical stage except to play the lead rôle in a tryout of a musical about the advertising business, *Jingle-Jangle*, which was not taken up for professional staging.

Wisdom wrote a number of songs, amongst which the successful 'Don't Laugh at Me' (w June Tremayne) featured in the film *Trouble in Store* (1952).

WISH YOU WERE HERE   Musical by Arthur Kober and Joshua Logan based on Kober's *Having Wonderful Time*. Music and lyrics by Harold Rome. Imperial Theater, New York, 25 June 1952.

A musical play set in a holiday camp, *Wish You Were Here* won itself celebrity by including a real swimming-pool, dug into the stage, as part of its setting. Based on the successful 1937 play *Having Wonderful Time* (Lyceum Theater, 20

February, 372 performances), which had in between times been made into a Hollywood film, the musical followed the love life of stenographer Teddy Stern (Patricia Marand) through a fortnight's holiday at Camp Karefree. She throws over Herman (Harry Clarke) for Chick (Jack Cassidy), losing him only temporarily when he thinks she's been up to no good with the medallion-man Pinky (Paul Valentine). Sheila Bond played soubrette Fay Fromkin, and Sidney Armus was the comical camp director who rejoiced in the name of 'Itchy'.

The little tale was illustrated by some suitably 'summer holiday' songs, and it was one of these, the gently lilting title-song, which (along with the swimming pool) helped assure the show's success. It needed assuring, for Leland Hayward and Joshua Logan's much ballyhooed production of *Wish You Were Here*, which was mounted directly on Broadway because of the problems of digging up out-of-town stages for the traditional tryout, had had a difficult birth and the opening had been several times postponed as director Logan tried to get the piece into shape. However, the delays allowed Eddie Fisher's happily crooned version of 'Wish You Were Here' to become popular and, in spite of a poor critical reception, the show galloped on to a run of 598 Broadway performances and a long life in regional theatres.

Logan continued to work on the show after it had opened and, in consequence, a London production mounted by Jack Hylton the following year included several amendments and one song not used at New York's opening. It was also largely de-Judaized, with popular comedian Dickie Henderson playing an anglicized Itchy called 'Dickie' and Bruce Trent (Chick), Elizabeth Larner (Teddy, still called Stern) and Shani Wallis (Fay) performing sometimes re-orientated lyrics. London's version played 282 performances.

UK: Casino Theatre 10 October 1953
Recordings: original cast (RCA Victor), London cast (Philips/DRG)

WITMARK, Isidore (b New York; d New York, 9 April 1941).

One of the foremost New York publishers of sheet music, including show music, for much of his 50 years in the music business, Witmark fostered and encouraged a number of successful stage writers of the early 20th century. He also put his own hand to both writing – his scenario for *Three Twins* was the basis for that successful adaptation, and Tony Pastor produced his play with songs, *The Broom-maker of Carlsbad* – and composing. He supplied the score for one Broadway musical, *The Chaperons* (49 performances), and for a spectacular piece put together for London and entitled *Shanghai* which was played for 131 performances in the vastness of the Theatre Royal, Drury Lane.

In days when the interpolation of songs into other folks' shows was both bread-and-butter to and a prized launching site for New York music publishers, publisher Witmark sued producers Klaw and Erlanger for uncontractually using other composers' songs in *The Chaperons*, but the show was gone before anything could be done, and what might have been an important and far-reaching case verdict wasn't handed down.

Witmark also authored a highly enjoyable autobio-graphy, with the rare ring (for a showbiz biography) of the truth to it. His publishing firm was eventually sold to Warner Brothers.

1902 **The Chaperons** (Frederick Ranken) New York Theater 5 June
1918 **Shanghai** (William Cary Duncan ad Lauri Wylie) Theatre Royal, Drury Lane 28 August
Autobiography: w Goldberg, I: *From Ragtime to Swingtime* (Lee Furman, New York, 1939)

WITTMANN, Hugo (b Ulm, 16 October 1839; d Vienna, 6 February 1923).

Journalist, author and stage writer, Wittmann enjoyed two decades of prominence as an operettic librettist, providing seven libretti to Carl Millöcker and several to each of Carl Weinberger and Adolf Müller jr during the 1880s and 1890s.

His first work in the musical theatre was in the field of adaptation and, although his name is now to be found attached, in this field, only to the German-language version of Lecocq's *Le Petit Duc*, it is probable that he provided others amongst the often uncredited adaptations of foreign shows of the 1870s to the Viennese stage. He found success with his first original libretto, Millöcker's *Der Feldprediger*, which went on to an international success after its initial run at the Theater an der Wien, and followed it up with two further successes at the same house: Adolf Müller's *Der Hofnarr* and Millöcker's *Die sieben Schwaben*, both written with the partner, Julius Bauer, with whom he would collaborate through much of the rest of his career.

The quaint, American tale of *Der arme Jonathan* won the pair their biggest international hit, and two further Millöcker Operetten, *Das Sonntagskind* (74 performances) and *Der Probekuss* (55 performances), a single collaboration with Johann Strauss on *Fürstin Ninetta* (76 performances) and the most successful of the pair's works with Weinberger, *Die Karlsschülerin* (59 performances) and *Adam und Eva* (52 performances), kept Wittmann firmly before the Vienna public through the 1890s. His last pieces for Millöcker, *Nordlicht* (38 performances) and the revised *Der Damenschneider* (11 performances), were not successful, and thereafter he supplied only one further text to the Vienna stage, *Der Kongress tanzt*, mounted by Emil Guttmann at the Wiener Stadttheater in 1918.

Early in his theatre career, Wittmann also wrote libretti for the operas *Heini der Steier* (C Bachrich, 1884) and *Der Papagei* (Anton Rubenstein, 1884) and in 1895 he adapted the text of Sullivan's *Ivanhoe* to the German stage (Königliches Opernhaus, Berlin 26 November 1895).

1878 **Der kleine Herzog** (*Le Petit Duc*) German version (Carltheater)
1884 **Der Feldprediger** (Carl Millöcker/w Alois Wohlmuth) Theater an der Wien 31 October
1886 **Der Botschafter** (Eduard Kremser/w Wohlmuth) Theater an der Wien 25 February
1886 **Der Hofnarr** (Adolf Müller jr/w Julius Bauer) Theater an der Wien 20 November
1887 **Die sieben Schwaben** (Millöcker/w Bauer) Theater an der Wien 29 October
1888 **Pagenstreiche** (Carl Weinberger) Theater an der Wien 28 April
1888 **Der Liebeshof** (A Müller jr/w Oskar Blumenthal) Theater an der Wien 11 November

1890 **Der arme Jonathan** (Millöcker/w Bauer) Theater an der Wien 4 January

1891 **Die Uhlanen** (Weinberger) Carltheater 5 December

1892 **Das Sonntagskind** (Millöcker/w Bauer) Theater an der Wien 16 January

1893 **Fürstin Ninetta** (Johann Strauss/w Bauer) Theater an der Wien 10 January

1894 **Der Probekuss** (Millöcker/w Bauer) Theater an der Wien 22 December

1895 **Die Karlsschülerin** (Weinberger) Theater an der Wien 21 March

1895 **Prima Ballerina** (Weinberger) Carltheater 23 November

1896 **General Gogo** (A Müller jr/w Gustav Davis) Theater an der Wien 1 February

1896 **Nordlicht** (*Der rote Graf*) (Millöcker) Theater an der Wien 22 December

1899 **Adam und Eva** (Weinberger/w Bauer) Carltheater 5 January

1901 **Der Damenschneider** (Millöcker/w Louis Herrmann) Carltheater 14 September

1918 **Der Kongress tanzt** (Karl Lafite/w Bauer) Neues Wiener Stadttheater 9 November

THE WIZ Musical in 2 acts by William F Brown based on *The Wonderful Wizard of Oz* by L Frank Baum. Music and lyrics by Charlie Smalls. Majestic Theater, New York, 5 January 1975.

An immensely energetic modern version of the long-loved *Wizard of Oz* tale, equipped with a driving, jazzy-to-gospelly 1970s score, *The Wiz* followed little Dorothy (Stephanie Mills) on the well-known route from Kansas to the land of Oz and its phoney wizard (André de Shields). On the way she meets a dancing scarecrow (Hinton Battle), a gruff Tin Man (Tiger Haynes) and the scaredy-cat lion (Ted Ross), the good witch Glinda (Dee Dee Bridgewater) and the howlingly horrid Evillene (Mabel King). Charlie Small's songs ranged from the move-it-along 'Ease on Down the Road' which set the friends out on what used to be the yellow-brick road to the wizard's palace, to the heroine's rangy, soulful thoughts of 'Home', a broken-glass-edged 'Don't Nobody Bring Me No Bad News' for the nasty witch and a warmly hopeful piece in which the lion tries to convince himself and everyone else that 'I'm a Mean Ol' Lion'.

Mounted with an all-black cast, staged with great pace and some eye-catching dance pieces (the tornado was a spankingly threatening dance-piece, and the scarecrow's introduction a thoroughly modern equivalent of the famous Ray Bolger film routine), the show caught on both with the normal Broadway audience and also with a new and inexperienced black audience unused to the Broadway theatre and inclined to arrive at any stage during the evening and to wander in, out and around the theatre during the performance in a manner reminiscent of the Gaiety and Alhambra gentleman patrons of Victorian times. As in those days, the entertainment in the stalls only gave atmosphere to the entertainment on the stage.

The Wiz was a first-rate success. It overcame unanimously negative notices with positive word of mouth and a touch of telly-push, took the year's Tony Award as Best Musical with additional citations for composer Smalls, director Geoffrey Holder and choreographer George Faison, and went on to play 1,672 performances at the Majestic and, later, the Broadway Theaters. The piece, however, did not continue as prosperously as it had begun.

A 1976 Australian production, cast on a colourblind basis, fared poorly, running a bare two months in Melbourne and just five weeks in Sydney (Her Majesty's Theatre, 1 May 1976), whilst in England, in spite of several attempts, the show was not picked up for an open-ended run. The first British production was seen at Sheffield's Crucible Theatre which, having succeeded in winning a London transfer with its mounting of *Chicago*, was looking for a second lucrative Broadway piece. Celena Duncan played Dorothy through a regular repertory theatre season, but the production did not go south. It was Miss Duncan, however, who was again Dorothy when the suburban Lyric Theatre in Hammersmith mounted the piece four years later for a Christmas season which, once again, had no tomorrow. There was also no success for an attempt to mount a Broadway revival in 1984. The production (24 May, Lunt-Fontanne Theater) folded in 13 performances.

A film version, which also featured an all-black cast, including a not-very-juvenile Diana Ross as Dorothy, Michael Jackson, Lena Horne and Richard Pryor alongside the original cast's Ross and Miss King, supplemented the main parts of the score with some additional pieces by Quincy Jones. It wasn't very successful either, and in the end the swingeing success of the original production was left as the show's only successful outing.

Australia: Her Majesty's Theatre, Melbourne 7 February 1976; UK: Crucible Theatre, Sheffield 3 September 1980, Lyric Theatre, Hammersmith 8 December 1984; Film: Universal 1978

Recordings: original cast (Atlantic), film soundtrack (MCA)

THE WIZARD OF OZ Musical extravaganza in 3 acts by L Frank Baum based on his book *The Wonderful Wizard of Oz*. Music by Paul Tietjens and A Baldwin Sloane. Majestic Theater, New York, 21 January 1903.

A fantasy spectacular mounted by producer Fred Hamlin for the opening of New York's Majestic Theater, *The Wizard of Oz* was adapted to the stage by the original author of the tale, Lyman Baum, as a picturesque extravaganza for the fabled children of all ages. Anna Laughlin played Dorothy Gale, caught up almost peripherally in the story of the deposed King Pastoria (Gilbert Clayton) and his girl-friend Trixie Tryfle (Grace Kimball) who are struggling to regain the throne of Oz from the usurping so-called Wizard (Bobby Gaylor) from the outside world. The King and Trixie are blown into Oz on the same tornado that brings Dorothy and her cow Imogene (Edwin J Stone), and Dorothy plods off through the scenery to seek the Wizard who can get her back home. The helpers she picks up en route include a nice witch, King Pastoria's ex-poet laureate (Bessie Wynn), a scarecrow without a brain (Fred Stone) and a tin woodsman without a heart (Dave Montgomery). In the end, it is the witch who forces the issue and gets the restored King to give Dorothy her ticket home.

The Wizard of Oz was not, as a piece, much thought of. The libretto was a rather rudimentary affair ('the book of the piece is very weak ... the lines consist almost entirely of old-fashioned puns'), with elements of the old English and French grand opéra-bouffe féerie of 30 years earlier cobbled together into what was little more than an excuse for some songs and scenery, and the songs which illustrated it were unremarkable ('the music is tuneful and there is plenty of it'). Of the pieces by the nominal composers,

Sloane's contribution included 'Niccolo's Piccolo', 'In Michigan' (ly: MacDonough) and a medley of all nations (ly: H B Smith), and Tietjens's share was topped by a ballad 'When You Love', but the best bits came from the added numbers: 'Hurrah for Baffin Bay' (written by Vincent Bryan and Theodore Morse of 'Hail, Hail, the Gang's All Here' fame), Cobb and Edwards's 'I Love Only One Girl in the Wide, Wide World' and a later addition, when Lotta Faust took over the leading rôle of Trixie, O'Dea and Hutchinson's 'Sammy'.

However, if neither the text nor the songs evoked much interest, there were other elements which were enough to ensure *The Wizard of Oz*'s success. The *Dramatic Mirror* reported 'to say the new piece made a hit is putting it mildly ... as a production *The Wizard of Oz* has never been excelled in this city'. Director Julian Mitchell and designer John Young had done their share of the work superbly and the piece's seven scenes – beginning with the Kansas town and its cyclone, portrayed with the aid of a stereopticon, moving via a transformation scene (again with the help of the aforesaid stereopticon) into Munchkinland in the best style of the Victorian British pantomime, then on to the road in the woods, the poppyfield ('one of the most beautiful ideas ever worked out by a scenic artist') with chorus girls at first as poppies dressed in green with big red hats, and then transformed by a change of millinery into the same field covered with snow, and finally to the wizard's palace – was a triumph of staging.

That staging was reinforced by two big, traditionally grotesque clown-comedy performances by Stone and Montgomery, performances which took the two men on to stardom, whilst *The Wizard of Oz* and its scenery were superseded by bigger and better productions in the following years. But the show was the hit of the 1902–3 season, running up 293 performances at the Majestic before Hamlin and Mitchell got ready to produce a successor in the same mould. It was, perhaps, the great success of that successor, *Babes in Toyland*, which partly led to *The Wizard of Oz* being largely forgotten.

The title and the tale – popular though both were in their time – might have gone the way of most turn-of-the-century children's fiction, but they didn't. *The Wizard of Oz* became internationally famous through the production of a different musical version, with a wholly different score by Harold Arlen, which was put together for the cinema by MGM in 1938. Judy Garland, Ray Bolger, Jack Haley, Bert Lahr, Billie Burke and Margaret Hamilton as a bad witch starred in this third film version (there had been silent ones in 1915 and 1925) which dumped King Pastoria and his soubrette, dumped the cow and the court poet, and concentrated on getting Dorothy to the Wizard in the company of her tin and straw companions and of the cowardly lion, who had been upped from an incidental part in the 1903 version to a much more important character. 'Follow the Yellow Brick Road', 'Over the Rainbow', 'We're Off to See the Wizard' and 'If I Only Had a Heart' gave the show the kind of accompaniment it had not previously had, and the score, along with the film, became a classic of its kind.

The film version was subsequently rewritten into a stage show which seems to have been first staged at St Louis's Municipal Opera in 1942. This version, with a libretto credited to Frank Gabrielsen, still hung on to some of the original stage score as well, mixing it with Arlen's songs, but, even though the initial London showing of the piece (Winter Garden 26 December 1946, w Walter Crisham as the Scarecrow and Claude Hulbert as the Lion) puzzlingly credited it as 'a play for children by Paul Tietjens, present version by Janet Green, lyrics by E Y Harburg, music by Harold Arlen), later versions soon abandoned the original music as varying versions of *The Wizard of Oz* went on to be played in theatres ranging from Australia's Tivoli circuit to Britain's Royal Shakespeare Theatre to the Radio City Music Hall as well as in such translations as the odd *Zauberer von Oss*.

Other inhabitants of Baum's *Oz* books have also made it to the stage, both in spectacular stagings like the American tour pieces *Ozma of Oz* and *The Tik-Tok Man of Oz* (Louis F Gottschalk/Baum Morosco Theater, Los Angeles, 30 March 1913) or on a more modest scale, as in the 1988 British piece, *The Patchwork Girl of Oz* (Andy Roberts/Adrian Mitchell, Palace Theatre, Watford, 16 December).

Recordings: (Arlen score) original film soundtrack (MGM/CBS), London cast (TER), selection (Decca)

THE WIZARD OF THE NILE Comic opera in 3 acts by Harry B Smith. Music by Victor Herbert. Casino Theater, New York, 4 November 1895.

The Wizard of the Nile brought the rising Victor Herbert his first Broadway success with the score to a comical Harry B Smith tale about a phoney rainmaker. The concept was scarcely new. It had been about – even in an Egyptian setting – since Joseph and Pharoah, it had been used for a comic opera called *The Rainmaker of Syria* and its remake as *The Woman King* just a couple of years earlier, and would still be around nearly 60 years further on in *110 in the Shade*. But the character of Kibosh, 'the wizard of the Nile', made up into a splendidly ridiculous rôle for Frank Daniels, the odd-looking and even more oddly made-up comedy star. Smith added several humorous turns to a low-comedy plot which had the wretched fellow getting into even worse trouble when he is unable to stop the rain once it has started and, in a burlesque of *Aida*, ends up being entombed alive for his troubles. His tomb-mate, however, is no adoring soprano but King Ptolomaeus (Walter Allen) himself, who has got on the wrong side of the sealing-up process. The soprano of the affair was Cleopatra (Dorothy Morgan) who was allowed to sing romantically with Ptarmigan (Edwin Isham) but not to wed him for, as all the world knows, history had other things in store for Cleopatra.

Herbert provided a delightful light-operetta score to go with the fooleries of the evening, and Daniels reaped some of the best of it with his pattering assertion that 'There's One Thing a Wizard Can Do' and a bouncing celebration of the very Un-Egyptian 'My Angeline', whilst the pretty music was topped by the waltz quintet 'Star Light, Star Bright' and the soprano 'Pure and White is the Lotus'. The whole mixture worked splendidly, and Kirk la Shelle and Arthur F Clark's production played out a fine 105-performance season on Broadway before going into the country, returning in 1897 (19 April) for a brief repeat run in New York.

Unusually for its time, *The Wizard of the Nile* found takers further afield than the American circuits. It made its way to Europe, and there it ran up a series of productions which would never be equalled by any other Victor Herbert work. The first of these was in Austria, where Franz Jauner's production of *Der Zauberer vom Nil* (ad Alexander Neumann) featured Julius Spielmann as Kibatschki, the wizard, Herr Frank in the rôle of the King, and Frln Sipos and Herr Bauer as the unconsummated romantic pair alongside no less than three female choruses – an Amazon guard, a bunch of noble ladies and another of dancing girls. *Der Zauberer* was by no means a hit, but it ran for 28 performances before being replaced by a new musical based on Meilhac and Halévy's *La Cigale*. When that did no better, Jauner pushed *Der Zauberer* back on for a few more performances. It was played for Christmas Day and again in the new year, but was dropped from the repertoire after 39 performances. It was well enough noticed, however, to get a production down the river at Budapest (ad Gyula Komor) the following year, and another German version (ad Julius Freund) was later played at Berlin's Metropoltheater and again in New York, produced by Adolf Philipp at the Terrace-Garten.

It was perhaps a simple trans-Atlantic difference in terminology that led London critics to find that the piece 'more resembles a burlesque than a comic opera', complaining that there was but a 'rudimentary plot' and that the fun was obtained by 'detached drollery rather than by a humorously culminating consistent scheme'. They conceded, however, that it was 'quite up to the standard of burlesque' and praised the 'tuneful and spirited' music. London's critics had obviously forgotten the days of opéra-bouffe, but opéra-bouffe and the crazy low comedy it had favoured still lay at the basis of what America called comic opera, and *The Wizard of the Nile* was of a very different flavour from the more sophisticated comic/romantic genre of the current hit of the London stage, *The Geisha*. London, however, didn't want to know about the forgotten joys of opéra-bouffe, and, in spite of a cast topped by Adele Ritchie (Cleopatra), J J Dallas (Kibosh), Charles Rock (Ptolemy), Amy Augarde (Simoona), Harrison Brockbank (Ptarmigan) and Ells Dagnall (Cheops), the show played only a few weeks in the West End.

Austria: Carltheater *Der Zauberer vom Nil* 16 September 1896; Hungary: Budai Színkör *A Nilusi Varázslo* 1 August 1897; UK: Shaftesbury Theatre 9 September 1897; Germany: Metropoltheater *Der Zauberer von Nil* 12 May 1900

WODEHOUSE, P[elham] G[renville] (b Guildford, Surrey, 15 October 1881; d Southampton, NY, 14 February 1975). British novelist, lyricist and sometime co-librettist for a decade of Broadway and London musical comedies which brought forth a couple of jolly, enduring hit shows and a couple more songs to match.

At first a journalist and from his earliest years a comic novelist, Wodehouse at the same time supplied a handful of lyrics to the West End musical comedy stage, adapting, co-writing and occasionally penning original words for songs used in such musicals as *Sergeant Brue* ('Put Me in My Little Cell' w Frederick Rosse), *The Beauty of Bath* (1905, 'The Frolic of the Breeze', 'Mr Chamberlain' w Jerome Kern, Clifford Harris), *My Darling* (1907, 'The Glowworm' w Haines, C H Taylor) and *The Gay Gordons*. As his career as a novelist, boosted by the creation of the comic character of Psmith, and as a journalist flourished, he had less to do with the theatre, although he had an adaptation of one of his books presented on Broadway (*A Gentleman of Leisure*) and a couple of quick flops in London.

All sorts of tales have been touted about concerning the beginning of Wodehouse's theatrical teaming with Guy Bolton (Bolton and Wodehouse told different ones, and even told differing ones themselves at different times). Whenever and however their meeting occurred, its first tangible product came when the two adapted the lyrics and book to the Hungarian musical *Zsuzsi kisasszony* for the New York stage. They followed this up over the next few years with a busy schedule of pieces. On the one, and often less successful, hand there were a number of other adaptations – another Kálmán hit, *Die Csárdásfürstin*, was turned into a flop as *The Riviera Girl*, and the French musical *Loute* which had been a play hit as *The Girl from Rectors* on Broadway closed on the way there twice as *See You Later*, but a version of another French hit, *Madame et son filleul*, made up successfully into *The Girl Behind the Gun* (aka *Kissing Time*) to become a hit around the English-speaking world.

The livelier part of their work was in their original musical comedies, on which, although the credits often read 'book and lyrics by Guy Bolton and P G Wodehouse' it was known that Wodehouse's department was principally that of songwords and his partner's that of the libretto. The earliest of this group of musical comedies were written in collaboration with Jerome Kern, Wodehouse's songwriting partner of one-and-a-half songs a dozen years earlier, who had also had an assignment as botcher-in-chief on *Zsuzsi kisasszony*. The team began tentatively with *Have a Heart* (78 performances), but had a fine hit with the comical *Oh, Boy!* (463 performances, 'Till the Clouds Roll By'), produced at the small Princess Theatre where Bolton had previously had a success with Kern with *Very Good Eddie*. It was a hit they didn't quite manage to repeat, for though an adaptation of George Ade's happy college play *The College Widow* as *Leave it to Jane* (167 performances, 'Siren's Song', 'Leave it to Jane') and their second piece for the Princess, *Oh, Lady! Lady!!* (219 performances) proved reasonably successful, the threesome's only other piece together, an attempt at a Ziegfeld revue called *Miss 1917*, did not.

Thereafter composer and authors went in separate directions – directions which would bring them individually together again, but only once more as a fully constituted team. Thus the 'Princess Theatre musicals of Bolton, Wodehouse and Kern' which have been so long and so glibly referred to by some commentators, actually come down to a total of two shows: the sizzling *Oh, Boy!* and the less sizzling *Oh, Lady! Lady!!*. Or three if *Leave it to Jane*, adapted and conceived in the same style, but staged elsewhere, is counted.

Bolton and Wodehouse went on to write shortlived shows with Louis Hirsch and Armand Vecsey and to the exportable hit of *Kissing Time*, before Wodehouse – now the author of a book about a butler called Jeeves – moved back to centre his activities in Britain. He left behind him in America a part-written musical called *The Little Thing* which Bolton and Kern later turned around and into a major hit without him. Wodehouse's songwords for 'The Church 'Round the Corner' and 'You Can't Keep a Good Girl Down' survived into the score of what became *Sally*.

Whilst Psmith and Jeeves continued to increase Wodehouse's success and fame quotient, he nevertheless kept in touch with the musical stage. He was involved in an almost-successful attempt to remake the famous 19th-century comic opera *Erminie* as a vehicle for London and comedian Bill Berry under the title of *The Golden Moth*, but he found more joy when he was called in by George Grossmith to work on two home-made 'American' musicals for his Winter Garden Theatre in the wake of the grand success there of *Sally*. A sort of transatlantic collaboration with Kern produced the successful *The Cabaret Girl* (361 performances) and the less successful *The Beauty Prize* (214 performances). Both, however, proved much more popular than the one reunion of the team of Bolton, Kern and Wodehouse: *Sitting Pretty* was a 95-performance failure on Broadway.

Thereafter, Wodehouse's musical-theatrical career was largely limited to adaptation, but the second highlight of that career – a decade after *Oh, Boy!* – was still to come. The Viennese hit *Der Orlow* (set in America!) became a London flop as *Hearts and Diamonds* and an attempt at a Jenny Lind biomusical to feature Bolton's wife (who then didn't play it) was a Broadway failure, but in the two collaborators' hands the famous French farce *La Présidente* became a deliciously constructed American comedy decorated with endearing George and Ira Gershwin songs and entitled *Oh, Kay!*. Wodehouse and Bolton's final text together, some years later, for *Anything Goes*, was (very?) largely replaced before the play was produced.

Over the years, Wodehouse contributed isolated lyrics to a number of other shows, the most famous of which was 'Bill' a cut-out from an earlier Wodehouse-Kern show which finally found itself a place in *Show Boat* and also a place as probably the best-known of all the writer's songs in later days. He also had a co-lyricist's credits on two Gershwin songs (w Ira Gershwin) in *Rosalie* ('Oh Gee! Oh Joy!', 'Say So!') and (although the printed score does not credit him) for some of the lyrics of Friml's *The Three Musketeers* (1928). In later years he also worked on the revamping of the *Oh, Kay!* score for an off-Broadway revival, adapting some lyrics and replacing some from Gershwin songs from other sources.

In 1975 Wodehouse's most famous creations, the butler Jeeves and his master Bertie Wooster, already famed on screens large and small, made their way onto the musical stage. However, a singing-dancing *Jeeves* (Andrew Lloyd Webber/Alyn Ayckbourn, Her Majesty's Theatre 20 March) did not bring the characters the same success that they had won in other areas.

'Plum' Wodehouse has, in recent years, become almost a cult figure, particularly amongst book and music collectors, but the details of his life in the theatre, now much pored-over, have been, at best, rather muddied. A 1982 biography billed as 'the authorized biography' does not much interest itself in Wodehouse's work for the musical theatre, and when it touches on it, more than once goes badly wrong. As for Bolton's *Bring on the Girls* – it may look like an autobiography, but to his friends he made no secret of the fact that he'd made up as much of it as he fancied sounded either good or better than the facts ... which it was a bit much to expect a chap to remember anyway.

1916 **Miss Springtime** (*Zsuzsi kisasszony*) English lyrics (New Amsterdam Theater)

1917 **Have a Heart** (Kern/w Bolton) Liberty Theater 11 January
1917 **Oh, Boy!** (Kern/w Bolton) Princess Theater 20 February
1917 **Leave it to Jane** (Kern/w Bolton) Longacre Theater 28 August
1917 **The Riviera Girl** (*Die Csárdásfürstin*) American version w Bolton (New Amsterdam Theater)
1917 **Kitty Darlin'** (Rudolf Friml/w Otto Harbach) Casino Theater 7 November
1918 **See You Later** (*Loute*) English lyrics (Academy of Music, Baltimore)
1918 **Oh, Lady! Lady!!** (Kern/w Bolton) Princess Theater 31 January
1918 **The Girl Behind the Gun** (Ivan Caryll/w Bolton) New Amsterdam Theater 16 September
1918 **The Canary** (Caryll/w others/H B Smith) Globe Theater 4 November
1918 **Oh, My Dear** (ex-*Ask Dad*) (Louis Hirsch/w Bolton) Princess Theater 26 November
1919 **The Rose of China** (Armand Vecsey/Bolton) Lyric Theater 25 November
1919 **Kissing Time** revised version of *The Girl Behind the Gun* Winter Garden Theatre, London 20 May
1921 **The Golden Moth** (Ivor Novello/w Adrian Ross/w Fred Thompson) Adelphi Theatre, London 5 October
1922 **The Cabaret Girl** (Kern/w George Grossmith) Winter Garden Theatre, London 19 September
1923 **The Beauty Prize** (Kern/w Grossmith) Winter Garden Theatre, London 5 September
1924 **Sitting Pretty** (Kern/w Bolton) Fulton Theater 8 April
1926 **Hearts and Diamonds** (*Der Orlow*) English libretto w Lauri Wylie (Strand Theatre)
1926 **Oh, Kay!** (George Gershwin/Ira Gershwin/w Bolton) Imperial Theater 8 November
1927 **The Nightingale** (Vecsey/w Bolton) Jolson Theater 3 January
1934 **Anything Goes** (Cole Porter/w Bolton ad Russel Crouse, Howard Lindsay) Alvin Theater 21 November

Autobiographies: *Performing Flea* (Jenkins, London, 1953), *Bring on the Girls* (fictionalized) (Simon & Schuster, New York, 1953) Biographies: Jasen, D J: *P G Wodehouse* (Mason & Lipscomb, New York, 1974), *The Theatre of P G Wodehouse* (Batsford Ltd, London, 1979), Green, B: *P G Wodehouse, A Literary Biography* (Pavilion Books, London, 1981), Donaldson, F: *P G Wodehouse* (Weidenfeld & Nicolson, London, 1982) etc

WO DIE LERCHE SINGT (*A pacsirta*) Operette in 3 acts by Ferenc Martos. Music by Franz Lehár. Király Színház, Budapest, 1 February 1918.

With *A pacsirta*, Lehár returned to his native Hungary to set, for the only time in his career, a libretto written in Hungarian for a show which was produced in Budapest. The tale told by Martos, one of the most experienced and best librettists of the Hungarian stage, was not his most original nor his most interesting, but it allowed Lehár to write music in which the strains of rural and city Hungary could be occasionally heard, rather than the unmingled bubbling Viennoiseries of the favourites amongst his previous works.

In a little Hungarian country village live the old peasant Török Pál (Dezső Gyárfás) and his pretty grand-daughter Juliska (Emmi Kosáry) who goes around singing like the carefree lark all day (hence the show's title) until the Budapest painter Sándor Zápolya (Ernő Király) comes to board. While he paints her, they fall in love. When the two of them go back to the city, Sándor's painting of his 'lark' wins a prize and he becomes famous, but now his old girfriend, the actress Vilma Garami (Juci Labáss/Ilona Dömötör), who was so horribly out of place in the country, shows up with all the suitable city graces that Juliska can't learn, and before long the country mouse decides she'd better go back to the village and her faithful Pista (Jenő Nádor).

The score, for all its Magyar intentions, was heavy with waltzes. Both Juliska ('Durch die weiten Felder') and Vilma ('Ein Hauch, wie von Blüten') made their first appearances in 3/4, and the final act took place largely in waltz time. One of the most successful numbers, however, was the jauntiest of the march-time pieces which numbered almost as many as the waltzes, 'Schau mich an und frag' nicht lang'. The lyric singing of the piece went to Vilma and to Sándor, whilst Juliska was the evening's soubrette and old Török had two numbers, the Marschlied von Temesvár ('Palikam, Palikam') and the brisk 'Was geh'n mich an die Leute' in croaking comic contrast.

The Budapest première was quickly followed by a Viennese one (ad A M Willner, Heinz Reichert) at the Theater an der Wien with Ernst Tautenhayn (Török), Luise Kartousch (Margit, ex-Juliska), Betty Fischer (Vilma), Hubert Marischka (Sándor) and Karl Meister (Pista) in the leading rôles. Boosted by those wartime conditions which favour long runs, *Wo die Lerche singt* became a solid ten-month success. Brought back occasionally thereafter in the repertoire, it ultimately played over 400 performances at the Theater an der Wien and, in consequence, it has become accepted as a Viennese Operette – its Hungarian origins (like Lehár's, often) quite forgotten.

The Vienna success was paralleled by a fine run in Germany, but there was no rush to take up the latest show of the composer of *Die lustige Witwe* elsewhere. Britain, which wasn't looking to Europe for shows in 1918, ignored it, France passed, and although Max Winter mounted a German-language version at New York's Lexington Opera House in 1920 as a hopeful shop-window for a sale to the English-speaking theatre, the show was not taken up there either.

Wo die Lerche singt did not precisely become a repertoire piece in the way that so many of Lehár's other – and even initially less popular – pieces did. However, it was given a major Vienna revival at the Raimundtheater in the 1970s.

Austria: Theater an der Wien *Wo die Lerche singt* 27 March 1918; Germany: Theater am Nollendorfplatz *Wo die Lerche singt* 21 February 1919; USA: Manhattan Opera House December 1920

WOMAN OF THE YEAR
Musical in 2 acts by Peter Stone based on the screenplay of the same title by Ring Lardner jr and Michael Kanin. Lyrics by Fred Ebb. Music by John Kander. Palace Theater, New York, 29 March 1981.

First seen as a 1942 MGM film with Katharine Hepburn and Spencer Tracy in its starring rôles, *Woman of the Year* underwent some modernization in its transfer to the musical stage of some 40 years later. Miss Hepburn's rôle of the upmarket woman of intelligence (a diplomat's daughter and current affairs reporter) was transmogrified into that of a more suitable heroine for the 1970 or 1980s, a television chat-show hostess, whilst Tracy's rumpled sports-page writer became, less obviously, a cartoonist. The nub of the story, however, remained the same.

When Tess Harding (Lauren Bacall) starts trashing 'the funnies' on her TV show, cartoonist Sam Craig (Harry Guardino) gets his own back by inserting a 'Tessie-Cat' character into his strip. The two meet, the sparks fly, and they fall in love. After the wedding, it doesn't work. In the course of the evening, Tess and Sam have to learn how to balance their private and professional lives, separately and together. Elvind Harum played a defected Soviet dancer and Marilyn Cooper the ordinary second wife of Tess's first husband, both of whom have something to teach Tess as she struggles to keep her marriage intact and work out why its going wrong. The Woman of the Year Award which Tess is seen accepting at the evening's opening epitomized her worldly success, soon to be contrasted with her home failure.

The score for the show was the work of Kander and Ebb, proven nonpareil experts at outfitting musically a 100-per-cent above-the-title Broadway star. Miss Bacall declared with gruff determination that – like Lulu Glaser, 70 years earlier – she was one of the girls who's just 'One of the Boys', quelled her querulous secretary (Roderick Cook) with no-nonsense imperiousness ('Shut Up, Gerald') and unshakeably announced 'When You're Right, You're Right'. She also moved momentarily into a more sentimental vein, but it was, uncharacteristically, a duet that proved to be the show's favourite number: Miss Bacall joined with the unspectacular homebody played by Miss Cooper to declare with mutual envy that 'The Grass is Always Greener' in other folks' lives.

Since it was a period where a substantial investment in a show could command a presentation credit, Miss Bacall shared her above-the-title billing with no fewer than six co-producers, the more active of whom ensured the show a slickly staged, eye-catching production that yet did not submerge the play, which was still the heart of the entertainment. The result was a run of 770 performances, for the last of which Miss Bacall was succeeded – to a surprised and pleased critical and public reaction – by another film star, Raquel Welch and, at the fag end of the run, by Debbie Reynolds.

The show was toured with Miss Bacall at its helm, and played regionally in America, and, although it did not find its way to London or to Paris, *Woman of the Year* did win a production in Budapest (ad István Hajnal) where Ági Voith and Janos Gávőlgyi starred in *Az év asszonya* at the Thalia Színház, and in Colombia.

Hungary: Thalia Színház *Az év asszonya* 15 December 1989
Recording: original cast (Arista), Colombian cast *El mujer del ano* (private label)

WONDERFUL TOWN
Musical comedy in 2 acts by Joseph Fields and Jerome Chodorov based on their play *My Sister Eileen*. Lyrics by Adolph Green and Betty Comden. Music by Leonard Bernstein. Winter Garden Theater, New York, 25 Februry 1953.

The play *My Sister Eileen*, adapted from a book by Ruth McKinney, was produced by Max Gordon at Broadway's Biltmore Theater in 1940 (26 December, 864 performances) with 42-year-old Shirley Booth and Jo Ann Sayers playing the two out-of-town sisters holed up amongst the endearing and quirky inhabitants of Greenwich Village, NYC whilst they strive for fame and fortune in the literary and theatrical worlds respectively. It was one of the longest-running comedy hits of its period and its Broadway success was followed by a 1942 film which starred Rosalind Russell and Janet Blair.

Slimmed tactfully into a libretto, without the loss of either plot or comedy, by its original authors, the show was set with songs by Betty Comden, Adolph Green and Leonard Bernstein, the trio who had been so successful a decade earlier with another jolly celebration of life in New York City in *On the Town*. Miss Russell, repeating her film rôle in this New York equivalent of a French Montmartre-musical, was a now glamorous and 40-plus Ruth Sherwood comically counting 'A Hundred Easy Ways to Lose a Man', leading a basketful of Brazilians in a wild 'Conga' through the streets of New York, and joining in glum harmonics with her blonde bombshell of a sister, Eileen (Edith Adams), in one of the show's most successful single numbers, wondering why on earth they left their home in 'Ohio' for an uncomfortable cellar in New York. Eileen had another winning number, assuring herself, to a delicate melody, that she is again 'A Little Bit in Love', next-door neighbour Wreck (Jordan Bentley) – an out-of-work football player with a talent for ironing – described his other talent in 'But I Could Pass a Football', a jailful of Irish policeman sang their praises of 'Darlin' Eileen' in burlesque shamrocky harmonies, the hero mumbled out his liking for 'A Quiet Girl' and, if *Wonderful Town*'s play-based nature meant that Bernstein had fewer opportunities for the orchestral and dance sections which were one of his particular fortes, he demonstrated his musical skills with a brilliantly babbling 'Conversation Piece' at an unfortunate, improvised dinner party for the men in the girls' lives (George Gaynes, Dort Clark, Cris Alexander).

Robert Fryer's production of *Wonderful Town* played a fine 559 performances at Broadway's Winter Garden Theater (during which time Carol Channing replaced Miss Russell to give a very different interpretation of the rôle of Ruth), and the show moved on to London where Pat Kirkwood and Shani Wallis took the featured rôles in the 207 performances played by Jack Hylton's production at the Prince's Theatre. At the same time, Hollywood mounted a fresh version of *My Sister Eileen* (1955), with Betty Garrett and Janet Leigh in its starring rôles, but with songs by Styne and Robin rather than Comden, Green and Bernstein.

Wonderful Town won regular regional productions following its initial run and it returned to New York at the City Center in 1957 (March) with Nancy Walker and Jo Sullivan featured, again in 1963 and for a third time in 1967 (May) with Elaine Stritch (the Ruth of the television series based on *My Sister Eileen*) starred. The show was also played on CBS television in 1958 with Miss Russell as an increasingly middle-aged Ruth now paired with Jacqueline McKeever. The most recent metropolitan revival was in London in 1986 (7 August) when a scaled-down production, sponsored by the King's Head Theatre and starring television actress Maureen Lipman as a gawkily comical young Ruth, was transferred to to the West End for a run of 264 performances.

UK: Prince's Theatre 23 February 1955
Recordings: original cast (Decca/MCA), TV soundtrack (Columbia), London 1986 revival (First Night), complete (DGG)

WONTNER, Arthur (b London, 21 January 1875; d Buckinghamshire, 10 July 1960).

A popular straight-theatre leading man who had played with Lewis Waller, Edward Compton and Beerbohm Tree, appearing on the London stage as Orsino, Laertes, Bassanio, as Raffles in the play of that title, Ben Hur, Voysey (*The Voysey Inheritance*), Robert Chiltern, and in many other major rôles, Wontner made a sidestep into the musical theatre in his early forties. He appeared first as the non-singing hero of Robert Evett's Daly's Theater production of *The Happy Day* (1916) and then of his *The Maid of the Mountains* (1917), creating the part of the songless brigand chief Baldasarre opposite José Collins. After several years back in the straight theatre he teamed with Evett and Miss Collins again, in their new enterprise at the Gaiety Theatre, taking over as Peter the Great opposite Miss Collins's *Catherine* and playing King Charles II to her Nell Gwynne (*Our Nell*). He later played Cardinal Richelieu to the D'Artagnan of Dennis King in the London production of Friml's *The Three Musketeers* (1930) and, after both many more fine stage rôles and the later part of a 40-year film career, he appeared one last time in the musical theatre as General Birabeau in a London revival of *The Desert Song* (1943).

WOOD, Arthur (b Heckmondwike, 24 January 1875; d London, 18 January 1953).

One of the most popular of British theatre conductors for 20 years and more, Wood led his first London show, Sidney Jones's comedy opera *My Lady Molly*, at Terry's Theatre in 1903. The following year he was musical director for George Edwardes's production of *Véronique* at the Apollo and in 1905 for the short-lived *The Gipsy Girl* before he joined Robert Courtneidge to conduct *The Dairymaids* (1906). This assignment began a long collaboration between Wood and the producer which saw him acting as musical director for the original production of *The Arcadians*, and for Courtneidge's *The Mousmé*, *Princess Caprice*, *Oh! Oh! Delphine*, *The Pearl Girl*, *The Cinema Star*, *My Lady Frayle* and *Young England*. When Courtneidge's fortunes declined, Wood also served him as composer and provided the scores for his touring shows *Oh, Caesar!*, *Petticoat Fair*, *Fancy Fair* and *Too Many Girls*.

Wood succeeded Percy Fletcher as the conductor of *Chu Chin Chow*, acted for several years as musical director at the Gaiety Theatre (*The Beauty Spot*, *Going Up*, *The Kiss Call*, *The Shop Girl*, *Faust on Toast*, *The Little Girl in Red*), took over at the head of *A Night Out* at the Winter Garden (1921), and conducted the short-lived London production of *Die Csárdásfürstin* (*The Gipsy Princess*), the flop *Jenny* (Empire) and *His Girl* (Gaiety). He spent several years under Jimmy White at Daly's Theatre conducting the producer's series of Continental musicals (*The Lady of the Rose*, *Madame Pompadour*, *Cleopatra*, *The Blue Mazurka*), and later conducted Stolz's *The Blue Train* (1927) and the London production of *Oh, Kay!* (1928) as well as some less well-made spectacular pieces (*The White Camellia*, *Eldorado*, *Kong*). He joined one last time with Courtneidge for the Chopin pasticcio *The Damask Rose* at the Savoy in 1931.

Wood's last West End appearances with the baton were for the vast *Casanova* at the London Coliseum in 1932 and an amateurish revival of *The Quaker Girl* in 1934, and he also headed the band for *The Gay Hussar* (later to become *Balalaika*) on its initial 1933 tour.

Wood's light orchestral music was extremely popular in its day, and has in one instance survived thoroughly to modern times, a fragment of his 'My Native Heath' being used as the theme tune for the long-running radio serial 'The Archers'. His theatre scores were entirely made for music halls and touring circuits, although he interpolated numbers into several West End shows and was much used as a theatrical orchestrator for the London stage.

1908 **His Living Image** (Stanley Cooke) 1 act Coronet Theatre 23 November

1916 **Oh, Caesar!** (w Nat D Ayer/Adrian Ross/Alexander M Thompson, Max Pemberton) Royal Lyceum, Edinburgh 23 December

1918 **Petticoat Fair** (Robert Courtneidge) Hippodrome, Newcastle 23 December

1919 **Fancy Fair** (G Hartley Milburn/Courtneidge) Hippodrome, Newcastle 14 April

1919 **Too Many Girls** (Hartley Milburn/Jack Hulbert, Harold Simpson, Courtneidge) Hippodrome, Liverpool 22 December

1922 **The Rose Garden** (Arthur Miller, Eustace Baynes) Hippodrome, Boscombe 1 May

1924 **The Sheik of Shepherd's Bush** (Harry Lowther/Arthur Shirley) Brixton Theatre 24 November

WOOD, David (b Sutton, 21 February 1944).

Britain's most successful author of juvenile musical plays, Wood led an early career as an actor (Bingo Little in *Jeeves*, the film *If* etc) and also had several adult musicals produced (*A Life in Bedrooms*, *A Present from the Corporation*, *Maudie*, *Rock Nativity*). Since the considerable and enduring success of *The Owl and the Pussycat Went to See ...*, his regular stream of lively and uncondescending plays with songs have been frequently played in theatres throughout Britain, and latterly toured under the banner of the Whirligig Theatre Company. The most successful of the group have been *The Owl and the Pussycat Went to See ...* and *The Gingerbread Man*. He has also authored a number of Christmas fairytale shows (*Mother Goose's Golden Christmas*, *Babes in the Magic Wood*, *Cinderella*, *Aladdin*, *Dick Whittington and the Wondercat*) as well as the plays *The BFG* (1991) and *The Witches* (1992).

1967 **A Life in Bedrooms** (w David Wright) Traverse Theatre, Edinburgh 11 April

1967 **A Present from the Corporation** (John Gould/Michael Sadler) Fortune Theatre 30 November

1967 **The Tinderbox** Swan Theatre, Worcester 26 December

1968 **The Owl and the Pussycat Went to See ...** (w Sheila Ruskin) Swan Theatre, Worcester 26 December; Jeanetta Cochrane Theatre, London 16 December 1969

1969 **Toytown** (*Larry the Lamb in Toytown*) (w Ruskin) Swan Theatre, Worcester 26 December; Shaw Theatre, London 12 December 1973

1969 **The Stiffkey Scandals of 1932** revised *A Life in Bedrooms* Queen's Theatre 12 June

1970 **The Plotters of Cabbage Patch Corner** Swan Theatre, Worcester 26 December; Shaw Theatre, London 15 December 1971

1971 **Flibberty and the Penguin** Swan Theatre, Worcester 26 December

1972 **The Papertown Paperchase** Swan Theatre, Worcester 26 December; Sadler's Wells Theatre, London 23 October 1984

1973 **Hi-Jack Over Hygenia** Swan Theatre, Worcester 26 December

1974 **Maudie** (w Iwan Williams) Thorndike Theatre, Leatherhead 12 November

1974 **Rock Nativity** (Tony Hatch, Jackie Trent) Newcastle University Theatre 18 December

1975 **Old Mother Hubbard** Queen's Theatre, Hornchurch 16 December

1976 **The Gingerbread Man** Towngate Theatre, Basildon 13 December; Old Vic, London 13 December 1977

1976 **Old Father Time** Queen's Theatre, Hornchurch 20 December

1977 **Nutcracker Sweet** Redgrave Theatre, Farnham 20 December; Sadler's Wells Theatre, London 14 October 1980

1979 **There Was an Old Woman** Haymarket Theatre, Leicester 25 July

1980 **The Ideal Gnome Exhibition** (*Chish and Fips*) Liverpool Playhouse 3 December; Sadler's Wells Theatre, London, 13 October 1981

1981 **Robin Hood** (w Dave Arthur, Toni Arthur) Nottingham Playhouse 29 May; Young Vic, London 9 December 1982

1981 **The Meg and Mog Show** Arts Theatre 10 December

1983 **The Selfish Shellfish** Redgrave Theatre, Farnham 29 March; Sadler's Wells Theatre 15 November

1983 **Abbacadabra** English version Lyric Theatre, Hammersmith 8 December

1984 **Jack the Lad** Library Theatre, Manchester 23 March

1986 **The See-Saw Tree** Redgrave Theatre, Farnham 18 March; Sadler's Wells Theatre, London 8 December 1987

1986 **Dinosaurs and all that Rubbish** Arts Centre Darlington, 20 October; Sadler's Wells Theatre, London 17 November

1986 **The Old Man of Lochnagar** Sadler's Wells Theatre 11 November

1988 **The Pied Piper** (w D Arthur, T Arthur) Octagon Theatre, Yeovil 16 November

1990 **Save the Human** Arts Theatre, Cambridge 15 February; Sadler's Wells Theatre, London 11 December

WOOD, Mrs John [née VINING, Matilda Charlotte] (b Liverpool, 6 November 1833; d Birchington-on-Sea, 10 January 1915). Internationally celebrated artist who also acted as manageress for her own and others' performances

A versatile actress of comedy, drama, musical burlesque and pantomime, Mrs John Wood (she was thus billed) spent most of her early career in America where, from 1854, she played in such extravaganzas and burlesques as *Shylock*, *The Corsair* (*Conrad and Medora*), *Cinderella*, *Fortunio*, *The Invisible Prince*, *Hiawatha*, John Brougham's *Pocahontas* (*La Belle Sauvage*) and was America's first Robin Luron in Offenbach's *King Carrot*, proving herself one of the country's foremost and most popular players. She managed theatres in San Francisco and New York and, on her eventual return to her native England, took over London's St James's Theatre where she performed several burlesques and produced Alfred Cellier's *The Sultan of Mocha* (1876). Her schedule at this house also included such musical pieces as *Treasure Trove* (*La Mariage aux lanternes*), *La Belle Sauvage*, *Jenny Lind at Last* and the burlesque *Vesta!*

Mrs Wood's daughter, Florence Wood, also took to the stage and was seen in London in *The Dashing Little Duke*, *Mitislaw* and *The Better 'Ole*.

WOOD, Peggy [WOOD, Margaret] (b Brooklyn, NY, 9 February 1892; d Stamford, Conn, 18 March 1978). Soprano and actress who created several important musical rôles on both sides of the Atlantic.

Miss Wood made her first stage appearance in the chorus of *Naughty Marietta* at the age of 18, and the following year had a small rôle in the briefly seen *Three Romeos* (Vera Steinway). She took over in the more successful Eddie Foy musical *Over the River* (t/o Sarah Parke) and in the Montgomery and Stone spectacular *The Lady of the Slipper* (t/o Valerie), played in a revival of *Mlle Modiste* (1913, Fanchette) with Fritzi Scheff, and in Victor Herbert's *The Madcap Duchess* (Gillette), before rising to her first leading rôle, touring in the title-part of Adolf Philipp's successful *Adele* (1914), created in New York by Nathalie Alt.

She appeared in New York in the revue *Hello, Broadway*, but away from the metropolis she played lead rôles in *The Firefly* (Nina), *The Girl of My Dreams* and *Naughty Marietta*, before returning to Broadway for a number-three rôle with a song ('A Little Lonesome Tune') and half a duet ('We'll See' w Alan Edwards) in *Love o' Mike* (1917, Peggy) and then, at 25, her first starring rôle as the three-generations heroine of *Maytime* (1917, Ottilie), introducing 'Will You Remember?' in duet with Charles Purcell.

Miss Wood followed up the Broadway and touring productions of this long-running success as the heroine of *Buddies* (1919, Julie), in the title-rôle of the musicalized *Pomander Walk* as *Marjolaine* (1922), and as Antoinette Allen, the new woman who pretends to be prettily weak, in Henry Savage's production of Zelda Sears's *The Clinging Vine* (1922), before tackling a number of non-musical rôles including Candida, Lady Percy, Imogen Parrott, and Portia to George Arliss's Shylock. She returned to the musical stage in 1926 to play Jenny Lind in a biomusical called *The Nightingale*, originally scheduled for librettist's wife Marguerite Namara, but was replaced after the New Haven tryout. In 1929 she created her second major musical rôle, Sarah Linden in Noël Coward's *Bitter-Sweet*, in London, introducing 'I'll See You Again', 'The Call of Life' and 'Zigeuner'.

Back in America she mixed musical and straight plays, getting away to a false start when E Ray Goetz's *Stardust* in which she was billed to star was abandoned in a flurry of lawsuits, but then creating the rôle of Shirley Sheridan in Kern's 1932 *The Cat and the Fiddle* ('She Didn't Say 'Yes''), playing Rosalinde in a version of *Die Fledermaus* christened *Champagne, Sec* (1933) and appearing on the west coast as Kálmán's *Countess Maritza*. In 1938 she returned to London to play another Coward rôle as Rozanne Gray, the heroine of *Operette*, but thereafter continued her career in non-musical pieces and, notably, on television where she played the eponymous heroine of *Mama* from 1949 to 1957.

In 1965 she appeared as the Mother Abbess in the film version of *The Sound of Music*, her voice dubbed by Margery McKay.

Memoirs: *Actors – and People* (Appleton, New York, 1930); *How Young You Look* (Farrar & Rinehart, New York, 1940), *Arts and Flowers* (Morrow, New York, 1963)

WOODS, A[lbert] H[erman] [HERMAN, Aladore] (b Budapest, 3 January 1870; d New York, 24 April 1951).

The picturesque, cigar-chomping, 'sweetheart'-ing Woods was the cliché Broadway producer of what ought to have been fiction. Born in Hungary and raised in New York, he at first worked in the theatre as an advance man for a touring company. He began producing on his own account in 1902, at first with road productions of highly coloured melodramas (w Paddy H Sullivan, Sam H Harris) of the *The Queen of the White Slaves* and *Dangers of Working Girls* ilk, and subsequently with slightly more sophisticated comedies and with musicals. He first mounted a piece on Broadway in 1909, and thereafter kept up a regular supply of productions, both straight (*Potash and Perlmutter*, *Up in Mabel's Room*, *The Trial of Mary Dugan*, *Twentieth Century*, *The Green Hat* etc) and musical, to the New York stage over some 20 years. He also built and operated the Eltinge Theater in New York and ran the Apollo and Adelphi Theaters in Chicago.

Amongst Woods's musical productions were numbered *The Girl in the Taxi*, the Julian Eltinge vehicles *The Crinoline Girl*, *The Fascinating Widow* and *Cousin Lucy*, the Sam Bernard show *All for the Ladies*, *Kick-In*, *Broadway and Buttermilk*, Lehár's *Gipsy Love*, the highly successful *Madame Sherry* (w H H Frazee and George Lederer), *Modest Suzanne* (*Die keusche Susanne* w Frazee), *The Woman Haters* (*Der Frauenfresser*) and *Tantalizing Tommy* as well as the unfortunate Avery Hopwood *I'll Say She Does*, *Under the Bamboo Tree* and a piece called *Naughty Diana* (1923) by the ever-failing Detroit-German composer Ortmann for which Woods brought Continental star Ilse Marvenga to America. He also presented New York with Sacha Guitry and Yvonne Printemps in *Mozart* in 1926.

Flattened by the onset of the depression, he discovered that his secret cache of rainy-day cash had been rifled by 'a friend', and he ended his career on Broadway broke.

WOOLF, Benjamin E[dward] (b London, 16 February 1836; d Boston, 7 February 1901).

Ben Woolf, whose grandfather had been 'a singer of some celebrity on the London stage', emigrated from England in his youth and settled in America where he became a theatre violinist, a conductor in Boston, Philadelphia and New Orleans and, after settling in Boston, music and theatre critic for the *Boston Globe*, the *Saturday Evening Gazette* and the *Herald*. An eclectic talent, he wrote and published poetry, painted to exhibition standards, and composed a considerable amount of chamber music, but he found his most enduring success as a theatrical author. His most notable efforts were his libretto to Julius Eichberg's *The Doctor of Alcantara*, the first American comic opera to win a production in Britain, and the play *The Mighty Dollar* (1875).

1862 **The Doctor of Alcantara** (Julius Eichberg) Boston Museum 7 April
1879 **Hobbies** (various) Lyceum Theater 6 October
1880 **Lawn Tennis, or Djack and Djill** (Woolf) Boston; Abbey's Park Theater, New York 20 September
1883 **Pounce and Company** Boston April
1884 **Fantine** (*François les bas-bleus*) American version w Roswell Martin Field (Boston Museum)
1894 **Westward Ho!** (R D Ware) Boston 31 December

Other titles attributed: *The King's Frolic*, *The Last of the Fairies*, *Once on a Time*, *The Village Orphan* and *Wapping Old Stairs*.

WOOLF, Edgar Allen (b Phalanx, NJ, 1881; d Beverly Hills, 9 December 1943).

The nephew of Ben Woolf, Edgar Allen had a more

prolific, if less quality, career than his uncle at first as an actor then a playwright and librettist, a director and, with the fading-away of the vaudeville field in which he largely operated, a screenwriter. Woolf had a stinging start to his Broadway career when the opening night of his University show, *Mamzelle Champagne*, taken up as a professional entertainment for the Madison Square Roof Garden, was the scene of the famous Harry Thaw murder, and the piece became a curiosity for scandal seekers through 60 performances. Its connotations even won it a revival years later. However, although Woolf went on to collaborate with both Jerome Kern and Sigmund Romberg during his musical-comedy career, he did not ever notch up a significant musical-stage hit. During his time as a contract scenarist to Metro films he managed to get his name on some rather happier ventures, including *The Wizard of Oz, The Night is Young, Everybody Sing* and *Ziegfeld Follies of 1939*.

1906 **Mamzelle Champagne** (Cass Freeborn) Madison Square Garden Roof 25 June
1911 **The Wife Hunters** (Anatol Friedland, Malvin Franklin/David Kempner) Herald Square Theater 2 November
1912 **A Persian Garden** (Friedland) Colonial Theatre 26 February
1912 **The Woman Who Wants** (Armand Kalisz) 1 scene Tivoli, London
1914 **Mon Désir** (Kalisz) 1 scene Finsbury Park Empire, London 9 March
1916 **The Bride Tamer** (Percy Wenrich) 1 act Colonial Theater 12 June
1917 **The Bride of the Nile** (Friedland) Royal Theater 2 April
1917 **Houp-La** (Jerome Kern) Parsons Theater, Hartford 25 June
1918 **Toot-Toot!** (Kern/Berton Braley) Cohan Theater 11 March
1918 **Rock-a-Bye Baby** (Kern/Herbert Reynolds/w Margaret Mayo) Astor Theater 22 May
1918 **Head Over Heels** (Kern) Cohan Theater 29 August
1919 **What's the Odds?** (Albert von Tilzer/Neville Leeson) Academy of Music, Baltimore 11 September
1919 **Roly Boly Eyes** (Eddy Brown, Louis Grünberg) Knickerbocker Theater 25 September
1921 **Love Birds** (Sigmund Romberg/Ballard MacDonald) Apollo Theater 14 March
1925 **The Daughter of Rosie O'Grady** (Joseph Santley/Cliff Hess) Walnut Street Theater, Philadelphia 14 September

WOOLF, Walter (b San Francisco, 2 November 1899; d Beverly Hills, 24 October 1984). Operetta hero who largely abandoned the stage for the singing and non-singing screen.

After first playing in vaudeville, in revue, and in Gilbert and Sullivan in Chicago, Woolf made his Broadway début in an edition of *The Passing Show* and took his first legit musical rôle in New York as Abercoed in the Shuberts' 1920 revival of *Florodora*. He subsequently played a series of strong-singing heroes in musically substantial shows, appearing as the star of Broadway's *The Last Waltz* (Jack Merrington), *The Lady in Ermine* (Belovar), *The Dream Girl* (Jack Warren), *Countess Mariza* (Tassilo), the sad *The Red Robe* (Gil de Béraud, 'it approaches being the worst thing the Shuberts have ever done') and the ill-fated American production of the London operetta *Dear Love* (1930) before visiting Hollywood for the first time to appear in the film version of Kálmán's *The Golden Dawn* (1930).

Thereafter he mixed film appearances with vaudeville

and straight plays, but he renounced the rôle intended for him in the musical version of *The Prisoner of Zenda* and instead made his return to the singing stage in Romberg's next operetta, the unfortunate *Melody* (1933, George Richards). He appeared on the West Coast in *Music in the Air*, and in New York (now calling himself, at filmland's behest, Walter Woolf King) in *May Wine* (1935, Baron Kuno). It proved to be his last such appearance, for he then returned to Hollywood where he appeared in the Marx Brothers' *A Night at the Opera, Go West*, as Sibirsky in *Balalaika* (1939) and in a number of other films both musical and, increasingly in later years, as a character actor in non-musical movies, and limited his stage appearances to the west coast (Danilo to the *Merry Widow* of Jarmila Novotna, 1940 etc).

WORSTER, [A] Howett (b London, 26 April 1882; d unknown). Staunchly baritonic hero of 1920s operetta.

A ten-year-old boy soprano in the Westminster Abbey choir, Worster studied music in Belgium and began his musical theatre career as a baritone chorister in George Edwardes's *Les P'tites Michus* and *Les Merveilleuses*. He went on to play in the original *Merry Widow*, as cover to Joe Coyne, appeared as Danilo in South Africa, toured as Fredy in *The Dollar Princess*, and then took time out from the theatre to try his hand at acting and directing for the Hepworth Film Company. He returned to singing two years later, joining Maurice Bandmann's company purveying musicals to the Orient.

Plate 295. **Howett Worster** *was Gaylord Ravenal to the Magnolia Hawkes of Edith Day in London's first* Show Boat.

When the First World War broke out, he spent a period serving in the Indian army's Rattray Sikhs and then, invalided out, worked in the army offices in Simla and Bombay before leaving India for Australia where he took a post as a singing teacher at the Albert Street Conservatory. When he played Figaro in a student production he was spotted by a representative of J C Williamson Ltd and, as a result, was cast as the Earl of Essex in the belated first production of *Merrie England* (1921) in Australia. He stayed down under for seven years altogether, playing in such pieces as *Dorothy* (Harry Sherwood), *The Naughty Princess* (Ladislas), the revue *Snap* (1925, producer/performer), *The Maid of the Mountains* (Baldasarre to the Maid of Gladys Moncrieff) and *The Lady of the Rose*, returning to England at the age of 44 to find himself shot quickly to the very forefront of fashionable musical theatre.

His first job was as the male star of London's *Wildflower*, and he followed up as the Red Shadow in an early revival of *The Desert Song*, as Gaylord Ravenal in London's original *Show Boat* and as the Robert Misson of *The New Moon* at the Theatre Royal, Drury Lane. He was quickly replaced in this last rôle by the younger and apparently slightly less stiff Harry Welchman, and he went back to the touring circuits as the Red Shadow, disappearing from the West End as suddenly and as wholly as he had come to it.

WRIGHT, Huntley (b London, 7 August 1869; d Bangor, 10 July 1943). Star comic of the Daly's Theatre series of musicals.

The son of Frederick Wright (1826–1911) who claimed in the early part of the new century to be 'the oldest living actor in active work', Huntley Wright worked in his father's touring companies from babyhood. He wrote and played in a burlesque, *Dashing Prince Hal*, under his father's management, appeared in other touring musicals and made his London musical-comedy début in a supporting rôle in *King Kodak* (1894, Hugh E Foote). He next appeared in *A Trip to Chinatown* and as a takeover from E M Robson as father Cripps in *An Artist's Model* before joining George Edwardes's company playing musical comedy in South Africa. On his return, he was engaged again at Daly's Theatre and there he created the decade-long series of rôles that gave him a star reputation second to none amongst musical comedians of his era: Wun-Hi in *The Geisha* (1896, introducing 'Chin Chin Chinaman'), the comical soothsayer Heliodorus in *A Greek Slave*, a second comic oriental, Li, in *San Toy*, Barry in *A Country Girl* ('Me and Mrs Brown'), Chambuddy Ram in *The Cingalee* and Bagnolet in *Les P'tites Michu*.

He left Daly's to play in comedy and then as his third George Edwardes oriental, Hang-Kee in *See See*, but he returned to the scene of his great successes to play St Amour in *Les Merveilleuses* before crossing the Atlantic to star as Joe Mivens in Broadway's version of *The Dairymaids*. He subsequently created the rôles of the terrified King of Alasia in *King of Cadonia* and Hans Hansen in *Dear Little Denmark* (1909) for Frank Curzon at the Prince of Wales Theatre, then returned to Edwardes's management for star comic rôles in *The Girl in the Train* (Van Eyck), *The Count of Luxemburg* (Grand Duke Rutzinov) and *Autumn Manoeuvres* (Captain Withers) before taking a turn in the halls playing a musical playlet called *Simple 'Earted Bill*.

After serving in the First World War, Wright returned to the West End to appear at the Gaiety in *The Kiss Call* and at his old stamping ground, Daly's, as the comical Poire in *Sybil*, Suitangi in *The Lady of the Rose* and Calicot to the *Madame Pompadour* of Evelyn Laye. Thereafter, he appeared more often in the straight theatre than the musical, but he reprised *The Lady of the Rose* and *Madame Pompadour*, played in the unfortunate romantic operetta *The White Camellia* and, in his early sixties, appeared as Gaspard in a revival of *Les Cloches de Corneville*. The last musical appearance in a career that had spanned several eras of the musical theatre, from burlesque to inter-war musical comedy, came when he replaced Will Fyffe in *Give Us a Ring* (1933).

Wright's brothers **Fred WRIGHT** (1871–1928) and Bertie Wright also appeared as comic actors in the musical theatre, and at one stage all three followed each other in the same rôle of Wun-Hi (*The Geisha*) at Daly's Theatre. Fred Wright (thanks to his father's longevity, originally Fred Wright jr) had an outstanding international career. Having begun, like Huntley, as a child with his father's companies, he toured with Horace Lingard in *Pepita*, *Falka*, *The Old Guard* and *La Fauvette du Temple*, then travelled through Europe with the Fanny Wentworth *Carmen Up-to-Data* (Don Jose) and *Faust Up-to-Date* company of 1892, appeared alongside Lillian Russell in London's edition of *The Queen of Brilliants* (1893, Max), at Daly's Theatre in *An Artist's Model* (t/o Cripps) and *The Geisha* (t/o Wun-Hi) and in major comic rôles at the Gaiety in *A Runaway Girl* (1898, Sir William Hake), *The Messenger Boy* (1900, Captain Pott), *The Toreador* (1901, Pettifer) and *The Orchid* (1903, Zaccary). In between times he succeeded

Plate 296. **Huntley Wright** *as soothsayer Heliodorus, the comedy of* A Greek Slave.

WUNDER-BAR

Sydney Paxton as Siroco in the Savoy's *The Lucky Star* (1899) and Courtice Pounds as Papillon in *The Duchess of Dantzic* (1904) before setting out on travels which no other musical comedian of the time equalled. He crossed to America to play in *The School Girl* (1904, General Marchmont) and *The Catch of the Season* (Mr William Gibson), returned to London for *Nelly Neil* (1907, t/o Nordheim), went to Paris to star in the French production of *The Prince of Pilsen* at the Moulin-Rouge and, after a brief return via London for the short-lived *The Antelope* (1908, Bennett Barker), disappeared back to the Continent, this time to Germany and Berlin's Metropoltheater where he starred in *Der oberen Zehntausend* and the local version of *Our Miss Gibbs*. He repeated his Timothy in *Our Miss Gibbs* in Vienna to the Mary of Mizzi Hajós, in Budapest and in America (August 1910), and then remained in America to play in *The Pink Lady* (1911, Benevol). The London season of that production took him home again, and he settled into variety and provincial musicals for a few years before the war called him abroad again, this time in uniform. He was home by 1916, touring as Tonio in *The Maid of the Mountains*, a rôle he later repeated in the Canadian production. His last appearances in a West End musical were in the spectacle *Shanghai* (1921, Ah Sing) and in *Katinka* (1923, Knopf).

Bertie Wright succeeded Huntley both as Wun-Hi and as Li at Daly's Theatre, but made the large part of his career in comic rôles in touring musical comedy (Cadeau in *Erminie* etc) and in such lesser pieces as *The Girl from Over the Border* (1908, Tubby Wiggles).

The Wrights were all married into other theatre familes. Huntley Wright himself was husband to Mary Fraser, sister to Savoy Theatre prima donna Agnes Fraser (herself wife to musical comedian Walter Passmore) and vocalist and actor Alec Fraser. His daughter, Betty Huntley Wright (b London 3 December 1911), also appeared in the musical theatre, being seen in *Bitter-Sweet*, *Clancarty* and *Six Pairs of Shoes* in London and in the title-rôle of *Sally Who?* on the road. Bertie Wright was first married to Madge Greet, who was a member of the pas de quatre in the 1892 Continental burlesque tour and who also played both in Edwardes's companies (Lucien in *An Artist's Model* on Broadway, t/o Juliette in *The Circus Girl*) and others (Milistra in *Florodora*, Alison in *My Lady Molly*, Princess Schowenhöhe-Hohenschowen in USA *Catch of The Season* etc). Her sister, Clare Greet, in a distinguished career as an actress dipped into the musical theatre in early years (Lady Walkover in *Morocco Bound* tour etc) and later created the rôles of Lisette in *The Duchess of Dantzic* (1904) and Lady Heldon in *My Darling* (1907).

WRIGHT, Robert [Craig] (b Daytona Beach 25 September 1914) *see* FORREST, GEORGE

DIE WUNDER-BAR Spiel in Nachtleben in 2 parts by Geza Herczeg and Karl Farkas. Music by Robert Katscher. Wiener Kammerspiele, Vienna, 17 February 1930.

A novelty piece which mixed conventional theatre with the fashionable jazz cabaret of the time, Franz Wenzler's production of *Die Wunder-Bar* was mounted in an auditorium which was done up throughout to represent the cabaret bar of the title, the 'Wunder-Bar' operated by

Sam Wunder (Fritz Wiesenthal). The strong, dramatic and cleverly worked-out story of the piece, in which the lead dancer of the club, Harry (Hans Unterkircher), gets himself involved in an unpleasant mess with some effectively stolen jewels and a touch of adultery (Friedl Haerlin), was shot through with opportunities for the various members of the cast to perform cabaret items. Vera Molnár as Harry's partner, star dancer Inez, Dolly the jazz-singer played by none other than jazz-singer Dolly, Trude Brionne as Elektra Pivonka 'the opening act', and the Sid Kay's Fellows as the bar's jazz band were listed on the programme along with the casting 'Guests of the Wunder Bar ... the public' (those members of the company invited, in their quality as stars, to dance, are requested to resume their seats when finished). But established star Otto Storm, in the rôle of Louis von Ferring, a flushed-out aristocrat out for a last night of entertainment at the bar before committing the suicide no-one believes he will, stole much of the limelight. He also provided the clever dénouement to the plot.

Die Wunder-Bar was a great success in its initial season at Vienna's Kammerspiele, moved on for five additional weeks to the Johann Strauss-Theater (23 January 1931), and was soon picked up for productions in Munich, and in Budapest (ad Zsolt Harsányi) where with Gyula Kabos (Wunder), Ferenc Delly (Harry), Teri Fejes (Inez) and Ilona Titkos (Erdy) featured it was again a hit. Whilst the German production continued on to Berlin, London too welcomed the *Wonder Bar* (ad Rowland Leigh) to no less than the august precincts of the Savoy Theatre. Joseph Greenwald directed the proceedings, Carl Brisson and Elsie Randolph were the dancers, Dorothy Dickson the 'other woman' Liane, Norah Blaney, Gwen Farrar and Giovanni were 'cabaret turns' and Katscher's score was lightly infiltrated with additional numbers. The entertainment proved popular and ran through 210 performances.

Morris Gest had a new version made for his Broadway production (ad Irving Caesar, Aben Kandel), partly because the show, subtitled 'a continental novelty of European night life', was used to bring Al Jolson back to Broadway, after five years in Hollywood, in the rôle of the chief of the now Parisian bar. But Jolson, here performing without his famous blackface, was old news, and Broadway theatregoers showed little interest in the show. It folded in 76 performances.

Farkas and/or Herczeg wrote and Katscher composed several further shows on similarly cabaret-revusical lines, whilst in London a show called *Get a Load of This*, produced in the larger London Hippodrome in 1941 (19 November), penned by James Hadley Chase as a vehicle for Austrian comic Vic Oliver, based itself very closely on the *Wunder-Bar* format and plot and came out with a run of nearly 700 performances.

A film version of *Wonder Bar*, with Jolson featured, also followed the outlines of the original show. It went perhaps unintentionally funny when the cabaret scenes opened out into vast Busby Berkeley numbers, and unintentionally unfunny when everything stopped to allow Jolson to fling out a ration of joey-joey jokes. When Ricardo Cortez (Harry), Dolores del Rio (Inez), Kay Francis (Liane) and Robert Barrat (Captain von Ferring) were on, the tale moved incisively. Dick Powell (Tommy) and Jolson – going blackface for a heavenly coon-cum-mule number – had the

1577

most of the six Harry Warren/Al Dubin songs which replaced Katscher's score.

Germany: Munich, Berlin; Hungary: Fővárosi Operettszinház *Csodabár* 15 September 1930; UK: Savoy Theater *Wonder Bar* 5 December 1930; USA: Nora Bayes Theater *Wonder Bar* 17 March 1931; Film: Warner Bros 1934

DER WUNDERKNABE Operette in 3 acts by Alexander Landesberg and Leo Stein. Music by Eugen von Taund. Theater an der Wien, Vienna, 28 March 1896.

The most widely played of von Taund's Operetten, *Der Wunderknabe* was written to a Stein and Landesberg libretto which was set in an original combination of locations: Edinburgh, Ostend and Aberdeen. Josef Joseffy played Patricio Gordoni, a showman about as Italian as his name, pushing a child prodigy violinist called Paolo (Annie Dirkens) through the houses of credulous Edinburgh society. Paolo is, of course, not a 15-year-old boy, but an 18-year-old girl, and, by the end of the evening, has been discovered to be the long-lost daughter of Graf Calmore, Lord von Aberdeen (Carl Lindau). The principal comic rôle was that of a musician called Tween, played by Alexander Girardi, a plagiaristic composer/pianist chasing after the daughter (Marie Ottmann) of a wealthy Scots mine-owner (Wallner), whilst real romance was represented by Karl Streitmann as the young Graf Edward Calmore.

Der Wunderknabe was given 27 times en suite at the Theater an der Wien and brought back for further performances later in the year and early the next to total 36 performances in all. In the meanwhile, it had been played in Berlin, and in London where Sir Augustus Harris produced an English version (ad Harris, Arthur Sturgess) which had to be postponed when its producer died shortly before opening night. Frln Dirkens came from Vienna to play the opening performances of a version which popped in some additional numbers by Landon Ronald and J M Glover, and which featured Arthur Williams (Patricio), Harrison Brockbank (Edward) and E J Lonnen (Tween) in the other leading rôles. In one of the busiest and richest London seasons in history, the show found it hard to make an effect. It was revised, recast (Ells Dagnall replaced Williams, Dirkens went home and was replaced by Florence St John), some variety turns including a quartet from the Moulin-Rouge headed by La Goulue popped into the Ostend Kursaal scene, new songs added, a 'second edition' announced, a group of midgets featured between the acts, and in the end the run stretched to 117 performances.

In Budapest (ad Gyula Komor), without the midgets and La Goulue, the run was rather shorter.

Germany: Theater Unter den Linden May 1896; UK: Shaftesbury Theatre *The Little Genius* 9 July 1896; Hungary: *A csodagyerek* 1896, Budai Színkör 22 May 1897

WYATT, Frank [WYATT, Francis Gunning] (b 7 November 1856; d London, 5 October 1926). Musical comedian who created two of the best British comicomusical rôles of his period.

At first an artist and illustrator, Wyatt soon moved to the theatre and made his ealiest appearances aged 20 in small parts in comedy with Charles Wyndham as 'Francis Wyatt'. Initially, his varying musical appearances – Don Pedro in *La Périchole* and the Zola burlesque *Another Drink*

(1879, Gouget) with Dolaro at the Folly, the inevitable *La Fille de Madame Angot* with Cornélie d'Anka at Holborn, the burlesque *Don Juan Jr* (1880, Baba), a tour with the Hanlon-Lees in *Le Voyage en Suisse* in America, the burlesques *Ariel* (Sebastian), *Valentine and Orson* (Hugo) and *Blue Beard* (Mustafa) at the Gaiety – were interleaved with non-musical assignments. That mixture continued, when, following his first major musical engagement, as Célestin to the *Nitouche* of American actress Lotta in 1884, he went on to play Shakespeare with Irving at the Lyceum (Aguecheek), comedy with the Bancrofts at the Haymarket and comic opera (silly-ass Captain Coqueluche in *The Grand Mogul*, Don Jose in *Manteaux Noirs*).

Then, in November 1885, Wyatt paired with Harry Paulton to create the suave thief to the author's low-comical one in the comic opera *Erminie* (Ravannes). The success he won there led to a list of major musical rôles over the following years: Alfred Pasha in *Our Diva* (*Joséphine vendue par ses soeurs*), Karl in *Mynheer Jan* (1887), Hippomenes in *Atalanta* (1888), Pedrillo in *Pepita* (1888), Don Trocadero in the Carl Rosa Light Opera's *Paul Jones* (1889), the Duke of Plaza-Toro in the original production of *The Gondoliers* (1889) and Baboo Currie in *The Nautch Girl* (1890) at the Savoy, Arrostino Annegato in *The Mountebanks* (1892) and Woodpecker Tapping in *Haste to the Wedding* (1892) for W S Gilbert, and Bouillon in *Ma mie Rosette* (1892).

The partner of his wife, *Erminie* producer Violet Melnotte, in the building of the Trafalgar Square Theater (later the Trafalgar and now the Duke of York's Theatre), Wyatt appeared there in *Dora, or Diplunacy*, *Nitouche* (1893, this time opposite May Yohé with his wife as Corinne) and in several of the unsuccessful new musicals produced there (Octopus Sharp in *The Taboo*, Count Acacia in *Baron Golosh*). He also played the title-rôle in Robert Buchanan's *The Pied Piper* (1893) and made a last West End musical appearance in the unfortunate *The Gay Pretenders* (Earl of Oxford) in 1905.

WYLIE, Julian [SAMUELSON, Julian] (b Southport, 1 August 1878; d London, 6 December 1934).

An accountant turned business manager turned theatrical agent turned director and producer, Wylie began his managerial career by touring musical productions through provincial variety houses before mounting first revues and then musical plays in London. Amongst the musicals which he produced or co-produced and directed were the early Weston and Lee piece *Mr Tickle MP* (tour, 1925), the musical version of *Turned Up* (w C B Cochran, J W Tate), the musical melodrama *The Yellow Mask* (w Laddie Cliff), the original pre-London *Mr Cinders* (which he then sold to J C Williamson Ltd for London), Arthur Schwartz's early musical, *Here Comes the Bride* (1929), the Binnie Hale vehicle *Nippy* (1930 w Moss' Empires), *Out of the Bottle* (1932) and the Eric Maschwitz spectacular *The Gay Hussar* (1933, for Moss's Empires and Howard & Wyndham). An indefatigable touring manager and producer of Christmas pantomime, Wylie's directorial style tended towards the latter genre in his love for scenic effects.

WYLIE, Lauri [SAMUELSON, Morris Laurence] (b Southport, 25 May 1880; d unknown).

Brother of Julian Wylie, Lauri entered the theatre at

around the same time, but in the capacity of author. He supplied a long list of revusical pieces and musical sketches to the provincial stage and, later, also the London theatre (*Bric à Brac, Vanity Fair, Peep Show, Brighter London, Dover Street to Dixie, Leap Year, Palladium Pleasures, Better Days* etc) and also adapted a number of Continental musicals, the most successful of which was Szirmai's *Alexandra*, the most unsuccessful a Swedish musical called *Serenade*, announced as the Scandinavian answer to *Oklahoma!*, but which never made it to London. Wylie's own most successful works, however, were the two musical plays which he wrote for (and apparently with) Lupino Lane, and which were produced at the Victoria Palace in the aftermath of the triumph of *Me and My Girl*.

1915 **Kiss Me, Sergeant** (James W Tate/Clifford Harris/w Alfred Parker) 1 act Leicester Palace 2 August

1917 **Sugar** (Louis Jerome/George Arthurs/w Alfred Parker) 1 act Oxford Theatre 16 July

1918 **Shanghai** English adaptation (Theatre Royal, Drury Lane)

1919 **A Good-Looking Lass** (Herman Darewski/w Leon Pollack) 1 act Chelsea Palace 11 August

1926 **Hearts and Diamonds** (*Der Orlow*) English version w P G Wodehouse (Strand Theatre)

1926 **Princess Charming** (*Alexandra*) English version w Arthur Wimperis (Palace Theatre)

1927 **The Grass Widow** (Vivian Ellis/William Helmore) Empire Theatre, Bristol 8 August

1927 **The Other Girl** (Ellis/Helmore, Collie Knox) Empire Theatre, Bristol 17 October

1928 **Song of the Sea** (*Lady Hamilton*) English version w Wimperis (His Majesty's Theatre)

1929 **Dear Love** (Haydn Wood, Joe Waller, Joseph Tunbridge/ w Herbert Clayton, Dion Titheradge) Palace Theatre 14 November

1930 **My Sister and I** (*Meine Schwester und ich*) English version (Shaftesbury Theatre)

1944 **Meet Me Victoria** (Noel Gay/Frank Eyton/w Lupino Lane) Victoria Palace 6 March

1946 **Sweetheart Mine** (Gay/Eyton/w Lane) Victoria Palace 1 July

1948 **Serenade** English version w Eric Maschwitz tour

WYNN, Ed [LEOPOLD, Isaiah Edwin] (b Philadelphia, 9 November 1886; d Beverly Hills, Calif, 19 June 1966).

'The Perfect Fool' of vaudeville made an early Broadway appearance in a book musical in 1910 in *The Deacon and the Lady* which lasted just two weeks. His next theatre appearances were in revues (*Ziegfeld Follies, The Passing Show* etc) but, in 1918, now established as a comedy star name, he was brought in, during try-out, to play Loney Bright, a throughly incidental highlight of Rudolf Friml's *Sometime*, a piece which almost certainly owed some of its success to his zany performance.

Wynn subsequently played Broadway in his own made-to-measure entertainments (*Ed Wynn Carnival, The Perfect Fool, The Grab Bag* etc), but ventured further book musicals in *Manhattan Mary* (1927), *Simple Simon* (1930) and *Hooray for What!* (1937) in between his own presentations and radio and, later, television successes. He also appeared in musical films, including the screen's *Manhattan Mary* (1930), and later, during his more celluloidly successful older character period, as the Toymaker in the 1961 version of *Babes in Toyland*, and as Uncle Albert ('I Love to Laugh') in *Mary Poppins* (1964).

Wynn also wrote and composed songs and other material for his own use, and co-wrote the libretto to his 1930 musical *Simple Simon*.

1930 **Simple Simon** (Richard Rodgers/Lorenz Hart/w Guy Bolton) Ziegfeld Theater 18 February

X

XANROF, Léon [FOURNEAU, Léon] (b Paris, 9 December 1867; d Paris, 17 May 1953).

A highly successful Parisian playwright, journalist (courrier des théâtres on *Gil Blas* etc) and literary figure, Xanrof first came to the notice of his contemporaries during his days as a law student, as the author and performer of some songs 'd'une ironie pincée, d'une gaîté un peu âpre (qui) chantaient, sur des modes sautillants, la vie des étudiants, leurs déboires, leurs faciles amours, leur existance insouciante ...' ('L'Hôtel du No 3', 'Les Quatre-z-étudiants' etc). He went on to become celebrated as a songwriter with pieces such as 'Le Fiacre', 'Encombrement' and 'Les Trottins', numbering Yvette Guilbert amongst his interpreters, before finding himself a place in the literary world at first as a writer of magazine pieces. He began his career in the theatre initially writing material for revue (*Paris en bateau* for La Cigale, *Revue intime* 1889, *Paris Nouveautés* 1892 etc) and saynètes and short plays for cafés-concerts and minor theatres, before going on to make a name as the author of such plays as *A Perpète*, *La Marmotte* and *Pour être aimée*, and of libretti.

Xanrof's first Parisian opérette, *Madame Putiphar*, won a good run in the French capital (64 performances) and a later production in Budapest (*Putifarné* ad Adolf Mérei, Magyar Színház 27 January 1905), but he had his most important theatrical success with the 1903 play *Le Prince-Consort* (w Jules Chancel, Théâtre de l'Athénée 25 November). After long runs in Paris, Berlin and London (*His Highness, My Husband*), and a production illustrated with songs and incidental music in Hungary (*A királynő férje* ad Jenő Heltai, mus: Lázsló Kun, 8 April 1904 Vigszinház) the piece was fully musicalized, five years on, by its authors, in collaboration with Ivan Caryll, under the title *S. A. R.* (*Son Altesse Royal*). If the musical piece was less popular than the play, it nevertheless had a good Parisian run and was produced in Germany as *Die kleine Königin*. Xanrof subsequently wrote several other musical scripts, the most enduring of which was his French version of the libretto for *Ein Walzertraum* – the main plotline of which was the same as that of *Le Prince Consort* – but late in life he collected perhaps his best music-based royalties from the song 'Le Fiacre', when it was popularized internationally by Jean Sablon who performed it in the New York revue *The Streets of Paris* (1939).

His play *L'Amorçage* (w Gaston Guérin) was used as the basis for George Edwardes's London musical *Peggy* (Leslie Stuart/C H Bovill/George Grossmith jr, Gaiety Theatre 4 March 1911), the text of *Madame Putiphar* was borrowed to become that of the highly successful zarzuela *La corte de Faraon* (1910, Vicente Lleo), whilst another of his works, unspecified, served as the source for the German musical *Die Lieben Ottos* (Jean Gilbert/Alfred Schönfeld/Jean Kren, Thalia-Theater 30 April 1910).

1892 **Cavalcada-Rastaquoera** (Nazy/w Malpertuis) Brussels April

1894 **Le Petit Chasseur alpin** (Pierre Brus) Villers-Cotterets 24 June
1897 **Madame Putiphar** (Edmond Diet/w Ernest Depré) Théâtre de l'Athénée-Comique 27 February
1898 **Feuilles à l'envers** (w Léon Garnier, Fabrice Lemon) 1 act Eldorado 13 October
1906 **La Plus Belle** (aka *Die schöne Vestalin*) (Viktor Holländer/w Pierre Veber) 1 act Casino de Paris 29 October
1908 **S. A. R.** (Ivan Caryll/w Jules Chancel) Théâtre des Bouffes-Parisiens 11 November
1909 **Mam'zelle Gogo** (Émile Pessard/w Maxime Boucheron) Théâtre Molière, Brussels February
1910 **Rêve de valse** (*Ein Walzertraum*) French version w Chancel (Théâtre Apollo)
1911 **Lysis rata** (w H Séré, Ondet) Casino de Paris 6 April
1911 **Les Petites Étoiles** (Henri Hirschmann/w Pierre Veber) Théâtre Apollo 23 December
1926 **Souris blonde** (François de Breteuil/w Alain Monjardin) Théâtre des Folies-Dramatiques May

Plate 297. **Léon Xanrof:** *Proof that the letter X can exist in an encyclopedia.*

Y

THE YANKEE CONSUL Comic opera in 2 acts by Henry M Blossom jr. Music by Alfred G Robyn. Broadway Theater, New York, 22 February 1904.

A vehicle for rising young comedian Raymond Hitchcock, the star of *King Dodo* of two seasons back, *The Yankee Consul* presented him as US diplomat Abijah Booze (the name said it all), based in the Ruramerican outpost of Puerta Plata. On his way to winning himself the hand of the local wealthy widow, Donna Teresa (Eva Davenport), 'Bi' (as he is dubiously called) gets himself entangled in incipient revolution and a devilish matrimonial agency and while he is doing so the evening's ingénue, Teresa's daughter Bonita (Flora Zabelle), is sweetly persuading the leader of the rebellion to postpone his attack so as not to spoil the governor's ball she has been so looking forward to. Her reward is Lieutenant Commander Jack Morrell of the US gunboat 'Vixen' (Harry Fairleigh) who arrives – as the British one had done a couple of seasons back in *A Chinese Honeymoon* – in time to turn that postponement into a cancellation.

Hitchcock sang in praise of 'In Old New York' and 'In Days of Old', and queried 'Ain't It Funny What Difference Just a Few Hours Make?' (with just a few topicalities), and joined with Rose Botti, in the piece's other principal female rôle to sing a smart duo about gossip ('The Hammers Will Go Rap, Rap, Rap'). Bonita had a 'Hola!' entrance number and a piece about a 'San Domingo Maid', Jack got into the first act (the tenor couldn't really wait until the dénouement to appear!) to sing soupily that 'Cupid Has Found My Heart' ('... a rapture o'er me stealing ...') and the male chorus, led by Captain Leopoldo of the Dominican Army (German baritone Hubert Wilke, no less) snarled 'We Come of Castilian Blood'. A 'San Domingo Dance' ensemble and military duo for Wilke and Miss Botti were other highlights.

Blossom's book, Hitchcock's comic style and George Marion's direction got some upmarket praise for using 'no horseplay, no local jibes, Rialtoisms or Tenderloin slang ...', and the recipe pleased the general public too. Henry Savage's production of *The Yankee Consul* played 115 performances on Broadway before going out to tour, returned to Wallack's Theater the following year for a second season, then went back to the country for three seasons on the road.

The 'Yankee' tag was picked up again by Hitchcock, Robyn and Mrs Hitchcock (Flora Zabelle) when they christened their next piece, a version of Richard Harding Davis's *The Galloper*, *The Yankee Tourist*. It too did well (103 performances on Broadway and much touring) as did two further Yankees in the next few seasons: *The Yankee Prince* (George M Cohan) and *The Yankee Girl* (Blanche Ring).

A film suggested by *The Yankee Consul* was made in 1924, directed by James W Horne and starring Douglas Maclean and Patsy Ruth Miller.

YARDLEY, William (b Bombay, 10 June 1849; d Kingston-on-Thames, 26 October 1900).

A cousin of George Sims, and a journalist on the *Sporting Times*, where he wrote dramatic criticism under the nom de plume of 'Bill of the Play', Yardley was also an occasional writer for the theatre, a sometime amateur performer (under the pseudonym 'William Wye'), on one occasion a producer for a revival of his friend 'Pot' Stephens's *Billee Taylor* (Crystal Palace, then Toole's) and briefly a theatre proprietor at the Garrick Theatre, Whitechapel. His principal contribution to the musical stage came when he collaborated with Stephens on the texts for the two burlesques, *The Vicar of Wide-awake-field* and *Little Jack Sheppard*, which were instrumental in beginning the fashion for 'new burlesque' that flourished in the hands of George Edwardes, Nellie Farren and Fred Leslie in the late 1880s at the Gaiety Theatre.

1876 **Our Doll's House** (Cotsford Dick) 1 act St George's Hall 26 December
1879 **A Cruise to China** (*Le Voyage en Chine*) English version (Garrick Theatre)
1881 **Herne the Hunted** (pasticcio/w Robert Breece) Gaiety Theatre 24 May
1884 **The Scalded Back** (pasticcio) Novelty Theatre 12 July
1884 **Very Little Hamlet** (pasticcio) Gaiety Theatre 29 November
1885 **Hobbies** (George Gear/w H Pottinger Stephens) 1 act St George's Hall 6 April
1885 **The Vicar of Wide-awake-field** (Florian Pascal/w Stephens) Gaiety Theatre 8 August
1885 **Little Jack Sheppard** (Meyer Lutz et al/w Stephens) Gaiety Theatre 26 December
1890 **Venus** new version w Augustus Harris (Prince of Wales Theatre, Liverpool)
1891 **Robinson Crusoe Esq** (Edward Solomon) Theatre Royal, Chelsea Barracks 11 April
1892 **The Wedding Eve** (*La Veillée de noces*) English version (Trafalgar Theatre)
1895 **A Modern Trilby** (Lutz/w C H E Brookfield) 1 act Opera Comique 16 November
1896 **On the March** (Edward Solomon, Frederick Clay, John Crook/w B C Stephenson, Cecil Clay) Theatre Royal, Sheffield 18 May
1899 **L'Amour mouillée** (*Cupid and the Princess*) English version w Henry Byatt (Lyric Theatre)

YEAMANS, Annie [née GRIFFITHS] (b Isle of Man, 19 November 1835; d New York, 4 March 1912).

Born into a family of entertainers, Mrs Yeamans began her performing life working as a bareback rider in a circus in Australia and on the Pacific circuits, a calling she followed until the death of her clown husband. She moved into the theatre in New York in the late 1860s and appeared in a variety of entertainments (*Humpty Dumpty* with G L Fox, the musical farce *Roughing It, Under the Gaslight* for Daly, the inevitable *Uncle Tom's Cabin* etc) until, in 1877, she joined Edward Harrigan's company to play a supporting rôle in *Old Lavender*. When, the following year, in *The Mulligan Guards' Ball*, Harrigan's Dan Mulligan acquired a wife, little, exuberantly funny Mrs Yeamans became the striving, social-climbing Cordelia Mulligan. Equipped with a red wig and an Irish brogue, she portrayed that lady through the next five years of Mulligan shows, winning a huge personal popularity in the process. In 1883, in one of the most successful of the series, she even made it to the title line of *Cordelia's Aspirations*. When the Mulligan shows were superseded by other Harrigan plays, Mrs Yeamans stayed on, as Harrigan's leading lady and foil, starring in all his musicals until the last in 1893.

She was later seen on Broadway in character rôles in the musical comedies *The Good Mr Best* (1897), *A Chinese Honeymoon* (1902, Mrs Brown), *The Maid and the Mummy* (1904, Astoria Dobbins), *The Hurdy Gurdy Girl* (1907, Mrs Sarah Otis, the sausage king's wife), *The Candy Shop* (1909), and for the last time, at the (probable) age of 74, in *The Echo* (1910).

In 1985 she was portrayed on the Broadway stage (as Mrs Yeamons) by Armelia McQueen in the biomusical *Harrigan and Hart* (Longacre Theater 31 January).

Her daughter **Jennie YEAMANS** [Eugenia Marguerite YEAMANS, b Sydney, Australia, 16 October 1862; d New York, 24 November 1906] followed her mother on to the stage (*The Regatta Girl* etc). She also became, for three years, the wife of producer Charles Dillingham.

THE YELLOW MASK Musical comedy drama in 2 acts by Edgar Wallace. Lyrics by Desmond Carter. Music by Vernon Duke. Additional numbers by Harry Acres. Additional lyrics by Eric Little. Carlton Theatre, London, 8 February 1928.

In the midst of the 1920s fashion for dancing-and-comedy musicals, the rising producer Laddie Cliff joined with pantomime- and spectacle-specialist Julian Wylie to mount an unusual 'musical comedy drama'. Thriller author Edgar Wallace provided the melodramatic tale of a diamond stolen from the crown jewels of Britain by a horrid Chinaman (Malcolm Keen) and the efforts of English John (Wilfred Temple) and Mary (Phyllis Dare) to avoid the yellow perils (Chinaman-specialist Frank Cochrane) and regain the stone. Top-billed Bobby Howes featured as a comical detective.

The songs with which they were provided, however, were the same waltzes, foxtrots and danced choruses to be found wedded to more suitable subjects in most of the rest of the shows in town, so that one officer of the crown was heard to sing about 'Blowing the Blues Away' whilst hero and heroine took time off to foxtrot through 'Half a Kiss' between drama in the Tower of London and Chinese tortures. The mixture of 'melodrama garnished with the froth and fribble of musical comedy', and most particularly the expanding comicalities of the young Howes, found themselves an audience, but had more difficulties with a theatre. After seven weeks the piece was booted out of the Carlton, which switched terminally to movies, and having found a new home down the street at His Majesty's, was

forced out of there three months later. It transferred to the (then) unlikely precincts of variety's London Palladium, and there ran out the last days of its 218-performance London run before going on the road.

A film version of the piece, made in 1930, used Temple and Cochrane in their stage rôles and Lupino Lane in Howes's rôle. It did not use the already forgotten music.

THE YEOMEN OF THE GUARD, or The Merryman and His Maid Opera in 2 acts by W S Gilbert. Music by Arthur Sullivan. Savoy Theatre, London 3 October 1888.

After the semi-setback of the melodrama burlesque of *Ruddigore*, Gilbert and Sullivan nevertheless turned back once again to older theatrical forms for the subject matter of their new musical. This time, it was the romantic English opera of the earlier part of the century which provided the librettist with his starting point, but, perhaps surprisingly, not for a burlesque of its conventions. Gilbert took the thread of the *Don Caesar de Bazan* tale which had been used as the basis for Vincent Wallace's hugely successful *Maritana* and remade it into a libretto that was much more in a conventional light-opera vein than in the very individual opéra-bouffe style that he had developed in his earlier pieces.

Lieutenant Fairfax (Courtice Pounds) has been condemned for witchcraft on the false witness of a relative who seeks to inherit his property. To balk that inheritance, Fairfax persuades the Governor of the Tower of London (Wallace Brownlow) to find him a bride. She will be married a few hours, and then become a wealthy widow. Sir Richard agrees, and he chooses Elsie Maynard (Geraldine Ulmar), a strolling player whose partner Jack Point (George Grossmith) agrees nervously to the exercise for the sake of the money. But after the wedding the Yeomen Sergeant Meryll (Richard Temple) and his daughter Phoebe (Jessie Bond) help Fairfax escape. He remains in the Tower, however, disguised as Meryll's son, Leonard, whilst waiting for the expected pardon to come, and in his disguise he woos and wins Elsie, who believes the false reports put out by Point and the culpable jailor Wilfred Shadbolt (W H Denny) that her husband was shot while escaping. When she is told that he is, in fact, alive and coming to claim his bride, she collapses, only to find that her lover and her husband are one and the same. And it is poor, silly, greedy Jack Point who, like *Patience*'s Bunthorne, is left alone at the final curtain.

In fact, the difference between Point's and Bunthorne's fate epitomized the difference between *The Yeomen of the Guard* and the earlier Gilbert libretti. In Point, the official 'comic' rôle of the show, Gilbert wrote a character which was wholly un-burlesque. Point had feelings, and whilst Bunthorne's wifeless end was humorous and ridiculous, Point's end was sentimental and even touching. So much so, indeed, that an over-enthusiastic touring Jack Point, George Thorne, decided that it would be correct to play the jester's final curtain collapse not as a despairing faint but as a broken-hearted death. Elsie, too, a conventional light-opera leading lady, was very different from the tongue-in-cheek star soubrettes of *Patience* or *The Mikado*, and what bitter witticisms there were in the script turned up largely in Point's repertoire of jestering jokes.

Sullivan wrote a score in the English opera style to match the tone Gilbert had taken. It exchanged the

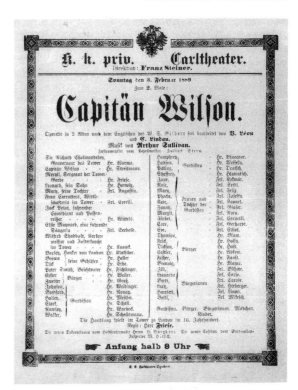

Plate 298. **The Yeomen of the Guard** *underwent some changes between the Savoy Theatre and its Austrian staging as* Capitän Wilson.

burlesque humour of the earlier shows for a straight-forward light-opera lyricism, and the soprano and tenor were the chief beneficiaries. Fairfax was equipped with two of the loveliest straight tenor melodies Sullivan ever wrote as he mused 'Is Life a Boon?' and wondered on his reck-less marriage in 'Free from His Fetters Grim', whilst Elsie's tuneful soprano showpiece, ''Tis Done, I Am a Bride' urged on into a driving chorus of operatic propor-tions. She also joined with Point in one of the popular highlights of the show, their 'act' of *The Merryman and the Maid*, played before the public in the utterly artless 'I Have a Song to Sing, O!' Jessie Bond's soubrette number 'Were I Thy Bride' and Rosina Brandram's heavy dame legend of the tower ('When Our Gallant Norman Foes') were in the same vein, whilst the comic pieces – Jack's disquisition on the arts of jesting, his duo with Wilfred inventing the details of the phoney death of Fairfax with rather less comical extravagance than the authors had shown in the same situation in *The Mikado* – though predictably excel-lent, rather took second place to the romantic tale and its music.

It was thus, perhaps, not surprising that Sullivan won all the praise for *The Yeomen of the Guard* and Gilbert, who had dared to go outside his usual style into something less showy, was less critically appreciated. The public, how-ever, had no doubts and *The Yeomen of the Guard* was a grand success at the Savoy through 423 performances before going out into the provinces and overseas. On Broadway, too, where local soprano Bertha Ricci played Elsie alongside Englishmen J H Ryley (Point), Henry Hal-lam (Fairfax) and Fred Solomon (Shadbolt) there were also initial queries, but New York audiences proved in 100 performances that they were unnecessary ones. J C

Williamson of Australia had *The Yeomen of the Guard* on the stage just six months after its London premiere. Jack Leumane (Fairfax), Nellie Stewart (Elsie), Ida Osborne (Phoebe), Wiliam Elton (Point) and Walter Marnock (Meryll) headed the cast, and the piece quickly installed itself amidst the Gilbert and Sullivan favourites. In later Australian revivals, Pounds and his fellow Savoyard Charles Kenningham were both seen as Fairfax, and Clara, Henry and Sydney Bracy all took turns in the cast.

On the Continent, however, where *The Mikado* had been a big success, the queries over the nature of *The Yeomen of the Guard* were given a pre-production answer. To Sul-livan's fury, the score of *Capitän Wilson* (ad Victor Léon, Carl Lindau) was topped up with a half-dozen pieces from *Patience, Iolanthe, The Mikado* and ... *Madame Favart*! When he complained, the botching practised on Viennese Oper-etten in London was meaningfully pointed out to him. Franz Steiner's production of *Capitän Wilson*, with Karl Streitmann starred as the Captain, Marie Seebold as Elsie, Wilhelm Knaack as Shadbolt, Carl Adolf Friese as Meryll and Herr Wittels as Point played just over two weeks (2–19 February) and said adieu to Vienna with a matinée the following 10 March. It turned up the following year in Prague (23 November 1890), by which time another ver-sion had found its way to Budapest (ad Lajos Evva, 'Imre Ukki') for seven performances at the Népszinház. Berlin ignored *Capitän Wilson* and mounted a less eccentric ver-sion by F Zell and Richard Genée under the title *Der Königsgardist* (the plural 'yeomen' had given place to a singular, presumably intended to mean the disguised Fairfax).

The original and unadulterated *Yeomen* found itself a solid place in the Savoy repertoire and in the English light-opera world, and it was played regularly throughout the existence of the original D'Oyly Carte Opera Company, and brought back in 1989 by the new company. In between, it was also mounted on four occasions at the Tower of London itself, most notably on the occasion of the edifice's 900th anniversary in 1978.

USA: Casino Theater 17 October 1888; Austria: Carltheater *Capitän Wilson* 2 February 1889; Australia: Princess Theatre, Melbourne 20 April 1889; Hungary: Népszinház *A gárdista* 26 April 1889; Germany: Krolls Theater *Der Königsgardist* 25 December 1889

Recordings: complete (Decca, HMV) etc

YES Comédie musicale in 3 acts by René Pujol and Pierre Soulaine adapted from *Totte et sa chance* by Soulaine. Additional lyrics by Paul Géraldy. Music by Maurice Yvain. Théâtre des Capucines, Paris, 26 January 1928.

Maxime (Louvigny), son of Gavard (Constant-Rémy) the 'roi de vermicelle', is horrified when his father arranges a useful marriage for him with the Chilean Marquita Négri (Lily Mounet), a little thing who apparently squashed a cobra in her bare hands at the age of five. Convinced that he is to be sacrificed to a vast negress, Maxime can think of only one way out of the marriage. He hurries to London with the little manicurist Totte (Renée Devillers) and for 50 francs gets her to say a quick 'yes' which can be undone for another 50 francs when Marquita is safely wed elsewhere. There are many quiproquos to be gone through between Touquet and Paris as father tries to get the marriage undone, but at the final curtain Maxime saves his second 50 francs, for Totte, it eventuates, is about to make him a father. Roger Tréville played a confident dreamboat singer called Roger, whilst alongside the main action Arletty appeared as a kooky maidservant with a hatred for work, and Georgé played a valet who dreams of nothing but standing for political office (he gets a feeble 341 votes when he does).

Yvain's score was in the best modern dance tradition of the times. Totte foxtrotted through the belief that 'La vie n'est faite que d'illusions' and went through all the different things that can be meant by the little word 'Yes' both before and after the one said before the clergyman; Marquita attacked 'Je suis de Valparaiso' with Latin vigour, Roger crooned out two pieces written as popular songs, Clémentine the maid asserted 'Moi, je cherche un emploi' with assorted conditions attached, and the deflated César, who had put forth his 'Profession de Foi' so eagerly in Act I, said goodbye to his 341 voters in a comical Valse d'Adieu in the final act, alongside a selection of rhythmic and highly effective ensembles.

Mounted by Armand Berthez at the tiny Théâtre des Capucines with a cast of 16 actors and a two-piano accompaniment, which was given a featured spot in an apropos-of-nothing song for Roger describing what 'Deux pianos' can do, *Yes* proved the hit of its season in a Paris which at that moment in time found much more entertainment in the intimate theatre and its sprightly humour and music than in lavish spectacle.

Like most pieces of its era, *Yes* was denied too much overseas travel by the sexuality of its lyrics and its tale, but Hungary – which alone seemed to share the French ease about such things – had a production (ad Adorján Stella, Imre Harmath) on the stage whilst Paris's *Yes* still ran.

Later, during the Second World War, a film version was made, with Suzy Delair and Paul Meurisse starred, under the title *Défense d'aimer*.

Hungary: Magyar Színház 18 May 1928; Film: *Défense d'aimer*

YES, MADAM? Musical comedy in 2 acts by R P Weston, Bert Lee and K R G Browne, based on the novel by Browne. Lyrics by Weston and Lee. Music by Jack Waller and Joseph Tunbridge. London Hippodrome, 27 September 1934.

Browne's novel, already used as the basis of a 1933 British Lion film, proved ideal material as the starting point for a musical comedy vehicle for comedian Bobby Howes, the enormously successful star of a series of musical farces since his singular hit in *Mr Cinders. Yes, Madam?* brought him back together with his co-star of that show, Binnie Hale, as little Bill and sweet Sally, obliged by the conditions of an *Oncle Célestin*-type musical comedy will to go into service for two months before they can inherit. There is, of course, a nasty cousin, Tony (Billy Leonard), who stands to benefit if he can make them throw it in before the time is up. Yorkshire button-manufacturer Peabody (Wylie Watson) and his dragonistic sister (Bertha Belmore) employ the pair, who get into all sorts of scrapes in their disguises. In the principal adventure, Bill is sent by Peabody to retrieve some incriminating love letters from the bosomy Pansy Beresford (Vera Pearce) at great risk to virtue and limb, but Pansy ends up entwined with the terrible Tony as Bill and Sally come through safely to richness and happiness.

Waller and Tunbridge supplied some happy songs to illustrate the tale. Bill and Sally sang sweetly of 'Sitting Beside o' You' and chirruped 'What Are You Going to Do?', Miss Pearce yodelled out her preference for 'Czechoslovakian Love' and a memorably lusty 'The Girl the Soldiers Always Leave Behind', and Watson and Howes, locked out when returning from a secret spree, made ghastly noises to a version of Rossini's 'Cat's Duet' as a signal to Sally to open the door to them. This touch of culture – a recurring item in the Waller shows – was compounded by a 'Shakespearian sextet' of dubious authenticity.

Yes, Madam? was a full-scale hit. The fine and favourite cast were all fitted with material which suited them splendidly, and Waller's production played at the Hippodrome for 302 performances before going out on the road for two seasons of touring and then into the film studios, where Howes, Watson, Miss Belmore and Miss Pearce repeated their stage rôles with Diana Churchill as Sally. Miss Pearce, however, did not return to her home country when *Yes, Madam?* was given its Australian production. Her rôle was taken by Ethel Morrison whilst Charles Heslop and Nellie Barnes played Bobby and Binnie, Marie La Varre the heavy lady, and Leo Franklyn, Cecil Kellaway, Robert Coote (who would, two decades later, be *My Fair Lady*'s Pickering) and Lois Green completed the leading players. The show played a satisfactory seven weeks in Sydney and two months in Melbourne.

Australia: Theatre Royal, Sydney 29 August 1936; Film: 1938

YES, UNCLE! Musical comedy in 2 acts by Austen Hurgon and George Arthurs based on *Le Truc de Brésilien* by Marcel Nancey and Paul Armont. Lyrics by Clifford

Grey. Music by Nat D Ayer. Prince of Wales Theatre, London, 29 December 1917.

Conceived by producers Grossmith and Laurillard as a follow-up to their successful French-farce-based musicals *Tonight's the Night* and *Theodore and Co*, *Yes, Uncle!* was scheduled for the Gaiety Theatre with Leslie Henson again as comic star. A coup d'état at the Gaiety sent them to the Prince of Wales Theatre, and the War almost deprived them of Henson who, anxious to join up, finally agreed to create the principal comedy rôle of the show before departing.

Henson played Bobby, a typical musical-comedy best-friend to the artist, G B Stark (Fred Leslie). Stark goes to a ball disguised as a French Count, and there he woos and wins his own wife, Joan (Margaret Bannerman) whilst disposing of his embarrassingly passionate and operatic model Lolita (Alexia Bassian) to his convenient uncle (Davy Burnaby). Henri Leoni sang tenorish ballads as a dashing Zouave who gets the household's maid (Lily St John), and Julia James was the widow Mabel Mannering who paired off at the final curtain with the bounding Henson. Their songs, written by Nat D Ayer of recent *Bing Boys* fame, included some attractive light pieces in the current dance-rhythmed fashion of which Leoni and Miss James's duet 'Think of Me (when the band is playing)' proved the much-plugged hit of the evening. Miss James also had the other success of the evening, a coy but catchy ballad insisting that 'Widows Are Wonderful'.

However, as intended, it was Henson who was the key to the entertainment, Henson and his 'working up' of the part of Bobby with his various bits of comic business. The producers knew this, and even though they knew they could only keep their star a short while, they agreed to pay him a royalty for the run of the show to rehearse and set up his rôle. Their idea worked, for when Henson handed over his rôle to his understudy, Norman Griffin, after two weeks of the show's run, the piece was in sufficiently good condition to last out the First World War, with 626 performances in over a year and a half in London prior to going on the road.

J C Williamson Ltd mounted the show in Australia with Dorothy Brunton (then Gracie Lavers) as Mabel, Cyril Ritchard and Madge Elliott as the Zouave and the maid, Marie Eaton (Lolita) and Alfred Frith in Henson's rôle. William Greene (Stark) performed Fred Fisher and Joseph McCarthy's 'They Go Wild over Me', Miss Brunton sang Maceo Pinkard and William Tracy's 'Mammy o' Mine' and joined Frith in Anita Elson's London revue hit 'I'm Getting Tired of Playing Second Fiddle', whilst Cecil Bradley (Joan) popped in Victor Jacobi's 'On Miami Shore' alongside a half-dozen bits of the original score. Even though the show was considered 'considerably short of the level of *Kissing Time*' which had preceded it, it did duty for a fine nine weeks in Melbourne and ten weeks in Sydney.

Australia: Theatre Royal, Melbourne 12 June 1920

YOHÉ, May [YOHÉ, Mary Augusta] (b Bethlehem, Pa, 6 April 1869; d Boston, 28 August 1938).

One of the more colourful and self-publicizing of the parade of musical-theatre performers who passed across the British and American stages of her era, though certainly not one of the more talented, May Yohé, who intermittently claimed to be bred from Narraganset Indian stock, was working in the chorus of a musical in Chicago when someone took a fancy to the very individual sound of 'one of the three notes in her voice' and decided she deserved to be featured.

She appeared in short trunks as the boy, Alphonse, in John McCaull's *Lorraine* and as Zal-am-Boo in *Aladdin*, featured on the bill at the Fifth Avenue Theater and the following year toured as the Princess in the Chicago extravaganza *The Arabian Nights*. She was again seen on Broadway playing in *Natural Gas* at the Bijou and around the country as a principal boy in the Eddie Foy spectacular *The Crystal Slipper* before, in 1890, she went out to Australia, billed as a 'baritone', performing with a minstrel company cheekily calling itself the Boston Ideal Company. The season was not a success, and May returned to San Francisco, announcing her arrival by having her carriage run away newspaperworthily with her in the local park.

It was London, however, that decided to make her, albeit very briefly, a star. She appeared in the Albéniz comic opera *The Magic Opal*, caught several eyes and, having been swiftly written out of that show, equally promptly got herself starred as *Mam'zelle Nitouche*. This time she walked out, but still got herself a new job – the title-rôle of *Little Christopher Columbus*. She also got a Lord for a husband. The Lord in question was the very questionable Lord Francis Hope, a weak gambler and womanizer who was heir to the Ducal seat of Newcastle and the infamous Hope Diamond. He was also the chief backer, to the tune of over £5,000, of *Little Christopher Columbus*, in which May herself had invested £1,000. However, even if the actress had bought herself her rôle, both *Little Christopher* and her performance of the songs written for her, within her wriggle-through range, by Ivan Caryll turned out a genuine hit.

These were May's peak months. The next year she starred in the title-rôle of the London production of the surefire *The Lady Slavey* which (apparently with a little help from her) misfired, and Hope was declared bankrupt. She was cast in *Christopher*'s follow-up, *Dandy Dick Whittington*, with less happy results, then, her notorious unprofessionalism having made her unemployable, took the Court Theatre to present herself first as *Mam'zelle Nitouche*, then as *The Belle of Cairo*. Then she was gone.

She later turned up in Australia, and in 1900 appeared on the stage in New York again, billing herself as Lady Francis Hope, in the rôle of Lady Muriel Despair in a piece called *The Giddy Throng* at the New York Theater. She sang two Ivan Caryll songs, was on stage for a total of 12 minutes, and prompted a critic to report 'When Miss Yohé left here she was said to have three notes in her voice. She has apparently lost two of them in her voyage across the Atlantic'. She also ended up being sued by producer A H Chamberlyn for breach of contract.

In 1901 she eloped with a gentleman called Captain Putnam B Strong and was divorced from Hope. She tried another comeback in 1907, attempting to add some scandal to her own faded notoriety by appearing as La Folaire in a revival of *Mamzelle Champagne*, the piece of which the opening night had been marked by the Harry Thaw murder. A critic remarked 'It would be harsh to speak of the efforts of Miss Yohé. It is sufficient to say that she was "featured".' She moved from New York to Japan

Plate 299. May Yohé *made up for having only three notes to her voice in other ways.*

and then back to England for yet another abortive return to the stage in the revue *Come Over Here* (1913), before trading Strong for a third husband, Captain John Smuts, who took her to a rubber plantation in the South Pacific. She later worked as a janitress, on a chicken ranch and in a tearoom, and tried yet again to return to the theatre, but her last years were spent working as a clerk in the Works Progress Administration.

YOUMANS, Vincent [Millie] (b New York, 27 September 1898; d Denver, Col, 5 April 1946). One of the most effective songwriters of the peak period of the Broadway dancing musical comedy.

The young Youmans got his first musical opportunities during a wartime period in the navy and, on his return home, worked as a song-plugger and rehearsal pianist whilst taking his first steps as a songwriter. He placed individual numbers in *Linger Longer Letty* and the E Ray Goetz revue *Vogues and Vanities* and had his first opportunity at a musical-comedy score, in collaboration with Paul Lannin and lyricist Ira Gershwin, on Abe Erlanger's production of *Two Little Girls in Blue*. A modest success through 135 performances on Broadway, but a pre-London flop when mounted in England, *Two Little Girls in Blue* did, however, bring Youmans sufficient Broadway exposure to make the favourite songs from the show ('Oh Me! Oh My! [Oh You!]', 'Who's Who with You?', 'Dolly') popular and to win him another opportunity, this time with top-drawer collaborators in Otto Harbach and Oscar Hammerstein II.

The show which they wrote together, *Wildflower*, was a fine success and Youmans's song 'Bambalina' proved the take-away hit of a score written in collaboration with operetta hardy Herbert Stothart. However, its success was

nothing compared to that which awaited Youmans's first solo effort as a musical comedy composer. Harry Frazee's production of *No, No, Nanette* opened in Detroit less than three months on from *Wildflower*'s début on Broadway, and the show soon became a Chicago hit as 'Tea for Two', 'I Want to Be Happy', 'Too Many Rings Around Rosie', 'You Can Dance with Any Girl At All' and much of the rest of its score became national song favourites. *No, No, Nanette* cleaned up around the country, and overseas, establishing itself as one of the greatest hits of its era before it was finally brought to Broadway, and in the meantime two other shows with songs by Youmans had appeared in New York. Neither *Mary Jane McKane* (151 performances) nor *Lollipop* (152 performances) was a disaster, but neither proved to be on *Wildflower*'s level. The latter show, however, did leave behind two songs which did not go down with the ship: 'Take a Little One Step' was later incorporated into *No, No, Nanette* and 'Tie a String around Your Finger' subsequently did the rounds of Europe, interpolated into the hugely successful *Mercenary Mary*.

Whilst *No, No, Nanette* continued to make its triumphant way around the world, Youmans produced the scores for a remake of the hit London musical version of *L'Hôtel du Libre Échange*, *A Night Out* – remade so badly that it flopped on the road – and for an unfortunate adaptation of another huge play hit, Veber and Hennequin's *La Présidente*, called *Oh, Please!* (75 performances). Unhappy with this lack of success and with the peremptory treatment handed out by producers, he then went into production himself to mount a musical version of the play *Shore Leave* under the lively title *Hit the Deck*. *Hit the Deck* gave its composer his third Broadway hit in three years, and 'Sometimes I'm Happy' (transferred from *A Night Out*) and 'Hallelujah!' (another trunk piece) found their way into the book of Youmans standards as the show followed *Nanette* around the world.

Thereafter, however, things went less well. An attempt to follow the path taken by Hammerstein and Kern in *Show Boat* resulted in a flop called *Rainbow* (29 performances); *Great Day*, in spite of a score which housed several numbers which would endure way beyond its out-of-town closure ('Without a Song', 'More Than You Know', 'Great Day'), vanished even more quickly; a Florenz Ziegfeld vehicle for Marilyn Miller and the Astaires called *Smiles* ('Time on My Hands') foundered in 63 nights, and an attempt to turn the famous old play *Smiling Through* into a musical, under the title *Through the Years*, lasted just 20 performances. Only a contribution to a remake of the revue-within-a-musical piece which was ultimately called *Take a Chance* won the composer an extended Broadway representation (243 performances). 'Rise and Shine', the most popular piece from his five-song share in this show's score, was later reused as the title song of a 1936 London flop for which Robert Stolz had the principal music credit, alongside another Youmans number, 'Leave it to Love'. On tour, the show became *Darling You* – the title of one of Stolz's songs – and Youmans's contribution, his last to the musical stage, was not detailed.

Youmans's last taste of success was in the film world, notably with his score to the 1934 *Flying Down to Rio* ('Orchids in the Moonlight', 'Carioca' etc), but precarious health and an inability to get to grips with work meant that for the last decade of a life which ended at age of 47, no new work came to the stage to add to the three big hits of the earliest years of his career. His name appeared on a bill for the last time as a producer when he mounted a dance compilation piece *Vincent Youmans' Ballet Revue* (Baltimore 27 January 1944) with music by Ravel, Rimsky-Korsakov Lecuona, some choreography by Massine, and utter failure.

Perhaps because of this narrow period of celebrity, it has been Youmans's fate – like the much more prolific Fall and Eysler in Austria, and Christiné in France – to have seen his reputation fritter away over the years. Although his music is still widely played, and *No, No, Nanette* regularly reproduced, he has not come in for the personal publicity and the sometimes exaggerated homage given to the more fashionable Broadway names of the pre-war era. But his contribution was considerable and the songs he gave to the musical theatre remain delightful examples of their genre 60 and 70 years on.

A compilation show of Youmans's works (ad Tom Taylor, Darwin Knight) was staged under the title *Oh Me, Oh My, Oh Youmans* at the Wonderhorse Theater, New York 14 January 1981.

1921 **Two Little Girls in Blue** (w Paul Lannin/Ira Gershwin/ Frederick Jackson) George M Cohan Theater 3 May
1923 **Wildflower** (w Herbert Stothart/Otto Harbach, Oscar Hammerstein) Casino Theater 7 February
1923 **No, No, Nanette** (Frank Mandel, Harbach, Irving Caesar) Garrick Theater, Detroit 23 April; Palace Theatre, London 11 March 1925
1923 **The Left Over** (Zelda Sears, Walter de Leon) Albany 24 September
1923 **Mary Jane McKane** (w Stothart/Hammerstein, William Cary Duncan) Imperial Theater 25 December
1924 **Lollipop** revised *The Left Over* Knickerbocker Theater 21 January
1925 **A Night Out** revised American version (Garrick Theater, Philadelphia)
1926 **Oh, Please!** (Anne Caldwell/Caldwell, Harbach) Fulton Theater 17 December
1927 **Hit the Deck!** (Leo Robin, Clifford Grey/Herbert Fields) Belasco Theater 25 April
1928 **Rainbow** (Hammerstein/Laurence Stallings, Hammerstein) Gallo Theater 21 November
1929 **Great Day** (Edward Eliscu, Billy Rose/William Cary Duncan, John Wells) Garrick Theater, Philadelphia 4 June; Cosmopolitan Theater 17 October
1930 **Smiles** (Harold Adamson, Grey/William Anthony McGuire et al) Ziegfeld Theater 18 November
1932 **Through the Years** (Edward Heyman/Brian Hooker) Manhattan Theater 28 January
1932 **Take a Chance** (w Nacio Herb Brown, Richard Whiting/ Buddy de Sylva/Schwab) Apollo Theater 26 November

Biography: Bordman, G: *Days to Be Happy, Days to Be Sad* (OUP, New York, 1982)

YOUNG, Rida Johnson [née JOHNSON, Ida R] (b Baltimore, 28 February ?1866; d Southfield Point, Conn, 8 May 1926). Broadway librettist and lyricist who scored a brace of major hits in the romantic musical theatre.

Daughter of a striving Baltimore middle-class family, Rida Johnson graduated from college in 1882 and decided on a career in the theatre. She spent several years as an actress in upmarket companies, married fellow actor, writer and subsequently film director James Young, then swapped the stage for a job in the press department at the music publishers Witmark. It was there that she began a career as a theatre writer. Mrs Young scored an early success with the play *Brown of Harvard* in 1906 and she made her first moves into the musical theatre four years later when she supplied the Shuberts with a text for Lulu Glaser (*Just One of the Boys*), and Augustus Pitou with a romantic Irish weepie-comedy for the perennial touring star Chauncey Olcott. Amongst the handful of lyrics that Mrs Young provided to composer Ernest Ball to set for the tenor hero of *Barry of Ballymore*, was one which gave her and them an enormous and international hit: 'Mother Machree'.

For several years, she continued to turn out variations on the Irish theme for Pitou and Olcott, but in the meanwhile she scored a major hit with her first attempt at a regular musical play, the picturesque New Orleans tale of *Naughty Marietta*, written with Victor Herbert around the members of Oscar Hammerstein's failed opera company. Along with her libretto, Mrs Young provided the lyrics to a score including 'Ah! Sweet Mystery of Life', 'Tramp, Tramp, Tramp', ''Neath the Southern Moon' and 'I'm Falling in Love with Someone'.

The Red Petticoat, a musical adaptation of her unsuccessful play *Next*, won some notice for its refreshingly unconventional choice of an unglamorous mining-town barber as its heroine, but there was nothing original about the glitzy *Lady Luxury*, a quick failure at the Casino Theater.

The War years brought the author several more successes. The two happiest of these were adaptations – americanized versions of the Hungarian military piece *Az obsitos*, and of the romantic Berlin hit *Wie einst im Mai* – and the second, as *Maytime*, gave its author a long-running stage success and yet another song hit with 'Do You Remember?'. An original script for a comical tale about mormons and multiple marriage, *His Little Widows*, had Broadway and London runs with good rather than great results, but Mrs Young's libretto was well enough thought-of by its British adapter, Firth Shephard, for him to borrow it a few years later and attach it to a different score under the title *Lady Luck* (Carlton Theatre 27 April 1927).

The *Maytime* flavour worked less well in a another time-shift script for Rudolf Friml's *Sometime*, a piece which nevertheless rode to a good run on its comedy, but a collaboration with British composer Augustus Barratt proved unfruitful and a fresh teaming with the partner of her first great Broadway success, Victor Herbert, on a musical version of another through-the-ages tale, *The Road to Yesterday*, turned up only medium results for the author's last musical play before her death at the age (although she admitted to much less) of 60.

1910 **Just One of the Boys** (William A Schroeder) Washington DC 3 July
1910 **Ragged Robin** (Chauncey Olcott et al/w Rita Olcott) Academy of Music 24 January
1910 **Barry of Ballymore** (Ernest Ball et al) Academy of Music 30 January 1911
1910 **Naughty Marietta** (Victor Herbert) New York Theater 7 November
1911 **Macushla** (Ernest Ball, C Olcott et al) Grand Opera House 5 February 1912
1912 **The Isle of Dreams** (C Olcott et al) McVickers Theater, Chicago 27 October; Grand Opera House 27 January 1913

1912 **The Red Petticoat** (aka *Look Who's Here*) (Jerome Kern/Paul West) Daly's Theater 13 November

1913 **Shameen Dhu** (C Olcott et al) Olympic Theater, Chicago 19 October

1913 **When Love is Young** (Schroeder) Cort Theater, Chicago 28 October

1914 **Lady Luxury** (Schroeder) His Majesty's Theater, Montreal 5 October; Casino Theater, New York, 25 December

1916 **Her Soldier Boy** (*Az obsitos*) American version w Sigmund Romberg (Astor Theater)

1917 **Captain Cupid** (Schroeder/w William Cary Duncan) Shubert Theater, Minneapolis 15 April

1917 **His Little Widows** (Schroeder/w Duncan) Astor Theater 30 April

1917 **Maytime** (*Wie einst im Mai*) American version w Romberg (Shubert Theater)

1918 **Miss I-don't know** (Augustus Barratt) Stamford, Conn, 14 September

1918 **Sometime** (Rudolf Friml) Shubert Theater 4 October

1918 **Little Simplicity** (Barratt) Astor Theater 4 November

1924 **Dream Girl** (Herbert/w Harold Atteridge) Ambassadors Theater 20 August

YOU NEVER KNOW   *see* BEI KERZENLICHT

YOU'RE A GOOD MAN, CHARLIE BROWN

Musical by John Gordon based on the comic strip *Peanuts* by Charles M Schulz. Music and lyrics by Clarke Gesner. Theater 80 St Marks, New York, 7 March 1967.

The songs which made up *You're a Good Man, Charlie Brown* were originally issued on record, as 'an original MGM Album Musical ... a series of delightful (and meaningful) new songs which portray the ups and downs of Charlie Brown, Lucy, Snoopy, Linus and Schroeder'. The piece was subsequently expanded – the ultimate cast was six – and made up into a stage show which was produced by Arthur Whitelaw and Gene Persson in a small off-Broadway venue. The favourite comic strip's characters appeared in a series of little strip-like scenes and songs, with Charlie Brown (Gary Burghoff) flying his 'Kite', Lucy (Reva Rose) putting on imperious airs as 'Queen Lucy' and dispensing blithely inaccurate 'Little Known Facts', Snoopy the dog (Bill Hinnant) – otherwise the fearless wartime flying ace, 'The Red Baron' – serenading his favourite pursuit of 'Suppertime', Linus (Bob Balaban) getting down to the nitty-gritty about 'My Blanket and Me' and everybody getting tied up in the all-important baseball game with predictable (to the millions of fans of the cartoon strip) results.

A long-running success in its New York production (1,597 performances), the show suffered the same fate as most other off-Broadway pieces mounted in a London with no comparable area of theatre. Even in the tiny Fortune Theatre, Harold Fielding and Bernard Delfont's production could not find the equivalent atmosphere and audience, and it folded in 115 performances. David Rhys-Anderson appeared as Charlie with Don Potter as Snoopy and Boni Enten as Lucy. The producers attempted to publicize their show by approaching a famous greetings card firm with the proposal that they publish 'Peanuts' greetings cards, but they were turned down with the answer that such a thing could never catch on.

In spite of its West End failure, *You're a Good Man, Charlie Brown* later (with a little help from 'Peanuts' greetings cards) established itself as a regular favourite in British provincial theatres in the same way that it did in smaller American houses and colleges. It also won productions elsewhere, including several in Australia. Sydney saw a first mounting in 1970, Harry M Miller and Melbourne's Actors' Theatre staged the piece three years later and Sydney's Phillips Street Theatre and Ensemble Theatre followed in 1981.

The show was televised in America in 1972, and a German-language version was produced in Hamburg in 1991 with Thomas Borchert (Snoopy), Goetz Fuhrmann (Charlie) and Sabine Steinke (Lucy) featured.

Another Peanuts musical, *Snoopy – the Musical* (Larry Grossman/Hal Hackady), was mounted in San Francisco in 1982 and subsequently played in New York (Lamb's Theater 20 December 1982, 152 performances) and in London (Duchess Theatre 20 September 1983) prior to winning a similar run of small-house productions.

UK: Fortune Theatre 1 February 1968; Australia: Playbox Theatre, Sydney 7 May 1970; Germany: Neues Theater, Hamburg *Du bist in Ordnung, Charlie Brown* 6 March 1991

Recordings: original concept disc (MGM), original cast (MGM), TV cast (Atlantic)

YOU'RE IN LOVE   Musical comedy in 2 acts by Otto Hauerbach and Edward Clark. Music by Rudolf Friml. Casino Theater, New York, 6 February 1917.

You're in Love was a musical comedy which was in many ways as conventional as could be – but it had one or two enjoyable little flavours of an almost French-comedy style of originality about it. It was not, for example, yet the fashion for a musical play to be set on a sea-going yacht (though it was by no means unprecedented), and it was almost always a wealthy uncle with dynastic or financial reasons who was, up till minutes from the final curtain, the bar to the marriage of the singing-dancing juveniles. *You're in Love* opened with a chorus of young San Francisco folk getting ready to sail off on a six months ocean cruise on the SS *High Hopes*, and the whole of the second act was spent on board, three days out of port. And the marriage between Georgina Payton (Marie Flynn) and Hobby Douglas (Harry Clarke) was celebrated before sailing time. It was not on this occasion forbidden – merely surrounded by all sorts of conditions laid down by auntie Payton (Florine Arnold), the nitty-gritty of which was – no physical contact for a year. By the time Georgina has gone sleepwalking on the ship's railings and on a boom which was swung gasp-makingly out over the audience, Auntie is ready to give in to the inevitable.

The score to the show was in Friml's most light-hearted vein. Georgina went sleepwalking to a shower of harp arpeggios and the song 'I'm Only Dreaming', serenaded 'Loveland' in waltz time, nodded through the pre-wedding quartet explaining 'Things That They Must Not Do' and commiserated with her Hobby over the fact that, under certain circumstances, 'A Year is a Long, Long Time'. The number-two couple Lacey Hart (Lawrence Wheat) and Dorothy (May Thompson) delivered several bright pieces ('Married Life', 'Be Sure it's Light', 'He Will Understand') and Lacey – who bore the brunt of the male music – joined Georgina to explain 'You're in Love'. Hauerbach and Clark had, however, their best time with the comedy numbers. Principal (and incidental) comedian Mr Wix (Al Roberts) burlesqued 'The Cradle of the Deep'

Plate 300.

in the sad tale of how he was 'Snatched from the Cradle (in my sleep)' to a youthful marriage, and demonstrated the dance the 'Boola Boo', whilst Mrs Payton sprayed out her mistrust of the male race in a 'Keep off the Grass' which was much more lyrically juicy than Gertie Millar's famous Gaiety song of the same title: 'I know the brutes, for I've had three, they're all alike as dollars, they differ merely in degree of waistbands, shirts or collars ... that's why I'm a grass widow, with a sign "Keep Off the Grass"!'

Arthur Hammerstein's production of You're in Love was warmed up in Stamford and Springfield and then moved to Broadway where it played for a fine 162 performances before heading for the regions dressed in success. In fact, it had further success awaiting it further afield for, although Britain did not take the show up, Australia's J C Williamson Ltd did, and Australia proved to like the show even better than America had. It was first produced in Sydney, understandably billed as 'by the author and composer of High Jinks' which had been one of the biggest musical-comedy hits of the era in Australia. It wasn't entirely by them by this time for 'Day Dream Isle', 'Naughty Times Three' and several other popular songs of the moment had made their way into the score in typical Williamson fashion. Talleur Andrews, Maud Fane, Field Fisher, Connie Ediss, Alfred Frith, Madge Elliott and William Greene headed the cast as the production moved to Melbourne (3 November–17 December), then back to Sydney after pantomime was done, then back again to Melbourne (7–25 March) as You're in Love established itself as a genuine favourite. It was revived in 1921–2 with Frith and Miss Fane again featured and, if it did not quite join the very favourites of its period – A Night Out, High

Jinks, Kissing Time – on the revival plan, it ended up holding a position not far behind them.

Australia: Her Majesty's Theatre, Sydney 7 September 1917

YOUR OWN THING Rock musical in 2 acts by Donald Driver suggested by Shakespeare's Twelfth Night. Music and lyrics by Hal Hester and Danny Apolinar. Orpheum Theater, New York, 13 January 1968.

A lively, up-to-date tale of pop people in the then 'Now Generation' which followed the outline of Twelfth Night and its tale of sexual ambiguities to a score of contemporary rock-and-roll music. If the girl-as-boy storyline was reminiscent of many Victorian musical plays, the manner of its telling (as reflected in the 1960s lingo of its title) put it squarely into its own time and place.

Sebastian (Rusty Thacker) and Viola (Leland Palmer) are identical pop-singing twins who get separated when they are involved in a shipwreck. The rescued Viola gets a job as a replacement singer in a rock quartet who have lost their vocalist to the draft, and soon afterwards the recovered Sebastian gets the same job. Orson (Tom Ligon), the manager of the group, who has been courting disco owner Olivia (Marian Mercer/Marcia Rodd), finds himself worryingly attracted by the new singer. He's not modern enough to be displeased when it turns out they are not one, but two, that Viola is a girl, and that Sebastian has been using his message-carrying moments between Orson and Olivia to win the disco lady for himself.

Several of the songs in the show were presented as the songs of the pop group ('Somethin's Happ'nin", 'Your Own Thing', 'What Do I Know?', The Apocalypse Fugue), whilst Shakespeare's words were set as lyrics for 'Come Away Death' (Sebastian in hospital) and 'She Never Told Her Love' (Viola on Orson).

Zev Bufman and Dorothy Love's off-Broadway production was a 937-performance success at the Orpheum Theater, and the show was subsequently mounted in London, under the same management. Misses Palmer and Rodd and composer Apolinar (who appeared as one of the Apocalypse rock group) from the New York production appeared alongside Gerry Glasier (Sebastian) and Les Carlson (Orson) for a run of six weeks. In Australia the response was equally negative, though better at Sydney's Phillip Street Theatre, where Lynn Rogers, Bunny Gibson, Bryan Davies and Kristen Mann featured, than in a brief subsequent season in Melbourne (Comedy Theatre, 8 June 1969). In France, where the trendy title apparently meant nothing, the piece was produced in the 1969–70 season with Arielle Semenoff and Jacques Tadieu featured, under the title Charlie.

UK: Comedy Theatre 6 February 1969; Australia: Phillip Street Theatre, Sydney 15 February 1969; France: Charlie 1969–70 season
Recording: original cast (RCA)

YVAIN, Maurice [Pierre Paul] (b Paris, 12 February 1891; d Suresne, 28 July 1965). One of the happiest composers of the French inter-war musical theatre through a long series of hits which mixed sprightly textual comedy with a touch of dance-musical class.

Trained at the Paris Conservatoire, Yvain made his first professional inroads into the world of music as a pianist and accompanist, playing the piano with Louis Ganne's well-respected orchestra in Monte-Carlo until military service called. That military service, however, turned into war and Yvain's musical career was forcibly postponed. After the war, a friendship struck up with Maurice Chevalier in the earliest days of his eight years in uniform proved highly useful, for the singer introduced Yvain to Albert Willemetz, author of the landmark musical *Phi-Phi*, and the two collaborated soon after on several songs which were performed at the Casino de Paris by Rose Amy (La Légende de la Violette), Dréan ('Cach' ton piano') and by Mistinguett. The last-named's performance of Yvain and Willemetz's 'Mon homme' proved the breakthrough for the neophyte composer, a breakthrough confirmed, in particular, by the Trio des épiciers in the revue *On peut monter!* Many other successful revue songs also followed: Mistinguett's 'J'en ai marre', Chevalier's 'Avec le sourire', 'L'Étrange Valse', 'Billets-doux', 'Le Gri-gri d'amour' (taken from an aborted opérette and turned into an 'Hawaiian' revue duo for Mistinguett and Boucot), 'En douce', 'Le Java' and 'La Belote'.

His songwriting success brought Yvain to the notice of wide-handed theatre magnate Gustave Quinson, who had produced Henri Christiné's *Phi-Phi* three years earlier and, in spite of the fact that the composer had not a full score to his name, Quinson signed him up for three musicals. It took only the first to establish Yvain at the top of the field. The winningly sexy *Ta bouche*, its bounding dance music no little assisted by a delicious Yves Mirande libretto, some amusing Willemetz lyrics and a fine cast of nine, followed behind and rendered nothing in popularity to Christiné's modern musical comedies. And whilst *Ta bouche* continued its Parisian, provincial, and its limited (by its subject matter) international career, Yvain followed up with the same collaborators on a second big success, *Là-haut*, with Chevalier and Dranem as stars.

La Dame en décolleté, which leaned slightly less on the popular dance rhythms of the age than its hit predecessors, won more praise than run (three months), but another up-to-date piece, *Gosse de riche*, did much more than a little better, and a collaboration with André Barde – hitherto best known as the librettist to Charles Cuvillier and the author of some superior revues – brought forth Yvain's fourth musical comedy hit in less than three years. In *Pas sur la bouche*, as illustration to another sparklingly sexy libretto, Yvain turned out a fresh selection of numbers in the light, dancing style of *Ta bouche*'s songs, and Benoît-Léon Deutsch's production at the Théâtre des Nouveautés gave the new team an enormous and enduring success both in the theatre and, for Yvain's most popular numbers, outside it. Continuing with the 'bouche' titles, the pair then wrote *Bouche à bouche*, a piece which took a pot-shot at the pretensions of the inevitably noble Russian émigrés, which managed a round 100 nights, and had a further grand success with another vehicle for that piece's comic star, Georges Milton, *Un bon garçon*, which followed a more than useful Paris career of over a year with provincial and overseas showings.

The small-scale *Yes*, produced at the tiny Théâtre des Capucines with just a two-piano accompaniment, added to the total of successes, *Elle est à vous* and *Kadubec* to the semi-successes, and if *Jean V*, a second collaboration with the authors of *Gosse de riche*, was a month and a bit's flop, the very few failures were heavily outweighed by the suc-

cesses as versions of Yvain's works – their libretti bowdlerized for more maidenly audiences – found their way to the stages of the world. London saw *Pas sur la bouche*, New York *Ta bouche* and *Un bon garçon*, Berlin got a Germanned *Ta bouche* whilst in Budapest where, for a period, the French musical comedy and in particular the works of Yvain and Christiné became all the rage, *Ta bouche*, *Gosse de riche*, *Pas sur la bouche*, *Un bon garçon* and *Yes* were all shown.

Yvain's fine record of the 1920s got a little reinforcement in the 1930s with *Oh! Papa...* and the composer's first collaboration with Christiné in a two-handed score for *Encore cinquante centimes* – both pieces successful at home and both subsequently played in Budapest – but other productions, ranging from the Puss-in-boots fairytale *La Belle Histoire* to a one-act 'modern féerie' and the musical comedy *Pépé*, failed to make a mark. The fashion for the French jazz-age musical comedy of which Yvain had been one of the earliest and most successful purveyors had gone its way and, in the years that followed, the composer found himself more successful in the world of the cinema and, subsequently, in the newly re-fashionable opérette à grand spectacle.

Yvain's approach to the large-scale opérette was less conquering than the entrance he had made more than a decade earlier onto the musical comedy stage. He supplied a couple of additional songs to the grandiose production of a De Sylva, Brown and Henderson piece mounted as *Miami* (1930) and found failure with *Coup de veine* at the Porte-Saint-Martin, but the spectacular and romantic *Au soleil du Mexique* won a good run at the Châtelet before its composer found it advisable to blush behind the pseudonym of 'Jean Sautreuil' for a new musical version of Louis Verneuil's *Le Coffre-fort vivant*, which played during the early days of the war, and *Le Beau Voyage d'un enfant de Paris* which was seen in its last days. The change of name did not, however, save him from being prosecuted and banned for collaborating by permitting his works to be 'used' by the invaders.

Yvain returned to his own name for the production of *Monseigneur*, a final effort in the small-scale musical field at the Daunou (a house which had not been lucky for the composer since *Gosse de riche*) before he switched modes again to compose the score for *Chanson gitane* in 1946. Following behind the enormous success won by Raymond Vincy, Maurice Vandair and Francis Lopez with *La Belle de Cadix*, Yvain turned out a lushly romantic and colourful score in the same postwar opérette vein. It was a score which was a little 'better made' than that of Lopez's landmark show, without perhaps having quite the same unerringly popular ring to it, but, just as Yvain had successfully followed *Phi-Phi* with *Ta bouche*, he again took the newest fashion and made his mark on it with a show which proved not only a long-running hit in its first run but which, although it did not follow *Ta bouche* and its sisters abroad, was to have a long and continued life in the French musical theatre.

In spite of this success, Yvain found that there was less of a place for him in the postwar theatre than there had been before the hostilities and, although he was only in his mid-fifties, he had in fact made his last contribution to the Parisian stage. His underexposed talents as a writer of soigné romantic musicals were given one last showing in *Le Corsaire noir*, another colourful costume piece, produced at Marseille and played through the French provinces for a number of years, but denied a Parisian production. Yvain's handful of opérettes à grand spectacle still make regular appearances on French stages, but his principal achievement remains his shapely, rhythmical and sparkling scores to the musical comedies of the années folles, the principal of which stand alongside Christiné's best works as the enduring representatives of a particularly attractive era in musical theatre.

Yvain's film scores included music for such screen pieces as *Paris-Béguin*, *Sans famille* ('Ma Lola'), *Les Deux Gamines*, *La Belle Équipe*, *La Chanson de Paris* with Tino Rossi, Suzy Delair and Milton, *Carthacala* and *La Fausse Maîtresse* as well as a film version of *Yes* under the title *Défense d'aimer* again with Suzy Delair. *Ta bouche* and *Pas sur la bouche* were also remade for the screen.

1922 **Ta bouche** (Albert Willemetz/Yves Mirande, Gustave Quinson) Théâtre Daunou 1 April

1923 **Là-haut** (Willemetz/Mirande, Quinson) Théâtre des Bouffes-Parisiens 31 March

1923 **La Dame en décolleté** (Mirande, Lucien Boyer) Théâtre des Bouffes-Parisiens 23 December-March

1924 **Gosse de riche** (Jacques Bousquet, Henri Falk) Théâtre Daunou 2 May

1925 **Pas sur la bouche** (André Barde) Théâtre des Nouveautés 17 February

1925 **Bouche à bouche** (Barde) Théâtre de l'Apollo 8 October

1926 **Un bon garçon** (Barde) Théâtre des Nouveautés 13 November

1928 **Yes** (Willemetz/Pierre Soulaine, René Pujol) Théâtre des Capucines 26 January

1929 **Elle est à vous** (Barde) Théâtre des Nouveautés 22 January

1929 **Jean V** (Jacques Bousquet, Henri Falk) Théâtre Daunou 2 March

1929 **Kadubec** (Barde) Théâtre des Nouveautés 12 December

1930 **Pépé** (Barde) Théâtre Daunou 25 October

1931 **Encore cinquante centimes** (w Christiné/Barde) Théâtre des Nouveautés 17 September

1933 **Oh! Papa ...** (Barde) Théâtre des Nouveautés 2 February

1934 **La Belle Histoire** (Henri-Georges Clouzot) Théâtre de la Madeleine 25 April

1934 **Un, deux, trois** (René Bizet, Jean Barreyre) 1 act Moulin de la Chanson

1934 **Vacances** (Henri Duvernois, Barde) Théâtre des Nouveautés 20 December

1935 **Un coup de veine** (Willemetz, Mouëzy-Éon) Théâtre de la Porte-Saint-Martin 11 October

1935 **Au soleil du Mexique** (Mouëzy-Éon, Willemetz) Théâtre du Châtelet 18 December

1938 **Le Coffre-fort vivant** (w Joseph Szulc, as Jean Sautreuil/Henri Wernert/Georges Berr, Louis Verneuil) Théâtre du Châtelet 17 December

1944 **Le Beau Voyage d'un enfant de Paris** (as Jean Sautreuil/Wernert/Ernest Morel) Théâtre du Châtelet 15 January

1945 **Monseigneur** Théâtre Daunou

1946 **Chanson gitane** (Mouëzy-Éon, Louis Poterat) Théâtre de la Gaîté-Lyrique 13 December

1958 **Le Corsaire noir** (Jean Valmy) Marseille 24 February

Autobiography: *Ma belle opérette* (La Table Ronde, Paris, 1962)

Z

ZABELLE, Flora (b Constantinople, ?1880; d New York, 7 October 1968).

Flora Zabelle began her stage career as a soubrette in Chicago, and first came to notice playing the rôle of Poppy in New York's version of *San Toy* and as Isabel Blythe in another British musical comedy, *The Messenger Boy*. She played alongside her husband, comedian Raymond Hitchcock, in his successful *King Dodo* (1902, Annette), *The Yankee Consul* (1903, Bonita), *A Yankee Tourist* (1907, Grace Whitney) and *The Man Who Owns Broadway* (1909, Sylvia Bridwell), appeared at Weber's Music Hall (*Twiddle Twaddle*) and in revue, and paired with Hitchcock again in the title-rôle of a Broadway revival of *La Mascotte* (1909). She played the rôle of Nella in Broadway's *The Kiss Waltz* (*Liebeswalzer*) and later moved into character rôles in *Have a Heart* (1917, tour), *Toot-Toot!* (1918, Mrs James Wellington) and *The Girl from Home* (1920, Juanita Arguilla), her last rôle before retiring from the stage. After her husband's death she worked as a designer.

ZAMARA, Alfred [Marie Victor] (b Vienna, 1863; d 1940).

The musically-trained son of a musician – his father was a well-known harpist – Zamara had his first short Operette produced when he was 21 years of age, and his first full-length work two years later. *Der Doppelgänger*, first produced in Munich, was seen soon after both in Berlin (Friedrich-Wilhelmstädtisches Theater 16 March 1887) and in Vienna (Theater an der Wien 1 October 1887, 15 performances), and subsequently in many provincial German and Austrian theatres. The young composer's next work from *Doppelgänger* librettist Léon was to have been his version of *Simplicius*, but that text was instead given to Johann Strauss and Zamara turned out *Der Sänger von Palermo* to a version of *Ne touchez pas à la reine* libretticized by Buchbinder. After a fortnight's first run at the Carltheater, it was seen in Budapest and in the regions.

Zamara's subsequent works, all written with collaborators of the quality of Léon, von Waldberg, Genée or Willner, were produced in Munich and in Hamburg, but only *Die Debütantin*, a musical version of the hit comedy *Le Mari de la débutante*, was taken up for Vienna (Carltheater, 4 October 1901) where it failed in ten performances. Zamara's last work, *Die Frauenjäger*, produced at the Theater an der Wien, was another failure (14 performances), and the promise of his earliest work was never fulfilled.

Zamara worked with Julius Stern on the completion of Suppé's posthumous *Das Modell* (Carltheater 4 October 1895) and again on the arrangement of the score of *Der Goldschmied von Toledo* (w Stern, lib Karl Georg Zwerenz) from the works of Offenbach.

1883 **Die Königin von Arragon** (Victor Léon) 1 act Möling 30 August, Ronacher, Vienna, 1 May 1884

1886 **Der Doppelgänger** (Léon) Theater am Gärtnerplatz, Munich 18 September

1888 **Der Sänger von Palermo** (ad Bernhard Buchbinder) Carltheater 14 February

1889 **Der Herr Abbé** (Léon, Franz Josef Brakl) Theater am Gärtnerplatz, Munich 10 August

1890 **Der bleiche Gast** (w Josef Hellmesberger/Léon, Heinrich von Waldberg) Carl-Schultze Theater, Hamburg 6 September

1894 **Die Welfenbraut** (Richard Genée, Max Tull) Stadttheater, Hamburg 20 March

1901 **Die Debütantin** (A M Willner, Waldberg) Theater am Gärtnerplatz, Munich 17 January

1908 **Die Frauenjäger** (Waldberg, Hans Liebstöckl) Theater an der Wien 16 October

1911 **Die vertauschte Braut** (von Waldberg, Felix Ujhély) Theater am Gärtnerplatz, Munich 20 January

1919 **Der Goldschmied von Toledo** (Jacques Offenbach arr w Julius Stern/Karl Georg Zwerenz) Nationaltheater, Mannheim 7 February

ZAPPERT, Bruno (b Sechshaus bei Wien, 28 January 1845; d Vienna, 31 January 1892).

A prolific author of Possen and some Operetten for the Viennese stage of the 1870s and 1880s, Zappert had his biggest success with the Gesangsburleske *Ein Böhm in Amerika*, an oft-revived piece which ran some 250 performances in its first decade at the Theater in der Josefstadt. His two principal contributions to the Operette stage, Czibulka's *Der Glücksritter* and Suppé's *Die Jagd nach dem Glück* both went on to overseas productions, being seen in America as *The May Queen* and *Clover* respectively.

1878 **Eine Hochgeborene** (Henrik Delin) Theater in der Josefstadt 19 January

1878 **Ninicherl** (Ludwig Gothov-Gruneke) 1 act Theater in der Josefstadt 7 November

1879 **Eine Gumpoldskirchnerin** (*Les Noces de Bouchencoeur*) Theater in der Josefstadt 1 March

1879 **Die Glöckerln von Kornfeld** (Gothov-Grünecke) 1 act Komische Oper 10 October

1880 **Eine Parforcejagd durch Europa** (Julius Hopp) Theater in der Josefstadt 14 February

1881 **Ein Böhm in Amerika** (Gothov-Grüneke) Theater in der Josefstadt 29 January

1881 **Unser Schatzerl** (Josef Reiter/Leon Treptow ad) Theater in der Josefstadt 17 December

1882 **Moderne Weiber** (Gothov-Grüneke) Theater in der Josefstadt 8 February

1884 **Der Herr Dr Schimmel** (Louis Roth) Theater in der Josefstadt 29 March

1885 **Johann Nestroy** (pasticcio) Graz 17 January

1885 **Sein Spetzl** (Franz Roth/Julius Findeisen ad) Carltheater 21 February

1885 **Der Walzerkönig** (Johann Brandl/Wilhelm Mannstädt, Karl Costa) Carltheater 9 October (additional lyrics)

1886 **Die Susi ihr G'spusi** (F Roth/w Bruno Hartl-Mitius) Carltheater 7 May

1886 **Ein gemachter Mann** (L Roth/w Jacobson) Theater in der Josefstadt 8 May

1886 **Das fünfte Rad** (L Roth/Treptow, Louis Herrmann ad) Carltheater 15 October

1887 **Der Glücksritter** (Alfons Czibulka/w Richard Genée, Mannstädt) Carltheater 22 December

1888 **Der Freibuter** (*Surcouf*) German version w Genée (Carltheater)

1888 **Die Jagd nach dem Glück** (Franz von Suppé/w Genée) Carltheater 27 October

1888 **Ein Deutschmeister** (Carl Michael Ziehrer/w Richard Genée) Carltheater 30 November

1891 **Im Fluge um die Welt** (Adolf Gisser) Fürsttheater

1892 **Die Tugendwachter** (Aurel Schwimmer) Ödenburg

DER ZAREWITSCH Operette in 3 acts by Béla Jenbach and Heinz Reichert based on the play *A csárevics* by Gabryela Zapolska. Music by Franz Lehár. Deutsches Künstlertheater, Berlin, 21 February 1927.

Perhaps the most thoroughly gloomy of the line of more or less gloomily romantic tales which were elaborated to make libretti for Franz Lehár in the later part of his writing career, *Der Zarewitsch*, whilst purporting to be based on a real incident in the life of the Russian Tsarevitch Alexis, followed the already clichéd formula of Lehár's librettists through its blighted love affair between tenor (extremely large rôle) and soprano (less large rôle) up to the fashionable unhappy ending.

Aljoscha, an apparently homosexual tsarevitch (Richard Tauber), will have nothing to do with women until, with his marriage and the dynasty needing to be secured, his uncle is forced into a plot to change his tastes. A dancer called Sonja (Rita Georg) is set up as bait. Disguised as a young male athlete, she attracts his attention, surmounts his horror at learning her real sex and wins from him first friendship and then love. However, when it is time for Aljoscha to assume the crown, she has to be renounced in favour of an unknown royal bride. Such lighter moments as the piece held were provided by the tsarevitch's servant, Iwan (Paul Heidemann), and his wife Mascha (Charlotte Ander). At first kept away from her flirtatious husband by the tsarevitch's anti-woman rules, she later becomes the despair of his life when she learns to flirt herself.

The score to *Der Zarewitsch*, tinted with a little balalaika music, was made to the measure of its tenor star. Apart from two or three light-hearted intrusions by the soubret pair ('Schaukle, Liebchen, schaukle', the one-step 'Heute Abend komm' ich zu dir', 'Ich bin bereit zu jeder Zeit'/ 'Täglich frische, heisse Liebe'), and an optional piece for the Grand Duke, it was devoted almost wholly to the tenor (a great deal) and soprano (quite a lot). Aljoscha waxed lonely in the Wolgalied ('Allein! Wieder allein!'), fell in love ('Herz, warum schlägst du so bang') and fell in love more thoroughly ('Willst du?', 'Ich bin verliebt!'), but still felt depressed at the thought that it was too good to go on (Napolitana: 'Warum hat der Frühling, ach, nur einen Mai?'). He also joined in a series of duets and sung scenes with the soprano, moving into tango time in the first-act finale as he sang in praise of champagne, but into more standard rhythms for the big duets, the waltzing 'Hab' nur dich allein' and 'Liebe mich, küsse mich'. It was to Sonja,

Plate 301. **Der Zarewitsch**: *The heir to the czardom (Andrea Poddigre) is about to find out that his companion (Eva-Maria Kaufmann) is a girl and not a boy (Bielefeld, 1986).*

however, that the most successful single number fell with a wondering solo 'Einer wird kommen' in the first act – before her part in the tale became more intense.

Der Zarewitsch was first produced in Berlin, and it was over a year before Vienna mounted its version at the Johann Strauss-Theater with Hans Heinz Bollmann and Emmi Kosáry starred, and with a Russian dance duo speciality, the Original Don-Kosakentruppe, and a Tcherkessentanz billed as large as they. Tauber took over from Bollmann for two weeks, and Sergei Abranowicz then saw the piece through to its 146th performance. A Hungarian-American pop-music piece called *Spektakel* took over and flopped violently, so three weeks later the theatre brought *Der Zarewitsch* back. It went through three more tenors before the 221st performance ended its run. In the meantime, Budapest had seen János Halmos and Hilda Harmath introduce the piece at the Városi Színház (ad Ernő Kulinyi).

The following year *Le Tzarévitch* (ad Robert de Mackiels, Bertal-Maubon) was mounted in France. The Lyon production, which alternated a high baritone and a tenor in the lead rôle, inspired several other provincial productions, but Paris was not tempted to take it up until 1935 when Maurice Lehmann mounted a version at the Théâtre de la Porte-Saint-Martin. Roger Bourdin continued the French tradition of playing Lehár tenor rôles with a baritone, alongside Fanély Revoil as Sonja. It survived less than a month.

If the French version was unfortunate, an English one simply did not take place. In spite of the appeal of the leading rôle to operatic tenors, *Der Zarewitsch* played neither Broadway nor London. That same tenor-appeal has, however, led to the piece being thoroughly represented on record, and it has also been the subject of three film versions. The first, in 1929, was actually a silent version of Zapolska's tale, the second, with Hans Söhnker and Marta Eggerth starred, was produced by Victor Janson in 1933, and a third, with a rather uncomfortably cast Luis Mariano opposite Sonja Ziemann, was made by Arthur Maria Rabenalt as late as 1954.

A version of *Der Zarewitsch* was mounted at the Volksoper in 1978 (11 December) with Adolf Dallapozza and Bettina Schoeller featured and the piece continues to find its way onto German-language stages when a star tenor is in need of a vehicle.

Austria: Johann Strauss-Theater 18 May 1928; Hungary: Városi Színház *A cárevics* 25 May 1928; France: Théâtre des Célestins, Lyon *Le Tsarévitch* 16 April 1929, Théâtre de la Porte-Saint-Martin *Rêve d'un soir* 30 January 1935; Films: 1929 (silent), 1933, 1954

Recordings: complete (EMI), complete variant version (Eurodisc), selections (Telefunken, London, Decca, Philips, Amadeo, Polydor etc)

ZAYTZ, Giovanni von [ZAJC, Iván] (b Fiume, 3 August 1831; d Zagreb, 16 December 1914). One of the most successful of the earliest contributors to the Viennese Operette stage.

The son of a military bandmaster, Iván Zajc was musically taught by his father and began composing at a young age, turning out an operatic *Maria Theresia* at the age of 12. He was sent to Milan to study, metamorphosed there from Zajc into Giovanni von Zaytz, and had his first full opera, *La Tirolese*, produced on stage there in 1855 (4 May). He continued to work in the operatic field and another opera, *Amelia*, was produced in Fiume in 1860, but he also ventured into the lighter musical theatre and after moving to Vienna to work as a theatre conductor in 1862 provided two of the most popular of the earliest Viennese Operetten to the Carltheater stage.

Mannschaft an Bord was a little nautical piece in which the composer made effective use of English sea shanties, even though it had a French setting. It held its own amongst the flood of newly popular Offenbach opérettes and other French works and it was maintained in the repertoire in Vienna for more than a decade as a forepiece and an item in spectacles coupés. It was also liberally played on Hungarian stages (*Matrozok a fedelzeten*). *Der Meisterschuss von Pottenstein* was scarcely less popular, holding a place in the Carltheater and Theater an der Wien repertoires for many years, whilst the little Zauberposse *Fitzliputzli* was also reprised at the Carltheater up to five years after its initial production. Amongst this series of short pieces, Zaytz also composed a three-act romantic opéra-bouffe, *Die Hexe von Boissy*, played both in Vienna and Budapest (*A Boissy Boszorkány* ad Endre Latabár, Budai Népszinház, 1 February 1868) without achieving quite the popularity of the best of his smaller works.

In 1870 he left Vienna and moved to Zagreb, as conductor at the local theatre, and returned to mainly operatic composition. His opera *Nikola Šubíc Zrinjki* (lib: Hugo Badaić, Zagreb, 4 November 1876), said to be the first written in the Croatian language, won a number of productions in Yugoslavia. In 1889 he became director of the Zagreb Conservatoire, a post he retained until 1908.

Alongside his operettic and operatic work, Zaytz composed incidental music to more than twenty plays, plus a large amount of vocal, instrumental and, particularly, choral music.

1861 **I funerali del karnevale** (Ivan Prodan) Teatro Civico, Fiume
1863 **Mannschaft an Bord** (J L Harisch) 1 act Carltheater 15 December
1864 **Fitzliputzli, oder die Teufelchen der Ehe** ('from the French') 1 act Carltheater 5 November

1865 **Die Lazzaroni von Neapel** (Hans Max) 1 act Carltheater 4 May
1866 **Die Hexe von Boissy** (Karl Costa) Carltheater 24 April
1866 **Nachtschwärmer** (Erik Nessl) 1 act Carltheater 10 November
1867 **Ein Rendezvous in der Schweiz** (Gustav Neuhaus) 1 act Carltheater 3 April
1867 **Das Gaugericht** (Carl Julius Folnes) 1 act Carltheater 14 September
1868 **Nach Mekka** (Nessl) 1 act Harmonietheater 11 January
1868 **Sonnambule** (Nessl) 1 act Harmonietheater 25 January
1868 **Der Meisterschuss von Pottenstein** (Anton Langer) 1 act Carltheater 25 July
1869 **Meister Puff** (Nessl) 1 act Theater an der Wien 22 May
1870 **Der Raub der Sabinerinnen** (Betty Young) Friedrich-Wilhelmstädtisches Theater, Berlin 6 August
1874 **Der gefangene Amor** (Wieland ad) 1 act Vaudeville Theater 12 September
1888 **Afrodita** (Nicola Milan) National Theatre, Zagreb 8 January
1906 **Die Nihilsten** (Wilhelm Otto) National Theatre, Zagreb 15 December

Biography: Pettan, H: *Popis Skladbi Ivana Zajca* (Jugoslavenska Akademija Znanosti i Umjetnosti, Zagreb, 1956)

ZEHN MÄDCHEN UND KEIN MANN Komische Operette in 1 act by 'W Friedrich' [ie Wilhelm Friedrich Riese] based on the libretto *Six demoiselles à marier* by Adolphe Jaime and Adolphe Choler. Music by Franz von Suppé. Theater am Franz-Josefs-Kai, Vienna, 25 October 1862.

Previously set in its original French by Delibes, *Six demoiselles à marier*, first produced in Paris in 1856, had been played at Theater an der Wien (*Sechs Mädchen zu heiraten* ad J F Niemetz) in 1860 (13 October). The libretto was remade by Riese, and set by Suppé for production at Karl Treumann's Theater am Franz-Josefs-Kai where it proved a thorough confirmation of his first little work in the same Viennese-French vein, *Das Pensionat*.

Herr von Schönhahn (Treumann) had a son by his first wife. But she went off and left him, and his two subsequent wives provided him with nothing but daughters. Ten of them. Getting this gaggle married off is a problem, and the over-proud father has put up a sign outside the door inviting visitors. If an unmarried man comes in, he is given a tour of the daughters. When the young veterinarian Agamemnon Paris (F Markwordt) ventures in, following a pretty girl, he is given the full display, rehearsed to a tee. Papa has it worked out neatly, and in order to appeal to all probable tastes each daughter displays her accomplishments in a different national style – Austrian, Castilian, English, Bavarian, Portuguese, Tyrolean, Italian, Mexican, Bohemian and Aragonese. However, the girl Paris is after is none of them but the housekeeper, Sidonia (Anna Grobecker), and since it turns out that he is the long-lost son of Schönhahn's first marriage, the old fellow ends up with ten daughters … and a daughter-in-law.

Suppé had great fun with the score for the little piece, of which the clou was the series of national numbers sung by the daughters, beginning with a Tirolienne for Almina and Maschinka, highlighted by a burlesque Italian aria for Limonia (Anna Marek) which gambolled up to a D in alt, then an 'Englische Ariette' for Britta, a dance quartet for four of the less vocal daughters, and (as alternatives and additions, depending on the daughters available) a Holz-

und-Stroh Polka, a Trinklied, an Italienisches Volkslied for soprano and alto, a Böhmische Volkslied for two of each, and a Guilleaume Walzer with florid cadenzas. The whole ended up in a massed family concert. Paris did his singing before the concert started, being equipped with a lively entrance song ('Der Frühling ist kommen') and a duo with Schönhahn in which he performed a lot of laughing on repeated high Bs. Sidonia, too, did her singing in the first part of the night, with a Stiefel-Putzer Lied and a Complimentier-Lied, and the father introduced his daughters and saw the action along in song as well as word.

Zehn Mädchen was a great success. It was played 32 times over the seven months' remaining life of the Kai-Theater, and Treumann took it with him when he removed to the Carltheater where Karl Blasel and Josef Matras both succeeded to the rôle of the father, Hermine Meyerhoff was Limonia but Anna Grobecker retained her part of Sidonia (17 June 1870). The piece later reappeared both there (20 September 1879, 19 December 1873 as *25 Mädchen und kein Mann*) and in other Viennese houses.

One of the earliest Viennese piece to travel to any extent, *Zehn Mädchen* was quickly played throughout Austria and Germany, and also in Hungary where Endre Latabár's vernacular version included the son in the title 'ten girls and one man' – instead of no man. Both London and New York first saw the piece in its original German, London as performed by a visiting German troupe and New York from Theodore L'Arronge who played it during his 1867–8 season at the local German-speaking theatre with Auguste Steglich-Fuchs as Sidonia and Rosa Zerboni as Limonia, and again the following year with his wife, Hedwig L'Arronge as his daughter, Limonia. The Terrace-Garten also played the piece which became a familiar part of New York German spectacles coupés.

An English-language version was played at London's Theatre Royal, Drury Lane (ad Arthur Matthison) in 1874, and another appeared in the New York repertoire of the Kelly and Leon Minstrels in which Leon featured as Sidonia but altered things so that he also performed the Italian aria and a dance routine. This version was the first to be seen in Australia when Kelly and Leon introduced it there in their repertoire in 1880.

The number of daughters in poor (overworked?) Herr von Schönhahn's family varied from production to production, depending on the number available, or the number wishing to interpolate a national song. The Italians avoided the issue and entitled the piece with a slightly different emphasis as *Le Amazzoni* (ad A Scalvini), whilst a certain A von Bayer and Karl Kleiber produced a contemporary comic-opera-parody in which there were *Zehn Männer und keine Frau*.

Germany: Friedrich-Wilhelmstädtisches Theater 3 May 1863, Nationaltheater *Vierzehn Mädchen und kein Mann* 12 July 1881; Hungary: Budai Népszinház *Tiz lány, egy férj sem* 20 June 1863, Budai Szinkör (Ger) 5 July 1863; UK: Opera Comique (Ger) 7 November 1871, Theatre Royal, Drury Lane *Ten of 'Em* 2 December 1874; USA: Stadttheater (Ger) 24 April 1867; Australia: Opera House, Sydney *Six Brides and No Bridegroom* 25 September 1880

ZELL, F[riedrich] [WALZEL, Camillo] (b Magdeburg, 11 February 1829; d Vienna, 17 March 1895). The most important librettist of the 19th-century Viennese stage.

Born in Magdeburg whilst his mother, the singer Fortunata Franchetti-Walzel, was engaged at the local theatre, Walzel was educated in Leipzig and in Pest and, as a young man, joined the Austrian army, where he rose to the rank of lieutenant. When he resigned his commission he joined the Danube Steamship Company, became a Captain, and in that capacity he served in the war of 1866. In the off-sailing season he found plenty of time to indulge his literary and journalistic predilections and in the early 1860s he began to work intermittently in the theatre, adapting French playlets and opérettes for Karl Treumann at the Theater am Franz-Josefs-Kai and at the Carltheater. As often happened in those days, however, his name did not appear on the playbills and it seems not to have been until 1863 that his first credited musical works, a pasticcio burlesque, a 1-performance Genrebild 'from the French' and, an adaptation of Offenbach's *Une demoiselle en loterie*, were played at the Theater an der Wien.

Sent to Paris to spy out adaptable material for the Viennese theatre, Walzel became friendly there with a number of prominent theatrical personalities, notably Offenbach, and, as a result, he became thoroughly orientated towards a theatrical rather than a nautical career, and one in which his texts, much like those of H B Farnie in Britain, were very often based – admittedly or not – on 'borrowed' French originals. He had his first significant success, however, with a piece on which there was no source doubt – collaborating with Julius Hopp on the Viennese version of *La Belle Hélène* for the Theater an der Wien. He subsequently wrote a sequel to Meilhac and Halévy's piece, dealing with the events of the Siege of Troy.

Walzel wrote several burlesques and satires (*Elegante Tini*, the parody of Patti entitled *Aböllina, oder ein Schwager für alles*, *Sarah und Bernhardt*) and some straight comedies, and dipped again into the area of opérette with a translation of Lecocq's *Fleur de thé* for the Vienna stage, before he came together with the Theater an der Wien's resident adapter and conductor, Richard Genée, to form a working partnership which would produce both men's most memorable work over a period of some 20 years.

The pair collaborated on both the adaptation of many of the principal imports of the period and also on the texts for many of the most important Viennese Operetten of the 1870s and 1880s a number of which were, again, adaptations of French libretti: Suppé's *Fatinitza*, *Boccaccio* and *Donna Juanita*, Millöcker's *Apajune, der Wassermann*, *Der Bettelstudent* and *Gasparone*, and Strauss's *Der lustige Krieg*, *Eine Nacht in Venedig*, *Cagliostro in Wien*, *Carneval in Rom* and *Das Spitzentuch der Königin*. Walzel also supplied the libretti for Genée's own musical compositions, notably his two international Operette successes *Der Seekadett* and *Nanon*, both of which were, once more, versions of established French texts.

Thoroughly established in his 'alternative' career, he eventually resigned from the Steamship Company in 1883, and devoted himself wholly to his theatrical occupations, often carrying on his collaboration with Genée, who in later days moved away from Vienna to live at Pressbaum, by post, either from Vienna or from his estate at Weissenbach. The division of their labour left much of the plot and dialogue to Walzel and the bulk of the lyric-writing to Genée, but such a division was by no means automatic.

Both (but Genée in particular) also worked alone or with other partners, and Walzel was responsible, alone, for the adaptation of several French vaudevilles as musical comedies for the Vienna stage, as well as for the straight adaptation of pieces such as the successful comedy *Décoré* (1889).

In 1884 Walzel became part of a syndicate under Alexandrine von Schönerer put together to run the Theater an der Wien, and between 1884 and 1889 he was the effective manager of the house. His management was initiated with the successful Vienna production of Strauss's *Eine Nacht in Venedig* and during the next five years his most important productions included Planquette's *Rip van Winkle*, *Gasparone*, *Der Feldprediger*, *Der Zigeunerbaron*, *Der Hofnarr*, *Die Wienerstadt in Wort und Bild*, *Die sieben Schwaben*, *Simplicius* and *Der Mikado*.

Following his withdrawal from the management and the managerial syndicate, Walzel continued to write for the theatre, but the last years of his life did not bring any hits comparable to those of the earlier part of his career.

1863 **Abällina, oder Ein Schwager für Alles** (pasticcio) Theater an der wien 16 May

1863 **Die Schwaben in Wien** (Adolf Müller/J Méry ad) Theater an der Wien 12 August

1864 **Die Kunstreiterin** (*Une demoiselle en loterie*) German version (Theater an der Wien)

1864 **Des Nachbars Äpfel** (*Les Pommes du voisin*) German version w O F Berg and music by Adolf Müller (Theater an der Wien)

1865 **Die schöne Helena** (*La Belle Hélène*) German version w Julius Hopp (Theater an der Wien)

1867 **Die Federschlange** (Carlo di Barbieri) 1 act Deutsches Theater, Budapest 16 February

1869 **Theeblüthe** (*Fleur de thé*) German version (Theater an der Wien)

1873 **Der Carneval in Rom** (Johann Strauss/w Josef Braun, Richard Genée) Theater an der Wien 1 March

1873 **Die Wilderer** (*Les Braconniers*) German version w Genée (Theater an der Wien)

1874 **Die Japanesin** (Émile Jonas/Eugène Grangé, Victor Bernard) German version w Genée (Theater an der Wien)

1874 **Angot und der blauen Donau** (Karl Pleininger) Strampfertheater 13 November

1875 **Cagliostro in Wien** (Strauss/w Genée) Theater an der Wien 27 February

1876 **Fatinitza** (Franz von Suppé/w Genée) Carltheater 5 January

1876 **Nach dem Mond und unterm Meer** (Suppé/Verne ad Adolphe L'Arronge ad) Carltheater March

1876 **Der Seekadet** (Genée) Theater an der Wien 24 October

1877 **Im Wunderland der Pyramiden** (Genée/w Genée) Komische Oper (Ringtheater) 25 December

1877 **Die Porträt-Dame** (*Die Profezeiungen des Quiribi*) (Max Wolf/w Genée) Theater an der Wien 5 March

1877 **Nanon (die Wirtin von goldenen Lamm)** (Genée/w Genée) Theater an der Wien 10 March

1878 **Die letzten Mohikaner** (Genée) Theater am Gärtnerplatz, Munich; Theater an der Wien 4 January 1879

1878 **Vom Touristen Kränzchen** (Franz Roth) 1 act Stadttheater 28 November

1878 **Niniche** German version w new music by Brandl (Carltheater)

1879 **Boccaccio** (Suppé/w Genée) Carltheater 1 February

1879 **Die Fornarina** (Karl Zeller/w Genée) Theater am Gärtnerplatz, Munich 18 October

1879 **Gräfin Dubarry** (Carl Millöcker/w Genée) Theater an der Wien 31 October

1879 **Der grosse Casimir** (*Le Grand Casimir*) German version (Carltheater)

1880 **Papas Frau** (*La Femme à papa*) German version w new music by Brandl (Carltheater)

1880 **Die hübsche Perserin** (*La Jolie Persane*) German version w Genée (Theater an der Wien)

1880 **Donna Juanita** (Suppé/w Genée) Carltheater 21 February

1880 **Die Carbonari** (Karl Zeller/w Moritz West) Carltheater 27 November

1880 **Nisida** (Genée/w Moritz West) Carltheater 9 October

1880 **Apajune der Wassermann** (Millöcker/w Genée) Theater an der Wien 18 December

1881 **Der Gascogner** (Suppé/w Genée) Carltheater 22 March

1881 **Jean de Nivelle** German version (Hofopern-Theater)

1881 **Der lustige Krieg** (Strauss/w Genée) Theater an der Wien 25 November

1881 **Die Jungfrau von Belleville** (Millöcker/w Genée) Theater an der Wien 29 October

1882 **Lili** German version (Theater an der Wien)

1882 **Der Bettelstudent** (Millöcker/w Genée) Theater an der Wien 6 December

1883 **Königin Mariette** (Ignaz Brüll/w Genée) Munich 16 June

1883 **Eine Nacht in Venedig** (Strauss/w Genée) Friedrich-Wilhelmstädtisches Theater, Berlin, 3 October

1884 **Gasparone** (Millöcker/w Genée) Theater an der Wien 26 January

1885 **Die Zwillinge** (Genée, Louis Roth/w Genée) Theater an der Wien 14 February

1885 **Die Kindsfrau** (Julius Stern arr/Hennequin ad) Theater an der Wien 7 May

1885 **Der Jagdjunker der Kaiserin** (Alfons Czibulka/w Genée) Walhalla Theater, Berlin 3 December; revised version Carltheater 20 March 1886

1886 **Die Novize** (Wilhelm Rab) Theater an der Wien 21 January

1886 **Der Nachtwandler** (Roth/w Genée) Friedrich-Wilhelmstädtisches Theater, Berlin, 25 September

1886 **Der Vice-Admiral** (Millöcker/w Genée) Theater an der Wien 9 October

1886 **Die Piraten** (Genée/w Genée) Walhalla-Theater, Berlin 9 October

1887 **Die Wienerstadt in Wort und Bild** (Adolf Müller jr, Julius Stern et al/w Isidor Fuchs, Julius Bauer) Theater an der Wien 10 April

1887 **Die Dreizehn** (Genée/w Genée) Carltheater 14 November

1888 **Die Hochzeit des Reservisten** (Julius Stern/w Hoffmann, Isidor Fuchs) Theater an der Wien 28 January

1888 **Der Mikado** German version w Genée (Theater an der Wien)

1888 **Wolf und Lampel** (*Cocard et Bicoquet*) (Stern/w Hoffmann) Theater an der Wien 13 October

1888 **Gil Blas von Santillana** (Czibulka/w West) Carl-Schultze Theater, Hamburg 23 November

1889 **Die indische Witwe** (Gustav Geiringer/w Genée) Hoftheater 9 February

1889 **Der schöne Kaspar** (Josef Bayer) Theater am Gärtnerplatz, Munich 6 April

1889 **Capitän Fracassa** (Rudolf Dellinger/w Genée) Hamburg, Theater an der Wien 21 September

1889 **Der Königsgardist** (*The Yeomen of the Guard*) German version w Genée (Krolls Theater, Berlin)

1889 **Die Piraten** (*The Pirates of Penzance*) German version (Theater an der Wien)

1890 **Die Gondoliere** (*The Gondoliers*) w Genée (Theater an der Wien)

1890 **Erminy** (*Erminie*) German version w Victor Léon (Carltheater)

1892 **Wiener Ausstellungs-G'schichten, oder Das Rendezvous der Strohwitwer** (Fritz Lehner) Theater in der Josefstadt 14 October

1892 **Der Millionen-Onkel** (Adolf Muller jr/w Genée) Theater and der Wien 5 November

1893 **Das Mädchen von Mirano** (*La Stupida*) 1 act (Alexander Neumann/w Genée) Carltheater 6 April

1893 **Der Schwiegerpapa** (Alfred Strasser, Max von Wienzierl/w Wilhelm Ascher) Brünn 22 April; Adolf Ernst-Theater, Berlin 10 June

1894 **Fürst Malachoff** (Stern/fr Fr) Carltheater 22 September

1894 **Sein erster Walzer** (Johann Strauss arr) Carltheater 15 October

1894 **Die Königin von Gamara** (Neumann/w Genée) Carltheater 27 October

1894 **Tata-Toto** (*Toto*) German version w Léon (Theater in der Josefstadt)

ZELLER, Carl [Johann Adam] (b St Peter-in-der-Au, 19 June 1842; d Baden-bei-Wien, 17 August 1898). The composer of some of the happiest music of the Golden Age Vienna stage, and of one of its most enduring Operetten.

Carl Zeller led, throughout his working life, separate careers as a civil servant and as a musician. Having been, from the age of 11, a chorister in the Vienna Boys' Choir, he led parallel studies in law and in music and, on his graduation, took up a post in the civic administration. In 1873 he was made an artistic consultant under the umbrella of the department of Education.

Although he had already turned his hand to composition, notably of choral and instrumental music, in earlier years, it was not until 1876 that he turned out his first work for the stage, the 'comic opera' *Joconde* produced by Maximilian Steiner at the Theater an der Wien 'in collaboration with members of the Gesang-Verein'. A Scottish Roundheads-and-Cavaliers piece, with Carl Adolf Friese featured as the 1650s Lord Dunstan Meredith of Killarnock Castle, Bertha Steinher in the title-rôle as the Cromwellian Governor of the area, and young Alexander Girardi in the rôle of Bob Calladwader (sic), the Laird's steward, *Joconde* was played 20 times.

For his second work, Zeller collaborated with the Theater an der Wien's accredited text-writers, Zell and Genée, but the resultant work, *Die Fornarina*, did not make it back to Vienna from its Munich presentation. A much more widespread future, however, was reserved for *Die Carbonari*. Produced at Vienna's Carltheater, it was remounted the following year in a revised version at Berlin's Friedrich-Wilhelmstädtisches Theater under the title *Capitän Nicol*, and that version found its way to other German houses and as far afield as America where it was given by Marie Geistinger's company with Adolf Link, Emma Seebold and Ernst Schütz at the Thalia-Theater. The show lasted well enough that it was reproduced in 1891 at New York's Amberg Theater, rather confusingly in its original *Die Carbonari* form.

The real breakthrough for Zeller the composer came in 1886, a decade after the first promises of *Joconde*, when the Carltheater produced the first of his collaborations with the new pairing of his faithful Moritz West and Ludwig Held, the successful author of *Die Näherin*. *Der Vagabund*'s 37 performances at the Carltheater may have looked statistically light, but they were the beginning of a series of productions throughout the world for the Operette, and the foundation of a team which five years later turned out the piece which was the triumph of its times and would become one of the most endearing classics of the 19th-century Viennese repertoire, *Der Vogelhändler* ('Ich bin die Christel von der Post', 'Fröhlich Pfalz', 'Schenkt man sich Rosen in Tirol' etc). With Alexander Girardi, now the darling of the Viennese theatre public, introducing the starring rôle of the little bird-seller, the show and its glorious music were launched on a career which has kept it to the front of the repertoire to this day.

Zeller, West and Held followed *Der Vogelhändler* with *Der Obersteiger* which, if it attempted rather openly to reproduce all the winning elements of the previous show, nevertheless turned out to be another delightful and successful musical-comical evening and, with its Girardi-waltz, the delicious 'Sei nicht bös', it produced the song which would become Zeller's most internationally known number.

At the height of his fame as a musician, Zeller met his downfall in his public position. Convicted of perjury in a damages case, he was sentenced to 12 months' prison. Forced to resign from his civil service post, he died soon after, at the age of 56. There was, however, one more Zeller musical produced on the Viennese stage. The uncompleted *Der Kellermeister*, put together from music left by the composer by Johann Brandl, was mounted in 1901 under the management of Ernst Gettke at the Raimundtheater. Girardi appeared as the hotelier, Urban, alongside Toni Braun and Oskar Braun, and the composer won another, posthumous, song hit with the star's 'Lass dir Zeit'.

His son, Karl Zeller jr, also composed for the musical stage (*Das Haremsmädel* etc).

1876 **Joconde** (West, Moret) Theater an der Wien 18 March

1879 **Die Fornarina** (Richard Genée, F Zell) Theater am Gärtnerplatz, Munich 18 October

1880 **Die Carbonari** (Moritz West, Zell) Carltheater 27 November

1881 **Capitän Nicol** revised *Die Carbonari* by West and Hermann Hirschel, Friedrich-Wilhelmstädtisches Theater, Berlin, 5 November

1886 **Der Vagabund** (West, Ludwig Held) Carltheater 30 October

1891 **Der Vogelhändler** (West, Held) Theater an der Wien 10 January

1894 **Der Obersteiger** (West, Held) Theater an der Wien 6 January

1901 **Der Kellermeister** (arr Johann Brandl/West) Raimundtheater 21 December

Biography: Zeller, K W: *Mein Vater Karl Zeller* (St Poltner Zeitungs-Verlag, St Pölten, 1942)

ZERKOVITZ, Béla (b Szeged, 11 July 1882; d Budapest, 23 October 1948). Popular songwriter who turned out scores to a large number of musical plays and scored a full ration of hometown hits.

Béla Zerkovitz studied music in his youth, but he paired those studies with more practical ones and qualified as an architectural engineer. Whilst continuing a career in his 'proper job', he made his first ventures as a songwriter and his songs were regularly interpolated into Hungarian musical shows of the early years of the 20th century. His first full score for the musical stage seems to have been that to Adolf Mérei's 1911 *A kék róka*, whilst in 1913 he successfully supplied the full scores to two operetts, *Aranyeso* and *Katonadolog* (a soldier's tale), written to texts by Izor Béldi, the librettist of Budapest's first 100-performance Operette *Katalin* a decade earlier.

Over the following years, Zerkovitz became hugely popular as a songwriter – the most famous of his many hits being the gently rhythmic 1914 song 'Hulló falevél' for which he wrote both music and lyric – and he won himself the reputation of being the 'national songsmith of Pest'. He ranged from opera to revue in his stage writings, from strongly lyrical music to many pieces which sounded like British music-hall numbers with an intermittent national flavouring, as he turned out a regular supply of songs in particular as house composer for the variegated productions at the Royal Orfeum. However, he won his chief success with the scores for a line of musical comedies produced both in Hungary and Austria after he had finally retired from his architectural work in 1919 and devoted himself wholly to music.

The highly successful *A csókos asszony*, a reset version of the French libretto to *Clary-Clara* (originally composed in its French version by Victor Roger) and *Aranymadár* (the golden bird) ('Párizsban huncut a lány') which totalled some 300 Budapest performances, set the scene for their composer to provide the scores for a series of popular musical plays, written with such top local writers as László Bús-Fekete, László Szilágyi and Imre Harmath, a series which gave Zerkovitz a regular run of stage success right through the late 1920s.

With Bús-Fekete he wrote *Árvácska* (pansy), which, with Ilona Vaály in the title-rôle, ran for over 100 consecutive nights on its production at the Budai Szinkör and produced a hit with the java 'Egyszer volt, hol nem volt ...', and *A nóta vége* (the end of the song), a musical adaptation of the playwright's internationally successful 1921 play *Buzavirág* (cornflower), set to a score featuring the foxtrots ('Kaderabek!') and tangos ('Tango d'amour') which were as de rigeur in Budapest as in the rest of the world. *A nóta vége*, similarly, had a fine run at the Budai Színkör before going on to pile up some 300 performances in the repertoire of the Városi Színház.

Harmath's *Postás Katica* was another success, and a set of four pieces with the young librettist Szilágyi in the late 1920s maintained the composer's career at its peak through its later stages with a fresh lot of fine runs and hit songs: a new version of *A csókos asszony*, with Hanna Honthy and Gyula Kompóthy starred, *Muzsikus Ferkó* (Ferko, the musician), mounted with Ferenc Kiss in the title-rôle alongside Irén Biller, Hanna Honthy and Gyula Kabos for more than 50 performances at the Budai Színkör, *A legkisebbik Horváth lány* (the littlest Horvath girl) and the happy *Eltörött a hegedüm* (the violin is broken), which mixed modern, jazzy dance numbers with traditional Hungarian melodies as illustration to a tale in which Juci Lábass played a country girl who turns vamp to win back a husband tempted by city lights and Oszkár Dénes and Rózsi Bársony tripped through the lighter numbers to triumph.

The 1930 *Meluzsina*, a circus musical which had the prima donna performing a rope-dance, was the last of his major works, although a 1936 piece *Hulló falevél*, mounted at the Városi Színház, had Hanna Honthy leading the company in its composer's most famous song as a finale. After his death, a score was arranged from his works as a musical accompaniment to Molnár's play *Doktor úr*. First staged in 1957 (Kis Színpad 8 February), it was revived in Budapest in 1990.

Alongside his composing career, Zerkovitz latterly led a second as a theatre manager. In the mid 1920s he became director of the Városi Színház, which in the pre-1917 era, when it was known as the Népopera, had housed his first hits, and in the early 1930s he took over at the head of the Royal Orfeum (1930), the other house which had supplied him with his early work.

1911 **A kék róka** (Adolf Mérei) Royal Orfeum 29 September
1912 **Die schöne Marietta** (Lantsch) 1 act Wiener Kolosseum 1 December
1913 **Finom familia** (*Eine feine Familie*) 1 act Royal Orfeum 31 January
1913 **Aranyeső** (Mérei/Izor Béldi) Népopera 21 February
1913 **Katonadolog** (Mérei/Béldi) Népopera 25 October
1914 **Die Wundermühle** (Bernhard Buchbinder) Theater in der Josefstadt, Vienna 24 March
1915 **Vándorfecskék** (Mérei) Télikert 1 March; Royal Orfeum, Budapest 2 October
1915 **Das Finanzgenie** (Felix Dörmann, Hans Kottow) Apollo-theater, Vienna 29 October
1917 **A szegény Golem** (Endre Nagy) Royal Orfeum 2 January
1917 **A mondur fiatalít** (Nagy) Royal Orfeum February
1917 **A porcellán-őrült** (Nagy) Royal Orfeum 31 March
1917 **A Balaton Romeoja** (Béla Szenes) Royal Orfeum ? August
1917 **Háron Határ Hotel** (Nagy) Royal Orfeum 1 October
1917 **Az utolsó Dankó-nóta** (Nagy) Royal Orfeum 1 November
1918 **Pambu** (Nagy) Royal Orfeum 1 January
1918 **A zsámbéki földesúr** (Nagy) Royal Orfeum 1 March
1918 **Pitypalaty kisasszony** (Jenő Faragó) Royal Orfeum 1 June
1918 **Páratlan menyeckse** (Jenő Faragó) Royal Orfeum 1 October
1918 **Aranykalitka** (Imre Harmath) Royal Orfeum 1 December
1919 **Százszorszép** (Faragó) Városi Színház 28 November
1919 **Beppo** (Harmath) 1 act Royal Orfeum 1 February
1919 **Kalandor kisasszony** (Harmath) Royal Orfeum 2 November
1920 **Csillagok csillaga** (Harmath) Royal Orfeum 1 January
1920 **Zsuzsu** (Harmath) Royal Orfeum 1 April
1920 **Lucia** (Harmath) Royal Orfeum 1 September
1920 **Csalogánydal** (Harmath) Royal Orfeum 1 November
1921 **A csókos asszony** (*Clary-Clara*) Hungarian version with new songs Eskü Téri Színház 11 March
1921 **Kvitt** (Harmath) Royal Orfeum 2 April
1921 **A 28-as** (lászlö Bús-Fekete) Royal Orfeum 1 October
1921 **A főúr** (Bús-Fekete) Royal Orfeum 1 December
1922 **Aranymadár** (Harmath) 1 act Royal Orfeum 1 April
1922 **A szép Sara** (ad István Zagon) Royal Orfeum 1 October
1922 **A vörös majom** (László Bķeffy) Royal Orfeum 2 November
1923 **A hattyúlovag** (Harmath) Royal Orfeum 1 April
1924 **Árvácska** (Ernő Kulinyi/Bús-Fekete) Budai Színkör 1 July; Király Színhaz 13 September
1924 **Postás Katica** (Harmath) Lujza Blaha Színház 19 December
1925 **A nóta vége** (Bús-Fekete, Kulinyi) Budai Színkör 24 June
1926 **A csókos asszony** (new version ad Lázsló Szilágyi) Városi Színház 27 February
1926 **Csuda Mihaly szerencséje** (Kulinyi/Bús-Fekete) Magyar Színház 22 May
1926 **Muzsikus Ferkó** (Szilágyi) Budai Színkör 18 June
1927 **A Zsiványkiraly** (Harmath) Royal Orfeum 1 January
1927 **A legkisebbik Horváth lány** (Szilágyi) Király Színház 21 May
1928 **Balról a harmadik** (Béla Szilágyi) Royal Orfeum 1 January
1928 **Eltörött a hegedüm** (Szilágyi) Király Színház 3 November
1930 **Meluzina**

1931 **Falu végén kurta kocsma** (Harmath) Bethlen-Téri Színház 10 April

1936 **Hulló falevél** (Dezső Kellér/Szilágyi, Ernő Andai) Városi Színház 23 December

ZIEGFELD, Florenz jr (b Chicago, 21 March 1867; d Los Angeles, 22 July 1932). Flamboyant Broadway producer of revue and musical plays whose name and fame have, with a little help from Hollywood, become legend.

Originally a variety producer, Florenz Ziegfeld ventured into the musical theatre when he produced a series of mostly made-over vehicles for his sometime wife, French soubrette Anna Held. Beginning with a remake of the old Charles Hoyt farce-comedy *A Parlour Match*, he followed up with chopped-up versions of the Judic shows *La Femme à papa*, *Mam'zelle Nitouche* and *Niniche* (*Papa's Wife*, *The Little Duchess*), a *Mam'selle Napoléon* which gave Jean Richepin as its source, *The Parisian Model* and *Miss Innocence* (which was not *Mam'zelle Nitouche*). He also mounted a vehicle apiece for the soprano Grace van Studdiford (the romantic comic opera *The Red Feather*) and ballerina Adeline Genée (*The Soul Kiss*) and was involved with Weber and Fields on *Higgledy Piggledy* in what should have been another star outing for Miss Held but from which she withdrew when it turned out not to be.

In 1907 Ziegfeld produced his first *Follies* variety show, and in the next two decades these ever-more-grandiose mixtures of dance, spectacle, comedy and song comprised the main part of his career as a producer. He did, however, venture a pair of musicals in 1912, of which the variety-based *Over the River* did better than another attempt to revive a Hoyt farce comedy: the transformation of the megahit *A Trip to Chinatown* into the flop *A Winsome Widow*.

Ziegfeld had his first real success as a musical-comedy producer in 1920 when he produced *Sally* as a vehicle for his *Follies* star Marilyn(n) Miller, and thereafter book musicals featured much more prominently amongst his works. In the final decade of his producing career, he presented 14 new musicals on Broadway, from which the comical *Kid Boots*, the colourful spectacular *Rio Rita*, *Show Boat* (1927), *Rosalie* (1928), Friml's *The Three Musketeers* (1928) and *Whoopee* (1928) were all successes.

The name of Florenz Ziegfeld has gone down in Broadway's theatrical history as the epitome of glamour and glitter, of showmanship and showbusiness hype. He was the man who wanted to put a line of up-to-date chorus girls in *Bitter-Sweet*. Yet he was also the producer – and by no means the silent producer – of one piece in *Show Boat* which has survived through the decades since as a classic of the substantial musical stage.

After his divorce from Anna Held, Ziegfeld was married to another leading lady, Billie Burke, who also spent a part of her career on the musical stage.

In 1988 an extravaganza based on the life of *Ziegfeld* was presented at the London Palladium (arr Michael Reed/Ned Sherrin, Alistair Beaton). Len Cariou, Marc Urquhart and Topol respectively played the part of the producer. A version of the piece was later seen in the American regions. On film, *The Great Ziegfeld* was represented by William Powell.

Biographies: Higham, C: *Ziegfeld* (Regnery, Chicago 1972), Carter, R; *The World of Flo Ziegfeld* (Elek, London, 1974) etc

ZIEHRER, Carl Michael (b Vienna, 2 May 1843; d Vienna, 14 November 1922). Composer of much popular Viennese music, including a number of scores for the Operette stage.

Born into a well-off Viennese family, the young Ziehrer studied music in his home town and was launched, at his family's expense, at the head of his own dance orchestra when only 20 years of age. Throughout a busy, prolific and highly successful career of some 40 years as a composer and conductor of orchestral dance music and military band music, Ziehrer also contributed, at first spasmodically but later more purposefully, to the Operette stage.

His first work for the Carltheater, *Wiener Kinder*, was produced in 1881 and was brought back for further showings in the following season, whilst the subsequent *Ein Deutschmeister*, a military piece allowing the composer to indulge in his now famous march music, played for several weeks at the same theatre, seven years later. A score for a remade Posse, *Wiener Luft*, at the Theater an der Wien was heard 26 times. However, the breakthrough for Ziehrer as a theatre composer finally came in 1898, when Gabor Steiner produced *Der schöne Rigo*, a piece which – in a manner practised normally only after a composer's death – re-used some of Ziehrer's earlier music to make up a score for the libretto by Venedig in Wien house writers Leopold Krenn and Carl Lindau. With Rudolf del Zopp, Arthur Guttmann and Karl Tuschl in the cast, it proved, if scarcely a hit, successful enough to go on to a production in Leipzig (Carola Theater 25 December 1898) and for Steiner to produce a further piece from the same writers for the next season.

Die Landstreicher was something different altogether. Not only was it a custom-written piece, it was easily Ziehrer's best stage work up to that time, and would remain one of his best of all time. It was a great summer success at the theatre at the Englisch Garten in the Prater, was brought back the following season, played at Steiner's Danzers Orpheum, at the Theater an der Wien in 1902, and then beyond Vienna for many years to come. The success of *Die Landstreicher* opened up top-drawer theatrical opportunities for the composer. He and his librettists had their next piece, *Die drei Wünsche*, mounted at the Carltheater with Mizzi Günther and Louis Treumann heading the cast and, although it managed a first run of only 27 performances, the following season the Theater an der Wien took up their *Der Fremdenführer*. A 40-night run was prefatory to productions in Germany and Hungary, and the show remained sufficiently alive to be revived at the Raimundtheater in a suitably altered wartime version and, again, in an even more altered state, at the Volksoper in 1978.

Back at the Carltheater, *Der Schätzmeister* saw Günther and Treumann featured in a second Ziehrer piece, but one which once again could manage only an indifferent first run of 31 performances and limited engagements in Germany and Hungary (*A Becsüs*, Budai Színkör, 1 May 1906), and Ziehrer returned to Steiner and his summer theatre with *Fesche Geister*. His second great hit, however, was not mounted in Vienna. He supplied the music for Kraatz, Stobitzer and Wilhelm Sterk's *Ein tolles Mädel*, a female star-vehicle musical comedy produced at Wiesbaden, and saw it score the biggest success he had known in his career as it moved on to Steiner's Danzers Orpheum in Vienna and then to productions around the world (*Mlle Mischief*, *Fuzsitus kisasszony* etc).

Ziehrer's *Liebeswalzer*, produced by Karczag as the first new Operette under his management of the Raimund-theater in 1908, also did well, being played in repertoire there for more than 150 performances over six years (100th 28 October 1909), and winning a botched Broadway production as *The Kiss Waltz*. Another collaboration with Sterk produced *Ball bei Hof*, which also travelled (*Bal az udvarnal* Budapesti Színház, 21 March 1912), but neither *Fürst Kasimir* played at the Carltheater with Mizzi Zwerenz and the aged Karl Blasel as chief comic (40 performances) nor a revised version of the summertime *Manöverkind* as *Husarengeneral*, played at the Raimund-theater with Betty Fischer and Franz Glawatsch featured (51 performances), nor a further collaboration with Sterk on *Das dumme Herz* (68 performances) at the Johann Strauss-Theater proved able to win the same kind of popularity.

Ziehrer's theatre pieces did not find the same success that his dances, marches and Viennese songs did, but even though many of his Operetten had indifferent runs in Vienna most were mounted in Germany, several in Hungary, and even a small handful in America. Today, it is for his non-theatre musical that the composer is celebrated in his home town, where even the most successful of his Operetten remain at best on the fringe of the repertoire.

1866 **Mahomeds Paradies** 1 act Harmonietheater 26 February
1872 **Das Orakel zu Delphi** (Karl Costa) Linz 21 September
1875 **Kleopatra** (w Richard Genée/Josef Steinher) Komische Oper 13 November
1878 **König Jerome** (Adolf Schirmer) Ringtheater 28 November
1879 **Alexander der Grosse** (Costa) Marburg January
1879 **Ein kleiner Don Juan** (Ludwig Ernst Pollhammer) Deutsches Theater, Budapest 21 November
1881 **Wiener Kinder** (Leopold Krenn, Carl Wolff) Carltheater 16 January
1888 **Ein Deutschmeister** (Richard Genée, Bruno Zappert) Carltheater 30 November
1889 **Wiener Luft** (Carl Lindau, Heinrich Thalboth) Theater an der Wien 10 May
1890 **Der bleiche Zauberer** (Isidor Fuchs) 1 act Theater an der Wien 20 September
1898 **Der schöne Rigo** (Krenn, Lindau) Venedig in Wien 24 May
1899 **Die Landstreicher** (Krenn, Lindau) Venedig in Wien 29 July
1901 **Die drei Wünsche** (Krenn, Lindau) Carltheater 9 March
1902 **Der Fremdenführer** (Krenn, Lindau) Theater an der Wien 11 October
1904 **Der Schätzmeister** (Alexander Engel, Julius Horst) Carltheater 10 December
1905 **Fesche Geister** (Krenn, Lindau) Venedig in Wien 7 July
1907 **Am Lido** (Ottokar Tann-Bergler, Alfred Deutsch-German) Budapester Orpheum 31 August
1907 **Ein tolles Mädel** (Wilhelm Sterk/Kurt Kraatz, Heinrich Stobitzer) Walhalla Theater, Wiesbaden 24 August; Danzers Orpheum, Vienna 8 November
1908 **Liebeswalzer** (Robert Bodanzky, Alfred Grünbaum) Raimundtheater October 24
1909 **Herr und Frau Biedermaier** (Sterk) 1 act Lustspieltheater, Munich 10 January
1909 **Der Gaukler** (Emil Golz, Arnold Golz) 1 act Apollotheater 6 September
1911 **In funfzig Jähren** (arr/Krenn, Lindau) Ronacher 7 January

1911 **Ball bei Hof** (Sterk) Stadttheater, Stettin 22 January
1912 **Manöverkind** (Oskar Friedmann, Fritz Lunzer) Venedig in Wien 22 June
1913 **Fürst Kasimir** (Max Neal, Max Ferner) Carltheater 13 September
1913 **Husarengeneral** revised *Manöverkind* (Friedmann, Lunzer) Raimundtheater 3 October
1914 **Das dumme Herz** (Rudolf Österreicher, Peter Herz) Johann Strauss-Theater 27 February
1916 **Im siebenten Himmel** (Neal, Ferner) Theater am Gärtnerplatz, Munich 26 February
1920 **Der verliebte Eskadron** (arr Karl Paupsertl/Sterk) Johann Strauss-Theater 11 July

Biography: Schönherr, M: *Carl Michael Ziehrer* (Österreiches Bundesverlag, Vienna, 1974)

DER ZIGEUNERBARON Comic opera in 3 acts by Ignaz Schnitzer based on the story *Sáffi* by Mór Jókai. Music by Johann Strauss. Theater an der Wien, Vienna, 24 October 1885.

Second only to *Die Fledermaus*, *Der Zigeunerbaron* has proved itself to be steadily the most popular of Johann Strauss's Operetten both in the theatre and outside it, and it has been played continually on European stages – and occasionally elsewhere – over the century and more since its first production in Vienna.

The genesis of the show apparently came in a meeting in Budapest between Strauss and the respected Hungarian author Mór Jókai, at which the latter suggested – amongst other possibilities – that of his novella *Sáffi* as the basis for an Operette libretto. It was also said to be Jókai who suggested that the Vienna-based Hungarian journalist and stage-writer Ignaz Schnitzer, who also did a successful job on his *Aranyember* (*Goldmensch*), be asked to write the stage adaptation. In contrast to the bubbling comedy of *Der lustige Krieg* and the Italianate pageantry and highish-jinks of *Eine Nacht in Venedig*, the subject matter and principal plotline of *Der Zigeunerbaron* (Jókai suggested the title as well) were in a strongly romantic and sentimental vein, and it was even announced at one stage that Strauss's new piece would be staged at the Vienna Hofoper. However, Schnitzer's adaptation, although it was a little lumpy in some respects, ultimately dosed the romance with just sufficient comedy to keep the show, though still palpably different in tone from its predecessors, safely in the operettic field.

The young Sándor Barinkay (Karl Streitmann) is brought back to Temesvár by the government official, Carnero (Carl Adolf Friese), to have restored to him the lands of which his father was dispossessed. He has barely arrived when his new neighbour, the pig-farmer Zsupán (Alexander Girardi), is hustling him into a tactical betrothal with his daughter, Arsena, but Arsena is in love with Ottokar, the son of her governess Mirabella (Therese Schäfer), and she refuses the match, claiming by way of an excuse that she must have at least a Baron for a husband. Barinkay soon discovers the truth and, to the anger of Zsupán and his family, plights himself instead to the gipsy maiden Sáffi (Ottilie Collin). Sáffi and her mother, Czipra (Antonie Hartmann), lead Barinkay to the ruin of his family home, and there they discover the treasure hidden by his fleeing father. Zsupán and Carnero are both anxious to lay claim to the gold, but when the governor, Graf Homonay (Josef Joseffy), comes by to recruit for the war against Spain,

Plate 302. **Der Zigeunerbaron:** *Claus Klincke as Zsupán gathers his pigs about him in the Theater Hof's 1986 production.*

Barinkay gives him the treasure towards the war effort. Zsupán and Ottokar unknowingly drink the recruiting wine and are taken for the army, and the distraught Barinkay joins up too when Czipra reveals that Sáffi is truthfully no child of hers, but the daughter of Hungary's last pasha ... a veritable gipsy princess. When the men return, two years later, with Barinkay a real hero and Zsupán a phoney one, the young man hands Arsena over to Ottokar and, his scruples over her rank now gone, weds Sáffi.

The romantic backbone of the score centred on the character of Sáffi, who was equipped with a powerful gipsy song, 'Habet acht!', and joined rapturously in duet with Barinkay in the bullfinch duet 'Wer uns getraut?', justifying their unofficial marriage before the Morality Commission regulations put forward by the fussy Carnero. Barinkay's own big moment came with his lively introductory 'Als flotter Geist', describing the occupations he has gone through since his father's dispossession, whilst a baritone recruiting song for Homonay was another of the strongly-sung vocal highlights. The soubret side was represented by Arsena and Ottokar, and the comic headed by Zsupán with a famously farmyard entrance piece ('Ja, das Schreiben und das Lesen') and by Mirabella, relating to the booming of orchestral cannons, the disastrous tale of how she lost her husband in the middle of a war ('Just sind es vierund-zwanzig Jahre'). That husband is Carnero, the representative of that overworked Operette convention the Morality Commission whose tenets are related in a song which was possibly funnier in its time than it is now. Alongside the solo pieces, some fine ensemble music was highlighted by a treasure trio for the two gipsy women and Barinkay ('Ha, seht es winkt').

Der Zigeunerbaron was produced at the Theater in der Wien with great success. It was played 87 times consecu-

tively in its first series, and it remained a regular part of the theatre's repertoire for many years thereafter, passing its 150th performance on 19 February 1887, and its 300th on 23 October 1903 with Karl Meister and Gisela Noris playing alongside Girardi in his original rôle. The show was produced at the Raimundtheater in 1908, in the earliest days of Karczag and Wallner's management, played there in repertoire for three years, and it was there that it passed its 1,000th Viennese night on 19 April 1909. In 1915 Streitmann and Girardi – both of whom repeated their rôles for very many years – appeared in a new revival there. In 1910 the show entered both the Volksoper (23 March) and the Hofoper (26 December), and it was played in 1925 at the Carltheater, with Albin Mittersheim and Ilona Kelmay. It returned to the Theater an der Wien in 1921 with Richard Tauber and Betty Fischer featured, and again in 1935, and it has been reproduced at the Volksoper in various versions since, remaining there in the current repertoire to the present day.

In 1886 the show was mounted for the first time in Germany, in Munich and then in Berlin, where it raced to its 200th performance by the end of the year, and also at Budapest's Népszinház, which it had originally been intended should share the première of Strauss's 'Hungarian Operette'. The show (ad Károly Gerő, Antal Rádó) had already been seen in Kolozsvár, with tenor János Kápolnai as Barinkay, but the metropolitan version followed the fashion of travesty casting, and displayed the city's favourite soubrette, Ilka Pálmay, as the gipsy baron, to the Sáffi of Aranka Hegyi and the Zsupán of József Németh. *A cigánybáró* was played a remarkable 42 times in its first year, and 156 times in all, placing it amongst the top shows at Budapest's most important musical house. Like Vienna, Budapest later took the show into its opera house and in 1905 (27 May), *A cigánybáró* was produced at the Magyar Királyi Operaház with Dezső Arányi as a male Barinkay and Teréz Krammer as Sáffi.

New York followed with the first English-language production (ad Sydney Rosenfeld) only a few weeks after these, when Rudolf Aronson produced the show at the Casino Theater. William Castle and the darkly beautiful Pauline Hall played the romantic leads, with Francis Wilson as Zsupán and Billie Barlow playing Ottokar in travesty. New York didn't care for the show as Continental audiences had, and it was soon removed. However, local audiences had a chance to hear the piece in the original German shortly after when the Thalia Theater mounted *Der Zigeunerbaron* with Ernst Schütz and Franziska Raberg for an excellent four-week run. The German house reprised the show through several seasons, and in the 1889–90 season New Yorkers had the opportunity to see Streitmann in his original rôle. As in Europe, if a little more tardily, the show also made its way into the opera houses, being produced at the New York City Opera in 1944 with William Horne and Polyna Stoska, and, with little success, at the Metropolitan Opera in 1957 with Lisa della Casa, Nicolai Gedda and Walter Slezak. There was even less success, however, for an embarrassing version produced on America's west coast in the 1938–9 season (ad George Marion, Ann Ronell) with John Charles Thomas as Barinkay (now a lion-tamer), which squeezed out more than half the score and made up the difference by plugging the piece full of spare Strauss waltzes and new music by Ms Ronell, composer of 'Who's Afraid of the Big, Bad Wolf?'. This nasty bit of botching later called itself *The Open Road* (1944, ad Milton Lazarus).

The show was first seen in Italian in 1890, but it was nearly a decade after the Vienna première before a production was mounted in France (ad Armand Lafrique). That production was in Le Havre, but it clearly did well enough, for later the same year the show was produced at the Paris Théâtre des Folies-Dramatiques, with Monteux (Barinkay), Jane Pernyn (Sáffi), Mlle Paulin (Arsena), Mlle Maya (Czipra) and the comic Paul Hittemans (Zsupán) in the principal rôles. One critic noted that it was 'tastefully mounted, and in spite of the wretched libretto I shall not be surprised if it becomes popular'. It stayed for a run of 60 performances.

Australia bypassed *Der Zigeunerbaron* in the 19th century and it was not until 1953, in the midst of the blossoming fashion for American musical plays (not to mention a sudden passion for ice shows) that J C Williamson Ltd, for some reason, decided to mount *The Gypsy Baron*. It proved a bad, unprofitable idea and was not long persevered with. Similarly, in England, where Strauss's works had originally created little interest, *Der Zigeunerbaron* failed to find a contemporary production, and, although performances were played by visiting German-language troupes, it was not until 1964 that *The Gipsy Baron* (ad Geoffrey Dunn) was first seen in London professionally performed in English, in a production at the Sadler's Wells Opera with Nigel Douglas and June Bronhill starred.

A number of German-language films have been made of versions of the work, the first in 1931 by Karl Hartl, with Adolf Wohlbrück, Hansi Knotek and Fritz Kampers in the lead rôles, a second in 1935 and the most recent by Kurt Wilhelm in 1962 with Carlos Thompson, Danièle Gaubert and Willy Millowitsch. In 1954 Arthur Maria Rabenalt produced simultaneous German and French versions, with Margit Saad (Sáffi) and Harald Paulsen (Zsupán) appearing alongside Gerhard Riemann for the German version and Georges Guétary for the French.

One of the most popular of all 19th-century Viennese Operetten in central European theatres of both yesteryear and the present day, *Der Zigeunerbaron*, in spite of its composer's saleable name and of a widespread familiarity through recordings, remains today, as it has from the start, altogether less popular in translation.

Germany: Munich January 1886, Friedrich-Wilhelmstädtisches Theater 24 January 1886; Hungary: Kolozsvár 2 March 1886, Népszinház *Cigánybáró* 26 March 1886; USA: Casino Theater *The Gipsy Baron* 15 February 1886, Thalia-Theater (Ger) 1 April 1886; France: Le Havre 13 January 1895, Théâtre des Folies-Dramatiques *Le Baron tzigane* 20 December 1895; Australia: Theatre Royal, Sydney *The Gipsy Baron* 4 July 1953; UK: Sadler's Wells Theatre *The Gipsy Baron* 9 June 1964

Recordings: complete (Decca, Vanguard, EMI, Eurodisc etc), complete in Russian (Melodiya), selection in English (HMV, RCA), selections in French (Musidisc, Véga, EMI), selection in Hungarian (Qualiton), etc

ZIGEUNERLIEBE Romantic Operette in 3 acts by A M Willner and Robert Bodanzky. Music by Franz Lehár. Carltheater, Vienna, 8 January 1910.

The era of the bubbling *Die lustige Witwe* and *Der Graf von Luxemburg* put firmly, if not finally, behind him, Lehár turned with the score for the 1910 *Zigeunerliebe* to what was to be his most genuine and substantial romantic Operette. Willner and Bodanzky's passionate Hungarian tale, which was lightened only briefly by some unforcedly amusing moments in a style which had but little of the traditional soubret to it, drew from the composer a score of sometimes darkly dramatic power, as it moved on through a plot of more than usual verisimilitude to a positive ending much more convincing than the glum parade of final-curtain partings-for-ever which a self-made fashion and his librettists would later impose on him.

On the day that Zorika (Grete Holm), the daughter of the well-off Dragotin (Karl Blasel), is to be affianced to Jonel Bolescu (Max Rohr) she encounters his gipsy half-brother, Józsi (Willi Strehl). Józsi speaks to her of love in a way that has nothing to do with the well-mannered relationship between Zorika and her husband-to-be, and when the moment comes for the now confused Zorika to commit herself to the betrothal she refuses. She runs to the river, drinks from the waters, which legend says allow you to see into the future, and she dreams. She sees herself passionately following Józsi to the gipsy life, whilst he plays the field and shares glances with Dragotin's rich neighbour, Ilona von Köröshaza (Mizzi Zwerenz), on the very day of the gipsy wedding which should bind him to Zorika. Rejected by her family, longing for a proper church wedding and the other conventional parts of married life that have been shared by her bright little cousin Jolán (Littl Koppel) and the mayor's shy son, Kajétan (Hubert Marischka), Zorika realizes the gipsy life is not for her. She awakes to go thankfully to her betrothal with Jonel. At the same time, Ilona, casting a liberated look at Józsi as he heads insouciantly back to his gipsy folk, brings together the impatient Jolán and the backward Kajétan.

The score to *Zigeunerliebe* showed its intentions from the very start, when the first-act curtain rose on a dramatic storm scene, with a soaring solo for Zorika ('Heissa, heissa!'). The rôle of Zorika was endowed with a rapturous second-act number 'Gib mir dort von Himmelszeit', and with a series of duos, beginning with the troubling 'Es liegt in blauen Fernen' with Józsi in the first act and ending with her safe in the arms of Jonel at the show's conclusion. However, the part of Ilona – Mizzi Zwerenz had the star-billing in the original production – was also well equipped, with a set of pieces which ranged from the charming 'Nur die Liebe macht uns jung' with Dragotin to the light-hearted love lesson 'Zuerst sucht man Gelegenheit'. In later years, the Lehár song 'Hör' ich Cymbalklänge' was added to make Ilona's rôle even more important. The two men – tenors both, as is the third male rôle of Kajétan – were also well-supplied, Jonel reaping one of the gems of the score in his waltzing dream-plea to Zorika to return to him ('Zorika, Zorika kehre zurück'), and Józsi with his defiant hymn to the a-responsible life, 'Ich bin ein Ziegunerkind'.

Zigeunerliebe was mounted at the Carltheater whilst *Der Graf von Luxemburg* dominated the stage of the city's other main house, the Theater an der Wien, and it gave Lehár a second simultaneous hit. The show ran non-stop through ten months and 232 performances, and continued in the house's repertoire well into the 1920s. Budapest was swift to pick up this most Hungarian of Lehár's Viennese Operetten, and *Cigányszerelem* (ad Andor Gábor) was produced at the Király Színház with Sári Fedák in the rôle of

Plate 303. **Zigeunerliebe:** *The life that Zorika (Gudrun Schäfer) would lead with the easy-going gipsy Józsi (Jörg Vorpahl) would not be like the conventional and comfortable one of Jolán (Lisbeth Brittain) and Kajétan (Kenneth Bannon) (Theater Dortmund, 1986).*

Zorika, racing past its 100th performance on 14 February 1911 before confirming itself on the Hungarian stage in such a fashion that it is still to be seen in the Fővárosi Operettszinház repertoire to the present day.

A visit by the Carltheater company to Paris resulted in a French version (ad Jean Bénédict, Henri Gauthier-Villars ie 'Willy') being mounted in Brussels in January 1911 with Germaine Huber starred, but it was a second French version (ad Saugey), produced at Marseille in the same year with Suzanne Cesbron and Louise Mantoue sharing the lead rôle, which was subsequently played at Paris's modest Trianon-Lyrique with Jane de Poumayrac featured. In Berlin, Martha Winternitz-Dorda (Zorika), Mary Hagen (Ilona) and Jean Nadolovitch (Józsi) starred in *Zigeunerliebe* at the Komische Oper, whilst the first English-language performance was staged not by Lehár's most effective promoter – George Edwardes – but in New York (ad Harry B Smith, Robert B Smith), under the management of A H Woods. The production was dogged by bad luck which climaxed on the opening night when prima donna Marguerite Namara broke down during the performance and understudy Phyllis Partington was thrust on. Although she actually knew the rôle, and acquitted herself well, the evening was not what it might have been and *Gipsy Love* left town after 31 performances.

Edwardes gave the piece rather more solid service, although the *Gipsy Love* heard in London was rather different from that which had been played in Vienna. The libretto was vastly rewritten (ad Basil Hood, Adrian Ross), with the rôle of Ilona reworked as one Lady Babby to feature resident star Gertie Millar in a tale with most of the passion taken out and replaced by more harmless emotions. The score, too, was torn apart. The storm opening vanished, Lady Babby primped about being 'Cosmopolitan' (possibly to explain what she was doing in Hungary instead of in *Florodora*), and the rôle of Jonel (Webster Miller) all but vanished. His waltz melody was given to the soprano, Hungarian prima donna Sári Petráss, whose rôle

– now called Ilona – had become decidedly secondary to the ubiquitous Lady Babby. Jolan (Mabel Russell) and Kajetan (Lauri de Frece) were played soubret-comic, Bill Berry made Dragotin low-comic, Józsi (Robert Michaelis) was a baritone, and, with Lehár's assistance on some new musical pieces, *Gipsy Love* was remade as near to conventional musical comedy lines as was thought desirable. However, although this emasculation meant that Britain saw a show that resembled *Zigeunerliebe* only superficially, Edwardes clearly knew his audience. His *Gipsy Love*, without getting anywhere near the success of *The Merry Widow*, did almost as well as *The Count of Luxemburg* with a run of 299 London performances. It then took to the road and also to the Australian stage, being produced by J C Williamson Ltd with a cast including Gertrude Glyn (Lady Babby), Elsie Spain (Ilona), Field Fisher (Dragotin), Phil Smith (Kajetan) and Dorothy Brunton (Jolan) for eight weeks in Sydney prior to Brisbane and Melbourne (Her Majesty's Theatre 5 September 1914).

If London remade *Zigeunerliebe* as a conventional musical comedy, Hungary's Ernő Innocent Vincze preferred to take it diametrically the opposite way: in 1943 an operatic version of *Zigeunerliebe* was mounted at the Budapest opera with Tibor Udvardy and Julia Orosz starred under the title *Garabonciás diák*. The 'versions' did not end there either. In some productions the Act II dream was put aside, and its doings depicted as reality in a scenario where Zorika runs away with Józsi, and a 1930 Hollywood film called *Rogue Song*, allegedly based on *Zigeunerliebe*, used only a little of Lehár's music set to an entirely different story. However, the show's worst fate came in an American production of the 1930s where one Kay Kenny turned out a 'version' which interpolated both some additional 'comic relief' and some vaudeville songs. Produced as *The Moon Rises* (Shubert Theater, Boston, 14 April 1934) Ms Kenny's piece was an unmitigated and salutory failure.

In an age where it is no longer obligatory for a piece to be either frankly opera or frankly musical comedy, when there are no vaudeville songs to interpolate, and when the romantic Operette is much in style, the rare modern productions of this show – which has undergone a surprising amount of fiddling-with when its great initial success is considered – have ('Hör' ich Cymbalklänge' apart) largely returned to the original script and score.

Germany: Komische Oper 11 February 1910; Hungary: Király Színház *Ciganyszerelem* 12 November 1910, revised version as *Garaboncias diák* Opera Színház 20 February 1943; USA: Globe Theater *Gipsy Love* 17 October 1911; UK: Daly's Theatre *Gipsy Love* 1 June 1912; France: Théâtre du Vaudeville (Ger) 1911, Théâtre de l'Opéra, Marseille *L'Amour tsigane* 16 December 1911, Trianon-Lyrique, Paris 1911; Australia: Her Majesty's Theatre, Sydney 13 June 1914

Recordings: two-record set (Urania), in Russian (Melodiya), selection (Ariola-Eurodisc) etc

DER ZIGEUNERPRIMÁS   Operette in 3 acts by Julius Wilhelm and Fritz Grünbaum. Music by Emmerich Kálmán. Johann Strauss-Theater, Vienna, 11 October 1912.

Emmerich Kálmán's *Der Zigeunerprimás* (the gipsy violinist) has had a curious career. Highly successful in those centres where it was produced (Vienna, Berlin, New York, Budapest), it was completely ignored elsewhere (London, Paris), and now, whilst others of its composer's works continue to be played, it seems to have wholly slipped from the repertoire even in central Europe.

The story of *Der Zigeunerprimás* purported to be about the famous 19th-century gipsy violinist Pali Rácz and his equally historical son, Laczi, but it had a decided ring to it of the tale used for the Strauss biomusicals – the famous musician father who has no confidence that his son can follow him in his profession, but who is ultimately outdone and replaced by that son. Alexander Girardi played ageing Pali Rácz, cared for quietly by his eldest daughter, Sári (Gerda Walde), at loggerheads with his son Laczi (Willy Strehl) over the young man's preference for the music of Wagner, Bach and Händel over the old gipsy melodies which made his father's fame, and itching for a fourth wife in his young niece, Juliska (Grete Holm). Gaston, Count Irini (Josef Victora) persuades the old man to leave his Hungarian home and travel to Paris to play once more before King Herbert VII (Paul Harden) but, on the big night, Rácz misses his cue, and Laczi steps in to replace him to enormous applause. When the old gipsy follows his son's bravura modern performance with his country tunes, he seems old-fashioned. He will return home, retire for good and wed Juliska. But, away from the constraints of his father's home, Laczi has finally found the courage to speak his heart to Juliska. With the help of Gaston's grandmother (Alma Sorel), a love of Rácz's youth, the violinist is persuaded to ruefully but gracefully let the young people go into the future together: Laczi and Juliska, Sári and Gaston. As for the comical Cadeau (Max Brod), who has lingered a little too long in his choice of a bride, he will have to wait until the youngest of Rácz's 16 children grows up.

Girardi had the big number of the evening in the gipsy's description of his love for his violin – 'Mein alter Stradivari' – in a Hungarian-flavoured Kálmán score which included numbers of spirit for Juliska ('Du, du, du, lieber Gott schaust du') and of gentler charm for Sári ('So ein armes, dummes, kleines Ding vom Land') prior to each becoming romantic with her tenor in duet.

Plate 304. **Der Zigeunerprimás**: *Girardi as Páli Racz.*

Erich Müller's production at the Johann Strauss-Theater was a hit. Only a handful of performances of another current hit, *Die Förster-Christl*, intervened in an effectively continuous run of 180 performances between October 1912 and 10 April 1913 and the show was still to be seen in the repertoire at the Johann Strauss-Theater in 1924. Budapest's Király Színház production (ad Zsolt Harsányi) starred Antal Nyárai (Rácz), Sári Fedak (Sári), Sári Perczel (Juliska), Márton Rátkai (Gaston) and Jenő Nádor (Laczi), with the great star of earlier years, Ilka Pálmay, as the old countess, and scored a comparable success, being brought back for a second run the following year. In New York, too, the show was a hit. Henry Savage's production of *Sari* (ad C C S Cushing, E P Heath) with the little Hungarian soubrette Mizzi Hajós in the title-rôle alongside one-time juvenile leading man van Rensslaer Wheeler as Rácz, J Humbird Duffy as Laczi and Blanche Duffield (Juliska), played 151 New York performances, giving the producer his biggest Broadway success since *The Merry Widow* prior to touring for many years. The show was even brought back to Broadway in 1930 (29 January, Liberty Theater) with a rather older Mitzi (as she was now called) and Duffy repeating their rôles.

Given this unsmudged record of success, it was clearly wartime considerations which stopped Britain, France and Australia from getting a glimpse of *Der Zigeunerprimás*. But after having missed it first time round, none of these countries thought to look at it a little later, and, apart from the odd song in the heart of an elderly American, it remains virtually unknown outside central Europe.

Hungary: Király Színház *Ciganyprimás* 21 January 1913; Germany: 8 March 1913; USA: Liberty Theater *Sári* 13 January 1914

Recording: selection in Hungarian (Qualiton)

ZIP GOES A MILLION Musical extravaganza in 2 acts by Eric Maschwitz adapted from *Brewster's Millions* by George Barr McCutcheon, Winchell Smith and Byron Ongley. Music by George Posford. Palace Theatre, London, 20 October 1951.

The successful 1906 play *Brewster's Millions* (New Amsterdam Theater, New York 31 December) made up from McCutcheon's novel about a fellow who has to spend a million in order to inherit several, long defied attempts to make it into a musical comedy. Broadway's Comstock and Gest were the first to try, with a piece called variously *Maid o' Millions*, *Maid of Money* and *Zip Goes a Million*, and written by Guy Bolton, Buddy De Sylva and Jerome Kern. Produced at the Worcester Theater, Worcester, 8 December 1919, it failed to make Broadway. The composer, however, rescued 'Look for the Silver Lining' and 'Whip-Poor-Will' from the score and re-used them with more success in his *Sally*. The story too was re-used. The second try, this time under the title *Bubbling Over*, had a libretto by Clifford Grey and songs by Richard Myers and Leo Robin. Produced at the Garrick Theatre, Philadelphia with the young Jeanette MacDonald and certified stars Cecil Lean and Cleo Mayfield in its cast (2 August 1926), it ran out a good season and moved on to Chicago where it expired a fortnight later. Myers rescued 'I'm a One-Man Girl' and 'True to Two', the first of which became a song hit when used in Britain's *Mr Cinders* a couple of seasons later. And still the story went begging.

The third version, put together in Britain a quarter of a century later, had less weighty names attached to it. Producer Emile Littler mounted a jolly, unpretentious version of the tale with the rôle of Brewster northern-anglicized as little window-cleaner Percy Piggott for ukelele-strumming singing star George Formby. Percy went through New York and the South Seas in his attempts to get rid of his million secretly and hurry home to his Sally (Sara Gregory), passing on the way such folk as the shady banker Van Norden (Frank Tilton) and his predatory daughter (Phoebe Kershaw) and a musical-comedy couple (Wade Donovan, Barbara Perry) whose awful show seems like a certain way to lose a fortune. George Posford's songs allowed him to insist 'I'm Saving Up for Sally' and that they are 'Ordinary People' in the simplest of music-hall style, whilst Donovan and Perry aped Broadway musical comedy (notably the current *South Pacific*) in the show within a show.

Formby was forced to withdraw from the production six months into the run after a heart-attack, but comedian Reg Dixon replaced him to good effect and *Zip Goes a Million* ran for 544 performances in 16 months in London prior to going on the road for several seasons and winning productions in venues as far apart as Norway and Australia. Australia's production, mounted by David N Martin, featured Roy Barbour in Formby's rôle in satisfactory seasons in Sydney and in Melbourne (Tivoli 30 October 1954, two months).

Australia: Tivoli, Sydney 17 April 1954

Recording: London cast recordings (Columbia, Encore)

ZIRKUS AIMÉE Operette in 3 acts by Kurt Goetze and Ralph Benatzky. Music by Ralph Benatzky. Stadttheater, Basel, 5 March 1932.

Goetze starred in his own show as a well-born army lieutenant, stationed in an out-of-the-way town, who falls in love with little Aimée (Valerie von Martens) from the circus. To be with her, he flings in his commission and joins the circus, but his horrified family is won over when they actually come and see the pair in action.

Following on behind *Die Dame vom Zirkus*, *Das Zirkuskind* and *Die Zirkusprinzessin*, Aimée gave further lie to the myth that circus musicals were unlucky as it followed up its first production in Basel by transferring to the Berlin Metropoltheater for a good run.

DIE ZIRKUSPRINZESSIN Operette in 3 acts by Julius Brammer and Alfred Grünwald. Music by Emmerich Kálmán. Theater an der Wien, Vienna, 26 March 1926.

Prince Sergius (Richard Waldemar) has had his honourable offers rejected by the rich, widowed and beautiful Fedora Palinska (Betty Fischer) and, in revenge, he tricks her into a marriage with a supposed nobleman who is, in fact, the circus star Mister X (Hubert Marischka) in disguise. Sergius is discomforted when it eventuates that Mister X is actually the very aristocratic Fedor Palinski, the young man Fedora disinherited by her first marriage, and after pride has been assuaged all round, the two find they are happy to be wed. The romantic story, was counterpointed by the adventures and the winsome wooing of the soubret pair, hotelier's son Toni Schlumberger (Fritz Steiner) and the little circus girl, Miss Mabel Gibson (Elsie Altmann), and the show's third act, which abandoned the aristocratic lovers until it was time to tie up their story, concentrated instead on life at the hotel run by Toni's mother (Mizzi Zwerenz) and contained an extended comic scene for the elderly waiter Pelikan, a rôle created to fit comedy star Hans Moser, a famous specialist in comic servants and functionaries.

The bon-bon of Kálmán's score was the romantic tenor hymn to 'Zwei Märchenaugen', a piece which went on to become a recital and recording favourite, and the hero also got to serenade Vienna ('Wo ist der Himmel so blau wie in Wien') and to join with his lady to murmur romantically 'My Darling, My Darling', but the music of *Die Zirkusprinzessin* also contained a number of distinctly lively pieces ranging from the march song 'Mädel gib acht!' to a set of bouncing melodies for Toni and Mabel – he slavering over the charms of 'Die kleinen Mäderln im Trikot', and joining with her in 'Liese, Liese komm mit mir auf die Wiese', as well as a moving little semi-spoken piece for Frau Schlumberger in the final act.

If it did not quite equal the record of *Der Orlow*, its predecessor at the Theater an der Wien, *Die Zirkusprinzessin* was nevertheless a fine Vienna hit, playing 311 performances as Erik Wirl, Ernst Nadherny, Harry Bauer and Karl Ziegler all took a turn behind the hero's mask. It moved quickly to Germany, and was played 75 times in Breslau and 50 in Hamburg before reaching Berlin where it was produced with Wirl repeating the rôle he had played in Vienna alongside Lori Leux (Fedora), Max Hansen (Toni) and Szőke Szakall – later better known to filmgoers as 'Cuddles' – in the rôle of Pelikan. In Hungary, the Király Színház production (ad Imre Liptai, Ernő Kulinyi) with Juci Lábass, Márton Rátkái, Tibor Halmay, Jenő Nador and Vilma Orosz added further to the run of success.

The Shuberts took up the show for Broadway (ad Harry B Smith) and there, too, it won success with Guy Robertson sporting the hero's mask in a version which stretched and fiddled with the plot to make it 'both more explicit and more conventional' than the original, alongside Désirée Tabor (Fedora), Ted Doner (Toni), Gloria Foy (Fritzi Burgstaller), George Hassell (Grand Duke Sergius), and Jesse Greer and Raymond Kalges's song 'What D'Ya Say?', through 192 performances. A 1931–2 West Coast revival with Robertson again featured called itself *The Blue Mask*, but a Jones Beach production in 1937 went back to being *The Circus Princess*. The show was presented with great success in Milan, but a tardy French version (ad Max Eddy, Jean Marietti), produced at Le Havre, with Vidal and Maguy Dalcy featured, did not make it to Paris, and London failed to see *Die Zirkusprinzessin* at all. Two film versions were produced, a silent one in 1925, and a sound one in 1928 with Harry Liedtke and Vera Schmitterlöw starred.

Back home, the show was given a 1957 revival at the Raimundtheater, and in 1988 a curiously altered version – which compared unfavourably with that being played down the river at the Budapest Fővárosi Operettszinház – was taken into the repertoire of the Volksoper (15 February 1988). The Hungarian company visited Paris in 1991 to give the first Paris performances of *A cirkuszhercegnő* ... in German. Perhaps at least partly because of its colourful circus atmosphere, its one big tenor bon-bon, and the fine opportunities it gives to its soubret players in particular, *Die Zirkusprinzessin* has remained staunchly in the modern European repertoire alongside Kálmán's *Gräfin Mariza* and *Die Csárdásfürstin*, whilst others of the composer's works which might have been considered more, or at least equally, eligible for revival are rarely if ever seen.

Germany: Breslau, Metropoltheater, Berlin; Hungary: Király Színház *A cirkuszhercegnő* 24 September 1926; USA: Winter Garden Theater *The Circus Princess* 25 April 1927; France: Théâtre du Havre *La Princesse du Cirque* 24 March 1934, Opéra-Comique (Ger) 20 March 1991; Films: Adolf Gärtner 1925, Victor Janson 1928

Recording: selection (Ariola-Eurodisc), selection in Hungarian (Qualiton)

THE ZOO Musical folly (musical absurdity) in 1 act by 'Bolton Rowe' (B C Stephenson). Music by Arthur Sullivan. St James's Theatre, London, 5 June 1875.

A comical little burlesque piece in which a disguised duke (Edgar Bruce) finds true love with Eliza, the refreshment stall lady at the Zoo (Henrietta Hodson), whilst a lovesick pharmacist (Carlos Florentine) tries to commit suicide in the bear-pit for love of his Laetitia (Gertrude Ashton). Sullivan's comicalities and intermittent parodies of opera provided a lively accompaniment to the humorous little text and the show was given several London productions as a forepiece. Pauline Markham, later to be a famous Lydia Thompson blonde, appeared as Eliza, whilst Richard Temple, later of the Savoy produced, directed and played the duke in another production, and W S Penley,

the original *Charley's Aunt*, was Letitia's nasty dad in a third version.

The Zoo was exhumed, published and recorded in the 1980s and has since been staged by a number of groups and colleges without having made its way back to the professional stage.

Recordings: D'Oyly Carte Co (Decca), amateur cast (RRE)

ZORBA Musical in 2 acts by Joseph Stein based on the novel by Nicos Kazantzakis. Lyrics by Fred Ebb. Music by John Kander. Imperial Theater, New York, 17 November 1968.

At first a novel, then the celebrated Michael Cacoyannis film of 1965 in which Antony Quinn played *Zorba the Greek* alongside Lila Kedrova and Alan Bates and the famous bouzouki music of Mikos Theodorakis's 'Zorba's Dance', the tale of Kazantzakis's exuberant Greek was finally made into a musical play in 1968 by the author of *Fiddler on the Roof* and the songwriters of *Cabaret*.

Framed within the kind of play-within-a-play setting which *Man of La Mancha* had recently re-re-popularized, the tale of Zorba (Herschel Bernardi) was narrated by the leader of a bouzouki group (Lorraine Serabian). That tale begins in a Piraeus café where the 'hero' of the story encounters young Nikos (John Cunningham), who is on his way to the islands to open up a mine he has inherited. Zorba attaches himself to the venture and the two men go off to Crete. There Zorba sets himself up with the sweet, ageing cocotte, Hortense (Maria Karnilova), whilst Nikos becomes involved with the Widow (Carmen Alvarez). But Nikos's relationship leads to tragedy, when an unstable boy (Richard Dmitri) who fancies himself in love with the woman commits suicide, leading his father revengefully to stab the Widow to death. The mine turns out to be useless, and when Hortense dies, happy with the pretence of a betrothal she has gone through with Zorba, the two men leave the island, each going his own separate way on to the next stage of life, that life which, in Zorba's philosophy and that of the islanders, leads uncomplicatedly and inevitably to death.

The score to the show was not made up of obvious 'numbers', but the musical part was a strongly effective support to the story and its characters. There were set pieces for the group leader, written in an ethnic style, one musical scene for Nikos and the Widow, a Zorba's Dance which was not the famous one of the same name, and some delicate songs for the self-deluding Hortense, whether telling of how she saved Crete by an arrangement between all the admirals who were her lovers ('No Boom Boom'), bidding temporary farewell to Zorba ('Goodbye Canavaro') or, in the haze of death, movingly reliving a childish 'Happy Birthday'.

Zorba had a 305-performance run on Broadway in Harold Prince and Ruth Mitchell's original production, and 15 years later it was given a major touring revival under the management of Barry and Fran Weissler and Kenneth-Mark Productions, with Cacoyannis directing the two stars of his film, repeating their performances in the musical version. The convention of the framework was discarded, and an additional song for Zorba added, and this time the show – with a 354-performance Broadway run – made money.

The show did not play the West End, a British production with Alfred Marks featured as Zorba stopping short at the Greenwich Theatre, but *Zorba* found great popularity in central Europe. It was produced (ad Robert Gilbert, Gerhard Bronner) at Vienna's Theater an der Wien – which had staged both *Anatevka* (ie *Fiddler on the Roof*) and *Cabaret* in the two previous years – with Yossi Yadin (another *Fiddler* star, like Bernardi and Karnilova, following up in *Zorba*) in the title-rôle alongside Luise Ulrich, Dagmar Koller, Peter Fröhlich and Olivia Molina through a series of 80 performances, and went on from there both to regular performances in German-speaking houses and also to Hungary where a local version (ad Ágnes György) was first produced in 1973.

UK: Greenwich Theatre 1973; Austria: Theater an der Wien *Sorbas* 28 January 1971; Hungary: Fertőrákosi Barlangszinház 5 July 1973; Germany: nd
Recordings: original cast (Capitol) revival cast (RCA), Hungarian cast (Hungaraton), Austrian cast (Preiser)

ZORINA, Vera [HARTWIG, Eva Brigitta] (b Berlin, 2 January 1917).

At first a ballet dancer in Norway and later with the Ballet Russe de Monte Carlo (1934–6), Vera Zorina made her first appearance on the musical stage in the rôle of the ballerina Vera Barnova in the short-lived London production of *On Your Toes* in 1937. She made her Broadway début as the Angel of Rodgers and Hart's subsequent *I Married an Angel* – another rôle with a large dance content – and later appeared as the sexy Marina van Linden in another successful musical, *Louisiana Purchase* (1940) and as a dream-Scheherazade in the very much less successful *Dream with Music* (1944). Each of these productions was choreographed by her sometime husband, George Balanchine.

Miss Zorina appeared in the film versions of *On Your Toes* (1939) and *Louisiana Purchase* (1941), and also in *The Goldwyn Follies*, *I Was an Adventuress* (1940), *Star Spangled Rhythm* (1943) and *Follow the Boys* (1944) and finally, after a decade's absence from the New York theatre, returned to Broadway to repeat her *On Your Toes* rôle in the show's 1954 revival, before retiring from the stage.

Miss Zorina was latterly married to Columbia Records executive Goddard Lieberson.

Autobiography: *Zorina* (Farrar, Straus, Giroux, New York, 1986)

ZSUZSI KISASSZONY Operett in 3 acts by Ferenc Martos and Miksa Bródy. Music by Emmerich Kálmán. Vigszinház, Budapest 27 February 1915.

Emmerich Kálmán's *Zsuzsi kisasszony* did not achieve the same kind of international coverage as the pieces with which he had preceded it (*Az obsitos*, *Der Zigeunerprimás*, *Die Csárdásfürstin*) or those with which he followed it (*Das Hollandweibchen*, *Die Bajadere*, *Gräfin Mariza* etc), but there was a reason.

Produced at Budapest's Vigszinház, the story of Miss Susy (Nusi Diósi) who gets all starry-eyed over her village's long-departed most famous inhabitant when he returns home for a local festival, only to find the man is a stand-in, was decorated with a typically lively score made up of predominantly waltz and march rhythms. It was well received, passed its 50th performance on 3 May 1915 and finally totalled a very respectable 78 nights. America's Klaw and Erlanger were quickest off the mark as buyers

Plate 305. **Zsuzsi kisasszony**: *Nusi Diósy as the heroine of Kálmán's operette.*

for the newest work by the composer of *Die Csárdásfürstin*, and *Miss Springtime* (ad Guy Bolton, P G Wodehouse) was produced on Broadway with Hungary's Sári Petráss starred 18 months after its Budapest première. Susy had become Rosita, Kálmán's score had been infiltrated by three numbers by Jerome Kern, and the resultant show ran for nearly 230 performances before going to the country.

In spite of such success, however, *Zsuzsi kisasszony* went nowhere else. The reason became apparent – so the story goes – when the Viennese hit *Die Faschingsfee* was transported to Hungary. It was due to go into rehearsal when someone recognized one of the tunes. The producer telegraphed Kálmán asking if the music of *Die Faschingsfee* was not that of *Zsuzsi kisasszony*, and the composer blithely telegraphed back that it was. But it had gone much better with its new Viennese libretto. In fact, virtually all the principal numbers of *Zsuzsi kisasszony* had been used either in whole, or partially made over, for the later work, effectively ending any further life for Susy or for Miss Springtime.

USA: New Amsterdam Theater *Miss Springtime* 25 September 1916

ZUMPE, Hermann (b Oppach [Taubenheim], 9 April 1850; d Munich, 4 September 1903).

Conductor and composer Zumpe was, in the former capacity, associated in particular with the works of Wagner, and in the latter wrote the scores for several operas, including *Des Teufels Anteil*, *Anahna* (Viktoria-Theater, Berlin, 23 December 1881) and *Sawitri* (Hoftheater, 8 November 1907), and for three well-considered Operetten which were premièred at Hamburg's Carl-Schultze Theater in the 1880s.

The first of these, *Farinelli*, a textual mix of the Scribe libretto for Auber's *Carlo Broschi* and a Hamburg play called *Farinelli* by one Teigmann, had a considerable success, being played throughout Germany and Austria (Carltheater 22 September 1888, 35 performances) and even in the German Amberg Theater in New York (20 December

1888), where Ernst Schütz appeared in the title-rôle, through a successful Christmas and new-year season. The second, *Karin*, does not seem to have progressed far beyond Hamburg, but the third, *Polnische Wirtschaft*, made its way to Berlin's Friedrich-Wilhelmstädtisches Theater in 1891 (26 November).

1886 **Farinelli** (Friedrich Willibald Wulff, Charles Cassmann) Carl-Schultze Theater, Hamburg 28 November
1888 **Karin** (Wulff, Eduard Pochmann) Carl-Schultze Theater, Hamburg 1 December
1889 **Polnische Wirtschaft** (Moritz West, Richard Genée) Carl-Schultze Theater, Hamburg

ZWAR, Charles (b Broadford, Vic, 10 April 1914; d Oxford, 2 December 1989). Australian-born composer of revue and musical comedy.

Zwar was not long out of university when he was offered the oportunity to compose the score for the musical play *Blue Mountain Melody*, one of several attempts in the 1930s to find a native musical comedy vehicle for home stars, in this case Cyril Ritchard and Madge Elliott. The show, a piece about a boxer and a dancer, set in Sydney, won certain local attention before Zwar moved on to Britain where he became pianist/md for the little Gate Theatre, accompanying and supplying music for their memorable run of intimate revues. He subsequently composed the music for a long run of small-scale London revues including *Sweeter and Lower*, *Sweetest and Lowest*, *One, Two, Three, Four, Five, Six*, *À la Carte*, *The Lyric Revue*, *The Globe Revue* and *Airs on a Shoestring*, and continued to write for revue long after that form of entertainment had been deflated by television. He also supplied the scores for two West End musical plays, the Arthur Askey comedy piece *Bet Your Life* (w Kenneth Leslie-Smith) which had a good 362-performance run as a twice-nightly entertainment, and a musical adaptation of the successful romantic Scottish play *Marigold* (77 performances). He also composed the songs for a tentatively politico-topical provincial piece *The Station Master's Daughter*.

1934 **Blue Mountain Melody** (J C Bancks) Theatre Royal, Sydney 15 September
1952 **Bet Your Life** (w Kenneth Leslie-Smith/Alan Melville) London Hippodrome 18 February
1959 **Marigold** (Melville) Savoy Theatre 27 May
1968 **The Station Master's Daughter** (Frank Harvey) Yvonne Arnaud Theatre, Guildford 11 April

ZWEI HERZEN IM DREIVIERTELTAKT [aka *Der verlorene Walzer*] Operette in 3 acts (8 scenes) by Paul Knepler and Ignaz M Welleminsky based on the screenplay of the same name by Walter Reisch and Franz Schulz. Music by Robert Stolz. Stadttheater, Zurich, 30 September 1933.

One of Robert Stolz's most successful film scores was that for the prettily-titled 1930 *Zwei Herzen im Dreivierteltakt* (two hearts in 3/4 time), produced by Géza von Bolvary and richly cast with Gretl Theimer, Walter Janssen, Oscar Karlweis, Willi Forst, Szőke Szakall and Paul Hörbiger. Three years later, when the film was adapted to the stage, Stolz composed virtually an entirely new score for the occasion, only the film's two major song hits – the title number and 'Auch du wirst mich einmal einmal betrügen' (better known for having been interpolated into

London's *Im weissen Rössl* under the title 'You Too') – being remade for the occasion.

The lost waltz of the sometime title of the stage show is the tune that composer-star Toni Hofer needs for his new Operette. He also may need a new leading lady, for his co-star/lover Anny Lohmayer is threatening to abandon ship, especially as the Hofer recipe for musical inspiration is apparently a new love affair. His librettists plan to send him a juicily willing soubrette, but their teenage sister, Hedi, takes her place and the result is a winning waltz. It disappears when she does, but returns in time for a happy ending for the new production and the new lovers.

The new score placed several other attractive numbers alongside the film score's hits, several of which were presented as parts of the Operette within the Operette ('Das ist der Schmerz beim ersten Kuss') and one as a straightforward Heurige number ('Das ist kein Zufall, dass das Glück in Wien wohnt').

The Zurich première (as *Zwei Herzen*) was followed by a production in Dresden of a version given the title *Der verlorene Walzer*, but it was the more familiar and catchy title which was used when the show was produced in Austria, both in its initial showing at the Titania-Theater and at the Volksoper, where it was mounted on 29 March 1975 with Peter Minich (Toni), Sylvia Holzmayer (Anny) and Helga Papouschek (Hedi). An English-language version (ad Dailey Paskman, William A Drake) was staged at the St Louis Muny in 1938 with Eric Mattson (Toni), Gladys Baxter (Anny), Nancy McCord (Hedi) and the Three Olympics roller-skating speciality. It was repeated there in 1939 and 1946 and played again at Los Angeles and at the Greek Theater in Hollywood in 1946 with Kenny Baker, Irene Manning and Pamela Caveness featured.

Germany: Centraltheater, Dresden *Der verlorene Walzer* 23 December 1933; USA: Municipal Opera, St Louis *The Lost Waltz* 11 July 1938; Austria: Titania-Theater 15 May 1948
Recording: selection (Ariola-Eurodisc, Remington)

ZWERENZ, Mizzi (b Pistyán, Hungary, 13 July 1876; d Vienna, 14 June 1947). Longtime star soubrette of the Vienna stage who matured into a fine second career as a character player.

The daughter of Karl Ludwig Zwerenz, an actor who subsequently became a theatre director in Bucharest and Pressburg, Mizzi made her first stage appearances at Baden bei Wien and at Berlin's Friedrich-Wilhelmstädtisches Theater before joining the company at the Vienna Carltheater in 1901 at the start of what was to be one of the most remarkable careers in the history of the Viennese musical stage. She made her earliest appearances at the Carltheater covering Therese Biedermann and playing in such new pieces as Millöcker's *Der Damenschneider* (1901, Marinka) and *Das gewisse Etwas* (1902, Cascarette Joujou), in the Vienna version of *Der kleine Günstling* (1902, Anita) and as Nelli in *Der Obersteiger*, before moving on to play leading rôles in the Operetten at Gabor Steiner's summer theater, Venedig in Wien – *Gräfin Pepi* (1902, Pepi), *Frühlingsluft* (1903, Hanni), Edna May's rôle of Olga in *The Girl from Up There* (*Die Eisjungfrau*, 1904), *Jung Heidelberg* (1904), Ziehrer's *Fesche Geister* (1905), *Wien bei Nacht* (1905, Mizzi) and the Parisian *Die Ringstrassen-Prinzessin* (1905, t/o Milli).

Plate 306. **Mizzi Zwerenz** *as Franzi in* Ein Walzertraum.

Zwerenz had grown to star-billing when she appeared opposite Girardi at the Carltheater in 1905 in the title-rôle of Eysler's hit *Die Schützenliesel*, and she held the top of the bill when she subsequently appeared in the travesty rôle of von Reif-Reiflingen in Reinhardt's Operette version of the famous comedy *Krieg im Frieden*, then as Fifine in *Mutzi*, Hugdietrich in *Hugdietrichs Brautfahrt* and in Kobler's short-lived *Der Rosenjüngling* (1906). She paired with Girardi as Nelli in *Künstlerblut*, and again as Gusti Fröhlich in *Der selige Vincenz* (1907) and then created one of her most memorable rôles when she played the part of the little violinist, Fritzi Steingruber, in *Ein Walzertraum* (1907) introducing the comedy duo 'Piccolo, Piccolo, tsin, tsin, tsin' with her husband Arthur Guttmann. She starred in a 1908 revival of Suppé's *Donna Juanita*, was billed large above the title in the less fortunate new pieces *Der schwarze Tenor* (Henriette), *Johann der Zweite* (Elly) and *Der Glücksnarr* (Friedel), but found another fine rôle as the memorable un-wronged wife of the major hit that was *Die geschiedene Frau* (Jana).

In 1909 she starred in the title-rôle of Oscar Straus's *Didi* (Lydia Garousse), and a major revival of Genée's *Nanon* featured her in the title-rôle to the Ninon of Dora Keplinger, before in 1910 she won another memorable rôle as the high-spirited Ilona von Köröshaza in Lehár's *Zigeunerliebe*. She created the rôles of Rosalilla in Fall's

Das Puppenmädel (1910) and of Granichstädten's *Majestät Mimi*, played, with notable success, the Viennese version of Jean Gilbert's *Die keusche Susanne* (1911, Susanne), appeared as Lini Stöckl, the little heroine of the Lanner pasticcio *Alt-Wien* (1911), Louison Duval in *Die kleine Freundin* and scored yet another singular hit as Princess Helene, the mixed-up non-Princess of *Der liebe Augustin* (1912).

Later in 1912 she appeared in the title-rôles of a revival of *Boccaccio* and of the Hungarian operett *Susi* (*A kis gróf*), in Ziehrer's unsuccessful *Fürst Casimir*, and scored again when she created the rôle of the wily Helena, who wins her raffish Count, in the Viennese production of Nedbal's highly successful *Polenblut* (1913). She played in travesty in the shortlived *Der erste Kuss* (1914, Harry), in a revival of the Posse *Zwei Mann von Hess* with Karl Blasel and appeared as Karl von Stigler's less-than-memorable *Mädchen im Mond* (1914, Hedwig Hübner), as Oscar Straus's *Schöne Unbekannte* (1915, Elly) and as Reinhardt's *Die erste Frau* (the little model, Seffi) in the same year. Other wartime rôles included the vocally dazzling Princess (otherwise Maria Theresia) in Fall's magnificent *Fürstenliebe*, Lola Brandt in the Posse *Man steigt nicht!*, and the filmstar Delia Gill in Vienna's version of the Berlin musical *Die Kino-Königin* (1915) before, in 1916 she ended her long-starring run with the Carltheater and moved to the Apollotheater.

There she turned out a further series of leading rôles, starring in *Hanni geht tanzen* (Hanni), the title-rôle of *Urschula*, *Graf Toni* (1916, Fritzi Paradeiser), as Richard Fall's *Die Dame von Welt* and *Die Puppen-Baronessen*, in Eysler's *Der Aushilfsgatte* (1917), Granichstädten's *Walzerliebe*, Lehár's *Rosenstock und Edelweiss*, Jean Gilbert's *Die Fahrt ins Glück* (1918), Stolz's *Der Favorit* (Pauline Villinger), Ascher's *Der Künstlerpreis* (Etelka von Vasarhely) and the Vienna production of *Die Dame vom Zirkus* (1919).

She was back at the Carltheater in 1921 as Josepha Freisinger in *Der Herzog von Reichstadt*, still heading the bill as she had done for 15 years, and the following year was seen in *Die Csárdásfürstin* at the Johann Strauss-Theater, but after some 20 years as a prima donna/soubrette she now gave way to others.

Her career as a leading lady had been one of the most remarkable in the Viennese Operette, but Mizzi Zwerenz was not finished yet. She was to have a second career, as a character player. Over the next decade she appeared in such komische Alte rôles as Portschunkula in *Die gold'ne Meisterin* (1926), the splendid Frau Schlumberger in *Die Zirkusprinzessin* (1926), Die Oberin in *Mam'zelle Nitouche* (1927), the hostess of 'Zum Blauen Insel' in a Bürgertheater rewrite of Strauss's *Cagliostro in Wien* (1927), Maria von Kirschstätt in *Prinzessin Ti-Ti-Pa* (1928), Cyprienne in Paul Ábrahám's jazz show *Spektakel* (1928), Jeanette in *Ihr erste Ball* (1929), Frau Kratochwill in *Walzer aus Wien* (1930), Die Fürstin-Mutter in the revised version of *Das Spitzentuch der Königin* (1931) and Madame Labile in *Die Dubarry* (1935) in a career only a little less memorable than her first, before finally going into retirement.

Her son, Fritz Zwerenz (b Baden bei Wien, 3 October 1895; d 12 October 1970), was a musical director, for a time at the Raimundtheater.

Illustration acknowledgements

The illustrations in these volumes are drawn from the British Musical Theatre Collection and from the following sources, who have generously given permission for their reproduction:

Agence de Presse Bernard (Plates 171, 231);
The Australian Opera, photography by Branco Gaica (Plates 16, 91, 113, 182, 207, 278);
Martin Büttner (Plate 301);
Joe Cantlin (Plate 289);
Fotofleck Presse und Buhnenfotograf (Plate 230);
Free Library of Philadelphia, Theater Collection (Plates 5, 33, 49, 59, 80, 117, 130, 142, 146, 163, 174, 186, 189, 197, 206, 222, 224);
Gordon Frost Organisation, Sydney, Australia (Plates 22, 150);
Vera von Glasner (Plate 190);
Theo Gröne (Plate 19);
Harrogate Opera House (Plate 188);
Klaus Hofman (Plate 302);
Hubert Huber (Plates 99, 292);
Tom Hustler (Plates 68, 119, 228, 234, 260);
Herbert Jager (Plate 63);
Helga Kirchberger (Plate 303);
Michael le Poer Trench (Plate 170);
Gerhard Kolb (Plate 200);
Manfred Kortmann (Plate 239);
Library Theatre Company, photograph by Gerry Murray (Plate 259);
Magyar Színházi Intézet (Plates 31a, 84, 90, 93, 122, 138, 143, 191, 204, 263b, 284, 305);
National Library of Australia (Plates 221, 288);
H Remmer (Plate 32);
Gunter Schreckenberg (Plate 283);
St Louis Municipal Opera (Plates 42, 98, 133, 134, 223, 265, 287);
Staatsoperette, Dresden (Plates 57, 66, 157, 193, 290);
Uwe Stratmann (Plate 114);
Volksoper, Wien (Plates 21, 152, 168, 211, 286);
Karlheinz Weinmann (Plate 279);
Reg Wilson (Plates 4, 20, 24, 62, 111, 139, 169, 173, 198, 199, 225, 242, 251).

Every effort has been made by the Publisher to trace the copyright holder of all the illustrations in this publication. If copyright has been infringed, we will be pleased to make proper acknowledgement, on being satisfied as to the owner's title, in future editions.